STATUTORY SUPPLE...

THE LAW OF BUSINESS ORGANIZATIONS

CASES, MATERIALS, AND PROBLEMS

Fourteenth Edition

■ ■ ■

Jonathan R. Macey
Sam Harris Professor of Corporate Law,
Corporate Finance and Securities Law
Yale Law School

Douglas K. Moll
Beirne, Maynard & Parsons, L.L.P. Professor of Law
University of Houston Law Center

**WEST
ACADEMIC**
PUBLISHING

The publisher is not engaged in rendering legal or other professional advice, and this publication is not a substitute for the advice of an attorney. If you require legal or other expert advice, you should seek the services of a competent attorney or other professional.

COPYRIGHT © 1990, 1994 WEST PUBLISHING CO.
© West, a Thomson business, 1998, 2001, 2005, 2007
© 2010 Thomson Reuters
© 2014, 2017 LEG, Inc. d/b/a West Academic
© 2020 LEG, Inc. d/b/a West Academic
    444 Cedar Street, Suite 700
    St. Paul, MN 55101
    1-877-888-1330

Printed in the United States of America

ISBN: 978-1-68467-765-8

[No claim of copyright is made for official U.S. government statutes, rules or regulations.]

PREFACE

This statutory supplement is designed for use in law school courses covering agency, partnerships, corporations, and other limited liability entities. In particular, the supplement compiles the statutes, regulations, and uniform or model acts needed for the use of our casebook, THE LAW OF BUSINESS ORGANIZATIONS: CASES, MATERIALS, AND PROBLEMS (14th ed. 2020).

The materials included in this supplement are generally presented in one of three manners. First, for state and federal statutes and regulations that have no accompanying comments, the statutory text is reprinted in its entirety. Examples of such materials include the Delaware General Corporation Law, the Delaware Limited Liability Company Act, and selected sections of the New York Business Corporation Law. Second, for some uniform or model acts, the statutory text and comments are reprinted in their entirety. Such materials include the Revised Uniform Partnership Act (1997 and 2013), the Revised Uniform Limited Partnership Act (1976 with 1985 amendments), the Uniform Limited Partnership Act (2001 and 2013), the Uniform Limited Liability Company Act (1996), and the Revised Uniform Limited Liability Company Act (2006 and 2013). Third, for Restatements and some uniform or model acts, the statutory text is reprinted in its entirety, but only selected comments (if any) are included. Examples of such materials include the Restatement (Second) of Agency (1958), the Restatement (Third) of Agency (2006), the Uniform Partnership Act (1914), and the Model Business Corporation Act.

We very much welcome your feedback on this supplement. Please call or e-mail us with any comments, suggestions, or insights. If you notice errors or omissions, please bring them to our attention as well. We'll incorporate as much as we can into the next edition.

JONATHAN R. MACEY
DOUGLAS K. MOLL

New Haven, Connecticut
Houston, Texas
May 20, 2020

TABLE OF CONTENTS

TABLE OF CONTENTS

STATUTORY SUPPLEMENT TO
THE LAW OF BUSINESS ORGANIZATIONS

CASES, MATERIALS, AND PROBLEMS

Fourteenth Edition

RESTATEMENT (SECOND) OF AGENCY (1958)

Table of Sections

Chapter 1

INTRODUCTORY MATTERS

TOPIC 1. DEFINITIONS

TOPIC 2. KNOWLEDGE AND NOTICE

TOPIC 3. ESSENTIAL CHARACTERISTICS OF RELATION

TOPIC 4. AGENCY DISTINGUISHED FROM OTHER RELATIONS

RESTATEMENT (SECOND) OF AGENCY (1958)

RESTATEMENT (SECOND) OF AGENCY (1958)

RESTATEMENT (SECOND) OF AGENCY (1958)

TITLE F. INTERPRETATION OF AUTHORIZATION TO MANAGE A BUSINESS

TITLE G. AUTHORIZATION TO BORROW

TITLE H. AUTHORIZATION TO MAKE NEGOTIABLE INSTRUMENTS

TITLE I. AUTHORIZATION TO DELEGATE OR TO APPOINT AGENTS AND SUBAGENTS

Chapter 4

RATIFICATION

TOPIC 1. DEFINITIONS

TOPIC 2. WHEN AFFIRMANCE RESULTS IN RATIFICATION

TOPIC 3. WHAT CONSTITUTES AFFIRMANCE

TOPIC 4. LIABILITIES

Chapter 5

TERMINATION OF AGENCY POWERS

TOPIC 1. TERMINATION OF AUTHORITY

TITLE A. INFERRED FROM ORIGINAL MANIFESTATION IN LIGHT OF SUBSEQUENT EVENTS

TITLE B. TERMINATION BY MUTUAL CONSENT, REVOCATION, OR RENUNCIATION

TITLE C. LOSS OF CAPACITY AND IMPOSSIBILITY

TITLE D. EFFECT OF TERMINATION OF AUTHORITY

TOPIC 2. TERMINATION OF APPARENT AUTHORITY

RESTATEMENT (SECOND) OF AGENCY (1958)

RESTATEMENT (SECOND) OF AGENCY (1958)

Chapter 7

LIABILITY OF PRINCIPAL TO THIRD PERSON; TORTS

TOPIC 1. LIABILITY FOR PERSONAL VIOLATION OF DUTY

TOPIC 2. LIABILITY FOR AUTHORIZED CONDUCT OR CONDUCT INCIDENTAL THERETO

TITLE A. IN GENERAL

TITLE B. TORTS OF SERVANTS

WHO IS A SERVANT

RESTATEMENT (SECOND) OF AGENCY (1958)

RESTATEMENT (SECOND) OF AGENCY (1958)

RESTATEMENT (SECOND) OF AGENCY (1958)

Chapter 10

LIABILITY OF THIRD PERSON TO PRINCIPAL

TOPIC 1. CONTRACTS; DISCLOSED AGENCY

TOPIC 2. CONTRACTS; UNDISCLOSED AGENCY

TOPIC 3. NON-CONTRACTUAL LIABILITY

TOPIC 4. SERVANTS, SUBSERVANTS AND OTHER SUBAGENTS

TOPIC 5. EFFECT OF RATIFICATION

RESTATEMENT (SECOND) OF AGENCY (1958)

Chapter 11

LIABILITY OF AGENT TO THIRD PERSONS

TOPIC 1. CONTRACTS AND CONVEYANCES

TITLE A. AGENT A PARTY TO A TRANSACTION CONDUCTED BY HIMSELF

TITLE B. AGENT NOT PARTY TO TRANSACTION CONDUCTED BY HIMSELF

TITLE C. DEFENSES AND EFFECTS OF SUBSEQUENT EVENTS

TOPIC 2. THINGS RECEIVED FROM OR FOR PRINCIPAL

TITLE A. THINGS RECEIVED FROM THIRD PERSON

TITLE B. THINGS RECEIVED FROM PRINCIPAL

TOPIC 3. TORTS

RESTATEMENT (SECOND) OF AGENCY (1958)

RESTATEMENT (SECOND) OF AGENCY (1958)

Chapter 13

DUTIES AND LIABILITIES OF AGENT TO PRINCIPAL

TOPIC 1. DUTIES

TITLE A. EFFECT OF MANIFESTATIONS OF CONSENT BETWEEN PRINCIPAL AND AGENT

TITLE B. DUTIES OF SERVICE AND OBEDIENCE

TITLE C. DUTIES OF LOYALTY

TOPIC 2. LIABILITIES

RESTATEMENT (SECOND) OF AGENCY (1958)

TOPIC 3. DEFENSES

TOPIC 4. DUTIES AND LIABILITIES OF PARTICULAR KINDS OF AGENTS

Chapter 14

DUTIES AND LIABILITIES OF PRINCIPAL TO AGENT

TOPIC 1. CONTRACTUAL AND RESTITUTIONAL DUTIES AND LIABILITIES

TITLE A. INTERPRETATION OF CONTRACTS AND LIABILITIES THEREUNDER

TITLE B. REMEDIES OF AGENT

TITLE C. DEFENSES

TOPIC 2. LIABILITY IN TORT FOR HIS OWN MISCONDUCT

TOPIC 3. LIABILITY TO AGENTS NOT SERVANTS FOR TORTS OF SERVANTS, OTHER AGENTS, AND CONTRACTORS

TOPIC 4. LIABILITY TO SERVANTS FOR TORTS OF SERVANTS, OTHER AGENTS, AND CONTRACTORS

TITLE A. GENERAL RULE

TITLE B. THE FELLOW SERVANT RULE

RESTATEMENT (SECOND) OF AGENCY (1958)

Chapter 1

INTRODUCTORY MATTERS

TOPIC 1.   DEFINITIONS

§ 1.   Agency; Principal; Agent

(1)   Agency is the fiduciary relation which results from the manifestation of consent by one person to another that the other shall act on his behalf and subject to his control, and consent by the other so to act.

(2)   The one for whom action is to be taken is the principal.

(3)   The one who is to act is the agent.

Comment b. Agency a legal concept. Agency is a legal concept which depends upon the existence of required factual elements: the manifestation by the principal that the agent shall act for him, the agent's acceptance of the undertaking and the understanding of the parties that the principal is to be in control of the undertaking. The relation which the law calls agency does not depend upon the intent of the parties to create it, nor their belief that they have done so. To constitute the relation, there must be an agreement, but not necessarily a contract, between the parties; if the agreement results in the factual relation between them to which are attached the legal consequences of agency, an agency exists although the parties did not call it agency and did not intend the legal consequences of the relation to follow. Thus, when one who asks a friend to do a slight service for him, such as to return for credit goods recently purchased from a store, neither one may have any realization that they are creating an agency relation or be aware of the legal obligations which would result from performance of the service. On the other hand, one may believe that he has created an agency when in fact the relation is that of seller and buyer. See § 14J. The distinction between agency and other relations, such as those of trust, buyer and seller, and others are stated in Sections 14A to 14O. The distinction between the kind of agent called a servant and a non-servant agent is stated in Section 2.

When it is doubtful whether a representative is the agent of one or the other of two contracting parties, the function of the court is to ascertain the factual relation of the parties to each other and in so doing can properly disregard a statement in the agreement that the agent is to be the agent of one rather than of the other, or a statement by the parties as to the legal relations which are thereby created. See § 14L. The agency relation results if, but only if, there is an understanding between the parties which, as interpreted by the court, creates a fiduciary relation in which the fiduciary is subject to the directions of the one on whose account he acts. It is the element of continuous subjection to the will of the principal which distinguishes the agent from other fiduciaries and the agency agreement from other agreements. The characteristics which tend to indicate an agency or a non-agency relation are stated in Sections 12 to 14O.

§ 2.   Master; Servant; Independent Contractor

(1)   A master is a principal who employs an agent to perform service in his affairs and who controls or has the right to control the physical conduct of the other in the performance of the service.

(2)   A servant is an agent employed by a master to perform service in his affairs whose physical conduct in the performance of the service is controlled or is subject to the right to control by the master.

(3)   An independent contractor is a person who contracts with another to do something for him but who is not controlled by the other nor subject to the other's right to control with respect to his physical conduct in the performance of the undertaking. He may or may not be an agent.

Comment a. Servants and non-servant agents. A master is a species of principal, and a servant is a species of agent. The words "master" and "servant" are herein used to indicate the relation from which arises both the liability of an employer for the physical harm caused to third persons by the tort of an employee (see §§ 219–249) and the special duties and immunities of an employer to the employee. See §§ 473–528. Although for brevity the definitions in this Section refer only to the control or right to control the physical conduct of the servant, there are many factors which are considered by the courts in defining the relation. These factors which distinguish a servant from an independent contractor are stated in Section 220. The distinction between servants and agents who are not servants is of importance for the purposes of the Sections referred to. Statements made in the Restatement of this Subject as applicable to principals or agents are, unless otherwise stated, applicable to masters and servants. The rules as to liability of a principal for the torts of agents who are not servants are stated in Sections 250–267, and those with respect to his liability in tort to such agents in Sections 470–472. The duties of servants to masters and their liabilities to third persons are in general the same as those of agents who are not servants. However, servants may have only custody, as distinguished from possession of goods entrusted to them by the master (see § 339, Comment *g* and § 349), and a servant, because of his position, may not be responsible for mistakes made by him as to facts upon which his authority depends, whereas an agent who is not a servant would be responsible. See Comment *c* on § 383.

§ 3.   General Agent; Special Agent

(1)   A general agent is an agent authorized to conduct a series of transactions involving a continuity of service.

(2)   A special agent is an agent authorized to conduct a single transaction or a series of transactions not involving continuity of service.

§ 4.   Disclosed Principal; Partially Disclosed Principal; Undisclosed Principal

(1)   If, at the time of a transaction conducted by an agent, the other party thereto has notice that the agent is acting for a principal and of the principal's identity, the principal is a disclosed principal.

(2)   If the other party has notice that the agent is or may be acting for a principal but has no notice of the principal's identity, the principal for whom the agent is acting is a partially disclosed principal.

(3)   If the other party has no notice that the agent is acting for a principal, the one for whom he acts is an undisclosed principal.

§ 5.   Subagents and Subservants

(1)   A subagent is a person appointed by an agent empowered to do so, to perform functions undertaken by the agent for the principal, but for whose conduct the agent agrees with the principal to be primarily responsible.

(2)   A subservant is a person appointed by a servant empowered to do so, to perform functions undertaken by the servant for the master and subject to the control as to his physical conduct both by the master and by the servant, but for whose conduct the servant agrees with the principal to be primarily responsible.

Comment a. An agent may be authorized to appoint another person to perform for the principal an act which the agent is authorized to perform or to have performed. The agreement may be that upon the appointment of such a person the agent's function as agent is performed, and that thereafter the person so appointed is not to be the representative of the agent but is to act solely on account of the principal, in which case the one so appointed is an agent and not a subagent. On the other hand, the agreement may be that the appointing agent is to undertake the performance of the authorized act either by himself or by someone else and that the person so appointed while doing the act on account of the principal is also, in so doing, to be the agent of the appointing agent, who consequently will have the responsibility of a principal with respect to such person. If this is the agreement, the person so appointed is a subagent. What the agreement is depends, as do other agreements, upon the manifestations of the parties as interpreted by the usages between them, the customs of business, and all other circumstances. See §§ 77–81.

A person may be a subagent although the appointing agent has no authority to appoint him. This is so if the agent has apparent authority to make the appointment, or if he otherwise has power to bind the principal, as where he is a general agent and the appointment of a subagent is an ordinary incident of his position, although forbidden in the particular instance. See §§ 161, 194.

b.   Reasons for distinguishing "agent" from "subagent". A subagent, as defined herein, is a person for whose conduct the appointing agent is responsible to the principal (see § 406), and in some cases is responsible to the person with whom the subagent deals. See § 362. These legal consequences do not follow when the appointing agent's function is merely to appoint a person to act for the principal, in which case the appointing agent is liable only if negligent in making the appointment. See § 405. In such a case, the person so appointed is not different from any other agent of the principal, and the fact that he was appointed by a superior agent rather than by the principal becomes immaterial. It is useful, therefore, to have a term which applies solely to the special type of relation where the appointed person is both an agent of the principal and an agent of the superior, appointing agent.

The courts have sometimes used the term subagent to describe both subagents as defined herein and also persons who, although appointed by superior agents, are not agents of such superior agents. This difference in usage has not resulted in improper decisions, but it has made the problem of citation difficult, since in noting cases in digests and encyclopedias the cases have to be read carefully to be sure that the court was referring to the kind of person described in this Section as a subagent.

Where an agent has no power to bind P by an appointment of a subagent, the one so appointed is the agent of the agent only, and the latter is responsible both to the principal for any improper delegation or/and to third persons for his agent's conduct. As to the authority to appoint an agent or subagent see Sections 77–81.

Comment e. Subagents in series. There may be a series of subagents, as where an attorney, authorized to collect a debt and appoint a subagent, sends it to a correspondent with a request for him to appoint another for whose conduct the correspondent is to be responsible.

§ 6.   Power

A power is an ability on the part of a person to produce a change in a given legal relation by doing or not doing a given act.

§ 7.   Authority

Authority is the power of the agent to affect the legal relations of the principal by acts done in accordance with the principal's manifestations of consent to him.

§ 8.   Apparent Authority

Apparent authority is the power to affect the legal relations of another person by transactions with third persons, professedly as agent for the other, arising from and in accordance with the other's manifestations to such third persons.

§ 8A.   Inherent Agency Power

Inherent agency power is a term used in the restatement of this subject to indicate the power of an agent which is derived not from authority, apparent authority or estoppel, but solely from the agency relation and exists for the protection of persons harmed by or dealing with a servant or other agent.

§ 8B.   Estoppel; Change of Position

(1)   A person who is not otherwise liable as a party to a transaction purported to be done on his account, is nevertheless subject to liability to persons who have changed their positions because of their belief that the transaction was entered into by or for him, if

  (a)   he intentionally or carelessly caused such belief, or

(b)   knowing of such belief and that others might change their positions because of it, he did not take reasonable steps to notify them of the facts.

(2)   An owner of property who represents to third persons that another is the owner of the property or who permits the other so to represent, or who realizes that third persons believe that another is the owner of the property, and that he could easily inform the third persons of the facts, is subject to the loss of the property if the other disposes of it to third persons who, in ignorance of the facts, purchase the property or otherwise change their position with reference to it.

(3)   Change of position, as the phrase is used in the restatement of this subject, indicates payment of money, expenditure of labor, suffering a loss or subjection to legal liability.

§ 8C.   Restitution

A person who has been unjustly enriched at the expense of another is required to make restitution to the other.

§ 8D.   Reformation

If by mistake of fact as to the contents of a written agreement or conveyance, or by mistake of law as to its legal effect, the writing does not conform to the agreement of the parties to it, the writing can be reformed to accord with the agreement.

TOPIC 2.   KNOWLEDGE AND NOTICE

§ 9.   Notice

(1)   A person has notice of a fact if he knows the fact, has reason to know it, should know it, or has been given notification of it.

(2)   A person is given notification of a fact by another if the latter

(a)   informs him of the fact by adequate or specified means or of other facts from which he has reason to know or should know the facts: or

(b)   does an act which, under the rules applicable to the transaction, has the same effect on the legal relations of the parties as the acquisition of knowledge or reason to know.

(3)   A person has notice of a fact if his agent has knowledge of the fact, reason to know it or should know it, or has been given a notification of it, under circumstances coming within the rules applying to the liability of a principal because of notice to his agent.

Comment d. Reason to know. A person has reason to know of a fact if he has information from which a person of ordinary intelligence, or of the superior intelligence which such person may have, would infer that the fact in question exists or that there is such a substantial chance of its existence that, if exercising reasonable care with reference to the matter in question, his action would be predicated upon the assumption of its possible existence. The inference drawn need not be that the fact exists; it is sufficient that the likelihood of its existence is so great that a person of ordinary intelligence, or of the superior intelligence which the person in question has, would, if exercising ordinary prudence under the circumstances, govern his conduct as if the fact existed, until he could ascertain its existence or non-existence. The words "reason to know" do not necessarily import the existence of a duty to others to ascertain facts; the words are used both where the actor has a duty to another and where he would not be acting adequately in the protection of his own interests were he not to act with reference to the facts which he has reason to know. One may have reason to know a fact although he does not make the inference of its existence which would be made by a reasonable person in his position and with his knowledge, whether his failure to make such inference is due to inferior intelligence or to a failure properly to exercise such intelligence as he has. A person of superior intelligence or training has reason to know a fact if a person with his mental capacity and attainments would draw such an inference from the facts known to him. On the other hand, "reason to know" imports no duty to ascertain facts not to be deduced as inferences from facts already known;

one has reason to know a fact only if a reasonable person in his position would infer such fact from other facts already known to him.

Further, a person has reason to know facts only if the circumstances are such that any unconscious knowledge would be made conscious if such person were to meet the required standards with reference to memory, consideration for the interests of others, or, in some instances, consideration for one's own interests. Thus, one who had no reason to remember facts once known would not at a later time have reason to know the facts. See Sections 276 and 277, which deal with situations in which this distinction may be crucial in determining the liability of the principal because of what an agent has reason to know.

§ 10.   Knowledge Which Principal or Agent Should Have Inter Se

Unless the parties have otherwise agreed, a principal or agent, with respect to the other, should know what a person of ordinary experience and intelligence would know, and in addition, what he would know if, having the knowledge and intelligence which he has or which he purports to have, he were to use due care in the performance of his duties to the other.

§ 11.   Notification by Principal or Agent to the Other

Unless otherwise agreed, there is a notification of a fact by the principal to the agent or by the agent to the principal:

(a)   when one of them states such fact to the other; or

(b)   when a reasonable time has elapsed after a writing stating such fact has been delivered

(i)   to the other personally,

(ii)   to the other's place of business,

(iii)   to a place designated by the other as a place for the receipt of business communications, or

(iv)   to a place which, in view of business customs or the relations between the parties, is reasonably believed to be the place for the receipt of such communications by the other.

TOPIC 3.   ESSENTIAL CHARACTERISTICS
OF RELATION

§ 12.   Agent as Holder of a Power

An agent or apparent agent holds a power to alter the legal relations between the principal and third persons and between the principal and himself.

§ 13.   Agent as a Fiduciary

An agent is a fiduciary with respect to matters within the scope of his agency.

§ 14.   Control by Principal

A principal has the right to control the conduct of the agent with respect to matters entrusted to him.

Comment a. The right of control by the principal may be exercised by prescribing what the agent shall or shall not do before the agent acts, or at the time when he acts, or at both times. The principal's right to control is continuous and continues as long as the agency relation exists, even though the principal agreed that he would not exercise it. Thus, the agent is subject to a duty not to act contrary to the principal's directions, although the principal has agreed not to give such directions. See § 33. Further, the principal has power to revoke the agent's authority, although this would constitute a breach of his contract with him. See § 118. The agent cannot obtain specific performance of the principal's agreement. If the agent has notice of facts from which he should infer that the principal does not wish him to act as originally specified, the agent's authority is terminated, suspended, or modified accordingly. See § 108. The control of the principal does not, however, include control at every moment; its exercise may be very attenuated and, as where the principal is physically absent, may be ineffective.

The extent of the right to control the physical acts of the agent is an important factor in determining whether or not a master-servant relation between them exists. See § 220.

Comment b. If it is otherwise clear that there is an agency relation, as in the case of recognized agents such as attorneys at law, factors, or auctioneers, the principal, although he has contracted with the agent not to exercise control and to permit the agent the free exercise of his discretion, nevertheless has power to give lawful directions which the agent is under a duty to obey if he continues to act as such. See § 385. If the existence of an agency relation is not otherwise clearly shown, as where the issue is whether a trust or an agency has been created, the fact that it is understood that the person acting is not to be subject to the control of the other as to the manner of performance determines that the relation is not that of agency. See § 14B.

TOPIC 4.   AGENCY DISTINGUISHED FROM OTHER RELATIONS

§ 14A.   Agent and Partner

A partnership is an association of two or more persons to carry on as co-owners a business for profit.

§ 14B.   Agency and Trust

One who has title to property which he agrees to hold for the benefit and subject to the control of another is an agent-trustee and is subject to the rules of agency.

§ 14C.   Agent or Director

Neither the board of directors nor an individual director of a business is, as such, an agent of the corporation or of its members.

§ 14D.   Agent or Escrow Holder

An escrow holder is not as such an agent of either party to the transaction until the event occurs which terminates the escrow relation.

§ 14E.   Agent and Interpreter or Amanuensis

Interpreters and amanuenses are agents for those who have employed them to interpret or to write; if selected by both or neither of the parties to a transaction, they are agents of neither.

§ 14F.   Judicially Appointed Fiduciaries

A person appointed by a court to manage the affairs of others is not an agent of the others.

§ 14G.   Agent or Assignee

An assignee of a claim is an agent of the assignor only if the latter retains an interest in, and control over, the claim.

§ 14H.   Agents or Holders of a Power Given for Their Benefit

One who holds a power created in the form of an agency authority, but given for the benefit of the power holder or of a third person, is not an agent of the one creating the power.

§ 14I.   Agent or Holder of a Restitutional Power

A person who has a power created by law to subject another to liability for the protection of the other's person or property or for the performance of the other's obligations is not an agent but is the holder of a power to create restitutional rights.

§ 14J.   Agent or Buyer

One who receives goods from another for resale to a third person is not thereby the other's agent in the transaction: whether he is an agent for this purpose or is himself a buyer depends upon whether the parties agree that his duty is to act primarily for the benefit of the one delivering the goods to him or is to act primarily for his own benefit.

§ 14K.   Agent or Supplier

One who contracts to acquire property from a third person and convey it to another is the agent of the other only if it is agreed that he is to act primarily for the benefit of the other and not for himself.

Comment a. Typical situations to which the rule stated in this Section apply are the purchase of shares in a corporation through a dealer or the purchase of land through a broker. Factors indicating that the one who is to acquire the property and transfer it to the other is selling to, and not acting as agent for, the other are: (1) That he is to receive a fixed price for the property, irrespective of the price paid by him. This is the most important. (2) That he acts in his own name and receives the title to the property which he thereafter is to transfer. (3) That he has an independent business in buying and selling similar property. None of these factors is conclusive. The question arises in a variety of ways. Thus the issue may be whether or not the supplier is entitled to keep the difference between what he paid for the goods and what it was agreed he should receive from the transferee; if there is an agency, normally this amount must be accounted for. However, a principal may agree that his buying agent is to retain the amount. The issue may arise because of the Statute of Frauds, because an oral order to an agent is not within the Statute, whereas an oral order to a seller, if above the statutory amount, must be in writing. Comment *c* on Section 14J states a number of other ways in which it may be important to determine whether a transaction creates a contract of sale or an agency relation.

§ 14L.   Ambiguous Principal

(1)   A person who conducts a transaction between two others may be an agent of both of them in the transaction, or the agent of one of them only, although the agent of the other for other transactions, or the agent of one for part of the transaction and the agent of the other for the remainder.

(2)   Unless otherwise agreed, one who has received money or other property from another to be paid or transferred to a creditor of the other is the agent of the other and not of the creditor.

§ 14M.   Corporate Subsidiaries

A corporation does not become an agent of another corporation merely because a majority of its voting shares is held by the other.

§ 14N.   Agent and Independent Contractor

One who contracts to act on behalf of another and subject to the other's control except with respect to his physical conduct is an agent and also an independent contractor.

§ 14O.   Security Holder Becoming a Principal

A creditor who assumes control of his debtor's business for the mutual benefit of himself and his debtor, may become a principal, with liability for the acts and transactions of the debtor in connection with the business.

Comment a. A security holder who merely exercises a veto power over the business acts of his debtor by preventing purchases or sales above specified amounts does not thereby become a principal. However, if he takes over the management of the debtor's business either in person or through an agent, and directs what contracts may or may not be made, he becomes a principal, liable as any principal for the obligations incurred thereafter in the normal course of business by the debtor who has now become his general agent. The point at which the creditor becomes a principal is that at which he assumes de facto control over the conduct of his debtor, whatever the terms of the formal contract with his debtor may be.

Where there is an assignment for the benefit of creditors, the latter may become the principals of the assignee if they exercise control over transactions entered into by him on their behalf.

Chapter 2

CREATION OF RELATION

TOPIC 1. MUTUAL CONSENT AND CONSIDERATION

§ 15. Manifestations of Consent

An agency relation exists only if there has been a manifestation by the principal to the agent that the agent may act on his account, and consent by the agent so to act.

§ 16. Consideration

The relation of principal and agent can be created although neither party receives consideration.

TOPIC 2. DELEGABLE ACTS AND POWERS

§ 17. What Acts are Delegable

A person privileged, or subject to a duty, to perform an act or accomplish a result can properly appoint an agent to perform the act or accomplish the result, unless public policy or the agreement with another requires personal performance; if personal performance is required, the doing of the act by another on his behalf does not constitute performance by him.

§ 18. Delegation of Powers Held by Agent

Unless otherwise agreed, an agent cannot properly delegate to another the exercise of discretion in the use of a power held for the benefit of the principal.

§ 19. Appointment to Perform Illegal Acts

The appointment of an agent to do an act is illegal if an agreement to do such an act or the doing of the act itself would be criminal, tortious, or otherwise opposed to public policy.

TOPIC 3. CAPACITY OF PARTIES TO RELATION

§ 20. Capacity of Principal

A person who has capacity to affect his legal relations by giving consent to a delegable act or transaction has capacity to authorize an agent to do such act or to conduct such transaction for him with the same effect as if he were to act in person.

§ 21. Capacity of Agent; In General

(1) Any person has capacity to hold a power to act on behalf of another.

(2)　The extent to which the person holding such power is a fiduciary and is subject to duties and liabilities to the principal depends upon his capacity.

§ 22.　Husband and Wife as Principal and Agent

A husband or wife can be authorized to act for the other party to the marital relation.

§ 23.　Agent Having Interests Adverse to Principal

One whose interests are adverse to those of another can be authorized to act on behalf of the other; it is a breach of duty for him so to act without revealing the existence and extent of such adverse interests.

§ 24.　Adverse Party to Transaction as Agent

One party to a transaction can be authorized to act as agent for the other party thereto, except for the purpose of satisfying the requirements of the Statute of Frauds.

TOPIC 4.　MASTER AND SERVANT

§ 25.　Applicability of General Agency Rules

The rules applicable generally to principal and agent as to the creation of the relation, delegability and capacity of the parties apply to master and servant.

Chapter 3

CREATION AND INTERPRETATION OF AUTHORITY AND APPARENT AUTHORITY

TOPIC 1.　METHODS OF MANIFESTING CONSENT

§ 26.　Creation of Authority; General Rule

Except for the execution of instruments under seal or for the performance of transactions required by statute to be authorized in a particular way, authority to do an act can be created by written or spoken words or other conduct of the principal which, reasonably interpreted, causes the agent to believe that the principal desires him so to act on the principal's account.

§ 27.　Creation of Apparent Authority: General Rule

Except for the execution of instruments under seal or for the conduct of transactions required by statute to be authorized in a particular way, apparent authority to do an act is created as to a third person by written or spoken words or any other conduct of the principal which, reasonably interpreted, causes the third person to believe that the principal consents to have the act done on his behalf by the person purporting to act for him.

§ 28.　Authority to Execute Sealed Instruments

(1)　Except as stated in Subsection (2), an instrument executed by an agent as a sealed instrument does not operate as such unless authority or apparent authority to execute it has been conferred by an instrument under seal.

(2)　Sealed authority is not necessary to execute an instrument under seal where:

(a)　the instrument is executed in the principal's presence and by his direction;

(b)　the instrument is authorized by a corporation or partnership in accordance with the rules relating to the authorization of such instruments by such associations; or

(c)   a statute deprives seals of their legal significance.

§ 29.   Defectively Authorized Deed as Memorandum of Contract

(1)   Where a statute requires a memorandum of a transaction to be evidenced by the signature of a party to be charged, a sealed instrument signed by an agent, ineffective as a deed because the agent's authority was not under seal, satisfies the requirements of the statute if the instrument is sufficiently definite and the agent is otherwise properly authorized.

(2)   A sealed instrument incapable of taking effect as a covenant because made by an agent not authorized under seal is effective as a simple contract if the agent is otherwise authorized and the elements of a simple contract are present.

§ 30.   Authority to Execute Writings

(1)   Unless so provided by statute, a written authorization is not necessary for the execution of a writing.

(2)   A statutory requirement that a memorandum of a transaction be signed by the parties in order to make it effective does not of itself impose a requirement of written authorization to execute such a memorandum.

§ 31.   Estoppel to Deny Authorization

(1)   A person who manifests to a third person that he has authorized an agent by an instrument under seal or by other formality is subject to liability to such third person as if the authorization had been by such means, if the third person changes his position in reasonable reliance upon the manifestation.

(2)   If a principal entrusts to an agent an executed document containing blanks, and the agent fills the blanks without authority and delivers the document to a third person, who changes his position in reliance thereon without notice that the principal did not fill the blanks before execution of the instrument, the principal is subject to liability to the third person as if the instrument had been completed by the principal or by an agent properly authorized to fill the blanks.

TOPIC 2.   INTERPRETATION OF AUTHORITY AND APPARENT AUTHORITY

TITLE A.   AUTHORITY

§ 32.   Applicability of Rules for Interpretation of Agreements

Except to the extent that the fiduciary relation between principal and agent requires special rules, the rules for the interpretation of contracts apply to the interpretation of authority.

§ 33.   General Principle of Interpretation

An agent is authorized to do, and to do only, what it is reasonable for him to infer that the principal desires him to do in the light of the principal's manifestations and the facts as he knows or should know them at the time he acts.

§ 34.   Circumstances Considered in Interpreting Authority

An authorization is interpreted in light of all accompanying circumstances, including among other matters:

(a)   the situation of the parties, their relations to one another, and the business in which they are engaged;

(b) the general usages of business, the usages of trades or employments of the kind to which the authorization relates, and the business methods of the principal;

(c) facts of which the agent has notice respecting the objects which the principal desires to accomplish;

(d) the nature of the subject matter, the circumstances under which the act is to be performed and the legality or illegality of the act; and

(e) the formality or informality, and the care, or lack of it, with which an instrument evidencing the authority is drawn.

§ 35.   When Incidental Authority Is Inferred

Unless otherwise agreed, authority to conduct a transaction includes authority to do acts which are incidental to it, usually accompany it, or are reasonably necessary to accomplish it.

§ 36.   Usage in Interpretation of Authority

Unless otherwise agreed, an agent is authorized to comply with relevant usages of business if the principal has notice that usages of such a nature may exist.

§ 37.   General Expressions and Particularized Authorizations

(1) Unless otherwise agreed, general expressions used in authorizing an agent are limited in application to acts done in connection with the act or business to which the authority primarily relates.

(2) The specific authorization of particular acts tends to show that a more general authority is not intended.

§ 38.   Interpretation as to Duration of Authority

Authority exists only during the period in which, from the manifestations of the principal and the happening of events of which the agent has notice, the agent reasonably believes that the principal desires him to act.

§ 39.   Inference That Agent Is to Act Only for Principal's Benefit

Unless otherwise agreed, authority to act as agent includes only authority to act for the benefit of the principal.

§ 40.   Inference as to Authority to Disclose Principal

Unless otherwise agreed, an agent is authorized to disclose the existence and identity of his principal; if, as the agent should know, non-disclosure of the principal's existence or identity would subject the principal to disadvantage, the agent has authority only if he makes the proper disclosure.

§ 41.   Interpretation of Authority Where Principals or Agents Are Joint

(1) Unless otherwise agreed, authority given by two or more principals jointly includes only authority to act for their joint account.

(2) Unless otherwise agreed, authority given in one authorization to two or more persons to act as agents includes only authority to act jointly, except in the execution of a properly delegable authority.

§ 42.   Interpretation by the Parties

If the authorization is ambiguous, the interpretation acted upon by the parties controls.

§43. Acquiescence by Principal in Agent's Conduct

(1) Acquiescence by the principal in conduct of an agent whose previously conferred authorization reasonably might include it, indicates that the conduct was authorized; if clearly not included in the authorization, acquiescence in it indicates affirmance.

(2) Acquiescence by the principal in a series of acts by the agent indicates authorization to perform similar acts in the future.

§44. Interpretation of Ambiguous Instructions

If an authorization is ambiguous because of facts of which the agent has no notice, he has authority to act in accordance with what he reasonably believes to be the intent of the principal although this is contrary to the principal's intent; if the agent should realize its ambiguity, his authority, except in the case of an emergency, is only to act in accordance with the principal's intent. If an authorization is not ambiguous, the agent is authorized to act only in accordance with its reasonable interpretation.

§45. Mistake by Agent as to Facts upon Which Authority Depends

If authority is stated to be conditioned upon the existence of specified facts, whether or not the agent is authorized to act when he reasonably believes that such facts exist, depends upon the agreement of the parties as to whether the agent or the principal shall bear the risk of mistake.

§46. Inference of Authority to Disclose Facts upon Which Authority Depends

Unless otherwise agreed, authority to enter into transactions with third persons includes authority to disclose to them such documents or facts indicating authority as it is reasonable for the principal to anticipate they will desire to see or know of for their own protection.

§47. Inference of Authority to Act in an Emergency

Unless otherwise agreed, if after the authorization is given, an unforeseen situation arises for which the terms of the authorization make no provision and it is impracticable for the agent to communicate with the principal, he is authorized to do what he reasonably believes to be necessary in order to prevent substantial loss to the principal with respect to the interests committed to his charge.

§48. Parol Evidence Rule

The rules applicable to the contradiction or alteration of an integrated contract by extrinsic evidence apply to an integrated agreement between principal and agent as to the agent's authority.

TITLE B. INTERPRETATION OF APPARENT AUTHORITY

§49. Interpretation of Apparent Authority Compared with Interpretation of Authority

The rules applicable to the interpretation of authority are applicable to the interpretation of apparent authority except that:

(a) manifestations of the principal to the other party to the transaction are interpreted in light of what the other party knows or should know instead of what the agent knows or should know, and

(b) if there is a latent ambiguity in the manifestations of the principal for which he is not at fault, the interpretation of apparent authority is based on the facts known to the principal.

TOPIC 3. INTERPRETATION OF PARTICULAR AUTHORIZATIONS

TITLE A. AUTHORIZATION TO CONTRACT

§ 50.   When Authority to Contract Inferred

Unless otherwise agreed, authority to make a contract is inferred from authority to conduct a transaction, if the making of such a contract is incidental to the transaction, usually accompanies such a transaction, or is reasonably necessary to accomplish it.

§ 51.   Authority Inferred from Authorizing Making of Contract

Unless otherwise agreed, authority to make a specified contract includes authority:

(a)   to make it in a usual form and with usual terms or, if there are no usual forms or terms, in an appropriate way; and

(b)   to do other acts incidental to its making which are usually done or which, if not usually done, are reasonably necessary for making it.

TITLE B. AUTHORIZATION TO BUY OR TO SELL

§ 52.   When Authority to Buy or to Sell Inferred

Unless otherwise agreed, authority to buy property for the principal or to sell his property is inferred from authority to conduct transactions for the principal, if such purchase or sale is incidental to such transactions, usually accompanies them, or is reasonably necessary in accomplishing them.

§ 53.   Meanings of "to Buy" and "to Sell"

Authorization "to buy" or "to sell" may be interpreted as meaning that the agent shall:

(a)   find a seller or a purchaser from whom or to whom the principal may buy or sell;

(b)   make a contract for purchase or sale; or

(c)   accept or make a conveyance for the principal.

§ 54.   Authority to Find Seller or Purchaser

Unless otherwise agreed, it is inferred that authority to find a seller or a purchaser includes authority to state the terms upon which the principal is willing to buy or to sell; to solicit offers in accordance therewith; and, in the case of agents to sell, to describe the subject matter.

§ 55.   Authority to Contract for Purchase or Sale

Unless otherwise agreed, authority to contract for a purchase or sale includes authority to enter into negotiations for and to complete the purchase or sale, including therein usual or other appropriate terms, and, if a writing is required or is usual, to execute such writing.

§ 56.   Authority to Acquire Property by Purchase, or to Convey

Unless otherwise agreed, authority to acquire property for the principal by purchase or to transfer the principal's property by sale includes authority to agree upon the terms; to demand or to make the usual representations and warranties; to receive or execute instruments required for the transfer or manifesting it in the usual form; to pay or receive so much of the purchase price as is to be paid at the time of the transfer; and to receive possession of the subject matter or the documents of title, or, in case of a selling agent, to surrender possession if he has been entrusted with it.

§ 57. Limitation of Authority to Identified Subject Matter

(1)   Authority to buy or to sell is limited to authority to deal with a subject matter which is sufficiently described to be identified with reasonable certainty by the agent in the light of facts of which he has notice, or which the principal intended to describe.

(2)   Unless otherwise agreed, authority to buy or sell a particular thing includes authority to buy or sell that which is appurtenant to it.

§ 58. Authority to Make Unspecified Terms

Unless otherwise agreed, the specification of particular terms in an authorization to buy or to sell does not exclude authority to make additional terms not inconsistent with those prescribed, nor terms which diminish the duties or increase the rights of the principal beyond those specified.

§ 59. Duration of Authority to Buy or to Sell

Authority to buy or to sell exists only when, from the manifestations of the principal or from the happening of events of which the agent has notice, the agent reasonably believes that the principal desires him to buy or to sell.

§ 60. Authorized Methods of Buying or Selling

Unless otherwise agreed, authority to sell includes only authority to sell at private sale and not at auction; authority to purchase includes authority to purchase at private sale or auction.

§ 61. Amount of Price to Be Paid or Received

(1)   Unless otherwise agreed, authority to buy or sell with no price specified in terms includes authority to buy or sell at the market price if any; otherwise at a reasonable price.

(2)   Unless the agent has notice that the principal has a fixed-price policy or unless other facts indicate that the principal's directions are to be followed implicitly, an agent authorized to buy or sell at a fixed price or at the market price is authorized to buy or sell at a price more advantageous to the principal.

§ 62. Authority to Pay or to Receive Purchase Price

(1)   Unless otherwise agreed, authority to contract for a purchase or sale or to make or to receive a conveyance on terms by which part or all of the price is payable at the time when the contract or conveyance is made includes authority to pay or to receive so much of the price as is payable at such time.

(2)   Unless otherwise agreed, authority to purchase chattels or choses in action includes authority to pay for them if, but only if, the agent is authorized to receive possession of them or of the documents representing them; authority to sell chattels or choses in action does not include authority to receive the purchase price unless the agent has been entrusted with them or with the documents representing them.

§ 63. Authority to Warrant or to Represent

(1)   Unless otherwise agreed, authority to sell includes authority to make such promises operating as warranties, and only such, as are usual in such a transaction; authority to buy is limited to purchases accompanied by such warranties.

(2)   Unless otherwise agreed, authority to sell includes authority to make such, and only such, representations as the agent reasonably believes to be true and as are usual with reference to such a subject matter or, in the absence of usage, representations concerning qualities of the subject matter which, at the time, are not open to inspection and as to which the principal has reason to know the buyer will desire to be informed; authority to buy on credit includes authority to make such representations concerning the credit of the buyer as the buyer has reason to know will be required by the seller.

§ 64. Employment of Assistants

Unless otherwise agreed, it is inferred that authority to buy or to sell includes authority to secure such professional or other assistants as the proper performance of the transaction requires.

§ 65. Giving or Receiving Cash or Credit

(1) Unless otherwise agreed, authority to sell includes only authority to sell for money or the customary medium of payment, payable at the time of the transfer of title.

(2) Unless otherwise agreed, authority to purchase includes:

(a) authority to buy for money only and not on credit if the principal supplies the funds: or

(b) authority to pledge the principal's credit upon usual or reasonable terms if the principal does not supply the funds.

§ 66. Authority After Purchase or Sale

Unless otherwise agreed, authority to buy or to sell does not include authority to rescind or modify the terms of the sale after its completion nor to act further with reference to the subject matter except to undo fraud or to correct mistake.

TITLE C. AUTHORIZATION TO LEASE

§ 67. When Authority to Lease Is Inferred

(1) Unless otherwise agreed, authority to lease land or chattels is inferred from authority to manage the subject matter if leasing is the usual method of dealing with it or if, in view of the principal's business and other circumstances, leasing is a reasonable method of dealing with it.

(2) Authority to lease land or chattels is not inferred merely from an authority to sell the subject matter, to take charge of it, or to receive rents from it.

§ 68. Authority Inferred from Authority to Lease

The rules of interpretation which are applicable to authority to sell are applicable to authority to lease.

TITLE D. AUTHORIZATION TO TAKE CHARGE
OF LAND, CHATTELS, OR INVESTMENTS

§ 69. Authority of Agent in Charge of Things

Unless otherwise agreed, authority to take charge of land, chattels, or securities includes authority to take reasonable measures appropriate to the subject matter, to protect the subject matter against destruction or loss, to keep it in reasonable repair, to recover it if lost or stolen, and, if the subject matter is ordinarily insured by owners, to insure it.

§ 70. Authority to Make Investments

Unless otherwise agreed, an agent authorized to make or manage investments is authorized to invest in, and only in, such securities as would be obtained by a prudent man for his own account, having regard both to safety and income considering his means and purposes; and, if the agent's duties include management, to change investments in accordance with changes in the security of the investments, or the condition of the principal sum.

TITLE E. AUTHORIZATION TO RECEIVE PAYMENT

§ 71. When Authority Is Inferred

Unless otherwise agreed, authority to receive payment is inferred from authority to conduct a transaction if the receipt of payment is incidental to such a transaction, usually accompanies it, or is a reasonably necessary means for accomplishing it.

§ 72. Authority Inferred from Authority to Receive Payment

Unless otherwise agreed, authority to receive payment includes authority:

(a) to receive payment in full in money or other customary medium of exchange when the debt is due; and

(b) to surrender to the payer any security for or evidence of the debt to which he is entitled and to give him such receipt as it is usual to give

TITLE F. INTERPRETATION OF AUTHORIZATION TO MANAGE A BUSINESS

§ 73. What Authority Is Inferred

Unless otherwise agreed, authority to manage a business includes authority:

(a) to make contracts which are incidental to such business, are usually made in it, or are reasonably necessary in conducting it;

(b) to procure equipment and supplies and to make repairs reasonably necessary for the proper conduct of the business;

(c) to employ, supervise, or discharge employees as the course of business may reasonably require;

(d) to sell or otherwise dispose of goods or other things in accordance with the purposes for which the business is operated;

(e) to receive payment of sums due the principal and to pay debts due from the principal arising out of the business enterprise; and

(f) to direct the ordinary operations of the business.

§ 74. When Authority Is Inferred

Unless otherwise agreed, an agent is not authorized to borrow unless such borrowing is usually incident to the performance of acts which he is authorized to perform for the principal.

§ 75. Authority Inferred from Authority to Borrow

Unless otherwise agreed, authority to borrow includes authority:

(a) to borrow from any lender, for delivery to or for the use of the principal, a reasonable amount in view of the purposes of the borrowing if no amount is specified, upon the terms which are usual, if any, or otherwise upon reasonable terms; if no time is specified, for a reasonable time;

(b) to execute in the name of the principal such evidences of debt as are usually given; and

(c) to make reasonably necessary representations concerning the credit of the principal which the agent reasonably believes to be true.

TITLE H. AUTHORIZATION TO MAKE NEGOTIABLE INSTRUMENTS

§ 76.   When Authority Is Inferred

Unless otherwise agreed, an agent is not authorized to execute or to endorse negotiable paper unless such execution or endorsement is usually incident to the performance of the acts which he is authorized to perform for the principal.

TITLE I.   AUTHORIZATION TO DELEGATE OR TO APPOINT AGENTS AND SUBAGENTS

§ 77.   General Rule

The authority to appoint agents, subagents or subservants of the principal can be conferred in the same manner as authority to do other acts for the principal, and the interpretation of the manifestations of the principal is governed by the rules generally applicable to the interpretation of authority.

§ 78.   Inference as to Authority to Delegate Authority

Unless otherwise agreed, authority to conduct a transaction does not include authority to delegate to another the performance of acts incidental thereto which involve discretion or the agent's special skill; such authority, however, includes authority to delegate to a subagent the performance of incidental mechanical and ministerial acts.

§ 79.   When Authority to Appoint an Agent Is Inferred

Unless otherwise agreed, an agent is authorized to appoint another agent for the principal if:

(a)   the agent is appointed to a position which, in view of business customs, ordinarily includes authority to appoint other agents; or

(b)   the proper conduct of the principal's business in the contemplated manner reasonably requires the employment of other agents; or

(c)   the agent is employed to act at a place where or in a business in which it is customary to employ other agents for the performance of such acts; or

(d)   an unforeseen contingency arises making it impracticable to communicate with the principal and making such an appointment reasonably necessary for the protection of the interests of the principal entrusted to the agent.

§ 80.   When Authority to Appoint a Subagent Is Inferred

Unless otherwise agreed, authority to appoint a subagent is inferred from authority to conduct a transaction for the principal for the performance of which the agent is to be responsible to the principal if:

(a)   the authorized transaction cannot lawfully be performed by the agent in person;

(b)   the agent is a corporation, partnership or other organization;

(c)   the business is of such a nature or is to be conducted in such a place that it is impracticable for the agent to perform it in person;

(d)   the appointment of subagents for the performance of such transactions is usual, or the principal has reason to know that the agent employs subagents; or

(e)   an unforeseen contingency arises in which it is impracticable to communicate with the principal and in which such an appointment is necessary in order to protect the interests of the principal entrusted to the agent.

§ 81.   Authority of Servant to Delegate

(1)   A servant is not authorized to permit, or to employ another, to perform acts of service which he is employed to perform unless it is so agreed between the master and the servant.

(2)   The master and the servant may agree that

(a)   the servant is to employ another for the master, or that

(b)   the servant is to employ a subservant for whose conduct the servant is responsible to the master, or that

(c)   the servant is to employ an independent contractor.

Chapter 4

RATIFICATION

TOPIC 1. DEFINITIONS

§ 82.   Ratification

Ratification is the affirmance by a person of a prior act which did not bind him but which was done or professedly done on his account, whereby the act, as to some or all persons, is given effect as if originally authorized by him.

Comment c. A unique concept. The concept of ratification is not a legal fiction, but denotes the legal consequences which result from a series of events beginning with a transaction inoperative as to the principal, and ending in an act of validation. The statement that there is a relation back to the time of the original act is fictitious in form, but in effect, it is a statement of liabilities. The concept is unique. It does not conform to the rules of contracts, since it can be accomplished without consideration to or manifestation by the purported principal and without fresh consent by the other party. Further, it operates as if the transaction were complete at the time and place of the first event, rather than the last, as in the normal case of offer and acceptance. It does not conform to the rules of torts, since the ratifier may become responsible for a harm which was not caused by him, his property or his agent. It can not be justified on a theory of restitution, since the ratifier may not have received a benefit, nor the third person a deprivation. Nor is ratification dependent upon a doctrine of estoppel, since there may be ratification although neither the agent nor the other party suffer a loss resulting from a statement of affirmance or a failure to disavow. However, in some cases in which ratification is claimed, the principal's liability can be based upon unjust enrichment or estoppel, either in addition to or as alternative to his liability based on ratification. See §§ 103, 104.

§ 83.   Affirmance

Affirmance is either

(a)   a manifestation of an election by one on whose account an unauthorized act has been done to treat the act as authorized, or

(b)   conduct by him justifiable only if there were such an election.

TOPIC 2. WHEN AFFIRMANCE RESULTS IN RATIFICATION

§ 84.   What Acts Can Be Ratified

(1)   An act which, when done, could have been authorized by a purported principal, or if an act of service by an intended principal, can be ratified if, at the time of affirmance, he could authorize such an act.

(2) An act which, when done, the purported or intended principal could not have authorized, he cannot ratify, except an act affirmed by a legal representative whose appointment relates back to or before the time of such act.

§ 85. Purporting to Act as Agent as a Requisite for Ratification

(1) Ratification does not result from the affirmance of a transaction with a third person unless the one acting purported to be acting for the ratifier.

(2) An act of service not involving a transaction with a third person is subject to ratification if, but only if, the one doing the act intends or purports to perform it as the servant of another.

§ 86. Illegality or Lack of Capacity at Time of Affirmance

(1) A transaction capable of ratification can be ratified if, but only if, the purported principal can authorize such a transaction at the time of affirmance, except as stated in Subsection (2).

(2) If, by a change in law, a transaction, lawful when done, has become so unlawful that an attempt thereafter to authorize it would be void, the transaction can nevertheless be ratified if it is not against the present public policy to enforce rights resulting from it.

§ 87. Who Can Affirm

To become effective as ratification, the affirmance must be by the person identified as the principal at the time of the original act or, if no person was then identified, by the one for whom the agent intended to act.

§ 88. Affirmance After Withdrawal of Other Party or Other Termination of Original Transaction

To constitute ratification, the affirmance of a transaction must occur before the other party has manifested his withdrawal from it either to the purported principal or to the agent, and before the offer or agreement has otherwise terminated or been discharged.

§ 89. Affirmance After Change of Circumstances

If the affirmance of a transaction occurs at a time when the situation has so materially changed that it would be inequitable to subject the other party to liability thereon, the other party has an election to avoid liability.

§ 90. Affirmance After Rights Have Crystallized

If an act to be effective in creating a right against another or to deprive him of a right must be performed before a specific time, an affirmance is not effective against the other unless made before such time.

§ 91. Knowledge of Principal at Time of Affirmance

(1) If, at the time of affirmance, the purported principal is ignorant of material facts involved in the original transaction, and is unaware of his ignorance, he can thereafter avoid the effect of the affirmance.

(2) Material facts are those which substantially affect the existence or extent of the obligations involved in the transaction, as distinguished from those which affect the values or inducements involved in the transaction.

§ 92. Events Not Required for and Not Preventing Ratification

An affirmance by the principal of a transaction with a third person is not prevented from resulting in ratification by the fact:

(a)   that the other does not give fresh consent to the transaction at or after the affirmance, or does not change his position because of it; or

(b)   that the purported principal, before affirming, had repudiated the transaction, if the other party has not acted or has failed to act in reliance upon the repudiation; or

(c)   that the other party had a cause of action against the agent because of a breach of warranty or a misrepresentation by the agent as to his authority to conduct the original transaction; or

(d)   that the agent conducting the transaction has died or lost capacity; or

(e)   that the principal is subject to liability without receiving consideration; or

(f)   that the agent or the other party knew the agent to be unauthorized; or

(g)   that the principal does not communicate with anyone.

TOPIC 3.   WHAT CONSTITUTES AFFIRMANCE

§ 93.   Methods and Formalities of Affirmance

(1)   Except as stated in Subsection (2), affirmance can be established by any conduct of the purported principal manifesting that he consents to be a party to the transaction, or by conduct justifiable only if there is ratification.

(2)   Where formalities are requisite for the authorization of an act, its affirmance must be by the same formalities in order to constitute a ratification.

(3)   The affirmance can be made by an agent authorized so to do.

§ 94.   Failure to Act as Affirmance

An affirmance of an unauthorized transaction can be inferred from a failure to repudiate it.

§ 95.   Necessity of Communicating Manifestation of Affirmance

The manifestation of a definitive election by the principal constitutes affirmance without communication to the agent, to the other party, or to other persons.

§ 96.   Effect of Affirming Part of a Transaction

A contract or other single transaction must be affirmed in its entirety in order to effect its ratification.

§ 97.   Bringing Suit or Basing Defense as Affirmance

There is affirmance if the purported principal, with knowledge of the facts, in an action in which the third person or the purported agent is an adverse party:

(a)   brings suit to enforce promises which were part of the unauthorized transaction or to secure interests which were the fruit of such transaction and to which he would be entitled only if the act had been authorized; or

(b)   bases a defense upon the unauthorized transaction as though it were authorized; or

(c)   continues to maintain such suit or base such defense.

§ 98.   Receipt of Benefits as Affirmance

The receipt by a purported principal, with knowledge of the facts, of something to which he would not be entitled unless an act purported to be done for him were affirmed, and to which he makes no claim except through such act, constitutes an affirmance unless at the time of such receipt he repudiates the act. If he repudiates the act, his receipt of benefits constitutes an affirmance at the election of the other party to the transaction.

§ 99.   Retention of Benefits as Affirmance

The retention by a purported principal, with knowledge of the facts and before he has changed his position, of something which he is not entitled to retain unless an act purported to be done on his account is affirmed, and to which he makes no claim except through such act, constitutes an affirmance unless at the time of such retention he repudiates the act. Even if he repudiates the act, his retention constitutes an affirmance at the election of the other party to the transaction.

TOPIC 4.   LIABILITIES

§ 100.   Effect of Ratification; In General

Except as stated in Section 101, the liabilities resulting from ratification are the same as those resulting from authorization if, between the time when the original act was performed and when it was affirmed, there has been no change in the capacity of the principal or third person or in the legality of authorizing or performing the original act.

§ 100A.   Relation Back in Time and Place

The liabilities of the parties to a ratified act or contract are determined in accordance with the law governing the act or contract at the time and place it was done or made. Whether the conduct of the purported principal is an affirmance depends upon the law at the time and place when and where the principal consents or acts.

§ 101.   Exceptions to Normal Effect of Ratification

Ratification is not effective:

    (a)   in favor of a person who, by misrepresentation or duress, has caused the affirmance;

    (b)   in favor of the agent against the principal if the principal is obliged to affirm in order to protect his own interests; or

    (c)   in diminution of the rights or other interests of persons not parties to the transaction which were acquired in the subject matter before affirmance.

§ 102.   Revocability of Ratification

An affirmance not voidable for fraud, duress, illegality, or lack of capacity; and which cannot be avoided by the principal for lack of knowledge, or by the other party because of a change of position or other similar cause, is not affected by the subsequent attempted withdrawal of either party; an agreement between the principal and the other party to rescind the affirmance does not affect the rights of the agent, and such an agreement between the principal and agent does not affect the rights of the other party.

§ 103.   Estoppel to Deny Ratification

A person may be estopped to deny that he has ratified an act or transaction.

§ 104.   Liability Because of Adoption, Novation, or Restitution

Although there is no ratification, a person on whose account another acts or purports to act may become a party to a transaction similar to the original transaction by manifesting consent, or he may become subject to liability for the value of benefits received as a result of the original transaction.

Chapter 5

TERMINATION OF AGENCY POWERS

TOPIC 1. TERMINATION OF AUTHORITY

TITLE A. INFERRED FROM ORIGINAL MANIFESTATION IN LIGHT OF SUBSEQUENT EVENTS

§ 105. Lapse of Time

Authority conferred for a specified time terminates at the expiration of that period; if no time is specified, authority terminates at the end of a reasonable period.

§ 106. Accomplishment of Authorized Act

The authority of an agent to perform a specified act or to accomplish a specified result terminates when the act is done or the result is accomplished by the agent or by another, except that if the act is done or the result is accomplished by a person other than the agent, the manifestations of the principal to the agent determine whether the authority terminates at once or when the agent has notice of it.

§ 107. Happening of Specified Events

If the terms of the authorization specifically provide that an authority is to continue until a specified event happens or during the continuance of specified conditions, whether the authority terminates at once upon the happening of the event or the cessation of the condition or only when the agent has notice of such happening or cessation depends upon the interpretation of the principal's manifestation in light of all circumstances.

§ 108. Happening of Unspecified Events or Changes; In General

(1) The authority of an agent terminates or is suspended when the agent has notice of the happening of an event or of a change in circumstances from which he should reasonably infer that the principal does not consent to the further exercise of authority or would not consent if he knew the facts.

(2) The agent's authority revives upon the restoration of the original situation within a reasonable time if the agent has no notice that the principal's position has been changed.

§ 109. Change in Value or Business Conditions

The authority of an agent terminates or is suspended when he has notice of a change in value of the subject matter or a change in business conditions from which he should infer that the principal, if he knew of it, would not consent to the further exercise of the authority.

§ 110. Loss or Destruction of Subject Matter

Unless otherwise agreed, the loss or destruction of the subject matter of the authority or the termination of the principal's interest therein terminates the agent's authority to deal with reference to it, either at once or when the agent has notice of it, dependent upon the manifestation of the principal to the agent.

§ 111. Loss of Qualification of Principal or Agent

The loss of or failure to acquire a qualification by the agent without which it is illegal to do an authorized act, or a similar loss or failure by the principal, of which the agent has notice, terminates the agent's authority to act if thereafter he should infer that the principal, if he knew the facts, would not consent to the further exercise of the authority.

§ 112.   Disloyalty of Agent

Unless otherwise agreed, the authority of an agent terminates if, without knowledge of the principal, he acquires adverse interests or if he is otherwise guilty of a serious breach of loyalty to the principal.

§ 113.   Bankruptcy of Agent

The bankruptcy or insolvency of an agent terminates his authority to conduct transactions in which the state of his credit would so affect the interests of the principal that the agent should infer that the principal, if he knew the facts, would not consent to the further exercise of the authority.

§ 114.   Bankruptcy of Principal

The bankruptcy or the substantial impairment of the assets of the principal, of which the agent has notice, terminates his authority as to transactions which he should infer the principal no longer consents to have conducted for him.

§ 115.   War

The outbreak of a war of which the agent has notice terminates his authority if the conditions are thereby so changed that he should infer that the principal, if he knew the facts, would not consent to the further exercise of the authority.

§ 116.   Change of Law

A change of law of which the agent has notice and which causes the execution of his authority to be illegal, or which otherwise materially changes the effect of its execution, terminates his authority, if he should infer that the principal, if he knew the circumstances, would not consent to the further exercise of the authority.

TITLE B.   TERMINATION BY MUTUAL CONSENT, REVOCATION, OR RENUNCIATION

§ 117.   Mutual Consent

The authority of an agent terminates in accordance with the terms of an agreement between the principal and agent so to terminate it.

§ 118.   Revocation or Renunciation

Authority terminates if the principal or the agent manifests to the other dissent to its continuance.

§ 119.   Manner of Revocation or Renunciation

Authority created in any manner terminates when either party in any manner manifests to the other dissent to its continuance or, unless otherwise agreed, when the other has notice of dissent.

TITLE C.   LOSS OF CAPACITY AND IMPOSSIBILITY

§ 120.   Death of Principal

(1)   The death of the principal terminates the authority of the agent without notice to him, except as stated in subsections (2) and (3) and in the caveat.

(2)   Until notice of a depositor's death, a bank has authority to pay checks drawn by him or by agents authorized by him before death.

(3)   Until notice of the death of the holder of a check deposited for collection, the bank in which it is deposited and those to which the check is sent for collection have authority to go forward with the process of collection.

Caveat:

No inference is to be drawn from the rule stated in this Section that an agent does not have power to bind the estate of a deceased principal in transactions dependent upon a special relation between the agent and the principal, such as trustee and beneficiary, or in transactions in which special rules are applicable, as in dealings with negotiable instruments.

§ 121.   Death of Agent

The death of the agent terminates the authority.

§ 122.   Loss of Capacity of Principal or Agent

(1)   Except as stated in the caveat, the loss of capacity by the principal has the same effect upon the authority of the agent during the period of incapacity as has the principal's death.

(2)   The agent's loss of capacity to do an act for the principal terminates or suspends his authority.

Caveat:

The Institute expresses no opinion as to the effect of the principal's temporary incapacity due to a mental disease.

§ 123.   Death or Loss of Capacity of Joint Principals or Agents

The death or loss of capacity of one of two or more joint principals terminates the authority of an agent to act on their joint account to the same extent as the loss of capacity of a single principal. The death or loss of capacity of one of two or more agents authorized to act only jointly terminates the authority of the survivor.

§ 124.   Impossibility

There is a termination of the agent's authority:

(a)   to create interests in or otherwise deal with a particular subject matter, when it is destroyed;

(b)   to affect the interests of the principal in a particular subject matter, when the principal has lost his interests in it;

(c)   to enter into transactions with particular persons when they die or lose capacity to become parties to such transactions; or

(d)   to effectuate results when, by a change of law or other circumstances, the transactions which the agent is authorized to conduct do not effectuate such results.

TITLE D.   EFFECT OF TERMINATION OF AUTHORITY

§ 124A.   Effect of Termination of Authority upon Apparent Authority and Other Powers

The termination of authority does not thereby terminate apparent authority. All other powers of the agent resulting from the relation terminate except powers necessary for the protection of his interests or of those of the principal.

TOPIC 2. TERMINATION OF APPARENT AUTHORITY

§ 125.   By Notice of Termination of Authority, or of Principal's Consent, or of a Basic Error

Apparent authority, not otherwise terminated, terminates when the third person has notice of:

    (a)   the termination of the agent's authority;

    (b)   a manifestation by the principal that he no longer consents; or

    (c)   facts, the failure to reveal which, were the transaction with the principal in person, would be ground for rescission by the principal.

Comment b. Apparent authority can exist only as long as the third person, to whom the principal has made a manifestation of authority, continues reasonably to believe that the agent is authorized. He does not have this reasonable belief if he has reason to know that the principal has revoked, or that the agent has renounced the authority, or that such time has elapsed or such events have happened after the authorization as to require the reasonable inference that the agent's authority has terminated. If the authority terminated only because the agent has notice of the happening of an event, the apparent authority may not terminate although the third person has notice of the event (see Comment *d*); it is terminated, however, if he knows that the agent has notice of it. In such case, it would be a breach of duty to the principal for the agent to act, and a third person having notice of this can acquire no rights against the principal by thereafter dealing with the agent. The third person has notice of the termination of authority, although he does not know the facts, if he has reason to know them or if, knowing the facts, he would, if reasonable, draw the inference that the authority is terminated, although in fact he unreasonably infers that it is not. He is also bound by a notification given him by the principal in accordance with the rules stated in Section 136.

§ 126.   Apparent Authority Conditioned by Time or Events

Apparent authority conditioned as to time or the happening of events terminates when the time has elapsed or the events have happened, either at once or when the third person has notice thereof, dependent upon the manifestation of the principal to him.

§ 127.   Apparent Authority of General Agent

Unless otherwise agreed, if the principal has manifested that an agent is a general agent, the apparent authority thereby created is not terminated by the termination of the agent's authority by a cause other than incapacity or impossibility, unless the third person has notice thereof.

§ 128.   Apparent Authority of Specially Accredited Agent

Unless otherwise agreed, if the principal has specially accredited an agent to a third person, the apparent authority thereby created is not terminated by the termination of the agent's authority by causes other than incapacity or impossibility, unless the third person has notice thereof.

§ 129.   Apparent Authority of Agent Who Has Begun to Deal

Unless otherwise agreed, if the agent properly begins to deal with a third person and the principal has notice of this, the apparent authority to conduct the transaction is not terminated by the termination of the agent's authority by a cause other than incapacity or impossibility, unless the third person has notice of it.

§ 130.   Apparent Authority of Agent Having Indicia of Authority

If the principal entrusts to the agent a power of attorney or other writing which manifests that the agent has authority and which is intended to be shown to third persons, and this is retained by the agent and exhibited to third persons, the termination of the agent's authority by causes other than incapacity or impossibility does not prevent him from having apparent authority as to persons to whom he exhibits the document and who have no notice of the termination of the authority.

§ 131. Agent Has Apparent Authority to Represent Nonexistence of Terminating Events

If, as a third person has notice, the agent's authority terminates upon the happening of an event other than the occurrence of incapacity or impossibility, the occurrence of the event does not terminate apparent authority if the agent is apparently authorized to represent its nonoccurrence and so represents to the third person, who has no notice that the event has occurred.

§ 132. Apparent Authority of Special Agent

Unless otherwise agreed, if the principal has manifested to the third person that the agent is to do a single act or perform a single transaction, the apparent authority terminates with the termination of the agent's authority, unless:

(a) the principal has specially accredited the agent to the third person;

(b) the agent has begun to deal with the third person as the principal has notice;

(c) the agent is in possession of indicia of authority entrusted to him by the principal and shown by him to the third person; or

(d) the principal has manifested that the agent has authority to represent the nonexistence of the terminating event and the agent does so represent.

§ 133. Incapacity of Parties or Other Impossibility

The apparent authority of an agent terminates upon the happening of an event which destroys the capacity of the principal to give the power, or an event which otherwise makes the authorized transaction impossible.

TOPIC 3. NOTICE OF TERMINATION OF AUTHORITY AND APPARENT AUTHORITY

§ 134. When Principal or Agent Has Notice of Termination of Authority

Unless the parties have manifested otherwise to each other, a principal or agent has notice that authority to do an act has terminated or is suspended if he knows, has reason to know, should know, or has been given a notification of the occurrence of an event from which the inference reasonably would be drawn:

(a) by the principal, that the agent does not consent to act;

(b) by the agent, that the principal does not consent to the act or would not if he knew the facts;

(c) by either, that the transaction has become impossible of execution because of incapacity of the parties, destruction of the subject matter, or illegality.

§ 135. When Third Persons Have Notice of Termination of Authority

A third person to whom a principal has manifested that an agent has authority to do an act has notice of the termination of authority when he knows, has reason to know, should know, or has been given a notification of the occurrence of an event from which, if reasonable, he would draw the inference that the principal does not consent to have the agent so act for him, that the agent does not consent so to act for the principal, or that the transaction has become impossible of execution.

§ 136. Notification Terminating Apparent Authority

(1) Unless otherwise agreed, there is a notification by the principal to the third person of revocation of an agent's authority or other fact indicating its termination:

(a) when the principal states such fact to the third person; or

(b) when a reasonable time has elapsed after a writing stating such fact has been delivered by the principal

(i)   to the other personally;

(ii)   to the other's place of business;

(iii) to a place designated by the other as one in which business communications are received; or

(iv)   to a place which, in view of the business customs or relations between the parties is reasonably believed to be the place for the receipt of such communications by the other.

(2)   Unless otherwise agreed, a notification to be effective in terminating apparent authority must be given by the means stated in Subsection (1) with respect to a third person:

(a)   who has previously extended credit to or received credit from the principal through the agent in reliance upon a manifestation from the principal of continuing authority in the agent;

(b)   to whom the agent has been specially accredited;

(c)   with whom the agent has begun to deal, as the principal should know; or

(d)   who relies upon the possession by the agent of indicia of authority entrusted to him by the principal.

(3)   Except as to the persons included in Subsection (2), the principal can properly give notification of the termination of the agent's authority by:

(a)   advertising the fact in a newspaper of general circulation in the place where the agency is regularly carried on; or

(b)   giving publicity by some other method reasonably adapted to give the information to such third person.

TOPIC 4. SUBAGENTS

§ 137.   Termination of Powers of Subagents

The principles applicable to the termination of an agent's authority or apparent authority are applicable also to the termination of the authority or apparent authority of a subagent or subservant.

Comment b. Notice to agent or subagent. If, in situations not involving subagency, authority would terminate because the agent has knowledge of facts or should know of them (see §§ 105–116), the authority of a subagent terminates under similar circumstances when either he or the intermediate agent acquires knowledge of or should know of such facts; except that where such knowledge is acquired by the intermediate agent it does not become operative as to the subagent until the agent has had time to communicate with him, and except that the agent may have apparent authority or other power to continue to authorize him to act for the principal. The agent and subagent are not, however, to be charged with their combined knowledge, if the knowledge had by each is not sufficient to create an inference of termination, unless the agent has failed in his duty to the principal to communicate to the subagent the knowledge which he has, or the subagent has failed in his duty to communicate facts to the agent. If, in situations not involving subagency, the authority of an agent terminates by notification by the principal to him, the authority of a subagent under similar circumstances terminates by notification by the principal either to the agent or the subagent. If the notification is given to the agent, the subagent's authority terminates only when the agent has had an opportunity to communicate with him. If the notification is to the subagent, it is ineffective if the subagent does not know that he is transacting the principal's business, as would be true when he is employed by an agent for an undisclosed principal, unless the principal can reasonably satisfy the subagent of his identification with the transaction. After the agent's authority to authorize a subagent to act for the principal has terminated, he may have apparent authority or other power to do so. If he has this and continues to direct the subagent to act, the latter's authority does not terminate.

The authority of the subagent may terminate because of the death or incapacity of the principal, the agent, or himself. In accordance with the rules generally applicable to agents (see §§ 120–123), no notice of such death or incapacity is necessary for the termination of authority or apparent authority, except as stated in Section 120. If the subagent continues to act after the death of the agent, he alone is responsible to the principal; the estate of the agent is not liable for his unauthorized acts, unless it had been so agreed between the principal and agent. His authority terminates without notice when the authorized act becomes impossible of execution. See § 124.

TOPIC 5. TERMINATION OF POWERS GIVEN AS SECURITY

§ 138. Definition

A power given as security is a power to affect the legal relations of another, created in the form of an agency authority, but held for the benefit of the power holder or a third person and given to secure the performance of a duty or to protect a title, either legal or equitable, such power being given when the duty or title is created or given for consideration.

§ 139. Termination of Powers Given as Security

(1) Unless otherwise agreed, a power given as security is not terminated by:

(a) revocation by the creator of the power;

(b) surrender by the holder of the power, if he holds for the benefit of another;

(c) the loss of capacity during the lifetime of either the creator of the power or the holder of the power; or

(d) the death of the holder of the power, or, if the power is given as security for a duty which does not terminate at the death of the creator of the power, by his death.

(2) A power given as security is terminated by its surrender by the beneficiary, if of full capacity; or by the happening of events which, by its terms, discharges the obligations secured by it, or which makes its execution illegal or impossible.

Chapter 6

LIABILITY OF PRINCIPAL TO THIRD PERSONS; CONTRACTS AND CONVEYANCES

TOPIC 1. GENERAL PRINCIPLES

§ 140. Liability Based upon Agency Principles

The liability of the principal to a third person upon a transaction conducted by an agent, or the transfer of his interests by an agent, may be based upon the fact that:

(a) the agent was authorized;

(b) the agent was apparently authorized; or

(c) the agent had a power arising from the agency relation and not dependent upon authority or apparent authority.

§ 141. Liability Based on Other Than Agency Principles

A principal, although not subject to liability because of principles of agency, may be liable to a third person on account of a transaction with an agent, because of the principles of estoppel, restitution or negotiability.

§ 142.   Liability for Acts of Servants and Subagents

The rules as to the power of an agent to subject the principal to liability are applicable to the power of a servant and of a subservant or other subagent.

§ 143.   Effect of Ratification

Upon ratification with knowledge of the material facts, the principal becomes responsible for contracts and conveyances made for him by one purporting to act on his account as if the transaction had been authorized, if there has been no supervening loss of capacity by the principal or change in the law which would render illegal the authorization or performance of such a transaction.

TOPIC 2.   DISCLOSED OR PARTIALLY DISCLOSED PRINCIPAL

TITLE A.   CREATION OF LIABILITY BY AUTHORIZED ACTS

§ 144.   General Rule

A disclosed or partially disclosed principal is subject to liability upon contracts made by an agent acting within his authority if made in proper form and with the understanding that the principal is a party.

§ 145.   Authorized Representations

In actions brought upon a contract or to rescind a contract or conveyance to which he is a party, a disclosed or partially disclosed principal is responsible for authorized representations of an agent made in connection with it as if made by himself, subject to the rules as to the effect of knowledge of, and notifications given to, the agent.

§ 146.   Manifestations by Agent Determining Parties

If an agent of a disclosed or partially disclosed principal makes an authorized contract with a third person, the liability of the principal thereon depends upon the agreement between the agent and the other party as to the parties to the transaction.

§ 147.   Inference That Principal Is a Party; Simple Contracts

Unless otherwise agreed, a disclosed or partially disclosed principal is a party to a contract, if not negotiable or sealed, made by his agent within his authority.

§ 148.   Orders of Several Principals Combined

Unless otherwise agreed between the principal and the agent, no one of two or more disclosed or partially disclosed principals, each of whom independently authorizes the same agent to make a contract, is liable upon a single contract made by the agent which combines the orders of the principals and calls for a single performance.

§ 149.   Written Contracts Not Containing Principal's Name

A disclosed or partially disclosed principal is subject to liability upon an authorized contract in writing, if not negotiable or sealed, although it purports to be the contract of the agent, unless the principal is excluded as a party by the terms of the instrument or by the agreement of the parties.

§ 150. Contracts Specifically Including or Excluding Principal

If an integrated contract by its specific terms excludes the principal as a party, extrinsic evidence is inadmissible to show that he is a party; if the integrated contract by its specific terms makes the principal a party, extrinsic evidence is not admissible to show that it was agreed that he should not become a party.

§ 151. Sealed Instruments

In the absence of statute, a disclosed or partially disclosed principal is not a covenantor or grantor in a sealed contract or conveyance unless he appears upon the instrument to be such.

§ 152. Negotiable Instruments

A disclosed or partially disclosed principal is not liable as a party to a negotiable instrument in which he is not named.

§ 153. Transactions Required to Be in Writing

For the purpose of satisfying the provisions of a statute requiring a note or memorandum to be signed by the party to be charged or by his agent, a memorandum signed by a properly authorized agent with or without indication of the existence or identity of the principal is sufficient to charge the principal.

TITLE B. INTERPRETATION OF WRITTEN INSTRUMENTS AS TO PARTIES

§ 154. General Rule

In determining the parties to an integrated contract made by an agent on account of his principal, the rules dealing with interpretation stated in the Restatement of Contracts apply.

§ 155. Instrument in Which Principal Appears as Such

In the absence of manifestations to the contrary therein, an unsealed written instrument is interpreted as the instrument of the principal and not of the agent if, from a consideration of it as a whole, it appears that the agent is acting as agent for a principal whose name appears therein as such.

§ 156. Instrument in Which Fact of Agency or Name of Principal Appears

In the absence of a manifestation to the contrary therein, an unsealed written instrument is interpreted as the instrument of the principal and not of the agent if, in the signature or description of the parties, the name of the principal and agent both appear, the agent indicating his agency. The addition of the word "agent" to the signature or description of the signer does not of itself prevent the inference that such person is a party to the contract.

§ 157. Instrument in Which Agency Shown Only in One Part

An unsealed written instrument, in one portion of which there is a manifestation that the agent is acting only for the principal, is interpreted as the instrument of the principal and not of the agent, although in other portions of the instrument or in the signature the agent's name appears without designation.

§ 158. Interpretation of Sealed Instruments as to Parties

The rules which determine the interpretation of unsealed instruments as to parties, are applicable to the interpretation of sealed instruments as to parties, except that:

(a) in order that a person should be bound as a covenantor or grantor in a sealed instrument he must be named as such therein, and the instrument must purport to be sealed by him; and (b)　in order that a person should be a covenantee or grantee in a sealed instrument he must appear as such in the instrument.

TITLE C.　CREATION OF LIABILITY BY UNAUTHORIZED ACTS

§ 159.　Apparent Authority

A disclosed or partially disclosed principal is subject to liability upon contracts made by an agent acting within his apparent authority if made in proper form and with the understanding that the apparent principal is a party. The rules as to the liability of a principal for authorized acts, are applicable to unauthorized acts which are apparently authorized.

§ 160.　Violation of Secret Instructions

A disclosed or partially disclosed principal authorizing an agent to make a contract, but imposing upon him limitations as to incidental terms intended not to be revealed, is subject to liability upon a contract made in violation of such limitations with a third person who has no notice of them.

§ 161.　Unauthorized Acts of General Agent

A general agent for a disclosed or partially disclosed principal subjects his principal to liability for acts done on his account which usually accompany or are incidental to transactions which the agent is authorized to conduct if, although they are forbidden by the principal, the other party reasonably believes that the agent is authorized to do them and has no notice that he is not so authorized.

§ 161A.　Unauthorized Acts of Special Agents

A special agent for a disclosed or partly disclosed principal has no power to bind his principal by contracts or conveyances which he is not authorized or apparently authorized to make, unless the principal is estopped, or unless:

    (a)　the agent's only departure from his authority or apparent authority is

        (i)　in naming or disclosing the principal, or

        (ii)　in having an improper motive, or

        (iii)　in being negligent in determining the facts upon which his authority is based, or

        (iv)　in making misrepresentations; or

    (b)　the agent is given possession of goods or commercial documents with authority to deal with them.

§ 162.　Unauthorized Representations

Except as to statements with relation to the agent's authority, in actions brought upon a contract or to rescind a contract, a disclosed or partially disclosed principal is responsible for unauthorized representations of the agent made incidental to it, if the contract is otherwise authorized and if true representations as to the same matter are within the authority or the apparent authority of the agent, unless the other party thereto has notice that the representations are untrue or unauthorized.

§ 163.　Disobedience as to Naming or Disclosing Principal

(1)　A principal who directs an agent to make a contract in the principal's name is subject to liability upon such a contract although made in the agent's name, unless the principal is excluded from it by its form or terms.

(2)   If a principal directs the agent to make a contract in the agent's name, concealing the existence or identity of the principal, he is subject to liability upon such a contract although the agent discloses the existence or identity of the principal or makes the contract in his name, except as stated in the Caveat.

Caveat:

No statement is made as to the principal's liability if the disclosure of his existence or identity may defeat his purposes.

§ 164.   Contracts Unauthorized in Part

(1)   Except as stated in subsection (2), an agent for a disclosed or partially disclosed principal who exceeds his powers in making an unauthorized contract with a third person does not bind the principal either by the contract as made or by the contract as it would have been made had he acted in accordance with his authority.

(2)   Where the only difference between the contract as authorized and the contract as made is a difference as to amount, or the inclusion or exclusion of a separable part, the principal is liable upon the contract as it was authorized to be made, provided that the other party seasonably manifests his willingness to accept the contract as it was authorized.

§ 165.   Agent Acts for Improper Purpose

A disclosed or partially disclosed principal is subject to liability upon a contract purported to be made on his account by an agent authorized to make it for the principal's benefit, although the agent acts for his own or other improper purposes, unless the other party has notice that the agent is not acting for the principal's benefit.

§ 165A.   Mistaken Exercise of Conditional Authority

If the authority of an agent of a disclosed or partially disclosed principal is stated to be conditioned upon determination by the agent of specified facts, the principal is bound by such determination although the agent was negligent in making it.

§ 166.   Persons Having Notice of Limitations of Agent's Authority

A person with notice of a limitation of an agent's authority cannot subject the principal to liability upon a transaction with the agent if he should know that the agent is acting improperly.

§ 167.   Persons Having Notice of Limitations of Written Authorizations

If a person dealing with an agent has notice that the agent's authority is created or described in a writing which is intended for his inspection, he is affected by limitations upon the authority contained in the writing, unless misled by conduct of the principal.

§ 168.   Power of Agent as to Statements of His Authority

A disclosed or partially disclosed principal is not thereby subject to liability because of untrue representations by an agent as to the existence or extent of his authority or the facts upon which it depends.

§ 169.   Agent Authorized to Disclose Terms

A disclosed or partially disclosed principal who invites third persons to deal with the agent on terms to be disclosed by the agent is subject to liability upon contracts made with them by the agent, although the terms are not within the authority of the agent, unless they have notice that the terms are not authorized.

§ 170.   Agent's Statements of Facts on Which His Authority Depends

A disclosed or partially disclosed principal who invites third persons to rely upon the representation of an agent as to the happening of a contingency upon which the authority of the agent depends is subject to liability upon contracts made with the agent by such third persons in reasonable reliance upon unauthorized and untrue representations of the agent that the contingency has happened.

§ 171. Authority Dependent on Facts Within Agent's Peculiar Knowledge

Unless otherwise agreed, a disclosed or partially disclosed principal who manifests to third persons that a general agent is authorized to make a contract if an event happens or if a specified fact exists, the happening or existence of which is peculiarly within the agent's knowledge, is subject to liability as a party to a contract made with such persons who rely upon the untruthful representations of the agent that the event has happened or that the fact exists; unless otherwise agreed, the principal is not subject to liability for such statements by a special agent.

§ 172. General Agent Authorized to Issue Commercial Documents

Unless otherwise agreed, a disclosed or partially disclosed principal who authorizes a general agent in the regular course of his employment to issue documents representing chattels or choses in action if an event happens or a specified fact exists, the happening or existence of which is peculiarly within the knowledge of the agent, is subject to liability to purchasers of such documents who have no notice that the agent has improperly issued them.

§ 173. Unauthorized Issue of Negotiable Instrument

A disclosed or partially disclosed principal who employs a general agent in a position in which it is usual for such agents to issue negotiable instruments is subject to liability to a holder in due course of such an instrument issued by the agent in the name of the principal, although contrary to the principal's directions, as if the instrument were authorized.

§ 174. Agent Entrusted with Possession of a Chattel

Aside from statute, a disclosed or partially disclosed principal who entrusts an agent with the possession of a chattel, other than a commercial document representing a chattel or chose in action, but who does not authorize him to sell it, display it for sale, or otherwise affect the principal's interest in it, is not thereby bound by an unauthorized transaction with reference to the chattel between the agent and a third person.

§ 175. Agent Authorized to Deal with Chattel Entrusted to Him

(1) Apart from statute, and except as stated in Subsection (3), the interests of a disclosed or partially disclosed principal who entrusts an agent with the possession of a chattel, other than a commercial document representing a chattel or chose in action, with directions to deal with it in a particular manner, as by sale, barter, pledge or mortgage, are not thereby affected by a transaction of a kind different from that authorized.

(2) The interests of the principal are affected by an unauthorized transaction of the same kind as that authorized, if conducted by an agent with one who reasonably believes him to be authorized and who pays value.

(3) If the principal delivers a chattel to a dealer in such chattels to be sold or exhibited for sale, an unauthorized sale of the chattel in accordance with the normal business practices to one who reasonably believes the dealer to be authorized to sell the chattel, binds the owner although the dealer was not authorized to sell it without the consent of the owner, or was not authorized to sell it to the person to whom it was sold, or at the price at which it was sold.

§ 176. Agent Entrusted with Commercial Document

A disclosed or partially disclosed principal who entrusts an agent with possession of, and a limited authority to deal with, a document representing a chattel or a chose in action in such form that possession of it is commonly regarded as indicating a general power to dispose of it, is subject to the loss of his interests in it by the agent's unauthorized disposition of it if it comes to the hands of a purchaser without notice that the agent was not authorized to dispose of it.

§ 177.   Agent Entrusted with Negotiable Instruments

A disclosed or partially disclosed principal who entrusts an agent with the possession of a negotiable instrument not payable to bearer or endorsed to the agent is not thereby subject to the loss of his interests therein by the collection of the claim or the transfer of the document by the agent.

§ 177A.   Agent Authorized to Fill Blanks

Where a principal entrusts an agent with an executed document containing blanks with authority to fill the blanks, and the agent fills the blanks in an unauthorized way, a person receiving the document from the agent

> (a)   is not entitled to hold the principal thereon, if he had notice that the agent filled the blanks.

> (b)   is entitled to hold the principal, if without notice that the blanks were unfilled when given to the agent.

§ 178.   Agent Authorized to Collect a Debt

(1)   If an agent, authorized to receive only money in payment of a debt, receives a check or other thing from the debtor and obtains the amount of the debt from the negotiation or sale of the thing received, the debt is paid.

(2)   If an agent who is authorized to receive a check payable to the principal as conditional payment forges the principal's endorsement to such a check, the maker is relieved of liability to the principal if the drawee bank pays the check and charges the amount to the maker.

(3)   An agent authorized to state to a debtor the amount of a debt, the amount of which is ordinarily determined or ascertained by the creditor, binds the principal by the receipt of a larger amount than that due resulting from the agent's misrepresentation.

§ 178A.   Where Agent Authorized to Pay Debts Makes a Mistaken Payment

An agent authorized to pay his principal's debts binds the principal by a mistaken payment, whether of fact or law, to the same extent as if the principal had made the payment.

TITLE D. DEFENSES AND LIABILITY AFFECTED BY SUBSEQUENT EVENTS

§ 179.   Rights Between Third Person and Agent

Unless otherwise agreed, the liability of a disclosed or partially disclosed principal is not affected by any rights or liabilities existing between the other party and the agent at the time the contract is made.

§ 180.   Defenses of Principal; In General

A disclosed or partially disclosed principal is entitled to all defenses arising out of a transaction between his agent and a third person. He is not entitled to defenses which are personal to the agent.

§ 181.   Subsequent Dealings Between Agent and Other Party

Where an agent for a disclosed or partially disclosed principal has entered into a transaction on behalf of the principal, subsequent dealings between the agent and the other party:

> (a)   may increase or diminish the principal's liability because of the further exercise of the agent's power, or

(b)   may diminish the principal's liability because the dealings are in derogation of the principal's rights.

§ 182.   Performance by Other Party Believing Agent Authorized

A disclosed or partially disclosed principal on whose account an agent purports to make a contract does not become liable as a party to the contract by reason of the fact that the other party performs the contract believing that the agent is authorized nor, unless there is ratification, by reason of the fact that the principal receives a benefit as the result of such a performance.

§ 183.   Settlement with Agent by Principal

A disclosed or partially disclosed principal is not discharged from liability to the other party to a transaction conducted by an agent by payment to, or settlement of accounts with, the agent, unless he does so in reasonable reliance upon conduct of the other party which is not induced by the agent's misrepresentations and which indicates that the agent has settled the account.

§ 184.   Judgment for or Against Agent

(1)   Recovery of judgment against the agent of a disclosed or partially disclosed principal for failure of performance of a contract to which the agent is a party does not thereby discharge the principal unless the agent and principal were joint contractors.

(2)   The existence and extent of the liability of a disclosed or partially disclosed principal upon a contract to which the agent is a party may be determined by a judgment for or against the agent in an action between the agent and the other party to the contract, in accordance with the rules of res judicata.

§ 184A.   Joinder of Principal and Agent

If a disclosed or partially disclosed principal and his agent are joined in an action on a contract to which both are parties and a judgment on the merits is rendered for one and against the other, or a judgment for a larger amount is rendered against one than against the other, the judgments are erroneous.

§ 185.   Satisfaction of Claim by Agent

A disclosed or partially disclosed principal ceases to be liable to the other party upon a contract to the extent that the claim against him has been satisfied by an agent who has been authorized to do so or who is a party to the contract.

TOPIC 3.   UNDISCLOSED PRINCIPAL

TITLE A.   CREATION OF LIABILITY
BY AUTHORIZED ACTS

§ 186.   General Rule

An undisclosed principal is bound by contracts and conveyances made on his account by an agent acting within his authority, except that the principal is not bound by a contract which is under seal or which is negotiable, or upon a contract which excludes him.

§ 187.   Orders of Several Principals Combined

Unless otherwise agreed between the principals and the agent, no one of two or more undisclosed principals, each of whom independently authorizes the same agent to make a contract, is liable upon a single contract made by the agent which combines the orders of the principals and calls for a single performance.

§ 188. Authorized Representations

In actions brought upon a contract or to rescind a contract or conveyance made by an agent for an undisclosed principal, the principal is responsible for authorized representations of the agent made in connection therewith as if made by himself, subject to the rules with regard to notice to the principal because of notifications given to the agent or of his knowledge of facts.

§ 189. Contracts Specifically Excluding Principal

An undisclosed principal does not become liable upon a contract which provides that he or any undisclosed principal shall not be a party to it.

§ 190. Simple Contracts in Writing

An undisclosed principal may be liable upon a simple contract in writing, although it purports to be the contract of the agent.

§ 191. Sealed Instruments

In the absence of statute, an undisclosed principal is not liable as a party to a sealed instrument.

§ 192. Negotiable Instruments

An undisclosed principal is not liable as a party to a negotiable instrument.

§ 193. Transactions Required to Be in Writing

For the purpose of satisfying the provisions of a statute requiring a note or memorandum to be signed by the party to be charged or by his agent, a memorandum signed by a properly authorized agent on account of an undisclosed principal is sufficient to charge the principal.

TITLE B. CREATION OF LIABILITY BY UNAUTHORIZED ACTS

§ 194. Acts of General Agents

A general agent for an undisclosed principal authorized to conduct transactions subjects his principal to liability for acts done on his account, if usual or necessary in such transactions, although forbidden by the principal to do them.

§ 195. Acts of Manager Appearing to Be Owner

An undisclosed principal who entrusts an agent with the management of his business is subject to liability to third persons with whom the agent enters into transactions usual in such businesses and on the principal's account, although contrary to the directions of the principal.

§ 195A. Unauthorized Acts of Special Agents

A special agent for an undisclosed principal has no power to bind his principal by contracts or conveyances which he is not authorized to make unless:

    (a) the agent's only departure from his authority is

        (i) in not disclosing his principal, or

        (ii) in having an improper motive, or

        (iii) in being negligent in determining the facts upon which his authority is based, or

        (iv) in making misrepresentations; or

(b)   the agent is given possession of goods or commercial documents with authority to deal with them.

§ 196.   Unauthorized Representations

In actions brought upon a contract or to rescind a contract, an undisclosed principal is subject to liability for unauthorized representations of the agent made incidental to it, if the contract is otherwise authorized and if true representations as to the same matter are within the authority of the agent, unless the other party has reason to know that they are untrue.

§ 196A.   Mistaken Exercise of Conditional Authority

If the authority of an agent of an undisclosed principal is stated to be conditioned upon the determination by the agent of specific facts, the principal is bound by such determination although the agent was negligent in making it.

§ 197.   Disobedience as to Disclosing Principal

A principal who directs an agent to make a contract in the principal's name or to reveal the principal's existence becomes liable upon the contract although made by the agent in his own name with another who has no reason to know that a principal exists, if the contract is one to which an undisclosed principal can be a party.

§ 198.   Contracts Unauthorized in Part

(1)   Except as stated in Subsection (2), an agent for an undisclosed principal who exceeds his powers in making an unauthorized contract with a third person does not bind the principal either by the contract as made or by the contract as it would have been had the agent acted in accordance with his authority.

(2)   Where the only difference between the contract as authorized and the contract as made is a difference as to amount or the inclusion or exclusion of a separable part, the principal is liable upon the contract as it was authorized to be made, if the other party seasonably manifests his willingness to accept the contract as it was authorized.

Caveat:

The rule stated herein does not include the situation in which the agent, in making the unauthorized terms, intends to act in fraud of the principal, as to which no statement is made.

§ 199.   Acts Not on Account of Principal or Done with an Improper Motive

An undisclosed principal who authorizes an agent to make a particular contract on his account and in his business is not liable upon such contract if the agent makes the very contract authorized but does not intend to act on account of the principal. If the agent intends to act for the principal, the fact that he has an improper motive does not prevent the principal from being liable.

§ 200.   Agent Entrusted with Possession of a Chattel

Apart from statute, an undisclosed principal who entrusts an agent with the possession of a chattel, other than a commercial document representing a chattel or chose in action, but who does not authorize him to sell it, display it for sale or otherwise affect the principal's interest in it, is not thereby bound by a transaction with respect to the chattel between the agent and a third person who believes the agent to be the owner.

§ 201.   Agent Authorized to Deal with Chattel Entrusted to Him

(1)   Apart from statute and except as stated in Subsection (3), the interests of an undisclosed principal who entrusts an agent with a chattel other than a commercial document representing a chattel or chose in

action with directions to deal with it in a particular way, as by sale, barter, pledge or mortgage, is not thereby affected by a transaction of a kind different from that authorized.

(2)   The interests of the principal are affected by an unauthorized transaction of the same kind as that authorized if it is conducted in the usual and ordinary course of business by an agent with one who reasonably believes the agent to be the owner and who pays value.

(3)   If the principal delivers a chattel to a dealer in such chattels to be sold or exhibited for sale, an unauthorized sale of the chattel by such dealer in accordance with the normal business practices to one who reasonably believes the dealer to be the owner, binds the owner, although the dealer was not authorized to sell it without the consent of the owner or was not authorized to sell it to the person to whom it was sold or at the price at which it was sold.

§ 202.   Agent Entrusted with Commercial Document

An undisclosed principal who entrusts an agent with possession of, and a limited authority to deal with, a document representing a chattel or a chose in action in such form that the possession thereof is commonly regarded as indicating a general power to dispose of it is subject to the loss of his interests therein by the agent's unauthorized disposition of it if it comes to the hands of a purchaser who takes it, reasonably believing that the agent is the owner.

TITLE C.   DEFENSES AND LIABILITY AFFECTED BY SUBSEQUENT EVENTS

§ 203.   Defenses of Undisclosed Principal; In General

An undisclosed principal is entitled to all defenses arising out of a transaction with an agent, but not defenses which are personal to the agent.

§ 204.   Notice to Principal or Agent

The liability of an undisclosed principal is affected by the knowledge which he acquires or by notification given to him which is relevant to his liability, and also by knowledge acquired or notification given to the agent with which he is chargeable.

§ 205.   Power of Agent to Modify Contract Before Disclosure of Principal

Until the existence of the principal is disclosed, an agent who has made a contract for an undisclosed principal has power to cancel the contract and to modify it with binding effect upon the principal if the contract or conveyance, as modified, is authorized or is within the inherent power of the agent to make.

§ 206.   Power of Agent as to Performance of or Defaults in Contract Before Disclosure of Principal

Until his existence is disclosed, the principal is affected by performance rendered by the third person to the agent, by notifications given to the agent with respect to the contract, and by the performance or default of the agent.

§ 207.   Dealings Between Other Party and Agent After Disclosure of Principal

Dealings between the agent of an undisclosed principal and the other party to a transaction subsequent to the disclosure of the existence or identity of the principal:

(a)   may increase or diminish the principal's liability because of the further exercise of the agent's power; or

(b)   may diminish the principal's liability because the dealings are in derogation of the principal's rights.

§ 208. Settlement with Agent by Principal

An undisclosed principal is not discharged from liability to the other party to a transaction conducted by an agent by payment to, or settlement of accounts with, the agent, unless he does so in reasonable reliance upon conduct of the other party which is not induced by the agent's misrepresentations and which indicates that the agent has settled the account.

§ 209. Choice by Third Person to Look Only to Agent

An undisclosed principal is not discharged from liability upon a contract made for him by an agent by the fact that, after the discovery of his existence or identity, the other party looks only to the agent for payment or performance.

§ 210. Judgment for or Against Agent

(1) An undisclosed principal is discharged from liability upon a contract if, with knowledge of the identity of the principal, the other party recovers judgment against the agent who made the contract, for breach of the contract.

(2) The principal is not discharged by a recovery of judgment against the agent by the other party before knowledge of the identity of the principal.

(3) The existence and extent of the liability of an undisclosed principal upon a contract made by an agent may be determined by a judgment for or against the agent in an action between the agent and the other party in accordance with the rules of res judicata stated in the Restatement of Judgments.

§ 210A. Joinder of Undisclosed Principal and Agent

A principal, initially undisclosed, and his agent can properly be joined in one action based upon a contract made by the agent; but if either defendant objects, the plaintiff can secure judgment only against the one whom he elects to hold.

§ 211. Satisfaction of Claim by Agent

An undisclosed principal ceases to be liable upon a contract made on his account by an agent if the claim of the other party against the agent has been satisfied.

Chapter 7

LIABILITY OF PRINCIPAL TO THIRD PERSON; TORTS

TOPIC 1. LIABILITY FOR PERSONAL VIOLATION OF DUTY

§ 212. Principal Intends Conduct or Consequences

A person is subject to liability for the consequences of another's conduct which results from his directions as he would be for his own personal conduct if, with knowledge of the conditions, he intends the conduct, or if he intends its consequences, unless the one directing or the one acting has a privilege or immunity not available to the other.

§ 213. Principal Negligent or Reckless

A person conducting an activity through servants or other agents is subject to liability for harm resulting from his conduct if he is negligent or reckless:

    (a) in giving improper or ambiguous orders of in failing to make proper regulations; or

(b) in the employment of improper persons or instrumentalities in work involving risk of harm to others:

(c) in the supervision of the activity; or

(d) in permitting, or failing to prevent, negligent or other tortious conduct by persons, whether or not his servants or agents, upon premises or with instrumentalities under his control.

§ 214. Failure of Principal to Perform Non-Delegable Duty

A master or other principal who is under a duty to provide protection for or to have care used to protect others or their property and who confides the performance of such duty to a servant or other person is subject to liability to such others for harm caused to them by the failure of such agent to perform the duty.

TOPIC 2. LIABILITY FOR AUTHORIZED CONDUCT OR CONDUCT INCIDENTAL THERETO

TITLE A. IN GENERAL

§ 215. Conduct Authorized but Unintended by Principal

A master or other principal who unintentionally authorizes conduct of a servant or other agent which constitutes a tort to a third person is subject to liability to such person.

§ 216. Unauthorized Tortious Conduct

A master or other principal may be liable to another whose interests have been invaded by the tortious conduct of a servant or other agent, although the principal does not personally violate a duty to such other or authorize the conduct of the agent causing the invasion.

§ 217. Where Principal or Agent Has Immunity or Privilege

In an action against a principal based on the conduct of a servant in the course of employment:

(a) The principal has a defense if:

    (i) he had an immunity from liability to the person harmed, or

    (ii) he had a delegable privilege so to act, or

    (iii) the agent had a privilege which he properly exercised on his principal's behalf, or

    (iv) the agent did not fall below the duty of care owed by the principal to the third person.

(b) The principal has no defense because of the fact that:

    (i) he had a non-delegable privilege to do the act, or

    (ii) the agent had an immunity from civil liability as to the act.

§ 217A. Dealings and Actions Between Injured Party and Agent

The liability of a principal for the tort of a servant or other agent may be affected by:

(a) dealings between the injured party and the agent, or

(b) a judgment for or against the agent in an action between the injured party and the agent.

§ 217B. Joinder of Principal and Agent

(1) Principal and agent can be joined in an action for a wrong resulting from the tortious conduct of an agent or that of agent and principal, and a judgment can be rendered against each.

(2)   If the action is based solely upon the tortious conduct of the agent, judgments on the merits for the agent and against the principal, or judgments of varying amounts for compensatory damages are erroneous.

§ 217C.   Punitive Damages

Punitive damages can properly be awarded against a master or other principal because of an act by an agent if, but only if:

(a)   the principal authorized the doing and the manner of the act, or

(b)   the agent was unfit and the principal was reckless in employing him, or

(c)   the agent was employed in a managerial capacity and was acting in the scope of employment, or

(d)   the principal or a managerial agent of the principal ratified or approved the act.

§ 217D.   Penalties

A principal may be subject to penalties enforced under the rules of the criminal law, for acts done by a servant or other agent.

§ 218.   Effect of Ratification

Upon ratification, a purported master or other principal becomes subject to liability for injuries caused by the tortious act of one acting or purporting to act as his agent as if the act had been authorized, if there has been no loss of capacity by the principal.

TITLE B.   TORTS OF SERVANTS

§ 219.   When Master Is Liable for Torts of His Servants

(1)   A master is subject to liability for the torts of his servants committed while acting in the scope of their employment.

(2)   A master is not subject to liability for the torts of his servants acting outside the scope of their employment, unless:

(a)   the master intended the conduct or the consequences, or

(b)   the master was negligent or reckless, or

(c)   the conduct violated a non-delegable duty of the master, or

(d)   the servant purported to act or to speak on behalf of the principal and there was reliance upon apparent authority, or he was aided in accomplishing the tort by the existence of the agency relation.

WHO IS A SERVANT

§ 220.   Definition of Servant

(1)   A servant is a person employed to perform services in the affairs of another and who with respect to the physical conduct in the performance of the services is subject to the other's control or right to control.

(2)   In determining whether one acting for another is a servant or an independent contractor, the following matters of fact, among others, are considered:

(a)   the extent of control which, by the agreement, the master may exercise over the details of the work;

(b)   whether or not the one employed is engaged in a distinct occupation or business;

(c) the kind of occupation, with reference to whether, in the locality, the work is usually done under the direction of the employer or by a specialist without supervision;

(d) the skill required in the particular occupation;

(e) whether the employer or the workman supplies the instrumentalities, tools, and the place of work for the person doing the work;

(f) the length of time for which the person is employed;

(g) the method of payment, whether by the time or by the job;

(h) whether or not the work is a part of the regular business of the employer;

(i) whether or not the parties believe they are creating the relation of master and servant; and

(j) whether the principal is or is not in business.

§ 221. Master's Consent to Service

To constitute the relation of master and servant, the one for whom the service is rendered must consent or manifest his consent to receive the services as a master.

§ 222. Servants of Agent of Undisclosed Principal

An undisclosed principal is subject to liability to third persons for conduct within the scope of employment of servants and of subservants employed for him by a servant or other agent empowered to employ them.

§ 223. Servant Required to be Taken from a Limited Class

The relation of master and servant may exist although the law requires the selection of persons for the particular work to be made from a limited class irrespective of how limited the class is, and the master is subject to liability for torts committed within the scope of employment by servants selected from such a class.

§ 224. Persons Compelled to Serve

One compelled by law or duress to render services to another has power to subject the other to liability as if there were a master and servant relation.

§ 225. Person Serving Gratuitously

One who volunteers services without an agreement for or expectation of reward may be a servant of the one accepting such services.

§ 226. Servant Acting for Two Masters

A person may be the servant of two masters, not joint employers, at one time as to one act, if the service to one does not involve abandonment of the service to the other.

§ 227. Servant Lent to Another Master

A servant directed or permitted by his master to perform services for another may become the servant of such other in performing the services. He may become the other's servant as to some acts and not as to others.

SCOPE OF EMPLOYMENT

§ 228. General Statement

(1) Conduct of a servant is within the scope of employment if, but only if:

(a)   it is of the kind he is employed to perform;

(b)   it occurs substantially within the authorized time and space limits;

(c)   it is actuated, at least in part, by a purpose to serve the master; and

(d)   if force is intentionally used by the servant against another, the use of force is not unexpectable by the master.

(2)   Conduct of a servant is not within the scope of employment if it is different in kind from that authorized, far beyond the authorized time or space limits, or too little actuated by a purpose to serve the master.

§ 229.   Kind of Conduct Within Scope of Employment

(1)   To be within the scope of the employment, conduct must be of the same general nature as that authorized, or incidental to the conduct authorized.

(2)   In determining whether or not the conduct, although not authorized, is nevertheless so similar to or incidental to the conduct authorized as to be within the scope of employment, the following matters of fact are to be considered:

(a)   whether or not the act is one commonly done by such servants;

(b)   the time, place and purpose of the act;

(c)   the previous relations between the master and the servant;

(d)   the extent to which the business of the master is apportioned between different servants;

(e)   whether or not the act is outside the enterprise of the master or, if within the enterprise, has not been entrusted to any servant;

(f)   whether or not the master has reason to expect that such an act will be done;

(g)   the similarity in quality of the act done to the act authorized;

(h)   whether or not the instrumentality by which the harm is done has been furnished by the master to the servant;

(i)   the extent of departure from the normal method of accomplishing an authorized result; and

(j)   whether or not the act is seriously criminal.

Comment a. As stated in Section 212, a master is responsible for an act or result which he intends the servant to perform or achieve if the servant acts because of his directions. Also, as stated in Section 215, a master is responsible for authorized but unintended conduct. Thus, a servant is authorized to do anything which is reasonably regarded as incidental to the work specifically directed or which is usually done in connection with such work. The scope of employment includes not only such acts but also other acts which, as between the master and servant, the servant is not privileged to do. The limits of the scope of employment are dependent upon the facts of the particular case, and no more definite statement can profitably be made concerning them than that made in Subsection (2). Since the phrase "scope of the employment," is used for the purpose of determining the liability of the master for the conduct of servants, the ultimate question is whether or not it is just that the loss resulting from the servant's acts should be considered as one of the normal risks to be borne by the business in which the servant is employed.

The factors here stated have primary reference to the physical activities of servants. The special rules which deal with situations in which the master may be liable for deceit, false arrest or attachment and similar matters are stated in Sections 246–264.

§ 230.   Forbidden Acts

An act, although forbidden, or done in a forbidden manner, may be within the scope of employment.

§ 231. Criminal or Tortious Acts

An act may be within the scope of employment although consciously criminal or tortious.

§ 232. Failure to Act

The failure of a servant to act may be conduct within the scope of employment.

§ 233. Time of Service

Conduct of a servant is within the scope of employment only during a period which has a reasonable connection with the authorized period.

§ 234. Area of Service

Conduct is within the scope of employment only in the authorized area or in a locality not unreasonably distant from it.

§ 235. Conduct Not for Purpose of Serving Master

An act of a servant is not within the scope of employment if it is done with no intention to perform it as a part of or incident to a service on account of which he is employed.

§ 236. Conduct Actuated by Dual Purpose

Conduct may be within the scope of employment, although done in part to serve the purposes of the servant or of a third person.

§ 237. Re-Entry into Employment

A servant who has temporarily departed in space or time from the scope of employment does not re-enter it until he is again reasonably near the authorized space and time limits and is acting with the intention of serving his master's business.

USE OF INSTRUMENTALITIES BY SERVANTS

§ 238. Instrumentalities Not Used in Employment

Except where he is at fault or fails to perform a nondelegable duty, a master is not liable for harm caused by the use of instrumentalities entrusted by him to a servant when they are not used in the scope of employment.

§ 239. Use of Unauthorized Instrumentality

A master is not liable for injuries caused by the negligence of a servant in the use of an instrumentality which if of a substantially different kind from that authorized as a means of performing the master's service, or over the use of which it is understood that the master is to have no right of control.

§ 240. Servant Leaves Instrumentality in Dangerous Situation

A master is subject to liability for the resulting harm if his servant, entrusted with the possession of an instrumentality, leaves it while within the scope of employment under such circumstances that an undue risk of harm to third persons is created, although the servant leaves it to serve some purpose of his own.

§ 241. Unauthorized Transfer of Custody of Instrumentality

A master who has entrusted a servant with an instrumentality is subject to liability for harm caused by its negligent management by one to whom the servant entrusts its custody to do the work the servant was employed to perform, if the servant should realize that there is an undue risk that such person will harm others by its management.

§ 242. Liability to Invitee of Servant

A master is not subject to liability for the conduct of a servant towards a person harmed as the result of accepting or soliciting from the servant an invitation, not binding upon the master, to enter or remain upon the master's premises or vehicle, although the conduct which immediately causes the harm is within the scope of the servant's employment.

SPECIFIC TORTS OF SERVANTS

§ 243. Negligence

A master is subject to liability for physical harm caused by the negligent conduct of servants within the scope of employment.

§ 244. Trespass and Conversion

A master is subject to liability for a trespass or a conversion caused by an act done by a servant within the scope of employment.

§ 245. Use of Force

A master is subject to liability for the intended tortious harm by a servant to the person or things of another by an act done in connection with the servant's employment, although the act was unauthorized, if the act was not unexpectable in view of the duties of the servant.

§ 246. Tortious Institution or Conduct of Legal Proceedings

A master is subject to liability for the tortious institution or conduct of legal proceedings by a servant acting within the scope of employment.

§ 247. Defamation

A master is subject to liability for defamatory statements made by a servant acting within the scope of his employment, or, as to those hearing or reading the statement, within his apparent authority.

§ 248. Interference with Business Relations

A master is subject to liability to third persons injured in their business relations by the tortious conduct of a servant acting within the scope of employment or, if apparent authority is relevant, acting within his apparent authority.

§ 249. Misrepresentations

A master is subject to liability for the misrepresentations of a servant causing pecuniary loss as he is for the misrepresentations of an agent who is not a servant.

TITLE C. AGENTS' TORTS; LIABILITY NOT DEPENDENT UPON RELATION OF MASTER AND SERVANT

IN GENERAL

§ 250.   Non-Liability for Physical Harm by Non-Servant Agents

A principal is not liable for physical harm caused by the negligent physical conduct of a non-servant agent during the performance of the principal's business, if he neither intended nor authorized the result nor the manner of performance, unless he was under a duty to have the act performed with due care.

§ 251.   Liability for Physical Harm Caused by a Servant or a Non-Servant Agent

A principal is subject to liability for physical harm to the person or the tangible things of another caused by the negligence of a servant or a non-servant agent:

(a)   in the performance of an act which the principal is under a duty to have performed with care; and

(b)   in the making of a representation which the agent is authorized or apparently authorized to make or which is within the power of the agent to make for the principal.

§ 252.   Mistaken Action by Agents

If a servant or other agent, authorized to do an act provided certain conditions exist, and to determine whether or not such conditions exist, does the act in the erroneous belief that such conditions do exist and thereby commits a tort, the principal is subject to liability for the act.

§ 253.   Tortious Institution or Conduct of Legal Proceedings

A principal who authorizes a servant or other agent to institute or conduct such legal proceedings as in his judgment are lawful and desirable for the protection of the principal's interests is subject to liability to a person against whom proceedings reasonably adapted to accomplish the principal's purposes are tortiously brought by the agent.

§ 254.   Defamation

A principal is subject to liability for a defamatory statement by a servant or other agent if the agent was authorized, or if, as to the person to whom he made the statement, he was apparently authorized to make it.

§ 255.   Acts of Subservants and Other Subagents

The rules applicable to the liability of a principal for the acts of agents, are applicable to his liability for subservants and other subagents insofar as their conduct has relation to the principal's affairs.

MISREPRESENTATIONS

§ 256.   Knowledge of Principal When Agent Innocently Makes a Misrepresentation

If a principal knows facts unknown to a servant or other agent and which are relevant to a transaction which the agent is authorized to conduct, and, because of his justifiable ignorance, the agent makes a material misstatement of facts, the principal:

(a)   is subject to liability for an intentional misrepresentation, if he believed the agent would make the statement, or for a negligent misrepresentation, if he had reason to know the agent would make the statement.

(b) is not subject to liability in tort if he had no reason to know that the agent would enter into such a transaction, or if, after acquiring the information, he had no way of communicating with the agent.

§ 257. Misrepresentations; In General

A principal is subject to liability for loss caused to another by the other's reliance upon a tortious representation of a servant or other agent, if the representation is:

(a) authorized;

(b) apparently authorized; or

(c) within the power of the agent to make for the principal.

Comment g. Physical harm. The rule stated in this Section applies to physical harm resulting from the misrepresentation, as well as to economic loss. Thus, an agent authorized to direct travelers causes his employer to be liable if he negligently directs them to a dangerous place in which they are harmed.

§ 258. Incidental Misrepresentations

In the absence of an exculpatory agreement, a principal authorizing a servant or other agent to enter into negotiations to which representations concerning the subject matter thereof are usually incident is subject to liability for loss caused to the other party to the transaction by tortious misrepresentations of the agent upon matters which the principal might reasonably expect would be the subject of representations, provided the other party has no notice that the representations are unauthorized.

§ 259. Rescission of Transaction for Misrepresentations of Agent

(1) A transaction into which one is induced to enter by reliance upon untrue and material representations as to the subject matter, made by a servant or other agent entrusted with its preliminary or final negotiations, is subject to rescission at the election of the person deceived.

(2) Change of position by the principal:

(a) is a defense if the agent has no power to bind the principal by the misrepresentations;

(b) is not a defense if the principal was liable for the misrepresentations.

Caveat:

No statement is made as to the defense of change of position if the misrepresentation, although within the power of the agent to make for the principal, was not tortious.

§ 260. Contracts Limiting Liability for Agent's Misrepresentations

(1) An innocent principal can, by contract with another, relieve himself of liability for deceit because of unauthorized fraud by a servant or other agent upon the other party.

(2) A contract with, or a conveyance to, the principal obtained by his agent through misrepresentations can be rescinded by the other party to the contract or conveyance prior to a change of position by the principal, even though the contract provides that "it shall not be affected by misrepresentations not contained therein" and includes a statement that the agent has made no representations.

Caveat:

The rule stated in Subsection (2) is not intended to deny the possibility that the principal and the other party can make a binding agreement that the other party shall not be able to avoid the transaction because of his reliance upon misrepresentations made by the agent.

§ 261. Agent's Position Enables Him to Deceive

A principal who puts a servant or other agent in a position which enables the agent, while apparently acting within his authority, to commit a fraud upon third persons is subject to liability to such third persons for the fraud.

Comment a. The principal is subject to liability under the rule stated in this Section although he is entirely innocent, has received no benefit from the transaction, and, as stated in Section 262, although the agent acted solely for his own purposes. Liability is based upon the fact that the agent's position facilitates the consummation of the fraud, in that from the point of view of the third person the transaction seems regular on its face and the agent appears to be acting in the ordinary course of the business confided to him.

§ 262. Agent Acts for His Own Purposes

A person who otherwise would be liable to another for the misrepresentations of one apparently acting for him is not relieved from liability by the fact that the servant or other agent acts entirely for his own purposes, unless the other has notice of this.

§ 263. Property Acquired for Principal by Fraud of Agent

Unless he has changed his position, a principal whose servant or other agent has fraudulently acquired property for him, holds it subject to the interests of the defrauded person. If the principal is liable in tort for the fraud of the agent, his change of position after acquiring the property is not a defense.

§ 264. Misrepresentations by Subservants and Other Subagents

The rules applicable to representations by servants and other agents are applicable to representations by subservants and other subagents made in connection with transactions conducted for the principal.

TITLE D. CONDUCT WITHIN APPARENT AUTHORITY OR EMPLOYMENT

§ 265. General Rule

(1) A master or other principal is subject to liability for torts which result from reliance upon, or belief in, statements or other conduct within an agent's apparent authority.

(2) Unless there has been reliance, the principal is not liable in tort for conduct of a servant or other agent merely because it is within his apparent authority or apparent scope of employment.

§ 266. Physical Harm Caused by Reliance Upon Representations

A purported master or other principal is subject to liability for physical harm caused to others or to their belongings by their reasonable reliance upon the tortious representations of one acting within his apparent authority or apparent scope of employment.

§ 267. Reliance upon Care or Skill of Apparent Servant or Other Agent

One who represents that another is his servant or other agent and thereby causes a third person justifiably to rely upon the care or skill of such apparent agent is subject to liability to the third person for harm caused by the lack of care or skill of the one appearing to be a servant or other agent as if he were such.

Chapter 8

LIABILITY OF PRINCIPAL TO THIRD PERSONS; NOTICE THROUGH AGENT

TOPIC 1. NOTIFICATION TO OR BY AGENTS

§ 268. General Rule

(1) Unless the notifier has notice that the agent has an interest adverse to the principal, a notification given to an agent is notice to the principal if it is given:

(a) to an agent authorized to receive it;

(b) to an agent apparently authorized to receive it;

(c) to an agent authorized to conduct a transaction, with respect to matters connected with it as to which notice is usually given to such an agent, unless the one giving the notification has notice that the agent is not authorized to receive it;

(d) to an agent to whom by the terms of a contract notification is to be given, with reference to matters in connection with the contract; or

(e) to the agent of an unidentified or undisclosed principal with reference to transactions entered into by such agent within his powers, until discovery of the identity of the principal; thereafter as in the case of a disclosed principal.

(2) The rules as to the giving of notification to an agent apply to the giving of notification by an agent.

§ 269. Time When Notification Must Be Given

To be effective as notice, a notification must be given to or by an agent during the time when the agent I as power to affect his principal by giving or receiving such notification.

§ 270. Time When Notice Results

Notice results when the act or event constituting notification is performed or happens.

§ 271. Notification; Agent's Interests Adverse to Principal's

A notification by or to a third person to or by an agent is not prevented from being notice to or by the principal because of the fact that the agent, when receiving or giving the notification, is acting adversely to the principal, unless the third person has notice of the agent's adverse purposes.

TOPIC 2. KNOWLEDGE OF AGENTS

§ 272. General Rule

In accordance with and subject to the rules stated in this Topic, the liability of a principal is affected by the knowledge of an agent concerning a matter as to which he acts within his power to bind the principal or upon which it is his duty to give the principal information.

Comment b. Where agent has reason to know or should know. In situations in which knowledge of a particular fact is relevant to the legal liability of participants in an event, their liability is often affected by their having knowledge of other facts from which persons of ordinary intelligence and prudence would infer the existence of the fact in question or would be led to make such inquiries as would give them knowledge of it. In such cases they have reason to know the fact in question or they should know of it. The Comment on Section 9 indicates the meaning of these phrases and gives illustrations of situations in which knowledge is important in a variety of situations. If an agent has reason to know or should know a particular fact, the principal is affected as if the circumstances were such that the principal would have reason to know or should know the fact, subject to the rules stated in Sections 274–282.

§ 273.   Agent Having Apparent Authority

Except where there is reliance upon the appearance of agency, a principal is not bound by knowledge of an agent concerning matters as to which he has only apparent authority.

§ 274.   Agent Acquiring Property for Principal

The knowledge of an agent who acquires property for his principal affects the interests of his principal in the subject matter to the same extent as if the principal had acquired it with the same knowledge, except where the agent is privileged not to disclose or to act upon the knowledge, or a change in conditions makes it inequitable thus to affect the principal.

§ 275.   Agent Having Duty to Reveal Knowledge

Except where the agent is acting adversely to the principal or where knowledge as distinguished from reason to know is important, the principal is affected by the knowledge which an agent has a duty to disclose to the principal or to another agent of the principal to the same extent as if the principal had the information.

§ 276.   Time, Place or Manner of Acquisition of Agent's Knowledge

Except for knowledge acquired confidentially, the time, place, or manner in which knowledge is acquired by a servant or other agent is immaterial in determining the liability of his principal because of it.

§ 277.   Agent Who Should, but Does Not, Have Knowledge

The principal is not affected by the knowledge which an agent should have acquired in the performance of the agent's duties to the principal or to others, except where the principal or master has a duty to others that care shall be exercised in obtaining information.

§ 278.   Time When Agent's Knowledge Affects Principal

The principal is affected by the knowledge which the agent has when acting for him or, if it is the duty of the agent to communicate the information and not otherwise to act, the principal is affected after the lapse of such time as is reasonable for its communication.

§ 279.   Agent Dealing with Principal as Adverse Party

The principal is not affected by the knowledge of an agent as to matters involved in a transaction in which the agent deals with the principal or another agent of the principal as, or on account of, an adverse party.

§ 280.   Agent's Knowledge of His Own Unauthorized Acts

If an agent has done an unauthorized act or intends to do one, the principal is not affected by the agent's knowledge that he has done or intends to do the act.

§ 281.   Agent Privileged Not to Disclose Knowledge

A principal is not affected by the knowledge of an agent who is privileged not to disclose or act upon it and who does not disclose or act upon it.

§ 282.   Agent Acting Adversely to Principal

(1)   A principal is not affected by the knowledge of an agent in a transaction in which the agent secretly is acting adversely to the principal and entirely for his own or another's purposes, except as stated in Subsection (2).

(2)   The principal is affected by the knowledge of an agent who acts adversely to the principal:

(a)   if the failure of the agent to act upon or to reveal the information results in a violation of a contractual or relational duty of the principal to a person harmed thereby;

(b)   if the agent enters into negotiations within the scope of his powers and the person with whom he deals reasonably believes him to be authorized to conduct the transaction; or

(c)   if, before he has changed his position, the principal knowingly retains a benefit through the act of the agent which otherwise he would not have received.

TOPIC 3.   SERVANTS AND SUBAGENTS

§ 283.   General Rule

The rules stated in this chapter which state the rules which apply to the liability of a principal because of notice through an agent apply to the liability:

(a)   of a master or other principal because of the knowledge of, or notification to, a servant, subservant or other subagent which the servant or subagent had a duty to act upon or to communicate to the agent or to the principal because of his employment or apparent employment.

(b)   of a master or other principal because of a notification given by a servant, subservant or other subagent.

Chapter 9

ADMISSIBILITY IN EVIDENCE OF STATEMENTS OF AGENTS

§ 284.   Operative and Relevant Statements

In actions between the principal and third persons, evidence of a statement by an agent is admissible for or against either party for the purpose of proving that such statement was made, if the fact that the statement was made constitutes, or is relevant in the proof of, one of the ultimate facts required to be established in order to maintain a cause of action or defense.

§ 285.   Statements as to Authority

Evidence of a statement by an agent concerning the existence or extent of his authority is not admissible against the principal to prove its existence or extent, unless it appears by other evidence that the making of such statement was within the authority of the agent or, as to persons dealing with the agent, within the apparent authority or other power of the agent.

§ 286.   Statement to Third Persons Constituting Admissions

In an action between the principal and a third person, statements of an agent to a third person are admissible in evidence against the principal to prove the truth of facts asserted in them as though made by the principal, if the agent was authorized to make the statement or was authorized to make, on the principal's behalf, any statements concerning the subject matter.

§ 287. Reports to Principal

Statements by an agent to the principal or to another agent of the principal are not admissible against the principal as admissions; such statements may be admissible in evidence under other rules of evidence.

§ 288. When Agent Has Authority to Make Statements

(1) The general rules concerning the interpretation of authority are applicable in determining whether an agent has authority to make statements concerning operative or other facts.

(2) Authority to do an act or to conduct a transaction does not of itself include authority to make statements concerning the act or transaction.

(3) Authority to make statements of fact does not of itself include authority to make statements admitting liability because of such facts.

§ 289. Statements Admissible Under General Rules of Evidence

Evidence of statements of agents, whether or not such statements are authorized, is admissible in favor of and against the principal, if admissible under the general rules of evidence as to the admissibility of such statements by persons not agents.

§ 290. Ratification of Agent's Statements

If a statement would be admissible in evidence because made in the course of authorized conduct, such a statement made by a person purporting to act for another or intending to serve another, is admissible if the person on whose behalf the statement was made or was purported to have been made, ratifies the conduct.

§ 291. Statements of Servants and Subagents

The rules dealing with the admissibility of statements by agents apply to the admissibility of statements by servants, subservants and other subagents with reference to transactions conducted for the principal by them.

Chapter 10

LIABILITY OF THIRD PERSON TO PRINCIPAL

TOPIC 1. CONTRACTS; DISCLOSED AGENCY

§ 292. General Rule

The other party to a contract made by an agent for a disclosed or partially disclosed principal, acting within his authority, apparent authority or other agency power, is liable to the principal as if he had contracted directly with the principal, unless the principal is excluded as a party by the form or terms of the contract.

§ 293. Principal Excluded from Transaction

The other party to a contract made by an agent on behalf of a disclosed or partially disclosed principal does not become liable to such principal upon it in an action at law if the principal is excluded as a party by the form or terms of the contract.

§ 294. Orders of Several Principals Combined

Unless otherwise agreed between the principals and the agent, the other party to a contract made by an agent who has been authorized by several disclosed or partially disclosed principals to act for them separately, but who combines their orders and purports to contract for them jointly, is not liable in an action at law brought upon the contract by one of them alone.

§ 295. Negotiable Instruments

An obligor upon a negotiable instrument given to an agent on account of a principal not named or described therein is not liable to the principal in an action at law upon the instrument, unless the principal is an endorsee or otherwise becomes a holder.

§ 296. Sealed Instruments

In the absence of statute, an obligor named in a sealed instrument given to an agent on behalf of the principal is not liable to the principal upon it in an action at law unless the principal appears therein as a covenantee.

§ 297. Interpretation of Written Instruments as to Parties

The rules with respect to the interpretation of written instruments as to the parties to them in actions brought against the principal by the person with whom the agent dealt are applicable in actions brought by the principal against the third person.

§ 298. Defenses of Other Party

The other party to a contract made by an agent on behalf of a disclosed or partially disclosed principal has all the defenses which he would have had against the principal if the principal had made the contract under the same circumstances.

§ 299. Rights Between Other Party and Agent

Unless otherwise agreed, the liability of the other party to a disclosed or partially disclosed principal upon a contract made by an agent is not affected by any rights or liabilities then existing between the other party and the agent.

§ 300. Dealings and Actions Between Agent and Other Party Subsequent to the Transaction

The liability of one who has contracted with an agent for a disclosed or partially disclosed principal is affected by:

    (a)   subsequent dealings between him and the agent

        (i)   which bind the principal because of the agent's authority or other power, or

        (ii)   which are in derogation of the principal's rights as a contracting party.

    (b)   a judgment in an action between him and the agent.

§ 301. Unauthorized Assignment of Contract by Agent

If a document evidencing a contract which an agent has made with another on behalf of the principal is in such form that the principal has reason to believe that third persons may reasonably believe the agent to be the owner of the contract or to have power of disposition of it, and if the agent had power to bind the principal by a contract in that form, the claim of the principal against the other party is destroyed by the agent's unauthorized transfer to a bona fide purchaser of the rights against the other party under the contract.

TOPIC 2. CONTRACTS; UNDISCLOSED AGENCY

§ 302.   General Rule

A person who makes a contract with an agent of an undisclosed principal, intended by the agent to be on account of his principal and within the power of such agent to bind his principal, is liable to the principal as if the principal himself had made the contract with him, unless he is excluded by the form or terms of the contract, unless his existence is fraudulently concealed or unless there is set-off or a similar defense against the agent.

§ 303.   Principal Excluded from Transaction

A person with whom an agent makes a contract on account of an undisclosed principal is not liable in an action at law brought upon the contract by such principal:

(a)   if the contract is in the form of a sealed or negotiable instrument; or

(b)   if the terms of the contract exclude liability to any undisclosed principal or to the particular principal.

§ 304.   Agent Misrepresents Existence of Principal

A person with whom an agent contracts on account of an undisclosed principal can rescind the contract if he was induced to enter into it by a representation that the agent was not acting for a principal and if, as the agent or principal had notice, he would not have dealt with the principal.

§ 305.   Orders of Several Principals Combined

Unless otherwise agreed between the principal and the agent, the other party to a contract made by an agent for several undisclosed principals who have not jointly authorized him is not liable in an action at law upon the contract brought by one of them alone.

§ 306.   Rights Between Other Party and Agent

(1)   If the agent has been authorized to conceal the existence of the principal, the liability to an undisclosed principal of a person dealing with the agent within his power to bind the principal is diminished by any claim which such person may have against the agent at the time of making the contract and until the existence of the principal becomes known to him, if he could set off such claim in an action against the agent.

(2)   If the agent is authorized only to contract in the principal's name, the other party does not have set-off for a claim due him from the agent unless the agent has been entrusted with the possession of chattels which he disposes of as directed or unless the principal has otherwise misled the third person into extending credit to the agent.

§ 307.   Dealings and Actions Between Agent and Other Party Subsequent to Transaction

(1)   When an agent has made a contract for an undisclosed principal:

(a)   until the existence of the principal is known, the agent has power to rescind, perform and receive performance of the contract and to modify it with binding effect, if the contract or conveyance, as modified, is within his agency powers.

(b)   after the principal's existence is known, the agent has the same powers with reference to the contract as if the principal had been originally disclosed or partially disclosed.

(2)   A judgment for or against the agent either before or after the principal's existence is known may increase, decrease or terminate the claim of the principal.

§ 307A.   Unauthorized Assignment by Agent

If an agent assigns an assignable contract which he has made for an undisclosed principal to one who pays value and has no notice of the principal's interests, the transferee is entitled to the contract.

§ 308.   Defenses of Other Party

In an action by an undisclosed principal against the other party to a contract, the other party has all the defenses, except those of a purely procedural nature:

    (a)   which he would have had against the principal if the principal had made the contract under the same circumstances,

    (b)   which he had against the agent until the discovery of the principal, unless the agent was authorized to contract only in the principal's name.

§ 309.   Principal Cannot or Does Not Give Required Performance

Acts done or offered to be done by an undisclosed principal which, if performed by a person other than the agent, are not substantially those which the contract contemplates, are not effective as a performance or as a tender of performance of the contract.

§ 310.   When Performance Must Be Rendered to Principal

An undisclosed principal upon whose account an agent has acted within his power to bind the principal in making a contract, unless he is excluded by its terms, can require the other party to render performance to him instead of to the agent, except in the case of personal services or where performance to the principal would subject the other to a substantially different liability from that contemplated.

TOPIC 3.   NON-CONTRACTUAL LIABILITY

§ 311.   Mistaken Dealing with Unauthorized Agent

A person with whom an agent deals in excess of his power to subject the principal to liability or to affect the principal's interests is not relieved from liability to the principal for interference with the principal's interests by such dealing because of a reasonable belief that the agent was authorized or was the owner of the subject matter.

§ 312.   Intentionally Causing or Assisting Agent to Violate Duty

A person who, without being privileged to do so, intentionally causes or assists an agent to violate a duty to his principal is subject to liability to the principal.

§ 313.   Adversely Employing Agent of Another

(1)   A person who, knowing that the other party to a transaction has employed an agent to conduct a transaction for him, employs the agent on his own account in such transaction is subject to liability to the other party, unless he reasonably believes that the other party acquiesces in the double employment.

(2)   If without knowledge of the common agency, two persons employ the same agent to conduct a transaction between them, the transaction is voidable at the election of either.

§ 314.   Restitutional Liability

A person who receives the principal's property from an agent of another, with notice that the agent is thereby committing a breach of fiduciary duty to the principal, holds the property thus acquired as a constructive trustee, or at the election of the principal, is subject to liability for its value; one who receives such property, non-tortiously and without notice, but who is not a bona fide purchaser, is subject to liability to the extent to which he has been unjustly enriched.

§ 315.   Third Person Fraudulent

A person who fraudulently obtains a contract through, or enters into a transaction with, an agent acting within the scope of his power to bind the principal, or who by fraud causes the agent to do what would be a violation of his duty to the principal if the agent knew the facts, is subject to liability to the principal whether the fraud is practiced upon the agent or upon the principal.

§ 316.   Interference with, or Harm Caused to, Servants or Other Agents

(1)   A person who, not being privileged to do so, intentionally interferes with the performance of the principal's business by the agent is subject to liability to the principal for the harm thereby caused to him.

(2)   A person who tortiously causes physical harm to an agent not a servant is not thereby liable to the principal for the harm thereby caused to him.

§ 317.   Contributory Negligence of Agent

The contributory negligence of an agent acting within the scope of his power to bind his principal by his conduct bars the principal from recovery against a third person to the same extent as if the principal had been negligent.

§ 317A.   Indemnity and Contribution from Another Principal

(1)   Unless otherwise agreed between them, one of two principals who has made expenditures because of the conduct of a common agent is entitled to

(a)   contribution from the other principal if, as between the two, each was equally responsible for the agent's conduct, or

(b)   indemnity from the other principal if the agent's conduct was the result of a breach of duty to the plaintiff by the other principal.

(2)   If the negligence or fraud of two servants or other agents of different principals unites in causing injury to a third person, one of the principals is entitled to indemnity or contribution from the other for amounts paid in compensation for the injury, in accordance with the rules stated in the Restatement of Restitution.

TOPIC 4.   SERVANTS, SUBSERVANTS AND OTHER SUBAGENTS

§ 318.   General Rule

The rules which apply to the liability of a third person to principals generally are applicable to his liability to a master or other principal on whose account a servant, subservant or other subagent has acted or purported to act.

TOPIC 5.   EFFECT OF RATIFICATION

§ 319.   General Rule

Where a purported servant or other agent has entered into a transaction with a third person, its ratification by the purported master or other principal has the same effect upon the liabilities of the third person to the principal as an original authorization.

Chapter 11

LIABILITY OF AGENT TO THIRD PERSONS

TOPIC 1. CONTRACTS AND CONVEYANCES

TITLE A. AGENT A PARTY TO A TRANSACTION CONDUCTED BY HIMSELF

§ 320. Principal Disclosed

Unless otherwise agreed, a person making or purporting to make a contract with another as agent for a disclosed principal does not become a party to the contract.

§ 321. Principal Partially Disclosed

Unless otherwise agreed, a person purporting to make a contract with another for a partially disclosed principal is a party to the contract.

§ 322. Principal Undisclosed

An agent purporting to act upon his own account, but in fact making a contract on account of an undisclosed principal, is a party to the contract.

§ 323. Integrated Contracts

(1)   If it appears unambiguously in an integrated contract that the agent is a party or is not a party, extrinsic evidence is not admissible to show a contrary intent, except for the purpose of reforming the contract.

(2)   If the fact of agency appears in an integrated contract, not sealed or negotiable, and there is no unambiguous expression of an intention either to make the agent a party thereto or not to make him a party thereto, extrinsic evidence can be introduced to show the intention of the parties.

(3)   If the fact of agency does not appear in an integrated contract, an agent who appears to be a party thereto can not introduce extrinsic evidence to show that he is not a party, except:

(a)   for the purpose of reforming the contract; or

(b)   to establish that his name was signed as the business name of the principal and that it was so agreed by the parties.

§ 324. Negotiable Instruments

(1)   In the absence of reformation, an agent signing a negotiable instrument in his own name is a party to it although the fact of agency appears upon it, unless the name of the principal also appears.

(2)   An agent is not liable as a party to a negotiable instrument on which the name of the principal appears if it is interpreted as being executed by the agent only on behalf of such principal and if the agent has power to bind the principal.

(3)   If the name of the principal appears upon a negotiable instrument and the agent does not appear unambiguously as a party, extrinsic evidence of an understanding that the agent shall not be a party to it is admissible as against any holder of the instrument who has notice of the agreement or who is not a holder in due course.

74

§ 325. Sealed Instruments

An agent is not liable as a party to a sealed instrument unless he is named as covenantor in the instrument which also purports to be sealed by him. If these facts appear unambiguously, extrinsic evidence is not admissible to show that it was agreed that he should be a party, except for the purpose of reforming the instrument.

§ 326. Principal Known to Be Nonexistent or Incompetent

Unless otherwise agreed, a person who, in dealing with another, purports to act as agent for a principal whom both know to be nonexistent or wholly incompetent, becomes a party to such a contract.

§ 327. Interpretation of Written Instruments as to Parties

The rules with respect to the interpretation of written instruments as to the parties thereto in actions brought against the principal by the third person are applicable in actions brought by the third person against the agent.

TITLE B. AGENT NOT PARTY TO TRANSACTION CONDUCTED BY HIMSELF

§ 328. Liability of Authorized Agent for Performance of Contract

An agent, by making a contract only on behalf of a competent disclosed or partially disclosed principal whom he has power so to bind, does not thereby become liable for its nonperformance.

§ 329. Agent Who Warrants Authority

A person who purports to make a contract, conveyance or representation on behalf of another who has full capacity but whom he has no power to bind, thereby becomes subject to liability to the other party thereto upon an implied warranty of authority, unless he has manifested that he does not make such warranty or the other party knows that the agent is not so authorized.

§ 330. Liability for Misrepresentation of Authority

A person who tortiously misrepresents to another that he has authority to make a contract, conveyance, or representation on behalf of a principal whom he has no power to bind, is subject to liability to the other in an action of tort for loss caused by reliance upon such misrepresentation.

§ 331. Agent Making No Warranty or Representation of Authority

A person who purports to make a contract, conveyance or representation on behalf of a principal whom he has no power to bind thereby is not subject to liability to the other party thereto if he sufficiently manifests that he does not warrant his authority and makes no tortious misrepresentation.

§ 332. Agent of Partially Incompetent Principal

An agent making a contract for a disclosed principal whose contracts are voidable because of lack of full capacity to contract, or for a principal who, although having capacity to contract generally, is incompetent to enter into the particular transaction, is not thereby liable to the other party. He does not become liable by reason of the failure of the principal to perform, unless he contracts or represents that the principal has capacity or unless he has reason to know of the principal's lack of capacity and of the other party's ignorance thereof.

TITLE C. DEFENSES AND EFFECTS OF
SUBSEQUENT EVENTS

§ 333.　Rights Between Other Party and Principal

Unless otherwise agreed, the liability of an agent upon a contract between a third person and the principal to which the agent is a party is not affected by any rights or liabilities existing between the third person and the principal not arising from the transaction, except that, with the consent of the principal, the agent can set off a claim which the principal would have in an action brought against him.

§ 334.　Defenses of Agent; In General

In an action against an agent upon a contract between a third person and the principal to which the agent is a party, the agent has all the defenses which arise out of the transaction itself and also those which he has personally against the third person; defenses which are personal to the principal are not available to the agent.

§ 335.　Agent Surety for Principal

In an action brought against an agent upon a contract to which the agent is a party but under which the primary duty of performance rests upon the principal, the agent has the defenses available to a surety.

§ 336.　Election by Other Party to Hold Principal; Agency Disclosed

Unless otherwise agreed, the agent of a disclosed or partially disclosed principal who is a party to a contract made by another with such principal is not relieved from liability upon the contract by the determination of the other party to look to the principal alone, nor, unless the agent and the principal are joint contractors, by the fact that the other gets a judgment against the principal. He is relieved from liability to the extent that he is prejudiced thereby if he changes his position in justifiable reliance upon a manifestation of the other that he will look solely to the principal for performance.

§ 337.　Election by Other Party to Hold Principal; Agency Undisclosed

An agent who has made a contract on behalf of an undisclosed principal is not relieved from liability by the determination of the other party thereto to look to the principal alone for the performance of the contract. He is discharged from liability if the other obtains a judgment against the principal, or, to the extent that he is prejudiced thereby, if he changes his position in justifiable reliance upon the other's manifestation that he will look solely to the principal for payment.

§ 338.　Effect of Ratification

Ratification by a principal of a contract which an agent without authority purported to make for the principal terminates the liability of the agent to the other party for the breach of warranty or misrepresentation of authority.

TOPIC 2. THINGS RECEIVED FROM
OR FOR PRINCIPAL

TITLE A. THINGS RECEIVED FROM THIRD PERSON

§ 339.　Other Party Rescinds for Cause Existing at Time of Transaction; Principal Disclosed or Partially Disclosed

An agent who has received things from another for a disclosed or partially disclosed principal in a transaction conducted by him has a duty to return them or their proceeds if the other rescinds the transaction for a cause existing at the time of their receipt, to the extent that the agent has not, before notice of rescission and in good faith, changed his position.

§ 340. Other Party Rescinds for Cause Arising After Transaction; Principal Disclosed or Partially Disclosed

If an agent receives things on behalf of a disclosed or partially disclosed principal by a transaction to which he is not a party and the other party rescinds the transaction for a cause arising after the things have been received, the agent does not thereby have a duty to return them.

§ 341. Other Party Rescinds; Principal Undisclosed

An agent who has received things from another on behalf of an undisclosed principal has a duty to return them or their proceeds upon rescission of the transaction, under the same circumstances as if the agent had acted upon his own account, except that payment by the agent to the principal does not constitute such a change of position as relieves the agent from liability to the other.

TITLE B. THINGS RECEIVED FROM PRINCIPAL

§ 342. General Rule

(1) An agent who receives money or other thing from his principal to pay or transfer to another person is not thereby liable to the other.

(2) An agent whose promise to pay is primarily for the benefit of a third person may be liable in an action of contract to the third person for his failure to perform his promise.

(3) If an agent receives money in trust from the principal for the benefit of another, the agent is liable as a trustee to the other.

TOPIC 3. TORTS

§ 343. General Rule

An agent who does an act otherwise a tort is not relieved from liability by the fact that he acted at the command of the principal or on account of the principal, except where he is exercising a privilege of the principal, or a privilege held by him for the protection of the principal's interests, or where the principal owes no duty or less than the normal duty of care to the person harmed.

§ 344. Liability for Directed Conduct or Consequences

An agent is subject to liability, as he would be for his own personal conduct, for the consequences of another's conduct which results from his directions if, with knowledge of the circumstances, he intends the conduct, or its consequences, except where the agent or the one acting has a privilege or immunity not available to the other.

§ 345. Agent Exercising Privileges of Principal

An agent is privileged to do what otherwise would constitute a tort if his principal is privileged to have an agent do it and has authorized the agent to do it.

§ 346. Privilege to Protect Principal's Interests

An agent is privileged to give such protection to the person or property of his principal as is authorized by the principal to the same extent as the principal is privileged to act in the protection of himself or his property.

§ 347.   Immunities and Standard of Care of Principal

(1)   An agent does not have the immunities of his principal although acting at the direction of the principal.

(2)   Where, because of his relation to a third person, a master owes no duty, or a diminished duty, of care, a servant in the performance of his master's work owes no greater duty, unless there has been reliance by the master or by a third person upon a greater undertaking by the servant.

§ 348.   Fraud and Duress

An agent who fraudulently makes representations, uses duress, or knowingly assists in the commission of tortious fraud or duress by his principal or by others is subject to liability in tort to the injured person although the fraud or duress occurs in a transaction on behalf of the principal.

§ 348A.   Trespass to Land

An agent who enters the land of another is not relieved from liability for trespass by the fact that he acted on account of the principal and reasonably believed that the principal had possession or the right to possession of the land, or the right to authorize the agent to enter.

§ 349.   Conversion

An agent who does acts which would otherwise constitute trespass to or conversion of a chattel is not relieved from liability by the fact that he acts on account of his principal and reasonably, although mistakenly, believes that the principal is entitled to possession of the chattels.

§ 350.   Negligent Action

An agent is subject to liability if, by his acts, he creates an unreasonable risk of harm to the interests of others protected against negligent invasion.

§ 351.   Directing or Permitting Negligent Conduct of Others

An agent who directs or permits conduct of another under such circumstances that he should realize that there is an unreasonable risk of physical harm to others or to their belongings is subject to liability for harm resulting from a risk which his direction or permission creates.

§ 352.   Agent's Failure to Perform Duties to Principal; In General

An agent is not liable for harm to a person other than his principal because of his failure adequately to perform his duties to his principal, unless physical harm results from reliance upon performance of the duties by the agent, or unless the agent has taken control of land or other tangible things.

§ 353.   Failure to Act Intending to Cause Physical Harm

An agent entrusted by his principal with a duty to act for the protection of others or their tangible things is subject to liability to such others for physical harm caused to them or to their things by his assumption of duty and subsequent unprivileged failure so to act intending harm to result, if the result would not have happened but for his assumption of the duty.

§ 354.   Agent's Negligent Failure After Undertaking Protection of Others

An agent who, by promise or otherwise, undertakes to act for his principal under such circumstances that some action is necessary for the protection of the person or tangible things of another, is subject to liability to the other for physical harm to him or to his things caused by the reliance of the principal or of the other upon his undertaking and his subsequent unexcused failure to act, if such failure creates an unreasonable risk of harm to him and the agent should so realize.

Caveat:

If the agent has not entered upon performance, it is not clear that liability will result from the agent's subsequent failure of performance.

§ 355. Agent as Custodian

An agent who has the custody of land or chattels and who should realize that there is an undue risk that their condition will cause harm to the person, land, or chattels of others is subject to liability for such harm caused during the continuance of his custody, by his failure to use care to take such reasonable precautions as he is authorized to take.

§ 356. Agent in Control of Third Persons

An agent who has taken control over the conduct of another who, as he should realize, is likely to cause physical harm to the person or tangible belongings of third persons unless the conduct of the other is controlled, is under a duty to use reasonable care to take such measures of control as he is authorized to take.

§ 357. Conduct Causing Harm to Pecuniary Interests of Third Persons

An agent who intentionally or negligently fails to perform duties to his principal is not thereby liable to a person whose economic interests are thereby harmed.

§ 358. Liability for Conduct of Other Agents

(1) The agent of a disclosed or partially disclosed principal is not subject to liability for the conduct of other agents unless he is at fault in appointing, supervising, or cooperating with them.

(2) An agent employing servants or other agents for the principal not revealing to them the existence of the principal, is subject to liability to third persons for their torts as is any other principal; if he reveals the existence of a principal to them, but not to third persons, he is subject to liability for their torts only to persons who have dealt with such agents in reliance upon their apparent employment.

§ 359. Liability to Other Agents

The liability of a servant or other agent to a fellow servant or other agent employed by the employer is the same as to third persons.

§ 359A. Liability of Agents for Crimes

A servant or other agent is not relieved from criminal liability for conduct otherwise a crime because of a command by his principal.

TOPIC 4. SUBSEQUENT EVENTS

§ 359B. Dealings and Actions Between Injured Party and Principal

The liability of an agent for tortious conduct for which his principal is liable may be affected by:

(a) dealings between the injured party and the principal, or

(b) a judgment for or against the principal.

§ 359C. Joinder of Principal and Agent

(1) Principal and agent can be joined in one action for a wrong resulting from the tortious conduct of an agent or that of agent and principal, and a judgment can issue against each.

(2)   If the action is based solely upon the tortious conduct of the agent, a judgment on the merits for the agent and against the principal, or a smaller judgment for compensatory damages against the agent than against the principal, is erroneous.

§ 360.   Effect of Ratification

Ratification releases a purported agent from liability to a third person for conduct which was tortious with respect to him only because the agent had no power to bind the principal thereby; ratification does not release the agent from liability for conduct which would have been tortious although authorized.

TOPIC 5.   SERVANTS, SUBSERVANTS AND OTHER SUBAGENTS

§ 361.   Liability of Servants, Subservants and Other Subagents

The rules as to the liability of agents to third persons are applicable to the liability of servants, subservants and other subagents.

§ 362.   Liability of Agent for Conduct of Servants, Subservants and Other Subagents

The liability of an agent to third persons for the conduct of his servants, subservants and other subagents is the same as that of a master or other principal for the conduct of his servants and other agents.

Chapter 12

LIABILITY OF THIRD PERSON TO AGENT

TOPIC 1.   ACTIONS BY AGENT ON BEHALF OF PRINCIPAL

TITLE A.   WHEN AGENT CAN SUE IN HIS OWN

§ 363.   Contracts; General Rule

An agent who makes a contract on behalf of a principal cannot maintain an action thereon in his own name on behalf of the principal although authorized by the principal to bring suit, unless the agent is a promisee or transferee.

§ 364.   Contracts; Agent a Party Promisee

A person with whom an agent makes a contract on behalf of a principal is subject to liability in an action brought thereon by the agent in his own name on behalf of the principal if the agent is a party promisee.

§ 365.   Agent as Transferee of Contract

Subject to defenses, an agent to whom a negotiable instrument or other contract has been transferred can maintain an action upon it for the principal's benefit as any other transferee can do, unless this is prevented by statutes providing that only the real party in interest can maintain an action.

§ 366.   Rescission or Reformation of Contracts

The other party to a contract of which the agent is a party promisee is subject to liability in an action brought by the agent in his own name on behalf of the principal for its rescission or reformation, or in other actions based upon its rescission.

§ 367.   Possessory Actions

A person who tortiously interferes with the possession or right to possession of chattels held by an agent on behalf of his principal is subject to liability in an action brought by the agent in his own name.

§ 367A.   Misdelivery by Agent

An agent authorized to deliver goods for his principal to a third person and who by mistake delivers them to one not entitled to them can maintain an action against such person for their recovery or value.

TITLE B.   DEFENSES

§ 368.   General Rule

In an action brought by an agent in his own name on behalf of his principal, the other party to the contract has all the defenses which would be available to him if the action were brought by the principal, except procedural defenses based upon the personal inability of the principal to maintain the action or, in the case of contracts, defenses based upon the fact that the principal is excluded as a party thereto by its form or terms.

§ 369.   Agent Who Has Acted Without Authority

A person who, without power to do so, purports to bind a disclosed or partially disclosed principal as a party to a contract cannot, even though he is a party thereto and offers to perform it, maintain an action thereon against the other party to it, unless the purported principal ratifies it.

§ 370.   Agent Without Authority to Maintain Suit

In an action upon a contract brought by an agent for the benefit of the principal, it is a defense that the agent does not have authority from the principal to sue or to continue the action.

§ 371.   Set-Off Against Agent

In an action upon a contract brought by an agent for the benefit of a disclosed or partially disclosed principal, the other party to the contract can set off claims which he could set off against the principal if the action were brought by him; and only such claims.

TOPIC 2.   ACTIONS BY AGENT ON HIS OWN BEHALF

§ 372.   Agent as Owner of Contract Right

(1)   Unless otherwise agreed, an agent who has or who acquires an interest in a contract which he makes on behalf of his principal can, although not a promisee, maintain such action thereon as might a transferee having a similar interest.

(2)   An agent does not have such an interest in a contract as to entitle him to maintain an action at law upon it in his own name merely because he is entitled to a portion of the proceeds as compensation for making it or because he is liable for its breach.

§ 373.   Actions for Restitution

A person to whom an agent delivers money or goods belonging to his principal, or on account of his principal, is subject to liability to the agent for their retention if such person is thereby unjustly enriched at the expense of the agent.

§ 374.   Actions of Tort by Agents Against Third Persons

(1)   The fact that an act, otherwise a tort upon an agent, is committed by another while the agent is conducting the affairs of the principal, or because of the agency relation, does not prevent the agent from maintaining an action against the other on his own account.

(2)   A servant or other agent has no action of tort because another has tortiously harmed the principal or destroyed his business, unless the other acted for the purpose of harming the agent's interests.

(3)   A servant or other agent has a cause of action against one who, without privilege, purposely causes the principal not to perform his contract of employment or not to continue the employment.

§ 375.   Defenses

(1)   An agent who acquires the beneficial interest in a contract which he has made or purported to make for a principal is subject to the same defenses by the other party thereto, as is any assignee of such contract.

(2)   The agreement of an agent with another, in violation of his duties of loyalty to his principal, is unenforceable.

Chapter 13

DUTIES AND LIABILITIES OF AGENT TO PRINCIPAL

TOPIC 1.   DUTIES

TITLE A.   EFFECT OF MANIFESTATIONS OF CONSENT BETWEEN PRINCIPAL AND AGENT

§ 376.   General Rule

The existence and extent of the duties of the agent to the principal are determined by the terms of the agreement between the parties, interpreted in light of the circumstances under which it is made, except to the extent that fraud, duress, illegality, or the incapacity of one or both of the parties to the agreement modifies it or deprives it of legal effect.

TITLE B.   DUTIES OF SERVICE AND OBEDIENCE

§ 377.   Contractual Duties

A person who makes a contract with another to perform services as an agent for him is subject to a duty to act in accordance with his promise.

§ 378.   Gratuitous Undertakings

One who, by a gratuitous promise or other conduct which he should realize will cause another reasonably to rely upon the performance of definite acts of service by him as the other's agent, causes the other to refrain from having such acts done by other available means is subject to a duty to use care to perform such service or, while other means are available, to give notice that he will not perform.

Caveat:

When the gratuitous agent has not entered upon performance, it is not clear that liability will be imposed.

§ 379. Duty of Care and Skill

(1) Unless otherwise agreed, a paid agent is subject to a duty to the principal to act with standard care and with the skill which is standard in the locality for the kind of work which he is employed to perform and, in addition, to exercise any special skill that he has.

(2) Unless otherwise agreed, a gratuitous agent is under a duty to the principal to act with the care and skill which is required of persons not agents performing similar gratuitous undertakings for others.

§ 380. Duty of Good Conduct

Unless otherwise agreed, an agent is subject to a duty not to conduct himself with such impropriety that he brings disrepute upon the principal or upon the business in which he is engaged. If the service involves personal relations, he has a duty not to act in such a way as to make continued friendly relations with the principal impossible.

§ 381. Duty to Give Information

Unless otherwise agreed, an agent is subject to a duty to use reasonable efforts to give his principal information which is relevant to affairs entrusted to him and which, as the agent has notice, the principal would desire to have and which can be communicated without violating a superior duty to a third person.

§ 382. Duty to Keep and Render Accounts

Unless otherwise agreed, an agent is subject to a duty to keep, and render to his principal, an account of money or other things which he has received or paid out on behalf of the principal.

§ 383. Duty to Act Only as Authorized

Except when he is privileged to protect his own or another's interests, an agent is subject to a duty to the principal not to act in the principal's affairs except in accordance with the principal's manifestation of consent.

§ 384. Duty Not to Attempt the Impossible or Impracticable

Unless otherwise agreed, an agent is subject to a duty to the principal not to continue to render service which subjects the principal to risk of expense if it reasonably appears to him to be impossible or impracticable for him to accomplish the objects of the principal and if he cannot communicate with the principal.

§ 385. Duty to Obey

(1) Unless otherwise agreed, an agent is subject to a duty to obey all reasonable directions in regard to the manner of performing a service that he has contracted to perform.

(2) Unless he is privileged to protect his own or another's interests, an agent is subject to a duty not to act in matters entrusted to him on account of the principal contrary to the directions of the principal, even though the terms of the employment prescribe that such directions shall not be given.

§ 386. Duties After Termination of Authority

Unless otherwise agreed, an agent is subject to a duty not to act as such after the termination of his authority.

TITLE C. DUTIES OF LOYALTY

§ 387. General Principle

Unless otherwise agreed, an agent is subject to a duty to his principal to act solely for the benefit of the principal in all matters connected with his agency.

§ 388. Duty to Account for Profits Arising Out of Employment

Unless otherwise agreed, an agent who makes a profit in connection with transactions conducted by him on behalf of the principal is under a duty to give such profit to the principal.

§ 389. Acting as Adverse Party Without Principal's Consent

Unless otherwise agreed, an agent is subject to a duty not to deal with his principal as an adverse party in a transaction connected with his agency without the principal's knowledge.

§ 390. Acting as Adverse Party with Principal's Consent

An agent who, to the knowledge of the principal, acts on his own account in a transaction in which he is employed has a duty to deal fairly with the principal and to disclose to him all facts which the agent knows or should know would reasonably affect the principal's judgment, unless the principal has manifested that he knows such facts or that he does not care to know them.

§ 391. Acting for Adverse Party Without Principal's Consent

Unless otherwise agreed, an agent is subject to a duty to his principal not to act on behalf of an adverse party in a transaction connected with his agency without the principal's knowledge.

Comment b. Where act not inconsistent with agent's duty. An agent can properly deal with the other party to a transaction if such dealing is not inconsistent with his duties to the principal. Thus, an agent employed to sell can properly lend money to the buyer to complete the purchase or he may "split" his commission with the buyer, unless because of business policy or otherwise it is understood that he is not to do so.

§ 392. Acting for Adverse Party with Principal's Consent

An agent who, to the knowledge of two principals, acts for both of them in a transaction between them, has a duty to act with fairness to each and to disclose to each all facts which he knows or should know would reasonably affect the judgment of each in permitting such dual agency, except as to a principal who has manifested that he knows such facts or does not care to know them.

§ 393. Competition as to Subject Matter of Agency

Unless otherwise agreed, an agent is subject to a duty not to compete with the principal concerning the subject matter of his agency.

§ 394. Acting for One with Conflicting Interests

Unless otherwise agreed, an agent is subject to a duty not to act or to agree to act during the period of his agency for persons whose interests conflict with those of the principal in matters in which the agent is employed.

§ 395. Using or Disclosing Confidential Information

Unless otherwise agreed, an agent is subject to a duty to the principal not to use or to communicate information confidentially given him by the principal or acquired by him during the course of or on account of his agency or in violation of his duties as agent, in competition with or to the injury of the principal, on his own account or on behalf of another, although such information does not relate to the transaction in which he is then employed, unless the information is a matter of general knowledge.

§ 396. Using Confidential Information After Termination of Agency

Unless otherwise agreed, after the termination of the agency, the agent:

(a)   has no duty not to compete with the principal;

(b)   has a duty to the principal not to use or to disclose to third persons, on his own account or on account of others, in competition with the principal or to his injury, trade secrets, written lists of names, or other similar confidential matters given to him only for the principal's use or acquired by the agent in violation of duty. The agent is entitled to use general information concerning the method of business of the principal and the names of the customers retained in his memory, if not acquired in violation of his duty as agent;

(c)   has a duty to account for profits made by the sale or use of trade secrets and other confidential information, whether or not in competition with the principal;

(d)   has a duty to the principal not to take advantage of a still subsisting confidential relation created during the prior agency relation.

§ 397. When Agent Has Right to Patents

Unless otherwise agreed, a person employed by another to do noninventive work is entitled to patents which are the result of his invention although the invention is due to the work for which he is employed.

§ 398. Confusing or Appearing to Own Principal's Things

Unless otherwise agreed, an agent receiving or holding things on behalf of the principal is subject to a duty to the principal not to receive or deal with them so that they will appear to be his own, and not so to mingle them with his own things as to destroy their identity.

TOPIC 2.   LIABILITIES

§ 399. Remedies of Principal

A principal whose agent has violated or threatens to violate his duties has an appropriate remedy for such violation. Such remedy may be:

(a)   an action on the contract of service;

(b)   an action for losses and for the misuse of property;

(c)   an action in equity to enforce the provisions of an express trust undertaken by the agent;

(d)   an action for restitution, either at law or in equity;

(e)   an action for an accounting;

(f)   an action for an injunction;

(g)   set-off or counterclaim;

(h)   causing the agent to be made party to an action brought by a third person against the principal;

(i)   self-help;

(j)   discharge; or

(k)   refusal to pay compensation or rescission of the contract of employment.

§ 400.   Liability for Breach of Contract

An agent who commits a breach of his contract with his principal is subject to liability to the principal in accordance with the principles stated in the Restatement of Contracts.

§ 401.   Liability for Loss Caused

An agent is subject to liability for loss caused to the principal by any breach of duty.

§ 402.   Liability for Misuse of Principal's Property

(1)   An agent is subject to liability to the principal for the value of a chattel, a chose in action, or money which he holds for the principal and to the immediate possession of which the principal is entitled, together with interest thereon if the amount is liquidated, or damages, if the agent:

   (a)   intentionally or negligently destroys it or causes its loss;

   (b)   uses it for his own purposes under an adverse claim;

   (c)   unreasonably refuses to surrender it on demand;

   (d)   manifests that he will not surrender it except on conditions which he is not privileged to exact;

   (e)   makes delivery of it to a person to whom he is not authorized to deliver it;

   (f)   improperly causes the title or indicia of title to be placed in his own name, if either this is done in bad faith or the thing substantially depreciates in value while the title is so held because of his wrongful conduct;

   (g)   deviates substantially from his authority in its transfer to a third person in a sale or purchase; or

   (h)   intentionally and substantially deviates from his authority in dealing with the possession of the thing, and the chattel suffers substantial harm during the course of such wrongful dealing or because of it.

(2)   An agent who deviates substantially from his authority in the transfer of land belonging to the principal or who, in bad faith, causes the title of such land to be placed in his own name, is subject to liability to the principal for the value of the land.

§ 403.   Liability for Things Received in Violation of Duty of Loyalty

If an agent receives anything as a result of his violation of a duty of loyalty to the principal, he is subject to a liability to deliver it, its value, or its proceeds, to the principal.

§ 404.   Liability for Use of Principal's Assets

An agent who, in violation of duty to his principal, uses for his own purposes or those of a third person assets of the principal's business is subject to liability to the principal for the value of the use. If the use predominates in producing a profit he is subject to liability, at the principal's election, for such profit; he is not, however, liable for profits made by him merely by the use of time which he has contracted to devote to the principal unless he violates his duty not to act adversely or in competition with the principal.

§ 404A.   Restitutional Liability of Agent to Principal

Although the agent has committed no breach of duty to the principal, he is liable in an action for restitution for any enrichment which it is unjust for him to retain.

§ 405. Liability for Conduct of Other Agents

(1)   Except as stated in Subsections (2) and (3), an agent is not subject to liability to the principal for the conduct of other agents who are not his subagents.

(2)   An agent is subject to liability to the principal if, having a duty to appoint or to supervise other agents, he has violated his duty through lack of care or otherwise in the appointment or supervision, and harm thereby results to the principal in a foreseeable manner. He is also subject to liability if he directs, permits, or otherwise takes part in the improper conduct of other agents.

(3)   An agent is subject to liability to a principal for the failure of another agent to perform a service which he and such other have jointly contracted to perform for the principal.

§ 406. Liability for Conduct of Subagent

Unless otherwise agreed, an agent is responsible to the principal for the conduct of a subservant or other subagent with reference to the principal's affairs entrusted to the subagent, as the agent is for his own conduct; and as to other matters, as a principal is for the conduct of a servant or other agent.

Comment b. An agent who employs a subagent is the latter's principal and is responsible both to third persons (see § 362) and to his principal for the subagent's derelictions. Thus the agent is subject to liability to the principal for harm to the principal's property or business caused by the subagent's negligence or other wrong to the principal's interests. The agent is also under a duty to indemnify the principal for payments made by the latter to third persons resulting from the agent's misrepresentations or other tortious conduct or from transactions binding the principal but beyond the authority of the subagent.

§ 407. Principal's Choice of Remedies

(1)   If an agent has received a benefit as a result of violating his duty of loyalty, the principal is entitled to recover from him what he has so received, its value, or its proceeds, and also the amount of damage thereby caused; except that, if the violation consists of the wrongful disposal of the principal's property, the principal cannot recover its value and also what the agent received in exchange therefor.

(2)   A principal who has recovered damages from a third person because of an agent's violation of his duty of loyalty is entitled nevertheless to obtain from the agent any profit which the agent improperly received as a result of the transaction.

§ 408. Liability Created by Principal's Ratification

The ratification of the act of a purported agent subjects him to liability to account to the person for whom he intended or purported to act for profits made by him to which the purported principal would have been entitled if the act had been authorized.

§ 409. When Principal Can Properly Terminate Employment; Condonation

(1)   A principal is privileged to discharge before the time fixed by the contract of employment an agent who has committed such a violation of duty that his conduct constitutes a material breach of contract or who, without committing a violation of duty, fails to perform or reasonably appears to be unable to perform a material part of the promised service, because of physical or mental disability.

(2)   The election by the principal not to discharge the agent for a breach of duty does not of itself release the agent from liability for loss caused by the breach nor, if the agent commits subsequent breaches of duty, is the principal prevented from electing subsequently to treat the first breach as cause for discharge.

TOPIC 3. DEFENSES

§ 410.　Incapacity of Agent

Whether or not an agent who lacks full capacity is subject to liability to the principal for conduct which, but for such lack of capacity, would be a breach of duty, depends upon the extent of his incapacity and the character of his conduct.

§ 411.　Illegality as a Defense for Nonperformance of Service

In accordance with and subject to the conditions stated in the Restatement of Contracts, one who undertakes to perform service as the agent of another is not liable for failing to perform such service if, at the time of the undertaking or of performance, such service is illegal.

§ 412.　Criminality as Defense for Failure to Account

(1)　Except as stated in Subsections (2) and (3), the fact that money or other thing received by the agent from or on behalf of the principal is the proceeds of a crime by the principal or by another, or was given to the agent to accomplish an unlawful purpose, does not relieve the agent from a duty to account for it or its proceeds.

(2)　An agent who has received money or other thing from or on behalf of the principal is under no duty to deliver the same to the principal or to account for the use thereof:

　　(a)　if the delivery to the principal would be, or would aid in, the commission of a criminal act; or

　　(b)　if the thing was obtained by the agent without his fraud, duress, or undue influence, and

　　　　(i)　the thing was given for the purpose of accomplishing a very serious crime, or

　　　　(ii)　a crime involving more than a minor offense has been accomplished by the delivery to the agent of the thing or by its use.

(3)　An agent who has received the proceeds or profits of an act committed by him on behalf of and at the direction of the principal and for which the principal is criminally responsible is under no duty to deliver them to the principal if the crime is more than a minor offense.

§ 413.　Impossibility as Defense

Subject to and in accordance with the rules stated in the Restatement of Contracts, an agent is under no duty to render services, the performance of which is impossible or impracticable if, when he promises to perform them, he has no reason to know that they are then impossible or impracticable or to anticipate that they will become such before the time for performance.

§ 414.　Statutes of Frauds as Defense

(1)　If a statute provides that no action shall be brought upon an agreement not capable of performance within a year unless the promise is in writing signed by the party to be charged, a person who orally promises to act as an agent for a period which cannot terminate within a year from the promise is not thereby subject to liability in an action upon the agreement for a failure to perform it.

(2)　Although a statute requires the creation of a trust in land or other thing to be manifested and proved by a writing signed by the party to be charged, an agent who is authorized and who agrees orally to acquire such thing for the principal, and who acquires it in his own name, holds the thing thus acquired upon a constructive or resulting trust for the principal.

(3)　If the principal is not bound to compensate the agent for his services because the principal has not signed a memorandum as required by a statute, the agent is not liable for failing to render promised services if, having been requested to do so, the principal refuses to sign a memorandum.

§ 415. Principal's Contributory Fault as Defense

The liability of the agent to the principal can be avoided, terminated, or reduced by a breach of contract by the principal, his contributory fault, or his failure to mitigate damages.

§ 416. Ratification or Affirmance as Defense

The ratification or other affirmance by the principal of an unauthorized act done by an agent acting in excess of his power to bind the principal releases the agent from liability in damages to the principal for having violated a duty to him, except when the principal:

(a) is obliged to affirm the act in order to protect his own interests; or

(b) is caused to ratify by the misrepresentation or duress of the agent.

§ 417. Rights of Third Persons as Defense

An agent who has received anything on account of his principal cannot defeat the claim of the principal upon the ground that a third person has a right superior to the principal's unless:

(a) the agent has been divested of it by, or has delivered it to, the holder of the paramount title; or

(b) the title of the principal has terminated after receipt by the agent, by a voluntary transfer or otherwise; or

(c) the agent interpleads the third person.

§ 418. Privilege of Agent to Protect His Own Interests

An agent is privileged to protect interests of his own which are superior to those of the principal, even though he does so at the expense of the principal's interests or in disobedience to his orders.

§ 419. Discharge by Release or Contract

An agent who has committed a breach of duty to the principal is discharged from liability by an effective release given by the principal or a contract with the principal having the effect of a discharge.

§ 420. Judicial Declaration of Insolvency or Bankruptcy of Agent

(1) The agent's bankruptcy or a judicial declaration of insolvency may discharge him from liability to the principal.

(2) The rights of the principal in property held for him by the agent or held by the agent in breach of trust are not affected by the agent's bankruptcy or discharge in insolvency proceedings.

§ 421. Set-Off and Counterclaim

Rights of set-off or counterclaim may be available to an agent in an action brought against him by the principal.

§ 421A. Other Events Terminating or Diminishing Agent's Liability

The principal's cause of action against the agent may be terminated or diminished because of:

(a) the rules as to the effect of judgments;

(b) the discharge of or satisfaction of a claim against a co-obligor;

(c) the statute of limitations; or

(d) laches.

TOPIC 4. DUTIES AND LIABILITIES OF PARTICULAR KINDS OF AGENTS

§ 422.   Agents in Charge of Land or Chattels

Unless otherwise agreed, an agent who has charge of land or chattels for his principal is subject to a duty to the principal to use reasonable care in their protection, to use them only in accordance with the directions of the principal and for his benefit, and to surrender them upon demand or upon the termination of the agency.

§ 423.   Agents Holding a Title

Unless otherwise agreed, an agent who holds the title to something for the principal is subject to a duty to the principal to use reasonable care in the protection of the title which he so holds, to act in accordance with the directions of the principal, to use it only for the principal's benefit, and to transfer it upon demand or upon the termination of the agency.

§ 424.   Agents to Buy or to Sell

Unless otherwise agreed, an agent employed to buy or to sell is subject to a duty to the principal, within the limits set by the principal's directions, to be loyal to the principal's interests and to use reasonable care to obtain terms which best satisfy the manifested purposes of the principal.

§ 425.   Agents to Make Investments

Unless otherwise agreed, an agent employed to make or to manage investments has a duty to the principal:

(a)   to use care to invest promptly;

(b)   to invest only in such securities as would be obtained by a prudent investor for his own account, having in view both safety and income, in the light of the principal's means and purposes; and

(c)   to change investments in accordance with changes in the security of the investments or the condition of the principal, if his duties include management.

§ 426.   Agents to Make Collections

Unless otherwise agreed, an agent employed to collect from others goods or money due the principal has a duty of using reasonable care and skill in making such collections in accordance with the directions of the principal.

§ 427.   Agents Who Have Made Collections

Unless otherwise agreed, an agent who has received goods or money for the principal has a duty to use care to keep them safely until they are remitted or delivered to the principal, and to deliver them to the principal upon his demand when the amount due him has been ascertained. The agent may also have a duty to use care to notify the principal of the collection, or to remit the goods or money to him within a reasonable time.

§ 428.   Subservants and Other Subagents

(1)   Unless otherwise agreed, a subagent who knows of the existence of the ultimate principal owes him the duties owed by an agent to a principal, except the duties dependent upon the existence of a contract.

(2)   Unless otherwise agreed, a subagent owes the agent the duties of an agent to his principal.

(3)   The rules stated in Subsections (1) and (2) apply to a subservant.

Comment b. Loyalty to principal and agent. The subagent is subject to a duty, as is the agent (see § 385), not to act contrary to what he knows to be the principal's orders. Although he has a duty of loyalty and obedience to the agent who is his immediate principal, the subagent is subject to liability to the ultimate principal for participating in a breach of duty by the agent to the principal if he has notice that the agent's conduct constitutes a breach of duty. He also may be subject to liability for unauthorized dealing with the principal's lands or chattels under the rule stated in Section 402; his justifiable mistake as to the power of his superior, the agent, to bind the principal does not necessarily excuse him.

The subagent has the delegable privileges of the agent, so that, in a conflict of interests between the agent and the principal, the subagent is both entitled and required to prefer the interests of the agent if, under the circumstances, the agent would be entitled to prefer his own interests to those of the principal.

§ 429. Servants

The rules as to the duties and liabilities to the principal of agents who are not servants apply to servants.

§ 430. Purported Agents

One who, without the consent or manifestation of consent of another, purports to act as the agent for such other is subject to liability for loss occasioned to the other by such conduct or for the value of anything belonging to the purported principal which he has improperly used. If the other ratifies, the liability of the purported agent to the other is the same as if he originally had been an agent who had acted without authority and whose conduct the principal ratified.

§ 431. Agents and Subagents Employed for Undisclosed Principal

(1) If an agent employs another agent for an undisclosed principal, the person so employed is subject to liability to the principal for a failure to perform duties due to the employing agent, in accordance with the rules generally applicable to undisclosed principals.

(2) If an agent employs a subagent to perform services for an undisclosed principal, the subagent is as subject to liability to the principal for his conduct as if the principal were disclosed, except that, until his discovery of the principal's existence, conduct which is privileged as to the agent is privileged as to the principal.

(3) The rules stated in Subsections (1) and (2) as to agents and subagents apply to servants and subservants employed by the agent.

Chapter 14

DUTIES AND LIABILITIES OF
PRINCIPAL TO AGENT

TOPIC 1. CONTRACTUAL AND RESTITUTIONAL
DUTIES AND LIABILITIES

TITLE A. INTERPRETATION OF CONTRACTS
AND LIABILITIES THEREUNDER

§ 432. Duty to Perform Contract

A principal is subject to a duty to an agent to perform the contract which he has made with the agent.

§ 433.   Duty to Furnish Opportunity for Work

A principal does not, by contracting to employ an agent, thereby promise to provide him with an opportunity for work, but the circumstances under which the agreement for employment is made or the nature of the employment may warrant an inference of such a promise.

§ 434.   Duty Not to Interfere with Agent's Work

A principal who has contracted to afford an agent an opportunity to work has a duty to refrain from unreasonably interfering with his work.

§ 435.   Duty to Give Agent Information

Unless otherwise agreed, it is inferred that a principal contracts to use care to inform the agent of risks of physical harm or pecuniary loss which, as the principal has reason to know, exist in the performance of authorized acts and which he has reason to know are unknown to the agent. His duty to give other information depends upon the agreement between them.

§ 436.   Duty to Keep and Render Accounts

Unless otherwise agreed, a master has a duty to keep and render accounts of the amount due from him to a servant; whether principals of other agents have such a duty depends upon the method of compensation, the fact that the agent operates or does not operate an independent enterprise, the customs of business and other similar factors.

§ 437.   Duty of Good Conduct

Unless otherwise agreed, a principal who has contracted to employ an agent has a duty to conduct himself so as not to harm the agent's reputation nor to make it impossible for the agent, consistently with his reasonable self-respect or personal safety, to continue in the employment.

§ 438.   Duty of Indemnity; The Principle

(1) A principal is under a duty to indemnify the agent in accordance with the terms of the agreement with him.

(2) In the absence of terms to the contrary in the agreement of employment, the principal has a duty to indemnify the agent where the agent

(a) makes a payment authorized or made necessary in executing the principal's affairs or, unless he is officious, one beneficial to the principal, or

(b) suffers a loss which, because of their relation, it is fair that the principal should bear.

§ 439.   When Duty of Indemnity Exists

Unless otherwise agreed, a principal is subject to a duty to exonerate an agent who is not barred by the illegality of his conduct to indemnify him for:

(a) authorized payments made by the agent on behalf of the principal;

(b) payments upon contracts upon which the agent is authorized to make himself liable, and upon obligations arising from the possession or ownership of things which he is authorized to hold on account of the principal;

(c) payments of damages to third persons which he is required to make on account of the authorized performance of an act which constitutes a tort or a breach of contract;

(d) expenses of defending actions by third persons brought because of the agent's authorized conduct, such actions being unfounded but not brought in bad faith; and

(e)   payments resulting in benefit to the principal, made by the agent under such circumstances that it would be inequitable for indemnity not to be made.

§ 440.   When No Duty of Indemnity

Unless otherwise agreed, the principal is not subject to a duty to indemnify an agent:

(a)   for pecuniary loss or other harm, not of benefit to the principal, arising from the performance of unauthorized acts or resulting solely from the agent's negligence or other fault; or

(b)   if the principal has otherwise performed his duties to the agent, for physical harm caused by the performance of authorized acts, for harm suffered as a result of torts, other than the tortious institution of suits, committed upon the agent by third persons because of his employment, or for harm suffered by the refusal of third persons to deal with him; or

(c)   if the agent's loss resulted from an enterprise which he knew to be illegal.

§ 441.   Duty to Pay Compensation

Unless the relation of the parties, the triviality of the services, or other circumstances, indicate that the parties have agreed otherwise, it is inferred that a person promises to pay for services which he requests or permits another to perform for him as his agent.

§ 442.   Period of Employment

Unless otherwise agreed, mutual promises by principal and agent to employ and to serve create obligations to employ and to serve which are terminable upon notice by either party; if neither party terminates the employment, it may terminate by lapse of time or by supervening events.

§ 442A.   Death or Incapacity of Principal or Agent

(1)   Unless otherwise agreed, the death of either principal or agent terminates the liabilities for nonperformance of a contract of employment.

(2)   Unless otherwise agreed, the mental incapacity of the principal, or the mental or physical incapacity of the agent, to perform services, terminates the liabilities for nonperformance of a contract of employment.

§ 443.   Amount of Compensation

If the contract of employment provides for compensation to the agent, he is entitled to receive for the full performance of the agreed service:

(a)   the definite amount agreed upon and no more, if the agreement is definite as to amount; or

(b)   the fair value of his services, if there is no agreement for a definite amount.

§ 444.   Compensation for Extra Services

If an agent is employed for specified hours or for specified work at a specified rate, and upon request he performs services outside of the agreed hours or performs other than the agreed services, it is inferred that he is not to receive compensation for such additional services, unless his compensation is based upon the number of his working hours, or for such different services, unless his compensation is based upon the results which he accomplishes.

§ 445.   Compensation Dependent upon Specified Result

Except where there is revocation in bad faith, an agent whose compensation is conditional upon the performance by him of specified services, or his accomplishment of a specified result, is not entitled to the agreed compensation unless he renders the specified services or achieves the result.

§ 446.　　Compensation Dependent upon Specified Result in Limited Time

An agent whose compensation is conditional upon his performance of specified services or his accomplishment of a specified result within a specified time is not entitled to the agreed compensation unless he renders the services or achieves the result within such time, unless the principal, in bad faith, has prevented him from doing so.

§ 447.　　Compensation Dependent upon Securing Specified Price or Other Terms

An agent whose compensation is conditional upon procuring a transaction on specified terms is not entitled to such compensation if, as a result of his efforts, a transaction is effected on different or modified terms, although the principal thereby benefits.

§ 448.　　Compensation; Agent as Effective Cause

An agent whose compensation is conditional upon his accomplishment of a specified result is entitled to the agreed compensation if, and only if, he is the effective cause of accomplishing the result.

§ 449.　　Compensation When Principal Competes

The principal does not, by contracting to pay compensation contingent upon the agent's success in accomplishing a definite result, thereby promise that he will not compete either personally or through another agent.

§ 450.　　Duty Not to Terminate Employment

A principal has a duty not to repudiate or terminate the employment in violation of the contract of employment.

§ 451.　　Compensation and Indemnity for Acts Performed After Termination

Unless otherwise agreed, upon termination of the agency relation, whether or not in breach of contract by either party, the principal has no duty to compensate the agent for subsequent services or to indemnify him for obligations subsequently assumed, unless otherwise the principal would be unjustly enriched.

§ 452.　　Compensation upon Termination Without Breach by Either Party; Services Part of Agreed Exchange

Unless otherwise agreed, if the principal has contracted to pay the agent for his services and the relation terminates without breach of contract by either party, the principal is subject to liability to pay to the agent for services previously performed and which are part of the agreed exchange:

(a)　the agreed compensation for services for which compensation is apportioned in the contract; and

(b)　the value, not exceeding the agreed ratable compensation, of services for which the compensation is not apportioned.

§ 453.　　Compensation upon Termination Without Breach by Either Party; Services Not Part of Agreed Exchange

(1)　Unless otherwise agreed, an agent whose compensation is dependent upon the accomplishment of a specified result is not entitled to compensation for services rendered in an unsuccessful effort to accomplish that result before the rightful termination of the agency, although the principal is thereby benefited, if the services are not part of the agreed exchange.

(2)　If the agent's compensation is not proportioned to the extent of his efforts in successfully accomplishing the result, it is inferred that his services are not part of the agreed exchange.

§ 454. Revocation in Bad Faith of Offer of Compensation

An agent to whom the principal has made a revocable offer of compensation if he accomplishes a specified result is entitled to the promised amount if the principal, in order to avoid payment of it, revokes the offer and thereafter the result is accomplished as the result of the agent's prior efforts.

§ 455. Damages Where Termination Results from Principal's Breach of Contract

If in violation of the contract of employment, the principal terminates or repudiates the employment, or the agent properly terminates it because of breach of contract by the principal, the agent is entitled at his election to receive either:

(a)   the amount of the net losses caused and gains prevented by the principal's breach or, if there are no such losses or gains, a small sum as nominal damages; or

(b)   the reasonable value of the services previously rendered the principal, not limited by the contract price, except that for services for which a price is apportioned by the terms of the contract he is entitled to receive the contract price and no more.

§ 456. Revocation for Breach of Contract or Renunciation in Breach of Contract

If a principal properly discharges an agent for breach of contract, or the agent wrongfully renounces the employment, the principal is subject to liability to pay to the agent, with a deduction for the loss caused the principal by the breach of contract:

(a)   the agreed compensation for services properly rendered for which the compensation is apportioned in the contract, whether or not the agent's breach is wilful and deliberate; and

(b)   the value, not exceeding the agreed ratable compensation, of services properly rendered for which the compensation is not apportioned if, but only if, the agent's breach is not wilful and deliberate.

§ 457. Restitutional Liability Where No Contract or Voidable Contract

A principal for whom an agent has performed services in accordance with a voidable contract which is avoided by one of the parties, or for whom an agent or purported agent has performed services without a promise by the principal to pay, is subject to liability to the agent to the extent that he has been unjustly enriched by such services.

§ 458. Liability of Principal to Subagent

The authorized employment of a subservant or other subagent does not thereby subject the principal to contractual liability to the subagent but the principal is subject to the same tort liability and has the same duty of indemnity to him as to agents directly employed.

§ 459. Liability of Agents to Subagents

An agent who employs a subservant or other subagent has the duties and liabilities of a principal to him.

§ 460. Liability of Undisclosed Principal and Agent to Person Employed by Agent

(1)   A principal on whose behalf an agent employs other agents and subagents without disclosing the principal's existence is liable to those thus employed in accordance with the rules which determine the liability of an undisclosed principal to third persons.

(2)   The employing agent has the same liabilities to those employed as he would have if acting on his own account.

§ 461.　Servants and Subservants

(1)　A master as to his servants, and a servant as to his subservants are subject to the same contractual and restitutional duties as to their agents who are not servants.

(2)　A master is not subject to contractual liability to a subservant, but he has the same tort and restitutional liability to a subservant as to his other servants.

§ 462.　Effect of Ratification

Upon ratification, an agent or other person who without power to bind the principal, has purported to do so is entitled to the same rights against the principal as if the act had been authorized, unless the principal:

(a)　is induced to affirm by the misrepresentation or duress of the agent; or

(b)　is obliged to affirm in order to protect his own interests.

TITLE B.　REMEDIES OF AGENT

§ 463.　General Rule

An agent whose principal violates or threatens to violate a contractual or restitutional duty to him has an appropriate remedy. He can, in a proper case:

(a)　maintain an action at law;

(b)　obtain a decree for an accounting or other equitable relief;

(c)　maintain a claim to a set-off or a counterclaim in an action brought by the principal;

(d)　refuse to render further services;

(e)　exercise the rights of a lien holder; or

(f)　stop in transit goods shipped to the principal.

§ 464.　When Agent Has Lien

Unless he undertakes duties inconsistent with such a right or otherwise agrees that it is not to exist:

(a)　an agent has a right to retain possession of money, goods, or documents of the principal, of which he has gained possession in the proper execution of his agency, until he is paid the amount due him from the principal as compensation for services performed or as indemnity for money advanced or liability incurred by him in connection with such things;

(b)　a factor, banker, or attorney-at-law has the further right to retain possession of money, goods, or documents until he is paid the amount due him upon the general balance of accounts created by transactions conducted by him as such factor, banker, or attorney;

(c)　a factor who has made advances or incurred liability with respect to goods received by him for sale has a right to sell them contrary to directions of the principal, after notice to the principal, if the reasonable protection of the factor's interest so requires;

(d)　an agent to whom goods have been consigned but not received, and who advances money in anticipation of their receipt, has a right to their possession and thereafter, under the circumstances stated in Clauses (a), (b), and (c), to the rights therein stated; and

(e)　an attorney of record who has obtained a judgment has an interest therein, as security for his fees in the case and for proper payments made and liabilities incurred during the course of the proceedings.

§ 465.   When Subagent Has Lien

(1)   Against the agent who employed him, a subagent has a lien under the circumstances under which other agents have liens, subject, however, to the rights of the principal.

(2)   Unless otherwise agreed, the lien of a subagent on things of a disclosed or partially disclosed principal is limited to the rights between the principal and the agent, except where the agent bound the principal by a transaction with the subagent in excess of his authority.

(3)   Against an undisclosed principal, a subagent has a lien under the same circumstances as if the agent were the principal, except where the agent has acted in excess of his authority.

§ 466.   When Agent Has Right of Stoppage in Transit

Unless otherwise agreed, an agent who has a security interest in goods of the principal because of money paid by him for them, liability incurred in their purchase, or advances made to the principal upon their security, is entitled to stop them when in transit to the principal upon learning of the principal's insolvency.

TITLE C.   DEFENSES

§ 467.   Illegality as Defense

An agent who makes an illegal agreement with the principal to act for him, or whose services for the principal are illegal under the rules stated in the Restatement of Contracts, is entitled neither to compensation for his services nor indemnity for losses sustained by him in performing them, except as therein stated.

§ 468.   Statutes of Frauds as Defense

(1)   If a statute provides that no action shall be brought upon an agreement not capable of performance within a year unless the promise is in writing signed by the party to be charged, a person who, by a bilateral contract, orally promises to employ another as an agent for such a period that the contract is not capable of performance within a year from the time of the promise, is not thereby liable in an action upon the agreement for failure to perform it.

(2)   If a statute provides that a person employing another for a specified purpose shall not be liable to the other for compensation although the other renders the promised performance, unless the employer has signed a memorandum in writing, a person has no duty to pay to another whom he orally employs for such purpose either the promised compensation or the reasonable value of services rendered.

(3)   Except as stated in Subsection (2), an agent who has partially or fully performed a contract which is not enforceable because a memorandum thereof has not been signed is entitled to the fair value of services rendered if the principal refuses to perform the contract or to sign a memorandum.

§ 469.   Disloyalty or Insubordination as Defense

An agent is entitled to no compensation for conduct which is disobedient or which is a breach of his duty of loyalty; if such conduct constitutes a wilful and deliberate breach of his contract of service, he is not entitled to compensation even for properly performed services for which no compensation is apportioned.

§ 469A.   Other Events Terminating or Diminishing Agent's Claim

The claim of the agent against the principal may be terminated or diminished because of:

    (a)   discharge or release by contract with the principal,

    (b)   the discharge of the principal in bankruptcy,

    (c)   set-off or counterclaim,

     (d)   the rules as to the effect of judgments,

     (e)   the discharge or satisfaction of claim against a co-obligor,

     (f)   the statute of limitations,

     (g)   laches.

TOPIC 2. LIABILITY IN TORT FOR HIS OWN MISCONDUCT

§ 470.   General Rule

A principal is subject to the same liability to an agent for his own conduct as he is to third persons for similar conduct, except that a master has nondelegable duties of care with respect to working conditions of his servants.

§ 471.   Duty of Warning

A principal is subject to liability in an action of tort for failing to use care to warn an agent of an unreasonable risk involved in the employment, if the principal should realize that it exists and that the agent is likely not to become aware of it, thereby suffering harm.

TOPIC 3. LIABILITY TO AGENTS NOT SERVANTS FOR TORTS OF SERVANTS, OTHER AGENTS, AND CONTRACTORS

§ 472.   General Rule

A principal is subject to the same liability to an agent who is not a servant for damage caused by the tortious conduct of his servants, of other agents, and of other persons doing work for him, as he is to third persons.

TOPIC 4. LIABILITY TO SERVANTS FOR TORTS OF SERVANTS, OTHER AGENTS, AND CONTRACTORS

TITLE A. GENERAL RULE

§ 473.   Statement of Rule

A master is subject to the same liability to a servant for damage caused by the tortious conduct of his other servants, of his agents who are not servants, and of other persons doing work for him, as he is to third persons, except where he is not liable for the conduct of fellow servants, in accordance with the fellow servant rule and except that he has non-delegable duties of care to servants acting in the scope of employment.

TITLE B. THE FELLOW SERVANT RULE

§ 474.   Statement of Rule

A master is not liable to a servant or subservant who, while acting within the scope of his employment or in connection therewith, is injured solely by the negligence of a fellow servant in the performance of acts not involving a violation of the master's non-delegable duties, unless the servant was coerced or deceived into serving, was too young to appreciate the risks, or was employed in violation of statute.

§ 475. Definition of Fellow Servant

Fellow servants are servants employed by the same master in the same enterprise or household and so related in their labor that, because of proximity or otherwise, there is a special risk of harm to one of them if the other is negligent.

§ 476. Fellow Servant Rule; Different Masters

Two servants employed by different masters are not fellow servants, although both servants are engaged upon the same piece of work and are subject to special risks from the negligence of each other.

§ 477. Fellow Servant Rule; Same Enterprise

Servants of the same master are fellow servants only if they are employed in the same enterprise or household.

§ 478. Fellow Servant Rule; Separate Departments

Servants employed in the same enterprise by the same master are not fellow servants unless they are so related in their labor that they are regularly or are likely to be in proximity to each other, or there is a special risk of harm to one of them if the other is negligent; but one may be a fellow servant of another even though the other is employed in a separate department.

§ 479. Fellow Servant Rule; Difference in Rank

One may be a fellow servant of another although the other is a superior or inferior servant.

§ 480. Fellow Servant Rule; Different Services

One may be a fellow servant of another although the two are performing different kinds of work.

§ 481. Fellow Servant Rule; Persons Compelled to Serve

(1) A servant compelled by law or by duress to enter the employment is not subject to the disabilities created by the fellow servant rule.

(2) Compulsion of law to continue in an employment voluntarily entered does not prevent the disabilities of the fellow servant rule from applying.

§ 482. Fellow Servant Rule; Non-Disclosure of Master or of Common Employment

(1) The fellow servant rule does not prevent a servant from having a cause of action against a master for an injury caused by the conduct of another servant employed by the same master if the injured servant, as the master should know, reasonably believes that the person injuring him is employed by a different master.

(2) Servants employed by the agent of an undisclosed principal are subject to the disabilities of the fellow servant rule in actions against the principal for the negligence of other servants employed in the same enterprise.

§ 483. Fellow Servant Rule; Illegal Employment

A servant employed in violation of a statute passed for the protection of the class to which he belongs against the risks arising from the conduct of fellow servants is not subject to the disabilities created by the fellow servant rule.

§ 484. Fellow Servant Rule; Incapacity of Servant

(1)   A person too young to appreciate the risks of the employment is not subject to the disabilities created by the fellow servant rule.

(2)   The fact that a person does not have capacity to contract does not prevent the application of the fellow servant rule.

§ 485. Fellow Servant Rule; Volunteer Assistants

A person who, without the consent of the master, acts as a servant in assisting a servant to perform the master's business primarily for the purpose of aiding the servant or the business of the master is subject to the disabilities created by the fellow servant rule.

§ 486. Fellow Servant Rule; Time and Place

The immunity of the master from liability to a servant for conduct of a fellow servant continues while the servant:

(a)   is acting within the scope of his employment or in connection therewith; or

(b)   is upon the premises or vehicle of his master, in connection with the work for which he is employed.

§ 487. Fellow Servant Rule; Assaults

A master is subject to liability to a servant for the unprivileged use of force directed against him, or for defamation, by another servant of the same master, acting within the scope of his authority in the enforcement of commands or in the protection of the principal's interests.

§ 488. Fellow Servant Rule; Belongings of Servants

The immunity created by the fellow servant rule applies not only to physical harm suffered by a servant, but also to damage to implements supplied by and used by him within the scope of his employment.

§ 489. Fellow Servant Rule; Families of Servants

Except in an action by members of a servant's family based upon an injury to him, the disabilities created by the fellow servant rule do not extend to the members of a servant's family who are harmed by another servant of the same master or by such servant himself.

§ 490. Fellow Servant Rule; Third Persons Suffering Loss

(1)   The disabilities of the fellow servant rule apply to a person suffering pecuniary loss from harm to a servant caused by a fellow servant, except a parent of an unemancipated minor employed without the parent's consent.

(2)   A parent who has consented to the illegal employment of his minor child cannot recover for harm to the child caused by his fellow servants even though the minor could recover.

§ 491. Fellow Servant Rule; Statutory Modifications

The immunity of the master from liability for the conduct of fellow servants may be diminished or terminated by statute.

TITLE C. NON-DELEGABLE DUTIES OF MASTER

§ 492. General Rule

A master is subject to a duty that care be used either to provide working conditions which are reasonably safe for his servants and subservants, considering the nature of the employment, or to warn them of risks of unsafe conditions which he should realize they may not discover by the exercise of due care.

Caveat:

No opinion is expressed as to whether or not the master is subject to liability to a servant harmed by the intentional failure of a person to whom the master has entrusted the duty of making working conditions safe, if the failure to make safe results from the intention of such person to cause harm.

§ 493. Extent of Duty of Care

In creating and maintaining the conditions of employment, the master has a duty to his servants to have precautions taken which reasonable care, intelligence, and regard for the safety of his servants require.

§ 494. Duty of Care to Children

Except as provided by statute, the standard of care as to working conditions with respect to children is the same as that with respect to adults, but in the application of the standard, the youth and inexperience of the child are considered.

§ 495. Knowledge Which Master is Required to Have

A master is subject to a duty to his servants to conduct his business in the light of knowledge which he has, and of such knowledge as to the conditions likely to harm his servants as persons experienced in the business and having special acquaintance with the subject matter have.

§ 496. Notice to Master of Dangerous Conditions

For the purpose of determining whether or not due care has been used in the performance of the non-delegable duties of the master to his servants, the master has notice of facts affecting the safety of his servants if notice of such facts comes to him, or to a servant or other person whose duty it is to act upon them in the performance of the master's duty to protect his servants.

§ 497. Time When and Place Where Duty Exists

The duty of the master to a servant to furnish reasonably safe conditions exists only while the servant is properly acting within the scope of his employment or while, in connection therewith, he is in a place or vehicle in the control of the master in which he is then required to be by reason of his employment or which has been provided for use incidental to his employment.

§ 498. Applicability of Tort Principles as to Risk and Causation

A master is not subject to liability to a servant harmed by the negligent breach of the master's duty to his servants, unless:

    (a)   the servant harmed is one to whom the master owed the duty of care;

    (b)   the harm suffered is within the risk created by the breach of duty; and

    (c)   the negligent conduct is the responsible cause of the harm.

§ 499. Risks Inherent in Enterprise

A master who has performed his duties of care is not liable to a servant harmed by a risk incident to the nature of the work.

§ 500.   Transitory Dangers

The master's liability for unsafe working conditions does not extend to temporary dangerous conditions of which the conduct of fellow servants in the performance of operative details of the work is the sole responsible cause.

§ 501.   Structures or Instrumentalities Made by Master

A master who, by his servants, erects structures or manufactures instrumentalities for use in his business is subject to liability to his servants who subsequently occupy or use them in their employment and who are harmed by defects therein which care in the erection or manufacture would have prevented.

§ 502.   Structures, Instrumentalities, or Materials Acquired from Others

A master who uses in his business a completed structure, instrumentality, or materials not made by his servants:

(a)   is subject to liability for harm caused to his servants by a failure to use reasonable care in the purchase or inspection thereof;

(b)   is not subject to liability for harm caused to his servants by unknown defects due to negligence in manufacture or upkeep prior to the time of purchase which reasonable care in the acquisition or inspection thereof would not reveal.

§ 503.   Maintenance, Inspection, and Repair

The duty of a master as to working conditions extends to the maintenance, inspection, and repair of the premises in his control upon which his servants are employed and of the implements which they use, and to the control of the conduct of fellow servants with whom they work.

§ 504.   Harm Caused by Third Persons or upon Premises Not in Master's Control

The master's duty as to working conditions does not extend to the condition of premises not in his control, or to the conduct of third persons with whom the servants are to be brought into contact during the course of the work, except that he has a duty to disclose dangerous conditions of which he should know.

§ 505.   Number and Quality of Servants

The duty of the master as to working conditions includes a duty of care to provide a sufficient number of competent fellow servants so that the conditions of employment are not unreasonably dangerous.

§ 506.   General Plan of Work

The duty of the master as to working conditions includes a duty of care so to plan the work that the servants employed therein are not subjected to unreasonable risks.

§ 507.   Duty to Provide Supervisors

The duty of the master as to working conditions includes a duty of care to supply competent supervisors of the operative details of the business where this is reasonably necessary to prevent undue risk of harm to his servants in the performance of such details.

§ 508.   Duty to Make and Enforce Rules

In work dangerous to servants employed in it unless rules are made for its conduct, the duty of the master as to working conditions includes a duty that care be used to promulgate and enforce suitable rules.

§ 509. Liability for Improper Orders

The duty of the master as to working conditions includes a duty of care as to orders given as acts of management and not in connection with the operative details of the work.

§ 510. Duties to Instruct, Warn, and Give Suitable Work to Servant

The master's duty as to working conditions includes a duty that care be used to give such instruction to servants employed by him as, from what the master should know concerning them and the work they are employed to do, is necessary to prevent unreasonable risk to them and to other servants during the progress of the work, and to give them work suitable to their apparent capacities.

§ 511. Liability for Harm from Forces of Nature

The master's duty as to working conditions includes a duty that care be used to guard against reasonably foreseeable harm from natural forces against which he should know the servants cannot protect themselves.

§ 512. Duty to Protect Endangered or Hurt Employee

(1) If a servant, while acting within the scope of his employment, comes into a position of imminent danger of serious harm and this is known to the master or to a person who has duties of management, the master is subject to liability for a failure by himself or by such person to exercise reasonable care to avert the threatened harm.

(2) If a servant is hurt and thereby becomes helpless when acting within the scope of employment and this is known to the master or to a person having duties of management, the master is subject to liability for his negligent failure or that of such person to give first aid to the servant and to care for him until he can be cared for by others.

§ 513. Liability to Servants Having Duty of Inspection

A master who has satisfied his duties as to warning and the selection of fellow servants is not liable to servants employed to make an inspection for harm caused during such employment by the condition which they were employed to discover.

§ 514. Liability to Servants Completing Things

A servant engaged in continuing the process of manufacture of a structure, instrumentality, or other thing does not have a cause of action against the master because of the negligence of a fellow servant in the prior construction or inspection of such thing, if the master has performed his duties of care as to materials, organization, and the selection of fellow servants.

§ 515. Liability to Servants Manufacturing Their Own Instrumentalities

If a master supplies a group of servants with carefully selected materials out of which they manufacture a structure or appliance to be used by them for temporary construction purposes, the master is not liable to one of them for harm caused during such use by the negligence of another member of the group in its construction, if the master has performed his duties of care as to planning, supervision, and the selection of fellow servants.

§ 516. Liability to Volunteer Assistants of Servants and to Servants of Independent Contractors

The duties of a master to his servants do not extend to those who assist his servants in the performance of the master's work, but who are not his servants.

§ 517.   Liability to Lent Servants

A servant knowing that he has been lent by his master to serve another as his servant has the rights of a servant against the second master but not those of a servant against the first.

§ 518.   Liability of Apparent Master and Undisclosed Master

(1)   One who employs another as his servant is subject to liability to him for unsafe working conditions although the employment is on behalf of an undisclosed principal.

(2)   An undisclosed principal is subject to liability for unsafe working conditions to a servant or subservant employed for him by a servant or other agent empowered to employ such servant or subservant.

§ 519.   Liability of Master Required to Employ Servants From a Specified Class

The master's liability for unsafe working conditions does not extend to conditions of which the responsible cause is the negligence of a person to whom he is required to confide the control of such conditions and over whose directions he has no control, unless the master has notice of the conditions or of the incompetency of such person.

§ 520.   Statutory Duties

A master is subject to liability to his servants for harm caused to them by his failure to perform duties imposed upon him by statute for their protection.

TITLE D.   DEFENSES

§ 521.   Servant's Assumption of Risk

In the absence of a statute or an agreement to the contrary, a master is not liable to a servant for harm caused by the unsafe state of the premises or other conditions of the employment, if the servant, with knowledge of the facts and understanding of the risks, voluntarily enters or continues in the employment.

§ 522.   Assumption of Risk; Master Promises to Make Safe

Unless otherwise agreed, if a master manifests his intention to remedy dangerous conditions of employment for which he would be responsible to servants having no notice of them, he is subject to liability to a servant harmed by such conditions who reasonably believes that the conditions will be made safe, until such time as the servant has reason to believe that the conditions will not be changed.

§ 523.   Assumption of Risk; Service Coerced

Although a servant enters or continues in his employment with the knowledge that the conditions of his employment are unsafe, he is not barred from recovery for harm caused by the failure of the employer to make the conditions safe if, at the time when he so enters or remains, he is compelled by law to do so, or if he is coerced to act in the protection of his own interests or of the interests of others by a situation created through a breach of the master's duty.

§ 524.   Servant's Assumption of Risks Within Protection of Statutes

Whether or not a servant is barred from recovery against his master because the servant voluntarily encounters a known risk from which a statute requires the master to protect him depends upon the construction placed upon the statute.

§ 525.   Servant's Contributory Negligence

A servant harmed by a violation of the master's duty of care is subject to the defense of contributory negligence if his own negligence is a contributing cause of the harm.

§ 526.   Servant's Disobedience of Orders

Unless a statute provides otherwise, a servant harmed by the concurrence of his own wilful and unjustified violation of orders and the negligence of the master has no cause of action against his master for such harm.

§ 527.   Illegal Employment

A servant knowingly assisting in an illegal enterprise conducted by the master is barred from recovery against the master for harm received as the result of a failure by the master to perform what would otherwise be his non-delegable duties, under the conditions which bar any person assisting another in the commission of illegal acts from recovery for the harmful conduct of the other.

§ 528.   Workmen's Compensation Acts

The freedom of a master from liability to a servant for the conduct of a fellow servant, his liability for personal fault, and his liability for failure to perform his non-delegable duties may be diminished or terminated by statutes providing for compensation to be paid to servants for harm arising out of and in the course of their employment, irrespective of fault.

RESTATEMENT (THIRD) OF AGENCY (2006)

Table of Sections

Chapter 1

INTRODUCTORY MATTERS

TOPIC 1. DEFINITIONS AND TERMINOLOGY

Chapter 2

PRINCIPLES OF ATTRIBUTION

TOPIC 1. ACTUAL AUTHORITY

TOPIC 2. APPARENT AUTHORITY

TOPIC 3. RESPONDEAT SUPERIOR

TOPIC 4. RELATED DOCTRINES

Chapter 3

CREATION AND TERMINATION OF AUTHORITY AND AGENCY RELATIONSHIPS

TOPIC 1. CREATING AND EVIDENCING ACTUAL AUTHORITY

TOPIC 2. CREATING APPARENT AUTHORITY

RESTATEMENT (THIRD) OF AGENCY (2006)

TOPIC 3.   CAPACITY TO ACT AS PRINCIPAL OR AGENT

TOPIC 4.   TERMINATION OF AGENT'S POWER

TITLE A.   TERMINATION OF ACTUAL AUTHORITY

TITLE B.   TERMINATION OF APPARENT AUTHORITY

TITLE C.   IRREVOCABLE POWERS

TOPIC 5.   AGENTS WITH MULTIPLE PRINCIPALS

Chapter 4

RATIFICATION

Chapter 5

NOTIFICATIONS AND NOTICE

Chapter 6

CONTRACTS AND OTHER TRANSACTIONS
WITH THIRD PARTIES

TOPIC 1.   PARTIES TO CONTRACTS

RESTATEMENT (THIRD) OF AGENCY (2006)

Chapter 1

INTRODUCTORY MATTERS

TOPIC 1. DEFINITIONS AND TERMINOLOGY

§ 1.01   Agency Defined

Agency is the fiduciary relationship that arises when one person (a "principal") manifests assent to another person (an "agent") that the agent shall act on the principal's behalf and subject to the principal's control, and the agent manifests assent or otherwise consents so to act.

Comment f. Principal's power and right of interim control

(1). Principal's power and right of interim control—in general. An essential element of agency is the principal's right to control the agent's actions. Control is a concept that embraces a wide spectrum of meanings, but within any relationship of agency the principal initially states what the agent shall and shall not do, in specific or general terms. Additionally, a principal has the right to give interim instructions or directions to the agent once their relationship is established. Within an organization the right to control its agents is essential to the organization's ability to function, regardless of its size, structure, or degree of hierarchy or complexity. In an organization, it is often another agent, one holding a supervisory position, who gives the directions. For definitions of the terms "superior" and "subordinate" coagents, see § 1.04(9). A principal may exercise influence over an agent's actions in other ways as well. Incentive structures that reward the agent for achieving results affect the agent's actions. In an organization, assigning a specified function with a functionally descriptive title to a person tends to control activity because it manifests what types of activity are approved by the principal to all who know of the function and title, including their holder.

A relationship of agency is not present unless the person on whose behalf action is taken has the right to control the actor. Thus, if a person is appointed by a court to act as a receiver, the receiver is not the agent of the person whose affairs the receiver manages because the appointing court retains the power to control the receiver.

A principal's control over an agent will as a practical matter be incomplete because no agent is an automaton who mindlessly but perfectly executes commands. A principal's power to give instructions, created by the agency relationship, does not mean that all instructions the principal gives are proper. An agent's duty of obedience does not require the agent to obey instructions to commit a crime or a tort or to violate established professional standards. See § 8.09(2). Moreover, an agent's duty of obedience does not supersede the agent's power to resign and terminate the agency relationship. See § 3.10.

The power to give interim instructions distinguishes principals in agency relationships from those who contract to receive services provided by persons who are not agents. In many agreements to provide services, the agreement between the service provider and the recipient specifies terms and conditions creating contractual obligations that, if enforceable, prescribe or delimit the choices that the service provider has the right to make. In particular, if the service provider breaches a contractual obligation, the service recipient has a claim for breach of contract. The service provider may be constrained by both the existence of such an obligation and the prospect of remedies for breach of contract. The fact that such an agreement imposes constraints on the service provider does not mean that the service recipient has an interim right to give instructions to the provider. Thus, setting standards in an agreement for acceptable service quality does not of itself create a right of control. Additionally, if a service provider is retained to give an independent assessment, the expectation of independence is in tension with a right of control in the service recipient.

To the extent the parties have created a relationship of agency, however, the principal has a power of control even if the principal has previously agreed with the agent that the principal will not give interim instructions to the agent or will not otherwise interfere in the agent's exercise of discretion. However, a principal who has made such an agreement but then subsequently exercises its power of control may breach contractual duties owed to the agent, and the agent may have remedies available for the breach.

If an agent disregards or contravenes an instruction, the doctrine of actual authority, defined in § 2.01, governs the consequences as between the principal and the agent. Section 8.09 states an agent's duties to act only within the scope of actual authority and to comply with lawful instructions. The rights and obligations of the third party with whom the agent interacts are governed by the doctrines of actual authority and apparent authority. Doctrines of estoppel, restitution, and ratification are also relevant under some circumstances. See §§ 2.03, 2.05–2.07, and 4.01–4.08.

The principal's right of control in an agency relationship is a narrower and more sharply defined concept than domination or influence more generally. Many positions and relationships give one person the ability to dominate or influence other persons but not the right to control their actions. Family ties, friendship, perceived expertise, and religious beliefs are often the source of influence or dominance, as are the variety of circumstances that create a strong position in bargaining. A position of dominance or influence does not in itself mean that a person is a principal in a relationship of agency with the person over whom dominance or influence may be exercised. A relationship is one of agency only if the person susceptible to dominance or influence has consented to act on behalf of the other and the other has a right of control, not simply an ability to bring influence to bear.

The right to veto another's decisions does not by itself create the right to give affirmative directives that action be taken, which is integral to the right of control within common-law agency. Thus, a debtor does not become a creditor's agent when a loan agreement gives the creditor veto rights over decisions the debtor may make. Moreover, typically a debtor does not consent to act on behalf of the creditor as opposed to acting in its own interests.

The principal's right of control presupposes that the principal retains the capacity throughout the relationship to assess the agent's performance, provide instructions to the agent, and terminate the agency relationship by revoking the agent's authority. See § 3.10 on the principal's power to revoke authority. Under the common law of agency, as stated in Restatement Second, Agency § 122(1), a durable agency power, one that survives the principal's loss of mental competence, was not feasible because of the loss of control by the principal. Section 3.08(2), like statutes in all states, recognizes the efficacy of durable powers, which enable an agent to act on behalf of a principal incapable of exercising control. Legitimating the power does not eliminate the risks for the principal that are inherent when the agent is not subject to direction or termination by the principal.

(2). Principal's power and right of interim control—corporate context. Many questions testing the nature of the right of control arise as a result of the legal consequences of incorporating or creating a juridical or legal person distinct from its shareholders, its governing body, and its agents. A corporation's agents are its own because it is a distinct legal person; they are not the agents of other affiliated corporations unless, separately, an agency relation has been created between the agents and the affiliated corporation. Similarly, the hierarchical link between a local union and its international affiliate does not by itself create a relationship of agency between the local and the international.

Although a corporation's shareholders elect its directors and may have the right to remove directors once elected, the directors are neither the shareholders' nor the corporation's agents as defined in this section, given the treatment of directors within contemporary corporation law in the United States.

Directors' powers originate as the legal consequence of their election and are not conferred or delegated by shareholders. Although corporation statutes require shareholder approval for specific fundamental transactions, corporation law generally invests managerial authority over corporate affairs in a board of directors, not in shareholders, providing that management shall occur by or under the board of directors. Thus, shareholders ordinarily do not have a right to control directors by giving binding instructions to them. If the statute under which a corporation has been incorporated so permits, shareholders may be allocated power to give binding instructions to directors through a provision in the corporation's articles or through a validly adopted shareholder agreement. The fact that a corporation statute may refer to directors as the corporation's "agents" for a particular purpose does not place directors in an agency relationship with shareholders for purposes of the common law of agency. In any event, directors' ability to bind the corporation is invested in the directors as a board, not in individual directors acting unilaterally. A director may, of course, also be an employee or officer (who may or may not be an employee) of the corporation, giving the director an additional and separate conventional position or role as an agent. Fellow directors may, with that director's consent, appoint a director as an agent to act on behalf of the corporation in some respect or matter.

Comment g. Acting on behalf of. The common-law definition of agency requires as an essential element that the agent consent to act on the principal's behalf, as well as subject to the principal's control. From the standpoint of the principal, this is the purpose for creating the relationship. The common law of agency encompasses employment as well as nonemployment relations. Employee and nonemployee agents who represent their principal in transactions with third parties act on the principal's account and behalf. Employee-agents whose work does not involve transactional interactions with third parties also act "on behalf of" their employer-principal. By consenting to act on behalf of the principal, an agent who is an employee consents to do the work that the employer directs and to do it subject to the employer's instructions. In either case, actions "on behalf of" a principal do not necessarily entail that the principal will benefit as a result.

In any relationship created by contract, the parties contemplate a benefit to be realized through the other party's performance. Performing a duty created by contract may well benefit the other party but the performance is that of an agent only if the elements of agency are present. A purchaser is not "acting on behalf of" a supplier in a distribution relationship in which goods are purchased from the supplier for resale. A purchaser who resells goods supplied by another is acting as a principal, not an agent. However, courts may treat a trademark licensee as the agent of the licensor in certain situations, with the result that the licensor is liable to third parties for defective goods produced by licensees.

An actor who acts under the immediate control of another person is not that person's agent unless the actor has agreed to act on the person's behalf. For example, a foreman or supervisor in charge of a crew of laborers exercises full and detailed control over the laborers' work activities. The relationship between the foreman and the laborers is not an agency relationship despite the foreman's full control, nor is their relationship one of subagency. Section 1.04(8) defines subagency. The foreman and the laborers are coagents of a common employer who occupy different strata within an organizational hierarchy. See § 1.04(9), which defines "superior" and "subordinate" coagents. The foreman's role of direction, defined by the organization, does not make the laborers the foreman's own agents. The laborers act on behalf of their common employer, not the foreman. Likewise, the captain of a ship and its crew are coagents, hierarchically stratified, who have consented to act on behalf of their common principal, the ship's owner.

It is possible to create a power to affect a person's legal relations to be exercised for the benefit of the holder of the power. Such powers typically are created as security for the interests of the holder or otherwise to benefit a person other than the person who creates the power. Consequently, the holder of such a power is not an agent as defined in this section, even though the power has the form of agency and, if exercised, will result in some of agency's legal consequences. The creator does not have a right to control the power holder's use of the power, and the power holder is not under a duty to use it in the interests of the creator. Sections 3.12–3.13 specifically treat powers given as security.

Relationships of agency are among the larger family of relationships in which one person acts to further the interests of another and is subject to fiduciary obligations. Agency is not antithetical to these other relationships, and whether a fiduciary is, additionally, an agent of another depends on the circumstances of the particular relationship. For example, as defined in Restatement Third, Trusts § 2, a trust is a fiduciary relationship with respect to property that arises from a manifestation of intention to create that relationship; a trustee is not an agent of the settlor or beneficiaries unless the term trustee to the control of either the settlor or the beneficiaries. Principals in agency to terminate authority and thus remove the agent; trust beneficiaries, in cont remove the trustee.

As agents, all employees owe duties of loyalty to their employers. The specific implicatic the position the employee occupies, the nature of the employer's assets to which the employee has and the degree of discretion that the employee's work requires. However ministerial or routinized a work assignment may be, no agent, whether or not an employee, is simply a pair of hands, legs, or eyes. All are sentient and, capable of disloyal action, all have the duty to act loyally. For further discussion of the scope of fiduciary duty, see § 8.01, Comment *c*.

§ 1.02 Parties' Labeling and Popular Usage Not Controlling

An agency relationship arises only when the elements stated in § 1.01 are present. Whether a relationship is characterized as agency in an agreement between parties or in the context of industry or popular usage is not controlling.

§ 1.03 Manifestation

A person manifests assent or intention through written or spoken words or other conduct.

§ 1.04 Terminology

(1) *Coagents.* Coagents have agency relationships with the same principal. A coagent may be appointed by the principal or by another agent actually or apparently authorized by the principal to do so.

(2) *Disclosed, undisclosed, and unidentified principals.*

(a) *Disclosed principal.* A principal is disclosed if, when an agent and a third party interact, the third party has notice that the agent is acting for a principal and has notice of the principal's identity.

(b) *Undisclosed principal.* A principal is undisclosed if, when an agent and a third party interact, the third party has no notice that the agent is acting for a principal.

(c) *Unidentified principal.* A principal is unidentified if, when an agent and a third party interact, the third party has notice that the agent is acting for a principal but does not have notice of the principal's identity.

(3) *Gratuitous agent.* A gratuitous agent acts without a right to compensation.

(4) *Notice.* A person has notice of a fact if the person knows the fact, has reason to know the fact, has received an effective notification of the fact, or should know the fact to fulfill a duty owed to another person. Notice of a fact that an agent knows or has reason to know is imputed to the principal as stated in §§ 5.03 and 5.04. A notification given to or by an agent is effective as notice to or by the principal as stated in § 5.02.

(5) *Person.* A person is (a) an individual; (b) an organization or association that has legal capacity to possess rights and incur obligations; (c) a government, political subdivision, or instrumentality or entity created by government; or (d) any other entity that has legal capacity to possess rights and incur obligations.

(6) *Power given as security.* A power given as security is a power to affect the legal relations of its creator that is created in the form of a manifestation of actual authority and held for the benefit of the holder or a third person. It is given to protect a legal or equitable title or to secure the performance of a duty apart from any duties owed the holder of the power by its creator that are incident to a relationship of agency under § 1.01.

(7) *Power of attorney.* A power of attorney is an instrument that states an agent's authority.

(8) *Subagent.* A subagent is a person appointed by an agent to perform functions that the agent has consented to perform on behalf of the agent's principal and for whose conduct the appointing agent is responsible to the principal. The relationship between an appointing agent and a subagent is one of agency, created as stated in § 1.01.

(9) *Superior and subordinate coagents.* A superior coagent has the right, conferred by the principal, direct a subordinate coagent.

(10) *Trustee and agent-trustee.* A trustee is a holder of property who is subject to fiduciary duties to deal with the property for the benefit of charity or for one or more persons, at least one of whom is not the sole trustee. An agent-trustee is a trustee subject to the control of the settlor or of one or more beneficiaries.

Chapter 2

PRINCIPLES OF ATTRIBUTION

TOPIC 1. ACTUAL AUTHORITY

§ 2.01   Actual Authority

An agent acts with actual authority when, at the time of taking action that has legal consequences for the principal, the agent reasonably believes, in accordance with the principal's manifestations to the agent, that the principal wishes the agent so to act.

Comment b. Terminology. As defined in this section, "actual authority" is a synonym for "true authority," a term used in some opinions. The definition in this section does not attempt to classify different types of actual authority on the basis of the degree of detail in the principal's manifestation, which may consist of written or spoken words or other conduct. See § 1.03. As commonly used, the term "express authority" often means actual authority that a principal has stated in very specific or detailed language.

The term "implied authority" has more than one meaning. "Implied authority" is often used to mean actual authority either (1) to do what is necessary, usual, and proper to accomplish or perform an agent's express responsibilities or (2) to act in a manner in which an agent believes the principal wishes the agent to act based on the agent's reasonable interpretation of the principal's manifestation in light of the principal's objectives and other facts known to the agent. These meanings are not mutually exclusive. Both fall within the definition of actual authority. Section 2.02, which delineates the scope of actual authority, subsumes the practical consequences of implied authority.

The term "inherent agency power," used in Restatement Second, Agency, and defined therein by § 8A, is not used in this Restatement. Inherent agency power is defined as "a term used . . . to indicate the power of an agent which is derived not from authority, apparent authority or estoppel, but solely from the agency relation and exists for the protection of persons harmed by or dealing with a servant or other agent." Other doctrines stated in this Restatement encompass the justifications underpinning § 8A, including the importance of interpretation by the agent in the agent's relationship with the principal, as well as the doctrines of apparent authority, estoppel, and restitution.

§ 2.02   Scope of Actual Authority

(1) An agent has actual authority to take action designated or implied in the principal's manifestations to the agent and acts necessary or incidental to achieving the principal's objectives, as the agent reasonably understands the principal's manifestations and objectives when the agent determines how to act.

(2) An agent's interpretation of the principal's manifestations is reasonable if it reflects any meaning known by the agent to be ascribed by the principal and, in the absence of any meaning known to the agent, as a reasonable person in the agent's position would interpret the manifestations in light of the context, including circumstances of which the agent has notice and the agent's fiduciary duty to the principal.

(3) An agent's understanding of the principal's objectives is reasonable if it accords with the principal's manifestations and the inferences that a reasonable person in the agent's position would draw from the circumstances creating the agency.

TOPIC 2. APPARENT AUTHORITY

§ 2.03 Apparent Authority

Apparent authority is the power held by an agent or other actor to affect a principal's legal relations with third parties when a third party reasonably believes the actor has authority to act on behalf of the principal and that belief is traceable to the principal's manifestations.

TOPIC 3. RESPONDEAT SUPERIOR

§ 2.04 Respondeat Superior

An employer is subject to liability for torts committed by employees while acting within the scope of their employment.

TOPIC 4. RELATED DOCTRINES

§ 2.05 Estoppel to Deny Existence of Agency Relationship

A person who has not made a manifestation that an actor has authority as an agent and who is not otherwise liable as a party to a transaction purportedly done by the actor on that person's account is subject to liability to a third party who justifiably is induced to make a detrimental change in position because the transaction is believed to be on the person's account, if

(1)   the person intentionally or carelessly caused such belief, or

(2)   having notice of such belief and that it might induce others to change their positions, the person did not take reasonable steps to notify them of the facts.

§ 2.06 Liability of Undisclosed Principal

(1)   An undisclosed principal is subject to liability to a third party who is justifiably induced to make a detrimental change in position by an agent acting on the principal's behalf and without actual authority if the principal, having notice of the agent's conduct and that it might induce others to change their positions, did not take reasonable steps to notify them of the facts.

(2)   An undisclosed principal may not rely on instructions given an agent that qualify or reduce the agent's authority to less than the authority a third party would reasonably believe the agent to have under the same circumstances if the principal had been disclosed.

Comment c. Rationale. The principle stated in this section will result in liability in a relatively small number of cases in which a third party deals with an agent but has no notice that the agent represents the interests of another. Under subsection (1), a principal is subject to liability to a third party who is justifiably induced to make a detrimental change in position by the conduct of an agent acting without actual authority when the principal has notice of the agent's conduct and its likely impact on third parties and fails to take reasonable steps to inform them of the facts. The underlying principle is consistent with the estoppel doctrine stated in § 2.05. Under subsection (2), a principal is subject to liability to a third party when the third party would have no reason to inquire into the scope of the agent's authority if the third party knew the agent acted on behalf of a principal. The principal may not rely on qualifications or reductions to the agent's authority when the doctrine of apparent authority would make the qualification or restriction ineffective as to an agent acting on behalf of a disclosed or an unidentified principal. In such cases, the principal has chosen to place the agent in a position in which it is reasonable for third parties to believe that the agent has authority consistent with the position.

The rule stated in this section, like the doctrine of apparent authority, protects third parties by backstopping actual authority when circumstances might otherwise permit the principal opportunistically to speculate at the expense of third parties. See § 2.03, Comment *c.* Apparent authority does not arise when a principal is undisclosed because no manifestation has been made that the actor with whom the third party interacts has authority to act as an agent.

A further rationale for the doctrine stated in this section is protection of the reasonable expectations of third parties who deal with an ongoing enterprise following an undisclosed sale to a new owner, whether or not affiliated in some manner with the former owner, when the former owner continues to operate the enterprise as agent on behalf of the new owner. The enterprise's new owner, as undisclosed principal, would or reasonably should expect that third parties will continue to deal with the now-agent as if no change had occurred. If the agent operates a business under the agent's name, the appearance to the third party may be that the agent owns the business and that its assets will be available to satisfy business-related obligations incurred by the agent. The opportunity for speculation provided the principal would emerge when the principal has limited the agent's authority and the agent enters into a contract that exceeds the agent's actual authority. Then, if the contract is advantageous to the principal, neither the principal nor the agent will raise the agent's lack of authority and the third party will not know of it. On the other hand, if the contract then is disadvantageous to the principal, the principal may assert lack of authority as a defense.

The doctrine allocates to the principal the risk that the agent will deviate from the principal's instructions while doing acts that are consistent with the apparent position the agent occupies, which are acts that third parties would anticipate an agent in such a position would have authority to do and may well be acts that are foreseeable to the principal. Such acts are especially likely to be foreseeable when they are consistent with the agent's position although they contravene the principal's instructions.

A third party who deals with an actor, lacking notice that the actor is someone's agent, does not expect the liability of any person in addition to the immediate actor with whom the third party deals. Estoppel's perspective is broader but less well defined. The question is whether it is unjust, in particular circumstances, to permit a principal who has chosen to deal through an agent but to remain undisclosed to have the benefit of restrictions on the agent's authority. In the instance in which the rule is applicable, it is unlikely that the third party will inquire into the status of the immediate actor or seek to identify the existence of restrictions on that actor's right to interact with legal consequences for the third party. The need to make such inquiries, in the circumstances to which this doctrine applies, is unlikely to occur to a reasonable third party, and making the inquiry may be difficult or its cost may seem excessive relative to the magnitude of the particular transaction. When a third party previously dealt with the agent as the owner of the business now managed by the agent, the third party may assume that inquiry is unnecessary for transactions similar to prior transactions. Separately, if an undisclosed principal has notice of an agent's unauthorized actions and notice that a third party will as a consequence be induced to make a detrimental change in position, the undisclosed principal may be estopped to deny the agent's authority. The undisclosed principal may avoid estoppel by disclosing the agent's status and the extent of the agent's authority.

The doctrine encompasses deviations from actual authority of a sort that would not lead a reasonable third party to inquire separately into the scope of the agent's authority. Such deviations are foreseeable to the principal and are likely not to be contested by any principal, whether or not undisclosed, when they appear likely to benefit the principal.

§ 2.07   Restitution of Benefit

If a principal is unjustly enriched at the expense of another person by the action of an agent or a person who appears to be an agent, the principal is subject to a claim for restitution by that person.

Chapter 3

CREATION AND TERMINATION OF AUTHORITY AND AGENCY RELATIONSHIPS

TOPIC 1. CREATING AND EVIDENCING ACTUAL AUTHORITY

§ 3.01 Creation of Actual Authority

Actual authority, as defined in § 2.01, is created by a principal's manifestation to an agent that, as reasonably understood by the agent, expresses the principal's assent that the agent take action on the principal's behalf.

§ 3.02 Formal Requirements

If the law requires a writing or record signed by the principal to evidence an agent's authority to bind a principal to a contract or other transaction, the principal is not bound in the absence of such a writing or record. A principal may be estopped to assert the lack of such a writing or record when a third party has been induced to make a detrimental change in position by the reasonable belief that an agent has authority to bind the principal that is traceable to a manifestation made by the principal.

Comment b. Equal-dignity requirements. Creating actual authority under § 3.01 does not require a writing or other formality. However, legislation in many states imposes what is often termed an "equal dignity" requirement for the creation of authority or agency applicable to specific types of agreements. As with the Statute of Frauds more generally, the purpose is to prevent fraud and perjury by safeguarding the principal against agreements made by an agent who lacks authority. Under an equal-dignity rule, if a transaction is unenforceable unless the party to be charged has agreed in writing to be bound, an agent's authority to enter into such a transaction on behalf of a principal must likewise be in writing. Such rules also apply to ratification. See § 4.02, Comment *e.* If an agent acted with apparent authority as defined in § 2.03 but no writing or record evidences the agent's authority, the principal is not bound to contracts or other transactions to which an equal-dignity rule applies.

A writing includes "any intentional reduction to tangible form," see Restatement Second, Contracts § 131, Comment *d.* A record includes an electronic record that is given the legal effect of a writing. Electronic records are given the legal effect of paper-and-ink writings by legislation, including the Uniform Electronic Transactions Act § 7 (1999) and the federal Electronic Signatures in Global and National Commerce Act § 101(a) (2000). A writing is signed by the principal by affixing a symbol that evidences intention to authenticate the writing. See Restatement Second, Contracts § 134. Similarly, an electronic record is signed by attaching to it an electronic sound, symbol, or process that is adopted with the intention of signing the record. See Uniform Electronic Transactions Act § 2(8).

Equal-dignity rules are either elements in a statute of frauds or are stated in separate statutes. Equal-dignity rules apply when a statute of frauds requires the underlying agreement to be evidenced by a writing signed by the party to be charged, including agreements for the sale or lease of land and suretyship agreements. On the scope of contracts to which statutes of frauds apply, see Restatement Second, Contracts § 110. Equal-dignity rules are inapplicable when a writing is required by agreement but not by law. However, a contract may not be binding when a contractual provision itself requires that the principal sign personally.

Equal-dignity rules have been applied with some stringency. For example, when one spouse acts as the agent of the other who owns property, or as an agent when both spouses own property jointly, the equal-dignity rule requires the agent-spouse's authorization to be in writing. If a principal executes a contract but leaves blanks that are completed by the agent, the contract may not be enforceable against the principal if the third party has notice that the agent may fill in the blanks only when the agent is authorized in writing to do so.

Nevertheless, the application of equal-dignity rules should not outrun their purpose. Equal-dignity rules do not apply when an action on a contract is brought by the principal against a third party. An equal-dignity rule may be satisfied by a writing or record executed by a principal following the agent's execution of the contract or transaction. Moreover, if an agent has acted without actual authority, as well as without prior written authorization, the principal would be able to ratify the transaction by a signed writing, see § 4.01, Comment *e*, so long as the principal ratifies prior to a manifestation from the third party that the third party has withdrawn from the transaction, see § 4.05(1). Additionally, an equal-dignity rule does not create a defense that an agent may assert against the third party, such as when the agent misrepresents authority. On an agent's warranties of authority, see § 6.10. On an agent's representations, see § 6.11.

TOPIC 2.   CREATING APPARENT AUTHORITY

§ 3.03   Creation of Apparent Authority

Apparent authority, as defined in § 2.03, is created by a person's manifestation that another has authority to act with legal consequences for the person who makes the manifestation, when a third party reasonably believes the actor to be authorized and the belief is traceable to the manifestation.

TOPIC 3.   CAPACITY TO ACT AS PRINCIPAL OR AGENT

§ 3.04   Capacity to Act as Principal

(1)   An individual has capacity to act as principal in a relationship of agency as defined in § 1.01 if, at the time the agent takes action, the individual would have capacity if acting in person.

(2)   The law applicable to a person that is not an individual governs whether the person has capacity to be a principal in a relationship of agency as defined in § 1.01, as well as the effect of the person's lack or loss of capacity on those who interact with it.

(3)   If performance of an act is not delegable, its performance by an agent does not constitute performance by the principal.

§ 3.05   Capacity to Act as Agent

Any person may ordinarily be empowered to act so as to affect the legal relations of another. The actor's capacity governs the extent to which, by so acting, the actor becomes subject to duties and liabilities to the person whose legal relations are affected or to third parties.

TOPIC 4.   TERMINATION OF AGENT'S POWER

TITLE A.   TERMINATION OF ACTUAL AUTHORITY

§ 3.06   Termination of Actual Authority—In General

An agent's actual authority may be terminated by:

(1)   the agent's death, cessation of existence, or suspension of powers as stated in § 3.07(1) and (3); or

(2)   the principal's death, cessation of existence, or suspension of powers as stated in § 3.07(2) and (4); or

(3)   the principal's loss of capacity, as stated in § 3.08(1) and (3); or

(4)   an agreement between the agent and the principal or the occurrence of circumstances on the basis of which the agent should reasonably conclude that the principal no longer would assent to the agent's taking action on the principal's behalf, as stated in § 3.09; or

(5)   a manifestation of revocation by the principal to the agent, or of renunciation by the agent to the principal, as stated in § 3.10(1); or

(6)   the occurrence of circumstances specified by statute.

Comment b. Agreement between principal and agent and changes in circumstances. The basis for actual authority is a manifestation of assent made by a principal to an agent. See § 3.01. When the manifestation is embodied in an agreement that specifies circumstances under which the agent's actual authority shall terminate, occurrence of a specified circumstance effects termination of the principal's expressed assent. Regardless of whether the initial agreement contains a termination provision, mutual agreement to terminate the agency relationship is always effective to terminate the agent's actual authority. See § 3.09.

Following the principal's manifestation of assent to an agent, circumstances may change such that, at the time the agent takes action, it is not reasonable for the agent to believe that the principal at that time consents to the action being taken on the principal's behalf even though the principal has not manifested dissent to the action by that time. For example, the agent may become insolvent and have notice that it is important to the principal to be represented by a solvent agent. The agent may lose capacity to bind itself by a contract or to become subject to other obligations and have notice that it is important to the principal that the agent retain such capacity. Events that are totally outside the control of the agent or the principal may also make it unreasonable for the agent to believe that the principal consents to the agent's action. For example, if the principal retains the agent to sell goods in a particular geographically defined market, the occurrence of war or widespread civil unrest may so impair the value of the agent's efforts to the principal that the agent would not be reasonable in believing the principal wishes the agent to sell into the territory. The agent then lacks actual authority so to act but would have acted with actual authority had the agent acted prior to the change in circumstances. The focal point for determining whether an agent acted with actual authority is the time of action, not the time of the principal's manifestation, which may be earlier. See §§ 2.01 and 2.02.

An alternate analysis of the impact of changed circumstances, as set forth in Restatement Second, Agency, requires the use of at least two distinct focal points. First, it is posited that an agent has actual authority up until the agent receives notice of the changed circumstances. Notice that circumstances have changed, beyond those operative when the principal manifested consent to the agent, then implicitly modifies either the principal's manifestation of consent or the actual authority it engenders on the basis of the agent's reasonable belief in the principal's consent. See Restatement Second, Agency, Introductory Note to Chapter 5. Moreover, if circumstances thereafter revert to those present originally, the agent's actual authority, having once existed but thereafter having been terminated, is again revived. See Restatement Second, Agency § 108(2). This Restatement does not follow this alternate pattern of analysis because it is unnecessary in light of the nature of actual authority and the rules that determine whether an agent acted with actual authority. See §§ 2.01–2.02.

§ 3.07   Death, Cessation of Existence, and Suspension of Powers

(1)   The death of an individual agent terminates the agent's actual authority.

(2)   The death of an individual principal terminates the agent's actual authority. The termination is effective only when the agent has notice of the principal's death. The termination is also effective as against a third party with whom the agent deals when the third party has notice of the principal's death.

(3)   When an agent that is not an individual ceases to exist or commences a process that will lead to cessation of existence or when its powers are suspended, the agent's actual authority terminates except as provided by law.

(4)   When a principal that is not an individual ceases to exist or commences a process that will lead to cessation of its existence or when its powers are suspended, the agent's actual authority terminates except as provided by law.

§ 3.08   Loss of Capacity

(1)   An individual principal's loss of capacity to do an act terminates the agent's actual authority to do the act. The termination is effective only when the agent has notice that the principal's loss of capacity is permanent or that the principal has been adjudicated to lack capacity. The termination is also effective as against a third party with whom the agent deals when the third party has notice that the principal's loss of capacity is permanent or that the principal has been adjudicated to lack capacity.

(2)   A written instrument may make an agent's actual authority effective upon a principal's loss of capacity, or confer it irrevocably regardless of such loss.

(3)   If a principal that is not an individual loses capacity to do an act, its agent's actual authority to do the act is terminated.

§ 3.09   Termination by Agreement or by Occurrence of Changed Circumstances

An agent's actual authority terminates (1) as agreed by the agent and the principal, subject to the provisions of § 3.10; or (2) upon the occurrence of circumstances on the basis of which the agent should reasonably conclude that the principal no longer would assent to the agent's taking action on the principal's behalf.

§ 3.10   Manifestation Terminating Actual Authority

(1)   Notwithstanding any agreement between principal and agent, an agent's actual authority terminates if the agent renounces it by a manifestation to the principal or if the principal revokes the agent's actual authority by a manifestation to the agent. A revocation or a renunciation is effective when the other party has notice of it.

(2)   A principal's manifestation of revocation is, unless otherwise agreed, ineffective to terminate a power given as security or to terminate a proxy to vote securities or other membership or ownership interests that is made irrevocable in compliance with applicable legislation. See §§ 3.12–3.13.

TITLE B.   TERMINATION OF APPARENT AUTHORITY

§ 3.11   Termination of Apparent Authority

(1)   The termination of actual authority does not by itself end any apparent authority held by an agent.

(2)   Apparent authority ends when it is no longer reasonable for the third party with whom an agent deals to believe that the agent continues to act with actual authority.

TITLE C.   IRREVOCABLE POWERS

§ 3.12   Power Given as Security; Irrevocable Proxy

(1)   A power given as security is a power to affect the legal relations of its creator that is created in the form of a manifestation of actual authority and held for the benefit of the holder or a third person. This power is given to protect a legal or equitable title or to secure the performance of a duty apart from any duties owed the holder of the power by its creator that are incident to a relationship of agency under § 1.01. It is given upon the creation of the duty or title or for consideration. It is distinct from actual authority that the holder may exercise if the holder is an agent of the creator of the power.

(2)   A power to exercise voting rights associated with securities or a membership interest may be conferred on a proxy through a manifestation of actual authority. The power may be given as security under (1) and may be made irrevocable in compliance with applicable legislation.

§ 3.13   Termination of Power Given as Security or Irrevocable Proxy

(1)   A power given as security or an irrevocable proxy is terminated by an event that

(a)   discharges the obligation secured by the power or terminates the interest secured or supported by the proxy, or

(b)   makes its execution illegal or impossible, or

(c)   constitutes an effective surrender of the power or proxy by the person for whose benefit it was created or conferred.

(2)   Unless otherwise agreed, neither a power given as security nor a proxy made irrevocable as provided in § 3.12(2) is terminated by:

(a)   a manifestation revoking the power or proxy made by the person who created it; or

(b)   surrender of the power or proxy by its holder if it is held for the benefit of another person, unless that person consents; or

(c)   loss of capacity by the creator or the holder of the power or proxy; or

(d)   death of the holder of the power or proxy, unless the holder's death terminates the interest secured or supported by the power or proxy; or

(e)   death of the creator of the power or proxy, if the power or proxy is given as security for the performance of a duty that does not terminate with the death of its creator.

TOPIC 5.   AGENTS WITH MULTIPLE PRINCIPALS

§ 3.14   Agents with Multiple Principals

An agent acting in the same transaction or matter on behalf of more than one principal may be one or both of the following:

(a)   a subagent, as stated in § 3.15; or

(b)   an agent for coprincipals, as stated in § 3.16.

§ 3.15   Subagency

(1)   A subagent is a person appointed by an agent to perform functions that the agent has consented to perform on behalf of the agent's principal and for whose conduct the appointing agent is responsible to the principal. The relationships between a subagent and the appointing agent and between the subagent and the appointing agent's principal are relationships of agency as stated in § 1.01.

(2)   An agent may appoint a subagent only if the agent has actual or apparent authority to do so.

Comment b. Subagency contrasted with coagency. Agency creates a personal relationship between principal and agent; an agent's delegation of power to another person to act on behalf of the principal is inconsistent with the undertaking made when a person consents to act as agent on behalf of a principal. However, a principal may empower an agent to appoint another agent to act on the principal's behalf. The second agent may be a subagent or a coagent. See Comment *d* for discussion of the consequences that follow if the second agent is characterized as a subagent.

An agent who appoints a subagent delegates to the subagent power to act on behalf of the principal that the principal has conferred on the agent. A subagent acts subject to the control of the appointing agent, and the principal's legal position is affected by action taken by the subagent as if the action had been taken by the appointing agent. Thus, a subagent has two principals, the appointing agent and that agent's principal. Although an appointing agent has the right and duty to control a subagent, the interests and instructions of the appointing agent's principal are paramount. See Comment *d*.

In contrast, an agent who appoints a coagent does not delegate power held by the agent to the coagent. By empowering an agent to appoint a coagent, the principal creates a mechanism through which to generate additional relationships of agency between the principal and persons chosen by the agent. Coagents, although they may occupy dominant and subordinate positions within an organizational hierarchy, share a common principal.

A person appointed by an agent to act on behalf of the agent's principal is a subagent if the appointing agent has agreed with the principal that the appointing agent shall be responsible to the principal for the agent's conduct. Such agreement may be express or implied. For example, employees of an appointing agent whom the agent designates to act on behalf of the appointing agent's principal are presumed to be subagents, not coagents of the appointing agent. When an agent is itself a corporation or other legal person, its officers, employees, partners, or members who are designated to work on the principal's account are subagents. In contrast, when a manager within an organization hires persons as employees of the organization, those hired are presumed to be the hiring manager's coagents and not subagents. Employees of a single organization are presumed to be coagents of that organization, not subagents.

Comment c. Creation of subagency. An agent has actual authority to create a relationship of subagency when the agent reasonably believes, based on a manifestation from the principal, that the principal consents to the appointment of a subagent. For the definition of actual authority, see § 2.01. For the means by which a principal creates it, see § 3.01.

A principal's consent to the appointment of a subagent may be express or implied. For example, a principal's consent to the appointment of subagents may be implied when the principal retains an individual as agent to carry out a number of transactions and has notice that the amount of work involved exceeds the agent's individual capability or requires action that the agent may not legally perform, such as action for which the law requires a license. Implied consent to appoint subagents is also present when an agent is itself a person that is not an individual, such as a corporation.

Subagents may be appointed in series. This would occur when a subagent has actual or apparent authority to appoint another for whose conduct the appointing subagent is responsible.

An agent may have apparent authority to appoint a subagent if the principal has made a manifestation to third parties that the agent has such authority. Section 1.03 defines manifestation. Section 2.03 defines apparent authority; § 3.03 states how it is created. A principal may make a manifestation that an agent has actual authority to appoint subagents by placing the agent in a position in which agents customarily have such authority without notice to third parties that the agent's authority does not include the appointment of subagents. A subagent appointed by an agent acting with only apparent authority may act on behalf of the principal with actual authority. See Comment *d*.

If an agent acts without actual or apparent authority in purporting to appoint a subagent, the person so appointed is the agent solely of the appointing agent and is not the principal's subagent unless the principal ratifies the appointment. On the requisites for ratification, see Chapter 4.

In emergencies and other unforeseen circumstances, when communication between agent and principal is not feasible, an agent's actual authority to take action to protect the principal's interests may permit the agent to appoint a subagent although the principal has not previously manifested consent to the agent to make such an appointment. See § 2.02, Comment *d*.

A person may be appointed as a subagent even though the person does not expect to be compensated for actions taken.

Comment d. Consequences of subagency. As between a principal and third parties, it is immaterial that an action was taken by a subagent as opposed to an agent directly appointed by the principal. In this respect, subagency is governed by a principle of transparency that looks from the subagent to the principal and through the appointing agent. As to third parties, an action taken by a subagent carries the legal consequences for the principal that would follow were the action instead taken by the appointing agent. . . .

When a subagent works on a principal's account, notifications received by the subagent are effective as notifications to the principal to the same extent as if the principal had appointed the subagent directly. Likewise, notice of facts the subagent knows or has reason to know is imputed to the principal to the same extent as if the principal had appointed the subagent directly. . . .

As among a principal, an appointing agent, and a subagent, the fact that action is taken by a subagent may carry different or additional legal consequences than if the action were taken directly by the appointing agent or by a coagent of the appointing agent. The legal consequences of subagency reflect the distinct significance of (1) the relationship between an appointing agent and a subagent; (2) the relationship between a principal and an appointing agent; and (3) the relationship between a principal and a subagent. An appointing agent is responsible to the principal for the subagent's conduct. This may subject an appointing agent to liability for loss incurred by the principal as a consequence of misconduct by a subagent. A contract between the principal and the appointing agent that requires or permits the appointment of subagents will often delineate the extent of the appointing agent's liability and will require indemnification by the principal of the appointing agent. In contrast, an agent is subject to liability stemming from a coagent's conduct only when the agent's own conduct subjects the agent to liability. See § 7.01, Comments *b* and *d*.

Statutes may change the results that would otherwise follow when a subagent takes action. For example, under Article 4 of the Uniform Commercial Code, when the owner of an item deposits it with a bank for collection, the depositary bank is treated as the agent of the item's owner. If the depositary bank sends the item for collection to another bank, the collecting bank is treated as the owner's subagent. See U.C.C. § 4–201(a). However, under U.C.C. § 4–202, although a depositary bank has a duty to use ordinary care in selecting intermediaries and in giving proper instructions to them, it is not liable for another bank's "insolvency, neglect, misconduct, mistake, or default. . . ."

Although an appointing agent is responsible for a subagent's action and has the right and duty to control the subagent, the principal's interests and instructions are nonetheless paramount. Several specific doctrines reflect this general point. If a subagent acts without actual or apparent authority, only the principal may ratify the subagent's action; ratification by an appointing agent is effective only when the principal has authorized the appointing agent to ratify on its behalf. Moreover, a subagent is a fiduciary, as is any agent. See § 1.01. A subagent owes duties of loyalty to the principal as well as to the appointing agent. See §§ 8.01–8.06, which state the specifics of these duties. A subagent owes a duty of obedience to the principal as well as to the appointing agent. See § 8.09(2). However, the principal's rights as to the subagent are superior to rights of the appointing agent, even in the event of conflict or disagreement between principal and appointing agent.

If a subagent is appointed by an agent who acts with only apparent authority, the subagent is privileged to act on behalf of the principal because the subagent, on the basis of the principal's manifestation, reasonably believes that the appointing agent acted with the principal's consent in appointing the subagent. As a consequence, the principal is subject to liability to the subagent to indemnify the subagent as stated in § 8.14. The appointing agent, having acted without actual authority in appointing the subagent, is subject to liability to the principal as stated in § 8.09(1). The subagent is not subject to liability to third parties on the basis that the subagent breached warranties of authority. See § 6.10.

A principal's duties to a subagent are those owed to any agent, but the principal is not subject to duties created by agreement between the appointing agent and the subagent, including the appointing agent's agreement to compensate the subagent. See § 8.13, Comment d. A subagent may have set-off rights against the principal. See § 6.06.

Comment e. Termination of subagent's actual and apparent authority. Whether a subagent acts with actual authority depends on three separate consensual relationships: (1) between principal and appointing agent; (2) between appointing agent and subagent; and (3) between principal and subagent. A subagent's actual authority terminates upon notice to the subagent that any of these relationships is severed.

Additionally, circumstances that terminate an agent's actual authority by operation of law likewise terminate a subagent's authority. Thus, notice of the death of a principal or of an appointing agent terminates a subagent's actual authority, as does notice that the principal has revoked an appointing agent's actual authority. See §§ 3.07(2) and 3.10(1). If the relationship between an appointing agent and a subagent is severed, for example by notice of the appointing agent's death or loss of capacity, the subagent no longer acts under the control of the appointing agent who had responsibility for the subagent's acts. If a subagent is a lawyer who represents a client having diminished capacity, the lawyer's duties are as stated in Restatement Third, The Law Governing Lawyers § 24.

Additionally, a principal may terminate a subagent's actual authority by making a manifestation of revocation directly to the subagent or to the appointing agent. A manifestation revoking a subagent's actual authority made by the principal to the appointing agent should not be effective, in most circumstances, as to the subagent until the subagent has notice of it. A principal has rights and responsibilities of ultimate control, including ultimate control over chains of command and channels of communication. A principal may choose how best to communicate with a subagent, including how best to convey notice that the subagent's actual authority has been revoked. If the principal chooses to rely exclusively on the appointing agent as the channel of communication with the subagent, the principal at least ordinarily should bear the risk that the appointing agent will not duly deliver notice of revocation to the subagent.

In contrast, under the rule stated in Restatement Second, Agency § 137, Comment b, when a principal terminates a subagent's authority by giving notice of termination to the appointing agent, "the subagent's authority terminates only when the agent has had an opportunity to communicate with him." If the appointing agent, having had the opportunity to communicate with the subagent, does not do so, or does not do so effectively, the rule as stated in Restatement Second allocates to the subagent the risk of acting without actual authority, although the subagent lacks notice that the principal wishes to terminate the subagent's authority. The notice requirement stated in this Restatement instead allocates to the principal the risk that notice of revocation communicated only to the appointing agent may not reach the subagent. So allocating the risk is supported by a well-reasoned case in the real-estate context. The principal should bear this risk because the principal has consented to the appointment of subagents and because a subagent should be under no greater risk than is an agent of unwittingly taking an unauthorized action following the termination of actual authority.

A subagent may continue to act with apparent authority following termination of the subagent's actual authority when third parties reasonably believe that the subagent continues to act with actual authority on the basis of manifestations traceable to the appointing agent or the principal. See § 3.11.

Comment f. Transactions in real estate. Under the common-law rule in most states, a real-estate broker or salesperson associated with a broker who successfully markets property to a prospective buyer (hereinafter the "showing broker") is treated as the subagent of the broker with whom a prospective seller has listed the property (hereinafter the "listing broker"), even if the showing broker is not the listing broker's employee or associate. Conventional terminology applies the term "broker" or "real-estate broker" to a person holding a license to provide brokerage services. A broker may use the services of salespeople, who may be employees of the broker or the broker's nonemployee associates. Except where the context otherwise requires, the remainder of this Comment refers to all as "brokers."

The better rule, followed in a minority of states, characterizes a showing broker as the agent of the prospective buyer, and not the seller's subagent, when the terms of the relationship between the showing broker and the prospective buyer reasonably reflect the buyer's expectation that the showing broker represents the buyer. The minority rule is consistent with the policy reflected in legislation in a majority of states that explicitly permits a prospective buyer to appoint a real-estate broker to act as the buyer's agent.

A showing broker may be characterized as: (1) the seller's subagent, regardless of whether the broker has a relationship with the buyer that constitutes a relationship of agency as defined by § 1.01; (2) the buyer's agent when the relationship between buyer and broker constitutes a relationship of agency as defined by § 1.01; or (3) neither the agent nor the subagent of buyer or seller. If a showing broker is characterized as acting as agent for both buyer and seller, or as agent for buyer and subagent for seller, the agent is in a position of dual agency because the showing broker represents adverse parties to the same transaction. See § 8.03.

As the seller's subagent, a showing broker is presumed not to have a relationship of agency with the buyer and does not owe an agent's fiduciary duties to the buyer. It is well-settled, as a matter of industry practice and regulation as well as common-law agency, that a broker in a single real-estate transaction may not represent both buyer and seller unless both know of and consent to the dual representation. Unless such consent is given, a broker who represents both buyer and seller may forfeit any commission otherwise payable to the broker. See § 8.03, Comment *d.* In a transaction involving the same property, buyer and seller have interests that are adverse. The benefit that a seller will receive through a higher sales price will be paid by the buyer. Moreover, a broker who represents a prospective seller or buyer of property may have material information that, if disclosed to the other party, will disadvantage the broker's client. For example, information about the seller's reservation price—the lowest price at which the seller may be willing to sell—is material to price negotiations between the seller and prospective buyers. For further treatment of dual agency, see § 8.03.

The mechanism through which a relationship of subagency arises is an offer of a unilateral contract of subagency, made by the listing broker to showing brokers, that is accepted by the showing broker who produces a buyer able and willing to purchase the property at the listing price and terms or at other terms acceptable to the seller. Such an offer is often made when a listing broker lists property with a multiple listing service ("MLS"). A multiple listing service is an agreement among brokers in a particular geographic market to pool information about their listings. A showing broker may also become a subagent in the absence of MLS participation through a relationship of cooperation with the listing broker. When a showing broker produces an offer from a buyer to purchase at the seller's stated listing price and on terms otherwise consistent with the listing agreement, conventional MLS terms require that the listing broker split the commission to be paid by the seller with the successful showing broker.

The legal consequences of how a showing broker is characterized carry corresponding advantages as well as disadvantages from the standpoint of buyers and sellers of real estate. Characterizing a showing broker as the seller's subagent orients the showing broker's duties exclusively to the seller, with the implication that the broker must disclose to the seller all material information the broker learns about the buyer. This disadvantages a buyer if the showing broker discloses information the buyer has provided to the seller or the listing broker, such as the maximum price the buyer is willing to pay to acquire property. However, this characterization may be advantageous to the buyer if the showing broker induces the buyer to purchase a property through fraud because the buyer may rescind the transaction. For the circumstances under which a misrepresentation makes a contract voidable, see Restatement Second, Contracts § 164(1). To be sure, a seller may not perceive this consequence to be fair when the seller has had no contact with a showing broker who induces a purchase through fraud. In contrast, if a showing broker acts as a buyer's agent, the buyer will be limited to remedies against the broker if the seller is innocent of the fraud and has in good faith given value or changed position in reliance on the transaction. See Restatement Second, Contracts § 164(2). Neither buyer nor seller benefits if a showing broker is not characterized as either the seller's subagent or the buyer's agent because the duties of a nonagent showing broker are indeterminate. However, principals in real-estate transactions may benefit if nonagent showing brokers charge lower commissions than brokers who act as agents and subagents.

The common-law rule applicable to agency relationships in this context should reflect the reasonable expectations of prospective buyers and sellers of property and the real-estate professionals who act on their behalf. If a broker has agreed to assist a prospective buyer, it is reasonable for the prospective buyer to expect that the broker does not owe duties of loyalty to the seller of property that the buyer purchases. Treating a showing broker as the seller's subagent is likely to conflict with the expectations of a buyer to whom the showing broker has given guidance and, in many instances, advice. Moreover, a seller may reasonably expect that, as the seller's subagent, the showing broker will be loyal to the seller's interests and will not compromise them through advice or information that the showing broker may share with buyers. If a showing broker is treated as a buyer's agent, although the buyer loses the availability of rescission as a remedy in some situations, the buyer gains the advantages of representation by a professional whom the buyer is free to choose. Real-estate professionals are best served by rules that clarify the identity of parties to whom particular duties are owed and that do not create the risk of inadvertently acting as a dual agent for buyer and seller.

Empirical results confirm the significance to buyers of retaining the services of an agent who has clearly defined duties to represent the buyer, even when the agent is compensated by splitting a commission that will be payable from the proceeds of a sale and that will be augmented the greater the sale price. In Georgia, following the enactment of a statute that encourages buyers to retain their own agents, the average time required to sell a house fell, as did reported sale prices of expensive houses. Additionally, a large majority of buyers chose to be represented by their own agent.

Statutes in many states expressly permit prospective buyers to retain licensed real-estate brokers as agents. Since 1993, the Realtors' Association has permitted listing brokers to offer showing brokers, as an alternative to a relationship of subagency, a relationship of "cooperation and compensation" that is compatible both with a showing broker who acts as a buyer's agent as well as with a showing broker who acts as the seller's subagent.

Unless a statute so requires, a writing should not be necessary to establish that a prospective buyer and a real-estate broker have consented to create a relationship of agency. See § 3.02, Comment *e*, for discussion of statutes that impose a writing requirement on agreements to pay commissions to brokers. Statutes in some states require a written agreement to create a relationship of agency with either a listing broker or a buyer's agent.

If a prospective buyer does not create a relationship of agency as defined in § 1.01 with a showing broker, the showing broker should be treated as the seller's subagent if the seller has expressly or impliedly consented to the appointment of subagents by the listing broker. The showing broker should not be treated as the buyer's agent when no relationship of agency as defined in § 1.01 has been created between the buyer and the showing broker, nor should the showing broker be treated as an intermediary who acts as no one's agent, unless a statute so requires.

If a prospective buyer consents to a relationship of agency as defined in § 1.01 with a particular real-estate broker, it is incompatible with the duties thereby created for that broker additionally to act as subagent for the seller of property that the buyer purchases unless the buyer knows of the subagency and consents to it and unless the seller knows of and consents to the broker's relationship with the buyer. On consent by a principal to conduct by an agent that would otherwise breach the agent's duties of loyalty to the principal, see § 8.06. A broker retained by a prospective buyer would become a dual agent if the broker also acts as subagent on behalf of the seller of the property purchased by the buyer who is represented by the broker. This would occur if the property's owner lists it with the buyer's broker or if the buyer's broker is also characterized as the subagent of the property's owner. If the property in which a buyer is interested is listed in a MLS under terms that designate a successful showing broker as the seller's subagent, that designation should not be operative without the consent of a buyer who has previously retained the showing broker as the buyer's agent.

However, an agent is not a dual agent if there is no substantial risk that the agent's action on behalf of one principal will materially and adversely affect the agent's action on behalf of another principal. See § 8.03. An agent retained by a buyer does not become a dual agent by taking ministerial actions on behalf of a seller. Dual agency, as noted above, results when the broker whom a buyer has retained to act as the buyer's agent also serves as listing agent for the property purchased by the buyer, whether at the outset of the buyer's relationship with the broker or thereafter if the owner of the property lists it for sale with that broker. Under the common-law rule in most states, a broker has a relationship of agency with each of the broker's clients although the clients have agreed to be represented by individuals among the broker's cohort of employees and associates. Thus, a broker would be characterized as a dual agent when one employee or associate serves as the designated agent of a buyer and another serves as the seller's designated agent. Statutes in some states explicitly permit the practice of designated dual agency and impose specific writing and disclosure requirements. In contrast, a few statutes categorically prohibit dual agency in transactions but permit the use of nonagent intermediaries, as described below.

Relationships among brokers, sellers, and buyers have been recharacterized by statutes enacted by many states since the late 1980s. Statutes in many states expressly permit prospective buyers to retain licensed real-estate brokers to act as their agents. However, these statutes are disparate in specifying the default rule that characterizes a showing broker when a buyer has not appointed that broker as agent. Several statutes provide that subagency shall not be deemed to be created automatically or through participation in a MLS. Some statutes provide that, if no written agreement establishes a relationship of agency or subagency, a broker is treated as a "transaction broker," "transaction coordinator," or "facilitator" who does not act as either party's agent or subagent. Some statutes that permit the use of such nonagent intermediaries specify the duties owed by the intermediary. Many statutes make subagency the default characterization, either explicitly or implicitly by not specifying an alternative. Other statutes require specific types of disclosure, such as disclosure to a prospective buyer that a seller's agent represents the seller. Several statutes permit the parties to create a relationship of "designated dual agency" not subject to the usual consequences of dual agency, in which one sales associate in a real-estate brokerage represents the seller of a property and the other its buyer. Some statutes characterize such brokers as "limited agents," specifying their duties. Some statutes explicitly prohibit "designated dual agency." Statutes in a few states explicitly abrogate the common law of agency.

§ 3.16   Agent for Coprincipals

Two or more persons may as coprincipals appoint an agent to act for them in the same transaction or matter.

Chapter 4

RATIFICATION

§ 4.01   Ratification Defined

(1)   Ratification is the affirmance of a prior act done by another, whereby the act is given effect as if done by an agent acting with actual authority.

(2)   A person ratifies an act by

    (a)   manifesting assent that the act shall affect the person's legal relations, or

    (b)   conduct that justifies a reasonable assumption that the person so consents.

(3)   Ratification does not occur unless

    (a)   the act is ratifiable as stated in § 4.03,

    (b)   the person ratifying has capacity as stated in § 4.04,

    (c)   the ratification is timely as stated in § 4.05, and

    (d)   the ratification encompasses the act in its entirety as stated in § 4.07.

Comment b. The nature and effect of ratification. As the term is used in agency law, ratification is both an act and a set of effects. The act of ratification consists of an externally observable manifestation of assent to be bound by the prior act of another person. When the prior act did not otherwise affect the legal relations of the ratifier, ratification provides the basis on which the ratifier's legal relations are affected by the act. The set of effects that ratification creates are the consequences of actual authority. That is, when a person ratifies another's act, the legal consequence is that the person's legal relations are affected as they would have been had the actor been an agent acting with actual authority at the time of the act.

In most jurisdictions, ratification may create a relationship of agency when none existed between the actor and the ratifier at the time of the act. It is necessary that the actor have acted or purported to act on behalf of the ratifier. See § 4.03. This limits the range of ratifiable acts to those done by an actor who is an agent or who is not an agent but pretends to be.

Ratification often serves the function of clarifying situations of ambiguous or uncertain authority. A principal's ratification confirms or validates an agent's right to have acted as the agent did. That is, an agent's action may have been effective to bind the principal to the third party, and the third party to the principal, because the agent acted with apparent authority. See § 2.03. If the principal ratifies the agent's act, it is thereafter not necessary to establish that the agent acted with apparent authority. Moreover, by replicating the effects of actual authority, the principal's ratification eliminates claims the principal would otherwise have against the agent for acting without actual authority. See § 8.09, Comment *b*. The principal's ratification may also eliminate claims that third parties could assert against the agent when the agent has purported to be authorized to bind the principal but the principal is not bound. See § 6.10. Ratification is effective even when the third party knew that the agent lacked authority to bind the principal but nonetheless dealt with the agent.

Much of the doctrine applicable to ratification either determines the validity and significance of the principal's assent or makes ratification unavailable or limits its effects when unfair consequences otherwise would follow. Although ratification creates the legal effects of actual authority, it reverses in time the sequence between an agent's conduct and the principal's manifestation of assent. If the principal ratifies, the relevant time for determining legal consequences is the time of the agent's act. See § 4.02, Comment *b*. Thus, if the agent purported to commit the principal to a transaction, the principal and third party become bound as of the time of the agent's commitment when the principal ratifies. If the agent's act constituted a tort, the time of the act is the time as of which the principal becomes vicariously liable, if the principal ratifies the agent's act. If the agent receives a notification, or learns information relevant to the action the agent takes, the notification is effective as to the principal, and knowledge of the information is imputed to the principal, as of the time of the agent's act if the principal ratifies it. See § 5.02, which covers notifications.

The sole requirement for ratification is a manifestation of assent or other conduct indicative of consent by the principal. To be effective as a ratification, the principal's assent need not be communicated to the agent or to third parties whose legal relations will be affected by the ratification. See Comment *d*. The principal is not bound by a ratification made without knowledge of material facts about the agent's act unless the principal chose to ratify with awareness that such knowledge was lacking. See § 4.06. When there are two or more coprincipals, each must ratify to be bound. In most cases in which the outcome turns on whether a principal has ratified, the claim of ratification is asserted by a third party who seeks to bind the principal in the absence of other bases to attribute the legal consequences of an agent's act to the principal. It is fair to hold the principal to such consequences when the principal has, after the fact, assented to the agent's act. The principal's ability to ratify also enables the principal to create a clear basis on which to hold the third party to transactions that are desirable from the principal's perspective. The doctrines stated in §§ 4.05, 4.07, and 4.08 deny the principal the power to ratify when the result of ratification would be unfair. Absent such circumstances, it is not unfair to bind the third party when the principal elects to ratify a transaction because the result binds the third party only as originally anticipated or hoped, which is to the terms of a transaction with the principal.

The effects of the principal's ratification are also fair to the agent because by assenting to the agent's act the principal usually eliminates claims that the principal or the third party might otherwise assert against the agent. Ratification is an all-or-nothing proposition in two basic respects. First, in most cases, by ratifying the principal eliminates claims the principal might otherwise have against the agent for acting without actual authority. See § 4.02(2) for exceptions to this general principle. Were the doctrine otherwise, the principal could speculate at the agent's expense by ratifying a transaction as against the third party, but holding the agent accountable if, after the time of ratification, the transaction turned out to be a losing proposition for the principal. Second, a principal must ratify a single transaction in its entirety, thereby becoming subject to its burdens as well as enjoying its benefits. See § 4.07.

§ 4.02   Effect of Ratification

(1)   Subject to the exceptions stated in subsection (2), ratification retroactively creates the effects of actual authority.

(2)   Ratification is not effective:

(a)   in favor of a person who causes it by misrepresentation or other conduct that would make a contract voidable;

(b)   in favor of an agent against a principal when the principal ratifies to avoid a loss; or

(c)   to diminish the rights or other interests of persons, not parties to the transaction, that were acquired in the subject matter prior to the ratification.

§ 4.03   Acts That May Be Ratified

A person may ratify an act if the actor acted or purported to act as an agent on the person's behalf.

§ 4.04   Capacity to Ratify

(1)   A person may ratify an act if

(a)   the person existed at the time of the act, and

(b)   the person had capacity as defined in § 3.04 at the time of ratifying the act.

(2)   At a later time, a principal may avoid a ratification made earlier when the principal lacked capacity as defined in § 3.04.

§ 4.05   Timing of Ratification

A ratification of a transaction is not effective unless it precedes the occurrence of circumstances that would cause the ratification to have adverse and inequitable effects on the rights of third parties. These circumstances include:

(1)   any manifestation of intention to withdraw from the transaction made by the third party;

(2)   any material change in circumstances that would make it inequitable to bind the third party, unless the third party chooses to be bound; and

(3)   a specific time that determines whether a third party is deprived of a right or subjected to a liability.

§ 4.06 Knowledge Requisite to Ratification

A person is not bound by a ratification made without knowledge of material facts involved in the original act when the person was unaware of such lack of knowledge.

§ 4.07 No Partial Ratification

A ratification is not effective unless it encompasses the entirety of an act, contract, or other single transaction.

§ 4.08 Estoppel to Deny Ratification

If a person makes a manifestation that the person has ratified another's act and the manifestation, as reasonably understood by a third party, induces the third party to make a detrimental change in position, the person may be estopped to deny the ratification.

Chapter 5

NOTIFICATIONS AND NOTICE

§ 5.01 Notifications and Notice—In General

(1) A notification is a manifestation that is made in the form required by agreement among parties or by applicable law, or in a reasonable manner in the absence of an agreement or an applicable law, with the intention of affecting the legal rights and duties of the notifier in relation to rights and duties of persons to whom the notification is given.

(2) A notification given to or by an agent is effective as notification to or by the principal as stated in § 5.02.

(3) A person has notice of a fact if the person knows the fact, has reason to know the fact, has received an effective notification of the fact, or should know the fact to fulfill a duty owed to another person.

(4) Notice of a fact that an agent knows or has reason to know is imputed to the principal as stated in §§ 5.03 and 5.04.

§ 5.02 Notification Given by or to an Agent

(1) A notification given to an agent is effective as notice to the principal if the agent has actual or apparent authority to receive the notification, unless the person who gives the notification knows or has reason to know that the agent is acting adversely to the principal as stated in § 5.04.

(2) A notification given by an agent is effective as notification given by the principal if the agent has actual or apparent authority to give the notification, unless the person who receives the notification knows or has reason to know that the agent is acting adversely to the principal as stated in § 5.04.

§ 5.03 Imputation of Notice of Fact to Principal

For purposes of determining a principal's legal relations with a third party, notice of a fact that an agent knows or has reason to know is imputed to the principal if knowledge of the fact is material to the agent's duties to the principal, unless the agent

(a) acts adversely to the principal as stated in § 5.04, or

(b) is subject to a duty to another not to disclose the fact to the principal.

Comment c. Imputation within organizational principals. Imputation doctrines, like common-law agency in general, treat a juridical person that is an organization as one legal person. Organizations generally function by subdividing work or activities into specific functions that are assigned to different people. See § 1.03, Comment *c*. Within an organization, the work done by some agents consists of obtaining information on the basis of which coagents take action. Imputation recognizes that an organization constitutes one legal person and that its link to the external world is through its agents, including those whose assigned function is to receive, collect, report, or record information for organizational purposes. . . .

The nature and scope of the duties assigned to an agent are key to imputation within an organization. . . .

An organization's large size does not in itself defeat imputation, nor does the fact that an organization has structured itself internally into separate departments or divisions. Organizations are treated as possessing the collective knowledge of their employees and other agents, when that knowledge is material to the agents' duties, however the organization may have configured itself or its internal practices for transmission of information.

If an agent has learned a fact under circumstances that impose a duty on the agent not to reveal it to a principal, notice of that fact is not imputed to that principal. Thus, notice of a fact that an agent learns in confidence from one principal is not imputed to another principal. For further discussion, see Comment *e*.

An organization may put in place internal restrictions on how information is handled and transmitted to assist in fulfilling duties of confidentiality owed to its clients. Such restrictions are common in multifunction financial-services firms.

If information is communicated within an organization contrary to a prohibition imposed by an internal barrier on communication, the firm is charged with notice of the information. . . . Prior communications that contravene an organization's internal barrier call the barrier's general effectiveness into question. A barrier is not likely to be effective or to appear credible when personnel who possess nonpublic information work on shared projects with personnel whose job functions involve trading or other activity that would be aided by access to nonpublic information. Indicia of commitment to the barrier at an organization's highest levels enhance its credibility, as does consistent imposition of sanctions when violations are known to have occurred. A barrier's credibility will also be enhanced by regular review of its efficacy by a suitable organ of internal governance, such as an internal audit or regulatory department or an independent audit or other committee of a board of directors.

Barriers on intra-organization transmission of nonpublic information may also be strongly encouraged or required by law or regulation, which evolves as circumstances require. For example, the SEC's Rule 14e–3(b), promulgated under § 14(e) of the Securities Exchange Act, provides that a person (other than a natural person) will not be subject to liability for trading on the basis of nonpublic information about an impending tender offer if the person has established reasonable policies to ensure that individuals who make decisions to trade in securities of the target corporation do not receive information about the bid possessed by other individuals within the same firm. Such barriers may also be required by law. For example, the Insider Trading and Securities Fraud Enforcement Act of 1988 requires broker-dealers and investment advisers to establish and maintain written procedures to prevent misuse of inside information. See 15 U.S.C. § 78*o*(f). National banks are required by the Office of the Comptroller of the Currency to use internal barriers to prevent bank trust departments from unlawfully obtaining nonpublic information from other bank departments. See 12 C.F.R. § 9.5.

An internal barrier on communication of nonpublic information does not provide a defense to the legal consequences of a failure to take action in light of information that is otherwise freely available. . . .

§ 5.04   An Agent Who Acts Adversely to a Principal

For purposes of determining a principal's legal relations with a third party, notice of a fact that an agent knows or has reason to know is not imputed to the principal if the agent acts adversely to the principal in a transaction or matter, intending to act solely for the agent's own purposes or those of another person. Nevertheless, notice is imputed

    (a)   when necessary to protect the rights of a third party who dealt with the principal in good faith; or

    (b)   when the principal has ratified or knowingly retained a benefit from the agent's action.

A third party who deals with a principal through an agent, knowing or having reason to know that the agent acts adversely to the principal, does not deal in good faith for this purpose.

Comment b. Exception to imputation—in general. The doctrine stated in this section is an exception to the general rule, stated in § 5.03, that notice is imputed to a principal of a fact that an agent knows or has reason to know if knowledge of the fact is material to the agent's duties to the principal and to the principal's legal relations with third parties. The exception stated in this section is often termed the "adverse interest" exception. There is no imputation if an agent acts adversely to the principal. The adverse-interest exception is subject to two exclusions or exceptions. First, as stated in subsection (a), notice is imputed to the principal of facts that an agent who acts adversely knows or has reason to know when necessary to protect the rights of a third party who has dealt with the principal in good faith. Second, as stated in subsection (b), notice is imputed to a principal when the principal ratifies the agent's action or knowingly retains a benefit from the agent's action, although the agent acted adversely to the principal.

A third party who knows or has reason to know that an agent acts adversely to the principal, and who deals with the principal through the agent, has not dealt in good faith and may not rely on the adverse-interest exception. Thus, imputation protects innocent third parties but not those who know or have reason to know that an agent is not likely to transmit material information to the principal.

The rule stated in this section, like the rule stated in § 5.03, is applicable only for purposes of determining a principal's legal relations with a third party. Thus, notice is not imputed for purposes of determining rights and liabilities as between principal and agent. As a consequence, imputation does not furnish a basis on which an agent may defend against a claim by the principal.

If a principal ratifies action taken by an agent, the principal is bound by the legal consequences of that action as if the principal had knowledge of all the facts known by the agent. Section 4.01(2) states how a principal may ratify an agent's action, including by retaining a benefit produced by the agent's action. See Comment *d* for further discussion.

This section states a well-established doctrine. Partnership legislation has long incorporated the principle that a partnership is not charged with the knowledge of a partner who acts adversely to it. Under § 12 of the Uniform Partnership Act (1914) and § 102(f) of the Uniform Partnership Act (1997), a partnership is charged with a partner's knowledge, "except in the case of a fraud on the partnership committed by or with the consent of that partner."

However, as stated above, in order to protect third parties who deal with the principal in good faith, common-law agency doctrine encompasses exclusions to the exception to imputation when an agent acts adversely. As stated in subsection (a), the adverse-interest exception to imputation does not defeat the rights of a third party who dealt in good faith with the principal through an agent. Common-law agency also recognizes that a principal may elect to ratify the actions of an adversely acting agent. Taken as a whole, the common-law doctrine reflects a balance among factors that, if pressed in isolation to their respective extremes, would lead to divergent outcomes.

Ordinarily, an agent's failure to disclose a material fact to a principal does not defeat imputation, nor does the fact that the agent's action otherwise constitutes a breach of a duty owed the principal. See § 5.03, Comment *b*. For an agent's duty to provide information to the principal, see § 8.11. A principal's opportunity to monitor an agent and create incentives for the proper handling of information warrant imputing an agent's knowledge to the principal even when the agent has breached duties of disclosure to the principal. Moreover, imputation does not rest on an identification between principal and agent but rather on the fact that a principal's agents link it to the external world for purposes of obtaining and conveying information as well as taking action.

When an agent acts for the agent's own purposes or those of another person, the principal may be subject to liability to third parties because the agent may reasonably appear to be acting as the principal's representative with actual authority. See § 2.03. Likewise, notice of material facts known to an agent is imputed to the principal when the agent deals with a third party who reasonably believes the agent to be authorized so to act for the principal. However, this section does not protect a third party who knows or has reason to know that an agent acts adversely to the principal. If the third party colludes with the agent against the principal or otherwise knows or has reason to know that the agent is acting adversely to the principal, the third party should not expect that the agent will fulfill duties of disclosure owed to the principal.

Chapter 6

CONTRACTS AND OTHER TRANSACTIONS
WITH THIRD PARTIES

TOPIC 1.   PARTIES TO CONTRACTS

Fully Disclosed

§ 6.01   Agent for Disclosed Principal

When an agent acting with actual or apparent authority makes a contract on behalf of a disclosed principal,

(1)   the principal and the third party are parties to the contract; and

(2)   the agent is not a party to the contract unless the agent and third party agree otherwise.

§ 6.02   Agent for Unidentified Principal   Partially Disclosed

When an agent acting with actual or apparent authority makes a contract on behalf of an unidentified principal,

(1)   the principal and the third party are parties to the contract; and

(2)   the agent is a party to the contract unless the agent and the third party agree otherwise.

§ 6.03   Agent for Undisclosed Principal   Undisclosed

When an agent acting with actual authority makes a contract on behalf of an undisclosed principal,

(1)   unless excluded by the contract, the principal is a party to the contract;

(2)   the agent and the third party are parties to the contract; and

(3)   the principal, if a party to the contract, and the third party have the same rights, liabilities, and defenses against each other as if the principal made the contract personally, subject to §§ 6.05–6.09.

Comment d. Circumstances that affect rights or liabilities of undisclosed principal; contract excluding undisclosed principal as party. An undisclosed principal does not become a party to a contract if the contract excludes the principal. An explicit exclusion limits the third party's manifestation of assent to be bound. Such an explicit exclusion provides a simple device through which a third party may exclude the interests of persons other than those identified as parties to the contract. An undisclosed principal is not excluded from a contract by language stating that the contract is not assignable.

In contrast, an undisclosed principal and an agent may agree that the agent alone shall be liable on a contract. An agreement between an undisclosed principal and an agent cannot effectively exclude the principal as a party to the contract because the third party has not assented to such exclusion.

By dealing on behalf of an undisclosed principal, an agent does not implicitly represent that the agent is not acting for a principal. This is because it is usually not material to a third party whether the person with whom the third party deals, and who becomes subject to liability on contracts made with the third party, acts as an agent for an undisclosed principal. See § 6.11, Comment *d*. If an agent falsely represents that the agent does not act on behalf of a principal, the third party may avoid a contract made with the agent under the circumstances stated in § 6.11(4). A third party may avoid a contract made by an agent acting for an undisclosed principal if the agent or the principal knows or has reason to know that the third party would not have dealt with the principal as a party to the contract. See id. See also § 6.02, Comment *c*.

The nature of the performance that a contract requires determines whether performance by an undisclosed principal will be effective as performance under the contract and whether an undisclosed principal can require that the third party render performance to the principal. Performance by an undisclosed principal is not effective as performance under a contract if the third party has a substantial

interest in receiving performance from the agent who made the contract. This limit cor
on delegability of performance of a duty as stated in Restatement Second, Contracts §

The nature of the performance that a contract requires from a third party determines w..
undisclosed principal is entitled to receive that performance. An undisclosed principal may not require tu...
a third party render performance to the principal if rendering performance to the principal would materially
change the nature of the third party's duty, materially increase the burden or risk imposed on the third
party, or materially impair the third party's chance of receiving return performance. These limits correspond
to the limits imposed on assignment of a contractual right. See Restatement Second, Contracts § 317(2).

§ 6.04   Principal Does Not Exist or Lacks Capacity

Unless the third party agrees otherwise, a person who makes a contract with a third party purportedly
as an agent on behalf of a principal becomes a party to the contract if the purported agent knows or has
reason to know that the purported principal does not exist or lacks capacity to be a party to a contract.

TOPIC 2.   RIGHTS, LIABILITIES, AND DEFENSES

TITLE A.   GENERAL

§ 6.05   Contract That Is Unauthorized in Part or That Combines Orders of Several Principals

(1)   If an agent makes a contract with a third party that differs from the contract that the agent had
actual or apparent authority to make only in an amount or by the inclusion or exclusion of a separable part,
the principal is subject to liability to the third party to the extent of the contract that the agent had actual
or apparent authority to make if

(a)   the third party seasonably makes a manifestation to the principal of willingness to be bound;
and

(b)   the principal has not changed position in reasonable reliance on the belief that no contract
bound the principal and the third party.

(2)   Two or more principals may authorize the same agent to make separate contracts for them. If the
agent makes a single contract with a third party on the principals' behalves that combines the principals'
separate orders or interests and calls for a single performance by the third party,

(a)   if the agent purports to make the combined contract on behalf of disclosed principals, the
agent is subject to liability to the third party for breach of the agent's warranty of authority as stated
in § 6.10, unless the separate principals are bound by the combined contract;

(b)   if the principals are unidentified or undisclosed, the third party and the agent are the only
parties to the combined contract; and

(c)   unless the agent acted with actual or apparent authority to bind each of the principals to
the combined contract,

(i)   subject to (1), none of the separate principals is subject to liability on the combined
contract; and

(ii)   the third party is not subject to liability on the combined contract to any of the separate
principals.

§ 6.06   Setoff

(1)   When an agent makes a contract on behalf of a disclosed or unidentified principal, unless the
principal and the third party agree otherwise,

(a)   the third party may not set off any amount that the agent independently owes the third
party against an amount the third party owes the principal under the contract; and

(b)   the principal may not set off any amount that the third party independently owes the agent against an amount the principal owes the third party under the contract.

(2)   When an agent makes a contract on behalf of an undisclosed principal,

(a)   the third party may set off

(i)   any amount that the agent independently owed the third party at the time the agent made the contract and

(ii)   any amount that the agent thereafter independently comes to owe the third party until the third party has notice that the agent acts on behalf of a principal against an amount the third party owes the principal under the contract;

(b)   after the third party has notice that the agent acts on behalf of a principal, the third party may not set off any amount that the agent thereafter independently comes to owe the third party against an amount the third party owes the principal under the contract unless the principal consents; and

(c)   the principal may not set off any amount that the third party independently owes the agent against an amount that the principal owes the third party under the contract, unless the principal and the third party agree otherwise.

(3)   Unless otherwise agreed, an agent who is a party to a contract may not set off any amount that the principal independently owes the agent against an amount that the agent owes the third party under the contract. However, with the principal's consent, the agent may set off any amount that the principal could set off against an amount that the principal owes the third party under the contract.

TITLE B. SUBSEQUENT DEALINGS BETWEEN THIRD PARTY AND PRINCIPAL OR AGENT

§ 6.07   Settlement with Agent by Principal or Third Party

(1)   A principal's payment to or settlement of accounts with an agent discharges the principal's liability to a third party with whom the agent has made a contract on the principal's behalf only when the principal acts in reasonable reliance on a manifestation by the third party, not induced by misrepresentation by the agent, that the agent has settled the account with the third party.

(2)   A third party's payment to or settlement of accounts with an agent discharges the third party's liability to the principal if the agent acts with actual or apparent authority in accepting the payment or settlement.

(3)   When an agent has made a contract on behalf of an undisclosed principal,

(a)   until the third party has notice of the principal's existence, the third party's payment to or settlement of accounts with the agent discharges the third party's liability to the principal;

(b)   after the third party has notice of the principal's existence, the third party's payment to or settlement of accounts with the agent discharges the third party's liability to the principal if the agent acts with actual or apparent authority in accepting the payment or settlement; and

(c)   after receiving notice of the principal's existence, the third party may demand reasonable proof of the principal's identity and relationship to the agent. Until such proof is received, the third party's payment to or settlement of accounts in good faith with the agent discharges the third party's liability to the principal.

§ 6.08   Other Subsequent Dealings Between Third Party and Agent

(1)   When an agent has made a contract with a third party on behalf of a disclosed or unidentified principal, subsequent dealings between the agent and the third party may increase or diminish the principal's rights or liabilities to the third party if the agent acts with actual or apparent authority or the principal ratifies the agent's action.

134

(2)   When an agent has made a contract with a third party on behalf of an undisclosed principal,

(a)   until the third party has notice of the principal's existence, subsequent dealings between the third party and the agent may increase or diminish the rights or liabilities of the principal to the third party if the agent acts with actual authority, or the principal ratifies the agent's action; and

(b)   after the third party has notice of the principal's existence, subsequent dealings between the third party and the agent may increase or diminish the principal's rights or liabilities to the third party if the agent acts with actual or apparent authority or the principal ratifies the agent's action.

§ 6.09   Effect of Judgment Against Agent or Principal

When an agent has made a contract with a third party on behalf of a principal, unless the contract provides otherwise,

(1)   the liability, if any, of the principal or the agent to the third party is not discharged if the third party obtains a judgment against the other; and

(2)   the liability, if any, of the principal or the agent to the third party is discharged to the extent a judgment against the other is satisfied.

TITLE C.   AGENT'S WARRANTIES AND REPRESENTATIONS

§ 6.10   Agent's Implied Warranty of Authority

A person who purports to make a contract, representation, or conveyance to or with a third party on behalf of another person, lacking power to bind that person, gives an implied warranty of authority to the third party and is subject to liability to the third party for damages for loss caused by breach of that warranty, including loss of the benefit expected from performance by the principal, unless

(1)   the principal or purported principal ratifies the act as stated in § 4.01; or

(2)   the person who purports to make the contract, representation, or conveyance gives notice to the third party that no warranty of authority is given; or

(3)   the third party knows that the person who purports to make the contract, representation, or conveyance acts without actual authority.

§ 6.11   Agent's Representations

(1)   When an agent for a disclosed or unidentified principal makes a false representation about the agent's authority to a third party, the principal is not subject to liability unless the agent acted with actual or apparent authority in making the representation and the third party does not have notice that the agent's representation is false.

(2)   A representation by an agent made incident to a contract or conveyance is attributed to a disclosed or unidentified principal as if the principal made the representation directly when the agent had actual or apparent authority to make the contract or conveyance unless the third party knew or had reason to know that the representation was untrue or that the agent acted without actual authority in making it.

(3)   A representation by an agent made incident to a contract or conveyance is attributed to an undisclosed principal as if the principal made the representation directly when

(a)   the agent acted with actual authority in making the representation, or

(b)   the agent acted without actual authority in making the representation but had actual authority to make true representations about the same matter.

The agent's representation is not attributed to the principal when the third party knew or had reason to know it was untrue.

(4)   When an agent who makes a contract or conveyance on behalf of an undisclosed principal falsely represents to the third party that the agent does not act on behalf of a principal, the third party may avoid

135

the contract or conveyance if the principal or agent had notice that the third party would not have dealt with the principal.

Chapter 7

TORTS—LIABILITY OF AGENT AND PRINCIPAL

TOPIC 1. AGENT'S LIABILITY

§ 7.01   Agent's Liability to Third Party

An agent is subject to liability to a third party harmed by the agent's tortious conduct. Unless an applicable statute provides otherwise, an actor remains subject to liability although the actor acts as an agent or an employee, with actual or apparent authority, or within the scope of employment.

§ 7.02   Duty to Principal; Duty to Third Party

An agent's breach of a duty owed to the principal is not an independent basis for the agent's tort liability to a third party. An agent is subject to tort liability to a third party harmed by the agent's conduct only when the agent's conduct breaches a duty that the agent owes to the third party.

TOPIC 2. PRINCIPAL'S LIABILITY

§ 7.03   Principal's Liability—In General

(1) A principal is subject to direct liability to a third party harmed by an agent's conduct when

    (a) as stated in § 7.04, the agent acts with actual authority or the principal ratifies the agent's conduct and

        (i) the agent's conduct is tortious, or

        (ii) the agent's conduct, if that of the principal, would subject the principal to tort liability;

or

    (b) as stated in § 7.05, the principal is negligent in selecting, supervising, or otherwise controlling the agent; or

    (c) as stated in § 7.06, the principal delegates performance of a duty to use care to protect other persons or their property to an agent who fails to perform the duty.

(2) A principal is subject to vicarious liability to a third party harmed by an agent's conduct when

    (a) as stated in § 7.07, the agent is an employee who commits a tort while acting within the scope of employment; or

    (b) as stated in § 7.08, the agent commits a tort when acting with apparent authority in dealing with a third party on or purportedly on behalf of the principal.

Comment d. Agents with multiple principals. An agent who commits a tort may have more than one principal for at least some purposes. On agents with multiple principals in general, see Chapter 3, Topic 5. In the context of a principal's liability on the basis of an agent's tort, it is helpful to distinguish among three different types of relationships: (1) subagency; (2) employees who are "borrowed" by one employer from another employer; and (3) officers of interrelated entities.

    (1) Subagency. A subagent is a person appointed by an agent to perform functions that the agent has consented to perform on behalf of the principal. See § 3.15(1). For general discussion of the consequences of subagency, see § 3.15, Comment *d.* A subagent may be an employee of the appointing agent. When a subagent is an employee, as defined in § 7.07(3), of the appointing agent, the appointing agent is subject to vicarious liability for torts committed by the subagent within the scope of employment. See § 7.07. Both the appointing agent and the principal are subject to vicarious liability when a subagent acts with apparent

authority in committing a tort, as stated in § 7.08. An appointing agent may be subject to liability for torts of a subagent who is not an employee. For example, when a law firm assigns work on behalf of a client to a "temporary" lawyer who is neither a member of the firm nor its employee, the firm creates a relationship of subagency with the "temporary" lawyer that subjects it to liability to its client for acts and omissions of the "temporary" lawyer. See Restatement Third, The Law Governing Lawyers § 58, Comment e.

A relationship of subagency does not result when an agent appoints a coagent. Coagents share a common principal, although they may occupy dominant and subordinate positions in an organizational hierarchy. See § 3.15, Comment b. An agent who has authority to hire a coagent is not subject to vicarious liability for the coagent's tortious conduct.

(2) "Lent employees," or "borrowed servants." When work requires specialized skills or equipment or requires that an actor perform a task on less than a full-time basis, it is not unusual that the actor who performs the work is employed by a firm that contracts to provide the actor's services to another firm. The types of actors who work through such arrangements vary greatly, as does the nature of the work they do. These arrangements span the range of highly skilled professionals, including nurses, lawyers, and other members of licensed professions; office workers; skilled construction workers; and unskilled manual laborers. The risks of injury to third parties posed by such work vary, as do the settings in which work is performed. Moreover, the specifics of such arrangements vary in several respects. These include the duration of an actor's placement in a particular workplace and the provision of supervision, training, and tools needed to perform work. An actor's employer may provide requisite training, furnish the actor with specialized equipment needed for work, and reassign the actor with frequency. Alternatively, the actor may work on a long-term basis within a particular firm using tools and receiving training provided by that firm.

When an actor negligently injures a third party while performing work for the firm that has contracted for the actor's services, the question is whether that firm (often termed the "special employer") or the initial employer (often termed the "general employer"), or both, should be subject to liability to the third party. Liability should be allocated to the employer in the better position to take measures to prevent the injury suffered by the third party. An employer is in that position if the employer has the right to control an employee's conduct. When both a general and special employer have the right to control an employee's conduct, the practical history of direction may establish that one employer in fact ceded its right of control to the other, whether through its failure to exercise the right or otherwise.

It is a question of fact whether a general or a special employer, or both, have the right to control an employee's conduct. Factors that a court may consider in making this determination include the extent of control that an employer may exercise over the details of an employee's work and the timing of the work; the relationship between the employee's work and the nature of the special employer's business; the nature of the employee's work, the skills required to perform it, and the degree of supervision customarily associated with the work; the duration of the employee's work in the special employer's firm; the identity of the employer who furnishes equipment or other instrumentalities requisite to performing the work; and the method of payment for the work.

Many cases allocate liability in this context on the basis that a general employer has an exclusive right of control over employees assigned to work for clients of the general employer. This presupposes that ties between a general employer and an assigned employee will remain strong despite the employee's emplacement in the special employer's workplace where the employee's performance will often be subject to some degree of direction and monitoring by members of the special employer's management. It may also reflect assumptions about links between the general employer and the risk that third parties will be injured when work is done in a special employer's workplace. A general employer is in a position to screen prospective employees to determine their general aptitude and fitness; a general employer may also provide training to those it selects for employment. If a general employer assigns an employee and furnishes the employee with equipment to use in performing assigned work, the general employer is also in a position to impose requirements for the proper usage and maintenance of the equipment. A general employer may also be in a better position to provide insurance coverage for an employee's actions. Any presumption that a general employer has the right to control an employee may be rebutted by proving factual indicia that the right has been assumed by a special employer. Even within the same jurisdiction, it may be difficult to predict whether a given set of indicia will demonstrate that a special employer has assumed the right of control.

However, a significant number of cases allocate liability to a special employer on the basis of its right and ability to direct a borrowed employee's specific actions in its workplace. A justification for this approach is that a borrowed employee may retain only formal ties to a general employer, depending on the duration and nature of the borrowed employee's relationship with the special employer, which weakens the likelihood that the general employer retains any practical capacity to control the borrowed employee's conduct. This approach also reflects the possibility that a special employer may in fact be in the better position to exercise control in a manner that reduces the risk of injury to third parties. This possibility may be especially likely when the nature of a borrowed employee's work requires coordinated effort as part of a skilled team and close direction or supervision by the team's leader. Some cases allocate liability to both general and special employer on the basis that both exercised control over the employee and both benefited to some degree from the employee's work.

A related question, arising when the third party injured by an actor's negligence is an employee of the special employer, is the applicability of workers'-compensation insurance law to the employee's claims. Although these questions may often be related as a practical matter, workers'-compensation questions are beyond the scope of this Restatement.

(3) Officers of interrelated entities. The fact that a corporation or other entity owns a majority of the voting equity in another entity does not create a relationship of agency between them or between each entity and the other's agents. Likewise, common ownership of multiple entities does not create relationships of agency among them. See § 1.01, Comment *f(2)*. An entity becomes the agent of another entity, and an individual becomes an entity's agent, only when they are linked by the elements of an agency relationship as stated in § 1.01.

Within a related group of corporations or other entities the same individuals may serve as officers or directors of more than one entity. An overlapping cast in multiple organizational roles does not in itself create relationships of agency that are not otherwise present.

When the same individuals serve multiple entities as their officers, directors, or employees, it may become necessary to determine the entity to which an individual's conduct should be attributed. There is a general presumption that contracts and other transactions entered into by a shared officer are attributed to the entity for which the officer purports to be acting. A rationale for this presumption is that the identity of the party who will be bound by a contract or transaction is often material to the other party to the contract or transaction. See § 6.01, Comment *b*. This rationale does not support applying the same presumption when a shared officer's conduct is tortious, especially when the party injured by the conduct has not chosen to engage in a transaction conducted by the shared officer. Moreover, that an officer purports to act on behalf of a particular entity does not create a basis for attribution that corresponds to policies and objectives that underlie contemporary tort law. When harm is caused negligently, these objectives include remedying an injustice that has been inflicted on a plaintiff by a defendant and providing a defendant with appropriate safety incentives. See Restatement Third, Torts: Liability for Physical Harm § 6, Comment *d* (Proposed Final Draft No. 1, 2005). On harm that is caused intentionally, see id. § 5, Comment *a*. Likewise, the contract-based presumption is inapt when a shared officer's conduct violates a statute that proscribes or regulates conduct, particularly conduct outside a transactional context.

§ 7.04   Agent Acts with Actual Authority

A principal is subject to liability to a third party harmed by an agent's conduct when the agent's conduct is within the scope of the agent's actual authority or ratified by the principal; and

    (1)   the agent's conduct is tortious, or

    (2)   the agent's conduct, if that of the principal, would subject the principal to tort liability.

§ 7.05   Principal's Negligence in Conducting Activity Through Agent; Principal's Special Relationship with Another Person

    (1)   A principal who conducts an activity through an agent is subject to liability for harm to a third party caused by the agent's conduct if the harm was caused by the principal's negligence in selecting, training, retaining, supervising, or otherwise controlling the agent.

(2)   When a principal has a special relationship with another person, the principal owes that person a duty of reasonable care with regard to risks arising out of the relationship, including the risk that agents of the principal will harm the person with whom the principal has such a special relationship.

§ 7.06   Failure in Performance of Principal's Duty of Protection

A principal required by contract or otherwise by law to protect another cannot avoid liability by delegating performance of the duty, whether or not the delegate is an agent.

§ 7.07   Employee Acting Within Scope of Employment

(1)   An employer is subject to vicarious liability for a tort committed by its employee acting within the scope of employment.

(2)   An employee acts within the scope of employment when performing work assigned by the employer or engaging in a course of conduct subject to the employer's control. An employee's act is not within the scope of employment when it occurs within an independent course of conduct not intended by the employee to serve any purpose of the employer.

(3)   For purposes of this section,

(a)   an employee is an agent whose principal controls or has the right to control the manner and means of the agent's performance of work, and

(b)   the fact that work is performed gratuitously does not relieve a principal of liability.

Comment c. Conduct in the performance of work and scope of employment. An employee's conduct is within the scope of employment when it constitutes performance of work assigned to the employee by the employer. The fact that the employee performs the work carelessly does not take the employee's conduct outside the scope of employment, nor does the fact that the employee otherwise makes a mistake in performing the work. Likewise, conduct is not outside the scope of employment merely because an employee disregards the employer's instructions.

. . . [T]he fact that an employee's action violates a generally applicable law, such as a speeding limit, does not by itself place the employee's conduct outside the scope of employment. These results are not surprising. An employee may believe that the employer wishes the employee to disregard an inconvenient constraint when the employee fears that compliance would jeopardize completing the employee's assigned mission at all or completing it on or ahead of schedule. Although the employee's belief may be mistaken, it is compatible with acting in an assigned role to do an assigned task. However, the character, extreme nature, or other circumstances accompanying an employee's actions may demonstrate that the employee's course of conduct is independent of performing work assigned by the employer and intended solely to further the employee's own purposes. . . .

An employee's failure to take action may also be conduct within the scope of employment. For example, an employee's failure to do work assigned by the employer, when harm to a third party results, under some circumstances may constitute negligence. A negligent action "frequently involves a failure to take a reasonable precaution. . . . [which] can be described as an omission, and it hence can be said that the omission is itself negligent." Restatement Third, Torts: Liability for Physical Harm § 3, Comment *c* (Proposed Final Draft No. 1, 2005).

An employee's assigned work may include tasks that contemplate the necessity of using physical force to complete the assigned work. . . . An employee's assigned duties may also place the employee in situations in which physical consequences may follow in an uninterrupted sequence from verbal exchanges with third parties. An escalation in the pitch of an employee's conduct does not by itself transform the conduct into an independent course of conduct that represents a departure not within the scope of employment. It is a question of fact what motivated an employee's conduct as verbal exchanges escalate or when an employee's use of physical force becomes more pronounced.

In determining whether an employee's tortious conduct is within the scope of employment, the nature of the tort is relevant, as is whether the conduct also constitutes a criminal act. An employee's intentionally criminal conduct may indicate a departure from conduct within the scope of employment, not a simple escalation. The nature and magnitude of the conduct are relevant to determining the employee's intention at the time. . . .

The determinative question is whether the course of conduct in which the tort occurred is within the scope of employment. Intentional torts and other intentional wrongdoing may be within the scope of employment. For example, if an employee's job duties include determining the prices at which the employer's output will be sold to customers, the employee's agreement with a competitor to fix prices is within the scope of employment unless circumstances establish a departure from the scope of employment. Likewise, when an employee's job duties include making statements to prospective customers to induce them to buy from the employer, intentional misrepresentations made by the employee are within the scope of employment unless circumstances establish that the employee has departed from it.

An employee may engage in conduct, part of which is within the scope of employment and part of which is not. . . .

When an employee's tortious conduct is outside the scope of employment, alternate theories of liability may be available against the employer. . . .

§ 7.08   Agent Acts with Apparent Authority

A principal is subject to vicarious liability for a tort committed by an agent in dealing or communicating with a third party on or purportedly on behalf of the principal when actions taken by the agent with apparent authority constitute the tort or enable the agent to conceal its commission.

Chapter 8

DUTIES OF AGENT AND PRINCIPAL TO EACH OTHER

TOPIC 1.   AGENT'S DUTIES TO PRINCIPAL

TITLE A.   GENERAL FIDUCIARY PRINCIPLE

§ 8.01   General Fiduciary Principle

An agent has a fiduciary duty to act loyally for the principal's benefit in all matters connected with the agency relationship.

TITLE B.   DUTIES OF LOYALTY

§ 8.02   Material Benefit Arising Out of Position

An agent has a duty not to acquire a material benefit from a third party in connection with transactions conducted or other actions taken on behalf of the principal or otherwise through the agent's use of the agent's position.

Comment e. Remedies. When an agent breaches the duty stated in this section, the principal may recover monetary relief from the agent and, in appropriate circumstances, from any third party who participated in the agent's breach. A principal may avoid a contract entered into by the agent with a third party who participated in the agent's breach of duty. The principal may recover any material benefit received by the agent through the agent's breach, the value of the benefit, or proceeds of the benefit retained by the agent. The principal may also recover damages for any harm caused by the agent's breach. If an agent's breach of duty involves a wrongful disposal of assets of the principal, the principal cannot recover both the value of the asset and what the agent received in exchange. If a principal recovers damages from a third party as a consequence of an agent's breach of fiduciary duty, the principal remains entitled to recover from the agent any benefit that the agent improperly received from the transaction.

If a principal seeks to recover a material benefit received by an agent, the value of the benefit, or its proceeds, the principal's recovery is not subject to a deduction for expenses incurred by the agent to induce a third party to confer the benefit on the agent.

However, if an agent breaches the agent's fiduciary duty by taking personal advantage of a business opportunity as discussed in Comment *d*, the principal may recover property that the agent acquired through the breach only if the principal reimburses the agent. The amount of reimbursement is either the amount paid by the agent for the property or the amount for which the principal could have obtained the property, whichever is less. See Restatement of Restitution §§ 194, 195; Principles of Corporate Governance: Analysis and Recommendations, Comment to § 5.05(e) and Illustration 13.

§ 8.03   Acting as or on Behalf of an Adverse Party

An agent has a duty not to deal with the principal as or on behalf of an adverse party in a transaction connected with the agency relationship.

Comment b. Rationale. As a fiduciary, an agent has a duty to the principal to act loyally in the principal's interest in all matters in connection with the agency relationship. See § 8.01. The rule stated in this section is a specific application of this general principle. When an agent deals with the principal on the agent's own account, the agent's own interests are irreconcilably in tension with the principal's interests because the interest of each is furthered by action—negotiating a higher or a lower price, for example—that is incompatible with the interests of the other. If an agent acts on behalf of the principal in a transaction with the agent, the agent's duty to act loyally in the principal's interest conflicts with the agent's self-interest. Even if the agent's divided loyalty does not result in demonstrable harm to the principal, the agent has breached the agent's duty of undivided loyalty. Likewise, an agent who acts on behalf of more than one principal in a transaction between or among the principals has breached the agent's duty of loyalty to each principal through undertaking service to multiple principals that divides the agent's loyalty.

A principal may consent to conduct by an agent that would otherwise constitute a breach of the agent's duty. See § 8.06. On consent by multiple principals when an agent conducts a transaction between or among the principals, see § 8.06(2).

The duty stated in this section is formulated broadly. So long as the transaction in which an agent acts as or on behalf of an adverse party is connected with the agency relationship, the agent is subject to the duty although the agent does not have direct or indirect responsibility for conducting the transaction on behalf of the principal. The breadth of this formulation requires that an agent disclose adverse interests to the principal so that the principal may evaluate, as only the principal is situated to do, how best to protect its interests in light of the agent's interest. See § 8.06. The breadth of the formulation also makes it unnecessary for a principal to prescribe its agents' duties and prohibit outside interests that its agents may have or acquire with great specificity in formulating the initial terms of its relationship with its agents.

A principal's knowledge that an agent deals as or on behalf of an adverse party does not relieve the agent of duties to the principal in connection with that transaction. Under the rule stated in § 8.06, the agent has a duty to deal fairly with the principal and to disclose to the principal all facts of which the agent has notice that are reasonably relevant to the principal's exercise of judgment, unless the principal has manifested that the principal already knows them or does not wish to know them. Thus, a principal's knowledge that its agent acts as or on behalf of an adverse party does not convert the relationship between principal and agent into an arm's-length relationship. Moreover, as stated in § 8.11, an agent has a duty to use reasonable effort to furnish information to the principal although the agent does not deal as or on behalf of an adverse party.

It is, of course, possible that an agent may assume an adverse position in which the agent may not legally discharge the duties of disclosure that the agent owes to the principal because the agent owes a duty to another person not to disclose a fact that §§ 8.06 and 8.11 require be disclosed to the principal. In Illustration 3, for example, A's duties to T Corporation may prohibit A's disclosure of new product developments to T Corporation's customer, P Corporation. Unless it is possible for T Corporation to shield A from access to facts that A will have a duty to disclose to P Corporation, A's position is not tenable, and consequently A must withdraw as P Corporation's agent.

However, an agent whose acts on behalf of a party consist solely of ministerial acts that require no exercise of discretion, judgment, or skill does not act on behalf of that party for purposes of determining whether the agent acts adversely to another principal. Thus, one principal's agent who performs only ministerial acts for another does not become a dual agent.

A custom in an industry that permits self-dealing by agents, if unknown to the principal, does not relieve the agent of the duty to refrain from self-dealing. If an agreement between principal and agent grants the agent discretion to take such adverse action, the agent is subject to a contract-law duty of good faith and fair dealing in exercising the discretion. See § 8.01, Comment *b*.

Many business-organization statutes contain provisions that address self-dealing conduct on the part of specified organizational actors. Under contemporary partnership legislation, a partner has a duty to "refrain from dealing with the partnership in the conduct or winding up of the partnership business as or on behalf of a party having an interest adverse to the partnership. . . ." Rev. Unif. Partnership Act § 404(b)(2). Similarly, a manager of a limited-liability company (LLC) has a comparable duty, as does a member of a member-managed LLC. See Unif. Limited Liability Company Act § 409(b)(2). Many corporation statutes have provisions applicable to transactions between a corporation and a director, or between a corporation and an officer, in which mechanisms are specified through which the director or officer may fulfill duties owed to the corporation in connection with the transaction. See Principles of Corporate Governance: Analysis and Recommendations § 5.02.

§ 8.04　Competition

Throughout the duration of an agency relationship, an agent has a duty to refrain from competing with the principal and from taking action on behalf of or otherwise assisting the principal's competitors. During that time, an agent may take action, not otherwise wrongful, to prepare for competition following termination of the agency relationship.

§ 8.05　Use of Principal's Property; Use of Confidential Information

An agent has a duty

(1)　not to use property of the principal for the agent's own purposes or those of a third party; and

(2)　not to use or communicate confidential information of the principal for the agent's own purposes or those of a third party.

§ 8.06　Principal's Consent

(1)　Conduct by an agent that would otherwise constitute a breach of duty as stated in §§ 8.01, 8.02, 8.03, 8.04, and 8.05 does not constitute a breach of duty if the principal consents to the conduct, provided that

(a)　in obtaining the principal's consent, the agent

(i)　acts in good faith,

(ii)　discloses all material facts that the agent knows, has reason to know, or should know would reasonably affect the principal's judgment unless the principal has manifested that such facts are already known by the principal or that the principal does not wish to know them, and

(iii)　otherwise deals fairly with the principal; and

(b)　the principal's consent concerns either a specific act or transaction, or acts or transactions of a specified type that could reasonably be expected to occur in the ordinary course of the agency relationship.

(2)　An agent who acts for more than one principal in a transaction between or among them has a duty

(a)　to deal in good faith with each principal,

(b)　to disclose to each principal

(i)   the fact that the agent acts for the other principal or principals, and

(ii)   all other facts that the agent knows, has reason to know, or should know would reasonably affect the principal's judgment unless the principal has manifested that such facts are already known by the principal or that the principal does not wish to know them, and

(c)   otherwise to deal fairly with each principal.

TITLE C. DUTIES OF PERFORMANCE

§ 8.07   Duty Created by Contract

An agent has a duty to act in accordance with the express and implied terms of any contract between the agent and the principal.

§ 8.08   Duties of Care, Competence, and Diligence

Subject to any agreement with the principal, an agent has a duty to the principal to act with the care, competence, and diligence normally exercised by agents in similar circumstances. Special skills or knowledge possessed by an agent are circumstances to be taken into account in determining whether the agent acted with due care and diligence. If an agent claims to possess special skills or knowledge, the agent has a duty to the principal to act with the care, competence, and diligence normally exercised by agents with such skills or knowledge.

Comment b. Common-law and statutory duties of care; regulatory duties. A principal and an agent may establish benchmarks or other measures for the effort and skill to be expected from the agent. For example, a contract between principal and agent may specify measures for the effort that the agent has a duty to expend in pursuing the principal's objectives. An agent may also guarantee by contract that the agent's work will be successful in achieving an objective or that the agent's work will be satisfactory to the principal. On conditions that an obligor be satisfied with an obligee's performance, see Restatement Second, Contracts § 228. A contract may also, in appropriate circumstances, raise or lower the standard of performance to be expected of an agent or specify the remedies or mechanisms of dispute resolution available to the principal. Regardless of their content, contractually shaped or contractually created duties are grounded in the mutual assent of agent and principal.

In contrast to § 8.06, the rule stated in this section articulates a broader role for general agreements that a principal and an agent may make in advance. If an agreement between principal and agent is otherwise enforceable, it may define the standard of performance applicable to the agent across the board in general terms and without the specificity required under § 8.06(1)(b) for consent by a principal to conduct by an agent that would otherwise breach a duty of loyalty owed to the principal under §§ 8.01, 8.02, 8.03, 8.04, or 8.05. Moreover, a principal's consent under § 8.06 is ineffective unless in obtaining the consent the agent acted consistently with the requirements stated in § 8.06(1)(a) or (2).

The duties stated in this section will often overlap with an agent's duties of performance that are express or implied terms of a contract between principal and agent. However, the duties stated in this section are tort-law duties because they "denote the fact that the actor is required to conduct himself in a particular manner at the risk that if he does not do so he becomes subject to liability to another to whom the duty is owed for any injury sustained by such other, of which that actor's conduct is a legal cause." Restatement Second, Torts § 4. Tort law imposes duties of care on an agent because the agent undertakes to act on behalf of the principal, because the principal's reliance on that undertaking is foreseeable by the agent, and because it is often socially useful that an agent fulfill the agent's undertaking to the principal. See Restatement Second, Torts § 323; Restatement Third, Torts: Liability for Physical Harm § 42 (Proposed Final Draft No. 1, 2005).

The overlap between duties derived from tort law and from an agent's contract with the principal will often provide the principal with alternative remedies when a breach of duty subjects the agent to liability. In particular, an agent is subject to liability to the principal for all harm, whether past, present, or prospective, caused the principal by the agent's breach of the duties stated in this section. See Restatement Second, Torts § 910. The agent's liability includes an obligation to indemnify the principal when a wrongful act by the agent subjects the principal to vicarious liability to a third person. See §§ 7.07 and 7.08. One agent's breach of the duties stated in this section does not bar an innocent principal from recovery against another agent who is also subject to liability.

Statutory provisions may also be relevant in determining the duties of care owed by an agent. For example, some organizational statutes establish standards of conduct for officers and others who act on behalf of an organization. Under § 8.42(a)(2) of the Model Business Corporation Act, an officer must act, in performing the officer's duties, "with the care that a person in like position would reasonably exercise under similar circumstances. . . ." The Revised Uniform Partnership Act states that a partner owes a duty of care to the partnership and to other partners "in the conduct and winding up of the partnership business" that is limited to "refraining from engaging in grossly negligent or reckless conduct, intentional misconduct, or a knowing violation of law." Rev. Unif. Partnership Act § 404(c). The Uniform Limited Liability Company Act imposes a comparable standard on an LLC's managers and members who are also managers. Unif. Limited Liability Co. Act § 409(c) and (h)(2).

An agent's conduct may be subject to regulation by statutes, administrative rules, or rules of a particular profession. An agent's violation of such a statute or rule does not in itself establish that the agent breached the agent's duty to the principal stated in this section. If the statute or rule is designed to protect persons in the principal's position, the trier of fact may consider the agent's violation of the statute in defining and applying the standard stated in this section.

§ 8.09   Duty to Act Only Within Scope of Actual Authority and to Comply with Principal's Lawful Instructions

(1)   An agent has a duty to take action only within the scope of the agent's actual authority.

(2)   An agent has a duty to comply with all lawful instructions received from the principal and persons designated by the principal concerning the agent's actions on behalf of the principal.

§ 8.10   Duty of Good Conduct

An agent has a duty, within the scope of the agency relationship, to act reasonably and to refrain from conduct that is likely to damage the principal's enterprise.

§ 8.11   Duty to Provide Information

An agent has a duty to use reasonable effort to provide the principal with facts that the agent knows, has reason to know, or should know when

(1)   subject to any manifestation by the principal, the agent knows or has reason to know that the principal would wish to have the facts or the facts are material to the agent's duties to the principal; and

(2)   the facts can be provided to the principal without violating a superior duty owed by the agent to another person.

§ 8.12   Duties Regarding Principal's Property—Segregation, Record-Keeping, and Accounting

An agent has a duty, subject to any agreement with the principal,

(1)   not to deal with the principal's property so that it appears to be the agent's property;

(2)   not to mingle the principal's property with anyone else's; and

(3)   to keep and render accounts to the principal of money or other property received or paid out on the principal's account.

TOPIC 2. PRINCIPAL'S DUTIES TO AGENT

§ 8.13 Duty Created by Contract

A principal has a duty to act in accordance with the express and implied terms of any contract between the principal and the agent.

Comment d. Compensation—other issues. Unless an agreement between a principal and an agent indicates otherwise, a principal has a duty to pay compensation to an agent for services that the agent provides. An agreement that an agent will not have a right to compensation for services provided may be implied from the agent's relationship to the principal or from the trivial nature of the services requested. The amount of compensation due may be determined by the terms of agreement between principal and agent and may be fixed in amount or made contingent on whether the agent achieves stated outcomes or on other criteria. An agreement between a principal and an agent may also set the agent's right to compensation at an amount or rate that is standard or customary in a particular industry. If an agent has a right to be paid compensation by a principal but the amount due cannot be determined on the basis of the terms of the parties' agreement, the agent is entitled to the value of the services provided by the agent.

A principal's duty to pay compensation to an agent does not extend to fulfilling an agent's duties to pay compensation to subagents engaged by the agent, unless the principal so agrees. See § 3.15, Comment *d*, for an extended discussion of the consequences of subagency relationships. Thus, unless a principal agrees otherwise, the principal is not a guarantor of obligations undertaken by its agent to pay subagents appointed by the agent. Were the rule otherwise, a principal would bear the risk that an appointing agent would make generous arrangements with a subagent in exchange for payments by the subagent or would be tempted for other reasons to disregard the principal's interests in making arrangements with a subagent.

In contrast, a principal's duties of indemnity extend to subagents appointed by agents of the principal. See § 8.14, Comment *b*.

§ 8.14 Duty to Indemnify

A principal has a duty to indemnify an agent

(1) in accordance with the terms of any contract between them; and

(2) unless otherwise agreed,

    (a) when the agent makes a payment

        (i) within the scope of the agent's actual authority, or

        (ii) that is beneficial to the principal, unless the agent acts officiously in making the payment; or

    (b) when the agent suffers a loss that fairly should be borne by the principal in light of their relationship.

§ 8.15 Principal's Duty to Deal Fairly and in Good Faith

A principal has a duty to deal with the agent fairly and in good faith, including a duty to provide the agent with information about risks of physical harm or pecuniary loss that the principal knows, has reason to know, or should know are present in the agent's work but unknown to the agent.

Comment d. Duty to refrain from conduct likely to injure agent's business reputation or reasonable self-respect. This duty is the reciprocal of an agent's duty of good conduct as stated in § 8.10. Although a principal is not subject to a duty of loyalty to an agent, the principal's duty to deal with an agent fairly and in good faith requires that the principal refrain from conduct that is likely to injure the agent's business reputation through the agent's association with the principal. Likewise, a principal has a duty to refrain from conduct that will injure the agent's reasonable self-respect if the association continues.

The nature of the agent's work and other circumstances of the relationship between principal and agent are relevant to whether a principal's conduct breaches this duty.

UNIFORM PARTNERSHIP ACT (1914)

Part I

PRELIMINARY PROVISIONS

§ 1.   Name of Act

This act may be cited as Uniform Partnership Act.

§ 2.   Definition of Terms

In this act, "Court" includes every court and judge having jurisdiction in the case.

"Business" includes every trade, occupation, or profession.

"Person" includes individuals, partnerships, corporations, and other associations.

"Bankrupt" includes bankrupt under the Federal Bankruptcy Act or insolvent under any state insolvent act.

"Conveyance" includes every assignment, lease, mortgage, or encumbrance.

"Real property" includes land and any interest or estate in land.

§ 3. Interpretation of Knowledge and Notice

(1)   A person has "knowledge" of a fact within the meaning of this act not only when he has actual knowledge thereof, but also when he has knowledge of such other facts as in the circumstances shows bad faith.

(2)   A person has "notice" of a fact within the meaning of this act when the person who claims the benefit of the notice:

(a)   States the fact to such person, or

(b)   Delivers through the mail, or by other means of communication, a written statement of the fact to such person or to a proper person at his place of business or residence.

§ 4. Rules of Construction

(1)   The rule that statutes in derogation of the common law are to be strictly construed shall have no application to this act.

(2)   The law of estoppel shall apply under this act.

(3)   The law of agency shall apply under this act.

(4)   This act shall be so interpreted and construed as to effect its general purpose to make uniform the law of those states which enact it.

(5)   This act shall not be construed so as to impair the obligations of any contract existing when the act goes into effect, nor to affect any action or proceedings begun or right accrued before this act takes effect.

§ 5. Rules for Cases Not Provided for in This Act

In any case not provided for in this act the rules of law and equity, including the law merchant, shall govern.

Part II

NATURE OF A PARTNERSHIP

§ 6. Partnership Defined

(1)   A partnership is an association of two or more persons to carry on as co-owners a business for profit.

(2)   But any association formed under any other statute of this state, or any statute adopted by authority, other than the authority of this state, is not a partnership under this act, unless such association would have been a partnership in this state prior to the adoption of this act; but this act shall apply to limited partnerships except in so far as the statutes relating to such partnerships are inconsistent herewith.

COMMENT

Subdivision (1). Explanation of the Reason for the Words Employed in the Definition. The first inquiry is, Why say a partnership is "an association of two or more persons"? In view of the fact that the word "association" itself implies the acting together of two or more persons, why not merely say that a partnership is an association to carry on business in which the members are co-owners of the business? The word person includes, as stated in section 2, supra, "individuals, partnerships, corporations, and other associations." The definition as worded thus asserts, what would be doubtful if the words "of two or more persons" were omitted, namely, that any one of these associations may become members of a partnership. It is true that if two or more corporations attempt to form a partnership the contract may be ultra vires as to both (Boyd v. American Carbon Black Co. (1897) 37 Atl. 937, 182 Pa.St. 206); but the capacity of corporations to contract is a question of corporation law. Under the present law it appears that a partnership can, as such, be a member of another partnership, if that was the intent of the parties. [Raymond v. Putnam (1862) 44 N.H. 160; Cheap v. Cramond (1821), 4 Barn. & Ald. 663, 6 E.C.L. 645; In re Hamilton (1880) 1 Fed. 800; Riddle v. Whitehill (1890) 10 S.Ct. 924, 135 U.S. 621, 34 U.S. (L.Ed.) 282.]

The words "to carry on as co-owners a business" remove any doubt in the following case: A and B sign partnership articles and make their agreed contributions to the common fund. A refuses to carry on business as agreed. Is there a partnership to be wound up in accordance with the provisions of Part VI "Dissolution and Winding-up"? The words quoted require an affirmative answer to this question. If the words "carrying on business" had been used, in the case given, no partnership would exist, and Part VI would not apply.

The definition asserts that the associates are "co-owners" of the business. This distinguishes a partnership from an agency—an association of principal and agent. A business is a series of acts directed toward an end. Ownership involves the power of ultimate control. To state that partners are co-owners of a business is to state that they each have the power of ultimate control.

Lastly, the definition asserts that the business is for profit. Partnership is a branch of our commercial law; it has developed in connection with a particular business association, and it is, therefore, essential that the operation of the act should be confined to associations organized for profit.

In view of the many definitions of a partnership which have been proposed, it is desirable to note the reasons for the omission of certain ideas expressed in some of the definitions cited by Lindley in his work on Partnership, pp. 11, 12.

It is not indicated that the association must be a voluntary one. In the domain of private law the term association necessarily involves the idea that the association is voluntary.

To say that the association must be created by contract, is not only unnecessary, but in view of the varied use of the word "contract" in our law, if the word is used an explanation would have to be made as to whether the contract could be implied, and if so, whether it could be implied in law or only implied as a fact. By merely saying that it is an association these difficulties are avoided.

Again, it is not said that the business must be lawful business. The effect of the unlawfulness of the business is dealt with under Part VI "Dissolution and Winding-up." Section 31(3), infra, provides that dissolution is produced "By any event which makes it unlawful for the business of the partnership to be carried on or for the members to carry it on in partnership." If the business is wholly unlawful, then the partnership is dissolved the moment it is created. The omission of the word "lawful" in the definition does not prevent this result. Very often, however, a business may be in part lawful and in part unlawful. Hotel-keepers may run a "dive." Placing the word "lawful" before the word business in the definition would tend to throw a doubt on the propriety of the orderly winding up of such a business as a partnership.

§ 7.   Rules for Determining the Existence of a Partnership

In determining whether a partnership exists, these rules shall apply:

(1)   Except as provided by section 16 persons who are not partners as to each other are not partners as to third persons.

(2)   Joint tenancy, tenancy in common, tenancy by the entireties, joint property, common property, or part ownership does not of itself establish a partnership, whether such co-owners do or do not share any profits made by the use of the property.

(3)   The sharing of gross returns does not of itself establish a partnership, whether or not the persons sharing them have a joint or common right or interest in any property from which the returns are derived.

(4)   The receipt by a person of a share of the profits of a business is prima facie evidence that he is a partner in the business, but no such inference shall be drawn if such profits were received in payment:

    (a)   As a debt by installments or otherwise,

    (b)   As wages of an employee or rent to a landlord,

    (c)   As an annuity to a widow or representative of a deceased partner,

    (d)   As interest on a loan, though the amount of payment vary with the profits of the business,

    (e)   As the consideration for the sale of the good-will of a business or other property by installments or otherwise.

§ 8. Partnership Property

(1) All property originally brought into the partnership stock or subsequently acquired by purchase or otherwise, on account of the partnership, is partnership property.

(2) Unless the contrary intention appears, property acquired with partnership funds is partnership property.

(3) Any estate in real property may be acquired in the partnership name. Title so acquired can be conveyed only in the partnership name.

(4) A conveyance to a partnership in the partnership name, though without words of inheritance, passes the entire estate of the grantor unless a contrary intent appears.

Part III

RELATIONS OF PARTNERS TO PERSONS DEALING WITH THE PARTNERSHIP

§ 9. Partner Agent of Partnership as to Partnership Business

(1) Every partner is an agent of the partnership for the purpose of its business, and the act of every partner, including the execution in the partnership name of any instrument, for apparently carrying on in the usual way the business of the partnership of which he is a member binds the partnership, unless the partner so acting has in fact no authority to act for the partnership in the particular matter, and the person with whom he is dealing has knowledge of the fact that he has no such authority.

(2) An act of a partner which is not apparently for the carrying on of the business of the partnership in the usual way does not bind the partnership unless authorized by the other partners.

(3) Unless authorized by the other partners or unless they have abandoned the business, one or more but less than all the partners have no authority to:

(a) Assign the partnership property in trust for creditors or on the assignee's promise to pay the debts of the partnership,

(b) Dispose of the good-will of the business,

(c) Do any other act which would make it impossible to carry on the ordinary business of a partnership,

(d) Confess a judgment,

(e) Submit a partnership claim or liability to arbitration or reference.

(4) No act of a partner in contravention of a restriction on authority shall bind the partnership to persons having knowledge of the restriction.

§ 10. Conveyance of Real Property of the Partnership

(1) Where title to real property is in the partnership name, any partner may convey title to such property by a conveyance executed in the partnership name; but the partnership may recover such property unless the partner's act binds the partnership under the provisions of paragraph (1) of section 9, or unless such property has been conveyed by the grantee or a person claiming through such grantee to a holder for value without knowledge that the partner, in making the conveyance, has exceeded his authority.

(2) Where title to real property is in the name of the partnership, a conveyance executed by a partner, in his own name, passes the equitable interest of the partnership, provided the act is one within the authority of the partner under the provisions of paragraph (1) of section 9.

(3) Where title to real property is in the name of one or more but not all the partners, and the record does not disclose the right of the partnership, the partners in whose name the title stands may convey title to such property, but the partnership may recover such property if the partners' act does not bind the

partnership under the provisions of paragraph (1) of section 9, unless the purchaser or his assignee, is a holder for value, without knowledge.

(4)   Where the title to real property is in the name of one or more or all the partners, or in a third person in trust for the partnership, a conveyance executed by a partner in the partnership name, or in his own name, passes the equitable interest of the partnership, provided the act is one within the authority of the partner under the provisions of paragraph (1) of section 9.

(5)   Where the title to real property is in the names of all the partners a conveyance executed by all the partners passes all their rights in such property.

§ 11.   Partnership Bound by Admission of Partner

An admission or representation made by any partner concerning partnership affairs within the scope of his authority as conferred by this act is evidence against the partnership.

§ 12.   Partnership Charged with Knowledge of or Notice to Partner

Notice to any partner of any matter relating to partnership affairs, and the knowledge of the partner acting in the particular matter, acquired while a partner or then present to his mind, and the knowledge of any other partner who reasonably could and should have communicated it to the acting partner, operate as notice to or knowledge of the partnership, except in the case of a fraud on the partnership committed by or with the consent of that partner.

§ 13.   Partnership Bound by Partner's Wrongful Act

Where, by any wrongful act or omission of any partner acting in the ordinary course of the business of the partnership or with the authority of his co-partners, loss or injury is caused to any person, not being a partner in the partnership, or any penalty is incurred, the partnership is liable therefor to the same extent as the partner so acting or omitting to act.

§ 14.   Partnership Bound by Partner's Breach of Trust

The partnership is bound to make good the loss:

(a)   Where one partner acting within the scope of his apparent authority receives money or property of a third person and misapplies it; and

(b)   Where the partnership in the course of its business receives money or property of a third person and the money or property so received is misapplied by any partner while it is in the custody of the partnership.

§ 15.   Nature of Partner's Liability

All partners are liable

(a)   Jointly and severally for everything chargeable to the partnership under sections 13 and 14.

(b)   Jointly for all other debts and obligations of the partnership; but any partner may enter into a separate obligation to perform a partnership contract.

§ 16.   Partner by Estoppel

(1)   When a person, by words spoken or written or by conduct, represents himself, or consents to another representing him to any one, as a partner in an existing partnership or with one or more persons not actual partners, he is liable to any such person to whom such representation has been made, who has, on the faith of such representation, given credit to the actual or apparent partnership, and if he has made such representation or consented to its being made in a public manner he is liable to such person, whether the representation has or has not been made or communicated to such person so giving credit by or with the knowledge of the apparent partner making the representation or consenting to its being made.

(a)   When a partnership liability results, he is liable as though he were an actual member of the partnership.

(b)   When no partnership liability results, he is liable jointly with the other persons, if any, so consenting to the contract or representation as to incur liability, otherwise separately.

(2)   When a person has been thus represented to be a partner in an existing partnership, or with one or more persons not actual partners, he is an agent of the persons consenting to such representation to bind them to the same extent and in the same manner as though he were a partner in fact, with respect to persons who rely upon the representation. Where all the members of the existing partnership consent to the representation, a partnership act or obligation results; but in all other cases it is the joint act or obligation of the person acting and the persons consenting to the representation.

§ 17.   Liability of Incoming Partner

A person admitted as a partner into an existing partnership is liable for all the obligations of the partnership arising before his admission as though he had been a partner when such obligations were incurred, except that this liability shall be satisfied only out of partnership property.

Part IV

RELATIONS OF PARTNERS TO ONE ANOTHER

Summers case

§ 18.   Rules Determining Rights and Duties of Partners

The rights and duties of the partners in relation to the partnership shall be determined, subject to any agreement between them, by the following rules:

(a)   Each partner shall be repaid his contributions, whether by way of capital or advances to the partnership property and share equally in the profits and surplus remaining after all liabilities, including those to partners, are satisfied; and must contribute towards the losses, whether of capital or otherwise, sustained by the partnership according to his share in the profits.

(b)   The partnership must indemnify every partner in respect of payments made and personal liabilities reasonably incurred by him in the ordinary and proper conduct of its business, or for the preservation of its business or property.

(c)   A partner, who in aid of the partnership makes any payment or advance beyond the amount of capital which he agreed to contribute, shall be paid interest from the date of the payment or advance.

(d)   A partner shall receive interest on the capital contributed by him only from the date when repayment should be made.

(e)   All partners have equal rights in the management and conduct of the partnership business.

(f)   No partner is entitled to remuneration for acting in the partnership business, except that a surviving partner is entitled to reasonable compensation for his services in winding up the partnership affairs.

(g)   No person can become a member of a partnership without the consent of all the partners.

(h)   Any difference arising as to ordinary matters connected with the partnership business may be decided by a majority of the partners; but no act in contravention of any agreement between the partners may be done rightfully without the consent of all the partners.

§ 19.   Partnership Books

The partnership books shall be kept, subject to any agreement between the partners, at the principal place of business of the partnership, and every partner shall at all times have access to and may inspect and copy any of them.

§ 20.   Duty of Partners to Render Information

Partners shall render on demand true and full information of all things affecting the partnership to any partner or the legal representative of any deceased partner or partner under legal disability.

§ 21.   Partner Accountable as a Fiduciary

(1)   Every partner must account to the partnership for any benefit, and hold as trustee for it any profits derived by him without the consent of the other partners from any transaction connected with the formation, conduct, or liquidation of the partnership or from any use by him of its property.

(2)   This section applies also to the representatives of a deceased partner engaged in the liquidation of the affairs of the partnership as the personal representatives of the last surviving partner.

§ 22.   Right to an Account

Any partner shall have the right to a formal account as to partnership affairs:

(a)   If he is wrongfully excluded from the partnership business or possession of its property by his co-partners,

(b)   If the right exists under the terms of any agreement,

(c)   As provided by section 21,

(d)   Whenever other circumstances render it just and reasonable.

§ 23.   Continuation of Partnership Beyond Fixed Term

(1)   When a partnership for a fixed term or particular undertaking is continued after the termination of such term or particular undertaking without any express agreement, the rights and duties of the partners remain the same as they were at such termination, so far as is consistent with a partnership at will.

(2)   A continuation of the business by the partners or such of them as habitually acted therein during the term, without any settlement or liquidation of the partnership affairs, is prima facie evidence of a continuation of the partnership.

Part V

PROPERTY RIGHTS OF A PARTNER

§ 24.   Extent of Property Rights of a Partner

The property rights of a partner are (1) his rights in specific partnership property, (2) his interest in the partnership, and (3) his right to participate in the management.

§ 25.   Nature of a Partner's Right in Specific Partnership Property

(1)   A partner is co-owner with his partners of specific partnership property holding as a tenant in partnership.

(2)   The incidents of this tenancy are such that:

(a)   A partner, subject to the provisions of this act and to any agreement between the partners, has an equal right with his partners to possess specific partnership property for partnership purposes; but he has no right to possess such property for any other purpose without the consent of his partners.

(b)   A partner's right in specific partnership property is not assignable except in connection with the assignment of rights of all the partners in the same property.

(c)   A partner's right in specific partnership property is not subject to attachment or execution, except on a claim against the partnership. When partnership property is attached for a partnership debt the partners, or any of them, or the representatives of a deceased partner, cannot claim any right under the homestead or exemption laws.

(d)   On the death of a partner his right in specific partnership property vests in the surviving partner or partners, except where the deceased was the last surviving partner, when his right in such property vests in his legal representative. Such surviving partner or partners, or the legal representative of the last surviving partner, has no right to possess the partnership property for any but a partnership purpose.

(e)   A partner's right in specific partnership property is not subject to dower, curtesy, or allowances to widows, heirs, or next of kin.

§ 26.   Nature of Partner's Interest in the Partnership

A partner's interest in the partnership is his share of the profits and surplus, and the same is personal property.

§ 27.   Assignment of Partner's Interest

(1)   A conveyance by a partner of his interest in the partnership does not of itself dissolve the partnership, nor, as against the other partners in the absence of agreement, entitle the assignee, during the continuance of the partnership, to interfere in the management or administration of the partnership business or affairs, or to require any information or account of partnership transactions, or to inspect the partnership books; but it merely entitles the assignee to receive in accordance with his contract the profits to which the assigning partner would otherwise be entitled.

(2)   In case of a dissolution of the partnership, the assignee is entitled to receive his assignor's interest and may require an account from the date only of the last account agreed to by all the partners.

§ 28.   Partner's Interest Subject to Charging Order

(1)   On due application to a competent court by any judgment creditor of a partner, the court which entered the judgment, order, or decree, or any other court, may charge the interest of the debtor partner with payment of the unsatisfied amount of such judgment debt with interest thereon; and may then or later appoint a receiver of his share of the profits, and of any other money due or to fall due to him in respect of the partnership, and make all other orders, directions, accounts and inquiries which the debtor partner might have made, or which the circumstances of the case may require.

(2)   The interest charged may be redeemed at any time before foreclosure, or in case of a sale being directed by the court may be purchased without thereby causing a dissolution:

(a)   With separate property, by any one or more of the partners, or

(b)   With partnership property, by any one or more of the partners with the consent of all the partners whose interests are not so charged or sold.

(3)   Nothing in this act shall be held to deprive a partner of his right, if any, under the exemption laws, as regards his interest in the partnership.

Part VI

DISSOLUTION AND WINDING UP

§ 29.   Dissolution Defined

The dissolution of a partnership is the change in the relation of the partners caused by any partner ceasing to be associated in the carrying on as distinguished from the winding up of the business.

§ 30.   Partnership Not Terminated by Dissolution

On dissolution the partnership is not terminated, but continues until the winding up of partnership affairs is completed.

§ 31.   Causes of Dissolution

Dissolution is caused:

(1)   Without violation of the agreement between the partners,

(a)   By the termination of the definite term or particular undertaking specified in the agreement,

(b)   By the express will of any partner when no definite term or particular undertaking is specified,

(c)   By the express will of all the partners who have not assigned their interests or suffered them to be charged for their separate debts, either before or after the termination of any specified term or particular undertaking,

(d)   By the expulsion of any partner from the business bona fide in accordance with such a power conferred by the agreement between the partners;

(2)   In contravention of the agreement between the partners, where the circumstances do not permit a dissolution under any other provision of this section, by the express will of any partner at any time;

(3)   By any event which makes it unlawful for the business of the partnership to be carried on or for the members to carry it on in partnership;

(4)   By the death of any partner;

(5)   By the bankruptcy of any partner or the partnership;

(6)   By decree of court under section 32.

§ 32.   Dissolution by Decree of Court

(1)   On application by or for a partner the court shall decree a dissolution whenever:

(a)   A partner has been declared a lunatic in any judicial proceeding or is shown to be of unsound mind,

(b)   A partner becomes in any other way incapable of performing his part of the partnership contract,

(c)   A partner has been guilty of such conduct as tends to affect prejudicially the carrying on of the business,

(d)   A partner wilfully or persistently commits a breach of the partnership agreement, or otherwise so conducts himself in matters relating to the partnership business that it is not reasonably practicable to carry on the business in partnership with him,

(e)   The business of the partnership can only be carried on at a loss,

(f)   Other circumstances render a dissolution equitable.

(2)   On the application of the purchaser of a partner's interest under sections 27 or 28:

(a)   After the termination of the specified term or particular undertaking,

(b)   At any time if the partnership was a partnership at will when the interest was assigned or when the charging order was issued.

§ 33.   General Effect of Dissolution on Authority of Partner

Except so far as may be necessary to wind up partnership affairs or to complete transactions begun but not then finished, dissolution terminates all authority of any partner to act for the partnership,

(1)   With respect to the partners,

    (a)   When the dissolution is not by the act, bankruptcy or death of a partner; or

    (b)   When the dissolution is by such act, bankruptcy or death of a partner, in cases where section 34 so requires.

(2)   With respect to persons not partners, as declared in section 35.

§ 34.   Right of Partner to Contribution from Co-Partners After Dissolution

Where the dissolution is caused by the act, death or bankruptcy of a partner, each partner is liable to his co-partners for his share of any liability created by any partner acting for the partnership as if the partnership had not been dissolved unless

    (a)   The dissolution being by act of any partner, the partner acting for the partnership had knowledge of the dissolution, or

    (b)   The dissolution being by the death or bankruptcy of a partner, the partner acting for the partnership had knowledge or notice of the death or bankruptcy.

§ 35.   Power of Partner to Bind Partnership to Third Persons After Dissolution

(1)   After dissolution a partner can bind the partnership except as provided in Paragraph (3).

    (a)   By any act appropriate for winding up partnership affairs or completing transactions unfinished at dissolution;

    (b)   By any transaction which would bind the partnership if dissolution had not taken place, provided the other party to the transaction

        (i)   Had extended credit to the partnership prior to dissolution and had no knowledge or notice of the dissolution; or

        (ii)   Though he had not so extended credit, had nevertheless known of the partnership prior to dissolution, and, having no knowledge or notice of dissolution, the fact of dissolution had not been advertised in a newspaper of general circulation in the place (or in each place if more than one) at which the partnership business was regularly carried on.

(2)   The liability of a partner under Paragraph (1b) shall be satisfied out of partnership assets alone when such partner had been prior to dissolution

    (a)   Unknown as a partner to the person with whom the contract is made; and

    (b)   So far unknown and inactive in partnership affairs that the business reputation of the partnership could not be said to have been in any degree due to his connection with it.

(3)   The partnership is in no case bound by any act of a partner after dissolution

    (a)   Where the partnership is dissolved because it is unlawful to carry on the business, unless the act is appropriate for winding up partnership affairs; or

    (b)   Where the partner has become bankrupt; or

    (c)   Where the partner has no authority to wind up partnership affairs; except by a transaction with one who

        (i)   Had extended credit to the partnership prior to dissolution and had no knowledge or notice of his want of authority; or

        (ii)   Had not extended credit to the partnership prior to dissolution, and; having no knowledge or notice of his want of authority, the fact of his want of authority has not been advertised in the manner provided for advertising the fact of dissolution in Paragraph (1b II).

(4)   Nothing in this section shall affect the liability under Section 16 of any person who after dissolution represents himself or consents to another representing him as a partner in a partnership engaged in carrying on business.

§ 36.   Effect of Dissolution on Partner's Existing Liability

(1)   The dissolution of the partnership does not of itself discharge the existing liability of any partner.

(2)   A partner is discharged from any existing liability upon dissolution of the partnership by an agreement to that effect between himself, the partnership creditor and the person or partnership continuing the business; and such agreement may be inferred from the course of dealing between the creditor having knowledge of the dissolution and the person or partnership continuing the business.

(3)   Where a person agrees to assume the existing obligations of a dissolved partnership, the partners whose obligations have been assumed shall be discharged from any liability to any creditor of the partnership who, knowing of the agreement, consents to a material alteration in the nature or time of payment of such obligations.

(4)   The individual property of a deceased partner shall be liable for all obligations of the partnership incurred while he was a partner but subject to the prior payment of his separate debts.

§ 37.   Right to Wind up

Unless otherwise agreed the partners who have nor wrongfully dissolved the partnership or the legal representative of the last surviving partner, not bankrupt, has the right to wind up the partnership affairs; provided, however, that any partner, his legal representative or his assignee, upon cause shown, may obtain winding up by the court.

§ 38.   Rights of Partners to Application of Partnership Property

(1)   When dissolution is caused in any way, except in contravention of the partnership agreement, each partner, as against his co-partners and all persons claiming through them in respect of their interests in the partnership, unless otherwise agreed, may have the partnership property applied to discharge its liabilities, and the surplus applied to pay in cash the net amount owing to the respective partners. But if dissolution is caused by expulsion of a partner, bona fide under the partnership agreement and if the expelled partner is discharged from all partnership liabilities, either by payment or agreement under section 36(2), he shall receive in cash only the net amount due him from the partnership.

(2)   When dissolution is caused in contravention of the partnership agreement the rights of the partners shall be as follows:

(a)   Each partner who has not caused dissolution wrongfully shall have,

(i) All the rights specified in paragraph (1) of this section, and

(ii) The right, as against each partner who has caused the dissolution wrongfully, to damages for breach of the agreement.

(b)   The partners who have not caused the dissolution wrongfully, if they all desire to continue the business in the same name, either by themselves or jointly with others, may do so, during the agreed term for the partnership and for that purpose may possess the partnership property, provided they secure the payment by bond approved by the court, or pay to any partner who has caused the dissolution wrongfully, the value of his interest in the partnership at the dissolution, less any damages recoverable under clause (2a II) of this section, and in like manner indemnify him against all present or future partnership liabilities.

(c)   A partner who has caused the dissolution wrongfully shall have:

(i)   If the business is not continued under the provisions of paragraph (2b) all the rights of a partner under paragraph (1), subject to clause (2a II), of this section,

(ii)   If the business is continued under paragraph (2b) of this section the right as against his co-partners and all claiming through them in respect of their interests in the partnership, to have the value of his interest in the partnership, less any damages caused to his co-partners by the dissolution, ascertained and paid to him in cash, or the payment secured by bond approved by the court, and to be released from all existing liabilities of the partnership; but in ascertaining the value of the partner's interest the value of the good-will of the business shall not be considered.

§ 39. Rights Where Partnership is Dissolved for Fraud or Misrepresentation

Where a partnership contract is rescinded on the ground of the fraud or misrepresentation of one of the parties thereto, the party entitled to rescind is, without prejudice to any other right, entitled,

(a)   To a lien on, or a right of retention of, the surplus of the partnership property after satisfying the partnership liabilities to third persons for any sum of money paid by him for the purchase of an interest in the partnership and for any capital or advances contributed by him; and

(b)   To stand, after all liabilities to third persons have been satisfied, in the place of the creditors of the partnership for any payments made by him in respect of the partnership liabilities; and

(c)   To be indemnified by the person guilty of the fraud or making the representation against all debts and liabilities of the partnership.

§ 40. Rules for Distribution

In settling accounts between the partners after dissolution, the following rules shall be observed, subject to any agreement to the contrary:

(a)   The assets of the partnership are:

(i)   The partnership property,

(ii)   The contributions of the partners necessary for the payment of all the liabilities specified in clause (b) of this paragraph.

(b)   The liabilities of the partnership shall rank in order of payment, as follows:

(i)   Those owing to creditors other than partners,

(ii)   Those owing to partners other than for capital and profits,

(iii)   Those owing to partners in respect of capital,

(iv)   Those owing to partners in respect of profits.

(c)   The assets shall be applied in the order of their declaration in clause (a) of this paragraph to the satisfaction of the liabilities.

(d)   The partners shall contribute, as provided by section 18(a) the amount necessary to satisfy the liabilities; but if any, but not all, of the partners are insolvent, or, not being subject to process, refuse to contribute, the other partners shall contribute their share of the liabilities, and, in the relative proportions in which they share the profits, the additional amount necessary to pay the liabilities.

(e)   An assignee for the benefit of creditors or any person appointed by the court shall have the right to enforce the contributions specified in clause (d) of this paragraph.

(f)   Any partner or his legal representative shall have the right to enforce the contributions specified in clause (d) of this paragraph, to the extent of the amount which he has paid in excess of his share of the liability.

(g)   The individual property of a deceased partner shall be liable for the contributions specified in clause (d) of this paragraph.

(h)   When partnership property and the individual properties of the partners are in possession of a court for distribution, partnership creditors shall have priority on partnership property and separate creditors on individual property, saving the rights of lien or secured creditors as heretofore.

(i)   Where a partner has become bankrupt or his estate insolvent the claims against his separate property shall rank in the following order:

    (i)   Those owing to separate creditors,

    (ii)   Those owing to partnership creditors,

    (iii) Those owing to partners by way of contribution.

§ 41.   Liability of Persons Continuing the Business in Certain Cases

(1)   When any new partner is admitted into an existing partnership, or when any partner retires and assigns (or the representative of the deceased partner assigns) his rights in partnership property to two or more of the partners, or to one or more of the partners and one or more third persons, if the business is continued without liquidation of the partnership affairs, creditors of the first or dissolved partnership are also creditors of the partnership so continuing the business.

(2)   When all but one partner retire and assign (or the representative of a deceased partner assigns) their rights in partnership property to the remaining partner, who continues the business without liquidation of partnership affairs, either alone or with others, creditors of the dissolved partnership are also creditors of the person or partnership so continuing the business.

(3)   When any partner retires or dies and the business of the dissolved partnership is continued as set forth in paragraphs (1) and (2) of this section, with the consent of the retired partners or the representative of the deceased partner, but without any assignment of his right in partnership property, rights of creditors of the dissolved partnership and of the creditors of the person or partnership continuing the business shall be as if such assignment had been made.

(4)   When all the partners or their representatives assign their rights in partnership property to one or more third persons who promise to pay the debts and who continue the business of the dissolved partnership, creditors of the dissolved partnership are also creditors of the person or partnership continuing the business.

(5)   When any partner wrongfully causes a dissolution and the remaining partners continue the business under the provisions of section 38(2b), either alone or with others, and without liquidation of the partnership affairs, creditors of the dissolved partnership are also creditors of the person or partnership continuing the business.

(6)   When a partner is expelled and the remaining partners continue the business either alone or with others, without liquidation of the partnership affairs, creditors of the dissolved partnership are also creditors of the person or partnership continuing the business.

(7)   The liability of a third person becoming a partner in the partnership continuing the business, under this section, to the creditors of the dissolved partnership shall be satisfied out of partnership property only.

(8)   When the business of a partnership after dissolution is continued under any conditions set forth in this section the creditors of the dissolved partnership, as against the separate creditors of the retiring or deceased partner or the representative of the deceased partner, have a prior right to any claim of the retired partner or the representative of the deceased partner against the person or partnership continuing the business, on account of the retired or deceased partner's interest in the dissolved partnership or on account of any consideration promised for such interest or for his right in partnership property.

(9)   Nothing in this section shall be held to modify any right of creditors to set aside any assignment on the ground of fraud.

(10) The use by the person or partnership continuing the business of the partnership name, or the name of a deceased partner as part thereof, shall not of itself make the individual property of the deceased partner liable for any debts contracted by such person or partnership.

§ 42.   Rights of Retiring or Estate of Deceased Partner When the Business is Continued

When any partner retires or dies, and the business is continued under any of the conditions set forth in section 41 (1, 2, 3, 5, 6), or section 38(2b) without any settlement of accounts as between him or his estate and the person or partnership continuing the business, unless otherwise agreed, he or his legal representative as against such persons or partnership may have the value of his interest at the date of dissolution ascertained, and shall receive as an ordinary creditor an amount equal to the value of his interest in the dissolved partnership with interest, or, at his option or at the option of his legal representative, in lieu of interest, the profits attributable to the use of his right in the property of the dissolved partnership; provided that the creditors of the dissolved partnership as against the separate creditors, or the representative of the retired or deceased partner, shall have priority on any claim arising under this section, as provided by section 41(8) of this act.

§ 43.   Accrual of Actions

The right to an account of his interest shall accrue to any partner, or his legal representative, as against the winding up partners or the surviving partners or the person or partnership continuing the business, at the date of dissolution, in the absence of any agreement to the contrary.

Part VII

MISCELLANEOUS PROVISIONS

§ 44.   When Act Takes Effect

This act shall take effect on the _____ day of _____ one thousand nine hundred and _____.

§ 45.   Legislation Repealed

All acts or parts of acts inconsistent with this act are hereby repealed.

REVISED UNIFORM PARTNERSHIP ACT (1997)

———————

Table of Sections

REVISED UNIFORM PARTNERSHIP ACT (1997)

Article 5

TRANSFEREES AND CREDITORS OF PARTNER

Article 6

PARTNER'S DISSOCIATION

Article 7

PARTNER'S DISSOCIATION WHEN BUSINESS NOT WOUND UP

Article 8

WINDING UP PARTNERSHIP BUSINESS

Article 9

CONVERSIONS AND MERGERS

Article 10

LIMITED LIABILITY PARTNERSHIP

Article 1

GENERAL PROVISIONS

§ 101.　Definitions

In this [Act]:

(1)　"Business" includes every trade, occupation, and profession.

(2)　"Debtor in bankruptcy" means a person who is the subject of:

(i)　an order for relief under Title 11 of the United States Code or a comparable order under a successor statute of general application; or

(ii)　a comparable order under federal, state, or foreign law governing insolvency.

(3)　"Distribution" means a transfer of money or other property from a partnership to a partner in the partner's capacity as a partner or to the partner's transferee.

(4)　"Foreign limited liability partnership" means a partnership that:

(i)　is formed under laws other than the laws of this State; and

(ii)　has the status of a limited liability partnership under those laws.

(5)　"Limited liability partnership" means a partnership that has filed a statement of qualification under Section 1001 and does not have a similar statement in effect in any other jurisdiction.

(6)　"Partnership" means an association of two or more persons to carry on as co-owners a business for profit formed under Section 202, predecessor law, or comparable law of another jurisdiction.

(7) "Partnership agreement" means the agreement, whether written, oral, or implied, among the partners concerning the partnership, including amendments to the partnership agreement.

(8) "Partnership at will" means a partnership in which the partners have not agreed to remain partners until the expiration of a definite term or the completion of a particular undertaking.

(9) "Partnership interest" or "partner's interest in the partnership" means all of a partner's interests in the partnership, including the partner's transferable interest and all management and other rights.

(10) "Person" means an individual, corporation, business trust, estate, trust, partnership, association, joint venture, government, governmental subdivision, agency, or instrumentality, or any other legal or commercial entity.

(11) "Property" means all property, real, personal, or mixed, tangible or intangible, or any interest therein.

(12) "State" means a State of the United States, the District of Columbia, the Commonwealth of Puerto Rico, or any territory or insular possession subject to the jurisdiction of the United States.

(13) "Statement" means a statement of partnership authority under Section 303, a statement of denial under Section 304, a statement of dissociation under Section 704, a statement of dissolution under Section 805, a statement of merger under Section 907, a statement of qualification under Section 1001, a statement of foreign qualification under Section 1102, or an amendment or cancellation of any of the foregoing.

(14) "Transfer" includes an assignment, conveyance, lease, mortgage, deed, and encumbrance.

COMMENT

These Comments include the original Comments to the Revised Uniform Partnership Act (RUPA or the Act) and the new Comments to the Limited Liability Partnership Act Amendments to the Uniform Partnership Act (1994). The new Comments regarding limited liability partnerships are integrated into the RUPA Comments.

The RUPA continues the definition of "business" from Section 2 of the Uniform Partnership Act (UPA).

RUPA uses the more contemporary term "debtor in bankruptcy" instead of "bankrupt." The definition is adapted from the new Georgia Partnership Act, Ga. Code Ann. § 14–8–2(1). The definition does not distinguish between a debtor whose estate is being liquidated under Chapter 7 of the Bankruptcy Code and a debtor who is being rehabilitated under Chapter 11, 12, or 13 and includes both. The filing of a voluntary petition under Section 301 of the Bankruptcy Code constitutes an order for relief, but the debtor is entitled to notice and an opportunity to be heard before the entry of an order for relief in an involuntary case under Section 303 of the Code. The term also includes a debtor who is the subject of a comparable order under state or foreign law.

The definition of "distribution" is new and adds precision to the accounting rules established in Sections 401 and 807 and related sections. Transfers to a partner in the partner's capacity as a creditor, lessor, or employee of the partnership, for example, are not "distributions."

The definition of a "foreign limited liability partnership" includes a partnership formed under the laws of another State, foreign country, or other jurisdiction provided it has the status of a limited liability partnership in the other jurisdiction. Since the scope and nature of foreign limited liability partnership liability shields may vary in different jurisdictions, the definition avoids reference to similar or comparable laws. Rather, the definition incorporates the concept of a limited liability partnership in the foreign jurisdiction, however defined in that jurisdiction. The reference to formation "under laws other than the laws of this State" makes clear that the definition includes partnerships formed in foreign countries as well as in another State.

The definition of a "limited liability partnership" makes clear that a partnership may adopt the special liability shield characteristics of a limited liability partnership simply by filing a statement of qualification under Section 1001. A partnership may file the statement in this State regardless of where formed. When coupled with the governing law provisions of Section 106(b), this definition simplifies the choice of law issues applicable to partnerships with multi-state activities and contacts. Once a statement of qualification is filed, a partnership's internal affairs and the liability of its partners are determined by the law of the State where the statement is filed. See Section 106(b). The partnership may not vary this particular requirement. See Section 103(b)(9).

The reference to a "partnership" in the definition of a limited liability partnership makes clear that the RUPA definition of the term rather than the UPA concept controls for purposes of a limited liability partnership. Section 101(6) defines a "partnership" as "an association of two or more persons to carry on as co-owners a business for profit formed under Section 202, predecessor law, or comparable law of another jurisdiction." Section 202(b) further provides that "an association formed under a statute other than this [Act], a predecessor statute, or a comparable statute of another jurisdiction is not a partnership under this [Act]." This language was intended to clarify that a limited partnership is not a RUPA general partnership. It was not intended to preclude the application of any RUPA general partnership rules to limited partnerships where limited partnership law otherwise adopts the RUPA rules. See Comments to Section 202(b) and Prefatory Note.

The effect of these definitions leaves the scope and applicability of RUPA to limited partnerships to limited partnership law, not to sever the linkage between the two Acts in all cases. Certain provisions of RUPA will continue to govern limited partnerships by virtue of Revised Uniform Limited Partnership Act (RULPA) Section 1105 which provides that "in any case not provided for in this [Act] the provisions of the Uniform Partnership Act govern." The RUPA partnership definition includes partnerships formed under the UPA. Therefore, the limited liability partnership rules will govern limited partnerships "in any case not provided for" in RULPA. Since RULPA does not provide for any rules applicable to a limited partnership becoming a limited liability partnership, the limited liability partnership rules should apply to limited partnerships that file a statement of qualification.

Partner liability deserves special mention. RULPA Section 403(b) provides that a general partner of a limited partnership "has the liabilities of a partner in a partnership without limited partners." Thus limited partnership law expressly references general partnership law for general partner liability and does not separately consider the liability of such partners. The liability of a general partner of a limited partnership that becomes a LLLP would therefore be the liability of a general partner in an LLP and would be governed by Section 306. The liability of a limited partner in a LLLP is a more complicated matter. RULPA Section 303(a) separately considers the liability of a limited partner. Unless also a general partner, a limited partner is not liable for the obligations of a limited partnership unless the partner participates in the control of the business and then only to persons reasonably believing the limited partner is a general partner. Therefore, arguably limited partners in a LLLP will have the specific RULPA Section 303(c) liability shield while general partners will have a superior Section 306(c) liability shield. In order to clarify limited partner liability and other linkage issues, States that have adopted RUPA, these limited liability partnership rules, and RULPA may wish to consider an amendment to RULPA. A suggested form of such an amendment is:

SECTION 1107. LIMITED LIABILITY LIMITED PARTNERSHIP.

(a) A limited partnership may become a limited liability partnership by:

(1) obtaining approval of the terms and conditions of the limited partnership becoming a limited liability limited partnership by the vote necessary to amend the limited partnership agreement except, in the case of a limited partnership agreement that expressly considers contribution obligations, the vote necessary to amend those provisions;

(2) filing a statement of qualification under Section 1001(c) of the Uniform Partnership Act (1994); and

(3) complying with the name requirements of Section 1002 of the Uniform Partnership Act (1994).

(b) A limited liability limited partnership continues to be the same entity that existed before the filing of a statement of qualification under Section 1001(c) of the Uniform Partnership Act (1994).

(c) Sections 306(c) and 307(b) of the Uniform Partnership Act (1994) apply to both general and limited partners of a limited liability limited partnership.

"Partnership" is defined to mean an association of two or more persons to carry on as co-owners a business for profit formed under Section 202 (or predecessor law or comparable law of another jurisdiction), that is, a general partnership. Thus, as used in RUPA, the term "partnership" does not encompass limited partnerships, contrary to the use of the term in the UPA. Section 901(3) defines "limited partnership" for the purpose of Article 9, which deals with conversions and mergers of general and limited partnerships.

The definition of "partnership agreement" is adapted from Section 101(9) of RULPA. The RUPA definition is intended to include the agreement among the partners, including amendments, concerning either the affairs of the partnership or the conduct of its business. It does not include other agreements between some or all of the partners, such as a lease or loan agreement. The partnership agreement need not be written; it may be oral or inferred from the conduct of the parties.

Any partnership in which the partners have not agreed to remain partners until the expiration of a definite term or the completion of a particular undertaking is a "partnership at will." The distinction between an "at-will" partnership and a partnership for "a definite term or the completion of a particular undertaking" is important in determining the rights of dissociating and continuing partners following the dissociation of a partner. See Sections 601, 602, 701(b), 801(a), 802(b), and 803.

It is sometimes difficult to determine whether a partnership is at will or is for a definite term or the completion of a particular undertaking. Presumptively, every partnership is an at-will partnership. *See, e.g., Stone v. Stone*, 292 So. 2d 686 (La. 1974); *Frey v. Hauke*, 171 Neb. 852, 108 N.W.2d 228 (1961). To constitute a partnership for a term or a particular undertaking, the partners must agree (i) that the partnership will continue for a definite term or until a particular undertaking is completed and (ii) that they will remain partners until the expiration of the term or the completion of the undertaking. Both are necessary for a term partnership; if the partners have the unrestricted right, as distinguished from the power, to withdraw from a partnership formed for a term or particular undertaking, the partnership is one at will, rather than a term partnership.

To find that the partnership is formed for a definite term or a particular undertaking, there must be clear evidence of an agreement among the partners that the partnership (i) has a minimum or maximum duration or (ii) terminates at the conclusion of a particular venture whose time is indefinite but certain to occur. *See, e.g., Stainton v. Tarantino*, 637 F. Supp. 1051 (E.D. Pa. 1986) (partnership to dissolve no later than December 30, 2020); *Abel v. American Art Analog, Inc.*, 838 F.2d 691 (3d Cir. 1988) (partnership purpose to market an art book); *68th Street Apts., Inc. v. Lauricella*, 362 A.2d 78 (N.J. Super. Ct. 1976) (partnership purpose to construct an apartment building). A partnership to conduct a business which may last indefinitely, however, is an at-will partnership, even though there may be an obligation of the partnership, such as a mortgage, which must be repaid by a certain date, absent a specific agreement that no partner can rightfully withdraw until the obligation is repaid. *See, e.g., Page v. Page*, 55 Cal. 2d. 192, 359 P.2d 41 (1961) (partnership purpose to operate a linen supply business); *Frey v. Hauke, supra* (partnership purpose to contract and operate a bowling alley); *Girard Bank v. Haley*, 460 Pa. 237, 332 A.2d 443 (1975) (partnership purpose to maintain and lease buildings).

"Partnership interest" or "partner's interest in the partnership" is defined to mean all of a partner's interests in the partnership, including the partner's transferable interest and all management and other rights. A partner's "transferable interest" is a more limited concept and means only his share of the profits and losses and right to receive distributions, that is, the partner's economic interests. See Section 502 and Comment. Compare RULPA § 101(10) ("partnership interest" includes partner's economic interests only).

The definition of "person" is the usual definition used by the National Conference of Commissioners on Uniform State Laws (NCCUSL or the Conference). The definition includes other legal or commercial entities such as limited liability companies.

"Property" is defined broadly to include all types of property, as well as any interest in property.

The definition of "State" is the Conference's usual definition.

The definition of "statement" is new and refers to one of the various statements authorized by RUPA to enhance or limit the agency authority of a partner, to deny the authority or status of a partner, or to give notice of certain events, such as the dissociation of a partner or the dissolution of the partnership. See Sections 303, 304, 704, 805, and 907. Generally, Section 105 governs the execution, filing, and recording of all statements. The definition also makes clear that a statement of qualification under Section 1001 and a statement of foreign qualification under Section 1102 are considered statements. Both qualification statements are therefore subject to the execution, filing, and recordation rules of Section 105.

"Transfer" is defined broadly to include all manner of conveyances, including leases and encumbrances.

§ 102. Knowledge and Notice

(a) A person knows a fact if the person has actual knowledge of it.

(b) A person has notice of a fact if the person:

    (1) knows of it;

    (2) has received a notification of it; or

    (3) has reason to know it exists from all of the facts known to the person at the time in question.

(c)   A person notifies or gives a notification to another by taking steps reasonably required to inform the other person in ordinary course, whether or not the other person learns of it.

(d)   A person receives a notification when the notification:

(1)   comes to the person's attention; or

(2)   is duly delivered at the person's place of business or at any other place held out by the person as a place for receiving communications.

(e)   Except as otherwise provided in subsection (f), a person other than an individual knows, has notice, or receives a notification of a fact for purposes of a particular transaction when the individual conducting the transaction knows, has notice, or receives a notification of the fact, or in any event when the fact would have been brought to the individual's attention if the person had exercised reasonable diligence. The person exercises reasonable diligence if it maintains reasonable routines for communicating significant information to the individual conducting the transaction and there is reasonable compliance with the routines. Reasonable diligence does not require an individual acting for the person to communicate information unless the communication is part of the individual's regular duties or the individual has reason to know of the transaction and that the transaction would be materially affected by the information.

(f)   A partner's knowledge, notice, or receipt of a notification of a fact relating to the partnership is effective immediately as knowledge by, notice to, or receipt of a notification by the partnership, except in the case of a fraud on the partnership committed by or with the consent of that partner.

COMMENT

The concepts and definitions of "knowledge," "notice," and "notification" draw heavily on Section 1–201(25) to (27) of the Uniform Commercial Code (UCC). The UCC text has been altered somewhat to improve clarity and style, but in general no substantive changes are intended from the UCC concepts. "A notification" replaces the UCC's redundant phrase, "a notice or notification," throughout the Act.

A person "knows" a fact only if that person has actual knowledge of it. Knowledge is cognitive awareness. That is solely an issue of fact. This is a change from the UPA Section 3(1) definition of "knowledge" which included the concept of "bad faith" knowledge arising from other known facts.

"Notice" is a lesser degree of awareness than "knows" and is based on a person's: (i) actual knowledge; (ii) receipt of a notification; or (iii) reason to know based on actual knowledge of other facts and the circumstances at the time. The latter is the traditional concept of inquiry notice.

Generally, under RUPA, statements filed pursuant to Section 105 do not constitute constructive knowledge or notice, except as expressly provided in the Act. *See* Section 301(1) (generally requiring knowledge of limitations on partner's apparent authority). Properly recorded statements of limitation on a partner's authority, on the other hand, generally constitute constructive knowledge with respect to the transfer of real property held in the partnership name. *See* Sections 303(d)(1), 303(e), 704(b), and 805(b). The other exceptions are Sections 704(c) (statement of dissociation effective 90 days after filing) and 805(c) (statement of dissolution effective 90 days after filing).

A person "receives" a notification when (i) the notification is delivered to the person's place of business (or other place for receiving communications) or (ii) the recipient otherwise actually learns of its existence.

The sender "notifies" or gives a notification by making an effort to inform the recipient, which is reasonably calculated to do so in ordinary course, even if the recipient does not actually learn of it.

The Official Comment to UCC Section 1–201(26), on which this subsection is based, explains that "notifies" is the word used when the essential fact is the proper dispatch of the notice, not its receipt. When the essential fact is the other party's receipt of the notice, that is stated.

A notification is not required to be in writing. That is a change from UPA Section 3(2)(b). As under the UCC, the time and circumstances under which a notification may cease to be effective are not determined by RUPA.

Subsection (e) determines when an agent's knowledge or notice is imputed to an organization, such as a corporation. In general, only the knowledge or notice of the agent conducting the particular transaction is imputed to the organization. Organizations are expected to maintain reasonable internal routines to insure that important information reaches the individual agent handling a transaction. If, in the exercise of reasonable diligence on the part of the organization, the agent should have known or had notice of a fact, or received a notification of it, the organization is bound. The Official Comment to UCC Section 1–201(27) explains:

This makes clear that reason to know, knowledge, or a notification, although "received" for instance by a clerk in Department A of an organization, is effective for a transaction conducted in Department B only from the time when it was or should have been communicated to the individual conducting that transaction.

Subsection (e) uses the phrase "person other than an individual" in lieu of the UCC term "organization."

Subsection (f) continues the rule in UPA Section 12 that a partner's knowledge or notice of a fact relating to the partnership is imputed to the partnership, except in the case of fraud on the partnership. Limited partners, however, are not "partners" within the meaning of RUPA. *See* Comment 4 to Section 202. It is anticipated that RULPA will address the issue of whether notice to a limited partner is imputed to a limited partnership.

§ 103.   Effect of Partnership Agreement; Nonwaivable Provisions

(a)   Except as otherwise provided in subsection (b), relations among the partners and between the partners and the partnership are governed by the partnership agreement. To the extent the partnership agreement does not otherwise provide, this [Act] governs relations among the partners and between the partners and the partnership.

(b)   The partnership agreement may not:

(1)   vary the rights and duties under Section 105 except to eliminate the duty to provide copies of statements to all of the partners;

(2)   unreasonably restrict the right of access to books and records under Section 403(b);

(3)   eliminate the duty of loyalty under Section 404(b) or 603(b)(3), but:

(i)   the partnership agreement may identify specific types or categories of activities that do not violate the duty of loyalty, if not manifestly unreasonable; or

(ii)   all of the partners or a number or percentage specified in the partnership agreement may authorize or ratify, after full disclosure of all material facts, a specific act or transaction that otherwise would violate the duty of loyalty;

(4)   unreasonably reduce the duty of care under Section 404(c) or 603(b)(3);

(5)   eliminate the obligation of good faith and fair dealing under Section 404(d), but the partnership agreement may prescribe the standards by which the performance of the obligation is to be measured, if the standards are not manifestly unreasonable;

(6)   vary the power to dissociate as a partner under Section 602(a), except to require the notice under Section 601(1) to be in writing;

(7)   vary the right of a court to expel a partner in the events specified in Section 601(5);

(8)   vary the requirement to wind up the partnership business in cases specified in Section 801(4), (5), or (6);

(9)   vary the law applicable to a limited liability partnership under Section 106(b); or

(10)   restrict rights of third parties under this [Act].

COMMENT

1.   The general rule under Section 103(a) is that relations among the partners and between the partners and the partnership are governed by the partnership agreement. *See* Section 101(5). To the extent that the partners fail to agree upon a contrary rule, RUPA provides the default rule. Only the rights and duties listed in Section 103(b), and implicitly the corresponding liabilities and remedies under Section 405, are mandatory and cannot be waived or varied by agreement beyond what is authorized. Those are the only exceptions to the general principle that the provisions of RUPA with respect to the rights of the partners *inter se* are merely default rules, subject to modification by the partners. All modifications must also, of course, satisfy the general standards of contract validity. See Section 104.

2.   Under subsection (b)(1), the partnership agreement may not vary the requirements for executing, filing, and recording statements under Section 105, except the duty to provide copies to all the partners. A statement that is not executed, filed, and recorded in accordance with the statutory requirements will not be accorded the effect prescribed in the Act, except as provided in Section 303(d).

3.   Subsection (b)(2) provides that the partnership agreement may not unreasonably restrict a partner or former partner's access rights to books and records under Section 403(b). It is left to the courts to determine what restrictions are reasonable. See Comment 2 to Section 403. Other information rights in Section 403 can be varied or even eliminated by agreement.

4.   Subsection (b)(3) through (5) are intended to ensure a fundamental core of fiduciary responsibility. Neither the fiduciary duties of loyalty or care, nor the obligation of good faith and fair dealing, may be eliminated entirely. However, the statutory requirements of each can be modified by agreement, subject to the limitation stated in subsection (b)(3) through (5).

There has always been a tension regarding the extent to which a partner's fiduciary duty of loyalty can be varied by agreement, as contrasted with the other partners' consent to a particular and known breach of duty. On the one hand, courts have been loathe to enforce agreements broadly "waiving" in advance a partner's fiduciary duty of loyalty, especially where there is unequal bargaining power, information, or sophistication. For this reason, a very broad provision in a partnership agreement in effect negating any duty of loyalty, such as a provision giving a managing partner complete discretion to manage the business with no liability except for acts and omissions that constitute willful misconduct, will not likely be enforced. *See, e.g., Labovitz v. Dolan*, 189 Ill. App. 3d 403, 136 Ill. Dec. 780, 545 N.E.2d 304 (1989). On the other hand, it is clear that the remaining partners can "consent" to a particular conflicting interest transaction or other breach of duty, after the fact, provided there is full disclosure.

RUPA attempts to provide a standard that partners can rely upon in drafting exculpatory agreements. It is not necessary that the agreement be restricted to a particular transaction. That would require bargaining over every transaction or opportunity, which would be excessively burdensome. The agreement may be drafted in terms of types or categories of activities or transactions, but it should be reasonably specific.

A provision in a real estate partnership agreement authorizing a partner who is a real estate agent to retain commissions on partnership property bought and sold by that partner would be an example of a "type or category" of activity that is not manifestly unreasonable and thus should be enforceable under the Act. Likewise, a provision authorizing that partner to buy or sell real property for his own account without prior disclosure to the other partners or without first offering it to the partnership would be enforceable as a valid category of partnership activity.

Ultimately, the courts must decide the outer limits of validity of such agreements, and context may be significant. It is intended that the risk of judicial refusal to enforce manifestly unreasonable exculpatory clauses will discourage sharp practices while accommodating the legitimate needs of the parties in structuring their relationship.

5.   Subsection (b)(3)(i) permits the partners, in their partnership agreement, to identify specific types or categories of partnership activities that do not violate the duty of loyalty. A modification of the statutory standard must not, however, be manifestly unreasonable. This is intended to discourage overreaching by a partner with superior bargaining power since the courts may refuse to enforce an overly broad exculpatory clause. *See, e.g., Vlases v. Montgomery Ward & Co.*, 377 F.2d 846, 850 (3d Cir. 1967) (limitation prohibits unconscionable agreements); *PPG Industries, Inc. v. Shell Oil Co.*, 919 F.2d 17, 19 (5th Cir. 1990) (apply limitation deferentially to agreements of sophisticated parties).

Subsection (b)(3)(ii) is intended to clarify the right of partners, recognized under general law, to consent to a known past or anticipated violation of duty and to waive their legal remedies for redress of that violation. This is intended to cover situations where the conduct in question is not specifically authorized by the partnership agreement. It can also be used to validate conduct that might otherwise not satisfy the "manifestly unreasonable" standard. Clause (ii) provides that, after full disclosure of all material facts regarding a specific act or transaction that otherwise would violate the duty of loyalty, it may be authorized or ratified by the partners. That authorization or ratification must be unanimous unless a lesser number or percentage is specified for this purpose in the partnership agreement.

6.   Under subsection (b)(4), the partners' duty of care may not be unreasonably reduced below the statutory standard set forth in Section 404(d), that is, to refrain from engaging in grossly negligent or reckless conduct, intentional misconduct, or a knowing violation of law.

For example, partnership agreements frequently contain provisions releasing a partner from liability for actions taken in good faith and in the honest belief that the actions are in the best interests of the partnership and indemnifying the partner against any liability incurred in connection with the business of the partnership if the partner acts in a good faith belief that he has authority to act. Many partnership agreements reach this same result by listing various activities and stating that the performance of these activities is deemed not to constitute gross negligence or willful misconduct. These types of provisions are intended to come within the modifications authorized by subsection (b)(4). On the other hand, absolving partners of intentional misconduct is probably unreasonable. As with contractual standards of loyalty, determining the outer limit in reducing the standard of care is left to the courts.

The standard may, of course, be increased by agreement to one of ordinary care or an even higher standard of care.

7.   Subsection (b)(5) authorizes the partners to determine the standards by which the performance of the obligation of good faith and fair dealing is to be measured. The language of subsection (b)(5) is based on UCC Section 1–102(3). The partners can negotiate and draft specific contract provisions tailored to their particular needs (*e.g.*, five days notice of a partners' meeting is adequate notice), but blanket waivers of the obligation are unenforceable. *See, e.g., PPG Indus., Inc. v. Shell Oil Co.*, 919 F.2d 17 (5th Cir. 1990); *First Security Bank v. Mountain View Equip. Co.*, 112 Idaho 158, 730 P.2d 1078 (Ct. App. 1986), *aff'd*, 112 Idaho 1078, 739 P.2d 377 (1987); *American Bank of Commerce v. Covolo*, 88 N.M. 405, 540 P.2d 1294 (1975).

8.   Section 602(a) continues the traditional UPA Section 31(2) rule that every partner has the power to withdraw from the partnership at any time, which power can not be bargained away. Section 103(b)(6) provides that the partnership agreement may not vary the power to dissociate as a partner under Section 602(a), except to require that the notice of withdrawal under Section 601(1) be in writing. The UPA was silent with respect to requiring a written notice of withdrawal.

9.   Under subsection (b)(7), the right of a partner to seek court expulsion of another partner under Section 601(5) can not be waived or varied (e.g., requiring a 90-day notice) by agreement. Section 601(5) refers to judicial expulsion on such grounds as misconduct, breach of duty, or impracticability.

10.   Under subsection (b)(8), the partnership agreement may not vary the right of partners to have the partnership dissolved and its business wound up under Section 801(4), (5), or (6). Section 801(4) provides that the partnership must be wound up if its business is unlawful. Section 801(5) provides for judicial winding up in such circumstances as frustration of the firm's economic purpose, partner misconduct, or impracticability. Section 801(6) accords standing to transferees of an interest in the partnership to seek judicial dissolution of the partnership in specified circumstances.

11.   Subsection (b)(9) makes clear that a limited liability partnership may not designate the law of a State other than the State where it filed its statement of qualification to govern its internal affairs and the liability of its partners. See Sections 101(5), 106(b), and 202(a). Therefore, the selection of a State within which to file a statement of qualification has important choice of law ramifications, particularly where the partnership was formed in another State. See Comments to Section 106(b).

12.   Although stating the obvious, subsection(b)(10) provides expressly that the rights of a third party under the Act may not be restricted by an agreement among the partners to which the third party has not agreed. A non-partner who is a party to an agreement among the partners is, of course, bound. *Cf.* Section 703(c) (creditor joins release).

13.   The Article 9 rules regarding conversions and mergers are not listed in Section 103(b) as mandatory. Indeed, Section 907 states expressly that partnerships may be converted and merged in any other manner provided by law. The effect of compliance with Article 9 is to provide a "safe harbor" assuring the legal validity of such conversions and mergers. Although not immune from variation in the partnership agreement, noncompliance with the requirements of Article 9 in effecting a conversion or merger is to deny that "safe harbor" validity to the transaction. In this regard, Sections 903(b) and 905(c)(2) require that the conversion or merger of a limited partnership be approved by all of the partners, notwithstanding a contrary provision in the limited partnership agreement. Thus, in effect, the agreement can not vary the voting requirement without sacrificing the benefits of the "safe harbor."

§ 104.   Supplemental Principles of Law

(a)   Unless displaced by particular provisions of this [Act], the principles of law and equity supplement this [Act].

(b)   If an obligation to pay interest arises under this [Act] and the rate is not specified, the rate is that specified in [applicable statute].

COMMENT

The principles of law and equity supplement RUPA unless displaced by a particular provision of the Act. This broad statement combines the separate rules contained in UPA Sections 4(2), 4(3), and 5. These supplementary principles encompass not only the law of agency and estoppel and the law merchant mentioned in the UPA, but all of the other principles listed in UCC Section 1–103: the law relative to capacity to contract, fraud, misrepresentation, duress, coercion, mistake, bankruptcy, and other common law validating or invalidating causes, such as unconscionability. No substantive change from either the UPA or the UCC is intended.

It was thought unnecessary to repeat the UPA Section 4(1) admonition that statutes in derogation of the common law are not to be strictly construed. This principle is now so well established that it is not necessary to so state in the Act. No change in the law is intended. See the Comment to RUPA Section 1101.

Subsection (b) is new. It is based on the definition of "interest" in Section 14–8–2(5) of the Georgia act and establishes the applicable rate of interest in the absence of an agreement among the partners. Adopting States can select the State's legal rate of interest or other statutory interest rate, such as the rate for judgments.

§ 105.   Execution, Filing, and Recording of Statements

(a)   A statement may be filed in the office of [the Secretary of State]. A certified copy of a statement that is filed in an office in another State may be filed in the office of [the Secretary of State]. Either filing has the effect provided in this [Act] with respect to partnership property located in or transactions that occur in this State.

(b)   A certified copy of a statement that has been filed in the office of the [Secretary of State] and recorded in the office for recording transfers of real property has the effect provided for recorded statements in this [Act]. A recorded statement that is not a certified copy of a statement filed in the office of the [Secretary of State] does not have the effect provided for recorded statements in this [Act].

(c)   A statement filed by a partnership must be executed by at least two partners. Other statements must be executed by a partner or other person authorized by this [Act]. An individual who executes a statement as, or on behalf of, a partner or other person named as a partner in a statement shall personally declare under penalty of perjury that the contents of the statement are accurate.

(d)   A person authorized by this [Act] to file a statement may amend or cancel the statement by filing an amendment or cancellation that names the partnership, identifies the statement, and states the substance of the amendment or cancellation.

(e)   A person who files a statement pursuant to this section shall promptly send a copy of the statement to every nonfiling partner and to any other person named as a partner in the statement. Failure to send a copy of a statement to a partner or other person does not limit the effectiveness of the statement as to a person not a partner.

(f)   The [Secretary of State] may collect a fee for filing or providing a certified copy of a statement. The [officer responsible for recording transfers of real property] may collect a fee for recording a statement.

COMMENT

1.   Section 105 is new. It mandates the procedural rules for the execution, filing, and recording of the various "statements" (see Section 101(11)) authorized by RUPA. Section 101(13) makes clear that a statement of qualification filed by a partnership to become a limited liability partnership is included in the definition of a statement. Therefore, the execution, filing, and recording rules of this section must be followed except that the decision to file the statement of qualification must be approved by the vote of the partners necessary to amend the partnership agreement as to contribution requirements. See Section 1001(b) and Comments.

No filings are mandatory under RUPA. In all cases, the filing of a statement is optional and voluntary. A system of mandatory filing and disclosure for partnerships, similar to that required for corporations and limited partnerships, was rejected for several reasons. First, RUPA is designed to accommodate the needs of small partnerships, which often have unwritten or sketchy agreements and limited resources. Furthermore, inadvertent

173

partnerships are also governed by the Act, as the default form of business organization, in which case filing would be unlikely.

The RUPA filing provisions are, however, likely to encourage the voluntary use of partnership statements. There are a number of strong incentives for the partnership or the partners to file statements or for third parties, such as lenders or transferees of partnership property, to compel them to do so.

Only statements that are executed, filed, and, if appropriate (such as the authority to transfer real property), recorded in conformity with Section 105 have the legal consequences accorded statements by RUPA. The requirements of Section 105 cannot be varied in the partnership agreement, except the duty to provide copies of statements to all the partners. *See* Section 103(b)(1).

In most States today, the filing and recording of statements requires written documents. As technology advances, alternatives suitable for filing and recording may be developed. RUPA itself does not impose any requirement that statements be in writing. It is intended that the form or medium for filing and recording be left to the general law of adopting States.

2.   Section 105(a) provides for a single, central filing of all statements, as is the case with corporations, limited partnerships, and limited liability companies. The expectation is that most States will assign to the Secretary of State the responsibility of maintaining the filing system for partnership statements. Since a partnership is an entity under RUPA, all statements should be indexed by partnership name, not by the names of the individual partners.

Partnerships transacting business in more than one State will want to file copies of statements in each State because subsection (a) limits the legal effect of filed statements to property located or transactions occurring within the State. The filing of a certified copy of a statement originally filed in another State is permitted, and indeed encouraged, in order to avoid inconsistencies between statements filed in different States.

3.   Subsection (b), in effect, mandates the use of certified copies of filed statements for local recording in the real estate records by limiting the legal effect of recorded statements under the Act to those copies. The reason for recording only certified copies of filed statements is to eliminate the possibility of inconsistencies affecting the title to real property.

Subsection (c) requires that statements filed on behalf of a partnership, that is, the entity, be executed by at least two partners. Individual partners and other persons authorized by the Act to file a statement may execute it on their own behalf. To protect the partners and the partnership from unauthorized or improper filings, an individual who executes a statement as a partner must personally declare under penalty of perjury that the statement is accurate.

The amendment or cancellation of statements is authorized by subsection (d).

As a further safeguard against inaccurate or unauthorized filings, subsection (e) requires that a copy of every statement filed be sent to each partner, although the failure to do so does not limit the effectiveness of the statement. This requirement may, however, be eliminated in the partnership agreement. *See* Section 103(b)(1). Partners may also file a statement of denial under Section 304.

4.   A filed statement may be amended or canceled by any person authorized by the Act to file an original statement. The amendment or cancellation must state the name of the partnership so that it can be properly indexed and found, identify the statement being amended or canceled, and the substance of the amendment or cancellation. An amendment generally has the same operative effect as an original statement. A cancellation of extraordinary authority terminates that authority. A cancellation of a limitation on authority revives a previous grant of authority. *See* Section 303(d). The subsequent filing of a statement similar in kind to a statement already of record is treated as an amendment, even if not so denominated. Any substantive conflict between filed statements operates as a cancellation of authority under Section 303.

§ 106.   Governing Law

(a)   Except as otherwise provided in subsection (b), the law of the jurisdiction in which a partnership has its chief executive office governs relations among the partners and between the partners and the partnership.

(b)   The law of this State governs relations among the partners and between the partners and the partnership and the liability of partners for an obligation of a limited liability partnership.

COMMENT

The subsection (a) internal relations rule is new. *Cf.* RULPA § 901 (internal affairs governed by law of State in which limited partnership organized).

RUPA looks to the jurisdiction in which a partnership's chief executive office is located to provide the law governing the internal relations among the partners and between the partners and the partnership. The concept of the partnership's "chief executive office" is drawn from UCC Section 9–103(3)(d). It was chosen in lieu of the State of organization because no filing is necessary to form a general partnership, and thus the situs of its organization is not always clear, unlike a limited partnership, which is organized in the State where its certificate is filed.

The term "chief executive office" is not defined in the Act, nor is it defined in the UCC. Paragraph 5 of the Official Comment to UCC Section 9–103(3)(d) explains:

"Chief executive office" . . . means the place from which in fact the debtor manages the main part of his business operations. . . . Doubt may arise as to which is the "chief executive office" of a multi-state enterprise, but it would be rare that there could be more than two possibilities. . . . [The rule] will be simple to apply in most cases. . . .

In the absence of any other clear rule for determining a partnership's legal situs, it seems convenient to use that rule for choice of law purposes as well.

The choice-of-law rule provided by subsection (a) is only a default rule, and the partners may by agreement select the law of another State to govern their internal affairs, subject to generally applicable conflict of laws requirements. For example, where the partners may not resolve a particular issue by an explicit provision of the partnership agreement, such as the rights and duties set forth in Section 103(b), the law chosen will not be applied if the partners or the partnership have no substantial relationship to the chosen State or other reasonable basis for their choice or if application of the law of the chosen State would be contrary to a fundamental policy of a State that has a materially greater interest than the chosen State. *See* Restatement (Second) of Conflict of Laws § 187(2) (1971). The partners must, however, select only one State to govern their internal relations. They cannot select one State for some aspects of their internal relations and another State for others.

Contrasted with the variable choice-of-law rule provided by subsection (a), the law of the State where a limited liability partnership files its statement of qualification applies to such a partnership and may not be varied by the agreement of the partners. See Section 103(b)(9). Also, a partnership that files a statement of qualification in another State is not defined as a limited liability partnership in this State. See Section 101(5). Unlike a general partnership which may be formed without any filing, a partnership may only become a limited liability partnership by filing a statement of qualification. Therefore, the situs of its organization is clear. Because it is often unclear where a general partnership is actually formed, the decision to file a statement of qualification in a particular State constitutes a choice-of-law for the partnership which cannot be altered by the partnership agreement. See Comments to Section 103(b)(9). If the partnership agreement of an existing partnership specifies the law of a particular State as its governing law, and the partnership thereafter files a statement of qualification in another State, the partnership agreement choice is no longer controlling. In such cases, the filing of a statement of qualification "amends" the partnership agreement on this limited matter. Accordingly, if a statement of qualification is revoked or canceled for a limited liability partnership, the law of the State of filing would continue to apply unless the partnership agreement thereafter altered the applicable law rule.

§ 107. Partnership Subject to Amendment or Repeal of [Act]

A partnership governed by this [Act] is subject to any amendment to or repeal of this [Act].

COMMENT

The reservation of power provision is new. It is adapted from Section 1.02 of the Revised Model Business Corporation Act (RMBCA) and Section 1106 of RULPA.

As explained in the Official Comment to the RMBCA, the genesis of those provisions is *Trustees of Dartmouth College v. Woodward*, 17 U.S. (4 Wheat) 518 (1819), which held that the United States Constitution prohibits the application of newly enacted statutes to existing corporations, while suggesting the efficacy of a reservation of power provision. Its purpose is to avoid any possible argument that a legal entity created pursuant to statute or its members have a contractual or vested right in any specific statutory provision and to ensure that the State

re modify its enabling statute as it deems appropriate and require existing entities to comply with
nodified.

Article 2

NATURE OF PARTNERSHIP

§ 201.   Partnership as Entity

✳   (a)   A partnership is an entity distinct from its partners.

(b)   A limited liability partnership continues to be the same entity that existed before the filing of a
statement of qualification under Section 1001.

COMMENT

RUPA embraces the entity theory of the partnership. In light of the UPA's ambivalence on the nature of
partnerships, the explicit statement provided by subsection (a) is deemed appropriate as an expression of the
increased emphasis on the entity theory as the dominant model. *But see* Section 306 (partners' liability joint and
several unless the partnership has filed a statement of qualification to become a limited liability partnership).

Giving clear expression to the entity nature of a partnership is intended to allay previous concerns stemming
from the aggregate theory, such as the necessity of a deed to convey title from the "old" partnership to the "new"
partnership every time there is a change of cast among the partners. Under RUPA, there is no "new" partnership
just because of membership changes. That will avoid the result in cases such as *Fairway Development Co. v. Title
Insurance Co.*, 621 F. Supp. 120 (N.D. Ohio 1985), which held that the "new" partnership resulting from a partner's
death did not have standing to enforce a title insurance policy issued to the "old" partnership.

Subsection (b) makes clear that the explicit entity theory provided by subsection (a) applies to a partnership
both before and after it files a statement of qualification to become a limited liability partnership. Thus, just as
there is no "new" partnership resulting from membership changes, the filing of a statement of qualification does
not create a "new" partnership. The filing partnership continues to be the same partnership entity that existed
before the filing. Similarly, the amendment or cancellation of a statement of qualification under Section 105(d) or
the revocation of a statement of qualification under Section 1003(c) does not terminate the partnership and create
a "new" partnership. See Section 1003(d). Accordingly, a partnership remains the same entity regardless of a filing,
cancellation, or revocation of a statement of qualification.

§ 202.   Formation of Partnership

(a)   Except as otherwise provided in subsection (b), the association of two or more persons to carry on
as co-owners a business for profit forms a partnership, whether or not the persons intend to form a
partnership.

(b)   An association formed under a statute other than this [Act], a predecessor statute, or a
comparable statute of another jurisdiction is not a partnership under this [Act].

(c)   In determining whether a partnership is formed, the following rules apply:

(1)   Joint tenancy, tenancy in common, tenancy by the entireties, joint property, common
property, or part ownership does not by itself establish a partnership, even if the co-owners share
profits made by the use of the property.

(2)   The sharing of gross returns does not by itself establish a partnership, even if the persons
sharing them have a joint or common right or interest in property from which the returns are derived.

(3)   A person who receives a share of the profits of a business is presumed to be a partner in the
business, unless the profits were received in payment:

(i)   of a debt by installments or otherwise;

(ii)   for services as an independent contractor or of wages or other compensation to an
employee;

(iii)   of rent;

(iv)   of an annuity or other retirement or health benefit to a beneficiary, representative, or designee of a deceased or retired partner;

(v)   of interest or other charge on a loan, even if the amount of payment varies with the profits of the business, including a direct or indirect present or future ownership of the collateral, or rights to income, proceeds, or increase in value derived from the collateral; or

(vi)   for the sale of the goodwill of a business or other property by installments or otherwise.

COMMENT

1.   Section 202 combines UPA Sections 6 and 7. The traditional UPA Section 6(1) "definition" of a partnership is recast as an operative rule of law. No substantive change in the law is intended. The UPA "definition" has always been understood as an operative rule, as well as a definition. The addition of the phrase, "whether or not the persons intend to form a partnership," merely codifies the universal judicial construction of UPA Section 6(1) that a partnership is created by the association of persons whose intent is to carry on as co-owners a business for profit, regardless of their subjective intention to be "partners." Indeed, they may inadvertently create a partnership despite their expressed subjective intention not to do so. The new language alerts readers to this possibility.

As under the UPA, the attribute of co-ownership distinguishes a partnership from a mere agency relationship. A business is a series of acts directed toward an end. Ownership involves the power of ultimate control. To state that partners are co-owners of a business is to state that they each have the power of ultimate control. See Official Comment to UPA § 6(1). On the other hand, as subsection (c)(1) makes clear, passive co-ownership of property by itself, as distinguished from the carrying on of a business, does not establish a partnership.

2.   Subsection (b) provides that business associations organized under other statutes are not partnerships. Those statutory associations include corporations, limited partnerships, and limited liability companies. That continues the UPA concept that general partnership is the residual form of for profit business association, existing only if another form does not.

A limited partnership is not a partnership under this definition. Nevertheless, certain provisions of RUPA will continue to govern limited partnerships because RULPA itself, in Section 1105, so requires "in any case not provided for" in RULPA. For example, the rules applicable to a limited liability partnership will generally apply to limited partnerships. See Comment to Section 101(5) (definition of a limited liability partnership). In light of that RULPA Section 1105, UPA Section 6(2), which provides that limited partnerships are governed by the UPA, is redundant and has not been carried over to RUPA. It is also more appropriate that the applicability of RUPA to limited partnerships be governed exclusively by RULPA. For example, a RULPA amendment may clarify certain linkage questions regarding the application of the limited liability partnership rules to limited partnerships. See Comment to Section 101(5) for a suggested form of such an amendment.

It is not intended that RUPA change any common law rules concerning special types of associations, such as mining partnerships, which in some jurisdictions are not governed by the UPA.

Relationships that are called "joint ventures" are partnerships if they otherwise fit the definition of a partnership. An association is not classified as a partnership, however, simply because it is called a "joint venture."

An unincorporated nonprofit organization is not a partnership under RUPA, even if it qualifies as a business, because it is not a "for profit" organization.

3.   Subsection (c) provides three rules of construction that apply in determining whether a partnership has been formed under subsection (a). They are largely derived from UPA Section 7, and to that extent no substantive change is intended. The sharing of profits is recast as a rebuttable presumption of a partnership, a more contemporary construction, rather than as prima facie evidence thereof. The protected categories, in which receipt of a share of the profits is not presumed to create a partnership, apply whether the profit share is a single flat percentage or a ratio which varies, for example, after reaching a dollar floor or different levels of profits.

Like its predecessor, RUPA makes no attempt to answer in every case whether a partnership is formed. Whether a relationship is more properly characterized as that of borrower and lender, employer and employee, or landlord and tenant is left to the trier of fact. As under the UPA, a person may function in both partner and nonpartner capacities.

Paragraph (3)(v) adds a new protected category to the list. It shields from the presumption a share of the profits received in payment of interest or other charges on a loan, "including a direct or indirect present or future ownership in the collateral, or rights to income, proceeds, or increase in value derived from the collateral." The quoted language is taken from Section 211 of the Uniform Land Security Interest Act. The purpose of the new language is to protect shared-appreciation mortgages, contingent or other variable or performance-related mortgages, and other equity participation arrangements by clarifying that contingent payments do not presumptively convert lending arrangements into partnerships.

4.　　Section 202(e) of the 1993 Act stated that partnerships formed under RUPA are general partnerships and that the partners are general partners. That section has been deleted as unnecessary. Limited partners are not "partners" within the meaning of RUPA, however.

§ 203.　Partnership Property

Property acquired by a partnership is property of the partnership and not of the partners individually.

COMMENT

All property acquired by a partnership, by transfer or otherwise, becomes partnership property and belongs to the partnership as an entity, rather than to the individual partners. This expresses the substantive result of UPA Sections 8(1) and 25.

Neither UPA Section 8(1) nor RUPA Section 203 provides any guidance concerning when property is "acquired by" the partnership. That problem is dealt with in Section 204.

UPA Sections 25(2)(c) and (e) also provide that partnership property is not subject to exemptions, allowances, or rights of a partner's spouse, heirs, or next of kin. Those provisions have been omitted as unnecessary. No substantive change is intended. Those exemptions and rights inure to the property of the partners, and not to partnership property.

§ 204.　When Property Is Partnership Property

(a)　Property is partnership property if acquired in the name of:

　　(1)　the partnership; or

　　(2)　one or more partners with an indication in the instrument transferring title to the property of the person's capacity as a partner or of the existence of a partnership but without an indication of the name of the partnership.

(b)　Property is acquired in the name of the partnership by a transfer to:

　　(1)　the partnership in its name; or

　　(2)　one or more partners in their capacity as partners in the partnership, if the name of the partnership is indicated in the instrument transferring title to the property.

(c)　Property is presumed to be partnership property if purchased with partnership assets, even if not acquired in the name of the partnership or of one or more partners with an indication in the instrument transferring title to the property of the person's capacity as a partner or of the existence of a partnership.

(d)　Property acquired in the name of one or more of the partners, without an indication in the instrument transferring title to the property of the person's capacity as a partner or of the existence of a partnership and without use of partnership assets, is presumed to be separate property, even if used for partnership purposes.

COMMENT

1.　　Section 204 sets forth the rules for determining when property is acquired by the partnership and, hence, becomes partnership property. It is based on UPA Section 8(3), as influenced by the recent Alabama and Georgia modifications. The rules govern the acquisition of personal property, as well as real property, that is held in the partnership name. See Section 101(9).

2.　　Subsection (a) governs the circumstances under which property becomes "partnership property," and subsection (b) clarifies the circumstances under which property is acquired "in the name of the partnership." The concept of record title is emphasized, although the term itself is not used. Titled personal property, as well as all transferable interests in real property acquired in the name of the partnership, are covered by this section.

Property becomes partnership property if acquired (1) in the name of the partnership or (2) in the name of one or more of the partners with an indication in the instrument transferring title of either (i) their capacity as partners or (ii) of the existence of a partnership, even if the name of the partnership is not indicated. Property acquired "in the name of the partnership" includes property acquired in the name of one or more partners in their capacity as partners, but only if the name of the partnership is indicated in the instrument transferring title.

Property transferred to a partner is partnership property, even though the name of the partnership is not indicated, if the instrument transferring title indicates either (i) the partner's capacity as a partner or (ii) the existence of a partnership. This is consonant with the entity theory of partnership and resolves the troublesome issue of a conveyance to fewer than all the partners but which nevertheless indicates their partner status.

3.   Ultimately, it is the intention of the partners that controls whether property belongs to the partnership or to one or more of the partners in their individual capacities, at least as among the partners themselves. RUPA sets forth two rebuttable presumptions that apply when the partners have failed to express their intent.

First, under subsection (c), property purchased with partnership funds is presumed to be partnership property, notwithstanding the name in which title is held. The presumption is intended to apply if partnership credit is used to obtain financing, as well as the use of partnership cash or property for payment. Unlike the rule in subsection (b), under which property is deemed to be partnership property if the partnership's name or the partner's capacity as a partner is disclosed in the instrument of conveyance, subsection (c) raises only a presumption that the property is partnership property if it is purchased with partnership assets.

That presumption is also subject to an important caveat. Under Section 302(b), partnership property held in the name of individual partners, without an indication of their capacity as partners or of the existence of a partnership, that is transferred by the partners in whose name title is held to a purchaser without knowledge that it is partnership property is free of any claims of the partnership.

Second, under subsection (d), property acquired in the name of one or more of the partners, without an indication of their capacity as partners and without use of partnership funds or credit, is presumed to be the partners' separate property, even if used for partnership purposes. In effect, it is presumed in that case that only the use of the property is contributed to the partnership.

4.   Generally, under RUPA, partners and third parties dealing with partnerships will be able to rely on the record to determine whether property is owned by the partnership. The exception is property purchased with partnership funds without any reference to the partnership in the title documents. The inference concerning the partners' intent from the use of partnership funds outweighs any inference from the State of the title, subject to the overriding reliance interest in the case of a purchaser without notice of the partnership's interest. This allocation of risk should encourage the partnership to eliminate doubt about ownership by putting title in the partnership.

5.   UPA Section 8(4) provides, "A transfer to a partnership in the partnership name, even without words of inheritance, passes the entire estate or interest of the grantor unless a contrary intent appears." It has been omitted from RUPA as unnecessary because modern conveyancing law deems all transfers to pass the entire estate or interest of the grantor unless a contrary intent appears.

Article 3

RELATIONS OF PARTNERS TO PERSONS DEALING WITH PARTNERSHIP

§ 301.   Partner Agent of Partnership

Subject to the effect of a statement of partnership authority under Section 303:

(1)   Each partner is an agent of the partnership for the purpose of its business. An act of a partner, including the execution of an instrument in the partnership name, for apparently carrying on in the ordinary course the partnership business or business of the kind carried on by the partnership binds the partnership, unless the partner had no authority to act for the partnership in the particular matter and the person with whom the partner was dealing knew or had received a notification that the partner lacked authority.

(2) An act of a partner which is not apparently for carrying on in the ordinary course the partnership business or business of the kind carried on by the partnership binds the partnership only if the act was authorized by the other partners.

COMMENT

1. Section 301 sets forth a partner's power, as an agent of the firm, to bind the partnership entity to third parties. The rights of the partners among themselves, including the right to restrict a partner's authority, are governed by the partnership agreement and by Section 401.

The agency rules set forth in Section 301 are subject to an important qualification. They may be affected by the filing or recording of a statement of partnership authority. The legal effect of filing or recording a statement of partnership authority is set forth in Section 303.

2. Section 301(1) retains the basic principles reflected in UPA Section 9(1). It declares that each partner is an agent of the partnership and that, by virtue of partnership status, each partner has apparent authority to bind the partnership in ordinary course transactions. The effect of Section 301(1) is to characterize a partner as a general managerial agent having both actual and apparent authority co-extensive in scope with the firm's ordinary business, at least in the absence of a contrary partnership agreement.

Section 301(1) effects two changes from UPA Section 9(1). First, it clarifies that a partner's apparent authority includes acts for carrying on in the ordinary course "business of the kind carried on by the partnership," not just the business of the particular partnership in question. The UPA is ambiguous on this point, but there is some authority for an expanded construction in accordance with the so-called English rule. *See, e.g., Burns v. Gonzalez*, 439 S.W.2d 128, 131 (Tex. Civ. App. 1969) (dictum); *Commercial Hotel Co. v. Weeks*, 254 S.W. 521 (Tex. Civ. App. 1923). No substantive change is intended by use of the more customary phrase "carrying on in the ordinary course" in lieu of the UPA phrase "in the usual way." The UPA and the case law use both terms without apparent distinction.

The other change from the UPA concerns the allocation of risk of a partner's lack of authority. RUPA draws the line somewhat differently from the UPA.

Under UPA Section 9(1) and (4), only a person with knowledge of a restriction on a partner's authority is bound by it. Section 301(1) provides that a person who has received a notification of a partner's lack of authority is also bound. The meaning of "receives a notification" is explained in Section 102(d). Thus, the partnership may protect itself from unauthorized acts by giving a notification of a restriction on a partner's authority to a person dealing with that partner. A notification may be effective upon delivery, whether or not it actually comes to the other person's attention. To that extent, the risk of lack of authority is shifted to those dealing with partners.

On the other hand, as used in the UPA, the term "knowledge" embodies the concept of "bad faith" knowledge arising from other known facts. As used in RUPA, however, "knowledge" is limited to actual knowledge. *See* Section 102(a). Thus, RUPA does not expose persons dealing with a partner to the greater risk of being bound by a restriction based on their purported reason to know of the partner's lack of authority from all the facts they did know. Compare Section 102(b)(3) (notice).

With one exception, this result is not affected even if the partnership files a statement of partnership authority containing a limitation on a partner's authority. Section 303(f) makes clear that a person dealing with a partner is not deemed to know of such a limitation merely because it is contained in a filed statement of authority. Under Section 303(e), however, all persons are deemed to know of a limitation on the authority of a partner to transfer real property contained in a recorded statement. Thus, a recorded limitation on authority concerning real property constitutes constructive knowledge of the limitation to the whole world.

3. Section 301(2) is drawn directly from UPA Section 9(2), with conforming changes to mirror the new language of subsection (1). Subsection (2) makes it clear that the partnership is bound by a partner's actual authority, even if the partner has no apparent authority. Section 401(j) requires the unanimous consent of the partners for a grant of authority outside the ordinary course of business, unless the partnership agreement provides otherwise. Under general agency principles, the partners can subsequently ratify a partner's unauthorized act. See Section 104(a).

4. UPA Section 9(3) contains a list of five extraordinary acts that require unanimous consent of the partners before the partnership is bound. RUPA omits that section. That leaves it to the courts to decide the outer limits of the agency power of a partner. Most of the acts listed in UPA Section 9(3) probably remain outside the apparent authority of a partner under RUPA, such as disposing of the goodwill of the business, but elimination of a statutory rule will afford more flexibility in some situations specified in UPA Section 9(3). In particular, it seems

180

archaic that the submission of a partnership claim to arbitration always requires unanimous consent. *See* UPA § 9(3)(e).

5.   Section 301(1) fully reflects the principle embodied in UPA Section 9(4) that the partnership is not bound by an act of a partner in contravention of a restriction on his authority known to the other party.

§ 302.   Transfer of Partnership Property

(a)   Partnership property may be transferred as follows:

(1)   Subject to the effect of a statement of partnership authority under Section 303, partnership property held in the name of the partnership may be transferred by an instrument of transfer executed by a partner in the partnership name.

(2)   Partnership property held in the name of one or more partners with an indication in the instrument transferring the property to them of their capacity as partners or of the existence of a partnership, but without an indication of the name of the partnership, may be transferred by an instrument of transfer executed by the persons in whose name the property is held.

(3)   Partnership property held in the name of one or more persons other than the partnership, without an indication in the instrument transferring the property to them of their capacity as partners or of the existence of a partnership, may be transferred by an instrument of transfer executed by the persons in whose name the property is held.

(b)   A partnership may recover partnership property from a transferee only if it proves that execution of the instrument of initial transfer did not bind the partnership under Section 301 and:

(1)   as to a subsequent transferee who gave value for property transferred under subsection (a)(1) and (2), proves that the subsequent transferee knew or had received a notification that the person who executed the instrument of initial transfer lacked authority to bind the partnership; or

(2)   as to a transferee who gave value for property transferred under subsection (a)(3), proves that the transferee knew or had received a notification that the property was partnership property and that the person who executed the instrument of initial transfer lacked authority to bind the partnership.

(c)   A partnership may not recover partnership property from a subsequent transferee if the partnership would not have been entitled to recover the property, under subsection (b), from any earlier transferee of the property.

(d)   If a person holds all of the partners' interests in the partnership, all of the partnership property vests in that person. The person may execute a document in the name of the partnership to evidence vesting of the property in that person and may file or record the document.

COMMENT

1.   Section 302 replaces UPA Section 10 and provides rules for the transfer and recovery of partnership property. The language is adapted in part from Section 14–8–10 of the Georgia partnership statute.

2.   Subsection (a)(1) deals with the transfer of partnership property held in the name of the partnership and subsection (a)(2) with property held in the name of one or more of the partners with an indication either of their capacity as partners or of the existence of a partnership. Subsection (a)(3) deals with partnership property held in the name of one or more of the partners without an indication of their capacity as partners or of the existence of a partnership. Like the general agency rules in Section 301, the power of a partner to transfer partnership property under subsection (a)(1) is subject to the effect under Section 303 of the filing or recording of a statement of partnership authority. These rules are intended to foster reliance on record title.

UPA Section 10 covers only real property. Section 302, however, also governs the transfer of partnership personal property acquired by instrument and held in the name of the partnership or one or more of the partners.

3.   Subsection (b) deals with the right of the partnership to recover partnership property transferred by a partner without authority. Subsection (b)(1) deals with the recovery of property held in either the name of the partnership or the name of one or more of the partners with an indication of their capacity as partners or of the

existence of a partnership, while subsection (b)(2) deals with the recovery of property held in the name of one or more persons without an indication of their capacity as partners or of the existence of a partnership.

In either case, a transfer of partnership property may be avoided only if the partnership proves that it was not bound under Section 301 by the execution of the instrument of initial transfer. Under Section 301, the partnership is bound by a transfer in the ordinary course of business, unless the transferee actually knew or had received a notification of the partner's lack of authority. See Section 102(a) and (d). The reference to Section 301, rather than Section 301(1), is intended to clarify that a partner's actual authority is not revoked by Section 302. Compare UPA § 10(1) (refers to partner's authority under Section 9(1)).

The burden of proof is on the partnership to prove the partner's lack of authority and, in the case of a subsequent transferee, the transferee's knowledge or notification thereof. Thus, even if the transfer to the initial transferee could be avoided, the partnership may not recover the property from a subsequent purchaser or other transferee for value unless it also proves that the subsequent transferee knew or had received a notification of the partner's lack of authority with respect to the initial transfer. Since knowledge is required, rather than notice, a remote purchaser has no duty to inquire as to the authority for the initial transfer, even if he knows it was partnership property.

The burden of proof is on the transferee to show that value was given. Value, as used in this context, is synonymous with valuable consideration and means any consideration sufficient to support a simple contract.

The burden of proof on all other issues is allocated to the partnership because it is generally in a better position than the transferee to produce the evidence. Moreover, the partnership may protect itself against unauthorized transfers by ensuring that partnership real property is held in the name of the partnership and that a statement of partnership authority is recorded specifying any limitations on the partners' authority to convey real property. Under Section 303(e), transferees of real property held in the partnership name are conclusively bound by those limitations. On the other hand, transferees can protect themselves by insisting that the partnership record a statement specifying who is authorized to transfer partnership property. Under Section 303(d), transferees for value, without actual knowledge to the contrary, may rely on that grant of authority.

4.   Subsection (b)(2) replaces UPA Section 10(3) and provides that partners who hold partnership property in their own names, without an indication in the record of their capacity as partners or of the existence of a partnership, may transfer good title to a transferee for value without knowledge or a notification that it was partnership property. To recover the property under this subsection, the partnership has the burden of proving that the transferee knew or had received a notification of the partnership's interest in the property, as well as of the partner's lack of authority for the initial transfer.

5.   Subsection (c) is new and provides that property may not be recovered by the partnership from a remote transferee if any intermediate transferee of the property would have prevailed against the partnership. *Cf.* Uniform Fraudulent Transfer Act, §§ 8(a) (subsequent transferee from bona fide purchaser protected), 8(b)(2) (same).

6.   Subsection (d) is new. The UPA does not have a provision dealing with the situation in which all of the partners' interests in the partnership are held by one person, such as a surviving partner or a purchaser of all the other partners' interests. Subsection (d) allows for clear record title, even though the partnership no longer exists as a technical matter. When a partnership becomes a sole proprietorship by reason of the dissociation of all but one of the partners, title vests in the remaining "partner," although there is no "transfer" of the property. The remaining "partner" may execute a deed or other transfer of record in the name of the non-existent partnership to evidence vesting of the property in that person's individual capacity.

7.   UPA Section 10(2) provides that, where title to real property is in the partnership name, a conveyance by a partner in his own name transfers the partnership's equitable interest in the property. It has been omitted as was done in Georgia and Florida. In this situation, the conveyance is clearly outside the chain of title and so should not pass title or any interest in the property. UPA Section 10(2) dilutes, albeit slightly, the effect of record title and is, therefore, inconsistent with RUPA's broad policy of fostering reliance on the record.

UPA Section 10(4) and (5) have also been omitted. Those situations are now adequately covered by Section 302(a).

§ 303.   Statement of Partnership Authority

(a)   A partnership may file a statement of partnership authority, which:

    (1)   must include:

(i)   the name of the partnership;

(ii)   the street address of its chief executive office and of one office in this State, if there is one;

(iii)   the names and mailing addresses of all of the partners or of an agent appointed and maintained by the partnership for the purpose of subsection (b); and

(iv)   the names of the partners authorized to execute an instrument transferring real property held in the name of the partnership; and

(2)   may state the authority, or limitations on the authority, of some or all of the partners to enter into other transactions on behalf of the partnership and any other matter.

(b)   If a statement of partnership authority names an agent, the agent shall maintain a list of the names and mailing addresses of all of the partners and make it available to any person on request for good cause shown.

(c)   If a filed statement of partnership authority is executed pursuant to Section 105(c) and states the name of the partnership but does not contain all of the other information required by subsection (a), the statement nevertheless operates with respect to a person not a partner as provided in subsections (d) and (e).

(d)   Except as otherwise provided in subsection (g), a filed statement of partnership authority supplements the authority of a partner to enter into transactions on behalf of the partnership as follows:

(1)   Except for transfers of real property, a grant of authority contained in a filed statement of partnership authority is conclusive in favor of a person who gives value without knowledge to the contrary, so long as and to the extent that a limitation on that authority is not then contained in another filed statement. A filed cancellation of a limitation on authority revives the previous grant of authority.

(2)   A grant of authority to transfer real property held in the name of the partnership contained in a certified copy of a filed statement of partnership authority recorded in the office for recording transfers of that real property is conclusive in favor of a person who gives value without knowledge to the contrary, so long as and to the extent that a certified copy of a filed statement containing a limitation on that authority is not then of record in the office for recording transfers of that real property. The recording in the office for recording transfers of that real property of a certified copy of a filed cancellation of a limitation on authority revives the previous grant of authority.

(e)   A person not a partner is deemed to know of a limitation on the authority of a partner to transfer real property held in the name of the partnership if a certified copy of the filed statement containing the limitation on authority is of record in the office for recording transfers of that real property.

(f)   Except as otherwise provided in subsections (d) and (e) and Sections 704 and 805, a person not a partner is not deemed to know of a limitation on the authority of a partner merely because the limitation is contained in a filed statement.

(g)   Unless earlier canceled, a filed statement of partnership authority is canceled by operation of law five years after the date on which the statement, or the most recent amendment, was filed with the [Secretary of State].

COMMENT

1.   Section 303 is new. It provides for an optional statement of partnership authority specifying the names of the partners authorized to execute instruments transferring real property held in the name of the partnership. It may also grant supplementary authority to partners, or limit their authority, to enter into other transactions on behalf of the partnership. The execution, filing, and recording of statements is governed by Section 105.

RUPA follows the lead of California and Georgia in authorizing the optional filing of statements of authority. Filing a statement of partnership authority may be deemed to satisfy the disclosure required by a State's fictitious name statute, if the State so chooses.

Section 105 provides for the central filing of statements, rather than local filing. However, to be effective in connection with the transfer of real property, a statement of partnership authority must also be recorded locally with the land records.

2.   The most important goal of the statement of authority is to facilitate the transfer of real property held in the name of the partnership. A statement must specify the names of the partners authorized to execute an instrument transferring that property.

Under subsection (d)(2), a recorded grant of authority to transfer real property held in the name of the partnership is conclusive in favor of a transferee for value without actual knowledge to the contrary. A partner's authority to transfer partnership real property is affected by a recorded statement only if the property is held in the name of the partnership. A recorded statement has no effect on the partners' authority to transfer partnership real property that is held other than in the name of the partnership. In that case, by definition, the record will not indicate the name of the partnership, and thus the partnership's interest would not be disclosed by a title search. *See* Section 204. To be effective, the statement recorded with the land records must be a certified copy of the original statement filed with the Secretary of State. *See* Section 105(b).

The presumption of authority created by subsection (d)(2) operates only so long as and to the extent that a limitation on the partner's authority is not contained in another recorded statement. This is intended to condition reliance on the record to situations where there is no conflict among recorded statements, amendments, or denials of authority. See Section 304. If the record is in conflict regarding a partner's authority, transferees must go outside the record to determine the partners' actual authority. This rule is modified slightly in the case of a cancellation of a limitation on a partner's authority, which revives the previous grant of authority.

Under subsection (e), third parties are deemed to know of a recorded limitation on the authority of a partner to transfer real property held in the partnership name. Since transferees are bound under Section 301 by knowledge of a limitation on a partner's authority, they are bound by such a recorded limitation. Of course, a transferee with actual knowledge of a limitation on a partner's authority is bound under Section 301, whether or not there is a recorded statement of limitation.

3.   A statement of partnership authority may have effect beyond the transfer of real property held in the name of the partnership. Under subsection (a)(2), a statement of authority may contain any other matter the partnership chooses, including a grant of authority, or a limitation on the authority, of some or all of the partners to enter into other transactions on behalf of the partnership. Since Section 301 confers authority on all partners to act for the partnership in ordinary matters, the real import of such a provision is to grant extraordinary authority, or to limit the ordinary authority, of some or all of the partners.

The effect given to such a provision is different from that accorded a provision regarding the transfer of real property. Under subsection (d)(1), a filed grant of authority is binding on the partnership, in favor of a person who gives value without actual knowledge to the contrary, unless limited by another filed statement. That is the same rule as for statements involving real property under subsection 301(d)(2). There is, however, no counterpart to subsection (e) regarding a filed limitation of authority. To the contrary, subsection (f) makes clear that filing a limitation of authority does not operate as constructive knowledge of a partner's lack of authority with respect to non-real property transactions.

Under Section 301, only a third party who knows or has received a notification of a partner's lack of authority in an ordinary course transaction is bound. Thus, a limitation on a partner's authority to transfer personal property or to enter into other non-real property transactions on behalf of the partnership, contained in a filed statement of partnership authority, is effective only against a third party who knows or has received a notification of it. The fact of the statement being filed has no legal significance in those transactions, although the filed statement is a potential source of actual knowledge to third parties.

4.   It should be emphasized that Section 303 concerns the authority of partners to bind the partnership to third persons. As among the partners, the authority of a partner to take any action is governed by the partnership agreement, or by the provisions of RUPA governing the relations among partners, and is not affected by the filing or recording of a statement of partnership authority.

5.   The exercise of the option to file a statement of partnership authority imposes a further disclosure obligation on the partnership. Under subsection (a)(1), a filed statement must include the street address of its chief executive office and of an office in the State (if any), as well as the names and mailing addresses of all of the partners or, alternatively, of an agent appointed and maintained by the partnership for the purpose of maintaining such a list. If an agent is appointed, subsection (b) provides that the agent shall maintain a list of all of the partners

and make it available to any person on request for good cause shown. Under subsection (c), the failure to make all of the required disclosures does not affect the statement's operative effect, however.

6.   Under subsection (g), a statement of authority is canceled by operation of law five years after the date on which the statement, or the most recent amendment, was filed.

7.   Section 308(c) makes clear that a person does not become a partner solely because he is named as a partner in a statement of partnership authority filed by another person. See also Section 304 ("person named as a partner" may file statement of denial).

§ 304.   Statement of Denial

A partner or other person named as a partner in a filed statement of partnership authority or in a list maintained by an agent pursuant to Section 303(b) may file a statement of denial stating the name of the partnership and the fact that is being denied, which may include denial of a person's authority or status as a partner. A statement of denial is a limitation on authority as provided in Section 303(d) and (e).

COMMENT

Section 304 is new and complements Section 303. It provides partners (and persons named as partners) an opportunity to deny any fact asserted in a statement of partnership authority, including denial of a person's status as a partner or of another person's authority as a partner. A statement of denial must be executed, filed, and recorded pursuant to the requirements of Section 105.

Section 304 does not address the consequences of a denial of partnership. No adverse inference should be drawn from the failure of a person named as a partner to deny such status, however. See Section 308(c) (person not liable as a partner merely because named in statement as a partner).

A statement of denial operates as a limitation on a partner's authority to the extent provided in Section 303. Section 303(d) provides that a filed or recorded statement of partnership authority is conclusive, in favor of purchasers without knowledge to the contrary, so long as and to the extent that a limitation on that authority is not contained in another filed or recorded statement. A filed or recorded statement of denial operates as such a limitation on authority, thereby precluding reliance on an inconsistent grant of authority. Under Section 303(d), a filed or recorded cancellation of a statement of denial that operates as a limitation on authority revives the previous grant of authority.

Under Section 303(e), a recorded statement of denial of a partner's authority to transfer partnership real property held in the partnership name constitutes constructive knowledge of that limitation.

§ 305.   Partnership Liable for Partner's Actionable Conduct

(a)   A partnership is liable for loss or injury caused to a person, or for a penalty incurred, as a result of a wrongful act or omission, or other actionable conduct, of a partner acting in the ordinary course of business of the partnership or with authority of the partnership.

(b)   If, in the course of the partnership's business or while acting with authority of the partnership, a partner receives or causes the partnership to receive money or property of a person not a partner, and the money or property is misapplied by a partner, the partnership is liable for the loss.

COMMENT

Section 305(a), which is derived from UPA Section 13, imposes liability on the partnership for the wrongful acts of a partner acting in the ordinary course of the partnership's business or otherwise within the partner's authority. The scope of the section has been expanded by deleting from UPA Section 13, "not being a partner in the partnership." This is intended to permit a partner to sue the partnership on a tort or other theory during the term of the partnership, rather than being limited to the remedies of dissolution and an accounting. See also Comment 2 to Section 405.

The section has also been broadened to cover no-fault torts by the addition of the phrase, "or other actionable conduct."

The partnership is liable for the actionable conduct or omission of a partner acting in the ordinary course of its business or "with the authority of the partnership." This is intended to include a partner's apparent, as well as actual, authority, thereby bringing within Section 305(a) the situation covered in UPA Section 14(a).

The phrase in UPA Section 13, "to the same extent as the partner so acting or omitting to act," has been deleted to prevent a partnership from asserting a partner's immunity from liability. This is consistent with the general agency rule that a principal is not entitled to its agent's immunities. *See* Restatement (Second) of Agency § 217(b) (1957). The deletion is not intended to limit a partnership's contractual rights.

Section 305(b) is drawn from UPA Section 14(b), but has been edited to improve clarity. It imposes strict liability on the partnership for the misapplication of money or property received by a partner in the course of the partnership's business or otherwise within the scope of the partner's actual authority.

§ 306.   Partner's Liability

(a)   Except as otherwise provided in subsections (b) and (c), all partners are liable jointly and severally for all obligations of the partnership unless otherwise agreed by the claimant or provided by law.

(b)   A person admitted as a partner into an existing partnership is not personally liable for any partnership obligation incurred before the person's admission as a partner.

(c)   An obligation of a partnership incurred while the partnership is a limited liability partnership, whether arising in contract, tort, or otherwise, is solely the obligation of the partnership. A partner is not personally liable, directly or indirectly, by way of contribution or otherwise, for such an obligation solely by reason of being or so acting as a partner. This subsection applies notwithstanding anything inconsistent in the partnership agreement that existed immediately before the vote required to become a limited liability partnership under Section 1001(b).

COMMENT

1.   Section 306(a) changes the UPA rule by imposing joint and several liability on the partners for all partnership obligations where the partnership is not a limited liability partnership. Under UPA Section 15, partners' liability for torts is joint and several, while their liability for contracts is joint but not several. About ten States that have adopted the UPA already provide for joint and several liability. The UPA reference to "debts and obligations" is redundant, and no change is intended by RUPA's reference solely to "obligations."

Joint and several liability under RUPA differs, however, from the classic model, which permits a judgment creditor to proceed immediately against any of the joint and several judgment debtors. Generally, Section 307(d) requires the judgment creditor to exhaust the partnership's assets before enforcing a judgment against the separate assets of a partner.

2.   RUPA continues the UPA scheme of liability with respect to an incoming partner, but states the rule more clearly and simply. Under Section 306(a), an incoming partner becomes jointly and severally liable, as a partner, for all partnership obligations, except as otherwise provided in subsection (b). That subsection eliminates an incoming partner's personal liability for partnership obligations incurred before his admission as a partner. In effect, a new partner has no personal liability to existing creditors of the partnership, and only his investment in the firm is at risk for the satisfaction of existing partnership debts. That is presently the rule under UPA Sections 17 and 41(7), and no substantive change is intended. As under the UPA, a new partner's personal assets are at risk with respect to partnership liabilities incurred after his admission as a partner.

3.   Subsection (c) alters classic joint and several liability of general partners for obligations of a partnership that is a limited liability partnership. Like shareholders of a corporation and members of a limited liability company, partners of a limited liability partnership are not personally liable for partnership obligations incurred while the partnership liability shield is in place solely because they are partners. As with shareholders of a corporation and members of a limited liability company, partners remain personally liable for their personal misconduct.

In cases of partner misconduct, Section 401(c) sets forth a partnership's obligation to indemnify the culpable partner where the partner's liability was incurred in the ordinary course of the partnership's business. When indemnification occurs, the assets of both the partnership and the culpable partner are available to a creditor. However, Sections 306(c), 401(b), and 807(b) make clear that a partner who is not otherwise liable under Section 306(c) is not obligated to contribute assets to the partnership in excess of agreed contributions to share the loss with the culpable partner. (See Comments to Sections 401(b) and 807(b). regarding a slight variation in the context of priority of payment of partnership obligations.) Accordingly, Section 306(c) makes clear that an innocent partner is not personally liable for specified partnership obligations, directly or indirectly, by way of contribution or otherwise.

Although the liability shield protections of Section 306(c) may be modified in part or in full in a partnership agreement (and by way of private contractual guarantees), the modifications must constitute an intentional waiver of the liability protections. See Sections 103(b), 104(a), and 902(b). Since the mere act of filing a statement of qualification reflects the assumption that the partners intend to modify the otherwise applicable partner liability rules, the final sentence of subsection (c) makes clear that the filing negates inconsistent aspects of the partnership agreement that existed immediately before the vote to approve becoming a limited liability partnership. The negation only applies to a partner's personal liability for future partnership obligations. The filing however has no effect as to previously created partner obligations to the partnership in the form of specific capital contribution requirements.

Inter se contribution agreements may erode part or all of the effects of the liability shield. For example, Section 807(f) provides that an assignee for the benefit of creditors of a partnership or a partner may enforce a partner's obligation to contribute to the partnership. The ultimate effect of such contribution obligations may make each partner jointly and severally liable for all partnership obligations—even those incurred while the partnership is a limited liability partnership. Although the final sentence of subsection (c) negates such provisions existing before a statement of qualification is filed, it will have no effect on any amendments to the partnership agreement after the statement is filed.

The connection between partner status and personal liability for partnership obligations is severed only with respect to obligations incurred while the partnership is a limited liability partnership. Partnership obligations incurred before a partnership becomes a limited liability partnership or incurred after limited liability partnership status is revoked or canceled are treated as obligations of an ordinary partnership. See Sections 1001 (filing), 1003 (revocation), and 1006 (cancellation). Obligations incurred by a partnership during the period when its statement of qualification is administratively revoked will be considered as incurred by a limited liability partnership provided the partnership's status as such is reinstated within two years under Section 1003(e). See Section 1003(f).

When an obligation is incurred is determined by other law. See Section 104(a). Under that law, and for the limited purpose of determining when partnership contract obligations are incurred, the reasonable expectations of creditors and the partners are paramount. Therefore, partnership obligations under or relating to a note, contract, or other agreement generally are incurred when the note, contract, or other agreement is made. Also, an amendment, modification, extension, or renewal of a note, contract, or other agreement should not affect or otherwise reset the time at which a partnership obligation under or relating to that note, contract, or other agreement is incurred, even as to a claim that relates to the subject matter of the amendment, modification, extension, or renewal. A note, contract, or other agreement may expressly modify these rules and fix the time a partnership obligation is incurred thereunder.

For the limited purpose of determining when partnership tort obligations are incurred, a distinction is intended between injury and the conduct causing that injury. The purpose of the distinction is to prevent unjust results. Partnership obligations under or relating to a tort generally are incurred when the tort conduct occurs rather than at the time of the actual injury or harm. This interpretation prevents a culpable partnership from engaging in wrongful conduct and then filing a statement of qualification to sever the vicarious responsibility of its partners for future injury or harm caused by conduct that occurred prior to the filing.

§ 307. Actions by and Against Partnership and Partners

(a) A partnership may sue and be sued in the name of the partnership.

(b) An action may be brought against the partnership and, to the extent not inconsistent with Section 306, any or all of the partners in the same action or in separate actions.

(c) A judgment against a partnership is not by itself a judgment against a partner. A judgment against a partnership may not be satisfied from a partner's assets unless there is also a judgment against the partner.

(d) A judgment creditor of a partner may not levy execution against the assets of the partner to satisfy a judgment based on a claim against the partnership unless the partner is personally liable for the claim under Section 306 and:

(1)   a judgment based on the same claim has been obtained against the partnership and a writ of execution on the judgment has been returned unsatisfied in whole or in part;

(2)   the partnership is a debtor in bankruptcy;

(3)   the partner has agreed that the creditor need not exhaust partnership assets;

(4)   a court grants permission to the judgment creditor to levy execution against the assets of a partner based on a finding that partnership assets subject to execution are clearly insufficient to satisfy the judgment, that exhaustion of partnership assets is excessively burdensome, or that the grant of permission is an appropriate exercise of the court's equitable powers; or

(5)   liability is imposed on the partner by law or contract independent of the existence of the partnership.

(e)   This section applies to any partnership liability or obligation resulting from a representation by a partner or purported partner under Section 308.

COMMENT

1.   Section 307 is new. Subsection (a) provides that a partnership may sue and be sued in the partnership name. That entity approach is designed to simplify suits by and against a partnership.

At common law, a partnership, not being a legal entity, could not sue or be sued in the firm name. The UPA itself is silent on this point, so in the absence of another enabling statute, it is generally necessary to join all the partners in an action against the partnership.

Most States have statutes or rules authorizing partnerships to sue or be sued in the partnership name. Many of those statutes, however, are found in the state provisions dealing with civil procedure rather than in the partnership act.

2.   Subsection (b) provides that suit generally may be brought against the partnership and any or all of the partners in the same action or in separate actions. It is intended to clarify that the partners need not be named in an action against the partnership. In particular, in an action against a partnership, it is not necessary to name a partner individually in addition to the partnership. This will simplify and reduce the cost of litigation, especially in cases of small claims where there are known to be significant partnership assets and thus no necessity to collect the judgment out of the partners' assets.

Where the partnership is a limited liability partnership, the limited liability partnership rules clarify that a partner not liable for the alleged partnership obligation may not be named in the action against the partnership unless the action also seeks to establish personal liability of the partner for the obligation. See subsections (b) and (d).

3.   Subsection (c) provides that a judgment against the partnership is not, standing alone, a judgment against the partners, and it cannot be satisfied from a partner's personal assets unless there is a judgment against the partner. Thus, a partner must be individually named and served, either in the action against the partnership or in a later suit, before his personal assets may be subject to levy for a claim against the partnership.

RUPA leaves it to the law of judgments, as did the UPA, to determine the collateral effects to be accorded a prior judgment for or against the partnership in a subsequent action against a partner individually. See Section 60 of the Second Restatement of Judgments (1982) and the Comments thereto.

4.   Subsection (d) requires partnership creditors to exhaust the partnership's assets before levying on a judgment debtor partner's individual property where the partner is personally liable for the partnership obligation under Section 306. That rule respects the concept of the partnership as an entity and makes partners more in the nature of guarantors than principal debtors on every partnership debt. It is already the law in some States.

As a general rule, a final judgment against a partner cannot be enforced by a creditor against the partner's separate assets unless a writ of execution against the partnership has been returned unsatisfied. Under subsection (d), however, a creditor may proceed directly against the partner's assets if (i) the partnership is a debtor in bankruptcy (see Section 101(2)); (ii) the partner has consented; or (iii) the liability is imposed on the partner independently of the partnership. For example, a judgment creditor may proceed directly against the assets of a partner who is liable independently as the primary tortfeasor, but must exhaust the partnership's assets before proceeding against the separate assets of the other partners who are liable only as partners.

There is also a judicial override provision in subsection (d)(4). A court may authorize execution against the partner's assets on the grounds that (i) the partnership's assets are clearly insufficient; (ii) exhaustion of the partnership's assets would be excessively burdensome; or (iii) it is otherwise equitable to do so. For example, if the partners who are parties to the action have assets located in the forum State, but the partnership does not, a court might find that exhaustion of the partnership's assets would be excessively burdensome.

5. Although subsection (d) is silent with respect to pre-judgment remedies, the law of pre-judgment remedies already adequately embodies the principle that partnership assets should be exhausted before partners' assets are attached or garnished. Attachment, for example, typically requires a showing that the partnership's assets are being secreted or fraudulently transferred or are otherwise inadequate to satisfy the plaintiff's claim. A showing of some exigent circumstance may also be required to satisfy due process. *See Connecticut v. Doehr*, 501 U.S. 1, 16 (1991).

6. Subsection (e) clarifies that actions against the partnership under Section 308, involving representations by partners or purported partners, are subject to Section 307.

§ 308. Liability of Purported Partner

(a) If a person, by words or conduct, purports to be a partner, or consents to being represented by another as a partner, in a partnership or with one or more persons not partners, the purported partner is liable to a person to whom the representation is made, if that person, relying on the representation, enters into a transaction with the actual or purported partnership. If the representation, either by the purported partner or by a person with the purported partner's consent, is made in a public manner, the purported partner is liable to a person who relies upon the purported partnership even if the purported partner is not aware of being held out as a partner to the claimant. If partnership liability results, the purported partner is liable with respect to that liability as if the purported partner were a partner. If no partnership liability results, the purported partner is liable with respect to that liability jointly and severally with any other person consenting to the representation.

(b) If a person is thus represented to be a partner in an existing partnership, or with one or more persons not partners, the purported partner is an agent of persons consenting to the representation to bind them to the same extent and in the same manner as if the purported partner were a partner, with respect to persons who enter into transactions in reliance upon the representation. If all of the partners of the existing partnership consent to the representation, a partnership act or obligation results. If fewer than all of the partners of the existing partnership consent to the representation, the person acting and the partners consenting to the representation are jointly and severally liable.

(c) A person is not liable as a partner merely because the person is named by another in a statement of partnership authority.

(d) A person does not continue to be liable as a partner merely because of a failure to file a statement of dissociation or to amend a statement of partnership authority to indicate the partner's dissociation from the partnership.

(e) Except as otherwise provided in subsections (a) and (b), persons who are not partners as to each other are not liable as partners to other persons.

COMMENT

Section 308 continues the basic principles of partnership by estoppel from UPA Section 16, now more accurately entitled "Liability of Purported Partner." Subsection (a) continues the distinction between representations made to specific persons and those made in a public manner. It is the exclusive basis for imposing liability as a partner on persons who are not partners in fact. As under the UPA, there is no duty of denial, and thus a person held out by another as a partner is not liable unless he actually consents to the representation. See the Official Comment to UPA Section 16. Also see Section 308(c) (no duty to file statement of denial) and Section 308(d) (no duty to file statement of dissociation or to amend statement of partnership authority).

Subsection (b) emphasizes that the persons being protected by Section 308 are those who enter into transactions in reliance upon a representation. If all of the partners of an existing partnership consent to the representation, a partnership obligation results. Apart from Section 308, the firm may be bound in other situations under general principles of apparent authority or ratification.

If a partnership liability results under Section 308, the creditor must exhaust the partnership's assets before seeking to satisfy the claim from the partners. See Section 307.

Subsections (c) and (d) are new and deal with potential negative inferences to be drawn from a failure to correct inaccurate or outdated filed statements. Subsection (c) makes clear that an otherwise innocent person is not liable as a partner for failing to deny his partnership status as asserted by a third person in a statement of partnership authority. Under subsection (d), a partner's liability as a partner does not continue after dissociation solely because of a failure to file a statement of dissociation.

Subsection (e) is derived from UPA Section 7(1). It means that only those persons who are partners as among themselves are liable as partners to third parties for the obligations of the partnership, except for liabilities incurred by purported partners under Section 308(a) and (b).

Article 4

RELATIONS OF PARTNERS TO EACH OTHER AND TO PARTNERSHIP

§ 401. Partner's Rights and Duties

(a) Each partner is deemed to have an account that is:

(1) credited with an amount equal to the money plus the value of any other property, net of the amount of any liabilities, the partner contributes to the partnership and the partner's share of the partnership profits; and

(2) charged with an amount equal to the money plus the value of any other property, net of the amount of any liabilities, distributed by the partnership to the partner and the partner's share of the partnership losses.

(b) Each partner is entitled to an equal share of the partnership profits and is chargeable with a share of the partnership losses in proportion to the partner's share of the profits.

(c) A partnership shall reimburse a partner for payments made and indemnify a partner for liabilities incurred by the partner in the ordinary course of the business of the partnership or for the preservation of its business or property.

(d) A partnership shall reimburse a partner for an advance to the partnership beyond the amount of capital the partner agreed to contribute.

(e) A payment or advance made by a partner which gives rise to a partnership obligation under subsection (c) or (d) constitutes a loan to the partnership which accrues interest from the date of the payment or advance.

(f) Each partner has equal rights in the management and conduct of the partnership business.

(g) A partner may use or possess partnership property only on behalf of the partnership.

(h) A partner is not entitled to remuneration for services performed for the partnership, except for reasonable compensation for services rendered in winding up the business of the partnership.

(i) A person may become a partner only with the consent of all of the partners.

(j) A difference arising as to a matter in the ordinary course of business of a partnership may be decided by a majority of the partners. An act outside the ordinary course of business of a partnership and an amendment to the partnership agreement may be undertaken only with the consent of all of the partners.

(k) This section does not affect the obligations of a partnership to other persons under Section 301.

COMMENT

1. Section 401 is drawn substantially from UPA Section 18. It establishes many of the default rules that govern the relations among partners. All of these rules are, however, subject to contrary agreement of the partners as provided in Section 103.

2.   Subsection (a) provides that each partner is deemed to have an account that is credited with the partner's contributions and share of the partnership profits and charged with distributions to the partner and the partner's share of partnership losses. In the absence of another system of partnership accounts, these rules establish a rudimentary system of accounts for the partnership. The rules regarding the settlement of the partners' accounts upon the dissolution and winding up of the partnership business are found in Section 807.

3.   Subsection (b) establishes the default rules for the sharing of partnership profits and losses. The UPA Section 18(a) rules that profits are shared equally and that losses, whether capital or operating, are shared in proportion to each partner's share of the profits are continued. Thus, under the default rule, partners share profits per capita and not in proportion to capital contribution as do corporate shareholders or partners in limited partnerships. Compare RULPA Section 504. With respect to losses, the qualifying phrase, "whether capital or operating," has been deleted as inconsistent with contemporary partnership accounting practice and terminology; no substantive change is intended.

If partners agree to share profits other than equally, losses will be shared similarly to profits, absent agreement to do otherwise. That rule, carried over from the UPA, is predicated on the assumption that partners would likely agree to share losses on the same basis as profits, but may fail to say so. Of course, by agreement, they may share losses on a different basis from profits.

The default rules apply, as does UPA Section 18(a), where one or more of the partners contribute no capital, although there is case law to the contrary. *See, e.g., Kovacik v. Reed,* 49 Cal. 2d 166, 315 P.2d 314 (1957); *Becker v. Killarney,* 177 Ill. App. 3d 793, 523 N.E.2d 467 (1988). It may seem unfair that the contributor of services, who contributes little or no capital, should be obligated to contribute toward the capital loss of the large contributor who contributed no services. In entering a partnership with such a capital structure, the partners should foresee that application of the default rule may bring about unusual results and take advantage of their power to vary by agreement the allocation of capital losses.

Subsection (b) provides that each partner "is chargeable" with a share of the losses, rather than the UPA formulation that each partner shall "contribute" to losses. Losses are charged to each partner's account as provided in subsection (a)(2). It is intended to make clear that a partner is not obligated to contribute to partnership losses before his withdrawal or the liquidation of the partnership, unless the partners agree otherwise. In effect, unless related to an obligation for which the partner is not personally liable under Section 306(c), a partner's negative account represents a debt to the partnership unless the partners agree to the contrary. Similarly, each partner's share of the profits is credited to his account under subsection (a)(1). Absent an agreement to the contrary, however, a partner does not have a right to receive a current distribution of the profits credited to his account, the interim distribution of profits being a matter arising in the ordinary course of business to be decided by majority vote of the partners.

However, where a liability to contribute at dissolution and winding up relates to a partnership obligation governed by the limited liability rule of Section 306(c), a partner is not obligated to contribute additional assets even at dissolution and winding up. See Section 807(b). In such a case, although a partner is not personally liable for the partnership obligation, that partner's interest in the partnership remains at risk. See also Comment to Section 401(c) relating to indemnification.

In the case of an operating limited liability partnership, the Section 306 liability shield may be partially eroded where the limited liability partnership incurs both shielded and unshielded liabilities. Where the limited liability partnership uses its assets to pay shielded liabilities before paying unshielded liabilities, each partner's obligation to contribute to the limited liability partnership for that partner's share of the unpaid and unshielded obligations at dissolution and winding up remains intact. The same issue is less likely to occur in the context of the termination of a limited liability partnership since a partner's contribution obligation is based only on that partner's share of unshielded obligations and the partnership will ordinarily use the contributed assets to pay unshielded claims first as they were the basis of the contribution obligations. See Comments to Section 807(b).

4.   Subsection (c) is derived from UPA Section 18(b) and provides that the partnership shall reimburse partners for payments made and indemnify them for liabilities incurred in the ordinary course of the partnership's business or for the preservation of its business or property. Reimbursement and indemnification is an obligation of the partnership. Indemnification may create a loss toward which the partners must contribute. Although the right to indemnification is usually enforced in the settlement of accounts among partners upon dissolution and winding up of the partnership business, the right accrues when the liability is incurred and thus may be enforced during the term of the partnership in an appropriate case. *See* Section 405 and Comment. A partner's right to indemnification under this Act is not affected by the partnership becoming a limited liability partnership. Accordingly, partners continue to share partnership losses to the extent of partnership assets.

5.   Subsection (d) is based on UPA Section 18(c). It makes explicit that the partnership must reimburse a partner for an advance of funds beyond the amount of the partner's agreed capital contribution, thereby treating the advance as a loan.

6.   Subsection (e), which is also drawn from UPA Section 18(c), characterizes the partnership's obligation under subsection (c) or (d) as a loan to the partnership which accrues interest from the date of the payment or advance. See Section 104(b) (default rate of interest).

7.   Under subsection (f), each partner has equal rights in the management and conduct of the business. It is based on UPA Section 18(e), which has been interpreted broadly to mean that, absent contrary agreement, each partner has a continuing right to participate in the management of the partnership and to be informed about the partnership business, even if his assent to partnership business decisions is not required. There are special rules regarding the partner vote necessary to approve a partnership becoming (or canceling its status as) a limited liability partnership. See Section 1001(b).

8.   Subsection (g) provides that partners may use or possess partnership property only for partnership purposes. That is the edited remains of UPA Section 25(2)(a), which deals in detail with the incidents of tenancy in partnership. That tenancy is abolished as a consequence of the entity theory of partnerships. *See* Section 501 and Comments.

9.   Subsection (h) continues the UPA Section 18(f) rule that a partner is not entitled to remuneration for services performed, except in winding up the partnership. Subsection (h) deletes the UPA reference to a "surviving" partner. That means any partner winding up the business is entitled to compensation, not just a surviving partner winding up after the death of another partner. The exception is not intended to apply in the hypothetical winding up that takes place if there is a buyout under Article 7.

10.   Subsection (i) continues the substance of UPA Section 18(g) that no person can become a partner without the consent of all the partners.

11.   Subsection (j) continues with one important clarification the UPA Section 18(h) scheme of allocating management authority among the partners. In the absence of an agreement to the contrary, matters arising in the ordinary course of the business may be decided by a majority of the partners. Amendments to the partnership agreement and matters outside the ordinary course of the partnership business require unanimous consent of the partners. Although the text of the UPA is silent regarding extraordinary matters, courts have generally required the consent of all partners for those matters. *See, e.g., Paciaroni v. Crane*, 408 A.2d 946 (Del. Ch. 1989); *Thomas v. Marvin E. Jewell & Co.*, 232 Neb. 261, 440 N.W.2d 437 (1989); *Duell v. Hancock*, 83 A.D.2d 762, 443 N.Y.S.2d 490 (1981).

It is not intended that subsection (j) embrace a claim for an objection to a partnership decision that is not discovered until after the fact. There is no cause of action based on that after-the-fact second-guessing.

12.   Subsection (k) is new and was added to make it clear that Section 301 governs partners' agency power to bind the partnership to third persons, while Section 401 governs partners' rights among themselves.

§ 402.   Distributions in Kind

A partner has no right to receive, and may not be required to accept, a distribution in kind.

COMMENT

Section 402 provides that a partner has no right to demand and receive a distribution in kind and may not be required to take a distribution in kind. That continues the "in kind" rule of UPA Section 38(*l*). The new language is suggested by RULPA Section 605.

This section is complemented by Section 807(a) which provides that, in winding up the partnership business on dissolution, any surplus after the payment of partnership obligations must be applied to pay in cash the net amount distributable to each partner.

§ 403.   Partner's Rights and Duties with Respect to Information

(a)   A partnership shall keep its books and records, if any, at its chief executive office.

(b)   A partnership shall provide partners and their agents and attorneys access to its books and records. It shall provide former partners and their agents and attorneys access to books and records pertaining to the period during which they were partners. The right of access provides the opportunity to inspect and copy books and records during ordinary business hours. A partnership may impose a reasonable charge, covering the costs of labor and material, for copies of documents furnished.

(c)   Each partner and the partnership shall furnish to a partner, and to the legal representative of a deceased partner or partner under legal disability:

(1)   without demand, any information concerning the partnership's business and affairs reasonably required for the proper exercise of the partner's rights and duties under the partnership agreement or this [Act]; and

(2)   on demand, any other information concerning the partnership's business and affairs, except to the extent the demand or the information demanded is unreasonable or otherwise improper under the circumstances.

COMMENT

1.   Subsection (a) provides that the partnership's books and records, if any, shall be kept at its chief executive office. It continues the UPA Section 19 rule, modified to include partnership records other than its "books," i.e., financial records. The concept of "chief executive office" comes from UCC Section 9–103(3)(d). See the Comment to Section 106.

Since general partnerships are often informal or even inadvertent, no books and records are enumerated as mandatory, such as that found in RULPA Section 105. Any requirement in UPA Section 19 that the partnership keep books is oblique at best, since it states merely where the books shall be kept, not that they shall be kept. Under RUPA, there is no liability to either partners or third parties for the failure to keep partnership books. A partner who undertakes to keep books, however, must do so accurately and adequately.

In general, a partnership should, at a minimum, keep those books and records necessary to enable the partners to determine their share of the profits and losses, as well as their rights on withdrawal. An action for an accounting provides an adequate remedy in the event adequate records are not kept. The partnership must also maintain any books and records required by state or federal taxing or other governmental authorities.

2.   Under subsection (b), partners are entitled to access to the partnership books and records. Former partners are expressly given a similar right, although limited to the books and records pertaining to the period during which they were partners. The line between partners and former partners is not a bright one for this purpose, however, and should be drawn in light of the legitimate interests of a dissociated partner in the partnership. For example, a withdrawing partner's liability is ongoing for pre-withdrawal liabilities and will normally be extended to new liabilities for at least 90 days. It is intended that a former partner be accorded access to partnership books and records as reasonably necessary to protect that partner's legitimate interests during the period his rights and liabilities are being wound down.

The right of access is limited to ordinary business hours, and the right to inspect and copy by agent or attorney is made explicit. The partnership may impose a reasonable charge for furnishing copies of documents. *Accord*, RULPA § 105(b).

A partner's right to inspect and copy the partnership's books and records is not conditioned on the partner's purpose or motive. Compare RMBCA Section 16.02(c)(*l*) (shareholder must have proper purpose to inspect certain corporate records). A partner's unlimited personal liability justifies an unqualified right of access to the partnership books and records. An abuse of the right to inspect and copy might constitute a violation of the obligation of good faith and fair dealing for which the other partners would have a remedy. See Sections 404(d) and 405.

Under Section 103(b)(2), a partner's right of access to partnership books and records may not be unreasonably restricted by the partnership agreement. Thus, to preserve a partner's core information rights despite unequal bargaining power, an agreement limiting a partner's right to inspect and copy partnership books and records is subject to judicial review. Nevertheless, reasonable restrictions on access to partnership books and records by agreement are authorized. For example, a provision in a partnership agreement denying partners access to the compensation of other partners should be upheld, absent any abuse such as fraud or duress.

3.   Subsection (c) is a significant revision of UPA Section 20 and provides a more comprehensive, although not exclusive, statement of partners' rights and duties with respect to partnership information other than books and records. Both the partnership and the other partners are obligated to furnish partnership information.

Paragraph (1) is new and imposes an affirmative disclosure obligation on the partnership and partners. There is no express UPA provision imposing an affirmative obligation to disclose any information other than the partnership books. Under some circumstances, however, an affirmative disclosure duty has been inferred from other sections of the Act, as well as from the common law, such as the fiduciary duty of good faith. Under UPA Section 18(e), for example, all partners enjoy an equal right in the management and conduct of the partnership business, absent contrary agreement. That right has been construed to require that every partner be provided with ongoing information concerning the partnership business. See Comment 7 to Section 401. Paragraph (1) provides expressly that partners must be furnished, without demand, partnership information reasonably needed for them to exercise their rights and duties as partners. In addition, a disclosure duty may, under some circumstances, also spring from the Section 404(d) obligation of good faith and fair dealing. See Comment 4 to Section 404.

Paragraph (2) continues the UPA rule that partners are entitled, on demand, to any other information concerning the partnership's business and affairs. The demand may be refused if either the demand or the information demanded is unreasonable or otherwise improper. That qualification is new to the statutory formulation. The burden is on the partnership or partner from whom the information is requested to show that the demand is unreasonable or improper. The UPA admonition that the information furnished be "true and full" has been deleted as unnecessary, and no substantive change is intended.

The Section 403(c) information rights can be waived or varied by agreement of the partners, since there is no Section 103(b) limitation on the variation of those rights as there is with respect to the Section 403(b) access rights to books and records. *See* Section 103(b)(2).

§ 404. General Standards of Partner's Conduct

(a) The only fiduciary duties a partner owes to the partnership and the other partners are the duty of loyalty and the duty of care set forth in subsections (b) and (c).

(b) A partner's duty of loyalty to the partnership and the other partners is limited to the following:

(1) to account to the partnership and hold as trustee for it any property, profit, or benefit derived by the partner in the conduct and winding up of the partnership business or derived from a use by the partner of partnership property, including the appropriation of a partnership opportunity;

(2) to refrain from dealing with the partnership in the conduct or winding up of the partnership business as or on behalf of a party having an interest adverse to the partnership; and

(3) to refrain from competing with the partnership in the conduct of the partnership business before the dissolution of the partnership.

(c) A partner's duty of care to the partnership and the other partners in the conduct and winding up of the partnership business is limited to refraining from engaging in grossly negligent or reckless conduct, intentional misconduct, or a knowing violation of law.

(d) A partner shall discharge the duties to the partnership and the other partners under this [Act] or under the partnership agreement and exercise any rights consistently with the obligation of good faith and fair dealing.

(e) A partner does not violate a duty or obligation under this [Act] or under the partnership agreement merely because the partner's conduct furthers the partner's own interest.

(f) A partner may lend money to and transact other business with the partnership, and as to each loan or transaction the rights and obligations of the partner are the same as those of a person who is not a partner, subject to other applicable law.

(g) This section applies to a person winding up the partnership business as the personal or legal representative of the last surviving partner as if the person were a partner.

COMMENT

1. Section 404 is new. The title, "General Standards of Partner's Conduct," is drawn from RMBCA Section 8.30. Section 404 is both comprehensive and exclusive. In that regard, it is structurally different from the UPA which touches only sparingly on a partner's duty of loyalty and leaves any further development of the fiduciary duties of partners to the common law of agency. Compare UPA Sections 4(3) and 21.

Section 404 begins by stating that the only fiduciary duties a partner owes to the partnership and the other partners are the duties of loyalty and care set forth in subsections (b) and (c) of the Act. Those duties may not be waived or eliminated in the partnership agreement, but the agreement may identify activities and determine standards for measuring performance of the duties, if not manifestly unreasonable. *See* Sections 103(b)(3)–(5).

Section 404 continues the term "fiduciary" from UPA Section 21, which is entitled "Partner Accountable as a Fiduciary." Arguably, the term "fiduciary" is inappropriate when used to describe the duties of a partner because a partner may legitimately pursue self-interest (see Section 404(e)) and not solely the interest of the partnership and the other partners, as must a true trustee. Nevertheless, partners have long been characterized as fiduciaries. *See, e.g., Meinhard v. Salmon*, 249 N.Y. 458, 463, 164 N.E. 545, 546 (1928) (Cardozo, J.). Indeed, the law of partnership reflects the broader law of principal and agent, under which every agent is a fiduciary. *See* Restatement (Second) of Agency § 13 (1957).

2.   Section 404(b) provides three specific rules that comprise a partner's duty of loyalty. Those rules are exclusive and encompass the entire duty of loyalty.

Subsection (b)(*l*) is based on UPA Section 21(1) and continues the rule that partnership property usurped by a partner, including the misappropriation of a partnership opportunity, is held in trust for the partnership. The express reference to the appropriation of a partnership opportunity is new, but merely codifies case law on the point. *See, e.g., Meinhard v. Salmon, supra; Fouchek v. Janicek*, 190 Ore. 251, 225 P.2d 783 (1950). Under a constructive trust theory, the partnership can recover any money or property in the partner's hands that can be traced to the partnership. *See, e.g., Yoder v. Hooper*, 695 P.2d 1182 (Colo. App. 1984), *aff'd*, 737 P.2d 852 (Colo. 1987); *Fortugno v. Hudson Manure Co.*, 51 N.J. Super. 482, 144 A.2d 207 (1958); *Harestad v. Weitzel*, 242 Or. 199, 536 P.2d 522 (1975). As a result, the partnership's claim is greater than that of an ordinary creditor. See Official Comment to UPA Section 21.

UPA Section 21(1) imposes the duty on partners to account for profits and benefits in all transactions connected with "the formation, conduct, or liquidation of the partnership." Reference to the "formation" of the partnership has been eliminated by RUPA because of concern that the duty of loyalty could be inappropriately extended to the pre-formation period when the parties are really negotiating at arm's length. *Compare Herring v. Offutt*, 295 A.2d 876 (Ct. App. Md. 1972), *with Phoenix Mutual Life Ins. Co. v. Shady Grove Plaza Limited Partnership*, 734 F. Supp. 1181 (D. Md. 1990), *aff'd*, 937 F.2d 603 (4th Cir. 1991). Once a partnership is agreed to, each partner becomes a fiduciary in the "conduct" of the business. Pre-formation negotiations are, of course, subject to the general contract obligation to deal honestly and without fraud.

Upon a partner's dissociation, Section 603(b)(3) limits the application of the duty to account for personal profits to those derived from matters arising or events occurring before the dissociation, unless the partner participates in winding up the partnership's business. Thus, after withdrawal, a partner is free to appropriate to his own benefit any new business opportunity thereafter coming to his attention, even if the partnership continues.

Subsection (b)(2) provides that a partner must refrain from dealing with the partnership as or on behalf of a party having an interest adverse to the partnership. This rule is derived from Sections 389 and 391 of the Restatement (Second) of Agency. Comment c to Section 389 explains that the rule is not based upon the harm caused to the principal, but upon avoiding a conflict of opposing interests in the mind of an agent whose duty is to act for the benefit of his principal.

Upon a partner's dissociation, Section 603(b)(3) limits the application of the duty to refrain from representing interests adverse to the partnership to the same extent as the duty to account. Thus, after withdrawal, a partner may deal with the partnership as an adversary with respect to new matters or events.

Section 404(b)(3) provides that a partner must refrain from competing with the partnership in the conduct of its business. This rule is derived from Section 393 of the Restatement (Second) of Agency and is an application of the general duty of an agent to act solely on his principal's behalf.

The duty not to compete applies only to the "conduct" of the partnership business; it does not extend to winding up the business, as do the other loyalty rules. Thus, a partner is free to compete immediately upon an event of dissolution under Section 801, unless the partnership agreement otherwise provides. A partner who dissociates without a winding up of the business resulting is also free to compete, because Section 603(b)(2) provides that the duty not to compete terminates upon dissociation. A dissociated partner is not, however, free to use confidential partnership information after dissociation. *See* Restatement (Second) of Agency § 393 cmt. e (1957). Trade secret law also may apply. See the Uniform Trade Secrets Act.

Under Section 103(b)(3), the partnership agreement may not "eliminate" the duty of loyalty. Section 103(b)(3)(i) expressly empowers the partners, however, to identify specific types or categories of activities that do not violate the duty of loyalty, if not manifestly unreasonable. As under UPA Section 21, the other partners may also consent to a specific act or transaction that otherwise violates one of the rules. For the consent to be effective under Section 103(b)(3)(ii), there must be full disclosure of all material facts regarding the act or transaction and the partner's conflict of interest. See Comment 5 to Section 103.

3.   Subsection (c) is new and establishes the duty of care that partners owe to the partnership and to the other partners. There is no statutory duty of care under the UPA, although a common law duty of care is recognized by some courts. *See, e.g., Rosenthal v. Rosenthal*, 543 A.2d 348, 352 (Me. 1988) (duty of care limited to acting in a manner that does not constitute gross negligence or willful misconduct).

The standard of care imposed by RUPA is that of gross negligence, which is the standard generally recognized by the courts. *See, e.g., Rosenthal v. Rosenthal, supra.* Section 103(b)(4) provides that the duty of care may not be eliminated entirely by agreement, but the standard may be reasonably reduced. See Comment 6 to Section 103.

4.   Subsection (d) is also new. It provides that partners have an obligation of good faith and fair dealing in the discharge of all their duties, including those arising under the Act, such as their fiduciary duties of loyalty and care, and those arising under the partnership agreement. The exercise of any rights by a partner is also subject to the obligation of good faith and fair dealing. The obligation runs to the partnership and to the other partners in all matters related to the conduct and winding up of the partnership business.

The obligation of good faith and fair dealing is a contract concept, imposed on the partners because of the consensual nature of a partnership. See Restatement (Second) of Contracts § 205 (1981). It is not characterized, in RUPA, as a fiduciary duty arising out of the partners' special relationship. Nor is it a separate and independent obligation. It is an ancillary obligation that applies whenever a partner discharges a duty or exercises a right under the partnership agreement or the Act.

The meaning of "good faith and fair dealing" is not firmly fixed under present law. "Good faith" clearly suggests a subjective element, while "fair dealing" implies an objective component. It was decided to leave the terms undefined in the Act and allow the courts to develop their meaning based on the experience of real cases. Some commentators, moreover, believe that good faith is more properly understood by what it excludes than by what it includes. See Robert S. Summers, *"Good Faith" in General Contract Law and the Sales Provisions of the Uniform Commercial Code*, 54 Va. L. Rev. 195, 262 (1968):

Good faith, as judges generally use the term in matters contractual, is best understood as an "excluder"—a phrase with no general meaning or meanings of its own. Instead, it functions to rule out many different forms of bad faith. It is hard to get this point across to persons used to thinking that every word must have one or more general meanings of its own—must be either univocal or ambiguous.

The UCC definition of "good faith" is honesty in fact and, in the case of a merchant, the observance of reasonable commercial standards of fair dealing in the trade. *See* UCC §§ 1–201(19), 2–103(b). Those definitions were rejected as too narrow or not applicable.

In some situations the obligation of good faith includes a disclosure component. Depending on the circumstances, a partner may have an affirmative disclosure obligation that supplements the Section 403 duty to render information.

Under Section 103(b)(5), the obligation of good faith and fair dealing may not be eliminated by agreement, but the partners by agreement may determine the standards by which the performance of the obligation is to be measured, if the standards are not manifestly unreasonable. See Comment 7 to Section 103.

5.   Subsection (e) is new and deals expressly with a very basic issue on which the UPA is silent. A partner as such is not a trustee and is not held to the same standards as a trustee. Subsection (e) makes clear that a partner's conduct is not deemed to be improper merely because it serves the partner's own individual interest.

That admonition has particular application to the duty of loyalty and the obligation of good faith and fair dealing. It underscores the partner's rights as an owner and principal in the enterprise, which must always be balanced against his duties and obligations as an agent and fiduciary. For example, a partner who, with consent, owns a shopping center may, under subsection (e), legitimately vote against a proposal by the partnership to open a competing shopping center.

6.   Subsection (f) authorizes partners to lend money to and transact other business with the partnership and, in so doing, to enjoy the same rights and obligations as a nonpartner. That language is drawn from RULPA Section 107. The rights and obligations of a partner doing business with the partnership as an outsider are expressly made subject to the usual laws governing those transactions. They include, for example, rules limiting or qualifying the rights and remedies of inside creditors, such as fraudulent transfer law, equitable subordination,

and the law of avoidable preferences, as well as general debtor-creditor law. The reference to "other applicable law" makes clear that subsection (f) is not intended to displace those laws, and thus they are preserved under Section 104(a).

It is unclear under the UPA whether a partner may, for the partner's own account, purchase the assets of the partnership at a foreclosure sale or upon the liquidation of the partnership. Those purchases are clearly within subsection (f)'s broad approval. It is also clear under that subsection that a partner may purchase partnership assets at a foreclosure sale, whether the partner is the mortgagee or the mortgagee is an unrelated third party. Similarly, a partner may purchase partnership property at a tax sale. The obligation of good faith requires disclosure of the partner's interest in the transaction, however.

7. Subsection (g) provides that the prescribed standards of conduct apply equally to a person engaged in winding up the partnership business as the personal or legal representative of the last surviving partner, as if the person were a partner. This is derived from UPA Section 21(2), but now embraces the duty of care and the obligation of good faith and fair dealing, as well as the duty of loyalty.

§ 405. Actions by Partnership and Partners

(a) A partnership may maintain an action against a partner for a breach of the partnership agreement, or for the violation of a duty to the partnership, causing harm to the partnership.

(b) A partner may maintain an action against the partnership or another partner for legal or equitable relief, with or without an accounting as to partnership business, to:

(1) enforce the partner's rights under the partnership agreement;

(2) enforce the partner's rights under this [Act], including:

(i) the partner's rights under Sections 401, 403, or 404;

(ii) the partner's right on dissociation to have the partner's interest in the partnership purchased pursuant to Section 701 or enforce any other right under Article 6 or 7; or

(iii) the partner's right to compel a dissolution and winding up of the partnership business under Section 801 or enforce any other right under Article 8; or

(3) enforce the rights and otherwise protect the interests of the partner, including rights and interests arising independently of the partnership relationship.

(c) The accrual of, and any time limitation on, a right of action for a remedy under this section is governed by other law. A right to an accounting upon a dissolution and winding up does not revive a claim barred by law.

COMMENT

1. Section 405(a) is new and reflects the entity theory of partnership. It provides that the partnership itself may maintain an action against a partner for any breach of the partnership agreement or for the violation of any duty owed to the partnership, such as a breach of fiduciary duty.

2. Section 405(b) is the successor to UPA Section 22, but with significant changes. At common law, an accounting was generally not available before dissolution. That was modified by UPA Section 22 which specifies certain circumstances in which an accounting action is available without requiring a partner to dissolve the partnership. Section 405(b) goes far beyond the UPA rule. It provides that, during the term of the partnership, partners may maintain a variety of legal or equitable actions, including an action for an accounting, as well as a final action for an accounting upon dissolution and winding up. It reflects a new policy choice that partners should have access to the courts during the term of the partnership to resolve claims against the partnership and the other partners, leaving broad judicial discretion to fashion appropriate remedies.

Under RUPA, an accounting is not a prerequisite to the availability of the other remedies a partner may have against the partnership or the other partners. That change reflects the increased willingness courts have shown to grant relief without the requirement of an accounting, in derogation of the so-called "exclusivity rule." *See*, *e.g.*, *Farney v. Hauser*, 109 Kan. 75, 79, 198 Pac. 178, 180 (1921) ("[For] all practical purposes a partnership may be considered as a business entity"); *Auld v. Estridge*, 86 Misc. 2d 895, 901, 382 N.Y.S.2d 897, 901 (1976) ("No purpose of justice is served by delaying the resolution here on empty procedural grounds").

Under subsection (b), a partner may bring a direct suit against the partnership or another partner for almost any cause of action arising out of the conduct of the partnership business. That eliminates the present procedural barriers to suits between partners filed independently of an accounting action. In addition to a formal account, the court may grant any other appropriate legal or equitable remedy. Since general partners are not passive investors like limited partners, RUPA does not authorize derivative actions, as does RULPA Section 1001.

Subsection (b)(3) makes it clear that a partner may recover against the partnership and the other partners for personal injuries or damage to the property of the partner caused by another partner. *See, e.g., Duffy v. Piazza Construction Co.*, 815 P.2d 267 (Wash. App. 1991); *Smith v. Hensley*, 354 S.W.2d 744 (Ky. App.). One partner's negligence is not imputed to bar another partner's action. *See, e.g., Reeves v. Harmon*, 475 P.2d 400 (Okla. 1970); *Eagle Star Ins. Co. v. Bean*, 134 F.2d 755 (9th Cir. 1943) (fire insurance company not subrogated to claim against partners who negligently caused fire that damaged partnership property).

3.   Generally, partners may limit or contract away their Section 405 remedies. They may not, however, eliminate entirely the remedies for breach of those duties that are mandatory under Section 103(b). See Comment 1 to Section 103.

4.   Section 405(c) replaces UPA Section 43 and provides that other (i.e., non-partnership) law governs the accrual of a cause of action for which subsection (b) provides a remedy. The statute of limitations on such claims is also governed by other law, and claims barred by a statute of limitations are not revived by reason of the partner's right to an accounting upon dissolution, as they were under the UPA. The effect of those rules is to compel partners to litigate their claims during the life of the partnership or risk losing them. Because an accounting is an equitable proceeding, it may also be barred by laches where there is an undue delay in bringing the action. Under general law, the limitations periods may be tolled by a partner's fraud.

5.   UPA Section 39 grants ancillary remedies to a person who rescinds his participation in a partnership because it was fraudulently induced, including the right to a lien on surplus partnership property for the amount of that person's interest in the partnership. RUPA has no counterpart provision to UPA Section 39, and leaves it to the general law of rescission to determine the rights of a person fraudulently induced to invest in a partnership. See Section 104(a).

§ 406.   Continuation of Partnership Beyond Definite Term or Particular Undertaking

(a)   If a partnership for a definite term or particular undertaking is continued, without an express agreement, after the expiration of the term or completion of the undertaking, the rights and duties of the partners remain the same as they were at the expiration or completion, so far as is consistent with a partnership at will.

(b)   If the partners, or those of them who habitually acted in the business during the term or undertaking, continue the business without any settlement or liquidation of the partnership, they are presumed to have agreed that the partnership will continue.

COMMENT

Section 406 continues UPA Section 23, with no substantive change. Subsection (a) provides that, if a term partnership is continued without an express agreement beyond the expiration of its term or the completion of the undertaking, the partners' rights and duties remain the same as they were, so far as is consistent with a partnership at will.

Subsection (b) provides that if the partnership is continued by the partners without any settlement or liquidation of the business, it is presumed that the partners have agreed not to wind up the business. The presumption is rebuttable. If the partnership is continued under this subsection, there is no dissolution under (2)(iii). As a partnership at will, however, the partnership may be dissolved under (1) at any time.

Article 5

TRANSFEREES AND CREDITORS OF PARTNER

§ 501.   Partner Not Co-Owner of Partnership Property

A partner is not a co-owner of partnership property and has no interest in partnership property which can be transferred, either voluntarily or involuntarily.

COMMENT

Section 501 provides that a partner is not a co-owner of partnership property and has no interest in partnership property that can be transferred, either voluntarily or involuntarily. Thus, the section abolishes the UPA Section 25(1) concept of tenants in partnership and reflects the adoption of the entity theory. Partnership property is owned by the entity and not by the individual partners. See also Section 203, which provides that property transferred to or otherwise acquired by the partnership is property of the partnership and not of the partners individually.

RUPA also deletes the references in UPA Sections 24 and 25 to a partner's "right in specific partnership property," although those rights are largely defined away by the detailed rules of UPA Section 25 itself. Thus, it is clear that a partner who misappropriates partnership property is guilty of embezzlement the same as a shareholder who misappropriates corporate property.

Adoption of the entity theory also has the effect of protecting partnership property from execution or other process by a partner's personal creditors. That continues the result under UPA Section 25(2)(c). Those creditors may seek a charging order under Section 504 to reach the partner's transferable interest in the partnership.

RUPA does not interfere with a partner's exemption claim in nonpartnership property. As under the UPA, disputes over whether specific property belongs to the partner or to the firm will likely arise in the context of an exemption claim by a partner.

A partner's spouse, heirs, or next of kin are not entitled to allowances or other rights in partnership property. That continues the result under UPA Section 25(2)(e).

§ 502. Partner's Transferable Interest in Partnership

The only transferable interest of a partner in the partnership is the partner's share of the profits and losses of the partnership and the partner's right to receive distributions. The interest is personal property.

COMMENT

Section 502 continues the UPA Section 26 concept that a partner's only transferable interest in the partnership is the partner's share of profits and losses and right to receive distributions, that is, the partner's financial rights. The term "distribution" is defined in Section 101(3). Compare RULPA Section 101(10) ("partnership interest").

The partner's transferable interest is deemed to be personal property, regardless of the nature of the underlying partnership assets.

Under Section 503(b)(3), a transferee of a partner's transferable interest has standing to seek judicial dissolution of the partnership business.

A partner has other interests in the partnership that may not be transferred, such as the right to participate in the management of the business. Those rights are included in the broader concept of a "partner's interest in the partnership." See Section 101(9).

§ 503. Transfer of Partner's Transferable Interest

(a) A transfer, in whole or in part, of a partner's transferable interest in the partnership:

(1) is permissible;

(2) does not by itself cause the partner's dissociation or a dissolution and winding up of the partnership business; and

(3) does not, as against the other partners or the partnership, entitle the transferee, during the continuance of the partnership, to participate in the management or conduct of the partnership business, to require access to information concerning partnership transactions, or to inspect or copy the partnership books or records.

(b) A transferee of a partner's transferable interest in the partnership has a right:

(1) to receive, in accordance with the transfer, distributions to which the transferor would otherwise be entitled;

(2)   to receive upon the dissolution and winding up of the partnership business, in accordance with the transfer, the net amount otherwise distributable to the transferor; and

(3)   to seek under Section 801(6) a judicial determination that it is equitable to wind up the partnership business.

(c)   In a dissolution and winding up, a transferee is entitled to an account of partnership transactions only from the date of the latest account agreed to by all of the partners.

(d)   Upon transfer, the transferor retains the rights and duties of a partner other than the interest in distributions transferred.

(e)   A partnership need not give effect to a transferee's rights under this section until it has notice of the transfer.

(f)   A transfer of a partner's transferable interest in the partnership in violation of a restriction on transfer contained in the partnership agreement is ineffective as to a person having notice of the restriction at the time of transfer.

COMMENT

1.   Section 503 is derived from UPA Section 27. Subsection (a)(1) states explicitly that a partner has the right to transfer his transferable interest in the partnership. The term "transfer" is used throughout RUPA in lieu of the term "assignment." See Section 101(10).

Subsection (a)(2) continues the UPA Section 27(1) rule that an assignment of a partner's interest in the partnership does not of itself cause a winding up of the partnership business. Under Section 601(4)(ii), however, a partner who has transferred substantially all of his partnership interest may be expelled by the other partners.

Subsection (a)(3), which is also derived from UPA Section 27(*l*), provides that a transferee is not, as against the other partners, entitled (i) to participate in the management or conduct of the partnership business; (ii) to inspect the partnership books or records; or (iii) to require any information concerning or an account of partnership transactions.

2.   The rights of a transferee are set forth in subsection (b). Under subsection (b)(1), which is derived from UPA Section 27(*l*), a transferee is entitled to receive, in accordance with the terms of the assignment, any distributions to which the transferor would otherwise have been entitled under the partnership agreement before dissolution. After dissolution, the transferee is also entitled to receive, under subsection (b)(2), the net amount that would otherwise have been distributed to the transferor upon the winding up of the business.

Subsection (b)(3) confers standing on a transferee to seek a judicial dissolution and winding up of the partnership business as provided in Section 801(6), thus continuing the rule of UPA Section 32(2).

Section 504(b) accords the rights of a transferee to the purchaser at a sale foreclosing a charging order. The same rule should apply to creditors or other purchasers who acquire partnership interests by pursuing UCC remedies or statutory liens under federal or state law.

3.   Subsection (c) is based on UPA Section 27(2). It grants to transferees the right to an account of partnership transactions, limited to the period since the date of the last account agreed to by all of the partners.

4.   Subsection (d) is new. It makes clear that unless otherwise agreed the partner whose interest is transferred retains all of the rights and duties of a partner, other than the right to receive distributions. That means the transferor is entitled to participate in the management of the partnership and remains personally liable for all partnership obligations, unless and until he withdraws as a partner, is expelled under Section 601(4)(ii), or is otherwise dissociated under Section 601.

A divorced spouse of a partner who is awarded rights in the partner's partnership interest as part of a property settlement is entitled only to the rights of a transferee. The spouse may instead be granted a money judgment in the amount of the property award, enforceable by a charging order in the same manner as any other money judgment against a partner. In neither case, however, would the spouse become a partner by virtue of the property settlement or succeed to any of the partner's management rights. *See, e.g., Warren v. Warren*, 12 Ark. App. 260, 675 S.W.2d 371 (1984).

5.   Subsection (e) is new and provides that the partnership has no duty to give effect to the transferee's rights until the partnership receives notice of the transfer. This is consistent with UCC Section 9–318(3), which provides that an "account debtor" is authorized to pay the assignor until the account debtor receives notification

that the amount due or to become due has been assigned and that payment is to be made to the assignee. It further provides that the assignee, on request, must furnish reasonable proof of the assignment.

6.   Subsection (f) is new and provides that a transfer of a partner's transferable interest in the partnership in violation of a restriction on transfer contained in a partnership agreement is ineffective as to a person with timely notice of the restriction. Under Section 103(a), the partners may agree among themselves to restrict the right to transfer their partnership interests. Subsection (f) makes explicit that a transfer in violation of such a restriction is ineffective as to a transferee with notice of the restriction. See Section 102(b) for the meaning of "notice." RUPA leaves to general law and the UCC the issue of whether a transfer in violation of a valid restriction is effective as to a transferee without notice of the restriction.

Whether a particular restriction will be enforceable, however, must be considered in light of other law. *See* 11 U.S.C. § 541(c)(1) (property owned by bankrupt passes to trustee regardless of restrictions on transfer); UCC § 9–318(4) (agreement between account debtor and assignor prohibiting creation of security interest in a general intangible or requiring account debtor's consent is ineffective); *Battista v. Carlo*, 57 Misc. 2d 495, 293 N.Y.S.2d 227 (1968) (restriction on transfer of partnership interest subject to rules against unreasonable restraints on alienation of property) (dictum); *Tupper v. Kroc*, 88 Nev. 146, 494 P.2d 1275 (1972) (partnership interest subject to charging order even if partnership agreement prohibits assignments). *Cf. Tu-Vu Drive-In Corp. v. Ashkins*, 61 Cal. 2d 283, 38 Cal. Rptr. 348, 391 P.2d 828 (1964) (restraints on transfer of corporate stock must be reasonable). Even if a restriction on the transfer of a partner's transferable interest in a partnership were held to be unenforceable, the transfer might be grounds for expelling the partner-transferor from the partnership under Section 601(5)(ii).

7.   Other rules that apply in the case of transfers include Section 601(4)(ii) (expulsion of partner who transfers substantially all of partnership interest); Section 601(6) (dissociation of partner who makes an assignment for benefit of creditors); and Section 801(6) (transferee has standing to seek judicial winding up).

§ 504.   Partner's Transferable Interest Subject to Charging Order

(a)   On application by a judgment creditor of a partner or of a partner's transferee, a court having jurisdiction may charge the transferable interest of the judgment debtor to satisfy the judgment. The court may appoint a receiver of the share of the distributions due or to become due to the judgment debtor in respect of the partnership and make all other orders, directions, accounts, and inquiries the judgment debtor might have made or which the circumstances of the case may require.

(b)   A charging order constitutes a lien on the judgment debtor's transferable interest in the partnership. The court may order a foreclosure of the interest subject to the charging order at any time. The purchaser at the foreclosure sale has the rights of a transferee.

(c)   At any time before foreclosure, an interest charged may be redeemed:

(1)   by the judgment debtor;

(2)   with property other than partnership property, by one or more of the other partners; or

(3)   with partnership property, by one or more of the other partners with the consent of all of the partners whose interests are not so charged.

(d)   This [Act] does not deprive a partner of a right under exemption laws with respect to the partner's interest in the partnership.

(e)   This section provides the exclusive remedy by which a judgment creditor of a partner or partner's transferee may satisfy a judgment out of the judgment debtor's transferable interest in the partnership.

COMMENT

1.   Section 504 continues the UPA Section 28 charging order as the proper remedy by which a judgment creditor of a partner may reach the debtor's transferable interest in a partnership to satisfy the judgment. Subsection (a) makes the charging order available to the judgment creditor of a transferee of a partnership interest. Under Section 503(b), the transferable interest of a partner or transferee is limited to the partner's right to receive distributions from the partnership and to seek judicial liquidation of the partnership. The court may appoint a receiver of the debtor's share of the distributions due or to become due and make all other orders that may be required.

2.   Subsection (b) is new and codifies the case law under the UPA holding that a charging order constitutes a lien on the debtor's transferable interest. The lien may be foreclosed by the court at any time, and the purchaser at the foreclosure sale has the Section 503(b) rights of a transferee. For a general discussion of the charging order remedy, see *I Alan R. Bromberg & Larry E. Ribstein, Partnership* (1988), at 3:69.

3.   Subsection (c) continues the UPA Section 28(2) right of the debtor or other partners to redeem the partnership interest before the foreclosure sale. Redemption by the partnership (i.e., with partnership property) requires the consent of all the remaining partners. Neither the UPA nor RUPA provide a statutory procedural framework for the redemption.

4.   Subsection (d) provides that nothing in RUPA deprives a partner of his rights under the State's exemption laws. That is essentially the same as UPA Section 28(3).

5.   Subsection (e) provides that the charging order is the judgment creditor's exclusive remedy. Although the UPA nowhere states that a charging order is the exclusive process for a partner's individual judgment creditor, the courts have generally so interpreted it. *See, e.g., Matter of Pischke,* 11 B.R. 913 (E.D. Va. 1981); *Baum v. Baum,* 51 Cal. 2d 610, 335 P.2d 481 (1959); *Atlantic Mobile Homes, Inc. v. LeFever,* 481 So. 2d 1002 (Fla. App. 1986).

Notwithstanding subsection (e), there may be an exception for the enforcement of family support orders. Some States have unique statutory procedures for the enforcement of support orders. In Florida, for example, a court may issue an "income deduction order" requiring any person or entity providing "income" to the obligor of a support order to remit to the obligee or a depository, as directed by the court, a specified portion of the income. Fla. Stat. § 61.1301 (1993). "Income" is broadly defined to include any form of payment to the obligor, including wages, salary, compensation as an independent contractor, dividends, interest, or other payment, regardless of source. Fla. Stat. § 61.046(4) (1993). That definition includes distributions payable to an obligor partner. A charging order under RUPA would still be necessary to reach the obligor's entire partnership interest, however.

Article 6

PARTNER'S DISSOCIATION

§ 601.   Events Causing Partner's Dissociation

A partner is dissociated from a partnership upon the occurrence of any of the following events:

(1)   the partnership's having notice of the partner's express will to withdraw as a partner or on a later date specified by the partner;

(2)   an event agreed to in the partnership agreement as causing the partner's dissociation;

(3)   the partner's expulsion pursuant to the partnership agreement;

(4)   the partner's expulsion by the unanimous vote of the other partners if:

(i)   it is unlawful to carry on the partnership business with that partner;

(ii)   there has been a transfer of all or substantially all of that partner's transferable interest in the partnership, other than a transfer for security purposes, or a court order charging the partner's interest, which has not been foreclosed;

(iii)   within 90 days after the partnership notifies a corporate partner that it will be expelled because it has filed a certificate of dissolution or the equivalent, its charter has been revoked, or its right to conduct business has been suspended by the jurisdiction of its incorporation, there is no revocation of the certificate of dissolution or no reinstatement of its charter or its right to conduct business; or

(iv)   a partnership that is a partner has been dissolved and its business is being wound up;

(5)   on application by the partnership or another partner, the partner's expulsion by judicial determination because:

(i)   the partner engaged in wrongful conduct that adversely and materially affected the partnership business;

(ii) the partner willfully or persistently committed a material breach of the partnership agreement or of a duty owed to the partnership or the other partners under Section 404; or

(iii) the partner engaged in conduct relating to the partnership business which makes it not reasonably practicable to carry on the business in partnership with the partner;

(6) the partner's:

(i) becoming a debtor in bankruptcy;

(ii) executing an assignment for the benefit of creditors;

(iii) seeking, consenting to, or acquiescing in the appointment of a trustee, receiver, or liquidator of that partner or of all or substantially all of that partner's property; or

(iv) failing, within 90 days after the appointment, to have vacated or stayed the appointment of a trustee, receiver, or liquidator of the partner or of all or substantially all of the partner's property obtained without the partner's consent or acquiescence, or failing within 90 days after the expiration of a stay to have the appointment vacated;

(7) in the case of a partner who is an individual:

(i) the partner's death;

(ii) the appointment of a guardian or general conservator for the partner; or

(iii) a judicial determination that the partner has otherwise become incapable of performing the partner's duties under the partnership agreement;

(8) in the case of a partner that is a trust or is acting as a partner by virtue of being a trustee of a trust, distribution of the trust's entire transferable interest in the partnership, but not merely by reason of the substitution of a successor trustee;

(9) in the case of a partner that is an estate or is acting as a partner by virtue of being a personal representative of an estate, distribution of the estate's entire transferable interest in the partnership, but not merely by reason of the substitution of a successor personal representative; or

(10) termination of a partner who is not an individual, partnership, corporation, trust, or estate.

COMMENT

1. RUPA dramatically changes the law governing partnership breakups and dissolution. An entirely new concept, "dissociation," is used in lieu of the UPA term "dissolution" to denote the change in the relationship caused by a partner's ceasing to be associated in the carrying on of the business. "Dissolution" is retained but with a different meaning. See Section 802. The entity theory of partnership provides a conceptual basis for continuing the firm itself despite a partner's withdrawal from the firm.

Under RUPA, unlike the UPA, the dissociation of a partner does not necessarily cause a dissolution and winding up of the business of the partnership. Section 801 identifies the situations in which the dissociation of a partner causes a winding up of the business. Section 701 provides that in all other situations there is a buyout of the partner's interest in the partnership, rather than a windup of the partnership business. In those other situations, the partnership entity continues, unaffected by the partner's dissociation.

A dissociated partner remains a partner for some purposes and still has some residual rights, duties, powers, and liabilities. Although Section 601 determines when a partner is dissociated from the partnership, the consequences of the partner's dissociation do not all occur at the same time. Thus, it is more useful to think of a dissociated partner as a partner for some purposes, but as a former partner for others. For example, see Section 403(b) (former partner's access to partnership books and records). The consequences of a partner's dissociation depend on whether the partnership continues or is wound up, as provided in Articles 6, 7, and 8.

Section 601 enumerates all of the events that cause a partner's dissociation. Section 601 is similar in approach to RULPA Section 402, which lists the events resulting in a general partner's withdrawal from a limited partnership.

2. Section 601(1) provides that a partner is dissociated when the partnership has notice of the partner's express will to withdraw as a partner, unless a later date is specified by the partner. If a future date is specified

by the partner, other partners may dissociate before that date; specifying a future date does not bind the others to remain as partners until that date. See also Section 801(2)(i).

Section 602(a) provides that a partner has the power to withdraw at any time. The power to withdraw is immutable under Section 103(b)(6), with the exception that the partners may agree the notice must be in writing. This continues the present rule that a partner has the power to withdraw at will, even if not the right. See UPA Section 31(2). Since no writing is required to create a partner relationship, it was felt unnecessarily formalistic, and a trap for the unwary, to require a writing to end one. If a written notification is given, Section 102(d) clarifies when it is deemed received.

RUPA continues the UPA "express will" concept, thus preserving existing case law. Section 601(1) clarifies existing law by providing that the partnership must have notice of the partner's expression of will before the dissociation is effective. See Section 102(b) for the meaning of "notice."

3.   Section 601(2) provides expressly that a partner is dissociated upon an event agreed to in the partnership agreement as causing dissociation. There is no such provision in the UPA, but that result has been assumed.

4.   Section 601(3) provides that a partner may be expelled by the other partners pursuant to a power of expulsion contained in the partnership agreement. That continues the basic rule of UPA Section 31(1)(d). The expulsion can be with or without cause. As under existing law, the obligation of good faith under Section 404(d) does not require prior notice, specification of cause, or an opportunity to be heard. *See Holman v. Coie*, 11 Wash. App. 195, 522 P.2d 515, *cert. denied*, 420 U.S. 984 (1974).

5.   Section 601(4) empowers the partners, by unanimous vote, to expel a partner for specified causes, even if not authorized in the partnership agreement. This changes the UPA Section 31(1)(d) rule that authorizes expulsion only if provided in the partnership agreement. A partner may be expelled from a term partnership, as well as from a partnership at will. Under Section 103(a), the partnership agreement may change or abolish the partners' power of expulsion.

Subsection (4)(i) is derived from UPA Section 31(3). A partner may be expelled if it is unlawful to carry on the business with that partner. Section 801(4), on the other hand, provides that the partnership itself is dissolved and must be wound up if substantially all of the business is unlawful.

Subsection (4)(ii) provides that a partner may be expelled for transferring substantially all of his transferable interest in the partnership, other than as security for a loan. (He may, however, be expelled upon foreclosure.) This rule is derived from UPA Section 31(1)(c). To avoid the presence of an unwelcome transferee, the remaining partners may dissolve the partnership under Section 801(2)(ii), after first expelling the transferor partner. A transfer of a partner's entire interest may, in some circumstances, evidence the transferor's intention to withdraw under Section 601(1).

Subsection (4)(iii) provides for the expulsion of a corporate partner if it has filed a certificate of dissolution, its charter has been revoked, or its right to conduct business has been suspended, unless cured within 90 days after notice. This provision is derived from RULPA Section 402(9). The cure proviso is important because charter revocation is very common in some States and partner status should not end merely because of a technical noncompliance with corporate law that can easily be cured. Withdrawal of a voluntarily filed notice of dissolution constitutes a cure.

Subsection (4)(iv) is the partnership analogue of paragraph (iii) and is suggested by RULPA Section 402(8). It provides that a partnership that is a partner may be expelled if it has been dissolved and its business is being wound up. It is intended that the right of expulsion not be triggered solely by the dissolution event, but only upon commencement of the liquidation process.

6.   Section 601(5) empowers a court to expel a partner if it determines that the partner has engaged in specified misconduct. The enumerated grounds for judicial expulsion are based on the UPA Section 32(1) grounds for judicial dissolution. The application for expulsion may be brought by the partnership or any partner. The phrase "judicial determination" is intended to include an arbitration award, as well as any final court order or decree.

Subsection (5)(i) provides for the partner's expulsion if the court finds that the partner has engaged in wrongful conduct that adversely and materially affected the partnership business. That language is derived from UPA Section 32(1)(c).

Subsection (5)(ii) provides for expulsion if the court determines that the partner willfully or persistently committed a material breach of the partnership agreement or of a duty owed to the partnership or to the other partners under Section 404. That would include a partner's breach of fiduciary duty. Paragraph (ii), together with paragraph (iii), carry forward the substance of UPA Section 32(1)(d).

Subsection (5)(iii) provides for judicial expulsion of a partner who engaged in conduct relating to the partnership business that makes it not reasonably practicable to carry on the business in partnership with that partner. Expulsion for such misconduct makes the partner's dissociation wrongful under Section 602(a)(ii) and may also support a judicial decree of dissolution under Section 801(5)(ii).

7.   Section 601(6) provides that a partner is dissociated upon becoming a debtor in bankruptcy or upon taking or suffering other action evidencing the partner's insolvency or lack of financial responsibility.

Subsection (6)(i) is derived from UPA Section 31(5), which provides for dissolution upon a partner's bankruptcy. *Accord* RULPA § 402(4)(ii). There is some doubt as to whether UPA Section 31(1) is limited to so-called "straight bankruptcy" under Chapter 7 or includes other bankruptcy relief, such as Chapter 11. Under RUPA Section 101(2), however, "debtor in bankruptcy" includes a person who files a voluntary petition, or against whom relief is ordered in an involuntary case, under any chapter of the Bankruptcy Code.

Initially, upon the filing of the bankruptcy petition, the debtor partner's transferable interest in the partnership will pass to the bankruptcy trustee as property of the estate under Section 541(a)(1) of the Bankruptcy Code, notwithstanding any restrictions on transfer provided in the partnership agreement. In most Chapter 7 cases, that will result in the eventual buyout of the partner's interest.

The application of various provisions of the federal Bankruptcy Code to Section 601(6)(i) is unclear. In particular, there is uncertainty as to the validity of UPA Section 31(5), and thus its RUPA counterpart, under Sections 365(e) and 541(c)(1) of the Bankruptcy Code. Those sections generally invalidate so-called *ipso facto* laws that cause a termination or modification of the debtor's contract or property rights because of the bankruptcy filing. As a consequence, RUPA Section 601(6)(i), which provides for a partner's dissociation by operation of law upon becoming a debtor in bankruptcy, may be invalid under the Supremacy Clause. *See, e.g., In the Matter of Phillips*, 966 F.2d 926 (5th Cir. 1992); *In re Cardinal Industries, Inc.*, 105 B.R. 385 (Bankr. S.D. Ohio 1989), 116 B.R. 964 (Bankr. S.D. Ohio 1990); *In re Corky Foods Corp.*, 85 B.R. 903 (Bankr. S.D. Fla. 1988). *But see, In re Catron*, 158 B.R. 629 (E.D. Va. 1993) (partnership agreement could not be assumed by debtor under Bankruptcy Code § 365(c)(1) because other partners excused by UPA from accepting performance by or rendering performance to party other than debtor and buyout option not invalid *ipso facto* clause under Code § 365 (e)), *aff'd per curiam*, 25 F.3d 1038 (4th Cir. 1994). RUPA reflects the policy choice, as a matter of state partnership law, that a partner be dissociated upon becoming a debtor in bankruptcy.

Subsection (6)(ii) is new and provides for dissociation upon a general assignment for the benefit of a partner's creditors. The UPA says nothing about an assignment for the benefit of creditors or the appointment of a trustee, receiver, or liquidator. Subsection (6)(iii) and (iv) cover the latter and are based substantially on RULPA Section 402(4) and (5).

8.   UPA Section 31(4) provides for the dissolution of a partnership upon the death of any partner, although by agreement the remaining partners may continue the partnership business. RUPA Section 601(7)(i), on the other hand, provides for dissociation upon the death of a partner who is an individual, rather than dissolution of the partnership. That changes existing law, except in those States previously adopting a similar non-uniform provision, such as California, Georgia, and Texas. Normally, under RUPA, the deceased partner's transferable interest in the partnership will pass to his estate and be bought out under Article 7.

Section 601(7)(ii) replaces UPA Section 32(1)(a) and provides for dissociation upon the appointment of a guardian or general conservator for partner who is an individual. The appointment itself operates as the event of dissociation, and no further order of the court is necessary.

Section 601(7)(iii) is based on UPA Section 32(1)(b) and provides for dissociation upon a judicial determination that an individual partner has in any other way become incapable of performing his duties under the partnership agreement. The intent is to include physical incapacity.

9.   Section 601(8) is new and provides for the dissociation of a partner that is a trust, or is acting as a partner by virtue of being a trustee of a trust, upon the distribution by the trust of its entire transferable interest in the partnership, but not merely upon the substitution of a successor trustee. The provision is inspired by RULPA Section 402(7).

10.   Section 601(9) is new and provides for the dissociation of a partner that is an estate, or is acting as a partner by virtue of being a personal representative of an estate, upon the distribution of the estate's entire transferable interest in the partnership, but not merely the substitution of a successor personal representative. It

is based on RULPA Section 402(10). Under Section 601(7), a partner is dissociated upon death, however, and the estate normally becomes a transferee, not a partner.

11.   Section 601(10) is new and provides that a partner that is not an individual, partnership, corporation, trust, or estate is dissociated upon its termination. It is the comparable "death" analogue for other types of entity partners, such as a limited liability company.

§ 602.   Partner's Power to Dissociate; Wrongful Dissociation

(a)   A partner has the power to dissociate at any time, rightfully or wrongfully, by express will pursuant to Section 601(1).

(b)   A partner's dissociation is wrongful only if:

     (1)   it is in breach of an express provision of the partnership agreement; or

     (2)   in the case of a partnership for a definite term or particular undertaking, before the expiration of the term or the completion of the undertaking:

         (i)   the partner withdraws by express will, unless the withdrawal follows within 90 days after another partner's dissociation by death or otherwise under Section 601(6) through (10) or wrongful dissociation under this subsection;

         (ii)   the partner is expelled by judicial determination under Section 601(5);

         (iii)   the partner is dissociated by becoming a debtor in bankruptcy; or

         (iv)   in the case of a partner who is not an individual, trust other than a business trust, or estate, the partner is expelled or otherwise dissociated because it willfully dissolved or terminated.

(c)   A partner who wrongfully dissociates is liable to the partnership and to the other partners for damages caused by the dissociation. The liability is in addition to any other obligation of the partner to the partnership or to the other partners.

COMMENT

1.   Subsection (a) states explicitly what is implicit in UPA Section 31(2) and RUPA Section 601(1)—that a partner has the power to dissociate at any time by expressing a will to withdraw, even in contravention of the partnership agreement. The phrase "rightfully or wrongfully" reflects the distinction between a partner's power to withdraw in contravention of the partnership agreement and a partner's right to do so. In this context, although a partner can not be enjoined from exercising the power to dissociate, the dissociation may be wrongful under subsection (b).

2.   Subsection (b) provides that a partner's dissociation is wrongful only if it results from one of the enumerated events. The significance of a wrongful dissociation is that it may give rise to damages under subsection (c) and, if it results in the dissolution of the partnership, the wrongfully dissociating partner is not entitled to participate in winding up the business under Section 804.

Under subsection (b), a partner's dissociation is wrongful if (1) it breaches an express provision of the partnership agreement or (2), in a term partnership, before the expiration of the term or the completion of the undertaking (i) the partner voluntarily withdraws by express will, except a withdrawal following another partner's wrongful dissociation or dissociation by death or otherwise under Section 601(6) through (10); (ii) the partner is expelled for misconduct under Section 601(5); (iii) the partner becomes a debtor in bankruptcy (see Section 101(2)); or (iv) a partner that is an entity (other than a trust or estate) is expelled or otherwise dissociated because its dissolution or termination was willful. Since subsection (b) is merely a default rule, the partnership agreement may eliminate or expand the dissociations that are wrongful or modify the effects of wrongful dissociation.

The exception in subsection (b)(2)(i) is intended to protect a partner's reactive withdrawal from a term partnership after the premature departure of another partner, such as the partnership's rainmaker or main supplier of capital, under the same circumstances that may result in the dissolution of the partnership under Section 801(2)(i). Under that section, a term partnership is dissolved 90 days after the bankruptcy, incapacity, death (or similar dissociation of a partner that is an entity), or wrongful dissociation of any partner, unless a majority in interest (see Comment 5(i) to Section 801 for a discussion of the term "majority in interest") of the remaining partners agree to continue the partnership. Under Section 602(b)(2)(i), a partner's exercise of the right of withdrawal by express will under those circumstances is rendered "rightful," even if the partnership is continued by others, and does not expose the withdrawing partner to damages for wrongful dissociation under Section 602(c).

A partner wishing to withdraw prematurely from a term partnership for any other reason, such as another partner's misconduct, can avoid being treated as a wrongfully dissociating partner by applying to a court under Section 601(5)(iii) to have the offending partner expelled. Then, the partnership could be dissolved under Section 801(2)(i) or the remaining partners could, by unanimous vote, dissolve the partnership under Section 801(2)(ii).

3.   Subsection (c) provides that a wrongfully dissociating partner is liable to the partnership and to the other partners for any damages caused by the wrongful nature of the dissociation. That liability is in addition to any other obligation of the partner to the partnership or to the other partners. For example, the partner would be liable for any damage caused by breach of the partnership agreement or other misconduct. The partnership might also incur substantial expenses resulting from a partner's premature withdrawal from a term partnership, such as replacing the partner's expertise or obtaining new financing. The wrongfully dissociating partner would be liable to the partnership for those and all other expenses and damages that are causally related to the wrongful dissociation.

Section 701(c) provides that any damages for wrongful dissociation may be offset against the amount of the buyout price due to the partner under Section 701(a), and Section 701(h) provides that a partner who wrongfully dissociates from a term partnership is not entitled to payment of the buyout price until the term expires.

Under UPA Section 38(2)(c)(II), in addition to an offset for damages, the goodwill value of the partnership is excluded in determining the value of a wrongfully dissociating partner's partnership interest. Under RUPA, however, unless the partnership's goodwill is damaged by the wrongful dissociation, the value of the wrongfully dissociating partner's interest will include any goodwill value of the partnership. If the firm's goodwill is damaged, the amount of the damages suffered by the partnership and the remaining partners will be offset against the buyout price. See Section 701 and Comments.

§ 603.   Effect of Partner's Dissociation

(a)   If a partner's dissociation results in a dissolution and winding up of the partnership business, Article 8 applies; otherwise, Article 7 applies.

(b)   Upon a partner's dissociation:

(1)   the partner's right to participate in the management and conduct of the partnership business terminates, except as otherwise provided in Section 803;

(2)   the partner's duty of loyalty under Section 404(b)(3) terminates; and

(3)   the partner's duty of loyalty under Section 404(b)(1) and (2) and duty of care under Section 404(c) continue only with regard to matters arising and events occurring before the partner's dissociation, unless the partner participates in winding up the partnership's business pursuant to Section 803.

COMMENT

1.   Section 603(a) is a "switching" provision. It provides that, after a partner's dissociation, the partner's interest in the partnership must be purchased pursuant to the buyout rules in Article 7 unless there is a dissolution and winding up of the partnership business under Article 8. Thus, a partner's dissociation will always result in either a buyout of the dissociated partner's interest or a dissolution and winding up of the business.

By contrast, under the UPA, every partner dissociation results in the dissolution of the partnership, most of which trigger a right to have the business wound up unless the partnership agreement provides otherwise. *See* UPA § 38. The only exception in which the remaining partners have a statutory right to continue the business is when a partner wrongfully dissolves the partnership in breach of the partnership agreement. *See* UPA § 38(2)(b).

2.   Section 603(b) is new and deals with some of the internal effects of a partner's dissociation. Subsection (b)(1) makes it clear that one of the consequences of a partner's dissociation is the immediate loss of the right to participate in the management of the business, unless it results in a dissolution and winding up of the business. In that case, Section 804(a) provides that all of the partners who have not wrongfully dissociated may participate in winding up the business.

Subsection (b)(2) and (3) clarify a partner's fiduciary duties upon dissociation. No change from current law is intended. With respect to the duty of loyalty, the Section 404(b)(3) duty not to compete terminates upon dissociation, and the dissociated partner is free immediately to engage in a competitive business, without any further consent. With respect to the partner's remaining loyalty duties under Section 404(b) and duty of care under Section 404(c), a withdrawing partner has a continuing duty after dissociation, but it is limited to matters that arose or events that occurred before the partner dissociated. For example, a partner who leaves a brokerage firm may immediately compete with the firm for new clients, but must exercise care in completing on-going client transactions and must account to the firm for any fees received from the old clients on account of those transactions. As the last clause makes clear, there is no contraction of a dissociated partner's duties under subsection (b)(3) if the partner thereafter participates in the dissolution and winding up the partnership's business.

Article 7

PARTNER'S DISSOCIATION WHEN BUSINESS NOT WOUND UP

§ 701.   Purchase of Dissociated Partner's Interest

(a)   If a partner is dissociated from a partnership without resulting in a dissolution and winding up of the partnership business under Section 801, the partnership shall cause the dissociated partner's interest in the partnership to be purchased for a buyout price determined pursuant to subsection (b).

(b)   The buyout price of a dissociated partner's interest is the amount that would have been distributable to the dissociating partner under Section 807(b) if, on the date of dissociation, the assets of the partnership were sold at a price equal to the greater of the liquidation value or the value based on a sale of the entire business as a going concern without the dissociated partner and the partnership were wound up as of that date. Interest must be paid from the date of dissociation to the date of payment.

(c)   Damages for wrongful dissociation under Section 602(b), and all other amounts owing, whether or not presently due, from the dissociated partner to the partnership, must be offset against the buyout price. Interest must be paid from the date the amount owed becomes due to the date of payment.

(d)   A partnership shall indemnify a dissociated partner whose interest is being purchased against all partnership liabilities, whether incurred before or after the dissociation, except liabilities incurred by an act of the dissociated partner under Section 702.

(e)   If no agreement for the purchase of a dissociated partner's interest is reached within 120 days after a written demand for payment, the partnership shall pay, or cause to be paid, in cash to the dissociated partner the amount the partnership estimates to be the buyout price and accrued interest, reduced by any offsets and accrued interest under subsection (c).

(f)   If a deferred payment is authorized under subsection (h), the partnership may tender a written offer to pay the amount it estimates to be the buyout price and accrued interest, reduced by any offsets under subsection (c), stating the time of payment, the amount and type of security for payment, and the other terms and conditions of the obligation.

(g)   The payment or tender required by subsection (e) or (f) must be accompanied by the following:

(1)   a statement of partnership assets and liabilities as of the date of dissociation;

(2)   the latest available partnership balance sheet and income statement, if any;

(3)   an explanation of how the estimated amount of the payment was calculated; and

(4)   written notice that the payment is in full satisfaction of the obligation to purchase unless, within 120 days after the written notice, the dissociated partner commences an action to determine the buyout price, any offsets under subsection (c), or other terms of the obligation to purchase.

(h)   A partner who wrongfully dissociates before the expiration of a definite term or the completion of a particular undertaking is not entitled to payment of any portion of the buyout price until the expiration of the term or completion of the undertaking, unless the partner establishes to the satisfaction of the court that earlier payment will not cause undue hardship to the business of the partnership. A deferred payment must be adequately secured and bear interest.

(i) A dissociated partner may maintain an action against the partnership, pursuant to Section 405(b)(2)(ii), to determine the buyout price of that partner's interest, any offsets under subsection (c), or other terms of the obligation to purchase. The action must be commenced within 120 days after the partnership has tendered payment or an offer to pay or within one year after written demand for payment if no payment or offer to pay is tendered. The court shall determine the buyout price of the dissociated partner's interest, any offset due under subsection (c), and accrued interest, and enter judgment for any additional payment or refund. If deferred payment is authorized under subsection (h), the court shall also determine the security for payment and other terms of the obligation to purchase. The court may assess reasonable attorney's fees and the fees and expenses of appraisers or other experts for a party to the action, in amounts the court finds equitable, against a party that the court finds acted arbitrarily, vexatiously, or not in good faith. The finding may be based on the partnership's failure to tender payment or an offer to pay or to comply with subsection (g).

COMMENT

1. Article 7 is new and provides for the buyout of a dissociated partner's interest in the partnership when the partner's dissociation does not result in a dissolution and winding up of its business under Article 8. *See* Section 603(a). If there is no dissolution, the remaining partners have a right to continue the business and the dissociated partner has a right to be paid the value of his partnership interest. These rights can, of course, be varied in the partnership agreement. *See* Section 103. A dissociated partner has a continuing relationship with the partnership and third parties as provided in Sections 603(b), 702, and 703. See also Section 403(b) (former partner's access to partnership books and records).

2. Subsection (a) provides that, if a partner's dissociation does not result in a windup of the business, the partnership shall cause the interest of the dissociating partner to be purchased for a buyout price determined pursuant to subsection (b). The buyout is mandatory. The "cause to be purchased" language is intended to accommodate a purchase by the partnership, one or more of the remaining partners, or a third party.

For federal income tax purposes, a payment to a partner for his interest can be characterized either as a purchase of the partner's interest or as a liquidating distribution. The two have different tax consequences. RUPA permits either option by providing that the payment may come from either the partnership, some or all of the continuing partners, or a third party purchaser.

3. Subsection (b) provides how the "buyout price" is to be determined. The terms "fair market value" or "fair value" were not used because they are often considered terms of art having a special meaning depending on the context, such as in tax or corporate law. "Buyout price" is a new term. It is intended that the term be developed as an independent concept appropriate to the partnership buyout situation, while drawing on valuation principles developed elsewhere.

Under subsection (b), the buyout price is the amount that would have been distributable to the dissociating partner under Section 807(b) if, on the date of dissociation, the assets of the partnership were sold at a price equal to the greater of liquidation value or going concern value without the departing partner. Liquidation value is not intended to mean distress sale value. Under general principles of valuation, the hypothetical selling price in either case should be the price that a willing and informed buyer would pay a willing and informed seller, with neither being under any compulsion to deal. The notion of a minority discount in determining the buyout price is negated by valuing the business as a going concern. Other discounts, such as for a lack of marketability or the loss of a key partner, may be appropriate, however.

Since the buyout price is based on the value of the business at the time of dissociation, the partnership must pay interest on the amount due from the date of dissociation until payment to compensate the dissociating partner for the use of his interest in the firm. Section 104(b) provides that interest shall be at the legal rate unless otherwise provided in the partnership agreement. The UPA Section 42 option of electing a share of the profits in lieu of interest has been eliminated.

UPA Section 38(2)(c)(II) provides that the good will of the business not be considered in valuing a wrongfully dissociating partner's interest. The forfeiture of good will rule is implicitly rejected by RUPA. See Section 602(c) and Comment 3.

The Section 701 rules are merely default rules. The partners may, in the partnership agreement, fix the method or formula for determining the buyout price and all of the other terms and conditions of the buyout right.

Indeed, the very right to a buyout itself may be modified, although a provision providing for a complete forfeiture would probably not be enforceable. *See* Section 104(a).

4.   Subsection (c) provides that the partnership may offset against the buyout price all amounts owing by the dissociated partner to the partnership, whether or not presently due, including any damages for wrongful dissociation under Section 602(c). This has the effect of accelerating payment of amounts not yet due from the departing partner to the partnership, including a long-term loan by the partnership to the dissociated partner. Where appropriate, the amounts not yet due should be discounted to present value. A dissociating partner, on the other hand, is not entitled to an add-on for amounts owing to him by the partnership. Thus, a departing partner who has made a long-term loan to the partnership must wait for repayment, unless the terms of the loan agreement provide for acceleration upon dissociation.

It is not intended that the partnership's right of setoff be construed to limit the amount of the damages for the partner's wrongful dissociation and any other amounts owing to the partnership to the value of the dissociated partner's interest. Those amounts may result in a net sum due to the partnership from the dissociated partner.

5.   Subsection (d) follows the UPA Section 38 rule and provides that the partnership must indemnify a dissociated partner against all partnership liabilities, whether incurred before or after the dissociation, except those incurred by the dissociated partner under Section 702.

6.   Subsection (e) provides that, if no agreement for the purchase of the dissociated partner's interest is reached within 120 days after the dissociated partner's written demand for payment, the partnership must pay, or cause to be paid, in cash the amount it estimates to be the buyout price, adjusted for any offsets allowed and accrued interest. Thus, the dissociating partner will receive in cash within 120 days of dissociation the undisputed minimum value of the partner's partnership interest. If the dissociated partner claims that the buyout price should be higher, suit may thereafter be brought as provided in subsection (i) to have the amount of the buyout price determined by the court. This is similar to the procedure for determining the value of dissenting shareholders' shares under RMBCA Sections 13.20–13.28.

The "cause to be paid" language of subsection (a) is repeated here to permit either the partnership, one or more of the continuing partners, or a third-party purchaser to tender payment of the estimated amount due.

7.   Subsection (f) provides that, when deferred payment is authorized in the case of a wrongfully dissociating partner, a written offer stating the amount the partnership estimates to be the purchase price should be tendered within the 120-day period, even though actual payment of the amount may be deferred, possibly for many years. See Comment 8. The dissociated partner is entitled to know at the time of dissociation what amount the remaining partners think is due, including the estimated amount of any damages allegedly caused by the partner's wrongful dissociation that may be offset against the buyout price.

8.   Subsection (g) provides that the payment of the estimated price (or tender of a written offer under subsection (f)) by the partnership must be accompanied by (1) a statement of the partnership's assets and liabilities as of the date of the partner's dissociation; (2) the latest available balance sheet and income statement, if the partnership maintains such financial statements; (3) an explanation of how the estimated amount of the payment was calculated; and (4) a written notice that the payment will be in full satisfaction of the partnership's buyout obligation unless the dissociated partner commences an action to determine the price within 120 days of the notice. Subsection (g) is based in part on the dissenters' rights provisions of RMBCA Section 13.25(b).

Those disclosures should serve to identify and narrow substantially the items of dispute between the dissociated partner and the partnership over the valuation of the partnership interest. They will also serve to pin down the parties as to their claims of partnership assets and values and as to the existence and amount of all known liabilities. See Comment 4. Lastly, it will force the remaining partners to consider thoughtfully the difficult and important questions as to the appropriate method of valuation under the circumstances, and in particular, whether they should use going concern or liquidation value. Simply getting that information on the record in a timely fashion should increase the likelihood of a negotiated resolution of the parties' differences during the 120-day period within which the dissociated partner must bring suit.

9.   Subsection (h) replaces UPA Section 38(2)(c) and provides a somewhat different rule for payment to a partner whose dissociation before the expiration of a definite term or the completion of a particular undertaking is wrongful under Section 602(b). Under subsection (h), a wrongfully dissociating partner is not entitled to receive any portion of the buyout price before the expiration of the term or completion of the undertaking, unless the dissociated partner establishes to the satisfaction of the court that earlier payment will not cause undue hardship to the business of the partnership. In all other cases, there must be an immediate payment in cash.

10.   Subsection (i) provides that a dissociated partner may maintain an action against the partnership to determine the buyout price, any offsets, or other terms of the purchase obligation. The action must be commenced within 120 days after the partnership tenders payment of the amount it estimates to be due or, if deferred payment is authorized, its written offer. This provision creates a 120-day "cooling off" period. It also allows the parties an opportunity to negotiate their differences after disclosure by the partnership of its financial statements and other required information.

If the partnership fails to tender payment of the estimated amount due (or a written offer, if deferred payment is authorized), the dissociated partner has one year after written demand for payment in which to commence suit.

If the parties fail to reach agreement, the court must determine the buyout price of the partner's interest, any offsets, including damages for wrongful dissociation, and the amount of interest accrued. If payment to a wrongfully dissociated partner is deferred, the court may also require security for payment and determine the other terms of the obligation.

Under subsection (i), attorney's fees and other costs may be assessed against any party found to have acted arbitrarily, vexatiously, or not in good faith in connection with the valuation dispute, including the partnership's failure to tender payment of the estimated price or to make the required disclosures. This provision is based in part on RMBCA Section 13.31(b).

§ 702.   Dissociated Partner's Power to Bind and Liability to Partnership

(a)   For two years after a partner dissociates without resulting in a dissolution and winding up of the partnership business, the partnership, including a surviving partnership under Article 9, is bound by an act of the dissociated partner which would have bound the partnership under Section 301 before dissociation only if at the time of entering into the transaction the other party:

(1)   reasonably believed that the dissociated partner was then a partner;

(2)   did not have notice of the partner's dissociation; and

(3)   is not deemed to have had knowledge under Section 303(e) or notice under Section 704(c).

(b)   A dissociated partner is liable to the partnership for any damage caused to the partnership arising from an obligation incurred by the dissociated partner after dissociation for which the partnership is liable under subsection (a).

COMMENT

1.   Section 702 deals with a dissociated partner's lingering apparent authority to bind the partnership in ordinary course partnership transactions and the partner's liability to the partnership for any loss caused thereby. It also applies to partners who withdraw incident to a merger under Article 9. *See* Section 906(e).

A dissociated partner has no actual authority to act for the partnership. *See* Section 603(b)(1). Nevertheless, in order to protect innocent third parties, Section 702(a) provides that the partnership remains bound, for two years after a partner's dissociation, by that partner's acts that would, before his dissociation, have bound the partnership under Section 301 if, and only if, the other party to the transaction reasonably believed that he was still a partner, did not have notice of the partner's dissociation, and is not deemed to have had knowledge of the dissociation under Section 303(e) or notice thereof under Section 704(c).

Under Section 301, every partner has apparent authority to bind the partnership by any act for carrying on the partnership business in the ordinary course, unless the other party knows that the partner has no actual authority to act for the partnership or has received a notification of the partner's lack of authority. Section 702(a) continues that general rule for two years after a partner's dissociation, subject to three modifications.

After a partner's dissociation, the general rule is modified, first, by requiring the other party to show reasonable reliance on the partner's status as a partner. Section 301 has no explicit reliance requirement, although the partnership is bound only if the partner purports to act on its behalf. Thus, the other party will normally be aware of the partnership and presumably the partner's status as such.

The second modification is that, under Section 702(a), the partnership is not bound if the third party has notice of the partner's dissociation, while under the general rule of Section 301 the partnership is bound unless the third party knows of the partner's lack of authority. Under Section 102(b), a person has "notice" of a fact if he knows or has reason to know it exists from all the facts that are known to him or he has received a notification of it. Thus, the partnership may protect itself by sending a notification of the dissociation to a third party, and a third party may, in any event, have a duty to inquire further based on what is known. That provides the partnership with greater protection from the unauthorized acts of a dissociated partner than from those of partners generally.

The third modification of the general apparent authority rule under Section 702(a) involves the effect of a statement of dissociation. Section 704(c) provides that, for the purposes of Sections 702(a)(3) and 703(b)(3), third parties are deemed to have notice of a partner's dissociation 90 days after the filing of a statement of dissociation. Thus, the filing of a statement operates as constructive notice of the dissociated partner's lack of authority after 90 days, conclusively terminating the dissociated partner's Section 702 apparent authority.

With respect to a dissociated partner's authority to transfer partnership real property, Section 303(e) provides that third parties are deemed to have knowledge of a limitation on a partner's authority to transfer real property held in the partnership name upon the proper recording of a statement containing such a limitation. Section 704(b) provides that a statement of dissociation operates as a limitation on the dissociated partner's authority for the purposes of Section 303(e). Thus, a properly recorded statement of dissociation operates as constructive knowledge of a dissociated partner's lack of authority to transfer real property held in the partnership name, effective immediately upon recording.

Under RUPA, therefore, a partnership should notify all known creditors of a partner's dissociation and may, by filing a statement of dissociation, conclusively limit to 90 days a dissociated partner's lingering agency power. Moreover, under Section 703(b), a dissociated partner's lingering liability for post-dissociation partnership liabilities may be limited to 90 days by filing a statement of dissociation. These incentives should encourage both partnerships and dissociating partners to file statements routinely. Those transacting substantial business with partnerships can protect themselves from the risk of dealing with dissociated partners, or relying on their credit, by checking the partnership records at least every 90 days.

2.   Section 702(b) is a corollary to subsection (a) and provides that a dissociated partner is liable to the partnership for any loss resulting from an obligation improperly incurred by the partner under subsection (a). In effect, the dissociated partner must indemnify the partnership for any loss, meaning a loss net of any gain from the transaction. The dissociated partner is also personally liable to the third party for the unauthorized obligation.

§ 703.   Dissociated Partner's Liability to Other Persons

(a)   A partner's dissociation does not of itself discharge the partner's liability for a partnership obligation incurred before dissociation. A dissociated partner is not liable for a partnership obligation incurred after dissociation, except as otherwise provided in subsection (b).

(b)   A partner who dissociates without resulting in a dissolution and winding up of the partnership business is liable as a partner to the other party in a transaction entered into by the partnership, or a surviving partnership under Article 9, within two years after the partner's dissociation, only if the partner is liable for the obligation under Section 306 and at the time of entering into the transaction the other party:

(1)   reasonably believed that the dissociated partner was then a partner;

(2)   did not have notice of the partner's dissociation; and

(3)   is not deemed to have had knowledge under Section 303(e) or notice under Section 704(c).

(c)   By agreement with the partnership creditor and the partners continuing the business, a dissociated partner may be released from liability for a partnership obligation.

(d)   A dissociated partner is released from liability for a partnership obligation if a partnership creditor, with notice of the partner's dissociation but without the partner's consent, agrees to a material alteration in the nature or time of payment of a partnership obligation.

COMMENT

Section 703(a) is based on UPA Section 36(1) and continues the basic rule that the departure of a partner does not of itself discharge the partner's liability to third parties for any partnership obligation incurred before dissociation. The word "obligation" is used instead of "liability" and is intended to include broadly both tort and contract liability incurred before dissociation. The second sentence states affirmatively that a dissociating partner is not liable for any partnership obligation incurred after dissociation except as expressly provided in subsection (b).

Section 703(b) is new and deals with the problem of protecting third parties who extend credit to the partnership after a partner's dissociation, believing that he is still a partner. It provides that the dissociated partner remains liable as a partner for transactions entered into by the partnership within two years after departure, if the other party does not have notice of the partner's dissociation and reasonably believes when entering the transaction that the dissociated partner is still a partner. The dissociated partner is not personally liable, however, if the other party is deemed to know of the dissociation under Section 303(e) or to have notice thereof under Section 704(c). Also, a dissociated partner is not personally liable for limited liability partnership obligations for which the partner is not personally liable under Section 306.

Section 703(b) operates similarly to Section 702(a) in that it requires reliance on the departed partner's continued partnership status, as well as lack of notice. Under Section 704(c), a statement of dissociation operates conclusively as constructive notice 90 days after filing for the purposes of Section 703(b)(3) and, under Section 704(b), as constructive knowledge when recorded for the purposes of Section 303(d) and (e).

Section 703(c) continues the rule of UPA Section 36(2) that a departing partner can bargain for a contractual release from personal liability for a partnership obligation, but it requires the consent of both the creditor and the remaining partners.

Section 703(d) continues the rule of UPA Section 36(3) that a dissociated partner is released from liability for a partnership obligation if the creditor, with notice of the partner's departure, agrees to a material alteration in the nature or time of payment, without that partner's consent. This rule covers all partner dissociations and is not limited, as is the UPA rule, to situations in which a third party "agrees to assume the existing obligations of a dissolved partnership."

In general under RUPA, as a result of the adoption of the entity theory, relationships between a partnership and its creditors are not affected by the dissociation of a partner or by the addition of a new partner, unless otherwise agreed. Therefore, there is no need under RUPA, as there is under the UPA, for an elaborate provision deeming the new partnership to assume the liabilities of the old partnership. See UPA Section 41.

The "dual priority" rule in UPA Section 36(4) is eliminated to reflect the abolition of the "jingle rule," providing that separate debts have first claim on separate property, in order to conform to the Bankruptcy Code. See Comment 2 to Section 807. A deceased partner's estate, and thus all of his individual property, remains liable for partnership obligations incurred while he was a partner, however.

§ 704.   Statement of Dissociation

(a)   A dissociated partner or the partnership may file a statement of dissociation stating the name of the partnership and that the partner is dissociated from the partnership.

(b)   A statement of dissociation is a limitation on the authority of a dissociated partner for the purposes of Section 303(d) and (e).

(c)   For the purposes of Sections 702(a)(3) and 703(b)(3), a person not a partner is deemed to have notice of the dissociation 90 days after the statement of dissociation is filed.

COMMENT

Section 704 is new and provides for a statement of dissociation and its effects. Subsection (a) authorizes either a dissociated partner or the partnership to file a statement of dissociation. Like other RUPA filings, the statement of dissociation is voluntary. Both the partnership and the departing partner have an incentive to file, however, and it is anticipated that those filings will become routine upon a partner's dissociation. The execution, filing, and recording of the statement is governed by Section 105.

Filing or recording a statement of dissociation has threefold significance:

(1)   It is a statement of limitation on the dissociated partner's authority to the extent provided in Section 303(d) and (e). Under Section 303(d), a filed or recorded limitation on the authority of a partner destroys the conclusive effect of a prior grant of authority to the extent it contradicts the prior grant. Under Section 303(e), nonpartners are conclusively bound by a limitation on the authority of a partner to transfer real property held in the partnership name, if the statement is properly recorded in the real property records.

(2)   Ninety days after the statement is filed, nonpartners are deemed to have notice of the dissociation and thus conclusively bound for purposes of cutting off the partner's apparent authority under Sections 301 and 702(a)(3).

(3)   Ninety days after the statement is filed, third parties are conclusively bound for purposes of cutting off the dissociated partner's continuing liability under Section 703(b)(3) for transactions entered into by the partnership after dissociation.

§ 705.   Continued Use of Partnership Name

Continued use of a partnership name, or a dissociated partner's name as part thereof, by partners continuing the business does not of itself make the dissociated partner liable for an obligation of the partners or the partnership continuing the business.

COMMENT

Section 705 is an edited version of UPA Section 41(10) and provides that a dissociated partner is not liable for the debts of the continuing business simply because of continued use of the partnership name or the dissociated partner's name as a part thereof. That prevents forcing the business to forego the good will associated with its name.

Article 8

WINDING UP PARTNERSHIP BUSINESS

§ 801.   Events Causing Dissolution and Winding up of Partnership Business

A partnership is dissolved, and its business must be wound up, only upon the occurrence of any of the following events:

(1)   in a partnership at will, the partnership's having notice from a partner, other than a partner who is dissociated under Section 601(2) through (10), of that partner's express will to withdraw as a partner, or on a later date specified by the partner;

(2)   in a partnership for a definite term or particular undertaking:

(i)   within 90 days after a partner's dissociation by death or otherwise under Section 601(6) through (10) or wrongful dissociation under Section 602(b), the express will of at least half of the remaining partners to wind up the partnership business, for which purpose a partner's rightful dissociation pursuant to Section 602(b)(2)(i) constitutes the expression of that partner's will to wind up the partnership business;

(ii)   the express will of all of the partners to wind up the partnership business; or

(iii)   the expiration of the term or the completion of the undertaking;

(3)   an event agreed to in the partnership agreement resulting in the winding up of the partnership business;

(4)   an event that makes it unlawful for all or substantially all of the business of the partnership to be continued, but a cure of illegality within 90 days after notice to the partnership of the event is effective retroactively to the date of the event for purposes of this section;

(5)   on application by a partner, a judicial determination that:

(i)   the economic purpose of the partnership is likely to be unreasonably frustrated;

(ii)   another partner has engaged in conduct relating to the partnership business which makes it not reasonably practicable to carry on the business in partnership with that partner; or

(iii)   it is not otherwise reasonably practicable to carry on the partnership business in conformity with the partnership agreement; or

(6) on application by a transferee of a partner's transferable interest, a judicial determination that it is equitable to wind up the partnership business:

(i) after the expiration of the term or completion of the undertaking, if the partnership was for a definite term or particular undertaking at the time of the transfer or entry of the charging order that gave rise to the transfer; or

(ii) at any time, if the partnership was a partnership at will at the time of the transfer or entry of the charging order that gave rise to the transfer.

COMMENT

1. Under UPA Section 29, a partnership is dissolved every time a partner leaves. That reflects the aggregate nature of the partnership under the UPA. Even if the business of the partnership is continued by some of the partners, it is technically a new partnership. The dissolution of the old partnership and creation of a new partnership causes many unnecessary problems.

Under RULPA, limited partnerships dissolve far less readily than do general partnerships under the UPA. A limited partnership does not dissolve on the withdrawal of a limited partner, nor does it necessarily dissolve on the withdrawal of a general partner. *See* RULPA § 801(4).

RUPA's move to the entity theory is driven in part by the need to prevent a technical dissolution or its consequences. Under RUPA, not every partner dissociation causes a dissolution of the partnership. Only certain departures trigger a dissolution. The basic rule is that a partnership is dissolved, and its business must be wound up, only upon the occurrence of one of the events listed in Section 801. All other dissociations result in a buyout of the partner's interest under Article 7 and a continuation of the partnership entity and business by the remaining partners. *See* Section 603(a).

With only three exceptions, the provisions of Section 801 are merely default rules and may by agreement be varied or eliminated as grounds for dissolution. The first exception is dissolution under Section 801(4) resulting from carrying on an illegal business. The other two exceptions cover the power of a court to dissolve a partnership under Section 801(5) on application of a partner and under Section 801(6) on application of a transferee. See Comments 6–8 for further explanation of these provisions.

2. Under RUPA, "dissolution" is merely the commencement of the winding up process. The partnership continues for the limited purpose of winding up the business. In effect, that means the scope of the partnership business contracts to completing work in process and taking such other actions as may be necessary to wind up the business. Winding up the partnership business entails selling its assets, paying its debts, and distributing the net balance, if any, to the partners in cash according to their interests. The partnership entity continues, and the partners are associated in the winding up of the business until winding up is completed. When the winding up is completed, the partnership entity terminates.

3. Section 801 continues two basic rules from the UPA. First, it continues the rule that any member of an at-will partnership has the right to force a liquidation. Second, by negative implication, it continues the rule that the partners who wish to continue the business of a term partnership can not be forced to liquidate the business by a partner who withdraws prematurely in violation of the partnership agreement.

Those rules are gleaned from the separate UPA provisions governing dissolution and its consequences. Under UPA Section 31(1)(b), dissolution is caused by the express will of any partner when no definite term or particular undertaking is specified. UPA Section 38(1) provides that upon dissolution any partner has the right to have the business wound up. That is a default rule and applies only in the absence of an agreement affording the other partners a right to continue the business.

UPA Section 31(2) provides that a term partnership may be dissolved at any time, in contravention of the partnership agreement, by the express will of any partner. In that case, however, UPA Section 38(2)(b) provides that the nonbreaching partners may by unanimous consent continue the business. If the business is continued, they must buy out the breaching partner.

4. Section 801(1) provides that a partnership at will is dissolved and its business must be wound up upon the partnership's having notice of a partner's express will to withdraw as a partner, unless a later effective date is specified by the partner. A partner at will who has already been dissociated in some other manner, such as a partner who has been expelled, does not thereafter have a right to cause the partnership to be dissolved and its business wound up.

If, after dissolution, none of the partners wants the partnership wound up, Section 802(b) provides that, with the consent of all the partners, including the withdrawing partner, the remaining partners may continue the business. In that event, although there is a technical dissolution of the partnership and, at least in theory, a temporary contraction of the scope of the business, the partnership entity continues and the scope of its business is restored. See Section 802(b) and Comment 2.

5.   Section 801(2) provides three ways in which a term partnership may be dissolved before the expiration of the term:

(i)   Subsection (2)(i) provides for dissolution after a partner's dissociation by death or otherwise under Section 601(6) to (10) or wrongful dissociation under Section 602(b), if within 90 days after the dissociation at least half of the remaining partners express their will to dissolve the partnership. Thus if a term partnership had six partners and one of the partners dies or wrongfully dissociates before the end of the term, the partnership will, as a result of the dissociation, be dissolved only if three of the remaining five partners affirmatively vote in favor of dissolution within 90 days after the dissociation.[*] This reactive dissolution of a term partnership protects the remaining partners where the dissociating partner is crucial to the successful continuation of the business. The corresponding UPA Section 38(2)(b) rule requires unanimous consent of the remaining partners to continue the business, thus giving each partner an absolute right to a reactive liquidation. Under UPA 1994, if the partnership is continued by the majority, any dissenting partner who wants to withdraw may do so rightfully under the exception to Section 602(b)(2)(i), in which case his interest in the partnership will be bought out under Article 7. By itself, however, a partner's vote not to continue the business is not necessarily an expression of the partner's will to withdraw, and a dissenting partner may still elect to remain a partner and continue in the business.

The Section 601 dissociations giving rise to a reactive dissolution are: (6) a partner's bankruptcy or similar financial impairment; (7) a partner's death or incapacity; (8) the distribution by a trust-partner of its entire partnership interest; (9) the distribution by an estate-partner of its entire partnership interest; and (10) the termination of an entity-partner. Any dissociation during the term of the partnership that is wrongful under Section 602(b), including a partner's voluntary withdrawal, expulsion or bankruptcy, also gives rise to a reactive dissolution. Those statutory grounds may be varied by agreement or the reactive dissolution may be abolished entirely.

Under Section 601(6)(i), a partner is dissociated upon becoming a debtor in bankruptcy. The bankruptcy of a partner or of the partnership is not, however, an event of dissolution under Section 801. That is a change from UPA Section 31(5). A partner's bankruptcy does, however, cause dissolution of a term partnership under Section 801(2)(i), unless a majority in interest of the remaining partners thereafter agree to continue the partnership. Affording the other partners the option of buying out the bankrupt partner's interest avoids the necessity of winding up a term partnership every time a partner becomes a debtor in bankruptcy.

Similarly, under Section 801(2)(i), the death of any partner will result in the dissolution of a term partnership, only if at least half of the remaining partners express their will to wind up the partnership's business. If dissolution does occur, the deceased partner's transferable interest in the partnership passes to his estate and must be bought out under Article 7. See Comment 8 to Section 601.

(ii)   Section 801(2)(ii) provides that a term partnership may be dissolved and wound up at any time by the express will of all the partners. That is merely an expression of the general rule that the partnership agreement may override the statutory default rules and that the partnership agreement, like any contract, can be amended at any time by unanimous consent.

UPA Section 31(1)(c) provides that a term partnership may be wound up by the express will of all the partners whose transferable interests have not been assigned or charged for a partner's separate debts. That rule reflects the belief that the remaining partners may find transferees very intrusive. This provision has been deleted, however, because the liquidation is easily accomplished under Section 801(2)(ii) by first expelling the transferor partner under Section 601(4)(ii).

---

[*]   Prior to August 1997, Section 801(2)(i) provided that upon the dissociation of a partner in a term partnership by death or otherwise under Section 601(6) through (10) or wrongful dissociation under 602(b) the partnership would dissolve unless "a majority in interest of the remaining partners (including partners who have rightfully dissociated pursuant to Section 602(b)(2)(i)) agree to continue the partnership." This language was thought to be necessary for a term partnership to lack continuity of life under the Internal Revenue Act tax classification regulations. These regulations were repealed effective January 1, 1997. The current language, approved at the 1997 annual meeting of the National Conference of Commissioners on Uniform State Laws, allows greater continuity in a term partnership than the prior version of this subsection and UPA Section 38(2)(b).

(iii) Section 801(2)(iii) is based on UPA Section 31(1)(a) and provides for winding up a term partnership upon the expiration of the term or the completion of the undertaking.

Subsection (2)(iii) must be read in conjunction with Section 406. Under Section 406(a), if the partners continue the business after the expiration of the term or the completion of the undertaking, the partnership will be treated as a partnership at will. Moreover, if the partners continue the business without any settlement or liquidation of the partnership, under Section 406(b) they are presumed to have agreed that the partnership will continue, despite the lack of a formal agreement. The partners may also agree to ratify all acts taken since the end of the partnership's term.

6. Section 801(3) provides for dissolution upon the occurrence of an event specified in the partnership agreement as resulting in the winding up of the partnership business. The partners may, however, agree to continue the business and to ratify all acts taken since dissolution.

7. Section 801(4) continues the basic rule in UPA Section 31(3) and provides for dissolution if it is unlawful to continue the business of the partnership, unless cured. The "all or substantially all" proviso is intended to avoid dissolution for insubstantial or innocent regulatory violations. If the illegality is cured within 90 days after notice to the partnership, it is effective retroactively for purposes of this section. The requirement that an uncured illegal business be wound up cannot be varied in the partnership agreement. *See* Section 103(b)(8).

8. Section 801(5) provides for judicial dissolution on application by a partner. It is based in part on UPA Section 32(1), and the language comes in part from RULPA Section 802. A court may order a partnership dissolved upon a judicial determination that: (i) the economic purpose of the partnership is likely to be unreasonably frustrated; (ii) another partner has engaged in conduct relating to the partnership business which makes it not reasonably practicable to carry on the business in partnership with that partner; or (iii) it is not otherwise reasonably practicable to carry on the partnership business in conformity with the partnership agreement. The court's power to wind up the partnership under Section 801(5) cannot be varied in the partnership agreement. *See* Section 103(b)(8).

RUPA deletes UPA Section 32(1)(e) which provides for dissolution when the business can only be carried on at a loss. That provision might result in a dissolution contrary to the partners' expectations in a start-up or tax shelter situation, in which case "book" or "tax" losses do not signify business failure. Truly poor financial performance may justify dissolution under subsection (5)(i) as a frustration of the partnership's economic purpose.

RUPA also deletes UPA Section 32(1)(f) which authorizes a court to order dissolution of a partnership when "other circumstances render a dissolution equitable." That provision was regarded as too open-ended and, given RUPA's expanded remedies for partners, unnecessary. No significant change in result is intended, however, since the interpretation of UPA Section 32(1)(f) is comparable to the specific grounds expressed in subsection (5). *See, e.g., Karber v. Karber*, 145 Ariz. 293, 701 P.2d 1 (Ct. App. 1985) (partnership dissolved on basis of suspicion and ill will, citing UPA §§ 32(1)(d) and (f)); *Fuller v. Brough*, 159 Colo. 147, 411 P.2d 18 (1966) (not equitable to dissolve partnership for trifling causes or temporary grievances that do not render it impracticable to carry on partnership business); *Lau v. Wong*, 1 Haw. App. 217, 616 P.2d 1031 (1980) (partnership dissolved where business operated solely for benefit of managing partner).

9. Section 801(6) provides for judicial dissolution on application by a transferee of a partner's transferable interest in the partnership, including the purchaser of a partner's interest upon foreclosure of a charging order. It is based on UPA Section 32(2) and authorizes dissolution upon a judicial determination that it is equitable to wind up the partnership business (i) after the expiration of the partnership term or completion of the undertaking or (ii) at any time, if the partnership were a partnership at will at the time of the transfer or when the charging order was issued. The requirement that the court determine that it is equitable to wind up the business is new. The rights of a transferee under this section cannot be varied in the partnership agreement. *See* Section 103(b)(8).

§ 802. Partnership Continues After Dissolution

(a) Subject to subsection (b), a partnership continues after dissolution only for the purpose of winding up its business. The partnership is terminated when the winding up of its business is completed.

(b) At any time after the dissolution of a partnership and before the winding up of its business is completed, all of the partners, including any dissociating partner other than a wrongfully dissociating partner, may waive the right to have the partnership's business wound up and the partnership terminated. In that event:

(1)   the partnership resumes carrying on its business as if dissolution had never occurred, and any liability incurred by the partnership or a partner after the dissolution and before the waiver is determined as if dissolution had never occurred; and

(2)   the rights of a third party accruing under Section 804(1) or arising out of conduct in reliance on the dissolution before the third party knew or received a notification of the waiver may not be adversely affected.

COMMENT

1.   Section 802(a) is derived from UPA Section 30 and provides that a partnership continues after dissolution only for the purpose of winding up its business, after which it is terminated. RUPA continues the concept of "termination" to mark the completion of the winding up process. Since no filing or other formality is required, the date will often be determined only by hindsight. No legal rights turn on the partnership's termination or the date thereof. Even after termination, if a previously unknown liability is asserted, all of the partners are still liable.

2.   Section 802(b) makes explicit the right of the remaining partners to continue the business after an event of dissolution if all of the partners, including the dissociating partner or partners, waive the right to have the business wound up and the partnership terminated. Only those "dissociating" partners whose dissociation was the immediate cause of the dissolution must waive the right to have the business wound up. The consent of wrongfully dissociating partners is not required.

3.   Upon waiver of the right to have the business wound up, Paragraph (1) of the subsection provides that the partnership entity may resume carrying on its business as if dissolution had never occurred, thereby restoring the scope of its business to normal. "Resumes" is intended to mean that acts appropriate to winding up, authorized when taken, are in effect ratified, and the partnership remains liable for those acts, as provided explicitly in paragraph (2).

If the business is continued following a waiver of the right to dissolution, any liability incurred by the partnership or a partner after the dissolution and before the waiver is to be determined as if dissolution had never occurred. That has the effect of validating transactions entered into after dissolution that might not have been appropriate for winding up the business, because, upon waiver, any liability incurred by either the partnership or a partner in those transactions will be determined under Sections 702 and 703, rather than Sections 804 and 806.

As to the liability for those transactions among the partners themselves, the partners by agreement may provide otherwise. Thus, a partner who, after dissolution, incurred an obligation appropriate for winding up, but not appropriate for continuing the business, may protect himself by conditioning his consent to the continuation of the business on the ratification of the transaction by the continuing partners.

Paragraph (2) of the subsection provides that the rights of third parties accruing under Section 804(1) before they knew (or were notified) of the waiver may not be adversely affected by the waiver. That is intended to mean the partnership is bound, notwithstanding a subsequent waiver of dissolution and resumption of its business, by a transaction entered into after dissolution that was appropriate for winding up the partnership business, even if not appropriate for continuing the business. Similarly, any rights of a third party arising out of conduct in reliance on the dissolution are protected, absent knowledge (or notification) of the waiver. Thus, for example, a partnership loan, callable upon dissolution, that has been called is not reinstated by a subsequent waiver. If the loan has not been called before the lender learns (or is notified) of the waiver, however, it may not thereafter be called because of the dissolution. On the other hand, a waiver does not reinstate a lease that is terminated by the dissolution itself.

§ 803.   Right to Wind up Partnership Business

(a)   After dissolution, a partner who has not wrongfully dissociated may participate in winding up the partnership's business, but on application of any partner, partner's legal representative, or transferee, the [designate the appropriate court], for good cause shown, may order judicial supervision of the winding up.

(b)   The legal representative of the last surviving partner may wind up a partnership's business.

(c)   A person winding up a partnership's business may preserve the partnership business or property as a going concern for a reasonable time, prosecute and defend actions and proceedings, whether civil, criminal, or administrative, settle and close the partnership's business, dispose of and transfer the partnership's property, discharge the partnership's liabilities, distribute the assets of the partnership pursuant to Section 807, settle disputes by mediation or arbitration, and perform other necessary acts.

COMMENT

Section 803(a) is drawn from UPA Section 37. It provides that the partners who have not wrongfully dissociated may participate in winding up the partnership business. Wrongful dissociation is defined in Section 602. On application of any partner, a court may for good cause judicially supervise the winding up.

Section 803(b) continues the rule of UPA Section 25(2)(d) that the legal representative of the last surviving partner may wind up the business. It makes clear that the representative of the last surviving partner will not be forced to go to court for authority to wind up the business. On the other hand, the legal representative of a deceased partner, other than the last surviving partner, has only the rights of a transferee of the deceased partner's transferable interest. See Comment 8 to Section 601.

Section 803(c) is new and provides further guidance on the powers of a person who is winding up the business. It is based on Delaware Laws, Title 6, Section 17–803. The powers enumerated are not intended to be exclusive.

Subsection (c) expressly authorizes the preservation of the partnership's business or property as a going concern for a reasonable time. Some courts have reached that result without benefit of statutory authority. *See, e.g., Paciaroni v. Crane,* 408 A.2d 946 (Del. Ch. 1979). An agreement to continue the partnership business in order to preserve its going-concern value until sale is not a waiver of a partner's right to have the business liquidated.

The authorization of mediation and arbitration implements Conference policy to encourage alternative dispute resolution.

A partner's fiduciary duties of care and loyalty under Section 404 extend to winding up the business, except as modified by Section 603(b).

§ 804. Partner's Power to Bind Partnership After Dissolution

Subject to Section 805, a partnership is bound by a partner's act after dissolution that:

    (1)   is appropriate for winding up the partnership business; or

    (2)   would have bound the partnership under Section 301 before dissolution, if the other party to the transaction did not have notice of the dissolution.

COMMENT

Section 804 is the successor to UPA Sections 33(2) and 35, which wind down the authority of partners to bind the partnership to third persons.

Section 804(1) provides that partners have the authority to bind the partnership after dissolution in transactions that are appropriate for winding-up the partnership business. Section 804(2) provides that partners also have the power after dissolution to bind the partnership in transactions that are inconsistent with winding up. The partnership is bound in a transaction not appropriate for winding up, however, only if the partner's act would have bound the partnership under Section 301 before dissolution and the other party to the transaction did not have notice of the dissolution. *See* Section 102(b) (notice). Compare Section 301(1) (partner has apparent authority unless other party knows or has received a notification of lack of authority).

Section 804(2) attempts to balance the interests of the partners to terminate their mutual agency authority against the interests of outside creditors who have no notice of the partnership's dissolution. Even if the partnership is not bound under Section 804, the faithless partner who purports to act for the partnership after dissolution may be liable individually to an innocent third party under the law of agency. See Section 330 of the Restatement (Second) of Agency (agent liable for misrepresentation of authority), applicable under RUPA as provided in Section 104(a).

RUPA eliminates the special and confusing UPA rules limiting the authority of partners after dissolution. The special protection afforded by UPA Section 35(1)(b)(I) to former creditors and the lesser special protection afforded by UPA Section 35(1)(b)(II) to other parties who knew of the partnership before dissolution are both abolished. RUPA eschews these cumbersome notice provisions in favor of the general apparent authority rules of Section 301, subject to the effect of a filed or recorded statement of dissolution under Section 805. This enhances the protection of innocent third parties and imposes liability on the partnership and the partners who choose their fellow partner-agents and are in the best position to protect others by providing notice of the dissolution.

Also deleted are the special rules for unknown partners in UPA Section 35(2) and for certain causes of dissolution in UPA Section 35(3). Those, too, are inconsistent with RUPA's policy of adhering more closely to the general agency rules of Section 301.

Section 804 should be contrasted with Section 702, which winds down the power of a partner being bought out. The power of a dissociating partner is limited to transactions entered into within two years after the partner's dissociation. Section 804 has no time limitation. However, the apparent authority of partners in both situations is now subject to the filing of a statement of dissociation or dissolution, as the case may be, which operates to cut off such authority after 90 days.

§ 805. Statement of Dissolution

(a)   After dissolution, a partner who has not wrongfully dissociated may file a statement of dissolution stating the name of the partnership and that the partnership has dissolved and is winding up its business.

(b)   A statement of dissolution cancels a filed statement of partnership authority for the purposes of Section 303(d) and is a limitation on authority for the purposes of Section 303(e).

(c)   For the purposes of Sections 301 and 804, a person not a partner is deemed to have notice of the dissolution and the limitation on the partners' authority as a result of the statement of dissolution 90 days after it is filed.

(d)   After filing and, if appropriate, recording a statement of dissolution, a dissolved partnership may file and, if appropriate, record a statement of partnership authority which will operate with respect to a person not a partner as provided in Section 303(d) and (e) in any transaction, whether or not the transaction is appropriate for winding up the partnership business.

COMMENT

1.   Section 805 is new. Subsection (a) provides that, after an event of dissolution, any partner who has not wrongfully dissociated may file a statement of dissolution on behalf of the partnership. The filing and recording of a statement of dissolution is optional. The execution, filing, and recording of the statement is governed by Section 105. The legal consequences of filing a statement of dissolution are similar to those of a statement of dissociation under Section 704.

2.   Subsection (b) provides that a statement of dissolution cancels a filed statement of partnership authority for the purposes of Section 303(d), thereby terminating any extraordinary grant of authority contained in that statement.

A statement of dissolution also operates as a limitation on authority for the purposes of Section 303(e). That section provides that third parties are deemed to know of a limitation on the authority of a partner to transfer real property held in the name of the partnership if a certified copy of the statement containing the limitation is recorded with the real estate records. In effect, a properly recorded statement of dissolution restricts the authority of all partners to real property transfers that are appropriate for winding up the business. Thus, third parties must inquire of the partnership whether a contemplated real property transfer is appropriate for winding up. After dissolution, the partnership may, however, file and record a new statement of authority that will bind the partnership under Section 303(d).

3.   Subsection (c) operates in conjunction with Sections 301 and 804 to wind down partners' apparent authority after dissolution. It provides that, for purposes of those sections, 90 days after the filing of a statement of dissolution nonpartners are deemed to have notice of the dissolution and the corresponding limitation on the authority of all partners. Sections 301 and 804 provide that a partner's lack of authority is binding on persons with notice thereof. Thus, after 90 days the statement of dissolution operates as constructive notice conclusively limiting the apparent authority of partners to transactions that are appropriate for winding up the business.

4.   Subsection (d) provides that, after filing and, if appropriate, recording a statement of dissolution, the partnership may file and record a new statement of partnership authority that will operate as provided in Section 303(d). A grant of authority contained in that statement is conclusive and may be relied upon by a person who gives value without knowledge to the contrary, whether or not the transaction is appropriate for winding up the

partnership business. That makes the partners' record authority conclusive after dissolution, and precludes going behind the record to inquire into whether or not the transaction was appropriate for winding up.

§ 806. Partner's Liability to Other Partners After Dissolution

(a)   Except as otherwise provided in subsection (b) and Section 306, after dissolution a partner is liable to the other partners for the partner's share of any partnership liability incurred under Section 804.

(b)   A partner who, with knowledge of the dissolution, incurs a partnership liability under Section 804(2) by an act that is not appropriate for winding up the partnership business is liable to the partnership for any damage caused to the partnership arising from the liability.

COMMENT

Section 806 is the successor to UPA Sections 33(1) and 34, which govern the rights of partners among themselves with respect to post-dissolution liability.

Subsection (a) provides that, except as provided in Section 306(a) and subsection (b), after dissolution each partner is liable to the other partners by way of contribution for his share of any partnership liability incurred under Section 804. That includes not only obligations that are appropriate for winding up the business, but also obligations that are inappropriate if within the partner's apparent authority. Consistent with other provisions of this Act, Section 806(a) makes clear that a partner does not have a contribution obligation with regard to limited liability partnership obligations for which the partner is not liable under Section 306. See Comments to Section 401(b).

Subsection (a) draws no distinction as to the cause of dissolution. Thus, as among the partners, their liability is treated alike in all events of dissolution. That is a change from UPA Section 33(*l*).

Subsection (b) creates an exception to the general rule in subsection (a). It provides that a partner, who with knowledge of the winding up nevertheless incurs a liability binding on the partnership by an act that is inappropriate for winding up the business, is liable to the partnership for any loss caused thereby.

Section 806 is merely a default rule and may be varied in the partnership agreement. *See* Section 103(a).

§ 807. Settlement of Accounts and Contributions Among Partners

(a)   In winding up a partnership's business, the assets of the partnership, including the contributions of the partners required by this section, must be applied to discharge its obligations to creditors, including, to the extent permitted by law, partners who are creditors. Any surplus must be applied to pay in cash the net amount distributable to partners in accordance with their right to distributions under subsection (b).

(b)   Each partner is entitled to a settlement of all partnership accounts upon winding up the partnership business. In settling accounts among the partners, profits and losses that result from the liquidation of the partnership assets must be credited and charged to the partners' accounts. The partnership shall make a distribution to a partner in an amount equal to any excess of the credits over the charges in the partner's account. A partner shall contribute to the partnership an amount equal to any excess of the charges over the credits in the partner's account but excluding from the calculation charges attributable to an obligation for which the partner is not personally liable under Section 306.

(c)   If a partner fails to contribute the full amount required under subsection (b), all of the other partners shall contribute, in the proportions in which those partners share partnership losses, the additional amount necessary to satisfy the partnership obligations for which they are personally liable under Section 306. A partner or partner's legal representative may recover from the other partners any contributions the partner makes to the extent the amount contributed exceeds that partner's share of the partnership obligations for which the partner is personally liable under Section 306.

(d)   After the settlement of accounts, each partner shall contribute, in the proportion in which the partner shares partnership losses, the amount necessary to satisfy partnership obligations that were not known at the time of the settlement and for which the partner is personally liable under Section 306.

(e)   The estate of a deceased partner is liable for the partner's obligation to contribute to the partnership.

(f)   An assignee for the benefit of creditors of a partnership or a partner, or a person appointed by a court to represent creditors of a partnership or a partner, may enforce a partner's obligation to contribute to the partnership.

COMMENT

1.   Section 807 provides the default rules for the settlement of accounts and contributions among the partners in winding up the business. It is derived in part from UPA Sections 38(1) and 40.

2.   Subsection (a) continues the rule in UPA Section 38(*l*) that, in winding up the business, the partnership assets must first be applied to discharge partnership liabilities to creditors. For this purpose, any required contribution by the partners is treated as an asset of the partnership. After the payment of all partnership liabilities, any surplus must be applied to pay in cash the net amount due the partners under subsection (b) by way of a liquidating distribution.

RUPA continues the "in-cash" rule of UPA Section 38(1) and is consistent with Section 402, which provides that a partner has no right to receive, and may not be required to accept, a distribution in kind, unless otherwise agreed. The in-cash rule avoids the valuation problems that afflict unwanted in-kind distributions.

The partnership must apply its assets to discharge the obligations of partners who are creditors on a parity with other creditors. See Section 404(f) and Comment 6. In effect, that abolishes the priority rules in UPA Section 40(b) and (c) which subordinate the payment of inside debt to outside debt. Both RULPA and the RMBCA do likewise. *See* RULPA § 804; RMBCA §§ 6.40(f), 14.05(a). Ultimately, however, a partner whose "debt" has been repaid by the partnership is personally liable, as a partner, for any outside debt remaining unsatisfied, unlike a limited partner or corporate shareholder. Accordingly, the obligation to contribute sufficient funds to satisfy the claims of outside creditors may result in the equitable subordination of inside debt when partnership assets are insufficient to satisfy all obligations to non-partners.

RUPA in effect abolishes the "dual priority" or "jingle" rule of UPA Section 40(h) and (i). Those sections gave partnership creditors priority as to partnership property and separate creditors priority as to separate property. The jingle rule has already been preempted by the Bankruptcy Code, at least as to Chapter 7 partnership liquidation proceedings. Under Section 723(c) of the Bankruptcy Code, and under RUPA, partnership creditors share pro rata with the partners' individual creditors in the assets of the partners' estates.

3.   Subsection (b) provides that each partner is entitled to a settlement of all partnership accounts upon winding up. It also establishes the default rules for closing out the partners' accounts. First, the profits and losses resulting from the liquidation of the partnership assets must be credited or charged to the partners' accounts, according to their respective shares of profits and losses. Then, the partnership must make a final liquidating distribution to those partners with a positive account balance. That distribution should be in the amount of the excess of credits over the charges in the account. Any partner with a negative account balance must contribute to the partnership an amount equal to the excess of charges over the credits in the account provided the excess relates to an obligation for which the partner is personally liable under Section 306. The partners may, however, agree that a negative account does not reflect a debt to the partnership and need not be repaid in settling the partners' accounts.

Section 807(b) makes clear that a partner's contribution obligation to a partnership in dissolution only considers the partner's share of obligations for which the partner was personally liable under Section 306 ("unshielded obligations"). See Comments to Section 401(b) (partner contribution obligation to an operating partnership). Properly determined under this Section, the total required partner contributions will be sufficient to satisfy the partnership's total unshielded obligations. In special circumstances where a partnership has both shielded and unshielded obligations and the partner required contributions are used to first pay shielded partnership obligations, the partners may be required to make further contributions to satisfy the partnership unpaid unshielded obligations. The proper resolution of this matter is left to debtor-creditor law as well as the law governing the fiduciary obligations of the partners. See Section 104(a).

RUPA eliminates the distinction in UPA Section 40(b) between the liability owing to a partner in respect of capital and the liability owing in respect of profits. Section 807(b) speaks simply of the right of a partner to a liquidating distribution. That implements the logic of RUPA Sections 401(a) and 502 under which contributions to capital and shares in profits and losses combine to determine the right to distributions. The partners may, however, agree to share "operating" losses differently from "capital" losses, thereby continuing the UPA distinction.

4. Subsection (c) continues the UPA Section 40(d) rule that solvent partners share proportionately in the shortfall caused by insolvent partners who fail to contribute their proportionate share. The partnership may enforce a partner's obligation to contribute. *See* Section 405(a). A partner is entitled to recover from the other partners any contributions in excess of that partner's share of the partnership's liabilities. *See* Section 405(b)(iii).

5. Subsection (d) provides that, after settling the partners' accounts, each partner must contribute, in the proportion in which he shares losses, the amount necessary to satisfy partnership obligations that were not known at the time of the settlement. That continues the basic rule of UPA Section 40(d) and underscores that the obligation to contribute exists independently of the partnership's books of account. It specifically covers the situation of a partnership liability that was unknown when the partnership books were closed.

6. Under subsection (e), the estate of a deceased partner is liable for the partner's obligation to contribute to partnership losses. That continues the rule of UPA Section 40(g).

7. Subsection (f) provides that an assignee for the benefit of creditors of the partnership or of a partner (or other court appointed creditor representative) may enforce any partner's obligation to contribute to the partnership. That continues the rules of UPA Sections 36(4) and 40(e).

Article 9

CONVERSIONS AND MERGERS

§ 901.   Definitions

In this article:

(1) "General partner" means a partner in a partnership and a general partner in a limited partnership.

(2) "Limited partner" means a limited partner in a limited partnership.

(3) "Limited partnership" means a limited partnership created under the [State Limited Partnership Act], predecessor law, or comparable law of another jurisdiction.

(4) "Partner" includes both a general partner and a limited partner.

COMMENT

1. Article 9 is new. The UPA is silent with respect to the conversion or merger of partnerships, and thus it is necessary under the UPA to structure those types of transactions as asset transfers. RUPA provides specific statutory authority for conversions and mergers. It provides for continuation of the partnership entity, thereby simplifying those transactions and adding certainty to the legal consequences.

A number of States currently authorize the merger of limited partnerships, and some authorize them to merge with other business entities such as corporations and limited liability companies. A few States currently authorize the merger of a general and a limited partnership or the conversion of a general to a limited partnership.

2. As Section 908 makes clear, the requirements of Article 9 are not mandatory, and a partnership may convert or merge in any other manner provided by law. Article 9 is merely a "safe harbor." If the requirements of the article are followed, the conversion or merger is legally valid. Since most States have no other established procedure for the conversion or merger of partnerships, it is likely that the Article 9 procedures will be used in virtually all cases.

3. Article 9 does not restrict the provisions authorizing conversions and mergers to domestic partnerships. Since no filing is required for the creation of a partnership under RUPA, it is often unclear where a partnership is domiciled. Moreover, a partnership doing business in the State satisfies the definition of a partnership created under this Act since it is an association of two or more co-owners carrying on a business for profit. Even a partnership clearly domiciled in another State could easily amend its partnership agreement to provide that its internal affairs are to be governed by the laws of a jurisdiction that has enacted Article 9 of RUPA. No harm is likely to result from extending to foreign partnerships the right to convert or merge under local law.

4. Because Article 9 deals with the conversion and merger of both general and limited partnerships, Section 901 sets forth four definitions distinguishing between the two types of partnerships solely for the purposes

of Article 9. "Partner" includes both general and limited partners, and "general partner" includes general partners in both general and limited partnerships.

§ 902.   Conversion of Partnership to Limited Partnership

(a)   A partnership may be converted to a limited partnership pursuant to this section.

(b)   The terms and conditions of a conversion of a partnership to a limited partnership must be approved by all of the partners or by a number or percentage specified for conversion in the partnership agreement.

(c)   After the conversion is approved by the partners, the partnership shall file a certificate of limited partnership in the jurisdiction in which the limited partnership is to be formed. The certificate must include:

    (1)   a statement that the partnership was converted to a limited partnership from a partnership;

    (2)   its former name; and

    (3)   a statement of the number of votes cast by the partners for and against the conversion and, if the vote is less than unanimous, the number or percentage required to approve the conversion under the partnership agreement.

(d)   The conversion takes effect when the certificate of limited partnership is filed or at any later date specified in the certificate.

(e)   A general partner who becomes a limited partner as a result of the conversion remains liable as a general partner for an obligation incurred by the partnership before the conversion takes effect. If the other party to a transaction with the limited partnership reasonably believes when entering the transaction that the limited partner is a general partner, the limited partner is liable for an obligation incurred by the limited partnership within 90 days after the conversion takes effect. The limited partner's liability for all other obligations of the limited partnership incurred after the conversion takes effect is that of a limited partner as provided in the [State Limited Partnership Act].

COMMENT

Section 902(a) authorizes the conversion of a "partnership" to a "limited partnership." Section 202(b) limits the usual RUPA definition of "partnership" to general partnerships. That definition is applicable to Article 9. If a limited partnership is contemplated, Article 9 uses the term "limited partnership." See Section 901(3).

Subsection (b) provides that the terms and conditions of the conversion must be approved by all the partners, unless the partnership agreement specifies otherwise for a conversion.

Subsection (c) provides that, after approval, the partnership must file a certificate of limited partnership which includes the requisite information concerning the conversion.

Subsection (d) provides that the conversion takes effect when the certificate is filed, unless a later effective date is specified.

Subsection (e) establishes the partners' liabilities following a conversion. A partner who becomes a limited partner as a result of the conversion remains fully liable as a general partner for any obligation arising before the effective date of the conversion, both to third parties and to other partners for contribution. Third parties who transact business with the converted partnership unaware of a partner's new status as a limited partner are protected for 90 days after the conversion. Since RULPA Section 201(a)(3) requires the certificate of limited partnership to name all of the general partners, and under RUPA Section 902(c) the certificate must also include a statement of the conversion, parties transacting business with the converted partnership can protect themselves by checking the record of the State where the limited partnership is formed (the State where the conversion takes place). A former general partner who becomes a limited partner as a result of the conversion can avoid the lingering 90-day exposure to liability as a general partner by notifying those transacting business with the partnership of his limited partner status.

Although Section 902 does not expressly provide that a partner's withdrawal upon a term partnership's conversion to a limited partnership is rightful, it was assumed that the unanimity requirement for the approval of a conversion would afford a withdrawing partner adequate opportunity to protect his interest as a condition of approval. This question is left to the partnership agreement if it provides for conversion without the approval of all the partners.

§ 903.   Conversion of Limited Partnership to Partnership

(a)   A limited partnership may be converted to a partnership pursuant to this section.

(b)   Notwithstanding a provision to the contrary in a limited partnership agreement, the terms and conditions of a conversion of a limited partnership to a partnership must be approved by all of the partners.

(c)   After the conversion is approved by the partners, the limited partnership shall cancel its certificate of limited partnership.

(d)   The conversion takes effect when the certificate of limited partnership is canceled.

(e)   A limited partner who becomes a general partner as a result of the conversion remains liable only as a limited partner for an obligation incurred by the limited partnership before the conversion takes effect. Except as otherwise provided in Section 306, the partner is liable as a general partner for an obligation of the partnership incurred after the conversion takes effect.

COMMENT

Section 903(a) authorizes the conversion of a limited partnership to a general partnership.

Subsection (b) provides that the conversion must be approved by all of the partners, even if the partnership agreement provides to the contrary. That includes all of the general and limited partners. *See* Section 901(4). The purpose of the unanimity requirement is to protect a limited partner from exposure to personal liability as a general partner without clear and knowing consent at the time of conversion. Despite a general voting provision to the contrary in the partnership agreement, conversion to a general partnership may never have been contemplated by the limited partner when the partnership investment was made.

Subsection (c) provides that, after approval of the conversion, the converted partnership must cancel its certificate of limited partnership. *See* RULPA § 203.

Subsection (d) provides that the conversion takes effect when the certificate of limited partnership is canceled.

Subsection (e) provides that a limited partner who becomes a general partner is liable as a general partner for all partnership obligations for which a general partner would otherwise be personally liable for if incurred after the effective date of the conversion, but still has only limited liability for obligations incurred before the conversion.

§ 904.   Effect of Conversion; Entity Unchanged

(a)   A partnership or limited partnership that has been converted pursuant to this article is for all purposes the same entity that existed before the conversion.

(b)   When a conversion takes effect:

(1)   all property owned by the converting partnership or limited partnership remains vested in the converted entity;

(2)   all obligations of the converting partnership or limited partnership continue as obligations of the converted entity; and

(3)   an action or proceeding pending against the converting partnership or limited partnership may be continued as if the conversion had not occurred.

COMMENT

Section 904 sets forth the effect of a conversion on the partnership. Subsection (a) provides that the converted partnership is for all purposes the same entity as before the conversion.

Subsection (b) provides that upon conversion: (1) all partnership property remains vested in the converted entity; (2) all obligations remain the obligations of the converted entity; and (3) all pending legal actions may be continued as if the conversion had not occurred. The term "entity" as used in Article 9 refers to either or both general and limited partnerships as the context requires.

Under subsection (b)(1), title to partnership property remains vested in the converted partnership. As a matter of general property law, title remains vested without further act or deed and without reversion or impairment.

§ 905. Merger of Partnerships

(a)   Pursuant to a plan of merger approved as provided in subsection (c), a partnership may be merged with one or more partnerships or limited partnerships.

(b)   The plan of merger must set forth:

(1)   the name of each partnership or limited partnership that is a party to the merger;

(2)   the name of the surviving entity into which the other partnerships or limited partnerships will merge;

(3)   whether the surviving entity is a partnership or a limited partnership and the status of each partner;

(4)   the terms and conditions of the merger;

(5)   the manner and basis of converting the interests of each party to the merger into interests or obligations of the surviving entity, or into money or other property in whole or part; and

(6)   the street address of the surviving entity's chief executive office.

(c)   The plan of merger must be approved:

(1)   in the case of a partnership that is a party to the merger, by all of the partners, or a number or percentage specified for merger in the partnership agreement; and

(2)   in the case of a limited partnership that is a party to the merger, by the vote required for approval of a merger by the law of the State or foreign jurisdiction in which the limited partnership is organized and, in the absence of such a specifically applicable law, by all of the partners, notwithstanding a provision to the contrary in the partnership agreement.

(d)   After a plan of merger is approved and before the merger takes effect, the plan may be amended or abandoned as provided in the plan.

(e)   The merger takes effect on the later of:

(1)   the approval of the plan of merger by all parties to the merger, as provided in subsection (c);

(2)   the filing of all documents required by law to be filed as a condition to the effectiveness of the merger; or

(3)   any effective date specified in the plan of merger.

COMMENT

Section 905 provides a "safe harbor" for the merger of a general partnership and one or more general or limited partnerships. The surviving entity may be either a general or a limited partnership.

The plan of merger must set forth the information required by subsection (b), including the status of each partner and the manner and basis of converting the interests of each party to the merger into interests or obligations of the surviving entity.

Subsection (c) provides that the plan of merger must be approved: (1) by all the partners of each general partnership that is a party to the merger, unless its partnership agreement specifically provides otherwise for mergers; and (2) by all the partners, including both general and limited partners, of each limited partnership that is a party to the merger, notwithstanding a contrary provision in its partnership agreement, unless specifically authorized by the law of the jurisdiction in which that limited partnership is organized. Like Section 902(b), the purpose of the unanimity requirement is to protect limited partners from exposure to liability as general partners without their clear and knowing consent.

Subsection (d) provides that the plan of merger may be amended or abandoned at any time before the merger takes effect, if the plan so provides.

Subsection (e) provides that the merger takes effect on the later of: (1) approval by all parties to the merger; (2) filing of all required documents; or (3) the effective date specified in the plan. The surviving entity must file all notices and documents relating to the merger required by other applicable statutes governing the entities that are parties to the merger, such as articles of merger or a certificate of limited partnership. It may also amend or cancel a statement of partnership authority previously filed by any party to the merger.

§ 906. Effect of Merger

(a) When a merger takes effect:

(1) the separate existence of every partnership or limited partnership that is a party to the merger, other than the surviving entity, ceases;

(2) all property owned by each of the merged partnerships or limited partnerships vests in the surviving entity;

(3) all obligations of every partnership or limited partnership that is a party to the merger become the obligations of the surviving entity; and

(4) an action or proceeding pending against a partnership or limited partnership that is a party to the merger may be continued as if the merger had not occurred, or the surviving entity may be substituted as a party to the action or proceeding.

(b) The [Secretary of State] of this State is the agent for service of process in an action or proceeding against a surviving foreign partnership or limited partnership to enforce an obligation of a domestic partnership or limited partnership that is a party to a merger. The surviving entity shall promptly notify the [Secretary of State] of the mailing address of its chief executive office and of any change of address. Upon receipt of process, the [Secretary of State] shall mail a copy of the process to the surviving foreign partnership or limited partnership.

(c) A partner of the surviving partnership or limited partnership is liable for:

(1) all obligations of a party to the merger for which the partner was personally liable before the merger;

(2) all other obligations of the surviving entity incurred before the merger by a party to the merger, but those obligations may be satisfied only out of property of the entity; and

(3) except as otherwise provided in Section 306, all obligations of the surviving entity incurred after the merger takes effect, but those obligations may be satisfied only out of property of the entity if the partner is a limited partner.

(d) If the obligations incurred before the merger by a party to the merger are not satisfied out of the property of the surviving partnership or limited partnership, the general partners of that party immediately before the effective date of the merger shall contribute the amount necessary to satisfy that party's obligations to the surviving entity, in the manner provided in Section 807 or in the [Limited Partnership Act] of the jurisdiction in which the party was formed, as the case may be, as if the merged party were dissolved.

(e) A partner of a party to a merger who does not become a partner of the surviving partnership or limited partnership is dissociated from the entity, of which that partner was a partner, as of the date the merger takes effect. The surviving entity shall cause the partner's interest in the entity to be purchased under Section 701 or another statute specifically applicable to that partner's interest with respect to a merger. The surviving entity is bound under Section 702 by an act of a general partner dissociated under this subsection, and the partner is liable under Section 703 for transactions entered into by the surviving entity after the merger takes effect.

COMMENT

Section 906 states the effect of a merger on the partnerships that are parties to the merger and on the individual partners.

Subsection (a) provides that when the merger takes effect: (1) the separate existence of every partnership that is a party to the merger (other than the surviving entity) ceases; (2) all property owned by the parties to the merger vests in the surviving entity; (3) all obligations of every party to the merger become the obligations of the surviving entity; and (4) all legal actions pending against a party to the merger may be continued as if the merger had not occurred or the surviving entity may be substituted as a party. Title to partnership property vests in the surviving entity without further act or deed and without reversion or impairment.

Subsection (b) makes the Secretary of State the agent for service of process in any action against the surviving entity, if it is a foreign entity, to enforce an obligation of a domestic partnership that is a party to the merger. The purpose of this rule is to make it more convenient for local creditors to sue a foreign surviving entity when the credit was extended to a domestic partnership that has disappeared as a result of the merger.

Subsection (c) provides that a general partner of the surviving entity is liable for (1) all obligations for which the partner was personally liable before the merger; (2) all other obligations of the surviving entity incurred before the merger by a party to the merger, which obligations may be satisfied only out of the surviving entity's partnership property; and (3) all obligations incurred by the surviving entity after the merger, limited to the surviving entity's property in the case of limited partners and also limited to obligations of the partnership for which the partner was personally liable under Section 306.

This scheme of liability is similar to that of an incoming partner under Section 306(b). Only the surviving partnership itself is liable for all obligations, including obligations incurred by every constituent party before the merger. A general partner of the surviving entity is personally liable for obligations of the surviving entity incurred before the merger by the partnership of which he was a partner and those incurred by the surviving entity after the merger. Thus, a general partner of the surviving entity is liable only to the extent of his partnership interest for obligations incurred before the merger by a constituent party of which he was not a general partner.

Subsection (d) requires general partners to contribute the amount necessary to satisfy all obligations for which they were personally liable before the merger, if such obligations are not satisfied out of the partnership property of the surviving entity, in the same manner as provided in Section 807 or the limited partnership act of the applicable jurisdiction, as if the merged party were then dissolved. *See* RULPA §§ 502, 608.

Subsection (e) provides for the dissociation of a partner of a party to the merger who does not become a partner in the surviving entity. The surviving entity must buy out that partner's interest in the partnership under Section 701 or other specifically applicable statute. If the state limited partnership act has a dissenter's rights provision providing a different method of determining the amount due a dissociating limited partner, it would apply, rather than Section 701, since the two statutes should be read *in pari materia*.

Although subsection (e) does not expressly provide that a partner's withdrawal upon the merger of a term partnership is rightful, it was assumed that the unanimity requirement for the approval of a merger would afford a withdrawing partner adequate opportunity to protect his interest as a condition of approval. This question is left to the partnership agreement if it provides for merger without the approval of all the partners.

Under subsection (e), a dissociating general partner's lingering agency power is wound down, pursuant to Section 702, the same as in any other dissociation. Moreover, a dissociating general partner may be liable, under Section 703, for obligations incurred by the surviving entity for up to two years after the merger. A dissociating general partner can, however, limit to 90 days his exposure to liability by filing a statement of dissociation under Section 704.

§ 907.   Statement of Merger

(a)   After a merger, the surviving partnership or limited partnership may file a statement that one or more partnerships or limited partnerships have merged into the surviving entity.

(b)   A statement of merger must contain:

(1)   the name of each partnership or limited partnership that is a party to the merger;

(2)   the name of the surviving entity into which the other partnerships or limited partnership were merged;

(3)   the street address of the surviving entity's chief executive office and of an office in this State, if any; and

(4)   whether the surviving entity is a partnership or a limited partnership.

(c)   Except as otherwise provided in subsection (d), for the purposes of Section 302, property of the surviving partnership or limited partnership which before the merger was held in the name of another party to the merger is property held in the name of the surviving entity upon filing a statement of merger.

(d)   For the purposes of Section 302, real property of the surviving partnership or limited partnership which before the merger was held in the name of another party to the merger is property held in the name of the surviving entity upon recording a certified copy of the statement of merger in the office for recording transfers of that real property.

(e)   A filed and, if appropriate, recorded statement of merger, executed and declared to be accurate pursuant to Section 105(c), stating the name of a partnership or limited partnership that is a party to the merger in whose name property was held before the merger and the name of the surviving entity, but not containing all of the other information required by subsection (b), operates with respect to the partnerships or limited partnerships named to the extent provided in subsections (c) and (d).

COMMENT

Section 907(a) provides that the surviving entity may file a statement of merger. The execution, filing, and recording of the statement are governed by Section 105.

Subsection (b) requires the statement to contain the name of each party to the merger, the name and address of the surviving entity, and whether it is a general or limited partnership.

Subsection (c) provides that, for the purpose of the Section 302 rules regarding the transfer of partnership property, all personal and intangible property which before the merger was held in the name of a party to the merger becomes, upon the filing of the statement of merger with the Secretary of State, property held in the name of the surviving entity.

Subsection (d) provides a similar rule for real property, except that real property does not become property held in the name of the surviving entity until a certified copy of the statement of merger is recorded in the office for recording transfers of that real property under local law.

Subsection (e) is a savings provision in the event a statement of merger fails to contain all of the information required by subsection (b). The statement will have the operative effect provided in subsections (c) and (d) if it is executed and declared to be accurate pursuant to Section 105(e) and correctly states the name of the party to the merger in whose name the property was held before the merger, so that it would be found by someone searching the record. Compare Section 303(c) (statement of partnership authority).

§ 908.   Nonexclusive

This article is not exclusive. Partnerships or limited partnerships may be converted or merged in any other manner provided by law.

COMMENT

Section 908 provides that Article 9 is not exclusive. It is merely a "safe harbor." Partnerships may be converted or merged in any other manner provided by statute or common law. Existing statutes in a few States already authorize the conversion or merger of general partnerships and limited partnerships. See Comment 1 to Section 901. Those procedures may be followed in lieu of Article 9.

Article 10

LIMITED LIABILITY PARTNERSHIP

§ 1001.   Statement of Qualification

(a)   A partnership may become a limited liability partnership pursuant to this section.

(b)   The terms and conditions on which a partnership becomes a limited liability partnership must be approved by the vote necessary to amend the partnership agreement except, in the case of a partnership agreement that expressly considers obligations to contribute to the partnership, the vote necessary to amend those provisions.

(c)   After the approval required by subsection (b), a partnership may become a limited liability partnership by filing a statement of qualification. The statement must contain:

(1)   the name of the partnership;

(2)   the street address of the partnership's chief executive office and, if different, the street address of an office in this State, if any;

(3)   if the partnership does not have an office in this State, the name and street address of the partnership's agent for service of process;

(4)   a statement that the partnership elects to be a limited liability partnership; and

(5)   a deferred effective date, if any.

(d)   The agent of a limited liability partnership for service of process must be an individual who is a resident of this State or other person authorized to do business in this State.

(e)   The status of a partnership as a limited liability partnership is effective on the later of the filing of the statement or a date specified in the statement. The status remains effective, regardless of changes in the partnership, until it is canceled pursuant to Section 105(d) or revoked pursuant to Section 1003.

(f)   The status of a partnership as a limited liability partnership and the liability of its partners is not affected by errors or later changes in the information required to be contained in the statement of qualification under subsection (c).

(g)   The filing of a statement of qualification establishes that a partnership has satisfied all conditions precedent to the qualification of the partnership as a limited liability partnership.

(h)   An amendment or cancellation of a statement of qualification is effective when it is filed or on a deferred effective date specified in the amendment or cancellation.

COMMENT

Any partnership may become a limited liability partnership by filing a statement of qualification. See Comments to Sections 101(6) and 202(b) regarding a limited partnership filing a statement of qualification to become a limited liability limited partnership. Section 1001 sets forth the required contents of a statement of qualification. The section also sets forth requirements for the approval of a statement of qualification, establishes the effective date of the filing (and any amendments) which remains effective until canceled or revoked, and provides that the liability of the partners of a limited liability partnership is not affected by errors or later changes in the statement information.

Subsection (b) provides that the terms and conditions on which a partnership becomes a limited liability partnership must be generally be approved by the vote necessary to amend the partnership agreement. This means that the act of becoming a limited liability partnership is equivalent to an amendment of the partnership agreement. Where the partnership agreement is silent as to how it may be amended, the subsection (b) vote requires the approval of every partner. Since the limited liability partnership rules are not intended to increase the vote necessary to amend the partnership agreement, where the partnership agreement specifically sets forth an amendment process, that process may be used. Where a partnership agreement sets forth several amendment procedures depending upon the nature of the amendment, the required vote will be that necessary to amend the contribution obligations of the partners. The specific "contribution" vote is preferred because the filing of the statement directly affects partner contribution obligations. Therefore, the language "considers contribution" should be broadly interpreted to include any amendment vote that indirectly affects any partner's contribution obligation such as a partner's obligation to "indemnify" other partners.

The unanimous vote default rule reflects the significance of a partnership becoming a limited liability partnership. In general, upon such a filing each partner is released from the personal contribution obligation imposed under this Act in exchange for relinquishing the right to enforce the contribution obligations of other partners under this Act. See Comments to Sections 306(c) and 401(b). The wisdom of this bargain will depend on many factors including the relative risks of the partners' duties and the assets of the partnership.

Subsection (c) sets forth the information required in a statement of qualification. The must include the name of the partnership which must comply with Section 1002 to identify the partnership as a limited liability partnership. The statement must also include the address of the partnership's chief executive office and, if different, the street address of any other office in this State. A statement must include the name and street address of an agent for service of process only if it does not have any office in this State.

As with other statements, a statement of qualification must be filed in the office of the Secretary of State. See Sections 101(13) and 105(a). Accordingly, a statement of qualification is executed, filed, and otherwise regarded as a statement under this Act. For example, a copy of a filed statement must be sent to every nonfiling partner unless otherwise provided in the partnership agreement. See Sections 105(e) and 103(b)(1). A statement of qualification must be executed by at least two partners under penalties of perjury that the contents of the statement are accurate. See Section 105(c). A person who files the statement must promptly send a copy of the statement to every nonfiling partner but failure to send the copy does not limit the effectiveness of the filed statement to a nonpartner. Section 105(e). The filing must be accompanied by the fee required by the Secretary of State. Section 105(f).

Subsection (d) makes clear that once a statement is filed and effective, the status of the partnership as a limited liability partnership remains effective until the partnership status is either canceled or revoked "regardless of changes in the partnership." Accordingly, a partnership that dissolves but whose business is continued under a business continuation agreement retains its status as a limited liability partnership without the need to refile a new statement. Also, limited liability partnership status remains even though a partnership may be dissolved, wound up, and terminated. Even after the termination of the partnership, the former partners of a terminated partnership would not be personally liable for partnership obligations incurred while the partnership was a limited liability partnership.

Subsection (d) also makes clear that limited liability partnership status remains effective until actual cancellation under Section 1003 or revocation under Section 105(d). Ordinarily the terms and conditions of becoming a limited liability partnership must be approved by the vote necessary to amend the partnership agreement. See Sections 1001(b), 306(c), and 401(j). Since the statement of cancellation may be filed by a person authorized to file the original statement of qualification, the same vote necessary to approve the filing of the statement of qualification must be obtained to file the statement of cancellation. See Section 105(d).

Subsection (f) provides that once a statement of qualification is executed and filed under subsection (c) and Section 105, the partnership assumes the status of a limited liability partnership. This status is intended to be conclusive with regard to third parties dealing with the partnership. It is not intended to affect the rights of partners. For example, a properly executed and filed statement of qualification conclusively establishes the limited liability shield described in Section 306(c). If the partners executing and filing the statement exceed their authority, the internal abuse of authority has no effect on the liability shield with regard to third parties. Partners may challenge the abuse of authority for purposes of establishing the liability of the culpable partners but may not [a]ffect the liability shield as to third parties. Likewise, third parties may not challenge the existence of the liability shield because the decision to file the statement lacked the proper vote. As a result, the filing of the statement creates the liability shield even when the required subsection (b) vote is not obtained.

§ 1002.   Name

The name of a limited liability partnership must end with "Registered Limited Liability Partnership", "Limited Liability Partnership", "R.L.L.P.", "L.L.P.", "RLLP," or "LLP".

COMMENT

The name provisions are intended to alert persons dealing with a limited liability partnership of the presence of the liability shield. Because many jurisdictions have adopted the naming concept of a "registered" limited liability partnership, this aspect has been retained. These name requirements also distinguish limited partnerships and general partnerships that become limited liability partnerships because the new name must be at the end of and in addition to the general or limited partnership's regular name. See Comments to Section 101(6). Since the name identification rules of this section do not alter the regular name of the partnership, they do not disturb historic notions of apparent authority of partners in both general and limited partnerships.

§ 1003.   Annual Report

(a)   A limited liability partnership, and a foreign limited liability partnership authorized to transact business in this State, shall file an annual report in the office of the [Secretary of State] which contains:

(1)   the name of the limited liability partnership and the State or other jurisdiction under whose laws the foreign limited liability partnership is formed;

(2)   the street address of the partnership's chief executive office and, if different, the street address of an office of the partnership in this State, if any; and

(3)   if the partnership does not have an office in this State, the name and street address of the partnership's current agent for service of process.

(b)   An annual report must be filed between [January 1 and April 1] of each year following the calendar year in which a partnership files a statement of qualification or a foreign partnership becomes authorized to transact business in this State.

(c)   The [Secretary of State] may revoke the statement of qualification of a partnership that fails to file an annual report when due or pay the required filing fee. To do so, the [Secretary of State] shall provide the partnership at least 60 days' written notice of intent to revoke the statement. The notice must be mailed to the partnership at its chief executive office set forth in the last filed statement of qualification or annual report. The notice must specify the annual report that has not been filed, the fee that has not been paid, and the effective date of the revocation. The revocation is not effective if the annual report is filed and the fee is paid before the effective date of the revocation.

(d)   A revocation under subsection (c) only affects a partnership's status as a limited liability partnership and is not an event of dissolution of the partnership.

(e)   A partnership whose statement of qualification has been revoked may apply to the [Secretary of State] for reinstatement within two years after the effective date of the revocation.

The application must state:

(1)   the name of the partnership and the effective date of the revocation; and

(2)   that the ground for revocation either did not exist or has been corrected.

(f)   A reinstatement under subsection (e) relates back to and takes effect as of the effective date of the revocation, and the partnership's status as a limited liability partnership continues as if the revocation had never occurred.

COMMENT

Section 1003 sets forth the requirements of an annual report that must be filed by all limited liability partnerships and any foreign limited liability partnership authorized to transact business in this State. See Sections 101(5)(definition of a limited liability partnership) and 101(4)(definition of a foreign limited liability partnership). The failure of a limited liability partnership to file an annual report is a basis for the Secretary of State to administratively revoke its statement of qualification. See Section 1003(c). A foreign limited liability partnership that fails to file an annual report may not maintain an action or proceeding in this State. See Section 1103(a).

Subsection (a) generally requires that an annual report contain the same information required in a statement of qualification. Compare Sections 1001(a) and 1003(a). The differences are that the annual report requires disclosure of the State of formation of a foreign limited liability partnership but deletes the delayed effective date and limited liability partnership election statement provisions of a statement of qualification. As such, the annual report serves to update the information required in a statement of qualification. Under subsection (b), the annual report must be filed between January 1 and April 1 of each calendar year following the year in which a statement of qualification was filed or a foreign limited liability partnership becomes authorized to transact business. This timing requirement means that a limited liability partnership must make an annual filing and may not profile multiple annual reports in a single year.

Subsection (c) sets forth the procedure for the Secretary of State to administratively revoke a partnership's statement of qualification for the failure to file an annual report when due or pay the required filing fee. The Secretary of State must provide a partnership at least 60 days' written notice of the intent to revoke the statement. The notice must be mailed to the partnership at the address of its chief executive office set forth in the last filed statement or annual report and must state the grounds for revocation as well as the effective date of revocation. The revocation is not effective if the stated problem is cured before the stated effective date.

Under subsection (d), a revocation only terminates the partnership's status as a limited liability partnership but is not an event of dissolution of the partnership itself. Where revocation occurs, a partnership may apply for reinstatement under subsection (e) within two years after the effective date of the revocation. The application must state that the grounds for revocation either did not exist or have been corrected. The Secretary of State may grant the application on the basis of the statements alone or require proof of correction. Under subsection (f), when the application is granted, the reinstatement relates back to and takes effect as of the effective date of the revocation. The relation back doctrine prevents gaps in a reinstated partnership's liability shield. See Comments to Section 306(c).

Article 11

FOREIGN LIMITED LIABILITY PARTNERSHIP

§ 1101. Law Governing Foreign Limited Liability Partnership

(a) The law under which a foreign limited liability partnership is formed governs relations among the partners and between the partners and the partnership and the liability of partners for obligations of the partnership.

(b) A foreign limited liability partnership may not be denied a statement of foreign qualification by reason of any difference between the law under which the partnership was formed and the law of this State.

(c) A statement of foreign qualification does not authorize a foreign limited liability partnership to engage in any business or exercise any power that a partnership may not engage in or exercise in this State as a limited liability partnership.

COMMENT

Section 1101 provides that the laws where a foreign limited liability partnership is formed rather than the laws of this State govern both the internal relations of the partnership and liability of its partners for the obligations of the partnership. See Section 101(4)(definition of a foreign limited liability partnership). Section 106(b) provides that the laws of this State govern the internal relations of a domestic limited liability and the liability of its partners for the obligations of the partnership. See Sections 101(5)(definition of a domestic limited liability partnership). A partnership may therefore chose the laws of a particular jurisdiction by filing a statement of qualification in that jurisdiction. But there are limitations on this choice.

Subsections (b) and (c) together make clear that although a foreign limited liability partnership may not be denied a statement of foreign qualification simply because of a difference between the laws of its foreign jurisdiction and the laws of this State, it may not engage in any business or exercise any power in this State that a domestic limited liability partnership may not engage in or exercise. Under subsection (c), a foreign limited liability partnership that engages in a business or exercises a power in this State that a domestic may not engage in or exercise, does so only as [an] ordinary partnership without the benefit of the limited liability partnership liability shield set forth in Section 306(c). In this sense, a foreign limited liability partnership is treated the same as a domestic limited liability partnership. Also, the Attorney General may maintain an action to restrain a foreign limited liability partnership from transacting an unauthorized business in this State. See Section 1105.

§ 1102. Statement of Foreign Qualification

(a) Before transacting business in this State, a foreign limited liability partnership must file a statement of foreign qualification. The statement must contain:

(1) the name of the foreign limited liability partnership which satisfies the requirements of the State or other jurisdiction under whose law it is formed and ends with "Registered Limited Liability Partnership", "Limited Liability Partnership", "R.L.L.P.", "L.L.P.", "RLLP," or "LLP";

(2) the street address of the partnership's chief executive office and, if different, the street address of an office of the partnership in this State, if any;

(3) if there is no office of the partnership in this State, the name and street address of the partnership's agent for service of process; and

(4) a deferred effective date, if any.

(b) The agent of a foreign limited liability company for service of process must be an individual who is a resident of this State or other person authorized to do business in this State.

233

(c)   The status of a partnership as a foreign limited liability partnership is effective on the later of the filing of the statement of foreign qualification or a date specified in the statement. The status remains effective, regardless of changes in the partnership, until it is canceled pursuant to Section 105(d) or revoked pursuant to Section 1003.

(d)   An amendment or cancellation of a statement of foreign qualification is effective when it is filed or on a deferred effective date specified in the amendment or cancellation.

COMMENT

Section 1102 provides that a foreign limited liability partnership must file a statement of foreign qualification before transacting business in this State. The section also sets forth the information required in the statement. As with other statements, a statement of foreign qualification must be filed in the office of the Secretary of State. See Sections 101(13), 105(a), and 1001(c). Accordingly, a statement of foreign qualification is executed, filed, and otherwise regarded as a statement under this Act. See Section 101(13)(definition of a statement includes a statement of foreign qualification).

Subsection (a) generally requires the same information in a statement of foreign qualification as is required in a statement of qualification. Compare Section 1001(c). The statement of foreign qualification must include a name that complies with the requirements for domestic limited liability partnership under Section 1002 and must include the address of the partnership's chief executive office and, if different, the street address of any other office in this State. If a foreign limited liability partnership does not have any office in this State, the statement of foreign qualification must include the name and street address of an agent for service of process.

As with a statement of qualification, a statement of foreign qualification (and amendments) is effective when filed or at a later specified filing date. Compare Sections 1102(b) and (c) with Sections 1001(e) and (h). Likewise, a statement of foreign qualification remains effective until canceled by the partnership or revoked by the Secretary of State, regardless of changes in the partnership. See Sections 105(d) (statement cancellation) and Section 1003 (revocation for failure to file annual report or pay annual filing fee) and Compare Sections 1102(b) and 1001(e). Statement of qualification provisions regarding the relationship of the status of a foreign partnership relative to its initial filing of a statement are governed by foreign law and are therefore omitted from this section. See Sections 1001(f)(effect of errors and omissions) and (g)(filing establishes all conditions precedent to qualification).

§ 1103.   Effect of Failure to Qualify

(a)   A foreign limited liability partnership transacting business in this State may not maintain an action or proceeding in this State unless it has in effect a statement of foreign qualification.

(b)   The failure of a foreign limited liability partnership to have in effect a statement of foreign qualification does not impair the validity of a contract or act of the foreign limited liability partnership or preclude it from defending an action or proceeding in this State.

(c)   A limitation on personal liability of a partner is not waived solely by transacting business in this State without a statement of foreign qualification.

(d)   If a foreign limited liability partnership transacts business in this State without a statement of foreign qualification, the [Secretary of State] is its agent for service of process with respect to a right of action arising out of the transaction of business in this State.

COMMENT

Section 1103 makes clear that the only consequence of a failure to file a statement of foreign qualification is that the foreign limited liability partnership will not be able to maintain an action or proceeding in this State. The partnership's contracts remain valid, it may defend an action or proceeding, personal liability of the partners is not waived, and the Secretary of State is the agent for service of process with respect to claims arising out of transacting business in this State. Sections 1103(b)–(d). Once a statement of foreign qualification is filed, the Secretary of State may revoke the statement for failure to file an annual report but the partnership has the right to cure the failure for two years. See Section 1003(c) and (e). Since the failure to file a statement of foreign qualification has no impact on the liability shield of the partners, a revocation of a statement of foreign qualification also has no impact on the liability shield created under foreign laws. Compare Sections 1103(c) and 1003(f)(revocation of the statement of qualification of a domestic limited liability partnership removes partner liability shield unless filing problems cured within two years).

§ 1104. Activities Not Constituting Transacting Business

(a)   Activities of a foreign limited liability partnership which do not constitute transacting business for the purpose of this article include:

(1)   maintaining, defending, or settling an action or proceeding;

(2)   holding meetings of its partners or carrying on any other activity concerning its internal affairs;

(3)   maintaining bank accounts;

(4)   maintaining offices or agencies for the transfer, exchange, and registration of the partnership's own securities or maintaining trustees or depositories with respect to those securities;

(5)   selling through independent contractors;

(6)   soliciting or obtaining orders, whether by mail or through employees or agents or otherwise, if the orders require acceptance outside this State before they become contracts;

(7)   creating or acquiring indebtedness, with or without a mortgage, or other security interest in property;

(8)   collecting debts or foreclosing mortgages or other security interests in property securing the debts, and holding, protecting, and maintaining property so acquired;

(9)   conducting an isolated transaction that is completed within 30 days and is not one in the course of similar transactions; and

(10) transacting business in interstate commerce.

(b)   For purposes of this article, the ownership in this State of income-producing real property or tangible personal property, other than property excluded under subsection (a), constitutes transacting business in this State.

(c)   This section does not apply in determining the contacts or activities that may subject a foreign limited liability partnership to service of process, taxation, or regulation under any other law of this State.

COMMENT

Because the Attorney General may restrain a foreign limited liability partnership from transacting an unauthorized business in this State and a foreign partnership may not maintain an action or proceeding in this State, the concept of "transacting business" in this State is important. To provide more certainty, subsection (a) sets forth ten separate categories of activities that do not constitute transacting business. Subsection (c) makes clear that the section only considers the definition of "transacting business" and as no impact on whether a foreign limited liability partnership's activities in this State subject it to service of process, taxation, or regulation under any other law of this State.

§ 1105. Action by [Attorney General]

The [Attorney General] may maintain an action to restrain a foreign limited liability partnership from transacting business in this State in violation of this article.

COMMENT

Section 1105 makes clear that the Attorney General may restrain a foreign limited liability from transacting an unauthorized business in this State. As a threshold matter, a foreign limited liability partnership must be "transacting business" in this State within the meaning of Section 1104. Secondly, the business transacted in this State must be that which could not be engaged in by a domestic limited liability partnership. See Section 1101(c). The fact that a foreign limited liability partnership has a statement of foreign qualification does not permit it to engage in any unauthorized business in this State or impair the power of the Attorney General to restrain the foreign partnership from engaging in the unauthorized business. See Section 1101(c).

Article 12

MISCELLANEOUS PROVISIONS

§ 1201.   Uniformity of Application and Construction

This [Act] shall be applied and construed to effectuate its general purpose to make uniform the law with respect to the subject of this [Act] among States enacting it.

§ 1202.   Short Title

This [Act] may be cited as the Uniform Partnership Act (1997).

§ 1203.   Severability Clause

If any provision of this [Act] or its application to any person or circumstance is held invalid, the invalidity does not affect other provisions or applications of this [Act] which can be given effect without the invalid provision or application, and to this end the provisions of this [Act] are severable.

§ 1204.   Effective Date

This [Act] takes effect . . . .

COMMENT

The effective date of the Act established by an adopting State has operative effects under Section 1206, which defers mandatory application of the Act to existing partnerships.

§ 1205.   Repeals

Effective January 1, 199___, the following acts and parts of acts are repealed: [the State Partnership Act as amended and in effect immediately before the effective date of this [Act]].

COMMENT

This section repeals the adopting State's present general partnership act. The effective date of the repealer should not be any earlier than the date selected by that State in Section 1206(b) for the application of the Act to all partnerships.

§ 1206.   Applicability

(a)   Before January 1, 199___, this [Act] governs only a partnership formed:

(1)   after the effective date of this [Act], except a partnership that is continuing the business of a dissolved partnership under [Section 41 of the superseded Uniform Partnership Act]; and

(2)   before the effective date of this [Act], that elects, as provided by subsection (c), to be governed by this [Act].

(b)   On and after January 1, 199___, this [Act] governs all partnerships.

(c)   Before January 1, 199___, a partnership voluntarily may elect, in the manner provided in its partnership agreement or by law for amending the partnership agreement, to be governed by this [Act]. The provisions of this [Act] relating to the liability of the partnership's partners to third parties apply to limit those partners' liability to a third party who had done business with the partnership within one year before the partnership's election to be governed by this [Act] only if the third party knows or has received a notification of the partnership's election to be governed by this [Act].

COMMENT

This section provides for a transition period in the applicability of the Act to existing partnerships, similar to that provided in the revised Texas partnership act. *See* Tex. Rev. Civ. Stat. Ann. art. 6132b–10.03 (Vernon Supp. 1994). Subsection (a) makes application of the Act mandatory for all partnerships formed after the effective date of the Act and permissive, by election, for existing partnerships. That affords existing partnerships and partners an opportunity to consider the changes effected by RUPA and to amend their partnership agreements, if appropriate.

Under subsection (b), application of the Act becomes mandatory for all partnerships, including existing partnerships that did not previously elect to be governed by it, upon a future date to be established by the adopting State. Texas, for example, deferred for five years mandatory compliance by existing partnerships.

Subsection (c) provides that an existing partnership may voluntarily elect to be governed by RUPA in the manner provided for amending its partnership agreement. Under UPA Section 18(h), that requires the consent of all the partners, unless otherwise agreed. Third parties doing business with the partnership must know or be notified of the election before RUPA's rules limiting a partner's liability become effective as to them. Those rules would include, for example, the provisions of Section 704 limiting the liability of a partner 90 days after the filing of a statement of dissociation. Without knowledge of the partnership's election, third parties would not be aware that they must check the record to ascertain the extent of a dissociated partner's personal liability.

§ 1207. Savings Clause

This [Act] does not affect an action or proceeding commenced or right accrued before this [Act] takes effect.

COMMENT

This section continues the prior law after the effective date of the Act with respect to a pending action or proceeding or a right accrued at the time of the effective date. Since courts generally apply the law that exists at the time an action is commenced, in many circumstances the new law of this Act would displace the old law, but for this section.

Almost all States have general savings statutes, usually as part of their statutory construction acts. These are often very broad. Compare Uniform Statute and Rule Construction Act § 16(a) (narrow savings clause). As RUPA is remedial, the more limited savings provisions in Section 1207 are more appropriate than the broad savings provisions of the usual general savings clause. *See generally*, Comment to Uniform Statute and Rule Construction Act § 16.

Pending "action" refers to a judicial proceeding, while "proceeding" is broader and includes administrative proceedings. Although it is not always clear whether a right has "accrued," the term generally means that a cause of action has matured and is ripe for legal redress. *See, e.g., Estate of Hoover v. Iowa Dept. of Social Services*, 299 Iowa 702, 251 N.W.2d 529 (1977); *Nielsen v. State of Wisconsin*, 258 Wis. 1110, 141 N.W.2d 194 (1966). An inchoate right is not enough, and thus, for example, there is no accrued right under a contract until it is breached.

[Sections 1208 through 1211 are necessary only for jurisdictions adopting Uniform Limited Liability Partnership Act Amendments after previously adopting Uniform Partnership Act (1994)]

§ 1208. Effective Date

These [Amendments] take effect . . . .

§ 1209. Repeals

Effective January 1, 199__, the following acts and parts of acts are repealed: [the Limited Liability Partnership amendments to the State Partnership Act as amended and in effect immediately before the effective date of these [Amendments]].

§ 1210. Applicability

(a) Before January 1, 199__, these [Amendments] govern only a limited liability partnership formed:

(1)   on or after the effective date of these [Amendments], unless that partnership is continuing the business of a dissolved limited liability partnership; and

(2)   before the effective date of these [Amendments], that elects, as provided by subsection (c), to be governed by these [Amendments].

(b)   On and after January 1, 199__, these [Amendments] govern all partnerships.

(c)   Before January 1, 199__, a partnership voluntarily may elect, in the manner provided in its partnership agreement or by law for amending the partnership agreement, to be governed by these [Amendments]. The provisions of these [Amendments] relating to the liability of the partnership's partners to third parties apply to limit those partners' liability to a third party who had done business with the partnership within one year before the partnership's election to be governed by these [Amendments], only if the third party knows or has received a notification of the partnership's election to be governed by these [Amendments].

(d)   The existing provisions for execution and filing a statement of qualification of a limited liability partnership continue until either the limited liability partnership elects to have this [Act] apply or January 1, 199__.

§ 1211.   Savings Clause

These [Amendments] do not affect an action or proceeding commenced or right accrued before these [Amendments] take effect.

REVISED UNIFORM PARTNERSHIP ACT (2013)

Table of Sections

RUPA (2013)

[ARTICLE] 4. RELATIONS OF PARTNERS TO EACH OTHER AND TO PARTNERSHIP

[ARTICLE] 5. TRANSFERABLE INTERESTS AND RIGHTS OF TRANSFEREES AND CREDITORS

[ARTICLE] 6. DISSOCIATION

[ARTICLE] 7. PERSON'S DISSOCIATION AS A PARTNER WHEN BUSINESS NOT WOUND UP

[ARTICLE] 8. DISSOLUTION AND WINDING UP

[ARTICLE] 9. LIMITED LIABILITY PARTNERSHIP

* * *

PREFATORY NOTE TO 2011 AND 2013 HARMONIZATION AMENDMENTS

From 2009 to 2013, the Uniform Law Conference undertook an intensive effort to harmonize, to the extent possible, all uniform acts pertaining to unincorporated organizations. As part of that effort, the Uniform Partnership Act (1997) underwent four types of changes: substantive; major improvements in language; minor revisions in language for the sake of harmonization; and relocation within this particular "spoke" of provisions that are part of the "HUB" in the new Uniform Business Organizations Code ("UBOC").

Substantive Changes

The most significant substantive changes are:

- simplifying the section on "knowledge" and "notice," Section 103;

- centralizing constructive notice provisions, Section 103(d);

- revising and expanding provisions pertaining to the partnership agreement, Sections 105–107;

- updating various filing provisions pertaining to limited liability partnerships, Sections 108–118;

- providing that, in the context of a claim to "pierce the veil" of a limited liability partnership, "[t]he failure of [the] limited liability partnership to observe formalities relating to the exercise of its powers or management of its business is not a ground for imposing liability on a partner for a debt, obligation, or other liability of the partnership," Section 306(d);

- providing rules on unlawful distributions, Sections 406–407;

242

- "uncabining" (*i.e.*, making non-exhaustive) the codification of fiduciary duties, Section 409 (a)–(b);

- making clear that the act's obligation of good faith and fair dealing is the common law obligation of contract law, Section 409(d);

- adding as an event causing dissolution "the passage of 90 consecutive days during which the partnership does not have at least two partners," Section 801(6); and

- adding the comprehensive provisions of the Model Entity Transactions Act, Article 11.

Substantial Improvements to Language

The most significant improvements in language appear in Section 105 (formerly Section 103), the first of three sections addressing the partnership agreement. The structure of Section 105 is far less complicated than the structure of former Section 103.

Harmonization-Based Language Changes

Minor changes in language for the sake of harmonization appear throughout the act.

Relocation and Renumbering of HUB-Based Provisions

The Harmonization Project included both the harmonization of various stand-alone acts and the compilation of UBOC, which comprises a "HUB" (somewhat analogous to Article 1 of the Uniform Commercial Code) and various spokes. Each spoke pertains to a different type of organization (*e.g.*, general partnership, limited partnership, limited liability company, statutory trust entity). Naturally, spokes in the Code do not repeat the provisions from the HUB. In contrast, each stand-alone act includes provisions that appear in the HUB in the Code.

So that the section numbers of this "spoke" correspond with the spoke provisions in the Code, HUB-based provisions of this Act have been renumbered to appear at the end of articles. *See, e.g.*, Sections 112–121.

* * *

[ARTICLE] 1.   GENERAL PROVISIONS

§ 101.   Short Title

This [act] may be cited as the Uniform Partnership Act.

COMMENT

This act is drafted to replace a state's current general partnership statute, whether or not that statute is based on UPA (1914) or UPA (1997). Section 110 contains transition provisions.

§ 102.   Definitions

In this [act]:

(1)   "Business" includes every trade, occupation, and profession.

(2)   "Contribution", except in the phrase "right of contribution", means property or a benefit described in Section 403 which is provided by a person to a partnership to become a partner or in the person's capacity as a partner.

(3)   "Debtor in bankruptcy" means a person that is the subject of:

(A)   an order for relief under Title 11 of the United States Code or a comparable order under a successor statute of general application; or

(B)   a comparable order under federal, state, or foreign law governing insolvency.

(4) "Distribution" means a transfer of money or other property from a partnership to a person on account of a transferable interest or in a person's capacity as a partner. The term:

    (A) includes:

        (i) a redemption or other purchase by a partnership of a transferable interest; and

        (ii) a transfer to a partner in return for the partner's relinquishment of any right to participate as a partner in the management or conduct of the partnership's business or have access to records or other information concerning the partnership's business; and

    (B) does not include amounts constituting reasonable compensation for present or past service or payments made in the ordinary course of business under a bona fide retirement plan or other bona fide benefits program.

(5) "Foreign limited liability partnership" means a foreign partnership whose partners have limited liability for the debts, obligations, or other liabilities of the foreign partnership under a provision similar to Section 306(c).

(6) "Foreign partnership" means an unincorporated entity formed under the law of a jurisdiction other than this state which would be a partnership if formed under the law of this state. The term includes a foreign limited liability partnership.

(7) "Jurisdiction", used to refer to a political entity, means the United States, a state, a foreign country, or a political subdivision of a foreign country.

(8) "Jurisdiction of formation" means the jurisdiction whose law governs the internal affairs of an entity.

(9) "Limited liability partnership", except in the phrase "foreign limited liability partnership" and in [Article] 11, means a partnership that has filed a statement of qualification under Section 901 and does not have a similar statement in effect in any other jurisdiction.

(10) "Partner" means a person that:

    (A) has become a partner in a partnership under Section 402 or was a partner in a partnership when the partnership became subject to this [act] under Section 110; and

    (B) has not dissociated as a partner under Section 601.

(11) "Partnership", except in [Article] 11, means an association of two or more persons to carry on as co-owners a business for profit formed under this [act] or that becomes subject to this [act] under [Article] 11 or Section 110. The term includes a limited liability partnership.

(12) "Partnership agreement" means the agreement, whether or not referred to as a partnership agreement and whether oral, implied, in a record, or in any combination thereof, of all the partners of a partnership concerning the matters described in Section 105(a). The term includes the agreement as amended or restated.

(13) "Partnership at will" means a partnership in which the partners have not agreed to remain partners until the expiration of a definite term or the completion of a particular undertaking.

(14) "Person" means an individual, business corporation, nonprofit corporation, partnership, limited partnership, limited liability company, [general cooperative association,] limited cooperative association, unincorporated nonprofit association, statutory trust, business trust, common-law business trust, estate, trust, association, joint venture, public corporation, government or governmental subdivision, agency, or instrumentality, or any other legal or commercial entity.

(15) "Principal office" means the principal executive office of a partnership or a foreign limited liability partnership, whether or not the office is located in this state.

(16) "Property" means all property, whether real, personal, or mixed or tangible or intangible, or any right or interest therein.

(17) "Record", used as a noun, means information that is inscribed on a tangible medium or that is stored in an electronic or other medium and is retrievable in perceivable form.

(18) "Registered agent" means an agent of a limited liability partnership or foreign limited liability partnership which is authorized to receive service of any process, notice, or demand required or permitted by law to be served on the partnership.

(19) "Registered foreign limited liability partnership" means a foreign limited liability partnership that is registered to do business in this state pursuant to a statement of registration filed by the [Secretary of State].

(20) "Sign" means, with present intent to authenticate or adopt a record:

    (A)   to execute or adopt a tangible symbol; or

    (B)   to attach to or logically associate with the record an electronic symbol, sound, or process.

(21) "State" means a state of the United States, the District of Columbia, Puerto Rico, the United States Virgin Islands, or any territory or insular possession subject to the jurisdiction of the United States.

(22) "Transfer" includes:

    (A)   an assignment;

    (B)   a conveyance;

    (C)   a sale;

    (D)   a lease;

    (E)   an encumbrance, including a mortgage or security interest;

    (F)   a gift; and

    (G)   a transfer by operation of law.

(23) "Transferable interest" means the right, as initially owned by a person in the person's capacity as a partner, to receive distributions from a partnership, whether or not the person remains a partner or continues to own any part of the right. The term applies to any fraction of the interest, by whomever owned.

(24) "Transferee" means a person to which all or part of a transferable interest has been transferred, whether or not the transferor is a partner.

COMMENT

UPA (1997) section 101 defined fourteen terms. This section defines twenty-four terms. The increase is generally due to harmonization and more particularly to changes made to bring the LLP provisions pertaining to limited liability and filings into line with the corresponding provisions of ULPA (2001) (Last Amended 2013) and ULLCA (2006) (Last Amended 2013). *See, e.g.*, Sections 111–117 (provisions pertaining to filings), 407 (liability for improper distributions).

This section contains definitions for terms used throughout the act; it is important to remember that "partnership" means solely a domestic general partnership, except when "partnership" is used as part of a multiword-term (*e.g.*, "foreign partnership"). Section 1101 contains definitions specific to Article 11's provisions on mergers, conversions, interest exchanges, and domestications.

"Business" [(1)]—This definition originated in UPA (1914) § 2 and is fundamentally important; a general partnership must have a business purpose. *See* Section 202(a) (referring to the association of two or more persons to carry on as co-owners a business for profit). *Compare* Section 102(1), *with* ULPA (2001) (Last Amended 2013) § 110(b) ("A limited partnership may have any lawful purpose, regardless of whether for profit."), *and* ULLCA (2006) (Last Amended 2013) § 108(a) (same as to a limited liability company).

"Contribution" [(2)]—This definition is based on ULPA (2001) § 102(2) ("Contribution", except in the phrase "right of contribution", means any benefit provided by a person to a limited partnership in order to become a partner or in the person's capacity as a partner."). UPA (1997) did not define "contribution." The Harmonization Project added this definition.

This definition serves to distinguish capital contributions from other circumstances under which a partner or would-be partner might provide benefits to a general partnership (*e.g.*, providing services to the partnership as an employee or independent contractor, leasing property to the partnership).

This definition also distinguishes "contributions" from capital raised from transferees who invest; to be a contribution, the property or benefit must be "provided by a person . . . to become a partner or in the person's capacity as a partner. This distinction is ubiquitous in the law of unincorporated business organizations. See, e.g., ULPA (2001) § 102(2) definition (quoted above); N.Y. LTD. LIAB. CO. LAW § 102(f) (McKinney 2013) (" 'Contribution' means any cash, property, services rendered, or a promissory note or other binding obligation to contribute cash or property or to render services that a member contributes to a limited liability company in his or her capacity as a member.")

In contrast, partnership agreements sometimes provide for contributions from transferees. In such circumstances, the default rules for liquidating distributions should be altered accordingly. *See* Section 806(b)(1) (referring to distributions to be made "to each person owning a transferable interest that reflects *contributions* made and not previously returned.") (emphasis added).

"Distribution" [(4)(A)—redemptions included]—This provision specifically refers to transactions between a general partnership and one of its partners, which in the corporate context would be labeled "redemption." The paragraph has subparts because ownership interests in a partnership are conceptually bifurcated into economic rights ("transferable interest"), and governance and information rights.

Under Section 405(a), "[a]ny distribution made by a partnership before its dissolution and winding up must be in equal shares among partners, except to the extent necessary to comply with a transfer effective under Section 503 or charging order in effect under Section 504." Since a redemption is a distribution, absent authorization in the partnership agreement a partnership may not redeem the interest of one partner or transferee without redeeming (or at least offering to redeem) the interests of all other partners and transferees to a comparable extent.

The law of close corporations has flirted with a similar notion. *See, e.g., Donahue v. Rodd Electrotype Co. of New England, Inc.*, 328 N.E.2d 505, 518 (Mass. 1975) (stating, with regard to closely held corporations, "if the stockholder whose shares were purchased was a member of the controlling group, the controlling stockholders must cause the corporation to offer each stockholder an equal opportunity to sell a ratable number of his shares to the corporation at an identical price"); *cf. Wilkes v. Springside Nursing Home, Inc.*, 353 N.E.2d 657, 663 (Mass. 1976) (stating that "untempered application of the strict good faith standard enunciated in *Donahue* . . . will result in the imposition of limitations on legitimate action by the controlling group in a close corporation which will unduly hamper its effectiveness in managing the corporation in the best interests of all concerned"). *See also Toner v. Baltimore Envelope Co.*, 498 A.2d 642, 650 (Md. 1985) (rejecting the "per se breach of duty" approach).

A partnership agreement can override Section 405(a)'s equal treatment requirement without specifically mentioning redemptions.

Example: Ryan Company is a general partnership whose partnership agreement: (i) includes a list (the "protected list") of decisions or actions that may be taken only with the consent of all partners; and (ii) provides that all other decisions and acts may be taken as the Management Committee determines. The protected list does not include redemptions. The partnership agreement overrides the Section 404(a)'s equal treatment requirement.

[(4)(B)—exclusion]—This exclusion affects the reach of: (i) the charging order remedy under Section 504; and (ii) Section 407's clawback provision applicable to distributions made by a limited liability partnership. The effect on the clawback provision reflects the law in several states, *see, e.g.,* DEL. CODE ANN. tit. 6, § 15–309(a) (2014); VA. CODE ANN. § 13.1–1036 (2014), and makes sense conceptually and as a matter of policy. *See In re Tri-River Trading, L.L.C.*, 329 B.R. 252, 266 (B.A.P. 8th Cir. 2005), *aff'd*, 452 F.3d 756 (8th Cir. 2006) ("We know of no principle of law which suggests that a manager of a company is required to give up agreed upon salary to pay creditors when business turns bad."). UPA (1997) provides no clawback provision, an omission that disadvantaged creditors of an LLP compared to creditors of other entities with a liability shield.

"Foreign limited liability partnership" and "Foreign partnership" [(5) and (6)]—These definitions intend a flexible, comparative approach. Under Paragraph 6, if a particular type of foreign entity has key legal characteristics that approximate the essential legal characteristics of a domestic general partnership, that particular type of foreign entity is a foreign partnership under this act. Likewise, under Paragraph 5, if a foreign partnership has a liability shield similar to the shield provided under this act for a domestic LLP, the foreign partnership is a foreign limited liability partnership.

As further explained in the comment to Section 306(c), this act provides a full liability shield (*i.e.*, the shield applies regardless of the law giving rise to a claim against an LLP). A few jurisdictions provide only a partial shield. *See, e.g.,* 15 PA. CONS. STAT. ANN. § 8204 (West 2013) (providing the partners of an LLP a shield for claims against the partnership "whether sounding in contract or tort or otherwise," but only the claims that "arise from any negligent or wrongful acts or misconduct committed by another partner or other representative of the partnership"). The resulting partial shield does not protect partners against liability for the partnership's ordinary commercial debts, such as liability for lease payments. Nonetheless, a partial-shield foreign LLP would be a "foreign limited liability partnership" under Paragraph 6.

"Jurisdiction of formation" [(8)]—This definition" is not limited to United States jurisdictions.

"Limited liability partnership" [(9)]—Under this act (and most, if not all, LLP statutes), a general partnership obtains its LLP status from only one jurisdiction. The resulting LLP is "domestic" with regard to that jurisdiction and "foreign" with regard to all others.

Sections 901(f) (cancellation of statement of qualification) and 903 (administrative revocation of statement of qualification) limit this paragraph's open-ended definition of a "limited liability partnership" as "a partnership that has filed a statement of qualification under Section 901." Under this act, LLP status depends on a statement of qualification being in effect. *See* Section 903(d) and its comment.

"Partner" [(10)]—Under Section 202(a), any "person" can be a partner. Paragraph 14 of this section defines "person" very broadly to include individuals and "any . . . legal or commercial entity." At common law, "[t]he general rule . . . [was] that every person of sound mind, *sui juris*, and not otherwise restrained by law, may enter into a contract of partnership." JOSEPH STORY, COMMENTARIES ON THE LAW ON PARTNERSHIP § 7, at 10 (2d ed. 1850). The phrase "sound mind" and the term "*sui juris*" suggest that at common law a partner was necessarily an individual. *See* BLACK'S LAW DICTIONARY (9th ed. 2009) (defining *sui juris* as one "[o]f full age and capacity"). UPA (1914) § 2 defined "person" to include "partnerships, corporations, and other associations." *See, e.g., Williams v. Mammoth of Alaska, Inc.,* 890 P.2d 581, 584 n.8 (Alaska 1995*)* (stating that under UPA (1914) "[a] partner need not be a natural person").

After a person has been dissociated as a partner under Section 602, the term "partner" continues to apply to the person's conduct while a partner. *See* Section 603(b).

"Partnership" [(11)]—This definition, combined with Section 202(a), makes clear that a general partnership is a *business* organization. This definition makes no reference to a partnership having partners upon formation, but Section 202(a) does.

"Partnership agreement" [(12)]—This definition must be read in conjunction with Sections 105 through 107, which further describe the partnership agreement. In particular, although this definition refers to "the agreement . . . of all the partners," the partnership itself is bound by and may enforce the agreement. Section 106(a).

A partnership agreement is a contract, and therefore all statutory language pertaining to the partnership agreement must be understood in the context of the law of contracts.

The definition in Paragraph 12 is very broad and recognizes a wide scope of authority for the partnership agreement: "the matters described in Section 105(a)." Those matters include not only all relations *inter se* the partners and the partnership but also "the business of the partnership and the conduct of that business." Section 105(a)(2). Moreover, the definition puts no limits on the form of the partnership agreement. To the contrary, the definition contains the phrase "whether oral, implied, in a record, or in any combination thereof."

Unless the partnership agreement itself provides otherwise:

- A partnership agreement may comprise a number of separate documents (or records), however denominated; and

- Subject to Section 106(b) (deeming new partners to assent to the then-existing partnership agreement), a document, record, understanding, etc. can be part of the partnership agreement only with the assent of all persons then partners.

An agreement among less than all partners might well be enforceable among those partners as parties, but would not be part of the partnership agreement. However, under Section 105(a)(3), an amendment to a partnership agreement can be made with less than unanimous consent if the partnership agreement itself so provides.

An agreement to form a partnership is not itself a partnership agreement. The term "partnership agreement" presupposes "partners," and a person cannot be a partner in a partnership before the partnership exists. However, as soon as a partnership comes into existence, it perforce has a partnership agreement. For example, suppose: (i) two persons orally and informally agree to join their activities in a manner that satisfies Section 202 (formation of partnership); (ii) the partnership is thus formed; and (iii) without further ado or agreement, the persons become the partnership's initial partners. A partnership agreement exists. In the words of Paragraph 12 "all the partners" have agreed who the partners are and that, as "all the partners," they will conduct a business. That agreement—no matter how informal or rudimentary—is an agreement "concerning the matters described in Section 105(a)." To the extent the agreement does not provide the *inter se* "rules of the game," the "default rules" of this act "fill in the gaps." Section 105(b).

This act states no rule as to whether the statute of frauds applies to partnership agreements. Case law suggests that the answer is yes:

> Partnership agreements, like other contracts, are subject to the Statute of Frauds. A contract of partnership for a term exceeding one year is within the Statute of Frauds and is void unless it is in writing [and signed by the party to be bound]; however, a contract establishing a partnership terminable at the will of any partner is generally held to be capable of performance by its terms within one year of its making and, therefore, to be outside the Statute of Frauds.

Abbott v. Hurst, 643 So. 2d 589, 592 (Ala. 1994) (citations omitted).

Likewise, the land provision of the statute of frauds:

> applies to an oral contract to transfer or convey partnership real property, and the interest of the other partners therein, to one partner as an individual, as well as to a parol contract by one of the parties to convey certain land owned by him individually to the partnership, or to another partner, or to put it into the partnership stock.

Froiseth v. Nowlin, 287 P. 55, 56 (Wash. 1930) (quoting 27 C.J.S. § 220); *see also E. Piedmont 120 Associates, L.P. v. Sheppard*, 434 S.E.2d 101, 102 (Ga. Ct. App. 1993) (same, stating that "the fact that promises covered by the Statute of Frauds are made in the context of a partnership or joint venture agreement does not render the statute inapplicable"); *Filippi v. Filippi*, 818 A.2d 608, 618 (R.I. 2003) (applying the statute of frauds to an alleged oral agreement to transfer land owned by a limited partnership to one of its partners).

In contrast, the land provision does not apply to a partner's interest in a partnership, no matter how much the partnership owns or deals in real property. Interests in a partnership are personal property and reflect no direct interest in the entity's assets. *See* Sections 102(23), 501. Thus, the real property issues pertaining to a partnership ownership of land do not "flow through" to the partners and partnership interests. *See, e.g., Wooten v. Marshall*, 153 F. Supp. 759, 763–64 (S.D.N.Y. 1957) (involving an "oral agreement for a joint venture concerning the purchase, exploitation and eventual disposition of this 160 acre tract" and stating "[t]he real property acquired and dealt with by the venturers takes on the character of personal property as between the partners in the enterprise, and hence is not covered by [the Statute of Frauds]"); *see also Wade v. DeHart*, 1926 WL 2944 (Ohio Misc. 1926), *aff'd sub nom., Wade v. De Hart*, 159 N.E. 838 (Ohio Ct. App. 1927) (same).

On the question of how far a written (or "in a record") partnership agreement can go to prevent oral or implied-in-fact terms, see Section 105(a)(3), comment. For the effect of a pre-formation agreement, see Section 106(c). For the partnership's status viz-a-viz the partnership agreement, see Section 106(a).

"Partnership at will" [(13)]—This paragraph defines "partnership at will" in the negative (*i.e.*, by stating what the defined term is not). A partnership is "at will" if the partners' agreement does not obligate them to remain in the partnership until the passage of a specified time (a term) or the completion of a specified task, job, project, etc. (an undertaking).

"Partnership at will" is thus the default mode under this act; that is, a partnership is "at will" unless the partners have agreed otherwise. Absent such agreement, a partner may rightfully leave the partnership at any time (dissociate), Sections 601(1), 602(b)(2), and rightfully cause or seek the winding up of the partnership and its business (dissolution), Section 801(1); *see Fleming v. Hagen Estate*, 702 N.W.2d 786, 789 (Minn. Ct. App. 2005) (rejecting "the [appellant] estate's assertion that the district court erred by not concluding that [a partner's] counterclaim unilaterally dissolved the agreement pursuant to [Minnesota Statutes section 323A.0801]"; noting that "section 323A.0801(1) is applicable only to an at-will partnership").

This act does not directly define "partnership for a term" and "partnership for an undertaking," but their respective meanings are clear from this paragraph's wording and the case law. *E.g., Girard Bank v. Haley*, 332 A.2d 443, 447 (Pa. 1975) ("A 'particular undertaking' under the statute must be capable of accomplishment at some time, although the exact time may be unknown and unascertainable at the date of the agreement."). This paragraph thus suggests that a partnership under this act will fit into one of three conveniently labeled categories: at-will, for a term, for an undertaking. However, hybrid structures are possible.

Example: The partnership agreement of a general partnership:

- states a minimum term of ten years;

- permits one particular partner to leave the partnership at any time upon thirty days advance written notice; and

- provides that that person's dissociation as a partner will neither cause the partnership to dissolve nor entitle any other person to dissociate.

Hybrid structures cause no trouble, if the partnership agreement: (i) clearly and completely details the partners' understanding as to dissociation and dissolution; and (ii) does not confuse matters by inaccurately labeling the partnership as if it were a pure form of one of the three categories.

"Principal office" [(15)]—This term appears mostly in provisions pertaining to court proceedings, *e.g.*, Section 809(a), or delivery or service of information; *e.g.*, Sections 117(f)(3), 912(b). The term also helps determine the governing law for a partnership that is not a limited liability partnership. Section 104(2).

UPA (1997) referred to a partnership's "chief executive office," *e.g.*, UPA (1997) § 106(a), but did not define the term. *Id.*, cmt. The Harmonization Project substituted "principal office," as a more traditional and better-understood term in business entity statutes. In most cases, a partnership's principal office will be the same as the partnership's chief executive office (however defined). With regard to LLPs and foreign LLPs registered to do business in this state, the annual/biennial report will record the LLP's view on where the LLP's principal office is located. *See* Sections 913(a)(3) (domestic LLP), 1003(4) (foreign LLP).

"Property" [(16)]—This definition encompasses every form of property. For rules determining when property belongs to the partnership, see Section 204.

"Transfer" [(22)]—The term "transfer" is broadly defined to include all types of conveyances of interests in property. The reference to "transfer by operation of law" is significant in connection with Section 502 (Transfer of Transferable Interest). That section severely restricts a transferee's rights (absent the consent of the partners), and this definition makes those restrictions applicable; for example, to transfers ordered by a family court as part of a divorce proceeding and transfers resulting from the death of a partner. The restrictions also apply to transfers in the context of a partner's bankruptcy, except to the extent that bankruptcy law supersedes this act.

"Transferable interest" [(23)]—Absent a contrary provision in the partnership agreement or the consent of the partners, a "transferable interest" is the only interest in a partnership which can be transferred to a non-partner. *See* the comment to Section 502. This act does not define any term to encompass the entirety of a partner's rights in a partnership (*i.e.*, governance and information rights as well as economic rights).

UPA (1997) took a different approach, defining the entirety of a partner's rights directly and identifying the economic aspect through a limit on transferability. *See* UPA (1997) §§ 101(9) (defining "[p]artnership interest" or "partner's interest in the partnership" as "all of a partner's interests in the partnership, including the partner's transferable interest and all management and other rights"), 502 (stating that "the only transferable interest of a partner in the partnership is the partner's share of the profits and losses of the partnership and the partner's right to receive distributions").

This act defines "[t]ransferable interest" as an interest "initially owned by a person in the person's capacity as a partner," because this act does not contemplate a partnership directly creating interests that comprise only economic rights. *See* Sections 402 (addressing how a person becomes a partner), 503 (addressing how a person becomes a transferee).

§ 103.   Knowledge; Notice

(a)   A person knows a fact if the person:

     (1)   has actual knowledge of it; or

     (2)   is deemed to know it under subsection (d)(1)   or law other than this [act].

(b)   A person has notice of a fact if the person:

     (1)   has reason to know the fact from all the facts known to the person at the time in question; or

     (2)   is deemed to have notice of the fact under subsection (d)(2).

(c)   Subject to Section 117(f), a person notifies another person of a fact by taking steps reasonably required to inform the other person in ordinary course, whether or not those steps cause the other person to know the fact.

(d)   A person not a partner is deemed:

(1)   to know of a limitation on authority to transfer real property as provided in Section 303(g); and

(2)   to have notice of:

(A)   a person's dissociation as a partner 90 days after a statement of dissociation under Section 704 becomes effective; and

(B)   a partnership's:

(i)   dissolution 90 days after a statement of dissolution under Section 802 becomes effective;

(ii)   termination 90 days after a statement of termination under Section 802 becomes effective; and

(iii)   participation in a merger, interest exchange, conversion, or domestication, 90 days after articles of merger, interest exchange, conversion, or domestication under [Article] 11 become effective.

(e)   A partner's knowledge or notice of a fact relating to the partnership is effective immediately as knowledge of or notice to the partnership, except in the case of a fraud on the partnership committed by or with the consent of that partner.

COMMENT

The Harmonization Project made two important changes to this section. First, unlike UPA (1997), this act contains no generally applicable provisions determining when an organization other than a partnership is charged with knowledge or notice, because those imputation rules: (i) comprise core topics within the law of agency; (ii) are very complicated; (iii) should not have any different content under this act than in other circumstances; and (iv) are the subject of considerable attention in the Restatement (Third) of Agency (2006). However, Subsection (e) does provide a rule for attributing to a partnership knowledge or notice possessed by a partner.

Second, this act does not define "notice" to include "knowledge." Although conceptualizing the latter as giving the former makes logical sense and has a long pedigree, that conceptualization is counter-intuitive for the uninitiated. In ordinary usage, notice has a meaning separate from knowledge. This act follows ordinary usage and therefore contains some references to "knowledge or notice."

Subsection (a)(2)—In this context, the most important source of "law other than this [act]" is the common law of agency.

Subsection (b)(1)—The "facts known to the person at the time in question" include facts the person is deemed to know under Subsection (a)(2).

Subsection (c)—If a person "notifies" another person of a fact, the other person has "reason to know" the fact and therefore has notice under Subsection (b)(1). However, a person can have "notice" of a fact without having been "notifie[d]" of the fact.

Section 117(f) pertains to delivery of records *by* the filing office.

Subsection (d)—Following the pioneering approach of UPA (1997), this subsection provides constructive notice of facts stated in specified filed public records. The subsection works in conjunction with other sections of this act to curtail the power to bind and personal liability of partners and persons dissociated as partners. *See* Sections 702, 703, 804, 805. The constructive notice begins ninety days after the effective date of the filed record. For this act's rules on delayed effective dates, see Section 114.

UPA (1997) used an oblique and decentralized approach to constructive notice. *See, e.g.,* UPA (1997) § 704(c) (stating that "for the purposes of Sections 702(a)(3) [pertaining to the lingering power to bind the partnership of a person dissociated as a partner] and 703(b)(3) [pertaining to a the lingering liability for partnership obligations of a person dissociated as a partner], a person not a partner is deemed to have notice of the dissociation 90 days after

[a] statement of dissociation is filed"). As revised by the Harmonization Project, this subsection provides directly for constructive notice and centralizes all of this act's constructive notice provisions except for those pertaining to statements of authority under Section 303.

Subsection (e)—This subsection states the rule for imputing a partner's knowledge or notice to the partnership. The rule was part of the common law. *Peoples' Bank of Baltimore v. Keech*, 26 Md. 521, 533 (Md. 1867) (holding that "the firm is bound by notice to one of the co-partners; because each represents the firm and is general agent of all"). UPA (1914) § 12 codified the rule, and UPA (1997) § 102(f) carried forward the codified rule with some modification. The Harmonization Project did not change UPA (1997) § 102(f), except to delete "receipt of a notification"; the phrase "receipt of a notification" is no longer a term of art in the LLC and partnership acts.

§ 104. Governing Law

The internal affairs of a partnership and the liability of a partner as a partner for a debt, obligation, or other liability of the partnership are governed by:

(1)   in the case of a limited liability partnership, the law of this state; and

(2)   in the case of a partnership that is not a limited liability partnership, the law of the jurisdiction in which the partnership has its principal office.

COMMENT

This section states two choice-of-law rules: an invariable rule for limited liability partnerships, Paragraph 1, and a default rule for non-LLPs, Paragraph 2. Both rules address "internal affairs" and "the liability of a partner as a partner for the debts, obligations, or other liabilities of the partnership."

Like any other legal concept, "internal affairs" may be indeterminate at its edges. However, the concept certainly includes interpretation and enforcement of the partnership agreement, relations among the partners as partners, and relations between the partnership and a partner as a partner. *Compare* Section 104, *with* RESTATEMENT (SECOND) OF CONFLICT OF LAWS § 302, cmt. a (1971) (defining "internal affairs" with reference to a corporation as "the relations inter se of the corporation, its shareholders, directors, officers or agents").

"Internal affairs" do not encompass the power *vel non* of a person to bind a partnership. RESTATEMENT (SECOND) OF CONFLICT OF LAWS §§ 292(2) (1971) ("The principal will be held bound by the agent's action if he would so be bound under the local law of the state where the agent dealt with the third person, provided at least that the principal had authorized the agent to act on his behalf in that state or had led the third person reasonably to believe that the agent had such authority."), 295(1) ("Whether a partnership is bound by action taken on its behalf by an agent in dealing with a third person is determined by the local law of the state selected by application of the rule of § 292."); RESTATEMENT (FIRST) OF CONFLICT OF LAWS § 345, cmt. c (1934) (Law Governing Effect of Act of Agent or Partner) ("If . . . the principal or partner sends the agent or other partner into a state to act on his behalf, he assumes the risk of liability not only for authorized but for unauthorized conduct of the agent or partner in accordance with the law of that state."); *see also Farm & Ranch Services, Ltd. v. LT Farm & Ranch, L.L.C.*, 779 F. Supp. 2d 949, 960 (S.D. Iowa 2011).

"Internal affairs" and the "liability of a partner as a partner" are mentioned separately, because it can be argued that the liability of partners to third parties is not an internal affair. *See, e.g.*, RESTATEMENT (SECOND) OF CONFLICT OF LAWS § 307 (1971) (treating shareholders' liability separately from the internal affairs doctrine). A few cases subsume owner/manager liability into internal affairs. *See, e.g., Kalb, Voorhis & Co. v. American Fin. Corp.*, 8 F.3d 130, 132 (2d Cir. 1993) (holding that the corporation's "primary purpose is to insulate shareholders from legal liability" and therefore "the state of incorporation has the greater interest in determining when and if that insulation is to be stripped away" (quoting *Soviet Pan Am Travel Effort v. Travel Comm., Inc.*, 756 F. Supp. 126, 131 (S.D.N.Y. 1991) (internal quotation marks omitted).

In any event, neither "internal affairs" nor the "liability of a partner as a partner" encompass a claim that a partner is liable to a third party for: (i) having purported inaccurately to have the actual authority to bind a partnership to the third party; or (ii) having committed a tort against the third party while acting on the partnership's behalf or in the course of the partnership's business. That liability is not by status (*i.e.*, not "as a partner") but rather results from function or conduct.

Treating "liability of a partner as a partner" as a matter of domestic law comports generally with the law of business entities. For example, some (if not all) limited liability partnership statutes so provide. *E.g.*, DEL. CODE

ANN. tit. 6, § 15–1101(a) (2013) (stating that "[t]he law under which a foreign limited liability partnership is formed governs . . . the liability of partners for obligations of the partnership"); N.Y. P'SHIP LAW § 121–1502(*l*) (2014) (stating that "[t]he laws of the jurisdiction that govern a foreign limited liability partnership shall determine . . . the liability of partners for debts, obligations and liabilities of, or chargeable to, the foreign limited liability partnership").

Moreover, "[t]he general rule [from the case law] is that a plaintiff's alter ego theory is governed by the law of the state in which the business at issue is organized." *Rual Trade Ltd. v. Viva Trade L.L.C.*, 549 F. Supp. 2d 1067, 1077 (E.D. Wis. 2008); *see also In re Gulf Fleet Holdings, Inc.*, 491 B.R. 747, 787 (Bankr. W.D. La. 2013) (stating both conceptual and policy rationales for choosing the law of the state of formation)*; In re Saba Enters., Inc.*, 421 B.R. 626, 648–51 (Bankr. S.D.N.Y. 2009) (examining the issue in detail and applying the state of formation rule).

Paragraph 1—The partnership agreement cannot alter this paragraph. *See* Section 105(c)(1). In essence, when a partnership chooses where to deliver for filing a statement of qualification, the partnership chooses its governing law. This approach comports with the law of other businesses entities whose formation or legal status depends at least in part on a publicly filed record. *See, e.g.,* ULPA (2001) (Last Amended 2013) § 104 (stating that the law of the state of formation is the domestic entity's governing law); ULLCA (2006) (Last Amended 2013) § 104 (same).

However, a partnership agreement may lawfully incorporate by reference the provisions of another state's partnership act. If done correctly, this incorporation makes the foreign statutory language part of the partnership agreement, and the incorporated terms (together with the rest of the partnership agreement) then govern the partners (and those claiming through the partners) to the extent not prohibited by this act. *See* Section 105. This approach: (i) does not switch the limited liability partnership's governing law to that of another state; (ii) instead takes the provisions of another state's law and incorporates them by reference into the contract among the partners; (iii) raises complex drafting issues—*e.g.*, how to address subsequent changes to the incorporated law (whether occurring by statutory amendment or court decision); and (iv) thus is rarely, if ever, a good idea.

Paragraph 2—Section 102(15) defines "principal office."

The partnership agreement may change the rule stated in this paragraph, although other law may limit a partnership's options. *See* RESTATEMENT (SECOND) OF CONFLICT OF LAWS §§ 294 (1971) (Relationship of Partners Inter Se), 187(2) (stating the limited bases for disregarding a contractual choice of law).

When a statement of qualification becomes effective under Section 901: (i) this paragraph no longer applies; and (ii) neither the partnership's principal office nor the partnership agreement is relevant to determining the law governing the partnership's internal affairs. Section 105(c)(1) (stating that the partnership agreement may not "vary the law applicable under Section 104(1)").

§ 105. Partnership Agreement; Scope, Function, and Limitations

(a) Except as otherwise provided in subsections (c) and (d), the partnership agreement governs:

(1) relations among the partners as partners and between the partners and the partnership;

(2) the business of the partnership and the conduct of that business; and

(3) the means and conditions for amending the partnership agreement.

(b) To the extent the partnership agreement does not provide for a matter described in subsection (a), this [act] governs the matter.

(c) A partnership agreement may not:

(1) vary the law applicable under Section 104(1);

(2) vary the provisions of Section 110;

(3) vary the provisions of Section 307;

(4) unreasonably restrict the duties and rights under Section 408, but the partnership agreement may impose reasonable restrictions on the availability and use of information obtained under that section and may define appropriate remedies, including liquidated damages, for a breach of any reasonable restriction on use;

(5)   alter or eliminate the duty of loyalty or the duty of care, except as otherwise provided in subsection (d);

(6)   eliminate the contractual obligation of good faith and fair dealing under Section 409(d), but the partnership agreement may prescribe the standards, if not manifestly unreasonable, by which the performance of the obligation is to be measured;

(7)   unreasonably restrict the right of a person to maintain an action under Section 410(b);

(8)   relieve or exonerate a person from liability for conduct involving bad faith, willful or intentional misconduct, or knowing violation of law;

(9)   vary the power of a person to dissociate as a partner under Section 602(a), except to require that the notice under Section 601(1) to be in a record;

(10) vary the grounds for expulsion specified in Section 601(5);

(11) vary the causes of dissolution specified in Section 801(4) or (5);

(12) vary the requirement to wind up the partnership's business as specified in Section 802(a), (b)(1), and (d);

(13) vary the right of a partner under Section 901(f) to vote on or consent to a cancellation of a statement of qualification;

(14) vary the right of a partner to approve a merger, interest exchange, conversion, or domestication under Section 1123(a)(2), 1133(a)(2), 1143(a)(2), or 1153(a)(2);

(15) vary the required contents of a plan of merger under Section 1122(a), plan of interest exchange under Section 1132(a), plan of conversion under Section 1142(a), or plan of domestication under Section 1152(a);

(16) vary any requirement, procedure, or other provision of this [act] pertaining to:

(A)   registered agents; or

(B)   the [Secretary of State], including provisions pertaining to records authorized or required to be delivered to the [Secretary of State] for filing under this [act]; or

(17) except as otherwise provided in Sections 106 and 107(b), restrict the rights under this [act] of a person other than a partner.

(d)   Subject to subsection (c)(8), without limiting other terms that may be included in a partnership agreement, the following rules apply:

(1)   The partnership agreement may:

(A)   specify the method by which a specific act or transaction that would otherwise violate the duty of loyalty may be authorized or ratified by one or more disinterested and independent persons after full disclosure of all material facts; and

(B)   alter the prohibition in Section 406(a)(2) so that the prohibition requires only that the partnership's total assets not be less than the sum of its total liabilities.

(2)   To the extent the partnership agreement expressly relieves a partner of a responsibility that the partner would otherwise have under this [act] and imposes the responsibility on one or more other partners, the agreement also may eliminate or limit any fiduciary duty of the partner relieved of the responsibility which would have pertained to the responsibility.

(3)   If not manifestly unreasonable, the partnership agreement may:

(A)   alter or eliminate the aspects of the duty of loyalty stated in Section 409(b);

(B)   identify specific types or categories of activities that do not violate the duty of loyalty;

(C)   alter the duty of care, but may not authorize conduct involving bad faith, willful or intentional misconduct, or knowing violation of law; and

(D)   alter or eliminate any other fiduciary duty.

(e)   The court shall decide as a matter of law whether a term of a partnership agreement is manifestly unreasonable under subsection (c)(6) or (d)(3). The court:

(1)   shall make its determination as of the time the challenged term became part of the partnership agreement and by considering only circumstances existing at that time; and

(2)   may invalidate the term only if, in light of the purposes and business of the partnership, it is readily apparent that:

(A)   the objective of the term is unreasonable; or

(B)   the term is an unreasonable means to achieve the term's objective.

COMMENT

The Harmonization Project re-wrote this section, for the most part conforming this section to the corresponding section of ULLCA (2006).

Principal Provisions of the Act Concerning the Partnership Agreement

The partnership agreement is pivotal to a partnership, and Sections 105 through 107 are pivotal to this act. They must be read together, along with Section 102(12) (defining the partnership agreement).

This section performs five essential functions. Subsection (a) establishes the primacy of the partnership agreement in establishing *inter se* relations among the partners and partnership. Subsection (b) recognizes this act as comprising mostly default rules (i.e., gap fillers for issues as to which the partnership agreement provides no rule). Subsection (c) lists the few mandatory provisions of the act. Subsection (d) lists some provisions frequently found in partnership agreements, authorizing some unconditionally and others so long as "not manifestly unreasonable." Subsection (e) delineates in detail both the meaning of "not manifestly unreasonable" and the information relevant to determining a claim that a provision of a partnership agreement is manifestly unreasonable.

Section 106 details the effect of a partnership agreement on the partnership and on persons becoming partners. Section 107 concerns the effect of a partnership agreement on third parties.

Role and Inevitability of Partnership Agreement

Section 102(12) delineates a very broad scope for "partnership agreement." As a result, once a partnership comes into existence, a partnership agreement necessarily exists. *See* the comment to Section 102(12). Accordingly, this act refers to "the partnership agreement" rather than "a partnership agreement." This phrasing should not, however, be read to require a partnership or its partners to take any formal action to adopt a partnership agreement.

The partnership agreement is the exclusive consensual process for modifying this act's various default rules pertaining to relationships *inter se* the partners and between the partners and the partnership. Section 105(a). The partnership agreement also has power over "the obligations of a partnership and its partners to a person in the person's capacity as a transferee or person dissociated as a partner." Section 107(b). For the relationship between the partnership agreement and public records in the filing office, see Section 107(d).

The Partnership Agreement and the Fiduciary and Other Duties of Those Who Manage

One of the most complex questions in the law of unincorporated business organizations is the extent to which an agreement among the organization's owners can affect the fiduciary and other duties of those who have ultimate power to manage the organization—in a general partnership, the partners themselves. As explained in detail in the comment to Subsection (d)(3), this act rejects the notion that a contract can completely transform an inherently fiduciary relationship into a merely arm's length association. Within that limitation, however, this section provides substantial power to the partnership agreement to reshape, limit, and eliminate fiduciary and other managerial duties.

Subsection (a) recognizes that the partnership agreement is the map to the parties' deal and that any claim by a partner of managerial misconduct must be assessed first under the relevant terms of the partnership agreement. Subsection (d) specifically validates arrangements commonly used to reshape managerial duties and limit the consequences of breaching those duties. Subsection (c) contains relevant limitations, but those limitations: (i) must be read together with Subsection (d); and (ii) do not preclude the partnership agreement fundamentally redesigning the duties applicable to the partners. For the act's design of those duties, see Sections 408 and 409.

Subsection (a)—This section describes the very broad scope of a partnership's partnership agreement, which includes all matters constituting "internal affairs." *Compare* Section 105(a), with Section 104 (using the phrase "internal affairs" in stating a choice of law rule). This broad grant of authority is subject to the restrictions stated in Subsection (c), including the broad restriction stated in Subsection (c)(17) (concerning the rights of third parties under this act).

Subsection (a)(1)—This paragraph encompasses all the rights and duties of each partner, including rights and duties pertaining to transactions under Article 11.

Subsection (a)(3)—Under this provision, the partnership agreement can control both the quantum of consent required (*e.g.*, majority of partners) and the means by which the consent is manifested (*e.g.*, prohibiting modifications except when consented to in writing). *See* the comment to Section 107(a).

If the partnership agreement does not address the issue, Section 401(k) applies and requires the affirmative vote or consent of all the partners. Under Section 119 (supplemental principles of law), the parol evidence rule will apply to a written partnership agreement when appropriate under contract law.

Subsection (b)—To the extent the partnership agreement does not determine an *inter se* matter, this act determines the matter. The partnership agreement may vary any provision of this act pertaining to inter se matters, except as provided in Subsections (c) and (d).

Sometimes—but not always—the comments to this act refer to a variable provision as a "default rule" and a non-waivable provision as "mandatory." These references are merely to draw attention to the default/mandatory distinction in particular contexts and have neither the intent nor the power to affect the default/mandatory status of provisions of this act whose comments lack a comparable reference.

Subsection (c)—This subsection lists provisions of this act whose respective effects cannot be varied or may be varied subject to a stated limitation. For historical reasons, this subsection uses the words "vary" and "alter" interchangeably. No difference in meaning is intended.

If a person claims that a term of the partnership agreement violates this subsection, as a matter of ordinary procedural law the burden of proof is on the person making the claim.

Subsection (c)(1)—"[T]he law applicable under Section 104(1)" establishes the governing law for the internal affairs of a partnership. The organizers of a partnership make this choice of law by choosing to form a partnership under this act. Domestication to another jurisdiction will re-set the choice of law, see Sections 1151–56, but the partnership agreement cannot. *See* the comment to Section 104(1).

Subsection (c) contains no parallel prohibition on varying Section 901 (stating the governing law for foreign limited liability partnerships), because a prohibition is unnecessary. As a matter of fundamental contract law, an agreement among partners of one partnership is powerless to govern the affairs of another partnership.

Subsection (c)(3)—Under this act, a partnership is emphatically an entity, and the partners lack the power to alter that characteristic.

The cited section pertains to "actions by and against partnership and partners," arguably comes within Subsection (c)(17) (prohibiting the partnership agreement from "restrict[ing] the rights under this [act] of a person other than a partner"), but is specifically noted for the avoidance of doubt.

Subsection (c)(4)—Although phrased as a restriction, this provision grants substantial power to the partnership agreement.

Example: A law firm operates as a partnership, and the partnership agreement provides that a "Compensation Committee" periodically decides each partner's compensation. The agreement also states that only partners who are on the Compensation Committee may have access to the Committee's compensation decisions pertaining to other partners. This restriction is reasonable.

The act also empowers the partnership "as a matter within the ordinary course of its business [to] impose reasonable restrictions and conditions on access to and use of information" obtained under Section 408. *See* Section 408(j).

In determining whether a restriction is reasonable, a court might consider: (i) the danger or other problem the restriction seeks to avoid; (ii) the purpose for which the information is sought; and (iii) whether, in light of both the problem and the purpose, the restriction is reasonably tailored.

Subsection (c)(5)—This limitation is less powerful than might first appear, because Subsection (d) specifically authorizes substantial alterations to the duties of loyalty and care, including restricting and substantially eliminating those duties.

Subsection (c)(6)—Section 409(d) refers to the "contractual obligation of good faith and fair dealing," which contract law implies in every contract. The partnership agreement cannot eliminate this obligation, neither in whole (*i.e.*, generally) nor in part (*i.e.*, as applicable to specified situations).

However, a partnership agreement may "prescribe the standards . . . by which the performance of [that] obligation is to be measured."

Example: A partnership agreement designates a managing partner, provides that partner almost total control of the partnership's operations, and grants the partner the discretion to cause the partnership to enter into contracts with affiliates of the partner (so-called "Conflict Transactions"). The agreement further provides: "When causing the Company to enter into a Conflict Transaction, the Managing Partner complies with Section 409(d) of [this act] if a disinterested person, knowledgeable in the subject matter, states in writing that the terms and conditions of the Conflict Transaction are equivalent to the terms and conditions that would be agreed to by persons at arm's length in comparable circumstances." This provision "prescribes[s] the standards by which the performance of the [Section 409(d)] obligation is to be measured."

Example: Same facts as the previous example, except that, during the performance of a Conflict Transaction, the managing partner causes the partnership to waive material protections under the applicable contract. The standard stated in the previous example is inapposite to this conduct. Section 409(d) therefore applies to the conduct without any direct contractual delineation. (However, other terms of the agreement may be relevant to determining whether the conduct violates Section 409(d). *See* the comment to Section 409(d).)

Example: A partnership agreement designates a managing partner and gives that partner "sole discretion" to make various decisions. The agreement further provides: "Whenever this agreement requires or permits the Managing Partner to make a decision that has the potential to benefit one class of partners to the detriment of another class, the Managing Partner complies with Section 409(d) of [this act] if the Managing Partner makes the decision with:

    a.   the honest belief that the decision:

        i.   serves the best interests of the Partnership; or

        ii.   at least does not injure or otherwise disserve those interests; and

    b.   the reasonable belief that the decision breaches no partner's rights under this agreement."

This provision "prescribe[s] the standards by which the performance of the [Section 409(d)] obligation is to be measured." *Compare* Section 105(c)(6), with *Nemec v. Shrader*, 991 A.2d 1120 (Del. 2010) (considering such a situation in the context of the right to call preferred stock and deciding by a three-two vote that exercising the call did not breach the implied covenant of good faith and fair dealing).

A partnership agreement that seeks to prescribe standards for measuring the contractual obligation of good faith and fair dealing under Section 409(d) should expressly refer to the obligation. *See Gerber v. Enter. Prods. Hldgs., L.L.C.*, 67 A.3d 400, 418 (Del. 2013) (distinguishing between the implied contractual covenant and an express contractual obligation of "good faith" as stated in a limited partnership agreement).

For an explanation of the function and role of the covenant of good faith and fair dealing, see the comment to Section 409(d). For the rules delimiting the "not manifestly unreasonable" requirement, see Subsection (e).

Subsection (c)(7)—Section 410(b) delineates a partner's rights to "maintain an action against the partnership or another partner." It would be unreasonable to frustrate these rights but not unreasonable to channel their exercise. For example, the partnership agreement might select a forum, require pre-suit mediation, provide for arbitration, or require a pre-suit demand on a management committee before a partner files suit against the partnership. Similarly, it is not unreasonable to provide for liquidated damages consonant with the law of contracts. In contrast, it would be unreasonable for a partnership agreement to both: (i) require a partner intending to sue the partnership to make demand on a management committee before filing suit against the partnership regardless of futility; and (ii) bar taking the claim to court no matter how long the management committee ponders the demand.

Subsection (c)(8)—These restrictions are ubiquitous in the law of business entities and, in conjunction with other provisions of this section, control the otherwise very broad power of a partnership agreement to affect fiduciary and other duties. The restrictions are central to the raft of exculpatory provisions that sprung up in corporate statutes in response to *Smith v. Van Gorkum*, 488 A.2d 858 (Del. 1985), *overruled on other grounds by Gantler v. Stephens*, 965 A.2d 695 (Del. 2009). Delaware led the response with Delaware Code Annotated title 8, section 102(b)(7), and a number of LLC statutes have similar provisions. E.g., GA. CODE ANN. § 14–11–305(4)(A) (2011). For an extreme example, see Virginia Code Annotated section 13.1–1025(B) (2012). In this context, "conduct" includes both acts and omissions. BLACK'S LAW DICTIONARY (9th ed. 2009) (defining conduct as "[p]ersonal behavior, whether by action or inaction").

The term "bad faith" has multiple meanings, and the context determines which meaning applies. In the context of the duty of loyalty, "bad faith" includes conduct motivated by ill will or other intent purposely to harm another person. The concept also includes conduct from which a person derives an improper personal benefit. See, e.g., *Mroz v. Hoaloha Na Eha, Inc.*, 410 F. Supp. 2d 919, 936–37 (D. Haw. 2005) (denying a motion to dismiss a claim that "the Majority Partners" were personally liable for the partnership's wrongful termination of the plaintiff; quoting the complaint as alleging that "the Majority Partners, individually and as a group, acted with malice and/or ill will, and/or with an intent to serve their own personal interests and/or without an intent to serve company interests, and/or outside of the scope of their authority and/or without justification"); *BOGNC, LLC v. Cornelius NC Self-Storage L.L.C.*, 10 CVS 19072, 2013 WL 1867065, at *9 (N.C. Super. [Business Court] May 1, 2013) (noting that "no . . . [exculpatory] provision may limit a manager's liability for acts known to be in conflict with the interests of the limited liability company, or for acts from which the manager derived an improper personal benefit") (citing N.C. Gen. Stat. § 57C–3–32(b)); *Lasica v. Savers Grp. of Minn., L.L.C.*, A12-0092, 2012 WL 3553246, at *2 (Minn. Ct. App. Aug. 20, 2012) (noting that an "individual seeking indemnification [under statute providing for indemnification)] must have acted in good faith and must not have received an improper personal benefit") (citing MINN. STAT. § 322B.699, subdivs. 2(a)(2), (3) (2010)).

In the context of the duty of care, the concept of bad faith comes primarily from corporate law and means an extreme breach of the duty (i.e., "the failure to exercise "honest judgment in the lawful and legitimate furtherance of corporate purposes"). *Deblinger v. Sani-Pine Products Co., Inc.*, 107 A.D.3d 659, 661 (N.Y. 2013) (quoting *Auerbach v. Bennett*, 393 N.E.2d 994 (N.Y. 1979)) (emphasis added) (internal quotation marks omitted).

Thus, when a plaintiff alleges bad faith as pertaining to the duty of care, "[t]he burden . . . is to show irrationality: a plaintiff must demonstrate that no reasonable business person could possibly authorize the action in good faith. Put positively, the decision must go so far beyond the bounds of reasonable business judgment that its only explanation is bad faith." *In re Tower Air, Inc.*, 416 F.3d 229, 238 (3d Cir. 2005) (discussing then prevailing Delaware law) (citation omitted); *see also KDW Restructuring & Liquidation Servs. L.L.C. v. Greenfield*, 874 F. Supp. 2d 213, 226 (S.D.N.Y. 2012) (referring to a lack of "a rationale corporate purpose" and "a disregard for the duty to examine all available information—*information that was readily at hand*") (emphasis added).

With regard to both the duty of loyalty and the duty of care, "bad faith" is entirely distinct from the meaning of "good faith" in the contractual covenant of good faith and fair dealing. *See* the comment to Section 409(d).

Subsection (c)(8) pertains to indirect as well as direct efforts to "relieve or exonerate" and thus limits how far a partnership agreement can go in providing for indemnification. *See* Section 401(c) (stating a default rule for indemnification).

Although this paragraph does not expressly address contracts between a partnership and a partner, the stated constraints must also apply to such contracts. If not, those constraints are effectively meaningless.

Example: A general partnership enters into a management contract with its sole managing partner, and the contract provides the partner exoneration for liability to the partnership even for willful and intentional misconduct. Most likely, contract law will treat the provision as against public policy and therefore unenforceable. RESTATEMENT (SECOND) OF CONTRACTS § 195(1) (1981) ("A term exempting a party from tort liability for harm caused intentionally or recklessly is unenforceable on grounds of public policy."). If not, a court should hold the provision unenforceable to avoid evisceration of Subsection (c)(8). (Or, the court could invoke the policy expressed in Subsection (c)(8) as grounds for holding the provision unenforceable under contract law.)

Subsection (c)(9)—As a result of this restriction, a partner always has the power to dissociate; the partnership agreement can only negate the right. This approach is consistent with the notions that: (i) a partnership is a voluntary association, see, e.g., *Gangl v. Gangl*, 281 N.W.2d 574, 580 (N.D. 1979) (stating that "[t]he term [association] connotes not only a group of two or more persons but also voluntariness"); (ii) the partnership relationship is essentially contractual, *see, e.g., Wallner v. Schmitz*, 239 Minn. 93, 95, 57 N.W.2d 821, 823 (1953) (stating that "[a] partnership is a contractual relationship as between the parties"); and (iii) only in exceptional circumstances does a party to a contract lack the power to breach, and courts will not enjoin a person to remain in an ongoing contractual relationship that involves trust and confidence. E. ALLAN FARNSWORTH, CONTRACTS § 12.7, at 781 (3d ed.1999) ("A court will not grant specific performance of a contract to provide a service that is personal in nature. This refusal . . . is based [in part] of the undesirability of compelling the continuance of personal relations after disputes have arisen and confidence and loyalty have been shaken and the undesirability, in some instances, of imposing what might seem like involuntary servitude.") (footnote omitted).

Subsection (c)(10)—The partnership agreement may not change the stated grounds for expulsion but may determine the forum in which a claim for expulsion under Section 601(5) is determined.

Subsection (c)(11)—The partnership agreement may not change the stated grounds for dissolution but may determine the forum in which a claim for dissolution under Section 801(4) or (5) is determined. For example, arbitration and forum selection clauses are commonplace in business relationships in general and in partnership agreements in particular.

The approach of this paragraph differs from the law of Delaware. *See Huatuco v. Satellite Healthcare*, CV 8465-VCG, 2013 WL 6460898, at *1, n.2 (Del. Ch. Dec. 9, 2013) (stating that "the right to judicial dissolution is a default right which the parties may eschew by contract" but reserving the question of "[w]hether the parties may, by contract, divest this Court of its authority to order a dissolution in all circumstances, even where it appears manifest that equity so requires—leaving, for instance, irreconcilable members locked away together forever like some alternative entity version of Sartre's *Huis Clos*").

Subsection (c)(12)—The cited provisions comprise the non-waivable aspects of winding up a dissolved partnership. The other provisions of Section 802 are default rules and therefore waivable.

Subsection (c)(13)—Section 901(f) requires the "the affirmative vote or consent of all the partners." The requirement is non-waivable, because canceling a statement of qualification eliminates the LLP liability shield and makes each partner automatically liable for partnership's obligations subsequently incurred.

Subsection (c)(14)—Sections 1123(a)(1), 1133(a)(1), 1143(a)(1), and 1153(a)(1) each requires the consent or the affirmative vote of all partners. The partnership agreement may modify these requirements. In contrast, under the sections stated in this subsection:

- each partner is protected from being merged, exchanged, converted, or domesticated "into" the status of a partner in a general partnership that is not a limited liability partnership (or a comparable "unshielded" position in some other organization) without the partner having *directly* consented to either:

  o the merger, interest exchange, conversion, or domestication; or

  o a partnership agreement provision that permits such transactions to occur with less than unanimous consent of the partners; and

- merely consenting to a partnership agreement provision that permits amendment of the partnership agreement with less than unanimous consent of the partners does not qualify as the requisite direct consent.

Subsection (c)(15)—Because these plans are the basic "deal documents" for each of the organic transactions contemplated in Article 11, the partnership agreement may not vary the contents of these plans.

Subsection (c)(16)—This prohibition is arguably implicit in Subsection (c)(17) (affecting rights under this act of third parties) but is stated expressly to avoid any doubt.

Subsection (c)(17)—This limitation pertains only to "the rights under this [act] of" third parties" other than partners. Moreover, the limitation is subject to two major exceptions: Section 106 (pertaining to the partnership agreement's relationship to the partnership itself and to persons becoming partners) and Section 107(b) (pertaining to the partnership agreement's power over the rights of transferees).

Subsection (d)—The partnership agreement has plenipotentiary power over the matters described in Subsection (a), except as specifically limited by Subsections (c) and (d)(3). However, for the convenience of practitioners and the courts, Paragraphs 1 and 2 list various terms often found in partnership agreements. No negative inference should be drawn about terms not listed; the listing is provided "without limiting other terms that may be included in a partnership agreement."

Paragraph 3 lists arrangements subject to the "not manifestly unreasonable" standard. Subsection (e) delineates that standard. The same standard applies to terms of a partnership agreement which seek to "prescribe the standards . . . by which the performance of the [contractual] obligation [of good faith and fair dealing under Section 409(d)] is to be measured." Subsection (c)(6).

Subsection (d)(1)(A)—An arrangement *not* involving "one or more disinterested and independent persons" acting "after full disclosure of all material facts" would "alter . . . the aspects of the duty of loyalty stated in Section 409(b)" and would therefore be subject to the "not manifestly unreasonable standard" of Subsection (d)(3)(A).

For the meaning of "material" as applied to information, see the comment to Section 409(f).

Subsection (d)(1)(B)—Section 405(a)(2) prohibits distributions by a limited liability partnership:

- *not merely* when, after the distribution, "the partnership's total assets would be less than the sum of its total liabilities";

- *but also* when, after the distribution, the assets would less than the total liabilities "plus the amount that would be needed, if the partnership were to be dissolved and wound up at the time of the distribution, to satisfy the preferential rights upon dissolution and winding up of partners and transferees whose preferential rights are superior to the rights of persons receiving the distribution."

The second part of the solvency test pertains to preferential rights to distributions, is thus a matter *inter se* the partners and any transferees, and is therefore subject to change in the partnership agreement.

In contrast, the first part of the solvency test protects third parties—creditors of the partnership—and therefore cannot be changed by the partnership agreement. Section 105(c)(17). Likewise, the partnership agreement cannot change the solvency test stated in Section 406(a)(1) (that "the partnership would not be able to pay its debts as they become due in the ordinary course of the partnership's business").

Subsection (d)(2)—The "not manifestly unreasonable" standard does not apply to partnership agreement provisions within this paragraph.

Example: ABC Company ("ABC") has three partners. ABC has two entirely separate lines of business, the Alpha business and the Beta business. Under ABC's partnership agreement:

- Partner 1's responsibilities pertain exclusively to the Alpha business, while responsibility for:

    o the Beta business is allocated exclusively to Partner 2; and

    o ABC's overall operation is allocated exclusively to Partner 3.

- Partner 2's responsibilities pertain exclusively to the Beta business, while responsibility for:

    o the Alpha business is allocated exclusively to Partner 1; and

    o ABC's overall operation is allocated exclusively to Partner 3.

- Partner 1 has no fiduciary duties pertaining to the Beta business.

- Partner 2 has no fiduciary duties pertaining to the Alpha business.

The elimination of Partner 1's fiduciary duties with regard to the Beta business and Partner 2's fiduciary duties with regard to the Alpha business are enforceable, without regard to the "manifestly unreasonable" standard of Subsection (d)(3).

Section (d)(3)—This act rejects the ultra-contractarian notion that fiduciary duty within a business organization is merely a set of default rules and seeks instead to balance the virtues of "freedom of contract" against the dangers that inescapably exist when some persons have power over the interests of others.

Nonetheless, a properly drafted partnership agreement may substantially alter and even eliminate fiduciary duties. Two important limitations exist. First, arrangements subject to this subsection may not be "manifestly unreasonable." *See* Subsection (e) (delineating this standard).

Second, the partnership agreement may not transform the relationship inter se partners and the partnership into an entirely arm's length arrangement. For example, displacement of fiduciary duties is effective only to the extent that the displacement is stated clearly and with particularity. This rule is fundamental in the jurisprudence of fiduciary duty. *See, e.g., Paige Capital Mgmt., L.L.C. v. Lerner Master Fund, L.L.C.*, Civ. A. No. 5502-CS, 2011 WL 3505355, at *31 (Del. Ch. Aug. 8, 2011) (stating that, even under a statute that "permits the waiver of fiduciary duties . . . such waivers must be set forth clearly"); *Kelly v. Blum*, Civ. A. No. 4516-VCP, 2010 WL 629850, at *10 n.70 (Del. Ch. Feb. 24, 2010) ("Having been granted great contractual freedom by the LLC Act, drafters of or parties to an LLC agreement should be expected to provide . . . clear and unambiguous provisions when they desire to expand, restrict or eliminate the operation of traditional fiduciary duties"). It would therefore be manifestly unreasonable for a partnership agreement to negate this rule.

Although Subsection (d)(3) does not expressly address contracts between a partnership and a partner, the stated constraints must also apply to such contracts. If not, those constraints are effectively meaningless.

Example: A general partnership enters into a management contract with its sole managing partner, and the contract provides that the duties of loyalty stated in Section 409(b) are entirely eliminated. If the partnership agreement were to so provide, the provision would be subject to the "manifestly unreasonable standard." Section 105(d)(3)(A). Absent the authorization provided by Section 105(d)(3)(A), the management contract's attempt to waive fiduciary duties may be unenforceable as a matter of public policy and contract law. *See Neubauer v. Goldfarb*, 108 Cal. App. 4th 47, 57, 133 Cal. Rptr. 2d 218 (2003) (stating that "waiver of corporate directors' and majority shareholders' fiduciary duties to minority shareholders in private close corporations is against public policy and a contract provision in a buy-sell agreement purporting to effect such a waiver is void"). If not, a court should hold the provision unenforceable nonetheless so as to avoid eviscerating Subsection (d)(3).

Subsection (d)(3)(A)—Subject to the "not manifestly unreasonable" standard, this paragraph empowers the partnership agreement to eliminate all aspects of the duty of loyalty listed in Section 409(b). The obligation of good faith and fair dealing, Section 409(d), would remain. *See* Subsection (c)(6). As to any other, uncodified aspects of the duty of loyalty, see Subsection (d)(3)(D) (empowering the partnership agreement to "alter or eliminate any other fiduciary duty").

Example: Joint Venture Partnership ("JV") is a general partnership, with two partners, Kappa, Inc. ("Kappa") and Lambda, LLC ("Lambda"). The partnership agreement provides that:

- JV is managed by a "board" consisting of one person appointed by Kappa and one person appointed by Lambda;

- each appointee:

  o owes fiduciary and any other duties exclusively to the partner that made the appointment; and

  o owes no duties to the other partner and the partnership.

The "not manifestly unreasonable" standard applies to these provisions under Subsection (d)(3)(A) and (D), and the provisions are not manifestly unreasonable. Note that the provisions do not affect the duties of Kappa and Lambda to each other.

Subsection (d)(3)(B)—Under this paragraph, a partnership agreement might provide that an affiliate of a partner will provide compensated services to the partnership at a price not exceeding market price, or that the partner may pursue opportunities that otherwise would be partnership opportunities. Such arrangements are commonplace and permissible.

Subsection (d)(3)(C)—In this context, "conduct" includes both acts and omissions. BLACK'S LAW DICTIONARY (9th ed. 2009) (defining conduct as "[p]ersonal behavior, whether by action or inaction"). Subject to the "not manifestly unreasonable" standard and the bedrock requirements stated here and in Subsection (c)(8), the partnership agreement can reduce the duty of care substantially. In particular, the partnership agreement can eliminate the aspects of the duty of care pertaining to gross negligence and recklessness.

This provision replicates in a particular context the general rule stated in Subsection (c)(8). For the meaning of "bad faith" in the context of the duty of care, see Subsection (c)(8), comment.

Subsection (e)—The "not manifestly unreasonable" concept became part of uniform business entity statutes when UPA (1997) imported the concept from the Uniform Commercial Code. (In the current version of the Uniform Commercial Code, the concept appears in Section 1–302(b).)

This subsection provides rules for applying the concept, specifying:

- who decides the issue of "manifestly unreasonable"

  - "the court . . . as a matter of law," Subsection (e);

- the framework for determining the issue

- ▪ determination to be made "in light of the purposes, activities, and affairs of the partnership," Subsection (e)(2);

- the temporal setting for determining the issue

  - ▪ "[d]etermination [to be made] as of the time the challenged term became part of the partnership agreement," Subsection (e)(1); and

- what information is admissible for determining the issue

  - ▪ "[o]nly circumstances existing" when "the challenged term became part of the partnership agreement," Subsection (e)(1).

The subsection also provides a very demanding standard for persons claiming that a term of a partnership agreement is "manifestly unreasonable." "The court . . . may invalidate the term only if, in light of the purposes, and business of the partnership, it is *readily apparent* that: (A) the objective of the term is unreasonable; or (B) the term is an unreasonable means to achieve the term's objective." Subsection (e)(2) (emphasis added).

Subsection (e) is fundamental to this act, because: (i) this act generally defers to the agreement among the partners; and (ii) Subsection (e) safeguards the partnership agreement in at least four ways:

- Determining manifest unreasonableness *inter se* owners of an organization is a different task than doing so in a commercial context, where concepts like "usages of trade" are available to inform the analysis. Each business organization must be understood in its own terms and context.

- If loosely applied, the concept of "manifestly unreasonable" would permit a court to rewrite the partners' agreement, which would destroy the balance this act seeks to establish between freedom of contract and fiduciary duty.

- Case law has not adequately delineated the concept. *See, e.g., In re Brobeck, Phleger & Harrison L.L.P.*, 408 B.R. 318, 335 (Bankr. N.D. Cal. 2009) ("RUPA [UPA (1997)] does not define what is 'manifestly unreasonable' and the parties have not cited, nor can the court locate, a decision that defines the term. Absent case law or even a dictionary definition, the court must rely on its common sense to recognize something as manifestly unreasonable.").

- In the context of statutes permitting stock transfer restrictions unless "manifestly unreasonable," courts have often ignored the word "manifestly." *See, e.g., Brandt v. Somerville*, 692 N.W.2d 144, 152 (N.D. 2005) (stating that "in close corporations, a majority of courts have sustained restrictions that are determined to be reasonable in light of the relevant circumstances"); *Roof Depot, Inc. v. Ohman*, 638 N.W.2d 782, 786 (Minn. Ct. App. 2002) (stating that "the restrictions [on share transfer] are not 'manifestly unreasonable' because they are reasonable means to ensure that the management and control of the business remains in the group of investors or with people well known to them"); *Castriota v. Castriota*, 633 A.2d 1024, 1027–28 (N.J. App. Div. 1993) ("We are obliged to apply the statute in a manner consonant with its essential purpose to permit reasonable restrictions upon alienation.").

Subsection (e)(1)—The significance of the phrase "as of the time the term as challenged became part of the partnership agreement" is best shown by example.

Example: When a particular partnership comes into existence, its business plan is quite unusual and its success depends on the willingness of a particular individual to serve as the partnership's sole managing partner. This individual has a rare combination of skills, experiences, and contacts, which are particularly appropriate for the partnership's start-up. In order to induce the individual to accept the position of sole managing partner, the other partners are willing to have the partnership agreement significantly limit the managing partner's fiduciary duties. Several years later, when the partnership's operations have turned prosaic and the managing partner's talents and background are not nearly so crucial, a partner challenges the fiduciary duty limitations as manifestly unreasonable. The relevant time under Subsection (e)(1) is when the partnership began. Subsequent developments are not relevant, except as they might inferentially bear on the circumstances in existence at the relevant time.

Example: As initially adopted, a partnership agreement identifies a category of decisions ordinarily subject to the duty of loyalty and provides that "the managing partner's sole, reasonable discretion" satisfies the duty. A year later, the agreement is amended to delete the word "reasonable." Later, a partner claims that, without the word "reasonable," the provision is manifestly unreasonable. The relevant time under Subsection (e)(1) is when the agreement was amended, not when the agreement was initially adopted.

Subsection (e)(2)—If a person claims that a term of the partnership agreement is manifestly unreasonable under Subsections (c)(6) or (d)(3), as a matter of ordinary procedural law the person making the claim has the burden of proof.

§ 106. Partnership Agreement; Effect on Partnership and Person Becoming Partner; Preformation Agreement

(a) A partnership is bound by and may enforce the partnership agreement, whether or not the partnership has itself manifested assent to the agreement.

(b) A person that becomes a partner is deemed to assent to the partnership agreement.

(c) Two or more persons intending to become the initial partners of a partnership may make an agreement providing that upon the formation of the partnership the agreement will become the partnership agreement.

COMMENT

Subsection (a)—This subsection resolves twin questions that have troubled some courts—namely, whether an unincorporated entity that has not signed its foundational agreement nonetheless is bound by and may enforce the agreement. The questions have been particularly troubling in the context of agreements to arbitrate. *See, e.g., Elkjer v. Scheef & Stone, L.L.P.*, 3:13-CV-1655-K, 2014 WL 1255844, at *5–6 (N.D. Tex. Mar. 27, 2014) (concluding that a limited liability partnership "is a party to the Partnership Agreement," even though the partnership itself never signed or otherwise assented to the agreement; enforcing arbitration provision to the benefit of the LLP). *Contra Trover v. 419 OCR, Inc.*, 921 N.E.2d 1249, 1255 (2010) (finding that "neither FODG [an LLC] nor the Golf Club [a related LLC] was a party to the operating agreements and that they are therefore not bound by the arbitration clauses therein").

Developments pertaining to the Virginia LLC Act further illustrate the difficulties. In *Mission Residential, L.L.C. v. Triple Net Properties, L.L.C.*, 654 S.E.2d 888, 891 (Va. 2008), the Virginia Supreme Court held that an LLC member's derivative claim was not subject to the arbitration provision in the operating agreement, because: (i) the LLC was "the real party in interest"; (ii) the LLC had not signed the operating agreement; and (iii) requiring the claim to be arbitrated would "ignore[ ] the separate existence of Holdings [the LLC]." The Virginia legislature promptly disagreed and amended the LLC act to state: "A limited liability company is bound by its operating agreement whether or not the limited liability company executes the operating agreement." 2009 VA. ACTS 763 (S.B. 1241), codified as VA. CODE ANN. § 13.1–1023.A.1 (2012). The legislature left open the question of a limited liability company's power to enforce an operating agreement that the company has not executed.

This subsection answers the twin questions, categorically and in the affirmative.

This subsection does not consider whether a partnership is an indispensable party to a suit concerning the partnership agreement. That question is one of procedural law, and the answer can determine whether federal diversity jurisdiction exists.

Subsection (b)—Given the possibility of oral and implied-in-fact terms in the partnership agreement, a person becoming a partner of an existing partnership should take precautions to ascertain fully the contents of the partnership agreement. *See* Section 105(a)(3), cmt.

Subsection (c)—A pre-formation arrangement is not a partnership agreement. A partnership agreement is among "partners," and, under this act, the earliest a person can become a partner is upon the formation of the partnership. *See* Section 402.

§ 107. Partnership Agreement; Effect on Third Parties and Relationship to Records Effective on Behalf of Partnership

(a) A partnership agreement may specify that its amendment requires the approval of a person that is not a party to the agreement or the satisfaction of a condition. An amendment is ineffective if its adoption does not include the required approval or satisfy the specified condition.

(b) The obligations of a partnership and its partners to a person in the person's capacity as a transferee or person dissociated as a partner are governed by the partnership agreement. Subject only to a court order issued under Section 504(b)(2) to effectuate a charging order, an amendment to the partnership agreement made after a person becomes a transferee or is dissociated as a partner:

(1)   is effective with regard to any debt, obligation, or other liability of the partnership or its partners to the person in the person's capacity as a transferee or person dissociated as a partner; and

(2)   is not effective to the extent the amendment:

(A)   imposes a new debt, obligation, or other liability on the transferee or person dissociated as a partner; or

(B)   prejudices the rights under Section 701 of a person that dissociated as a partner before the amendment was made.

(c)   If a record delivered by a partnership to the [Secretary of State] for filing becomes effective and contains a provision that would be ineffective under Section 105(c) or (d)(3) if contained in the partnership agreement, the provision is ineffective in the record.

(d)   Subject to subsection (c), if a record delivered by a partnership to the [Secretary of State] for filing becomes effective and conflicts with a provision of the partnership agreement:

(1)   the agreement prevails as to partners, persons dissociated as partners, and transferees; and

(2)   the record prevails as to other persons to the extent they reasonably rely on the record.

COMMENT

Subsection (a)—This subsection, derived from Delaware Code Annotated title 6, § 18–302(e), permits the partnership agreement to: (i) accord a non-partner veto rights over amendments to the agreement; and (ii) establish other preconditions for amendments. An amendment made in derogation of a veto right or precondition is ineffective.

Veto rights are likely to be sought by lenders but may also be attractive to non-partner managers.

Example: A non-partner manager enters into a management contract with a partnership, and that agreement provides in part that the partnership may remove the manager without cause only with the consent of partners holding two-thirds of the profits interests. The partnership agreement contains a parallel provision (the "quantum provision"), but the non-partner manager is not a party to the partnership agreement. Later, the partners amend the quantum provision to reduce the quantum to a simple majority of profits interests and thereafter purport to remove the manager without cause. Although the partnership has undoubtedly breached its contract with the manager and subjected itself to a damage claim, the partnership has the *power* under Section 105(a)(2) to effect the removal—unless the partnership agreement provides the manager a veto right over changes in the partnership agreement's quantum provision.

This subsection does not refer to partner veto rights because, unless otherwise provided in the partnership agreement, the consent of each partner is necessary to effect an amendment. *See* Section 401(k).

Because "[a] partnership agreement may specify that its amendment requires . . . the satisfaction of a condition," a partnership agreement can require that any amendment be made through a writing or a record signed by each partner. *See* Section 105(a)(3) (empowering the partnership agreement to determine "the means and conditions for amending the partnership agreement").

Subsection (b)—The law of unincorporated business organizations is only beginning to grapple in a modern way with the tension between the rights of an organization's owners to carry on their activities as they see fit (or have agreed) and the rights of transferees of the organization's economic interests. If, as is often the situation, the partnership agreement overrides Section 701 (Purchase of Interest of Person Dissociated as Partner), such transferees can include the heirs of the partnership's founders as well as former partners who, by agreement, are "locked in" as transferees of their own interests.

If the law categorically favors the owners, there is a serious risk of expropriation and other abuse. On the other hand, if the law grants former owners and other transferees the right to seek judicial protection, that specter can "freeze the deal" as of the moment an owner leaves the enterprise or a third party obtains an economic interest.

There is little case law in this area, and almost all of it pertains to limited rather than general partnerships. The case law clearly favors the remaining owners over former owners and other transferees. *See, e.g., Bauer v. Blomfield Co./Holden Joint Venture*, 849 P.2d 1365, 1367 n.2 (Alaska 1993) (holding that a mere assignee "was not entitled to complain about a decision made with the consent of all the partners" and stating "[w]e are unwilling to hold that partners owe a duty of good faith and fair dealing to assignees of a partner's interest"); *Bynum v. Frisby*, 311 P.2d 972, 975 (Nev. 1957) ("[A]n assignment of a partnership interest from one partner to a stranger does not bring that stranger into fiduciary relationship with the remaining partners nor require them to resort to dissolution in order to prevent such a relationship from arising. The stranger remains a stranger entitled only to share in the partnership's worth and to demand an accounting upon dissolution.") (applying UPA (1914) § 27, which pertains to rights of an assignee). *See generally* Daniel S. Kleinberger, *The Plight of the Bare Naked Assignee*, 42 SUFFOLK L. REV. 587 (2009).

This subsection follows *Bauer* and other cases by expressly subjecting transferees (including a person dissociated as a partner) to partnership agreement amendments made after the transfer or dissociation, except amendments that increase obligations on transferees. For example, an amendment might extend the duration of a partnership but may not institute a new capital call obligation on transferees.

The issue of whether, in extreme and sufficiently harsh circumstances, transferees might be able to claim some type of duty or obligation to protect against expropriation awaits development in the case law. An unreported LLC case suggests the answer might be yes, but the decision rests primarily on the wording of the LLC's operating agreement. In *Kohannim v. Katoli*, 08-11-00155-CV, 2013 WL 3943078, at *10–11 (Tex. App. July 24, 2013), the court: (i) noted that a limited liability company's "[r]egulations provide[ ] for the distribution of 'available cash' to members quarterly provided that the available cash is not needed for a reasonable working capital reserve"; (ii) also noted that "Jacob [the defendant member] paid himself $100,000 for management services that were not performed and failed to make any profit distributions to Mike [former member and ex-spouse of the plaintiff Parvaneh] or Parvaneh [ex-spouse of Mike, who became Mike's transferee as part of their divorce proceeding] even though more than $250,000 in undistributed profit had accumulated in the company's accounts since the mortgage on the property had been paid off in February 2007"; and (iii) concluded that "more than a scintilla of evidence supports the trial court's finding that Jacob failed to make profit distributions to [Parvaneh]." In essence, the court upheld a finding that Jacob had breached (or caused the partnership to breach) a contractual obligation to make distributions. But the court went further: "We also agree with the trial court's conclusion that the established facts demonstrated Jacob engaged in wrongful conduct and exhibited a lack of fair dealing in the company's affairs to the prejudice of Parvaneh." *Id.* at *11.

For the very limited statutory rights of transferees, see Section 503.

Subsection (b)(1)—This provision is inapposite when "a partner or transferee becomes entitled to receive a distribution." Section 405(d). In that circumstance:

- "the partner or transferee has the status of . . . a creditor of the partnership with respect to the distribution," *id.*; and

- the relevant obligation is not owed to "a person in the person's capacity as a transferee or person dissociated as a partner," Subsection (b), but rather to the person in the person's capacity as a creditor.

Subsection (c)—This provision precludes using a filed record (*e.g.*, a statement of authority) to make an end run around the strictures of Section 105(c) and (d)(3).

Subsection (d)—It will be possible, albeit improvident, for a partnership agreement to be inconsistent with a public filing pertaining to the partnership. For those circumstances, this subsection provides rules for determining which source of information prevails.

- For partners and transferees, the partnership agreement is paramount.

- Third parties may invoke the public record upon a showing of reasonable reliance, which presupposes actual knowledge—*i.e.*, deemed knowledge under Section 103(d) does not suffice.

The mere fact that a term is present in a publicly filed record and not in the partnership agreement, or *vice versa*, does not automatically establish a conflict. This subsection does not expressly cover a situation in which: (i) one of the specified filed records contains information in addition to, but not inconsistent with, the partnership agreement, and (ii) a person, other than a partner or transferee, reasonably relies on the additional information. However, the policy reflected in this subsection seems equally applicable to that situation. Moreover, to argue that the partnership agreement prevails over the filed record is to argue that the additional term does conflict with the partnership agreement, at least in effect.

Section 105(a)(3) might also be relevant to the subject matter of this subsection. Absent a contrary provision in the partnership agreement, language in a record delivered to the filing office for filing on behalf of the partnership might be evidence of the partners' agreement and might thereby constitute or at least imply a term of the partnership agreement.

This subsection does not apply to records delivered to the filing office for filing on behalf of persons other than a partnership.

§ 108. Signing of Records to Be Delivered for Filing to [Secretary of State]

(a)   A record delivered to the [Secretary of State] for filing pursuant to this [act] must be signed as follows:

(1)   Except as otherwise provided in paragraphs (2) and (3), a record signed by a partnership must be signed by a person authorized by the partnership.

(2)   A record filed on behalf of a dissolved partnership that has no partner must be signed by the person winding up the partnership's business under Section 802(c) or a person appointed under Section 802(d) to wind up the business.

(3)   A statement of denial by a person under Section 304 must be signed by that person.

(4)   Any other record delivered on behalf of a person to the [Secretary of State] for filing must be signed by that person.

(b)   A record filed under this [act] may be signed by an agent. Whenever this [act] requires a particular individual to sign a record and the individual is deceased or incompetent, the record may be signed by a legal representative of the individual.

(c)   A person that signs a record as an agent or legal representative affirms as a fact that the person is authorized to sign the record.

COMMENT

Subsection (a)—Section 102(20) defines "sign" broadly, including "an electronic symbol, sound, or process."

Subsection (a)(1)—From the perspective of the filing office, it is not necessary that a partner sign a record delivered for filing on behalf of a partnership. The partnership agreement can impose such a requirement as an *inter se* matter, but the requirement would not affect this provision. *See* Section 105(c)(16)(B) (stating that the partnership agreement may not "vary any requirement, procedure, or other provision of this [act] pertaining to . . . the [Secretary of State], including provisions pertaining to records authorized or required to be delivered to the [Secretary of State] for filing under this [act]").

The filing office will not check whether a person who purports to be authorized to sign a record on behalf of a partnership actually has that authority, even if a statement of authority pertaining to the matter is in effect. Indeed, even if the filing office somehow "knows" of a statement limiting authority, the office lacks the authority to reject a record on that basis. *See* the comment to Section 117(a) (stating the requirements for filing and noting that the filing office's review is ministerial and limited to information pertaining to the stated requirements), and the comment to Section 117(c) (explaining why such a statement of authority does not affect the filing office).

Subsection (b)—The filing office will not check the bona fides of a person purporting to have signed a record in a representative capacity. This subsection expressly authorizes taking action through an agent to provide context for Subsection (c) and for the avoidance of doubt. No negative inference should be drawn about using agents to take other action under this act.

Subsection (c)—As a matter of agency law, a person who signs in a representative capacity gives a "warranty of authority." RESTATEMENT (THIRD) OF AGENCY § 6.10 (2006). This subsection has criminal law implications. Under Section 109(c), "[a]n individual who signs a record authorized or required to be filed under this [act] affirms under penalty of perjury that the information stated in the record is accurate."

§ 109. Liability for Inaccurate Information in Filed Record

(a)   If a record delivered to the [Secretary of State] for filing under this [act] and filed by the [Secretary of State] contains inaccurate information, a person that suffers loss by reliance on the information may recover damages for the loss from:

(1)   a person that signed the record, or caused another to sign it on the person's behalf, and knew the information to be inaccurate at the time the record was signed; and

(2)   subject to subsection (b), a partner if:

(A)   the record was delivered for filing on behalf of the partnership; and

(B)   the partner knew or had notice of the inaccuracy for a reasonably sufficient time before the information was relied upon so that, before the reliance, the partner reasonably could have:

(i)   effected an amendment under Section 901(f);

(ii)   filed a petition under Section 112; or

(iii) delivered to the [Secretary of State] for filing a statement of change under Section 909 or a statement of correction under Section 116.

(b)   To the extent the partnership agreement expressly relieves a partner of responsibility for maintaining the accuracy of information contained in records delivered on behalf of the partnership to the [Secretary of State] for filing under this [act] and imposes that responsibility on one or more other partners, the liability stated in subsection (a)(2) applies to those other partners and not to the partner that the partnership agreement relieves of the responsibility.

(c)   An individual who signs a record authorized or required to be filed under this [act] affirms under penalty of perjury that the information stated in the record is accurate.

COMMENT

Subsection (a)—This subsection relates to liability to third parties for inaccurate information in a filed record. Paragraph 1 requires actual knowledge because the paragraph can inculpate a person who is not a partner. Under Paragraph 2(B), notice suffices, because: (i) the provision applies only to partners; (ii) by status partners have overall management authority; and (iii) therefore, it is reasonable to impose liability when a partner either knows or "has reason to know . . . from all the facts known to the person at the time in question." Section 103(b)(1) (defining notice). For the same reason, Paragraph 1 applies only to "information [known] to be inaccurate at the time the record was signed," while Paragraph 2 applies whenever a "partner knew or had notice of the inaccuracy for a reasonably sufficient time before the information was relied upon so that, before the reliance, the partner reasonably could have [taken corrective action]." Paragraph (2)(B).

Subsection (a)(2)—Although this act establishes the avoidance of gross negligence as the standard of care for partners viz-a-viz the partnership, this subsection encompasses liability to third parties. Accordingly, the standard here is more demanding. The phrases "reasonably sufficient time" and "reasonably could have" indicate a standard of ordinary care. "[N]otice of the inaccuracy" involves "reason to know." Section 103(b)(1).

Subsection (b)—Section 105(d)(2) authorizes the partnership agreement to establish an analogous rule *inter se* the partners. This subsection goes where the partnership agreement cannot reach and affects the rights of third parties.

Subsection (c)—This subsection provides criminal liability. The elements of perjury are a matter for the criminal law of the jurisdiction.

§ 110.   Application to Existing Relationships

(a)   Before [all-inclusive date], this [act] governs only:

(1)   a partnership formed on or after [the effective date of this [act]]; and

(2)   except as otherwise provided in subsection (c), a partnership formed before [the effective date of this [act]] which elects, in the manner provided in its partnership agreement or by law for amending the partnership agreement, to be subject to this [act].

(b)   Except as otherwise provided in subsection (c), on and after [all-inclusive date] this [act] governs all partnerships.

(c)   With respect to a partnership that elects pursuant to subsection (a)(2) to be subject to this [act], after the election takes effect the provisions of this [act] relating to the liability of the partnership's partners to third parties apply:

(1)   before [all-inclusive date], to:

(A)   a third party that had not done business with the partnership in the year before the election took effect; and

(B) a third party that had done business with the partnership in the year before the election took effect only if the third party knows or has been notified of the election; and

(2) on and after [all-inclusive date], to all third parties, but those provisions remain inapplicable to any obligation incurred while those provisions were inapplicable under paragraph (1)(B).

Legislative Note:

For states that have previously enacted UPA (1997): For these states this section is unnecessary. There is no need for a delayed effective date, even with regard to pre-existing partnerships. (Presumably, the "linkage" issue [discussed below] was addressed when UPA (1997) was enacted.)

For states that have not previously enacted UPA (1997): Each enacting jurisdiction should consider whether: (i) this act makes material changes to the "default" (or "gap filler") rules of the predecessor statute; and (ii) if so, whether Subsection (c) should carry forward any of those rules for pre-existing partnerships. In this assessment, the focus is on pre-existing partnerships that have left default rules in place, whether advisedly or not. The central question is whether, for such partnerships, expanding Subsection (c) is necessary to prevent material changes to the partners' "deal."

The "all-inclusive" date should be at least one year after the effective date of this act, Section 1206, but no more than two years.

The "linkage" issue—for states that still have ULPA (1976) or ULPA (1976/1985) in effect: These states should enact ULPA (2001) (Last Amended 2013) to take effect in conjunction with this act. If not, a state's current limited partnership act must be amended to link to this act.

§ 111.   Delivery of Record

(a) Except as otherwise provided in this [act], permissible means of delivery of a record include delivery by hand, mail, conventional commercial practice, and electronic transmission.

(b) Delivery to the [Secretary of State] is effective only when a record is received by the [Secretary of State].

COMMENT

Subsection (a)—Permissible means of delivery are not limited to those listed in this subsection, because this subsection by its terms is a non-exclusive list. Conventional commercial practice includes the use of private delivery or courier services. What constitutes conventional commercial practice may change over time.

Subsection (b)—This section lists permissible means of delivery but, except for delivery to the filing office, does not determine when delivery occurs. Delivery to the filing office is effective only upon actual receipt.

§ 112.   Signing and Filing Pursuant to Judicial Order

(a) If a person required by this [act] to sign a record or deliver a record to the [Secretary of State] for filing under this [act] does not do so, any other person that is aggrieved may petition [the appropriate court] to order:

(1) the person to sign the record;

(2) the person to deliver the record to the [Secretary of State] for filing; or

(3) the [Secretary of State] to file the record unsigned.

(b) If a petitioner under subsection (a) is not the partnership or foreign limited liability partnership to which the record pertains, the petitioner shall make the partnership or foreign partnership a party to the action.

(c) A record filed under subsection (a)(3) is effective without being signed.

COMMENT

This section gives the court the flexibility to order either that a record be signed or that the record be filed by the filing office unsigned. The latter circumstance may arise; for example, in a situation where the person who should sign the record is not subject to the jurisdiction of the court. This section also makes clear that the court may order a person with control over a record that has been signed to deliver the record to the filing office for filing.

§ 113.   Filing Requirements

(a)   To be filed by the [Secretary of State] pursuant to this [act], a record must be received by the [Secretary of State], comply with this [act], and satisfy the following:

(1)   The filing of the record must be required or permitted by this [act].

(2)   The record must be physically delivered in written form unless and to the extent the [Secretary of State] permits electronic delivery of records.

(3)   The words in the record must be in English, and numbers must be in Arabic or Roman numerals, but the name of an entity need not be in English if written in English letters or Arabic or Roman numerals.

(4)   The record must be signed by a person authorized or required under this [act] to sign the record.

(5)   The record must state the name and capacity, if any, of each individual who signed it, either on behalf of the individual or the person authorized or required to sign the record, but need not contain a seal, attestation, acknowledgment, or verification.

(b)   If law other than this [act] prohibits the disclosure by the [Secretary of State] of information contained in a record delivered to the [Secretary of State] for filing, the [Secretary of State] shall file the record if the record otherwise complies with this [act] but may redact the information.

(c)   When a record is delivered to the [Secretary of State] for filing, any fee required under this [act] and any fee, tax, interest, or penalty required to be paid under this [act] or law other than this [act] must be paid in a manner permitted by the [Secretary of State] or by that law.

(d)   The [Secretary of State] may require that a record delivered in written form be accompanied by an identical or conformed copy.

(e)   The [Secretary of State] may provide forms for filings required or permitted to be made by this [act], but, except as otherwise provided in subsection (f), their use is not required.

(f)   The [Secretary of State] may require that a cover sheet for a filing be on a form prescribed by the [Secretary of State].

COMMENT

The filing office's duty under this section is ministerial, Section 117(a), and the office's assessment of a record delivered for filing is limited to conformity with this section. The filing office *must* file a record delivered for filing if the record contains the information required by this act and is accompanied by the required filing fee. The filing office is authorized to provide forms but not require their use, and, as a result, may not reject records delivered for filing on the basis of form (except to the very limited extent permitted by Subsections (d) and (f)).

In view of the very limited discretion granted to the filing office under this section and Section 117(a), "[t]he filing of . . . a record does not create a presumption that . . . the information contained in the record is correct . . . ." Section 117(e).

Subsection (a)—The first requisite for having a record filed is to cause the record actually to be received by the filing office. Section 111(b) reiterates this point.

Subsection (a)(2)—A record delivered for filing must be in typewritten or printed form unless the filing office permits delivery by electronic transmission. The types of electronic transmission that may be used will be determined by the filing office and is intended to include the evolving methods of electronic delivery, including facsimile transmissions, electronic transmissions between computers, and filings through delivery of storage media.

Subsection (a)(3)—The text of an entity filing must be in the English language, except to the limited extent permitted by this paragraph.

Subsection (a)(4)—To be filed a record must be signed by the appropriate person. See the definition of "sign" in Section 102(20) for a description of the manner in which a record may be "signed." Who is an appropriate person is determined under Section 108, but the filing office will not check to determine whether a person purportedly authorized to sign is in fact authorized. *See* the comment to Section 108(a)–(c).

The requirement in some state statutes that records delivered for filing on behalf of an entity must be acknowledged or verified as a condition for filing has been rejected. These requirements serve little purpose in connection with entity filings. On the other hand, many organizations, like lenders or title companies, may desire that specific records include acknowledgements, verifications, or seals; Subsection (a)(4) does not prohibit the addition of these forms of execution and their use does not affect the eligibility of the record for filing.

Subsection (b)—Under this subsection, a confidentiality obligation does not affect the filing office's duty to file, and the filing office is authorized but not required to redact. This act does not affect any confidentiality-related obligations the filing office may have under other law.

§ 114. Effective Date and Time

Except as otherwise provided in Section 115 and subject to Section 116(c), a record filed under this [act] is effective:

(1)   on the date and at the time of its filing by the [Secretary of State], as provided in Section 117(b);

(2)   on the date of filing and at the time specified in the record as its effective time, if later than the time under paragraph (1);

(3)   at a specified delayed effective date and time, which may not be more than 90 days after the date of filing; or

(4)   if a delayed effective date is specified, but no time is specified, at 12:01 a.m. on the date specified, which may not be more than 90 days after the date of filing.

COMMENT

Records accepted for filing become effective at the date and time of filing as recorded by the filing office, or at another specified time on that date, unless a permissible delayed effective date is stated in the record.

Section 117(b) requires the filing office to maintain some means of recording the date and time of delivery of a record and requires that office to record that date and time as the date and time of filing. That provision gives express statutory authority to the common practice of most filing offices of ignoring processing time and treating a record as filed as of the date and time it

is delivered for filing even though it may not be reviewed and accepted for filing until several days after delivery. That section contemplates that time of delivery, as well as the date, will be routinely recorded.

Paragraph (1)—In the absence of provision for a delayed effective date, a record delivered for filing becomes effective on the date and time of filing by the filing office. Since under Section 117(b) the date and time of filing is the recorded date and time of delivery of the record to the filing office (which under Section 117(b) is the date and time of actual receipt), together these provisions eliminate any doubt about situations involving same-day transactions in which a record, for example, a statement of merger, is delivered for filing on the morning of the day the merger is to become effective.

Paragraph (3)—This paragraph does not authorize or contemplate the retroactive establishment of an effective date before the date of filing.

Paragraphs (3) and (4)—A record that states an effective date beyond the ninety-day limit is not a record that "satisfies this [act]," Section 117(a), and will properly be rejected by the filing office.

§ 115. Withdrawal of Filed Record Before Effectiveness

(a)   Except as otherwise provided in Sections 1124, 1134, 1144, and 1154, a record delivered to the [Secretary of State] for filing may be withdrawn before it takes effect by delivering to the [Secretary of State] for filing a statement of withdrawal.

(b)   A statement of withdrawal must:

(1) be signed by each person that signed the record being withdrawn, except as otherwise agreed by those persons;

(2) identify the record to be withdrawn; and

(3) if signed by fewer than all the persons that signed the record being withdrawn, state that the record is withdrawn in accordance with the agreement of all the persons that signed the record.

(c) On filing by the [Secretary of State] of a statement of withdrawal, the action or transaction evidenced by the original record does not take effect.

COMMENT

Only records that have not yet taken effect may be withdrawn under this section. If a record has taken effect, it may be corrected under Section 116 if the requirements of that section are satisfied. Otherwise, the record must be amended in accordance with this act.

Subsection (b)(1)—This provision is subject to Section 108(b) ("Whenever this [act] requires a particular individual to sign a record and the individual is deceased or incompetent, the record may be signed by a legal representative of the individual.").

§ 116. Correcting Filed Record

(a) A person on whose behalf a filed record was delivered to the [Secretary of State] for filing may correct the record if:

(1) the record at the time of filing was inaccurate;

(2) the record was defectively signed; or

(3) the electronic transmission of the record to the [Secretary of State] was defective.

(b) To correct a filed record, a person on whose behalf the record was delivered to the [Secretary of State] must deliver to the [Secretary of State] for filing a statement of correction.

(c) A statement of correction:

(1) may not state a delayed effective date;

(2) must be signed by the person correcting the filed record;

(3) must identify the filed record to be corrected;

(4) must specify the inaccuracy or defect to be corrected; and

(5) must correct the inaccuracy or defect.

(d) A statement of correction is effective as of the effective date of the filed record that it corrects except for purposes of Section 103(d) and as to persons relying on the uncorrected filed record and adversely affected by the correction. For those purposes and as to those persons, the statement of correction is effective when filed.

COMMENT

This section permits making corrections in filed records without re-submitting the entire record.

Subsection (a)(1) and (2)—A filed record may be corrected because it contains an inaccuracy or because it was defectively signed (including defects in optional forms of execution that do not affect the eligibility of the original record for filing).

Subsection (a)(3)—In addition, a filed record may be corrected if its electronic transmission was defective (*i.e.*, where an electronic delivery is made but, due to a defect in transmission, the filed record is later discovered to be inconsistent with the record intended to be filed). If no delivery is made because of a defect in transmission, a statement of correction may not be used to make a retroactive filing effective. Therefore, a partnership making an electronic delivery should take steps to confirm that the filing office receives the transmission.

Subsection (c)—A provision in a filed record setting an effective date may be corrected under this section, but the corrected effective date must comply with Section 114, which limits delayed effective dates to within ninety days after filing. A corrected effective date is thus measured from the date of the original filing of the record being corrected (*i.e.*, it cannot be before the date of filing of the record or more than ninety days thereafter).

Subsection (d)—The correction relates back to the original effective date of the record being corrected, except as to persons relying on the original entity filing and adversely affected by the correction. As to these persons, the effective date of the statement of correction is the date the statement is filed.

§ 117. Duty of [Secretary of State] to File; Review of Refusal to File; Delivery of Record by [Secretary of State]

(a) The [Secretary of State] shall file a record delivered to the [Secretary of State] for filing which satisfies this [act]. The duty of the [Secretary of State] under this section is ministerial.

(b) When the [Secretary of State] files a record, the [Secretary of State] shall record it as filed on the date and at the time of its delivery. After filing a record, the [Secretary of State] shall deliver to the person that submitted the record a copy of the record with an acknowledgment of the date and time of filing and, in the case of a statement of denial, also to the partnership to which the statement pertains.

(c) If the [Secretary of State] refuses to file a record, the [Secretary of State] shall, not later than [15] business days after the record is delivered:

(1) return the record or notify the person that submitted the record of the refusal; and

(2) provide a brief explanation in a record of the reason for the refusal.

(d) If the [Secretary of State] refuses to file a record, the person that submitted the record may petition [the appropriate court] to compel filing of the record. The record and the explanation of the [Secretary of State] of the refusal to file must be attached to the petition. The court may decide the matter in a summary proceeding.

(e) The filing of or refusal to file a record does not:

(1) affect the validity or invalidity of the record in whole or in part; or

(2) create a presumption that the information contained in the record is correct or incorrect.

(f) Except as otherwise provided by Section 909 or by law other than this [act], the [Secretary of State] may deliver any record to a person by delivering it:

(1) in person to the person that submitted it;

(2) to the address of the person's registered agent;

(3) to the principal office of the person; or

(4) to another address the person provides to the [Secretary of State] for delivery.

COMMENT

Subsection (a)—Under this subsection the filing office is required to file a record if it "satisfies this [act]." The purpose of this language is to limit the discretion of the filing office to a ministerial role in reviewing the contents of records. If the record submitted is in the form prescribed, contains the information required by this act, and the appropriate filing fee is tendered, the filing office must file the record. Consistent with this approach, this subsection states explicitly that the filing duty of the filing office is ministerial. *See* Subsection (e) (pertaining to presumptions not created).

Subsection (b)—This subsection provides that when the filing office files a record, the filing office records it as filed on the date and time of delivery to the filing office, retains the original record for the office's records, and delivers a copy of the record to the person who delivered the record for filing with an acknowledgement of the date and time of filing. In the case of a statement of denial, Section 304, the filing office will also send a copy of the record and acknowledgment to the partnership.

In the case of a record transmitted electronically to the filing office that office may deliver by electronic transmission. The copy returned will be the exact or conformed copy if the filing office has required one, or will be a copy made by the filing office if an exact or conformed copy was not required.

Under this subsection the acceptance of a filing is evidenced merely by the filing office's delivery of a copy of the record with an acknowledgment of the date and time of filing. The act does not provide for the filing office to issue a formal certificate of filing. A copy of the filed record together with an acknowledgment of the date and time of filing should sufficiently indicate that the filing has been accepted for filing and been filed.

Subsection (c)—Because of the simplification of formal filing requirements and the limited discretion granted to the filing office by this act, it is probable that rejection of records delivered to the filing office for filing will occur only rarely. This subsection provides that if the filing office does reject a record delivered for filing, the filing office must return the record to the person that submitted the filing within fifteen days together with a brief written explanation of the reason for rejection. In the case of a record delivered by electronic transmission, rejection of the record may be made electronically by the filing office or by a mailing to the person that submitted the record.

Subsection (e)—This subsection provides that the filing of a record by the filing office does not affect the validity or invalidity of any provision contained in the record and does not create any presumption with respect to any information in the record. Likewise, the refusal of the filing office to file a record creates no presumption that any of the information in the record is incorrect. Persons adversely affected by a statement in a filed record may contest the statement in a proceeding appropriate for that purpose, including a damage action under Section 109.

§ 118.   Reservation of Power to Amend or Repeal

The [legislature of this state] has power to amend or repeal all or part of this [act] at any time, and all limited liability partnerships and foreign limited liability partnerships subject to this [act] are governed by the amendment or repeal.

COMMENT

Provisions similar to this section have their genesis in *Trustees of Dartmouth College v. Woodward*, 17 U.S. (4 Wheat) 518 (1819), which held that the United States Constitution prohibited the application of newly enacted statutes to existing corporations while suggesting the efficacy of a reservation of power similar to this section. This section is a generalized form of the type of provision found in many entity organic laws, the purpose of which is to avoid any possible argument that an entity has contractual or vested rights in any specific statutory provision of its organic law and to ensure that the state may in the future modify its entity statutes as it deems appropriate and require existing entities to comply with the statutes as modified.

This section applies to changes in mandatory provisions of this act; the section does not pertain to changes in default rules.

Example: Having enacted this act, State A later amends Section 402(b)(3) (affirmative vote or consent of all partners required for a person to become a partner) to reduce, as a default rule, the necessary quantum of consent to consent from partners owning in the aggregate at least two-third of the interests in current profits owned by partners at the time of the consent. XYZ is a partnership formed under State A's act before the amendment. XYZ's partnership agreement is silent on this issue, leaving in place the act's default rule. Whether the act's amended default rule applies depends on whether the partners initially: (i) agreed (whether expressly or implicitly) to accept the then-applicable default rule requiring unanimous consent; (ii) agreed (whether expressly or implicitly) to adopt whatever rule the act provided; or (iii) never considered the issue. In short, the change in a default rule occasions an inquiry into the partners' express or implied agreement as to the role of the default rule in their mutual understanding. In the first instance, the old rule would continue in effect. In the second and third instances, the new rule would apply.

§ 119.   Supplemental Principles of Law

Unless displaced by particular provisions of this [act], the principles of law and equity supplement this [act].

COMMENT

For this act, the common law rules of contract and agency are among the most important supplemental "principles of law." With regard to transactions under Article 11, noteworthy principles include the rights of creditors following leveraged buyouts, spinoffs, asset purchases, or other similar transactions; and creditors' rights under other laws.

[ARTICLE] 2.   NATURE OF PARTNERSHIP

§ 201.   Partnership as Entity

(a)   A partnership is an entity distinct from its partners.

(b)   A partnership is the same entity regardless of whether the partnership has a statement of qualification in effect under Section 901.

COMMENT

Subsection (a)—The law of general partnerships long struggled with the question of whether a partnership is merely an aggregate of its partners or an entity distinct from its partners.

The common law took the aggregate approach. *X-L Liquors v. Taylor*, 111 A.2d 753, 759 (1955) (stating that "the common law did not recognize the separate existence of partnerships"); *Watson v. G.C. Associates Ltd. P'ship*, 691 P.2d 417, 418 (1984) (referring to the "common law or aggregate theory of partnership"); *McKinney v. Truck Ins. Exch.*, 324 S.W.2d 773, 776 (Mo. Ct. App. 1959) (referring to "the aggregate or common-law theory as to partnerships").

Under UPA (1914), a general partnership had both entity and aggregate characteristics, in part because that act's first reporter, who died during the lengthy drafting process, strongly favored the entity approach, while his replacement just as strongly favored the aggregate construct. *New England Herald Dev. Grp. v. Town of Falmouth*, 521 A.2d 693, 697 (Me. 1987) ("The draftsmen of the uniform act were divided over what effect it should have on the common law [aggregate] rule . . . . The result is the Act contains language that supports application of either [the entity or aggregate] theory.").

According to the comment to this section, UPA (1997) "embrace[d] the entity theory of the partnership," characterized "the entity theory as the dominant model" for the act, and highlighted a key problem arising from the aggregate aspect of UPA (1914)—namely, "the necessity of a deed to convey title from the 'old' partnership to the 'new' partnership every time there is a change of cast among the partners." Under UPA (1997), "there [was] no 'new' partnership just because of membership changes," thereby "avoid[ing] the result in cases such as *Fairway Development Co. v. Title Insurance Co.*, 621 F. Supp. 120 (N.D. Ohio 1985), which held that the 'new' partnership resulting from a partner's death did not have standing to enforce a title insurance policy issued to the 'old' partnership."

The Harmonization process made no changes to this aspect of UPA (1997). Note, however, that UPA (1997) retained several aspects of the aggregate construct: (i) joint and several liability of the partners for the obligations of a partnership that is not an LLP, Section 306(a); (ii) the concept of a partnership at-will, under which dissociation of any partner by "express will" dissolves the partnership, Section 801(1); and (iii) the susceptibility to dissolution of a partnership for a term or undertaking following the dissociation of a person as a partner. Section 801(2). Those vestiges continue under the Harmonization amendments adopted in 2011 and 2013.

Subsection (b)—Neither becoming nor ceasing to be a limited liability partnership affects a partnership's entity status. These changes merely add or subtract a characteristic. *Compare* Section 201(b), *with* Section 1146(a)(1) (stating that "[w]hen a conversion becomes effective [ ] (1) the converted entity is: (A) organized under and subject to the organic law of the converted entity [and therefore a different type of entity]; and (B) the same entity without interruption as the converting entity").

[handwritten: ✳ "partnership"]

§ 202.   Formation of Partnership

(a)   Except as otherwise provided in subsection (b), the association of two or more persons to carry on as co-owners a business for profit forms a partnership, whether or not the persons intend to form a partnership.

(b)   An association formed under a statute other than this [act], a predecessor statute, or a comparable statute of another jurisdiction is not a partnership under this [act].

(c)   In determining whether a partnership is formed, the following rules apply:

(1)   Joint tenancy, tenancy in common, tenancy by the entireties, joint property, common property, or part ownership does not by itself establish a partnership, even if the co-owners share profits made by the use of the property.

(2)   The sharing of gross returns does not by itself establish a partnership, even if the persons sharing them have a joint or common right or interest in property from which the returns are derived.

(3)   A person who receives a share of the profits of a business is presumed to be a partner in the business, unless the profits were received in payment:

smith v. kelley

(A)   of a debt by installments or otherwise;

(B)   for services as an independent contractor or of wages or other compensation to an employee;

(C)   of rent;

(D)   of an annuity or other retirement or health benefit to a deceased or retired partner or a beneficiary, representative, or designee of a deceased or retired partner;

(E)   of interest or other charge on a loan, even if the amount of payment varies with the profits of the business, including a direct or indirect present or future ownership of the collateral, or rights to income, proceeds, or increase in value derived from the collateral; or

(F)   for the sale of the goodwill of a business or other property by installments or otherwise.

COMMENT

UPA (1997) § 202 combined UPA (1914) §§ 6 and 7, recasting the "definition" of a partnership in UPA (1914) § 6(1) "as an operative rule of law—*i.e.*, "[a] partnership is an association of two or more persons. . . ." became "the association of two or more persons . . . forms." The change was stylistic and made no substantive change in the law. The Harmonization Project made no substantive change to this section, except to clarify that this act is not linked to the uniform limited partnership act. *See* Subsection (b), cmt.

The addition of the phrase, "whether or not the persons intend to form a partnership," merely codifies the universal judicial construction of UPA (1914) § 6(1) that a partnership is created by the association of persons whose intent is to carry on as co-owners a business for profit, regardless of their subjective intention to be "partners." Indeed, they may inadvertently create a partnership despite their expressed subjective intention not to do so. The language of Section 202 alerts readers to this possibility.

Subsection (a)—Consistent with the common law and UPA (1914), under this act "co-ownership" is a key concept. Ownership involves the power of ultimate control (albeit a power that can be substantially diminished by agreement) and a right to share in the profits of the co-owned business. To state that partners are co-owners of a business is to state that: (i) they share in the profits (if any) of the enterprise; and (ii) *ab initio* at least, they collectively have the power of ultimate control. Consequently:

- mere passive co-ownership of property, as distinguished from using the property to carry on a business, does not establish a partnership, Subsection (c)(1); and

- merely sharing gross revenues is likewise insufficient, Subsection (c)(2).

UPA (1997) added, "whether or not the persons intend to form a partnership" to the UPA (1914) formulation, thereby codifying a rule uniformly applied by courts: Subjective intent to create the legal relationship of "partnership" is irrelevant. What matters is the intent *vel non* to establish the business relationship that the law labels a "partnership." Thus, a disclaimer of partnership status is ineffective to the extent the parties' intended arrangements meet the criteria stated in this subsection.

Subsection (b)—This subsection continues the UPA (1914) concept that the general partnership is the residual form of business association. Accordingly, partnership-like organizations formed under specially applicable statutes are not within this act. *E.g.*, MONT. CODE ANN. §§ 35–13–101 to 102 (pertaining to mining partnerships).

An arrangement labeled a "joint venture" is a partnership if the arrangement meets the criteria stated in Subsection (a). In fact, in many jurisdictions, the law of general partnerships applies almost without analysis to joint ventures in which the co-venturers share profits. *See Jonathan Woodner Co. v. Laufer*, 531 A.2d 280, 285 n.7 (D.C. 1987) (stating that: (i) "[s]trictly speaking, a joint venture is not the same as a partnership, but there is 'very little law . . . applicable to one that does not apply to the other' "; (ii) "the rights and liabilities of joint venturers among themselves are generally governed by the laws of partnership"; and (iii) "[p]rinciples of partnership law, in particular the Uniform Partnership act, apply in most instances to joint ventures") (quoting 46 AM. JUR. 2D JOINT VENTURES § 4, at 25 (1969) and collecting cases).

A limited partnership is not a partnership under this act; a limited partnership is "formed under a statute other than this [act]" (*i.e.*, ULPA (2001) (Last Amended 2013) § 201). Moreover, ULPA (2001) delinked the uniform limited partnership act from the uniform general partnership act. *See* ULPA (2001) (Last Amended 2013) Prefatory Note, *The Decision to "De-Link" and Create a Stand Alone Act.*

An unincorporated nonprofit organization is not a partnership under this act, because the organization is limited to "nonprofit purposes" and therefore cannot "carry on a business" in the traditional sense of that concept. *See* UUNA (2008) (Last Amended 2013) § 102(11) (defining "unincorporated nonprofit association").

Subsection (c)—UPA (1997) derived this subsection from UPA (1914) § 7 and with one exception, made no substantive change to the law. The substantive change pertains to the sharing of profits, which UPA (1997) recast as creating a rebuttable presumption of partnership rather merely constituting *prima facie* evidence. *"Prima facie"* means that the party with the burden of proof has adduced sufficient evidence to carry that burden, subject to the finder of fact's view of any contrary evidence. The burden of persuasion is unchanged. In contrast, "rebuttable presumption" switches the burden of persuasion.

Subsection (c)(3)—The protected categories listed in this paragraph apply regardless of whether the profit share is a single, unvarying percentage or a ratio that varies; for example, after reaching a dollar floor or different levels of profits. Like UPA (1914), this act makes no attempt to answer in every case whether a partnership is formed. Whether a relationship is more properly characterized as that of borrower and lender, employer and employee, or landlord and tenant is left to the trier of fact. As under UPA (1914), a person may function in both partner and non-partner capacities.

Subsection (c)(3)(E)—UPA (1997) added this protected category, excepting from the rebuttable presumption a share of the profits received in payment of interest or other charges on a loan, "including a direct or indirect present or future ownership in the collateral, or rights to income, proceeds, or increase in value derived from the collateral." The quoted language was taken from Section 211 of the Uniform Land Security Interest Act and is intended to protect shared-appreciation mortgages, contingent or other variable or performance-related mortgages, and other equity participation arrangements by clarifying that contingent payments do not presumptively convert lending arrangements into partnerships.

§ 203. Partnership Property

Property acquired by a partnership is property of the partnership and not of the partners individually.

COMMENT

Although phrased differently, this section, which originated in UPA (1997), produces the same result as do UPA (1914) §§ 8(1) and 25. All property acquired by a partnership, by whatever manner acquired, becomes partnership property and belongs to the partnership as an entity, rather than to the individual partners.

Section 204 provides guidance concerning when property is "acquired by" the partnership.

UPA (1914) § 25(2)(c) and (e) also provides that partnership property is not subject to exemptions, allowances, or rights of a partner's spouse, heirs, or next of kin. UPA (1997) omitted those provisions as unnecessary, because the exemptions and rights inure to the property of the partners, and not to partnership property.

§ 204. When Property Is Partnership Property

(a) Property is partnership property if acquired in the name of:

    (1) the partnership; or

    (2) one or more partners with an indication in the instrument transferring title to the property of the person's capacity as a partner or of the existence of a partnership but without an indication of the name of the partnership.

(b) Property is acquired in the name of the partnership by a transfer to:

    (1) the partnership in its name; or

    (2) one or more partners in their capacity as partners in the partnership, if the name of the partnership is indicated in the instrument transferring title to the property.

(c)   Property is presumed to be partnership property if purchased with partnership assets, even if not acquired in the name of the partnership or of one or more partners with an indication in the instrument transferring title to the property of the person's capacity as a partner or of the existence of a partnership.

(d)   Property acquired in the name of one or more of the partners, without an indication in the instrument transferring title to the property of the person's capacity as a partner or of the existence of a partnership and without use of partnership assets, is presumed to be separate property, even if used for partnership purposes.

COMMENT

Section 204 states the rules *inter se the partners and partnership* for determining when property is acquired by the partnership and so becomes partnership property. These rules apply to "all property, whether real, personal, or mixed or tangible or intangible, or any right or interest therein." Section 102(16) (defining "property").

These rules provide three separate approaches—according to:

- the name or names used in acquiring the property;

- when a partner's name appears as a transferee, the capacity in which the partner is acting; and

- for property acquired by purchase, whether the partnership provided the consideration for the property.

These approaches are complementary, not mutually exclusive.

This section omits any provision corresponding to UPA (1914) § 8(4), which states: "A conveyance to a partnership in the partnership name, even without words of inheritance, passes the entire estate of the grantor unless a contrary intent appears." UPA (1997) omitted the provision as unnecessary because under modern conveyancing law all transfers pass the entire estate or interest of the grantor unless a contrary intent appears.

To what extent this section's *inter se* rules affect third party rights is a matter for other law, but in any event these rules yield automatically to statutes providing record title for particular types of property. For an example, see Subsection (c), comment.

Subsection (a) and (b)—These subsections act in combination to provide the first two of the approaches listed above. Under these subsections, property becomes partnership property if acquired:

- in the name of the partnership; or

- in the name of one or more of the partners with an indication in the instrument transferring title of either:

  o   their capacity as partners; or

  o   of the existence of a partnership, even if the name of the partnership is not indicated.

Property acquired "in the name of the partnership" includes property acquired in the name of one or more partners in their capacity as partners, but only if the name of the partnership is indicated in the instrument transferring title.

Property transferred to a partner is partnership property, even though the name of the partnership is not indicated, if the instrument transferring title indicates either: (i) the partner's capacity as a partner; or (ii) the existence of a partnership. This approach is consonant with the entity theory of partnership and resolves the troublesome issue of a conveyance to fewer than all the partners but that nevertheless indicates their partner status.

Subsections (c) and (d)—At least *inter se* the partners and partnership, it is the intention of the partners that controls whether property belongs to the partnership or to one or more of the partners in their individual capacities. These subsections each contain a rebuttable presumption as to the partners' intent.

When applicable, the presumptions switch the burden of persuasion but are subject to an important limitation in favor of third parties. *See* Section 302(a)(3) ("Partnership property held in the name of one or more persons other than the partnership, without an indication in the instrument transferring the property to them of their capacity as partners or of the existence of a partnership, may be transferred by an instrument of transfer executed signed by the persons in whose name the property is held.").

Subsection (c)—Under this subsection, property purchased with partnership property is presumed to be partnership property, notwithstanding the name in which title is held or any other indicia. In this context, a promise made by a partnership in exchange for property triggers the presumption, including a promise to perform services or to guarantee another person's obligation with regard to the purchase of the property.

The presumption is entirely ineffective against third parties with regard to property with record title.

Example: Using partnership funds, a partner purchases realty in the partner's own name and records the purchase in the appropriate land records. The partner later transfers title to the realty to a third party that has neither knowledge nor notice of any rights the partnership may have in the property. The relevant real estate statute is the applicable law; this subsection is entirely inapposite.

Subsection (d)—Under this subsection, property acquired in the name of one or more of the partners, without an indication of their capacity as partners and without use of partnership funds or credit, is presumed to be the partners' separate property, even if used for partnership purposes. In effect, this subsection presumes that only the use of the property is contributed to the partnership.

[ARTICLE] 3. RELATIONS OF PARTNERS TO PERSONS DEALING WITH PARTNERSHIP

[handwritten: General or ordinary partnership]

§ 301. Partner Agent of Partnership

Subject to the effect of a statement of partnership authority under Section 303, the following rules apply:

(1) Each partner is an agent of the partnership for the purpose of its business. An act of a partner, including the signing of an instrument in the partnership name, for apparently carrying on in the ordinary course the partnership business or business of the kind carried on by the partnership binds the partnership, unless the partner did not have authority to act for the partnership in the particular matter and the person with which the partner was dealing knew or had notice that the partner lacked authority.

(2) An act of a partner which is not apparently for carrying on in the ordinary course the partnership's business or business of the kind carried on by the partnership binds the partnership only if the act was actually authorized by all the other partners.

COMMENT

At common law, a general partner was considered a general agent of the partnership. Joseph Story, COMMENTARIES ON THE LAW ON PARTNERSHIP § 101, at 153 (2d ed. 1850); RESTATEMENT (SECOND) OF AGENCY § 14A, cmt. a (1958). The mere status of a general partner "clothes" a person with apparent authority to carry on the partnership business. *Stockwell v. U.S.*, 80 U.S. 531, 567 (1871); *Lincoln Nat'l Bank v. Schoen*, 56 Mo. App. 160, 164 (Mo. Ct. App. 1894); *Kansallis Fin. Ltd. v. Fern*, 659 N.E.2d 731, 733, 740 (Mass. 1996). In 1914, the UPA codified this principle, UPA (1914) § 9, and "statutory apparent authority" has been part of uniform partnerships acts ever since. *See* UPA (1997) § 301 (1997) (Partnership Agent of Partnership); ULPA (2001) § 402 (General Partner Agent of Limited Partnership).

This section's principal purpose is to delineate a partner's statutory apparent authority. The partnership agreement and Section 401 govern the rights of the partners among themselves, including the right to restrict a partner's actual authority.

Section 301(1)—This paragraph retains the basic principles reflected in UPA (1914) § 9(1) and in effect characterizes a partner as a general managerial agent. Such agents have both actual and apparent authority, and this section delineates the apparent authority. For a discussion of the scope of actual authority, see Section 401(h), comment.

The agency law origins of statutory apparent authority has informed courts' application of UPA (1914) § 9(1), and that case law is equally applicable under this act. For example, although the statutory language does not appear to require that the appearance of authority be reasonable, the case law does so routinely. *See, e.g., In re Fox Hill Office Invs., Ltd.*, 101 B.R. 1007, 1019 (Bankr. W.D. Mo. 1989) (stating a third-party lender in possession of a copy of a limited partnership's partnership agreement was on notice of the general partner's lack of authority and therefore should have inquired as to the partner's authority), *aff'd*, 926 F.2d 752 (8th Cir. 1991); *Investors Title Ins. Co. v. Herzig*, 360 S.E.2d 786, 789 (N.C. 1987) (stating that "in order to hold the [partnership] liable, [a third party] must show that in the exercise of reasonable care under the circumstances, it was justified in believing that the principal had conferred . . . authority to [act] on behalf of the partnership"); *First Interstate Bank of Oregon, N.A. v. Bergendahl*, 723 P.2d 1005, 1010 (Or. Ct. App. 1986) (stating that bank in possession of management agreement was on notice of general partner's restricted authority and could not rely on a theory of apparent authority).

Likewise, per the law of apparent authority, a partner can bind a partnership under this section even if the partner intends to take and does take the resulting benefits for the partner's own benefit. *See Wolfe v. Harms*, 413 S.W.2d 204, 216 (Mo. 1967) (stating that partnership is liable for partner's acts "even if the predominant motive of the partner was to benefit himself or third persons"); *Rouse v. Pollard*, 18 A.2d 5, 7 (N.J. Eq. 1941) ("All the partners are responsible for the act of one of their number as agent, even though he acts for some secret purpose of his own, and not really for the benefit of the [partnership]."), *aff'd*, 21 A.2d 801 (N.J. Eq. 1941); *Investors Title Ins. Co. v. Herzig*, 360 S.E.2d 786, 788 (N.C. 1987) (stating that the mere fact that the partner's act was for personal gain was not enough to justify summary judgment for the partnership on the subject of the partnership's liability for the act).

UPA (1997) § 301(1) effected three changes from UPA (1914) § 9(1). First, Section 301(1) clarified that a partner's apparent authority includes acts for carrying on in the ordinary course "business of the kind carried on by the partnership," not just the business of the particular partnership in question. UPA (1914) is ambiguous on this point, but the drafters of UPA (1997) found some authority for an expanded construction in accordance with the so-called English rule. *See, e.g., Burns v. Gonzalez*, 439 S.W.2d 128, 131 (Tex. Civ. App. 1969) (dictum); *Comm'l Hotel v. Weeks*, 254 S.W. 521 (Tex. Civ. App. 1923).

The Harmonization Project preserved this UPA (1997) change, the significance of which depends on how broadly courts construe "business of the kind carried on by the partnership." For example, does a partnership that acts as a grain broker (never taking a position in grain) do business "of the kind carried on" by a partnership that buys grain for resale?

Second, UPA (1997) used "carrying on in the ordinary course" in lieu of the UPA (1914) phrase "in the usual way." The 1997 comments stated that: (i) "[t]he UPA and the case law use both terms without apparent distinction"; and (ii) "[n]o substantive change [was] intended by use of the more customary phrase."

The change in language had the benefit of aligning Section 301(1) with Section 305 (establishing attribution rules for a partner's wrongful conduct and referring to "ordinary course of business of the partnership" and "the ordinary course of the partnership's business"). The Harmonization Project also preserved this UPA (1997) change. For a discussion of the relationship between the ordinary course of the partnership's business and a partner's ordinary duties, see Section 305(a), comment.

UPA (1997)'s third change to UPA (1914) § 9(1) concerned the allocation of risk of a partner's lack of authority. Under UPA (1914) § 9(1) and (4), a restriction on a partner's authority binds only a person with knowledge of the restriction. In contrast, UPA (1997) § 301(1) provides that a person who has received a notification of a restriction is also bound. Thus, UPA (1997) shifted the risk of lack of authority somewhat away from the partnership and somewhat toward third parties dealing with partners.

The Harmonization Project shifted the risk a bit further, binding third parties who know or *have reason to know* of a restriction. Section 301(1). (However, it is arguable that the Harmonization Project merely made explicit a rule implicit in the case law. As noted above, the case law requires a third party to show a *reasonable* belief in the partner's authority. A third party who has reason to know of a partner's lack of authority will be hard pressed to make that showing.)

Statements of partnership authority, Section 303, affect the application of this paragraph only in two ways. First, under Section 303(e) all persons (other than partners) are deemed to know of a limitation on the authority of a partner to transfer real property contained in a statement recorded in the appropriate land records. Second, a person (other than a partner) with actual knowledge of a grant or limitation of a partner's authority may rely on that knowledge.

Section 301(2)—UPA (1997) drew this paragraph directly from UPA (1914) § 9(2), with conforming changes to mirror the new language of Paragraph (1). Consistent with the law of agency, a partnership is bound by a partner's actual authority, even if the partner lacks apparent authority. Under general agency principles, a partnership can subsequently ratify a partner's unauthorized act. *See* Section 119.

UPA (1914) § 9(3) and (4)—UPA (1997) omitted UPA (1914) § 9(3), which lists five acts requiring unanimous consent of the partners to bind the partnership. Most of the listed acts probably remain outside the apparent authority of a partner under this act, such as disposing of the goodwill of the business, but the drafters of UPA (1997) believed that eliminating categorical rules affords useful flexibility. In particular, it seemed "archaic to always require unanimous consent to submit a partnership claim to arbitration." UPA (1997) § 301, cmt.

UPA (1914) § 9(4) provides that a partnership is not bound by an act of a partner in contravention of a restriction on a partner's authority known to the other party. UPA (1997) omitted that provision as being entirely redundant of UPA (1997) § 301(1).

The Harmonization Project preserved UPA (1997)'s approach to both UPA (1914) § 9(3) and (4).

§ 302. Transfer of Partnership Property

(a) Partnership property may be transferred as follows:

(1) Subject to the effect of a statement of partnership authority under Section 303, partnership property held in the name of the partnership may be transferred by an instrument of transfer signed by a partner in the partnership name.

(2) Partnership property held in the name of one or more partners with an indication in the instrument transferring the property to them of their capacity as partners or of the existence of a partnership, but without an indication of the name of the partnership, may be transferred by an instrument of transfer signed by the persons in whose name the property is held.

(3) Partnership property held in the name of one or more persons other than the partnership, without an indication in the instrument transferring the property to them of their capacity as partners or of the existence of a partnership, may be transferred by an instrument of transfer signed by the persons in whose name the property is held.

(b) A partnership may recover partnership property from a transferee only if it proves that signing of the instrument of initial transfer did not bind the partnership under Section 301 and:

(1) as to a subsequent transferee who gave value for property transferred under subsection (a)(1) and (2), proves that the subsequent transferee knew or had been notified that the person who signed the instrument of initial transfer lacked authority to bind the partnership; or

(2) as to a transferee who gave value for property transferred under subsection (a)(3), proves that the transferee knew or had been notified that the property was partnership property and that the person who signed the instrument of initial transfer lacked authority to bind the partnership.

(c) A partnership may not recover partnership property from a subsequent transferee if the partnership would not have been entitled to recover the property, under subsection (b), from any earlier transferee of the property.

(d) If a person holds all the partners' interests in the partnership, all the partnership property vests in that person. The person may sign a record in the name of the partnership to evidence vesting of the property in that person and may file or record the record.

COMMENT

UPA (1997) § 302 replaced UPA (1914) § 10 and provides rules for the transfer and recovery of partnership property. While UPA (1914) § 10 covers only real property, this section applies also to personal property acquired by instrument and held in the name of the partnership or one or more of the partners.

The language of this section was adapted in part from the Georgia partnership statute in effect during the UPA (1997) drafting process. *See* GA. CODE ANN. § 14–8–10. Rules stated in this section necessarily parallel the rules stated in Section 203.

Subsection (a)—Subsection (a)(1) deals with the transfer of partnership property held in the name of the partnership and Subsection (a)(2) deals with property held in the name of one or more of the partners with an indication either of their capacity as partners or of the existence of a partnership. Subsection (a)(3) deals with partnership property held in the name of one or more of the partners without an indication of their capacity as partners or of the existence of a partnership. Like Section 301, Subsection (a)(1) is subject to statements of partnership authority under Section 303. *See* the comment to Section 301(1).

Subsection (b)—This subsection deals with the right of a partnership to recover partnership property transferred by a partner without actual authority. The subsection's structure corresponds to the structure of Subsection (a).

Subsection (b)(1)—This paragraph deals with the recovery of "property transferred under subsection (a)(1) [or] (2)."

Subsection (b)(2)—This paragraph deals with the recovery of "property transferred under subsection (a)(3)."

Subsection (c)—UPA (1997) added this subsection, which parallels Uniform Fraudulent Transfer Act, section 8(a) (subsequent transferee from bona fide purchaser protected), 8(b)(2) (same).

Subsection (d)—UPA (1997) added this subsection. So that this provision does not destroy transferee rights, "all the partners interests" must be read to mean "each interest that originated as a partner interest—which includes all transferable interests, by whomever owned."

The UPA (1997) comment to this subsection took a noteworthy position on the consequences of all the partners' interests in the partnership being held by one person:

> Subsection (d) allows for clear record title, even though the partnership no longer exists as a technical matter. When a partnership becomes a sole proprietorship by reason of the dissociation of all but one of the partners, title vests in the remaining "partner," although there is no "transfer" of the property. The remaining "partner" may execute a deed or other transfer of record in the name of the non-existent partnership to evidence vesting of the property in that person's individual capacity.

Section 801(6), added during the Harmonization Project, changes the analysis. The paragraph states that dissolution is caused by "the passage of 90 consecutive days during which the partnership does not have at least two partners." Consequently, for at least eighty-nine consecutive days a partnership remains un-dissolved although having only one partner, and even at ninety days the partnership remains a partnership, albeit dissolved and compelled to wind up its business. Subsection (d) remains quite useful if the sole remaining partner winds up the partnership by becoming a sole proprietor, but it is no longer accurate to state that a partnership with only one partner "no longer exists as a technical matter."

§ 303.   Statement of Partnership Authority

(a)   A partnership may deliver to the [Secretary of State] for filing a statement of partnership authority. The statement:

     (1)   must include the name of the partnership and:

         (A)   if the partnership is not a limited liability partnership, the street and mailing addresses of its principal office; or

         (B)   if the partnership is a limited liability partnership, the name and street and mailing addresses of its registered agent;

     (2)   with respect to any position that exists in or with respect to the partnership, may state the authority, or limitations on the authority, of all persons holding the position to:

         (A)   sign an instrument transferring real property held in the name of the partnership; or

         (B)   enter into other transactions on behalf of, or otherwise act for or bind, the partnership; and

     (3)   may state the authority, or limitations on the authority, of a specific person to:

         (A)   sign an instrument transferring real property held in the name of the partnership; or

         (B)   enter into other transactions on behalf of, or otherwise act for or bind, the partnership.

(b)   To amend or cancel a statement of authority filed by the [Secretary of State], a partnership must deliver to the [Secretary of State] for filing an amendment or cancellation stating:

     (1)   the name of the partnership;

     (2)   if the partnership is not a limited liability partnership, the street and mailing addresses of the partnership's principal office;

     (3)   if the partnership is a limited liability partnership, the name and street and mailing addresses of its registered agent;

(4)   the date the statement being affected became effective; and

(5)   the contents of the amendment or a declaration that the statement is canceled.

(c)   A statement of authority affects only the power of a person to bind a partnership to persons that are not partners.

(d)   Subject to subsection (c) and Section 103(d)(1), and except as otherwise provided in subsections (f), (g), and (h), a limitation on the authority of a person or a position contained in an effective statement of authority is not by itself evidence of any person's knowledge or notice of the limitation.

(e)   Subject to subsection (c), a grant of authority not pertaining to transfers of real property and contained in an effective statement of authority is conclusive in favor of a person that gives value in reliance on the grant, except to the extent that if the person gives value:

(1)   the person has knowledge to the contrary;

(2)   the statement has been canceled or restrictively amended under subsection (b); or

(3)   a limitation on the grant is contained in another statement of authority that became effective after the statement containing the grant became effective.

(f)   Subject to subsection (c), an effective statement of authority that grants authority to transfer real property held in the name of the partnership, a certified copy of which statement is recorded in the office for recording transfers of the real property, is conclusive in favor of a person that gives value in reliance on the grant without knowledge to the contrary, except to the extent that when the person gives value:

(1)   the statement has been canceled or restrictively amended under subsection (b), and a certified copy of the cancellation or restrictive amendment has been recorded in the office for recording transfers of the real property; or

(2)   a limitation on the grant is contained in another statement of authority that became effective after the statement containing the grant became effective, and a certified copy of the later-effective statement is recorded in the office for recording transfers of the real property.

(g)   Subject to subsection (c), if a certified copy of an effective statement containing a limitation on the authority to transfer real property held in the name of a partnership is recorded in the office for recording transfers of that real property, all persons are deemed to know of the limitation.

(h)   Subject to subsection (i), an effective statement of dissolution is a cancellation of any filed statement of authority for the purposes of subsection (f) and is a limitation on authority for purposes of subsection (g).

(i)   After a statement of dissolution becomes effective, a partnership may deliver to the [Secretary of State] for filing and, if appropriate, may record a statement of authority that is designated as a post-dissolution statement of authority. The statement operates as provided in subsections (f) and (g).

(j)   Unless canceled earlier, an effective statement of authority is canceled by operation of law five years after the date on which the statement, or its most recent amendment, becomes effective. The cancellation is effective without recording under subsection (f) or (g).

(k)   An effective statement of denial operates as a restrictive amendment under this section and may be recorded by certified copy for purposes of subsection (f)(1).

COMMENT

UPA (1997) § 303 pioneered this concept, which was refined in ULLCA (2006) and further refined in the Harmonization Project. This section is conceptually divided into two realms: (i) statements pertaining to the power to transfer interests in the partnership real property; and (ii) statements pertaining to other matters. In the latter realm, statements are filed only in the records of the filing office and operate only to the extent the statements are actually known and relied on by a third party. Section 303(d), (e).

As to interests in real property, in contrast, this section: (i) requires double filing—with the filing office and in the appropriate land records; and (ii) provides for constructive knowledge of statements limiting authority. Thus, a properly filed and recorded statement can protect the partnership, Section 303(g), and, in order for a statement pertaining to real property to be a sword in the hands of a third party, the statement must have been both filed and properly recorded, Section 303(f). Experience suggests that statements of authority will most often be used in connection with transactions in real estate.

By its terms, this section applies only to domestic general partnerships. The section refers throughout to "partnership," which means a domestic general partnership. *See* Section 102(11) (" 'Partnership' . . . means an association of two or more persons to carry on as co-owners a business for profit formed under this [act] or that becomes subject to this [act] under [Article] 11 [mergers and other organic transactions] or Section 110 [transition provision that eventually makes pre-existing general partnerships subject to this act]."). *Cf. Fannie Mae v. Heather Apartments Ltd. P'ship*, A13-0562, 2013 WL 6223564, at *6 (Minn. Ct. App. Dec. 2, 2013) (considering the remedies available to a judgment creditor with respect to the judgment debtor's interest in a Cook Islands LLC; rejecting the debtor's argument that the creditor's "only remedy is to obtain a charging order under" [the Minnesota LLC statute]; explaining that "this argument fails because that statute only applies to Minnesota limited liability companies" which that statute "defines . . . as 'a limited liability company, other than a foreign limited liability company, *organized or governed by this chapter*' ") (emphasis added) (statutory citations omitted).

Subsection (a)(2)—This paragraph permits a statement to designate authority by position (or office) rather than by specific person, thus avoiding the need to file anew whenever a new person assumes the position or the office. This type of a statement will enable partnerships to provide evidence of ongoing power to enter into transactions without having to disclose to third parties the entirety of the partnership agreement.

Here and elsewhere in the section, the phrase "real property" includes all types of interests in real property, such as mortgages, easements, etc.

Subsection (a)(2)(A) and (a)(3)(A)—The authority to "sign" an instrument includes the authority to commit the partnership to the transfer reflected in the agreement. *See* Subsection (f) (referring not merely to signing but also to "an effective statement of authority that grants authority to transfer real property").

Subsection (c)—This subsection expresses a very important limitation—*i.e.*, that this section's rules do not operate viz-a-viz partners. For partners, the partnership agreement is controlling. Section 107(d). However, like any other record delivered for filing on behalf of a partnership, a statement of authority might be some evidence of the contents of the partnership agreement. *See* the comment to Section 107(d).

Another important limitation exists. The filing office is not affected by a statement of authority that purports to delineate the authority of persons to sign documents to be delivered for filing of behalf of a partnership. The act does define "[p]erson" to include a "government or governmental subdivision, agency, or instrumentality," Section 102(14), but "a limitation on the authority of a person or a position contained in an effective statement of authority is not by itself evidence of knowledge or notice of the limitation by any person," Subsection (d).

Moreover, even if an employee of the filing office happened to see that a statement of authority purported to delineate the authority of persons to sign records to be delivered on behalf of a partnership, that information would not pertain to a "fact [that] is material to the agent's duties to the principal" and therefore would not be attributed to the filing office. RESTATEMENT (THIRD) OF AGENCY § 5.03 (2006).

Subsection (d)—The phrase "by itself" is important, because the existence of a limitation of authority could be evidence if, for example, the person in question reviewed the public record at a time when the limitation was of record.

Subsection (e)(2)—This paragraph by its terms does not affect a claim of lingering apparent authority. A person could: (i) assert knowledge of a statement of authority as the statement existed before a cancellation or restrictive amendment; and (ii) characterize the original statement as a manifestation of authority traceable to the partnership. RESTATEMENT (THIRD) OF AGENCY § 3.03, cmt. b (2006) ("Apparent authority is present only when a third party's belief is traceable to manifestations of the principal.").

However, for apparent authority to exist, the purported agent must *reasonably* appear to be authorized. RESTATEMENT (THIRD) OF AGENCY § 2.03 (2006) (stating that apparent authority can only exist when "a third party reasonably believes the actor has authority to act on behalf of the principal"). Given the possibility of cancellation or restrictive amendment, how reasonable can it be for a person to know of a statement of authority, let time pass, and then rely on the statement without re-checking the public record?

Subsections (f)–(h)—These subsections: (i) pertain to transactions in real property; (ii) provide a mechanism by which authority to transfer a partnership's real property can be made to appear in the real estate records; and (iii) thus address the principal concerns (raised by real estate lawyers) that led the drafters of UPA (1997) to provide for statements of authority.

Subsection (f)—This subsection provides a sword for a vendee of real property. If the vendee has "give[n] value in reliance on the grant without knowledge to the contrary," the statement of authority protects the vendee against claims that contradict the grant.

Subsection (f)(1) and (2)—As to a claim of lingering apparent authority, see Section (e)(2), comment. The analysis stated there applies even more strongly in the context of customary practices involving land transfers.

Subsection (g)—This subsection provides a shield for the partnership as alleged vendor. If a vendee's claim contradicts the stated limitation, constructive notice knowledge ("deemed to know") defeats the claim even if the vendee gave value and lacked actual knowledge.

Subsection (h)—This subsection integrates statements of dissolution, Section 802(b)(2)(A), and termination, Section 802(b)(2)(F), into the operation of this section.

The effect of a statement of dissolution depends on the circumstances.

Example: ABC, a general partnership, has in effect a properly filed and recorded statement of authority authorizing ABC's CEO to transfer real estate owned by the partnership. The proper filing and recording by ABC of a statement of dissolution cancels the statement of authority. Subsequently, Buyer gives value in return for a deed signed by the CEO on behalf of ABC. Due to Subsections (h) and (f)(1), Subsection (f) does not protect Buyer. Moreover, under Subsections (g) and (h), Buyer is "deemed to know" of the dissolution. Whether that deemed knowledge functions to deprive the CEO of authority to bind ABC depends on agency law and additional facts. For example, the CEO might have had actual or apparent authority to transfer the real estate despite the dissolution of the partnership.

In contrast, the effect of a statement of termination, Section 802(b)(2)(f), is categorical. If properly filed with the filing office and properly recorded in the office for land records, the statement eliminates the power of any person to transfer real property owned in the name of the partnership. No one can have the authority to act for a non-existent entity. Cf. RESTATEMENT (THIRD) OF AGENCY § 4.04(1)(a) (2006) (precluding ratification by a principal that did not exist at the time of the unauthorized act).

Subsection (i)—This provision permits a partnership to use statements of authority during winding up. As an additional protection for third parties, a statement must be "designated as a post-dissolution statement of authority" to be effective under this provision.

Subsection (k)—Presumably, when real property is involved, a person who obtains the filing of a statement of denial under Section 304 will cause a certified copy of the statement to be "recorded by certified copy for purposes of subsection (f)(1)" [undercutting constructive notice as to authority to transfer real property]. However, nothing in this subsection prevents the partnership from causing a certified copy to appear in the land records; due to the section's use of the passive voice ("may be recorded"), the act does not delimit who has the authority to act under this subsection.

§ 304. Statement of Denial

A person named in a filed statement of authority granting that person authority may deliver to the [Secretary of State] for filing a statement of denial that:

(1) provides the name of the partnership and the caption of the statement of authority to which the statement of denial pertains; and

(2) denies the grant of authority.

COMMENT

A person whose powers are delineated in the public record by another person should have the right to dissent from that delineation. This section takes an "all or nothing" approach; a person may not deny in part and confirm in part. For the effect of a statement of denial, see Section 303(c), comment, and Section 303(k).

Section 308(c) makes clear that a person does not become a partner solely because he is named as a partner in a statement of partnership authority filed by another person.

§ 305.　　Partnership Liable for Partner's Actionable Conduct

(a)　A partnership is liable for loss or injury caused to a person, or for a penalty incurred, as a result of a wrongful act or omission, or other actionable conduct, of a partner acting in the ordinary course of business of the partnership or with the actual or apparent authority of the partnership.

(b)　If, in the course of the partnership's business or while acting with actual or apparent authority of the partnership, a partner receives or causes the partnership to receive money or property of a person not a partner, and the money or property is misapplied by a partner, the partnership is liable for the loss.

COMMENT

Subsection (a)—This provision is derived from UPA (1914) § 13 (Partnership Bound by Partner's Wrongful Act), as modernized by UPA (1997) § 305(a) (Partnership Liable for Partner's Actionable Conduct) and for the most part parallels the agency law doctrine of *respondeat superior*. *See* RESTATEMENT (SECOND) OF AGENCY § 14A, cmt. a (1958) ("When one of the partners is in active management of the business or is otherwise regularly employed in the business, he is a servant of the partnership."). The liability is vicarious and without regard to the fault of those managing the partnership.

UPA (1997) expanded this attribution rule in two ways. First, the 1997 language omitted the 1914 phrase "not being a partner in the partnership," thereby permitting a partner to sue the partnership under this subsection during the term of the partnership, rather than being limited to the remedies of dissolution and an accounting. This change was consistent with UPA(1997) § 410(b) (stating "[a] partner may maintain an action against the partnership or another partner, with or without an accounting as to partnership business, to enforce the partner's rights and protect the partner's interests"). Second, adding "or other actionable conduct" broadens the subsection to cover no-fault torts.

To successfully invoke this provision, a plaintiff must show: (i) "a wrongful act or omission or other actionable conduct" by a partner; (ii) that caused "loss or injury"; and (iii) that at the relevant moment, the partner was acting with actual authority, apparent authority (if relevant), or within "the ordinary course of business of the partnership."

Extrapolating from agency law, apparent authority is relevant only when the appearance of authority augments the impact of the wrongful act. *See* RESTATEMENT (THIRD) OF AGENCY, § 7.8 (2006) ("A principal is subject to vicarious liability for a tort committed by an agent in dealing or communicating with a third party on or purportedly on behalf of the principal when actions taken by the agent with apparent authority constitute the tort or enable the agent to conceal its commission.").

An act or omission may be "in the ordinary course of business of the partnership" even though the act is wrongful. Any other interpretation would vitiate the "ordinary course" element. "The proper question . . . is not whether the specific wrongful act is 'ordinary course' . . . , but rather whether that type of act, if done rightfully, would be." DANIEL S. KLEINBERGER, AGENCY, PARTNERSHIP AND LLCS: EXAMPLES AND EXPLANATIONS § 10.5.1, at 350 (4th ed. 2012) (emphasis omitted)

However, in *Jackson v. Jackson*, 201 S.E.2d 722, 724 (N.C. App. 1974), the North Carolina Court of Appeals stated that, while "[a]dvising the initiation of a criminal prosecution is clearly within the normal range of activities for a typical law partnership, . . . taking such action maliciously and without probable cause is quite a different matter." The court held that "[i]n view of [ethics] rules, which clearly forbid any attempt by a lawyer to prosecute a person without cause, it cannot be held that malicious prosecution is within the ordinary course of business of a law partnership." *Id.* It is difficult to identify a reasonable limit to this approach. Presumably, at least, a partner's "plain vanilla" malpractice is within a law firm's ordinary course of business despite the ethical rules requiring lawyers to act zealously and competently.

In any event, Subsection (a) refers to "the ordinary course of business of the *partnership*" (emphasis added); thus, the proper question is whether the conduct is in the ordinary course for the partnership and not whether the particular partner ordinarily plays a role in that part of the partnership's business. *See Vanacore v. Kennedy*, 86 F. Supp. 2d 42, 51 (D. Conn. 1998), *aff'd sub nom.*, *Vanacore v. Space Realty, Inc.*, 208 F.3d 204 (2d Cir. 2000) (stating that "Kennedy [a partner] committed his misdeeds, which led directly to plaintiff's injuries, within the ordinary course of the business of E & K [the partnership]"); *Sheridan v. Desmond*, 697 A.2d 1162, 1166 (Conn. App. Ct.1997) (stating that to be considered "in ordinary course of the business," a partner's action must be "the kind of thing a . . . partner would do") (emphasis added); *In Moren ex. rel. Moren v. JAX Rest.*, 679 N.W.2d 165, 167–68 (Minn. Ct. App. 2004) (stating, as part of its analysis under UPA (1997) § 305, that "[i]t is undisputed that one of the cooks scheduled to work that evening [at the partnership's restaurant] did not come in, and that [one] partner asked [another partner] to help in the kitchen . . . [and] that [the other partner] was making pizzas for the partnership when" her negligence injured the plaintiff).

Subsection (b)—This provision is derived from UPA (1914) § 14 (Partnership Bound by Partner's Breach of Trust) and UPA (1997) § 305(b) (Partnership Liable for Partner's Actionable Conduct). It is not necessary that the partner "receiv[ing] or caus[ing] the partnership to receive money or property" do so wrongfully. Culpability is necessary at the second phase—*i.e.* when "the money or property is misapplied by a partner."

§ 306. Partner's Liability

(a) Except as otherwise provided in subsections (b) and (c), all partners are liable jointly and severally for all debts, obligations, and other liabilities of the partnership unless otherwise agreed by the claimant or provided by law.

(b) A person that becomes a partner is not personally liable for a debt, obligation, or other liability of the partnership incurred before the person became a partner.

(c) A debt, obligation, or other liability of a partnership incurred while the partnership is a limited liability partnership is solely the debt, obligation, or other liability of the limited liability partnership. A partner is not personally liable, directly or indirectly, by way of contribution or otherwise, for a debt, obligation, or other liability of the limited liability partnership solely by reason of being or acting as a partner. This subsection applies:

(1) despite anything inconsistent in the partnership agreement that existed immediately before the vote or consent required to become a limited liability partnership under Section 901(b); and

(2) regardless of the dissolution of the limited liability partnership.

(d) The failure of a limited liability partnership to observe formalities relating to the exercise of its powers or management of its business is not a ground for imposing liability on a partner for a debt, obligation, or other liability of the partnership.

(e) The cancellation or administrative revocation of a limited liability partnership's statement of qualification does not affect the limitation in this section on the liability of a partner for a debt, obligation, or other liability of the partnership incurred while the statement was in effect.

COMMENT

Derivation—This section was derived from UPA (1997) § 306, which was also the source for ULPA (2001) § 404 and ULLCA (2006) § 304. The Harmonization Project brought the two partnership acts and the limited liability company act into accord to the extent the three acts overlap.

Subsection (a)—Until the advent of limited liability partnerships and limited liability limited partnerships, one hallmark of general partner status was strict, vicarious liability for the debts, obligations, and other liabilities of the partnership. This subsection states that venerable rule, albeit with two changes:

- Under UPA (1914) § 15, the nature of the general partners' liability depended on the claim, giving rise to the partnership's liability. If the partnership's liability sounded in tort, the general partners' liability was joint and several. If the partnership's liability sounded in contract, the general partners' liability was only several. UPA (1997) § 306(a) dispensed with that distinction.

- UPA (1997) § 307(d) generally requires a judgment creditor to exhaust the partnership's assets before enforcing a judgment against the separate assets of a partner. Prior law was to the contrary.

The Harmonization Project made no substantive changes to this subsection.

Subsection (b)—UPA (1997) continued the approach of UPA (1914) §§ 17 and 41(7) to the vicarious liability of an incoming partner, but used a simpler and clearer formulation. The Harmonization Project made no substantive changes to this subsection.

With regard to when a partnership incurs a debt, obligation, or other liability, the case law is scant and concerns only contractual and similar obligations. The leading case is *Conklin Farm v. Leibowitz*, 658 A.2d 1257 (N.J. 1995), which holds that: (i) obligations on a loan, whether for interest or principal, are incurred when the loan is made, not when each particular payment is due; and (ii) obligations for lease payments are incurred when each rental payment is due, not when the lease is made.

Conklin concerned a partnership loan obligation that was: (i) entered into before a particular partner joined the partnership; but (ii) for the most part, was payable afterwards. The court held that "interest is part of the contractual debt, and the obligation to pay interest on a loan *arises,* if at all, at the time that the parties execute the note or other debt instrument. *Conklin,* 658 A.2d at 1261. The court indicated that the same analysis applies to the obligation to repay principal. *Id.* at 1263 (stating that "the decisive issue before this court . . . [is that] [p]ayment of interest, like repayment of advances, is an obligation that arises at the time the debt instrument is executed").

Conklin discussed the lease issue in response to the creditor's argument that "just as a rent obligation arises for current use of property, an interest obligation arises for current use of principal." *Id.* at 1261. Rejecting that argument, the court: (i) noted "the *common-law* obligation to pay rent based on current tenancy [which] . . . arises with each period of tenancy, and . . . arises even in the absence of a lease"; (ii) described "the common-law obligation to pay rent [as] entirely independent of the contractual obligation under the lease"; and (iii) held that, for purposes of partnership law, the rule for "incurring" a lease obligation rests on the common law duty in tenancy and not on the lease as a contract. *Id.* at 1262 (citing *Ellingson v. Walsh, O'Connor & Barneson,* 104 P.2d 507, 508 (Cal. 1940)).

As to when a partnership incurs a tort liability, the answer might be found by analogy to statute of limitation rules, another area of law concerned with when claims arise. "Although the courts have not been consistent . . . , the interpretation of [when] a . . . statute [of limitations begins to run] as applied to torts has been such that the statute does not usually begin to run until the tort is complete . . . . A tort is ordinarily not complete until there has been an invasion of a legally protected interest of the plaintiff." RESTATEMENT (SECOND) OF TORTS § 899, cmt c (1979); *see also Loehr v. Ventura Cnty. Cmty. Coll. Dist.,* 147 Cal. App. 3d 1071, 1078 (Cal. Ct. App. 1983). By analogy, a partnership would incur liability for a tort when the harm occurs. *See, e.g., Jones v. Cox,* 828 P.2d 218, 224 (Colo. 1992) ("A cause of action has commonly been understood to 'accrue' when a suit may be maintained thereon.") (quoting BLACK'S LAW DICTIONARY 19 (5th ed. 1979)); *Loehr,* 147 Cal. App. 3d at 1078.

However, a policy argument exists to the contrary. Vicarious liability for a partnership's torts should be confined to persons who are partners when the wrongful conduct occurs. It is the conduct, not the consequences, that is wrongful; therefore, the occurrence of the wrongful conduct should determine which set of partners is liable for the conduct's consequences.

For further discussion of the "incurred" issue, see Subsection (c), comment (The Temporal Nexus—When Claim Incurred).

Subsection (c)—This subsection provides a corporate/LLC-like liability shield for partners, protecting them from (and only from) the debts, obligations and liabilities of the partnership—*i.e.,* against a partner's alleged vicarious liability for the obligations of the entity.

Full Liability Shield

This act provides a full liability shield—*i.e.,* the shield applies regardless of the law giving rise to a claim against an LLP. A few jurisdictions provide only a partial shield. *See, e.g.,* 15 PA. CONS. STAT. ANN. § 8204 (West 2013) (providing the partners of an LLP a shield for claims against the partnership "whether sounding in contract or tort or otherwise," but only the claims that "arise from any negligent or wrongful acts or misconduct committed by another partner or other representative of the partnership"). The resulting partial shield does not protect partners against liability for the partnership's ordinary commercial debts, such as liability for lease payments.

Shield Applicable Regardless of the Identity of the Plaintiff

What makes the shield relevant is the nature of the claim. If the complaint seeks to hold a partner vicariously liability for the LLP's obligations, the shield applies. If not, not. Thus, there is no distinction among a claim arising from an LLP's debt to a commercial creditor, a partner's claim that the LLP has failed to return a contribution as required by the partnership agreement, and a claim by a former partner that the LLP has failed to follow through on a buy-out agreement. *See Rappaport v. Gelfand,* 197 Cal. App. 4th 1213, 1230–32 (Cal. Ct. App. 2011) (involving a claim by a former partner). *Accord Ederer v. Gursky,* 881 N.E.2d 204, 212–13 (N.Y. 2007) (Smith, J., dissenting).

Shield Inapposite for Claims Arising from a Partner's Own Conduct

Because the partner liability at issue is solely vicarious, the LLP shield is irrelevant to claims seeking to hold a partner directly liable on account of the partner's own conduct. Case law on this issue comes from the analogous context of limited liability companies, and in that context a few judges have failed to understand this point. *See* ULLCA (2006) (Last Amended 2013) § 304(c), cmt. (Shield Inapposite for Claims Arising from a Member's or Manager's Own Conduct). However, the overwhelming weight of case law is contrary, as are the actual words of shield provisions (immunizing only for obligations of the entity and making no reference to direct obligations of an owner or manager) and public policy (which recoils from the idea of immunizing a person's misconduct solely because the person acts on behalf of an organization).

Example: A partner personally guarantees a debt of a limited liability partnership. Subsection (c) is irrelevant to the partner's liability as guarantor.

Example: A partner purports to bind a limited liability partnership while lacking any agency law power to do so. The LLP is not bound, but the partner is liable for having breached the "warranty of authority" (an agency law doctrine). Subsection (c) does not apply. The liability is not *for* a debt, obligation, or other liability of the LLP, but is rather the partner's own, direct liability. Indeed, the liability exists because the LLP is *not* indebted, obligated or liable. RESTATEMENT (THIRD) OF AGENCY § 6.10 (2006).

Example: A partner of a limited liability partnership defames a third party in circumstances that render an LLP vicariously liable under Section 305(a). Under Subsection (c), the third party cannot hold the partner accountable for the *partnership's* liability, but that protection is immaterial. The partner is the tortfeasor and in that role is directly liable to the third party.

Example: A limited liability partnership provides professional services, and one of its partners commits malpractice. The liability shield is irrelevant to the partner's direct liability in tort. However, if the partner's malpractice liability is attributed to the partnership under Section 305(a), the liability shield will protect the other partners against a claim that they must make good on the LLP's liability. The same analysis applies if the plaintiff also successfully claims that another partner was negligent in supervising the first partner.

Example: A limited liability partnership with two partners enters into a contract to build a home, and the partners perform substantial amounts of the work. The homeowner sues both the LLP and the partners for allegedly defective work, but the complaint sounds in contract rather than in tort. The LLP may be liable, but the partners are not. *See Ogea v. Merritt*, 130 So. 3d 888, 905 (La. 2013).

Subsection (c) pertains only to claims based on the LLP's liability and is irrelevant to claims by a limited liability partnership or a partner against another partner and *vice versa*. *See* Sections 307 (pertaining to actions by partners), 409 (pertaining to management duties).

Shield Inapposite to Role Liability Claims

Provisions of regulatory law may impose liability on a partner of an LLP due to a role the partner plays in the partnership. *See, e.g., Food Team Intern., Ltd. v. Unilink, L.L.C.*, 872 F. Supp. 2d 405, 424 (E.D Pa. 2012) (holding several individuals "subject to secondary individual liability under PACA [Perishable Agricultural Commodities Act]" because their roles within a limited liability company enabled them to control the relevant assets) (citing *Bear Mountain Orchards, Inc. v. Mich-Kim, Inc.*, 623 F.3d 163, 172 (3d Cir. 2010)). Subsection (c) does not affect this "role liability."

The Temporal Nexus—When Claim Incurred

The LLP shield functions only with respect to obligations incurred while the partnership is a limited liability partnership. The shield does not protect partners from vicarious liability for partnership obligations incurred before a partnership becomes an LLP or after the partnership cancels its LLP status. *See* Section 903(d). The same is true initially when LLP status has been administratively revoked, but reinstatement of LLP status resurrects the shield retroactively, except as to persons who relied on the revocation. Section 903(d).

For a preliminary discussion of when a partnership obligation is incurred, see Subsection (b), comment. It could well be argued that "incurred" under Subsection (c) has the same meaning as "incurred" under Subsection (b). *IBP, Inc. v. Alvarez*, 546 U.S. 21, 34 (2005) (referring to "the normal rule of statutory interpretation that identical words used in different parts of the same statute are generally presumed to have the same meaning"); *Timberline Air Serv., Inc. v. Bell Helicopter-Textron, Inc.*, 884 P.2d 920, 925 (1994) (stating that "[w]hen the same words are used in different parts of the same statute, it is presumed that the Legislature intended that the words have the same meaning").

However, the argument should yield if the subsections' different contexts raise different issues of policy. 1A SUTHERLAND STATUTES AND STATUTORY CONSTRUCTION § 45:12 (7th ed.) (stating that "departure from the literal construction of a statute is justified when such a construction would produce an absurd and unjust result and would clearly be inconsistent with the purposes and policies of the act in question"); *see, e.g., S.V. v. R.V.*, 933 S.W.2d 1, 4 (Tex. 1996) ("[W]e have held that a cause of action accrues when a wrongful act causes some legal injury, even if the fact of injury is not discovered until later, and even if all resulting damages have not yet occurred. We have not applied this rule without exception, however, and have sometimes held that an action does not accrue until the plaintiff knew or in the exercise of reasonable diligence should have known of the wrongful act and resulting injury.") (citations omitted).

The case law concerning contractual obligations (incurred when the contract is made) applies appropriately in the context of the LLP shield. However, the lease case law is problematic. If an obligation is incurred each time rent is due, subsection(c) is a trap for the unwary landlord.

> **Example:** Ordinary general partnership enters into a lease with a commercial landlord. Knowing that each partner is automatically liable for the partnership's debt, the landlord does not obtain personal guarantees. Subsequently, the partnership becomes an LLP. If future rent payments are incurred when due, and not as of when the lease was made, the landlord loses a very important part of the bargain.

Thus, for the purposes of Subsection (c), lease obligations should be treated as contractual obligations, incurred when the contract is made.

A similar issue exists with regard to tort liability. Courts must look to when the conduct causing the injury takes place and not to when actual injury occurs. Otherwise, a partnership could: (i) engage in wrongful conduct that does not cause immediate injury; (ii) come to realize that the conduct has occurred; (iii) subsequently file a statement of qualification; (iv) thereby become an LLP; and (v) thereby eliminate the vicarious liability of its partners for all harm subsequently arising from the misconduct. *Cf. Savini v. Univ. of Haw.*, 153 P.3d 1144, 1150 (Haw. 2007) (addressing the question of when a statute of limitations begins to run for bodily injury, when another statute precludes bringing a claim until the amount of damages has reached a specified threshold).

In general, courts should determine the "incurred" question under Subsection (c) so that the LLP shield protects the partners of an LLP to the same extent that the corporate and LLC shields protect corporate shareholders and LLC members. From that perspective, LLP status obtained after a partnership commits a wrongful act should provide no greater protection for the partners than a sole proprietor obtains by forming an LLC after committing a wrongful—*i.e.*, none. *See, e.g., Foxchase, L.L.L.P. v. Cliatt*, 562 S.E.2d 221, 224 (Ga. Ct. App. 2002) (holding that a partnership's liability shield did not protect partners from claims of property damage caused by the construction of a golf course, where the jury could have found that the "damage . . . occurred when they, not the partnership, owned the course").

From the same perspective, *Evanston Ins. Co. v. Dillard Dept. Stores, Inc.*, 602 F.3d 610 (5th Cir. 2010) makes no sense. Interpreting the Texas LLP statute, the court held that a partner's liability for a partnership debit is incurred only when judgment is entered against the partnership. Although the decision itself benefitted creditors, the holding invites the type of gamesmanship shown in the leasing example, above. Moreover, the decision: (i) has been criticized by the Texas Court of Appeals, *Am. Star Energy & Minerals Corp. v. Stowers*, 405 S.W.3d 905, 907 (Tex. App. 2013); (ii) ignores the precedent discussed in Subsection (b), comment and Section 307(c), comment; and (iii) can be distinguished as depending on the particular (non-uniform) language of the Texas statute. *Evanston Ins. Co v. Dillard Dep't Stores, Inc.*, 602 F.3d 610, 615–16 (5th Cir. 2010) (contrasting "incurred" with "committed").

Effect of LLP Status on Relations Inter Se the Partners

Although the most noticeable consequence of LLP status is the corporate/LLC-like liability shield, there are two *inter se* consequences as well. One is straightforward; the other is complex.

- When a partnership chooses the jurisdiction in which to deliver for filing a statement of qualification, the partnership chooses its governing law. Section 104(1). The partnership agreement cannot override that choice. Section 105(c)(1).

- When a partnership becomes a limited liability partnership, several related default rules change (going forward):

    o Partners no longer share losses. Capital losses "lay where they fall."

    o Except for contributions promised but not made, partners no longer have

    o contribution obligations.

        ▪ Due to:

            • the liability shield, partners are no longer required to contribute capital to enable the partnership to meet its obligations to creditors; and

            • the elimination of loss sharing, partners are no longer required to contribute capital to adjust capital losses *inter se*.

In this context, a partnership's obligations include a duty to indemnify partners (and others). Thus, indemnification provisions (whether as provided by this act, Section 401(c), or the partnership agreement) are no longer "backstopped" by the partners. *See* the comment to Subsection (c)(1).

Subsection (c)(1)—The main part of Subsection (c) overrides contribution obligations under this act. Paragraph 1 overrides contribution obligations created by the partnership agreement.

Example: The partnership agreement of a non-LLP partnership requires partners to contribute additional capital as necessary to fund the partnership's obligations to indemnify partners. When the partnership becomes an LLP, Paragraph 1 overrides that requirement.

Paragraph 1 does not, however, override contribution and indemnification requirements running directly from partner to partner. These obligations are not obligations of the LLP but rather personal to each partner. If such obligations remain in the partnership agreement, they might disable the shield as to partnership liability arising from the misconduct of a partner.

Example: The partnership agreement of a non-LLP partnership requires partners to contribute additional capital as necessary to fund the partnership's obligations to indemnify the Managing Partner and also states:

> To the extent the partnership lacks sufficient funds to perform the partnership's indemnification obligation, each partner shall indemnify the Managing Partner to the same extent and under the same conditions as the partnership. As among themselves, the indemnifying partners shall share the indemnification obligation proportional to their rights to distributions of then current profits as of the time the Managing Partner's conduct gave rise to the claim for which the Managing Partner is to be indemnified.

The partnership becomes an LLP. Subsequently, the Managing Partner is held liable in tort for conduct within the scope of the Managing Partner's responsibility and the partnership is held liable under Section 305(a). The partnership has no funds to pay the judgment or indemnify the Managing Partner. Paragraph 1 overrides the contribution requirement but does not change each partner's obligation to indemnify the Managing Partner. The Managing Partner's right to be indemnified is an asset of the Managing Partner, and the judgment creditor can levy on that asset, thereby defeating the liability shield in effect if not in form.

Subsection (c)(2)—*The Shield and Dissolution.* The rule stated here is inherent in the nature of partnership dissolution. "[D]issolution does not end a partnership's existence but rather changes the purpose of that existence." Section 801, cmt. "A dissolved partnership shall wind up its business and . . . continues after dissolution . . . for the purpose of winding up." Section 802(a). Put another way: dissolution and winding up are part of the life cycle of a partnership—sometimes the most complicated part. There is no logical reason to remove the shield during the last part of an LLP's life cycle.

This subsection makes this point expressly, because it is possible to misinterpret some outlying cases as holding to the contrary. *See, e.g., Carolina Cas. Ins. Co. v. L.M. Ross Law Grp., LLP*, 151 Cal. Rptr. 3d 628, 635 (2012) (affirming the trial court's decision to hold an LLP's named partner liable for a judgment against his limited ability partnership; noting that "[c]entral to the decision to amend the judgment to add Ross [the named partner] as a judgment debtor . . . is the trial court's finding that Ross Law Group dissolved"; recognizing, however, that, before the partnership incurred the liability, Ross had signed and filed with the California Secretary of State a form stating that the law firm had "cease[d] to be a registered limited liability partnership and is hereby filing this notice with the California Secretary of State that [it] is no longer a registered limited partnership") (quotation marks omitted).

The Shield and Termination. This subsection does not expressly provide that, when a limited liability partnership's existence terminates, the LLP shield remains in place as to any debt, obligation, or other liability of the partnership incurred before the termination. However, the point follows ineluctably from Subsection 306(b). That subsection adopts an "occurrence" rather than a "claims made" basis for determining whether the shield applies. *See* the comment to Subsection (b). (The Temporal Nexus—When Claim Incurred).

Moreover, any other result would: (i) create huge holes in the shield; (ii) put the law of unincorporated businesses at odds with the law of corporations; (iii) render surplus this act's distribution recapture provision, Section 407; (iv) render meaningless the exception to the notice requirement as stated in Sections 807(b)(5) and 808(b)(4); and (v) render nonsensical the otherwise logical extension of the equitable trust fund theory to limited liability partnerships. *Cf. Velasquez v. Franz*, 589 A.2d 143, 146 (N.J. 1991) (explaining that "the trust-fund doctrine . . . renders shareholders who receive distributed assets of the corporation liable as 'trustees' for claims of the corporation's creditors").

Subsection (d)—This subsection was added during the Harmonization Project and pertains to the equitable doctrine of "piercing the veil"—*i.e.*, conflating an entity and its owners to hold one liable for the obligations of the other. The doctrine of "piercing the corporate veil" is well established, and courts should apply the doctrine to limited liability partnerships for the same reasons that courts have regularly (and sometimes almost reflexively) applied the doctrine to limited liability companies. *Cf. Axtmann v. Chillemi*, 740 N.W.2d 838, 847 (N.D. 2007) (stating that "the shield of a limited liability partnership may be pierced under 'the case law that states the conditions and circumstances under which the corporate veil or limited liability shield of a corporation may be pierced under North Dakota law . . . .' ") (quoting N.D.C.C. § 45–22–09(1)).

However, as with LLC piercing, LLP piercing involves one important distinction from the corporate realm. While under corporate law "disregard of corporate formalities" is a key piercing factor, that factor is inapposite in the law of unincorporated organizations. Corporate formalities reflect statutory mandates. LLP formalities derive for the most part from the agreement among the partners. From a policy perspective, disregarding formalities adopted by agreement differs substantially from disregarding formalities imposed by law. *See e.g. In re Packer*, Bankruptcy No. 13–41304, 2014 WL 5100095 (Bankr. E.D. Tex. Oct. 10, 2014) (noting the informality of LLC governance, recognizing that "the disregard of corporate formalities . . . [is] one of the key factors in [corporate] veil-piercing determinations"; but holding that " 'it makes no sense to imperil the shield simply because the members do not undergo meaningless formalities such as formal meetings' ") (citing Carter G. Bishop & Daniel S. Kleinberger, LIMITED LIABILITY COMPANIES: TAX AND BUSINESS LAW ¶ 6.03 at *3 (Thomson Reuters Tax and Accounting 2014)).

Moreover, because the terms of a partnership agreement may be "implied," Section 102(12), an LLP's ongoing disregard of formalities may well constitute an amendment to the partnership agreement. If so, disregard equals amendment, and the concept of "disregard of formalities" makes no sense.

In contrast, this subsection is inapposite to another key piercing factor—disregard of the separateness between entity and owner. *Cf. Vanderford Co. v. Knudson*, 165 P.3d 261, 271 (Idaho 2007) (noting that managing member and "his accountant testified that the LLC's checking account was so confusing that the accountant could not be sure whose money was in the account at what times"); *Utzler v. Braca*, 972 A.2d 743 (Conn. App. Ct. 2009) (holding that veil piercing was appropriate under alter-ego theory when owner deposited LLC funds into a commingled bank account from which he made withdrawals for personal needs and unrelated projects).

Example: A partner in a limited liability partnership uses a car titled in the partnership's name for personal purposes and writes checks on the partnership's account to pay for personal expenses. These facts are relevant to a piercing claim; they pertain to economic separateness, not Subsection (b) formalities.

This subsection addresses claims to "impos[e] liability on a partner for a debt, obligation, or other liability of the partnership"—*i.e.*, for what is sometimes termed a "direct pierce." Whether the same approach should apply to claims for a "reverse pierce" is a question for the courts. *See Comm'r of Envtl. Prot. v. State Five Indus. Park, Inc.*, 37 A.3d 724, 732–33 (Conn. 2012) (stating that "[a]lthough some courts have adopted reverse veil piercing with little distinction as a logical corollary of traditional veil piercing, because the two share the same equitable goals, others wisely have recognized important differences between them").

This subsection is inapposite to a member's claim that the disregard of agreed-upon formalities is a breach of the partnership agreement.

Subsection (e)—The rule stated here is implicit in Subsection (c) but is stated expressly for the avoidance of doubt.

§ 307. Actions By and Against Partnership and Partners

(a)   A partnership may sue and be sued in the name of the partnership.

(b)   To the extent not inconsistent with Section 306, a partner may be joined in an action against the partnership or named in a separate action.

(c)   A judgment against a partnership is not by itself a judgment against a partner. A judgment against a partnership may not be satisfied from a partner's assets unless there is also a judgment against the partner.

(d)   A judgment creditor of a partner may not levy execution against the assets of the partner to satisfy a judgment based on a claim against the partnership unless the partner is personally liable for the claim under Section 306 and:

(1)   a judgment based on the same claim has been obtained against the partnership and a writ of execution on the judgment has been returned unsatisfied in whole or in part;

(2)   the partnership is a debtor in bankruptcy;

(3)   the partner has agreed that the creditor need not exhaust partnership assets;

(4)   a court grants permission to the judgment creditor to levy execution against the assets of a partner based on a finding that partnership assets subject to execution are clearly insufficient to satisfy the judgment, that exhaustion of partnership assets is excessively burdensome, or that the grant of permission is an appropriate exercise of the court's equitable powers; or

(5)   liability is imposed on the partner by law or contract independent of the existence of the partnership.

(e)   This section applies to any debt, liability, or other obligation of a partnership which results from a representation by a partner or purported partner under Section 308.

COMMENT

Section 307 reflects the entity construct, Section 201(a), was new in UPA (1997), and cannot be varied by the partnership agreement. *See* Section 105(c)(3). The Harmonization Project made no substantive changes to this section.

Subsection (a)—UPA (1997) § 307 clarified and simplified an "entity versus aggregate" question that had been at best complicated under the common law and UPA (1914) (*i.e.*, whether a general partnership could sue and be sued in its own name and without joining all the partners).

"[A]t common law, . . . a partnership could neither sue or be sued in its name. The individual partners were required to be named as plaintiffs in an action brought by the partnership and as defendants in an action against a partnership." *Telamarketing Commc'ns, Inc. v. Liberty Partners*, 798 S.W.2d 462, 463 (Ky. 1990) (discussing Kentucky law); *see also* JOSEPH STORY, COMMENTARIES ON THE LAW ON PARTNERSHIP § 241, at 373–74 (2d ed. 1850) ("It is a general rule, that in all such suits at law [between a partnership and a third party] all the partners should join.").

UPA (1914) was silent on the point, although some courts inferred capacity to sue (and presumably to be sued) from other entity-like characteristics reflected in that act. *E.g.*, *Decker Coal Co. v. Commonwealth Edison Co.*, 714 P.2d 155, 157 (Mont. 1986) (agreeing with a party's contention that "[a]lthough . . . the UPA does not expressly deal with the question of a partnership's capacity to sue, . . . the UPA does show the modern tendency to treat a partnership as a legal entity distinct from and independent of the individuals composing it"; citing as an example, a partnership's ability to "own property in its own name"; and holding that "it is clear that a partnership is indeed a legal entity distinct from its partners [and] [t]herefore, . . . has the capacity to sue in its own name").

The situation was further complicated by "common name" statutes enacted in many states. *See Silliman v. DuPont*, 302 A.2d 327, 331 (Del. Super. 1972), *aff'd sub nom.*, *F. I. Du Pont, Glore Forgan & Co. v. Silliman*, 310 A.2d 128 (Del. 1973) ("The basic purpose of [common name] statutes was to permit a non-corporate entity to be sued in the name it presented to the public without the necessity of joining the many individuals who composed it.").

The rule stated here is perhaps implicit in Section 201(a) ("A partnership is an entity distinct from its partners."). It is a hallmark of a legal entity that it can sue and be sued. In any event, this subsection leaves no room for doubt.

Subsection (b)—The phrase "not inconsistent with Section 306" means:

- *•*   If a debt, obligation, or other liability is incurred by a limited liability partnership, this subsection does not permit joinder of a partner.

- •   Likewise, if a debt, obligation, or other liability is incurred by an ordinary partnership before a person becomes a partner, this subsection does not permit joinder of that person.

As for when a claim is incurred, see Section 307(c) and (d), comments.

The reference to "not inconsistent with Section 306" is the procedural analog to the substantive protections of Section 306(b) (incoming partner not liable for pre-existing partnership obligations) and (c) (partners not liable for partnership obligations incurred by an LLP). When a partner has personally guaranteed a partnership obligation, naming that partner in a suit against the partnership is "not inconsistent with Section 306." *See* the comment to Section 306(c) (Shield Inapposite for Claims Arising from a Partner's Conduct); *cf. Bank of Bos. Conn. v. Schlesinger*, 595 A.2d 872, 875 (Conn. 1991) (upholding pre-judgment attachment of a partner's assets, where the partner had personally guaranteed the partnership's obligations).

Subsection (c)—Reflecting the entity construct, Section 201(a), this subsection provides that a judgment against the partnership: (i) is not, standing alone, a judgment against the partners; and (ii) cannot be satisfied from a partner's personal assets absent a judgment against the partner.

As did UPA (1914) and UPA (1997), this act leaves to the law of judgments to determine the collateral effects to be accorded a prior judgment for or against the partnership in a subsequent action against a partner individually. *See* RESTATEMENT (SECOND) OF JUDGMENTS § 60, cmts. (1982); *see also Detrio v. U.S.*, 264 F.2d 658 (5th Cir. 1959); *Brunsoman v. Seltz*, 414 N.W.2d 547 (Minn. Ct. App. 1987) (Lansing, J.). *Contra Evanston Ins. Co. v. Dillard Dep't Stores, Inc.*, 602 F.3d 610, 618 (5th Cir. 2010) (disregarding *sub silentio* the separateness of partner and partnership, overlooking therefore the issue of collateral estoppel, discussing with approval a bankruptcy case in which "the trustee sought to enforce the partnership judgment against [partners] simply by virtue of their status as partner"; and quoting with approval that case's holding that "[o]nce the liability of the partnership became fixed, the only issue remaining was whether the Defendants are partners of [the partnership]" (quoting *In re Jones*, 161 B.R. 180, 183–84 (Bankr. N.D. Tex. 1993)).

This subsection and Subsection (d) combine to create a trap for the unwary. For statute of limitations purposes, a creditor's claim against the partners accrues simultaneously with the claim against the partnership. If a creditor chooses not to sue the partners in its suit against the partnership, the statute of limitations may run before the creditor commences suit against the partners. *Am. Star Energy & Minerals Corp. v. Stowers*, 405 S.W.3d 905, 907 (Tex. App. 2013) (holding that the partnership creditor "was obligated to sue the partners of S & J . . . within the same limitations period it had to sue S & J, the partnership" and that "[b]ecause, [the creditor] did not, the trial court correctly held that limitations ran"); *Sunseri v. Proctor*, 487 F. Supp. 2d 905, 908 (E.D. Mich. 2007), *aff'd*, 286 F. App'x 930 (6th Cir. 2008) ("While the plaintiff may use collateral estoppel to prevent the partner from relitigating the issue of liability, the plaintiff must still bring suit within the applicable limitations period for the underlying wrong.")

Subsection (d)—Subject to the five listed exceptions, this subsection prevents a partner's assets from being the first recourse for a judgment creditor of the partnership, even if the partner is liable for the judgment debt under Section 306.

Although this subsection is silent with respect to pre-judgment remedies, as a matter of policy the subsection should guide courts as they apply the law of pre-judgment remedies. *Compare Sec. Pac. Nat'l Bank v. Matek*, 175 Cal. App. 3d 1071, 1077 (Cal. Ct. App. 1985) (granting a pre-judgment remedy against a partner because there is "no distinction between those sued individually as partners and those sued as sole proprietors"), *with Bank of Bos. Conn. v. Schlesinger*, 595 A.2d 872, 875 (Conn. 1991) (upholding pre-judgment attachment of a partner's assets, because the partner had personally guaranteed the partnership's obligations).

Subsection (e)—The effect of this subsection depends on whether Section 308 applies to produce a partnership obligation or a joint and several obligation. *See* Section 308(a) ("If partnership liability results [under the subsection], the purported partner is liable with respect to that liability as if the purported partner were a partner. If no partnership liability results, the purported partner is liable with respect to that liability jointly and severally with any other person consenting to the representation."), (b) ("If all the partners of the existing partnership consent to the representation, a partnership act or obligation results. If fewer than all the partners of the existing partnership consent to the representation, the person acting and the partners consenting to the representation are jointly and severally liable.").

§ 308.   Liability of Purported Partner

(a)   If a person, by words or conduct, purports to be a partner, or consents to being represented by another as a partner, in a partnership or with one or more persons not partners, the purported partner is liable to a person to whom the representation is made, if that person, relying on the representation, enters into a transaction with the actual or purported partnership. If the representation, either by the purported partner or by a person with the purported partner's consent, is made in a public manner, the purported partner is liable to a person who relies upon the purported partnership even if the purported partner is not aware of being held out as a partner to the claimant. If partnership liability results, the purported partner is liable with respect to that liability as if the purported partner were a partner. If no partnership liability results, the purported partner is liable with respect to that liability jointly and severally with any other person consenting to the representation.

(b)   If a person is thus represented to be a partner in an existing partnership, or with one or more persons not partners, the purported partner is an agent of persons consenting to the representation to bind them to the same extent and in the same manner as if the purported partner were a partner with respect to persons who enter into transactions in reliance upon the representation. If all the partners of the existing partnership consent to the representation, a partnership act or obligation results. If fewer than all the partners of the existing partnership consent to the representation, the person acting and the partners consenting to the representation are jointly and severally liable.

(c)   A person is not liable as a partner merely because the person is named by another as a partner in a statement of partnership authority.

(d)   A person does not continue to be liable as a partner merely because of a failure to file a statement of dissociation or to amend a statement of partnership authority to indicate the person's dissociation as a partner.

(e)   Except as otherwise provided in subsections (a) and (b), persons who are not partners as to each other are not liable as partners to other persons.

COMMENT

UPA (1997) § 308 continued the basic principles of partnership by estoppel stated in UPA (1914) § 16. To the extent a partnership liability results under Section 308, Section 307 applies. *See* Section 307(e). The Harmonization Project made no substantive changes to this section.

Subsections (a) and (b)—Even though these subdivisions refer to "reliance" without expressly imposing a reasonableness requirement, the requirement exists in the case law. *See, e.g., In re Cay Clubs*, 319 P.3d 625, 633 (Nev. 2014) (adopting the requirement and stating that, although the requirement is not explicitly stated in [the statute,] [g]enerally, jurisdictions provide that the partnership-by-estoppel doctrine conditions liability on the plaintiff having reasonably relied on the representation of partnership, which often involves an exercise of due diligence to ascertain the facts").

Subsection (a)—This subsection continues the distinction between representations made to specific persons and those made in a public manner. In both circumstances, the claimant must show reliance.

Like UPA (1914) § 16, this section imposes no duty of denial; thus, a person held out by another as a partner is not liable without having actually consented to the representation. *See* Subsection (c) (no duty to file statement of denial); Subsection (d) (no duty to file statement of dissociation or to amend statement of partnership authority).

Subsections (c) and (d)—These subsections were new in UPA (1997) and preclude negative inferences from outdated information in filed statements.

Subsection (e)—Derived from UPA (1914) § 7(1), this subsection circumscribes the circumstances in which a person can be liable as a partner to third parties for the obligations of the partnership—*i.e.*, only if (i) the person is a partner in the partnership; or (ii) the person is liable under Section 308(a) or (b).

[ARTICLE] 4.   RELATIONS OF PARTNERS TO EACH OTHER AND TO PARTNERSHIP

If there is nothing drafted ↑

§ 401.   Partner's Rights and Duties

(a)   Each partner is entitled to an equal share of the partnership distributions and, except in the case of a limited liability partnership, is chargeable with a share of the partnership losses in proportion to the partner's share of the distributions.

(b)   A partnership shall reimburse a partner for any payment made by the partner in the course of the partner's activities on behalf of the partnership, if the partner complied with this section and Section 409 in making the payment.

(c)   A partnership shall indemnify and hold harmless a person with respect to any claim or demand against the person and any debt, obligation, or other liability incurred by the person by reason of the person's former or present capacity as a partner, if the claim, demand, debt, obligation, or other liability does not arise from the person's breach of this section or Section 407 or 409.

(d)   In the ordinary course of its business, a partnership may advance reasonable expenses, including attorney's fees and costs, incurred by a person in connection with a claim or demand against the person by reason of the person's former or present capacity as a partner, if the person promises to repay the partnership if the person ultimately is determined not to be entitled to be indemnified under subsection (c).

(e)   A partnership may purchase and maintain insurance on behalf of a partner against liability asserted against or incurred by the partner in that capacity or arising from that status even if, under Section 105(c)(7), the partnership agreement could not eliminate or limit the person's liability to the partnership for the conduct giving rise to the liability.

(f)   A partnership shall reimburse a partner for an advance to the partnership beyond the amount of capital the partner agreed to contribute.

(g)   A payment or advance made by a partner which gives rise to a partnership obligation under subsection (b) or (f) constitutes a loan to the partnership which accrues interest from the date of the payment or advance.

(h)   Each partner has equal rights in the management and conduct of the partnership's business.

(i)   A partner may use or possess partnership property only on behalf of the partnership.

(j)   A partner is not entitled to remuneration for services performed for the partnership, except for reasonable compensation for services rendered in winding up the business of the partnership.

(k)   A difference arising as to a matter in the ordinary course of business of a partnership may be decided by a majority of the partners. An act outside the ordinary course of business of a partnership and an amendment to the partnership agreement may be undertaken only with the affirmative vote or consent of all the partners.

 Summers Case

COMMENT

For the most part, Section 401 merely restates the rules of UPA (1914) § 18, thereby establishing many of the default rules that govern the relations among partners. All of these rules are, however, subject to contrary agreement of the partners as provided in Sections 105 through 107.

UPA (1997) § 401(a) experimented with providing a default configuration for capital accounts. For the reasons stated in Section 405, comment, the Harmonization Project ended the experiment and eliminated the configuration.

Subsection (a)—This subsection continues the approach of UPA (1914) § 18(a), although for the reasons stated in Section 405, comment, the Harmonization Project substituted "distribution" for "profits." Distributions are shared equally and losses are shared in proportion to each partner's share of distributions. Thus, under this default rule, partners share distributions per capita and not in proportion to capital contribution (per capital).

If partners agree to share distributions other than equally, losses will be shared in the same proportion as distributions, absent agreement to do otherwise. This rule, carried over from UPA (1914) rests on the assumption that partners would likely agree to share losses on the same basis as distributions, but may fail to say so. Of course, by agreement, they may share losses on a different basis from distributions.

Subject to contrary agreement and the effect of Section 806(e), this subsection's loss sharing rules apply, even where one or more of the partners contribute no capital. The rule was the same under UPA (1914) § 18(a), although there is some case law to the contrary. *See, e.g., Kovacik v. Reed,* 315 P.2d 314 (Cal. 1957); *Becker v. Killarney,* 523 N.E.2d 467 (Ill. App. Ct. 1988). It may seem unfair that the contributor of services, who contributes little or no capital, should be obligated to contribute toward the capital loss of the large contributor who contributed no services. In entering a partnership with such a capital structure, the partners should foresee that application of the default rule might bring about unusual results and take advantage of their power to vary by agreement the allocation of capital losses.

Subsections (b) and (c)—A partnership's obligation, if any, to reimburse or indemnify others (*e.g.,* employees, other agents, and independent contractors) is a question for other law, including the law of agency, contract, and restitution. The fact a person has dissociated as a partner does not affect any obligations incurred by the partnership under these subsections for conduct occurring before the dissociation.

To the extent a partnership agreement modifies or displaces the default rules stated in Sections 401 and 409, the agreement should also address these sections. For example, if the partnership agreement establishes a duty of ordinary care (modifying Section 409(c)), the agreement should specify which level of care is necessary to satisfy Subsections (b) and (c). It is not necessary that the levels of care be the same, only that the partnership agreement make the situation clear and thereby avoid difficult issues of interpretation.

Subsection (b)—UPA (1997) derived this subsection from UPA (1914) § 18(b). The Harmonization Project made two changes: (i) deleting "for the preservation of its business or property" as a separate category for reimbursement, because that category is a subset of the category of "payments made . . . in the course of the partner's activities on behalf of the partnership"; and (ii) conditioning reimbursement on the partner's having complied with the duties stated in Section 409.

The reimbursement obligation stated here is a default rule and roughly parallels a rule of agency law. Restatement (Third) of Agency § 8.14(2) (2006) (stating that "[a] principal has a duty to indemnify an agent . . . when the agent makes a payment (i) within the scope of the agent's actual authority, or (ii) that is beneficial to the principal, unless the agent acts officiously in making the payment").

Subsection (c)—This subsection provides for indemnification, but the provision is a default rule.

The rule's eligibility requirements correspond to the default rules on management duties, which is appropriate because otherwise the statutory default rule on indemnification could undercut or even vitiate the statutory default rules on duty. However, subject only to Section 105(c)(8), the partnership agreement can substantially relax the eligibility requirements. The agreement can also impose stricter preconditions.

Although referring broadly to any "person," this subsection is actually limited to present and former partners. The indemnification obligation applies to only a "debt, obligation, or other liability incurred by the person by reason of the person's former or present capacity as a partner." Thus, by its terms this subsection does not apply to a person in the capacity of an officer, manager, etc.

Of course, the partnership agreement may mandate indemnification to persons in such positions, as well as to other persons providing services to or acting for the partnership. Within the limitations stated in Section 105(c)(8), a partnership agreement may obligate a partnership to indemnify a person even though the person has breached a duty to the partnership.

A separate agreement between a partnership and another person may also provide for indemnification. For example, a management contract between a partnership and its managing partner may contain an indemnification provision. The limitations stated in Section 105(c)(8) apply to such separate agreements, for the reasons stated in the comment to that paragraph.

Subsection (d)—This subsection authorizes but does not require a partnership to provide advances to cover expenses. *Cf. Majkowski v. Am. Imaging Mgmt. Servs., L.L.C.*, 913 A.2d 572, 589 (Del. Ch. 2006) ("Because rights to indemnification and advancement differ in important ways, our courts have refused to recognize claims for advancement not granted in specific language clearly suggesting such rights."). The phrase "hold harmless" likewise does not encompass advances. *Id.* The authorization applies only to those persons eligible for indemnification under Subsection (c), but the partnership agreement certainly can authorize a broader scope and can also make advances obligatory.

The reference to "ordinary course" pertains to Subsection (k) (stating that any "difference arising in the ordinary course of the business of the partnership may be decided by a majority of the partners").

Subsection (e)—This subsection's language is very broad and authorizes a partnership to purchase insurance to cover (*e.g.*, a partner's intentional misconduct). It is unlikely that such insurance would be available. This authorization comes from the act, not the partnership agreement, and therefore is not subject to Section 105(c)(8) (precluding the partnership agreement from "reliev[ing] or exonerate[ing] a person from liability for conduct involving bad faith, willful or intentional misconduct, or knowing violation of law").

Subsection (f)—This subsection was UPA (1997) § 401(d) and is based on UPA (1914) § 18(c).

Subsection (g)—This subsection was UPA (1997) § 401(c) and is based on UPA (1914) § 18(c).

Subsection (h)—This subsection was UPA (1997) § 401(f) and is based on UPA (1914) § 18(e). UPA (1997) § 401, comment 7, suggests that UPA (1914) § 18(e) case law continues to be relevant and notes that Section 18(e) "has been interpreted broadly to mean that, absent contrary agreement, each partner has a continuing right to participate in the management of the partnership and to be informed about the partnership business, even if, per the partnership agreement, the partner's assent to partnership business decisions is not required."

Note also that for some decisions this act requires the affirmative vote or consent of all partners. *See, e.g.*, Subsection (k) ("an act outside the ordinary course of business of a partnership and an amendment to the partnership agreement"); Section 402(b)(3) (becoming a partner after formation of the partnership).

The subsection has important implications for a partner's actual authority to act on behalf of the partnership. The actual authority of a partner is a question of agency law and depends fundamentally on the contents of the partnership agreement. If, however, the partnership agreement is silent on the issue, this subsection helps delineate that actual authority. Acting individually, a partner:

- has no actual authority to commit the partnership to any matter for which this act requires the affirmative vote or consent of all partners;

- has the actual authority to commit the partnership to usual and customary matters, unless the partner has reason to know that: (i) other partners might disagree; or (ii) for some other reason consultation with fellow partners is appropriate; and

- has no actual authority to take unusual or non-customary actions that will have a substantial effect on the partnership.

The first point follows self-evidently from the language of this act. Where this act requires unanimity, no partner could reasonably believe to the contrary (unless the partnership agreement provided otherwise).

The second point follows because:

- Subsection (h) serves as the gap-filler manifestation from the partnership to its partners and does *not* require partners to act *only* in concert or after consultation. To the contrary, subject to the partnership agreement, this subsection expressly provides that "each partner has equal rights in the management and conduct of the partnership's business."

- It would be impractical to require collective action on even the smallest of decisions.

- However, to the extent a partner has reason to know of a possible difference of opinion among the partner, Subsection (k) requires a decision by at least "a majority of the partners" and by unanimous consent if the matter is "outside the ordinary course of the business."

The third point is a matter of common sense. The more serious the matter, the less likely it is that a partner has actual authority to act unilaterally. *Cf.* RESTATEMENT (THIRD) OF AGENCY § 3.03, cmt. c (2006) (noting the unreasonableness of believing, without more facts, that an individual has "an unusual degree of unilateral authority over a matter fraught with enduring consequences for the institution" and stating that "[t]he gravity of the matter from the standpoint of the organization is relevant to whether a third party could reasonably believe that the manager has authority to proceed unilaterally").

Finally, the authority granted by this subsection includes the authority to delegate. Delegation does not relieve the delegating partner or partners of their duties under Section 409. However, the fact of delegation is a fact relevant to any breach of duty analysis.

Example: A partner personally handles all important paperwork for a partnership. The partner neglects to renew the fire insurance coverage on a building owned by the partnership, despite having received and read a warning notice from the insurance company. The building subsequently burns to the ground and is a total loss. The partner might be liable for breach of the duty of care under Section 409(c) (gross negligence).

Example: A partner delegates responsibility for insurance renewals to the partnership's office manager, and that manager neglects to renew the fire insurance coverage on the building. Even assuming that the office manager has been grossly negligent, the partner is not necessarily liable under Section 409(c). The office manager's gross negligence is not automatically attributed to the partner. Under Section 409(c), the question is whether the partner was grossly negligent (or worse) in selecting the office manager, delegating insurance renewal matters to the office manager, and supervising the general manager after the delegation.

The partnership agreement may also provide for delegation and, subject to Section 105(c), may modify a partner's duties under Section 409 accordingly.

Subsection (i)—This subsection states directly what UPA (1914) § 25(2)(a) provides indirectly, through the "tenancy in partnership." That tenancy reflected the aggregate view of partnership (in the extreme), stated management rights as property rights, and was eliminated by UPA (1997) 401(g). The Harmonization Project relocated the UPA (1997) provision into this subsection.

The substance of UPA (1997) § 401(i), which continued the substance of UPA (1914) § 18(g), now appears in Section 402(b)(3) (providing that no person can become a partner without the affirmative vote or consent of all partners).

Subsection (j)—This subsection (i) follows the default rule of UPA (1914) § 18(f) (providing that a partner is not entitled to remuneration for services performed, except in winding up the partnership); while (ii) expanding the exception to include any partner who undertakes winding up. "[R]easonable compensation" includes reimbursement for reasonable expenses. *Moran v. Willensky*, 339 S.W.3d 651, 663 (Tenn. Ct. App. 2010) (stating that "the winding up partner . . . [is] entitled to recover costs associated with the winding up process); *see also O'Reilly's Adm'r v. Brady*, 28 Ala. 530, 535 (1856) (holding that "the surviving partner is entitled, at least, to an allowance and deduction for 'tavern bills,' [sic] and 'other expenses incurred' in the adjustment and settling up' of the affairs of the partnership."). Reasonable expenses include reasonable attorney's fees, even when the winding up partner has (rightfully) caused the partnership to sue one of the partners. *Moran*, 339 S.W.3d at 663 ("Because Mr. Willensky's capital account had a negative balance, Ms. Moran was well within her rights to sue him to make up that balance.").

In UPA (1997), this subsection was Subsection (h). The Harmonization Project made no change except to relocate the provision.

Subsection (k)—UPA (1997) continued the allocation of management authority stated by UPA (1914) § 18(h), with one important clarification. UPA (1914) § 18(h) requires majority consent for ordinary matters and unanimous consent for amending the partnership but is silent regarding extraordinary matters. Courts have generally required the consent of all partners for those matters. *See, e.g., Paciaroni v. Crane*, 408 A.2d 946 (Del. Ch. 1989); *Thomas v. Marvin E. Jewell & Co.*, 440 N.W.2d 437(Neb. 1989); *Duell v. Hancock*, 83 A.D.2d 762 (N.Y. 1981). UPA (1997) codified those cases in § 401(j). The Harmonization Project made no substantive change but relocated the provision to Subsection (k).

Other provisions of this act also contain default rules providing for unanimous consent. *E.g.*, Sections 402(b)(3) (for a person to become a partner), 504(c) (for compromising a person's obligation to make a contribution). In addition, absent a contrary provision in the partnership agreement, the transactions authorized under Article 11 each require unanimous consent.

§ 402. Becoming Partner

(a) Upon formation of a partnership, a person becomes a partner under Section 202(a).

(b) After formation of a partnership, a person becomes a partner:

    (1) as provided in the partnership agreement;

    (2) as a result of a transaction effective under [Article] 11; or

    (3) with the affirmative vote or consent of all the partners.

(c) A person may become a partner without:

    (1) acquiring a transferable interest; or

    (2) making or being obligated to make a contribution to the partnership.

COMMENT

This section was adopted in the 2011 and 2013 Harmonization amendments and changes UPA (1997) both in style and substance.

Subsection (b)(2)—Article 11 deals with entity transactions (*e.g.*, mergers and conversions). This reference is new, although UPA (1997) Article 9 did contemplate mergers and conversions.

Subsection (b)(3)—A partnership being a creature of contract, consent is determined on an objective basis (*i.e.*, contract law's "reasonable person" standard). Depending on the terms of the partnership agreement, the partners' manifestation of consent might involve detailed formalities, entirely informal activities, or anything in between. Moreover, the partnership agreement might reduce the quantum of consent necessary or shift the consent right to the management committee or managing partners.

A partnership being a voluntary association, a person cannot become a partner without manifesting consent to do so. That consent also is judged objectively.

Under Section 106(b), "[a] person that becomes a partner is deemed to assent to the partnership agreement," and the agreement binds the partner regardless of whether the partner has actually indicated assent in any way.

Subsection (c)(1)—To accommodate business practices, this provision permits so-called "non-economic partners."

§ 403.   Form of Contribution

A contribution may consist of property transferred to, services performed for, or another benefit provided to the partnership or an agreement to transfer property to, perform services for, or provide another benefit to the partnership.

COMMENT

This section is derived from ULLCA (2006) § 402, was adopted as part of the 2011 and 2013 Harmonization amendments, is intentionally quite broad, and encompasses past, present, and promised benefits.

Partnership law and practice are in accord. *E.g.*, *Canet v. Gooch Ware Travelstead*, 917 F. Supp. 969, 974 (E.D.N.Y. 1996) (referring to "Travelstead's acknowledged use of 'sweat equity' participations" in two projects); *In re Jones*, 445 B.R. 677, 717 (Bankr. N.D. Tex. 2011) (stating that "Ex-Mrs. Mullen essentially put 'sweat equity' (*i.e.*, the provision of modeling services and related consultation) into Simple Beaute and not a significant monetary investment"); *Tumminaro v. Tumminaro*, 556 N.E.2d 293, 299 (Ill. App. Ct. 1990) ("A partner's contribution to the partnership may consist of 'services, skill, know-how, or "sweat equity." ' ") (quoting *Becker v. Killarney*, 532 N.E.2d 931 (Ill. App. Ct. 1988)).

This act does not contain a statute of frauds specifically applicable to promised contributions. Generally applicable statutes of fraud might apply, however. For example, a promise to contribute land to a partnership would be subject to the statute of frauds pertaining to land transfers. Likewise, a promise that by its terms requires performance that extends beyond one year from the making of the contract would be subject to the one-year provision of the statute of frauds. *See* the comment to Section 102(12).

§ 404.   Liability for Contribution

(a)   A person's obligation to make a contribution to a partnership is not excused by the person's death, disability, termination, or other inability to perform personally.

(b)   If a person does not fulfill an obligation to make a contribution other than money, the person is obligated at the option of the partnership to contribute money equal to the value of the part of the contribution which has not been made.

(c)   The obligation of a person to make a contribution may be compromised only by the affirmative vote or consent of all the partners. If a creditor of a limited liability partnership extends credit or otherwise acts in reliance on an obligation described in subsection (a) without knowledge or notice of a compromise under this subsection, the creditor may enforce the obligation.

COMMENT

Subsection (a)—Under common law principles of impracticability, an individual's death or incapacity will sometimes discharge a duty to render performance. RESTATEMENT (SECOND) OF CONTRACTS §§ 261 (Discharge by Supervening Impracticability), 262 (Death or Incapacity of Person Necessary For Performance) (1981). This subsection overrides those principles. Moreover, the reference to "perform personally" is not limited to individuals but rather may refer to any legal person (including an entity) that has a non-delegable duty.

Subsection (b)—This subsection is a statutory liquidated damage provision, exercisable at the option of the partnership, with the damage amount set according to the value of the promised, non-monetary contribution.

Example: In order to become a partner, a person promises to contribute to the partnership various assets "free and clear," which the partnership agreement values at $150,000. In return for the person's promise, and in light of the agreed value, the partnership admits the person as a partnership with a right to receive twenty-five percent of the partnership's distributions.

However, the promised assets are subject to a security agreement, and, before the partner can contribute the assets, the secured party forecloses on the security interest and sells the assets at a public sale for $75,000. Even if the $75,000 reflects the actual fair market value of the assets, under this subsection the partnership has a claim against the partner for "money equal to the value of the part of the contribution which has not been made"—*i.e.*, $150,000.

Example: Same facts as the previous example, except that the public sale brings $225,000. The limited liability company is neither obliged to invoke this subsection nor limited to the $150,000. The LLC may instead sue for breach of the promise to make the contribution, asserting the $225,000 figure as evidence of the actual loss suffered as a result of the breach.

Subsection (c)—The unanimity requirement expressed in the first sentence might indirectly benefit creditors, but the requirement is nonetheless a default rule and therefore may be varied in the partnership agreement. The right of each partner to consent is not a "right[ ] under this [act] of a person other than a partner." *See* Section 105(c)(17) (preventing the partnership agreement from affecting such rights). In contrast, the right stated in the second sentence fits squarely within Section 105(c)(17) and therefore may not be varied by the partnership agreement.

§ 405.   Sharing of and Right to Distributions Before Dissolution

(a)   Any distribution made by a partnership before its dissolution and winding up must be in equal shares among partners, except to the extent necessary to comply with a transfer effective under Section 503 or charging order in effect under Section 504.

(b)   Subject to Section 701, a person has a right to a distribution before the dissolution and winding up of a partnership only if the partnership decides to make an interim distribution.

(c)   A person does not have a right to demand or receive a distribution from a partnership in any form other than money. Except as otherwise provided in Section 806, a partnership may distribute an asset in kind only if each part of the asset is fungible with each other part and each person receives a percentage of the asset equal in value to the person's share of distributions.

(d)   If a partner or transferee becomes entitled to receive a distribution, the partner or transferee has the status of, and is entitled to all remedies available to, a creditor of the partnership with respect to the distribution. However, the partnership's obligation to make a distribution is subject to offset for any amount owed to the partnership by the partner or a person dissociated as partner on whose account the distribution is made.

COMMENT

Past uniform unincorporated entity acts and many current limited liability company acts provide default rules for allocation of profits, and UPA (1997) even provides a default configuration for maintaining capital accounts. For the following reasons, this act, incorporating changes made by the Harmonization Project, provides a default rule only for rights to share in distributions:

- Capital accounts are maintained for one purpose, to determine how distributions will be made to partners. The rules for maintenance of capital accounts can be very complex. Generally, however, profits increase capital account balances (and increase the amounts that will be distributed to the partners) and losses reduce capital account balances (and reduce the amounts that will be distributed to the partners). If the statute has a simple default rule for how distributions are to be made to the partners, providing an additional set of default profit and loss allocation provisions and capital account rules will be, at best, duplicative and, at worse, inconsistent with the distribution rules.

- Some argue that capital account rules and profit and loss allocation provisions are necessary to comply with tax requirements. Tax income or loss is allocated to partners according to the partners' economic interests in the partnership, and these interests are based on distributions that would be made to partners on liquidation of the partnership. By including default distribution provisions, the act includes the information necessary to make these tax determinations. To the extent the tax law allows partners to make further tax elections or satisfy alternative safe harbors, the partners may look to the tax law for guidance and include necessary provisions in their agreements.

Subsection (a)—The rule stated applies to redemptions as well as operating distributions but is a default rule in both contexts. *See* the comment to Section 102(4)(A).

Subsection (b)—Section 701 provides a default rule for buying out a person dissociated as a partner when the dissociation does not lead to dissolution of the partnership.

Subsection (d)—For the rights of partners and transferees that receive a distribution in the form of indebtedness, see Section 406(d).

§ 406.   Limitations on Distributions by Limited Liability Partnership

(a)   A limited liability partnership may not make a distribution, including a distribution under Section 806, if after the distribution:

     (1)   the partnership would not be able to pay its debts as they become due in the ordinary course of the partnership's business; or

     (2)   the partnership's total assets would be less than the sum of its total liabilities plus the amount that would be needed, if the partnership were to be dissolved and wound up at the time of the distribution, to satisfy the preferential rights upon dissolution and winding up of partners and transferees whose preferential rights are superior to the rights of persons receiving the distribution.

(b)   A limited liability partnership may base a determination that a distribution is not prohibited under subsection (a) on:

     (1)   financial statements prepared on the basis of accounting practices and principles that are reasonable in the circumstances; or

     (2)   a fair valuation or other method that is reasonable under the circumstances.

(c)   Except as otherwise provided in subsection (e), the effect of a distribution under subsection (a) is measured:

     (1)   in the case of a distribution as defined in Section 102(4)(A), as of the earlier of:

         (A)   the date money or other property is transferred or debt is incurred by the limited liability partnership; or

         (B)   the date the person entitled to the distribution ceases to own the interest or rights being acquired by the partnership in return for the distribution;

     (2)   in the case of any other distribution of indebtedness, as of the date the indebtedness is distributed; and

     (3)   in all other cases, as of the date:

         (A)   the distribution is authorized, if the payment occurs not later than 120 days after that date; or

         (B)   the payment is made, if the payment occurs more than 120 days after the distribution is authorized.

(d)   A limited liability partnership's indebtedness to a partner or transferee incurred by reason of a distribution made in accordance with this section is at parity with the partnership's indebtedness to its general, unsecured creditors, except to the extent subordinated by agreement.

(e)   A limited liability partnership's indebtedness, including indebtedness issued as a distribution, is not a liability for purposes of subsection (a) if the terms of the indebtedness provide that payment of principal and interest is made only if and to the extent that a payment of a distribution could then be made under this section. If the indebtedness is issued as a distribution, each payment of principal or interest is treated as a distribution, the effect of which is measured on the date the payment is made.

(f)   In measuring the effect of a distribution under Section 806, the liabilities of a dissolved limited liability partnership do not include any claim that has been disposed of under Section 807, 808, or 809.

COMMENT

Both this section and Section 407 were derived essentially from the Model Business Corporation Act section 6.40, and were added during the Harmonization Project. Both sections are necessary and appropriate because a limited liability partnership provides the partners a corporate-like liability shield. With the exception noted in the comment to Subsection (a)(2), the provisions of this section are non-waivable. Section 105(c)(17).

"Distribution" does not include "amounts constituting reasonable compensation for present or past service or payments made in the ordinary course of business under a bona fide retirement plan or other bona fide benefits program." Section 102(4)(B).

Subsection (a)—Insolvency is a fundamental issue under this section, and this subsection provides two tests of insolvency. The tests are disjunctive; a distribution violates this section if after the distribution the LLP fails either of the tests. The subsection applies both to interim and liquidating distributions.

Solvency is also a fundamental issue under bankruptcy and fraudulent transfer law, which provide their own respective definitions of the concept.

Subsection (a)(2)—The reference to "preferential rights upon dissolution and winding up" is a default rule, because removing this protection for preferred partners or transferees is an *inter se* matter. *See* Section 105(d)(1)(B). The rest of the section is not subject to change in the partnership agreement. Section 105(c)(17).

Subsection (b)—This subsection states a standard of ordinary care, in contrast with the generally applicable standard stated in Section 409(c) (gross negligence).

Subsection (b)(2)—This alternative valuation provision is likely to be both useful and fair when the partnership has appreciated assets but for accounting purposes these assets are valued at book value less depreciation.

Subsection (c)—This subsection provides three alternative rules for determining the point(s) in time of as which to apply the solvency tests stated in Subsection (a). The timing depends on which of three categories encompasses a distribution: (i) a distribution in the nature of a redemption (regardless of whether the distribution includes a distribution of indebtedness); (ii) any distribution of indebtedness other than a distribution in the nature of a redemption; and (iii) any distribution that involves neither a redemption nor a distribution of indebtedness. A requirement for additional solvency testing pertaining to distributions of indebtedness appears in Subsection (e).

Subsection (c)(1)—Section 102(4)(A) encompasses distributions in the nature of a redemption.

Subsection (c)(1)(A) and (B)—Under Subparagraph (A), any beginning of payment activity triggers the rule and sets the date as of when to apply the solvency tests. Under Subparagraph (B), the partnership's complete acquisition of the rights is necessary to trigger the rule.

Subsection (c)(2)—This provision states the general rule for distributions in the form of debt and which are not connected with a redemption.

Subsection (c)(3)—This provision states alternative rules for all distributions of money or property (*i.e.*, not debt). The measuring date depends on the length of time between the authorization and payment of the distribution.

Subsection (d)—For a related provision, characterizing as a creditor a person who has become entitled to receive a distribution, see Section 405(d).

Subsection (e)—This subsection contains two rules pertaining to indebtedness issued as part of a distribution and the Subsection (a) solvency tests. The first sentence states the sensible rule that indebtedness that is essentially subordinated to the solvency requirement (*i.e.*, not payable if making payment would transgress that requirement) is not counted in determining liabilities for purposes of the solvency tests. The second sentence applies the solvency tests to each payment of principal and interest on any indebtedness issued as a distribution, in addition to any previous testing required by Subsection (c)(1)(A) or (c)(2).

Example: A limited liability partnership and one of its partners agree that the LLP will buy out the person's entire ownership interest in the LLP in return for a promissory note from the LLP, payable in installments. Under the redemption agreement: (i) on January 15 the person surrenders all its interests and rights and dissociates as a partner; and (ii) the LLP signs and delivers the note to the person on February 15. Under the note, payment of interest is due monthly beginning March 15, with a balloon payment of the principal due December 30.

Under Subsection (c)(1)(B), the solvency tests are applied as of January 15. Under Subsection (e), the solvency tests are again applied on the March 15, April 15, etc., and again on December 30.

Subsection (f)—The cited sections provide methods for extinguishing or limiting the debts of an LLP that is winding up its affairs and activities and thus any debt affected by any of the cited sections is irrelevant for purposes of solvency testing.

§ 407. Liability for Improper Distributions by Limited Liability Partnership

(a) Except as otherwise provided in subsection (b), if a partner of a limited liability partnership consents to a distribution made in violation of Section 406 and in consenting to the distribution fails to comply with Section 409, the partner is personally liable to the partnership for the amount of the distribution which exceeds the amount that could have been distributed without the violation of Section 406.

(b) To the extent the partnership agreement of a limited liability partnership expressly relieves a partner of the authority and responsibility to consent to distributions and imposes that authority and responsibility on one or more other partners, the liability stated in subsection (a) applies to the other partners and not to the partner that the partnership agreement relieves of the authority and responsibility.

(c) A person that receives a distribution knowing that the distribution violated Section 406 is personally liable to the limited liability partnership but only to the extent that the distribution received by the person exceeded the amount that could have been properly paid under Section 406.

(d) A person against which an action is commenced because the person is liable under subsection (a) may:

(1) implead any other person that is liable under subsection (a) and seek to enforce a right of contribution from the person; and

(2) implead any person that received a distribution in violation of subsection (c) and seek to enforce a right of contribution from the person in the amount the person received in violation of subsection (c).

(e) An action under this section is barred unless commenced not later than two years after the distribution.

COMMENT

This section and Section 406 were derived essentially from Model Business Corporation Act section 6.40. The provisions of this section are non-waivable. Section 105(c)(17).

This section contemplates two categories of liability: liability of those who have authorized improper distributions (Subsection (a)—*i.e.*, the partners) and the liability of those who have received improper distributions (Subsection (c)—*i.e.*, partners and transferees). Neither dissociating as a partner nor ceasing to be a transferee affects liability previously incurred under this section.

The liability is to the LLP, not to the creditors of an insolvent LLP. *Weinstein v. Colborne Foodbotics, L.L.C.*, 302 P.3d 263, 268 (Colo. 2013); *Rev O, Inc. v. Woo*, 725 S.E.2d 45, 52 (N.C. Ct. App. 2012).

This section does not preclude or interfere with claims for fraudulent transfer. *See* the comment to Subsection (e).

Subsection (a)—The liability is not strict liability but rather attaches only to the extent a decision maker has failed to comply with the duties stated in Section 409. To the extent those duties have been permissibly revised by the partnership agreement, the revised standards apply to this subsection. *See* Section 406(b)(1) (permitting reasonable reliance on specified financial information).

Subsection (b)—*Compare* Section 407(b), *with* Section 105(d)(2) (generally permitting provisions of this type).

Subsection (c)—Actual knowledge is necessary to impose liability. Reason to know does not suffice. *Compare* Section 407(c), *with* Section 103(a), (b).

Subsections (c) and (d)(2)—Liability could apply to a person who receives a distribution under a charging order, but only if the person meets the knowledge requirement. That situation is very unlikely unless the person with the charging order is also a partner.

Subsection (e)—When the distribution is in the form of indebtedness, the distribution may occur on several different dates. *See* the comment to Section 406(e).

This statute of limitations applies only to actions "under this section" and does not affect claims under other applicable law, which most often is fraudulent transfer law. For a different approach, see Delaware Code Annotated title 6, section 15–309(c) (West 2013) (applying a three-year statute of limitations to claims "under this chapter or other applicable law"); New York Limited Liability Company section 508(c) (2013) (same). *But see, e.g., In re The Heritage Org., L.L.C.*, 413 B.R. 438, 461 (Bankr. ND Tex. 2009) (invoking the Texas Uninform Fraudulent Act (TUFTA) to recover distributions made by a Delaware LLC headquartered in Texas; rejecting Delaware Code title 6, section 18–607(c) on choice of law grounds; stating that "the Delaware legislature cannot limit the reach of TUFTA").

§ 408. Rights to Information of Partners and Persons Dissociated as Partner

(a)   A partnership shall keep its books and records, if any, at its principal office.

(b)   On reasonable notice, a partner may inspect and copy during regular business hours, at a reasonable location specified by the partnership, any record maintained by the partnership regarding the partnership's business, financial condition, and other circumstances, to the extent the information is material to the partner's rights and duties under the partnership agreement or this [act].

(c)   The partnership shall furnish to each partner:

(1)   without demand, any information concerning the partnership's business, financial condition, and other circumstances which the partnership knows and is material to the proper exercise of the partner's rights and duties under the partnership agreement or this [act], except to the extent the partnership can establish that it reasonably believes the partner already knows the information; and

(2)   on demand, any other information concerning the partnership's business, financial condition, and other circumstances, except to the extent the demand or the information demanded is unreasonable or otherwise improper under the circumstances.

(d)   The duty to furnish information under subsection (c) also applies to each partner to the extent the partner knows any of the information described in subsection (c).

(e)   Subject to subsection (j), on 10 days' demand made in a record received by a partnership, a person dissociated as a partner may have access to information to which the person was entitled while a partner if:

(1)   the information pertains to the period during which the person was a partner;

(2)   the person seeks the information in good faith; and

(3)   the person satisfies the requirements imposed on a partner by subsection (b).

(f)   Not later than 10 days after receiving a demand under subsection (e), the partnership in a record shall inform the person that made the demand of:

(1)   the information that the partnership will provide in response to the demand and when and where the partnership will provide the information; and

(2)   the partnership's reasons for declining, if the partnership declines to provide any demanded information.

(g)   A partnership may charge a person that makes a demand under this section the reasonable costs of copying, limited to the costs of labor and material.

(h)   A partner or person dissociated as a partner may exercise the rights under this section through an agent or, in the case of an individual under legal disability, a legal representative. Any restriction or condition imposed by the partnership agreement or under subsection (j) applies both to the agent or legal representative and to the partner or person dissociated as a partner.

(i)   Subject to Section 505, the rights under this section do not extend to a person as transferee.

(j)   In addition to any restriction or condition stated in its partnership agreement, a partnership, as a matter within the ordinary course of its business, may impose reasonable restrictions and conditions on access to and use of information to be furnished under this section, including designating information confidential and imposing nondisclosure and safeguarding obligations on the recipient. In a dispute concerning the reasonableness of a restriction under this subsection, the partnership has the burden of proving reasonableness.

COMMENT

Subsections (a) and (c) derive from UPA (1997). The other subsections are derived from the ULPA (2001) § 401 (rights to information of general partners and former general partners) and were adopted as part of the 2011 and 2103 Harmonization amendments. The rules stated here might be termed "quasi-default rules"—subject to some change by the partnership agreement. *See* Section 105(c)(4) (prohibiting unreasonable restrictions on the information rights stated in this section).

Although the rights and duties stated in this section are extensive, they are not necessarily all-inclusive. This act's statement of fiduciary duties is not exhaustive, *see* the comment to Section 409(a), and some cases characterize owners' information rights as reflecting a fiduciary duty of those with management power. *E.g. Bakerman v. Sidney Frank Importing Co., Inc.*, No. Civ.A. 1844-N, 2006 WL 3927242, at *14 (Del. Ch. Oct. 16, 2006) (holding that an LLC manager owed "certain duties to members of the LLC" and stating that "[w]hen fiduciaries communicate with their beneficiaries in the context of asking the beneficiary to make a discretionary decision—such as whether to consent to a sale of substantially all the assets of an LLC—the fiduciary has a duty to disclose all material facts bearing on the decision at issue") (citing *Loudon v. Archer-Daniels-Midland Co.*, 700 A.2d 135, 137 (Del. 1997)).

Subsection (a)—A general partnership is often a very informal organization. Accordingly, this subsection states a default-required location for any books and records a partnership may have but does not require that books and records be kept. Other law may so require, however—particularly tax law. This subsection applies to any books and records kept to satisfy other law.

Subsection (b)—This subsection states the rule pertaining to information memorialized in "any record maintained by the partnership." For the meaning of "material" as applied to information, see Section 409(f), comment.

Subsections (c) and (d)—In appropriate circumstances, violation of either or both of these provisions might cause a court to enjoin or even rescind action taken by the partnership, especially when the violation has interfered with an approval or veto mechanism involving partner consent. *E.g., Blue Chip Emerald L.L.C. v. Allied Partners Inc.*, 299 A.D.2d 278, 279–80 (N.Y. App. Div. 2002) (invoking partnership law precedent as reflecting a duty of full disclosure and holding that "[a]bsent such full disclosure, the transaction is voidable").

Subsection (c)—This subsection imposes a duty on the partnership, not the partners. However, a partner could be liable in damages if the partner were to: (i) breach a duty under Section 409 or the partnership agreement; and (ii) in doing so cause or suffer the partnership to breach the duty stated in this paragraph.

Subsection (c)(1)—This provision imposes an affirmative duty to volunteer information. However, given the assumption that each partner will be active in management, the obligation ceases "to the extent the partnership can establish that it reasonably believes the partner already knows the information."

In any event, the obligation is limited to information that is both material and known by the partnership. "Knowledge" is viewed subjectively (*i.e.*, actual knowledge). Section 103(a)(1). Materiality is viewed objectively. Thus, the duty applies to known, material information, even if the partnership does not know that the information is material.

A partnership will "know" what its partners know. Under Section 103(e), "[a] partner's knowledge . . . of a fact relating to the partnership is effective immediately as knowledge of or notice to the partnership." As to others acting or reasonably appearing to act on behalf of the partnership, common law agency rules will apply. RESTATEMENT (THIRD) OF AGENCY § 5.03 (2006) (Imputation of Notice of Fact to Principal).

Typically a partner's duties are continuous, and therefore a partner's right to information is not just transaction-specific. Ongoing managerial responsibilities require ongoing information—both periodically and *ad hoc* when a situation warrants.

For the meaning of "material" as applied to information, see Section 409(f), comment.

Subsection (c)(2)—Other law determines which party has the burden of proof as to the stated exception.

Subsection (d)—This subsection imposes a duty directly on each partner, "except to the extent the [partner] can establish that it reasonably believes [another] partner already knows the information."

Example: A partnership has two partners: each of which is regularly engaged in conducting the partnership's activities; both of which are aware of and have regular access to all significant partnership records; and neither of which has special responsibility for or knowledge of any particular aspect of those activities or the relevant partnership records. Most likely, neither partner is obliged to draw the other general partner's attention to information apparent in the partnership's records.

Example: Although a partnership has three partners, one is the managing partner with day-to-day responsibility for running the partnership's activities. The other two meet periodically with the managing partner and together with that partner function in a manner analogous to a corporate board of directors. Most likely, the managing partner has a duty to draw the attention of the other partners to important information, even if that information would be apparent from a review of the partnership's records.

Because this subsection imposes duties directly on partner, the duties are in the nature of a contractual obligation, and breach is a matter of strict liability. For example, it is no defense for a partner under this section to assert that, although the partner failed to furnish required information, the failure did not amount to gross negligence under Section 409(c).

Subsection (e)—Codifying the information rights of former owners began with UPA (1997) § 403(b).

For the additional information rights of the legal representative of a deceased partner, see Section 505.

Subsection (e)(1)—A person dissociated as a partner has information rights in that capacity only as to the period during which the person was a partner. To the extent that further information is accessible under Section 505(2) (providing access to the legal representative of a deceased partner), that access is limited both in purpose ("for purposes of settling the estate") and in scope ("the rights the deceased partner had under Section 408").

Subsection (e)(2)—A duty of good faith is needed here, because a person claiming access under this subsection is no longer a partner and is no longer subject to a partner's obligation of good faith and fair dealing under Section 409(d). *See* Section 603(b)(2) (stating a person's dissociation as a partner terminates as to subsequent events the person's duties under Section 409, including the contractual obligation of good faith). *But see id.*, cmt (noting that the common law implied covenant will continue to be relevant if the partnership agreement provides continuing rights and obligations for a person dissociated as a partner).

In the context of Subsection (e)(2), "good faith" is properly understood to mean an honest belief that the request is made for a proper purpose. *Associated Indem. Corp. v. CAT Contracting, Inc.*, 964 S.W.2d 276, 285 (Tex. 1998) (holding that " 'good faith' in the surety agreement before us refers to conduct which is honest in fact, free of improper motive or wilful ignorance of the facts at hand"); Andrews v. Bible, 812 S.W.2d 284, 288 (Tenn. 1991) (describing "subjective good faith" as "[a] pure heart but an empty head") (quoting *Whittington v. Ohio River Co.*, 115 F.R.D. 201, 209 (E.D.Ky.1987)). Willful ignorance includes being an ostrich. "While 'honesty' may require no more than a pure heart, it is questionable that a pure heart can co-exist with closed eyes. It is not honest to close one's eyes so as to maintain an empty head." *J.R. Hale Contracting Co. v. United New Mexico Bank at Albuquerque*, 799 P.2d 581, 591 (NM 1990). *See also* UPA (1914) § (3)(1) ("A person has 'knowledge' of a fact within the meaning of this act not only when he has actual knowledge thereof, but also when he has knowledge of such other facts as in the circumstances shows bad faith.").

Subsection (h)—For the avoidance of doubt, this subsection expressly authorizes taking action through an agent. The doubt might arise from old corporate cases in which the parties contested a shareholder's right to exercise inspection rights through another person. *White v. Coeur D'Alene Big Creek Mining Co.*, 55 P.2d 720, 723 (Idaho 1936) (stating that "[t]he refusal to permit respondent [shareholder] to appoint his own attorney or agent to make the examination [of the corporation's books] was in effect a denial of his right" of inspection); *State v. Monida & Yellowstone Stage Co.*, 124 N.W. 971, 972 (Minn. 1910) (upholding a trial court's mandamus order, "which shall provide that [the shareholder complainant], or such attorney or agent as he may select, . . . shall be allowed to inspect the books, records, and papers of the defendant [corporation]").

No negative inference should be drawn about using agents to take other action under this act.

Subsection (j)—This subsection provides fallback protection for gaps in the partnership agreement. For example, the partners may protect trade secrets from disclosure and prohibit various misuses of confidential information even if the partnership agreement omits to do so.

The reference to "ordinary course" pertains to Section 401(k) (stating that any "matter in the ordinary course of business of a partnership may be decided by a majority of the partners"). This approach is necessary, lest a requesting partner have the power to block imposition of a reasonable restriction or condition needed to prevent the requestor from abusing the partnership.

The burden of persuasion under this subsection contrasts with the burden of persuasion under Section 105(c)(4) (prohibiting unreasonable limitations on the information rights provided by this section). Under that paragraph, as a matter of ordinary procedural law the burden is on the person making the claim.

§ 409. Standards of Conduct for Partners

(a)   A partner owes to the partnership and the other partners the duties of loyalty and care stated in subsections (b) and (c).

(b)   The fiduciary duty of loyalty of a partner includes the duties:

(1)   to account to the partnership and hold as trustee for it any property, profit, or benefit derived by the partner:

(A)   in the conduct or winding up of the partnership's business;

(B)   from a use by the partner of the partnership's property; or

(C)   from the appropriation of a partnership opportunity;

(2)   to refrain from dealing with the partnership in the conduct or winding up of the partnership business as or on behalf of a person having an interest adverse to the partnership; and

(3)   to refrain from competing with the partnership in the conduct of the partnership's business before the dissolution of the partnership.

(c)   The duty of care of a partner in the conduct or winding up of the partnership business is to refrain from engaging in grossly negligent or reckless conduct, willful or intentional misconduct, or a knowing violation of law.

(d)   A partner shall discharge the duties and obligations under this [act] or under the partnership agreement and exercise any rights consistently with the contractual obligation of good faith and fair dealing.

(e)   A partner does not violate a duty or obligation under this [act] or under the partnership agreement solely because the partner's conduct furthers the partner's own interest.

(f)   All the partners may authorize or ratify, after full disclosure of all material facts, a specific act or transaction by a partner that otherwise would violate the duty of loyalty.

(g)   It is a defense to a claim under subsection (b)(2) and any comparable claim in equity or at common law that the transaction was fair to the partnership.

(h)   If, as permitted by subsection (f) or the partnership agreement, a partner enters into a transaction with the partnership which otherwise would be prohibited by subsection (b)(2), the partner's rights and obligations arising from the transaction are the same as those of a person that is not a partner.

COMMENT

This section originated as UPA (1997) § 404. The 2011 and 2013 Harmonization amendments made one major substantive change; they "un-cabined" fiduciary duty. UPA (1997) § 404 had deviated substantially from UPA (1914) by purporting to codify all fiduciary duties owed by partners. This approach had a number of problems. Most notably, the exhaustive list of fiduciary duties left no room for the fiduciary duty owed by partners to each other—i.e., "the punctilio of an honor the most sensitive". *Meinhard v. Salmon*, 164 N.E. 545, 546 (N.Y. 1928). Although UPA (1997) § 404(b) purported to state "[a] partner's duty of loyalty to the partnership *and the other partners*" (emphasis added), the three listed duties each protected the partnership and not the partners.

"Un-cabining" harmonized this act to ULLCA (2006), and this section states some of the core aspects of the fiduciary duty of loyalty, provides a duty of care, and incorporates the contractual obligation of good faith and fair dealing. The duties stated in this section are subject to the partnership agreement, but Sections 105(c) and (d) contain important limitations on the power of the partnership agreement to affect fiduciary and other duties and the obligation of good faith and fair dealing.

For the effect of dissociation on a person's duties under this section, see Section 603(b)(2).

Subsection (a)—This subsection recognizes two core managerial duties but, unlike UPA (1997), does not purport to be exhaustive. For example, many cases characterize a manager's duty to disclose as a fiduciary duty.

E.g., Lonergan v. EPE Holdings, L.L.C., 5 A.3d 1008, 1023 (Del. Ch. 2010) (stating that "in the limited partnership context, absent contractual modification, a general partner owes fiduciary duties that include a duty of full disclosure") (quotation marks omitted) (citation omitted); *Exxon Corp. v. Burglin*, 4 F.3d 1294, 1298 (5th Cir. 1993) ("Under Alaska law, a general partner stands in a fiduciary relationship with the limited partnership and thereby owes 'a fiduciary duty . . . to disclose information concerning partnership affairs.'") (quoting *Parker v. N. Mixing Co.*, 756 P.2d 881, 894 (Alaska 1988)).

Subsection (b)—This subsection states three core aspects of the fiduciary duty of loyalty: (i) not "usurping" partnership opportunities or otherwise wrongly benefiting from the partnership's operations or property; (ii) avoiding conflict of interests in dealing with the partnership (whether directly or on behalf of another); and (iii) refraining from competing with the partnership. Essentially the same duties exist in agency law and under the law of all types of business organizations.

This subsection applies beginning with "the partnership's business," which by definition cannot exist before the partnership does; thus the stated duties do not apply to pre-formation activities.

The stated duties comprise a default rule. Under Section 105(d)(3)(A): "If not manifestly unreasonable, the partnership agreement may . . . alter or eliminate the aspects of the duty of loyalty stated in Section 409(b)."

Subsection (b)(1)—The phrase "hold as trustee" dates back to UPA (1914) § 21 and reflects the availability of disgorgement remedies, such as a constructive trust. In contrast to an actual trustee, a person subject to this duty does not: (i) face the special obstacles to consent characteristic of trust law; or (ii) enjoy protection for decisions taken in reliance on the governing instrument and other sources of information. *Cf.* Uniform Statutory Trust Entity Act (2009) (Last Amended 2013) § 506 ("A trustee [of a statutory trust] . . . is not liable to the trust or to a beneficial owner for breach of any duty, *including a fiduciary duty*, to the extent the breach results from reasonable reliance on: (i) a term of the governing instrument; (ii) a record of the statutory trust; or (iii) an opinion, report, or statement of another person that the person to which the opinion, report, or statement is made or delivered reasonably believes is within the other person's professional or expert competence and is made or delivered to the trustee . . . .") (emphasis added).

Subsection (b)(1)(A)—This provision is consistent with a basic principle of agency law—namely, that an agent may not benefit at all from the performance of the agency unless the principal consents. RESTATEMENT (THIRD) OF AGENCY § 8.06, cmt. c. (2006). Typically, however, the partnership agreement will legitimize particular benefits—*e.g.*, a management fee paid to a managing partner in addition to that partner's share of distributions. Also, an agreed allocation of distributions takes those benefits outside the reach of this provision.

Subsection (b)(1)(B)—For the expansive meaning of "property," see Section 102(16). The term includes confidential information.

Subsection (b)(1)(C)—This act does not specify what constitutes "a partnership opportunity," but ample case law exists. See, e.g., *Triple Five of Minn., Inc. v. Simon*, 404 F.3d 1088, 1096 (8th Cir. 2005) ("An opportunity that is closely related to the entity's existing or prospective line of business, would competitively advantage the partnership, and is one that the partnership has the financial ability, knowledge and experience to pursue is a partnership opportunity."); *Knudson v. Kyllo*, 831 N.W.2d 763, 767 (N.D. 2013) (explaining why conducting farming operations on land owned by others was a partnership opportunity while purchasing farmland was not).

The duty stated here continues through winding up, although in that context the scope of partnership opportunities inevitably narrows.

In most, if not all, situations, usurping a partnership opportunity also breaches the duty not to compete, Paragraph (b)(3), but not vice versa.

Subsection (b)(2)—In this context, the phrase "adverse interest" is a term of art, meaning "to be on the other side of the table" in some dealing with the partnership. Absent informed consent by the partnership, this duty is breached by the mere existence of the conflict of interest and the partnership need not prove that the outcome of the dealing was adverse to the partnership. *But see* Subsection (g) (permitting the defense of fairness).This duty continues through winding up.

Subsection (b)(3)—Although competition is often thought of in terms of potential customers, this duty applies equally to competition for resources, including employees. This duty ends when the partnership dissolves.

Subsection (c)—This act no longer refers to the duty of care as a fiduciary duty, because: the duty of care applies in many non-fiduciary situations; and (ii) breach of the duty of care is remediable in damages while breach of a fiduciary duty gives rise also to equitable remedies, including disgorgement, constructive trust, and rescission.

The change in label is consistent with the Restatement (Third) of Agency section 8.02 (2006), which refers to the agent's "fiduciary duty" to act loyally, but eschews the word "fiduciary" when stating the agent's duties of "care, competence, and diligence." *Id.* § 8.08. However, the label change is merely semantics; no change in the law is intended.

The partnership agreement can raise the standard of care, or subject to Sections 105(c)(8) and (d)(3)(C), lower it. A person's practical exposure for breaching the duty of care involves not only the standard of care but also any partnership agreement provision that: (i) exonerates the person from liability for breach of the duty of care, Section 105(c)(8); or (ii) entitles the person to indemnification despite such breach, Section 408(b), cmt.

Subsection (d)—This subsection refers to the *"contractual* obligation of good faith and fair dealing" (emphasis added) and thereby invokes the implied obligation that exists in every contract. *See* RESTATEMENT (SECOND) CONTRACTS § 205 (1981) ("Every contract imposes upon each party a duty of good faith and fair dealing in its performance and its enforcement."). The adjective ("contractual") should help avoid decisions like *Phelps v. Frampton*, 170 P.3d 474, 483 (Mont. 2007) (holding that Montana's version of UPA (1997) creates a statutory obligation of good faith and fair dealing separate from the implied contractual covenant).

At first glance, it may seem strange to apply a contractual obligation to statutory duties and rights—*i.e.,* duties and rights "under this [act]." However, for the most part those duties and rights apply to relationships *inter se* the partners and the partnership and function only to the extent not displaced by the partnership agreement. Those statutory default rules are thus intended to function like a contract; applying the contractual notion of good faith and fair dealing therefore makes sense.

The contractual obligation of "good faith" has nothing to do with the corporate concept of good faith that for years bedeviled courts and attorneys trying to understand: (i) Delaware's famous corporate law exoneration provision; and (ii) that provision's exception "for acts or omissions not in good faith." DEL. CODE ANN. tit. 8, § 102(b)(7) (2012). In that context, good faith is an aspect of the duty of loyalty. *See Stone ex rel. AmSouth Bancorporation v. Ritter,* 911 A.2d 362, 369–70 (Del. 2006).

Likewise, the contractual obligation of good faith and fair dealing has nothing to do with the "utmost good faith" sometimes used to describe the fiduciary duties that owners of closely held businesses owe each other. *See, e.g., Meinhard v. Salmon,* 477, 164 N.E. 545, 551 (NY 1928) ("[W]here parties engage in a joint enterprise each owes to the other the duty of the utmost good faith in all that relates to their common venture. Within its scope they stand in a fiduciary relationship."); *Donahue v. Rodd Electrotype Co. of New England, Inc.,* 328 N.E.2d 505, 515 (Mass. 1975) ("[S]tockholders in the close corporation owe one another substantially the same fiduciary duty in the operation of the enterprise that partners owe to one another. In our previous decisions, we have defined the standard of duty owed by partners to one another as the utmost good faith and loyalty.") (footnotes omitted) (citations omitted) (internal quotations omitted).

To the contrary, the contractual obligation of good faith and fair dealing is not a fiduciary duty, does not command altruism or self-abnegation, and does not prevent a partner from acting in the partner's own self-interest:

> "Fair dealing" is not akin to the fair process component of entire fairness, *i.e.,* whether the fiduciary acted fairly when engaging in the challenged transaction as measured by duties of loyalty and care . . . . It is rather a commitment to deal "fairly" in the sense of consistently with the terms of the parties' agreement and its purpose. Likewise "good faith" does not envision loyalty to the contractual counterparty, but rather faithfulness to the scope, purpose, and terms of the parties' contract. Both necessarily turn on the contract itself and what the parties would have agreed upon had the issue arisen when they were bargaining originally.

Gerber v. Enter. Prods. Holdings, L.L.C., 67 A.3d 400, 418–19 (Del. 2013) (quoting *ASB Allegiance Real Estate Fund v. Scion Breckenridge Managing Member, L.L.C.,* 50 A.3d 434, 440–42 (Del. Ch. 2012), *aff'd in part, rev'd in part on other grounds,* 68 A.3d 665 (Del. 2013); *see also* Subsection (e).

Courts should not use the contractual obligation to change *ex post facto* the parties' or this act's allocation of risk and power. To the contrary, the obligation should be used only to protect agreed-upon arrangements from conduct that is manifestly beyond what a reasonable person could have contemplated when the arrangements were made.

The partnership agreement or this act may grant discretion to a partner, and the contractual obligation of good faith and fair dealing is especially salient when discretion is at issue. However, a partner may properly exercise discretion even though another partner suffers as a consequence. Conduct does not violate the obligation of good faith and fair dealing merely because that conduct substantially prejudices a party. Indeed, parties allocate risk precisely because prejudice may occur.

The exercise of discretion constitutes a breach of the obligation of good faith and fair dealing only when the party claiming breach shows that the conduct has no honestly held purpose that legitimately comports with the parties' agreed-upon arrangements:

> An implied covenant claim . . . looks to the past. It is not a free-floating duty unattached to the underlying legal documents. It does not ask what duty the law should impose on the parties given their relationship at the time of the wrong, but *rather what the parties would have agreed to themselves had they considered the issue in their original bargaining positions at the time of contracting.*

Gerber v. Enter. Prods. Holdings, L.L.C., 67 A.3d 400, 418 (Del. 2013) (quoting *ASB Allegiance Real Estate Fund v. Scion Breckenridge Managing Member, L.L.C.,* 50 A.3d 434, 440–42 (Del. Ch. 2012), *aff'd in part, rev'd in part on other grounds,* 68 A.3d 665 (Del. 2013)).

In sum, the purpose of the contractual obligation of good faith and fair dealing is to protect the arrangement the partners have chosen for themselves, not to restructure that arrangement under the guise of safeguarding it.

As to the power of the partnership agreement to affect the contractual obligation of good faith and fair dealing, see Section 105(c)(6) (prohibiting elimination but allowing the agreement to "prescribe standards, if not manifestly unreasonable, by which the performance of the obligation is to be measured"). For examples, see Section 105(c)(6), comment. As to whether the obligation stated in this subsection applies to the benefit of transferees, see Section 107(b), comment.

Subsection (e)—A partner in a general partnership has at least two different roles: (i) as a party to the partnership agreement, with rights and obligations under that agreement; and (ii) as co-manager of the enterprise. This provision pertains to the first role. A partner's exercise of rights under the partnership agreement is subject to the obligation of good faith and fair dealing, Subsection (d), but a partner does not breach that contractual obligation "solely because the partner's conduct furthers the partner's own interest." In contrast, this provision is ineffective with regard to a partner's duties as co-manager. For example, a partner's liability under Section 409(b)(3) (prohibiting competition) is not "solely because the partner's conduct furthers the partner's own interest." Rather, the liability results from the breach of a specific obligation—*i.e.,* the codified aspect of the duty of loyalty that prohibits competition.

Subsection (f)—Here and elsewhere in this act, information "is material if there is a substantial likelihood that a reasonable [decision maker] would consider it important in deciding how to vote" or take other action under this act or the partnership agreements. See *Basic Inc. v. Levinson,* 485 U.S. 224, 231–32 (1988) (quoting *TSC Indus., Inc. v. Northway, Inc.,* 426 U.S. 438, 449 (1976)).

The partnership agreement can provide additional or different methods of authorization or ratification, subject to the strictures of Section 105(c)(5), (d)(1), and (d)(3)(A)(B) and (D).

Subsection (g)—This subsection codifies judge-made law applicable to all business entities. See, e.g., *Kahn v. Lynch Commc'n Sys., Inc.,* 638 A.2d 1110, 1116 (Del. 1994) (discussing "entire fairness" in the context of a corporation's merger with an affiliate); *Lonergan EPE Holdings, L.L.C.,* 5 A.3d 1008, 1019 (Del. Ch. 2010) (discussing "entire fairness" in the context of a limited partnership); *Gottsacker v. Monnier,* 697 N.W.2d 436, 444 (Wis. 2005) (referring to "a willful failure to deal fairly with the LLC or its other members").

Subsection (h)—This subsection is the modern, reformulated version of a language that sought to overturn the now-defunct notion that debts to partners were categorically inferior to debts to non-partner creditors. *See, e.g.,* ULPA (2001) § 112 ("A partner may lend money to and transact other business with the limited partnership and has the same rights and obligations with respect to the loan or other transaction as a person that is not a partner."). The reformulation makes clear that this provision has nothing to do with the fiduciary duty pertaining to conflict of interests. *See BT-I v. Equitable Life Assurance Soc'y of the U.S.,* 75 Cal. App. 4th 1406, 1415 (Cal. Ct. App. 1999) (examining the prior formulation, explaining its history and stating "[w]e cannot discern anything in the purpose of [the prior formulation] that suggests an intent to affect a general partner's fiduciary duty to limited partners").

This subsection states a default rule. The partnership agreement may provide that debt to a partner (or partners generally) is subordinate to other partnership obligations. The agreement that creates the debt may do likewise.

§ 410.   Actions by Partnership and Partners

(a)   A partnership may maintain an action against a partner for a breach of the partnership agreement, or for the violation of a duty to the partnership, causing harm to the partnership.

(b)   A partner may maintain an action against the partnership or another partner, with or without an accounting as to partnership business, to enforce the partner's rights and protect the partner's interests, including rights and interests under the partnership agreement or this [act] or arising independently of the partnership relationship.

(c)   A right to an accounting on dissolution and winding up does not revive a claim barred by law.

COMMENT

In UPA (1997) this section was Section 405. The Harmonization Project did not change the section other than to renumber it.

Subsection (a)—This subsection originated in UPA (1997) § 405(a) and reflects the entity theory of partnership.

Subsection (b)—This subsection is the successor to UPA (1914) § 22 but with significant changes.

UPA (1914) § 22 itself had made significant changes to the common law. "It . . . generally was established at common law that an equitable accounting was a condition precedent to an action in law between partners," *Thompson v. Coughlin*, 997 P.2d 191, 194 (Or. 2000), and an accounting was generally not available before dissolution. Thus, claims among partners pertaining the partnership could not be asserted except through an action for dissolution and accounting. UPA (1914) § 22 modified this "exclusivity rule," specifying certain circumstances in which an accounting action is available without requiring an action to dissolve the partnership.

UPA (1997) eliminated the "exclusivity rule" entirely; an action of dissolution and accounting remains available but is no longer "a condition precedent" to other claims.

This subsection authorizes a partner to bring claims "to enforce the partner's rights and protect the partner's interests"—*i.e.*, direct claims. The statutory language does not contemplate derivative claims; thus, this act neither authorizes nor precludes such claims. *See Tzolis v. Wolff*, 884 N.E.2d 1005 (N.Y. 2008) (rejecting the argument that "members of a limited liability company (LLC) may [not] bring derivative suits on the LLC's behalf, . . . [because] there are no provisions governing such suits in the Limited Liability Company Law").

The case law does generally recognize the direct/derivative distinction in the context of general partnerships, and some cases permit a partner to sue derivatively. *E.g., Hill v. Vanderbilt Capital Advisors, L.L.C.*, 834 F. Supp. 2d 1228, 1246 (D.N.M. 2011) (stating that "[t]he Supreme

Court of New Mexico extended the scope of derivative suits beyond the corporate context . . . and allowed a partner's derivative suit on behalf of a general partnership") (citations omitted).

In general, however, the cases are conflicting and somewhat confused. A decision of the Maryland Court of Special Appeals illustrates the situation. At one point the court states:

We agree that the term "derivative" is an inappropriate and confusing term to use in the general partnership context. "Derivative" actions are necessary in the corporate and limited partnership context, where the shareholders and limited partners have no managerial rights and thus must "derive" the right to sue from the entity itself. Unlike shareholders and limited partners, however, general partners all have the ability to act on behalf of the partnership, and all have management rights [citations omitted]. Thus, general partners have no need for "derivative" action.

George Wasserman & Janice Wasserman Goldsten Family L.L.C. v. Kay, 14 A.3d 1193, 1215 (Md. Ct. Spec. App. 2011) (citing the comment to the UPA (1997) version of this section). However, later in the opinion the court recognizes that the partners' "ability to act on behalf of the partnership, and . . . [the partners'] management rights" are ineffective when a partner with a controlling interest declines to cause the partnership to sue the controlling partner for alleged misconduct.

The court concludes that such a "partnership claim may be enforced by all of the *disinterested* partners." *Wasserman*, 14 A.3d at 1216. In addition, the court cites with approval *Cates v. International Tel. & Tel. Corp.*, 756 F.2d 1161 (5th Cir.1985), which includes a lengthy discussion of circumstances in which a partner in a general partnership might be entitled to bring a derivative claim on behalf of the partnership. *Cates*, 756 F.2d at 1178 (referring to the possible "availability of a derivative action" but cautioning "[w]e do not hold that Texas law would *necessarily* allow a derivative action on the part of a minority partner") (emphasis added).

Despite the conflict and confusion in the cases, one proposition does appears reasonably certain: A minority partner in a general partnership must have some right to sue "where the controlling partners, for improper, ulterior motives and not because of what they in good faith believe to be the best interests of the partnership, decline to sue on a valid, valuable *partnership cause of action* which it is advantageous to the partnership to pursue." *Cates*, F.2d at 1179 (emphasis added).

Subsection (c)—This subsection originated as UPA (1997) § 405(c) and reversed the rule stated in UPA (1914) § 43. This subsection inevitably implies that other law governs the accrual of a claim under Subsection (b) as well as the statute of limitations applicable to those claims. As a result, partners must take care not to "to sit on their claims" waiting for the partnership to dissolve. *Veloski v. State Farm Mut. Auto Ins. Co.*, 719 N.E.2d 574, 576 (Ohio Ct. App. 1998).

§ 411. Continuation of Partnership Beyond Definite Term or Particular Undertaking

(a) If a partnership for a definite term or particular undertaking is continued, without an express agreement, after the expiration of the term or completion of the undertaking, the rights and duties of the partners remain the same as they were at the expiration or completion, so far as is consistent with a partnership at will.

(b) If the partners, or those of them who habitually acted in the business during the term or undertaking, continue the business without any settlement or liquidation of the partnership, they are presumed to have agreed that the partnership will continue.

COMMENT

This section originated as UPA (1997) § 406 and continues the approach of UPA (1997) (1914) § 23, with no substantive change.

Subsection (a)—Continuation beyond an agreed term or undertaking results in a partnership at will, not an automatic renewal of the term or extension of the undertaking. *See* the comment to Section 102(13 (partnership at will).

Subsection (b)—In general, a pattern of conduct can imply a term in a partnership agreement. Section 102(12) (defining partnership agreement and referring to an agreement among all the partners, "whether oral, implied, in a record, or in any combination thereof"). In particular, this subsection creates a presumption that by their conduct the partners have agreed to continue the business. The presumption shifts the burden of persuasion to the person claiming that the partnership is dissolved.

[ARTICLE] 5. TRANSFERABLE INTERESTS AND RIGHTS OF TRANSFEREES AND CREDITORS

§ 501. Partner Not Co-Owner of Partnership Property

A partner is not a co-owner of partnership property and has no interest in partnership property which can be transferred, either voluntarily or involuntarily.

COMMENT

This section originated in UPA (1997), followed ineluctably from the concept of a partnership as an entity, Section 201, abolished the UPA (1914) construct of "partnership in tenancy," and was retained during the Harmonization Project as a "belt and suspenders" approach to reinforcing the entity construct. *See* Section 203 (providing that property transferred to or otherwise acquired by the partnership is property of the partnership and not of the partners individually).

§ 502. Nature of Transferable Interest

A transferable interest is personal property.

COMMENT

For the definition of transferable interest, see Section 102(23). Absent a contrary provision in the partnership agreement or the consent of the partners, a "transferable interest" is the only interest in a partnership that can be transferred to a person not already a partner. *See* Section 503. As to whether a partner may transfer governance rights to a fellow partner, the question is moot absent a provision in the partnership agreement changing the default rule, *see* Section 401(h) (allocating governance rights *per capita*). In the default mode, a partner's transfer of governance rights to another partner: (i) does not increase the transferee's governance rights; (ii) eliminates the transferor's governance rights; (iii) and thereby changes the denominator but not the numerator in calculating governance rights.

> **Example:** LCN Company is a general partnership with three partners, Laura, Charles, and Nora. The partnership agreement does not displace this act's default rule on the allocation of governance rights among general partners. Thus, each partner has 1/3 of those rights. Laura transfers her entire ownership interest to Charles. The transfer does not increase Charles's governance rights but does eliminate Laura's. After the transfer, Laura has no governance rights (regardless of whether Charles and Nora agree to expel Laura under Section 601(4)(B)). As a result, Charles and Nora each have 1/2 of the governance rights.

Whether a transferable interest pledged as security is governed by Article 8 or 9 of the Uniform Commercial Code depends on the rules stated in those Articles.

§ 503.   Transfer of Transferable Interest

(a)   A transfer, in whole or in part, of a transferable interest:

   (1)   is permissible;

   (2)   does not by itself cause a person's dissociation as a partner or a dissolution and winding up of the partnership business; and

   (3)   subject to Section 505, does not entitle the transferee to:

      (A)   participate in the management or conduct of the partnership's business; or

      (B)   except as otherwise provided in subsection (c), have access to records or other information concerning the partnership's business.

(b)   A transferee has the right to:

   (1)   receive, in accordance with the transfer, distributions to which the transferor would otherwise be entitled; and

   (2)   seek under Section 801(5) a judicial determination that it is equitable to wind up the partnership business.

(c)   In a dissolution and winding up of a partnership, a transferee is entitled to an account of the partnership's transactions only from the date of dissolution.

(d)   A partnership need not give effect to a transferee's rights under this section until the partnership knows or has notice of the transfer.

(e)   A transfer of a transferable interest in violation of a restriction on transfer contained in the partnership agreement is ineffective if the intended transferee has knowledge or notice of the restriction at the time of transfer.

(f)   Except as otherwise provided in Section 601(4)(B), if a partner transfers a transferable interest, the transferor retains the rights of a partner other than the transferable interest transferred and retains all the duties and obligations of a partner.

(g)   If a partner transfers a transferable interest to a person that becomes a partner with respect to the transferred interest, the transferee is liable for the partner's obligations under Sections 404 and 407 known to the transferee when the transferee becomes a partner.

COMMENT

One of the most fundamental characteristics of partnership law is its fidelity to the "pick your partner" principle. *See, e.g., Bynum v. Frisby*, 311 P.2d 972, 975 (Nev. 1957) (stating that (i) "the assignment of a partnership interest from one partner to a stranger does not bring that stranger into fiduciary relationship with the remaining partners"; and (ii) absent consent by the remaining partners "[t]he stranger remains a stranger" with no rights to management or even information). This section is the core of the act's provisions reflecting and protecting that principle. A partner's rights in a partnership are bifurcated into economic rights (the transferable interest) and governance rights (including management rights, consent rights, rights to information, rights to seek judicial intervention). Unless the partnership agreement otherwise provides, a partner acting without the consent of all other partners lacks both the power and the right to: (i) bestow partnership on a non-partner, Section 402(b)(3); or (ii) transfer to a non-partner anything other than some or all of the partner's transferable interest, Section 503(a)(3). The rights of a mere transferee are quite limited (*i.e.,* to receive distributions), Section 503(b), and, if the partnership dissolves and winds up, to receive specified information pertaining to the partnership from the date of dissolution, Section 503(c).

This section applies regardless of whether the transferor is a partner, a transferee of a partner, a transferee of a transferee, etc. *See* Section 102(23) (defining "transferable interest" in terms of a right "initially owned by a person in the person's capacity as a partner" regardless of "whether or not the person remains a partner or continues to own any part of the right").

This section does not directly consider whether a partner may transfer governance rights to another partner without obtaining consent from all the other partners. As noted in Section 502, comment, the question is moot under this act's default rule for allocating governance rights.

However, the question can be pivotal when the partnership agreement displaces the default rule on governance rights but does not determine whether transfer restrictions (whether contractual, statutory, or both) apply to transfers of governance rights from one partner to another. Case law is scant and pertains to limited liability companies. Nonetheless, the cases suggest that this act does not protect partners from control shifts that result from transfers among partners. *Blythe v. Bell*, No. 11 CVS 933, 2012 WL 7807800, at ¶ 6 (N.C. Dist. Dec. 10, 2012) (holding in a case of "first impression in North Carolina" that "in the absence of articles of incorporation or an operating agreement to the contrary . . . the assignment of control [*i.e.,* governance] interests between members is effective without unanimous member consent"); *Achaian, Inc. v. Leemon Family LLC*, 25 A.3d 800, 810 (Del. Ch. 2011) (Strine, Ch.) (holding that the terms of the LLC agreement did not preclude one member of a three-member LLC from transferring the member's entire interest (including governance rights) to a second member without first having the consent of the third member; stating that the third member's "argument relies on a very thinly sliced version of [the "pick-your-partner" principle, the strained version being] . . . that once one chooses his initial co-members, one continues to hold a veto over how much additional voting power they may acquire" explaining that "[t]he problem for [the third member] is that nothing in the LLC Agreement supports [that member's] reading of it that would require an already admitted Member, like [the acquirer—*i.e.,* the second member], to be become once, twice (or even three times) a Member each and every time that Member acquires an additional block of Interests").

Other law may affect the applicability of this section. *See* 11 U.S.C. § 541(c)(1) (providing that, initially at least, all property of a debtor becomes part of the bankruptcy estate regardless of restrictions on transfer); UCC §§ 9–406, 9–408 (overriding specified restrictions on assignment in specified circumstances, regardless of whether state law or a contract imposes the restrictions).

In any event, this section does not apply to the transfer of ownership interests in a partner that is an entity.

Example: ABC, Partnership ("ABC") has three partners: Ralph (an individual), Alice, Inc. ("Alice"), and Norton, LLC ("Norton"). Section 502 applies to any attempt by Ralph, Alice, or Norton to transfer their respective partnership interest in ABC. Section 502 is inapplicable, however, to a change in control of Alice or Norton or even a complete change in their respective ownership.

Subsection (a)—The definition of "transfer," Section 102(22), and this subsection's reference to "in whole or in part" combine to mean that this section encompasses not only unconditional, permanent, and complete transfers but also temporary, contingent, and partial ones. Thus, for example, a charging order under Section 504 effects a transfer of part of the judgment debtor's transferable interest, as does the pledge of a transferable interest as collateral for a loan and the gift of a life-interest in a partner's rights to distribution.

Subsection (a)(2)—The phrase "by itself" contemplates Section 601(4)(B), which creates a risk of dissociation via expulsion when a partner transfers all of the partner's transferable interest.

Subsection (a)(3)—Mere transferees have no right to participate in management or otherwise intrude as the partners carry on the business of the partnership and their activities as partners.

Because Section 102(22)(G) defines "transfer" to include "a transfer by operation of law," this section affects the power of other law to effect transfers of a partner's ownership interest. For example, a divorce court lacks the power to award a partner's spouse anything beyond the partner's transferable interest. Nor does the partner have the power to enter into a property settlement purporting to effect any greater transfer.

For the divorce court, the best solution is to value the partner's complete ownership interest (*i.e.*, the transferable interest as enhanced by the management and information rights and the standing to sue) and: (i) if possible, award the partner's spouse marital property of equal value; or (ii) if not possible, award the partner's spouse a money judgment and a charging order to enforce the judgment.

Granting the non-partner any part of a partner's transferable interest is almost always imprudent; marital discord will almost inevitably carry over into the business relationship. Granting the partner's ex-spouse the entire transferable interest is rarely a viable alternative. If the partner is active participant in the partnership, the approach is impossible. The partner's transferable interest will typically constitute much or all of the partner's remuneration for the partner's activity. Even if the partner is essentially passive, granting the transferable interest to the ex-spouse puts him or her at great risk as a "bare naked assignee." *See* the comment to Section 107(b).

When a partner dies, subject to the partnership agreement other law may effect a transfer of the partner's transferable interest to the partner's estate or personal representative. However, for the reasons just stated, other law lacks the power to transfer anything more than a transferable interest. (Section 505 does provide extra information rights for the purposes of settling the estate of the deceased partner.)

Subsection (a)(3)(B)—For a related provision, providing that that section's information rights do not apply to transferees, see Section 408(i).

Subsection (b)—Amounts due under this subsection are of course subject to offset for any amount owed to the partnership by the partner or person dissociated as a partner on whose account the distribution is made. Section 405(d). As to whether a partnership may properly offset for claims against a transferor that was never a partner is matter for other law, specifically the law of contracts dealing with assignments.

Subsection (c)—This very limited grant of information rights encompasses only transactions occurring at or after the date of the partnership's dissolution. The transferee has only the right to information as to the allocation of net assets among the partnership's creditors, partners, and transferees—and only from the date of dissolution.

This subsection does not prevent a transferee from contracting with a partner-transferor to require the partner-transferor to disclose further information to the transferee. Whether such an agreement would breach the partnership agreement, the implied contractual obligation of good faith and fair dealing, Section 409(d), or a fiduciary duty depends on the circumstances.

If a dissolved partnership rescinds its dissolution, Section 803, this subsection no longer applies.

Subsection (e)—This provision originated as UPA (1997) § 503(e), was then consistent with Uniform Commercial Code section 9–318(3), and is now consistent with section 9–406(a) (stating that "an account debtor . . . may discharge its obligation by paying the assignor until, but not after, the account debtor receives a notification, authenticated by the assignor or the assignee, that the amount due or to become due has been assigned and that payment is to be made to the assignee").

The term "notice" includes "reason to know," Section 103(b)(1), and ordinarily a potential transferee has reason to inquire about transfer restrictions that might be contained in the partnership agreement.

Subsection (f)—Under this subsection, a partner remains a partner (with all attendant rights and obligations) even after permanently transferring the entirety of the transferable interest, unless: (i) the other partners opt for expulsion under Section 601(4)(B); or (ii) as otherwise provided in the partnership agreement.

§ 504.   Charging Order

(a)   On application by a judgment creditor of a partner or transferee, a court may enter a charging order against the transferable interest of the judgment debtor for the unsatisfied amount of the judgment. A charging order constitutes a lien on a judgment debtor's transferable interest and requires the partnership to pay over to the person to which the charging order was issued any distribution that otherwise would be paid to the judgment debtor.

(b)   To the extent necessary to effectuate the collection of distributions pursuant to a charging order in effect under subsection (a), the court may:

(1)   appoint a receiver of the distributions subject to the charging order, with the power to make all inquiries the judgment debtor might have made; and

(2)   make all other orders necessary to give effect to the charging order.

(c)   Upon a showing that distributions under a charging order will not pay the judgment debt within a reasonable time, the court may foreclose the lien and order the sale of the transferable interest. The purchaser at the foreclosure sale obtains only the transferable interest, does not thereby become a partner, and is subject to Section 503.

(d)   At any time before foreclosure under subsection (c), the partner or transferee whose transferable interest is subject to a charging order under subsection (a) may extinguish the charging order by satisfying the judgment and filing a certified copy of the satisfaction with the court that issued the charging order.

(e)   At any time before foreclosure under subsection (c), a partnership or one or more partners whose transferable interests are not subject to the charging order may pay to the judgment creditor the full amount due under the judgment and thereby succeed to the rights of the judgment creditor, including the charging order.

(f)   This [act] does not deprive any partner or transferee of the benefit of any exemption law applicable to the transferable interest of the partner or transferee.

(g)   This section provides the exclusive remedy by which a person seeking in the capacity of a judgment creditor to enforce a judgment against a partner or transferee may satisfy the judgment from the judgment debtor's transferable interest.

COMMENT

The charging order concept dates back to the English Partnership Act of 1890 and in the United States has been a fundamental part of law of unincorporated business organizations since 1914. *See* UPA (1914) § 28. As much a remedy limitation as a remedy, the charging order is the sole method by which a person acting as judgment creditor of a partner or transferee can extract value from the partner's or transferee's ownership interest in a partnership. *See* the comment to Subsection (g).

Under this section, the judgment creditor of a partner or transferee is entitled to a charging order against the relevant transferable interest. While in effect, that order entitles the judgment creditor to whatever distributions would otherwise be due to the partner or transferee whose interest is subject to the order. However, the judgment creditor has no say in the timing or amount of those distributions. The charging order does not entitle the judgment creditor to accelerate any distributions or to otherwise interfere with the management and activities of the partnership.

By its terms, this section does not apply to foreign partnerships. *See* Section 102(11) (defining "partnership" to mean "an association of two or more persons to carry on as co-owners a business for profit *formed under this [act]*") (emphasis added). *See also Fannie Mae v. Heather Apartments Ltd. P'ship*, A13-0562, 2013 WL 6223564, at *6 (Minn. Ct. App. Dec. 2, 2013) (considering the remedies available to a judgment creditor with respect to the judgment debtor's interest in a Cook Islands LLC; rejecting the debtor's argument that the creditor's "only remedy is to obtain a charging order under" the Minnesota LLC statute; explaining that "this argument fails because that statute only applies to Minnesota limited liability companies" which that statute "defines . . . as 'a limited liability company, other than a foreign limited liability company, *organized or governed by this chapter*'") (emphasis added) (statutory citations omitted).

The partnership agreement has no power to alter the provisions of this section to the prejudice of third parties. Section 105(c)(17).

Subsection (a)—The phrase "judgment debtor" encompasses both partners and transferees. The lien pertains only to a distribution, which excludes "amounts constituting reasonable compensation for present or past service or payments made in the ordinary course of business under a bona fide retirement plan or other bona fide benefits program." Section 102(4)(B). A judgment creditor that wishes to levy on such amounts should use the appropriate creditor's remedy, such as garnishment (which may be subject to exemptions or exclusions not relevant to a charging order). *Cf. PB Real Estate, Inc. v. Dem II Props.*, 719 A.2d 73, 76 (Conn. Ct. App. 1998) (rejecting the contention of an LLC's two members that "payments of $28,000 to each of them" should be treated "as expenses for wages" rather than as distributions).

Whether an application for a charging order must be served on the partnership, the judgment debtor, or both is a matter for other law, principally the law of remedies and civil procedure. The order itself must be served on the partnership. Whether the order must also be served on the judgment debtor is a matter for other law.

If a distribution consists of rights to acquire interests in a partnership, the charging order applies only to those rights within the definition of transferable interest. *See* Section 102(23) (defining transferable interest).

Subsection (b)—Paragraph (2) refers to "other orders" rather than "additional orders." Therefore, given appropriate circumstances, a court may invoke Paragraph (1), Paragraph (2), or both.

Subsection (b)(1)—The receiver contemplated here is emphatically not a receiver for the partnership, but rather a receiver for the distributions subject to the charging order. The principal advantage provided by this paragraph is an expanded right to information. However, that right goes no further than "the extent necessary to effectuate the collections of distributions pursuant to a charging order." For a correctly narrow reading of this provision, see *Wells Fargo Bank, Nat. Ass'n v. Continuous Control Solutions, Inc.*, No. 11–1285, 2012 WL 3195759 (Iowa Ct. App. Aug. 8, 2012).

Subsection (b)(2)—This paragraph must be understood in the context of: (i) the very limited nature of the charging order; and (ii) the importance of preventing overreaching on behalf of a person that is not a judgment creditor of the partnership, has no claim on the partnership's assets, and has no right to interfere in the activities, affairs, and management of the partnership. In particular, the court's power to make "all other orders" is limited to "orders necessary to give effect to the charging order."

Example: A judgment creditor with a charging order believes that the partnership should invest less of its surplus in operations, leaving more funds for distributions. The creditor moves the court for an order directing the partnership to restrict re-investment. Subsection (b)(2) does not authorize the court to grant the motion.

Example: A judgment creditor with a judgment for $10,000 against a partner obtains a charging order against the partner's transferable interest. Having been properly served with the order, the partnership nonetheless fails to comply and makes a $3000 distribution to the partner. The court has the power to order the partnership to pay $3000 to the judgment creditor to "give effect to the charging order."

Under Subsection (b)(2), the court has the power to decide whether a particular payment is a distribution, because that decision determines whether the payment is part of a transferable interest subject to a charging order.

Example: Partner A of ABC, a general partnership, has for some years received distributions form the partnership. However, when a judgment creditor of Partner A obtains a charging order against Partner A's transferable interest, the partnership ceases to make distributions to Partner A and instead provides a salary to Partner A equivalent to former distributions. A court might deem this salary a disguised distribution. (In any event, the salary will be subject to garnishment.)

This act has no specific rules for determining the fate or effect of a charging order when the partnership undergoes a merger, conversion, interest exchange, or domestication under Article 11. In the proper circumstances, such an organic change might trigger an order under Subsection (b)(2).

Subsection (c)—The phrase "that distributions under the charging order will not pay the judgment debt within a reasonable period of time" comes from case law. *See, e.g., Nigri v. Lotz*, 453 S.E.2d 780, 783 (Ga. Ct. App. 1995); *Stewart v. Lanier Park Med. Office Bldg., Ltd.*, 578 S.E.2d 572, 574 (Ga. Ct. App. 2003) ("Judicial sale may be appropriate where . . . it is apparent that distributions under the charging order will not pay the judgment debt within a reasonable amount of time."). A purchaser at a foreclosure sale obtains only the very limited rights of a transferee under Section 503 and is in some ways more vulnerable and less powerful than the holder of a charging order. After foreclosure and sale, Subsection (b) no longer applies. More generally, the court is no longer involved in the matter. For the vulnerability of a transferee, see Sections 503(a)(3) comment; 107(b), comment.

Subsection (d)—This provision allows the judgment debtor to end the charging order without need for a hearing.

Subsection (e)—Traditionally, charging order provisions referred to the possibility of "redeeming" an interest subject to a charging order. That usage was confusing, leaving several important questions unanswered. This act substitutes a far simpler approach, contemplating the partnership or its partners buying the underlying judgment and thereby dispensing with any interference the judgment creditor might seek to inflict on the partnership.

In many circumstances, buying the judgment is superior to the mechanism provided by this subsection, because: (i) this subsection requires full satisfaction of the underlying judgment; and (ii) the partnership or the other partners might be able to buy the judgment for less than face value. On the other hand, this subsection operates without need for the judgment creditor's consent, so it remains a valuable protection in the event a judgment creditor seeks to do mischief to the partnership.

Whether a partnership's decision to invoke this subsection is "ordinary course" or "outside the ordinary course," Section 401(k), depends on the circumstances. However, the involvement of this subsection does not by itself make the decision "outside the ordinary course."

Subsection (f)—This subsection preserves otherwise applicable exemptions but does not create any. *In re Foos*, 405 B.R. 604, 609 (Bankr. N. D. Ohio 2009) (interpreting the comparable provision in UPA (1997) and stating that "it is clear that [the provision] does not create an exemption").

Subsection (g)—This subsection does not override Uniform Commercial Code, Article 9, which may provide different remedies for a secured creditor acting in that capacity. A secured creditor with a judgment might decide to proceed under Article 9 alone, under this section alone, or under both Article 9 and this section. In the last-mentioned circumstance, the constraints of this section would apply to the charging order but not to the Article 9 remedies.

This subsection is not intended to prevent a court from effecting a "reverse pierce" where appropriate. In a reverse pierce, the court conflates the entity and its owner to hold the entity liable for a debt of the owner. *Litchfield Asset Mgmt. Corp. v. Howell*, 799 A.2d 298, 312 (Conn. App. Ct. 2002) (approving a reverse pierce where a judgment debtor had established a partnership in a patent attempt to frustrate the judgment creditor), *overruled on other grounds by*, *Robinson v. Coughlin*, 830 A.2d 1114 (Conn. 2003). Likewise, this subsection does not supplant fraudulent transfer law.

§ 505.　Power of Legal Representative of Deceased

If a partner dies, the deceased partner's legal representative may exercise:

(1)　the rights of a transferee provided in Section 503(c); and

(2)　for purposes of settling the estate, the rights the deceased partner had under Section 408.

COMMENT

The estate and those claiming through the estate are transferees, and as such they have very limited rights to information. This section provides temporary, additional information rights to the legal representative of the estate. Sections 408 and 503(c) pertain only to information rights.

[ARTICLE] 6.　DISSOCIATION

§ 601.　Events Causing Dissociation

A person is dissociated as a partner when:

(1)　the partnership knows or has notice of the person's express will to withdraw as a partner, but, if the person has specified a withdrawal date later than the date the partnership knew or had notice, on that later date;

(2)　an event stated in the partnership agreement as causing the person's dissociation occurs;

(3)　the person is expelled as a partner pursuant to the partnership agreement;

(4)　the person is expelled as a partner by the affirmative vote or consent of all the other partners if:

(A)　it is unlawful to carry on the partnership business with the person as a partner;

(B) there has been a transfer of all of the person's transferable interest in the partnership, other than:

(i) a transfer for security purposes; or

(ii) a charging order in effect under Section 504 which has not been foreclosed;

(C) the person is an entity and:

(i) the partnership notifies the person that it will be expelled as a partner because the person has filed a statement of dissolution or the equivalent, the person has been administratively dissolved, the person's charter or the equivalent has been revoked, or the person's right to conduct business has been suspended by the person's jurisdiction of formation; and

(ii) not later than 90 days after the notification, the statement of dissolution or the equivalent has not been withdrawn, rescinded, or revoked, or the person's charter or the equivalent or right to conduct business has not been reinstated; or

(D) the person is an unincorporated entity that has been dissolved and whose activities and affairs are being wound up;

(5) on application by the partnership or another partner, the person is expelled as a partner by judicial order because the person:

(A) has engaged or is engaging in wrongful conduct that has affected adversely and materially, or will affect adversely and materially, the partnership's business;

(B) has committed willfully or persistently, or is committing willfully or persistently, a material breach of the partnership agreement or a duty or obligation under Section 409; or

(C) has engaged or is engaging in conduct relating to the partnership's business which makes it not reasonably practicable to carry on the business with the person as a partner;

(6) the person:

(A) becomes a debtor in bankruptcy;

(B) signs an assignment for the benefit of creditors; or

(C) seeks, consents to, or acquiesces in the appointment of a trustee, receiver, or liquidator of the person or of all or substantially all the person's property;

(7) in the case of an individual:

(A) the individual dies;

(B) a guardian or general conservator for the individual is appointed; or

(C) a court orders that the individual has otherwise become incapable of performing the individual's duties as a partner under this [act] or the partnership agreement;

(8) in the case of a person that is a testamentary or inter vivos trust or is acting as a partner by virtue of being a trustee of such a trust, the trust's entire transferable interest in the partnership is distributed;

(9) in the case of a person that is an estate or is acting as a partner by virtue of being a personal representative of an estate, the estate's entire transferable interest in the partnership is distributed;

(10) in the case of a person that is not an individual, the existence of the person terminates;

(11) the partnership participates in a merger under [Article] 11 and:

(A) the partnership is not the surviving entity; or

(B) otherwise as a result of the merger, the person ceases to be a partner;

(12) the partnership participates in an interest exchange under [Article] 11 and, as a result of the interest exchange, the person ceases to be a partner;

(13) the partnership participates in a conversion under [Article] 11;

(14) the partnership participates in a domestication under [Article] 11 and, as a result of the domestication, the person ceases to be a partner; or

(15) the partnership dissolves and completes winding up.

COMMENT

This section mostly states default rules, which the partnership agreement may vary. However, it makes no sense to vary some of the rules—*e.g.*, that the death of a partner who is an individual does *not* cause the individual's dissociation as a partner, Paragraph (7)(A), or that an entity remains a partner even *after* the existence of the entity has terminated, Paragraph (10).

Paragraph (1)—Partnership agreements often require notice of dissociation to be in writing and to specify the effective date of the dissociation. The partnership cannot eliminate the power of a partner to dissociate by express will, Section 110(c)(9), but can eliminate the right and thereby make the dissociation wrongful.

Paragraph (3)—General partnership agreements often provide for "no cause" expulsion, and courts differ somewhat in how they approach such provisions. *Compare Gelder Med. Grp. v. Webber*, 363 N.E.2d 573, 576 (N.Y. 1977), *with Winston & Strawn v. Nosal*, 664 N.E.2d 239, 245 (Ill. App. Ct. 1996). *See also* the comment to Section 409(d) (stating and explaining the implied contractual covenant of good faith and fair dealing).

Paragraph (4)(B)—This paragraph permits expulsion when a partner no longer has any "skin in the game." Although Article 7 provides for the buy-out of a dissociated partner's transferable interest, in this context the dissociated partner has no transferable interest.

Paragraph (5)—For examples of conduct warranting an expulsion order, see *Della Ratta v. Dyas*, 961 A.2d 629, 642 (Md. Ct. Spec. App. 2008), *aff'd*, 996 A.2d 382 (Md. 2010) (noting that "[t]he trial court expressly found that [two major capital] calls 'were issued in bad faith' . . . [and the] court also found that, '[by] another improper accounting movement" in [the partnership], $580,000 was taken 'for executive office expenses which was improper' "); *Brennan v. Brennan Assocs.*, 977 A.2d 107, 117–18 (Conn. 2009) (referring to the expelled partner's "moral turpitude, criminal fraud, and failure to be honest in court as to the extent of his criminal wrongdoing" as well as "his baseless claims of fraud" against a fellow partner; stating "he has rung the bell and it cannot be unrung").

For an analysis that helps distinguish Paragraph (5)(C) from Paragraphs (5)(A) and (B), *see All Saints University of Medicine Aruba v. Chilana*, A-2628-09T1, 2012 WL 6652510, at *15 (N.J. Super. Ct. App. Div. Dec. 24, 2012) (interpreting predecessor law and noting that the "not reasonably practicable standard" does not require a showing of wrongful conduct). *Cf. Dunnagan v. Watson*, 204 S.W.3d 30, 40 (Tex. Ct. App. 2006) (same issue in the context of dissolution).

Where grounds exist for both dissociation and dissolution, a court has the discretion to choose between the alternatives. *Robertson v. Jacobs Cattle Co.*, 830 N.W.2d 191, 201–02 (Neb. 2013). "[T]here is no textual basis for imposing a higher burden of proof for dissociation than dissolution." *Brennan v. Brennan Assocs.*, 977 A.2d 107, 121 (Conn. 2009).

The partnership agreement cannot vary the stated grounds for expulsion, Section 105(c)(10), but can choose an alternate forum—*e.g.*, arbitration. *Compare* Section 801(a)(4) (containing analogous grounds for dissolution by court order), *with* Section 105(c)(11) (making the Section 701(a)(4) grounds non-waivable).

Paragraph (6)(A)—This provision is subject to bankruptcy law. *See, e.g.,* 11 U.S.C.A. § 365(e) (invalidating "ipso facto" clauses, subject to some exceptions).

Paragraphs (8) and (9)—A change in trustee or personal representative does not cause dissociation.

Paragraph (11)(A)—If a partnership disappears as part of a merger, no person can continue as a partner of the partnership. When the merger takes effect, those partners of the disappearing company are perforce dissociated. Depending on the plan of merger, those persons may become partners of a surviving partnership. In those circumstances, the merger will have dissociated them from one partnership and admitted them into partnership in the surviving partnership. *See* Sections 402(b)(2) and 1126(a)(10).

Paragraph (11)(B)—It is possible for a plan of merger to "shuffle the equity" of the surviving entity, even to the extent of "taking out" some or all of the owners of the surviving entity. A reverse triangular merger involving a partnership as the surviving entity would dissociate all the partners of the partnership.

Paragraph (13)—By definition, a partnership that converts ceases to be a partnership. *See* Section 1146. Thus, when the plan of conversion takes effect, all the partners of the converted entity are dissociated from that entity. In many cases, those persons will all be owners of the converted entity. In some cases, the conversion will "shuffle the equity" and "take out"

some of the partners of the converting partnership.

Paragraph (14)—Domestication does not by itself dissociate a partner, because the domesticated entity remains both a partnership and "the same entity without interruption as the domesticating company." Section 1156(a)(1)(B). However, an "equity shuffle" could dissociate a partner.

§ 602. Power to Dissociate as Partner; Wrongful Dissociation

(a) A person has the power to dissociate as a partner at any time, rightfully or wrongfully, by withdrawing as a partner by express will under Section 601(1).

(b) A person's dissociation as a partner is wrongful only if the dissociation:

    (1) is in breach of an express provision of the partnership agreement; or

    (2) in the case of a partnership for a definite term or particular undertaking, occurs before the expiration of the term or the completion of the undertaking and:

        (A) the person withdraws as a partner by express will, unless the withdrawal follows not later than 90 days after another person's dissociation by death or otherwise under Section 601(6) through (10) or wrongful dissociation under this subsection;

        (B) the person is expelled as a partner by judicial order under Section 601(5);

        (C) the person is dissociated under Section 601(6); or

        (D) in the case of a person that is not a trust other than a business trust, an estate, or an individual, the person is expelled or otherwise dissociated because it willfully dissolved or terminated.

(c) A person that wrongfully dissociates as a partner is liable to the partnership and to the other partners for damages caused by the dissociation. The liability is in addition to any debt, obligation, or other liability of the partner to the partnership or the other partners.

COMMENT

Subsection (a)—A general partnership is a voluntary association, *see* Section 105(c)(9), and voluntary in this context means "proceeding from the will or from one's own choice or consent . . . having power of free choice." BLACK'S LAW DICTIONARY (9th ed. 2009). Necessarily therefore, a general partner always has the power to dissociate by express will. Accordingly, the partnership agreement cannot vary this subsection except to the extent of requiring the notice of dissociation to be in writing. Section 105(c)(9).

The phrase "rightfully or wrongfully" reflects the distinction between a partner's *power* to withdraw in contravention of the partnership agreement and a partner's *right* to do so. Thus, although a partner cannot be enjoined from exercising the power to dissociate, the dissociation may be wrongful under Subsection (b).

Subsection (b)—This subsection list exhaustively ("only if") the dissociations that are "wrongful." The label has three consequences:

- under Subsection (c) liability for resulting damages, which, under Section 701(c), may be offset against the amount of the buyout price due to the partner under Section 701(a);

- under Section 701(h) postponement of payment of the buyout price until the term expires or the undertaking is completed; and

- under Section 804, exclusion from the winding up process, if the dissociation results in dissolution of the partnership.

This subsection states a default rule. The partnership agreement can expand the list (*e.g.*, by making wrongful a dissociation that beaches the implied contractual covenant of good faith and fair dealing). In theory, the partnership agreement can provide for liquidated damages (subject to the requirements of contract law) and, in theory, can also shrink or even eliminate the list of wrongful dissociations.

Subsection (b)(2)(A)—This paragraph protects a partner's reactive withdrawal from a term partnership after the premature departure of another partner, such as the partnership's rainmaker or main supplier of capital, under the same circumstances that may result in the dissolution of the partnership under Section 801(2)(A). Under that provision, a term partnership is dissolved ninety days after the bankruptcy, incapacity, death (or similar dissociation of a partner that is an entity), or wrongful dissociation of any partner, unless a majority in interest of the remaining partners agree to continue the partnership. Under this provision, a partner's exercise of the right of withdrawal by express will under those circumstances is rendered "rightful," even if the partnership is continued by others, and does not expose the withdrawing partner to damages for wrongful dissociation under Section 602(c).

Subsection (b)(2)(C)—This provision refers to Section 601(6), which involves *inter alia* dissociation on account of bankruptcy, which in turn is subject to bankruptcy law. *See, e.g.*, 11 U.S.C.A. § 365(e) (invalidating "ipso facto" clauses, subject to some exceptions).

Subsection (c)—A partner who prematurely dissociates from a partnership for an agreed term or undertaking risks liability for any resulting damages. For example, the partnership might incur substantial expenses in replacing the general partner's expertise, reputation, or creditworthiness.

In effect, this subsection equates wrongful dissociation with breach of contract. Accordingly, courts should look to contract law to determine what consequential damages are recoverable. *See Hadley v. Baxendale*, 9 Exch. 341 (1854); RESTATEMENT (SECOND) OF CONTRACTS § 351 (1981); *see also Williams v. Hildebrand*, 247 S.W.2d 356, 358 (Ark. 1952) (interpreting UPA (1914) § 38(2)(a)(II), pertaining to wrongful dissolution, and stating that "the measure of damages, when the partnership was to have continued for a fixed term, is the profits that the injured partner would have received").

§ 603.   Effect of Dissociation

(a)   If a person's dissociation results in a dissolution and winding up of the partnership business, [Article] 8 applies; otherwise, [Article] 7 applies.

(b)   If a person is dissociated as a partner:

(1)   the person's right to participate in the management and conduct of the partnership's business terminates, except as otherwise provided in Section 802(c); and

(2)   the person's duties and obligations under Section 409 end with regard to matters arising and events occurring after the person's dissociation, except to the extent the partner participates in winding up the partnership's business pursuant to Section 802.

(c)   A person's dissociation does not of itself discharge the person from any debt, obligation, or other liability to the partnership or the other partners which the person incurred while a partner.

COMMENT

Subsection (a)—This subsection is a "switching" provision, invoking either Article 7 or 8 depending on whether a person's dissociation as a partner results in dissolution.

Subsection (b)—This section originated as UPA (1997) § 603(b) and deals with some of the internal effects of a person's dissociation as a partner.

Subsection (b)(1)—A person's dissociation as a partner ends immediately the person's right to participate in the management of the business, unless the dissociation results in dissolution of the partnership. *See* Section 802(c) ("A person whose dissociation as a partner resulted in dissolution may participate in winding up as if still a partner, unless the dissociation was wrongful.").

Subsection (b)(2)—Unless a person's dissociation as a partner results in dissolution and the person participates in winding up, Section 802(c), this provision establishes a dividing line, separating out "matters arising and events occurring after the person's dissociation." If the partnership has continuing projects with clients, ongoing relationships with clients, or both, the dividing line requires special attention with regard to non-competition and partnership opportunities duties. *See* Section 409(b)(1), (3).

Disputes involving law firms have generated much of the relevant case law. *See, e.g., Meehan v. Shaughnessy*, 535 N.E.2d 1255, 1257 (Mass. 1989); *Jewel v. Boxer*, 156 Cal. App. 3d 171, 175 (Cal. Ct. App. 1984). To a large extent a well-drawn partnership agreement can delineate the parties' respective rights and responsibilities and thereby avoid problems. However, if the partnership becomes insolvent, the bankruptcy court may well scrutinize the partners' *inter se* arrangements. *See Geron v. Robinson & Cole L.L.P.*, 476 B.R. 732, 743 (Bankr. S.D.N.Y.

2012) (considering whether a law firm had "fraudulently transferred . . . assets when its partners adopted the Jewel Waiver [releasing rights recognized by *Jewel v. Boxer*] on the eve of dissolution without consideration").

This provision does not determine the effect of a person's dissociation as a partner on the person's future obligations or rights under the partnership agreement. Some contractual obligations typically extend beyond dissociation—*e.g.*, non-competition agreements, buyout arrangements. To the extent provisions of the partnership agreement continue to apply, the common law obligation of good faith continues to apply as well. *See* the comment to Section 409(d) (explaining that the subsection "invokes the implied obligation that exists in every contract" as a matter of common law).

Subsection (c)—A partner's obligation to safeguard trade secrets and other confidential or proprietary information is incurred when the partner learns or otherwise obtains the information. This subsection preserves the obligation post-dissociation.

[ARTICLE] 7. PERSON'S DISSOCIATION AS A PARTNER WHEN BUSINESS NOT WOUND UP

§ 701. Purchase of Interest of Person Dissociated as Partner

(a) If a person is dissociated as a partner without the dissociation resulting in a dissolution and winding up of the partnership business under Section 801, the partnership shall cause the person's interest in the partnership to be purchased for a buyout price determined pursuant to subsection (b).

(b) The buyout price of the interest of a person dissociated as a partner is the amount that would have been distributable to the person under Section 806(b) if, on the date of dissociation, the assets of the partnership were sold and the partnership were wound up, with the sale price equal to the greater of:

(1) the liquidation value; or

(2) the value based on a sale of the entire business as a going concern without the person.

(c) Interest accrues on the buyout price from the date of dissociation to the date of payment, but damages for wrongful dissociation under Section 602(b), and all other amounts owing, whether or not presently due, from the person dissociated as a partner to the partnership, must be offset against the buyout price.

(d) A partnership shall defend, indemnify, and hold harmless a person dissociated as a partner whose interest is being purchased against all partnership liabilities, whether incurred before or after the dissociation, except liabilities incurred by an act of the person under Section 702.

(e) If no agreement for the purchase of the interest of a person dissociated as a partner is reached not later than 120 days after a written demand for payment, the partnership shall pay, or cause to be paid, in money to the person the amount the partnership estimates to be the buyout price and accrued interest, reduced by any offsets and accrued interest under subsection (c).

(f) If a deferred payment is authorized under subsection (h), the partnership may tender a written offer to pay the amount it estimates to be the buyout price and accrued interest, reduced by any offsets under subsection (c), stating the time of payment, the amount and type of security for payment, and the other terms and conditions of the obligation.

(g) The payment or tender required by subsection (e) or (f) must be accompanied by the following:

(1) a statement of partnership assets and liabilities as of the date of dissociation;

(2) the latest available partnership balance sheet and income statement, if any;

(3) an explanation of how the estimated amount of the payment was calculated; and

(4) written notice that the payment is in full satisfaction of the obligation to purchase unless, not later than 120 days after the written notice, the person dissociated as a partner commences an action to determine the buyout price, any offsets under subsection (c), or other terms of the obligation to purchase.

(h) A person that wrongfully dissociates as a partner before the expiration of a definite term or the completion of a particular undertaking is not entitled to payment of any part of the buyout price until the expiration of the term or completion of the undertaking, unless the person establishes to the satisfaction of the court that earlier payment will not cause undue hardship to the business of the partnership. A deferred payment must be adequately secured and bear interest.

(i)   A person dissociated as a partner may maintain an action against the partnership, pursuant to Section 410(b)(2), to determine the buyout price of that person's interest, any offsets under subsection (c), or other terms of the obligation to purchase. The action must be commenced not later than 120 days after the partnership has tendered payment or an offer to pay or within one year after written demand for payment if no payment or offer to pay is tendered. The court shall determine the buyout price of the person's interest, any offset due under subsection (c), and accrued interest, and enter judgment for any additional payment or refund. If deferred payment is authorized under subsection (h), the court shall also determine the security for payment and other terms of the obligation to purchase. The court may assess reasonable attorney's fees and the fees and expenses of appraisers or other experts for a party to the action, in amounts the court finds equitable, against a party that the court finds acted arbitrarily, vexatiously, or not in good faith. The finding may be based on the partnership's failure to tender payment or an offer to pay or to comply with subsection (g).

COMMENT

Article 7 originated in UPA (1997) and provides for the buyout of the interest of a person dissociated as a partner if the dissociation does not result in a dissolution and winding up of the partnership's business under Article 8. *See* Section 603(a). If there is no dissolution, the remaining partners have a right to continue the business and the person dissociated as a partner has a right to be bought out. These rights can, of course, be varied in the partnership agreement. *See* Section 105. A person dissociated as a partner has a continuing relationship with the partnership and third parties as provided in Sections 603(b), 702, and 703. *See* Section 408(e) (access to information of person dissociated as a partner).

The rules in this section are merely default rules. The partners may, in the partnership agreement, fix the method or formula for determining the buyout price and all of the other terms and conditions of the buyout right. Indeed, the very right to a buyout itself may be modified, although a provision providing for a complete forfeiture would probably not be enforceable. *See* Section 119 (Supplemental Principles of Law).

Subsection (a)—This subsection provides that, if a person's dissociation as a partner does not result in a windup of the business, the partnership shall cause the interest of the dissociating partner to be purchased for a buyout price determined pursuant to Subsection (b). The buyout is mandatory, unless the partnership provides otherwise. The "cause to be purchased" language is intended to accommodate a purchase by the partnership, one or more of the remaining partners, or a third party.

Subsection (b)—This subsection provides how the "buyout price" is to be determined. The terms "fair market value" or "fair value" were not used because they are often considered terms of art having a special meaning depending on the context, such as in tax or corporate law. "Buyout price" was a new term in UPA (1997). Under Subsection (b), the buyout price is the amount that would have been distributable to the dissociating partner under Section 807(b) if, on the date of dissociation, the assets of the partnership were sold at a price equal to the greater of liquidation value or going concern value without the departing partner. Liquidation value is not intended to mean distress sale value. Under general principles of valuation, the hypothetical selling price in either case should be the price that a willing and informed buyer would pay a willing and informed seller, with neither being under any compulsion to deal. The notion of a minority discount in determining the buyout price is negated by valuing the business as a going concern. Other discounts, such as for a lack of marketability or the loss of a key partner, may be appropriate, however. For a case applying the concept, see *Fotouhi v. Mansdorf*, 427 B.R. 798, 803–05 (Bankr. N.D. Cal. 2010)

Since the buyout price is based on the value of the business at the time of dissociation, the partnership must pay interest on the amount due from the date of dissociation until payment to compensate the dissociating partner for the use of his interest in the firm. Under UPA (1914) § 42, the person dissociated as a partner could elect a share of the profits in lieu of interest. UPA (1997) eliminated that option.

UPA (1914) § 38(2)(c)(II) provides that the good will of the business not be considered in valuing a wrongfully dissociating partner's interest. UPA (1997) implicitly rejected that approach. Under this section, unless the partnership's goodwill is damaged by the wrongful dissociation, the value of the wrongfully dissociating partner's interest will include any goodwill value of the partnership. If the firm's goodwill is damaged, the amount of the damages suffered by the partnership and the remaining partners will be offset against the buyout price.

Subsection (c)—This subsection provides that the partnership may offset against the buyout price all amounts owing by the person dissociated as a partner to the partnership, whether or not presently due, including any damages for wrongful dissociation under Section 602(c). This rule has the effect of accelerating payment of amounts not yet due from the former partner to the partnership, including a long-term loan by the partnership to the former partner. Where appropriate, the amounts not yet due should be discounted to present value. A dissociating partner, on the other hand, is not entitled to an add-on for amounts owing to him by the partnership. Thus, a departing partner who has made a long-term loan to the partnership must wait for repayment, unless the terms of the loan agreement provide for acceleration upon dissociation.

The partnership's right of setoff does not limit the amount of damages the partnership may claim for the wrongful dissociation and does not alter any other amounts owed to the partnership. Those amounts may result in a net sum due to the partnership from the person dissociated as a partner.

Subsection (d)—Following the rule stated in UPA (1914) § 38, this section requires the partnership to indemnify a person dissociated as a partner against all partnership liabilities, whether incurred before or after the dissociation, except those incurred by the person under Section 702. The rationale for covering post-dissociation liabilities is the fact of dissociation; the person dissociated as a partner is no longer a co-owner of the enterprise. As for pre-existing liabilities, the determination of the buyout price necessarily assumes that these liabilities will be paid. Thus, in effect the person's share of these liabilities has already been paid through the valuation process.

Subsection (e)—If a person dissociated as a partner makes a written demand for payment and no agreement for the purchase of the interest is reached within 120 days after the demand, the partnership must pay, or cause to be paid, in cash the amount it estimates to be the buyout price, adjusted for any offsets allowed and accrued interest. Thus, the person dissociated as a partner will receive in cash within 120 days of dissociation the undisputed minimum value of the person's partnership interest. If the person claims that the buyout price should be higher, suit may thereafter be brought as provided in Subsection (i) to have the amount of the buyout price determined by the court. This is similar to the procedure for determining the value of dissenting shareholders' shares under the Model Business Corporation Act §§ 13.20–13.28.

The "cause to be paid" language of Subsection (a) is repeated here to permit either the partnership, one or more of the continuing partners, or a third-party purchaser to tender payment of the estimated amount due.

Subsection (f)—Under this subsection, when deferred payment is authorized in the case of a wrongfully dissociating partner, a written offer stating the amount the partnership estimates to be the purchase price should be tendered within the 120-day period, even though actual payment of the amount may be deferred, possibly for many years. *See* the comment to Subsection (h). The dissociated partner is entitled to know at the time of dissociation what amount the remaining partners think is due, including the estimated amount of any damages allegedly caused by the partner's wrongful dissociation that may be offset against the buyout price.

Subsection (g)—This subsection provides that the payment of the estimated price (or tender of a written offer under Subsection (f)) by the partnership must be accompanied by: (i) a statement of the partnership's assets and liabilities as of the date of the person's dissociation as a partner; (ii) the latest available balance sheet and income statement, if the partnership maintains such financial statements; (iii) an explanation of how the estimated amount of the payment was calculated; and (iv) a written notice that the payment will be in full satisfaction of the partnership's buyout obligation unless the person dissociated as a partner commences an action to determine the price within 120 days of the notice. Subsection (g) is based in part on the dissenters' rights provisions of Model Business Corporation Act Section 13.25(b).

Those disclosures should serve to identify and narrow substantially the items of dispute between the person dissociated as a partner and the partnership over the valuation of the partnership interest. The disclosures will also serve to pin down the parties as to their claims of partnership assets and values and as to the existence and amount of all known liabilities. Lastly, the disclosures will force the remaining partners to consider thoughtfully the difficult and important questions as to the appropriate method of valuation under the circumstances, and in particular, whether they should use going concern or liquidation value. Simply getting that information on the record in a timely fashion should increase the likelihood of a negotiated resolution of the parties' differences during the 120-day period within which the person dissociated as a partner must bring suit.

Subsection (h)—UPA (1914) § 38 contemplates a buyout in the context of the partnership business being continued after a partner's wrongful dissociation has (inevitably) caused dissolution. UPA (1914) § 38(2)(c) entitles the wrongfully dissociating partner to have the buyout price "paid to him in cash, or the payment secured by bond approved by the court." UPA (1997) took a different approach, which the Harmonization Project did not change. Under Subsection (h), a wrongfully dissociating partner is not entitled to receive any portion of the buyout price before the expiration of the term or completion of the undertaking, unless the person dissociated as a partner establishes to the satisfaction of the court that earlier payment will not cause undue hardship to the business of the partnership.

Subsection (i)—This subsection provides that a person dissociated as a partner may maintain an action against the partnership to determine the buyout price, any offsets, or other terms of the purchase obligation. The action must be commenced within 120 days after the partnership tenders payment of the amount it estimates to be due or, if deferred payment is authorized, its written offer. This provision creates a 120-day "cooling off" period. It also allows the parties an opportunity to negotiate their differences after disclosure by the partnership of its financial statements and other required information.

If the partnership fails to tender payment of the estimated amount due (or a written offer, if deferred payment is authorized), the person dissociated as a partner has one year after written demand for payment in which to commence suit.

§ 702. Power to Bind and Liability of Person Dissociated as Partner

(a)   After a person is dissociated as a partner without the dissociation resulting in a dissolution and winding up of the partnership business and before the partnership is merged out of existence, converted, or domesticated under [Article] 11, or dissolved, the partnership is bound by an act of the person only if:

(1)   the act would have bound the partnership under Section 301 before dissociation; and

(2)   at the time the other party enters into the transaction:

(A)   less than two years has passed since the dissociation; and

(B)   the other party does not know or have notice of the dissociation and reasonably believes that the person is a partner.

(b)   If a partnership is bound under subsection (a), the person dissociated as a partner which caused the partnership to be bound is liable:

(1)   to the partnership for any damage caused to the partnership arising from the obligation incurred under subsection (a); and

(2)   if a partner or another person dissociated as a partner is liable for the obligation, to the partner or other person for any damage caused to the partner or other person arising from the liability.

COMMENT

A person's dissociation as a partner ends immediately the person's actual authority to act for the partnership, unless the dissociation results in a dissolution and winding up of the business of the partnership. *See* Section 603(b)(1). However, the person's apparent authority may linger.

This section does not affect a person's power to bind a partnership in another capacity—*e.g.*, as an employee with actual authority.

Subsection (a)—This subsection codifies and constrains the lingering apparent authority of a person dissociated as a partner. The constraint is in the phrase "only if."

The provision applies until the partnership dissolves or under Article 11 ceases to be governed by this act. Once a partnership dissolves, Section 804 applies.

With respect to authority of a person dissociated as a partner to transfer partnership real property, Section 303(e) provides that third parties are deemed to have knowledge of a limitation on the person's authority to transfer real property held in the partnership name upon the proper recording of a statement containing such a limitation. Section 704(b) provides that a statement of dissociation operates as a limitation on the person's authority for the purposes of Section 303(e).

Thus, a properly recorded statement of dissociation provides, immediately upon recording, constructive knowledge of the lack of authority of a person dissociated as a partner to transfer real property held in the partnership name.

Subsection (a)(1)—It is the statutory apparent authority from Section 301 which lingers.

Subsection (a)(2)(A)—In any event, any lingering apparent authority ends two years after the dissociation.

Subsection **(a)(2)(B)**—A person might have notice under Section 103(d)(2)(A) (statement of dissociation) as well as under Section 103(b)(1) (person "ha[ving] reason to know the fact from all the facts known to the person at the time in question").

Subsection **(b)**—The liability stated in this subsection is not exhaustive. For example, if a person dissociated as a partner causes a partnership to be bound under Subsection (a) and, due to a guaranty, some other person—not a partner nor a person dissociated as a partner—is liable on the resulting obligation, that other person may have a claim under other law against the person dissociated as a partner.

§ 703. Liability of Person Dissociated as Partner to Other Persons

(a) Except as otherwise provided in subsection (b), a person dissociated as a partner is not liable for a partnership obligation incurred after dissociation.

(b) A person that is dissociated as a partner is liable on a transaction entered into by the partnership after the dissociation only if:

    (1) a partner would be liable on the transaction; and

    (2) at the time the other party enters into the transaction:

        (A) less than two years has passed since the dissociation; and

        (B) the other party does not have knowledge or notice of the dissociation and reasonably believes that the person is a partner.

(c) By agreement with a creditor of a partnership and the partnership, a person dissociated as a partner may be released from liability for a debt, obligation, or other liability of the partnership.

(d) A person dissociated as a partner is released from liability for a debt, obligation, or other liability of the partnership if the partnership's creditor, with knowledge or notice of the person's dissociation but without the person's consent, agrees to a material alteration in the nature or time of payment of the debt, obligation, or other liability.

COMMENT

To the extent a partnership has been a limited liability partnership throughout its existence, the liability rules stated in this section are moot. *See* Subsection (b)(1).

This section parallels Section 805.

Subsection **(a)**—As stated in Section 306(b), comment and 306(c), comment, other law determines when a partnership obligation is "incurred."

Subsection **(b)**—The rule stated here for the "lingering liability" of a person dissociated a partner parallels the rule stated in Section 702 for the lingering apparent authority of a person dissociated as a partner.

Subsection **(b)(2)(A)**—In any event, the lingering liability ends two years after the dissociation.

Subsection **(b)(2)(B)**—A person might have notice under Section 103(d)(2)(A) (statement of dissociation) as well as under Section 103(b)(1) (person "ha[ving] reason to know the fact from all the facts known to the person at the time in question").

Subsections **(c) and (d)**—These provisions trace back to UPA (1914) § 36(2), (3).

§ 704. Statement of Dissociation

(a) A person dissociated as a partner or the partnership may deliver to the [Secretary of State] for filing a statement of dissociation stating the name of the partnership and that the person has dissociated from the partnership.

(b) A statement of dissociation is a limitation on the authority of a person dissociated as a partner for the purposes of Section 303.

COMMENT

A partnership and a person dissociated as a partner each have the right (but not an obligation) to deliver to the filing office a statement of dissociation, and each has an incentive to do so. *See* Sections 702(a)(2)(B) (extinguishing the lingering apparent authority of a person dissociated as a partner as to any party that has notice of the dissociation), 703(b)(2)(B) (extinguishing the lingering liability of a person dissociated as a partner as to any party that has notice of the dissociation).

This section originated as UPA (1997) § 704 and was unchanged by the Harmonization Project.

Subsection (a)—"A person not a partner is deemed . . . to have notice of a person's dissociation as a partner 90 days after a statement of dissociation under Section 704 becomes effective." Section 103(d)(2)(A). This constructive notice ends both the lingering apparent authority and lingering liability exposure of the person dissociated as a partner. *See* Sections 702(a)(2)(B), 703(b)(2)(B).

Subsection (b)—This subsection interrelates a statement of dissociation with the act's intricate section on statements of authority. *See* Section 303.

§ 705. Continued Use of Partnership Name

Continued use of a partnership name, or the name of a person dissociated as a partner as part of the partnership name, by partners continuing the business does not of itself make the person dissociated as a partner liable for an obligation of the partners or the partnership continuing the business.

COMMENT

Section 705 originated in UPA (1997) and is an edited version of UPA (1914) § 41(10). The section merely protects a person dissociated as a person from liability in case the partnership continues to use the person's name. Whether a partnership has a right to the continued use is a matter for the partnership agreement; this act states no rule on the subject.

If the partnership agreement does not expressly address the issue, custom may imply a term. *See Gignilliat v. Gignilliat, Savitz & Bettis, L.L.P.*, 684 S.E.2d 756, 762, n.6 (S.C. 2009) ("This Court takes judicial notice of the custom and practice in this state of law firms continuing to use the names of deceased members in their firm names. Heretofore, the basis has been the taking for granted that the deceased partner would consent. Hereafter, it is presumed, unless proven otherwise, that the deceased partner consented to the continued use of his or her name in the partnership's name.").

[ARTICLE] 8. DISSOLUTION AND WINDING UP

§ 801. Events Causing Dissolution

A partnership is dissolved, and its business must be wound up, upon the occurrence of any of the following:

(1) in a partnership at will, the partnership knows or has notice of a person's express will to withdraw as a partner, other than a partner that has dissociated under Section 601(2) through (10), but, if the person has specified a withdrawal date later than the date the partnership knew or had notice, on the later date;

(2) in a partnership for a definite term or particular undertaking:

(A) within 90 days after a person's dissociation by death or otherwise under Section 601(6) through (10) or wrongful dissociation under Section 602(b), the affirmative vote or consent of at least half of the remaining partners to wind up the partnership business, for which purpose a person's rightful dissociation pursuant to Section 602(b)(2)(A) constitutes that partner's consent to wind up the partnership business;

(B) the affirmative vote or consent of all the partners to wind up the partnership business; or

(C) the expiration of the term or the completion of the undertaking;

(3) an event or circumstance that the partnership agreement states causes dissolution;

(4) on application by a partner, the entry by [the appropriate court] of an order dissolving the partnership on the grounds that:

(A)   the conduct of all or substantially all the partnership's business is unlawful;

(B)   the economic purpose of the partnership is likely to be unreasonably frustrated;

(C)   another partner has engaged in conduct relating to the partnership business which makes it not reasonably practicable to carry on the business in partnership with that partner; or

(D)   it is otherwise not reasonably practicable to carry on the partnership business in conformity with the partnership agreement;

(5)   on application by a transferee, the entry by [the appropriate court] of an order dissolving the partnership on the ground that it is equitable to wind up the partnership business:

(A)   after the expiration of the term or completion of the undertaking, if the partnership was for a definite term or particular undertaking at the time of the transfer or entry of the charging order that gave rise to the transfer; or

(B)   at any time, if the partnership was a partnership at will at the time of the transfer or entry of the charging order that gave rise to the transfer; or

(6)   the passage of 90 consecutive days during which the partnership does not have at least two partners.

COMMENT

"Dissolution" has been a term of art in the law of unincorporated business organizations since at least the time of Roman law. JOSEPH STORY, COMMENTARIES ON THE LAW OF PARTNERSHIP § 266, at 408 (2d ed. 1850) ("The Roman law . . . declared, that partnership might be dissolved in various ways . . . ."). Dissolution does not end a partnership's existence but rather changes the purpose of that existence: "A dissolved partnership shall wind up its business and . . . the partnership continues after dissolution only for the purpose of winding up." Section 802(a). The partnership may, but need not, file a statement of dissolution. Section 802(b)(2)(A). The partnership terminates when winding up is complete. The partnership may, but need not, file a statement of termination. Section 802(b)(2)(F).

UPA (1914) took a strictly aggregate approach to dissolution; under UPA (1914) § 29, the departure of any partner under any circumstances inevitably caused the partnership to dissolve. A partnership agreement had no power to avoid this result, although many partnership agreements purported to do so. A partnership agreement could provide for the continuation of the partnership business in a successor partnership, UPA (1914) § 38(2)(b), but that approach was often problematic. *See* the comment to Section 201(a).

UPA (1997) fundamentally changed this aspect of the law of general partnerships, making the partnership entity much more durable than the UPA (1914) aggregate. For example, expelling a partner does not cause the partnership to dissolve, even if the partnership is at-will. Section 801(1). More generally, the grounds for dissolution stated in Section 801 are exhaustive, unless the partnership agreement states otherwise.

Given this act's built-in transfer restrictions, Section 503, increasing the partnership's durability necessarily decreases each partner's exit rights. Under UPA (1914), each partner has a non-waivable power to exit the enterprise; dissociation inevitably causes dissolution, which in most instances will lead to a buyout of the dissociating partner, subject to any damages for wrongful dissolution. UPA (1914) § 38. Eliminating that power creates a risk of "lock-in."

UPA (1997) addressed the lock-in issue through UPA (1997) § 701. When a person dissociates as a partner, whether rightfully or wrongfully, the partnership is obligated to buy out the person's interest. Note, however, that Section 701, like UPA (1997) § 701, is a default rule.

Except for Paragraphs 4 and 5, this section comprises default rules. Paragraphs 4 and 5 are mandatory only with regard to the stated grounds for dissolution. *See* the comment to Section 105(c)(11). Variations to the statutory causes of dissolution are commonplace.

Section 803 permits rescission of dissolution in some circumstances. In some circumstances, an amendment to the partnership agreement might avert dissolution—*e.g.*, by revising an agreed-upon deadline for selling the partnership assets and winding up the business. A retroactive amendment may also be possible. *See Kindred Ltd. P'ship v. Screen Actors Guild, Inc.*, CV082220PSGPJWX, 2009 WL 279080, at *5–6 (C.D. Cal. Feb. 3, 2009) (giving effect to an amendment that retroactively eliminated an event of dissolution; noting that UPA (1997) § 802(b) permitted a partnership to rescind dissolution).

The Harmonization Project added Paragraph 6 but otherwise made no significant changes to this section.

Paragraph (1)—This paragraph: (i) recognizes the power of any partner in a partnership at will to dissolve the partnership at any time "by express will"; and (ii) provides that a partner who has already been dissociated under some other provision of this section lacks the power to dissolve the partnership. The latter proposition seems self-evident; a person dissociated as a partner is no longer a partner.

Paragraph (2)—This paragraph provides three ways in which a term partnership may be dissolved before the expiration of the term.

Paragraph (2)(A)—This provision: (i) originated in UPA (1997); (ii) helps make the partnership entity more durable; (iii) protects the remaining partners where the dissociating partner is crucial to the successful continuation of the business; and (iv) reverses the approach of UPA (1914).

Under UPA (1914), any dissociation dissolves the partnership, and unanimous consent of the remaining partners to continue the business. Thus each partner has the right to cause liquidation. *See* UPA (1914) § 38(2)(b). Under this act, a term partnership is more durable.

A person's dissociation as a partner by death or otherwise under Section 601(6) to (10) or wrongful dissociation under Section 602(b), makes a term partnership *susceptible* to dissolution. If within ninety days after the dissociation at least half of the remaining partners express their will to dissolve the partnership, the partnership dissolves. Section 601(6) to (10) pertain, respectively, to a partner's bankruptcy or similar financial impairment (6); a partner's death or incapacity (7); the distribution by a trust-partner of its entire transferable interest (8); the distribution by an estate-partner of its entire transferable interest; and the termination of an entity-partner (10).

During the same ninety-day window, Section 602(b)(2)(A) permits each remaining partner to withdraw rightfully by express will. A partner does not express a desire to withdraw solely by reason of voting for or consenting to the winding up of the partnership business. However, the converse is true: "[A] person's rightful dissociation pursuant to Section 602(b)(2)(A) constitutes the expression of that partner's consent to wind up the partnership business." Section 801(2)(A).

Example: A term partnership has seven partners, and one of the partners dissociates by dying before the end of the term. Section 601(7). The partnership will dissolve if within ninety days after the dissociation three of the remaining five partners affirmatively vote or consent to dissolution.

Example: Same facts, except the partner dissociates in breach of the partnership agreement. Same result.

Example: Same facts, except that the partner is "a person that . . . is acting as a partner by virtue of being a trustee of . . . a trust, [and] the trust's entire transferable interest in the partnership [has been] distributed. Section 601(8). Same result.

Paragraph (2)(B)—This provision states that a term partnership may be dissolved and wound up at any time by the express will of all the partners. The provision merely reflects the general rule that the partnership agreement may override the statutory default rules and that the partnership agreement, like any contract, can be amended at any time by unanimous consent.

Paragraph (2)(C)—This rule is inherent in the concept of a partnership for a specified term or undertaking. This provision must be read in conjunction with Section 411. Under Section 411(a), if the partners continue the business after the expiration of the term or the completion of the undertaking, the partnership will be treated as a partnership at will. Moreover, if the partners continue the business without any settlement or liquidation of the partnership, under Section 411(b) they are presumed to have agreed that the partnership will continue, despite the lack of a formal agreement.

Paragraph (3)—The partners can avoid the effects of this paragraph either by amending the partnership agreement before dissolution occurs or using Section 803 to rescind dissolution. A retroactive amendment may also be possible. *See Kindred Ltd. P'ship v. Screen Actors Guild, Inc.*, CV082220PSGPJWX, 2009 WL 279080, at *5–6 (C.D. Cal. Feb. 3, 2009) (giving effect to an amendment that retroactively eliminated an event of dissolution; noting that UPA (1997) § 802(b) permitted a partnership to rescind dissolution).

Paragraph (4)—The partnership agreement cannot vary the stated grounds for dissolution.

Paragraph (4)(A)—The "all or substantially all" proviso is intended to avoid dissolution for insubstantial or innocent regulatory violations.

Paragraph (4)(B)–(D)—The Virginia Supreme Court has referred to "these statutory bases for judicial dissolution as the economic purpose test, the partner conduct test, and the business operations test, respectively." *Russell Realty Assocs. v. Russell*, 724 S.E.2d 690, 693 (Va. 2012). These tests somewhat overlap and are often pled together. *E.g., Wood v. Apodaca,* 375 F. Supp. 2d 942, 948 (N.D. Cal. 2005).

Some courts have held that, if the trial court finds grounds for dissolution under one or more of these provisions, that court has no power to order a lesser remedy, such as a buyout. *Pankratz Farms, Inc. v. Pankratz*, 95 P.3d 671, 679–80 (Mont. 2004) (so holding even though: (i) "judicial dissolution of the Partnership would trigger significant adverse tax consequences to all the parties involved, including Marvin [who commenced the action seeking dissolution"; and (ii) "Marvin [had] requested monetary damages as an alternative to dissolution"); *Navarro v. Perron*, 122 Cal. App. 4th 797, 801, 19 Cal. Rptr. 3d 198, 201 (2004) ("Where the court determines it is not reasonably practical to carry on the partnership, the court has no discretion to deny a partner's application to dissolve it.").

Paragraph (4)(B)—"[P]oor financial performance" is neither sufficient nor necessary to satisfy this provision. *Russell Realty Assocs. v. Russell*, 724 S.E.2d 690, 694 (Va. 2012). The provision's history substantiates the first point (not by itself sufficient). *See* UPA (1997) § 801, cmt. 8 ("RUPA deletes UPA Section 32(1)(e) which provides for dissolution when the business can only be carried on at a loss. That provision might result in a dissolution contrary to the partners' expectations in a start-up or tax shelter situation, in which case 'book' or 'tax' losses do not signify business failure.").

As for the second point (not always necessary), see *Russell Realty Assocs. v. Russell*, 724 S.E.2d 690, 694–55 (Va. 2012) (noting that the partnership's purpose was "to acquire, hold, invest in, and lease and sell investment properties"; stating with regard to the Virginia analog to Paragraph 4(B) that "[t]he partners' expectations for realizing these purposes included not only expectations of economic success, but also the ability to undertake these activities in an efficient and productive manner to maximize return to the partnership"; and listing numerous ways in which the relationship between the partners frustrated the economic purpose of the partnership).

Paragraph (4)(C)—A partner can trigger this provision without necessarily breaching the partnership agreement. *E.g., Robertson v. Jacobs Cattle Co.*, 830 N.W.2d 191, 202 (Neb. 2013) (stating that "the somewhat autocratic manner in which Ardith conducted the affairs of the partnership in recent years, even if not in violation of the partnership agreement, would constitute grounds for dissolution under [the UPA (1997) version of] this provision").

Paragraph (4)(D)—The specific terms of the partnership agreement are the frame of reference for applying this provision. *Sriram v. Preferred Income Fund III Ltd. P'ship*, 22 F.3d 498, 502 (2d Cir. 1994) ("The issue is not whether the partnerships can effectively carry out the general purpose of the Agreements after considerable modification of their terms. Rather, the query . . . is whether the purpose of the Agreements can be carried out 'in conformity with the partnership agreement,' that is, in conformity with the terms and conditions of the Agreements to which the limited partners ascribed and on which they relied when choosing to part with their capital.") (applying the provision of RULPA (1976/1985) that is analogous to Paragraph (4)(C)).

Paragraph (5)—This paragraph gives a transferee rights comparable to a partner who seeks dissolution because the other partners are continuing the business in derogation of the partner's rights to obtain dissolution. The paragraph is based on UPA (1914) § 32(2) but UPA (1997) added the requirement that the court determine that it is equitable to wind up the business. The rights of a transferee under this section cannot be varied in the partnership agreement. *See* Section 105(c)(11). Neither ULPA (2001) (Last Amended 2013) nor ULLCA (2006) (Last Amended 2013) have a comparable provision, because both those acts provide for perpetual existence. *See* ULPA (2001) (Last Amended 2013) § 110 and ULLCA (2006) (Last Amended 2013) § 108.

Paragraph (6)—The Harmonization Project added this provision, which is consistent with Section 202(a) (stating that "the association of two or more persons to carry on as co-owners a business for profit forms a partnership"). *See* the comment to Section 302(d); *Pemstein v. Pemstein*, G030217, 2004 WL 1260034 (Cal. Ct. App. June 9, 2004) (" 'Can one person carry on a partnership?' In short, the answer is no . . . . Just as it takes two to form a marriage, it takes a minimum of two to run a viable partnership. We were unable to find any contrary authority, and appellants fail to provide any, holding a partnership can be carried on by less than two persons.")

§ 802.   Winding Up

(a)   A dissolved partnership shall wind up its business and, except as otherwise provided in Section 803, the partnership continues after dissolution only for the purpose of winding up.

this will be termination

(b)   In winding up its business, the partnership:

(1)   shall discharge the partnership's debts, obligations, and other liabilities, [settle and close the partnership's business,] and marshal and distribute the assets of the partnership; and

(2)   may:

(A)   deliver to the [Secretary of State] for filing a statement of dissolution stating the name of the partnership and that the partnership is dissolved;

(B)   preserve the partnership business and property as a going concern for a reasonable time;

(C)   prosecute and defend actions and proceedings, whether civil, criminal, or administrative;

(D)   transfer the partnership's property;

(E)   settle disputes by mediation or arbitration;

(F)   deliver to the [Secretary of State] for filing a statement of termination stating the name of the partnership and that the partnership is terminated; and

(G)   perform other acts necessary or appropriate to the winding up.

(c)   A person whose dissociation as a partner resulted in dissolution may participate in winding up as if still a partner, unless the dissociation was wrongful.

(d)   If a dissolved partnership does not have a partner and no person has the right to participate in winding up under subsection (c), the personal or legal representative of the last person to have been a partner may wind up the partnership's business. If the representative does not exercise that right, a person to wind up the partnership's business may be appointed by the affirmative vote or consent of transferees owning a majority of the rights to receive distributions at the time the consent is to be effective. A person appointed under this subsection has the powers of a partner under Section 804 but is not liable for the debts, obligations, and other liabilities of the partnership solely by reason of having or exercising those powers or otherwise acting to wind up the partnership's business.

(e)   On the application of any partner or person entitled under subsection (c) to participate in winding up, the [appropriate court] may order judicial supervision of the winding up of a dissolved partnership, including the appointment of a person to wind up the partnership's business, if:

(1)   the partnership does not have a partner and within a reasonable time following the dissolution no person has been appointed under subsection (d); or

(2)   the applicant establishes other good cause.

COMMENT

Under the default rules of this act, dissolution does not change governance arrangements. However, dissolution does change the context for determining whether a matter is in or outside "the ordinary course of business of [the] partnership." Section 401(k). In addition, dissolution triggers a default rule entitling each partner to "reasonable compensation for services rendered in winding up the business of the partnership." Section 401(j).

Section 804 governs the post-dissolution power of a partner to bind the partnership, and Section 805 governs the "liability after dissolution of partner and person dissociated as general partner."

Subsection (a)—For more information on the impact of a partnership's dissolution, see Section 801, comment.

Subsection (b)—The particular circumstances determine how long winding up may continue without giving "good cause" for court intervention under Section 802(e). There is no "hard and fast" rule. *See, e.g., Mathis v. Meyeres*, 574 P.2d 447, 450 (Alaska 1978) (stating "we are aware of [no authority] requiring that deadlines be set in the winding up of a partnership"); *8182 Md. Assocs., Ltd. P'ship v. Sheehan*, 14 S.W.3d 576, 581 (Mo. 2000) ("The Uniform Partnership Law contemplates that dissolved partnerships may continue in business for a short, long or indefinite period of time.") (quoting *Schoeller v. Schoeller*, 497 S.W.2d 860, 867 (Mo. Ct. App. 1973)).

"Winding up usually entails the time necessary for the partners to finish old business, collect and pay debts, and finally distribute remaining assets to the partners." *Gibson v. Deuth*, 270 N.W.2d 632, 635 (Iowa 1978). "Generally the best interests of the partnership will be served by winding up the partnership affairs as quickly as possible." *Doting v. Trunk*, 856 P.2d 536, 540 (Mont. 1993). However, in some circumstances, a long period of winding up is not only appropriate but necessary. *Lebanon Trotting Ass'n v. Battista*, 306 N.E.2d 769, 772 (Ohio Ct. App. 1972) ("[I]f the only means of availing the partners of the benefit of the value of the lease would be to continue to operate under such lease until its expiration, then such operation may continue as part of the winding up of the partnership affairs after dissolution. It is not necessary that a partnership, in the absence of the consent of all the partners, abandon a valuable asset upon dissolution merely because it may have no ready market value, but the value of such asset can continue to inure to the benefit of the partners through the continuation of the partnership after dissolution.").

Subsection (b)(2)(A) and (F)—For the constructive notice effect of a statement of dissolution or termination, see Sections 103(d)(2)(A) and (B) and 303.

Subsection (c)—This provision applies only to "[a] partner whose [rightful] dissociation resulted in dissolution."

> **Example:** Partner A dissociates from the Killarney Company ("Killarney"), a general partnership. Partner A's dissociation does not result in dissolution, and, per the Killarney partnership agreement, Partner A's transferable interest is being redeemed over five years. One year after Partner A's dissociation, Partner B dissociates rightfully, and dissolution results. Partner B may participate in Killarney's winding up; Partner A may not.

> **Example:** Partner A wrongfully dissociates from Killarney, and the dissociation results in the dissolution of Killarney. Partner A may not participate in winding up.

A partner's duties and obligation under Section 409 extend to winding up. Section 603(b)(2). However, under Section 409(b)(3), each partner's duty not to compete ends when the partnership dissolves.

Subsection (d)—A person appointed under this section will normally be an agent of the dissolved partnership, acting pursuant to a contract. Agency and contract law will determine the person's duties; by its terms Section 409 does not apply.

§ 803. Rescinding Dissolution

(a) A partnership may rescind its dissolution, unless a statement of termination applicable to the partnership has become effective or [the appropriate court] has entered an order under Section 801(4) or (5) dissolving the partnership.

(b) Rescinding dissolution under this section requires:

    (1) the affirmative vote or consent of each partner; and

    (2) if the partnership has delivered to the [Secretary of State] for filing a statement of dissolution and:

        (A) the statement has not become effective, delivery to the [Secretary of State] for filing of a statement of withdrawal under Section 115 applicable to the statement of dissolution; or

        (B) the statement of dissolution has become effective, delivery to the [Secretary of State] for filing of a statement of rescission stating the name of the partnership and that dissolution has been rescinded under this section.

(c) If a partnership rescinds its dissolution:

    (1) the partnership resumes carrying on its business as if dissolution had never occurred;

    (2) subject to paragraph (3), any liability incurred by the partnership after the dissolution and before the rescission has become effective is determined as if dissolution had never occurred; and

    (3) the rights of a third party arising out of conduct in reliance on the dissolution before the third party knew or had notice of the rescission may not be adversely affected.

COMMENT

The Harmonization Project added this section, replacing UPA (1997) § 802(b) (permitting the partners to "waive the right to have the partnership's business wound up and the partnership terminated" after which "the partnership resumes carrying on its business as if dissolution had never occurred").

Subsection (a)—The first exclusion results inevitably from the effect of a statement of termination, Section 802(b)(2)(F)—*i.e.*, the partnership ceases to exist. A "dead" entity lacks both the capacity and power to bring itself back from the dead.

The second and third exclusions pertain to dissolutions effected by outsiders—*i.e.*, the court and the filing office.

Subsections (b)(1)—The requirement of unanimous consent protects any vested rights or reliance by partners. However, the partnership agreement may vary this provision.

Subsection (c)(3)—This paragraph protects third parties. *E.g.*, *Neurobehavorial Associates, P.A. v. Cypress Creek Hosp., Inc.*, 995 S.W.2d 326, 331 (Tex. App. 1999) ("If the Hospital had the right to terminate the Agreement when it did because the Association was then dissolved, then even though the Association can revoke articles of dissolution and have that relate back to the date of dissolution, it would be grossly unfair to let the Association assert its ex post facto change as a defense. Surely the Association would be estopped from doing so, having created the very conditions that gave the Hospital the correct impression that it was then dissolved.").

§ 804. Power to Bind Partnership After Dissolution

(a)   A partnership is bound by a partner's act after dissolution which:

    (1)   is appropriate for winding up the partnership business; or

    (2)   would have bound the partnership under Section 301 before dissolution if, at the time the other party enters into the transaction, the other party does not know or have notice of the dissolution.

(b)   A person dissociated as a partner binds a partnership through an act occurring after dissolution if:

    (1)   at the time the other party enters into the transaction:

        (A)   less than two years has passed since the dissociation; and

        (B)   the other party does not know or have notice of the dissociation and reasonably believes that the person is a partner; and

    (2)   the act:

        (A)   is appropriate for winding up the partnership's business; or

        (B)   would have bound the partnership under Section 301 before dissolution and at the time the other party enters into the transaction the other party does not know or have notice of the dissolution.

COMMENT

This section provides the "power to bind" rules applicable once dissolution occurs. The section originated in UPA (1997), which significantly departed from the approach of UPA (1914). The Harmonization Project revised this section to conform to ULPA (2001). However, the revisions are essentially stylistic.

In general, this section parallels Section 702 (power to bind of a person dissociated as partner when dissolution does not result from the dissociation). However, one significant difference exists. Section 702(a)(2)(A) contains a provision analogous to a statute of repose. A person's power to bind the partnership terminates two years after the date of dissociation. Subsection (b) contains a comparable provision, but Subsection (a) does not.

Subsections (a) and (b)—Subsection (a) states the power-to-bind rules for persons still partners when dissolution occurs. Subsection (b) pertains to persons dissociated before dissolution, including a partner whose dissociation results in dissolution. *Compare* Section 804, *with* Section 802(c) (stating that as an *inter se* matter a person whose rightful dissociation results in dissolution may participate in winding up "as if still a partner.").

Subsection (a)(1)—This paragraph states a rule of inherent agency power. *See* RESTATEMENT (SECOND) OF AGENCY § 8A (defining "inherent agency power" as "the power of an agent which is derived not from authority, apparent authority or estoppel, but solely from the agency relation and exists for the protection of persons harmed by or dealing with a servant or other agent"). Thus, a partner might act without actual or apparent authority and still bind the partnership. The partnership agreement cannot change the stated rule because the rule pertains to the rights under this act of third parties. *See* Section 105(c)(17).

If a partner's words or conduct trigger this paragraph, thereby binding the partnership, and the partner lacks the actual authority to do so, the partner breaches an agent's duty to act within authority, and is liable to the partnership for any resulting damages. RESTATEMENT (THIRD) OF AGENCY § 8.09(1) ("An agent has a duty to take action only within the scope of the agent's actual authority"). The partner might also be liable for breach of the partnership agreement.

Subsection (a)(2)—A person might have notice under Section 103(d)(2)(B)(i) (statement of dissolution) as well as under Section 103(b)(1) (reason to know).

Subsection (b)—This subsection deals with the post-dissolution power to bind of a person dissociated as a partner. For the most part: (i) Paragraph 1 replicates Section 702, pertaining to the pre-dissolution power to bind of a person dissociated as a partner; and (ii) Paragraph 2 replicates Subsection (a) of this section, which states the post-dissolution power to bind of a person is still a partner.

For a person dissociated as a partner to bind a dissolved partnership:

- the person's dissociation must have:
  - been rightful; and
  - resulted in dissolution; and
- the person's act must satisfy both Paragraphs 1 and 2.

Subsection (b)(1)(B)—A person might have notice under Section 103(d)(2)(B)(i) (statement of dissolution) as well as under Section 103(b)(1) (reason to know).

Subsection (b)(2)(B)—A person might have notice under Section 103(d)(2)(B)(i) (statement of dissolution) as well as under Section 103(b)(1) (reason to know).

§ 805. Liability After Dissolution of Partner and Person Dissociated as Partner

(a) If a partner having knowledge of the dissolution causes a partnership to incur an obligation under Section 804(a) by an act that is not appropriate for winding up the partnership business, the partner is liable:

(1) to the partnership for any damage caused to the partnership arising from the obligation; and

(2) if another partner or person dissociated as a partner is liable for the obligation, to that other partner or person for any damage caused to that other partner or person arising from the liability.

(b) Except as otherwise provided in subsection (c), if a person dissociated as a partner causes a partnership to incur an obligation under Section 804(b), the person is liable:

(1) to the partnership for any damage caused to the partnership arising from the obligation; and

(2) if a partner or another person dissociated as a partner is liable for the obligation, to the partner or other person for any damage caused to the partner or other person arising from the obligation.

(c) A person dissociated as a partner is not liable under subsection (b) if:

(1) Section 802(c) permits the person to participate in winding up; and

(2) the act that causes the partnership to be bound under Section 804(b) is appropriate for winding up the partnership's business.

COMMENT

This section parallels Section 702. It is possible for more than one person to be liable under this section on account of the same partnership obligation. This act does not provide any rule for apportioning liability in that circumstance.

Subsection (a)(2)—If the partnership is not a limited liability partnership, the liability created by this paragraph includes liability under Sections 306(a) and 703(b). The paragraph also applies when a partner or person dissociated as a general partner suffers damage due to a contract of guaranty.

Other law determines liability (if any) to a person that is neither a partner nor dissociated as a partner.

§ 806.   Disposition of Assets in Winding Up; When Contributions Required

(a)   In winding up its business, a partnership shall apply its assets, including the contributions required by this section, to discharge the partnership's obligations to creditors, including partners that are creditors.

(b)   After a partnership complies with subsection (a), any surplus must be distributed in the following order, subject to any charging order in effect under Section 504:

(1)   to each person owning a transferable interest that reflects contributions made and not previously returned, an amount equal to the value of the unreturned contributions; and

(2)   among persons owning transferable interests in proportion to their respective rights to share in distributions immediately before the dissolution of the partnership.

(c)   If a partnership's assets are insufficient to satisfy all its obligations under subsection (a), with respect to each unsatisfied obligation incurred when the partnership was not a limited liability partnership, the following rules apply:

(1)   Each person that was a partner when the obligation was incurred and that has not been released from the obligation under Section 703(c) and (d) shall contribute to the partnership for the purpose of enabling the partnership to satisfy the obligation. The contribution due from each of those persons is in proportion to the right to receive distributions in the capacity of a partner in effect for each of those persons when the obligation was incurred.

(2)   If a person does not contribute the full amount required under paragraph (1) with respect to an unsatisfied obligation of the partnership, the other persons required to contribute by paragraph (1) on account of the obligation shall contribute the additional amount necessary to discharge the obligation. The additional contribution due from each of those other persons is in proportion to the right to receive distributions in the capacity of a partner in effect for each of those other persons when the obligation was incurred.

(3)   If a person does not make the additional contribution required by paragraph (2), further additional contributions are determined and due in the same manner as provided in that paragraph.

(d)   A person that makes an additional contribution under subsection (c)(2) or (3) may recover from any person whose failure to contribute under subsection (c)(1) or (2) necessitated the additional contribution. A person may not recover under this subsection more than the amount additionally contributed. A person's liability under this subsection may not exceed the amount the person failed to contribute.

(e)   If a partnership does not have sufficient surplus to comply with subsection (b)(1), any surplus must be distributed among the owners of transferable interests in proportion to the value of the respective unreturned contributions.

(f)   All distributions made under subsections (b) and (c) must be paid in money.

COMMENT

Subsection (a)—This subsection is non-waivable as to creditors who are not partners. *See* Section 105(c)(17) (stating that the partnership agreement may not "restrict the rights under this [act] of a person other than a partner "). However, if a creditor is willing, a dissolved partnership may certainly make agreements with the creditor specifying the terms under which the partnership will "discharge its obligations" to the creditor. If under

Section 306(a) one or more partners are also liable on a partnership obligation, any agreement between the partnership and the creditor should take in account Section 703(d).

Subsection (b)—For the most part, this subsection states default rules. For example, partnership agreements often provide for different distribution rights upon liquidation than during operations. However, distributions under this subsection (or otherwise under the partnership agreement) are subject to Section 504 (charging orders). As to the extent the partnership agreement can be amended to affect the distribution rights of persons already transferees, see Section 107(b).

Subsection (c)—This section applies obligation by obligation, because a person—*qua* partner or person dissociated as a partner—is required to contribute to the partnership to satisfy a partnership obligation only if, when the obligation was incurred: (i) the person was a partner; and (ii) the partnership was not an LLP. *See* Section 306(b), (c). As for when a partnership obligation is incurred, see Section 306(b) and (c), comments.

The allocation of contribution obligations parallels the default rule stated in Section 401(a) (providing that, "except in the case of a limited liability partnership, [each partner] is chargeable with a share of the partnership losses in proportion to the partner's share of the profits"). The partnership agreement can change the allocation *inter se* partners and persons dissociated as partners but cannot prejudice the rights of non-partner creditors.

Example: The A-B Partnership (the "Partnership") owes Creditor $150, an obligation incurred when Partners A and B were the only partners, sharing distributions equally, and the Partnership was not an LLP. The Partnership has no funds to pay Creditor. Although Subsection (c)(1) would require Partners A and B each to contribute equally (*i.e.*, $75), the A-B Partnership Agreement provides that Partner A has the entire contribution obligation and Partner B has none. As between Partners A and B, Partner A is obligated to contribute $150 and Partner B nothing. However, as to Creditor, Partner B still has a contribution obligation of $75.

This formal distinction will have practical consequences only if A does not contribute the full $150. Also, Creditor may have problems establishing standing. *Cf.* the comment to Section 407.

Subsection (c)(2) and (3)—These provisions are analogous to buy-sell provisions that: (i) provide that an owner's effort to sell the ownership interest triggers an option to purchase allocated among all the other owners; (ii) make the option conditional on the entire interest being purchased; and (iii) provide for successive allocations to take up any previous allocations that were not unexercised.

Subsection (e)—If a partnership has been a limited liability partnership throughout the partnership's existence, this subsection is consistent with this act's approach to loss sharing. If a partnership has been a limited liability partnership during only part of the partnership's existence, the issue of loss sharing upon dissolution: (i) can be exceedingly complicated, varying radically depending on the circumstances; (ii) is therefore not amenable to a statutory "gap filler"; and (iii) thus should always be addressed in the partnership agreement.

However, in case the partnership agreement does not address the issue, this act must provide a default rule. *See* the comment to Section 105(b) ("To the extent the partnership agreement does not determine an inter se matter, this act determines the matter."). This subsection applies to fill the gap. This approach has the virtues of simplicity and certainty but in no way resembles what "typical" partners might agree if they were to consider the matter *ab initio*, especially if the partnership was never an LLP. *Cf.* Robert W. Hillman, *Private Ordering Within Partnerships*, 41 U. MIAMI L. REV. 425, 448 (1987) ("[T]he various norms established by the Act, applicable in the absence of agreements to the contrary, represent the supposed understandings partners most likely reach if they choose to bargain on the various issues.").

§ 807.   Known Claims Against Dissolved Limited Liability Partnership

(a)   Except as otherwise provided in subsection (d), a dissolved limited liability partnership may give notice of a known claim under subsection (b), which has the effect provided in subsection (c).

(b)   A dissolved limited liability partnership may in a record notify its known claimants of the dissolution. The notice must:

     (1)   specify the information required to be included in a claim;

     (2)   state that a claim must be in writing and provide a mailing address to which the claim is to be sent;

     (3)   state the deadline for receipt of a claim, which may not be less than 120 days after the date the notice is received by the claimant;

(4) state that the claim will be barred if not received by the deadline; and

(5) unless the partnership has been throughout its existence a limited liability partnership, state that the barring of a claim against the partnership will also bar any corresponding claim against any partner or person dissociated as a partner which is based on Section 306.

(c) A claim against a dissolved limited liability partnership is barred if the requirements of subsection (b) are met and:

(1) the claim is not received by the specified deadline; or

(2) if the claim is timely received but rejected by the limited liability partnership:

(A) the partnership causes the claimant to receive a notice in a record stating that the claim is rejected and will be barred unless the claimant commences an action against the partnership to enforce the claim not later than 90 days after the claimant receives the notice; and

(B) the claimant does not commence the required action not later than 90 days after the claimant receives the notice.

(d) This section does not apply to a claim based on an event occurring after the date of dissolution or a liability that on that date is contingent.

COMMENT

Source—Added during the Harmonization Project, this section is derived almost verbatim from Model Business Corporation Act section 14.06.

Subsection (b)(5)—For additional information on when a claim against a partnership is barred, see Section 810, comment.

§ 808. Other Claims Against Dissolved Limited Liability Partnership

(a) A dissolved limited liability partnership may publish notice of its dissolution and request persons having claims against the partnership to present them in accordance with the notice.

(b) A notice under subsection (a) must:

(1) be published at least once in a newspaper of general circulation in the [county] in this state in which the dissolved limited liability partnership's principal office is located or, if the principal office is not located in this state, in the [county] in which the office of the partnership's registered agent is or was last located;

(2) describe the information required to be contained in a claim, state that the claim must be in writing, and provide a mailing address to which the claim is to be sent;

(3) state that a claim against the partnership is barred unless an action to enforce the claim is commenced not later than three years after publication of the notice; and

(4) unless the partnership has been throughout its existence a limited liability partnership, state that the barring of a claim against the partnership will also bar any corresponding claim against any partner or person dissociated as a partner which is based on Section 306.

(c) If a dissolved limited liability partnership publishes a notice in accordance with subsection (b), the claim of each of the following claimants is barred unless the claimant commences an action to enforce the claim against the partnership not later than three years after the publication date of the notice:

(1) a claimant that did not receive notice in a record under Section 807;

(2) a claimant whose claim was timely sent to the partnership but not acted on; and

(3) a claimant whose claim is contingent at, or based on an event occurring after, the date of dissolution.

(d) A claim not barred under this section or Section 807 may be enforced:

(1) against a dissolved limited liability partnership, to the extent of its undistributed assets;

337

(2) except as otherwise provided in Section 809, if assets of the partnership have been distributed after dissolution, against a partner or transferee to the extent of that person's proportionate share of the claim or of the partnership's assets distributed to the partner or transferee after dissolution, whichever is less, but a person's total liability for all claims under this paragraph may not exceed the total amount of assets distributed to the person after dissolution; and

(3) against any person liable on the claim under Sections 306, 703, and 805.

COMMENT

Source—Added during the Harmonization Project, this section is derived almost verbatim from Model Business Corporation Act section 14.07.

Subsection (b)(4)—For additional information on when a claim against a partnership is barred, see Section 810, comment

Subsection (d)(2)—Liability under this paragraph extends to those who have received distributions under a charging order. *See* the comment to Section 504(a) (explaining that the beneficiary of a charging order is a transferee). Unlike Section 407(c) (recapture of improper distributions), this paragraph contains no "knowledge" element.

Subsection (d)(3)—The referenced sections address the vicarious liability of partners and persons dissociated as partners for obligations of a partnership that is not an LLP.

§ 809.   Court Proceedings

(a) A dissolved limited liability partnership that has published a notice under Section 808 may file an application with [the appropriate court] in the [county] where the partnership's principal office is located or, if the principal office is not located in this state, where the office of its registered agent is or was last located, for a determination of the amount and form of security to be provided for payment of claims that are reasonably expected to arise after the date of dissolution based on facts known to the partnership and:

(1) at the time of the application:

(A) are contingent; or

(B) have not been made known to the partnership; or

(2) are based on an event occurring after the date of dissolution.

(b) Security is not required for any claim that is or is reasonably anticipated to be barred under Section 807.

(c) Not later than 10 days after the filing of an application under subsection (a), the dissolved limited liability partnership shall give notice of the proceeding to each claimant holding a contingent claim known to the partnership.

(d) In any proceeding under this section, the court may appoint a guardian ad litem to represent all claimants whose identities are unknown. The reasonable fees and expenses of the guardian, including all reasonable expert witness fees, must be paid by the dissolved limited liability partnership.

(e) A dissolved limited liability partnership that provides security in the amount and form ordered by the court under subsection (a) satisfies the partnership's obligations with respect to claims that are contingent, have not been made known to the partnership, or are based on an event occurring after the date of dissolution, and such claims may not be enforced against a partner or transferee on account of assets received in liquidation.

COMMENT

Source—Added during the Harmonization Project, this section is derived almost verbatim from Model Business Corporation Act section14.08.

§ 810. Liability of Partner and Person Dissociated as Partner When Claim Against Partnership Barred

If a claim against a dissolved partnership is barred under Section 807, 808, or 809, any corresponding claim under Section 306, 703, or 805 is also barred.

COMMENT

A partner's liability under Sections 306, 703 and 805 is vicarious liability—liability solely by status and solely for the "debts, obligations, and other liabilities of the partnership." To the extent a claim pertaining to the underlying debt, obligation, or other liability is barred, a claim pertaining to the corresponding vicarious liability should likewise be barred.

[ARTICLE] 9. LIMITED LIABILITY PARTNERSHIP

§ 901. Statement of Qualification

(a) A partnership may become a limited liability partnership pursuant to this section.

(b) The terms and conditions on which a partnership becomes a limited liability partnership must be approved by the affirmative vote or consent necessary to amend the partnership agreement except, in the case of a partnership agreement that expressly addresses obligations to contribute to the partnership, the affirmative vote or consent necessary to amend those provisions.

(c) After the approval required by subsection (b), a partnership may become a limited liability partnership by delivering to the [Secretary of State] for filing a statement of qualification. The statement must contain:

(1) the name of the partnership;

(2) the street and mailing addresses of the partnership's principal office and, if different, the street address of an office in this state, if any;

(3) the name and street and mailing addresses in this state of the partnership's registered agent; and

(4) a statement that the partnership elects to become a limited liability partnership.

(d) A partnership's status as a limited liability partnership remains effective, regardless of changes in the partnership, until it is canceled pursuant to subsection (f) or administratively revoked pursuant to Section 903.

(e) The status of a partnership as a limited liability partnership and the protection against liability of its partners for the debts, obligations, or other liabilities of the partnership while it is a limited liability partnership is not affected by errors or later changes in the information required to be contained in the statement of qualification.

(f) A limited liability partnership may amend or cancel its statement of qualification by delivering to the [Secretary of State] for filing a statement of amendment or cancellation. The statement must be approved by the affirmative vote or consent of all the partners and state the name of the limited liability partnership and in the case of:

(1) an amendment, state the text of the amendment; and

(2) a cancellation, state that the statement of qualification is canceled.

COMMENT

Subsection (a)—Every partnership governed by this act may become a limited liability partnership, and the necessary formalities are straightforward: approval of the decision by the partners and delivering to the filing office for filing a simple statement of qualification. A partnership becomes a limited liability partnership when the filing office files the statement of qualification and the statement takes effect. For the consequences of LLP status, see Section 306(c), comment.

Subsection (b)—In the default mode, becoming a limited liability partnership requires the agreement of all partners, because in the default mode amending the partnership agreement requires the affirmative vote or consent of all partners, Section 401(k) (stating the voting/consent requirement to amend the partnership agreement). The unanimous vote/consent default rule reflects the significance of the transformation *inter se* the partners. *See* the comment to Section 306(c) (Effect of LLP Status on Relations Inter Se the Partners).

In the event a partnership agreement provides different quanta of consent for different matters, this subsection chooses (as a default rule) "the affirmative vote or consent necessary to amend those provisions" of "partnership agreement that expressly addresses obligations to contribute to the partnership." This choice makes good sense, given the effect of LLP status on contribution obligations. *See* the comment to Section 306(c).

Subsection (c)—Although a statement of qualification does not create a new entity, Section 201(b), the requirements stated here are comparable to the requirements for a certificate of formation for a limited liability company, ULLCA (2006) (Last Amended 2013), and a certificate of limited partnership, ULPA (2001) (Last Amended 2013). The liability shield—a privilege granted by state—justifies requiring an LLP to meet these requirements.

Subsection (d)—Under some early LLP statutes, an LLP's failure to file an annual renewal ended LLP status and terminated the shield. This subsection eschews that draconian result. However, an LLP's failure to file an annual/biennial report, Section 913, is grounds for administrative revocation. *See* Section 903(d); *see also* Section 306(c)(2) (stating that the liability shield continues despite dissolution).

Neither this subsection nor Section 306(c)(2) expressly addresses the effect of an LLP's termination on the liability shield. However, neither logic nor policy supports the retroactive destruction of the shield.

Subsection (f)—The unanimity requirement for amending a statement of qualification is a default rule. The unanimity requirement for cancelling a statement of qualification is mandatory. Section 105(c)(13). The difference reflects the very different consequences of amendment and cancellation. Subsection (b) requires very little information in a statement of qualification and does not contemplate additional information. *Compare* Section 901(f), *with* ULLCA (2006) (Last Amended 2013) § 201(c) (authorizing a certificate of formation to include additional information) *and* ULPA (2001) (Last Amended 2013) § 201(c) (same). Therefore, an amendment can do no substantial harm to any partner's interest. In contrast, cancelling a statement of qualification makes every partner vicariously liable for all partnership obligations. *Compare* Section 901(f), *with* Section 105(c)(14) (stating that the partnership agreement may not "vary the right of a partner to approve a merger, interest exchange, conversion, or domestication" the result of which is to impose vicarious liability on the person for the obligations of the resulting entity).

§ 902. Permitted Names

(a) The name of a partnership that is not a limited liability partnership may not contain the phrase "Registered Limited Liability Partnership" or "Limited Liability Partnership" or the abbreviation "R.L.L.P.", "L.L.P.", "RLLP", or "LLP".

(b) The name of a limited liability partnership must contain the phrase "Registered Limited Liability Partnership" or "Limited Liability Partnership" or the abbreviation "R.L.L.P.", "L.L.P.", "RLLP", or "LLP".

(c) Except as otherwise provided in subsection (f), the name of a limited liability partnership, and the name under which a foreign limited liability partnership may register to do business in this state, must be distinguishable on the records of the [Secretary of State] from any:

(1) name of an existing person whose formation required the filing of a record by the [Secretary of State] and which is not at the time administratively dissolved;

(2) name of a limited liability partnership whose statement of qualification is in effect;

(3) name under which a person that is registered to do business in this state by the filing of a record by the [Secretary of State];

(4) name that is reserved under Section 903 or other law of this state providing for the reservation of a name by a filing of a record by the [Secretary of State];

(5) name that is registered under Section 904 or other law of this state providing for the registration of a name by a filing of a record by the [Secretary of State]; and

(6) a name registered under [this state's assumed or fictitious name statute].

(d)   If a person consents in a record to the use of its name and submits an undertaking in a form satisfactory to the [Secretary of State] to change its name to a name that is distinguishable on the records of the [Secretary of State] from any name in any category of names in subsection (c), the name of the consenting person may be used by the person to which the consent was given.

(e)   Except as otherwise provided in subsection (f), in determining whether a name is the same as or not distinguishable on the records of the [Secretary of State] from the name of another person, words, phrases, or abbreviations indicating a type of entity, such as "corporation", "corp.", "incorporated", "Inc.", "professional corporation", "PC", "P.C.", "professional association", "PA", "P.A.", "Limited", "Ltd.", "limited partnership", "LP", "L.P.", "limited liability partnership", "LLP", "L.L.P.", "registered limited liability partnership", "RLLP", "R.L.L.P.", "limited liability limited partnership", "LLLP", "L.L.L.P.", "registered limited liability limited partnership", "RLLLP", "R.L.L.L.P.", "limited liability company", "LLC", or "L.L.C.", "limited cooperative association", "limited cooperative", "LCA", or "L.C.A." may not be taken into account.

(f)   A person may consent in a record to the use of a name that is not distinguishable on the records of the [Secretary of State] from its name except for the addition of a word, phrase, or abbreviation indicating the type of person as provided in subsection (e). In such a case, the person need not change its name pursuant to subsection (d).

(g)   The name of a limited liability partnership or foreign limited liability partnership may not contain the words [insert prohibited words or words that may be used only with approval by an appropriate state agency].

(h)   A limited liability partnership or foreign limited liability partnership may use a name that is not distinguishable from a name described in subsection (c)(1) through (6) if the partnership delivers to the [Secretary of State] a certified copy of a final judgment of a court of competent jurisdiction establishing the right of the partnership to use the name in this state.

COMMENT

This section adopts the "distinguishable on the records" test for name availability and rejects the "deceptively similar" test widely used in the past in business entity statutes.

For name requirements for foreign registered limited partnerships, see Section 1003(1).

§ 903.   Administrative Revocation of Statement of Qualification

(a)   The [Secretary of State] may commence a proceeding under subsection (b) to revoke the statement of qualification of a limited liability partnership administratively if the partnership does not:

(1)   pay any fee, tax, interest, or penalty required to be paid to the [Secretary of State] not later than [six months] after it is due;

(2)   deliver [an annual] [a biennial] report to the [Secretary of State] not later than [six months] after it is due; or

(3)   have a registered agent in this state for [60] consecutive days.

(b)   If the [Secretary of State] determines that one or more grounds exist for administratively revoking a statement of qualification, the [Secretary of State] shall serve the partnership with notice in a record of the [Secretary of State's] determination.

(c)   If a limited liability partnership, not later than [60] days after service of the notice under subsection (b), does not cure or demonstrate to the satisfaction of the [Secretary of State] the nonexistence of each ground determined by the [Secretary of State], the [Secretary of State] shall administratively revoke the statement of qualification by signing a statement of administrative revocation that recites the grounds for revocation and the effective date of the revocation. The [Secretary of State] shall file the statement and serve a copy on the partnership pursuant to Section 116.

(d)   An administrative revocation under subsection (c) affects only a partnership's status as a limited liability partnership and is not an event causing dissolution of the partnership.

(e)   The administrative revocation of a statement of qualification of a limited liability partnership does not terminate the authority of its registered agent.

COMMENT

Many failures to comply with statutory requirements that may give rise to administrative revocation occur because of oversight or inadvertence and are usually corrected promptly when brought to the LLP's attention. Subsections (b) and (c) therefore provide a mandatory notice by the filing office to each LLP whose statement of qualification is subject to administrative revocation and a sixty-day grace period following the notice before the statement of administrative revocation may be filed.

In most instances, the issue whether a statement of qualification is subject to administrative revocation will not be controverted. If an LLP's statement of qualification is administratively revoked, the statement is no longer in effect. However, the partnership may petition the filing office for reinstatement under Section 904 and, i f reinstatement is denied, the company may appeal to the courts under Section 905.

As a practical matter, administrative revocation permits the filing office to clear the record of "dead wood" and free up names.

However, the consequences for the partners can be quite serious. The liability shield remains effective for debts, liabilities, and other obligations incurred before revocation but disappears as to those incurred subsequently. A reinstated statement of qualification has retroactive effect generally, but exceptions can exist with regard to partnership obligations incurred before reinstatement. *See* Section 904(d)(3). For a discussion of when a partnership obligation is incurred, see the comment to Section 304(c) (The Temporal Nexus—When Claim Incurred).

Subsection (d)—This rule follows from Section 201(b) ("A partnership is the same entity regardless of whether the partnership has a statement of qualification in effect under Section 901.").

§ 904.   Reinstatement

(a)   A partnership whose statement of qualification has been revoked administratively under Section 903 may apply to the [Secretary of State] for reinstatement of the statement of qualification [not later than [two] years after the effective date of the revocation]. The application must state:

(1)   the name of the partnership at the time of the administrative revocation of its statement of qualification and, if needed, a different name that satisfies Section 902;

(2)   the address of the principal office of the partnership and the name and street and mailing addresses of its registered agent;

(3)   the effective date of administrative revocation of the partnership's statement of qualification; and

(4)   that the grounds for revocation did not exist or have been cured.

(b)   To have its statement of qualification reinstated, a partnership must pay all fees, taxes, interest, and penalties that were due to the [Secretary of State] at the time of the administrative revocation and all fees, taxes, interest, and penalties that would have been due to the [Secretary of State] while the partnership's statement of qualification was revoked administratively.

(c)   If the [Secretary of State] determines that an application under subsection (a) contains the required information, is satisfied that the information is correct, and determines that all payments required to be made to the [Secretary of State] by subsection (b) have been made, the [Secretary of State] shall:

(1)   cancel the statement of revocation and prepare a statement of reinstatement that states the [Secretary of State's] determination and the effective date of reinstatement; and

(2)   file the statement of reinstatement and serve a copy on the partnership.

(d) When reinstatement under this section has become effective, the following rules apply:

(1)   The reinstatement relates back to and takes effect as of the effective date of the administrative revocation.

(2)   The partnership's status as a limited liability partnership continues as if the revocation had not occurred.

(3)   The rights of a person arising out of an act or omission in reliance on the revocation before the person knew or had notice of the reinstatement are not affected.

COMMENT

This section is analogous to statutes authorizing reinstatement following administrative dissolution. *See* ULLCA (2006) (Last Amended 2013) § 709; ULPA (2001) (Last Amended 2013) § 812. In that context:

- some states require that reinstatement be sought within two years of administrative dissolution;

- other states provide a longer time, or do not impose any time limit;

- imposing no limit risks abuse by unscrupulous people seeking to reinstate and appropriate for improper ends a dormant entity that has been abandoned by its owners; but

- on the other hand, reinstatement is intended as a safety net for the inattentive and, if the deadline comes too soon, the safety net may be gone before the inattentive even learn that administrative dissolution has occurred.

Subsection (a)(1)—This provision will apply if, before the statement of qualification is reinstated, another entity has taken the company's name. *See* Section 902(c)(2).

Subsection (d)(3)—This paragraph provides an exception to the retroactive effect provided by Paragraphs (1) and (2). The greatest risk resulting from the exception is a creditor's claim of having entered into a contract with the partnership, knowing of the revocation and relying on the vicarious liability of each partner. The exception could also preclude a reinstated LLP's use of its own name. *See* Section 902(c)(2) (indirectly permitting an LLP to use the name of another partnership whose statement of qualification has been administratively revoked). Comparable provisions exist in other uniform acts pertaining to entities. *E.g.*, ULLCA (2006) (Last Amended 2013) § 112(b)(1).

§ 905.   Judicial Review of Denial of Reinstatement

(a)   If the [Secretary of State] denies a partnership's application for reinstatement following administrative revocation of the partnership's statement of qualification, the [Secretary of State] shall serve the partnership with a notice in a record that explains the reasons for the denial.

(b)   A partnership may seek judicial review of denial of reinstatement in [the appropriate court] not later than [30] days after service of the notice of denial.

COMMENT

Because the grounds for administrative revocation under Section 904 are limited and straight forward, it is unlikely there will be a dispute about whether a partnership has corrected the reasons for the administrative revocation of the partnership's statement of qualification. But in the event a partnership disagrees with a determination by the filing office to deny the partnership's application for reinstatement, this section gives the partnership a limited right to seek judicial review of the denial of reinstatement.

§ 906.   Reservation of Name

(a)   A person may reserve the exclusive use of a name that complies with Section 902 by delivering an application to the [Secretary of State] for filing. The application must state the name and address of the applicant and the name to be reserved. If the [Secretary of State] finds that the name is available, the [Secretary of State] shall reserve the name for the applicant's exclusive use for [120] days.

(b)   The owner of a reserved name may transfer the reservation to another person by delivering to the [Secretary of State] a signed notice in a record of the transfer which states the name and address of the person to which the reservation is being transferred.

COMMENT

This section does not provide for the renewal of a name reservation for successive 120-day periods. A new reservation may be filed upon the expiration of a reservation, but by requiring a new filing this section creates the possibility that another party may timely submit a reservation for the same name. It was considered appropriate to allow for that possibility so that the procedure in this section cannot be used to block a name indefinitely. *Compare* Section 906, *with* Section 907(d) (authorizing a renewable registration of certain names).

§ 907. Registration of Name

(a) A foreign limited liability partnership not registered to do business in this state under [Article] 10 may register its name, or an alternate name adopted pursuant to Section 902, if the name is distinguishable on the records of the [Secretary of State] from the names that are not available under Section 902.

(b) To register its name or an alternate name adopted pursuant to Section 902, a foreign limited liability partnership must deliver to the [Secretary of State] for filing an application stating the partnership's name, the jurisdiction and date of its formation, and any alternate name adopted pursuant to Section 902. If the [Secretary of State] finds that the name applied for is available, the [Secretary of State] shall register the name for the applicant's exclusive use.

(c) The registration of a name under this section is effective for [one year] after the date of registration.

(d) A foreign limited liability partnership whose name registration is effective may renew the registration for successive [one-year] periods by delivering, not earlier than [three months] before the expiration of the registration, to the [Secretary of State] for filing a renewal application that complies with this section. When filed, the renewal application renews the registration for a succeeding [one-year] period.

(e) A foreign limited liability partnership whose name registration is effective may register as a foreign limited liability partnership under the registered name or consent in a signed record to the use of that name by another person that is not an individual.

COMMENT

Unlike the reservation of a name under Section 906, a registration of a name under this section may be renewed for successive periods thus permitting a name to be protected for a period longer than the initial registration period. Use of the procedure in this section is limited, however, to the names of foreign limited partnerships, which are not registered to do business in the state. The purpose of this section is to permit a foreign entity to make sure its name will be available if the entity chooses to register in the state in the future.

§ 908. Registered Agent

(a) Each limited liability partnership and each registered foreign limited liability partnership shall designate and maintain a registered agent in this state. The designation of a registered agent is an affirmation of fact by the partnership or foreign partnership that the agent has consented to serve.

(b) A registered agent for a limited liability partnership or registered foreign limited liability partnership must have a place of business in this state.

(c) The only duties under this [act] of a registered agent that has complied with this [act] are:

(1) to forward to the limited liability partnership or registered foreign limited liability partnership at the address most recently supplied to the agent by the partnership or foreign partnership any process, notice, or demand pertaining to the partnership or foreign partnership which is served on or received by the agent;

(2) if the registered agent resigns, to provide the notice required by Section 907(c) to the partnership or foreign partnership at the address most recently supplied to the agent by the partnership or foreign partnership; and

(3) to keep current the information with respect to the agent in the statement of qualification or foreign registration statement.

COMMENT

This section is limited to prescribing the duties of a registered agent under this act. The partnership agreement cannot vary this section. Section 105(c)(16)(A). However, an agent may undertake other responsibilities to a represented limited liability partnership or foreign limited liability partnership, such as by contract or course of dealing, but those duties will be determined under other law.

§ 909. Change of Registered Agent or Address for Registered Agent by Limited Liability Partnership

(a) A limited liability partnership or registered foreign limited liability partnership may change its registered agent or the address of its registered agent by delivering to the [Secretary of State] for filing a statement of change that states:

(1) the name of the partnership or foreign partnership; and

(2) the information that is to be in effect as a result of the filing of the statement of change.

(b) The partners of a limited liability partnership need not approve the delivery to the [Secretary of State] for filing of:

(1) a statement of change under this section; or

(2) a similar filing changing the registered agent or registered office, if any, of the partnership in any other jurisdiction.

(c) A statement of change under this section designating a new registered agent is an affirmation of fact by the limited liability partnership or registered foreign limited liability partnership that the agent has consented to serve.

(d) As an alternative to using the procedure in this section, a limited liability partnership may amend its statement of qualification.

COMMENT

A change in the identity of the registered agent of an LLP or registered foreign LLP or a change of the office address of a partnership's registered agent are usually routine matters that do not affect the rights of the partners of the represented LLP. This section permits those changes to be made without: (i) amendment of an LLP's statement of qualification or a registered foreign LLPs registration; and (ii) any approval by an LLP's partners. For the registered agent's power to resign, see Section 910. For the registered agent's power to change its name, address, or both, see Section 911.

Subsection (c)—This subsection avoids the need to file with a statement of change consent of the new registered agent being designated.

Subsection (d)—This subsection makes clear that the procedures in this section are not exclusive. A common way in which a limited liability partnership changes its registered agent is to include the change in its annual/biennial report. *See* Section 913(e).

§ 910. Resignation of Registered Agent

(a) A registered agent may resign as an agent for a limited liability partnership or registered foreign limited liability partnership by delivering to the [Secretary of State] for filing a statement of resignation that states:

(1) the name of the partnership or foreign partnership;

(2) the name of the agent;

(3) that the agent resigns from serving as registered agent for the partnership or foreign partnership; and

(4) the address of the partnership or foreign partnership to which the agent will send the notice required by subsection (c).

(b)   A statement of resignation takes effect on the earlier of:

(1)   the 31st day after the day on which it is filed by the [Secretary of State]; or

(2)   the designation of a new registered agent for the limited liability partnership or registered foreign limited liability partnership.

(c)   A registered agent promptly shall furnish to the limited liability partnership or registered foreign limited liability partnership notice in a record of the date on which a statement of resignation was filed.

(d)   When a statement of resignation takes effect, the registered agent ceases to have responsibility under this [act] for any matter thereafter tendered to it as agent for the limited liability partnership or registered foreign limited liability partnership. The resignation does not affect any contractual rights the partnership or foreign partnership has against the agent or that the agent has against the partnership or foreign partnership.

(e)   A registered agent may resign with respect to a limited liability partnership or registered foreign limited liability partnership whether or not the partnership or foreign partnership is in good standing.

COMMENT

Resignation under this section may be accomplished solely by action of the registered agent and does not require the cooperation or consent of the represented LLP or registered foreign LLP. Whether a resignation violates a contract between the registered agent and the partnership is beyond the scope of this act, and Subsection (d) preserves whatever claims a represented LLC may have against its registered agent for a wrongful termination. Even if a resignation were to violate such a contract, the resignation would still be effective if the provisions of this section were followed.

Subsection (b)—This subsection delays the effectiveness of a statement of resignation for thirty-one days to allow the notice of the resignation that must be sent under Subsection (c) to reach the represented LLP or registered foreign LLP and to allow the represented LLP to arrange for a substitute registered agent.

Subsection (e)—This subsection makes clear that a registered agent may resign with respect to an LLP or registered foreign LLP that is not in good standing and supersedes the contrary administrative practice in some states of refusing to accept any filings with respect to an entity that is not in good standing until the problem with the entity's standing is cured.

§ 911.   Change of Name or Address by Registered Agent

(a)   If a registered agent changes its name or address, the agent may deliver to the [Secretary of State] for filing a statement of change that states:

(1)   the name of the limited liability partnership or registered foreign limited liability partnership represented by the registered agent;

(2)   the name of the agent as currently shown in the records of the [Secretary of State] for the partnership or foreign partnership;

(3)   if the name of the agent has changed, its new name; and

(4)   if the address of the agent has changed, its new address.

(b)   A registered agent promptly shall furnish notice to the represented limited liability partnership or registered foreign limited liability partnership of the filing by the [Secretary of State] of the statement of change and the changes made by the statement.

Legislative Note: Many registered agents act in that capacity for many entities, and the Model Registered Agents Act (2006) (Last Amended 2013) provides a streamlined method through which a commercial registered agent can make a single filing to change its information for all represented entities. The single filing does not prevent an enacting state from assessing filing fees on the basis of the number of entity records affected. Alternatively the fees can be set on an incremental sliding fee or capitated amount based upon potential economies of costs for a bulk filing.

COMMENT

This section permits a registered agent to change the name and address of the agent that appears in the registered agent filing of an LLP or registered foreign LLP represented by the agent. This act does not provide for commercial registered agents, *contra* UBOC (2011) (Last Amended 2013) §§ 1–405, 1–406, 1–409. As a result, a registered agent will need to make a separate filing under this section for each LLP and registered foreign LLP represented by the agent, unless, if authorized by rule or administrative policy, the filing office establishes procedures for a bulk filing with one filing listing the names of all the registered agent's represented entities.

§ 912.   Service of Process, Notice, or Demand

(a)   A limited liability partnership or registered foreign limited liability partnership may be served with any process, notice, or demand required or permitted by law by serving its registered agent.

(b)   If a limited liability partnership or registered foreign limited liability partnership ceases to have a registered agent, or if its registered agent cannot with reasonable diligence be served, the partnership or foreign partnership may be served by registered or certified mail, return receipt requested, or by similar commercial delivery service, addressed to the partnership or foreign partnership at its principal office. The address of the principal office must be as shown in the partnership's or foreign partnership's most recent [annual] [biennial] report filed by the [Secretary of State]. Service is effected under this subsection on the earliest of:

(1)   the date the partnership or foreign partnership receives the mail or delivery by the commercial delivery service;

(2)   the date shown on the return receipt, if signed by the partnership or foreign partnership; or

(3)   five days after its deposit with the United States Postal Service, or with the commercial delivery service, if correctly addressed and with sufficient postage or payment.

(c)   If process, notice, or demand cannot be served on a limited liability partnership or registered foreign limited liability partnership pursuant to subsection (a) or (b), service may be made by handing a copy to the individual in charge of any regular place of business of the partnership or foreign partnership if the individual served is not a plaintiff in the action.

(d)   Service of process, notice, or demand on a registered agent must be in a written record.

(e)   Service of process, notice, or demand may be made by other means under law other than this [act].

COMMENT

Subsection (b)—This subsection offers three alternative methods for establishing the date service is effected, a date important for determining the time within which an LLP or registered foreign LLP must respond to the process, notice, or demand served. Under Subsection (b)(1), service is effected on the date of receipt by the partnership of the mail or commercial delivery. Under Subsection (b)(2), service is effected on the date shown on the return receipt, if signed on behalf of the partnership. Under Subsection (b)(3), service is effected five days after it is deposited with the Postal Service or with a similar commercial delivery service, if correctly addressed and with correct postage or payment. Service is effective at the earliest of the three listed circumstances.

However, for the party effecting service there are difficulties of proof under the first two circumstances. Under Subsection (b)(1) the exact date of the receipt by the LLP or registered foreign LLP of mail or commercial delivery is peculiarly within the knowledge of the partnership. Under Subsection (b)(2) the return receipt must be signed on behalf of the partnership. That requirement is designed to assure that the service is actually received by the partnership, but the signature on the return receipt may not always show unambiguously that the signer was acting for the partnership and was authorized to do so. As a practical matter, therefore, parties effecting service under Subsection (b) may find it most convenient to rely on Subsection (b)(3) and to maintain their own records so that the date of deposit in the mails or with a commercial delivery service can easily be established.

Subsection (c)—This subsection provides a means for serving process on an LLP or registered foreign LLP that cannot be served under Subsection (a) or (b). In such circumstances, some statutes require or permit service of process to be made on the filing office.

Subsection (e)—For an example, see, *e.g.*, FED. R. CIV. P. 4(h)(1)(B) (authorizing service on "a domestic or foreign corporation, or a partnership or other unincorporated association that is subject to suit under a common name" to be made on "an officer, a managing or general agent, or any other agent authorized by appointment or by law to receive service of process").

§ 913.   [Annual] [Biennial] Report for [Secretary of State]

(a)   A limited liability partnership or registered foreign limited liability partnership shall deliver to the [Secretary of State] for filing [an annual] [a biennial] report that states:

(1)   the name of the partnership or registered foreign partnership;

(2)   the name and street and mailing addresses of its registered agent in this state;

(3)   the street and mailing addresses of its principal office;

(4)   the name of at least one partner; and

(5)   in the case of a foreign partnership, its jurisdiction of formation and any alternate name adopted under Section 1006.

(b)   Information in the [annual] [biennial] report must be current as of the date the report is signed by the limited liability partnership or registered foreign limited liability partnership.

(c)   The first [annual] [biennial] report must be delivered to the [Secretary of State] for filing after [January 1] and before [April 1] of the year following the calendar year in which the limited liability partnership's statement of qualification became effective or the registered foreign limited liability partnership registered to do business in this state. Subsequent [annual] [biennial] reports must be delivered to the [Secretary of State] for filing after [January 1] and before [April 1] of each [second] calendar year thereafter.

(d)   If [an annual] [a biennial] report does not contain the information required by this section, the [Secretary of State] promptly shall notify the reporting limited liability partnership or registered foreign limited liability partnership in a record and return the report for correction.

(e)   If [an annual] [a biennial] report contains the name or address of a registered agent which differs from the information shown in the records of the [Secretary of State] immediately before the report becomes effective, the differing information is considered a statement of change under Section 909.

COMMENT

In some states, an annual or biennial report by a limited liability partnership or a registered foreign limited liability partnership will be a new requirement.

Subsection (a)(4)—The requirement that the report include the name of at least one partner will be a new requirement in some states. There has been increasing pressure from law enforcement agencies for access to more information about the ownership and control of legal entities. This requirement will enable law enforcement to contact a person with some knowledge about the affairs of the limited liability partnership. Members of the public will also have that ability.

[ARTICLE] 10.   FOREIGN LIMITED LIABILITY PARTNERSHIP

§ 1001.   Governing Law

(a)   The law of the jurisdiction of formation of a foreign limited liability partnership governs:

(1)   the internal affairs of the partnership; and

(2)   the liability of a partner as partner for a debt, obligation, or other liability of the foreign partnership.

(b)   A foreign limited liability partnership is not precluded from registering to do business in this state because of any difference between the law of its jurisdiction of formation and the law of this state.

(c)   Registration of a foreign limited liability partnership to do business in this state does not authorize the foreign partnership to engage in any business or exercise any power that a limited liability partnership may not engage in or exercise in this state.

COMMENT

For the purposes of this section, "jurisdiction of formation" refers to the jurisdiction under whose law a foreign partnership became a limited liability partnership. Strictly speaking, becoming an LLP involves transforming an already existing entity, not forming a new one. *Cf.* Section 201(b) (making this point as to domestic LLPs).

Subsection (a)—This subsection provides that the laws of the jurisdiction of formation of a foreign LLP, rather than the laws of this state, govern both the internal affairs of the foreign LLP and the liability of its partners for the obligations of the LLP. A partnership agreement cannot change this provision. Section 105(c)(17).

This subdivision parallels Section 104(1) (pertaining to the governing law for domestic LLPs). *See* the comment to Section 104(1).

Subsections (b) and (c)—These sections together make clear that, although a foreign LLP may not be denied registration simply because of a difference between the laws of its jurisdiction of formation and the laws of this state, the foreign limited liability partnership "may not engage in any activity or exercise any power a domestic LLP may not engage in or exercise in this state." Subsection (c).

§ 1002.   Registration to Do Business in This State

(a)   A foreign limited liability partnership may not do business in this state until it registers with the [Secretary of State] under this [article].

(b)   A foreign limited liability partnership doing business in this state may not maintain an action or proceeding in this state unless it has registered to do business in this state.

(c)   The failure of a foreign limited liability partnership to register to do business in this state does not impair the validity of a contract or act of the foreign partnership or preclude it from defending an action or proceeding in this state.

(d)   A limitation on the liability of a partner of a foreign limited liability partnership is not waived solely because the foreign partnership does business in this state without registering to do business in this state.

(e)   Section 1001(a) and (b) applies even if a foreign limited liability partnership fails to register under this [article].

COMMENT

Subsection (a)—Following a long-established tradition, this act does not state what constitutes "do[ing] business in this state." Instead, Section 1005 provides a non-exhaustive list of "[a]ctivities of a foreign limited liability partnership which do not constitute doing business in this state."

Subsection (b)—The purpose of this subsection is to induce foreign limited liability partnerships to register without imposing harsh or erratic sanctions. Often the failure to register is a result of inadvertence or bona fide disagreement as to the scope of Section 1005, which is necessarily imprecise. Thus, the imposition of harsh sanctions in those situations is inappropriate. The sanction of closing the courts of the state to suits brought by foreign LLPs that should have registered is not a punitive one. If a foreign LLP should have registered and failed to do so, it may still enforce its contractual and other rights simply by registering.

However, if a court dismisses a case under this subsection rather than staying the proceedings pending the foreign LLP's registration, a statute of limitations problem may occur. *Corco, Inc. v. Ledar Transport, Inc.* 946 P.2d 1009, 1010 (Kan. Ct. App. 1997) ("[T]he proper remedy was to dismiss [the unregistered entity's] counterclaim without prejudice rather than with prejudice. This would leave [the entity] the opportunity to comply with the statutes and then reassert its claim against [the defendant]. On the other hand, it would also leave the risk that the statute of limitations might run against [the entity].").

This subsection does not prevent a foreign LLP that has failed to register from "defending" an action or proceeding. The distinction between "maintaining" an action or proceeding under this subsection and "defending" an action or proceeding under Subsection (c) is determined on the basis of whether affirmative relief is sought. A nonregistered foreign LLP may interpose any defense or permissive or mandatory counterclaim to defeat a claimed recovery, but may not obtain an affirmative judgment based on the counterclaim without first registering.

Subsection (c)—In addition to permitting a non-registered foreign LLP doing business in this state to defend (but not maintain) an action or proceeding, this section makes clear that failure to register does not impair the validity of a foreign LLP's acts.

Subsection (d)—This subsection preserves the effectiveness of a foreign LLP's liability shield applicable under the LLP's governing law.

§ 1003.　Foreign Registration Statement

To register to do business in this state, a foreign limited liability partnership must deliver a foreign registration statement to the [Secretary of State] for filing. The statement must state:

(1)　the name of the partnership and, if the name does not comply with Section 902, an alternate name adopted pursuant to Section 1006(a);

(2)　that the partnership is a foreign limited liability partnership;

(3)　the partnership's jurisdiction of formation;

(4)　the street and mailing addresses of the partnership's principal office and, if the law of the partnership's jurisdiction of formation requires the partnership to maintain an office in that jurisdiction, the street and mailing addresses of the required office; and

(5)　the name and street and mailing addresses of the partnership's registered agent in this state.

COMMENT

The foreign registration statement provides certain basic information about the foreign limited liability partnership to ensure that citizens of the state have access to that information in their dealings with the foreign partnership. The statement also facilitates making the foreign partnership subject to the jurisdiction of the courts of the state.

Once registered, a foreign limited liability partnership must file an annual/biennial report. Section 913.

For the purposes of this section, "jurisdiction of formation" refers to the jurisdiction under whose law a foreign partnership became a limited liability partnership. Strictly speaking, becoming an LLP involves transforming an already existing entity, not forming a new one. *See* Section 201(b).

§ 1004.　Amendment of Foreign Registration Statement

A registered foreign limited liability partnership shall deliver to the [Secretary of State] for filing an amendment to its foreign registration statement if there is a change in:

(1)　the name of the partnership;

(2)　the partnership's jurisdiction of formation;

(3)　an address required by Section 1003(4); or

(4)　the information required by Section 1003(5).

COMMENT

This section works in tandem with the annual/biennial report required by Section 913 to keep up to date the information of record in the filing office about a registered foreign limited partnership.

§ 1005.　Activities Not Constituting Doing Business

(a)　Activities of a foreign limited liability partnership which do not constitute doing business in this state under this [article] include:

(1)　maintaining, defending, mediating, arbitrating, or settling an action or proceeding;

(2)   carrying on any activity concerning its internal affairs, including holding meetings of its partners;

(3)   maintaining accounts in financial institutions;

(4)   maintaining offices or agencies for the transfer, exchange, and registration of securities of the partnership or maintaining trustees or depositories with respect to those securities;

(5)   selling through independent contractors;

(6)   soliciting or obtaining orders by any means if the orders require acceptance outside this state before they become contracts;

(7)   creating or acquiring indebtedness, mortgages, or security interests in property;

(8)   securing or collecting debts or enforcing mortgages or security interests in property securing the debts and holding, protecting, or maintaining property;

(9)   conducting an isolated transaction that is not in the course of similar transactions;

(10) owning, without more, property; and

(11) doing business in interstate commerce.

(b)   A person does not do business in this state solely by being a partner of a foreign limited liability partnership that does business in this state.

(c)   This section does not apply in determining the contacts or activities that may subject a foreign limited liability partnership to service of process, taxation, or regulation under law of this state other than this [act].

COMMENT

This act does not attempt to formulate an inclusive definition of what constitutes doing business in a state. Rather, the concept is defined in a negative fashion by Subsections (a) and (b), which state that certain activities do not constitute doing business.

In general terms, any conduct more regular, systematic, or extensive than that described in Subsection (a) constitutes doing business and requires the foreign limited liability partnership to register to do business. Typical conduct requiring registration includes maintaining an office to conduct local intrastate business, selling personal property not in interstate commerce, entering into contracts relating to the local business or sales, and owning or using real estate for general purposes. But the passive owning of real estate for investment purposes does not constitute doing business. *See* Subsection (a)(10).

The test of "doing business" defined in a negative way in Subsections (a) and (b) applies only to the question whether a foreign limited liability partnership 's contacts with the state are such that it must register under this section. The test is not applicable to other questions such as whether the foreign LLP is amenable to service of process under state "long-arm" statutes or liable for state or local taxes. A foreign LLP that has registered (or is required to register) will generally be subject to suit and state taxation in the state, while a foreign LLP that is subject to service of process or state taxation in a state will not necessarily be required to register.

Subsection (a)—The list of activities set forth in this subsection is not exhaustive.

Subsection (a)(1)—A foreign limited liability partnership is not "doing business" solely because it resorts to the courts of the state to recover an indebtedness, enforce an obligation, recover possession of personal property, obtain the appointment of a receiver, intervene in a pending proceeding, bring a petition to compel arbitration, file an appeal bond, or pursue appellate remedies. Similarly, a foreign LLP is not required to register merely because it files a complaint with a governmental agency or participates in an administrative proceeding within the state.

Subsection (a)(2)—A foreign limited liability partnership does not "do business" within a state under this section merely because some of its internal affairs occur within a state. Thus, a foreign LLP may hold meetings of its partners within a state without first registering. A foreign LLP also may maintain offices or agencies within a state relating solely to the transfer, exchange or registration of its interests without registering. Other activities relating to the internal affairs of the foreign LLP that do not constitute doing business under this section include having officers or representatives who reside within or are physically present in the state; while there, the officers or representatives may make executive decisions relating to the internal affairs of the foreign LLP without imposing on the foreign LLP the requirement that it register, if these activities are not so regular and systematic as to cause the residence to be viewed as a business office.

Subsection (a)(5)—Under this paragraph, a foreign limited liability partnership need not register if it sells goods in the state through independent contractors. These transactions are viewed as transactions by the independent contractors, not by the foreign LLP itself even though the foreign LLP sets some limits or ground rules for its contractors. If these controls are sufficiently pervasive, however, the foreign LLP may be deemed to be selling for itself in intrastate commerce, and not through the independent contractors and therefore engaged in doing business in the state.

Subsection (a)(7) and (8)—The mere act of making a loan by a foreign limited liability partnership that is not in the business of making loans does not constitute doing business in the state in which the loan is made. On the same theory, a foreign LLP may obtain security for the repayment of a loan, and foreclose or enforce the lien or security interest to collect the loan, without being deemed to be doing business. Similarly, a refunding or "roll over" of a loan or its adjustment or compromise does not involve doing business.

Subsection (a)(9)—The concept of "doing business" involves regular, repeated, and continuing business contacts of a local nature. A single agreement or isolated transaction within a state does not constitute doing business if there is no intention to repeat the transaction or engage in similar transactions. This act does not impose the limitation found in some statutes, such as Section 15.01(b)(10) of the Model Business Corporation Act, that the isolated transaction be completed within thirty days. A foreign LLP should not be required to register simply because it engages in an isolated transaction that takes longer than thirty days to complete.

Subsection (a)(11)—A foreign limited liability partnership is not "doing business" within the meaning of this section if it is transacting business in interstate commerce. *See* Subsection (a)(6) (stating that soliciting or obtaining orders that must be accepted outside the state before they become contracts is not "doing business" within the meaning of this section).

These exclusions reflect the provisions of the United States Constitution that grant to the United States Congress exclusive power over interstate commerce, and preclude states from imposing restrictions or conditions upon this commerce. This subsection should be construed in a manner consistent with judicial decisions under the United States Constitution. Under these decisions, a foreign entity is not required to register even though it sells goods within the state if they are shipped to the purchasers in interstate commerce. Thus a foreign LLP need not register even if it also does work and performs acts within the state incidental to the interstate business (*e.g.,* if it takes or enforces a security interest incidental to these transactions). Nor is it required to register merely because it sends traveling salespeople or solicitors into a state so long as contracts are not made within the state. Similarly, an office may be maintained by a foreign LLP in this state without registering if the office's functions relate solely to interstate commerce. Purchases of goods may of course be in interstate commerce as readily as sales. Thus, the purchase of personal property in this state by a foreign limited liability partnership for shipment in interstate commerce out of the state does not require the entity to register.

§ 1006.   Noncomplying Name of Foreign Limited Liability Partnership

(a)   A foreign limited liability partnership whose name does not comply with Section 902 may not register to do business in this state until it adopts, for the purpose of doing business in this state, an alternate name that complies with Section 902. A partnership that registers under an alternate name under this subsection need not comply with [this state's assumed or fictitious name statute]. After registering to do business in this state with an alternate name, a partnership shall do business in this state under:

(1)   the alternate name;

(2)   the partnership's name, with the addition of its jurisdiction of formation; or

(3)   a name the partnership is authorized to use under [this state's assumed or fictitious name statute].

(b)   If a registered foreign limited liability partnership changes its name to one that does not comply with Section 902, it may not do business in this state until it complies with subsection (a) by amending its registration to adopt an alternate name that complies with Section 902.

COMMENT

A foreign limited liability partnership must register under its true name if that name satisfies the requirements of Section 902. If the true name is unavailable because it is not distinguishable upon the records of the filing office from a name already in use or reserved or registered, the foreign LLP may use an alternate name.

A foreign limited liability partnership that registers to do business in the state may do business under a fictitious name to the same extent as a domestic entity.

§ 1007. Withdrawal Deemed on Conversion to Domestic Filing Entity or Domestic Limited Liability Partnership

A registered foreign limited liability partnership that converts to a domestic limited liability partnership or to a domestic entity whose formation requires the delivery of a record to the [Secretary of State] for filing is deemed to have withdrawn its registration on the effective date of the conversion.

COMMENT

When a registered foreign limited liability partnership has converted to a domestic "filing entity" or domestic limited liability partnership, information about the entity in its capacity as a domestic entity will continue to be of record in the filing office. At that point, there is no further reason for the entity to be registered as a foreign LLP, and this section automatically treats its prior registration as withdrawn.

§ 1008. Withdrawal on Dissolution or Conversion to Nonfiling Entity Other than Limited Liability Partnership

(a)   A registered foreign limited liability partnership that has dissolved and completed winding up or has converted to a domestic or foreign entity whose formation does not require the public filing of a record, other than a limited liability partnership, shall deliver a statement of withdrawal to the [Secretary of State] for filing. The statement must state:

(1)   in the case of a partnership that has completed winding up:

(A)   its name and jurisdiction of formation;

(B)   that the partnership surrenders its registration to do business in this state; and

(2)   in the case of a partnership that has converted:

(A)   the name of the converting partnership and its jurisdiction of formation;

(B)   the type of entity to which the partnership has converted and its jurisdiction of formation;

(C)   that the converted entity surrenders the converting partnership's registration to do business in this state and revokes the authority of the converting partnership's registered agent to act as registered agent in this state on behalf of the partnership or the converted entity; and

(D)   a mailing address to which service of process may be made under subsection (b).

(b)   After a withdrawal under this section becomes effective, service of process in any action or proceeding based on a cause of action arising during the time the foreign limited liability partnership was registered to do business in this state may be made pursuant to Section 909.

COMMENT

When a registered foreign limited liability partnership has dissolved and completed winding up, or has converted to a "nonfiling entity" other than a limited liability partnership, there is no further reason for information about the entity to appear in the records of the filing office. This section thus requires delivery of a statement of withdrawal for the purpose of removing the foreign LLP from the rolls of registered foreign entities.

Subsection (a)—The exclusion of limited liability partnerships from this provision is merely technical; Section 1007 covers conversion to a domestic LLP.

§ 1009.   Transfer of Registration

(a)   When a registered foreign limited liability partnership has merged into a foreign entity that is not registered to do business in this state or has converted to a foreign entity required to register with the [Secretary of State] to do business in this state, the foreign entity shall deliver to the [Secretary of State] for filing an application for transfer of registration. The application must state:

(1)   the name of the registered foreign limited partnership before the merger or conversion;

(2)   that before the merger or conversion the registration pertained to a foreign limited liability partnership;

(3)   the name of the applicant foreign entity into which the foreign limited liability partnership has merged or to which it has been converted and, if the name does not comply with Section 902, an alternate name adopted pursuant to Section 1006(a);

(4)   the type of entity of the applicant foreign entity and its jurisdiction of formation;

(5)   the street and mailing addresses of the principal office of the applicant foreign entity and, if the law of that entity's jurisdiction of formation requires the entity to maintain an office in that jurisdiction, the street and mailing addresses of that office; and

(6)   the name and street and mailing addresses of the applicant foreign entity's registered agent in this state.

(b)   When an application for transfer of registration takes effect, the registration of the foreign limited liability limited partnership to do business in this state is transferred without interruption to the foreign entity into which the partnership has merged or to which it has been converted.

COMMENT

The purpose of this section is to clarify the status of the foreign limited liability partnership in the public records of the state. A filing under this section has the two-fold effect of canceling the authority of the foreign LLP to do business in the state while at the same time reregistering the former foreign LLP as the new type of foreign entity. If the reregistered foreign entity subsequently wishes to cancel its registration to do business in the state, it may do so under the statute of this state pertaining the registration of the new type of foreign entity.

§ 1010.   Termination of Registration

(a)   The [Secretary of State] may terminate the registration of a registered foreign limited liability partnership in the manner provided in subsections (b) and (c) if the partnership does not:

(1)   pay, not later than [60] days after the due date, any fee, tax, interest, or penalty required to be paid to the [Secretary of State] under this [act] or law other than this [act];

(2)   deliver to the [Secretary of State] for filing, not later than [60] days after the due date, [an annual] [a biennial] report required under Section 913;

(3)   have a registered agent as required by Section 908; or

(4)   deliver to the [Secretary of State] for filing a statement of a change under Section 909 not later than [30] days after a change has occurred in the name or address of the registered agent.

(b)   The [Secretary of State] may terminate the registration of a registered foreign limited liability partnership by:

(1)   filing a notice of termination or noting the termination in the records of the [Secretary of State]; and

(2)   delivering a copy of the notice or the information in the notation to the partnership's registered agent or, if the partnership does not have a registered agent, to the partnership's principal office.

(c)   A notice or information in a notation under subsection (b) must include:

(1)   the effective date of the termination, which must be at least [60] days after the date the [Secretary of State] delivers the copy; and

(2)   the grounds for termination under subsection (a).

(d)   The authority of a registered foreign limited liability partnership to do business in this state ceases on the effective date of the notice of termination or notation under subsection (b), unless before that date the partnership cures each ground for termination stated in the notice or notation. If the partnership cures each ground, the [Secretary of State] shall file a record so stating.

COMMENT

This section is analogous to the procedures for administrative revocation under Section 903.

§ 1011.   Withdrawal of Registration of Registered Foreign Limited Liability Partnership

(a)   A registered foreign limited liability partnership may withdraw its registration by delivering a statement of withdrawal to the [Secretary of State] for filing. The statement of withdrawal must state:

(1)   the name of the partnership and its jurisdiction of formation;

(2)   that the partnership is not doing business in this state and that it withdraws its registration to do business in this state;

(3)   that the partnership revokes the authority of its registered agent to accept service on its behalf in this state; and

(4)   an address to which service of process may be made under subsection (b).

(b)   After the withdrawal of the registration of a foreign limited liability partnership, service of process in any action or proceeding based on a cause of action arising during the time the partnership was registered to do business in this state may be made pursuant to Section 909.

COMMENT

The statement of withdrawal must set forth an address where service of process may be made on the foreign limited liability partnership pursuant to Section 912. There is no limit on how long the withdrawn partnership must keep that address up to date.

§ 1012.   Action by [Attorney General]

The [Attorney General] may maintain an action to enjoin a foreign limited liability partnership from doing business in this state in violation of this [article].

COMMENT

The authority stated here has been part of corporate law for more than a century and has been carried over into the law of unincorporated business entities. Nowadays, the authority is rarely if ever invoked in either realm of entity law.

[ARTICLE] 11.   MERGER, INTEREST EXCHANGE, CONVERSION, AND DOMESTICATION

INTRODUCTORY COMMENT

This article deals comprehensively with both same-type and cross-type mergers and interest exchanges and with conversions and domestications. For this article to apply, at least one participant organization must be a domestic general partnership (regardless of whether the partnership is an LLP). For a foreign organization to be involved, its organic law must permit the organization's participation.

Part 1 contains definitions specific to this article as well as provisions applicable to all transactions authorized by this article.

Part 2 governs mergers and is an amalgamation of existing entity law, both unincorporated and incorporated.

Part 3 governs interest exchanges, previously a feature only of corporate law. Part 3 is derived from the share exchange provisions in Chapter 11 of the Model Business Corporation Act.

Part 4 governs conversions, a one-step procedure by which an entity changes from one type of entity to another type while nonetheless continuing in existence as the same legal entity.

Part 5 governs domestications, a procedure by a domestic limited liability partnership can become a foreign limited liability partnership or vice versa, in each instance with the partnership remaining the same legal entity.

Part 2 sets the paradigm for Parts 3, 4, and 5, because mergers are long established, and merger rules and concepts are familiar to business lawyers. Moreover, conversions and domestications could formerly be accomplished via mergers (with a new entity), and an interest exchange produces the same result as a triangular merger. The comments to Part 2 are thus relevant to understanding Parts 3, 4, and 5.

This article contemplates transactions in which the surviving entity is neither a filing entity nor otherwise of record in the filing office (*e.g.*, the merger of an LLC into a non-LLP general partnership). As a result, a filing under this article may be the first time that a filing office takes cognizance of an entity's existence.

[PART] 1.   GENERAL PROVISIONS

§ 1101.   Definitions

(1)   "Acquired entity" means the entity, all of one or more classes or series of interests of which are acquired in an interest exchange.

(2)   "Acquiring entity" means the entity that acquires all of one or more classes or series of interests of the acquired entity in an interest exchange.

(3)   "Conversion" means a transaction authorized by [Part] 4.

(4)   "Converted entity" means the converting entity as it continues in existence after a conversion.

(5)   "Converting entity" means the domestic entity that approves a plan of conversion pursuant to Section 1143 or the foreign entity that approves a conversion pursuant to the law of its jurisdiction of formation.

(6)   "Distributional interest" means the right under an unincorporated entity's organic law and organic rules to receive distributions from the entity.

(7)   "Domestic", with respect to an entity, means governed as to its internal affairs by the law of this state.

(8)   "Domesticated limited liability partnership" means a domesticating limited liability partnership as it continues in existence after a domestication.

(9)   "Domesticating limited liability partnership" means the domestic limited liability partnership that approves a plan of domestication pursuant to Section 1153 or the foreign limited liability partnership that approves a domestication pursuant to the law of its jurisdiction of formation.

(10)   "Domestication" means a transaction authorized by [Part] 5.

(11)   "Entity":

    (A)   means:

        (i)   a business corporation;

        (ii)   a nonprofit corporation;

        (iii)   a general partnership, including a limited liability partnership;

        (iv)   a limited partnership, including a limited liability limited partnership;

        (v)   a limited liability company;

        [(vi) a general cooperative association;]

(vii) a limited cooperative association;

(viii) an unincorporated nonprofit association;

(ix) a statutory trust, business trust, or common-law business trust; or

(x) any other person that has:

(I) a legal existence separate from any interest holder of that person; or

(II) the power to acquire an interest in real property in its own name; and

(B) does not include:

(i) an individual;

(ii) a trust with a predominantly donative purpose or a charitable trust;

(iii) an association or relationship that is not an entity listed in subparagraph (A) and is not a partnership under the rules stated in [Section 202(c) of the Uniform Partnership Act (1997) (Last Amended 2013)] [Section 7 of the Uniform Partnership Act (1914)] or a similar provision of the law of another jurisdiction;

(iv) a decedent's estate; or

(v) a government or a governmental subdivision, agency, or instrumentality.

(12) "Filing entity" means an entity whose formation requires the filing of a public organic record. The term does not include a limited liability partnership.

(13) "Foreign", with respect to an entity, means an entity governed as to its internal affairs by the law of a jurisdiction other than this state.

(14) "Governance interest" means a right under the organic law or organic rules of an unincorporated entity, other than as a governor, agent, assignee, or proxy, to:

(A) receive or demand access to information concerning, or the books and records of, the entity;

(B) vote for or consent to the election of the governors of the entity; or

(C) receive notice of or vote on or consent to an issue involving the internal affairs of the entity.

(15) "Governor" means:

(A) a director of a business corporation;

(B) a director or trustee of a nonprofit corporation;

(C) a general partner of a general partnership;

(D) a general partner of a limited partnership;

(E) a manager of a manager-managed limited liability company;

(F) a member of a member-managed limited liability company;

[(G) a director of a general cooperative association;]

(H) a director of a limited cooperative association;

(I) a manager of an unincorporated nonprofit association;

(J) a trustee of a statutory trust, business trust, or common-law business trust; or

(K) any other person under whose authority the powers of an entity are exercised and under whose direction the activities and affairs of the entity are managed pursuant to the organic law and organic rules of the entity.

(16) "Interest" means:

(A) a share in a business corporation;

(B) a membership in a nonprofit corporation;

    (C)   a partnership interest in a general partnership;

    (D)   a partnership interest in a limited partnership;

    (E)   a membership interest in a limited liability company;

    [(F)   a share in a general cooperative association;]

    (G)   a member's interest in a limited cooperative association;

    (H)   a membership in an unincorporated nonprofit association;

    (I)   a beneficial interest in a statutory trust, business trust, or common-law business trust; or

    (J)   a governance interest or distributional interest in any other type of unincorporated entity.

(17) "Interest Exchange" means a transaction authorized by [Part] 3.

(18) "Interest holder" means:

    (A)   a shareholder of a business corporation;

    (B)   a member of a nonprofit corporation;

    (C)   a general partner of a general partnership;

    (D)   a general partner of a limited partnership;

    (E)   a limited partner of a limited partnership;

    (F)   a member of a limited liability company;

    [(G)   a shareholder of a general cooperative association;]

    (H)   a member of a limited cooperative association;

    (I)   a member of an unincorporated nonprofit association;

    (J)   a beneficiary or beneficial owner of a statutory trust, business trust, or common-law business trust; or

    (K)   any other direct holder of an interest.

(19) "Interest holder liability" means:

    (A)   personal liability for a liability of an entity which is imposed on a person:

        (i)   solely by reason of the status of the person as an interest holder; or

        (ii)   by the organic rules of the entity which make one or more specified interest holders or categories of interest holders liable in their capacity as interest holders for all or specified liabilities of the entity; or

    (B)   an obligation of an interest holder under the organic rules of an entity to contribute to the entity.

(20) "Merger" means a transaction authorized by [Part] 2.

(21) "Merging entity" means an entity that is a party to a merger and exists immediately before the merger becomes effective.

(22) "Organic law" means the law of an entity's jurisdiction of formation governing the internal affairs of the entity.

(23) "Organic rules" means the public organic record and private organic rules of an entity.

(24) "Plan" means a plan of merger, plan of interest exchange, plan of conversion, or plan of domestication.

(25) "Plan of conversion" means a plan under Section 1142.

(26) "Plan of domestication" means a plan under Section 1152.

(27) "Plan of interest exchange" means a plan under Section 1132.

(28) "Plan of merger" means a plan under Section 1122.

(29) "Private organic rules" means the rules, whether or not in a record, that govern the internal affairs of an entity, are binding on all its interest holders, and are not part of its public organic record, if any. The term includes:

(A) the bylaws of a business corporation;

(B) the bylaws of a nonprofit corporation;

(C) the partnership agreement of a general partnership;

(D) the partnership agreement of a limited partnership;

(E) the operating agreement of a limited liability company;

[(F) the bylaws of a general cooperative association;]

(G) the bylaws of a limited cooperative association;

(H) the governing principles of an unincorporated nonprofit association; and

(I) the trust instrument of a statutory trust or similar rules of a business trust or common-law business trust.

(30) "Protected agreement" means:

(A) a record evidencing indebtedness and any related agreement in effect on [the effective date of this [act]];

(B) an agreement that is binding on an entity on [the effective date of this [act]];

(C) the organic rules of an entity in effect on [the effective date of this [act]]; or

(D) an agreement that is binding on any of the governors or interest holders of an entity on [the effective date of this [act]].

(31) "Public organic record" means the record the filing of which by the [Secretary of State] is required to form an entity and any amendment to or restatement of that record. The term includes:

(A) the articles of incorporation of a business corporation;

(B) the articles of incorporation of a nonprofit corporation;

(C) the certificate of limited partnership of a limited partnership;

(D) the certificate of organization of a limited liability company;

[(E) the articles of incorporation of a general cooperative association;]

(F) the articles of organization of a limited cooperative association; and

(G) the certificate of trust of a statutory trust or similar record of a business trust.

(32) "Registered foreign entity" means a foreign entity that is registered to do business in this state pursuant to a record filed by the [Secretary of State].

(33) "Statement of conversion" means a statement under Section 1145.

(34) "Statement of domestication" means a statement under Section 1155.

(35) "Statement of interest exchange" means a statement under Section 1135.

(36) "Statement of merger" means a statement under Section 1125.

(37) "Surviving entity" means the entity that continues in existence after or is created by a merger.

(38) "Type of entity" means a generic form of entity:

(A) recognized at common law; or

(B)   formed under an organic law, whether or not some entities formed under that organic law are subject to provisions of that law that create different categories of the form of entity.

COMMENT

This section defines the terms that are used in this article. Many of the definitions describe attributes that are significant in some forms of entity and not in others. For example, the concept of separate "distributional" and "governance" interests are inherent in unincorporated entities but have no counterpart in corporations. In addition, because some statutes use different terms to describe the same transaction, the definitions are intended to be broad enough to encompass those similar transactions, regardless of how described. *See, e.g.,* the comment to Paragraph 8.

"Acquired entity" [(1)]—This definition recognizes that an interest exchange may involve only the acquisition of a particular "class" or "series" of interests in an entity. Model Business Corporation Act section 6.01 does not expressly define "classes" or "series." Because the interests of members in an unincorporated business organization often tend to be distinctive, it may be that each member's interest will comprise a separate class or series. For an explanation of a new and different meaning of the word "series," see Section 1131, comment. The term "acquired entity" does not encompass series under that new meaning.

"Acquiring entity" [(2)]—An "acquiring entity" is an entity that acquires the interests of the acquired entity in an interest exchange governed by Part 3 of this article.

"Conversion" [(3)]—The term "conversion" means a transaction authorized by Part 4 pursuant to which an entity of one type is converted into an entity of another type. As used in this act, the term "conversion" does not include a transaction in which an entity changes the jurisdiction in which it is organized but does not change to a different form of entity; that type of transaction is referred to in this act as a "domestication" and is governed by Article 5.

"Converted entity" [(4)]—This term is used in Part 4 to refer to the entity that results from a conversion.

"Converting entity" [(5)]—A converting entity is the entity that becomes the converted entity under Part 4.

"Distributional interest" [(6)]—This term is similar to the concept of a "transferable interest" found in this act and the organic laws of several other types of unincorporated entities, but has a broader meaning because the scope of this act includes entities in addition to those whose organic law uses the term "transferable interest."

"Domestic" [(7)]—The term "domestic", when used in this article with respect to an entity, refers to an entity whose internal affairs are governed by the organic laws of this state. In the case of a general partnership organized under UPA (1997) (Last Amended 2013), the term will mean a general partnership whose governing law under UPA (1997) § 104 is the law of the adopting state. Under that section, the governing law is determined by the location of the partnership's principal office, except for limited liability partnerships whose governing law is the law of the state where the LLP's statement of qualification is filed.

"Domesticated limited liability partnership" [(8)]—This term is used in Part 5 and means the entity limited liability partnership that is domesticated pursuant to Part 5. By the nature of the transaction, the domesticated entity will be of the same type as the domesticating entity—*i.e.,* a limited liability partnership.

"Domesticating limited liability partnership" [(9)]—This term is used in Part 5 and means the entity that is domesticated pursuant to Part 5.

Sections 1101(8) and (9) and 1151(a) exclude non-LLP general partnerships from domestications. However, a non-LLP general partnership that seeks to change its governing law may obtain that result through other means. *See* the comment to Section1151(a).

"Domestication" [(10)]—The term "domestication" means a transaction of the kind authorized by Part 5 pursuant to which an entity may change its *jurisdiction* of formation *but not its type* so long as the laws of the foreign jurisdiction permit the domestication. The legal effect of the domestication of an LLP out of this state will be governed by the laws of both this state and the foreign jurisdiction. Some statutes include what is described in this act as "domestication" in their definition of a "conversion." *See, e.g.,* COLO. REV. STAT. § 7–90–201. It is intended that the domestication provisions of this act will apply to a transaction that may be characterized under another act as a "conversion" if the transaction meets the definition of "domestication" under this act.

"Entity" [(11)]—This definition determines the overall scope of the act because only an "entity" may participate in the transactions authorized by Parts 2 (mergers), 3 (interest exchanges), 4 (conversions), and 5 (domestications). *See* Sections 1121 (authorization of mergers), 1131 (authorization of interest exchanges), 1141 (authorization of conversions), 1151 (authorization of domestications).

Subparagraph (A)(x) is a "catch-all" provision that includes within the definition of "entity" any type of organization recognized under the law of this state which is not listed specifically in the preceding paragraphs of this definition. Subparagraph (A)(x) is intended to include all forms of private organizations, regardless of whether organized for profit, and artificial legal persons other than those excluded by Subparagraph (B). This definition does not exclude regulated entities such as public utilities, banks, and insurance companies. Should a state desire to exclude certain types of regulated entities or any of the entities listed in Subparagraph (A)(i)–(x) from participating in transactions permitted by this act for policy reasons, that may be done by listing those types of entities in Section 1107(a), or by permitting those type of entities to engage in transactions under this act generally but prohibiting certain types of transactions by listing those transactions in Section 1107(b).

Unincorporated nonprofit associations are treated as a type of entity in Subparagraph (A)(viii) because Section 5 of the Uniform Unincorporated Nonprofit Association Act (2008) (Last Amended 2013) specifically states that an unincorporated nonprofit association is an entity. In many states, the status of a nonprofit association may not be clear. Nevertheless, in most states a nonprofit association has the power to acquire an interest in real property in its own name and therefore would qualify as an "entity" under Subparagraph (A)(x). *See* UUNAA § 6 (giving an unincorporated nonprofit association the power to acquire in its own name an interest in real property).

Subparagraph (B)(i) of this definition excludes a sole proprietorship from the concept of an "entity."

Trusts with a predominately donative purpose, such as inter vivos and testamentary trusts and charitable trusts, are treated in many states as having a separate legal existence, but they have been excluded from the definition of "entity" (and thus are not within the scope of this article) under Subparagraph (B)(ii) because they should not be able to engage in transactions under this act as a matter of public policy. Trusts that carry on a business, however, such as business and statutory entity trusts, are "entities." *See* Subparagraph (A)(ix).

Subparagraph (B)(iii) of this definition excludes from the concept of an "entity" any form of co-ownership of property or sharing of returns from property that is not listed in Subparagraph (A) and is not a partnership under this act. In that connection, Section 202(c) of this act provides in part:

In determining whether a partnership is formed, the following rules apply:

(1) Joint tenancy, tenancy in common, tenancy by the entireties, joint property, common property, or part ownership does not by itself establish a partnership, even if the co-owners share profits made by the use of the property.

(2) The sharing of gross returns does not by itself establish a partnership, even if the persons sharing them have a joint or common right or interest in property from which the returns are derived.

Limited liability partnerships and limited liability limited partnerships are "entities" because they are general partnerships and limited partnerships respectively that have taken the necessary steps to obtain LLP or LLLP status. A limited liability partnership is not, therefore, a separate type of entity from the underlying general or limited partnership that has elected limited liability partnership status. Thus, for example, the election of a general partnership to become a limited liability partnership is not a conversion subject to Article 4.

Under Subparagraph (B)(iv), decedent's estates are excluded from the definition of an entity for the same policy reason as trusts with a predominately donative purpose and charitable trusts.

This same public policy rationale is the justification for the exclusion of governmental subdivisions, agencies, or instrumentalities in Subparagraph (B)(v).

"Filing entity" [Paragraph (12)]—Whether an entity is a filing entity is determined by reference to whether its legal existence requires the filing of a document with the state filing officer. To fit within this definition, the filing must be necessary but need not be sufficient to form the entity. *See, e.g.*, ULLCA (2006) (Last Amended 2013) § 201(d) ("A limited liability company is formed when the company's certificate of organization becomes effective *and* at least one person becomes a member.") (emphasis added).

While the statute refers to the "formation" of an entity, the term is intended to encompass corporations that are "incorporated," as well as other filing entities whose statutes refer to them as being "organized." Business trusts present a special problem. In some states a business trust could be a filing entity or a common law relationship, while in other states business trusts are only recognized at common law. A statutory trust entity formed under the Uniform Statutory Trust Entity Act (2009) (Last Amended 2013) § 201(a) is a filing entity, because a statutory trust entity is formed by the filing office filing a certificate of trust pertaining to the entity.

The term "filing entity" does not include a limited liability partnership because, while a filed document is precondition to LLP status, that document (a statement of qualification under Section 901) does not form the underlying entity. A limited liability limited partnership, on the other hand, is a filing entity because the underlying limited partnership is formed by filing a certificate of limited partnership. ULPA (2001) (Last Amended 2013) § 201(a).

"Foreign" [(13)]—The term "foreign entity" includes any non-domestic entity of any type. Where a foreign entity is a filing entity, the entity is governed by the laws of the state of filing. A nonfiling foreign entity is governed by the laws governing its internal affairs. It is a factual question whether a general partnership whose internal affairs are governed by UPA (1914) is a domestic or foreign partnership. A UPA (1914) partnership will likely be deemed to be a domestic entity where the greatest nexus of contacts are found. The domestic or foreign characterization of partnerships under this act that are not limited liability partnerships will be governed by Section 104(2) ("the law of the jurisdiction in which the partnership has its principal office") or the partnership agreement. (Section 104(2) is a default rule.)

"Governance interest" [(14)]—A governance interest is typically only part of the interest that a person will hold in an unincorporated entity and is usually coupled with a distributional interest (or economic rights). Memberships in some nonprofit corporations and unincorporated nonprofit associations consist solely of governance interests and memberships in other nonprofit entities may not include either governance interests or distributional interests. In some unincorporated business entities, including partnerships, there is a more limited right to transfer governance interests than there is to transfer distributional interests. An interest holder in such an unincorporated business entity who transfers only a distributional interest and retains the governance interest will also retain the status of an interest holder. Whether a transferee who acquires only a distributional interest will acquire the status of an interest holder is determined by the definition of "interest holder."

Governors of an entity have the kinds of rights listed in the definition of "governance interest" by reason of their position with the entity. For a governor to have a "governance interest," however, requires that the governor also have those rights for a reason other than the governor's status as such. A manager who is not a member in a limited liability company, for example, will not have a governance interest, but a manager who is a member will have a governance interest arising from the ownership of a membership interest.

"Governor" [(15)]—This term has been chosen to provide a way of referring to a person who has the authority under an entity's organic law to make management decisions regarding the entity that is different from any of the existing terms used in connection with particular types of entities. Depending on the type of entity or its organic rules, the governors of an entity may have the power to act on their own authority, or they may be organized as a board or similar group and have only the power to act collectively, and then only through a designated agent. In other words, a person having only the power to bind the organization pursuant to the instruction of the governors is not a governor. Under the organic rules, particularly those of unincorporated entities, most or all of the management decisions may be reserved to the members or partners. Thus, if a manager of a limited liability company were limited to having authority to execute management decisions made by the members and did not have any authority to make independent management decisions, the manager would not be a governor under this definition.

"Interest" [(16)]—In the usual case, the interest held by an interest holder will include both a governance interest and a distributional interest. Members in nonprofit corporations or unincorporated nonprofit associations generally do not have any distributional interest because they do not receive distributions, but they nonetheless may hold a governance interest in which case they would have the status of interest holders under this article.

"Interest exchange" [(17)]—The term "interest exchange" means a transaction authorized by Part 3 pursuant to which an entity may acquire interests in another entity. The consideration that may be provided to the interest holders whose interests are being acquired in an exchange may consist in whole or part of interests in a third party that is not one of the two parties to the exchange itself. *See* Section 1131(a).

"Interest holder" [(18)]—This article does not refer to "equity" interests or "equity" owners or holders because the term "equity" could be confusing in the case of a nonprofit entity whose members do not have an interest in the assets or results of operations of the entity but have only a right to vote on its internal affairs.

"Interest holder liability" [(19)]—This term is used to describe the vicarious liability of an interest holder, by virtue of being an interest holder, for liabilities of the entity. The term includes only personal liability of an interest holder for a debt of the entity imposed on the interest holder either by statute or by the organic rules to the extent authorized pursuant to the organic law. Liabilities that an interest holder incurs in any other fashion are not interest holder liabilities for purposes of this act. Thus, for example, if a state's business corporation law makes shareholders personally liable for unpaid wages because of their status as shareholders, that liability would be an "interest holder liability." If, on the other hand, a shareholder were to guarantee payment of an obligation of a corporation, that liability would not be an "interest holder liability" because it is a direct liability and not based on the status of being a shareholder. Similarly, the liability to return an improper distribution is not an interest holder liability because it is a direct liability of the interest holder based on receipt of the distribution.

"Merger" [(20)]—The term means a transaction in which two or more entities are combined into a single entity pursuant to a filing by the filing office. The term "merger" in this act includes the transaction known as a consolidation in which a new entity results from the combination of two or more pre-existing entities.

"Merging entity" [(21)]—The term "merging entity" refers to each entity that is in existence immediately before a merger and is a party to the merger. It will include the surviving entity if the surviving entity exists before the merger becomes effective. It does not include an entity that provides consideration to be received by interest holders if that entity is not a party to the merger.

"Organic law" [(22)]—Organic law means statutes that govern the internal affairs of an entity. For example, this act is the organic law of a limited liability partnership whose statement of qualification is filed under this act.

Entity laws in a few states purport to require that some of their internal governance rules applicable to a domestic entity also apply to a foreign entity with significant ties to the state. *See, e.g.*, CAL. CORP. CODE § 2115 (Foreign Corporations); N.Y. NOT-FOR-PROFIT-CORP. §§ 1318–21 (Liabilities of Directors and Officers of Foreign Corporations); 15 PA.CONS. STAT. § 6145 (Applicability of Certain Safeguards to Foreign Corporations). Such a "sticky fingers" law is not included within the definition of "organic law" for purposes of this act because those laws are not part of the law of the entity's jurisdiction of formation.

"Organic rules" [(23)]—The term "organic rules" means an entity's public organic record and the private organic rules. The organic rules, together with this act, the organic law, and the common law, provide the rules governing the internal affairs of the entity. For example, this act and the partnership agreement comprise the organic rules of a limited liability partnership formed under this act.

"Plan" [(24)]—The term "plan" is a short-hand way of referring to the plan of merger, interest exchange, conversion, or domestication, as the case may be, depending on which form of transaction is taking place. *See* Sections 1122 (plan of merger), 1132 (plan of interest exchange), 1142 (plan of conversion), 1152 (plan of domestication).

"Private organic rules" [(29)]—The term private "organic rules" is intended to include all governing rules of an entity that are binding on all of its interest holders, whether or not in record form, except for the provisions of the entity's public organic record, if any. The term is intended to include agreements in "record" form such as corporate bylaws, as well as oral partnership agreements and oral operating agreements among LLC members.

"Protected agreement" [(30)]—The term "protected agreement" refers to evidences of indebtedness and agreements binding on the entity or any of its governors or interest holders that are unpaid or executory in whole or in part on the effective date of the act. Thus a revolving line of credit from a bank to a corporation would constitute a protected agreement even if advances were not made until after the effective date of the act. Likewise, a partnership agreement in effect under this act or a predecessor to this act is a "protected agreement."

If a protected agreement has provisions that apply if an entity merges, those provisions will apply if the entity enters into an interest exchange, conversion, or domestication even though the agreement does not mention those other types of transactions. *See* Sections 1131(c) (interest exchange), 1141(c) (conversion), 1151(c) (domestication).

"Public organic record" [(31)]—A "public organic record" is a record that is filed publicly to form, organize, incorporate, or otherwise create an entity. The term does not include a statement of authority under this act or any of the other statements that may be filed under this act since those statements do not create a new entity. Thus, a statement of qualification filed under Section 1003 is not a "public organic record." The limited liability partnership that results from the filing is the same entity as the partnership that delivered the statement to the filing office.

Similarly, the term does not include a statement of authority filed under Section 7 of the Revised Uniform Unincorporated Nonprofit Association Act (2008) (Last Amended 2013), a statement appointing a registered agent filed under Section 31 of that act, or any of the various statements filed under the ULLCA (2006) (Last Amended 2013).

In those states where a deed of trust or other instrument is publicly filed to create a business trust, that filing will constitute a public organic record. But in those states where a business trust is not created by a public filing, the deed of trust or similar record will be part of the private organic rules of the business trust.

Where a public organic document has been amended or restated, the term means the public organic document as last amended or restated.

"Registered foreign entity" [(32]—This term refers to a foreign entity that is registered to transact business in this state pursuant to a public filing.

"Surviving entity" [(37)]—The term "surviving entity" refers to either a merging entity that survives the merger or the new entity created by the merger.

"Type of entity" [(38]—The term "type of entity" has been developed in an attempt to distinguish different legal forms of entities. It is sometimes difficult to decide whether one is dealing with a different form of entity or a variation of the same form. For example, a limited partnership, although it has long been characterized or even defined as a partnership, is a different type of entity from a general partnership, while a limited liability partnership is not a different type of entity from a general partnership. In some states cooperatives are categories of business corporations or nonprofit corporations, while in other states cooperatives are a separate type of entity.

§ 1102. Relationship of [Article] to Other Laws

(a)   This [article] does not authorize an act prohibited by, and does not affect the application or requirements of, law other than this [article].

(b)   A transaction effected under this [act] may not create or impair a right, duty, or obligation of a person under the statutory law of this state relating to a change in control, takeover, business combination, control-share acquisition, or similar transaction involving a domestic merging, acquired, converting, or domesticating business corporation unless:

     (1)   if the corporation does not survive the transaction, the transaction satisfies any requirements of the law; or

     (2)   if the corporation survives the transaction, the approval of the plan is by a vote of the shareholders or directors which would be sufficient to create or impair the right, duty, or obligation directly under the law.

COMMENT

This section preserves existing regulatory law in an adopting state in general terms. Adopting states should consider more carefully integrating this act with their various regulatory laws. For example, in some states certain professions are limited in their use of limited liability entities. *See* Section 1103.

Laws other than this act that will apply to transactions under the act include, for example, uniform fraudulent transfer and fraudulent conveyance acts, state insolvency statutes, federal bankruptcy law, and Articles 8 and 9 of the Uniform Commercial Code.

Subsection (b)—Many states have enacted "antitakeover" statutes intended to make it more difficult to acquire control of a publicly traded corporation. Those statutes often provide that their application to a particular corporation cannot be changed unless the corporation obtains certain specified approvals, such as a vote of disinterested directors or a supermajority vote by the shareholders. The purpose of the special requirements in this subsection on varying the application of an antitakeover statute is to protect against a hostile acquirer or group of shareholders seeking to use the act to avoid the application of the antitakeover statute.

This subsection protects the application of antitakeover statutes from being affected by a transaction under this act by requiring that the transaction be approved in a manner that would be sufficient to approve changing the application of the antitakeover statute. If a transaction is approved in that manner, there is no policy reason to prohibit the application of the antitakeover statute from being varied by a transaction under this act. If the application of an antitakeover statute cannot be varied by action of an entity subject to it, then a transaction under this act will be permissible only if the antitakeover provision continues to apply after the transaction or the transaction itself is permissible under the antitakeover statute.

§ 1103. Required Notice or Approval

(a) A domestic or foreign entity that is required to give notice to, or obtain the approval of, a governmental agency or officer of this state to be a party to a merger must give the notice or obtain the approval to be a party to an interest exchange, conversion, or domestication.

(b) Property held for a charitable purpose under the law of this state by a domestic or foreign entity immediately before a transaction under this [article] becomes effective may not, as a result of the transaction, be diverted from the objects for which it was donated, granted, devised, or otherwise transferred unless, to the extent required by or pursuant to the law of this state concerning cy pres or other law dealing with nondiversion of charitable assets, the entity obtains an appropriate order of [the appropriate court] [the Attorney General] specifying the disposition of the property.

(c) A bequest, devise, gift, grant, or promise contained in a will or other instrument of donation, subscription, or conveyance which is made to a merging entity that is not the surviving entity and which takes effect or remains payable after the merger inures to the surviving entity.

(d) A trust obligation that would govern property if transferred to a nonsurviving entity applies to property that is transferred to the surviving entity under this section.

Legislative Note: As an alternative to enacting Subsection (a), a state may identify each of its regulatory laws that requires prior approval for a merger of a regulated entity, decide whether regulatory approval should be required for an interest exchange, conversion, or domestication, and make amendments as appropriate to those laws.

As with Subsection (a), an adopting state may choose to amend its various laws with respect to the nondiversion of charitable property to cover the various transactions authorized by this act as an alternative to enacting Subsection (b).

COMMENT

Subsection (a)—Because at least some of the provisions of this act will be new in most states, it is likely that existing state laws that require regulatory approval of transactions by businesses such as banks, insurance companies, or public utilities may not be worded in a fashion that will include at least some of the transactions authorized by this act. The purpose of this subsection is to ensure that transactions under this act will be subject to the same regulatory approval as mergers. This subsection is based on whether a merger by a regulated entity requires prior approval because the transactions authorized by this act may be effectuated indirectly in many cases under existing law by establishing a wholly owned subsidiary of the desired type and then merging into it.

The consequence of violating this subsection should be the same as in the case of a merger consummated without the required approval.

Subsection (b)—This act applies generally to nonprofit corporations and unincorporated nonprofit associations. As in the case of laws regulating particular industries, a state's laws governing the nondiversion of charitable property to other uses may not cover some of the transactions authorized by this act. To prevent the procedures in this act from being used to avoid restrictions on the use of such charitable property, this subsection requires approval of the effect of transactions under this act by the appropriate arm of government having supervision of nonprofit entities.

An approval or order obtained under this section may impose conditions or specify the disposition of assets or liabilities in a manner different than would otherwise be the case. In such an instance, the approval or order will control over the provisions of this act specifying the effects of a transaction. *See* Sections 1126 (effect of merger), 1136 (effect of interest exchange), 1146 (effect of conversion), 1156 (effect of domestication).

Subsection (c)—This subsection clarifies the legal effect of a merger on bequests, etc. that were originally made to an entity that does not survive the merger. This issue does not arise in an interest exchange, conversion, or domestication transaction because the entity to which the bequest, etc. was made survives in some form after the transaction.

§ 1104. Nonexclusivity

The fact that a transaction under this [article] produces a certain result does not preclude the same result from being accomplished in any other manner permitted by law other than this [article].

COMMENT

This section allows a transaction that has the same end result as one of the transactions governed by this act, but that is accomplished in a manner not within the scope of this act, to be exempt from this act. For example, a sale of assets and transfer of liabilities by two entities to a third entity followed by the liquidation of the two transferring entities can be accomplished pursuant to statutory provisions pertaining to sale of assets rather than under Part 2 of this article, even though the end result of the transaction is essentially the same as if the two entities had merged into a third entity.

§ 1105. Reference to External Facts

A plan may refer to facts ascertainable outside the plan if the manner in which the facts will operate upon the plan is specified in the plan. The facts may include the occurrence of an event or a determination or action by a person, whether or not the event, determination, or action is within the control of a party to the transaction.

COMMENT

This section is based on, but more concise than, section 1.20(k) of the Model Business Corporation Act.

§ 1106. Appraisal Rights

An interest holder of a domestic merging, acquired, converting, or domesticating partnership is entitled to contractual appraisal rights in connection with a transaction under this [article] to the extent provided in:

    (1)   the partnership's organic rules; or

    (2)   the plan.

COMMENT

In corporate law, appraisal rights developed when corporate statutes were amended to permit mergers with less than unanimous consent of the shareholders. This article provides no appraisal rights, because as a default rule transactions under this article require the consent or affirmative vote of all the partners. Where the partnership agreement changes this default rule, parties may wish to consider contractual appraisal rights.

This subsection validates the grant of such contractual appraisal rights. *Cf.* 6 DEL. CODE ANN. §§ 15–120 (general partnerships), 17–212 (limited partnerships), 18–210 (limited liability companies) (validating "contractual appraisal rights"); MODEL BUS. CORP. ACT § 13.02(5) (permitting the articles of incorporation, bylaws, or a resolution of the board of directors to confer appraisal rights in contexts in which they would otherwise not be available). Legislative authorization in this subsection of the grant of contractual appraisal rights removes any question as to whether a court would have jurisdiction to hear a case in which the parties were attempting to create jurisdiction in the court by private agreement.

In this section, the term "appraisal rights" refers to any arrangement, either in the partnership agreement or the plan, providing for the buy-out of partners that object to a transaction under this article.

[§ 1107. Excluded Entities and Transactions

    (a)   The following entities may not participate in a transaction under this [article]:

        (1)

        (2).

    (b)   This [article] may not be used to effect a transaction that:

        (1)

        (2).]

Legislative Note: *Subsection (a) may be used by states that have special statutes restricted to the organization of certain types of entities. A common example is banking statutes that prohibit banks from engaging in transactions other than pursuant to those statutes.*

Nonprofit entities may participate in transactions under this act with for-profit entities, subject to compliance with Section 1103. If a state desires, however, to exclude entities with a charitable purpose or to exclude other types of entities from the scope of this article, that may be done by referring to those entities in Subsection (a).

Subsection (b) may be used to exclude certain types of transactions governed by more specific statutes. A common example is the conversion of an insurance company from mutual to stock form. There may be other types of transactions that vary greatly among the states.

[PART] 2. MERGER

§ 1121. Merger Authorized

(a) By complying with this [part]:

(1) one or more domestic partnerships may merge with one or more domestic or foreign entities into a domestic or foreign surviving entity; and

(2) two or more foreign entities may merge into a domestic partnership.

(b) By complying with the provisions of this [part] applicable to foreign entities, a foreign entity may be a party to a merger under this [part] or may be the surviving entity in such a merger if the merger is authorized by the law of the foreign entity's jurisdiction of formation.

COMMENT

The merger transaction authorized by this act involves the combination of one or more domestic general partnerships with or into one or more other domestic or foreign entities. It also contemplates the consolidation of two or more foreign entities into a single domestic general partnership. Upon the effective date of the merger, all the assets and liabilities of the constituent entities vest in the surviving entity as a matter of law. As such, mergers require the existence of at least two separate entities before the transaction and only one entity may survive the merger. If independent existence of the constituent entities is desired following the conclusion of the transaction, a restructuring transaction other than a merger must be used to accomplish the transfer of assets and liabilities.

This act authorizes a merger for state entity law purposes. Federal law and other state law will independently determine how a merger transaction will be taxed.

Subsection (a)(1)—This paragraph states the general rule that subject to Subsection (b) one or more domestic general partnerships may merge with or into a domestic or foreign surviving entity.

Subsection (a)(2)—This paragraph provides that two or more foreign entities may merge into a domestic surviving general partnership so long as the requirements of Subsection (b) are met.

Subsection (b)—This subsection provides that a foreign entity may be a party to a merger or may be the surviving entity in a merger only if the merger is authorized by the laws of the foreign entity's jurisdiction of formation.

§ 1122. Plan of Merger

(a) A domestic partnership may become a party to a merger under this [part] by approving a plan of merger. The plan must be in a record and contain:

(1) as to each merging entity, its name, jurisdiction of formation, and type of entity;

(2) if the surviving entity is to be created in the merger, a statement to that effect and the entity's name, jurisdiction of formation, and type of entity;

(3) the manner of converting the interests in each party to the merger into interests, securities, obligations, money, other property, rights to acquire interests or securities, or any combination of the foregoing;

(4) if the surviving entity exists before the merger, any proposed amendments to:

(A) its public organic record, if any; or

(B) its private organic rules that are, or are proposed to be, in a record;

    (5)   if the surviving entity is to be created in the merger:

        (A)   its proposed public organic record, if any; and

        (B)   the full text of its private organic rules that are proposed to be in a record;

    (6)   the other terms and conditions of the merger; and

    (7)   any other provision required by the law of a merging entity's jurisdiction of formation or the organic rules of a merging entity.

(b)   In addition to the requirements of subsection (a), a plan of merger may contain any other provision not prohibited by law.

COMMENT

Subsection (a)—This subsection states the requirements for the plan of merger. They are similar to plan of merger provisions in corporation statutes. *See* MODEL BUS. CORP. ACT § 11.02(c). The requirements stated in this subsection are mandatory. *See* Section 105(c)(15).

Subsection (a)(1)—This paragraph requires that the plan of merger identify the parties to the merger. The name of a merging entity as it appears in the plan of merger will be its name in its jurisdiction of formation.

Subsection (a)(3)—The language of this paragraph is similar to Model Business Corporation Act § 11.02(c)(3). What may be done under this paragraph with respect to providing for continuing interests in the surviving entity for some holders of interests of a class or series of a party to the merger while paying some other form of consideration to other holders of the same class or series of interests in that entity will vary depending on the type of entity involved and the extent to which its organic rules provide for non-uniform treatment of interest holders in a manner that is permissible under its organic law. Similarly the ability to use a merger to reorganize the capital structure of the surviving entity will vary depending on the type of entity involved and whether the entity has appropriately adopted relevant provisions in its organic rules.

If the organic law and organic rules of an unincorporated entity permit a non-uniform "equity shuffle" to be accomplished in a merger involving the unincorporated entity, the minority owners of the unincorporated entity will not necessarily be entitled to the statutory appraisal rights currently afforded to minority stockholders in merging corporate entities. Any perceived unfairness in the shuffle would be addressed either: (i) under principles of fiduciary duties and the contractual obligations of good faith and fair dealing, assuming, of course, that such duties and obligations have not been contractually modified or eliminated to the extent permitted by the applicable organic law, or (ii) by the exercise of whatever rights the minority owners may have to veto the transaction or to withdraw or to dissociate and be paid the value of their interests.

The Model Business Corporation Act generally requires that shares of the same class or series be treated in the same manner in a merger unless the corporation has adopted an applicable provision of its articles of incorporation pursuant to section 6.01(e) of that act providing for variations in the treatment of holders of the same class or series of shares. Thus, a determination of what may be done by way of an equity shuffle in the case of a corporation will require reference to its organic law and organic rules.

The consideration paid to the interest holders of the merging parties may be supplied in whole or part by a person who is not a party to the merger.

Subsection (b)—This subsection provides the statutory authority for a merging party to include a provision in a plan of merger that is not specifically listed in Subsection (a). One such possibility is contractual appraisal rights as provided in Section 1106(2).

§ 1123. Approval of Merger

(a)   A plan of merger is not effective unless it has been approved:

    (1)   by a domestic merging partnership, by all the partners of the partnership entitled to vote on or consent to any matter; and

    (2)   in a record, by each partner of a domestic merging partnership which will have interest holder liability for debts, obligations, and other liabilities that are incurred after the merger becomes effective, unless:

(A)   the partnership agreement of the partnership provides in a record for the approval of a merger in which some or all of its partners become subject to interest holder liability by the affirmative vote or consent of fewer than all the partners; and

(B)   the partner consented in a record to or voted for that provision of the partnership agreement or became a partner after the adoption of that provision.

(b)   A merger involving a domestic merging entity that is not a partnership is not effective unless the merger is approved by that entity in accordance with its organic law.

(c)   A merger involving a foreign merging entity is not effective unless the merger is approved by the foreign entity in accordance with the law of the foreign entity's jurisdiction of formation.

COMMENT

Subsection (a)—In the uniform acts pertaining to unincorporated business organizations, unanimity is the default rule for approving a merger. The partnership agreement certainly can change this rule, but care should be taken in doing so. For example, a merger can revise the partnership agreement. Section 1122(a)(4). Thus, if a merger requires less-than-unanimous consent, the partnership agreement is subject to amendment by the same quantum of consent. "Exit rights" also require consideration. This act does not provide appraisal rights, because those rights are inapposite when unanimous consent is required. *See* the comment to Section 1106.

Subsection (a)(2)—This provision is not a default rule, Section 105(c)(14), and deals with the situation in which a partner of a general partnership that is a party to a merger will have "interest holder liability" for the liabilities of the surviving entity which are incurred after the merger becomes effective. This provision applies regardless of whether the partnership is an LLP. The issue is not whether the partners have "interest holder liability" in their current partnership but rather whether they will have that liability in the surviving entity. Thus, for example, if general partnership Alpha merges into general partnership Beta, which is not an LLP, the special approval requirement in Subsection (a)(2) will be applicable to each Alpha partner who will become a Beta partner—regardless of whether Alpha is a limited liability partnership.

The consent of a partner required by Subsection (a)(2)(B) may be given either by: (i) signing or agreeing generally to the terms of a partnership agreement that includes the required provision permitting less than unanimous approval of a merger in which partners become subject to "interest holder liability," or (ii) voting for or consenting to an amendment to the partnership agreement to add such a provision.

Subsection (b)—Where a domestic entity other than a general partnership is a party to a merger under this act, this subsection defers to that entity's organic law for the requirements for approval of the merger by that entity.

Subsection (c)—Where a foreign entity is a party to a merger under this act, this subsection defers to the laws of the foreign jurisdiction for the requirements for approval of the merger by the foreign entity. Those laws will include the organic law of the foreign entity and other applicable laws. The laws of the foreign jurisdiction will also control the application of any special approval requirements found in the organic rules of the foreign entity.

§ 1124.   Amendment or Abandonment of Plan of Merger

(a)   A plan of merger may be amended only with the consent of each party to the plan, except as otherwise provided in the plan.

(b)   A domestic merging partnership may approve an amendment of a plan of merger:

(1)   in the same manner as the plan was approved, if the plan does not provide for the manner in which it may be amended; or

(2)   by its partners in the manner provided in the plan, but a partner that was entitled to vote on or consent to approval of the merger is entitled to vote on or consent to any amendment of the plan that will change:

(A)   the amount or kind of interests, securities, obligations, money, other property, rights to acquire interests or securities, or any combination of the foregoing, to be received by the interest holders of any party to the plan;

     (B)   the public organic record, if any, or private organic rules of the surviving entity that will be in effect immediately after the merger be effective, except for changes that do not require approval of the interest holders of the surviving entity under its organic law or organic rules; or

     (C)   any other terms or conditions of the plan, if the change would adversely affect the partner in any material respect.

    (c)   After a plan of merger has been approved and before a statement of merger becomes effective, the plan may be abandoned as provided in the plan. Unless prohibited by the plan, a domestic merging partnership may abandon the plan in the same manner as the plan was approved.

    (d)   If a plan of merger is abandoned after a statement of merger has been delivered to the [Secretary of State] for filing and before the statement becomes effective, a statement of abandonment, signed by a party to the plan, must be delivered to the [Secretary of State] for filing before the statement of merger becomes effective. The statement of abandonment takes effect on filing, and the merger is abandoned and does not become effective. The statement of abandonment must contain:

    (1)   the name of each party to the plan of merger;

    (2)   the date on which the statement of merger was filed by the [Secretary of State]; and

    (3)   a statement that the merger has been abandoned in accordance with this section.

COMMENT

    This section sets out the requirements for amending or abandoning the plan of merger. They are similar to provisions for amending or abandoning mergers found in existing corporation merger statutes. *See* MODEL BUS.CORP. ACT §§ 11.02(e), 11.08.

§ 1125.   Statement of Merger; Effective Date of Merger

    (a)   A statement of merger must be signed by each merging entity and delivered to the [Secretary of State] for filing.

    (b)   A statement of merger must contain:

    (1)   the name, jurisdiction of formation, and type of entity of each merging entity that is not the surviving entity;

    (2)   the name, jurisdiction of formation, and type of entity of the surviving entity;

    (3)   a statement that the merger was approved by each domestic merging entity, if any, in accordance with this [part] and by each foreign merging entity, if any, in accordance with the law of its jurisdiction of formation;

    (4)   if the surviving entity exists before the merger and is a domestic filing entity, any amendment to its public organic record approved as part of the plan of merger;

    (5)   if the surviving entity is created by the merger and is a domestic filing entity, its public organic record, as an attachment; and

    (6)   if the surviving entity is created by the merger and is a domestic limited liability partnership, its statement of qualification, as an attachment.

    (c)   In addition to the requirements of subsection (b), a statement of merger may contain any other provision not prohibited by law.

    (d)   If the surviving entity is a domestic entity, its public organic record, if any, must satisfy the requirements of the law of this state, except that the public organic record does not need to be signed.

    (e)   A plan of merger that is signed by all the merging entities and meets all the requirements of subsection (b) may be delivered to the [Secretary of State] for filing instead of a statement of merger and on filing has the same effect. If a plan of merger is filed as provided in this subsection, references in this [article] to a statement of merger refer to the plan of merger filed under this subsection.

(f) If the surviving entity is a domestic partnership, the merger becomes effective when the statement of merger is effective. In all other cases, the merger becomes effective on the later of:

(1) the date and time provided by the organic law of the surviving entity; and

(2) when the statement is effective.

COMMENT

The filing of a statement of merger makes the transaction a matter of public record.

Subsection (a)—This subsection pertains to all merging entities involved in a merger, not merely any merging domestic general partnership. Other filings may be required by the organic law of other entities participating in the merger.

Subsection (b)(1) and (2)—The names of foreign entities set forth in the statement of merger will generally be their names in their jurisdiction of formation, except that if a foreign entity has been required to adopt a different name in order to register to do business in this state, the foreign qualification statute will likely require that, when the entity does business in this state, the entity must use the name adopted for the purposes of registering to do business. Engaging in a merger under this act will be part of the business done by the entity in this state and the name of the entity set forth in the statement of merger will thus need to be the name under which the entity has registered to do business. Use of the name under which the entity has registered to do business will allow the records in the filing office to associate the registration of the entity to do business with the statement of merger.

Subsection (b)(3)—For more information on the statement of merger, see Subsection (f), comment.

Subsection (b)(4)—The statement in this paragraph that the plan of merger was approved by each entity in accordance with this article necessarily presupposes that the plan was approved in accordance with any valid, special requirements in the organic rules of each merging entity.

Subsection (b)(5) and (6)—The public organic record of a domestic surviving entity created by the merger that is attached to the statement of merger becomes the original, officially filed text of the public organic record of the surviving entity when the statement of merger takes effect. It is not necessary, or appropriate, to make any other filing to create the surviving entity.

Similarly, a statement of qualification for a domestic limited liability partnership created by the merger that is attached to the statement of merger does not need to be filed separately.

Subsection (d)—Organic laws typically require that an initial filing that creates an entity be signed by the person serving as the incorporator or other organizer. This subsection, however, provides that the public organic record of the surviving entity does not need to be signed since the record is attached to a signed record.

This subsection also permits the public organic record of the surviving entity to omit any provision that is not required to be included in a restatement of the public organic record. Pursuant to this provision, for example, the public organic record of a business corporation created as the surviving entity in the merger would not need to state the name and address of each incorporator even though that information would be required by section 2.02(a)(4) of the Model Business Corporation Act if the corporation were being incorporated outside the context of the merger.

Subsection (e)—A plan of merger that contains all the information required in the statement of merger may be filed instead of the statement of merger. The plan must be in a record and signed by each merging party.

Subsection (f)—A merger in which the surviving entity is a domestic general partnership takes effect when the statement of merger takes effect. A merger in which the surviving entity is

a foreign entity will usually also take effect when the statement of merger takes effect because the practice is to coordinate the filings that need to be made when a merger involves both a domestic entity and also a foreign entity so that the filings in each jurisdiction take effect at the same time.

However, when the surviving general partnership is a foreign general partnership, it is possible that the filing in the foreign jurisdiction will take effect at a different time. For that reason, this subsection provides that the merger will take effect at the later of: (i) when the statement of merger takes effect; and (ii) when the merger takes effect under the law of the foreign jurisdiction. This rule avoids the possibility that the merger will take effect in this state before it takes effect in the foreign jurisdiction, which would produce the undesirable result that the merging domestic general partnership would cease to appear as an active entity on the records of this state before the records of the foreign jurisdiction reflect a completed merger.

It is necessary for the filing office to record only the effective date of the statement of merger, and the filing office does not need to be concerned with the effective date of the merger itself. Persons wishing to determine the effective date of a merger involving both a domestic and a foreign entity will be able to do so by consulting the records of the filing offices in each jurisdiction.

§ 1126. Effect of Merger

(a) When a merger becomes effective:

(1) the surviving entity continues or comes into existence;

(2) each merging entity that is not the surviving entity ceases to exist;

(3) all property of each merging entity vests in the surviving entity without transfer, reversion, or impairment;

(4) all debts, obligations, and other liabilities of each merging entity are debts, obligations, and other liabilities of the surviving entity;

(5) except as otherwise provided by law or the plan of merger, all the rights, privileges, immunities, powers, and purposes of each merging entity vest in the surviving entity;

(6) if the surviving entity exists before the merger:

(A) all its property continues to be vested in it without transfer, reversion, or impairment;

(B) it remains subject to all its debts, obligations, and other liabilities; and

(C) all its rights, privileges, immunities, powers, and purposes continue to be vested in it;

(7) the name of the surviving entity may be substituted for the name of any merging entity that is a party to any pending action or proceeding;

(8) if the surviving entity exists before the merger:

(A) its public organic record, if any, is amended as provided in the statement of merger; and

(B) its private organic rules that are to be in a record, if any, are amended to the extent provided in the plan of merger;

(9) if the surviving entity is created by the merger, its private organic rules become effective and:

(A) if it is a filing entity, its public organic record becomes effective; and

(B) if it is a limited liability partnership, its statement of qualification becomes effective; and

(10) the interests in each merging entity which are to be converted in the merger are converted, and the interest holders of those interests are entitled only to the rights provided to them under the plan of merger and to any appraisal rights they have under Section 1106 and the merging entity's organic law.

(b) Except as otherwise provided in the organic law or organic rules of a merging entity, the merger does not give rise to any rights that an interest holder, governor, or third party would have upon a dissolution, liquidation, or winding up of the merging entity.

(c) When a merger becomes effective, a person that did not have interest holder liability with respect to any of the merging entities and becomes subject to interest holder liability with respect to a domestic entity as a result of the merger has interest holder liability only to the extent provided by the organic law of that entity and only for those debts, obligations, and other liabilities that are incurred after the merger becomes effective.

(d)   When a merger becomes effective, the interest holder liability of a person that ceases to hold an interest in a domestic merging partnership with respect to which the person had interest holder liability is subject to the following rules:

(1)   The merger does not discharge any interest holder liability under this [act] to the extent the interest holder liability was incurred before the merger became effective.

(2)   The person does not have interest holder liability under this [act] for any debt, obligation, or other liability that is incurred after the merger becomes effective.

(3)   This [act] continues to apply to the release, collection, or discharge of any interest holder liability preserved under paragraph (1) as if the merger had not occurred and the surviving entity were the domestic merging entity.

(4)   The person has whatever rights of contribution from any other person as are provided by this [act], law other than this [act], or the partnership agreement of the domestic merging partnership with respect to any interest holder liability preserved under paragraph (1) as if the merger had not occurred.

(e)   When a merger has become effective, a foreign entity that is the surviving entity may be served with process in this state for the collection and enforcement of any debts, obligations, or other liabilities of a domestic merging partnership as provided in Section 119.

(f)   When a merger has become effective, the registration to do business in this state of any foreign merging entity that is not the surviving entity is canceled.

COMMENT

With the exception of Subsections (c) and (d), this section is similar to statutory provisions on the effect of a merger of a corporation with a corporation. *See* MODEL BUS. CORP. ACT § 11.07.

Subsection (a)—This subsection states the general understanding that in a merger the assets and liabilities of the merging entities automatically vest in the surviving entity. The surviving entity becomes the owner of all real and personal property of the merged entities and is subject to all debts, obligations, and liabilities of the merging entities. A merger does not constitute a transfer, assignment, or conveyance of any property held by the merging entities before the merger. A merger also does not give rise to a claim that a contract with a merging entity is no longer in effect on the ground of nonassignability, unless the contract specifically provides that it does not survive a merger. The contract rights that are vested in the surviving entity include the right to enforce subscription agreements for interests and obligations to make capital contributions entered into or incurred before the merger. *See* Section 1103(c) (dealing with the surviving entity's rights in trust obligations of a nonsurviving party in a merger and transactions such as bequests made to a nonsurviving party to a merger that take effect after the merger).

After a merger has become effective, the law of the surviving entity's jurisdiction of formation governs the surviving entity. *See* Sections 1103(a) and (b) (modifying the provisions of this section with respect to the effects of a merger to the extent a regulatory law provides otherwise or any of the parties holds property committed to charitable purposes).

Subsection (a)(2)—A merger cannot have the effect of making an interest holder of a domestic merging general partnership subject to interest holder liability for the debts, obligations, or other liabilities of any other person or entity unless the interest holder has signed a separate written consent to become subject to such liability or previously agreed to the effectuation of a transaction having that effect without the interest holder's consent. The partnership agreement cannot change this provision. Section 105(c)(14).

Subsection (a)(7)—All pending proceedings involving either the survivor or a party whose separate existence ceased as a result of the merger are continued. Under this paragraph, the name of the survivor may be, but need not be, substituted in any pending proceeding for the name of a party to the merger whose separate existence ceased as a result of the merger. The substitution may be made whether the survivor is a complainant or a respondent, and may be made at the instance of either the survivor or an opposing party. That substitution has no substantive effect because, whether or not the survivor's name is substituted, the survivor succeeds to the claims, and is subject to the liabilities, of any party to the merger whose separate existence ceased as a result of the merger.

Subsection (a)(8)(B)—The private organic rules of an unincorporated entity typically may be either oral or written. The plan of merger is not required to set forth amendments to oral provisions of the private organic rules of the surviving entity, and thus this provision is limited in scope to amendments to the private organic rules that are to be in a record, if any.

Subsection (a)(10)—For more information on appraisal rights, see Section 1106, comment.

Subsections (c) and (d)—These subsections set forth rules for two circumstances that typically do not exist in a merger where all the entities involved are corporations. Subsection (c) deals with the situation where an interest holder that does not have vicarious liability for the obligations of a merging entity before the merger has interest holder liability after the merger. An example would be a corporate shareholder who agrees to be the general partner in a limited partnership that is the surviving entity in a merger between a corporation and a limited partnership that is not a limited liability limited partnership. Subsection (d) deals with the situation where an interest holder has vicarious liability for the obligations of one of the merging parties before the merger but ceases to have any interest holder liability for the obligations of the surviving entity after the merger becomes effective. An example would be a general partner in a general partnership that merges into a corporation.

The effects of Subsections (c) and (d) will depend on when a liability is incurred, which is determined by other law. For a discussion of the issue, see the comment to Section 404(c) (The Temporal Nexus—When Claim Incurred).

These subsections apply not only to merging domestic general partnerships but also to any other domestic entity involved in the merger.

Subsection (c)—This subsection sets forth the general rule that an interest holder that was not liable for the liabilities of a merging entity before the merger but will have personal liability for the obligations of the surviving entity after the merger will be personally liable only for the liabilities of a domestic surviving entity that are incurred after the effective date of a merger.

Subsection (d)—This subsection uses "arose" as its term of art, while Section 306(b) and (c) use "incur." The difference is historical, and no difference in meaning is intended. For a discussion of case law interpreting "incurred," see Section 306(b), comment.

This subsection provides four rules with respect to an interest holder who ceases to have interest holder liability after the effective date of the merger:

(1)   the interest holder remains personally liable for any obligations that were incurred before the effective date of the merger;

(2)   the interest holder does not have any personal liability for obligations of the surviving entity;

(3)   the pre-existing personal liability of the interest holder is enforced against the interest holder on the same basis as if the merger had not taken place; and

(4)   the interest holder has the same rights of contribution from other interest holders of the merging entity as the interest holder would have had if the merger had not occurred.

See the comment to Section 1146(d).

Subsection (e)—When a merger has become effective, this subsection provides that a foreign entity that is the surviving entity may be served with process in this state. The proceedings covered by this subsection include a proceeding to enforce the rights of any interest holders of each domestic merging entity who are entitled to and exercise appraisal rights. One of the liabilities that a foreign surviving entity succeeds to is the obligation of a merging entity to pay the amount, if any, to which its interest holders who assert appraisal rights are entitled.

[PART] 3.   INTEREST EXCHANGE

§ 1131.   Interest Exchange Authorized

(a)   By complying with this [part]:

(1)   a domestic partnership may acquire all of one or more classes or series of interests of another domestic entity or a foreign entity in exchange for interests, securities, obligations, money, other property, rights to acquire interests or securities, or any combination of the foregoing; or

(2) all of one or more classes or series of interests of a domestic partnership may be acquired by another domestic entity or a foreign entity in exchange for interests, securities, obligations, money, other property, rights to acquire interests or securities, or any combination of the foregoing.

(b) By complying with the provisions of this [part] applicable to foreign entities, a foreign entity may be the acquiring or acquired entity in an interest exchange under this [part] if the interest exchange is authorized by the law of the foreign entity's jurisdiction of formation.

(c) If a protected agreement contains a provision that applies to a merger of a domestic partnership but does not refer to an interest exchange, the provision applies to an interest exchange in which the domestic partnership is the acquired entity as if the interest exchange were a merger until the provision is amended after [the effective date of this [act]].

COMMENT

An interest exchange is the same type of transaction as the share exchange provided for in section 11.03 of the Model Business Corporation Act. The effect of an interest exchange is that: (i) the separate existence of the acquired entity is not affected; and (ii) the acquiring entity acquires all of the interests of one or more classes of the acquired entity. An interest exchange also allows an indirect acquisition through the use of consideration in the exchange that is not provided by the acquiring entity (*e.g.*, consideration from another or related entity).

Neither share exchanges nor interest exchanges are universally recognized in either corporation or unincorporated entity laws. The effect of an interest exchange can be achieved through a triangular merger in which the acquiring entity forms a new subsidiary and the acquired entity is then merged into the new subsidiary. Part 3 allows the interest exchange to be accomplished directly in a single step, rather than indirectly through the triangular merger route.

The "series" referenced in Subsection (a) are not the series contemplated by the Uniform Statutory Entity Trust Act §§ 401–405 and some LLC statutes. *See, e.g.*, DEL. CODE ANN. tit. 6, § 18–215 (2012); 805 ILL. COMP. STAT. 180/37–40 (2012). Instead, in this context "series" refers to a subset of a class, which is a meaning commonly found in corporation law. *See, e.g.*, MODEL BUS. CORP. ACT § 6.02. Specific provisions authorizing classes and series are less common in unincorporated entity law but do exist. *See, e.g.*, MINN. STAT. § 322B.155 (2012). In any event, a partnership agreement certainly has the power to create classes and series as contemplated by this section.

Subsection (a)—For this section to apply, a domestic limited liability partnership must be either the acquiring or acquired entity.

The acquiring entity is not required to acquire all of the interests in the acquired entity. For example, assume that a general partnership with three classes of partnership interests enters into an interest exchange with an acquiring entity. The acquiring entity need acquire only all of the partnership interests of one or more classes of the partnership interests.

Subsection (b)—This subsection allows a foreign entity to effectuate an interest exchange with a domestic general partnership if the interest exchange is authorized by the organic law of the foreign entity.

Subsection (c)—This subsection deals with rights of parties to protected agreements, Section 1101(30), when an interest exchange takes place. Because the concept of an interest exchange is relatively new, a person contracting with a domestic general partnership or loaning it money who drafted and negotiated special rights relating to the transaction before the enactment of this article should not be charged with the consequences of not having dealt with the concept of an interest exchange in the context of those special rights. Similarly, when the governance structure of an entity has been negotiated before the enactment of this act, the concept of an interest exchange may not have been reflected in any special governance arrangements; for example, special approval rights may have been provided for fundamental transactions, but those rights fail to include language that would make them applicable to an interest exchange.

Accordingly, this subsection provides a transitional rule that is intended to protect those special rights. If, for example, a general partnership is a party to a contract that provides that the partnership cannot participate in a merger without the consent of the other party to the contract, the requirement to obtain the consent of the other party will apply also to an interest exchange in which the partnership is the acquired entity. If the partnership fails to obtain the consent, the result will be that the other party will have the same rights it would have had if the entity were to participate in a merger without the required consent.

The transitional rule in this subsection ceases to make sense at the time the provisions of the agreement giving rise to the special rights are first amended after the effective date of this article because at that time the provision may be amended to address expressly an interest exchange. The transitional rule will continue to apply, however, if a provision other than the specific provisions giving rise to the special rights is amended.

§ 1132. Plan of Interest Exchange

(a)   A domestic partnership may be the acquired entity in an interest exchange under this [part] by approving a plan of interest exchange. The plan must be in a record and contain:

(1)   the name of the acquired entity;

(2)   the name, jurisdiction of formation, and type of entity of the acquiring entity;

(3)   the manner of converting the interests in the acquired entity into interests, securities, obligations, money, other property, rights to acquire interests or securities, or any combination of the foregoing;

(4)   any proposed amendments to the partnership agreement that are, or are proposed to be, in a record of the acquired entity;

(5)   the other terms and conditions of the interest exchange; and

(6)   any other provision required by the law of this state or the partnership agreement of the acquired entity.

(b)   In addition to the requirements of subsection (a), a plan of interest exchange may contain any other provision not prohibited by law.

COMMENT

This section sets forth the requirements for the plan of interest exchange, which must be approved by the acquired entity in accordance with Section 1131. The content of the plan of interest exchange is similar to the content of a plan of merger. *See* Section 1122.

The plan of interest exchange may, but need not, be filed instead of the statement of interest exchange, Section 1135, so long as the plan contains all the information required to be in the statement and is delivered to the filing office for filing after the plan has been adopted and approved. *See* Section 1135(d).

Subsection (a)—The requirements stated in this subsection are mandatory. *See* Section 105(c)(15).

Subsection (a)(3)—Under this paragraph, interest holders in the acquired entity may receive interests or securities of the acquiring entity or of a party other than the acquiring entity, obligations, rights to acquire interests or securities, cash, or other property. *See* the comment to Section 1122(a)(3).

Subsection (b)—This subsection authorizes the plan to contain any other provision the parties wish to include, unless the provision is prohibited by law.

§ 1133. Approval of Interest Exchange

(a)   A plan of interest exchange is not effective unless it has been approved:

(1)   by all the partners of a domestic acquired partnership entitled to vote on or consent to any matter; and

(2)   in a record, by each partner of the domestic acquired partnership that will have interest holder liability for debts, obligations, and other liabilities that are incurred after the interest exchange becomes effective, unless:

(A)   the partnership agreement of the partnership provides in a record for the approval of an interest exchange or a merger in which some or all its partners become subject to interest holder liability by the affirmative vote or consent of fewer than all the partners; and

(B)   the partner consented in a record to or voted for that provision of the partnership agreement or became a partner after the adoption of that provision.

(b)   An interest exchange involving a domestic acquired entity that is not a partnership is not effective unless it is approved by the domestic entity in accordance with its organic law.

(c)   An interest exchange involving a foreign acquired entity is not effective unless it is approved by the foreign entity in accordance with the law of the foreign entity's jurisdiction of formation.

(d)   Except as otherwise provided in its organic law or organic rules, the interest holders of the acquiring entity are not required to approve the interest exchange.

COMMENT

This section sets forth the required approval of an interest exchange. An interest exchange transaction governed by this article requires approval only by the acquired entity, unless the applicable organic law or the organic rules of the acquiring entity otherwise provide, Subsection (d), a condition that rarely exists.

Subsection (a)(2)—For an explanation of this interest holder liability provision, see Section 1123(a)(2), comment.

§ 1134. Amendment or Abandonment of Plan of Interest Exchange

(a)   A plan of interest exchange may be amended only with the consent of each party to the plan, except as otherwise provided in the plan.

(b)   A domestic acquired partnership may approve an amendment of a plan of interest exchange:

(1)   in the same manner as the plan was approved, if the plan does not provide for the manner in which it may be amended; or

(2)   by its partners in the manner provided in the plan, but a partner that was entitled to vote on or consent to approval of the interest exchange is entitled to vote on or consent to any amendment of the plan that will change:

(A)   the amount or kind of interests, securities, obligations, money, other property, rights to acquire interests or securities, or any combination of the foregoing, to be received by any of the partners of the acquired partnership under the plan;

(B)   the partnership agreement of the acquired partnership that will be in effect immediately after the interest exchange becomes effective, except for changes that do not require approval of the partners of the acquired partnership under this [act] or the partnership agreement; or

(C)   any other terms or conditions of the plan, if the change would adversely affect the partner in any material respect.

(c)   After a plan of interest exchange has been approved and before a statement of interest exchange becomes effective, the plan may be abandoned as provided in the plan. Unless prohibited by the plan, a domestic acquired partnership may abandon the plan in the same manner as the plan was approved.

(d)   If a plan of interest exchange is abandoned after a statement of interest exchange has been delivered to the [Secretary of State] for filing and before the statement becomes effective, a statement of abandonment, signed by the acquired partnership, must be delivered to the [Secretary of State] for filing before the statement of interest exchange becomes effective. The statement of abandonment takes effect on filing, and the interest exchange is abandoned and does not become effective. The statement of abandonment must contain:

(1)   the name of the acquired partnership;

(2)   the date on which the statement of interest exchange was filed by the [Secretary of State]; and

(3)   a statement that the interest exchange has been abandoned in accordance with this section.

COMMENT

This section parallels provisions in Parts 2 (mergers), 4 (conversions), and 5 (domestications). *See* Sections 1124, 1144, 1154.

§ 1135.   Statement of Interest Exchange; Effective Date of Interest Exchange

(a)   A statement of interest exchange must be signed by a domestic acquired partnership and delivered to the [Secretary of State] for filing.

(b)   A statement of interest exchange must contain:

(1)   the name of the acquired partnership;

(2)   the name, jurisdiction of formation, and type of entity of the acquiring entity; and

(3)   a statement that the plan of interest exchange was approved by the acquired partnership in accordance with this [part].

(c)   In addition to the requirements of subsection (b), a statement of interest exchange may contain any other provision not prohibited by law.

(d)   A plan of interest exchange that is signed by a domestic acquired partnership and meets all the requirements of subsection (b) may be delivered to the [Secretary of State] for filing instead of a statement of interest exchange and on filing has the same effect. If a plan of interest exchange is filed as provided in this subsection, references in this [article] to a statement of interest exchange refer to the plan of interest exchange filed under this subsection.

(e)   An interest exchange becomes effective when the statement of interest exchange is effective.

COMMENT

This section applies only when the acquired entity is a domestic general partnership. The filing makes the transaction a matter of public record.

This act has no filing requirement when the only domestic general partnership involved is the acquiring entity.

Subsection (b)—This subsection states the requirements for a statement of interest exchange, which are essentially the same as the requirements for a statement of merger under Section 1125(b).

Subsection (d)—A plan of interest exchange can be used as a substitute for the statement of interest exchange so long as the plan satisfies the requirements in Subsection (b).

Subsection (e)—This subsection applies when the acquiring entity is a domestic general partnership, and Section 114 determines when a record delivered for filing under this act becomes effective. A statement of interest exchange may specify a delayed effective time and date, subject to the ninety-day limit stated in Section 114(3) and (4).

If the acquiring entity is not a domestic general partnership, the effectiveness of the interest exchange will occur when provided by the law of the jurisdiction of formation of the acquiring entity.

§ 1136.   Effect of Interest Exchange

(a)   When an interest exchange in which the acquired entity is a domestic partnership becomes effective:

(1)   the interests in the acquired partnership which are the subject of the interest exchange are converted, and the partners holding those interests are entitled only to the rights provided to them under the plan of interest exchange and to any appraisal rights they have under Section 1106;

(2)   the acquiring entity becomes the interest holder of the interests in the acquired partnership stated in the plan of interest exchange to be acquired by the acquiring entity; and

(3)   the provisions of the partnership agreement of the acquired partnership that are to be in a record, if any, are amended to the extent provided in the plan of interest exchange.

(b)   Except as otherwise provided in the partnership agreement of a domestic acquired partnership, the interest exchange does not give rise to any rights that a partner or third party would have upon a dissolution, liquidation, or winding up of the acquired partnership.

(c)   When an interest exchange becomes effective, a person that did not have interest holder liability with respect to a domestic acquired partnership and becomes subject to interest holder liability with respect to a domestic entity as a result of the interest exchange has interest holder liability only to the extent provided by the organic law of the entity and only for those debts, obligations, and other liabilities that are incurred after the interest exchange becomes effective.

(d)   When an interest exchange becomes effective, the interest holder liability of a person that ceases to hold an interest in a domestic acquired partnership with respect to which the person had interest holder liability is subject to the following rules:

(1)   The interest exchange does not discharge any interest holder liability under this [act] to the extent the interest holder liability was incurred before the interest exchange became effective.

(2)   The person does not have interest holder liability under this [act] for any debt, obligation, or other liability that is incurred after the interest exchange becomes effective.

(3)   This [act] continues to apply to the release, collection, or discharge of any interest holder liability preserved under paragraph (1) as if the interest exchange had not occurred.

(4)   The person has whatever rights of contribution from any other person as are provided by this [act], law other than this [act], or the partnership agreement of the domestic acquired partnership with respect to any interest holder liability preserved under paragraph (1) as if the interest exchange had not occurred.

COMMENT

This section applies only when the *acquired* entity is a domestic general partnership, and this part states no rule for the effect of an interest exchange when the only domestic general partnership involved is the *acquiring* entity. For that situation, other provisions of this act must be consulted, because this act is the organic law of the acquiring entity.

Subsection (a)—In contrast to a merger, an interest exchange does not in and of itself affect the separate existence of the parties, vest in the acquiring entity the assets of the acquired entity, or render the acquiring entity liable for the liabilities of the acquired entity. Thus, Subsection (a) is significantly simpler than Section 1126(a) with respect to the effects of a merger.

When an interest exchange becomes effective: (i) the interests of the acquired domestic general partnership are exchanged, converted, or canceled as provided in the plan; (ii) the only rights of the former partners and transferees of the acquired partnership whose interests are affected by the interest exchange are those rights related to the exchange, conversion, or cancellation; (iii) the acquiring entity becomes the owner of the acquired partnership's interests as provided in the plan; and (iv) the provisions of the partnership agreement of the acquired partnership that are to be in a record, if any, are amended to the extent provided in the plan of interest exchange.

Subsection (c)—This subsection provides the rule for future interest holder liability pertaining to domestic entities and parallels analogous provisions in Parts 2 (mergers), 4 (conversions), and 5 (domestications). *See* the comment to Section 1126.

Subsection (d)—This subsection provides the rule for past interest holder liability and parallels analogous provisions in Parts 2 (mergers), 4 (conversions), and 5 (domestications). *See* the comments to Sections 1126(d) and 1146(d).

[PART] 4.   CONVERSION

§ 1141.   Conversion Authorized

(a)   By complying with this [part], a domestic partnership may become:

(1)   a domestic entity that is a different type of entity; or

(2)   a foreign entity that is a different type of entity, if the conversion is authorized by the law of the foreign entity's jurisdiction of formation.

(b)   By complying with the provisions of this [part] applicable to foreign entities, a foreign entity that is not a foreign partnership may become a domestic partnership if the conversion is authorized by the law of the foreign entity's jurisdiction of formation.

(c)   If a protected agreement contains a provision that applies to a merger of a domestic partnership but does not refer to a conversion, the provision applies to a conversion of the partnership as if the conversion were a merger until the provision is amended after [the effective date of this [act]].

COMMENT

This part of Article 11 permits an entity to change to a different type of entity. A transaction in which an entity changes its jurisdiction of organization but does not change its type is a domestication and is the subject of Part 5.

Subsection (a)(2)—For this provision to apply, this type of conversion must be authorized by the law of the foreign jurisdiction. If this is not the case, it may be possible to achieve the same result by forming an entity of the type desired in the foreign jurisdiction and then merging the domestic entity into the new foreign entity under Part 2 of Article 11.

Subsection (b)—This subsection allows a foreign entity to effectuate a conversion into a domestic general partnership, but only if the conversion is permitted by the laws of the foreign entity's jurisdiction of formation. When a foreign entity becomes a domestic general partnership pursuant to this part of Article 11, the effect of the conversion will be as provided in Section 1146. The procedures by which the conversion is approved, however, will be determined by the laws of the foreign entity's jurisdiction of formation. See Section 102(8) for the definition of "jurisdiction of formation."

Subsection (c)—For more information on an authorized interest exchange, see Section 1131(c), comment.

§ 1142.   Plan of Conversion

(a)   A domestic partnership may convert to a different type of entity under this [part] by approving a plan of conversion. The plan must be in a record and contain:

(1)   the name of the converting partnership;

(2)   the name, jurisdiction of formation, and type of entity of the converted entity;

(3)   the manner of converting the interests in the converting partnership into interests, securities, obligations, money, other property, rights to acquire interests or securities, or any combination of the foregoing;

(4)   the proposed public organic record of the converted entity if it will be a filing entity;

(5)   the full text of the private organic rules of the converted entity which are proposed to be in a record;

(6)   the other terms and conditions of the conversion; and

(7)   any other provision required by the law of this state or the partnership agreement of the converting partnership.

(b)   In addition to the requirements of subsection (a), a plan of conversion may contain any other provision not prohibited by law.

COMMENT

This section sets forth the requirements for the plan of conversion, which must be approved by the converting entity in accordance with Section 1143. The content of a plan of conversion is similar to the content of a plan of merger. *See* Section 1122.

Subsection (a)—The requirements stated in this subsection are mandatory. *See* Section 105(c)(15).

Subsection (a)(3)—Interest holders in the converting entity may receive interests or other securities of the converted entity or of any other person, obligations, rights to acquire interests or other securities, cash, or other property. *See* Sections 1122(a)(3) (mergers), 1132(a)(3) (interest exchanges), 1152(a)(3) (domestications).

Subsection (b)—This subsection authorizes the plan to contain any other provision the parties wish to include, unless the provision is prohibited by law.

§ 1143. Approval of Conversion

(a)　A plan of conversion is not effective unless it has been approved:

(1)　by a domestic converting partnership, by all the partners of the partnership entitled to vote on or consent to any matter; and

(2)　in a record, by each partner of a domestic converting partnership which will have interest holder liability for debts, obligations, and other liabilities that are incurred after the conversion becomes effective, unless:

(A)　the partnership agreement of the partnership provides in a record for the approval of a conversion or a merger in which some or all of its partners become subject to interest holder liability by the affirmative vote or consent of fewer than all the partners; and

(B)　the partner voted for or consented in a record to that provision of the partnership agreement or became a partner after the adoption of that provision.

(b)　A conversion involving a domestic converting entity that is not a partnership is not effective unless it is approved by the domestic converting entity in accordance with its organic law.

(c)　A conversion of a foreign converting entity is not effective unless it is approved by the foreign entity in accordance with the law of the foreign entity's jurisdiction of formation.

COMMENT

Subsection (a)(1)—This provision is a default rule, subject to change in the partnership agreement.

Subsection (a)(2)—This provision is not a default rule. Section 105(c)(14). For an explanation of this interest holder liability provision, see Section 1123(a)(2), comment.

§ 1144. Amendment or Abandonment of Plan of Conversion

(a)　A plan of conversion of a domestic converting partnership may be amended:

(1)　in the same manner as the plan was approved, if the plan does not provide for the manner in which it may be amended; or

(2)　by its partners in the manner provided in the plan, but a partner that was entitled to vote on or consent to approval of the conversion is entitled to vote on or consent to any amendment of the plan that will change:

(A)　the amount or kind of interests, securities, obligations, money, other property, rights to acquire interests or securities, or any combination of the foregoing, to be received by any of the partners of the converting partnership under the plan;

(B)　the public organic record, if any, or private organic rules of the converted entity which will be in effect immediately after the conversion becomes effective, except for changes that do not require approval of the interest holders of the converted entity under its organic law or organic rules; or

(C)　any other terms or conditions of the plan, if the change would adversely affect the partner in any material respect.

(b)　After a plan of conversion has been approved by a domestic converting partnership and before a statement of conversion becomes effective, the plan may be abandoned as provided in the plan. Unless prohibited by the plan, a domestic converting partnership may abandon the plan in the same manner as the plan was approved.

(c)   If a plan of conversion is abandoned after a statement of conversion has been delivered to the [Secretary of State] for filing and before the statement becomes effective, a statement of abandonment, signed by the converting entity, must be delivered to the [Secretary of State] for filing before the statement of conversion becomes effective. The statement of abandonment takes effect on filing, and the conversion is abandoned and does not become effective. The statement of abandonment must contain:

(1)   the name of the converting partnership;

(2)   the date on which the statement of conversion was filed by the [Secretary of State]; and

(3)   a statement that the conversion has been abandoned in accordance with this section.

COMMENT

This section parallels analogous provisions in Parts 2 (mergers), 3 (interest exchanges), and 5 (domestications). *See* Sections 1124, 1134, 1154.

§ 1145.   Statement of Conversion; Effective Date of Conversion

(a)   A statement of conversion must be signed by the converting entity and delivered to the [Secretary of State] for filing.

(b)   A statement of conversion must contain:

(1)   the name, jurisdiction of formation, and type of entity of the converting entity;

(2)   the name, jurisdiction of formation, and type of entity of the converted entity;

(3)   if the converting entity is a domestic partnership, a statement that the plan of conversion was approved in accordance with this [part] or, if the converting entity is a foreign entity, a statement that the conversion was approved by the foreign entity in accordance with the law of its jurisdiction of formation;

(4)   if the converted entity is a domestic filing entity, its public organic record, as an attachment; and

(5)   if the converted entity is a domestic limited liability partnership, its statement of qualification, as an attachment.

(c)   In addition to the requirements of subsection (b), a statement of conversion may contain any other provision not prohibited by law.

(d)   If the converted entity is a domestic entity, its public organic record, if any, must satisfy the requirements of the law of this state, except that the public organic record does not need to be signed.

(e)   A plan of conversion that is signed by a domestic converting partnership and meets all the requirements of subsection (b) may be delivered to the [Secretary of State] for filing instead of a statement of conversion and on filing has the same effect. If a plan of conversion is filed as provided in this subsection, references in this [article] to a statement of conversion refer to the plan of conversion filed under this subsection.

(f)   If the converted entity is a domestic partnership, the conversion becomes effective when the statement of conversion is effective. In all other cases, the conversion becomes effective on the later of:

(1)   the date and time provided by the organic law of the converted entity; and

(2)   when the statement is effective.

COMMENT

This section applies regardless of whether a domestic general partnership is the converting or converted entity. A foreign entity seeking to convert to a domestic general partnership must therefore comply with this section.

If either the converting or converted entity is a foreign entity, the organic law of the foreign entity's jurisdiction must also be consulted.

The filing of a statement of conversion makes the transaction a matter of public record.

Subsection (b)—This subsection sets forth the requirements for a statement of conversion. They are essentially the same as the requirements for a statement of merger in Section 1125.

Subsection (e)—A plan of conversion can be used as a substitute for the statement of conversion so long as the plan satisfies the requirements in Subsection (b).

Subsection (f)—Section 114 determines when a record delivered for filing under this act becomes effective. A statement of conversion may specify a delayed effective time and date, subject to the ninety-day limit stated in Section 114(3) and (4).

When the statement of conversion has become effective under this subsection, the conversion transaction occurs if the converted entity is a domestic general partnership. A conversion in which the converted entity is a foreign entity will usually also take effect when the statement of conversion takes effect because the best practice will be to coordinate the filings that need to be made when a conversion involves both a domestic entity and also a foreign entity so that the filings in each jurisdiction take effect at the same time.

However, when the converting general partnership is a foreign general partnership, it is possible that the filing in the foreign jurisdiction will take effect at a different time. For that reason, this subsection provides that the conversion will take effect at the later of: (i) when the statement of conversion takes effect; and (ii) when the conversion takes effect under the law of the foreign jurisdiction. This rule avoids the possibility that the conversion will take effect in this state before it takes effect in the foreign jurisdiction, which would produce the undesirable result that the converting domestic general partnership would cease to appear as an active entity on the records of this state before appearing as its active, converted self on the records of the foreign jurisdiction.

It is necessary for the filing office to record only the effective date of the statement of conversion, and the filing office does not need to be concerned with the effective date of the conversion itself. Persons wishing to determine the effective date of a conversion involving both a domestic general partnership and a foreign entity will be able to do so by consulting the records of the filing offices in each jurisdiction.

§ 1146.   Effect of Conversion

(a)   When a conversion becomes effective:

    (1)   the converted entity is:

        (A)   organized under and subject to the organic law of the converted entity; and

        (B)   the same entity without interruption as the converting entity;

    (2)   all property of the converting entity continues to be vested in the converted entity without transfer, reversion, or impairment;

    (3)   all debts, obligations, and other liabilities of the converting entity continue as debts, obligations, and other liabilities of the converted entity;

    (4)   except as otherwise provided by law or the plan of conversion, all the rights, privileges, immunities, powers, and purposes of the converting entity remain in the converted entity;

    (5)   the name of the converted entity may be substituted for the name of the converting entity in any pending action or proceeding;

    (6)   if the converted entity is a limited liability partnership, its statement of qualification becomes effective;

    (7)   the provisions of the partnership agreement of the converted entity which are to be in a record, if any, approved as part of the plan of conversion become effective; and

    (8)   the interests in the converting entity are converted, and the interest holders of the converting entity are entitled only to the rights provided to them under the plan of conversion and to any appraisal rights they have under Section 1106.

(b)   Except as otherwise provided in the partnership agreement of a domestic converting partnership, the conversion does not give rise to any rights that a partner or third party would have upon a dissolution, liquidation, or winding up of the converting entity.

(c)   When a conversion becomes effective, a person that did not have interest holder liability with respect to the converting entity and becomes subject to interest holder liability with respect to a domestic entity as a result of the conversion has interest holder liability only to the extent provided by the organic law of the entity and only for those debts, obligations, and other liabilities that are incurred after the conversion becomes effective.

(d)   When a conversion becomes effective, the interest holder liability of a person that ceases to hold an interest in a domestic converting partnership with respect to which the person had interest holder liability is subject to the following rules:

(1)   The conversion does not discharge any interest holder liability under this [act] to the extent the interest holder liability was incurred before the conversion became effective.

(2)   The person does not have interest holder liability under this [act] for any debt, obligation, or other liability that is incurred after the conversion becomes effective.

(3)   This [act] continues to apply to the release, collection, or discharge of any interest holder liability preserved under paragraph (1) as if the conversion had not occurred.

(4)   The person has whatever rights of contribution from any other person as are provided by this [act], law other than this [act], or the organic rules of the converting entity with respect to any interest holder liability preserved under paragraph (1) as if the conversion had not occurred.

(e)   When a conversion has become effective, a foreign entity that is the converted entity may be served with process in this state for the collection and enforcement of any of its debts, obligations, and other liabilities as provided in Section 119.

(f)   If the converting entity is a registered foreign entity, its registration to do business in this state is canceled when the conversion becomes effective.

(g)   A conversion does not require the entity to wind up its affairs and does not constitute or cause the dissolution of the entity.

COMMENT

A converted entity is the same entity as it was before the conversion; the entity just has a different legal form.

Subsection (a)—This subsection states the principal legal effects of a conversion. The converted entity remains the owner of all real and personal property and remains subject to all the liabilities, actual or contingent, of the converted entity. A conversion is not a conveyance, transfer, or assignment. A conversion does not give rise to: (i) claims of reverter or impairment of title based on a prohibited conveyance or transfer; or (ii) to a claim that a contract with the converting entity is no longer in effect on the ground of nonassignability, unless the contract specifically provides that it does not survive a conversion. The contract rights that remain in the converted entity include, without limitation, the right to enforce subscription agreements for interests and obligations to make capital contributions entered into or incurred before the conversion.

When a conversion becomes effective, the internal affairs of the converting entity are no longer governed by its former organic law but instead by the organic law of the converted entity. As a result, filings that may have been made under the organic law of the converting entity, such as the following, will no longer be effective: a statement of qualification as a limited liability partnership under UPA (1997) (Last Amended 2013) § 901, a statement of partnership authority under Section 303 of that act, a statement of authority under Section of the ULLCA (2006) (Last Amended 2013) § 302, or under Uniform Unincorporated Nonprofit Association Act (2008) (Last Amended 2013) § 7.

Subsection (a)(5)—All pending proceedings involving the converting entity are continued. The name of the converted entity may be, but need not be, substituted in any pending proceeding for the name of the converting entity.

Subsection (c)—This subsection provides the rule for future interest holder liability and parallels provisions in Parts 2 (mergers), 3 (interest exchanges), and 5 (domestications). *See* the comment to Section 1126(c).

Subsection (d)—Subsection (d) provides the rule for past interest holder liability and parallels analogous provisions in Parts 2 (mergers), 3 (interest exchanges), and 5 (domestications). *See* the comment to Section 1126(d).

Subsection (e)—For this provision to apply, the converting entity must have been a domestic general partnership. When a domestic general partnership becomes a foreign entity as a result of a conversion, some mechanism is needed to facilitate the enforcement of claims by the creditors and interest holders of the converting partnership. This subsection, which parallels analogous provisions in Parts 2 (mergers) and 5 (domestications), authorizes service of process for all such claims in this state.

Subsection (g)—When a conversion takes effect, the entity continues to exist—simply in a different form. This subsection thus makes clear that the conversion does not require the entity to wind up its affairs and does not constitute or cause the dissolution of the entity.

[PART] 5. DOMESTICATION

§ 1151. Domestication Authorized

(a) By complying with this [part], a domestic limited liability partnership may become a foreign limited liability partnership if the domestication is authorized by the law of the foreign jurisdiction.

(b) By complying with the provisions of this [part] applicable to foreign limited liability partnerships, a foreign limited liability partnership may become a domestic limited liability partnership if the domestication is authorized by the law of the foreign limited liability partnership's jurisdiction of formation.

(c) If a protected agreement contains a provision that applies to a merger of a domestic limited liability partnership but does not refer to a domestication, the provision applies to a domestication of the limited liability partnership as if the domestication were a merger until the provision is amended after [the effective date of this [act]].

COMMENT

A domestication authorized by Part 5 of Article 11 differs from a conversion in that a domestication requires that the domesticating entity be the same type of entity as the domesticated entity. In a conversion, by contrast, the converting entity changes its type.

As with a conversion, all rights and privileges, debts, obligations and other liabilities, and actions or proceedings of a domesticating entity remain vested in the domesticated entity. A domestication is not a sale, transfer, assignment, or conveyance and does not give rise to a claim of reverter or impairment of title. *See* the comment to Section 1146(a).

Part 5 of Article 11 governs the legal effect of a foreign limited liability partnership domesticating in this state. On the other hand, the organic laws of the foreign jurisdiction, and not Part 5, will govern the legal effect of most aspects of a domestication of a domestic limited liability partnership in another jurisdiction. In the latter scenario, Part 5 authorizes the domestication of the domestic entity in the foreign jurisdiction, but Part 5 does not create a right in the domestic entity to be received in the foreign jurisdiction. Similarly, this section does not provide a right on the part of a foreign limited liability partnership to become a domestic limited liability partnership if the domestication is not authorized by the laws of the foreign jurisdiction. If the foreign jurisdiction does not authorize a domestication transaction, the same results can be accomplished by forming a new limited liability partnership in this state and merging the existing foreign limited liability partnership into the new domestic limited liability partnership.

Subsection (a)—Unlike the Parts 2 (merger), 3 (interest exchange), and 4 (conversion), Part 5 applies only to limited liability partnerships. However, a non-LLP general partnership that seeks to change its governing law may:

• amend its partnership agreement to specify the governing law of the desired jurisdiction, if the partnership intends to remain non-LLP; or

• deliver to the filing office in the desired jurisdiction a statement of qualification, if the partnership intends not only to change its governing law but also to become an LLP.

Subsection (c)—For the parallel provision pertaining to mergers, see Section 1131(c).

§ 1152. Plan of Domestication

(a) A domestic limited liability partnership may become a foreign limited liability partnership in a domestication by approving a plan of domestication. The plan must be in a record and contain:

(1)   the name of the domesticating limited liability partnership;

(2)   the name and jurisdiction of formation of the domesticated limited liability partnership;

(3)   the manner of converting the interests in the domesticating limited liability partnership into interests, securities, obligations, money, other property, rights to acquire interests or securities, or any combination of the foregoing;

(4)   the proposed statement of qualification of the domesticated limited liability partnership;

(5)   the full text of the provisions of the partnership agreement of the domesticated limited liability partnership that are proposed to be in a record;

(6)   the other terms and conditions of the domestication; and

(7)   any other provision required by the law of this state or the partnership agreement of the domesticating limited liability partnership.

(b)   In addition to the requirements of subsection (a), a plan of domestication may contain any other provision not prohibited by law.

COMMENT

This section sets forth the requirements for the plan of domestication for a domestic limited liability partnership seeking to become a limited liability partnership existing under the law of another jurisdiction. For a foreign limited liability partnership seeking to become a domestic limited liability partnership, the organic law of the foreign limited liability partnership governs the requirements for a plan of domestication. The content of a plan of domestication is similar to the content of a plan of merger. *See* Section 1122.

Subsection (a)—The requirements stated in this subsection are mandatory. *See* Section 105(c)(15).

Subsection (a)(3)—Interest holders in the domesticating limited liability partnership may receive interests or other securities of the domesticated limited liability partnership or any other entity, obligations, rights to acquire interests or other securities, cash, or other property. *See* the comment to Section 1122(a)(3).

Subsection (b)—This subsection authorizes the plan to contain any other provision the parties wish to include, unless the provision is prohibited by law.

§ 1153.   Approval of Domestication

(a)   A plan of domestication of a domestic domesticating limited liability partnership is not effective unless it has been approved:

(1)   by all the partners entitled to vote on or consent to any matter; and

(2)   in a record, by each partner that will have interest holder liability for debts, obligations, and other liabilities that are incurred after the domestication becomes effective, unless:

(A)   the partnership agreement of the domesticating partnership in a record provides for the approval of a domestication or merger in which some or all of its partners become subject to interest holder liability by the affirmative vote or consent of fewer than all the partners; and

(B)   the partner voted for or consented in a record to that provision of the partnership agreement or became a partner after the adoption of that provision.

(b)   A domestication of a foreign domesticating limited liability partnership is not effective unless it is approved in accordance with the law of the foreign limited liability partnership's jurisdiction of formation.

COMMENT

Subsection (a)(1)—This provision is a default rule, subject to change in the partnership agreement.

Subsection (a)(2)—This provision is mandatory. Section 105(c)(14). For an explanation of the provision, see Section 1123(a)(2), comment.

Subsection (b)—In the case of a foreign limited liability partnership that is domesticating in this state, this subsection provides that the required approval is determined by the laws of the foreign limited liability partnership's jurisdiction of formation (which in this context means the jurisdiction in which the foreign LLP's statement of qualification is filed).

§ 1154. Amendment or Abandonment of Plan of Domestication

(a)   A plan of domestication of a domestic domesticating limited liability partnership may be amended:

(1)   in the same manner as the plan was approved, if the plan does not provide for the manner in which it may be amended; or

(2)   by its partners in the manner provided in the plan, but a partner that was entitled to vote on or consent to approval of the domestication is entitled to vote on or consent to any amendment of the plan that will change:

(A)   the amount or kind of interests, securities, obligations, money, other property, rights to acquire interests or securities, or any combination of the foregoing, to be received by any of the partners of the domesticating limited liability partnership under the plan;

(B)   the partnership agreement of the domesticated limited liability partnership that will be in effect immediately after the domestication becomes effective, except for changes that do not require approval of the partners of the domesticated limited liability partnership under its organic law or partnership agreement; or

(C)   any other terms or conditions of the plan, if the change would adversely affect the partner in any material respect.

(b)   After a plan of domestication has been approved by a domestic domesticating limited liability partnership and before a statement of domestication becomes effective, the plan may be abandoned as provided in the plan. Unless prohibited by the plan, a domestic domesticating limited liability partnership may abandon the plan in the same manner as the plan was approved.

(c)   If a plan of domestication is abandoned after a statement of domestication has been delivered to the [Secretary of State] for filing and before the statement becomes effective, a statement of abandonment, signed by the domesticating limited liability partnership, must be delivered to the [Secretary of State] for filing before the statement of domestication becomes effective. The statement of abandonment takes effect on filing, and the domestication is abandoned and does not become effective. The statement of abandonment must contain:

(1)   the name of the domesticating limited liability partnership;

(2)   the date on which the statement of domestication was filed by the [Secretary of State]; and

(3)   a statement that the domestication has been abandoned in accordance with this section.

COMMENT

This section parallels provisions in Parts 2 (mergers), 3 (interest exchanges), and 4 (conversions). *See* Sections 1124 (mergers), 1134 (interest exchanges), 1144 (conversions).

§ 1155. Statement of Domestication; Effective Date of Domestication

(a)   A statement of domestication must be signed by the domesticating limited liability partnership and delivered to the [Secretary of State] for filing.

(b)   A statement of domestication must contain:

(1)   the name and jurisdiction of formation of the domesticating limited liability partnership;

(2)   the name and jurisdiction of formation of the domesticated limited liability partnership;

(3)   if the domesticating limited liability partnership is a domestic limited liability partnership, a statement that the plan of domestication was approved in accordance with this [part] or, if the domesticating limited liability partnership is a foreign limited liability partnership, a statement that the domestication was approved in accordance with the law of its jurisdiction of formation; and

(4)   the statement of qualification of the domesticated limited liability partnership, as an attachment.

(c)   In addition to the requirements of subsection (b), a statement of domestication may contain any other provision not prohibited by law.

(d)   The statement of qualification of a domesticated domestic limited liability partnership must satisfy the requirements of this [act], but the statement does not need to be signed.

(e)   A plan of domestication that is signed by a domesticating domestic limited liability partnership and meets all the requirements of subsection (b) may be delivered to the [Secretary of State] for filing instead of a statement of domestication and on filing has the same effect. If a plan of domestication is filed as provided in this subsection, references in this [article] to a statement of domestication refer to the plan of domestication filed under this subsection.

(f)   If the domesticated entity is a domestic partnership, the domestication becomes effective when the statement of domestication is effective. If the domesticated entity is a foreign partnership, the domestication becomes effective on the later of:

(1)   the date and time provided in the organic law of the domesticated entity; and

(2)   when the statement is effective.

COMMENT

Regardless of whether a domestic limited liability partnership is the domesticating or domesticated entity:

- This section applies and, therefore, a foreign limited liability partnership seeking to domesticate and thereby become a domestic LLP must comply with this section.

- The organic law of the foreign LLP's jurisdiction must also be consulted.

The filing of a statement of domestication makes the transaction a matter of public record.

Subsection (b)—This subsection sets forth the requirements for a statement of domestication. They are essentially the same as the requirements for a statement of merger in Section 1125.

Subsection (e)—A plan of domestication can be used as a substitute for the statement of domestication so long as the plan satisfies the requirements in Subsection (b).

Subsection (f)—Section 114 determines when a record delivered for filing under this act becomes effective. A statement of domestication may specify a delayed effective time and date, subject to the ninety-day limit stated in Section 114(3) and (4).

When the statement of domestication becomes effective under this subsection, the domestication transaction occurs if the domesticated entity is a domestic limited liability partnership. A domestication in which the domesticated entity is a foreign limited liability partnership will usually also take effect when the statement of domestication takes effect because the best practice will be to coordinate the filings that need to be made in each jurisdiction so that they take effect at the same time.

However, when the domesticated general partnership is a foreign general partnership, it is possible that the filing in the foreign jurisdiction will take effect at a different time. For that reason, this subsection provides that the domestication will take effect at the later of: (i) when the statement of domestication takes effect; and (ii) when the domestication takes effect under the law of the foreign jurisdiction. This rule avoids the possibility that the domestication will take effect in this state before it takes effect in the foreign jurisdiction, which would produce the undesirable result that the domesticating domestic general partnership would cease to appear as an active entity on the records of this state before appearing as its active, domesticated self on the records of the foreign jurisdiction.

It is necessary for the filing office to record only the effective date of the statement of domestication, and the filing office does not need to be concerned with the effective date of the domestication itself. Persons wishing to determine the effective date of a domestication will be able to do so by consulting the records of the filing offices in each jurisdiction.

§ 1156. Effect of Domestication

(a)   When a domestication becomes effective:

(1)   the domesticated entity is:

(A)   organized under and subject to the organic law of the domesticated entity; and

(B)   the same entity without interruption as the domesticating entity;

(2)   all property of the domesticating entity continues to be vested in the domesticated entity without transfer, reversion, or impairment;

(3)   all debts, obligations, and other liabilities of the domesticating entity continue as debts, obligations, and other liabilities of the domesticated entity;

(4)   except as otherwise provided by law or the plan of domestication, all the rights, privileges, immunities, powers, and purposes of the domesticating entity remain in the domesticated entity;

(5)   the name of the domesticated entity may be substituted for the name of the domesticating entity in any pending action or proceeding;

(6)   the statement of qualification of the domesticated entity becomes effective;

(7)   the provisions of the partnership agreement of the domesticated entity that are to be in a record, if any, approved as part of the plan of domestication become effective; and

(8)   the interests in the domesticating entity are converted to the extent and as approved in connection with the domestication, and the partners of the domesticating entity are entitled only to the rights provided to them under the plan of domestication and to any appraisal rights they have under Section 1106.

(b)   Except as otherwise provided in the organic law or partnership agreement of the domesticating limited liability partnership, the domestication does not give rise to any rights that a partner or third party would otherwise have upon a dissolution, liquidation, or winding up of the domesticating partnership.

(c)   When a domestication becomes effective, a person that did not have interest holder liability with respect to the domesticating limited liability partnership and becomes subject to interest holder liability with respect to a domestic limited liability partnership as a result of the domestication has interest holder liability only to the extent provided by this [act] and only for those debts, obligations, and other liabilities that are incurred after the domestication becomes effective.

(d)   When a domestication becomes effective, the interest holder liability of a person that ceases to hold an interest in a domestic domesticating limited liability partnership with respect to which the person had interest holder liability is subject to the following rules:

(1)   The domestication does not discharge any interest holder liability under this [act] to the extent the interest holder liability was incurred before the domestication became effective.

(2)   A person does not have interest holder liability under this [act] for any debt, obligation, or other liability that is incurred after the domestication becomes effective.

(3)   This [act] continues to apply to the release, collection, or discharge of any interest holder liability preserved under paragraph (1) as if the domestication had not occurred.

(4)   A person has whatever rights of contribution from any other person as are provided by this [act], law other than this [act], or the partnership agreement of the domestic domesticating limited liability partnership with respect to any interest holder liability preserved under paragraph (1) as if the domestication had not occurred.

(e)   When a domestication becomes effective, a foreign limited liability partnership that is the domesticated partnership may be served with process in this state for the collection and enforcement of any of its debts, obligations, and other liabilities as provided in Section 119.

(f)   If the domesticating limited liability partnership is a registered foreign entity, the registration of the partnership is canceled when the domestication becomes effective.

(g)   A domestication does not require a domestic domesticating limited liability partnership to wind up its business and does not constitute or cause the dissolution of the partnership.

COMMENT

Subsection (a)(1)—The domesticated entity is the same entity as the domesticating entity; it has merely changed its jurisdiction of formation.

Subsection (a)(2)—A domestication is not a sale, conveyance, transfer, or assignment and does not give rise to claims of reverter or impairment of title that may be based on a prohibition on transfer, assignment, or conveyance.

Subsection (a)(4)—All pending proceedings involving the domesticating entity are continued. The name of the domesticated entity may be, but need not be, substituted in any pending proceeding for the name of the domesticating entity.

Subsection (a)(8)—The interests of the domesticating limited liability partnership are reclassified into whatever rights were negotiated in the domestication and the partners and transferees of the domesticating LLP are entitled only to those rights. Paragraph 8, on its face, allows for certain partners of the domesticating LLP to be entitled to a continuing equity interest in the domesticated LLP whereas other partners of the domesticating LLP may be cashed out as a result of the transaction.

Subsection (c)—This subsection provides the rule for future interest holder liability and parallels analogous provisions in Parts 2 (mergers), 3 (interest exchanges), and 4 (conversions). *See* the comment to Section 1126(c).

Subsection (d)—This subsection provides the rule for past interest holder liability and parallels analogous provisions in Parts 2 (mergers), 3 (interest exchanges), and 4 (conversions). *See* the comments to Sections 1126(d) and 1146(d).

Subsection (e)—When a domestic domesticating limited liability partnership becomes a foreign LLP as a result of a domestication, some mechanism is needed to facilitate the enforcement of claims by the creditors and interest holders of the domesticating LLP. This subsection, which parallels analogous provisions in Parts 2 (mergers) and 4 (conversions), authorizes service of process for all such claims in this state.

Subsection (g)—When a domestication takes effect, the entity continues to exist—simply as a domestic entity under the laws of a different state. This subsection thus makes clear that the domestication does not require the limited liability partnership to wind up its affairs and does not constitute or cause the dissolution of the limited liability partnership.

[ARTICLE] 12.   MISCELLANEOUS PROVISIONS

§ 1201.   Uniformity of Application and Construction

In applying and construing this uniform act, consideration must be given to the need to promote uniformity of the law with respect to its subject matter among states that enact it.

§ 1202.   Relation to Electronic Signatures in Global and National Commerce Act

This [act] modifies, limits, and supersedes the Electronic Signatures in Global and National Commerce Act, 15 U.S.C. Section 7001 et seq., but does not modify, limit, or supersede Section 101(c) of that act, 15 U.S.C. Section 7001(c), or authorize electronic delivery of any of the notices described in Section 103(b) of that act, 15 U.S.C. Section 7003(b).

COMMENT

This section responds to specific language of the Electronic Signatures in Global and National Commerce Act and is designed to avoid preemption of state law under that federal legislation.

§ 1203.   Savings Clause

This [act] does not affect an action commenced, proceeding brought, or right accrued before [the effective date of this [act]].

COMMENT

This section continues prior law after the effective date of this act with respect to rights accrued and proceedings. But for this section, the new law of this act would displace the old laws in some circumstances. The power of a new act to displace the old statute with respect to conduct occurring before the new act's enactment is substantial. Millard H. Ruud, *The Savings Clause—Some Problems in Construction and Drafting*, 33 TEX. L. REV. 285, 286–93 (1955). A court generally applies the law that exists at the time it acts.

Eventually, this act will apply all to pre-existing general partnerships—whether by choice under Section 110(a)(2) (permitting an early opt-in), or without choice on the "all-inclusive date." Section 110(b). In this context, the phrase "before [the effective date of this [act]]" should be understood as referring to the date upon which this act becomes applicable to the particular general partnership at issue.

§ 1204. Severability Clause

If any provision of this [act] or its application to any person or circumstance is held invalid, the invalidity does not affect other provisions or applications of this [act] which can be given effect without the invalid provision or application, and to this end the provisions of this [act] are severable.]

Legislative Note: Include this section only if this state lacks a general severability statute or decision by the highest court of this state stating a general rule of severability.

§ 1205. Repeals

The following are repealed:

(1)   [the state partnership act as [amended, and as] in effect immediately before [the effective date of this [act]]].

(2)   . . . .

(3)   . . . .

§ 1206. Effective Date

This [act] takes effect. . . .

COMMENT

For the effect of the act's effective date on pre-existing partnerships, see Section 110.

DELAWARE GENERAL CORPORATION LAW

Delaware Code, Title 8, Chapter 1

Table of Contents

SUBCHAPTER I. FORMATION

SUBCHAPTER II. POWERS

SUBCHAPTER III. REGISTERED OFFICE AND REGISTERED AGENT

DELAWARE GENERAL CORPORATION LAW

SUBCHAPTER IV.   DIRECTORS AND OFFICERS

SUBCHAPTER V.   STOCK AND DIVIDENDS

SUBCHAPTER VI.   STOCK TRANSFERS

SUBCHAPTER VII.   MEETINGS, ELECTIONS, VOTING AND NOTICE

DELAWARE GENERAL CORPORATION LAW

DELAWARE GENERAL CORPORATION LAW

SUBCHAPTER I.   FORMATION

§ 101.   Incorporators; how corporation formed; purposes.

(a)   Any person, partnership, association or corporation, singly or jointly with others, and without regard to such person's or entity's residence, domicile or state of incorporation, may incorporate or organize a corporation under this chapter by filing with the Division of Corporations in the Department of State a certificate of incorporation which shall be executed, acknowledged and filed in accordance with § 103 of this title.

(b)   A corporation may be incorporated or organized under this chapter to conduct or promote any lawful business or purposes, except as may otherwise be provided by the Constitution or other law of this State.

(c)   Corporations for constructing, maintaining and operating public utilities, whether in or outside of this State, may be organized under this chapter, but corporations for constructing, maintaining and operating public utilities within this State shall be subject to, in addition to this chapter, the special provisions and requirements of Title 26 applicable to such corporations.

§ 102.   Contents of certificate of incorporation.

(a)   The certificate of incorporation shall set forth:

(1)   The name of the corporation, which (i) shall contain 1 of the words "association," "company," "corporation," "club," "foundation," "fund," "incorporated," "institute," "society," "union," "syndicate," or "limited," (or abbreviations thereof, with or without punctuation), or words (or abbreviations thereof, with or without punctuation) of like import of foreign countries or jurisdictions (provided they are written in roman characters or letters); provided, however, that the Division of Corporations in the Department of State may waive such requirement (unless it determines that such name is, or might otherwise appear to be, that of a natural person) if such corporation executes, acknowledges and files with the Secretary of State in accordance with § 103 of this title a certificate stating that its total assets, as defined in § 503(i) of this title, are not less than $10,000,000, or, in the sole discretion of the Division of Corporations in the Department of State, if the corporation is both a nonprofit nonstock corporation and an association of professionals, (ii) shall be such as to distinguish it upon the records in the office of the Division of Corporations in the Department of State from the names that are

reserved on such records and from the names on such records of each other corporation, partnership, limited partnership, limited liability company, registered series of a limited liability company or statutory trust organized or registered as a domestic or foreign corporation, partnership, limited partnership, limited liability company, registered series of a limited liability company or statutory trust under the laws of this State, except with the written consent of the person who has reserved such name or such other foreign corporation or domestic or foreign partnership, limited partnership, limited liability company, registered series of a limited liability company or statutory trust, executed, acknowledged and filed with the Secretary of State in accordance with § 103 of this title, or except that, without prejudicing any rights of the person who has reserved such name or such other foreign corporation or domestic or foreign partnership, limited partnership, limited liability company, registered series of a limited liability company or statutory trust, the Division of Corporations in the Department of State may waive such requirement if the corporation demonstrates to the satisfaction of the Secretary of State that the corporation or a predecessor entity previously has made substantial use of such name or a substantially similar name, that the corporation has made reasonable efforts to secure such written consent, and that such waiver is in the interest of the State, (iii) except as permitted by § 395 of this title, shall not contain the word "trust," and (iv) shall not contain the word "bank," or any variation thereof, except for the name of a bank reporting to and under the supervision of the State Bank Commissioner of this State or a subsidiary of a bank or savings association (as those terms are defined in the Federal Deposit Insurance Act, as amended, at 12 U.S.C. § 1813), or a corporation regulated under the Bank Holding Company Act of 1956, as amended, 12 U.S.C. § 1841 et seq., or the Home Owners' Loan Act, as amended, 12 U.S.C. § 1461 et seq.; provided, however, that this section shall not be construed to prevent the use of the word "bank," or any variation thereof, in a context clearly not purporting to refer to a banking business or otherwise likely to mislead the public about the nature of the business of the corporation or to lead to a pattern and practice of abuse that might cause harm to the interests of the public or the State as determined by the Division of Corporations in the Department of State;

(2) The address (which shall be stated in accordance with § 131(c) of this title) of the corporation's registered office in this State, and the name of its registered agent at such address;

(3) The nature of the business or purposes to be conducted or promoted. It shall be sufficient to state, either alone or with other businesses or purposes, that the purpose of the corporation is to engage in any lawful act or activity for which corporations may be organized under the General Corporation Law of Delaware, and by such statement all lawful acts and activities shall be within the purposes of the corporation, except for express limitations, if any;

(4) If the corporation is to be authorized to issue only 1 class of stock, the total number of shares of stock which the corporation shall have authority to issue and the par value of each of such shares, or a statement that all such shares are to be without par value. If the corporation is to be authorized to issue more than 1 class of stock, the certificate of incorporation shall set forth the total number of shares of all classes of stock which the corporation shall have authority to issue and the number of shares of each class and shall specify each class the shares of which are to be without par value and each class the shares of which are to have par value and the par value of the shares of each such class. The certificate of incorporation shall also set forth a statement of the designations and the powers, preferences and rights, and the qualifications, limitations or restrictions thereof, which are permitted by § 151 of this title in respect of any class or classes of stock or any series of any class of stock of the corporation and the fixing of which by the certificate of incorporation is desired, and an express grant of such authority as it may then be desired to grant to the board of directors to fix by resolution or resolutions any thereof that may be desired but which shall not be fixed by the certificate of incorporation. The foregoing provisions of this paragraph shall not apply to nonstock corporations. In the case of nonstock corporations, the fact that they are not authorized to issue capital stock shall be stated in the certificate of incorporation. The conditions of membership, or other criteria for identifying members, of nonstock corporations shall likewise be stated in the certificate of incorporation or the bylaws. Nonstock corporations shall have members, but failure to have members shall not affect otherwise valid corporate acts or work a forfeiture or dissolution of the corporation. Nonstock corporations may provide for classes or groups of members having relative rights, powers and duties, and may make provision for the future creation of additional classes or groups of members having such relative rights, powers and duties as may from time to time be established, including rights, powers

and duties senior to existing classes and groups of members. Except as otherwise provided in this chapter, nonstock corporations may also provide that any member or class or group of members shall have full, limited, or no voting rights or powers, including that any member or class or group of members shall have the right to vote on a specified transaction even if that member or class or group of members does not have the right to vote for the election of the members of the governing body of the corporation. Voting by members of a nonstock corporation may be on a per capita, number, financial interest, class, group, or any other basis set forth. The provisions referred to in the 3 preceding sentences may be set forth in the certificate of incorporation or the bylaws. If neither the certificate of incorporation nor the bylaws of a nonstock corporation state the conditions of membership, or other criteria for identifying members, the members of the corporation shall be deemed to be those entitled to vote for the election of the members of the governing body pursuant to the certificate of incorporation or bylaws of such corporation or otherwise until thereafter otherwise provided by the certificate of incorporation or the bylaws;

(5)   The name and mailing address of the incorporator or incorporators;

(6)   If the powers of the incorporator or incorporators are to terminate upon the filing of the certificate of incorporation, the names and mailing addresses of the persons who are to serve as directors until the first annual meeting of stockholders or until their successors are elected and qualify.

(b)   In addition to the matters required to be set forth in the certificate of incorporation by subsection (a) of this section, the certificate of incorporation may also contain any or all of the following matters:

(1)   Any provision for the management of the business and for the conduct of the affairs of the corporation, and any provision creating, defining, limiting and regulating the powers of the corporation, the directors, and the stockholders, or any class of the stockholders, or the governing body, members, or any class or group of members of a nonstock corporation; if such provisions are not contrary to the laws of this State. Any provision which is required or permitted by any section of this chapter to be stated in the bylaws may instead be stated in the certificate of incorporation;

(2)   The following provisions, in haec verba, (i), for a corporation other than a nonstock corporation, viz:

"Whenever a compromise or arrangement is proposed between this corporation and its creditors or any class of them and/or between this corporation and its stockholders or any class of them, any court of equitable jurisdiction within the State of Delaware may, on the application in a summary way of this corporation or of any creditor or stockholder thereof or on the application of any receiver or receivers appointed for this corporation under § 291 of Title 8 of the Delaware Code or on the application of trustees in dissolution or of any receiver or receivers appointed for this corporation under § 279 of Title 8 of the Delaware Code order a meeting of the creditors or class of creditors, and/or of the stockholders or class of stockholders of this corporation, as the case may be, to be summoned in such manner as the said court directs. If a majority in number representing three fourths in value of the creditors or class of creditors, and/or of the stockholders or class of stockholders of this corporation, as the case may be, agree to any compromise or arrangement and to any reorganization of this corporation as consequence of such compromise or arrangement, the said compromise or arrangement and the said reorganization shall, if sanctioned by the court to which the said application has been made, be binding on all the creditors or class of creditors, and/or on all the stockholders or class of stockholders, of this corporation, as the case may be, and also on this corporation"; or

(ii), for a nonstock corporation, viz:

"Whenever a compromise or arrangement is proposed between this corporation and its creditors or any class of them and/or between this corporation and its members or any class of them, any court of equitable jurisdiction within the State of Delaware may, on the application in a summary way of this corporation or of any creditor or member thereof or on the application of any receiver or receivers appointed for this corporation under § 291 of Title 8 of the Delaware Code or on the application of trustees in dissolution or of any receiver or receivers appointed for this corporation under § 279 of Title 8 of the Delaware Code order a meeting of the creditors or class of creditors, and/or of the members or class of members of this corporation, as the case may be, to be summoned in such manner as the said court directs. If a majority in number representing three fourths in value of the creditors or class of creditors, and/or of the members or class of members of this corporation, as the case may be, agree to any compromise or arrangement and to any reorganization of this corporation as consequence of such compromise or arrangement, the said compromise or arrangement and the said reorganization shall, if sanctioned by the court to which the said application has been made, be binding on all the creditors or class of creditors, and/or on all the members or class of members, of this corporation, as the case may be, and also on this corporation";

(3) Such provisions as may be desired granting to the holders of the stock of the corporation, or the holders of any class or series of a class thereof, the preemptive right to subscribe to any or all additional issues of stock of the corporation of any or all classes or series thereof, or to any securities of the corporation convertible into such stock. No stockholder shall have any preemptive right to subscribe to an additional issue of stock or to any security convertible into such stock unless, and except to the extent that, such right is expressly granted to such stockholder in the certificate of incorporation. All such rights in existence on July 3, 1967, shall remain in existence unaffected by this paragraph unless and until changed or terminated by appropriate action which expressly provides for the change or termination;

(4) Provisions requiring for any corporate action, the vote of a larger portion of the stock or of any class or series thereof, or of any other securities having voting power, or a larger number of the directors, than is required by this chapter;

(5) A provision limiting the duration of the corporation's existence to a specified date; otherwise, the corporation shall have perpetual existence;

(6) A provision imposing personal liability for the debts of the corporation on its stockholders to a specified extent and upon specified conditions; otherwise, the stockholders of a corporation shall not be personally liable for the payment of the corporation's debts except as they may be liable by reason of their own conduct or acts;

(7) A provision eliminating or limiting the personal liability of a director to the corporation or its stockholders for monetary damages for breach of fiduciary duty as a director, provided that such provision shall not eliminate or limit the liability of a director: (i) For any breach of the director's duty of loyalty to the corporation or its stockholders; (ii) for acts or omissions not in good faith or which involve intentional misconduct or a knowing violation of law; (iii) under § 174 of this title; or (iv) for any transaction from which the director derived an improper personal benefit. No such provision shall eliminate or limit the liability of a director for any act or omission occurring prior to the date when such provision becomes effective. All references in this paragraph to a director shall also be deemed to refer to such other person or persons, if any, who, pursuant to a provision of the certificate of incorporation in accordance with § 141(a) of this title, exercise or perform any of the powers or duties otherwise conferred or imposed upon the board of directors by this title.

(c) It shall not be necessary to set forth in the certificate of incorporation any of the powers conferred on corporations by this chapter.

(d) Except for provisions included pursuant to paragraphs (a)(1), (a)(2), (a)(5), (a)(6), (b)(2), (b)(5), (b)(7) of this section, and provisions included pursuant to paragraph (a)(4) of this section specifying the classes, number of shares, and par value of shares a corporation other than a nonstock corporation is authorized to issue, any provision of the certificate of incorporation may be made dependent upon facts ascertainable outside such instrument, provided that the manner in which such facts shall operate upon the provision is clearly and explicitly set forth therein. The term "facts," as used in this subsection, includes, but is not limited to, the occurrence of any event, including a determination or action by any person or body, including the corporation.

(e) The exclusive right to the use of a name that is available for use by a domestic or foreign corporation may be reserved by or on behalf of:

(1) Any person intending to incorporate or organize a corporation with that name under this chapter or contemplating such incorporation or organization;

(2)   Any domestic corporation or any foreign corporation qualified to do business in the State of Delaware, in either case, intending to change its name or contemplating such a change;

(3)   Any foreign corporation intending to qualify to do business in the State of Delaware and adopt that name or contemplating such qualification and adoption; and

(4)   Any person intending to organize a foreign corporation and have it qualify to do business in the State of Delaware and adopt that name or contemplating such organization, qualification and adoption.

The reservation of a specified name may be made by filing with the Secretary of State an application, executed by the applicant, certifying that the reservation is made by or on behalf of a domestic corporation, foreign corporation or other person described in paragraphs (e)(1)–(4) of this section above, and specifying the name to be reserved and the name and address of the applicant. If the Secretary of State finds that the name is available for use by a domestic or foreign corporation, the Secretary shall reserve the name for the use of the applicant for a period of 120 days. The same applicant may renew for successive 120-day periods a reservation of a specified name by filing with the Secretary of State, prior to the expiration of such reservation (or renewal thereof), an application for renewal of such reservation, executed by the applicant, certifying that the reservation is renewed by or on behalf of a domestic corporation, foreign corporation or other person described in paragraphs (e)(1)–(4) of this section above and specifying the name reservation to be renewed and the name and address of the applicant. The right to the exclusive use of a reserved name may be transferred to any other person by filing in the office of the Secretary of State a notice of the transfer, executed by the applicant for whom the name was reserved, specifying the name reservation to be transferred and the name and address of the transferee. The reservation of a specified name may be cancelled by filing with the Secretary of State a notice of cancellation, executed by the applicant or transferee, specifying the name reservation to be cancelled and the name and address of the applicant or transferee. Unless the Secretary of State finds that any application, application for renewal, notice of transfer, or notice of cancellation filed with the Secretary of State as required by this subsection does not conform to law, upon receipt of all filing fees required by law the Secretary of State shall prepare and return to the person who filed such instrument a copy of the filed instrument with a notation thereon of the action taken by the Secretary of State. A fee as set forth in § 391 of this title shall be paid at the time of the reservation of any name, at the time of the renewal of any such reservation and at the time of the filing of a notice of the transfer or cancellation of any such reservation.

(f)   The certificate of incorporation may not contain any provision that would impose liability on a stockholder for the attorneys' fees or expenses of the corporation or any other party in connection with an internal corporate claim, as defined in § 115 of this title.

§ 103.   Execution, acknowledgment, filing, recording and effective date of original certificate of incorporation and other instruments; exceptions.

(a)   Whenever any instrument is to be filed with the Secretary of State or in accordance with this section or chapter, such instrument shall be executed as follows:

(1)   The certificate of incorporation, and any other instrument to be filed before the election of the initial board of directors if the initial directors were not named in the certificate of incorporation, shall be signed by the incorporator or incorporators (or, in the case of any such other instrument, such incorporator's or incorporators' successors and assigns). If any incorporator is not available then any such other instrument may be signed, with the same effect as if such incorporator had signed it, by any person for whom or on whose behalf such incorporator, in executing the certificate of incorporation, was acting directly or indirectly as employee or agent, provided that such other instrument shall state that such incorporator is not available and the reason therefor, that such incorporator in executing the certificate of incorporation was acting directly or indirectly as employee or agent for or on behalf of such person, and that such person's signature on such instrument is otherwise authorized and not wrongful.

(2)   All other instruments shall be signed:

     a.   By any authorized officer of the corporation; or

b.   If it shall appear from the instrument that there are no such officers, then by a majority of the directors or by such directors as may be designated by the board; or

c.   If it shall appear from the instrument that there are no such officers or directors, then by the holders of record, or such of them as may be designated by the holders of record, of a majority of all outstanding shares of stock; or

d.   By the holders of record of all outstanding shares of stock.

(b)   Whenever this chapter requires any instrument to be acknowledged, such requirement is satisfied by either:

(1)   The formal acknowledgment by the person or 1 of the persons signing the instrument that it is such person's act and deed or the act and deed of the corporation, and that the facts stated therein are true. Such acknowledgment shall be made before a person who is authorized by the law of the place of execution to take acknowledgments of deeds. If such person has a seal of office such person shall affix it to the instrument.

(2)   The signature, without more, of the person or persons signing the instrument, in which case such signature or signatures shall constitute the affirmation or acknowledgment of the signatory, under penalties of perjury, that the instrument is such person's act and deed or the act and deed of the corporation, and that the facts stated therein are true.

(c)   Whenever any instrument is to be filed with the Secretary of State or in accordance with this section or chapter, such requirement means that:

(1)   The signed instrument shall be delivered to the office of the Secretary of State;

(2)   All taxes and fees authorized by law to be collected by the Secretary of State in connection with the filing of the instrument shall be tendered to the Secretary of State; and

(3)   Upon delivery of the instrument, the Secretary of State shall record the date and time of its delivery. Upon such delivery and tender of the required taxes and fees, the Secretary of State shall certify that the instrument has been filed in the Secretary of State's office by endorsing upon the signed instrument the word "Filed", and the date and time of its filing. This endorsement is the "filing date" of the instrument, and is conclusive of the date and time of its filing in the absence of actual fraud. The Secretary of State shall file and index the endorsed instrument. Except as provided in paragraph (c)(4) of this section and in subsection (i) of this section, such filing date of an instrument shall be the date and time of delivery of the instrument.

(4)   Upon request made upon or prior to delivery, the Secretary of State may, to the extent deemed practicable, establish as the filing date of an instrument a date and time after its delivery. If the Secretary of State refuses to file any instrument due to an error, omission or other imperfection, the Secretary of State may hold such instrument in suspension, and in such event, upon delivery of a replacement instrument in proper form for filing and tender of the required taxes and fees within 5 business days after notice of such suspension is given to the filer, the Secretary of State shall establish as the filing date of such instrument the date and time that would have been the filing date of the rejected instrument had it been accepted for filing. The Secretary of State shall not issue a certificate of good standing with respect to any corporation with an instrument held in suspension pursuant to this subsection. The Secretary of State may establish as the filing date of an instrument the date and time at which information from such instrument is entered pursuant to paragraph (c)(8) of this section if such instrument is delivered on the same date and within 4 hours after such information is entered.

(5)   The Secretary of State, acting as agent for the recorders of each of the counties, shall collect and deposit in a separate account established exclusively for that purpose a county assessment fee with respect to each filed instrument and shall thereafter weekly remit from such account to the recorder of each of the said counties the amount or amounts of such fees as provided for in paragraph (c)(6) of this section or as elsewhere provided by law. Said fees shall be for the purposes of defraying certain costs incurred by the counties in merging the information and images of such filed documents with the document information systems of each of the recorder's offices in the counties and in retrieving, maintaining and displaying such information and images in the offices of the recorders and at remote locations in each of such counties. In consideration for its acting as the agent for the recorders

with respect to the collection and payment of the county assessment fees, the Secretary of State shall retain and pay over to the General Fund of the State an administrative charge of 1 percent of the total fees collected.

(6) The assessment fee to the counties shall be $24 for each 1-page instrument filed with the Secretary of State in accordance with this section and $9.00 for each additional page for instruments with more than 1 page. The recorder's office to receive the assessment fee shall be the recorder's office in the county in which the corporation's registered office in this State is, or is to be, located, except that an assessment fee shall not be charged for either a certificate of dissolution qualifying for treatment under § 391(a)(5)b. of this title or a document filed in accordance with subchapter XVI of this chapter.

(7) The Secretary of State, acting as agent, shall collect and deposit in a separate account established exclusively for that purpose a courthouse municipality fee with respect to each filed instrument and shall thereafter monthly remit funds from such account to the treasuries of the municipalities designated in § 301 of Title 10. Said fees shall be for the purposes of defraying certain costs incurred by such municipalities in hosting the primary locations for the Delaware courts. The fee to such municipalities shall be $20 for each instrument filed with the Secretary of State in accordance with this section. The municipality to receive the fee shall be the municipality designated in § 301 of Title 10 in the county in which the corporation's registered office in this State is, or is to be, located, except that a fee shall not be charged for a certificate of dissolution qualifying for treatment under § 391(a)(5)b. of this title, a resignation of agent without appointment of a successor under § 136 of this title, or a document filed in accordance with subchapter XVI of this chapter.

(8) The Secretary of State shall cause to be entered such information from each instrument as the Secretary of State deems appropriate into the Delaware Corporation Information System or any system which is a successor thereto in the office of the Secretary of State, and such information and a copy of each such instrument shall be permanently maintained as a public record on a suitable medium. The Secretary of State is authorized to grant direct access to such system to registered agents subject to the execution of an operating agreement between the Secretary of State and such registered agent. Any registered agent granted such access shall demonstrate the existence of policies to ensure that information entered into the system accurately reflects the content of instruments in the possession of the registered agent at the time of entry.

(d) Any instrument filed in accordance with subsection (c) of this section shall be effective upon its filing date. Any instrument may provide that it is not to become effective until a specified time subsequent to the time it is filed, but such time shall not be later than a time on the ninetieth day after the date of its filing. If any instrument filed in accordance with subsection (c) of this section provides for a future effective date or time and if the transaction is terminated or its terms are amended to change the future effective date or time prior to the future effective date or time, the instrument shall be terminated or amended by the filing, prior to the future effective date or time set forth in such instrument, of a certificate of termination or amendment of the original instrument, executed in accordance with subsection (a) of this section, which shall identify the instrument which has been terminated or amended and shall state that the instrument has been terminated or the manner in which it has been amended.

(e) If another section of this chapter specifically prescribes a manner of executing, acknowledging or filing a specified instrument or a time when such instrument shall become effective which differs from the corresponding provisions of this section, then such other section shall govern.

(f) Whenever any instrument authorized to be filed with the Secretary of State under any provision of this title, has been so filed and is an inaccurate record of the corporate action therein referred to, or was defectively or erroneously executed, sealed or acknowledged, the instrument may be corrected by filing with the Secretary of State a certificate of correction of the instrument which shall be executed, acknowledged and filed in accordance with this section. The certificate of correction shall specify the inaccuracy or defect to be corrected and shall set forth the portion of the instrument in corrected form. In lieu of filing a certificate of correction the instrument may be corrected by filing with the Secretary of State a corrected instrument which shall be executed, acknowledged and filed in accordance with this section. The corrected instrument shall be specifically designated as such in its heading, shall specify the inaccuracy or defect to be corrected, and shall set forth the entire instrument in corrected form. An instrument corrected in accordance with this section shall be effective as of the date the original instrument was filed, except as to those persons who are substantially and adversely affected by the correction and as to those persons the instrument as corrected shall be effective from the filing date.

(g) Notwithstanding that any instrument authorized to be filed with the Secretary of State under this title is when filed inaccurately, defectively or erroneously executed, sealed or acknowledged, or otherwise defective in any respect, the Secretary of State shall have no liability to any person for the preclearance for filing, the acceptance for filing or the filing and indexing of such instrument by the Secretary of State.

(h) Any signature on any instrument authorized to be filed with the Secretary of State under this title may be a facsimile, a conformed signature or an electronically transmitted signature.

(i)(1) If:

a. Together with the actual delivery of an instrument and tender of the required taxes and fees, there is delivered to the Secretary of State a separate affidavit (which in its heading shall be designated as an "affidavit of extraordinary condition") attesting, on the basis of personal knowledge of the affiant or a reliable source of knowledge identified in the affidavit, that an earlier effort to deliver such instrument and tender such taxes and fees was made in good faith, specifying the nature, date and time of such good faith effort and requesting that the Secretary of State establish such date and time as the filing date of such instrument; or

b. Upon the actual delivery of an instrument and tender of the required taxes and fees, the Secretary of State in the Secretary's discretion provides a written waiver of the requirement for such an affidavit stating that it appears to the Secretary of State that an earlier effort to deliver such instrument and tender such taxes and fees was made in good faith and specifying the date and time of such effort; and

c. The Secretary of State determines that an extraordinary condition existed at such date and time, that such earlier effort was unsuccessful as a result of the existence of such extraordinary condition, and that such actual delivery and tender were made within a reasonable period (not to exceed 2 business days) after the cessation of such extraordinary condition,

then the Secretary of State may establish such date and time as the filing date of such instrument. No fee shall be paid to the Secretary of State for receiving an affidavit of extraordinary condition.

(2) For purposes of this subsection, an "extraordinary condition" means: any emergency resulting from an attack on, invasion or occupation by foreign military forces of, or disaster, catastrophe, war or other armed conflict, revolution or insurrection, or rioting or civil commotion in, the United States or a locality in which the Secretary of State conducts its business or in which the good faith effort to deliver the instrument and tender the required taxes and fees is made, or the immediate threat of any of the foregoing; or any malfunction or outage of the electrical or telephone service to the Secretary of State's office, or weather or other condition in or about a locality in which the Secretary of State conducts its business, as a result of which the Secretary of State's office is not open for the purpose of the filing of instruments under this chapter or such filing cannot be effected without extraordinary effort. The Secretary of State may require such proof as it deems necessary to make the determination required under paragraph (i)(1)c. of this section, and any such determination shall be conclusive in the absence of actual fraud.

(3) If the Secretary of State establishes the filing date of an instrument pursuant to this subsection, the date and time of delivery of the affidavit of extraordinary condition or the date and time of the Secretary of State's written waiver of such affidavit shall be endorsed on such affidavit or waiver and such affidavit or waiver, so endorsed, shall be attached to the filed instrument to which it relates. Such filed instrument shall be effective as of the date and time established as the filing date by the Secretary of State pursuant to this subsection, except as to those persons who are substantially and adversely affected by such establishment and, as to those persons, the instrument shall be effective from the date and time endorsed on the affidavit of extraordinary condition or written waiver attached thereto.

(j) Notwithstanding any other provision of this chapter, it shall not be necessary for any corporation to amend its certificate of incorporation, or any other document, that has been filed prior to August 1, 2011, to comply with § 131(c) of this title, provided that any certificate or other document filed under this chapter on or after August 1, 2011, and changing the address of a registered office shall comply with § 131(c) of this title.

§ 104. Certificate of incorporation; definition.

The term "certificate of incorporation," as used in this chapter, unless the context requires otherwise, includes not only the original certificate of incorporation filed to create a corporation but also all other certificates, agreements of merger or consolidation, plans of reorganization, or other instruments, howsoever designated, which are filed pursuant to § 102, §§ 133–136, § 151, §§ 241–243, § 245, §§ 251–258, §§ 263–264, § 267, § 303, §§ 311–313, or any other section of this title, and which have the effect of amending or supplementing in some respect a corporation's certificate of incorporation.

§ 105. Certificate of incorporation and other certificates; evidence.

A copy of a certificate of incorporation, or a restated certificate of incorporation, or of any other certificate which has been filed in the office of the Secretary of State as required by any provision of this title shall, when duly certified by the Secretary of State, be received in all courts, public offices and official bodies as prima facie evidence of:

(1) Due execution, acknowledgment and filing of the instrument;

(2) Observance and performance of all acts and conditions necessary to have been observed and performed precedent to the instrument becoming effective; and

(3) Any other facts required or permitted by law to be stated in the instrument.

§ 106. Commencement of corporate existence.

Upon the filing with the Secretary of State of the certificate of incorporation, executed and acknowledged in accordance with § 103 of this title, the incorporator or incorporators who signed the certificate, and such incorporator's or incorporators' successors and assigns, shall, from the date of such filing, be and constitute a body corporate, by the name set forth in the certificate, subject to § 103(d) of this title and subject to dissolution or other termination of its existence as provided in this chapter.

§ 107. Powers of incorporators.

If the persons who are to serve as directors until the first annual meeting of stockholders have not been named in the certificate of incorporation, the incorporator or incorporators, until the directors are elected, shall manage the affairs of the corporation and may do whatever is necessary and proper to perfect the organization of the corporation, including the adoption of the original bylaws of the corporation and the election of directors.

§ 108. Organization meeting of incorporators or directors named in certificate of incorporation.

(a) After the filing of the certificate of incorporation an organization meeting of the incorporator or incorporators, or of the board of directors if the initial directors were named in the certificate of incorporation, shall be held, either within or without this State, at the call of a majority of the incorporators or directors, as the case may be, for the purposes of adopting bylaws, electing directors (if the meeting is of the incorporators) to serve or hold office until the first annual meeting of stockholders or until their successors are elected and qualify, electing officers if the meeting is of the directors, doing any other or further acts to perfect the organization of the corporation, and transacting such other business as may come before the meeting.

(b) The persons calling the meeting shall give to each other incorporator or director, as the case may be, at least 2 days' notice thereof in writing or by electronic transmission by any usual means of communication, which notice shall state the time, place and purposes of the meeting as fixed by the persons calling it. Notice of the meeting need not be given to anyone who attends the meeting or who waives notice either before or after the meeting.

(c)   Any action permitted to be taken at the organization meeting of the incorporators or directors, as the case may be, may be taken without a meeting if each incorporator or director, where there is more than 1, or the sole incorporator or director where there is only 1, consents thereto in writing or by electronic transmission. Any person (whether or not then an incorporator or director) may provide, whether through instruction to an agent or otherwise, that a consent to action will be effective at a future time (including a time determined upon the happening of an event), no later than 60 days after such instruction is given or such provision is made and such consent shall be deemed to have been given for purposes of this subsection at such effective time so long as such person is then an incorporator or director, as the case may be, and did not revoke the consent prior to such time. Any such consent shall be revocable prior to its becoming effective.

(d)   If any incorporator is not available to act, then any person for whom or on whose behalf the incorporator was acting directly or indirectly as employee or agent, may take any action that such incorporator would have been authorized to take under this section or § 107 of this title; provided that any instrument signed by such other person, or any record of the proceedings of a meeting in which such person participated, shall state that such incorporator is not available and the reason therefor, that such incorporator was acting directly or indirectly as employee or agent for or on behalf of such person, and that such person's signature on such instrument or participation in such meeting is otherwise authorized and not wrongful.

§ 109.   Bylaws.

(a)   The original or other bylaws of a corporation may be adopted, amended or repealed by the incorporators, by the initial directors of a corporation other than a nonstock corporation or initial members of the governing body of a nonstock corporation if they were named in the certificate of incorporation, or, before a corporation other than a nonstock corporation has received any payment for any of its stock, by its board of directors. After a corporation other than a nonstock corporation has received any payment for any of its stock, the power to adopt, amend or repeal bylaws shall be in the stockholders entitled to vote. In the case of a nonstock corporation, the power to adopt, amend or repeal bylaws shall be in its members entitled to vote. Notwithstanding the foregoing, any corporation may, in its certificate of incorporation, confer the power to adopt, amend or repeal bylaws upon the directors or, in the case of a nonstock corporation, upon its governing body. The fact that such power has been so conferred upon the directors or governing body, as the case may be, shall not divest the stockholders or members of the power, nor limit their power to adopt, amend or repeal bylaws.

(b)   The bylaws may contain any provision, not inconsistent with law or with the certificate of incorporation, relating to the business of the corporation, the conduct of its affairs, and its rights or powers or the rights or powers of its stockholders, directors, officers or employees. The bylaws may not contain any provision that would impose liability on a stockholder for the attorneys' fees or expenses of the corporation or any other party in connection with an internal corporate claim, as defined in § 115 of this title.

§ 110.   Emergency bylaws and other powers in emergency.

(a)   The board of directors of any corporation may adopt emergency bylaws, subject to repeal or change by action of the stockholders, which shall notwithstanding any different provision elsewhere in this chapter or in Chapters 3 [repealed] and 5 [repealed] of Title 26, or in Chapter 7 of Title 5, or in the certificate of incorporation or bylaws, be operative during any emergency resulting from an attack on the United States or on a locality in which the corporation conducts its business or customarily holds meetings of its board of directors or its stockholders, or during any nuclear or atomic disaster, or during the existence of any catastrophe, or other similar emergency condition, as a result of which a quorum of the board of directors or a standing committee thereof cannot readily be convened for action. The emergency bylaws may make any provision that may be practical and necessary for the circumstances of the emergency, including provisions that:

(1)   A meeting of the board of directors or a committee thereof may be called by any officer or director in such manner and under such conditions as shall be prescribed in the emergency bylaws;

(2)   The director or directors in attendance at the meeting, or any greater number fixed by the emergency bylaws, shall constitute a quorum; and

(3)   The officers or other persons designated on a list approved by the board of directors before the emergency, all in such order of priority and subject to such conditions and for such period of time (not longer than reasonably necessary after the termination of the emergency) as may be provided in the emergency bylaws or in the resolution approving the list, shall, to the extent required to provide a quorum at any meeting of the board of directors, be deemed directors for such meeting.

(b)   The board of directors, either before or during any such emergency, may provide, and from time to time modify, lines of succession in the event that during such emergency any or all officers or agents of the corporation shall for any reason be rendered incapable of discharging their duties.

(c)   The board of directors, either before or during any such emergency, may, effective in the emergency, change the head office or designate several alternative head offices or regional offices, or authorize the officers so to do.

(d)   No officer, director or employee acting in accordance with any emergency bylaws shall be liable except for wilful misconduct.

(e)   To the extent not inconsistent with any emergency bylaws so adopted, the bylaws of the corporation shall remain in effect during any emergency and upon its termination the emergency bylaws shall cease to be operative.

(f)   Unless otherwise provided in emergency bylaws, notice of any meeting of the board of directors during such an emergency may be given only to such of the directors as it may be feasible to reach at the time and by such means as may be feasible at the time, including publication or radio.

(g)   To the extent required to constitute a quorum at any meeting of the board of directors during such an emergency, the officers of the corporation who are present shall, unless otherwise provided in emergency bylaws, be deemed, in order of rank and within the same rank in order of seniority, directors for such meeting.

(h)   Nothing contained in this section shall be deemed exclusive of any other provisions for emergency powers consistent with other sections of this title which have been or may be adopted by corporations created under this chapter.

§ 111. Jurisdiction to interpret, apply, enforce or determine the validity of corporate instruments and provisions of this title. [For application of this section, see 80 Del. Laws, c. 265, § 17]

(a)   Any civil action to interpret, apply, enforce or determine the validity of the provisions of:

(1)   The certificate of incorporation or the bylaws of a corporation;

(2)   Any instrument, document or agreement (i) by which a corporation creates or sells, or offers to create or sell, any of its stock, or any rights or options respecting its stock, or (ii) to which a corporation and 1 or more holders of its stock are parties, and pursuant to which any such holder or holders sell or offer to sell any of such stock, or (iii) by which a corporation agrees to sell, lease or exchange any of its property or assets, and which by its terms provides that 1 or more holders of its stock approve of or consent to such sale, lease or exchange;

(3)   Any written restrictions on the transfer, registration of transfer or ownership of securities under § 202 of this title;

(4)   Any proxy under § 212 or § 215 of this title;

(5)   Any voting trust or other voting agreement under § 218 of this title;

(6)   Any agreement, certificate of merger or consolidation, or certificate of ownership and merger governed by §§ 251–253, §§ 255–258, §§ 263–264, or § 267 of this title;

(7)   Any certificate of conversion under § 265 or § 266 of this title;

(8)   Any certificate of domestication, transfer or continuance under § 388, § 389 or § 390 of this title; or

(9)   Any other instrument, document, agreement, or certificate required by any provision of this title;

may be brought in the Court of Chancery, except to the extent that a statute confers exclusive jurisdiction on a court, agency or tribunal other than the Court of Chancery.

(b)   Any civil action to interpret, apply or enforce any provision of this title may be brought in the Court of Chancery.

$\S$ 112.   Access to proxy solicitation materials.

The bylaws may provide that if the corporation solicits proxies with respect to an election of directors, it may be required, to the extent and subject to such procedures or conditions as may be provided in the bylaws, to include in its proxy solicitation materials (including any form of proxy it distributes), in addition to individuals nominated by the board of directors, 1 or more individuals nominated by a stockholder. Such procedures or conditions may include any of the following:

(1)   A provision requiring a minimum record or beneficial ownership, or duration of ownership, of shares of the corporation's capital stock, by the nominating stockholder, and defining beneficial ownership to take into account options or other rights in respect of or related to such stock;

(2)   A provision requiring the nominating stockholder to submit specified information concerning the stockholder and the stockholder's nominees, including information concerning ownership by such persons of shares of the corporation's capital stock, or options or other rights in respect of or related to such stock;

(3)   A provision conditioning eligibility to require inclusion in the corporation's proxy solicitation materials upon the number or proportion of directors nominated by stockholders or whether the stockholder previously sought to require such inclusion;

(4)   A provision precluding nominations by any person if such person, any nominee of such person, or any affiliate or associate of such person or nominee, has acquired or publicly proposed to acquire shares constituting a specified percentage of the voting power of the corporation's outstanding voting stock within a specified period before the election of directors;

(5)   A provision requiring that the nominating stockholder undertake to indemnify the corporation in respect of any loss arising as a result of any false or misleading information or statement submitted by the nominating stockholder in connection with a nomination; and

(6)   Any other lawful condition.

$\S$ 113.   Proxy expense reimbursement.

(a)   The bylaws may provide for the reimbursement by the corporation of expenses incurred by a stockholder in soliciting proxies in connection with an election of directors, subject to such procedures or conditions as the bylaws may prescribe, including:

(1)   Conditioning eligibility for reimbursement upon the number or proportion of persons nominated by the stockholder seeking reimbursement or whether such stockholder previously sought reimbursement for similar expenses;

(2)   Limitations on the amount of reimbursement based upon the proportion of votes cast in favor of 1 or more of the persons nominated by the stockholder seeking reimbursement, or upon the amount spent by the corporation in soliciting proxies in connection with the election;

(3)   Limitations concerning elections of directors by cumulative voting pursuant to $\S$ 214 of this title; or

(4)   Any other lawful condition.

(b)   No bylaw so adopted shall apply to elections for which any record date precedes its adoption.

§ 114. Application of chapter to nonstock corporations.

(a) Except as otherwise provided in subsections (b) and (c) of this section, the provisions of this chapter and of chapter 5 of this title shall apply to nonstock corporations in the manner specified in the following paragraphs (a)(1)–(4) of this section:

(1) All references to stockholders of the corporation shall be deemed to refer to members of the corporation;

(2) All references to the board of directors of the corporation shall be deemed to refer to the governing body of the corporation;

(3) All references to directors or to members of the board of directors of the corporation shall be deemed to refer to members of the governing body of the corporation; and

(4) All references to stock, capital stock, or shares thereof of a corporation authorized to issue capital stock shall be deemed to refer to memberships of a nonprofit nonstock corporation and to membership interests of any other nonstock corporation.

(b) Subsection (a) of this section shall not apply to:

(1) Sections 102(a)(4), (b)(1) and (2), 109(a), 114, 141, 154, 215, 228, 230(b), 241, 242, 253, 254, 255, 256, 257, 258, 271, 276, 311, 312, 313, 390, and 503 of this title, which apply to nonstock corporations by their terms;

(2) Sections 102(f), 109(b) (last sentence), 151, 152, 153, 155, 156, 157(d), 158, 161, 162, 163, 164, 165, 166, 167, 168, 203, 211, 212, 213, 214, 216, 219, 222, 231, 243, 244, 251, 252, 267, 274, 275, 324, 364, 366(a), 391 and 502(a)(5) of this title; and

(3) Subchapter XIV and subchapter XVI of this chapter.

(c) In the case of a nonprofit nonstock corporation, subsection (a) of this section shall not apply to:

(1) The sections and subchapters listed in subsection (b) of this section;

(2) Sections 102(b)(3), 111(a)(2) and (3), 144(a)(2), 217, 218(a) and (b), and 262 of this title; and

(3) Subchapter V, subchapter VI (other than §§ 204 and 205 of this title) and subchapter XV of this chapter.

(d) For purposes of this chapter:

(1) A "charitable nonstock corporation" is any nonprofit nonstock corporation that is exempt from taxation under § 501(c)(3) of the United States Internal Revenue Code [26 U.S.C. § 501(c)(3)], or any successor provisions.

(2) A "membership interest" is, unless otherwise provided in a nonstock corporation's certificate of incorporation, a member's share of the profits and losses of a nonstock corporation, or a member's right to receive distributions of the nonstock corporation's assets, or both;

(3) A "nonprofit nonstock corporation" is a nonstock corporation that does not have membership interests; and

(4) A "nonstock corporation" is any corporation organized under this chapter that is not authorized to issue capital stock.

§ 115. Forum selection provisions.

The certificate of incorporation or the bylaws may require, consistent with applicable jurisdictional requirements, that any or all internal corporate claims shall be brought solely and exclusively in any or all of the courts in this State, and no provision of the certificate of incorporation or the bylaws may prohibit bringing such claims in the courts of this State. "Internal corporate claims" means claims, including claims in the right of the corporation, (i) that are based upon a violation of a duty by a current or former director or officer or stockholder in such capacity, or (ii) as to which this title confers jurisdiction upon the Court of Chancery.

§ 116. Document form, signature and delivery.

(a)   Except as provided in subsection (b) of this section, without limiting the manner in which any act or transaction may be documented, or the manner in which a document may be signed or delivered:

(1)   Any act or transaction contemplated or governed by this chapter or the certificate of incorporation or bylaws may be provided for in a document, and an electronic transmission shall be deemed the equivalent of a written document. "Document" means:

a.   Any tangible medium on which information is inscribed, and includes handwritten, typed, printed or similar instruments, and copies of such instruments; and

b.   An electronic transmission.

(2)   Whenever this chapter or the certificate of incorporation or bylaws requires or permits a signature, the signature may be a manual, facsimile, conformed or electronic signature. "Electronic signature" means an electronic symbol or process that is attached to, or logically associated with, a document and executed or adopted by a person with an intent to authenticate or adopt the document.

(3)   Unless otherwise agreed between the sender and recipient, an electronic transmission shall be deemed delivered to a person for purposes of this chapter and the certificate of incorporation and bylaws when it enters an information processing system that the person has designated for the purpose of receiving electronic transmissions of the type delivered, so long as the electronic transmission is in a form capable of being processed by that system and such person is able to retrieve the electronic transmission. Whether a person has so designated an information processing system is determined by the certificate of incorporation, the bylaws or from the context and surrounding circumstances, including the parties' conduct. An electronic transmission is delivered under this section even if no person is aware of its receipt. Receipt of an electronic acknowledgement from an information processing system establishes that an electronic transmission was received but, by itself, does not establish that the content sent corresponds to the content received.

This chapter shall not prohibit 1 or more persons from conducting a transaction in accordance with Chapter 12A of Title 6 so long as the part or parts of the transaction that are governed by this chapter are documented, signed and delivered in accordance with this subsection or otherwise in accordance with this chapter. This subsection shall apply solely for purposes of determining whether an act or transaction has been documented, and the document has been signed and delivered, in accordance with this chapter, the certificate of incorporation and the bylaws.

(b)   Subsection (a) of this section shall not apply to:

(1)   A document filed with or submitted to the Secretary of State, the Register in Chancery, or a court or other judicial or governmental body of this State;

(2)   A document comprising part of the stock ledger;

(3)   A certificate representing a security;

(4)   Any document expressly referenced as a notice (or waiver of notice) by this chapter, the certificate of incorporation or bylaws;

(5)   A consent in lieu of a meeting given by a director, stockholder or incorporator;

(6)   A ballot to vote on actions at a meeting of stockholders; and

(7)   An act or transaction effected pursuant to § 280 of this title or subchapters III, XIII or XVI of this chapter.

The foregoing shall not create any presumption about the lawful means to document a matter addressed by this subsection, or the lawful means to sign or deliver a document addressed by this subsection. A provision of the certificate of incorporation or bylaws shall not limit the application of subsection (a) of this section unless the provision expressly restricts one or more of the means of documenting an act or transaction, or of signing or delivering a document, permitted by subsection (a) of this section.

(c)   In the event that any provision of this chapter is deemed to modify, limit or supersede the Electronic Signatures in Global and National Commerce Act, (15 U.S.C. § 7001 et. seq.), the provisions of this chapter shall control to the fullest extent permitted by § 7002(a)(2) of such act [15 U.S.C. § 7002(a)(2)].

SUBCHAPTER II.   POWERS

§ 121.   General powers.

(a)   In addition to the powers enumerated in § 122 of this title, every corporation, its officers, directors and stockholders shall possess and may exercise all the powers and privileges granted by this chapter or by any other law or by its certificate of incorporation, together with any powers incidental thereto, so far as such powers and privileges are necessary or convenient to the conduct, promotion or attainment of the business or purposes set forth in its certificate of incorporation.

(b)   Every corporation shall be governed by the provisions and be subject to the restrictions and liabilities contained in this chapter.

§ 122.   Specific powers.

Every corporation created under this chapter shall have power to:

(1)   Have perpetual succession by its corporate name, unless a limited period of duration is stated in its certificate of incorporation;

(2)   Sue and be sued in all courts and participate, as a party or otherwise, in any judicial, administrative, arbitrative or other proceeding, in its corporate name;

(3)   Have a corporate seal, which may be altered at pleasure, and use the same by causing it or a facsimile thereof, to be impressed or affixed or in any other manner reproduced;

(4)   Purchase, receive, take by grant, gift, devise, bequest or otherwise, lease, or otherwise acquire, own, hold, improve, employ, use and otherwise deal in and with real or personal property, or any interest therein, wherever situated, and to sell, convey, lease, exchange, transfer or otherwise dispose of, or mortgage or pledge, all or any of its property and assets, or any interest therein, wherever situated;

(5)   Appoint such officers and agents as the business of the corporation requires and to pay or otherwise provide for them suitable compensation;

(6)   Adopt, amend and repeal bylaws;

(7)   Wind up and dissolve itself in the manner provided in this chapter;

(8)   Conduct its business, carry on its operations and have offices and exercise its powers within or without this State;

(9)   Make donations for the public welfare or for charitable, scientific or educational purposes, and in time of war or other national emergency in aid thereof;

(10)   Be an incorporator, promoter or manager of other corporations of any type or kind;

(11)   Participate with others in any corporation, partnership, limited partnership, joint venture or other association of any kind, or in any transaction, undertaking or arrangement which the participating corporation would have power to conduct by itself, whether or not such participation involves sharing or delegation of control with or to others;

(12)   Transact any lawful business which the corporation's board of directors shall find to be in aid of governmental authority;

(13)   Make contracts, including contracts of guaranty and suretyship, incur liabilities, borrow money at such rates of interest as the corporation may determine, issue its notes, bonds and other obligations, and secure any of its obligations by mortgage, pledge or other encumbrance of all or any of its property, franchises and income, and make contracts of guaranty and suretyship which are necessary or convenient to the conduct, promotion or attainment of the business of (a) a corporation all

of the outstanding stock of which is owned, directly or indirectly, by the contracting corporation, or (b) a corporation which owns, directly or indirectly, all of the outstanding stock of the contracting corporation, or (c) a corporation all of the outstanding stock of which is owned, directly or indirectly, by a corporation which owns, directly or indirectly, all of the outstanding stock of the contracting corporation, which contracts of guaranty and suretyship shall be deemed to be necessary or convenient to the conduct, promotion or attainment of the business of the contracting corporation, and make other contracts of guaranty and suretyship which are necessary or convenient to the conduct, promotion or attainment of the business of the contracting corporation;

(14) Lend money for its corporate purposes, invest and reinvest its funds, and take, hold and deal with real and personal property as security for the payment of funds so loaned or invested;

(15) Pay pensions and establish and carry out pension, profit sharing, stock option, stock purchase, stock bonus, retirement, benefit, incentive and compensation plans, trusts and provisions for any or all of its directors, officers and employees, and for any or all of the directors, officers and employees of its subsidiaries;

(16) Provide insurance for its benefit on the life of any of its directors, officers or employees, or on the life of any stockholder for the purpose of acquiring at such stockholder's death shares of its stock owned by such stockholder.

(17) Renounce, in its certificate of incorporation or by action of its board of directors, any interest or expectancy of the corporation in, or in being offered an opportunity to participate in, specified business opportunities or specified classes or categories of business opportunities that are presented to the corporation or 1 or more of its officers, directors or stockholders.

§ 123.   Powers respecting securities of other corporations or entities.

Any corporation organized under the laws of this State may guarantee, purchase, take, receive, subscribe for or otherwise acquire; own, hold, use or otherwise employ; sell, lease, exchange, transfer or otherwise dispose of; mortgage, lend, pledge or otherwise deal in and with, bonds and other obligations of, or shares or other securities or interests in, or issued by, any other domestic or foreign corporation, partnership, association or individual, or by any government or agency or instrumentality thereof. A corporation while owner of any such securities may exercise all the rights, powers and privileges of ownership, including the right to vote.

§ 124.   Effect of lack of corporate capacity or power; ultra vires.

No act of a corporation and no conveyance or transfer of real or personal property to or by a corporation shall be invalid by reason of the fact that the corporation was without capacity or power to do such act or to make or receive such conveyance or transfer, but such lack of capacity or power may be asserted:

(1)   In a proceeding by a stockholder against the corporation to enjoin the doing of any act or acts or the transfer of real or personal property by or to the corporation. If the unauthorized acts or transfer sought to be enjoined are being, or are to be, performed or made pursuant to any contract to which the corporation is a party, the court may, if all of the parties to the contract are parties to the proceeding and if it deems the same to be equitable, set aside and enjoin the performance of such contract, and in so doing may allow to the corporation or to the other parties to the contract, as the case may be, such compensation as may be equitable for the loss or damage sustained by any of them which may result from the action of the court in setting aside and enjoining the performance of such contract, but anticipated profits to be derived from the performance of the contract shall not be awarded by the court as a loss or damage sustained;

(2)   In a proceeding by the corporation, whether acting directly or through a receiver, trustee or other legal representative, or through stockholders in a representative suit, against an incumbent or former officer or director of the corporation, for loss or damage due to such incumbent or former officer's or director's unauthorized act;

(3)   In a proceeding by the Attorney General to dissolve the corporation, or to enjoin the corporation from the transaction of unauthorized business.

§ 125.   Conferring academic or honorary degrees.

No corporation organized after April 18, 1945, shall have power to confer academic or honorary degrees unless the certificate of incorporation or an amendment thereof shall so provide and unless the certificate of incorporation or an amendment thereof prior to its being filed in the office of the Secretary of State shall have endorsed thereon the approval of the Department of Education of this State. No corporation organized before April 18, 1945, any provision in its certificate of incorporation to the contrary notwithstanding, shall possess the power aforesaid without first filing in the office of the Secretary of State a certificate of amendment so providing, the filing of which certificate of amendment in the office of the Secretary of State shall be subject to prior approval of the Department of Education, evidenced as hereinabove provided. Approval shall be granted only when it appears to the reasonable satisfaction of the Department of Education that the corporation is engaged in conducting a bona fide institution of higher learning, giving instructions in arts and letters, science or the professions, or that the corporation proposes, in good faith, to engage in that field and has or will have the resources, including personnel, requisite for the conduct of an institution of higher learning. Upon dissolution, all such corporations shall comply with § 8530 of Title 14. Notwithstanding any provision herein to the contrary, no corporation shall have the power to conduct a private business or trade school unless the certificate of incorporation or an amendment thereof, prior to its being filed in the office of the Secretary of State, shall have endorsed thereon the approval of the Department of Education pursuant to Chapter 85 of Title 14.

Notwithstanding the foregoing provisions, any corporation conducting a law school, which has its principal place of operation in Delaware, and which intends to meet the standards of approval of the American Bar Association, may, after it has been in actual operation for not less than 1 year, retain at its own expense a dean or dean emeritus of a law school fully approved by the American Bar Association to make an on-site inspection and report concerning the progress of the corporation toward meeting the standards for approval by the American Bar Association. Such dean or dean emeritus shall be chosen by the Attorney General from a panel of 3 deans whose names are presented to the Attorney General as being willing to serve. One such dean on this panel shall be nominated by the trustees of said law school corporation; another dean shall be nominated by a committee of the Student Bar Association of said law school; and the other dean shall be nominated by a committee of lawyers who are parents of students attending such law school. If any of the above-named groups cannot find a dean, it may substitute 2 full professors of accredited law schools for the dean it is entitled to nominate, and in such a case if the Attorney General chooses 1 of such professors, such professor shall serve the function of a dean as herein prescribed. If the dean so retained shall report in writing that, in such dean's professional judgment, the corporation is attempting, in good faith, to comply with the standards for approval of the American Bar Association and is making reasonable progress toward meeting such standards, the corporation may file a copy of the report with the Secretary of Education and with the Attorney General. Any corporation which complies with these provisions by filing such report shall be deemed to have temporary approval from the State and shall be entitled to amend its certificate of incorporation to authorize the granting of standard academic law degrees. Thereafter, until the law school operated by the corporation is approved by the American Bar Association, the corporation shall file once during each academic year a new report, in the same manner as the first report. If, at any time, the corporation fails to file such a report, or if the dean retained to render such report states that, in such dean's opinion, the corporation is not continuing to make reasonable progress toward accreditation, the Attorney General, at the request of the Secretary of Education, may file a complaint in the Court of Chancery to suspend said temporary approval and degree-granting power until a further report is filed by a dean or dean emeritus of an accredited law school that the school has resumed its progress towards meeting the standards for approval. Upon approval of the law school by the American Bar Association, temporary approval shall become final, and shall no longer be subject to suspension or vacation under this section.

§ 126.   Banking power denied.

(a)   No corporation organized under this chapter shall possess the power of issuing bills, notes, or other evidences of debt for circulation as money, or the power of carrying on the business of receiving deposits of money.

(b)   Corporations organized under this chapter to buy, sell and otherwise deal in notes, open accounts and other similar evidences of debt, or to loan money and to take notes, open accounts and other similar evidences of debt as collateral security therefor, shall not be deemed to be engaging in the business of banking.

§ 127.   Private foundation; powers and duties.

A corporation of this State which is a private foundation under the United States internal revenue laws and whose certificate of incorporation does not expressly provide that this section shall not apply to it is required to act or to refrain from acting so as not to subject itself to the taxes imposed by 26 U.S.C. § 4941 (relating to taxes on self-dealing), § 4942 (relating to taxes on failure to distribute income), § 4943 (relating to taxes on excess business holdings), § 4944 (relating to taxes on investments which jeopardize charitable purpose), or § 4945 (relating to taxable expenditures), or corresponding provisions of any subsequent United States internal revenue law.

SUBCHAPTER III.   REGISTERED OFFICE AND REGISTERED AGENT

§ 131.   Registered office in State; principal office or place of business in State.

(a)   Every corporation shall have and maintain in this State a registered office which may, but need not be, the same as its place of business.

(b)   Whenever the term "corporation's principal office or place of business in this State" or "principal office or place of business of the corporation in this State," or other term of like import, is or has been used in a corporation's certificate of incorporation, or in any other document, or in any statute, it shall be deemed to mean and refer to, unless the context indicates otherwise, the corporation's registered office required by this section; and it shall not be necessary for any corporation to amend its certificate of incorporation or any other document to comply with this section.

(c)   As contained in any certificate of incorporation or other document filed with the Secretary of State under this chapter, the address of a registered office shall include the street, number, city, county and postal code.

§ 132.   Registered agent in State; resident agent.

(a)   Every corporation shall have and maintain in this State a registered agent, which agent may be any of:

(1)   The corporation itself;

(2)   An individual resident in this State;

(3)   A domestic corporation (other than the corporation itself), a domestic partnership (whether general (including a limited liability partnership) or limited (including a limited liability limited partnership)), a domestic limited liability company or a domestic statutory trust; or

(4)   A foreign corporation, a foreign partnership (whether general (including a limited liability partnership) or limited (including a limited liability limited partnership)), a foreign limited liability company or a foreign statutory trust.

(b)   Every registered agent for a domestic corporation or a foreign corporation shall:

(1)   If an entity, maintain a business office in this State which is generally open, or if an individual, be generally present at a designated location in this State, at sufficiently frequent times to accept service of process and otherwise perform the functions of a registered agent;

(2)   If a foreign entity, be authorized to transact business in this State;

(3)   Accept service of process and other communications directed to the corporations for which it serves as registered agent and forward same to the corporation to which the service or communication is directed;

(4)   Forward to the corporations for which it serves as registered agent the annual report required by § 502 of this title or an electronic notification of same in a form satisfactory to the Secretary of State ("Secretary"); and

(5)   Satisfy and adhere to regulations established by the Secretary regarding the verification of both the identity of the entity's contacts and individuals for which the registered agent maintains a record for the reduction of risk of unlawful business purposes.

(c)   Any registered agent who at any time serves as registered agent for more than 50 entities (a "commercial registered agent"), whether domestic or foreign, shall satisfy and comply with the following qualifications.

(1)   A natural person serving as a commercial registered agent shall:

a.   Maintain a principal residence or a principal place of business in this State;

b.   Maintain a Delaware business license;

c.   Be generally present at a designated location within this State during normal business hours to accept service of process and otherwise perform the functions of a registered agent as specified in subsection (b) of this section;

d.   Provide the Secretary upon request with such information identifying and enabling communication with such commercial registered agent as the Secretary shall require; and

e.   Satisfy and adhere to regulations established by the Secretary regarding the verification of both the identity of the entity's contacts and individuals for which the natural person maintains a record for the reduction of risk of unlawful business purposes.

(2)   A domestic or foreign corporation, a domestic or foreign partnership (whether general (including a limited liability partnership) or limited (including a limited liability limited partnership)), a domestic or foreign limited liability company, or a domestic or foreign statutory trust serving as a commercial registered agent shall:

a.   Have a business office within this State which is generally open during normal business hours to accept service of process and otherwise perform the functions of a registered agent as specified in subsection (b) of this section;

b.   Maintain a Delaware business license;

c.   Have generally present at such office during normal business hours an officer, director or managing agent who is a natural person;

d.   Provide the Secretary upon request with such information identifying and enabling communication with such commercial registered agent as the Secretary shall require; and

e.   Satisfy and adhere to regulations established by the Secretary regarding the verification of both the identity of the entity's contacts and individuals for which it maintains a record for the reduction of risk of unlawful business purposes.

(3)   For purposes of this subsection and paragraph (f)(2)a. of this section, a commercial registered agent shall also include any registered agent which has an officer, director or managing agent in common with any other registered agent or agents if such registered agents at any time during such common service as officer, director or managing agent collectively served as registered agents for more than 50 entities, whether domestic or foreign.

(d)   Every corporation formed under the laws of this State or qualified to do business in this State shall provide to its registered agent and update from time to time as necessary the name, business address and business telephone number of a natural person who is an officer, director, employee, or designated agent of the corporation, who is then authorized to receive communications from the registered agent. Such person shall be deemed the communications contact for the corporation. Every registered agent shall retain (in paper or electronic form) the above information concerning the current communications contact for each corporation for which he, she or it serves as a registered agent. If the corporation fails to provide the registered agent with a current communications contact, the registered agent may resign as the registered agent for such corporation pursuant to § 136 of this title.

(e)   The Secretary is fully authorized to issue such regulations, as may be necessary or appropriate to carry out the enforcement of subsections (b), (c) and (d) of this section, and to take actions reasonable and necessary to assure registered agents' compliance with subsections (b), (c) and (d) of this section. Such actions may include refusal to file documents submitted by a registered agent, including the refusal to file any documents regarding an entity's formation.

(f) Upon application of the Secretary, the Court of Chancery may enjoin any person or entity from serving as a registered agent or as an officer, director or managing agent of a registered agent.

(1) Upon the filing of a complaint by the Secretary pursuant to this section, the Court may make such orders respecting such proceeding as it deems appropriate, and may enter such orders granting interim or final relief as it deems proper under the circumstances.

(2) Any one or more of the following grounds shall be a sufficient basis to grant an injunction pursuant to this section:

a. With respect to any registered agent who at any time within 1 year immediately prior to the filing of the Secretary's complaint is a commercial registered agent, failure after notice and warning to comply with the qualifications set forth in subsection (b) of this section and/or the requirements of subsection (c) or (d) of this section above;

b. The person serving as a registered agent, or any person who is an officer, director or managing agent of an entity registered agent, has been convicted of a felony or any crime which includes an element of dishonesty or fraud or involves moral turpitude;

c. The registered agent has engaged in conduct in connection with acting as a registered agent that is intended to or likely to deceive or defraud the public.

(3) With respect to any order the court enters pursuant to this section with respect to an entity that has acted as a registered agent, the court may also direct such order to any person who has served as an officer, director, or managing agent of such registered agent. Any person who, on or after January 1, 2007, serves as an officer, director, or managing agent of an entity acting as a registered agent in this State shall be deemed thereby to have consented to the appointment of such registered agent as agent upon whom service of process may be made in any action brought pursuant to this section, and service as an officer, director, or managing agent of an entity acting as a registered agent in this State shall be a signification of the consent of such person that any process when so served shall be of the same legal force and validity as if served upon such person within this State, and such appointment of the registered agent shall be irrevocable.

(4) Upon the entry of an order by the Court enjoining any person or entity from acting as a registered agent, the Secretary shall mail or deliver notice of such order to each affected corporation at the address of its principal place of business as specified in its most recent franchise tax report or other record of the Secretary. If such corporation is a domestic corporation and fails to obtain and designate a new registered agent within 30 days after such notice is given, the Secretary shall declare the charter of such corporation forfeited. If such corporation is a foreign corporation, and fails to obtain and designate a new registered agent within 30 days after such notice is given, the Secretary shall forfeit its qualification to do business in this State. If the court enjoins a person or entity from acting as a registered agent as provided in this section and no new registered agent shall have been obtained and designated in the time and manner aforesaid, service of legal process against the corporation for which the registered agent had been acting shall thereafter be upon the Secretary in accordance with § 321 of this title. The Court of Chancery may, upon application of the Secretary on notice to the former registered agent, enter such orders as it deems appropriate to give the Secretary access to information in the former registered agent's possession in order to facilitate communication with the corporations the former registered agent served.

(g) The Secretary is authorized to make a list of registered agents available to the public, and to establish such qualifications and issue such rules and regulations with respect to such listing as the Secretary deems necessary or appropriate.

(h) Whenever the term "resident agent" or "resident agent in charge of a corporation's principal office or place of business in this State," or other term of like import which refers to a corporation's agent required by statute to be located in this State, is or has been used in a corporation's certificate of incorporation, or in any other document, or in any statute, it shall be deemed to mean and refer to, unless the context indicates otherwise, the corporation's registered agent required by this section; and it shall not be necessary for any corporation to amend its certificate of incorporation or any other document to comply with this section.

§ 133. Change of location of registered office; change of registered agent.

Any corporation may, by resolution of its board of directors, change the location of its registered office in this State to any other place in this State. By like resolution, the registered agent of a corporation may be changed to any other person or corporation including itself. In either such case, the resolution shall be as detailed in its statement as is required by § 102(a)(2) of this title. Upon the adoption of such a resolution, a certificate certifying the change shall be executed, acknowledged, and filed in accordance with § 103 of this title.

§ 134. Change of address or name of registered agent.

(a) A registered agent may change the address of the registered office of the corporation or corporations for which the agent is a registered agent to another address in this State by filing with the Secretary of State a certificate, executed and acknowledged by such registered agent, setting forth the address at which such registered agent has maintained the registered office for each of the corporations for which it is a registered agent, and further certifying to the new address to which each such registered office will be changed on a given day, and at which new address such registered agent will thereafter maintain the registered office for each of the corporations for which it is a registered agent. Thereafter, or until further change of address, as authorized by law, the registered office in this State of each of the corporations for which the agent is a registered agent shall be located at the new address of the registered agent thereof as given in the certificate.

(b) In the event of a change of name of any person or corporation acting as registered agent in this State, such registered agent shall file with the Secretary of State a certificate, executed and acknowledged by such registered agent, setting forth the new name of such registered agent, the name of such registered agent before it was changed, and the address at which such registered agent has maintained the registered office for each of the corporations for which it acts as a registered agent. A change of name of any person or corporation acting as a registered agent as a result of a merger or consolidation of the registered agent, with or into another person or corporation which succeeds to its assets by operation of law, shall be deemed a change of name for purposes of this section.

§ 135. Resignation of registered agent coupled with appointment of successor.

The registered agent of 1 or more corporations may resign and appoint a successor registered agent by filing a certificate with the Secretary of State, stating the name and address of the successor agent, in accordance with § 102(a)(2) of this title. There shall be attached to such certificate a statement of each affected corporation ratifying and approving such change of registered agent. Each such statement shall be executed and acknowledged in accordance with § 103 of this title. Upon such filing, the successor registered agent shall become the registered agent of such corporations as have ratified and approved such substitution and the successor registered agent's address, as stated in such certificate, shall become the address of each such corporation's registered office in this State. The Secretary of State shall then issue a certificate that the successor registered agent has become the registered agent of the corporations so ratifying and approving such change and setting out the names of such corporations.

§ 136. Resignation of registered agent not coupled with appointment of successor.

(a) The registered agent of a corporation, including a corporation which has become void pursuant to § 510 of this title, may resign without appointing a successor by filing a certificate of resignation with the Secretary of State, but such resignation shall not become effective until 30 days after the certificate is filed. The certificate shall be executed and acknowledged by the registered agent, shall contain a statement that written notice of resignation was given to the corporation at least 30 days prior to the filing of the certificate by mailing or delivering such notice to the corporation at its address last known to the registered agent and shall set forth the date of such notice. The certificate shall include such information last provided to the registered agent pursuant to § 132(d) of this title for a communications contact for the affected corporation.

Such information regarding the communications contact shall not be deemed public. A certificate filed pursuant to this section must be on the form prescribed by the Secretary of State.

(b)   After receipt of the notice of the resignation of its registered agent, provided for in subsection (a) of this section, the corporation for which such registered agent was acting shall obtain and designate a new registered agent to take the place of the registered agent so resigning in the same manner as provided in § 133 of this title for change of registered agent. If such corporation, being a corporation of this State, fails to obtain and designate a new registered agent as aforesaid prior to the expiration of the period of 30 days after the filing by the registered agent of the certificate of resignation, the Secretary of State shall declare the charter of such corporation forfeited. If such corporation, being a foreign corporation, fails to obtain and designate a new registered agent as aforesaid prior to the expiration of the period of 30 days after the filing by the registered agent of the certificate of resignation, the Secretary of State shall forfeit its authority to do business in this State.

(c)   After the resignation of the registered agent shall have become effective as provided in this section and if no new registered agent shall have been obtained and designated in the time and manner aforesaid, service of legal process against the corporation for which the resigned registered agent had been acting shall thereafter be upon the Secretary of State in accordance with § 321 of this title.

SUBCHAPTER IV.   DIRECTORS AND OFFICERS

§ 141.   Board of directors; powers; number, qualifications, terms and quorum; committees; classes of directors; nonstock corporations; reliance upon books; action without meeting; removal.

(a)   The business and affairs of every corporation organized under this chapter shall be managed by or under the direction of a board of directors, except as may be otherwise provided in this chapter or in its certificate of incorporation. If any such provision is made in the certificate of incorporation, the powers and duties conferred or imposed upon the board of directors by this chapter shall be exercised or performed to such extent and by such person or persons as shall be provided in the certificate of incorporation.

(b)   The board of directors of a corporation shall consist of 1 or more members, each of whom shall be a natural person. The number of directors shall be fixed by, or in the manner provided in, the bylaws, unless the certificate of incorporation fixes the number of directors, in which case a change in the number of directors shall be made only by amendment of the certificate. Directors need not be stockholders unless so required by the certificate of incorporation or the bylaws. The certificate of incorporation or bylaws may prescribe other qualifications for directors. Each director shall hold office until such director's successor is elected and qualified or until such director's earlier resignation or removal. Any director may resign at any time upon notice given in writing or by electronic transmission to the corporation. A resignation is effective when the resignation is delivered unless the resignation specifies a later effective date or an effective date determined upon the happening of an event or events. A resignation which is conditioned upon the director failing to receive a specified vote for reelection as a director may provide that it is irrevocable. A majority of the total number of directors shall constitute a quorum for the transaction of business unless the certificate of incorporation or the bylaws require a greater number. Unless the certificate of incorporation provides otherwise, the bylaws may provide that a number less than a majority shall constitute a quorum which in no case shall be less than ⅓ of the total number of directors. The vote of the majority of the directors present at a meeting at which a quorum is present shall be the act of the board of directors unless the certificate of incorporation or the bylaws shall require a vote of a greater number.

(c)(1)All corporations incorporated prior to July 1, 1996, shall be governed by this paragraph (c)(1) of this section, provided that any such corporation may by a resolution adopted by a majority of the whole board elect to be governed by paragraph (c)(2) of this section, in which case this paragraph (c)(1) of this section shall not apply to such corporation. All corporations incorporated on or after July 1, 1996, shall be governed by paragraph (c)(2) of this section. The board of directors may, by resolution passed by a majority of the whole board, designate 1 or more committees, each committee to consist of 1 or more of the directors of the corporation. The board may designate 1 or more directors as alternate members of any committee, who may replace any absent or disqualified member at any meeting of the committee. The bylaws may provide that in the absence or disqualification of a member of a committee, the member or members present at any meeting and not disqualified from voting, whether or not the member or members present constitute a quorum, may unanimously appoint another member of the board of directors to act at the meeting in the place of any such absent or disqualified member. Any such committee, to the extent provided in the resolution of the board of directors, or in the bylaws of the corporation, shall have and may exercise all the powers and authority of the board of directors in the management of the business and affairs of the corporation, and may authorize the seal of the corporation to be affixed to all papers which may require it; but no such committee shall have the power or authority in reference to amending the certificate of incorporation (except that a committee may, to the extent authorized in the resolution or resolutions providing for the issuance of shares of stock adopted by the board of directors as provided in § 151(a) of this title, fix the designations and any of the preferences or rights of such shares relating to dividends, redemption, dissolution, any distribution of assets of the corporation or the conversion into, or the exchange of such shares for, shares of any other class or classes or any other series of the same or any other class or classes of stock of the corporation or fix the number of shares of any series of stock or authorize the increase or decrease of the shares of any series), adopting an agreement of merger or consolidation under § 251, § 252, § 254, § 255, § 256, § 257, § 258, § 263 or § 264 of this title, recommending to the stockholders the sale, lease or exchange of all or substantially all of the corporation's property and assets, recommending to the stockholders a dissolution of the corporation or a revocation of a dissolution, or amending the bylaws of the corporation; and, unless the resolution, bylaws or certificate of incorporation expressly so provides, no such committee shall have the power or authority to declare a dividend, to authorize the issuance of stock or to adopt a certificate of ownership and merger pursuant to § 253 of this title.

(2)   The board of directors may designate 1 or more committees, each committee to consist of 1 or more of the directors of the corporation. The board may designate 1 or more directors as alternate members of any committee, who may replace any absent or disqualified member at any meeting of the committee. The bylaws may provide that in the absence or disqualification of a member of a committee, the member or members present at any meeting and not disqualified from voting, whether or not such member or members constitute a quorum, may unanimously appoint another member of the board of directors to act at the meeting in the place of any such absent or disqualified member. Any such committee, to the extent provided in the resolution of the board of directors, or in the bylaws of the corporation, shall have and may exercise all the powers and authority of the board of directors in the management of the business and affairs of the corporation, and may authorize the seal of the corporation to be affixed to all papers which may require it; but no such committee shall have the power or authority in reference to the following matter: (i) approving or adopting, or recommending to the stockholders, any action or matter (other than the election or removal of directors) expressly required by this chapter to be submitted to stockholders for approval or (ii) adopting, amending or repealing any bylaw of the corporation.

(3)   Unless otherwise provided in the certificate of incorporation, the bylaws or the resolution of the board of directors designating the committee, a committee may create 1 or more subcommittees, each subcommittee to consist of 1 or more members of the committee, and delegate to a subcommittee any or all of the powers and authority of the committee. Except for references to committees and members of committees in subsection (c) of this section, every reference in this chapter to a committee of the board of directors or a member of a committee shall be deemed to include a reference to a subcommittee or member of a subcommittee.

(4)   A majority of the directors then serving on a committee of the board of directors or on a subcommittee of a committee shall constitute a quorum for the transaction of business by the committee or subcommittee, unless the certificate of incorporation, the bylaws, a resolution of the board of directors or a resolution of a committee that created the subcommittee requires a greater or lesser number, provided that in no case shall a quorum be less than ⅓ of the directors then serving on the committee or subcommittee. The vote of the majority of the members of a committee or subcommittee present at a meeting at which a quorum is present shall be the act of the committee or subcommittee, unless the certificate of incorporation, the bylaws, a resolution of the board of directors or a resolution of a committee that created the subcommittee requires a greater number.

(d)   The directors of any corporation organized under this chapter may, by the certificate of incorporation or by an initial bylaw, or by a bylaw adopted by a vote of the stockholders, be divided into 1, 2 or 3 classes; the term of office of those of the first class to expire at the first annual meeting held after such classification becomes effective; of the second class 1 year thereafter; of the third class 2 years thereafter; and at each annual election held after such classification becomes effective, directors shall be chosen for a full term, as the case may be, to succeed those whose terms expire. The certificate of incorporation or bylaw provision dividing the directors into classes may authorize the board of directors to assign members of the board already in office to such classes at the time such classification becomes effective. The certificate of incorporation may confer upon holders of any class or series of stock the right to elect 1 or more directors who shall serve for such term, and have such voting powers as shall be stated in the certificate of incorporation. The terms of office and voting powers of the directors elected separately by the holders of any class or series of stock may be greater than or less than those of any other director or class of directors. In addition, the certificate of incorporation may confer upon 1 or more directors, whether or not elected separately by the holders of any class or series of stock, voting powers greater than or less than those of other directors. Any such provision conferring greater or lesser voting power shall apply to voting in any committee, unless otherwise provided in the certificate of incorporation or bylaws. If the certificate of incorporation provides that 1 or more directors shall have more or less than 1 vote per director on any matter, every reference in this chapter to a majority or other proportion of the directors shall refer to a majority or other proportion of the votes of the directors.

(e) A member of the board of directors, or a member of any committee designated by the board of directors, shall, in the performance of such member's duties, be fully protected in relying in good faith upon the records of the corporation and upon such information, opinions, reports or statements presented to the corporation by any of the corporation's officers or employees, or committees of the board of directors, or by any other person as to matters the member reasonably believes are within such other person's professional or expert competence and who has been selected with reasonable care by or on behalf of the corporation.

(f) Unless otherwise restricted by the certificate of incorporation or bylaws, any action required or permitted to be taken at any meeting of the board of directors or of any committee thereof may be taken without a meeting if all members of the board or committee, as the case may be, consent thereto in writing, or by electronic transmission. Any person (whether or not then a director) may provide, whether through instruction to an agent or otherwise, that a consent to action will be effective at a future time (including a time determined upon the happening of an event), no later than 60 days after such instruction is given or such provision is made and such consent shall be deemed to have been given for purposes of this subsection at such effective time so long as such person is then a director and did not revoke the consent prior to such time. Any such consent shall be revocable prior to its becoming effective. After an action is taken, the consent or consents relating thereto shall be filed with the minutes of the proceedings of the board of directors, or the committee thereof, in the same paper or electronic form as the minutes are maintained.

(g) Unless otherwise restricted by the certificate of incorporation or bylaws, the board of directors of any corporation organized under this chapter may hold its meetings, and have an office or offices, outside of this State.

(h) Unless otherwise restricted by the certificate of incorporation or bylaws, the board of directors shall have the authority to fix the compensation of directors.

(i) Unless otherwise restricted by the certificate of incorporation or bylaws, members of the board of directors of any corporation, or any committee designated by the board, may participate in a meeting of such board, or committee by means of conference telephone or other communications equipment by means of which all persons participating in the meeting can hear each other, and participation in a meeting pursuant to this subsection shall constitute presence in person at the meeting.

(j) The certificate of incorporation of any nonstock corporation may provide that less than ⅓ of the members of the governing body may constitute a quorum thereof and may otherwise provide that the business and affairs of the corporation shall be managed in a manner different from that provided in this section. Except as may be otherwise provided by the certificate of incorporation, this section shall apply to such a corporation, and when so applied, all references to the board of directors, to members thereof, and to stockholders shall be deemed to refer to the governing body of the corporation, the members thereof and the members of the corporation, respectively; and all references to stock, capital stock, or shares thereof shall be deemed to refer to memberships of a nonprofit nonstock corporation and to membership interests of any other nonstock corporation.

(k) Any director or the entire board of directors may be removed, with or without cause, by the holders of a majority of the shares then entitled to vote at an election of directors, except as follows:

(1)   Unless the certificate of incorporation otherwise provides, in the case of a corporation whose board is classified as provided in subsection (d) of this section, stockholders may effect such removal only for cause; or

(2)   In the case of a corporation having cumulative voting, if less than the entire board is to be removed, no director may be removed without cause if the votes cast against such director's removal would be sufficient to elect such director if then cumulatively voted at an election of the entire board of directors, or, if there be classes of directors, at an election of the class of directors of which such director is a part.

Whenever the holders of any class or series are entitled to elect 1 or more directors by the certificate of incorporation, this subsection shall apply, in respect to the removal without cause of a director or directors so elected, to the vote of the holders of the outstanding shares of that class or series and not to the vote of the outstanding shares as a whole.

§ 142.   Officers; titles, duties, selection, term; failure to elect; vacancies.

(a)   Every corporation organized under this chapter shall have such officers with such titles and duties as shall be stated in the bylaws or in a resolution of the board of directors which is not inconsistent with the bylaws and as may be necessary to enable it to sign instruments and stock certificates which comply with §§ 103(a)(2) and 158 of this title. One of the officers shall have the duty to record the proceedings of the meetings of the stockholders and directors in a book to be kept for that purpose. Any number of offices may be held by the same person unless the certificate of incorporation or bylaws otherwise provide.

(b)   Officers shall be chosen in such manner and shall hold their offices for such terms as are prescribed by the bylaws or determined by the board of directors or other governing body. Each officer shall hold office until such officer's successor is elected and qualified or until such officer's earlier resignation or removal. Any officer may resign at any time upon written notice to the corporation.

(c)   The corporation may secure the fidelity of any or all of its officers or agents by bond or otherwise.

(d)   A failure to elect officers shall not dissolve or otherwise affect the corporation.

(e)   Any vacancy occurring in any office of the corporation by death, resignation, removal or otherwise, shall be filled as the bylaws provide. In the absence of such provision, the vacancy shall be filled by the board of directors or other governing body.

§ 143.   Loans to employees and officers; guaranty of obligations of employees and officers.

Any corporation may lend money to, or guarantee any obligation of, or otherwise assist any officer or other employee of the corporation or of its subsidiary, including any officer or employee who is a director of the corporation or its subsidiary, whenever, in the judgment of the directors, such loan, guaranty or assistance may reasonably be expected to benefit the corporation. The loan, guaranty or other assistance may be with or without interest, and may be unsecured, or secured in such manner as the board of directors shall approve, including, without limitation, a pledge of shares of stock of the corporation. Nothing in this section contained shall be deemed to deny, limit or restrict the powers of guaranty or warranty of any corporation at common law or under any statute.

§ 144.   Interested directors; quorum.

(a)   No contract or transaction between a corporation and 1 or more of its directors or officers, or between a corporation and any other corporation, partnership, association, or other organization in which 1 or more of its directors or officers, are directors or officers, or have a financial interest, shall be void or voidable solely for this reason, or solely because the director or officer is present at or participates in the meeting of the board or committee which authorizes the contract or transaction, or solely because any such director's or officer's votes are counted for such purpose, if:

(1)   The material facts as to the director's or officer's relationship or interest and as to the contract or transaction are disclosed or are known to the board of directors or the committee, and the board or committee in good faith authorizes the contract or transaction by the affirmative votes of a

majority of the disinterested directors, even though the disinterested directors be less than a quorum; or

(2)   The material facts as to the director's or officer's relationship or interest and as to the contract or transaction are disclosed or are known to the stockholders entitled to vote thereon, and the contract or transaction is specifically approved in good faith by vote of the stockholders; or

(3)   The contract or transaction is fair as to the corporation as of the time it is authorized, approved or ratified, by the board of directors, a committee or the stockholders.

(b)   Common or interested directors may be counted in determining the presence of a quorum at a meeting of the board of directors or of a committee which authorizes the contract or transaction.

§ 145.   Indemnification of officers, directors, employees and agents; insurance.

(a)   A corporation shall have power to indemnify any person who was or is a party or is threatened to be made a party to any threatened, pending or completed action, suit or proceeding, whether civil, criminal, administrative or investigative (other than an action by or in the right of the corporation) by reason of the fact that the person is or was a director, officer, employee or agent of the corporation, or is or was serving at the request of the corporation as a director, officer, employee or agent of another corporation, partnership, joint venture, trust or other enterprise, against expenses (including attorneys' fees), judgments, fines and amounts paid in settlement actually and reasonably incurred by the person in connection with such action, suit or proceeding if the person acted in good faith and in a manner the person reasonably believed to be in or not opposed to the best interests of the corporation, and, with respect to any criminal action or proceeding, had no reasonable cause to believe the person's conduct was unlawful. The termination of any action, suit or proceeding by judgment, order, settlement, conviction, or upon a plea of nolo contendere or its equivalent, shall not, of itself, create a presumption that the person did not act in good faith and in a manner which the person reasonably believed to be in or not opposed to the best interests of the corporation, and, with respect to any criminal action or proceeding, had reasonable cause to believe that the person's conduct was unlawful.

(b)   A corporation shall have power to indemnify any person who was or is a party or is threatened to be made a party to any threatened, pending or completed action or suit by or in the right of the corporation to procure a judgment in its favor by reason of the fact that the person is or was a director, officer, employee or agent of the corporation, or is or was serving at the request of the corporation as a director, officer, employee or agent of another corporation, partnership, joint venture, trust or other enterprise against expenses (including attorneys' fees) actually and reasonably incurred by the person in connection with the defense or settlement of such action or suit if the person acted in good faith and in a manner the person reasonably believed to be in or not opposed to the best interests of the corporation and except that no indemnification shall be made in respect of any claim, issue or matter as to which such person shall have been adjudged to be liable to the corporation unless and only to the extent that the Court of Chancery or the court in which such action or suit was brought shall determine upon application that, despite the adjudication of liability but in view of all the circumstances of the case, such person is fairly and reasonably entitled to indemnity for such expenses which the Court of Chancery or such other court shall deem proper.

(c)   To the extent that a present or former director or officer of a corporation has been successful on the merits or otherwise in defense of any action, suit or proceeding referred to in subsections (a) and (b) of this section, or in defense of any claim, issue or matter therein, such person shall be indemnified against expenses (including attorneys' fees) actually and reasonably incurred by such person in connection therewith.

(d)   Any indemnification under subsections (a) and (b) of this section (unless ordered by a court) shall be made by the corporation only as authorized in the specific case upon a determination that indemnification of the present or former director, officer, employee or agent is proper in the circumstances because the person has met the applicable standard of conduct set forth in subsections (a) and (b) of this section. Such determination shall be made, with respect to a person who is a director or officer of the corporation at the time of such determination:

(1)   By a majority vote of the directors who are not parties to such action, suit or proceeding, even though less than a quorum; or

(2)   By a committee of such directors designated by majority vote of such directors, even though less than a quorum; or

(3)   If there are no such directors, or if such directors so direct, by independent legal counsel in a written opinion; or

(4)   By the stockholders.

(e)   Expenses (including attorneys' fees) incurred by an officer or director of the corporation in defending any civil, criminal, administrative or investigative action, suit or proceeding may be paid by the corporation in advance of the final disposition of such action, suit or proceeding upon receipt of an undertaking by or on behalf of such director or officer to repay such amount if it shall ultimately be determined that such person is not entitled to be indemnified by the corporation as authorized in this section. Such expenses (including attorneys' fees) incurred by former directors and officers or other employees and agents of the corporation or by persons serving at the request of the corporation as directors, officers, employees or agents of another corporation, partnership, joint venture, trust or other enterprise may be so paid upon such terms and conditions, if any, as the corporation deems appropriate.

(f)   The indemnification and advancement of expenses provided by, or granted pursuant to, the other subsections of this section shall not be deemed exclusive of any other rights to which those seeking indemnification or advancement of expenses may be entitled under any bylaw, agreement, vote of stockholders or disinterested directors or otherwise, both as to action in such person's official capacity and as to action in another capacity while holding such office. A right to indemnification or to advancement of expenses arising under a provision of the certificate of incorporation or a bylaw shall not be eliminated or impaired by an amendment to the certificate of incorporation or the bylaws after the occurrence of the act or omission that is the subject of the civil, criminal, administrative or investigative action, suit or proceeding for which indemnification or advancement of expenses is sought, unless the provision in effect at the time of such act or omission explicitly authorizes such elimination or impairment after such action or omission has occurred.

(g)   A corporation shall have power to purchase and maintain insurance on behalf of any person who is or was a director, officer, employee or agent of the corporation, or is or was serving at the request of the corporation as a director, officer, employee or agent of another corporation, partnership, joint venture, trust or other enterprise against any liability asserted against such person and incurred by such person in any such capacity, or arising out of such person's status as such, whether or not the corporation would have the power to indemnify such person against such liability under this section.

(h)   For purposes of this section, references to "the corporation" shall include, in addition to the resulting corporation, any constituent corporation (including any constituent of a constituent) absorbed in a consolidation or merger which, if its separate existence had continued, would have had power and authority to indemnify its directors, officers, and employees or agents, so that any person who is or was a director, officer, employee or agent of such constituent corporation, or is or was serving at the request of such constituent corporation as a director, officer, employee or agent of another corporation, partnership, joint venture, trust or other enterprise, shall stand in the same position under this section with respect to the resulting or surviving corporation as such person would have with respect to such constituent corporation if its separate existence had continued.

(i)   For purposes of this section, references to "other enterprises" shall include employee benefit plans; references to "fines" shall include any excise taxes assessed on a person with respect to any employee benefit plan; and references to "serving at the request of the corporation" shall include any service as a director, officer, employee or agent of the corporation which imposes duties on, or involves services by, such director, officer, employee or agent with respect to an employee benefit plan, its participants or beneficiaries; and a person who acted in good faith and in a manner such person reasonably believed to be in the interest of the participants and beneficiaries of an employee benefit plan shall be deemed to have acted in a manner "not opposed to the best interests of the corporation" as referred to in this section.

(j)   The indemnification and advancement of expenses provided by, or granted pursuant to, this section shall, unless otherwise provided when authorized or ratified, continue as to a person who has ceased to be a director, officer, employee or agent and shall inure to the benefit of the heirs, executors and administrators of such a person.

(k)   The Court of Chancery is hereby vested with exclusive jurisdiction to hear and determine all actions for advancement of expenses or indemnification brought under this section or under any bylaw, agreement, vote of stockholders or disinterested directors, or otherwise. The Court of Chancery may summarily determine a corporation's obligation to advance expenses (including attorneys' fees).

§ 146.   Submission of matters for stockholder vote.

A corporation may agree to submit a matter to a vote of its stockholders whether or not the board of directors determines at any time subsequent to approving such matter that such matter is no longer advisable and recommends that the stockholders reject or vote against the matter.

SUBCHAPTER V.   STOCK AND DIVIDENDS

§ 151.   Classes and series of stock; redemption; rights.

(a)   Every corporation may issue 1 or more classes of stock or 1 or more series of stock within any class thereof, any or all of which classes may be of stock with par value or stock without par value and which classes or series may have such voting powers, full or limited, or no voting powers, and such designations, preferences and relative, participating, optional or other special rights, and qualifications, limitations or restrictions thereof, as shall be stated and expressed in the certificate of incorporation or of any amendment thereto, or in the resolution or resolutions providing for the issue of such stock adopted by the board of directors pursuant to authority expressly vested in it by the provisions of its certificate of incorporation. Any of the voting powers, designations, preferences, rights and qualifications, limitations or restrictions of any such class or series of stock may be made dependent upon facts ascertainable outside the certificate of incorporation or of any amendment thereto, or outside the resolution or resolutions providing for the issue of such stock adopted by the board of directors pursuant to authority expressly vested in it by its certificate of incorporation, provided that the manner in which such facts shall operate upon the voting powers, designations, preferences, rights and qualifications, limitations or restrictions of such class or series of stock is clearly and expressly set forth in the certificate of incorporation or in the resolution or resolutions providing for the issue of such stock adopted by the board of directors. The term "facts," as used in this subsection, includes, but is not limited to, the occurrence of any event, including a determination or action by any person or body, including the corporation. The power to increase or decrease or otherwise adjust the capital stock as provided in this chapter shall apply to all or any such classes of stock.

(b)   Any stock of any class or series may be made subject to redemption by the corporation at its option or at the option of the holders of such stock or upon the happening of a specified event; provided however, that immediately following any such redemption the corporation shall have outstanding 1 or more shares of 1 or more classes or series of stock, which share, or shares together, shall have full voting powers. Notwithstanding the limitation stated in the foregoing proviso:

(1)   Any stock of a regulated investment company registered under the Investment Company Act of 1940 [15 U.S.C. § 80a–1 et seq.], as heretofore or hereafter amended, may be made subject to redemption by the corporation at its option or at the option of the holders of such stock.

(2)   Any stock of a corporation which holds (directly or indirectly) a license or franchise from a governmental agency to conduct its business or is a member of a national securities exchange, which license, franchise or membership is conditioned upon some or all of the holders of its stock possessing prescribed qualifications, may be made subject to redemption by the corporation to the extent necessary to prevent the loss of such license, franchise or membership or to reinstate it.

Any stock which may be made redeemable under this section may be redeemed for cash, property or rights, including securities of the same or another corporation, at such time or times, price or prices, or rate or rates, and with such adjustments, as shall be stated in the certificate of incorporation or in the resolution or resolutions providing for the issue of such stock adopted by the board of directors pursuant to subsection (a) of this section.

(c)   The holders of preferred or special stock of any class or of any series thereof shall be entitled to receive dividends at such rates, on such conditions and at such times as shall be stated in the certificate of incorporation or in the resolution or resolutions providing for the issue of such stock adopted by the board of directors as hereinabove provided, payable in preference to, or in such relation to, the dividends payable on any other class or classes or of any other series of stock, and cumulative or noncumulative as shall be so stated and expressed. When dividends upon the preferred and special stocks, if any, to the extent of the preference to which such stocks are entitled, shall have been paid or declared and set apart for payment, a dividend on the remaining class or classes or series of stock may then be paid out of the remaining assets of the corporation available for dividends as elsewhere in this chapter provided.

(d)   The holders of the preferred or special stock of any class or of any series thereof shall be entitled to such rights upon the dissolution of, or upon any distribution of the assets of, the corporation as shall be stated in the certificate of incorporation or in the resolution or resolutions providing for the issue of such stock adopted by the board of directors as hereinabove provided.

(e)   Any stock of any class or of any series thereof may be made convertible into, or exchangeable for, at the option of either the holder or the corporation or upon the happening of a specified event, shares of any other class or classes or any other series of the same or any other class or classes of stock of the corporation, at such price or prices or at such rate or rates of exchange and with such adjustments as shall be stated in the certificate of incorporation or in the resolution or resolutions providing for the issue of such stock adopted by the board of directors as hereinabove provided.

(f)   If any corporation shall be authorized to issue more than 1 class of stock or more than 1 series of any class, the powers, designations, preferences and relative, participating, optional, or other special rights of each class of stock or series thereof and the qualifications, limitations or restrictions of such preferences and/or rights shall be set forth in full or summarized on the face or back of the certificate which the corporation shall issue to represent such class or series of stock, provided that, except as otherwise provided in § 202 of this title, in lieu of the foregoing requirements, there may be set forth on the face or back of the certificate which the corporation shall issue to represent such class or series of stock, a statement that the corporation will furnish without charge to each stockholder who so requests the powers, designations, preferences and relative, participating, optional, or other special rights of each class of stock or series thereof and the qualifications, limitations or restrictions of such preferences and/or rights. Within a reasonable time after the issuance or transfer of uncertificated stock, the registered owner thereof shall be given a notice, in writing or by electronic transmission, containing the information required to be set forth or stated on certificates pursuant to this section or § 156, § 202(a), § 218(a) or § 364 of this title or with respect to this section a statement that the corporation will furnish without charge to each stockholder who so requests the powers, designations, preferences and relative participating, optional or other special rights of each class of stock or series thereof and the qualifications, limitations or restrictions of such preferences and/or rights. Except as otherwise expressly provided by law, the rights and obligations of the holders of uncertificated stock and the rights and obligations of the holders of certificates representing stock of the same class and series shall be identical.

(g)   When any corporation desires to issue any shares of stock of any class or of any series of any class of which the powers, designations, preferences and relative, participating, optional or other rights, if any, or the qualifications, limitations or restrictions thereof, if any, shall not have been set forth in the certificate of incorporation or in any amendment thereto but shall be provided for in a resolution or resolutions adopted by the board of directors pursuant to authority expressly vested in it by the certificate of incorporation or any amendment thereto, a certificate of designations setting forth a copy of such resolution or resolutions and the number of shares of stock of such class or series as to which the resolution or resolutions apply shall be executed, acknowledged, filed and shall become effective, in accordance with § 103 of this title. Unless otherwise provided in any such resolution or resolutions, the number of shares of stock of any such series to which such resolution or resolutions apply may be increased (but not above the total number of authorized shares of the class) or decreased (but not below the number of shares thereof then outstanding) by a certificate likewise executed, acknowledged and filed setting forth a statement that a specified increase or decrease therein had been authorized and directed by a resolution or resolutions likewise adopted by the board of directors. In case the number of such shares shall be decreased the number of shares so specified in the certificate shall resume the status which they had prior to the adoption of the first resolution or resolutions. When no shares of any such class or series are outstanding, either because none were issued or because no issued shares of any such class or series remain outstanding, a certificate setting forth a resolution or resolutions adopted by the board of directors that none of the authorized shares of such class or series are outstanding, and that none will be issued subject to the certificate of designations previously filed with respect to such class or series, may be executed, acknowledged and filed in accordance with § 103 of this title and, when such certificate becomes effective, it shall have the effect of eliminating from the certificate of incorporation all matters set forth in the certificate of designations with respect to such class or series of stock. Unless otherwise provided in the certificate of incorporation, if no shares of stock have been issued of a class or series of stock established by a resolution of the board of directors, the voting powers, designations, preferences and relative, participating, optional or other rights, if any, or the qualifications, limitations or restrictions thereof, may be amended by a resolution or resolutions adopted by the board of directors. A certificate which:

(1)   States that no shares of the class or series have been issued;

(2)   Sets forth a copy of the resolution or resolutions; and

(3)   If the designation of the class or series is being changed, indicates the original designation and the new designation,

shall be executed, acknowledged and filed and shall become effective, in accordance with § 103 of this title. When any certificate filed under this subsection becomes effective, it shall have the effect of amending the certificate of incorporation; except that neither the filing of such certificate nor the filing of a restated certificate of incorporation pursuant to § 245 of this title shall prohibit the board of directors from subsequently adopting such resolutions as authorized by this subsection.

§ 152.   Issuance of stock; lawful consideration; fully paid stock.

The consideration, as determined pursuant to § 153(a) and (b) of this title, for subscriptions to, or the purchase of, the capital stock to be issued by a corporation shall be paid in such form and in such manner as the board of directors shall determine. The board of directors may authorize capital stock to be issued for consideration consisting of cash, any tangible or intangible property or any benefit to the corporation, or any combination thereof. The resolution authorizing the issuance of capital stock may provide that any stock to be issued pursuant to such resolution may be issued in 1 or more transactions in such numbers and at such times as are set forth in or determined by or in the manner set forth in the resolution, which may include a determination or action by any person or body, including the corporation, provided the resolution fixes a maximum number of shares that may be issued pursuant to such resolution, a time period during which such shares may be issued and a minimum amount of consideration for which such shares may be issued. The board of directors may determine the amount of consideration for which shares may be issued by setting a minimum amount of consideration or approving a formula by which the amount or minimum amount of consideration is determined. The formula may include or be made dependent upon facts ascertainable outside the formula, provided the manner in which such facts shall operate upon the formula is clearly and expressly set forth in the formula or in the resolution approving the formula. In the absence of actual fraud in the transaction, the judgment of the directors as to the value of such consideration shall be conclusive. The capital stock so issued shall be deemed to be fully paid and nonassessable stock upon receipt by the corporation of such consideration; provided, however, nothing contained herein shall prevent the board of directors from issuing partly paid shares under § 156 of this title.

§ 153.   Consideration for stock.

(a)   Shares of stock with par value may be issued for such consideration, having a value not less than the par value thereof, as determined from time to time by the board of directors, or by the stockholders if the certificate of incorporation so provides.

(b)   Shares of stock without par value may be issued for such consideration as is determined from time to time by the board of directors, or by the stockholders if the certificate of incorporation so provides.

(c)   Treasury shares may be disposed of by the corporation for such consideration as may be determined from time to time by the board of directors, or by the stockholders if the certificate of incorporation so provides.

(d)   If the certificate of incorporation reserves to the stockholders the right to determine the consideration for the issue of any shares, the stockholders shall, unless the certificate requires a greater vote, do so by a vote of a majority of the outstanding stock entitled to vote thereon.

§ 154.   Determination of amount of capital; capital, surplus and net assets defined.

Any corporation may, by resolution of its board of directors, determine that only a part of the consideration which shall be received by the corporation for any of the shares of its capital stock which it shall issue from time to time shall be capital; but, in case any of the shares issued shall be shares having a par value, the amount of the part of such consideration so determined to be capital shall be in excess of the aggregate par value of the shares issued for such consideration having a par value, unless all the shares issued shall be shares having a par value, in which case the amount of the part of such consideration so determined to be capital need be only equal to the aggregate par value of such shares. In each such case the board of directors shall specify in dollars the part of such consideration which shall be capital. If the board of directors shall not have determined (1) at the time of issue of any shares of the capital stock of the corporation issued for cash or (2) within 60 days after the issue of any shares of the capital stock of the corporation issued for consideration other than cash what part of the consideration for such shares shall be capital, the capital of the corporation in respect of such shares shall be an amount equal to the aggregate par value of such shares having a par value, plus the amount of the consideration for such shares without par value. The amount of the consideration so determined to be capital in respect of any shares without par value shall be the stated capital of such shares. The capital of the corporation may be increased from time to time by resolution of the board of directors directing that a portion of the net assets of the corporation in excess of the amount so determined to be capital be transferred to the capital account. The board of directors may direct that the portion of such net assets so transferred shall be treated as capital in respect of any shares of the corporation of any designated class or classes. The excess, if any, at any given time, of the net assets of the corporation over the amount so determined to be capital shall be surplus. Net assets means the amount by which total assets exceed total liabilities. Capital and surplus are not liabilities for this purpose. Notwithstanding anything in this section to the contrary, for purposes of this section and §§ 160 and 170 of this title, the capital of any nonstock corporation shall be deemed to be zero.

§ 155.   Fractions of shares.

A corporation may, but shall not be required to, issue fractions of a share. If it does not issue fractions of a share, it shall (1) arrange for the disposition of fractional interests by those entitled thereto, (2) pay in cash the fair value of fractions of a share as of the time when those entitled to receive such fractions are determined or (3) issue scrip or warrants in registered form (either represented by a certificate or uncertificated) or in bearer form (represented by a certificate) which shall entitle the holder to receive a full share upon the surrender of such scrip or warrants aggregating a full share. A certificate for a fractional share or an uncertificated fractional share shall, but scrip or warrants shall not unless otherwise provided therein, entitle the holder to exercise voting rights, to receive dividends thereon and to participate in any of the assets of the corporation in the event of liquidation. The board of directors may cause scrip or warrants to be issued subject to the conditions that they shall become void if not exchanged for certificates representing the full shares or uncertificated full shares before a specified date, or subject to the conditions that the shares for which scrip or warrants are exchangeable may be sold by the corporation and the proceeds thereof distributed to the holders of scrip or warrants, or subject to any other conditions which the board of directors may impose.

§ 156.   Partly paid shares.

Any corporation may issue the whole or any part of its shares as partly paid and subject to call for the remainder of the consideration to be paid therefor. Upon the face or back of each stock certificate issued to represent any such partly paid shares, or upon the books and records of the corporation in the case of uncertificated partly paid shares, the total amount of the consideration to be paid therefor and the amount paid thereon shall be stated. Upon the declaration of any dividend on fully paid shares, the corporation shall declare a dividend upon partly paid shares of the same class, but only upon the basis of the percentage of the consideration actually paid thereon.

§ 157.   Rights and options respecting stock.

(a)   Subject to any provisions in the certificate of incorporation, every corporation may create and issue, whether or not in connection with the issue and sale of any shares of stock or other securities of the corporation, rights or options entitling the holders thereof to acquire from the corporation any shares of its capital stock of any class or classes, such rights or options to be evidenced by or in such instrument or instruments as shall be approved by the board of directors.

(b) The terms upon which, including the time or times which may be limited or unlimited in duration, at or within which, and the consideration (including a formula by which such consideration may be determined) for which any such shares may be acquired from the corporation upon the exercise of any such right or option, shall be such as shall be stated in the certificate of incorporation, or in a resolution adopted by the board of directors providing for the creation and issue of such rights or options, and, in every case, shall be set forth or incorporated by reference in the instrument or instruments evidencing such rights or options. A formula by which such consideration may be determined may include or be made dependent upon facts ascertainable outside the formula, provided the manner in which such facts shall operate upon the formula is clearly and expressly set forth in the formula or in the resolution approving the formula. In the absence of actual fraud in the transaction, the judgment of the directors as to the consideration for the issuance of such rights or options and the sufficiency thereof shall be conclusive.

(c) The board of directors may, by a resolution adopted by the board, authorize 1 or more officers of the corporation to do 1 or both of the following: (i) designate officers and employees of the corporation or of any of its subsidiaries to be recipients of such rights or options created by the corporation, and (ii) determine the number of such rights or options to be received by such officers and employees; provided, however, that the resolution so authorizing such officer or officers shall specify the total number of rights or options such officer or officers may so award. The board of directors may not authorize an officer to designate himself or herself as a recipient of any such rights or options.

(d) In case the shares of stock of the corporation to be issued upon the exercise of such rights or options shall be shares having a par value, the consideration so to be received therefor shall have a value not less than the par value thereof. In case the shares of stock so to be issued shall be shares of stock without par value, the consideration therefor shall be determined in the manner provided in § 153 of this title.

§ 158. Stock certificates; uncertificated shares.

The shares of a corporation shall be represented by certificates, provided that the board of directors of the corporation may provide by resolution or resolutions that some or all of any or all classes or series of its stock shall be uncertificated shares. Any such resolution shall not apply to shares represented by a certificate until such certificate is surrendered to the corporation. Every holder of stock represented by certificates shall be entitled to have a certificate signed by, or in the name of, the corporation by any 2 authorized officers of the corporation representing the number of shares registered in certificate form. Any or all the signatures on the certificate may be a facsimile. In case any officer, transfer agent or registrar who has signed or whose facsimile signature has been placed upon a certificate shall have ceased to be such officer, transfer agent or registrar before such certificate is issued, it may be issued by the corporation with the same effect as if such person were such officer, transfer agent or registrar at the date of issue. A corporation shall not have power to issue a certificate in bearer form.

§ 159. Shares of stock; personal property, transfer and taxation.

The shares of stock in every corporation shall be deemed personal property and transferable as provided in Article 8 of subtitle I of Title 6. No stock or bonds issued by any corporation organized under this chapter shall be taxed by this State when the same shall be owned by nonresidents of this State, or by foreign corporations. Whenever any transfer of shares shall be made for collateral security, and not absolutely, it shall be so expressed in the entry of transfer if, when the certificates are presented to the corporation for transfer or uncertificated shares are requested to be transferred, both the transferor and transferee request the corporation to do so.

§ 160. Corporation's powers respecting ownership, voting, etc., of its own stock; rights of stock called for redemption.

(a) Every corporation may purchase, redeem, receive, take or otherwise acquire, own and hold, sell, lend, exchange, transfer or otherwise dispose of, pledge, use and otherwise deal in and with its own shares; provided, however, that no corporation shall:

(1) Purchase or redeem its own shares of capital stock for cash or other property when the capital of the corporation is impaired or when such purchase or redemption would cause any impairment of the capital of the corporation, except that a corporation other than a nonstock corporation may purchase or redeem out of capital any of its own shares which are entitled upon any distribution of its assets, whether by dividend or in liquidation, to a preference over another class or series of its stock, or, if no shares entitled to such a preference are outstanding, any of its own shares, if such shares will be retired upon their acquisition and the capital of the corporation reduced in accordance with §§ 243 and 244 of this title. Nothing in this subsection shall invalidate or otherwise affect a note, debenture or other obligation of a corporation given by it as consideration for its acquisition by purchase, redemption or exchange of its shares of stock if at the time such note, debenture or obligation was delivered by the corporation its capital was not then impaired or did not thereby become impaired;

(2) Purchase, for more than the price at which they may then be redeemed, any of its shares which are redeemable at the option of the corporation; or

(3) a. In the case of a corporation other than a nonstock corporation, redeem any of its shares, unless their redemption is authorized by § 151(b) of this title and then only in accordance with such section and the certificate of incorporation, or

b. In the case of a nonstock corporation, redeem any of its membership interests, unless their redemption is authorized by the certificate of incorporation and then only in accordance with the certificate of incorporation.

(b) Nothing in this section limits or affects a corporation's right to resell any of its shares theretofore purchased or redeemed out of surplus and which have not been retired, for such consideration as shall be fixed by the board of directors.

(c) Shares of its own capital stock belonging to the corporation or to another corporation, if a majority of the shares entitled to vote in the election of directors of such other corporation is held, directly or indirectly, by the corporation, shall neither be entitled to vote nor be counted for quorum purposes. Nothing in this section shall be construed as limiting the right of any corporation to vote stock, including but not limited to its own stock, held by it in a fiduciary capacity.

(d) Shares which have been called for redemption shall not be deemed to be outstanding shares for the purpose of voting or determining the total number of shares entitled to vote on any matter on and after the date on which notice of redemption has been sent to holders thereof and a sum sufficient to redeem such shares has been irrevocably deposited or set aside to pay the redemption price to the holders of the shares upon surrender of certificates therefor.

§ 161. Issuance of additional stock; when and by whom.

The directors may, at any time and from time to time, if all of the shares of capital stock which the corporation is authorized by its certificate of incorporation to issue have not been issued, subscribed for, or otherwise committed to be issued, issue or take subscriptions for additional shares of its capital stock up to the amount authorized in its certificate of incorporation.

§ 162. Liability of stockholder or subscriber for stock not paid in full.

(a) When the whole of the consideration payable for shares of a corporation has not been paid in, and the assets shall be insufficient to satisfy the claims of its creditors, each holder of or subscriber for such shares shall be bound to pay on each share held or subscribed for by such holder or subscriber the sum necessary to complete the amount of the unpaid balance of the consideration for which such shares were issued or are to be issued by the corporation.

(b) The amounts which shall be payable as provided in subsection (a) of this section may be recovered as provided in § 325 of this title, after a writ of execution against the corporation has been returned unsatisfied as provided in said § 325.

(c) Any person becoming an assignee or transferee of shares or of a subscription for shares in good faith and without knowledge or notice that the full consideration therefor has not been paid shall not be personally liable for any unpaid portion of such consideration, but the transferor shall remain liable therefor.

(d) No person holding shares in any corporation as collateral security shall be personally liable as a stockholder but the person pledging such shares shall be considered the holder thereof and shall be so liable. No executor, administrator, guardian, trustee or other fiduciary shall be personally liable as a stockholder, but the estate or funds held by such executor, administrator, guardian, trustee or other fiduciary in such fiduciary capacity shall be liable.

(e) No liability under this section or under § 325 of this title shall be asserted more than 6 years after the issuance of the stock or the date of the subscription upon which the assessment is sought.

(f) In any action by a receiver or trustee of an insolvent corporation or by a judgment creditor to obtain an assessment under this section, any stockholder or subscriber for stock of the insolvent corporation may appear and contest the claim or claims of such receiver or trustee.

§ 163. Payment for stock not paid in full.

The capital stock of a corporation shall be paid for in such amounts and at such times as the directors may require. The directors may, from time to time, demand payment, in respect of each share of stock not fully paid, of such sum of money as the necessities of the business may, in the judgment of the board of directors, require, not exceeding in the whole the balance remaining unpaid on said stock, and such sum so demanded shall be paid to the corporation at such times and by such installments as the directors shall direct. The directors shall give notice of the time and place of such payments, which notice shall be given at least 30 days before the time for such payment, to each holder of or subscriber for stock which is not fully paid at such holder's or subscriber's last known address.

§ 164. Failure to pay for stock; remedies.

When any stockholder fails to pay any installment or call upon such stockholder's stock which may have been properly demanded by the directors, at the time when such payment is due, the directors may collect the amount of any such installment or call or any balance thereof remaining unpaid, from the said stockholder by an action at law, or they shall sell at public sale such part of the shares of such delinquent stockholder as will pay all demands then due from such stockholder with interest and all incidental expenses, and shall transfer the shares so sold to the purchaser, who shall be entitled to a certificate therefor.

Notice of the time and place of such sale and of the sum due on each share shall be given by advertisement at least 1 week before the sale, in a newspaper of the county in this State where such corporation's registered office is located, and such notice shall be mailed by the corporation to such delinquent stockholder at such stockholder's last known post-office address, at least 20 days before such sale.

If no bidder can be had to pay the amount due on the stock, and if the amount is not collected by an action at law, which may be brought within the county where the corporation has its registered office, within 1 year from the date of the bringing of such action at law, the said stock and the amount previously paid in by the delinquent stockholder on the stock shall be forfeited to the corporation.

§ 165. Revocability of preincorporation subscriptions.

Unless otherwise provided by the terms of the subscription, a subscription for stock of a corporation to be formed shall be irrevocable, except with the consent of all other subscribers or the corporation, for a period of 6 months from its date.

§ 166. Formalities required of stock subscriptions.

A subscription for stock of a corporation, whether made before or after the formation of a corporation, shall not be enforceable against a subscriber, unless in writing and signed by the subscriber or by such subscriber's agent.

§ 167.　　Lost, stolen or destroyed stock certificates; issuance of new certificate or uncertificated shares.

A corporation may issue a new certificate of stock or uncertificated shares in place of any certificate theretofore issued by it, alleged to have been lost, stolen or destroyed, and the corporation may require the owner of the lost, stolen or destroyed certificate, or such owner's legal representative to give the corporation a bond sufficient to indemnify it against any claim that may be made against it on account of the alleged loss, theft or destruction of any such certificate or the issuance of such new certificate or uncertificated shares.

§ 168.　　Judicial proceedings to compel issuance of new certificate or uncertificated shares.

(a)　　If a corporation refuses to issue new uncertificated shares or a new certificate of stock in place of a certificate theretofore issued by it, or by any corporation of which it is the lawful successor, alleged to have been lost, stolen or destroyed, the owner of the lost, stolen or destroyed certificate or such owner's legal representatives may apply to the Court of Chancery for an order requiring the corporation to show cause why it should not issue new uncertificated shares or a new certificate of stock in place of the certificate so lost, stolen or destroyed. Such application shall be by a complaint which shall state the name of the corporation, the number and date of the certificate, if known or ascertainable by the plaintiff, the number of shares of stock represented thereby and to whom issued, and a statement of the circumstances attending such loss, theft or destruction. Thereupon the court shall make an order requiring the corporation to show cause at a time and place therein designated, why it should not issue new uncertificated shares or a new certificate of stock in place of the one described in the complaint. A copy of the complaint and order shall be served upon the corporation at least 5 days before the time designated in the order.

(b)　　If, upon hearing, the court is satisfied that the plaintiff is the lawful owner of the number of shares of capital stock, or any part thereof, described in the complaint, and that the certificate therefor has been lost, stolen or destroyed, and no sufficient cause has been shown why new uncertificated shares or a new certificate should not be issued in place thereof, it shall make an order requiring the corporation to issue and deliver to the plaintiff new uncertificated shares or a new certificate for such shares. In its order the court shall direct that, prior to the issuance and delivery to the plaintiff of such new uncertificated shares or a new certificate, the plaintiff give the corporation a bond in such form and with such security as to the court appears sufficient to indemnify the corporation against any claim that may be made against it on account of the alleged loss, theft or destruction of any such certificate or the issuance of such new uncertificated shares or new certificate. No corporation which has issued uncertificated shares or a certificate pursuant to an order of the court entered hereunder shall be liable in an amount in excess of the amount specified in such bond.

§ 169.　　Situs of ownership of stock.

For all purposes of title, action, attachment, garnishment and jurisdiction of all courts held in this State, but not for the purpose of taxation, the situs of the ownership of the capital stock of all corporations existing under the laws of this State, whether organized under this chapter or otherwise, shall be regarded as in this State.

§ 170.　　Dividends; payment; wasting asset corporations.

(a)　　The directors of every corporation, subject to any restrictions contained in its certificate of incorporation, may declare and pay dividends upon the shares of its capital stock either:

(1)　　Out of its surplus, as defined in and computed in accordance with §§ 154 and 244 of this title; or

(2)　　In case there shall be no such surplus, out of its net profits for the fiscal year in which the dividend is declared and/or the preceding fiscal year.

If the capital of the corporation, computed in accordance with §§ 154 and 244 of this title, shall have been diminished by depreciation in the value of its property, or by losses, or otherwise, to an amount less than the aggregate amount of the capital represented by the issued and outstanding stock of all classes having a preference upon the distribution of assets, the directors of such corporation shall not declare and pay out of such net profits any dividends upon any shares of any classes of its capital stock until the deficiency in the amount of capital represented by the issued and outstanding stock of all classes having a preference upon the distribution of assets shall have been repaired. Nothing in this subsection shall invalidate or otherwise affect a note, debenture or other obligation of the corporation paid by it as a dividend on shares of its stock, or any payment made thereon, if at the time such note, debenture or obligation was delivered by the corporation, the corporation had either surplus or net profits as provided in (a)(1) or (2) of this section from which the dividend could lawfully have been paid.

(b) Subject to any restrictions contained in its certificate of incorporation, the directors of any corporation engaged in the exploitation of wasting assets (including but not limited to a corporation engaged in the exploitation of natural resources or other wasting assets, including patents, or engaged primarily in the liquidation of specific assets) may determine the net profits derived from the exploitation of such wasting assets or the net proceeds derived from such liquidation without taking into consideration the depletion of such assets resulting from lapse of time, consumption, liquidation or exploitation of such assets.

§ 171. Special purpose reserves.

The directors of a corporation may set apart out of any of the funds of the corporation available for dividends a reserve or reserves for any proper purpose and may abolish any such reserve.

§ 172. Liability of directors and committee members as to dividends or stock redemption.

A member of the board of directors, or a member of any committee designated by the board of directors, shall be fully protected in relying in good faith upon the records of the corporation and upon such information, opinions, reports or statements presented to the corporation by any of its officers or employees, or committees of the board of directors, or by any other person as to matters the director reasonably believes are within such other person's professional or expert competence and who has been selected with reasonable care by or on behalf of the corporation, as to the value and amount of the assets, liabilities and/or net profits of the corporation or any other facts pertinent to the existence and amount of surplus or other funds from which dividends might properly be declared and paid, or with which the corporation's stock might properly be purchased or redeemed.

§ 173. Declaration and payment of dividends.

No corporation shall pay dividends except in accordance with this chapter. Dividends may be paid in cash, in property, or in shares of the corporation's capital stock. If the dividend is to be paid in shares of the corporation's theretofore unissued capital stock the board of directors shall, by resolution, direct that there be designated as capital in respect of such shares an amount which is not less than the aggregate par value of par value shares being declared as a dividend and, in the case of shares without par value being declared as a dividend, such amount as shall be determined by the board of directors. No such designation as capital shall be necessary if shares are being distributed by a corporation pursuant to a split-up or division of its stock rather than as payment of a dividend declared payable in stock of the corporation.

§ 174. Liability of directors for unlawful payment of dividend or unlawful stock purchase or redemption; exoneration from liability; contribution among directors; subrogation.

(a) In case of any wilful or negligent violation of § 160 or § 173 of this title, the directors under whose administration the same may happen shall be jointly and severally liable, at any time within 6 years after paying such unlawful dividend or after such unlawful stock purchase or redemption, to the corporation, and to its creditors in the event of its dissolution or insolvency, to the full amount of the dividend unlawfully paid, or to the full amount unlawfully paid for the purchase or redemption of the corporation's stock, with interest from the time such liability accrued. Any director who may have been absent when the same was done, or who may have dissented from the act or resolution by which the same was done, may be exonerated from such liability by causing his or her dissent to be entered on the books containing the minutes of the proceedings of the directors at the time the same was done, or immediately after such director has notice of the same.

(b)   Any director against whom a claim is successfully asserted under this section shall be entitled to contribution from the other directors who voted for or concurred in the unlawful dividend, stock purchase or stock redemption.

(c)   Any director against whom a claim is successfully asserted under this section shall be entitled, to the extent of the amount paid by such director as a result of such claim, to be subrogated to the rights of the corporation against stockholders who received the dividend on, or assets for the sale or redemption of, their stock with knowledge of facts indicating that such dividend, stock purchase or redemption was unlawful under this chapter, in proportion to the amounts received by such stockholders respectively.

SUBCHAPTER VI.   STOCK TRANSFERS

§ 201.   Transfer of stock, stock certificates and uncertificated stock.

Except as otherwise provided in this chapter, the transfer of stock and the certificates of stock which represent the stock or uncertificated stock shall be governed by Article 8 of subtitle I of Title 6. To the extent that any provision of this chapter is inconsistent with any provision of subtitle I of Title 6, this chapter shall be controlling.

§ 202.   Restrictions on transfer and ownership of securities.

(a)   A written restriction or restrictions on the transfer or registration of transfer of a security of a corporation, or on the amount of the corporation's securities that may be owned by any person or group of persons, if permitted by this section and noted conspicuously on the certificate or certificates representing the security or securities so restricted or, in the case of uncertificated shares, contained in the notice or notices given pursuant to § 151(f) of this title, may be enforced against the holder of the restricted security or securities or any successor or transferee of the holder including an executor, administrator, trustee, guardian or other fiduciary entrusted with like responsibility for the person or estate of the holder. Unless noted conspicuously on the certificate or certificates representing the security or securities so restricted or, in the case of uncertificated shares, contained in the notice or notices given pursuant to § 151(f) of this title, a restriction, even though permitted by this section, is ineffective except against a person with actual knowledge of the restriction.

(b)   A restriction on the transfer or registration of transfer of securities of a corporation, or on the amount of a corporation's securities that may be owned by any person or group of persons, may be imposed by the certificate of incorporation or by the bylaws or by an agreement among any number of security holders or among such holders and the corporation. No restrictions so imposed shall be binding with respect to securities issued prior to the adoption of the restriction unless the holders of the securities are parties to an agreement or voted in favor of the restriction.

(c)   A restriction on the transfer or registration of transfer of securities of a corporation or on the amount of such securities that may be owned by any person or group of persons is permitted by this section if it:

(1)   Obligates the holder of the restricted securities to offer to the corporation or to any other holders of securities of the corporation or to any other person or to any combination of the foregoing, a prior opportunity, to be exercised within a reasonable time, to acquire the restricted securities; or

(2)   Obligates the corporation or any holder of securities of the corporation or any other person or any combination of the foregoing, to purchase the securities which are the subject of an agreement respecting the purchase and sale of the restricted securities; or

(3)   Requires the corporation or the holders of any class or series of securities of the corporation to consent to any proposed transfer of the restricted securities or to approve the proposed transferee of the restricted securities, or to approve the amount of securities of the corporation that may be owned by any person or group of persons; or

(4)   Obligates the holder of the restricted securities to sell or transfer an amount of restricted securities to the corporation or to any other holders of securities of the corporation or to any other person or to any combination of the foregoing, or causes or results in the automatic sale or transfer of an amount of restricted securities to the corporation or to any other holders of securities of the corporation or to any other person or to any combination of the foregoing; or

(5)   Prohibits or restricts the transfer of the restricted securities to, or the ownership of restricted securities by, designated persons or classes of persons or groups of persons, and such designation is not manifestly unreasonable.

(d)   Any restriction on the transfer or the registration of transfer of the securities of a corporation, or on the amount of securities of a corporation that may be owned by a person or group of persons, for any of the following purposes shall be conclusively presumed to be for a reasonable purpose:

(1)   Maintaining any local, state, federal or foreign tax advantage to the corporation or its stockholders, including without limitation:

a.   Maintaining the corporation's status as an electing small business corporation under subchapter S of the United States Internal Revenue Code [26 U.S.C. § 1371 et seq.], or

b.   Maintaining or preserving any tax attribute (including without limitation net operating losses), or

c.   Qualifying or maintaining the qualification of the corporation as a real estate investment trust pursuant to the United States Internal Revenue Code or regulations adopted pursuant to the United States Internal Revenue Code, or

(2)   Maintaining any statutory or regulatory advantage or complying with any statutory or regulatory requirements under applicable local, state, federal or foreign law.

(e)   Any other lawful restriction on transfer or registration of transfer of securities, or on the amount of securities that may be owned by any person or group of persons, is permitted by this section.

§ 203.   Business combinations with interested stockholders.

(a)   Notwithstanding any other provisions of this chapter, a corporation shall not engage in any business combination with any interested stockholder for a period of 3 years following the time that such stockholder became an interested stockholder, unless:

(1)   Prior to such time the board of directors of the corporation approved either the business combination or the transaction which resulted in the stockholder becoming an interested stockholder;

(2)   Upon consummation of the transaction which resulted in the stockholder becoming an interested stockholder, the interested stockholder owned at least 85% of the voting stock of the corporation outstanding at the time the transaction commenced, excluding for purposes of determining the voting stock outstanding (but not the outstanding voting stock owned by the interested stockholder) those shares owned (i) by persons who are directors and also officers and (ii) employee stock plans in which employee participants do not have the right to determine confidentially whether shares held subject to the plan will be tendered in a tender or exchange offer; or

(3)   At or subsequent to such time the business combination is approved by the board of directors and authorized at an annual or special meeting of stockholders, and not by written consent, by the affirmative vote of at least 66 2/3% of the outstanding voting stock which is not owned by the interested stockholder.

(b)   The restrictions contained in this section shall not apply if:

(1)   The corporation's original certificate of incorporation contains a provision expressly electing not to be governed by this section;

(2)   The corporation, by action of its board of directors, adopts an amendment to its bylaws within 90 days of February 2, 1988, expressly electing not to be governed by this section, which amendment shall not be further amended by the board of directors;

(3)   The corporation, by action of its stockholders, adopts an amendment to its certificate of incorporation or bylaws expressly electing not to be governed by this section; provided that, in addition to any other vote required by law, such amendment to the certificate of incorporation or bylaws must be adopted by the affirmative vote of a majority of the outstanding stock entitled to vote thereon. In the case of a corporation that both (i) has never had a class of voting stock that falls within any of the 2 categories set out in paragraph (b)(4) of this section, and (ii) has not elected by a provision in its original certificate of incorporation or any amendment thereto to be governed by this section, such amendment shall become effective upon (i) in the case of an amendment to the certificate of incorporation, the date and time at which the certificate filed in accordance with § 103 of this title becomes effective thereunder or (ii) in the case of an amendment to the bylaws, the date of the adoption of such amendment. In all other cases, an amendment adopted pursuant to this paragraph shall become effective (i) in the case of an amendment to the certificate of incorporation, 12 months after the date and time at which the certificate filed in accordance with § 103 of this title becomes effective thereunder or (ii) in the case of an amendment to the bylaws, 12 months after the date of the adoption of such amendment, and, in either case, the election not to be governed by this section shall not apply to any business combination between such corporation and any person who became an interested stockholder of such corporation on or before (A) in the case of an amendment to the certificate of incorporation, the date and time at which the certificate filed in accordance with § 103 of this title becomes effective thereunder; or (B) in the case of an amendment to the bylaws, the date of the adoption of such amendment. A bylaw amendment adopted pursuant to this paragraph shall not be further amended by the board of directors;

(4)   The corporation does not have a class of voting stock that is: (i) Listed on a national securities exchange; or (ii) held of record by more than 2,000 stockholders, unless any of the foregoing results from action taken, directly or indirectly, by an interested stockholder or from a transaction in which a person becomes an interested stockholder;

(5)   A stockholder becomes an interested stockholder inadvertently and (i) as soon as practicable divests itself of ownership of sufficient shares so that the stockholder ceases to be an interested stockholder; and (ii) would not, at any time within the 3-year period immediately prior to a business combination between the corporation and such stockholder, have been an interested stockholder but for the inadvertent acquisition of ownership;

(6)   The business combination is proposed prior to the consummation or abandonment of and subsequent to the earlier of the public announcement or the notice required hereunder of a proposed transaction which (i) constitutes 1 of the transactions described in the second sentence of this paragraph; (ii) is with or by a person who either was not an interested stockholder during the previous 3 years or who became an interested stockholder with the approval of the corporation's board of directors or during the period described in paragraph (b)(7) of this section; and (iii) is approved or not opposed by a majority of the members of the board of directors then in office (but not less than 1) who were directors prior to any person becoming an interested stockholder during the previous 3 years or were recommended for election or elected to succeed such directors by a majority of such directors. The proposed transactions referred to in the preceding sentence are limited to (x) a merger or consolidation of the corporation (except for a merger in respect of which, pursuant to § 251(f) of this title, no vote of the stockholders of the corporation is required); (y) a sale, lease, exchange, mortgage, pledge, transfer or other disposition (in 1 transaction or a series of transactions), whether as part of a dissolution or otherwise, of assets of the corporation or of any direct or indirect majority-owned subsidiary of the corporation (other than to any direct or indirect wholly-owned subsidiary or to the corporation) having an aggregate market value equal to 50% or more of either that aggregate market value of all of the assets of the corporation determined on a consolidated basis or the aggregate market value of all the outstanding stock of the corporation; or (z) a proposed tender or exchange offer for 50% or more of the outstanding voting stock of the corporation. The corporation shall give not less than 20 days' notice to all interested stockholders prior to the consummation of any of the transactions described in clause (x) or (y) of the second sentence of this paragraph; or

(7)   The business combination is with an interested stockholder who became an interested stockholder at a time when the restrictions contained in this section did not apply by reason of any of paragraphs (b)(1) through (4) of this section, provided, however, that this paragraph (b)(7) shall not

apply if, at the time such interested stockholder became an interested stockholder, the corporation's certificate of incorporation contained a provision authorized by the last sentence of this subsection (b).

Notwithstanding paragraphs (b)(1), (2), (3) and (4) of this section, a corporation may elect by a provision of its original certificate of incorporation or any amendment thereto to be governed by this section; provided that any such amendment to the certificate of incorporation shall not apply to restrict a business combination between the corporation and an interested stockholder of the corporation if the interested stockholder became such before the date and time at which the certificate filed in accordance with § 103 of this title becomes effective thereunder.

(c)   As used in this section only, the term:

(1)   "Affiliate" means a person that directly, or indirectly through 1 or more intermediaries, controls, or is controlled by, or is under common control with, another person.

(2)   "Associate," when used to indicate a relationship with any person, means: (i) Any corporation, partnership, unincorporated association or other entity of which such person is a director, officer or partner or is, directly or indirectly, the owner of 20% or more of any class of voting stock; (ii) any trust or other estate in which such person has at least a 20% beneficial interest or as to which such person serves as trustee or in a similar fiduciary capacity; and (iii) any relative or spouse of such person, or any relative of such spouse, who has the same residence as such person.

(3)   "Business combination," when used in reference to any corporation and any interested stockholder of such corporation, means:

(i)   Any merger or consolidation of the corporation or any direct or indirect majority-owned subsidiary of the corporation with (A) the interested stockholder, or (B) with any other corporation, partnership, unincorporated association or other entity if the merger or consolidation is caused by the interested stockholder and as a result of such merger or consolidation subsection (a) of this section is not applicable to the surviving entity;

(ii)   Any sale, lease, exchange, mortgage, pledge, transfer or other disposition (in 1 transaction or a series of transactions), except proportionately as a stockholder of such corporation, to or with the interested stockholder, whether as part of a dissolution or otherwise, of assets of the corporation or of any direct or indirect majority-owned subsidiary of the corporation which assets have an aggregate market value equal to 10% or more of either the aggregate market value of all the assets of the corporation determined on a consolidated basis or the aggregate market value of all the outstanding stock of the corporation;

(iii)   Any transaction which results in the issuance or transfer by the corporation or by any direct or indirect majority-owned subsidiary of the corporation of any stock of the corporation or of such subsidiary to the interested stockholder, except: (A) Pursuant to the exercise, exchange or conversion of securities exercisable for, exchangeable for or convertible into stock of such corporation or any such subsidiary which securities were outstanding prior to the time that the interested stockholder became such; (B) pursuant to a merger under § 251(g) of this title; (C) pursuant to a dividend or distribution paid or made, or the exercise, exchange or conversion of securities exercisable for, exchangeable for or convertible into stock of such corporation or any such subsidiary which security is distributed, pro rata to all holders of a class or series of stock of such corporation subsequent to the time the interested stockholder became such; (D) pursuant to an exchange offer by the corporation to purchase stock made on the same terms to all holders of said stock; or (E) any issuance or transfer of stock by the corporation; provided however, that in no case under items (C)–(E) of this subparagraph shall there be an increase in the interested stockholder's proportionate share of the stock of any class or series of the corporation or of the voting stock of the corporation;

(iv)   Any transaction involving the corporation or any direct or indirect majority-owned subsidiary of the corporation which has the effect, directly or indirectly, of increasing the proportionate share of the stock of any class or series, or securities convertible into the stock of any class or series, of the corporation or of any such subsidiary which is owned by the interested stockholder, except as a result of immaterial changes due to fractional share adjustments or as a result of any purchase or redemption of any shares of stock not caused, directly or indirectly, by the interested stockholder; or

(v)   Any receipt by the interested stockholder of the benefit, directly or indirectly (except proportionately as a stockholder of such corporation), of any loans, advances, guarantees, pledges or other financial benefits (other than those expressly permitted in paragraphs (c)(3)(i)–(iv) of this section) provided by or through the corporation or any direct or indirect majority-owned subsidiary.

(4)   "Control," including the terms "controlling," "controlled by" and "under common control with," means the possession, directly or indirectly, of the power to direct or cause the direction of the management and policies of a person, whether through the ownership of voting stock, by contract or otherwise. A person who is the owner of 20% or more of the outstanding voting stock of any corporation, partnership, unincorporated association or other entity shall be presumed to have control of such entity, in the absence of proof by a preponderance of the evidence to the contrary; Notwithstanding the foregoing, a presumption of control shall not apply where such person holds voting stock, in good faith and not for the purpose of circumventing this section, as an agent, bank, broker, nominee, custodian or trustee for 1 or more owners who do not individually or as a group have control of such entity.

(5)   "Interested stockholder" means any person (other than the corporation and any direct or indirect majority-owned subsidiary of the corporation) that (i) is the owner of 15% or more of the outstanding voting stock of the corporation, or (ii) is an affiliate or associate of the corporation and was the owner of 15% or more of the outstanding voting stock of the corporation at any time within the 3-year period immediately prior to the date on which it is sought to be determined whether such person is an interested stockholder, and the affiliates and associates of such person; provided, however, that the term "interested stockholder" shall not include (x) any person who (A) owned shares in excess of the 15% limitation set forth herein as of, or acquired such shares pursuant to a tender offer commenced prior to, December 23, 1987, or pursuant to an exchange offer announced prior to the aforesaid date and commenced within 90 days thereafter and either (I) continued to own shares in excess of such 15% limitation or would have but for action by the corporation or (II) is an affiliate or associate of the corporation and so continued (or so would have continued but for action by the corporation) to be the owner of 15% or more of the outstanding voting stock of the corporation at any time within the 3-year period immediately prior to the date on which it is sought to be determined whether such a person is an interested stockholder or (B) acquired said shares from a person described in item (A) of this paragraph by gift, inheritance or in a transaction in which no consideration was exchanged; or (y) any person whose ownership of shares in excess of the 15% limitation set forth herein is the result of action taken solely by the corporation; provided that such person shall be an interested stockholder if thereafter such person acquires additional shares of voting stock of the corporation, except as a result of further corporate action not caused, directly or indirectly, by such person. For the purpose of determining whether a person is an interested stockholder, the voting stock of the corporation deemed to be outstanding shall include stock deemed to be owned by the person through application of paragraph (9) of this subsection but shall not include any other unissued stock of such corporation which may be issuable pursuant to any agreement, arrangement or understanding, or upon exercise of conversion rights, warrants or options, or otherwise.

(6)   "Person" means any individual, corporation, partnership, unincorporated association or other entity.

(7)   "Stock" means, with respect to any corporation, capital stock and, with respect to any other entity, any equity interest.

(8)   "Voting stock" means, with respect to any corporation, stock of any class or series entitled to vote generally in the election of directors and, with respect to any entity that is not a corporation, any equity interest entitled to vote generally in the election of the governing body of such entity. Every reference to a percentage of voting stock shall refer to such percentage of the votes of such voting stock.

(9)   "Owner," including the terms "own" and "owned," when used with respect to any stock, means a person that individually or with or through any of its affiliates or associates:

(i)   Beneficially owns such stock, directly or indirectly; or

(ii) Has (A) the right to acquire such stock (whether such right is exercisable immediately or only after the passage of time) pursuant to any agreement, arrangement or understanding, or upon the exercise of conversion rights, exchange rights, warrants or options, or otherwise; provided, however, that a person shall not be deemed the owner of stock tendered pursuant to a tender or exchange offer made by such person or any of such person's affiliates or associates until such tendered stock is accepted for purchase or exchange; or (B) the right to vote such stock pursuant to any agreement, arrangement or understanding; provided, however, that a person shall not be deemed the owner of any stock because of such person's right to vote such stock if the agreement, arrangement or understanding to vote such stock arises solely from a revocable proxy or consent given in response to a proxy or consent solicitation made to 10 or more persons; or

(iii) Has any agreement, arrangement or understanding for the purpose of acquiring, holding, voting (except voting pursuant to a revocable proxy or consent as described in item (B) of subparagraph (ii) of this paragraph), or disposing of such stock with any other person that beneficially owns, or whose affiliates or associates beneficially own, directly or indirectly, such stock.

(d) No provision of a certificate of incorporation or bylaw shall require, for any vote of stockholders required by this section, a greater vote of stockholders than that specified in this section.

(e) The Court of Chancery is hereby vested with exclusive jurisdiction to hear and determine all matters with respect to this section.

§ 204. Ratification of defective corporate acts and stock. [For application of this section, see 80 Del. Laws, c. 40, § 16, and 81 Del. Laws, c. 354, § 16]

(a) Subject to subsection (f) of this section, no defective corporate act or putative stock shall be void or voidable solely as a result of a failure of authorization if ratified as provided in this section or validated by the Court of Chancery in a proceeding brought under § 205 of this title.

(b)(1) In order to ratify 1 or more defective corporate acts pursuant to this section (other than the ratification of an election of the initial board of directors pursuant to paragraph (b)(2) of this section), the board of directors of the corporation shall adopt resolutions stating:

(A) The defective corporate act or acts to be ratified;

(B) The date of each defective corporate act or acts;

(C) If such defective corporate act or acts involved the issuance of shares of putative stock, the number and type of shares of putative stock issued and the date or dates upon which such putative shares were purported to have been issued;

(D) The nature of the failure of authorization in respect of each defective corporate act to be ratified; and

(E) That the board of directors approves the ratification of the defective corporate act or acts.

Such resolutions may also provide that, at any time before the validation effective time in respect of any defective corporate act set forth therein, notwithstanding the approval of the ratification of such defective corporate act by stockholders, the board of directors may abandon the ratification of such defective corporate act without further action of the stockholders. The quorum and voting requirements applicable to the ratification by the board of directors of any defective corporate act shall be the quorum and voting requirements applicable to the type of defective corporate act proposed to be ratified at the time the board adopts the resolutions ratifying the defective corporate act; provided that if the certificate of incorporation or bylaws of the corporation, any plan or agreement to which the corporation was a party or any provision of this title, in each case as in effect as of the time of the defective corporate act, would have required a larger number or portion of directors or of specified directors for a quorum to be present or to approve the defective corporate act, such larger number or portion of such directors or such specified directors shall be required for a quorum to be present or to adopt the resolutions to ratify the defective corporate act, as applicable, except that the presence or approval of any director elected, appointed or nominated by holders of any class or series of which no shares are then outstanding, or by any person that is no longer a stockholder, shall not be required.

(2)   In order to ratify a defective corporate act in respect of the election of the initial board of directors of the corporation pursuant to § 108 of this title, a majority of the persons who, at the time the resolutions required by this paragraph (b)(2) of this section are adopted, are exercising the powers of directors under claim and color of an election or appointment as such may adopt resolutions stating:

(A)   The name of the person or persons who first took action in the name of the corporation as the initial board of directors of the corporation;

(B)   The earlier of the date on which such persons first took such action or were purported to have been elected as the initial board of directors; and

(C)   That the ratification of the election of such person or persons as the initial board of directors is approved.

(c)   Each defective corporate act ratified pursuant to paragraph (b)(1) of this section shall be submitted to stockholders for approval as provided in subsection (d) of this section, unless:

(1)(A)   No other provision of this title, and no provision of the certificate of incorporation or bylaws of the corporation, or of any plan or agreement to which the corporation is a party, would have required stockholder approval of such defective corporate act to be ratified, either at the time of such defective corporate act or at the time the board of directors adopts the resolutions ratifying such defective corporate act pursuant to paragraph (b)(1) of this section; and

(B)   Such defective corporate act did not result from a failure to comply with § 203 of this title; or

(2)   As of the record date for determining the stockholders entitled to vote on the ratification of such defective corporate act, there are no shares of valid stock outstanding and entitled to vote thereon, regardless of whether there then exist any shares of putative stock.

(d)   If the ratification of a defective corporate act is required to be submitted to stockholders for approval pursuant to subsection (c) of this section, due notice of the time, place, if any, and purpose of the meeting shall be given at least 20 days before the date of the meeting to each holder of valid stock and putative stock, whether voting or nonvoting, at the address of such holder as it appears or most recently appeared, as appropriate, on the records of the corporation. The notice shall also be given to the holders of record of valid stock and putative stock, whether voting or nonvoting, as of the time of the defective corporate act (or, in the case of any defective corporate act that involved the establishment of a record date for notice of or voting at any meeting of stockholders, for action by written consent of stockholders in lieu of a meeting, or for any other purpose, the record date for notice of or voting at such meeting, the record date for action by written consent, or the record date for such other action, as the case may be), other than holders whose identities or addresses cannot be determined from the records of the corporation. The notice shall contain a copy of the resolutions adopted by the board of directors pursuant to paragraph (b)(1) of this section or the information required by paragraphs (b)(1)(A) through (E) of this section and a statement that any claim that the defective corporate act or putative stock ratified hereunder is void or voidable due to the failure of authorization, or that the Court of Chancery should declare in its discretion that a ratification in accordance with this section not be effective or be effective only on certain conditions must be brought within 120 days from the applicable validation effective time. At such meeting, the quorum and voting requirements applicable to ratification of such defective corporate act shall be the quorum and voting requirements applicable to the type of defective corporate act proposed to be ratified at the time of the approval of the ratification, except that:

(1)   If the certificate of incorporation or bylaws of the corporation, any plan or agreement to which the corporation was a party or any provision of this title in effect as of the time of the defective corporate act would have required a larger number or portion of stock or of any class or series thereof or of specified stockholders for a quorum to be present or to approve the defective corporate act, the presence or approval of such larger number or portion of stock or of such class or series thereof or of such specified stockholders shall be required for a quorum to be present or to approve the ratification of the defective corporate act, as applicable, except that the presence or approval of shares of any class

or series of which no shares are then outstanding, or of any person that is no longer a stockholder, shall not be required;

    (2)   The approval by stockholders of the ratification of the election of a director shall require the affirmative vote of the majority of shares present at the meeting and entitled to vote on the election of such director, except that if the certificate of incorporation or bylaws of the corporation then in effect or in effect at the time of the defective election require or required a larger number or portion of stock or of any class or series thereof or of specified stockholders to elect such director, the affirmative vote of such larger number or portion of stock or of any class or series thereof or of such specified stockholders shall be required to ratify the election of such director, except that the presence or approval of shares of any class or series of which no shares are then outstanding, or of any person that is no longer a stockholder, shall not be required; and

    (3)   In the event of a failure of authorization resulting from failure to comply with the provisions of § 203 of this title, the ratification of the defective corporate act shall require the vote set forth in § 203(a)(3) of this title, regardless of whether such vote would have otherwise been required.

Shares of putative stock on the record date for determining stockholders entitled to vote on any matter submitted to stockholders pursuant to subsection (c) of this section (and without giving effect to any ratification that becomes effective after such record date) shall neither be entitled to vote nor counted for quorum purposes in any vote to ratify any defective corporate act.

    (e)   If a defective corporate act ratified pursuant to this section would have required under any other section of this title the filing of a certificate in accordance with § 103 of this title, then, whether or not a certificate was previously filed in respect of such defective corporate act and in lieu of filing the certificate otherwise required by this title, the corporation shall file a certificate of validation with respect to such defective corporate act in accordance with § 103 of this title. A separate certificate of validation shall be required for each defective corporate act requiring the filing of a certificate of validation under this section, except that (i) 2 or more defective corporate acts may be included in a single certificate of validation if the corporation filed, or to comply with this title would have filed, a single certificate under another provision of this title to effect such acts, and (ii) 2 or more overissues of shares of any class, classes or series of stock may be included in a single certificate of validation, provided that the increase in the number of authorized shares of each such class or series set forth in the certificate of validation shall be effective as of the date of the first such overissue. The certificate of validation shall set forth:

    (1)   Each defective corporate act that is the subject of the certificate of validation (including, in the case of any defective corporate act involving the issuance of shares of putative stock, the number and type of shares of putative stock issued and the date or dates upon which such putative shares were purported to have been issued), the date of such defective corporate act, and the nature of the failure of authorization in respect of such defective corporate act;

    (2)   A statement that such defective corporate act was ratified in accordance with this section, including the date on which the board of directors ratified such defective corporate act and the date, if any, on which the stockholders approved the ratification of such defective corporate act; and

    (3)   Information required by 1 of the following paragraphs:

    a.   If a certificate was previously filed under § 103 of this title in respect of such defective corporate act and no changes to such certificate are required to give effect to such defective corporate act in accordance with this section, the certificate of validation shall set forth (x) the name, title and filing date of the certificate previously filed and of any certificate of correction thereto and (y) a statement that a copy of the certificate previously filed, together with any certificate of correction thereto, is attached as an exhibit to the certificate of validation;

    b.   If a certificate was previously filed under § 103 of this title in respect of the defective corporate act and such certificate requires any change to give effect to the defective corporate act in accordance with this section (including a change to the date and time of the effectiveness of such certificate), the certificate of validation shall set forth (x) the name, title and filing date of the certificate so previously filed and of any certificate of correction thereto, (y) a statement that a certificate containing all of the information required to be included under the applicable section or sections of this title to give effect to the defective corporate act is attached as an exhibit to the certificate of validation, and (z) the date and time that such certificate shall be deemed to have become effective pursuant to this section; or

c. If a certificate was not previously filed under § 103 of this title in respect of the defective corporate act and the defective corporate act ratified pursuant to this section would have required under any other section of this title the filing of a certificate in accordance with § 103 of this title, the certificate of validation shall set forth (x) a statement that a certificate containing all of the information required to be included under the applicable section or sections of this title to give effect to the defective corporate act is attached as an exhibit to the certificate of validation, and (y) the date and time that such certificate shall be deemed to have become effective pursuant to this section.

A certificate attached to a certificate of validation pursuant to paragraph (e)(3)b. or c. of this section need not be separately executed and acknowledged and need not include any statement required by any other section of this title that such instrument has been approved and adopted in accordance with the provisions of such other section.

(f) From and after the validation effective time, unless otherwise determined in an action brought pursuant to § 205 of this title:

(1) Subject to the last sentence of subsection (d) of this section, each defective corporate act ratified in accordance with this section shall no longer be deemed void or voidable as a result of the failure of authorization described in the resolutions adopted pursuant to subsection (b) of this section and such effect shall be retroactive to the time of the defective corporate act; and

(2) Subject to the last sentence of subsection (d) of this section, each share or fraction of a share of putative stock issued or purportedly issued pursuant to any such defective corporate act shall no longer be deemed void or voidable and shall be deemed to be an identical share or fraction of a share of outstanding stock as of the time it was purportedly issued.

(g) In respect of each defective corporate act ratified by the board of directors pursuant to subsection (b) of this section, prompt notice of the ratification shall be given to all holders of valid stock and putative stock, whether voting or nonvoting, as of the date the board of directors adopts the resolutions approving such defective corporate act, or as of a date within 60 days after such date of adoption, as established by the board of directors, at the address of such holder as it appears or most recently appeared, as appropriate, on the records of the corporation. The notice shall also be given to the holders of record of valid stock and putative stock, whether voting or nonvoting, as of the time of the defective corporate act, other than holders whose identities or addresses cannot be determined from the records of the corporation. The notice shall contain a copy of the resolutions adopted pursuant to subsection (b) of this section or the information specified in paragraphs (b)(1)(A) through (E) or paragraphs (b)(2)(A) through (C) of this section, as applicable, and a statement that any claim that the defective corporate act or putative stock ratified hereunder is void or voidable due to the failure of authorization, or that the Court of Chancery should declare in its discretion that a ratification in accordance with this section not be effective or be effective only on certain conditions must be brought within 120 days from the later of the validation effective time or the time at which the notice required by this subsection is given. Notwithstanding the foregoing, (i) no such notice shall be required if notice of the ratification of the defective corporate act is to be given in accordance with subsection (d) of this section, and (ii) in the case of a corporation that has a class of stock listed on a national securities exchange, the notice required by this subsection and the second sentence of subsection (d) of this section may be deemed given if disclosed in a document publicly filed by the corporation with the Securities and Exchange Commission pursuant to § 13, § 14 or § 15(d) (15 U.S.C. § 78m, § 77n or § 78*o*(d)) of the Securities Exchange Act of 1934, as amended, and the rules and regulations promulgated thereunder, or the corresponding provisions of any subsequent United States federal securities laws, rules or regulations. If any defective corporate act has been approved by stockholders acting pursuant to § 228 of this title, the notice required by this subsection may be included in any notice required to be given pursuant to § 228(e) of this title and, if so given, shall be sent to the stockholders entitled thereto under § 228(e) and to all holders of valid and putative stock to whom notice would be required under this subsection if the defective corporate act had been approved at a meeting other than any stockholder who approved the action by consent in lieu of a meeting pursuant to § 228 of this title or any holder of putative stock who otherwise consented thereto in writing. Solely for purposes of subsection (d) of this section and this subsection, notice to holders of putative stock, and notice to holders of valid stock and putative stock as of the time of the defective corporate act, shall be treated as notice to holders of valid stock for purposes of §§ 222 and 228, 229, 230, 232 and 233 of this title.

(h) As used in this section and in § 205 of this title only, the term:

(1) "Defective corporate act" means an overissue, an election or appointment of directors that is void or voidable due to a failure of authorization, or any act or transaction purportedly taken by or on behalf of the corporation that is, and at the time such act or transaction was purportedly taken would have been, within the power of a corporation under subchapter II of this chapter (without regard to the failure of authorization identified in § 204(b)(1)(D) of this title), but is void or voidable due to a failure of authorization;

(2) "Failure of authorization" means: (i) the failure to authorize or effect an act or transaction in compliance with (A) the provisions of this title, (B) the certificate of incorporation or bylaws of the corporation, or (C) any plan or agreement to which the corporation is a party or the disclosure set forth in any proxy or consent solicitation statement, if and to the extent such failure would render such act or transaction void or voidable; or (ii) the failure of the board of directors or any officer of the corporation to authorize or approve any act or transaction taken by or on behalf of the corporation that would have required for its due authorization the approval of the board of directors or such officer;

(3) "Overissue" means the purported issuance of:

a. Shares of capital stock of a class or series in excess of the number of shares of such class or series the corporation has the power to issue under § 161 of this title at the time of such issuance; or

b. Shares of any class or series of capital stock that is not then authorized for issuance by the certificate of incorporation of the corporation;

(4) "Putative stock" means the shares of any class or series of capital stock of the corporation (including shares issued upon exercise of options, rights, warrants or other securities convertible into shares of capital stock of the corporation, or interests with respect thereto that were created or issued pursuant to a defective corporate act) that:

a. But for any failure of authorization, would constitute valid stock; or

b. Cannot be determined by the board of directors to be valid stock;

(5) "Time of the defective corporate act" means the date and time the defective corporate act was purported to have been taken;

(6) "Validation effective time" with respect to any defective corporate act ratified pursuant to this section means the latest of:

a. The time at which the defective corporate act submitted to the stockholders for approval pursuant to subsection (c) of this section is approved by such stockholders or if no such vote of stockholders is required to approve the ratification of the defective corporate act, the time at which the board of directors adopts the resolutions required by paragraph (b)(1) or (b)(2) of this section;

b. Where no certificate of validation is required to be filed pursuant to subsection (e) of this section, the time, if any, specified by the board of directors in the resolutions adopted pursuant to paragraph (b)(1) or (b)(2) of this section, which time shall not precede the time at which such resolutions are adopted; and

c. The time at which any certificate of validation filed pursuant to subsection (e) of this section shall become effective in accordance with § 103 of this title.

(7) "Valid stock" means the shares of any class or series of capital stock of the corporation that have been duly authorized and validly issued in accordance with this title.

In the absence of actual fraud in the transaction, the judgment of the board of directors that shares of stock are valid stock or putative stock shall be conclusive, unless otherwise determined by the Court of Chancery in a proceeding brought pursuant to § 205 of this title.

(i)   Ratification under this section or validation under § 205 of this title shall not be deemed to be the exclusive means of ratifying or validating any act or transaction taken by or on behalf of the corporation, including any defective corporate act, or any issuance of stock, including any putative stock, or of adopting or endorsing any act or transaction taken by or in the name of the corporation prior to the commencement of its existence, and the absence or failure of ratification in accordance with either this section or validation under § 205 of this title shall not, of itself, affect the validity or effectiveness of any act or transaction or the issuance of any stock properly ratified under common law or otherwise, nor shall it create a presumption that any such act or transaction is or was a defective corporate act or that such stock is void or voidable.

§ 205.   Proceedings regarding validity of defective corporate acts and stock. [For application of this section, see 80 Del. Laws, c. 40, § 16]

(a)   Subject to subsection (f) of this section, upon application by the corporation, any successor entity to the corporation, any member of the board of directors, any record or beneficial holder of valid stock or putative stock, any record or beneficial holder of valid or putative stock as of the time of a defective corporate act ratified pursuant to § 204 of this title, or any other person claiming to be substantially and adversely affected by a ratification pursuant to § 204 of this title, the Court of Chancery may:

(1)   Determine the validity and effectiveness of any defective corporate act ratified pursuant to § 204 of this title;

(2)   Determine the validity and effectiveness of the ratification of any defective corporate act pursuant to § 204 of this title;

(3)   Determine the validity and effectiveness of any defective corporate act not ratified or not ratified effectively pursuant to § 204 of this title;

(4)   Determine the validity of any corporate act or transaction and any stock, rights or options to acquire stock; and

(5)   Modify or waive any of the procedures set forth in § 204 of this title to ratify a defective corporate act.

(b)   In connection with an action under this section, the Court of Chancery may:

(1)   Declare that a ratification in accordance with and pursuant to § 204 of this title is not effective or shall only be effective at a time or upon conditions established by the Court;

(2)   Validate and declare effective any defective corporate act or putative stock and impose conditions upon such validation by the Court;

(3)   Require measures to remedy or avoid harm to any person substantially and adversely affected by a ratification pursuant to § 204 of this title or from any order of the Court pursuant to this section, excluding any harm that would have resulted if the defective corporate act had been valid when approved or effectuated;

(4)   Order the Secretary of State to accept an instrument for filing with an effective time specified by the Court, which effective time may be prior or subsequent to the time of such order, provided that the filing date of such instrument shall be determined in accordance with § 103(c)(3) of this title;

(5)   Approve a stock ledger for the corporation that includes any stock ratified or validated in accordance with this section or with § 204 of this title;

(6)   Declare that shares of putative stock are shares of valid stock or require a corporation to issue and deliver shares of valid stock in place of any shares of putative stock;

(7)   Order that a meeting of holders of valid stock or putative stock be held and exercise the powers provided to the Court under § 227 of this title with respect to such a meeting;

(8)   Declare that a defective corporate act validated by the Court shall be effective as of the time of the defective corporate act or at such other time as the Court shall determine;

(9)   Declare that putative stock validated by the Court shall be deemed to be an identical share or fraction of a share of valid stock as of the time originally issued or purportedly issued or at such other time as the Court shall determine; and

(10) Make such other orders regarding such matters as it deems proper under the circumstances.

(c)   Service of the application under subsection (a) of this section upon the registered agent of the corporation shall be deemed to be service upon the corporation, and no other party need be joined in order for the Court of Chancery to adjudicate the matter. In an action filed by the corporation, the Court may require notice of the action be provided to other persons specified by the Court and permit such other persons to intervene in the action.

(d)   In connection with the resolution of matters pursuant to subsections (a) and (b) of this section, the Court of Chancery may consider the following:

(1)   Whether the defective corporate act was originally approved or effectuated with the belief that the approval or effectuation was in compliance with the provisions of this title, the certificate of incorporation or bylaws of the corporation;

(2)   Whether the corporation and board of directors has treated the defective corporate act as a valid act or transaction and whether any person has acted in reliance on the public record that such defective corporate act was valid;

(3)   Whether any person will be or was harmed by the ratification or validation of the defective corporate act, excluding any harm that would have resulted if the defective corporate act had been valid when approved or effectuated;

(4)   Whether any person will be harmed by the failure to ratify or validate the defective corporate act; and

(5)   Any other factors or considerations the Court deems just and equitable.

(e)   The Court of Chancery is hereby vested with exclusive jurisdiction to hear and determine all actions brought under this section.

(f)   Notwithstanding any other provision of this section, no action asserting:

(1)   That a defective corporate act or putative stock ratified in accordance with § 204 of this title is void or voidable due to a failure of authorization identified in the resolution adopted in accordance with 204(b) of this title; or

(2)   That the Court of Chancery should declare in its discretion that a ratification in accordance with § 204 of this title not be effective or be effective only on certain conditions,

may be brought after the expiration of 120 days from the later of the validation effective time and the time notice, if any, that is required to be given pursuant to § 204(g) of this title is given with respect to such ratification, except that this subsection shall not apply to an action asserting that a ratification was not accomplished in accordance with § 204 of this title or to any person to whom notice of the ratification was required to have been given pursuant to § 204(d) or (g) of this title, but to whom such notice was not given.

SUBCHAPTER VII.   MEETINGS, ELECTIONS, VOTING AND NOTICE

§ 211.   Meetings of stockholders.

(a)(1)   Meetings of stockholders may be held at such place, either within or without this State as may be designated by or in the manner provided in the certificate of incorporation or bylaws, or if not so designated, as determined by the board of directors. If, pursuant to this paragraph or the certificate of incorporation or the bylaws of the corporation, the board of directors is authorized to determine the place of a meeting of stockholders, the board of directors may, in its sole discretion, determine that the meeting shall not be held at any place, but may instead be held solely by means of remote communication as authorized by paragraph (a)(2) of this section.

(2)　If authorized by the board of directors in its sole discretion, and subject to such guidelines and procedures as the board of directors may adopt, stockholders and proxyholders not physically present at a meeting of stockholders may, by means of remote communication:

a.　Participate in a meeting of stockholders; and

b.　Be deemed present in person and vote at a meeting of stockholders, whether such meeting is to be held at a designated place or solely by means of remote communication, provided that (i) the corporation shall implement reasonable measures to verify that each person deemed present and permitted to vote at the meeting by means of remote communication is a stockholder or proxyholder, (ii) the corporation shall implement reasonable measures to provide such stockholders and proxyholders a reasonable opportunity to participate in the meeting and to vote on matters submitted to the stockholders, including an opportunity to read or hear the proceedings of the meeting substantially concurrently with such proceedings, and (iii) if any stockholder or proxyholder votes or takes other action at the meeting by means of remote communication, a record of such vote or other action shall be maintained by the corporation.

(b)　Unless directors are elected by written consent in lieu of an annual meeting as permitted by this subsection, an annual meeting of stockholders shall be held for the election of directors on a date and at a time designated by or in the manner provided in the bylaws. Stockholders may, unless the certificate of incorporation otherwise provides, act by written consent to elect directors; provided, however, that, if such consent is less than unanimous, such action by written consent may be in lieu of holding an annual meeting only if all of the directorships to which directors could be elected at an annual meeting held at the effective time of such action are vacant and are filled by such action. Any other proper business may be transacted at the annual meeting.

(c)　A failure to hold the annual meeting at the designated time or to elect a sufficient number of directors to conduct the business of the corporation shall not affect otherwise valid corporate acts or work a forfeiture or dissolution of the corporation except as may be otherwise specifically provided in this chapter. If the annual meeting for election of directors is not held on the date designated therefor or action by written consent to elect directors in lieu of an annual meeting has not been taken, the directors shall cause the meeting to be held as soon as is convenient. If there be a failure to hold the annual meeting or to take action by written consent to elect directors in lieu of an annual meeting for a period of 30 days after the date designated for the annual meeting, or if no date has been designated, for a period of 13 months after the latest to occur of the organization of the corporation, its last annual meeting or the last action by written consent to elect directors in lieu of an annual meeting, the Court of Chancery may summarily order a meeting to be held upon the application of any stockholder or director. The shares of stock represented at such meeting, either in person or by proxy, and entitled to vote thereat, shall constitute a quorum for the purpose of such meeting, notwithstanding any provision of the certificate of incorporation or bylaws to the contrary. The Court of Chancery may issue such orders as may be appropriate, including, without limitation, orders designating the time and place of such meeting, the record date or dates for determination of stockholders entitled to notice of the meeting and to vote thereat, and the form of notice of such meeting.

(d)　Special meetings of the stockholders may be called by the board of directors or by such person or persons as may be authorized by the certificate of incorporation or by the bylaws.

(e)　All elections of directors shall be by written ballot unless otherwise provided in the certificate of incorporation; if authorized by the board of directors, such requirement of a written ballot shall be satisfied by a ballot submitted by electronic transmission, provided that any such electronic transmission must either set forth or be submitted with information from which it can be determined that the electronic transmission was authorized by the stockholder or proxy holder.

§ 212.　Voting rights of stockholders; proxies; limitations.

(a)　Unless otherwise provided in the certificate of incorporation and subject to § 213 of this title, each stockholder shall be entitled to 1 vote for each share of capital stock held by such stockholder. If the certificate of incorporation provides for more or less than 1 vote for any share, on any matter, every reference in this chapter to a majority or other proportion of stock, voting stock or shares shall refer to such majority or other proportion of the votes of such stock, voting stock or shares.

(b)   Each stockholder entitled to vote at a meeting of stockholders or to express consent or dissent to corporate action in writing without a meeting may authorize another person or persons to act for such stockholder by proxy, but no such proxy shall be voted or acted upon after 3 years from its date, unless the proxy provides for a longer period.

(c)   Without limiting the manner in which a stockholder may authorize another person or persons to act for such stockholder as proxy pursuant to subsection (b) of this section, the following shall constitute a valid means by which a stockholder may grant such authority:

(1)   A stockholder may execute a document authorizing another person or persons to act for such stockholder as proxy. Execution may be accomplished by the stockholder or such stockholder's authorized officer, director, employee or agent.

(2)   A stockholder may authorize another person or persons to act for such stockholder as proxy by transmitting or authorizing the transmission of an electronic transmission to the person who will be the holder of the proxy or to a proxy solicitation firm, proxy support service organization or like agent duly authorized by the person who will be the holder of the proxy to receive such transmission, provided that any such transmission must either set forth or be submitted with information from which it can be determined that the transmission was authorized by the stockholder. If it is determined that such transmissions are valid, the inspectors or, if there are no inspectors, such other persons making that determination shall specify the information upon which they relied.

(d)   Any copy, facsimile telecommunication or other reliable reproduction of the document (including any electronic transmission) created pursuant to subsection (c) of this section may be substituted or used in lieu of the original document for any and all purposes for which the original document could be used, provided that such copy, facsimile telecommunication or other reproduction shall be a complete reproduction of the entire original document.

(e)   A duly executed proxy shall be irrevocable if it states that it is irrevocable and if, and only as long as, it is coupled with an interest sufficient in law to support an irrevocable power. A proxy may be made irrevocable regardless of whether the interest with which it is coupled is an interest in the stock itself or an interest in the corporation generally.

§ 213.   Fixing date for determination of stockholders of record.

(a)   In order that the corporation may determine the stockholders entitled to notice of any meeting of stockholders or any adjournment thereof, the board of directors may fix a record date, which record date shall not precede the date upon which the resolution fixing the record date is adopted by the board of directors, and which record date shall not be more than 60 nor less than 10 days before the date of such meeting. If the board of directors so fixes a date, such date shall also be the record date for determining the stockholders entitled to vote at such meeting unless the board of directors determines, at the time it fixes such record date, that a later date on or before the date of the meeting shall be the date for making such determination. If no record date is fixed by the board of directors, the record date for determining stockholders entitled to notice of and to vote at a meeting of stockholders shall be at the close of business on the day next preceding the day on which notice is given, or, if notice is waived, at the close of business on the day next preceding the day on which the meeting is held. A determination of stockholders of record entitled to notice of or to vote at a meeting of stockholders shall apply to any adjournment of the meeting; provided, however, that the board of directors may fix a new record date for determination of stockholders entitled to vote at the adjourned meeting, and in such case shall also fix as the record date for stockholders entitled to notice of such adjourned meeting the same or an earlier date as that fixed for determination of stockholders entitled to vote in accordance with the foregoing provisions of this subsection (a) at the adjourned meeting.

(b)   In order that the corporation may determine the stockholders entitled to consent to corporate action in writing without a meeting, the board of directors may fix a record date, which record date shall not precede the date upon which the resolution fixing the record date is adopted by the board of directors, and which date shall not be more than 10 days after the date upon which the resolution fixing the record date is adopted by the board of directors. If no record date has been fixed by the board of directors, the record date for determining stockholders entitled to consent to corporate action in writing without a meeting, when no prior action by the board of directors is required by this chapter, shall be the first date on which a signed written consent setting forth the action taken or proposed to be taken is delivered to the corporation by delivery to its registered office in this State, its principal place of business or an officer or agent of the corporation having custody of the book in which proceedings of meetings of stockholders are recorded. Delivery made to a corporation's registered office shall be by hand or by certified or registered mail, return receipt requested. If no record date has been fixed by the board of directors and prior action by the board of directors is required by this chapter, the record date for determining stockholders entitled to consent to corporate action in writing without a meeting shall be at the close of business on the day on which the board of directors adopts the resolution taking such prior action.

(c)   In order that the corporation may determine the stockholders entitled to receive payment of any dividend or other distribution or allotment of any rights or the stockholders entitled to exercise any rights in respect of any change, conversion or exchange of stock, or for the purpose of any other lawful action, the board of directors may fix a record date, which record date shall not precede the date upon which the resolution fixing the record date is adopted, and which record date shall be not more than 60 days prior to such action. If no record date is fixed, the record date for determining stockholders for any such purpose shall be at the close of business on the day on which the board of directors adopts the resolution relating thereto.

§ 214.   Cumulative voting.

The certificate of incorporation of any corporation may provide that at all elections of directors of the corporation, or at elections held under specified circumstances, each holder of stock or of any class or classes or of a series or series thereof shall be entitled to as many votes as shall equal the number of votes which (except for such provision as to cumulative voting) such holder would be entitled to cast for the election of directors with respect to such holder's shares of stock multiplied by the number of directors to be elected by such holder, and that such holder may cast all of such votes for a single director or may distribute them among the number to be voted for, or for any 2 or more of them as such holder may see fit.

§ 215.   Voting rights of members of nonstock corporations; quorum; proxies.

(a)   Sections 211 through 214 and 216 of this title shall not apply to nonstock corporations, except that § 211(a) and (d) of this title and § 212(c), (d), and (e) of this title shall apply to such corporations, and, when so applied, all references therein to stockholders and to the board of directors shall be deemed to refer to the members and the governing body of a nonstock corporation, respectively; and all references to stock, capital stock, or shares thereof shall be deemed to refer to memberships of a nonprofit nonstock corporation and to membership interests of any other nonstock corporation.

(b)   Unless otherwise provided in the certificate of incorporation or the bylaws of a nonstock corporation, and subject to subsection (f) of this section, each member shall be entitled at every meeting of members to 1 vote on each matter submitted to a vote of members. A member may exercise such voting rights in person or by proxy, but no proxy shall be voted on after 3 years from its date, unless the proxy provides for a longer period.

(c)   Unless otherwise provided in this chapter, the certificate of incorporation or bylaws of a nonstock corporation may specify the number of members having voting power who shall be present or represented by proxy at any meeting in order to constitute a quorum for, and the votes that shall be necessary for, the transaction of any business. In the absence of such specification in the certificate of incorporation or bylaws of a nonstock corporation:

(1)   One-third of the members of such corporation shall constitute a quorum at a meeting of such members;

(2)   In all matters other than the election of the governing body of such corporation, the affirmative vote of a majority of such members present in person or represented by proxy at the meeting and entitled to vote on the subject matter shall be the act of the members, unless the vote of a greater number is required by this chapter;

(3)   Members of the governing body shall be elected by a plurality of the votes of the members of the corporation present in person or represented by proxy at the meeting and entitled to vote thereon; and

(4)   Where a separate vote by a class or group or classes or groups is required, a majority of the members of such class or group or classes or groups, present in person or represented by proxy, shall constitute a quorum entitled to take action with respect to that vote on that matter and, in all matters other than the election of members of the governing body, the affirmative vote of the majority of the members of such class or group or classes or groups present in person or represented by proxy at the meeting shall be the act of such class or group or classes or groups.

(d)   If the election of the governing body of any nonstock corporation shall not be held on the day designated by the bylaws, the governing body shall cause the election to be held as soon thereafter as convenient. The failure to hold such an election at the designated time shall not work any forfeiture or dissolution of the corporation, but the Court of Chancery may summarily order such an election to be held upon the application of any member of the corporation. At any election pursuant to such order the persons entitled to vote in such election who shall be present at such meeting, either in person or by proxy, shall constitute a quorum for such meeting, notwithstanding any provision of the certificate of incorporation or the bylaws of the corporation to the contrary.

(e)   If authorized by the governing body, any requirement of a written ballot shall be satisfied by a ballot submitted by electronic transmission, provided that any such electronic transmission must either set forth or be submitted with information from which it can be determined that the electronic transmission was authorized by the member or proxy holder.

(f)   Except as otherwise provided in the certificate of incorporation, in the bylaws, or by resolution of the governing body, the record date for any meeting or corporate action shall be deemed to be the date of such meeting or corporate action; provided, however, that no record date may precede any action by the governing body fixing such record date.

§ 216.   Quorum and required vote for stock corporations.

Subject to this chapter in respect of the vote that shall be required for a specified action, the certificate of incorporation or bylaws of any corporation authorized to issue stock may specify the number of shares and/or the amount of other securities having voting power the holders of which shall be present or represented by proxy at any meeting in order to constitute a quorum for, and the votes that shall be necessary for, the transaction of any business, but in no event shall a quorum consist of less than 1/3 of the shares entitled to vote at the meeting, except that, where a separate vote by a class or series or classes or series is required, a quorum shall consist of no less than 1/3 of the shares of such class or series or classes or series. In the absence of such specification in the certificate of incorporation or bylaws of the corporation:

(1)   A majority of the shares entitled to vote, present in person or represented by proxy, shall constitute a quorum at a meeting of stockholders;

(2)   In all matters other than the election of directors, the affirmative vote of the majority of shares present in person or represented by proxy at the meeting and entitled to vote on the subject matter shall be the act of the stockholders;

(3)   Directors shall be elected by a plurality of the votes of the shares present in person or represented by proxy at the meeting and entitled to vote on the election of directors; and

(4)   Where a separate vote by a class or series or classes or series is required, a majority of the outstanding shares of such class or series or classes or series, present in person or represented by proxy, shall constitute a quorum entitled to take action with respect to that vote on that matter and, in all matters other than the election of directors, the affirmative vote of the majority of shares of such class or series or classes or series present in person or represented by proxy at the meeting shall be the act of such class or series or classes or series.

A bylaw amendment adopted by stockholders which specifies the votes that shall be necessary for the election of directors shall not be further amended or repealed by the board of directors.

§ 217.   Voting rights of fiduciaries, pledgors and joint owners of stock.

(a)   Persons holding stock in a fiduciary capacity shall be entitled to vote the shares so held. Persons whose stock is pledged shall be entitled to vote, unless in the transfer by the pledgor on the books of the corporation such person has expressly empowered the pledgee to vote thereon, in which case only the pledgee, or such pledgee's proxy, may represent such stock and vote thereon.

(b)   If shares or other securities having voting power stand of record in the names of 2 or more persons, whether fiduciaries, members of a partnership, joint tenants, tenants in common, tenants by the entirety or otherwise, or if 2 or more persons have the same fiduciary relationship respecting the same shares, unless the secretary of the corporation is given written notice to the contrary and is furnished with a copy of the instrument or order appointing them or creating the relationship wherein it is so provided, their acts with respect to voting shall have the following effect:

(1)   If only 1 votes, such person's act binds all;

(2)   If more than 1 vote, the act of the majority so voting binds all;

(3)   If more than 1 vote, but the vote is evenly split on any particular matter, each faction may vote the securities in question proportionally, or any person voting the shares, or a beneficiary, if any, may apply to the Court of Chancery or such other court as may have jurisdiction to appoint an additional person to act with the persons so voting the shares, which shall then be voted as determined by a majority of such persons and the person appointed by the Court. If the instrument so filed shows that any such tenancy is held in unequal interests, a majority or even split for the purpose of this subsection shall be a majority or even split in interest.

§ 218.   Voting trusts and other voting agreements.

(a)   One stockholder or 2 or more stockholders may by agreement in writing deposit capital stock of an original issue with or transfer capital stock to any person or persons, or entity or entities authorized to act as trustee, for the purpose of vesting in such person or persons, entity or entities, who may be designated voting trustee, or voting trustees, the right to vote thereon for any period of time determined by such agreement, upon the terms and conditions stated in such agreement. The agreement may contain any other lawful provisions not inconsistent with such purpose. After delivery of a copy of the agreement to the registered office of the corporation in this State or the principal place of business of the corporation, which copy shall be open to the inspection of any stockholder of the corporation or any beneficiary of the trust under the agreement daily during business hours, certificates of stock or uncertificated stock shall be issued to the voting trustee or trustees to represent any stock of an original issue so deposited with such voting trustee or trustees, and any certificates of stock or uncertificated stock so transferred to the voting trustee or trustees shall be surrendered and cancelled and new certificates or uncertificated stock shall be issued therefore to the voting trustee or trustees. In the certificate so issued, if any, it shall be stated that it is issued pursuant to such agreement, and that fact shall also be stated in the stock ledger of the corporation. The voting trustee or trustees may vote the stock so issued or transferred during the period specified in the agreement. Stock standing in the name of the voting trustee or trustees may be voted either in person or by proxy, and in voting the stock, the voting trustee or trustees shall incur no responsibility as stockholder, trustee or otherwise, except for their own individual malfeasance. In any case where 2 or more persons or entities are designated as voting trustees, and the right and method of voting any stock standing in their names at any meeting of the corporation are not fixed by the agreement appointing the trustees, the right to vote the stock and the manner of voting it at the meeting shall be determined by a majority of the trustees, or if they be equally divided as to the right and manner of voting the stock in any particular case, the vote of the stock in such case shall be divided equally among the trustees.

(b)   Any amendment to a voting trust agreement shall be made by a written agreement, a copy of which shall be delivered to the registered office of the corporation in this State or principal place of business of the corporation.

(c)   An agreement between 2 or more stockholders, if in writing and signed by the parties thereto, may provide that in exercising any voting rights, the shares held by them shall be voted as provided by the agreement, or as the parties may agree, or as determined in accordance with a procedure agreed upon by them.

(d)   This section shall not be deemed to invalidate any voting or other agreement among stockholders or any irrevocable proxy which is not otherwise illegal.

§ 219.   List of stockholders entitled to vote; penalty for refusal to produce; stock ledger.

(a)   The corporation shall prepare, at least 10 days before every meeting of stockholders, a complete list of the stockholders entitled to vote at the meeting; provided, however, if the record date for determining the stockholders entitled to vote is less than 10 days before the meeting date, the list shall reflect the stockholders entitled to vote as of the tenth day before the meeting date, arranged in alphabetical order, and showing the address of each stockholder and the number of shares registered in the name of each stockholder. Nothing contained in this section shall require the corporation to include electronic mail addresses or other electronic contact information on such list. Such list shall be open to the examination of any stockholder for any purpose germane to the meeting for a period of at least 10 days prior to the meeting: (i) on a reasonably accessible electronic network, provided that the information required to gain access to such list is provided with the notice of the meeting, or (ii) during ordinary business hours, at the principal place of business of the corporation. In the event that the corporation determines to make the list available on an electronic network, the corporation may take reasonable steps to ensure that such information is available only to stockholders of the corporation. If the meeting is to be held at a place, then a list of stockholders entitled to vote at the meeting shall be produced and kept at the time and place of the meeting during the whole time thereof and may be examined by any stockholder who is present. If the meeting is to be held solely by means of remote communication, then such list shall also be open to the examination of any stockholder during the whole time of the meeting on a reasonably accessible electronic network, and the information required to access such list shall be provided with the notice of the meeting.

(b)   If the corporation, or an officer or agent thereof, refuses to permit examination of the list by a stockholder, such stockholder may apply to the Court of Chancery for an order to compel the corporation to permit such examination. The burden of proof shall be on the corporation to establish that the examination such stockholder seeks is for a purpose not germane to the meeting. The Court may summarily order the corporation to permit examination of the list upon such conditions as the Court may deem appropriate, and may make such additional orders as may be appropriate, including, without limitation, postponing the meeting or voiding the results of the meeting.

(c)   For purposes of this chapter, "stock ledger" means 1 or more records administered by or on behalf of the corporation in which the names of all of the corporation's stockholders of record, the address and number of shares registered in the name of each such stockholder, and all issuances and transfers of stock of the corporation are recorded in accordance with § 224 of this title. The stock ledger shall be the only evidence as to who are the stockholders entitled by this section to examine the list required by this section or to vote in person or by proxy at any meeting of stockholders.

§ 220.   Inspection of books and records.

(a)   As used in this section:

(1)   "Stockholder" means a holder of record of stock in a stock corporation, or a person who is the beneficial owner of shares of such stock held either in a voting trust or by a nominee on behalf of such person.

(2)   "Subsidiary" means any entity directly or indirectly owned, in whole or in part, by the corporation of which the stockholder is a stockholder and over the affairs of which the corporation directly or indirectly exercises control, and includes, without limitation, corporations, partnerships, limited partnerships, limited liability partnerships, limited liability companies, statutory trusts and/or joint ventures.

(3)   "Under oath" includes statements the declarant affirms to be true under penalty of perjury under the laws of the United States or any state.

(b)   Any stockholder, in person or by attorney or other agent, shall, upon written demand under oath stating the purpose thereof, have the right during the usual hours for business to inspect for any proper purpose, and to make copies and extracts from:

(1)   The corporation's stock ledger, a list of its stockholders, and its other books and records; and

(2)   A subsidiary's books and records, to the extent that:

a.   The corporation has actual possession and control of such records of such subsidiary; or

b.   The corporation could obtain such records through the exercise of control over such subsidiary, provided that as of the date of the making of the demand:

1.   The stockholder inspection of such books and records of the subsidiary would not constitute a breach of an agreement between the corporation or the subsidiary and a person or persons not affiliated with the corporation; and

2.   The subsidiary would not have the right under the law applicable to it to deny the corporation access to such books and records upon demand by the corporation.

In every instance where the stockholder is other than a record holder of stock in a stock corporation, or a member of a nonstock corporation, the demand under oath shall state the person's status as a stockholder, be accompanied by documentary evidence of beneficial ownership of the stock, and state that such documentary evidence is a true and correct copy of what it purports to be. A proper purpose shall mean a purpose reasonably related to such person's interest as a stockholder. In every instance where an attorney or other agent shall be the person who seeks the right to inspection, the demand under oath shall be accompanied by a power of attorney or such other writing which authorizes the attorney or other agent to so act on behalf of the stockholder. The demand under oath shall be directed to the corporation at its registered office in this State or at its principal place of business.

(c)   If the corporation, or an officer or agent thereof, refuses to permit an inspection sought by a stockholder or attorney or other agent acting for the stockholder pursuant to subsection (b) of this section or does not reply to the demand within 5 business days after the demand has been made, the stockholder may apply to the Court of Chancery for an order to compel such inspection. The Court of Chancery is hereby vested with exclusive jurisdiction to determine whether or not the person seeking inspection is entitled to the inspection sought. The Court may summarily order the corporation to permit the stockholder to inspect the corporation's stock ledger, an existing list of stockholders, and its other books and records, and to make copies or extracts therefrom; or the Court may order the corporation to furnish to the stockholder a list of its stockholders as of a specific date on condition that the stockholder first pay to the corporation the reasonable cost of obtaining and furnishing such list and on such other conditions as the Court deems appropriate. Where the stockholder seeks to inspect the corporation's books and records, other than its stock ledger or list of stockholders, such stockholder shall first establish that:

(1)   Such stockholder is a stockholder;

(2)   Such stockholder has complied with this section respecting the form and manner of making demand for inspection of such documents; and

(3)   The inspection such stockholder seeks is for a proper purpose.

Where the stockholder seeks to inspect the corporation's stock ledger or list of stockholders and establishes that such stockholder is a stockholder and has complied with this section respecting the form and manner of making demand for inspection of such documents, the burden of proof shall be upon the corporation to establish that the inspection such stockholder seeks is for an improper purpose. The Court may, in its discretion, prescribe any limitations or conditions with reference to the inspection, or award such other or further relief as the Court may deem just and proper. The Court may order books, documents and records, pertinent extracts therefrom, or duly authenticated copies thereof, to be brought within this State and kept in this State upon such terms and conditions as the order may prescribe.

(d)   Any director shall have the right to examine the corporation's stock ledger, a list of its stockholders and its other books and records for a purpose reasonably related to the director's position as a director. The Court of Chancery is hereby vested with the exclusive jurisdiction to determine whether a director is entitled to the inspection sought. The Court may summarily order the corporation to permit the director to inspect any and all books and records, the stock ledger and the list of stockholders and to make copies or extracts therefrom. The burden of proof shall be upon the corporation to establish that the inspection such director seeks is for an improper purpose. The Court may, in its discretion, prescribe any limitations or conditions with reference to the inspection, or award such other and further relief as the Court may deem just and proper.

§ 221.   Voting, inspection and other rights of bondholders and debenture holders.

Every corporation may in its certificate of incorporation confer upon the holders of any bonds, debentures or other obligations issued or to be issued by the corporation the power to vote in respect to the corporate affairs and management of the corporation to the extent and in the manner provided in the certificate of incorporation and may confer upon such holders of bonds, debentures or other obligations the same right of inspection of its books, accounts and other records, and also any other rights, which the stockholders of the corporation have or may have by reason of this chapter or of its certificate of incorporation. If the certificate of incorporation so provides, such holders of bonds, debentures or other obligations shall be deemed to be stockholders, and their bonds, debentures or other obligations shall be deemed to be shares of stock, for the purpose of any provision of this chapter which requires the vote of stockholders as a prerequisite to any corporate action and the certificate of incorporation may divest the holders of capital stock, in whole or in part, of their right to vote on any corporate matter whatsoever, except as set forth in § 242(b)(2) of this title.

§ 222.   Notice of meetings and adjourned meetings.

(a)   Whenever stockholders are required or permitted to take any action at a meeting, a notice of the meeting in the form of a writing or electronic transmission shall be given which shall state the place, if any, date and hour of the meeting, the means of remote communications, if any, by which stockholders and proxy holders may be deemed to be present in person and vote at such meeting, the record date for determining the stockholders entitled to vote at the meeting, if such date is different from the record date for determining stockholders entitled to notice of the meeting, and, in the case of a special meeting, the purpose or purposes for which the meeting is called.

(b)   Unless otherwise provided in this chapter, the notice of any meeting shall be given not less than 10 nor more than 60 days before the date of the meeting to each stockholder entitled to vote at such meeting as of the record date for determining the stockholders entitled to notice of the meeting.

(c)   When a meeting is adjourned to another time or place, unless the bylaws otherwise require, notice need not be given of the adjourned meeting if the time, place, if any, thereof, and the means of remote communications, if any, by which stockholders and proxy holders may be deemed to be present in person and vote at such adjourned meeting are announced at the meeting at which the adjournment is taken. At the adjourned meeting the corporation may transact any business which might have been transacted at the original meeting. If the adjournment is for more than 30 days, a notice of the adjourned meeting shall be given to each stockholder of record entitled to vote at the meeting. If after the adjournment a new record date for stockholders entitled to vote is fixed for the adjourned meeting, the board of directors shall fix a new record date for notice of such adjourned meeting in accordance with § 213(a) of this title, and shall give notice of the adjourned meeting to each stockholder of record entitled to vote at such adjourned meeting as of the record date fixed for notice of such adjourned meeting.

§ 223.   Vacancies and newly created directorships.

(a)   Unless otherwise provided in the certificate of incorporation or bylaws:

     (1)   Vacancies and newly created directorships resulting from any increase in the authorized number of directors elected by all of the stockholders having the right to vote as a single class may be filled by a majority of the directors then in office, although less than a quorum, or by a sole remaining director;

     (2)   Whenever the holders of any class or classes of stock or series thereof are entitled to elect 1 or more directors by the certificate of incorporation, vacancies and newly created directorships of such class or classes or series may be filled by a majority of the directors elected by such class or classes or series thereof then in office, or by a sole remaining director so elected.

If at any time, by reason of death or resignation or other cause, a corporation should have no directors in office, then any officer or any stockholder or an executor, administrator, trustee or guardian of a stockholder, or other fiduciary entrusted with like responsibility for the person or estate of a stockholder, may call a special meeting of stockholders in accordance with the certificate of incorporation or the bylaws, or may apply to the Court of Chancery for a decree summarily ordering an election as provided in § 211 or § 215 of this title.

(b)   In the case of a corporation the directors of which are divided into classes, any directors chosen under subsection (a) of this section shall hold office until the next election of the class for which such directors shall have been chosen, and until their successors shall be elected and qualified.

(c)   If, at the time of filling any vacancy or any newly created directorship, the directors then in office shall constitute less than a majority of the whole board (as constituted immediately prior to any such increase), the Court of Chancery may, upon application of any stockholder or stockholders holding at least 10 percent of the voting stock at the time outstanding having the right to vote for such directors, summarily order an election to be held to fill any such vacancies or newly created directorships, or to replace the directors chosen by the directors then in office as aforesaid, which election shall be governed by § 211 or § 215 of this title as far as applicable.

(d)   Unless otherwise provided in the certificate of incorporation or bylaws, when 1 or more directors shall resign from the board, effective at a future date, a majority of the directors then in office, including those who have so resigned, shall have power to fill such vacancy or vacancies, the vote thereon to take effect when such resignation or resignations shall become effective, and each director so chosen shall hold office as provided in this section in the filling of other vacancies.

§ 224.   Form of records.

Any records administered by or on behalf of the corporation in the regular course of its business, including its stock ledger, books of account, and minute books, may be kept on, or by means of, or be in the form of, any information storage device, method, or 1 or more electronic networks or databases (including 1 or more distributed electronic networks or databases), provided that the records so kept can be converted into clearly legible paper form within a reasonable time, and, with respect to the stock ledger, that the records so kept (i) can be used to prepare the list of stockholders specified in §§ 219 and 220 of this title, (ii) record the information specified in §§ 156, 159, 217(a) and 218 of this title, and (iii) record transfers of stock as governed by Article 8 of subtitle I of Title 6. Any corporation shall convert any records so kept into clearly legible paper form upon the request of any person entitled to inspect such records pursuant to any provision of this chapter. When records are kept in such manner, a clearly legible paper form prepared from or by means of the information storage device, method, or 1 or more electronic networks or databases (including 1 or more distributed electronic networks or databases) shall be valid and admissible in evidence, and accepted for all other purposes, to the same extent as an original paper record of the same information would have been, provided the paper form accurately portrays the record.

§ 225.   Contested election of directors; proceedings to determine validity.

(a)   Upon application of any stockholder or director, or any officer whose title to office is contested, the Court of Chancery may hear and determine the validity of any election, appointment, removal or resignation of any director or officer of any corporation, and the right of any person to hold or continue to hold such office, and, in case any such office is claimed by more than 1 person, may determine the person entitled thereto; and to that end make such order or decree in any such case as may be just and proper, with power to enforce the production of any books, papers and records of the corporation relating to the issue. In case it should be determined that no valid election has been held, the Court of Chancery may order an election to be held in accordance with § 211 or § 215 of this title. In any such application, service of copies of the application upon the registered agent of the corporation shall be deemed to be service upon the corporation and upon the person whose title to office is contested and upon the person, if any, claiming such office; and the registered agent shall forward immediately a copy of the application to the corporation and to the person whose title to office is contested and to the person, if any, claiming such office, in a postpaid, sealed, registered letter addressed to such corporation and such person at their post-office addresses last known to the registered agent or furnished to the registered agent by the applicant stockholder. The Court may make such order respecting further or other notice of such application as it deems proper under the circumstances.

(b)   Upon application of any stockholder or upon application of the corporation itself, the Court of Chancery may hear and determine the result of any vote of stockholders upon matters other than the election of directors or officers. Service of the application upon the registered agent of the corporation shall be deemed to be service upon the corporation, and no other party need be joined in order for the Court to adjudicate the result of the vote. The Court may make such order respecting notice of the application as it deems proper under the circumstances.

(c)   If 1 or more directors has been convicted of a felony in connection with the duties of such director or directors to the corporation, or if there has been a prior judgment on the merits by a court of competent jurisdiction that 1 or more directors has committed a breach of the duty of loyalty in connection with the duties of such director or directors to that corporation, then, upon application by the corporation, or derivatively in the right of the corporation by any stockholder, in a subsequent action brought for such purpose, the Court of Chancery may remove from office such director or directors if the Court determines that the director or directors did not act in good faith in performing the acts resulting in the prior conviction or judgment and judicial removal is necessary to avoid irreparable harm to the corporation. In connection with such removal, the Court may make such orders as are necessary to effect such removal. In any such application, service of copies of the application upon the registered agent of the corporation shall be deemed to be service upon the corporation and upon the director or directors whose removal is sought; and the registered agent shall forward immediately a copy of the application to the corporation and to such director or directors, in a postpaid, sealed, registered letter addressed to such corporation and such director or directors at their post office addresses last known to the registered agent or furnished to the registered agent by the applicant. The Court may make such order respecting further or other notice of such application as it deems proper under the circumstances.

§ 226.   Appointment of custodian or receiver of corporation on deadlock or for other cause.

(a)   The Court of Chancery, upon application of any stockholder, may appoint 1 or more persons to be custodians, and, if the corporation is insolvent, to be receivers, of and for any corporation when:

(1)   At any meeting held for the election of directors the stockholders are so divided that they have failed to elect successors to directors whose terms have expired or would have expired upon qualification of their successors; or

(2)   The business of the corporation is suffering or is threatened with irreparable injury because the directors are so divided respecting the management of the affairs of the corporation that the required vote for action by the board of directors cannot be obtained and the stockholders are unable to terminate this division; or

(3)   The corporation has abandoned its business and has failed within a reasonable time to take steps to dissolve, liquidate or distribute its assets.

(b)   A custodian appointed under this section shall have all the powers and title of a receiver appointed under § 291 of this title, but the authority of the custodian is to continue the business of the corporation and not to liquidate its affairs and distribute its assets, except when the Court shall otherwise order and except in cases arising under paragraph (a)(3) of this section or § 352(a)(2) of this title.

(c)   In the case of a charitable nonstock corporation, the applicant shall provide a copy of any application referred to in subsection (a) of this section to the Attorney General of the State of Delaware within 1 week of its filing with the Court of Chancery.

§ 227.   Powers of Court in elections of directors.

(a)   The Court of Chancery, in any proceeding instituted under § 211, § 215 or § 225 of this title may determine the right and power of persons claiming to own stock to vote at any meeting of the stockholders.

(b)   The Court of Chancery may appoint a Master to hold any election provided for in § 211, § 215 or § 225 of this title under such orders and powers as it deems proper; and it may punish any officer or director for contempt in case of disobedience of any order made by the Court; and, in case of disobedience by a corporation of any order made by the Court, may enter a decree against such corporation for a penalty of not more than $5,000.

§ 228.   **Consent of stockholders or members in lieu of meeting [for application of section, see 81 Del. Laws, c. 86, § 40].**

(a)   Unless otherwise provided in the certificate of incorporation, any action required by this chapter to be taken at any annual or special meeting of stockholders of a corporation, or any action which may be taken at any annual or special meeting of such stockholders, may be taken without a meeting, without prior notice and without a vote, if a consent or consents in writing, setting forth the action so taken, shall be signed by the holders of outstanding stock having not less than the minimum number of votes that would be necessary to authorize or take such action at a meeting at which all shares entitled to vote thereon were present and voted and shall be delivered to the corporation by delivery to its registered office in this State, its principal place of business or an officer or agent of the corporation having custody of the book in which proceedings of meetings of stockholders are recorded. Delivery made to a corporation's registered office shall be by hand or by certified or registered mail, return receipt requested.

(b)   Unless otherwise provided in the certificate of incorporation, any action required by this chapter to be taken at a meeting of the members of a nonstock corporation, or any action which may be taken at any meeting of the members of a nonstock corporation, may be taken without a meeting, without prior notice and without a vote, if a consent or consents in writing, setting forth the action so taken, shall be signed by members having not less than the minimum number of votes that would be necessary to authorize or take such action at a meeting at which all members having a right to vote thereon were present and voted and shall be delivered to the corporation by delivery to its registered office in this State, its principal place of business or an officer or agent of the corporation having custody of the book in which proceedings of meetings of members are recorded. Delivery made to a corporation's registered office shall be by hand or by certified or registered mail, return receipt requested.

(c)   No written consent shall be effective to take the corporate action referred to therein unless written consents signed by a sufficient number of holders or members to take action are delivered to the corporation in the manner required by this section within 60 days of the first date on which a written consent is so delivered to the corporation. Any person executing a consent may provide, whether through instruction to an agent or otherwise, that such a consent will be effective at a future time (including a time determined upon the happening of an event), no later than 60 days after such instruction is given or such provision is made, if evidence of such instruction or provision is provided to the corporation. Unless otherwise provided, any such consent shall be revocable prior to its becoming effective.

(d)(1)   An electronic transmission consenting to an action to be taken and transmitted by a stockholder, member or proxyholder, or by a person or persons authorized to act for a stockholder, member or proxyholder, shall be deemed to be written and signed for the purposes of this section, provided that any such electronic transmission sets forth or is delivered with information from which the corporation can determine (A) that the electronic transmission was transmitted by the stockholder, member or proxyholder or by a person or persons authorized to act for the stockholder, member or proxyholder and (B) the date on which such stockholder, member or proxyholder or authorized person or persons transmitted such electronic transmission. A consent given by electronic transmission is delivered to the corporation upon the earliest of: (i) when the consent enters an information processing system, if any, designated by the corporation for receiving consents, so long as the electronic transmission is in a form capable of being processed by that system and the corporation is able to retrieve that electronic transmission; (ii) when a paper reproduction of the consent is delivered to the corporation's principal place of business or an officer or agent of the corporation having custody of the book in which proceedings of meetings of stockholders or members are recorded; (iii) when a paper reproduction of the consent is delivered to the corporation's registered office in this State by hand or by certified or registered mail, return receipt requested; or (iv) when delivered in such other manner, if any, provided by resolution of the board of directors or governing body of the corporation. Whether the corporation has so designated an information processing system to receive consents is determined by the certificate of incorporation, the bylaws or from the context and surrounding circumstances, including the conduct of the corporation. A consent given by electronic transmission is delivered under this section even if no person is aware of its receipt. Receipt of an electronic acknowledgement from an information processing system establishes that a consent given by electronic transmission was received but, by itself, does not establish that the content sent corresponds to the content received.

(2)   Any copy, facsimile or other reliable reproduction of a consent in writing may be substituted or used in lieu of the original writing for any and all purposes for which the original writing could be used, provided that such copy, facsimile or other reproduction shall be a complete reproduction of the entire original writing.

(e)   Prompt notice of the taking of the corporate action without a meeting by less than unanimous written consent shall be given to those stockholders or members who have not consented in writing and who, if the action had been taken at a meeting, would have been entitled to notice of the meeting if the record date for notice of such meeting had been the date that written consents signed by a sufficient number of holders or members to take the action were delivered to the corporation as provided in this section. In the event that the action which is consented to is such as would have required the filing of a certificate under any other section of this title, if such action had been voted on by stockholders or by members at a meeting thereof, the certificate filed under such other section shall state, in lieu of any statement required by such section concerning any vote of stockholders or members, that written consent has been given in accordance with this section.

§ 229.   Waiver of notice.

Whenever notice is required to be given under any provision of this chapter or the certificate of incorporation or bylaws, a written waiver, signed by the person entitled to notice, or a waiver by electronic transmission by the person entitled to notice, whether before or after the time stated therein, shall be deemed equivalent to notice. Attendance of a person at a meeting shall constitute a waiver of notice of such meeting, except when the person attends a meeting for the express purpose of objecting at the beginning of the meeting, to the transaction of any business because the meeting is not lawfully called or convened. Neither the business to be transacted at, nor the purpose of, any regular or special meeting of the stockholders, directors or members of a committee of directors need be specified in any written waiver of notice or any waiver by electronic transmission unless so required by the certificate of incorporation or the bylaws.

§ 230.   Exception to requirements of notice.

(a)   Whenever notice is required to be given, under any provision of this chapter or of the certificate of incorporation or bylaws of any corporation, to any person with whom communication is unlawful, the giving of such notice to such person shall not be required and there shall be no duty to apply to any governmental authority or agency for a license or permit to give such notice to such person. Any action or meeting which shall be taken or held without notice to any such person with whom communication is unlawful shall have the same force and effect as if such notice had been duly given. In the event that the action taken by the corporation is such as to require the filing of a certificate under any of the other sections of this title, the certificate shall state, if such is the fact and if notice is required, that notice was given to all persons entitled to receive notice except such persons with whom communication is unlawful.

(b)   Whenever notice is required to be given, under any provision of this title or the certificate of incorporation or bylaws of any corporation, to any stockholder or, if the corporation is a nonstock corporation, to any member, to whom (1) notice of 2 consecutive annual meetings, and all notices of meetings or of the taking of action by written consent without a meeting to such person during the period between such 2 consecutive annual meetings, or (2) all, and at least 2, payments (if sent by first-class mail) of dividends or interest on securities during a 12-month period, have been mailed addressed to such person at such person's address as shown on the records of the corporation and have been returned undeliverable, the giving of such notice to such person shall not be required. Any action or meeting which shall be taken or held without notice to such person shall have the same force and effect as if such notice had been duly given. If any such person shall deliver to the corporation a written notice setting forth such person's then current address, the requirement that notice be given to such person shall be reinstated. In the event that the action taken by the corporation is such as to require the filing of a certificate under any of the other sections of this title, the certificate need not state that notice was not given to persons to whom notice was not required to be given pursuant to this subsection.

(c)   The exception in paragraph (b)(1) of this section to the requirement that notice be given shall not be applicable to any notice returned as undeliverable if the notice was given by electronic transmission. The exception in paragraph (b)(1) of this section to the requirement that notice be given shall not be applicable to any stockholder or member whose electronic mail address appears on the records of the corporation and to whom notice by electronic transmission is not prohibited by § 232 of this title.

§ 231.　　Voting procedures and inspectors of elections.

(a)　The corporation shall, in advance of any meeting of stockholders, appoint 1 or more inspectors to act at the meeting and make a written report thereof. The corporation may designate 1 or more persons as alternate inspectors to replace any inspector who fails to act. If no inspector or alternate is able to act at a meeting of stockholders, the person presiding at the meeting shall appoint 1 or more inspectors to act at the meeting. Each inspector, before entering upon the discharge of the duties of inspector, shall take and sign an oath faithfully to execute the duties of inspector with strict impartiality and according to the best of such inspector's ability.

(b)　The inspectors shall:

(1)　Ascertain the number of shares outstanding and the voting power of each;

(2)　Determine the shares represented at a meeting and the validity of proxies and ballots;

(3)　Count all votes and ballots;

(4)　Determine and retain for a reasonable period a record of the disposition of any challenges made to any determination by the inspectors; and

(5)　Certify their determination of the number of shares represented at the meeting, and their count of all votes and ballots.

The inspectors may appoint or retain other persons or entities to assist the inspectors in the performance of the duties of the inspectors.

(c)　The date and time of the opening and the closing of the polls for each matter upon which the stockholders will vote at a meeting shall be announced at the meeting. No ballot, proxies or votes, nor any revocations thereof or changes thereto, shall be accepted by the inspectors after the closing of the polls unless the Court of Chancery upon application by a stockholder shall determine otherwise.

(d)　In determining the validity and counting of proxies and ballots, the inspectors shall be limited to an examination of the proxies, any envelopes submitted with those proxies, any information provided in accordance with § 211(e) or § 212(c)(2) of this title, or any information provided pursuant to § 211(a)(2)b.(i) or (iii) of this title, ballots and the regular books and records of the corporation, except that the inspectors may consider other reliable information for the limited purpose of reconciling proxies and ballots submitted by or on behalf of banks, brokers, their nominees or similar persons which represent more votes than the holder of a proxy is authorized by the record owner to cast or more votes than the stockholder holds of record. If the inspectors consider other reliable information for the limited purpose permitted herein, the inspectors at the time they make their certification pursuant to paragraph (b)(5) of this section shall specify the precise information considered by them including the person or persons from whom they obtained the information, when the information was obtained, the means by which the information was obtained and the basis for the inspectors' belief that such information is accurate and reliable.

(e)　Unless otherwise provided in the certificate of incorporation or bylaws, this section shall not apply to a corporation that does not have a class of voting stock that is:

(1)　Listed on a national securities exchange;

(2)　Authorized for quotation on an interdealer quotation system of a registered national securities association; or

(3)　Held of record by more than 2,000 stockholders.

§ 232.　　Delivery of notice; notice by electronic transmission.

(a)　Without limiting the manner by which notice otherwise may be given effectively to stockholders, any notice to stockholders given by the corporation under any provision of this chapter, the certificate of incorporation, or the bylaws may be given in writing directed to the stockholder's mailing address (or by electronic transmission directed to the stockholder's electronic mail address, as applicable) as it appears on the records of the corporation and shall be given:

(1)   If mailed, when the notice is deposited in the U.S. mail, postage prepaid;

(2)   If delivered by courier service, the earlier of when the notice is received or left at such stockholder's address; or

(3)   If given by electronic mail, when directed to such stockholder's electronic mail address unless the stockholder has notified the corporation in writing or by electronic transmission of an objection to receiving notice by electronic mail or such notice is prohibited by subsection (e) of this section.

A notice by electronic mail must include a prominent legend that the communication is an important notice regarding the corporation.

(b)   Without limiting the manner by which notice otherwise may be given effectively to stockholders, but subject to subsection (e) of this section, any notice to stockholders given by the corporation under any provision of this chapter, the certificate of incorporation, or the bylaws shall be effective if given by a form of electronic transmission consented to by the stockholder to whom the notice is given. Any such consent shall be revocable by the stockholder by written notice or electronic transmission to the corporation.

(c)   Notice given pursuant to subsection (b) of this section shall be deemed given:

(1)   If by facsimile telecommunication, when directed to a number at which the stockholder has consented to receive notice;

(2)   If by a posting on an electronic network together with separate notice to the stockholder of such specific posting, upon the later of:

a.   Such posting; and

b.   The giving of such separate notice; and

(3)   If by any other form of electronic transmission, when directed to the stockholder.

(d)   For purposes of this chapter:

(1)   "Electronic transmission" means any form of communication, not directly involving the physical transmission of paper, including the use of, or participation in, 1 or more electronic networks or databases (including 1 or more distributed electronic networks or databases), that creates a record that may be retained, retrieved and reviewed by a recipient thereof, and that may be directly reproduced in paper form by such a recipient through an automated process;

(2)   "Electronic mail" means an electronic transmission directed to a unique electronic mail address (which electronic mail shall be deemed to include any files attached thereto and any information hyperlinked to a website if such electronic mail includes the contact information of an officer or agent of the corporation who is available to assist with accessing such files and information); and

(3)   "Electronic mail address" means a destination, commonly expressed as a string of characters, consisting of a unique user name or mailbox (commonly referred to as the "local part" of the address) and a reference to an internet domain (commonly referred to as the "domain part" of the address), whether or not displayed, to which electronic mail can be sent or delivered.

(e)   Notwithstanding the foregoing, a notice may not be given by an electronic transmission from and after the time that:

(1)   The corporation is unable to deliver by such electronic transmission 2 consecutive notices given by the corporation; and

(2)   Such inability becomes known to the secretary or an assistant secretary of the corporation or to the transfer agent, or other person responsible for the giving of notice, provided, however, the inadvertent failure to discover such inability shall not invalidate any meeting or other action.

(f)   An affidavit of the secretary or an assistant secretary or of the transfer agent or other agent of the corporation that notice has been given shall, in the absence of fraud, be prima facie evidence of the facts stated therein.

(g)   No provision of this section, except for paragraphs (a)(1), (d)(2) and (d)(3) of this section, shall apply to § 164, § 296, § 311, § 312, or § 324 of this title.

§ 233.   Notice to stockholders sharing an address.

(a)   Without limiting the manner by which notice otherwise may be given effectively to stockholders, any notice to stockholders given by the corporation under any provision of this chapter, the certificate of incorporation, or the bylaws shall be effective if given by a single written notice to stockholders who share an address if consented to by the stockholders at that address to whom such notice is given. Any such consent shall be revocable by the stockholder by written notice to the corporation.

(b)   Any stockholder who fails to object in writing to the corporation, within 60 days of having been given written notice by the corporation of its intention to send the single notice permitted under subsection (a) of this section, shall be deemed to have consented to receiving such single written notice.

(c)   [Repealed.]

(d)   This section shall not apply to § 164, § 296, § 311, § 312 or § 324 of this title.

SUBCHAPTER VIII.   AMENDMENT OF CERTIFICATE OF INCORPORATION; CHANGES IN CAPITAL AND CAPITAL STOCK

§ 241.   Amendment of certificate of incorporation before receipt of payment for stock.

(a)   Before a corporation has received any payment for any of its stock, it may amend its certificate of incorporation at any time or times, in any and as many respects as may be desired, so long as its certificate of incorporation as amended would contain only such provisions as it would be lawful and proper to insert in an original certificate of incorporation filed at the time of filing the amendment.

(b)   The amendment of a certificate of incorporation authorized by this section shall be adopted by a majority of the incorporators, if directors were not named in the original certificate of incorporation or have not yet been elected, or, if directors were named in the original certificate of incorporation or have been elected and have qualified, by a majority of the directors. A certificate setting forth the amendment and certifying that the corporation has not received any payment for any of its stock, or that the corporation has no members, as applicable, and that the amendment has been duly adopted in accordance with this section shall be executed, acknowledged and filed in accordance with § 103 of this title. Upon such filing, the corporation's certificate of incorporation shall be deemed to be amended accordingly as of the date on which the original certificate of incorporation became effective, except as to those persons who are substantially and adversely affected by the amendment and as to those persons the amendment shall be effective from the filing date.

(c)   This section will apply to a nonstock corporation before such a corporation has any members; provided, however, that all references to directors shall be deemed to be references to members of the governing body of the corporation.

§ 242.   Amendment of certificate of incorporation after receipt of payment for stock; nonstock corporations.

(a)   After a corporation has received payment for any of its capital stock, or after a nonstock corporation has members, it may amend its certificate of incorporation, from time to time, in any and as many respects as may be desired, so long as its certificate of incorporation as amended would contain only such provisions as it would be lawful and proper to insert in an original certificate of incorporation filed at the time of the filing of the amendment; and, if a change in stock or the rights of stockholders, or an exchange, reclassification, subdivision, combination or cancellation of stock or rights of stockholders is to be made, such provisions as may be necessary to effect such change, exchange, reclassification, subdivision, combination or cancellation. In particular, and without limitation upon such general power of amendment, a corporation may amend its certificate of incorporation, from time to time, so as:

(1)　To change its corporate name; or

(2)　To change, substitute, enlarge or diminish the nature of its business or its corporate powers and purposes; or

(3)　To increase or decrease its authorized capital stock or to reclassify the same, by changing the number, par value, designations, preferences, or relative, participating, optional, or other special rights of the shares, or the qualifications, limitations or restrictions of such rights, or by changing shares with par value into shares without par value, or shares without par value into shares with par value either with or without increasing or decreasing the number of shares, or by subdividing or combining the outstanding shares of any class or series of a class of shares into a greater or lesser number of outstanding shares; or

(4)　To cancel or otherwise affect the right of the holders of the shares of any class to receive dividends which have accrued but have not been declared; or

(5)　To create new classes of stock having rights and preferences either prior and superior or subordinate and inferior to the stock of any class then authorized, whether issued or unissued; or

(6)　To change the period of its duration; or

(7)　To delete:

　　a.　Such provisions of the original certificate of incorporation which named the incorporator or incorporators, the initial board of directors and the original subscribers for shares; and

　　b.　Such provisions contained in any amendment to the certificate of incorporation as were necessary to effect a change, exchange, reclassification, subdivision, combination or cancellation of stock, if such change, exchange, reclassification, subdivision, combination or cancellation has become effective.

Any or all such changes or alterations may be effected by 1 certificate of amendment.

(b)　Every amendment authorized by subsection (a) of this section shall be made and effected in the following manner:

(1)　If the corporation has capital stock, its board of directors shall adopt a resolution setting forth the amendment proposed, declaring its advisability, and either calling a special meeting of the stockholders entitled to vote in respect thereof for the consideration of such amendment or directing that the amendment proposed be considered at the next annual meeting of the stockholders; provided, however, that unless otherwise expressly required by the certificate of incorporation, no meeting or vote of stockholders shall be required to adopt an amendment that effects only changes described in paragraph (a)(1) or (7) of this section. Such special or annual meeting shall be called and held upon notice in accordance with § 222 of this title. The notice shall set forth such amendment in full or a brief summary of the changes to be effected thereby unless such notice constitutes a notice of internet availability of proxy materials under the rules promulgated under the Securities Exchange Act of 1934 [15 U.S.C. § 78a et seq.]. At the meeting a vote of the stockholders entitled to vote thereon shall be taken for and against any proposed amendment that requires adoption by stockholders. If no vote of stockholders is required to effect such amendment, or if a majority of the outstanding stock entitled to vote thereon, and a majority of the outstanding stock of each class entitled to vote thereon as a class has been voted in favor of the amendment, a certificate setting forth the amendment and certifying that such amendment has been duly adopted in accordance with this section shall be executed, acknowledged and filed and shall become effective in accordance with § 103 of this title.

(2)　The holders of the outstanding shares of a class shall be entitled to vote as a class upon a proposed amendment, whether or not entitled to vote thereon by the certificate of incorporation, if the amendment would increase or decrease the aggregate number of authorized shares of such class, increase or decrease the par value of the shares of such class, or alter or change the powers, preferences, or special rights of the shares of such class so as to affect them adversely. If any proposed amendment would alter or change the powers, preferences, or special rights of 1 or more series of any class so as to affect them adversely, but shall not so affect the entire class, then only the shares of the series so affected by the amendment shall be considered a separate class for the purposes of this paragraph. The number of authorized shares of any such class or classes of stock may be increased or decreased (but not below the number of shares thereof then outstanding) by the affirmative vote of the holders of a majority of the stock of the corporation entitled to vote irrespective of this subsection, if so provided in the original certificate of incorporation, in any amendment thereto which created such class or classes of stock or which was adopted prior to the issuance of any shares of such class or classes of stock, or in any amendment thereto which was authorized by a resolution or resolutions adopted by the affirmative vote of the holders of a majority of such class or classes of stock.

(3)   If the corporation is a nonstock corporation, then the governing body thereof shall adopt a resolution setting forth the amendment proposed and declaring its advisability. If a majority of all the members of the governing body shall vote in favor of such amendment, a certificate thereof shall be executed, acknowledged and filed and shall become effective in accordance with § 103 of this title. The certificate of incorporation of any nonstock corporation may contain a provision requiring any amendment thereto to be approved by a specified number or percentage of the members or of any specified class of members of such corporation in which event such proposed amendment shall be submitted to the members or to any specified class of members of such corporation in the same manner, so far as applicable, as is provided in this section for an amendment to the certificate of incorporation of a stock corporation; and in the event of the adoption thereof by such members, a certificate evidencing such amendment shall be executed, acknowledged and filed and shall become effective in accordance with § 103 of this title.

(4)   Whenever the certificate of incorporation shall require for action by the board of directors of a corporation other than a nonstock corporation or by the governing body of a nonstock corporation, by the holders of any class or series of shares or by the members, or by the holders of any other securities having voting power the vote of a greater number or proportion than is required by any section of this title, the provision of the certificate of incorporation requiring such greater vote shall not be altered, amended or repealed except by such greater vote.

(c)   The resolution authorizing a proposed amendment to the certificate of incorporation may provide that at any time prior to the effectiveness of the filing of the amendment with the Secretary of State, notwithstanding authorization of the proposed amendment by the stockholders of the corporation or by the members of a nonstock corporation, the board of directors or governing body may abandon such proposed amendment without further action by the stockholders or members.

§ 243.   Retirement of stock.

(a)   A corporation, by resolution of its board of directors, may retire any shares of its capital stock that are issued but are not outstanding.

(b)   Whenever any shares of the capital stock of a corporation are retired, they shall resume the status of authorized and unissued shares of the class or series to which they belong unless the certificate of incorporation otherwise provides. If the certificate of incorporation prohibits the reissuance of such shares, or prohibits the reissuance of such shares as a part of a specific series only, a certificate stating that reissuance of the shares (as part of the class or series) is prohibited identifying the shares and reciting their retirement shall be executed, acknowledged and filed and shall become effective in accordance with § 103 of this title. When such certificate becomes effective, it shall have the effect of amending the certificate of incorporation so as to reduce accordingly the number of authorized shares of the class or series to which such shares belong or, if such retired shares constitute all of the authorized shares of the class or series to which they belong, of eliminating from the certificate of incorporation all reference to such class or series of stock.

(c)   If the capital of the corporation will be reduced by or in connection with the retirement of shares, the reduction of capital shall be effected pursuant to § 244 of this title.

§ 244.   Reduction of capital.

(a)   A corporation, by resolution of its board of directors, may reduce its capital in any of the following ways:

(1)   By reducing or eliminating the capital represented by shares of capital stock which have been retired;

(2)   By applying to an otherwise authorized purchase or redemption of outstanding shares of its capital stock some or all of the capital represented by the shares being purchased or redeemed, or any capital that has not been allocated to any particular class of its capital stock;

(3)   By applying to an otherwise authorized conversion or exchange of outstanding shares of its capital stock some or all of the capital represented by the shares being converted or exchanged, or some or all of any capital that has not been allocated to any particular class of its capital stock, or both, to the extent that such capital in the aggregate exceeds the total aggregate par value or the stated capital of any previously unissued shares issuable upon such conversion or exchange; or

(4)   By transferring to surplus (i) some or all of the capital not represented by any particular class of its capital stock; (ii) some or all of the capital represented by issued shares of its par value capital stock, which capital is in excess of the aggregate par value of such shares; or (iii) some of the capital represented by issued shares of its capital stock without par value.

(b)   Notwithstanding the other provisions of this section, no reduction of capital shall be made or effected unless the assets of the corporation remaining after such reduction shall be sufficient to pay any debts of the corporation for which payment has not been otherwise provided. No reduction of capital shall release any liability of any stockholder whose shares have not been fully paid.

(c)   [Repealed.]

§ 245.   Restated certificate of incorporation.

(a)   A corporation may, whenever desired, integrate into a single instrument all of the provisions of its certificate of incorporation which are then in effect and operative as a result of there having theretofore been filed with the Secretary of State 1 or more certificates or other instruments pursuant to any of the sections referred to in § 104 of this title, and it may at the same time also further amend its certificate of incorporation by adopting a restated certificate of incorporation.

(b)   If the restated certificate of incorporation merely restates and integrates but does not further amend the certificate of incorporation, as theretofore amended or supplemented by any instrument that was filed pursuant to any of the sections mentioned in § 104 of this title, it may be adopted by the board of directors without a vote of the stockholders, or it may be proposed by the directors and submitted by them to the stockholders for adoption, in which case the procedure and vote required, if any, by § 242 of this title for amendment of the certificate of incorporation shall be applicable. If the restated certificate of incorporation restates and integrates and also further amends in any respect the certificate of incorporation, as theretofore amended or supplemented, it shall be proposed by the directors and adopted by the stockholders in the manner and by the vote prescribed by § 242 of this title or, if the corporation has not received any payment for any of its stock, in the manner and by the vote prescribed by § 241 of this title.

(c)   A restated certificate of incorporation shall be specifically designated as such in its heading. It shall state, either in its heading or in an introductory paragraph, the corporation's present name, and, if it has been changed, the name under which it was originally incorporated, and the date of filing of its original certificate of incorporation with the Secretary of State. A restated certificate shall also state that it was duly adopted in accordance with this section. If it was adopted by the board of directors without a vote of the stockholders (unless it was adopted pursuant to § 241 of this title or without a vote of members pursuant to 242(b)(3) of this title), it shall state that it only restates and integrates and does not further amend (except, if applicable, as permitted under § 242(a)(1) and § 242(b)(1) of this title) the provisions of the corporation's certificate of incorporation as theretofore amended or supplemented, and that there is no discrepancy between those provisions and the provisions of the restated certificate. A restated certificate of incorporation may omit (a) such provisions of the original certificate of incorporation which named the incorporator or incorporators, the initial board of directors and the original subscribers for shares, and (b) such provisions contained in any amendment to the certificate of incorporation as were necessary to effect a change, exchange, reclassification, subdivision, combination or cancellation of stock, if such change, exchange, reclassification, subdivision, combination or cancellation has become effective. Any such omissions shall not be deemed a further amendment.

(d)   A restated certificate of incorporation shall be executed, acknowledged and filed in accordance with § 103 of this title. Upon its filing with the Secretary of State, the original certificate of incorporation, as theretofore amended or supplemented, shall be superseded; thenceforth, the restated certificate of incorporation, including any further amendments or changes made thereby, shall be the certificate of incorporation of the corporation, but the original date of incorporation shall remain unchanged.

(e)   Any amendment or change effected in connection with the restatement and integration of the certificate of incorporation shall be subject to any other provision of this chapter, not inconsistent with this section, which would apply if a separate certificate of amendment were filed to effect such amendment or change.

§ 246.   [Reserved.]

SUBCHAPTER IX.   MERGER, CONSOLIDATION OR CONVERSION

§ 251.   Merger or consolidation of domestic corporations [For application of this section, see 79 Del. Laws, c. 327, § 8 and 80 Del. Laws, c. 265, § 17].

(a)   Any 2 or more corporations of this State may merge into a single surviving corporation, which may be any 1 of the constituent corporations or may consolidate into a new resulting corporation formed by the consolidation, pursuant to an agreement of merger or consolidation, as the case may be, complying and approved in accordance with this section.

(b)   The board of directors of each corporation which desires to merge or consolidate shall adopt a resolution approving an agreement of merger or consolidation and declaring its advisability. The agreement shall state:

(1)   The terms and conditions of the merger or consolidation;

(2)   The mode of carrying the same into effect;

(3)   In the case of a merger, such amendments or changes in the certificate of incorporation of the surviving corporation as are desired to be effected by the merger (which amendments or changes may amend and restate the certificate of incorporation of the surviving corporation in its entirety), or, if no such amendments or changes are desired, a statement that the certificate of incorporation of the surviving corporation shall be its certificate of incorporation;

(4)   In the case of a consolidation, that the certificate of incorporation of the resulting corporation shall be as is set forth in an attachment to the agreement;

(5)   The manner, if any, of converting the shares of each of the constituent corporations into shares or other securities of the corporation surviving or resulting from the merger or consolidation, or of cancelling some or all of such shares, and, if any shares of any of the constituent corporations are not to remain outstanding, to be converted solely into shares or other securities of the surviving or resulting corporation or to be cancelled, the cash, property, rights or securities of any other corporation or entity which the holders of such shares are to receive in exchange for, or upon conversion of such shares and the surrender of any certificates evidencing them, which cash, property, rights or securities of any other corporation or entity may be in addition to or in lieu of shares or other securities of the surviving or resulting corporation; and

(6)   Such other details or provisions as are deemed desirable, including, without limiting the generality of the foregoing, a provision for the payment of cash in lieu of the issuance or recognition of fractional shares, rights or other securities of the surviving or resulting corporation or of any other corporation or entity the shares, rights or other securities of which are to be received in the merger or consolidation, or for any other arrangement with respect thereto, consistent with § 155 of this title.

The agreement so adopted shall be executed by an authorized person, provided that if the agreement is filed, it shall be executed and acknowledged in accordance with § 103 of this title. Any of the terms of the agreement of merger or consolidation may be made dependent upon facts ascertainable outside of such agreement, provided that the manner in which such facts shall operate upon the terms of the agreement is clearly and expressly set forth in the agreement of merger or consolidation. The term "facts," as used in the preceding sentence, includes, but is not limited to, the occurrence of any event, including a determination or action by any person or body, including the corporation.

(c)   The agreement required by subsection (b) of this section shall be submitted to the stockholders of each constituent corporation at an annual or special meeting for the purpose of acting on the agreement. Due notice of the time, place and purpose of the meeting shall be given to each holder of stock, whether voting or nonvoting, of the corporation at the stockholder's address as it appears on the records of the corporation, at least 20 days prior to the date of the meeting. The notice shall contain a copy of the agreement or a brief summary thereof. At the meeting, the agreement shall be considered and a vote taken for its adoption or rejection. If a majority of the outstanding stock of the corporation entitled to vote thereon shall be voted for the adoption of the agreement, that fact shall be certified on the agreement by the secretary or assistant secretary of the corporation, provided that such certification on the agreement shall not be required if a certificate of merger or consolidation is filed in lieu of filing the agreement. If the agreement shall be so adopted and certified by each constituent corporation, it shall then be filed and shall become effective, in accordance with § 103 of this title. In lieu of filing the agreement of merger or consolidation required by this section, the surviving or resulting corporation may file a certificate of merger or consolidation, executed in accordance with § 103 of this title, which states:

(1)   The name and state of incorporation of each of the constituent corporations;

(2)   That an agreement of merger or consolidation has been approved, adopted, executed and acknowledged by each of the constituent corporations in accordance with this section;

(3)   The name of the surviving or resulting corporation;

(4)   In the case of a merger, such amendments or changes in the certificate of incorporation of the surviving corporation as are desired to be effected by the merger (which amendments or changes may amend and restate the certificate of incorporation of the surviving corporation in its entirety), or, if no such amendments or changes are desired, a statement that the certificate of incorporation of the surviving corporation shall be its certificate of incorporation;

(5)   In the case of a consolidation, that the certificate of incorporation of the resulting corporation shall be as set forth in an attachment to the certificate;

(6)   That the executed agreement of consolidation or merger is on file at an office of the surviving or resulting corporation, stating the address thereof; and

(7)   That a copy of the agreement of consolidation or merger will be furnished by the surviving or resulting corporation, on request and without cost, to any stockholder of any constituent corporation.

(d)   Any agreement of merger or consolidation may contain a provision that at any time prior to the time that the agreement (or a certificate in lieu thereof) filed with the Secretary of State becomes effective in accordance with § 103 of this title, the agreement may be terminated by the board of directors of any constituent corporation notwithstanding approval of the agreement by the stockholders of all or any of the constituent corporations; in the event the agreement of merger or consolidation is terminated after the filing of the agreement (or a certificate in lieu thereof) with the Secretary of State but before the agreement (or a certificate in lieu thereof) has become effective, a certificate of termination or merger or consolidation shall be filed in accordance with § 103 of this title. Any agreement of merger or consolidation may contain a provision that the boards of directors of the constituent corporations may amend the agreement at any time prior to the time that the agreement (or a certificate in lieu thereof) filed with the Secretary of State becomes effective in accordance with § 103 of this title, provided that an amendment made subsequent to the adoption of the agreement by the stockholders of any constituent corporation shall not (1) alter or change the amount or kind of shares, securities, cash, property and/or rights to be received in exchange for or on conversion of all or any of the shares of any class or series thereof of such constituent corporation, (2) alter or change any term of the certificate of incorporation of the surviving corporation to be effected by the merger or consolidation, or (3) alter or change any of the terms and conditions of the agreement if such alteration or change would adversely affect the holders of any class or series thereof of such constituent corporation; in the event the agreement of merger or consolidation is amended after the filing thereof with the Secretary of State but before the agreement has become effective, a certificate of amendment of merger or consolidation shall be filed in accordance with § 103 of this title.

(e)   In the case of a merger, the certificate of incorporation of the surviving corporation shall automatically be amended to the extent, if any, that changes in the certificate of incorporation are set forth in the agreement of merger.

(f)   Notwithstanding the requirements of subsection (c) of this section, unless required by its certificate of incorporation, no vote of stockholders of a constituent corporation surviving a merger shall be necessary to authorize a merger if (1) the agreement of merger does not amend in any respect the certificate of incorporation of such constituent corporation, (2) each share of stock of such constituent corporation outstanding immediately prior to the effective date of the merger is to be an identical outstanding or treasury share of the surviving corporation after the effective date of the merger, and (3) either no shares of common stock of the surviving corporation and no shares, securities or obligations convertible into such stock are to be issued or delivered under the plan of merger, or the authorized unissued shares or the treasury shares of common stock of the surviving corporation to be issued or delivered under the plan of merger plus those initially issuable upon conversion of any other shares, securities or obligations to be issued or delivered under such plan do not exceed 20% of the shares of common stock of such constituent corporation outstanding immediately prior to the effective date of the merger. No vote of stockholders of a constituent corporation shall be necessary to authorize a merger or consolidation if no shares of the stock of such corporation shall have been issued prior to the adoption by the board of directors of the resolution approving the agreement of merger or consolidation. If an agreement of merger is adopted by the constituent corporation surviving the merger, by action of its board of directors and without any vote of its stockholders pursuant to this subsection, the secretary or assistant secretary of that corporation shall certify on the agreement that the agreement has been adopted pursuant to this subsection and, (1) if it has been adopted pursuant to the first sentence of this subsection, that the conditions specified in that sentence have been satisfied, or (2) if it has been adopted pursuant to the second sentence of this subsection, that no shares of stock of such corporation were issued prior to the adoption by the board of directors of the resolution approving the agreement of merger or consolidation, provided that such certification on the agreement shall not be required if a certificate of merger or consolidation is filed in lieu of filing the agreement. The agreement so adopted and certified shall then be filed and shall become effective, in accordance with § 103 of this title. Such filing shall constitute a representation by the person who executes the agreement that the facts stated in the certificate remain true immediately prior to such filing.

(g)   Notwithstanding the requirements of subsection (c) of this section, unless expressly required by its certificate of incorporation, no vote of stockholders of a constituent corporation shall be necessary to authorize a merger with or into a single direct or indirect wholly-owned subsidiary of such constituent corporation if: (1) such constituent corporation and the direct or indirect wholly-owned subsidiary of such constituent corporation are the only constituent entities to the merger; (2) each share or fraction of a share of the capital stock of the constituent corporation outstanding immediately prior to the effective time of the merger is converted in the merger into a share or equal fraction of share of capital stock of a holding company having the same designations, rights, powers and preferences, and the qualifications, limitations and restrictions thereof, as the share of stock of the constituent corporation being converted in the merger; (3) the holding company and the constituent corporation are corporations of this State and the direct or indirect wholly-owned subsidiary that is the other constituent entity to the merger is a corporation or limited liability company of this State; (4) the certificate of incorporation and by-laws of the holding company immediately following the effective time of the merger contain provisions identical to the certificate of incorporation and by-laws of the constituent corporation immediately prior to the effective time of the merger (other than provisions, if any, regarding the incorporator or incorporators, the corporate name, the registered office and agent, the initial board of directors and the initial subscribers for shares and such provisions contained in any amendment to the certificate of incorporation as were necessary to effect a change, exchange, reclassification, subdivision, combination or cancellation of stock, if such change, exchange, reclassification, subdivision, combination, or cancellation has become effective); (5) as a result of the merger the constituent corporation or its successor becomes or remains a direct or indirect wholly-owned subsidiary of the holding company; (6) the directors of the constituent corporation become or remain the directors of the holding company upon the effective time of the merger; (7) the organizational documents of the surviving entity immediately following the effective time of the merger contain provisions identical to the certificate of incorporation of the constituent corporation immediately prior to the effective time of the merger (other than provisions, if any, regarding the incorporator or incorporators, the corporate or entity name, the registered office and agent, the initial board of directors and the initial subscribers for shares, references to members rather than stockholders or shareholders, references to interests, units or the like rather than stock or shares, references to managers, managing members or other members of the governing body rather than directors and such provisions contained in any amendment to the certificate of incorporation as were necessary to effect a change, exchange, reclassification, subdivision, combination or cancellation of stock, if such change, exchange, reclassification, subdivision, combination or cancellation has become effective); provided, however, that (i) if the organizational documents of the surviving entity do not contain the following provisions, they shall be amended in the merger to contain provisions requiring that (A) any act or transaction by or involving the surviving entity, other than the election or removal of directors or managers, managing members or other members of the governing body of the surviving entity, that requires for its adoption under this chapter or its organizational documents the approval of the stockholders or members of the surviving entity shall, by specific reference to this subsection, require, in addition, the approval of the stockholders of the holding company (or any successor by merger), by the same vote as is required by this chapter and/or by the organizational documents of the surviving entity; provided, however, that for purposes of this clause (i)(A), any surviving entity that is not a corporation shall include in such amendment a requirement that the approval of the stockholders of the holding company be obtained for any act or transaction by or involving the surviving entity, other than the election or removal of directors or managers, managing members or other members of the governing body of the surviving entity, which would require the approval of the stockholders of the surviving entity if the surviving entity were a corporation subject to this chapter; (B) any amendment of the organizational documents of a surviving entity that is not a corporation, which amendment would, if adopted by a corporation subject to this chapter, be required to be included in the certificate of incorporation of such corporation, shall, by specific reference to this subsection, require, in addition, the approval of the stockholders of the holding company (or any successor by merger), by the same vote as is required by this chapter and/or by the organizational documents of the surviving entity; and (C) the business and affairs of a surviving entity that is not a corporation shall be managed by or under the direction of a board of directors, board of managers or other governing body consisting of individuals who are subject to the same fiduciary duties applicable to, and who are liable for breach of such duties to the same extent as, directors of a corporation subject to this chapter; and (ii) the organizational documents of the surviving entity may be amended in the merger (A) to reduce the number of classes and shares of capital stock or other equity interests or units that the surviving entity is authorized to issue and (B) to eliminate any provision authorized by § 141(d) of this title; and (8) the stockholders of the constituent corporation do not recognize gain or loss for United States federal income tax purposes as determined by the board of directors of the constituent corporation. Neither paragraph (g)(7)(i) of this section nor any provision of a surviving entity's organizational documents required by paragraph (g)(7)(i) of this section shall be deemed or construed to require approval of the stockholders of the holding company to elect or remove directors or managers, managing members or other members of the governing body of the surviving entity. The term "organizational documents", as used in paragraph (g)(7) of this section and in the preceding sentence, shall, when used in reference to a corporation, mean the certificate of incorporation of such corporation, and when used in reference to a limited liability company, mean the limited liability company agreement of such limited liability company.

As used in this subsection only, the term "holding company" means a corporation which, from its incorporation until consummation of a merger governed by this subsection, was at all times a direct or indirect wholly-owned subsidiary of the constituent corporation and whose capital stock is issued in such merger. From and after the effective time of a merger adopted by a constituent corporation by action of its board of directors and without any vote of stockholders pursuant to this subsection: (i) to the extent the restrictions of § 203 of this title applied to the constituent corporation and its stockholders at the effective time of the merger, such restrictions shall apply to the holding company and its stockholders immediately after the effective time of the merger as though it were the constituent corporation, and all shares of stock of the holding company acquired in the merger shall for purposes of § 203 of this title be deemed to have been acquired at the time that the shares of stock of the constituent corporation converted in the merger were acquired, and provided further that any stockholder who immediately prior to the effective time of the merger was not an interested stockholder within the meaning of § 203 of this title shall not solely by reason of the merger become an interested stockholder of the holding company, (ii) if the corporate name of the holding company immediately following the effective time of the merger is the same as the corporate name of the constituent corporation immediately prior to the effective time of the merger, the shares of capital stock of the holding company into which the shares of capital stock of the constituent corporation are converted in the merger shall be represented by the stock certificates that previously represented shares of capital stock of the constituent corporation and (iii) to the extent a stockholder of the constituent corporation immediately prior to the merger had standing to institute or maintain derivative litigation on behalf of the constituent corporation, nothing in this section shall be deemed to limit or extinguish such standing. If an agreement of merger is adopted by a constituent corporation by action of its board of directors and without any vote of stockholders pursuant to this subsection, the secretary or assistant secretary of the constituent corporation shall certify on the agreement that the agreement has been adopted pursuant to this subsection and that the conditions specified in the first sentence of this subsection have been satisfied, provided that such certification on the agreement shall not be required if a certificate of merger or consolidation is filed in lieu of filing the agreement. The agreement so adopted and certified shall then be filed and become effective, in accordance with § 103 of this title. Such filing shall constitute a representation by the person who executes the agreement that the facts stated in the certificate remain true immediately prior to such filing.

(h) Notwithstanding the requirements of subsection (c) of this section, unless expressly required by its certificate of incorporation, no vote of stockholders of a constituent corporation that has a class or series of stock that is listed on a national securities exchange or held of record by more than 2,000 holders immediately prior to the execution of the agreement of merger by such constituent corporation shall be necessary to authorize a merger if:

(1) The agreement of merger expressly:

a. Permits or requires such merger to be effected under this subsection; and

b. Provides that such merger shall be effected as soon as practicable following the consummation of the offer referred to in paragraph (h)(2) of this section if such merger is effected under this subsection;

(2) A corporation consummates an offer for all of the outstanding stock of such constituent corporation on the terms provided in such agreement of merger that, absent this subsection, would be entitled to vote on the adoption or rejection of the agreement of merger; provided, however, that such offer may be conditioned on the tender of a minimum number or percentage of shares of the stock of such constituent corporation, or of any class or series thereof, and such offer may exclude any excluded stock and provided further that the corporation may consummate separate offers for separate classes or series of the stock of such constituent corporation;

a.–d. [Repealed.]

(3) Immediately following the consummation of the offer referred to in paragraph (h)(2) of this section, the stock irrevocably accepted for purchase or exchange pursuant to such offer and received by the depository prior to expiration of such offer, together with the stock otherwise owned by the consummating corporation or its affiliates and any rollover stock, equals at least such percentage of the shares of stock of such constituent corporation, and of each class or series thereof, that, absent this subsection, would be required to adopt the agreement of merger by this chapter and by the certificate of incorporation of such constituent corporation;

(4) The corporation consummating the offer referred to in paragraph (h)(2) of this section merges with or into such constituent corporation pursuant to such agreement; and

(5) Each outstanding share (other than shares of excluded stock) of each class or series of stock of such constituent corporation that is the subject of and is not irrevocably accepted for purchase or exchange in the offer referred to in paragraph (h)(2) of this section is to be converted in such merger into, or into the right to receive, the same amount and kind of cash, property, rights or securities to be paid for shares of such class or series of stock of such constituent corporation irrevocably accepted for purchase or exchange in such offer.

(6) As used in this section only, the term:

a. "Affiliate" means, in respect of the corporation making the offer referred to in paragraph (h)(2) of this section, any person that (i) owns, directly or indirectly, all of the outstanding stock of such corporation or (ii) is a direct or indirect wholly-owned subsidiary of such corporation or of any person referred to in clause (i) of this definition;

b. "Consummates" (and with correlative meaning, "consummation" and "consummating") means irrevocably accepts for purchase or exchange stock tendered pursuant to an offer;

c. "Depository" means an agent, including a depository, appointed to facilitate consummation of the offer referred to in paragraph (h)(2) of this section;

d. "Excluded stock" means (i) stock of such constituent corporation that is owned at the commencement of the offer referred to in paragraph (h)(2) of this section by such constituent corporation, the corporation making the offer referred to in paragraph (h)(2) of this section, any person that owns, directly or indirectly, all of the outstanding stock of the corporation making such offer, or any direct or indirect wholly-owned subsidiary of any of the foregoing and (ii) rollover stock;

e. "Person" means any individual, corporation, partnership, limited liability company, unincorporated association or other entity;

f. "Received" (solely for purposes of paragraph (h)(3) of this section) means (a) with respect to certificated shares, physical receipt of a stock certificate accompanied by an executed letter of transmittal, (b) with respect to uncertificated shares held of record by a clearing corporation as nominee, transfer into the depository's account by means of an agent's message, and (c) with respect to uncertificated shares held of record by a person other than a clearing corporation as nominee, physical receipt of an executed letter of transmittal by the depository; provided, however, that shares shall cease to be "received" (i) with respect to certificated shares, if the certificate representing such shares was canceled prior to consummation of the offer referred to in paragraph (h)(2) of this section, or (ii) with respect to uncertificated shares, to the extent such uncertificated shares have been reduced or eliminated due to any sale of such shares prior to consummation of the offer referred to in paragraph (h)(2) of this section; and

g. "Rollover stock" means any shares of stock of such constituent corporation that are the subject of a written agreement requiring such shares to be transferred, contributed or delivered to the consummating corporation or any of its affiliates in exchange for stock or other equity interests in such consummating corporation or an affiliate thereof; provided, however, that such shares of stock shall cease to be rollover stock for purposes of paragraph (h)(3) of this section if, immediately prior to the time the merger becomes effective under this chapter, such shares have not been transferred, contributed or delivered to the consummating corporation or any of its affiliates pursuant to such written agreement.

If an agreement of merger is adopted without the vote of stockholders of a corporation pursuant to this subsection, the secretary or assistant secretary of the surviving corporation shall certify on the agreement that the agreement has been adopted pursuant to this subsection and that the conditions specified in this subsection (other than the condition listed in paragraph (h)(4) of this section) have been satisfied; provided that such certification on the agreement shall not be required if a certificate of merger is filed in lieu of filing the agreement. The agreement so adopted and certified shall then be filed and shall become effective, in accordance with § 103 of this title. Such filing shall constitute a representation by the person who executes the agreement that the facts stated in the certificate remain true immediately prior to such filing.

§ 252. Merger or consolidation of domestic and foreign corporations; service of process upon surviving or resulting corporation.

(a) Any 1 or more corporations of this State may merge or consolidate with 1 or more foreign corporations, unless the laws of the jurisdiction or jurisdictions under which such foreign corporation or corporations are organized prohibit such merger or consolidation. The constituent corporations may merge into a single surviving corporation, which may be any 1 of the constituent corporations, or they may consolidate into a new resulting corporation formed by the consolidation, which may be a corporation of the jurisdiction of organization of any 1 of the constituent corporations, pursuant to an agreement of merger or consolidation, as the case may be, complying and approved in accordance with this section.

(b) All the constituent corporations shall enter into an agreement of merger or consolidation. The agreement shall state:

(1) The terms and conditions of the merger or consolidation;

(2) The mode of carrying the same into effect;

(3) In the case of a merger in which the surviving corporation is a corporation of this State, such amendments or changes in the certificate of incorporation of the surviving corporation as are desired to be effected by the merger (which amendments or changes may amend and restate the certificate of incorporation of the surviving corporation in its entirety), or, if no such amendments or changes are desired, a statement that the certificate of incorporation of the surviving corporation shall be its certificate of incorporation;

(4) In the case of a consolidation in which the resulting corporation is a corporation of this State, that the certificate of incorporation of the resulting corporation shall be as is set forth in an attachment to the agreement;

(5) The manner, if any, of converting the shares of each of the constituent corporations into shares or other securities of the corporation surviving or resulting from the merger or consolidation, or of cancelling some or all of such shares, and, if any shares of any of the constituent corporations are not to remain outstanding, to be converted solely into shares or other securities of the surviving or resulting corporation or to be cancelled, the cash, property, rights or securities of any other corporation or entity which the holders of such shares are to receive in exchange for, or upon conversion of, such shares and the surrender of any certificates evidencing them, which cash, property, rights or securities of any other corporation or entity may be in addition to or in lieu of the shares or other securities of the surviving or resulting corporation;

(6) Such other details or provisions as are deemed desirable, including, without limiting the generality of the foregoing, a provision for the payment of cash in lieu of the issuance or recognition of fractional shares, rights or other securities of the surviving or resulting corporation or of any other corporation or entity the shares, rights or other securities of which are to be received in the merger or consolidation, or for some other arrangement with respect thereto, consistent with § 155 of this title; and

(7) Such other provisions or facts as shall be required to be set forth in an agreement of merger or consolidation (including any provision for amendment of the certificate of incorporation (or equivalent document) of a surviving or resulting foreign corporation) by the laws of each jurisdiction under which any of the foreign corporations are organized.

Any of the terms of the agreement of merger or consolidation may be made dependent upon facts ascertainable outside of such agreement, provided that the manner in which such facts shall operate upon the terms of the agreement is clearly and expressly set forth in the agreement of merger or consolidation. The term "facts," as used in the preceding sentence, includes, but is not limited to, the occurrence of any event, including a determination or action by any person or body, including the corporation.

(c) The agreement shall be adopted, approved, certified, executed and acknowledged by each of the constituent corporations in accordance with the laws under which it is organized, and, in the case of a corporation of this State, in the same manner as is provided in § 251 of this title. The agreement shall be filed and shall become effective for all purposes of the laws of this State when and as provided in § 251 of this title with respect to the merger or consolidation of corporations of this State. In lieu of filing the agreement of merger or consolidation, the surviving or resulting corporation may file a certificate of merger or consolidation, executed in accordance with § 103 of this title, which states:

(1) The name and jurisdiction of organization of each of the constituent corporations;

(2) That an agreement of merger or consolidation has been approved, adopted, certified, executed and acknowledged by each of the constituent corporations in accordance with this subsection;

(3) The name of the surviving or resulting corporation;

(4) In the case of a merger in which the surviving corporation is a corporation of this State, such amendments or changes in the certificate of incorporation of the surviving corporation as are desired to be effected by the merger (which amendments or changes may amend and restate the certificate of incorporation of the surviving corporation in its entirety), or, if no such amendments or changes are desired, a statement that the certificate of incorporation of the surviving corporation shall be its certificate of incorporation;

(5)   In the case of a consolidation in which the resulting corporation is a corporation of this State, that the certificate of incorporation of the resulting corporation shall be as is set forth in an attachment to the certificate;

(6)   That the executed agreement of consolidation or merger is on file at an office of the surviving or resulting corporation and the address thereof;

(7)   That a copy of the agreement of consolidation or merger will be furnished by the surviving or resulting corporation, on request and without cost, to any stockholder of any constituent corporation;

(8)   If the corporation surviving or resulting from the merger or consolidation is a corporation of this State, the authorized capital stock of each constituent corporation which is not a corporation of this State; and

(9)   The agreement, if any, required by subsection (d) of this section.

(d)   If the corporation surviving or resulting from the merger or consolidation is a foreign corporation, it shall agree that it may be served with process in this State in any proceeding for enforcement of any obligation of any constituent corporation of this State, as well as for enforcement of any obligation of the surviving or resulting corporation arising from the merger or consolidation, including any suit or other proceeding to enforce the right of any stockholders as determined in appraisal proceedings pursuant to § 262 of this title, and shall irrevocably appoint the Secretary of State as its agent to accept service of process in any such suit or other proceedings and shall specify the address to which a copy of such process shall be mailed by the Secretary of State. Process may be served upon the Secretary of State under this subsection by means of electronic transmission but only as prescribed by the Secretary of State. The Secretary of State is authorized to issue such rules and regulations with respect to such service as the Secretary of State deems necessary or appropriate. In the event of such service upon the Secretary of State in accordance with this subsection, the Secretary of State shall forthwith notify such surviving or resulting corporation thereof by letter, directed to such surviving or resulting corporation at its address so specified, unless such surviving or resulting corporation shall have designated in writing to the Secretary of State a different address for such purpose, in which case it shall be mailed to the last address so designated. Such letter shall be sent by a mail or courier service that includes a record of mailing or deposit with the courier and a record of delivery evidenced by the signature of the recipient. Such letter shall enclose a copy of the process and any other papers served on the Secretary of State pursuant to this subsection. It shall be the duty of the plaintiff in the event of such service to serve process and any other papers in duplicate, to notify the Secretary of State that service is being effected pursuant to this subsection and to pay the Secretary of State the sum of $50 for the use of the State, which sum shall be taxed as part of the costs in the proceeding, if the plaintiff shall prevail therein. The Secretary of State shall maintain an alphabetical record of any such service setting forth the name of the plaintiff and the defendant, the title, docket number and nature of the proceeding in which process has been served, the fact that service has been effected pursuant to this subsection, the return date thereof, and the day and hour service was made. The Secretary of State shall not be required to retain such information longer than 5 years from receipt of the service of process.

(e)   Section 251(d) of this title shall apply to any merger or consolidation under this section; § 251(e) of this title shall apply to a merger under this section in which the surviving corporation is a corporation of this State; and § 251(f) and (h) of this title shall apply to any merger under this section.

§ 253.   Merger of parent corporation and subsidiary corporation or corporations.

(a)   In any case in which: (1) at least 90% of the outstanding shares of each class of the stock of a corporation or corporations (other than a corporation which has in its certificate of incorporation the provision required by § 251(g)(7)(i) of this title), of which class there are outstanding shares that, absent this subsection, would be entitled to vote on such merger, is owned by a corporation of this State or a foreign corporation, and (2) 1 or more of such corporations is a corporation of this State, unless the laws of the jurisdiction or jurisdictions under which the foreign corporation or corporations are organized prohibit such merger, the parent corporation may either merge the subsidiary corporation or corporations into itself and assume all of its or their obligations, or merge itself, or itself and 1 or more of such other subsidiary corporations, into 1 of the subsidiary corporations by executing, acknowledging and filing, in accordance with § 103 of this title, a certificate of such ownership and merger setting forth a copy of the resolution of its board of directors to so merge and the date of the adoption; provided, however, that in case the parent corporation shall not own all the outstanding stock of all the subsidiary corporations, parties to a merger as aforesaid, the resolution of the board of directors of the parent corporation shall state the terms and conditions of the merger, including the securities, cash, property, or rights to be issued, paid, delivered or granted by the surviving corporation upon surrender of each share of the subsidiary corporation or corporations not owned by the parent corporation, or the cancellation of some or all of such shares. Any of the terms of the resolution of the board of directors to so merge may be made dependent upon facts ascertainable outside of such resolution, provided that the manner in which such facts shall operate upon the terms of the resolution is clearly and expressly set forth in the resolution. The term "facts," as used in the preceding sentence, includes, but is not limited to, the occurrence of any event, including a determination or action by any person or body, including the corporation. If the parent corporation be not the surviving corporation, the resolution shall include provision for the pro rata issuance of stock of the surviving corporation to the holders of the stock of the parent corporation on surrender of any certificates therefor, and the certificate of ownership and merger shall state that the proposed merger has been approved by a majority of the outstanding stock of the parent corporation entitled to vote thereon at a meeting duly called and held after 20 days' notice of the purpose of the meeting given to each such stockholder at the stockholder's address as it appears on the records of the corporation if the parent corporation is a corporation of this State or state that the proposed merger has been adopted, approved, certified, executed and acknowledged by the parent corporation in accordance with the laws under which it is organized if the parent corporation is a foreign corporation. If the surviving corporation is a foreign corporation:

(1)   Section 252(d) of this title or § 258(c) of this title, as applicable, shall also apply to a merger under this section; and

(2)   The terms and conditions of the merger shall obligate the surviving corporation to provide the agreement, and take the actions, required by § 252(d) of this title or § 258(c) of this title, as applicable.

(b)   If the surviving corporation is a Delaware corporation, it may change its corporate name by the inclusion of a provision to that effect in the resolution of merger adopted by the directors of the parent corporation and set forth in the certificate of ownership and merger, and upon the effective date of the merger, the name of the corporation shall be so changed.

(c)   Section § 251(d) of this title shall apply to a merger under this section, and § 251(e) of this title shall apply to a merger under this section in which the surviving corporation is the subsidiary corporation and is a corporation of this State. References to "agreement of merger" in § 251(d) and (e) of this title shall mean for purposes of this subsection the resolution of merger adopted by the board of directors of the parent corporation. Any merger which effects any changes other than those authorized by this section or made applicable by this subsection shall be accomplished under § 251, § 252, § 257, or § 258 of this title. Section 262 of this title shall not apply to any merger effected under this section, except as provided in subsection (d) of this section.

(d)   In the event all of the stock of a subsidiary Delaware corporation party to a merger effected under this section is not owned by the parent corporation immediately prior to the merger, the stockholders of the subsidiary Delaware corporation party to the merger shall have appraisal rights as set forth in § 262 of this title.

(e)   This section shall apply to nonstock corporations if the parent corporation is such a corporation and is the surviving corporation of the merger; provided, however, that references to the directors of the parent corporation shall be deemed to be references to members of the governing body of the parent corporation, and references to the board of directors of the parent corporation shall be deemed to be references to the governing body of the parent corporation.

(f)   Nothing in this section shall be deemed to authorize the merger of a corporation with a charitable nonstock corporation, if the charitable status of such charitable nonstock corporation would thereby be lost or impaired.

§ 254.   **Merger or consolidation of domestic corporation and joint-stock or other association.**

(a)   The term "joint-stock association" as used in this section, includes any association of the kind commonly known as a joint-stock association or joint-stock company and any unincorporated association, trust or enterprise having members or having outstanding shares of stock or other evidences of financial or beneficial interest therein, whether formed or organized by agreement or under statutory authority or otherwise and whether formed or organized under the laws of this State or any other jurisdiction, but does not include a corporation, partnership or limited liability company. The term "stockholder" as used in this section, includes every member of such joint-stock association or holder of a share of stock or other evidence of financial or beneficial interest therein.

(b)   Any 1 or more corporations of this State may merge or consolidate with 1 or more joint-stock associations, unless the laws of the jurisdiction or jurisdictions under which such joint-stock association or associations are formed or organized prohibit such merger or consolidation. Such corporation or corporations and such 1 or more joint-stock associations may merge into a single surviving corporation or joint-stock association, which may be any 1 of such corporations or joint-stock associations, or they may consolidate into a new resulting corporation of this State or a joint-stock association, pursuant to an agreement of merger or consolidation, as the case may be, complying and approved in accordance with this section. The surviving or resulting entity may be organized for profit or not organized for profit, and if the surviving or resulting entity is a corporation, it may be a stock corporation of this State or a nonstock corporation of this State.

(c)   Each such corporation and joint-stock association shall enter into a written agreement of merger or consolidation. The agreement shall state:

(1)   The terms and conditions of the merger or consolidation;

(2)   The mode of carrying the same into effect;

(3)   In the case of a merger in which the surviving entity is a corporation of this State, such amendments or changes in the certificate of incorporation of the surviving corporation as are desired to be effected by the merger (which amendments or changes may amend and restate the certificate of incorporation of the surviving corporation in its entirety), or, if no such amendments or changes are desired, a statement that the certificate of incorporation of the surviving corporation shall be its certificate of incorporation;

(4)   In the case of a consolidation in which the resulting entity is a corporation of this State, that the certificate of incorporation of the resulting corporation shall be as is set forth in an attachment to the agreement;

(5)   The manner, if any, of converting the shares of stock of each stock corporation, the interest of members of each nonstock corporation, and the shares, membership or financial or beneficial interests in each of the joint-stock associations into shares or other securities of a stock corporation or membership interests of a nonstock corporation or into shares, memberships or financial or beneficial interests of the joint-stock association surviving or resulting from such merger or consolidation, or of cancelling some or all of such shares, memberships or financial or beneficial interests, and, if any shares of any such stock corporation, any membership interests of any such nonstock corporation or any shares, memberships or financial or beneficial interests in any such joint-stock association are not to remain outstanding, to be converted solely into shares or other securities of the stock corporation or membership interests of the nonstock corporation or into shares, memberships or financial or beneficial interests of the joint-stock association surviving or resulting from such merger or consolidation or to be cancelled, the cash, property, rights or securities of any other corporation or entity which the holders of shares of any such stock corporation, membership interests of any such nonstock corporation, or shares, memberships or financial or beneficial interests of any such joint-stock association are to receive in exchange for, or upon conversion of such shares, membership interests or shares, memberships or financial or beneficial interests, and the surrender of any certificates evidencing them, which cash, property, rights or securities of any other corporation or entity may be in addition to or in lieu of shares or other securities of the stock corporation or membership interests of the nonstock

corporation or shares, memberships or financial or beneficial interests of the joint-stock association surviving or resulting from such merger or consolidation;

(6) Such other details or provisions as are deemed desirable, including, without limiting the generality of the foregoing, a provision for the payment of cash in lieu of the issuance or recognition of fractional shares, rights, other securities or interests of the surviving or resulting entity or of fractional shares, rights, other securities or interests of any other corporation or entity the securities of which are to be received in the merger or consolidation, or for some other arrangement with respect thereto, consistent with § 155 of this title; and

(7) Such other provisions or facts as shall be required to be set forth in an agreement of merger or consolidation (including any provision for amendment of the governing documents of a surviving joint-stock association) or required to establish and maintain a joint-stock association by the laws under which the joint-stock association is formed or organized.

Any of the terms of the agreement of merger or consolidation may be made dependent upon facts ascertainable outside of such agreement, provided that the manner in which such facts shall operate upon the terms of the agreement is clearly and expressly set forth in the agreement of merger or consolidation. The term "facts," as used in the preceding sentence, includes, but is not limited to, the occurrence of any event, including a determination or action by any person or body, including the corporation.

(d) The agreement required by subsection (c) of this section shall be adopted, approved, certified, executed and acknowledged by each of the stock or nonstock corporations in the same manner as is provided in § 251 or § 255 of this title, respectively, and in the case of the joint-stock associations in accordance with the laws of the jurisdiction under which they are formed or organized. The agreement shall be filed and shall become effective for all purposes of the laws of this State when and as provided in § 251 of this title with respect to the merger or consolidation of corporations of this State. In lieu of filing the agreement of merger or consolidation, the surviving or resulting entity may file a certificate of merger or consolidation, executed in accordance with § 103 of this title, which states:

(1) The name, jurisdiction of formation or organization and type of entity of each of the constituent entities;

(2) That an agreement of merger or consolidation has been approved, adopted, certified, executed and acknowledged by each of the constituent entities in accordance with this subsection;

(3) The name of the surviving or resulting corporation or joint-stock association;

(4) In the case of a merger in which the surviving entity is a corporation of this State, such amendments or changes in the certificate of incorporation of the surviving corporation as are desired to be effected by the merger (which amendments or changes may amend and restate the certificate of incorporation of the surviving corporation in its entirety), or, if no such amendments or changes are desired, a statement that the certificate of incorporation of the surviving corporation shall be its certificate of incorporation;

(5) In the case of a consolidation in which the resulting entity is a corporation of this State, that the certificate of incorporation of the resulting corporation shall be as is set forth in an attachment to the certificate;

(6) That the executed agreement of consolidation or merger is on file at an office of the surviving or resulting corporation or joint-stock association and the address thereof;

(7) That a copy of the agreement of consolidation or merger will be furnished by the surviving or resulting corporation or joint-stock association, on request and without cost, to any stockholder or member of any constituent entity; and

(8) The agreement, if any, required by § 252(d) of this title.

(e) Sections 251(d), 251(e) to the extent the surviving entity is a corporation of this State, §§ 251(f), 252(d), 259 through 262 and 328 of this title shall, insofar as they are applicable, apply to mergers or consolidations between corporations and joint-stock associations; the word "corporation" where applicable, as used in those sections, being deemed to include joint-stock associations as defined herein. Where the surviving or resulting entity is a corporation, for purposes of the laws of this State, the personal liability, if any, of any stockholder of a joint-stock association existing at the time of such merger or consolidation shall not thereby be extinguished, shall remain personal to such stockholder and shall not become the liability of any subsequent transferee of any share of stock in such surviving or resulting corporation or of any other stockholder of such surviving or resulting corporation.

(f) Nothing in this section shall be deemed to authorize the merger of a charitable nonstock corporation or charitable joint-stock association into a stock corporation or joint-stock association if the charitable status of such nonstock corporation or joint-stock association would be thereby lost or impaired, but a stock corporation or a joint-stock association may be merged into a charitable nonstock corporation or charitable joint-stock association which shall continue as the surviving corporation or joint-stock association.

§ 255. Merger or consolidation of domestic nonstock corporations.

(a) Any 2 or more nonstock corporations of this State, whether or not organized for profit, may merge into a single surviving corporation, which may be any 1 of the constituent corporations, or they may consolidate into a new resulting nonstock corporation, whether or not organized for profit, formed by the consolidation, pursuant to an agreement of merger or consolidation, as the case may be, complying and approved in accordance with this section.

(b) Subject to subsection (d) of this section, the governing body of each corporation which desires to merge or consolidate shall adopt a resolution approving an agreement of merger or consolidation. The agreement shall state:

(1) The terms and conditions of the merger or consolidation;

(2) The mode of carrying the same into effect;

(3) In the case of a merger, such amendments or changes in the certificate of incorporation of the surviving corporation as are desired to be effected by the merger (which amendments or changes may amend and restate the certificate of incorporation of the surviving corporation in its entirety), or, if no such amendments or changes are desired, a statement that the certificate of incorporation of the surviving corporation shall be its certificate of incorporation;

(4) In the case of a consolidation, that the certificate of incorporation of the resulting corporation shall be as is set forth in an attachment to the agreement;

(5) The manner, if any, of converting the memberships or membership interests of each of the constituent corporations into memberships or membership interests of the corporation surviving or resulting from the merger or consolidation, or of cancelling some or all of such memberships or membership interests, and, if any memberships or membership interests of any of the constituent corporations are not to remain outstanding, to be converted solely into memberships or membership interests of the surviving or resulting corporation or to be cancelled, the cash, property, rights or securities of any other corporation or entity which the holders of such memberships or membership interests are to receive in exchange for, or upon conversion of, such memberships or membership interests, which cash, property, rights or securities of any other corporation or entity may be in addition to or in lieu of memberships or membership interests of the surviving or resulting corporation; and

(6) Such other details or provisions as are deemed desirable, including, without limiting the generality of the foregoing, a provision for the payment of cash in lieu of the issuance or recognition of fractional shares, rights or other securities of any other corporation or entity the shares, rights or other securities of which are to be received in the merger or consolidation, or for some other arrangement with respect thereto, consistent with § 155 of this title.

The agreement so adopted shall be executed by an authorized person, provided that if the agreement is filed, it shall be executed and acknowledged in accordance with § 103 of this title. Any of the terms of the agreement of merger or consolidation may be made dependent upon facts ascertainable outside of such agreement, provided that the manner in which such facts shall operate upon the terms of the agreement is clearly and expressly set forth in the agreement of merger or consolidation. The term "facts," as used in the preceding sentence, includes, but is not limited to, the occurrence of any event, including a determination or action by any person or body, including the corporation.

(c)   Subject to subsection (d) of this section, the agreement shall be submitted to the members of each constituent corporation, at an annual or special meeting thereof for the purpose of acting on the agreement. Due notice of the time, place and purpose of the meeting shall be given to each member of each such corporation who has the right to vote for the election of the members of the governing body of the corporation and to each other member who is entitled to vote on the merger under the certificate of incorporation or the bylaws of such corporation, at the member's address as it appears on the records of the corporation, at least 20 days prior to the date of the meeting. The notice shall contain a copy of the agreement or a brief summary thereof. At the meeting the agreement shall be considered and a vote, in person or by proxy, taken for the adoption or rejection of the agreement. If the agreement is adopted by a majority of the members of each such corporation entitled to vote for the election of the members of the governing body of the corporation and any other members entitled to vote on the merger under the certificate of incorporation or the bylaws of such corporation, then that fact shall be certified on the agreement by the officer of each such corporation performing the duties ordinarily performed by the secretary or assistant secretary of a corporation, provided that such certification on the agreement shall not be required if a certificate of merger or consolidation is filed in lieu of filing the agreement. If the agreement shall be adopted and certified by each constituent corporation in accordance with this section, it shall be filed and shall become effective in accordance with § 103 of this title. The provisions set forth in the last sentence of § 251(c) of this title shall apply to a merger under this section, and the reference therein to "stockholder" shall be deemed to include "member" hereunder.

(d)   Notwithstanding subsection (b) or (c) of this section, if, under the certificate of incorporation or the bylaws of any 1 or more of the constituent corporations, there shall be no members who have the right to vote for the election of the members of the governing body of the corporation, or for the merger, other than the members of the governing body themselves, no further action by the governing body or the members of such corporation shall be necessary if the resolution approving an agreement of merger or consolidation has been adopted by a majority of all the members of the governing body thereof, and that fact shall be certified on the agreement in the same manner as is provided in the case of the adoption of the agreement by the vote of the members of a corporation, provided that such certification on the agreement shall not be required if a certificate of merger or consolidation is filed in lieu of filing the agreement, and thereafter the same procedure shall be followed to consummate the merger or consolidation.

(e)   Section 251(d) of this title shall apply to a merger under this section; provided, however, that references to the board of directors, to stockholders, and to shares of a constituent corporation shall be deemed to be references to the governing body of the corporation, to members of the corporation, and to memberships or membership interests, as applicable, respectively.

(f)   Section 251(e) of this title shall apply to a merger under this section.

(g)   Nothing in this section shall be deemed to authorize the merger of a charitable nonstock corporation into a nonstock corporation if such charitable nonstock corporation would thereby have its charitable status lost or impaired; but a nonstock corporation may be merged into a charitable nonstock corporation which shall continue as the surviving corporation.

§ 256.   Merger or consolidation of domestic and foreign nonstock corporations; service of process upon surviving or resulting corporation.

(a)   Any 1 or more nonstock corporations of this State may merge or consolidate with 1 or more foreign nonstock corporations, unless the laws of the jurisdiction or jurisdictions under which such foreign nonstock corporation or corporations are organized prohibit such merger or consolidation. The constituent corporations may merge into a single surviving corporation, which may be any 1 of the constituent corporations, or they may consolidate into a new resulting nonstock corporation formed by the consolidation, which may be a corporation of the jurisdiction of organization of any 1 of the constituent corporations, pursuant to an agreement of merger or consolidation, as the case may be, complying and approved in accordance with this section. The term "foreign nonstock corporation" means a nonstock corporation organized under the laws of any jurisdiction other than this State.

(b)   All the constituent corporations shall enter into an agreement of merger or consolidation. The agreement shall state:

(1)   The terms and conditions of the merger or consolidation;

(2)   The mode of carrying the same into effect;

(3)   In the case of a merger in which the surviving corporation is a corporation of this State, such amendments or changes in the certificate of incorporation of the surviving corporation as are desired to be effected by the merger (which amendments or changes may amend and restate the certificate of incorporation of the surviving corporation in its entirety), or, if no such amendments or changes are desired, a statement that the certificate of incorporation of the surviving corporation shall be its certificate of incorporation;

(4)   In the case of a consolidation in which the resulting corporation is a corporation of this State, that the certificate of incorporation of the resulting corporation shall be as is set forth in an attachment to the agreement;

(5)   The manner, if any, of converting the memberships or membership interests of each of the constituent corporations into memberships or membership interests of the corporation surviving or resulting from the merger or consolidation, or of cancelling some or all of such memberships or membership interests, and, if any memberships or membership interests of any of the constituent corporations are not to remain outstanding, to be converted solely into memberships or membership interests of the surviving or resulting corporation or to be cancelled, the cash, property, rights or securities of any other corporation or entity which the holders of such memberships or membership interests are to receive in exchange for, or upon conversion of, such memberships or membership interests, which cash, property, rights or securities of any other corporation or entity may be in addition to or in lieu of memberships or membership interests of the surviving or resulting corporation;

(6)   Such other details or provisions as are deemed desirable, including, without limiting the generality of the foregoing, a provision for the payment of cash in lieu of the issuance or recognition of fractional shares, rights or other securities of any other corporation or entity the shares, rights or other securities of which are to be received in the merger or consolidation, or for some other arrangement with respect thereto, consistent with § 155 of this title; and

(7)   Such other provisions or facts as shall be required to be set forth in an agreement of merger or consolidation (including any provision for amendment of the certificate of incorporation (or equivalent document) of a surviving foreign nonstock corporation) by the laws of each jurisdiction under which any of the foreign nonstock corporations are organized.

Any of the terms of the agreement of merger or consolidation may be made dependent upon facts ascertainable outside of such agreement, provided that the manner in which such facts shall operate upon the terms of the agreement is clearly and expressly set forth in the agreement of merger or consolidation. The term "facts," as used in the preceding sentence, includes, but is not limited to, the occurrence of any event, including a determination or action by any person or body, including the corporation.

(c)   The agreement shall be adopted, approved, certified, executed and acknowledged by each of the constituent corporations in accordance with the laws under which it is organized and, in the case of a Delaware corporation, in the same manner as is provided in § 255 of this title. The agreement shall be filed and shall become effective for all purposes of the laws of this State when and as provided in § 255 of this title with respect to the merger of nonstock corporations of this State. Insofar as they may be applicable, the provisions set forth in the last sentence of § 252(c) of this title shall apply to a merger under this section, and the reference therein to "stockholder" shall be deemed to include "member" hereunder.

(d)   If the corporation surviving or resulting from the merger or consolidation is a foreign nonstock corporation, it shall agree that it may be served with process in this State in any proceeding for enforcement of any obligation of any constituent corporation of this State, as well as for enforcement of any obligation of the surviving or resulting corporation arising from the merger or consolidation and shall irrevocably appoint the Secretary of State as its agent to accept service of process in any suit or other proceedings and shall specify the address to which a copy of such process shall be mailed by the Secretary of State. Process may be served upon the Secretary of State under this subsection by means of electronic transmission but only as prescribed by the Secretary of State. The Secretary of State is authorized to issue such rules and regulations with respect to such service as the Secretary of State deems necessary or appropriate. In the event of such service upon the Secretary of State in accordance with this subsection, the Secretary of State shall forthwith notify such surviving or resulting corporation thereof by letter, directed to such corporation at its address so specified, unless such surviving or resulting corporation shall have designated in writing to the Secretary of State a different address for such purpose, in which case it shall be mailed to the last address so designated. Such letter shall be sent by a mail or courier service that includes a record of mailing or deposit with the courier and a record of delivery evidenced by the signature of the recipient. Such letter shall enclose a copy of the process and any other papers served upon the Secretary of State. It shall be the duty of the plaintiff in the event of such service to serve process and any other papers in duplicate, to notify the Secretary of State that service is being made pursuant to this subsection, and to pay the Secretary of State the sum of $50 for the use of the State, which sum shall be taxed as a part of the costs in the proceeding if the plaintiff shall prevail therein. The Secretary of State shall maintain an alphabetical record of any such service setting forth the name of the plaintiff and defendant, the title, docket number and nature of the proceeding in which process has been served upon the Secretary of State, the fact that service has been effected pursuant to this subsection, the return date thereof, and the day and hour when the service was made. The Secretary of State shall not be required to retain such information for a period longer than 5 years from receipt of the service of process.

(e)   Section § 251(e) of this title shall apply to a merger under this section if the corporation surviving the merger is a corporation of this State.

(f)   Section 251(d) of this title shall apply to a merger under this section; provided, however, that references to the board of directors, to stockholders, and to shares of a constituent corporation shall be deemed to be references to the governing body of the corporation, to members of the corporation, and to memberships or membership interests, as applicable, respectively.

(g)   Nothing in this section shall be deemed to authorize the merger of a charitable nonstock corporation into a nonstock corporation, if the charitable status of such charitable nonstock corporation would thereby be lost or impaired; but a nonstock corporation may be merged into a charitable nonstock corporation which shall continue as the surviving corporation.

§ 257.   Merger or consolidation of domestic stock and nonstock corporations.

(a)   Any 1 or more nonstock corporations of this State, whether or not organized for profit, may merge or consolidate with 1 or more stock corporations of this State, whether or not organized for profit. The constituent corporations may merge into a single surviving corporation, which may be any 1 of the constituent corporations, or they may consolidate into a new resulting corporation formed by the consolidation, pursuant to an agreement of merger or consolidation, as the case may be, complying and approved in accordance with this section. The surviving constituent corporation or the resulting corporation may be organized for profit or not organized for profit and may be a stock corporation or a nonstock corporation.

(b)   The board of directors of each stock corporation which desires to merge or consolidate and the governing body of each nonstock corporation which desires to merge or consolidate shall adopt a resolution approving an agreement of merger or consolidation. The agreement shall state:

(1)   The terms and conditions of the merger or consolidation;

(2)   The mode of carrying the same into effect;

(3)   In the case of a merger, such amendments or changes in the certificate of incorporation of the surviving corporation as are desired to be effected by the merger (which amendments or changes may amend and restate the certificate of incorporation of the surviving corporation in its entirety), or, if no such amendments or changes are desired, a statement that the certificate of incorporation of the surviving corporation shall be its certificate of incorporation;

(4)   In the case of a consolidation, that the certificate of incorporation of the resulting corporation shall be as is set forth in an attachment to the agreement;

(5)   The manner, if any, of converting the shares of stock of a stock corporation and the memberships or membership interests of a nonstock corporation into shares or other securities of a stock corporation or memberships or membership interests of a nonstock corporation surviving or resulting from such merger or consolidation or of cancelling some or all of such shares or memberships or membership interests, and, if any shares of any such stock corporation or memberships or

membership interests of any such nonstock corporation are not to remain outstanding, to be converted solely into shares or other securities of the stock corporation or memberships or membership interests of the nonstock corporation surviving or resulting from such merger or consolidation or to be cancelled, the cash, property, rights or securities of any other corporation or entity which the holders of shares of any such stock corporation or memberships or membership interests of any such nonstock corporation are to receive in exchange for, or upon conversion of such shares or memberships or membership interests, and the surrender of any certificates evidencing them, which cash, property, rights or securities of any other corporation or entity may be in addition to or in lieu of shares or other securities of any stock corporation or memberships or membership interests of any nonstock corporation surviving or resulting from such merger or consolidation; and

(6)   Such other details or provisions as are deemed desirable, including, without limiting the generality of the foregoing, a provision for the payment of cash in lieu of the issuance or recognition of fractional shares, rights or other securities of the surviving or resulting corporation or of any other corporation or entity the shares, rights or other securities of which are to be received in the merger or consolidation, or for some other arrangement with respect thereto, consistent with § 155 of this title.

Any of the terms of the agreement of merger or consolidation may be made dependent upon facts ascertainable outside of such agreement, provided that the manner in which such facts shall operate upon the terms of the agreement is clearly and expressly set forth in the agreement of merger or consolidation. The term "facts," as used in the preceding sentence, includes, but is not limited to, the occurrence of any event, including a determination or action by any person or body, including the corporation.

(c)   The agreement required by subsection (b) of this section, in the case of each constituent stock corporation, shall be adopted, approved, certified, executed and acknowledged by each constituent corporation in the same manner as is provided in § 251 of this title and, in the case of each constituent nonstock corporation, shall be adopted, approved, certified, executed and acknowledged by each of said constituent corporations in the same manner as is provided in § 255 of this title. The agreement shall be filed and shall become effective for all purposes of the laws of this State when and as provided in § 251 of this title with respect to the merger of stock corporations of this State. Insofar as they may be applicable, the provisions set forth in the last sentence of § 251(c) of this title shall apply to a merger under this section, and the reference therein to "stockholder" shall be deemed to include "member" hereunder.

(d)   Section 251(e) of this title shall apply to a merger under this section; § 251(d) of this title shall apply to any constituent stock corporation participating in a merger or consolidation under this section; and § 251(f) of this title shall apply to any constituent stock corporation participating in a merger under this section.

(e)   Section 251(d) of this title shall apply to a merger under this section; provided, however, that, for purposes of a constituent nonstock corporation, references to the board of directors, to stockholders, and to shares of a constituent corporation shall be deemed to be references to the governing body of the corporation, to members of the corporation, and to memberships or membership interests, as applicable, respectively.

(f)   Nothing in this section shall be deemed to authorize the merger of a charitable nonstock corporation into a stock corporation, if the charitable status of such nonstock corporation would thereby be lost or impaired; but a stock corporation may be merged into a charitable nonstock corporation which shall continue as the surviving corporation.

§ 258.   Merger or consolidation of domestic and foreign stock and nonstock corporations.

(a)   Any 1 or more corporations of this State, whether stock or nonstock corporations and whether or not organized for profit, may merge or consolidate with 1 or more foreign corporations, unless the laws of the jurisdiction or jurisdictions under which such foreign corporation or corporations are organized prohibit such merger or consolidation. The constituent corporations may merge into a single surviving corporation, which may be any 1 of the constituent corporations, or they may consolidate into a new resulting corporation formed by the consolidation, which may be a corporation of the jurisdiction of organization of any 1 of the constituent corporations, pursuant to an agreement of merger or consolidation, as the case may be, complying and approved in accordance with this section. The surviving or resulting corporation may be either a domestic or foreign stock corporation or a domestic or foreign nonstock corporation, as shall be specified in the agreement of merger or consolidation required by subsection (b) of this section. For purposes of this section, the term "foreign corporation" includes a nonstock corporation organized under the laws of any jurisdiction other than this State.

(b) The method and procedure to be followed by the constituent corporations so merging or consolidating shall be as prescribed in § 257 of this title in the case of Delaware corporations. The agreement of merger or consolidation shall be as provided in § 257 of this title and also set forth such other provisions or facts as shall be required to be set forth in an agreement of merger or consolidation (including any provision for amendment of the certificate of incorporation (or equivalent document) of a surviving foreign corporation) by the laws of the jurisdiction or jurisdictions which are stated in the agreement to be the laws under which the foreign corporation or corporations are organized. The agreement, in the case of foreign corporations, shall be adopted, approved, certified, executed and acknowledged in accordance with the laws under which each is organized.

(c) The requirements of § 252(d) of this title as to the appointment of the Secretary of State to receive process and the manner of serving the same in the event the surviving or resulting corporation is a foreign corporation shall also apply to mergers or consolidations effected under this section and such appointment, if any, shall be included in the certificate of merger or consolidation, if any, filed pursuant to subsection (b) of this section. Section 251(e) of this title shall apply to mergers effected under this section if the surviving corporation is a corporation of this State; § 251(d) of this title shall apply to any constituent corporation participating in a merger or consolidation under this section (provided, however, that for purposes of a constituent nonstock corporation, references to the board of directors, to stockholders, and to shares shall be deemed to be references to the governing body of the corporation, to members of the corporation, and to memberships or membership interests of the corporation, as applicable, respectively); and § 251(f) of this title shall apply to any constituent stock corporation of this State participating in a merger under this section.

(d) Nothing in this section shall be deemed to authorize the merger of a charitable nonstock corporation into a stock corporation, if the charitable status of such nonstock corporation would thereby be lost or impaired; but a stock corporation may be merged into a charitable nonstock corporation which shall continue as the surviving corporation.

§ 259. Status, rights, liabilities, of constituent and surviving or resulting corporations following merger or consolidation.

(a) When any merger or consolidation shall have become effective under this chapter, for all purposes of the laws of this State the separate existence of all the constituent corporations, or of all such constituent corporations except the one into which the other or others of such constituent corporations have been merged, as the case may be, shall cease and the constituent corporations shall become a new corporation, or be merged into 1 of such corporations, as the case may be, possessing all the rights, privileges, powers and franchises as well of a public as of a private nature, and being subject to all the restrictions, disabilities and duties of each of such corporations so merged or consolidated; and all and singular, the rights, privileges, powers and franchises of each of said corporations, and all property, real, personal and mixed, and all debts due to any of said constituent corporations on whatever account, as well for stock subscriptions as all other things in action or belonging to each of such corporations shall be vested in the corporation surviving or resulting from such merger or consolidation; and all property, rights, privileges, powers and franchises, and all and every other interest shall be thereafter as effectually the property of the surviving or resulting corporation as they were of the several and respective constituent corporations, and the title to any real estate vested by deed or otherwise, under the laws of this State, in any of such constituent corporations, shall not revert or be in any way impaired by reason of this chapter; but all rights of creditors and all liens upon any property of any of said constituent corporations shall be preserved unimpaired, and all debts, liabilities and duties of the respective constituent corporations shall thenceforth attach to said surviving or resulting corporation, and may be enforced against it to the same extent as if said debts, liabilities and duties had been incurred or contracted by it.

(b) In the case of a merger of banks or trust companies, without any order or action on the part of any court or otherwise, all appointments, designations, and nominations, and all other rights and interests as trustee, executor, administrator, registrar of stocks and bonds, guardian of estates, assignee, receiver, trustee of estates of persons mentally ill and in every other fiduciary capacity, shall be automatically vested in the corporation resulting from or surviving such merger; provided, however, that any party in interest shall have the right to apply to an appropriate court or tribunal for a determination as to whether the surviving corporation shall continue to serve in the same fiduciary capacity as the merged corporation, or whether a new and different fiduciary should be appointed.

§ 260. Powers of corporation surviving or resulting from merger or consolidation; issuance of stock, bonds or other indebtedness.

When 2 or more corporations are merged or consolidated, the corporation surviving or resulting from the merger may issue bonds or other obligations, negotiable or otherwise, and with or without coupons or interest certificates thereto attached, to an amount sufficient with its capital stock to provide for all the payments it will be required to make, or obligations it will be required to assume, in order to effect the merger or consolidation. For the purpose of securing the payment of any such bonds and obligations, it shall be lawful for the surviving or resulting corporation to mortgage its corporate franchise, rights, privileges and property, real, personal or mixed. The surviving or resulting corporation may issue certificates of its capital stock or uncertificated stock if authorized to do so and other securities to the stockholders of the constituent corporations in exchange or payment for the original shares, in such amount as shall be necessary in accordance with the terms of the agreement of merger or consolidation in order to effect such merger or consolidation in the manner and on the terms specified in the agreement.

§ 261. Effect of merger upon pending actions.

Any action or proceeding, whether civil, criminal or administrative, pending by or against any corporation which is a party to a merger or consolidation shall be prosecuted as if such merger or consolidation had not taken place, or the corporation surviving or resulting from such merger or consolidation may be substituted in such action or proceeding.

§ 262. Appraisal rights [for application of this section, see 79 Del. Laws, c. 72, § 22; 79 Del. Laws, c. 122, § 12; 80 Del. Laws, c. 265, § 18; 81 Del. Laws, c. 354, § 17; and 82 Del. Laws, c. 45, § 23].

(a) Any stockholder of a corporation of this State who holds shares of stock on the date of the making of a demand pursuant to subsection (d) of this section with respect to such shares, who continuously holds such shares through the effective date of the merger or consolidation, who has otherwise complied with subsection (d) of this section and who has neither voted in favor of the merger or consolidation nor consented thereto in writing pursuant to § 228 of this title shall be entitled to an appraisal by the Court of Chancery of the fair value of the stockholder's shares of stock under the circumstances described in subsections (b) and (c) of this section. As used in this section, the word "stockholder" means a holder of record of stock in a corporation; the words "stock" and "share" mean and include what is ordinarily meant by those words; and the words "depository receipt" mean a receipt or other instrument issued by a depository representing an interest in 1 or more shares, or fractions thereof, solely of stock of a corporation, which stock is deposited with the depository.

(b) Appraisal rights shall be available for the shares of any class or series of stock of a constituent corporation in a merger or consolidation to be effected pursuant to § 251 (other than a merger effected pursuant to § 251(g) of this title), § 252, § 254, § 255, § 256, § 257, § 258, § 263 or § 264 of this title:

(1) Provided, however, that, except as expressly provided in § 363(b) of this title, no appraisal rights under this section shall be available for the shares of any class or series of stock, which stock, or depository receipts in respect thereof, at the record date fixed to determine the stockholders entitled to receive notice of the meeting of stockholders to act upon the agreement of merger or consolidation (or, in the case of a merger pursuant to § 251(h), as of immediately prior to the execution of the agreement of merger), were either: (i) listed on a national securities exchange or (ii) held of record by more than 2,000 holders; and further provided that no appraisal rights shall be available for any shares of stock of the constituent corporation surviving a merger if the merger did not require for its approval the vote of the stockholders of the surviving corporation as provided in § 251(f) of this title.

(2) Notwithstanding paragraph (b)(1) of this section, appraisal rights under this section shall be available for the shares of any class or series of stock of a constituent corporation if the holders

thereof are required by the terms of an agreement of merger or consolidation pursuant to §§ 251, 252, 254, 255, 256, 257, 258, 263 and 264 of this title to accept for such stock anything except:

    a.   Shares of stock of the corporation surviving or resulting from such merger or consolidation, or depository receipts in respect thereof;

    b.   Shares of stock of any other corporation, or depository receipts in respect thereof, which shares of stock (or depository receipts in respect thereof) or depository receipts at the effective date of the merger or consolidation will be either listed on a national securities exchange or held of record by more than 2,000 holders;

    c.   Cash in lieu of fractional shares or fractional depository receipts described in the foregoing paragraphs (b)(2)a. and b. of this section; or

    d.   Any combination of the shares of stock, depository receipts and cash in lieu of fractional shares or fractional depository receipts described in the foregoing paragraphs (b)(2)a., b. and c. of this section.

(3)   In the event all of the stock of a subsidiary Delaware corporation party to a merger effected under § 253 or § 267 of this title is not owned by the parent immediately prior to the merger, appraisal rights shall be available for the shares of the subsidiary Delaware corporation.

(4)   In the event of an amendment to a corporation's certificate of incorporation contemplated by § 363(a) of this title, appraisal rights shall be available as contemplated by § 363(b) of this title, and the procedures of this section, including those set forth in subsections (d) and (e) of this section, shall apply as nearly as practicable, with the word "amendment" substituted for the words "merger or consolidation," and the word "corporation" substituted for the words "constituent corporation" and/or "surviving or resulting corporation."

(c)   Any corporation may provide in its certificate of incorporation that appraisal rights under this section shall be available for the shares of any class or series of its stock as a result of an amendment to its certificate of incorporation, any merger or consolidation in which the corporation is a constituent corporation or the sale of all or substantially all of the assets of the corporation. If the certificate of incorporation contains such a provision, the provisions of this section, including those set forth in subsections (d),(e), and (g) of this section, shall apply as nearly as is practicable.

(d)   Appraisal rights shall be perfected as follows:

(1)   If a proposed merger or consolidation for which appraisal rights are provided under this section is to be submitted for approval at a meeting of stockholders, the corporation, not less than 20 days prior to the meeting, shall notify each of its stockholders who was such on the record date for notice of such meeting (or such members who received notice in accordance with § 255(c) of this title) with respect to shares for which appraisal rights are available pursuant to subsection (b) or (c) of this section that appraisal rights are available for any or all of the shares of the constituent corporations, and shall include in such notice a copy of this section and, if 1 of the constituent corporations is a nonstock corporation, a copy of § 114 of this title. Each stockholder electing to demand the appraisal of such stockholder's shares shall deliver to the corporation, before the taking of the vote on the merger or consolidation, a written demand for appraisal of such stockholder's shares; provided that a demand may be delivered to the corporation by electronic transmission if directed to an information processing system (if any) expressly designated for that purpose in such notice. Such demand will be sufficient if it reasonably informs the corporation of the identity of the stockholder and that the stockholder intends thereby to demand the appraisal of such stockholder's shares. A proxy or vote against the merger or consolidation shall not constitute such a demand. A stockholder electing to take such action must do so by a separate written demand as herein provided. Within 10 days after the effective date of such merger or consolidation, the surviving or resulting corporation shall notify each stockholder of each constituent corporation who has complied with this subsection and has not voted in favor of or consented to the merger or consolidation of the date that the merger or consolidation has become effective; or

(2)   If the merger or consolidation was approved pursuant to § 228, § 251(h), § 253, or § 267 of this title, then either a constituent corporation before the effective date of the merger or consolidation

or the surviving or resulting corporation within 10 days thereafter shall notify each of the holders of any class or series of stock of such constituent corporation who are entitled to appraisal rights of the approval of the merger or consolidation and that appraisal rights are available for any or all shares of such class or series of stock of such constituent corporation, and shall include in such notice a copy of this section and, if 1 of the constituent corporations is a nonstock corporation, a copy of § 114 of this title. Such notice may, and, if given on or after the effective date of the merger or consolidation, shall, also notify such stockholders of the effective date of the merger or consolidation. Any stockholder entitled to appraisal rights may, within 20 days after the date of giving such notice or, in the case of a merger approved pursuant to § 251(h) of this title, within the later of the consummation of the offer contemplated by § 251(h) of this title and 20 days after the date of giving such notice, demand in writing from the surviving or resulting corporation the appraisal of such holder's shares; provided that a demand may be delivered to the corporation by electronic transmission if directed to an information processing system (if any) expressly designated for that purpose in such notice. Such demand will be sufficient if it reasonably informs the corporation of the identity of the stockholder and that the stockholder intends thereby to demand the appraisal of such holder's shares. If such notice did not notify stockholders of the effective date of the merger or consolidation, either (i) each such constituent corporation shall send a second notice before the effective date of the merger or consolidation notifying each of the holders of any class or series of stock of such constituent corporation that are entitled to appraisal rights of the effective date of the merger or consolidation or (ii) the surviving or resulting corporation shall send such a second notice to all such holders on or within 10 days after such effective date; provided, however, that if such second notice is sent more than 20 days following the sending of the first notice or, in the case of a merger approved pursuant to § 251(h) of this title, later than the later of the consummation of the offer contemplated by § 251(h) of this title and 20 days following the sending of the first notice, such second notice need only be sent to each stockholder who is entitled to appraisal rights and who has demanded appraisal of such holder's shares in accordance with this subsection. An affidavit of the secretary or assistant secretary or of the transfer agent of the corporation that is required to give either notice that such notice has been given shall, in the absence of fraud, be prima facie evidence of the facts stated therein. For purposes of determining the stockholders entitled to receive either notice, each constituent corporation may fix, in advance, a record date that shall be not more than 10 days prior to the date the notice is given, provided, that if the notice is given on or after the effective date of the merger or consolidation, the record date shall be such effective date. If no record date is fixed and the notice is given prior to the effective date, the record date shall be the close of business on the day next preceding the day on which the notice is given.

(e)   Within 120 days after the effective date of the merger or consolidation, the surviving or resulting corporation or any stockholder who has complied with subsections (a) and (d) of this section hereof and who is otherwise entitled to appraisal rights, may commence an appraisal proceeding by filing a petition in the Court of Chancery demanding a determination of the value of the stock of all such stockholders. Notwithstanding the foregoing, at any time within 60 days after the effective date of the merger or consolidation, any stockholder who has not commenced an appraisal proceeding or joined that proceeding as a named party shall have the right to withdraw such stockholder's demand for appraisal and to accept the terms offered upon the merger or consolidation. Within 120 days after the effective date of the merger or consolidation, any stockholder who has complied with the requirements of subsections (a) and (d) of this section hereof, upon request given in writing (or by electronic transmission directed to an information processing system (if any) expressly designated for that purpose in the notice of appraisal), shall be entitled to receive from the corporation surviving the merger or resulting from the consolidation a statement setting forth the aggregate number of shares not voted in favor of the merger or consolidation (or, in the case of a merger approved pursuant to § 251(h) of this title, the aggregate number of shares (other than any excluded stock (as defined in § 251(h)(6)d. of this title)) that were the subject of, and were not tendered into, and accepted for purchase or exchange in, the offer referred to in § 251(h)(2)), and, in either case, with respect to which demands for appraisal have been received and the aggregate number of holders of such shares. Such statement shall be given to the stockholder within 10 days after such stockholder's request for such a statement is received by the surviving or resulting corporation or within 10 days after expiration of the period for delivery of demands for appraisal under subsection (d) of this section hereof, whichever is later. Notwithstanding subsection (a) of this section, a person who is the beneficial owner of shares of such stock held either in a voting trust or by a nominee on behalf of such person may, in such person's own name, file a petition or request from the corporation the statement described in this subsection.

(f)   Upon the filing of any such petition by a stockholder, service of a copy thereof shall be made upon the surviving or resulting corporation, which shall within 20 days after such service file in the office of the Register in Chancery in which the petition was filed a duly verified list containing the names and addresses of all stockholders who have demanded payment for their shares and with whom agreements as to the value of their shares have not been reached by the surviving or resulting corporation. If the petition shall be filed by the surviving or resulting corporation, the petition shall be accompanied by such a duly verified list. The Register in Chancery, if so ordered by the Court, shall give notice of the time and place fixed for the hearing of such petition by registered or certified mail to the surviving or resulting corporation and to the stockholders shown on the list at the addresses therein stated. Such notice shall also be given by 1 or more publications at least 1 week before the day of the hearing, in a newspaper of general circulation published in the City of Wilmington, Delaware or such publication as the Court deems advisable. The forms of the notices by mail and by publication shall be approved by the Court, and the costs thereof shall be borne by the surviving or resulting corporation.

(g)   At the hearing on such petition, the Court shall determine the stockholders who have complied with this section and who have become entitled to appraisal rights. The Court may require the stockholders who have demanded an appraisal for their shares and who hold stock represented by certificates to submit their certificates of stock to the Register in Chancery for notation thereon of the pendency of the appraisal proceedings; and if any stockholder fails to comply with such direction, the Court may dismiss the proceedings as to such stockholder. If immediately before the merger or consolidation the shares of the class or series of stock of the constituent corporation as to which appraisal rights are available were listed on a national securities exchange, the Court shall dismiss the proceedings as to all holders of such shares who are otherwise entitled to appraisal rights unless (1) the total number of shares entitled to appraisal exceeds 1% of the outstanding shares of the class or series eligible for appraisal, (2) the value of the consideration provided in the merger or consolidation for such total number of shares exceeds $1 million, or (3) the merger was approved pursuant to § 253 or § 267 of this title.

(h)   After the Court determines the stockholders entitled to an appraisal, the appraisal proceeding shall be conducted in accordance with the rules of the Court of Chancery, including any rules specifically governing appraisal proceedings. Through such proceeding the Court shall determine the fair value of the shares exclusive of any element of value arising from the accomplishment or expectation of the merger or consolidation, together with interest, if any, to be paid upon the amount determined to be the fair value. In determining such fair value, the Court shall take into account all relevant factors. Unless the Court in its discretion determines otherwise for good cause shown, and except as provided in this subsection, interest from the effective date of the merger through the date of payment of the judgment shall be compounded quarterly and shall accrue at 5% over the Federal Reserve discount rate (including any surcharge) as established from time to time during the period between the effective date of the merger and the date of payment of the judgment. At any time before the entry of judgment in the proceedings, the surviving corporation may pay to each stockholder entitled to appraisal an amount in cash, in which case interest shall accrue thereafter as provided herein only upon the sum of (1) the difference, if any, between the amount so paid and the fair value of the shares as determined by the Court, and (2) interest theretofore accrued, unless paid at that time. Upon application by the surviving or resulting corporation or by any stockholder entitled to participate in the appraisal proceeding, the Court may, in its discretion, proceed to trial upon the appraisal prior to the final determination of the stockholders entitled to an appraisal. Any stockholder whose name appears on the list filed by the surviving or resulting corporation pursuant to subsection (f) of this section and who has submitted such stockholder's certificates of stock to the Register in Chancery, if such is required, may participate fully in all proceedings until it is finally determined that such stockholder is not entitled to appraisal rights under this section.

(i)   The Court shall direct the payment of the fair value of the shares, together with interest, if any, by the surviving or resulting corporation to the stockholders entitled thereto. Payment shall be so made to each such stockholder, in the case of holders of uncertificated stock forthwith, and the case of holders of shares represented by certificates upon the surrender to the corporation of the certificates representing such stock. The Court's decree may be enforced as other decrees in the Court of Chancery may be enforced, whether such surviving or resulting corporation be a corporation of this State or of any state.

(j)   The costs of the proceeding may be determined by the Court and taxed upon the parties as the Court deems equitable in the circumstances. Upon application of a stockholder, the Court may order all or a portion of the expenses incurred by any stockholder in connection with the appraisal proceeding, including, without limitation, reasonable attorney's fees and the fees and expenses of experts, to be charged pro rata against the value of all the shares entitled to an appraisal.

(k) From and after the effective date of the merger or consolidation, no stockholder who has demanded appraisal rights as provided in subsection (d) of this section shall be entitled to vote such stock for any purpose or to receive payment of dividends or other distributions on the stock (except dividends or other distributions payable to stockholders of record at a date which is prior to the effective date of the merger or consolidation); provided, however, that if no petition for an appraisal shall be filed within the time provided in subsection (e) of this section, or if such stockholder shall deliver to the surviving or resulting corporation a written withdrawal of such stockholder's demand for an appraisal and an acceptance of the merger or consolidation, either within 60 days after the effective date of the merger or consolidation as provided in subsection (e) of this section or thereafter with the written approval of the corporation, then the right of such stockholder to an appraisal shall cease. Notwithstanding the foregoing, no appraisal proceeding in the Court of Chancery shall be dismissed as to any stockholder without the approval of the Court, and such approval may be conditioned upon such terms as the Court deems just; provided, however that this provision shall not affect the right of any stockholder who has not commenced an appraisal proceeding or joined that proceeding as a named party to withdraw such stockholder's demand for appraisal and to accept the terms offered upon the merger or consolidation within 60 days after the effective date of the merger or consolidation, as set forth in subsection (e) of this section.

(l) The shares of the surviving or resulting corporation to which the shares of such objecting stockholders would have been converted had they assented to the merger or consolidation shall have the status of authorized and unissued shares of the surviving or resulting corporation.

§ 263. Merger or consolidation of domestic corporations and partnerships.

(a) Any 1 or more corporations of this State may merge or consolidate with 1 or more partnerships (whether general (including a limited liability partnership) or limited (including a limited liability limited partnership)), unless the laws of the jurisdiction or jurisdictions under which such partnership or partnerships are formed prohibit such merger or consolidation. Such corporation or corporations and such 1 or more partnerships may merge with or into a surviving corporation, which may be any 1 of such corporations, or they may merge with or into a surviving partnership, which may be any 1 of such partnerships, or they may consolidate into a new resulting corporation, which corporation shall be a corporation of this State, or a partnership formed pursuant to an agreement of merger or consolidation, as the case may be, complying and approved in accordance with this section. The term "partnership" as used in this section includes any partnership (whether general (including a limited liability partnership) or limited (including a limited liability limited partnership)) formed under the laws of this State or the laws of any other jurisdiction.

(b) Each such corporation and partnership shall enter into a written agreement of merger or consolidation. The agreement shall state:

(1) The terms and conditions of the merger or consolidation;

(2) The mode of carrying the same into effect;

(3) In the case of a merger in which the surviving entity is a corporation of this State, such amendments or changes in the certificate of incorporation of the surviving corporation as are desired to be effected by the merger (which amendments or changes may amend and restate the certificate of incorporation of the surviving corporation in its entirety), or, if no such amendments or changes are desired, a statement that the certificate of incorporation of the surviving corporation shall be its certificate of incorporation;

(4) In the case of a consolidation in which the resulting entity is a corporation of this State, that the certificate of incorporation of the resulting corporation shall be as is set forth in an attachment to the agreement;

(5) The manner, if any, of converting the shares of stock of each such corporation and the partnership interests of each such partnership into shares, partnership interests or other securities of the entity surviving or resulting from such merger or consolidation or of cancelling some or all of such

shares or interests, and if any shares of any such corporation or any partnership interests of any such partnership are not to remain outstanding, to be converted solely into shares, partnership interests or other securities of the entity surviving or resulting from such merger or consolidation or to be cancelled, the cash, property, rights or securities of any other corporation or entity which the holders of such shares or partnership interests are to receive in exchange for, or upon conversion of such shares or partnership interests and the surrender of any certificates evidencing them, which cash, property, rights or securities of any other corporation or entity may be in addition to or in lieu of shares, partnership interests or other securities of the entity surviving or resulting from such merger or consolidation;

(6)   Such other details or provisions as are deemed desirable, including, without limiting the generality of the foregoing, a provision for the payment of cash in lieu of the issuance or recognition of fractional shares, rights, other securities or interests of the surviving or resulting corporation or partnership or of any other corporation or entity the shares, rights, other securities or interests of which are to be received in the merger or consolidation, or for some other arrangement with respect thereto, consistent with § 155 of this title; and

(7)   Such other provisions or facts as shall be required to be set forth in an agreement of merger or consolidation (including any provision for amendment of the partnership agreement and statement of partnership existence or certificate of limited partnership (or equivalent documents) of the surviving partnership) by the laws of each jurisdiction under which any of the partnerships are formed.

Any of the terms of the agreement of merger or consolidation may be made dependent upon facts ascertainable outside of such agreement, provided that the manner in which such facts shall operate upon the terms of the agreement is clearly and expressly set forth in the agreement of merger or consolidation. The term "facts," as used in the preceding sentence, includes, but is not limited to, the occurrence of any event, including a determination or action by any person or body, including the corporation.

(c)   The agreement required by subsection (b) of this section shall be adopted, approved, certified, executed and acknowledged by each of the corporations in the same manner as is provided in § 251 or § 255 of this title and, in the case of the partnerships, in accordance with their partnership agreements and in accordance with the laws of the jurisdiction under which they are formed. If the surviving or resulting entity is a partnership, in addition to any other approvals, each stockholder of a merging corporation who will become a general partner of the surviving or resulting partnership must approve the agreement of merger or consolidation. The agreement shall be filed and shall become effective for all purposes of the laws of this State when and as provided in § 251 or § 255 of this title with respect to the merger or consolidation of corporations of this State. In lieu of filing the agreement of merger or consolidation, the surviving or resulting corporation or partnership may file a certificate of merger or consolidation, executed in accordance with § 103 of this title, if the surviving or resulting entity is a corporation, or by a general partner, if the surviving or resulting entity is a partnership, which states:

(1)   The name, jurisdiction of formation or organization and type of entity of each of the constituent entities;

(2)   That an agreement of merger or consolidation has been approved, adopted, certified, executed and acknowledged by each of the constituent entities in accordance with this subsection;

(3)   The name of the surviving or resulting corporation or partnership;

(4)   In the case of a merger in which a corporation is the surviving entity, such amendments or changes in the certificate of incorporation of the surviving corporation as are desired to be effected by the merger (which amendments or changes may amend and restate the certificate of incorporation of the surviving corporation in its entirety), or, if no such amendments or changes are desired, a statement that the certificate of incorporation of the surviving corporation shall be its certificate of incorporation;

(5)   In the case of a consolidation in which a corporation is the resulting entity, that the certificate of incorporation of the resulting corporation shall be as is set forth in an attachment to the certificate;

(6)   That the executed agreement of consolidation or merger is on file at an office of the surviving or resulting corporation or partnership and the address thereof;

(7)   That a copy of the agreement of consolidation or merger will be furnished by the surviving or resulting entity, on request and without cost, to any stockholder of any constituent corporation or any partner of any constituent partnership; and

(8)   The agreement, if any, required by subsection (d) of this section.

(d)   If the entity surviving or resulting from the merger or consolidation is a partnership formed under the laws of a jurisdiction other than this State, it shall agree that it may be served with process in this State in any proceeding for enforcement of any obligation of any constituent corporation or partnership of this State, as well as for enforcement of any obligation of the surviving or resulting corporation or partnership arising from the merger or consolidation, including any suit or other proceeding to enforce the right of any stockholders as determined in appraisal proceedings pursuant to § 262 of this title, and shall irrevocably appoint the Secretary of State as its agent to accept service of process in any such suit or other proceedings and shall specify the address to which a copy of such process shall be mailed by the Secretary of State. Process may be served upon the Secretary of State under this subsection by means of electronic transmission but only as prescribed by the Secretary of State. The Secretary of State is authorized to issue such rules and regulations with respect to such service as the Secretary of State deems necessary or appropriate. In the event of such service upon the Secretary of State in accordance with this subsection, the Secretary of State shall forthwith notify such surviving or resulting corporation or partnership thereof by letter, directed to such surviving or resulting corporation or partnership at its address so specified, unless such surviving or resulting corporation or partnership shall have designated in writing to the Secretary of State a different address for such purpose, in which case it shall be mailed to the last address so designated. Such letter shall be sent by a mail or courier service that includes a record of mailing or deposit with the courier and a record of delivery evidenced by the signature of the recipient. Such letter shall enclose a copy of the process and any other papers served on the Secretary of State pursuant to this subsection. It shall be the duty of the plaintiff in the event of such service to serve process and any other papers in duplicate, to notify the Secretary of State that service is being effected pursuant to this subsection and to pay the Secretary of State the sum of $50 for the use of the State, which sum shall be taxed as part of the costs in the proceeding, if the plaintiff shall prevail therein. The Secretary of State shall maintain an alphabetical record of any such service setting forth the name of the plaintiff and the defendant, the title, docket number and nature of the proceeding in which process has been served upon the Secretary of State, the fact that service has been effected pursuant to this subsection, the return date thereof, and the day and hour service was made. The Secretary of State shall not be required to retain such information longer than 5 years from receipt of the service of process.

(e)   Sections 251(d)–(f), 255(c) (second sentence) and (d)–(f), 259–261 and 328 of this title shall, insofar as they are applicable, apply to mergers or consolidations between corporations and partnerships.

(f)   Nothing in this section shall be deemed to authorize the merger of a charitable nonstock corporation into a partnership, if the charitable status of such nonstock corporation would thereby be lost or impaired; but a partnership may be merged into a charitable nonstock corporation which shall continue as the surviving corporation.

§ 264.   Merger or consolidation of domestic corporations and limited liability companies; service of process upon surviving or resulting corporation or limited liability company.

(a)   Any 1 or more corporations of this State may merge or consolidate with 1 or more limited liability companies, unless the laws of the jurisdiction or jurisdictions under which such limited liability company or limited liability companies are formed prohibit such merger or consolidation. Such corporation or corporations and such 1 or more limited liability companies may merge with or into a surviving corporation, which may be any 1 of such corporations, or they may merge with or into a surviving limited liability company, which may be any 1 of such limited liability companies, or they may consolidate into a new resulting corporation, which corporation shall be a corporation of this State, or a limited liability company formed pursuant to an agreement of merger or consolidation, as the case may be, complying and approved in accordance with this section. The term "limited liability company" as used in this section includes any limited liability company formed under the laws of this State or the laws of any other jurisdiction.

(b) Each such corporation and limited liability company shall enter into a written agreement of merger or consolidation. The agreement shall state:

(1) The terms and conditions of the merger or consolidation;

(2) The mode of carrying the same into effect;

(3) In the case of a merger in which the surviving entity is a corporation of this State, such amendments or changes in the certificate of incorporation of the surviving corporation as are desired to be effected by the merger (which amendments or changes may amend and restate the certificate of incorporation of the surviving corporation in its entirety), or, if no such amendments or changes are desired, a statement that the certificate of incorporation of the surviving corporation shall be its certificate of incorporation;

(4) In the case of a consolidation in which the resulting entity is a corporation of this State, that the certificate of incorporation of the resulting corporation shall be as is set forth in an attachment to the agreement;

(5) The manner, if any, of converting the shares of stock of each such corporation and the limited liability company interests of each such limited liability company into shares, limited liability company interests or other securities of the entity surviving or resulting from such merger or consolidation or of cancelling some or all of such shares or interests, and if any shares of any such corporation or any limited liability company interests of any such limited liability company are not to remain outstanding, to be converted solely into shares, limited liability company interests or other securities of the entity surviving or resulting from such merger or consolidation or to be cancelled, the cash, property, rights or securities of any other corporation or entity which the holders of such shares or limited liability company interests are to receive in exchange for, or upon conversion of such shares or limited liability company interests and the surrender of any certificates evidencing them, which cash, property, rights or securities of any other corporation or entity may be in addition to or in lieu of shares, limited liability company interests or other securities of the entity surviving or resulting from such merger or consolidation;

(6) Such other details or provisions as are deemed desirable, including, without limiting the generality of the foregoing, a provision for the payment of cash in lieu of the issuance or recognition of fractional shares, rights, other securities or interests of the surviving or resulting corporation or limited liability company or of any other corporation or entity the shares, rights, other securities or interests of which are to be received in the merger or consolidation, or for some other arrangement with respect thereto, consistent with § 155 of this title; and

(7) Such other provisions or facts as shall be required to be set forth in an agreement of merger or consolidation (including any provision for amendment of the limited liability company agreement and certificate of formation (or equivalent documents) of the surviving limited liability company) by the laws of each jurisdiction under which any of the limited liability companies are formed.

Any of the terms of the agreement of merger or consolidation may be made dependent upon facts ascertainable outside of such agreement, provided that the manner in which such facts shall operate upon the terms of the agreement is clearly and expressly set forth in the agreement of merger or consolidation. The term "facts," as used in the preceding sentence, includes, but is not limited to, the occurrence of any event, including a determination or action by any person or body, including the corporation.

(c) The agreement required by subsection (b) of this section shall be adopted, approved, certified, executed and acknowledged by each of the corporations in the same manner as is provided in § 251 or § 255 of this title and, in the case of the limited liability companies, in accordance with their limited liability company agreements and in accordance with the laws of the jurisdiction under which they are formed. The agreement shall be filed and shall become effective for all purposes of the laws of this State when and as provided in § 251 or § 255 of this title with respect to the merger or consolidation of corporations of this State. In lieu of filing the agreement of merger or consolidation, the surviving or resulting corporation or limited liability company may file a certificate of merger or consolidation, executed in accordance with § 103 of this title, if the surviving or resulting entity is a corporation, or by an authorized person, if the surviving or resulting entity is a limited liability company, which states:

(1)   The name and jurisdiction of formation or organization of each of the constituent entities;

(2)   That an agreement of merger or consolidation has been approved, adopted, certified, executed and acknowledged by each of the constituent entities in accordance with this subsection;

(3)   The name of the surviving or resulting corporation or limited liability company;

(4)   In the case of a merger in which a corporation is the surviving entity, such amendments or changes in the certificate of incorporation of the surviving corporation as are desired to be effected by the merger (which amendments or changes may amend and restate the certificate of incorporation of the surviving corporation in its entirety), or, if no such amendments or changes are desired, a statement that the certificate of incorporation of the surviving corporation shall be its certificate of incorporation;

(5)   In the case of a consolidation in which a corporation is the resulting entity, that the certificate of incorporation of the resulting corporation shall be as is set forth in an attachment to the certificate;

(6)   That the executed agreement of consolidation or merger is on file at an office of the surviving or resulting corporation or limited liability company and the address thereof;

(7)   That a copy of the agreement of consolidation or merger will be furnished by the surviving or resulting entity, on request and without cost, to any stockholder of any constituent corporation or any member of any constituent limited liability company; and

(8)   The agreement, if any, required by subsection (d) of this section.

(d)   If the entity surviving or resulting from the merger or consolidation is a limited liability company formed under the laws of a jurisdiction other than this State, it shall agree that it may be served with process in this State in any proceeding for enforcement of any obligation of any constituent corporation or limited liability company of this State, as well as for enforcement of any obligation of the surviving or resulting corporation or limited liability company arising from the merger or consolidation, including any suit or other proceeding to enforce the right of any stockholders as determined in appraisal proceedings pursuant to the provisions of § 262 of this title, and shall irrevocably appoint the Secretary of State as its agent to accept service of process in any such suit or other proceedings and shall specify the address to which a copy of such process shall be mailed by the Secretary of State. Process may be served upon the Secretary of State under this subsection by means of electronic transmission but only as prescribed by the Secretary of State. The Secretary of State is authorized to issue such rules and regulations with respect to such service as the Secretary of State deems necessary or appropriate. In the event of such service upon the Secretary of State in accordance with this subsection, the Secretary of State shall forthwith notify such surviving or resulting corporation or limited liability company thereof by letter, directed to such surviving or resulting corporation or limited liability company at its address so specified, unless such surviving or resulting corporation or limited liability company shall have designated in writing to the Secretary of State a different address for such purpose, in which case it shall be mailed to the last address so designated. Such letter shall be sent by a mail or courier service that includes a record of mailing or deposit with the courier and a record of delivery evidenced by the signature of the recipient. Such letter shall enclose a copy of the process and any other papers served on the Secretary of State pursuant to this subsection. It shall be the duty of the plaintiff in the event of such service to serve process and any other papers in duplicate, to notify the Secretary of State that service is being effected pursuant to this subsection and to pay the Secretary of State the sum of $50 for the use of the State, which sum shall be taxed as part of the costs in the proceeding, if the plaintiff shall prevail therein. The Secretary of State shall maintain an alphabetical record of any such service setting forth the name of the plaintiff and the defendant, the title, docket number and nature of the proceeding in which process has been served upon the Secretary of State, the fact that service has been effected pursuant to this subsection, the return date thereof, and the day and hour service was made. The Secretary of State shall not be required to retain such information longer than 5 years from receipt of the service of process.

(e)   Sections 251(d)–(f), 255(c) (second sentence) and (d)–(f), 259–261 and 328 of this title shall, insofar as they are applicable, apply to mergers or consolidations between corporations and limited liability companies.

(f)   Nothing in this section shall be deemed to authorize the merger of a charitable nonstock corporation into a limited liability company, if the charitable status of such nonstock corporation would thereby be lost or impaired; but a limited liability company may be merged into a charitable nonstock corporation which shall continue as the surviving corporation.

§ 265.   Conversion of other entities to a domestic corporation.

(a)   As used in this section, the term "other entity" means a limited liability company, statutory trust, business trust or association, real estate investment trust, common-law trust or any other unincorporated business including a partnership (whether general (including a limited liability partnership) or limited (including a limited liability limited partnership)), or a foreign corporation.

(b)   Any other entity may convert to a corporation of this State by complying with subsection (h) of this section and filing in the office of the Secretary of State:

(1)   A certificate of conversion to corporation that has been executed in accordance with subsection (i) of this section and filed in accordance with § 103 of this title; and

(2)   A certificate of incorporation that has been executed, acknowledged and filed in accordance with § 103 of this title.

Each of the certificates required by this subsection (b) shall be filed simultaneously in the office of the Secretary of State and, if such certificates are not to become effective upon their filing as permitted by § 103(d) of this title, then each such certificate shall provide for the same effective date or time in accordance with § 103(d) of this title.

(c)   The certificate of conversion to corporation shall state:

(1)   The date on which and jurisdiction where the other entity was first created, incorporated, formed or otherwise came into being and, if it has changed, its jurisdiction immediately prior to its conversion to a domestic corporation;

(2)   The name and type of entity of the other entity immediately prior to the filing of the certificate of conversion to corporation; and

(3)   The name of the corporation as set forth in its certificate of incorporation filed in accordance with subsection (b) of this section.

(4)   [Repealed.]

(d)   Upon the effective time of the certificate of conversion to corporation and the certificate of incorporation, the other entity shall be converted to a corporation of this State and the corporation shall thereafter be subject to all of the provisions of this title, except that notwithstanding § 106 of this title, the existence of the corporation shall be deemed to have commenced on the date the other entity commenced its existence in the jurisdiction in which the other entity was first created, formed, incorporated or otherwise came into being.

(e)   The conversion of any other entity to a corporation of this State shall not be deemed to affect any obligations or liabilities of the other entity incurred prior to its conversion to a corporation of this State or the personal liability of any person incurred prior to such conversion.

(f)   When an other entity has been converted to a corporation of this State pursuant to this section, the corporation of this State shall, for all purposes of the laws of the State of Delaware, be deemed to be the same entity as the converting other entity. When any conversion shall have become effective under this section, for all purposes of the laws of the State of Delaware, all of the rights, privileges and powers of the other entity that has converted, and all property, real, personal and mixed, and all debts due to such other entity, as well as all other things and causes of action belonging to such other entity, shall remain vested in the domestic corporation to which such other entity has converted and shall be the property of such domestic corporation and the title to any real property vested by deed or otherwise in such other entity shall not revert or be in any way impaired by reason of this chapter; but all rights of creditors and all liens upon any property of such other entity shall be preserved unimpaired, and all debts, liabilities and duties of the other entity that has converted shall remain attached to the corporation of this State to which such other entity has converted, and may be enforced against it to the same extent as if said debts, liabilities and duties had originally been incurred or contracted by it in its capacity as a corporation of this State. The rights, privileges, powers and interests in property of the other entity, as well as the debts, liabilities and duties of the other entity, shall not be deemed, as a consequence of the conversion, to have been transferred to the domestic corporation to which such other entity has converted for any purpose of the laws of the State of Delaware.

(g) Unless otherwise agreed for all purposes of the laws of the State of Delaware or as required under applicable non-Delaware law, the converting other entity shall not be required to wind up its affairs or pay its liabilities and distribute its assets, and the conversion shall not be deemed to constitute a dissolution of such other entity and shall constitute a continuation of the existence of the converting other entity in the form of a corporation of this State.

(h) Prior to filing a certificate of conversion to corporation with the office of the Secretary of State, the conversion shall be approved in the manner provided for by the document, instrument, agreement or other writing, as the case may be, governing the internal affairs of the other entity and the conduct of its business or by applicable law, as appropriate, and a certificate of incorporation shall be approved by the same authorization required to approve the conversion.

(i) The certificate of conversion to corporation shall be signed by any person who is authorized to sign the certificate of conversion to corporation on behalf of the other entity.

(j) In connection with a conversion hereunder, rights or securities of, or interests in, the other entity which is to be converted to a corporation of this State may be exchanged for or converted into cash, property, or shares of stock, rights or securities of such corporation of this State or, in addition to or in lieu thereof, may be exchanged for or converted into cash, property, or shares of stock, rights or securities of or interests in another domestic corporation or other entity or may be cancelled.

§ 266.   Conversion of a domestic corporation to other entities.

(a) A corporation of this State may, upon the authorization of such conversion in accordance with this section, convert to a limited liability company, statutory trust, business trust or association, real estate investment trust, common-law trust or any other unincorporated business including a partnership (whether general (including a limited liability partnership) or limited (including a limited liability limited partnership)) or a foreign corporation.

(b) The board of directors of the corporation which desires to convert under this section shall adopt a resolution approving such conversion, specifying the type of entity into which the corporation shall be converted and recommending the approval of such conversion by the stockholders of the corporation. Such resolution shall be submitted to the stockholders of the corporation at an annual or special meeting. Due notice of the time, and purpose of the meeting shall be given to each holder of stock, whether voting or nonvoting, of the corporation at the address of the stockholder as it appears on the records of the corporation, at least 20 days prior to the date of the meeting. At the meeting, the resolution shall be considered and a vote taken for its adoption or rejection. If all outstanding shares of stock of the corporation, whether voting or nonvoting, shall be voted for the adoption of the resolution, the conversion shall be authorized.

(1)–(4)   [Repealed.]

(c) If a corporation shall convert in accordance with this section to another entity organized, formed or created under the laws of a jurisdiction other than the State of Delaware, the corporation shall file with the Secretary of State a certificate of conversion executed in accordance with § 103 of this title, which certifies:

(1) The name of the corporation, and if it has been changed, the name under which it was originally incorporated;

(2) The date of filing of its original certificate of incorporation with the Secretary of State;

(3) The name and jurisdiction of the entity to which the corporation shall be converted;

(4)   That the conversion has been approved in accordance with the provisions of this section;

(5)   The agreement of the corporation that it may be served with process in the State of Delaware in any action, suit or proceeding for enforcement of any obligation of the corporation arising while it was a corporation of this State, and that it irrevocably appoints the Secretary of State as its agent to accept service of process in any such action, suit or proceeding; and

(6)   The address to which a copy of the process referred to in paragraph (c)(5) of this section shall be mailed to it by the Secretary of State. Process may be served upon the Secretary of State in accordance with paragraph (c)(5) of this section by means of electronic transmission but only as prescribed by the Secretary of State. The Secretary of State is authorized to issue such rules and regulations with respect to such service as the Secretary of State deems necessary or appropriate. In the event of such service upon the Secretary of State in accordance with paragraph (c)(5) of this section, the Secretary of State shall forthwith notify such corporation that has converted out of the State of Delaware by letter, directed to such corporation that has converted out of the State of Delaware at the address so specified, unless such corporation shall have designated in writing to the Secretary of State a different address for such purpose, in which case it shall be mailed to the last address designated. Such letter shall be sent by a mail or courier service that includes a record of mailing or deposit with the courier and a record of delivery evidenced by the signature of the recipient. Such letter shall enclose a copy of the process and any other papers served on the Secretary of State pursuant to this subsection. It shall be the duty of the plaintiff in the event of such service to serve process and any other papers in duplicate, to notify the Secretary of State that service is being effected pursuant to this subsection and to pay the Secretary of State the sum of $50 for the use of the State, which sum shall be taxed as part of the costs in the proceeding, if the plaintiff shall prevail therein. The Secretary of State shall maintain an alphabetical record of any such service setting forth the name of the plaintiff and the defendant, the title, docket number and nature of the proceeding in which process has been served, the fact that service has been effected pursuant to this subsection, the return date thereof, and the day and hour service was made. The Secretary of State shall not be required to retain such information longer than 5 years from receipt of the service of process.

(d)   Upon the filing in the Office of the Secretary of State of a certificate of conversion to non-Delaware entity in accordance with subsection (c) of this section or upon the future effective date or time of the certificate of conversion to non-Delaware entity and payment to the Secretary of State of all fees prescribed under this title, the Secretary of State shall certify that the corporation has filed all documents and paid all fees required by this title, and thereupon the corporation shall cease to exist as a corporation of this State at the time the certificate of conversion becomes effective in accordance with § 103 of this title. Such certificate of the Secretary of State shall be prima facie evidence of the conversion by such corporation out of the State of Delaware.

(e)   The conversion of a corporation out of the State of Delaware in accordance with this section and the resulting cessation of its existence as a corporation of this State pursuant to a certificate of conversion to non-Delaware entity shall not be deemed to affect any obligations or liabilities of the corporation incurred prior to such conversion or the personal liability of any person incurred prior to such conversion, nor shall it be deemed to affect the choice of law applicable to the corporation with respect to matters arising prior to such conversion.

(f)   Unless otherwise provided in a resolution of conversion adopted in accordance with this section, the converting corporation shall not be required to wind up its affairs or pay its liabilities and distribute its assets, and the conversion shall not constitute a dissolution of such corporation.

(g)   In connection with a conversion of a domestic corporation to another entity pursuant to this section, shares of stock, of the corporation of this State which is to be converted may be exchanged for or converted into cash, property, rights or securities of, or interests in, the entity to which the corporation of this State is being converted or, in addition to or in lieu thereof, may be exchanged for or converted into cash, property, shares of stock, rights or securities of, or interests in, another domestic corporation or other entity or may be cancelled.

(h)   When a corporation has been converted to another entity or business form pursuant to this section, the other entity or business form shall, for all purposes of the laws of the State of Delaware, be deemed to be the same entity as the corporation. When any conversion shall have become effective under this section, for all purposes of the laws of the State of Delaware, all of the rights, privileges and powers of the corporation that has converted, and all property, real, personal and mixed, and all debts due to such corporation, as well as all other things and causes of action belonging to such corporation, shall remain vested in the other entity or business form to which such corporation has converted and shall be the property of such other entity or business form, and the title to any real property vested by deed or otherwise in such corporation shall not revert or be in any way impaired by reason of this chapter; but all rights of creditors and all liens upon any property of such corporation shall be preserved unimpaired, and all debts, liabilities and duties of the corporation that has converted shall remain attached to the other entity or business form to which such corporation has converted, and may be enforced against it to the same extent as if said debts, liabilities and duties had originally been incurred or contracted by it in its capacity as such other entity or business form. The rights, privileges, powers and interest in property of the corporation that has converted, as well as the debts, liabilities and duties of such corporation, shall not be deemed, as a consequence of the conversion, to have been transferred to the other entity or business form to which such corporation has converted for any purpose of the laws of the State of Delaware.

(i) No vote of stockholders of a corporation shall be necessary to authorize a conversion if no shares of the stock of such corporation shall have been issued prior to the adoption by the board of directors of the resolution approving the conversion.

(j) Nothing in this section shall be deemed to authorize the conversion of a charitable nonstock corporation into another entity, if the charitable status of such charitable nonstock corporation would thereby be lost or impaired.

§ 267. Merger of parent entity and subsidiary corporation or corporations.

(a) In any case in which: (1) at least 90% of the outstanding shares of each class of the stock of a corporation or corporations (other than a corporation which has in its certificate of incorporation the provision required by § 251(g)(7)(i) of this title), of which class there are outstanding shares that, absent this subsection, would be entitled to vote on such merger, is owned by an entity, and (2) 1 or more of such corporations is a corporation of this State, unless the laws of the jurisdiction or jurisdictions under which such entity or such foreign corporations are formed or organized prohibit such merger, the entity having such stock ownership may either merge the corporation or corporations into itself and assume all of its or their obligations, or merge itself, or itself and 1 or more of such corporations, into 1 of the other corporations by (a) authorizing such merger in accordance with such entity's governing documents and the laws of the jurisdiction under which such entity is formed or organized and (b) acknowledging and filing with the Secretary of State, in accordance with § 103 of this title, a certificate of such ownership and merger certifying (i) that such merger was authorized in accordance with such entity's governing documents and the laws of the jurisdiction under which such entity is formed or organized, such certificate executed in accordance with such entity's governing documents and in accordance with the laws of the jurisdiction under which such entity is formed or organized and (ii) the type of entity of each constituent entity to the merger; provided, however, that in case the entity shall not own all the outstanding stock of all the corporations, parties to a merger as aforesaid, (A) the certificate of ownership and merger shall state the terms and conditions of the merger, including the securities, cash, property, or rights to be issued, paid, delivered or granted by the surviving constituent party upon surrender of each share of the corporation or corporations not owned by the entity, or the cancellation of some or all of such shares and (B) such terms and conditions of the merger may not result in a holder of stock in a corporation becoming a general partner in a surviving entity that is a partnership (other than a limited liability partnership or a limited liability limited partnership). Any of the terms of the merger may be made dependent upon facts ascertainable outside of the certificate of ownership and merger, provided that the manner in which such facts shall operate upon the terms of the merger is clearly and expressly set forth in the certificate of ownership and merger. The term "facts," as used in the preceding sentence, includes, but is not limited to, the occurrence of any event, including a determination or action by any person or body, including the entity. If the surviving constituent party is an entity formed or organized under the laws of a jurisdiction other than this State, (1) § 252(d) of this title shall also apply to a merger under this section; if the surviving constituent party is the entity, the word "corporation" where applicable, as used in § 252(d) of this title, shall be deemed to include an entity as defined herein; and (2) the terms and conditions of the merger shall obligate the surviving constituent party to provide the agreement, and take the actions, required by § 252(d) of this title.

(b) Sections 259, 261, and 328 of this title shall, insofar as they are applicable, apply to a merger under this section, and §§ 260 and 251(e) of this title shall apply to a merger under this section in which the surviving constituent party is a corporation of this State. For purposes of this subsection, references to "agreement of merger" in § 251(e) of this title shall mean the terms and conditions of the merger set forth in the certificate of ownership and merger, and references to "corporation" in §§ 259–261 of this title, and § 328 of this title shall be deemed to include the entity, as applicable. Section 262 of this title shall not apply to any merger effected under this section, except as provided in subsection (c) of this section.

(c) In the event all of the stock of a Delaware corporation party to a merger effected under this section is not owned by the entity immediately prior to the merger, the stockholders of such Delaware corporation party to the merger shall have appraisal rights as set forth in § 262 of this title.

(d) As used in this section only, the term:

(1) "Constituent party" means an entity or corporation to be merged pursuant to this section;

(2) "Entity" means a partnership (whether general (including a limited liability partnership) or limited (including a limited liability limited partnership)), limited liability company, any association of the kind commonly known as a joint-stock association or joint-stock company and any unincorporated association, trust or enterprise having members or having outstanding shares of stock or other evidences of financial or beneficial interest therein, whether formed or organized by agreement or under statutory authority or otherwise and whether formed or organized under the laws of this State or the laws of any other jurisdiction; and

(3) "Governing documents" means a partnership agreement, limited liability company agreement, articles of association or any other instrument containing the provisions by which an entity is formed or organized.

SUBCHAPTER X. SALE OF ASSETS, DISSOLUTION AND WINDING UP

§ 271. Sale, lease or exchange of assets; consideration; procedure.

(a) Every corporation may at any meeting of its board of directors or governing body sell, lease or exchange all or substantially all of its property and assets, including its goodwill and its corporate franchises, upon such terms and conditions and for such consideration, which may consist in whole or in part of money or other property, including shares of stock in, and/or other securities of, any other corporation or corporations, as its board of directors or governing body deems expedient and for the best interests of the corporation, when and as authorized by a resolution adopted by the holders of a majority of the outstanding stock of the corporation entitled to vote thereon or, if the corporation is a nonstock corporation, by a majority of the members having the right to vote for the election of the members of the governing body and any other members entitled to vote thereon under the certificate of incorporation or the bylaws of such corporation, at a meeting duly called upon at least 20 days' notice. The notice of the meeting shall state that such a resolution will be considered.

(b) Notwithstanding authorization or consent to a proposed sale, lease or exchange of a corporation's property and assets by the stockholders or members, the board of directors or governing body may abandon such proposed sale, lease or exchange without further action by the stockholders or members, subject to the rights, if any, of third parties under any contract relating thereto.

(c) For purposes of this section only, the property and assets of the corporation include the property and assets of any subsidiary of the corporation. As used in this subsection, "subsidiary" means any entity wholly-owned and controlled, directly or indirectly, by the corporation and includes, without limitation, corporations, partnerships, limited partnerships, limited liability partnerships, limited liability companies, and/or statutory trusts. Notwithstanding subsection (a) of this section, except to the extent the certificate of incorporation otherwise provides, no resolution by stockholders or members shall be required for a sale, lease or exchange of property and assets of the corporation to a subsidiary.

§ 272. Mortgage or pledge of assets.

The authorization or consent of stockholders to the mortgage or pledge of a corporation's property and assets shall not be necessary, except to the extent that the certificate of incorporation otherwise provides.

§ 273. Dissolution of joint venture corporation having 2 stockholders.

(a)   If the stockholders of a corporation of this State, having only 2 stockholders each of which own 50% of the stock therein, shall be engaged in the prosecution of a joint venture and if such stockholders shall be unable to agree upon the desirability of discontinuing such joint venture and disposing of the assets used in such venture, either stockholder may, unless otherwise provided in the certificate of incorporation of the corporation or in a written agreement between the stockholders, file with the Court of Chancery a petition stating that it desires to discontinue such joint venture and to dispose of the assets used in such venture in accordance with a plan to be agreed upon by both stockholders or that, if no such plan shall be agreed upon by both stockholders, the corporation be dissolved. Such petition shall have attached thereto a copy of the proposed plan of discontinuance and distribution and a certificate stating that copies of such petition and plan have been transmitted in writing to the other stockholder and to the directors and officers of such corporation. The petition and certificate shall be executed and acknowledged in accordance with § 103 of this title.

(b)   Unless both stockholders file with the Court of Chancery:

(1)   Within 3 months of the date of the filing of such petition, a certificate similarly executed and acknowledged stating that they have agreed on such plan, or a modification thereof, and

(2)   Within 1 year from the date of the filing of such petition, a certificate similarly executed and acknowledged stating that the distribution provided by such plan had been completed,

the Court of Chancery may dissolve such corporation and may by appointment of 1 or more trustees or receivers with all the powers and title of a trustee or receiver appointed under § 279 of this title, administer and wind up its affairs. Either or both of the above periods may be extended by agreement of the stockholders, evidenced by a certificate similarly executed, acknowledged and filed with the Court of Chancery prior to the expiration of such period.

(c)   In the case of a charitable nonstock corporation, the petitioner shall provide a copy of any petition referred to in subsection (a) of this section to the Attorney General of the State of Delaware within 1 week of its filing with the Court of Chancery.

§ 274. Dissolution before issuance of shares or beginning of business; procedure.

If a corporation has not issued shares or has not commenced the business for which the corporation was organized, a majority of the incorporators, or, if directors were named in the certificate of incorporation or have been elected, a majority of the directors, may surrender all of the corporation's rights and franchises by filing in the office of the Secretary of State a certificate, executed and acknowledged by a majority of the incorporators or directors, stating: that no shares of stock have been issued or that the business or activity for which the corporation was organized has not been begun; the date of filing of the corporation's original certificate of incorporation with the Secretary of State; that no part of the capital of the corporation has been paid, or, if some capital has been paid, that the amount actually paid in for the corporation's shares, less any part thereof disbursed for necessary expenses, has been returned to those entitled thereto; that if the corporation has begun business but it has not issued shares, all debts of the corporation have been paid; that if the corporation has not begun business but has issued stock certificates, all issued stock certificates, if any, have been surrendered and cancelled; and that all rights and franchises of the corporation are surrendered. Upon such certificate becoming effective in accordance with § 103 of this title, the corporation shall be dissolved.

§ 275. Dissolution generally; procedure.

(a)   If it should be deemed advisable in the judgment of the board of directors of any corporation that it should be dissolved, the board, after the adoption of a resolution to that effect by a majority of the whole board at any meeting called for that purpose, shall cause notice of the adoption of the resolution and of a meeting of stockholders to take action upon the resolution to be given to each stockholder entitled to vote thereon as of the record date for determining the stockholders entitled to notice of the meeting.

(b)   At the meeting a vote shall be taken upon the proposed dissolution. If a majority of the outstanding stock of the corporation entitled to vote thereon shall vote for the proposed dissolution, a certification of dissolution shall be filed with the Secretary of State pursuant to subsection (d) of this section.

(c)   Dissolution of a corporation may also be authorized without action of the directors if all the stockholders entitled to vote thereon shall consent in writing and a certificate of dissolution shall be filed with the Secretary of State pursuant to subsection (d) of this section.

(d)   If dissolution is authorized in accordance with this section, a certificate of dissolution shall be executed, acknowledged and filed, and shall become effective, in accordance with § 103 of this title. Such certificate of dissolution shall set forth:

(1)   The name of the corporation;

(2)   The date dissolution was authorized;

(3)   That the dissolution has been authorized by the board of directors and stockholders of the corporation, in accordance with subsections (a) and (b) of this section, or that the dissolution has been authorized by all of the stockholders of the corporation entitled to vote on a dissolution, in accordance with subsection (c) of this section;

(4)   The names and addresses of the directors and officers of the corporation; and

(5)   The date of filing of the corporation's original certificate of incorporation with the Secretary of State.

(e)   The resolution authorizing a proposed dissolution may provide that notwithstanding authorization or consent to the proposed dissolution by the stockholders, or the members of a nonstock corporation pursuant to § 276 of this title, the board of directors or governing body may abandon such proposed dissolution without further action by the stockholders or members.

(f)   Upon a certificate of dissolution becoming effective in accordance with § 103 of this title, the corporation shall be dissolved.

§ 276.   Dissolution of nonstock corporation; procedure.

(a)   Whenever it shall be desired to dissolve any nonstock corporation, the governing body shall perform all the acts necessary for dissolution which are required by § 275 of this title to be performed by the board of directors of a corporation having capital stock. If any members of a nonstock corporation are entitled to vote for the election of members of its governing body or are entitled to vote for dissolution under the certificate of incorporation or the bylaws of such corporation, such members shall perform all the acts necessary for dissolution which are contemplated by § 275 of this title to be performed by the stockholders of a corporation having capital stock, including dissolution without action of the members of the governing body if all the members of the corporation entitled to vote thereon shall consent in writing and a certificate of dissolution shall be filed with the Secretary of State pursuant to § 275(d) of this title. If there is no member entitled to vote thereon, the dissolution of the corporation shall be authorized at a meeting of the governing body, upon the adoption of a resolution to dissolve by the vote of a majority of members of its governing body then in office. In all other respects, the method and proceedings for the dissolution of a nonstock corporation shall conform as nearly as may be to the proceedings prescribed by § 275 of this title for the dissolution of corporations having capital stock.

(b)   If a nonstock corporation has not commenced the business for which the corporation was organized, a majority of the governing body or, if none, a majority of the incorporators may surrender all of the corporation rights and franchises by filing in the office of the Secretary of State a certificate, executed and acknowledged by a majority of the incorporators or governing body, conforming as nearly as may be to the certificate prescribed by § 274 of this title.

§ 277.   Payment of franchise taxes before dissolution, merger, transfer or conversion.

No corporation shall be dissolved, merged, transferred (without continuing its existence as a corporation of this State) or converted under this chapter until:

(1)   All franchise taxes due to or assessable by the State including all franchise taxes due or which would be due or assessable for the entire calendar month during which such dissolution, merger, transfer or conversion becomes effective have been paid by the corporation; and

(2)   All annual franchise tax reports including a final annual franchise tax report for the year in which such dissolution, merger, transfer or conversion becomes effective have been filed by the corporation;

notwithstanding the foregoing, if the Secretary of State certifies that an instrument to effect a dissolution, merger, transfer or conversion has been filed in the Secretary of State's office, such corporation shall be dissolved, merged, transferred or converted at the effective time of such instrument.

§ 278.   Continuation of corporation after dissolution for purposes of suit and winding up affairs.

All corporations, whether they expire by their own limitation or are otherwise dissolved, shall nevertheless be continued, for the term of 3 years from such expiration or dissolution or for such longer period as the Court of Chancery shall in its discretion direct, bodies corporate for the purpose of prosecuting and defending suits, whether civil, criminal or administrative, by or against them, and of enabling them gradually to settle and close their business, to dispose of and convey their property, to discharge their liabilities and to distribute to their stockholders any remaining assets, but not for the purpose of continuing the business for which the corporation was organized. With respect to any action, suit or proceeding begun by or against the corporation either prior to or within 3 years after the date of its expiration or dissolution, the action shall not abate by reason of the dissolution of the corporation; the corporation shall, solely for the purpose of such action, suit or proceeding, be continued as a body corporate beyond the 3-year period and until any judgments, orders or decrees therein shall be fully executed, without the necessity for any special direction to that effect by the Court of Chancery.

Sections 279 through 282 of this title shall apply to any corporation that has expired by its own limitation, and when so applied, all references in those sections to a dissolved corporation or dissolution shall include a corporation that has expired by its own limitation and to such expiration, respectively.

§ 279.   Trustees or receivers for dissolved corporations; appointment; powers; duties.

When any corporation organized under this chapter shall be dissolved in any manner whatever, the Court of Chancery, on application of any creditor, stockholder or director of the corporation, or any other person who shows good cause therefor, at any time, may either appoint 1 or more of the directors of the corporation to be trustees, or appoint 1 or more persons to be receivers, of and for the corporation, to take charge of the corporation's property, and to collect the debts and property due and belonging to the corporation, with power to prosecute and defend, in the name of the corporation, or otherwise, all such suits as may be necessary or proper for the purposes aforesaid, and to appoint an agent or agents under them, and to do all other acts which might be done by the corporation, if in being, that may be necessary for the final settlement of the unfinished business of the corporation. The powers of the trustees or receivers may be continued as long as the Court of Chancery shall think necessary for the purposes aforesaid.

§ 280.   Notice to claimants; filing of claims.

(a)(1) After a corporation has been dissolved in accordance with the procedures set forth in this chapter, the corporation or any successor entity may give notice of the dissolution, requiring all persons having a claim against the corporation other than a claim against the corporation in a pending action, suit or proceeding to which the corporation is a party to present their claims against the corporation in accordance with such notice. Such notice shall state:

a.   That all such claims must be presented in writing and must contain sufficient information reasonably to inform the corporation or successor entity of the identity of the claimant and the substance of the claim;

b.   The mailing address to which such a claim must be sent;

c.   The date by which such a claim must be received by the corporation or successor entity, which date shall be no earlier than 60 days from the date thereof; and

     d.   That such claim will be barred if not received by the date referred to in paragraph (a)(1)c. of this section; and

     e.   That the corporation or a successor entity may make distributions to other claimants and the corporation's stockholders or persons interested as having been such without further notice to the claimant; and

     f.   The aggregate amount, on an annual basis, of all distributions made by the corporation to its stockholders for each of the 3 years prior to the date the corporation dissolved.

Such notice shall also be published at least once a week for 2 consecutive weeks in a newspaper of general circulation in the county in which the office of the corporation's last registered agent in this State is located and in the corporation's principal place of business and, in the case of a corporation having $10,000,000 or more in total assets at the time of its dissolution, at least once in all editions of a daily newspaper with a national circulation. On or before the date of the first publication of such notice, the corporation or successor entity shall mail a copy of such notice by certified or registered mail, return receipt requested, to each known claimant of the corporation including persons with claims asserted against the corporation in a pending action, suit or proceeding to which the corporation is a party.

    (2)   Any claim against the corporation required to be presented pursuant to this subsection is barred if a claimant who was given actual notice under this subsection does not present the claim to the dissolved corporation or successor entity by the date referred to in paragraph (a)(1)c. of this section.

    (3)   A corporation or successor entity may reject, in whole or in part, any claim made by a claimant pursuant to this subsection by mailing notice of such rejection by certified or registered mail, return receipt requested, to the claimant within 90 days after receipt of such claim and, in all events, at least 150 days before the expiration of the period described in § 278 of this title; provided however, that in the case of a claim filed pursuant to § 295 of this title against a corporation or successor entity for which a receiver or trustee has been appointed by the Court of Chancery the time period shall be as provided in § 296 of this title, and the 30-day appeal period provided for in § 296 of this title shall be applicable. A notice sent by a corporation or successor entity pursuant to this subsection shall state that any claim rejected therein will be barred if an action, suit or proceeding with respect to the claim is not commenced within 120 days of the date thereof, and shall be accompanied by a copy of §§ 278–283 of this title and, in the case of a notice sent by a court-appointed receiver or trustee and as to which a claim has been filed pursuant to § 295 of this title, copies of §§ 295 and 296 of this title.

    (4)   A claim against a corporation is barred if a claimant whose claim is rejected pursuant to paragraph (a)(3) of this section does not commence an action, suit or proceeding with respect to the claim no later than 120 days after the mailing of the rejection notice.

(b)(1) A corporation or successor entity electing to follow the procedures described in subsection (a) of this section shall also give notice of the dissolution of the corporation to persons with contractual claims contingent upon the occurrence or nonoccurrence of future events or otherwise conditional or unmatured, and request that such persons present such claims in accordance with the terms of such notice. Provided however, that as used in this section and in § 281 of this title, the term "contractual claims" shall not include any implied warranty as to any product manufactured, sold, distributed or handled by the dissolved corporation. Such notice shall be in substantially the form, and sent and published in the same manner, as described in paragraph (a)(1) of this section.

    (2)   The corporation or successor entity shall offer any claimant on a contract whose claim is contingent, conditional or unmatured such security as the corporation or successor entity determines is sufficient to provide compensation to the claimant if the claim matures. The corporation or successor entity shall mail such offer to the claimant by certified or registered mail, return receipt requested, within 90 days of receipt of such claim and, in all events, at least 150 days before the expiration of the period described in § 278 of this title. If the claimant offered such security does not deliver in writing to the corporation or successor entity a notice rejecting the offer within 120 days after receipt of such offer for security, the claimant shall be deemed to have accepted such security as the sole source from which to satisfy the claim against the corporation.

(c)(1) A corporation or successor entity which has given notice in accordance with subsection (a) of this section shall petition the Court of Chancery to determine the amount and form of security that will be reasonably likely to be sufficient to provide compensation for any claim against the corporation which is the subject of a pending action, suit or proceeding to which the corporation is a party other than a claim barred pursuant to subsection (a) of this section.

(2) A corporation or successor entity which has given notice in accordance with subsections (a) and (b) of this section shall petition the Court of Chancery to determine the amount and form of security that will be sufficient to provide compensation to any claimant who has rejected the offer for security made pursuant to paragraph (b)(2) of this section.

(3) A corporation or successor entity which has given notice in accordance with subsection (a) of this section shall petition the Court of Chancery to determine the amount and form of security which will be reasonably likely to be sufficient to provide compensation for claims that have not been made known to the corporation or that have not arisen but that, based on facts known to the corporation or successor entity, are likely to arise or to become known to the corporation or successor entity within 5 years after the date of dissolution or such longer period of time as the Court of Chancery may determine not to exceed 10 years after the date of dissolution. The Court of Chancery may appoint a guardian ad litem in respect of any such proceeding brought under this subsection. The reasonable fees and expenses of such guardian, including all reasonable expert witness fees, shall be paid by the petitioner in such proceeding.

(d) The giving of any notice or making of any offer pursuant to this section shall not revive any claim then barred or constitute acknowledgment by the corporation or successor entity that any person to whom such notice is sent is a proper claimant and shall not operate as a waiver of any defense or counterclaim in respect of any claim asserted by any person to whom such notice is sent.

(e) As used in this section, the term "successor entity" shall include any trust, receivership or other legal entity governed by the laws of this State to which the remaining assets and liabilities of a dissolved corporation are transferred and which exists solely for the purposes of prosecuting and defending suits, by or against the dissolved corporation, enabling the dissolved corporation to settle and close the business of the dissolved corporation, to dispose of and convey the property of the dissolved corporation, to discharge the liabilities of the dissolved corporation and to distribute to the dissolved corporation's stockholders any remaining assets, but not for the purpose of continuing the business for which the dissolved corporation was organized.

(f) The time periods and notice requirements of this section shall, in the case of a corporation or successor entity for which a receiver or trustee has been appointed by the Court of Chancery, be subject to variation by, or in the manner provided in, the Rules of the Court of Chancery.

(g) In the case of a nonstock corporation, any notice referred to in the last sentence of paragraph (a)(3) of this section shall include a copy of § 114 of this title. In the case of a nonprofit nonstock corporation, provisions of this section regarding distributions to members shall not apply to the extent that those provisions conflict with any other applicable law or with that corporation's certificate of incorporation or bylaws.

§ 281. Payment and distribution to claimants and stockholders.

(a) A dissolved corporation or successor entity which has followed the procedures described in § 280 of this title:

(1) Shall pay the claims made and not rejected in accordance with § 280(a) of this title,

(2) Shall post the security offered and not rejected pursuant to § 280(b)(2) of this title,

(3) Shall post any security ordered by the Court of Chancery in any proceeding under § 280(c) of this title, and

(4) Shall pay or make provision for all other claims that are mature, known and uncontested or that have been finally determined to be owing by the corporation or such successor entity.

Such claims or obligations shall be paid in full and any such provision for payment shall be made in full if there are sufficient assets. If there are insufficient assets, such claims and obligations shall be paid or provided for according to their priority, and, among claims of equal priority, ratably to the extent of assets legally available therefor. Any remaining assets shall be distributed to the stockholders of the dissolved corporation; provided, however, that such distribution shall not be made before the expiration of 150 days from the date of the last notice of rejections given pursuant to § 280(a)(3) of this title. In the absence of actual fraud, the judgment of the directors of the dissolved corporation or the governing persons of such successor entity as to the provision made for the payment of all obligations under paragraph (a)(4) of this section shall be conclusive.

(b)   A dissolved corporation or successor entity which has not followed the procedures described in § 280 of this title shall, prior to the expiration of the period described in § 278 of this title, adopt a plan of distribution pursuant to which the dissolved corporation or successor entity (i) shall pay or make reasonable provision to pay all claims and obligations, including all contingent, conditional or unmatured contractual claims known to the corporation or such successor entity, (ii) shall make such provision as will be reasonably likely to be sufficient to provide compensation for any claim against the corporation which is the subject of a pending action, suit or proceeding to which the corporation is a party and (iii) shall make such provision as will be reasonably likely to be sufficient to provide compensation for claims that have not been made known to the corporation or that have not arisen but that, based on facts known to the corporation or successor entity, are likely to arise or to become known to the corporation or successor entity within 10 years after the date of dissolution. The plan of distribution shall provide that such claims shall be paid in full and any such provision for payment made shall be made in full if there are sufficient assets. If there are insufficient assets, such plan shall provide that such claims and obligations shall be paid or provided for according to their priority and, among claims of equal priority, ratably to the extent of assets legally available therefor. Any remaining assets shall be distributed to the stockholders of the dissolved corporation.

(c)   Directors of a dissolved corporation or governing persons of a successor entity which has complied with subsection (a) or (b) of this section shall not be personally liable to the claimants of the dissolved corporation.

(d)   As used in this section, the term "successor entity" has the meaning set forth in § 280(e) of this title.

(e)   The term "priority," as used in this section, does not refer either to the order of payments set forth in paragraph (a)(1)–(4) of this section or to the relative times at which any claims mature or are reduced to judgment.

(f)   In the case of a nonprofit nonstock corporation, provisions of this section regarding distributions to members shall not apply to the extent that those provisions conflict with any other applicable law or with that corporation's certificate of incorporation or bylaws.

§ 282.   Liability of stockholders of dissolved corporations.

(a)   A stockholder of a dissolved corporation the assets of which were distributed pursuant to § 281(a) or (b) of this title shall not be liable for any claim against the corporation in an amount in excess of such stockholder's pro rata share of the claim or the amount so distributed to such stockholder, whichever is less.

(b)   A stockholder of a dissolved corporation the assets of which were distributed pursuant to § 281(a) of this title shall not be liable for any claim against the corporation on which an action, suit or proceeding is not begun prior to the expiration of the period described in § 278 of this title.

(c)   The aggregate liability of any stockholder of a dissolved corporation for claims against the dissolved corporation shall not exceed the amount distributed to such stockholder in dissolution.

§ 283.   Jurisdiction.

The Court of Chancery shall have jurisdiction of any application prescribed in this subchapter and of all questions arising in the proceedings thereon, and may make such orders and decrees and issue injunctions therein as justice and equity shall require.

§ 284. Revocation or forfeiture of charter; proceedings.

(a) Upon motion by the Attorney General, the Court of Chancery shall have jurisdiction to revoke or forfeit the charter of any corporation for abuse, misuse or nonuse of its corporate powers, privileges or franchises. The Attorney General shall proceed for this purpose by complaint in the Court of Chancery.

(b) The Court of Chancery shall have power, by appointment of trustees, receivers or otherwise, to administer and wind up the affairs of any corporation whose charter shall be revoked or forfeited by the Court of Chancery under this section, and to make such orders and decrees with respect thereto as shall be just and equitable respecting its affairs and assets and the rights of its stockholders and creditors.

(c) No proceeding shall be instituted under this section for nonuse of any corporation's powers, privileges or franchises during the first 2 years after its incorporation.

§ 285. Dissolution or forfeiture of charter by decree of court; filing.

Whenever any corporation is dissolved or its charter forfeited by decree or judgment of the Court of Chancery, the decree or judgment shall be forthwith filed by the Register in Chancery of the county in which the decree or judgment was entered, in the office of the Secretary of State, and a note thereof shall be made by the Secretary of State on the corporation's charter or certificate of incorporation and on the index thereof.

SUBCHAPTER XI. INSOLVENCY; RECEIVERS AND TRUSTEES

§ 291. Receivers for insolvent corporations; appointment and powers.

Whenever a corporation shall be insolvent, the Court of Chancery, on the application of any creditor or stockholder thereof, may, at any time, appoint 1 or more persons to be receivers of and for the corporation, to take charge of its assets, estate, effects, business and affairs, and to collect the outstanding debts, claims, and property due and belonging to the corporation, with power to prosecute and defend, in the name of the corporation or otherwise, all claims or suits, to appoint an agent or agents under them, and to do all other acts which might be done by the corporation and which may be necessary or proper. The powers of the receivers shall be such and shall continue so long as the Court shall deem necessary.

§ 292. Title to property; filing order of appointment; exception.

(a) Trustees or receivers appointed by the Court of Chancery of and for any corporation, and their respective survivors and successors, shall, upon their appointment and qualification or upon the death, resignation or discharge of any co-trustee or co-receiver, be vested by operation of law and without any act or deed, with the title of the corporation to all of its property, real, personal or mixed of whatsoever nature, kind, class or description, and wheresoever situate, except real estate situate outside this State.

(b) Trustees or receivers appointed by the Court of Chancery shall, within 20 days from the date of their qualification, file in the office of the recorder in each county in this State, in which any real estate belonging to the corporation may be situated, a certified copy of the order of their appointment and evidence of their qualification.

(c) This section shall not apply to receivers appointed pendente lite.

§ 293. Notices to stockholders and creditors.

All notices required to be given to stockholders and creditors in any action in which a receiver or trustee for a corporation was appointed shall be given by the Register in Chancery, unless otherwise ordered by the Court of Chancery.

§ 294. Receivers or trustees; inventory; list of debts and report.

Trustees or receivers shall, as soon as convenient, file in the office of the Register in Chancery of the county in which the proceeding is pending, a full and complete itemized inventory of all the assets of the corporation which shall show their nature and probable value, and an account of all debts due from and to it, as nearly as the same can be ascertained. They shall make a report to the Court of their proceedings, whenever and as often as the Court shall direct.

§ 295.   Creditors' proofs of claims; when barred; notice.

All creditors shall make proof under oath of their respective claims against the corporation, and cause the same to be filed in the office of the Register in Chancery of the county in which the proceeding is pending within the time fixed by and in accordance with the procedure established by the rules of the Court of Chancery. All creditors and claimants failing to do so, within the time limited by this section, or the time prescribed by the order of the Court, may, by direction of the Court, be barred from participating in the distribution of the assets of the corporation. The Court may also prescribe what notice, by publication or otherwise, shall be given to the creditors of the time fixed for the filing and making proof of claims.

§ 296.   Adjudication of claims; appeal.

(a)   The Register in Chancery, immediately upon the expiration of the time fixed for the filing of claims, in compliance with § 295 of this title, shall notify the trustee or receiver of the filing of the claims, and the trustee or receiver, within 30 days after receiving the notice, shall inspect the claims, and if the trustee or receiver or any creditor shall not be satisfied with the validity or correctness of the same, or any of them, the trustee or receiver shall forthwith notify the creditors whose claims are disputed of such trustee's or receiver's decision. The trustee or receiver shall require all creditors whose claims are disputed to submit themselves to such examination in relation to their claims as the trustee or receiver shall direct, and the creditors shall produce such books and papers relating to their claims as shall be required. The trustee or receiver shall have power to examine, under oath or affirmation, all witnesses produced before such trustee or receiver touching the claims, and shall pass upon and allow or disallow the claims, or any part thereof, and notify the claimants of such trustee's or receiver's determination.

(b)   Every creditor or claimant who shall have received notice from the receiver or trustee that such creditor's or claimant's claim has been disallowed in whole or in part may appeal to the Court of Chancery within 30 days thereafter. The Court, after hearing, shall determine the rights of the parties.

§ 297.   Sale of perishable or deteriorating property.

Whenever the property of a corporation is at the time of the appointment of a receiver or trustee encumbered with liens of any character, and the validity, extent or legality of any lien is disputed or brought in question, and the property of the corporation is of a character which will deteriorate in value pending the litigation respecting the lien, the Court of Chancery may order the receiver or trustee to sell the property of the corporation, clear of all encumbrances, at public or private sale, for the best price that can be obtained therefor, and pay the net proceeds arising from the sale thereof after deducting the costs of the sale into the Court, there to remain subject to the order of the Court, and to be disposed of as the Court shall direct.

§ 298.   Compensation, costs and expenses of receiver or trustee.

The Court of Chancery, before making distribution of the assets of a corporation among the creditors or stockholders thereof, shall allow a reasonable compensation to the receiver or trustee for such receiver's or trustee's services, and the costs and expenses incurred in and about the execution of such receiver's or trustee's trust, and the costs of the proceedings in the Court, to be first paid out of the assets.

§ 299.   Substitution of trustee or receiver as party; abatement of actions.

A trustee or receiver, upon application by such receiver or trustee in the court in which any suit is pending, shall be substituted as party plaintiff in the place of the corporation in any suit or proceeding which was so pending at the time of such receiver's or trustee's appointment. No action against a trustee or receiver of a corporation shall abate by reason of such receiver's or trustee's death, but, upon suggestion of the facts on the record, shall be continued against such receiver's or trustee's successor or against the corporation in case no new trustee or receiver is appointed.

§ 300.   Employee's lien for wages when corporation insolvent.

Whenever any corporation of this State, or any foreign corporation doing business in this State, shall become insolvent, the employees doing labor or service of whatever character in the regular employ of the corporation, shall have a lien upon the assets thereof for the amount of the wages due to them, not exceeding

2 months' wages respectively, which shall be paid prior to any other debt or debts of the corporation. The word "employee" shall not be construed to include any of the officers of the corporation.

§ 301. Discontinuance of liquidation.

The liquidation of the assets and business of an insolvent corporation may be discontinued at any time during the liquidation proceedings when it is established that cause for liquidation no longer exists. In such event the Court of Chancery in its discretion, and subject to such condition as it may deem appropriate, may dismiss the proceedings and direct the receiver or trustee to redeliver to the corporation all of its remaining property and assets.

§ 302. Compromise or arrangement between corporation and creditors or stockholders.

(a) Whenever the provision permitted by § 102(b)(2) of this title is included in the original certificate of incorporation of any corporation, all persons who become creditors or stockholders thereof shall be deemed to have become such creditors or stockholders subject in all respects to that provision and the same shall be absolutely binding upon them. Whenever that provision is inserted in the certificate of incorporation of any such corporation by an amendment of its certificate all persons who become creditors or stockholders of such corporation after such amendment shall be deemed to have become such creditors or stockholders subject in all respects to that provision and the same shall be absolutely binding upon them.

(b) The Court of Chancery may administer and enforce any compromise or arrangement made pursuant to the provision contained in § 102(b)(2) of this title and may restrain, pendente lite, all actions and proceedings against any corporation with respect to which the Court shall have begun the administration and enforcement of that provision and may appoint a temporary receiver for such corporation and may grant the receiver such powers as it deems proper, and may make and enforce such rules as it deems necessary for the exercise of such jurisdiction.

§ 303. Proceeding under the Federal Bankruptcy Code of the United States; effectuation.

(a) Any corporation of this State, an order for relief with respect to which has been entered pursuant to the Federal Bankruptcy Code, 11 U.S.C. § 101 et seq., or any successor statute, may put into effect and carry out any decrees and orders of the court or judge in such bankruptcy proceeding and may take any corporate action provided or directed by such decrees and orders, without further action by its directors or stockholders. Such power and authority may be exercised, and such corporate action may be taken, as may be directed by such decrees or orders, by the trustee or trustees of such corporation appointed or elected in the bankruptcy proceeding (or a majority thereof), or if none be appointed or elected and acting, by designated officers of the corporation, or by a representative appointed by the court or judge, with like effect as if exercised and taken by unanimous action of the directors and stockholders of the corporation.

(b) Such corporation may, in the manner provided in subsection (a) of this section, but without limiting the generality or effect of the foregoing, alter, amend or repeal its bylaws; constitute or reconstitute and classify or reclassify its board of directors, and name, constitute or appoint directors and officers in place of or in addition to all or some of the directors or officers then in office; amend its certificate of incorporation, and make any change in its capital or capital stock, or any other amendment, change, or alteration, or provision, authorized by this chapter; be dissolved, transfer all or part of its assets, merge or consolidate as permitted by this chapter, in which case, however, no stockholder shall have any statutory right of appraisal of such stockholder's stock; change the location of its registered office, change its registered agent, and remove or appoint any agent to receive service of process; authorize and fix the terms, manner and conditions of, the issuance of bonds, debentures or other obligations, whether or not convertible into stock of any class, or bearing warrants or other evidences of optional rights to purchase or subscribe for stock of any class; or lease its property and franchises to any corporation, if permitted by law.

(c) A certificate of any amendment, change or alteration, or of dissolution, or any agreement of merger or consolidation, made by such corporation pursuant to the foregoing provisions, shall be filed with the Secretary of State in accordance with § 103 of this title, and, subject to § 103(d) of this title, shall thereupon become effective in accordance with its terms and the provisions hereof. Such certificate, agreement of merger or other instrument shall be made, executed and acknowledged, as may be directed by such decrees or orders, by the trustee or trustees appointed or elected in the bankruptcy proceeding (or a majority thereof), or, if none be appointed or elected and acting, by the officers of the corporation, or by a representative appointed by the court or judge, and shall certify that provision for the making of such certificate, agreement or instrument is contained in a decree or order of a court or judge having jurisdiction of a proceeding under such Federal Bankruptcy Code or successor statute.

(d) This section shall cease to apply to such corporation upon the entry of a final decree in the bankruptcy proceeding closing the case and discharging the trustee or trustees, if any; provided however, that the closing of a case and discharge of trustee or trustees, if any, will not affect the validity of any act previously performed pursuant to subsections (a) through (c) of this section.

(e) On filing any certificate, agreement, report or other paper made or executed pursuant to this section, there shall be paid to the Secretary of State for the use of the State the same fees as are payable by corporations not in bankruptcy upon the filing of like certificates, agreements, reports or other papers.

SUBCHAPTER XII. RENEWAL, REVIVAL, EXTENSION AND RESTORATION OF CERTIFICATE OF INCORPORATION OR CHARTER

§ 311. Revocation of voluntary dissolution; restoration of expired certificate of incorporation.

(a) At any time prior to the expiration of 3 years following the dissolution of a corporation pursuant to § 275 of this title or such longer period as the Court of Chancery may have directed pursuant to § 278 of this title, or at any time prior to the expiration of 3 years following the expiration of the time limited for the corporation's existence as provided in its certificate of incorporation or such longer period as the Court of Chancery may have directed pursuant to § 278 of this title, a corporation may revoke the dissolution theretofore effected by it or restore its certificate of incorporation after it has expired by its own limitation in the following manner:

(1) For purposes of this section, the term "stockholders" shall mean the stockholders of record on the date the dissolution became effective or the date of expiration by limitation.

(2) The board of directors shall adopt a resolution recommending that the dissolution be revoked in the case of a dissolution or that the certificate of incorporation be restored in the case of an expiration by limitation and directing that the question of the revocation or restoration be submitted to a vote at a special meeting of stockholders.

(3) Notice of the special meeting of stockholders shall be given in accordance with § 222 of this title to each of the stockholders.

(4) At the meeting a vote of the stockholders shall be taken on a resolution to revoke the dissolution in the case of a dissolution or to restore the certificate of incorporation in the case of an expiration by limitation. If a majority of the stock of the corporation which was outstanding and entitled to vote upon a dissolution at the time of its dissolution, in the case of a revocation of dissolution, or which was outstanding and entitled to vote upon an amendment to the certificate of incorporation to change the period of the corporation's duration at the time of its expiration by limitation, in the case of a restoration, shall be voted for the resolution, a certificate of revocation of dissolution or a certificate of restoration shall be executed, acknowledged and filed in accordance with § 103 of this title, which shall be specifically designated as a certificate of revocation of dissolution or a certificate of restoration in its heading and shall state:

a. The name of the corporation;

b. The address (which shall be stated in accordance with § 131(c) of this title) of the corporation's registered office in this State, and the name of its registered agent at such address;

c. The names and respective addresses of its officers;

d. The names and respective addresses of its directors;

e. That a majority of the stock of the corporation which was outstanding and entitled to vote upon a dissolution at the time of its dissolution have voted in favor of a resolution to revoke the dissolution, in the case of a revocation of dissolution, or that a majority of the stock of the corporation which was outstanding and entitled to vote upon an amendment to the certificate of incorporation to change the period of the corporation's duration at the time of its expiration by limitation, in the case of a restoration, have voted in favor of a resolution to restore the certificate of incorporation; or, if it be the fact, that, in lieu of a meeting and vote of stockholders, the stockholders have given their written consent to the revocation or restoration in accordance with § 228 of this title; and

       f.   In the case of a restoration, the new specified date limiting the duration of the corporation's existence or that the corporation shall have perpetual existence.

(b)   Upon the effective time of the filing in the office of the Secretary of State of the certificate of revocation of dissolution or the certificate of restoration, the revocation of the dissolution or the restoration of the corporation shall become effective and the corporation may again carry on its business.

(c)   Upon the effectiveness of the revocation of the dissolution or the restoration of the corporation as provided in subsection (b) of this section, the provisions of § 211(c) of this title shall govern, and the period of time the corporation was in dissolution or was expired by limitation shall be included within the calculation of the 30-day and 13-month periods to which § 211(c) of this title refers. An election of directors, however, may be held at the special meeting of stockholders to which subsection (a) of this section refers, and in that event, that meeting of stockholders shall be deemed an annual meeting of stockholders for purposes of § 211(c) of this title.

(d)   If after the dissolution became effective or after the expiration by limitation any other corporation organized under the laws of this State shall have adopted the same name as the corporation, or shall have adopted a name so nearly similar thereto as not to distinguish it from the corporation, or any foreign corporation shall have qualified to do business in this State under the same name as the corporation or under a name so nearly similar thereto as not to distinguish it from the corporation, then, in such case, the corporation shall not be reinstated under the same name which it bore when its dissolution became effective or it expired by limitation, but shall adopt and be reinstated or restored under some other name, and in such case the certificate to be filed under this section shall set forth the name borne by the corporation at the time its dissolution became effective or it expired by limitation and the new name under which the corporation is to be reinstated or restored.

(e)   Nothing in this section shall be construed to affect the jurisdiction or power of the Court of Chancery under § 279 or § 280 of this title.

(f)   At any time prior to the expiration of 3 years following the dissolution of a nonstock corporation pursuant to § 276 of this title or such longer period as the Court of Chancery may have directed pursuant to § 278 of this title, or at any time prior to the expiration of 3 years following the expiration of the time limited for a nonstock corporation's existence as provided in its certificate of incorporation or such longer period as the Court of Chancery may have directed pursuant to § 278 of this title, a nonstock corporation may revoke the dissolution theretofore effected by it or restore its certificate of incorporation after it has expired by limitation in a manner analogous to that by which the dissolution was authorized or, in the case of a restoration, in the manner in which an amendment to the certificate of incorporation to change the period of the corporation's duration would have been authorized at the time of its expiration by limitation including (i) if applicable, a vote of the members entitled to vote, if any, on the dissolution or the amendment and (ii) the filing of a certificate of revocation of dissolution or a certificate of restoration containing information comparable to that required by paragraph (a)(4) of this section. Notwithstanding the foregoing, only subsections (b), (d), and (e) of this section shall apply to nonstock corporations.

(g)   Any corporation that revokes its dissolution or restores its certificate of incorporation pursuant to this section shall file all annual franchise tax reports that the corporation would have had to file if it had not dissolved or expired and shall pay all franchise taxes that the corporation would have had to pay if it had not dissolved or expired. No payment made pursuant to this subsection shall reduce the amount of franchise tax due under Chapter 5 of this title for the year in which such revocation or restoration is effected.

§ 312.   Revival of certificate of incorporation.

(a)   As used in this section, the term "certificate of incorporation" includes the charter of a corporation organized under any special act or any law of this State.

(b)   Any corporation whose certificate of incorporation has become forfeited or void pursuant to this title or whose certificate of incorporation has been revived, but, through failure to comply strictly with the provisions of this chapter, the validity of whose revival has been brought into question, may at any time procure a revival of its certificate of incorporation, together with all the rights, franchises, privileges and immunities and subject to all of its duties, debts and liabilities which had been secured or imposed by its original certificate of incorporation and all amendments thereto, by complying with the requirements of this section. Notwithstanding the foregoing, this section shall not be applicable to a corporation whose certificate of incorporation has been revoked or forfeited pursuant to § 284 of this title.

(c)   The revival of the certificate of incorporation may be procured as authorized by the board of directors or members of the governing body of the corporation in accordance with subsection (h) of this section and by executing, acknowledging and filing a certificate of revival in accordance with § 103 of this title.

(d)   The certificate required by subsection (c) of this section shall state:

(1)   The date of filing of the corporation's original certificate of incorporation; the name under which the corporation was originally incorporated; the name of the corporation at the time its certificate of incorporation became forfeited or void pursuant to this title; and the new name under which the corporation is to be revived to the extent required by subsection (f) of this section;

(2)   The address (which shall be stated in accordance with § 131(c) of this title) of the corporation's registered office in this State and the name of its registered agent at such address;

(3)   That the corporation desiring to be revived and so reviving its certificate of incorporation was organized under the laws of this State;

(4)   The date when the certificate of incorporation became forfeited or void pursuant to this title, or that the validity of any revival has been brought into question; and

(5)   That the certificate of revival is filed by authority of the board of directors or members of the governing body of the corporation in accordance with subsection (h) of this section.

(e)   Upon the filing of the certificate in accordance with § 103 of this title the corporation shall be revived with the same force and effect as if its certificate of incorporation had not been forfeited or void pursuant to this title. Such revival shall validate all contracts, acts, matters and things made, done and performed within the scope of its certificate of incorporation by the corporation, its directors or members of its governing body, officers, agents and stockholders or members during the time when its certificate of incorporation was forfeited or void pursuant to this title, with the same force and effect and to all intents and purposes as if the certificate of incorporation had at all times remained in full force and effect. All real and personal property, rights and credits, which belonged to the corporation at the time its certificate of incorporation became forfeited or void pursuant to this title and which were not disposed of prior to the time of its revival, and all real and personal property, rights and credits acquired by the corporation after its certificate of incorporation became forfeited or void pursuant to this title shall be vested in the corporation, after its revival, as if its certificate of incorporation had at all times remained in full force and effect, and the corporation after its revival shall be as exclusively liable for all contracts, acts, matters and things made, done or performed in its name and on its behalf by its directors or members of its governing body, officers, agents and stockholders or members prior to its revival, as if its certificate of incorporation had at all times remained in full force and effect.

(f)   If, since the certificate of incorporation became forfeited or void pursuant to this title, any other corporation organized under the laws of this State shall have adopted the same name as the corporation sought to be revived or shall have adopted a name so nearly similar thereto as not to distinguish it from the corporation to be revived or any foreign corporation qualified in accordance with § 371 of this title shall have adopted the same name as the corporation sought to be revived or shall have adopted a name so nearly similar thereto as not to distinguish it from the corporation to be revived, then in such case the corporation to be revived shall not be revived under the same name which it bore when its certificate of incorporation became forfeited or void pursuant to this title, but shall be revived under some other name as set forth in the certificate to be filed pursuant to subsection (c) of this section.

(g)   Any corporation that revives its certificate of incorporation under this chapter shall pay to this State a sum equal to all franchise taxes, penalties and interest thereon due at the time its certificate of incorporation became forfeited or void pursuant to this title; provided, however, that any corporation that revives its certificate of incorporation under this chapter whose certificate of incorporation has been forfeited or void for more than 5 years shall, in lieu of the payment of the franchise taxes and penalties otherwise required by this subsection, pay a sum equal to 3 times the amount of the annual franchise tax that would be due and payable by such corporation for the year in which the revival is effected, computed at the then current rate of taxation. No payment made pursuant to this subsection shall reduce the amount of franchise tax due under Chapter 5 of this title for the year in which the revival is effected.

(h)   For purposes of this section and § 502(a) of this title, the board of directors or governing body of the corporation shall be comprised of the persons, who, but for the certificate of incorporation having become forfeited or void pursuant to this title, would be the duly elected or appointed directors or members of the governing body of the corporation. The requirement for authorization by the board of directors under subsection (c) of this section shall be satisfied if a majority of the directors or members of the governing body then in office, even though less than a quorum, or the sole director or member of the governing body then in office, authorizes the revival of the certificate of incorporation of the corporation and the filing of the certificate required by subsection (c) of this section. In any case where there shall be no directors of the corporation available for the purposes aforesaid, the stockholders may elect a full board of directors, as provided by the bylaws of the corporation, and the board so elected may then authorize the revival of the certificate of incorporation of the corporation and the filing of the certificate required by subsection (c) of this section. A special meeting of the stockholders for the purpose of electing directors may be called by any officer or stockholder upon notice given in accordance with § 222 of this title. For purposes of this section, the bylaws shall be the bylaws of the corporation that, but for the certificate of incorporation having become forfeited or void pursuant to this title, would be the duly adopted bylaws of the corporation.

(i)   After a revival of the certificate of incorporation of the corporation shall have been effected, the provisions of § 211(c) of this title shall govern and the period of time during which the certificate of incorporation of the corporation was forfeited or void pursuant to this title shall be included within the calculation of the 30-day and 13-month periods to which § 211(c) of this title refers. A special meeting of stockholders held in accordance with subsection (h) of this section shall be deemed an annual meeting of stockholders for purposes of § 211(c) of this title.

(j)   Except as otherwise provided in § 313 of this title, whenever it shall be desired to revive the certificate of incorporation of any nonstock corporation, the governing body shall perform all the acts necessary for the revival of the certificate of incorporation of the corporation which are performed by the board of directors in the case of a corporation having capital stock, and the members of any nonstock corporation who are entitled to vote for the election of members of its governing body and any other members entitled to vote for dissolution under the certificate of incorporation or the bylaws of such corporation, shall perform all the acts necessary for the revival of the certificate of incorporation of the corporation which are performed by the stockholders in the case of a corporation having capital stock. Except as otherwise provided in § 313 of this title, in all other respects, the procedure for the revival of the certificate of incorporation of a nonstock corporation shall conform, as nearly as may be applicable, to the procedure prescribed in this section for the revival of the certificate of incorporation of a corporation having capital stock; provided, however, that subsection (i) of this section shall not apply to nonstock corporations.

§ 313.   Revival of certificate of incorporation or charter of exempt corporations.

(a)   Every exempt corporation whose certificate of incorporation or charter has become forfeited, pursuant to § 136(b) of this title for failure to obtain a registered agent, or inoperative and void, by operation of § 510 of this title for failure to file annual franchise tax reports required, and for failure to pay taxes or penalties from which it would have been exempt if the reports had been filed, shall be deemed to have filed all the reports and be relieved of all the taxes and penalties, upon satisfactory proof submitted to the Secretary of State of its right to be classified as an exempt corporation pursuant to § 501(b) of this title, and upon filing with the Secretary of State a certificate of revival in manner and form as required by § 312 of this title.

(b)   Upon the filing by the corporation of the proof of classification as required by subsection (a) of this section, the filing of the certificate of revival and payment of the required filing fees, the corporation shall be revived with the same force and effect as provided in § 312(e) of this title for other corporations.

(c)   As used in this section, the term "exempt corporation" shall have the meaning given to it in § 501(b) of this title. Nothing contained in this section relieves any exempt corporation from filing the annual report required by § 502 of this title.

§ 314.   Status of corporation.

Any corporation desiring to renew, extend and continue its corporate existence shall, upon complying with applicable constitutional provisions of this State, continue as provided in its certificate effecting the foregoing as a corporation and shall, in addition to the rights, privileges and immunities conferred by its charter, possess and enjoy all the benefits of this chapter, which are applicable to the nature of its business, and shall be subject to the restrictions and liabilities by this chapter imposed on such corporations.

SUBCHAPTER XIII.   SUITS AGAINST CORPORATIONS, DIRECTORS, OFFICERS OR STOCKHOLDERS

§ 321.   Service of process on corporations.

(a)   Service of legal process upon any corporation of this State shall be made by delivering a copy personally to any officer or director of the corporation in this State, or the registered agent of the corporation in this State, or by leaving it at the dwelling house or usual place of abode in this State of any officer, director or registered agent (if the registered agent be an individual), or at the registered office or other place of business of the corporation in this State. If the registered agent be a corporation, service of process upon it as such agent may be made by serving, in this State, a copy thereof on the president, vice-president, secretary, assistant secretary or any director of the corporate registered agent. Service by copy left at the dwelling house or usual place of abode of any officer, director or registered agent, or at the registered office or other place of business of the corporation in this State, to be effective must be delivered thereat at least 6 days before the return date of the process, and in the presence of an adult person, and the officer serving the process shall distinctly state the manner of service in such person's return thereto. Process returnable forthwith must be delivered personally to the officer, director or registered agent.

(b)   In case the officer whose duty it is to serve legal process cannot by due diligence serve the process in any manner provided for by subsection (a) of this section, it shall be lawful to serve the process against the corporation upon the Secretary of State, and such service shall be as effectual for all intents and purposes as if made in any of the ways provided for in subsection (a) of this section. Process may be served upon the Secretary of State under this subsection by means of electronic transmission but only as prescribed by the Secretary of State. The Secretary of State is authorized to issue such rules and regulations with respect to such service as the Secretary of State deems necessary or appropriate. In the event that service is effected through the Secretary of State in accordance with this subsection, the Secretary of State shall forthwith notify the corporation by letter, directed to the corporation at its principal place of business as it appears on the records relating to such corporation on file with the Secretary of State or, if no such address appears, at its last registered office. Such letter shall be sent by a mail or courier service that includes a record of mailing or deposit with the courier and a record of delivery evidenced by the signature of the recipient. Such letter shall enclose a copy of the process and any other papers served on the Secretary of State pursuant to this subsection. It shall be the duty of the plaintiff in the event of such service to serve process and any other papers in duplicate, to notify the Secretary of State that service is being effected pursuant to this subsection, and to pay the Secretary of State the sum of $50 for the use of the State, which sum shall be taxed as part of the costs in the proceeding if the plaintiff shall prevail therein. The Secretary of State shall maintain an alphabetical record of any such service setting forth the name of the plaintiff and defendant, the title, docket number and nature of the proceeding in which process has been served upon the Secretary of State, the fact that service has been effected pursuant to this subsection, the return date thereof, and the day and hour when the service was made. The Secretary of State shall not be required to retain such information for a period longer than 5 years from receipt of the service of process.

(c)   Service upon corporations may also be made in accordance with § 3111 of Title 10 or any other statute or rule of court.

§ 322. Failure of corporation to obey order of court; appointment of receiver.

Whenever any corporation shall refuse, fail or neglect to obey any order or decree of any court of this State within the time fixed by the court for its observance, such refusal, failure or neglect shall be a sufficient ground for the appointment of a receiver of the corporation by the Court of Chancery. If the corporation be a foreign corporation, such refusal, failure or neglect shall be a sufficient ground for the appointment of a receiver of the assets of the corporation within this State.

§ 323. Failure of corporation to obey writ of mandamus; quo warranto proceedings for forfeiture of charter.

If any corporation fails to obey the mandate of any peremptory writ of mandamus issued by a court of competent jurisdiction of this State for a period of 30 days after the serving of the writ upon the corporation in any manner as provided by the laws of this State for the service of writs, any party in interest in the proceeding in which the writ of mandamus issued may file a statement of such fact prepared by such party or such party's attorney with the Attorney General of this State, and it shall thereupon be the duty of the Attorney General to forthwith commence proceedings of quo warranto against the corporation in a court of competent jurisdiction, and the court, upon competent proof of such state of facts and proper proceedings had in such proceeding in quo warranto, shall decree the charter of the corporation forfeited.

§ 324. Attachment of shares of stock or any option, right or interest therein; procedure; sale; title upon sale; proceeds.

(a) The shares of any person in any corporation with all the rights thereto belonging, or any person's option to acquire the shares, or such person's right or interest in the shares, may be attached under this section for debt, or other demands, if such person appears on the books of the corporation to hold or own such shares, option, right or interest. So many of the shares, or so much of the option, right or interest therein may be sold at public sale to the highest bidder, as shall be sufficient to satisfy the debt, or other demand, interest and costs, upon an order issued therefor by the court from which the attachment process issued, and after such notice as is required for sales upon execution process. Except as to an uncertificated security as defined in § 8–102 of Title 6, the attachment is not laid and no order of sale shall issue unless § 8–112 of Title 6 has been satisfied. No order of sale shall be issued until after final judgment shall have been rendered in any case. If the debtor lives out of the county, a copy of the order shall be sent by registered or certified mail, return receipt requested, to such debtor's last known address, and shall also be published in a newspaper published in the county of such debtor's last known residence, if there be any, 10 days before the sale; and if the debtor be a nonresident of this State shall be mailed as aforesaid and published at least twice for 2 successive weeks, the last publication to be at least 10 days before the sale, in a newspaper published in the county where the attachment process issued. If the shares of stock or any of them or the option to acquire shares or any such right or interest in shares, or any part of them, be so sold, any assignment, or transfer thereof, by the debtor, after attachment, shall be void.

(b) When attachment process issues for shares of stock, or any option to acquire such or any right or interest in such, a certified copy of the process shall be left in this State with any officer or director, or with the registered agent of the corporation. Within 20 days after service of the process, the corporation shall serve upon the plaintiff a certificate of the number of shares held or owned by the debtor in the corporation, with the number or other marks distinguishing the same, or in the case the debtor appears on the books of the corporation to have an option to acquire shares of stock or any right or interest in any shares of stock of the corporation, there shall be served upon the plaintiff within 20 days after service of the process a certificate setting forth any such option, right or interest in the shares of the corporation in the language and form in which the option, right or interest appears on the books of the corporation, anything in the certificate of incorporation or bylaws of the corporation to the contrary notwithstanding. Service upon a corporate registered agent may be made in the manner provided in § 321 of this title.

(c) If, after sale made and confirmed, a certified copy of the order of sale and return and the stock certificate, if any, be left with any officer or director or with the registered agent of the corporation, the purchaser shall be thereby entitled to the shares or any option to acquire shares or any right or interest in shares so purchased, and all income, or dividends which may have been declared, or become payable thereon since the attachment laid. Such sale, returned and confirmed, shall transfer the shares or the option to acquire shares or any right or interest in shares sold to the purchaser, as fully as if the debtor, or defendant, had transferred the same to such purchaser according to the certificate of incorporation or bylaws of the corporation, anything in the certificate of incorporation or bylaws to the contrary notwithstanding. The court which issued the levy and confirmed the sale shall have the power to make an order compelling the corporation, the shares of which were sold, to issue new certificates or uncertificated shares to the purchaser at the sale and to cancel the registration of the shares attached on the books of the corporation upon the giving of an open end bond by such purchaser adequate to protect such corporation.

(d)   The money arising from the sale of the shares or from the sale of the option or right or interest shall be applied and paid, by the public official receiving the same, as by law is directed as to the sale of personal property in cases of attachment.

§ 325.   Actions against officers, directors or stockholders to enforce liability of corporation; unsatisfied judgment against corporation.

(a)   When the officers, directors or stockholders of any corporation shall be liable by the provisions of this chapter to pay the debts of the corporation, or any part thereof, any person to whom they are liable may have an action, at law or in equity, against any 1 or more of them, and the complaint shall state the claim against the corporation, and the ground on which the plaintiff expects to charge the defendants personally.

(b)   No suit shall be brought against any officer, director or stockholder for any debt of a corporation of which such person is an officer, director or stockholder, until judgment be obtained therefor against the corporation and execution thereon returned unsatisfied.

§ 326.   Action by officer, director or stockholder against corporation for corporate debt paid.

When any officer, director or stockholder shall pay any debt of a corporation for which such person is made liable by the provisions of this chapter, such person may recover the amount so paid in an action against the corporation for money paid for its use, and in such action only the property of the corporation shall be liable to be taken, and not the property of any stockholder.

§ 327.   Stockholder's derivative action; allegation of stock ownership.

In any derivative suit instituted by a stockholder of a corporation, it shall be averred in the complaint that the plaintiff was a stockholder of the corporation at the time of the transaction of which such stockholder complains or that such stockholder's stock thereafter devolved upon such stockholder by operation of law.

§ 328.   Effect of liability of corporation on impairment of certain transactions.

The liability of a corporation of this State, or the stockholders, directors or officers thereof, or the rights or remedies of the creditors thereof, or of persons doing or transacting business with the corporation, shall not in any way be lessened or impaired by the sale of its assets, or by the increase or decrease in the capital stock of the corporation, or by its merger or consolidation with 1 or more corporations or by any change or amendment in its certificate of incorporation.

§ 329.   Defective organization of corporation as defense.

(a)   No corporation of this State and no person sued by any such corporation shall be permitted to assert the want of legal organization as a defense to any claim.

(b)   This section shall not be construed to prevent judicial inquiry into the regularity or validity of the organization of a corporation, or its lawful possession of any corporate power it may assert in any other suit or proceeding where its corporate existence or the power to exercise the corporate rights it asserts is challenged, and evidence tending to sustain the challenge shall be admissible in any such suit or proceeding.

§ 330.   Usury; pleading by corporation.

No corporation shall plead any statute against usury in any court of law or equity in any suit instituted to enforce the payment of any bond, note or other evidence of indebtedness issued or assumed by it.

SUBCHAPTER XIV.   CLOSE CORPORATIONS; SPECIAL PROVISIONS

§ 341.   Law applicable to close corporation.

(a)   This subchapter applies to all close corporations, as defined in § 342 of this title. Unless a corporation elects to become a close corporation under this subchapter in the manner prescribed in this subchapter, it shall be subject in all respects to this chapter, except this subchapter.

(b)   This chapter shall be applicable to all close corporations, as defined in § 342 of this title, except insofar as this subchapter otherwise provides.

§ 342.   Close corporation defined; contents of certificate of incorporation.

(a)   A close corporation is a corporation organized under this chapter whose certificate of incorporation contains the provisions required by § 102 of this title and, in addition, provides that:

(1)   All of the corporation's issued stock of all classes, exclusive of treasury shares, shall be represented by certificates and shall be held of record by not more than a specified number of persons, not exceeding 30; and

(2)   All of the issued stock of all classes shall be subject to 1 or more of the restrictions on transfer permitted by § 202 of this title; and

(3)   The corporation shall make no offering of any of its stock of any class which would constitute a "public offering" within the meaning of the United States Securities Act of 1933 [15 U.S.C. § 77a et seq.] as it may be amended from time to time.

(b)   The certificate of incorporation of a close corporation may set forth the qualifications of stockholders, either by specifying classes of persons who shall be entitled to be holders of record of stock of any class, or by specifying classes of persons who shall not be entitled to be holders of stock of any class or both.

(c)   For purposes of determining the number of holders of record of the stock of a close corporation, stock which is held in joint or common tenancy or by the entireties shall be treated as held by 1 stockholder.

§ 343.   Formation of a close corporation.

A close corporation shall be formed in accordance with §§ 101, 102 and 103 of this title, except that:

(1)   Its certificate of incorporation shall contain a heading stating the name of the corporation and that it is a close corporation; and

(2)   Its certificate of incorporation shall contain the provisions required by § 342 of this title.

§ 344.   Election of existing corporation to become a close corporation.

Any corporation organized under this chapter may become a close corporation under this subchapter by executing, acknowledging and filing, in accordance with § 103 of this title, a certificate of amendment of its certificate of incorporation which shall contain a statement that it elects to become a close corporation, the provisions required by § 342 of this title to appear in the certificate of incorporation of a close corporation, and a heading stating the name of the corporation and that it is a close corporation. Such amendment shall be adopted in accordance with the requirements of § 241 or 242 of this title, except that it must be approved by a vote of the holders of record of at least 2/3 of the shares of each class of stock of the corporation which are outstanding.

§ 345.   Limitations on continuation of close corporation status.

A close corporation continues to be such and to be subject to this subchapter until:

(1)   It files with the Secretary of State a certificate of amendment deleting from its certificate of incorporation the provisions required or permitted by § 342 of this title to be stated in the certificate of incorporation to qualify it as a close corporation; or

(2)   Any 1 of the provisions or conditions required or permitted by § 342 of this title to be stated in a certificate of incorporation to qualify a corporation as a close corporation has in fact been breached and neither the corporation nor any of its stockholders takes the steps required by § 348 of this title to prevent such loss of status or to remedy such breach.

§ 346.   Voluntary termination of close corporation status by amendment of certificate of incorporation; vote required.

(a)   A corporation may voluntarily terminate its status as a close corporation and cease to be subject to this subchapter by amending its certificate of incorporation to delete therefrom the additional provisions required or permitted by § 342 of this title to be stated in the certificate of incorporation of a close corporation. Any such amendment shall be adopted and shall become effective in accordance with § 242 of this title, except that it must be approved by a vote of the holders of record of at least 2/3 of the shares of each class of stock of the corporation which are outstanding.

(b)   The certificate of incorporation of a close corporation may provide that on any amendment to terminate its status as a close corporation, a vote greater than 2/3 or a vote of all shares of any class shall be required; and if the certificate of incorporation contains such a provision, that provision shall not be amended, repealed or modified by any vote less than that required to terminate the corporation's status as a close corporation.

§ 347.   Issuance or transfer of stock of a close corporation in breach of qualifying conditions.

(a)   If stock of a close corporation is issued or transferred to any person who is not entitled under any provision of the certificate of incorporation permitted by § 342(b) of this title to be a holder of record of stock of such corporation, and if the certificate for such stock conspicuously notes the qualifications of the persons entitled to be holders of record thereof, such person is conclusively presumed to have notice of the fact of such person's ineligibility to be a stockholder.

(b)   If the certificate of incorporation of a close corporation states the number of persons, not in excess of 30, who are entitled to be holders of record of its stock, and if the certificate for such stock conspicuously states such number, and if the issuance or transfer of stock to any person would cause the stock to be held by more than such number of persons, the person to whom such stock is issued or transferred is conclusively presumed to have notice of this fact.

(c)   If a stock certificate of any close corporation conspicuously notes the fact of a restriction on transfer of stock of the corporation, and the restriction is one which is permitted by § 202 of this title, the transferee of the stock is conclusively presumed to have notice of the fact that such person has acquired stock in violation of the restriction, if such acquisition violates the restriction.

(d)   Whenever any person to whom stock of a close corporation has been issued or transferred has, or is conclusively presumed under this section to have, notice either:

(1)   That such person is a person not eligible to be a holder of stock of the corporation, or

(2)   That transfer of stock to such person would cause the stock of the corporation to be held by more than the number of persons permitted by its certificate of incorporation to hold stock of the corporation, or

(3)   That the transfer of stock is in violation of a restriction on transfer of stock,

the corporation may, at its option, refuse to register transfer of the stock into the name of the transferee.

(e)   Subsection (d) of this section shall not be applicable if the transfer of stock, even though otherwise contrary to subsection (a), (b) or (c) of this section has been consented to by all the stockholders of the close corporation, or if the close corporation has amended its certificate of incorporation in accordance with § 346 of this title.

(f)   The term "transfer," as used in this section, is not limited to a transfer for value.

(g)   The provisions of this section do not in any way impair any rights of a transferee regarding any right to rescind the transaction or to recover under any applicable warranty express or implied.

§ 348.   Involuntary termination of close corporation status; proceeding to prevent loss of status.

(a)   If any event occurs as a result of which 1 or more of the provisions or conditions included in a close corporation's certificate of incorporation pursuant to § 342 of this title to qualify it as a close corporation has been breached, the corporation's status as a close corporation under this subchapter shall terminate unless:

(1)   Within 30 days after the occurrence of the event, or within 30 days after the event has been discovered, whichever is later, the corporation files with the Secretary of State a certificate, executed and acknowledged in accordance with § 103 of this title, stating that a specified provision or condition included in its certificate of incorporation pursuant to § 342 of this title to qualify it as a close corporation has ceased to be applicable, and furnishes a copy of such certificate to each stockholder; and

(2)   The corporation concurrently with the filing of such certificate takes such steps as are necessary to correct the situation which threatens its status as a close corporation, including, without limitation, the refusal to register the transfer of stock which has been wrongfully transferred as provided by § 347 of this title, or a proceeding under subsection (b) of this section.

(b)   The Court of Chancery, upon the suit of the corporation or any stockholder, shall have jurisdiction to issue all orders necessary to prevent the corporation from losing its status as a close corporation, or to restore its status as a close corporation by enjoining or setting aside any act or threatened act on the part of the corporation or a stockholder which would be inconsistent with any of the provisions or conditions required or permitted by § 342 of this title to be stated in the certificate of incorporation of a close corporation, unless it is an act approved in accordance with § 346 of this title. The Court of Chancery may enjoin or set aside any transfer or threatened transfer of stock of a close corporation which is contrary to the terms of its certificate of incorporation or of any transfer restriction permitted by § 202 of this title, and may enjoin any public offering, as defined in § 342 of this title, or threatened public offering of stock of the close corporation.

§ 349.   Corporate option where a restriction on transfer of a security is held invalid.

If a restriction on transfer of a security of a close corporation is held not to be authorized by § 202 of this title, the corporation shall nevertheless have an option, for a period of 30 days after the judgment setting aside the restriction becomes final, to acquire the restricted security at a price which is agreed upon by the parties, or if no agreement is reached as to price, then at the fair value as determined by the Court of Chancery. In order to determine fair value, the Court may appoint an appraiser to receive evidence and report to the Court such appraiser's findings and recommendation as to fair value.

§ 350.   Agreements restricting discretion of directors.

A written agreement among the stockholders of a close corporation holding a majority of the outstanding stock entitled to vote, whether solely among themselves or with a party not a stockholder, is not invalid, as between the parties to the agreement, on the ground that it so relates to the conduct of the business and affairs of the corporation as to restrict or interfere with the discretion or powers of the board of directors. The effect of any such agreement shall be to relieve the directors and impose upon the stockholders who are parties to the agreement the liability for managerial acts or omissions which is imposed on directors to the extent and so long as the discretion or powers of the board in its management of corporate affairs is controlled by such agreement.

§ 351.   Management by stockholders.

The certificate of incorporation of a close corporation may provide that the business of the corporation shall be managed by the stockholders of the corporation rather than by a board of directors. So long as this provision continues in effect:

(1)   No meeting of stockholders need be called to elect directors;

(2)   Unless the context clearly requires otherwise, the stockholders of the corporation shall be deemed to be directors for purposes of applying provisions of this chapter; and

(3)   The stockholders of the corporation shall be subject to all liabilities of directors.

Such a provision may be inserted in the certificate of incorporation by amendment if all incorporators and subscribers or all holders of record of all of the outstanding stock, whether or not having voting power, authorize such a provision. An amendment to the certificate of incorporation to delete such a provision shall be adopted by a vote of the holders of a majority of all outstanding stock of the corporation, whether or not otherwise entitled to vote. If the certificate of incorporation contains a provision authorized by this section, the existence of such provision shall be noted conspicuously on the face or back of every stock certificate issued by such corporation.

§ 352.   Appointment of custodian for close corporation.

(a)   In addition to § 226 of this title respecting the appointment of a custodian for any corporation, the Court of Chancery, upon application of any stockholder, may appoint 1 or more persons to be custodians, and, if the corporation is insolvent, to be receivers, of any close corporation when:

(1)   Pursuant to § 351 of this title the business and affairs of the corporation are managed by the stockholders and they are so divided that the business of the corporation is suffering or is threatened with irreparable injury and any remedy with respect to such deadlock provided in the certificate of incorporation or bylaws or in any written agreement of the stockholders has failed; or

(2)   The petitioning stockholder has the right to the dissolution of the corporation under a provision of the certificate of incorporation permitted by § 355 of this title.

(b)   In lieu of appointing a custodian for a close corporation under this section or § 226 of this title the Court of Chancery may appoint a provisional director, whose powers and status shall be as provided in § 353 of this title if the Court determines that it would be in the best interest of the corporation. Such appointment shall not preclude any subsequent order of the Court appointing a custodian for such corporation.

§ 353.   Appointment of a provisional director in certain cases.

(a)   Notwithstanding any contrary provision of the certificate of incorporation or the bylaws or agreement of the stockholders, the Court of Chancery may appoint a provisional director for a close corporation if the directors are so divided respecting the management of the corporation's business and affairs that the votes required for action by the board of directors cannot be obtained with the consequence that the business and affairs of the corporation can no longer be conducted to the advantage of the stockholders generally.

(b)   An application for relief under this section must be filed (1) by at least one half of the number of directors then in office, (2) by the holders of at least one third of all stock then entitled to elect directors, or, (3) if there be more than 1 class of stock then entitled to elect 1 or more directors, by the holders of two thirds of the stock of any such class; but the certificate of incorporation of a close corporation may provide that a lesser proportion of the directors or of the stockholders or of a class of stockholders may apply for relief under this section.

(c)   A provisional director shall be an impartial person who is neither a stockholder nor a creditor of the corporation or of any subsidiary or affiliate of the corporation, and whose further qualifications, if any, may be determined by the Court of Chancery. A provisional director is not a receiver of the corporation and does not have the title and powers of a custodian or receiver appointed under §§ 226 and 291 of this title. A provisional director shall have all the rights and powers of a duly elected director of the corporation, including the right to notice of and to vote at meetings of directors, until such time as such person shall be removed by order of the Court of Chancery or by the holders of a majority of all shares then entitled to vote to elect directors or by the holders of two thirds of the shares of that class of voting shares which filed the application for appointment of a provisional director. A provisional director's compensation shall be determined by agreement between such person and the corporation subject to approval of the Court of Chancery, which may fix such person's compensation in the absence of agreement or in the event of disagreement between the provisional director and the corporation.

(d) Even though the requirements of subsection (b) of this section relating to the number of directors or stockholders who may petition for appointment of a provisional director are not satisfied, the Court of Chancery may nevertheless appoint a provisional director if permitted by § 352(b) of this title.

§ 354. Operating corporation as partnership.

No written agreement among stockholders of a close corporation, nor any provision of the certificate of incorporation or of the bylaws of the corporation, which agreement or provision relates to any phase of the affairs of such corporation, including but not limited to the management of its business or declaration and payment of dividends or other division of profits or the election of directors or officers or the employment of stockholders by the corporation or the arbitration of disputes, shall be invalid on the ground that it is an attempt by the parties to the agreement or by the stockholders of the corporation to treat the corporation as if it were a partnership or to arrange relations among the stockholders or between the stockholders and the corporation in a manner that would be appropriate only among partners.

§ 355. Stockholders' option to dissolve corporation.

(a) The certificate of incorporation of any close corporation may include a provision granting to any stockholder, or to the holders of any specified number or percentage of shares of any class of stock, an option to have the corporation dissolved at will or upon the occurrence of any specified event or contingency. Whenever any such option to dissolve is exercised, the stockholders exercising such option shall give written notice thereof to all other stockholders. After the expiration of 30 days following the sending of such notice, the dissolution of the corporation shall proceed as if the required number of stockholders having voting power had consented in writing to dissolution of the corporation as provided by § 228 of this title.

(b) If the certificate of incorporation as originally filed does not contain a provision authorized by subsection (a) of this section, the certificate may be amended to include such provision if adopted by the affirmative vote of the holders of all the outstanding stock, whether or not entitled to vote, unless the certificate of incorporation specifically authorizes such an amendment by a vote which shall be not less than 2/3 of all the outstanding stock whether or not entitled to vote.

(c) Each stock certificate in any corporation whose certificate of incorporation authorizes dissolution as permitted by this section shall conspicuously note on the face thereof the existence of the provision. Unless noted conspicuously on the face of the stock certificate, the provision is ineffective.

§ 356. Effect of this subchapter on other laws.

This subchapter shall not be deemed to repeal any statute or rule of law which is or would be applicable to any corporation which is organized under this chapter but is not a close corporation.

SUBCHAPTER XV. PUBLIC BENEFIT CORPORATIONS

§ 361. Law applicable to public benefit corporations; how formed.

This subchapter applies to all public benefit corporations, as defined in § 362 of this title. If a corporation elects to become a public benefit corporation under this subchapter in the manner prescribed in this subchapter, it shall be subject in all respects to the provisions of this chapter, except to the extent this subchapter imposes additional or different requirements, in which case such requirements shall apply.

§ 362. Public benefit corporation defined; contents of certificate of incorporation.

(a) A "public benefit corporation" is a for-profit corporation organized under and subject to the requirements of this chapter that is intended to produce a public benefit or public benefits and to operate in a responsible and sustainable manner. To that end, a public benefit corporation shall be managed in a manner that balances the stockholders' pecuniary interests, the best interests of those materially affected by the corporation's conduct, and the public benefit or public benefits identified in its certificate of incorporation. In the certificate of incorporation, a public benefit corporation shall:

     (1)   Identify within its statement of business or purpose pursuant to § 102(a)(3) of this title 1 or more specific public benefits to be promoted by the corporation; and

     (2)   State within its heading that it is a public benefit corporation.

     (b)   "Public benefit" means a positive effect (or reduction of negative effects) on 1 or more categories of persons, entities, communities or interests (other than stockholders in their capacities as stockholders) including, but not limited to, effects of an artistic, charitable, cultural, economic, educational, environmental, literary, medical, religious, scientific or technological nature. "Public benefit provisions" means the provisions of a certificate of incorporation contemplated by this subchapter.

     (c)   The name of the public benefit corporation may contain the words "public benefit corporation," or the abbreviation "P.B.C.," or the designation "PBC," which shall be deemed to satisfy the requirements of § 102(a)(1)(i) of this title. If the name does not contain such language, the corporation shall, prior to issuing unissued shares of stock or disposing of treasury shares, provide notice to any person to whom such stock is issued or who acquires such treasury shares that it is a public benefit corporation; provided that such notice need not be provided if the issuance or disposal is pursuant to an offering registered under the Securities Act of 1933 [15 U.S.C. § 77r et seq.] or if, at the time of issuance or disposal, the corporation has a class of securities that is registered under the Securities Exchange Act of 1934 [15 U.S.C. § 78a et seq.].

§ 363.   Certain amendments and mergers; votes required; appraisal rights. [For application of this section, see 80 Del. Laws, c. 40, § 16]

     (a)   Notwithstanding any other provisions of this chapter, a corporation that is not a public benefit corporation, may not, without the approval of 2/3 of the outstanding stock of the corporation entitled to vote thereon:

     (1)   Amend its certificate of incorporation to include a provision authorized by § 362(a)(1) of this title; or

     (2)   Merge or consolidate with or into another entity if, as a result of such merger or consolidation, the shares in such corporation would become, or be converted into or exchanged for the right to receive, shares or other equity interests in a domestic or foreign public benefit corporation or similar entity.

The restrictions of this section shall not apply prior to the time that the corporation has received payment for any of its capital stock, or in the case of a nonstock corporation, prior to the time that it has members.

     (b)   Any stockholder of a corporation that is not a public benefit corporation that holds shares of stock of such corporation immediately prior to the effective time of:

     (1)   An amendment to the corporation's certificate of incorporation to include a provision authorized by § 362(a)(1) of this title; or

     (2)   A merger or consolidation that would result in the conversion of the corporation's stock into or exchange of the corporation's stock for the right to receive shares or other equity interests in a domestic or foreign public benefit corporation or similar entity;

and has neither voted in favor of such amendment or such merger or consolidation nor consented thereto in writing pursuant to § 228 of this title, shall be entitled to an appraisal by the Court of Chancery of the fair value of the stockholder's shares of stock; provided, however, that no appraisal rights under this section shall be available for the shares of any class or series of stock, which stock, or depository receipts in respect thereof, at the record date fixed to determine the stockholders entitled to receive notice of the meeting of stockholders to act upon the agreement of merger or consolidation, or amendment, were either: (i) listed on a national securities exchange or (ii) held of record by more than 2,000 holders, unless, in the case of a merger or consolidation, the holders thereof are required by the terms of an agreement of merger or consolidation to accept for such stock anything except (A) shares of stock of any other corporation, or depository receipts in respect thereof, which shares of stock (or depository receipts in respect thereof) or depository receipts at the effective date of the merger or consolidation will be either listed on a national securities exchange or held of record by more than 2,000 holders; (B) cash in lieu of fractional shares or fractional depository receipts described in the foregoing clause (A); or (C) any combination of the shares of stock, depository receipts and cash in lieu of fractional shares or fractional depository receipts described in the foregoing clauses (A) and (B).

(c) Notwithstanding any other provisions of this chapter, a corporation that is a public benefit corporation may not, without the approval of 2/3 of the outstanding stock of the corporation entitled to vote thereon:

(1) Amend its certificate of incorporation to delete or amend a provision authorized by § 362(a)(1) or § 366(c) of this title; or

(2) Merge or consolidate with or into another entity if, as a result of such merger or consolidation, the shares in such corporation would become, or be converted into or exchanged for the right to receive, shares or other equity interests in a domestic or foreign corporation that is not a public benefit corporation or similar entity and the certificate of incorporation (or similar governing instrument) of which does not contain the identical provisions identifying the public benefit or public benefits pursuant to § 362(a) of this title or imposing requirements pursuant to § 366(c) of this title.

(d) Notwithstanding the foregoing, a nonprofit nonstock corporation may not be a constituent corporation to any merger or consolidation governed by this section.

§ 364. Stock certificates; notices regarding uncertificated stock.

Any stock certificate issued by a public benefit corporation shall note conspicuously that the corporation is a public benefit corporation formed pursuant to this subchapter. Any notice given by a public benefit corporation pursuant to § 151(f) of this title shall state conspicuously that the corporation is a public benefit corporation formed pursuant to this subchapter.

§ 365. Duties of directors.

(a) The board of directors shall manage or direct the business and affairs of the public benefit corporation in a manner that balances the pecuniary interests of the stockholders, the best interests of those materially affected by the corporation's conduct, and the specific public benefit or public benefits identified in its certificate of incorporation.

(b) A director of a public benefit corporation shall not, by virtue of the public benefit provisions or § 362(a) of this title, have any duty to any person on account of any interest of such person in the public benefit or public benefits identified in the certificate of incorporation or on account of any interest materially affected by the corporation's conduct and, with respect to a decision implicating the balance requirement in subsection (a) of this section, will be deemed to satisfy such director's fiduciary duties to stockholders and the corporation if such director's decision is both informed and disinterested and not such that no person of ordinary, sound judgment would approve.

(c) The certificate of incorporation of a public benefit corporation may include a provision that any disinterested failure to satisfy this section shall not, for the purposes of § 102(b)(7) or § 145 of this title, constitute an act or omission not in good faith, or a breach of the duty of loyalty.

§ 366. Periodic statements and third-party certification.

(a) A public benefit corporation shall include in every notice of a meeting of stockholders a statement to the effect that it is a public benefit corporation formed pursuant to this subchapter.

(b) A public benefit corporation shall no less than biennially provide its stockholders with a statement as to the corporation's promotion of the public benefit or public benefits identified in the certificate of incorporation and of the best interests of those materially affected by the corporation's conduct. The statement shall include:

(1) The objectives the board of directors has established to promote such public benefit or public benefits and interests;

(2) The standards the board of directors has adopted to measure the corporation's progress in promoting such public benefit or public benefits and interests;

(3) Objective factual information based on those standards regarding the corporation's success in meeting the objectives for promoting such public benefit or public benefits and interests; and

(4) An assessment of the corporation's success in meeting the objectives and promoting such public benefit or public benefits and interests.

(c) The certificate of incorporation or bylaws of a public benefit corporation may require that the corporation:

(1) Provide the statement described in subsection (b) of this section more frequently than biennially;

(2) Make the statement described in subsection (b) of this section available to the public; and/or

(3) Use a third-party standard in connection with and/or attain a periodic third-party certification addressing the corporation's promotion of the public benefit or public benefits identified in the certificate of incorporation and/or the best interests of those materially affected by the corporation's conduct.

§ 367. Derivative suits.

Stockholders of a public benefit corporation owning individually or collectively, as of the date of instituting such derivative suit, at least 2% of the corporation's outstanding shares or, in the case of a corporation with shares listed on a national securities exchange, the lesser of such percentage or shares of at least $2,000,000 in market value, may maintain a derivative lawsuit to enforce the requirements set forth in § 365(a) of this title.

§ 368. No effect on other corporations.

This subchapter shall not affect a statute or rule of law that is applicable to a corporation that is not a public benefit corporation, except as provided in § 363 of this title.

SUBCHAPTER XVI.   FOREIGN CORPORATIONS

§ 371. Definition; qualification to do business in State; procedure.

(a) As used in this chapter, the words "foreign corporation" mean a corporation organized under the laws of any jurisdiction other than this State.

(b) No foreign corporation shall do any business in this State, through or by branch offices, agents or representatives located in this State, until it shall have paid to the Secretary of State of this State for the use of this State, $80, and shall have filed in the office of the Secretary of State:

(1) A certificate, as of a date not earlier than 6 months prior to the filing date, issued by an authorized officer of the jurisdiction of its incorporation evidencing its corporate existence. If such certificate is in a foreign language, a translation thereof, under oath of the translator, shall be attached thereto;

(2) A statement executed by an authorized officer of each corporation setting forth (i) the name and address of its registered agent in this State, which agent may be any of the foreign corporation itself, an individual resident in this State, a domestic corporation, a domestic partnership (whether general (including a limited liability partnership) or limited (including a limited liability limited partnership)), a domestic limited liability company, a domestic statutory trust, a foreign corporation (other than the foreign corporation itself), a foreign partnership (whether general (including a limited liability partnership) or limited (including a limited liability limited partnership)), a foreign limited liability company or a foreign statutory trust, (ii) a statement, as of a date not earlier than 6 months prior to the filing date, of the assets and liabilities of the corporation, and (iii) the business it proposes to do in this State, and a statement that it is authorized to do that business in the jurisdiction of its incorporation. The statement shall be acknowledged in accordance with § 103 of this title.

(c)   The certificate of the Secretary of State, under seal of office, of the filing of the certificates required by subsection (b) of this section, shall be delivered to the registered agent upon the payment to the Secretary of State of the fee prescribed for such certificates, and the certificate shall be prima facie evidence of the right of the corporation to do business in this State; provided, that the Secretary of State shall not issue such certificate unless the name of the corporation is such as to distinguish it upon the records in the office of the Division of Corporations in the Department of State from the names that are reserved on such records and from the names on such records of each other corporation, partnership, limited partnership, limited liability company or statutory trust organized or registered as a domestic or foreign corporation, partnership, limited partnership, limited liability company or statutory trust under the laws of this State, except with the written consent of the person who has reserved such name or such other corporation, partnership, limited partnership, limited liability company or statutory trust, executed, acknowledged and filed with the Secretary of State in accordance with § 103 of this title. If the name of the foreign corporation conflicts with the name of a corporation, partnership, limited partnership, limited liability company or statutory trust organized under the laws of this State, or a name reserved for a corporation, partnership, limited partnership, limited liability company or statutory trust to be organized under the laws of this State, or a name reserved or registered as that of a foreign corporation, partnership, limited partnership, limited liability company or statutory trust under the laws of this State, the foreign corporation may qualify to do business if it adopts an assumed name which shall be used when doing business in this State as long as the assumed name is authorized for use by this section.

§ 372.   Additional requirements in case of change of name, change of business purpose or merger or consolidation.

(a)   Every foreign corporation admitted to do business in this State which shall change its corporate name, or enlarge, limit or otherwise change the business which it proposes to do in this State, shall, within 30 days after the time said change becomes effective, file with the Secretary of State a certificate, which shall set forth:

(1)   The name of the foreign corporation as it appears on the records of the Secretary of State of this State;

(2)   The jurisdiction of its incorporation;

(3)   The date it was authorized to do business in this State;

(4)   If the name of the foreign corporation has been changed, a statement of the name relinquished, a statement of the new name and a statement that the change of name has been effected under the laws of the jurisdiction of its incorporation and the date the change was effected;

(5)   If the business it proposes to do in this State is to be enlarged, limited or otherwise changed, a statement reflecting such change and a statement that it is authorized to do in the jurisdiction of its incorporation the business which it proposes to do in this State.

(b)   Whenever a foreign corporation authorized to transact business in this State shall be the survivor of a merger permitted by the laws of the state or country in which it is incorporated, it shall, within 30 days after the merger becomes effective, file a certificate, issued by the proper officer of the state or country of its incorporation, attesting to the occurrence of such event. If the merger has changed the corporate name of such foreign corporation or has enlarged, limited or otherwise changed the business it proposes to do in this State, it shall also comply with subsection (a) of this section.

(c)   Whenever a foreign corporation authorized to transact business in this State ceases to exist because of a statutory merger or consolidation, it shall comply with § 381 of this title.

(d)   The Secretary of State shall be paid, for the use of the State, $50 for filing and indexing each certificate required by subsection (a) or (b) of this section, and in the event of a change of name an additional $50 shall be paid for a certificate to be issued as evidence of filing the change of name.

§ 373.   Exceptions to requirements.

(a)   No foreign corporation shall be required to comply with §§ 371 and 372 of this title, under any of the following conditions:

(1)   If it is in the mail order or a similar business, merely receiving orders by mail or otherwise in pursuance of letters, circulars, catalogs or other forms of advertising, or solicitation, accepting the orders outside this State, and filling them with goods shipped into this State;

(2)   If it employs salespersons, either resident or traveling, to solicit orders in this State, either by display of samples or otherwise (whether or not maintaining sales offices in this State), all orders being subject to approval at the offices of the corporation without this State, and all goods applicable to the orders being shipped in pursuance thereof from without this State to the vendee or to the seller or such seller's agent for delivery to the vendee, and if any samples kept within this State are for display or advertising purposes only, and no sales, repairs or replacements are made from stock on hand in this State;

(3)   If it sells, by contract consummated outside this State, and agrees, by the contract, to deliver into this State, machinery, plants or equipment, the construction, erection or installation of which within this State requires the supervision of technical engineers or skilled employees performing services not generally available, and as a part of the contract of sale agrees to furnish such services, and such services only, to the vendee at the time of construction, erection or installation;

(4)   If its business operations within this State, although not falling within the terms of paragraphs (a)(1), (2) and (3) of this section or any of them, are nevertheless wholly interstate in character;

(5)   If it is an insurance company doing business in this State;

(6)   If it creates, as borrower or lender, or acquires, evidences of debt, mortgages or liens on real or personal property;

(7)   If it secures or collects debts or enforces any rights in property securing the same.

(b)   This section shall have no application to the question of whether any foreign corporation is subject to service of process and suit in this State under § 382 of this title or any other law of this State.

§ 374.   Annual report.

Annually on or before June 30, a foreign corporation doing business in this State shall file a report with the Secretary of State. The report shall be made on a form designated by the Secretary of State and shall be signed by the corporation's president, secretary, treasurer or other proper officer duly authorized so to act, or by any of its directors, or if filing an initial report by any incorporator in the event its board of directors shall not have been elected. The fact that an individual's name is signed on a certification attached to a corporate report shall be prima facie evidence that such individual is authorized to certify the report on behalf of the corporation; however the official title or position of the individual signing the corporate report shall be designated. The report shall contain the following information:

(1)   The location of its registered office in this State, which shall include the street, number, city and postal code;

(2)   The name of the agent upon whom service of process against the corporation may be served;

(3)   The location of the principal place of business of the corporation, which shall include the street, number, city, state or foreign country; and

(4)   The names and addresses of all the directors as of the filing date of the report and the name and address of the officer who signs the report.

If any officer or director of a foreign corporation required to file an annual report with the Secretary of State shall knowingly make any false statement in the report, such officer or director shall be guilty of perjury.

§ 375.   Failure to file report.

Upon the failure, neglect or refusal of any foreign corporation to file an annual report as required by § 374 of this title, the Secretary of State may, in the Secretary of State's discretion, investigate the reasons therefor and shall terminate the right of the foreign corporation to do business within this State upon failure of the corporation to file an annual report within any 2-year period.

§ 376.   Service of process upon qualified foreign corporations.

(a)   All process issued out of any court of this State, all orders made by any court of this State, all rules and notices of any kind required to be served on any foreign corporation which has qualified to do business in this State may be served on the registered agent of the corporation designated in accordance with § 371 of this title, or, if there be no such agent, then on any officer, director or other agent of the corporation then in this State.

(b)   In case the officer whose duty it is to serve legal process cannot by due diligence serve the process in any manner provided for by subsection (a) of this section, it shall be lawful to serve the process against the corporation upon the Secretary of State, and such service shall be as effectual for all intents and purposes as if made in any of the ways provided for in subsection (a) of this section. Process may be served upon the Secretary of State under this subsection by means of electronic transmission but only as prescribed by the Secretary of State. The Secretary of State is authorized to issue such rules and regulations with respect to such service as the Secretary of State deems necessary or appropriate. In the event that service is effected through the Secretary of State in accordance with this subsection, the Secretary of State shall forthwith notify the corporation by letter, directed to the corporation at its principal place of business as it appears on the last annual report filed pursuant to § 374 of this title or, if no such address appears, at its last registered office. Such letter shall be sent by a mail or courier service that includes a record of mailing or deposit with the courier and a record of delivery evidenced by the signature of the recipient. Such letter shall enclose a copy of the process and any other papers served upon the Secretary of State pursuant to this subsection. It shall be the duty of the plaintiff in the event of such service to serve process and any other papers in duplicate, to notify the Secretary of State that service is being effected pursuant to this subsection, and to pay the Secretary of State the sum of $50 for the use of the State, which sum shall be taxed as a part of the costs in the proceeding if the plaintiff shall prevail therein. The Secretary of State shall maintain an alphabetical record of any such service setting forth the name of the plaintiff and the defendant, the title, docket number and nature of the proceeding in which process has been served upon the Secretary of State, the fact that service has been effected pursuant to this subsection, the return date thereof, and the day and hour when the service was made. The Secretary of State shall not be required to retain such information for a period longer than 5 years from receipt of such service.

§ 377.   Change of registered agent.

(a)   Any foreign corporation, which has qualified to do business in this State, may change its registered agent and substitute another registered agent by filing a certificate with the Secretary of State, acknowledged in accordance with § 103 of this title, setting forth:

    (1)   The name and address of its registered agent designated in this State upon whom process directed to said corporation may be served; and

    (2)   A revocation of all previous appointments of agent for such purposes.

Such registered agent shall comply with § 371(b)(2)(i) of this title.

(b)   Any individual or entity designated by a foreign corporation as its registered agent for service of process may resign by filing with the Secretary of State a signed statement that the registered agent is unwilling to continue to act as the registered agent of the corporation for service of process, including in the statement the post-office address of the main or headquarters office of the foreign corporation, but such resignation shall not become effective until 30 days after the statement is filed. The statement shall be acknowledged by the registered agent and shall contain a representation that written notice of resignation was given to the corporation at least 30 days prior to the filing of the statement by mailing or delivering such notice to the corporation at its address given in the statement.

(c)   If any agent designated and certified as required by § 371 of this title shall die or remove from this State, or resign, then the foreign corporation for which the agent had been so designated and certified shall, within 10 days after the death, removal or resignation of its agent, substitute, designate and certify to the Secretary of State, the name of another registered agent for the purposes of this subchapter, and all process, orders, rules and notices mentioned in § 376 of this title may be served on or given to the substituted agent with like effect as is prescribed in that section.

(d)   A foreign corporation whose qualification to do business in this State has been forfeited pursuant to § 132(f)(4) or § 136(b) of this title may be reinstated by filing a certificate of reinstatement with the Secretary of State, acknowledged in accordance with § 103 of this title, setting forth:

(1)   The name of the foreign corporation;

(2)   The effective date of the forfeiture; and

(3)   The name and address of the foreign corporation's registered agent required to be maintained by § 132 of this title.

(e)   Upon the filing of a certificate of reinstatement in accordance with subsection (d) of this section, the qualification of the foreign corporation to do business in this State shall be reinstated with the same force and effect as if it had not been forfeited pursuant to this title.

§ 378.   Penalties for noncompliance.

Any foreign corporation doing business of any kind in this State without first having complied with any section of this subchapter applicable to it, shall be fined not less than $200 nor more than $500 for each such offense. Any agent of any foreign corporation that shall do any business in this State for any foreign corporation before the foreign corporation has complied with any section of this subchapter applicable to it, shall be fined not less than $100 nor more than $500 for each such offense.

§ 379.   Banking powers denied.

(a)   No foreign corporation shall, within the limits of this State, by any implication or construction, be deemed to possess the power of discounting bills, notes or other evidence of debt, of receiving deposits, of buying and selling bills of exchange, or of issuing bills, notes or other evidences of debt upon loan for circulation as money, anything in its charter or articles of incorporation to the contrary notwithstanding, except as otherwise provided in subchapter VII of Chapter 7 or in Chapter 14 of Title 5.

(b)   All certificates issued by the Secretary of State under § 371 of this title shall expressly set forth the limitations and restrictions contained in this section.

§ 380.   Foreign corporation as fiduciary in this State.

A corporation organized and doing business under the laws of the District of Columbia or of any state of the United States other than Delaware, duly authorized by its certificate of incorporation or bylaws so to act, may be appointed by any last will and testament or other testamentary writing, probated within this State, or by a deed of trust, mortgage or other agreement, as executor, guardian, trustee or other fiduciary, and may act as such within this State, when and to the extent that the laws of the District of Columbia or of the state in which the foreign corporation is organized confer like powers upon corporations organized and doing business under the laws of this State.

§ 381.   Withdrawal of foreign corporation from State; procedure; service of process on Secretary of State.

(a)   Any foreign corporation which shall have qualified to do business in this State under § 371 of this title, may surrender its authority to do business in this State and may withdraw therefrom by filing with the Secretary of State:

(1)   A certificate executed in accordance with § 103 of this title, stating that it surrenders its authority to transact business in the state and withdraws therefrom; and stating the address to which the Secretary of State may mail any process against the corporation that may be served upon the Secretary of State, or

(2)   A copy of an order or decree of dissolution made by any court of competent jurisdiction or other competent authority of the State or other jurisdiction of its incorporation, certified to be a true copy under the hand of the clerk of the court or other official body, and the official seal of the court or official body or clerk thereof, together with a certificate executed in accordance with paragraph (a)(1)

of this section, stating the address to which the Secretary of State may mail any process against the corporation that may be served upon the Secretary of State.

(b)   The Secretary of State shall, upon payment to the Secretary of State of the fees prescribed in § 391 of this title, issue a sufficient number of certificates, under the Secretary of State's hand and official seal, evidencing the surrender of the authority of the corporation to do business in this State and its withdrawal therefrom. One of the certificates shall be furnished to the corporation withdrawing and surrendering its right to do business in this State.

(c)   Upon the issuance of the certificates by the Secretary of State, the appointment of the registered agent of the corporation in this State, upon whom process against the corporation may be served, shall be revoked, and the corporation shall be deemed to have consented that service of process in any action, suit or proceeding based upon any cause of action arising in this State, during the time the corporation was authorized to transact business in this State, may thereafter be made by service upon the Secretary of State. Process may be served upon the Secretary of State under this subsection by means of electronic transmission but only as prescribed by the Secretary of State. The Secretary of State is authorized to issue such rules and regulations with respect to such service as the Secretary of State deems necessary or appropriate.

(d)   In the event of service upon the Secretary of State in accordance with subsection (c) of this section, the Secretary of State shall forthwith notify the corporation by letter, directed to the corporation at the address stated in the certificate which was filed by the corporation with the Secretary of State pursuant to subsection (a) of this section. Such letter shall be sent by a mail or courier service that includes a record of mailing or deposit with the courier and a record of delivery evidenced by the signature of the recipient. Such letter shall enclose a copy of the process and any other papers served upon the Secretary of State. It shall be the duty of the plaintiff in the event of such service to serve process and any other papers in duplicate, to notify the Secretary of State that service is being made pursuant to this subsection, and to pay the Secretary of State the sum of $50 for the use of the State, which sum shall be taxed as part of the cost of the action, suit or proceeding if the plaintiff shall prevail therein. The Secretary of State shall maintain an alphabetical record of such service setting forth the name of the plaintiff and defendant, the title, docket number and nature of the proceeding in which the process has been served upon the Secretary of State, the fact that service has been effected pursuant to this subsection, the return date thereof, and the day and hour when the service was made. The Secretary of State shall not be required to retain such information for a period longer than 5 years from receipt of the service of process.

§ 382.   Service of process on nonqualifying foreign corporations.

(a)   Any foreign corporation which shall transact business in this State without having qualified to do business under § 371 of this title shall be deemed to have thereby appointed and constituted the Secretary of State of this State its agent for the acceptance of legal process in any civil action, suit or proceeding against it in any state or federal court in this State arising or growing out of any business transacted by it within this State. If any foreign corporation consents in writing to be subject to the jurisdiction of any state or federal court in this State for any civil action, suit or proceeding against it arising or growing out of any business or matter, and if the agreement or instrument setting forth such consent does not otherwise provide a manner of service of legal process in any such civil action, suit or proceeding against it, such foreign corporation shall be deemed to have thereby appointed and constituted the Secretary of State of this State its agent for the acceptance of legal process in any such civil action, suit or proceeding against it. The transaction of business in this State by such corporation and/or such consent by such corporation to the jurisdiction of any state or federal court in this State without provision for a manner of service of legal process shall be a signification of the agreement of such corporation that any process served upon the Secretary of State when so served shall be of the same legal force and validity as if served upon an authorized officer or agent personally within this State. Process may be served upon the Secretary of State under this subsection by means of electronic transmission but only as prescribed by the Secretary of State. The Secretary of State is authorized to issue such rules and regulations with respect to such service as the Secretary of State deems necessary or appropriate.

(b)   Section 373 of this title shall not apply in determining whether any foreign corporation is transacting business in this State within the meaning of this section; and "the transaction of business" or "business transacted in this State," by any such foreign corporation, whenever those words are used in this section, shall mean the course or practice of carrying on any business activities in this State, including, without limiting the generality of the foregoing, the solicitation of business or orders in this State. This section shall not apply to any insurance company doing business in this State.

(c)　In the event of service upon the Secretary of State in accordance with subsection (a) of this section, the Secretary of State shall forthwith notify the corporation thereof by letter, directed to the corporation at the address furnished to the Secretary of State by the plaintiff in such action, suit or proceeding. Such letter shall be sent by a mail or courier service that includes a record of mailing or deposit with the courier and a record of delivery evidenced by the signature of the recipient. Such letter shall enclose a copy of the process and any other papers served upon the Secretary of State. It shall be the duty of the plaintiff in the event of such service to serve process and any other papers in duplicate, to notify the Secretary of State that service is being made pursuant to this subsection, and to pay the Secretary of State the sum of $50 for the use of the State, which sum shall be taxed as a part of the costs in the proceeding if the plaintiff shall prevail therein. The Secretary of State shall maintain an alphabetical record of any such process setting forth the name of the plaintiff and defendant, the title, docket number and nature of the proceeding in which process has been served upon the Secretary of State, the fact that service has been effected pursuant to this subsection, the return date thereof, and the day and hour when the service was made. The Secretary of State shall not be required to retain such information for a period longer than 5 years from receipt of the service of process.

§ 383.　Actions by and against unqualified foreign corporations.

(a)　A foreign corporation which is required to comply with §§ 371 and 372 of this title and which has done business in this State without authority shall not maintain any action or special proceeding in this State unless and until such corporation has been authorized to do business in this State and has paid to the State all fees, penalties and franchise taxes for the years or parts thereof during which it did business in this State without authority. This prohibition shall not apply to any successor in interest of such foreign corporation.

(b)　The failure of a foreign corporation to obtain authority to do business in this State shall not impair the validity of any contract or act of the foreign corporation or the right of any other party to the contract to maintain any action or special proceeding thereon, and shall not prevent the foreign corporation from defending any action or special proceeding in this State.

§ 384.　Foreign corporations doing business without having qualified; injunctions.

The Court of Chancery shall have jurisdiction to enjoin any foreign corporation, or any agent thereof, from transacting any business in this State if such corporation has failed to comply with any section of this subchapter applicable to it or if such corporation has secured a certificate of the Secretary of State under § 371 of this title on the basis of false or misleading representations. The Attorney General shall, upon the Attorney General's own motion or upon the relation of proper parties, proceed for this purpose by complaint in any county in which such corporation is doing business.

§ 385.　Filing of certain instruments with recorder of deeds not required.

No instrument that is required to be filed with the Secretary of State of this State by this subchapter need be filed with the recorder of deeds of any county of this State in order to comply with this subchapter.

SUBCHAPTER XVII.　DOMESTICATION AND TRANSFER

§ 388.　Domestication of non-United States entities.

(a)　As used in this section, the term:

(1)　"Foreign jurisdiction" means any foreign country or other foreign jurisdiction (other than the United States, any state, the District of Columbia, or any possession or territory of the United States); and

(2)　"Non-United States entity" means a corporation, a limited liability company, a statutory trust, a business trust or association, a real estate investment trust, a common-law trust, or any other unincorporated business or entity, including a partnership (whether general (including a limited liability partnership) or limited (including a limited liability limited partnership)), formed, incorporated, created or that otherwise came into being under the laws of any foreign jurisdiction.

(b) Any non-United States entity may become domesticated as a corporation in this State by complying with subsection (h) of this section and filing with the Secretary of State:

(1) A certificate of corporate domestication which shall be executed in accordance with subsection (g) of this section and filed in accordance with § 103 of this title; and

(2) A certificate of incorporation, which shall be executed, acknowledged and filed in accordance with § 103 of this title.

Each of the certificates required by this subsection (b) shall be filed simultaneously with the Secretary of State and, if such certificates are not to become effective upon their filing as permitted by § 103(d) of this title, then each such certificate shall provide for the same effective date or time in accordance with § 103(d) of this title.

(c) The certificate of corporate domestication shall certify:

(1) The date on which and jurisdiction where the non-United States entity was first formed, incorporated, created or otherwise came into being;

(2) The name of the non-United States entity immediately prior to the filing of the certificate of corporate domestication;

(3) The name of the corporation as set forth in its certificate of incorporation filed in accordance with subsection (b) of this section; and

(4) The jurisdiction that constituted the seat, siege social, or principal place of business or central administration of the non-United States entity or any other equivalent thereto under applicable law, immediately prior to the filing of the certificate of corporate domestication; and

(5) That the domestication has been approved in the manner provided for by the document, instrument, agreement or other writing, as the case may be, governing the internal affairs of the non-United States entity and the conduct of its business or by applicable non-Delaware law, as appropriate.

(d) Upon the certificate of corporate domestication and the certificate of incorporation becoming effective in accordance with § 103 of this title, the non-United States entity shall be domesticated as a corporation in this State and the corporation shall thereafter be subject to all of the provisions of this title, except that notwithstanding § 106 of this title, the existence of the corporation shall be deemed to have commenced on the date the non-United States entity commenced its existence in the jurisdiction in which the non-United States entity was first formed, incorporated, created or otherwise came into being.

(e) The domestication of any non-United States entity as a corporation in this State shall not be deemed to affect any obligations or liabilities of the non-United States entity incurred prior to its domestication as a corporation in this State, or the personal liability of any person therefor.

(f) The filing of a certificate of corporate domestication shall not affect the choice of law applicable to the non-United States entity, except that, from the effective time of the domestication, the law of the State of Delaware, including this title, shall apply to the non-United States entity to the same extent as if the non-United States entity had been incorporated as a corporation of this State on that date.

(g) The certificate of corporate domestication shall be signed by any person who is authorized to sign the certificate of corporate domestication on behalf of the non-United States entity.

(h) Prior to the filing of a certificate of corporate domestication with the Secretary of State, the domestication shall be approved in the manner provided for by the document, instrument, agreement or other writing, as the case may be, governing the internal affairs of the non-United States entity and the conduct of its business or by applicable non-Delaware law, as appropriate, and the certificate of incorporation shall be approved by the same authorization required to approve the domestication.

(i) When a non-United States entity has become domesticated as a corporation pursuant to this section, for all purposes of the laws of the State of Delaware, the corporation shall be deemed to be the same entity as the domesticating non-United States entity and the domestication shall constitute a continuation of the existence of the domesticating non-United States entity in the form of a corporation of this State. When any domestication shall have become effective under this section, for all purposes of the laws of the State of Delaware, all of the rights, privileges and powers of the non-United States entity that has been domesticated, and all property, real, personal and mixed, and all debts due to such non-United States entity, as well as all other things and causes of action belonging to such non-United States entity, shall remain vested in the corporation to which such non-United States entity has been domesticated (and also in the non-United States entity, if and for so long as the non-United States entity continues its existence in the foreign jurisdiction in which it was existing immediately prior to the domestication) and shall be the property of such corporation (and also of the non-United States entity, if and for so long as the non-United States entity continues its existence in the foreign jurisdiction in which it was existing immediately prior to the domestication), and the title to any real property vested by deed or otherwise in such non-United States entity shall not revert or be in any way impaired by reason of this title; but all rights of creditors and all liens upon any property of such non-United States entity shall be preserved unimpaired, and all debts, liabilities and duties of the non-United States entity that has been domesticated shall remain attached to the corporation to which such non-United States entity has been domesticated (and also to the non-United States entity, if and for so long as the non-United States entity continues its existence in the foreign jurisdiction in which it was existing immediately prior to the domestication), and may be enforced against it to the same extent as if said debts, liabilities and duties had originally been incurred or contracted by it in its capacity as such corporation. The rights, privileges, powers and interests in property of the non-United States entity, as well as the debts, liabilities and duties of the non-United States entity, shall not be deemed, as a consequence of the domestication, to have been transferred to the corporation to which such non-United States entity has domesticated for any purpose of the laws of the State of Delaware.

(j)   Unless otherwise agreed or otherwise required under applicable non-Delaware law, the domesticating non-United States entity shall not be required to wind up its affairs or pay its liabilities and distribute its assets, and the domestication shall not be deemed to constitute a dissolution of such non-United States entity. If, following domestication, a non-United States entity that has become domesticated as a corporation of this State continues its existence in the foreign jurisdiction in which it was existing immediately prior to domestication, the corporation and such non-United States entity shall, for all purposes of the laws of the State of Delaware, constitute a single entity formed, incorporated, created or otherwise having come into being, as applicable, and existing under the laws of the State of Delaware and the laws of such foreign jurisdiction.

(k)   In connection with a domestication under this section, shares of stock, rights or securities of, or interests in, the non-United States entity that is to be domesticated as a corporation of this State may be exchanged for or converted into cash, property, or shares of stock, rights or securities of such corporation or, in addition to or in lieu thereof, may be exchanged for or converted into cash, property, or shares of stock, rights or securities of, or interests in, another corporation or other entity or may be cancelled.

§ 389.   Temporary transfer of domicile into this State.

(a)   As used in this section:

(1)   The term "emergency condition" shall be deemed to include but not be limited to any of the following:

    a.   War or other armed conflict;

    b.   Revolution or insurrection;

    c.   Invasion or occupation by foreign military forces;

    d.   Rioting or civil commotion of an extended nature;

    e.   Domination by a foreign power;

    f.   Expropriation, nationalization or confiscation of a material part of the assets or property of the non-United States entity;

    g.   Impairment of the institution of private property (including private property held abroad);

h. The taking of any action under the laws of the United States whereby persons resident in the jurisdiction, the law of which governs the internal affairs of the non-United States entity, might be treated as "enemies" or otherwise restricted under laws of the United States relating to trading with enemies of the United States;

i. The immediate threat of any of the foregoing; and

j. Such other event which, under the law of the jurisdiction governing the internal affairs of the non-United States entity, permits the non-United States entity to transfer its domicile.

(2) The term "foreign jurisdiction" and the term "non-United States entity" shall have the same meanings as set forth in § 388(a) of this title.

(3) The terms "officers" and "directors" include, in addition to such persons, trustees, managers, partners and all other persons performing functions equivalent to those of officers and directors, however named or described in any relevant instrument.

(b) Any non-United States entity may, subject to and upon compliance with this section, transfer its domicile (which term, as used in this section, shall be deemed to refer in addition to the seat, siege social or principal place of business or central administration of such entity, or any other equivalent thereto under applicable law) into this State, and may perform the acts described in this section, so long as the law by which the internal affairs of such entity are governed does not expressly prohibit such transfer.

(c) Any non-United States entity that shall propose to transfer its domicile into this State shall submit to the Secretary of State for the Secretary of State's review, at least 30 days prior to the proposed transfer of domicile, the following:

(1) A copy of its certificate of incorporation and bylaws (or the equivalent thereof under applicable law), certified as true and correct by the appropriate director, officer or government official;

(2) A certificate issued by an authorized official of the jurisdiction the law of which governs the internal affairs of the non-United States entity evidencing its existence;

(3) A list indicating the person or persons who, in the event of a transfer pursuant to this section, shall be the authorized officers and directors of the non-United States entity, together with evidence of their authority to act and their respective executed agreements in writing regarding service of process as set out in subsection (j) of this section;

(4) A certificate executed by the appropriate officer or director of the non-United States entity, setting forth:

a. The name and address of its registered agent in this State;

b. A general description of the business in which it is engaged;

c. That the filing of such certificate has been duly authorized by any necessary action and does not violate the certificate of incorporation or bylaws (or equivalent thereof under applicable law) or any material agreement or instrument binding on such entity;

d. A list indicating the person or persons authorized to sign the written communications required by subsection (e) of this section;

e. An affirmance that such transfer is not expressly prohibited under the law by which the internal affairs of the non-United States entity are governed; and

f. An undertaking that any transfer of domicile into this State will take place only in the event of an emergency condition in the jurisdiction the law of which governs the internal affairs of the non-United States entity and that such transfer shall continue only so long as such emergency condition, in the judgment of the non-United States entity's management, so requires; and

(5) The examination fee prescribed under § 391 of this title.

If any of the documents referred to in paragraphs (c)(1)–(5) of this section are not in English, a translation thereof, under oath of the translator, shall be attached thereto. If such documents satisfy the requirements of this section, and if the name of the non-United States entity meets the requirements of § 102(a)(1) of this title, the Secretary of State shall notify the non-United States entity that such documents have been accepted for filing, and the records of the Secretary of State shall reflect such acceptance and such notification. In addition, the Secretary of State shall enter the name of the non-United States entity on the Secretary of State's reserved list to remain there so long as the non-United States entity is in compliance with this section. No document submitted under this subsection shall be available for public inspection pursuant to Chapter 100 of Title 29 until, and unless, such entity effects a transfer of its domicile as provided in this section. The Secretary of State may waive the 30-day period and translation requirement provided for in this subsection upon request by such entity, supported by facts (including, without limitation, the existence of an emergency condition) justifying such waiver.

(d)   On or before March 1 in each year, prior to the transfer of its domicile as provided for in subsection (e) of this section, during any such transfer and, in the event that it desires to continue to be subject to a transfer of domicile under this section, after its domicile has ceased to be in this State, the non-United States entity shall file a certificate executed by an appropriate officer or director of the non-United States entity, certifying that the documents submitted pursuant to this section remain in full force and effect or attaching any amendments or supplements thereto and translated as required in subsection (c) of this section, together with the filing fee prescribed under § 391 of this title. In the event that any non-United States entity fails to file the required certificate on or before March 1 in each year, all certificates and filings made pursuant to this section shall become null and void on March 2 in such year, and any proposed transfer thereafter shall be subject to all of the required submissions and the examination fee set forth in subsection (c) of this section.

(e)   If the Secretary of State accepts the documents submitted pursuant to subsection (c) of this section for filing, such entity may transfer its domicile to this State at any time by means of a written communication to such effect addressed to the Secretary of State, signed by 1 of the persons named on the list filed pursuant to paragraph (c)(4)d. of this section, and confirming that the statements made pursuant to paragraph (c)(4) of this section remain true and correct; provided, that if emergency conditions have affected ordinary means of communication, such notification may be made by telegram, telex, telecopy or other form of writing so long as a duly signed duplicate is received by the Secretary of State within 30 days thereafter. The records of the Secretary of State shall reflect the fact of such transfer. Upon the payment to the Secretary of State of the fee prescribed under § 391 of this title, the Secretary of State shall certify that the non-United States entity has filed all documents and paid all fees required by this title. Such certificate of the Secretary of State shall be prima facie evidence of transfer by such non-United States entity of its domicile into this State.

(f)   Except to the extent expressly prohibited by the laws of this State, from and after the time that a non-United States entity transfers its domicile to this State pursuant to this section, the non-United States entity shall have all of the powers which it had immediately prior to such transfer under the law of the jurisdiction governing its internal affairs and the directors and officers designated pursuant to paragraph (c)(3) of this section, and their successors, may manage the business and affairs of the non-United States entity in accordance with the laws of such jurisdiction. Any such activity conducted pursuant to this section shall not be deemed to be doing business within this State for purposes of § 371 of this title. Any reference in this section to the law of the jurisdiction governing the internal affairs of a non-United States entity which has transferred its domicile into this State shall be deemed to be a reference to such law as in effect immediately prior to the transfer of domicile.

(g)   For purposes of any action in the courts of this State, no non-United States entity which has obtained the certificate of the Secretary of State referred to in subsection (e) of this section shall be deemed to be an "enemy" person or entity for any purpose, including, without limitation, in relation to any claim of title to its assets, wherever located, or to its ability to institute suit in said courts.

(h)   The transfer by any non-United States entity of its domicile into this State shall not be deemed to affect any obligations or liabilities of such non-United States entity incurred prior to such transfer.

(i)   The directors of any non-United States entity which has transferred its domicile into this State may withhold from any holder of equity interests in such entity any amounts payable to such holder on account of dividends or other distributions, if the directors shall determine that such holder will not have the full benefit of such payment, so long as the directors shall make provision for the retention of such withheld payment in escrow or under some similar arrangement for the benefit of such holder.

(j) All process issued out of any court of this State, all orders made by any court of this State and all rules and notices of any kind required to be served on any non-United States entity which has transferred its domicile into this State may be served on the non-United States entity pursuant to § 321 of this title in the same manner as if such entity were a corporation of this State. The directors of a non-United States entity which has transferred its domicile into this State shall agree in writing that they will be amenable to service of process by the same means as, and subject to the jurisdiction of the courts of this State to the same extent as are directors of corporations of this State, and such agreements shall be submitted to the Secretary of State for filing before the respective directors take office.

(k) Any non-United States entity which has transferred its domicile into this State may voluntarily return to the jurisdiction the law of which governs its internal affairs by filing with the Secretary of State an application to withdraw from this State. Such application shall be accompanied by a resolution of the directors of the non-United States entity authorizing such withdrawal and by a certificate of the highest diplomatic or consular official of such jurisdiction accredited to the United States indicating the consent of such jurisdiction to such withdrawal. The application shall also contain, or be accompanied by, the agreement of the non-United States entity that it may be served with process in this State in any proceeding for enforcement of any obligation of the non-United States entity arising prior to its withdrawal from this State, which agreement shall include the appointment of the Secretary of State as the agent of the non-United States entity to accept service of process in any such proceeding and shall specify the address to which a copy of process served upon the Secretary of State shall be mailed. Upon the payment of any fees and taxes owed to this State, the Secretary of State shall file the application and the non-United States entity's domicile shall, as of the time of filing, cease to be in this State.

§ 390. Transfer, domestication or continuance of domestic corporations.

(a) Upon compliance with the provisions of this section, any corporation existing under the laws of this State may transfer to or domesticate or continue in any foreign jurisdiction and, in connection therewith, may elect to continue its existence as a corporation of this State. As used in this section, the term:

(1) "Foreign jurisdiction" means any foreign country, or other foreign jurisdiction (other than the United States, any state, the District of Columbia, or any possession or territory of the United States); and

(2) "Resulting entity" means the entity formed, incorporated, created or otherwise coming into being as a consequence of the transfer of the corporation to, or its domestication or continuance in, a foreign jurisdiction pursuant to this section.

(b) The board of directors of the corporation which desires to transfer to or domesticate or continue in a foreign jurisdiction shall adopt a resolution approving such transfer, domestication or continuance specifying the foreign jurisdiction to which the corporation shall be transferred or in which the corporation shall be domesticated or continued and, if applicable, that in connection with such transfer, domestication or continuance the corporation's existence as a corporation of this State is to continue and recommending the approval of such transfer or domestication or continuance by the stockholders of the corporation. Such resolution shall be submitted to the stockholders of the corporation at an annual or special meeting. Due notice of the time, place and purpose of the meeting shall be given to each holder of stock, whether voting or nonvoting, of the corporation at the address of the stockholder as it appears on the records of the corporation, at least 20 days prior to the date of the meeting. At the meeting, the resolution shall be considered and a vote taken for its adoption or rejection. If all outstanding shares of stock of the corporation, whether voting or nonvoting, shall be voted for the adoption of the resolution, the corporation shall file with the Secretary of State a certificate of transfer if its existence as a corporation of this State is to cease or a certificate of transfer and domestic continuance if its existence as a corporation of this State is to continue, executed in accordance with § 103 of this title, which certifies:

(1) The name of the corporation, and if it has been changed, the name under which it was originally incorporated.

(2) The date of filing of its original certificate of incorporation with the Secretary of State.

(3)   The foreign jurisdiction to which the corporation shall be transferred or in which it shall be domesticated or continued and the name of the resulting entity.

(4)   That the transfer, domestication or continuance of the corporation has been approved in accordance with the provisions of this section.

(5)   In the case of a certificate of transfer, (i) that the existence of the corporation as a corporation of this State shall cease when the certificate of transfer becomes effective, and (ii) the agreement of the corporation that it may be served with process in this State in any proceeding for enforcement of any obligation of the corporation arising while it was a corporation of this State which shall also irrevocably appoint the Secretary of State as its agent to accept service of process in any such proceeding and specify the address (which may not be that of the corporation's registered agent without the written consent of the corporation's registered agent, such consent to be filed along with the certificate of transfer) to which a copy of such process shall be mailed by the Secretary of State. Process may be served upon the Secretary of State under this subsection by means of electronic transmission but only as prescribed by the Secretary of State. The Secretary of State is authorized to issue such rules and regulations with respect to such service as the Secretary of State deems necessary or appropriate. In the event of service upon the Secretary of State in accordance with this subsection, the Secretary of State shall forthwith notify such corporation that has transferred out of the State of Delaware by letter, directed to such corporation that has transferred out of the State of Delaware at the address so specified, unless such corporation shall have designated in writing to the Secretary of State a different address for such purpose, in which case it shall be mailed to the last address designated. Such letter shall be sent by a mail or courier service that includes a record of mailing or deposit with the courier and a record of delivery evidenced by the signature of the recipient. Such letter shall enclose a copy of the process and any other papers served on the Secretary of State pursuant to this subsection. It shall be the duty of the plaintiff in the event of such service to serve process and any other papers in duplicate, to notify the Secretary of State that service is being effected pursuant to this subsection and to pay the Secretary of State the sum of $50 for the use of the State, which sum shall be taxed as part of the costs in the proceeding, if the plaintiff shall prevail therein. The Secretary of State shall maintain an alphabetical record of any such service setting forth the name of the plaintiff and the defendant, the title, docket number and nature of the proceeding in which process has been served, the fact that service has been effected pursuant to this subsection, the return date thereof, and the day and hour service was made. The Secretary of State shall not be required to retain such information longer than 5 years from receipt of the service of process.

(6)   In the case of a certificate of transfer and domestic continuance, that the corporation will continue to exist as a corporation of this State after the certificate of transfer and domestic continuance becomes effective.

(c)   Upon the filing of a certificate of transfer in accordance with subsection (b) of this section and payment to the Secretary of State of all fees prescribed under this title, the Secretary of State shall certify that the corporation has filed all documents and paid all fees required by this title, and thereupon the corporation shall cease to exist as a corporation of this State at the time the certificate of transfer becomes effective in accordance with § 103 of this title. Such certificate of the Secretary of State shall be prima facie evidence of the transfer, domestication or continuance by such corporation out of this State.

(d)   The transfer, domestication or continuance of a corporation out of this State in accordance with this section and the resulting cessation of its existence as a corporation of this State pursuant to a certificate of transfer shall not be deemed to affect any obligations or liabilities of the corporation incurred prior to such transfer, domestication or continuance, the personal liability of any person incurred prior to such transfer, domestication or continuance, or the choice of law applicable to the corporation with respect to matters arising prior to such transfer, domestication or continuance. Unless otherwise agreed or otherwise provided in the certificate of incorporation, the transfer, domestication or continuance of a corporation out of the State of Delaware in accordance with this section shall not require such corporation to wind up its affairs or pay its liabilities and distribute its assets under this title and shall not be deemed to constitute a dissolution of such corporation.

(e)   If a corporation files a certificate of transfer and domestic continuance, after the time the certificate of transfer and domestic continuance becomes effective, the corporation shall continue to exist as a corporation of this State, and the law of the State of Delaware, including this title, shall apply to the corporation to the same extent as prior to such time. So long as a corporation continues to exist as a corporation of the State of Delaware following the filing of a certificate of transfer and domestic continuance, the continuing corporation and the resulting entity shall, for all purposes of the laws of the State of Delaware, constitute a single entity formed, incorporated, created or otherwise having come into being, as applicable, and existing under the laws of the State of Delaware and the laws of the foreign jurisdiction.

(f)   When a corporation has transferred, domesticated or continued pursuant to this section, for all purposes of the laws of the State of Delaware, the resulting entity shall be deemed to be the same entity as the transferring, domesticating or continuing corporation and shall constitute a continuation of the existence of such corporation in the form of the resulting entity. When any transfer, domestication or continuance shall have become effective under this section, for all purposes of the laws of the State of Delaware, all of the rights, privileges and powers of the corporation that has transferred, domesticated or continued, and all property, real, personal and mixed, and all debts due to such corporation, as well as all other things and causes of action belonging to such corporation, shall remain vested in the resulting entity (and also in the corporation that has transferred, domesticated or continued, if and for so long as such corporation continues its existence as a corporation of this State) and shall be the property of such resulting entity (and also of the corporation that has transferred, domesticated or continued, if and for so long as such corporation continues its existence as a corporation of this State), and the title to any real property vested by deed or otherwise in such corporation shall not revert or be in any way impaired by reason of this title; but all rights of creditors and all liens upon any property of such corporation shall be preserved unimpaired, and all debts, liabilities and duties of such corporation shall remain attached to the resulting entity (and also to the corporation that has transferred, domesticated or continued, if and for so long as such corporation continues its existence as a corporation of this State), and may be enforced against it to the same extent as if said debts, liabilities and duties had originally been incurred or contracted by it in its capacity as such resulting entity. The rights, privileges, powers and interests in property of the corporation, as well as the debts, liabilities and duties of the corporation, shall not be deemed, as a consequence of the transfer, domestication or continuance, to have been transferred to the resulting entity for any purpose of the laws of the State of Delaware.

(g)   In connection with a transfer, domestication or continuance under this section, shares of stock of the transferring, domesticating or continuing corporation may be exchanged for or converted into cash, property, or shares of stock, rights or securities of, or interests in, the resulting entity or, in addition to or in lieu thereof, may be exchanged for or converted into cash, property, or shares of stock, rights or securities of, or interests in, another corporation or other entity or may be cancelled.

(h)   No vote of the stockholders of a corporation shall be necessary to authorize a transfer, domestication or continuance if no shares of the stock of such corporation shall have been issued prior to the adoption by the board of directors of the resolution approving the transfer, domestication or continuance.

(i)   Whenever it shall be desired to transfer to or domesticate or continue in any foreign jurisdiction any nonstock corporation, the governing body shall perform all the acts necessary to effect a transfer, domestication or continuance which are required by this section to be performed by the board of directors of a corporation having capital stock. If the members of a nonstock corporation are entitled to vote for the election of members of its governing body or are entitled under the certificate of incorporation or the bylaws of such corporation to vote on such transfer, domestication or continuance or on a merger, consolidation, or dissolution of the corporation, they, and any other holder of any membership interest in the corporation, shall perform all the acts necessary to effect a transfer, domestication or continuance which are required by this section to be performed by the stockholders of a corporation having capital stock. If there is no member entitled to vote thereon, nor any other holder of any membership interest in the corporation, the transfer, domestication or continuance of the corporation shall be authorized at a meeting of the governing body, upon the adoption of a resolution to transfer or domesticate or continue by the vote of a majority of members of its governing body then in office. In all other respects, the method and proceedings for the transfer, domestication or continuance of a nonstock corporation shall conform as nearly as may be to the proceedings prescribed by this section for the transfer, domestication or continuance of corporations having capital stock. In the case of a charitable nonstock corporation, due notice of the corporation's intent to effect a transfer, domestication or continuance shall be mailed to the Attorney General of the State of Delaware 10 days prior to the date of the proposed transfer, domestication or continuance.

SUBCHAPTER XVIII.   MISCELLANEOUS PROVISIONS

§ 391.   Amounts payable to Secretary of State upon filing certificate or other paper.

(a)   The following fees and penalties shall be collected by and paid to the Secretary of State, for the use of the State:

(1)   Upon the receipt for filing of an original certificate of incorporation, the fee shall be computed on the basis of $0.02 for each share of authorized capital stock having par value up to and including 20,000 shares, $0.01 for each share in excess of 20,000 shares up to and including 200,000 shares, and $2/5$ of a $0.01 for each share in excess of 200,000 shares; $0.01 for each share of authorized capital stock without par value up to and including 20,000 shares, $1/2$ of $0.01 for each share in excess of 20,000 shares up to and including 2,000,000 shares, and $2/5$ of $0.01 for each share in excess of 2,000,000 shares. In no case shall the amount paid be less than $15. For the purpose of computing the fee on par value stock each $100 unit of the authorized capital stock shall be counted as 1 assessable share.

(2)   Upon the receipt for filing of a certificate of amendment of certificate of incorporation, or a certificate of amendment of certificate of incorporation before payment of capital, or a restated certificate of incorporation, increasing the authorized capital stock of a corporation, the fee shall be an amount equal to the difference between the fee computed at the foregoing rates upon the total authorized capital stock of the corporation including the proposed increase, and the fee computed at the foregoing rates upon the total authorized capital stock excluding the proposed increase. In no case shall the amount paid be less than $30.

(3)   Upon the receipt for filing of a certificate of amendment of certificate of incorporation before payment of capital and not involving an increase of authorized capital stock, or an amendment to the certificate of incorporation not involving an increase of authorized capital stock, or a restated certificate of incorporation not involving an increase of authorized capital stock, or a certificate of retirement of stock, the fee to be paid shall be $30. For all other certificates relating to corporations, not otherwise provided for, the fee to be paid shall be $5.00. In the case of exempt corporations no fee shall be paid under this paragraph.

(4)   Upon the receipt for filing of a certificate of merger or consolidation of 2 or more corporations, the fee shall be an amount equal to the difference between the fee computed at the foregoing rates upon the total authorized capital stock of the corporation created by the merger or consolidation, and the fee so computed upon the aggregate amount of the total authorized capital stock of the constituent corporations. In no case shall the amount paid be less than $75. The foregoing fee shall be in addition to any tax or fee required under any other law of this State to be paid by any constituent entity that is not a corporation in connection with the filing of the certificate of merger or consolidation.

(5)   Upon the receipt for filing of a certificate of dissolution, there shall be paid to and collected by the Secretary of State a fee of:

    a.   Forty dollars; or

    b.   Ten dollars in the case of a certificate of dissolution which certifies that:

        1.   The corporation has no assets and has ceased transacting business; and

        2.   The corporation, for each year since its incorporation in this State, has been required to pay only the minimum franchise tax then prescribed by § 503 of this title; and

        3.   The corporation has paid all franchise taxes and fees due to or assessable by this State through the end of the year in which said certificate of dissolution is filed.

(6)   Upon the receipt for filing of a certificate of reinstatement of a foreign corporation or a certificate of surrender and withdrawal from the State by a foreign corporation, there shall be collected by and paid to the Secretary of State a fee of $10.

(7)   For receiving and filing and/or indexing any certificate, affidavit, agreement or any other paper provided for by this chapter, for which no different fee is specifically prescribed, a fee of $115 in each case shall be paid to the Secretary of State. The fee in the case of a certificate of incorporation

filed as required by § 102 of this title shall be $25. For entering information from each instrument into the Delaware Corporation Information System in accordance with § 103(c)(8) of this title, the fee shall be $5.00.

a. A certificate of dissolution which meets the criteria stated in paragraph (a)(5)b. of this section shall not be subject to such fee; and

b. A certificate of incorporation filed in accordance with § 102 of this title shall be subject to a fee of $25.

(8) For receiving and filing and/or indexing the annual report of a foreign corporation doing business in this State, a fee of $125 shall be paid. In the event of neglect, refusal or failure on the part of any foreign corporation to file the annual report with the Secretary of State on or before June 30 each year, the corporation shall pay a penalty of $125.

(9) For recording and indexing articles of association and other papers required by this chapter to be recorded by the Secretary of State, a fee computed on the basis of $0.01 a line shall be paid.

(10) For certifying copies of any paper on file provided by this chapter, a fee of $50 shall be paid for each copy certified. In addition, a fee of $2.00 per page shall be paid in each instance where the Secretary of State provides the copies of the document to be certified.

(11) For issuing any certificate of the Secretary of State other than a certification of a copy under paragraph (a)(10) of this section, or a certificate that recites all of a corporation's filings with the Secretary of State, a fee of $50 shall be paid for each certificate. For issuing any certificate of the Secretary of State that recites all of a corporation's filings with the Secretary of State, a fee of $175 shall be paid for each certificate. For issuing any certificate via the Division's online services, a fee of up to $175 shall be paid for each certificate.

(12) For filing in the office of the Secretary of State any certificate of change of location or change of registered agent, as provided in § 133 of this title, there shall be collected by and paid to the Secretary of State a fee of $50, provided that no fee shall be charged pursuant to § 103(c)(6) and (c)(7) of this title.

(13) For filing in the office of the Secretary of State any certificate of change of address or change of name of registered agent, as provided in § 134 of this title, there shall be collected by and paid to the Secretary of State a fee of $50, plus the same fees for receiving, filing, indexing, copying and certifying the same as are charged in the case of filing a certificate of incorporation.

(14) For filing in the office of the Secretary of State any certificate of resignation of a registered agent and appointment of a successor, as provided in § 135 of this title, there shall be collected by and paid to the Secretary of State a fee of $50.

(15) For filing in the office of the Secretary of State, any certificate of resignation of a registered agent without appointment of a successor, as provided in §§ 136 and 377 of this title, there shall be collected by and paid to the Secretary of State a fee of $2.00 for each corporation whose registered agent has resigned by such certificate.

(16) For preparing and providing a written report of a record search, a fee of [up to $100] shall be paid.

(17) For preclearance of any document for filing, a fee of $250 shall be paid.

(18) For receiving and filing and/or indexing an annual franchise tax report of a corporation provided for by § 502 of this title, a fee of $25 shall be paid by exempt corporations and a fee of $50 shall be paid by all other corporations.

(19) For receiving and filing and/or indexing by the Secretary of State of a certificate of domestication and certificate of incorporation prescribed in § 388(d) of this title, a fee of $165, plus the fee payable upon the receipt for filing of an original certificate of incorporation, shall be paid.

(20) For receiving, reviewing and filing and/or indexing by the Secretary of State of the documents prescribed in § 389(c) of this title, a fee of $10,000 shall be paid.

(21) For receiving, reviewing and filing and/or indexing by the Secretary of State of the documents prescribed in § 389(d) of this title, an annual fee of $2,500 shall be paid.

(22) Except as provided in this section, the fees of the Secretary of State shall be as provided for in § 2315 of Title 29.

(23) In the case of exempt corporations, the total fees payable to the Secretary of State upon the filing of a Certificate of Change of Registered Agent and/or Registered Office or a Certificate of Revival shall be $5.00 and such filings shall be exempt from any fees or assessments pursuant to the requirements of § 103(c)(6) and (c)(7) of this title.

(24) For accepting a corporate name reservation application, an application for renewal of a corporate name reservation, or a notice of transfer or cancellation of a corporate name reservation, there shall be collected by and paid to the Secretary of State a fee of up to $75.

(25) For receiving and filing and/or indexing by the Secretary of State of a certificate of transfer or a certificate of continuance prescribed in § 390 of this title, a fee of $1,000 shall be paid.

(26) For receiving and filing and/or indexing by the Secretary of State of a certificate of conversion and certificate of incorporation prescribed in § 265 of this title, a fee of $115, plus the fee payable upon the receipt for filing of an original certificate of incorporation, shall be paid.

(27) For receiving and filing and/or indexing by the Secretary of State of a certificate of conversion prescribed in § 266 of this title, a fee of $165 shall be paid.

(28) For receiving and filing and/or indexing by the Secretary of State of a certificate of validation prescribed in § 204 of this title, a fee of $2,500 shall be paid; provided, that if the certificate of validation has the effect of increasing the authorized capital stock of a corporation, an additional fee, calculated in accordance with paragraph (a)(2) of this section, shall also be paid.

(b)(1) For the purpose of computing the fee prescribed in paragraphs (a)(1), (2), (4) and (28) of this section the authorized capital stock of a corporation shall be considered to be the total number of shares which the corporation is authorized to issue, whether or not the total number of shares that may be outstanding at any 1 time be limited to a less number.

(2) For the purpose of computing the fee prescribed in paragraphs (a)(2), (3) and (28) of this section, a certificate of amendment of certificate of incorporation, or an amended certificate of incorporation before payment of capital, or a restated certificate of incorporation, or a certificate of validation, shall be considered as increasing the authorized capital stock of a corporation provided it involves an increase in the number of shares, or an increase in the par value of shares, or a change of shares with par value into shares without par value, or a change of shares without par value into shares with par value, or any combination of 2 or more of the above changes, and provided further that the fee computed at the rates set forth in paragraph (a)(1) of this section upon the total authorized capital stock of the corporation including the proposed change or changes exceeds the fee so computed upon the total authorized stock of the corporation excluding such change or changes.

(c) The Secretary of State may issue photocopies or electronic image copies of instruments on file, as well as instruments, documents and other papers not on file, and for all such photocopies or electronic image copies which are not certified by the Secretary of State, a fee of $10 shall be paid for the first page and $2.00 for each additional page. Notwithstanding Delaware's Freedom of Information Act (Chapter 100 of Title 29) or any other provision of law granting access to public records, the Secretary of State upon request shall issue only photocopies or electronic image copies of public records in exchange for the fees described in this section, and in no case shall the Secretary of State be required to provide copies (or access to copies) of such public records (including without limitation bulk data, digital copies of instruments, documents and other papers, databases or other information) in an electronic medium or in any form other than photocopies or electronic image copies of such public records in exchange, as applicable, for the fees described in this section or § 2318 of Title 29 for each such record associated with a file number.

(d) No fees for the use of the State shall be charged or collected from any corporation incorporated for the drainage and reclamation of lowlands or for the amendment or renewal of the charter of such corporation.

(e)   The Secretary of State may in the Secretary of State's discretion permit the extension of credit for the fees required by this section upon such terms as the Secretary of State shall deem to be appropriate.

(f)   The Secretary of State shall retain from the revenue collected from the fees required by this section a sum sufficient to provide at all times a fund of at least $500, but not more than $1,500, from which the Secretary of State may refund any payment made pursuant to this section to the extent that it exceeds the fees required by this section. The fund shall be deposited in the financial institution which is the legal depository of state moneys to the credit of the Secretary of State and shall be disbursable on order of the Secretary of State.

(g)   The Secretary of State may in the Secretary of State's discretion charge a fee of $60 for each check received for payment of any fee or tax under Chapter 1 or Chapter 6 of this title that is returned due to insufficient funds or as the result of a stop payment order.

(h)   In addition to those fees charged under subsections (a) and (c) of this section, there shall be collected by and paid to the Secretary of State the following:

(1)   For all services described in subsection (a) of this section that are requested to be completed within 30 minutes on the same day as the day of the request, an additional sum of up to $7,500 and for all services described in subsections (a) and (c) of this section that are requested to be completed within 1 hour on the same day as the day of the request, an additional sum of up to $1,000 and for all services described in subsections (a) and (c) of this section that are requested to be completed within 2 hours on the same day as the day of the request, an additional sum of up to $500; and

(2)   For all services described in subsections (a) and (c) of this section that are requested to be completed within the same day as the day of the request, an additional sum of up to $300; and

(3)   For all services described in subsections (a) and (c) of this section that are requested to be completed within a 24-hour period from the time of the request, an additional sum of up to $150.

The Secretary of State shall establish (and may from time to time alter or amend) a schedule of specific fees payable pursuant to this subsection.

(i)   A domestic corporation or a foreign corporation registered to do business in this State that files with the Secretary of State any instrument or certificate, and in connection therewith, neglects, refuses or fails to pay any fee or tax under Chapter 1 or Chapter 6 of this title shall, after written demand therefor by the Secretary of State by mail addressed to such domestic corporation or foreign corporation in care of its registered agent in this State, cease to be in good standing as a domestic corporation or registered as a foreign corporation in this State on the ninetieth day following the date of mailing of such demand, unless such fee or tax and, if applicable, the fee provided for in subsection (g) of this section are paid in full prior to the ninetieth day following the date of mailing of such demand. A domestic corporation that has ceased to be in good standing or a foreign corporation that has ceased to be registered by reason of the neglect, refusal or failure to pay any such fee or tax shall be restored to and have the status of a domestic corporation in good standing or a foreign corporation that is registered in this State upon the payment of the fee or tax which such domestic corporation or foreign corporation neglected, refused or failed to pay together with the fee provided for in subsection (g) of this section, if applicable. The Secretary of State shall not accept for filing any instrument authorized to be filed with the Secretary of State under this title in respect of any domestic corporation that is not in good standing or any foreign corporation that has ceased to be registered by reason of the neglect, refusal or failure to pay any such fee or tax, and shall not issue any certificate of good standing with respect to such domestic corporation or foreign corporation, unless and until such domestic corporation or foreign corporation shall have been restored to and have the status of a domestic corporation in good standing or a foreign corporation duly registered in this State.

(j)   As used in this section, the term "exempt corporation" shall have the meaning given to it in § 501(b) of this title.

§ 392.   [Reserved.]

§ 393.　Rights, liabilities and duties under prior statutes.

All rights, privileges and immunities vested or accrued by and under any laws enacted prior to the adoption or amendment of this chapter, all suits pending, all rights of action conferred, and all duties, restrictions, liabilities and penalties imposed or required by and under laws enacted prior to the adoption or amendment of this chapter, shall not be impaired, diminished or affected by this chapter.

§ 394.　Reserved power of State to amend or repeal chapter; chapter part of corporation's charter or certificate of incorporation.

This chapter may be amended or repealed, at the pleasure of the General Assembly, but any amendment or repeal shall not take away or impair any remedy under this chapter against any corporation or its officers for any liability which shall have been previously incurred. This chapter and all amendments thereof shall be a part of the charter or certificate of incorporation of every corporation except so far as the same are inapplicable and inappropriate to the objects of the corporation.

§ 395.　Corporations using "trust" in name, advertisements and otherwise; restrictions; violations and penalties; exceptions.

(a)　Except as provided below in subsection (d) of this section, every corporation of this State using the word "trust" as part of its name, except a corporation regulated under the Bank Holding Company Act of 1956, 12 U.S.C. § 1841 et seq., or § 10 of the Home Owners' Loan Act, 12 U.S.C. § 1467a et seq., as those statutes shall from time to time be amended, shall be under the supervision of the State Bank Commissioner of this State and shall make not less than 2 reports during each year to the Commissioner, according to the form which shall be prescribed by the Commissioner, verified by the oaths or affirmations of the president or vice-president, and the treasurer or secretary of the corporation, and attested by the signatures of at least 3 directors.

(b)　Except as provided below in subsection (d) of this section, no corporation of this State shall use the word "trust" as part of its name, except a corporation reporting to and under the supervision of the State Bank Commissioner of this State or a corporation regulated under the Bank Holding Company Act of 1956, 12 U.S.C. § 1841 et seq., or § 10 of the Home Owners' Loan Act, 12 U.S.C. § 1467a et seq., as those statutes shall from time to time be amended. Except as provided below in subsection (d) of this section, the name of any such corporation shall not be amended so as to include the word "trust" unless such corporation shall report to and be under the supervision of the Commissioner, or unless it is regulated under the Bank Holding Company Act of 1956 or the Savings and Loan Holding Company Act.

(c)　No corporation of this State, except corporations reporting to and under the supervision of the State Bank Commissioner of this State or corporations regulated under the Bank Holding Company Act of 1956, 12 U.S.C. § 1841 et seq., or § 10 of the Home Owners' Loan Act, 12 U.S.C. § 1467a et seq., as those statutes shall from time to time be amended, shall advertise or put forth any sign as a trust company, or in any way solicit or receive deposits or transact business as a trust company.

(d)　The requirements and restrictions set forth above in subsections (a) and (b) of this section shall not apply to, and shall not be construed to prevent the use of the word "trust" as part of the name of, a corporation that is not subject to the supervision of the State Bank Commissioner of this State and that is not regulated under the Bank Holding Company Act of 1956, 12 U.S.C. § 1841 et seq., or § 10 of the Home Owners' Loan Act, 12 U.S.C. § 1467a et seq., where use of the word "trust" as part of such corporation's name clearly:

(1)　Does not refer to a trust business;

(2)　Is not likely to mislead the public into believing that the nature of the business of the corporation includes activities that fall under the supervision of the State Bank Commissioner of this State or that are regulated under the Bank Holding Company Act of 1956, 12 U.S.C. § 1841 et seq., or § 10 of the Home Owners' Loan Act, 12 U.S.C. § 1467a et seq.; and

(3)　Will not otherwise lead to a pattern and practice of abuse that might cause harm to the interests of the public or the State, as determined by the Director of the Division of Corporations and the State Bank Commissioner.

§ 396. Publication of chapter by Secretary of State; distribution.

The Secretary of State may have printed, from time to time as the Secretary of State deems necessary, pamphlet copies of this chapter, and the Secretary of State shall dispose of the copies to persons and corporations desiring the same for a sum not exceeding the cost of printing. The money received from the sale of the copies shall be disposed of as are other fees of the office of the Secretary of State. Nothing in this section shall prevent the free distribution of single pamphlet copies of this chapter by the Secretary of State, for the printing of which provision is made from time to time by joint resolution of the General Assembly.

§ 397. Penalty for unauthorized publication of chapter.

Whoever prints or publishes this chapter without the authority of the Secretary of State of this State, shall be fined not more than $500 or imprisoned not more than 3 months, or both.

§ 398. Short title.

This chapter shall be known and may be identified and referred to as the "General Corporation Law of the State of Delaware."

MODEL BUSINESS CORPORATION ACT

Table of Sections

CHAPTER 1.   GENERAL PROVISIONS

Subchapter A. Short Title and Reservation of Power

Subchapter B.   Filing Documents

Subchapter C.   Secretary of State

Subchapter D.   Definitions

Subchapter E.   Ratification of Defective Corporate Actions

CHAPTER 2.   INCORPORATION

MODEL BUSINESS CORPORATION ACT

MODEL BUSINESS CORPORATION ACT

CHAPTER 7. SHAREHOLDERS

Subchapter A. Meetings

Subchapter B. Voting

Subchapter C. Voting Trusts and Agreements

Subchapter D. Derivative Proceedings

Subchapter E. Judicial Proceedings

CHAPTER 8. DIRECTORS AND OFFICERS

Subchapter A. Board of Directors

MODEL BUSINESS CORPORATION ACT

Subchapter G.   Business Opportunities

CHAPTER 9.   DOMESTICATION AND CONVERSION

Subchapter A.   Preliminary Provisions

Subchapter B.   Domestication

Subchapter C.   Conversion

CHAPTER 10.   AMENDMENT OF ARTICLES OF INCORPORATION AND BYLAWS

Subchapter A.   Amendment of Articles of Incorporation

Subchapter B.   Amendment of Bylaws

CHAPTER 11.   MERGER AND SHARE EXCHANGES

MODEL BUSINESS CORPORATION ACT

———

CHAPTER 1

GENERAL PROVISIONS

Subchapter A.   Short Title and Reservation of Power

§ 1.01   Short Title

This Act shall be known and may be cited as the "[name of state] Business Corporation Act."

§ 1.02   Reservation of Power to Amend or Repeal

The [name of state legislature] has power to amend or repeal all or part of this Act at any time and all domestic and foreign corporations subject to this Act are governed by the amendment or repeal.

Subchapter B.   Filing Documents

§ 1.20   Requirements for Documents; Extrinsic Facts

(a)   A document must satisfy the requirements of this section, and of any other section that adds to or varies these requirements, to be entitled to filing by the secretary of state.

(b)   This Act must require or permit filing the document in the office of the secretary of state.

(c)   The document must contain the information required by this Act and may contain other information.

(d)   The document must be typewritten or printed or, if electronically transmitted, it must be in a format that can be retrieved or reproduced in typewritten or printed form.

(e)   The document must be in the English language. A corporate name need not be in English if written in English letters or Arabic or Roman numerals.

(f)   The document must be signed:

(1)   by the chairman of the board of directors of a domestic or foreign corporation, by its president, or by another of its officers;

(2)   if directors have not been selected or the corporation has not been formed, by an incorporator; or

(3)   if the corporation is in the hands of a receiver, trustee, or other court-appointed fiduciary, by that fiduciary.

(g)   The person executing the document shall sign it and state beneath or opposite the person's signature the person's name and the capacity in which the document is signed. The document may but need not contain a corporate seal, attestation, acknowledgment, or verification.

(h)   If the secretary of state has prescribed a mandatory form for the document under section 1.21(a), the document must be in or on the prescribed form.

(i)   The document must be delivered to the office of the secretary of state for filing. Delivery may be made by electronic transmission if and to the extent permitted by the secretary of state. If it is filed in typewritten or printed form and not transmitted electronically, the secretary of state may require one exact or conformed copy to be delivered with the document.

(j)   When the document is delivered to the office of the secretary of state for filing, the correct filing fee, and any franchise tax, license fee, or penalty required by this Act or other law to be paid at the time of delivery for filing must be paid or provision for payment made in a manner permitted by the secretary of state.

(k)   Whenever a provision of this Act permits any of the terms of a plan or a filed document to be dependent on facts objectively ascertainable outside the plan or filed document, the following provisions apply:

(1)   The manner in which the facts will operate upon the terms of the plan or filed document must be set forth in the plan or filed document.

(2)   The facts may include:

(i)   any of the following that is available in a nationally recognized news or information medium either in print or electronically: statistical or market indices, market prices of any security or group of securities, interest rates, currency exchange rates, or similar economic or financial data;

(ii)   a determination or action by any person or body, including the corporation or any other party to a plan or filed document; or

(iii)   the terms of, or actions taken under, an agreement to which the corporation is a party, or any other agreement or document.

(3)   As used in this subsection (k):

(i)   "filed document" means a document filed by the secretary of state under any provision of this Act except chapter 15 or section 16.21; and

(ii)   "plan" means a plan of domestication, conversion, merger, or share exchange.

(4)   The following provisions of a plan or filed document may not be made dependent on facts outside the plan or filed document:

(i)   the name and address of any person required in a filed document;

(ii)   the registered office of any entity required in a filed document;

(iii)   the registered agent of any entity required in a filed document;

(iv)   the number of authorized shares and designation of each class or series of shares;

(v)   the effective date of a filed document; and

(vi)   any required statement in a filed document of the date on which the underlying transaction was approved or the manner in which that approval was given.

(5)   If a provision of a filed document is made dependent on a fact ascertainable outside of the filed document, and that fact is neither ascertainable by reference to a source described in subsection (k)(2)(i) or a document that is a matter of public record, nor have the affected shareholders received notice of the fact from the corporation, then the corporation shall file with the secretary of state articles of amendment to the filed document setting forth the fact promptly after the time when the fact referred to is first ascertainable or thereafter changes. Articles of amendment under this subsection (k)(5) are deemed to be authorized by the authorization of the original filed document to which they relate and may be filed by the corporation without further action by the board of directors or the shareholders.

§ 1.21   Forms

(a)   The secretary of state may prescribe and furnish on request forms for: (i) an application for a certificate of existence, (ii) a foreign corporation's registration statement, (iii) a foreign corporation's statement of withdrawal, (iv) a foreign corporation's transfer of registration statement, and (v) the annual report. If the secretary of state so requires, use of these forms is mandatory.

(b)   The secretary of state may prescribe and furnish on request forms for other documents required or permitted to be filed by this Act but their use is not mandatory.

§ 1.22   Filing, Service, and Copying Fees

(a)   The secretary of state shall collect the following fees when the documents described in this subsection are delivered to the secretary of state for filing:

Document	Fee
Articles of incorporation	$_____.
Application for use of indistinguishable name	$_____.
Application for reserved name	$_____.
Notice of transfer of reserved name	$_____.
Application for registered name	$_____.
Application for renewal of registered name	$_____.
Corporation's statement of change of registered agent or registered office or both	$_____.
Agent's statement of change of registered office for each affected corporation not to exceed a total of $_____	$_____.
Agent's statement of resignation	No fee.
Articles of domestication	$_____.
Articles of conversion	$_____.
Amendment of articles of incorporation	$_____.
Restatement of articles of incorporation with amendment of articles	$_____.
Restatement of articles of incorporation without amendment of articles	$_____.
Articles of merger or share exchange	$_____.
Articles of dissolution	$_____.
Articles of revocation of dissolution	$_____.
Certificate of administrative dissolution	No fee.
Application for reinstatement following administrative dissolution	$_____.
Certificate of reinstatement	No fee.
Certificate of judicial dissolution	No fee.
Foreign registration statement	$_____.
Amendment of foreign registration statement	$_____.
Statement of withdrawal	$_____.
Transfer of foreign registration statement	$_____.
Notice of termination of registration	No fee.
Annual report	$_____.
Articles of correction	$_____.
Articles of validation	$_____.
Application for certificate of existence or foreign registration	$_____.
Any other document required or permitted to be filed by this Act	$_____.

(b)   The secretary of state shall collect a fee of $ _____ each time process is served on the secretary of state under this Act. The party to a proceeding causing service of process is entitled to recover this fee as costs if such party prevails in the proceeding.

(c)   The secretary of state shall collect the following fees for copying and certifying the copy of any filed document relating to a domestic or foreign corporation:

$ _____ a page for copying; and

$ _____ for the certificate.

§ 1.23   Effective Date of Filed Document

(a)   Except to the extent otherwise provided in section 1.24(c) and subchapter E of this chapter, a document accepted for filing is effective:

(1)   on the date and at the time of filing, as provided in section 1.25(b);

(2)   on the date of filing and at the time specified in the document as its effective time if later than the time under subsection (a)(1);

(3)   at a specified delayed effective date and time which may not be more than 90 days after filing; or

(4)   if a delayed effective date is specified, but no time is specified, at 12:01 a.m. on the date specified, which may not be more than 90 days after the date of filing.

(b)   If a filed document does not specify the time zone or place at which a date or time or both is to be determined, the date or time or both at which it becomes effective shall be those prevailing at the place of filing in this state.

§ 1.24   Correcting Filed Document

(a)   A document filed by the secretary of state pursuant to this Act may be corrected if (i) the document contains an inaccuracy, (ii) the document was defectively signed, attested, sealed, verified, or acknowledged, or (iii) the electronic transmission was defective.

(b)   A document is corrected:

(1)   by preparing articles of correction that

(i)   describe the document (including its filing date) or attach a copy of it to the articles of correction,

(ii)   specify the inaccuracy or defect to be corrected, and

(iii)   correct the inaccuracy or defect; and

(2)   by delivering the articles of correction to the secretary of state for filing.

(c)   Articles of correction are effective on the effective date of the document they correct except as to persons relying on the uncorrected document and adversely affected by the correction. As to those persons, articles of correction are effective when filed.

§ 1.25   Filing Duty of Secretary of State

(a)   If a document delivered to the office of the secretary of state for filing satisfies the requirements of section 1.20, the secretary of state shall file it.

(b)   The secretary of state files a document by recording it as filed on the date and time of receipt. After filing a document, the secretary of state shall return to the person who delivered the document for filing a copy of the document with an acknowledgement of the date and time of filing.

(c)   If the secretary of state refuses to file a document, it shall be returned to the person who delivered the document for filing within five days after the document was delivered, together with a brief, written explanation of the reason for the refusal.

(d)   The secretary of state's duty to file documents under this section is ministerial. The secretary of state's filing or refusing to file a document does not create a presumption that: (i) the document does or does not conform to the requirements of the Act; or (ii) the information contained in the document is correct or incorrect.

§ 1.26   Appeal from Secretary of State's Refusal to File Document

(a)   If the secretary of state refuses to file a document delivered for filing, the person that delivered the document for filing may petition [name or describe court] to compel its filing. The document and the explanation of the secretary of state of the refusal to file must be attached to the petition. The court may decide the matter in a summary proceeding.

(b)   The court may order the secretary of state to file the document or take other action the court considers appropriate.

(c)   The court's final decision may be appealed as in other civil proceedings.

§ 1.27   Evidentiary Effect of Certified Copy of Filed Document

A certificate from the secretary of state delivered with a copy of a document filed by the secretary of state is conclusive evidence that the original document is on file with the secretary of state.

§ 1.28   Certificate of Existence or Registration

(a)   Any person may apply to the secretary of state to furnish a certificate of existence for a domestic corporation or a certificate of registration for a foreign corporation.

(b)   A certificate of existence sets forth:

(1)   the domestic corporation's corporate name;

(2)   that the domestic corporation is duly incorporated under the law of this state, the date of its incorporation, and the period of its duration if less than perpetual;

(3)   that all fees, taxes, and penalties owed to this state have been paid, if

(i)   payment is reflected in the records of the secretary of state and

(ii)   nonpayment affects the existence of the domestic corporation;

(4)   that its most recent annual report required by section 16.21 has been filed with the secretary of state;

(5)   that articles of dissolution have not been filed;

(6)   that the corporation is not administratively dissolved and a proceeding is not pending under section 14.21; and

(7)   other facts of record in the office of the secretary of state that may be requested by the applicant.

(c)   A certificate of registration sets forth:

(1)   the foreign corporation's name used in this state;

(2)   that the foreign corporation is registered to do business in this state;

(3)   that all fees, taxes, and penalties owed to this state have been paid, if

(i)   payment is reflected in the records of the secretary of state and

(ii)   nonpayment affects the registration of the foreign corporation;

(4)   that its most recent annual report required by section 16.21 has been filed with the secretary of state; and

(5)   other facts of record in the office of the secretary of state that may be requested by the applicant.

(d)   Subject to any qualification stated in the certificate, a certificate of existence or registration issued by the secretary of state may be relied upon as conclusive evidence of the facts stated in the certificate.

§ 1.29   Penalty for Signing False Document

(a)   A person commits an offense by signing a document that the person knows is false in any material respect with intent that the document be delivered to the secretary of state for filing.

(b)   An offense under this section is a [_____] misdemeanor [punishable by a fine of not to exceed $ _____].

Subchapter C.   Secretary of State

§ 1.30   Powers

The secretary of state has the power reasonably necessary to perform the duties required of the secretary of state by this Act.

Subchapter D.   Definitions

§ 1.40   Act Definitions

In this Act, unless otherwise specified:

"Articles of incorporation" means the articles of incorporation described in section 2.02, all amendments to the articles of incorporation, and any other documents permitted or required to be delivered for filing by a domestic business corporation with the secretary of state under any provision of this Act that modify, amend, supplement, restate or replace the articles of incorporation. After an amendment of the articles of incorporation or any other document filed under this Act that restates the articles of incorporation in their entirety, the articles of incorporation shall not include any prior documents. When used with respect to a foreign corporation or a domestic or foreign nonprofit corporation, the "articles of incorporation" of such an entity means the document of such entity that is equivalent to the articles of incorporation of a domestic business corporation.

"Authorized shares" means the shares of all classes a domestic or foreign corporation is authorized to issue.

"Beneficial shareholder" means a person who owns the beneficial interest in shares, which may be a record shareholder or a person on whose behalf shares are registered in the name of an intermediary or nominee.

"Conspicuous" means so written, displayed, or presented that a reasonable person against whom the writing is to operate should have noticed it.

"Corporation," "domestic corporation," "business corporation" or "domestic business corporation" means a corporation for profit, which is not a foreign corporation, incorporated under this Act.

"Deliver" or "delivery" means any method of delivery used in conventional commercial practice, including delivery by hand, mail, commercial delivery, and, if authorized in accordance with section 1.41, by electronic transmission.

"Distribution" means a direct or indirect transfer of cash or other property (except a corporation's own shares) or incurrence of indebtedness by a corporation to or for the benefit of its shareholders in respect of any of its shares. A distribution may be in the form of a payment of a dividend; a purchase, redemption, or other acquisition of shares; a distribution of indebtedness; a distribution in liquidation; or otherwise.

"Document" means (i) any tangible medium on which information is inscribed, and includes handwritten, typed, printed or similar instruments, and copies of such instruments, or (ii) an electronic record.

"Domestic," with respect to an entity, means an entity governed as to its internal affairs by the law of this state.

"Effective date," when referring to a document accepted for filing by the secretary of state, means the time and date determined in accordance with section 1.23.

"Electronic" means relating to technology having electrical, digital, magnetic, wireless, optical, electromagnetic, or similar capabilities.

"Electronic record" means information that is stored in an electronic or other nontangible medium and is retrievable in paper form through an automated process used in conventional commercial practice, unless otherwise authorized in accordance with section 1.41(j).

"Electronic transmission" or "electronically transmitted" means any form or process of communication not directly involving the physical transfer of paper or another tangible medium, which (i) is suitable for the retention, retrieval, and reproduction of information by the recipient, and (ii) is retrievable in paper form by the recipient through an automated process used in conventional commercial practice, unless otherwise authorized in accordance with section 1.41(j).

"Eligible entity" means a domestic or foreign unincorporated entity or a domestic or foreign nonprofit corporation.

"Eligible interests" means interests or memberships.

"Employee" includes an officer but not a director. A director may accept duties that make the director also an employee.

"Entity" includes domestic and foreign business corporation; domestic and foreign nonprofit corporation; estate; trust; domestic and foreign unincorporated entity; and state, United States, and foreign government.

"Expenses" means reasonable expenses of any kind that are incurred in connection with a matter.

"Filing entity" means an unincorporated entity, other than a limited liability partnership, that is of a type that is created by filing a public organic record or is required to file a public organic record that evidences its creation.

"Foreign," with respect to an entity, means an entity governed as to its internal affairs by the organic law of a jurisdiction other than this state.

"Foreign corporation" or "foreign business corporation" means a corporation incorporated under a law other than the law of this state which would be a business corporation if incorporated under the law of this state.

"Foreign nonprofit corporation" means a corporation incorporated under a law other than the law of this state which would be a nonprofit corporation if incorporated under the law of this state.

"Foreign registration statement" means the foreign registration statement described in section 15.03.

"Governmental subdivision" includes authority, county, district, and municipality.

"Governor" means any person under whose authority the powers of an entity are exercised and under whose direction the activities and affairs of the entity are managed pursuant to the organic law governing the entity and its organic rules.

"Includes" and "including" denote a partial definition or a nonexclusive list.

"Individual" means a natural person.

"Interest" means either or both of the following rights under the organic law governing an unincorporated entity:

(i)   the right to receive distributions from the entity either in the ordinary course or upon liquidation; or

(ii)   the right to receive notice or vote on issues involving its internal affairs, other than as an agent, assignee, proxy or person responsible for managing its business and affairs.

"Interest holder" means a person who holds of record an interest.

"Interest holder liability" means:

(i)   personal liability for a debt, obligation, or other liability of a domestic or foreign corporation or eligible entity that is imposed on a person:

(A)   solely by reason of the person's status as a shareholder, member or interest holder; or

(B)   by the articles of incorporation of the domestic corporation or the organic rules of the eligible entity or foreign corporation that make one or more specified shareholders, members, or interest holders, or categories of shareholders, members, or interest holders, liable in their capacity as shareholders, members, or interest holders for all or specified liabilities of the corporation or eligible entity; or

(ii)   an obligation of a shareholder, member, or interest holder under the articles of incorporation of a domestic corporation or the organic rules of an eligible entity or foreign corporation to contribute to the entity.

For purposes of the foregoing, except as otherwise provided in the articles of incorporation of a domestic corporation or the organic law or organic rules of an eligible entity or a foreign corporation, interest holder liability arises under clause (i) when the corporation or eligible entity incurs the liability.

"Jurisdiction of formation" means the state or country the law of which includes the organic law governing a domestic or foreign corporation or eligible entity.

"Means" denotes an exhaustive definition.

"Membership" means the rights of a member in a domestic or foreign nonprofit corporation.

"Merger" means a transaction pursuant to section 11.02.

"Nonfiling entity" means an unincorporated entity that is of a type that is not created by filing a public organic record.

"Nonprofit corporation" or "domestic nonprofit corporation" means a corporation incorporated under the laws of this state and subject to the provisions of the [Model Nonprofit Corporation Act].

"Organic law" means the statute governing the internal affairs of a domestic or foreign business or nonprofit corporation or unincorporated entity.

"Organic rules" means the public organic record and private organic rules of a domestic or foreign corporation or eligible entity.

"Person" includes an individual and an entity.

"Principal office" means the office (in or out of this state) so designated in the annual report or foreign registration statement where the principal executive offices of a domestic or foreign corporation are located.

"Private organic rules" means (i) the bylaws of a domestic or foreign business or nonprofit corporation or (ii) the rules, regardless of whether in writing, that govern the internal affairs of an unincorporated entity, are binding on all its interest holders, and are not part of its public organic record, if any. Where private organic rules have been amended or restated, the term means the private organic rules as last amended or restated.

"Proceeding" includes civil suit and criminal, administrative, and investigatory action.

"Public organic record" means (i) the articles of incorporation of a domestic or foreign business or nonprofit corporation or (ii) the document, if any, the filing of which is required to create an unincorporated entity, or which creates the unincorporated entity and is required to be filed. Where a public organic record has been amended or restated, the term means the public organic record as last amended or restated.

"Record date" means the date fixed for determining the identity of the corporation's shareholders and their shareholdings for purposes of this Act. Unless another time is specified when the record date is fixed, the determination shall be made as of the close of business at the principal office of the corporation on the date so fixed.

*"Record shareholder" means (i) the person in whose name shares are registered in the records of the corporation or (ii) the person identified as the beneficial owner of shares in a beneficial ownership certificate pursuant to section 7.23 on file with the corporation to the extent of the rights granted by such certificate.

"Registered foreign corporation" means a foreign corporation registered to do business in the state pursuant to chapter 15.

"Secretary" means the corporate officer to whom the board of directors has delegated responsibility under section 8.40(c) to maintain the minutes of the meetings of the board of directors and of the shareholders and for authenticating records of the corporation.

"Share exchange" means a transaction pursuant to section 11.03.

*"Shareholder" means a record shareholder.

"Shares" means the units into which the proprietary interests in a domestic or foreign corporation are divided.

"Sign" or "signature" means, with present intent to authenticate or adopt a document:

(i)   to execute or adopt a tangible symbol to a document, and includes any manual, facsimile, or conformed signature; or

(ii)   to attach to or logically associate with an electronic transmission an electronic sound, symbol, or process, and includes an electronic signature in an electronic transmission.

"State," when referring to a part of the United States, includes a state and commonwealth (and their agencies and governmental subdivisions) and a territory and insular possession (and their agencies and governmental subdivisions) of the United States.

"Subscriber" means a person who subscribes for shares in a corporation, whether before or after incorporation.

"Type of entity" means a generic form of entity:

(i)   recognized at common law; or

(ii)   formed under an organic law, regardless of whether some entities formed under that law are subject to provisions of that law that create different categories of the form of entity.

"Unincorporated entity" means an organization or artificial legal person that either has a separate legal existence or has the power to acquire an estate in real property in its own name and that is not any of the following: a domestic or foreign business or nonprofit corporation, a series of a limited liability company or of another type of entity, an estate, a trust, a state, United States, or foreign government. The term includes a general partnership, limited liability company, limited partnership, business trust, joint stock association and unincorporated nonprofit association.

"United States" includes district, authority, bureau, commission, department, and any other agency of the United States.

"Unrestricted voting trust beneficial owner" means, with respect to any shareholder rights, a voting trust beneficial owner whose entitlement to exercise the shareholder right in question is not inconsistent with the voting trust agreement.

"Voting group" means all shares of one or more classes or series that under the articles of incorporation or this Act are entitled to vote and be counted together collectively on a matter at a meeting of shareholders. All shares entitled by the articles of incorporation or this Act to vote generally on the matter are for that purpose a single voting group.

"Voting power" means the current power to vote in the election of directors.

"Voting trust beneficial owner" means an owner of a beneficial interest in shares of the corporation held in a voting trust established pursuant to section 7.30(a).

"Writing" or "written" means any information in the form of a document.

§ 1.41   Notices and Other Communications

(a)   A notice under this Act must be in writing unless oral notice is reasonable in the circumstances. Unless otherwise agreed between the sender and the recipient, words in a notice or other communication under this Act must be in English.

(b)   A notice or other communication may be given by any method of delivery, except that electronic transmissions must be in accordance with this section. If the methods of delivery are impracticable, a notice or other communication may be given by means of a broad non-exclusionary distribution to the public (which may include a newspaper of general circulation in the area where published; radio, television, or other form of public broadcast communication; or other methods of distribution that the corporation has previously identified to its shareholders).

(c)   A notice or other communication to a domestic corporation or to a foreign corporation registered to do business in this state may be delivered to the corporation's registered agent at its registered office or to the secretary at the corporation's principal office shown in its most recent annual report or, in the case of a foreign corporation that has not yet delivered an annual report, in its foreign registration statement.

(d)   A notice or other communications may be delivered by electronic transmission if consented to by the recipient or if authorized by subsection (j).

(e)   Any consent under subsection (d) may be revoked by the person who consented by written or electronic notice to the person to whom the consent was delivered. Any such consent is deemed revoked if (i) the corporation is unable to deliver two consecutive electronic transmissions given by the corporation in accordance with such consent, and (ii) such inability becomes known to the secretary or an assistant secretary or to the transfer agent, or other person responsible for the giving of notice or other communications; provided, however, the inadvertent failure to treat such inability as a revocation shall not invalidate any meeting or other action.

(f)   Unless otherwise agreed between the sender and the recipient, an electronic transmission is received when:

(1)   it enters an information processing system that the recipient has designated or uses for the purposes of receiving electronic transmissions or information of the type sent, and from which the recipient is able to retrieve the electronic transmission; and

(2)   it is in a form capable of being processed by that system.

(g)   Receipt of an electronic acknowledgement from an information processing system described in subsection (f)(1) establishes that an electronic transmission was received but, by itself, does not establish that the content sent corresponds to the content received.

(h)   An electronic transmission is received under this section even if no person is aware of its receipt.

(i)   A notice or other communication, if in a comprehensible form or manner, is effective at the earliest of the following:

(1)   if in a physical form, the earliest of when it is actually received, or when it is left at:

(i)   a shareholder's address shown on the corporation's record of shareholders maintained by the corporation under section 16.01(d);

(ii)   a director's residence or usual place of business; or

(iii)   the corporation's principal office;

(2)   if mailed postage prepaid and correctly addressed to a shareholder, upon deposit in the United States mail;

(3)   if mailed by United States mail postage prepaid and correctly addressed to a recipient other than a shareholder, the earliest of when it is actually received, or:

(i)   if sent by registered or certified mail, return receipt requested, the date shown on the return receipt signed by or on behalf of the addressee; or

(ii)   five days after it is deposited in the United States mail;

(4)   if an electronic transmission, when it is received as provided in subsection (f); and

(5)   if oral, when communicated.

(j)   A notice or other communication may be in the form of an electronic transmission that cannot be directly reproduced in paper form by the recipient through an automated process used in conventional commercial practice only if (i) the electronic transmission is otherwise retrievable in perceivable form, and (ii) the sender and the recipient have consented in writing to the use of such form of electronic transmission.

(k)   If this Act prescribes requirements for notices or other communications in particular circumstances, those requirements govern. If articles of incorporation or bylaws prescribe requirements for notices or other communications, not inconsistent with this section or other provisions of this Act, those requirements govern. The articles of incorporation or bylaws may authorize or require delivery of notices of meetings of directors by electronic transmission.

(*l*)   In the event that any provisions of this Act are deemed to modify, limit, or supersede the federal Electronic Signatures in Global and National Commerce Act, 15 U.S.C. §§ 7001 et seq., the provisions of this Act shall control to the maximum extent permitted by section 102(a)(2) of that federal act.

(m)   Whenever notice would otherwise be required to be given under any provision of this Act to a shareholder, the notice need not be given if:

(1)   notices to shareholders of two consecutive annual meetings, and all notices of meetings during the period between such two consecutive annual meetings, have been sent, other than by electronic transmission, to such shareholder at such shareholder's address as shown on the records of the corporation and have been returned undeliverable or could not be delivered; or

(2)   all, but not less than two, distributions to shareholders during a 12-month period, or two consecutive distributions to shareholders during a period of more than 12 months, have been sent to such shareholder at such shareholder's address as shown on the records of the corporation and have been returned undeliverable or could not be delivered.

If any shareholder to which this subsection (m) applies delivers to the corporation a written notice setting forth such shareholder's then-current address, the requirement that notice be given to such shareholder shall be reinstated.

§ 1.42   Number of Shareholders

(a)   For purposes of this Act, the following identified as a shareholder in a corporation's current record of shareholders constitutes one shareholder:

(1)   three or fewer co-owners;

(2)   a corporation, partnership, trust, estate, or other entity; and

(3)   the trustees, guardians, custodians, or other fiduciaries of a single trust, estate, or account.

(b)   For purposes of this Act, shareholdings registered in substantially similar names constitute one shareholder if it is reasonable to believe that the names represent the same person.

§ 1.43   Qualified Director

(a)   A "qualified director" is a director who, at the time action is to be taken under:

(1)   section 2.02(b)(6), is not a director (i) to whom the limitation or elimination of the duty of an officer to offer potential business opportunities to the corporation would apply, or (ii) who has a material relationship with any other person to whom the limitation or elimination would apply;

(2)   section 7.44, does not have (i) a material interest in the outcome of the proceeding, or (ii) a material relationship with a person who has such an interest;

(3)   section 8.53 or 8.55, (i) is not a party to the proceeding, (ii) is not a director as to whom a transaction is a director's conflicting interest transaction or who sought a disclaimer of the corporation's interest in a business opportunity under section 8.70, which transaction or disclaimer is challenged in the proceeding, and (iii) does not have a material relationship with a director described in either clause (i) or clause (ii) of this subsection (a)(3);

(4)   section 8.62, is not a director (i) as to whom the transaction is a director's conflicting interest transaction, or (ii) who has a material relationship with another director as to whom the transaction is a director's conflicting interest transaction; or

(5)   section 8.70, is not a director who (i) pursues or takes advantage of the business opportunity, directly, or indirectly through or on behalf of another person, or (ii) has a material relationship with a director or officer who pursues or takes advantage of the business opportunity, directly, or indirectly through or on behalf of another person.

(b)   For purposes of this section:

(1)   "material relationship" means a familial, financial, professional, employment or other relationship that would reasonably be expected to impair the objectivity of the director's judgment when participating in the action to be taken; and

(2)   "material interest" means an actual or potential benefit or detriment (other than one which would devolve on the corporation or the shareholders generally) that would reasonably be expected to impair the objectivity of the director's judgment when participating in the action to be taken.

(c)   The presence of one or more of the following circumstances shall not automatically prevent a director from being a qualified director:

(1)   nomination or election of the director to the current board by any director who is not a qualified director with respect to the matter (or by any person that has a material relationship with that director), acting alone or participating with others;

(2)   service as a director of another corporation of which a director who is not a qualified director with respect to the matter (or any individual who has a material relationship with that director), is or was also a director; or

(3)   with respect to action to be taken under section 7.44, status as a named defendant, as a director against whom action is demanded, or as a director who approved the conduct being challenged.

§ 1.44   Householding

(a)   A corporation has delivered written notice or any other report or statement under this Act, the articles of incorporation or the bylaws to all shareholders who share a common address if:

(1)   the corporation delivers one copy of the notice, report or statement to the common address;

(2)　the corporation addresses the notice, report or statement to those shareholders either as a group or to each of those shareholders individually or to the shareholders in a form to which each of those shareholders has consented; and

(3)　each of those shareholders consents to delivery of a single copy of such notice, report or statement to the shareholders' common address.

(b)　Any such consent described in subsections (a)(2) or (a)(3) shall be revocable by any of such shareholders who deliver written notice of revocation to the corporation. If such written notice of revocation is delivered, the corporation shall begin providing individual notices, reports or other statements to the revoking shareholder no later than 30 days after delivery of the written notice of revocation.

(c)　Any shareholder who fails to object by written notice to the corporation, within 60 days of written notice by the corporation of its intention to deliver single copies of notices, reports or statements to shareholders who share a common address as permitted by subsection (a), shall be deemed to have consented to receiving such single copy at the common address; provided that the notice of intention explains that consent may be revoked and the method for revoking.

Subchapter E.　Ratification of Defective Corporate Actions

§ 1.45　Definitions

In this subchapter:

"Corporate action" means any action taken by or on behalf of the corporation, including any action taken by the incorporator, the board of directors, a committee of the board of directors, an officer or agent of the corporation or the shareholders.

"Date of the defective corporate action" means the date (or the approximate date, if the exact date is unknown) the defective corporate action was purported to have been taken.

"Defective corporate action" means (i) any corporate action purportedly taken that is, and at the time such corporate action was purportedly taken would have been, within the power of the corporation, but is void or voidable due to a failure of authorization, and (ii) an overissue.

"Failure of authorization" means the failure to authorize, approve or otherwise effect a corporate action in compliance with the provisions of this Act, the articles of incorporation or bylaws, a corporate resolution or any plan or agreement to which the corporation is a party, if and to the extent such failure would render such corporate action void or voidable.

"Overissue" means the purported issuance of:

(i)　shares of a class or series in excess of the number of shares of a class or series the corporation has the power to issue under section 6.01 at the time of such issuance; or

(ii)　shares of any class or series that is not then authorized for issuance by the articles of incorporation.

"Putative shares" means the shares of any class or series (including shares issued upon exercise of rights, options, warrants or other securities convertible into shares of the corporation, or interests with respect to such shares) that were created or issued as a result of a defective corporate action, that (i) but for any failure of authorization would constitute valid shares, or (ii) cannot be determined by the board of directors to be valid shares.

"Valid shares" means the shares of any class or series that have been duly authorized and validly issued in accordance with this Act, including as a result of ratification or validation under this subchapter.

"Validation effective time" with respect to any defective corporate action ratified under this subchapter means the later of:

(i)   the time at which the ratification of the defective corporate action is approved by the shareholders, or if approval of shareholders is not required, the time at which the notice required by section 1.49 becomes effective in accordance with section 1.41; and

(ii)   the time at which any articles of validation filed in accordance with section 1.51 become effective.

The validation effective time shall not be affected by the filing or pendency of a judicial proceeding under section 1.52 or otherwise, unless otherwise ordered by the court.

§ 1.46   Defective Corporate Actions

(a)   A defective corporate action shall not be void or voidable if ratified in accordance with section 1.47 or validated in accordance with section 1.52.

(b)   Ratification under section 1.47 or validation under section 1.52 shall not be deemed to be the exclusive means of ratifying or validating any defective corporate action, and the absence or failure of ratification in accordance with this subchapter shall not, of itself, affect the validity or effectiveness of any corporate action properly ratified under common law or otherwise, nor shall it create a presumption that any such corporate action is or was a defective corporate action or void or voidable.

(c)   In the case of an overissue, putative shares shall be valid shares effective as of the date originally issued or purportedly issued upon:

(1) the effectiveness under this subchapter and under chapter 10 of an amendment to the articles of incorporation authorizing, designating or creating such shares; or

(2)   the effectiveness of any other corporate action under this subchapter ratifying the authorization, designation or creation of such shares.

§ 1.47   Ratification of Defective Corporate Actions

(a)   To ratify a defective corporate action under this section (other than the ratification of an election of the initial board of directors under subsection (b)), the board of directors shall take action ratifying the action in accordance with section 1.48, stating:

(1)   the defective corporate action to be ratified and, if the defective corporate action involved the issuance of putative shares, the number and type of putative shares purportedly issued;

(2)   the date of the defective corporate action;

(3)   the nature of the failure of authorization with respect to the defective corporate action to be ratified; and

(4)   that the board of directors approves the ratification of the defective corporate action.

(b)   In the event that a defective corporate action to be ratified relates to the election of the initial board of directors of the corporation under section 2.05(a)(2), a majority of the persons who, at the time of the ratification, are exercising the powers of directors may take an action stating:

(1)   the name of the person or persons who first took action in the name of the corporation as the initial board of directors of the corporation;

(2)   the earlier of the date on which such persons first took such action or were purported to have been elected as the initial board of directors; and

(3)   that the ratification of the election of such person or persons as the initial board of directors is approved.

(c)   If any provision of this Act, the articles of incorporation or bylaws, any corporate resolution or any plan or agreement to which the corporation is a party in effect at the time action under subsection (a) is taken requires shareholder approval or would have required shareholder approval at the date of the occurrence of the defective corporate action, the ratification of the defective corporate action approved in the action taken by the directors under subsection (a) shall be submitted to the shareholders for approval in accordance with section 1.48.

(d)   Unless otherwise provided in the action taken by the board of directors under subsection (a), after the action by the board of directors has been taken and, if required, approved by the shareholders, the board of directors may abandon the ratification at any time before the validation effective time without further action of the shareholders.

§ 1.48   Action on Ratification

(a)   The quorum and voting requirements applicable to a ratifying action by the board of directors under section 1.47(a) shall be the quorum and voting requirements applicable to the corporate action proposed to be ratified at the time such ratifying action is taken.

(b)   If the ratification of the defective corporate action requires approval by the shareholders under section 1.47(c), and if the approval is to be given at a meeting, the corporation shall notify each holder of valid and putative shares, regardless of whether entitled to vote, as of the record date for notice of the meeting and as of the date of the occurrence of defective corporate action, provided that notice shall not be required to be given to holders of valid or putative shares whose identities or addresses for notice cannot be determined from the records of the corporation. The notice must state that the purpose, or one of the purposes, of the meeting, is to consider ratification of a defective corporate action and must be accompanied by (i) either a copy of the action taken by the board of directors in accordance with section 1.47(a) or the information required by sections 1.47(a)(1) through (a)(4), and (ii) a statement that any claim that the ratification of such defective corporate action and any putative shares issued as a result of such defective corporate action should not be effective, or should be effective only on certain conditions, shall be brought within 120 days from the applicable validation effective time.

(c)   Except as provided in subsection (d) with respect to the voting requirements to ratify the election of a director, the quorum and voting requirements applicable to the approval by the shareholders required by section 1.47(c) shall be the quorum and voting requirements applicable to the corporate action proposed to be ratified at the time of such shareholder approval.

(d)   The approval by shareholders to ratify the election of a director requires that the votes cast within the voting group favoring such ratification exceed the votes cast opposing such ratification of the election at a meeting at which a quorum is present.

(e)   Putative shares on the record date for determining the shareholders entitled to vote on any matter submitted to shareholders under section 1.47(c) (and without giving effect to any ratification of putative shares that becomes effective as a result of such vote) shall neither be entitled to vote nor counted for quorum purposes in any vote to approve the ratification of any defective corporate action.

(f)   If the approval under this section of putative shares would result in an overissue, in addition to the approval required by section 1.47, approval of an amendment to the articles of incorporation under chapter 10 to increase the number of shares of an authorized class or series or to authorize the creation of a class or series of shares so there would be no overissue shall also be required.

§ 1.49   Notice Requirements

(a)   Unless shareholder approval is required under section 1.47(c), prompt notice of an action taken under section 1.47 shall be given to each holder of valid and putative shares, regardless of whether entitled to vote, as of (i) the date of such action by the board of directors and (ii) the date of the defective corporate action ratified, provided that notice shall not be required to be given to holders of valid and putative shares whose identities or addresses for notice cannot be determined from the records of the corporation.

(b)   The notice must contain (i) either a copy of the action taken by the board of directors in accordance with section 1.47(a) or (b) or the information required by sections 1.47(a)(1) through (a)(4) or sections 1.47(b)(1) through (b)(3), as applicable, and (ii) a statement that any claim that the ratification of the defective corporate action and any putative shares issued as a result of such defective corporate action should not be effective, or should be effective only on certain conditions, shall be brought within 120 days from the applicable validation effective time.

(c)   No notice under this section is required with respect to any action required to be submitted to shareholders for approval under section 1.47(c) if notice is given in accordance with section 1.48(b).

(d)   A notice required by this section may be given in any manner permitted by section 1.41 and, for any corporation subject to the reporting requirements of Section 13 or 15(d) of the Securities Exchange Act of 1934, may be given by means of a filing or furnishing of such notice with the United States Securities and Exchange Commission.

§ 1.50   Effect of Ratification

From and after the validation effective time, and without regard to the 120-day period during which a claim may be brought under section 1.52:

(a)   Each defective corporate action ratified in accordance with section 1.47 shall not be void or voidable as a result of the failure of authorization identified in the action taken under section 1.47(a) or (b) and shall be deemed a valid corporate action effective as of the date of the defective corporate action;

(b)   The issuance of each putative share or fraction of a putative share purportedly issued pursuant to a defective corporate action identified in the action taken under section 1.47 shall not be void or voidable, and each such putative share or fraction of a putative share shall be deemed to be an identical share or fraction of a valid share as of the time it was purportedly issued; and

(c)   Any corporate action taken subsequent to the defective corporate action ratified in accordance with this subchapter in reliance on such defective corporate action having been validly effected and any subsequent defective corporate action resulting directly or indirectly from such original defective corporate action shall be valid as of the time taken.

§ 1.51   Filings

(a)   If the defective corporate action ratified under this subchapter would have required under any other section of this Act a filing in accordance with this Act, then, regardless of whether a filing was previously made in respect of such defective corporate action and in lieu of a filing otherwise required by this Act, the corporation shall file articles of validation in accordance with this section, and such articles of validation shall serve to amend or substitute for any other filing with respect to such defective corporate action required by this Act.

(b)   The articles of validation must set forth:

(1)   the defective corporate action that is the subject of the articles of validation (including, in the case of any defective corporate action involving the issuance of putative shares, the number and type of putative shares issued and the date or dates upon which such putative shares were purported to have been issued);

(2)   the date of the defective corporate action;

(3)   the nature of the failure of authorization in respect of the defective corporate action;

(4)   a statement that the defective corporate action was ratified in accordance with section 1.47, including the date on which the board of directors ratified such defective corporate action and the date, if any, on which the shareholders approved the ratification of such defective corporate action; and

(5)   the information required by subsection (c).

(c)   The articles of validation must also contain the following information:

(1)   if a filing was previously made in respect of the defective corporate action and no changes to such filing are required to give effect to the ratification of such defective corporate action in accordance with section 1.47, the articles of validation must set forth (i) the name, title and filing date of the filing previously made and any articles of correction to that filing and (ii) a statement that a copy of the filing

previously made, together with any articles of correction to that filing, is attached as an exhibit to the articles of validation;

(2)   if a filing was previously made in respect of the defective corporate action and such filing requires any change to give effect to the ratification of such defective corporate action in accordance with section 1.47, the articles of validation must set forth (i) the name, title and filing date of the filing previously made and any articles of correction to that filing and (ii) a statement that a filing containing all of the information required to be included under the applicable section or sections of the Act to give effect to such defective corporate action is attached as an exhibit to the articles of validation, and (iii) the date and time that such filing is deemed to have become effective; or

(3)   if a filing was not previously made in respect of the defective corporate action and the defective corporate action ratified under section 1.47 would have required a filing under any other section of the Act, the articles of validation must set forth (i) a statement that a filing containing all of the information required to be included under the applicable section or sections of the Act to give effect to such defective corporate action is attached as an exhibit to the articles of validation, and (ii) the date and time that such filing is deemed to have become effective.

§ 1.52   Judicial Proceedings Regarding Validity of Corporate Actions

(a)   Upon application by the corporation, any successor entity to the corporation, a director of the corporation, any shareholder, beneficial shareholder or unrestricted voting trust beneficial owner of the corporation, including any such shareholder, beneficial shareholder or unrestricted voting trust beneficial owner as of the date of the defective corporate action ratified under section 1.47, or any other person claiming to be substantially and adversely affected by a ratification under section 1.47, the [name or describe court] may:

(1)   determine the validity and effectiveness of any corporate action or defective corporate action;

(2)   determine the validity and effectiveness of any ratification under section 1.47;

(3)   determine the validity of any putative shares; and

(4)   modify or waive any of the procedures specified in section 1.47 or 1.48 to ratify a defective corporate action.

(b)   In connection with an action under this section, the court may make such findings or orders, and take into account any factors or considerations, regarding such matters as it deems proper under the circumstances.

(c)   Service of process of the application under subsection (a) on the corporation may be made in any manner provided by statute of this state or by rule of the applicable court for service on the corporation, and no other party need be joined in order for the court to adjudicate the matter. In an action filed by the corporation, the court may require notice of the action be provided to other persons specified by the court and permit such other persons to intervene in the action.

(d)   Notwithstanding any other provision of this section or otherwise under applicable law, any action asserting that the ratification of any defective corporate action and any putative shares issued as a result of such defective corporate action should not be effective, or should be effective only on certain conditions, shall be brought within 120 days of the validation effective time.

CHAPTER 2

INCORPORATION

§ 2.01   Incorporators

One or more persons may act as the incorporator or incorporators of a corporation by delivering articles of incorporation to the secretary of state for filing.

§ 2.02 Articles of Incorporation

(a) The articles of incorporation must set forth:

Mandatory

(1) a corporate name for the corporation that satisfies the requirements of section 4.01;

(2) the number of shares the corporation is authorized to issue;

(3) the street and mailing addresses of the corporation's initial registered office and the name of its initial registered agent at that office; and

(4) the name and address of each incorporator.

(b) The articles of incorporation may set forth:

(1) the names and addresses of the individuals who are to serve as the initial directors;

(2) provisions not inconsistent with law regarding:

(i) the purpose or purposes for which the corporation is organized;

(ii) managing the business and regulating the affairs of the corporation;

(iii) defining, limiting, and regulating the powers of the corporation, its board of directors, and shareholders;

(iv) a par value for authorized shares or classes of shares; or

(v) the imposition of interest holder liability on shareholders;

(3) any provision that under this Act is required or permitted to be set forth in the bylaws;

(4) a provision eliminating or limiting the liability of a director to the corporation or its shareholders for money damages for any action taken, or any failure to take any action, as a director, except liability for (i) the amount of a financial benefit received by a director to which the director is not entitled; (ii) an intentional infliction of harm on the corporation or the shareholders; (iii) a violation of section 8.32; or (iv) an intentional violation of criminal law;

(5) a provision permitting or making obligatory indemnification of a director for liability as defined in section 8.50 to any person for any action taken, or any failure to take any action, as a director, except liability for (i) receipt of a financial benefit to which the director is not entitled, (ii) an intentional infliction of harm on the corporation or the shareholders, (iii) a violation of section 8.32, or (iv) an intentional violation of criminal law; and

(6) a provision limiting or eliminating any duty of a director or any other person to offer the corporation the right to have or participate in any, or one or more classes or categories of, business opportunities, before the pursuit or taking of the opportunity by the director or other person; provided that any application of such a provision to an officer or a related person of that officer (i) also requires approval of that application by the board of directors, subsequent to the effective date of the provision, by action of qualified directors taken in compliance with the same procedures as are set forth in section 8.62, and (ii) may be limited by the authorizing action of the board.

(c) The articles of incorporation need not set forth any of the corporate powers enumerated in this Act.

(d) Provisions of the articles of incorporation may be made dependent upon facts objectively ascertainable outside the articles of incorporation in accordance with section 1.20(k).

(e) As used in this section, "related person" has the meaning specified in section 8.60.

OFFICIAL COMMENT

1. Introduction

A corporation will have perpetual duration unless a special provision is included in its articles of incorporation providing for a shorter period. See section 3.02. Similarly, a corporation with articles of incorporation which do not contain a purpose clause will have the purpose of engaging in any lawful business under section 3.01(a). The option of providing a narrower purpose clause is also preserved in sections 2.02(b)(2)(i) and 3.01, with the effect described in the Official Comment to section 3.01.

2.　*Required Provisions*

If a single class of shares is authorized, only the number of shares authorized need be stated; if more than one class of shares is authorized, however, both the number of authorized shares of each class and a description of the rights of each class must be included. See the Official Comment to sections 6.01 and 6.02. It is unnecessary to specify par value, expected minimum capitalization, or contemplated issue price.

The corporation's initial registered office and agent must be included, and a mailing address alone, such as a post office box, is not sufficient since the registered office is the designated location for service of process. See chapter 5.

No reference need be made to a variety of other matters such as preemptive rights. See section 6.30 and its Official Comment. Generally, no substantive effect should be given to the absence of a specific reference to such matters in section 2.02. They are referred to in other sections of the Act that usually provide an "opt in" privilege. See particularly the list of optional provisions set forth in parts 4 and 5 of this Official Comment.

3.　*Optional Provisions*

Section 2.02(b) allows the articles of incorporation to contain optional provisions deemed sufficiently important to be of public record or subject to amendment only by the processes applicable to amendments of articles of incorporation.

A.　BUSINESS OR AFFAIRS

Provisions relating to the business or affairs of the corporation that may be included in the articles may be subdivided into four general classes:

- provisions that under the Act may be elected only by specific inclusion in the articles of incorporation (a list of these provisions is set forth in part 4 of this Official Comment);

- provisions that under the Act may be elected by specific inclusion in either the articles of incorporation or the bylaws, as listed in part 5 of this Official Comment;

- other provisions not referred to in the Act, including any provision that the Act requires or permits to be set forth in the bylaws (see section 2.02(b)(3)); and

- other provisions that are inconsistent with one or more provisions of the Act but are nonetheless permitted by section 7.32 for inclusion in a shareholders' agreement, if the requirements of that section are met.

B.　CORPORATE POWERS

Section 2.02(c) makes it unnecessary to set forth any corporate powers in the articles of incorporation in view of the broad grant of power in section 3.02. This grant of power, however, may be overbroad for particular corporations; if so, it may be qualified or narrowed by appropriate provisions in the articles of incorporation.

C.　PAR VALUE

Although par value is no longer a mandatory statutory concept under the Act, section 2.02(b)(2)(iv) permits optional "par value" provisions with regard to shares. Other than being permitted by section 2.02(b)(2)(iv), however, "par value" is not mentioned in the Act. Special provisions may be included to give effect or meaning to "par value" essentially as a matter of contract between the parties. These provisions, whether appearing in the articles of incorporation or in other documents, have only the effect any permissible contractual provision has in the absence of a prohibition by statute. Provisions in the articles of incorporation establishing an optional par value may also be of use to corporations which are to be qualified or registered in foreign jurisdictions that compute franchise or other taxes upon the basis of par value.

For a general discussion of capitalization, see the Official Comment to section 6.21.

D. SHAREHOLDER LIABILITY

The basic tenet of corporation law is that shareholders are not liable for the corporation's liabilities by reason of their status as shareholders. Section 2.02(b)(2)(v) nevertheless permits a corporation to impose that liability under specified circumstances if that is desirable. If no provision of this type is included, shareholders have no liability for corporate liabilities except to the extent they become liable by reason of their own conduct or acts. See section 6.22(b).

E. LIMITATIONS OF DIRECTOR LIABILITY

Section 2.02(b)(4) authorizes the inclusion of a provision in the articles of incorporation eliminating or limiting, with certain exceptions, the liability of the directors to the corporation or its shareholders for money damages. This section is optional rather than self-executing and does not apply to equitable relief. Likewise, nothing in section 2.02(b)(4) in any way affects the right of the shareholders to remove directors, under section 8.08(a), with or without cause. The phrase "as a director" emphasizes that section 2.02(b)(4) applies to a director's actions or failures to take action in the director's capacity as a director and not in any other capacity, such as officer, employee or controlling shareholder. However, it is not intended to exclude coverage of conduct by individuals, even though they are also officers, employees or controlling shareholders, to the extent they are acting in their capacity as directors.

Shareholders are given considerable latitude in limiting directors' liability for money damages. The statutory exceptions to permitted limitations of director liability are few and narrow and are discussed below.

Financial Benefit

Corporate law subjects transactions from which a director could benefit personally to special scrutiny. The financial benefits exception is limited to the amount of the benefit actually received. Thus, liability for punitive damages could be eliminated, except in cases of intentional infliction of harm or for violation of criminal law (as described below) where, in a particular case (for example, theft), punitive damages may be available. The benefit must be financial rather than in less easily measured and more conjectural forms, such as business goodwill, personal reputation, or social ingratiation. The phrase "received by a director" is not intended to be a "bright line." As a director's conduct moves toward the edge of what may be exculpated, the director should bear the risk of miscalculation. Depending upon the circumstances, a director may be deemed to have received a benefit that the director caused to be directed to another person, for example, a relative, friend, or affiliate.

What constitutes a financial benefit "to which the director is not entitled" is left to judicial development. For example, a director is entitled to reasonable compensation for the performance of services or to an increase in the value of stock or stock options held by the director; on the other hand, a director is not entitled to a bribe, a kick-back, or the profits from a corporate opportunity improperly taken by the director. See section 8.70 as to procedures for disclaiming the corporation's interest in a business opportunity by action of qualified directors or shareholders. See section 2.02(b)(6) for optional provisions permitted in the articles of incorporation to limit or eliminate, in advance, any duty of directors and others to bring business opportunities to the corporation. If the corporation declines the opportunity after it has been presented to the corporation by the director in accordance with the provisions of section 8.70(a)(1)(i) or (ii), or if a provision under section 2.02(b)(6) limits or eliminates the duty to bring the particular opportunity to the corporation, the corporation will have no right to participate in any financial benefit arising from the opportunity if the director pursues or takes the opportunity.

Intentional Infliction of Harm

There may be situations in which a director intentionally causes harm to the corporation even though the director does not receive any improper benefit. The use of the word "intentional," rather than a less precise term such as "knowing," is meant to refer to the specific intent to perform, or fail to perform, the acts with actual knowledge that the director's action, or failure to act, will cause harm, rather than a general intent to perform the acts which cause the harm.

Unlawful Distributions

Section 8.32(a) indicates a strong policy in favor of liability for unlawful distributions approved by directors who have not complied with the standards of conduct of section 8.30. Accordingly, the exception in section 2.02(b)(4)(iii) prohibits the shareholders from eliminating or limiting the liability of directors for a violation of section 8.32.

Intentional Violation of Criminal Law

Even though a director committing a crime may intend to benefit the corporation, the shareholders should not be permitted to exculpate the director for any harm caused by an intentional violation of criminal law, including, for example, fines and legal expenses of the corporation in defending a criminal prosecution. The use of the word "intentional," rather than a less precise term such as "knowing," is meant to refer to the specific intent to perform, or fail to perform, the acts with actual knowledge that the director's action, or failure to act, constitutes a violation of criminal law.

F. DIRECTOR INDEMNIFICATION

Section 2.02(b)(5) specifically prohibits provisions for indemnification of director liability arising out of improper financial benefit received by a director, an intentional infliction of harm on the corporation or the shareholders, an unlawful distribution or an intentional violation of criminal law. These excepted liabilities parallel those a corporation is not permitted to limit or eliminate under section 2.02(b)(4). See "E. Limitations of Director Liability" above. Officers are not included in the language of section 2.02(b)(5) because the expansion of indemnification for directors that section permits must be set forth in the articles of incorporation as required by section 8.51(a)(2); section 8.56 allows a similar expansion of indemnification for officers to be set forth also in the bylaws, resolutions or contracts.

G. BUSINESS OPPORTUNITIES

Section 2.02 (b)(6) authorizes the inclusion of a provision in the articles of incorporation to limit or eliminate, in advance, the duty of a director or other person to bring a business opportunity to the corporation. The limitation or elimination may be blanket in nature and apply to any business opportunities, or it may extend only to one or more specified classes or categories of business opportunities. The adoption of such a provision constitutes a curtailment of the duty of loyalty which includes the doctrine of corporate opportunity. If such a provision is included in the articles, taking advantage of a business opportunity covered by the provision of the articles without offering it to the corporation will not expose the director or other person to whom it is made applicable either to monetary damages or to equitable or any other relief in favor of the corporation upon compliance with the requirements of section 2.02(b)(6).

This provision may be useful, for example, in the context of a private equity investor that wishes to have a nominee on the board but conditions its investment on an advance limitation or elimination of the corporate opportunity doctrine because of the uncertainty over the application of the corporate opportunity doctrine inherent when investments are made in multiple enterprises in specific industries. Another example is a joint venture in corporate form where the participants in the joint venture want to be sure that the corporate opportunity doctrine would not apply to their activities outside the joint venture.

The focus of the advance limitation or elimination is on the duty of the director which extends indirectly to the investor through the application of the related party definition in section 8.60. This provision also permits extension of the limitation or elimination of the duty to any other persons who might be deemed to have a duty to offer business opportunities to the corporation. For example, courts have held that the corporate opportunity doctrine extends to officers of the corporation. Although officers may be included in a provision under this subsection, the limitation or elimination of corporate opportunity obligations of officers must be addressed by the board of directors in specific cases or by the directors' authorizing provisions in employment agreements or other contractual arrangements with such officers. Accordingly, section 2.02(b)(6) requires that the application of an advance limitation or elimination of the duty to offer a business opportunity to the corporation to any person who is an officer of the corporation or a related person of an officer also requires action by the board of directors acting through qualified directors. This action must be taken subsequent to the inclusion of the provision in the articles of incorporation and may limit the application. This means that if the advance limitation or elimination of the duty of an officer to offer business opportunities to the corporation is included in the articles by an amendment recommended by the directors and approved by the shareholders, that recommendation of the directors does not serve as the required authorization by qualified directors; rather, separate authorization by qualified directors after the amendment is included in the articles is necessary to apply the provision to a particular officer or any related person of that officer. See sections 1.43(a)(1) and 8.60 for the definition of "qualified directors" and "related persons," respectively.

Whether a provision for advance limitation or elimination of duty in the articles of incorporation should be a broad "blanket" provision or one more tailored to specific categories or classes of transactions deserves careful consideration given the particular circumstances of the corporation.

Limitation or elimination of the duty of a director or officer to present a business opportunity to the corporation does not limit or eliminate the director's or officer's duty not to make unauthorized use of corporate property or information or to compete unfairly with the corporation.

4. *List of Options in the Act That May Be Elected Only in the Articles of Incorporation*

A. OPTIONS WITH RESPECT TO DIRECTORS

- Board of directors may be dispensed with entirely, § 7.32, or its functions may be restricted, § 8.01.
- Power to compensate directors may be restricted or eliminated, § 8.11.
- Election of directors by cumulative voting may be authorized, § 7.28.
- Election of directors by greater than plurality vote may be authorized, § 7.28.
- Directors may be elected by classes or series of shares, § 8.04.
- Director's term may be limited by failure to receive specified vote for election, § 8.05.
- Power to remove directors without cause may be restricted or eliminated, § 8.08.
- Terms of directors may be staggered so that all directors are not elected in the same year, § 8.06.
- Power to fill vacancies may be limited to the shareholders, § 8.10.
- Power to indemnify directors, officers, and employees may be limited, §§ 8.50 through 8.59.
- Prohibition on adoption of bylaw provision under § 10.22.

B. OPTIONS WITH RESPECT TO SHAREHOLDERS

- Action by shareholders may be taken without a meeting, § 7.04.
- Special voting groups of shareholders may be authorized, § 7.25.
- Elimination or restriction of separate voting groups for mergers and share exchanges, § 11.04, and for domestications, § 9.21.
- Quorum for voting groups of shareholders may be increased or reduced, §§ 7.25, 7.26, and 7.27.
- Quorum for voting by voting groups of shareholders may be prescribed, see § 7.26.
- Greater than majority vote may be required for action by voting groups of shareholders, § 7.27.

C. OPTIONS WITH RESPECT TO SHARES

- Shares may be divided into classes and classes into series, §§ 6.01 and 6.02.
- Cumulative voting for directors may be permitted, § 7.28.
- Distributions may be restricted, § 6.40.
- Share dividends may be restricted, § 6.23.
- Voting rights of classes or series of shares may be limited or denied, § 6.01.
- Classes or series of shares may be given more or less than one vote per share, § 7.21.

- Terms of a class or series of shares may vary among holders of the same class or series, so long as such variations are expressly set forth in the articles, § 6.01.

- The board of directors may allocate authorized but unissued shares of a class or series of shares to another class or series without shareholder approval, § 6.02.

- Shares may be redeemed at the option of the corporation or the shareholder, § 6.01.

- Reissue of acquired or redeemed shares may be prohibited, § 6.31.

- Shareholders may be given preemptive rights to acquire unissued shares, § 6.30.

- Redemption preferences may be ignored in determining lawfulness of distributions, § 6.40.

5. *List of Options in the Act That May Be Elected Either in the Articles of Incorporation or in the Bylaws*

A. OPTIONS WITH RESPECT TO DIRECTORS

- Number of directors may be fixed or changed within limits, § 8.03.

- Qualifications for directors may be prescribed, § 8.02.

- Notice of regular or special meetings of board of directors may be prescribed, § 8.22.

- Power of board of directors to act without meeting may be restricted, § 8.21.

- Quorum for meeting of board of directors may be increased or decreased (down to one-third) from majority, § 8.24.

- Action at meeting of board of directors may require a greater than majority vote, § 8.24.

- Power of directors to participate in meeting without being physically present may be prohibited, § 8.20.

- Board of directors may create board committees and specify their powers, § 8.25.

- Board of directors may create safe harbor for consideration of corporate opportunities, § 8.70.

- Power of board of directors to amend bylaws may be restricted, §§ 10.20 and 10.21.

- Election of directors may be governed by the optional rules under section 10.22.

B. OPTIONS WITH RESPECT TO SHARES

- Shares may be issued without certificates, § 6.26.

- Procedure for treating beneficial owner of street name shares as record owner may be prescribed, § 7.23.

- Transfer of shares may be restricted, § 6.27.

§ 2.03   Incorporation

(a)   Unless a delayed effective date is specified, the corporate existence begins when the articles of incorporation are filed.

(b)   The secretary of state's filing of the articles of incorporation is conclusive proof that the incorporators satisfied all conditions precedent to incorporation except in a proceeding by the state to cancel or revoke the incorporation or involuntarily dissolve the corporation.

§ 2.04   Liability for Preincorporation Transactions

All persons purporting to act as or on behalf of a corporation, knowing there was no incorporation under this Act, are jointly and severally liable for all liabilities created while so acting.

OFFICIAL COMMENT

Ordinarily, only the filing of articles of incorporation should create the privilege of limited liability. Situations may arise, however, in which the protection of limited liability arguably should be recognized even though the simple incorporation process established by the Act has not been completed.

As a result, the Act imposes liability only on persons who act as or on behalf of corporations "knowing" that no corporation exists. In addition, section 2.04 does not foreclose the possibility that persons who urge defendants to execute contracts in the corporate name knowing that no steps to incorporate have been taken may be estopped to impose personal liability on individual defendants. This estoppel may be based on the inequity perceived when persons, unwilling or reluctant to enter into a commitment under their own name, are persuaded to use the name of a nonexistent corporation, and then are sought to be held personally liable under section 2.04 by the party advocating execution in the name of the corporation.

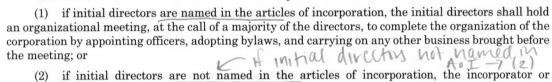

§ 2.05 Organization of Corporation

(a) After incorporation:

(1) if initial directors are named in the articles of incorporation, the initial directors shall hold an organizational meeting, at the call of a majority of the directors, to complete the organization of the corporation by appointing officers, adopting bylaws, and carrying on any other business brought before the meeting; or

(2) if initial directors are not named in the articles of incorporation, the incorporator or incorporators shall hold an organizational meeting at the call of a majority of the incorporators:

(i) to elect initial directors and complete the organization of the corporation; or

(ii) to elect a board of directors who shall complete the organization of the corporation.

(b) Action required or permitted by this Act to be taken by incorporators at an organizational meeting may be taken without a meeting if the action taken is evidenced by one or more written consents describing the action taken and signed by each incorporator.

(c) An organizational meeting may be held in or out of this state.

§ 2.06 Bylaws

(a) The incorporators or board of directors of a corporation shall adopt initial bylaws for the corporation.

(b) The bylaws of a corporation may contain any provision that is not inconsistent with law or the articles of incorporation.

(c) The bylaws may contain one or both of the following provisions:

(1) a requirement that if the corporation solicits proxies or consents with respect to an election of directors, the corporation include in its proxy statement and any form of its proxy or consent, to the extent and subject to such procedures or conditions as are provided in the bylaws, one or more individuals nominated by a shareholder in addition to individuals nominated by the board of directors; and

(2) a requirement that the corporation reimburse the expenses incurred by a shareholder in soliciting proxies or consents in connection with an election of directors, to the extent and subject to such procedures and conditions as are provided in the bylaws, provided that no bylaw so adopted shall apply to elections for which any record date precedes its adoption.

(d) Notwithstanding section 10.20(b)(2), the shareholders in amending, repealing, or adopting a bylaw described in subsection (c) may not limit the authority of the board of directors to amend or repeal any condition or procedure set forth in or to add any procedure or condition to such a bylaw to provide for a reasonable, practical, and orderly process.

§ 2.07　　Emergency Bylaws

(a)　Unless the articles of incorporation provide otherwise, the board of directors may adopt bylaws to be effective only in an emergency defined in subsection (d). The emergency bylaws, which are subject to amendment or repeal by the shareholders, may make all provisions necessary for managing the corporation during the emergency, including:

　　(1)　procedures for calling a meeting of the board of directors;

　　(2)　quorum requirements for the meeting; and

　　(3)　designation of additional or substitute directors.

(b)　All provisions of the regular bylaws not inconsistent with the emergency bylaws remain effective during the emergency. The emergency bylaws are not effective after the emergency ends.

(c)　Corporate action taken in good faith in accordance with the emergency bylaws:

　　(1)　binds the corporation; and

　　(2)　may not be used to impose liability on a director, officer, employee, or agent of the corporation.

(d)　An emergency exists for purposes of this section if a quorum of the board of directors cannot readily be assembled because of some catastrophic event.

§ 2.08　　Forum Selection Provisions

(a)　The articles of incorporation or the bylaws may require that any or all internal corporate claims shall be brought exclusively in any specified court or courts of this state and, if so specified, in any additional courts in this state or in any other jurisdictions with which the corporation has a reasonable relationship.

(b)　A provision of the articles of incorporation or bylaws adopted under subsection (a) shall not have the effect of conferring jurisdiction on any court or over any person or claim, and shall not apply if none of the courts specified by such provision has the requisite personal and subject matter jurisdiction. If the court or courts of this state specified in a provision adopted under subsection (a) do not have the requisite personal and subject matter jurisdiction and another court of this state does have such jurisdiction, then the internal corporate claim may be brought in such other court of this state, notwithstanding that such other court of this state is not specified in such provision, and in any other court specified in such provision that has the requisite jurisdiction.

(c)　No provision of the articles of incorporation or the bylaws may prohibit bringing an internal corporate claim in the courts of this state or require such claims to be determined by arbitration.

(d)　"Internal corporate claim" means, for the purposes of this section, (i) any claim that is based upon a violation of a duty under the laws of this state by a current or former director, officer, or shareholder in such capacity, (ii) any derivative action or proceeding brought on behalf of the corporation, (iii) any action asserting a claim arising pursuant to any provision of this Act or the articles of incorporation or bylaws, or (iv) any action asserting a claim governed by the internal affairs doctrine that is not included in (i) through (iii) above.

CHAPTER 3

PURPOSES AND POWERS

§ 3.01　　Purposes

(a)　Every corporation incorporated under this Act has the purpose of engaging in any lawful business unless a more limited purpose is set forth in the articles of incorporation.

(b)　A corporation engaging in a business that is subject to regulation under another statute of this state may incorporate under this Act only if permitted by, and subject to all limitations of, the other statute.

§ 3.02 General Powers

Unless its articles of incorporation provide otherwise, every corporation has perpetual duration and succession in its corporate name and has the same powers as an individual to do all things necessary or convenient to carry out its business and affairs, including power:

(a) to sue and be sued, complain and defend in its corporate name;

(b) to have a corporate seal, which may be altered at will, and to use it, or a facsimile of it, by impressing or affixing it or in any other manner reproducing it;

(c) to make and amend bylaws, not inconsistent with its articles of incorporation or with the laws of this state, for managing the business and regulating the affairs of the corporation;

(d) to purchase, receive, lease, or otherwise acquire, and own, hold, improve, use, and otherwise deal with, real or personal property, or any legal or equitable interest in property, wherever located;

(e) to sell, convey, mortgage, pledge, lease, exchange, and otherwise dispose of all or any part of its property;

(f) to purchase, receive, subscribe for, or otherwise acquire, own, hold, vote, use, sell, mortgage, lend, pledge, or otherwise dispose of, and deal in and with shares or other interests in, or obligations of, any other entity;

(g) to make contracts and guarantees, incur liabilities, borrow money, issue its notes, bonds, and other securities and obligations (which may be convertible into or include the option to purchase other securities of the corporation), and secure any of its obligations by mortgage or pledge of any of its property, franchises, or income;

(h) to lend money, invest and reinvest its funds, and receive and hold real and personal property as security for repayment;

(i) to be a promoter, partner, member, associate, or manager of any partnership, joint venture, trust, or other entity;

(j) to conduct its business, locate offices, and exercise the powers granted by this Act within or without this state;

(k) to elect directors and appoint officers, employees, and agents of the corporation, define their duties, fix their compensation, and lend them money and credit;

(l) to pay pensions and establish pension plans, pension trusts, profit sharing plans, share bonus plans, share option plans, and benefit or incentive plans for any or all of its current or former directors, officers, employees, and agents;

(m) to make donations for the public welfare or for charitable, scientific, or educational purposes;

(n) to transact any lawful business that will aid governmental policy; and

(o) to make payments or donations, or do any other act, not inconsistent with law, that furthers the business and affairs of the corporation.

OFFICIAL COMMENT

The general philosophy of section 3.02 is that corporations formed under the Act should be automatically authorized to engage in all acts and have all powers that an individual may have. Because broad grants of power of this nature may not be desired in some corporations, section 3.02 generally authorizes articles of incorporation to deny or limit specific powers to a corporation.

The powers of a corporation under the Act exist independently of whether a corporation has a broad or narrow purpose clause. A corporation with a narrow purpose clause nevertheless has the same powers as an individual to do all things necessary or convenient to carry out its business. Many actions are therefore within the corporation's powers even if they do not directly affect the limited purpose for which the corporation is formed. For example, a corporation may generally make charitable contributions without regard to the purpose for which the charity will use the funds or may invest money in shares of other corporations without regard to whether the corporate purpose of the other corporation is broader or narrower than the limited purpose clause of the investing corporation. In some instances, however, a limited or narrow purpose clause may be considered to be a restriction on corporate powers as well as a restriction on purposes. Since the same ultra vires rule is applicable to corporations that exceed their purposes or powers (see the Official Comment to section 3.04), it is not necessary to determine whether a narrow purpose clause also limits the powers of the corporation but simply whether the purpose of the transaction in question is consistent with the purpose clause. These issues do not arise in corporations with an "any lawful business" purpose clause.

§ 3.03　　Emergency Powers

(a)　In anticipation of or during an emergency defined in subsection (d), the board of directors of a corporation may:

(1)　modify lines of succession to accommodate the incapacity of any director, officer, employee, or agent; and

(2)　relocate the principal office, designate alternative principal offices or regional offices, or authorize the officers to do so.

(b)　During an emergency defined in subsection (d), unless emergency bylaws provide otherwise:

(1)　notice of a meeting of the board of directors need be given only to those directors whom it is practicable to reach and may be given in any practicable manner; and

(2)　one or more officers of the corporation present at a meeting of the board of directors may be deemed to be directors for the meeting, in order of rank and within the same rank in order of seniority, as necessary to achieve a quorum.

(c)　Corporate action taken in good faith during an emergency under this section to further the ordinary business affairs of the corporation:

(1)　binds the corporation; and

(2)　may not be used to impose liability on a director, officer, employee, or agent.

(d)　An emergency exists for purposes of this section if a quorum of the board of directors cannot readily be assembled because of some catastrophic event.

§ 3.04　　Lack of Power to Act

(a)　Except as provided in subsection (b), the validity of corporate action may not be challenged on the ground that the corporation lacks or lacked power to act.

(b)　A corporation's power to act may be challenged:

(1)　in a proceeding by a shareholder against the corporation to enjoin the act;

(2)　in a proceeding by the corporation, directly, derivatively, or through a receiver, trustee, or other legal representative, against an incumbent or former director, officer, employee, or agent of the corporation; or

(3)　in a proceeding by the attorney general under section 14.30.

(c)　In a shareholder's proceeding under subsection (b)(1) to enjoin an unauthorized corporate act, the court may enjoin or set aside the act, if equitable and if all affected persons are parties to the proceeding, and may award damages for loss (other than anticipated profits) suffered by the corporation or another party because of enjoining the unauthorized act.

CHAPTER 4

NAME

§ 4.01 Corporate Name

(a) A corporate name:

(1) must contain the word "corporation," "incorporated," "company," or "limited," or the abbreviation "corp.," "inc.," "co.," or "ltd.," or words or abbreviations of like import in another language; and

(2) may not contain language stating or implying that the corporation is organized for a purpose other than that permitted by section 3.01 and its articles of incorporation.

(b) Except as authorized by subsections (c) and (d), a corporate name must be distinguishable upon the records of the secretary of state from:

(1) the corporate name of a corporation incorporated in this state which is not administratively dissolved;

(2) a corporate name reserved or registered under section 4.02 or 4.03 or any similar provision of the law of this state;

(3) the name of a foreign corporation registered to do business in this state or an alternate name adopted by a foreign corporation registered to do business in this state because its corporate name is unavailable;

(4) the corporate name of a nonprofit corporation incorporated in this state which is not administratively dissolved;

(5) the name of a foreign nonprofit corporation registered to do business in this state or an alternate name adopted by a foreign nonprofit corporation registered to conduct activities in this state because its real name is unavailable;

(6) the name of a domestic filing entity or limited liability partnership which is not administratively dissolved;

(7) the name of a foreign unincorporated entity registered to do business in this state or an alternate name adopted by such an entity registered to conduct activities in this state because its real name is unavailable; and

(8) an assumed name registered under [state's assumed name statute].

(c) A corporation may apply to the secretary of state for authorization to use a name that is not distinguishable upon the secretary of state's records from one or more of the names described in subsection (b). The secretary of state shall authorize use of the name applied for if:

(1) the other corporation or unincorporated entity consents to the use in writing and submits an undertaking in form satisfactory to the secretary of state to change its name to a name that is distinguishable upon the records of the secretary of state from the name of the applying corporation; or

(2) the applicant delivers to the secretary of state a certified copy of the final judgment of a court of competent jurisdiction establishing the applicant's right to use the name applied for in this state.

(d) This Act does not control the use of fictitious names.

§ 4.02 Reserved Name

(a) A person may reserve the exclusive use of a corporate name, including a fictitious or alternate name for a foreign corporation whose corporate name is not available, by delivering an application to the secretary of state for filing. The application must set forth the name and address of the applicant and the name proposed to be reserved. If the secretary of state finds that the corporate name applied for is available, the secretary of state shall reserve the name for the applicant's exclusive use for a nonrenewable 120-day period.

(b)   The owner of a reserved corporate name may transfer the reservation to another person by delivering to the secretary of state a signed notice of the transfer that states the name and address of the transferee.

§ 4.03   Registered Name

(a)   A foreign corporation may register its corporate name (or its corporate name with the addition of any word or abbreviation listed in section 4.01(a)(1) if necessary for the corporate name to comply with section 4.01(a)(1)) if the name is distinguishable upon the records of the secretary of state from the corporate names that are not available under section 4.01(b).

(b)   A foreign corporation registers its corporate name (or its corporate name with any addition permitted by subsection (a)) by delivering to the secretary of state for filing an application setting forth that name, the state or country and date of its incorporation, and a brief description of the nature of the business which is to be conducted in this state.

(c)   The name is registered for the applicant's exclusive use upon the effective date of the application and for the remainder of the calendar year, unless renewed.

(d)   A foreign corporation whose name registration is effective may renew it for successive years by delivering to the secretary of state for filing a renewal application, which complies with the requirements of subsection (b), between October 1 and December 31 of the preceding year. The renewal application when filed renews the registration for the following calendar year.

(e)   A foreign corporation whose name registration is effective may thereafter (i) register to do business as a foreign corporation under the registered name (if it complies with section 4.01(a)(2)) or (ii) consent in writing to the use of that name by a domestic corporation thereafter incorporated under this Act or by another foreign corporation. The registration terminates when the domestic corporation is incorporated or the foreign corporation registers to do business under that name.

CHAPTER 5

OFFICE AND AGENT

§ 5.01   Registered Office and Agent of Domestic and Registered Foreign Corporations

(a)   Each corporation shall continuously maintain in this state:

    (1)   a registered office that may be the same as any of its places of business; and

    (2)   a registered agent, which may be:

        (i)   an individual who resides in this state and whose business office is identical with the registered office; or

        (ii)   a domestic or foreign corporation or other eligible entity whose business office is identical with the registered office and, in the case of a foreign corporation or foreign eligible entity, is registered to do business in this state.

(b)   As used in this chapter, "corporation" means both a domestic corporation and a registered foreign corporation.

§ 5.02   Change of Registered Office or Registered Agent

(a)   A corporation may change its registered office or registered agent by delivering to the secretary of state for filing a statement of change that sets forth:

(1)   the name of the corporation;

(2)   the street and mailing addresses of its current registered office;

(3)   if the current registered office is to be changed, the street and mailing addresses of the new registered office;

(4)   the name of its current registered agent;

(5)   if the current registered agent is to be changed, the name of the new registered agent and the new agent's written consent (either on the statement or attached to it) to the appointment; and

(6)   that after the change or changes are made, the street and mailing addresses of its registered office and of the business office of its registered agent will be identical.

(b)   If the street or mailing address of a registered agent's business office changes, the agent shall change the street or mailing address of the registered office of any corporation for which the agent is the registered agent by delivering a signed written notice of the change to the corporation and delivering to the secretary of state for filing a signed statement that complies with the requirements of subsection (a) and states that the corporation has been notified of the change.

§ 5.03   Resignation of Registered Agent

(a)   A registered agent may resign as agent for a corporation by delivering to the secretary of state for filing a statement of resignation signed by the agent which states:

(1)   the name of the corporation;

(2)   the name of the agent;

(3)   that the agent resigns from serving as registered agent for the corporation; and

(4)   the address of the corporation to which the agent will deliver the notice required by subsection (c).

(b)   A statement of resignation takes effect on the earlier of:

(1)   12:01 a.m. on the 31st day after the day on which it is filed by the secretary of state; or

(2)   the designation of a new registered agent for the corporation.

(c)   A registered agent promptly shall deliver to the corporation notice of the date on which a statement of resignation was delivered to the secretary of state for filing.

(d)   When a statement of resignation takes effect, the person that resigned ceases to have responsibility under this Act for any matter thereafter tendered to it as agent for the corporation. The resignation does not affect any contractual rights the corporation has against the agent or that the agent has against the corporation.

(e)   A registered agent may resign with respect to a corporation regardless of whether the corporation is in good standing.

§ 5.04   Service on Corporation

(a)   A corporation's registered agent is the corporation's agent for service of process, notice, or demand required or permitted by law to be served on the corporation.

(b)   If a corporation has no registered agent, or the agent cannot with reasonable diligence be served, the corporation may be served by registered or certified mail, return receipt requested, addressed to the secretary at the corporation's principal office. Service is perfected under this subsection at the earliest of:

(1)   the date the corporation receives the mail;

(2)   the date shown on the return receipt, if signed on behalf of the corporation; or

(3)   five days after its deposit in the U.S. mail, as evidenced by the postmark, if mailed postpaid and correctly addressed.

(c)   If process, notice, or demand (i) cannot be served on a corporation pursuant to subsection (a) or (b), or (ii) is to be served on a registered foreign corporation that has withdrawn its registration pursuant to section 15.07 or 15.09, or the registration of which has been terminated pursuant to section 15.11, then the secretary of state shall be an agent of the corporation upon whom process, notice, or demand may be served. Service of any process, notice, or demand on the secretary of state as agent for a corporation may be made by delivering to the secretary of state duplicate copies of the process, notice, or demand. If process, notice, or demand is served on the secretary of state, the secretary of state shall forward one of the copies by registered or certified mail, return receipt requested, to the corporation at the last address shown in the records of the secretary of state. Service is effected under this subsection (c) at the earliest of:

(1)   the date the corporation receives the process, notice, or demand;

(2)   the date shown on the return receipt, if signed on behalf of the corporation; or

(3)   five days after the process, notice, or demand is deposited with the United States mail by the secretary of state.

(d)   This section does not prescribe the only means, or necessarily the required means, of serving a corporation.

CHAPTER 6

SHARES AND DISTRIBUTIONS

Subchapter A.   Shares

§ 6.01   Authorized Shares

(a)   The articles of incorporation must set forth any classes of shares and series of shares within a class, and the number of shares of each class and series, that the corporation is authorized to issue. If more than one class or series of shares is authorized, the articles of incorporation must prescribe a distinguishing designation for each class or series and, before the issuance of shares of a class or series, describe the terms, including the preferences, rights, and limitations, of that class or series. Except to the extent varied as permitted by this section, all shares of a class or series must have terms, including preferences, rights, and limitations, that are identical with those of other shares of the same class or series.

(b)   The articles of incorporation must authorize:

(1)   one or more classes or series of shares that together have full voting rights, and

(2)   one or more classes or series of shares (which may be the same class, classes or series as those with voting rights) that together are entitled to receive the net assets of the corporation upon dissolution.

(c)   The articles of incorporation may authorize one or more classes or series of shares that:

(1)   have special, conditional, or limited voting rights, or no right to vote, except to the extent otherwise provided by this Act;

(2)   are redeemable or convertible as specified in the articles of incorporation:

(i)   at the option of the corporation, the shareholder, or another person or upon the occurrence of a specified event;

(ii)   for cash, indebtedness, securities, or other property; and

(iii)   at prices and in amounts specified or determined in accordance with a formula;

(3)   entitle the holders to distributions calculated in any manner, including dividends that may be cumulative, noncumulative, or partially cumulative; or

(4) have preference over any other class or series of shares with respect to distributions, including distributions upon the dissolution of the corporation.

(d) Terms of shares may be made dependent upon facts objectively ascertainable outside the articles of incorporation in accordance with section 1.20(k).

(e) Any of the terms of shares may vary among holders of the same class or series so long as such variations are expressly set forth in the articles of incorporation.

(f) The description of the preferences, rights, and limitations of classes or series of shares in subsection (c) is not exhaustive.

§ 6.02 Terms of Class or Series Determined by Board of Directors

(a) If the articles of incorporation so provide, the board of directors is authorized, without shareholder approval, to:

(1) classify any unissued shares into one or more classes or into one or more series within a class;

(2) reclassify any unissued shares of any class into one or more classes or into one or more series within one or more classes; or

(3) reclassify any unissued shares of any series of any class into one or more classes or into one or more series within a class.

(b) If the board of directors acts pursuant to subsection (a), it shall determine the terms, including the preferences, rights, and limitations, to the same extent permitted under section 6.01, of:

(1) any class of shares before the issuance of any shares of that class, or

(2) any series within a class before the issuance of any shares of that series.

(c) Before issuing any shares of a class or series created under this section, the corporation shall deliver to the secretary of state for filing articles of amendment setting forth the terms determined under subsection (a).

§ 6.03 Issued and Outstanding Shares

(a) A corporation may issue the number of shares of each class or series authorized by the articles of incorporation. Shares that are issued are outstanding shares until they are reacquired, redeemed, converted, or cancelled.

(b) The reacquisition, redemption, or conversion of outstanding shares is subject to the limitations of subsection (c) and to section 6.40.

(c) At all times that shares of the corporation are outstanding, one or more shares that together have full voting rights and one or more shares that together are entitled to receive the net assets of the corporation upon dissolution must be outstanding.

§ 6.04 Fractional Shares

(a) A corporation may issue fractions of a share or in lieu of doing so may:

(1) pay in cash the value of fractions of a share;

(2) issue scrip in registered or bearer form entitling the holder to receive a full share upon surrendering enough scrip to equal a full share; or

(3) arrange for disposition of fractional shares by the holders of such shares.

(b) Each certificate representing scrip must be conspicuously labeled "scrip" and must contain the information required by section 6.25(b).

(c)   The holder of a fractional share is entitled to exercise the rights of a shareholder, including the rights to vote, to receive dividends and to receive distributions upon dissolution. The holder of scrip is not entitled to any of these rights unless the scrip provides for them.

(d)   The board of directors may authorize the issuance of scrip subject to any condition, including that:

(1)   the scrip will become void if not exchanged for full shares before a specified date; and

(2)   the shares for which the scrip is exchangeable may be sold and the proceeds paid to the scripholders.

Subchapter B.   Issuance of Shares

§ 6.20   Subscription for Shares Before Incorporation

(a)   A subscription for shares entered into before incorporation is irrevocable for six months unless the subscription agreement provides a longer or shorter period or all the subscribers agree to revocation.

(b)   The board of directors may determine the payment terms of subscriptions for shares that were entered into before incorporation, unless the subscription agreement specifies them. A call for payment by the board of directors must be uniform so far as practicable as to all shares of the same class or series, unless the subscription agreement specifies otherwise.

(c)   Shares issued pursuant to subscriptions entered into before incorporation are fully paid and nonassessable when the corporation receives the consideration specified in the subscription agreement.

(d)   If a subscriber defaults in payment of cash or property under a subscription agreement entered into before incorporation, the corporation may collect the amount owed as any other debt. Alternatively, unless the subscription agreement provides otherwise, the corporation may rescind the agreement and may sell the shares if the debt remains unpaid for more than 20 days after the corporation delivers a written demand for payment to the subscriber.

§ 6.21   Issuance of Shares

(a)   The powers granted in this section to the board of directors may be reserved to the shareholders by the articles of incorporation.

(b)   The board of directors may authorize shares to be issued for consideration consisting of any tangible or intangible property or benefit to the corporation, including cash, promissory notes, services performed, contracts for services to be performed, or other securities of the corporation.

(c)   Before the corporation issues shares, the board of directors shall determine that the consideration received or to be received for shares to be issued is adequate. That determination by the board of directors is conclusive insofar as the adequacy of consideration for the issuance of shares relates to whether the shares are validly issued, fully paid, and nonassessable.

(d)   When the corporation receives the consideration for which the board of directors authorized the issuance of shares, the shares issued therefor are fully paid and nonassessable.

(e)   The corporation may place in escrow shares issued for a contract for future services or benefits or a promissory note, or make other arrangements to restrict the transfer of the shares, and may credit distributions in respect of the shares against their purchase price, until the services are performed, the benefits are received, or the note is paid. If the services are not performed, the benefits are not received, or the note is not paid, the shares escrowed or restricted and the distributions credited may be cancelled in whole or part.

(f)(1)   An issuance of shares or other securities convertible into or rights exercisable for shares in a transaction or a series of integrated transactions requires approval of the shareholders, at a meeting at which a quorum consisting of a majority (or such greater number as the articles of incorporation may prescribe) of the votes entitled to be cast on the matter exists, if:

(i)   the shares, other securities, or rights are to be issued for consideration other than cash or cash equivalents, and

(ii)   the voting power of shares that are issued and issuable as a result of the transaction or series of integrated transactions will comprise more than 20% of the voting power of the shares of the corporation that were outstanding immediately before the transaction.

(2)   In this subsection:

(i)   For purposes of determining the voting power of shares issued and issuable as a result of a transaction or series of integrated transactions, the voting power of shares or other securities convertible into or rights exercisable for shares shall be the greater of (A) the voting power of the shares to be issued, or (B) the voting power of the shares that would be outstanding after giving effect to the conversion of convertible shares and other securities and the exercise of rights to be issued.

(ii)   A series of transactions is integrated only if consummation of one transaction is made contingent on consummation of one or more of the other transactions.

§ 6.22   Liability of Shareholders

(a)   A purchaser from a corporation of the corporation's own shares is not liable to the corporation or its creditors with respect to the shares except to pay the consideration for which the shares were authorized to be issued or specified in the subscription agreement.

(b)   A shareholder of a corporation is not personally liable for any liabilities of the corporation (including liabilities arising from acts of the corporation) except (i) to the extent provided in a provision of the articles of incorporation permitted by section 2.02(b)(2)(v), and (ii) that a shareholder may become personally liable by reason of the shareholder's own acts or conduct.

§ 6.23   Share Dividends

(a)   Unless the articles of incorporation provide otherwise, shares may be issued pro rata and without consideration to the corporation's shareholders or to the shareholders of one or more classes or series of shares. An issuance of shares under this subsection is a share dividend.

(b)   Shares of one class or series may not be issued as a share dividend in respect of shares of another class or series unless (i) the articles of incorporation so authorize, (ii) a majority of the votes entitled to be cast by the class or series to be issued approve the issue, or (iii) there are no outstanding shares of the class or series to be issued.

(c)   The board of directors may fix the record date for determining shareholders entitled to a share dividend, which date may not be retroactive. If the board of directors does not fix the record date for determining shareholders entitled to a share dividend, the record date is the date the board of directors authorizes the share dividend.

§ 6.24   Share Rights, Options, Warrants and Awards

(a)   A corporation may issue rights, options, or warrants for the purchase of shares or other securities of the corporation. The board of directors shall determine (i) the terms and conditions upon which the rights, options, or warrants are issued and (ii) the terms, including the consideration for which the shares or other securities are to be issued. The authorization by the board of directors for the corporation to issue such rights, options, or warrants constitutes authorization of the issuance of the shares or other securities for which the rights, options or warrants are exercisable.

(b)   The terms and conditions of such rights, options or warrants may include restrictions or conditions that:

(1)   preclude or limit the exercise, transfer or receipt of such rights, options or warrants by any person or persons owning or offering to acquire a specified number or percentage of the outstanding

shares or other securities of the corporation or by any transferee or transferees of any such person or persons, or

(2)   invalidate or void such rights, options, or warrants held by any such person or persons or any such transferee or transferees.

(c)   The board of directors may authorize one or more officers to (i) designate the recipients of rights, options, warrants, or other equity compensation awards that involve the issuance of shares and (ii) determine, within an amount and subject to any other limitations established by the board of directors and, if applicable, the shareholders, the number of such rights, options, warrants, or other equity compensation awards and the terms of such rights, options, warrants or awards to be received by the recipients, provided that an officer may not use such authority to designate himself or herself or any other persons as the board of directors may specify as a recipient of such rights, options, warrants, or other equity compensation awards.

§ 6.25   Form and Content of Certificates

(a)   Shares may, but need not, be represented by certificates. Unless this Act or another statute expressly provides otherwise, the rights and obligations of shareholders are identical regardless of whether their shares are represented by certificates.

(b)   At a minimum each share certificate must state on its face:

(1)   the name of the corporation and that it is organized under the law of this state;

(2)   the name of the person to whom issued; and

(3)   the number and class of shares and the designation of the series, if any, the certificate represents.

(c)   If the corporation is authorized to issue different classes of shares or series of shares within a class, the front or back of each certificate must summarize (i) the preferences, rights, and limitations applicable to each class and series, (ii) any variations in preferences, rights, and limitations among the holders of the same class or series, and (iii) the authority of the board of directors to determine the terms of future classes or series. Alternatively, each certificate may state conspicuously on its front or back that the corporation will furnish the shareholder this information on request in writing and without charge.

(d)   Each share certificate must be signed by two officers designated in the bylaws.

(e)   If the person who signed a share certificate no longer holds office when the certificate is issued, the certificate is nevertheless valid.

§ 6.26   Shares Without Certificates

(a)   Unless the articles of incorporation or bylaws provide otherwise, the board of directors of a corporation may authorize the issuance of some or all of the shares of any or all of its classes or series without certificates. The authorization does not affect shares already represented by certificates until they are surrendered to the corporation.

(b)   Within a reasonable time after the issuance or transfer of shares without certificates, the corporation shall deliver to the shareholder a written statement of the information required on certificates by sections 6.25(b) and (c), and, if applicable, section 6.27.

§ 6.27   Restriction on Transfer of Shares

(a)   The articles of incorporation, the bylaws, an agreement among shareholders, or an agreement between shareholders and the corporation may impose restrictions on the transfer or registration of transfer of shares of the corporation. A restriction does not affect shares issued before the restriction was adopted unless the holders of the shares are parties to the restriction agreement or voted in favor of the restriction.

(b)   A restriction on the transfer or registration of transfer of shares is valid and enforceable against the holder or a transferee of the holder if the restriction is authorized by this section and its existence is noted conspicuously on the front or back of the certificate or is contained in the information statement required by section 6.26(b). Unless so noted or contained, a restriction is not enforceable against a person without knowledge of the restriction.

(c)   A restriction on the transfer or registration of transfer of shares is authorized:

(1)   to maintain the corporation's status when it is dependent on the number or identity of its shareholders;

(2)   to preserve exemptions under federal or state securities law; or

(3)   for any other reasonable purpose.

(d)   A restriction on the transfer or registration of transfer of shares may:

(1)   obligate the shareholder first to offer the corporation or other persons (separately, consecutively, or simultaneously) an opportunity to acquire the restricted shares;

(2)   obligate the corporation or other persons (separately, consecutively, or simultaneously) to acquire the restricted shares;

(3)   require the corporation, the holders of any class or series of its shares, or other persons to approve the transfer of the restricted shares, if the requirement is not manifestly unreasonable; or

(4)   prohibit the transfer of the restricted shares to designated persons or classes of persons, if the prohibition is not manifestly unreasonable.

(e)   For purposes of this section, "shares" includes a security convertible into or carrying a right to subscribe for or acquire shares.

OFFICIAL COMMENT

Share transfer restrictions are used by corporations for a variety of purposes. Section 6.27(c) enumerates certain purposes for which share transfer restrictions may be imposed, but does not limit the purposes given that section 6.27(c)(3) permits restrictions "for any other reasonable purpose." Examples of the "status" referred to in section 6.27(c)(1) include the subchapter S election under the Internal Revenue Code, and entitlement to a program or eligibility for a privilege administered by governmental agencies or national securities exchanges.

Examples of the uses of share transfer restrictions include:

- a corporation with few shareholders may impose share transfer restrictions to ensure that shareholders do not transfer their shares to a person not acceptable to the corporation or other shareholders;

- a corporation with few shareholders may impose share transfer restrictions to establish the value of the shares of deceased shareholders;

- a professional corporation may impose share transfer restrictions to ensure that its treatment of departing, retiring or deceased shareholders is consistent with rules applicable to the profession in question;

- a corporation may impose share transfer restrictions to ensure that its election of subchapter S treatment under the Internal Revenue Code will not be unexpectedly terminated; and

- a corporation issuing securities pursuant to an exemption from federal or state securities registration may impose share transfer restrictions to ensure that subsequent transfers of shares will not result in the loss of the exemption being relied upon.

Section 6.27(d) describes the types of restrictions that may be imposed. The types of restrictions referred to in sections 6.27(d)(1) (rights of first offer) and (d)(2) (buy-sell agreements) are imposed as a matter of contractual negotiation and do not prohibit the outright transfer of shares. Rather, they designate to whom shares or other securities must be offered at a price established in the agreement or by a formula or method agreed to in advance. By contrast, the restrictions described in clauses sections 6.27(d)(3) and (d)(4) may permanently limit the market for shares by disqualifying all or some potential purchasers. The restrictions imposed by these two provisions must not be "manifestly unreasonable."

Subchapter C.   Subsequent Acquisition of Shares By Shareholders and Corporation

§ 6.30   Shareholders' Preemptive Rights

(a)   The shareholders of a corporation do not have a preemptive right to acquire the corporation's unissued shares except to the extent the articles of incorporation so provide.

(b)   A statement included in the articles of incorporation that "the corporation elects to have preemptive rights" (or words of similar effect) means that the following principles apply except to the extent the articles of incorporation expressly provide otherwise:

    (1)   The shareholders of the corporation have a preemptive right, granted on uniform terms and conditions prescribed by the board of directors to provide a fair and reasonable opportunity to exercise the right, to acquire proportional amounts of the corporation's [unissued] shares upon the decision of the board of directors to issue them.

    (2)   A preemptive right may be waived by a shareholder. A waiver evidenced by a writing is irrevocable even though it is not supported by consideration.

    (3)   There is no preemptive right with respect to:

       (i)   shares issued as compensation to directors, officers, employees or agents of the corporation, its subsidiaries or affiliates;

       (ii)   shares issued to satisfy conversion or option rights created to provide compensation to directors, officers, employees or agents of the corporation, its subsidiaries or affiliates;

       (iii)   shares authorized in the articles of incorporation that are issued within six months from the effective date of incorporation; or

       (iv)   shares sold otherwise than for cash.

    (4)   Holders of shares of any class or series without voting power but with preferential rights to distributions have no preemptive rights with respect to shares of any class or series.

    (5)   Holders of shares of any class or series with voting power but without preferential rights to distributions have no preemptive rights with respect to shares of any class or series with preferential rights to distributions unless the shares with preferential rights are convertible into or carry a right to subscribe for or acquire the shares without preferential rights.

    (6)   Shares subject to preemptive rights that are not acquired by shareholders may be issued to any person for a period of one year after being offered to shareholders at a consideration set by the board of directors that is not lower than the consideration set for the exercise of preemptive rights. An offer at a lower consideration or after the expiration of one year is subject to the shareholders' preemptive rights.

(c)   For purposes of this section, "shares" includes a security convertible into or carrying a right to subscribe for or acquire shares.

§ 6.31   Corporation's Acquisition of Its Own Shares

(a)   A corporation may acquire its own shares, and shares so acquired constitute authorized but unissued shares.

(b)   If the articles of incorporation prohibit the reissue of the acquired shares, the number of authorized shares is reduced by the number of shares acquired.

Subchapter D. Distributions

§6.40 Distributions to Shareholders

(a) A board of directors may authorize and the corporation may make distributions to its shareholders subject to restriction by the articles of incorporation and the limitation in subsection (c).

(b) The board of directors may fix the record date for determining shareholders entitled to a distribution, which date may not be retroactive. If the board of directors does not fix a record date for determining shareholders entitled to a distribution (other than one involving a purchase, redemption, or other acquisition of the corporation's shares), the record date is the date the board of directors authorizes the distribution.

(c) No distribution may be made if, after giving it effect:

(1) the corporation would not be able to pay its debts as they become due in the usual course of business; or

(2) the corporation's total assets would be less than the sum of its total liabilities plus (unless the articles of incorporation permit otherwise) the amount that would be needed, if the corporation were to be dissolved at the time of the distribution, to satisfy the preferential rights upon dissolution of shareholders whose preferential rights are superior to those receiving the distribution.

(d) The board of directors may base a determination that a distribution is not prohibited under subsection (c) either on financial statements prepared on the basis of accounting practices and principles that are reasonable in the circumstances or on a fair valuation or other method that is reasonable in the circumstances.

(e) Except as provided in subsection (g), the effect of a distribution under subsection (c) is measured:

(1) in the case of distribution by purchase, redemption, or other acquisition of the corporation's shares, as of the earlier of (i) the date cash or other property is transferred or debt to a shareholder is incurred by the corporation or (ii) the date the shareholder ceases to be a shareholder with respect to the acquired shares;

(2) in the case of any other distribution of indebtedness, as of the date the indebtedness is distributed; and

(3) in all other cases, as of (i) the date the distribution is authorized if the payment occurs within 120 days after the date of authorization or (ii) the date the payment is made if it occurs more than 120 days after the date of authorization.

(f) A corporation's indebtedness to a shareholder incurred by reason of a distribution made in accordance with this section is at parity with the corporation's indebtedness to its general, unsecured creditors except to the extent subordinated by agreement.

(g) Indebtedness of a corporation, including indebtedness issued as a distribution, is not considered a liability for purposes of determinations under subsection (c) if its terms provide that payment of principal and interest are made only if and to the extent that payment of a distribution to shareholders could then be made under this section. If such indebtedness is issued as a distribution, each payment of principal or interest is treated as a distribution, the effect of which is measured on the date the payment is actually made.

(h) This section shall not apply to distributions in liquidation under chapter 14.

CHAPTER 7

SHAREHOLDERS

Subchapter A.   Meetings

§ 7.01   Annual Meeting

(a)   Unless directors are elected by written consent in lieu of an annual meeting as permitted by section 7.04, a corporation shall hold a meeting of shareholders annually at a time stated in or fixed in accordance with the bylaws at which directors shall be elected.

(b)   Unless the board of directors determines to hold the meeting solely by means of remote communication in accordance with section 7.09(c), annual meetings may be held (i) in or out of this state at the place stated in or fixed in accordance with the bylaws, or (ii) if no place is stated or fixed in accordance with the bylaws, at the corporation's principal office.

(c)   The failure to hold an annual meeting at the time stated in or fixed in accordance with a corporation's bylaws does not affect the validity of any corporate action.

§ 7.02   Special Meeting

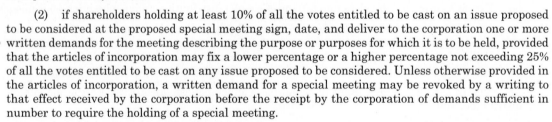

(a)   A corporation shall hold a special meeting of shareholders:

(1)   on call of its board of directors or the person or persons authorized to do so by the articles of incorporation or bylaws; or

(2)   if shareholders holding at least 10% of all the votes entitled to be cast on an issue proposed to be considered at the proposed special meeting sign, date, and deliver to the corporation one or more written demands for the meeting describing the purpose or purposes for which it is to be held, provided that the articles of incorporation may fix a lower percentage or a higher percentage not exceeding 25% of all the votes entitled to be cast on any issue proposed to be considered. Unless otherwise provided in the articles of incorporation, a written demand for a special meeting may be revoked by a writing to that effect received by the corporation before the receipt by the corporation of demands sufficient in number to require the holding of a special meeting.

(b)   If not otherwise fixed under section 7.03 or 7.07, the record date for determining shareholders entitled to demand a special meeting shall be the first date on which a signed shareholder demand is delivered to the corporation. No written demand for a special meeting shall be effective unless, within 60 days of the earliest date on which such a demand delivered to the corporation as required by this section was signed, written demands signed by shareholders holding at least the percentage of votes specified in or fixed in accordance with subsection (a)(2) have been delivered to the corporation.

(c)   Unless the board of directors determines to hold the meeting solely by remote participation in accordance with section 7.09(c), special meetings of shareholders may be held (i) in or out of this state at the place stated in or fixed in accordance with the bylaws, or (ii) if no place is stated in or fixed in accordance with the bylaws, at the corporation's principal office.

(d)   Only business within the purpose or purposes described in the meeting notice required by section 7.05(c) may be conducted at a special meeting of shareholders.

§ 7.03   Court-Ordered Meeting

(a)   The [name or describe court] may summarily order a meeting to be held:

(1)   on application of any shareholder of the corporation if an annual meeting was not held or action by written consent in lieu of an annual meeting did not become effective within the earlier of six months after the end of the corporation's fiscal year or 15 months after its last annual meeting; or

584

(2)   on application of one or more shareholders who signed a demand for a special meeting valid under section 7.02, if:

(i)   notice of the special meeting was not given within 30 days after the first day on which the requisite number of such demands have been delivered to the corporation; or

(ii)   the special meeting was not held in accordance with the notice.

(b)   The court may fix the time and place of the meeting, determine the shares entitled to participate in the meeting, specify a record date or dates for determining shareholders entitled to notice of and to vote at the meeting, prescribe the form and content of the meeting notice, fix the quorum required for specific matters to be considered at the meeting (or direct that the shares represented at the meeting constitute a quorum for action on those matters), and enter other orders necessary to accomplish the purpose or purposes of the meeting.

(c)   For purposes of subsection (a)(1), "shareholder" means a record shareholder, a beneficial shareholder, and an unrestricted voting trust beneficial owner.

§ 7.04   Action Without Meeting

(a)   Action required or permitted by this Act to be taken at a shareholders' meeting may be taken without a meeting if the action is taken by all the shareholders entitled to vote on the action. The action must be evidenced by one or more written consents bearing the date of signature and describing the action taken, signed by all the shareholders entitled to vote on the action and delivered to the corporation for filing by the corporation with the minutes or corporate records.

(b)   The articles of incorporation may provide that any action required or permitted by this Act to be taken at a shareholders' meeting may be taken without a meeting, and without prior notice, if consents in writing setting forth the action so taken are signed by the holders of outstanding shares having not less than the minimum number of votes that would be required to authorize or take the action at a meeting at which all shares entitled to vote on the action were present and voted; provided, however, that if a corporation's articles of incorporation authorize shareholders to cumulate their votes when electing directors pursuant to section 7.28, directors may not be elected by less than unanimous written consent. A written consent must bear the date of signature of the shareholder who signs the consent and be delivered to the corporation for filing by the corporation with the minutes or corporate records.

(c)   If not otherwise fixed under section 7.07 and if prior action by the board of directors is not required respecting the action to be taken without a meeting, the record date for determining the shareholders entitled to take action without a meeting shall be the first date on which a signed written consent is delivered to the corporation. If not otherwise fixed under section 7.07 and if prior action by the board of directors is required respecting the action to be taken without a meeting, the record date shall be the close of business on the day the resolution of the board of directors taking such prior action is adopted. No written consent shall be effective to take the corporate action referred to therein unless, within 60 days of the earliest date on which a consent delivered to the corporation as required by this section was signed, written consents signed by sufficient shareholders to take the action have been delivered to the corporation. A written consent may be revoked by a writing to that effect delivered to the corporation before unrevoked written consents sufficient in number to take the corporate action have been delivered to the corporation.

(d)   A consent signed pursuant to the provisions of this section has the effect of a vote taken at a meeting and may be described as such in any document. Unless the articles of incorporation, bylaws or a resolution of the board of directors provides for a reasonable delay to permit tabulation of written consents, the action taken by written consent shall be effective when written consents signed by sufficient shareholders to take the action have been delivered to the corporation.

(e)   If this Act requires that notice of a proposed action be given to nonvoting shareholders and the action is to be taken by written consent of the voting shareholders, the corporation shall give its nonvoting shareholders written notice of the action not more than 10 days after (i) written consents sufficient to take the action have been delivered to the corporation, or (ii) such later date that tabulation of consents is completed pursuant to an authorization under subsection (d). The notice must reasonably describe the action taken and contain or be accompanied by the same material that, under any provision of this Act, would have been required to be sent to nonvoting shareholders in a notice of a meeting at which the proposed action would have been submitted to the shareholders for action.

(f)   If action is taken by less than unanimous written consent of the voting shareholders, the corporation shall give its nonconsenting voting shareholders written notice of the action not more than 10 days after (i) written consents sufficient to take the action have been delivered to the corporation, or (ii) such later date that tabulation of consents is completed pursuant to an authorization under subsection (d). The notice must reasonably describe the action taken and contain or be accompanied by the same material that, under any provision of this Act, would have been required to be sent to voting shareholders in a notice of a meeting at which the action would have been submitted to the shareholders for action.

(g)   The notice requirements in subsections (e) and (f) shall not delay the effectiveness of actions taken by written consent, and a failure to comply with such notice requirements shall not invalidate actions taken by written consent, provided that this subsection shall not be deemed to limit judicial power to fashion any appropriate remedy in favor of a shareholder adversely affected by a failure to give such notice within the required time period.

§ 7.05   Notice of Meeting

(a)   A corporation shall notify shareholders of the date, time, and place, if any, of each annual and special shareholders' meeting no fewer than 10 nor more than 60 days before the meeting date. If the board of directors has authorized participation by means of remote communication pursuant to section 7.09 for holders of any class or series of shares, the notice to the holders of such class or series of shares must describe the means of remote communication to be used. The notice must include the record date for determining the shareholders entitled to vote at the meeting, if such date is different from the record date for determining shareholders entitled to notice of the meeting. Unless this Act or the articles of incorporation require otherwise, the corporation is required to give notice only to shareholders entitled to vote at the meeting as of the record date for determining the shareholders entitled to notice of the meeting.

(b)   Unless this Act or the articles of incorporation require otherwise, the notice of an annual meeting of shareholders need not include a description of the purpose or purposes for which the meeting is called.

(c)   Notice of a special meeting of shareholders must include a description of the purpose or purposes for which the meeting is called.

(d)   If not otherwise fixed under section 7.03 or 7.07, the record date for determining shareholders entitled to notice of and to vote at an annual or special shareholders' meeting is the day before the first notice is delivered to shareholders.

(e)   Unless the bylaws require otherwise, if an annual or special shareholders' meeting is adjourned to a different date, time, or place, if any, notice need not be given of the new date, time, or place, if any, if the new date, time, or place, if any, is announced at the meeting before adjournment. If a new record date for the adjourned meeting is or must be fixed under section 7.07, however, notice of the adjourned meeting shall be given under this section to shareholders entitled to vote at such adjourned meeting as of the record date fixed for notice of such adjourned meeting.

§ 7.06   Waiver of Notice

(a)   A shareholder may waive any notice required by this Act or the articles of incorporation or bylaws, before or after the date and time stated in the notice. The waiver must be in writing, be signed by the shareholder entitled to the notice, and be delivered to the corporation for filing by the corporation with the minutes or corporate records.

(b)   A shareholder's attendance at a meeting:

(1)   waives objection to lack of notice or defective notice of the meeting, unless the shareholder at the beginning of the meeting objects to holding the meeting or transacting business at the meeting; and

(2) waives objection to consideration of a particular matter at the meeting that is not within the purpose or purposes described in the meeting notice, unless the shareholder objects to considering the matter when it is presented.

§ 7.07 Record Date for Meeting

(a) The bylaws may fix or provide the manner of fixing the record date or dates for one or more voting groups to determine the shareholders entitled to notice of a shareholders' meeting, to demand a special meeting, to vote, or to take any other action. If the bylaws do not fix or provide for fixing a record date, the board of directors may fix the record date.

(b) A record date fixed under this section may not be more than 70 days before the meeting or action requiring a determination of shareholders and may not be retroactive.

(c) A determination of shareholders entitled to notice of or to vote at a shareholders' meeting is effective for any adjournment of the meeting unless the board of directors fixes a new record date or dates, which it shall do if the meeting is adjourned to a date more than 120 days after the date fixed for the original meeting.

(d) If a court orders a meeting adjourned to a date more than 120 days after the date fixed for the original meeting, it may provide that the original record date or dates continues in effect or it may fix a new record date or dates.

(e) The record dates for a shareholders' meeting fixed by or in the manner provided in the bylaws or by the board of directors shall be the record date for determining shareholders entitled both to notice of and to vote at the shareholders' meeting, unless in the case of a record date fixed by the board of directors and to the extent not prohibited by the bylaws, the board, at the time it fixes the record date for shareholders entitled to notice of the meeting, fixes a later record date on or before the date of the meeting to determine the shareholders entitled to vote at the meeting.

§ 7.08 Conduct of the Meeting

(a) At each meeting of shareholders, a chair shall preside. The chair shall be appointed as provided in the bylaws or, in the absence of such provision, by the board of directors.

(b) The chair, unless the articles of incorporation or bylaws provide otherwise, shall determine the order of business and shall have the authority to establish rules for the conduct of the meeting.

(c) Any rules adopted for, and the conduct of, the meeting shall be fair to shareholders.

(d) The chair of the meeting shall announce at the meeting when the polls close for each matter voted upon. If no announcement is made, the polls shall be deemed to have closed upon the final adjournment of the meeting. After the polls close, no ballots, proxies or votes nor any revocations or changes to such ballots, proxies or votes may be accepted.

§ 7.09 Remote Participation in Shareholders' Meetings; Meetings Held Solely by Remote Participation

(a) Shareholders of any class or series of shares may participate in any meeting of shareholders by means of remote communication to the extent the board of directors authorizes such participation for such class or series. Participation as a shareholder by means of remote communication shall be subject to such guidelines and procedures as the board of directors adopts, and shall be in conformity with subsection (b).

(b) Shareholders participating in a shareholders' meeting by means of remote communication shall be deemed present and may vote at such a meeting if the corporation has implemented reasonable measures:

(1) to verify that each person participating remotely as a shareholder is a shareholder; and

(2) to provide such shareholders a reasonable opportunity to participate in the meeting and to vote on matters submitted to the shareholders, including an opportunity to communicate, and to read or hear the proceedings of the meeting, substantially concurrently with such proceedings.

(c)   Unless the bylaws require the meeting of shareholders to be held at a place, the board of directors may determine that any meeting of shareholders shall not be held at any place and shall instead be held solely by means of remote communication, but only if the corporation implements the measures specified in subsection (b).

Subchapter B.   Voting

§ 7.20   Shareholders' List for Meeting

(a)   After fixing a record date for a meeting, a corporation shall prepare an alphabetical list of the names of all its shareholders who are entitled to notice of a shareholders' meeting. If the board of directors fixes a different record date under section 7.07(e) to determine the shareholders entitled to vote at the meeting, a corporation also shall prepare an alphabetical list of the names of all its shareholders who are entitled to vote at the meeting. A list must be arranged by voting group (and within each voting group by class or series of shares) and show the address of and number of shares held by each shareholder. Nothing contained in this subsection shall require the corporation to include on such list the electronic mail address or other electronic contact information of a shareholder.

(b)   The shareholders' list for notice shall be available for inspection by any shareholder, beginning two business days after notice of the meeting is given for which the list was prepared and continuing through the meeting, (i) at the corporation's principal office or at a place identified in the meeting notice in the city where the meeting will be held or (ii) on a reasonably accessible electronic network, provided that the information required to gain access to such list is provided with the notice of the meeting. In the event that the corporation determines to make the list available on an electronic network, the corporation may take reasonable steps to ensure that such information is available only to shareholders of the corporation. A shareholders' list for voting shall be similarly available for inspection promptly after the record date for voting. A shareholder, or the shareholder's agent or attorney, is entitled on written demand to inspect and, subject to the requirements of section 16.02(c), to copy a list, during regular business hours and at the shareholder's expense, during the period it is available for inspection.

(c)   If the meeting is to be held at a place, the corporation shall make the list of shareholders entitled to vote available at the meeting, and any shareholder, or the shareholder's agent or attorney, is entitled to inspect the list at any time during the meeting or any adjournment. If the meeting is to be held solely by means of remote communication, then such list shall also be open to such inspection during the meeting on a reasonably accessible electronic network, and the information required to access such list shall be provided with the notice of the meeting.

(d)   If the corporation refuses to allow a shareholder, or the shareholder's agent or attorney, to inspect a shareholders' list before or at the meeting (or copy a list as permitted by subsection (b)), the [name or describe court], on application of the shareholder, may summarily order the inspection or copying at the corporation's expense and may postpone the meeting for which the list was prepared until the inspection or copying is complete.

(e)   Refusal or failure to prepare or make available the shareholders' list does not affect the validity of action taken at the meeting.

§ 7.21   Voting Entitlement of Shares

(a)   Except as provided in subsections (b) and (d) or unless the articles of incorporation provide otherwise, each outstanding share, regardless of class or series, is entitled to one vote on each matter voted on at a shareholders' meeting. Only shares are entitled to vote.

(b)   Shares of a corporation are not entitled to vote if they are owned by or otherwise belong to the corporation directly, or indirectly through an entity of which a majority of the voting power is held directly or indirectly by the corporation or which is otherwise controlled by the corporation.

(c)   Shares held by the corporation in a fiduciary capacity for the benefit of any person are entitled to vote unless they are held for the benefit of, or otherwise belong to, the corporation directly, or indirectly through an entity of which a majority of the voting power is held directly or indirectly by the corporation or which is otherwise controlled by the corporation.

(d)   Redeemable shares are not entitled to vote after delivery of written notice of redemption is effective and a sum sufficient to redeem the shares has been deposited with a bank, trust company, or other financial institution under an irrevocable obligation to pay the holders the redemption price on surrender of the shares.

(e)   For purposes of this section, "voting power" means the current power to vote in the election of directors of a corporation or to elect, select or appoint governors of another entity.

§ 7.22   Proxies

An enforcement mechanism

(a)   A shareholder may vote the shareholder's shares in person or by proxy.

(b)   A shareholder, or the shareholder's agent or attorney-in-fact, may appoint a proxy to vote or otherwise act for the shareholder by signing an appointment form, or by an electronic transmission. An electronic transmission must contain or be accompanied by information from which the recipient can determine the date of the transmission and that the transmission was authorized by the sender or the sender's agent or attorney-in-fact.

(c)   An appointment of a proxy is effective when a signed appointment form or an electronic transmission of the appointment is received by the inspector of election or the officer or agent of the corporation authorized to count votes. An appointment is valid for the term provided in the appointment form, and, if no term is provided, is valid for 11 months unless the appointment is irrevocable under subsection (d).

(d)   An appointment of a proxy is revocable unless the appointment form or electronic transmission states that it is irrevocable and the appointment is coupled with an interest. Appointments coupled with an interest include the appointment of:

(1)   a pledgee;

(2)   a person who purchased or agreed to purchase the shares;

(3)   a creditor of the corporation who extended it credit under terms requiring the appointment;

(4)   an employee of the corporation whose employment contract requires the appointment; or

(5)   a party to a voting agreement created under section 7.31.

(e)   The death or incapacity of the shareholder appointing a proxy does not affect the right of the corporation to accept the proxy's authority unless notice of the death or incapacity is received by the secretary or other officer or agent authorized to tabulate votes before the proxy exercises authority under the appointment.

(f)   An appointment made irrevocable under subsection (d) is revoked when the interest with which it is coupled is extinguished.

(g)   Unless it otherwise provides, an appointment made irrevocable under subsection (d) continues in effect after a transfer of the shares and a transferee takes subject to the appointment, except that a transferee for value of shares subject to an irrevocable appointment may revoke the appointment if the transferee did not know of its existence when acquiring the shares and the existence of the irrevocable appointment was not noted conspicuously on the certificate representing the shares or on the information statement for shares without certificates.

(h)   Subject to section 7.24 and to any express limitation on the proxy's authority stated in the appointment form or electronic transmission, a corporation is entitled to accept the proxy's vote or other action as that of the shareholder making the appointment.

§ 7.23　Shares Held by Intermediaries and Nominees

(a)　A corporation's board of directors may establish a procedure under which a person on whose behalf shares are registered in the name of an intermediary or nominee may elect to be treated by the corporation as the record shareholder by filing with the corporation a beneficial ownership certificate. The terms, conditions, and limitations of this treatment shall be specified in the procedure. To the extent such person is treated under such procedure as having rights or privileges that the record shareholder otherwise would have, the record shareholder shall not have those rights or privileges.

(b)　The procedure must specify:

(1)　the types of intermediaries or nominees to which it applies;

(2)　the rights or privileges that the corporation recognizes in a person with respect to whom a beneficial ownership certificate is filed;

(3)　the manner in which the procedure is selected which must include that the beneficial ownership certificate be signed or assented to by or on behalf of the record shareholder and the person on whose behalf the shares are held;

(4)　the information that must be provided when the procedure is selected;

(5)　the period for which selection of the procedure is effective;

(6)　requirements for notice to the corporation with respect to the arrangement; and

(7)　the form and contents of the beneficial ownership certificate.

(c)　The procedure may specify any other aspects of the rights and duties created by the filing of a beneficial ownership certificate.

§ 7.24　Acceptance of Votes and Other Instruments

(a)　If the name signed on a vote, ballot, consent, waiver, shareholder demand, or proxy appointment corresponds to the name of a shareholder, the corporation, if acting in good faith, is entitled to accept the vote, ballot, consent, waiver, shareholder demand, or proxy appointment and give it effect as the act of the shareholder.

(b)　If the name signed on a vote, ballot, consent, waiver, shareholder demand, or proxy appointment does not correspond to the name of its shareholder, the corporation, if acting in good faith, is nevertheless entitled to accept the vote, ballot, consent, waiver, shareholder demand, or proxy appointment and give it effect as the act of the shareholder if:

(1)　the shareholder is an entity and the name signed purports to be that of an officer or agent of the entity;

(2)　the name signed purports to be that of an administrator, executor, guardian, or conservator representing the shareholder and, if the corporation requests, evidence of fiduciary status acceptable to the corporation has been presented with respect to the vote, ballot, consent, waiver, shareholder demand, or proxy appointment;

(3)　the name signed purports to be that of a receiver or trustee in bankruptcy of the shareholder and, if the corporation requests, evidence of this status acceptable to the corporation has been presented with respect to the vote, ballot, consent, waiver, shareholder demand, or proxy appointment;

(4)　the name signed purports to be that of a pledgee, beneficial owner, or attorney-in-fact of the shareholder and, if the corporation requests, evidence acceptable to the corporation of the signatory's authority to sign for the shareholder has been presented with respect to the vote, ballot, consent, waiver, shareholder demand, or proxy appointment; or

(5)　two or more persons are the shareholder as co-tenants or fiduciaries and the name signed purports to be the name of at least one of the co-owners and the person signing appears to be acting on behalf of all the co-owners.

(c)   The corporation is entitled to reject a vote, ballot, consent, waiver, shareholder demand, or proxy appointment if the person authorized to accept or reject such instrument, acting in good faith, has reasonable basis for doubt about the validity of the signature on it or about the signatory's authority to sign for the shareholder.

(d)   Neither the corporation or any person authorized by it, nor an inspector of election appointed under section 7.29, that accepts or rejects a vote, ballot, consent, waiver, shareholder demand, or proxy appointment in good faith and in accordance with the standards of this section 7.24 or section 7.22(b) is liable in damages to the shareholder for the consequences of the acceptance or rejection.

(e)   Corporate action based on the acceptance or rejection of a vote, ballot, consent, waiver, shareholder demand, or proxy appointment under this section is valid unless a court of competent jurisdiction determines otherwise.

(f)   If an inspector of election has been appointed under section 7.29, the inspector of election also has the authority to request information and make determinations under subsections (a), (b), and (c). Any determination made by the inspector of election under those subsections is controlling.

§ 7.25   Quorum and Voting Requirements for Voting Groups

(a)   Shares entitled to vote as a separate voting group may take action on a matter at a meeting only if a quorum of those shares exists with respect to that matter. Unless the articles of incorporation provide otherwise, shares representing a majority of the votes entitled to be cast on the matter by the voting group constitutes a quorum of that voting group for action on that matter. Whenever this Act requires a particular quorum for a specified action, the articles of incorporation may not provide for a lower quorum.

(b)   Once a share is represented for any purpose at a meeting, it is deemed present for quorum purposes for the remainder of the meeting and for any adjournment of that meeting unless a new record date is or must be fixed for that adjourned meeting.

(c)   If a quorum exists, action on a matter (other than the election of directors) by a voting group is approved if the votes cast within the voting group favoring the action exceed the votes cast opposing the action, unless the articles of incorporation require a greater number of affirmative votes.

(d)   An amendment of the articles of incorporation adding, changing, or deleting a quorum or voting requirement for a voting group greater than specified in subsection (a) or (c) is governed by section 7.27.

(e)   The election of directors is governed by section 7.28.

(f)   Whenever a provision of this Act provides for voting of classes or series as separate voting groups, the rules provided in section 10.04(c) for amendments of the articles of incorporation apply to that provision.

§ 7.26   Action by Single and Multiple Voting Groups

(a)   If the articles of incorporation or this Act provide for voting by a single voting group on a matter, action on that matter is taken when voted upon by that voting group as provided in section 7.25.

(b)   If the articles of incorporation or this Act provide for voting by two or more voting groups on a matter, action on that matter is taken only when voted upon by each of those voting groups counted separately as provided in section 7.25. Action may be taken by different voting groups on a matter at different times.

§ 7.27   Modifying Quorum or Voting Requirements

An amendment to the articles of incorporation that adds, changes, or deletes a quorum or voting requirement shall meet the same quorum requirement and be adopted by the same vote and voting groups required to take action under the quorum and voting requirements then in effect or proposed to be adopted, whichever is greater.

§ 7.28   Voting for Directors; Cumulative Voting

(a)   Unless otherwise provided in the articles of incorporation, directors are elected by a plurality of the votes cast by the shares entitled to vote in the election at a meeting at which a quorum is present.

(b)   Shareholders do not have a right to cumulate their votes for directors unless the articles of incorporation so provide.

(c)   A statement included in the articles of incorporation that "[all] [a designated voting group of] shareholders are entitled to cumulate their votes for directors" (or words of similar import) means that the shareholders designated are entitled to multiply the number of votes they are entitled to cast by the number of directors for whom they are entitled to vote and cast the product for a single candidate or distribute the product among two or more candidates.

(d)   Shares otherwise entitled to vote cumulatively may not be voted cumulatively at a particular meeting unless:

(1)   the meeting notice or proxy statement accompanying the notice states conspicuously that cumulative voting is authorized; or

(2)   a shareholder who has the right to cumulate the shareholder's votes gives notice to the corporation not less than 48 hours before the time set for the meeting of the shareholder's intent to cumulate votes during the meeting, and if one shareholder gives this notice all other shareholders in the same voting group participating in the election are entitled to cumulate their votes without giving further notice.

§ 7.29   Inspectors of Election

(a)   A corporation that has a class of equity securities registered pursuant to section 12 of the Securities Exchange Act of 1934 shall, and any other corporation may, appoint one or more inspectors to act at a meeting of shareholders in connection with determining voting results. Each inspector shall verify in writing that the inspector will faithfully execute the duties of inspector with strict impartiality and according to the best of the inspector's ability. An inspector may be an officer or employee of the corporation. The inspectors may appoint or retain other persons to assist the inspectors in the performance of the duties of inspector under subsection (b), and may rely on information provided by such persons and other persons, including those appointed to tabulate votes, unless the inspectors believe reliance is unwarranted.

(b)   The inspectors shall:

(1)   ascertain the number of shares outstanding and the voting power of each;

(2)   determine the shares represented at a meeting;

(3)   determine the validity of proxy appointments and ballots;

(4)   count the votes; and

(5)   make a written report of the results.

(c)   In performing their duties, the inspectors may examine (i) the proxy appointment forms and any other information provided in accordance with section 7.22(b), (ii) any envelope or related writing submitted with those appointment forms, (iii) any ballots, (iv) any evidence or other information specified in section 7.24 and (v) the relevant books and records of the corporation relating to its shareholders and their entitlement to vote, including any securities position list provided by a depository clearing agency.

(d)   The inspectors also may consider other information that they believe is relevant and reliable for the purpose of performing any of the duties assigned to them pursuant to subsection (b), including for the purpose of evaluating inconsistent, incomplete or erroneous information and reconciling information submitted on behalf of banks, brokers, their nominees or similar persons that indicates more votes being cast than a proxy authorized by the record shareholder is entitled to cast. If the inspectors consider other information allowed by this subsection, they shall in their report under subsection (b) specify the information considered by them, including the purpose or purposes for which the information was considered, the person or persons from whom they obtained the information, when the information was obtained, the means by which the information was obtained, and the basis for the inspectors' belief that such information is relevant and reliable.

(e)   Determinations of law by the inspectors of election are subject to de novo review by a court in a proceeding under section 7.49 or other judicial proceeding.

Subchapter C.   Voting Trusts and Agreements

§ 7.30   Voting Trusts

(a)   One or more shareholders may create a voting trust, conferring on a trustee the right to vote or otherwise act for them, by signing an agreement setting out the provisions of the trust (which may include anything consistent with its purpose) and transferring their shares to the trustee. When a voting trust agreement is signed, the trustee shall prepare a list of the names and addresses of all voting trust beneficial owners, together with the number and class of shares each transferred to the trust, and deliver copies of the list and agreement to the corporation at its principal office.

(b)   A voting trust becomes effective on the date the first shares subject to the trust are registered in the trustee's name.

(c)   Limits, if any, on the duration of a voting trust shall be as set forth in the voting trust. A voting trust that became effective when this Act provided a 10-year limit on its duration remains governed by the provisions of this section concerning duration then in effect, unless the voting trust is amended to provide otherwise by unanimous agreement of the parties to the voting trust.

§ 7.31   Voting Agreements

(a)   Two or more shareholders may provide for the manner in which they will vote their shares by signing an agreement for that purpose. A voting agreement created under this section is not subject to the provisions of section 7.30.

(b)   A voting agreement created under this section is specifically enforceable. *look @ lecture notes!!*

§ 7.32   Shareholder Agreements

(a)   An agreement among the shareholders of a corporation that complies with this section is effective among the shareholders and the corporation even though it is inconsistent with one or more other provisions of this Act in that it:

(1)   eliminates the board of directors or restricts the discretion or powers of the board of directors;

(2)   governs the authorization or making of distributions, regardless of whether they are in proportion to ownership of shares, subject to the limitations in section 6.40;

(3)   establishes who shall be directors or officers of the corporation, or their terms of office or manner of selection or removal;

(4)   governs, in general or in regard to specific matters, the exercise or division of voting power by or between the shareholders and directors or by or among any of them, including use of weighted voting rights or director proxies;

(5)   establishes the terms and conditions of any agreement for the transfer or use of property or the provision of services between the corporation and any shareholder, director, officer or employee of the corporation or among any of them;

(6)   transfers to one or more shareholders or other persons all or part of the authority to exercise the corporate powers or to manage the business and affairs of the corporation, including the resolution of any issue about which there exists a deadlock among directors or shareholders;

(7)   requires dissolution of the corporation at the request of one or more of the shareholders or upon the occurrence of a specified event or contingency; or

(8)   otherwise governs the exercise of the corporate powers or the management of the business and affairs of the corporation or the relationship among the shareholders, the directors and the corporation, or among any of them, and is not contrary to public policy.

(b)   An agreement authorized by this section shall be:

(1)   as set forth (i) in the articles of incorporation or bylaws and approved by all persons who are shareholders at the time of the agreement, or (ii) in a written agreement that is signed by all persons who are shareholders at the time of the agreement and is made known to the corporation; and

(2)   subject to amendment only by all persons who are shareholders at the time of the amendment, unless the agreement provides otherwise.

(c)   The existence of an agreement authorized by this section shall be noted conspicuously on the front or back of each certificate for outstanding shares or on the information statement required by section 6.26(b). If at the time of the agreement the corporation has shares outstanding represented by certificates, the corporation shall recall the outstanding certificates and issue substitute certificates that comply with this subsection. The failure to note the existence of the agreement on the certificate or information statement shall not affect the validity of the agreement or any action taken pursuant to it. Any purchaser of shares who, at the time of purchase, did not have knowledge of the existence of the agreement shall be entitled to rescission of the purchase. A purchaser shall be deemed to have knowledge of the existence of the agreement if its existence is noted on the certificate or information statement for the shares in compliance with this subsection and, if the shares are not represented by a certificate, the information statement is delivered to the purchaser at or before the time of purchase of the shares. An action to enforce the right of rescission authorized by this subsection shall be commenced within the earlier of 90 days after discovery of the existence of the agreement or two years after the time of purchase of the shares.

(d)   If the agreement ceases to be effective for any reason, the board of directors may, if the agreement is contained or referred to in the corporation's articles of incorporation or bylaws, adopt an amendment to the articles of incorporation or bylaws, without shareholder action, to delete the agreement and any references to it.

(e)   An agreement authorized by this section that limits the discretion or powers of the board of directors shall relieve the directors of, and impose upon the person or persons in whom such discretion or powers are vested, liability for acts or omissions imposed by law on directors to the extent that the discretion or powers of the directors are limited by the agreement.

(f)   The existence or performance of an agreement authorized by this section shall not be a ground for imposing personal liability on any shareholder for the acts or debts of the corporation even if the agreement or its performance treats the corporation as if it were a partnership or results in failure to observe the corporate formalities otherwise applicable to the matters governed by the agreement.

(g)   Incorporators or subscribers for shares may act as shareholders with respect to an agreement authorized by this section if no shares have been issued when the agreement is made.

(h)   Limits, if any, on the duration of an agreement authorized by this section must be set forth in the agreement. An agreement that became effective when this Act provided for a 10-year limit on duration of shareholder agreements, unless the agreement provided otherwise, remains governed by the provisions of this section concerning duration then in effect.

Subchapter D.   Derivative Proceedings

§ 7.40   Subchapter Definitions

In this subchapter:

"Derivative proceeding" means a civil suit in the right of a domestic corporation or, to the extent provided in section 7.47, in the right of a foreign corporation.

"Shareholder" means a record shareholder, a beneficial shareholder, and an unrestricted voting trust beneficial owner.

§7.41 Standing ✳

A shareholder may not commence or maintain a derivative proceeding unless the shareholder (i) was a shareholder of the corporation at the time of the act or omission complained of or became a shareholder through transfer by operation of law from one who was a shareholder at that time and (ii) fairly and adequately represents the interests of the corporation in enforcing the right of the corporation.

§7.42 Demand ✳

No shareholder may commence a derivative proceeding until (i) a written demand has been made upon the corporation to take suitable action and (ii) 90 days have expired from the date delivery of the demand was made unless the shareholder has earlier been notified that the demand has been rejected by the corporation or unless irreparable injury to the corporation would result by waiting for the expiration of the 90-day period.

§7.43 Stay of Proceedings

If the corporation commences an inquiry into the allegations made in the demand or complaint, the court may stay any derivative proceeding for such period as the court deems appropriate.

§7.44 Dismissal

(a) A derivative proceeding shall be dismissed by the court on motion by the corporation if one of the groups specified in subsection (b) or subsection (e) has determined in good faith, after conducting a reasonable inquiry upon which its conclusions are based, that the maintenance of the derivative proceeding is not in the best interests of the corporation.

(b) Unless a panel is appointed pursuant to subsection (e), the determination in subsection (a) shall be made by:

(1) a majority vote of qualified directors present at a meeting of the board of directors if the qualified directors constitute a quorum; or

(2) a majority vote of a committee consisting of two or more qualified directors appointed by majority vote of qualified directors present at a meeting of the board of directors, regardless of whether such qualified directors constitute a quorum.

(c) If a derivative proceeding is commenced after a determination has been made rejecting a demand by a shareholder, the complaint shall allege with particularity facts establishing either (1) that a majority of the board of directors did not consist of qualified directors at the time the determination was made or (2) that the requirements of subsection (a) have not been met.

(d) If a majority of the board of directors consisted of qualified directors at the time the determination was made, the plaintiff shall have the burden of proving that the requirements of subsection (a) have not been met; if not, the corporation shall have the burden of proving that the requirements of subsection (a) have been met.

(e) Upon motion by the corporation, the court may appoint a panel of one or more individuals to make a determination whether the maintenance of the derivative proceeding is in the best interests of the corporation. In such case, the plaintiff shall have the burden of proving that the requirements of subsection (a) have not been met.

§7.45 Discontinuance or Settlement

A derivative proceeding may not be discontinued or settled without the court's approval. If the court determines that a proposed discontinuance or settlement will substantially affect the interests of the corporation's shareholders or a class or series of shareholders, the court shall direct that notice be given to the shareholders affected.

§ 7.46   Payment of Expenses

On termination of the derivative proceeding the court may:

(1)   order the corporation to pay the plaintiff's expenses incurred in the proceeding if it finds that the proceeding has resulted in a substantial benefit to the corporation;

(2)   order the plaintiff to pay any defendant's expenses incurred in defending the proceeding if it finds that the proceeding was commenced or maintained without reasonable cause or for an improper purpose; or

(3)   order a party to pay an opposing party's expenses incurred because of the filing of a pleading, motion or other paper, if it finds that the pleading, motion or other paper (i) was not well grounded in fact, after reasonable inquiry, or warranted by existing law or a good faith argument for the extension, modification or reversal of existing law or (ii) was interposed for an improper purpose, such as to harass or cause unnecessary delay or needless increase in the cost of litigation.

§ 7.47   Applicability to Foreign Corporations

In any derivative proceeding in the right of a foreign corporation, the matters covered by this subchapter shall be governed by the laws of the jurisdiction of incorporation of the foreign corporation except for sections 7.43, 7.45, and 7.46.

Subchapter E.   Judicial Proceedings

§ 7.48   Shareholder Action to Appoint a Custodian or Receiver

(a)   The [name or describe court] may appoint one or more persons to be custodians, or, if the corporation is insolvent, to be receivers, of and for a corporation in a proceeding by a shareholder where it is established that:

(1)   the directors are deadlocked in the management of the corporate affairs, the shareholders are unable to break the deadlock, and irreparable injury to the corporation is threatened or being suffered; or

(2)   the directors or those in control of the corporation are acting fraudulently and irreparable injury to the corporation is threatened or being suffered.

(b)   The court:

(1)   may issue injunctions, appoint a temporary custodian or temporary receiver with all the powers and duties the court directs, take other action to preserve the corporate assets wherever located, and carry on the business of the corporation until a full hearing is held;

(2)   shall hold a full hearing, after notifying all parties to the proceeding and any interested persons designated by the court, before appointing a custodian or receiver; and

(3)   has jurisdiction over the corporation and all of its property, wherever located.

(c)   The court may appoint an individual or domestic or foreign corporation (registered to do business in this state) as a custodian or receiver and may require the custodian or receiver to post bond, with or without sureties, in an amount the court directs.

(d)   The court shall describe the powers and duties of the custodian or receiver in its appointing order, which may be amended from time to time. Among other powers:

(1)   a custodian may exercise all of the powers of the corporation, through or in place of its board of directors, to the extent necessary to manage the business and affairs of the corporation; and

(2)   a receiver (i) may dispose of all or any part of the assets of the corporation wherever located, at a public or private sale, if authorized by the court; and (ii) may sue and defend in the receiver's own name as receiver in all courts of this state.

(e)   The court during a custodianship may redesignate the custodian a receiver, and during a receivership may redesignate the receiver a custodian, if doing so is in the best interests of the corporation.

(f)   The court from time to time during the custodianship or receivership may order compensation paid and expense disbursements or reimbursements made to the custodian or receiver from the assets of the corporation or proceeds from the sale of its assets.

(g)   In this section, "shareholder" means a record shareholder, a beneficial shareholder, and an unrestricted voting trust beneficial owner.

§ 7.49   Judicial Determination of Corporate Offices and Review of Elections and Shareholder Votes

(a)   Upon application of or in a proceeding commenced by a person specified in subsection (b), the [name or describe court] may determine:

(1)   the result or validity of the election, appointment, removal or resignation of a director or officer of the corporation;

(2)   the right of an individual to hold the office of director or officer of the corporation;

(3)   the result or validity of any vote by the shareholders of the corporation;

(4)   the right of a director to membership on a committee of the board of directors; and

(5)   the right of a person to nominate or an individual to be nominated as a candidate for election or appointment as a director of the corporation, and any right under a bylaw adopted pursuant to section 2.06(c) or any comparable right under any provision of the articles of incorporation, contract, or applicable law.

(b)   An application or proceeding pursuant to subsection (a) of this section may be filed or commenced by any of the following persons:

(1)   the corporation;

(2)   any record shareholder, beneficial shareholder or unrestricted voting trust beneficial owner of the corporation;

(3)   a director of the corporation, an individual claiming the office of director, or a director whose membership on a committee of the board of directors is contested, in each case who is seeking a determination of his or her right to such office or membership;

(4)   an officer of the corporation or an individual claiming to be an officer of the corporation, in each case who is seeking a determination of his or her right to such office; and

(5)   a person claiming a right covered by subsection (a)(5) and who is seeking a determination of such right.

(c)   In connection with any application or proceeding under subsection (a), the following shall be named as defendants, unless such person made the application or commenced the proceeding:

(1)   the corporation;

(2)   any individual whose right to office or membership on a committee of the board of directors is contested;

(3)   any individual claiming the office or membership at issue; and

(4)   any person claiming a right covered by subsection (a)(5) that is at issue.

(d)   In connection with any application or proceeding under subsection (a), service of process may be made upon each of the persons specified in subsection (c) either by:

(1)   service of process on the corporation addressed to such person in any manner provided by statute of this state or by rule of the applicable court for service on the corporation; or

(2)   service of process on the person in any manner provided by statute of this state or by rule of the applicable court.

(e)   When service of process is made upon a person other than the corporation by service upon the corporation pursuant to subsection (d)(1), the plaintiff and the corporation or its registered agent shall promptly provide written notice of such service, together with copies of all process and the application or complaint, to the person at the person's last known residence or business address, or as permitted by statute of this state or by rule of the applicable court.

(f)   In connection with any application or proceeding under subsection (a), the court shall dispose of the application or proceeding on an expedited basis and also may:

(1)   order such additional or further notice as the court deems proper under the circumstances;

(2)   order that additional persons be joined as parties to the proceeding if the court determines that such joinder is necessary for a just adjudication of matters before the court;

(3)   order an election or meeting be held in accordance with the provisions of section 7.03(b) or otherwise;

(4)   appoint a master to conduct an election or meeting;

(5)   enter temporary, preliminary or permanent injunctive relief;

(6)   resolve solely for the purpose of this proceeding any legal or factual issues necessary for the resolution of any of the matters specified in subsection (a), including the right and power of persons claiming to own shares to vote at any meeting of the shareholders; and

(7)   order such other relief as the court determines is equitable, just and proper.

(g)   It is not necessary to make shareholders a party to a proceeding or application pursuant to this section unless the shareholder is a required defendant under subsection (c)(4), relief is sought against the shareholder individually, or the court orders joinder pursuant to subsection (f)(2).

(h)   Nothing in this section limits, restricts, or abolishes the subject matter jurisdiction or powers of the court as existed before the enactment of this section, and an application or proceeding pursuant to this section is not the exclusive remedy or proceeding available with respect to the matters specified in subsection (a).

CHAPTER 8

DIRECTORS AND OFFICERS

Subchapter A.   Board of Directors

§ 8.01   Requirement for and Functions of Board of Directors

(a)   Except as may be provided in an agreement authorized under section 7.32, each corporation shall have a board of directors.

(b)   Except as may be provided in an agreement authorized under section 7.32, and subject to any limitation in the articles of incorporation permitted by section 2.02(b), all corporate powers shall be exercised by or under the authority of the board of directors, and the business and affairs of the corporation shall be managed by or under the direction, and subject to the oversight, of the board of directors.

§ 8.02   Qualifications of Directors

(a)   The articles of incorporation or bylaws may prescribe qualifications for directors or for nominees for directors. Qualifications must be reasonable as applied to the corporation and be lawful.

(b)   A requirement that is based on a past, prospective, or current action, or expression of opinion, by a nominee or director that could limit the ability of a nominee or director to discharge his or her duties as a director is not a permissible qualification under this section. Notwithstanding the foregoing, qualifications may include not being or having been subject to specified criminal, civil, or regulatory sanctions or not having been removed as a director by judicial action or for cause.

(c)   A director need not be a resident of this state or a shareholder unless the articles of incorporation or bylaws so prescribe.

(d)   A qualification for nomination for director prescribed before a person's nomination shall apply to such person at the time of nomination. A qualification for nomination for director prescribed after a person's nomination shall not apply to such person with respect to such nomination.

(e)   A qualification for director prescribed before a director has been elected or appointed may apply only at the time an individual becomes a director or may apply during a director's term. A qualification prescribed after a director has been elected or appointed shall not apply to that director before the end of that director's term.

§ 8.03   Number and Election of Directors

(a)   A board of directors shall consist of one or more individuals, with the number specified in or fixed in accordance with the articles of incorporation or bylaws.

(b)   The number of directors may be increased or decreased from time to time by amendment to, or in the manner provided in, the articles of incorporation or bylaws.

(c)   Directors are elected at the first annual shareholders' meeting and at each annual shareholders' meeting thereafter unless elected by written consent in lieu of an annual meeting as permitted by section 7.04 or unless their terms are staggered under section 8.06.

§ 8.04   Election of Directors by Certain Classes or Series of Shares

If the articles of incorporation or action by the board of directors pursuant to section 6.02 authorize dividing the shares into classes or series, the articles of incorporation may also authorize the election of all or a specified number of directors by the holders of one or more authorized classes or series of shares. A class or series (or multiple classes or series) of shares entitled to elect one or more directors is a separate voting group for purposes of the election of directors.

§ 8.05   Terms of Directors Generally

(a)   The terms of the initial directors of a corporation expire at the first shareholders' meeting at which directors are elected.

(b)   The terms of all other directors expire at the next, or if their terms are staggered in accordance with section 8.06, at the applicable second or third, annual shareholders' meeting following their election, except to the extent (1) provided in section 10.22 if a bylaw electing to be governed by that section is in effect or (2) a shorter term is specified in the articles of incorporation in the event of a director nominee failing to receive a specified vote for election.

(c)   A decrease in the number of directors does not shorten an incumbent director's term.

(d)   The term of a director elected to fill a vacancy expires at the next shareholders' meeting at which directors are elected.

(e)   Except to the extent otherwise provided in the articles of incorporation or under section 10.22 if a bylaw electing to be governed by that section is in effect, despite the expiration of a director's term, the director continues to serve until the director's successor is elected and qualifies or there is a decrease in the number of directors.

§ 8.06   Staggered Terms for Directors

The articles of incorporation may provide for staggering the terms of directors by dividing the total number of directors into two or three groups, with each group containing half or one-third of the total, as near as may be practicable. In that event, the terms of directors in the first group expire at the first annual shareholders' meeting after their election, the terms of the second group expire at the second annual shareholders' meeting after their election, and the terms of the third group, if any, expire at the third annual shareholders' meeting after their election. At each annual shareholders' meeting held thereafter, directors shall be elected for a term of two years or three years, as the case may be, to succeed those whose terms expire.

§ 8.07   Resignation of Directors

(a)   A director may resign at any time by delivering a written notice of resignation to the board of directors, or its chair, or to the secretary.

(b)   A resignation is effective as provided in section 1.41(i) unless the resignation provides for a delayed effectiveness, including effectiveness determined upon a future event or events. A resignation that is conditioned upon failing to receive a specified vote for election as a director may provide that it is irrevocable.

§ 8.08   Removal of Directors by Shareholders

(a)   The shareholders may remove one or more directors with or without cause unless the articles of incorporation provide that directors may be removed only for cause.

(b)   If a director is elected by a voting group of shareholders, only the shareholders of that voting group may participate in the vote to remove that director.

(c)   A director may be removed if the number of votes cast to remove exceeds the number of votes cast not to remove the director, except to the extent the articles of incorporation or bylaws require a greater number; provided that if cumulative voting is authorized, a director may not be removed if, in the case of a meeting, the number of votes sufficient to elect the director under cumulative voting is voted against removal and, if action is taken by less than unanimous written consent, voting shareholders entitled to the number of votes sufficient to elect the director under cumulative voting do not consent to the removal.

(d)   A director may be removed by the shareholders only at a meeting called for the purpose of removing the director and the meeting notice must state that removal of the director is a purpose of the meeting.

§ 8.09   Removal of Directors by Judicial Proceeding

(a)   The [name or describe court] may remove a director from office or may order other relief, including barring the director from reelection for a period prescribed by the court, in a proceeding commenced by or in the right of the corporation if the court finds that (i) the director engaged in fraudulent conduct with respect to the corporation or its shareholders, grossly abused the position of director, or intentionally inflicted harm on the corporation; and (ii) considering the director's course of conduct and the inadequacy of other available remedies, removal or such other relief would be in the best interest of the corporation.

(b)   A shareholder proceeding on behalf of the corporation under subsection (a) shall comply with all of the requirements of subchapter 7D, except clause (i) of section 7.41.

§ 8.10   Vacancy on Board

(a)   Unless the articles of incorporation provide otherwise, if a vacancy occurs on a board of directors, including a vacancy resulting from an increase in the number of directors:

(1)   the shareholders may fill the vacancy;

(2)   the board of directors may fill the vacancy; or

(3)   if the directors remaining in office are less than a quorum, they may fill the vacancy by the affirmative vote of a majority of all the directors remaining in office.

(b)   If the vacant office was held by a director elected by a voting group of shareholders, only the holders of shares of that voting group are entitled to vote to fill the vacancy if it is filled by the shareholders, and only the remaining directors elected by that voting group, even if less than a quorum, are entitled to fill the vacancy if it is filled by the directors.

(c)   A vacancy that will occur at a specific later date (by reason of a resignation effective at a later date under section 8.07(b) or otherwise) may be filled before the vacancy occurs but the new director may not take office until the vacancy occurs.

§ 8.11   Compensation of Directors

Unless the articles of incorporation or bylaws provide otherwise, the board of directors may fix the compensation of directors.

Subchapter B.   Meetings and Action of the Board

§ 8.20   Meetings

(a)   The board of directors may hold regular or special meetings in or out of this state.

(b)   Unless restricted by the articles of incorporation or bylaws, any or all directors may participate in any meeting of the board of directors through the use of any means of communication by which all directors participating may simultaneously hear each other during the meeting. A director participating in a meeting by this means is deemed to be present in person at the meeting.

§ 8.21   Action Without Meeting

(a)   Except to the extent that the articles of incorporation or bylaws require that action by the board of directors be taken at a meeting, action required or permitted by this Act to be taken by the board of directors may be taken without a meeting if each director signs a consent describing the action to be taken and delivers it to the corporation.

(b)   Action taken under this section is the act of the board of directors when one or more consents signed by all the directors are delivered to the corporation. The consent may specify a later time as the time at which the action taken is to be effective. A director's consent may be withdrawn by a revocation signed by the director and delivered to the corporation before delivery to the corporation of unrevoked written consents signed by all the directors.

(c)   A consent signed under this section has the effect of action taken at a meeting of the board of directors and may be described as such in any document.

§ 8.22   Notice of Meeting

(a)   Unless the articles of incorporation or bylaws provide otherwise, regular meetings of the board of directors may be held without notice of the date, time, place, or purpose of the meeting.

(b)   Unless the articles of incorporation or bylaws provide for a longer or shorter period, special meetings of the board of directors shall be preceded by at least two days' notice of the date, time, and place of the meeting. The notice need not describe the purpose of the special meeting unless required by the articles of incorporation or bylaws.

§ 8.23   Waiver of Notice

(a)   A director may waive any notice required by this Act, the articles of incorporation or the bylaws before or after the date and time stated in the notice. Except as provided by subsection (b), the waiver must be in writing, signed by the director entitled to the notice and delivered to the corporation for filing by the corporation with the minutes or corporate records.

(b)   A director's attendance at or participation in a meeting waives any required notice to the director of the meeting unless the director at the beginning of the meeting (or promptly upon arrival) objects to holding the meeting or transacting business at the meeting and does not after objecting vote for or assent to action taken at the meeting.

§ 8.24   Quorum and Voting

(a)   Unless the articles of incorporation or bylaws provide for a greater or lesser number or unless otherwise expressly provided in this Act, a quorum of a board of directors consists of a majority of the number of directors specified in or fixed in accordance with the articles of incorporation or bylaws.

(b)   The quorum of the board of directors specified in or fixed in accordance with the articles of incorporation or bylaws may not consist of less than one-third of the specified or fixed number of directors.

(c)   If a quorum is present when a vote is taken, the affirmative vote of a majority of directors present is the act of the board of directors unless the articles of incorporation or bylaws require the vote of a greater number of directors or unless otherwise expressly provided in this Act.

(d)   A director who is present at a meeting of the board of directors or a committee when corporate action is taken is deemed to have assented to the action taken unless: (i) the director objects at the beginning of the meeting (or promptly upon arrival) to holding it or transacting business at the meeting; (ii) the dissent or abstention from the action taken is entered in the minutes of the meeting; or (iii) the director delivers written notice of the director's dissent or abstention to the presiding officer of the meeting before its adjournment or to the corporation immediately after adjournment of the meeting. The right of dissent or abstention is not available to a director who votes in favor of the action taken.

§ 8.25   Committees of the Board

(a)   Unless this Act, the articles of incorporation or the bylaws provide otherwise, a board of directors may establish one or more board committees composed exclusively of one or more directors to perform functions of the board of directors.

(b)   The establishment of a board committee and appointment of members to it shall be approved by the greater of (i) a majority of all the directors in office when the action is taken or (ii) the number of directors required by the articles of incorporation or bylaws to take action under section 8.24, unless, in either case, this Act or the articles of incorporation provide otherwise.

(c)   Sections 8.20 through 8.24 apply to board committees and their members.

(d)   A board committee may exercise the powers of the board of directors under section 8.01, to the extent specified by the board of directors or in the articles of incorporation or bylaws, except that a board committee may not:

(1)   authorize or approve distributions, except according to a formula or method, or within limits, prescribed by the board of directors;

(2)   approve or propose to shareholders action that this Act requires be approved by shareholders;

(3)   fill vacancies on the board of directors or, subject to subsection (e), on any board committees; or

(4)   adopt, amend, or repeal bylaws.

(e)   The board of directors may appoint one or more directors as alternate members of any board committee to replace any absent or disqualified member during the member's absence or dis-qualification. If the articles of incorporation, the bylaws, or the resolution creating the board committee so provide, the member or members present at any board committee meeting and not disqualified from voting may, by unanimous action, appoint another director to act in place of an absent or disqualified member during that member's absence or disqualification.

§ 8.26   Submission of Matters for Shareholder Vote

A corporation may agree to submit a matter to a vote of its shareholders even if, after approving the matter, the board of directors determines it no longer recommends the matter.

Subchapter C.   Directors

§ 8.30   Standards of Conduct for Directors

(a)   Each member of the board of directors, when discharging the duties of a director, shall act: (i) in good faith, and (ii) in a manner the director reasonably believes to be in the best interests of the corporation.

(b)   The members of the board of directors or a board committee, when becoming informed in connection with their decision-making function or devoting attention to their oversight function, shall discharge their duties with the care that a person in a like position would reasonably believe appropriate under similar circumstances.

(c)   In discharging board or board committee duties, a director shall disclose, or cause to be disclosed, to the other board or committee members information not already known by them but known by the director to be material to the discharge of their decision-making or oversight functions, except that disclosure is not required to the extent that the director reasonably believes that doing so would violate a duty imposed under law, a legally enforceable obligation of confidentiality, or a professional ethics rule.

(d)   In discharging board or board committee duties, a director who does not have knowledge that makes reliance unwarranted is entitled to rely on the performance by any of the persons specified in subsection (f)(1) or subsection (f)(3) to whom the board may have delegated, formally or informally by course of conduct, the authority or duty to perform one or more of the board's functions that are delegable under applicable law.

(e)   In discharging board or board committee duties, a director who does not have knowledge that makes reliance unwarranted is entitled to rely on information, opinions, reports or statements, including financial statements and other financial data, prepared or presented by any of the persons specified in subsection (f).

(f)   A director is entitled to rely, in accordance with subsection (d) or (e), on:

(1)   one or more officers or employees of the corporation whom the director reasonably believes to be reliable and competent in the functions performed or the information, opinions, reports or statements provided;

(2)   legal counsel, public accountants, or other persons retained by the corporation as to matters involving skills or expertise the director reasonably believes are matters (i) within the particular person's professional or expert competence or (ii) as to which the particular person merits confidence; or

(3)   a board committee of which the director is not a member if the director reasonably believes the committee merits confidence.

OFFICIAL COMMENT

Section 8.30 sets standards of conduct for directors that focus on the manner in which directors make their decisions, not the correctness of the decisions made. Section 8.30 should be read in light of the basic role of directors set forth in section 8.01(b), which provides that the "business and affairs of a corporation shall be managed by or under the direction and subject to the oversight of the board of directors," as supplemented by various provisions of the Act assigning specific powers or responsibilities to the board. The standards of conduct for directors established by section 8.30 are analogous to those generally articulated by courts in evaluating director conduct, often referred to as the duties of care and loyalty.

Section 8.30 addresses standards of conduct—the level of performance expected of directors undertaking the role and responsibilities of the office of director. The section does not address the liability of a director, although exposure to liability may result from a failure to honor the standards of conduct required to be observed. The issue of director liability is addressed in sections 8.31 and 8.32. Section 8.30 does, however, play an important role in evaluating a director's conduct and the effectiveness of board action. It has relevance in assessing, under section 8.31, the reasonableness of a director's belief. Similarly, it has relevance in assessing a director's timely attention to appropriate inquiry when particular facts and circumstances of significant concern materialize. It also serves as a frame of reference for determining, under section 8.32(a), liability for an unlawful distribution. Finally, section 8.30 compliance may influence a court's analysis where injunctive relief against a transaction is being sought. Directors act both individually and collectively as a board in performing their functions and discharging their duties. Section 8.30 addresses actions in both capacities.

Under the standards of section 8.30, the board may delegate or assign to appropriate officers or employees of the corporation the authority or duty to exercise powers that the law does not require the board to retain. Because the directors are entitled to rely on these persons absent knowledge making reliance unwarranted, the directors will not be in breach of the standards under section 8.30 as a result of their delegatees' actions or omissions so long as the board acted in good faith and complied with the other standards of conduct set forth in section 8.30 in delegating responsibility and, where appropriate, monitoring performance of the duties delegated. In addition, subsections (d), (e) and (f) permit a director to rely on enumerated third parties for specified purposes, although reliance is prohibited when a director has knowledge that makes reliance unwarranted. Section 8.30(a)'s standards of good faith and reasonable belief in the best interests of the corporation also apply to a director's reliance under subsections (d), (e) and (f).

1. *Section 8.30(a)*

Section 8.30(a) establishes the basic standards of conduct for all directors and its mandate governs all aspects of directors' conduct, including the requirements in other subsections. It includes concepts courts have used in defining the duty of loyalty. Two of the phrases used in section 8.30(a) deserve further comment:

- The phrase "reasonably believes" is both subjective and objective in character. Its first level of analysis is geared to what the particular director, acting in good faith, actually believes—not what objective analysis would lead another director (in a like position and acting in similar circumstances) to conclude. The second level of analysis is focused specifically on "reasonably." Although a director has wide discretion in gathering information and reaching conclusions, whether a director's belief is reasonable (*i.e.,* could—not would—a reasonable person in a like position and acting in similar circumstances, taking into account that director's knowledge and experience, have arrived at that belief) ultimately involves an overview that is objective in character.

- The phrase "best interests of the corporation" is key to an understanding of a director's duties. The term "corporation" is a surrogate for the business enterprise as well as a frame of reference encompassing the shareholder body. In determining the corporation's "best interests," the director has wide discretion in deciding how to weigh near-term opportunities versus long-term benefits as well as in making judgments where the interests of various groups of shareholders or other corporate constituencies may differ.

Section 8.30 operates as a "baseline" principle governing director conduct in circumstances uncomplicated by self-interest. The Act recognizes, however, that directors' personal interests may not always align with the corporation's best interests and provides procedures by which situations and transactions involving conflicts of interest can be processed. See subchapter D (derivative proceedings) of chapter 7 and subchapters E (indemnification and advance for expenses), F (directors' conflicting interest transactions), and G (business opportunities) of this chapter 8. Those procedures generally contemplate that the interested director will provide appropriate disclosure and will not be involved in taking action on the matter giving rise to the conflict of interest.

2. *Section 8.30(b)*

Section 8.30(b) establishes a general standard of care for directors in the context of their dealing with the board's decision-making and oversight functions. Although certain aspects will involve individual conduct (*e.g.,* preparation for meetings), these functions are generally performed by the board of directors through collective action, as recognized by the reference in subsection (b) to board and committee "members" and "their duties." In contrast with section 8.30(a)'s individual conduct mandate, section 8.30(b) has a two-fold thrust: it provides a standard of conduct for individual action and, more broadly, it states a conduct obligation—"shall discharge their duties"—concerning the degree of care to be used collectively by the directors when performing those functions. The standard is not what care a particular director might believe appropriate in the circumstances but what a person—in a like position and acting under similar circumstances—would reasonably believe to be appropriate. Thus, the degree of care that directors should employ under section 8.30(b) involves an objective standard.

The process by which a director becomes informed, in carrying out the decision-making and oversight functions, will vary. The directors' decision-making function is reflected in various sections of the Act, including: the issuance of shares (section 6.21); distributions (section 6.40); dismissal of derivative proceedings (section 7.44); indemnification (section 8.55); conflict of interest transaction authorization (section 8.62); articles of incorporation amendments (sections 10.02 and 10.03); bylaw amendments (section 10.20); mergers and share exchanges (section 11.04); asset dispositions (section 12.02); and dissolution (section 14.02). The directors' oversight function is established under section 8.01. In discharging the section 8.01 duties associated with the board's oversight function, the standard of care entails primarily a requirement of attention. In contrast with the board's decision-making function, which generally involves informed action at a point in time, the oversight function is concerned with a continuum and the attention of the directors accordingly involves participatory performance over a period of time.

Several of the phrases chosen to define the standard of conduct in section 8.30(b) deserve specific mention:

- The phrase "becoming informed," in the context of the decision—making function, refers to the process of gaining sufficient familiarity with the background facts and circumstances to make an informed judgment. Unless the circumstances would permit a reasonable director to conclude that he or she is already sufficiently informed, the standard of care requires every director to take steps to become informed about the background facts and circumstances before taking action on the matter at hand. The process typically involves review of written materials provided before or at the meeting and attention to or participation in the deliberations leading up to a vote. In addition to considering information and data on which a director is expressly entitled to rely under section 8.30(e), "becoming informed" can also involve consideration of information and data generated by other persons, for example, review of industry studies or research articles prepared by third parties. It can also involve direct communications, outside of the boardroom, with members of management or other directors. There is no one way for "becoming informed," and both the method and measure—"how to" and "how much"—are matters of reasonable judgment for the director to exercise.

- The phrase "devoting attention," in the context of the oversight function, refers to considering such matters as the corporation's information and reporting systems generally and not to an independent investigation into particular system inadequacies or noncompliance. Although directors typically give attention to future plans and trends as well as current activities, they should not be expected to anticipate any particular problems which the corporation may face except in those circumstances where something has occurred to make it obvious to the board that the corporation should be addressing a particular problem. The standard of care associated with the oversight function involves gaining assurances from management and advisers that appropriate systems have been established, such as those concerned with legal compliance, risk assessment or internal controls. Such assurances also should cover establishment of ongoing monitoring of the systems in place, with appropriate follow-up responses when alerted to the issues requiring attention.

- The reference to "person," without embellishment, is intended to avoid implying any qualifications, such as specialized expertise or experience requirements, beyond the basic attributes of common sense, practical wisdom, and informed judgment (however, see the last bullet below).

- The phrase "reasonably believe appropriate" refers to the array of possible options that a person possessing the basic attributes of common sense, practical wisdom and informed judgment would recognize to be available, in terms of the degree of care that might be appropriate, and from which a choice by such person would be made. The measure of care that such person might determine to be appropriate, in a given instance, would normally involve a selection from the range of options and any choice within the realm of reason would be an appropriate decision under the standard of care called for under section 8.30(b). However, a decision that is so removed from the realm of reason, or is so unreasonable, that it falls outside the permissible bounds of sound discretion, and thus is an abuse of discretion, will not satisfy the standard.

- The phrase "in a like position" recognizes that the "care" under consideration is that which would be used by the "person" if he or she were a director of the particular corporation.

- The combined phrase "in a like position . . . under similar circumstances" is intended to recognize that (i) the nature and extent of responsibilities will vary, depending upon such factors as the size, complexity, urgency, and location of activities carried on by the particular corporation, (ii) decisions must be made on the basis of the information known to the directors without the benefit of hindsight, and (iii) the special background, qualifications, and oversight responsibilities of a particular director may be relevant in evaluating that director's compliance with the standard of care.

3. Section 8.30(c)

A requirement to disclose to other directors information that a director knows to be material to the decision-making or oversight functions of the board of directors or a board committee is implicit in the standards of conduct set forth in sections 8.30(a) and (b), but section 8.30(c) makes this explicit. Thus, for example, when a member of the board of directors knows information that the director recognizes is material to a decision by the board but is not known to the other directors, the director is obligated to disclose that information to the other members of the board. Such disclosure can occur through direct statements in meetings of the board, or by any other timely means, including, for example, communicating the information to the chairman of the board or the chairman of a committee, or to the corporation's general counsel, and requesting that the recipient inform the other board or committee members of the information.

Section 8.30(c) recognizes that a duty of confidentiality to a third party can override a director's obligation to share with other directors information pertaining to a current corporate matter. In some circumstances, a duty of confidentiality to a third party may even prohibit disclosure of the nature or the existence of the duty itself. Ordinarily, however, a director who withholds material information based on a reasonable belief that a duty of confidentiality to a third party prohibits disclosure should advise the other directors of the existence and nature of that duty. Under the standards of conduct set forth in section 8.30(a), the withholding of material information may, depending on the nature of the material information and of the matter before the board of directors or a board committee, require that a director abstain or recuse himself or herself from all or a portion of the other directors' deliberation or vote on the matter to which the undisclosed information is material, or even resign as a director. See Official Comment to section 8.62.

In connection with a director's conflicting interest transaction, the required disclosure (as defined in section 8.60) that must be made under section 8.62(a) and the exceptions to the required disclosure in that context under section 8.62(b) have elements that parallel the disclosure obligation of directors under section 8.30(c). The demands of section 8.62, however, are more detailed and specific. They apply to just one situation—a director's conflicting interest transaction—while the requirements of section 8.30(c) apply generally to all other decision-making and oversight functions. For example, the specific requirements of section 8.62(a)(1) for deliberation and a vote outside the presence of the conflicted director are not imposed universally for all decision-making matters or for oversight matters that do not involve decisions. Although they may be different from the generally applicable provisions of section 8.30(c), the specific provisions of subchapter 8F control and are exclusive with respect to director conflicting interest transactions.

The requirement that a director disclose information to other directors as set forth in section 8.30(c) is different from any common law duty the board may have to cause the corporation to make disclosures to shareholders under certain circumstances. The Act does not seek to codify such a duty of disclosure, but leaves its existence and scope, the circumstances for its application, and the consequences of any failure to satisfy it, to be developed by courts on a case-by-case basis.

4. Section 8.30(d)

The delegation of authority and responsibility described in section 8.30(d) may take a variety of forms, including (i) formal action through a board resolution, (ii) implicit action through the election of corporate officers (*e.g.*, chief financial officer or controller) or the appointment of corporate managers (*e.g.*, credit manager), or (iii) informal action through a course of conduct (*e.g.*, involvement through corporate officers and managers in the management of a significant 50%-owned joint venture). Under section 8.30(d), a director may properly rely on those to whom authority has been delegated pursuant to section 8.30(d) respecting particular matters calling for specific action or attention in connection with the directors' decision-making function as well as matters on the board's continuing agenda, such as legal compliance and internal controls, in connection with the directors' oversight function. Delegation should be carried out in accordance with the standard of care set forth in section 8.30(b).

By identifying those persons upon whom a director may rely in connection with the discharge of duties, section 8.30(d) does not limit the ability of directors to delegate their powers under section 8.01(b) except where delegation is expressly prohibited by the Act or otherwise by applicable law. See section 8.25 and its Official Comment for discussion of delegation to committees of the authority of the board under section 8.01. By employing the concept of delegation, the Act does not limit the ability of directors to establish baseline principles as to management responsibilities. Specifically, section 8.01(b) provides that "all corporate powers shall be exercised by or under the authority of" the board, and a basic board function involves the allocation of management responsibilities and the related assignment (or delegation) of corporate powers. For example, a board can properly decide to retain a third party to assume responsibility for the administration of designated aspects of risk management for the corporation (*e.g.*, health insurance or disability claims).

Although the board of directors may delegate the authority or duty to perform one or more of its functions, delegation and reliance under section 8.30(d) may not alone constitute compliance with sections 8.30(a) and (b) and the action taken by the delegatee may not alone satisfy the directors or a noncommittee board member's section 8.01 responsibilities. On the other hand, failure of the board committee or the corporate officer or employee performing the function delegated to meet section 8.30(b)'s standard of care will not automatically result in violation by the board of section 8.01. Factors to be considered in determining whether a violation of section 8.01 has occurred will include the care used in the delegation to and supervision over the delegatee, and the amount of knowledge regarding the particular matter which is reasonably available to the particular director. Care in delegation and supervision includes appraisal of the capabilities and diligence of the delegatee in light of the subject and its relative importance and may be satisfied, in the usual case, by receipt of reports concerning the delegatee's activities. The enumeration of these factors is intended to emphasize that directors may not abdicate their responsibilities and avoid accountability simply by delegating authority to others. Rather, a director who is accountable for the acts of delegatees will fulfill the director's duties if the standards contained in section 8.30 are met.

5. Section 8.30(e)

Reliance under section 8.30(e) on a report, statement, opinion, or other information is permitted only if the director has read or heard orally presented the information, opinion, report or statement in question, or took other steps to become generally familiar with it. A director must comply with the general standard of care of section 8.30(b) in making a judgment as to the reliability and competence of the source of information upon which the director proposes to rely or, as appropriate, that it otherwise merits confidence.

6. Section 8.30(f)

In determining whether a corporate officer or employee is "reliable," for purposes of section 8.30(f)(1), the director would typically consider (i) the individual's background experience and scope of responsibility within the corporation in gauging the individual's familiarity and knowledge respecting the subject matter and (ii) the individual's record and reputation for honesty, care and ability in discharging responsibilities which he or she undertakes. In determining whether a person is "competent," the director would normally take into account the same considerations and, if expertise should be relevant, the director would consider the individual's technical skills as well. Recognition of the right of one director to rely on the expertise and experience of another director, in the context of board or committee deliberations, is unnecessary, for reliance on shared experience and wisdom of other board members is an implicit underpinning of collective board conduct. In relying on another member of the board, a director would quite properly take advantage of the colleague's knowledge and experience in becoming informed about the matter at hand before taking action; however, the director would be expected to exercise independent judgment when it comes time to vote.

Advisers on whom a director may rely under section 8.30(f)(2) include not only licensed professionals, such as lawyers, accountants, and engineers, but also those in other fields involving special experience and skills, such as investment bankers, geologists, management consultants, actuaries, and appraisers. The adviser could be an individual or an organization, such as a law or investment banking firm. Reliance on a nonmanagement director, who is specifically engaged (and, normally, additionally compensated) to undertake a special assignment or a particular consulting role, would fall within this outside adviser frame of reference. The concept of "expert competence" embraces a wide variety of qualifications and is not limited to the more precise and narrower recognition of experts under the Securities Act of 1933. In addition, a director may also rely on outside advisers where skills or expertise of a technical nature is not a prerequisite, or where the person's professional or expert competence has not been established, so long as the director reasonably believes the person merits confidence. For example, a board might choose to engage a private investigator to inquire into a particular matter (e.g., follow up on rumors about a senior executive's alleged misconduct) and properly rely on the private investigator's report.

Section 8.30(f)(3) permits reliance on a board committee when it is submitting recommendations for action by the full board of directors as well as when it is performing supervisory or other functions in instances where neither the full board of directors nor the committee takes dispositive action. For example, the compensation committee typically reviews proposals and makes recommendations for action by the full board of directors. There also might be reliance upon an investigation undertaken by a board committee and reported to the full board, which forms the basis for a decision by the board of directors not to take dispositive action. Another example is reliance on a board committee, such as an audit committee with respect to the board's ongoing role of oversight of the accounting and auditing functions of the corporation. In addition, where reliance on information or materials prepared or presented by a board committee is not involved in connection with board action, a director may properly rely on oversight monitoring or dispositive action by a board committee (of which the director is not a member) empowered to act pursuant to authority delegated under section 8.25 or acting with the acquiescence of the board of directors. See the Official Comment to section 8.25. In parallel with section 8.30(f)(2)(ii), the concept of "confidence" is used instead of "competence" to avoid any inference that technical skills are a prerequisite. In the usual case, the appointment of committee members or the reconstitution of the membership of a standing committee (e.g., the audit committee), following an annual shareholders' meeting, would alone manifest the noncommittee members' belief that the committee "merits confidence." Depending on the circumstances, the reliance contemplated by section 8.30(f)(3) is geared to the point in time when the board takes action or the period of time over which a committee is engaged in an oversight function; consequently, the judgment to be made (i.e., whether a committee "merits confidence") will arise at varying points in time. Ordinarily, after making an initial judgment that a committee (of which a director is not a member) merits confidence, a director may continue to rely on that committee so long as the director has no reason to believe that confidence is no longer warranted.

7. *Application to Officers*

Section 8.30 generally deals only with directors. Section 8.42 and its Official Comment explain the extent to which the principles set forth in section 8.30 apply to officers.

§ 8.31   Standards of Liability for Directors

(a)   A director shall not be liable to the corporation or its shareholders for any decision to take or not to take action, or any failure to take any action, as a director, unless the party asserting liability in a proceeding establishes that:

(1)   no defense interposed by the director based on (i) any provision in the articles of incorporation authorized by section 2.02(b)(4) or by section 2.02(b)(6), or (ii) the protection afforded by

section 8.61 (for action taken in compliance with section 8.62 or section 8.63), or (iii) the protection afforded by section 8.70, precludes liability; and

(2)   the challenged conduct consisted or was the result of:

     (i)   action not in good faith; or

     (ii)   a decision

         (A)   which the director did not reasonably believe to be in the best interests of the corporation, or

         (B)   as to which the director was not informed to an extent the director reasonably believed appropriate in the circumstances; or

     (iii)   a lack of objectivity due to the director's familial, financial or business relationship with, or a lack of independence due to the director's domination or control by, another person having a material interest in the challenged conduct

         (A)   which relationship or which domination or control could reasonably be expected to have affected the director's judgment respecting the challenged conduct in a manner adverse to the corporation, and

         (B)   after a reasonable expectation to such effect has been established, the director shall not have established that the challenged conduct was reasonably believed by the director to be in the best interests of the corporation; or

     (iv)   a sustained failure of the director to devote attention to ongoing oversight of the business and affairs of the corporation, or a failure to devote timely attention, by making (or causing to be made) appropriate inquiry, when particular facts and circumstances of significant concern materialize that would alert a reasonably attentive director to the need for such inquiry; or

     (v)   receipt of a financial benefit to which the director was not entitled or any other breach of the director's duties to deal fairly with the corporation and its shareholders that is actionable under applicable law.

(b)   The party seeking to hold the director liable:

(1)   for money damages, shall also have the burden of establishing that:

     (i)   harm to the corporation or its shareholders has been suffered, and

     (ii)   the harm suffered was proximately caused by the director's challenged conduct; or

(2)   for other money payment under a legal remedy, such as compensation for the unauthorized use of corporate assets, shall also have whatever persuasion burden may be called for to establish that the payment sought is appropriate in the circumstances; or

(3)   for other money payment under an equitable remedy, such as profit recovery by or disgorgement to the corporation, shall also have whatever persuasion burden may be called for to establish that the equitable remedy sought is appropriate in the circumstances.

(c)   Nothing contained in this section shall (i) in any instance where fairness is at issue, such as consideration of the fairness of a transaction to the corporation under section 8.61(b)(3), alter the burden of proving the fact or lack of fairness otherwise applicable, (ii) alter the fact or lack of liability of a director under another section of this Act, such as the provisions governing the consequences of an unlawful distribution under section 8.32 or a transactional interest under section 8.61, or (iii) affect any rights to which the corporation or a shareholder may be entitled under another statute of this state or the United States.

OFFICIAL COMMENT

Boards of directors and corporate managers make numerous decisions that involve the balancing of risks and benefits for the enterprise. Although some decisions turn out to have been unwise or the result of a mistake of judgment, it is not reasonable to impose liability for an informed decision made in good faith which with the benefit of hindsight turns out to be wrong or unwise. Therefore, as a general rule, a director is not exposed to personal liability for injury or damage caused by an unwise decision and conduct conforming with the standards of section 8.30 will almost always be protected regardless of the end result. Moreover, the fact that a director's performance fails to meet the standards of section 8.30 does not in itself establish personal liability for damages that the corporation or its shareholders may have suffered as a consequence. Nevertheless, a director can be held liable for misfeasance or nonfeasance in performing his or her duties. Section 8.31 sets forth the standards of liability of directors as distinct from the standards of conduct set forth in section 8.30.

Courts have developed the broad common law concept of the business judgment rule. Although formulations vary, in basic principle, a board of directors generally enjoys a presumption of sound business judgment and its decisions will not be disturbed by a court substituting its own notions of what is or is not sound business judgment if the board's decisions can be attributed to any rational business purpose. It is also presumed that, in making a business decision, directors act in good faith, on an informed basis, and in the honest belief that the action taken is in the best interests of the corporation. The elements of the business judgment rule and the circumstances for its application continue to be developed and refined by courts. Accordingly, it would not be desirable to freeze the concept in a statute. Thus, section 8.31 does not codify the business judgment rule as a whole, although certain of its principal elements, relating to personal liability issues, are reflected in section 8.31(a)(2).

* * * * *

Note on Directors' Liability

A director's exposure to financial liability (*e.g.*, in a lawsuit for money damages suffered by the corporation or its shareholders claimed to have resulted from misfeasance or nonfeasance in connection with the performance of the director's duties) can be analyzed as follows:

- *Articles of incorporation limitations.* If the corporation's articles of incorporation contain a provision eliminating its directors' liability to the corporation or its shareholders for money damages, adopted pursuant to section 2.02(b)(4), there is no liability unless the director's conduct involves one of the exceptions prescribed in that section that preclude the elimination of liability. If the matter involves a director's taking of a business opportunity and an articles of incorporation provision has been adopted under section 2.02(b)(6) eliminating directors' duties with respect to those opportunities, there also will be no liability. See section 2.02 and its Official Comment.

- *Director's conflicting interest transaction safe harbor.* If the matter at issue involves a director's conflicting interest transaction (as defined in section 8.60) and a safe harbor procedure under section 8.61 involving action taken in compliance with section 8.62 or 8.63 has been properly implemented, there is no liability for the interested director arising out of the transaction. See subchapter 8F.

- *Business opportunities safe harbors.* Similarly, if the matter involves a director's pursuit or taking of a business opportunity, there is no liability for that director if (i) an applicable limitation or elimination of any duty to offer that business opportunity has been adopted pursuant to section 2.02(b)(6), or (ii) a safe harbor procedure under section 8.70 has been properly implemented, even if the articles of incorporation contain no provision under section 2.02(b)(6). See subchapter 8G.

- *Business judgment rule.* If a provision in the articles of incorporation adopted pursuant to section 2.02(b)(4) or (6) or a safe harbor procedure under section 8.61 or 8.70 does not shield the director's conduct from liability, the presumptions, standards of judicial review and procedural matters related to the business judgment rule may insulate the director from liability for conduct in connection with a corporate decision.

- *Damages and proximate cause.* If the business judgment rule does not shield the directors' decision-making from liability, as a general rule it must be established that money damages were suffered by the corporation or its shareholders and those damages resulted from and were legally caused by the challenged act or omission of the director.

- *Other liability for money payment.* Aside from a claim for damages, the director may have monetary liability for other reasons, for example, if corporate resources have been used without proper authorization, or a claim for disgorgement of short-swing trading profits under section 16(b) of the Securities Exchange Act of 1934.

- *Equitable profit recovery or disgorgement.* An equitable remedy compelling the disgorgement of the director's improper financial gain or entitling the corporation to profit recovery, where directors' duties have been breached, may require the payment of money by the director to the corporation.

- *Corporate indemnification.* If the director is monetarily liable, the director may be indemnified by the corporation for any payments made and expenses incurred, depending upon the circumstances. See subchapter 8E.

- *Insurance.* To the extent that corporate indemnification is not available, the director may be reimbursed for the money damages for which the director is accountable, together with proceeding-related expenses, if the claim and grounds for liability come within the coverage under directors' and officers' liability insurance that has been purchased by the corporation as authorized under section 8.57.

* * * * *

1. *Section 8.31(a)*

A. SECTION 8.31(A)(1)—AFFIRMATIVE DEFENSES

Under section 8.31(a)(1), if a provision in the articles of incorporation (i) (adopted pursuant to section 2.02(b)(4)) shelters the director from liability for money damages, or (ii) (adopted pursuant to section 2.02(b)(6)) limits or eliminates any duty to offer the particular business opportunity to the corporation, or if a safe harbor procedure under sections 8.61(b)(1) or (b)(2) or section 8.70(a)(1) shelters the director's conduct in connection with a conflicting interest transaction or the pursuit or taking of a business opportunity, and such defense applies to all claims in plaintiff's complaint, there is no need to consider further the application of section 8.31's standards of liability. In that event, the court would presumably grant the defendant director's motion for dismissal or summary judgment (or the equivalent) and the proceeding would be ended. If the defense applies to some but not all of plaintiff's claims, dismissal or summary judgment would presumably be granted with respect to those claims. Termination of the proceeding or dismissal of claims on the basis of a provision in the articles of incorporation or a safe harbor procedure will not automatically follow, however, if the party challenging the director's conduct can assert any of the valid bases for contesting the availability of the liability shelter. Absent such a challenge, the relevant shelter provision is self-executing and the individual director's exoneration from liability is automatic. Further, under both sections 8.61 and 8.70, the directors approving the conflicting interest transaction or approving a director's taking of the business opportunity will presumably be protected as well, because compliance with the relevant standards of conduct under section 8.30 is important for their action to be effective and because, as noted above, conduct meeting section 8.30's standards will almost always be protected.

If a claim of liability arising out of a challenged act or omission of a director is not resolved and disposed of under section 8.31(a)(1), section 8.31(a)(2) provides the basis for evaluating whether the conduct in question can be challenged. One of the elements in section 8.31(a)(2) must be established for a director to have liability under section 8.31.

B. SECTION 8.31(A)(2)(I)—GOOD FAITH

It is a basic standard under section 8.31(a)(2)(i) that a director's conduct in performing his or her duties be in good faith. If a director's conduct can be successfully challenged pursuant to other clauses of section 8.31(a)(2), there is a substantial likelihood that the conduct in question will also present an issue of good faith implicating section 8.31(a)(2)(i). Similarly, if section 8.31(a)(2) included only subsection (i), much of the conduct with which the other clauses are concerned could still be considered under that subsection, on the basis that such conduct evidenced the director's lack of good faith. Where conduct has not been found deficient on other grounds, decision-making outside the bounds of reasonable judgment can give rise to an inference of bad faith. That form of conduct, sometimes characterized as "reckless indifference" or "deliberate disregard," giving rise to an inference of bad faith can also raise a question whether the director could have reasonably believed that the best interests of the corporation would be served. These issues could arise, for example, in approval of conflicting interest transactions. See the Official Comment to section 8.61.

C.   SECTION 8.31(A)(2)(II)—REASONABLE BELIEF

Liability under section 8.31(a)(2)(ii) turns on a director's reasonable belief with respect to the nature of his or her decision and the degree to which he or she has become informed. In each case, the director must have an actual subjective belief and, so long as it is his or her honest and good faith belief, a director has wide discretion. There is also an objective element to be met, in that the director's belief must also be reasonable. The inquiry is similar to that in section 8.30(a)—could a reasonable person in a like position and acting in similar circumstances have arrived at that belief? In the rare case where a decision respecting the corporation's best interests is so removed from the realm of reason (*e.g.,* corporate waste), or a belief as to the sufficiency of the director's preparation to make an informed judgment is so unreasonable as to fall outside the permissible bounds of sound discretion (*e.g.,* if the director has undertaken no preparation and is completely uninformed), the director's judgment will not be sustained.

D.   SECTION 8.31(A)(2)(III)—LACK OF OBJECTIVITY OR INDEPENDENCE

If the matter at issue involves a director's transactional interest, such as a "director's conflicting interest transaction" in which a "related person" is involved (see section 8.60), it will be governed by section 8.61; otherwise, a lack of objectivity due to a relationship's influence on the director's judgment will be evaluated, in the context of the pending challenge of director conduct, under section 8.31. If the matter at issue involves lack of independence, the proof of domination or control and its influence on the director's judgment will typically entail different (and perhaps more convincing) evidence than what may be involved in a lack of objectivity case. The variables are manifold, and the facts must be sorted out and weighed on a case-by-case basis. For example, the closeness or nature of the relationship with the person allegedly exerting influence on the director could be a factor. If the director is required under section 8.31(a)(2)(iii)(B) to establish that the action taken by him or her was reasonably believed to be in the best interests of the corporation, the inquiry will involve the elements of actual subjective belief and objective reasonableness similar to those found in section 8.31(a)(2)(ii) and section 8.30(a).

To call into question the director's objectivity or independence on the basis of a person's relationship with, or exertion of dominance over, the director, the person must have a material interest in the challenged conduct. In the typical case, analysis of another's interest would first consider the materiality of the transaction or conduct at issue—in most cases, any transaction or other action involving the attention of the board of directors or a board committee will cross the materiality threshold, but not always—and would then consider the materiality of that person's interest in the matter. The possibility that a director's judgment would be adversely affected by another's interest in a transaction or conduct that is not material, or another's immaterial interest in a transaction or conduct, is sufficiently remote that it should not be made subject to judicial review.

In situations where there may be a lack of objectivity, domination, a conflict of interest or divided loyalty, or even where there may be grounds for the issue to be raised, the better course to follow where board or committee action is required is usually for the director to disclose the facts and circumstances posing the possible issue, and then to withdraw from the meeting (or, in the alternative, to abstain from the deliberations and voting). The board members free of any possible taint may then take appropriate action as contemplated by section 8.30 (or section 8.61 if applicable). If this course is followed, the director's conduct respecting the matter in question should be beyond challenge.

E.   SECTION 8.31(A)(2)(IV)—FAILURE TO DEVOTE ATTENTION

The director's role involves two fundamental components: the decision-making function and the oversight function. In contrast with the decision-making function, which generally involves action taken at a point in time, the oversight function under section 8.01(b) involves ongoing monitoring of the corporation's business and affairs over a period of time. Although the facts will be outcome-determinative, deficient conduct involving a sustained failure to exercise oversight—where found actionable—has typically been characterized by the courts in terms of abdication and continued neglect by a director to devote attention, not a brief distraction or temporary interruption. Also embedded in the oversight function is the need to inquire when suspicions are aroused. This need to inquire is not a component of ongoing oversight, and does not entail proactive vigilance, but arises under section 8.31(a)(2)(iv) when, and only when, particular facts and circumstances of material concern (*e.g.*, evidence of embezzlement at a high level or the discovery of significant inventory shortages) surface.

F. SECTION 8.31(A)(2)(V)—IMPROPER FINANCIAL BENEFIT AND OTHER BREACHES OF DUTIES

Subchapter 8F deals in detail with directors' transactional interests. Its coverage of those interests is exclusive and its safe harbor procedures for director's conflicting interest transactions (as defined)—providing shelter from legal challenges based on interest conflicts, when properly observed—will establish a director's entitlement to any financial benefit gained from the transactional event. A director's conflicting interest transaction that is not protected by the fairness standard set forth in section 8.61(b)(3), pursuant to which the conflicted director may establish the transaction to have been fair to the corporation, would often involve receipt of a financial benefit to which the director was not entitled (*i.e.*, the transaction was not "fair" to the corporation). Unauthorized use of corporate assets, such as aircraft or hotel suites, would also provide a basis for the proper challenge of a director's conduct. There can be other forms of improper financial benefit not involving a transaction with the corporation or use of its facilities, such as where a director profits from unauthorized use of proprietary information.

There is no materiality threshold that applies to a financial benefit to which a director is not properly entitled. The Act observes this principle in several places, for example, the exception to liability elimination prescribed in section 2.02(b)(4)(i) and the indemnification restriction in section 8.51(d)(2), as well as the liability standard in section 8.31(a)(2)(v).

The second clause of section 8.31(a)(2)(v) is, in part, a catchall provision that implements the intention to make section 8.31 a generally inclusive provision but, at the same time, to recognize the existence of other breaches of common-law principles that can give rise to liability for directors. As developed in the case law, these actionable breaches may include unauthorized use of corporate property or information (which as noted above, might also be characterized as receipt of an improper financial benefit), unfair competition with the corporation or the taking of a corporate opportunity. In the case of corporate opportunity, if the director is alleged to have wrongfully diverted a business opportunity as to which the corporation had a prior right, the Act provides two possible safe harbors. First, any duty to offer the business opportunity to the corporation may have been limited or eliminated pursuant to a provision in the articles of incorporation authorized by section 2.02(b)(6). Second, section 8.70(a)(1) provides a safe harbor procedure for a director who wishes to pursue or take advantage of a business opportunity, regardless of whether such opportunity would be characterized as a "corporate opportunity" under existing case law. Note that section 8.70(b) provides that the fact that a director did not employ the safe harbor procedure of section 8.70(a)(1) does not create an implication that the opportunity should have first been presented to the corporation or alter the burden of proof otherwise applicable to establish a breach of the director's duty to the corporation.

2. Section 8.31(b)

Whether a corporation or its shareholders have suffered harm and whether a particular director's conduct was the proximate cause of that harm may be affected by the collective nature of board action. Proper performance of the relevant duty through the action taken by the director's colleagues can overcome the consequences of his or her deficient conduct. For example, where a director's conduct can be challenged under section 8.31(a)(2)(ii)(B) by reason of having been uninformed about the decision or not reading the materials distributed before the meeting, or arriving late at the board meeting just in time for the vote but, nonetheless, voting in favor solely because the others were in favor—the favorable action by a quorum of properly informed directors would ordinarily protect the director against liability, either because there was no harm or the offending director's actions were not the proximate cause of the harm. Although the concept of "proximate cause" is a term of art that is basic to tort law, for purposes of section 8.31(b)(1), a useful approach for the concept's application would be that the challenged conduct must have been a "substantial factor in producing the harm."

3.   Section 8.31(c)

Section 8.31(c) expressly disclaims any shift of the burden of proof otherwise applicable where the question of the fairness of a transaction or other challenged conduct is at issue. This is the case whether the question of fairness arises under another section of the Act, such as section 8.61, under existing case law, under a judicial requirement in a particular instance or otherwise. Similarly, section 8.31 does not affect liability under other sections of the Act. It also does not foreclose any rights of the corporation or its shareholders under other laws, for example, rights of shareholders or the corporation under applicable federal securities laws. In addition, directors can have liability to persons other than the corporation and its shareholders, such as liability to employee benefit plan participants and beneficiaries (who may or may not be shareholders), if the directors are determined to be fiduciaries under other applicable laws, to government agencies for regulatory violations or to individuals claiming damages for injury governed by tort-law concepts (*e.g.*, libel or slander). Section 8.31 is not intended to change the standards applicable under these other laws or legal principles.

§ 8.32   Directors' Liability for Unlawful Distributions

(a)   A director who votes for or assents to a distribution in excess of what may be authorized and made pursuant to section 6.40(a) or 14.09(a) is personally liable to the corporation for the amount of the distribution that exceeds what could have been distributed without violating section 6.40(a) or 14.09(a) if the party asserting liability establishes that when taking the action the director did not comply with section 8.30.

(b)   A director held liable under subsection (a) for an unlawful distribution is entitled to:

(1)   contribution from every other director who could be held liable under subsection (a) for the unlawful distribution; and

(2)   recoupment from each shareholder of the pro-rata portion of the amount of the unlawful distribution the shareholder accepted, knowing the distribution was made in violation of section 6.40(a) or 14.09(a).

(c)   A proceeding to enforce:

(1)   the liability of a director under subsection (a) is barred unless it is commenced within two years after the date (i) on which the effect of the distribution was measured under section 6.40(e) or (g), (ii) as of which the violation of section 6.40(a) occurred as the consequence of disregard of a restriction in the articles of incorporation, or (iii) on which the distribution of assets to shareholders under section 14.09(a) was made; or

(2)   contribution or recoupment under subsection (b) is barred unless it is commenced within one year after the liability of the claimant has been finally adjudicated under subsection (a).

Subchapter D.   Officers

§ 8.40   Officers

(a)   A corporation has the officers described in its bylaws or appointed by the board of directors in accordance with the bylaws.

(b)   The board of directors may elect individuals to fill one or more offices of the corporation. An officer may appoint one or more officers if authorized by the bylaws or the board of directors.

(c)   The bylaws or the board of directors shall assign to an officer responsibility for maintaining and authenticating the records of the corporation required to be kept under section 16.01(a).

(d)   The same individual may simultaneously hold more than one office in a corporation.

§ 8.41 Functions of Officers

Each officer has the authority and shall perform the functions set forth in the bylaws or, to the extent consistent with the bylaws, the functions prescribed by the board of directors or by direction of an officer authorized by the board of directors to prescribe the functions of other officers.

§ 8.42 Standards of Conduct for Officers

(a) An officer, when performing in such capacity, has the duty to act:

(1) in good faith;

(2) with the care that a person in a like position would reasonably exercise under similar circumstances; and

(3) in a manner the officer reasonably believes to be in the best interests of the corporation.

(b) The duty of an officer includes the obligation:

(1) to inform the superior officer to whom, or the board of directors or the board committee to which, the officer reports of information about the affairs of the corporation known to the officer, within the scope of the officer's functions, and known to the officer to be material to such superior officer, board or committee; and

(2) to inform his or her superior officer, or another appropriate person within the corporation, or the board of directors, or a board committee, of any actual or probable material violation of law involving the corporation or material breach of duty to the corporation by an officer, employee, or agent of the corporation, that the officer believes has occurred or is likely to occur.

(c) In discharging his or her duties, an officer who does not have knowledge that makes reliance unwarranted is entitled to rely on:

(1) the performance of properly delegated responsibilities by one or more employees of the corporation whom the officer reasonably believes to be reliable and competent in performing the responsibilities delegated; or

(2) information, opinions, reports or statements, including financial statements and other financial data, prepared or presented by one or more employees of the corporation whom the officer reasonably believes to be reliable and competent in the matters presented or by legal counsel, public accountants, or other persons retained by the corporation as to matters involving skills or expertise the officer reasonably believes are matters (i) within the particular person's professional or expert competence or (ii) as to which the particular person merits confidence.

(d) An officer shall not be liable to the corporation or its shareholders for any decision to take or not to take action, or any failure to take any action, as an officer, if the duties of the office are performed in compliance with this section. Whether an officer who does not comply with this section shall have liability will depend in such instance on applicable law, including those principles of section 8.31 that have relevance.

OFFICIAL COMMENT

Under section 8.42(a), an officer, when performing in such officer's official capacity, has to meet standards of conduct generally specified for directors under section 8.30. This section is not intended to modify, diminish or qualify the duties or standards of conduct that may be imposed upon specific officers by other law or regulation.

Common law has generally recognized a duty on the part of officers and key employees to disclose to their superiors material information relevant to the affairs of the corporation. This duty is implicit in, and embraced under, the broader standard of section 8.42(a), but section 8.42(b) sets forth this disclosure obligation explicitly. Section 8.42(b)(1) specifies that business information shall be transmitted through the officer's regular reporting channels. Section 8.42(b)(2) specifies the reporting responsibility differently with respect to actual or probable material violations of law or material breaches of duty. The use of the term "appropriate" in subsection (b)(2) accommodates any normative standard that the corporation may have prescribed for reporting potential violations of law or duty to a specified person, such as an ombudsperson, ethics officer, internal auditor, general counsel or the like, as well as situations where there is no designated person but the officer's immediate superior is not appropriate (for example, because the officer believes that individual is complicit in the unlawful activity or breach of duty).

Section 8.42(b)(1) should not be interpreted so broadly as to discourage efficient delegation of functions. It addresses the flow of information to the board of directors and to superior officers necessary to enable them to perform their decision-making and oversight functions. See the Official Comment to section 8.31. The officer's duties under subsection (b) may not be negated by agreement; however, their scope under section 8.42(b)(1) may be shaped by prescribing the scope of an officer's functional responsibilities.

With respect to the duties under section 8.42(b)(2), codes of conduct or codes of ethics may prescribe the circumstances in which and mechanisms by which officers and employees may discharge their duty to report material information to superior officers or the board of directors, or to other designated persons.

The term "material" modifying violations of law or breaches of duty in section 8.42(b)(2) denotes a qualitative as well as quantitative standard. It relates not only to the potential direct financial impact on the corporation, but also to the nature of the violation or breach. For example, an embezzlement of $10,000, or even less, would be material because of the seriousness of the offense, even though the amount involved would ordinarily not be material to the financial position or results of operations of the corporation.

The duty under section 8.42(b)(2) is triggered by an officer's subjective belief that a material violation of law or breach of duty actually or probably has occurred or is likely to occur. This duty is not triggered by objective knowledge concepts, such as whether the officer should have concluded that such misconduct was occurring. The subjectivity of the trigger under subsection (b)(2), however, does not excuse officers from their obligations under subsection (a) to act in good faith and with due care in the performance of the functions assigned to them, including oversight duties within their respective areas of responsibility. There may be occasions when the principles applicable under section 8.30(c) limiting the duty of disclosure by directors where a duty of confidentiality is overriding may also apply to officers. See the Official Comment to section 8.30(c).

An officer's ability to rely on others in meeting the standards prescribed in section 8.42 may be more limited, depending upon the circumstances of the particular case, than the measure and scope of reliance permitted a director under section 8.30, in view of the greater obligation the officer may have to be familiar with the affairs of the corporation. The proper delegation of responsibilities by an officer, separate and apart from the exercise of judgment as to the delegatee's reliability and competence, is concerned with the procedure employed. This will involve, in the usual case, sufficient communication such that the delegatee understands the scope of the assignment and, in turn, manifests to the officer a willingness and commitment to undertake its performance. The entitlement to rely upon employees assumes that a delegating officer will maintain a sufficient level of communication with the officer's subordinates to fulfill his or her supervisory responsibilities. The definition of "employee" in section 1.40 includes an officer; accordingly, section 8.42 contemplates the delegation of responsibilities to other officers as well as to non-officer employees.

Although under section 8.42(d), performance meeting that section's standards of conduct will eliminate an officer's exposure to any liability to the corporation or its shareholders, failure by an officer to meet that section's standards will not automatically result in liability. Deficient performance of duties by an officer, depending upon the facts and circumstances, will normally be dealt with through intracorporate disciplinary procedures, such as reprimand, compensation adjustment, delayed promotion, demotion or discharge. These procedures may be subject to (and limited by) the terms of an officer's employment agreement. See section 8.44.

In some cases, failure to observe relevant standards of conduct can give rise to an officer's liability to the corporation or its shareholders. A court review of challenged conduct will involve an evaluation of the particular facts and circumstances in light of applicable law. In this connection, section 8.42(d) recognizes that relevant principles of section 8.31, such as duties to deal fairly with the corporation and its shareholders and the challenger's burden of establishing proximately caused harm, should be taken into account. In addition, the business judgment rule will normally apply to decisions within an officer's discretionary authority. Liability to others can also arise from an officer's own acts or omissions (*e.g.*, violations of law or tort claims) and, in some cases, an officer with supervisory responsibilities can have risk exposure in connection with the acts or omissions of others.

The Official Comment to section 8.30 supplements this Official Comment to the extent that it can be appropriately viewed as generally applicable to officers as well as directors.

§ 8.43 Resignation and Removal of Officers

(a)   An officer may resign at any time by delivering a written notice to the board of directors, or its chair, or to the appointing officer or the secretary. A resignation is effective as provided in section 1.41(i) unless the notice provides for a delayed effectiveness, including effectiveness determined upon a future event or events. If effectiveness of a resignation is stated to be delayed and the board of directors or the appointing officer accepts the delay, the board of directors or the appointing officer may fill the pending vacancy before the delayed effectiveness but the new officer may not take office until the vacancy occurs.

(b)   An officer may be removed at any time with or without cause by: (i) the board of directors; (ii) the appointing officer, unless the bylaws or the board of directors provide otherwise; or (iii) any other officer if authorized by the bylaws or the board of directors.

(c)   In this section, "appointing officer" means the officer (including any successor to that officer) who appointed the officer resigning or being removed.

§ 8.44 Contract Rights of Officers

(a)   The election or appointment of an officer does not itself create contract rights.

(b)   An officer's removal does not affect the officer's contract rights, if any, with the corporation. An officer's resignation does not affect the corporation's contract rights, if any, with the officer.

Subchapter E.   Indemnification and Advance for Expenses

INTRODUCTORY COMMENT

1.   Policy Issues Raised by Indemnification and Advance for Expenses

Indemnification (including advance for expenses) provides financial protection by the corporation for its directors against exposure to expenses and liabilities that may be incurred by them in connection with legal proceedings based on an alleged breach of duty in their service to or on behalf of the corporation.

The concept of indemnification recognizes that there will be situations in which even though the director does not satisfy all of the elements of the standard of conduct set forth in section 8.30(a) or the requirements of some other applicable law, the corporation should nevertheless be permitted (or required) to absorb the economic costs incurred by the director in any ensuing litigation.

Subchapter 8E is an integrated treatment of indemnification and advance for expenses and strikes a balance among important public policies. It would be difficult to persuade responsible persons to serve as directors if they were compelled to bear personally the cost of vindicating the propriety of their conduct in every instance in which it might be challenged. If permitted too broadly, however, indemnification may violate equally basic tenets of public policy. For example, a director who intentionally inflicts harm on the corporation should not expect to receive assistance from the corporation for legal or other expenses and should be required to satisfy from his or her personal assets not only any adverse judgment but also expenses incurred in connection with the proceeding. A similar policy issue is raised in connection with indemnification against liabilities or sanctions imposed under state or federal civil or criminal statutes. A shift of the economic cost of these liabilities from the individual director to the corporation by way of indemnification may in some instances frustrate the public policy of those statutes.

Some of the same policy considerations apply to the indemnification of officers and, in many cases, employees and agents. The indemnification of officers, whose duties are specified in section 8.42, is dealt with separately in section 8.56. The indemnification of employees and agents, whose duties are prescribed by sources of law other than corporation law (e.g., contract and agency law), is beyond the scope of this subchapter. Section 8.58(d), however, makes clear that subchapter E does not limit a corporation's power to indemnify or advance expenses to employees and agents in accordance with applicable law.

2.   Relationship of Indemnification to Other Policies Established in the Act

Indemnification is closely related to the standards of conduct for directors and officers established elsewhere in chapter 8. The structure of the Act is based on the assumption that if a director acts consistently with the standards of conduct described in section 8.30 or with the standards of a liability-limitation provision in the articles of incorporation (as authorized by section 2.02(b)(4)), the director will not have exposure to liability to the corporation or to shareholders and any expenses necessary to establish a defense will be borne by the corporation (under section 8.52). The converse, however, is not necessarily true. The basic standards for indemnification set forth in section 8.51 for a civil action, in the absence of an indemnification provision in the articles of incorporation (as authorized by section 2.02(b)(5)), are good faith and reasonable belief that the conduct was in or not opposed to the best interests of the corporation. In some circumstances, a director or officer may be found to have violated a statutory or common law duty and yet be able to establish eligibility for indemnification under these standards of conduct. In addition, subchapter E permits a director or officer who is held liable for violating a statutory or common law duty, but who does not meet the relevant standard of conduct, to petition a court to order indemnification under section 8.54 if the court determines that it would be fair and reasonable to do so.

§ 8.50   Subchapter Definitions

In this subchapter:

"Corporation" includes any domestic or foreign predecessor entity of a corporation in a merger.

"Director" or "officer" means an individual who is or was a director or officer, respectively, of a corporation or who, while a director or officer of the corporation, is or was serving at the corporation's request as a director, officer, manager, partner, trustee, employee, or agent of another entity or employee benefit plan. A director or officer is considered to be serving an employee benefit plan at the corporation's request if the individual's duties to the corporation also impose duties on, or otherwise involve services by, the individual to the plan or to participants in or beneficiaries of the plan. "Director" or "officer" includes, unless the context requires otherwise, the estate or personal representative of a director or officer.

"Liability" means the obligation to pay a judgment, settlement, penalty, fine (including an excise tax assessed with respect to an employee benefit plan), or expenses incurred with respect to a proceeding.

"Official capacity" means: (i) when used with respect to a director, the office of director in a corporation; and (ii) when used with respect to an officer, as contemplated in section 8.56, the office in a corporation held by the officer. "Official capacity" does not include service for any other domestic or foreign corporation or any joint venture, trust, employee benefit plan, or other entity.

"Party" means an individual who was, is, or is threatened to be made, a defendant or respondent in a proceeding.

"Proceeding" means any threatened, pending, or completed action, suit, or proceeding, whether civil, criminal, administrative, arbitrative, or investigative and whether formal or informal.

§ 8.51   Permissible Indemnification

(a) Except as otherwise provided in this section, a corporation may indemnify an individual who is a party to a proceeding because the individual is a director against liability incurred in the proceeding if:

    (1)

        (i)   the director conducted himself or herself in good faith; and

        (ii)   the director reasonably believed:

           (A)   in the case of conduct in an official capacity, that his or her conduct was in the best interests of the corporation; and

           (B)   in all other cases, that his or her conduct was at least not opposed to the best interests of the corporation; and

        (iii)   in the case of any criminal proceeding, the director had no reasonable cause to believe his or her conduct was unlawful; or

(2)   the director engaged in conduct for which broader indemnification has been made permissible or obligatory under a provision of the articles of incorporation (as authorized by section 2.02(b)(5)).

(b)   A director's conduct with respect to an employee benefit plan for a purpose the director reasonably believed to be in the interests of the participants in, and the beneficiaries of, the plan is conduct that satisfies the requirement of subsection (a)(1)(ii)(B).

(c)   The termination of a proceeding by judgment, order, settlement, or conviction, or upon a plea of nolo contendere or its equivalent, is not, of itself, determinative that the director did not meet the relevant standard of conduct described in this section.

(d)   Unless ordered by a court under section 8.54(a)(3), a corporation may not indemnify a director:

(1)   in connection with a proceeding by or in the right of the corporation, except for expenses incurred in connection with the proceeding if it is determined that the director has met the relevant standard of conduct under subsection (a); or

(2)   in connection with any proceeding with respect to conduct for which the director was adjudged liable on the basis of receiving a financial benefit to which he or she was not entitled, regardless of whether it involved action in the director's official capacity.

§ 8.52   Mandatory Indemnification

A corporation shall indemnify a director who was wholly successful, on the merits or otherwise, in the defense of any proceeding to which the director was a party because he or she was a director of the corporation against expenses incurred by the director in connection with the proceeding.

§ 8.53   Advance for Expenses

(a)   A corporation may, before final disposition of a proceeding, advance funds to pay for or reimburse expenses incurred in connection with the proceeding by an individual who is a party to the proceeding because that individual is a director if the director delivers to the corporation a signed written undertaking of the director to repay any funds advanced if (i) the director is not entitled to mandatory indemnification under section 8.52 and (ii) it is ultimately determined under section 8.54 or section 8.55 that the director is not entitled to indemnification.

(b)   The undertaking required by subsection (a) must be an unlimited general obligation of the director but need not be secured and may be accepted without reference to the financial ability of the director to make repayment.

(c)   Authorizations under this section shall be made:

(1)   by the board of directors:

(i)   if there are two or more qualified directors, by a majority vote of all the qualified directors (a majority of whom shall for such purpose constitute a quorum) or by a majority of the members of a committee consisting solely of two or more qualified directors appointed by such a vote; or

(ii)   if there are fewer than two qualified directors, by the vote necessary for action by the board of directors in accordance with section 8.24(c), in which authorization directors who are not qualified directors may participate; or

(2)   by the shareholders, but shares owned by or voted under the control of a director who at the time is not a qualified director may not be voted on the authorization.

§ 8.54   Court-Ordered Indemnification and Advance for Expenses

(a)   A director who is a party to a proceeding because he or she is a director may apply for indemnification or an advance for expenses to the court conducting the proceeding or to another court of competent jurisdiction. After receipt of an application and after giving any notice it considers necessary, the court shall:

(1)   order indemnification if the court determines that the director is entitled to mandatory indemnification under section 8.52;

(2)   order indemnification or advance for expenses if the court determines that the director is entitled to indemnification or advance for expenses pursuant to a provision authorized by section 8.58(a); or

(3)   order indemnification or advance for expenses if the court determines, in view of all the relevant circumstances, that it is fair and reasonable (i) to indemnify the director, or (ii) to advance expenses to the director, even if, in the case of (i) or (ii), he or she has not met the relevant standard of conduct set forth in section 8.51(a), failed to comply with section 8.53 or was adjudged liable in a proceeding referred to in section 8.51(d)(1) or (d)(2), but if the director was adjudged so liable indemnification shall be limited to expenses incurred in connection with the proceeding.

(b)   If the court determines that the director is entitled to indemnification under subsection (a)(1) or to indemnification or advance for expenses under subsection (a)(2), it shall also order the corporation to pay the director's expenses incurred in connection with obtaining court-ordered indemnification or advance for expenses. If the court determines that the director is entitled to indemnification or advance for expenses under subsection (a)(3), it may also order the corporation to pay the director's expenses to obtain court-ordered indemnification or advance for expenses.

§ 8.55   Determination and Authorization of Indemnification

(a)   A corporation may not indemnify a director under section 8.51 unless authorized for a specific proceeding after a determination has been made that indemnification is permissible because the director has met the relevant standard of conduct set forth in section 8.51.

(b)   The determination shall be made:

(1)   if there are two or more qualified directors, by the board of directors by a majority vote of all the qualified directors (a majority of whom shall for such purpose constitute a quorum), or by a majority of the members of a committee of two or more qualified directors appointed by such a vote;

(2)   by special legal counsel:

(i)   selected in the manner prescribed in subsection (b)(1); or

(ii)   if there are fewer than two qualified directors, selected by the board of directors (in which selection directors who are not qualified directors may participate); or

(3)   by the shareholders, but shares owned by or voted under the control of a director who at the time is not a qualified director may not be voted on the determination.

(c)   Authorization of indemnification shall be made in the same manner as the determination that indemnification is permissible except that if there are fewer than two qualified directors, or if the determination is made by special legal counsel, authorization of indemnification shall be made by those entitled to select special legal counsel under subsection (b)(2)(ii).

§ 8.56   Indemnification of Officers

(a)   A corporation may indemnify and advance expenses under this subchapter to an officer who is a party to a proceeding because he or she is an officer

(1)   to the same extent as a director; and

(2)   if he or she is an officer but not a director, to such further extent as may be provided by the articles of incorporation or the bylaws, or by a resolution adopted or a contract approved by the board of directors or shareholders, except for

(i)   liability in connection with a proceeding by or in the right of the corporation other than for expenses incurred in connection with the proceeding, or

(ii)   liability arising out of conduct that constitutes

(A)   receipt by the officer of a financial benefit to which he or she is not entitled,

(B)   an intentional infliction of harm on the corporation or the shareholders, or

(C)   an intentional violation of criminal law.

(b)   Subsection (a)(2) shall apply to an officer who is also a director if he or she is made a party to the proceeding based on an act or omission solely as an officer.

(c)   An officer who is not a director is entitled to mandatory indemnification under section 8.52, and may apply to a court under section 8.54 for indemnification or an advance for expenses, in each case to the same extent to which a director may be entitled to indemnification or advance for expenses under those sections.

§ 8.57   Insurance

A corporation may purchase and maintain insurance on behalf of an individual who is a director or officer of the corporation, or who, while a director or officer of the corporation, serves at the corporation's request as a director, officer, partner, trustee, employee, or agent of another domestic or foreign corporation or a joint venture, trust, employee benefit plan, or other entity, against liability asserted against or incurred by the individual in that capacity or arising from the individual's status as a director or officer, regardless of whether the corporation would have power to indemnify or advance expenses to the individual against the same liability under this subchapter.

§ 8.58   Variation by Corporate Action; Application of Subchapter

(a)   A corporation may, by a provision in its articles of incorporation or bylaws or in a resolution adopted or a contract approved by the board of directors or shareholders, obligate itself in advance of the act or omission giving rise to a proceeding to provide indemnification in accordance with section 8.51 or advance funds to pay for or reimburse expenses in accordance with section 8.53. Any such obligatory provision shall be deemed to satisfy the requirements for authorization referred to in section 8.53(c) and in section 8.55(c). Any such provision that obligates the corporation to provide indemnification to the fullest extent permitted by law shall be deemed to obligate the corporation to advance funds to pay for or reimburse expenses in accordance with section 8.53 to the fullest extent permitted by law, unless the provision expressly provides otherwise.

(b)   A right of indemnification or to advances for expenses created by this subchapter or under subsection (a) and in effect at the time of an act or omission shall not be eliminated or impaired with respect to such act or omission by an amendment of the articles of incorporation or bylaws or a resolution of the board of directors or shareholders, adopted after the occurrence of such act or omission, unless, in the case of a right created under subsection (a), the provision creating such right and in effect at the time of such act or omission explicitly authorizes such elimination or impairment after such act or omission has occurred.

(c)   Any provision pursuant to subsection (a) shall not obligate the corporation to indemnify or advance expenses to a director of a predecessor of the corporation, pertaining to conduct with respect to the predecessor, unless otherwise expressly provided. Any provision for indemnification or advance for expenses in the articles of incorporation or bylaws, or a resolution of the board of directors or shareholders of a predecessor of the corporation in a merger or in a contract to which the predecessor is a party, existing at the time the merger takes effect, shall be governed by section 11.07(a)(4).

(d)   Subject to subsection (b), a corporation may, by a provision in its articles of incorporation, limit any of the rights to indemnification or advance for expenses created by or pursuant to this subchapter.

(e)   This subchapter does not limit a corporation's power to pay or reimburse expenses incurred by a director or an officer in connection with appearing as a witness in a proceeding at a time when he or she is not a party.

(f)   This subchapter does not limit a corporation's power to indemnify, advance expenses to or provide or maintain insurance on behalf of an employee or agent.

§ 8.59   Exclusivity of Subchapter

A corporation may provide indemnification or advance expenses to a director or an officer only as permitted by this subchapter.

Subchapter F.   Director's Conflicting Interest Transactions

§ 8.60   Subchapter Definitions

In this subchapter:

"Control" (including the term "controlled by") means (i) having the power, directly or indirectly, to elect or remove a majority of the members of the board of directors or other governing body of an entity, whether through the ownership of voting shares or interests, by contract, or otherwise, or (ii) being subject to a majority of the risk of loss from the entity's activities or entitled to receive a majority of the entity's residual returns.

"Director's conflicting interest transaction" means a transaction effected or proposed to be effected by the corporation (or by an entity controlled by the corporation)

(i)   to which, at the relevant time, the director is a party;

(ii)   respecting which, at the relevant time, the director had knowledge and a material financial interest known to the director; or

(iii)   respecting which, at the relevant time, the director knew that a related person was a party or had a material financial interest.

"Fair to the corporation" means, for purposes of section 8.61(b)(3), that the transaction as a whole was beneficial to the corporation, taking into appropriate account whether it was (i) fair in terms of the director's dealings with the corporation, and (ii) comparable to what might have been obtainable in an arm's length transaction, given the consideration paid or received by the corporation.

"Material financial interest" means a financial interest in a transaction that would reasonably be expected to impair the objectivity of the director's judgment when participating in action on the authorization of the transaction.

"Related person" means:

(i)   the individual's spouse;

(ii)   a child, stepchild, grandchild, parent, step parent, grandparent, sibling, step sibling, half sibling, aunt, uncle, niece or nephew (or spouse of any such person) of the individual or of the individual's spouse;

(iii)   a natural person living in the same home as the individual;

(iv)   an entity (other than the corporation or an entity controlled by the corporation) controlled by the individual or any person specified above in this definition;

(v)   a domestic or foreign (a) business or nonprofit corporation (other than the corporation or an entity controlled by the corporation) of which the individual is a director, (b) unincorporated entity of which the individual is a general partner or a member of the governing body, or (c) individual, trust or estate for whom or of which the individual is a trustee, guardian, personal representative or like fiduciary; or

(vi)   a person that is, or an entity that is controlled by, an employer of the individual.

"Relevant time" means (i) the time at which directors' action respecting the transaction is taken in compliance with section 8.62, or (ii) if the transaction is not brought before the board of directors (or a committee) for action under section 8.62, at the time the corporation (or an entity controlled by the corporation) becomes legally obligated to consummate the transaction.

"Required disclosure" means disclosure of (i) the existence and nature of the director's conflicting interest, and (ii) all facts known to the director respecting the subject matter of the transaction that a director free of such conflicting interest would reasonably believe to be material in deciding whether to proceed with the transaction.

§ 8.61   Judicial Action

(a)   A transaction effected or proposed to be effected by the corporation (or by an entity controlled by the corporation) may not be the subject of equitable relief, or give rise to an award of damages or other sanctions against a director of the corporation, in a proceeding by a shareholder or by or in the right of the corporation, on the ground that the director has an interest respecting the transaction, if it is not a director's conflicting interest transaction.

(b)   A director's conflicting interest transaction may not be the subject of equitable relief, or give rise to an award of damages or other sanctions against a director of the corporation, in a proceeding by a shareholder or by or in the right of the corporation, on the ground that the director has an interest respecting the transaction, if:

     (1)   directors' action respecting the transaction was taken in compliance with section 8.62 at any time; or

     (2)   shareholders' action respecting the transaction was taken in compliance with section 8.63 at any time; or

     (3)   the transaction, judged according to the circumstances at the relevant time, is established to have been fair to the corporation.

§ 8.62   Directors' Action

(a)   Directors' action respecting a director's conflicting interest transaction is effective for purposes of section 8.61(b)(1) if the transaction has been authorized by the affirmative vote of a majority (but no fewer than two) of the qualified directors who voted on the transaction, after required disclosure by the conflicted director of information not already known by such qualified directors, or after modified disclosure in compliance with subsection (b), provided that:

     (1)   the qualified directors have deliberated and voted outside the presence of and without the participation by any other director; and

     (2)   where the action has been taken by a board committee, all members of the committee were qualified directors, and either (i) the committee was composed of all the qualified directors on the board of directors or (ii) the members of the committee were appointed by the affirmative vote of a majority of the qualified directors on the board of directors.

(b)   Notwithstanding subsection (a), when a transaction is a director's conflicting interest transaction only because a related person described in clause (v) or (vi) of the definition of "related person" in section 8.60 is a party to or has a material financial interest in the transaction, the conflicted director is not obligated to make required disclosure to the extent that the director reasonably believes that doing so would violate a duty imposed under law, a legally enforceable obligation of confidentiality, or a professional ethics rule, provided that the conflicted director discloses to the qualified directors voting on the transaction:

     (1)   all information required to be disclosed that is not so violative,

     (2)   the existence and nature of the director's conflicting interest, and

     (3)   the nature of the conflicted director's duty not to disclose the confidential information.

(c)   A majority (but no fewer than two) of all the qualified directors on the board of directors, or on the board committee, constitutes a quorum for purposes of action that complies with this section.

(d)   Where directors' action under this section does not satisfy a quorum or voting requirement applicable to the authorization of the transaction by reason of the articles of incorporation or bylaws or a provision of law, independent action to satisfy those authorization requirements shall be taken by the board of directors or a board committee, in which action directors who are not qualified directors may participate.

§ 8.63   Shareholders' Action

(a)   Shareholders' action respecting a director's conflicting interest transaction is effective for purposes of section 8.61(b)(2) if a majority of the votes cast by the holders of all qualified shares are in favor of the transaction after (i) notice to shareholders describing the action to be taken respecting the transaction, (ii) provision to the corporation of the information referred to in subsection (b), and (iii) communication to the shareholders entitled to vote on the transaction of the information that is the subject of required disclosure, to the extent the information is not known by them. In the case of shareholders' action at a meeting, the shareholders entitled to vote shall be determined as of the record date for notice of the meeting.

(b)   A director who has a conflicting interest respecting the transaction shall, before the shareholders' vote, inform the secretary or other officer or agent of the corporation authorized to tabulate votes, in writing, of the number of shares that the director knows are not qualified shares under subsection (c), and the identity of the holders of those shares.

(c)   For purposes of this section: (i) "holder" means and "held by" refers to shares held by a record shareholder, a beneficial shareholder, and an unrestricted voting trust beneficial owner; and (ii) "qualified shares" means all shares entitled to be voted with respect to the transaction except for shares that the secretary or other officer or agent of the corporation authorized to tabulate votes either knows, or under subsection (b) is notified, are held by (A) a director who has a conflicting interest respecting the transaction or (B) a related person of the director (excluding a person described in clause (vi) of the definition of "related person" in section 8.60).

(d)   A majority of the votes entitled to be cast by the holders of all qualified shares constitutes a quorum for purposes of compliance with this section. Subject to the provisions of subsection (e), shareholders' action that otherwise complies with this section is not affected by the presence of holders, or by the voting, of shares that are not qualified shares.

(e)   If a shareholders' vote does not comply with subsection (a) solely because of a director's failure to comply with subsection (b), and if the director establishes that the failure was not intended to influence and did not in fact determine the outcome of the vote, the court may take such action respecting the transaction and the director, and may give such effect, if any, to the shareholders' vote, as the court considers appropriate in the circumstances.

(f)   Where shareholders' action under this section does not satisfy a quorum or voting requirement applicable to the authorization of the transaction by reason of the articles of incorporation or the bylaws or a provision of law, independent action to satisfy those authorization requirements shall be taken by the shareholders, in which action shares that are not qualified shares may participate.

Subchapter G.   Business Opportunities

§ 8.70   Business Opportunities

(a)   If a director or officer pursues or takes advantage of a business opportunity directly, or indirectly through or on behalf of another person, that action may not be the subject of equitable relief, or give rise to an award of damages or other sanctions against the director, officer or other person, in a proceeding by or in the right of the corporation on the ground that the opportunity should have first been offered to the corporation, if

(1)   before the director, officer or other person becomes legally obligated respecting the opportunity the director or officer brings it to the attention of the corporation and either:

(i)   action by qualified directors disclaiming the corporation's interest in the opportunity is taken in compliance with the same procedures as are set forth in section 8.62, or

(ii) shareholders' action disclaiming the corporation's interest in the opportunity is taken in compliance with the procedures set forth in section 8.63,

in either case as if the decision being made concerned a director's conflicting interest transaction, except that, rather than making "required disclosure" as defined in section 8.60, the director or officer shall have made prior disclosure to those acting on behalf of the corporation of all material facts concerning the business opportunity known to the director or officer; or

(2) the duty to offer the corporation the business opportunity has been limited or eliminated pursuant to a provision of the articles of incorporation adopted (and where required, made effective by action of qualified directors) in accordance with section 2.02(b)(6).

(b) In any proceeding seeking equitable relief or other remedies based upon an alleged improper pursuit or taking advantage of a business opportunity by a director or officer, directly, or indirectly through or on behalf of another person, the fact that the director or officer did not employ the procedure described in subsection (a)(1)(i) or (ii) before pursuing or taking advantage of the opportunity shall not create an implication that the opportunity should have been first presented to the corporation or alter the burden of proof otherwise applicable to establish that the director or officer breached a duty to the corporation in the circumstances.

CHAPTER 9

DOMESTICATION AND CONVERSION

INTRODUCTORY COMMENT

This chapter provides procedures by which a domestic corporation may become a foreign corporation or a different form of domestic or foreign entity and, conversely, a foreign corporation or an eligible entity may become a domestic corporation. These procedures are:

- **Domestication.** The procedures in subchapter 9B permit a corporation to change its state of incorporation, thus allowing a domestic corporation to become a foreign corporation or a foreign corporation to become a domestic corporation.

- **Conversion.** The procedures in subchapter 9C permit a domestic corporation to become a domestic or foreign eligible entity and also permit a domestic or foreign eligible entity to become a domestic corporation.

The provisions of this chapter apply only if a domestic corporation is present either immediately before or immediately after a domestication or conversion.

Note on Adoption: Some states may wish to generalize the provisions of this chapter so that they are not limited to transactions involving a domestic business corporation. For example, a state may wish to permit a domestic limited partnership to become a domestic limited liability company. The Model Entity Transactions Act prepared by the Uniform Law Commission is such a generalized statute. Some states have elected to include transactions that are described in chapter 9 as domestications in their definition of conversions and not to refer to domestication separately.

Subchapter A. Preliminary Provisions

§ 9.01 Definitions

As used in this chapter:

"Conversion" means a transaction pursuant to subchapter C.

"Converted entity" means the converting entity as it continues in existence after a conversion.

"Converting entity" means the domestic corporation or eligible entity that approves a plan of conversion pursuant to section 9.32 or the foreign eligible entity that approves a conversion pursuant to the organic law of the eligible entity.

"Domesticated corporation" means the domesticating corporation as it continues in existence after a domestication.

"Domesticating corporation" means the domestic corporation that approves a plan of domestication pursuant to section 9.21 or the foreign corporation that approves a domestication pursuant to the organic law of the foreign corporation.

"Domestication" means a transaction pursuant to subchapter B.

"Protected agreement" means:

      (i)   a document evidencing indebtedness of a domestic corporation or eligible entity and any related agreement in effect immediately before the enactment date;

      (ii)   an agreement that is binding on a domestic corporation or eligible entity immediately before the enactment date;

      (iii) the articles of incorporation or bylaws of a domestic corporation or the organic rules of a domestic eligible entity, in each case in effect immediately before the enactment date; or

      (iv) an agreement that is binding on any of the shareholders, members, interest holders, directors or other governors of a domestic corporation or eligible entity, in their capacities as such, immediately before the enactment date.

For purposes of this definition and sections 9.20 and 9.30, "enactment date" means the first date on which the law of this state authorized a transaction having the effect of a domestication or a conversion, as applicable.

Note on adoption: *When adopting the definition of "protected agreement," a state could consider setting out in the last sentence of the definition the actual dates when domestication and conversion statutes were first enacted in the state so those dates would be apparent on the face of the statute.*

§ 9.02   Excluded Transactions [Optional]

This chapter may not be used to effect a transaction that:

(a)   [converts a company organized on the mutual principle to one organized on the basis of share ownership]; or

(b)   [other examples]

Note on adoption: *A state should use this section to list those situations in which the state has enacted specific legislation governing the domestication or conversion of domestic corporations that engage in particular types of activities or that do business in a regulated industry. Mutual to share conversions (for instance, of an insurance company, bank, savings institution or credit union)) are examples of such transactions.*

§ 9.03   Required Approvals [Optional]

If a domestic or foreign corporation or eligible entity may not be a party to a merger without the approval of the [attorney general], the [department of banking], the [department of insurance] or the [public utility commission], and the applicable statutes or regulations do not specifically deal with transactions under this chapter but do require such approval for mergers, a corporation or eligible entity shall not be a party to a transaction under this chapter without the prior approval of that agency or official.

Note on adoption: *Section 9.03 is an optional provision that should be considered in states where corporations or other entities that conduct regulated activities, such as banking, insurance or the provision of public utility services, are incorporated or organized under general laws instead of under special laws applicable only to entities conducting the regulated activity. If this section is used, the list of officials and agencies should be conformed to the laws of the enacting state.*

§ 9.04 Relationship of Chapter to Other Laws [Optional]

A transaction effected under this chapter may not create or impair a right, duty or obligation of a person under the statutory law of this state other than this chapter relating to a change in control, business combination, control-share acquisition, or similar transaction involving a domesticating or converting domestic corporation, unless the approval of the plan of domestication or conversion is by a vote of the shareholders or the board of directors which would be sufficient to create or impair the right, duty or obligation directly under that law.

Subchapter B. Domestication

§ 9.20 Domestication

(a) By complying with the provisions of this subchapter applicable to foreign corporations, a foreign corporation may become a domestic corporation if the domestication is permitted by the organic law of the foreign corporation.

(b) By complying with the provisions of this subchapter, a domestic corporation may become a foreign corporation pursuant to a plan of domestication if the domestication is permitted by the organic law of the foreign corporation.

(c) The plan of domestication must include:

(1) the name of the domesticating corporation;

(2) the name and jurisdiction of formation of the domesticated corporation;

(3) the manner and basis of reclassifying the shares of the domesticating corporation into shares or other securities, obligations, rights to acquire shares or other securities, cash, other property, or any combination of the foregoing;

(4) the proposed articles of incorporation and bylaws of the domesticated corporation; and

(5) the other terms and conditions of the domestication.

(d) In addition to the requirements of subsection (c), a plan of domestication may contain any other provision not prohibited by law.

(e) The terms of a plan of domestication may be made dependent upon facts objectively ascertainable outside the plan in accordance with section 1.20(k).

(f) If a protected agreement of a domestic domesticating corporation in effect immediately before the domestication becomes effective contains a provision applying to a merger of the corporation and the agreement does not refer to a domestication of the corporation, the provision applies to a domestication of the corporation as if the domestication were a merger until such time as the provision is first amended after the enactment date.

§ 9.21 Action on a Plan of Domestication

In the case of a domestication of a domestic corporation into a foreign jurisdiction, the plan of domestication shall be adopted in the following manner:

(a) The plan of domestication shall first be adopted by the board of directors.

(b) The plan of domestication shall then be approved by the shareholders. In submitting the plan of domestication to the shareholders for approval, the board of directors shall recommend that the shareholders approve the plan, unless (i) the board of directors makes a determination that because of conflicts of interest or other special circumstances it should not make such a recommendation or (ii) section 8.26 applies. If either (i) or (ii) applies, the board shall inform the shareholders of the basis for its so proceeding.

(c) The board of directors may set conditions for approval of the plan of domestication by the shareholders or the effectiveness of the plan of domestication.

(d) If the approval of the shareholders is to be given at a meeting, the corporation shall notify each shareholder, regardless of whether entitled to vote, of the meeting of shareholders at which the plan of domestication is to be submitted for approval. The notice must state that the purpose, or one of the purposes, of the meeting is to consider the plan of domestication and must contain or be accompanied by a copy or summary of the plan. The notice must include or be accompanied by a copy of the articles of incorporation and the bylaws as they will be in effect immediately after the domestication.

(e) Unless the articles of incorporation, or the board of directors acting pursuant to subsection (c), require a greater vote or a greater quorum, approval of the plan of domestication requires (i) the approval of the shareholders at a meeting at which a quorum exists consisting of a majority of the votes entitled to be cast on the plan, and, (ii) except as provided in subsection (f), the approval of each class or series of shares voting as a separate voting group at a meeting at which a quorum of the voting group exists consisting of a majority of the votes entitled to be cast on the plan by that voting group.

(f) The articles of incorporation may expressly limit or eliminate the separate voting rights provided in subsection (e)(ii) as to any class or series of shares, except when the articles of incorporation of the foreign corporation resulting from the domestication include what would be in effect an amendment that would entitle the class or series to vote as a separate group under section 10.04 if it were a proposed amendment of the articles of incorporation of the domestic domesticating corporation.

(g) If as a result of a domestication one or more shareholders of a domestic domesticating corporation would become subject to interest holder liability, approval of the plan of domestication shall require the signing in connection with the domestication, by each such shareholder, of a separate written consent to become subject to such interest holder liability, unless in the case of a shareholder that already has interest holder liability with respect to the domesticating corporation, the terms and conditions of the interest holder liability with respect to the domesticated corporation are substantially identical to those of the existing interest holder liability (other than for changes that eliminate or reduce such interest holder liability).

§ 9.22 Articles of Domestication; Effectiveness

(a) After (i) a plan of domestication of a domestic corporation has been adopted and approved as required by this Act, or (ii) a foreign corporation that is the domesticating corporation has approved a domestication as required under its organic law, articles of domestication shall be signed by the domesticating corporation. The articles must set forth:

(1) the name of the domesticating corporation and its jurisdiction of formation;

(2) the name and jurisdiction of formation of the domesticated corporation; and

(3) if the domesticating corporation is a domestic corporation, a statement that the plan of domestication was approved in accordance with this chapter or, if the domesticating corporation is a foreign corporation, a statement that the domestication was approved in accordance with its organic law.

(b) If the domesticated corporation is a domestic corporation, the articles of domestication must attach articles of incorporation of the domesticated corporation that satisfy the requirements of section 2.02. Provisions that would not be required to be included in restated articles of incorporation may be omitted from the articles of incorporation attached to the articles of domestication.

(c) The articles of domestication shall be delivered to the secretary of state for filing, and shall take effect at the effective date determined in accordance with section 1.23.

(d) If the domesticated corporation is a domestic corporation, the domestication becomes effective when the articles of domestication are effective. If the domesticated corporation is a foreign corporation, the domestication becomes effective on the later of (i) the date and time provided by the organic law of the domesticated corporation, and (ii) when the articles of domestication are effective.

(e)   If the domesticating corporation is a foreign corporation that is registered to do business in this state under chapter 15, its registration statement shall be cancelled automatically when the domestication becomes effective.

§ 9.23   Amendment of Plan of Domestication; Abandonment

(a)   A plan of domestication of a domestic corporation may be amended:

(1)   in the same manner as the plan was approved, if the plan does not provide for the manner in which it may be amended; or

(2)   in the manner provided in the plan, except that a shareholder that was entitled to vote on or consent to approval of the plan is entitled to vote on or consent to any amendment of the plan that will change:

(i)   the amount or kind of shares or other securities, obligations, rights to acquire shares or other securities, cash, other property, or any combination of the foregoing, to be received by any of the shareholders of the domesticating corporation under the plan;

(ii)   the articles of incorporation or bylaws of the domesticated corporation that will be in effect immediately after the domestication becomes effective, except for changes that do not require approval of the shareholders of the domesticated corporation under its organic law or its proposed articles of incorporation or bylaws as set forth in the plan; or

(iii)   any of the other terms or conditions of the plan, if the change would adversely affect the shareholder in any material respect.

(b)   After a plan of domestication has been adopted and approved by a domestic corporation as required by this subchapter, and before the articles of domestication have become effective, the plan may be abandoned by the corporation without action by its shareholders in accordance with any procedures set forth in the plan or, if no such procedures are set forth in the plan, in the manner determined by the board of directors.

(c)   If a domestication is abandoned after the articles of domestication have been delivered to the secretary of state for filing but before the articles of domestication have become effective, articles of abandonment, signed by the domesticating corporation, must be delivered to the secretary of state for filing before the articles of domestication become effective. The articles of abandonment take effect upon filing, and the domestication shall be deemed abandoned and shall not become effective. The articles of abandonment must contain:

(1)   the name of the domesticating corporation;

(2)   the date on which the articles of domestication were filed by the secretary of state; and

(3)   a statement that the domestication has been abandoned in accordance with this section.

§ 9.24   Effect of Domestication

(a)   When a domestication becomes effective:

(1)   all property owned by, and every contract right possessed by, the domesticating corporation are the property and contract rights of the domesticated corporation without transfer, reversion or impairment;

(2)   all debts, obligations and other liabilities of the domesticating corporation are the debts, obligations and other liabilities of the domesticated corporation;

(3)   the name of the domesticated corporation may but need note be substituted for the name of the domesticating corporation in any pending proceeding;

(4)   the articles of incorporation and bylaws of the domesticated corporation become effective;

(5)   the shares of the domesticating corporation are reclassified into shares or other securities, obligations, rights to acquire shares or other securities, cash or other property in accordance with the

terms of the domestication, and the shareholders of the domesticating corporation are entitled only to the rights provided to them by those terms and to any appraisal rights they may have under the organic law of the domesticating corporation; and

    (6)   the domesticated corporation is:

        (i)   incorporated under and subject to the organic law of the domesticated corporation;

        (ii)   the same corporation without interruption as the domesticating corporation; and

        (iii)   deemed to have been incorporated on the date the domesticating corporation was originally incorporated.

(b)   When a domestication of a domestic corporation into a foreign jurisdiction becomes effective, the domesticated corporation is deemed to:

    (1)   appoint the secretary of state as its agent for service of process in a proceeding to enforce the rights of shareholders who exercise appraisal rights in connection with the domestication; and

    (2)   agree that it will promptly pay the amount, if any, to which such shareholders are entitled under chapter 13.

(c)   Except as otherwise provided in the organic law or organic rules of a domesticating foreign corporation, the interest holder liability of a shareholder in a foreign corporation that is domesticated into this state who had interest holder liability in respect of such domesticating corporation before the domestication becomes effective shall be as follows:

    (1)   The domestication does not discharge that prior interest holder liability with respect to any interest holder liabilities that arose before the domestication becomes effective.

    (2)   The provisions of the organic law of the domesticating corporation shall continue to apply to the collection or discharge of any interest holder liabilities preserved by subsection (c)(1), as if the domestication had not occurred.

    (3)   The shareholder shall have such rights of contribution from other persons as are provided by the organic law of the domesticating corporation with respect to any interest holder liabilities preserved by subsection (c)(1), as if the domestication had not occurred.

    (4)   The shareholder shall not, by reason of such prior interest holder liability, have interest holder liability with respect to any interest holder liabilities that are incurred after the domestication becomes effective.

(d)   A shareholder who becomes subject to interest holder liability in respect of the domesticated corporation as a result of the domestication shall have such interest holder liability only in respect of interest holder liabilities that arise after the domestication becomes effective.

(e)   A domestication does not constitute or cause the dissolution of the domesticating corporation.

(f)   Property held for charitable purposes under the laws of this state by a domestic or foreign corporation immediately before a domestication shall not, as a result of the transaction, be diverted from the objects for which it was donated, granted, devised, or otherwise transferred except and to the extent permitted by or pursuant to the laws of this state addressing cy près or dealing with nondiversion of charitable assets.

(g)   A bequest, devise, gift, grant, or promise contained in a will or other instrument of donation, subscription, or conveyance which is made to the domesticating corporation and which takes effect or remains payable after the domestication inures to the domesticated corporation.

(h)   A trust obligation that would govern property if transferred to the domesticating corporation applies to property that is transferred to the domesticated corporation after the domestication takes effect.

Subchapter C.   Conversion

§ 9.30   Conversion

(a) By complying with this chapter, a domestic corporation may become (i) a domestic eligible entity or (ii) a foreign eligible entity if the conversion is permitted by the organic law of the foreign entity.

(b) By complying with this subchapter and applicable provisions of its organic law, a domestic eligible entity may become a domestic corporation. If procedures for the approval of a conversion are not provided by the organic law or organic rules of a domestic eligible entity, the conversion shall be adopted and approved in the same manner as a merger of that eligible entity. If the organic law or organic rules of a domestic eligible entity do not provide procedures for the approval of either a conversion or a merger, a plan of conversion may nonetheless be adopted and approved by the unanimous consent of all the interest holders of such eligible entity. In either such case, the conversion thereafter may be effected as provided in the other provisions of this subchapter; and for purposes of applying this chapter in such a case:

    (1) the eligible entity, its members or interest holders, eligible interests and organic rules taken together, shall be deemed to be a domestic business corporation, shareholders, shares and articles of incorporation, respectively and vice versa, as the context may require; and

    (2) if the business and affairs of the eligible entity are managed by a person or persons that are not identical to the members or interest holders, that person or persons shall be deemed to be the board of directors.

(c) By complying with the provisions of this subchapter applicable to foreign entities, a foreign eligible entity may become a domestic corporation if the organic law of the foreign eligible entity permits it to become a business corporation in another jurisdiction.

(d) If a protected agreement of a domestic converting corporation in effect immediately before the conversion becomes effective contains a provision applying to a merger of the corporation that is a converting entity and the agreement does not refer to a conversion of the corporation, the provision applies to a conversion of the corporation as if the conversion were a merger, until such time as the provision is first amended after the enactment date.

§ 9.31   Plan of Conversion

(a) A domestic corporation may convert to a domestic or foreign eligible entity under this subchapter by approving a plan of conversion. The plan of conversion must include:

    (1) the name of the converting corporation;

    (2) the name, jurisdiction of formation and type of entity of the converted entity;

    (3) the manner and basis of converting the shares of the domestic corporation into eligible interests or other securities, obligations, rights to acquire eligible interests or other securities, cash, other property, or any combination of the foregoing;

    (4) the other terms and conditions of the conversion; and

    (5) the full text, as it will be in effect immediately after the conversion becomes effective, of the organic rules of the converted entity which are to be in writing.

(b) In addition to the requirements of subsection (a), a plan of conversion may contain any other provision not prohibited by law.

(c) The terms of a plan of conversion may be made dependent upon facts objectively ascertainable outside the plan in accordance with section 1.20(k).

§ 9.32   Action on a Plan of Conversion

In the case of a conversion of a domestic corporation to a domestic or foreign eligible entity, the plan of conversion shall be adopted in the following manner:

(a)　The plan of conversion shall first be adopted by the board of directors.

(b)　The plan of conversion shall then be approved by the shareholders. In submitting the plan of conversion to the shareholders for their approval, the board of directors must recommend that the shareholders approve the plan, unless (i) the board of directors makes a determination that because of conflicts of interest or other special circumstances it should not make such a recommendation, or (ii) section 8.26 applies. If either (i) or (ii) applies, the board of directors shall inform the shareholders of the basis for its so proceeding.

(c)　The board of directors may set conditions for approval of the plan of conversion by the shareholders or the effectiveness of the plan of conversion.

(d)　If the approval of the shareholders is to be given at a meeting, the corporation shall notify each shareholder, regardless of whether entitled to vote, of the meeting of shareholders at which the plan of conversion is to be submitted for approval. The notice must state that the purpose, or one of the purposes, of the meeting is to consider the plan of conversion and must contain or be accompanied by a copy or summary of the plan. The notice must include or be accompanied by a copy of the organic rules of the converted entity which are to be in writing as they will be in effect immediately after the conversion.

(e)　Unless the articles of incorporation, or the board of directors acting pursuant to subsection (c), require a greater vote or a greater quorum, approval of the plan of conversion requires (i) the approval of the shareholders at a meeting at which a quorum exists consisting of a majority of the votes entitled to be cast on the plan, and (ii) the approval of each class or series of shares voting as a separate voting group at a meeting at which a quorum of the voting group exists consisting of a majority of the votes entitled to be cast on the plan by that voting group.

(f)　If as a result of the conversion one or more shareholders of the converting domestic corporation would become subject to interest holder liability, approval of the plan of conversion shall require the signing in connection with the transaction, by each such shareholder, of a separate written consent to become subject to such interest holder liability.

§ 9.33　Articles of Conversion; Effectiveness

(a)　After (i) a plan of conversion of a domestic corporation has been adopted and approved as required by this Act, or (ii) a domestic or foreign eligible entity that is the converting entity has approved a conversion as required under its organic law, articles of conversion shall be signed by the converting entity and must:

(1)　state the name, jurisdiction of formation, and type of entity of the converting entity;

(2)　state the name, jurisdiction of formation, and type of entity of the converted entity;

(3)　if the converting entity is (i) a domestic corporation, state that the plan of conversion was approved in accordance with this subchapter; or (ii) an eligible entity, (A) state that the conversion was approved by the eligible entity in accordance with its organic law or (B) if the converting entity is a domestic eligible entity the organic law of which does not provide for approval of the conversion, state that the conversion was approved by the domestic eligible entity in accordance with this subchapter; and

(4)　if the converted entity is (i) a domestic business corporation, or a domestic nonprofit corporation or filing entity, have attached the public organic record of the converted entity, except that provisions that would not be required to be included in a restated public organic record may be omitted; or (ii) a domestic limited liability partnership, have attached the filing required to become a limited liability partnership.

(b)　If the converted entity is a domestic corporation, its articles of incorporation must satisfy the requirements of section 2.02, except that provisions that would not be required to be included in restated articles of incorporation may be omitted from the articles of incorporation. If the converted entity is a domestic eligible entity, its public organic record, if any, must satisfy the requirements of the organic law of this state, except that the public organic record does not need to be signed.

(c) The articles of conversion shall be delivered to the secretary of state for filing, and shall take effect at the effective date determined in accordance with section 1.23.

(d) If a converted entity is a domestic entity, the conversion becomes effective when the articles of conversion are effective. With respect to a conversion in which the converted entity is a foreign eligible entity, the conversion itself shall become effective at the later of (i) the date and time provided by the organic law of that eligible entity, and (ii) when the articles of conversion become effective.

(e) Articles of conversion under this section may be combined with any required conversion filing under the organic law of a domestic eligible entity that is the converting entity or converted entity if the combined filing satisfies the requirements of both this section and the other organic law.

(f) If the converting entity is a foreign eligible entity that is registered to do business in this state under a provision of law similar to chapter 15, its registration statement or other type of foreign qualification shall be cancelled automatically on the effective date of its conversion.

§ 9.34 Amendment of Plan of Conversion; Abandonment

(a) A plan of conversion of a converting entity that is a domestic corporation may be amended:

(1) in the same manner as the plan was approved, if the plan does not provide for the manner in which it may be amended; or

(2) in the manner provided in the plan, except that shareholders that were entitled to vote on or consent to approval of the plan are entitled to vote on or consent to any amendment of the plan that will change:

(i) the amount or kind of eligible interests or other securities, obligations, rights to acquire eligible interests or other securities, cash, other property, or any combination of the foregoing, to be received by any of the shareholders of the converting corporation under the plan;

(ii) the organic rules of the converted entity that will be in effect immediately after the conversion becomes effective, except for changes that do not require approval of the eligible interest holders of the converted entity under its organic law or organic rules; or

(iii) any other terms or conditions of the plan, if the change would adversely affect such shareholders in any material respect.

(b) After a plan of conversion has been approved by a converting entity that is a domestic corporation in the manner required by this subchapter and before the articles of conversion become effective, the plan may be abandoned by the corporation without action by its shareholders in accordance with any procedures set forth in the plan or, if no such procedures are set forth in the plan, in the manner determined by the board of directors.

(c) If a conversion is abandoned after the articles of conversion have been delivered to the secretary of state for filing and before the articles of conversion become effective, articles of abandonment, signed by the converting entity, must be delivered to the secretary of state for filing before the articles of conversion become effective. The articles of abandonment take effect on filing, and the conversion is abandoned and does not become effective. The articles of abandonment must contain:

(1) the name of the converting entity;

(2) the date on which the articles of conversion were filed by the secretary of state; and

(3) a statement that the conversion has been abandoned in accordance with this section.

§ 9.35 Effect of Conversion

(a) When a conversion becomes effective:

(1) all property owned by, and every contract right possessed by, the converting entity remain the property and contract rights of the converted entity without transfer, reversion or impairment;

(2)　all debts, obligations and other liabilities of the converting entity remain the debts, obligations and other liabilities of the converted entity;

(3)　the name of the converted entity may but need not be substituted for the name of the converting entity in any pending action or proceeding;

(4)　if the converted entity is a filing entity or a domestic business corporation or a domestic or foreign nonprofit corporation, its public organic record and its private organic rules become effective;

(5)　if the converted entity is a nonfiling entity, its private organic rules become effective;

(6)　if the converted entity is a limited liability partnership, the filing required to become a limited liability partnership and its private organic rules become effective;

(7)　the shares or eligible interests of the converting entity are reclassified into shares, eligible interests or other securities, obligations, rights to acquire shares, eligible interests or other securities, cash, or other property in accordance with the terms of the conversion, and the shareholders or interest holders of the converting entity are entitled only to the rights provided to them by those terms and to any appraisal rights they may have under the organic law of the converting entity; and

(8)　the converted entity is:

(i)　incorporated or organized under and subject to the organic law of the converted entity;

(ii)　the same entity without interruption as the converting entity; and

(iii)　deemed to have been incorporated or otherwise organized on the date that the converting entity was originally incorporated or organized.

(b)　When a conversion of a domestic corporation to a foreign eligible entity becomes effective, the converted entity is deemed to:

(1)　appoint the secretary of state as its agent for service of process in a proceeding to enforce the rights of shareholders who exercise appraisal rights in connection with the conversion; and

(2)　agree that it will promptly pay the amount, if any, to which such shareholders are entitled under chapter 13.

(c)　Except as otherwise provided in the articles of incorporation of a domestic corporation or the organic law or organic rules of a foreign corporation or a domestic or foreign eligible entity, a shareholder or eligible interest holder who becomes subject to interest holder liability in respect of a domestic corporation or eligible entity as a result of the conversion shall have such interest holder liability only in respect of interest holder liabilities that arise after the conversion becomes effective.

(d)　Except as otherwise provided in the organic law or the organic rules of the eligible entity, the interest holder liability of an interest holder in a converting eligible entity that converts to a domestic corporation who had interest holder liability in respect of such converting eligible entity before the conversion becomes effective shall be as follows:

(1)　The conversion does not discharge that prior interest holder liability with respect to any interest holder liabilities that arose before the conversion became effective.

(2)　The provisions of the organic law of the eligible entity shall continue to apply to the collection or discharge of any interest holder liabilities preserved by subsection (d)(1), as if the conversion had not occurred.

(3)　The eligible interest holder shall have such rights of contribution from other persons as are provided by the organic law of the eligible entity with respect to any interest holder liabilities preserved by subsection (d)(1), as if the conversion had not occurred.

(4)　The eligible interest holder shall not, by reason of such prior interest holder liability, have interest holder liability with respect to any interest holder liabilities that arise after the conversion becomes effective.

(e) A conversion does not require the converting entity to wind up its affairs and does not constitute or cause the dissolution or termination of the entity.

(f) Property held for charitable purposes under the laws of this state by a corporation or a domestic or foreign eligible entity immediately before a conversion shall not, as a result of the transaction, be diverted from the objects for which it was donated, granted, devised, or otherwise transferred except and to the extent permitted by or pursuant to the laws of this state addressing cy près or dealing with nondiversion of charitable assets.

(g) A bequest, devise, gift, grant, or promise contained in a will or other instrument of donation, subscription, or conveyance which is made to the converting entity and which takes effect or remains payable after the conversion inures to the converted entity.

(h) A trust obligation that would govern property if transferred to the converting entity applies to property that is transferred to the converted entity after the conversion takes effect.

CHAPTER 10

AMENDMENT OF ARTICLES OF INCORPORATION AND BYLAWS

Subchapter A. Amendment of Articles of Incorporation

§ 10.01   Authority to Amend

(a) A corporation may amend its articles of incorporation at any time to add or change a provision that is required or permitted in the articles of incorporation as of the effective date of the amendment or to delete a provision that is not required to be contained in the articles of incorporation.

(b) A shareholder of the corporation does not have a vested property right resulting from any provision in the articles of incorporation, including provisions relating to management, control, capital structure, dividend entitlement, or purpose or duration of the corporation.

§ 10.02   Amendment Before Issuance of Shares

If a corporation has not yet issued shares, its board of directors, or its incorporators if it has no board of directors, may adopt one or more amendments to the corporation's articles of incorporation.

§ 10.03   Amendment by Board of Directors and Shareholders

If a corporation has issued shares, an amendment to the articles of incorporation shall be adopted in the following manner:

(a) The proposed amendment shall first be adopted by the board of directors.

(b) Except as provided in sections 10.05, 10.07, and 10.08, the amendment shall then be approved by the shareholders. In submitting the proposed amendment to the shareholders for approval, the board of directors shall recommend that the shareholders approve the amendment, unless (i) the board of directors makes a determination that because of conflicts of interest or other special circumstances it should not make such a recommendation, or (ii) section 8.26 applies. If either (i) or (ii) applies, the board must inform the shareholders of the basis for its so proceeding.

(c) The board of directors may set conditions for the approval of the amendment by the shareholders or the effectiveness of the amendment.

(d) If the amendment is required to be approved by the shareholders, and the approval is to be given at a meeting, the corporation shall notify each shareholder, regardless of whether entitled to vote, of the meeting of shareholders at which the amendment is to be submitted for approval. The notice must state that the purpose, or one of the purposes, of the meeting is to consider the amendment. The notice must contain or be accompanied by a copy of the amendment.

(e)   Unless the articles of incorporation, or the board of directors acting pursuant to subsection (c), require a greater vote or a greater quorum, approval of the amendment requires the approval of the shareholders at a meeting at which a quorum consisting of a majority of the votes entitled to be cast on the amendment exists, and, if any class or series of shares is entitled to vote as a separate group on the amendment, except as provided in section 10.04(c), the approval of each such separate voting group at a meeting at which a quorum of the voting group exists consisting of a majority of the votes entitled to be cast on the amendment by that voting group.

(f)   If as a result of an amendment of the articles of incorporation one or more shareholders of a domestic corporation would become subject to new interest holder liability, approval of the amendment requires the signing in connection with the amendment, by each such shareholder, of a separate written consent to become subject to such new interest holder liability, unless in the case of a shareholder that already has interest holder liability the terms and conditions of the new interest holder liability (i) are substantially identical to those of the existing interest holder liability, or (ii) are substantially identical to those of the existing interest holder liability (other than changes that eliminate or reduce such interest holder liability).

(g)   For purposes of subsection (f) and section 10.09, "new interest holder liability" means interest holder liability of a person resulting from an amendment of the articles of incorporation if (i) the person did not have interest holder liability before the amendment becomes effective, or (ii) the person had interest holder liability before the amendment becomes effective, the terms and conditions of which are changed when the amendment becomes effective.

§ 10.04   Voting on Amendments by Voting Groups

(a)   The holders of the outstanding shares of a class are entitled to vote as a separate voting group (if shareholder voting is otherwise required by this Act) on a proposed amendment to the articles of incorporation if the amendment would:

(1)   effect an exchange or reclassification of all or part of the shares of the class into shares of another class;

(2)   effect an exchange or reclassification, or create the right of exchange, of all or part of the shares of another class into shares of the class;

(3)   change the rights, preferences, or limitations of all or part of the shares of the class;

(4)   change the shares of all or part of the class into a different number of shares of the same class;

(5)   create a new class of shares having rights or preferences with respect to distributions that are prior or superior to the shares of the class;

(6)   increase the rights, preferences, or number of authorized shares of any class that, after giving effect to the amendment, have rights or preferences with respect to distributions that are prior or superior to the shares of the class;

(7)   limit or deny an existing preemptive right of all or part of the shares of the class; or

(8)   cancel or otherwise affect rights to distributions that have accumulated but not yet been authorized on all or part of the shares of the class.

(b)   If a proposed amendment would affect a series of a class of shares in one or more of the ways described in subsection (a), the holders of shares of that series are entitled to vote as a separate voting group on the proposed amendment.

(c)   If a proposed amendment that entitles the holders of two or more classes or series of shares to vote as separate voting groups under this section would affect those two or more classes or series in the same or a substantially similar way, the holders of shares of all the classes or series so affected shall vote together as a single voting group on the proposed amendment, unless otherwise provided in the articles of incorporation or added as a condition by the board of directors pursuant to section 10.03(c).

(d)   A class or series of shares is entitled to the voting rights granted by this section even if the articles of incorporation provide that the shares are nonvoting shares.

§ 10.05   Amendment by Board of Directors

Unless the articles of incorporation provide otherwise, a corporation's board of directors may adopt amendments to the corporation's articles of incorporation without shareholder approval:

(a)   to extend the duration of the corporation if it was incorporated at a time when limited duration was required by law;

(b)   to delete the names and addresses of the initial directors;

(c)   to delete the name and address of the initial registered agent or registered office, if a statement of change is on file with the secretary of state;

(d)   if the corporation has only one class of shares outstanding:

(1)   to change each issued and unissued authorized share of the class into a greater number of whole shares of that class; or

(2)   to increase the number of authorized shares of the class to the extent necessary to permit the issuance of shares as a share dividend;

(e)   to change the corporate name by substituting the word "corporation," "incorporated," "company," "limited," or the abbreviation "corp.," "inc.," "co.," or "ltd.," for a similar word or abbreviation in the name, or by adding, deleting, or changing a geographical attribution for the name;

(f)   to reflect a reduction in authorized shares, as a result of the operation of section 6.31(b), when the corporation has acquired its own shares and the articles of incorporation prohibit the reissue of the acquired shares;

(g)   to delete a class of shares from the articles of incorporation, as a result of the operation of section 6.31(b), when there are no remaining shares of the class because the corporation has acquired all shares of the class and the articles of incorporation prohibit the reissue of the acquired shares; or

(h)   to make any change expressly permitted by section 6.02(a) or (b) to be made without shareholder approval.

§ 10.06   Articles of Amendment

(a)   After an amendment to the articles of incorporation has been adopted and approved in the manner required by this Act and by the articles of incorporation, the corporation shall deliver to the secretary of state for filing articles of amendment, which must set forth:

(1)   the name of the corporation;

(2)   the text of each amendment adopted, or the information required by section 1.20(k)(5);

(3)   if an amendment provides for an exchange, reclassification, or cancellation of issued shares, provisions for implementing the amendment if not contained in the amendment itself, (which may be made dependent upon facts objectively ascertainable outside the articles of amendment in accordance with section 1.20(k)(5);

(4)   the date of each amendment's adoption; and

(5)   if an amendment:

(i)   was adopted by the incorporators or board of directors without shareholder approval, a statement that the amendment was duly adopted by the incorporators or by the board of directors, as the case may be, and that shareholder approval was not required;

(ii)   required approval by the shareholders, a statement that the amendment was duly approved by the shareholders in the manner required by this Act and by the articles of incorporation; or

(iii) is being filed pursuant to section 1.20(k)(5), a statement to that effect.

(b)   Articles of amendment shall take effect at the effective date determined in accordance with section 1.23.

§ 10.07   Restated Articles of Incorporation

(a)   A corporation's board of directors may restate its articles of incorporation at any time, without shareholder approval, to consolidate all amendments into a single document.

(b)   If the restated articles include one or more new amendments that require shareholder approval, the amendments shall be adopted and approved as provided in section 10.03.

(c)   A corporation that restates its articles of incorporation shall deliver to the secretary of state for filing articles of restatement setting forth:

(1)   the name of the corporation;

(2)   the text of the restated articles of incorporation;

(3)   a statement that the restated articles consolidate all amendments into a single document; and

(4)   if a new amendment is included in the restated articles, the statements required under section 10.06 with respect to the new amendment.

(d)   Duly adopted restated articles of incorporation supersede the original articles of incorporation and all amendments to the articles of incorporation.

(e)   The secretary of state may certify restated articles of incorporation as the articles of incorporation currently in effect, without including the statements required by subsection (c)(4).

§ 10.08   Amendment Pursuant to Reorganization

(a)   A corporation's articles of incorporation may be amended without action by the board of directors or shareholders to carry out a plan of reorganization ordered or decreed by a court of competent jurisdiction under the authority of a law of the United States.

(b)   The individual or individuals designated by the court shall deliver to the secretary of state for filing articles of amendment setting forth:

(1)   the name of the corporation;

(2)   the text of each amendment approved by the court;

(3)   the date of the court's order or decree approving the articles of amendment;

(4)   the title of the reorganization proceeding in which the order or decree was entered; and

(5)   a statement that the court had jurisdiction of the proceeding under federal statute.

(c)   This section does not apply after entry of a final decree in the reorganization proceeding even though the court retains jurisdiction of the proceeding for limited purposes unrelated to consummation of the reorganization plan.

§ 10.09   Effect of Amendment

(a)   An amendment to the articles of incorporation does not affect a cause of action existing against or in favor of the corporation, a proceeding to which the corporation is a party, or the existing rights of persons other than the shareholders. An amendment changing a corporation's name does not affect a proceeding brought by or against the corporation in its former name.

(b)   A shareholder who becomes subject to new interest holder liability in respect of the corporation as a result of an amendment to the articles of incorporation shall have that new interest holder liability only in respect of interest holder liabilities that arise after the amendment becomes effective.

(c)   Except as otherwise provided in the articles of incorporation of the corporation, the interest holder liability of a shareholder who had interest holder liability in respect of the corporation before the amendment becomes effective and has new interest holder liability after the amendment becomes effective shall be as follows:

(1)   The amendment does not discharge that prior interest holder liability with respect to any interest holder liabilities that arose before the amendment becomes effective.

(2)   The provisions of the articles of incorporation of the corporation relating to interest holder liability as in effect immediately prior to the amendment shall continue to apply to the collection or discharge of any interest holder liabilities preserved by subsection (c)(1), as if the amendment had not occurred.

(3)   The shareholder shall have such rights of contribution from other persons as are provided by the articles of incorporation relating to interest holder liability as in effect immediately prior to the amendment with respect to any interest holder liabilities preserved by subsection (c)(1), as if the amendment had not occurred.

(4)   The shareholder shall not, by reason of such prior interest holder liability, have interest holder liability with respect to any interest holder liabilities that arise after the amendment becomes effective.

Subchapter B.   Amendment of Bylaws

§ 10.20   Authority of Amend

(a)   A corporation's shareholders may amend or repeal the corporation's bylaws.

(b)   A corporation's board of directors may amend or repeal the corporation's bylaws, unless:

(1)   the articles of incorporation, section 10.21 or, if applicable, section 10.22 reserve that power exclusively to the shareholders in whole or part; or

(2)   except as provided in section 2.06(d), the shareholders in amending, repealing, or adopting a bylaw expressly provide that the board of directors may not amend, repeal, or adopt that bylaw.

(c)   A shareholder of the corporation does not have a vested property right resulting from any provision in the bylaws.

§ 10.21   Bylaw Increasing Quorum or Voting Requirement for Directors or Requiring a Meeting Place

(a)   A bylaw that increases a quorum or voting requirement for the board of directors may be amended or repealed:

(1)   if originally adopted by the shareholders, only by the shareholders, unless the bylaw otherwise provides; or

(2)   if adopted by the board of directors, either by the shareholders or by the board of directors.

(b)   A bylaw adopted or amended by the shareholders that increases a quorum or voting requirement for the board of directors may provide that it can be amended or repealed only by a specified vote of either the shareholders or the board of directors.

(c)   Action by the board of directors under subsection (a) to amend or repeal a bylaw that changes a quorum or voting requirement for the board of directors shall meet the same quorum requirement and be adopted by the same vote required to take action under the quorum and voting requirement then in effect or proposed to be adopted, whichever is greater.

§ 10.22 Bylaw Provisions Relating to the Election of Directors

(a)   Unless the articles of incorporation (i) specifically prohibit the adoption of a bylaw pursuant to this section, (ii) alter the vote specified in section 7.28(a), or (iii) provide for cumulative voting, a corporation may elect in its bylaws to be governed in the election of directors as follows:

(1)   each vote entitled to be cast may be voted for or against up to that number of candidates that is equal to the number of directors to be elected, or a shareholder may indicate an abstention, but without cumulating the votes;

(2)   to be elected, a nominee shall have received a plurality of the votes cast by holders of shares entitled to vote in the election at a meeting at which a quorum is present, provided that a nominee who is elected but receives more votes against than for election shall serve as a director for a term that shall terminate on the date that is the earlier of (i) 90 days from the date on which the voting results are determined pursuant to section 7.29(b)(5) or (ii) the date on which an individual is selected by the board of directors to fill the office held by such director, which selection shall be deemed to constitute the filling of a vacancy by the board to which section 8.10 applies. Subject to subsection (a)(3), a nominee who is elected but receives more votes against than for election shall not serve as a director beyond the 90-day period referenced above; and

(3)   the board of directors may select any qualified individual to fill the office held by a director who received more votes against than for election.

(b)   Subsection (a) does not apply to an election of directors by a voting group if (i) at the expiration of the time fixed under a provision requiring advance notification of director candidates, or (ii) absent such a provision, at a time fixed by the board of directors which is not more than 14 days before notice is given of the meeting at which the election is to occur, there are more candidates for election by the voting group than the number of directors to be elected, one or more of whom are properly proposed by shareholders. An individual shall not be considered a candidate for purposes of this subsection if the board of directors determines before the notice of meeting is given that such individual's candidacy does not create a bona fide election contest.

(c)   A bylaw electing to be governed by this section may be repealed:

(1)   if originally adopted by the shareholders, only by the shareholders, unless the bylaw otherwise provides;

(2)   if adopted by the board of directors, by the board of directors or the shareholders.

CHAPTER 11

MERGERS AND SHARE EXCHANGES

INTRODUCTORY COMMENT

Transactions Permitted

Chapter 11 deals with mergers and share exchanges. A merger is the traditional form for combining entities by operation of law, and the range of merger transactions chapter 11 permits is broad. In a merger, a domestic business corporation may merge with one or more of the following domestic or foreign entities: (i) business corporations; (ii) unincorporated entities (including limited liability companies, general and limited partnerships and business trusts); and (iii) nonprofit corporations (which are defined together with unincorporated entities as "eligible entities;" neither is included in the defined term "corporation"). These and other relevant terms used in this chapter are defined in sections 1.40 and 11.01.

The entity resulting from the merger may be one of the parties to the merger, or a new corporation or eligible entity created by the merger. Chapter 11 therefore may apply to a merger in which none of the parties is a domestic corporation, as long as the resulting entity (defined in section 11.01 as the "survivor") is a new domestic corporation. In the case of any merger involving a corporation or eligible entity organized under the laws of a foreign jurisdiction, the Act recognizes that whether and how those foreign entities may merge are matters governed by the law of the foreign jurisdiction.

Chapter 11 also permits share exchanges in which either (i) a domestic corporation acquires all of the shares or eligible interests of one or more classes or series of another domestic or foreign corporation or eligible entity, or (ii) all of the shares of one of more classes or series of a domestic corporation are acquired by another domestic or foreign corporation or eligible entity. As a result, in a share exchange, the existence of the acquired entity (the entity whose shares are acquired) continues. If enough shares or eligible interests are acquired, the acquired entity may become a subsidiary of the acquiring entity. Each of these transactions is a share exchange, even if it involves no shares and only "eligible interests" (which are defined in section 1.40 as specified rights in unincorporated entities and memberships in nonprofit corporations). A foreign corporation or eligible entity may only be the acquired entity in a share exchange if it is permitted by the law governing the foreign corporation or eligible entity.

Other chapters of the Act permit transactions that once could only be effected by merger. For example, chapter 9 provides for domestications, in which corporations can reincorporate in another jurisdiction, and conversions, in which corporations may convert to eligible entities. The Act's approach is generally to provide similar procedures for effecting any of these types of transactions and certain other fundamental actions, such as amendments to the articles of incorporation under chapter 10 and sales of assets outside the usual and regular course of business under chapter 12.

Requirements and Effects

Section 11.02 generally authorizes mergers and sets out requirements for their approval. For a domestic corporation, the requirements usually include a plan or merger, adopted by the board of directors and recommended by the board of directors to the shareholders, and approved by the shareholders. Section 11.03 has similar provisions for share exchanges and plans of share exchange. These sections permit the holders of shares or eligible interests of a party to a merger or of an acquired class or series in a share exchange to receive a broad range of consideration for their shares or interests. Section 11.04 sets out the approval requirements for domestic corporations that are parties to mergers or acquired entities in share exchanges, although section 11.05 has special rules for certain parent-subsidiary transactions. Section 11.06 relates to the preparation and filing of articles of merger and share exchange, and section 11.07 states the effects of those transactions. Finally, section 11.08 provides how mergers and share exchanges may be abandoned after they are adopted and approved. Dissenting shareholders in certain mergers and share exchanges and certain other fundamental actions have appraisal rights under chapter 13.

§ 11.01   Definitions

As used in this chapter:

"Acquired entity" means the domestic or foreign corporation or eligible entity that will have all of one or more classes or series of its shares or eligible interests acquired in a share exchange.

"Acquiring entity" means the domestic or foreign corporation or eligible entity that will acquire all of one or more classes or series of shares or eligible interests of the acquired entity in a share exchange.

"New interest holder liability" means interest holder liability of a person, resulting from a merger or share exchange, that is (i) in respect of an entity which is different from the entity in which the person held shares or eligible interests immediately before the merger or share exchange became effective; or (ii) in respect of the same entity as the one in which the person held shares or eligible interests immediately before the merger or share exchange became effective if (A) the person did not have interest holder liability immediately before the merger or share exchange became effective, or (B) the person had interest holder liability immediately before the merger or share exchange became effective, the terms and conditions of which were changed when the merger or share exchange became effective.

"Party to a merger" means any domestic or foreign corporation or eligible entity that will merge under a plan of merger but does not include a survivor created by the merger.

"Survivor" in a merger means the domestic or foreign corporation or eligible entity into which one or more other corporations or eligible entities are merged.

§ 11.02　Merger

(a)　By complying with this chapter:

(1)　one or more domestic business corporations may merge with one or more domestic or foreign business corporations or eligible entities pursuant to a plan of merger, resulting in a survivor; and

(2)　two or more foreign business corporations or domestic or foreign eligible entities may merge, resulting in a survivor that is a domestic business corporation created in the merger.

(b)　By complying with the provisions of this chapter applicable to foreign entities, a foreign business corporation or a foreign eligible entity may be a party to a merger with a domestic business corporation, or may be created as the survivor in a merger in which a domestic business corporation is a party, but only if the merger is permitted by the organic law of the foreign business corporation or eligible entity.

(c)　If the organic law or organic rules of a domestic eligible entity do not provide procedures for the approval of a merger, a plan of merger may nonetheless be adopted and approved by the unanimous consent of all of the interest holders of such eligible entity, and the merger may thereafter by effected as provided in the other provisions of this chapter; and for the purposes of applying this chapter in such a case:

(1)　the eligible entity, its members or interest holders, eligible interests and articles of incorporation or other organic rules taken together shall be deemed to be a domestic business corporation, shareholders, shares and articles of incorporation, respectively and vice versa as the context may require; and

(2)　if the business and affairs of the eligible entity are managed by a person or persons that are not identical to the members or interest holders, that group shall be deemed to be the board of directors.

(d)　The plan of merger must include:

(1)　as to each party to the merger, its name, jurisdiction of formation, and type of entity;

(2)　the survivor's name, jurisdiction of formation, and type of entity, and, if the survivor is to be created in the merger, a statement to that effect;

(3)　the terms and conditions of the merger;

(4)　the manner and basis of converting the shares of each merging domestic or foreign business corporation and eligible interests of each merging domestic or foreign eligible entity into shares or other securities, eligible interests, obligations, rights to acquire shares, other securities or eligible interests, cash, other property, or any combination of the foregoing;

(5)　the articles of incorporation of any domestic or foreign business or nonprofit corporation, or the public organic record of any domestic or foreign unincorporated entity, to be created by the merger, or if a new domestic or foreign business or nonprofit corporation or unincorporated entity is not to be created by the merger, any amendments to the survivor's articles of incorporation or other public organic record; and

(6)　any other provisions required by the laws under which any party to the merger is organized or by which it is governed, or by the articles of incorporation or organic rules of any such party.

(e)　In addition to the requirements of subsection (d), a plan of merger may contain any other provision not prohibited by law.

(f)　Terms of a plan of merger may be made dependent on facts objectively ascertainable outside the plan in accordance with section 1.20(k).

(g)　A plan of merger may be amended only with the consent of each party to the merger, except as provided in the plan. A domestic party to a merger may approve an amendment to a plan:

(1)　in the same manner as the plan was approved, if the plan does not provide for the manner in which it may be amended; or

(2)   in the manner provided in the plan, except that shareholders, members, or interest holders that were entitled to vote on or consent to approval of the plan are entitled to vote on or consent to any amendment of the plan that will change:

(i)   the amount or kind of shares or other securities, eligible interests, obligations, rights to acquire shares, other securities or eligible interests, cash, or other property to be received under the plan by the shareholders, members, or interest holders of any party to the merger;

(ii)   the articles of incorporation of any domestic or foreign business or nonprofit corporation, or the organic rules of any unincorporated entity, that will be the survivor of the merger, except for changes permitted by section 10.05 or by comparable provisions of the organic law of any such foreign corporation or domestic or foreign nonprofit corporation or unincorporated entity; or

(iii)   any of the other terms or conditions of the plan if the change would adversely affect such shareholders, members, or interest holders in any material respect.

§ 11.03   Share Exchange

(a)   By complying with this chapter:

(1)   a domestic corporation may acquire all of the shares of one or more classes or series of shares of another domestic or foreign corporation, or all of the eligible interests of one or more classes or series of interests of a domestic or foreign eligible entity, in exchange for shares or other securities, eligible interests, obligations, rights to acquire shares or other securities or eligible interests, cash, other property, or any combination of the foregoing, pursuant to a plan of share exchange; or

(2)   all of the shares of one or more classes or series of shares of a domestic corporation may be acquired by another domestic or foreign corporation or eligible entity, in exchange for shares or other securities, eligible interests, obligations, rights to acquire shares or other securities or eligible interests, cash, other property, or any combination of the foregoing, pursuant to a plan of share exchange.

(b)   A foreign corporation or eligible entity may be the acquired entity in a share exchange only if the share exchange is permitted by the organic law of that corporation or other entity.

(c)   If the organic law or organic rules of a domestic eligible entity does not provide procedures for the approval of a share exchange, a plan of share exchange may be adopted and approved, and the share exchange effected, in accordance with the procedures, if any, for a merger. If the organic law or organic rules of a domestic eligible entity does not provide procedures for the approval of either a share exchange or a merger, a plan of share exchange may nonetheless be adopted and approved by the unanimous consent of all of the interest holders of such eligible entity whose interests will be exchanged under the plan of share exchange, and the share exchange may thereafter be effected as provided in the other provisions of this chapter; and for purposes of applying this chapter in such a case:

(1)   the eligible entity, its interest holders, interests and articles of incorporation or other organic rules taken together shall be deemed to be a domestic business corporation, shareholders, shares and articles of incorporation, respectively and vice versa as the context may require; and

(2)   if the business and affairs of the eligible entity are managed by a person or persons that are not identical to the members or interest holders, that person or those persons shall be deemed to be the board of directors.

(d)   The plan of share exchange must include:

(1)   the name of each domestic or foreign corporation or other eligible entity the shares or eligible interests of which will be acquired and the name of the domestic or foreign corporation or eligible entity that will acquire those shares or eligible interests;

(2)   the terms and conditions of the share exchange;

(3)   the manner and basis of exchanging shares of a domestic or foreign corporation or eligible interests in a domestic or foreign eligible entity the shares or eligible interests of which will be acquired under the share exchange for shares or other securities, eligible interests, obligations, rights to acquire shares, other securities, or eligible interests, cash, other property, or any combination of the foregoing; and

(4)   any other provisions required by the organic law governing the acquired entity or its articles of incorporation or organic rules.

(e)   Terms of a plan of share exchange may be made dependent on facts objectively ascertainable outside the plan in accordance with section 1.20(k).

(f)   A plan of share exchange may be amended only with the consent of each party to the share exchange, except as provided in the plan. A domestic entity may approve an amendment to a plan:

(1)   in the same manner as the plan was approved, if the plan does not provide for the manner in which it may be amended; or

(2)   in the manner provided in the plan, except that shareholders, members, or interest holders that were entitled to vote on or consent to approval of the plan are entitled to vote on or consent to any amendment of the plan that will change:

(i)   the amount or kind of shares or other securities, eligible interests, obligations, rights to acquire shares, other securities or eligible interests, cash, or other property to be received under the plan by the shareholders, members or interest holders of the acquired entity; or

(ii)   any of the other terms or conditions of the plan if the change would adversely affect such shareholders, members or interest holders in any material respect.

§ 11.04   Action on a Plan of Merger or Share Exchange

In the case of a domestic corporation that is a party to a merger or the acquired entity in a share exchange, the plan of merger or share exchange shall be adopted in the following manner:

(a)   The plan of merger or share exchange shall first be adopted by the board of directors.

(b)   Except as provided in subsections (h), (j) and (*l*) and in section 11.05, the plan of merger or share exchange shall then be approved by the shareholders. In submitting the plan of merger or share exchange to the shareholders for approval, the board of directors shall recommend that the shareholders approve the plan or, in the case of an offer referred to in subsection (j)(2), that the shareholders tender their shares to the offeror in response to the offer, unless (i) the board of directors makes a determination that because of conflicts of interest or other special circumstances it should not make such a recommendation or (ii) section 8.26 applies. If either (i) or (ii) applies, the board shall inform the shareholders of the basis for its so proceeding.

(c)   The board of directors may set conditions for the approval of the plan of merger or share exchange by the shareholders or the effectiveness of the plan of merger or share exchange.

(d)   If the plan of merger or share exchange is required to be approved by the shareholders, and if the approval is to be given at a meeting, the corporation shall notify each shareholder, regardless of whether entitled to vote, of the meeting of shareholders at which the plan is to be submitted for approval. The notice must state that the purpose, or one of the purposes, of the meeting is to consider the plan and must contain or be accompanied by a copy or summary of the plan. If the corporation is to be merged into an existing foreign or domestic corporation or eligible entity, the notice must also include or be accompanied by a copy or summary of the articles of incorporation and bylaws or the organic rules of that corporation or eligible entity. If the corporation is to be merged with a domestic or foreign corporation or eligible entity and a new domestic or foreign corporation or eligible entity is to be created pursuant to the merger, the notice must include or be accompanied by a copy or a summary of the articles of incorporation and bylaws or the organic rules of the new corporation or eligible entity.

(e)   Unless the articles of incorporation, or the board of directors acting pursuant to subsection (c), require a greater vote or a greater quorum, approval of the plan of merger or share exchange requires the approval of the shareholders at a meeting at which a quorum exists consisting of a majority of the votes entitled to be cast on the plan, and, if any class or series of shares is entitled to vote as a separate group on the plan of merger or share exchange, the approval of each such separate voting group at a meeting at which a quorum of the voting group is present consisting of a majority of the votes entitled to be cast on the merger or share exchange by that voting group.

(f)   Subject to subsection (g), separate voting by voting groups is required:

(1)   on a plan of merger, by each class or series of shares that:

(i)   are to be converted under the plan of merger into shares, other securities, eligible interests, obligations, rights to acquire shares, other securities or eligible interests, cash, other property, or any combination of the foregoing; or

(ii)   are entitled to vote as a separate group on a provision in the plan that constitutes a proposed amendment to the articles of incorporation of a surviving corporation that requires action by separate voting groups under section 10.04;

(2)   on a plan of share exchange, by each class or series of shares included in the exchange, with each class or series constituting a separate voting group; and

(3)   on a plan of merger or share exchange, if the voting group is entitled under the articles of incorporation to vote as a voting group to approve a plan of merger or share exchange, respectively.

(g)   The articles of incorporation may expressly limit or eliminate the separate voting rights provided in subsections (f)(1)(i) and (f)(2) as to any class or series of shares, except when the plan of merger or share exchange (i) includes what is or would be in effect an amendment subject to subsection (f)(1)(ii), and (ii) will not effect a substantive business combination.

(h)   Unless the articles of incorporation otherwise provide, approval by the corporation's shareholders of a plan of merger is not required if:

(1)   the corporation will survive the merger;

(2)   except for amendments permitted by section 10.05, its articles of incorporation will not be changed;

(3)   each shareholder of the corporation whose shares were outstanding immediately before the effective date of the merger or share exchange will hold the same number of shares, with identical preferences, rights and limitations, immediately after the effective date of the merger; and

(4)   the issuance in the merger of shares or other securities convertible into or rights exercisable for shares does not require a vote under section 6.21(f).

(i)   If as a result of a merger or share exchange one or more shareholders of a domestic corporation would become subject to new interest holder liability, approval of the plan of merger or share exchange requires the signing in connection with the transaction, by each such shareholder, of a separate written consent to become subject to such new interest holder liability, unless in the case of a shareholder that already has interest holder liability with respect to such domestic corporation, (i) the new interest holder liability is with respect to a domestic or foreign corporation (which may be a different or the same domestic corporation in which the person is a shareholder), and (ii) the terms and conditions of the new interest holder liability are substantially identical to those of the existing interest holder liability (other than for changes that eliminate or reduce such interest holder liability).

(j)   Unless the articles of incorporation otherwise provide, approval by the shareholders of a plan of merger or share exchange is not required if:

(1)   the plan of merger or share exchange expressly (i) permits or requires the merger or share exchange to be effected under this subsection and (ii) provides that, if the merger or share exchange is to be effected under this subsection, the merger or share exchange will be effected as soon as practicable following the satisfaction of the requirement set forth in subsection (j)(6);

(2)   another party to the merger, the acquiring entity in the share exchange, or a parent of another party to the merger or the acquiring entity in the share exchange, makes an offer to purchase,

on the terms provided in the plan of merger or share exchange, any and all of the outstanding shares of the corporation that, absent this subsection, would be entitled to vote on the plan of merger or share exchange, except that the offer may exclude shares of the corporation that are owned at the commencement of the offer by the corporation, the offeror, or any parent of the offeror, or by any wholly owned subsidiary of any of the foregoing;

(3)   the offer discloses that the plan of merger or share exchange provides that the merger or share exchange will be effected as soon as practicable following the satisfaction of the requirement set forth in subsection (j)(6) and that the shares of the corporation that are not tendered in response to the offer will be treated as set forth in subsection (j)(8);

(4)   the offer remains open for at least 10 days;

(5)   the offeror purchases all shares properly tendered in response to the offer and not properly withdrawn;

(6)   the shares listed below are collectively entitled to cast at least the minimum number of votes on the merger or share exchange that, absent this subsection, would be required by this chapter and by the articles of incorporation for the approval of the merger or share exchange by the shareholders and by any other voting group entitled to vote on the merger or share exchange at a meeting at which all shares entitled to vote on the approval were present and voted:

(i)   shares purchased by the offeror in accordance with the offer;

(ii)   shares otherwise owned by the offeror or by any parent of the offeror or any wholly owned subsidiary of any of the foregoing; and

(iii)   shares subject to an agreement that they are to be transferred, contributed or delivered to the offeror, any parent of the offeror, or any wholly owned subsidiary of any of the foregoing in exchange for shares or eligible interests in such offeror, parent or subsidiary;

(7)   the offeror or a wholly owned subsidiary of the offeror merges with or into, or effects a share exchange in which it acquires shares of, the corporation; and

(8)   each outstanding share of each class or series of shares of the corporation that the offeror is offering to purchase in accordance with the offer, and that is not purchased in accordance with the offer, is to be converted in the merger into, or into the right to receive, or is to be exchanged in the share exchange for, or for the right to receive, the same amount and kind of securities, eligible interests, obligations, rights, cash, or other property to be paid or exchanged in accordance with the offer for each share of that class or series of shares that is tendered in response to the offer, except that shares of the corporation that are owned by the corporation or that are described in clause (ii) or (iii) of subsection (j)(6) need not be converted into or exchanged for the consideration described in this subsection (j)(8).

(k)   As used in subsection (j):

(1)   "offer" means the offer referred to in subsection (j)(2);

(2)   "offeror" means the person making the offer;

(3)   "parent" of an entity means a person that owns, directly or indirectly (through one or more wholly owned subsidiaries), all of the outstanding shares of or eligible interests in that entity;

(4)   shares tendered in response to the offer shall be deemed to have been "purchased" in accordance with the offer at the earliest time as of which (i) the offeror has irrevocably accepted those shares for payment and (ii) either (A) in the case of shares represented by certificates, the offeror, or the offeror's designated depository or other agent, has physically received the certificates representing those shares or (B) in the case of shares without certificates, those shares have been transferred into the account of the offeror or its designated depository or other agent, or an agent's message relating to those shares has been received by the offeror or its designated depository or other agent; and

(5)   "wholly owned subsidiary" of a person means an entity of or in which that person owns, directly or indirectly (through one or more wholly owned subsidiaries), all of the outstanding shares or eligible interests.

(*l*)   Unless the articles of incorporation otherwise provide,

(1)   approval of a plan of share exchange by the shareholders of a domestic corporation is not required if the corporation is the acquiring entity in the share exchange; and

(2)   shares not to be exchanged under the plan of share exchange are not entitled to vote on the plan.

§ 11.05   Merger Between Parent and Subsidiary or Between Subsidiaries

(a)   A domestic or foreign parent entity that owns shares of a domestic corporation which carry at least 90% of the voting power of each class and series of the outstanding shares of the subsidiary that has voting power may (i) merge the subsidiary into itself (if it is a domestic or foreign corporation or eligible entity) or into another domestic or foreign corporation or eligible entity in which the parent entity owns at least 90% of the voting power of each class and series of the outstanding shares or eligible interests which have voting power, or (ii) merge itself (if it is a domestic or foreign corporation or eligible entity) into such subsidiary, in either case without the approval of the board of directors or shareholders of the subsidiary, unless the articles of incorporation or organic rules of the parent entity or the articles of incorporation of the subsidiary corporation otherwise provide. Section 11.04(i) applies to a merger under this section. The articles of merger relating to a merger under this section do not need to be signed by the subsidiary.

(b)   A parent entity shall, within 10 days after the effective date of a merger approved under subsection (a), notify each of the subsidiary's shareholders that the merger has become effective.

(c)   Except as provided in subsections (a) and (b), a merger between a parent entity and a domestic subsidiary corporation shall be governed by the provisions of chapter 11 applicable to mergers generally.

§ 11.06   Articles of Merger or Share Exchange

(a)   After (i) a plan of merger has been adopted and approved as required by this Act, or (ii) if the merger is being effected under section 11.02(a)(2), the merger has been approved as required by the organic law governing the parties to the merger, then articles of merger shall be signed by each party to the merger except as provided in section 11.05(a). The articles must set forth:

(1)   the name, jurisdiction of formation, and type of entity of each party to the merger;

(2)   the name, jurisdiction of formation, and type of entity of the survivor;

(3)   if the survivor of the merger is a domestic corporation and its articles of incorporation are amended, or if a new domestic corporation is created as a result of the merger:

(i)   the amendments to the survivor's articles of incorporation; or

(ii)   the articles of incorporation of the new corporation;

(4)   if the survivor of the merger is a domestic eligible entity and its public organic record is amended, or if a new domestic eligible entity is created as a result of the merger:

(i)   the amendments to the public organic record of the survivor; or

(ii)   the public organic record of the new eligible entity;

(5)   if the plan of merger required approval by the shareholders of a domestic corporation that is a party to the merger, a statement that the plan was duly approved by the shareholders and, if voting by any separate voting group was required, by each such separate voting group, in the manner required by this Act and the articles of incorporation;

(6)   if the plan of merger or share exchange did not require approval by the shareholders of a domestic corporation that is a party to the merger, a statement to that effect;

(7)   as to each foreign corporation that is a party to the merger, a statement that the participation of the foreign corporation was duly authorized as required by its organic law;

(8)   as to each domestic or foreign eligible entity that is a party to the merger, a statement that the merger was approved in accordance with its organic law or section 11.02(c); and

(9)   if the survivor is created by the merger and is a domestic limited liability partnership, the filing required to become a limited liability partnership, as an attachment.

(b)   After a plan of share exchange in which the acquired entity is a domestic corporation or eligible entity has been adopted and approved as required by this Act, articles of share exchange shall be signed by the acquired entity and the acquiring entity. The articles shall set forth:

(1)   the name of the acquired entity;

(2)   the name, jurisdiction of formation, and type of entity of the domestic or foreign corporation or eligible entity that is the acquiring entity; and

(3)   a statement that the plan of share exchange was duly approved by the acquired entity by:

(i)   the required vote or consent of each class or series of shares or eligible interests included in the exchange; and

(ii)   the required vote or consent of each other class or series of shares or eligible interests entitled to vote on approval of the exchange by the articles of incorporation or organic rules of the acquired entity or section 11.03(c).

(c)   In addition to the requirements of subsection (a) or (b), articles of merger or share exchange may contain any other provision not prohibited by law.

(d)   The articles of merger or share exchange shall be delivered to the secretary of state for filing and, subject to subsection (e), the merger or share exchange shall take effect at the effective date determined in accordance with section 1.23.

(e)   With respect to a merger in which one or more foreign entities is a party or a foreign entity created by the merger is the survivor, the merger itself shall become effective at the later of:

(1)   when all documents required to be filed in foreign jurisdictions to effect the merger have become effective, or

(2)   when the articles of merger take effect.

(f)   Articles of merger filed under this section may be combined with any filing required under the organic law governing any domestic eligible entity involved in the transaction if the combined filing satisfies the requirements of both this section and the other organic law.

§ 11.07   Effect of Merger or Share Exchange

(a)   When a merger becomes effective:

(1)   the domestic or foreign corporation or eligible entity that is designated in the plan of merger as the survivor continues or comes into existence, as the case may be;

(2)   the separate existence of every domestic or foreign corporation or eligible entity that is a party to the merger, other than the survivor, ceases;

(3)   all property owned by, and every contract right possessed by, each domestic or foreign corporation or eligible entity that is a party to the merger, other than the survivor, are the property and contract rights of the survivor without transfer, reversion or impairment;

(4)   all debts, obligations and other liabilities of each domestic or foreign corporation or eligible entity that is a party to the merger, other than the survivor, are debts, obligations or liabilities of the survivor;

(5)   the name of the survivor may, but need not be, substituted in any pending proceeding for the name of any party to the merger whose separate existence ceased in the merger;

(6)   if the survivor is a domestic entity, the articles of incorporation and bylaws or the organic rules of the survivor are amended to the extent provided in the plan of merger;

(7)   the articles of incorporation and bylaws or the organic rules of a survivor that is a domestic entity and is created by the merger become effective;

(8)   the shares of each domestic or foreign corporation that is a party to the merger, and the eligible interests in an eligible entity that is a party to a merger, that are to be converted in accordance with the terms of the merger into shares or other securities, eligible interests, obligations, rights to acquire shares, other securities, or eligible interests, cash, other property, or any combination of the foregoing, are converted, and the former holders of such shares or eligible interests are entitled only to the rights provided to them by those terms or to any rights they may have under chapter 13 or the organic law governing the eligible entity or foreign corporation;

(9)   except as provided by law or the terms of the merger, all the rights, privileges, franchises, and immunities of each entity that is a party to the merger, other than the survivor, are the rights, privileges, franchises, and immunities of the survivor; and

(10)   if the survivor exists before the merger:

(i)   all the property and contract rights of the survivor remain its property and contract rights without transfer, reversion, or impairment;

(ii)   the survivor remains subject to all its debts, obligations, and other liabilities; and

(iii) except as provided by law or the plan of merger, the survivor continues to hold all of its rights, privileges, franchises, and immunities.

(b)   When a share exchange becomes effective, the shares or eligible interests in the acquired entity that are to be exchanged for shares or other securities, eligible interests, obligations, rights to acquire shares, other securities or eligible interests, cash, other property, or any combination of the foregoing, are entitled only to the rights provided to them in the plan of share exchange or to any rights they may have under chapter 13 or under the organic law governing the acquired entity.

(c)   Except as otherwise provided in the articles of incorporation of a domestic corporation or the organic law governing or organic rules of a foreign corporation or a domestic or foreign eligible entity, the effect of a merger or share exchange on interest holder liability is as follows:

(1)   A person who becomes subject to new interest holder liability in respect of an entity as a result of a merger or share exchange shall have that new interest holder liability only in respect of interest holder liabilities that arise after the merger or share exchange becomes effective.

(2)   If a person had interest holder liability with respect to a party to the merger or the acquired entity before the merger or share exchange becomes effective with respect to shares or eligible interests of such party or acquired entity which were (i) exchanged in the merger or share exchange, (ii) were cancelled in the merger or (iii) the terms and conditions of which relating to interest holder liability were amended pursuant to the merger:

(i)   The merger or share exchange does not discharge that prior interest holder liability with respect to any interest holder liabilities that arose before the merger or share exchange becomes effective.

(ii)   The provisions of the organic law governing any entity for which the person had that prior interest holder liability shall continue to apply to the collection or discharge of any interest holder liabilities preserved by subsection (c)(2)(i), as if the merger or share exchange had not occurred.

(iii) The person shall have such rights of contribution from other persons as are provided by the organic law governing the entity for which the person had that prior interest holder liability with respect to any interest holder liabilities preserved by subsection (c)(2)(i), as if the merger or share exchange had not occurred.

(iv)   The person shall not, by reason of such prior interest holder liability, have interest holder liability with respect to any interest holder liabilities that arise after the merger or share exchange becomes effective.

(3)   If a person has interest holder liability both before and after a merger becomes effective with unchanged terms and conditions with respect to the entity that is the survivor by reason of owning the same shares or eligible interests before and after the merger becomes effective, the merger has no effect on such interest holder liability.

(4)   A share exchange has no effect on interest holder liability related to shares or eligible interests of the acquired entity that were not exchanged in the share exchange.

(d)   Upon a merger becoming effective, a foreign corporation, or a foreign eligible entity, that is the survivor of the merger is deemed to:

(1)   appoint the secretary of state as its agent for service of process in a proceeding to enforce the rights of shareholders of each domestic corporation that is a party to the merger who exercise appraisal rights; and

(2)   agree that it will promptly pay the amount, if any, to which such shareholders are entitled under chapter 13.

(e)   Except as provided in the organic law governing a party to a merger or in its articles of incorporation or organic rules, the merger does not give rise to any rights that an interest holder, governor, or third party would have upon a dissolution, liquidation, or winding up of that party. The merger does not require a party to the merger to wind up its affairs and does not constitute or cause its dissolution or termination.

(f)   Property held for a charitable purpose under the law of this state by a domestic or foreign corporation or eligible entity immediately before a merger becomes effective may not, as a result of the transaction, be diverted from the objects for which it was donated, granted, devised, or otherwise transferred except and to the extent permitted by or pursuant to the laws of this state addressing cy près or dealing with nondiversion of charitable assets.

(g)   A bequest, devise, gift, grant, or promise contained in a will or other instrument of donation, subscription, or conveyance which is made to an entity that is a party to a merger that is not the survivor and which takes effect or remains payable after the merger inures to the survivor.

(h)   A trust obligation that would govern property if transferred to a nonsurviving entity applies to property that is transferred to the survivor after a merger becomes effective

§ 11.08   Abandonment of a Merger or Share Exchange

(a)   After a plan of merger or share exchange has been adopted and approved as required by this chapter, and before articles of merger or share exchange have become effective, the plan may be abandoned by a domestic business corporation that is a party to the plan without action by its shareholders in accordance with any procedures set forth in the plan of merger or share exchange or, if no such procedures are set forth in the plan, in the manner determined by the board of directors.

(b)   If a merger or share exchange is abandoned under subsection (a) after articles of merger or share exchange have been delivered to the secretary of state for filing but before the merger or share exchange has become effective, a statement of abandonment signed by all the parties that signed the articles of merger or share exchange shall be delivered to the secretary of state for filing before the articles of merger or share exchange become effective. The statement shall take effect on filing and the merger or share exchange shall be deemed abandoned and shall not become effective. The statement of abandonment must contain:

(1)   the name of each party to the merger or the names of the acquiring and acquired entities in a share exchange;

(2)   the date on which the articles of merger or share exchange were filed by the secretary of state; and

(3) a statement that the merger or share exchange has been abandoned in accordance with this section.

CHAPTER 12

DISPOSITION OF ASSETS

§ 12.01 Disposition of Assets Not Requiring Shareholder Approval

No approval of the shareholders is required, unless the articles of incorporation otherwise provide:

(a) to sell, lease, exchange, or otherwise dispose of any or all of the corporation's assets in the usual and regular course of business;

(b) to mortgage, pledge, dedicate to the repayment of indebtedness (whether with or without recourse), or otherwise encumber any or all of the corporation's assets, regardless of whether in the usual and regular course of business;

(c) to transfer any or all of the corporation's assets to one or more domestic or foreign corporations or other entities all of the shares or interests of which are owned by the corporation; or

(d) to distribute assets pro rata to the holders of one or more classes or series of the corporation's shares.

§ 12.02 Shareholder Approval of Certain Dispositions

(a) A sale, lease, exchange, or other disposition of assets, other than a disposition described in section 12.01, requires approval of the corporation's shareholders if the disposition would leave the corporation without a significant continuing business activity. A corporation will conclusively be deemed to have retained a significant continuing business activity if it retains a business activity that represented, for the corporation and its subsidiaries on a consolidated basis, at least (i) 25% of total assets at the end of the most recently completed fiscal year, and (ii) either 25% of either income from continuing operations before taxes or 25% of revenues from continuing operations, in each case, for the most recently completed fiscal year.

(b) To obtain the approval of the shareholders under subsection (a) the board of directors shall first adopt a resolution authorizing the disposition. The disposition shall then be approved by the shareholders. In submitting the disposition to the shareholders for approval, the board of directors shall recommend that the shareholders approve the disposition, unless (i) the board of directors makes a determination that because of conflicts of interest or other special circumstances it should not make such a recommendation, or (ii) section 8.26 applies. If either (i) or (ii) applies, the board shall inform the shareholders of the basis for its so proceeding.

(c) The board of directors may set conditions for the approval by the shareholders of a disposition or the effectiveness of the disposition.

(d) If a disposition is required to be approved by the shareholders under subsection (a), and if the approval is to be given at a meeting, the corporation shall notify each shareholder, regardless of whether entitled to vote, of the meeting of shareholders at which the disposition is to be submitted for approval. The notice must state that the purpose, or one of the purposes, of the meeting is to consider the disposition and must contain a description of the disposition, including the terms and conditions of the disposition and the consideration to be received by the corporation.

(e) Unless the articles of incorporation or the board of directors acting pursuant to subsection (c) require a greater vote or a greater quorum, the approval of a disposition by the shareholders shall require the approval of the shareholders at a meeting at which a quorum exists consisting of a majority of the votes entitled to be cast on the disposition.

(f) After a disposition has been approved by the shareholders under this chapter, and at any time before the disposition has been consummated, it may be abandoned by the corporation without action by the shareholders, subject to any contractual rights of other parties to the disposition.

(g)   A disposition of assets in the course of dissolution under chapter 14 is not governed by this section.

(h)   The assets of a direct or indirect consolidated subsidiary shall be deemed to be the assets of the parent corporation for the purposes of this section.

CHAPTER 13

APPRAISAL RIGHTS

Subchapter A.   Right to Appraisal and Payment for Shares

§ 13.01   Definitions

In this chapter:

"Affiliate" means a person that directly or indirectly through one or more intermediaries controls, is controlled by, or is under common control with another person or is a senior executive of such person. For purposes of section 13.02(b)(4), a person is deemed to be an affiliate of its senior executives.

"Corporation" means the domestic corporation that is the issuer of the shares held by a shareholder demanding appraisal and, for matters covered in sections 13.22 through 13.31, includes the survivor of a merger.

"Fair value" means the value of the corporation's shares determined:

(i)   immediately before the effectiveness of the corporate action to which the shareholder objects;

(ii)   using customary and current valuation concepts and techniques generally employed for similar businesses in the context of the transaction requiring appraisal; and

(iii)   without discounting for lack of marketability or minority status except, if appropriate, for amendments to the articles of incorporation pursuant to section 13.02(a)(5).

"Interest" means interest from the date the corporate action becomes effective until the date of payment, at the rate of interest on judgments in this state on the effective date of the corporate action.

"Interested transaction" means a corporate action described in section 13.02(a), other than a merger pursuant to section 11.05, involving an interested person in which any of the shares or assets of the corporation are being acquired or converted. As used in this definition:

(i)   "Interested person" means a person, or an affiliate of a person, who at any time during the one-year period immediately preceding approval by the board of directors of the corporate action:

(A)   was the beneficial owner of 20% or more of the voting power of the corporation, other than as owner of excluded shares;

(B)   had the power, contractually or otherwise, other than as owner of excluded shares, to cause the appointment or election of 25% or more of the directors to the board of directors of the corporation; or

(C)   was a senior executive or director of the corporation or a senior executive of any affiliate of the corporation, and that senior executive or director will receive, as a result of the corporate action, a financial benefit not generally available to other shareholders as such, other than:

(I)   employment, consulting, retirement, or similar benefits established separately and not as part of or in contemplation of the corporate action;

(II)   employment, consulting, retirement, or similar benefits established in contemplation of, or as part of, the corporate action that are not more favorable than those existing before the corporate action or, if more favorable, that have been approved on behalf of the corporation in the same manner as is provided in section 8.62; or

(III) in the case of a director of the corporation who will, in the corporate action, become a director or governor of the acquiror or any of its affiliates, rights and benefits as a director or governor that are provided on the same basis as those afforded by the acquiror generally to other directors or governors of such entity or such affiliate.

(ii) "Beneficial owner" means any person who, directly or indirectly, through any contract, arrangement, or understanding, other than a revocable proxy, has or shares the power to vote, or to direct the voting of, shares; except that a member of a national securities exchange is not deemed to be a beneficial owner of securities held directly or indirectly by it on behalf of another person if the member is precluded by the rules of the exchange from voting without instruction on contested matters or matters that may affect substantially the rights or privileges of the holders of the securities to be voted. When two or more persons agree to act together for the purpose of voting their shares of the corporation, each member of the group formed thereby is deemed to have acquired beneficial ownership, as of the date of the agreement, of all shares having voting power of the corporation beneficially owned by any member of the group.

(iii) "Excluded shares" means shares acquired pursuant to an offer for all shares having voting power if the offer was made within one year before the corporate action for consideration of the same kind and of a value equal to or less than that paid in connection with the corporate action.

"Preferred shares" means a class or series of shares whose holders have preference over any other class or series of shares with respect to distributions.

"Senior executive" means the chief executive officer, chief operating officer, chief financial officer, and any individual in charge of a principal business unit or function.

"Shareholder" means a record shareholder, a beneficial shareholder, and a voting trust beneficial owner.

§ 13.02   Right to Appraisal

(a)   A shareholder is entitled to appraisal rights, and to obtain payment of the fair value of that shareholder's shares, in the event of any of the following corporate actions:

(1)   consummation of a merger to which the corporation is a party (i) if shareholder approval is required for the merger by section 11.04, or would be required but for the provisions of section 11.04(j), except that appraisal rights shall not be available to any shareholder of the corporation with respect to shares of any class or series that remain outstanding after consummation of the merger, or (ii) if the corporation is a subsidiary and the merger is governed by section 11.05;

(2)   consummation of a share exchange to which the corporation is a party the shares of which will be acquired, except that appraisal rights shall not be available to any shareholder of the corporation with respect to any class or series of shares of the corporation that is not acquired in the share exchange;

(3)   consummation of a disposition of assets pursuant to section 12.02 if the shareholder is entitled to vote on the disposition, except that appraisal rights shall not be available to any shareholder of the corporation with respect to shares of any class or series if (i) under the terms of the corporate action approved by the shareholders there is to be distributed to shareholders in cash the corporation's net assets, in excess of a reasonable amount reserved to meet claims of the type described in sections 14.06 and 14.07, (A) within one year after the shareholders' approval of the action and (B) in accordance with their respective interests determined at the time of distribution, and (ii) the disposition of assets is not an interested transaction;

(4)   an amendment of the articles of incorporation with respect to a class or series of shares that reduces the number of shares of a class or series owned by the shareholder to a fraction of a share if the corporation has the obligation or right to repurchase the fractional share so created;

(5)   any other merger, share exchange, disposition of assets or amendment to the articles of incorporation, in each case to the extent provided by the articles of incorporation, bylaws or a resolution of the board of directors;

(6)   consummation of a domestication pursuant to section 9.20 if the shareholder does not receive shares in the foreign corporation resulting from the domestication that have terms as favorable to the shareholder in all material respects, and represent at least the same percentage interest of the total voting rights of the outstanding shares of the foreign corporation, as the shares held by the shareholder before the domestication;

(7)   consummation of a conversion of the corporation to a nonprofit corporation pursuant to section 9.30; or

(8)   consummation of a conversion of the corporation to an unincorporated entity pursuant to section 9.30.

(b)   Notwithstanding subsection (a), the availability of appraisal rights under subsections (a)(1), (2), (3), (4), (6) and (8) shall be limited in accordance with the following provisions:

(1)   Appraisal rights shall not be available for the holders of shares of any class or series of shares which is:

(i)   a covered security under section 18(b)(1)(A) or (B) of the Securities Act of 1933;

(ii)   traded in an organized market and has at least 2,000 shareholders and a market value of at least $20 million (exclusive of the value of such shares held by the corporation's subsidiaries, senior executives and directors and by any beneficial shareholder and any voting trust beneficial owner owning more than 10% of such shares); or

(iii)   issued by an open end management investment company registered with the Securities and Exchange Commission under the Investment Company Act of 1940 and which may be redeemed at the option of the holder at net asset value.

(2)   The applicability of subsection (b)(1) shall be determined as of:

(i)   the record date fixed to determine the shareholders entitled to receive notice of the meeting of shareholders to act upon the corporate action requiring appraisal rights or, in the case of an offer made pursuant to section 11.04(j), the date of such offer; or

(ii)   if there is no meeting of shareholders and no offer made pursuant to section 11.04(j), the day before the consummation of the corporate action or effective date of the amendment of the articles of incorporation, as applicable.

(3)   Subsection (b)(1) shall not be applicable and appraisal rights shall be available pursuant to subsection (a) for the holders of any class or series of shares (i) who are required by the terms of the corporate action requiring appraisal rights to accept for such shares anything other than cash or shares of any class or any series of shares of any corporation, or any other proprietary interest of any other entity, that satisfies the standards set forth in subsection (b)(1) at the time the corporate action becomes effective, or (ii) in the case of the consummation of a disposition of assets pursuant to section 12.02, unless the cash, shares, or proprietary interests received in the disposition are, under the terms of the corporate action approved by the shareholders, to be distributed to the shareholders, as part of a distribution to shareholders of the net assets of the corporation in excess of a reasonable amount to meet claims of the type described in sections 14.06 and 14.07, (A) within one year after the shareholders' approval of the action, and (B) in accordance with their respective interests determined at the time of the distribution.

(4)   Subsection (b)(1) shall not be applicable and appraisal rights shall be available pursuant to subsection (a) for the holders of any class or series of shares where the corporate action is an interested transaction.

(c)   Notwithstanding any other provision of section 13.02, the articles of incorporation as originally filed or any amendment to the articles of incorporation may limit or eliminate appraisal rights for any class or series of preferred shares, except that (i) no such limitation or elimination shall be effective if the class or series does not have the right to vote separately as a voting group (alone or as part of a group) on the action or if the action is a conversion under section 9.30, or a merger having a similar effect as a conversion in which the converted entity is an eligible entity, and (ii) any such limitation or elimination contained in an amendment to the articles of incorporation that limits or eliminates appraisal rights for any of such shares that are outstanding immediately before the effective date of such amendment or that the corporation is or may be required to issue or sell thereafter pursuant to any conversion, exchange or other right existing immediately before the effective date of such amendment shall not apply to any corporate action that becomes effective within one year after the effective date of such amendment if such action would otherwise afford appraisal rights.

§ 13.03 Assertion of Rights by Nominees and Beneficial Shareholders

(a)   A record shareholder may assert appraisal rights as to fewer than all the shares registered in the record shareholder's name but owned by a beneficial shareholder or a voting trust beneficial owner only if the record shareholder objects with respect to all shares of a class or series owned by the beneficial shareholder or the voting trust beneficial owner and notifies the corporation in writing of the name and address of each beneficial shareholder or voting trust beneficial owner on whose behalf appraisal rights are being asserted. The rights of a record shareholder who asserts appraisal rights for only part of the shares held of record in the record shareholder's name under this subsection shall be determined as if the shares as to which the record shareholder objects and the record shareholder's other shares were registered in the names of different record shareholders.

(b)   A beneficial shareholder and a voting trust beneficial owner may assert appraisal rights as to shares of any class or series held on behalf of the shareholder only if such shareholder:

(1)   submits to the corporation the record shareholder's written consent to the assertion of such rights no later than the date referred to in section 13.22(b)(2)(ii); and

(2)   does so with respect to all shares of the class or series that are beneficially owned by the beneficial shareholder or the voting trust beneficial owner.

Subchapter B.   Procedure for Exercise of Appraisal Rights

§ 13.20   Notice of Appraisal Rights

(a)   Where any corporate action specified in section 13.02(a) is to be submitted to a vote at a shareholders' meeting, the meeting notice (or where no approval of such action is required pursuant to section 11.04(j), the offer made pursuant to section 11.04(j)), must state that the corporation has concluded that appraisal rights are, are not or may be available under this chapter. If the corporation concludes that appraisal rights are or may be available, a copy of this chapter must accompany the meeting notice or offer sent to those record shareholders entitled to exercise appraisal rights.

(b)   In a merger pursuant to section 11.05, the parent entity shall notify in writing all record shareholders of the subsidiary who are entitled to assert appraisal rights that the corporate action became effective. Such notice shall be sent within 10 days after the corporate action became effective and include the materials described in section 13.22.

(c)   Where any corporate action specified in section 13.02(a) is to be approved by written consent of the shareholders pursuant to section 7.04:

(1)   written notice that appraisal rights are, are not or may be available shall be sent to each record shareholder from whom a consent is solicited at the time consent of such shareholder is first solicited and, if the corporation has concluded that appraisal rights are or may be available, the notice must be accompanied by a copy of this chapter; and

(2)   written notice that appraisal rights are, are not or may be available must be delivered together with the notice to nonconsenting and nonvoting shareholders required by sections 7.04(e) and (f), may include the materials described in section 13.22 and, if the corporation has concluded that appraisal rights are or may be available, must be accompanied by a copy of this chapter.

(d)   Where corporate action described in section 13.02(a) is proposed, or a merger pursuant to section 11.05 is effected, the notice referred to in subsection (a) or (c), if the corporation concludes that appraisal rights are or may be available, and in subsection (b) must be accompanied by:

(1)   financial statements of the corporation that issued the shares that may be subject to appraisal, consisting of a balance sheet as of the end of a fiscal year ending not more than 16 months before the date of the notice, an income statement for that year, and a cash flow statement for that year; provided that, if such financial statements are not reasonably available, the corporation shall provide reasonably equivalent financial information; and

(2)   the latest interim financial statements of such corporation, if any.

(e)   The right to receive the information described in subsection (d) may be waived in writing by a shareholder before or after the corporate action.

§ 13.21   Notice of Intent to Demand Payment and Consequences of Voting or Consenting

(a)   If a corporate action specified in section 13.02(a) is submitted to a vote at a shareholders' meeting, a shareholder who wishes to assert appraisal rights with respect to any class or series of shares:

(1)   shall deliver to the corporation, before the vote is taken, written notice of the shareholder's intent to demand payment if the proposed action is effectuated; and

(2)   shall not vote, or cause or permit to be voted, any shares of such class or series in favor of the proposed action.

(b)   If a corporate action specified in section 13.02(a) is to be approved by written consent, a shareholder who wishes to assert appraisal rights with respect to any class or series of shares shall not sign a consent in favor of the proposed action with respect to that class or series of shares.

(c)   If a corporate action specified in section 13.02(a) does not require shareholder approval pursuant to section 11.04(j), a shareholder who wishes to assert appraisal rights with respect to any class or series of shares (i) shall deliver to the corporation before the shares are purchased pursuant to the offer written notice of the shareholder's intent to demand payment if the proposed action is effected; and (ii) shall not tender, or cause or permit to be tendered, any shares of such class or series in response to such offer.

(d)   A shareholder who fails to satisfy the requirements of subsection (a), (b) or (c) is not entitled to payment under this chapter.

§ 13.22   Appraisal Notice and Form

(a)   If a corporate action requiring appraisal rights under section 13.02(a) becomes effective, the corporation shall deliver a written appraisal notice and form required by subsection (b) to all shareholders who satisfy the requirements of sections 13.21(a), (b) or (c). In the case of a merger under section 11.05, the parent shall deliver an appraisal notice and form to all record shareholders who may be entitled to assert appraisal rights.

(b)   The appraisal notice shall be delivered no earlier than the date the corporate action specified in section 13.02(a) became effective, and no later than 10 days after such date, and must:

(1)   supply a form that (i) specifies the first date of any announcement to shareholders made before the date the corporate action became effective of the principal terms of the proposed corporate action, and (ii) if such announcement was made, requires the shareholder asserting appraisal rights to certify whether beneficial ownership of those shares for which appraisal rights are asserted was acquired before that date, and (iii) requires the shareholder asserting appraisal rights to certify that such shareholder did not vote for or consent to the transaction as to the class or series of shares for which appraisal is sought;

(2)   state:

(i)   where the form shall be sent and where certificates for certificated shares shall be deposited and the date by which those certificates must be deposited, which date may not be earlier than the date by which the corporation must receive the required form under subsection (b)(2)(ii);

(ii)   a date by which the corporation shall receive the form, which date may not be fewer than 40 nor more than 60 days after the date the subsection (a) appraisal notice is sent, and state that the shareholder shall have waived the right to demand appraisal with respect to the shares unless the form is received by the corporation by such specified date;

(iii)   the corporation's estimate of the fair value of the shares;

(iv)   that, if requested in writing, the corporation will provide, to the shareholder so requesting, within 10 days after the date specified in subsection (b)(2)(ii) the number of shareholders who return the forms by the specified date and the total number of shares owned by them; and

(v)   the date by which the notice to withdraw under section 13.23 shall be received, which date shall be within 20 days after the date specified in subsection (b)(2)(ii); and

(3)   be accompanied by a copy of this chapter.

§ 13.23   Perfection of Rights; Right to Withdraw

(a)   A shareholder who receives notice pursuant to section 13.22 and who wishes to exercise appraisal rights shall sign and return the form sent by the corporation and, in the case of certificated shares, deposit the shareholder's certificates in accordance with the terms of the notice by the date referred to in the notice pursuant to section 13.22(b)(2)(ii). In addition, if applicable, the shareholder shall certify on the form whether the beneficial owner of such shares acquired beneficial ownership of the shares before the date required to be set forth in the notice pursuant to section 13.22(b)(1)(i). If a shareholder fails to make this certification, the corporation may elect to treat the shareholder's shares as after-acquired shares under section 13.25. Once a shareholder deposits that shareholder's certificates or, in the case of uncertificated shares, returns the signed forms, that shareholder loses all rights as a shareholder, unless the shareholder withdraws pursuant to subsection (b).

(b)   A shareholder who has complied with subsection (a) may nevertheless decline to exercise appraisal rights and withdraw from the appraisal process by so notifying the corporation in writing by the date set forth in the appraisal notice pursuant to section 13.22(b)(2)(v). A shareholder who fails to so withdraw from the appraisal process may not thereafter withdraw without the corporation's written consent.

(c)   A shareholder who does not sign and return the form and, in the case of certificated shares, deposit that shareholder's share certificates where required, each by the date set forth in the notice described in section 13.22(b), shall not be entitled to payment under this chapter.

§ 13.24   Payment

(a)   Except as provided in section 13.25, within 30 days after the form required by section 13.22(b)(2)(ii) is due, the corporation shall pay in cash to those shareholders who complied with section 13.23(a) the amount the corporation estimates to be the fair value of their shares, plus interest.

(b)   The payment to each shareholder pursuant to subsection (a) must be accompanied by:

(1) (i)   financial statements of the corporation that issued the shares to be appraised, consisting of a balance sheet as of the end of a fiscal year ending not more than 16 months before the date of payment, an income statement for that year, and a cash flow statement for that year; provided that, if such annual financial statements are not reasonably available, the corporation shall provide reasonably equivalent financial information, and (ii) the latest interim financial statements of such corporation, if any;

(2)   a statement of the corporation's estimate of the fair value of the shares, which estimate shall equal or exceed the corporation's estimate given pursuant to section 13.22(b)(2)(iii); and

(3)   a statement that shareholders described in subsection (a) have the right to demand further payment under section 13.26 and that if any such shareholder does not do so within the time period specified in section 13.26(b), such shareholder shall be deemed to have accepted the payment under subsection (a) in full satisfaction of the corporation's obligations under this chapter.

§ 13.25   After-Acquired Shares

(a)   A corporation may elect to withhold payment required by section 13.24 from any shareholder who was required to, but did not certify that beneficial ownership of all of the shareholder's shares for which appraisal rights are asserted was acquired before the date set forth in the appraisal notice sent pursuant to section 13.22(b)(1).

(b)   If the corporation elected to withhold payment under subsection (a), it shall, within 30 days after the form required by section 13.22(b)(2)(ii) is due, notify all shareholders who are described in subsection (a):

(1)   of the information required by section 13.24(b)(1);

(2)   of the corporation's estimate of fair value pursuant to section 13.24(b)(2);

(3)   that they may accept the corporation's estimate of fair value, plus interest, in full satisfaction of their demands or demand appraisal under section 13.26;

(4)   that those shareholders who wish to accept such offer shall so notify the corporation of their acceptance of the corporation's offer within 30 days after receiving the offer; and

(5)   that those shareholders who do not satisfy the requirements for demanding appraisal under section 13.26 shall be deemed to have accepted the corporation's offer.

(c)   Within 10 days after receiving the shareholder's acceptance pursuant to subsection (b)(4), the corporation shall pay in cash the amount it offered under subsection (b)(2) plus interest to each shareholder who agreed to accept the corporation's offer in full satisfaction of the shareholder's demand.

(d)   Within 40 days after delivering the notice described in subsection (b), the corporation shall pay in cash the amount it offered to pay under subsection (b)(2) plus interest to each shareholder described in subsection (b)(5).

§ 13.26   Procedure if Shareholder Dissatisfied with Payment or Offer

(a)   A shareholder paid pursuant to section 13.24 who is dissatisfied with the amount of the payment shall notify the corporation in writing of that shareholder's estimate of the fair value of the shares and demand payment of that estimate (less any payment under section 13.24) plus interest. A shareholder offered payment under section 13.25 who is dissatisfied with that offer shall reject the offer and demand payment of the shareholder's stated estimate of the fair value of the shares plus interest.

(b)   A shareholder who fails to notify the corporation in writing of that shareholder's demand to be paid the shareholder's stated estimate of the fair value plus interest under subsection (a) within 30 days after receiving the corporation's payment or offer of payment under section 13.24 or section 13.25, respectively, waives the right to demand payment under this section and shall be entitled only to the payment made or offered pursuant to those respective sections.

Subchapter C.   Judicial Appraisal of Shares

§ 13.30   Court Action

(a)   If a shareholder makes demand for payment under section 13.26 which remains unsettled, the corporation shall commence a proceeding within 60 days after receiving the payment demand and petition the court to determine the fair value of the shares and accrued interest. If the corporation does not commence the proceeding within the 60-day period, it shall pay in cash to each shareholder the amount the shareholder demanded pursuant to section 13.26 plus interest.

(b)   The corporation shall commence the proceeding in the [name or describe court].

(c)   The corporation shall make all shareholders (regardless of whether they are residents of this state) whose demands remain unsettled parties to the proceeding as in an action against their shares, and all parties shall be served with a copy of the petition. Nonresidents may be served by registered or certified mail or by publication as provided by law.

(d)   The jurisdiction of the court in which the proceeding is commenced under subsection (b) is plenary and exclusive. The court may appoint one or more persons as appraisers to receive evidence and recommend a decision on the question of fair value. The appraisers shall have the powers described in the order appointing them, or in any amendment to it. The shareholders demanding appraisal rights are entitled to the same discovery rights as parties in other civil proceedings. There shall be no right to a jury trial.

(e)   Each shareholder made a party to the proceeding is entitled to judgment (i) for the amount, if any, by which the court finds the fair value of the shareholder's shares exceeds the amount paid by the corporation to the shareholder for such shares, plus interest, or (ii) for the fair value, plus interest, of the shareholder's shares for which the corporation elected to withhold payment under section 13.25.

§ 13.31   Court Costs and Expenses

(a)   The court in an appraisal proceeding commenced under section 13.30 shall determine all court costs of the proceeding, including the reasonable compensation and expenses of appraisers appointed by the court. The court shall assess the court costs against the corporation, except that the court may assess court costs against all or some of the shareholders demanding appraisal, in amounts which the court finds equitable, to the extent the court finds such shareholders acted arbitrarily, vexatiously, or not in good faith with respect to the rights provided by this chapter.

(b)   The court in an appraisal proceeding may also assess the expenses of the respective parties in amounts the court finds equitable:

(1)   against the corporation and in favor of any or all shareholders demanding appraisal if the court finds the corporation did not substantially comply with the requirements of sections 13.20, 13.22, 13.24, or 13.25; or

(2)   against either the corporation or a shareholder demanding appraisal, in favor of any other party, if the court finds the party against whom expenses are assessed acted arbitrarily, vexatiously, or not in good faith with respect to the rights provided by this chapter.

(c)   If the court in an appraisal proceeding finds that the expenses incurred by any shareholder were of substantial benefit to other shareholders similarly situated and that such expenses should not be assessed against the corporation, the court may direct that such expenses be paid out of the amounts awarded the shareholders who were benefited.

(d)   To the extent the corporation fails to make a required payment pursuant to sections 13.24, 13.25, or 13.26, the shareholder may sue directly for the amount owed, and to the extent successful, shall be entitled to recover from the corporation all expenses of the suit.

Subchapter D.   Other Remedies

§ 13.40   Other Remedies Limited

(a)   The legality of a proposed or completed corporate action described in section 13.02(a) may not be contested, nor may the corporate action be enjoined, set aside or rescinded, in a legal or equitable proceeding by a shareholder after the shareholders have approved the corporate action.

(b)   Subsection (a) does not apply to a corporate action that:

(1)   was not authorized and approved in accordance with the applicable provisions of:

(i)   chapter 9, 10, 11, or 12;

(ii)   the articles of incorporation or bylaws; or

(iii)   the resolution of the board of directors authorizing the corporate action;

(2)   was procured as a result of fraud, a material misrepresentation, or an omission of a material fact necessary to make statements made, in light of the circumstances in which they were made, not misleading;

(3)   is an interested transaction, unless it has been recommended by the board of directors in the same manner as is provided in section 8.62 and has been approved by the shareholders in the same manner as is provided in section 8.63 as if the interested transaction were a director's conflicting interest transaction; or

(4)   is approved by less than unanimous consent of the voting shareholders pursuant to section 7.04 if:

(i)   the challenge to the corporate action is brought by a shareholder who did not consent and as to whom notice of the approval of the corporate action was not effective at least 10 days before the corporate action was effected; and

(ii)   the proceeding challenging the corporate action is commenced within 10 days after notice of the approval of the corporate action is effective as to the shareholder bringing the proceeding.

CHAPTER 14

DISSOLUTION

Subchapter A.   Voluntary Dissolution

§ 14.01   Dissolution by Incorporators or Initial Directors

A majority of the incorporators or initial directors of a corporation that has not issued shares or has not commenced business may dissolve the corporation by delivering to the secretary of state for filing articles of dissolution that set forth:

(a)   the name of the corporation;

(b)   the date of its incorporation;

(c)   either (i) that none of the corporation's shares has been issued or (ii) that the corporation has not commenced business;

(d)   that no debt of the corporation remains unpaid;

(e)   that the net assets of the corporation remaining after winding up have been distributed to the shareholders, if shares were issued; and

(f)   that a majority of the incorporators or initial directors authorized the dissolution.

§ 14.02   Dissolution by Board of Directors and Shareholders

(a)   The board of directors may propose dissolution for submission to the shareholders by first adopting a resolution authorizing the dissolution.

(b)   For a proposal to dissolve to be adopted, it shall then be approved by the shareholders. In submitting the proposal to dissolve to the shareholders for approval, the board of directors shall recommend that the shareholders approve the dissolution, unless (i) the board of directors determines that because of conflict of interest or other special circumstances it should make no recommendation or (ii) section 8.26 applies. If either (i) or (ii) applies, the board shall inform the shareholders of the basis for its so proceeding.

(c)   The board of directors may set conditions for the approval of the proposal for dissolution by shareholders or the effectiveness of the dissolution.

(d)   If the approval of the shareholders is to be given at a meeting, the corporation shall notify each shareholder, regardless of whether entitled to vote, of the meeting of shareholders at which the dissolution is to be submitted for approval. The notice must state that the purpose, or one of the purposes, of the meeting is to consider dissolving the corporation.

(e)   Unless the articles of incorporation or the board of directors acting pursuant to subsection (c) require a greater vote, a greater quorum, or a vote by voting groups, adoption of the proposal to dissolve shall require the approval of the shareholders at a meeting at which a quorum exists consisting of a majority of the votes entitled to be cast on the proposal to dissolve.

§ 14.03   Articles of Dissolution

(a)   At any time after dissolution is authorized, the corporation may dissolve by delivering to the secretary of state for filing articles of dissolution setting forth:

(1)   the name of the corporation;

(2)   the date that dissolution was authorized; and

(3)   if dissolution was approved by the shareholders, a statement that the proposal to dissolve was duly approved by the shareholders in the manner required by this Act and by the articles of incorporation.

(b)   The articles of dissolution shall take effect at the effective date determined in accordance with section 1.23. A corporation is dissolved upon the effective date of its articles of dissolution.

(c)   For purposes of this subchapter, "dissolved corporation" means a corporation whose articles of dissolution have become effective and includes a successor entity to which the remaining assets of the corporation are transferred subject to its liabilities for purposes of liquidation.

§ 14.04   Revocation of Dissolution

(a)   A corporation may revoke its dissolution within 120 days after its effective date.

(b)   Revocation of dissolution shall be authorized in the same manner as the dissolution was authorized unless that authorization permitted revocation by action of the board of directors alone, in which event the board of directors may revoke the dissolution without shareholder action.

(c)   After the revocation of dissolution is authorized, the corporation may revoke the dissolution by delivering to the secretary of state for filing articles of revocation of dissolution, together with a copy of its articles of dissolution, that set forth:

(1)   the name of the corporation;

(2)   the effective date of the dissolution that was revoked;

(3)   the date that the revocation of dissolution was authorized;

(4)   if the corporation's board of directors (or incorporators) revoked the dissolution, a statement to that effect;

(5)   if the corporation's board of directors revoked a dissolution as authorized by the shareholders, a statement that revocation was permitted by action by the board of directors alone pursuant to that authorization; and

(6)   if shareholder action was required to revoke the dissolution, a statement that the revocation was duly approved by the shareholders in the manner required by this Act and by the articles of incorporation.

(d)   Revocation of dissolution is effective upon the effective date of the articles of revocation of dissolution.

(e)   When the revocation of dissolution is effective, it relates back to and takes effect as of the effective date of the dissolution and the corporation resumes carrying on its business as if dissolution had never occurred.

§ 14.05   Effect of Dissolution

(a)   A corporation that has dissolved continues its corporate existence but the dissolved corporation may not carry on any business except that appropriate to wind up and liquidate its business and affairs, including:

(1)   collecting its assets;

(2)   disposing of its properties that will not be distributed in kind to its shareholders;

(3)   discharging or making provision for discharging its liabilities;

(4)   making distributions of its remaining assets among its shareholders according to their interests; and

(5)   doing every other act necessary to wind up and liquidate its business and affairs.

(b)   Dissolution of a corporation does not:

(1)   transfer title to the corporation's property;

(2)   prevent transfer of its shares or securities;

(3)   subject its directors or officers to standards of conduct different from those prescribed in chapter 8;

(4)   change (i) quorum or voting requirements for its board of directors or shareholders; (ii) provisions for selection, resignation, or removal of its directors or officers or both; or (iii) provisions for amending its bylaws;

(5)   prevent commencement of a proceeding by or against the corporation in its corporate name;

(6)   abate or suspend a proceeding pending by or against the corporation on the effective date of dissolution; or

(7)   terminate the authority of the registered agent of the corporation.

(c)   A distribution in liquidation under this section may only be made by a dissolved corporation. For purposes of determining the shareholders entitled to receive a distribution in liquidation, the board of directors may fix a record date for determining shareholders entitled to a distribution in liquidation, which date may not be retroactive. If the board of directors does not fix a record date for determining shareholders entitled to a distribution in liquidation, the record date is the date the board of directors authorizes the distribution in liquidation.

§ 14.06   Known Claims Against Dissolved Corporation

(a)   A dissolved corporation may dispose of the known claims against it by notifying its known claimants in writing of the dissolution at any time after its effective date.

(b)   The written notice must:

(1)   describe information that must be included in a claim;

(2)   provide a mailing address where a claim may be sent;

(3)   state the deadline, which may not be fewer than 120 days after the written notice is effective, by which the dissolved corporation shall receive the claim; and

(4)   state that the claim will be barred if not received by the deadline.

(c) A claim against the dissolved corporation is barred:

(1) if a claimant who was given written notice under subsection (b) does not deliver the claim to the dissolved corporation by the deadline; or

(2) if a claimant whose claim was rejected by the dissolved corporation does not commence a proceeding to enforce the claim within 90 days after the rejection notice is effective.

(d) For purposes of this section, "claim" does not include a contingent liability or a claim based on an event occurring after the effective date of dissolution.

§ 14.07 Other Claims Against Dissolved Corporation

(a) A dissolved corporation may publish notice of its dissolution and request that persons with claims against the dissolved corporation present them in accordance with the notice.

(b) The notice must:

(1) be published (i) one time in a newspaper of general circulation in the county where the dissolved corporation's principal office (or, if none in this state, its registered office) is or was last located or (ii) be posted conspicuously for at least 30 days on the dissolved corporation's website;

(2) describe the information that must be included in a claim and provide a mailing address where the claim may be sent; and

(3) state that a claim against the dissolved corporation will be barred unless a proceeding to enforce the claim is commenced within three years after the publication of the notice.

(c) If the dissolved corporation publishes a notice in accordance with subsection (b), the claim of each of the following claimants is barred unless the claimant commences a proceeding to enforce the claim against the dissolved corporation within three years after the publication date of the notice:

(1) a claimant who was not given written notice under section 14.06;

(2) a claimant whose claim was timely sent to the dissolved corporation but not acted on by the corporation;

(3) a claimant whose claim is contingent or based on an event occurring after the effective date of dissolution.

(d) A claim that is not barred by section 14.06(c) or section 14.07(c) may be enforced:

(1) against the dissolved corporation, to the extent of its undistributed assets; or

(2) except as provided in section 14.08(d), if the assets have been distributed in liquidation, against a shareholder of the dissolved corporation to the extent of the shareholder's pro rata share of the claim or the corporate assets distributed to the shareholder in liquidation, whichever is less, but a shareholder's total liability for all claims under this section may not exceed the total amount of assets distributed to the shareholder.

§ 14.08 Court Proceedings

(a) A dissolved corporation that has published a notice under section 14.07 may file an application with the [name or describe court] for a determination of the amount and form of security to be provided for payment of claims that are contingent or have not been made known to the dissolved corporation or that are based on an event occurring after the effective date of dissolution but that, based on the facts known to the dissolved corporation, are reasonably estimated to arise after the effective date of dissolution. Provision need not be made for any claim that is or is reasonably anticipated to be barred under section 14.07(c).

(b) Within 10 days after the filing of the application, notice of the proceeding shall be given by the dissolved corporation to each claimant holding a contingent claim whose contingent claim is shown on the records of the dissolved corporation.

(c)   The court may appoint a guardian ad litem to represent all claimants whose identities are unknown in any proceeding brought under this section. The reasonable fees and expenses of such guardian, including all reasonable expert witness fees, shall be paid by the dissolved corporation.

(d)   Provision by the dissolved corporation for security in the amount and the form ordered by the court under section 14.08(a) shall satisfy the dissolved corporation's obligations with respect to claims that are contingent, have not been made known to the dissolved corporation or are based on an event occurring after the effective date of dissolution, and such claims may not be enforced against a shareholder who received assets in liquidation.

§ 14.09   Director Duties

(a)   Directors shall cause the dissolved corporation to discharge or make reasonable provision for the payment of claims and make distributions in liquidation of assets to shareholders after payment or provision for claims.

(b)   Directors of a dissolved corporation which has disposed of claims under sections 14.06, 14.07, or 14.08 shall not be liable for breach of section 14.09(a) with respect to claims against the dissolved corporation that are barred or satisfied under sections 14.06, 14.07 or 14.08.

Subchapter B.   Administrative Dissolution

§ 14.20   Grounds for Administrative Dissolution

The secretary of state may commence a proceeding under section 14.21 to dissolve a corporation administratively if:

(a)   the corporation does not pay within 60 days after they are due any fees, taxes, interest or penalties imposed by this Act or other laws of this state;

(b)   the corporation does not deliver its annual report to the secretary of state within 60 days after it is due;

(c)   the corporation is without a registered agent or registered office in this state for 60 days or more;

(d)   the secretary of state has not been notified within 60 days that the corporation's registered agent or registered office has been changed, that its registered agent has resigned, or that its registered office has been discontinued; or

(e)   the corporation's period of duration stated in its articles of incorporation expires.

§ 14.21   Procedure for and Effect of Administrative Dissolution

(a)   If the secretary of state determines that one or more grounds exist under section 14.20 for dissolving a corporation, the secretary of state shall serve the corporation with written notice of such determination under section 5.04.

(b)   If the corporation does not correct each ground for dissolution or demonstrate to the reasonable satisfaction of the secretary of state that each ground determined by the secretary of state does not exist within 60 days after service of the notice under section 5.04, the secretary of state shall administratively dissolve the corporation by signing a certificate of dissolution that recites the ground or grounds for dissolution and its effective date. The secretary of state shall file the original of the certificate and serve a copy on the corporation under section 5.04.

(c)   A corporation administratively dissolved continues its corporate existence but may not carry on any business except that necessary to wind up and liquidate its business and affairs under section 14.05 and notify claimants under sections 14.06 and 14.07.

(d)   The administrative dissolution of a corporation does not terminate the authority of its registered agent.

§ 14.22 Reinstatement Following Administrative Dissolution

(a) A corporation administratively dissolved under section 14.21 may apply to the secretary of state for reinstatement within two years after the effective date of dissolution. The application must:

(1) state the name of the corporation and the effective date of its administrative dissolution;

(2) state that the ground or grounds for dissolution either did not exist or have been eliminated;

(3) state that the corporation's name satisfies the requirements of section 4.01; and

(4) contain a certificate from the [taxing authority] reciting that all taxes owed by the corporation have been paid.

(b) If the secretary of state determines that the application contains the information required by subsection (a) and that the information is correct, the secretary of state shall cancel the certificate of dissolution and prepare a certificate of reinstatement that recites such determination and the effective date of reinstatement, file the original of the certificate, and serve a copy on the corporation under section 5.04.

(c) When the reinstatement is effective, it relates back to and takes effect as of the effective date of the administrative dissolution and the corporation resumes carrying on its business as if the administrative dissolution had never occurred.

§ 14.23 Appeal from Denial of Reinstatement

(a) If the secretary of state denies a corporation's application for reinstatement following administrative dissolution, the secretary of state shall serve the corporation under section 5.04 with a written notice that explains the reason or reasons for denial.

(b) The corporation may appeal the denial of reinstatement to the [name or describe court] within 30 days after service of the notice of denial is effected. The corporation appeals by petitioning the court to set aside the dissolution and attaching to the petition copies of the secretary of state's certificate of dissolution, the corporation's application for reinstatement, and the secretary of state's notice of denial.

(c) The court may summarily order the secretary of state to reinstate the dissolved corporation or may take other action the court considers appropriate.

(d) The court's final decision may be appealed as in other civil proceedings.

Subchapter C. Judicial Dissolution

§ 14.30 Grounds for Judicial Dissolution

(a) The [name or describe court or courts] may dissolve a corporation:

(1) in a proceeding by the attorney general if it is established that:

(i) the corporation obtained its articles of incorporation through fraud; or

(ii) the corporation has continued to exceed or abuse the authority conferred upon it by law;

(2) in a proceeding by a shareholder if it is established that:

(i) the directors are deadlocked in the management of the corporate affairs, the shareholders are unable to break the deadlock, and irreparable injury to the corporation is threatened or being suffered, or the business and affairs of the corporation can no longer be conducted to the advantage of the shareholders generally, because of the deadlock;

(ii) the directors or those in control of the corporation have acted, are acting, or will act in a manner that is illegal, oppressive, or fraudulent;

(iii) the shareholders are deadlocked in voting power and have failed, for a period that includes at least two consecutive annual meeting dates, to elect successors to directors whose terms have expired; or

(iv) the corporate assets are being misapplied or wasted;

(3) in a proceeding by a creditor if it is established that:

(i) the creditor's claim has been reduced to judgment, the execution on the judgment returned unsatisfied, and the corporation is insolvent; or

(ii) the corporation has admitted in writing that the creditor's claim is due and owing and the corporation is insolvent;

(4) in a proceeding by the corporation to have its voluntary dissolution continued under court supervision; or

(5) in a proceeding by a shareholder if the corporation has abandoned its business and has failed within a reasonable time to liquidate and distribute its assets and dissolve.

(b) Subsection (a)(2) shall not apply in the case of a corporation that, on the date of the filing of the proceeding, has shares which are:

(i) a covered security under section 18(b)(1)(A) or (B) of the Securities Act of 1933; or

(ii) not a covered security, but are held by at least 300 shareholders and the shares outstanding have a market value of at least $20 million (exclusive of the value of such shares held by the corporation's subsidiaries, senior executives, directors and beneficial shareholders and voting trust beneficial owners owning more than 10% of such shares).

(c) In subsection (a), "shareholder" means a record shareholder, a beneficial shareholder, and an unrestricted voting trust beneficial owner, and in subsection (b), "shareholder" means a record shareholder, a beneficial shareholder, and a voting trust beneficial owner.

§ 14.31   Procedure for Judicial Dissolution

(a) Venue for a proceeding by the attorney general to dissolve a corporation lies in [name or describe court]. Venue for a proceeding brought by any other party named in section 14.30(a) lies in [name or describe court].

(b) It is not necessary to make shareholders parties to a proceeding to dissolve a corporation unless relief is sought against them individually.

(c) A court in a proceeding brought to dissolve a corporation may issue injunctions, appoint a receiver or custodian during the proceeding with all powers and duties the court directs, take other action required to preserve the corporate assets wherever located, and carry on the business of the corporation until a full hearing can be held.

(d) Within 10 days of the commencement of a proceeding to dissolve a corporation under section 14.30(a)(2), the corporation shall deliver to all shareholders, other than the petitioner, a notice stating that the shareholders are entitled to avoid the dissolution of the corporation by electing to purchase the petitioner's shares under section 14.34 and accompanied by a copy of section 14.34.

§ 14.32   Receivership or Custodianship

(a) Unless an election to purchase has been filed under section 14.34, a court in a judicial proceeding brought to dissolve a corporation may appoint one or more receivers to wind up and liquidate, or one or more custodians to manage, the business and affairs of the corporation. The court shall hold a hearing, after notifying all parties to the proceeding and any interested persons designated by the court, before appointing a receiver or custodian. The court appointing a receiver or custodian has jurisdiction over the corporation and all of its property wherever located.

(b)   The court may appoint an individual or a domestic or foreign corporation or eligible entity as a receiver or custodian, which, if a foreign corporation or foreign eligible entity, must be registered to do business in this state. The court may require the receiver or custodian to post bond, with or without sureties, in an amount the court directs.

(c)   The court shall describe the powers and duties of the receiver or custodian in its appointing order, which may be amended from time to time. Among other powers:

(1)   the receiver (i) may dispose of all or any part of the assets of the corporation wherever located, at a public or private sale; and (ii) may sue and defend in the receiver's own name as receiver of the corporation in all courts of this state;

(2)   the custodian may exercise all of the powers of the corporation, through or in place of its board of directors, to the extent necessary to manage the affairs of the corporation in the best interests of its shareholders and creditors.

The receiver or custodian shall have such other powers and duties as the court may provide in the appointing order, which may be amended from time to time.

(d)   The court during a receivership may redesignate the receiver a custodian and during a custodianship may redesignate the custodian a receiver.

(e)   The court from time to time during the receivership or custodianship may order compensation paid and expenses paid or reimbursed to the receiver or custodian from the assets of the corporation or proceeds from the sale of the assets.

§ 14.33   Decree of Dissolution

(a)   If after a hearing the court determines that one or more grounds for judicial dissolution described in section 14.30 exist, it may enter a decree dissolving the corporation and specifying the effective date of the dissolution, and the clerk of the court shall deliver a certified copy of the decree to the secretary of state for filing.

(b)   After entering the decree of dissolution, the court shall direct the winding-up and liquidation of the corporation's business and affairs in accordance with section 14.05 and the notification of claimants in accordance with sections 14.06 and 14.07.

§ 14.34   Election to Purchase in Lieu of Dissolution

(a)   In a proceeding under section 14.30(a)(2) to dissolve a corporation, the corporation may elect or, if it fails to elect, one or more shareholders may elect to purchase all shares owned by the petitioning shareholder at the fair value of the shares. An election pursuant to this section shall be irrevocable unless the court determines that it is equitable to set aside or modify the election.

(b)   An election to purchase pursuant to this section may be filed with the court at any time within 90 days after the filing of the petition under section 14.30(a)(2) or at such later time as the court in its discretion may allow. If the election to purchase is filed by one or more shareholders, the corporation shall, within 10 days thereafter, give written notice to all shareholders, other than the petitioner. The notice must state the name and number of shares owned by the petitioner and the name and number of shares owned by each electing shareholder and must advise the recipients of their right to join in the election to purchase shares in accordance with this section. Shareholders who wish to participate shall file notice of their intention to join in the purchase no later than 30 days after the effectiveness of the notice to them. All shareholders who have filed an election or notice of their intention to participate in the election to purchase thereby become parties to the proceeding and shall participate in the purchase in proportion to their ownership of shares as of the date the first election was filed, unless they otherwise agree or the court otherwise directs. After an election has been filed by the corporation or one or more shareholders, the proceeding under section 14.30(a)(2) may not be discontinued or settled, nor may the petitioning shareholder sell or otherwise dispose of his or her shares, unless the court determines that it would be equitable to the corporation and the shareholders, other than the petitioner, to permit such discontinuance, settlement, sale, or other disposition.

(c)   If, within 60 days of the filing of the first election, the parties reach agreement as to the fair value and terms of purchase of the petitioner's shares, the court shall enter an order directing the purchase of the petitioner's shares upon the terms and conditions agreed to by the parties.

(d)   If the parties are unable to reach an agreement as provided for in subsection (c), the court, upon application of any party, shall stay the proceedings under section 14.30(a)(2) and determine the fair value of the petitioner's shares as of the day before the date on which the petition under section 14.30(a)(2) was filed or as of such other date as the court deems appropriate under the circumstances.

(e)   Upon determining the fair value of the shares, the court shall enter an order directing the purchase upon such terms and conditions as the court deems appropriate, which may include payment of the purchase price in installments, where necessary in the interests of equity, provision for security to assure payment of the purchase price and any additional expenses as may have been awarded, and, if the shares are to be purchased by shareholders, the allocation of shares among them. In allocating the petitioner's shares among holders of different classes or series of shares, the court should attempt to preserve the existing distribution of voting rights among holders of different classes or series insofar as practicable and may direct that holders of a specific class or classes or series shall not participate in the purchase. Interest may be allowed at the rate and from the date determined by the court to be equitable, but if the court finds that the refusal of the petitioning shareholder to accept an offer of payment was arbitrary or otherwise not in good faith, no interest shall be allowed. If the court finds that the petitioning shareholder had probable grounds for relief under sections 14.30(a)(2)(ii) or (iv), it may award expenses to the petitioning shareholder.

(f)   Upon entry of an order under subsections (c) or (e), the court shall dismiss the petition to dissolve the corporation under section 14.30(a)(2), and the petitioning shareholder shall no longer have any rights or status as a shareholder of the corporation, except the right to receive the amounts awarded by the order of the court which shall be enforceable in the same manner as any other judgment.

(g)   The purchase ordered pursuant to subsection (e) shall be made within 10 days after the date the order becomes final.

(h)   Any payment by the corporation pursuant to an order under subsections (c) or (e), other than an award of expenses pursuant to subsection (e), is subject to the provisions of section 6.40.

Subchapter D.   Miscellaneous

§ 14.40   Deposit with State Treasurer

Assets of a dissolved corporation that should be transferred to a creditor, claimant, or shareholder of the corporation who cannot be found or who is not competent to receive them shall be reduced to cash and deposited with the state treasurer or other appropriate state official for safekeeping. When the creditor, claimant, or shareholder furnishes satisfactory proof of entitlement to the amount deposited, the state treasurer or other appropriate state official shall pay such person or his or her representative that amount.

CHAPTER 15

FOREIGN CORPORATIONS

§ 15.01   Governing Law

(a)   The law of the jurisdiction of formation of a foreign corporation governs:

    (1)   the internal affairs of the foreign corporation; and

    (2)   the interest holder liability of its shareholders.

(b)   A foreign corporation is not precluded from registering to do business in this state because of any difference between the law of the foreign corporation's jurisdiction of formation and the law of this state.

(c) Registration of a foreign corporation to do business in this state does not permit the foreign corporation to engage in any business or affairs or exercise any power that a domestic corporation may not engage in or exercise in this state.

§ 15.02 Registration to Do Business in This State

(a) A foreign corporation may not do business in this state until it registers with the secretary of state under this chapter.

(b) A foreign corporation doing business in this state may not maintain a proceeding in any court of this state until it is registered to do business in this state.

(c) The failure of a foreign corporation to register to do business in this state does not impair the validity of a contract or act of the foreign corporation or preclude it from defending a proceeding in this state.

(d) A limitation on the liability of a shareholder or director of a foreign corporation is not waived solely because the foreign corporation does business in this state without registering.

(e) Section 15.01(a) applies even if a foreign corporation fails to register under this chapter.

§ 15.03 Foreign Registration Statement

To register to do business in this state, a foreign corporation shall deliver a foreign registration statement to the secretary of state for filing. The registration statement must be signed by the foreign corporation and state:

(a) the corporate name of the foreign corporation and, if the name does not comply with section 4.01, an alternate name as required by section 15.06;

(b) the foreign corporation's jurisdiction of formation;

(c) the street and mailing addresses of the foreign corporation's principal office and, if the law of the foreign corporation's jurisdiction of formation requires the foreign corporation to maintain an office in that jurisdiction, the street and mailing addresses of that office;

(d) the street and mailing addresses of the foreign corporation's registered office in this state and the name of its registered agent at that office;

(e) the names and business addresses of its directors and principal officers; and

(f) a brief description of the nature of its business to be conducted in this state.

§ 15.04 Amendment of Foreign Registration Statement

A registered foreign corporation shall sign and deliver to the secretary of state for filing an amendment to its foreign registration statement if there is a change in:

(a) its name or alternate name;

(b) its jurisdiction of formation, unless its registration is deemed to have been withdrawn under section 15.08 or transferred under section 15.10; or

(c) an address required by section 15.03(c).

§ 15.05 Activities Not Constituting Doing Business

(a) Activities of a foreign corporation that do not constitute doing business in this state for purposes of this chapter include:

(1) maintaining, defending, mediating, arbitrating, or settling a proceeding;

(2) carrying on any activity concerning the internal affairs of the foreign corporation, including holding meetings of its shareholders or board of directors;

(3) maintaining accounts in financial institutions;

(4)   maintaining offices or agencies for the transfer, exchange, and registration of securities of the foreign corporation or maintaining trustees or depositories with respect to those securities;

(5)   selling through independent contractors;

(6)   soliciting or obtaining orders by any means if the orders require acceptance outside this state before they become contracts;

(7)   creating or acquiring indebtedness, mortgages, or security interests in property;

(8)   securing or collecting debts or enforcing mortgages or security interests in property securing the debts, and holding, protecting, or maintaining property so acquired;

(9)   conducting an isolated transaction that is not in the course of similar transactions;

(10)   owning, protecting and maintaining property; and

(11)   doing business in interstate commerce.

(b)   This section does not apply in determining the contacts or activities that may subject a foreign corporation to service of process, taxation, or regulation under the laws of this state other than this Act.

§ 15.06   Noncomplying Name of Foreign Corporation

(a)   A foreign corporation whose name does not comply with section 4.01 may not register to do business in this state until it adopts, for the purpose of doing business in this state, an alternate name that complies with section 4.01 by filing a foreign registration statement under section 15.03, or if applicable, a transfer of registration statement under section 15.10, setting forth that alternate name. A foreign corporation adopting an alternate name as provided in this subsection need not file under this state's assumed or fictitious name statute with respect that alternate name. After registering to do business in this state with an alternate name, a foreign corporation shall do business in this state under:

(1)   the alternate name;

(2)   the foreign corporation's name, with the addition of its jurisdiction of formation; or

(3)   a name the foreign corporation is authorized to use under the assumed or fictitious name statute of this state.

(b)   If a registered foreign corporation changes its name after registration to a name that does not comply with section 4.01, it may not do business in this state until it complies with subsection (a) by amending its registration statement to adopt an alternate name that complies with section 4.01.

§ 15.07   Withdrawal of Registration of Registered Foreign Corporation

(a)   A registered foreign corporation may withdraw its registration by delivering a statement of withdrawal to the secretary of state for filing. The statement of withdrawal must be signed by the foreign corporation and state:

(1)   the name of the foreign corporation and its jurisdiction of formation;

(2)   that the foreign corporation is not doing business in this state and that it withdraws its registration to do business in this state;

(3)   that the foreign corporation revokes the authority of its registered agent in this state; and

(4)   an address to which process on the foreign corporation may be sent by the secretary of state under section 5.04(c).

(b)   After the withdrawal of the registration of a foreign corporation, service of process in any proceeding based on a cause of action arising during the time the entity was registered to do business in this state may be made as provided in section 5.04.

§ 15.08   Deemed Withdrawal Upon Domestication or Conversion to Certain Domestic Entities

A registered foreign corporation that domesticates to a domestic business corporation or converts to a domestic nonprofit corporation or any type of domestic filing entity or to a domestic limited liability partnership is deemed to have withdrawn its registration on the effectiveness of such event.

§ 15.09   Withdrawal Upon Dissolution or Conversion to Certain Nonfiling Entities

(a)   A registered foreign corporation that has dissolved and completed winding up or has converted to a domestic or foreign nonfiling entity other than a limited liability partnership shall deliver to the secretary of state for filing a statement of withdrawal. The statement must be signed by the dissolved corporation or the converted domestic or foreign nonfiling entity and state:

(1)   in the case of a foreign corporation that has completed winding up:

(i)   its name and jurisdiction of formation;

(ii)   that the foreign corporation withdraws its registration to do business in this state and revokes the authority of its registered agent to accept service on its behalf; and

(iii)   an address to which process on the foreign corporation may be sent by the secretary of state under section 5.04(c).

(2)   in the case of a foreign corporation that has converted to a domestic or foreign nonfiling entity other than a limited liability partnership:

(i)   the name of the converting foreign corporation and its jurisdiction of formation;

(ii)   the type of the nonfiling entity to which it has converted and its name and jurisdiction of formation;

(iii)   that it withdraws its registration to do business in this state and revokes the authority of its registered agent to accept service on its behalf; and

(iv)   an address to which process on the foreign corporation may be sent by the secretary of state under 5.04(c).

(b)   After the withdrawal of the registration of a foreign corporation, service of process in any proceeding based on a cause of action arising during the time the entity was registered to do business in this state may be made as provided in section 5.04.

§ 15.10   Transfer of Registration

(a)   If a registered foreign corporation merges into a nonregistered foreign corporation or converts to a foreign corporation required to register with the secretary of state to do business in this state, the foreign corporation shall deliver to the secretary of state for filing a transfer of registration statement. The transfer of registration statement must be signed by the surviving or converted foreign corporation and state:

(1)   the name of the registered foreign corporation and its jurisdiction of formation before the merger or conversion;

(2)   the name of the surviving or converted foreign corporation and its jurisdiction of formation after the merger or conversion and, if the name does not comply with section 4.01, an alternate name adopted pursuant to section 15.06; and

(3)   the following information regarding the surviving or converted foreign corporation after the merger or conversion:

(i)   the street and mailing addresses of the principal office of the foreign corporation and, if the law of the foreign corporation's jurisdiction of formation requires it to maintain an office in that jurisdiction, the street and mailing addresses of that office; and

(ii)   the street and mailing addresses of the foreign corporation's registered office in this state and the name of its registered agent at that office.

(b)   On the effective date of a transfer of registration statement as determined in accordance with section 1.23, the registration of the registered foreign corporation to do business in this state is transferred without interruption to the foreign corporation into which it has merged or to which it has been converted.

§ 15.11   Administrative Termination of Registration

(a)   The secretary of state may terminate the registration of a registered foreign corporation in the manner provided in subsections (b) and (c) if:

(1)   the foreign corporation does not pay within 60 days after they are due any fees, taxes, interest or penalties imposed by this Act or other laws of this state;

(2)   the foreign corporation does not deliver its annual report to the secretary of state within 60 days after it is due;

(3)   the foreign corporation is without a registered agent or registered office in this state for 60 days or more; or

(4)   the secretary of state has not been notified within 60 days that the foreign corporation's registered agent or registered office has been changed, that its registered agent has resigned, or that its registered office has been discontinued.

(b)   The secretary of state may terminate the registration of a registered foreign corporation by:

(1)   filing a certificate of termination; and

(2)   delivering a copy of the certificate of termination to the foreign corporation's registered agent or, if the foreign corporation does not have a registered agent, to the foreign corporation's principal office.

(c)   The certificate of termination must state:

(1)   the effective date of the termination, which must be not less than 60 days after the secretary of state delivers the copy of the certificate of termination as prescribed in subsection (b)(2); and

(2)   the grounds for termination under subsection (a).

(d)   The registration of a registered foreign corporation to do business in this state ceases on the effective date of the termination as set forth in the certificate of termination, unless before that date the foreign corporation cures each ground for termination stated in the certificate of termination. If the foreign corporation cures each ground, the secretary of state shall file a statement that the certificate of termination is withdrawn.

(e)   After the effective date of the termination as set forth in the certificate of termination, service of process in any proceeding based on a cause of action arising during the time the entity was registered to do business in this state may be made as provided in section 5.04.

§ 15.12   Action by [Attorney General]

The [Attorney General] may maintain an action to enjoin a foreign corporation from doing business in this state in violation of this Act.

CHAPTER 16

RECORDS AND REPORTS

Subchapter A.   Records

§ 16.01   Corporate Records

(a)   A corporation shall maintain the following records:

(1)   its articles of incorporation as currently in effect;

(2)   any notices to shareholders referred to in section 1.20(k)(5) specifying facts on which a filed document is dependent if those facts are not included in the articles of incorporation or otherwise available as specified in section 1.20(k)(5);

(3)   its bylaws as currently in effect;

(4)   all written communications within the past three years to shareholders generally;

(5)   minutes of all meetings of, and records of all actions taken without a meeting by, its shareholders, its board of directors, and board committees established under section 8.25;

(6)   a list of the names and business addresses of its current directors and officers; and

(7)   its most recent annual report delivered to the secretary of state under section 16.21.

(b)   A corporation shall maintain all annual financial statements prepared for the corporation for its last three fiscal years (or such shorter period of existence) and any audit or other reports with respect to such financial statements.

(c)   A corporation shall maintain accounting records in a form that permits preparation of its financial statements.

(d)   A corporation shall maintain a record of its current shareholders in alphabetical order by class or series of shares showing the address of, and the number and class or series of shares held by, each shareholder. Nothing contained in this subsection shall require the corporation to include in such record the electronic mail address or other electronic contact information of a shareholder.

(e)   A corporation shall maintain the records specified in this section in a manner so that they may be made available for inspection within a reasonable time.

§ 16.02   Inspection Rights of Shareholders

(a)   A shareholder of a corporation is entitled to inspect and copy, during regular business hours at the corporation's principal office, any of the records of the corporation described in section 16.01(a), excluding minutes of meetings of, and records of actions taken without a meeting by, the corporation's board of directors and board committees established under section 8.25, if the shareholder gives the corporation a signed written notice of the shareholder's demand at least five business days before the date on which the shareholder wishes to inspect and copy.

(b)   A shareholder of a corporation is entitled to inspect and copy, during regular business hours at a reasonable location specified by the corporation, any of the following records of the corporation if the shareholder meets the requirements of subsection (c) and gives the corporation a signed written notice of the shareholder's demand at least five business days before the date on which the shareholder wishes to inspect and copy:

(1)   the financial statements of the corporation maintained in accordance with section 16.01(b);

(2)   accounting records of the corporation;

(3)   excerpts from minutes of any meeting of, or records of any actions taken without a meeting by, the corporation's board of directors and board committees maintained in accordance with section 16.01(a); and

(4)   the record of shareholders maintained in accordance with section 16.01(d).

(c)   A shareholder may inspect and copy the records described in subsection (b) only if:

(1)   the shareholder's demand is made in good faith and for a proper purpose;

(2)   the shareholder's demand describes with reasonable particularity the shareholder's purpose and the records the shareholder desires to inspect; and

(3)   the records are directly connected with the shareholder's purpose.

(d)   The corporation may impose reasonable restrictions on the confidentiality, use or distribution of records described in subsection (b).

(e)   For any meeting of shareholders for which the record date for determining shareholders entitled to vote at the meeting is different than the record date for notice of the meeting, any person who becomes a shareholder subsequent to the record date for notice of the meeting and is entitled to vote at the meeting is entitled to obtain from the corporation upon request the notice and any other information provided by the corporation to shareholders in connection with the meeting, unless the corporation has made such information generally available to shareholders by posting it on its website or by other generally recognized means. Failure of a corporation to provide such information does not affect the validity of action taken at the meeting.

(f)   The right of inspection granted by this section may not be abolished or limited by a corporation's articles of incorporation or bylaws.

(g)   This section does not affect:

(1)   the right of a shareholder to inspect records under section 7.20 or, if the shareholder is in litigation with the corporation, to the same extent as any other litigant; or

(2)   the power of a court, independently of this Act, to compel the production of corporate records for examination and to impose reasonable restrictions as provided in section 16.04(c), provided that, in the case of production of records described in subsection (b) of this section at the request of a shareholder, the shareholder has met the requirements of subsection (c).

(h)   For purposes of this section, "shareholder" means a record shareholder, a beneficial shareholder, and an unrestricted voting trust beneficial owner.

§ 16.03   Scope of Inspection Right

(a)   A shareholder may appoint an agent or attorney to exercise the shareholder's inspection and copying rights under section 16.02.

(b)   The corporation may, if reasonable, satisfy the right of a shareholder to copy records under section 16.02 by furnishing to the shareholder copies by photocopy or other means chosen by the corporation, including furnishing copies through an electronic transmission.

(c)   The corporation may comply at its expense with a shareholder's demand to inspect the record of shareholders under section 16.02(b)(4) by providing the shareholder with a list of shareholders that was compiled no earlier than the date of the shareholder's demand.

(d)   The corporation may impose a reasonable charge to cover the costs of providing copies of documents to the shareholder, which may be based on an estimate of such costs.

§ 16.04   Court-Ordered Inspection

(a)   If a corporation does not allow a shareholder who complies with section 16.02(a) to inspect and copy any records required by that section to be available for inspection, the [name or describe court] may summarily order inspection and copying of the records demanded at the corporation's expense upon application of the shareholder.

(b)   If a corporation does not within a reasonable time allow a shareholder who complies with section 16.02(b) to inspect and copy the records required by that section, the shareholder who complies with section 16.02(c) may apply to the [name or describe court] for an order to permit inspection and copying of the records demanded. The court shall dispose of an application under this subsection on an expedited basis.

(c)   If the court orders inspection and copying of the records demanded under section 16.02(b), it may impose reasonable restrictions on their confidentiality, use or distribution by the demanding shareholder and it shall also order the corporation to pay the shareholder's expenses incurred to obtain the order unless the corporation establishes that it refused inspection in good faith because the corporation had:

(1)   a reasonable basis for doubt about the right of the shareholder to inspect the records demanded; or

(2)   required reasonable restrictions on the confidentiality, use or distribution of the records demanded to which the demanding shareholder had been unwilling to agree.

§ 16.05   Inspection Rights of Directors

(a)   A director of a corporation is entitled to inspect and copy the books, records and documents of the corporation at any reasonable time to the extent reasonably related to the performance of the director's duties as a director, including duties as a member of a board committee, but not for any other purpose or in any manner that would violate any duty to the corporation.

(b)   The [name or describe court] may order inspection and copying of the books, records and documents at the corporation's expense, upon application of a director who has been refused such inspection rights, unless the corporation establishes that the director is not entitled to such inspection rights. The court shall dispose of an application under this subsection on an expedited basis.

(c)   If an order is issued, the court may include provisions protecting the corporation from undue burden or expense, and prohibiting the director from using information obtained upon exercise of the inspection rights in a manner that would violate a duty to the corporation, and may also order the corporation to reimburse the director for the director's expenses incurred in connection with the application.

Subchapter B.   Reports

§ 16.20   Financial Statements for Shareholders

(a)   Upon the written request of a shareholder, a corporation shall deliver or make available to such requesting shareholder by posting on its website or by other generally recognized means annual financial statements for the most recent fiscal year of the corporation for which annual financial statements have been prepared for the corporation. If financial statements have been prepared for the corporation on the basis of generally accepted accounting principles for such specified period, the corporation shall deliver or make available such financial statements to the requesting shareholder. If the annual financial statements to be delivered or made available to the requesting shareholder are audited or otherwise reported upon by a public accountant, the report shall also be delivered or made available to the requesting shareholder.

(b)   A corporation shall deliver, or make available and provide written notice of availability of, the financial statements required under subsection (a) to the requesting shareholder within five business days of delivery of such written request to the corporation.

(c)   A corporation may fulfill its responsibilities under this section by delivering the specified financial statements, or otherwise making them available, in any manner permitted by the applicable rules and regulations of the United States Securities and Exchange Commission.

(d)   Notwithstanding the provisions of subsections (a), (b) and (c) of this section:

(1)   as a condition to delivering or making available financial statements to a requesting shareholder, the corporation may require the requesting shareholder to agree to reasonable restrictions on the confidentiality, use and distribution of such financial statements; and

(2)   the corporation may, if it reasonably determines that the shareholder's request is not made in good faith or for a proper purpose, decline to deliver or make available such financial statements to that shareholder.

(e)   If a corporation does not respond to a shareholder's request for annual financial statements pursuant to this section in accordance with subsection (b) within five business days of delivery of such request to the corporation:

(1)   The requesting shareholder may apply to the [name or describe court] for an order requiring delivery of or access to the requested financial statements. The court shall dispose of an application under this subsection on an expedited basis.

(2)   If the court orders delivery or access to the requested financial statements, it may impose reasonable restrictions on their confidentiality, use or distribution.

(3)   In such proceeding, if the corporation has declined to deliver or make available such financial statements because the shareholder had been unwilling to agree to restrictions proposed by the corporation on the confidentiality, use and distribution of such financials statements, the corporation shall have the burden of demonstrating that the restrictions proposed by the corporation were reasonable.

(4)   In such proceeding, if the corporation has declined to deliver or make available such financial statements pursuant to section 16.20(d)(2), the corporation shall have the burden of demonstrating that it had reasonably determined that the shareholder's request was not made in good faith or for a proper purpose.

(5)   If the court orders delivery or access to the requested financial statements it shall order the corporation to pay the shareholder's expenses incurred to obtain such order unless the corporation establishes that it had refused delivery or access to the requested financial statements because the shareholder had refused to agree to reasonable restrictions on the confidentiality, use or distribution of the financial statements or that the corporation had reasonably determined that the shareholder's request was not made in good faith or for a proper purpose.

§ 16.21   Annual Report for Secretary of State

(a)   Each domestic corporation shall deliver to the secretary of state for filing an annual report that sets forth:

(1)   the name of the corporation;

(2)   the street and mailing address of its registered office and the name of its registered agent at that office in this state;

(3)   the street and mailing address of its principal office;

(4)   the names and business addresses of its directors and principal officers;

(5)   a brief description of the nature of its business;

(6)   the total number of authorized shares, itemized by class and series, if any, within each class; and

(7)   the total number of issued and outstanding shares, itemized by class and series, if any, within each class.

(b)   Each foreign corporation registered to do business in this state shall deliver to the secretary of state for filing an annual report that sets forth:

(1)   the name of the foreign corporation and, if the name does not comply with section 4.01, an alternate name as required by section 15.06;

(2)   the foreign corporation's jurisdiction of formation;

(3)   the street and mailing addresses of the foreign corporation's principal office and, if the law of the foreign corporation's jurisdiction of formation requires the foreign corporation to maintain an office in that jurisdiction, the street and mailing addresses of that office;

(4)   the street and mailing addresses of the foreign corporation's registered office in this state and the name of its registered agent at that office;

(5)   the names and business addresses of its directors and principal officers; and

(6)   a brief description of the nature of its business conducted in this state.

(c)   Information in the annual report must be current as of the date the annual report is signed on behalf of the corporation.

(d)   The first annual report shall be delivered to the secretary of state between January 1 and April 1 of the year following the calendar year in which a domestic corporation was incorporated or a foreign corporation was registered to do business. Subsequent annual reports shall be delivered to the secretary of state between January 1 and April 1 of the following calendar years.

(e)   If an annual report does not contain the information required by this section, the secretary of state shall promptly notify the reporting domestic or foreign corporation in writing and return the report to it for correction. If the report is corrected to contain the information required by this section and delivered to the secretary of state within 30 days after the notice from the secretary of state becomes effective as determined in accordance with section 1.41, it is deemed to be timely filed.

CHAPTER 17.

BENEFIT CORPORATIONS

§ 17.01   Application of Chapter; Definitions

(a)   A corporation electing to become a benefit corporation under this chapter in the manner prescribed in this chapter is subject in all respects to the provisions of this Act, except to the extent this chapter imposes additional or different requirements, in which case such requirements apply. The inclusion of a provision in this chapter does not imply that a contrary or different rule of law applies to a corporation that is not a benefit corporation. This chapter does not affect a statute or rule of law that applies to a corporation that is not a benefit corporation.

(b)   As used in this chapter:

"Benefit corporation" means a corporation that includes in its articles of incorporation a statement that the corporation is subject to this chapter.

"Public benefit" means a positive effect, or reduction of negative effects, on one or more communities or categories of persons (other than shareholders solely in their capacity as shareholders) or on the environment, including effects of an artistic, charitable, economic, educational, cultural, literary, medical, religious, social, ecological, or scientific nature.

"Public benefit provision" means a provision in the articles of incorporation which states that the corporation shall pursue one or more identified public benefits.

"Responsible and sustainable manner" means a manner that:

(i)   pursues through the business of the corporation the creation of a positive effect on society and the environment, taken as a whole, that is material taking into consideration the corporation's size and the nature of its business; and

(ii)   considers, in addition to the interests of shareholders generally, the separate interests of stakeholders known to be affected by the conduct of the business of the corporation.

OFFICIAL COMMENT

Benefit Corporation

Chapter 17 does not create or imply any limitation on the factors or interests the board of directors of a corporation that is not a benefit corporation may take into account under section 8.30 of the Act.

Public Benefit

In addition to pursuing the creation of a positive effect on society and the environment, taken as a whole, the articles of incorporation of a benefit corporation may require a benefit corporation to pursue one or more identified public benefits. Public benefits are defined broadly. If the articles of incorporation include a public benefit provision, then directors also are required to act in a manner that pursues the identified public benefit or benefits in discharging their duties as provided in section 17.04. Pursuit of a public benefit may contribute to acting in a responsible and sustainable manner but, depending on the materiality to the corporation of the public benefit chosen, may or may not be sufficient by itself to satisfy that duty.

Responsible and Sustainable

The requirement in section 17.04(a) that directors act in a responsible and sustainable manner recognizes that corporate operations and business decisions may affect stakeholders other than shareholders. Such operations and decisions have the potential to affect, positively or negatively, critical resources, such as environmental capacities and social stability. The requirement that directors pursue, through the business of the corporation, creation of a positive effect on "society and the environment, taken as a whole" should be viewed in the context of the individual corporation and its ability to create a positive effect that is material considering its size and the nature of its business. It does not require the benefit corporation to create such an effect by itself. For many benefit corporations, pursuit of a positive effect may involve conduct that, in combination with similar conduct by others, can be expected to have a positive effect on society and the environment, taken as a whole. The requirement that the benefit be material makes clear that pursuit of more than a token or incidental benefit is required to satisfy the duty to act in a responsible and sustainable manner. The materiality requirement takes into account the size and nature of a business. It applies the same quantitative and qualitative considerations that would be applicable in other business contexts to determine whether an effect is "material" to the business of a particular corporation. The reference to "business of the corporation" encompasses both what the corporation does and how it conducts its business and operations.

Acting in a responsible and sustainable manner requires that directors consider the interests of shareholders as well as stakeholders known to be affected by the business of the corporation. Section 17.04(b) includes a nonexclusive list of stakeholder interests to be considered to the extent affected.

§ 17.02   Name; Share Certificates

(a)   The name of a benefit corporation may contain the words "benefit corporation," the abbreviation "B.C.," or the designation "BC," any of which shall be deemed to satisfy the requirements of section 4.01(a)(1).

(b)   Any share certificate issued by a benefit corporation, and any information statement delivered by a benefit corporation pursuant to section 6.26(b), must note conspicuously that the corporation is a benefit corporation subject to this chapter.

OFFICIAL COMMENT

A benefit corporation may, but need not, identify itself as such in its corporate name. In order to provide investors in a benefit corporation with notice they are investing in a corporation that does not operate solely for the benefit of its shareholders, share certificates and information statements evidencing shares in a benefit corporation must contain a legend identifying the corporation as a benefit corporation.

§ 17.03   Certain Amendments and Transactions; Votes Required

(a)   Unless the articles of incorporation require a greater vote, in addition to any other approval of shareholders required under this Act, the approval of at least two-thirds of the votes entitled to be cast thereon, and, if any class or series of shares is entitled to vote as a separate group thereon, the approval of at least two-thirds of the votes entitled to be cast by that voting group, shall be required for a corporation that is not a benefit corporation to:

    (1)   amend its articles of incorporation to include a statement that it is subject to this chapter; or

    (2)   merge with or into, or enter into a share exchange with, another entity, or effect a domestication or conversion, if, as a result of the merger, share exchange, domestication, or conversion, the shares of any voting group would become, or be converted into or exchanged for the right to receive, shares of a benefit corporation or shares or interests in an entity subject to provisions of organic law analogous to those in this chapter; provided, however, that in the case of this subsection (a)(2), if the shares of one or more, but not all, voting groups are so affected, then only the shares in the voting groups so affected shall be entitled to cast votes under this subsection (a).

(b)   Unless the articles of incorporation require a greater vote, in addition to any other approval of shareholders required under this Act, the approval of at least two-thirds of the votes entitled to be cast thereon, and, if any class or series of shares is entitled to vote as a separate group thereon, the approval of at least two-thirds of the votes entitled to be cast by that voting group, shall be required for a benefit corporation to:

    (1)   amend its articles of incorporation to eliminate a statement that the corporation is subject to this chapter; or

    (2)   merge with or into, or enter into a share exchange with, another entity, or effect a domestication or conversion if, as a result of the merger, share exchange, domestication, or conversion, the shares of any voting group would become, or be converted into or exchanged for the right to receive, shares or interests in an entity that is neither a benefit corporation nor an entity subject to provisions of organic law analogous to those in this chapter; provided, however, that in the case of this subsection (b)(2), if the shares of one or more, but not all, voting groups are so affected, then only the shares in the voting groups so affected shall be entitled to cast votes under this subsection (b).

OFFICIAL COMMENT

Section 17.03 does not eliminate any vote otherwise required under the Act. Section 17.03(a) increases the shareholder vote otherwise required under the Act for amendments or transactions by which a corporation becomes a benefit corporation or shares of a corporation are converted into shares of a benefit corporation or interests in an analogous domestic entity (e.g., a benefit limited liability company) or foreign entity (e.g., a foreign benefit corporation or benefit limited liability company). The vote is increased because the change from ownership of shares of a corporation to those of a benefit corporation significantly changes the nature of the shareholder's investment. For the same reason, section 17.03(b) increases the shareholder vote requirement for amendments or transactions by which a benefit corporation ceases to be a benefit corporation or shares of a benefit corporation are converted into shares of a corporation that is not a benefit corporation or interests in a domestic or foreign entity that is not subject to provisions of organic law analogous to those of this chapter. When a transaction described in subsections (a)(2) or (b)(2) has the indicated effects on the shares of only some voting groups, the increased votes called for in subsections (a) and (b) apply only to shares in the affected voting groups.

§ 17.04   Duties of Directors

(a)   Each member of the board of directors of a benefit corporation, when discharging the duties of a director, shall act: (i) in a responsible and sustainable manner, and (ii) in a manner that pursues the public benefit or benefits identified in any public benefit provision.

(b)   In fulfilling the duties under subsection (a), a director shall consider, to the extent affected, in addition to the interests of shareholders generally, the separate interests of stakeholders known to be affected by the business of the corporation including:

    (1)   the employees and work forces of the corporation, its subsidiaries, and its suppliers;

    (2)   customers;

(3)　communities or society, including those of each community in which offices or facilities of the corporation, its subsidiaries, or its suppliers are located; and

(4)　the local and global environment.

(c)　A director of a benefit corporation shall not, by virtue of the duties imposed by subsections (a) and (b), owe any duty to a person other than the benefit corporation due to any interest of the person in the status of the corporation as a benefit corporation or in any public benefit provision.

(d)　Unless otherwise provided in the articles of incorporation, the violation by a director of the duties imposed by subsections (a) and (b) shall not constitute an intentional infliction of harm on the corporation or the shareholders for purposes of sections 2.02(b)(4) and (5).

OFFICIAL COMMENT

Section 17.04 is the heart of the benefit corporation provisions. In addition to the duties imposed on directors of all corporations under section 8.30, section 17.04 requires directors of a benefit corporation to pursue through the business of the corporation a positive impact on society and the environment, taken as a whole, and to consider the interests of stakeholders in addition to the interests of shareholders generally. As noted in the Official Comment to section 17.01, the "business of the corporation" encompasses both what the corporation does and how it conducts its business and operations.

The list in section 17.04(b) of stakeholders to be considered is not exclusive, and stakeholders not specifically named but known to be affected by the corporation's business must be considered. The list is not a checklist and the interests of listed stakeholders need be considered only to the extent they are known to be affected by the decision in question. In considering the interests of stakeholders known to be affected, the extent to which an action or decision affects different stakeholders should also be considered.

The standards of director conduct and liability in sections 8.30 and 8.31 apply to actions of directors of a benefit corporation under sections 17.04(a) and (b). Likewise, the presumptions and standards of judicial review, including those related to the common law business judgment rule, described in the Official Comment to section 8.31, apply to director decisions under sections 17.04(a) and (b), including, as part of such decisions, the weighting and reconciliation of competing or inconsistent shareholder and stakeholder interests. A director being a shareholder of the corporation would not, by itself, be expected to constitute a material financial interest (as defined in section 8.60) when performing the duties of a director under sections 17.04(a) or (b), or prevent the business judgment rule from applying to decisions under sections 17.04(a) or (b). Thus, if directors take into account shareholder and relevant stakeholder interests, the business judgment rule would be expected to apply to any business decision that can rationally be viewed as being consistent with the board's duty to act in a responsible and sustainable manner and in furtherance of identified public benefit or benefits. This would be the case no matter how much weight is ultimately given to shareholder and to particular stakeholder interests.

For example, in exercising their duty to act in a responsible and sustainable manner, directors of a benefit corporation considering whether to close a facility would be required to consider the effects of closing the facility not only on shareholder interests but also on the separate interests of, among others, the workforce and community. However, after considering those effects, the directors, consistent with their duties under sections 17.04(a) and (b), could decide to close or not close the facility. This would be the case as long as their decision, taking those effects, and the interests of shareholders and other relevant stakeholders into account, can rationally be viewed as consistent with their duty to act in a responsible and sustainable manner, even if adverse to shareholder or stakeholder interests.

Sections 17.04(a) and (b) provide that all directors of a benefit corporation have the duty to act in a responsible and sustainable manner and does not provide for the creation of a "benefit director" with special duties. However, a benefit corporation may choose to assign oversight of responsibility and sustainability to a board committee. Many benefit corporations will have a chief sustainability officer or other officer with a similar role within management.

The provisions of section 17.04(c) make clear that benefit corporation duties may be enforced only by the corporation or by shareholders in a derivative proceeding brought under section 17.06.

Under section 17.04(d), if a corporation has a section 2.02(b)(4) provision in its articles of incorporation limiting the availability of money damages against directors except in certain enumerated circumstances, relief for violation of a director's duties under section 17.04 will be limited to non-monetary equitable relief, absent a financial benefit to a director to which the director is not entitled, an unlawful distribution, or an intentional violation of criminal law. Similarly, section 17.04(d) protects mandatory director indemnification rights granted in the articles of incorporation pursuant to section 2.02(b)(5) by providing that the limitations on indemnification of directors who intentionally harm either the corporation or shareholders are not applicable in the case of violations of sections 17.04(a) and (b).

§ 17.05   Annual Benefit Report

(a)   No less than annually, a benefit corporation shall prepare a benefit report addressing the efforts of the corporation during the preceding year to operate in a responsible and sustainable manner, to pursue any public benefit or benefits identified in any public benefit provision, and to consider the interests described in section 17.04(b). The annual benefit report must include:

(1)   the objectives that the board of directors has established for the corporation to operate in a responsible and sustainable manner, to pursue the public benefit or benefits identified in any public benefit provision, and to consider the interests described in section 17.04(b);

(2)   the standards the board of directors has adopted to measure the corporation's progress in operating in a responsible and sustainable manner, in pursuing the public benefit or benefits identified in any public benefit provision, and in considering the interests described in section 17.04(b);

(3)   if the articles of incorporation or bylaws require that the corporation use an independent third-party standard in reporting on the corporation's progress in operating in a responsible and sustainable manner, in pursuing the public benefit or benefits identified in any public benefit provision, or in considering the interests described in section 17.04(b), or if the board of directors has chosen to use such a standard, the applicable standard so required or chosen; and

(4)   an assessment of the corporation's success in meeting the objectives and standards identified in subsections (a)(1) and (a)(2) and, if applicable, subsection (a)(3), and the basis for that assessment.

(b)   The benefit corporation shall deliver to each shareholder, or make available and provide written notice to each shareholder of the availability of, the annual benefit report required by subsection (a) on or before the earlier of:

(1)   120 days following the end of the fiscal year of the benefit corporation; or

(2)   the time that the benefit corporation delivers any other annual reports or annual financial statements to its shareholders.

(c)   Any shareholder that has not received or been given access to an annual benefit report within the time required by subsection (b) may make a written request that the corporation deliver or make available the annual benefit report to the shareholder. If a benefit corporation does not deliver or make available an annual benefit report to the shareholder within five business days of receiving such request, the requesting shareholder may apply to the [name or describe court] for an order requiring delivery of or access to the annual benefit report. The court shall dispose of an action under this subsection (c) on an expedited basis.

(d)   A benefit corporation shall post all of its annual benefit reports on the public portion of its website, if any. If a benefit corporation does not have a website, the benefit corporation shall provide a copy of its most recent annual benefit report, without charge, to any person that requests a copy in writing.

OFFICIAL COMMENT

The purpose of the annual benefit report is to provide a minimum level of visibility into the benefit corporation's efforts so that shareholders may determine how successful the corporation has been in operating in a responsible and sustainable manner and pursuing the public benefit or benefits identified in any public benefit provision.

Benefit corporations and their shareholders may find that measuring sustainability results against a third-party standard, as referenced in subsection (a)(3), provides added credibility to the corporation's sustainability efforts. A provision requiring measurement against a third-party standard may identify a particular third-party standard or may require that a third-party standard be utilized without specifying the particular third-party standard to be used. Absent such a provision in the articles of incorporation or bylaws, a benefit corporation is not required to measure its progress against a third-party standard, but is required to disclose the standard it has adopted to assess its progress in operating in a responsible and sustainable manner, in pursuing the public benefit or benefits identified in any public benefit provision, and in considering the interests described in section 17.04(b).

Section 17.05(c) provides a summary remedy to a shareholder that has not received or been given access to an annual benefit report after request, similar to the remedy provided under section 16.20(e)(1) for failure to provide financial statements upon request. Unlike section 16.20(e)(5), section 17.05(c) does not impose on the corporation the expenses incurred by the shareholder in a successful proceeding under section 17.05(e). However, such expenses could be awarded by a court in an appropriate case.

§ 17.06　Rights of Action

(a)　Except in a proceeding authorized under section 17.05(c) or this section, no person other than the corporation, or a shareholder in the right of the corporation pursuant to subsection (b), may bring an action or assert a claim with respect to the violation of any duty applicable to a benefit corporation or any of its directors under this chapter.

(b)　Except for a proceeding brought under section 17.05(c), a proceeding by a shareholder of a benefit corporation claiming violation of any duty applicable to a benefit corporation or any of its directors under this chapter:

(1)　must be brought in a derivative proceeding pursuant to subchapter 7D; and

(2)　may be brought only by a shareholder of the benefit corporation that at the time of the act or omission complained of either individually, or together with other shareholders bringing such action collectively, owned directly or indirectly at least five percent of a class of the corporation's outstanding shares or, in the case of a corporation with shares traded on an organized market as described in section 13.02(b)(1)(ii), either that percentage of shares or shares with a market value of at least $5 million at the time the proceeding is commenced.

(c)　A suit under subsection (b) may not be maintained if, during the pendency of the suit, the shareholder individually fails, or the shareholders collectively fail, to continue to own directly or indirectly the lesser of (i) the number of shares owned at the time the proceeding is commenced, (ii) a number of shares representing five percent of a class of the corporation's shares, or (iii) a number of shares with a market value of at least $5 million.

OFFICIAL COMMENT

In addition to the standing and demand requirements for bringing a derivative suit under sections 7.41 and 7.42, section 17.06(b) adds a minimum ownership threshold for shareholders to be permitted to bring a derivative proceeding for violation of the duties under chapter 17. The minimum ownership requirement does not apply in a suit under section 17.05(c) to receive or be given access to an annual benefit report. In addition, section 17.06(c) imposes a continuous ownership requirement for a shareholder to be able to maintain a derivative proceeding under section 17.06(b).

CHAPTER 18

TRANSITION PROVISIONS

NOTE ON ADOPTION OF THE ACT

Chapter 18 addresses various transitional and interpretational issues that merit consideration by the legislature adopting the Act, especially as an entirety. This Note summarizes and explains some of those issues. Each adopting state will need to consider the differences between the Act and its existing corporation statute to determine if additional transitional provisions will be necessary.

Special Circumstances Warranting Delayed Effectiveness

The Act has been drafted to apply to domestic business corporations in existence on its effective date. See section 18.01. To the extent that some of the provisions of the Act differ in significant respects from earlier laws, it may be appropriate to delay the effective date of such provisions to give existing corporations adequate time to revise controlling corporate documents to take into account the provisions of the Act, or in unusual circumstances, to allow existing corporations to continue to be governed by a preexisting law until a later election to be governed by the pertinent provision of the Act. Two examples of such transitional problems are discussed below.

- Changes in Voting Requirements

The Act, unlike some corporation statutes, requires by virtue of section 7.25 only that votes cast in favor exceed votes cast against, in a meeting at which a quorum is present, to approve transactions such as mergers, sale of substantially all the assets, important amendments to the articles of incorporation, and dissolution. When considering adoption of the Act's voting requirements, it is important to recognize that specific control arrangements may have been established on the assumption that the existing statutory voting requirements would not be reduced. Rather than defeat those reasonable assumptions by effectively eliminating a shareholder's power to veto changes when there was a higher statutory vote requirement, a state that adopts the Act's lesser voting requirement may wish to consider "grandfathering" existing corporations and afford them an option to elect to be governed by the new requirement.

- Increased Power of the Board of Directors

The Act generally grants the board of directors authority to increase or decrease its own size without specific authority (section 8.03) unless the articles of incorporation restrict this power. Some corporation statutes do not grant this power to the board of directors unless express provision is made in the articles or bylaws. Corporations that have not granted this express power to the board of directors may in effect do so when they become subject to the Act, and a delayed effective date therefore may be appropriate.

Foreign Corporations

Although chapter 15 of the Act may change the rules applicable to foreign corporations in some states, these changes are not of a type that requires a transition period. It is therefore recommended that only a single effective date be provided for the application of the Act to foreign corporations and that delayed effective dates for specific provisions in this regard are unnecessary. See section 18.02.

Savings and Severability Provisions

The Act contains its own savings and severability provisions, in sections 18.03 and 18.04, respectively. If the state has a savings statute of general application, however, it may be unnecessary to adopt section 18.03. Likewise, if the state has a severability provision of general application, or if the state's highest court has established a general rule of severability, it may be unnecessary to adopt section 18.04.

Repeal

Although section 18.05 provides for repeal of previously enacted general corporation statutes that are specified, such repeal is generally unnecessary with regard to statutes providing special incorporation and regulatory provisions for corporations engaged in specific businesses, like banking and insurance. If these specialized statutes expressly incorporate by reference provisions from the general business corporation act, however, these statutes should be amended to refer specifically to the present Act rather than to an earlier statute; an appropriate provision would apply this Act to all these corporations except to the extent the specialized statute expressly provides that a different principle should apply.

§ 18.01   Application to Existing Domestic Corporations

This Act applies to all domestic corporations in existence on its effective date that were incorporated under any general statute of this state providing for incorporation of corporations for profit if power to amend or repeal the statute under which the corporation was incorporated was reserved.

§ 18.02 Application to Existing Foreign Corporations

A foreign corporation registered or authorized to do business in this state on the effective date of this Act is subject to this Act, is deemed to be registered to do business in this state, and is not required to file a foreign registration statement under this Act.

§ 18.03 Saving Provisions

(a) Except as to procedural provisions, this Act does not affect a pending action or proceeding or a right accrued before the effective date of this Act, and a pending civil action or proceeding may be completed, and a right accrued may be enforced, as if this Act had not become effective.

(b) If a penalty or punishment for violation of a statute or rule is reduced by this Act, the penalty, if not already imposed, shall be imposed in accordance with this Act.

§ 18.04 Severability

If any provision of this Act or its application to any person or circumstance is held invalid by a court of competent jurisdiction, the invalidity does not affect other provisions or applications of this Act that can be given effect without the invalid provision or application.

§ 18.05 Repeal

The following laws and parts of laws are repealed: [to be inserted by the adopting state].

MODEL BUSINESS CORPORATION ACT (1969)

(Selected Provisions)

Per Value and Legal Capital Provisions

Historical Commentary

A number of states retain historical concepts of par value and legal capital. The MBCA (1969) incorporates these concepts, which have been eliminated from the MBCA.

Table of Sections

---

§ 2. Definitions

As used in this Act, unless the context otherwise requires, the term: * * *

(h) "Treasury shares" means shares of a corporation which have been issued, have been subsequently acquired by and belong to the corporation, and have not, either by reason of the acquisition or thereafter, been cancelled or restored to the status of authorized but unissued shares. Treasury shares shall be deemed to be "issued" shares, but not "outstanding" shares.

(i) "Net assets" means the amount by which the total assets of a corporation exceed the total debts of the corporation.

(j) "Stated capital" means, at any particular time, the sum of (1) the par value of all shares of the corporation having a par value that have been issued, (2) the amount of the consideration received by the corporation for all shares of the corporation without par value that have been issued, except such part of the consideration therefor as may have been allocated to capital surplus in a manner permitted by law, and (3) such amounts not included in clauses (1) and (2) of this paragraph as have been transferred to stated capital of the corporation, whether upon the issue of shares as a share dividend or otherwise, minus all reductions from such sum as have been effected in a manner permitted by law. Irrespective of the manner of designation thereof by the laws under which a foreign corporation is organized, the stated capital of a foreign corporation shall be determined on the same basis and in the same manner as the stated capital of a domestic corporation, for the purpose of computing fees, franchise taxes and other charges imposed by this Act.

(k)   "Surplus" means the excess of the net assets of a corporation over its stated capital.

(*l*)   "Earned surplus" means the portion of the surplus of a corporation equal to the balance of its net profits, income, gains and losses from the date of incorporation, or from the latest date when a deficit was eliminated by an application of its capital surplus or stated capital or otherwise, after deducting subsequent distributions to shareholders and transfers to stated capital and capital surplus to the extent such distributions and transfers are made out of earned surplus. Earned surplus shall include also any portion of surplus allocated to earned surplus in mergers, consolidations or acquisitions of all or substantially all of the outstanding shares or of the property and assets of another corporation, domestic or foreign.

(m)   "Capital surplus" means the entire surplus of a corporation other than its earned surplus.

(n)   "Insolvent" means inability of a corporation to pay its debts as they become due in the usual course of its business.

§ 6. Right of Corporation to Acquire and Dispose of Its Own Shares

A corporation shall have the right to purchase, take, receive or otherwise acquire, hold, own, pledge, transfer or otherwise dispose of its own shares, but purchases of its own shares, whether direct or indirect, shall be made only to the extent of unreserved and unrestricted earned surplus available therefor, and, if the articles of incorporation so permit or with the affirmative vote of the holders of a majority of all shares entitled to vote thereon, to the extent of unreserved and unrestricted capital surplus available therefor.

To the extent that earned surplus or capital surplus is used as the measure of the corporation's right to purchase its own shares, such surplus shall be restricted so long as such shares are held as treasury shares, and upon the disposition or cancellation of any such shares the restriction shall be removed pro tanto.

Notwithstanding the foregoing limitation, a corporation may purchase or otherwise acquire its own shares for the purpose of:

(a)   Eliminating fractional shares.

(b)   Collecting or compromising indebtedness to the corporation.

(c)   Paying dissenting shareholders entitled to payment for their shares under the provisions of this Act.

(d)   Effecting, subject to the other provisions of this Act, the retirement of its redeemable shares by redemption or by purchase at not to exceed the redemption price.

No purchase of or payment for its own shares shall be made at a time when the corporation is insolvent or when such purchase or payment would make it insolvent.

§ 15. Authorized Shares

Each corporation shall have power to create and issue the number of shares stated in its articles of incorporation. Such shares may be divided into one or more classes, any or all of which classes may consist of shares with par value or shares without par value, with such designations, preferences, limitations, and relative rights as shall be stated in the articles of incorporation. The articles of incorporation may limit or deny the voting rights of or provide special voting rights for the shares of any class to the extent not inconsistent with the provisions of this Act.

Without limiting the authority herein contained, a corporation, when so provided in its articles of incorporation, may issue shares of preferred or special classes:

(a) Subject to the right of the corporation to redeem any of such shares at the price fixed by the articles of incorporation for the redemption thereof.

(b) Entitling the holders thereof to cumulative, noncumulative or partially cumulative dividends.

(c) Having preference over any other class or classes of shares as to the payment of dividends.

(d) Having preference in the assets of the corporation over any other class or classes of shares upon the voluntary or involuntary liquidation of the corporation.

(e) Convertible into shares of any other class or into shares of any series of the same or any other class, except a class having prior or superior rights and preferences as to dividends or distribution of assets upon liquidation, but shares without par value shall not be converted into shares with par value unless that part of the stated capital of the corporation represented by such shares without par value is, at the time of conversion, at least equal to the aggregate par value of the shares into which the shares without par value are to be converted or the amount of any such deficiency is transferred from surplus to stated capital.

§ 18. Consideration for Shares

Shares having a par value may be issued for such consideration expressed in dollars, not less than the par value thereof, as shall be fixed from time to time by the board of directors.

Shares without par value may be issued for such consideration expressed in dollars as may be fixed from time to time by the board of directors unless the articles of incorporation reserve to the shareholders the right to fix the consideration. In the event that such right be reserved as to any shares, the shareholders shall, prior to the issuance of such shares, fix the consideration to be received for such shares, by a vote of the holders of a majority of all shares entitled to vote thereon.

Treasury shares may be disposed of by the corporation for such consideration expressed in dollars as may be fixed from time to time by the board of directors.

That part of the surplus of a corporation which is transferred to stated capital upon the issuance of shares as a share dividend shall be deemed to be the consideration for the issuance of such shares.

In the event of the issuance of shares upon the conversion or exchange of indebtedness or shares, the consideration for the shares so issued shall be (1) the principal sum of, and accrued interest on, the indebtedness so exchanged or converted, or the stated capital then represented by the shares so exchanged or converted, and (2) that part of surplus, if any, transferred to stated capital upon the issuance of shares for the shares so exchanged or converted, and (3) any additional consideration paid to the corporation upon the issuance of shares for the indebtedness or shares so exchanged or converted.

§ 19. Payment for Shares

The consideration for the issuance of shares may be paid, in whole or in part, in cash, in other property, tangible or intangible, or in labor or services actually performed for the corporation. When payment of the consideration for which shares are to be issued shall have been received by the corporation, such shares shall be deemed to be fully paid and non-assessable.

Neither promissory notes nor future services shall constitute payment or part payment for the issuance of shares of a corporation.

In the absence of fraud in the transaction, the judgment of the board of directors or the shareholders, as the case may be, as to the value of the consideration received for shares shall be conclusive.

§ 20. Stock Rights and Options

Subject to any provisions in respect thereof set forth in its articles of incorporation, a corporation may create and issue, whether or not in connection with the issuance and sale of any of its shares or other securities, rights or options entitling the holders thereof to purchase from the corporation shares of any class or classes. * * *

The price or prices to be received for any shares having a par value, other than treasury shares to be issued upon the exercise of such rights or options, shall not be less than the par value thereof.

§ 21. Determination of Amount of Stated Capital

In case of the issuance by a corporation of shares having a par value, the consideration received therefor shall constitute stated capital to the extent of the par value of such shares, and the excess, if any, of such consideration shall constitute capital surplus.

In case of the issuance by a corporation of shares without par value, the entire consideration received therefor shall constitute stated capital unless the corporation shall determine as provided in this section that only a part thereof shall be stated capital. Within a period of sixty days after the issuance of any shares without par value, the board of directors may allocate to capital surplus any portion of the consideration received for the issuance of such shares. No such allocation shall be made of any portion of the consideration received for shares without par value having a preference in the assets of the corporation in the event of involuntary liquidation except the amount, if any, of such consideration in excess of such preference.

If shares have been or shall be issued by a corporation in merger or consolidation or in acquisition of all or substantially all of the outstanding shares or of the property and assets of another corporation, whether domestic or foreign, any amount that would otherwise constitute capital surplus under the foregoing provisions of this section may instead be allocated to earned surplus by the board of directors of the issuing corporation except that its aggregate earned surplus shall not exceed the sum of the earned surpluses as defined in this Act of the issuing corporation and of all other corporations, domestic or foreign, that were merged or consolidated or of which the shares or assets were acquired.

The stated capital of a corporation may be increased from time to time by resolution of the board of directors directing that all or a part of the surplus of the corporation be transferred to stated capital. The board of directors may direct that the amount of the surplus so transferred shall be deemed to be stated capital in respect of any designated class of shares.

§ 22. Expenses of Organization, Reorganization and Financing

The reasonable charges and expenses of organization or reorganization of a corporation, and the reasonable expenses of and compensation for the sale or underwriting of its shares, may be paid or allowed by such corporation out of the consideration received by it in payment for its shares without thereby rendering such shares not fully paid or assessable.

§ 23. Certificates Representing Shares * * *

Each certificate representing shares shall state upon the face thereof: * * *

    (c)   The number and class of shares, and the designation of the series, if any, which such certificate represents.

    (d)   The par value of each share represented by such certificate, or a statement that the shares are without par value.

No certificate shall be issued for any share until such share is fully paid.

§ 25. Liability of Subscribers and Shareholders

A holder of or subscriber to shares of a corporation shall be under no obligation to the corporation or its creditors with respect to such shares other than the obligation to pay to the corporation the full consideration for which such shares were issued or to be issued.

Any person becoming an assignee or transferee of shares or of a subscription for shares in good faith and without knowledge or notice that the full consideration therefor has not been paid shall not be personally liable to the corporation or its creditors for any unpaid portion of such consideration.

An executor, administrator, conservator, guardian, trustee, assignee for the benefit of creditors, or receiver shall not be personally liable to the corporation as a holder of or subscriber to shares of a corporation but the estate and funds in his hands shall be so liable.

No pledgee or other holder of shares as collateral security shall be personally liable as a shareholder.

§ 45. Dividends

The board of directors of a corporation may, from time to time, declare and the corporation may pay dividends in cash, property, or its own shares, except when the corporation is insolvent or when the payment thereof would render the corporation insolvent or when the declaration or payment thereof would be contrary to any restriction contained in the articles of incorporation, subject to the following provisions:

(a) Dividends may be declared and paid in cash or property only out of the unreserved and unrestricted earned surplus of the corporation, except as otherwise provided in this section.

[Alternative] (a) Dividends may be declared and paid in cash or property only out of the unreserved and unrestricted earned surplus of the corporation, or out of the unreserved and unrestricted net earnings of the current fiscal year and the next preceding fiscal year taken as a single period, except as otherwise provided in this section.

(b) If the articles of incorporation of a corporation engaged in the business of exploiting natural resources so provide, dividends may be declared and paid in cash out of the depletion reserves, but each such dividend shall be identified as a distribution of such reserves and the amount per share paid from such reserves shall be disclosed to the shareholders receiving the same concurrently with the distribution thereof.

(c) Dividends may be declared and paid in its own treasury shares.

(d) Dividends may be declared and paid in its own authorized but unissued shares out of any unreserved and unrestricted surplus of the corporation upon the following conditions:

(1) If a dividend is payable in its own shares having a par value, such shares shall be issued at not less than the par value thereof and there shall be transferred to stated capital at the time such dividend is paid an amount of surplus equal to the aggregate par value of the shares to be issued as a dividend.

(2) If a dividend is payable in its own shares without par value, such shares shall be issued at such stated value as shall be fixed by the board of directors by resolution adopted at the time such dividend is declared, and there shall be transferred to stated capital at the time such dividend is paid an amount of surplus equal to the aggregate stated value so fixed in respect of such shares; and the amount per share so transferred to stated capital shall be disclosed to the shareholders receiving such dividend concurrently with the payment thereof.

(e) No dividend payable in shares of any class shall be paid to the holders of shares of any other class unless the articles of incorporation so provide or such payment is authorized by the affirmative vote or the written consent of the holders of at least a majority of the outstanding shares of the class in which the payment is to be made.

A split-up or division of the issued shares of any class into a greater number of shares of the same class without increasing the stated capital of the corporation shall not be construed to be a share dividend within the meaning of this section.

§ 46. Distributions from Capital Surplus

The board of directors of a corporation may, from time to time, distribute to its shareholders out of capital surplus of the corporation a portion of its assets, in cash or property, subject to the following provisions:

(a)   No such distribution shall be made at a time when the corporation is insolvent or when such distribution would render the corporation insolvent.

(b)   No such distribution shall be made unless the articles of incorporation so provide or such distribution is authorized by the affirmative vote of the holders of a majority of the outstanding shares of each class whether or not entitled to vote thereon by the provisions of the articles of incorporation of the corporation.

(c)   No such distribution shall be made to the holders of any class of shares unless all cumulative dividends accrued on all preferred or special classes of shares entitled to preferential dividends shall have been fully paid.

(d)   No such distribution shall be made to the holders of any class of shares which would reduce the remaining net assets of the corporation below the aggregate preferential amount payable in event of involuntary liquidation to the holders of shares having preferential rights to the assets of the corporation in the event of liquidation.

(e)   Each such distribution, when made, shall be identified as a distribution from capital surplus and the amount per share disclosed to the shareholders receiving the same concurrently with the distribution thereof.

The board of directors of a corporation may also, from time to time, distribute to the holders of its outstanding shares having a cumulative preferential right to receive dividends, in discharge of their cumulative dividend rights, dividends payable in cash out of the capital surplus of the corporation, if at the time the corporation has no earned surplus and is not insolvent and would not thereby be rendered insolvent. Each such distribution when made, shall be identified as a payment of cumulative dividends out of capital surplus.

§ 48. Liability of Directors in Certain Cases

In addition to any other liabilities, a director shall be liable in the following circumstances unless he complies with the standard provided in this Act for the performance of the duties of directors:

(a)   A director who votes for or assents to the declaration of any dividend or other distribution of the assets of a corporation to its shareholders contrary to the provisions of this Act or contrary to any restrictions contained in the articles of incorporation, shall be liable to the corporation, jointly and severally with all other directors so voting or assenting, for the amount of such dividend which is paid or the value of such assets which are distributed in excess of the amount of such dividend or distribution which could have been paid or distributed without a violation of the provisions of this Act or the restrictions in the articles of incorporation.

(b)   A director who votes for or assents to the purchase of the corporation's own shares contrary to the provisions of this Act shall be liable to the corporation, jointly and severally with all other directors so voting or assenting, for the amount of consideration paid for such shares which is in excess of the maximum amount which could have been paid therefor without a violation of the provisions of this Act.

(c)   A director who votes for or assents to any distribution of assets of a corporation to its shareholders during the liquidation of the corporation without the payment and discharge of, or making adequate provision for, all known debts, obligations, and liabilities of the corporation shall be liable to the corporation, jointly and severally with all other directors so voting or assenting, for the value of such assets which are distributed, to the extent that such debts, obligations and liabilities of the corporation are not thereafter paid and discharged.

Any director against whom a claim shall be asserted under or pursuant to this section for the payment of a dividend or other distribution of assets of a corporation and who shall be held liable thereon, shall be entitled to contribution from the shareholders who accepted or received any such dividend or assets, knowing such dividend or distribution to have been made in violation of this Act, in proportion to the amounts received by them.

Any director against whom a claim shall be asserted under or pursuant to this section shall be entitled to contribution from the other directors who voted for or assented to the action upon which the claim is asserted.

§ 54. Articles of Incorporation

The articles of incorporation shall set forth: * * *

(d)   The aggregate number of shares which the corporation shall have authority to issue; if such shares are to consist of one class only, the par value of each of such shares, or a statement that all of such shares are without par value; or, if such shares are to be divided into classes, the number of shares of each such class, and a statement of the par value of the shares of each such class or that such shares are to be without par value.

§ 58. Right to Amend Articles of Incorporation

A corporation may amend its articles of incorporation, from time to time, in any and as many respects as may be desired, so long as its articles of incorporation as amended contain only such provisions as might be lawfully contained in original articles of incorporation at the time of making such amendment, and, if a change in shares or the rights of shareholders, or an exchange, reclassification or cancellation of shares or rights of shareholders is to be made, such provisions as may be necessary to effect such change, exchange, reclassification or cancellation.

In particular, and without limitation upon such general power of amendment, a corporation may amend its articles of incorporation, from time to time, so as: * * *

(e)   To increase or decrease the par value of the authorized shares of any class having a par value, whether issued or unissued.

(f)   To exchange, classify, reclassify or cancel all or any part of its shares, whether issued or unissued.

(g)   To change the designation of all or any part of its shares, whether issued or unissued, and to change the preferences, limitations, and the relative rights in respect of all or any part of its shares, whether issued or unissued.

(h)   To change shares having the par value, whether issued or unissued, into the same or a different number of shares without par value, and to change shares without par value, whether issued or unissued, into the same or a different number of shares having a par value.

(i)   To change the shares of any class, whether issued or unissued, and whether with or without par value, into a different number of shares of the same class or into the same or a different number of shares, either with or without par value, of other classes. * * *

§ 60. Class Voting on Amendments

The holders of the outstanding shares of a class shall be entitled to vote as a class upon a proposed amendment, whether or not entitled to vote thereon by the provisions of the articles of incorporation, if the amendment would:

(a)   Increase or decrease the aggregate number of authorized shares of such class.

(b)   Increase or decrease the par value of the shares of such class.

(c)   Effect an exchange, reclassification or cancellation of all or part of the shares of such class.

(d)   Effect an exchange, or create a right of exchange, of all or any part of the shares of another class into the shares of such class.

(e)   Change the designations, preferences, limitations or relative rights of the shares of such class.

(f) Change the shares of such class, whether with or without par value, into the same or a different number of shares, either with or without par value, of the same class or another class or classes. * * *

§ 66. Restriction on Redemption or Purchase of Redeemable Shares

No redemption or purchase of redeemable shares shall be made by a corporation when it is insolvent or when such redemption or purchase would render it insolvent, or which would reduce the net assets below the aggregate amount payable to the holders of shares having prior or equal rights to the assets of the corporation upon involuntary dissolution.

§ 67. Cancellation of Redeemable Shares by Redemption or Purchase

When redeemable shares of a corporation are redeemed or purchased by the corporation, the redemption or purchase shall effect a cancellation of such shares, and a statement of cancellation shall be filed as provided in this section. Thereupon such shares shall be restored to the status of authorized but unissued shares, unless the articles of incorporation provide that such shares when redeemed or purchased shall not be reissued, in which case the filing of the statement of cancellation shall constitute an amendment to the articles of incorporation and shall reduce the number of shares of the class so cancelled which the corporation is authorized to issue by the number of shares so cancelled.

The statement of cancellation shall be executed in duplicate by the corporation by its president or a vice president and by its secretary or an assistant secretary, and verified by one of the officers signing such statement, and shall set forth:

(a) The name of the corporation.

(b) The number of redeemable shares cancelled through redemption or purchase, itemized by classes and series.

(c) The aggregate number of issued shares, itemized by classes and series, after giving effect to such cancellation.

(d) The amount, expressed in dollars, of the stated capital of the corporation after giving effect to such cancellation.

(e) If the articles of incorporation provide that the cancelled shares shall not be reissued, the number of shares which the corporation will have authority to issue itemized by classes and series, after giving effect to such cancellation. * * *

Upon the filing of such statement of cancellation, the stated capital of the corporation shall be deemed to be reduced by that part of the stated capital which was, at the time of such cancellation, represented by the shares so cancelled.

Nothing contained in this section shall be construed to forbid a cancellation of shares or a reduction of stated capital in any other manner permitted by this Act.

§ 68. Cancellation of Other Reacquired Shares

A corporation may at any time, by resolution of its board of directors, cancel all or any part of the shares of the corporation of any class reacquired by it, other than redeemable shares redeemed or purchased, and in such event a statement of cancellation shall be filed as provided in this section.

The statement of cancellation shall be executed in duplicate by the corporation by its president or a vice president and by its secretary or an assistant secretary, and verified by one of the officers signing such statement, and shall set forth:

(a) The name of the corporation.

(b) The number of reacquired shares cancelled by resolution duly adopted by the board of directors, itemized by classes and series, and the date of its adoption.

(c)   The aggregate number of issued shares, itemized by classes and series, after giving effect to such cancellation.

(d)   The amount, expressed in dollars, of the stated capital of the corporation after giving effect to such cancellation. * * *

Upon the filing of such statement of cancellation, the stated capital of the corporation shall be deemed to be reduced by that part of the stated capital which was, at the time of such cancellation, represented by the shares so cancelled, and the shares so cancelled shall be restored to the status of authorized but unissued shares.

Nothing contained in this section shall be construed to forbid a cancellation of shares or a reduction of stated capital in any other manner permitted by this Act.

§ 69. Reduction of Stated Capital in Certain Cases

A reduction of the stated capital of a corporation, where such reduction is not accompanied by any action requiring an amendment of the articles of incorporation and not accompanied by a cancellation of shares, may be made in the following manner:

(A)   The board of directors shall adopt a resolution setting forth the amount of the proposed reduction and the manner in which the reduction shall be effected, and directing that the question of such reduction be submitted to a vote at a meeting of shareholders, which may be either an annual or a special meeting.

(B)   Written notice, stating that the purpose or one of the purposes of such meeting is to consider the question of reducing the stated capital of the corporation in the amount and manner proposed by the board of directors, shall be given to each shareholder of record entitled to vote thereon within the time and in the manner provided in this Act for the giving of notice of meetings of shareholders.

(C)   At such meeting a vote of the shareholders entitled to vote thereon shall be taken on the question of approving the proposed reduction of stated capital, which shall require for its adoption the affirmative vote of the holders of a majority of the shares entitled to vote thereon.

When a reduction of the stated capital of a corporation has been approved as provided in this section, a statement shall be executed in duplicate by the corporation by its president or a vice president and by its secretary or an assistant secretary, and verified by one of the officers signing such statement, and shall set forth: * * *

(e)   A statement of the manner in which such reduction is effected, and a statement, expressed in dollars, of the amount of stated capital of the corporation after giving effect to such reduction. * * *

Upon the filing of such statement, the stated capital of the corporation shall be reduced as therein set forth.

No reduction of stated capital shall be made under the provisions of this section which would reduce the amount of the aggregate stated capital of the corporation to an amount equal to or less than the aggregate preferential amounts payable upon all issued shares having a preferential right in the assets of the corporation in the event of involuntary liquidation, plus the aggregate par value of all issued shares having a par value but no preferential right in the assets of the corporation in the event of involuntary liquidation.

§ 70. Special Provisions Relating to Surplus and Reserves

The surplus, if any, created by or arising out of a reduction of the stated capital of a corporation shall be capital surplus.

The capital surplus of a corporation may be increased from time to time by resolution of the board of directors directing that all or a part of the earned surplus of the corporation be transferred to capital surplus.

A corporation may, by resolution of its board of directors, apply any part or all of its capital surplus to the reduction or elimination of any deficit arising from losses, however incurred, but only after first eliminating the earned surplus, if any, of the corporation by applying such losses against earned surplus and only to the extent that such losses exceed the earned surplus, if any. Each such application of capital surplus shall, to the extent thereof, effect a reduction of capital surplus.

A corporation may, by resolution of its board of directors, create a reserve or reserves out of its earned surplus for any proper purpose or purposes, and may abolish any such reserve in the same manner. Earned surplus of the corporation to the extent so reserved shall not be available for the payment of dividends or other distributions by the corporation except as expressly permitted by this Act.

NEW YORK BUSINESS CORPORATION LAW

(Selected Provisions)

Table of Sections

---

§ 609.   Proxies

(a)   Every shareholder entitled to vote at a meeting of shareholders or to express consent or dissent without a meeting may authorize another person or persons to act for him by proxy.

(b)   No proxy shall be valid after the expiration of eleven months from the date thereof unless otherwise provided in the proxy. Every proxy shall be revocable at the pleasure of the shareholder executing it, except as otherwise provided in this section.

(c)   The authority of the holder of a proxy to act shall not be revoked by the incompetence or death of the shareholder who executed the proxy unless, before the authority is exercised, written notice of an adjudication of such incompetence or of such death is received by the corporate officer responsible for maintaining the list of shareholders.

(d)   Except when other provision shall have been made by written agreement between the parties, the record holder of shares which he holds as pledgee or otherwise as security or which belong to another, shall issue to the pledgor or to such owner of such shares, upon demand therefor and payment of necessary expenses thereof, a proxy to vote or take other action thereon.

(e)   A shareholder shall not sell his vote or issue a proxy to vote to any person for any sum of money or anything of value, except as authorized in this section and section 620 (Agreements as to voting; provision in certificate of incorporation as to control of directors); provided, however, that this paragraph shall not apply to votes, proxies or consents given by holders of preferred shares in connection with a proxy or consent solicitation made available on identical terms to all holders of shares of the same class or series and remaining open for acceptance for at least twenty business days.

(f)   A proxy which is entitled "irrevocable proxy" and which states that it is irrevocable, is irrevocable when it is held by any of the following or a nominee of any of the following:

(1)   A pledgee;

(2)   A person who has purchased or agreed to purchase the shares;

(3)   A creditor or creditors of the corporation who extend or continue credit to the corporation in consideration of the proxy if the proxy states that it was given in consideration of such extension or continuation of credit, the amount thereof, and the name of the person extending or continuing credit;

(4)   A person who has contracted to perform services as an officer of the corporation, if a proxy is required by the contract of employment, if the proxy states that it was given in consideration of such contract of employment, the name of the employee and the period of employment contracted for;

(5)   A person designated by or under an agreement under paragraph (a) of section 620.

(g)   Notwithstanding a provision in a proxy, stating that it is irrevocable, the proxy becomes revocable after the pledge is redeemed, or the debt of the corporation is paid, or the period of employment provided for in the contract of employment has terminated, or the agreement under paragraph (a) of section 620 has terminated; and, in a case provided for in subparagraphs (f)(3) or (4), becomes revocable three years after the date of the proxy or at the end of the period, if any, specified therein, whichever period is less, unless the period of irrevocability is renewed from time to time by the execution of a new irrevocable proxy as provided in this section. This paragraph does not affect the duration of a proxy under paragraph (b).

(h)   A proxy may be revoked, notwithstanding a provision making it irrevocable, by a purchaser of shares without knowledge of the existence of the provision unless the existence of the proxy and its irrevocability is noted conspicuously on the face or back of the certificate representing such shares.

(i)   Without limiting the manner in which a shareholder may authorize another person or persons to act for him as proxy pursuant to paragraph (a) of this section, the following shall constitute a valid means by which a shareholder may grant such authority.

(1)   A shareholder may execute a writing authorizing another person or persons to act from him as proxy. Execution may be accomplished by the shareholder or the shareholder's authorized officer, director, employee or agent signing such writing or causing his or her signature to be affixed to such writing by any reasonable means including, but not limited to, by facsimile signature.

(2)   A shareholder may authorize another person or persons to act for the shareholder as proxy by transmitting or authorizing the transmission of a telegram, cablegram or other means of electronic transmission to the person who will be the holder of the proxy or to a proxy solicitation firm, proxy support service organization or like agent duly authorized by the person who will be the holder of the proxy to receive such transmission, provided that any such telegram, cablegram or other means of electronic transmission must either set forth or be submitted with information from which it can be reasonably determined that the telegram, cablegram or other electronic transmission was authorized by the shareholder. If it is determined that such telegrams, cablegrams or other electronic transmissions are valid, the inspectors or, if there are no inspectors, such other persons making that determination shall specify the nature of the information upon which they relied.

(j)   Any copy, facsimile telecommunication or other reliable reproduction of the writing or transmission created pursuant to paragraph (i) of this section may be substituted or used in lieu of the original writing or transmission for any and all purposes for which the original writing or transmission could be used, provided that such copy, facsimile telecommunication or other reproduction shall be a complete reproduction of the entire original writing or transmission.

§ 620.   Agreements as to Voting; Provision in Certificate of Incorporation as to Control of Directors

(a)   An agreement between two or more shareholders, if in writing and signed by the parties thereto, may provide that in exercising any voting rights, the shares held by them shall be voted as therein provided, or as they may agree, or as determined in accordance with a procedure agreed upon by them.

(b)   A provision in the certificate of incorporation otherwise prohibited by law because it improperly restricts the board in its management of the business of the corporation, or improperly transfers to one or more shareholders or to one or more persons or corporations to be selected by him or them, all or any part of such management otherwise within the authority of the board under this chapter, shall nevertheless be valid:

(1)   If all the incorporators or holders of record of all outstanding shares, whether or not having voting power, have authorized such provision in the certificate of incorporation or an amendment thereof; and

(2)   If, subsequent to the adoption of such provision, shares are transferred or issued only to persons who had knowledge or notice thereof or consented in writing to such provision.

(c)   A provision authorized by paragraph (b) shall be valid only so long as no shares of the corporation are listed on a national securities exchange or regularly quoted in an over-the-counter market by one or more members of a national or affiliated securities association.

(d)(1)   Except as provided in paragraph (e), an amendment to strike out a provision authorized by paragraph (b) shall be authorized at a meeting of shareholders by (A) (i) for any corporation in existence on the effective date of subparagraph (2) of this paragraph, two-thirds of the votes of the shares entitled to vote thereon and (ii) for any corporation in existence on the effective date of this clause the certificate of incorporation of which expressly provides such and for any corporation incorporated after the effective date of subparagraph (2) of this paragraph, a majority of the votes of the shares entitled to vote thereon or (B) in either case, by such greater proportion of votes of shares as may be required by the certificate of incorporation for that purpose.

(2)   Any corporation may adopt an amendment of the certificate of incorporation in accordance with the applicable clause or subclause of subparagraph (1) of this paragraph to provide that any further amendment of the certificate of incorporation that strikes out a provision authorized by paragraph (b) of this section shall be authorized at a meeting of the shareholders by a specified proportion of votes of the shares, or votes of a particular class or series of shares, entitled to vote thereon, provided that such proportion may not be less than a majority.

(e)   Alternatively, if a provision authorized by paragraph (b) shall have ceased to be valid under this section, the board may authorize a certificate of amendment under section 805 (Certificate of amendment; contents) striking out such provision. Such certificate shall set forth the event by reason of which the provision ceased to be valid.

(f)   The effect of any such provision authorized by paragraph (b) shall be to relieve the directors and impose upon the shareholders authorizing the same or consenting thereto the liability for managerial acts or omissions that is imposed on directors by this chapter to the extent that and so long as the discretion or powers of the board in its management of corporate affairs is controlled by any such provision.

(g)   If the certificate of incorporation of any corporation contains a provision authorized by paragraph (b), the existence of such provision shall be noted conspicuously on the face or back of every certificate for shares issued by such corporation.

§ 1104–a. Petition for Judicial Dissolution Under Special Circumstances

(a)   The holders of shares representing twenty percent or more of the votes of all outstanding shares of a corporation, other than a corporation registered as an investment company under an act of congress entitled "Investment Company Act of 1940", no shares of which are listed on a national securities exchange or regularly quoted in an over-the-counter market by one or more members of a national or an affiliated securities association, entitled to vote in an election of directors may present a petition of dissolution on one or more of the following grounds:

(1)   The directors or those in control of the corporation have been guilty of illegal, fraudulent or oppressive actions toward the complaining shareholders;

(2)   The property or assets of the corporation are being looted, wasted, or diverted for non-corporate purposes by its directors, officers or those in control of the corporation.

(b)   The court, in determining whether to proceed with involuntary dissolution pursuant to this section, shall take into account:

(1)   Whether liquidation of the corporation is the only feasible means whereby the petitioners may reasonably expect to obtain a fair return on their investment; and

(2)   Whether liquidation of the corporation is reasonably necessary for the protection of the rights and interests of any substantial number of shareholders or of the petitioners.

(c)   In addition to all other disclosure requirements, the directors or those in control of the corporation, no later than thirty days after the filing of a petition hereunder, shall make available for inspection and copying to the petitioners under reasonable working conditions the corporate financial books and records for the three preceding years.

(d)   The court may order stock valuations be adjusted and may provide for a surcharge upon the directors or those in control of the corporation upon a finding of wilful or reckless dissipation or transfer of assets or corporate property without just or adequate compensation therefor.

§ 1118.   Purchase of Petitioner's Shares; Valuation

(a)   In any proceeding brought pursuant to section eleven hundred four-a of this chapter, any other shareholder or shareholders or the corporation may, at any time within ninety days after the filing of such petition or at such later time as the court in its discretion may allow, elect to purchase the shares owned by the petitioners at their fair value and upon such terms and conditions as may be approved by the court, including the conditions of paragraph (c) herein. An election pursuant to this section shall be irrevocable unless the court, in its discretion, for just and equitable considerations, determines that such election be revocable.

(b)   If one or more shareholders or the corporation elect to purchase the shares owned by the petitioner but are unable to agree with the petitioner upon the fair value of such shares, the court, upon the application of such prospective purchaser or purchasers or the petitioner, may stay the proceedings brought pursuant to section 1104–a of this chapter and determine the fair value of the petitioner's shares as of the day prior to the date on which such petition was filed, exclusive of any element of value arising from such filing but giving effect to any adjustment or surcharge found to be appropriate in the proceeding under section 1104– a of this chapter. In determining the fair value of the petitioner's shares, the court, in its discretion, may award interest from the date the petition is filed to the date of payment for the petitioner's share at an equitable rate upon judicially determined fair value of his shares.

(c)   In connection with any election to purchase pursuant to this section:

(1)   If such election is made beyond ninety days after the filing of the petition, and the court allows such petition, the court, in its discretion, may award the petitioner his reasonable expenses incurred in the proceeding prior to such election, including reasonable attorneys' fees;

(2)   The court, in its discretion, may require, at any time prior to the actual purchase of petitioner's shares, the posting of a bond or other acceptable security in an amount sufficient to secure petitioner for the fair value of his shares.

ALI PRINCIPLES OF CORPORATE GOVERNANCE

(As quoted in the Appendix to Cuker v. Mikalauskas,
692 A.2d 1042 (Pa. 1997))

---

§ 7.02   Standing to Commence and Maintain a Derivative Action

(a)   A holder of an equity security has standing to commence and maintain a derivative action if the holder:

(1)   Acquired the equity security either (A) before the material facts relating to the alleged wrong were publicly disclosed or were known by, or specifically communicated to, the holder, or (B) by devolution of law, directly or indirectly, from a prior holder who acquired the security as described in the preceding clause (A);

(2)   Continues to hold the equity security until the time of judgment, unless the failure to do so is the result of corporate action in which the holder did not acquiesce, and either (A) the derivative action was commenced prior to the corporate action terminating the holder's status, or (B) the court finds that the holder is better able to represent the interests of the shareholders than any other holder who has brought suit;

(3)   Has complied with the demand requirement of § 7.03 (Exhaustion of Intracorporate Remedies; The Demand Rule) or was excused by its terms; and

(4)   Is able to represent fairly and adequately the interests of the shareholders.

(b)   On a timely motion, a holder of an equity security should be permitted to intervene in a derivative action, unless the court finds that the interests to be represented by the intervenor are already fairly and adequately represented or that the intervenor is unable to represent fairly and adequately the interests of the shareholders.

(c)   A director of a corporation has standing to commence and maintain a derivative action unless the court finds that the director is unable to represent fairly and adequately the interest of the shareholders.

§ 7.03   Exhaustion of Intracorporate Remedies: The Demand Rule

(a)   Before commencing a derivative action, a holder or a director should be required to make a written demand upon the board of directors of the corporation, requesting it to prosecute the action or take suitable corrective measures, unless demand is excused under § 7.03(b). The demand should give notice to the board, with reasonable specificity, of the essential facts relied upon to support each of the claims made therein.

(b)   Demand on the board should be excused only if the plaintiff makes a specific showing that irreparable injury to the corporation would otherwise result, and in such instances demand should be made promptly after commencement of the action.

(c)   Demand on shareholders should not be required.

(d)   Except as provided in § 7.03(b), the court should dismiss a derivative action that is commenced prior to the response of the board or a committee thereof to the demand required by § 7.03(a), unless the board or committee fails to respond within a reasonable time.

§ 7.04   Pleading, Demand Rejection, Procedure, and Costs in a Derivative Action

The legal standards applicable to a derivative action should provide that:

(a)   Particularity; Demand Rejection.

(1) In General. The complaint shall plead with particularity facts that, if true, raise a significant prospect that the transaction or conduct complained of did not meet the applicable requirements of Parts IV (Duty of Care and the Business Judgment Rule), V (Duty of Fair Dealing), or VI (Role of Directors and Shareholders in Transactions in Control and Tender Offers), in light of any approvals of the transaction or conduct communicated to the plaintiff by the corporation.

(2) Demand Rejection. If the corporation rejects the demand made on the board pursuant to § 7.03, and if, at or following the rejection, the corporation delivers to the plaintiff a written reply to the demand which states that the demand was rejected by directors who were not interested in the transaction or conduct described in and forming the basis for the demand and that those directors constituted a majority of the entire board and were capable as a group of objective judgment in the circumstances, and which provides specific reasons for those statements, then the complaint shall also plead with particularity facts that, if true, raise a significant prospect that either:

(A) The statements in the reply are not correct;

(B) If Part IV, V, or VI provides that the underlying transaction or conduct would be reviewed under a standard other than the business judgment rule, either (i) that the disinterested directors who rejected the demand did not satisfy the good faith and informational requirements (§ 4.01(c)(2)) of the business judgment rule or (ii) that disinterested directors could not reasonably have determined that rejection of the demand was in the best interests of the corporation.

If the complaint fails to set forth sufficiently such particularized facts, defendants shall be entitled to dismissal of the complaint prior to discovery.

(b) Attorney's Certification. Each party's attorney of record shall sign every pleading, motion, and other paper filed on behalf of the party, and such signature shall constitute the attorney's certification that (i) to the best of the attorney's knowledge, information, and belief, formed after reasonable inquiry, the pleading, motion, or other paper is well grounded in fact and is warranted by existing law or by a good faith argument for the extension, modification, or reversal of existing law, and (ii) the pleading, motion, or other paper is not interposed for any improper purpose, such as to harass or to cause unnecessary delay or needless increase in the cost of litigation.

(c) Security for Expenses. Except as authorized by statute or judicial rule applicable to civil actions generally, no bond, undertaking, or other security for expenses shall be required.

(d) Award of Costs. The court may award applicable costs, including reasonable attorney's fees and expenses, against a party, or a party's counsel:

(1) At any time, if the court finds that any specific claim for relief or defense was asserted or any pleading, motion, request for discovery, or other action was made or taken in bad faith or without reasonable cause; or

(2) Upon final judgment, if the court finds, in light of all the evidence, and considering both the state and trend of the substantive law, that the action taken as a whole was brought, prosecuted, or defended in bad faith or in an unreasonable manner.

§ 7.05 Board or Committee Authority in Regard to a Derivative Action

(a) The board of a corporation in whose name or right a derivative action is brought has standing on behalf of the corporation to:

(1) Move to dismiss the action on account of the plaintiff's lack of standing under § 7.02 (Standing to Commence and Maintain a Derivative Action) or the plaintiff's failure to comply with § 7.03 (Exhaustion of Intracorporate Remedies: The Demand Rule) or § 7.04(a) or (b) (Pleading, Demand Rejection, Procedure, and Costs in a Derivative Action) or move for dismissal of the complaint or for summary judgment;

(2) Move for a stay of the action, including discovery, as provided by § 7.06 (Authority of Court to Stay a Derivative Action);

(3) Move to dismiss the action as contrary to the best interests of the corporation, as provided in §§ 7.07–7.12 (dismissal of a derivative action based on a motion requesting dismissal by the board, a board committee, the shareholders, or a special panel);

(4) Oppose injunctive or other relief materially affecting the corporation's interests;

(5) Adopt or pursue the action in the corporation's right;

(6) Comment on, object to, or recommend any proposed settlement, discontinuance, compromise, or voluntary dismissal by agreement between the plaintiff and any defendant under § 7.14 (Settlement of a Derivative Action by Agreement Between the Plaintiff and a Defendant), or any award of attorney's fees and other expenses under § 7.17 (Plaintiff's attorney's Fees and Expenses); and

(7) Seek to settle the action without agreement of the plaintiff under § 7.15 (Settlement of a Derivative Action Without the Agreement of the Plaintiff).

Except as provided above, the corporation may not otherwise defend the action in the place of, or raise defenses on behalf of, other defendants.

(b) The board of a corporation in whose name or right a derivative action is brought may:

(1) Delegate its authority to take any action specified in § 7.05(a) to a committee of directors; or

(2) Request the court to appoint a special panel in lieu of a committee of directors, or a special member of a committee, under § 7.12 (Special Panel or Special Committee Members).

§ 7.06 Authority of Court to Stay a Derivative Action

In the absence of special circumstances, the court should stay discovery and all further proceedings by the plaintiff in a derivative action on the motion of the corporation and upon such conditions as the court deems appropriate pending the court's determination of any motion made by the corporation under § 7.04(a)(2) and the completion within a reasonable period of any review and evaluation undertaken and diligently pursued pursuant to § 7.09 (Procedures for Requesting Dismissal of a Derivative Action). On the same basis the court may stay discovery and further proceedings pending (a) the resolution of a related action or (b) such other event or development as the interests of justice may require.

§ 7.07 Dismissal of a Derivative Action Based on a Motion Requesting Dismissal by the Board or a Committee: General Statement

(a) The court having jurisdiction over a derivative action should dismiss the action as against one or more of the defendants based on a motion by the board or a properly delegated committee requesting dismissal of the action as in the best interests of the corporation, if:

(1) In the case of an action against a person other than a director, senior executive, or person in control of the corporation, or an associate of any such person, the determinations of the board or committee underlying the motion satisfy the requirements of the business judgment rule as specified in § 4.01;

(2) In the case of an action against a director, senior executive, or person in control of the corporation, or an associate of any such person, the conditions specified in § 7.08 (Dismissal of a Derivative Action Against Directors, Senior Executives, Controlling Persons, or Associates Based on a Motion Requesting Dismissal by the Board or a Committee) are satisfied; or

(3) In any case, the shareholders approve a resolution requesting dismissal of the action in the manner provided in § 7.11 (Dismissal of a Derivative Action Based Upon Action by the Shareholders).

(b) Regardless of whether a corporation chooses to proceed under § 7.08 or § 7.11, it is free to make any other motion available to it under the law, including a motion to dismiss the complaint or for summary judgment.

§ 7.08   Dismissal of a Derivative Action Against Directors, Senior Executives, Controlling Persons, or Associates Based on a Motion Requesting Dismissal by the Board or a Committee

The court should, subject to the provisions of § 7.10(b) (retention of significant improper benefit), dismiss a derivative action against a defendant who is a director, a senior executive, or a person in control of the corporation, or an associate of any such person, if:

(a)   The board of directors or a properly delegated committee thereof (either in response to a demand or following commencement of the action) has determined that the action is contrary to the best interests of the corporation and has requested dismissal of the action;

(b)   The procedures specified in § 7.09 (Procedures for Requesting Dismissal of a Derivative Action) for the conduct of a review and evaluation of the action were substantially complied with (either in response to a demand or following commencement of the action), or any material departures therefrom were justified under the circumstances; and

(c)   The determinations of the board or committee satisfy the applicable standard of review set forth in § 7.10(a) (Standard of Judicial Review with Regard to a Board of Committee Motion Requesting Dismissal of a Derivative Action Under § 7.08).

§ 7.09   Procedures for Requesting Dismissal of a Derivative Action

(a)   The following procedural standards should apply to the review and evaluation of a derivative action by the board or committee under § 7.08 (Dismissal of a Derivative Action Against Directors, Senior Executives, Controlling Persons, or Associates Based on a Motion Requesting Dismissal by the Board or a Committee) or § 7.11 (Dismissal of a Derivative Action Based Upon Action by the Shareholders):

(1)   The board or a committee should be composed of two or more persons, no participating member of which was interested in the action, and should as a group be capable of objective judgment in the circumstances;

(2)   The board or committee should be assisted by counsel of its choice and such other agents as it reasonably considers necessary;

(3)   The determinations of the board or committee should be based upon a review and evaluation that was sufficiently informed to satisfy the standards applicable under § 7.10(a); and

(4)   If the board or committee determines to request dismissal of the derivative action, it shall prepare and file with the court a report or other written submission setting forth its determinations in a manner sufficient to enable the court to conduct the review required under § 7.10 (Standard of Judicial Review with Regard to a Board or Committee Motion Requesting Dismissal of a Derivative Action Under § 7.08).

(b)   If the court is unwilling to grant a motion to dismiss under § 7.08 or § 7.11 because the procedures followed by the board or committee departed materially from the standards specified in § 7.09(a), the court should permit the board or committee to supplement its procedures, and make such further reports or other written submissions, as will satisfy the standards specified in § 7.09(a), unless the court decides that (i) the board or committee did not act on the basis of a good faith belief that its procedures and report were justified in the circumstances; (ii) unreasonable delay or prejudice would result; or (iii) there is no reasonable prospect that such further steps would support dismissal of the action.

§ 7.10   Standard of Judicial Review with Regard to a Board or Committee Motion Requesting Dismissal of a Derivative Action Under § 7.08

(a)   Standard of Review. In deciding whether an action should be dismissed under § 7.08 (Dismissal of a Derivative Action Against Directors, Senior Executives, Controlling Persons, or Associates Based on a Motion Requesting Dismissal by the Board or a Committee), the court should apply the following standards of review:

(1) If the gravamen of the claim is that the defendant violated a duty set forth in Part IV (Duty of Care and the Business Judgment Rule), other than by committing a knowing and culpable violation of law that is alleged with particularity, or if the underlying transaction or conduct would be reviewed under the business judgment rule under § 5.03, § 5.04, § 5.05, § 5.06, § 5.08, or § 6.02, the court should dismiss the claim unless it finds that the board's or committee's determinations fail to satisfy the requirements of the business judgment rule as specified in § 4.01(c).

(2) In other cases governed by Part V (Duty of Fair Dealing) or Part VI (Role of Directors and Shareholders in Transactions in Control and Tender Offers), or to which the business judgment rule is not applicable, including cases in which the gravamen of the claim is that defendant committed a knowing and culpable violation of law in breach of Part IV, the court should dismiss the action if the court finds, in light of the applicable standards under Part IV, V, or VI that the board or committee was adequately informed under the circumstances and reasonably determined that dismissal was in the best interests of the corporation, based on grounds that the court deems to warrant reliance.

(3) In cases arising under either Subsection (a)(1) or (a)(2), the court may substantively review and determine any issue of law.

(b) Retention of Significant Improper Benefit. The court shall not dismiss an action if the plaintiff establishes that dismissal would permit a defendant, or an associate, to retain a significant improper benefit where:

(1) The defendant, either alone or collectively with others who are also found to have received a significant improper benefit arising out of the same transaction, possesses control of the corporation; or

(2) Such benefit was obtained:

(A) As the result of a knowing and material misrepresentation or omission or other fraudulent act; or

(B) Without advance authorization or the requisite ratification of such benefit by disinterested directors (or, in the case of a nondirector senior executive, advance authorization by a disinterested superior), or authorization or ratification by disinterested shareholders, and in breach of § 5.02 (Transactions with the Corporation) or § 5.04 (Use by a Director or Senior Executive of Corporate Property, Material Non-Public Corporate Information, or Corporate Position); unless the court determines, in light of specific reasons advanced by the board or committee, that the likely injury to the corporation from continuation of the action convincingly outweighs any adverse impact on the public interest from dismissal of the action.

(c) Subsequent Developments. In determining whether the standards of § 7.10(a) are satisfied or whether § 7.10(b) or any of the exceptions set forth therein are applicable, the court may take into account considerations set forth by the board or committee (or otherwise brought to the court's attention) that reflect material developments subsequent to the time of the underlying transaction or conduct or to the time of the motion by the board or committee requesting dismissal.

§ 7.13 Judicial Procedures on Motions to Dismiss a Derivative Action Under § 7.08 or § 7.11

(a) Filing of Report or Other Written Submission. Upon a motion to dismiss an action under § 7.08 (Dismissal of a Derivative Action Against Directors, Senior Executives, Controlling Persons, or Associates Based on a Motion Requesting Dismissal by the Board or a Committee) or § 7.11 (Dismissal of a Derivative Action Based Upon Action by the Shareholders), the corporation shall file with the court a report or other written submission setting forth the procedures and determinations of the board or committee, or the resolution of the shareholders. A copy of the report or other written submission, including any supporting documentation filed by the corporation, shall be given to the plaintiff's counsel.

(b) Protective Order. The court may issue a protective order concerning such materials, where appropriate.

(c) Discovery. Subject to § 7.06 (Authority of Court to Stay a Derivative Action), if the plaintiff has demonstrated that a substantial issue exists whether the applicable standards of § 7.08, § 7.09, § 7.10, § 7.11, or § 7.12 have been satisfied and if the plaintiff is unable without undue hardship to obtain the information by other means, the court may order such limited discovery or limited evidentiary hearing, as to issues specified by the court, as the court finds to be (i) necessary to enable it to render a decision on the motion under the applicable standards of § 7.08, § 7.09, § 7.10, § 7.11, or § 7.12, and (ii) consistent with an expedited resolution of the motion. In the absence of special circumstances, the court should limit on a similar basis any discovery that is sought by the plaintiff in response to a motion for summary judgment by the corporation or any defendant to those facts likely to be in dispute. The results of any such discovery may be made subject to a protective order on the same basis as under § 7.13(b).

(d) Burdens of Proof. The plaintiff has the burden of proof in the case of a motion (1) under § 7.08 where the standard of judicial review is determined under § 7.10(a)(1) because the basis of the claim involves a breach of a duty set forth in Part IV (Duty of Care and the Business Judgment Rule) or because the underlying transaction would be reviewed under the business judgment rule, or (2) under § 7.07(a)(1) (suits against third parties and lesser corporate officials). The corporation has the burden of proof in the case of a motion under § 7.08 where the standard of judicial review is determined under § 7.10(a)(2) because the underlying transaction would be reviewed under a standard other than the business judgment rule, except that the plaintiff retains the burden of proof in all cases to show (i) that a defendant's conduct involved a knowing and culpable violation of law, (ii) that the board or committee as a group was not capable of objective judgment in the circumstances as required by § 7.09(a)[1], and (iii) that dismissal of the action would permit a defendant or an associate thereof to retain a significant improper benefit under § 7.10(b). The corporation shall also have the burden of proving under § 7.10(b) that the likely injury to the corporation from continuation of the action convincingly outweighs any adverse impact on the public interest from dismissal of the action. In the case of a motion under § 7.11 (Dismissal of a Derivative Action Based Upon Action by the Shareholders), the plaintiff has the burden of proof with respect to § 7.11(b), (c), and (d), and the corporation has the burden of proof with respect to § 7.11(a).

(e) Privilege. The plaintiff's counsel should be furnished a copy of related legal opinions received by the board or committee if any opinion is tendered to the court under § 7.13(a). Subject to that requirement, communications, both oral and written, between the board or committee and its counsel with respect to the subject matter of the action do not forfeit their privileged character, and documents, memoranda, or other material qualifying as attorney's work product do not become subject to discovery, on the grounds that the action is derivative or that the privilege was waived by the production to the plaintiff or the filing with the court of a report, other written submission, or supporting documents pursuant to § 7.13.

SAMPLE MINUTES OF ORGANIZATIONAL MEETING

MINUTES OF ORGANIZATIONAL MEETING OF
DIRECTORS OF ABC CORPORATION

The organizational meeting of the Board of Directors of ABC Corporation was duly convened in _____, _____ on _____, __, 20__, at _____ __.M.

All directors were present at the meeting and each director waived notice of the time, place of the meeting, and of the purposes for which it was held, as evidenced by execution of a waiver of notice, which is attached hereto.

By unanimous consent, Ms. Barbara Brown served as chairperson of the meeting and Mr. Walter White served as secretary of the meeting.

The secretary presented and read to the meeting a copy of the articles of incorporation of the corporation. He reported that an original and a copy of the articles of incorporation had been duly filed with the office of the Secretary of State, together with the required filing fee, and that the Secretary of State had issued a fee receipt dated _____.

The secretary presented to the meeting a minute book for the corporation. Thereupon motion duly made, seconded, and unanimously adopted, it was:

RESOLVED, That the minute book presented to this meeting be adopted as the minute book for this corporation, and that the secretary of this meeting be instructed to place therein the articles of incorporation and certificate of incorporation of the corporation.

The chairperson then read to the meeting a draft of the bylaws which had been prepared for the regulation and management of the affairs of the corporation. On motion duly made, seconded, and unanimously adopted, it was:

RESOLVED, That the bylaws submitted at and read to this meeting are hereby approved as the bylaws of this corporation, and the secretary of this meeting is hereby instructed to copy such bylaws, at length, in the minute book of the corporation.

The chairperson then presented a form of stock certificate to be used to represent shares issued by the corporation. On motion duly made, seconded, and unanimously adopted, it was:

RESOLVED, That the form of stock certificate presented to this meeting is hereby approved and adopted, and the secretary of this meeting is hereby instructed to insert a specimen of such stock certificate in the minute book of the corporation.

The chairperson then presented to the meeting a form of corporate seal for use by the corporation. On motion duly made, seconded, and unanimously adopted, it was:

RESOLVED, That the corporate seal, an impression of which is affixed in the margin of the bylaws, is hereby approved and adopted as the official corporate seal of this corporation.

The chairperson then called for the election of officers of the corporation. On motion duly made, seconded, and unanimously adopted, the following persons were elected to the offices set opposite their respective names:

Barbara Brown	President
George Green	Vice President and Treasurer
Walter White	Vice President and Secretary

SAMPLE MINUTES OF ORGANIZATIONAL MEETING

each such officer to serve in accordance with the provisions of the bylaws and until his or her successor shall have been elected and shall have qualified.

Thereupon, on motion duly made, seconded, and unanimously adopted, Ms. Brown not voting, it was resolved that Ms. Brown be paid a salary of $_____ per month, payable monthly, but that the other officers of the corporation not be paid any regular salary.

Barbara Brown, George Green and Walter White each submitted written offers to purchase one thousand (1,000) shares of the corporation at a price of ten dollars ($10) per share. On motion duly made, seconded, and unanimously adopted, it was:

RESOLVED, That this corporation accept the following offers to purchase shares of the corporation:

these ppl made offers to buy shares in the corporation

Name	Number of Shares	Total Price
Barbara Brown	1,000	$10,000.00
George Green	1,000	$10,000.00
Walter White	1,000	$10,000.00

FURTHER RESOLVED, That upon payment to this corporation of the respective sums payable to this corporation, the officers of this corporation are hereby authorized and directed to issue to the respective purchasers certificates representing fully paid and nonassessable shares of this corporation for the shares so purchased.

Ms. Brown reported to the meeting that she had incurred and paid the following sums to the following persons for the following purposes in connection with the formation of the corporation:

$100.00   to the secretary of state of _____ as the statutory fee for filing the articles of incorporation.

$277.20   to Mr. Jones for legal services in connection with drafting the articles of incorporation, bylaws, and other matters directly related to the formation of the corporation.

It was thereupon resolved that Ms. Brown should be reimbursed for such expenses in the total sum of $377.20 and the treasurer was instructed to pay Ms. Brown such sum as soon as possible out of corporate funds.

On motion duly made, seconded, and unanimously adopted, it was:

RESOLVED that the _____ Bank be chosen as the depository of the funds of the corporation, and the _____ and the _____ were each authorized to draw checks on the corporation's bank account in such bank. A form of resolution furnished by such bank was then presented to the meeting and, after being read and fully understood, such form of resolution was adopted and is attached to these minutes as an exhibit.

There being no further business, on motion duly made, seconded, and unanimously adopted, the meeting was adjourned.

_____

SECRETARY

We consent to the foregoing actions

_____

_____

_____

SAMPLE MINUTES OF ORGANIZATIONAL MEETING

WAIVER OF NOTICE

We, the undersigned, being all the original directors of ABC Corporation named in the articles of incorporation, do hereby waive notice and the call by the incorporators of said corporation of the organizational meeting of the directors of said corporation, and agree that the organizational meeting shall be held at _____, in the city of _____, _____ _____ o'clock __.M. on the _____ day of _____, 20__.

_____

_____

_____

SAMPLE BYLAWS

(Selected Provisions)[a]

ARTICLE III. BOARD OF DIRECTORS

Section 1. *General Powers.* The business and affairs of the corporation shall be managed by its board of directors.

Section 2. *Number, Tenure, and Qualifications.* The number of directors of the corporation shall be _____. Directors shall be elected at the annual meeting of stockholders, and the term of office of each director shall be until the next annual meeting of stockholders and the election and qualification of his or her successor. Directors need not be residents of the State of _____, _____ *[but shall be stockholders of the corporation] [and need not be stockholders of the corporation].*

Section 3. *Regular Meetings.* A regular meeting of the board of directors shall be held without notice other than this bylaw immediately after and at the same place as the annual meeting of stockholders. The board of directors may provide, by resolution, the time and place for holding additional regular meetings without other notice than such resolution. Additional regular meetings shall be held at the principal office of the corporation in the absence of any designation in the resolution.

Section 4. *Special Meetings.* Special meetings of the board of directors may be called by or at the request of the president or any _____ *[two]* directors, and shall be held at the principal office of the corporation or at such other place as the directors may determine.

Section 5. *Notice.* Notice of any special meeting shall be given at least _____ *[48 hours or as the case may be]* before the time fixed for the meeting, by written notice delivered personally or mailed to each director at his or her business address, or by telegram. If mailed, such notice shall be deemed to be delivered when deposited in the United States mail so addressed, with postage thereon prepaid, not less than _____ days prior to the commencement of the above-stated notice period. If notice is given by telegram, such notice shall be deemed to be delivered when the telegram is delivered to the telegraph company. Any director may waive notice of any meeting. The attendance of a director at a meeting shall constitute a waiver of notice of such meeting, except where a director attends a meeting for the express purpose of objecting to the transaction of any business because the meeting is not lawfully called or convened. Neither the business to be transacted at, nor the purpose of, any regular or special meeting of the board of directors need be specified in the notice or waiver of notice of such meeting.

Section 6. *Quorum.* A majority of the number of directors fixed by these bylaws shall constitute a quorum for the transaction of business at any meeting of the board of directors, but if less than such majority is present at a meeting, a majority of the directors present may adjourn the meeting from time to time without further notice.

Section 7. *Board Decisions.* The act of the majority of the directors present at a meeting at which a quorum is present shall be the act of the board of directors _____ *[except that vote of not less than _____ (fraction) of all the members of the board shall be required for the amendment of or addition to these bylaws or as the case may be].*

Section 8. *Vacancies.* Any vacancy occurring in the board of directors may be filled by the affirmative vote of a majority of the remaining directors though less than a quorum of the board of directors. A director elected to fill a vacancy shall be elected for the unexpired term of his or her predecessor in office. Any directorship to be filled by reason of an increase in the number of directors shall be filled by election at an annual meeting or at a special meeting of stockholders called for that purpose.

Section 9. *Compensation.* By resolution of the board of directors, the directors may be paid their expenses, if any, of attendance at each meeting of the board of directors, and may be paid a fixed sum for

----

attendance at each meeting of the board of directors or a stated salary as director. No such payment shall preclude any director from serving the corporation in any other capacity and receiving compensation therefor.

Section 10. *Presumption of Assent.* A director of the corporation who is present at a meeting of the board of directors at which action on any corporate matter is taken shall be presumed to have assented to the action taken unless his or her dissent shall be entered in the minutes of the meeting or unless he or she shall file his or her written dissent to such action with the person acting as the secretary of the meeting before the adjournment thereof or shall forward such dissent by registered mail to the secretary of the corporation immediately after the adjournment of the meeting. Such right to dissent shall not apply to a director who voted in favor of such action.

SECURITIES WITHOUT REGISTRATION UNDER THE SECURITIES ACT OF 1933 (REGULATION D)

(17 C.F.R. § 230.500 et seq.)

(Selected Provisions)

Table of Sections

§ 230.500 Use of Regulation D.

Users of Regulation D (§§ 230.500 *et seq.*) should note the following:

(a) Regulation D relates to transactions exempted from the registration requirements of section 5 of the Securities Act of 1933 (the Act) (15 U.S.C.77a *et seq.*, as amended). Such transactions are not exempt from the antifraud, civil liability, or other provisions of the federal securities laws. Issuers are reminded of their obligation to provide such further material information, if any, as may be necessary to make the information required under Regulation D, in light of the circumstances under which it is furnished, not misleading.

(b) Nothing in Regulation D obviates the need to comply with any applicable state law relating to the offer and sale of securities. Regulation D is intended to be a basic element in a uniform system of federal-state limited offering exemptions consistent with the provisions of sections 18 and 19(c) of the Act (15 U.S.C. 77r and 77(s)(c)). In those states that have adopted Regulation D, or any version of Regulation D, special attention should be directed to the applicable state laws and regulations, including those relating to registration of persons who receive remuneration in connection with the offer and sale of securities, to disqualification of issuers and other persons associated with offerings based on state administrative orders or judgments, and to requirements for filings of notices of sales.

(c) Attempted compliance with any rule in Regulation D does not act as an exclusive election; the issuer can also claim the availability of any other applicable exemption. For instance, an issuer's failure to satisfy all the terms and conditions of rule 506(b) (§ 230.506(b)) shall not raise any presumption that the exemption provided by section 4(a)(2) of the Act (15 U.S.C. 77d(2)) is not available.

(d) Regulation D is available only to the issuer of the securities and not to any affiliate of that issuer or to any other person for resales of the issuer's securities. Regulation D provides an exemption only for the transactions in which the securities are offered or sold by the issuer, not for the securities themselves.

(e) Regulation D may be used for business combinations that involve sales by virtue of rule 145(a) (§ 230.145(a)) or otherwise.

(f)   In view of the objectives of Regulation D and the policies underlying the Act, Regulation D is not available to any issuer for any transaction or chain of transactions that, although in technical compliance with Regulation D, is part of a plan or scheme to evade the registration provisions of the Act. In such cases, registration under the Act is required.

(g)   Securities offered and sold outside the United States in accordance with Regulation S (§ 230.901 through 905) need not be registered under the Act. See Release No. 33-6863. Regulation S may be relied upon for such offers and sales even if coincident offers and sales are made in accordance with Regulation D inside the United States. Thus, for example, persons who are offered and sold securities in accordance with Regulation S would not be counted in the calculation of the number of purchasers under Regulation D. Similarly, proceeds from such sales would not be included in the aggregate offering price. The provisions of this paragraph (g), however, do not apply if the issuer elects to rely solely on Regulation D for offers or sales to persons made outside the United States.

§ 230.501 Definitions and terms used in Regulation D.

As used in Regulation D (§ 230.500 *et seq.* of this chapter), the following terms shall have the meaning indicated:

(a)   *Accredited investor. Accredited investor* shall mean any person who comes within any of the following categories, or who the issuer reasonably believes comes within any of the following categories, at the time of the sale of the securities to that person:

(1)   Any bank as defined in section 3(a)(2) of the Act, or any savings and loan association or other institution as defined in section 3(a)(5)(A) of the Act whether acting in its individual or fiduciary capacity; any broker or dealer registered pursuant to section 15 of the Securities Exchange Act of 1934; any insurance company as defined in section 2(a)(13) of the Act; any investment company registered under the Investment Company Act of 1940 or a business development company as defined in section 2(a)(48) of that Act; any Small Business Investment Company licensed by the U.S. Small Business Administration under section 301(c) or (d) of the Small Business Investment Act of 1958; any plan established and maintained by a state, its political subdivisions, or any agency or instrumentality of a state or its political subdivisions, for the benefit of its employees, if such plan has total assets in excess of $5,000,000; any employee benefit plan within the meaning of the Employee Retirement Income Security Act of 1974 if the investment decision is made by a plan fiduciary, as defined in section 3(21) of such act, which is either a bank, savings and loan association, insurance company, or registered investment adviser, or if the employee benefit plan has total assets in excess of $5,000,000 or, if a self-directed plan, with investment decisions made solely by persons that are accredited investors;

(2)   Any private business development company as defined in section 202(a)(22) of the Investment Advisers Act of 1940;

(3)   Any organization described in section 501(c)(3) of the Internal Revenue Code, corporation, Massachusetts or similar business trust, or partnership, not formed for the specific purpose of acquiring the securities offered, with total assets in excess of $5,000,000;

(4)   Any director, executive officer, or general partner of the issuer of the securities being offered or sold, or any director, executive officer, or general partner of a general partner of that issuer;

(5)   Any natural person whose individual net worth, or joint net worth with that person's spouse, exceeds $1,000,000.

(i)   Except as provided in paragraph (a)(5)(ii) of this section, for purposes of calculating net worth under this paragraph (a)(5):

(A)   The person's primary residence shall not be included as an asset;

(B)   Indebtedness that is secured by the person's primary residence, up to the estimated fair market value of the primary residence at the time of the sale of securities, shall not be included as a liability (except that if the amount of such indebtedness outstanding at the time of sale of securities exceeds the amount outstanding 60 days before such time, other than as a result of the acquisition of the primary residence, the amount of such excess shall be included as a liability); and

(C)   Indebtedness that is secured by the person's primary residence in excess of the estimated fair market value of the primary residence at the time of the sale of securities shall be included as a liability;

(ii)   Paragraph (a)(5)(i) of this section will not apply to any calculation of a person's net worth made in connection with a purchase of securities in accordance with a right to purchase such securities, provided that:

(A)   Such right was held by the person on July 20, 2010;

(B)   The person qualified as an accredited investor on the basis of net worth at the time the person acquired such right; and

(C)   The person held securities of the same issuer, other than such right, on July 20, 2010.

(6)   Any natural person who had an individual income in excess of $200,000 in each of the two most recent years or joint income with that person's spouse in excess of $300,000 in each of those years and has a reasonable expectation of reaching the same income level in the current year;

(7)   Any trust, with total assets in excess of $5,000,000, not formed for the specific purpose of acquiring the securities offered, whose purchase is directed by a sophisticated person as described in § 230.506(b)(2)(ii); and

(8) Any entity in which all of the equity owners are accredited investors.

(b)   *Affiliate.* An *affiliate* of, or person *affiliated* with, a specified person shall mean a person that directly, or indirectly through one or more intermediaries, controls or is controlled by, or is under common control with, the person specified.

(c)   *Aggregate offering price. Aggregate offering price* shall mean the sum of all cash, services, property, notes, cancellation of debt, or other consideration to be received by an issuer for issuance of its securities. Where securities are being offered for both cash and non-cash consideration, the aggregate offering price shall be based on the price at which the securities are offered for cash. Any portion of the aggregate offering price attributable to cash received in a foreign currency shall be translated into United States currency at the currency exchange rate in effect at a reasonable time prior to or on the date of the sale of the securities. If securities are not offered for cash, the aggregate offering price shall be based on the value of the consideration as established by bona fide sales of that consideration made within a reasonable time, or, in the absence of sales, on the fair value as determined by an accepted standard. Such valuations of non-cash consideration must be reasonable at the time made.

(d)   *Business combination. Business combination* shall mean any transaction of the type specified in paragraph (a) of Rule 145 under the Act (17 CFR 230.145) and any transaction involving the acquisition by one issuer, in exchange for all or a part of its own or its parent's stock, of stock of another issuer if, immediately after the acquisition, the acquiring issuer has control of the other issuer (whether or not it had control before the acquisition).

(e)   *Calculation of number of purchasers.* For purposes of calculating the number of purchasers under [§ 230.506(b)] only, the following shall apply:

(1)   The following purchasers shall be excluded:

(i)   Any relative, spouse or relative of the spouse of a purchaser who has the same primary residence as the purchaser;

(ii)   Any trust or estate in which a purchaser and any of the persons related to him as specified in paragraph (e)(1)(i) or (e)(1)(iii) of this section collectively have more than 50 percent of the beneficial interest (excluding contingent interests);

(iii)   Any corporation or other organization of which a purchaser and any of the persons related to him as specified in paragraph (e)(1)(i) or (e)(1)(ii) of this section collectively are beneficial owners of more than 50 percent of the equity securities (excluding directors' qualifying shares) or equity interests; and

(iv)   Any accredited investor.

(2)   A corporation, partnership or other entity shall be counted as one purchaser. If, however, that entity is organized for the specific purpose of acquiring the securities offered and is not an accredited investor under paragraph (a)(8) of this section, then each beneficial owner of equity securities or equity interests in the entity shall count as a separate purchaser for all provisions of Regulation D (§§ 230.501–230.508), except to the extent provided in paragraph (e)(1) of this section.

(3)   A non-contributory employee benefit plan within the meaning of Title I of the Employee Retirement Income Security Act of 1974 shall be counted as one purchaser where the trustee makes all investment decisions for the plan.

NOTE: The issuer must satisfy all the other provisions of Regulation D for all purchasers whether or not they are included in calculating the number of purchasers. Clients of an investment adviser or customers of a broker or dealer shall be considered the "purchasers" under Regulation D regardless of the amount of discretion given to the investment adviser or broker or dealer to act on behalf of the client or customer.

(f)   *Executive officer. Executive officer* shall mean the president, any vice president in charge of a principal business unit, division or function (such as sales, administration or finance), any other officer who performs a policy making function, or any other person who performs similar policy making functions for the issuer. Executive officers of subsidiaries may be deemed executive officers of the issuer if they perform such policy making functions for the issuer.

(g)   *Final order. Final order* shall mean a written directive or declaratory statement issued by a federal or state agency described in § 230.506(d)(1)(iii) under applicable statutory authority that provides for notice and an opportunity for hearing, which constitutes a final disposition or action by that federal or state agency.

(h)   *Issuer.* The definition of the term *issuer* in section 2(a)(4) of the Act shall apply, except that in the case of a proceeding under the Federal Bankruptcy Code (11 U.S.C. 101 *et seq.*), the trustee or debtor in possession shall be considered the issuer in an offering under a plan or reorganization, if the securities are to be issued under the plan.

(i)   *Purchaser representative. Purchaser representative* shall mean any person who satisfies all of the following conditions or who the issuer reasonably believes satisfies all of the following conditions:

(1)   Is not an affiliate, director, officer or other employee of the issuer, or beneficial owner of 10 percent or more of any class of the equity securities or 10 percent or more of the equity interest in the issuer, except where the purchaser is:

(i)   A relative of the purchaser representative by blood, marriage or adoption and not more remote than a first cousin;

(ii)   A trust or estate in which the purchaser representative and any persons related to him as specified in paragraph (h)(1)(i) or (h)(1)(iii) of this section collectively have more than 50 percent of the beneficial interest (excluding contingent interest) or of which the purchaser representative serves as trustee, executor, or in any similar capacity; or

(iii)   A corporation or other organization of which the purchaser representative and any persons related to him as specified in paragraph (h)(1)(i) or (h)(1)(ii) of this section collectively are the beneficial owners of more than 50 percent of the equity securities (excluding directors' qualifying shares) or equity interests;

(2)   Has such knowledge and experience in financial and business matters that he is capable of evaluating, alone, or together with other purchaser representatives of the purchaser, or together with the purchaser, the merits and risks of the prospective investment;

(3)   Is acknowledged by the purchaser in writing, during the course of the transaction, to be his purchaser representative in connection with evaluating the merits and risks of the prospective investment; and

(4)   Discloses to the purchaser in writing a reasonable time prior to the sale of securities to that purchaser any material relationship between himself or his affiliates and the issuer or its affiliates

that then exists, that is mutually understood to be contemplated, or that has existed at any time during the previous two years, and any compensation received or to be received as a result of such relationship.

NOTE 1 TO § 230.501: A person acting as a purchaser representative should consider the applicability of the registration and antifraud provisions relating to brokers and dealers under the Securities Exchange Act of 1934 (*Exchange Act*) (15 U.S.C. 78a *et seq.*, as amended) and relating to investment advisers under the Investment Advisers Act of 1940.

NOTE 2 TO § 230.501: The acknowledgment required by paragraph (h)(3) and the disclosure required by paragraph (h)(4) of this section must be made with specific reference to each prospective investment. Advance blanket acknowledgment, such as for *all securities transactions* or *all private placements*, is not sufficient.

NOTE 3 TO § 230.501: Disclosure of any material relationships between the purchaser representative or his affiliates and the issuer or its affiliates does not relieve the purchaser representative of his obligation to act in the interest of the purchaser.

§ 230.502 General conditions to be met.

The following conditions shall be applicable to offers and sales made under Regulation D (§ 230.500 *et seq.* of this chapter):

(a) *Integration.* All sales that are part of the same Regulation D offering must meet all of the terms and conditions of Regulation D. Offers and sales that are made more than six months before the start of a Regulation D offering or are made more than six months after completion of a Regulation D offering will not be considered part of that Regulation D offering, so long as during those six month periods there are no offers or sales of securities by or for the issuer that are of the same or a similar class as those offered or sold under Regulation D, other than those offers or sales of securities under an employee benefit plan as defined in rule 405 under the Act (17 CFR 230.405).

NOTE: The term *offering* is not defined in the Act or in Regulation D. If the issuer offers or sells securities for which the safe harbor rule in paragraph (a) of this § 230.502 is unavailable, the determination as to whether separate sales of securities are part of the same offering (*i.e.*, are considered *integrated*) depends on the particular facts and circumstances. Generally, transactions otherwise meeting the requirements of an exemption will not be integrated with simultaneous offerings being made outside the United States in compliance with Regulation S. See Release No. 33-6863.

The following factors should be considered in determining whether offers and sales should be integrated for purposes of the exemptions under Regulation D:

(a) Whether the sales are part of a single plan of financing;

(b) Whether the sales involve issuance of the same class of securities;

(c) Whether the sales have been made at or about the same time;

(d) Whether the same type of consideration is being received; and

(e) Whether the sales are made for the same general purpose.

See Release 33-4552 (November 6, 1962) [27 FR 11316].

(b) *Information requirements*—(1) *When information must be furnished.* If the issuer sells securities under § 230.506(b) to any purchaser that is not an accredited investor, the issuer shall furnish the information specified in paragraph (b)(2) of this section to such purchaser a reasonable time prior to sale. The issuer is not required to furnish the specified information to purchasers when it sells securities under § 230.504, or to any accredited investor.

NOTE: When an issuer provides information to investors pursuant to paragraph (b)(1), it should consider providing such information to accredited investors as well, in view of the anti-fraud provisions of the federal securities laws.

(2) *Type of information to be furnished.* (i) If the issuer is not subject to the reporting requirements of section 13 or 15(d) of the Exchange Act, at a reasonable time prior to the sale of

securities the issuer shall furnish to the purchaser, to the extent material to an understanding of the issuer, its business and the securities being offered:

(A) *Non-financial statement information.* If the issuer is eligible to use Regulation A (§ 230.251–263), the same kind of information as would be required in Part II of Form 1-A (§ 239.90 of this chapter). If the issuer is not eligible to use Regulation A, the same kind of information as required in Part I of a registration statement filed under the Securities Act on the form that the issuer would be entitled to use.

(B) *Financial statement information—(1) Offerings up to $2,000,000.* The information required in Article 8 of Regulation S-X (§ 210.8 of this chapter), except that only the issuer's balance sheet, which shall be dated within 120 days of the start of the offering, must be audited.

(*2*) *Offerings up to $7,500,000.* The financial statement information required in Form S-1 (§ 239.10 of this chapter) for smaller reporting companies. If an issuer, other than a limited partnership, cannot obtain audited financial statements without unreasonable effort or expense, then only the issuer's balance sheet, which shall be dated within 120 days of the start of the offering, must be audited. If the issuer is a limited partnership and cannot obtain the required financial statements without unreasonable effort or expense, it may furnish financial statements that have been prepared on the basis of Federal income tax requirements and examined and reported on in accordance with generally accepted auditing standards by an independent public or certified accountant.

(*3*) *Offerings over $7,500,000.* The financial statement as would be required in a registration statement filed under the Act on the form that the issuer would be entitled to use. If an issuer, other than a limited partnership, cannot obtain audited financial statements without unreasonable effort or expense, then only the issuer's balance sheet, which shall be dated within 120 days of the start of the offering, must be audited. If the issuer is a limited partnership and cannot obtain the required financial statements without unreasonable effort or expense, it may furnish financial statements that have been prepared on the basis of Federal income tax requirements and examined and reported on in accordance with generally accepted auditing standards by an independent public or certified accountant.

(C) If the issuer is a foreign private issuer eligible to use Form 20-F (§ 249.220f of this chapter), the issuer shall disclose the same kind of information required to be included in a registration statement filed under the Act on the form that the issuer would be entitled to use. The financial statements need be certified only to the extent required by paragraph (b)(2)(i) (B) (*1*), (*2*) or (*3*) of this section, as appropriate.

(ii) If the issuer is subject to the reporting requirements of section 13 or 15(d) of the Exchange Act, at a reasonable time prior to the sale of securities the issuer shall furnish to the purchaser the information specified in paragraph (b)(2)(ii)(A) or (B) of this section, and in either event the information specified in paragraph (b)(2)(ii)(C) of this section:

(A) The issuer's annual report to shareholders for the most recent fiscal year, if such annual report meets the requirements of Rules 14a–3 or 14c–3 under the Exchange Act (§ 240.14a–3 or § 240.14c–3 of this chapter), the definitive proxy statement filed in connection with that annual report, and if requested by the purchaser in writing, a copy of the issuer's most recent Form 10-K (§ 249.310 of this chapter) under the Exchange Act.

(B) The information contained in an annual report on Form 10-K (§ 249.310 of this chapter) under the Exchange Act or in a registration statement on Form S-1 (§ 239.11 of this chapter) or S-11 (§ 239.18 of this chapter) under the Act or on Form 10 (§ 249.210 of this chapter) under the Exchange Act, whichever filing is the most recent required to be filed.

(C) The information contained in any reports or documents required to be filed by the issuer under sections 13(a), 14(a), 14(c), and 15(d) of the Exchange Act since the distribution or filing of the report or registration statement specified in paragraphs (b)(2)(ii) (A) or (B), and a brief description of the securities being offered, the use of the proceeds from the offering, and any material changes in the issuer's affairs that are not disclosed in the documents furnished.

(D) If the issuer is a foreign private issuer, the issuer may provide in lieu of the information specified in paragraph (b)(2)(ii) (A) or (B) of this section, the information contained in its most recent filing on Form 20-F or Form F-1 (§ 239.31 of the chapter).

(iii) Exhibits required to be filed with the Commission as part of a registration statement or report, other than an annual report to shareholders or parts of that report incorporated by reference in a Form 10-K report, need not be furnished to each purchaser that is not an accredited investor if the contents of material exhibits are identified and such exhibits are made available to a purchaser, upon his or her written request, a reasonable time before his or her purchase.

(iv) At a reasonable time prior to the sale of securities to any purchaser that is not an accredited investor in a transaction under § 230.506(b), the issuer shall furnish to the purchaser a brief description in writing of any material written information concerning the offering that has been provided by the issuer to any accredited investor but not previously delivered to such unaccredited purchaser. The issuer shall furnish any portion or all of this information to the purchaser, upon his written request a reasonable time prior to his purchase.

(v) The issuer shall also make available to each purchaser at a reasonable time prior to his purchase of securities in a transaction under § 230.506(b) the opportunity to ask questions and receive answers concerning the terms and conditions of the offering and to obtain any additional information which the issuer possesses or can acquire without unreasonable effort or expense that is necessary to verify the accuracy of information furnished under paragraph (b)(2) (i) or (ii) of this section.

(vi) For business combinations or exchange offers, in addition to information required by Form S-4 (17 CFR 239.25), the issuer shall provide to each purchaser at the time the plan is submitted to security holders, or, with an exchange, during the course of the transaction and prior to sale, written information about any terms or arrangements of the proposed transactions that are materially different from those for all other security holders. For purposes of this subsection, an issuer which is not subject to the reporting requirements of section 13 or 15(d) of the Exchange Act may satisfy the requirements of Part I.B. or C. of Form S-4 by compliance with paragraph (b)(2)(i) of this § 230.502.

(vii) At a reasonable time prior to the sale of securities to any purchaser that is not an accredited investor in a transaction under § 230.506(b), the issuer shall advise the purchaser of the limitations on resale in the manner contained in paragraph (d)(2) of this section. Such disclosure may be contained in other materials required to be provided by this paragraph.

(c) *Limitation on manner of offering.* Except as provided in § 230.504(b)(1) or § 230.506(c), neither the issuer nor any person acting on its behalf shall offer or sell the securities by any form of general solicitation or general advertising, including, but not limited to, the following:

(1) Any advertisement, article, notice or other communication published in any newspaper, magazine, or similar media or broadcast over television or radio; and

(2) Any seminar or meeting whose attendees have been invited by any general solicitation or general advertising; *Provided, however*, that publication by an issuer of a notice in accordance with § 230.135c or filing with the Commission by an issuer of a notice of sales on Form D (17 CFR 239.500) in which the issuer has made a good faith and reasonable attempt to comply with the requirements of such form, shall not be deemed to constitute general solicitation or general advertising for purposes of this section; *Provided further*, that, if the requirements of § 230.135e are satisfied, providing any journalist with access to press conferences held outside of the United States, to meetings with issuer or selling security holder representatives conducted outside of the United States, or to written press-related materials released outside the United States, at or in which a present or proposed offering of securities is discussed, will not be deemed to constitute general solicitation or general advertising for purposes of this section.

(d)   *Limitations on resale.* Except as provided in § 230.504(b)(1), securities acquired in a transaction under Regulation D shall have the status of securities acquired in a transaction under section 4(a)(2) of the Act and cannot be resold without registration under the Act or an exemption therefrom. The issuer shall exercise reasonable care to assure that the purchasers of the securities are not underwriters within the meaning of section 2(a)(11) of the Act, which reasonable care may be demonstrated by the following:

    (1)   Reasonable inquiry to determine if the purchaser is acquiring the securities for himself or for other persons;

    (2)   Written disclosure to each purchaser prior to sale that the securities have not been registered under the Act and, therefore, cannot be resold unless they are registered under the Act or unless an exemption from registration is available; and

    (3)   Placement of a legend on the certificate or other document that evidences the securities stating that the securities have not been registered under the Act and setting forth or referring to the restrictions on transferability and sale of the securities.

While taking these actions will establish the requisite reasonable care, it is not the exclusive method to demonstrate such care. Other actions by the issuer may satisfy this provision. In addition, § 230.502(b)(2)(vii) requires the delivery of written disclosure of the limitations on resale to investors in certain instances.

§ 230.503 Filing of notice of sales.

    (a)   *When notice of sales on Form D is required and permitted to be filed.* (1) An issuer offering or selling securities in reliance on § 230.504 or § 230.506 must file with the Commission a notice of sales containing the information required by Form D (17 CFR 239.500) for each new offering of securities no later than 15 calendar days after the first sale of securities in the offering, unless the end of that period falls on a Saturday, Sunday or holiday, in which case the due date would be the first business day following.

    (2)   An issuer may file an amendment to a previously filed notice of sales on Form D at any time.

    (3)   An issuer must file an amendment to a previously filed notice of sales on Form D for an offering:

        (i)   To correct a material mistake of fact or error in the previously filed notice of sales on Form D, as soon as practicable after discovery of the mistake or error;

        (ii)   To reflect a change in the information provided in the previously filed notice of sales on Form D, as soon as practicable after the change, except that no amendment is required to reflect a change that occurs after the offering terminates or a change that occurs solely in the following information:

            (A)   The address or relationship to the issuer of a related person identified in response to Item 3 of the notice of sales on Form D;

            (B)   An issuer's revenues or aggregate net asset value;

            (C)   The minimum investment amount, if the change is an increase, or if the change, together with all other changes in that amount since the previously filed notice of sales on Form D, does not result in a decrease of more than 10%;

            (D)   Any address or state(s) of solicitation shown in response to Item 12 of the notice of sales on Form D;

            (E)   The total offering amount, if the change is a decrease, or if the change, together with all other changes in that amount since the previously filed notice of sales on Form D, does not result in an increase of more than 10%;

            (F)   The amount of securities sold in the offering or the amount remaining to be sold;

            (G)   The number of non-accredited investors who have invested in the offering, as long as the change does not increase the number to more than 35;

            (H)   The total number of investors who have invested in the offering; or

(I)   The amount of sales commissions, finders' fees or use of proceeds for payments to executive officers, directors or promoters, if the change is a decrease, or if the change, together with all other changes in that amount since the previously filed notice of sales on Form D, does not result in an increase of more than 10%; and

(iii)   Annually, on or before the first anniversary of the filing of the notice of sales on Form D or the filing of the most recent amendment to the notice of sales on Form D, if the offering is continuing at that time.

(4)   An issuer that files an amendment to a previously filed notice of sales on Form D must provide current information in response to all requirements of the notice of sales on Form D regardless of why the amendment is filed.

(b)   *How notice of sales on Form D must be filed and signed.* (1) A notice of sales on Form D must be filed with the Commission in electronic format by means of the Commission's Electronic Data Gathering, Analysis, and Retrieval System (EDGAR) in accordance with EDGAR rules set forth in Regulation S-T (17 CFR Part 232).

(2)   Every notice of sales on Form D must be signed by a person duly authorized by the issuer.

§ 230.504 Exemption for limited offerings and sales of securities not exceeding $5,000,000.

(a)   *Exemption.* Offers and sales of securities that satisfy the conditions in paragraph (b) of this § 230.504 by an issuer that is not:

(1)   Subject to the reporting requirements of section 13 or 15(d) of the Exchange Act,;

(2)   An investment company; or

(3)   A development stage company that either has no specific business plan or purpose or has indicated that its business plan is to engage in a merger or acquisition with an unidentified company or companies, or other entity or person, shall be exempt from the provision of section 5 of the Act under section 3(b) of the Act.

(b)   *Conditions to be met—(1) General conditions.* To qualify for exemption under this § 230.504, offers and sales must satisfy the terms and conditions of §§ 230.501 and 230.502 (a), (c) and (d), except that the provisions of § 230.502 (c) and (d) will not apply to offers and sales of securities under this § 230.504 that are made:

(i)   Exclusively in one or more states that provide for the registration of the securities, and require the public filing and delivery to investors of a substantive disclosure document before sale, and are made in accordance with those state provisions;

(ii)   In one or more states that have no provision for the registration of the securities or the public filing or delivery of a disclosure document before sale, if the securities have been registered in at least one state that provides for such registration, public filing and delivery before sale, offers and sales are made in that state in accordance with such provisions, and the disclosure document is delivered before sale to all purchasers (including those in the states that have no such procedure); or

(iii)   Exclusively according to state law exemptions from registration that permit general solicitation and general advertising so long as sales are made only to "accredited investors" as defined in § 230.501(a).

(2)   The aggregate offering price for an offering of securities under this § 230.504, as defined in § 230.501(c), shall not exceed $5,000,000, less the aggregate offering price for all securities sold within the twelve months before the start of and during the offering of securities under this § 230.504 or in violation of section 5(a) of the Securities Act.

Instruction to paragraph (b)(2): If a transaction under § 230.504 fails to meet the limitation on the aggregate offering price, it does not affect the availability of this § 230.504 for the other transactions considered in applying such limitation. For example, if an issuer sold $5,000,000 of its securities on January

1, 2014 under this § 230.504 and an additional $500,000 of its securities on July 1, 2014, this § 230.504 would not be available for the later sale, but would still be applicable to the January 1, 2014 sale.

(3) *Disqualifications.* No exemption under this section shall be available for the securities of any issuer if such issuer would be subject to disqualification under § 230.506(d) on or after January 20, 2017; provided that disclosure of prior "bad actor" events shall be required in accordance with § 230.506(e).

Instruction to paragraph (b)(3): For purposes of disclosure of prior "bad actor" events pursuant to § 230.506(e), an issuer shall furnish to each purchaser, a reasonable time prior to sale, a description in writing of any matters that would have triggered disqualification under this paragraph (b)(3) but occurred before January 20, 2017.

§ 230.505 [Reserved].

§ 230.506 Exemption for limited offers and sales without regard to dollar amount of offering.

(a) *Exemption.* Offers and sales of securities by an issuer that satisfy the conditions in paragraph (b) or (c) of this section shall be deemed to be transactions not involving any public offering within the meaning of section 4(a)(2) of the Act.

(b) *Conditions to be met in offerings subject to limitation on manner of offering*—(1) *General conditions.* To qualify for an exemption under this section, offers and sales must satisfy all the terms and conditions of §§ 230.501 and 230.502.

(2) *Specific conditions*—(i) *Limitation on number of purchasers.* There are no more than or the issuer reasonably believes that there are no more than 35 purchasers of securities from the issuer in any offering under this section.

NOTE TO PARAGRAPH (b)(2)(i): See § 230.501(e) for the calculation of the number of purchasers and § 230.502(a) for what may or may not constitute an offering under paragraph (b) of this section.

(ii) *Nature of purchasers.* Each purchaser who is not an accredited investor either alone or with his purchaser representative(s) has such knowledge and experience in financial and business matters that he is capable of evaluating the merits and risks of the prospective investment, or the issuer reasonably believes immediately prior to making any sale that such purchaser comes within this description.

(c) *Conditions to be met in offerings not subject to limitation on manner of offering*—(1) *General conditions.* To qualify for exemption under this section, sales must satisfy all the terms and conditions of §§ 230.501 and 230.502(a) and (d).

(2) *Specific conditions*—(i) *Nature of purchasers.* All purchasers of securities sold in any offering under paragraph (c) of this section are accredited investors.

(ii) *Verification of accredited investor status.* The issuer shall take reasonable steps to verify that purchasers of securities sold in any offering under paragraph (c) of this section are accredited investors. The issuer shall be deemed to take reasonable steps to verify if the issuer uses, at its option, one of the following non-exclusive and non-mandatory methods of verifying that a natural person who purchases securities in such offering is an accredited investor; provided, however, that the issuer does not have knowledge that such person is not an accredited investor:

(A) In regard to whether the purchaser is an accredited investor on the basis of income, reviewing any Internal Revenue Service form that reports the purchaser's income for the two most recent years (including, but not limited to, Form W-2, Form 1099, Schedule K-1 to Form 1065, and Form 1040) and obtaining a written representation from the purchaser that he or she has a reasonable expectation of reaching the income level necessary to qualify as an accredited investor during the current year;

(B)   In regard to whether the purchaser is an accredited investor on the basis of net worth, reviewing one or more of the following types of documentation dated within the prior three months and obtaining a written representation from the purchaser that all liabilities necessary to make a determination of net worth have been disclosed:

(*1*)   With respect to assets: Bank statements, brokerage statements and other statements of securities holdings, certificates of deposit, tax assessments, and appraisal reports issued by independent third parties; and

(*2*)   With respect to liabilities: A consumer report from at least one of the nationwide consumer reporting agencies; or

(C)   Obtaining a written confirmation from one of the following persons or entities that such person or entity has taken reasonable steps to verify that the purchaser is an accredited investor within the prior three months and has determined that such purchaser is an accredited investor:

(*1*)   A registered broker-dealer;

(*2*)   An investment adviser registered with the Securities and Exchange Commission;

(*3*)   A licensed attorney who is in good standing under the laws of the jurisdictions in which he or she is admitted to practice law; or

(*4*)   A certified public accountant who is duly registered and in good standing under the laws of the place of his or her residence or principal office.

(D)   In regard to any person who purchased securities in an issuer's Rule 506(b) offering as an accredited investor prior to September 23, 2013 and continues to hold such securities, for the same issuer's Rule 506(c) offering, obtaining a certification by such person at the time of sale that he or she qualifies as an accredited investor.

Instructions to paragraph (c)(2)(ii)(A) through (D) of this section:

1.   The issuer is not required to use any of these methods in verifying the accredited investor status of natural persons who are purchasers. These methods are examples of the types of non-exclusive and non-mandatory methods that satisfy the verification requirement in §230.506(c)(2)(ii).

2.   In the case of a person who qualifies as an accredited investor based on joint income with that person's spouse, the issuer would be deemed to satisfy the verification requirement in §230.506(c)(2)(ii)(A) by reviewing copies of Internal Revenue Service forms that report income for the two most recent years in regard to, and obtaining written representations from, both the person and the spouse.

3.   In the case of a person who qualifies as an accredited investor based on joint net worth with that person's spouse, the issuer would be deemed to satisfy the verification requirement in §230.506(c)(2)(ii)(B) by reviewing such documentation in regard to, and obtaining written representations from, both the person and the spouse.

(d)   *"Bad Actor" disqualification.* (1) No exemption under this section shall be available for a sale of securities if the issuer; any predecessor of the issuer; any affiliated issuer; any director, executive officer, other officer participating in the offering, general partner or managing member of the issuer; any beneficial owner of 20% or more of the issuer's outstanding voting equity securities, calculated on the basis of voting power; any promoter connected with the issuer in any capacity at the time of such sale; any investment manager of an issuer that is a pooled investment fund; any person that has been or will be paid (directly or indirectly) remuneration for solicitation of purchasers in connection with such sale of securities; any general partner or managing member of any such investment manager or solicitor; or any director, executive officer or other officer participating in the offering of any such investment manager or solicitor or general partner or managing member of such investment manager or solicitor:

(i)   Has been convicted, within ten years before such sale (or five years, in the case of issuers, their predecessors and affiliated issuers), of any felony or misdemeanor:

(A)   In connection with the purchase or sale of any security;

(B)   Involving the making of any false filing with the Commission; or

(C)   Arising out of the conduct of the business of an underwriter, broker, dealer, municipal securities dealer, investment adviser or paid solicitor of purchasers of securities;

(ii)   Is subject to any order, judgment or decree of any court of competent jurisdiction, entered within five years before such sale, that, at the time of such sale, restrains or enjoins such person from engaging or continuing to engage in any conduct or practice:

(A)   In connection with the purchase or sale of any security;

(B)   Involving the making of any false filing with the Commission; or

(C)   Arising out of the conduct of the business of an underwriter, broker, dealer, municipal securities dealer, investment adviser or paid solicitor of purchasers of securities;

(iii)   Is subject to a final order of a state securities commission (or an agency or officer of a state performing like functions); a state authority that supervises or examines banks, savings associations, or credit unions; a state insurance commission (or an agency or officer of a state performing like functions); an appropriate federal banking agency; the U.S. Commodity Futures Trading Commission; or the National Credit Union Administration that:

(A)   At the time of such sale, bars the person from:

(*1*)   Association with an entity regulated by such commission, authority, agency, or officer;

(*2*)   Engaging in the business of securities, insurance or banking; or

(*3*)   Engaging in savings association or credit union activities; or

(B)   Constitutes a final order based on a violation of any law or regulation that prohibits fraudulent, manipulative, or deceptive conduct entered within ten years before such sale;

(iv)   Is subject to an order of the Commission entered pursuant to section 15(b) or 15B(c) of the Securities Exchange Act of 1934 (15 U.S.C. 78*o*(b) or 78*o*–4(c)) or section 203(e) or (f) of the Investment Advisers Act of 1940 (15 U.S.C. 80b–3(e) or (f)) that, at the time of such sale:

(A)   Suspends or revokes such person's registration as a broker, dealer, municipal securities dealer or investment adviser;

(B)   Places limitations on the activities, functions or operations of such person; or

(C)   Bars such person from being associated with any entity or from participating in the offering of any penny stock;

(v)   Is subject to any order of the Commission entered within five years before such sale that, at the time of such sale, orders the person to cease and desist from committing or causing a violation or future violation of:

(A)   Any scienter-based anti-fraud provision of the federal securities laws, including without limitation section 17(a)(1) of the Securities Act of 1933 (15 U.S.C. 77q(a)(1)), section 10(b) of the Securities Exchange Act of 1934 (15 U.S.C. 78j(b)) and 17 CFR 240.10b–5, section 15(c)(1) of the Securities Exchange Act of 1934 (15 U.S.C. 78*o*(c)(1)) and section 206(1) of the Investment Advisers Act of 1940 (15 U.S.C. 80b–6(1)), or any other rule or regulation thereunder; or

(B)   Section 5 of the Securities Act of 1933 (15 U.S.C. 77e).

(vi)   Is suspended or expelled from membership in, or suspended or barred from association with a member of, a registered national securities exchange or a registered national or affiliated securities association for any act or omission to act constituting conduct inconsistent with just and equitable principles of trade;

(vii)   Has filed (as a registrant or issuer), or was or was named as an underwriter in, any registration statement or Regulation A offering statement filed with the Commission that, within five years before such sale, was the subject of a refusal order, stop order, or order suspending the Regulation A exemption, or is, at the time of such sale, the subject of an investigation or proceeding to determine whether a stop order or suspension order should be issued; or

(viii) Is subject to a United States Postal Service false representation order entered within five years before such sale, or is, at the time of such sale, subject to a temporary restraining order or preliminary injunction with respect to conduct alleged by the United States Postal Service to constitute a scheme or device for obtaining money or property through the mail by means of false representations.

(2)   Paragraph (d)(1) of this section shall not apply:

(i)   With respect to any conviction, order, judgment, decree, suspension, expulsion or bar that occurred or was issued before September 23, 2013;

(ii)   Upon a showing of good cause and without prejudice to any other action by the Commission, if the Commission determines that it is not necessary under the circumstances that an exemption be denied;

(iii)   If, before the relevant sale, the court or regulatory authority that entered the relevant order, judgment or decree advises in writing (whether contained in the relevant judgment, order or decree or separately to the Commission or its staff) that disqualification under paragraph (d)(1) of this section should not arise as a consequence of such order, judgment or decree; or

(iv)   If the issuer establishes that it did not know and, in the exercise of reasonable care, could not have known that a disqualification existed under paragraph (d)(1) of this section.

Instruction to paragraph (d)(2)(iv). An issuer will not be able to establish that it has exercised reasonable care unless it has made, in light of the circumstances, factual inquiry into whether any disqualifications exist. The nature and scope of the factual inquiry will vary based on the facts and circumstances concerning, among other things, the issuer and the other offering participants.

(3)   For purposes of paragraph (d)(1) of this section, events relating to any affiliated issuer that occurred before the affiliation arose will be not considered disqualifying if the affiliated entity is not:

(i)   In control of the issuer; or

(ii)   Under common control with the issuer by a third party that was in control of the affiliated entity at the time of such events.

(e)   *Disclosure of prior "bad actor" events.* The issuer shall furnish to each purchaser, a reasonable time prior to sale, a description in writing of any matters that would have triggered disqualification under paragraph (d)(1) of this section but occurred before September 23, 2013. The failure to furnish such information timely shall not prevent an issuer from relying on this section if the issuer establishes that it did not know and, in the exercise of reasonable care, could not have known of the existence of the undisclosed matter or matters.

Instruction to paragraph (e). An issuer will not be able to establish that it has exercised reasonable care unless it has made, in light of the circumstances, factual inquiry into whether any disqualifications exist. The nature and scope of the factual inquiry will vary based on the facts and circumstances concerning, among other things, the issuer and the other offering participants.

§230.507 Disqualifying provision relating to exemptions under §§230.504 and 230.506.

(a)   No exemption under §230.504 or §230.506 shall be available for an issuer if such issuer, any of its predecessors or affiliates have been subject to any order, judgment, or decree of any court of competent jurisdiction temporarily, preliminary or permanently enjoining such person for failure to comply with §230.503.

(b)   Paragraph (a) of this section shall not apply if the Commission determines, upon a showing of good cause, that it is not necessary under the circumstances that the exemption be denied.

§ 230.508 Insignificant deviations from a term, condition or requirement of Regulation D.

(a)   A failure to comply with a term, condition or requirement of § 230.504 or § 230.506 will not result in the loss of the exemption from the requirements of section 5 of the Act for any offer or sale to a particular individual or entity, if the person relying on the exemption shows:

(1)   The failure to comply did not pertain to a term, condition or requirement directly intended to protect that particular individual or entity; and

(2)   The failure to comply was insignificant with respect to the offering as a whole, provided that any failure to comply with paragraph (c) of § 230.502, paragraph (b)(2) of § 230.504 and paragraph (b)(2)(i) of § 230.506 shall be deemed to be significant to the offering as a whole; and

(3)   A good faith and reasonable attempt was made to comply with all applicable terms, conditions and requirements of § 230.504 or § 230.506.

(b)   A transaction made in reliance on § 230.504 or § 230.506 shall comply with all applicable terms, conditions and requirements of Regulation D. Where an exemption is established only through reliance upon paragraph (a) of this section, the failure to comply shall nonetheless be actionable by the Commission under section 20 of the Act.

SARBANES-OXLEY

Public Law 107–204

107th Congress

To protect investors by improving the accuracy and reliability of corporate disclosures made pursuant to the securities laws, and for other purposes.

Be it enacted by the Senate and House of Representatives of the United States of America in Congress assembled,

§ 1. Short Title; Table of Contents

(a) Short Title.—This Act may be cited as the "Sarbanes-Oxley Act of 2002".

(b) Table of Contents.—The table of contents for this Act is as follows:

Table of Sections

---

§ 2.   Definitions

(a)   In General.—In this Act, the following definitions shall apply:

(1)   Appropriate state regulatory authority.—The term "appropriate State regulatory authority" means the State agency or other authority responsible for the licensure or other regulation of the practice of accounting in the State or States having jurisdiction over a registered public accounting firm or associated person thereof, with respect to the matter in question.

(2)   Audit.—The term "audit" means an examination of the financial statements of any issuer by an independent public accounting firm in accordance with the rules of the Board or the Commission (or, for the period preceding the adoption of applicable rules of the Board under section 103, in accordance with then-applicable generally accepted auditing and related standards for such purposes), for the purpose of expressing an opinion on such statements.

(3)   Audit committee.—The term "audit committee" means—

(A)   a committee (or equivalent body) established by and amongst the board of directors of an issuer for the purpose of overseeing the accounting and financial reporting processes of the issuer and audits of the financial statements of the issuer; and

(B)   if no such committee exists with respect to an issuer, the entire board of directors of the issuer.

(4)   Audit report.—The term "audit report" means a document or other record—

(A)   prepared following an audit performed for purposes of compliance by an issuer with the requirements of the securities laws; and

(B)   in which a public accounting firm either—

(i)   sets forth the opinion of that firm regarding a financial statement, report, or other document; or

(ii)   asserts that no such opinion can be expressed.

(5)   Board.—The term "Board" means the Public Company Accounting Oversight Board established under section 101.

(6)   Commission.—The term "Commission" means the Securities and Exchange Commission.

(7)   Issuer.—The term "issuer" means an issuer (as defined in section 3 of the Securities Exchange Act of 1934 (15 U.S.C. 78c)), the securities of which are registered under section 12 of that Act (15 U.S.C. 78*l*), or that is required to file reports under section 15(d) (15 U.S.C. 78o(d)), or that files or has filed a registration statement that has not yet become effective under the Securities Act of 1933 (15 U.S.C. 77a et seq.), and that it has not withdrawn.

(8) Non-audit services.—The term "non-audit services" means any professional services provided to an issuer by a registered public accounting firm, other than those provided to an issuer in connection with an audit or a review of the financial statements of an issuer.

(9) Person associated with a public accounting firm.—

(A) In general.—The terms "person associated with a public accounting firm" (or with a "registered public accounting firm") and "associated person of a public accounting firm" (or of a "registered public accounting firm") mean any individual proprietor, partner, shareholder, principal, accountant, or other professional employee of a public accounting firm, or any other independent contractor or entity that, in connection with the preparation or issuance of any audit report—

(i) shares in the profits of, or receives compensation in any other form from, that firm; or

(ii) participates as agent or otherwise on behalf of such accounting firm in any activity of that firm.

(B) Exemption authority.—The Board may, by rule, exempt persons engaged only in ministerial tasks from the definition in subparagraph (A), to the extent that the Board determines that any such exemption is consistent with the purposes of this Act, the public interest, or the protection of investors.

(10) Professional standards.—The term "professional standards" means—

(A) accounting principles that are—

(i) established by the standard setting body described in section 19(b) of the Securities Act of 1933, as amended by this Act, or prescribed by the Commission under section 19(a) of that Act (15 U.S.C. 17a(s)) or section 13(b) of the Securities Exchange Act of 1934 (15 U.S.C. 78a(m)); and

(ii) relevant to audit reports for particular issuers, or dealt with in the quality control system of a particular registered public accounting firm; and

(B) auditing standards, standards for attestation engagements, quality control policies and procedures, ethical and competency standards, and independence standards (including rules implementing title II) that the Board or the Commission determines—

(i) relate to the preparation or issuance of audit reports for issuers; and

(ii) are established or adopted by the Board under section 103(a), or are promulgated as rules of the Commission.

(11) Public accounting firm.—The term "public accounting firm" means—

(A) a proprietorship, partnership, incorporated association, corporation, limited liability company, limited liability partnership, or other legal entity that is engaged in the practice of public accounting or preparing or issuing audit reports; and

(B) to the extent so designated by the rules of the Board, any associated person of any entity described in subparagraph (A).

(12) Registered public accounting firm.—The term "registered public accounting firm" means a public accounting firm registered with the Board in accordance with this Act.

(13) Rules of the board.—The term "rules of the Board" means the bylaws and rules of the Board (as submitted to, and approved, modified, or amended by the Commission, in accordance with section 107), and those stated policies, practices, and interpretations of the Board that the Commission, by rule, may deem to be rules of the Board, as necessary or appropriate in the public interest or for the protection of investors.

(14) Security.—The term "security" has the same meaning as in section 3(a) of the Securities Exchange Act of 1934 (15 U.S.C. 78c(a)).

(15) Securities laws.—The term "securities laws" means the provisions of law referred to in section 3(a)(47) of the Securities Exchange Act of 1934 (15 U.S.C. 78c(a)(47)), as amended by this Act, and includes the rules, regulations, and orders issued by the Commission thereunder.

(16) State.—The term "State" means any State of the United States, the District of Columbia, Puerto Rico, the Virgin Islands, or any other territory or possession of the United States.

(b) Conforming Amendment.—Section 3(a)(47) of the Securities Exchange Act of 1934 (15 U.S.C. 78c(a)(47)) is amended by inserting "the Sarbanes-Oxley Act of 2002," before "the Public".

§ 3. Commission Rules and Enforcement

(a) Regulatory Action.—The Commission shall promulgate such rules and regulations, as may be necessary or appropriate in the public interest or for the protection of investors, and in furtherance of this Act.

(b) Enforcement.—

(1) In general.—A violation by any person of this Act, any rule or regulation of the Commission issued under this Act, or any rule of the Board shall be treated for all purposes in the same manner as a violation of the Securities Exchange Act of 1934 (15 U.S.C. 78a et seq.) or the rules and regulations issued thereunder, consistent with the provisions of this Act, and any such person shall be subject to the same penalties, and to the same extent, as for a violation of that Act or such rules or regulations.

(2) Investigations, injunctions, and prosecution of offenses.—Section 21 of the Securities Exchange Act of 1934 (15 U.S.C. 78u) is amended—

(A) in subsection (a)(1), by inserting "the rules of the Public Company Accounting Oversight Board, of which such person is a registered public accounting firm or a person associated with such a firm," after "is a participant,";

(B) in subsection (d)(1), by inserting "the rules of the Public Company Accounting Oversight Board, of which such person is a registered public accounting firm or a person associated with such a firm," after "is a participant,";

(C) in subsection (e), by inserting "the rules of the Public Company Accounting Oversight Board, of which such person is a registered public accounting firm or a person associated with such a firm," after "is a participant,"; and

(D) in subsection (f), by inserting "or the Public Company Accounting Oversight Board" after "self-regulatory organization" each place that term appears.

(3) Cease-and-desist proceedings.—Section 21C(c)(2) of the Securities Exchange Act of 1934 (15 U.S.C. 78u–3(c)(2)) is amended by inserting "registered public accounting firm (as defined in section 2 of the Sarbanes-Oxley Act of 2002)," after "government securities dealer,".

(4) Enforcement by federal banking agencies.—Section 12(i) of the Securities Exchange Act of 1934 (15 U.S.C. 78l(i)) is amended by—

(A) striking "sections 12," each place it appears and inserting "sections 10A(m), 12,"; and

(B) striking "and 16," each place it appears and inserting "and 16 of this Act, and sections 302, 303, 304, 306, 401(b), 404, 406, and 407 of the Sarbanes-Oxley Act of 2002,".

(c) Effect on Commission Authority.—Nothing in this Act or the rules of the Board shall be construed to impair or limit—

(1) the authority of the Commission to regulate the accounting profession, accounting firms, or persons associated with such firms for purposes of enforcement of the securities laws;

(2) the authority of the Commission to set standards for accounting or auditing practices or auditor independence, derived from other provisions of the securities laws or the rules or regulations thereunder, for purposes of the preparation and issuance of any audit report, or otherwise under applicable law; or

(3) the ability of the Commission to take, on the initiative of the Commission, legal, administrative, or disciplinary action against any registered public accounting firm or any associated person thereof.

TITLE I.   PUBLIC COMPANY ACCOUNTING OVERSIGHT BOARD

§ 101.   Establishment; Administrative Provisions

(a) Establishment of Board.—There is established the Public Company Accounting Oversight Board, to oversee the audit of public companies that are subject to the securities laws, and related matters, in order to protect the interests of investors and further the public interest in the preparation of informative, accurate, and independent audit reports for companies the securities of which are sold to, and held by and for, public investors. The Board shall be a body corporate, operate as a nonprofit corporation, and have succession until dissolved by an Act of Congress.

(b) Status.—The Board shall not be an agency or establishment of the United States Government, and, except as otherwise provided in this Act, shall be subject to, and have all the powers conferred upon a nonprofit corporation by, the District of Columbia Nonprofit Corporation Act. No member or person employed by, or agent for, the Board shall be Deemed to be an officer or employee of or agent for the Federal Government by reason of such service.

(c) Duties of the Board.—The Board shall, subject to action by the Commission under section 107, and once a determination is made by the Commission under subsection (d) of this section—

(1) register public accounting firms that prepare audit reports for issuers, in accordance with section 102;

(2) establish or adopt, or both, by rule, auditing, quality control, ethics, independence, and other standards relating to the preparation of audit reports for issuers, in accordance with section 103;

(3) conduct inspections of registered public accounting firms, in accordance with section 104 and the rules of the Board;

(4) conduct investigations and disciplinary proceedings concerning, and impose appropriate sanctions where justified upon, registered public accounting firms and associated persons of such firms, in accordance with section 105;

(5) perform such other duties or functions as the Board (or the Commission, by rule or order) determines are necessary or appropriate to promote high professional standards among, and improve the quality of audit services offered by, registered public accounting firms and associated persons thereof, or otherwise to carry out this Act, in order to protect investors, or to further the public interest;

(6) enforce compliance with this Act, the rules of the Board, professional standards, and the securities laws relating to the preparation and issuance of audit reports and the obligations and liabilities of accountants with respect thereto, by registered public accounting firms and associated persons thereof; and

(7) set the budget and manage the operations of the Board and the staff of the Board.

(d) Commission Determination.—The members of the Board shall take such action (including hiring of staff, proposal of rules, and adoption of initial and transitional auditing and other professional standards) as may be necessary or appropriate to enable the Commission to determine, not later than 270 days after the date of enactment of this Act, that the Board is so organized and has the capacity to carry out the requirements of this title, and to enforce compliance with this title by registered public accounting firms and associated persons thereof. The Commission shall be responsible, prior to the appointment of the Board, for the planning for the establishment and administrative transition to the Board's operation.

(e) Board Membership.—

(1) Composition.—The Board shall have 5 members, appointed from among prominent individuals of integrity and reputation who have a demonstrated commitment to the interests of

investors and the public, and an understanding of the responsibilities for and nature of the financial disclosures required of issuers under the securities laws and the obligations of accountants with respect to the preparation and issuance of audit reports with respect to such disclosures.

(2) Limitation.—Two members, and only 2 members, of the Board shall be or have been certified public accountants pursuant to the laws of 1 or more States, provided that, if 1 of those 2 members is the chairperson, he or she may not have been a practicing certified public accountant for at least 5 years prior to his or her appointment to the Board.

(3) Full-time independent service.—Each member of the Board shall serve on a full-time basis, and may not, concurrent with service on the Board, be employed by any other person or engage in any other professional or business activity. No member of the Board may share in any of the profits of, or receive payments from, a public accounting firm (or any other person, as determined by rule of the Commission), other than fixed continuing payments, subject to such conditions as the Commission may impose, under standard arrangements for the retirement of members of public accounting firms.

(4) Appointment of board members.—

(A) Initial board.—Not later than 90 days after the date of enactment of this Act, the Commission, after consultation with the Chairman of the Board of Governors of the Federal Reserve System and the Secretary of the Treasury, shall appoint the chairperson and other initial members of the Board, and shall designate a term of service for each.

(B) Vacancies.—A vacancy on the Board shall not affect the powers of the Board, but shall be filled in the same manner as provided for appointments under this section.

(5) Term of service.—

(A) In general.—The term of service of each Board member shall be 5 years, and until a successor is appointed, except that—

(i) the terms of office of the initial Board members (other than the chairperson) shall expire in annual increments, 1 on each of the first 4 anniversaries of the initial date of appointment; and

(ii) any Board member appointed to fill a vacancy occurring before the expiration of the term for which the predecessor was appointed shall be appointed only for the remainder of that term.

(B) Term limitation.—No person may serve as a member of the Board, or as chairperson of the Board, for more than 2 terms, whether or not such terms of service are consecutive.

(6) Removal from office.—A member of the Board may be removed by the Commission from office, in accordance with section 107(d)(3), for good cause shown before the expiration of the term of that member.

(f) Powers of the Board.—In addition to any authority granted to the Board otherwise in this Act, the Board shall have the power, subject to section 107—

(1) to sue and be sued, complain and defend, in its corporate name and through its own counsel, with the approval of the Commission, in any Federal, State, or other court;

(2) to conduct its operations and maintain offices, and to exercise all other rights and powers authorized by this Act, in any State, without regard to any qualification, licensing, or other provision of law in effect in such State (or a political subdivision thereof);

(3) to lease, purchase, accept gifts or donations of or otherwise acquire, improve, use, sell, exchange, or convey, all of or an interest in any property, wherever situated;

(4) to appoint such employees, accountants, attorneys, and other agents as may be necessary or appropriate, and to determine their qualifications, define their duties, and fix their salaries or other compensation (at a level that is comparable to private sector self-regulatory, accounting, technical, supervisory, or other staff or management positions);

(5)   to allocate, assess, and collect accounting support fees established pursuant to section 109, for the Board, and other fees and charges imposed under this title; and

(6)   to enter into contracts, execute instruments, incur liabilities, and do any and all other acts and things necessary, appropriate, or incidental to the conduct of its operations and the exercise of its obligations, rights, and powers imposed or granted by this title.

(g)   Rules of the Board.—The rules of the Board shall, subject to the approval of the Commission—

(1)   provide for the operation and administration of the Board, the exercise of its authority, and the performance of its responsibilities under this Act;

(2)   permit, as the Board determines necessary or appropriate, delegation by the Board of any of its functions to an individual member or employee of the Board, or to a division of the Board, including functions with respect to hearing, determining, ordering, certifying, reporting, or otherwise acting as to any matter, except that—

(A)   the Board shall retain a discretionary right to review any action pursuant to any such delegated function, upon its own motion;

(B)   a person shall be entitled to a review by the Board with respect to any matter so delegated, and the decision of the Board upon such review shall be deemed to be the action of the Board for all purposes (including appeal or review thereof); and

(C)   if the right to exercise a review described in subparagraph (A) is declined, or if no such review is sought within the time stated in the rules of the Board, then the action taken by the holder of such delegation shall for all purposes, including appeal or review thereof, be deemed to be the action of the Board;

(3)   establish ethics rules and standards of conduct for Board members and staff, including a bar on practice before the Board (and the Commission, with respect to Board-related matters)   of   1 year for former members of the Board, and appropriate periods (not to exceed 1 year) for former staff of the Board; and

(4)   provide as otherwise required by this Act.

(h)   Annual Report to the Commission.—The Board shall submit an annual report (including its audited financial statements) to the Commission, and the Commission shall transmit a copy of that report to the Committee on Banking, Housing, and Urban Affairs of the Senate, and the Committee on Financial Services of the House of Representatives, not later than 30 days after the date of receipt of that report by the Commission.

§ 102.   Registration with the Board

(a)   Mandatory Registration.—Beginning 180 days after the date of the determination of the Commission under section 101(d), it shall be unlawful for any person that is not a registered public accounting firm to prepare or issue, or to participate in the preparation or issuance of, any audit report with respect to any issuer.

(b)   Applications for Registration.—

(1)   Form of application.—A public accounting firm shall use such form as the Board may prescribe, by rule, to apply for registration under this section.

(2)   Contents of applications.—Each public accounting firm shall submit, as part of its application for registration, in such detail as the Board shall specify—

(A)   the names of all issuers for which the firm prepared or issued audit reports during the immediately preceding calendar year, and for which the firm expects to prepare or issue audit reports during the current calendar year;

(B)   the annual fees received by the firm from each such issuer for audit services, other accounting services, and non-audit services, respectively;

(C) such other current financial information for the most recently completed fiscal year of the firm as the Board may reasonably request;

(D) a statement of the quality control policies of the firm for its accounting and auditing practices;

(E) a list of all accountants associated with the firm who participate in or contribute to the preparation of audit reports, stating the license or certification number of each such person, as well as the State license numbers of the firm itself;

(F) information relating to criminal, civil, or administrative actions or disciplinary proceedings pending against the firm or any associated person of the firm in connection with any audit report;

(G) copies of any periodic or annual disclosure filed by an issuer with the Commission during the immediately preceding calendar year which discloses accounting disagreements between such issuer and the firm in connection with an audit report furnished or prepared by the firm for such issuer; and

(H) such other information as the rules of the Board or the Commission shall specify as necessary or appropriate in the public interest or for the protection of investors.

(3) Consents.—Each application for registration under this subsection shall include—

(A) a consent executed by the public accounting firm to cooperation in and compliance with any request for testimony or the production of documents made by the Board in the furtherance of its authority and responsibilities under this title (and an agreement to secure and enforce similar consents from each of the associated persons of the public accounting firm as a condition of their continued employment by or other association with such firm); and

(B) a statement that such firm understands and agrees that cooperation and compliance, as described in the consent required by subparagraph (A), and the securing and enforcement of such consents from its associated persons, in accordance with the rules of the Board, shall be a condition to the continuing effectiveness of the registration of the firm with the Board.

(c) Action on Applications.—

(1) Timing.—The Board shall approve a completed application for registration not later than 45 days after the date of receipt of the application, in accordance with the rules of the Board, unless the Board, prior to such date, issues a written notice of disapproval to, or requests more information from, the prospective registrant.

(2) Treatment.—A written notice of disapproval of a completed application under paragraph (1) for registration shall be treated as a disciplinary sanction for purposes of sections 105(d) and 107(c).

(d) Periodic Reports.—Each registered public accounting firm shall submit an annual report to the Board, and may be required to report more frequently, as necessary to update the information contained in its application for registration under this section, and to provide to the Board such additional information as the Board or the Commission may specify, in accordance with subsection (b)(2).

(e) Public Availability.—Registration applications and annual reports required by this subsection, or such portions of such applications or reports as may be designated under rules of the Board, shall be made available for public inspection, subject to rules of the Board or the Commission, and to applicable laws relating to the confidentiality of proprietary, personal, or other information contained in such applications or reports, provided that, in all events, the Board shall protect from public disclosure information reasonably identified by the subject accounting firm as proprietary information.

(f) Registration and Annual Fees.—The Board shall assess and collect a registration fee and an annual fee from each registered public accounting firm, in amounts that are sufficient to recover the costs of processing and reviewing applications and annual reports.

§ 103. Auditing, Quality Control, and Independence Standards and Rules

(a) Auditing, Quality Control, and Ethics Standards.—

(1) In general.—The Board shall, by rule, establish, including, to the extent it determines appropriate, through adoption of standards proposed by 1 or more professional groups of accountants designated pursuant to paragraph (3)(A) or advisory groups convened pursuant to paragraph (4), and amend or otherwise modify or alter, such auditing and related attestation standards, such quality control standards, and such ethics standards to be used by registered public accounting firms in the preparation and issuance of audit reports, as required by this Act or the rules of the Commission, or as may be necessary or appropriate in the public interest or for the protection of investors.

(2) Rule requirements.—In carrying out paragraph (1), the Board—

(A) shall include in the auditing standards that it adopts, requirements that each registered public accounting firm shall—

(i) prepare, and maintain for a period of not less than 7 years, audit work papers, and other information related to any audit report, in sufficient detail to support the conclusions reached in such report;

(ii) provide a concurring or second partner review and approval of such audit report (and other related information), and concurring approval in its issuance, by a qualified person (as prescribed by the Board) associated with the public accounting firm, other than the person in charge of the audit, or by an independent reviewer (as prescribed by the Board); and

(iii) describe in each audit report the scope of the auditor's testing of the internal control structure and procedures of the issuer, required by section 404(b), and present (in such report or in a separate report)—

(I) the findings of the auditor from such testing;

(II) an evaluation of whether such internal control structure and procedures—

(aa) include maintenance of records that in reasonable detail accurately and fairly reflect the transactions and dispositions of the assets of the issuer;

(bb) provide reasonable assurance that transactions are recorded as necessary to permit preparation of financial statements in accordance with generally accepted accounting principles, and that receipts and expenditures of the issuer are being made only in accordance with authorizations of management and directors of the issuer; and

(III) a description, at a minimum, of material weaknesses in such internal controls, and of any material noncompliance found on the basis of such testing.

(B) shall include, in the quality control standards that it adopts with respect to the issuance of audit reports, requirements for every registered public accounting firm relating to—

(i) monitoring of professional ethics and independence from issuers on behalf of which the firm issues audit reports;

(ii) consultation within such firm on accounting and auditing questions;

(iii) supervision of audit work;

(iv) hiring, professional development, and advancement of personnel;

(v) the acceptance and continuation of engagements;

(vi) internal inspection; and

(vii) such other requirements as the Board may prescribe, subject to subsection (a)(1).

(3) Authority to adopt other standards.—

(A) In general.—In carrying out this subsection, the Board—

(i) may adopt as its rules, subject to the terms of section 107, any portion of any statement of auditing standards or other professional standards that the Board determines satisfy the requirements of paragraph (1), and that were proposed by 1 or more professional groups of accountants that shall be designated or recognized by the Board, by rule, for such purpose, pursuant to this paragraph or 1 or more advisory groups convened pursuant to paragraph (4); and

(ii) notwithstanding clause (i), shall retain full authority to modify, supplement, revise, or subsequently amend, modify, or repeal, in whole or in part, any portion of any statement described in clause (i).

(B) Initial and transitional standards.—The Board shall adopt standards described in subparagraph (A)(i) as initial or transitional standards, to the extent the Board determines necessary, prior to a determination of the Commission under section 101(d), and such standards shall be separately approved by the Commission at the time of that determination, without regard to the procedures required by section 107 that otherwise would apply to the approval of rules of the Board.

(4) Advisory groups.—The Board shall convene, or authorize its staff to convene, such expert advisory groups as may be appropriate, which may include practicing accountants and other experts, as well as representatives of other interested groups, subject to such rules as the Board may prescribe to prevent conflicts of interest, to make recommendations concerning the content (including proposed drafts) of auditing, quality control, ethics, independence, or other standards required to be established under this section.

(b) Independence Standards and Rules.—The Board shall establish such rules as may be necessary or appropriate in the public interest or for the protection of investors, to implement, or as authorized under, title II of this Act.

(c) Cooperation With Designated Professional Groups of Accountants and Advisory Groups.—

(1) In general.—The Board shall cooperate on an ongoing basis with professional groups of accountants designated under subsection (a)(3)(A) and advisory groups convened under subsection (a)(4) in the examination of the need for changes in any standards subject to its authority under subsection (a), recommend issues for inclusion on the agendas of such designated professional groups of accountants or advisory groups, and take such other steps as it deems appropriate to increase the effectiveness of the standard setting process.

(2) Board responses.—The Board shall respond in a timely fashion to requests from designated professional groups of accountants and advisory groups referred to in paragraph (1) for any changes in standards over which the Board has authority.

(d) Evaluation of Standard Setting Process.—The Board shall include in the annual report required by section 101(h) the results of its standard setting responsibilities during the period to which the report relates, including a discussion of the work of the Board with any designated professional groups of accountants and advisory groups described in paragraphs (3)(A) and (4) of subsection (a), and its pending issues agenda for future standard setting projects.

§ 104. Inspections of Registered Public Accounting Firms

(a) In General.—The Board shall conduct a continuing program of inspections to assess the degree of compliance of each registered public accounting firm and associated persons of that firm with this Act, the rules of the Board, the rules of the Commission, or professional standards, in connection with its performance of audits, issuance of audit reports, and related matters involving issuers.

(b) Inspection Frequency.—

(1) In general.—Subject to paragraph (2), inspections required by this section shall be conducted—

(A) annually with respect to each registered public accounting firm that regularly provides audit reports for more than 100 issuers; and

(B) not less frequently than once every 3 years with respect to each registered public accounting firm that regularly provides audit reports for 100 or fewer issuers.

(2) Adjustments to schedules.—The Board may, by rule, adjust the inspection schedules set under paragraph (1) if the Board finds that different inspection schedules are consistent with the purposes of this Act, the public interest, and the protection of investors. The Board may conduct special inspections at the request of the Commission or upon its own motion.

(c) Procedures.—The Board shall, in each inspection under this section, and in accordance with its rules for such inspections—

(1) identify any act or practice or omission to act by the registered public accounting firm, or by any associated person thereof, revealed by such inspection that may be in violation of this Act, the rules of the Board, the rules of the Commission, the firm's own quality control policies, or professional standards;

(2) report any such act, practice, or omission, if appropriate, to the Commission and each appropriate State regulatory authority; and

(3) begin a formal investigation or take disciplinary action, if appropriate, with respect to any such violation, in accordance with this Act and the rules of the Board.

(d) Conduct of Inspections.—In conducting an inspection of a registered public accounting firm under this section, the Board shall—

(1) inspect and review selected audit and review engagements of the firm (which may include audit engagements that are the subject of ongoing litigation or other controversy between the firm and 1 or more third parties), performed at various offices and by various associated persons of the firm, as selected by the Board;

(2) evaluate the sufficiency of the quality control system of the firm, and the manner of the documentation and communication of that system by the firm; and

(3) perform such other testing of the audit, supervisory, and quality control procedures of the firm as are necessary or appropriate in light of the purpose of the inspection and the responsibilities of the Board.

(e) Record Retention.—The rules of the Board may require the retention by registered public accounting firms for inspection purposes of records whose retention is not otherwise required by section 103 or the rules issued thereunder.

(f) Procedures for Review.—The rules of the Board shall provide a procedure for the review of and response to a draft inspection report by the registered public accounting firm under inspection. The Board shall take such action with respect to such response as it considers appropriate (including revising the draft report or continuing or supplementing its inspection activities before issuing a final report), but the text of any such response, appropriately redacted to protect information reasonably identified by the accounting firm as confidential, shall be attached to and made part of the inspection report.

(g) Report.—A written report of the findings of the Board for each inspection under this section, subject to subsection (h), shall be—

(1) transmitted, in appropriate detail, to the Commission and each appropriate State regulatory authority, accompanied by any letter or comments by the Board or the inspector, and any letter of response from the registered public accounting firm; and

(2) made available in appropriate detail to the public (subject to section 105(b)(5)(A), and to the protection of such confidential and proprietary information as the Board may determine to be appropriate, or as may be required by law), except that no portions of the inspection report that deal with criticisms of or potential defects in the quality control systems of the firm under inspection shall be made public if those criticisms or defects are addressed by the firm, to the satisfaction of the Board, not later than 12 months after the date of the inspection report.

(h) Interim Commission Review.—

(1) Reviewable matters.—A registered public accounting firm may seek review by the Commission, pursuant to such rules as the Commission shall promulgate, if the firm—

(A) has provided the Board with a response, pursuant to rules issued by the Board under subsection (f), to the substance of particular items in a draft inspection report, and disagrees with the assessments contained in any final report prepared by the Board following such response; or

(B) disagrees with the determination of the Board that criticisms or defects identified in an inspection report have not been addressed to the satisfaction of the Board within 12 months of the date of the inspection report, for purposes of subsection (g)(2).

(2) Treatment of review.—Any decision of the Commission with respect to a review under paragraph (1) shall not be reviewable under section 25 of the Securities Exchange Act of 1934 (15 U.S.C. 78y), or deemed to be "final agency action" for purposes of section 704 of title 5, United States Code.

(3) Timing.—Review under paragraph (1) may be sought during the 30-day period following the date of the event giving rise to the review under subparagraph (A) or (B) of paragraph (1).

§ 105. Investigations and Disciplinary Proceedings

(a) In General.—The Board shall establish, by rule, subject to the requirements of this section, fair procedures for the investigation and disciplining of registered public accounting firms and associated persons of such firms.

(b) Investigations.—

(1) Authority.—In accordance with the rules of the Board, the Board may conduct an investigation of any act or practice, or omission to act, by a registered public accounting firm, any associated person of such firm, or both, that may violate any provision of this Act, the rules of the Board, the provisions of the securities laws relating to the preparation and issuance of audit reports and the obligations and liabilities of accountants with respect thereto, including the rules of the Commission issued under this Act, or professional standards, regardless of how the act, practice, or omission is brought to the attention of the Board.

(2) Testimony and document production.—In addition to such other actions as the Board determines to be necessary or appropriate, the rules of the Board may—

(A) require the testimony of the firm or of any person associated with a registered public accounting firm, with respect to any matter that the Board considers relevant or material to an investigation;

(B) require the production of audit work papers and any other document or information in the possession of a registered public accounting firm or any associated person thereof, wherever domiciled, that the Board considers relevant or material to the investigation, and may inspect the books and records of such firm or associated person to verify the accuracy of any documents or information supplied;

(C) request the testimony of, and production of any document in the possession of, any other person, including any client of a registered public accounting firm that the Board considers relevant or material to an investigation under this section, with appropriate notice, subject to the needs of the investigation, as permitted under the rules of the Board; and

(D) provide for procedures to seek issuance by the Commission, in a manner established by the Commission, of a subpoena to require the testimony of, and production of any document in the possession of, any person, including any client of a registered public accounting firm, that the Board considers relevant or material to an investigation under this section.

(3) Noncooperation with investigations.—

(A) In general.—If a registered public accounting firm or any associated person thereof refuses to testify, produce documents, or otherwise cooperate with the Board in connection with an investigation under this section, the Board may—

(i) suspend or bar such person from being associated with a registered public accounting firm, or require the registered public accounting firm to end such association;

(ii) suspend or revoke the registration of the public accounting firm; and

(iii) invoke such other lesser sanctions as the Board considers appropriate, and as specified by rule of the Board.

(B) Procedure.—Any action taken by the Board under this paragraph shall be subject to the terms of section 107(c).

(4) Coordination and referral of investigations.—

(A) Coordination.—The Board shall notify the Commission of any pending Board investigation involving a potential violation of the securities laws, and thereafter coordinate its work with the work of the Commission's Division of Enforcement, as necessary to protect an ongoing Commission investigation.

(B) Referral.—The Board may refer an investigation under this section—

(i) to the Commission;

(ii) to any other Federal functional regulator (as defined in section 509 of the Gramm-Leach-Bliley Act (15 U.S.C. 6809)), in the case of an investigation that concerns an audit report for an institution that is subject to the jurisdiction of such regulator; and

(iii) at the direction of the Commission, to—

(I) the Attorney General of the United States;

(II) the attorney general of 1 or more States; and

(III) the appropriate State regulatory authority.

(5) Use of documents.—

(A) Confidentiality.—Except as provided in subparagraph (B), all documents and information prepared or received by or specifically for the Board, and deliberations of the Board and its employees and agents, in connection with an inspection under section 104 or with an investigation under this section, shall be confidential and privileged as an evidentiary matter (and shall not be subject to civil discovery or other legal process) in any proceeding in any Federal or State court or administrative agency, and shall be exempt from disclosure, in the hands of an agency or establishment of the Federal Government, under the Freedom of Information Act (5 U.S.C. 552a), or otherwise, unless and until presented in connection with a public proceeding or released in accordance with subsection (c).

(B) Availability to government agencies.—Without the loss of its status as confidential and privileged in the hands of the Board, all information referred to in subparagraph (A) may—

(i) be made available to the Commission; and

(ii) in the discretion of the Board, when determined by the Board to be necessary to accomplish the purposes of this Act or to protect investors, be made available to—

(I) the Attorney General of the United States;

(II) the appropriate Federal functional regulator (as defined in section 509 of the Gramm-Leach-Bliley Act (15 U.S.C. 6809)), other than the Commission, with respect to an audit report for an institution subject to the jurisdiction of such regulator;

(III) State attorneys general in connection with any criminal investigation; and

(IV) any appropriate State regulatory authority, each of which shall maintain such information as confidential and privileged.

(6) Immunity.—Any employee of the Board engaged in carrying out an investigation under this Act shall be immune from any civil liability arising out of such investigation in the same manner and to the same extent as an employee of the Federal Government in similar circumstances.

(c) Disciplinary Procedures.—

(1) Notification; recordkeeping.—The rules of the Board shall provide that in any proceeding by the Board to determine whether a registered public accounting firm, or an associated person thereof, should be disciplined, the Board shall—

(A) bring specific charges with respect to the firm or associated person;

(B) notify such firm or associated person of, and provide to the firm or associated person an opportunity to defend against, such charges; and

(C) keep a record of the proceedings.

(2) Public hearings.—Hearings under this section shall not be public, unless otherwise ordered by the Board for good cause shown, with the consent of the parties to such hearing.

(3) Supporting statement.—A determination by the Board to impose a sanction under this subsection shall be supported by a statement setting forth—

(A) each act or practice in which the registered public accounting firm, or associated person, has engaged (or omitted to engage), or that forms a basis for all or a part of such sanction;

(B) the specific provision of this Act, the securities laws, the rules of the Board, or professional standards which the Board determines has been violated; and

(C) the sanction imposed, including a justification for that sanction.

(4) Sanctions.—If the Board finds, based on all of the facts and circumstances, that a registered public accounting firm or associated person thereof has engaged in any act or practice, or omitted to act, in violation of this Act, the rules of the Board, the provisions of the securities laws relating to the preparation and issuance of audit reports and the obligations and liabilities of accountants with respect thereto, including the rules of the Commission issued under this Act, or professional standards, the Board may impose such disciplinary or remedial sanctions as it determines appropriate, subject to applicable limitations under paragraph (5), including—

(A) temporary suspension or permanent revocation of registration under this title;

(B) temporary or permanent suspension or bar of a person from further association with any registered public accounting firm;

(C) temporary or permanent limitation on the activities, functions, or operations of such firm or person (other than in connection with required additional professional education or training);

(D) a civil money penalty for each such violation, in an amount equal to—

(i) not more than $100,000 for a natural person or $2,000,000 for any other person; and

(ii) in any case to which paragraph (5) applies, not more than $750,000 for a natural person or $15,000,000 for any other person;

(E) censure;

(F) required additional professional education or training; or

(G) any other appropriate sanction provided for in the rules of the Board.

(5) Intentional or other knowing conduct.—The sanctions and penalties described in subparagraphs (A) through (C) and (D)(ii) of paragraph (4) shall only apply to—

(A) intentional or knowing conduct, including reckless conduct, that results in violation of the applicable statutory, regulatory, or professional standard; or

(B) repeated instances of negligent conduct, each resulting in a violation of the applicable statutory, regulatory, or professional standard.

(6)   Failure to supervise.—

(A)   In general.—The Board may impose sanctions under this section on a registered accounting firm or upon the supervisory personnel of such firm, if the Board finds that—

(i)   the firm has failed reasonably to supervise an associated person, either as required by the rules of the Board relating to auditing or quality control standards, or otherwise, with a view to preventing violations of this Act, the rules of the Board, the provisions of the securities laws relating to the preparation and issuance of audit reports and the obligations and liabilities of accountants with respect thereto, including the rules of the Commission under this Act, or professional standards; and

(ii)   such associated person commits a violation of this Act, or any of such rules, laws, or standards.

(B)   Rule of construction.—No associated person of a registered public accounting firm shall be deemed to have failed reasonably to supervise any other person for purposes of subparagraph (A), if—

(i)   there have been established in and for that firm procedures, and a system for applying such procedures, that comply with applicable rules of the Board and that would reasonably be expected to prevent and detect any such violation by such associated person; and

(ii)   such person has reasonably discharged the duties and obligations incumbent upon that person by reason of such procedures and system, and had no reasonable cause to believe that such procedures and system were not being complied with.

(7)   Effect of suspension.—

(A)   Association with a public accounting firm.—It shall be unlawful for any person that is suspended or barred from being associated with a registered public accounting firm under this subsection willfully to become or remain associated with any registered public accounting firm, or for any registered public accounting firm that knew, or, in the exercise of reasonable care should have known, of the suspension or bar, to permit such an association, without the consent of the Board or the Commission.

(B)   Association with an issuer.—It shall be unlawful for any person that is suspended or barred from being associated with an issuer under this subsection willfully to become or remain associated with any issuer in an accountancy or a financial management capacity, and for any issuer that knew, or in the exercise of reasonable care should have known, of such suspension or bar, to permit such an association, without the consent of the Board or the Commission.

(d)   Reporting of Sanctions.—

(1)   Recipients.—If the Board imposes a disciplinary sanction, in accordance with this section, the Board shall report the sanction to—

(A)   the Commission;

(B)   any appropriate State regulatory authority or any foreign accountancy licensing board with which such firm or person is licensed or certified; and

(C)   the public (once any stay on the imposition of such sanction has been lifted).

(2)   Contents.—The information reported under paragraph (1) shall include—

(A)   the name of the sanctioned person;

(B)   a description of the sanction and the basis for its imposition; and

(C)   such other information as the Board deems appropriate.

(e)   Stay of Sanctions.—

(1)   In general.—Application to the Commission for review, or the institution by the Commission of review, of any disciplinary action of the Board shall operate as a stay of any such disciplinary action,

unless and until the Commission orders (summarily or after notice and opportunity for hearing on the question of a stay, which hearing may consist solely of the submission of affidavits or presentation of oral arguments) that no such stay shall continue to operate.

(2) Expedited procedures.—The Commission shall establish for appropriate cases an expedited procedure for consideration and determination of the question of the duration of a stay pending review of any disciplinary action of the Board under this subsection.

§ 106. Foreign Public Accounting Firms

(a) Applicability to Certain Foreign Firms.—

(1) In general.—Any foreign public accounting firm that prepares or furnishes an audit report with respect to any issuer, shall be subject to this Act and the rules of the Board and the Commission issued under this Act, in the same manner and to the same extent as a public accounting firm that is organized and operates under the laws of the United States or any State, except that registration pursuant to section 102 shall not by itself provide a basis for subjecting such a foreign public accounting firm to the jurisdiction of the Federal or State courts, other than with respect to controversies between such firms and the Board.

(2) Board authority.—The Board may, by rule, determine that a foreign public accounting firm (or a class of such firms) that does not issue audit reports nonetheless plays such a substantial role in the preparation and furnishing of such reports for particular issuers, that it is necessary or appropriate, in light of the purposes of this Act and in the public interest or for the protection of investors, that such firm (or class of firms) should be treated as a public accounting firm (or firms) for purposes of registration under, and oversight by the Board in accordance with, this title.

(b) Production of Audit Workpapers.—

(1) Consent by foreign firms.—If a foreign public accounting firm issues an opinion or otherwise performs material services upon which a registered public accounting firm relies in issuing all or part of any audit report or any opinion contained in an audit report, that foreign public accounting firm shall be deemed to have consented—

(A) to produce its audit workpapers for the Board or the Commission in connection with any investigation by either body with respect to that audit report; and

(B) to be subject to the jurisdiction of the courts of the United States for purposes of enforcement of any request for production of such workpapers.

(2) Consent by domestic firms.—A registered public accounting firm that relies upon the opinion of a foreign public accounting firm, as described in paragraph (1), shall be deemed—

(A) to have consented to supplying the audit workpapers of that foreign public accounting firm in response to a request for production by the Board or the Commission; and

(B) to have secured the agreement of that foreign public accounting firm to such production, as a condition of its reliance on the opinion of that foreign public accounting firm.

(c) Exemption Authority.—The Commission, and the Board, subject to the approval of the Commission, may, by rule, regulation, or order, and as the Commission (or Board) determines necessary or appropriate in the public interest or for the protection of investors, either unconditionally or upon specified terms and conditions exempt any foreign public accounting firm, or any class of such firms, from any provision of this Act or the rules of the Board or the Commission issued under this Act.

(d) Definition.—In this section, the term "foreign public accounting firm" means a public accounting firm that is organized and operates under the laws of a foreign government or political subdivision thereof.

§ 107. Commission Oversight of the Board

(a) General Oversight Responsibility.—The Commission shall have oversight and enforcement authority over the Board, as provided in this Act. The provisions of section 17(a)(1) of the Securities Exchange Act of 1934 (15 U.S.C. 78q(a)(1)), and of section 17(b)(1) of the Securities Exchange Act of 1934

(15 U.S.C. 78q(b)(1)) shall apply to the Board as fully as if the Board were a "registered securities association" for purposes of those sections 17(a)(1) and 17(b)(1).

(b) Rules of the Board.—

(1) Definition.—In this section, the term "proposed rule" means any proposed rule of the Board, and any modification of any such rule.

(2) Prior approval required.—No rule of the Board shall become effective without prior approval of the Commission in accordance with this section, other than as provided in section 103(a)(3)(B) with respect to initial or transitional standards.

(3) Approval criteria.—The Commission shall approve a proposed rule, if it finds that the rule is consistent with the requirements of this Act and the securities laws, or is necessary or appropriate in the public interest or for the protection of investors.

(4) Proposed rule procedures.—The provisions of paragraphs (1) through (3) of section 19(b) of the Securities Exchange Act of 1934 (15 U.S.C. 78s(b)) shall govern the proposed rules of the Board, as fully as if the Board were a "registered securities association" for purposes of that section 19(b), except that, for purposes of this paragraph—

(A) the phrase "consistent with the requirements of this title and the rules and regulations thereunder applicable to such organization" in section 19(b)(2) of that Act shall be deemed to read "consistent with the requirements of title I of the Sarbanes-Oxley Act of 2002, and the rules and regulations issued thereunder applicable to such organization, or as necessary or appropriate in the public interest or for the protection of investors"; and

(B) the phrase "otherwise in furtherance of the purposes of this title" in section 19(b)(3)(C) of that Act shall be deemed to read "otherwise in furtherance of the purposes of title I of the Sarbanes-Oxley Act of 2002".

(5) Commission authority to amend rules of the board.—The provisions of section 19(c) of the Securities Exchange Act of 1934 (15 U.S.C. 78s(c)) shall govern the abrogation, deletion, or addition to portions of the rules of the Board by the Commission as fully as if the Board were a "registered securities association" for purposes of that section 19(c), except that the phrase "to conform its rules to the requirements of this title and the rules and regulations thereunder applicable to such organization, or otherwise in furtherance of the purposes of this title" in section 19(c) of that Act shall, for purposes of this paragraph, be deemed to read "to assure the fair administration of the Public Company Accounting Oversight Board, conform the rules promulgated by that Board to the requirements of title I of the Sarbanes-Oxley Act of 2002, or otherwise further the purposes of that Act, the securities laws, and the rules and regulations thereunder applicable to that Board".

(c) Commission Review of Disciplinary Action Taken by the Board.—

(1) Notice of sanction.—The Board shall promptly file notice with the Commission of any final sanction on any registered public accounting firm or on any associated person thereof, in such form and containing such information as the Commission, by rule, may prescribe.

(2) Review of sanctions.—The provisions of sections 19(d)(2) and 19(e)(1) of the Securities Exchange Act of 1934 (15 U.S.C. 78s (d)(2) and (e)(1)) shall govern the review by the Commission of final disciplinary sanctions imposed by the Board (including sanctions imposed under section 105(b)(3) of this Act for noncooperation in an investigation of the Board), as fully as if the Board were a self-regulatory organization and the Commission were the appropriate regulatory agency for such organization for purposes of those sections 19(d)(2) and 19(e)(1), except that, for purposes of this paragraph—

(A) section 105(e) of this Act (rather than that section 19(d)(2)) shall govern the extent to which application for, or institution by the Commission on its own motion of, review of any disciplinary action of the Board operates as a stay of such action;

(B) references in that section 19(e)(1) to "members" of such an organization shall be deemed to be references to registered public accounting firms;

(C) the phrase "consistent with the purposes of this title" in that section 19(e)(1) shall be deemed to read "consistent with the purposes of this title and title I of the Sarbanes-Oxley Act of 2002";

(D) references to rules of the Municipal Securities Rulemaking Board in that section 19(e)(1) shall not apply; and

(E) the reference to section 19(e)(2) of the Securities Exchange Act of 1934 shall refer instead to section 107(c)(3) of this Act.

(3) Commission modification authority.—The Commission may enhance, modify, cancel, reduce, or require the remission of a sanction imposed by the Board upon a registered public accounting firm or associated person thereof, if the Commission, having due regard for the public interest and the protection of investors, finds, after a proceeding in accordance with this subsection, that the sanction—

(A) is not necessary or appropriate in furtherance of this Act or the securities laws; or

(B) is excessive, oppressive, inadequate, or otherwise not appropriate to the finding or the basis on which the sanction was imposed.

(d) Censure of the Board; Other Sanctions.—

(1) Rescission of board authority.—The Commission, by rule, consistent with the public interest, the protection of investors, and the other purposes of this Act and the securities laws, may relieve the Board of any responsibility to enforce compliance with any provision of this Act, the securities laws, the rules of the Board, or professional standards.

(2) Censure of the board; limitations.—The Commission may, by order, as it determines necessary or appropriate in the public interest, for the protection of investors, or otherwise in furtherance of the purposes of this Act or the securities laws, censure or impose limitations upon the activities, functions, and operations of the Board, if the Commission finds, on the record, after notice and opportunity for a hearing, that the Board—

(A) has violated or is unable to comply with any provision of this Act, the rules of the Board, or the securities laws; or

(B) without reasonable justification or excuse, has failed to enforce compliance with any such provision or rule, or any professional standard by a registered public accounting firm or an associated person thereof.

(3) Censure of board members; removal from office.—The Commission may, as necessary or appropriate in the public interest, for the protection of investors, or otherwise in furtherance of the purposes of this Act or the securities laws, remove from office or censure any member of the Board, if the Commission finds, on the record, after notice and opportunity for a hearing, that such member—

(A) has willfully violated any provision of this Act, the rules of the Board, or the securities laws;

(B) has willfully abused the authority of that member; or

(C) without reasonable justification or excuse, has failed to enforce compliance with any such provision or rule, or any professional standard by any registered public accounting firm or any associated person thereof.

§ 108. Accounting Standards

(a) Amendment to Securities Act of 1933.—Section 19 of the Securities Act of 1933 (15 U.S.C. 77s) is amended—

(1) by redesignating subsections (b) and (c) as subsections (c) and (d), respectively; and

(2) by inserting after subsection (a) the following:

"(b) Recognition of Accounting Standards.—

"(1) In general.—In carrying out its authority under subsection (a) and under section 13(b) of the Securities Exchange Act of 1934, the Commission may recognize, as 'generally accepted' for purposes of the securities laws, any accounting principles established by a standard setting body—

"(A) that—

"(i) is organized as a private entity;

"(ii) has, for administrative and operational purposes, a board of trustees (or equivalent body) serving in the public interest, the majority of whom are not, concurrent with their service on such board, and have not been during the 2-year period preceding such service, associated persons of any registered public accounting firm;

"(iii) is funded as provided in section 109 of the Sarbanes-Oxley Act of 2002;

"(iv) has adopted procedures to ensure prompt consideration, by majority vote of its members, of changes to accounting principles necessary to reflect emerging accounting issues and changing business practices; and

"(v) considers, in adopting accounting principles, the need to keep standards current in order to reflect changes in the business environment, the extent to which international convergence on high quality accounting standards is necessary or appropriate in the public interest and for the protection of investors; and

"(B) that the Commission determines has the capacity to assist the Commission in fulfilling the requirements of subsection (a) and section 13(b) of the Securities Exchange Act of 1934, because, at a minimum, the standard setting body is capable of improving the accuracy and effectiveness of financial reporting and the protection of investors under the securities laws.

"(2) Annual report.—A standard setting body described in paragraph (1) shall submit an annual report to the Commission and the public, containing audited financial statements of that standard setting body.".

(b) Commission Authority.—The Commission shall promulgate such rules and regulations to carry out section 19(b) of the Securities Act of 1933, as added by this section, as it deems necessary or appropriate in the public interest or for the protection of investors.

(c) No Effect on Commission Powers.—Nothing in this Act, including this section and the amendment made by this section, shall be construed to impair or limit the authority of the Commission to establish accounting principles or standards for purposes of enforcement of the securities laws.

(d) Study and Report on Adopting Principles-Based Accounting.—

(1) Study.—

(A) In general.—The Commission shall conduct a study on the adoption by the United States financial reporting system of a principles-based accounting system.

(B) Study topics.—The study required by subparagraph (A) shall include an examination of—

(i) the extent to which principles-based accounting and financial reporting exists in the United States;

(ii) the length of time required for change from a rules-based to a principles-based financial reporting system;

(iii) the feasibility of and proposed methods by which a principles-based system may be implemented; and

(iv) a thorough economic analysis of the implementation of a principles-based system.

(2) Report.—Not later than 1 year after the date of enactment of this Act, the Commission shall submit a report on the results of the study required by paragraph (1) to the Committee on Banking, Housing, and Urban Affairs of the Senate and the Committee on Financial Services of the House of Representatives.

§ 109. Funding

(a) In General.—The Board, and the standard setting body designated pursuant to section 19(b) of the Securities Act of 1933, as amended by section 108, shall be funded as provided in this section.

(b) Annual Budgets.—The Board and the standard setting body referred to in subsection (a) shall each establish a budget for each fiscal year, which shall be reviewed and approved according to their respective internal procedures not less than 1 month prior to the commencement of the fiscal year to which the budget pertains (or at the beginning of the Board's first fiscal year, which may be a short fiscal year). The budget of the Board shall be subject to approval by the Commission. The budget for the first fiscal year of the Board shall be prepared and approved promptly following the appointment of the initial five Board members, to permit action by the Board of the organizational tasks contemplated by section 101(d).

(c) Sources and Uses of Funds.—

(1) Recoverable budget expenses.—The budget of the Board (reduced by any registration or annual fees received under section 102(e) for the year preceding the year for which the budget is being computed), and all of the budget of the standard setting body referred to in subsection (a), for each fiscal year of each of those 2 entities, shall be payable from annual accounting support fees, in accordance with subsections (d) and (e). Accounting support fees and other receipts of the Board and of such standard-setting body shall not be considered public monies of the United States.

(2) Funds generated from the collection of monetary penalties.—Subject to the availability in advance in an appropriations Act, and notwithstanding subsection (i), all funds collected by the Board as a result of the assessment of monetary penalties shall be used to fund a merit scholarship program for undergraduate and graduate students enrolled in accredited accounting degree programs, which program is to be administered by the Board or by an entity or agent identified by the Board.

(d) Annual Accounting Support Fee for the Board.—

(1) Establishment of fee.—The Board shall establish, with the approval of the Commission, a reasonable annual accounting support fee (or a formula for the computation thereof), as may be necessary or appropriate to establish and maintain the Board. Such fee may also cover costs incurred in the Board's first fiscal year (which may be a short fiscal year), or may be levied separately with respect to such short fiscal year.

(2) Assessments.—The rules of the Board under paragraph (1) shall provide for the equitable allocation, assessment, and collection by the Board (or an agent appointed by the Board) of the fee established under paragraph (1), among issuers, in accordance with subsection (g), allowing for differentiation among classes of issuers, as appropriate.

(e) Annual Accounting Support Fee for Standard Setting Body.—The annual accounting support fee for the standard setting body referred to in subsection (a)—

(1) shall be allocated in accordance with subsection (g), and assessed and collected against each issuer, on behalf of the standard setting body, by 1 or more appropriate designated collection agents, as may be necessary or appropriate to pay for the budget and provide for the expenses of that standard setting body, and to provide for an independent, stable source of funding for such body, subject to review by the Commission; and

(2) may differentiate among different classes of issuers.

(f) Limitation on Fee.—The amount of fees collected under this section for a fiscal year on behalf of the Board or the standards setting body, as the case may be, shall not exceed the recoverable budget expenses of the Board or body, respectively (which may include operating, capital, and accrued items), referred to in subsection (c)(1).

(g)　Allocation of Accounting Support Fees Among Issuers.—Any amount due from issuers (or a particular class of issuers) under this section to fund the budget of the Board or the standard setting body referred to in subsection (a) shall be allocated among and payable by each issuer (or each issuer in a particular class, as applicable) in an amount equal to the total of such amount, multiplied by a fraction—

(1)　the numerator of which is the average monthly equity market capitalization of the issuer for the 12-month period immediately preceding the beginning of the fiscal year to which such budget relates; and

(2)　the denominator of which is the average monthly equity market capitalization of all such issuers for such 12-month period.

(h)　Conforming Amendments.—Section 13(b)(2) of the Securities Exchange Act of 1934 (15 U.S.C. 78m(b)(2)) is amended—

(1)　in subparagraph (A), by striking "and" at the end; and

(2)　in subparagraph (B), by striking the period at the end and inserting the following:"; and

"(C) notwithstanding any other provision of law, pay the allocable share of such issuer of a reasonable annual accounting support fee or fees, determined in accordance with section 109 of the Sarbanes-Oxley Act of 2002.".

(i)　Rule of Construction.—Nothing in this section shall be construed to render either the Board, the standard setting body referred to in subsection (a), or both, subject to procedures in Congress to authorize or appropriate public funds, or to prevent such organization from utilizing additional sources of revenue for its activities, such as earnings from publication sales, provided that each additional source of revenue shall not jeopardize, in the judgment of the Commission, the actual and perceived independence of such organization.

(j)　Start-Up Expenses of the Board.—From the unexpended balances of the appropriations to the Commission for fiscal year 2003, the Secretary of the Treasury is authorized to advance to the Board not to exceed the amount necessary to cover the expenses of the Board during its first fiscal year (which may be a short fiscal year).

TITLE II.　AUDITOR INDEPENDENCE

§ 201.　Services Outside the Scope of Practice of Auditors

(a)　Prohibited Activities.—Section 10A of the Securities Exchange Act of 1934 (15 U.S.C. 78j–1) is amended by adding at the end the following:

"(g) Prohibited Activities.—Except as provided in subsection (h), it shall be unlawful for a registered public accounting firm (and any associated person of that firm, to the extent determined appropriate by the Commission) that performs for any issuer any audit required by this title or the rules of the Commission under this title or, beginning 180 days after the date of commencement of the operations of the Public Company Accounting Oversight Board established under section 101 of the Sarbanes-Oxley Act of 2002 (in this section referred to as the 'Board'), the rules of the Board, to provide to that issuer, contemporaneously with the audit, any non-audit service, including—

"(1)　bookkeeping or other services related to the accounting records or financial statements of the audit client;

"(2)　financial information systems design and implementation;

"(3)　appraisal or valuation services, fairness opinions, or contribution-in-kind reports;

"(4)　actuarial services;

"(5)　internal audit outsourcing services;

"(6)　management functions or human resources;

"(7)　broker or dealer, investment adviser, or investment banking services;

"(8) legal services and expert services unrelated to the audit; and

"(9) any other service that the Board determines, by regulation, is impermissible.

"(h) Preapproval Required for Non-Audit Services.—A registered public accounting firm may engage in any non-audit service, including tax services, that is not described in any of paragraphs (1) through (9) of subsection (g) for an audit client, only if the activity is approved in advance by the audit committee of the issuer, in accordance with subsection (i).".

(b) Exemption Authority.—The Board may, on a case by case basis, exempt any person, issuer, public accounting firm, or transaction from the prohibition on the provision of services under section 10A(g) of the Securities Exchange Act of 1934 (as added by this section), to the extent that such exemption is necessary or appropriate in the public interest and is consistent with the protection of investors, and subject to review by the Commission in the same manner as for rules of the Board under section 107.

§ 202. Preapproval Requirements

Section 10A of the Securities Exchange Act of 1934 (15 U.S.C. 78j–1), as amended by this Act, is amended by adding at the end the following:

"(i) Preapproval Requirements.—

"(1) In general.—

"(A) Audit committee action.—All auditing services (which may entail providing comfort letters in connection with securities underwritings or statutory audits required for insurance companies for purposes of State law) and non-audit services, other than as provided in subparagraph (B), provided to an issuer by the auditor of the issuer shall be preapproved by the audit committee of the issuer.

"(B) De minimus exception.—The preapproval requirement under subparagraph (A) is waived with respect to the provision of non-audit services for an issuer, if—

"(i) the aggregate amount of all such non-audit services provided to the issuer constitutes not more than 5 percent of the total amount of revenues paid by the issuer to its auditor during the fiscal year in which the nonaudit services are provided;

"(ii) such services were not recognized by the issuer at the time of the engagement to be non-audit services; and

"(iii) such services are promptly brought to the attention of the audit committee of the issuer and approved prior to the completion of the audit by the audit committee or by 1 or more members of the audit committee who are members of the board of directors to whom authority to grant such approvals has been delegated by the audit committee.

"(2) Disclosure to investors.—Approval by an audit committee of an issuer under this subsection of a non-audit service to be performed by the auditor of the issuer shall be disclosed to investors in periodic reports required by section 13(a).

"(3) Delegation authority.—The audit committee of an issuer may delegate to 1 or more designated members of the audit committee who are independent directors of the board of directors, the authority to grant preapprovals required by this subsection. The decisions of any member to whom authority is delegated under this paragraph to preapprove an activity under this subsection shall be presented to the full audit committee at each of its scheduled meetings.

"(4) Approval of audit services for other purposes.—In carrying out its duties under subsection (m)(2), if the audit committee of an issuer approves an audit service within the scope of the engagement of the auditor, such audit service shall be deemed to have been preapproved for purposes of this subsection.".

§ 203.   Audit Partner Rotation

Section 10A of the Securities Exchange Act of 1934 (15 U.S.C. 78j–1), as amended by this Act, is amended by adding at the end the following:

"(j) Audit Partner Rotation.—It shall be unlawful for a registered public accounting firm to provide audit services to an issuer if the lead (or coordinating) audit partner (having primary responsibility for the audit), or the audit partner responsible for reviewing the audit, has performed audit services for that issuer in each of the 5 previous fiscal years of that issuer.".

§ 204.   Auditor Reports to Audit Committees

Section 10A of the Securities Exchange Act of 1934 (15 U.S.C. 78j–1), as amended by this Act, is amended by adding at the end the following:

"(k) Reports to Audit Committees.—Each registered public accounting firm that performs for any issuer any audit required by this title shall timely report to the audit committee of the issuer—

"(1) all critical accounting policies and practices to be used;

"(2) all alternative treatments of financial information within generally accepted accounting principles that have been discussed with management officials of the issuer, ramifications of the use of such alternative disclosures and treatments, and the treatment preferred by the registered public accounting firm; and

"(3) other material written communications between the registered public accounting firm and the management of the issuer, such as any management letter or schedule of unadjusted differences.".

§ 205.   Conforming Amendments

(a) Definitions.—Section 3(a) of the Securities Exchange Act of 1934 (15 U.S.C. 78c(a)) is amended by adding at the end the following:

"(58) Audit committee.—The term 'audit committee' means—

"(A) a committee (or equivalent body) established by and amongst the board of directors of an issuer for the purpose of overseeing the accounting and financial reporting processes of the issuer and audits of the financial statements of the issuer; and

"(B) if no such committee exists with respect to an issuer, the entire board of directors of the issuer.

"(59) Registered public accounting firm.—The term 'registered public accounting firm' has the same meaning as in section 2 of the Sarbanes-Oxley Act of 2002.".

(b) Auditor Requirements.—Section 10A of the Securities Exchange Act of 1934 (15 U.S.C. 78j–1) is amended—

(1) by striking "an independent public accountant" each place that term appears and inserting "a registered public accounting firm";

(2) by striking "the independent public accountant" each place that term appears and inserting "the registered public accounting firm";

(3) in subsection (c), by striking "No independent public accountant" and inserting "No registered public accounting firm"; and

(4) in subsection (b)—

(A) by striking "the accountant" each place that term appears and inserting "the firm";

(B) by striking "such accountant" each place that term appears and inserting "such firm"; and

(C)   in paragraph (4), by striking "the accountant's report" and inserting "the report of the firm".

(c)   Other References.—The Securities Exchange Act of 1934 (15 U.S.C. 78a et seq.) is amended—

(1)   in section 12(b)(1) (15 U.S.C. 78*l*(b)(1)), by striking "independent public accountants" each place that term appears and inserting "a registered public accounting firm"; and

(2)   in subsections (e) and (i) of section 17 (15 U.S.C. 78q), by striking "an independent public accountant" each place that term appears and inserting "a registered public accounting firm".

(d)   Conforming Amendment.—Section 10A(f) of the Securities Exchange Act of 1934 (15 U.S.C. 78k(f)) is amended—

(1)   by striking "Definition" and inserting "Definitions"; and

(2)   by adding at the end the following: "As used in this section, the term 'issuer' means an issuer (as defined in section 3), the securities of which are registered under section 12, or that is required to file reports pursuant to section 15(d), or that files or has filed a registration statement that has not yet become effective under the Securities Act of 1933 (15 U.S.C. 77a et seq.), and that it has not withdrawn.".

§ 206.   Conflicts of Interest

Section 10A of the Securities Exchange Act of 1934 (15 U.S.C. 78j–1), as amended by this Act, is amended by adding at the end the following:

"(*l*) Conflicts of Interest.—It shall be unlawful for a registered public accounting firm to perform for an issuer any audit service required by this title, if a chief executive officer, controller, chief financial officer, chief accounting officer, or any person serving in an equivalent position for the issuer, was employed by that registered independent public accounting firm and participated in any capacity in the audit of that issuer during the 1-year period preceding the date of the initiation of the audit.".

§ 207.   Study of Mandatory Rotation of Registered Public Accounting Firms

(a)   Study and Review Required.—The Comptroller General of the United States shall conduct a study and review of the potential effects of requiring the mandatory rotation of registered public accounting firms.

(b)   Report Required.—Not later than 1 year after the date of enactment of this Act, the Comptroller General shall submit a report to the Committee on Banking, Housing, and Urban Affairs of the Senate and the Committee on Financial Services of the House of Representatives on the results of the study and review required by this section.

(c)   Definition.—For purposes of this section, the term "mandatory rotation" refers to the imposition of a limit on the period of years in which a particular registered public accounting firm may be the auditor of record for a particular issuer.

§ 208.   Commission Authority

(a)   Commission Regulations.—Not later than 180 days after the date of enactment of this Act, the Commission shall issue final regulations to carry out each of subsections (g) through (*l*) of section 10A of the Securities Exchange Act of 1934, as added by this title.

(b)   Auditor Independence.—It shall be unlawful for any registered public accounting firm (or an associated person thereof, as applicable) to prepare or issue any audit report with respect to any issuer, if the firm or associated person engages in any activity with respect to that issuer prohibited by any of subsections (g) through (*l*) of section 10A of the Securities Exchange Act of 1934, as added by this title, or any rule or regulation of the Commission or of the Board issued thereunder.

§ 209.   Considerations by Appropriate State Regulatory Authorities

In supervising nonregistered public accounting firms and their associated persons, appropriate State regulatory authorities should make an independent determination of the proper standards applicable, particularly taking into consideration the size and nature of the business of the accounting firms they supervise and the size and nature of the business of the clients of those firms. The standards applied by the Board under this Act should not be presumed to be applicable for purposes of this section for small and medium sized nonregistered public accounting firms.

TITLE III.   CORPORATE RESPONSIBILITY

§ 301.   Public Company Audit Committees

Section 10A of the Securities Exchange Act of 1934 (15 U.S.C. 78f) is amended by adding at the end the following:

"(m) Standards Relating to Audit Committees.—

"(1) Commission rules.—

"(A) In general.—Effective not later than 270 days after the date of enactment of this subsection, the Commission shall, by rule, direct the national securities exchanges and national securities associations to prohibit the listing of any security of an issuer that is not in compliance with the requirements of any portion of paragraphs (2) through (6).

"(B) Opportunity to cure defects.—The rules of the Commission under subparagraph (A) shall provide for appropriate procedures for an issuer to have an opportunity to cure any defects that would be the basis for a prohibition under subparagraph (A), before the imposition of such prohibition.

"(2) Responsibilities relating to registered public accounting firms.—The audit committee of each issuer, in its capacity as a committee of the board of directors, shall be directly responsible for the appointment, compensation, and oversight of the work of any registered public accounting firm employed by that issuer (including resolution of disagreements between management and the auditor regarding financial reporting) for the purpose of preparing or issuing an audit report or related work, and each such registered public accounting firm shall report directly to the audit committee.

"(3) Independence.—

"(A) In general.—Each member of the audit committee of the issuer shall be a member of the board of directors of the issuer, and shall otherwise be independent.

"(B) Criteria.—In order to be considered to be independent for purposes of this paragraph, a member of an audit committee of an issuer may not, other than in his or her capacity as a member of the audit committee, the board of directors, or any other board committee—

"(i)   accept any consulting, advisory, or other compensatory fee from the issuer; or

"(ii) be an affiliated person of the issuer or any subsidiary thereof.

"(C) Exemption authority.—The Commission may exempt from the requirements of subparagraph (B) a particular relationship with respect to audit committee members, as the Commission determines appropriate in light of the circumstances.

"(4) Complaints.—Each audit committee shall establish procedures for—

"(A) the receipt, retention, and treatment of complaints received by the issuer regarding accounting, internal accounting controls, or auditing matters; and

"(B) the confidential, anonymous submission by employees of the issuer of concerns regarding questionable accounting or auditing matters.

"(5) Authority to engage advisers.—Each audit committee shall have the authority to engage independent counsel and other advisers, as it determines necessary to carry out its duties.

"(6) Funding.—Each issuer shall provide for appropriate funding, as determined by the audit committee, in its capacity as a committee of the board of directors, for payment of compensation—

"(A) to the registered public accounting firm employed by the issuer for the purpose of rendering or issuing an audit report; and

"(B) to any advisers employed by the audit committee under paragraph (5).".

§ 302. Corporate Responsibility for Financial Reports

(a) Regulations Required.—The Commission shall, by rule, require, for each company filing periodic reports under section 13(a) or 15(d) of the Securities Exchange Act of 1934 (15 U.S.C. 78m, 78o(d)), that the principal executive officer or officers and the principal financial officer or officers, or persons performing similar functions, certify in each annual or quarterly report filed or submitted under either such section of such Act that—

(1) the signing officer has reviewed the report;

(2) based on the officer's knowledge, the report does not contain any untrue statement of a material fact or omit to state a material fact necessary in order to make the statements made, in light of the circumstances under which such statements were made, not misleading;

(3) based on such officer's knowledge, the financial statements, and other financial information included in the report, fairly present in all material respects the financial condition and results of operations of the issuer as of, and for, the periods presented in the report;

(4) the signing officers—

(A) are responsible for establishing and maintaining internal controls;

(B) have designed such internal controls to ensure that material information relating to the issuer and its consolidated subsidiaries is made known to such officers by others within those entities, particularly during the period in which the periodic reports are being prepared;

(C) have evaluated the effectiveness of the issuer's internal controls as of a date within 90 days prior to the report; and

(D) have presented in the report their conclusions about the effectiveness of their internal controls based on their evaluation as of that date;

(5) the signing officers have disclosed to the issuer's auditors and the audit committee of the board of directors (or persons fulfilling the equivalent function)—

(A) all significant deficiencies in the design or operation of internal controls which could adversely affect the issuer's ability to record, process, summarize, and report financial data and have identified for the issuer's auditors any material weaknesses in internal controls; and

(B) any fraud, whether or not material, that involves management or other employees who have a significant role in the issuer's internal controls; and

(6) the signing officers have indicated in the report whether or not there were significant changes in internal controls or in other factors that could significantly affect internal controls subsequent to the date of their evaluation, including any corrective actions with regard to significant deficiencies and material weaknesses.

(b) Foreign Reincorporations Have No Effect.—Nothing in this section 302 shall be interpreted or applied in any way to allow any issuer to lessen the legal force of the statement required under this section 302, by an issuer having reincorporated or having engaged in any other transaction that resulted in the transfer of the corporate domicile or offices of the issuer from inside the United States to outside of the United States.

(c) Deadline.—The rules required by subsection (a) shall be effective not later than 30 days after the date of enactment of this Act.

§ 303.   Improper Influence on Conduct of Audits

(a) Rules To Prohibit.—It shall be unlawful, in contravention of such rules or regulations as the Commission shall prescribe as necessary and appropriate in the public interest or for the protection of investors, for any officer or director of an issuer, or any other person acting under the direction thereof, to take any action to fraudulently influence, coerce, manipulate, or mislead any independent public or certified accountant engaged in the performance of an audit of the financial statements of that issuer for the purpose of rendering such financial statements materially misleading.

(b) Enforcement.—In any civil proceeding, the Commission shall have exclusive authority to enforce this section and any rule or regulation issued under this section.

(c) No Preemption of Other Law.—The provisions of subsection (a) shall be in addition to, and shall not supersede or preempt, any other provision of law or any rule or regulation issued thereunder.

(d) Deadline for Rulemaking.—The Commission shall—

(1) propose the rules or regulations required by this section, not later than 90 days after the date of enactment of this Act; and

(2) issue final rules or regulations required by this section, not later than 270 days after that date of enactment.

§ 304.   Forfeiture of Certain Bonuses and Profits

(a) Additional Compensation Prior to Noncompliance with Commission Financial Reporting Requirements.—If an issuer is required to prepare an accounting restatement due to the material noncompliance of the issuer, as a result of misconduct, with any financial reporting requirement under the securities laws, the chief executive officer and chief financial officer of the issuer shall reimburse the issuer for—

(1) any bonus or other incentive-based or equity-based compensation received by that person from the issuer during the 12-month period following the first public issuance or filing with the Commission (whichever first occurs) of the financial document embodying such financial reporting requirement; and

(2) any profits realized from the sale of securities of the issuer during that 12-month period.

(b) Commission Exemption Authority.—The Commission may exempt any person from the application of subsection (a), as it deems necessary and appropriate.

§ 305.   Officer and Director Bars and Penalties

(a) Unfitness Standard.—

(1) Securities exchange act of 1934.—Section 21(d)(2) of the Securities Exchange Act of 1934 (15 U.S.C. 78u(d)(2)) is amended by striking "substantial unfitness" and inserting "unfitness".

(2) Securities act of 1933.—Section 20(e) of the Securities Act of 1933 (15 U.S.C. 77t(e)) is amended by striking "substantial unfitness" and inserting "unfitness".

(b) Equitable Relief.—Section 21(d) of the Securities Exchange Act of 1934 (15 U.S.C. 78u(d)) is amended by adding at the end the following:

"(5) Equitable Relief.—In any action or proceeding brought or instituted by the Commission under any provision of the securities laws, the Commission may seek, and any Federal court may grant, any equitable relief that may be appropriate or necessary for the benefit of investors.".

§ 306.   Insider Trades During Pension Fund Blackout Periods

(a)   Prohibition of Insider Trading During Pension Fund Blackout Periods.—

(1)   In general.—Except to the extent otherwise provided by rule of the Commission pursuant to paragraph (3), it shall be unlawful for any director or executive officer of an issuer of any equity security (other than an exempted security), directly or indirectly, to purchase, sell, or otherwise acquire or transfer any equity security of the issuer (other than an exempted security) during any blackout period with respect to such equity security if such director or officer acquires such equity security in connection with his or her service or employment as a director or executive officer.

(2)   Remedy.—

(A)   In general.—Any profit realized by a director or executive officer referred to in paragraph (1) from any purchase, sale, or other acquisition or transfer in violation of this subsection shall inure to and be recoverable by the issuer, irrespective of any intention on the part of such director or executive officer in entering into the transaction.

(B)   Actions to recover profits.—An action to recover profits in accordance with this subsection may be instituted at law or in equity in any court of competent jurisdiction by the issuer, or by the owner of any security of the issuer in the name and in behalf of the issuer if the issuer fails or refuses to bring such action within 60 days after the date of request, or fails diligently to prosecute the action thereafter, except that no such suit shall be brought more than 2 years after the date on which such profit was realized.

(3)   Rulemaking Authorized.—The Commission shall, in consultation with the Secretary of Labor, issue rules to clarify the application of this subsection and to prevent evasion thereof. Such rules shall provide for the application of the requirements of paragraph (1) with respect to entities treated as a single employer with respect to an issuer under section 414(b), (c), (m), or (o) of the Internal Revenue Code of 1986 to the extent necessary to clarify the application of such requirements and to prevent evasion thereof. Such rules may also provide for appropriate exceptions from the requirements of this subsection, including exceptions for purchases pursuant to an automatic dividend reinvestment program or purchases or sales made pursuant to an advance election.

(4)   Blackout period.—For purposes of this subsection, the term "blackout period", with respect to the equity securities of any issuer—

(A)   means any period of more than 3 consecutive business days during which the ability of not fewer than 50 percent of the participants or beneficiaries under all individual account plans maintained by the issuer to purchase, sell, or otherwise acquire or transfer an interest in any equity of such issuer held in such an individual account plan is temporarily suspended by the issuer or by a fiduciary of the plan; and

(B)   does not include, under regulations which shall be prescribed by the Commission—

(i)   a regularly scheduled period in which the participants and beneficiaries may not purchase, sell, or otherwise acquire or transfer an interest in any equity of such issuer, if such period is—

(I)   incorporated into the individual account plan; and

(II)   timely disclosed to employees before becoming participants under the individual account plan or as a subsequent amendment to the plan; or

(ii)   any suspension described in subparagraph

(A)   that is imposed solely in connection with persons becoming participants or beneficiaries, or ceasing to be participants or beneficiaries, in an individual account plan by reason of a corporate merger, acquisition, divestiture, or similar transaction involving the plan or plan sponsor.

(5)   Individual account plan.—For purposes of this subsection, the term "individual account plan" has the meaning provided in section 3(34) of the Employee Retirement Income Security Act of

1974 (29 U.S.C. 1002(34), except that such term shall not include a one-participant retirement plan (within the meaning of section 101(i)(8)(B) of such Act (29 U.S.C. 1021(i)(8)(B)).

(6)   Notice to directors, executive officers, and the commission.—In any case in which a director or executive officer is subject to the requirements of this subsection in connection with a blackout period (as defined in paragraph (4)) with respect to any equity securities, the issuer of such equity securities shall timely notify such director or officer and the Securities and Exchange Commission of such blackout period.

(b)   Notice Requirements to Participants and Beneficiaries under ERISA.—

(1)   In general.—Section 101 of the Employee Retirement Income Security Act of 1974 (29 U.S.C. 1021) is amended by redesignating the second subsection (h) as subsection (j), and by inserting after the first subsection (h) the following new subsection:

"(i)   Notice of Blackout Periods to Participant or Beneficiary Under Individual Account Plan.—

"(1)   Duties of plan administrator.—In advance of the commencement of any blackout period with respect to an individual account plan, the plan administrator shall notify the plan participants and beneficiaries who are affected by such action in accordance with this subsection.

"(2)   Notice requirements.—

"(A)   In general.—The notices described in paragraph (1) shall be written in a manner calculated to be understood by the average plan participant and shall include—

"(i)   the reasons for the blackout period,

"(ii)   an identification of the investments and other rights affected,

"(iii)   the expected beginning date and length of the blackout period,

"(iv)   in the case of investments affected, a statement that the participant or beneficiary should evaluate the appropriateness of their current investment decisions in light of their inability to direct or diversify assets credited to their accounts during the blackout period, and

"(v)   such other matters as the Secretary may require by regulation.

"(B)   Notice to participants and beneficiaries.—Except as otherwise provided in this subsection, notices described in paragraph (1) shall be furnished to all participants and beneficiaries under the plan to whom the blackout period applies at least 30 days in advance of the blackout period.

"(C)   Exception to 30-day notice requirement.—In any case in which—

"(i)   a deferral of the blackout period would violate the requirements of subparagraph (A) or (B) of section 404(a)(1), and a fiduciary of the plan reasonably so determines in writing, or

"(ii)   the inability to provide the 30-day advance notice is due to events that were unforeseeable or circumstances beyond the reasonable control of the plan administrator, and a fiduciary of the plan reasonably so determines in writing, subparagraph (B) shall not apply, and the notice shall be furnished to all participants and beneficiaries under the plan to whom the blackout period applies as soon as reasonably possible under the circumstances unless such a notice in advance of the termination of the blackout period is impracticable.

"(D)   Written notice.—The notice required to be provided under this subsection shall be in writing, except that such notice may be in electronic or other form to the extent that such form is reasonably accessible to the recipient.

"(E) Notice to issuers of employer securities subject to blackout period.—In the case of any blackout period in connection with an individual account plan, the plan administrator shall provide timely notice of such blackout period to the issuer of any employer securities subject to such blackout period.

"(3) Exception for blackout periods with limited applicability.—In any case in which the blackout period applies only to 1 or more participants or beneficiaries in connection with a merger, acquisition, divestiture, or similar transaction involving the plan or plan sponsor and occurs solely in connection with becoming or ceasing to be a participant or beneficiary under the plan by reason of such merger, acquisition, divestiture, or transaction, the requirement of this subsection that the notice be provided to all participants and beneficiaries shall be treated as met if the notice required under paragraph (1) is provided to such participants or beneficiaries to whom the blackout period applies as soon as reasonably practicable.

"(4) Changes in length of blackout period.—If, following the furnishing of the notice pursuant to this subsection, there is a change in the beginning date or length of the blackout period (specified in such notice pursuant to paragraph (2)(A)(iii)), the administrator shall provide affected participants and beneficiaries notice of the change as soon as reasonably practicable. In relation to the extended blackout period, such notice shall meet the requirements of paragraph (2)(D) and shall specify any material change in the matters referred to in clauses (i) through (v) of paragraph (2)(A).

"(5) Regulatory exceptions.—The Secretary may provide by regulation for additional exceptions to the requirements of this subsection which the Secretary determines are in the interests of participants and beneficiaries.

"(6) Guidance and model notices.—The Secretary shall issue guidance and model notices which meet the requirements of this subsection.

"(7) Blackout period.—For purposes of this subsection—

"(A) In general.—The term 'blackout period' means, in connection with an individual account plan, any period for which any ability of participants or beneficiaries under the plan, which is otherwise available under the terms of such plan, to direct or diversify assets credited to their accounts, to obtain loans from the plan, or to obtain distributions from the plan is temporarily suspended, limited, or restricted, if such suspension, limitation, or restriction is for any period of more than 3 consecutive business days.

"(B) Exclusions.—The term 'blackout period' does not include a suspension, limitation, or restriction—

"(i) which occurs by reason of the application of the securities laws (as defined in section 3(a)(47) of the Securities Exchange Act of 1934),

"(ii) which is a change to the plan which provides for a regularly scheduled suspension, limitation, or restriction which is disclosed to participants or beneficiaries through any summary of material modifications, any materials describing specific investment alternatives under the plan, or any changes thereto, or

"(iii) which applies only to 1 or more individuals, each of whom is the participant, an alternate payee (as defined in section 206(d)(3)(K)), or any other beneficiary pursuant to a qualified domestic relations order (as defined in section 206(d)(3)(B)(i)).

"(8) Individual account plan.—

"(A) In general.—For purposes of this subsection, the term 'individual account plan' shall have the meaning provided such term in section 3(34), except that such term shall not include a one-participant retirement plan.

"(B) One-participant retirement plan.—For purposes of subparagraph (A), the term 'one-participant retirement plan' means a retirement plan that—

"(i) on the first day of the plan year—

"(I) covered only the employer (and the employer's spouse) and the employer owned the entire business (whether or not incorporated), or

"(II) covered only one or more partners (and their spouses) in a business partnership (including partners in an S or C corporation (as defined in section 1361(a) of the Internal Revenue Code of 1986)),

"(ii) meets the minimum coverage requirements of section 410(b) of the Internal Revenue Code of 1986 (as in effect on the date of the enactment of this paragraph) without being combined with any other plan of the business that covers the employees of the business,

"(iii) does not provide benefits to anyone except the employer (and the employer's spouse) or the partners (and their spouses),

"(iv) does not cover a business that is a member of an affiliated service group, a controlled group of corporations, or a group of businesses under common control, and

"(v) does not cover a business that leases employees.".

(2) Issuance of initial guidance and model notice.—The Secretary of Labor shall issue initial guidance and a model notice pursuant to section 101(i)(6) of the Employee Retirement Income Security Act of 1974 (as added by this subsection) not later than January 1, 2003. Not later than 75 days after the date of the enactment of this Act, the Secretary shall promulgate interim final rules necessary to carry out the amendments made by this subsection.

(3) Civil penalties for failure to provide notice.—Section 502 of such Act (29 U.S.C. 1132) is amended—

(A) in subsection (a)(6), by striking "(5), or (6)" and inserting "(5), (6), or (7)";

(B) by redesignating paragraph (7) of subsection (c) as paragraph (8); and

(C) by inserting after paragraph (6) of subsection (c) the following new paragraph:

"(7) The Secretary may assess a civil penalty against a plan administrator of up to $100 a day from the date of the plan administrator's failure or refusal to provide notice to participants and beneficiaries in accordance with section 101(i). For purposes of this paragraph, each violation with respect to any single participant or beneficiary shall be treated as a separate violation.".

(3) Plan amendments.—If any amendment made by this subsection requires an amendment to any plan, such plan amendment shall not be required to be made before the first plan year beginning on or after the effective date of this section, if—

(A) during the period after such amendment made by this subsection takes effect and before such first plan year, the plan is operated in good faith compliance with the requirements of such amendment made by this subsection, and

(B) such plan amendment applies retroactively to the period after such amendment made by this subsection takes effect and before such first plan year.

(c) Effective Date.—The provisions of this section (including the amendments made thereby) shall take effect 180 days after the date of the enactment of this Act. Good faith compliance with the requirements of such provisions in advance of the issuance of applicable regulations thereunder shall be treated as compliance with such provisions.

§ 307. Rules of Professional Responsibility for Attorneys

Not later than 180 days after the date of enactment of this Act, the Commission shall issue rules, in the public interest and for the protection of investors, setting forth minimum standards of professional conduct for attorneys appearing and practicing before the Commission in any way in the representation of issuers, including a rule—

(1) requiring an attorney to report evidence of a material violation of securities law or breach of fiduciary duty or similar violation by the company or any agent thereof, to the chief legal counsel or the chief executive officer of the company (or the equivalent thereof); and

(2) if the counsel or officer does not appropriately respond to the evidence (adopting, as necessary, appropriate remedial measures or sanctions with respect to the violation), requiring the attorney to report the evidence to the audit committee of the board of directors of the issuer or to another committee of the board of directors comprised solely of directors not employed directly or indirectly by the issuer, or to the board of directors.

§ 308. Fair Funds for Investors

(a) Civil Penalties Added to Disgorgement Funds for the Relief of Victims.—If in any judicial or administrative action brought by the Commission under the securities laws (as such term is defined in section 3(a)(47) of the Securities Exchange Act of 1934 (15 U.S.C. 78c(a)(47))) the Commission obtains an order requiring disgorgement against any person for a violation of such laws or the rules or regulations thereunder, or such person agrees in settlement of any such action to such disgorgement, and the Commission also obtains pursuant to such laws a civil penalty against such person, the amount of such civil penalty shall, on the motion or at the direction of the Commission, be added to and become part of the disgorgement fund for the benefit of the victims of such violation.

(b) Acceptance of Additional Donations.—The Commission is authorized to accept, hold, administer, and utilize gifts, bequests and devises of property, both real and personal, to the United States for a disgorgement fund described in subsection (a). Such gifts, bequests, and devises of money and proceeds from sales of other property received as gifts, bequests, or devises shall be deposited in the disgorgement fund and shall be available for allocation in accordance with subsection (a).

(c) Study Required.—

(1) Subject of study.—The Commission shall review and analyze—

(A) enforcement actions by the Commission over the five years preceding the date of the enactment of this Act that have included proceedings to obtain civil penalties or disgorgements to identify areas where such proceedings may be utilized to efficiently, effectively, and fairly provide restitution for injured investors; and

(B) other methods to more efficiently, effectively, and fairly provide restitution to injured investors, including methods to improve the collection rates for civil penalties and disgorgements.

(2) Report Required.—The Commission shall report its findings to the Committee on Financial Services of the House of Representatives and the Committee on Banking, Housing, and Urban Affairs of the Senate within 180 days after of the date of the enactment of this Act, and shall use such findings to revise its rules and regulations as necessary. The report shall include a discussion of regulatory or legislative actions that are recommended or that may be necessary to address concerns identified in the study.

(d) Conforming Amendments.—Each of the following provisions is amended by inserting ", except as otherwise provided in section 308 of the Sarbanes-Oxley Act of 2002" after "Treasury of the United States":

(1) Section 21(d)(3)(C)(i) of the Securities Exchange Act of 1934 (15 U.S.C. 78u(d)(3)(C)(i)).

(2) Section 21A(d)(1) of such Act (15 U.S.C. 78u–1(d)(1)).

(3) Section 20(d)(3)(A) of the Securities Act of 1933 (15 U.S.C. 77t(d)(3)(A)).

(4) Section 42(e)(3)(A) of the Investment Company Act of 1940 (15 U.S.C. 80a–41(e)(3)(A)).

(5)   Section 209(e)(3)(A) of the Investment Advisers Act of 1940 (15 U.S.C. 80b–9(e)(3)(A)).

(e)   Definition.—As used in this section, the term "disgorgement fund" means a fund established in any administrative or judicial proceeding described in subsection (a).

TITLE IV.   ENHANCED FINANCIAL DISCLOSURES

§ 401.   Disclosures in Periodic Reports

(a)   Disclosures Required.—Section 13 of the Securities Exchange Act of 1934 (15 U.S.C. 78m) is amended by adding at the end the following:

"(i)   Accuracy of Financial Reports.—Each financial report that contains financial statements, and that is required to be prepared in accordance with (or reconciled to) generally accepted accounting principles under this title and filed with the Commission shall reflect all material correcting adjustments that have been identified by a registered public accounting firm in accordance with generally accepted accounting principles and the rules and regulations of the Commission.

"(j)   Off-Balance Sheet Transactions.—Not later than 180 days after the date of enactment of the Sarbanes-Oxley Act of 2002, the Commission shall issue final rules providing that each annual and quarterly financial report required to be filed with the Commission shall disclose all material off-balance sheet transactions, arrangements, obligations (including contingent obligations), and other relationships of the issuer with unconsolidated entities or other persons, that may have a material current or future effect on financial condition, changes in financial condition, results of operations, liquidity, capital expenditures, capital resources, or significant components of revenues or expenses.".

(b)   Commission Rules on Pro Forma Figures.—Not later than 180 days after the date of enactment of the Sarbanes-Oxley Act of 2002, the Commission shall issue final rules providing that pro forma financial information included in any periodic or other report filed with the Commission pursuant to the securities laws, or in any public disclosure or press or other release, shall be presented in a manner that—

(1)   does not contain an untrue statement of a material fact or omit to state a material fact necessary in order to make the pro forma financial information, in light of the circumstances under which it is presented, not misleading; and

(2)   reconciles it with the financial condition and results of operations of the issuer under generally accepted accounting principles.

(c)   Study and Report on Special Purpose Entities.—

(1)   Study required.—The Commission shall, not later than 1 year after the effective date of adoption of off-balance sheet disclosure rules required by section 13(j) of the Securities Exchange Act of 1934, as added by this section, complete a study of filings by issuers and their disclosures to determine—

(A)   the extent of off-balance sheet transactions, including assets, liabilities, leases, losses, and the use of special purpose entities; and

(B)   whether generally accepted accounting rules result in financial statements of issuers reflecting the economics of such off-balance sheet transactions to investors in a transparent fashion.

(2)   Report and recommendations.—Not later than 6 months after the date of completion of the study required by paragraph (1), the Commission shall submit a report to the President, the Committee on Banking, Housing, and Urban Affairs of the Senate, and the Committee on Financial Services of the House of Representatives, setting forth—

(A)   the amount or an estimate of the amount of off-balance sheet transactions, including assets, liabilities, leases, and losses of, and the use of special purpose entities by, issuers filing periodic reports pursuant to section 13 or 15 of the Securities Exchange Act of 1934;

(B)   the extent to which special purpose entities are used to facilitate off-balance sheet transactions;

(C) whether generally accepted accounting principles or the rules of the Commission result in financial statements of issuers reflecting the economics of such transactions to investors in a transparent fashion;

(D) whether generally accepted accounting principles specifically result in the consolidation of special purpose entities sponsored by an issuer in cases in which the issuer has the majority of the risks and rewards of the special purpose entity; and

(E) any recommendations of the Commission for improving the transparency and quality of reporting off-balance sheet transactions in the financial statements and disclosures required to be filed by an issuer with the Commission.

§ 402. Enhanced Conflict of Interest Provisions

(a) Prohibition on Personal Loans to Executives.—Section 13 of the Securities Exchange Act of 1934 (15 U.S.C. 78m), as amended by this Act, is amended by adding at the end the following:

"(k) Prohibition on Personal Loans to Executives.—

"(1) In general.—It shall be unlawful for any issuer (as defined in section 2 of the Sarbanes-Oxley Act of 2002), directly or indirectly, including through any subsidiary, to extend or maintain credit, to arrange for the extension of credit, or to renew an extension of credit, in the form of a personal loan to or for any director or executive officer (or equivalent thereof) of that issuer. An extension of credit maintained by the issuer on the date of enactment of this subsection shall not be subject to the provisions of this subsection, provided that there is no material modification to any term of any such extension of credit or any renewal of any such extension of credit on or after that date of enactment.

"(2) Limitation.—Paragraph (1) does not preclude any home improvement and manufactured home loans (as that term is defined in section 5 of the Home Owners' Loan Act (12 U.S.C. 1464)), consumer credit (as defined in section 103 of the Truth in Lending Act (15 U.S.C. 1602)), or any extension of credit under an open end credit plan (as defined in section 103 of the Truth in Lending Act (15 U.S.C. 1602)), or a charge card (as defined in section 127(c)(4)(e) of the Truth in Lending Act (15 U.S.C. 1637(c)(4)(e)), or any extension of credit by a broker or dealer registered under section 15 of this title to an employee of that broker or dealer to buy, trade, or carry securities, that is permitted under rules or regulations of the Board of Governors of the Federal Reserve System pursuant to section 7 of this title (other than an extension of credit that would be used to purchase the stock of that issuer), that is—

"(A) made or provided in the ordinary course of the consumer credit business of such issuer;

"(B) of a type that is generally made available by such issuer to the public; and

"(C) made by such issuer on market terms, or terms that are no more favorable than those offered by the issuer to the general public for such extensions of credit.

"(3) Rule of construction for certain loans.—Paragraph (1) does not apply to any loan made or maintained by an insured depository institution (as defined in section 3 of the Federal Deposit Insurance Act (12 U.S.C. 1813)), if the loan is subject to the insider lending restrictions of section 22(h) of the Federal Reserve Act (12 U.S.C. 375b).".

§ 403. Disclosures of Transactions Involving Management and Principal Stockholders

(a) Amendment.—Section 16 of the Securities Exchange Act of 1934 (15 U.S.C. 78p) is amended by striking the heading of such section and subsection (a) and inserting the following:

"§ 16. Directors, Officers, and Principal Stockholders.

"(a) Disclosures Required.—

"(1) Directors, officers, and principal stockholders required to file.—Every person who is directly or indirectly the beneficial owner of more than 10 percent of any class of any equity security (other than an exempted security) which is registered pursuant to section 12, or who is a director or an officer of the issuer of such security, shall file the statements required by this subsection with the Commission (and, if such security is registered on a national securities exchange, also with the exchange).

"(2) Time of filing.—The statements required by this subsection shall be filed—

"(A) at the time of the registration of such security on a national securities exchange or by the effective date of a registration statement filed pursuant to section 12(g);

"(B) within 10 days after he or she becomes such beneficial owner, director, or officer;

"(C) if there has been a change in such ownership, or if such person shall have purchased or sold a security-based swap agreement (as defined in section 206(b) of the Gramm-Leach-Bliley Act (15 U.S.C. 78c note)) involving such equity security, before the end of the second business day following the day on which the subject transaction has been executed, or at such other time as the Commission shall establish, by rule, in any case in which the Commission determines that such 2-day period is not feasible.

"(3) Contents of statements.—A statement filed—

"(A) under subparagraph (A) or (B) of paragraph (2) shall contain a statement of the amount of all equity securities of such issuer of which the filing person is the beneficial owner; and

"(B) under subparagraph (C) of such paragraph shall indicate ownership by the filing person at the date of filing, any such changes in such ownership, and such purchases and sales of the security-based swap agreements as have occurred since the most recent such filing under such subparagraph.

"(4) Electronic filing and availability.—Beginning not later than 1 year after the date of enactment of the Sarbanes-Oxley Act of 2002—

"(A) a statement filed under subparagraph (C) of paragraph (2) shall be filed electronically;

"(B) the Commission shall provide each such statement on a publicly accessible Internet site not later than the end of the business day following that filing; and

"(C) the issuer (if the issuer maintains a corporate website) shall provide that statement on that corporate website, not later than the end of the business day following that filing.".

(b) Effective Date.—The amendment made by this section shall be effective 30 days after the date of the enactment of this Act.

§ 404.   Management Assessment of Internal Controls

(a) Rules Required.—The Commission shall prescribe rules requiring each annual report required by section 13(a) or 15(d) of the Securities Exchange Act of 1934 (15 U.S.C. 78m or 78o(d)) to contain an internal control report, which shall—

(1) state the responsibility of management for establishing and maintaining an adequate internal control structure and procedures for financial reporting; and

(2) contain an assessment, as of the end of the most recent fiscal year of the issuer, of the effectiveness of the internal control structure and procedures of the issuer for financial reporting.

(b) Internal Control Evaluation and Reporting.—With respect to the internal control assessment required by subsection (a), each registered public accounting firm that prepares or issues the audit report for the issuer shall attest to, and report on, the assessment made by the management of the issuer. An attestation made under this subsection shall be made in accordance with standards for attestation engagements issued or adopted by the Board. Any such attestation shall not be the subject of a separate engagement.

§ 405. Exemption

Nothing in section 401, 402, or 404, the amendments made by those sections, or the rules of the Commission under those sections shall apply to any investment company registered under section 8 of the Investment Company Act of 1940 (15 U.S.C. 80a–8).

§ 406. Code of Ethics for Senior Financial Officers

(a) Code of Ethics Disclosure.—The Commission shall issue rules to require each issuer, together with periodic reports required pursuant to section 13(a) or 15(d) of the Securities Exchange Act of 1934, to disclose whether or not, and if not, the reason therefor, such issuer has adopted a code of ethics for senior financial officers, applicable to its principal financial officer and comptroller or principal accounting officer, or persons performing similar functions.

(b) Changes in Codes of Ethics.—The Commission shall revise its regulations concerning matters requiring prompt disclosure on Form 8-K (or any successor thereto) to require the immediate disclosure, by means of the filing of such form, dissemination by the Internet or by other electronic means, by any issuer of any change in or waiver of the code of ethics for senior financial officers.

(c) Definition.—In this section, the term "code of ethics" means such standards as are reasonably necessary to promote—

(1) honest and ethical conduct, including the ethical handling of actual or apparent conflicts of interest between personal and professional relationships;

(2) full, fair, accurate, timely, and understandable disclosure in the periodic reports required to be filed by the issuer; and

(3) compliance with applicable governmental rules and regulations.

(d) Deadline for Rulemaking.—The Commission shall—

(1) propose rules to implement this section, not later than 90 days after the date of enactment of this Act; and

(2) issue final rules to implement this section, not later than 180 days after that date of enactment.

§ 407. Disclosure of Audit Committee Financial Expert

(a) Rules Defining "Financial Expert".—The Commission shall issue rules, as necessary or appropriate in the public interest and consistent with the protection of investors, to require each issuer, together with periodic reports required pursuant to sections 13(a) and 15(d) of the Securities Exchange Act of 1934, to disclose whether or not, and if not, the reasons therefor, the audit committee of that issuer is comprised of at least 1 member who is a financial expert, as such term is defined by the Commission.

(b) Considerations.—In defining the term "financial expert" for purposes of subsection (a), the Commission shall consider whether a person has, through education and experience as a public accountant or auditor or a principal financial officer, comptroller, or principal accounting officer of an issuer, or from a position involving the performance of similar functions—

(1) an understanding of generally accepted accounting principles and financial statements;

(2) experience in—

(A) the preparation or auditing of financial statements of generally comparable issuers; and

(B) the application of such principles in connection with the accounting for estimates, accruals, and reserves;

(3) experience with internal accounting controls; and

(4) an understanding of audit committee functions.

(c)   Deadline for Rulemaking.—The Commission shall—

(1)   propose rules to implement this section, not later than 90 days after the date of enactment of this Act; and

(2)   issue final rules to implement this section, not later than 180 days after that date of enactment.

§ 408.   Enhanced Review of Periodic Disclosures by Issuers

(a)   Regular and Systematic Review.—The Commission shall review disclosures made by issuers reporting under section 13(a) of the Securities Exchange Act of 1934 (including reports filed on Form 10-K), and which have a class of securities listed on a national securities exchange or traded on an automated quotation facility of a national securities association, on a regular and systematic basis for the protection of investors. Such review shall include a review of an issuer's financial statement.

(b)   Review Criteria.—For purposes of scheduling the reviews required by subsection (a), the Commission shall consider, among other factors—

(1)   issuers that have issued material restatements of financial results;

(2)   issuers that experience significant volatility in their stock price as compared to other issuers;

(3)   issuers with the largest market capitalization;

(4)   emerging companies with disparities in price to earning[s] ratios;

(5)   issuers whose operations significantly affect any material sector of the economy; and

(6)   any other factors that the Commission may consider relevant.

(c)   Minimum Review Period.—In no event shall an issuer required to file reports under section 13(a) or 15(d) of the Securities Exchange Act of 1934 be reviewed under this section less frequently than once every 3 years.

§ 409.   Real Time Issuer Disclosures

Section 13 of the Securities Exchange Act of 1934 (15 U.S.C. 78m), as amended by this Act, is amended by adding at the end the following:

"(*l*) Real Time Issuer Disclosures.—Each issuer reporting under section 13(a) or 15(d) shall disclose to the public on a rapid and current basis such additional information concerning material changes in the financial condition or operations of the issuer, in plain English, which may include trend and qualitative information and graphic presentations, as the Commission determines, by rule, is necessary or useful for the protection of investors and in the public interest.".

TITLE V.   ANALYST CONFLICTS OF INTEREST

§ 501.   Treatment of Securities Analysts by Registered Securities Associations and National Securities Exchanges

(a)   Rules Regarding Securities Analysts.—The Securities Exchange Act of 1934 (15 U.S.C. 78a et seq.) is amended by inserting after section 15C the following new section:

"Sec. 15D. Securities Analysts and Research Reports.

"(a) Analyst Protections.—The Commission, or upon the authorization and direction of the Commission, a registered securities association or national securities exchange, shall have adopted, not later than 1 year after the date of enactment of this section, rules reasonably designed to address conflicts of interest that can arise when securities analysts recommend equity securities in research reports and public appearances, in order to improve the objectivity of research and provide investors with more useful and reliable information, including rules designed—

"(1) to foster greater public confidence in securities research, and to protect the objectivity and independence of securities analysts, by—

"(A) restricting the prepublication clearance or approval of research reports by persons employed by the broker or dealer who are engaged in investment banking activities, or persons not directly responsible for investment research, other than legal or compliance staff;

"(B) limiting the supervision and compensatory evaluation of securities analysts to officials employed by the broker or dealer who are not engaged in investment banking activities; and

"(C) requiring that a broker or dealer and persons employed by a broker or dealer who are involved with investment banking activities may not, directly or indirectly, retaliate against or threaten to retaliate against any securities analyst employed by that broker or dealer or its affiliates as a result of an adverse, negative, or otherwise unfavorable research report that may adversely affect the present or prospective investment banking relationship of the broker or dealer with the issuer that is the subject of the research report, except that such rules may not limit the authority of a broker or dealer to discipline a securities analyst for causes other than such research report in accordance with the policies and procedures of the firm;

"(2) to define periods during which brokers or dealers who have participated, or are to participate, in a public offering of securities as underwriters or dealers should not publish or otherwise distribute research reports relating to such securities or to the issuer of such securities;

"(3) to establish structural and institutional safeguards within registered brokers or dealers to assure that securities analysts are separated by appropriate informational partitions within the firm from the review, pressure, or oversight of those whose involvement in investment banking activities might potentially bias their judgment or supervision; and

"(4) to address such other issues as the Commission, or such association or exchange, determines appropriate.

"(b) Disclosure.—The Commission, or upon the authorization and direction of the Commission, a registered securities association or national securities exchange, shall have adopted, not later than 1 year after the date of enactment of this section, rules reasonably designed to require each securities analyst to disclose in public appearances, and each registered broker or dealer to disclose in each research report, as applicable, conflicts of interest that are known or should have been known by the securities analyst or the broker or dealer, to exist at the time of the appearance or the date of distribution of the report, including—

"(1) the extent to which the securities analyst has debt or equity investments in the issuer that is the subject of the appearance or research report;

"(2) whether any compensation has been received by the registered broker or dealer, or any affiliate thereof, including the securities analyst, from the issuer that is the subject of the appearance or research report, subject to such exemptions as the Commission may determine appropriate and necessary to prevent disclosure by virtue of this paragraph of material non-public information regarding specific potential future investment banking transactions of such issuer, as is appropriate in the public interest and consistent with the protection of investors;

"(3) whether an issuer, the securities of which are recommended in the appearance or research report, currently is, or during the 1-year period preceding the date of the appearance or date of distribution of the report has been, a client of the registered broker or dealer, and if so, stating the types of services provided to the issuer;

"(4) whether the securities analyst received compensation with respect to a research report, based upon (among any other factors) the investment banking revenues (either generally or specifically earned from the issuer being analyzed) of the registered broker or dealer; and

"(5) such other disclosures of conflicts of interest that are material to investors, research analysts, or the broker or dealer as the Commission, or such association or exchange, determines appropriate.

"(c) Definitions.—In this section—

"(1) the term 'securities analyst' means any associated person of a registered broker or dealer that is principally responsible for, and any associated person who reports directly or indirectly to a securities analyst in connection with, the preparation of the substance of a research report, whether or not any such person has the job title of 'securities analyst'; and

"(2) the term 'research report' means a written or electronic communication that includes an analysis of equity securities of individual companies or industries, and that provides information reasonably sufficient upon which to base an investment decision.".

(b) Enforcement.—Section 21B(a) of the Securities Exchange Act of 1934 (15 U.S.C. 78u–2(a)) is amended by inserting "15D," before "15B".

(c) Commission Authority.—The Commission may promulgate and amend its regulations, or direct a registered securities association or national securities exchange to promulgate and amend its rules, to carry out section 15D of the Securities Exchange Act of 1934, as added by this section, as is necessary for the protection of investors and in the public interest.

TITLE VI. COMMISSION RESOURCES AND AUTHORITY

§ 601. Authorization of Appropriations

Section 35 of the Securities Exchange Act of 1934 (15 U.S.C. 78kk) is amended to read as follows:

"Sec. 35. Authorization of Appropriations.

"In addition to any other funds authorized to be appropriated to the Commission, there are authorized to be appropriated to carry out the functions, powers, and duties of the Commission, $776,000,000 for fiscal year 2003, of which—

"(1) $102,700,000 shall be available to fund additional compensation, including salaries and benefits, as authorized in the Investor and Capital Markets Fee Relief Act (Public Law 107–123; 115 Stat. 2390 et seq.);

"(2) $108,400,000 shall be available for information technology, security enhancements, and recovery and mitigation activities in light of the terrorist attacks of September 11, 2001; and

"(3) $98,000,000 shall be available to add not fewer than an additional 200 qualified professionals to provide enhanced oversight of auditors and audit services required by the Federal securities laws, and to improve Commission investigative and disciplinary efforts with respect to such auditors and services, as well as for additional professional support staff necessary to strengthen the programs of the Commission involving Full Disclosure and Prevention and Suppression of Fraud, risk management, industry technology review, compliance, inspections, examinations, market regulation, and investment management.".

§ 602. Appearance and Practice Before the Commission

The Securities Exchange Act of 1934 (15 U.S.C. 78a et seq.) is amended by inserting after section 4B the following:

"Sec. 4c. Appearance and Practice Before the Commission.

"(a) Authority To Censure.—The Commission may censure any person, or deny, temporarily or permanently, to any person the privilege of appearing or practicing before the Commission in any way, if that person is found by the Commission, after notice and opportunity for hearing in the matter—

"(1) not to possess the requisite qualifications to represent others;

"(2) to be lacking in character or integrity, or to have engaged in unethical or improper professional conduct; or

"(3) to have willfully violated, or willfully aided and abetted the violation of, any provision of the securities laws or the rules and regulations issued thereunder.

(b) Definition.—With respect to any registered public accounting firm or associated person, for purposes of this section, the term 'improper professional conduct' means—

"(1) intentional or knowing conduct, including reckless conduct, that results in a violation of applicable professional standards; and

"(2) negligent conduct in the form of—

"(A) a single instance of highly unreasonable conduct that results in a violation of applicable professional standards in circumstances in which the registered public accounting firm or associated person knows, or should know, that heightened scrutiny is warranted; or

"(B) repeated instances of unreasonable conduct, each resulting in a violation of applicable professional standards, that indicate a lack of competence to practice before the Commission.".

§ 603. Federal Court Authority to Impose Penny Stock Bars

(a) Securities Exchange Act of 1934.—Section 21(d) of the Securities Exchange Act of 1934 (15 U.S.C. 78u(d)), as amended by this Act, is amended by adding at the end the following:

"(6) Authority of a court to prohibit persons from participating in an offering of penny stock.—

"(A) In general.—In any proceeding under paragraph (1) against any person participating in, or, at the time of the alleged misconduct who was participating in, an offering of penny stock, the court may prohibit that person from participating in an offering of penny stock, conditionally or unconditionally, and permanently or for such period of time as the court shall determine.

"(B) Definition.—For purposes of this paragraph, the term 'person participating in an offering of penny stock' includes any person engaging in activities with a broker, dealer, or issuer for purposes of issuing, trading, or inducing or attempting to induce the purchase or sale of, any penny stock. The Commission may, by rule or regulation, define such term to include other activities, and may, by rule, regulation, or order, exempt any person or class of persons, in whole or in part, conditionally or unconditionally, from inclusion in such term.".

(b) Securities Act of 1933.—Section 20 of the Securities Act of 1933 (15 U.S.C. 77t) is amended by adding at the end the following:

"(g) Authority of a Court To Prohibit Persons From Participating in an Offering of Penny Stock.—

"(1) In general.—In any proceeding under subsection (a) against any person participating in, or, at the time of the alleged misconduct, who was participating in, an offering of penny stock, the court may prohibit that person from participating in an offering of penny stock, conditionally or unconditionally, and permanently or for such period of time as the court shall determine.

"(2) Definition.—For purposes of this subsection, the term 'person participating in an offering of penny stock' includes any person engaging in activities with a broker, dealer, or issuer for purposes of issuing, trading, or inducing or attempting to induce the purchase or sale of, any penny stock. The Commission may, by rule or regulation, define such term to include other activities, and may, by rule, regulation, or order, exempt any person or class of persons, in whole or in part, conditionally or unconditionally, from inclusion in such term.".

§ 604. Qualifications of Associated Persons of Brokers and Dealers

(a) Brokers and Dealers.—Section 15(b)(4) of the Securities Exchange Act of 1934 (15 U.S.C. 78o) is amended—

(1) by striking subparagraph (F) and inserting the following:

"(F) is subject to any order of the Commission barring or suspending the right of the person to be associated with a broker or dealer;"; and

(2) in subparagraph (G), by striking the period at the end and inserting the following: "; or

"(H) is subject to any final order of a State securities commission (or any agency or officer performing like functions), State authority that supervises or examines banks, savings associations, or credit unions, State insurance commission (or any agency or office performing like functions), an appropriate Federal banking agency (as defined in section 3 of the Federal Deposit Insurance Act (12 U.S.C. 1813(q))), or the National Credit Union Administration, that—

"(i) bars such person from association with an entity regulated by such commission, authority, agency, or officer, or from engaging in the business of securities, insurance, banking, savings association activities, or credit union activities; or

"(ii) constitutes a final order based on violations of any laws or regulations that prohibit fraudulent, manipulative, or deceptive conduct.".

(b) Investment Advisers.—Section 203(e) of the Investment Advisers Act of 1940 (15 U.S.C. 80b–3(e)) is amended—

(1) by striking paragraph (7) and inserting the following:

"(7) is subject to any order of the Commission barring or suspending the right of the person to be associated with an investment adviser;";

(2) in paragraph (8), by striking the period at the end and inserting "; or"; and

(3) by adding at the end the following:

"(9) is subject to any final order of a State securities commission (or any agency or officer performing like functions), State authority that supervises or examines banks, savings associations, or credit unions, State insurance commission (or any agency or office performing like functions), an appropriate Federal banking agency (as defined in section 3 of the Federal Deposit Insurance Act (12 U.S.C. 1813(q))), or the National Credit Union Administration, that—

"(A) bars such person from association with an entity regulated by such commission, authority, agency, or officer, or from engaging in the business of securities, insurance, banking, savings association activities, or credit union activities; or

"(B) constitutes a final order based on violations of any laws or regulations that prohibit fraudulent, manipulative, or deceptive conduct.".

(c) Conforming Amendments.—

(1) Securities exchange act of 1934.—The Securities Exchange Act of 1934 (15 U.S.C. 78a et seq.) is amended—

(A) in section 3(a)(39)(F) (15 U.S.C. 78c(a)(39)(F))—

(i) by striking "or (G)" and inserting "(H), or (G)"; and

(ii) by inserting ", or is subject to an order or finding," before "enumerated";

(B) in each of section 15(b)(6)(A)(i) (15 U.S.C. 78o(b)(6)(A)(i)), paragraphs (2) and (4) of section 15B(c) (15 U.S.C. 78o–4(c)), and subparagraphs (A) and

(C) of section 15C(c)(1) (15 U.S.C. 78o–5(c)(1))—

(i) by striking "or (G)" each place that term appears and inserting "(H), or (G)"; and

    (ii) by striking "or omission" each place that term appears, and inserting ", or is subject to an order or finding,"; and

    (C) in each of paragraphs (3)(A) and (4)(C) of section 17A(c) (15 U.S.C. 78q–1(c))—

        (i) by striking "or (G)" each place that term appears and inserting "(H), or (G)"; and

        (ii) by inserting ", or is subject to an order or finding," before "enumerated" each place that term appears.

    (2) Investment advisers act of 1940.—Section 203(f) of the Investment Advisers Act of 1940 (15 U.S.C. 80b–3(f)) is amended—

    (A) by striking "or (8)" and inserting "(8), or (9)"; and

    (B) by inserting "or (3)" after "paragraph (2)".

TITLE VII. STUDIES AND REPORTS

§ 701. GAO Study and Report Regarding Consolidation of Public Accounting Firms

    (a) Study Required.—The Comptroller General of the United States shall conduct a study—

    (1) to identify—

        (A) the factors that have led to the consolidation of public accounting firms since 1989 and the consequent reduction in the number of firms capable of providing audit services to large national and multi-national business organizations that are subject to the securities laws;

        (B) the present and future impact of the condition described in subparagraph (A) on capital formation and securities markets, both domestic and international; and

        (C) solutions to any problems identified under subparagraph (B), including ways to increase competition and the number of firms capable of providing audit services to large national and multinational business organizations that are subject to the securities laws;

    (2) of the problems, if any, faced by business organizations that have resulted from limited competition among public accounting firms, including—

        (A) higher costs;

        (B) lower quality of services;

        (C) impairment of auditor independence; or

        (D) lack of choice; and

    (3) whether and to what extent Federal or State regulations impede competition among public accounting firms.

    (b) Consultation.—In planning and conducting the study under this section, the Comptroller General shall consult with—

    (1) the Commission;

    (2) the regulatory agencies that perform functions similar to the Commission within the other member countries of the Group of Seven Industrialized Nations;

    (3) the Department of Justice; and

    (4) any other public or private sector organization that the Comptroller General considers appropriate.

    (c) Report Required.—Not later than 1 year after the date of enactment of this Act, the Comptroller General shall submit a report on the results of the study required by this section to the Committee on Banking, Housing, and Urban Affairs of the Senate and the Committee on Financial Services of the House of Representatives.

§ 702. Commission Study and Report Regarding Credit Rating Agencies

(a) Study Required.—

(1) In general.—The Commission shall conduct a study of the role and function of credit rating agencies in the operation of the securities market.

(2) Areas of consideration.—The study required by this subsection shall examine—

(A) the role of credit rating agencies in the evaluation of issuers of securities;

(B) the importance of that role to investors and the functioning of the securities markets;

(C) any impediments to the accurate appraisal by credit rating agencies of the financial resources and risks of issuers of securities;

(D) any barriers to entry into the business of acting as a credit rating agency, and any measures needed to remove such barriers;

(E) any measures which may be required to improve the dissemination of information concerning such resources and risks when credit rating agencies announce credit ratings; and

(F) any conflicts of interest in the operation of credit rating agencies and measures to prevent such conflicts or ameliorate the consequences of such conflicts.

(b) Report Required.—The Commission shall submit a report on the study required by subsection (a) to the President, the Committee on Financial Services of the House of Representatives, and the Committee on Banking, Housing, and Urban Affairs of the Senate not later than 180 days after the date of enactment of this Act.

§ 703. Study and Report on Violators and Violations

(a) Study.—The Commission shall conduct a study to determine, based upon information for the period from January 1, 1998, to December 31, 2001—

(1) the number of securities professionals, defined as public accountants, public accounting firms, investment bankers, investment advisers, brokers, dealers, attorneys, and other securities professionals practicing before the Commission—

(A) who have been found to have aided and abetted a violation of the Federal securities laws, including rules or regulations promulgated thereunder (collectively referred to in this section as "Federal securities laws"), but who have not been sanctioned, disciplined, or otherwise penalized as a primary violator in any administrative action or civil proceeding, including in any settlement of such an action or proceeding (referred to in this section as "aiders and abettors"); and

(B) who have been found to have been primary violators of the Federal securities laws;

(2) a description of the Federal securities laws violations committed by aiders and abettors and by primary violators, including—

(A) the specific provision of the Federal securities laws violated;

(B) the specific sanctions and penalties imposed upon such aiders and abettors and primary violators, including the amount of any monetary penalties assessed upon and collected from such persons;

(C) the occurrence of multiple violations by the same person or persons, either as an aider or abettor or as a primary violator; and

(D) whether, as to each such violator, disciplinary sanctions have been imposed, including any censure, suspension, temporary bar, or permanent bar to practice before the Commission; and

(3) the amount of disgorgement, restitution, or any other fines or payments that the Commission has assessed upon and collected from, aiders and abettors and from primary violators.

(b) Report.—A report based upon the study conducted pursuant to subsection (a) shall be submitted to the Committee on Banking, Housing, and Urban Affairs of the Senate, and the Committee on Financial Services of the House of Representatives not later than 6 months after the date of enactment of this Act.

§ 704. Study of Enforcement Actions

(a) Study Required.—The Commission shall review and analyze all enforcement actions by the Commission involving violations of reporting requirements imposed under the securities laws, and restatements of financial statements, over the 5-year period preceding the date of enactment of this Act, to identify areas of reporting that are most susceptible to fraud, inappropriate manipulation, or inappropriate earnings management, such as revenue recognition and the accounting treatment of off-balance sheet special purpose entities.

(b) Report Required.—The Commission shall report its findings to the Committee on Financial Services of the House of Representatives and the Committee on Banking, Housing, and Urban Affairs of the Senate, not later than 180 days after the date of enactment of this Act, and shall use such findings to revise its rules and regulations, as necessary. The report shall include a discussion of regulatory or legislative steps that are recommended or that may be necessary to address concerns identified in the study.

§ 705. Study of Investment Banks

(a) GAO Study.—The Comptroller General of the United States shall conduct a study on whether investment banks and financial advisers assisted public companies in manipulating their earnings and obfuscating their true financial condition. The study should address the rule of investment banks and financial advisers—

(1) in the collapse of the Enron Corporation, including with respect to the design and implementation of derivatives transactions, transactions involving special purpose vehicles, and other financial arrangements that may have had the effect of altering the company's reported financial statements in ways that obscured the true financial picture of the company;

(2) in the failure of Global Crossing, including with respect to transactions involving swaps of fiberoptic cable capacity, in the designing transactions that may have had the effect of altering the company's reported financial statements in ways that obscured the true financial picture of the company; and

(3) generally, in creating and marketing transactions which may have been designed solely to enable companies to manipulate revenue streams, obtain loans, or move liabilities off balance sheets without altering the economic and business risks faced by the companies or any other mechanism to obscure a company's financial picture.

(b) Report.—The Comptroller General shall report to Congress not later than 180 days after the date of enactment of this Act on the results of the study required by this section. The report shall include a discussion of regulatory or legislative steps that are recommended or that may be necessary to address concerns identified in the study.

TITLE VIII.   CORPORATE AND CRIMINAL FRAUD ACCOUNTABILITY

§ 801.   Short Title

This title may be cited as the "Corporate and Criminal Fraud Accountability Act of 2002".

§ 802.   Criminal Penalties for Altering Documents

(a) In General.—Chapter 73 of title 18, United States Code, is amended by adding at the end the following:

"Sec. 1519. Destruction, alteration, or falsification of records in Federal investigations and bankruptcy "Whoever knowingly alters, destroys, mutilates, conceals, covers up, falsifies, or makes a false entry in any record, document, or tangible object with the intent to impede, obstruct, or influence the investigation or proper administration of any matter within the jurisdiction of any department or agency of the United States or any case filed under title 11, or in relation to or contemplation of any such matter or case, shall be fined under this title, imprisoned not more than 20 years, or both.

"Sec. 1520. Destruction of corporate audit records "(a)(1) Any accountant who conducts an audit of an issuer of securities to which section 10A(a) of the Securities Exchange Act of 1934 (15 U.S.C. 78j–1(a)) applies, shall maintain all audit or review workpapers for a period of 5 years from the end of the fiscal period in which the audit or review was concluded.

"(2) The Securities and Exchange Commission shall promulgate, within 180 days, after adequate notice and an opportunity for comment, such rules and regulations, as are reasonably necessary, relating to the retention of relevant records such as workpapers, documents that form the basis of an audit or review, memoranda, correspondence, communications, other documents, and records (including electronic records) which are created, sent, or received in connection with an audit or review and contain conclusions, opinions, analyses, or financial data relating to such an audit or review, which is conducted by any accountant who conducts an audit of an issuer of securities to which section 10A(a) of the Securities Exchange Act of 1934 (15 U.S.C. 78j–1(a)) applies. The Commission may, from time to time, amend or supplement the rules and regulations that it is required to promulgate under this section, after adequate notice and an opportunity for comment, in order to ensure that such rules and regulations adequately comport with the purposes of this section.

"(b) Whoever knowingly and willfully violates subsection (a)(1), or any rule or regulation promulgated by the Securities and Exchange Commission under subsection (a)(2), shall be fined under this title, imprisoned not more than 10 years, or both.

"(c) Nothing in this section shall be deemed to diminish or relieve any person of any other duty or obligation imposed by Federal or State law or regulation to maintain, or refrain from destroying, any document.".

(b) Clerical Amendment.—The table of sections at the beginning of chapter 73 of title 18, United States Code, is amended by adding at the end the following new items:

"1519. Destruction, alteration, or falsification of records in Federal investigations and bankruptcy.

"1520. Destruction of corporate audit records.".

§ 803.   Debts Nondischargeable If Incurred in Violation of Securities Fraud Laws

Section 523(a) of title 11, United States Code, is amended—

    (1)   in paragraph (17), by striking "or" after the semicolon;

    (2)   in paragraph (18), by striking the period at the end and inserting "; or"; and

    (3)   by adding at the end, the following:

        "(19) that—

            "(A) is for—

                "(i)   the violation of any of the Federal securities laws (as that term is defined in section 3(a)(47) of the Securities Exchange Act of 1934), any of the State securities laws, or any regulation or order issued under such Federal or State securities laws; or

                "(ii) common law fraud, deceit, or manipulation in connection with the purchase or sale of any security; and

            "(B) results from—

                "(i)   any judgment, order, consent order, or decree entered in any Federal or State judicial or administrative proceeding;

                "(ii) any settlement agreement entered into by the debtor; or "(iii) any court or administrative order for any damages, fine, penalty, citation, restitutionary payment, disgorgement payment, attorney fee, cost, or other payment owed by the debtor.".

§ 804. Statute of Limitations for Securities Fraud

(a) In General.—Section 1658 of title 28, United States Code, is amended—

(1) by inserting "(a)" before "Except"; and

(2) by adding at the end the following:

"(b) Notwithstanding subsection (a), a private right of action that involves a claim of fraud, deceit, manipulation, or contrivance in contravention of a regulatory requirement concerning the securities laws, as defined in section 3(a)(47) of the Securities Exchange Act of 1934 (15 U.S.C. 78c(a)(47)), may be brought not later than the earlier of—

"(1) 2 years after the discovery of the facts constituting the violation; or

"(2) 5 years after such violation.".

(b) Effective Date.—The limitations period provided by section 1658(b) of title 28, United States Code, as added by this section, shall apply to all proceedings addressed by this section that are commenced on or after the date of enactment of this Act.

(c) No Creation of Actions.—Nothing in this section shall create a new, private right of action.

§ 805. Review of Federal Sentencing Guidelines for Obstruction of Justice and Extensive Criminal Fraud

(a) Enhancement of Fraud and Obstruction of Justice Sentences.—Pursuant to section 994 of title 28, United States Code, and in accordance with this section, the United States Sentencing Commission shall review and amend, as appropriate, the Federal Sentencing Guidelines and related policy statements to ensure that—

(1) the base offense level and existing enhancements contained in United States Sentencing Guideline 2J1.2 relating to obstruction of justice are sufficient to deter and punish that activity;

(2) the enhancements and specific offense characteristics relating to obstruction of justice are adequate in cases where—

(A) the destruction, alteration, or fabrication of evidence involves—

(i) a large amount of evidence, a large number of participants, or is otherwise extensive;

(ii) the selection of evidence that is particularly probative or essential to the investigation; or

(iii) more than minimal planning; or

(B) the offense involved abuse of a special skill or a position of trust;

(3) the guideline offense levels and enhancements for violations of section 1519 or 1520 of title 18, United States Code, as added by this title, are sufficient to deter and punish that activity;

(4) a specific offense characteristic enhancing sentencing is provided under United States Sentencing Guideline 2B1.1 (as in effect on the date of enactment of this Act) for a fraud offense that endangers the solvency or financial security of a substantial number of victims; and

(5) the guidelines that apply to organizations in United States Sentencing Guidelines, chapter 8, are sufficient to deter and punish organizational criminal misconduct.

(b) Emergency Authority and Deadline for Commission Action.—The United States Sentencing Commission is requested to promulgate the guidelines or amendments provided for under this section as soon as practicable, and in any event not later than 180 days after the date of enactment of this Act, in accordance with the procedures set forth in section 219(a) of the Sentencing Reform Act of 1987, as though the authority under that Act had not expired.

§ 806.   Protection for Employees of Publicly Traded Companies Who Provide Evidence of Fraud

(a)   In General.—Chapter 73 of title 18, United States Code, is amended by inserting after section 1514 the following:

"Sec. 1514A. Civil action to protect against retaliation in fraud cases

"(a)   Whistleblower Protection for Employees of Publicly Traded Companies.—No company with a class of securities registered under section 12 of the Securities Exchange Act of 1934 (15 U.S.C. 78*l*), or that is required to file reports under section 15(d) of the Securities Exchange Act of 1934 (15 U.S.C. 78*o*(d)), or any officer, employee, contractor, subcontractor, or agent of such company, may discharge, demote, suspend, threaten, harass, or in and other manner discriminate against an employee in the terms and conditions of employment because of any lawful act done by the employee—

"(1)   to provide information, cause information to be provided, or otherwise assist in an investigation regarding any conduct which the employee reasonably believes constitutes a violation of section 1341, 1343, 1344, or 1348, any rule or regulation of the Securities and Exchange Commission, or any provision of Federal law relating to fraud against shareholders, when the information or assistance is provided to or the investigation is conducted by—

"(A)   a Federal regulatory or law enforcement agency;

"(B)   any Member of Congress or any committee of Congress; or

"(C)   a person with supervisory authority over the employee (or such other person working for the employer who has the authority to investigate, discover, or terminate misconduct); or

"(2)   to file, cause to be filed, testify, participate in, or otherwise assist in a proceeding filed or about to be filed (with any knowledge of the employer) relating to an alleged violation of section 1341, 1343, 1344, or 1348, any rule or regulation of the Securities and Exchange Commission, or any provision of Federal law relating to fraud against shareholders.

"(b)   Enforcement Action.—

"(1)   In general.—A person who alleges discharge or other discrimination by any person in violation of subsection (a) may seek relief under subsection (c), by—

"(A)   filing a complaint with the Secretary of Labor; or

"(B)   if the Secretary has not issued a final decision within 180 days of the filing of the complaint and there is no showing that such delay is due to the bad faith of the claimant, bringing an action at law or equity for de novo review in the appropriate district court of the United States, which shall have jurisdiction over such an action without regard to the amount in controversy.

"(2)   Procedure.—

"(A)   In general.—An action under paragraph (1)(A) shall be governed under the rules and procedures set forth in section 42121(b) of title 49, United States Code.

"(B)   Exception.—Notification made under section 42121(b)(1) of title 49, United States Code, shall be made to the person named in the complaint and to the employer.

"(C)   Burdens of proof.—An action brought under paragraph (1)(B) shall be governed by the legal burdens of proof set forth in section 42121(b) of title 49, United States Code.

"(D) Statute of limitations.—An action under paragraph (1) shall be commenced not later than 90 days after the date on which the violation occurs.

"(c) Remedies.—

"(1) In general.—An employee prevailing in any action under subsection (b)(1) shall be entitled to all relief necessary to make the employee whole.

"(2) Compensatory damages.—Relief for any action under paragraph (1) shall include—

"(A) reinstatement with the same seniority status that the employee would have had, but for the discrimination;

"(B) the amount of back pay, with interest; and

"(C) compensation for any special damages sustained as a result of the discrimination, including litigation costs, expert witness fees, and reasonable attorney fees.

"(d) Rights Retained by Employee.—Nothing in this section shall be deemed to diminish the rights, privileges, or remedies of any employee under any Federal or State law, or under any collective bargaining agreement.".

(b) Clerical Amendment.—The table of sections at the beginning of chapter 73 of title 18, United States Code, is amended by inserting after the item relating to section 1514 the following new item:

"1514A. Civil action to protect against retaliation in fraud cases.".

§ 807. Criminal Penalties for Defrauding Shareholders of Publicly Traded Companies

(a) In General.—Chapter 63 of title 18, United States Code, is amended by adding at the end the following:

"Sec. 1348. Securities fraud

"Whoever knowingly executes, or attempts to execute, a scheme or artifice—

"(1) to defraud any person in connection with any security of an issuer with a class of securities registered under section 12 of the Securities Exchange Act of 1934 (15 U.S.C. 78*l*) or that is required to file reports under section 15(d) of the Securities Exchange Act of 1934 (15 U.S.C. 78*o*(d)); or

"(2) to obtain, by means of false or fraudulent pretenses, representations, or promises, any money or property in connection with the purchase or sale of any security of an issuer with a class of securities registered under section 12 of the Securities Exchange Act of 1934 (15 U.S.C. 78*l*) or that is required to file reports under section 15(d) of the Securities Exchange Act of 1934 (15 U.S.C. 78*o*(d)); shall be fined under this title, or imprisoned not more than 25 years, or both.".

(b) Clerical Amendment.—The table of sections at the beginning of chapter 63 of title 18, United States Code, is amended by adding at the end the following new item:

"1348. Securities fraud.".

TITLE IX. WHITE-COLLAR CRIME PENALTY ENHANCEMENTS

§ 901. Short Title

This title may be cited as the "White-Collar Crime Penalty Enhancement Act of 2002".

§ 902. Attempts and Conspiracies to Commit Criminal Fraud Offenses

(a) In General.—Chapter 63 of title 18, United States Code, is amended by inserting after section 1348 as added by this Act the following:

"Sec. 1349. Attempt and conspiracy

"Any person who attempts or conspires to commit any offense under this chapter shall be subject to the same penalties as those prescribed for the offense, the commission of which was the object of the attempt or conspiracy.

(b)   Clerical Amendment.—The table of sections at the beginning of chapter 63 of title 18, United States Code, is amended by adding at the end the following new item:

"1349. Attempt and conspiracy.".

§ 903.   Criminal Penalties for Mail and Wire Fraud

(a)   Mail Fraud.—Section 1341 of title 18, United States Code, is amended by striking "five" and inserting "20".

(b)   Wire Fraud.—Section 1343 of title 18, United States Code, is amended by striking "five" and inserting "20".

§ 904.   Criminal Penalties for Violations of the Employee Retirement Income Security Act of 1974

Section 501 of the Employee Retirement Income Security Act of 1974 (29 U.S.C. 1131) is amended—

(1)   by striking "$5,000" and inserting "$100,000";

(2)   by striking "one year" and inserting "10 years"; and

(3)   by striking "$100,000" and inserting "$500,000".

§ 905.   Amendment to Sentencing Guidelines Relating to Certain White-Collar Offenses

(a)   Directive to the United States Sentencing Commission.—Pursuant to its authority under section 994(p) of title 18, United States Code, and in accordance with this section, the United States Sentencing Commission shall review and, as appropriate, amend the Federal Sentencing Guidelines and related policy statements to implement the provisions of this Act.

(b)   Requirements.—In carrying out this section, the Sentencing Commission shall—

(1)   ensure that the sentencing guidelines and policy statements reflect the serious nature of the offenses and the penalties set forth in this Act, the growing incidence of serious fraud offenses which are identified above, and the need to modify the sentencing guidelines and policy statements to deter, prevent, and punish such offenses;

(2)   consider the extent to which the guidelines and policy statements adequately address whether the guideline offense levels and enhancements for violations of the sections amended by this Act are sufficient to deter and punish such offenses, and specifically, are adequate in view of the statutory increases in penalties contained in this Act;

(3)   assure reasonable consistency with other relevant directives and sentencing guidelines;

(4)   account for any additional aggravating or mitigating circumstances that might justify exceptions to the generally applicable sentencing ranges;

(5)   make any necessary conforming changes to the sentencing guidelines; and

(6)   assure that the guidelines adequately meet the purposes of sentencing, as set forth in section 3553(a)(2) of title 18, United States Code.

(c)   Emergency Authority and Deadline for Commission Action.—The United States Sentencing Commission is requested to promulgate the guidelines or amendments provided for under this section as soon as practicable, and in any event not later than 180 days after the date of enactment of this Act, in accordance with the procedures set forth in section 219(a) of the Sentencing Reform Act of 1987, as though the authority under that Act had not expired.

§ 906. Corporate Responsibility for Financial Reports

(a) In General.—Chapter 63 of title 18, United States Code, is amended by inserting after section 1349, as created by this Act, the following:

"Sec. 1350. Failure of corporate officers to certify financial reports

(a) Certification of Periodic Financial Reports.—Each periodic report containing financial statements filed by an issuer with the Securities Exchange Commission pursuant to section 13(a) or 15(d) of the Securities Exchange Act of 1934 (15 U.S.C. 78m(a) or 78o(d)) shall be accompanied by a written statement by the chief executive officer and chief financial officer (or equivalent thereof) of the issuer.

"(b) Content.—The statement required under subsection (a) shall certify that the periodic report containing the financial statements fully complies with the requirements of section 13(a) or 15(d) of the Securities Exchange Act of 1934 (15 U.S.C. 78m or 78o(d)) and that information contained in the periodic report fairly presents, in all material respects, the financial condition and results of operations of the issuer.

"(c) Criminal Penalties.—Whoever—

"(1) certifies any statement as set forth in subsections (a) and (b) of this section knowing that the periodic report accompanying the statement does not comport with all the requirements set forth in this section shall be fined not more than $1,000,000 or imprisoned not more than 10 years, or both; or

"(2) willfully certifies any statement as set forth in subsections (a) and (b) of this section knowing that the periodic report accompanying the statement does not comport with all the requirements set forth in this section shall be fined not more than $5,000,000, or imprisoned not more than 20 years, or both.".

(b) Clerical Amendment.—The table of sections at the beginning of chapter 63 of title 18, United States Code, is amended by adding at the end the following:

"1350. Failure of corporate officers to certify financial reports.".

TITLE X. CORPORATE TAX RETURNS

§ 1001. Sense of the Senate Regarding the Signing of Corporate Tax Returns by Chief Executive Officers

It is the sense of the Senate that the Federal income tax return of a corporation should be signed by the chief executive officer of such corporation.

TITLE XI. CORPORATE FRAUD ACCOUNTABILITY

§ 1101. Short Title

This title may be cited as the "Corporate Fraud Accountability Act of 2002".

§ 1102. Tampering with a Record or Otherwise Impeding an Official Proceeding

Section 1512 of title 18, United States Code, is amended—

(1) by redesignating subsections (c) through (i) as subsections (d) through (j), respectively; and

(2) by inserting after subsection (b) the following new subsection:

"(c) Whoever corruptly—

"(1) alters, destroys, mutilates, or conceals a record, document, or other object, or attempts to do so, with the intent to impair the object's integrity or availability for use in an official proceeding; or

"(2) otherwise obstructs, influences, or impedes any official proceeding, or attempts to do so, shall be fined under this title or imprisoned not more than 20 years, or both.".

§ 1103.   Temporary Freeze Authority for the Securities and Exchange Commission

(a) In General.—Section 21C(c) of the Securities Exchange Act of 1934 (15 U.S.C. 78u–3(c)) is amended by adding at the end the following:

"(3) Temporary freeze.—

"(A) In general.—

"(i) Issuance of temporary order.—Whenever, during the course of a lawful investigation involving possible violations of the Federal securities laws by an issuer of publicly traded securities or any of its directors, officers, partners, controlling persons, agents, or employees, it shall appear to the Commission that it is likely that the issuer will make extraordinary payments (whether compensation or otherwise) to any of the foregoing persons, the commission may petition a Federal district court for a temporary order requiring the issuer to escrow, subject to court supervision, those payments in an interest-bearing account for 45 days.

"(ii) Standard.—A temporary order shall be entered under clause (i), only after notice and opportunity for a hearing, unless the court determines that notice and hearing prior to entry of the order would be impracticable or contrary to the public interest.

"(iii) Effective period.—A temporary order issued under clause (i) shall—

"(I) become effective immediately;

"(II) be served upon the parties subject to it; and

"(III) unless set aside, limited or suspended by a court of competent jurisdiction, shall remain effective and enforceable for 45 days.

"(iv) Extensions authorized.—The effective period of an order under this subparagraph may be extended by the court upon good cause shown for not longer than 45 additional days, provided that the combined period of the order shall not exceed 90 days.

"(B) Process on Determination of violations.—

"(i) Violations charged.—If the issuer or other person described in subparagraph (A) is charged with any violation of the Federal securities laws before the expiration of the effective period of a temporary order under subparagraph (A) (including any applicable extension period), the order shall remain in effect, subject to court approval, until the conclusion of any legal proceedings related thereto, and the affected issuer or other person, shall have the right to petition the court for review of the order.

"(ii) Violations not charged.—If the issuer or other person described in subparagraph (A) is not charged with any violation of the Federal securities laws before the expiration of the effective period of a temporary order under subparagraph (A) (including any applicable extension period), the escrow shall terminate at the expiration of the 45-day effective period (or the expiration of any extension period, as applicable), and the disputed payments (with accrued interest) shall be returned to the issuer or other affected person.".

(b) Technical Amendment.—Section 21C(c)(2) of the Securities Exchange Act of 1934 (15 U.S.C. 78u–3(c)(2)) is amended by striking "This" and inserting "paragraph (1)".

§ 1104. Amendment to the Federal Sentencing Guidelines

(a) Request for Immediate Consideration by The United States Sentencing Commission.—Pursuant to its authority under section 994(p) of title 28, United States Code, and in accordance with this section, the United States Sentencing Commission is requested to—

(1) promptly review the sentencing guidelines applicable to securities and accounting fraud and related offenses;

(2) expeditiously consider the promulgation of new sentencing guidelines or amendments to existing sentencing guidelines to provide an enhancement for officers or directors of publicly traded corporations who commit fraud and related offenses; and

(3) submit to Congress an explanation of actions taken by the Sentencing Commission pursuant to paragraph (2) and any additional policy recommendations the Sentencing Commission may have for combating offenses described in paragraph (1).

(b) Considerations in Review.—In carrying out this section, the Sentencing Commission is requested to—

(1) ensure that the sentencing guidelines and policy statements reflect the serious nature of securities, pension, and accounting fraud and the need for aggressive and appropriate law enforcement action to prevent such offenses;

(2) assure reasonable consistency with other relevant directives and with other guidelines;

(3) account for any aggravating or mitigating circumstances that might justify exceptions, including circumstances for which the sentencing guidelines currently provide sentencing enhancements;

(4) ensure that guideline offense levels and enhancements for an obstruction of justice offense are adequate in cases where documents or other physical evidence are actually destroyed or fabricated;

(5) ensure that the guideline offense levels and enhancements under United States Sentencing Guideline 2B1.1 (as in effect on the date of enactment of this Act) are sufficient for a fraud offense when the number of victims adversely involved is significantly greater than 50;

(6) make any necessary conforming changes to the sentencing guidelines; and

(7) assure that the guidelines adequately meet the purposes of sentencing as set forth in section 3553 (a)(2) of title 18, United States Code.

(c) Emergency Authority and Deadline For Commission Action.—The United States Sentencing Commission is requested to promulgate the guidelines or amendments provided for under this section as soon as practicable, and in any event not later than the 180 days after the date of enactment of this Act, in accordance with the procedures sent forth in section 21(a) of the Sentencing Reform Act of 1987, as though the authority under that Act had not expired.

§ 1105. Authority of the Commission to Prohibit Persons from Serving as Officers or Directors

(a) Securities Exchange Act of 1934.—Section 21C of the Securities Exchange Act of 1934 (15 U.S.C. 78u–3) is amended by adding at the end the following:

"(f) Authority of the Commission to Prohibit Persons From Serving as Officers or Directors.—In any cease-and-desist proceeding under subsection (a), the Commission may issue an order to prohibit, conditionally or unconditionally, and permanently or for such period of time as it shall determine, any person who has violated section 10(b) or the rules or regulations thereunder, from acting as an officer or director of any issuer that has a class of securities registered pursuant to section 12, or that is required to file reports pursuant to section 15(d), if the conduct of that person demonstrates unfitness to serve as an officer or director of any such issuer.".

(b) Securities Act of 1933.—Section 8A of the Securities Act of 1933 (15 U.S.C. 77h–1) is amended by adding at the end of the following:

"(f)   Authority of the Commission to Prohibit Persons From Serving as Officers or Directors.—In any cease-and-desist proceeding under subsection (a), the Commission may issue an order to prohibit, conditionally or unconditionally, and permanently or for such period of time as it shall determine, any person who has violated section 17(a)(1) or the rules or regulations thereunder, from acting as an officer or director of any issuer that has a class of securities registered pursuant to section 12 of the Securities Exchange Act of 1934, or that is required to file reports pursuant to section 15(d) of that Act, if the conduct of that person demonstrates unfitness to serve as an officer or director of any such issuer.".

§ 1106.   Increased Criminal Penalties Under Securities Exchange Act of 1934

Section 32(a) of the Securities Exchange Act of 1934 (15 U.S.C. 78ff(a)) is amended—

(1)   by striking "$1,000,000, or imprisoned not more than 10 years" and inserting "$5,000,000, or imprisoned not more than 20 years"; and

(2)   by striking "$2,500,000" and inserting "$25,000,000".

§ 1107.   Retaliation Against Informants

(a)   In General.—Section 1513 of title 18, United States Code, is amended by adding at the end the following:

"(e)   Whoever knowingly, with the intent to retaliate, takes any action harmful to any person, including interference with the lawful employment or livelihood of any person, for providing to a law enforcement officer any truthful information relating to the commission or possible commission of any Federal offense, shall be fined under this title or imprisoned not more than 10 years, or both.".

Approved July 30, 2002.

REGULATION 14A. SOLICITATION OF PROXIES (RULES 14a–7, 14a–8)

17 C.F.R. §§ 240.14a–7, 240.14a–8

─────────────

Table of Sections

─────────────

§ 240.14a–7   Obligations of Registrants to Provide a List of, or Mail Soliciting Material to, Security Holders

(a)   If the registrant has made or intends to make a proxy solicitation in connection with a security holder meeting or action by consent or authorization, upon the written request by any record or beneficial holder of securities of the class entitled to vote at the meeting or to execute a consent or authorization to provide a list of security holders or to mail the requesting security holder's materials, regardless of whether the request references this section, the registrant shall:

(1)   Deliver to the requesting security holder within five business days after receipt of the request:

(i)   Notification as to whether the registrant has elected to mail the security holder's soliciting materials or provide a security holder list if the election under paragraph (b) of this section is to be made by the registrant;

(ii)   A statement of the approximate number of record holders and beneficial holders, separated by type of holder and class, owning securities in the same class or classes as holders which have been or are to be solicited on management's behalf, or any more limited group of such holders designated by the security holder if available or retrievable under the registrant's or its transfer agent's security holder data systems; and

(iii)   The estimated cost of mailing a proxy statement, form of proxy or other communication to such holders, including to the extent known or reasonably available, the estimated costs of any bank, broker, and similar person through whom the registrant has solicited or intends to solicit beneficial owners in connection with the security holder meeting or action;

(2)   Perform the acts set forth in either paragraphs (a)(2)(i) or (a)(2)(ii) of this section, at the registrant's or requesting security holder's option, as specified in paragraph (b) of this section:

(i)   Send copies of any proxy statement, form of proxy, or other soliciting material, including a Notice of Internet Availability of Proxy Materials (as described in § 240.14a–16), furnished by the security holder to the record holders, including banks, brokers, and similar entities, designated by the security holder. A sufficient number of copies must be sent to the banks, brokers, and similar entities for distribution to all beneficial owners designated by the security holder. The security holder may designate only record holders and/or beneficial owners who have not requested paper and/ or e-mail copies of the proxy statement. If the registrant has received affirmative written or implied consent to deliver a single proxy statement to security holders at a shared address in accordance with the procedures in § 240.14a–3(e)(1), a single copy of the proxy statement or Notice of Internet Availability of Proxy Materials furnished by the security holder shall be sent to that address, provided that if multiple copies of the Notice of Internet Availability of Proxy Materials are furnished by the security holder for that address, the registrant shall deliver those copies in a single envelope to that address. The registrant shall send the security holder material with reasonable promptness after tender of the material to be sent, envelopes or other containers therefore, postage or payment for postage and other reasonable expenses of effecting such distribution. The registrant shall not be responsible for the content of the material; or

(ii)   Deliver the following information to the requesting security holder within five business days of receipt of the request:

(A)   A reasonably current list of the names, addresses and security positions of the record holders, including banks, brokers and similar entities holding securities in the same class or classes as holders which have been or are to be solicited on management's behalf, or any more limited group of such holders designated by the security holder if available or retrievable under the registrant's or its transfer agent's security holder data systems;

(B)   The most recent list of names, addresses and security positions of beneficial owners as specified in § 240.14a–13(b), in the possession, or which subsequently comes into the possession, of the registrant;

(C)   The names of security holders at a shared address that have consented to delivery of a single copy of proxy materials to a shared address, if the registrant has received written or implied consent in accordance with § 240.14a–3(e)(1); and

(D)   If the registrant has relied on § 240.14a–16, the names of security holders who have requested paper copies of the proxy materials for all meetings and the names of security holders who, as of the date that the registrant receives the request, have requested paper copies of the proxy materials only for the meeting to which the solicitation relates.

(iii)   All security holder list information shall be in the form requested by the security holder to the extent that such form is available to the registrant without undue burden or expense. The registrant shall furnish the security holder with updated record holder information on a daily basis or, if not available on a daily basis, at the shortest reasonable intervals; provided, however, the registrant need not provide beneficial or record holder information more current than the record date for the meeting or action.

(b)(1)   The requesting security holder shall have the options set forth in paragraph (a)(2) of this section, and the registrant shall have corresponding obligations, if the registrant or general partner or sponsor is soliciting or intends to solicit with respect to:

(i)   A proposal that is subject to § 240.13e–3;

(ii)   A roll-up transaction as defined in Item 901(c) of Regulation S-K (§ 229.901(c) of this chapter) that involves an entity with securities registered pursuant to Section 12 of the Act (15 U.S.C. 78*l*); or

(iii)   A roll-up transaction as defined in Item 901(c) of Regulation S-K (§ 229.901(c) of this chapter) that involves a limited partnership, unless the transaction involves only:

(A)   Partnerships whose investors will receive new securities or securities in another entity that are not reported under a transaction reporting plan declared effective before December 17, 1993 by the Commission under Section 11A of the Act (15 U.S.C. 78k–1); or

(B)   Partnerships whose investors' securities are reported under a transaction reporting plan declared effective before December 17, 1993 by the Commission under Section 11A of the Act (15 U.S.C. 78k–1).

(2)   With respect to all other requests pursuant to this section, the registrant shall have the option to either mail the security holder's material or furnish the security holder list as set forth in this section.

(c)   At the time of a list request, the security holder making the request shall:

(1)   If holding the registrant's securities through a nominee, provide the registrant with a statement by the nominee or other independent third party, or a copy of a current filing made with the Commission and furnished to the registrant, confirming such holder's beneficial ownership; and

(2)   Provide the registrant with an affidavit, declaration, affirmation or other similar document provided for under applicable state law identifying the proposal or other corporate action that will be the subject of the security holder's solicitation or communication and attesting that:

(i)   The security holder will not use the list information for any purpose other than to solicit security holders with respect to the same meeting or action by consent or authorization for which the registrant is soliciting or intends to solicit or to communicate with security holders with respect to a solicitation commenced by the registrant; and

(ii)   The security holder will not disclose such information to any person other than a beneficial owner for whom the request was made and an employee or agent to the extent necessary to effectuate the communication or solicitation.

(d)   The security holder shall not use the information furnished by the registrant pursuant to paragraph (a)(2)(ii) of this section for any purpose other than to solicit security holders with respect to the same meeting or action by consent or authorization for which the registrant is soliciting or intends to solicit or to communicate with security holders with respect to a solicitation commenced by the registrant; or disclose such information to any person other than an employee, agent, or beneficial owner for whom a request was made to the extent necessary to effectuate the communication or solicitation. The security holder shall return the information provided pursuant to paragraph (a)(2)(ii) of this section and shall not retain any copies thereof or of any information derived from such information after the termination of the solicitation.

(e)   The security holder shall reimburse the reasonable expenses incurred by the registrant in performing the acts requested pursuant to paragraph (a) of this section.

Note 1 to § 240.14a–7. Reasonably prompt methods of distribution to security holders may be used instead of mailing. If an alternative distribution method is chosen, the costs of that method should be considered where necessary rather than the costs of mailing.

Note 2 to § 240.14a–7. When providing the information required by § 240.14a–7(a)(1)(ii), if the registrant has received affirmative written or implied consent to delivery of a single copy of proxy materials to a shared address in accordance with § 240.14a–3(e)(1), it shall exclude from the number of record holders those to whom it does not have to deliver a separate proxy statement.

§ 240.14a–8   Shareholder Proposals

This section addresses when a company must include a shareholder's proposal in its proxy statement and identify the proposal in its form of proxy when the company holds an annual or special meeting of shareholders. In summary, in order to have your shareholder proposal included on a company's proxy card, and included along with any supporting statement in its proxy statement, you must be eligible and follow certain procedures. Under a few specific circumstances, the company is permitted to exclude your proposal, but only after submitting its reasons to the Commission. We structured this section in a question-and-answer format so that it is easier to understand. The references to "you" are to a shareholder seeking to submit the proposal.

(a)   Question 1: What is a proposal? A shareholder proposal is your recommendation or requirement that the company and/or its board of directors take action, which you intend to present at a meeting of the company's shareholders. Your proposal should state as clearly as possible the course of action that you believe the company should follow. If your proposal is placed on the company's proxy card, the company must also provide in the form of proxy means for shareholders to specify by boxes a choice between approval or disapproval, or abstention. Unless otherwise indicated, the word "proposal" as used in this section refers both to your proposal, and to your corresponding statement in support of your proposal (if any).

(b)   Question 2: Who is eligible to submit a proposal, and how do I demonstrate to the company that I am eligible?

(1)   In order to be eligible to submit a proposal, you must have continuously held at least $2,000 in market value, or 1%, of the company's securities entitled to be voted on the proposal at the meeting for at least one year by the date you submit the proposal. You must continue to hold those securities through the date of the meeting.

(2)   If you are the registered holder of your securities, which means that your name appears in the company's records as a shareholder, the company can verify your eligibility on its own, although you will still have to provide the company with a written statement that you intend to continue to hold the securities through the date of the meeting of shareholders. However, if like many shareholders you are not a registered holder, the company likely does not know that you are a shareholder, or how many shares you own. In this case, at the time you submit your proposal, you must prove your eligibility to the company in one of two ways:

(i)   The first way is to submit to the company a written statement from the "record" holder of your securities (usually a broker or bank) verifying that, at the time you submitted your proposal, you continuously held the securities for at least one year. You must also include your own written statement that you intend to continue to hold the securities through the date of the meeting of shareholders; or

(ii)   The second way to prove ownership applies only if you have filed a Schedule 13D (§ 240.13d–101), Schedule 13G (§ 240.13d–102), Form 3 (§ 249.103 of this chapter), Form 4 (§ 249.104 of this chapter) and/or Form 5 (§ 249.105 of this chapter), or amendments to those documents or updated forms, reflecting your ownership of the shares as of or before the date on which the one-year eligibility period begins. If you have filed one of these documents with the SEC, you may demonstrate your eligibility by submitting to the company:

(A)   A copy of the schedule and/or form, and any subsequent amendments reporting a change in your ownership level;

(B)   Your written statement that you continuously held the required number of shares for the one-year period as of the date of the statement; and

(C)   Your written statement that you intend to continue ownership of the shares through the date of the company's annual or special meeting.

(c)   Question 3: How many proposals may I submit? Each shareholder may submit no more than one proposal to a company for a particular shareholders' meeting.

(d)   Question 4: How long can my proposal be? The proposal, including any accompanying supporting statement, may not exceed 500 words.

(e)   Question 5: What is the deadline for submitting a proposal?

(1)   If you are submitting your proposal for the company's annual meeting, you can in most cases find the deadline in last year's proxy statement. However, if the company did not hold an annual meeting last year, or has changed the date of its meeting for this year more than 30 days from last year's meeting, you can usually find the deadline in one of the company's quarterly reports on Form 10-Q (§ 249.308a of this chapter), or in shareholder reports of investment companies under § 270.30d–1 of this chapter of the Investment Company Act of 1940. In order to avoid controversy, shareholders should submit their proposals by means, including electronic means, that permit them to prove the date of delivery.

(2)   The deadline is calculated in the following manner if the proposal is submitted for a regularly scheduled annual meeting. The proposal must be received at the company's principal executive offices not less than 120 calendar days before the date of the company's proxy statement released to shareholders in connection with the previous year's annual meeting. However, if the company did not hold an annual meeting the previous year, or if the date of this year's annual meeting has been changed by more than 30 days from the date of the previous year's meeting, then the deadline is a reasonable time before the company begins to print and send its proxy materials.

(3)   If you are submitting your proposal for a meeting of shareholders other than a regularly scheduled annual meeting, the deadline is a reasonable time before the company begins to print and send its proxy materials.

(f)   Question 6: What if I fail to follow one of the eligibility or procedural requirements explained in answers to Questions 1 through 4 of this section?

(1) The company may exclude your proposal, but only after it has notified you of the problem, and you have failed adequately to correct it. Within 14 calendar days of receiving your proposal, the company must notify you in writing of any procedural or eligibility deficiencies, as well as of the time frame for your response. Your response must be postmarked, or transmitted electronically, no later than 14 days from the date you received the company's notification. A company need not provide you such notice of a deficiency if the deficiency cannot be remedied, such as if you fail to submit a proposal by the company's properly determined deadline. If the company intends to exclude the proposal, it will later have to make a submission under § 240.14a–8 and provide you with a copy under Question 10 below, § 240.14a–8(j).

(2) If you fail in your promise to hold the required number of securities through the date of the meeting of shareholders, then the company will be permitted to exclude all of your proposals from its proxy materials for any meeting held in the following two calendar years.

(g) Question 7: Who has the burden of persuading the Commission or its staff that my proposal can be excluded? Except as otherwise noted, the burden is on the company to demonstrate that it is entitled to exclude a proposal.

(h) Question 8: Must I appear personally at the shareholders' meeting to present the proposal?

(1) Either you, or your representative who is qualified under state law to present the proposal on your behalf, must attend the meeting to present the proposal. Whether you attend the meeting yourself or send a qualified representative to the meeting in your place, you should make sure that you, or your representative, follow the proper state law procedures for attending the meeting and/or presenting your proposal.

(2) If the company holds its shareholder meeting in whole or in part via electronic media, and the company permits you or your representative to present your proposal via such media, then you may appear through electronic media rather than traveling to the meeting to appear in person.

(3) If you or your qualified representative fail to appear and present the proposal, without good cause, the company will be permitted to exclude all of your proposals from its proxy materials for any meetings held in the following two calendar years.

(i) Question 9: If I have complied with the procedural requirements, on what other bases may a company rely to exclude my proposal?

(1) Improper under state law: If the proposal is not a proper subject for action by shareholders under the laws of the jurisdiction of the company's organization;

Note to paragraph (i)(1): Depending on the subject matter, some proposals are not considered proper under state law if they would be binding on the company if approved by shareholders. In our experience, most proposals that are cast as recommendations or requests that the board of directors take specified action are proper under state law. Accordingly, we will assume that a proposal drafted as a recommendation or suggestion is proper unless the company demonstrates otherwise.

(2) Violation of law: If the proposal would, if implemented, cause the company to violate any state, federal, or foreign law to which it is subject;

Note to paragraph (i)(2): We will not apply this basis for exclusion to permit exclusion of a proposal on grounds that it would violate foreign law if compliance with the foreign law would result in a violation of any state or federal law.

(3) Violation of proxy rules: If the proposal or supporting statement is contrary to any of the Commission's proxy rules, including § 240.14a–9, which prohibits materially false or misleading statements in proxy soliciting materials;

(4) Personal grievance; special interest: If the proposal relates to the redress of a personal claim or grievance against the company or any other person, or if it is designed to result in a benefit to you, or to further a personal interest, which is not shared by the other shareholders at large;

(5) Relevance: If the proposal relates to operations which account for less than 5 percent of the company's total assets at the end of its most recent fiscal year, and for less than 5 percent of its net

earnings and gross sales for its most recent fiscal year, and is not otherwise significantly related to the company's business;

(6)   Absence of power/authority: If the company would lack the power or authority to implement the proposal;

(7)   Management functions: If the proposal deals with a matter relating to the company's ordinary business operations;

(8)   Director elections: If the proposal:

(i)   Would disqualify a nominee who is standing for election;

(ii)   Would remove a director from office before his or her term expired;

(iii)   Questions the competence, business judgment, or character of one or more nominees or directors;

(iv)   Seeks to include a specific individual in the company's proxy materials for election to the board of directors; or

(v)   Otherwise could affect the outcome of the upcoming election of directors.

(9)   Conflicts with company's proposal: If the proposal directly conflicts with one of the company's own proposals to be submitted to shareholders at the same meeting;

Note to paragraph (i)(9): A company's submission to the Commission under this section should specify the points of conflict with the company's proposal.

(10)   Substantially implemented: If the company has already substantially implemented the proposal;

Note to paragraph (i)(10): A company may exclude a shareholder proposal that would provide an advisory vote or seek future advisory votes to approve the compensation of executives as disclosed pursuant to Item 402 of Regulation S-K (§ 229.402 of this chapter) or any successor to Item 402 (a "say-on-pay vote") or that relates to the frequency of say-on-pay votes, provided that in the most recent shareholder vote required by § 240.14a–21(b) of this chapter a single year (i.e., one, two, or three years) received approval of a majority of votes cast on the matter and the company has adopted a policy on the frequency of say-on-pay votes that is consistent with the choice of the majority of votes cast in the most recent shareholder vote required by § 240.14a–21(b) of this chapter.

(11)   Duplication: If the proposal substantially duplicates another proposal previously submitted to the company by another proponent that will be included in the company's proxy materials for the same meeting;

(12)   Resubmissions: If the proposal deals with substantially the same subject matter as another proposal or proposals that has or have been previously included in the company's proxy materials within the preceding 5 calendar years, a company may exclude it from its proxy materials for any meeting held within 3 calendar years of the last time it was included if the proposal received:

(i)   Less than 3% of the vote if proposed once within the preceding 5 calendar years;

(ii)   Less than 6% of the vote on its last submission to shareholders if proposed twice previously within the preceding 5 calendar years; or

(iii)   Less than 10% of the vote on its last submission to shareholders if proposed three times or more previously within the preceding 5 calendar years; and

(13)   Specific amount of dividends: If the proposal relates to specific amounts of cash or stock dividends.

(j)   Question 10: What procedures must the company follow if it intends to exclude my proposal?

(1)   If the company intends to exclude a proposal from its proxy materials, it must file its reasons with the Commission no later than 80 calendar days before it files its definitive proxy statement and form of proxy with the Commission. The company must simultaneously provide you with a copy of its submission. The Commission staff may permit the company to make its submission later than 80 days

before the company files its definitive proxy statement and form of proxy, if the company demonstrates good cause for missing the deadline.

(2) The company must file six paper copies of the following:

(i) The proposal;

(ii) An explanation of why the company believes that it may exclude the proposal, which should, if possible, refer to the most recent applicable authority, such as prior Division letters issued under the rule; and

(iii) A supporting opinion of counsel when such reasons are based on matters of state or foreign law.

(k) Question 11: May I submit my own statement to the Commission responding to the company's arguments?

Yes, you may submit a response, but it is not required. You should try to submit any response to us, with a copy to the company, as soon as possible after the company makes its submission. This way, the Commission staff will have time to consider fully your submission before it issues its response. You should submit six paper copies of your response.

(*l*) Question 12: If the company includes my shareholder proposal in its proxy materials, what information about me must it include along with the proposal itself?

(1) The company's proxy statement must include your name and address, as well as the number of the company's voting securities that you hold. However, instead of providing that information, the company may instead include a statement that it will provide the information to shareholders promptly upon receiving an oral or written request.

(2) The company is not responsible for the contents of your proposal or supporting statement.

(m) Question 13: What can I do if the company includes in its proxy statement reasons why it believes shareholders should not vote in favor of my proposal, and I disagree with some of its statements?

(1) The company may elect to include in its proxy statement reasons why it believes shareholders should vote against your proposal. The company is allowed to make arguments reflecting its own point of view, just as you may express your own point of view in your proposal's supporting statement.

(2) However, if you believe that the company's opposition to your proposal contains materially false or misleading statements that may violate our anti-fraud rule, § 240.14a–9, you should promptly send to the Commission staff and the company a letter explaining the reasons for your view, along with a copy of the company's statements opposing your proposal. To the extent possible, your letter should include specific factual information demonstrating the inaccuracy of the company's claims. Time permitting, you may wish to try to work out your differences with the company by yourself before contacting the Commission staff.

(3) We require the company to send you a copy of its statements opposing your proposal before it sends its proxy materials, so that you may bring to our attention any materially false or misleading statements, under the following timeframes:

(i) If our no-action response requires that you make revisions to your proposal or supporting statement as a condition to requiring the company to include it in its proxy materials, then the company must provide you with a copy of its opposition statements no later than 5 calendar days after the company receives a copy of your revised proposal; or

(ii) In all other cases, the company must provide you with a copy of its opposition statements no later than 30 calendar days before its files definitive copies of its proxy statement and form of proxy under § 240.14a–6.

REVISED UNIFORM LIMITED PARTNERSHIP ACT (1976) WITH 1985 AMENDMENTS

(The 1985 Amendments are Indicated by
Underscore and Strikeout)

———————

Table of Sections

ARTICLE 1.   GENERAL PROVISIONS

ARTICLE 2.   FORMATION: CERTIFICATE OF LIMITED PARTNERSHIP

ARTICLE 3.   LIMITED PARTNERS

ARTICLE 4.   GENERAL PARTNERS

RULPA (1976/1985)

ARTICLE 5.   FINANCE

ARTICLE 6.   DISTRIBUTIONS AND WITHDRAWAL

ARTICLE 7.   ASSIGNMENT OF PARTNERSHIP INTERESTS

ARTICLE 8.   DISSOLUTION

ARTICLE 9.   FOREIGN LIMITED PARTNERSHIPS

ARTICLE 10.   DERIVATIVE ACTIONS

ARTICLE 11.   MISCELLANEOUS

ARTICLE 1
GENERAL PROVISIONS

§ 101.   Definitions

As used in this [Act], unless the context otherwise requires:

(1)   "Certificate of limited partnership" means the certificate referred to in Section 201, and the certificate as amended or restated.

(2)   "Contribution" means any cash, property, services rendered, or a promissory note or other binding obligation to contribute cash or property or to perform services, which a partner contributes to a limited partnership in his capacity as a partner.

(3)   "Event of withdrawal of a general partner" means an event that causes a person to cease to be a general partner as provided in Section 402.

(4)   "Foreign limited partnership" means a partnership formed under the laws of any State state other than this State and having as partners one or more general partners and one or more limited partners.

(5)   "General partner" means a person who has been admitted to a limited partnership as a general partner in accordance with the partnership agreement and named in the certificate of limited partnership as a general partner.

(6)   "Limited partner" means a person who has been admitted to a limited partnership as a limited partner in accordance with the partnership agreement and named in the certificate of limited partnership as a limited partner.

(7)   "Limited partnership" and "domestic limited partnership" mean a partnership formed by two or more persons under the laws of this State and having one or more general partners and one or more limited partners.

(8)   "Partner" means a limited or general partner.

(9)   "Partnership agreement" means any valid agreement, written or oral, of the partners as to the affairs of a limited partnership and the conduct of its business.

(10)   "Partnership interest" means a partner's share of the profits and losses of a limited partnership and the right to receive distributions of partnership assets.

(11)   "Person" means a natural person, partnership, limited partnership (domestic or foreign), trust, estate, association, or corporation.

(12)   "State" means a state, territory, or possession of the United States, the District of Columbia, or the Commonwealth of Puerto Rico.

COMMENT

The definitions in this section clarify a number of uncertainties in the law existing law prior to the 1976 Act, and also make certain changes in such prior law. The 1985 Act makes very few additional changes in Section 101.

Contribution: this definition makes it clear that a present contribution of services and a promise to make a future payment of cash, contribution of property or performance of services are permissible forms for a contribution. Accordingly, the present Section 502 of the 1985 Act provides that a limited partner's promise to make a contribution is enforceable only when set out in a writing signed by the limited partner. (This result is not dissimilar from that under the 1976 Act, which required all promises of future contributions to be described in the certificate of limited partnership, which was to be signed by, among others, the partners making such promises.) The property or services contributed presently or promise promised to be contributed in the future must be accorded a value in the certificate of limited partnership (Section 201(5)) partnership agreement or the partnership records required to be kept pursuant to Section 105, and, in the case of a promise, that value may determine the liability of a partner who fails to honor his agreement (Section 502). Section 3 of the ~~prior uniform law~~ 1916 Act did not permit a limited partner's contribution to be in the form of services, although that inhibition did not apply to general partners.

Foreign limited partnership: the Act only deals with foreign limited partnerships formed under the laws of another ~~"State"~~ "state" of the United States (see subdivision 12 of Section 101), and any adopting ~~State~~ state that desires to deal by statute with the status of entities formed under the laws of foreign countries must make appropriate changes throughout the Act. The exclusion of such entities from the Act was not intended to suggest that their "limited partners" should not be accorded limited liability by the courts of a ~~State~~ state adopting the Act. That question would be resolved by the choice-of-law rules of the forum ~~State~~ state.

General partner: this definition recognizes the separate functions of the partnership agreement and the certificate of limited partnership. The partnership agreement establishes the basic grant of management power to the persons named as general partners; but because of the passive role played by the limited partners, the separate, formal step of ~~embodying~~ memorializing that grant of power in the certificate of limited partnership has been preserved to emphasize its importance and to provide notice of the identity of the partnership's general partners to persons dealing with the partnership.

Limited partner: ~~as in~~ unlike the ~~case of~~ definition of general partners, this definition provides for admission of limited partners through the partnership agreement ~~and solemnization in the certificate of limited partnership. In addition, the definition makes it clear that being named in the certificate of limited partnership is a prerequisite to limited partner status. Failure to file does not, however, mean that the participant is a general partner or that he has general liability. See Sections 202(c) and 303~~ alone and does not require identification of any limited partner in the certificate of limited partnership (Section 201). Under the 1916 and the 1976 Acts, being named as a limited partner in the certificate of limited partnership was a statutory requirement and, in most if not all cases, probably also a prerequisite to limited partner status. By eliminating the requirement that the certificate of limited partnership contain the name, address, and capital contribution of each limited partner, the 1985 Act all but eliminates any risk that a person intended to be a limited partner may be exposed to liability as a general partner as a result of the inadvertent omission of any of that information from the certificate of limited partnership, and also dispenses with the need to amend the certificate of limited partnership upon the admission or withdrawal of, transfer of an interest by, or change in the address or capital contribution of, any limited partner.

Partnership agreement: the ~~prior uniform law~~ 1916 Act did not refer to the partnership agreement, assuming that all important matters affecting limited partners would be set forth in the certificate of limited partnership. Under modern practice, however, it has been common for the partners to enter into a comprehensive partnership agreement, only part of which was required to be included or summarized in the certificate of limited partnership. As reflected in Section 201 of the 1985 Act, the certificate of limited partnership is confined principally to matters respecting the partnership itself and the ~~addition and withdrawal~~ identity of general partners ~~and of capital~~, and other important issues are left to the partnership agreement. Most of the information formerly provided by, but no longer required to be included in, the certificate of limited partnership is now required to be kept in the partnership records (Section 105).

Partnership interest: this definition ~~is new~~ first appeared in the 1976 Act and is intended to define what it is that is transferred when a partnership interest is assigned.

§ 102.   Name

The name of each limited partnership as set forth in its certificate of limited partnership:

(1)   shall contain without abbreviation the words "limited partnership";

(2)   may not contain the name of a limited partner unless (i) it is also the name of a general partner or the corporate name of a corporate general partner, or (ii) the business of the limited partnership had been carried on under that name before the admission of that limited partner;

~~(3)   may not contain any word or phrase indicating or implying that it is organized other than for a purpose stated in its certificate of limited partnership;~~

~~(4)~~ (3) may not be the same as, or deceptively similar to, the name of any corporation or limited partnership organized under the laws of this State or licensed or registered as a foreign corporation or limited partnership in this State; and

(5) (4) may not contain the following words [here insert prohibited words].

COMMENT

Subdivision (2) of Section 102 has been carried over from Section 5 of the ~~prior uniform law~~ 1916 Act with certain editorial changes. The remainder of Section 102 ~~is new~~ first appeared in the 1976 Act and primarily reflects the intention to integrate the registration of limited partnership names with that of corporate names. Accordingly, Section 201 provides for central, ~~State-wide~~ state-wide filing of certificates of limited partnership, and subdivisions (3)~~,~~ and (4) ~~and (5)~~ of Section 102 contain standards to be applied by the filing officer in determining whether the certificate should be filed. Subdivision (1) requires that the proper name of a limited partnership contain the words "limited partnership" in full. Subdivision (3) of the 1976 Act has been deleted, to reflect the deletion from Section 201 of any requirement that the certificate of limited partnership describe the partnership's purposes or the character of its business.

§ 103. Reservation of Name

(a) The exclusive right to the use of a name may be reserved by:

(1) any person intending to organize a limited partnership under this [Act] and to adopt that name;

(2) any domestic limited partnership or any foreign limited partnership registered in this State which, in either case, intends to adopt that name;

(3) any foreign limited partnership intending to register in this State and adopt that name; and

(4) any person intending to organize a foreign limited partnership and intending to have it register in this State and adopt that name.

(b) The reservation shall be made by filing with the Secretary of State an application, executed by the applicant, to reserve a specified name. If the Secretary of State finds that the name is available for use by a domestic or foreign limited partnership, he [or she] shall reserve the name for the exclusive use of the applicant for a period of 120 days. Once having so reserved a name, the same applicant may not again reserve the same name until more than 60 days after the expiration of the last 120-day period for which that applicant reserved that name. The right to the exclusive use of a reserved name may be transferred to any other person by filing in the office of the Secretary of State a notice of the transfer, executed by the applicant for whom the name was reserved and specifying the name and address of the transferee.

COMMENT

Section 103 ~~is new~~ first appeared in the 1976 Act. The ~~prior uniform law~~ 1916 Act did not provide for registration of names.

§ 104. Specified Office and Agent

Each limited partnership shall continuously maintain in this State:

(1) an office, which may but need not be a place of its business in this State, at which shall be kept the records required by Section 105 to be maintained; and

(2) an agent for service of process on the limited partnership, which agent must be an individual resident of this State, a domestic corporation, or a foreign corporation authorized to do business in this State.

COMMENT

Section 104 ~~is new~~ first appeared in the 1976 Act. It requires that a limited partnership have certain minimum contacts with its State of organization, i.e., an office at which the constitutive documents and basic financial information is kept and an agent for service of process.

§ 105. Records to Be Kept

(a) Each limited partnership shall keep at the office referred to in Section 104(1) the following:

(1)   a current list of the full name and last known business address of each partner ~~set forth~~, separately identifying the general partners (in alphabetical order) and the limited partners (in alphabetical order~~,~~);

(2)   a copy of the certificate of limited partnership and all certificates of amendment thereto, together with executed copies of any powers of attorney pursuant to which any certificate has been executed~~,~~;

(3)   copies of the limited partnership's federal, state and local income tax returns and reports, if any, for the three most recent years~~, and~~;

(4)   copies of any then effective written partnership agreements and of any financial statements of the limited partnership for the three most recent years; and

(5)   unless contained in a written partnership agreement, a writing setting out:

(i)   the amount of cash and a description and statement of the agreed value of the other property or services contributed by each partner and which each partner has agreed to contribute;

(ii)   the times at which or events on the happening of which any additional contributions agreed to be made by each partner are to be made;

(iii)   any right of a partner to receive, or of a general partner to make, distributions to a partner which include a return of all or any part of the partner's contribution; and

(iv)   any events upon the happening of which the limited partnership is to be dissolved and its affairs wound up.

(b)   ~~Those records~~ Records kept under this section are subject to inspection and copying at the reasonable request and at the expense of any partner during ordinary business hours.

COMMENT

Section 105 ~~is new~~ first appeared in the 1976 Act. In view of the passive nature of the limited partner's position, it has been widely felt that limited partners are entitled to access to certain basic documents and information, including the certificate of limited partnership ~~and~~, any partnership agreement, and a writing setting out certain important matters which, under the 1916 and 1976 Acts, were required to be set out in the certificate of limited partnership. In view of the great diversity among limited partnerships, it was thought inappropriate to require a standard form of financial report, and Section 105 does no more than require retention of tax returns and any other financial statements that are prepared. The names and addresses of the general partners are made available to the general public in the certificate of limited partnership.

§ 106.   Nature of Business

A limited partnership may carry on any business that a partnership without limited partners may carry on except [here designate prohibited activities].

COMMENT

Section 106 is identical to Section 3 of the ~~prior uniform law~~ 1916 Act. Many states require that certain regulated industries, such as banking, may be carried on only by entities organized pursuant to special statutes, and it is contemplated that the prohibited activities would be confined to the matters covered by those statutes.

§ 107.   Business Transactions of Partner with Partnership

Except as provided in the partnership agreement, a partner may lend money to and transact other business with the limited partnership and, subject to other applicable law, has the same rights and obligations with respect thereto as a person who is not a partner.

COMMENT

Section 107 makes a number of important changes in Section 13 of the ~~prior uniform law~~ 1916 Act. Section 13, in effect, created a special fraudulent conveyance provision applicable to the making of secured loans by limited partners and the repayment by limited partnerships of loans from limited partners. Section 107 leaves that question to a ~~State's~~ state's general fraudulent conveyance statute. In addition, Section 107 eliminates the prohibition in ~~former~~ Section 13 against a general ~~partner (as opposed to a limited partner)~~ partner's sharing pro rata with general creditors in the case of an unsecured loan. Of course, other doctrines developed under bankruptcy and insolvency laws may require the subordination of loans by partners under appropriate circumstances.

ARTICLE 2
FORMATION: CERTIFICATE OF LIMITED PARTNERSHIP

§ 201.   Certificate of Limited Partnership

(a)   In order to form a limited partnership, ~~two or more persons must execute~~ a certificate of limited partnership. ~~The certificate shall be~~ must be executed and filed in the office of the Secretary of State. ~~and~~ The certificate shall set forth:

(1)   the name of the limited partnership;

~~(2)   the general character of its business;~~

~~(3)~~ (2) the address of the office and the name and address of the agent for service of process required to be maintained by Section 104;

~~(4)~~ (3) the name and the business address of each general partner ~~(specifying separately the general partners and limited partners)~~;

~~(5)   the amount of cash and a description and statement of the agreed value of the other property or services contributed by each partner and which each partner has agreed to contribute in the future;~~

~~(6)   the times at which or events on the happening of which any additional contributions agreed to be made by each partner are to be made;~~

~~(7)   any power of a limited partner to grant the right to become a limited partner to an assignee of any part of his partnership interest, and the terms and conditions of the power;~~

~~(8)   if agreed upon, the time at which or the events on the happening of which a partner may terminate his membership in the limited partnership and the amount of, or the method of determining, the distribution to which he may be entitled respecting his partnership interest, and the terms and conditions of the termination and distribution;~~

~~(9)   any right of a partner to receive distributions of property, including cash from the limited partnership;~~

~~(10)   any right of a partner to receive, or of a general partner to make, distributions to a partner which include a return of all or any part of the partner's contribution;~~

~~(11)   any time at which or events upon the happening of which the limited partnership is to be dissolved and its affairs wound up;~~

~~(12)   any right of the remaining general partners to continue the business on the happening of an event of withdrawal of a general partner; and~~

(4)   the latest date upon which the limited partnership is to dissolve; and

~~(13)~~ (5) any other matters the general partners determine to include therein.

(b)   A limited partnership is formed at the time of the filing of the certificate of limited partnership in the office of the Secretary of State or at any later time specified in the certificate of limited partnership if, in either case, there has been substantial compliance with the requirements of this section.

COMMENT

The 1985 Act requires far fewer matters ~~required~~ to be set forth in the certificate of limited partnership ~~are not different in kind from those required by~~ than did Section 2 of the ~~prior uniform law, although certain additions and deletions have been made and the description has been revised to conform with the rest of the Act. In general,~~

the certificate is intended to serve two functions: first, to place creditors on notice of the 1916 Act and Section 201 of the 1976 Act. This is in recognition of the fact that the partnership agreement, not the certificate of limited partnership, has become the authoritative and comprehensive document for most limited partnerships, and that creditors and potential creditors of the partnership do and should refer to the partnership agreement and to other information furnished to them directly by the partnership and by others, not to the certificate of limited partnership, to obtain facts concerning the capital and finances of the partnership and the rules regarding additional contributions to and withdrawals from the partnership; second, to clearly delineate the time at which persons become general partners and limited partners other matters of concern. Subparagraph (b), which is based upon the prior uniform law 1916 Act, has been retained to make it clear that the existence of the limited partnership depends only upon compliance with this section. Its continued existence is not dependent upon compliance with other provisions of this Act.

§ 202.   Amendment to Certificate

(a)   A certificate of limited partnership is amended by filing a certificate of amendment thereto in the office of the Secretary of State. The certificate shall set forth:

(1)   the name of the limited partnership;

(2)   the date of filing the certificate; and

(3)   the amendment to the certificate.

(b)   Within 30 days after the happening of any of the following events, an amendment to a certificate of limited partnership reflecting the occurrence of the event or events shall be filed:

(1)   a change in the amount or character of the contribution of any partner, or in any partner's obligation to make a contribution;

(2)   (1) the admission of a new general partner;

(3)   (2) the withdrawal of a general partner; or

(4)   (3) the continuation of the business under Section 801 after an event of withdrawal of a general partner.

(c)   A general partner who becomes aware that any statement in a certificate of limited partnership was false when made or that any arrangements or other facts described have changed, making the certificate inaccurate in any respect, shall promptly amend the certificate, but an amendment to show a change of address of a limited partner need be filed only once every 12 months.

(d)   A certificate of limited partnership may be amended at any time for any other proper purpose the general partners determine.

(e)   No person has any liability because an amendment to a certificate of limited partnership has not been filed to reflect the occurrence of any event referred to in subsection (b) of this Section section if the amendment is filed within the 30-day period specified in subsection (b).

(f)   A restated certificate of limited partnership may be executed and filed in the same manner as a certificate of amendment.

COMMENT

Section 202 makes of the 1976 Act made substantial changes in Section 24 of the prior uniform law 1916 Act. Further changes in this section are made by the 1985 Act. Paragraph (b) lists the basic events—the addition or withdrawal of partners or capital or capital obligations a general partner—that are so central to the function of the certificate of limited partnership that they require prompt amendment. With the elimination of the requirement that the certificate of limited partnership include the names of all limited partners and the amount and character of all capital contributions, the requirement of the 1916 and 1976 Acts that the certificate be amended upon the admission or withdrawal of limited partners or on any change in the partnership capital must also be eliminated. This change should greatly reduce the frequency and complexity of amendments to the certificate of limited partnership. Paragraph (c) makes it clear, as it was not clear under subdivision (2)(g) of former Section 24 24(2)(g) of the 1916 Act, that the certificate of limited partnership is intended to be an accurate description of the facts to which it relates at all times and does not speak merely as of the date it is executed.

Paragraph (e) provides a "safe harbor" against claims of creditors or others who assert that they have been misled by the failure to amend the certificate of limited partnership to reflect changes in any of the important facts referred to in paragraph (b); if the certificate of limited partnership is amended within 30 days of the occurrence of the event, no creditor or other person can recover for damages sustained during the interim. Additional protection is afforded by the provisions of Section 304. The elimination of the requirement that the certificate of limited partnership identify all limited partners and their respective capital contributions may have rendered paragraph (e) an obsolete and unnecessary vestige. The principal, if not the sole, purpose of paragraph (e) in the 1976 Act was to protect limited partners newly admitted to a partnership from being held liable as general partners when an amendment to the certificate identifying them as limited partners and describing their contributions was not filed contemporaneously with their admission to the partnership. Such liability cannot arise under the 1985 Act because such information is not required to be stated in the certificate. Nevertheless, the 1985 Act retains paragraph (e) because it is protective of partners, shielding them from liability to the extent its provisions apply, and does not create or impose any liability.

Paragraph (f) is added in the 1985 Act to provide explicit statutory recognition of the common practice of restating an amended certificate of limited partnership. While a limited partnership seeking to amend its certificate of limited partnership may do so by recording a restated certificate which incorporates the amendment, that is by no means the only purpose or function of a restated certificate, which may be filed for the sole purpose of restating in a single integrated instrument all the provisions of a limited partnership's certificate of limited partnership which are then in effect.

§ 203. Cancellation of Certificate

A certificate of limited partnership shall be cancelled upon the dissolution and the commencement of winding up of the partnership or at any other time there are no limited partners. A certificate of cancellation shall be filed in the office of the Secretary of State and set forth:

(1)   the name of the limited partnership;

(2)   the date of filing of its certificate of limited partnership;

(3)   the reason for filing the certificate of cancellation;

(4)   the effective date (which shall be a date certain) of cancellation if it is not to be effective upon the filing of the certificate; and

(5)   any other information the general partners filing the certificate determine.

COMMENT

Section 203 changes Section 24 of the ~~prior uniform law~~ 1916 Act by making it clear that the certificate of cancellation should be filed upon the commencement of winding up of the limited partnership. Section 24 provided for cancellation "when the partnership is dissolved."

§ 204. Execution of Certificates

(a)   Each certificate required by this Article to be filed in the office of the Secretary of State shall be executed in the following manner:

(1)   an original certificate of limited partnership must be signed by all general partners ~~named therein~~;

(2)   a certificate of amendment must be signed by at least one general partner and by each other general partner designated in the certificate as a new general partner ~~or whose contribution is described as having been increased~~; and

(3)   a certificate of cancellation must be signed by all general partners~~;~~.

(b)   Any person may sign a certificate by an attorney-in-fact, but a power of attorney to sign a certificate relating to the admission~~, or increased contribution,~~ of a general partner must specifically describe the admission ~~or increase~~.

(c)   The execution of a certificate by a general partner constitutes an affirmation under the penalties of perjury that the facts stated therein are true.

COMMENT

Section 204 collects in one place the formal requirements for the execution of certificates which were set forth in Sections 2 and 25 of the ~~prior uniform law~~ 1916 Act. Those sections required that each certificate be signed by all partners, and there developed an unnecessarily cumbersome practice of having each limited partner sign powers of attorney to authorize the general partners to execute certificates of amendment on their behalf. ~~Section 204 insures that each partner must sign a certificate when he becomes a partner or when the certificates reflect any increase in his obligation to make contributions.~~ The 1976 Act, while simplifying the execution requirements, nevertheless required that an original certificate of limited partnership be signed by all partners and a certificate of amendment by all new partners being admitted to the limited partnership. However, the certificate of limited partnership is no longer required to include the name or capital contribution of any limited partner. Therefore, while the 1985 Act still requires all general partners to sign the original certificate of limited partnership, no limited partner is required to sign any certificate. Certificates of amendment are required to be signed by only one general partner and all general partners must sign certificates of cancellation. ~~Section 204 prohibits blanket powers of attorney for the execution of certificates in many cases, since those conditions under which a partner is required to sign have been narrowed to circumstances of special importance to that partner.~~ The ~~former~~ requirement in the 1916 Act that all certificates be sworn ~~has been confined to statements by the general partners, recognizing that the limited partner's role is a limited one~~ was deleted in the 1976 and 1985 Acts as potentially an unfair trap for the unwary (see, e.g., Wisniewski v. Johnson, 223 Va. 141, 286 S.E.2d 223 (1982)); in its place, paragraph (c) now provides, as a matter of law, that the execution of a certificate by a general partner subjects him to the penalties of perjury for inaccuracies in the certificate.

§ 205.   ~~Amendment or Cancellation~~ Execution by Judicial Act

If a person required by Section 204 to execute ~~a~~ any certificate ~~of amendment or cancellation~~ fails or refuses to do so, any other ~~partner, and any assignee of a partnership interest,~~ person who is adversely affected by the failure or refusal~~,~~ may petition the [designate the appropriate court] to direct the ~~amendment or cancellation~~ execution of the certificate. If the court finds that ~~the amendment or cancellation is proper~~ it is proper for the certificate to be executed and that any person so designated has failed or refused to execute the certificate, it shall order the Secretary of State to record an appropriate certificate ~~of amendment or cancellation~~.

COMMENT

Section 205 ~~changes~~ of the 1976 Act changed subdivisions (3) and (4) of Section 25 of the ~~prior uniform law~~ 1916 Act by confining the persons who have standing to seek judicial intervention to partners and to those assignees who ~~are~~ were adversely affected by the failure or refusal of the appropriate persons to file a certificate of amendment or cancellation. Section 205 of the 1985 Act reverses that restriction, and provides that any person adversely affected by a failure or refusal to file any certificate (not only a certificate of cancellation or amendment) has standing to seek judicial intervention.

§ 206.   Filing in Office of Secretary of State

(a)   Two signed copies of the certificate of limited partnership and of any certificates of amendment or cancellation (or of any judicial decree of amendment or cancellation) shall be delivered to the Secretary of State. A person who executes a certificate as an agent or fiduciary need not exhibit evidence of his [or her] authority as a prerequisite to filing. Unless the Secretary of State finds that any certificate does not conform to law, upon receipt of all filing fees required by law he [or she] shall:

(1)   endorse on each duplicate original the word "Filed" and the day, month and year of the filing thereof;

(2)   file one duplicate original in his [or her] office; and

(3)   return the other duplicate original to the person who filed it or his [or her] representative.

(b)   Upon the filing of a certificate of amendment (or judicial decree of amendment) in the office of the Secretary of State, the certificate of limited partnership shall be amended as set forth therein, and upon the effective date of a certificate of cancellation (or a judicial decree thereof), the certificate of limited partnership is cancelled.

COMMENT

Section 206 ~~is new~~ <u>first appeared in the 1976 Act</u>. In addition to providing mechanics for the central filing system, the second sentence of this section does away with the requirement, formerly imposed by some local filing officers, that persons who have executed certificates under a power of attorney exhibit executed copies of the power of attorney itself. Paragraph (b) changes subdivision (5) of Section 25 of the ~~prior uniform law~~ <u>1916 Act</u> by providing that certificates of cancellation are effective upon their effective date under Section 203.

§ 207.   Liability for False Statement in Certificate

If any certificate of limited partnership or certificate of amendment or cancellation contains a false statement, one who suffers loss by reliance on the statement may recover damages for the loss from:

(1)   any person who executes the certificate, or causes another to execute it on his behalf, and knew, and any general partner who knew or should have known, the statement to be false at the time the certificate was executed; and

(2)   any general partner who thereafter knows or should have known that any arrangement or other fact described in the certificate has changed, making the statement inaccurate in any respect within a sufficient time before the statement was relied upon reasonably to have enabled that general partner to cancel or amend the certificate, or to file a petition for its cancellation or amendment under Section 205.

COMMENT

Section 207 changes Section 6 of the ~~prior uniform law~~ <u>1916 Act</u> by providing explicitly for the liability of persons who sign a certificate as agent under a power of attorney and by confining the obligation to amend a certificate of limited partnership in light of future events to general partners.

§ 208.   <u>Scope of</u> Notice

The fact that a certificate of limited partnership is on file in the office of the Secretary of State is notice that the partnership is a limited partnership and the persons designated therein as ~~limited~~ <u>general</u> partners are ~~limited~~ <u>general</u> partners, but it is not notice of any other fact.

COMMENT

Section 208 ~~is new~~ <u>first appeared in the 1976 Act, and referred to the certificate's providing constructive notice of the status as limited partners of those so identified therein. The 1985 Act's deletion of any requirement that the certificate name limited partners required that Section 208 be modified accordingly.</u>

By stating that the filing of a certificate of limited partnership only results in notice of the ~~limited~~ <u>general</u> liability of the ~~limited~~ <u>general</u> partners, ~~it~~ <u>Section 208</u> obviates the concern that third parties may be held to have notice of special provisions set forth in the certificate. While this section is designed to preserve <u>by implication</u> the limited liability of limited partners, the ~~notice~~ <u>implicit protection</u> provided is not intended to change any liability of a limited partner which may be created by his action or inaction under the law of estoppel, agency, fraud, or the like.

§ 209.   Delivery of Certificates to Limited Partners

Upon the return by the Secretary of State pursuant to Section 206 of a certificate marked "Filed", the general partners shall promptly deliver or mail a copy of the certificate of limited partnership and each certificate of amendment or cancellation to each limited partner unless the partnership agreement provides otherwise.

COMMENT

This section ~~is new~~ <u>first appeared in the 1976 Act</u>.

ARTICLE 3
LIMITED PARTNERS

§ 301.   Admission of ~~Additional~~ Limited Partners

(a)   A person becomes a limited partner:

     (1)   at the time the limited partnership is formed; or

     (2)   at any later time specified in the records of the limited partnership for becoming a limited partner.

~~(a)~~ (b) After the filing of a limited partnership's original certificate of limited partnership, a person may be admitted as an additional limited partner:

     (1)   in the case of a person acquiring a partnership interest directly from the limited partnership, upon compliance with the partnership agreement or, if the partnership agreement does not so provide, upon the written consent of all partners; and

     (2)   in the case of an assignee of a partnership interest of a partner who has the power, as provided in Section 704, to grant the assignee the right to become a limited partner, upon the exercise of that power and compliance with any conditions limiting the grant or exercise of the power.

~~(b) In each case under subsection (a), the person acquiring the partnership interest becomes a limited partner only upon amendment of the certificate of limited partnership reflecting that fact.~~

COMMENT

Section 301(a) is new; no counterpart was found in the 1916 or 1976 Acts. This section imposes on the partnership an obligation to maintain in its records the date each limited partner becomes a limited partner. Under the 1976 Act, one could not become a limited partner until an appropriate certificate reflecting his status as such was filed with the Secretary of State. Because the 1985 Act eliminates the need to name limited partners in the certificate of limited partnership, an alternative mechanism had to be established to evidence the fact and date of a limited partner's admission. The partnership records required to be maintained under Section 105 now serve that function, subject to the limitation that no person may become a limited partner before the partnership is formed (Section 201(b)).

Subdivision (1) of Section ~~301(a)~~ 301(b) adds to Section 8 of the ~~prior uniform law~~ 1916 Act an explicit recognition of the fact that unanimous consent of all partners is required for admission of new limited partners unless the partnership agreement provides otherwise. Subdivision (2) is derived from Section 19 of the ~~prior uniform law~~ 1916 Act but abandons the former terminology of "substituted limited partner."

§ 302.   Voting

Subject to Section 303, the partnership agreement may grant to all or a specified group of the limited partners the right to vote (on a per capita or other basis) upon any matter.

COMMENT

Section 302 ~~is new~~ first appeared in the 1976 Act, and must be read together with subdivision ~~(b)(5)~~ (b)(6) of Section 303. Although the ~~prior uniform law~~ 1916 Act did not speak specifically of the voting powers of limited partners, it ~~is~~ was not uncommon for partnership agreements to grant such ~~power~~ powers to limited partners. Section 302 is designed only to make it clear that the partnership agreement may grant such power to limited partners. If such powers are granted to limited partners beyond the "safe harbor" of subdivision (6) or (8) of Section ~~303(b)(5)~~ 303(b), a court may (but of course need not) hold that, under the circumstances, the limited partners have participated in "control of the business" within the meaning of Section 303(a). Section 303(c) ~~simply means~~ makes clear that the exercise of powers beyond the ambit of Section 303(b) is not ipso facto to be taken as taking part in the control of the business.

§ 303.   Liability to Third Parties

(a)   Except as provided in subsection (d), a limited partner is not liable for the obligations of a limited partnership unless he [or she] is also a general partner or, in addition to the exercise of his [or her] rights and powers as a limited partner, he [or she] ~~takes part~~ participates in the control of the business. However, if the limited ~~partner's participation~~ partner participates in the control of the business ~~is not substantially the same as the exercise of the powers of a general partner~~, he [or she] is liable only to persons who transact business with the limited partnership ~~with actual knowledge of his participation in control~~ reasonably believing, based upon the limited partner's conduct, that the limited partner is a general partner.

(b)   A limited partner does not participate in the control of the business within the meaning of subsection (a) solely by doing one or more of the following:

(1)   being a contractor for or an agent or employee of the limited partnership or of a general partner or being an officer, director, or shareholder of a general partner that is a corporation;

(2)   consulting with and advising a general partner with respect to the business of the limited partnership;

(3)   acting as surety for the limited partnership or guaranteeing or assuming one or more specific obligations of the limited partnership;

(4)   ~~approving or disapproving an amendment to the partnership agreement~~ taking any action required or permitted by law to bring or pursue a derivative action in the right of the limited partnership; ~~or~~

(5)   ~~voting on one or more of the following matters:~~

(5)   requesting or attending a meeting of partners;

(6)   proposing, approving, or disapproving, by voting or otherwise, one or more of the following matters:

(i)   the dissolution and winding up of the limited partnership;

(ii)   the sale, exchange, lease, mortgage, pledge, or other transfer of all or substantially all of the assets of the limited partnership ~~other than in the ordinary course of its business~~;

(iii)   the incurrence of indebtedness by the limited partnership other than in the ordinary course of its business;

(iv)   a change in the nature of the business; ~~or~~

(v)   the admission or removal of a general partner~~.~~;

(vi)   the admission or removal of a limited partner;

(vii)   a transaction involving an actual or potential conflict of interest between a general partner and the limited partnership or the limited partners;

(viii)   an amendment to the partnership agreement or certificate of limited partnership; or

(ix)   matters related to the business of the limited partnership not otherwise enumerated in this subsection (b), which the partnership agreement states in writing may be subject to the approval or disapproval of limited partners;

(7)   winding up the limited partnership pursuant to Section 803; or

(8)   exercising any right or power permitted to limited partners under this [Act] and not specifically enumerated in this subsection (b).

(c)   The enumeration in subsection (b) does not mean that the possession or exercise of any other powers by a limited partner constitutes participation by him [or her] in the business of the limited partnership.

(d)   A limited partner who knowingly permits his [or her] name to be used in the name of the limited partnership, except under circumstances permitted by Section 102(2), is liable to creditors who extend credit to the limited partnership without actual knowledge that the limited partner is not a general partner.

COMMENT

Section 303 makes several important changes in Section 7 of the ~~prior uniform law~~ 1916 Act. The first sentence of Section 303(a) ~~carries over the basic test from former Section 7—whether the limited partner "takes part in the control of the business"—in order to insure that judicial decisions under the prior uniform law remain applicable to the extent not expressly changed~~ differs from the text of Section 7 of the 1916 Act in that it speaks of participating (rather than taking part) in the control of the business; this was done for the sake of consistency with the second sentence of Section 303(a), not to change the meaning of the text. It is intended that judicial decisions interpreting the phrase "takes part in the control of the business" under the prior uniform law will remain applicable to the extent that a different result is not called for by other provisions of Section 303 and other provisions of the Act. The second sentence of Section 303(a) reflects a wholly new concept. ~~Because~~ in the 1976 Act that has been further modified in the 1985 Act. It was adopted partly because of the difficulty of determining when the "control" line has been overstepped, ~~it was thought it unfair to impose general partner's liability on a limited partner except to the extent that a third party had knowledge of his participation in control of the business. On the other hand, in order to avoid permitting a limited partner to exercise all of the powers of a general partner while avoiding any direct dealings with third parties, the "is not substantially the same as" test was introduced~~ but also (and more importantly) because of a determination that it is not sound public policy to hold a limited partner who is not also a general partner liable for the obligations of the partnership except to persons who have done business with the limited partnership reasonably believing, based on the limited partner's conduct, that he is a general partner. Paragraph (b) is intended to provide a "safe harbor" by enumerating certain activities which a limited partner may carry on for the partnership without being deemed to have taken part in control of the business. This "safe harbor" list has been expanded beyond that set out in the 1976 Act to reflect case law and statutory developments and more clearly to assure that limited partners are not subjected to general liability where such liability is inappropriate. Paragraph (d) is derived from Section 5 of the ~~prior uniform law~~ 1916 Act, but adds as a condition to the limited partner's liability the ~~fact~~ requirement that a limited partner must have knowingly permitted his name to be used in the name of the limited partnership.

§ 304.   Person Erroneously Believing Himself [or Herself] Limited Partner

(a)   Except as provided in subsection (b), a person who makes a contribution to a business enterprise and erroneously but in good faith believes that he [or she] has become a limited partner in the enterprise is not a general partner in the enterprise and is not bound by its obligations by reason of making the contribution, receiving distributions from the enterprise, or exercising any rights of a limited partner, if, on ascertaining the mistake, he [or she]:

(1)   causes an appropriate certificate of limited partnership or a certificate of amendment to be executed and filed; or

(2)   withdraws from future equity participation in the enterprise by executing and filing in the office of the Secretary of State a certificate declaring withdrawal under this section.

(b)   A person who makes a contribution of the kind described in subsection (a) is liable as a general partner to any third party who transacts business with the enterprise (i) before the person withdraws and an appropriate certificate is filed to show withdrawal, or (ii) before an appropriate certificate is filed to show ~~his status as a limited partner and, in the case of an amendment, after expiration of the 30-day period for filing an amendment relating to the person as a limited partner under Section 202~~ that he [or she] is not a general partner, but in either case only if the third party actually believed in good faith that the person was a general partner at the time of the transaction.

COMMENT

Section 304 is derived from Section 11 of the ~~prior uniform law~~ 1916 Act. The "good faith" requirement has been added in the first sentence of Section 304(a). The provisions of subdivision (2) of Section 304(a) are intended to clarify an ambiguity in the prior law by providing that a person who chooses to withdraw from the enterprise in order to protect himself from liability is not required to renounce any of his then current interest in the enterprise so long as he has no further participation as an equity participant. Paragraph (b) preserves the liability of the equity participant prior to withdrawal ~~(and after the time for appropriate amendment in the case of a limited partnership)~~ by such person from the limited partnership or amendment to the certificate demonstrating that such person is not a general partner to any third party who has transacted business with the person believing in good faith that he was a general partner.

Evidence strongly suggests that Section 11 of the 1916 Act and Section 304 of the 1976 Act were rarely used, and one might expect that Section 304 of the 1985 Act may never have to be used. Section 11 of the 1916 Act and Section 304 of the 1976 Act could have been used by a person who invested in a limited partnership believing he would be a limited partner but who was not identified as a limited partner in the certificate of limited partnership. However, because the 1985 Act does not require limited partners to be named in the certificate, the only situation to which Section 304 would now appear to be applicable is one in which a person intending to be a limited partner was erroneously identified as a general partner in the certificate.

§ 305. Information

Each limited partner has the right to:

(1)   inspect and copy any of the partnership records required to be maintained by Section 105; and

(2)   obtain from the general partners from time to time upon reasonable demand (i) true and full information regarding the state of the business and financial condition of the limited partnership, (ii) promptly after becoming available, a copy of the limited partnership's federal, state and local income tax returns for each year, and (iii) other information regarding the affairs of the limited partnership as is just and reasonable.

COMMENT

Section 305 changes and restates the rights of limited partners to information about the partnership formerly provided by Section 10 of the ~~prior uniform law~~ 1916 Act. Its importance has increased as a result of the 1985 Act's substituting the records of the partnership for the certificate of limited partnership as the place where certain categories of information are to be kept.

Section 305, which should be read together with Section 105(b), provides a mechanism for limited partners to obtain information about the partnership useful to them in making decisions concerning the partnership and their investments in it. Its purpose is not to provide a mechanism for competitors of the partnership or others having interests or agendas adverse to the partnership's to subvert the partnership's business. It is assumed that courts will protect limited partnerships from abuses and attempts to misuse Section 305 for improper purposes.

ARTICLE 4
GENERAL PARTNERS

§ 401.   Admission of Additional General Partners

After the filing of a limited partnership's original certificate of limited partnership, additional general partners may be admitted ~~only~~ as provided in writing in the partnership agreement or, if the partnership agreement does not provide in writing for the admission of additional general partners, with the ~~specific~~ written consent of ~~each partner~~ all partners.

COMMENT

Section 401 is derived from, but represents a significant departure from, Section 9(1)(e) of the ~~prior law and carries over the unwaivable requirement that all limited partners must consent~~ 1916 Act and Section 401 of the 1976 Act, which required, as a condition to the admission of an additional general partner, that all limited partners consent and that such consent ~~must~~ specifically identify the general partner involved. Section 401 of the 1985 Act provides that the written partnership agreement determines the procedure for authorizing the admission of additional general partners, and that the written consent of all partners is required only when the partnership agreement fails to address the question.

§ 402.   Events of Withdrawal

Except as approved by the specific written consent of all partners at the time, a person ceases to be a general partner of a limited partnership upon the happening of any of the following events:

    (1)   the general partner withdraws from the limited partnership as provided in Section 602;

    (2)   the general partner ceases to be a member of the limited partnership as provided in Section 702;

    (3)   the general partner is removed as a general partner in accordance with the partnership agreement;

    (4)   unless otherwise provided in writing in the ~~certificate of limited~~ partnership agreement, the general partner: (i) makes an assignment for the benefit of creditors; (ii) files a voluntary petition in bankruptcy; (iii) is adjudicated a bankrupt or insolvent; (iv) files a petition or answer seeking for himself [or herself] any reorganization, arrangement, composition, readjustment, liquidation, dissolution or similar relief under any statute, law, or regulation; (v) files an answer or other pleading admitting or failing to contest the material allegations of a petition filed against him [or her] in any proceeding of this nature; or (vi) seeks, consents to, or acquiesces in the appointment of a trustee, receiver, or liquidator of the general partner or of all or any substantial part of his [or her] properties;

    (5)   unless otherwise provided in writing in the ~~certificate of limited~~ partnership agreement, [120] days after the commencement of any proceeding against the general partner seeking reorganization, arrangement, composition, readjustment, liquidation, dissolution or similar relief under any statute, law, or regulation, the proceeding has not been dismissed, or if within [90] days after the appointment without his [or her] consent or acquiescence of a trustee, receiver, or liquidator of the general partner or of all or any substantial part of his [or her] properties, the appointment is not vacated or stayed or within [90] days after the expiration of any such stay, the appointment is not vacated;

    (6)   in the case of a general partner who is a natural person,

        (i)   his [or her] death; or

        (ii)   the entry of an order by a court of competent jurisdiction adjudicating him [or her] incompetent to manage his [or her] person or his [or her] estate;

    (7)   in the case of a general partner who is acting as a general partner by virtue of being a trustee of a trust, the termination of the trust (but not merely the substitution of a new trustee);

    (8)   in the case of a general partner that is a separate partnership, the dissolution and commencement of winding up of the separate partnership;

    (9)   in the case of a general partner that is a corporation, the filing of a certificate of dissolution, or its equivalent, for the corporation or the revocation of its charter; or

    (10)   in the case of an estate, the distribution by the fiduciary of the estate's entire interest in the partnership.

COMMENT

Section 402 expands considerably the provisions of Section 20 of the ~~prior uniform law~~ 1916 Act which provided for dissolution in the event of the retirement, death or insanity of a general partner. Subdivisions (1), (2) and (3) recognize that the general partner's agency relationship is terminable at will, although it may result in a breach of the partnership agreement giving rise to an action for damages. Subdivisions (4) and (5) reflect a judgment that, unless the limited partners agree otherwise, they ought to have the power to rid themselves of a general partner who is in such dire financial straits that he is the subject of proceedings under the National Bankruptcy ~~Act~~ Code or a similar provision of law. Subdivisions (6) through (10) simply elaborate on the notion of death in the case of a general partner who is not a natural person. ~~Of course, the addition of the words "and in the partnership statement" was not intended to suggest that liabilities to third parties could be affected by provisions in the partnership agreement.~~ Subdivisions (4) and (5) differ from their counterparts in the 1976 Act, reflecting the policy underlying the 1985 revision of Section 201, that the partnership agreement, not the certificate of limited partnership, is the appropriate document for setting out most provisions relating to the respective powers, rights, and obligations of the partners inter se. Although the partnership agreement need not be written, the 1985 Act provides that, to protect the partners from fraud, these and certain other particularly significant provisions must be set out in a written partnership agreement to be effective for the purposes described in the Act.

§ 403. General Powers and Liabilities

(a)   Except as provided in this [Act] or in the partnership agreement, a general partner of a limited partnership has the rights and powers and is subject to the restrictions of a partner in a partnership without limited partners.

(b)   Except as provided in this [Act], a general partner of a limited partnership has the liabilities of a partner in a partnership without limited partners to persons other than the partnership and the other partners. Except as provided in this [Act] or in the partnership agreement, a general partner of a limited partnership has the liabilities of a partner in a partnership without limited partners to the partnership and to the other partners.

COMMENT

Section 403 is derived from Section 9(1) of the prior uniform law 1916 Act.

§ 404. Contributions by General Partner

A general partner of a limited partnership may make contributions to the partnership and share in the profits and losses of, and in distributions from, the limited partnership as a general partner. A general partner also may make contributions to and share in profits, losses, and distributions as a limited partner. A person who is both a general partner and a limited partner has the rights and powers, and is subject to the restrictions and liabilities, of a general partner and, except as provided in the partnership agreement, also has the powers, and is subject to the restrictions, of a limited partner to the extent of his [or her] participation in the partnership as a limited partner.

COMMENT

Section 404 is derived from Section 12 of the prior uniform law 1916 Act and makes clear that the partnership agreement may provide that a general partner who is also a limited partner may exercise all of the powers of a limited partner.

§ 405. Voting

The partnership agreement may grant to all or certain identified general partners the right to vote (on a per capita or any other basis), separately or with all or any class of the limited partners, on any matter.

COMMENT

Section 405 is new first appeared in the 1976 Act and is intended to make it clear that the Act does not require that the limited partners have any right to vote on matters as a separate class.

ARTICLE 5
FINANCE

§ 501. Form of Contribution

The contribution of a partner may be in cash, property, or services rendered, or a promissory note or other obligation to contribute cash or property or to perform services.

COMMENT

As noted in the comment to Section 101, the explicit permission to make contributions of services expands Section 4 of the prior uniform law 1916 Act.

§ 502.   Liability for Contribution

(a)   A promise by a limited partner to contribute to the limited partnership is not enforceable unless set out in a writing signed by the limited partner.

~~(a)~~ (b) Except as provided in the ~~certificate of limited~~ partnership agreement, a partner is obligated to the limited partnership to perform any enforceable promise to contribute cash or property or to perform services, even if he [or she] is unable to perform because of death, disability, or any other reason. If a partner does not make the required contribution of property or services, he [or she] is obligated at the option of the limited partnership to contribute cash equal to that portion of the value, as stated in the ~~certificate of limited~~ partnership records required to be kept pursuant to Section 105, of the stated contribution which has not been made.

~~(b)~~ (c) Unless otherwise provided in the partnership agreement, the obligation of a partner to make a contribution or return money or other property paid or distributed in violation of this [Act] may be compromised only by consent of all partners. Notwithstanding the compromise, a creditor of a limited partnership who extends credit~~,~~ or ~~whose claim arises,~~ otherwise acts in reliance on that obligation after the ~~filing of the certificate of limited partnership or an amendment thereto~~ partner signs a writing which~~,~~ ~~in either case,~~ reflects the obligation~~,~~ and before the amendment or cancellation thereof to reflect the compromise~~,~~ may enforce the original obligation.

COMMENT

Section 502(a) is new; it has no counterpart in the 1916 or 1976 Act. Because, unlike the prior uniform acts, the 1985 Act does not require that promises to contribute cash, property, or services be described in the limited partnership certificate, to protect against fraud it requires instead that such important promises be in a signed writing.

Although Section 17(1) of the ~~prior uniform law~~ 1916 Act required a partner to fulfill his promise to make contributions, the addition of contributions in the form of a promise to render services means that a partner who is unable to perform those services because of death or disability as well as because of an intentional default is required to pay the cash value of the services unless the ~~certificate of limited partnership~~ partnership agreement provides otherwise.

Subdivision ~~(b)~~ (c) is derived from, but expands upon, Section 17(3) of the ~~prior uniform law~~ 1916 Act.

§ 503.   Sharing of Profits and Losses

The profits and losses of a limited partnership shall be allocated among the partners, and among classes of partners, in the manner provided in writing in the partnership agreement. If the partnership agreement does not so provide in writing, profits and losses shall be allocated on the basis of the value, as stated in the ~~certificate of limited~~ partnership records required to be kept pursuant to Section 105, of the contributions made by each partner to the extent they have been received by the partnership and have not been returned.

COMMENT

Section 503 ~~is new~~ first appeared in the 1976 Act. The ~~prior uniform law~~ 1916 Act did not provide ~~for~~ the basis on which partners would share profits and losses in the absence of agreement. The 1985 Act differs from its counterpart in the 1976 Act by requiring that, to be effective, the partnership agreement provisions concerning allocation of profits and losses be in writing, and by its reference to records required to be kept pursuant to Section 105, the latter reflecting the 1985 changes in Section 201.

§ 504.   Sharing of Distributions

Distributions of cash or other assets of a limited partnership shall be allocated among the partners and among classes of partners in the manner provided in writing in the partnership agreement. If the partnership agreement does not so provide in writing, distributions shall be made on the basis of the value, as stated in the ~~certificate of limited~~ partnership records required to be kept pursuant to Section 105, of the contributions made by each partner to the extent they have been received by the partnership and have not been returned.

COMMENT

Section 504 ~~is new~~ first appeared in the 1976 Act. The ~~prior uniform law~~ 1916 Act did not provide ~~for~~ the basis on which partners would share distributions in the absence of agreement. Section 504 also differs from its counterpart in the 1976 Act by requiring that, to be effective, the partnership agreement provisions concerning allocation of distributions be in writing, and in its reference to records required to be kept pursuant to Section 105, the latter reflecting the 1985 changes in Section 201. This section also recognizes that partners may choose to share in ~~distribution~~ distributions on a ~~different~~ basis ~~than~~ different from that on which they share in profits and losses.

ARTICLE 6
DISTRIBUTIONS AND WITHDRAWAL

§ 601. Interim Distributions

Except as provided in this Article, a partner is entitled to receive distributions from a limited partnership before his [or her] withdrawal from the limited partnership and before the dissolution and winding up thereof~~:~~

~~(1)~~ to the extent and at the times or upon the happening of the events specified in the partnership agreement~~; and~~

~~(2)   if any distribution constitutes a return of any part of his contribution under Section 608(c), to the extent and at the times or upon the happening of the events specified in the certificate of limited partnership.~~

COMMENT

Section 601 ~~is new~~ first appeared in the 1976 Act. The 1976 Act provisions have been modified to reflect the 1985 changes made in Section 201.

§ 602. Withdrawal of General Partner

A general partner may withdraw from a limited partnership at any time by giving written notice to the other partners, but if the withdrawal violates the partnership agreement, the limited partnership may recover from the withdrawing general partner damages for breach of the partnership agreement and offset the damages against the amount otherwise distributable to him [or her].

COMMENT

Section 602 ~~is new~~ first appeared in the 1976 Act, but is generally derived from Section 38 of the Uniform Partnership Act.

§ 603. Withdrawal of Limited Partner

A limited partner may withdraw from a limited partnership at the time or upon the happening of events specified ~~in the certificate of limited partnership and in accordance with~~ in writing in the partnership agreement. If the ~~certificate~~ agreement does not specify in writing the time or the events upon the happening of which a limited partner may withdraw or a definite time for the dissolution and winding up of the limited partnership, a limited partner may withdraw upon not less than six months' prior written notice to each general partner at his [or her] address on the books of the limited partnership at its office in this State.

COMMENT

Section 603 is derived from Section ~~16(c)~~ 16 of the ~~prior uniform law~~ 1916 Act. The 1976 Act provision has been modified to reflect the 1985 changes made in Section 201. This section additionally reflects the policy determination, also embodied in certain other sections of the 1985 Act, that to avoid fraud, agreements concerning certain matters of substantial importance to the partners will be enforceable only if in writing. If the partnership agreement does provide, in writing, whether a limited partner may withdraw and, if he may, when and on what terms and conditions, those provisions will control.

§ 604.   Distribution upon Withdrawal

Except as provided in this Article, upon withdrawal any withdrawing partner is entitled to receive any distribution to which he [or she] is entitled under the partnership agreement and, if not otherwise provided in the agreement, he [or she] is entitled to receive, within a reasonable time after withdrawal, the fair value of his [or her] interest in the limited partnership as of the date of withdrawal based upon his [or her] right to share in distributions from the limited partnership.

COMMENT

Section 604 is new first appeared in the 1976 Act. It fixes the distributive share of a withdrawing partner in the absence of an agreement among the partners.

§ 605.   Distribution in Kind

Except as provided in writing in the certificate of limited partnership agreement, a partner, regardless of the nature of his [or her] contribution, has no right to demand and receive any distribution from a limited partnership in any form other than cash. Except as provided in writing in the partnership agreement, a partner may not be compelled to accept a distribution of any asset in kind from a limited partnership to the extent that the percentage of the asset distributed to him [or her] exceeds a percentage of that asset which is equal to the percentage in which he [or she] shares in distributions from the limited partnership.

COMMENT

The first sentence of Section 605 is derived from Section 16(3) of the prior uniform law 1916 Act; it also differs from its counterpart in the 1976 Act, reflecting the 1985 changes made in Section 201. The second sentence is new first appeared in the 1976 Act, and is intended to protect a limited partner (and the remaining partners) against a distribution in kind of more than his share of particular assets.

§ 606.   Right to Distribution

At the time a partner becomes entitled to receive a distribution, he [or she] has the status of, and is entitled to all remedies available to, a creditor of the limited partnership with respect to the distribution.

COMMENT

Section 606 is new first appeared in the 1976 Act and is intended to make it clear that the right of a partner to receive a distribution, as between the partners, is not subject to the equity risks of the enterprise. On the other hand, since partners entitled to distributions have creditor status, there did not seem to be a need for the extraordinary remedy of Section 16(4)(a) of the prior uniform law 1916 Act, which granted a limited partner the right to seek dissolution of the partnership if he was unsuccessful in demanding the return of his contribution. It is more appropriate for the partner to simply sue as an ordinary creditor and obtain a judgment.

§ 607.   Limitations on Distribution

A partner may not receive a distribution from a limited partnership to the extent that, after giving effect to the distribution, all liabilities of the limited partnership, other than liabilities to partners on account of their partnership interests, exceed the fair value of the partnership assets.

COMMENT

Section 607 is derived from Section 16(1)(a) of the prior uniform law 1916 Act.

§ 608.   Liability upon Return of Contribution

(a)   If a partner has received the return of any part of his [or her] contribution without violation of the partnership agreement or this [Act], he [or she] is liable to the limited partnership for a period of one year thereafter for the amount of the returned contribution, but only to the extent necessary to discharge the limited partnership's liabilities to creditors who extended credit to the limited partnership during the period the contribution was held by the partnership.

(b)   If a partner has received the return of any part of his [or her] contribution in violation of the partnership agreement or this [Act], he [or she] is liable to the limited partnership for a period of six years thereafter for the amount of the contribution wrongfully returned.

(c)   A partner receives a return of his [or her] contribution to the extent that a distribution to him [or her] reduces his [or her] share of the fair value of the net assets of the limited partnership below the value, as set forth in the ~~certificate of limited~~ partnership records required to be kept pursuant to Section 105, of his contribution which has not been distributed to him [or her].

COMMENT

Paragraph (a) is derived from Section 17(4) of the ~~prior uniform law~~ 1916 Act, but the one year statute of limitations has been added. Paragraph (b) is derived from Section 17(2)(b) of the ~~prior uniform law~~ 1916 Act but, again, a statute of limitations has been added.

Paragraph (c) ~~is new~~ first appeared in the 1976 Act. The provisions of former Section 17(2) that referred to the partner holding as "trustee" any money or specific property wrongfully returned to him have been eliminated. Paragraph (c) in the 1985 Act also differs from its counterpart in the 1976 Act to reflect the 1985 changes made in Sections 105 and 201.

ARTICLE 7
ASSIGNMENT OF PARTNERSHIP INTERESTS

§ 701.   Nature of Partnership Interest

A partnership interest is personal property.

COMMENT

This section is derived from Section 18 of the ~~prior uniform law~~ 1916 Act.

§ 702.   Assignment of Partnership Interest

Except as provided in the partnership agreement, a partnership interest is assignable in whole or in part. An assignment of a partnership interest does not dissolve a limited partnership or entitle the assignee to become or to exercise any rights of a partner. An assignment entitles the assignee to receive, to the extent assigned, only the distribution to which the assignor would be entitled. Except as provided in the partnership agreement, a partner ceases to be a partner upon assignment of all his [or her] partnership interest.

COMMENT

Section 19(1) of the ~~prior uniform law~~ 1916 Act provided simply that "a limited partner's interest is assignable," raising a question whether any limitations on the right of assignment were permitted. While the first sentence of Section 702 recognizes that the power to assign may be restricted in the partnership agreement, there was no intention to affect in any way the usual rules regarding restraints on alienation of personal property. The second and third sentences of Section 702 are derived from Section 19(3) of the ~~prior uniform law~~ 1916 Act. The last sentence ~~is new~~ first appeared in the 1976 Act.

§ 703.   Rights of Creditor

On application to a court of competent jurisdiction by any judgment creditor of a partner, the court may charge the partnership interest of the partner with payment of the unsatisfied amount of the judgment with interest. To the extent so charged, the judgment creditor has only the rights of an assignee of the partnership interest. This [Act] does not deprive any partner of the benefit of any exemption laws applicable to his [or her] partnership interest.

COMMENT

Section 703 is derived from Section 22 of the ~~prior uniform law~~ 1916 Act but has not carried over some provisions that were thought to be superfluous. For example, references in Section 22(1) to specific remedies have been omitted, as has a prohibition in Section 22(2) against discharge of the lien with partnership property. Ordinary rules governing the remedies available to a creditor and the fiduciary obligations of general partners will determine those matters.

§ 704.   Right of Assignee to Become Limited Partner

(a)   An assignee of a partnership interest, including an assignee of a general partner, may become a limited partner if and to the extent that ~~(1)~~ (i) the assignor gives the assignee that right in accordance with authority described in the ~~certificate of limited~~ partnership agreement, or ~~(2)~~ (ii) all other partners consent.

(b)   An assignee who has become a limited partner has, to the extent assigned, the rights and powers, and is subject to the restrictions and liabilities, of a limited partner under the partnership agreement and this [Act]. An assignee who becomes a limited partner also is liable for the obligations of his [or her] assignor to make and return contributions as provided in ~~Article~~ Articles 5 and 6. However, the assignee is not obligated for liabilities unknown to the assignee at the time he [or she] became a limited partner ~~and which could not be ascertained from the certificate of limited partnership~~.

(c)   If an assignee of a partnership interest becomes a limited partner, the assignor is not released from his [or her] liability to the limited partnership under Sections 207 and 502.

COMMENT

Section 704 is derived from Section 19 of the ~~prior uniform law~~ 1916 Act, but paragraph (b) defines more narrowly than Section 19 the obligations of the assignor that are automatically assumed by the assignee. Section 704 of the 1985 Act also differs from the 1976 Act to reflect the 1985 changes made in Section 201.

§ 705.   Power of Estate of Deceased or Incompetent Partner

If a partner who is an individual dies or a court of competent jurisdiction adjudges him [or her] to be incompetent to manage his [or her] person or his [or her] property, the partner's executor, administrator, guardian, conservator, or other legal representative may exercise all the partner's rights for the purpose of settling his [or her] estate or administering his [or her] property, including any power the partner had to give an assignee the right to become a limited partner. If a partner is a corporation, trust, or other entity and is dissolved or terminated, the powers of that partner may be exercised by its legal representative or successor.

COMMENT

Section 705 is derived from Section 21(1) of the ~~prior uniform law~~ 1916 Act. Former Section 21(2), making a deceased limited partner's estate liable for his liabilities as a limited partner was deleted as superfluous, with no intention of changing the liability of the estate.

ARTICLE 8
DISSOLUTION

§ 801.   Nonjudicial Dissolution

A limited partnership is dissolved and its affairs shall be wound up upon the happening of the first to occur of the following:

(1)   at the time specified in the certificate of limited partnership;

(2)   ~~or~~ upon the happening of events specified in writing in the ~~certificate of limited~~ partnership agreement;

~~(2)~~ (3) written consent of all partners;

(3)—(4) an event of withdrawal of a general partner unless at the time there is at least one other general partner and the ~~certificate of limited~~ written provisions of the partnership agreement ~~permits~~ permit the business of the limited partnership to be carried on by the remaining general partner and that partner does so, but the limited partnership is not dissolved and is not required to be wound up by reason of any event of withdrawal, if, within 90 days after the withdrawal, all partners agree in writing to continue the business of the limited partnership and to the appointment of one or more additional general partners if necessary or desired; or

(4)—(5) entry of a decree of judicial dissolution under Section 802.

COMMENT

Section 801 merely collects in one place all of the events causing dissolution. Paragraph (3) is derived from Sections 9(1)(g) and 20 of the ~~prior uniform law~~ 1916 Act, but adds the 90-day grace period. Section 801 also differs from its counterpart in the 1976 Act to reflect the 1985 changes made in Section 201.

§ 802. Judicial Dissolution

On application by or for a partner the [designate the appropriate court] court may decree dissolution of a limited partnership whenever it is not reasonably practicable to carry on the business in conformity with the partnership agreement.

COMMENT

Section 802 ~~is new~~ first appeared in the 1976 Act.

§ 803. Winding up

Except as provided in the partnership agreement, the general partners who have not wrongfully dissolved a limited partnership or, if none, the limited partners, may wind up the limited partnership's affairs; but the [designate the appropriate court] court may wind up the limited partnership's affairs upon application of any partner, his [or her] legal representative, or assignee.

COMMENT

Section 803 ~~is new~~ first appeared in the 1976 Act and is derived in part from Section 37 of the Uniform ~~General~~ Partnership Act.

§ 804. Distribution of Assets

Upon the winding up of a limited partnership, the assets shall be distributed as follows:

(1) to creditors, including partners who are creditors, to the extent permitted by law, in satisfaction of liabilities of the limited partnership other than liabilities for distributions to partners under Section 601 or 604;

(2) except as provided in the partnership agreement, to partners and former partners in satisfaction of liabilities for distributions under Section 601 or 604; and

(3) except as provided in the partnership agreement, to partners first for the return of their contributions and secondly respecting their partnership interests, in the proportions in which the partners share in distributions.

COMMENT

Section 804 revises Section 23 of the ~~prior uniform law~~ 1916 Act by providing that (1) to the extent partners are also creditors, other than in respect of their interests in the partnership, they share with other creditors, (2) once the partnership's obligation to make a distribution accrues, it must be paid before any other distributions of an "equity" nature are made, and (3) general and limited partners rank on the same level except as otherwise provided in the partnership agreement.

ARTICLE 9
FOREIGN LIMITED PARTNERSHIPS

§ 901.   Law Governing

Subject to the Constitution of this State, (i) the laws of the state under which a foreign limited partnership is organized govern its organization and internal affairs and the liability of its limited partners, and (ii) a foreign limited partnership may not be denied registration by reason of any difference between those laws and the laws of this State.

COMMENT

Section 901 is new first appeared in the 1976 Act.

§ 902.   Registration

Before transacting business in this State, a foreign limited partnership shall register with the Secretary of State. In order to register, a foreign limited partnership shall submit to the Secretary of State, in duplicate, an application for registration as a foreign limited partnership, signed and sworn to by a general partner and setting forth:

(1)   the name of the foreign limited partnership and, if different, the name under which it proposes to register and transact business in this State;

(2)   the state State and date of its formation;

(3)   the general character of the business it proposes to transact in this State;

(4) (3) the name and address of any agent for service of process on the foreign limited partnership whom the foreign limited partnership elects to appoint; the agent must be an individual resident of this state State, a domestic corporation, or a foreign corporation having a place of business in, and authorized to do business in, this State;

(5) (4) a statement that the Secretary of State is appointed the agent of the foreign limited partnership for service of process if no agent has been appointed under paragraph (4) (3) or, if appointed, the agent's authority has been revoked or if the agent cannot be found or served with the exercise of reasonable diligence;

(6) (5) the address of the office required to be maintained in the State state of its organization by the laws of that State state or, if not so required, of the principal office of the foreign limited partnership; and

(7) if the certificate of limited partnership filed in the foreign limited partnership's state of organization is not required to include the names and business addresses of the partners, a list of the names and addresses.

(6)   the name and business address of each general partner; and

(7)   the address of the office at which is kept a list of the names and addresses of the limited partners and their capital contributions, together with an undertaking by the foreign limited partnership to keep those records until the foreign limited partnership's registration in this State is cancelled or withdrawn.

COMMENT

Section 902 is new first appeared in the 1976 Act. It was thought that requiring a full copy of the certificate of limited partnership and all amendments thereto to be filed in each state in which the partnership does business would impose an unreasonable burden on interstate limited partnerships and that the information on file was Section 902 required to be filed would be sufficient to tell interested persons where they could write to obtain copies of those basic documents. Subdivision (3) of the 1976 Act has been omitted, and subdivisions (6) and (7) differ from their counterparts in the 1976 Act, to conform these provisions relating to the registration of foreign limited partnerships to the corresponding changes made by the Act in the provisions relating to domestic limited partnerships. The requirement that an application for registration be sworn to by a general partner is simply intended to produce the same result as is provided for in Section 204(c) with respect to certificates of domestic limited partnerships; the acceptance and endorsement by the Secretary of State (or equivalent authority) of an application which was not sworn by a general partner should be deemed a mere technical and insubstantial shortcoming, and should not result in the limited partners' being subjected to general liability for the obligations of the foreign limited partnership (see Section 907(c)).

§ 903.   Issuance of Registration

(a)   If the Secretary of State finds that an application for registration conforms to law and all requisite fees have been paid, he [or she] shall:

(1)   endorse on the application the word "Filed," and the month, day and year of the filing thereof;

(2)   file in his [or her] office a duplicate original of the application; and

(3)   issue a certificate of registration to transact business in this State.

(b)   The certificate of registration, together with a duplicate original of the application, shall be returned to the person who filed the application or his [or her] representative.

COMMENT

Section 903 first appeared in the 1976 Act.

§ 904.   Name

A foreign limited partnership may register with the Secretary of State under any name, whether or not it is the name under which it is registered in its state of organization, that includes without abbreviation the words "limited partnership" and that could be registered by a domestic limited partnership.

COMMENT

Section 904 ~~is new~~ first appeared in the 1976 Act.

§ 905.   Changes and Amendments

If any statement in the application for registration of a foreign limited partnership was false when made or any arrangements or other facts described have changed, making the application inaccurate in any respect, the foreign limited partnership shall promptly file in the office of the Secretary of State a certificate, signed and sworn to by a general partner, correcting such statement.

COMMENT

Section 905 ~~is new~~ first appeared in the 1976 Act. It corresponds to the provisions of Section 202(c) relating to domestic limited partnerships.

§ 906.   Cancellation of Registration

A foreign limited partnership may cancel its registration by filing with the Secretary of State a certificate of cancellation signed and sworn to by a general partner. A cancellation does not terminate the authority of the Secretary of State to accept service of process on the foreign limited partnership with respect to [claims for relief] [causes of action] arising out of the transactions of business in this State.

COMMENT

Section 906 ~~is new~~ first appeared in the 1976 Act.

§ 907.   Transaction of Business Without Registration

(a)   A foreign limited partnership transacting business in this State may not maintain any action, suit, or proceeding in any court of this State until it has registered in this State.

(b)   The failure of a foreign limited partnership to register in this State does not impair the validity of any contract or act of the foreign limited partnership or prevent the foreign limited partnership from defending any action, suit, or proceeding in any court of this State.

(c)   A limited partner of a foreign limited partnership is not liable as a general partner of the foreign limited partnership solely by reason of having transacted business in this State without registration.

(d)   A foreign limited partnership, by transacting business in this State without registration, appoints the Secretary of State as its agent for service of process with respect to [claims for relief] [causes of action] arising out of the transaction of business in this State.

COMMENT

Section 907 is new first appeared in the 1976 Act.

§ 908.   Action by [Appropriate Official]

The [designate the appropriate official] may bring an action to restrain a foreign limited partnership from transacting business in this State in violation of this Article.

COMMENT

Section 908 is new first appeared in the 1976 Act.

ARTICLE 10
DERIVATIVE ACTIONS

§ 1001.   Right of Action

A limited partner may bring an action in the right of a limited partnership to recover a judgment in its favor if general partners with authority to do so have refused to bring the action or if an effort to cause those general partners to bring the action is not likely to succeed.

COMMENT

Section 1001 is new first appeared in the 1976 Act.

§ 1002.   Proper Plaintiff

In a derivative action, the plaintiff must be a partner at the time of bringing the action and (i) must have been a partner at the time of the transaction of which he [or she] complains or (ii) his [or her] status as a partner had must have devolved upon him [or her] by operation of law or pursuant to the terms of the partnership agreement from a person who was a partner at the time of the transaction.

COMMENT

Section 1002 is new first appeared in the 1976 Act.

§ 1003.   Pleading

In a derivative action, the complaint shall set forth with particularity the effort of the plaintiff to secure initiation of the action by a general partner or the reasons for not making the effort.

COMMENT

Section 1003 is new first appeared in the 1976 Act.

§ 1004. Expenses

If a derivative action is successful, in whole or in part, or if anything is received by the plaintiff as a result of a judgment, compromise or settlement of an action or claim, the court may award the plaintiff reasonable expenses, including reasonable attorney's fees, and shall direct him [or her] to remit to the limited partnership the remainder of those proceeds received by him [or her].

COMMENT

Section 1004 is new first appeared in the 1976 Act.

ARTICLE 11
MISCELLANEOUS

§ 1101. Construction and Application

This [Act] shall be so applied and construed to effectuate its general purpose to make uniform the law with respect to the subject of this [Act] among states enacting it.

COMMENT

Because the principles set out in Sections 28(1) and 29 of the 1916 Act have become so universally established, it was felt that the 1976 and 1985 Acts need not contain express provisions to the same effect. However, it is intended that the principles enunciated in those provisions of the 1916 Act also apply to this Act.

§ 1102. Short Title

This [Act] may be cited as the Uniform Limited Partnership Act.

§ 1103. Severability

If any provision of this [Act] or its application to any person or circumstance is held invalid, the invalidity does not affect other provisions or applications of the [Act] which can be given effect without the invalid provision or application, and to this end the provisions of this [Act] are severable.

§ 1104. Effective Date, Extended Effective Date and Repeal

Except as set forth below, the effective date of this [Act] is _____ and the following acts [list prior existing limited partnership acts] are hereby repealed:

(1) The existing provisions for execution and filing of certificates of limited partnerships and amendments thereunder and cancellations thereof continue in effect until [specify time required to create central filing system], the extended effective date, and Sections 102, 103, 104, 105, 201, 202, 203, 204 and 206 are not effective until the extended effective date.

(2) Section 402, specifying the conditions under which a general partner ceases to be a member of a limited partnership, is not effective until the extended effective date, and the applicable provisions of existing law continue to govern until the extended effective date.

(3) Sections 501, 502 and 608 apply only to contributions and distributions made after the effective date of this [Act].

(4) Section 704 applies only to assignments made after the effective date of this [Act].

(5) Article 9, dealing with registration of foreign limited partnerships, is not effective until the extended effective date.

(6) Unless otherwise agreed by the partners, the applicable provisions of existing law governing allocation of profits and losses (rather than the provisions of Section 503), distributions to a withdrawing partner (rather than the provisions of Section 604), and distribution of assets upon the

winding up of a limited partnership (rather than the provisions of Section 804) govern limited partnerships formed before the effective date of this [Act].

COMMENT

Subdivisions (6) and (7) did not appear in Section 1104 of the 1976 Act. They are included in the 1985 Act to ensure that the application of the Act to limited partnerships formed and existing before the Act becomes effective would not violate constitutional prohibitions against the impairment of contracts.

§ 1105.   Rules for Cases Not Provided for in This [Act]

In any case not provided for in this [Act] the provisions of the Uniform Partnership Act govern.

COMMENT

The result provided for in Section 1105 would obtain even in its absence in a jurisdiction which had adopted the Uniform Partnership Act, by operation of Section 6 of that act.

§ 1106.   Savings Clause

The repeal of any statutory provision by this [Act] does not impair, or otherwise affect, the organization or the continued existence of a limited partnership existing at the effective date of this [Act], nor does the repeal of any existing statutory provision by this [Act] impair any contract or affect any right accrued before the effective date of this [Act].

COMMENT

Section 1106 did not appear in the 1976 Act. It was included in the 1985 Act to ensure that the application of the Act to limited partnerships formed and existing before the Act becomes effective would not violate constitutional prohibitions against the impairment of contracts.

UNIFORM LIMITED PARTNERSHIP ACT (2001)

———

Table of Sections

[ARTICLE] 1.   GENERAL PROVISIONS

[ARTICLE] 2.   FORMATION; CERTIFICATE OF LIMITED PARTNERSHIP AND OTHER FILINGS

[ARTICLE] 3.   LIMITED PARTNERS

ULPA (2001)

[ARTICLE] 4. GENERAL PARTNERS

[ARTICLE] 5. CONTRIBUTIONS AND DISTRIBUTIONS

[ARTICLE] 6. DISSOCIATION

[ARTICLE] 7. TRANSFERABLE INTERESTS AND RIGHTS OF TRANSFEREES AND CREDITORS

[ARTICLE] 8. DISSOLUTION

ULPA (2001)

UNIFORM LIMITED PARTNERSHIP ACT (2001)

PREFATORY NOTE

The Act's Overall Approach

The new Limited Partnership Act is a "stand alone" act, "de-linked" from both the original general partnership act ("UPA") and the Revised Uniform Partnership Act ("RUPA"). To be able to stand alone, the Limited Partnership incorporates many provisions from RUPA and some from the Uniform Limited Liability Company Act ("ULLCA"). As a result, the new Act is far longer and more complex than its immediate predecessor, the Revised Uniform Limited Partnership Act ("RULPA").

The new Act has been drafted for a world in which limited liability partnerships and limited liability companies can meet many of the needs formerly met by limited partnerships. This Act therefore targets two types of enterprises that seem largely beyond the scope of LLPs and LLCs: (i) sophisticated, manager-entrenched commercial deals whose participants commit for the long term, and (ii) estate planning arrangements (family limited partnerships). This Act accordingly assumes that, more often than not, people utilizing it will want:

- strong centralized management, strongly entrenched, and
- passive investors with little control over or right to exit the entity

The Act's rules, and particularly its default rules, have been designed to reflect these assumptions.

The Decision to "De-Link" and Create a Stand Alone Act

Unlike this Act, RULPA is not a stand alone statute. RULPA was drafted to rest on and link to the UPA. RULPA Section 1105 states that "In any case not provided for in this [Act] the provisions of the Uniform Partnership Act govern." UPA Section 6(2) in turn provides that "this Act shall apply to limited partnerships except in so far as the statutes relating to such partnerships are inconsistent herewith." More particularly, RULPA Section 403 defines the rights, powers, restrictions and liabilities of a "general partner of a limited partnership" by equating them to the rights, powers, restrictions and liabilities of "a partner in a partnership without limited partners."

This arrangement has not been completely satisfactory, because the consequences of linkage are not always clear. *See, e.g., Frye v. Manacare Ltd.*, 431 So.2d 181, 183–84 (Fla. Dist. Ct. App. 1983) (applying UPA Section 42 in favor of a limited partner), *Porter v. Barnhouse*, 354 N.W.2d 227, 232–33 (Iowa 1984) (declining to apply UPA Section 42 in favor of a limited partner) and *Baltzell-Wolfe Agencies, Inc. v. Car Wash Investments No. 1, Ltd.*, 389 N.E.2d 517, 518–20 (Ohio App. 1978) (holding that neither the specific provisions of the general partnership statute nor those of the limited partnership statute determined the liability of a person who had withdrawn as general partner of a limited partnership). Moreover, in some instances the "not inconsistent" rules of the UPA can be inappropriate for the fundamentally different relations involved in a limited partnership.

In any event, the promulgation of RUPA unsettled matters. RUPA differs substantially from the UPA, and the drafters of RUPA expressly declined to decide whether RUPA provides a suitable base and link for the limited partnership statute. According to RUPA's Prefatory Note:

> Partnership law no longer governs limited partnerships pursuant to the provisions of RUPA itself. First, limited partnerships are not "partnerships" within the RUPA definition. Second, UPA Section 6(2), which provides that the UPA governs limited partnerships in cases not provided for in the Uniform Limited Partnership Act (1976) (1985) ("RULPA") has been deleted. No substantive change in result is intended, however. Section 1105 of RULPA already provides that the UPA governs in any case not provided for in RULPA, and thus the express linkage in RUPA is unnecessary. Structurally, it is more appropriately left to RULPA to determine the applicability of RUPA to limited partnerships. It is contemplated that the Conference will review the linkage question carefully, although no changes in RULPA may be necessary despite the many changes in RUPA.

The linkage question was the first major issue considered and decided by this Act's Drafting Committee. Since the Conference has recommended the repeal of the UPA, it made no sense to recommend retaining the UPA as the base and link for a revised or new limited partnership act. The Drafting Committee therefore had to choose between recommending linkage to the new general partnership act (i.e., RUPA) or recommending de-linking and a stand alone act.

The Committee saw several substantial advantages to de-linking. A stand alone statute would:

- be more convenient, providing a single, self-contained source of statutory authority for issues pertaining to limited partnerships;

- eliminate confusion as to which issues were solely subject to the limited partnership act and which required reference (i.e., linkage) to the general partnership act; and

- rationalize future case law, by ending the automatic link between the cases concerning partners in a general partnership and issues pertaining to general partners in a limited partnership.

Thus, a stand alone act seemed likely to promote efficiency, clarity, and coherence in the law of limited partnerships.

In contrast, recommending linkage would have required the Drafting Committee to (1) consider each provision of RUPA and determine whether the provision addressed a matter provided for in RULPA; (2) for each RUPA provision which addressed a matter not provided for in RULPA, determine whether the provision stated an appropriate rule for limited partnerships; and (3) for each matter addressed both by RUPA and RULPA, determine whether RUPA or RULPA stated the better rule for limited partnerships.

That approach was unsatisfactory for at least two reasons. No matter how exhaustive the Drafting Committee's analysis might be, the Committee could not guarantee that courts and practitioners would reach the same conclusions. Therefore, in at least some situations linkage would have produced ambiguity. In addition, the Drafting Committee could not guarantee that all currently appropriate links would remain appropriate as courts begin to apply and interpret RUPA. Even if the Committee recommended linkage, RUPA was destined to be interpreted primarily in the context of general partnerships. Those interpretations might not make sense for limited partnership law, because the modern limited partnership involves fundamentally different relations than those involved in "the small, often informal, partnership" that is "[t]he primary focus of RUPA." RUPA, Prefatory Note.

The Drafting Committee therefore decided to draft and recommend a stand alone act.

Availability of LLLP Status

Following the example of a growing number of States, this Act provides for limited liability limited partnerships. In a limited liability limited partnership ("LLLP"), no partner—whether general or limited—is liable on account of partner status for the limited partnership's obligations. Both general and limited partners benefit from a full, status-based liability shield that is equivalent to the shield enjoyed by corporate shareholders, LLC members, and partners in an LLP.

This Act is designed to serve preexisting limited partnerships as well as limited partnerships formed after the Act's enactment. Most of those preexisting limited partnership will not be LLLPs, and accordingly the Act does not prefer or presume LLLP status. Instead, the Act makes LLLP status available through a simple statement in the certificate of limited partnership. See Sections 102(9), 201(a)(4) and 404(c).

Liability Shield for Limited Partners

RULPA provides only a restricted liability shield for limited partners. The shield is at risk for any limited partner who "participates in the control of the business." RULPA Section 303(a). Although this "control rule" is subject to a lengthy list of safe harbors, RULPA Section 303(b), in a world with LLPs, LLCs and, most importantly, LLLPs, the rule is an anachronism. This Act therefore eliminates the control rule and provides a full, status-based shield against limited partner liability for entity obligations. The shield applies whether or not the limited partnership is an LLLP. See Section 303.

Transition Issues

Following RUPA's example, this Act provides (i) an effective date, after which all newly formed limited partnerships are subject to this Act; (ii) an optional period, during which limited partnerships formed under a predecessor statute may elect to become subject to this Act; and (iii) a mandatory date, on which all preexisting limited partnerships become subject to this Act by operation of law.

ULPA (2001)

A few provisions of this Act differ so substantially from prior law that they should not apply automatically to a preexisting limited partnership. Section 1206(c) lists these provisions and states that each remains inapplicable to a preexisting limited partnership, unless the limited partnership elects for the provision to apply.

Comparison of RULPA and this Act

The following table compares some of the major characteristics of RULPA and this Act. In most instances, the rules involved are "default" rules—i.e., subject to change by the partnership agreement.

Characteristic	RULPA	This Act
relationship to general partnership act	linked, Sections 1105, 403; UPA Section 6(2)	de-linked (but many RUPA provisions incorporated)
Permitted purposes	subject to any specified exceptions, "any business that a partnership without limited partners may carry on, "Section 106	any lawful purpose, Section 104(b)
Constructive notice via publicly filed documents	only that limited partnership exists and that designated general partners are general partners, Section 208	RULPA constructive notice provisions carried forward, Section 103(c), plus constructive notice, 90 days after appropriate filing, of: general partner dissociation and of limited partnership dissolution, termination, merger and conversion, Section 103(d)
duration	specified in certificate of limited partnership, Section 201(a)(4)	perpetual, Section 104(c); subject to change in partnership agreement
use of limited partner name in entity name	prohibited, except in unusual circumstances, Section 102(2)	permitted, Section 108(a)
annual report	none	required, Section 210
limited partner liability for entity debts	none unless limited partner "participates in the control of the business" and person "transact[s] business with the limited partnership reasonably believing . . . that the limited partner is a general partner," Section 303(a); safe harbor lists many activities that do not constitute participating in the control of the business, Section 303(b)	none, regardless of whether the limited partnership is an LLLP, "even if the limited partner participates in the management and control of the limited partnership," Section 303
limited partner duties	none specified	no fiduciary duties "solely by reason of being a limited partner," Section 305(a); each limited partner is obliged to "discharge duties . . . and exercise rights consistently with the obligation of good faith and fair dealing," Section 305(b)

ULPA (2001)

Characteristic	RULPA	This Act
partner access to information—required records/ information	all partners have right of access; no requirement of good cause; Act does not state whether partnership agreement may limit access; Sections 105(b) and 305(1)	list of required information expanded slightly; Act expressly states that partner does not have to show good cause; Sections 304(a), 407(a); however, the partnership agreement may set reasonable restrictions on access to and use of required information, Section 110(b)(4), and limited partnership may impose reasonable restrictions on the use of information, Sections 304(g) and 407(f)
partner access to information—other information	limited partners have the right to obtain other relevant information "upon reasonable demand," Section 305(2); general partner rights linked to general partnership act, Section 403	for limited partners, RULPA approach essentially carried forward, with procedures and standards for making a reasonable demand stated in greater detail, plus requirement that limited partnership supply known material information when limited partner consent sought, Section 304; general partner access rights made explicit, following ULLCA and RUPA, including obligation of limited partnership and general partners to volunteer certain information, Section 407; access rights provided for former partners, Sections 304 and 407
general partner liability for entity debts	complete, automatic and formally inescapable, Section 403(b) (n.b.—in practice, most modern limited partnerships have used a general partner that has its own liability shield; *e.g.*, a corporation or limited liability company)	LLLP status available via a simple statement in the certificate of limited partnership, Sections 102(9), 201(a)(4); LLLP status provides a full liability shield to all general partners, Section 404(c); if the limited partnership is not an LLLP, general partners are liable just as under RULPA, Section 404(a)
general partner duties	linked to duties of partners in a general partnership, Section 403	RUPA general partner duties imported, Section 408; general partner's non-compete duty continues during winding up, Section 408(b)(3)
allocation of profits, losses and distributions	provides separately for sharing of profits and losses, Section 503, and for sharing of distributions, Section 504; allocates each according to contributions made and not returned	eliminates as unnecessary the allocation rule for profits and losses; allocates distributions according to contributions made, Section 503 (n.b.—in the default mode, the Act's

Characteristic	RULPA	This Act
		formulation produces the same result as RULPA formulation)
partner liability for distributions	recapture liability if distribution involved "the return of . . . contribution"; one year recapture liability if distribution rightful, Section 608(a); six year recapture liability if wrongful, Section 608(b)	following ULLCA Sections 406 and 407, the Act adopts the RMBCA approach to improper distributions, Sections 508 and 509
limited partner voluntary dissociation	theoretically, limited partner may withdraw on six months notice unless partnership agreement specifies a term for the limited partnership or withdrawal events for limited partner, Section 603; practically, virtually every partnership agreement specifies a term, thereby eliminating the right to withdraw (n.b.—due to estate planning concerns, several States have amended RULPA to prohibit limited partner withdrawal unless otherwise provided in the partnership agreement)	no "right to dissociate as a limited partner before the termination of the limited partnership," Section 601(a); power to dissociate expressly recognized, Section 601(b)(1), but can be eliminated by the partnership agreement
limited partner involuntary dissociation	not addressed	lengthy list of causes, Section 601(b), taken with some modification from RUPA
limited partner dissociation—payout	"fair value . . . based upon [the partner's] right to share in distributions," Section 604	no payout; person becomes transferee of its own transferable interest, Section 602(3)
general partner voluntary dissociation	right exists unless otherwise provided in partnership agreement, Section 602; power exists regardless of partnership agreement, Section 602	RULPA rule carried forward, although phrased differently, Section 604(a); dissociation before termination of the limited partnership is defined as wrongful, Section 604(b)(2)
general partner involuntary dissociation	Section 402 lists causes	following RUPA, Section 603 expands the list of causes, including expulsion by court order, Section 603(5)

ULPA (2001)

Characteristic	RULPA	This Act
general partner dissociation—payout	"fair value . . . based upon [the partner's] right to share in distributions," Section 604, subject to offset for damages caused by wrongful withdrawal, Section 602	no payout; person becomes transferee of its own transferable interest, Section 605(5)
transfer of partner interest—nomenclature	"Assignment of Partnership Interest," Section 702	"Transfer of Partner's Transferable Interest," Section 702
transfer of partner interest—substance	economic rights fully transferable, but management rights and partner status are not transferable, Section 702	same rule, but Sections 701 and 702 follow RUPA's more detailed and less oblique formulation
rights of creditor of partner	limited to charging order, Section 703	essentially the same rule, but, following RUPA and ULLCA, the Act has a more elaborate provision that expressly extends to creditors of transferees, Section 703
dissolution by partner consent	requires unanimous written consent, Section 801(3)	requires consent of "all general partners and of limited partners owning a majority of the rights to receive distributions as limited partners at the time the consent is to be effective," Section 801(2)
Dissolution following dissociation of a general partner	occurs automatically unless all partners agree to continue the business and, if there is no remaining general partner, to appoint a replacement general partner, Section 801(4)	if at least one general partner remains, no dissolution unless "within 90 days after the dissociation . . . partners owning a majority of the rights to receive distributions as partners" consent to dissolve the limited partnership; Section 801(3)(A); if no general partner remains, dissolution occurs upon the passage of 90 days after the dissociation, unless before that deadline limited partners owning a majority of the rights to receive distributions owned by limited partners consent to continue the business and admit at least one new general partner and a new general partner is admitted, Section 801(3)(B)
filings related to entity termination	certificate of limited partnership to be cancelled when limited partnership dissolves and begins winding up, Section 203	limited partnership may amend certificate to indicate dissolution, Section 803(b)(1), and may file statement of termination indicating that winding up has been completed

Characteristic	RULPA	This Act
		and the limited partnership is terminated, Section 203
procedures for barring claims against dissolved limited partnership	none	following ULLCA Sections 807 and 808, the Act adopts the RMBCA approach providing for giving notice and barring claims, Sections 806 and 807
conversions and mergers	no provision	Article 11 permits conversions to and from and mergers with any "organization," defined as "a general partnership, including a limited liability partnership; limited partnership, including a limited liability limited partnership; limited liability company; business trust; corporation; or any other entity having a governing statute . . . [including] domestic and foreign entities regardless of whether organized for profit." Section 1101(8)
Writing requirements	some provisions pertain only to written understandings; *see, e.g.,* Sections 401 (partnership agreement may "provide in writing for the admission of additional general partners"; such admission also permitted "with the written consent of all partners"), 502(a) (limited partner's promise to contribute "is not enforceable unless set out in a writing signed by the limited partner"), 801(2) and (3) (dissolution occurs "upon the happening of events specified in writing in the partnership agreement" and upon "written consent of all partners"), 801(4) (dissolution avoided following withdrawal of a general partner if "all partners agree in writing")	removes virtually all writing requirements; but does require that certain information be maintained in record form, Section 111

[ARTICLE] 1.   GENERAL PROVISIONS

§ 101.   Short Title

This [Act] may be cited as the Uniform Limited Partnership Act [year of enactment].

§ 102.   Definitions

In this [Act]:

(1)   "Certificate of limited partnership" means the certificate required by Section 201. The term includes the certificate as amended or restated.

(2)   "Contribution", except in the phrase "right of contribution," means any benefit provided by a person to a limited partnership in order to become a partner or in the person's capacity as a partner.

(3)   "Debtor in bankruptcy" means a person that is the subject of:

    (A)   an order for relief under Title 11 of the United States Code or a comparable order under a successor statute of general application; or

    (B)   a comparable order under federal, state, or foreign law governing insolvency.

(4)   "Designated office" means:

    (A)   with respect to a limited partnership, the office that the limited partnership is required to designate and maintain under Section 114; and

    (B)   with respect to a foreign limited partnership, its principal office.

(5)   "Distribution" means a transfer of money or other property from a limited partnership to a partner in the partner's capacity as a partner or to a transferee on account of a transferable interest owned by the transferee.

(6)   "Foreign limited liability limited partnership" means a foreign limited partnership whose general partners have limited liability for the obligations of the foreign limited partnership under a provision similar to Section 404(c).

(7)   "Foreign limited partnership" means a partnership formed under the laws of a jurisdiction other than this State and required by those laws to have one or more general partners and one or more limited partners. The term includes a foreign limited liability limited partnership.

(8)   "General partner" means:

(A)   with respect to a limited partnership, a person that:

    (i)   becomes a general partner under Section 401; or

    (ii)   was a general partner in a limited partnership when the limited partnership became subject to this [Act] under Section 1206(a) or (b); and

(B)   with respect to a foreign limited partnership, a person that has rights, powers, and obligations similar to those of a general partner in a limited partnership.

(9)   "Limited liability limited partnership", except in the phrase "foreign limited liability limited partnership", means a limited partnership whose certificate of limited partnership states that the limited partnership is a limited liability limited partnership.

(10)   "Limited partner" means:

(A)   with respect to a limited partnership, a person that:

    (i)   becomes a limited partner under Section 301; or

    (ii)   was a limited partner in a limited partnership when the limited partnership became subject to this [Act] under Section 1206(a) or (b); and

(B)   with respect to a foreign limited partnership, a person that has rights, powers, and obligations similar to those of a limited partner in a limited partnership.

(11)   "Limited partnership", except in the phrases "foreign limited partnership" and "foreign limited liability limited partnership", means an entity, having one or more general partners and one or more limited partners, which is formed under this [Act] by two or more persons or becomes subject to this [Act] under [Article] 11 or Section 1206(a) or (b). The term includes a limited liability limited partnership.

(12)   "Partner" means a limited partner or general partner.

(13)   "Partnership agreement" means the partners' agreement, whether oral, implied, in a record, or in any combination, concerning the limited partnership. The term includes the agreement as amended.

(14) "Person" means an individual, corporation, business trust, estate, trust, partnership, limited liability company, association, joint venture, government; governmental subdivision, agency, or instrumentality; public corporation, or any other legal or commercial entity.

(15) "Person dissociated as a general partner" means a person dissociated as a general partner of a limited partnership.

(16) "Principal office" means the office where the principal executive office of a limited partnership or foreign limited partnership is located, whether or not the office is located in this State.

(17) "Record" means information that is inscribed on a tangible medium or that is stored in an electronic or other medium and is retrievable in perceivable form.

(18) "Required information" means the information that a limited partnership is required to maintain under Section 111.

(19) "Sign" means:

(A)   to execute or adopt a tangible symbol with the present intent to authenticate a record; or

(B)   to attach or logically associate an electronic symbol, sound, or process to or with a record with the present intent to authenticate the record.

(20) "State" means a State of the United States, the District of Columbia, Puerto Rico, the United States Virgin Islands, or any territory or insular possession subject to the jurisdiction of the United States.

(21) "Transfer" includes an assignment, conveyance, deed, bill of sale, lease, mortgage, security interest, encumbrance, gift, and transfer by operation of law.

(22) "Transferable interest" means a partner's right to receive distributions.

(23) "Transferee" means a person to which all or part of a transferable interest has been transferred, whether or not the transferor is a partner.

COMMENT

This section contains definitions applicable throughout the Act. Section 1101 provides additional definitions applicable within Article 11.

Paragraph 8(A)(i) [General partner]—A partnership agreement may vary Section 401 and provide a process or mechanism for becoming a general partner which is different from or additional to the rules stated in that section. For the purposes of this definition, a person who becomes a general partner pursuant to a provision of the partnership agreement "becomes a general partner under Section 401."

Paragraph 10(A)(i) [Limited partner]—The Comment to Paragraph 8(A)(i) applies here as well. For the purposes of this definition, a person who becomes a limited partner pursuant to a provision of the partnership agreement "becomes a limited partner under Section 301."

Paragraph (11) [Limited partnership]—This definition pertains to what is commonly termed a "domestic" limited partnership. The definition encompasses: (i) limited partnerships originally formed under this Act, including limited partnerships formed under Section 1101(11) to be the surviving organization in a merger; (ii) any entity that becomes subject to this Act by converting into a limited partnership under Article 11; (iii) any preexisting domestic limited partnership that elects pursuant to Section 1206(a) to become subject to this Act; and (iv) all other preexisting domestic limited partnerships when they become subject to this Act under Section 1206(b).

Following the approach of predecessor law, RULPA Section 101(7), this definition contains two substantive requirements. First, it is of the essence of a limited partnership to have two classes of partners. Accordingly, under Section 101(11) a limited partnership must have at least one general and one limited partner. Section 801(3)(B) and (4) provide that a limited partnership dissolves if its sole general partner or sole limited partner dissociates and the limited partnership fails to admit a replacement within 90 days of the dissociation. The 90 day limitation is a default rule, but, in light of Section 101(11), a limited partnership may not indefinitely delay "having one or more general partners and one or more limited partners."

It is also of the essence of a limited partnership to have at least two partners. Section 101(11) codifies this requirement by referring to a limited partnership as "an entity . . . which is formed under this [Act] by two or more persons." Thus, while the same person may be both a general and limited partner, Section 113 (Dual Capacity), one person alone cannot be the "two persons" contemplated by this definition. However, nothing in this definition prevents two closely affiliated persons from satisfying the two person requirement.

Paragraph (13) [Partnership agreement]—Section 110 is essential to understanding the significance of the partnership agreement. See also Section 201(d) (resolving inconsistencies between the certificate of limited partnership and the partnership agreement).

Paragraph (21) [Transfer]—Following RUPA, this Act uses the words "transfer" and "transferee" rather than the words "assignment" and "assignee." See RUPA Section 503.

The reference to "transfer by operation of law" is significant in connection with Section 702 (Transfer of Partner's Transferable Interest). That section severely restricts a transferee's rights (absent the consent of the partners), and this definition makes those restrictions applicable, for example, to transfers ordered by a family court as part of a divorce proceeding and transfers resulting from the death of a partner.

Paragraph (23) [Transferee]—See comment to Paragraph 21 for an explanation of why this Act refers to "transferee" rather than "assignee."

§ 103. Knowledge and Notice

(a)   A person knows a fact if the person has actual knowledge of it.

(b)   A person has notice of a fact if the person:

    (1)   knows of it;

    (2)   has received a notification of it;

    (3)   has reason to know it exists from all of the facts known to the person at the time in question; or

    (4)   has notice of it under subsection (c) or (d).

(c)   A certificate of limited partnership on file in the [office of the Secretary of State] is notice that the partnership is a limited partnership and the persons designated in the certificate as general partners are general partners. Except as otherwise provided in subsection (d), the certificate is not notice of any other fact.

(d)   A person has notice of:

    (1)   another person's dissociation as a general partner, 90 days after the effective date of an amendment to the certificate of limited partnership which states that the other person has dissociated or 90 days after the effective date of a statement of dissociation pertaining to the other person, whichever occurs first;

    (2)   a limited partnership's dissolution, 90 days after the effective date of an amendment to the certificate of limited partnership stating that the limited partnership is dissolved;

    (3)   a limited partnership's termination, 90 days after the effective date of a statement of termination;

    (4)   a limited partnership's conversion under [Article] 11, 90 days after the effective date of the articles of conversion; or

    (5)   a merger under [Article] 11, 90 days after the effective date of the articles of merger.

(e)   A person notifies or gives a notification to another person by taking steps reasonably required to inform the other person in ordinary course, whether or not the other person learns of it.

(f)   A person receives a notification when the notification:

    (1)   comes to the person's attention; or

    (2)   is delivered at the person's place of business or at any other place held out by the person as a place for receiving communications.

(g)   Except as otherwise provided in subsection (h), a person other than an individual knows, has notice, or receives a notification of a fact for purposes of a particular transaction when the individual conducting the transaction for the person knows, has notice, or receives a notification of the fact, or in any event when the fact would have been brought to the individual's attention if the person had exercised reasonable diligence. A person other than an individual exercises reasonable diligence if it maintains reasonable routines for communicating significant information to the individual conducting the transaction for the person and there is reasonable compliance with the routines. Reasonable diligence does not require an individual acting for the person to communicate information unless the communication is part of the individual's regular duties or the individual has reason to know of the transaction and that the transaction would be materially affected by the information.

(h) A general partner's knowledge, notice, or receipt of a notification of a fact relating to the limited partnership is effective immediately as knowledge of, notice to, or receipt of a notification by the limited partnership, except in the case of a fraud on the limited partnership committed by or with the consent of the general partner. A limited partner's knowledge, notice, or receipt of a notification of a fact relating to the limited partnership is not effective as knowledge of, notice to, or receipt of a notification by the limited partnership.

COMMENT

Source—RUPA Section 102; RULPA Section 208.

Notice and the relationship among subsections (b), (c) and (d)—These subsections provide separate and independent avenues through which a person can have notice of a fact. A person has notice of a fact as soon as any of the avenues applies.

Example: A limited partnership dissolves and amends its certificate of limited partnership to indicate dissolution. The amendment is effective on March 1. On March 15, Person #1 has reason to know of the dissolution and therefore has "notice" of the dissolution under Section 103(b)(3) even though Section 103(d)(2) does not yet apply. Person #2 does not have actual knowledge of the dissolution until June 15. Nonetheless, under Section 103(d)(2) Person #2 has "notice" of the dissolution on May 30.

Subsection (c)—This subsection provides what is commonly called constructive notice and comes essentially verbatim from RULPA Section 208. As for the significance of constructive notice "that the partnership is a limited partnership," see *Water, Waste & Land, Inc. v. Lanham*, 955 P.2d 997, 1001–1003 (Colo. 1998) (interpreting a comparable provision of the Colorado LLC statute and holding the provision ineffective to change common law agency principles, including the rules relating to the liability of an agent that transacts business for an undisclosed principal).

As for constructive notice that "the persons designated in the certificate as general partners are general partners," Section 201(a)(3) requires the initial certificate of limited partnership to name each general partner, and Section 202(b) requires a limited partnership to promptly amend its certificate of limited partnership to reflect any change in the identity of its general partners. Nonetheless, it will be possible, albeit improper, for a person to be designated in the certificate of limited partnership as a general partner without having become a general partner as contemplated by Section 401. Likewise, it will be possible for a person to have become a general partner under Section 401 without being designated as a general partner in the certificate of limited partnership. According to the last clause of this subsection, the fact that a person is **not** listed . . . in the certificate as a general partner is **not** notice that the person is **not** a general partner. For further discussion of this point, see the Comment to Section 401.

If the partnership agreement and the public record are inconsistent, Section 201(d) applies (partnership agreement controls *inter se*; public record controls as to third parties who have relied). See also Section 202(b) (requiring the limited partnership to amend its certificate of limited partnership to keep accurate the listing of general partners), 202(c) (requiring a general partner to take corrective action when the general partner knows that the certificate of limited partnership contains false information), and 208 (imposing liability for false information in *inter alia* the certificate of limited partnership).

Subsection (d)—This subsection also provides what is commonly called constructive notice and works in conjunction with other sections of this Act to curtail the power to bind and personal liability of general partners and persons dissociated as general partners. See Sections 402, 606, 607, 804, 805, 1111, and 1112. Following RUPA (in substance, although not in form), the constructive notice begins 90 days after the effective date of the filed record. For the Act's rules on delayed effective dates, see Section 206(c).

The 90-day delay applies only to the constructive notice and not to the event described in the filed record.

Example: On March 15, X dissociates as a general partner from XYZ Limited Partnership by giving notice to XYZ. See Section 603(1). On March 20, XYZ amends its certificate of limited partnership to remove X's name from the list of general partners. See Section 202(b)(2).

X's **dissociation** is effective March 15. If on March 16 X purports to be a general partner of XYZ and under Section 606(a) binds XYZ to some obligation, X will be liable under Section 606(b) as a "person dissociated as a general partner."

On June 13 (90 days after March 15), the world has constructive notice of X's dissociation as a general partner. Beginning on that date, X will lack the power to bind XYZ. See Section 606(a)(2)(B) (person dissociated as a general partner can bind the limited partnership only if, *inter alia*, "at the time the other party enters into the transaction . . . the other party does not have notice of the dissociation").

Constructive notice under this subsection applies to partners and transferees as well as other persons.

Subsection (e)—The phrase "person learns of it" in this subsection is equivalent to the phrase "knows of it" in subsection (b)(1).

Subsection (h)—Under this subsection and Section 302, information possessed by a person that is only a limited partner is not attributable to the limited partnership. However, information possessed by a person that is both a general partner and a limited partner is attributable to the limited partnership. See Section 113 (Dual Capacity).

§ 104. Nature, Purpose, and Duration of Entity

(a) A limited partnership is an entity distinct from its partners. A limited partnership is the same entity regardless of whether its certificate states that the limited partnership is a limited liability limited partnership.

(b) A limited partnership may be organized under this [Act] for any lawful purpose.

(c) A limited partnership has a perpetual duration.

COMMENT

Subsection (a)—Acquiring or relinquishing an LLLP shield changes only the rules governing a general partner's liability for subsequently incurred obligations of the limited partnership. The underlying entity is unaffected.

Subsection (b)—In contrast with RULPA Section 106, this Act does not require a limited partnership to have a business purpose. However, many of the Act's default rules presuppose at least a profit-making purpose. See, e.g., Section 503 (providing for the sharing of distributions in proportion to the value of contributions), 701 (defining a transferable interest in terms of the right to receive distributions), 801 (allocating the right to consent to cause or avoid dissolution in proportion to partners' rights to receive distributions), and 812 (providing that, after a dissolved limited partnership has paid its creditors, "[a]ny surplus remaining . . . must be paid in cash as a distribution" to partners and transferees). If a limited partnership is organized for an essentially non-pecuniary purpose, the organizers should carefully review the Act's default rules and override them as necessary via the partnership agreement.

Subsection (c)—The partnership agreement has the power to vary this subsection, either by stating a definite term or by specifying an event or events which cause dissolution. Sections 110(a) and 801(1). Section 801 also recognizes several other occurrences that cause dissolution. Thus, the public record pertaining to a limited partnership will not necessarily reveal whether the limited partnership actually has a perpetual duration.

The public record might also fail to reveal whether the limited partnership has in fact dissolved. A dissolved limited partnership may amend its certificate of limited partnership to indicate dissolution but is not required to do so. Section 803(b)(1).

Predecessor law took a somewhat different approach. RULPA Section 201(4) required the certificate of limited partnership to state "the latest date upon which the limited partnership is to dissolve." Although RULPA Section 801(2) provided for a limited partnership to dissolve "upon the happening of events specified in writing in the partnership agreement," RULPA Section 203 required the limited partnership to file a certificate of cancellation to indicate that dissolution had occurred.

§ 105.   Powers

A limited partnership has the powers to do all things necessary or convenient to carry on its activities, including the power to sue, be sued, and defend in its own name and to maintain an action against a partner for harm caused to the limited partnership by a breach of the partnership agreement or violation of a duty to the partnership.

COMMENT

This Act omits as unnecessary any detailed list of specific powers. The power to sue and be sued is mentioned specifically so that Section 110(b)(1) can prohibit the partnership agreement from varying that power. The power to maintain an action against a partner is mentioned specifically to establish that the limited partnership itself has standing to enforce the partnership agreement.

§ 106.   Governing Law

The law of this State governs relations among the partners of a limited partnership and between the partners and the limited partnership and the liability of partners as partners for an obligation of the limited partnership.

COMMENT

To partially define its scope, this section uses the phrase "relations among the partners of a limited partnership and between the partners and the limited partnership." Section 110(a) uses essentially identical language in defining the proper realm of the partnership agreement: "relations among the partners and between the partners and the partnership."

Despite the similarity of language, this section has no bearing on the power of a partnership agreement to vary other provisions of this Act. It is quite possible for a provision of this Act to involve "relations among the partners of a limited partnership and between the partners and the limited partnership" and thus come within this section, and yet not be subject to variation by the partnership agreement. Although Section 110(a) grants plenary authority to the partnership agreement to regulate "relations among the partners and between the partners and the partnership," that authority is subject to Section 110(b).

For example, Section 408 (General Standards of General Partner's Conduct) certainly involves "relations among the partners of a limited partnership and between the partners and the limited partnership." Therefore, according to this section, Section 408 applies to a limited partnership formed or otherwise subject to this Act. Just as certainly, Section 408 pertains to "relations among the partners and between the partners and the partnership" for the purposes of Section 110(a), and therefore the partnership agreement may properly address matters covered by Section 408. However, Section 110(b)(5), (6), and (7) limit the power of the partnership agreement to vary the rules stated in Section 408. See also, e.g., Section 502(c) (stating creditor's rights, which are protected under Section 110(b)(13) from being restricted by the partnership agreement) and Comment to Section 509.

This section also applies to "the liability of partners as partners for an obligation of a limited partnership." The phrase "as partners" contemplates the liability shield for limited partners under Section 303 and the rules for general partner liability stated in Section 404. Other grounds for liability can be supplied by other law, including the law of some other jurisdiction. For example, a partner's contractual guaranty of a limited partnership obligation might well be governed by the law of some other jurisdiction.

Transferees derive their rights and status under this Act from partners and accordingly this section applies to the relations of a transferee to the limited partnership.

The partnership agreement may not vary the rule stated in this section. See Section 110(b)(2).

§ 107.   Supplemental Principles of Law; Rate of Interest

(a)   Unless displaced by particular provisions of this [Act], the principles of law and equity supplement this [Act].

(b)   If an obligation to pay interest arises under this [Act] and the rate is not specified, the rate is that specified in [applicable statute].

COMMENT

Subsection (a)—This language comes from RUPA Section 104 and does not address an important question raised by the de-linking of this Act from the UPA and RUPA—namely, to what extent is the case law of general partnerships relevant to limited partnerships governed by this Act?

Predecessor law, RULPA Section 403, expressly equated the rights, powers, restrictions, and liabilities of a general partner in a limited partnership with the rights, powers, restrictions, and liabilities of a partner in a general partnership. This Act has no comparable provision. See Prefatory Note. Therefore, a court should not assume that a case concerning a general partnership is automatically relevant to a limited partnership governed by this Act. A general partnership case may be relevant by analogy, especially if (1) the issue in dispute involves a provision of this Act for which a comparable provision exists under the law of general partnerships; and (2) the fundamental differences between a general partnership and limited partnership are immaterial to the disputed issue.

§ 108.   Name

(a)   The name of a limited partnership may contain the name of any partner.

(b)   The name of a limited partnership that is not a limited liability limited partnership must contain the phrase "limited partnership" or the abbreviation "L.P." or "LP" and may not contain the phrase "limited liability limited partnership" or the abbreviation "LLLP" or "L.L.L.P."

(c)   The name of a limited liability limited partnership must contain the phrase "limited liability limited partnership" or the abbreviation "LLLP" or "L.L.L.P." and must not contain the abbreviation "L.P." or "LP."

(d)   Unless authorized by subsection (e), the name of a limited partnership must be distinguishable in the records of the [Secretary of State] from:

(1)   the name of each person other than an individual incorporated, organized, or authorized to transact business in this State; and

(2)   each name reserved under Section 109 [or other state laws allowing the reservation or registration of business names, including fictitious name statutes].

(e)   A limited partnership may apply to the [Secretary of State] for authorization to use a name that does not comply with subsection (d). The [Secretary of State] shall authorize use of the name applied for if, as to each conflicting name:

(1)   the present user, registrant, or owner of the conflicting name consents in a signed record to the use and submits an undertaking in a form satisfactory to the [Secretary of State] to change the conflicting name to a name that complies with subsection (d) and is distinguishable in the records of the [Secretary of State] from the name applied for;

(2)   the applicant delivers to the [Secretary of State] a certified copy of the final judgment of a court of competent jurisdiction establishing the applicant's right to use in this State the name applied for; or

(3)   the applicant delivers to the [Secretary of State] proof satisfactory to the [Secretary of State] that the present user, registrant, or owner of the conflicting name:

(A)   has merged into the applicant;

(B)   has been converted into the applicant; or

(C)   has transferred substantially all of its assets, including the conflicting name, to the applicant.

(f)   Subject to Section 905, this section applies to any foreign limited partnership transacting business in this State, having a certificate of authority to transact business in this State, or applying for a certificate of authority.

COMMENT

Subsection (a)—Predecessor law, RULPA Section 102, prohibited the use of a limited partner's name in the name of a limited partnership except in unusual circumstances. That approach derived from the 1916 Uniform Limited Partnership Act and has become antiquated. In 1916, most business organizations were either unshielded (*e.g.*, general partnerships) or partially shielded (*e.g.*, limited partnerships), and it was reasonable for third parties to believe that an individual whose own name appeared in the name of a business would "stand behind" the business. Today most businesses have a full shield (*e.g.*, corporations, limited liability companies, most limited liability partnerships), and corporate, LLC and LLP statutes generally pose no barrier to the use of an owner's name in the name of the entity. This Act eliminates RULPA's restriction and puts limited partnerships on equal footing with these other "shielded" entities.

Subsection (d)(1)—If a sole proprietor registers or reserves a business name under a fictitious name statute, that name comes within this provision. For the purposes of this provision, a sole proprietor doing business under a registered or reserved name is a "person other than an individual."

Subsection (f)—Section 905 permits a foreign limited partnership to obtain a certificate of authority under an alternate name if the foreign limited partnership's actual name does not comply with this section.

§ 109.   Reservation of Name

(a)   The exclusive right to the use of a name that complies with Section 108 may be reserved by:

     (1)   a person intending to organize a limited partnership under this [Act] and to adopt the name;

     (2)   a limited partnership or a foreign limited partnership authorized to transact business in this State intending to adopt the name;

     (3)   a foreign limited partnership intending to obtain a certificate of authority to transact business in this State and adopt the name;

     (4)   a person intending to organize a foreign limited partnership and intending to have it obtain a certificate of authority to transact business in this State and adopt the name;

     (5)   a foreign limited partnership formed under the name; or

     (6)   a foreign limited partnership formed under a name that does not comply with Section 108(b) or (c), but the name reserved under this paragraph may differ from the foreign limited partnership's name only to the extent necessary to comply with Section 108(b) and (c).

(b)   A person may apply to reserve a name under subsection (a) by delivering to the [Secretary of State] for filing an application that states the name to be reserved and the paragraph of subsection (a) which applies. If the [Secretary of State] finds that the name is available for use by the applicant, the [Secretary of State] shall file a statement of name reservation and thereby reserve the name for the exclusive use of the applicant for a 120 days.

(c)   An applicant that has reserved a name pursuant to subsection (b) may reserve the same name for additional 120-day periods. A person having a current reservation for a name may not apply for another 120-day period for the same name until 90 days have elapsed in the current reservation.

(d)   A person that has reserved a name under this section may deliver to the [Secretary of State] for filing a notice of transfer that states the reserved name, the name and street and mailing address of some other person to which the reservation is to be transferred, and the paragraph of subsection (a) which applies to the other person. Subject to Section 206(c), the transfer is effective when the [Secretary of State] files the notice of transfer.

§ 110.   Effect of Partnership Agreement; Nonwaivable Provisions

(a)   Except as otherwise provided in subsection (b), the partnership agreement governs relations among the partners and between the partners and the partnership. To the extent the partnership agreement does not otherwise provide, this [Act] governs relations among the partners and between the partners and the partnership.

(b)   A partnership agreement may not:

(1)   vary a limited partnership's power under Section 105 to sue, be sued, and defend in its own name;

(2)   vary the law applicable to a limited partnership under Section 106;

(3)   vary the requirements of Section 204;

(4)   vary the information required under Section 111 or unreasonably restrict the right to information under Sections 304 or 407, but the partnership agreement may impose reasonable restrictions on the availability and use of information obtained under those sections and may define appropriate remedies, including liquidated damages, for a breach of any reasonable restriction on use;

(5)   eliminate the duty of loyalty under Section 408, but the partnership agreement may:

(A)   identify specific types or categories of activities that do not violate the duty of loyalty, if not manifestly unreasonable; and

(B)   specify the number or percentage of partners which may authorize or ratify, after full disclosure to all partners of all material facts, a specific act or transaction that otherwise would violate the duty of loyalty;

(6)   unreasonably reduce the duty of care under Section 408(c);

(7)   eliminate the obligation of good faith and fair dealing under Sections 305(b) and 408(d), but the partnership agreement may prescribe the standards by which the performance of the obligation is to be measured, if the standards are not manifestly unreasonable;

(8)   vary the power of a person to dissociate as a general partner under Section 604(a) except to require that the notice under Section 603(1) be in a record;

(9)   vary the power of a court to decree dissolution in the circumstances specified in Section 802;

(10) vary the requirement to wind up the partnership's business as specified in Section 803;

(11) unreasonably restrict the right to maintain an action under [Article] 10;

(12) restrict the right of a partner under Section 1110(a) to approve a conversion or merger or the right of a general partner under Section 1110(b) to consent to an amendment to the certificate of limited partnership which deletes a statement that the limited partnership is a limited liability limited partnership; or

(13) restrict rights under this [Act] of a person other than a partner or a transferee.

COMMENT

Source—RUPA Section 103.

Subject only to subsection (b), the partnership agreement has plenary power to structure and regulate the relations of the partners *inter se*. Although the certificate of limited partnership is a limited partnership's foundational document, among the partners the partnership agreement controls. See Section 201(d).

The partnership agreement has the power to control the manner of its own amendment. In particular, a provision of the agreement prohibiting oral modifications is enforceable, despite any common law antagonism to "no oral modification" provisions. Likewise, a partnership agreement can impose "made in a record" requirements on other aspects of the partners' relationship, such as requiring consents to be made in a record and signed, or rendering unenforceable oral promises to make contributions or oral understandings as to "events upon the happening of which the limited partnership is to be dissolved," Section 111(9)(D). See also Section 801(1).

Subsection (b)(3)—The referenced section states who must sign various documents.

Subsection (b)(4)—In determining whether a restriction is reasonable, a court might consider: (i) the danger or other problem the restriction seeks to avoid; (ii) the purpose for which the information is sought; and (iii) whether, in light of both the problem and the purpose, the restriction is reasonably tailored. Restricting access to or use of the names and addresses of limited partners is not per se unreasonable.

Under this Act, general and limited partners have sharply different roles. A restriction that is reasonable as to a limited partner is not necessarily reasonable as to a general partner.

Sections 304(g) and 407(f) authorize the limited partnership (as distinguished from the partnership agreement) to impose restrictions on the use of information. For a comparison of restrictions contained in the partnership agreement and restrictions imposed unilaterally by the limited partnership, see the Comment to Section 304(g).

Subsection (b)(5)(A)—It is not per se manifestly unreasonable for the partnership agreement to permit a general partner to compete with the limited partnership.

Subsection (b)(5)(B)—The Act does not require that the authorization or ratification be by **disinterested** partners, although the partnership agreement may so provide. The Act does require that the disclosure be made to all partners, even if the partnership agreement excludes some partners from the authorization or ratification process. An interested partner that participates in the authorization or ratification process is subject to the obligation of good faith and fair dealing. Sections 305(b) and 408(d).

Subsection (b)(8)—This restriction applies only to the power of a person to dissociate as a general partner. The partnership agreement may eliminate the power of a person to dissociate as a limited partner.

Subsection (b)(9)—This provision should not be read to limit a partnership agreement's power to provide for arbitration. For example, an agreement to arbitrate all disputes—including dissolution disputes—is enforceable. Any other interpretation would put this Act at odds with federal law. *See Southland Corp. v. Keating*, 465 U.S. 1 (1984) (holding that the Federal Arbitration Act preempts state statutes that seek to invalidate agreements to arbitrate) and *Allied-Bruce Terminix Cos., Inc. v. Dobson*, 513 U.S. 265 (1995) (same). This provision does prohibit any narrowing of the substantive grounds for judicial dissolution as stated in Section 802.

> **Example:** A provision of a partnership agreement states that no partner may obtain judicial dissolution without showing that a general partner is in material breach of the partnership agreement. The provision is ineffective to prevent a court from ordering dissolution under Section 802.

Subsection (b)(11)—Section 1001 codifies a partner's right to bring a direct action, and the rest of Article 10 provides for derivative actions. The partnership agreement may not restrict a partner's right to bring either type of action if the effect is to undercut or frustrate the duties and rights protected by Section 110(b).

The reasonableness of a restriction on derivative actions should be judged in light of the history and purpose of derivative actions. They originated as an equitable remedy, intended to protect passive owners against management abuses. A partnership agreement may not provide that all derivative claims will be subject to final determination by a special litigation committee appointed by the limited partnership, because that provision would eliminate, not merely restrict, a partner's right to bring a derivative *action*.

Subsection (b)(12)—Section 1110 imposes special consent requirements with regard to transactions that might make a partner personally liable for entity debts.

Subsection (b)(13)—The partnership agreement is a contract, and this provision reflects a basic notion of contract law—namely, that a contract can **directly** restrict rights only of parties to the contract and of persons who derive their rights from the contract. A provision of a partnership agreement can be determined to be unenforceable against third parties under paragraph (b)(13) without therefore and automatically being unenforceable *inter se* the partners and any transferees. How the former determination affects the latter question is a matter of other law.

§ 111.   Required Information

A limited partnership shall maintain at its designated office the following information:

(1) a current list showing the full name and last known street and mailing address of each partner, separately identifying the general partners, in alphabetical order, and the limited partners, in alphabetical order;

(2) a copy of the initial certificate of limited partnership and all amendments to and restatements of the certificate, together with signed copies of any powers of attorney under which any certificate, amendment, or restatement has been signed;

(3) a copy of any filed articles of conversion or merger;

(4) a copy of the limited partnership's federal, state, and local income tax returns and reports, if any, for the three most recent years;

(5)   a copy of any partnership agreement made in a record and any amendment made in a record to any partnership agreement;

(6)   a copy of any financial statement of the limited partnership for the three most recent years;

(7)   a copy of the three most recent annual reports delivered by the limited partnership to the [Secretary of State] pursuant to Section 210;

(8)   a copy of any record made by the limited partnership during the past three years of any consent given by or vote taken of any partner pursuant to this [Act] or the partnership agreement; and

(9)   unless contained in a partnership agreement made in a record, a record stating:

(A)   the amount of cash, and a description and statement of the agreed value of the other benefits, contributed and agreed to be contributed by each partner;

(B)   the times at which, or events on the happening of which, any additional contributions agreed to be made by each partner are to be made;

(C)   for any person that is both a general partner and a limited partner, a specification of what transferable interest the person owns in each capacity; and

(D)   any events upon the happening of which the limited partnership is to be dissolved and its activities wound up.

COMMENT

Source—RULPA Section 105.

Sections 304 and 407 govern access to the information required by this section, as well as to other information pertaining to a limited partnership.

Paragraph (5)—This requirement applies to superseded as well as current agreements and amendments. An agreement or amendment is "made in a record "to the extent the agreement is "integrated" into a record and consented to in that memorialized form. It is possible for a partnership agreement to be made in part in a record and in part otherwise. See Comment to Section 110. An oral agreement that is subsequently inscribed in a record (but not consented to as such) was not "made in a record" and is not covered by paragraph (5). However, if the limited partnership happens to have such a record, Section 304(b) might and Section 407(a)(2) will provide a right of access.

Paragraph (8)—This paragraph does not require a limited partnership to make a record of consents given and votes taken. However, if the limited partnership has made such a record, this paragraph requires that the limited partnership maintain the record for three years. The requirement applies to any record made by the limited partnership, not just to records made contemporaneously with the giving of consent or voting. The three year period runs from when the record was made and not from when the consent was given or vote taken.

Paragraph (9)—Information is "contained in a partnership agreement made in a record" only to the extent that the information is "integrated" into a record and, in that memorialized form, has been consented to as part of the partnership agreement.

This paragraph is not a statute of frauds provision. For example, failure to comply with paragraph (9)(A) or (B) does not render unenforceable an oral promise to make a contribution. Likewise, failure to comply with paragraph (9)(D) does not invalidate an oral term of the partnership specifying "events upon the happening of which the limited partnership is to be dissolved and its activities wound up." See also Section 801(1).

Obversely, the mere fact that a limited partnership maintains a record in purported compliance with paragraph (9)(A) or (B) does not prove that a person has actually promised to make a contribution. Likewise, the mere fact that a limited partnership maintains a record in purported compliance with paragraph (9)(D) does not prove that the partnership agreement actually includes the specified events as causes of dissolution.

Consistent with the partnership agreement's plenary power to structure and regulate the relations of the partners *inter se*, a partnership agreement can impose "made in a record" requirements which render unenforceable oral promises to make contributions or oral understandings as to "events upon the happening of which the limited partnership is to be dissolved." See Comment to Section 110.

Paragraph (9)(A) and (B)—Often the partnership agreement will state in record form the value of contributions made and promised to be made. If not, these provisions require that the value be stated in a record maintained as part of the limited partnership's required information. The Act does not authorize the limited partnership or the general partners to set the value of a contribution without the concurrence of the person who has made or promised the contribution, although the partnership agreement itself can grant that authority.

Paragraph (9)(C)—The information required by this provision is essential for determining what happens to the transferable interests of a person that is both a general partner and a limited partner and that dissociates in one of those capacities but not the other. See Sections 602(3) and 605(5).

§ 112.   Business Transactions of Partner with Partnership

A partner may lend money to and transact other business with the limited partnership and has the same rights and obligations with respect to the loan or other transaction as a person that is not a partner.

COMMENT

Source—RULPA Section 107. See also RUPA Section 404(f) and ULLCA Section 409(f).

This section has no impact on a general partner's duty under Section 408(b)(2) (duty of loyalty includes refraining from acting as or for an adverse party) and means rather that this Act does not discriminate against a creditor of a limited partnership that happens also to be a partner. *See, e.g., BT-I v. Equitable Life Assurance Society of the United States*, 75 Cal.App.4th 1406, 1415, 89 Cal.Rptr.2d 811, 814 (Cal.App. 4 Dist.1999). and *SEC v. DuPont, Homsey & Co.*, 204 F. Supp. 944, 946 (D. Mass. 1962), vacated and remanded on other grounds, 334 F.2d 704 (1st Cir. 1964). This section does not, however, override other law, such as fraudulent transfer or conveyance acts.

§ 113.   Dual Capacity

A person may be both a general partner and a limited partner. A person that is both a general and limited partner has the rights, powers, duties, and obligations provided by this [Act] and the partnership agreement in each of those capacities. When the person acts as a general partner, the person is subject to the obligations, duties and restrictions under this [Act] and the partnership agreement for general partners. When the person acts as a limited partner, the person is subject to the obligations, duties and restrictions under this [Act] and the partnership agreement for limited partners.

COMMENT

Source—RULPA Section 404, redrafted for reasons of style.

§ 114.   Office and Agent for Service of Process

(a)   A limited partnership shall designate and continuously maintain in this State:

     (1)   an office, which need not be a place of its activity in this State; and

     (2)   an agent for service of process.

(b)   A foreign limited partnership shall designate and continuously maintain in this State an agent for service of process.

(c)   An agent for service of process of a limited partnership or foreign limited partnership must be an individual who is a resident of this State or other person authorized to do business in this State.

COMMENT

Subsection (a)—The initial designation occurs in the original certificate of limited partnership. Section 201(a)(2). A limited partnership may change the designation in any of three ways: a statement of change, Section 115, an amendment to the certificate, Section 202, and the annual report, Section 210(e). If a limited partnership fails to maintain an agent for service of process, substituted service may be made on the Secretary of State. Section 117(b). Although a limited partnership's failure to maintain an agent for service of process is not immediate grounds for administrative dissolution, Section 809(a), the failure will prevent the limited partnership from delivering to the Secretary of State for filing an annual report that complies with Section 210(a)(2). Failure to deliver a proper annual report is grounds for administrative dissolution. Section 809(a)(2).

Subsection (b)—The initial designation occurs in the application for a certificate of authority. See Section 902(a)(4). A foreign limited partnership may change the designation in either of two ways: a statement of change, Section 115, and the annual report, Section 210(e). If a foreign limited partnership fails to maintain an agent for service of process, substituted service may be made on the Secretary of State. Section 117(b). A foreign limited partnership's failure to maintain an agent for service of process is grounds for administrative revocation of the certificate of authority. Section 906(a)(3).

A foreign limited partnership need not maintain an office in this State.

§ 115. Change of Designated Office or Agent for Service of Process

(a) In order to change its designated office, agent for service of process, or the address of its agent for service of process, a limited partnership or a foreign limited partnership may deliver to the [Secretary of State] for filing a statement of change containing:

(1) the name of the limited partnership or foreign limited partnership;

(2) the street and mailing address of its current designated office;

(3) if the current designated office is to be changed, the street and mailing address of the new designated office;

(4) the name and street and mailing address of its current agent for service of process; and

(5) if the current agent for service of process or an address of the agent is to be changed, the new information.

(b) Subject to Section 206(c), a statement of change is effective when filed by the [Secretary of State].

COMMENT

Source—ULLCA Section 109.

Subsection (a)—The Act uses "may" rather than "shall" here because other avenues exist. A limited partnership may also change the information by an amendment to its certificate of limited partnership, Section 202, or through its annual report. Section 210(e). A foreign limited partnership may use its annual report. Section 210(e). However, neither a limited partnership nor a foreign limited partnership may wait for the annual report if the information described in the public record becomes inaccurate. See Sections 208 (imposing liability for false information in record) and 117(b) (providing for substitute service).

§ 116. Resignation of Agent for Service of Process

(a) In order to resign as an agent for service of process of a limited partnership or foreign limited partnership, the agent must deliver to the [Secretary of State] for filing a statement of resignation containing the name of the limited partnership or foreign limited partnership.

(b) After receiving a statement of resignation, the [Secretary of State] shall file it and mail a copy to the designated office of the limited partnership or foreign limited partnership and another copy to the principal office if the address of the office appears in the records of the [Secretary of State] and is different from the address of the designated office.

(c) An agency for service of process is terminated on the 31st day after the [Secretary of State] files the statement of resignation.

COMMENT

Source—ULLCA Section 110.

This section provides the only way an agent can resign without cooperation from the limited partnership or foreign limited partnership and the only way the agent, rather than the limited partnership or foreign limited partnership, can effect a change in the public record. See Sections 115(a) (Statement of Change), 202 (Amendment or Restatement of Certificate), and 210(e) (Annual Report), all of which involve the limited partnership or foreign limited partnership designating a replacement agent for service of process.

Subsection (c)—In contrast to most records authorized or required to be delivered to the filing officer for filing under this Act, a statement of resignation may not provide for a delayed effective date. This subsection mandates the effective date, and an effective date included in a statement of resignation is disregarded. See also Section 206(c).

§ 117.   Service of Process

(a)   An agent for service of process appointed by a limited partnership or foreign limited partnership is an agent of the limited partnership or foreign limited partnership for service of any process, notice, or demand required or permitted by law to be served upon the limited partnership or foreign limited partnership.

(b)   If a limited partnership or foreign limited partnership does not appoint or maintain an agent for service of process in this State or the agent for service of process cannot with reasonable diligence be found at the agent's address, the [Secretary of State] is an agent of the limited partnership or foreign limited partnership upon whom process, notice, or demand may be served.

(c)   Service of any process, notice, or demand on the [Secretary of State] may be made by delivering to and leaving with the [Secretary of State] duplicate copies of the process, notice, or demand. If a process, notice, or demand is served on the [Secretary of State], the [Secretary of State] shall forward one of the copies by registered or certified mail, return receipt requested, to the limited partnership or foreign limited partnership at its designated office.

(d)   Service is effected under subsection (c) at the earliest of:

(1)   the date the limited partnership or foreign limited partnership receives the process, notice, or demand;

(2)   the date shown on the return receipt, if signed on behalf of the limited partnership or foreign limited partnership; or

(3)   five days after the process, notice, or demand is deposited in the mail, if mailed postpaid and correctly addressed.

(e)   The [Secretary of State] shall keep a record of each process, notice, and demand served pursuant to this section and record the time of, and the action taken regarding, the service.

(f)   This section does not affect the right to serve process, notice, or demand in any other manner provided by law.

COMMENT

Source—ULLCA Section 111.

Requiring a foreign limited partnership to name an agent for service of process is a change from RULPA. See RULPA Section 902(3).

§ 118.   Consent and Proxies of Partners

Action requiring the consent of partners under this [Act] may be taken without a meeting, and a partner may appoint a proxy to consent or otherwise act for the partner by signing an appointment record, either personally or by the partner's attorney in fact.

COMMENT

Source—ULLCA Section 404(d) and (e).

This Act imposes no meeting requirement and does not distinguish among oral, record, express and tacit consent. The partnership agreement may establish such requirements and make such distinctions.

[ARTICLE] 2.   FORMATION; CERTIFICATE OF LIMITED PARTNERSHIP AND OTHER FILINGS

§ 201.   Formation of Limited Partnership; Certificate of Limited Partnership

(a)   In order for a limited partnership to be formed, a certificate of limited partnership must be delivered to the [Secretary of State] for filing. The certificate must state:

(1)   the name of the limited partnership, which must comply with Section 108;

(2)   the street and mailing address of the initial designated office and the name and street and mailing address of the initial agent for service of process;

(3)   the name and the street and mailing address of each general partner;

(4)   whether the limited partnership is a limited liability limited partnership; and

(5)   any additional information required by [Article] 11.

(b)   A certificate of limited partnership may also contain any other matters but may not vary or otherwise affect the provisions specified in Section 110(b) in a manner inconsistent with that section.

(c)   If there has been substantial compliance with subsection (a), subject to Section 206(c) a limited partnership is formed when the [Secretary of State] files the certificate of limited partnership.

(d)   Subject to subsection (b), if any provision of a partnership agreement is inconsistent with the filed certificate of limited partnership or with a filed statement of dissociation, termination, or change or filed articles of conversion or merger:

(1)   the partnership agreement prevails as to partners and transferees; and

(2)   the filed certificate of limited partnership, statement of dissociation, termination, or change or articles of conversion or merger prevail as to persons, other than partners and transferees, that reasonably rely on the filed record to their detriment.

COMMENT

Source—RULPA Section 201.

A limited partnership is a creature of statute, and this section governs how a limited partnership comes into existence. A limited partnership is formed only if (i) a certificate of limited partnership is prepared and delivered to the specified public official for filing, (ii) the public official files the certificate, and (iii) the certificate, delivery and filing are in "substantial compliance" with the requirements of subsection (a). Section 206(c) governs when a limited partnership comes into existence.

Despite its foundational importance, a certificate of limited partnership is far less powerful than a corporation's articles of incorporation. Among partners and transferees, for example, the partnership agreement is paramount. See Section 201(d).

Subsection (a)(1)—Section 108 contains name requirements. To be acceptable for filing, a certificate of limited partnership must state a name for the limited partnership which complies with Section 108.

Subsection (a)(3)—This provision should be read in conjunction with Section 103(c) and Section 401. See the Comment to those sections.

Subsection (a)(4)—This Act permits a limited partnership to be a limited liability limited partnership ("LLLP"), and this provision requires the certificate of limited partnership to state whether the limited partnership is an LLLP. The requirement is intended to force the organizers of a limited partnership to decide whether the limited partnership is to be an LLLP.

Subject to Sections 406(b)(2) and 1110, a limited partnership may amend its certificate of limited partnership to add or delete a statement that the limited partnership is a limited liability limited partnership. An amendment deleting such a statement must be accompanied by an amendment stating that the limited partnership is **not** a limited liability limited partnership. Section 201(a)(4) does not permit a certificate of limited partnership to be silent on this point, except for pre-existing partnerships that become subject to this Act under Section 1206. See Section 1206(c)(2).

Subsection (d)—Source: ULLCA Section 203(c).

A limited partnership is a creature of contract as well as a creature of statute. It will be possible, albeit improper, for the partnership agreement to be inconsistent with the certificate of limited partnership or other specified public filings relating to the limited partnership. For those circumstances, this subsection provides the rule for determining which source of information prevails.

For partners and transferees, the partnership agreement is paramount. For third parties seeking to invoke the public record, actual knowledge of that record is necessary and notice under Section 103(c) or (d) is irrelevant. A third party wishing to enforce the public record over the partnership agreement must show reasonable reliance on the public record, and reliance presupposes knowledge.

This subsection does not expressly cover a situation in which (i) one of the specified filed records contains information in addition to, but not inconsistent with, the partnership agreement, and (ii) a person, other than a partner or transferee, detrimentally relies on the additional information. However, the policy reflected in this subsection seems equally applicable to that situation.

Responsibility for maintaining a limited partnership's public record rests with the general partner or partners. Section 202(c). A general partner's failure to meet that responsibility can expose the general partner to liability to third parties under Section 208(a)(2) and might constitute a breach of the general partner's duties under Section 408. In addition, an aggrieved person may seek a remedy under Section 205 (Signing and Filing Pursuant to Judicial Order).

§ 202.   Amendment or Restatement of Certificate

(a)   In order to amend its certificate of limited partnership, a limited partnership must deliver to the [Secretary of State] for filing an amendment or, pursuant to [Article] 11, articles of merger stating:

(1)   the name of the limited partnership;

(2)   the date of filing of its initial certificate; and

(3)   the changes the amendment makes to the certificate as most recently amended or restated.

(b)   A limited partnership shall promptly deliver to the [Secretary of State] for filing an amendment to a certificate of limited partnership to reflect:

(1)   the admission of a new general partner;

(2)   the dissociation of a person as a general partner; or

(3)   the appointment of a person to wind up the limited partnership's activities under Section 803(c) or (d).

(c)   A general partner that knows that any information in a filed certificate of limited partnership was false when the certificate was filed or has become false due to changed circumstances shall promptly:

(1)   cause the certificate to be amended; or

(2)   if appropriate, deliver to the [Secretary of State] for filing a statement of change pursuant to Section 115 or a statement of correction pursuant to Section 207.

(d)   A certificate of limited partnership may be amended at any time for any other proper purpose as determined by the limited partnership.

(e)   A restated certificate of limited partnership may be delivered to the [Secretary of State] for filing in the same manner as an amendment.

(f)   Subject to Section 206(c), an amendment or restated certificate is effective when filed by the [Secretary of State].

COMMENT

Source—RULPA Section 202.

Subsection (b)—This subsection lists changes in circumstances which require an amendment to the certificate. Neither a statement of change, Section 115, nor the annual report, Section 210(e), suffice to report the addition or deletion of a general partner or the appointment of a person to wind up a limited partnership that has no general partner.

This subsection states an obligation of the limited partnership. However, so long as the limited partnership has at least one general partner, the general partner or partners are responsible for managing the limited partnership's activities. Section 406(a). That management responsibility includes maintaining accuracy in the limited partnership's public record. Moreover, subsection (c) imposes direct responsibility on any general partner that knows that the filed certificate of limited partnership contains false information.

Acquiring or relinquishing LLLP status also requires an amendment to the certificate. See Sections 201(a)(4), 406(b)(2), and 1110(b)(2).

Subsection (c)—This provision imposes an obligation directly on the general partners rather than on the limited partnership. A general partner's failure to meet that responsibility can expose the general partner to liability to third parties under Section 208(a)(2) and might constitute a breach of the general partner's duties under Section 408. In addition, an aggrieved person may seek a remedy under Section 205 (Signing and Filing Pursuant to Judicial Order).

Subsection (d)—A limited partnership that desires to change its name will have to amend its certificate of limited partnership. The new name will have to comply with Section 108. See Section 201(a)(1).

§ 203. Statement of Termination

A dissolved limited partnership that has completed winding up may deliver to the [Secretary of State] for filing a statement of termination that states:

(1) the name of the limited partnership;

(2) the date of filing of its initial certificate of limited partnership; and

(3) any other information as determined by the general partners filing the statement or by a person appointed pursuant to Section 803(c) or (d).

COMMENT

Under Section 103(d)(3), a filed statement of termination provides constructive notice, 90 days after the statement's effective date, that the limited partnership is terminated. That notice effectively terminates any apparent authority to bind the limited partnership.

However, this section is permissive. Therefore, it is not possible to use Section 205 (Signing and Filing Pursuant to Judicial Order) to cause a statement of termination to be filed.

This section differs from predecessor law, RULPA Section 203, which required the filing of a certificate of cancellation when a limited partnership dissolved.

§ 204. Signing of Records

(a) Each record delivered to the [Secretary of State] for filing pursuant to this [Act] must be signed in the following manner:

(1) An initial certificate of limited partnership must be signed by all general partners listed in the certificate.

(2) An amendment adding or deleting a statement that the limited partnership is a limited liability limited partnership must be signed by all general partners listed in the certificate.

(3) An amendment designating as general partner a person admitted under Section 801(3)(B) following the dissociation of a limited partnership's last general partner must be signed by that person.

(4) An amendment required by Section 803(c) following the appointment of a person to wind up the dissolved limited partnership's activities must be signed by that person.

(5) Any other amendment must be signed by:

(A)   at least one general partner listed in the certificate;

(B)   each other person designated in the amendment as a new general partner; and

(C)   each person that the amendment indicates has dissociated as a general partner, unless:

(i)   the person is deceased or a guardian or general conservator has been appointed for the person and the amendment so states; or

(ii)   the person has previously delivered to the [Secretary of State] for filing a statement of dissociation.

(6)   A restated certificate of limited partnership must be signed by at least one general partner listed in the certificate, and, to the extent the restated certificate effects a change under any other paragraph of this subsection, the certificate must be signed in a manner that satisfies that paragraph.

(7)   A statement of termination must be signed by all general partners listed in the certificate or, if the certificate of a dissolved limited partnership lists no general partners, by the person appointed pursuant to Section 803(c) or (d) to wind up the dissolved limited partnership's activities.

(8)   Articles of conversion must be signed by each general partner listed in the certificate of limited partnership.

(9)   Articles of merger must be signed as provided in Section 1108(a).

(10)   Any other record delivered on behalf of a limited partnership to the [Secretary of State] for filing must be signed by at least one general partner listed in the certificate.

(11)   A statement by a person pursuant to Section 605(a)(4) stating that the person has dissociated as a general partner must be signed by that person.

(12)   A statement of withdrawal by a person pursuant to Section 306 must be signed by that person.

(13)   A record delivered on behalf of a foreign limited partnership to the [Secretary of State] for filing must be signed by at least one general partner of the foreign limited partnership.

(14)   Any other record delivered on behalf of any person to the [Secretary of State] for filing must be signed by that person.

(b)   Any person may sign by an attorney in fact any record to be filed pursuant to this [Act].

COMMENT

Source—ULLCA Section 205.

This section pertains only to signing requirements and implies nothing about approval requirements. For example, Section 204(a)(2) requires that an amendment changing a limited partnership's LLLP status be signed by all **general** partners listed in the certificate, but under Section 406(b)(2) **all** partners must consent to that change unless otherwise provided in the partnership agreement.

A person who signs a record without ascertaining that the record has been properly authorized risks liability under Section 208.

Subsection (a)—The recurring reference to general partners "listed in the certificate" recognizes that a person might be admitted as a general partner under Section 401 without immediately being listed in the certificate of limited partnership. Such persons may have rights, powers and obligations despite their unlisted status, but they cannot act as general partners for the purpose of affecting the limited partnership's public record. See the Comment to Section 103(c) and the Comment to Section 401.

§ 205.   Signing and Filing Pursuant to Judicial Order

(a)   If a person required by this [Act] to sign a record or deliver a record to the [Secretary of State] for filing does not do so, any other person that is aggrieved may petition the [appropriate court] to order:

(1)   the person to sign the record;

(2)   deliver the record to the [Secretary of State] for filing; or

(3)   the [Secretary of State] to file the record unsigned.

(b)   If the person aggrieved under subsection (a) is not the limited partnership or foreign limited partnership to which the record pertains, the aggrieved person shall make the limited partnership or foreign limited partnership a party to the action. A person aggrieved under subsection (a) may seek the remedies provided in subsection (a) in the same action in combination or in the alternative.

(c)   A record filed unsigned pursuant to this section is effective without being signed.

COMMENT

Source—RULPA Section 205.

§ 206.   Delivery to and Filing of Records by [Secretary of State]; Effective Time and Date

(a)   A record authorized or required to be delivered to the [Secretary of State] for filing under this [Act] must be captioned to describe the record's purpose, be in a medium permitted by the [Secretary of State], and be delivered to the [Secretary of State]. Unless the [Secretary of State] determines that a record does not comply with the filing requirements of this [Act], and if all filing fees have been paid, the [Secretary of State] shall file the record and:

(1)   for a statement of dissociation, send:

(A)   a copy of the filed statement and a receipt for the fees to the person which the statement indicates has dissociated as a general partner; and

(B)   a copy of the filed statement and receipt to the limited partnership;

(2)   for a statement of withdrawal, send:

(A)   a copy of the filed statement and a receipt for the fees to the person on whose behalf the record was filed; and

(B)   if the statement refers to an existing limited partnership, a copy of the filed statement and receipt to the limited partnership; and

(3)   for all other records, send a copy of the filed record and a receipt for the fees to the person on whose behalf the record was filed.

(b)   Upon request and payment of a fee, the [Secretary of State] shall send to the requester a certified copy of the requested record.

(c)   Except as otherwise provided in Sections 116 and 207, a record delivered to the [Secretary of State] for filing under this [Act] may specify an effective time and a delayed effective date. Except as otherwise provided in this [Act], a record filed by the [Secretary of State] is effective:

(1)   if the record does not specify an effective time and does not specify a delayed effective date, on the date and at the time the record is filed as evidenced by the [Secretary of State's] endorsement of the date and time on the record;

(2)   if the record specifies an effective time but not a delayed effective date, on the date the record is filed at the time specified in the record;

(3)   if the record specifies a delayed effective date but not an effective time, at 12:01 a.m. on the earlier of:

(A)   the specified date; or

(B)   the 90th day after the record is filed; or

(4)   if the record specifies an effective time and a delayed effective date, at the specified time on the earlier of:

(A)   the specified date; or

843

(B)   the 90th day after the record is filed.

COMMENT

Source—ULLCA Section 206.

In order for a record prepared by a private person to become part of the public record under this Act, (i) someone must put a properly prepared version of the record into the possession of the public official specified in the Act as the appropriate filing officer, and (ii) that filing officer must determine that the record complies with the filing requirements of this Act and then officially make the record part of the public record. This Act refers to the first step as *delivery to the [Secretary of State] for filing* and refers to the second step as *filing*. Thus, under this Act "filing" is an official act.

Subsection (a)—The caption need only indicate the title of the record; *e.g.*, Certificate of Limited Partnership, Statement of Change for Limited Partnership.

Filing officers typically note on a filed record the fact, date and time of filing. The copies provided by the filing officer under this subsection should contain that notation.

This Act does not provide a remedy if the filing officer wrongfully fails or refuses to file a record.

Subsection (c)—This subsection allows most records to have a delayed effective date, up to 90 days after the date the record is filed by the filing officer. A record specifying a longer delay will **not** be rejected. Instead, under paragraph (c)(3) and (4), the delayed effective date is adjusted by operation of law to the "90th day after the record is filed." The Act does not require the filing officer to notify anyone of the adjustment.

§ 207.   Correcting Filed Record

(a)   A limited partnership or foreign limited partnership may deliver to the [Secretary of State] for filing a statement of correction to correct a record previously delivered by the limited partnership or foreign limited partnership to the [Secretary of State] and filed by the [Secretary of State], if at the time of filing the record contained false or erroneous information or was defectively signed.

(b)   A statement of correction may not state a delayed effective date and must:

(1)   describe the record to be corrected, including its filing date, or attach a copy of the record as filed;

(2)   specify the incorrect information and the reason it is incorrect or the manner in which the signing was defective; and

(3)   correct the incorrect information or defective signature.

(c)   When filed by the [Secretary of State], a statement of correction is effective retroactively as of the effective date of the record the statement corrects, but the statement is effective when filed:

(1)   for the purposes of Section 103(c) and (d); and

(2)   as to persons relying on the uncorrected record and adversely affected by the correction.

COMMENT

Source—ULLCA Section 207.

A statement of correction is appropriate only to correct inaccuracies that existed or signatures that were defective "at the time of filing." A statement of correction may not be used to correct a record that was accurate when filed but has become inaccurate due to subsequent events.

Subsection (c)—Generally, a statement of correction "relates back." However, there is no retroactive effect: (1) for the purposes of constructive notice under Section 103(c) and (d); and (2) against persons who have relied on the uncorrected record and would be adversely affected if the correction related back.

844

§ 208. Liability for False Information in Filed Record

(a)   If a record delivered to the [Secretary of State] for filing under this [Act] and filed by the [Secretary of State] contains false information, a person that suffers loss by reliance on the information may recover damages for the loss from:

(1)   a person that signed the record, or caused another to sign it on the person's behalf, and knew the information to be false at the time the record was signed; and

(2)   a general partner that has notice that the information was false when the record was filed or has become false because of changed circumstances, if the general partner has notice for a reasonably sufficient time before the information is relied upon to enable the general partner to effect an amendment under Section 202, file a petition pursuant to Section 205, or deliver to the [Secretary of State] for filing a statement of change pursuant to Section 115 or a statement of correction pursuant to Section 207.

(b)   Signing a record authorized or required to be filed under this [Act] constitutes an affirmation under the penalties of perjury that the facts stated in the record are true.

COMMENT

This section pertains to both limited partnerships and foreign limited partnerships.

LLLP status is irrelevant to this section. The LLLP shield protects only to the extent that (i) the obligation involved is an obligation of the limited partnership or foreign limited partnership, and (ii) a partner is claimed to be liable for that obligation by reason of being a partner. This section does not address the obligations of a limited partnership or foreign limited partnership and instead imposes direct liability on signers and general partners.

Subsection (a)—This subsection's liability rules apply only to records (i) created by private persons ("delivered to the [Secretary of State] for filing"), (ii) which actually become part of the public record ("filed by the [Secretary of State]"). This subsection does not preempt other law, which might provide remedies for misleading information contained, for example, in a record that is delivered to the filing officer for filing but withdrawn before the filing officer takes the official action of filing the record.

Records filed under this Act are signed subject to the penalties for perjury. See subsection (b). This subsection therefore does not require a party who relies on a record to demonstrate that the reliance was reasonable. Contrast Section 201(d)(2), which provides that, if the partnership agreement is inconsistent with the public record, the public record prevails in favor of a person that is neither a partner nor a transferee and that reasonably relied on the record.

§ 209. Certificate of Existence or Authorization

(a)   The [Secretary of State], upon request and payment of the requisite fee, shall furnish a certificate of existence for a limited partnership if the records filed in the [office of the Secretary of State] show that the [Secretary of State] has filed a certificate of limited partnership and has not filed a statement of termination. A certificate of existence must state:

(1)   the limited partnership's name;

(2)   that it was duly formed under the laws of this State and the date of formation;

(3)   whether all fees, taxes, and penalties due to the [Secretary of State] under this [Act] or other law have been paid;

(4)   whether the limited partnership's most recent annual report required by Section 210 has been filed by the [Secretary of State];

(5)   whether the [Secretary of State] has administratively dissolved the limited partnership;

(6)   whether the limited partnership's certificate of limited partnership has been amended to state that the limited partnership is dissolved;

(7)   that a statement of termination has not been filed by the [Secretary of State]; and

(8)   other facts of record in the [office of the Secretary of State] which may be requested by the applicant.

(b)   The [Secretary of State], upon request and payment of the requisite fee, shall furnish a certificate of authorization for a foreign limited partnership if the records filed in the [office of the Secretary of State] show that the [Secretary of State] has filed a certificate of authority, has not revoked the certificate of authority, and has not filed a notice of cancellation. A certificate of authorization must state:

(1)   the foreign limited partnership's name and any alternate name adopted under Section 905(a) for use in this State;

(2)   that it is authorized to transact business in this State;

(3)   whether all fees, taxes, and penalties due to the [Secretary of State] under this [Act] or other law have been paid;

(4)   whether the foreign limited partnership's most recent annual report required by Section 210 has been filed by the [Secretary of State];

(5)   that the [Secretary of State] has not revoked its certificate of authority and has not filed a notice of cancellation; and

(6)   other facts of record in the [office of the Secretary of State] which may be requested by the applicant.

(c)   Subject to any qualification stated in the certificate, a certificate of existence or authorization issued by the [Secretary of State] may be relied upon as conclusive evidence that the limited partnership or foreign limited partnership is in existence or is authorized to transact business in this State.

COMMENT

Source—ULLCA Section 208.

A certificate of existence can reveal only information present in the public record, and under this Act significant information bearing on the status of a limited partnership may be outside the public record. For example, while this Act provides for a limited partnership to have a perpetual duration, Section 104(c), the partnership agreement may set a definite term or designate particular events whose occurrence will cause dissolution. Section 801(1). Dissolution is also possible by consent, Section 801(2), and, absent a contrary provision in the partnership agreement, will at least be at issue whenever a general partner dissociates. Section 801(3). Nothing in this Act requires a limited partnership to deliver to the filing officer for filing a record indicating that the limited partnership has dissolved.

A certificate of authorization furnished under this section is different than a certificate of authority filed under Section 904.

§ 210.   Annual Report for [Secretary of State]

(a)   A limited partnership or a foreign limited partnership authorized to transact business in this State shall deliver to the [Secretary of State] for filing an annual report that states:

(1)   the name of the limited partnership or foreign limited partnership;

(2)   the street and mailing address of its designated office and the name and street and mailing address of its agent for service of process in this State;

(3)   in the case of a limited partnership, the street and mailing address of its principal office; and

(4)   in the case of a foreign limited partnership, the State or other jurisdiction under whose law the foreign limited partnership is formed and any alternate name adopted under Section 905(a).

(b)   Information in an annual report must be current as of the date the annual report is delivered to the [Secretary of State] for filing.

(c)   The first annual report must be delivered to the [Secretary of State] between [January 1 and April 1] of the year following the calendar year in which a limited partnership was formed or a foreign limited partnership was authorized to transact business. An annual report must be delivered to the [Secretary of State] between [January 1 and April 1] of each subsequent calendar year.

(d)   If an annual report does not contain the information required in subsection (a), the [Secretary of State] shall promptly notify the reporting limited partnership or foreign limited partnership and return the report to it for correction. If the report is corrected to contain the information required in subsection (a) and delivered to the [Secretary of State] within 30 days after the effective date of the notice, it is timely delivered.

(e)   If a filed annual report contains an address of a designated office or the name or address of an agent for service of process which differs from the information shown in the records of the [Secretary of State] immediately before the filing, the differing information in the annual report is considered a statement of change under Section 115.

COMMENT

Source—ULLCA Section 211.

Subsection (d)—This subsection's rule affects only Section 809(a)(2) (late filing of annual report grounds for administrative dissolution) and any late fees that the filing officer might have the right to impose. For the purposes of subsection (e), the annual report functions as a statement of change only when "filed" by the filing officer. Likewise, a person cannot rely on subsection (d) to escape liability arising under Section 208.

[ARTICLE] 3.   LIMITED PARTNERS

§ 301.   Becoming Limited Partner

A person becomes a limited partner:

    (1)   as provided in the partnership agreement;

    (2)   as the result of a conversion or merger under [Article] 11; or

    (3)   with the consent of all the partners.

COMMENT

Source—RULPA Section 301.

Although Section 801(4) contemplates the admission of a limited partner to avoid dissolution, that provision does not itself authorize the admission. Instead, this section controls. Contrast Section 801(3)(B), which itself authorizes the admission of a general partner in order to avoid dissolution.

§ 302.   No Right or Power as Limited Partner to Bind Limited Partnership

A limited partner does not have the right or the power as a limited partner to act for or bind the limited partnership.

COMMENT

In this respect a limited partner is analogous to a shareholder in a corporation; status as owner provides neither the right to manage nor a reasonable appearance of that right.

The phrase "as a limited partner" is intended to recognize that: (i) this section does not disable a general partner that also owns a limited partner interest; (ii) the partnership agreement may as a matter of contract allocate managerial rights to one or more limited partners; and (iii) a separate agreement can empower and entitle a person that is a limited partner to act for the limited partnership in another capacity; *e.g.*, as an agent. See Comment to Section 305.

The fact that a limited partner *qua* limited partner has no power to bind the limited partnership means that, subject to Section 113 (Dual Capacity), information possessed by a limited partner is not attributed to the limited partnership. See Section 103(h).

This Act specifies various circumstances in which limited partners have consent rights, including:

- admission of a limited partner, Section 301(3)

- admission of a general partner, Section 401(4)

- amendment of the partnership agreement, Section 406(b)(1)

- the decision to amend the certificate of limited partnership so as to obtain or relinquish LLLP status, Section 406(b)(2)

- the disposition of all or substantially all of the limited partnership's property, outside the ordinary course, Section 406(b)(3)

- the compromise of a partner's obligation to make a contribution or return an improper distribution, Section 502(c)

- expulsion of a limited partner by consent of the other partners, Section 601(b)(4)

- expulsion of a general partner by consent of the other partners, Section 603(4)

- redemption of a transferable interest subject to charging order, using limited partnership property, Section 703(c)(3)

- causing dissolution by consent, Section 801(2)

- causing dissolution by consent following the dissociation of a general partner, when at least one general partner remains, Section 801(3)(A)

- avoiding dissolution and appointing a successor general partner, following the dissociation of the sole general partner, Section 801(3)(B)

- appointing a person to wind up the limited partnership when there is no general partner, Section 803(C)

- approving, amending or abandoning a plan of conversion, Section 1103(a) and (b)(2)

- approving, amending or abandoning a plan of merger, Section 1107(a) and (b)(2).

§ 303. No Liability as Limited Partner for Limited Partnership Obligations

An obligation of a limited partnership, whether arising in contract, tort, or otherwise, is not the obligation of a limited partner. A limited partner is not personally liable, directly or indirectly, by way of contribution or otherwise, for an obligation of the limited partnership solely by reason of being a limited partner, even if the limited partner participates in the management and control of the limited partnership.

COMMENT

This section provides a full, status-based liability shield for each limited partner, "even if the limited partner participates in the management and control of the limited partnership." The section thus eliminates the so-called "control rule" with respect to personal liability for entity obligations and brings limited partners into parity with LLC members, LLP partners and corporate shareholders.

The "control rule" first appeared in an uniform act in 1916, although the concept is much older. Section 7 of the original Uniform Limited Partnership Act provided that "A limited partner shall not become liable as a general partner [i.e., for the obligations of the limited partnership] unless . . . he takes part in the control of the business." The 1976 Uniform Limited Partnership Act (ULPA–1976) "carrie[d] over the basic test from former Section 7," but recognized "the difficulty of determining when the 'control' line has been overstepped." Comment to ULPA–1976, Section 303. Accordingly, ULPA–1976 tried to buttress the limited partner's shield by (i) providing a safe harbor for a lengthy list of activities deemed not to constitute participating in control, ULPA–1976, Section 303(b), and (ii) limiting a limited partner's "control rule" liability "only to persons who transact business with the limited partnership with actual knowledge of [the limited partner's] participation in control." ULPA–1976, Section 303(a). However, these protections were complicated by a countervailing rule which made a limited partner generally liable for the limited partnership's obligations "if the limited partner's participation in the control of the business is . . . substantially the same as the exercise of the powers of a general partner." ULPA–1976, Section 303(a).

The 1985 amendments to ULPA–1976 (i.e., RULPA) further buttressed the limited partner's shield, removing the "substantially the same" rule, expanding the list of safe harbor activities and limiting "control rule" liability "only to persons who transact business with the limited partnership reasonably believing, based upon the limited partner's conduct, that the limited partner is a general partner."

In a world with LLPs, LLCs and, most importantly, LLLPs, the control rule has become an anachronism. This Act therefore takes the next logical step in the evolution of the limited partner's liability shield and renders the control rule extinct.

The shield established by this section protects only against liability for the limited partnership's obligations and only to the extent that the limited partner is claimed to be liable on account of being a limited partner. Thus, a person that is both a general and limited partner will be liable as a general partner for the limited partnership's obligations. Moreover, this section does not prevent a limited partner from being liable as a result of the limited partner's own conduct and is therefore inapplicable when a third party asserts that a limited partner's own wrongful conduct has injured the third party. This section is likewise inapplicable to claims by the limited partnership or another partner that a limited partner has breached a duty under this Act or the partnership agreement.

This section does not eliminate a limited partner's liability for promised contributions, Section 502 or improper distributions. Section 509. That liability pertains to a person's status as a limited partner but is **not** liability for an obligation of the limited partnership.

The shield provided by this section applies whether or not a limited partnership is a limited liability limited partnership.

§ 304. Right of Limited Partner and Former Limited Partner to Information

(a)   On 10 days' demand, made in a record received by the limited partnership, a limited partner may inspect and copy required information during regular business hours in the limited partnership's designated office. The limited partner need not have any particular purpose for seeking the information.

(b)   During regular business hours and at a reasonable location specified by the limited partnership, a limited partner may obtain from the limited partnership and inspect and copy true and full information regarding the state of the activities and financial condition of the limited partnership and other information regarding the activities of the limited partnership as is just and reasonable if:

(1)   the limited partner seeks the information for a purpose reasonably related to the partner's interest as a limited partner;

(2)   the limited partner makes a demand in a record received by the limited partnership, describing with reasonable particularity the information sought and the purpose for seeking the information; and

(3)   the information sought is directly connected to the limited partner's purpose.

(c)   Within 10 days after receiving a demand pursuant to subsection (b), the limited partnership in a record shall inform the limited partner that made the demand:

(1)   what information the limited partnership will provide in response to the demand;

(2)   when and where the limited partnership will provide the information; and

(3)   if the limited partnership declines to provide any demanded information, the limited partnership's reasons for declining.

(d)   Subject to subsection (f), a person dissociated as a limited partner may inspect and copy required information during regular business hours in the limited partnership's designated office if:

(1)   the information pertains to the period during which the person was a limited partner;

(2)   the person seeks the information in good faith; and

(3)   the person meets the requirements of subsection (b).

(e)   The limited partnership shall respond to a demand made pursuant to subsection (d) in the same manner as provided in subsection (c).

(f)   If a limited partner dies, Section 704 applies.

(g)   The limited partnership may impose reasonable restrictions on the use of information obtained under this section. In a dispute concerning the reasonableness of a restriction under this subsection, the limited partnership has the burden of proving reasonableness.

(h)   A limited partnership may charge a person that makes a demand under this section reasonable costs of copying, limited to the costs of labor and material.

(i)   Whenever this [Act] or a partnership agreement provides for a limited partner to give or withhold consent to a matter, before the consent is given or withheld, the limited partnership shall, without demand, provide the limited partner with all information material to the limited partner's decision that the limited partnership knows.

(j)   A limited partner or person dissociated as a limited partner may exercise the rights under this section through an attorney or other agent. Any restriction imposed under subsection (g) or by the partnership agreement applies both to the attorney or other agent and to the limited partner or person dissociated as a limited partner.

(k)   The rights stated in this section do not extend to a person as transferee, but may be exercised by the legal representative of an individual under legal disability who is a limited partner or person dissociated as a limited partner.

COMMENT

This section balances two countervailing concerns relating to information: the need of limited partners and former limited partners for access versus the limited partnership's need to protect confidential business data and other intellectual property. The balance must be understood in the context of fiduciary duties. The general partners are obliged through their duties of care and loyalty to protect information whose confidentiality is important to the limited partnership or otherwise inappropriate for dissemination. See Section 408 (general standards of general partner conduct). A limited partner, in contrast, "does not have any fiduciary duty to the limited partnership or to any other partner solely by reason of being a limited partner." Section 305(a). (Both general partners and limited partners are subject to a duty of good faith and fair dealing. Section 305(b) and 408(d)).

Like predecessor law, this Act divides limited partner access rights into two categories—required information and other information. However, this Act builds on predecessor law by:

- expanding slightly the category of required information and stating explicitly that a limited partner may have access to that information without having to show cause

- specifying a procedure for limited partners to follow when demanding access to other information

- specifying how a limited partnership must respond to such a demand and setting a time limit for the response

- retaining predecessor law's "just and reasonable" standard for determining a limited partner's right to other information, while recognizing that, to be "just and reasonable," a limited partner's demand for other information must meet at minimum standards of relatedness and particularity

- expressly requiring the limited partnership to volunteer known, material information when seeking or obtaining consent from limited partners

- codifying (while limiting) the power of the partnership agreement to vary limited partner access rights

- permitting the limited partnership to establish other reasonable limits on access

- providing access rights for former limited partners.

The access rights stated in this section are personal to each limited partner and are enforceable through a direct action under Section 1001(a). These access rights are in addition to whatever discovery rights a party has in a civil suit.

Subsection (a)—The phrase "required information" is a defined term. See Sections 102(18) and 111. This subsection's broad right of access is subject not only to reasonable limitations in the partnership agreement, Section 110(b)(4), but also to the power of the limited partnership to impose reasonable limitations on use. Unless the partnership agreement provides otherwise, it will be the general partner or partners that have the authority to use that power. See Section 406(a).

Subsection (b)—The language describing the information to be provided comes essentially verbatim from RULPA Section 305(a)(2)(i) and (iii). The procedural requirements derive from RMBCA Section 16.02(c). This subsection does not impose a requirement of good faith, because Section 305(b) contains a generally applicable obligation of good faith and fair dealing for limited partners.

Subsection (d)—The notion that former owners should have information rights comes from RUPA Section 403(b) and ULLCA Section 408(a). The access is limited to the required information and is subject to certain conditions.

Example: A person dissociated as a limited partner seeks data which the limited partnership has compiled, which relates to the period when the person was a limited partner, but which is beyond the scope of the information required by Section 111. No matter how reasonable the person's purpose and how well drafted the person's demand, the limited partnership is not obliged to provide the data.

Example: A person dissociated as a limited partner seeks access to required information pertaining to the period during which the person was a limited partner. The person makes a bald demand, merely stating a desire to review the required information at the limited partnership's designated office. In particular, the demand does not describe "with reasonable particularity the information sought and the purpose for seeking the information." See subsection (b)(2). The limited partnership is not obliged to allow access. The person must first comply with subsection (d), which incorporates by reference the requirements of subsection (b).

Subsection (f) and Section 704 provide greater access rights for the estate of a deceased limited partner.

Subsection (d)(2)—A duty of good faith is needed here, because a person claiming access under this subsection is no longer a limited partner and is no longer subject to Section 305(b). See Section 602(a)(2) (dissociation as a limited partner terminates duty of good faith as to subsequent events).

Subsection (g)—This subsection permits the limited partnership—as distinguished from the partnership agreement—to impose use limitations. Contrast Section 110(b)(4). Under Section 406(a), it will be the general partner or partners that decide whether the limited partnership will impose use restrictions.

The limited partnership bears the burden of proving the reasonableness of any restriction imposed under this subsection. In determining whether a restriction is reasonable, a court might consider: (i) the danger or other problem the restriction seeks to avoid; (ii) the purpose for which the information is sought; and (iii) whether, in light of both the problem and the purpose, the restriction is reasonably tailored. Restricting use of the names and addresses of limited partners is not per se unreasonable.

The following table compares the limitations available through the partnership agreement with those available under this subsection.

	partnership agreement	Section 304(g)
how restrictions adopted	by the consent of partners when they adopt or amend the partnership agreement, unless the partnership agreement provides another method of amendment	by the general partners, acting under Section 406(a)
what restrictions may be imposed	"reasonable restrictions on the availability and use of information obtained," Section 110(b)(4)	"reasonable restrictions on the use of information obtained"

	partnership agreement	Section 304(g)
burden of proof	the person challenging the restriction must prove that the restriction will "unreasonably restrict the right of information," Section 110(b)(4)	"the limited partnership has the burden of proving reasonableness"

Subsection (h)—Source: RUPA Section 403(b) and ULLCA Section 408(a).

Subsection (i)—Source: ULLCA Section 408(b).

The duty stated in this subsection is at the core of the duties owed the limited partners by a limited partnership and its general partners. This subsection imposes an affirmative duty to volunteer information, but that obligation is limited to information which is both material and known by the limited partnership. The duty applies to known, material information, even if the limited partnership does not know that the information is material.

A limited partnership will "know" what its general partners know. Section 103(h). A limited partnership may also know information known by the "individual conducting the transaction for the [limited partnership]." Section 103(g).

A limited partner's right to information under this subsection is enforceable through the full panoply of "legal or equitable relief" provided by Section 1001(a), including in appropriate circumstances the withdrawal or invalidation of improperly obtained consent and the invalidation or recis[s]ion of action taken pursuant to that consent.

Subsection (k)—Section 304 provides no information rights to a transferee as transferee. Transferee status brings only the very limited information rights stated in Section 702(c).

It is nonetheless possible for a person that happens to be a transferee to have rights under this section. For example, under Section 602(a)(3) a person dissociated as a limited partner becomes a "mere transferee" of its own transferable interest. While that status provides the person no rights under this section, the status of person dissociated as a limited partner triggers rights under subsection (d).

§ 305.   Limited Duties of Limited Partners

(a)   A limited partner does not have any fiduciary duty to the limited partnership or to any other partner solely by reason of being a limited partner.

(b)   A limited partner shall discharge the duties to the partnership and the other partners under this [Act] or under the partnership agreement and exercise any rights consistently with the obligation of good faith and fair dealing.

(c)   A limited partner does not violate a duty or obligation under this [Act] or under the partnership agreement merely because the limited partner's conduct furthers the limited partner's own interest.

COMMENT

Subsection (a)—Fiduciary duty typically attaches to a person whose status or role creates significant power for that person over the interests of another person. Under this Act, limited partners have very limited power of any sort in the regular activities of the limited partnership and no power whatsoever justifying the imposition of fiduciary duties either to the limited partnership or fellow partners. It is possible for a partnership agreement to allocate significant managerial authority and power to a limited partner, but in that case the power exists not as a matter of status or role but rather as a matter of contract. The proper limit on such contract-based power is the obligation of good faith and fair dealing, not fiduciary duty, unless the partnership agreement itself expressly imposes a fiduciary duty or creates a role for a limited partner which, as a matter of other law, gives rise to a fiduciary duty. For example, if the partnership agreement makes a limited partner an agent for the limited partnership as to particular matters, the law of agency will impose fiduciary duties on the limited partner with respect to the limited partner's role as agent.

Subsection (b)—Source: RUPA Section 404(d). The same language appears in Section 408(d), pertaining to general partners.

The obligation of good faith and fair dealing is *not* a fiduciary duty, does not command altruism or self-abnegation, and does not prevent a partner from acting in the partner's own self-interest. Courts should not use the obligation to change *ex post facto* the parties' or this Act's allocation of risk and power. To the contrary, in light of the nature of a limited partnership, the obligation should be used only to protect agreed-upon arrangements from conduct that is manifestly beyond what a reasonable person could have contemplated when the arrangements were made.

The partnership agreement or this Act may grant discretion to a partner, and that partner may properly exercise that discretion even though another partner suffers as a consequence. Conduct does not violate the obligation of good faith and fair dealing merely because that conduct substantially prejudices a party. Indeed, parties allocate risk precisely because prejudice may occur. The exercise of discretion constitutes a breach of the obligation of good faith and fair dealing only when the party claiming breach shows that the conduct has no honestly-held purpose that legitimately comports with the parties' agreed-upon arrangements. Once such a purpose appears, courts should not second guess a party's choice of method in serving that purpose, unless the party invoking the obligation of good faith and fair dealing shows that the choice of method itself lacks any honestly-held purpose that legitimately comports with the parties' agreed-upon arrangements.

In sum, the purpose of the obligation of good faith and fair dealing is to protect the arrangement the partners have chosen for themselves, not to restructure that arrangement under the guise of safeguarding it.

§ 306. Person Erroneously Believing Self to Be Limited Partner

(a)   Except as otherwise provided in subsection (b), a person that makes an investment in a business enterprise and erroneously but in good faith believes that the person has become a limited partner in the enterprise is not liable for the enterprise's obligations by reason of making the investment, receiving distributions from the enterprise, or exercising any rights of or appropriate to a limited partner, if, on ascertaining the mistake, the person:

(1)   causes an appropriate certificate of limited partnership, amendment, or statement of correction to be signed and delivered to the [Secretary of State] for filing; or

(2)   withdraws from future participation as an owner in the enterprise by signing and delivering to the [Secretary of State] for filing a statement of withdrawal under this section.

(b)   A person that makes an investment described in subsection (a) is liable to the same extent as a general partner to any third party that enters into a transaction with the enterprise, believing in good faith that the person is a general partner, before the [Secretary of State] files a statement of withdrawal, certificate of limited partnership, amendment, or statement of correction to show that the person is not a general partner.

(c)   If a person makes a diligent effort in good faith to comply with subsection (a)(1) and is unable to cause the appropriate certificate of limited partnership, amendment, or statement of correction to be signed and delivered to the [Secretary of State] for filing, the person has the right to withdraw from the enterprise pursuant to subsection (a)(2) even if the withdrawal would otherwise breach an agreement with others that are or have agreed to become co-owners of the enterprise.

COMMENT

Source—RULPA Section 304, substantially redrafted for reasons of style.

Subsection (a)(2)—The requirement that a person "withdraw[ ] from future participation as an owner in the enterprise" means, in part, that the person refrain from taking any further profit from the enterprise. The requirement does not mean, however, that the person is required to return previously obtained profits or forfeit any investment.

[ARTICLE] 4.   GENERAL PARTNERS

§ 401.   Becoming General Partner

A person becomes a general partner:

(1)   as provided in the partnership agreement;

(2)   under Section 801(3)(B) following the dissociation of a limited partnership's last general partner;

(3)   as the result of a conversion or merger under [Article] 11; or

(4)   with the consent of all the partners.

COMMENT

This section does not make a person's status as a general partner dependent on the person being so designated in the certificate of limited partnership. If a person does become a general partner under this section without being so designated:

- the limited partnership is obligated to promptly and appropriately amend the certificate of limited partnership, Section 202(b)(1);

- each general partner that knows of the anomaly is personally obligated to cause the certificate to be promptly and appropriately amended, Section 202(c)(1), and is subject to liability for failing to do so, Section 208(a)(2);

- the "non-designated" general partner has:

  — all the rights and duties of a general partner to the limited partnership and the other partners, and

  — the powers of a general partner to bind the limited partnership under Sections 402 and 403, but

  — no power to sign records which are to be filed on behalf of the limited partnership under this Act

Example: By consent of the partners of XYZ Limited Partnership, G is admitted as a general partner. However, XYZ's certificate of limited partnership is not amended accordingly. Later, G—acting without actual authority—purports to bind XYZ to a transaction with Third Party. Third Party does not review the filed certificate of limited partnership before entering into the transaction. XYZ might be bound under Section 402.

Section 402 attributes to a limited partnership "[a]n act of a general partner . . . for apparently carrying on in the ordinary course the limited partnership's activities or activities of the kind carried on by the limited partnership." The limited partnership's liability under Section 402 does not depend on the "act of a general partner" being the act of a general partner designated in the certificate of limited partnership. Moreover, the notice provided by Section 103(c) does not undercut G's appearance of authority. Section 402 refers only to notice under Section 103(d) and, in any event, according to the second sentence of Section 103(c), the fact that a person is **not** listed as in the certificate as a general partner is **not** notice that the person is **not** a general partner. See Comment to Section 103(c).

Example: Same facts, except that Third Party does review the certificate of limited partnership before entering into the transaction. The result might still be the same.

The omission of a person's name from the certificate's list of general partners is **not** notice that the person is **not** a general partner. Therefore, Third Party's review of the certificate does not mean that Third Party knew, had received a notification or had notice that G lacked authority. At most, XYZ could argue that, because Third Party knew that G was not listed in the certificate, a transaction entered into by G could not appear to Third Party to be for apparently carrying on the limited partnership's activities in the ordinary course.

§ 402.   General Partner Agent of Limited Partnership

(a)   Each general partner is an agent of the limited partnership for the purposes of its activities. An act of a general partner, including the signing of a record in the partnership's name, for apparently carrying on in the ordinary course the limited partnership's activities or activities of the kind carried on by the limited partnership binds the limited partnership, unless the general partner did not have authority to act for the limited partnership in the particular matter and the person with which the general partner was dealing knew, had received a notification, or had notice under Section 103(d) that the general partner lacked authority.

(b)   An act of a general partner which is not apparently for carrying on in the ordinary course the limited partnership's activities or activities of the kind carried on by the limited partnership binds the limited partnership only if the act was actually authorized by all the other partners.

COMMENT

Source—RUPA Section 301. For the meaning of "authority" in subsection (a) and "authorized" in subsection (b), see RUPA Section 301, Comment 3 (stating that "Subsection (2) [of RUPA Section 301] makes it clear that the partnership is bound by a partner's *actual* authority, even if the partner has no apparent authority"; emphasis added).

The fact that a person is not listed in the certificate of limited partnership as a general partner is **not** notice that the person is **not** a partner and is **not** notice that the person lacks authority to act for the limited partnership. See Comment to Section 103(c) and Comment to Section 401.

Section 103(f) defines receipt of notification. Section 103(d) lists various public filings, each of which provides notice 90 days after its effective date.

Example: For the past ten years, X has been a general partner of XYZ Limited Partnership and has regularly conducted the limited partnership's business with Third Party. However, 100 days ago the limited partnership expelled X as a general partner and the next day delivered for filing an amendment to XYZ's certificate of limited partnership which stated that X was no longer a general partner. On that same day, the filing officer filed the amendment.

Today X approaches Third Party, purports [to still be] a general partner of XYZ and purports to enter into a transaction with Third Party on XYZ's behalf. Third Party is unaware that X has been expelled and has no reason to doubt . . . X's bona fides. Nonetheless, XYZ is not liable on the transaction. Under Section 103(d), Third Party has notice that X is dissociated and perforce has notice that X is not a general partner authorized to bind XYZ.

§ 403.   Limited Partnership Liable for General Partner's Actionable Conduct

(a)   A limited partnership is liable for loss or injury caused to a person, or for a penalty incurred, as a result of a wrongful act or omission, or other actionable conduct, of a general partner acting in the ordinary course of activities of the limited partnership or with authority of the limited partnership.

(b)   If, in the course of the limited partnership's activities or while acting with authority of the limited partnership, a general partner receives or causes the limited partnership to receive money or property of a person not a partner, and the money or property is misapplied by a general partner, the limited partnership is liable for the loss.

COMMENT

Source—RUPA Section 305. For the meaning of "authority" in subsections (a) and (b), see RUPA Section 305, Comment. The third-to-last paragraph of that Comment states:

The partnership is liable for the actionable conduct or omission of a partner acting in the ordinary course of its business or "with the authority of the partnership." This is intended to include a partner's apparent, as well as actual, authority, thereby bringing within Section 305(a) the situation covered in UPA Section 14(a).

The last paragraph of that Comment states:

Section 305(b) is drawn from UPA Section 14(b), but has been edited to improve clarity. It imposes strict liability on the partnership for the misapplication of money or property received by a partner in the course of the partnership's business or otherwise within the scope of the partner's actual authority.

Section 403(a) of this Act is taken essentially verbatim from RUPA Section 305(a), and Section 403(b) of this Act is taken essentially verbatim from RUPA Section 305(b).

This section makes the limited partnership vicariously liable for a partner's misconduct. That vicarious[ ] liability in no way discharges or diminishes the partner's direct liability for the partner's own misconduct.

A general partner can cause a limited partnership to be liable under this section, even if the general partner is not designated as a general partner in the certificate of limited partnership. See Comment to Section 401.

§ 404.   General Partner's Liability

(a)   Except as otherwise provided in subsections (b) and (c), all general partners are liable jointly and severally for all obligations of the limited partnership unless otherwise agreed by the claimant or provided by law.

(b)   A person that becomes a general partner of an existing limited partnership is not personally liable for an obligation of a limited partnership incurred before the person became a general partner.

(c)   An obligation of a limited partnership incurred while the limited partnership is a limited liability limited partnership, whether arising in contract, tort, or otherwise, is solely the obligation of the limited partnership. A general partner is not personally liable, directly or indirectly, by way of contribution or otherwise, for such an obligation solely by reason of being or acting as a general partner. This subsection applies despite anything inconsistent in the partnership agreement that existed immediately before the consent required to become a limited liability limited partnership under Section 406(b)(2).

COMMENT

Source—RUPA Section 306.

Following RUPA and the UPA, this Act leaves to other law the question of when a limited partnership obligation is incurred.

Subsection (c)—For an explanation of the decision to provide for limited liability limited partnerships, see the Prefatory Note.

§ 405.   Actions by and Against Partnership and Partners

(a)   To the extent not inconsistent with Section 404, a general partner may be joined in an action against the limited partnership or named in a separate action.

(b)   A judgment against a limited partnership is not by itself a judgment against a general partner. A judgment against a limited partnership may not be satisfied from a general partner's assets unless there is also a judgment against the general partner.

(c)   A judgment creditor of a general partner may not levy execution against the assets of the general partner to satisfy a judgment based on a claim against the limited partnership, unless the partner is personally liable for the claim under Section 404 and:

(1)   a judgment based on the same claim has been obtained against the limited partnership and a writ of execution on the judgment has been returned unsatisfied in whole or in part;

(2)   the limited partnership is a debtor in bankruptcy;

(3)   the general partner has agreed that the creditor need not exhaust limited partnership assets;

(4)   a court grants permission to the judgment creditor to levy execution against the assets of a general partner based on a finding that limited partnership assets subject to execution are clearly insufficient to satisfy the judgment, that exhaustion of limited partnership assets is excessively burdensome, or that the grant of permission is an appropriate exercise of the court's equitable powers; or

(5)   liability is imposed on the general partner by law or contract independent of the existence of the limited partnership.

COMMENT

Source—RUPA Section 307.

If a limited partnership is a limited liability limited partnership throughout its existence, this section will bar a creditor of a limited partnership from impleading, suing or reaching the assets of a general partner unless the creditor can satisfy subsection (c)(5).

§ 406. Management Rights of General Partner

(a)   Each general partner has equal rights in the management and conduct of the limited partnership's activities. Except as expressly provided in this [Act], any matter relating to the activities of the limited partnership may be exclusively decided by the general partner or, if there is more than one general partner, by a majority of the general partners.

(b)   The consent of each partner is necessary to:

(1)   amend the partnership agreement;

(2)   amend the certificate of limited partnership to add or, subject to Section 1110, delete a statement that the limited partnership is a limited liability limited partnership; and

(3)   sell, lease, exchange, or otherwise dispose of all, or substantially all, of the limited partnership's property, with or without the good will, other than in the usual and regular course of the limited partnership's activities.

(c)   A limited partnership shall reimburse a general partner for payments made and indemnify a general partner for liabilities incurred by the general partner in the ordinary course of the activities of the partnership or for the preservation of its activities or property.

(d)   A limited partnership shall reimburse a general partner for an advance to the limited partnership beyond the amount of capital the general partner agreed to contribute.

(e)   A payment or advance made by a general partner which gives rise to an obligation of the limited partnership under subsection (c) or (d) constitutes a loan to the limited partnership which accrues interest from the date of the payment or advance.

(f)   A general partner is not entitled to remuneration for services performed for the partnership.

COMMENT

Source—RUPA Section 401 and ULLCA Section 404.

Subsection (a)—As explained in the Prefatory Note, this Act assumes that, more often than not, people utilizing the Act will want (i) strong centralized management, strongly entrenched, and (ii) passive investors with little control over the entity. Section 302 essentially excludes limited partners from the ordinary management of a limited partnership's activities. This subsection states affirmatively the general partners' commanding role. Only the partnership agreement and the express provisions of this Act can limit that role.

The authority granted by this subsection includes the authority to delegate. Delegation does not relieve the delegating general partner or partners of their duties under Section 408. However, the fact of delegation is a fact relevant to any breach of duty analysis.

Example: A sole general partner personally handles all "important paperwork" for a limited partnership. The general partner neglects to renew the fire insurance coverage on the a building owned by the limited partnership, despite having received and read a warning notice from the insurance company. The building subsequently burns to the ground and is a total loss. The general partner might be liable for breach of the duty of care under Section 408(c) (gross negligence).

Example: A sole general partner delegates responsibility for insurance renewals to the limited partnership's office manager, and that manager neglects to renew the fire insurance coverage on the building. Even assuming that the office manager has been grossly negligent, the general partner is not necessarily liable under Section 408(c). The office manager's gross negligence is not automatically attributed to the general partner. Under Section 408(c), the question is whether the general partner was grossly negligent (or worse) in selecting the general manager, delegating insurance renewal matters to the general manager and supervising the general manager after the delegation.

For the consequences of delegating authority to a person that is a limited partner, see the Comment to Section 305.

The partnership agreement may also provide for delegation and, subject to Section 110(b)(5)–(7), may modify a general partner's Section 408 duties.

Subsection (b)—This subsection limits the managerial rights of the general partners, requiring the consent of each general and limited partner for the specified actions. The subsection is subject to change by the partnership agreement, except as provided in Section 110(b)(12) (pertaining to consent rights established by Section 1110).

Subsection (c)—This Act does not include any parallel provision for limited partners, because they are assumed to be passive. To the extent that by contract or other arrangement a limited partner has authority to act on behalf of the limited partnership, agency law principles will create an indemnity obligation. In other situations, principles of restitution might apply.

Subsection (f)—Unlike RUPA Section 401(h), this subsection provides no compensation for winding up efforts. In a limited partnership, winding up is one of the tasks for which the limited partners depend on the general partner. There is no reason for the Act to single out this particular task as giving rise to compensation.

§ 407.   Right of General Partner and Former General Partner to Information

(a)   A general partner, without having any particular purpose for seeking the information, may inspect and copy during regular business hours:

(1)   in the limited partnership's designated office, required information; and

(2)   at a reasonable location specified by the limited partnership, any other records maintained by the limited partnership regarding the limited partnership's activities and financial condition.

(b)   Each general partner and the limited partnership shall furnish to a general partner:

(1)   without demand, any information concerning the limited partnership's activities and activities reasonably required for the proper exercise of the general partner's rights and duties under the partnership agreement or this [Act]; and

(2)   on demand, any other information concerning the limited partnership's activities, except to the extent the demand or the information demanded is unreasonable or otherwise improper under the circumstances.

(c)   Subject to subsection (e), on 10 days' demand made in a record received by the limited partnership, a person dissociated as a general partner may have access to the information and records described in subsection (a) at the location specified in subsection (a) if:

(1)   the information or record pertains to the period during which the person was a general partner;

(2)   the person seeks the information or record in good faith; and

(3)   the person satisfies the requirements imposed on a limited partner by Section 304(b).

(d)   The limited partnership shall respond to a demand made pursuant to subsection (c) in the same manner as provided in Section 304(c).

(e)   If a general partner dies, Section 704 applies.

(f)   The limited partnership may impose reasonable restrictions on the use of information under this section. In any dispute concerning the reasonableness of a restriction under this subsection, the limited partnership has the burden of proving reasonableness.

(g)   A limited partnership may charge a person dissociated as a general partner that makes a demand under this section reasonable costs of copying, limited to the costs of labor and material.

(h)   A general partner or person dissociated as a general partner may exercise the rights under this section through an attorney or other agent. Any restriction imposed under subsection (f) or by the partnership agreement applies both to the attorney or other agent and to the general partner or person dissociated as a general partner.

(i)   The rights under this section do not extend to a person as transferee, but the rights under subsection (c) of a person dissociated as a general may be exercised by the legal representative of an individual who dissociated as a general partner under Section 603(7)(B) or (C).

COMMENT

This section's structure parallels the structure of Section 304 and the Comment to that section may be helpful in understanding this section.

Subsection (b)—Source: RUPA Section 403(c).

Subsection (b)(1)—If a particular item of material information is apparent in the limited partnership's records, whether a general partner is obliged to disseminate that information to fellow general partners depends on the circumstances.

Example: A limited partnership has two general partners: each of which is regularly engaged in conducting the limited partnership's activities; both of which are aware of and have regular access to all significant limited partnership records; and neither of which has special responsibility for or knowledge about any particular aspect of those activities or the partnership records pertaining to any particular aspect of those activities. Most likely, neither general partner is obliged to draw the other general partner's attention to information apparent in the limited partnership's records.

Example: Although a limited partnership has three general partners, one is the managing partner with day-to-day responsibility for running the limited partnership's activities. The other two meet periodically with the managing general partner, and together with that partner function in a manner analogous to a corporate board of directors. Most likely, the managing general partner has a duty to draw the attention of the other general partners to important information, even if that information would be apparent from a review of the limited partnership's records.

In all events under subsection (b)(1), the question is whether the disclosure by one general partner is "reasonably required for the proper exercise" of the other general partner's rights and duties.

Subsection (f)—This provision is identical to Section 304(g) and the Comment to Section 304(g) is applicable here. Under this Act, general and limited partners have sharply different roles. A restriction that is reasonable as to a limited partner is not necessarily reasonable as to a general partner.

Subsection (g)—No charge is allowed for current general partners, because in almost all cases they would be entitled to reimbursement under Section 406(c). Contrast Section 304(h), which authorizes charges to current limited partners.

Subsection (i)—The Comment to Section 304(k) is applicable here.

§ 408.   General Standards of General Partner's Conduct

(a)   The only fiduciary duties that a general partner has to the limited partnership and the other partners are the duties of loyalty and care under subsections (b) and (c).

(b)   A general partner's duty of loyalty to the limited partnership and the other partners is limited to the following:

(1)   to account to the limited partnership and hold as trustee for it any property, profit, or benefit derived by the general partner in the conduct and winding up of the limited partnership's activities or derived from a use by the general partner of limited partnership property, including the appropriation of a limited partnership opportunity;

(2)   to refrain from dealing with the limited partnership in the conduct or winding up of the limited partnership's activities as or on behalf of a party having an interest adverse to the limited partnership; and

(3)   to refrain from competing with the limited partnership in the conduct or winding up of the limited partnership's activities.

(c)   A general partner's duty of care to the limited partnership and the other partners in the conduct and winding up of the limited partnership's activities is limited to refraining from engaging in grossly negligent or reckless conduct, intentional misconduct, or a knowing violation of law.

(d)   A general partner shall discharge the duties to the partnership and the other partners under this [Act] or under the partnership agreement and exercise any rights consistently with the obligation of good faith and fair dealing.

(e)   A general partner does not violate a duty or obligation under this [Act] or under the partnership agreement merely because the general partner's conduct furthers the general partner's own interest.

COMMENT

Source—RUPA Section 404.

This section does not prevent a general partner from delegating one or more duties, but delegation does not discharge the duty. For further discussion, see the Comment to Section 406(a).

If the partnership agreement removes a particular responsibility from a general partner, that general partner's fiduciary duty must be judged according to the rights and powers the general partner retains. For example, if the partnership agreement denies a general partner the right to act in a particular matter, the general partner's compliance with the partnership agreement cannot be a breach of fiduciary duty. However, the general partner may still have a duty to provide advice with regard to the matter. That duty could arise from the fiduciary duty of care under Section 408(c) and the duty to provide information under Sections 304(i) and 407(b).

For the partnership agreement's power directly to circumscribe a general partner's fiduciary duty, see Section 110(b)(5) and (6).

Subsection (a)—The reference to "the other partners" does not affect the distinction between direct and derivative claims. See Section 1001(b) (prerequisites for a partner bringing a direct claim).

Subsection (b)—A general partner's duty under this subsection continues through winding up, since the limited partners' dependence on the general partner does not end at dissolution. See Comment to Section 406(f) (explaining why this Act provides no remuneration for a general partner's winding up efforts).

Subsection (d)—This provision is identical to Section 305(b) and the Comment to Section 305(b) is applicable here.

[ARTICLE] 5.   CONTRIBUTIONS AND DISTRIBUTIONS

§ 501.   Form of Contribution

A contribution of a partner may consist of tangible or intangible property or other benefit to the limited partnership, including money, services performed, promissory notes, other agreements to contribute cash or property, and contracts for services to be performed.

COMMENT

Source—ULLCA Section 401.

§ 502.   Liability for Contribution

(a)   A partner's obligation to contribute money or other property or other benefit to, or to perform services for, a limited partnership is not excused by the partner's death, disability, or other inability to perform personally.

(b)   If a partner does not make a promised non-monetary contribution, the partner is obligated at the option of the limited partnership to contribute money equal to that portion of the value, as stated in the required information, of the stated contribution which has not been made.

(c)   The obligation of a partner to make a contribution or return money or other property paid or distributed in violation of this [Act] may be compromised only by consent of all partners. A creditor of a limited partnership which extends credit or otherwise acts in reliance on an obligation described in subsection (a), without notice of any compromise under this subsection, may enforce the original obligation.

COMMENT

In contrast with predecessor law, RULPA Section 502(a), this Act does not include a statute of frauds provision covering promised contributions. Section 111(9)(A) does require that the value of a promised contribution be memorialized, but that requirement does not affect enforceability. See Comment to Section 111(9).

Subsection (a)—Source: RULPA Section 502(b).

Under common law principles of impracticability, an individual's death or incapacity will sometimes discharge a duty to render performance. Restatement (Second) of Contracts, Sections 261 and 262. This subsection overrides those principles.

Subsection (b)—RULPA Section 502(b).

This subsection is a statutory liquidated damage provision, exercisable at the option of the limited partnership, with the damage amount set according to the value of the promised, non-monetary contribution as stated in the required information.

Example: In order to become a limited partner, a person promises to contribute to the limited partnership various assets which the partnership agreement values at $150,000. In return for the person's promise, and in light of the agreed value, the limited partnership admits the person as a limited partner with a right to receive 25% of the limited partnership's distributions.

The promised assets are subject to a security agreement, but the limited partner promises to contribute them "free and clear." Before the limited partner can contribute the assets, the secured party forecloses on the security interest and sells the assets at a public sale for $75,000. Even if the $75,000 reflects the actual fair market value of the assets, under this subsection the limited partnership has a claim against the limited partner for "the value, as stated in the required information, of the stated contribution which has not been made"—i.e., $150,000.

This section applies "at the option of the limited partnership" and does not affect other remedies which the limited partnership may have under other law.

Example: Same facts as the previous example, except that the public sale brings $225,000. The limited partnership is not obliged to invoke this subsection and may instead sue for breach of the promise to make the contribution, asserting the $225,000 figure as evidence of the actual loss suffered as a result of the breach.

Subsection (c)—Source: ULLCA Section 402(b); RULPA Section 502(c). The first sentence of this subsection applies not only to promised contributions but also to improper distributions. See Sections 508 and 509. The second sentence, pertaining to creditor's rights, applies only to promised contributions.

§ 503. Sharing of Distributions

A distribution by a limited partnership must be shared among the partners on the basis of the value, as stated in the required records when the limited partnership decides to make the distribution, of the contributions the limited partnership has received from each partner.

COMMENT

This Act has no provision allocating profits and losses among the partners. Instead, the Act directly apportions the right to receive distributions.

Nearly all limited partnerships will choose to allocate profits and losses in order to comply with applicable tax, accounting and other regulatory requirements. Those requirements, rather than this Act, are the proper source of guidance for that profit and loss allocation.

Unlike predecessor law, this section apportions distributions in relation to the value of contributions received from each partner without regard to whether the limited partnership has returned any of those contributions. Compare RULPA Sections 503 and 504. This Act's approach produces the same result as predecessor law, so long as the limited partnership does not vary this section's approach to apportioning distributions.

This section's rule for sharing distributions is subject to change under Section 110. A limited partnership that does vary the rule should be careful to consider not only the tax and accounting consequences but also the "ripple" effect on other provisions of this Act. See, e.g., Sections 801 and 803(c) (apportioning consent power in relation to the right to receive distributions).

§ 504. Interim Distributions

A partner does not have a right to any distribution before the dissolution and winding up of the limited partnership unless the limited partnership decides to make an interim distribution.

COMMENT

Under Section 406(a), the general partner or partners make this decision for the limited partnership.

§ 505.   No Distribution on Account of Dissociation

A person does not have a right to receive a distribution on account of dissociation.

COMMENT

This section varies substantially from predecessor law. RULPA Sections 603 and 604 permitted a limited partner to withdraw on six months notice and receive the fair value of the limited partnership interest, unless the partnership agreement provided the limited partner with some exit right or stated a definite duration for the limited partnership.

Under this Act, a partner that dissociates becomes a transferee of its own transferable interest. See Sections 602(a)(3) (person dissociated as a limited partner) and 605(a)(5) (person dissociated as a general partner).

§ 506.   Distribution in Kind

A partner does not have a right to demand or receive any distribution from a limited partnership in any form other than cash. subject to Section 812(b), a limited partnership may distribute an asset in kind to the extent each partner receives a percentage of the asset equal to the partner's share of distributions.

COMMENT

Source—RULPA Section 605.

§ 507.   Right to Distribution

When a partner or transferee becomes entitled to receive a distribution, the partner or transferee has the status of, and is entitled to all remedies available to, a creditor of the limited partnership with respect to the distribution. However, the limited partnership's obligation to make a distribution is subject to offset for any amount owed to the limited partnership by the partner or dissociated partner on whose account the distribution is made.

COMMENT

Source—RULPA Section 606.

This section's first sentence refers to distributions generally. Contrast Section 508(e), which refers to indebtedness issued as a distribution.

The reference in the second sentence to "dissociated partner" encompasses circumstances in which the partner is gone and the dissociated partner's transferable interest is all that remains.

§ 508.   Limitations on Distribution

(a)   A limited partnership may not make a distribution in violation of the partnership agreement.

(b)   A limited partnership may not make a distribution if after the distribution:

(1)   the limited partnership would not be able to pay its debts as they become due in the ordinary course of the limited partnership's activities; or

(2)   the limited partnership's total assets would be less than the sum of its total liabilities plus the amount that would be needed, if the limited partnership were to be dissolved, wound up, and terminated at the time of the distribution, to satisfy the preferential rights upon dissolution, winding up, and termination of partners whose preferential rights are superior to those of persons receiving the distribution.

(c)   A limited partnership may base a determination that a distribution is not prohibited under subsection (b) on financial statements prepared on the basis of accounting practices and principles that are reasonable in the circumstances or on a fair valuation or other method that is reasonable in the circumstances.

(d)   Except as otherwise provided in subsection (g), the effect of a distribution under subsection (b) is measured:

(1)   in the case of distribution by purchase, redemption, or other acquisition of a transferable interest in the limited partnership, as of the date money or other property is transferred or debt incurred by the limited partnership; and

(2)   in all other cases, as of the date:

(A)   the distribution is authorized, if the payment occurs within120 days after that date; or

(B)   the payment is made, if payment occurs more than120 days after the distribution is authorized.

(e)   A limited partnership's indebtedness to a partner incurred by reason of a distribution made in accordance with this section is at parity with the limited partnership's indebtedness to its general, unsecured creditors.

(f)   A limited partnership's indebtedness, including indebtedness issued in connection with or as part of a distribution, is not considered a liability for purposes of subsection (b) if the terms of the indebtedness provide that payment of principal and interest are made only to the extent that a distribution could then be made to partners under this section.

(g)   If indebtedness is issued as a distribution, each payment of principal or interest on the indebtedness is treated as a distribution, the effect of which is measured on the date the payment is made.

COMMENT

Source—ULLCA Section 406. See also RMBCA Section 6.40.

Subsection (c)—This subsection appears to impose a standard of ordinary care, in contrast with the general duty of care stated in Section 408(c). For a reconciliation of these two provisions, see Comment to Section 509(a).

§ 509.   Liability for Improper Distributions

(a)   A general partner that consents to a distribution made in violation of Section 508 is personally liable to the limited partnership for the amount of the distribution which exceeds the amount that could have been distributed without the violation if it is established that in consenting to the distribution the general partner failed to comply with Section 408.

(b)   A partner or transferee that received a distribution knowing that the distribution to that partner or transferee was made in violation of Section 508 is personally liable to the limited partnership but only to the extent that the distribution received by the partner or transferee exceeded the amount that could have been properly paid under Section 508.

(c)   A general partner against which an action is commenced under subsection (a) may:

(1)   implead in the action any other person that is liable under subsection (a) and compel contribution from the person; and

(2)   implead in the action any person that received a distribution in violation of subsection (b) and compel contribution from the person in the amount the person received in violation of subsection (b).

(d)   An action under this section is barred if it is not commenced within two years after the distribution.

COMMENT

Source—ULLCA Section 407. See also RMBCA Section 8.33.

In substance and effect this section protects the interests of creditors of the limited partnership. Therefore, according to Section 110(b)(13), the partnership agreement may not change this section in a way that restricts the rights of those creditors. As for a limited partnership's power to compromise a claim under this section, see Section 502(c).

Subsection (a)—This subsection refers both to Section 508, which includes in its subsection (c) a standard of ordinary care ("reasonable in the circumstances"), and to Section 408, which includes in its subsection (c) a general duty of care that is limited to "refraining from engaging in grossly negligent or reckless conduct, intentional misconduct, or a knowing violation of law."

A limited partnership's failure to meet the standard of Section 508(c) cannot by itself cause a general partner to be liable under Section 509(a). *Both* of the following would have to occur before a failure to satisfy Section 508(c) could occasion personal liability for a general partner under Section 509(a):

- the limited partnership "base[s] a determination that a distribution is not prohibited . . . on financial statements prepared on the basis of accounting practices and principles that are [not] reasonable in the circumstances or on a [not] fair valuation or other method that is [not] reasonable in the circumstances" [Section 508(c)]

AND

- the general partner's decision to rely on the improper methodology in consenting to the distribution constitutes "grossly negligent or reckless conduct, intentional misconduct, or a knowing violation of law" [Section 408(c)] or breaches some other duty under Section 408.

To serve the protective purpose of Sections 508 and 509, in this subsection "consent" must be understood as encompassing any form of approval, assent or acquiescence, whether formal or informal, express or tacit.

Subsection (d)—The subsection's limitation applies to the commencement of an action under subsection (a) or (b) and not to subsection (c), under which a general partner may implead other persons.

[ARTICLE] 6. DISSOCIATION

§ 601. Dissociation as Limited Partner

(a)   A person does not have a right to dissociate as a limited partner before the termination of the limited partnership.

(b)   A person is dissociated from a limited partnership as a limited partner upon the occurrence of any of the following events:

(1)   the limited partnership's having notice of the person's express will to withdraw as a limited partner or on a later date specified by the person;

(2)   an event agreed to in the partnership agreement as causing the person's dissociation as a limited partner;

(3)   the person's expulsion as a limited partner pursuant to the partnership agreement;

(4)   the person's expulsion as a limited partner by the unanimous consent of the other partners if:

(A)   it is unlawful to carry on the limited partnership's activities with the person as a limited partner;

(B)   there has been a transfer of all of the person's transferable interest in the limited partnership, other than a transfer for security purposes, or a court order charging the person's interest, which has not been foreclosed;

(C)   the person is a corporation and, within 90 days after the limited partnership notifies the person that it will be expelled as a limited partner because it has filed a certificate of dissolution or the equivalent, its charter has been revoked, or its right to conduct business has been suspended by the jurisdiction of its incorporation, there is no revocation of the certificate of dissolution or no reinstatement of its charter or its right to conduct business; or

(D) the person is a limited liability company or partnership that has been dissolved and whose business is being wound up;

(5) on application by the limited partnership, the person's expulsion as a limited partner by judicial order because:

(A) the person engaged in wrongful conduct that adversely and materially affected the limited partnership's activities;

(B) the person willfully or persistently committed a material breach of the partnership agreement or of the obligation of good faith and fair dealing under Section 305(b); or

(C) the person engaged in conduct relating to the limited partnership's activities which makes it not reasonably practicable to carry on the activities with the person as limited partner;

(6) in the case of a person who is an individual, the person's death;

(7) in the case of a person that is a trust or is acting as a limited partner by virtue of being a trustee of a trust, distribution of the trust's entire transferable interest in the limited partnership, but not merely by reason of the substitution of a successor trustee;

(8) in the case of a person that is an estate or is acting as a limited partner by virtue of being a personal representative of an estate, distribution of the estate's entire transferable interest in the limited partnership, but not merely by reason of the substitution of a successor personal representative;

(9) termination of a limited partner that is not an individual, partnership, limited liability company, corporation, trust, or estate;

(10) the limited partnership's participation in a conversion or merger under [Article] 11, if the limited partnership:

(A) is not the converted or surviving entity; or

(B) is the converted or surviving entity but, as a result of the conversion or merger, the person ceases to be a limited partner.

COMMENT

Source—RUPA Section 601.

This section adopts RUPA's dissociation provision essentially verbatim, except for provisions inappropriate to limited partners. For example, this section does not provide for the dissociation of a person as a limited partner on account of bankruptcy, insolvency or incompetency.

This Act refers to *a person's dissociation as a limited partner* rather than to the *dissociation of a limited partner*, because the same person may be both a general and a limited partner. See Section 113 (Dual Capacity). It is possible for a dual capacity partner to dissociate in one capacity and not in the other.

Subsection (a)—This section varies substantially from predecessor law. See Comment to Section 505.

Subsection (b)(1)—This provision gives a person the power to dissociate as a limited partner even though the dissociation is wrongful under subsection (a). See, however, Section 110(b)(8) (prohibiting the partnership agreement from eliminating the power of a person to dissociate as a *general* partner but imposing no comparable restriction with regard to a person's dissociation as a *limited* partner).

Subsection (b)(5)—In contrast to RUPA, this provision may be varied or even eliminated by the partnership agreement.

§ 602. Effect of Dissociation as Limited Partner

(a) Upon a person's dissociation as a limited partner:

(1) subject to Section 704, the person does not have further rights as a limited partner;

(2) the person's obligation of good faith and fair dealing as a limited partner under Section 305(b) continues only as to matters arising and events occurring before the dissociation; and

(3)   subject to Section 704 and [Article] 11, any transferable interest owned by the person in the person's capacity as a limited partner immediately before dissociation is owned by the person as a mere transferee.

(b)   A person's dissociation as a limited partner does not of itself discharge the person from any obligation to the limited partnership or the other partners which the person incurred while a limited partner.

COMMENT

Source—RUPA Section 603(b).

Subsection (a)(1)—In general, when a person dissociates as a limited partner, the person's rights as a limited partner disappear and, subject to Section 113 (Dual Status), the person's status degrades to that of a mere transferee. However, Section 704 provides some special rights when dissociation is caused by an individual's death.

Subsection (a)(3)—For any person that is both a general partner and a limited partner, the required records must state which transferable interest is owned in which capacity. Section 111(9)(C).

Article 11 provides for conversions and mergers. A plan of conversion or merger may provide for the dissociation of a person as a limited partner and may override the rule stated in this paragraph.

§ 603.   Dissociation as General Partner

A person is dissociated from a limited partnership as a general partner upon the occurrence of any of the following events:

(1)   the limited partnership's having notice of the person's express will to withdraw as a general partner or on a later date specified by the person;

(2)   an event agreed to in the partnership agreement as causing the person's dissociation as a general partner;

(3)   the person's expulsion as a general partner pursuant to the partnership agreement;

(4)   the person's expulsion as a general partner by the unanimous consent of the other partners if:

(A)   it is unlawful to carry on the limited partnership's activities with the person as a general partner;

(B)   there has been a transfer of all or substantially all of the person's transferable interest in the limited partnership, other than a transfer for security purposes, or a court order charging the person's interest, which has not been foreclosed;

(C)   the person is a corporation and, within 90 days after the limited partnership notifies the person that it will be expelled as a general partner because it has filed a certificate of dissolution or the equivalent, its charter has been revoked, or its right to conduct business has been suspended by the jurisdiction of its incorporation, there is no revocation of the certificate of dissolution or no reinstatement of its charter or its right to conduct business; or

(D)   the person is a limited liability company or partnership that has been dissolved and whose business is being wound up;

(5)   on application by the limited partnership, the person's expulsion as a general partner by judicial determination because:

(A)   the person engaged in wrongful conduct that adversely and materially affected the limited partnership activities;

(B)   the person willfully or persistently committed a material breach of the partnership agreement or of a duty owed to the partnership or the other partners under Section 408; or

(C)   the person engaged in conduct relating to the limited partnership's activities which makes it not reasonably practicable to carry on the activities of the limited partnership with the person as a general partner;

(6)   the person's:

    (A)   becoming a debtor in bankruptcy;

    (B)   execution of an assignment for the benefit of creditors;

    (C)   seeking, consenting to, or acquiescing in the appointment of a trustee, receiver, or liquidator of the person or of all or substantially all of the person's property; or

    (D)   failure, within 90 days after the appointment, to have vacated or stayed the appointment of a trustee, receiver, or liquidator of the general partner or of all or substantially all of the person's property obtained without the person's consent or acquiescence, or failing within 90 days after the expiration of a stay to have the appointment vacated;

(7)   in the case of a person who is an individual:

    (A)   the person's death;

    (B)   the appointment of a guardian or general conservator for the person; or

    (C)   a judicial determination that the person has otherwise become incapable of performing the person's duties as a general partner under the partnership agreement;

(8)   in the case of a person that is a trust or is acting as a general partner by virtue of being a trustee of a trust, distribution of the trust's entire transferable interest in the limited partnership, but not merely by reason of the substitution of a successor trustee;

(9)   in the case of a person that is an estate or is acting as a general partner by virtue of being a personal representative of an estate, distribution of the estate's entire transferable interest in the limited partnership, but not merely by reason of the substitution of a successor personal representative;

(10)   termination of a general partner that is not an individual, partnership, limited liability company, corporation, trust, or estate; or

(11)   the limited partnership's participation in a conversion or merger under [Article] 11, if the limited partnership:

    (A)   is not the converted or surviving entity; or

    (B)   is the converted or surviving entity but, as a result of the conversion or merger, the person ceases to be a general partner.

COMMENT

Source—RUPA Section 601.

This section adopts RUPA's dissociation provision essentially verbatim. This Act refers to *a person's dissociation as a general partner* rather than to the *dissociation of a general partner*, because the same person may be both a general and a limited partner. See Section 113 (Dual Capacity). It is possible for a dual capacity partner to dissociate in one capacity and not in the other.

Paragraph (1)—The partnership agreement may not eliminate this power to dissociate. See Section 110(b)(8).

Paragraph (5)—In contrast to RUPA, this provision may be varied or even eliminated by the partnership agreement.

§ 604.   Person's Power to Dissociate as General Partner; Wrongful Dissociation

(a)   A person has the power to dissociate as a general partner at any time, rightfully or wrongfully, by express will pursuant to Section 603(1).

(b)   A person's dissociation as a general partner is wrongful only if:

(1)   it is in breach of an express provision of the partnership agreement; or

(2)   it occurs before the termination of the limited partnership, and:

(A)   the person withdraws as a general partner by express will;

(B)   the person is expelled as a general partner by judicial determination under Section 603(5);

(C)   the person is dissociated as a general partner by becoming a debtor in bankruptcy; or

(D)   in the case of a person that is not an individual, trust other than a business trust, or estate, the person is expelled or otherwise dissociated as a general partner because it willfully dissolved or terminated.

(c)   A person that wrongfully dissociates as a general partner is liable to the limited partnership and, subject to Section 1001, to the other partners for damages caused by the dissociation. The liability is in addition to any other obligation of the general partner to the limited partnership or to the other partners.

COMMENT

Source—RUPA Section 602.

Subsection (a)—The partnership agreement may not eliminate this power. See Section 110(b)(8).

Subsection (b)(1)—The reference to "an express provision of the partnership agreement" means that a person's dissociation as a general partner in breach of the obligation of good faith and fair dealing is not wrongful dissociation for the purposes of this section. The breach might be actionable on other grounds.

Subsection (b)(2)—The reference to "before the termination of the limited partnership" reflects the expectation that each general partner will shepherd the limited partnership through winding up. See Comment to Section 406(f). A person's obligation to remain as general partner through winding up continues even if another general partner dissociates and even if that dissociation leads to the limited partnership's premature dissolution under Section 801(3)(A).

Subsection (c)—The language "subject to Section 1001" is intended to preserve the distinction between direct and derivative claims.

§ 605.   Effect of Dissociation as General Partner

(a)   Upon a person's dissociation as a general partner:

(1)   the person's right to participate as a general partner in the management and conduct of the partnership's activities terminates;

(2)   the person's duty of loyalty as a general partner under Section 408(b)(3) terminates;

(3)   the person's duty of loyalty as a general partner under Section 408(b)(1) and (2) and duty of care under Section 408(c) continue only with regard to matters arising and events occurring before the person's dissociation as a general partner;

(4)   the person may sign and deliver to the [Secretary of State] for filing a statement of dissociation pertaining to the person and, at the request of the limited partnership, shall sign an amendment to the certificate of limited partnership which states that the person has dissociated; and

(5)   subject to Section 704 and [Article] 11, any transferable interest owned by the person immediately before dissociation in the person's capacity as a general partner is owned by the person as a mere transferee.

(b)   A person's dissociation as a general partner does not of itself discharge the person from any obligation to the limited partnership or the other partners which the person incurred while a general partner.

COMMENT

Source—RUPA Section 603(b).

Subsection (a)(1)—Once a person dissociates as a general partner, the person loses all management rights as a general partner regardless of what happens to the limited partnership. This rule contrasts with RUPA Section 603(b)(1), which permits a dissociated general partner to participate in winding up in some circumstances.

Subsection (a)(4)—Both records covered by this paragraph have the same effect under Section 103(d)—namely, to give constructive notice that the person has dissociated as a general partner. The notice benefits the person by curtailing any further personal liability under Sections 607, 805, and 1111. The notice benefits the limited partnership by curtailing any lingering power to bind under Sections 606, 804, and 1112.

The limited partnership is in any event obligated to amend its certificate of limited partnership to reflect the dissociation of a person as general partner. See Section 202(b)(2). In most circumstances, the amendment requires the signature of the person that has dissociated. Section 204(a)(5)(C). If that signature is required and the person refuses or fails to sign, the limited partnership may invoke Section 205 (Signing and Filing Pursuant to Judicial Order).

Subsection (a)(5)—In general, when a person dissociates as a general partner, the person's rights as a general partner disappear and, subject to Section 113 (Dual Status), the person's status degrades to that of a mere transferee. For any person that is both a general partner and a limited partner, the required records must state which transferable interest is owned in which capacity. Section 111(9)(C).

Section 704 provides some special rights when an individual dissociates by dying. Article 11 provides for conversions and mergers. A plan of conversion or merger may provide for the dissociation of a person as a general partner and may override the rule stated in this paragraph.

§ 606. Power to Bind and Liability to Limited Partnership Before Dissolution of Partnership of Person Dissociated as General Partner

(a)   After a person is dissociated as a general partner and before the limited partnership is dissolved, converted under [Article] 11, or merged out of existence under [Article 11], the limited partnership is bound by an act of the person only if:

>   (1)   the act would have bound the limited partnership under Section 402 before the dissociation; and

>   (2)   at the time the other party enters into the transaction:

>>   (A)   less than two years has passed since the dissociation; and

>>   (B)   the other party does not have notice of the dissociation and reasonably believes that the person is a general partner.

(b)   If a limited partnership is bound under subsection (a), the person dissociated as a general partner which caused the limited partnership to be bound is liable:

>   (1)   to the limited partnership for any damage caused to the limited partnership arising from the obligation incurred under subsection (a); and

>   (2)   if a general partner or another person dissociated as a general partner is liable for the obligation, to the general partner or other person for any damage caused to the general partner or other person arising from the liability.

COMMENT

Source—RUPA Section 702.

This Act contains three sections pertaining to the lingering power to bind of a person dissociated as a general partner:

- this section, which applies until the limited partnership dissolves, converts to another form of organization under Article 11, or is merged out of existence under Article 11;

- Section 804(b), which applies after a limited partnership dissolves; and

- Section 1112(b), which applies after a conversion or merger.

Subsection (a)(2)(B)—A person might have notice under Section 103(d)(1) as well as under Section 103(b).

Subsection (b)—The liability provided by this subsection is not exhaustive. For example, if a person dissociated as a general partner causes a limited partnership to be bound under subsection (a) and, due to a guaranty, some other person is liable on the resulting obligation, that other person may have a claim under other law against the person dissociated as a general partner.

§ 607. Liability to Other Persons of Person Dissociated as General Partner

(a) A person's dissociation as a general partner does not of itself discharge the person's liability as a general partner for an obligation of the limited partnership incurred before dissociation. Except as otherwise provided in subsections (b) and (c), the person is not liable for a limited partnership's obligation incurred after dissociation.

(b) A person whose dissociation as a general partner resulted in a dissolution and winding up of the limited partnership's activities is liable to the same extent as a general partner under Section 404 on an obligation incurred by the limited partnership under Section 804.

(c) A person that has dissociated as a general partner but whose dissociation did not result in a dissolution and winding up of the limited partnership's activities is liable on a transaction entered into by the limited partnership after the dissociation only if:

(1) a general partner would be liable on the transaction; and

(2) at the time the other party enters into the transaction:

(A) less than two years has passed since the dissociation; and

(B) the other party does not have notice of the dissociation and reasonably believes that the person is a general partner.

(d) By agreement with a creditor of a limited partnership and the limited partnership, a person dissociated as a general partner may be released from liability for an obligation of the limited partnership.

(e) A person dissociated as a general partner is released from liability for an obligation of the limited partnership if the limited partnership's creditor, with notice of the person's dissociation as a general partner but without the person's consent, agrees to a material alteration in the nature or time of payment of the obligation.

COMMENT

Source—RUPA Section 703.

A person's dissociation as a general partner does not categorically prevent the person from being liable as a general partner for subsequently incurred obligations of the limited partnership. If the dissociation results in dissolution, subsection (b) applies and the person will be liable as a general partner on any partnership obligation incurred under Section 804. In these circumstances, neither filing a statement of dissociation nor amending the certificate of limited partnership to state that the person has dissociated as a general partner will curtail the person's lingering exposure to liability.

If the dissociation does not result in dissolution, subsection (c) applies. In this context, filing a statement of dissociation or amending the certificate of limited partnership to state that the person has dissociated as a general partner will curtail the person's lingering liability. See subsection (c)(2)(B).

If the limited partnership subsequently dissolves as the result of some other occurrence (i.e., not a result of the person's dissociation as a general partner), subsection (c) continues to apply. In that situation, Section 804 will determine whether, for the purposes of subsection (c), the limited partnership has entered into a transaction after dissolution.

If the limited partnership is a limited liability limited partnership, these liability rules are moot.

Subsection (a)—The phrase "liability as a general partner for an obligation of the limited partnership" refers to liability under Section 404. Following RUPA and the UPA, this Act leaves to other law the question of when a limited partnership obligation is incurred.

Subsection (c)(2)(B)—A person might have notice under Section 103(d)(1) as well as under Section 103(b).

[ARTICLE] 7.   TRANSFERABLE INTERESTS AND RIGHTS OF TRANSFEREES AND CREDITORS

§ 701.   Partner's Transferable Interest

The only interest of a partner which is transferable is the partner's transferable interest. A transferable interest is personal property.

COMMENT

Source—RUPA Section 502.

Like all other partnership statutes, this Act dichotomizes each partner's rights into economic rights and other rights. The former are freely transferable, as provided in Section 702. The latter are not transferable at all, unless the partnership agreement so provides.

Although a partner or transferee owns a transferable interest as a present right, that right only entitles the owner to distributions if and when made. See Sections 504 (subject to any contrary provision in the partnership agreement, no right to interim distribution unless the limited partnership decides to make an interim distribution) and the Comment to Section 812 (subject to any contrary provision in the partnership agreement, no partner obligated to contribute for the purpose of equalizing or otherwise allocating capital losses).

§ 702.   Transfer of Partner's Transferable Interest

(a)   A transfer, in whole or in part, of a partner's transferable interest:

(1)   is permissible;

(2)   does not by itself cause the partner's dissociation or a dissolution and winding up of the limited partnership's activities; and

(3)   does not, as against the other partners or the limited partnership, entitle the transferee to participate in the management or conduct of the limited partnership's activities, to require access to information concerning the limited partnership's transactions except as otherwise provided in subsection (c), or to inspect or copy the required information or the limited partnership's other records.

(b)   A transferee has a right to receive, in accordance with the transfer:

(1)   distributions to which the transferor would otherwise be entitled; and

(2)   upon the dissolution and winding up of the limited partnership's activities the net amount otherwise distributable to the transferor.

(c)   In a dissolution and winding up, a transferee is entitled to an account of the limited partnership's transactions only from the date of dissolution.

(d)   Upon transfer, the transferor retains the rights of a partner other than the interest in distributions transferred and retains all duties and obligations of a partner.

(e)   A limited partnership need not give effect to a transferee's rights under this section until the limited partnership has notice of the transfer.

(f)   A transfer of a partner's transferable interest in the limited partnership in violation of a restriction on transfer contained in the partnership agreement is ineffective as to a person having notice of the restriction at the time of transfer.

(g)   A transferee that becomes a partner with respect to a transferable interest is liable for the transferor's obligations under Sections 502 and 509. However, the transferee is not obligated for liabilities unknown to the transferee at the time the transferee became a partner.

Source—RUPA Section 503, except for subsection (g), which derives from RULPA Section 704(b). Following RUPA, this Act uses the words "transfer" and "transferee" rather than the words "assignment" and "assignee." See RUPA Section 503.

Subsection (a)(2)—The phrase "by itself" is significant. A transfer of all of a person's transferable interest could lead to dissociation via expulsion, Sections 601(b)(4)(B) and 603(4)(B).

Subsection (a)(3)—Mere transferees have no right to intrude as the partners carry on their activities as partners. Moreover, a partner's obligation of good faith and fair dealing under Sections 305(b) and 408(d) is framed in reference to "the limited partnership and the other partners." See also Comment to Section 1102(b)(3) and Comment to Section 1106(b)(3).

§ 703.   Rights of Creditor of Partner or Transferee

(a)   On application to a court of competent jurisdiction by any judgment creditor of a partner or transferee, the court may charge the transferable interest of the judgment debtor with payment of the unsatisfied amount of the judgment with interest. To the extent so charged, the judgment creditor has only the rights of a transferee. The court may appoint a receiver of the share of the distributions due or to become due to the judgment debtor in respect of the partnership and make all other orders, directions, accounts, and inquiries the judgment debtor might have made or which the circumstances of the case may require to give effect to the charging order.

(b)   A charging order constitutes a lien on the judgment debtor's transferable interest. The court may order a foreclosure upon the interest subject to the charging order at any time. The purchaser at the foreclosure sale has the rights of a transferee.

(c)   At any time before foreclosure, an interest charged may be redeemed:

(1)   by the judgment debtor;

(2)   with property other than limited partnership property, by one or more of the other partners; or

(3)   with limited partnership property, by the limited partnership with the consent of all partners whose interests are not so charged.

(d)   This [Act] does not deprive any partner or transferee of the benefit of any exemption laws applicable to the partner's or transferee's transferable interest.

(e)   This section provides the exclusive remedy by which a judgment creditor of a partner or transferee may satisfy a judgment out of the judgment debtor's transferable interest.

Source—RUPA Section 504 and ULLCA Section 504.

This section balances the needs of a judgment creditor of a partner or transferee with the needs of the limited partnership and non-debtor partners and transferees. The section achieves that balance by allowing the judgment creditor to collect on the judgment through the transferable interest of the judgment debtor while prohibiting interference in the management and activities of the limited partnership.

Under this section, the judgment creditor of a partner or transferee is entitled to a charging order against the relevant transferable interest. While in effect, that order entitles the judgment creditor to whatever distributions would otherwise be due to the partner or transferee whose interest is subject to the order. The creditor has no say in the timing or amount of those distributions. The charging order does not entitle the creditor to accelerate any distributions or to otherwise interfere with the management and activities of the limited partnership.

Foreclosure of a charging order effects a permanent transfer of the charged transferable interest to the purchaser. The foreclosure does not, however, create any rights to participate in the management and conduct of the limited partnership's activities. The purchaser obtains nothing more than the status of a transferee.

Subsection (a)—The court's power to appoint a receiver and "make all other orders, directions, accounts, and inquiries the judgment debtor might have made or which the circumstances of the case may require" must be understood in the context of the balance described above. In particular, the court's power to make orders "which the circumstances may require" is limited to "giv[ing] effect to the charging order."

Example: A judgment creditor with a charging order believes that the limited partnership should invest less of its surplus in operations, leaving more funds for distributions. The creditor moves the court for an order directing the general partners to restrict re-investment. This section does not authorize the court to grant the motion.

Example: A judgment creditor with a judgment for $10,000 against a partner obtains a charging order against the partner's transferable interest. The limited partnership is duly served with the order. However, the limited partnership subsequently fails to comply with the order and makes a $3000 distribution to the partner. The court has the power to order the limited partnership to turn over $3000 to the judgment creditor to "give effect to the charging order."

The court also has the power to decide whether a particular payment is a distribution, because this decision determines whether the payment is part of a transferable interest subject to a charging order. (To the extent a payment is not a distribution, it is not part of the transferable interest and is not subject to subsection (e). The payment is therefore subject to whatever other creditor remedies may apply.)

Subsection (c)(3)—This provision requires the consent of all the limited as well as general partners.

§ 704. Power of Estate of Deceased Partner

If a partner dies, the deceased partner's personal representative or other legal representative may exercise the rights of a transferee as provided in section 702 and, for the purposes of settling the estate, may exercise the rights of a current limited partner under section 304.

COMMENT

Section 702 strictly limits the rights of transferees. In particular, a transferee has no right to participate in management in any way, no voting rights and, except following dissolution, no information rights. Even after dissolution, a transferee's information rights are limited. See Section 702(c).

This section provides special informational rights for a deceased partner's legal representative for the purposes of settling the estate. For those purposes, the legal representative may exercise the informational rights of a current limited partner under Section 304. Those rights are of course subject to the limitations and obligations stated in that section—*e.g.*, Section 304 (g) (restrictions on use) and (h) (charges for copies)—as well as any generally applicable limitations stated in the partnership agreement.

[ARTICLE] 8. DISSOLUTION

§ 801. Nonjudicial Dissolution

Except as otherwise provided in Section 802, a limited partnership is dissolved, and its activities must be wound up, only upon the occurrence of any of the following:

(1) the happening of an event specified in the partnership agreement;

(2) the consent of all general partners and of limited partners owning a majority of the rights to receive distributions as limited partners at the time the consent is to be effective;

(3) after the dissociation of a person as a general partner:

(A) if the limited partnership has at least one remaining general partner, the consent to dissolve the limited partnership given within 90 days after the dissociation by partners owning a majority of the rights to receive distributions as partners at the time the consent is to be effective; or

(B) if the limited partnership does not have a remaining general partner, the passage of 90 days after the dissociation, unless before the end of the period:

   (i) consent to continue the activities of the limited partnership and admit at least one general partner is given by limited partners owning a majority of the rights to receive distributions as limited partners at the time the consent is to be effective; and

   (ii) at least one person is admitted as a general partner in accordance with the consent;

  (4) the passage of 90 days after the dissociation of the limited partnership's last limited partner, unless before the end of the period the limited partnership admits at least one limited partner; or

  (5) the signing and filing of a declaration of dissolution by the [Secretary of State] under Section 809(c).

COMMENT

 This Act does not require that any of the consents referred to in this section be given in the form of a signed record. The partnership agreement has the power to impose that requirement. See Comment to Section 110.

 In several provisions, this section provides for consent in terms of rights to receive distributions. Distribution rights of non-partner transferees are not relevant. Mere transferees have no consent rights, and their distribution rights are not counted in determining whether majority consent has been obtained.

 Paragraph (1)—There is no requirement that the relevant provision of the partnership agreement be made in a record, unless the partnership agreement creates that requirement. However, if the relevant provision is not "contained in a partnership agreement made in a record," Section 111(9)(D) includes among the limited partnership's required information "a record stating . . . any events upon the happening of which the limited partnership is to be dissolved and its activities wound up."

 Paragraph (2)—Rights to receive distributions owned by a person that is both a general and a limited partner figure into the limited partner determination only to the extent those rights are owned in the person's capacity as a limited partner. See Section 111(9)(C).

 Example: XYZ is a limited partnership with three general partners, each of whom is also a limited partner, and 5 other limited partners. Rights to receive distributions are allocated as follows:

Partner #1 as general partner—3%

Partner #2 as general partner—2%

Partner #3 as general partner—1%

Partner #1 as limited partner—7%

Partner #2 as limited partner—3%

Partner #3 as limited partner—4%

Partner #4 as limited partner—5%

Partner #5 as limited partner—5%

Partner #6 as limited partner—5%

Partner #7 as limited partner—5%

Partner #8 as limited partner—5%

Several non-partner transferees, in the aggregate—55%

Distribution rights owned by persons as limited partners amount to 39% of total distribution rights. A majority is therefore anything greater than 19.5%. If only Partners 1, 2, 3 and 4 consent to dissolve, the limited partnership is not dissolved. Together these partners own as limited partners 19% of the distribution rights owned by persons as limited partners—just short of the necessary majority. For purposes of this calculation, distribution rights owned by non-partner transferees are irrelevant. So, too, are distribution rights owned by persons as general partners. (However, dissolution under this provision requires "the consent of all general partners.")

 Paragraph (3)(A)—Unlike paragraph (2), this paragraph makes no distinction between distribution rights owned by persons as general partners and distribution rights owned by persons as limited partners. Distribution rights owned by non-partner transferees are irrelevant.

874

§ 802. Judicial Dissolution

On application by a partner the [appropriate court] may order dissolution of a limited partnership if it is not reasonably practicable to carry on the activities of the limited partnership in conformity with the partnership agreement.

COMMENT

Source—RULPA Section 802.

Section 110(b)(9) limits the power of the partnership agreement with regard to this section.

§ 803. Winding up

(a)   A limited partnership continues after dissolution only for the purpose of winding up its activities.

(b)   In winding up its activities, the limited partnership:

(1)   may amend its certificate of limited partnership to state that the limited partnership is dissolved, preserve the limited partnership business or property as a going concern for a reasonable time, prosecute and defend actions and proceedings, whether civil, criminal, or administrative, transfer the limited partnership's property, settle disputes by mediation or arbitration, file a statement of termination as provided in Section 203, and perform other necessary acts; and

(2)   shall discharge the limited partnership's liabilities, settle and close the limited partnership's activities, and marshal and distribute the assets of the partnership.

(c)   If a dissolved limited partnership does not have a general partner, a person to wind up the dissolved limited partnership's activities may be appointed by the consent of limited partners owning a majority of the rights to receive distributions as limited partners at the time the consent is to be effective. A person appointed under this subsection:

(1)   has the powers of a general partner under Section 804; and

(2)   shall promptly amend the certificate of limited partnership to state:

(A)   that the limited partnership does not have a general partner;

(B)   the name of the person that has been appointed to wind up the limited partnership; and

(C)   the street and mailing address of the person.

(d)   On the application of any partner, the [appropriate court] may order judicial supervision of the winding up, including the appointment of a person to wind up the dissolved limited partnership's activities, if:

(1)   a limited partnership does not have a general partner and within a reasonable time following the dissolution no person has been appointed pursuant to subsection (c); or

(2)   the applicant establishes other good cause.

COMMENT

Source—RUPA Sections 802 and 803.

Subsection (b)(2)—A limited partnership may satisfy its duty to "discharge" a liability either by paying or by making an alternative arrangement satisfactory to the creditor.

Subsection (c)—The method for determining majority consent is analogous to the method applicable under Section 801(2). See the Comment to that paragraph.

A person appointed under this subsection is **not** a general partner and therefore is not subject to Section 408.

§ 804.   Power of General Partner and Person Dissociated as General Partner to Bind Partnership After Dissolution

(a)   A limited partnership is bound by a general partner's act after dissolution which:

    (1)   is appropriate for winding up the limited partnership's activities; or

    (2)   would have bound the limited partnership under Section 402 before dissolution, if, at the time the other party enters into the transaction, the other party does not have notice of the dissolution.

(b)   A person dissociated as a general partner binds a limited partnership through an act occurring after dissolution if:

    (1)   at the time the other party enters into the transaction:

        (A)   less than two years has passed since the dissociation; and

        (B)   the other party does not have notice of the dissociation and reasonably believes that the person is a general partner; and

    (2)   the act:

        (A)   is appropriate for winding up the limited partnership's activities; or

        (B)   would have bound the limited partnership under Section 402 before dissolution and at the time the other party enters into the transaction the other party does not have notice of the dissolution.

COMMENT

Subsection (a)—Source: RUPA Section 804.

Subsection (a)(2)—A person might have notice under Section 103(d)(2) (amendment of certificate of limited partnership to indicate dissolution) as well as under Section 103(b).

Subsection (b)—This subsection deals with the post-dissolution power to bind of a person dissociated as a general partner. Paragraph (1) replicates the provisions of Section 606, pertaining to the pre-dissolution power to bind of a person dissociated as a general partner. Paragraph (2) replicates the provisions of subsection (a), which state the post-dissolution power to bind of a general partner. For a person dissociated as a general partner to bind a dissolved limited partnership, the person's act will have to satisfy both paragraph (1) and paragraph (2).

Subsection (b)(1)(B)—A person might have notice under Section 103(d)(1) as well as under Section 103(b).

Subsection (b)(2)(B)—A person might have notice under Section 103(d)(2) (amendment of certificate of limited partnership to indicate dissolution) as well as under Section 103(b).

§ 805.   Liability After Dissolution of General Partner and Person Dissociated as General Partner to Limited Partnership, Other General Partners, and Persons Dissociated as General Partner

(a)   If a general partner having knowledge of the dissolution causes a limited partnership to incur an obligation under Section 804(a) by an act that is not appropriate for winding up the partnership's activities, the general partner is liable:

    (1)   to the limited partnership for any damage caused to the limited partnership arising from the obligation; and

    (2)   if another general partner or a person dissociated as a general partner is liable for the obligation, to that other general partner or person for any damage caused to that other general partner or person arising from the liability.

(b)   If a person dissociated as a general partner causes a limited partnership to incur an obligation under Section 804(b), the person is liable:

    (1)   to the limited partnership for any damage caused to the limited partnership arising from the obligation; and

(2)   if a general partner or another person dissociated as a general partner is liable for the obligation, to the general partner or other person for any damage caused to the general partner or other person arising from the liability.

COMMENT

Source—RUPA Section 806.

It is possible for more than one person to be liable under this section on account of the same limited partnership obligation. This Act does not provide any rule for apportioning liability in that circumstance.

Subsection (a)(2)—If the limited partnership is not a limited liability limited partnership, the liability created by this paragraph includes liability under Sections 404(a), 607(b), and 607(c). The paragraph also applies when a partner or person dissociated as a general partner suffers damage due to a contract of guaranty.

§ 806.   Known Claims Against Dissolved Limited Partnership

(a)   A dissolved limited partnership may dispose of the known claims against it by following the procedure described in subsection (b).

(b)   A dissolved limited partnership may notify its known claimants of the dissolution in a record. The notice must:

(1)   specify the information required to be included in a claim;

(2)   provide a mailing address to which the claim is to be sent;

(3)   state the deadline for receipt of the claim, which may not be less than 120 days after the date the notice is received by the claimant;

(4)   state that the claim will be barred if not received by the deadline; and

(5)   unless the limited partnership has been throughout its existence a limited liability limited partnership, state that the barring of a claim against the limited partnership will also bar any corresponding claim against any general partner or person dissociated as a general partner which is based on Section 404.

(c)   A claim against a dissolved limited partnership is barred if the requirements of subsection (b) are met and:

(1)   the claim is not received by the specified deadline; or

(2)   in the case of a claim that is timely received but rejected by the dissolved limited partnership, the claimant does not commence an action to enforce the claim against the limited partnership within 90 days after the receipt of the notice of the rejection.

(d)   This section does not apply to a claim based on an event occurring after the effective date of dissolution or a liability that is contingent on that date.

COMMENT

Source—ULLCA Section 807. See also RMBCA Section 14.06.

Paragraph (b)(5)—If the limited partnership has always been a limited liability limited partnership, there can be no liability under Section 404 for any general partner or person dissociated as a general partner.

§ 807.   Other Claims Against Dissolved Limited Partnership

(a)   A dissolved limited partnership may publish notice of its dissolution and request persons having claims against the limited partnership to present them in accordance with the notice.

(b)   The notice must:

(1)   be published at least once in a newspaper of general circulation in the [county] in which the dissolved limited partnership's principal office is located or, if it has none in this State, in the [county] in which the limited partnership's designated office is or was last located;

877

(2)   describe the information required to be contained in a claim and provide a mailing address to which the claim is to be sent;

(3)   state that a claim against the limited partnership is barred unless an action to enforce the claim is commenced within five years after publication of the notice; and

(4)   unless the limited partnership has been throughout its existence a limited liability limited partnership, state that the barring of a claim against the limited partnership will also bar any corresponding claim against any general partner or person dissociated as a general partner which is based on Section 404.

(c)   If a dissolved limited partnership publishes a notice in accordance with subsection (b), the claim of each of the following claimants is barred unless the claimant commences an action to enforce the claim against the dissolved limited partnership within five years after the publication date of the notice:

(1)   a claimant that did not receive notice in a record under Section 806;

(2)   a claimant whose claim was timely sent to the dissolved limited partnership but not acted on; and

(3)   a claimant whose claim is contingent or based on an event occurring after the effective date of dissolution.

(d)   A claim not barred under this section may be enforced:

(1)   against the dissolved limited partnership, to the extent of its undistributed assets;

(2)   if the assets have been distributed in liquidation, against a partner or transferee to the extent of that person's proportionate share of the claim or the limited partnership's assets distributed to the partner or transferee in liquidation, whichever is less, but a person's total liability for all claims under this paragraph does not exceed the total amount of assets distributed to the person as part of the winding up of the dissolved limited partnership; or

(3)   against any person liable on the claim under Section 404.

COMMENT

Source—ULLCA Section 808.   See also RMBCA Section 14.07.

Paragraph (b)(4)—If the limited partnership has always been a limited liability limited partnership, there can be no liability under Section 404 for any general partner or person dissociated as a general partner.

§ 808. Liability of General Partner and Person Dissociated as General Partner When Claim Against Limited Partnership Barred

If a claim against a dissolved limited partnership is barred under Section 806 or 807, any corresponding claim under Section 404 is also barred.

COMMENT

The liability under Section 404 of a general partner or person dissociated as a general partner is merely liability for the obligations of the limited partnership.

§ 809. Administrative Dissolution

(a)   The [Secretary of State] may dissolve a limited partnership administratively if the limited partnership does not, within 60 days after the due date:

(1)   pay any fee, tax, or penalty due to the [Secretary of State] under this [Act] or other law; or

(2)   deliver its annual report to the [Secretary of State].

(b)   If the [Secretary of State] determines that a ground exists for administratively dissolving a limited partnership, the [Secretary of State] shall file a record of the determination and serve the limited partnership with a copy of the filed record.

(c)   If within 60 days after service of the copy the limited partnership does not correct each ground for dissolution or demonstrate to the reasonable satisfaction of the [Secretary of State] that each ground determined by the [Secretary of State] does not exist, the [Secretary of State] shall administratively dissolve the limited partnership by preparing, signing and filing a declaration of dissolution that states the grounds for dissolution. The [Secretary of State] shall serve the limited partnership with a copy of the filed declaration.

(d)   A limited partnership administratively dissolved continues its existence but may carry on only activities necessary to wind up its activities and liquidate its assets under Sections 803 and 812 and to notify claimants under Sections 806 and 807.

(e)   The administrative dissolution of a limited partnership does not terminate the authority of its agent for service of process.

COMMENT

Source—ULLCA Sections 809 and 810. See also RMBCA Sections 14.20 and 14.21.

Subsection (a)(1)—This provision refers solely to money due the specified filing officer and does not apply to other money due to the State.

Subsection (c)—The filing of a declaration of dissolution does not provide notice under Section 103(d).

§ 810.   Reinstatement Following Administrative Dissolution

(a)   A limited partnership that has been administratively dissolved may apply to the [Secretary of State] for reinstatement within two years after the effective date of dissolution. The application must be delivered to the [Secretary of State] for filing and state:

(1)   the name of the limited partnership and the effective date of its administrative dissolution;

(2)   that the grounds for dissolution either did not exist or have been eliminated; and

(3)   that the limited partnership's name satisfies the requirements of Section 108.

(b)   If the [Secretary of State] determines that an application contains the information required by subsection (a) and that the information is correct, the [Secretary of State] shall prepare a declaration of reinstatement that states this determination, sign, and file the original of the declaration of reinstatement, and serve the limited partnership with a copy.

(c)   When reinstatement becomes effective, it relates back to and takes effect as of the effective date of the administrative dissolution and the limited partnership may resume its activities as if the administrative dissolution had never occurred.

COMMENT

Source—ULLCA Section 811. See also RMBCA Section 14.22.

§ 811.   Appeal from Denial of Reinstatement

(a)   If the [Secretary of State] denies a limited partnership's application for reinstatement following administrative dissolution, the [Secretary of State] shall prepare, sign and file a notice that explains the reason or reasons for denial and serve the limited partnership with a copy of the notice.

(b)   Within 30 days after service of the notice of denial, the limited partnership may appeal from the denial of reinstatement by petitioning the [appropriate court] to set aside the dissolution. The petition must be served on the [Secretary of State] and contain a copy of the [Secretary of State's] declaration of dissolution, the limited partnership's application for reinstatement, and the [Secretary of State's] notice of denial.

(c)   The court may summarily order the [Secretary of State] to reinstate the dissolved limited partnership or may take other action the court considers appropriate.

Source—ULLCA Section 812.

§ 812.　Disposition of Assets; When Contributions Required

(a)　In winding up a limited partnership's activities, the assets of the limited partnership, including the contributions required by this section, must be applied to satisfy the limited partnership's obligations to creditors, including, to the extent permitted by law, partners that are creditors.

(b)　Any surplus remaining after the limited partnership complies with subsection (a) must be paid in cash as a distribution.

(c)　If a limited partnership's assets are insufficient to satisfy all of its obligations under subsection (a), with respect to each unsatisfied obligation incurred when the limited partnership was not a limited liability limited partnership, the following rules apply:

(1)　Each person that was a general partner when the obligation was incurred and that has not been released from the obligation under Section 607 shall contribute to the limited partnership for the purpose of enabling the limited partnership to satisfy the obligation. The contribution due from each of those persons is in proportion to the right to receive distributions in the capacity of general partner in effect for each of those persons when the obligation was incurred.

(2)　If a person does not contribute the full amount required under paragraph (1) with respect to an unsatisfied obligation of the limited partnership, the other persons required to contribute by paragraph (1) on account of the obligation shall contribute the additional amount necessary to discharge the obligation. The additional contribution due from each of those other persons is in proportion to the right to receive distributions in the capacity of general partner in effect for each of those other persons when the obligation was incurred.

(3)　If a person does not make the additional contribution required by paragraph (2), further additional contributions are determined and due in the same manner as provided in that paragraph.

(d)　A person that makes an additional contribution under subsection (c)(2) or (3) may recover from any person whose failure to contribute under subsection (c)(1) or (2) necessitated the additional contribution. A person may not recover under this subsection more than the amount additionally contributed. A person's liability under this subsection may not exceed the amount the person failed to contribute.

(e)　The estate of a deceased individual is liable for the person's obligations under this section.

(f)　An assignee for the benefit of creditors of a limited partnership or a partner, or a person appointed by a court to represent creditors of a limited partnership or a partner, may enforce a person's obligation to contribute under subsection (c).

In some circumstances, this Act requires a partner to make payments to the limited partnership. See, e.g., Sections 502(b), 509(a), 509(b), and 812(c). In other circumstances, this Act requires a partner to make payments to other partners. See, e.g., Sections 509(c) and 812(d). In no circumstances does this Act require a partner to make a payment for the purpose of equalizing or otherwise reallocating capital losses incurred by partners.

Example: XYZ Limited Partnership ("XYZ") has one general partner and four limited partners. According to XYZ's required information, the value of each partner's contributions to XYZ are:

General partner—$5,000

Limited partner #1—$10,000

Limited partner #2—$15,000

Limited partner #3—$20,000

Limited partner #4—$25,000

XYZ is unsuccessful and eventually dissolves without ever having made a distribution to its partners. XYZ lacks any assets with which to return to the partners the value of their respective contributions. No partner is obliged to make any payment either to the limited partnership or to fellow partners to adjust these capital losses. These losses are not part of "the limited partnership's obligations to creditors." Section 812(a).

Example: Same facts, except that Limited Partner #4 loaned $25,000 to XYZ when XYZ was not a limited liability limited partnership, and XYZ lacks the assets to repay the loan. The general partner must contribute to the limited partnership whatever funds are necessary to enable XYZ to satisfy the obligation owned to Limited Partner #4 on account of the loan. Section 812(a) and (c).

Subsection (c)—Following RUPA and the UPA, this Act leaves to other law the question of when a limited partnership obligation is incurred.

[ARTICLE] 9. FOREIGN LIMITED PARTNERSHIPS

§ 901. Governing Law

(a) The laws of the State or other jurisdiction under which a foreign limited partnership is organized govern relations among the partners of the foreign limited partnership and between the partners and the foreign limited partnership and the liability of partners as partners for an obligation of the foreign limited partnership.

(b) A foreign limited partnership may not be denied a certificate of authority by reason of any difference between the laws of the jurisdiction under which the foreign limited partnership is organized and the laws of this State.

(c) A certificate of authority does not authorize a foreign limited partnership to engage in any business or exercise any power that a limited partnership may not engage in or exercise in this State.

COMMENT

Source—ULLCA Section 1001 for subsections (b) and (c).

Subsection (a)—This subsection parallels and is analogous in scope and effect to Section 106 (choice of law for domestic limited partnerships).

§ 902. Application for Certificate of Authority

(a) A foreign limited partnership may apply for a certificate of authority to transact business in this State by delivering an application to the [Secretary of State] for filing. The application must state:

(1) the name of the foreign limited partnership and, if the name does not comply with Section 108, an alternate name adopted pursuant to Section 905(a).

(2) the name of the State or other jurisdiction under whose law the foreign limited partnership is organized;

(3) the street and mailing address of the foreign limited partnership's principal office and, if the laws of the jurisdiction under which the foreign limited partnership is organized require the foreign limited partnership to maintain an office in that jurisdiction, the street and mailing address of the required office;

(4) the name and street and mailing address of the foreign limited partnership's initial agent for service of process in this State;

(5) the name and street and mailing address of each of the foreign limited partnership's general partners; and

(6) whether the foreign limited partnership is a foreign limited liability limited partnership.

(b) A foreign limited partnership shall deliver with the completed application a certificate of existence or a record of similar import signed by the [Secretary of State] or other official having custody of the foreign limited partnership's publicly filed records in the State or other jurisdiction under whose law the foreign limited partnership is organized.

COMMENT

Source—ULLCA Section 1002.

A certificate of authority applied for under this section is different than a certificate of authorization furnished under Section 209.

§ 903.   Activities Not Constituting Transacting Business

(a)   Activities of a foreign limited partnership which do not constitute transacting business in this State within the meaning of this [article] include:

(1)   maintaining, defending, and settling an action or proceeding;

(2)   holding meetings of its partners or carrying on any other activity concerning its internal affairs;

(3)   maintaining accounts in financial institutions;

(4)   maintaining offices or agencies for the transfer, exchange, and registration of the foreign limited partnership's own securities or maintaining trustees or depositories with respect to those securities;

(5)   selling through independent contractors;

(6)   soliciting or obtaining orders, whether by mail or electronic means or through employees or agents or otherwise, if the orders require acceptance outside this State before they become contracts;

(7)   creating or acquiring indebtedness, mortgages, or security interests in real or personal property;

(8)   securing or collecting debts or enforcing mortgages or other security interests in property securing the debts, and holding, protecting, and maintaining property so acquired;

(9)   conducting an isolated transaction that is completed within 30 days and is not one in the course of similar transactions of a like manner; and

(10)   transacting business in interstate commerce.

(b)   For purposes of this [article], the ownership in this State of income-producing real property or tangible personal property, other than property excluded under subsection (a), constitutes transacting business in this State.

(c)   This section does not apply in determining the contacts or activities that may subject a foreign limited partnership to service of process, taxation, or regulation under any other law of this State.

COMMENT

Source—ULLCA Section 1003.

§ 904.   Filing of Certificate of Authority

Unless the [Secretary of State] determines that an application for a certificate of authority does not comply with the filing requirements of this [Act], the [Secretary of State], upon payment of all filing fees, shall file the application, prepare, sign and file a certificate of authority to transact business in this state, and send a copy of the filed certificate, together with a receipt for the fees, to the foreign limited partnership or its representative.

COMMENT

Source—ULLCA Section 1004 and RULPA Section 903.

A certificate of authority filed under this section is different than a certificate of authorization furnished under Section 209.

§ 905. Noncomplying Name of Foreign Limited Partnership

(a) A foreign limited partnership whose name does not comply with Section 108 may not obtain a certificate of authority until it adopts, for the purpose of transacting business in this State, an alternate name that complies with Section 108. A foreign limited partnership that adopts an alternate name under this subsection and then obtains a certificate of authority with the name need not comply with [fictitious name statute]. After obtaining a certificate of authority with an alternate name, a foreign limited partnership shall transact business in this State under the name unless the foreign limited partnership is authorized under [fictitious name statute] to transact business in this State under another name.

(b) If a foreign limited partnership authorized to transact business in this State changes its name to one that does not comply with Section 108, it may not thereafter transact business in this State until it complies with subsection (a) and obtains an amended certificate of authority.

COMMENT

Source—ULLCA Section 1005.

§ 906. Revocation of Certificate of Authority

(a) A certificate of authority of a foreign limited partnership to transact business in this State may be revoked by the [Secretary of State] in the manner provided in subsections (b) and (c) if the foreign limited partnership does not:

(1) pay, within 60 days after the due date, any fee, tax or penalty due to the [Secretary of State] under this [Act] or other law;

(2) deliver, within 60 days after the due date, its annual report required under Section 210;

(3) appoint and maintain an agent for service of process as required by Section 114(b); or

(4) deliver for filing a statement of a change under Section 115 within 30 days after a change has occurred in the name or address of the agent.

(b) In order to revoke a certificate of authority, the [Secretary of State] must prepare, sign, and file a notice of revocation and send a copy to the foreign limited partnership's agent for service of process in this State, or if the foreign limited partnership does not appoint and maintain a proper agent in this State, to the foreign limited partnership's designated office. The notice must state:

(1) the revocation's effective date, which must be at least 60 days after the date the [Secretary of State] sends the copy; and

(2) the foreign limited partnership's failures to comply with subsection (a) which are the reason for the revocation.

(c) The authority of the foreign limited partnership to transact business in this State ceases on the effective date of the notice of revocation unless before that date the foreign limited partnership cures each failure to comply with subsection (a) stated in the notice. If the foreign limited partnership cures the failures, the [Secretary of State] shall so indicate on the filed notice.

COMMENT

Source—ULLCA Section 1006.

§ 907. Cancellation of Certificate of Authority; Effect of Failure to Have Certificate

(a) In order to cancel its certificate of authority to transact business in this State, a foreign limited partnership must deliver to the [Secretary of State] for filing a notice of cancellation. The certificate is canceled when the notice becomes effective under Section 206.

(b) A foreign limited partnership transacting business in this State may not maintain an action or proceeding in this State unless it has a certificate of authority to transact business in this State.

(c)   The failure of a foreign limited partnership to have a certificate of authority to transact business in this State does not impair the validity of a contract or act of the foreign limited partnership or prevent the foreign limited partnership from defending an action or proceeding in this State.

(d)   A partner of a foreign limited partnership is not liable for the obligations of the foreign limited partnership solely by reason of the foreign limited partnership's having transacted business in this State without a certificate of authority.

(e)   If a foreign limited partnership transacts business in this State without a certificate of authority or cancels its certificate of authority, it appoints the [Secretary of State] as its agent for service of process for rights of action arising out of the transaction of business in this State.

COMMENT

Source—RULPA Section 907(d); ULLCA Section 1008.

§ 908.   Action by [Attorney General]

The [Attorney General] may maintain an action to restrain a foreign limited partnership from transacting business in this state in violation of this [article].

COMMENT

Source—RULPA Section 908; ULLCA Section 1009.

[ARTICLE] 10.   ACTIONS BY PARTNERS

§ 1001.   Direct Action by Partner

(a)   Subject to subsection (b), a partner may maintain a direct action against the limited partnership or another partner for legal or equitable relief, with or without an accounting as to the partnership's activities, to enforce the rights and otherwise protect the interests of the partner, including rights and interests under the partnership agreement or this [Act] or arising independently of the partnership relationship.

(b)   A partner commencing a direct action under this section is required to plead and prove an actual or threatened injury that is not solely the result of an injury suffered or threatened to be suffered by the limited partnership.

(c)   The accrual of, and any time limitation on, a right of action for a remedy under this section is governed by other law. A right to an accounting upon a dissolution and winding up does not revive a claim barred by law.

COMMENT

Subsection (a)—Source: RUPA Section 405(b).

Subsection (b)—In ordinary contractual situations it is axiomatic that each party to a contract has standing to sue for breach of that contract. Within a limited partnership, however, different circumstances may exist. A partner does not have a direct claim against another partner merely because the other partner has breached the partnership agreement. Likewise a partner's violation of this Act does not automatically create a direct claim for every other partner. To have standing in his, her, or its own right, a partner plaintiff must be able to show a harm that occurs independently of the harm caused or threatened to be caused to the limited partnership.

The reference to "threatened" harm is intended to encompass claims for injunctive relief and does not relax standards for proving injury.

§ 1002.   Derivative Action

A partner may maintain a derivative action to enforce a right of a limited partnership if:

(1)   the partner first makes a demand on the general partners, requesting that they cause the limited partnership to bring an action to enforce the right, and the general partners do not bring the action within a reasonable time; or

(2)   a demand would be futile.

COMMENT

Source—RULPA Section 1001.

§ 1003.   Proper Plaintiff

A derivative action may be maintained only by a person that is a partner at the time the action is commenced and:

(1)   that was a partner when the conduct giving rise to the action occurred; or

(2)   whose status as a partner devolved upon the person by operation of law or pursuant to the terms of the partnership agreement from a person that was a partner at the time of the conduct.

COMMENT

Source—RULPA Section 1002.

§ 1004.   Pleading

In a derivative action, the complaint must state with particularity:

(1)   the date and content of plaintiff's demand and the general partners' response to the demand; or

(2)   why demand should be excused as futile.

COMMENT

Source—RULPA Section 1003.

§ 1005.   Proceeds and Expenses

(a)   Except as otherwise provided in subsection (b):

(1)   any proceeds or other benefits of a derivative action, whether by judgment, compromise, or settlement, belong to the limited partnership and not to the derivative plaintiff;

(2)   if the derivative plaintiff receives any proceeds, the derivative plaintiff shall immediately remit them to the limited partnership.

(b)   If a derivative action is successful in whole or in part, the court may award the plaintiff reasonable expenses, including reasonable attorney's fees, from the recovery of the limited partnership.

COMMENT

Source—RULPA Section 1004.

[ARTICLE] 11.   CONVERSION AND MERGER

§ 1101.   Definitions

In this [article]:

(1)   "Constituent limited partnership" means a constituent organization that is a limited partnership.

(2)   "Constituent organization" means an organization that is party to a merger.

(3)   "Converted organization" means the organization into which a converting organization converts pursuant to Sections 1102 through 1105.

(4)   "Converting limited partnership" means a converting organization that is a limited partnership.

(5)   "Converting organization" means an organization that converts into another organization pursuant to Section 1102.

(6)   "General partner" means a general partner of a limited partnership.

(7)   "Governing statute" of an organization means the statute that governs the organization's internal affairs.

(8)   "Organization" means a general partnership, including a limited liability partnership; limited partnership, including a limited liability limited partnership; limited liability company; business trust; corporation; or any other person having a governing statute. The term includes domestic and foreign organizations whether or not organized for profit.

(9)   "Organizational documents" means:

(A)   for a domestic or foreign general partnership, its partnership agreement;

(B)   for a limited partnership or foreign limited partnership, its certificate of limited partnership and partnership agreement;

(C)   for a domestic or foreign limited liability company, its articles of organization and operating agreement, or comparable records as provided in its governing statute;

(D)   for a business trust, its agreement of trust and declaration of trust;

(E)   for a domestic or foreign corporation for profit, its articles of incorporation, bylaws, and other agreements among its shareholders which are authorized by its governing statute, or comparable records as provided in its governing statute; and

(F)   for any other organization, the basic records that create the organization and determine its internal governance and the relations among the persons that own it, have an interest in it, or are members of it.

(10) "Personal liability" means personal liability for a debt, liability, or other obligation of an organization which is imposed on a person that co-owns, has an interest in, or is a member of the organization:

(A)   by the organization's governing statute solely by reason of the person co-owning, having an interest in, or being a member of the organization; or

(B)   by the organization's organizational documents under a provision of the organization's governing statute authorizing those documents to make one or more specified persons liable for all or specified debts, liabilities, and other obligations of the organization solely by reason of the person or persons co-owning, having an interest in, or being a member of the organization.

(11) "Surviving organization" means an organization into which one or more other organizations are merged. A surviving organization may preexist the merger or be created by the merger.

COMMENT

This section contains definitions specific to this Article.

§ 1102.   Conversion

(a)   An organization other than a limited partnership may convert to a limited partnership, and a limited partnership may convert to another organization pursuant to this section and Sections 1103 through 1105 and a plan of conversion, if:

(1)   the other organization's governing statute authorizes the conversion;

(2)   the conversion is not prohibited by the law of the jurisdiction that enacted the governing statute; and

(3)   the other organization complies with its governing statute in effecting the conversion.

(b) A plan of conversion must be in a record and must include:

    (1) the name and form of the organization before conversion;

    (2) the name and form of the organization after conversion; and

    (3) the terms and conditions of the conversion, including the manner and basis for converting interests in the converting organization into any combination of money, interests in the converted organization, and other consideration; and

    (4) the organizational documents of the converted organization.

COMMENT

In a statutory conversion an existing entity changes its form, the jurisdiction of its governing statute or both. For example, a limited partnership organized under the laws of one jurisdiction might convert to:

- a limited liability company (or other form of entity) organized under the laws of the same jurisdiction,

- a limited liability company (or other form of entity) organized under the laws of another jurisdiction, or

- a limited partnership organized under the laws of another jurisdiction (referred to in some statutes as "domestication").

In contrast to a merger, which involves at least two entities, a conversion involves only one. The converting and converted organization are the same entity. See Section 1105(a). For this Act to apply to a conversion, either the converting or converted organization must be a limited partnership subject to this Act. If the converting organization is a limited partnership subject to this Act, the partners of the converting organization are subject to the duties and obligations stated in this Act, including Sections 304 (informational rights of limited partners), 305(b) (limited partner's obligation of good faith and fair dealing), 407 (informational rights of general partners), and 408 (general partner duties).

Subsection (a)(2)—Given the very broad definition of "organization," Section 1101(8), this Act authorizes conversions involving non-profit organizations. This provision is intended as an additional safeguard for that context.

Subsection (b)(3)—A plan of conversion may provide that some persons with interests in the converting organization will receive interests in the converted organization while other persons with interests in the converting organization will receive some other form of consideration. Thus, a "squeeze out" conversion is possible. As noted above, if the converting organization is a limited partnership subject to this Act, the partners of the converting organization are subject to the duties and obligations stated in this Act. Those duties would apply to the process and terms under which a squeeze out conversion occurs.

If the converting organization is a limited partnership, the plan of conversion will determine the fate of any interests held by mere transferees. This Act does not state any duty or obligation owed by a converting limited partnership or its partners to mere transferees. That issue is a matter for other law.

§ 1103. Action on Plan of Conversion by Converting Limited Partnership

(a) Subject to Section 1110, a plan of conversion must be consented to by all the partners of a converting limited partnership.

(b) Subject to Section 1110 and any contractual rights, after a conversion is approved, and at any time before a filing is made under Section 1104, a converting limited partnership may amend the plan or abandon the planned conversion:

    (1) as provided in the plan; and

    (2) except as prohibited by the plan, by the same consent as was required to approve the plan.

COMMENT

Section 1110 imposes special consent requirements for transactions which might cause a partner to have "personal liability," as defined in Section 1101(10) for entity debts. The partnership agreement may not restrict the rights provided by Section 1110. See Section 110(b)(12).

Subsection (a)—Like many of the rules stated in this Act, this subsection's requirement of unanimous consent is a default rule. Subject only to Section 1110, the partnership agreement may state a different quantum of consent or provide a completely different approval mechanism. Varying this subsection's rule means that a partner might be subject to a conversion (including a "squeeze out" conversion) without consent and with no appraisal remedy. If the converting organization is a limited partnership subject to this Act, the partners of the converting organization are subject to the duties and obligations stated in this Act. Those duties would apply to the process and terms under which the conversion occurs. However, if the partnership agreement allows for a conversion with less than unanimous consent, the mere fact a partner objects to a conversion does not mean that the partners favoring, arranging, consenting to or effecting the conversation have breached a duty under this Act.

§ 1104.   Filings Required for Conversion; Effective Date

(a)   After a plan of conversion is approved:

(1)   a converting limited partnership shall deliver to the [Secretary of State] for filing articles of conversion, which must include:

(A)   a statement that the limited partnership has been converted into another organization;

(B)   the name and form of the organization and the jurisdiction of its governing statute;

(C)   the date the conversion is effective under the governing statute of the converted organization;

(D)   a statement that the conversion was approved as required by this [Act];

(E)   a statement that the conversion was approved as required by the governing statute of the converted organization; and

(F)   if the converted organization is a foreign organization not authorized to transact business in this State, the street and mailing address of an office which the [Secretary of State] may use for the purposes of Section 1105(c); and

(2)   if the converting organization is not a converting limited partnership, the converting organization shall deliver to the [Secretary of State] for filing a certificate of limited partnership, which must include, in addition to the information required by Section 201:

(A)   a statement that the limited partnership was converted from another organization;

(B)   the name and form of the organization and the jurisdiction of its governing statute; and

(C)   a statement that the conversion was approved in a manner that complied with the organization's governing statute.

(b)   A conversion becomes effective:

(1)   if the converted organization is a limited partnership, when the certificate of limited partnership takes effect; and

(2)   if the converted organization is not a limited partnership, as provided by the governing statute of the converted organization.

COMMENT

Subsection (b)—The effective date of a conversion is determined under the governing statute of the converted organization.

§ 1105.   Effect of Conversion

(a)   An organization that has been converted pursuant to this [article] is for all purposes the same entity that existed before the conversion.

(b)   When a conversion takes effect:

(1)   all property owned by the converting organization remains vested in the converted organization;

(2) all debts, liabilities, and other obligations of the converting organization continue as obligations of the converted organization;

(3) an action or proceeding pending by or against the converting organization may be continued as if the conversion had not occurred;

(4) except as prohibited by other law, all of the rights, privileges, immunities, powers, and purposes of the converting organization remain vested in the converted organization;

(5) except as otherwise provided in the plan of conversion, the terms and conditions of the plan of conversion take effect; and

(6) except as otherwise agreed, the conversion does not dissolve a converting limited partnership for the purposes of [Article] 8.

(c) A converted organization that is a foreign organization consents to the jurisdiction of the courts of this State to enforce any obligation owed by the converting limited partnership, if before the conversion the converting limited partnership was subject to suit in this State on the obligation. A converted organization that is a foreign organization and not authorized to transact business in this State appoints the [Secretary of State] as its agent for service of process for purposes of enforcing an obligation under this subsection. Service on the [Secretary of State] under this subsection is made in the same manner and with the same consequences as in Section 117(c) and (d).

COMMENT

Subsection (a)—A conversion changes an entity's legal type, but does not create a new entity.

Subsection (b)—Unlike a merger, a conversion involves a single entity, and the conversion therefore does not transfer any of the entity's rights or obligations.

§ 1106.   Merger

(a) A limited partnership may merge with one or more other constituent organizations pursuant to this section and Sections 1107 through 1109 and a plan of merger, if:

(1) the governing statute of each the other organizations authorizes the merger;

(2) the merger is not prohibited by the law of a jurisdiction that enacted any of those governing statutes; and

(3) each of the other organizations complies with its governing statute in effecting the merger.

(b) A plan of merger must be in a record and must include:

(1) the name and form of each constituent organization;

(2) the name and form of the surviving organization and, if the surviving organization is to be created by the merger, a statement to that effect;

(3) the terms and conditions of the merger, including the manner and basis for converting the interests in each constituent organization into any combination of money, interests in the surviving organization, and other consideration;

(4) if the surviving organization is to be created by the merger, the surviving organization's organizational documents; and

(5) if the surviving organization is not to be created by the merger, any amendments to be made by the merger to the surviving organization's organizational documents.

COMMENT

For this Act to apply to a merger, at least one of the constituent organizations must be a limited partnership subject to this Act. The partners of any such limited partnership are subject to the duties and obligations stated in this Act, including Sections 304 (informational rights of limited partners), 305(b) (limited partner's obligation of good faith and fair dealing), 407 (informational rights of general partners), and 408 (general partner duties).

Subsection (a)(2)—Given the very broad definition of "organization," Section 1101(8), this Act authorizes mergers involving non-profit organizations. This provision is intended as an additional safeguard for that context.

Subsection (b)(3)—A plan of merger may provide that some persons with interests in a constituent organization will receive interests in the surviving organization, while other persons with interests in the same constituent organization will receive some other form of consideration. Thus, a "squeeze out" merger is possible. As noted above, the duties and obligations stated in this Act apply to the partners of a constituent organization that is a limited partnership subject to this Act. Those duties would apply to the process and terms under which a squeeze out merger occurs.

If a constituent organization is a limited partnership, the plan of merger will determine the fate of any interests held by mere transferees. This Act does not state any duty or obligation owed by a constituent limited partnership or its partners to mere transferees. That issue is a matter for other law.

§ 1107.   Action on Plan of Merger by Constituent Limited Partnership

(a)   Subject to Section 1110, a plan of merger must be consented to by all the partners of a constituent limited partnership.

(b)   Subject to Section 1110 and any contractual rights, after a merger is approved, and at any time before a filing is made under Section 1108, a constituent limited partnership may amend the plan or abandon the planned merger:

    (1)   as provided in the plan; and

    (2)   except as prohibited by the plan, with the same consent as was required to approve the plan.

COMMENT

Section 1110 imposes special consent requirements for transactions which might make a partner personally liable for entity debts. The partnership agreement may not restrict the rights provided by Section 1110. See Section 110(b)(12).

Subsection (a)—Like many of the rules stated in this Act, this subsection's requirement of unanimous consent is a default rule. Subject only to Section 1110, the partnership agreement may state a different quantum of consent or provide a completely different approval mechanism. Varying this subsection's rule means that a partner might be subject to a merger (including a "squeeze out" merger) without consent and with no appraisal remedy. The partners of a constituent limited partnership are subject to the duties and obligations stated in this Act, and those duties would apply to the process and terms under which the merger occurs. However, if the partnership agreement allows for a merger with less than unanimous consent, the mere fact a partner objects to a merger does not mean that the partners favoring, arranging, consenting to or effecting the merger have breached a duty under this Act.

§ 1108.   Filings Required for Merger; Effective Date

(a)   After each constituent organization has approved a merger, articles of merger must be signed on behalf of:

    (1)   each preexisting constituent limited partnership, by each general partner listed in the certificate of limited partnership; and

    (2)   each other preexisting constituent organization, by an authorized representative.

(b)   The articles of merger must include:

    (1)   the name and form of each constituent organization and the jurisdiction of its governing statute;

    (2)   the name and form of the surviving organization, the jurisdiction of its governing statute, and, if the surviving organization is created by the merger, a statement to that effect;

    (3)   the date the merger is effective under the governing statute of the surviving organization;

    (4)   if the surviving organization is to be created by the merger:

(A) if it will be a limited partnership, the limited partnership's certificate of limited partnership; or

(B) if it will be an organization other than a limited partnership, the organizational document that creates the organization;

(5) if the surviving organization preexists the merger, any amendments provided for in the plan of merger for the organizational document that created the organization;

(6) a statement as to each constituent organization that the merger was approved as required by the organization's governing statute;

(7) if the surviving organization is a foreign organization not authorized to transact business in this State, the street and mailing address of an office which the [Secretary of State] may use for the purposes of Section 1109(b); and

(8) any additional information required by the governing statute of any constituent organization.

(c) Each constituent limited partnership shall deliver the articles of merger for filing in the [office of the Secretary of State].

(d) A merger becomes effective under this [article]:

(1) if the surviving organization is a limited partnership, upon the later of:

(i) compliance with subsection (c); or

(ii) subject to Section 206(c), as specified in the articles of merger; or

(2) if the surviving organization is not a limited partnership, as provided by the governing statute of the surviving organization.

COMMENT

Subsection (b)—The effective date of a merger is determined under the governing statute of the surviving organization.

§ 1109. Effect of Merger

(a) When a merger becomes effective:

(1) the surviving organization continues or comes into existence;

(2) each constituent organization that merges into the surviving organization ceases to exist as a separate entity;

(3) all property owned by each constituent organization that ceases to exist vests in the surviving organization;

(4) all debts, liabilities, and other obligations of each constituent organization that ceases to exist continue as obligations of the surviving organization;

(5) an action or proceeding pending by or against any constituent organization that ceases to exist may be continued as if the merger had not occurred;

(6) except as prohibited by other law, all of the rights, privileges, immunities, powers, and purposes of each constituent organization that ceases to exist vest in the surviving organization;

(7) except as otherwise provided in the plan of merger, the terms and conditions of the plan of merger take effect; and

(8) except as otherwise agreed, if a constituent limited partnership ceases to exist, the merger does not dissolve the limited partnership for the purposes of [Article] 8;

(9) if the surviving organization is created by the merger:

(A) if it is a limited partnership, the certificate of limited partnership becomes effective; or

(B)   if it is an organization other than a limited partnership, the organizational document that creates the organization becomes effective; and

(10) if the surviving organization preexists the merger, any amendments provided for in the articles of merger for the organizational document that created the organization become effective.

(b)   A surviving organization that is a foreign organization consents to the jurisdiction of the courts of this State to enforce any obligation owed by a constituent organization, if before the merger the constituent organization was subject to suit in this State on the obligation. A surviving organization that is a foreign organization and not authorized to transact business in this State appoints the [Secretary of State] as its agent for service of process for the purposes of enforcing an obligation under this subsection. Service on the [Secretary of State] under this subsection is made in the same manner and with the same consequences as in Section 117(c) and (d).

§ 1110. Restrictions on Approval of Conversions and Mergers and on Relinquishing LLLP Status

(a)   If a partner of a converting or constituent limited partnership will have personal liability with respect to a converted or surviving organization, approval and amendment of a plan of conversion or merger are ineffective without the consent of the partner, unless:

(1)   the limited partnership's partnership agreement provides for the approval of the conversion or merger with the consent of fewer than all the partners; and

(2)   the partner has consented to the provision of the partnership agreement.

(b)   An amendment to a certificate of limited partnership which deletes a statement that the limited partnership is a limited liability limited partnership is ineffective without the consent of each general partner unless:

(1)   the limited partnership's partnership agreement provides for the amendment with the consent of less than all the general partners; and

(2)   each general partner that does not consent to the amendment has consented to the provision of the partnership agreement.

(c)   A partner does not give the consent required by subsection (a) or (b) merely by consenting to a provision of the partnership agreement which permits the partnership agreement to be amended with the consent of fewer than all the partners.

COMMENT

This section imposes special consent requirements for transactions that might make a partner personally liable for entity debts. The partnership agreement may not restrict the rights provided by this section. See Section 110(b)(12).

Subsection (c)—This subsection prevents circumvention of the consent requirements of subsections (a) and (b).

Example: As initially . . . consented to, the partnership agreement of a limited partnership leaves in place the Act's rule requiring unanimous consent for a conversion or merger. The partnership agreement does provide, however, that the agreement may be amended with the affirmative vote of general partners owning 2/3 of the rights to receive distributions as general partners and of limited partners owning 2/3 of the rights to receive distributions as limited partners. The required vote is obtained for an amendment that permits approval of a conversion or merger by the same vote necessary to amend the partnership agreement. Partner X votes for the amendment. Partner Y votes against. Partner Z does not vote.

Subsequently the limited partnership proposes to convert to a limited partnership (not an LLLP) organized under the laws of another state, with Partners X, Y and Z each receiving interests as general partners. Under the amended partnership agreement, approval of the conversion does not require unanimous consent. However, since after the conversion, Partners X, Y and Z will each have "personal liability with respect to [the] converted . . . organization," Section 1110(a) applies.

As a result, the approval of the plan of conversion will require the consent of Partner Y and Partner Z. They did not consent to the amendment that provided for non-unanimous approval of a conversion or merger. Their initial consent to the partnership agreement, with its provision permitting non-unanimous consent for amendments, does <u>not</u> satisfy the consent requirement of Subsection 1110(a)(2).

In contrast, Partner X's consent is not required. Partner X lost its Section 1110(a) veto right by consenting directly to the amendment to the partnership agreement which permitted non-unanimous consent to a conversion or merger.

§ 1111. Liability of General Partner After Conversion or Merger

(a)   A conversion or merger under this [article] does not discharge any liability under Sections 404 and 607 of a person that was a general partner in or dissociated as a general partner from a converting or constituent limited partnership, but:

(1)   the provisions of this [Act] pertaining to the collection or discharge of the liability continue to apply to the liability;

(2)   for the purposes of applying those provisions, the converted or surviving organization is deemed to be the converting or constituent limited partnership; and

(3)   if a person is required to pay any amount under this subsection:

(A)   the person has a right of contribution from each other person that was liable as a general partner under Section 404 when the obligation was incurred and has not been released from the obligation under Section 607; and

(B)   the contribution due from each of those persons is in proportion to the right to receive distributions in the capacity of general partner in effect for each of those persons when the obligation was incurred.

(b)   In addition to any other liability provided by law:

(1)   a person that immediately before a conversion or merger became effective was a general partner in a converting or constituent limited partnership that was not a limited liability limited partnership is personally liable for each obligation of the converted or surviving organization arising from a transaction with a third party after the conversion or merger becomes effective, if, at the time the third party enters into the transaction, the third party:

(A)   does not have notice of the conversion or merger; and

(B)   reasonably believes that:

(i)   the converted or surviving business is the converting or constituent limited partnership;

(ii)   the converting or constituent limited partnership is not a limited liability limited partnership; and

(iii)   the person is a general partner in the converting or constituent limited partnership; and

(2)   a person that was dissociated as a general partner from a converting or constituent limited partnership before the conversion or merger became effective is personally liable for each obligation of the converted or surviving organization arising from a transaction with a third party after the conversion or merger becomes effective, if:

(A)   immediately before the conversion or merger became effective the converting or surviving limited partnership was a not a limited liability limited partnership; and

(B)   at the time the third party enters into the transaction less than two years have passed since the person dissociated as a general partner and the third party:

(i)   does not have notice of the dissociation;

(ii)   does not have notice of the conversion or merger; and

(iii) reasonably believes that the converted or surviving organization is the converting or constituent limited partnership, the converting or constituent limited partnership is not a limited liability limited partnership, and the person is a general partner in the converting or constituent limited partnership.

COMMENT

This section extrapolates the approach of Section 607 into the context of a conversion or merger involving a limited partnership.

Subsection (a)—This subsection pertains to general partner liability for obligations which a limited partnership incurred before a conversion or merger. Following RUPA and the UPA, this Act leaves to other law the question of when a limited partnership obligation is incurred.

If the converting or constituent limited partnership was a limited liability limited partnership at all times before the conversion or merger, this subsection will not apply because no person will have any liability under Section 404 or 607.

Subsection (b)—This subsection pertains to entity obligations incurred after a conversion or merger and creates lingering exposure to personal liability for general partners and persons previously dissociated as general partners. In contrast to subsection (a)(3), this subsection does not provide for contribution among persons personally liable under this section for the same entity obligation. That issue is left for other law.

Subsection (b)(1)—If the converting or constituent limited partnership was a limited liability limited partnership immediately before the conversion or merger, there is no lingering exposure to personal liability under this subsection.

Subsection (b)(1)(A)—A person might have notice under Section 103(d)(4) or (5) as well as under Section 103(b).

Subsection (b)(2)(B)(i)—A person might have notice under Section 103(d)(1) as well as under Section 103(b).

Subsection (b)(2)(B)(ii)—A person might have notice under Section 103(d)(4) or (5) as well as under Section 103(b).

§ 1112. Power of General Partners and Persons Dissociated as General Partners to Bind Organization After Conversion or Merger

(a) An act of a person that immediately before a conversion or merger became effective was a general partner in a converting or constituent limited partnership binds the converted or surviving organization after the conversion or merger becomes effective, if:

(1) before the conversion or merger became effective, the act would have bound the converting or constituent limited partnership under Section 402; and

(2) at the time the third party enters into the transaction, the third party:

(A) does not have notice of the conversion or merger; and

(B) reasonably believes that the converted or surviving business is the converting or constituent limited partnership and that the person is a general partner in the converting or constituent limited partnership.

(b) An act of a person that before a conversion or merger became effective was dissociated as a general partner from a converting or constituent limited partnership binds the converted or surviving organization after the conversion or merger becomes effective, if:

(1) before the conversion or merger became effective, the act would have bound the converting or constituent limited partnership under Section 402 if the person had been a general partner; and

(2) at the time the third party enters into the transaction, less than two years have passed since the person dissociated as a general partner and the third party:

(A) does not have notice of the dissociation;

    (B)   does not have notice of the conversion or merger; and

    (C)   reasonably believes that the converted or surviving organization is the converting or constituent limited partnership and that the person is a general partner in the converting or constituent limited partnership.

(c)   If a person having knowledge of the conversion or merger causes a converted or surviving organization to incur an obligation under subsection (a) or (b), the person is liable:

    (1)   to the converted or surviving organization for any damage caused to the organization arising from the obligation; and

    (2)   if another person is liable for the obligation, to that other person for any damage caused to that other person arising from the liability.

COMMENT

This section extrapolates the approach of Section 606 into the context of a conversion or merger involving a limited partnership.

Subsection (a)(2)(A)—A person might have notice under Section 103(d)(4) or (5) as well as under Section 103(b).

Subsection (b)(2)(A)—A person might have notice under Section 103(d)(1) as well as under Section 103(b).

Subsection (b)(2)(B)—A person might have notice under Section 103(d)(4) or (5) as well as under Section 103(b).

§ 1113.   [Article] Not Exclusive

This [article] does not preclude an entity from being converted or merged under other law.

[ARTICLE] 12. MISCELLANEOUS PROVISIONS

§ 1201.   Uniformity of Application and Construction

In applying and construing this Uniform Act, consideration must be given to the need to promote uniformity of the law with respect to its subject matter among States that enact it.

§ 1202.   Severability Clause

If any provision of this [Act] or its application to any person or circumstance is held invalid, the invalidity does not affect other provisions or applications of this [Act] which can be given effect without the invalid provision or application, and to this end the provisions of this [Act] are severable.

§ 1203.   Relation to Electronic Signatures in Global and National Commerce Act

This [Act] modifies, limits, or supersedes the federal Electronic Signatures in Global and National Commerce Act, 15 U.S.C. Section 7001 et seq., but this [Act] does not modify, limit, or supersede Section 101(c) of that Act or authorize electronic delivery of any of the notices described in Section 103(b) of that act.

§ 1204.   Effective Date

This [Act] takes effect [effective date].

COMMENT

Section 1206 specifies how this Act affects domestic limited partnerships, with special provisions pertaining to domestic limited partnerships formed before the Act's effective date. Section 1206 contains no comparable provisions for foreign limited partnerships. Therefore, once this Act is effective, it applies immediately to all foreign limited partnerships, whether formed before or after the Act's effective date.

§ 1205. Repeals

Effective [all-inclusive date], the following acts and parts of acts are repealed: [the State Limited Partnership Act as amended and in effect immediately before the effective date of this [Act]].

§ 1206. Application to Existing Relationships

(a) Before [all-inclusive date], this [Act] governs only:

(1) a limited partnership formed on or after [the effective date of this [Act]]; and

(2) except as otherwise provided in subsections (c) and (d), a limited partnership formed before [the effective date of this [Act]] which elects, in the manner provided in its partnership agreement or by law for amending the partnership agreement, to be subject to this [Act].

(b) Except as otherwise provided in subsection (c), on and after [all-inclusive date] this [Act] governs all limited partnerships.

(c) With respect to a limited partnership formed before [the effective date of this [Act]], the following rules apply except as the partners otherwise elect in the manner provided in the partnership agreement or by law for amending the partnership agreement:

(1) Section 104(c) does not apply and the limited partnership has whatever duration it had under the law applicable immediately before [the effective date of this [Act]].

(2) the limited partnership is not required to amend its certificate of limited partnership to comply with Section 201(a)(4).

(3) Sections 601 and 602 do not apply and a limited partner has the same right and power to dissociate from the limited partnership, with the same consequences, as existed immediately before [the effective date of this [Act]].

(4) Section 603(4) does not apply.

(5) Section 603(5) does not apply and a court has the same power to expel a general partner as the court had immediately before [the effective date of this [Act]].

(6) Section 801(3) does not apply and the connection between a person's dissociation as a general partner and the dissolution of the limited partnership is the same as existed immediately before [the effective date of this [Act]].

(d) With respect to a limited partnership that elects pursuant to subsection (a)(2) to be subject to this [Act], after the election takes effect the provisions of this [Act] relating to the liability of the limited partnership's general partners to third parties apply:

(1) before [all-inclusive date], to:

(A) a third party that had not done business with the limited partnership in the year before the election took effect; and

(B) a third party that had done business with the limited partnership in the year before the election took effect only if the third party knows or has received a notification of the election; and

(2) on and after [all-inclusive date], to all third parties, but those provisions remain inapplicable to any obligation incurred while those provisions were inapplicable under paragraph (1)(B).

Legislative Note: In a State that has previously amended its existing limited partnership statute to provide for limited liability limited partnerships (LLLPs), this Act should include transition provisions specifically applicable to preexisting limited liability limited partnerships. The precise wording of those provisions must depend on the wording of the State's previously enacted LLLP provisions. However, the following principles apply generally:

1. In Sections 806(b)(5) and 807(b)(4) (notice by dissolved limited partnership to claimants), the phrase "the limited partnership has been throughout its existence a limited liability limited partnership" should be revised to encompass a limited partnership that was a limited liability limited partnership under the State's previously enacted LLLP provisions.

    2.   *Section 1206(d) should provide that, if a preexisting limited liability limited partnership elects to be subject to this Act, this Act's provisions relating to the liability of general partners to third parties apply immediately to all third parties, regardless of whether a third party has previously done business with the limited liability limited partnership.*

    3.   *A preexisting limited liability limited partnership that elects to be subject to this Act should have to comply with Sections 201(a)(4) (requiring the certificate of limited partnership to state whether the limited partnership is a limited liability limited partnership) and 108(c) (establishing name requirements for a limited liability limited partnership).*

    4.   *As for Section 1206(b) (providing that, after a transition period, this Act applies to all preexisting limited partnerships):*

        a.   if a State's previously enacted LLLP provisions have requirements essentially the same as Sections 201(a)(4) and 108(c), preexisting limited liability limited partnerships should automatically retain LLLP status under this Act.

        b.   if a State's previously enacted LLLP provisions have name requirements essentially the same as Section 108(c) and provide that a public filing other than the certificate of limited partnership establishes a limited partnership's status as a limited liability limited partnership:

            i.   that filing can be deemed to an amendment to the certificate of limited partnership to comply with Section 201(a)(4), and

            ii. preexisting limited liability limited partnerships should automatically retain LLLP status under this Act.

        c.   if a State's previously enacted LLLP provisions do not have name requirements essentially the same as Section 108(c), it will be impossible both to enforce Section 108(c) and provide for automatic transition to LLLP status under this Act.

COMMENT

Source: RUPA Section 1206.

    This section pertains exclusively to domestic limited partnerships—i.e., to limited partnerships formed under this Act or a predecessor statute enacted by the same jurisdiction. For foreign limited partnerships, see the Comment to Section 1204.

    This Act governs all limited partnerships formed on or after the Act's effective date. As for pre-existing limited partnerships, this section establishes an optional "elect in" period and a mandatory, all-inclusive date. The "elect in" period runs from the effective date, stated in Section 1204, until the all-inclusive date, stated in both subsection(a) and (b).

    During the "elect in" period, a pre-existing limited partnership may elect to become subject to this Act. Subsection (d) states certain important consequences for a limited partnership that elects in. Beginning on the all-inclusive date, each pre-existing limited partnership that has not previously elected in becomes subject to this Act by operation of law.

    Subsection (c)—This subsection specifies six provisions of this Act which never automatically apply to any pre-existing limited partnership. Except for subsection (c)(2), the list refers to provisions governing the relationship of the partners *inter se* and considered too different than predecessor law to be fairly applied to a preexisting limited partnership without the consent of its partners. Each of these *inter se* provisions is subject to change in the partnership agreement. However, many pre-existing limited partnerships may have taken for granted the analogous provisions of predecessor law and may therefore not have addressed the issues in their partnership agreements.

    Subsection (c)(1)—Section 104(c) provides that a limited partnership has a perpetual duration.

    Subsection (c)(2)—Section 201(a)(4) requires the certificate of limited partnership to state "whether the limited partnership is a limited liability limited partnership." The requirement is intended to force the organizers of a limited partnership to decide whether the limited partnership is to be an LLLP and therefore is inapposite to pre-existing limited partnerships. Moreover, applying the requirement to pre-existing limited partnerships would create a significant administrative burden both for limited partnerships and the filing officer and probably would result in many pre-existing limited partnerships being in violation of the requirement.

Subsection (c)(3)—Section 601 and 602 concern a person's dissociation as a limited partner.

Subsection (c)(4)—Section 603(4) provides for the expulsion of a general partner by the unanimous consent of the other partners in specified circumstances.

Subsection (c)(5)—Section 603(5) provides for the expulsion of a general partner by a court in specified circumstances.

Subsection (c)(6)—Section 801(3) concerns the continuance or dissolution of a limited partnership following a person's dissociation as a general partner.

Subsection (d)—Following RUPA Section 1206(c), this subsection limits the efficacy of the Act's liability protections for partners of an "electing in" limited partnership. The limitation:

- applies only to the benefit of "a third party that had done business with the limited partnership in the year before the election took effect," and

- ceases to apply when "the third party knows or has received a notification of the election" or on the "all-inclusive" date, whichever occurs first.

If the limitation causes a provision of this Act to be inapplicable with regard to a third party, the comparable provision of predecessor law applies.

Example: A pre-existing limited partnership elects to be governed by this Act before the "all-inclusive" date. Two months before the election, Third Party provided services to the limited partnership. Third Party neither knows nor has received a notification of the election. Until the "all inclusive" date, with regard to Third Party, Section 303's full liability shield does not apply to each limited partner. Instead, each limited partner has the liability shield applicable under predecessor law.

Subsection (d)(2)—To the extent subsection (d) causes a provision of this Act to be inapplicable when an obligation is incurred, the inapplicability continues as to that obligation even after the "all inclusive" date.

§ 1207.　Savings Clause

This [Act] does not affect an action commenced, proceeding brought, or right accrued before this [Act] takes effect.

UNIFORM LIMITED PARTNERSHIP ACT (2013)

Table of Sections

[ARTICLE] 1. GENERAL PROVISIONS

[ARTICLE] 2. FORMATION; CERTIFICATE OF LIMITED PARTNERSHIP AND OTHER FILINGS

ULPA (2013)

[ARTICLE] 9.   ACTIONS BY PARTNERS

[ARTICLE] 10.   FOREIGN LIMITED PARTNERSHIPS

[ARTICLE] 11.   MERGER, INTEREST EXCHANGE, CONVERSION, AND DOMESTICATION

[PART] 1.   GENERAL PROVISIONS

[PART] 2.   MERGER

ULPA (2013)

* * *

PREFATORY NOTE TO 2011 AND 2013 HARMONIZATION AMENDMENTS

From 2009 to 2011, the Uniform Law Conference undertook an intensive effort to harmonize, to the extent possible, all uniform acts pertaining to unincorporated organizations. As part of that effort, the Uniform Limited Partnership Act ("ULPA") underwent four types of changes: substantive, major improvements in language, minor revisions in language for the sake of harmonization; and relocation within this particular "spoke" of provisions that are part of the "HUB" in the new Uniform Business Organizations Code ("UBOC").

Substantive Changes

The most significant substantive changes is the "un-cabining" fiduciary duty; *i.e.*, ceasing to characterize the Act's codification of fiduciary duty as exhaustive, Section 409.

Other substantive changes include: (i) providing a narrow exception to the rule that the amendments to the partnership agreement control the rights of persons previously dissociated as partners and of persons that had previously become transferees, Section 107(b)(2); (ii) eliminating the requirement that a domestic limited partnership designate and maintain an in-state office, Section 201; (iii) requiring that the annual report list the name of at least one general partner, Section 212(a)(4); and (iv) expressly authorizing a limited partnership to provide advancements to a person entitled to indemnification, Section 408(c).

Substantial Improvements to Language

The most significant improvements in language appear in Section 105 (formerly Section 110), the first of three sections addressing the partnership agreement. The structure of Section 105 is far less complicated than the structure of former Section 110.

Harmonization-Based Language Changes

Minor changes in language for the sake of harmonization appear throughout the act. For example, Section 202(b) is revised as follows:

(b)   ~~In order to~~ To amend its certificate of limited partnership, a limited partnership must deliver to the [Secretary of State] for filing an amendment ~~or, pursuant to [Article] 11, articles of merger~~ stating:

(1)   the name of the ~~limited~~ partnership;

(2)   the date of filing of its initial certificate of limited partnership; and

(3)   ~~the changes~~ the amendment ~~makes to the certificate as most recently~~ amended or restated.

Relocation and Renumbering of HUB-Based Provisions

The harmonization process included both the harmonization of various stand-alone acts and UBOC, which comprises a "HUB" (somewhat analogous to Article 1 of the Uniform Commercial Code) and various spokes. Each spoke pertains to a different type of organization (*e.g.*, limited partnership, statutory entity trust). Naturally, spokes in the Code do not repeat the provisions from the HUB. In contrast, each stand-alone act includes provisions that appear in the HUB in the Code.

So that the section numbers this "spoke" correspond with the spoke provisions in the Code, "HUB"-based provisions of this Act have been renumbered to appear at the end of articles. *See, e.g.*, Sections 112 through 122.

* * *

[ARTICLE] 1.   GENERAL PROVISIONS

§ 101.   Short Title

This [act] may be cited as the Uniform Limited Partnership Act.

COMMENT

This act is drafted to replace a state's current limited partnership statute, whether or not that statute is based on the ULPA (1916), ULPA (1976/1985), or ULPA (2001). Section 112 contains transition provisions.

§ 102.   Definitions

In this [act]:

(1)   "Certificate of limited partnership" means the certificate required by Section 201. The term includes the certificate as amended or restated.

(2)   "Contribution", except in the phrase "right of contribution", means property or a benefit described in Section 501 which is provided by a person to a limited partnership to become a partner or in the person's capacity as a partner.

(3) "Debtor in bankruptcy" means a person that is the subject of:

(A) an order for relief under Title 11 of the United States Code or a comparable order under a successor statute of general application; or

(B) a comparable order under federal, state, or foreign law governing insolvency.

(4) "Distribution" means a transfer of money or other property from a limited partnership to a person on account of a transferable interest or in the person's capacity as a partner. The term:

(A) includes:

(i) a redemption or other purchase by a limited partnership of a transferable interest; and

(ii) a transfer to a partner in return for the partner's relinquishment of any right to participate as a partner in the management or conduct of the partnership's activities and affairs or to have access to records or other information concerning the partnership's activities and affairs; and

(B) does not include amounts constituting reasonable compensation for present or past service or payments made in the ordinary course of business under a bona fide retirement plan or other bona fide benefits program.

(5) "Foreign limited liability limited partnership" means a foreign limited partnership whose general partners have limited liability for the debts, obligations, or other liabilities of the foreign partnership under a provision similar to Section 404(c).

(6) "Foreign limited partnership" means an unincorporated entity formed under the law of a jurisdiction other than this state which would be a limited partnership if formed under the law of this state. The term includes a foreign limited liability limited partnership.

(7) "General partner" means a person that:

(A) has become a general partner under Section 401 or was a general partner in a partnership when the partnership became subject to this [act] under Section 112; and

(B) has not dissociated as a general partner under Section 603.

(8) "Jurisdiction", used to refer to a political entity, means the United States, a state, a foreign country, or a political subdivision of a foreign country.

(9) "Jurisdiction of formation" means the jurisdiction whose law governs the internal affairs of an entity.

(10) "Limited liability limited partnership", except in the phrase "foreign limited liability limited partnership" and in [Article] 11, means a limited partnership whose certificate of limited partnership states that the partnership is a limited liability limited partnership.

(11) "Limited partner" means a person that:

(A) has become a limited partner under Section 301 or was a limited partner in a limited partnership when the partnership became subject to this [act] under Section 112; and

(B) has not dissociated under Section 601.

(12) "Limited partnership", except in the phrase "foreign limited partnership" and in [Article] 11, means an entity formed under this [act] or which becomes subject to this [act] under [Article] 11 or Section 112. The term includes a limited liability limited partnership.

(13) "Partner" means a limited partner or general partner.

(14) "Partnership agreement" means the agreement, whether or not referred to as a partnership agreement and whether oral, implied, in a record, or in any combination thereof, of all the partners of a limited partnership concerning the matters described in Section 105(a). The term includes the agreement as amended or restated.

(15) "Person" means an individual, business corporation, nonprofit corporation, partnership, limited partnership, limited liability company, [general cooperative association,] limited cooperative association,

unincorporated nonprofit association, statutory trust, business trust, common-law business trust, estate, trust, association, joint venture, public corporation, government or governmental subdivision, agency, or instrumentality, or any other legal or commercial entity.

(16) "Principal office" means the principal executive office of a limited partnership or foreign limited partnership, whether or not the office is located in this state.

(17) "Property" means all property, whether real, personal, or mixed or tangible or intangible, or any right or interest therein.

(18) "Record", used as a noun, means information that is inscribed on a tangible medium or that is stored in an electronic or other medium and is retrievable in perceivable form.

(19) "Registered agent" means an agent of a limited partnership or foreign limited partnership which is authorized to receive service of any process, notice, or demand required or permitted by law to be served on the partnership.

(20) "Registered foreign limited partnership" means a foreign limited partnership that is registered to do business in this state pursuant to a statement of registration filed by the [Secretary of State].

(21) "Required information" means the information that a limited partnership is required to maintain under Section 108.

(22) "Sign" means, with present intent to authenticate or adopt a record:

(A)   to execute or adopt a tangible symbol; or

(B)   to attach to or logically associate with the record an electronic symbol, sound, or process.

(23) "State" means a state of the United States, the District of Columbia, Puerto Rico, the United States Virgin Islands, or any territory or insular possession subject to the jurisdiction of the United States.

(24) "Transfer" includes:

(A)   an assignment;

(B)   a conveyance;

(C)   a sale;

(D)   a lease;

(E)   an encumbrance, including a mortgage or security interest;

(F)   a gift; and

(G)   a transfer by operation of law.

(25) "Transferable interest" means the right, as initially owned by a person in the person's capacity as a partner, to receive distributions from a limited partnership, whether or not the person remains a partner or continues to own any part of the right. The term applies to any fraction of the interest, by whomever owned.

(26) "Transferee" means a person to which all or part of a transferable interest has been transferred, whether or not the transferor is a partner. The term includes a person that owns a transferable interest under Section 602(a)(3) or 605(a)(4).

COMMENT

This section contains definitions for terms used throughout the act, while Section 1011 contains definitions specific to Article 11's provisions on mergers, conversions, interest exchanges, and domestications.

"Certificate of limited partnership" [(1)]—Until the 1985 amendments to the Revised Uniform Limited Partnership Act (1976), the certificate of limited partnership contained significant information about the limited partnership and the relationship among the partners. Consistent with the 1985 amendments and ULPA (2001), under this act the certificate: (i) merely reflects the existence of a limited partnership (rather than being the locus for important governance rules); and (ii) is significantly different from articles of incorporation, which have a

905

substantially greater power to affect *inter se* rules for the corporate entity and its owners. For the relationship between the certificate of limited partnership and the partnership agreement, see Section 107(d).

"Contribution" [(2)]—This definition serves to distinguish capital contributions from other circumstances under which a partner or would-be partner might provide benefits to a limited partnership (*e.g.*, providing services to the partnership as an employee or independent contractor, leasing property to the partnership).

This definition also distinguishes "contributions" from capital raised from transferees who invest; to be a contribution, the property or benefit must be "provided by a person . . . to become a partner or in the person's capacity as a partner." This distinction is ubiquitous in the law of unincorporated business organizations. *See, e.g.,* N.Y. LTD. LIAB. CO. LAW § 102(f) (McKinney 2013) (" 'Contribution' means any cash, property, services rendered, or a promissory note or other binding obligation to contribute cash or property or to render services that a member contributes to a limited liability company in his or her capacity as a member.").

In contrast, partnership agreements sometimes provide for contributions from transferees. In such circumstances, the default rules for liquidating distributions should be altered accordingly. *See* Section 810(b)(1) (referring to distributions to be made "to each person owning a transferable interest that reflects *contributions* made and not previously returned") (emphasis added).

"Distribution" [(4)(A)—redemptions included]—This provision specifically refers to transactions between a limited partnership and one of its partners, which in the corporate context would be labeled a "redemption." This paragraph has subparts because ownership interests in a partnership are conceptually bifurcated into economic rights ("transferable interest") and governance and information rights.

Under Section 503(a), "[a]ny distribution made by a limited partnership before its dissolution and winding up must be shared among the partners on the basis of the value, as stated in the required information when the limited partnership decides to make the distribution, of the contributions the limited partnership has received from each partner. . . ." Since a redemption is a distribution, absent authorization in the partnership agreement a limited partnership may not redeem the interest of one partner or transferee without redeeming (or at least offering to redeem) the interests of all other partners and transferees to a comparable extent.

The law of close corporations has flirted with a similar notion. *See, e.g., Donahue v. Rodd Electrotype Co. of New England, Inc.*, 367 Mass. 578, 598, 328 N.E.2d 505, 518 (1975) (stating, with regard to closely held corporations, "if the stockholder whose shares were purchased was a member of the controlling group, the controlling stockholders must cause the corporation to offer each stockholder an equal opportunity to sell a ratable number of his shares to the corporation at an identical price"); *Toner v. Baltimore Envelope Co.*, 304 Md. 256, 273, 498 A.2d 642, 650 (1985) (rejecting the "per se breach of duty" approach); *Wilkes v. Springside Nursing Home, Inc.*, 370 Mass. 842, 850, 353 N.E.2d 657, 663 (1976) (stating that "untempered application of the strict good faith standard enunciated in *Donahue* to . . . will result in the imposition of limitations on legitimate action by the controlling group in a close corporation which will unduly hamper its effectiveness in managing the corporation in the best interests of all concerned").

A partnership agreement can override Section 503(a)'s proportional treatment requirement without specifically mentioning redemptions.

    Example: A limited partnership agreement: (i) includes a list (the "protected list") of decisions or actions that may be taken only with the consent of all the general partners and 2/3 of the interests owned by the limited partners; and (ii) provides that all other decisions and acts may be taken as the general partners determine. The protected list does not include redemptions. The partnership agreement overrides Section 503(a)'s proportional treatment requirement.

[(4)(B)—exclusion]—This exclusion affects the reach of: (i) Section 505's clawback provisions; and (ii) the charging order remedy under Section 703. The effect on the clawback provision reflects the law in several states, *see, e.g.,* DEL. CODE ANN. tit. 6 § 17–607(a) (2012) and V.A. CODE § 153.210(b) (2012), and makes sense conceptually and as a matter of policy. *See In re Tri-River Trading, LLC*, 329 B.R. 252, 266 (B.A.P. 8th Cir. 2005), *aff'd.* 452 F.3d 756 (8th Cir. 2006) ("We know of no principle of law which suggests that a manager of a company is required to give up agreed upon salary to pay creditors when business turns bad.").

Affecting the charging order remedy is novel. For further explanation, see Section 703(a), comment.

"Foreign limited partnership" [(6)]—This definition intends a flexible, comparative approach. If a particular type of foreign entity has key legal characteristics that approximate the essential legal characteristics of a domestic limited partnership, that particular type of foreign entity is a foreign limited partnership under this act.

"General partner" [(7)]—A partnership agreement may vary Section 401 and provide a process or mechanism for becoming a general partner that is different from or additional to the rules stated in that section. *See* Section 401(b)(1). For the purposes of this definition, a person who becomes a general partner pursuant to a provision of the partnership agreement "become[s] a general partner under Section 401." After a person has been dissociated as a general partner, Section 603, the term "general partner" continues to apply to the person's conduct while a general partner. *See* Section 605(b).

"Jurisdiction of formation" [(9)]—This definition is not limited to United States jurisdictions.

"Limited liability limited partnership" [(10)]—Typically, a general partnership becomes a limited liability partnership when the filing office files a statement of qualification submitted by the partnership. In contrast, LLLP status results from a statement in a limited partnership's certificate of limited partnership. Section 201(b)(5) requires a limited partnership's certificate of limited partnership to state "whether the limited partnership is a limited liability limited partnership."

The definition makes an exception for Article 11, because in that article the phrase "limited liability limited partnership" encompasses both domestic and foreign LLLPs.

"Limited partner" [(11)]—This definition parallels the definition of "general partner" and the comment to Paragraph 7 applies here as well.

"Limited partnership" [(12)]—This definition makes no reference to a limited partnership having partners upon formation, but Section 201(d) does.

"Partnership agreement" [(14)]—This definition must be read in conjunction with Sections 105 through 107, which further describe the partnership agreement. In particular, although this definition refers to "the agreement . . . of all the partners," the limited partnership itself is bound by and may enforce the agreement. Section 106(a).

A partnership agreement is a contract, and therefore all statutory language pertaining to the partnership agreement must be understood in the context of the law of contracts.

The definition in Paragraph 14 is very broad and recognizes a wide scope of authority for the partnership agreement: "the matters described in Section 105(a)." Those matters include not only all relations *inter se* the partners and the partnership but also "the activities and affairs of the partnership and the conduct of those activities and affairs." Section 105(a)(2). Moreover, the definition puts no limits on the form of the partnership agreement. To the contrary, the definition contains the phrase "whether oral, implied, in a record, or in any combination thereof."

Unless the partnership agreement itself provides otherwise:

- a partnership agreement may comprise a number of separate documents (or records), however denominated; and

- subject to Section 106(b) (deeming new partners to assent to the then-existing partnership agreement), a document, record, understanding, etc. can be part of the partnership agreement only with the assent of all persons then partners.

An agreement among less than all partners might well be enforceable among those partners as parties, but would not be part of the partnership agreement. However, under Section 105(a)(3), an amendment to a partnership agreement can be made with less than unanimous consent if the partnership agreement itself so provides.

An agreement to form a limited partnership is not itself a partnership agreement. The term "partnership agreement" presupposes "partners," and a person cannot be a partner in a partnership before the partnership exists. However, as soon as a limited partnership comes into existence, it perforce has a partnership agreement. For example, suppose: (i) two persons, Gamma and Lambda, orally and informally agree to join their activities through a limited partnership, in which Gamma will be the general partner and Lambda the limited partner; (ii) an appropriate certification of limited partnership is delivered to the filing office, which files the certificate; (iii) Gamma and Lambda become respectively the general and limited partner; and (iv) the limited partnership is thus formed under Section 201(d). A partnership agreement exists. In the words of Paragraph 14 "all the partners" have agreed who the partners are, that, as "all the partners" they will conduct a business, and that Gamma will be the managing partner and Lambda will be more or less passive. That agreement—no matter how informal or rudimentary—is an agreement "concerning the matters described in Section 105(a)." To the extent the agreement does not provide the *inter se* "rules of the game," the "default rules" of this act "fill in the gaps." Section 105(b).

This act states no rule as to whether the statute of frauds applies to partnership agreements. Case law suggests that the answer is yes:

> Partnership agreements, like other contracts, are subject to the Statute of Frauds. A contract of partnership for a term exceeding one year is within the Statute of Frauds and is void unless it is in writing [and signed by the party to be bound]; however, a contract establishing a partnership terminable at the will of any partner is generally held to be capable of performance by its terms within one year of its making and, therefore, to be outside the Statute of Frauds.

Abbott v. Hurst, 643 So.2d 589, 592 (Ala. 1994) (citations omitted). *See also Chase Pratt, LLC v. Aetna Life Ins. Co.*, CV 960560740S, 1999 WL 229214 at *4 (Conn. Super. Ct. Mar. 26, 1999) (recognizing that the one-year provision applies to limited partnership agreements but holding the provision inapplicable to a stated "99-year term," because the agreement permitted dissolution at any time "earlier by mutual consent of the Partners") (quoting the partnership agreement).

Likewise, the land provision of the statute of frauds:

> applies to an oral contract to transfer or convey partnership real property, and the interest of the other partners therein, to one partner as an individual, as well as to a parol contract by one of the parties to convey certain land owned by him individually to the partnership, or to another partner, or to put it into the partnership stock.

Froiseth v. Nowlin, 156 Wash. 314, 316, 287 P. 55, 56 (Wash. 1930) (quoting 27 C.J.S. § 220). *See also E. Piedmont 120 Associates, L.P. v. Sheppard*, 209 Ga. App. 664, 665, 434 S.E.2d 101, 102 (Ga. Ct. App. 1993) (same, stating that "the fact that promises covered by the Statute of Frauds are made in the context of a partnership or joint venture agreement does not render the statute inapplicable"); *Filippi v. Filippi*, 818 A.2d 608, 618 (R.I. 2003) (applying the statute of frauds to an alleged oral agreement to transfer land owned by a limited partnership to one of its partners).

In contrast, the land provision does not apply to a partner's interest in a partnership, no matter how much the partnership owns or deals in real property. Interests in a partnership are personal property and reflect no direct interest in the entity's assets. See Sections 102(24) and 701. Thus, the real property issues pertaining to a partnership ownership of land do not "flow through" to the partners and partnership interests. *See, e.g., Wooten v. Marshall*, 153 F. Supp. 759, 763–764 (S.D.N.Y. 1957) (involving an "oral agreement for a joint venture concerning the purchase, exploitation and eventual disposition of this 160 acre tract" and stating "[t]he real property acquired and dealt with by the venturers takes on the character of personal property as between the partners in the enterprise, and hence is not covered by [the Statute of Frauds]"). *See also Wade v. DeHart*, 26 Ohio N.P. 560 (Ohio Com. Pl. 1926), *aff'd sub nom., Wade v. De Hart*, 26 Ohio App. 177, 159 N.E. 838 (Ohio Ct. App. 1927) (same).

On the question of how far a written (or "in a record") partnership agreement can go to prevent oral or implied-in-fact terms, see Section 105(a)(3), comment. For the effect of a pre-formation agreement, see Section 106(c).

"Property" [(17)]—This definition encompasses every form of property.

"Transfer" [(24)]—The term "transfer" is broadly defined to include all types of conveyances of interests in property. The reference to "transfer by operation of law" is significant in connection with Section 702 (Transfer of Transferable Interest). That section severely restricts a transferee's rights (absent the consent of the partners), and this definition makes those restrictions applicable, for example, to transfers ordered by a family court as part of a divorce proceeding and transfers resulting from the death of a partner. The restrictions also apply to transfers in the context of a partner's bankruptcy, except to the extent that bankruptcy law supersedes this act.

"Transferable interest" [(25)]—Absent a contrary provision in the partnership agreement or the consent of the partners, a "transferable interest" is the only interest in a limited partnership which can be transferred. *See* Section 702.

This act defines "[t]ransferable interest" as an interest "initially owned by a person in the person's capacity as a partner," because this act does not contemplate a limited partnership directly creating interests that comprise only economic rights. *See* Sections 301 and 401 (addressing how a person becomes a limited and general partner) and 702 (addressing how a person becomes a transferee).

"Transferee" [(26)]—This definition should be read in light of Sections 602(a)(3) and 605(a)(4), which subject to limited exceptions provide that "any transferable interest owned by [a general or limited partner] in the person's capacity as a [general or limited] partner immediately before dissociation is owned by the person solely as a transferee."

§ 103.   Knowledge; Notice

(a)   A person knows a fact if the person:

(1)   has actual knowledge of it; or

(2)   is deemed to know it under law other than this [act].

(b)   A person has notice of a fact if the person:

(1)   has reason to know the fact from all the facts known to the person at the time in question; or

(2)   is deemed to have notice of the fact under subsection (c) or (d).

(c)   A certificate of limited partnership on file in the office of the [Secretary of State] is notice that the partnership is a limited partnership and the persons designated in the certificate as general partners are general partners. Except as otherwise provided in subsection (d), the certificate is not notice of any other fact.

(d)   A person not a partner is deemed to have notice of:

(1)   a person's dissociation as a general partner 90 days after an amendment to the certificate of limited partnership which states that the other person has dissociated becomes effective or 90 days after a statement of dissociation pertaining to the other person becomes effective, whichever occurs first;

(2)   a limited partnership's:

(A)   dissolution 90 days after an amendment to the certificate of limited partnership stating that the limited partnership is dissolved becomes effective;

(B)   termination 90 days after a statement of termination under Section 802(b)(2)(F) becomes effective; and

(C)   participation in a merger, interest exchange, conversion, or domestication, 90 days after articles of merger, interest exchange, conversion, or domestication under [Article] 11 become effective.

(e)   Subject to Section 210(f), a person notifies another person of a fact by taking steps reasonably required to inform the other person in ordinary course, whether or not those steps cause the other person to know the fact.

(f)   A general partner's knowledge or notice of a fact relating to the limited partnership is effective immediately as knowledge of or notice to the partnership, except in the case of a fraud on the partnership committed by or with the consent of the general partner. A limited partner's knowledge or notice of a fact relating to the partnership is not effective as knowledge of or notice to the partnership.

COMMENT

Three aspects of this section warrant particular note. First, this section is substantially slimmer than the corresponding provisions of previous uniform acts pertaining to business organizations: UPA (1997), ULLCA (1996), and ULPA (2001). Each of those acts borrowed heavily from the comparable provision of the Uniform Commercial Code. This act relies instead on generally applicable principles of agency law, see Section 113, although Subsection (f) does provide a rule for attributing to a partnership knowledge or notice possessed by a general partner.

Second, the section contains no generally applicable provisions determining when an organization is charged with knowledge or notice, because those imputation rules: (i) comprise core topics within the law of agency; (ii) are very complicated; (iii) should not have any different content under this act than in other circumstances; and (iv) are the subject of considerable attention in the RESTATEMENT (THIRD) OF AGENCY (2006).

Third, this act does not define "notice" to include "knowledge." Although conceptualizing the latter as giving the former makes logical sense and has a long pedigree, that conceptualization is counter-intuitive for the uninitiated. In ordinary usage, notice has a meaning separate from knowledge. This act follows ordinary usage and therefore contains some references to "knowledge or notice."

Subsection (a)(2)—In this context, the most important source of "law other than this [act]" is the common law of agency.

Subsection (b)(1)—The "facts known to the person at the time in question" include facts the person is deemed to know under Subsection (a)(2).

Subsection (c)—As for the significance of constructive notice "that the partnership is a limited partnership," see *Water, Waste & Land, Inc. v. Lanham*, 955 P.2d 997, 1001 1003 (Colo. 1998) (interpreting a comparable provision of the Colorado LLC statute and holding the provision ineffective to change common law agency principles, including the rules relating to the liability of an agent that transacts business for an undisclosed principal).

As for constructive notice that "the persons designated in the certificate as general partners are general partners," Section 201(b)(4) requires the initial certificate of limited partnership to name each general partner, and Section 202(d) requires a limited partnership to promptly amend its certificate of limited partnership to reflect any change in the identity of its general partners. Nonetheless, it will be possible, albeit improper, for a person to be designated in the certificate of limited partnership as a general partner without having become a general partner as contemplated by Section 401. Likewise, it will be possible for a person to have become a general partner under Section 401 without being designated as a general partner in the certificate of limited partnership. According to the last clause of this subsection, the fact that a person is not listed in the certificate as a general partner is not notice that the person is not a general partner. For further discussion of this point, see Section 401, comment.

If the partnership agreement and the public record are inconsistent, the partnership agreement prevails as to *inter se* matters and the record prevails as to third parties who have reasonably relied on it. Section 107(d). *See also* Sections 202(d) (requiring the limited partnership to amend its certificate of limited partnership to keep accurate the listing of general partners), 202(e) (requiring a general partner to take corrective action when the general partner knows that the certificate of limited partnership contains false information), and 205 (imposing liability for false information in, *inter alia*, the certificate of limited partnership).

Subsection (d)—This subsection provides constructive notice of facts stated in specified filed public records. The subsection works in conjunction with other sections of this act to curtail the power to bind and personal liability of general partners and persons dissociated as general partners. *See* Sections 402, 606, 607, 804, and 805. The constructive notice begins ninety days after the effective date of the filed record. For the act's rules on delayed effective dates, see Section 207.

The 90-day delay applies only to the constructive notice and not to the event described in the filed record.

Example: On March 15, X dissociates as a general partner from XYZ Limited Partnership by giving notice to XYZ. *See* Section 603(1). On March 20, XYZ amends its certificate of limited partnership to remove X's name from the list of general partners. *See* Section 202(d)(2).

X's dissociation is effective March 15. If on March 16 X purports to be a general partner of XYZ and under Section 606(a) binds XYZ to some obligation, X will be liable under Section 606(b) as a "person dissociated as a general partner."

On June 19 (90 days after March 20), the world has constructive notice of X's dissociation as a general partner. Beginning on that date, X will lack the power to bind XYZ. *See* Section 606(a)(2)(B) (providing that a person dissociated as a general partner can bind the limited partnership only if, *inter alia*, "at the time the other party enters into the transaction . . . the other party does not know or have notice of the dissociation").

Constructive notice under this subsection applies to partners and transferees as well as other persons.

Subsection (e)—If a person "notifies" another person of a fact, the other person has "reason to know" the fact and therefore has notice under Subsection (b)(1). However, a person can have "notice" of a fact without having been "notifie[d]" of the fact.

Section 210(f) pertains to delivery of records *by* the filing office.

Subsection (f)—This subsection states the rule for imputing a partner's knowledge or notice to the partnership. Under this subsection and Section 302, information possessed by a person that is only a limited partner is not attributable to the limited partnership. However, information possessed by a person that is both a general partner and a limited partner is attributable to the limited partnership. *See* Section 109 (Dual Capacity). For a discussion of agency law principles analogous to "fraud on the partnership," see RESTATEMENT (THIRD) OF AGENCY § 5.04 cmt. b (2006).

§ 104. Governing Law

The law of this state governs:

(1) the internal affairs of a limited partnership; and

(2) the liability of a partner as partner for a debt, obligation, or other liability of a limited partnership.

COMMENT

Paragraph (1)—Like any other legal concept, "internal affairs" may be indeterminate at its edges. However, the concept certainly includes interpretation and enforcement of the partnership agreement, relations among the partners as partners, and relations between the limited partnership and its partners. *Compare* Section 104, *with* RESTATEMENT (SECOND) OF CONFLICT OF LAWS § 302 cmt. a (1971) (defining "internal affairs" with reference to a corporation as "the relations inter se of the corporation, its shareholders, directors, officers or agents").

"Internal affairs" do not encompass the power *vel non* of a person to bind a limited partnership. RESTATEMENT (SECOND) OF CONFLICT OF LAWS § 292(2) (1971) ("The principal will be held bound by the agent's action if he would so be bound under the local law of the state where the agent dealt with the third person, provided at least that the principal had authorized the agent to act on his behalf in that state or had led the third person reasonably to believe that the agent had such authority."); *Id.* § 295(1) ("Whether a partnership is bound by action taken on its behalf by an agent in dealing with a third person is determined by the local law of the state selected by application of the rule of § 292."); RESTATEMENT (FIRST) OF CONFLICT OF LAWS § 345 cmt. c (1934) (Law Governing Effect of Act of Agent or Partner) ("If . . . the principal or partner sends the agent or other partner into a state to act on his behalf, he assumes the risk of liability not only for authorized but for unauthorized conduct of the agent or partner in accordance with the law of that state."). *See also Farm & Ranch Services, Ltd. v. LT Farm & Ranch, LLC*, 779 F. Supp.2d 949, 960 (S.D. Iowa 2011).

The partnership agreement cannot alter this Section. *See* Section 105(c)(1). However, partnership agreement may lawfully incorporate by reference the provisions of another state's limited partnership statute. If done correctly, this incorporation makes the foreign statutory language part of the partnership agreement, and the incorporated terms (together with the rest of the partnership agreement) then govern the partners (and those claiming through the partners) to the extent not prohibited by this act. *See* Section 105. This approach: (i) does not switch the limited partnership's governing law to that of another state; (ii) instead takes the provisions of another state's law and incorporates them by reference into the contract among the partners; (iii) raises complex drafting issues—*e.g.*, how to address subsequent changes to the incorporated law (whether occurring by statutory amendment or court decision); and (iv) thus is rarely, if ever, a good idea.

Paragraph (2)—This paragraph obviously encompasses Sections 303 (the liability shield for limited partners) and 404(c) (the shield for general partners in a limited liability limited partnership), but does not necessarily encompass a claim that a partner is liable to a third party for: (i) having purported to bind a limited partnership to the third party; or (ii) having committed a tort against the third party while acting on a limited partnership's behalf or in the course of the partnership's business. That liability is not by status (*i.e.*, not partner as a partner) but rather results from function or conduct. *Cf.* § 302(b) (stating that, although this act does not make a limited partner as limited partner the agent of a limited partnership, other law may make a limited partnership liable for the conduct of a limited partner).

"Internal affairs" and the "liability of a partner as a partner" are mentioned separately because it can be argued that the liability of partners to third parties is not an internal affair. *See, e.g.*, RESTATEMENT (SECOND) OF CONFLICT OF LAWS, § 307 (1971) (treating shareholders' liability separately from the internal affairs doctrine). A few cases subsume owner/manager liability into internal affairs, but many do not. *See, e.g., Kalb, Voorhis & Co. v. American Fin. Corp.*, 8 F.3d 130, 132 (2nd Cir. 1993) (holding that the corporation's "primary purpose is to insulate shareholders from legal liability" and therefore "the state of incorporation has the greater interest in determining when and if that insulation is to be stripped away") (quoting *Soviet Pan Am Travel Effort v. Travel Comm., Inc.*, 756 F.Supp. 126, 131 (S.D.N.Y. 1991) (internal quotation marks omitted).

In any event, most (if not all) limited partnership statutes follow the rule stated in this paragraph. *See* RULPA (1976/1985) § 901 (stating that "the laws of the state under which a foreign limited partnership is organized govern its organization and internal affairs and the liability of its limited partners"); ULPA (2001) § 901 (same, but as to all partners).

Moreover, "[t]he general rule [from the case law] is that a plaintiff's alter ego theory is governed by the law of the state in which the business at issue is organized." *Rual Trade Ltd. v. Viva Trade LLC*, 549 F. Supp. 2d 1067, 1077 (E.D. Wis. 2008). *See also, e.g., In re Gulf Fleet Holdings, Inc.*, 491 B.R. 747, 787 (Bankr. W.D. La. 2013) (stating both conceptual and policy rationales for choosing the law of the state of formation); *In re Saba Enters.*, 421 B.R. 626, 648–51 (Bankr. S.D.N.Y. 2009) (examining the issue in detail and applying the state of formation rule).

§ 105.   Partnership Agreement; Scope, Function, and Limitations

(a)   Except as otherwise provided in subsections (c) and (d), the partnership agreement governs:

(1)   relations among the partners as partners and between the partners and the limited partnership;

(2)   the activities and affairs of the partnership and the conduct of those activities and affairs; and

(3)   the means and conditions for amending the partnership agreement.

(b)   To the extent the partnership agreement does not provide for a matter described in subsection (a), this [act] governs the matter.

(c)   A partnership agreement may not:

(1)   vary the law applicable under Section 104;

(2)   vary a limited partnership's capacity under Section 111 to sue and be sued in its own name;

(3)   vary any requirement, procedure, or other provision of this [act] pertaining to:

(A)   registered agents; or

(B)   the [Secretary of State], including provisions pertaining to records authorized or required to be delivered to the [Secretary of State] for filing under this [act];

(4)   vary the provisions of Section 204;

(5)   vary the right of a general partner under Section 406(b)(2) to vote on or consent to an amendment to the certificate of limited partnership which deletes a statement that the limited partnership is a limited liability limited partnership;

(6)   alter or eliminate the duty of loyalty or the duty of care except as otherwise provided in subsection (d);

(7)   eliminate the contractual obligation of good faith and fair dealing under Sections 305(a) and 409(d), but the partnership agreement may prescribe the standards, if not manifestly unreasonable, by which the performance of the obligation is to be measured;

(8)   relieve or exonerate a person from liability for conduct involving bad faith, willful or intentional misconduct, or knowing violation of law;

(9)   vary the information required under Section 108 or unreasonably restrict the duties and rights under Section 304 or 407, but the partnership agreement may impose reasonable restrictions on the availability and use of information obtained under those sections and may define appropriate remedies, including liquidated damages, for a breach of any reasonable restriction on use;

(10)   vary the grounds for expulsion specified in Section 603(5)(B);

(11)   vary the power of a person to dissociate as a general partner under Section 604(a), except to require that the notice under Section 603(1) be in a record;

(12)   vary the causes of dissolution specified in Section 801(a)(6);

(13)   vary the requirement to wind up the partnership's activities and affairs as specified in Section 802(a), (b)(1), and (d);

(14)   unreasonably restrict the right of a partner to maintain an action under [Article] 9;

(15) vary the provisions of Section 905, but the partnership agreement may provide that the partnership may not have a special litigation committee;

(16) vary the right of a partner to approve a merger, interest exchange, conversion, or domestication under Section 1123(a)(2), 1133(a)(2), 1143(a)(2), or 1153(a)(2);

(17) vary the required contents of a plan of merger under Section 1122(a), plan of interest exchange under Section 1132(a), plan of conversion under Section 1142(a), or plan of domestication under Section 1152(a); or

(18) except as otherwise provided in Sections 106 and 107(b), restrict the rights under this [act] of a person other than a partner.

(d) Subject to subsection (c)(8), without limiting other terms that may be included in a partnership agreement, the following rules apply:

(1) The partnership agreement may:

(A) specify the method by which a specific act or transaction that would otherwise violate the duty of loyalty may be authorized or ratified by one or more disinterested and independent persons after full disclosure of all material facts; and

(B) alter the prohibition in Section 504(a)(2) so that the prohibition requires only that the partnership's total assets not be less than the sum of its total liabilities.

(2) If not manifestly unreasonable, the partnership agreement may:

(A) alter or eliminate the aspects of the duty of loyalty stated in Section 409(b);

(B) identify specific types or categories of activities that do not violate the duty of loyalty;

(C) alter the duty of care, but may not authorize conduct involving bad faith, willful or intentional misconduct, or knowing violation of law; and

(D) alter or eliminate any other fiduciary duty.

(e) The court shall decide as a matter of law whether a term of a partnership agreement is manifestly unreasonable under subsection (c)(7) or (d)(2). The court:

(1) shall make its determination as of the time the challenged term became part of the partnership agreement and by considering only circumstances existing at that time; and

(2) may invalidate the term only if, in light of the purposes, activities, and affairs of the limited partnership, it is readily apparent that:

(A) the objective of the term is unreasonable; or

(B) the term is an unreasonable means to achieve its objective.

COMMENT

The Harmonization Project rewrote this section to conform, for the most part, to the corresponding section of ULLCA (2006) (Last Amended).

Principal Provisions of the Act Concerning the Partnership Agreement

The partnership agreement is pivotal to a limited partnership, and Sections 105 through 107 are pivotal to this act. They must be read together, along with Section 102(14) (defining the partnership agreement).

This Section performs five essential functions. Subsection (a) establishes the primacy of the partnership agreement in establishing relations *inter se* the limited partnership and its partners. Subsection (b) recognizes this act as comprising mostly default rules—*i.e.*, gap fillers for issues as to which the partnership agreement provides no rule. Subsection (c) lists the few mandatory provisions of the act. Subsection (d) lists some provisions frequently found in partnership agreements, authorizing some provisions unconditionally and other provisions so long as "not manifestly unreasonable." Subsection (e) delineates in detail both the meaning of "not manifestly unreasonable" and the information relevant to a determining a claim that a provision of a partnership agreement is manifestly unreasonable.

Section 106 details the effect of a partnership agreement on the limited partnership and on persons becoming partners. Section 107 concerns the effect of a partnership agreement on third parties.

Role and Inevitability of Partnership Agreement

"A limited partnership is a creature of both statute and contract." *Cantor Fitzgerald, L.P. Cantor*, CIV.A. 18101, 2001 WL 1456494 at *5 (Del. Ch. Nov. 5, 2001); *Gottsacker v. Monnier*, 281 Wis. 2d 361, 370, 697 N.W.2d 436, 440 (2005) (stating that "from the partnership form, the LLC borrows . . . internal governance by contract"), and Section 102(14) delineates a very broad scope for "partnership agreement." As a result, once a limited partnership comes into existence and has at least one general partner and one limited partner, a partnership agreement necessarily exists. See Section 102(14), cmt. Accordingly, this act refers to "the partnership agreement" rather than "a partnership agreement." This phrasing should not, however, be read to require a limited partnership or its partners to take any formal action to adopt a partnership agreement.

Subject only to Subsections (c) and (d), the partnership agreement has plenary power to structure and regulate the relations of the partners *inter se*. Although the certificate of limited partnership is a limited partnership's foundational document, among the partners the partnership agreement controls.

The partnership agreement is the exclusive consensual process for modifying this act's various default rules pertaining to relationships *inter se* the partners and between the partners and the limited partnership. Section 105(b). The partnership agreement also has power over "[t]he obligations of a limited partnership and its partners to a person in the person's capacity as a transferee or a person dissociated as a partner." Section 107(b). For the relationship between the partnership agreement and certificate of limited partnership, see Section 107(d).

The Partnership Agreement and the Fiduciary and Other Duties of the General Partner

One of the most complex questions in the law of unincorporated business organizations is the extent to which an agreement among the organization's owners can affect the fiduciary and other duties of those who manage the organization—in the case of a limited partnership, the general partner (or partners). As explained in detail in the comment to Subsection (d)(3), this act rejects the notion that a contract can completely transform an inherently fiduciary relationship into a merely arm's length association. Within that limitation, however, this section provides substantial power to the partnership agreement to reshape, limit, and eliminate fiduciary and other managerial duties.

Subsection (a) recognizes that the partnership agreement is the map to the parties' deal and that any claim by a partner of managerial misconduct must be assessed first under the relevant terms of the partnership agreement. Subsection (d) specifically validates arrangements commonly used to reshape managerial duties and limit the consequences of breaching those duties. Subsection (c) contains relevant limitations, but those limitations: (i) must be read together with Subsection (d); and (ii) do not preclude the partnership agreement fundamentally redesigning the duties applicable to the general partners. For the act's design of those duties, see Sections 304, 407, and 409.

Subsection (a)—This subsection describes the very broad scope of a limited partnership's partnership agreement, which includes all matters constituting "internal affairs." Compare Section 105(a), with Section 104(1) (using the phrase "internal affairs" in stating a choice of law rule). This broad grant of authority is subject to the restrictions stated in Subsection (c), including the broad restriction stated in Paragraph (c)(18) (concerning the rights of third parties under this act).

Subsection (a)(1)—This paragraph encompasses all the rights and duties of each partner, including rights and duties pertaining to transactions under Article 11.

Subsection (a)(3)—Under this provision, the partnership agreement can control both the quantum of consent required (*e.g.*, majority of partners) and the means by which the consent is manifested (*e.g.*, prohibiting modifications except when consented to in writing). *See also* Section 107(a), cmt.

If the partnership agreement does not address the issue, this act provides the rule. Section 407(b)(4)(C) (requiring the affirmative vote or consent of all the partners) and 407(c)(3)(C) (same). Under Section 111 (supplemental principles of law), the parol evidence rule will apply to a written partnership agreement when appropriate under contract law.

Subsection (b)—To the extent the partnership agreement does not determine an inter se matter, this act determines the matter. The partnership agreement may vary any provision of this act pertaining to *inter se* matters, except as provided in Subsections (c) and (d).

Sometimes—but not always—the Comments to this act refer to a variable provision as a "default rule" and a non-waivable provision as "mandatory." These references are merely to draw attention to the default/mandatory distinction in particular contexts and have neither the intent nor the power to affect the default/mandatory status of provisions of this act whose comments lack a comparable reference.

Subsection (c)—This subsection lists provisions of this act whose respective effects cannot be varied or may be varied subject to a stated limitation. For historical reasons, this subsection uses the words "vary" and "alter" interchangeably. No difference in meaning is intended.

If a person claims that a term of the partnership agreement violates this subsection, as a matter of ordinary procedural law the burden of proof is on the person making the claim.

Subsection (c)(1)—Section 104 states that this act provides the law applicable to: (i) the internal affairs of a limited partnership formed under this act; and (ii) the liability of partners for obligations of the limited partnership. The organizers of a limited partnership make this choice of law by choosing to form a limited partnership under this act. Domestication to another jurisdiction will re-set the choice of law, *see* Sections 1151–56, but the partnership agreement cannot. The partnership agreement may incorporate wholesale and by reference the provisions of another jurisdiction's limited partnership statute, but that approach raises complex drafting issues—*e.g.*, how to address future revisions to that statute—and in any event is subject to the strictures of Section 105(c) and (d). *See also* Section 104(1), cmt.

Subsection (c) contains no parallel prohibition on varying Section 1001 (stating the governing law for foreign limited partnerships), because a prohibition is unnecessary. As a matter of fundamental contract law, an agreement among partners of one limited partnership is powerless to govern the affairs of another limited partnership.

Subsection (c)(2)—Under this act, a limited partnership is emphatically an entity, and the partners lack the power to alter that characteristic.

Subsection (c)(3)—This prohibition is arguably implicit in Subsection (c)(18) (affecting rights of third parties under this act) but is stated expressly to avoid any doubt.

Subsection (c)(4)—This provision means that the partnership agreement cannot affect the right of an "aggrieved" person to seek the court's help when "a person required by this [act] to sign a record or deliver a record to the filing office for filing under this [act] does not do so." Section 204(a).

Subsection (c)(5)—Because deleting the specified statement exposes each general partner to unlimited liability for each debt, liability, or other obligation of the limited partnership accrued after the deletion: (i) Section 406(b)(2) gives each general partner veto power; and (ii) this subsection makes that power non-waivable.

Subsection (c)(6)—This limitation is less powerful than might first appear, because Subsection (d) specifically authorizes substantial alterations to the duties of loyalty and care, including restricting and substantially eliminating those duties.

Subsection (c)(7)—Sections 305(a) and 409(d) refer to the "contractual obligation of good faith and fair dealing," which contract law implies in every contract. The partnership agreement cannot eliminate this obligation, neither in whole (*i.e.*, generally) nor in part (*i.e.*, as applicable to specified situations).

However, a partnership agreement may "prescribe the standards . . . by which the performance of the obligation is to be measured."

Example: The partnership agreement of a limited partnership gives the general partner the discretion to cause the limited partnership to enter into contracts with affiliates of the general partner (so-called "Conflict Transactions"). The agreement further provides: "When causing the Limited Partnership to enter into a Conflict Transaction, the general partner complies with Section 409(d) of [this act] if a disinterested person, knowledgeable in the subject matter, states in writing that the terms and conditions of the Transaction are equivalent to the terms and conditions that would be agreed to by persons at arm's length in comparable circumstances." This provision "prescribe[s] the standards by which the performance of the [Section 409(d)] obligation is to be measured."

Example: Same facts as the previous example, except that, during the performance of a Conflict Transaction, the general partner causes the limited partnership to waive material protections under the applicable contract. The standard stated in the previous example is inapposite to this conduct. Section 409(d) therefore applies to the conduct without any direct contractual delineation. (However, other terms of the agreement may be relevant to determining whether the conduct violates Section 409(d). See Section 409(d), cmt.)

Example: The partnership agreement of a limited partnership gives the general partner "sole discretion" to make various decisions. The agreement further provides: "Whenever this agreement requires or permits a general partner to make a decision that has the potential to benefit one class of partners to the detriment of another class, the general partner complies with Section 409(d) of [this act] if the general partner makes the decision with:

    a.   the honest belief that the decision:

        i.   serves the best interests of the Limited Partnership; or

        ii.   at least does not injure or otherwise disserve those interests; and

    b.   the reasonable belief that the decision breaches no partner's rights under this agreement."

This provision "prescribe[s] the standards by which the performance of the [Section 409(d)] obligation is to be measured." Compare Section 105(c)(7), with *Nemec v. Shrader*, 991 A.2d 1120 (Del. 2010) (considering such a situation in the context of the right to call preferred stock and deciding by a 3–2 vote that exercising the call did not breach the implied covenant of good faith and fair dealing).

A partnership agreement that seeks to prescribe standards for measuring the contractual obligation of good faith and fair dealing under Section 409(d) should expressly refer to the obligation. *See Gerber v. Enter. Prods. Hldgs., LLC*, 67 A.3d 400, 418 (Del. 2013) (distinguishing between the implied contractual covenant and an express contractual obligation of "good faith" as stated in a limited partnership agreement).

For an explanation of the function and role of the covenant of good faith and fair dealing, see Section 409(d), comment. For the rules delimiting the "not manifestly unreasonable" requirement, see Subsection (e).

Subsection (c)(8)—These restrictions are ubiquitous in the law of business entities and, in conjunction with other provisions of this section, control the otherwise very broad power of a partnership agreement to affect fiduciary and other duties. The restrictions are central to the raft of exculpatory provisions that sprung up in corporate statutes in response to *Smith v. Van Gorkum*, 488 A.2d 858 (Del. 1985). Delaware led the response with DEL. CODE ANN. tit. 8, § 102(b)(7), and a number of LLC statutes have similar provisions. *E.g.* GA. CODE ANN. § 14–11–305(4)(A) (2011). For an extreme example, see VA. CODE ANN. § 13.1–1025(B) (2012). In this context, "conduct" includes both acts and omissions. BLACK'S LAW DICTIONARY (9th ed. 2009) (defining conduct as "[p]ersonal behavior, whether by action or inaction").

The term "bad faith" has multiple meanings, and the context determines which meaning applies. In the context of the duty of loyalty, "bad faith" includes conduct motivated by ill will or other intent purposely to harm another person. The concept also includes conduct from which a person derives an improper personal benefit. *See, e.g., Mroz v. Hoaloha Na Eha, Inc.*, 410 F. Supp. 2d 919, 936–37 (D. Haw. 2005) (denying a motion to dismiss a claim that "the Majority Partners" were personally liable for the partnership's wrongful termination of the plaintiff; quoting the complaint as alleging that "the Majority Partners, individually and as a group, acted with malice and/or ill will, and or with an intent to serve their own personal interests and/or without an intent to serve company interests, and/or outside of the scope of their authority and/or without justification"); *BOGNC, LLC v. Cornelius NC Self-Storage LLC*, 10 CVS 19072, 2013 WL 1867065 at *9 (N.C. Super. [Business Court] May 1, 2013) (noting that "no . . . [exculpatory] provision may limit a manager's liability for acts known to be in conflict with the interests of the limited liability company, or for acts from which the manager derived an improper personal benefit") (citing N.C. GEN. STAT. § 57C–3–32(b)); *Lasica v. Savers Grp. of Minnesota, LLC*, A12-0092, 2012 WL 3553246 at *2 (Minn. Ct. App. Aug. 20, 2012) (noting that an "individual seeking indemnification [under statute providing for indemnification] must have acted in good faith and must not have received an improper personal benefit") (citing MINN. STAT. § 322B.69, subds. 2(a)(2), (3) (2010)).

In the context of the duty of care, the concept of bad faith comes primarily from corporate law and means an extreme breach of the duty—*i.e.*, "the failure to exercise "*honest judgment* in the lawful and legitimate furtherance of corporate purposes." *Deblinger v. Sani-Pine Products Co., Inc.*, 107 A.D.3d 659, 661, 967 N.Y.S.2d 394 (2013) (quoting *Auerbach v. Bennett*, 47 N.Y.2d 619, 629, 393 N.E.2d 994 (1979) (emphasis added) (internal quotation marks omitted).

Thus, when a plaintiff alleges bad faith as pertaining to the duty of care, "[t]he burden . . . is to show irrationality: a plaintiff must demonstrate that no reasonable business person could possibly authorize the action in good faith. Put positively, the decision must go so far beyond the bounds of reasonable business judgment that its only explanation is bad faith." *In re Tower Air, Inc.*, 416 F.3d 229, 238 (3d Cir. 2005) (discussing then prevailing

Delaware law) (citation omitted). *See also KDW Restructuring & Liquidation Servs. LLC v. Greenfield*, 874 F. Supp. 2d 213, 226 (S.D.N.Y. 2012) (referring to a lack of "a rationale corporate purpose" and "a disregard for the duty to examine all available information—*information that was readily at hand*") (emphasis added).

With regard to both the duty of loyalty and the duty of care, "bad faith" is entirely distinct from the meaning of "good faith" in the contractual covenant of good faith and fair dealing. *See* Section 409(d), cmt.

Subsection (c)(8) pertains to indirect as well as direct efforts to "relieve or exonerate" and thus limits how far a partnership agreement can go in providing for indemnification. *See* Section 408(b) (stating a default rule for indemnification).

Although this paragraph does not expressly address contracts between a limited partnership and a general partner, the stated constraints must also apply to such contracts. If not, those constraints are effectively meaningless.

Example: A limited partnership enters into a management contract with its general partner, and the contract provides the general partner exoneration for liability to the limited partnership even for willful and intentional misconduct. Most likely, contract law will treat the provision as against public policy and therefore unenforceable. RESTATEMENT (SECOND) OF CONTRACTS § 195(1) (1981) ("A term exempting a party from tort liability for harm caused intentionally or recklessly is unenforceable on grounds of public policy."). If not, a court should hold the provision unenforceable to avoid evisceration of Subsection (c)(8). (Or, the court could invoke the policy expressed in Subsection (c)(8) as grounds for holding the provision unenforceable under contract law.)

Subsection (c)(9)—Although phrased as a restriction, this provision grants substantial power to the partnership agreement.

Example: The partnership agreement of a limited partnership states "No limited partner may have access to information constituting a trade secret of the Partnership." This restriction is reasonable.

The information required under Section 108 is skeletal, and the partnership agreement can impose reasonable limitations on access to and use of other information.

The act also empowers the limited partnership "as a matter within the ordinary course of its activities and affairs [to] impose reasonable restrictions and conditions on access to and use of information" obtained under Section 304 or 407. *See* Sections 304(j) and 407(j), cmts.

In determining whether a restriction is reasonable, a court might consider: (i) the danger or other problem the restriction seeks to avoid; (ii) the purpose for which the information is sought; and (iii) whether, in light of both the problem and the purpose, the restriction is reasonably tailored. Under this act, general and limited partners have sharply different roles. A restriction that is reasonable as to a limited partner is not necessarily reasonable as to a general partner. Restricting a limited partner's access to or use of the names and addresses of other limited partners is not per se unreasonable.

Subsection (c)(11)—A partnership agreement certainly may make a person's dissociation as a general partner a breach of contract, but eliminating even the *power* to dissociate would contradict the essence of the limited partnership. General partners in a limited partnership are analogous to partners in a general partnership, and the relationship among general partners is at its core a *voluntary* association.

Moreover, general partners in a limited partnership provide services not only as fiduciaries but also pursuant to a contract. *See* Section 105, cmt. (Role and Inevitability of Partnership Agreement). Only in exceptional circumstances does a party to a contract lack the power to breach, and such circumstances do not exist as to general partners of a limited partnership. Indeed, courts will not enjoin a person to remain in an ongoing contractual relationship that involves trust and confidence. E. ALLAN FARNSWORTH, CONTRACTS § 12.7 at 781 (3rd ed. 1999) ("A court will not grant specific performance of a contract to provide a service that is personal in nature. This refusal . . . is based [in part] of the undesirability of compelling the continuance of personal relations after disputes have arisen and confidence and loyalty have been shaken and the undesirability, in some instances, of imposing what might seem like involuntary servitude.") (footnote omitted).

For two reasons this act treats limited partners quite differently. First, to make possible the act a suitable vehicle for family limited partnerships, "[a] person does not have a right to dissociate as a limited partner before the completion of the winding up of the limited partnership." Section 601(a). *See also* Prefatory Note to 2011 Act, *"The Act's Overall Approach."*

Second, the partnership agreement may eliminate a limited partner's power to dissociate, because limited partners do not resemble contract obligors. Limited partners *qua* limited partners provide no services to the limited partnership, and therefore the analysis stated in the second paragraph of this comment does not apply. Moreover, limited partners have no fiduciary duties, Section 305(b), and therefore the analysis stated in the first paragraph of this comment is inapposite as well.

Subsection (c)(12)—The partnership agreement may not change the stated grounds for judicial dissolution but may determine the forum in which a claim for dissolution under Section 801(a)(6) is determined. For example, arbitration and forum selection clauses are commonplace in business relationships in general and in partnership agreements in particular.

The approach of this paragraph differs from the law of Delaware. *See Huatuco v. Satellite Healthcare*, CV 8465-VCG, 2013 WL 6460898 at *1 and n.2 (Del. Ch. Dec. 9, 2013) (stating that "the right to judicial dissolution is a default right which the parties may eschew by contract" but reserving the question of "[w]hether the parties may, by contract, divest this Court of its authority to order a dissolution in all circumstances, even where it appears manifest that equity so requires—leaving, for instance, irreconcilable members locked away together forever like some alternative entity version of Sartre's *Huis Clos*").

Subsection (c)(13)—The cited provisions comprise the non-waivable aspects of winding up a dissolved limited partnership. The other provisions of Section 802 are default rules.

Subsection (c)(14)—Article 9 delineates a partner's rights to bring direct and derivative actions. It would be unreasonable to frustrate these rights but not unreasonable to channel their exercise. For example, the partnership agreement might select a forum, require pre-suit mediation, provide for arbitration of both direct and derivative claims, or override Section 902 and require "universal demand" in all derivative cases. Similarly, it is not unreasonable to provide for liquidated damages consonant with the law of contracts. In contrast, it would be unreasonable for a partnership agreement to both: (i) require a would-be derivative plaintiff to make demand regardless of futility; and (ii) bar taking the claim to court no matter how long the general partners ponder the demand.

Subsection (c)(15)—A partnership agreement may not alter the act's rules for a special litigation committee but may preclude entirely the use of such a committee.

Subsection (c)(16)—Section 1123(a)(1), 1133(a)(1), 1143(a)(1), and 1153(a)(1) each requires the consent or the affirmative vote of all partners. The partnership agreement may modify these requirements. In contrast, under the sections stated in this subsection:

- each partner is protected from being merged, exchanged, converted, or domesticated "into" the status of a partner in a general partnership that is not a limited liability partnership (or a comparable "unshielded" position in some other organization) without the member having directly consented to either:

  o the merger, interest exchange, conversion, or domestication; or

  o a partnership agreement provision that permits such transactions to occur with less than unanimous consent of the partners; and

- merely consenting to a partnership agreement provision that permits amendment of the agreement with less than unanimous consent of the partners does not qualify as the requisite direct consent.

Subsection (c)(17)—Because these plans are the basic "deal documents" for each of the organic transactions contemplated in Article 11, the partnership agreement may not vary the contents of these plans.

Subsection (c)(18)—This limitation pertains only to "the rights under this [act] of" third parties other than partners. Moreover, the limitation is subject to two substantial exceptions: Section 106 (pertaining to the partnership agreement's relationship to the limited partnership itself and to persons becoming partners) and Section 107(b) (pertaining to the partnership agreement's power over the rights of transferees).

Subsection (d)—The partnership agreement has plenipotentiary power over the matters described in Subsection (a), except as specifically limited by Subsections (c). However, for the convenience of practitioners and the courts, Paragraphs 1 and 2 list various terms often found in partnership agreements. No negative inference should be drawn about terms not listed; the listing is provided "without limiting other terms that may be included in a partnership agreement."

Paragraph 2 lists arrangements subject to the "not manifestly unreasonable standard." Subsection (e) delineates that standard. The same standard applies to terms of a partnership agreement which seek to "prescribe the standards . . . by which the performance of the [contractual] obligation [of good faith and fair dealing] is to be measured." Subsection (c)(7).

Subsection (d)(1)(A)—An arrangement *not* involving "one or more disinterested and independent persons" acting "after full disclosure of all material facts" would "alter . . . the aspects of the duty of loyalty stated in Section 409(b)" and would therefore be subject to the "not manifestly unreasonable standard" of Subsection (d)(2)(A).

For the meaning of "material" as applied to information, see Section 409(f), comment.

Subsection (d)(1)(B)—Section 504(a)(2) prohibits distributions:

- *not merely* when, after the distribution, "the partnership's total assets would be less than the sum of its total liabilities,"

- *but also* when, after the distribution, the assets would less than the total liabilities "plus the amount that would be needed, if the partnership were to be dissolved and wound up at the time of the distribution, to satisfy the preferential rights upon dissolution and winding up of partners and transferees whose preferential rights are superior to those of persons receiving the distribution."

The second part of the solvency test pertains to preferential rights to distributions, is thus a matter *inter se* the partners and any transferees, and is therefore subject to change in the partnership agreement.

In contrast, the first part of the solvency test protects third parties—creditors of the limited partnership—and therefore cannot be changed by the partnership agreement. Section 105(c)(18). Likewise, the partnership agreement cannot change solvency test stated in Section 504(a)(1) (that "the partnership would not be able to pay its debts as they become due in the ordinary course of the partnership's activities and affairs").

Section (d)(2)—This act rejects the ultra-contractarian notion that fiduciary duty within a business organization is merely a set of default rules and seeks instead to balance the virtues of "freedom of contract" against the dangers that inescapably exist when some have power over the interests of others.

Nonetheless, a properly drafted partnership agreement may substantially alter and even eliminate fiduciary duties. Two important limitations exist. First, arrangements subject to this subsection may not be "manifestly unreasonable." *See* Subsection (e) (delineating this standard).

Second, the partnership agreement may not transform the relationship inter se the general partners to the limited partnership and limited partners into an entirely arm's length arrangement. For example, displacement of fiduciary duties is effective only to the extent that the displacement is stated clearly and with particularity. This rule is fundamental in the jurisprudence of fiduciary duty. *See, e.g., Paige Capital Mgmt., LLC v. Lerner Master Fund, LLC*, Civ. A. No. 5502-CS, 2011 WL 3505355 at *31 (Del. Ch. Aug. 8 2011) (stating that, even under a statute that "permits the waiver of fiduciary duties . . . such waivers must be set forth clearly"); *Kelly v. Blum*, Civ. A. No. 4516-VCP, 2010 WL 629850, at *10 n.70 (Del. Ch. Feb. 24, 2010) ("Having been granted great contractual freedom by the LLC Act, drafters of or parties to an LLC agreement should be expected to provide . . . clear and unambiguous provisions when they desire to expand, restrict or eliminate the operation of traditional fiduciary duties"). It would therefore be manifestly unreasonable for a partnership agreement to negate this rule.

Although Subsection (d)(2) does not expressly address contracts between a limited partnership and general partner, the stated constraints must also apply to such contracts. If not, those constraints are effectively meaningless.

Example: A limited partnership enters into a management contract with its sole general partner, and the contract provides that the duties of loyalty stated in Section 409(b) are entirely eliminated. If the partnership agreement were to so provide, the provision would be subject to the "manifestly unreasonable standard." Section 105(d)(2)(A). Absent the authorization provided by Section 105(d)(2)(A), the management contract's attempt to waive fiduciary duties may be unenforceable as a matter of public policy and contract law. *See Neubauer v. Goldfarb*, 108 Cal. App. 4th 47, 57, 133 Cal. Rptr. 2d 218 (2003) (stating that "waiver of corporate directors' and majority shareholders' fiduciary duties to minority shareholders in private close corporations is against public policy and a contract provision in a buy-sell agreement purporting to effect such a waiver is void"). If not, a court should hold the provision unenforceable nonetheless so as to avoid eviscerating Subsection (d)(2).

Subsection (d)(2)(A)—Subject to the "not manifestly unreasonable" standard, this paragraph empowers the partnership agreement to eliminate *all* aspects of the duty of loyalty listed in Section 409(b). The obligation of good faith and fair dealing, Section 409(d), would remain. See Subsection (c)(6). As to any other, uncodified aspects of the duty of loyalty, see Subsection (d)(2)(D) (empowering the partnership agreement to "alter or eliminate any other fiduciary duty").

Example: Joint Venture Limited Partnership ("JV") is a limited partnership, with two general partners, Kappa, Inc. ("Kappa") and Lambda, LLC ("Lambda"). The partnership agreement provides that:

- JV is managed by a "board" consisting of one person appointed by Kappa and one person appointed by Lambda;

- each appointee:

   o owes fiduciary and any other duties exclusively to the general partner that made the appointment; and

   o owes no duties to:

      - the other general partner;

      - the limited partners; and

      - the limited partnership itself.

The "not manifestly unreasonable" standard applies to these provisions under Subsection (d)(2)(A) and (D), and the provisions are not manifestly unreasonable. Note that the provisions do not affect the duties of Kappa and Lambda as general partners.

Example: ABC Limited Partnership ("ABC") is a limited partnership with three general partners. ABC has two entirely separate lines of business, the Alpha business and the Beta business. Under ABC's partnership agreement:

- General Partner 1's responsibilities pertain exclusively to the Alpha business, while responsibility for:

   o the Beta business is allocated exclusively to General Partner 2; and

   o ABC's overall operations is allocated exclusively to General Partner 3.

- General Partner 2's responsibilities pertain exclusively to the Beta business, while responsibility for:

   o the Alpha business is allocated exclusively to General Partner 1; and

   o ABC's overall operations is allocated exclusively to General Partner 3.

- General Partner 1 has no fiduciary duties pertaining to the Beta business.

- General Partner 2 has no fiduciary duties pertaining to the Alpha business.

The "not manifestly unreasonable" standard applies to these provisions under Subsection (d)(2)(A) and (D), and the provisions are not manifestly unreasonable.

Subsection (d)(2)(B)—Under this paragraph, a partnership agreement might provide that an affiliate of a general partner will provide compensated services to the limited partnership at a price not exceeding market price, or that a general partner may pursue opportunities that otherwise would be partnership opportunities. Such arrangements are commonplace and permissible.

Subsection (d)(2)(C)—In this context, "conduct" includes both acts and omissions. Black's Law Dictionary (9th ed. 2009), conduct (defining conduct as "[p]ersonal behavior, whether by action or inaction"). Subject to the "not manifestly unreasonable" standard and the bedrock requirements stated here and in Subsection (c)(8), the partnership agreement can reduce the duty of care substantially. In particular, the partnership agreement can eliminate the aspects of the duty of care pertaining to gross negligence and recklessness.

This provision replicates in a particular context the general rule stated in Subsection (c)(8). For the meaning of "bad faith" in the context of the duty of care, see Subsection (c)(8), comment.

Subsection (e)—The "not manifestly unreasonable" concept became part of uniform business entity statutes when UPA (1997) imported the concept from the Uniform Commercial Code. (In the current version of the Uniform Commercial Code, the concept appears in Section 1–302(b).)

This subsection provides rules for applying the concept, specifying:

- who decides the issue of "manifestly unreasonable"
  - "the court . . . as a matter of law," Subsection (e);
- the framework for determining the issue
  - determination to be made "in light of the purposes, activities, and affairs of the limited partnership," Subsection (e)(2);
- the temporal setting for determining the issue
  - "determination [to be made] as of the time the challenged term became part of the partnership agreement," Subsection (e)(1); and
- what information is admissible for determining the issue
  - "only circumstances existing" when "the challenged term became part of the partnership agreement," Subsection (e)(1).

The subsection also provides a very demanding standard for persons claiming that a term of a partnership agreement is "manifestly unreasonable." "The court . . . may invalidate the term only if, in light of the purposes, activities, and affairs of the limited partnership it is *readily apparent* that: (A) the objective of the term is unreasonable; or (B) the term is an unreasonable means to achieve the term's objective." Subsection (e)(2) (emphasis added).

Subsection (e) is fundamental to this act, because: (i) this act generally defers to the agreement among the partners; and (ii) Subsection (e) safeguards the partnership agreement in at least four ways:

- Determining manifest unreasonableness inter se partners of an organization is a different task than doing so in a commercial context, where concepts like "usages of trade" are available to inform the analysis. Each business organization must be understood in its own terms and context.

- If loosely applied, the concept of "manifestly unreasonable" would permit a court to rewrite the partners' agreement, which would destroy the balance this act seeks to establish between freedom of contract and fiduciary duty.

- Case law has not adequately delineated the concept. *See, e.g., In re Brobeck, Phleger & Harrison LLP*, 408 B.R. 318, 335 (Bankr. N.D. Cal. 2009) ("RUPA [UPA (1997)] does not define what is 'manifestly unreasonable' and the parties have not cited, nor can the court locate, a decision that defines the term. Absent case law or even a dictionary definition, the court must rely on its common sense to recognize something as manifestly unreasonable.").

- In the context of statutes permitting stock transfer restrictions unless "manifestly unreasonable," courts have often ignored the word "manifestly." *See, e.g., Brandt v. Somerville*, 692 N.W.2d 144, 152 (N.D. 2005) (stating that "in close corporations, a majority of courts have sustained restrictions that are determined to be reasonable in light of the relevant circumstances"); *Roof Depot, Inc. v. Ohman*, 638 N.W.2d 782, 786 (Minn. Ct. App. 2002) (stating that "the restrictions [on share transfer] are not 'manifestly unreasonable' because they are reasonable means to ensure that the management and control of the business remains in the group of investors or with people well known to them"); *Castriota v. Castriota*, 268 N.J. Super. 417, 423–24, 633 A.2d 1024, 1027–28 (App. Div. 1993) ("We are obliged to apply the statute in a manner consonant with its essential purpose to permit reasonable restrictions upon alienation.").

Subsection (e)(1)—The significance of the phrase "as of the time the term as challenged became part of the partnership agreement" is best shown by example.

Example: When a particular limited partnership comes into existence, its business plan is quite unusual and its success depends on the willingness of a particular individual to serve as the limited partnership's sole general partner. This individual has a rare combination of skills, experiences, and contacts, which are particularly appropriate for the partnership's start-up. In order to induce the individual to accept the position of sole general partner, the other partners are willing to have the partnership agreement significantly limit the general partner's fiduciary duties. Several years later, when the limited partnership's operations have turned prosaic and the general partner's talents and background are not nearly so crucial, a limited partner challenges the fiduciary duty limitations as manifestly unreasonable. The relevant time under Subsection (e)(1) is when the limited partnership began. Subsequent developments are not relevant, except as they might inferentially bear on the circumstances in existence at the relevant time.

Example: As initially adopted, a partnership agreement identifies a category of decisions ordinarily subject to the duty of loyalty and provides that "the general partner's sole, reasonable discretion" satisfies the duty. A year later, the agreement is amended to delete the word "reasonable." Later, a partner claims that, without the word "reasonable," the provision is manifestly unreasonable. The relevant time under Subsection (e)(1) is when the agreement was amended, not when the agreement was initially adopted.

Subsection (e)(2)—If a person claims that a term of the partnership agreement is manifestly unreasonable under Subsections (c)(7) or (d)(2), as a matter of ordinary procedural law the person making the claim has the burden of proof.

§ 106.   Partnership Agreement; Effect on Limited Partnership and Person Becoming Partner; Preformation Agreement

(a)   A limited partnership is bound by and may enforce the partnership agreement, whether or not the partnership has itself manifested assent to the agreement.

(b)   A person that becomes a partner is deemed to assent to the partnership agreement.

(c)   Two or more persons intending to become the initial partners of a limited partnership may make an agreement providing that upon the formation of the partnership the agreement will become the partnership agreement.

COMMENT

Subsection (a)—This subsection resolves twin questions that have troubled some courts—namely, whether an unincorporated entity that has not signed its foundational agreement nonetheless is bound by and may enforce the agreement. The questions have been particularly troubling in the context of agreements to arbitrate. *See, e.g., Elkjer v. Scheef & Stone, L.L.P.*, 3:13-CV-1655-K, ___ F. Supp. 2d ___, 2014 WL 1255844 at *5–6 (N.D. Tex. Mar. 27, 2014) (concluding that a limited liability partnership "is a party to the Partnership Agreement," even though the partnership itself never signed or otherwise assented to the agreement; enforcing arbitration provision to the benefit of the LLP). *Contra Trover v. 419 OCR, Inc.*, 397 Ill. App. 3d 403, 409, 921 N.E.2d 1249, 1255 (2010) (finding that "neither FODG [an LLC] nor the Golf Club [a related LLC] was a party to the operating agreements and that they are therefore not bound by the arbitration clauses therein").

Developments pertaining to the Virginia LLC Act further illustrate the difficulties. In *Mission Residential, LLC v. Triple Net Properties, LLC*, 275 Va. 157, 161–62, 654 S.E.2d 888, 891 (2008), the Virginia Supreme Court held that an LLC member's derivative claim was not subject to the arbitration provision in the operating agreement, because: (i) the LLC was "the real party in interest;" (ii) the LLC had not signed the operating agreement; and (iii) requiring the claim to be arbitrated would "ignore[ ] the separate existence of Holdings [the LLC]." The Virginia legislature promptly disagreed and amended the LLC act to state: "A limited liability company is bound by its operating agreement whether or not the limited liability company executes the operating agreement." VA. CODE ANN. § 13.1–1023.A.1 (2012). The legislature left open the question of a limited liability company's power to enforce an operating agreement that the company has not executed.

This subsection answers the twin questions, categorically and in the affirmative.

This subsection does not consider whether a limited partnership is an indispensable party to a suit concerning the partnership agreement. That is a question of procedural law, and the answer can determine whether federal diversity jurisdiction exists.

Subsection (b)—Given the possibility of oral and implied-in-fact terms in the partnership agreement, a person becoming a partner of an existing limited partnership should take precautions to ascertain fully the contents of the partnership agreement. *See* Section 105(a)(3), comment.

Subsection (c)—A preformation agreement is not a partnership agreement. A partnership agreement is among "partners," and, under this act, the earliest a person can become a partner is upon the formation of the limited partnership. Section 401.

§ 107. Partnership Agreement; Effect on Third Parties and Relationship to Records Effective on Behalf of Limited Partnership

(a) A partnership agreement may specify that its amendment requires the approval of a person that is not a party to the agreement or the satisfaction of a condition. An amendment is ineffective if its adoption does not include the required approval or satisfy the specified condition.

(b) The obligations of a limited partnership and its partners to a person in the person's capacity as a transferee or person dissociated as a partner are governed by the partnership agreement. Subject only to a court order issued under Section 703(b)(2) to effectuate a charging order, an amendment to the partnership agreement made after a person becomes a transferee or is dissociated as a partner:

(1) is effective with regard to any debt, obligation, or other liability of the partnership or its partners to the person in the person's capacity as a transferee or person dissociated as a partner; and

(2) is not effective to the extent the amendment imposes a new debt, obligation, or other liability on the transferee or person dissociated as a partner.

(c) If a record delivered by a limited partnership to the [Secretary of State] for filing becomes effective and contains a provision that would be ineffective under Section 105(c) or (d)(2) if contained in the partnership agreement, the provision is ineffective in the record.

(d) Subject to subsection (c), if a record delivered by a limited partnership to the [Secretary of State] for filing becomes effective and conflicts with a provision of the partnership agreement:

(1) the agreement prevails as to partners, persons dissociated as partners, and transferees; and

(2) the record prevails as to other persons to the extent they reasonably rely on the record.

COMMENT

Subsection (a)—This subsection, derived from DEL. CODE ANN. tit. 6, § 18–302(e), permits the partnership agreement to: (i) accord a non-partner veto rights over amendments to the agreement; and (ii) establish other preconditions for amendments. An amendment made in derogation of a veto right or precondition is ineffective.

Veto rights are likely to be sought by lenders but may also be attractive to non-partner managers.

Example: A non-partner manager enters into a management contract with a limited partnership, and that agreement provides in part that the limited partnership may remove the manager without cause only with the consent of partners holding 2/3 of the profits interests. The partnership agreement contains a parallel provision (the "partnership agreement's quantum provision"), but the non-partner manager is not a party to the partnership agreement. Later, the partners amend the partnership agreement's quantum provision to reduce the quantum to a simple majority of profits interests and thereafter purport to remove the manager without cause. Although the limited partnership has undoubtedly breached its contract with the manager and subjected itself to a damage claim, the limited partnership has the *power* under Section 105(a)(2) to effect the removal—unless the partnership agreement provides the manager a veto right over changes in the partnership agreement's quantum provision.

This subsection does not refer to partner veto rights because, unless otherwise provided in the partnership agreement, the consent of each partner is necessary to effect an amendment. *See* Section 406(b)(1). Because "[a] partnership agreement may specify that its amendment requires . . . the satisfaction of a condition," a partnership agreement can require that any amendment be made through a writing or a record signed by each partner. *See also* Section 105(a)(3) (empowering the partnership agreement to determine "the means and conditions for amending the partnership agreement").

Subsection (b)—The law of unincorporated business organizations is only beginning to grapple in a modern way with the tension between the rights of an organization's owners to carry on their activities as they see fit (or have agreed) and the rights of transferees of the organization's economic interests. Such transferees can include the heirs of business founders as well as former owners who are "locked in" as transferees of their own interests. *See* Section 602(a)(3) and 605(a)(4).

If the law categorically favors the owners, there is a serious risk of expropriation and other abuse. On the other hand, if the law grants former owners and other transferees the right to seek judicial protection, that specter can "freeze the deal" as of the moment an owner leaves the enterprise or a third party obtains an economic interest.

The scant case law in this area clearly favors the remaining partners over former partners and other transferees. *See, e.g., Bauer v. Blomfield Co./Holden Joint Venture*, 849 P2d 1365, 1367 n.2 (Alaska 1993) (holding that a mere assignee "was not entitled to complain about a decision made with the consent of all the partners" and stating "[w]e are unwilling to hold that partners owe a duty of good faith and fair dealing to assignees of a partner's interest"); *Bynum v. Frisby*, 73 Nev. 145, 149–50, 311 P.2d 972, 975 (1957) ("[A]n assignment of a partnership interest from one partner to a stranger does not bring that stranger into fiduciary relationship with the remaining partners nor require them to resort to dissolution in order to prevent such a relationship from arising. The stranger remains a stranger entitled only to share in the partnership's worth and to demand an accounting upon dissolution.") (applying UPA (1914) § 27, pertaining to rights of an assignee). *See generally* Daniel S. Kleinberger, *The Plight of the Bare Naked Assignee*, 42 SUFFOLK L. REV. 587 (2009).

This subsection follows *Bauer* and other cases by expressly subjecting transferees (including a person dissociated as a partner) to partnership agreement amendments made after the transfer or dissociation, except amendments that increase obligations on transferees. For example, an amendment might extend the duration of a limited partnership but may not institute a new capital call obligation on transferees.

The question of whether, in extreme and sufficiently harsh circumstances, transferees might be able to claim some type of duty or obligation to protect against expropriation awaits development in the case law. An unreported LLC case suggests the answer might be yes, but the decision rests primarily on the wording of the LLC's operating agreement. In *Kohannim v. Katoli*, 08-11-00155-CV, 2013 WL 3943078 at *10–11 (Tex. App. July 24, 2013), the court: (i) noted an LLC's "Regulations provide[ ] for the distribution of 'available cash' to members quarterly provided that the available cash is not needed for a reasonable working capital reserve"; (ii) noted that "Jacob [the defendant member] paid himself $100,000 for management services that were not performed and failed to make any profit distributions to Mike [former member and ex-spouse of the plaintiff Parvaneh] or Parvaneh [ex-spouse of Mike, who became Mike's transferee as part of their divorce proceeding] even though more than $250,000 in undistributed profit had accumulated in the company's accounts since the mortgage on the property had been paid off in February 2007"; and (iii) concluded that "more than a scintilla of evidence supports the trial court's finding that Jacob failed to make profit distributions to Parvaneh." In essence, the court upheld a finding that Jacob had breached (or caused the LLC to breach) a contractual obligation to make distributions. But the court went further: "We also agree with the trial court's conclusion that the established facts demonstrated Jacob engaged in wrongful conduct and exhibited a lack of fair dealing in the company's affairs to the prejudice of Parvaneh." *Id.* at *11.

For the very limited rights of transferees, see Section 702.

Subsection (b)(1)—This provision is inapposite when "a partner or transferee becomes entitled to receive a distribution." Section 503(d). In that circumstance:

- "the partner or transferee has the status of . . . a creditor of the limited partnership with respect to the distribution," *Id.*; and

- the relevant obligation is not owed to "a person in the person's capacity as a transferee or person dissociated as a partner," Subsection (b), but rather to the person in the person's capacity as a creditor.

Subsection (c)—This provision precludes using the certificate of limited partnership to make an end run around the strictures of Section 105(c) and (d)(2).

Subsection (d)—It will be possible, albeit improvident, for a limited partnership agreement to be inconsistent with the certificate of limited partnership or other public filings pertaining to the partnership. For those circumstances, this subsection provides rules for determining which source of information prevails:

- For partners, persons dissociated as partners, and transferees, the partnership agreement is paramount.

- Third parties may invoke the public record upon a showing of reasonable reliance, which presupposes actual knowledge—*i.e.*, deemed knowledge under Section 103(d) does not suffice.

The mere fact that a term is present in a publicly-filed record and not in the partnership agreement, or *vice versa*, does not automatically establish a conflict. This subsection does not expressly cover a situation in which: (i) one of the specified filed records contains information in addition to, but not inconsistent with, the partnership agreement; and (ii) a person, other than a partner or transferee, reasonably relies on the additional information. However, the policy reflected in this subsection seems equally applicable to that situation. Moreover, to argue that the partnership agreement prevails over the filed record is to argue that the additional term does conflict with the partnership agreement, at least in effect.

Section 105(a)(3) might also be relevant to the subject matter of this subsection. Absent a contrary provision in the partnership agreement, language in a certificate of limited partnership or other record delivered to the filing office for filing on behalf of the limited partnership might be evidence of the partners' agreement and thereby constitute or at least imply a term of the partnership agreement.

This subsection does not apply to records delivered to the filing office for filing on behalf of a person other than a limited partnership.

§ 108.   Required Information

A limited partnership shall maintain at its principal office the following information:

(1)   a current list showing the full name and last known street and mailing address of each partner, separately identifying the general partners, in alphabetical order, and the limited partners, in alphabetical order;

(2)   a copy of the initial certificate of limited partnership and all amendments to and restatements of the certificate, together with signed copies of any powers of attorney under which any certificate, amendment, or restatement has been signed;

(3)   a copy of any filed articles of merger, interest exchange, conversion, or domestication;

(4)   a copy of the partnership's federal, state, and local income tax returns and reports, if any, for the three most recent years;

(5)   a copy of any partnership agreement made in a record and any amendment made in a record to any partnership agreement;

(6)   a copy of any financial statement of the partnership for the three most recent years;

(7)   a copy of the three most recent [annual] [biennial] reports delivered by the partnership to the [Secretary of State] pursuant to Section 212;

(8)   a copy of any record made by the partnership during the past three years of any consent given by or vote taken of any partner pursuant to this [act] or the partnership agreement; and

(9)   unless contained in a partnership agreement made in a record, a record stating:

(A)   a description and statement of the agreed value of contributions other than money made and agreed to be made by each partner;

(B)   the times at which, or events on the happening of which, any additional contributions agreed to be made by each partner are to be made;

(C)   for any person that is both a general partner and a limited partner, a specification of what transferable interest the person owns in each capacity; and

(D)   any events upon the happening of which the partnership is to be dissolved and its activities and affairs wound up.

COMMENT

A required information section first appeared in ULPA (1976) § 105, although the notion of information rights traces back to the original uniform limited partnership act, ULPA (1916) § 10.

The partnership agreement cannot vary this section. However, subject to Section 105(c)(9), the agreement can vary Sections 304 and 407, which govern access to and use of the information required by this section.

Paragraph (5)—This requirement applies to both superseded and current agreements and amendments. An agreement or amendment is "made in a record" to the extent the agreement is integrated into a record and consented to in that memorialized form. It is possible for a partnership agreement to be made in part in a record and in part otherwise. *See* Section 102(14), cmt. An oral agreement that is subsequently inscribed in a record (but not consented to as such) was not "made in a record" and is not covered by this paragraph. However, if the limited partnership happens to have such a record, Section 304(b) might and Section 407(a)(2) will provide a right of access.

Paragraph (8)—This paragraph does not require a limited partnership to make a record of consents given and votes taken. However, if the limited partnership has made such a record, this paragraph requires that the limited partnership maintain the record for three years. The requirement applies to any record made by the limited partnership, not just to records made contemporaneously with the giving of consent or voting. The three-year period runs from when the record was made and not from when the consent was given or vote taken.

Paragraph (9)—Information is "contained in a partnership agreement made in a record" only to the extent that the information is integrated into a record and, in that memorialized form, has been consented to as part of the partnership agreement.

This paragraph is not a statute of frauds provision. For example, failure to comply with Paragraph (9)(A) or (B) does not render unenforceable an oral promise to make a contribution. Likewise, failure to comply with Paragraph (9)(D) does not invalidate an oral term of the partnership specifying "events upon the happening of which the limited partnership is to be dissolved and its activities wound up." *See also* Section 801(a).

Conversely, the mere fact that a limited partnership maintains a record in purported compliance with Paragraph (9)(A) or (B) does not prove that a person has actually promised to make a contribution. Likewise, the mere fact that a limited partnership maintains a record in purported compliance with Paragraph (9)(D) does not prove that the partnership agreement actually includes the specified events as causes of dissolution.

Consistent with the partnership agreement's plenary power to structure and regulate the relations of the partners *inter se*, a partnership agreement can impose "made in a record" requirements which render unenforceable oral promises to make contributions or oral understandings as to "events upon the happening of which the limited partnership is to be dissolved."

Paragraph (9)(A) and (B)—Often a partnership agreement will state in record form the value of contributions made and promised to be made. If not, these provisions require that the value be stated in a record maintained as part of the limited partnership's required information. This act does not authorize the limited partnership or the general partners to set the value of a contribution without the concurrence of the person who has made or promised the contribution, although the partnership agreement itself can grant that authority.

Paragraph (9)(C)—The information required by this provision is essential for determining what happens to the transferable interests of a person that is both a general partner and a limited partner and that dissociates in one of those capacities but not the other. *See* Sections 602(a)(3) and 605(a)(5).

§ 109. Dual Capacity

A person may be both a general partner and a limited partner. A person that is both a general and limited partner has the rights, powers, duties, and obligations provided by this [act] and the partnership agreement in each of those capacities. When the person acts as a general partner, the person is subject to the obligations, duties, and restrictions under this [act] and the partnership agreement for general partners. When the person acts as a limited partner, the person is subject to the obligations, duties, and restrictions under this [act] and the partnership agreement for limited partners.

COMMENT

It may be to the advantage of a general partner to own some of its interests as a limited partner, especially interests connected to voting rights. *See* Section 305(b) (providing that, except for the implied contractual covenant of good faith and fair dealing, "a limited partner does not have any duty to the limited partnership or to any other partner solely by reason of acting as a limited partner").

§ 110. Nature, Purpose, and Duration of Limited Partnership

(a) <u>A limited partnership is an entity distinct from its partners.</u> A limited partnership is the same entity regardless of whether its certificate states that the limited partnership is a limited liability limited partnership.

(b) A limited partnership may have any lawful purpose, regardless of whether for profit.

(c) A limited partnership has perpetual duration.

COMMENT

Subsection (a)—The "separate entity" characteristic is fundamental to a limited partnership and is inextricably connected to both the liability shield, Sections 303 and 404(b), and the inability of creditors of a partner or transferee to reach the assets of the limited partnership, absent a "reverse pierce" or a claim of fraudulent transfer. *See, e.g., C.F. Trust, Inc. v. First Flight, L.P.,* 580 S.E.2d 806, 810 (Va. 2003) ("hold[ing] that Virginia does recognize the concept of outsider reverse piercing and that this concept can be applied to a Virginia limited partnership"); *In re Flanagan,* 373 B.R. 216, 223, n.6 (Bankr. D. Conn. 2007) (stating that "[r]everse piercing claims have been recognized as viable causes of action in Connecticut" and "[t]he fact that [an entity] is a limited partnership does not alter the analysis"); *Egle v. Egle,* 817 So. 2d 136, 140 (La. Ct. App. 2002) (allowing plaintiff to proceed with claims that transfers made by her ex-spouse inter alia to an LLC were sham transactions).

Acquiring or relinquishing an LLLP shield changes only the rules governing a general partner's liability for subsequently incurred obligations of the limited partnership. The underlying entity is unaffected.

Subsection (b)—Although some limited partnership statutes continue to require a business purpose, this act follows the current trend and takes a more expansive approach. The phrase "any lawful purpose, regardless of whether for profit" encompasses even charitable activities, but this act does not include any comprehensive protections pertaining to charitable assets and purposes. Section 1104(b) does contain a "nondiversion" provision, but the provision applies only to the organic transactions contemplated by Article 11. Comprehensive protections must be (and typically are) found in other law, although sometimes that "other law" appears within a state's non-profit corporation statute. *See, e.g.,* MINN. STAT. § 317A.811 (2012) (providing restrictions on charitable organizations that seek to "dissolve, merge, or consolidate, or to transfer all or substantially all of their assets" but imposing those restrictions only on "corporations," which are elsewhere defined as corporations incorporated under the non-profit corporation act).

Subsection (c)—The word "perpetual" is a misnomer, albeit one commonplace in limited partnership and limited liability company statutes. In this context, "perpetual" means merely that the act: (i) does not require a definite term; and (ii) creates no immediate nexus between the dissociation of a partner and the dissolution of the entity.

Moreover, the public record pertaining to a limited partnership will not necessarily reveal whether the limited partnership actually has a perpetual duration or has in fact dissolved, because: (i) this act, like all limited partnership statutes, provides several consent-based methods to dissolve a limited partnership; and (ii) none of those methods involve a public filing. For example, dissolution and winding up of a limited partnership may result from a term specified in the partnership agreement, an event specified in the partnership agreement, or the affirmative vote or consent of all partners. *See* Sections 801 (events causing dissolution) and 802 (winding up required upon dissolution). A partnership agreement is not a publicly-filed document, and a partner vote to dissolve a limited partnership is not a public event. A dissolved limited partnership may deliver to the filing office for filing an amendment to the certificate of limited partnership stating that the partnership is dissolved, Section 802(b)(2)(A), and later a statement of termination, Section 802(b)(2)(F), or both, but the filing of such statements is permissive rather than mandatory. *Id.*

Likewise, the public record will not reveal when (or even whether) a limited partnership has come into existence. *See* Section 201(d) (providing that the formation of a limited partnership requires both that the certificate of limited partnership become effective and that at least two separate persons become partners, with at least one being a general partner and one being a limited partner).

§ 111.   Powers

A limited partnership has the capacity to sue and be sued in the name of the partnership and the power to do all things necessary or convenient to carry on the partnership's activities and affairs.

COMMENT

Continuing the approach initiated in ULPA (2001) § 105, this act omits as unnecessary any detailed list of specific powers.

The partnership agreement cannot vary a limited partnership's capacity to sue and be sued. Section 105(c)(2). A limited partnership's standing to enforce the partnership agreement is a separate matter, which is covered by Section 106(a) (stating, as a default rule, that the limited partnership "may enforce the partnership agreement").

§ 112. Application to Existing Relationships

(a)   Before [all-inclusive date], this [act] governs only:

(1)   a limited partnership formed on or after [the effective date of this [act]]; and

(2)   except as otherwise provided in subsections (c) and (d), a limited partnership formed before [the effective date of this [act]] which elects, in the manner provided in its partnership agreement or by law for amending the partnership agreement, to be subject to this [act].

(b)   Except as otherwise provided in subsections (c) and (d), on and after [all-inclusive date] this [act] governs all limited partnerships.

(c)   With respect to a limited partnership formed before [the effective date of this [act]], the following rules apply except as the partners otherwise elect in the manner provided in the partnership agreement or by law for amending the partnership agreement:

(1)   Section 110(c) does not apply and the limited partnership has whatever duration it had under the law applicable immediately before [the effective date of this [act]].

(2)   the limited partnership is not required to amend its certificate of limited partnership to comply with Section 201(b)(5).

(3)   Sections 601 and 602 do not apply and a limited partner has the same right and power to dissociate from the limited partnership, with the same consequences, as existed immediately before [the effective date of this [act]].

(4)   Section 603(4) does not apply.

(5)   Section 603(5) does not apply and a court has the same power to expel a general partner as the court had immediately before [the effective date of this [act]].

(6)   Section 801(a)(3) does not apply and the connection between a person's dissociation as a general partner and the dissolution of the limited partnership is the same as existed immediately before [the effective date of this [act]].

(d)   With respect to a limited partnership that elects pursuant to subsection (a)(2) to be subject to this [act], after the election takes effect the provisions of this [act] relating to the liability of the limited partnership's general partners to third parties apply:

(1)   before [all-inclusive date], to:

(A)   a third party that had not done business with the limited partnership in the year before the election took effect; and

(B)   a third party that had done business with the limited partnership in the year before the election took effect only if the third party knows or has been notified of the election; and

(2)   on and after [all-inclusive date], to all third parties, but those provisions remain inapplicable to any obligation incurred while those provisions were inapplicable under paragraph (1)(B).

Legislative Note: Subsection 112(c) presupposes that this act is replacing ULPA (1976) (Last Amended 1985). If this act is replacing a substantially different limited partnership act, the enacting jurisdiction should consider whether: (i) this act makes material changes to the "default" (or "gap filler") rules of the predecessor statute; and (ii) if so, whether Subsection (c) should carry forward any of those rules for pre-existing limited partnerships. In this assessment, the focus is on pre-existing limited partnerships that have left default rules in place, whether advisedly or not. The central question is whether, for such limited partnerships, expanding Subsection (c) is necessary to prevent material changes to the partners' "deal."

In an enacting jurisdiction that has previously amended its existing limited partnership statute to provide for limited liability limited partnerships (LLLPs), this act should include transition provisions specifically applicable to pre-existing limited liability limited partnerships. The precise wording of those provisions must depend on the wording of the State's previously enacted LLLP provisions. However, the following principles apply generally:

1.   In Sections 806(b)(5) and 807(b)(4) (notice by dissolved limited partnership to claimants), the phrase "the limited partnership has been throughout its existence a limited liability limited partnership" should be revised to encompass a limited partnership that was a limited liability limited partnership under the State's previously enacted LLLP provisions.

2.   Section 112(d) should provide that, if a pre-existing limited liability limited partnership elects to be subject to this act, this act's provisions relating to the liability of general partners to third parties apply immediately to all third parties, regardless of whether a third party has previously done business with the limited liability limited partnership.

3.   A pre-existing limited liability limited partnership that elects to be subject to this act should have to comply with Sections 201(b)(5) (requiring the certificate of limited partnership to state whether the limited partnership is a limited liability limited partnership) and 114(c) (establishing name requirements for a limited liability limited partnership).

4.   As for Section 112(b) (providing that, after a transition period, this act applies to all preexisting limited partnerships):

a.   if a State's previously enacted LLLP provisions have requirements essentially the same as Sections 201(b)(5) and 114(c), pre-existing limited liability limited partnerships should automatically retain LLLP status under this act.

b.   if a State's previously enacted LLLP provisions have name requirements essentially the same as Section 114(c) and provide that a public filing other than the certificate of limited partnership establishes a limited partnership's status as a limited liability limited partnership:

i.   that filing can be deemed to an amendment to the certificate of limited partnership to comply with Section 201(b)(5), and

ii.   pre-existing limited liability limited partnerships should automatically retain LLLP status under this act.

c.   if a State's previously enacted LLLP provisions do not have name requirements essentially the same as Section 114(c), it will be impossible both to enforce Section 114(c) and provide for automatic transition to LLLP status under this act.

It is recommended that the "all-inclusive" date should be at least one year after the effective date of this act, Section 1206, but no more than two years.

COMMENT

Subsection (c)—For the effective date of this act, see Section 1206.

§ 113.   Supplemental Principles of Law

Unless displaced by particular provisions of this [act], the principles of law and equity supplement this [act].

COMMENT

For this act, the common law rules of contract and agency are among the most important supplemental "principles of law." With regard to transactions under Article 11, noteworthy principles include the rights of creditors following leveraged buyouts, spinoffs, asset purchases, or other similar transactions; and creditors' rights under other laws.

§ 114.   Permitted Names

(a)   The name of a limited partnership may contain the name of any partner.

(b)   The name of a limited partnership that is not a limited liability limited partnership must contain the phrase "limited partnership" or the abbreviation "LP" or "L.P." and may not contain the phrase "limited liability limited partnership" or the abbreviation "LLLP" or "L.L.L.P.".

(c)   The name of a limited liability limited partnership must contain the phrase "limited liability limited partnership" or the abbreviation "LLLP" or "L.L.L.P." and must not contain the abbreviation "LP" or "L.P.".

(d)   Except as otherwise provided in subsection (g), the name of a limited partnership, and the name under which a foreign limited partnership may register to do business in this state, must be distinguishable on the records of the [Secretary of State] from any:

(1)   name of an existing person whose formation required the filing of a record by the [Secretary of State] and which is not at the time administratively dissolved;

(2)   name of a limited liability partnership whose statement of qualification is in effect;

(3)   name under which a person is registered to do business in this state by the filing of a record by the [Secretary of State];

(4)   name reserved under Section 115 or other law of this state providing for the reservation of a name by the filing of a record by the [Secretary of State];

(5)   name registered under Section 116 or other law of this state providing for the registration of a name by the filing of a record by the [Secretary of State]; and

(6)   name registered under [this state's assumed or fictitious name statute].

(e)   If a person consents in a record to the use of its name and submits an undertaking in a form satisfactory to the [Secretary of State] to change its name to a name that is distinguishable on the records of the [Secretary of State] from any name in any category of names in subsection (d), the name of the consenting person may be used by the person to which the consent was given.

(f)   Except as otherwise provided in subsection (g), in determining whether a name is the same as or not distinguishable on the records of the [Secretary of State] from the name of another person, words, phrases, or abbreviations indicating the type of person, such as "corporation", "corp.", "incorporated", "Inc.", "professional corporation", "PC", "P.C.", "professional association", "PA", "P.A.", "Limited", "Ltd.", "limited partnership", "LP", "L.P.", "limited liability partnership", "LLP", "L.L.P.", "registered limited liability partnership", "RLLP", "R.L.L.P.", "limited liability limited partnership", "LLLP", "L.L.L.P.", "registered limited liability limited partnership", "RLLLP", "R.L.L.L.P.", "limited liability company", "LLC", "L.L.C.", "limited cooperative association", "limited cooperative", "LCA", or "L.C.A." may not be taken into account.

(g)   A person may consent in a record to the use of a name that is not distinguishable on the records of the [Secretary of State] from its name except for the addition of a word, phrase, or abbreviation indicating the type of person as provided in subsection (f). In such a case, the person need not change its name pursuant to subsection (e).

(h)   The name of a limited partnership or foreign limited partnership may not contain the words [insert prohibited words or words that may be used only with approval by an appropriate state agency].

(i)   A limited partnership or foreign limited partnership may use a name that is not distinguishable from a name described in subsection (d)(1) through (6) if the partnership delivers to the [Secretary of State] a certified copy of a final judgment of a court of competent jurisdiction establishing the right of the partnership to use the name in this state.

COMMENT

This section adopts the "distinguishable on the records" test for name availability and rejects the "deceptively similar" test widely used in the past.

For name requirements for foreign registered limited partnerships, see Section 1003(1).

§ 115.   Reservation of Name

(a)   A person may reserve the exclusive use of a name that complies with Section 114 by delivering an application to the [Secretary of State] for filing. The application must state the name and address of the applicant and the name to be reserved. If the [Secretary of State] finds that the name is available, the [Secretary of State] shall reserve the name for the applicant's exclusive use for [120] days.

(b)   The owner of a reserved name may transfer the reservation to another person by delivering to the [Secretary of State] a signed notice in a record of the transfer which states the name and address of the person to which the reservation is being transferred.

COMMENT

This section does not provide for the renewal of a name reservation for successive 120 day periods. A new reservation may be filed upon the expiration of a reservation, but by requiring a new filing this section creates the possibility that another party may timely submit a reservation for the same name. It was considered appropriate to allow for that possibility so that the procedure in this section cannot be used to block a name indefinitely. *Compare* Section 115, *with* Section 116(d) (authorizing a renewable registration of certain names).

§ 116.   Registration of Name

(a)   A foreign limited partnership not registered to do business in this state under [Article] 10 may register its name, or an alternate name adopted pursuant to Section 1006, if the name is distinguishable on the records of the [Secretary of State] from the names that are not available under Section 114.

(b)   To register its name or an alternate name adopted pursuant to Section 1006, a foreign limited partnership must deliver to the [Secretary of State] for filing an application stating the partnership's name, the jurisdiction and date of its formation, and any alternate name adopted pursuant to Section 1006. If the [Secretary of State] finds that the name applied for is available, the [Secretary of State] shall register the name for the applicant's exclusive use.

(c)   The registration of a name under this section is effective for [one year] after the date of registration.

(d)   A foreign limited partnership whose name registration is effective may renew the registration for successive [one-year] periods by delivering, not earlier than [three months] before the expiration of the registration, to the [Secretary of State] for filing a renewal application that complies with this section. When filed, the renewal application renews the registration for a succeeding [one-year] period.

(e)   A foreign limited partnership whose name registration is effective may register as a foreign limited partnership under the registered name or consent in a signed record to the use of that name by another person that is not an individual.

COMMENT

Unlike the reservation of a name under Section 115, a registration of a name under this section may be renewed for successive periods thus permitting a name to be protected for a period longer than the initial registration period. Use of the procedure in this section is limited, however, to the names of foreign limited partnerships which are not registered to do business in the state. The purpose of this section is to permit a foreign entity to make sure its name will be available if it chooses to register in the state in the future.

§ 117.   Registered Agent

(a)   Each limited partnership and each registered foreign limited partnership shall designate and maintain a registered agent in this state. The designation of a registered agent is an affirmation of fact by the limited partnership or registered foreign limited partnership that the agent has consented to serve.

(b)   A registered agent for a limited partnership or registered foreign limited partnership must have a place of business in this state.

(c)   The only duties under this [act] of a registered agent that has complied with this [act] are:

(1)   to forward to the limited partnership or registered foreign limited partnership at the address most recently supplied to the agent by the partnership or foreign partnership any process, notice, or demand pertaining to the partnership or foreign partnership which is served on or received by the agent;

(2)   if the registered agent resigns, to provide the notice required by Section 119(c) to the partnership or foreign partnership at the address most recently supplied to the agent by the partnership or foreign partnership; and

(3)   to keep current the information with respect to the agent in the certificate of limited partnership.

COMMENT

This section is limited to prescribing the duties of a registered agent under this act. The partnership agreement cannot vary this section. Section 105(c)(3)(A). However, an agent may undertake other responsibilities to a represented limited partnership or foreign limited partnership, such as by contract or course of dealing, but those duties will be determined under other law.

§ 118.   Change of Registered Agent or Address for Registered Agent by Limited Partnership

(a)   A limited partnership or registered foreign limited partnership may change its registered agent or the address of its registered agent by delivering to the [Secretary of State] for filing a statement of change that states:

(1)   the name of the partnership or foreign partnership; and

(2)   the information that is to be in effect as a result of the filing of the statement of change.

(b)   The general or limited partners of a limited partnership need not approve the [delivery to the Secretary of State] for filing of:

(1)   a statement of change under this section; or

(2)   a similar filing changing the registered agent or registered office, if any, of the partnership in any other jurisdiction.

(c)   A statement of change under this section designating a new registered agent is an affirmation of fact by the limited partnership or registered foreign limited partnership that the agent has consented to serve.

(d)   As an alternative to using the procedure in this section, a limited partnership may amend its certificate of limited partnership.

COMMENT

A change in the identity of the registered agent of a limited partnership or foreign limited partnership or a change of the office address of a partnership's registered agent are usually routine matters that do not affect the rights of the partners of the represented limited partnership. This section permits those changes to be made without: (i) amendment of the certificate of limited partnership; (ii) formal approval by the general partners; and (iii) any approval by the limited partners. For the registered agent's power to resign, see Section 119. For the registered agent's power to change its name, address, or both, see Section 120.

Subsection (c)—This subsection avoids the need to file with a statement of change consent of the new registered agent being designated.

Subsection (d)—This subsection makes clear that the procedures in this section are not exclusive. A common way in which a limited partnership changes its registered agent is to include the change in an amendment of its certificate of limited partnership or in its annual/biennial report. *See* Section 212(e).

§ 119.   Resignation of Registered Agent

(a)   A registered agent may resign as an agent for a limited partnership or registered foreign limited partnership by delivering to the [Secretary of State] for filing a statement of resignation that states:

(1)   the name of the partnership or foreign partnership;

(2)   the name of the agent;

(3)   that the agent resigns from serving as registered agent for the partnership or foreign partnership; and

(4)   the address of the partnership or foreign partnership to which the agent will send the notice required by subsection (c).

(b)   A statement of resignation takes effect on the earlier of:

(1)   the 31st day after the day on which it is filed by the [Secretary of State]; or

(2)   the designation of a new registered agent for the limited partnership or registered foreign limited partnership.

(c)   A registered agent promptly shall furnish to the limited partnership or registered foreign limited partnership notice in a record of the date on which a statement of resignation was filed.

(d)   When a statement of resignation takes effect, the registered agent ceases to have responsibility under this [act] for any matter thereafter tendered to it as agent for the limited partnership or registered foreign limited partnership. The resignation does not affect any contractual rights the partnership or foreign partnership has against the agent or that the agent has against the partnership or foreign partnership.

(e)   A registered agent may resign with respect to a limited partnership or registered foreign limited partnership whether or not the partnership or foreign partnership is in good standing.

COMMENT

Resignation under this section may be accomplished solely by action of the registered agent and does not require the cooperation or consent of the represented limited partnership or registered foreign limited partnership. Whether a resignation violates a contract between the registered agent and the partnership is beyond the scope of this act, and Subsection (d) preserves whatever claims a represented partnership may have against its registered agent for a wrongful termination. Even if a resignation were to violate such a contract, the resignation would still be effective if the provisions of this section were followed.

Subsection (b)—This subsection delays the effectiveness of a statement of resignation for thirty one days to allow the notice of the resignation that must be sent under Subsection (c) to reach the represented limited partnership or registered foreign limited partnership and to allow the partnership to arrange for a substitute registered agent.

Subsection (e)—This subsection makes clear that a registered agent may resign with respect to limited partnership or registered foreign limited partnership that is not in good standing and supersedes the contrary administrative practice in some states of refusing to accept any filings with respect to an entity that is not in good standing until the problem with the entity's standing is cured.

§ 120.   Change of Name or Address by Registered Agent

(a)   If a registered agent changes its name or address, the agent may deliver to the [Secretary of State] for filing a statement of change that states:

(1)   the name of the limited partnership or registered foreign limited partnership represented by the registered agent;

(2)   the name of the agent as currently shown in the records of the [Secretary of State] for the partnership or foreign partnership;

(3)   if the name of the agent has changed, its new name; and

(4)   if the address of the agent has changed, its new address.

(b)   A registered agent promptly shall furnish notice to the represented limited partnership or registered foreign limited partnership of the filing by the [Secretary of State] of the statement of change and the changes made by the statement.

Legislative Note: Many registered agents act in that capacity for many entities, and the Model Registered Agents Act (2006) (Last Amended 2013) provides a streamlined method through which a commercial registered agent can make a single filing to change its information for all represented entities. The single filing does not prevent an enacting state from assessing filing fees on the basis of the number of entity records affected. Alternatively the fees can be set on an incremental sliding fee or capitated amount based upon potential economies of costs for a bulk filing.

COMMENT

This section permits a registered agent to change the name and address of the agent that appears in the registered agent filing of a limited partnership or foreign limited partnership represented by the agent. This act does not provide for commercial registered agents. *Cf.* UBOC (2011) (Last Amended 2013) §§ 1–405, 1–406, 1–409. As a result, a registered agent will need to make a separate filing under this section for each limited partnership and foreign limited partnership represented by the agent, unless, if authorized by rule or administrative policy, the filing office establishes procedures for a bulk filing with one filing listing the names of all the registered agent's represented entities.

§ 121. Service of Process, Notice, or Demand

(a) A limited partnership or registered foreign limited partnership may be served with any process, notice, or demand required or permitted by law by serving its registered agent.

(b) If a limited partnership or registered foreign limited partnership ceases to have a registered agent, or if its registered agent cannot with reasonable diligence be served, the partnership or foreign partnership may be served by registered or certified mail, return receipt requested, or by similar commercial delivery service, addressed to the partnership or foreign partnership at its principal office. The address of the principal office must be as shown in the partnership's or foreign partnership's most recent [annual] [biennial] report filed by the [Secretary of State]. Service is effected under this subsection on the earliest of:

(1) the date the partnership or foreign partnership receives the mail or delivery by the commercial delivery service;

(2) the date shown on the return receipt, if signed by the partnership or foreign partnership; or

(3) five days after its deposit with the United States Postal Service, or with the commercial delivery service, if correctly addressed and with sufficient postage or payment.

(c) If process, notice, or demand cannot be served on a limited partnership or registered foreign limited partnership pursuant to subsection (a) or (b), service may be made by handing a copy to the individual in charge of any regular place of business or activity of the partnership or foreign partnership if the individual served is not a plaintiff in the action.

(d) Service of process, notice, or demand on a registered agent must be in a written record.

(e) Service of process, notice, or demand may be made by other means under law other than this [act].

COMMENT

Subsection (b)—This subsection offers three alternative methods for establishing the date service is effected, a date important for determining the time within which a limited partnership or registered foreign limited partnership must respond to the process, notice, or demand served. Under Subsection (b)(1), service is effected on the date or receipt by the partnership of the mail or commercial delivery. Under Subsection (b)(2), service is effected on the date shown on the return receipt, if signed on behalf of the partnership. Under Subsection (b)(3), service is effected five days after it is deposited with the Postal Service or with a similar commercial delivery service, if correctly addressed and with correct postage or payment. Service is effective at the earliest of the three listed circumstances.

However, for the party effecting service there are difficulties of proof under the first two circumstances. Under Subsection (b)(1) the exact date of the receipt by the limited partnership or registered foreign limited partnership of mail or commercial delivery is peculiarly within the knowledge of the limited partnership. Under Subsection (b)(2) the return receipt must be signed on behalf of the partnership. That requirement is designed to assure that the service is actually received by the partnership, but the signature on the return receipt may not always show unambiguously that the signer was acting for the partnership and was authorized to do so. As a practical matter, therefore, parties effecting service under Subsection (b) may find it most convenient to rely on Subsection (c) and to maintain their own records so that the date of deposit in the mails or with a commercial delivery service can easily be established.

Subsection (c)—This subsection provides a means for serving process on a limited partnership or foreign limited partnership that cannot be served under Subsection (a) or (b). Some limited partnership statutes require or permit service of process in that circumstance be made on the filing office.

Subsection (e)—*See, e.g.,* Fed. R. Civ. P. 4(h)(1)(B) (authorizing service on "a domestic or foreign corporation, or a partnership or other unincorporated association that is subject to suit under a common name" to be made on "an officer, a managing or general agent, or any other agent authorized by appointment or by law to receive service of process").

§ 122. Delivery of Record

(a) Except as otherwise provided in this [act], permissible means of delivery of a record include delivery by hand, mail, conventional commercial practice, and electronic transmission.

(b) Delivery to the [Secretary of State] is effective only when a record is received by the [Secretary of State].

COMMENT

Subsection (a)—Permissible means of delivery are not limited to those listed in this subsection, because this subsection by its terms is a non-exclusive list. Conventional commercial practice includes the use of private delivery or courier services. What constitutes conventional commercial practice may change over time.

Subsection (b)—This section lists permissible means of delivery but, except for delivery to the filing office, does not determine when delivery occurs. Delivery to the filing office is effective only upon actual receipt.

§ 123. Reservation of Power to Amend or Repeal

The [legislature of this state] has power to amend or repeal all or part of this [act] at any time, and all limited partnerships and foreign limited partnerships subject to this [act] are governed by the amendment or repeal.

COMMENT

Provisions similar to this section have their genesis in *Trustees of Dartmouth College v. Woodward*, 17 U.S. (4 Wheat) 518 (1819), which held that the United States Constitution prohibited the application of newly enacted statutes to existing corporations while suggesting the efficacy of a reservation of power similar to this section. This section is a generalized form of the type of provision found in many entity organic laws, the purpose of which is to avoid any possible argument that an entity has contractual or vested rights in any specific statutory provision of its organic law and to ensure that the state may in the future modify its entity statutes as it deems appropriate and require existing entities to comply with the statutes as modified.

This section applies to changes in mandatory provisions of this act; the section does not pertain to changes in default rules.

Example: Having enacted this act, State A later amends Section 401(b)(3) (affirmative vote or consent of all partners required for a person to become a general partner) to reduce, as a default rule, the necessary quantum of consent to consent from partners owning in the aggregate at least two-third of the interests in current profits owned by partners at the time of the consent. XYZ, LP is a limited partnership formed under State A's act before the amendment. XYZ's partnership agreement is silent on this issue, leaving in place the act's default rule. Whether the act's amended default rule applies depends on whether the partners initially: (i) agreed (whether expressly or implicitly) to accept the then-applicable default rule requiring unanimous consent; (ii) agreed (whether expressly or implicitly) to adopt whatever rule the act provided; or (iii) never considered the issue. In short, the change in a default rule occasions an inquiry into the partners' express or implied agreement as to the role of the default rule in their mutual understanding. In the first instance, the old rule would continue in effect. In the second and third instances, the new rule would apply.

[ARTICLE] 2.   FORMATION; CERTIFICATE OF LIMITED PARTNERSHIP AND OTHER FILINGS

§ 201.   Formation of Limited Partnership; Certificate of Limited Partnership

(a)   To form a limited partnership, a person must deliver a certificate of limited partnership to the [Secretary of State] for filing.

(b)   A certificate of limited partnership must state:

Mandatory provisions

(1)   the name of the limited partnership, which must comply with Section 114;

(2)   the street and mailing addresses of the partnership's principal office;

(3)   the name and street and mailing addresses in this state of the partnership's registered agent;

(4)   the name and street and mailing addresses of each general partner; and

(5)   whether the limited partnership is a limited liability limited partnership.

(c)   A certificate of limited partnership may contain statements as to matters other than those required by subsection (b), but may not vary or otherwise affect the provisions specified in Section 105(c) and (d) in a manner inconsistent with that section.

(d)   A limited partnership is formed when:

(1)   the certificate of limited partnership becomes effective:

(2)   at least two persons have become partners;

(3)   at least one person has become a general partner; and

(4)   at least one person has become a limited partner.

COMMENT

For a limited partnership to be formed (*i.e.*, to come into existence), four conditions must be met: (i) a certificate of limited partnership must become effective; (ii) at least two persons must become * * * partners; (iii) at least one person must become a general partner; and (iv) at least one person must become a limited partner.

By definition, the earliest a person can become a limited partner is when the certificate of limited partnership takes effect. *See* Section 102(11) (defining "limited partner" as a person that "has become a limited partner under Section 301"). However, a certificate of limited partnership can take effect long before any person becomes a limited partner, and the act does not require any public filing to indicate that a person has become a limited partner. Therefore, the public record will not reflect when (and even whether) a limited partnership has come into existence. *See also* Section 211, cmt.

Subsection (b)—Consistent with the modern trend, this act requires only the most "bare bones" of disclosure.

Subsection (b)(4)—The requirement to identify all general partners dates back to 1916. ULPA (1916) § 2. When a person dissociates as a general partner or a person becomes a new general partner, the certificate must be amended. *See* Section 202(d). However, a person can become a general partner for many purposes without being listed as such on the certificate. *See* Section 401, cmt.

Section (b)(5)—This act permits a limited partnership to be a limited liability limited partnership ("LLLP"), and this provision requires the certificate of limited partnership to state whether the limited partnership is an LLLP. The requirement is intended to force the organizers of a limited partnership to decide whether the limited partnership is to be an LLLP.

Subject to Sections 406(b)(2) and 105(c)(5), a limited partnership may amend its certificate of limited partnership to add or delete a statement that the limited partnership is a limited liability limited partnership. An amendment deleting such a statement must be accompanied by an amendment stating that the limited partnership is *not* a limited liability limited partnership. Section 201(b)(5) does not permit a certificate of limited partnership to be silent on this point, except for pre-existing partnerships that become subject to this act under Section 112. *See* Section 112(c)(2).

Subsection (c)—This provision permits the certificate of limited partnership to contain information beyond that required in Subsection (b). A limited partnership should have good reason, however, before choosing to include additional information. Such information: (i) is available to the public (including competitors); (ii) increases the chances of a conflict between the certificate of limited partnership and the partnership agreement, *see* Section 107(d); (iii) permits the argument that the additional information is part of the partnership agreement, *see* Section 102(14), cmt. (stating that "[t]he partnership agreement may comprise a number of separate documents (or records), however denominated, unless the partnership agreement itself provides otherwise"); and (iv) can be confusing to the extent the information appears to delineate the power of persons to act for the limited partnership. In any event, placing additional information in the certificate of limited partnership does not enable a limited partnership to "end run" the provisions of Section 105(c) and (d) (limiting the power of the partnership agreement to vary specified provisions of this act).

§ 202. Amendment or Restatement of Certificate of Limited Partnership

(a)   A certificate of limited partnership may be amended or restated at any time.

(b)   To amend its certificate of limited partnership, a limited partnership must deliver to the [Secretary of State] for filing an amendment stating:

   (1)   the name of the partnership;

   (2)   the date of filing of its initial certificate; and

   (3)   the text of the amendment.

(c)   To restate its certificate of limited partnership, a limited partnership must deliver to the [Secretary of State] for filing a restatement, designated as such in its heading.

(d)   A limited partnership shall promptly deliver to the [Secretary of State] for filing an amendment to a certificate of limited partnership to reflect:

   (1)   the admission of a new general partner;

   (2)   the dissociation of a person as a general partner; or

   (3)   the appointment of a person to wind up the limited partnership's activities and affairs under Section 802(c) or (d).

(e)   If a general partner knows that any information in a filed certificate of limited partnership was inaccurate when the certificate was filed or has become inaccurate due to changed circumstances, the general partner shall promptly:

   (1)   cause the certificate to be amended; or

   (2)   if appropriate, deliver to the [Secretary of State] for filing a statement of change under Section 118 or a statement of correction under Section 209.

COMMENT

Like other provisions of the act requiring records to be delivered to the filing officer for filing, this section is not subject to change by the partnership agreement. *See* Section 105(c)(3). Except for Subsection (d), this section is essentially mechanical.

Subsection (d)—This subsection lists changes in circumstances which require an amendment to the certificate. Neither a statement of change, Section 118, nor the annual/biennial report, Section 212, suffice to report the addition or deletion of a general partner or the appointment of a person to wind up a limited partnership that has no general partner.

Acquiring or relinquishing LLLP status also requires an amendment to the certificate. *See* Sections 105(c)(5), 201(b)(5), 406(b)(2).

This subsection states an obligation of the limited partnership. However, so long as the limited partnership has at least one general partner, the general partner or partners are responsible for managing the limited partnership's activities. Section 406(a). That management responsibility includes maintaining accuracy in the limited partnership's public record.

Moreover, Subsection (e) imposes direct responsibility on any general partner that knows that the filed certificate of limited partnership contains false information.

Subsection (e)—This subsection imposes an obligation directly on the general partners rather than on the limited partnership. A general partner's failure to meet the obligation can expose the general partner to liability to third parties under Section 205(a)(2) and might constitute a breach of the general partner's duties under Section 409(c). In addition, an aggrieved person may seek a remedy under Sections 204 (Signing and Filing Pursuant to Judicial Order) and 205(Liability for Inaccurate Information in Filed Record).

§ 203. Signing of Records to be Delivered for Filing to [Secretary of State]

(a)   A record delivered to the [Secretary of State] for filing pursuant to this [act] must be signed as follows:

(1)   An initial certificate of limited partnership must be signed by all general partners listed in the certificate.

(2)   An amendment to the certificate of limited partnership adding or deleting a statement that the limited partnership is a limited liability limited partnership must be signed by all general partners listed in the certificate.

(3)   An amendment to the certificate of limited partnership designating as general partner a person admitted under Section 801(a)(3)(B) following the dissociation of a limited partnership's last general partner must be signed by that person.

(4)   An amendment to the certificate of limited partnership required by Section 802(c) following the appointment of a person to wind up the dissolved limited partnership's activities and affairs must be signed by that person.

(5)   Any other amendment to the certificate of limited partnership must be signed by:

(A)   at least one general partner listed in the certificate;

(B)   each person designated in the amendment as a new general partner; and

(C)   each person that the amendment indicates has dissociated as a general partner, unless:

(i)   the person is deceased or a guardian or general conservator has been appointed for the person and the amendment so states; or

(ii)   the person has previously delivered to the [Secretary of State] for filing a statement of dissociation.

(6)   A restated certificate of limited partnership must be signed by at least one general partner listed in the certificate, and, to the extent the restated certificate effects a change under any other paragraph of this subsection, the certificate must be signed in a manner that satisfies that paragraph.

(7)   A statement of termination must be signed by all general partners listed in the certificate of limited partnership or, if the certificate of a dissolved limited partnership lists no general partners, by the person appointed pursuant to Section 802(c) or (d) to wind up the dissolved limited partnership's activities and affairs.

(8)   Any other record delivered by a limited partnership to the [Secretary of State] for filing must be signed by at least one general partner listed in the certificate of limited partnership.

(9)   A statement by a person pursuant to Section 605(a)(3) stating that the person has dissociated as a general partner must be signed by that person.

(10)   A statement of negation by a person pursuant to Section 306 must be signed by that person.

(11)   Any other record delivered on behalf of a person to the [Secretary of State] for filing must be signed by that person.

(b)   Any record delivered for filing under this [act] may be signed by an agent. Whenever this [act] requires a particular individual to sign a record and the individual is deceased or incompetent, the record may be signed by a legal representative of the individual.

(c)   A person that signs a record as an agent or legal representative thereby affirms as a fact that the person is authorized to sign the record.

COMMENT

Subsection (a)—Section 102(22) defines "sign" broadly, including "an electronic symbol, sound, or process."

Subsection (b)—The filing office will not check the bona fides of a person purporting to have signed a record in a representative capacity. This subsection expressly authorizes taking action through an agent so as to provide context for Subsection (c) and for the avoidance of doubt. No negative inference should be drawn about using agents to take other action under this act.

Subsection (c)—As a matter of agency law, a person who signs in a representative capacity gives a "warranty of authority." RESTATEMENT (THIRD) OF AGENCY § 6.10 (2006) (Agent's Implied Warranty of Authority). This subsection also has criminal law implications. Under Section 205(b), "[a]n individual who signs a record authorized or required to be filed under this [act] affirms under penalty of perjury that the information stated in the record is accurate."

§ 204.   Signing and Filing Pursuant to Judicial Order

(a)   If a person required by this [act] to sign a record or deliver a record to the [Secretary of State] for filing under this [act] does not do so, any other person that is aggrieved may petition [the appropriate court] to order:

(1)   the person to sign the record;

(2)   the person to deliver the record to the [Secretary of State] for filing; or

(3)   the [Secretary of State] to file the record unsigned.

(b)   If a petitioner under subsection (a) is not the limited partnership or foreign limited partnership to which the record pertains, the petitioner shall make the partnership or foreign partnership a party to the action.

(c)   A record filed under subsection (a)(3) is effective without being signed.

COMMENT

This section gives the court the flexibility to order either that a record be signed or that the record be filed by the filing office unsigned. The latter circumstance may arise, for example, in a situation where the person who should sign the record is not subject to the jurisdiction of the court. This section also makes clear that the court may order a person with control over a record that has been signed to deliver the record to the filing office for filing.

§ 205.   Liability for Inaccurate Information in Filed Record

(a)   If a record delivered to the [Secretary of State] for filing under this [act] and filed by the [Secretary of State] contains inaccurate information, a person that suffers loss by reliance on the information may recover damages for the loss from:

(1)   a person that signed the record, or caused another to sign it on the person's behalf, and knew the information to be inaccurate at the time the record was signed; and

(2)   a general partner if:

(A)   the record was delivered for filing on behalf of the partnership; and

(B)   the general partner knew or had notice of the inaccuracy for a reasonably sufficient time before the information was relied upon so that, before the reliance, the general partner reasonably could have:

(i)   effected an amendment under Section 202;

(ii)   filed a petition under Section 204; or

939

(iii)   delivered to the [Secretary of State] for filing a statement of change under Section 118 or a statement of correction under Section 209.

(b)   An individual who signs a record authorized or required to be filed under this [act] affirms under penalty of perjury that the information stated in the record is accurate.

COMMENT

Subsection (a)—This subsection relates to liability to third parties for inaccurate information in a filed record. Paragraph 1 requires actual knowledge because the paragraph can inculpate a person who is not a general partner. Under Paragraph 2(B), notice suffices, because: (i) the provision applies only to general partners; (ii) by status these persons have overall management authority; and (iii) therefore it is reasonable to impose liability when a person either knows or "has reason to know . . . from all the facts known to the person at the time in question." Section 103(b)(1) (defining notice). For the same reason, Paragraph 1 applies only to "information [known] to be inaccurate at the time the record was signed," while Paragraph 2 applies whenever a "general partner knew or had notice of the inaccuracy for a reasonably sufficient time before the information was relied upon so that, before the reliance, the general partner reasonably could have [taken corrective action]." Paragraph (2)(B).

Subsection (a)(2)—Although this act establishes the avoidance of gross negligence as the standard of care for general partners viz-a-viz the limited partnership, this provision encompasses liability to third parties. Accordingly, the standard here is more demanding. The phrases "reasonably sufficient time" and "reasonably could have" indicate a standard of ordinary care. "[N]otice of the inaccuracy" involves "reason to know." Section 103(b)(1)

Subsection (b)—This subsection provides criminal liability. The elements of perjury are a matter for the criminal law of the jurisdiction of formation.

§ 206.   Filing Requirements

(a)   To be filed by the [Secretary of State] pursuant to this [act], a record must be received by the [Secretary of State], must comply with this [act], and satisfy the following:

(1)   The filing of the record must be required or permitted by this [act].

(2)   The record must be physically delivered in written form unless and to the extent the [Secretary of State] permits electronic delivery of records.

(3)   The words in the record must be in English, and numbers must be in Arabic or Roman numerals, but the name of an entity need not be in English if written in English letters or Arabic or Roman numerals.

(4)   The record must be signed by a person authorized or required under this [act] to sign the record.

(5)   The record must state the name and capacity, if any, of each individual who signed it, either on behalf of the individual or the person authorized or required to sign the record, but need not contain a seal, attestation, acknowledgment, or verification.

(b)   If law other than this [act] prohibits the disclosure by the [Secretary of State] of information contained in a record delivered to the [Secretary of State] for filing, the [Secretary of State] shall file the record if the record otherwise complies with this [act] but may redact the information.

(c)   When a record is delivered to the [Secretary of State] for filing, any fee required under this [act] and any fee, tax, interest, or penalty required to be paid under this [act] or law other than this [act] must be paid in a manner permitted by the [Secretary of State] or by that law.

(d)   The [Secretary of State] may require that a record delivered in written form be accompanied by an identical or conformed copy.

(e)   The [Secretary of State] may provide forms for filings required or permitted to be made by this [act], but, except as otherwise provided in subsection (f), their use is not required.

(f)   The [Secretary of State] may require that a cover sheet for a filing be on a form prescribed by the [Secretary of State].

COMMENT

The filing office's duty under this section is ministerial, Section 210(a), and the office's assessment of a record delivered for filing is limited to conformity with this section. The filing office *must* file a record delivered for filing if the record contains the information required by this act and is accompanied by the required filing fee. The filing office is authorized to provide forms but not require their use, and, as a result, may not reject records delivered for filing on the basis of form (except to the very limited extent permitted by Subsections (d) and (f)).

In view of the very limited discretion granted to the filing office under this section and Section 210(a), "[t]he filing of . . . a record does not create a presumption that the information contained in the record is correct. . . ." Section 210(e).

Subsection (a)—The first requisite for having a record filed is to cause the record actually to be received by the filing office. Section 122(b) reiterates this point.

Subsection (a)(2)—A record delivered for filing must be in typewritten or printed form unless the filing office permits delivery by electronic transmission. The types of electronic transmission that may be used will be determined by the filing office and is intended to include the evolving methods of electronic delivery, including facsimile transmissions, electronic transmissions between computers and filings through delivery of storage media.

Subsection (a)(3)—The text of an entity filing must be in the English language, except to the limited extent permitted by this paragraph.

Subsection (a)(4)—To be filed a record must be signed by the appropriate person. For a description of the manner in which a record may be "signed," see Section 102(22) (defining "sign"). Who is an appropriate person is determined under Section 203, but the filing office will not check to determine whether a person purportedly authorized to sign is in fact authorized.

The requirement in some state statutes that records delivered for filing on behalf of an entity must be acknowledged or verified as a condition for filing has been rejected. These requirements serve little purpose in connection with entity filings. On the other hand, many organizations, like lenders or title companies, may desire that specific records include acknowledgements, verifications, or seals; Subsection (a)(4) does not prohibit the addition of these forms of execution and their use does not affect the eligibility of the record for filing.

Subsection (b)—Under this subsection, a confidentiality obligation does not affect the filing office's duty to file, and the filing office is authorized but not required to redact. This act does not affect any confidentiality-related obligations the filing office may have under other law.

§ 207. Effective Date and Time

Except as otherwise provided in Section 208 and subject to Section 209(d), a record filed under this [act] is effective:

(1) on the date and at the time of its filing by the [Secretary of State], as provided in Section 210(b);

(2) on the date of filing and at the time specified in the record as its effective time, if later than the time under paragraph (1);

(3) at a specified delayed effective date and time, which may not be more than 90 days after the date of filing; or

(4) if a delayed effective date is specified, but no time is specified, at 12:01 a.m. on the date specified, which may not be more than 90 days after the date of filing.

COMMENT

Records accepted for filing become effective at the date and time of filing as recorded by the filing office, or at another specified time on that date, unless a permissible delayed effective date is stated in the record.

Section 210(b) requires the filing office to maintain some means of recording the date and time of delivery of a record and requires that office to record that date and time as the date and time of filing. That provision gives express statutory authority to the common practice of most filing offices of ignoring processing time and treating a record as filed as of the date and time it is delivered for filing even though it may not be reviewed and accepted for filing until several days after delivery. That section contemplates that time of delivery, as well as the date, will be routinely recorded.

Paragraph (1)—In the absence of provision for a delayed effective date, a record delivered for filing becomes effective on the date and time of filing by the filing office. Since under 210(b) the date and time of filing is the recorded date and time of delivery of the record to the filing office (which under Section 210(b) is the date and time of actual receipt), together these provisions eliminate any doubt about situations involving same-day transactions in which a record, for example, a statement of merger, is delivered for filing on the morning of the day the merger is to become effective.

Paragraph (3)—This paragraph does not authorize or contemplate the retroactive establishment of an effective date before the date of filing.

Paragraphs (3) and (4)—A record that states an effective date beyond the 90-day limit is not a record that "satisfies this [act]," Section 210(a), and will properly be rejected by the filing office.

§ 208.   Withdrawal of Filed Record Before Effectiveness

(a)   Except as otherwise provided in Sections 1124, 1134, 1144, and 1154, a record delivered to the [Secretary of State] for filing may be withdrawn before it takes effect by delivering to the [Secretary of State] for filing a statement of withdrawal.

(b)   A statement of withdrawal must:

     (1)   be signed by each person that signed the record being withdrawn, except as otherwise agreed by those persons;

     (2)   identify the record to be withdrawn; and

     (3)   if signed by fewer than all the persons that signed the record being withdrawn, state that the record is withdrawn in accordance with the agreement of all the persons that signed the record.

(c)   On filing by the [Secretary of State] of a statement of withdrawal, the action or transaction evidenced by the original record does not take effect.

COMMENT

Only records that have not yet taken effect may be withdrawn under this section. If a record has taken effect, it may be corrected under Section 209 if the requirements of that section are satisfied. Otherwise, the record must be amended in accordance with this act or, if the record is a certificate of limited partnership, the resulting limited partnership may be dissolved and terminated in accordance with Article 8.

Subsection (b)(1)—This provision is subject to Section 203(b) ("Whenever this [act] requires a particular individual to sign a record and the individual is deceased or incompetent, the record may be signed by a legal representative of the individual.").

§ 209.   Correcting Filed Record

(a)   A person on whose behalf a filed record was delivered to the [Secretary of State] for filing may correct the record if:

     (1)   the record at the time of filing was inaccurate;

     (2)   the record was defectively signed; or

     (3)   the electronic transmission of the record to the [Secretary of State] was defective.

(b)   To correct a filed record, a person on whose behalf the record was delivered to the [Secretary of State] must deliver to the [Secretary of State] for filing a statement of correction.

(c)   A statement of correction:

     (1)   may not state a delayed effective date;

     (2)   must be signed by the person correcting the filed record;

     (3)   must identify the filed record to be corrected;

     (4)   must specify the inaccuracy or defect to be corrected; and

     (5)   must correct the inaccuracy or defect.

(d)   A statement of correction is effective as of the effective date of the filed record that it corrects except for purposes of Section 103(d) and as to persons relying on the uncorrected filed record and adversely affected by the correction. For those purposes and as to those persons, the statement of correction is effective when filed.

COMMENT

This section permits making corrections in filed records without re-submitting the entire record.

Subsection (a)(1) and (2)—A filed record may be corrected because it contains an inaccuracy or because it was defectively executed (including defects in optional forms of execution that do not affect the eligibility of the original record for filing).

Subsection (a)(3)—In addition, a filed record may be corrected if its electronic transmission was defective—*i.e.*, where an electronic delivery is made but, due to a defect in transmission, the filed record is later discovered to be inconsistent with the record intended to be filed. If no delivery is made because of a defect in transmission, a statement of correction may not be used to effect a retroactive filing. Therefore, a limited partnership making an electronic delivery should take steps to confirm that the transmission was received by the filing office.

Subsection (c)—A provision in a filed record setting an effective date may be corrected under this section, but the corrected effective date must comply with Section 207, which limits delayed effective dates to within ninety days after filing. A corrected effective date is thus measured from the date of the original filing of the record being corrected, *i.e.*, it cannot be before the date of filing of the record or more than ninety days thereafter.

Subsection (d)—The correction relates back to the original effective date of the record being corrected, except as to persons relying on the original entity filing and adversely affected by the correction. As to these persons, the effective date of the statement of correction is the date the statement is filed.

§ 210.   Duty of [Secretary of State] to File; Review of Refusal to File; Delivery of Record by [Secretary of State]

(a)   The [Secretary of State] shall file a record delivered to the [Secretary of State] for filing which satisfies this [act]. The duty of the [Secretary of State] under this section is ministerial.

(b)   When the [Secretary of State] files a record, the [Secretary of State] shall record it as filed on the date and at the time of its delivery. After filing a record, the [Secretary of State] shall deliver to the person that submitted the record a copy of the record with an acknowledgment of the date and time of filing.

(c)   If the [Secretary of State] refuses to file a record, the [Secretary of State] shall, not later than [15] business days after the record is delivered:

(1)   return the record or notify the person that submitted the record of the refusal; and

(2)   provide a brief explanation in a record of the reason for the refusal.

(d)   If the [Secretary of State] refuses to file a record, the person that submitted the record may petition [the appropriate court] to compel filing of the record. The record and the explanation of the [Secretary of State] of the refusal to file must be attached to the petition. The court may decide the matter in a summary proceeding.

(e)   The filing of or refusal to file a record does not:

(1)   affect the validity or invalidity of the record in whole or in part; or

(2)   create a presumption that the information contained in the record is correct or incorrect.

(f)   Except as otherwise provided by Section 121 or by law other than this [act], the [Secretary of State] may deliver any record to a person by delivering it:

(1)   in person to the person that submitted it;

(2)   to the address of the person's registered agent;

(3)   to the principal office of the person; or

(4)   to another address the person provides to the [Secretary of State] for delivery.

COMMENT

Subsection (a)—Under this subsection the filing office is required to file a record if it "satisfies this [act]." The purpose of this language is to limit the discretion of the filing office to a ministerial role in reviewing the contents of records. If the record submitted is in the form prescribed, contains the information required by this act, and the appropriate filing fee is tendered, the filing office must file the record. Consistent with this approach, this subsection states explicitly that the filing duty of the filing office is ministerial. *See also* Subsection (e) (pertaining to presumptions not created).

Subsection (b)—This subsection provides that when the filing office files a record, the filing office records it as filed on the date and time of delivery to the filing office, retains the original record for the office's records, and delivers a copy of the record to the person who delivered the record for filing with an acknowledgement of the date and time of filing.

In the case of a record transmitted electronically to the filing office, that office may make delivery by electronic transmission. The copy returned will be the exact or conformed copy if one has been required by the filing office, or will be a copy made by the filing office if an exact or conformed copy was not required.

Under this subsection the acceptance of a filing is evidenced merely by the filing office's delivery of a copy of the record with an acknowledgment of the date and time of filing. The act does not provide for the filing office to issue a formal certificate of filing. A copy of the filed record together with an acknowledgment of the date and time of filing should sufficiently indicate that the filing has been accepted for filing and been filed.

Subsection (c)—Because of the simplification of formal filing requirements and the limited discretion granted to the filing office by this act, it is probable that rejection of records delivered to the filing office for filing will occur only rarely. This subsection provides that if the filing office does reject a record delivered for filing, the filing office must return the record to the person that submitted the filing within fifteen days together with a brief written explanation of the reason for rejection. In the case of a record delivered by electronic transmission, rejection of the record may be made electronically by the filing office or by a mailing to the person that submitted the record.

Subsection (e)—This subsection provides that the filing of a record by the filing office does not affect the validity or invalidity of any provision contained in the record and does not create any presumption with respect to any information in the record. Likewise, the refusal of the filing office to file a record creates no presumption that any of the information in the record is incorrect. Persons adversely affected by a statement in a filed record may contest the statement in a proceeding appropriate for that purpose, including a damage action under Section 205.

§ 211. Certificate of Good Standing or Registration

(a) On request of any person, the [Secretary of State] shall issue a certificate of good standing for a limited partnership or a certificate of registration for a registered foreign limited partnership.

(b) A certificate under subsection (a) must state:

(1) the limited partnership's name or the registered foreign limited partnership's name used in this state;

(2) in the case of a limited partnership:

(A) that a certificate of limited partnership has been filed and has taken effect;

(B) the date the certificate became effective;

(C) the period of the partnership's duration if the records of the [Secretary of State] reflect that its period of duration is less than perpetual; and

(D) that:

(i) no statement of administrative dissolution, or statement of termination has been filed;

(ii) the records of the [Secretary to State] do not otherwise reflect that the partnership has been dissolved or terminated; and

(iii) a proceeding is not pending under Section 811;

(3)   in the case of a registered foreign limited partnership, that it is registered to do business in this state;

(4)   that all fees, taxes, interest, and penalties owed to this state by the limited partnership or the foreign partnership and collected through the [Secretary of State] have been paid, if:

     (A)   payment is reflected in the records of the [Secretary of State]; and

     (B)   nonpayment affects the good standing or registration of the partnership or foreign partnership;

(5)   that the most recent [annual] [biennial] report required by Section 212 has been delivered to the [Secretary of State] for filing; and

(6)   other facts reflected in the records of the [Secretary of State] pertaining to the limited partnership or foreign limited partnership which the person requesting the certificate reasonably requests.

(c)   Subject to any qualification stated in the certificate, a certificate issued by the [Secretary of State] under subsection (a) may be relied on as conclusive evidence of the facts stated in the certificate.

COMMENT

This section establishes a procedure by which anyone may obtain a conclusive certificate from the filing office that, among other things, the records of the filing office either (i) do not indicate that a particular domestic limited partnership has ceased to exist; or (ii) indicate that a particular foreign limited partnership is registered to do business in the state. The certificate will probably be a standardized form. The filing office is to make those determinations from public records only and is neither expected nor permitted to make a more extensive investigation.

Thus, the certificate of good standing will state whether a certificate has been filed and become effective but not that the limited partnership has been formed. For two reasons, a certificate concerning a domestic limited partnership can never conclusively indicate whether the limited partnership has actually been formed and, if formed, whether the limited partnership has been dissolved. Formation depends in part on the occurrence of an act "not of record." *See* Section 201(d) (providing that a limited partnership is formed only when the certificate of limited partnership becomes effective *and* the requisite number of persons have become partners, general partners, and limited partners). Similarly, causes of dissolution are typically "not of record." *See* Section 801. A dissolved limited partnership may deliver for filing an amendment to the certificate of limited partnership stating that the partnership is dissolved, Section 802(b)(2)(A), and the filing of such an amendment would preclude the issuance of a certificate of good standing, Subsection (b)(2)(D)(ii). However, such an amendment is permissive as is a statement of termination. *See* Section 802(b)(2)(F). Thus, the public record might not reflect either the dissolution or termination of a limited partnership.

Subsection (b)(4)—This provision refers only to fees, taxes, interest, and penalties collected by the filing office. In some states other agencies may report to the filing office that franchise or other taxes have been paid; in those states, this information may be included in the certificate. In states where this procedure does not unduly delay the issuance of certificates, this section may be revised appropriately. Subsection (b)(4)(B) limits the scope of the statement in the certificate that all fees, taxes, interest, and penalties have been paid to those where nonpayment affects the existence or authorization to do business of the entity.

Subsection (b)(2)(D)(ii)—The most likely application of this provision is an amendment to a "certificate of limited partnership to state that the partnership is dissolved." Section 802(b)(2)(A).

§ 212.   [Annual] [Biennial] Report for [Secretary of State]

(a)   A limited partnership or registered foreign limited partnership shall deliver to the [Secretary of State] for filing [an annual] [a biennial] report that states:

(1)   the name of the partnership or foreign partnership;

(2)   the name and street and mailing addresses of its registered agent in this state;

(3)   the street and mailing addresses of its principal office;

(4)   the name of at least one general partner; and

(5)   in the case of a foreign partnership, its jurisdiction of formation and any alternate name adopted under Section 1006(a).

(b)   Information in the [annual] [biennial] report must be current as of the date the report is signed by the limited partnership or registered foreign limited partnership.

(c)   The first [annual] [biennial] report must be delivered to the [Secretary of State] for filing after [January 1] and before [April 1] of the year following the calendar year in which the limited partnership's certificate of limited partnership became effective or the registered foreign limited partnership registered to do business in this state. Subsequent [annual] [biennial] reports must be delivered to the [Secretary of State] for filing after [January 1] and before [April 1] of each [second] calendar year thereafter.

(d)   If [an annual] [a biennial] report does not contain the information required by this section, the [Secretary of State] promptly shall notify the reporting limited partnership or registered foreign limited partnership in a record and return the report for correction.

(e)   If [an annual] [a biennial] report contains the name or address of a registered agent which differs from the information shown in the records of the [Secretary of State] immediately before the report becomes effective, the differing information is considered a statement of change under Section 118.

COMMENT

In some states, an annual or biennial report by a limited partnership or registered foreign limited partnership will be a new requirement.

Subsection (a)(4)—The requirement that the report include the name of at least one general partner will be a new requirement in some states. There has been increasing pressure from law enforcement agencies for access to more information about the ownership and control of legal entities. This requirement will enable law enforcement to contact a person with some knowledge about the affairs of the limited partnership. Members of the public will also have that ability.

This requirement is separate from the requirement that the certificate of limited partnership always list all current general partners. *See* Sections 201(b)(4), 202(d), 401, cmt.

[ARTICLE] 3.   LIMITED PARTNERS

§ 301.   Becoming Limited Partner

(a)   Upon formation of a limited partnership, a person becomes a limited partner as agreed among the persons that are to be the initial partners.

(b)   After formation, a person becomes a limited partner:

(1)   as provided in the partnership agreement;

(2)   as the result of a transaction effective under [Article] 11;

(3)   with the affirmative vote or consent of all the partners; or

(4)   as provided in Section 801(a)(4) or (a)(5).

(c)   A person may become a limited partner without:

(1)   acquiring a transferable interest; or

(2)   making or being obligated to make a contribution to the limited partnership.

COMMENT

Subsection (b)(3)—A limited partnership being in part a creature of contract, consent is determined on an objective basis (*i.e.*, contract law's "reasonable person" standard). Depending on the terms of a limited partnership agreement, the partners' manifestation of consent might involve detailed formalities, entirely informal activities, or anything in between. Moreover, the partnership agreement might reduce the quantum of consent necessary or shift the consent exclusively to the general partners.

Given that a limited partnership is a voluntary association, a person cannot become a partner of a limited partnership without manifesting consent to do so. That consent also is judged objectively.

Under Section 106(b), "[a] person that becomes a partner is deemed to assent to the partnership agreement," and the agreement binds the partner regardless of whether the partner has actually indicated assent in any way.

Subsection (d)—To accommodate business practices and also because a limited partnership need not have a business purpose, this subsection permits so-called "non-economic partners."

§ 302.　No Agency Power of Limited Partner as Limited Partner

(a)　A limited partner is not an agent of a limited partnership solely by reason of being a limited partner.

(b)　A person's status as a limited partner does not prevent or restrict law other than this [act] from imposing liability on a limited partnership because of the person's conduct.

COMMENT

Subsection (a)—In this respect a limited partner is analogous to a shareholder in a corporation; in each case, status as owner provides neither the right to manage nor a reasonable appearance of that right. The phrase "solely by reason of being a limited partner" conforms to Subsection (b).

Subsection (b)—The phrase "as a limited partner" indicates that: (i) this section does not disable a general partner that also owns a limited partner interest; (ii) the partnership agreement may as a matter of contract allocate managerial rights to one or more limited partners; and (iii) a separate agreement can empower and entitle a person that is a limited partner to act for the limited partnership in another capacity, *e.g.*, as an agent. *See* Section 305(a), cmt.

The fact that a limited partner *qua* limited partner has no power to bind the limited partnership means that, subject to Section 109 (Dual Capacity), information possessed by a limited partner is not attributed to the limited partnership. *See* Section 103(f).

This act specifies various circumstances in which limited partners have consent rights, including:

- admission of a limited partner, Section 301(b)(3)
- admission of a general partner, Section 401(b)(3)
- amendment of the partnership agreement, Section 406(b)(1)
- the decision to amend the certificate of limited partnership so as to obtain or relinquish LLLP status, Section 406(b)(2)
- the disposition of all or substantially all of the limited partnership's property, outside the usual and regular course of its activities and affairs, Section 406(b)(3)
- the compromise of a partner's obligation to make a contribution or return an improper distribution, Section 502(c)
- expulsion of a limited partner by consent of the other partners, Section 601(b)(4)
- expulsion of a general partner by consent of the other partners, Section 603(4)
- causing dissolution by consent, Section 801(a)(2)
- causing dissolution by consent following the dissociation of a general partner, when at least one general partner remains, Section 801(a)(3)(A)
- avoiding dissolution and appointing a successor general partner, following the dissociation of the sole general partner, Section 801(a)(3)(B)(i)
- appointing a person to wind up the limited partnership when there is no general partner, Section 802(c)
- rescinding dissolution, Section 803(b)(1)
- approving, amending or abandoning a plan of:
  - merger, Sections 1123–24;

    ○   interest exchange, Sections 1133–34;

    ○   conversion, Sections 1143–44; and

    ○   domestication, Sections 1153–54.

§ 303. No Liability as Limited Partner for Limited Partnership Obligations

(a)   A debt, obligation, or other liability of a limited partnership is not the debt, obligation, or other liability of a limited partner. A limited partner is not personally liable, directly or indirectly, by way of contribution or otherwise, for a debt, obligation, or other liability of the partnership solely by reason of being or acting as a limited partner, even if the limited partner participates in the management and control of the limited partnership. This subsection applies regardless of the dissolution of the partnership.

(b)   The failure of a limited partnership to observe formalities relating to the exercise of its powers or management of its activities and affairs is not a ground for imposing liability on a limited partner for a debt, obligation, or other liability of the partnership.

COMMENT

Elimination of the "Control Rule"

ULPA (2001) eliminated the so-called "control rule," which had impaired the liability protection accorded limited partners and had become an anachronism in a world with LLPs, LLCs and, most importantly, LLLPs.

The "control rule" first appeared in a uniform act in 1916, although the concept is much older. Section 7 of the original Uniform Limited Partnership Act provided that "a limited partner shall not become liable as a general partner [*i.e.*, for the obligations of the limited partnership] unless . . . he takes part in the control of the business."

ULPA (1976) "carrie[d] over the basic test from former Section 7," but recognized "the difficulty of determining when the control line has been overstepped." ULPA (1976) § 303, cmt. Accordingly, ULPA (1976) tried to buttress the limited partner's shield by: (i) providing a safe harbor for a lengthy list of activities deemed not to constitute participating in control, Section 303(b); and (ii) limiting a limited partner's "control rule" liability "only to persons who transact business with the limited partnership with actual knowledge of [the limited partner's] participation in control," Section 303(a). However, these protections were complicated by a countervailing rule which made a limited partner generally liable for the limited partnership's obligations "if the limited partner's participation in the control of the business is . . . substantially the same as the exercise of the powers of a general partner." Section 303(a).

The 1985 amendments to ULPA (1976) further buttressed the limited partner's shield, removing the "substantially the same" rule, expanding the list of safe harbor activities and limiting "control rule" liability "only to persons who transact business with the limited partnership reasonably believing, based upon the limited partner's conduct, that the limited partner is a general partner." ULPA (1976/1985) § 303(a).

ULPA (2001) took the logical next step, bringing limited partners into parity with corporate shareholders, LLC members, and LLP partners.

Subsection (a)—This subsection provides a corporate-like liability shield for limited partners, protecting them against the debts, obligations and other liabilities of the limited partnership—*i.e.*, against vicarious liability for the obligations of the entity. Because a dissolved limited partnership is nonetheless an entity formed under this act, dissolution has no effect on the liability shield.

For further comments on the nature of the shield, see Section 404(c), comment.

Subsection (b)—For an explanation of this subsection, see Section 404(d), comment.

§ 304. Rights to Information of Limited Partner and Person Dissociated as Limited Partner

(a)   On 10 days' demand, made in a record received by the limited partnership, a limited partner may inspect and copy required information during regular business hours in the limited partnership's principal office. The limited partner need not have any particular purpose for seeking the information.

(b)   During regular business hours and at a reasonable location specified by the limited partnership, a limited partner may inspect and copy information regarding the activities, affairs, financial condition, and other circumstances of the limited partnership as is just and reasonable if:

(1)   the limited partner seeks the information for a purpose reasonably related to the partner's interest as a limited partner;

(2)   the limited partner makes a demand in a record received by the limited partnership, describing with reasonable particularity the information sought and the purpose for seeking the information; and

(3)   the information sought is directly connected to the limited partner's purpose.

(c)   Not later than 10 days after receiving a demand pursuant to subsection (b), the limited partnership shall inform in a record the limited partner that made the demand of:

(1)   what information the partnership will provide in response to the demand and when and where the partnership will provide the information; and

(2)   the partnership's reasons for declining, if the partnership declines to provide any demanded information.

(d)   Whenever this [act] or a partnership agreement provides for a limited partner to vote on or give or withhold consent to a matter, before the vote is cast or consent is given or withheld, the limited partnership shall, without demand, provide the limited partner with all information that is known to the partnership and is material to the limited partner's decision.

(e)   Subject to subsection (j), on 10 days' demand made in a record received by a limited partnership, a person dissociated as a limited partner may have access to information to which the person was entitled while a limited partner if:

(1)   the information pertains to the period during which the person was a limited partner;

(2)   the person seeks the information in good faith; and

(3)   the person satisfies the requirements imposed on a limited partner by subsection (b).

(f)   A limited partnership shall respond to a demand made pursuant to subsection (e) in the manner provided in subsection (c).

(g)   A limited partnership may charge a person that makes a demand under this section reasonable costs of copying, limited to the costs of labor and material.

(h)   A limited partner or person dissociated as a limited partner may exercise the rights under this section through an agent or, in the case of an individual under legal disability, a legal representative. Any restriction or condition imposed by the partnership agreement or under subsection (j) applies both to the agent or legal representative and to the limited partner or person dissociated as a limited partner.

(i)   Subject to Section 704, the rights under this section do not extend to a person as transferee.

(j)   In addition to any restriction or condition stated in its partnership agreement, a limited partnership, as a matter within the ordinary course of its activities and affairs, may impose reasonable restrictions and conditions on access to and use of information to be furnished under this section, including designating information confidential and imposing nondisclosure and safeguarding obligations on the recipient. In a dispute concerning the reasonableness of a restriction under this subsection, the partnership has the burden of proving reasonableness.

COMMENT

This section balances two countervailing concerns relating to information: the need of limited partners and former limited partners for access versus the limited partnership's need to protect confidential business data and other intellectual property. The balance must be understood in the context of fiduciary duties. The general partners are obliged through their duties of care and loyalty to protect information whose confidentiality is important to the limited partnership or otherwise inappropriate for dissemination. *See* Section 409 (general standards of general partner conduct). A limited partner, in contrast, "does not have any [fiduciary] duty to the limited partnership or to any other partner solely by reason of acting as a limited partner." Section 305(b).

Like predecessor law, this act divides limited partner access rights into two categories: required information and other information. However, this act builds on predecessor law by:

- expanding slightly the category of required information and stating explicitly that a limited partner may have access to that information without having to show cause;

- specifying a procedure for limited partners to follow when demanding access to other information;

- specifying how a limited partnership must respond to such a demand and setting a time limit for the response;

- retaining predecessor law's "just and reasonable" standard for determining a limited partner's right to other information, while recognizing that, to be "just and reasonable," a limited partner's demand for other information must meet minimum standards of relatedness and particularity;

- expressly requiring the limited partnership to volunteer known, material information when seeking or obtaining consent from limited partners;

- codifying (while limiting) the power of the partnership agreement to vary limited partner access rights;

- permitting the limited partnership to establish other reasonable limits on access; and

- providing access rights for former limited partners.

Although the rights and duties stated in this section are extensive, they are not necessarily all-inclusive. This act's statement of fiduciary duties is not exhaustive. *See* Section 409(a), cmt., and some cases characterize owners' information rights as reflecting a fiduciary duty of those with management power. *E.g., Fate v. Owens*, 130 N.M. 503, 511, 27 P.3d 990, 998 (2001) (stating that "[a] partner, as a fiduciary, is required to fully disclose material facts and information relating to partnership affairs to the other partners," including limited partners); *Konover Dev. Corp. v. Zeller*, 228 Conn. 206, 218–19, 635 A.2d 798, 804–05 (1994) (stating that "the general partner of a limited partnership has the fiduciary duty of rendering true accounts and full information about anything which affects the partnership") (quoting *Williams v. Bartlett*, 189 Conn. 471, 482 n. 8, 457 A.2d 290 (1983) (internal quotations omitted). Also, the rights stated in this section are in addition to whatever discovery rights a party has in a civil suit.

In contrast, the rights of transferees are limited to those stated in this section and Subsection 702(c); general partners do not owe fiduciary duties to transferees.

The rights stated in this section are personal to limited partners and transferees, and are enforceable through a direct action. *See* Section 901(b), cmt.

Subsection (a)—The phrase "required information" is a defined term. *See* Sections 102(21) and 108. This subsection's broad right of access is subject not only to reasonable limitations in the partnership agreement, Section 105(c)(9), but also to the power of the limited partnership to impose reasonable limitations on use, Subsection (j). Unless the partnership agreement provides otherwise, general partners have the authority to use that power. *See* Section 406(a).

Subsection (b)—The language describing the information to be provided comes essentially verbatim from ULPA (1976/1985) § 305 (2)(i) and (iii). The procedural requirements derive from the Model Business Corporation Act section 16.02(c) (2011). This subsection does not itself impose a requirement of good faith because Section 305(a) contains a generally applicable obligation of good faith and fair dealing for limited partners. *But see* Subsection (e)(2) (establishing a duty of good faith applicable to a former limited partner).

Subsection (d)—The duty stated in this subsection is at the core of the duties owed by a limited partnership and its general partners to the limited partners, and imposes an affirmative duty to volunteer information. The obligation is limited to information which is both material and known by the limited partnership.

"Knowledge" is viewed subjectively—*i.e.*, actual knowledge. Section 103(a)(1). A limited partnership will "know" what its general partners know. Under Section 103(f), "[a] general partner's knowledge . . . of a fact relating to the limited partnership is effective immediately as knowledge of or notice to the partnership." As to others acting or reasonably appearing to act on behalf of the limited partnership, common law agency rules will apply. RESTATEMENT (THIRD) OF AGENCY § 5.03 (2006) (Imputation of Notice of Fact to Principal).

In contrast, materiality is viewed objectively. Thus, this subsection applies to known, material information, even if the limited partnership does not know that the information is material.

If a violation of this subsection causes harm to a limited partner, the limited partnership is answerable in damages. In appropriate circumstances, a violation might cause a court to enjoin or even rescind an action of a limited partnership, especially when the violation has interfered with an approval or veto mechanism involving limited partner consent. *E.g., Blue Chip Emerald LLC v. Allied Partners Inc.*, 299 A.D.2d 278, 279–280 (N.Y. App. Div. 2002) (invoking partnership law precedent as reflecting a duty of full disclosure and holding that "[a]bsent such full disclosure, the transaction is voidable"), abrogated on other grounds by *Centro Empresarial Cempresa S.A. v. Am. Movil, S.A.B. de C.V.*, 17 N.Y.3d 269, 952 N.E.2d 995 (N.Y. 2011). In addition, a limited partnership's violation of this paragraph could give rise to a claim for damages against a general partner who, through the breach of a duty stated in Section 409, causes or suffers the limited partnership to violate this paragraph. *See Anthony v. Padmar, Inc.*, 465 S.E.2d 745, 755 (S.C. Ct. App. 1995) (finding general partners made a defective disclosure prior to a vote and were therefore liable for resulting pecuniary damages to limited partners).

Subsection (e)—Codifying the information rights of former partners began with UPA (1997) § 403(b). Access is limited and subject to conditions.

Example: A person dissociated as a limited partner seeks access to information pertaining to the period during which the person was a limited partner and to which the person would have access while a limited partner. The person makes a bald demand, merely stating a desire to review the information at the limited partnership's principal office. In particular, the demand does not describe "with reasonable particularity the information sought and the purpose for seeking the information." *See* Subsection (b)(2). The limited partnership is not obliged to allow access. The person must first comply with Subsection (e), which incorporates by reference the requirements of Subsection (b).

See also Subsection (i) (pertaining to information rights of the legal representative of a deceased limited partner).

Subsection (e)(2)—A duty of good faith is needed here because a person claiming access under this subsection is no longer a limited partner and is no longer subject to Section 305(a). *See* Section 602(a)(2) (dissociation as a limited partner terminates duty of good faith as to subsequent events). *But see id.*, cmt (noting that the common law implied covenant will continue to be relevant if the partnership agreement provides continuing rights and obligations for a person dissociated as a limited partner).

As for the meaning of "good faith" in this context, see Section 407(e)(2), cmt.

Subsection (h)—Some old cases involved conflicts over whether a shareholder could exercise inspection rights through another person. *White v. Coeur D'Alene Big Creek Mining Co.*, 55 P.2d 720, 723 (Idaho 1936) (stating that "[t]he refusal to permit respondent [shareholder] to appoint his own attorney or agent to make the examination [of the corporation's books] was in effect a denial of his right" of inspection); *State v. Monida & Yellowstone Stage Co.*, 124 N.W. 971, 972 (Minn. 1910) (upholding a trial court's mandamus order, "which shall provide that [the shareholder complainant], or such attorney or agent as he may select, . . . shall be allowed to inspect the books, records, and papers of the defendant [corporation]"). In light of that history, for the avoidance of doubt, this subsection expressly authorizes taking action through an agent. No negative inference should be drawn about using agents to take other action under this act.

Subsection (i)—This section provides no information rights to a person as transferee. Transferee status brings only the very limited information rights stated in Section 702(c). However, a transferee that is a person dissociated as a limited partner has rights in the latter capacity under Subsection (e).

Subsection (j)—This subsection permits the limited partnership—as distinguished from the partnership agreement—to impose access and use limitations. *See* Section 105(c)(9) (providing that the partnership agreement may impose reasonable restrictions). Under Section 406(a), it will be the general partners that decide whether the limited partnership will impose access and use restrictions.

The limited partnership bears the burden of proving the reasonableness of any restriction imposed under this subsection. In determining whether a restriction is reasonable, a court might consider: (i) the danger or other problem the restriction seeks to avoid; (ii) the purpose for which the information is sought; and (iii) whether, in light of both the problem the restriction seeks to avoid and the purpose for which information is sought, the restriction is reasonably tailored. Restricting use of the names and addresses of limited partners is not *per se* unreasonable.

§ 305. Limited Duties of Limited Partners

(a)   A limited partner shall discharge any duties to the partnership and the other partners under the partnership agreement and exercise any rights under this [act] or the partnership agreement consistently with the contractual obligation of good faith and fair dealing.

(b)   Except as otherwise provided in subsection (a), a limited partner does not have any duty to the limited partnership or to any other partner solely by reason of acting as a limited partner.

(c)   If a limited partner enters into a transaction with a limited partnership, the limited partner's rights and obligations arising from the transaction are the same as those of a person that is not a partner.

COMMENT

Subsection (a)—Fiduciary duty typically attaches to a person whose status or role creates significant power for that person over the interests of another person. Under this act, limited partners have very limited power of any sort in the regular activities of the limited partnership and no power whatsoever justifying the imposition of fiduciary duties either to the limited partnership or fellow partners. *See, e.g., Lichtyger v. Franchard Corp.*, 223 N.E.2d 869, 873 (N.Y. 1966) ("the limited partner is in a position analogous to that of a corporate shareholder, an investor who likewise has limited liability and no voice in the operation of an enterprise") (internal quotation omitted).

It is possible for a partnership agreement to allocate significant managerial authority and power to a limited partner, but in that case the power exists not as a matter of status or role but rather as a matter of contract. *E.g., DV Realty Advisors LLC v. Policemen's Annuity & Ben. Fund of Chicago*, 75 A.3d 101, 111 (Del. 2013) (pertaining to a limited partnership agreement that allowed the limited partners to remove the general partner). The proper limit on such contract-based power is the contract itself (including the implied obligation of good faith and fair dealing), not fiduciary duty, unless the partnership agreement itself: (i) expressly imposes a fiduciary duty; or (ii) creates a role for a limited partner which, as a matter of other law, gives rise to a fiduciary duty. For example, if the partnership agreement makes a limited partner an agent for the limited partnership as to particular matters, the law of agency will impose fiduciary duties on the limited partner with respect to the limited partner's role as agent.

This subsection refers to the "contractual obligation of good faith and fair dealing" to emphasize that the obligation is not an invitation to re-write agreements among the partners. At first glance, it may seem strange to apply a contractual obligation to statutory duties and rights—*i.e.*, duties and rights "under this [act]." However, for the most part those duties and rights apply to relationships *inter se* the partners and the limited partnership and function only to the extent not displaced by the partnership agreement. Those statutory default rules are thus intended to function like a contract; applying the contractual notion of good faith and fair dealing therefore makes sense.

For a detailed discussion of the implied contractual obligation of good faith and fair dealing, see Section 409(d), comment. As to the power of the partnership agreement to affect the obligation, see Section 105(c)(7) (prohibiting elimination but allowing the agreement to "prescribe the standards, if not manifestly unreasonable, by which the performance of the obligation is to be measured").

§ 306. Person Erroneously Believing Self to be Limited Partner

(a)   Except as otherwise provided in subsection (b), a person that makes an investment in a business enterprise and erroneously but in good faith believes that the person has become a limited partner in the enterprise is not liable for the enterprise's obligations by reason of making the investment, receiving distributions from the enterprise, or exercising any rights of or appropriate to a limited partner, if, on ascertaining the mistake, the person:

(1)   causes an appropriate certificate of limited partnership, amendment, or statement of correction to be signed and delivered to the [Secretary of State] for filing; or

(2)   withdraws from future participation as an owner in the enterprise by signing and delivering to the [Secretary of State] for filing a statement of negation under this section.

(b)   A person that makes an investment described in subsection (a) is liable to the same extent as a general partner to any third party that enters into a transaction with the enterprise, believing in good faith that the person is a general partner, before the [Secretary of State] files a statement of negation, certificate of limited partnership, amendment, or statement of correction to show that the person is not a general partner.

(c) If a person makes a diligent effort in good faith to comply with subsection (a)(1) and is unable to cause the appropriate certificate of limited partnership, amendment, or statement of correction to be signed and delivered to the [Secretary of State] for filing, the person has the right to withdraw from the enterprise pursuant to subsection (a)(2) even if the withdrawal would otherwise breach an agreement with others that are or have agreed to become co-owners of the enterprise.

COMMENT

This section deals with the somewhat rare situation in which a person intending in good faith to be a limited partner invests in an enterprise, but:

- the enterprise is not a limited partnership (*i.e.*, no certificate of limited partnership has become effective); or

- the certificate of limited partnership has become effective but lists the person as a general partner.

Subsection (a)—In this subsection, "good faith" does not refer to the implied contractual covenant under Section 409(d). By hypothesis, a person invoking this section is not a partner under this act. In this context, "good faith" is properly understood as referring to the notion of "clean heart, [even if] empty head." Thus, the good faith standard here is entirely subjective, pertaining to the person's actual state of mind regardless of whether that statement of mind is objectively reasonable.

Subsection (a)(2)—The requirement that a person "withdraw[ ] from future participation as an owner in the enterprise" means, in part, that the person refrain from taking any further profit from the enterprise. However, the person is not required to return previously obtained profits or forfeit the investment.

[ARTICLE] 4. GENERAL PARTNERS

§ 401. Becoming General Partner

(a) Upon formation of a limited partnership, a person becomes a general partner as agreed among the persons that are to be the initial partners.

(b) After formation of a limited partnership, a person becomes a general partner:

    (1) as provided in the partnership agreement;

    (2) as the result of a transaction effective under [Article] 11;

    (3) with the affirmative vote or consent of all the partners; or

    (4) as provided in Section 801(a)(3)(B).

(c) A person may become a general partner without:

    (1) acquiring a transferable interest; or

    (2) making or being obligated to make a contribution to the partnership.

COMMENT

A person's status as a general partner is not dependent on the person being so designated in the certificate of limited partnership. If a person does become a general partner under this section without being so designated:

- the limited partnership is obligated to promptly and appropriately amend the certificate of limited partnership, Section 202(d)(1);

- each general partner that knows of the discrepancy is personally obligated to cause the certificate to be promptly and appropriately amended, Section 202(e)(1), and is subject to liability for failing to do so, Section 205(a)(2);

- the "non-designated" general partner has no right to sign records which are to be filed on behalf of the limited partnership under this act, Section 203(a), except the right to sign an amendment to the

953

certificate of limited partnership in the capacity of a person newly designated as a general partner, *see* Section 203(a)(5)(B);

- the "non-designated" general partner has nonetheless:

  ○ the powers of a general partner to bind the limited partnership under Sections 402 and 403; and

  ○ the rights and duties of a general partner viz-a-viz the limited partnership and the other partners.

A limited partnership's liability under Section 402 does not depend on the "act of a general partner" being the act of a general partner designated in the certificate of limited partnership. Moreover, the notice provided by Section 103(c) does not undercut any appearance of authority. Section 402 refers only to notice under Section 103(d) and, in any event, according to the second sentence of Section 103(c), the fact that a person is not listed as in the certificate as a general partner is not notice that the person is not a general partner.

Example: By consent of the partners of XYZ Limited Partnership, Partner G is admitted as a general partner. However, XYZ's certificate of limited partnership is not amended accordingly. Later, Partner G—acting without actual authority—purports to bind XYZ to a transaction with Third Party. Third Party does not review the filed certificate of limited partnership before entering into the transaction. XYZ will be bound under Section 402, assuming that Partner G's action is "for apparently carrying on in the ordinary course the partnership's activities and affairs or activities and affairs of the kind carried on by the partnership."

Example: Same facts, except that Third Party does review the certificate of limited partnership before entering into the transaction. The result might still be the same. The omission of a person's name from the certificate's list of general partners is not notice that the person is not a general partner. Therefore, Third Party's review of the certificate does not mean that Third Party knew, had received a notification or had notice that Partner G lacked authority. At most, XYZ could argue that, because Third Party knew that Partner G was not listed in the certificate, a transaction entered into by Partner G could not reasonably appear to Third Party to be for apparently carrying on the limited partnership's activities in the ordinary course. For a discussion of the reasonableness requirement, see Section 402(a), comment.

Subsection (b)(3)—A limited partnership being in part a creature of contract, consent is determined on an objective basis (*i.e.*, contract law's "reasonable person" standard). Depending on the terms of the partnership agreement, the partners' manifestation of consent might involve detailed formalities, entirely informal activities, or anything in between. Moreover, the partnership agreement might reduce the quantum of consent necessary or shift the consent right to the general partners.

A limited partnership being a voluntary association, a person cannot become a partner without manifesting consent to do so. That consent also is judged objectively.

Under Section 106(b), "[a] person that becomes a partner is deemed to assent to the partnership agreement," and the agreement binds the partner regardless of whether the partner has actually indicated assent in any way.

Subsection (c)(1)—To accommodate business practices and also because a limited partnership need not have a business purpose, this provision permits so-called "non-economic partners."

§ 402.   General Partner Agent of Limited Partnership

(a)   Each general partner is an agent of the limited partnership for the purposes of its activities and affairs. An act of a general partner, including the signing of a record in the partnership's name, for apparently carrying on in the ordinary course the partnership's activities and affairs or activities and affairs of the kind carried on by the partnership binds the partnership, unless the general partner did not have authority to act for the partnership in the particular matter and the person with which the general partner was dealing knew or had notice that the general partner lacked authority.

(b)   An act of a general partner which is not apparently for carrying on in the ordinary course the limited partnership's activities and affairs or activities and affairs of the kind carried on by the partnership binds the partnership only if the act was actually authorized by all the other partners.

COMMENT

Derivation—ULPA (2001) derived this section from UPA (1997) § 301(1), which was derived from UPA (1914) § 9. For further information on the derivation, see UPA (1997) (Last Amended 2013) § 301, comment.

At common law, a general partner was considered a general agent of the partnership. JOSEPH STORY, COMMENTARIES ON THE LAW OF PARTNERSHIP § 101 at 153 (2nd ed. 1850); RESTATEMENT (SECOND) OF AGENCY § 14A cmt. a (1958), and the mere status of a general partner "clothes" a person with apparent authority to carry on the partnership business. *Stockwell v. U.S.*, 80 U.S. 531, 567 (1871); *Lincoln Nat. Bank v. Schoen*, 56 Mo. App. 160, 1894 WL 1879 (1894); *Kansallis Finance Ltd. v. Fern*, 659 N.E.2d 731, 733, 740 (Mass. 1996). In 1914, the Uniform Partnership Act codified this principle, UPA (1914) § 9 (Partner Agent of Partnership as to Partnership Business), and "statutory apparent authority" has been part of uniform partnerships acts ever since. *See* UPA (1997) § 301 (Partner Agent of Partnership; ULPA (2001) § 402 (General Partner Agent of Limited Partnership).

This section's principal purpose is to delineate a general partner's statutory apparent authority. The partnership agreement and Section 406 govern the rights of the partners among themselves, including the right to restrict a general partner's actual authority.

Subsection (a)—This subsection reflects the basic common law principles, as first codified in UPA (1914) § 9(1) and later in UPA (1997) § 301(1). In effect, the subsection characterizes a general partner as a general managerial agent of the limited partnership. Such agents have both actual and apparent authority, and this section delineates the apparent authority. For a discussion of the scope of actual authority, see Section 406(a) and (b), cmt.

The agency law origins of statutory apparent authority have informed courts' application of UPA (1914) § 9(1), and that case law is equally applicable under this act. For example, although the statutory language does not appear to require that the appearance of authority be reasonable, the case law does so routinely. *See, e.g., In re Fox Hill Office Invs., Ltd.*, 101 B.R. 1007, 1019 (Bankr. W.D. Mo. 1989) (stating a third-party lender in possession of a copy of a limited partnership's partnership agreement was on notice of the general partner's lack of authority and therefore should have inquired as to the partner's authority), *aff'd*, 926 F.2d 752 (8th Cir. 1991); *Investors Title Ins. Co. v. Herzig*, 360 S.E.2d 786, 789 (N.C. 1987) (stating that "in order to hold the [partnership] liable, [a third party] must show that in the exercise of reasonable care under the circumstances, it was justified in believing that the principal had conferred . . . authority to [act] on behalf of the partnership"); *First Interstate Bank of Oregon, N.A. v. Bergendahl*, 723 P.2d 1005, 1010 (Or. Ct. App. 1986) (stating that bank in possession of management agreement was on notice of general partner's restricted authority and could not rely on a theory of apparent authority).

Likewise, per the law of apparent authority, a general partner can bind a partnership under this section even if the partner intends to take and does take the resulting benefits for the partner's own benefit. *See Wolfe v. Harms*, 413 S.W.2d 204, 216 (Mo. 1967) (stating that partnership is liable for partner's acts "even if the predominant motive of the partner was to benefit himself or third persons"); *Rouse v. Pollard*, 18 A.2d 5, 7 (N.J. Eq. 1941) ("All the partners are responsible for the act of one of their number as agent, even though he acts for some secret purpose of his own, and not really for the benefit of the [partnership]."), *aff'd*, 21 A.2d 801 (N.J. Eq. 1941); *Investors Title Ins. Co. v. Herzig*, 360 S.E.2d 786, 788 (N.C. 1987) (stating that the mere fact that the partner's act was for personal gain was not enough to justify summary judgment for the partnership on the subject of the partnership's liability for the act).

The fact that a person is not listed in the certificate of limited partnership as a general partner is not notice that the person is not a partner and is not notice that the person lacks authority to act for the limited partnership. *See* Section 103(c) and Section 401, cmt. In contrast, several filings under Section 103(d) may provide notice "to the world" that a person lacks authority to bind a limited partnership.

Example: For the past ten years, Partner X has been a general partner of XYZ Limited Partnership and has regularly conducted the limited partnership's business with Third Party. However, 100 days ago the limited partnership expelled Partner X as a general partner and the next day delivered for filing an amendment to XYZ's certificate of limited partnership which stated that Partner X was no longer a general partner. On that same day, the filing officer filed the amendment.

Today Partner X approaches Third Party, purports still be to a general partner of XYZ and purports to enter into a transaction with Third Party on XYZ's behalf. Third Party is unaware that Partner X has been expelled and has no reason to doubt Partner X's bona fides. Nonetheless, XYZ is not liable on the transaction. Under Section 103(d)(1), Third Party has notice that Partner X is dissociated and perforce has notice that Partner X is not a general partner authorized to bind XYZ because Third Party is deemed to have notice ninety days after the amendment became effective.

The reference to "signing of a record in the partnership's name" encompasses records that purport to convey title to realty.

Subsection (b)—Under this provision, a general partner that lacks both actual and statutory apparent authority entirely lacks the power to bind the entity. *Accord* RESTATEMENT (THIRD) OF AGENCY, ch. 2, Introductory Note (2006) (stating that "this Restatement . . . does not use the concept of inherent agency power"). *But see* Section 403, cmt. (explaining that, under that section, a general partner may bind a limited partnership by unauthorized and wrongful conduct as to which the apparent authority *vel non* is irrelevant).

Agency law determines whether a general partner has actual authority in any particular situation. *See* RESTATEMENT (THIRD) OF AGENCY § 3.01 (2006) (Creation of Actual Authority). For delineation of a general partner's actual authority when this act's default management rules remain in effect, see Section 406(a), (b), cmt. However, the partnership agreement will typically be the primary source of a general partner's actual authority.

This subsection does not affect a limited partnership's power to ratify a general partner's unauthorized act. *See* RESTATEMENT (THIRD) OF AGENCY (2006), Chapter 4 (Ratification).

§ 403.   Limited Partnership Liable for General Partner's Actionable Conduct

(a)   A limited partnership is liable for loss or injury caused to a person, or for a penalty incurred, as a result of a wrongful act or omission, or other actionable conduct, of a general partner acting in the ordinary course of activities and affairs of the partnership or with the actual or apparent authority of the partnership.

(b)   If, in the course of a limited partnership's activities and affairs or while acting with actual or apparent authority of the partnership, a general partner receives or causes the partnership to receive money or property of a person not a partner, and the money or property is misapplied by a general partner, the partnership is liable for the loss.

COMMENT

Subsection (a)—This provision is derived from UPA (1914) § 13 (Partnership Bound by Partner's Wrongful Act) as modernized by UPA (1997) § 305(a) (Partnership Liable for Partner's Actionable Conduct) and for the most part parallels the agency law doctrine of *respondeat superior*. *See* RESTATEMENT (SECOND) OF AGENCY § 14A cmt. a (1958) ("When one of the partners is in active management of the business or is otherwise regularly employed in the business, he is a servant of the partnership."). The liability is vicarious and without regard to the fault of those managing the partnership. For more information on the historical development of this section, see UPA (1997) (Last Amended 2013) 305(a), comment.

To successfully invoke this provision, a plaintiff must show: (i) "a wrongful act or omission, or other actionable conduct" by a general partner; (ii) that caused "loss or injury"; and (iii) that at the relevant moment, the general partner was acting with actual authority, apparent authority (if relevant), or within "the ordinary course of activities and affairs of the partnership." Extrapolating from agency law, apparent authority is relevant only when the appearance of authority augments the impact of the wrongful act. *See* RESTATEMENT (THIRD) OF AGENCY, § 7.08 (2006) ("A principal is subject to vicarious liability for a tort committed by an agent in dealing or communicating with a third party on or purportedly on behalf of the principal when actions taken by the agent with apparent authority constitute the tort or enable the agent to conceal its commission.").

An act or omission may be "in the ordinary course of activities and affairs of the partnership" even though the act is wrongful. Any other interpretation would vitiate the "ordinary course" element. "The proper question . . . is not whether the specific wrongful act is 'ordinary course' . . . , but rather whether that type of act, if done rightfully, would be." DANIEL S. KLEINBERGER, AGENCY, PARTNERSHIP AND LLCS: EXAMPLES AND EXPLANATIONS § 10.5.1 at 350 (4th ed., Wolters Kluwer, 2012) (emphasis omitted).

However, in *Jackson v. Jackson*, 20 N.C.App. 406, 408, 201 S.E.2d 722, 724 (N.C.App. 1974), the North Carolina Court of Appeals stated that, while "[a]dvising the initiation of a criminal prosecution is clearly within the normal range of activities for a typical law partnership, . . . taking such action maliciously and without probable cause is quite a different matter." The court held that "[i]n view of [ethics] rules, which clearly forbid any attempt by a lawyer to prosecute a person without cause, it cannot be held that malicious prosecution is within the ordinary course of business of a law partnership." *Id.* It is difficult to identify a reasonable limit to this approach. Presumably, at least, a partner's "plain vanilla" malpractice is within a law firm's ordinary course of business despite the ethical rules requiring lawyers to act zealously and competently.

In any event, Subsection (a) refers to "the ordinary course of activities and affairs of the *partnership*" (emphasis added); thus the proper question is whether the conduct is in the ordinary course for the partnership and not whether the particular general partner ordinarily plays a role in that part of the partnership's business. *See In Moren ex. rel. Moren v. JAX Rest.*, 679 N.W.2d 165, 167–168 (Minn. Ct. App. 2004) (stating, as part of its analysis under UPA (1997) § 305, that "[i]t is undisputed that one of the cooks scheduled to work that evening [at the partnership's restaurant] did not come in, and that [one] partner asked [another partner] to help in the kitchen . . . [and] that [the other partner] was making pizzas for the partnership when" her negligence injured the plaintiff); *Vanacore v. Kennedy*, 86 F. Supp. 2d 42, 51 (D. Conn. 1998), *aff'd sub nom., Vanacore v. Space Realty, Inc.*, 208 F.3d 204 (2d Cir. 2000) (stating that "Kennedy [a partner] committed his misdeeds, which led directly to plaintiff's injuries, within the ordinary course of the business of E & K [the partnership]"); *Sheridan v. Desmond*, 697 A.2d 1162, 1166 (Conn. App. Ct. 1997) (stating that to be considered "in ordinary course of the business," a partner's action must be "the kind of thing *a* . . . partner would do") (emphasis added).

Subsection (b)—This provision is derived from UPA (1914) § 14 (Partnership Bound by Partner's Breach of Trust) and UPA (1997) § 305(b) (Partnership Liable for Partner's Actionable Conduct). It is not necessary that the general partner "receiv[ing] or caus[ing] the partnership to receive money or property" do so wrongfully. Culpability is necessary at the second phase—*i.e.*, when "the money or property is misapplied by a general partner."

§ 404. General Partner's Liability

(a)   Except as otherwise provided in subsections (b) and (c), all general partners are liable jointly and severally for all debts, obligations, and other liabilities of the limited partnership unless otherwise agreed by the claimant or provided by law.

(b)   A person that becomes a general partner is not personally liable for a debt, obligation, or other liability of the limited partnership incurred before the person became a general partner.

(c)   A debt, obligation, or other liability of a limited partnership incurred while the partnership is a limited liability limited partnership is solely the debt, obligation, or other liability of the limited liability limited partnership. A general partner is not personally liable, directly or indirectly, by way of contribution or otherwise, for a debt, obligation, or other liability of the limited liability limited partnership solely by reason of being or acting as a general partner. This subsection applies:

(1)   despite anything inconsistent in the partnership agreement that existed immediately before the vote or consent required to become a limited liability limited partnership under Section 406(b)(2); and

(2)   regardless of the dissolution of the partnership.

(d)   The failure of a limited liability limited partnership to observe formalities relating to the exercise of its powers or management of its activities and affairs is not a ground for imposing liability on a general partner for a debt, obligation, or other liability of the partnership.

(e)   An amendment of a certificate of limited partnership which deletes a statement that the limited partnership is a limited liability limited partnership does not affect the limitation in this section on the liability of a general partner for a debt, obligation, or other liability of the limited partnership incurred before the amendment became effective.

COMMENT

Derivation—ULPA (2001) derived this section from UPA (1997) § 306, which was also the source for ULLCA (2006) § 304. The Harmonization Project brought the two partnership acts and the limited liability company act into accord to the extent the three acts overlap.

Subsection (a)—Until the advent of limited liability partnerships and limited liability limited partnerships, one hallmark of general partner status was strict, vicarious liability for the debts, obligations, and other liabilities of the partnership. This subsection states a modern version of that venerable rule. The Harmonization Project made no substantive changes to this subsection.

Subsection (b)—UPA (1997) continued the approach of UPA (1914) §§ 17 and 41(7) to the vicarious liability of an incoming partner, but used a simpler and clearer formulation. ULPA (2001) followed UPA (1997), and the Harmonization Project made no substantive changes to this subsection.

With regard to when a limited partnership incurs a debt, obligation, or other liability, the case law is scant and concerns contractual and similar obligations. The leading case is *Conklin Farm v. Leibowitz*, 140 N.J. 417, 658 A.2d 1257 (1995), which holds that: (i) obligations on a loan, whether for interest or principal, are incurred when the loan is made, not when each particular payment is due; and (ii) obligations for lease payments are incurred when each rental payment is due, not when the lease is made.

Conklin concerned a partnership loan obligation that was: (i) entered into before a particular partner joined the partnership; but (ii) for the most part, was payable afterwards. The court held that "interest is part of the contractual debt, and the obligation to pay interest on a loan *arises,* if at all, at the time that the parties execute the note or other debt instrument." *Conklin,* 140 N.J. at 423,425, 658 A.2d at 1261 (emphasis in original). The court indicated that the same analysis applies to the obligation to repay principal. 140 N.J. at 429, 658 A.2d at 1263 (stating that "the decisive issue before this court . . . [is that] [p]ayment of interest, like repayment of advances, is an obligation that arises at the time the debt instrument is executed").

Conklin discussed the lease issue in response to the creditor's argument that "just as a rent obligation arises for current use of property, an interest obligation arises for current use of principal." *Conklin,* 140 N.J. at 425, 658 A.2d at 1261. Rejecting that argument, the court: (i) noted "the *common-law* obligation to pay rent based on current tenancy [which] . . . arises with each period of tenancy, and . . . arises even in the absence of a lease"; (ii) described "the common-law obligation to pay rent [as] entirely independent of the contractual obligation under the lease"; and (iii) held that, for purposes of partnership law, the rule for "incurring" a lease obligation rests on the common law duty in tenancy and not on the lease as a contract. *Conklin,* 140 N.J. at 426, 658 A.2d at 1262 (citing *Ellingson v. Walsh, O'Connor & Barneson,* 15 Cal. 2d 673, 104 P.2d 507, 508 (1940)). *Conklin* involved a general partnership but, in this context, that difference is immaterial.

As to when a partnership incurs a tort liability, the answer might be found by analogy to statute of limitation rules, another area of law concerned with when claims arise. "Although the courts have not been consistent . . . the interpretation of [when] a . . . statute [of limitations begins to run] as applied to torts has been such that the statute does not usually begin to run until the tort is complete. . . . A tort is ordinarily not complete until there has been an invasion of a legally protected interest of the plaintiff." RESTATEMENT (SECOND) OF TORTS § 899 cmt c. (1979); *Loehr v. Ventura Cnty. Cmty. Coll. Dist.,* 147 Cal. App. 3d 1071, 1078, 195 Cal. Rptr. 576 (Ct. App. 1983). By analogy, a limited partnership would incur liability for a tort when the harm occurs. *See, e.g., Jones v. Cox,* 828 P.2d 218, 224 (Colo. 1992) ("A cause of action has commonly been understood to 'accrue' when a suit may be maintained thereon.") (quoting BLACK'S LAW DICTIONARY 19 (5th ed. 1979)); *Loehr v. Ventura Cnty. Cmty. Coll. Dist.,* 147 Cal. App. 3d 1071, 1078, 195 Cal. Rptr. 576 (Ct. App. 1983).

However, a policy argument exists to the contrary. Vicarious liability for a limited partnership's torts should be confined to persons who are general partners when the wrongful conduct occurs. It is the conduct, not the consequences, that is wrongful; therefore, the occurrence of the wrongful conduct should determine which set of general partners are liable for the conduct's consequences.

For further discussion of the "incurred" issue, see Subsection (c), comment (The Temporal Nexus—When Claim Incurred).

Subsection (c)—This subsection provides a corporate/LLC-like liability shield for general partners, protecting them from (and only from) the debts, obligations and liabilities of the limited partnership—*i.e.,* against a partner's alleged vicarious liability for the obligations of the entity.

Shield Applicable Regardless of the Identity of the Plaintiff

What makes the shield relevant is the nature of the claim. If the complaint seeks to hold a partner vicariously liability for the LLLP's obligations, the shield applies. If not, not. Thus, there is no distinction among a claim arising from an LLLP's debt to a commercial creditor, a partner's claim that the LLLP has failed to return a contribution as required by the partnership agreement, and a claim by a former partner that the LLLP has failed to follow through on a buy-out agreement. *See Rappaport v. Gelfand,* 197 Cal. App. 4th 1213, 1230–1232, 129 Cal. Rptr. 3d 670, 682–84 (Cal.App. 2 Dist. 2011) (involving a claim by a former partner). *Accord Ederer v. Gursky,* 9 N.Y.3d 514, 526, 881 N.E.2d 204, 212–213 (N.Y. 2007) (Smith, J., dissenting).

Shield Inapposite for Claims Arising from a Partner's Own Conduct

Because the partner liability at issue is solely vicarious, the LLLP shield is irrelevant to claims seeking to hold a partner directly liable on account of the partner's own conduct. Case law on this issue comes from the analogous context of limited liability companies, and in that context a few judges have failed to understand this point. *See* ULLCA (2006) (Last Amended 2013) § 304(a), cmt. (Shield Inapposite for Claims Arising from a Member's or Manager's Own Conduct). However, the overwhelming weight of case law is contrary, as are the actual words of shield provisions (immunizing only for obligations of the entity and making no reference to direct obligations of an owner or manager) and public policy (which recoils from the idea of immunizing a person's misconduct solely because the person acts on behalf of an organization).

Example: A general partner personally guarantees a debt of a limited liability limited partnership. Subsection (c) is irrelevant to the general partner's liability as guarantor.

Example: A general partner purports to bind a limited liability limited partnership while lacking any agency law power to do so. The LLLP is not bound, but the partner is liable for having breached the "warranty of authority" (an agency law doctrine). Subsection (c) does not apply. The liability is not *for* a debt, obligation, or other liability of the LLLP, but is rather the partner's own, direct liability. Indeed, the liability exists because the LLLP is *not* indebted, obligated or liable. RESTATEMENT (THIRD) OF AGENCY § 6.10 (2006).

Example: A general partner of a limited liability limited partnership defames a third party in circumstances that render the LLLP vicariously liable under Section 403(a). Under Subsection (c), the third party cannot hold the partner accountable for the *partnership's* liability, but that protection is immaterial. The partner is the tortfeasor and in that role is directly liable to the third party.

Example: An LLLP provides professional services, and one of its general partners commits malpractice. The liability shield is irrelevant to the partner's direct liability in tort. However, if the partner's malpractice liability is attributed to the partnership under Section 403(a), the liability shield will protect the other general partners against a claim that they must make good on the LLLP's liability. The same analysis applies if the plaintiff also successfully claims that another general partner was negligent in supervising the first partner.

Subsection (c) pertains only to claims based on the LLLP's liability and is irrelevant to claims by a limited liability limited partnership or a partner against a general partner and *vice versa*. *See* Sections 409 (pertaining to management duties) and 901 (pertaining to direct claims by a partner).

Shield Inapposite to Role Liability Claims

Provisions of regulatory law may impose liability on a general partner of an LLLP due to a role the general partner plays in the limited partnership. *See, e.g., Food Team Intern., Ltd. v. Unilink, LLC*, 872 F. Supp. 2d 405, 424 (E.D. Pa. 2012) (holding several individuals "subject to secondary individual liability under PACA [Perishable Agricultural Commodities Act]" because their roles within a limited liability company enabled them to control the relevant assets) (citing *Bear Mountain Orchards, Inc. v. Mich-Kim, Inc.*, 623 F.3d 163, 172 (3d Cir. 2010)). Subsection (c) does not affect this "role liability."

The Temporal Nexus—When Claim Incurred

The LLLP shield functions only with respect to obligations incurred while the partnership is a limited liability limited partnership. The shield does not protect general partners from vicarious liability for partnership obligations incurred before a partnership becomes an LLLP or after the partnership ends its LLLP status. Sections 201(b)(5) and 406(b)(2).

For a preliminary discussion of when a partnership obligation is incurred, see Subsection (b), comment. It could well be argued that "incurred" under Subsection (c) has the same meaning as "incurred" under Subsection (b). *IBP, Inc. v. Alvarez*, 546 U.S. 21, 34, 126 S.Ct. 514, 523 (2005) (referring to "the normal rule of statutory interpretation that identical words used in different parts of the same statute are generally presumed to have the same meaning"); *Timberline Air Serv., Inc. v. Bell Helicopter-Textron, Inc.*, 125 Wash. 2d 305, 313, 884 P.2d 920, 925 (1994) (stating that "[w]hen the same words are used in different parts of the same statute, it is presumed that the Legislature intended that the words have the same meaning").

However, the argument should yield if the subsections' different contexts raise different issues of policy. 1A SUTHERLAND STATUTES AND STATUTORY CONSTRUCTION § 45:12 (7th ed.) (stating that "departure from the literal construction of a statute is justified when such a construction would produce an absurd and unjust result and would clearly be inconsistent with the purposes and policies of the act in question"). *See, e.g., S.V. v. R.V.*, 933 S.W.2d 1, 4 (Tex. 1996) ("[W]e have held that a cause of action accrues when a wrongful act causes some legal injury, even if the fact of injury is not discovered until later, and even if all resulting damages have not yet occurred. We have not applied this rule without exception, however, and have sometimes held that an action does not accrue until the plaintiff knew or in the exercise of reasonable diligence should have known of the wrongful act and resulting injury.") (citations omitted).

The case law concerning contractual obligations (incurred when the contract is made) applies appropriately in the context of the LLLP shield. However, the lease case law is problematic. If an obligation is incurred each time rent is due, subsection(c) is a trap for the unwary landlord.

Example: Ordinary limited partnership enters into a lease with a commercial landlord. Knowing that each general partner is automatically liable for the partnership's debt, the landlord does not obtain personal guarantees. Subsequently, the partnership becomes an LLLP. If future rent payments are incurred when due, and not as of when the lease was made, the landlord loses a very important part of the bargain.

Thus, for the purposes of Subsection (c), lease obligations should be treated as contractual obligations, incurred when the contract is made.

A similar issue exists with regard to tort liability. Courts must look to when the conduct causing the injury takes place and not to when actual injury occurs. Otherwise, a limited partnership could: (i) engage in wrongful conduct that does not cause immediate injury; (ii) come to realize that the conduct has occurred; (iii) subsequently amend its certificate of limited partnership to become a limited liability limited partnership; and (iv) thereby eliminate the vicarious liability of its general partners for all harm subsequently arising from the misconduct. *Cf. Savini v. Univ. of Hawaii*, 113 Haw. 459, 465, 153 P.3d 1144, 1150 (2007) (addressing the question of when a statute of limitations begins to run for bodily injury, when another statute precludes bringing a claim until the amount of damages has reach a specified threshold).

In general, courts should determine the "incurred" question under Subsection (c) so that the LLLP shield protects the general partners of an LLLP to the same extent that the corporate and LLC shields protect corporate shareholders and LLC members. From that perspective, LLLP status obtained after a limited partnership commits a wrongful act should provide no greater protection for the general partners than the protection a sole proprietor obtains by forming an LLC after committing a wrongful act—*i.e.*, none. *See, e.g., Foxchase, LLP v. Cliatt*, 562 S.E. 2d 221, 224 (Ga. Ct. App. 2002) (holding that a partnership's liability shield did not protect partners from claims of property damage caused by the construction of a golf course, where the jury could have found that the "damage . . . occurred when they, not the partnership, owned the course").

Subsection (c)(2)—*The Shield and Dissolution*. The rule stated here is inherent in the nature of partnership dissolution. "[D]issolution does not end a limited partnership's existence but rather changes the purpose of that existence." Section 801, cmt. "A dissolved limited partnership shall wind up its business and . . . continues after dissolution . . . for the purpose of winding up." Section 802(a). Put another way: dissolution and winding up are part of the life cycle of a limited liability limited partnership—sometimes the most complicated part. There is no logical reason to remove the shield during the last part of a LLLP's partnership's life cycle.

This subsection makes this point expressly, because it is possible to misinterpret some outlying LLP cases as holding to the contrary. *See, e.g., Carolina Cas. Ins. Co. v. L.M. Ross Law Grp., LLP*, 151 Cal. Rptr. 3d 628, 635 (2012) (affirming the trial court's decision to hold an LLP's named partner liable for a judgment against his limited ability partnership; noting that "[c]entral to the decision to amend the judgment to add Ross [the named partner] as a judgment debtor . . . is the trial court's finding that Ross Law Group dissolved"; recognizing, however, that, before the partnership incurred the liability, Ross had signed and filed with the California Secretary of State a form stating that the law firm had "cease[d] to be a registered limited liability partnership and is hereby filing this notice with the California Secretary of State that [it] is no longer a registered limited partnership") (quotation marks omitted).

The Shield and Termination. This subsection does not expressly provide that, when a limited liability limited partnership's existence terminates, the liability shield remains in place as to any debt, obligation, or other liability of the partnership incurred before the termination. However, the point follows ineluctably from this subsection, which adopts an "occurrence" rather than a "claims made" basis for determining whether the shield applies. See the comment to Subsection (c), above (The Temporal Nexus—When Claim Incurred).

Moreover, any other result would: (i) create huge holes in the shield; (ii) put the law of unincorporated businesses at odds with the law of corporations; (iii) render surplus this act's distribution recapture provision, Section 407; (iv) render meaningless the exception to the notice requirement as stated in Sections 806b)(5) and 807(b)(4); and (v) render nonsensical the otherwise logical extension of the equitable trust fund theory to limited liability limited partnerships. *Cf. Velasquez v. Franz*, 589 A.2d 143, 146 (N.J. 1991) (explaining that "the trust-fund doctrine . . . renders shareholders who receive distributed assets of the corporation liable as 'trustees' for claims of the corporation's creditors").

Subsection (d)—This subsection was added during the Harmonization Project and pertains to the equitable doctrine of "piercing the veil"—*i.e.*, conflating an entity and its owners to hold one liable for the obligations of the other. The doctrine of "piercing the corporate veil" is well-established, and courts should apply the doctrine to limited liability limited partnership for the same reasons that courts have regularly (and sometimes almost reflexively) applied the doctrine to limited liability companies. *Cf. Axtmann v. Chillemi*, 2007 ND 179, 740 N.W.2d 838, 847 (stating that "the shield of a limited liability partnership may be pierced under 'the case law that states the conditions and circumstances under which the corporate veil or limited liability shield of a corporation may be pierced under North Dakota law. . . .' ") (quoting N.D.C.C. § 45–22–09(1)).

However, LLLP piercing involves one important distinction from the corporate realm. While under corporate law "disregard of corporate formalities" is a key piercing factor, that factor is inapposite in the law of unincorporated organizations. Corporate formalities reflect statutory mandates. LLLP formalities derive for the most part from the agreement among the partners. From a policy perspective, disregarding formalities adopted by agreement differs substantially from disregarding formalities imposed by law.

Moreover, because the terms of a partnership agreement may be "implied," Section 102(14), an LLLP's ongoing disregard of formalities may well constitute an amendment to the partnership agreement. If so, disregard equals amendment, and the concept of "disregard of formalities" makes no sense.

In contrast, this subsection is inapposite to another key piercing factor—disregard of the separateness between entity and owner. *Cf. Vanderford Co. v. Knudson*, 165 P.3d 261, 271 (Idaho 2007) (noting that managing member and "his accountant testified that the LLC's checking account was so confusing that the accountant could not be sure whose money was in the account at what times"); *Utzler v. Braca*, 972 A.2d 743 (Conn. App. 2009) (holding that veil piercing was appropriate under alter-ego theory when owner deposited LLC funds into a commingled bank account from which he made withdrawals for personal needs and unrelated projects).

Example: The sole general partner of a limited liability limited partnership uses a car titled in the partnership's name for personal purposes and writes checks on the partnership's account to pay for personal expenses. These facts are relevant to a piercing claim; they pertain to economic separateness, not Subsection (b) formalities.

This subsection addresses claims to "impos[e] liability on a general partner for a debt, obligation, or other liability of the partnership"—*i.e.*, for what is sometimes termed a "direct pierce." Whether the same approach should apply to claims for a "reverse pierce" is a question for the courts. *See Comm'r of Envtl. Prot. v. State Five Indus. Park, Inc.*, 304 Conn. 128, 140, 37 A.3d 724, 732–33 (2012) (stating that "[a]lthough some courts have adopted reverse veil piercing with little distinction as a logical corollary of traditional veil piercing, because the two share the same equitable goals, others wisely have recognized important differences between them").

This subsection has no relevance to a partner's claim that the disregard of agreed-upon formalities is a breach of the limited partnership agreement.

Subsection (e)—The rule stated here is implicit in Subsection (c) but is stated expressly for the avoidance of doubt.

§ 405.   Actions by and Against Partnership and Partners

(a)   To the extent not inconsistent with Section 404, a general partner may be joined in an action against the limited partnership or named in a separate action.

(b)   A judgment against a limited partnership is not by itself a judgment against a general partner. A judgment against a partnership may not be satisfied from a general partner's assets unless there is also a judgment against the general partner.

(c)   A judgment creditor of a general partner may not levy execution against the assets of the general partner to satisfy a judgment based on a claim against the limited partnership, unless the partner is personally liable for the claim under Section 404 and:

(1)   a judgment based on the same claim has been obtained against the limited partnership and a writ of execution on the judgment has been returned unsatisfied in whole or in part;

(2)   the partnership is a debtor in bankruptcy;

(3)   the general partner has agreed that the creditor need not exhaust partnership assets;

(4)   a court grants permission to the judgment creditor to levy execution against the assets of a general partner based on a finding that partnership assets subject to execution are clearly insufficient to satisfy the judgment, that exhaustion of assets is excessively burdensome, or that the grant of permission is an appropriate exercise of the court's equitable powers; or

(5)   liability is imposed on the general partner by law or contract independent of the existence of the partnership.

COMMENT

Subsection (a)—If a debt, obligation, or other liability is incurred against a limited liability limited partnership, joining a general partner would be improper. Likewise, if a debt, obligation, or other liability against an ordinary limited partnership is incurred before a person becomes a general partner, it would be improper to join that person. As for when a claim is incurred, see Section 404(b) and (c), comments.

The reference to "not inconsistent with Section 404" is the procedural analog to the substantive protections of Section 404(b) (incoming general partner not liable for pre-existing limited partnership obligations) and (c) (general partner not liable for partnership obligations incurred by an LLLP). When a general partner has personally guaranteed a limited partnership obligation, naming that general partner in a suit against the limited partnership is "not inconsistent with Section 404." *See* Section 404, cmt. (Shield Inapposite for Claims Arising from a Partner's Conduct). *Cf. Bank of Boston Connecticut v. Schlesinger*, 220 Conn. 152, 157–58, 595 A.2d 872, 875 (1991) (upholding pre-judgment attachment of a partner's assets, where the partner had personally guaranteed the partnership's obligations).

Subsection (b)—Reflecting the entity construct, Section 110(a), this subsection provides that a judgment against the limited partnership: (i) is not, standing alone, a judgment against the general partners; and (ii) cannot be satisfied from a general partner's personal assets absent a judgment against the general partner.

This act leaves to the law of judgments to determine the collateral effects to be accorded a prior judgment for or against the limited partnership in a subsequent action against a general partner individually. *See* RESTATEMENT (SECOND) OF JUDGMENTS § 60 (1982) and cmts. *E.g., Detrio v. U.S.*, 264 F.2d 658 (5th Cir. 1959); *Brunsoman v. Seltz*, 414 N.W.2d 547 (Minn. App. 1987) (Lansing, J.). *Contra Evanston Ins. Co. v. Dillard Dep't Stores, Inc.*, 602 F.3d 610, 618 (5th Cir. 2010) (disregarding *sub silentio* the separateness of partner and partnership, overlooking therefore the issue of collateral estoppel, discussing with approval a bankruptcy case in which "the trustee sought to enforce the partnership judgment against [partners] simply by virtue of their status as partner"; and quoting with approval that case's holding that "[o]nce the liability of the partnership became fixed, the only issue remaining was whether the Defendants are partners of [the partnership]") (quoting *In re Jones*, 161 B.R. 180, 183–184 (Bankr. N.D. Tex. 1993)) (second brackets in original).

This subsection and Subsection (c) combine to create a trap for the unwary. For statute of limitations purposes, a creditor's claim against the general partners accrues simultaneously with the claim against the limited partnership. If a creditor chooses not to sue the general partners in its suit against the limited partnership, the statute of limitations may run before the creditor commences suit against the general partners. *Am. Star Energy & Minerals Corp. v. Stowers*, 405 S.W.3d 905, 907 (Tex. App. 2013) (holding that the partnership creditor "was obligated to sue the partners of S & J . . . within the same limitations period it had to sue S & J, the partnership" and that "[b]ecause, [the creditor] did not, the trial court correctly held that limitations ran"); *Sunseri v. Proctor*, 487 F. Supp. 2d 905, 908 (E.D. Mich. 2007), *aff'd*, 286 F. App'x 930 (6th Cir. 2008) ("While the plaintiff may use collateral estoppel to prevent the partner from relitigating the issue of liability, the plaintiff must still bring suit within the applicable limitations period for the underlying wrong.").

Subsection (c)—Subject to the five listed exceptions, this subsection prevents a general partner's assets from being the first recourse for a judgment creditor of the limited partnership, even if the partner is liable for the judgment debt under Section 404.

Although this subsection is silent with respect to pre-judgment remedies, as a matter of policy the subsection should guide courts as they apply the law of pre-judgment remedies. *Compare Sec. Pac. Nat. Bank v. Matek,* 175 Cal. App. 3d 1071, 1077, 223 Cal. Rptr. 288 (Ct. App. 1985) (granting a pre-judgment remedy against a partner because there is "no distinction between those sued individually as partners and those sued as sole proprietors"), *with Bank of Boston Connecticut v. Schlesinger*, 220 Conn. 152, 157–58, 595 A.2d 872, 875 (1991) (upholding pre-judgment attachment of a partner's assets, because the partner had personally guaranteed the partnership's obligations).

§ 406.   Management Rights of General Partner

(a)   Each general partner has equal rights in the management and conduct of the limited partnership's activities and affairs. Except as otherwise provided in this [act], any matter relating to the activities and affairs of the partnership is decided exclusively by the general partner or, if there is more than one general partner, by a majority of the general partners.

(b)   The affirmative vote or consent of all the partners is required to:

(1)   amend the partnership agreement;

(2)   amend the certificate of limited partnership to add or delete a statement that the limited partnership is a limited liability limited partnership; and

(3)   sell, lease, exchange, or otherwise dispose of all, or substantially all, of the limited partnership's property, with or without the good will, other than in the usual and regular course of the limited partnership's activities and affairs.

(c)   A limited partnership shall reimburse a general partner for an advance to the partnership beyond the amount of capital the general partner agreed to contribute.

(d)   A payment or advance made by a general partner which gives rise to a limited partnership obligation under subsection (c) or Section 408(a) constitutes a loan to the limited partnership which accrues interest from the date of the payment or advance.

(e)   A general partner is not entitled to remuneration for services performed for the limited partnership.

COMMENT

Subsection (a)—As explained in the Prefatory Note to ULPA (2001), this act assumes that, more often than not, people utilizing the act will want: (i) strong centralized management, strongly entrenched; and (ii) passive investors with little control over the entity. Section 302 essentially excludes limited partners from the ordinary management of a limited partnership's activities and affairs, unless the partnership agreement provides otherwise.

This subsection states affirmatively the general partners' commanding role. Only the partnership agreement and the express provisions of this act can limit that role.

The authority granted by this subsection includes the authority to delegate. Delegation does not relieve the delegating general partner or partners of their duties under Section 409. However, the fact of delegation is a fact relevant to any breach of duty analysis.

Example: A sole general partner personally handles all important paperwork for a limited partnership. The general partner neglects to renew the fire insurance coverage on a building owned by the limited partnership, despite having received and read a warning notice from the insurance company. The building subsequently burns to the ground and is a total loss. The general partner might be liable for breach of the duty of care under Section 409(c) (gross negligence).

Example: A sole general partner delegates responsibility for insurance renewals to the limited partnership's office manager, and that manager neglects to renew the fire insurance coverage on the building. Even assuming that the office manager has been grossly negligent, the general partner is not necessarily liable under Section 409(c). The office manager's gross negligence is not automatically attributed to the general partner. Under Section 409(c), the question is whether the general partner was grossly negligent (or worse) in selecting the office manager, delegating insurance renewal matters to the office manager, and supervising the office manager after the delegation.

The partnership agreement may also provide for delegation and, subject to Section 105(c)(6)–(8) and (d)(2), may modify a general partner's duties under Section 409.

For limited partnerships that have more than one general partner, this act provides that in most circumstances a "matter relating to the activities and affairs of the partnership is decided . . . by a majority of the general partners." However, unlike corporate statutes, this act does not provide a rule for the quantum of participation necessary to constitute "a majority." *Cf., e.g.,* MINN. STAT. § 302A.237 (2014) (providing rules for determining the votes need to constitute "an act of the board"). If a limited partnership has more than one general partner, the partnership agreement should consider what "a majority" means in the event a general partner position is vacant. Note also that for some decisions this act requires the affirmative vote or consent of all partners. *See* Section 406(b), cmt.

Subsection (b)—Other provisions of this act also contain default rules providing for unanimous consent. *E.g.,* Sections 301(b)(3) (for a person to become a limited partner after formation of the limited partnership), 401(b)(3) (same as to becoming a general partner), and 502(3) (for compromising a person's obligation to make a contribution). In addition, the transactions authorized under Article 11 each have a default unanimous consent requirement.

Subsections (a) and (b)—These subsections have important implications for a partner's actual authority to act on behalf of the partnership. The actual authority of a general partner is a question of agency law, *see* RESTATEMENT (THIRD) OF AGENCY § 3.01 (2006) (Creation of Actual Authority), and depends fundamentally on the contents of the partnership agreement. If, however, the partnership agreement is silent on the issue, this subsection helps delineate that actual authority. Acting individually, a general partner:

- has no actual authority to commit the limited partnership to any matter for which this act require requires the affirmative vote or consent of all partners;

- has the actual authority to commit the limited partnership to usual and customary matters, unless the general partner has reason to know that: (i) other general partners might disagree; or (ii) for some other reason consultation with fellow general partners is appropriate; and

- has no actual authority to take unusual or non-customary actions that will have a substantial effect on the limited partnership.

The first point follows self-evidently from the language of this act. Where this act requires unanimity of all partners, no general partner could reasonably believe to the contrary (unless the partnership agreement provided otherwise).

The second point follows because:

- Subsection (a) serves as the gap-filler manifestation from the limited partnership to its general partners and does <u>not</u> require partners to act <u>only</u> in concert or after consultation. To the contrary, subject to the partnership agreement, this subsection expressly provides that "[e]ach general partner has equal rights in the management and conduct of the limited partnership's activities and affairs."

- It would be impractical to require collective action on even the smallest of decisions.

- However, to the extent a general partner has reason to know of a possible difference of opinion among the general partners, this subsection requires a decision by "a majority of the general partners."

A third point is a matter of common sense. The more serious the matter, the less likely it is that a general partner has actual authority to act unilaterally. *Cf.* RESTATEMENT (THIRD) OF AGENCY § 3.03, cmt. c (2006) (noting the unreasonableness of believing, without more facts, that an individual has "an unusual degree of unilateral authority over a matter fraught with enduring consequences for the institution" and stating that "[t]he gravity of the matter from the standpoint of the organization is relevant to whether a third party could reasonably believe that the manager has authority to proceed unilaterally").

Subsection (e)—In a limited partnership, winding up is one of the tasks for which the limited partners depend on the general partner. There is no reason for this act to single out this particular task as giving rise to compensation.

§ 407.   Rights to Information of General Partner and Person Dissociated as General Partner

(a)   A general partner may inspect and copy required information during regular business hours in the limited partnership's principal office, without having any particular purpose for seeking the information.

(b)   On reasonable notice, a general partner may inspect and copy during regular business hours, at a reasonable location specified by the limited partnership, any record maintained by the partnership regarding the partnership's activities, affairs, financial condition, and other circumstances, to the extent the information is material to the general partner's rights and duties under the partnership agreement or this [act].

(c)   A limited partnership shall furnish to each general partner:

(1)   without demand, any information concerning the partnership's activities, affairs, financial condition, and other circumstances which the partnership knows and is material to the proper exercise of the general partner's rights and duties under the partnership agreement or this [act], except to the extent the partnership can establish that it reasonably believes the general partner already knows the information; and

(2) on demand, any other information concerning the partnership's activities, affairs, financial condition, and other circumstances, except to the extent the demand or the information demanded is unreasonable or otherwise improper under the circumstances.

(d) The duty to furnish information under subsection (c) also applies to each general partner to the extent the general partner knows any of the information described in subsection (b).

(e) Subject to subsection (j), on 10 days' demand made in a record received by a limited partnership, a person dissociated as a general partner may have access to the information and records described in subsections (a) and (b) at the locations specified in those subsections if:

(1) the information or record pertains to the period during which the person was a general partner;

(2) the person seeks the information or record in good faith; and

(3) the person satisfies the requirements imposed on a limited partner by Section 304(b).

(f) A limited partnership shall respond to a demand made pursuant to subsection (e) in the manner provided in Section 304(c).

(g) A limited partnership may charge a person that makes a demand under this section the reasonable costs of copying, limited to the costs of labor and material.

(h) A general partner or person dissociated as a general partner may exercise the rights under this section through an agent or, in the case of an individual under legal disability, a legal representative. Any restriction or condition imposed by the partnership agreement or under subsection (j) applies both to the agent or legal representative and to the general partner or person dissociated as a general partner.

(i) The rights under this section do not extend to a person as transferee, but if:

(1) a general partner dies, Section 704 applies; and

(2) an individual dissociates as a general partner under Section 603(6)(B) or (C), the legal representative of the individual may exercise the rights under subsection (c) of a person dissociated as a general partner.

(j) In addition to any restriction or condition stated in its partnership agreement, a limited partnership, as a matter within the ordinary course of its activities and affairs, may impose reasonable restrictions and conditions on access to and use of information to be furnished under this section, including designating information confidential and imposing nondisclosure and safeguarding obligations on the recipient. In a dispute concerning the reasonableness of a restriction under this subsection, the partnership has the burden of proving reasonableness.

COMMENT

Subsection (a)—The phrase "required information" is a defined term. *See* Sections 102(21) and 108. This subsection's broad right of access is subject both to reasonable limitations in the partnership agreement, Section 105(c)(9), and also the power of the limited partnership to impose reasonable limitations on use, Subsection (j). However, limiting a general partner's access to this information or any other information would be quite unusual.

Subsection (b)—This subsection states the rule pertaining to information memorialized in "any record maintained by the partnership." Except in unusual circumstances (*e.g.*, a back-up general partner with no ongoing responsibilities), all of the information encompassed by this provision will be "material to the general partner's rights and duties under the partnership agreement or this [act]." For further discussion of the meaning of "material" as applied to information, see Section 409(f), comment.

Subsection (c)—Because a limited partnership is an entity, this subsection imposes a duty on the partnership, not the partners. However, the general partners are typically responsible for seeing that the limited partnership fulfills this obligation. For the limited partnership, breaching this obligation is a matter of strict liability (analogous to breaching a contract). In contrast, Section 409 provides the standard for evaluating a general partner's conduct in this context. Subsection (d) establishes a separate duty for the general partners.

A general partner's right to information under this subsection is personal to the general partner and enforceable under Section 901(a). These rights are in addition to whatever discovery rights a party has in a civil suit.

Subsection (c)(1)—This provision imposes an affirmative duty to volunteer information. However, given the assumption that each general partner will be active in management, the obligation ceases "to the extent the partnership can establish that it reasonably believes the general partner already knows the information."

In any event, the obligation is limited to information which is both material and known by the limited partnership. "Knowledge" is viewed subjectively—*i.e.,* actual knowledge. Section 103(a)(1). Materiality is viewed objectively. Thus, the duty applies to known, material information, even if the limited partnership does not know that the information is material.

A limited partnership will "know" what its general partners know. Under Section 103(f), "[a] general partner's knowledge . . . of a fact relating to the limited partnership is effective immediately as knowledge of or notice to the partnership." As to others acting or reasonably appearing to act on behalf of the limited partnership, common law agency rules will apply. RESTATEMENT (THIRD) OF AGENCY § 5.03 (2006) (Imputation of Notice of Fact to Principal).

Typically a general partner's duties are continuous, and therefore a general partner's right to information is not just transaction-specific. Ongoing managerial responsibilities require ongoing information—both periodically and *ad hoc* when a situation warrants.

For the meaning of "material" as applied to information, see Section 409(f), comment.

Subsection (c)(2)—Other law determines which party has the burden of proof as to the stated exception.

Subsection (d)—This subsection imposes a duty directly on each general partner. The duty is both narrower and more demanding than the duty placed on general partners as the typically responsible parties under Subsection (c). The duty is narrower because the relevant information is confined to "the information [pertaining to records] described in subsection (b)," rather than the wide scope of "any information" delineated by Subsection (c). The duty is more demanding because it applies directly to the general partners, is therefore in the nature of a contractual obligation, and its breach is a matter of strict liability. For example, it is no defense for a general partner under this section to assert that, although the partner failed to furnish required information, the failure did not amount to gross negligence under Section 409(c).

Example: A limited partnership has two general partners: each of which is regularly engaged in conducting the limited partnership's activities; both of which are aware of and have regular access to all significant limited partnership records; and neither of which has special responsibility for or knowledge of any particular aspect of those activities or the relevant partnership records. Most likely, neither general partner is obliged to draw the other general partner's attention to information apparent in the limited partnership's records.

Example: Although a limited partnership has three general partners, one is the managing partner with day-to-day responsibility for running the limited partnership's activities. The other two meet periodically with the managing general partner, and together with that partner function in a manner analogous to a corporate board of directors. Most likely, the managing general partner has a duty to draw the attention of the other general partners to important information, even if that information would be apparent from a review of the limited partnership's records.

As with Subsection (c), a general partner's right to information under this subsection is personal to the general partner and enforceable under Section 901(a). These rights are in addition to whatever discovery rights a party has in a civil suit.

Subsection (e)—Codifying the information rights of former owners began with RUPA (1997) § 403(b). Access is limited and subject to conditions, most of which are drawn from Section 304 (pertaining to the information rights of limited partners). *See also* Subsection (i) (providing information rights to the legal representative of a deceased general partner); Section 704 (providing additional information rights to the legal representative of the deceased partner).

Subsection (e)(1)—A person dissociated as a general partner has information rights in that capacity only as to the period during which the person was a general partner. To the extent that further information is accessible under Section 704(2) (providing access to the legal representative of a deceased partner's estate), that access is limited both in purpose ("for purposes of settling the estate") and in scope ("the rights of a current limited partner under Section 304").

Subsection (e)(2)—A duty of good faith is needed here, because a person claiming access under this subsection is no longer a general partner and no longer subject to a general partner's duties and obligations under Section 409. Section 605(a)(2) (dissociation as a partner terminates duty of good faith as to subsequent events). *But see id.*, cmt (noting that the common law implied covenant will continue to be relevant if the partnership agreement provides continuing rights and obligations for a person dissociated as a general partner).

In the context of Subsection (e)(2), "good faith" is properly understood to mean an honest belief that the request is made for a proper purpose. *Associated Indem. Corp. v. CAT Contracting, Inc.*, 964 S.W.2d 276, 285 (Tex. 1998) (holding that " 'good faith' in the surety agreement before us refers to conduct which is honest in fact, free of improper motive or wilful ignorance of the facts at hand"); Andrews v. Bible, 812 S.W.2d 284, 288 (Tenn. 1991) (describing "subjective good faith" as "[a] pure heart but an empty head") (quoting *Whittington v. Ohio River Co.*, 115 F.R.D. 201, 209 (E.D.Ky.1987)). Willful ignorance includes being an ostrich. "While 'honesty' may require no more than a pure heart, it is questionable that a pure heart can co-exist with closed eyes. It is not honest to close one's eyes so as to maintain an empty head." *J.R. Hale Contracting Co. v. United New Mexico Bank at Albuquerque*, 799 P.2d 581, 591 (NM 1990). *See also* UPA (1914) § (3)(1) ("A person has 'knowledge' of a fact within the meaning of this act not only when he has actual knowledge thereof, but also when he has knowledge of such other facts as in the circumstances shows bad faith.").

Subsection (e)(3)—Applying the limited partner standard Section 304(b) to a person dissociated as a general partner makes sense, because the person has no further management role. Theoretically, an even stricter standard might apply, because limited partners have at least some governance role. However, this act already has several different standards applicable to information rights. *See* Sections 304(b) (limited partner), Section 304(e) (person dissociated as a limited partner), 407(b), (c)(2) (general partner), 407(e) (person dissociated as a general partner). This act applies Section 304(b) to a person dissociated as a general partner to avoid having to create another standard.

Subsection (h)—Some old cases involved conflicts over whether a shareholder could exercise inspection rights through another person. *White v. Coeur D'Alene Big Creek Mining Co.*, 55 P.2d 720, 723 (Idaho 1936) (stating that "[t]he refusal to permit respondent [shareholder] to appoint his own attorney or agent to make the examination [of the corporation's books] was in effect a denial of his right" of inspection); *State v. Monida & Yellowstone Stage Co.*, 124 N.W. 971, 972 (Minn. 1910) (upholding a trial court's mandamus order, "which shall provide that [the shareholder complainant], or such attorney or agent as he may select, . . . shall be allowed to inspect the books, records, and papers of the defendant [corporation]"). In light of that history, for the avoidance of doubt, this subsection expressly authorizes taking action through an agent. No negative inference should be drawn about using agents to take other action under this act.

Subsection (i)—This section provides no information rights to a person as transferee. Transferee status brings only the very limited information rights stated in Section 702(c). However, a transferee that is a person dissociated as a limited partner has rights in the latter capacity under Subsection (e).

Subsection (j)—This subsection provides fallback protection for gaps in the partnership agreement. For example, the general partners may protect trade secrets from disclosure and prohibit various misuses of confidential information even if the partnership agreement omits to do so.

Strictly speaking, the reference to "ordinary course" is unnecessary. *See* Section 406(a) (providing generally that "any matter relating to the activities and affairs of the partnership is decided exclusively" by the general partners). The phrase is included merely for the avoidance of doubt.

The limited partnership bears the burden of proving the reasonableness of any restriction imposed under this subsection. In determining whether a restriction is reasonable, a court might consider: (i) the danger or other problem the restriction seeks to avoid; (ii) the purpose for which the information is sought; and (iii) whether, in light of both the problem and the purpose, the restriction is reasonably tailored.

The burden of persuasion under this subsection contrasts with the burden of persuasion under Section 105(c)(9) (prohibiting unreasonable limitations on the information rights provided by this section). Under that paragraph, as a matter of ordinary procedural law the burden is on the person making the claim.

§ 408. Reimbursement; Indemnification; Advancement; and Insurance

(a) A limited partnership shall reimburse a general partner for any payment made by the general partner in the course of the general partner's activities on behalf of the partnership, if the general partner complied with Sections 406, 409, and 504 in making the payment.

(b)   A limited partnership shall indemnify and hold harmless a person with respect to any claim or demand against the person and any debt, obligation, or other liability incurred by the person by reason of the person's former or present capacity as a general partner, if the claim, demand, debt, obligation, or other liability does not arise from the person's breach of Section 406, 409, or 504.

(c)   In the ordinary course of its activities and affairs, a limited partnership may advance reasonable expenses, including attorney's fees and costs, incurred by a person in connection with a claim or demand against the person by reason of the person's former or present capacity as a general partner, if the person promises to repay the partnership if the person ultimately is determined not to be entitled to be indemnified under subsection (b).

(d)   A limited partnership may purchase and maintain insurance on behalf of a general partner against liability asserted against or incurred by the general partner in that capacity or arising from that status even if, under Section 105(c)(8), the partnership agreement could not eliminate or limit the person's liability to the partnership for the conduct giving rise to the liability.

COMMENT

Subsections (a) and (b)—These subsections apply only to general partners. A limited partnership's obligation, if any, to reimburse or indemnify others (*e.g.,* employees, independent contractors, other agents) is a question for other law, including the law of agency, contract and restitution. The fact a person has dissociated as a partner does not affect any obligations incurred by the partnership under these subsections for conduct occurring before the dissociation.

To the extent a partnership agreement modifies or displaces the default rules stated in Sections 406 and 409, the agreement should also address these sections. For example, if the partnership agreement establishes a duty of ordinary care (modifying Section 409(c)), the agreement should specify which level of care is necessary to satisfy Subsections (a) and (b). It is not necessary that the levels of care be the same, only that the partnership agreement make the situation clear and thereby avoid difficult issues of interpretation.

Subsection (a)—The reimbursement obligation stated here is a default rule and roughly parallels a rule of agency law. RESTATEMENT (THIRD) OF AGENCY § 8.14(2)(a) (2006) (stating that "[a] principal has a duty to indemnify an agent . . . when the agent makes a payment (i) within the scope of the agent's actual authority, or (ii) that is beneficial to the principal, unless the agent acts officiously in making the payment").

Subsection (b)—This subsection provides for indemnification but only as a default rule. Subject only to Section 105(c)(8), the partnership agreement can relax these preconditions substantially. The agreement can also impose stricter preconditions.

The rule's eligibility requirements correspond to the default rules on management duties, which is appropriate because otherwise the statutory default rule on indemnification could undercut or even vitiate the statutory default rules on duty.

Although referring broadly to any "person," this subsection is actually limited to present and former general partners. The indemnification obligation applies to only to a "debt, obligation, or other liability incurred by the person by reason of the person's former or present capacity as a general partner." Thus, by its terms this subsection does not apply to a person in the capacity of an officer, manager, CEO, etc.

Of course, the partnership agreement may mandate indemnification to officers, managers, employees, and other persons providing services to or acting for the limited partnership. Within the limitations stated in Section 105(c)(8), a limited partnership agreement may obligate a limited partnership to indemnify a person even when the person has breached a managerial duty or the partnership agreement itself.

Subsection (c)—This subsection authorizes but does not require a limited partnership to provide advances to cover expenses. *Cf. Majkowski v. American Imaging Mgmt. Servs., LLC*, 913 A.2d 572, 589 (Del. Ch. 2006) ("Because rights to indemnification and advancement differ in important ways, our courts have refused to recognize claims for advancement not granted in specific language clearly suggesting such rights."). The phrase "hold harmless" likewise does not encompass advances. *Id.* The authorization applies only to those persons eligible for indemnification under Subsection (b), but the partnership agreement certainly can authorize a broader scope and even make advances obligatory.

The reference to "ordinary course" pertains to Section 406(a) (stating that "any matter relating to the activities and affairs of the partnership is decided exclusively by the general partner or, if there is more than one general partner, by a majority of the general partners.")

Subsection (d)—This subsection's language is very broad and authorizes a limited partnership to purchase insurance to cover, *e.g.*, a general partner's intentional misconduct. It is unlikely that such insurance would be available. This authorization comes from the act, not the partnership agreement, and therefore is not subject to restrictions stated in Section 105(c)(8) (precluding the partnership agreement from "reliev[ing] or exonerat[ing] a person from liability for conduct involving bad faith, willful or intentional misconduct, or knowing violation of law").

§ 409. Standards of Conduct for General Partners

(a) A general partner owes to the limited partnership and, subject to Section 901, the other partners the duties of loyalty and care stated in subsections (b) and (c).

(b) The fiduciary duty of loyalty of a general partner includes the duties:

(1) to account to the limited partnership and hold as trustee for it any property, profit, or benefit derived by the general partner:

(A) in the conduct or winding up of the partnership's activities and affairs;

(B) from a use by the general partner of the partnership's property; or

(C) from the appropriation of a partnership opportunity;

(2) to refrain from dealing with the partnership in the conduct or winding up of the partnership's activities and affairs as or on behalf of a person having an interest adverse to the partnership; and

(3) to refrain from competing with the partnership in the conduct or winding up of the partnership's activities and affairs.

(c) The duty of care of a general partner in the conduct or winding up of the limited partnership's activities and affairs is to refrain from engaging in grossly negligent or reckless conduct, willful or intentional misconduct, or knowing violation of law.

(d) A general partner shall discharge the duties and obligations under this [act] or under the partnership agreement and exercise any rights consistently with the contractual obligation of good faith and fair dealing.

(e) A general partner does not violate a duty or obligation under this [act] or under the partnership agreement solely because the general partner's conduct furthers the general partner's own interest.

(f) All the partners of a limited partnership may authorize or ratify, after full disclosure of all material facts, a specific act or transaction by a general partner that otherwise would violate the duty of loyalty.

(g) It is a defense to a claim under subsection (b)(2) and any comparable claim in equity or at common law that the transaction was fair to the limited partnership.

(h) If, as permitted by subsection (f) or the partnership agreement, a general partner enters into a transaction with the limited partnership which otherwise would be prohibited by subsection (b)(2), the general partner's rights and obligations arising from the transaction are the same as those of a person that is not a general partner.

COMMENT

ULPA (2001) derived this section from UPA (1997) § 404. The 2011 and 2013 Harmonization amendments made one major substantive change; they "un-cabined" fiduciary duty. UPA (1997) § 404 had deviated substantially from UPA (1914) by purporting to codify all fiduciary duties owed by partners. This approach had a number of problems. Most notably, the exhaustive list of fiduciary duties left no room for the fiduciary duty owed by partners to each other—*i.e.*, "the punctilio of an honor the most sensitive." *Meinhard v. Salmon*, 164 N.E. 545, 546 (N.Y. 1928). Although UPA (1997) § 404(b) purported to state "[a] partner's duty of loyalty to the partnership *and the other partners*" (emphasis added), the three listed duties each protected the partnership and not the partners.

The 2011 and 2013 Harmonization amendments "un-cabined" fiduciary duty in both partnership acts, thereby harmonizing them to ULLCA (2006). As harmonized, this section states some of the core aspects of the fiduciary duty of loyalty, provides a duty of care, and incorporates the contractual obligation of good faith and fair dealing. The duties stated in this section are subject to the limited partnership agreement, but Section 105(c) and (d) contain important limitations on the power of the partnership agreement to affect fiduciary and other duties and the obligation of good faith and fair dealing.

For the effect of dissociation on a person's duties under this section, see Sections 602(a)(2) (limited partners) and 605(a)(2) (general partners).

Subsection (a)—This subsection recognizes two core managerial duties but, unlike UPA (1997) and ULPA (2001), does not purport to be exhaustive. For example, many cases characterize a manager's duty to disclose as a fiduciary duty. *E.g., Lonergan v. EPE Holdings, LLC*, 5 A.3d 1008, 1023 (Del. Ch. 2010) (stating that "in the limited partnership context, absent contractual modification, a general partner owes fiduciary duties that include a duty of full disclosure") (quotation marks and citation omitted); *Exxon Corp. v. Burglin*, 4 F.3d 1294, 1298 (5th Cir. 1993) ("Under Alaska law, a general partner stands in a fiduciary relationship with the limited partnership and thereby owes 'a fiduciary duty . . . to disclose information concerning partnership affairs.' ") (quoting *Parker v. Northern Mixing Co.*, 756 P.2d 881, 894 (Alaska 1988)).

Subsection (b)—This subsection states three core aspects of the fiduciary duty of loyalty: (i) not "usurping" partnership opportunities or otherwise wrongly benefiting from the limited partnership's operations or property; (ii) avoiding conflict of interests in dealing with the limited partnership (whether directly or on behalf of another); and (iii) refraining from competing with the limited partnership. Essentially the same duties exist in agency law and under the law of all types of business organizations.

The duties apply beginning with "the conduct of the partnership's activities and affairs," which by definition cannot exist before the partnership does; thus the stated duties do not apply to pre-formation activities.

The duties stated in this subsection comprise a default rule. Under Section 105(d)(3)(A): "If not manifestly unreasonable, the partnership agreement may . . . alter or eliminate the aspects of the duty of loyalty stated in Section 409(b)."

Subsection (b)(1)—The phrase "hold as trustee" dates back to UPA (1914) § 21 and reflects the availability of disgorgement remedies, such as a constructive trust. In contrast to an actual trustee, a person subject to this duty does not: (i) face the special obstacles to consent characteristic of trust law; or (ii) enjoy protection for decisions taken in reliance on the governing instrument and other sources of information. *Cf.* Uniform Statutory Trust Entity Act (2009) (Last Amended 2013) § 506 ("A trustee [of a statutory trust] . . . is not liable to the trust or to a beneficial owner for breach of any duty, *including a fiduciary duty*, to the extent the breach results from reasonable reliance on: (1) a term of the governing instrument; (2) a record of the statutory trust; or (3) an opinion, report, or statement of another person that the person to which the opinion, report, or statement is made or delivered reasonably believes is within the other person's professional or expert competence and is made or delivered to the trustee.") (emphasis added).

Subsection (b)(1)(A)—This provision is consistent with a basic principle of agency law—namely, that an agent may not benefit at all from the performance of the agency unless the principal consents. RESTATEMENT (THIRD) OF AGENCY § 8.06, cmt. c. (2006). Typically, however, the limited partnership agreement legitimizes particular benefits—*e.g.*, a management fee paid to a general partner in addition to that partner's share of distributions. Also, an agreed allocation of distributions takes those benefits outside the reach of this provision.

Subsection (b)(1)(B)—For the expansive meaning of "property," see Section 102(17). The term includes confidential information.

Subsection (b)(1)(C)—This act does not specify what constitutes "a partnership opportunity," but ample case law exists. *See, e.g., In re Monetary Grp.*, 159 B.R. 964 (M.D. Fla. 1990) (discussing the usurpation of a limited partnership opportunity"), *aff'd in part, rev'd in part*, 2 F.3d 1098 (11th Cir. 1993); *Lichtyger v. Franchard Corp.*, 18 N.Y.2d 528, 223 N.E.2d 869, 873 (1966) ("There is no basis or warrant for distinguishing the fiduciary relationship of corporate director and shareholder from that of general partner and limited partner.")

In the context of winding up, the scope of partnership opportunities inevitably narrows.

In most, if not all, situations, usurping a partnership opportunity also breaches the duty not to compete, Paragraph (b)(3), but not *vice versa*.

Subsection (b)(2)—In this context, the phrase "adverse interest" is a term of art, meaning "to be on the other side of the table" in some dealing with the limited partnership. Absent informed consent by the limited partnership, this duty is breached by the mere existence of the conflict of interest; the limited partnership need not prove that the outcome of the dealing was adverse to the partnership. *But see* Subsection (g) (permitting the defense of fairness).

Subsection (b)(3)—Although competition is often thought of in terms of potential customers, this duty applies equally to competition for resources, including employees.

Subsection (c)—This act no longer refers to the duty of care as a fiduciary duty, because: the duty of care applies in many non-fiduciary situations; and (ii) breach of the duty of care is remediable only in damages while breach of a fiduciary duty gives rise also to equitable remedies, including disgorgement, constructive trust, and rescission.

The change in label is consistent with the RESTATEMENT (THIRD) OF AGENCY § 8.02 (2006), which refers to the agent's "fiduciary duty" to act loyally, but eschews the word "fiduciary" when stating the agent's duties of "care, competence, and diligence." *Id.* § 8.08. However, the label change is merely semantics; no change is the law is intended.

The partnership agreement can raise the standard of care, or subject to Sections 105(c)(8) and (d)(2)(C), lower it. A person's practical exposure for breaching the duty of care involves not only the standard of care but also any partnership agreement provision that: (i) exonerates the person from liability for breach of the duty of care, Section 105(c)(8); or (ii) entitles the person to indemnification despite such breach, Section 408(b), comment.

Subsection (d)—This subsection refers to the "*contractual* obligation of good faith and fair dealing" (emphasis added) and thereby invokes the implied obligation that exists in every contract. *See* RESTATEMENT (SECOND) CONTRACTS § 205 (1981) ("Every contract imposes upon each party a duty of good faith and fair dealing in its performance and its enforcement."). The adjective ("contractual") should help avoid decisions like *Phelps v. Frampton*, 2007 MT 263, 339 Mont. 330, 342–43, 170 P.3d 474, 483 (2007) (holding that Montana's version of UPA (1997) creates a statutory obligation of good faith and fair dealing separate from the implied contractual covenant).

At first glance, it may seem strange to apply a contractual obligation to statutory duties and rights—*i.e.*, duties and rights "under this [act]." However, for the most part those duties and rights apply to relationships *inter se* the partners and the limited partnership and function only to the extent not displaced by the partnership agreement. Those statutory default rules are thus intended to function like a contract; applying the contractual notion of good faith and fair dealing therefore makes sense.

The contractual obligation of "good faith" has nothing to do with the corporate concept of good faith that for years bedeviled courts and attorneys trying to understand: (i) Delaware's famous corporate law exoneration provision; and (ii) that provision's exception "for acts or omissions not in good faith." DEL. CODE ANN. tit. 8, § 102(b)(7) (2012). In that context, good faith is an aspect of the duty of loyalty. *See Stone ex rel. AmSouth Bancorporation v. Ritter*, 911 A.2d 362, 369–70 (Del. 2006).

Likewise, the contractual obligation of good faith and fair dealing has nothing to do with the "utmost good faith" sometimes used to describe the fiduciary duties that owners of closely held businesses owe each other. *See, e.g., Meinhard v. Salmon*, 249 N.Y. 458, 477, 164 N.E. 545, 551 (1928) ("[W]here parties engage in a joint enterprise each owes to the other the duty of the utmost good faith in all that relates to their common venture. Within its scope they stand in a fiduciary relationship."); *Donahue v. Rodd Electrotype Co. of New England, Inc.*, 367 Mass. 578, 593, 328 N.E.2d 505, 515 (1975) ("[S]tockholders in the close corporation owe one another substantially the same fiduciary duty in the operation of the enterprise that partners owe to one another. In our previous decisions, we have defined the standard of duty owed by partners to one another as the utmost good faith and loyalty.") (footnotes omitted) (citations omitted) (internal quotations omitted).

To the contrary, the contractual obligation of good faith and fair dealing is not a fiduciary duty, does not command altruism or self-abnegation, and does not prevent a general partner from acting in the general partner's own self-interest:

"Fair dealing" is not akin to the fair process component of entire fairness, *i.e.*, whether the fiduciary acted fairly when engaging in the challenged transaction as measured by duties of loyalty and care . . . It is rather a commitment to deal "fairly" in the sense of consistently with the terms of the parties' agreement and its purpose. Likewise "good faith" does not envision loyalty to the contractual counterparty, but rather faithfulness to the scope, purpose, and terms of the parties' contract. Both necessarily turn on the contract itself and what the parties would have agreed upon had the issue arisen when they were bargaining originally.

Gerber v. Enter. Products Holdings, LLC, 67 A.3d 400, 418–19 (Del. 2013) (quoting *ASB Allegiance Real Estate Fund v. Scion Breckenridge Managing Member, LLC*, 50 A.3d 434, 440–42 (Del. Ch. 2012), *aff'd in part, rev'd in part on other grounds*, 68 A.3d 665 (Del. 2013)) (footnotes omitted) (citations omitted) (internal quotations omitted). *See also* Subsection (e).

Courts should not use the contractual obligation to change ex post facto the parties' or this act's allocation of risk and power. To the contrary, the obligation should be used only to protect agreed-upon arrangements from conduct that is manifestly beyond what a reasonable person could have contemplated when the arrangements were made.

The partnership agreement or this act may grant discretion to a general partner, and the contractual obligation of good faith and fair dealing is especially salient when discretion is at issue. However, a general partner may properly exercise discretion even though another partner (whether general or limited) suffers as a consequence. Conduct does not violate the obligation of good faith and fair dealing merely because that conduct substantially prejudices a party. Indeed, parties allocate risk precisely because prejudice may occur.

The exercise of discretion constitutes a breach of the obligation of good faith and fair dealing only when the party claiming breach shows that the conduct has no honestly-held purpose that legitimately comports with the parties' agreed-upon arrangements:

> An implied covenant claim . . . looks to the past. It is not a free-floating duty unattached to the underlying legal documents. It does not ask what duty the law should impose on the parties given their relationship at the time of the wrong, but *rather what the parties would have agreed to themselves had they considered the issue in their original bargaining positions at the time of contracting.*

Gerber v. Enter. Prods. Holdings, LLC, 67 A.3d 400, 418 (Del. 2013) (quoting *ASB Allegiance Real Estate Fund v. Scion Breckenridge Managing Member, LLC*, 50 A.3d 434, 440–42 (Del. Ch. 2012), *aff'd in part, rev'd in part on other grounds*, 68 A.3d 665 (Del. 2013)) (emphasis added) (footnotes omitted) (citations omitted) (internal quotations omitted by *Gerber*).

In sum, the purpose of the contractual obligation of good faith and fair dealing is to protect the arrangement the partners have chosen for themselves, not to restructure that arrangement under the guise of safeguarding it.

As to the power of the partnership agreement to affect the contractual obligation of good faith and fair dealing, see Section 105(c)(7) (prohibiting elimination but allowing the agreement to "prescribe the standards, if not manifestly unreasonable, by which the performance of the obligation is to be measured"). For examples, see Section 105(c)(7), comment. As to whether the obligation stated in this subsection applies to the benefit of transferees, see Section 107(b), comment.

Subsection (e)—A general partner in a limited partnership has at least two different roles: (i) as a party to the limited partnership agreement, with rights and obligations under that agreement; and (ii) as manager or co-manager of the enterprise. This provision pertains to the first role. A general partner's exercise of rights under the partnership agreement is subject to the obligation of good faith and fair dealing, Subsection (d), but a general partner does not breach that contractual obligation "solely because the general partner's conduct furthers the general partner's own interest." In contrast, this provision is ineffective with regard to a general partner's duties as manager or co-manager. For example, a general partner's liability under Section 409(b)(3) (prohibiting competition) is not "solely because the general partner's conduct furthers the general partner's own interest." Rather, the liability results from the breach of a specific obligation—*i.e.*, the codified aspect of the duty of loyalty that prohibits competition.

Subsection (f)—Here and elsewhere in this act, information "is material if there is a substantial likelihood that a reasonable [decision maker] would consider it important in deciding how to vote" or take other action under this act or the partnership agreements. *See TSC Industries, Inc. v. Northway, Inc.*, 426 U.S. 438, 449, 96 S.Ct. 2126, 2132 (1976).

The partnership agreement can provide additional or different methods of authorization or ratification, subject to the strictures of Section 105(c)(5), (d)(1), and (d)(3)(A)(B) and (D).

Subsection (g)—This subsection codifies judge-made law applicable to all business entities. *See, e.g., Lonergan v. EPE Holdings, LLC*, 5 A.3d 1008, 1019 (Del. Ch. 2010) (discussing "entire fairness" in the context of a limited partnership"); *Gottsacker v. Monnier*, 281 Wis. 2d 361, 379, 697 N.W.2d 436, 444 (Wisc. 2005) (referring to "a willful failure to deal fairly with the LLC or its other members"); *Kahn v. Lynch Commc'n Sys., Inc.*, 638 A.2d 1110, 1116 (Del. 1994) (discussing "entire fairness" in the context of a corporation's merger with an affiliate).

Subsection (h)—This subsection is the modern, reformulated version of a language that sought to overturn the now-defunct notion that debts to partners were categorically inferior to debts to non-partner creditors. *See, e.g.,* ULPA (2001) § 112 ("A partner may lend money to and transact other business with the limited partnership and has the same rights and obligations with respect to the loan or other transaction as a person that is not a partner."). The reformulation makes clear that this provision has nothing to do with the fiduciary duty pertaining to conflict of interests. *See BT-I v. Equitable Life Assurance Soc'y of the United States,* 75 Cal. App. 4th 1406, 1415, 89 Cal. Rptr. 2d 811 (1999) (examining the prior formulation, explaining its history and stating "[w]e cannot discern anything in the purpose of [the prior formulation] that suggests an intent to affect a general partner's fiduciary duty to limited partners").

This subsection states a default rule. The partnership agreement may provide that debt to a general partner (or general partners generally) is subordinate to other partnership obligations. The agreement that creates the debt may do likewise.

[ARTICLE] 5. CONTRIBUTIONS AND DISTRIBUTIONS

INTRODUCTORY COMMENT

With the exception of Section 505, this Article applies in the same way to both general and limited partners.

§ 501.   Form of Contribution

A contribution may consist of property transferred to, services performed for, or another benefit provided to the limited partnership or an agreement to transfer property to, perform services for, or provide another benefit to the partnership.

COMMENT

This section is intentionally quite broad, encompassing past, present, and promised benefits. Comparable language exists in most, if not all, limited partnership statutes, and case law recognizes the intended broadness of this approach. *See, e.g., Rival 1981-IV Drilling Program, Ltd. v. Guar. Bank & Trust,* 732 P.2d 1233, 1234 (Colo. Ct. App. 1986) (letter of credit as contribution); *Rehfuss v. Moore,* 19 A. 756, 757 (Pa. 1890) (patent rights); *Belgard v. Manchac Technologies, LLC,* 92 So.3d 660, 664 (La. Ct. App. 3d Cir. 2012) (establishing a line of credit).

This act does not contain a statute of frauds specifically applicable to promised contributions. Generally applicable statutes of fraud might apply, however. For example, a promise to contribute land to the limited partnership would be subject to the statute of frauds pertaining to land transfers. *See Gunsorek v. Heartland Bank,* 707 N.E.2d 557, 564 (Ohio 1997) (holding that where terms of oral partnership agreement required limited partner to contribute real property, statute of frauds barred enforceability of the agreement). Likewise, a promise that by its terms requires performance that extends beyond one year from the making of the contract would be subject to the one-year provision of the statute of frauds. *See* Section 102(14), cmt.

§ 502.   Liability for Contribution

(a)   A person's obligation to make a contribution to a limited partnership is not excused by the person's death, disability, termination, or other inability to perform personally.

(b)   If a person does not fulfill an obligation to make a contribution other than money, the person is obligated at the option of the limited partnership to contribute money equal to the value, as stated in the required information, of the part of the contribution which has not been made.

(c)   The obligation of a person to make a contribution may be compromised only by the affirmative vote or consent of all the partners. If a creditor of a limited partnership extends credit or otherwise acts in reliance on an obligation described in subsection (a) without knowledge or notice of a compromise under this subsection, the creditor may enforce the obligation.

COMMENT

Subsection (a)—Under common law principles of impracticability, an individual's death or incapacity will sometimes discharge a duty to render performance. RESTATEMENT (SECOND) OF CONTRACTS §§ 261 (Discharge by Supervening Impracticability), 262 (Death or Incapacity of Person Necessary For Performance).

(1981). This subsection overrides those principles. Moreover, the reference to "perform personally" is not limited to individuals but rather may refer to any legal person (including an entity) that has a non-delegable duty.

Subsection (b)—This subsection is a statutory liquidated damage provision, exercisable at the option of the limited partnership, with the damage amount set according to the value of the promised, non-monetary contribution.

Example: In order to become a partner, a person promises to contribute to the limited partnership various assets which the partnership agreement values at $150,000. In return for the person's promise, and in light of the agreed value, the limited partnership admits the person as a partner with a right to receive 25% of the limited partnership's distributions.

The promised assets are subject to a security agreement, but the partner promises to contribute them "free and clear." Before the partner can contribute the assets, the secured party forecloses on the security interest and sells the assets at a public sale for $75,000. Even if the $75,000 reflects the actual fair market value of the assets, under this subsection the limited partnership has a claim against the partner for "money equal to the value . . . of the part of the contribution which has not been made"—*i.e.*, $150,000.

Example: Same facts as the previous example, except that the public sale brings $225,000. The limited partnership is neither obliged to invoke this subsection nor limited to the $150,000 valuation. The limited partnership may instead sue for breach of the promise to make the contribution, asserting the $225,000 figure as evidence of the actual loss suffered as a result of the breach.

Subsection (c)—The unanimity requirement expressed in the first sentence might indirectly benefit creditors, but the requirement is nonetheless a default rule and therefore may be varied by the partnership agreement. The right of each partner to consent is not a "right[ ] under this [act] of a person other than a partner." *See* Section 105(c)(18) (preventing the partnership agreement from affecting such rights). In contrast, the creditor right stated in the second sentence fits squarely within Section 105(c)(18) and therefore may not be varied by the partnership agreement.

§ 503.   Sharing of and Right to Distributions Before Dissolution

(a)   Any distribution made by a limited partnership before its dissolution and winding up must be shared among the partners on the basis of the value, as stated in the required information when the limited partnership decides to make the distribution, of the contributions the limited partnership has received from each partner, except to the extent necessary to comply with a transfer effective under Section 702 or charging order in effect under Section 703.

(b)   A person has a right to a distribution before the dissolution and winding up of a limited partnership only if the partnership decides to make an interim distribution. A person's dissociation does not entitle the person to a distribution.

(c)   A person does not have a right to demand or receive a distribution from a limited partnership in any form other than money. Except as otherwise provided in Section 810(f), a partnership may distribute an asset in kind only if each part of the asset is fungible with each other part and each person receives a percentage of the asset equal in value to the person's share of distributions.

(d)   If a partner or transferee becomes entitled to receive a distribution, the partner or transferee has the status of, and is entitled to all remedies available to, a creditor of the limited partnership with respect to the distribution. However, the partnership's obligation to make a distribution is subject to offset for any amount owed to the partnership by the partner or a person dissociated as a partner on whose account the distribution is made.

COMMENT

Past uniform unincorporated entity acts and many current limited partnership acts provide default rules for allocation of profits, and UPA (1997) even provided a default structure for maintaining capital accounts. For the following reasons, this act, incorporating changes made by the Harmonization Project, provides a default rule only for rights to share in distributions:

- Capital accounts are maintained for one purpose, to determine how distributions will be made to partners. The rules for maintenance of capital accounts can be very complex. Generally, however, profits increase capital account balances (and increase the amounts that will be distributed to the partners) and losses reduce capital account balances (and reduce the amounts that will be distributed to the partners). If the statute has a simple default rule for how distributions are to be made to the partners, providing an additional set of default profit and loss allocation provisions and capital account rules will be, at best, duplicative and, at worse, inconsistent with the distribution rules.

- Some argue that capital account rules and profit and loss allocation provisions are necessary to comply with tax requirements. Tax income or loss is allocated to partners according to the partners' economic interests in the partnership, and these interests are based on distributions that would be made to partners on liquidation of the partnership. By including default distribution provisions, the act includes the information necessary to make these tax determinations. To the extent the tax law allows partners to make further tax elections or satisfy alternative safe harbors, the partners may look to the tax law for guidance and include necessary provisions in their agreements.

Subsection (a)—The rule stated applies to redemptions as well as operating distributions but is a default rule in both contexts. *See* 102(4)(A), cmt.

Subsection (b)—The second sentence of this subsection accords with Section 602(a)(3)—upon dissociation a partner is treated as a mere transferee of the partner's own transferable interest. Like most *inter se* rules in this act, this one is subject to the limited partnership agreement. *See* Section 602(a)(3), cmt. and 605(a)(3).

Subsection (d)—*See also* Section 504(d) (pertaining to the rights of partners and transferees that receive a distribution in the form of indebtedness) and 504(e) (pertaining to solvency testing for payments on indebtedness issued to redeem an interest).

§ 504. Limitations on Distributions

(a)   A limited partnership may not make a distribution, including a distribution under Section 810, if after the distribution:

(1)   the partnership would not be able to pay its debts as they become due in the ordinary course of the partnership's activities and affairs; or

(2)   the partnership's total assets would be less than the sum of its total liabilities plus the amount that would be needed, if the partnership were to be dissolved and wound up at the time of the distribution, to satisfy the preferential rights upon dissolution and winding up of partners and transferees whose preferential rights are superior to the rights of persons receiving the distribution.

(b)   A limited partnership may base a determination that a distribution is not prohibited under subsection (a) on:

(1)   financial statements prepared on the basis of accounting practices and principles that are reasonable in the circumstances; or

(2)   a fair valuation or other method that is reasonable under the circumstances.

(c)   Except as otherwise provided in subsection (e), the effect of a distribution under subsection (a) is measured:

(1)   in the case of a distribution as defined in Section 102(4)(A), as of the earlier of:

(A)   the date money or other property is transferred or debt is incurred by the limited partnership; or

(B)   the date the person entitled to the distribution ceases to own the interest or right being acquired by the partnership in return for the distribution;

(2)   in the case of any other distribution of indebtedness, as of the date the indebtedness is distributed; and

(3)   in all other cases, as of the date:

(A)   the distribution is authorized, if the payment occurs not later than 120 days after that date; or

(B)   the payment is made, if the payment occurs more than 120 days after the distribution is authorized.

(d) A limited partnership's indebtedness to a partner or transferee incurred by reason of a distribution made in accordance with this section is at parity with the partnership's indebtedness to its general, unsecured creditors, except to the extent subordinated by agreement.

(e) A limited partnership's indebtedness, including indebtedness issued as a distribution, is not a liability for purposes of subsection (a) if the terms of the indebtedness provide that payment of principal and interest is made only if and to the extent that payment of a distribution could then be made under this section. If the indebtedness is issued as a distribution, each payment of principal or interest is treated as a distribution, the effect of which is measured on the date the payment is made.

(f) In measuring the effect of a distribution under Section 810, the liabilities of a dissolved limited partnership do not include any claim that has been disposed of under Section 806, 807, or 808.

COMMENT

Both this section and Section 505 were derived essentially from the Model Business Corporation Act section 6.40. Both sections are necessary and appropriate because a limited partnership provides its limited partners a corporate-like liability shield and a limited liability limited partnership provides the shield to general partners as well. With the exception noted in the comment to Subsection (a)(2), the provisions of this section are non-waivable. Section 105(c)(18).

"Distribution" does not include "amounts constituting reasonable compensation for present or past service or payments made in the ordinary course of business under a bona fide retirement plan or other bona fide benefits program." Section 102(4)(B).

Subsection (a)—Insolvency is a fundamental issue under this section, and this subsection provides two tests of insolvency. The tests are disjunctive; a distribution violates this section if after the distribution the limited partnership fails either of the tests. The subsection applies both to interim and liquidating distributions.

Solvency is also a fundamental issue under bankruptcy and fraudulent transfer law, which provide their own respective definitions of the concept.

Subsection (a)(2)—The reference to "preferential rights upon dissolution and winding up" is a default rule, because removing this protection for preferred partners or transferees is an *inter se* matter. *See* Section 105(d)(1)(B). The rest of the section is not subject to change in the partnership agreement. Section 105(c)(18).

Subsection (b)—This subsection states a standard of ordinary care, in contrast with the generally-applicable standard stated in Section 409(c) (gross negligence).

Subsection (b)(2)—This alternative valuation provision is likely to be both useful and fair when the limited partnership has appreciated assets but for accounting purposes these assets are valued at book value less depreciation.

Subsection (c)—This subsection provides three alternative rules for determining the point(s) in time of as which to apply the Subsection (a) solvency tests. The timing depends on which of three categories encompasses a distribution: (i) a distribution in the nature of a redemption (regardless of whether the distribution includes a distribution of indebtedness); (ii) any distribution of indebtedness other than a distribution in the nature of a redemption; and (iii) any distribution that involves neither a redemption nor a distribution of indebtedness. A requirement for additional solvency testing pertaining to distributions of indebtedness appears in Subsection (e).

Subsection (c)(1)—Section 102(4)(A) encompasses distributions in the nature of a redemption.

Subsection (c)(1)(A) and (B)—Under Subparagraph (A), any beginning of payment activity triggers to the rule and sets the date as of when to apply the solvency tests. Under Subparagraph (B), the limited partnership's complete acquisition of the rights is necessary to trigger the rule.

Subsection (c)(2)—This provision states the general rule for distributions that are in the form of debt and which are not connected with a redemption.

Subsection (c)(3)—This provision states alternative rules for all distribution of money or property (*i.e.*, not debt). The measuring date depends on the length of time between the authorization and payment of the distribution.

Subsection (d)—*Compare* Subsection (d), *with* Section 503(d) (characterizing as a creditor a person who has become entitled to receive a distribution).

Subsection (e)—This subsection contains two rules pertaining to indebtedness issued as part of a distribution and the solvency tests of Subsection (a). The first sentence states the sensible rule that indebtedness that is essentially subordinated to the solvency requirement—*i.e.*, not payable if making payment would transgress that requirement—is not counted in determining liabilities for purposes of the solvency tests. The second sentence applies the solvency tests to each payment of principal and interest on any indebtedness issued as a distribution, in addition to any previous testing required by Subsection (c)(1)(A) or (c)(2).

Example: A limited partnership and one of its partners agree that the limited partnership will buy out the partner's entire ownership interest in the partnership in return for a promissory note from the partnership, payable in installments. Under the redemption agreement, the partner yields up all its interests and rights on January 15 and the partnership signs and delivers the note to the dissociated partner on February 15. Under the note, payment of interest is due monthly beginning March 15, with a balloon payment of the principal due December 30.

Under Subsection (c)(1)(B), the solvency tests are applied as of January 15. Under Subsection (e), the solvency tests are again applied on the March 15, April 15, etc., and again on December 30.

Subsection (f)—The cited sections provide methods for extinguishing or limiting the debts of a limited partnership that is winding up its affairs and activities and thus any debt affected by any of the cited sections is irrelevant for purposes of solvency testing.

§ 505. Liability for Improper Distributions

(a) If a general partner consents to a distribution made in violation of Section 504 and in consenting to the distribution fails to comply with Section 409, the general partner is personally liable to the limited partnership for the amount of the distribution which exceeds the amount that could have been distributed without the violation of Section 504.

(b) A person that receives a distribution knowing that the distribution violated Section 504 is personally liable to the limited partnership but only to the extent that the distribution received by the person exceeded the amount that could have been properly paid under Section 504.

(c) A general partner against which an action is commenced because the general partner is liable under subsection (a) may:

(1) implead any other person that is liable under subsection (a) and seek to enforce a right of contribution from the person; and

(2) implead any person that received a distribution in violation of subsection (b) and seek to enforce a right of contribution from the person in the amount the person received in violation of subsection (b).

(d) An action under this section is barred unless commenced not later than two years after the distribution.

COMMENT

This section and Section 504 were derived essentially from Model Business Corporation Act section 6.40. As with Section 504, this section is appropriate and necessary due to the liability shield of a limited partnership. The provisions of this section are non-waivable. Section 105(c)(18).

This section contemplates two categories of liability: liability of those who have authorized improper distributions, Subsection (a), and the liability of those who have received improper distributions, Subsection (c). Liability that has accrued under this section is not affected by a person subsequently ceasing to be a partner or transferee.

The liability is to the entity, not to the creditors of an insolvent entity. *See Hullett v. Cousin,* 63 P.3d 1029, 1036 (Ariz. 2003) (holding that where limited partners had no intent to defraud creditors, and had no reason to know the partnership was insolvent at the time, return of the partners' contributions was not an improper distribution and could not be used to satisfy creditor's claim against the partnership). However, some cases accord a creditor standing to invoke the statute. *See, e.g., Henkels & McCoy, Inc. v. Adochio,* 906 F.Supp. 244, 249–50 (E.D. Pa. 1995), *aff'd,* 138 F.3d 491, 503–04 (3d Cir. 1998) (holding limited partners liable to creditor where general partner knew or should have known the distributions were in violation of partnership agreement).

This section does not preclude or interfere with claims for fraudulent transfer. *See* Subsection (d), cmt.

Subsection (a)—The liability is not strict liability but rather attaches only to the extent a decision maker has failed to comply with the duties stated in Section 409. To the extent those duties have been permissibly revised by the partnership agreement, the revised standards apply to this subsection. *See also* Section 504(b)(1) (permitting reasonable reliance on specified financial information).

Subsection (b)—Actual knowledge is necessary to impose liability. Reason to know does not suffice. *Compare* Subsection (b), *with* Section 103(a)–(b).

Subsections (b) and (c)(2)—Liability could apply to a person who receives a distribution under a charging order, but only if the person meets the knowledge requirement. That situation is very unlikely unless the person with the charging order is also a general partner.

Subsection (e)—When the distribution is in the form of indebtedness, the distribution may occur on several different dates. *See* Section 504(e), cmt.

This statute of limitations applies only to actions "under this section" and does not affect claims under other applicable law, which most often is fraudulent transfer law. For a different approach, see DEL. CODE ANN. tit. 6, § 18–607(c) (West 2013) (applying a 3-year statute of limitations to claims "under this chapter or other applicable law"); N.Y. PTR. LAW § 121–607(c) (same). *But see, e.g., In re The Heritage Org., LLC*, 413 BR 438, 461 (Bankr. ND Tex. 2009) (invoking the Texas Uniform Fraudulent Act [TUFTA] to recover distributions made by a Delaware LLC headquartered in Texas; rejecting DEL. CODE ANN. tit. 6, § 18–607(c) on choice of law grounds; stating that "the Delaware legislature cannot limit the reach of TUFTA").

[ARTICLE] 6.   DISSOCIATION

§ 601.   Dissociation as Limited Partner

(a)   A person does not have a right to dissociate as a limited partner before the completion of the winding up of the limited partnership.

(b)   A person is dissociated as a limited partner when:

(1)   the limited partnership knows or has notice of the person's express will to withdraw as a limited partner, but, if the person has specified a withdrawal date later than the date the partnership knew or had notice, on that later date;

(2)   an event stated in the partnership agreement as causing the person's dissociation as a limited partner occurs;

(3)   the person is expelled as a limited partner pursuant to the partnership agreement;

(4)   the person is expelled as a limited partner by the affirmative vote or consent of all the other partners if:

(A)   it is unlawful to carry on the limited partnership's activities and affairs with the person as a limited partner;

(B)   there has been a transfer of all the person's transferable interest in the partnership, other than:

(i)   a transfer for security purposes; or

(ii)   a charging order in effect under Section 703 which has not been foreclosed;

(C)   the person is an entity and:

(i)   the partnership notifies the person that it will be expelled as a limited partner because the person has filed a statement of dissolution or the equivalent, the person has been administratively dissolved, the person's charter or the equivalent has been revoked, or the person's right to conduct business has been suspended by the person's jurisdiction of formation; and

(ii)   not later than 90 days after the notification, the statement of dissolution or the equivalent has not been withdrawn, rescinded, or revoked, the person has not been reinstated, or the person's charter or the equivalent or right to conduct business has not been reinstated; or

(D)   the person is an unincorporated entity that has been dissolved and whose activities and affairs are being would up;

(5)   on application by the limited partnership or a partner in a direct action under Section 901, the person is expelled as a limited partner by judicial order because the person:

(A)   has engaged or is engaging in wrongful conduct that has affected adversely and materially, or will affect adversely and materially, the partnership's activities and affairs;

(B)   has committed willfully or persistently, or is committing willfully and persistently, a material breach of the partnership agreement or the contractual obligation of good faith and fair dealing under Section 305(a); or

(C)   has engaged or is engaging in conduct relating to the partnership's activities and affairs which makes it not reasonably practicable to carry on the activities and affairs with the person as a limited partner;

(6)   in the case of an individual, the individual dies;

(7)   in the case of a person that is a testamentary or inter vivos trust or is acting as a limited partner by virtue of being a trustee of such a trust, the trust's entire transferable interest in the limited partnership is distributed;

(8)   in the case of a person that is an estate or is acting as a limited partner by virtue of being a personal representative of an estate, the estate's entire transferable interest in the limited partnership is distributed;

(9)   in the case of a person that is not an individual, the existence of the person terminates;

(10)   the limited partnership participates in a merger under [Article] 11 and:

(A)   the partnership is not the surviving entity; or

(B)   otherwise as a result of the merger, the person ceases to be a limited partner;

(11)   the limited partnership participates in an interest exchange under [Article] 11 and, as a result of the interest exchange, the person ceases to be a limited partner;

(12)   the limited partnership participates in a conversion under [Article] 11;

(13)   the limited partnership participates in a domestication under [Article] 11 and, as a result of the domestication, the person ceases to be a limited partner; or

(14)   the limited partnership dissolves and completes winding up.

COMMENT

Subsection (a)—This provision states a default rule.

Subsection (b)—This subsection states default rules, which the partnership agreement may vary. However, it would be nonsensical to vary some of the rules—*e.g.,* to provide that the death of a partner who is an individual does not cause the individual's dissociation as a partner, Subsection (b)(6), or that an entity remains a partner even after the existence of the entity has terminated, Subsection (b)(9).

Subsection (b)(1)—The partnership agreement may vary this provision, even to the extent of eliminating a person's power to dissociate as a limited partner. Section 105(c)(11) prohibits the limited partnership agreement from eliminating the power to dissociate of a person as a *general* partner, but neither Section 105(c) nor (d) preserve as mandatory the power of a person to dissociate as a *limited* partner.

Subsection (b)(4)(B)—This provision permits expulsion when a limited partner no longer has any "skin in the game." Under this subparagraph (unless the limited partnership agreement provides otherwise), a limited partner's transferee can protect itself from the vulnerability of "bare naked transferee" status by obligating the partner/transferor to retain a 1% interest and exercise the partner's contract and governance rights (including the right to bring a derivative suit) to protect the transferee's interests.

Subsection (b)(5)—By its terms, this provision does not permit a partner to bring a direct action for expulsion even if the partner could establish standing under Section 901(b). Dealing with a misbehaving limited partner is a management duty, properly reserved to the general partners. *Cf.* Section 603(5) (permitting an "application by the limited partnership or a partner in a direct action under Section 901" for a judicial order expelling a general partner).

Although the partnership agreement can revise or eliminate the possibility of judicial expulsion, doing so requires careful planning. *Cf. Huatuco v. Satellite Healthcare,* CV 8465-VCG, 2013 WL 6460898, at *1, n.2 (Del. Ch. Dec. 9, 2013) (stating that "the right to judicial dissolution is a default right which the parties may eschew by contract" while reserving the question of "[w]hether the parties may, by contract, divest this Court of its authority to order a dissolution in all circumstances, even where it appears manifest that equity so requires—leaving, for instance, irreconcilable members locked away together forever like some alternative entity version of Sartre's Huis Clos").

For examples of conduct warranting an expulsion order in various contexts, see *All Saints Univ. of Med. Aruba v. Chilana,* A-2628-09T1, 2012 WL 6652510 (N.J. Super. Ct. App. Div. Dec. 24, 2012) (discussing a pattern of conduct); *Sherwood Park Bus. Ctr., L.L.C. v. Taggart,* 323 P.3d 551, 561 (Or. Ct. App. 2014) (upholding expulsion of a member who "had stolen a large amount of money from [the limited liability company], had intentionally failed to provide financial information, and had made himself unavailable to carry on the business"); *CCD, L.C. v. Millsap,* 116 P.3d 366, 373 (Utah 2005) (holding that a member's "misappropriat[ion of] trust account funds totaling at least $11,540.06 for his personal use" warranted expulsion, where the member's "misconduct continued the pattern of behavior that [had previously] resulted in losses to the company of $625,000[, where the new misconduct] . . . took place after [the member's] prior wrongdoing had been discovered and after [the limited liability company] had assented to permit [the member] to atone for his misdeeds by fulfilling the terms of the amended operating agreement").

For an analysis that helps distinguish Paragraph (5)(C) from Paragraphs (5)(A) and (B), see *All Saints Univ. of Med. Aruba v. Chilana,* A-2628-09T1, 2012 WL 6652510, at *15 (N.J. Super. Ct. App. Div. Dec. 24, 2012) (interpreting predecessor law and noting that the "not reasonably practicable standard" does not require a showing of wrongful conduct). *Cf. Dunnagan v. Watson,* 204 S.W.3d 30, 40 (Tex. Ct. App. 2006) (same issue in the context of dissolution). Where grounds exist for both dissociation and dissolution, a court has the discretion to choose between the alternatives. *Robertson v. Jacobs Cattle Co.,* 830 N.W.2d 191, 201–02 (Neb. 2013) (discussing analogous provisions of UPA (1997)). "[T]here is no textual basis for imposing a higher burden of proof for dissociation than dissolution." *Brennan v. Brennan Assocs.,* 977 A.2d 107, 121 (Conn. 2009) (general partnership).

Subsection (b)(7) and (8)—A change in trustee or personal representative does not cause dissociation.

Subsection (b)(9)—This provision is the entity analog to Subsection (b)(6) (death of an individual). Although in theory the partnership agreement could change this rule, doing so would be nonsensical. *See* Section 803(a), cmt. (noting that a terminated limited liability company cannot rescind its dissolution because "a 'dead' entity lacks both the capacity and power to bring itself back from the dead"). *See also* Subsection (b)(14).

Subsection (b)(10)(A)—If a limited partnership disappears as part of a merger, no person can continue as a partner of the limited partnership. When the merger takes effect, the partners of the disappearing entity are perforce dissociated. Depending on the plan of merger, those persons may become partners of a surviving limited partnership. In those circumstances, the merger will have dissociated them from one limited partnership and admitted them into partnership in the surviving entity. *See* Section 301(b)(2).

Subsection (b)(10)(B)—It is possible for a plan of merger to "shuffle the equity" of the surviving entity, even to the extent of "taking out" some or all of the owners of the surviving entity. A reverse triangular merger involving a limited partnership as the surviving entity would dissociate all the pre-merger partners of the partnership.

Subsection (b)(12)—By definition, a limited partnership that converts ceases to be a limited partnership. Thus, when the plan of conversion takes effect, all the partners of the converted entity are dissociated from that entity. In many cases, those persons will all be owners of the converted entity. In some cases, the conversion will "shuffle the equity" and "take out" some of the partners of the converting limited partnership.

Subsection (b)(13)—Domestication does not by itself dissociate a partner, because the domesticated entity remains both a limited partnership and "the same entity without interruption as the domesticating company." Section 1156(a)(1)(B). However, an "equity shuffle" could dissociate a partner.

§ 602. **Effect of Dissociation as Limited Partner**

(a)   If a person is dissociated as a limited partner:

(1)   subject to Section 704, the person does not have further rights as a limited partner;

(2)   the person's contractual obligation of good faith and fair dealing as a limited partner under Section 305(a) ends with regard to matters arising and events occurring after the person's dissociation; and

(3)   subject to Section 704 and [Article] 11, any transferable interest owned by the person in the person's capacity as a limited partner immediately before dissociation is owned by the person solely as a transferee.

(b)   A person's dissociation as a limited partner does not of itself discharge the person from any debt, obligation, or other liability to the limited partnership or the other partners which the person incurred while a limited partner.

COMMENT

Subsection (a)—This provision makes no reference to power-to-bind matters, because the act provides that a limited partner *qua* limited partner has no power to bind the limited partnership. Section 302(a).

Subsection (a)(2)—This provision does not determine the effect of a person's dissociation as a limited partner on the person's future obligations or rights under the partnership agreement. Some contractual obligations typically extend beyond dissociation—*e.g.*, buyout arrangements. To the extent provisions of the partnership agreement continue to apply, the common law obligation of good faith continues to apply as well. *See* 409(d), cmt. (explaining that the subsection "invokes the implied obligation that exists in every contract" as a matter of common law).

Subsection (a)(3)—This paragraph accords with Section 503(b)—dissociation does not entitle a person to any distribution, even if dissociation takes the form of expulsion. *All Saints Univ. of Med. Aruba v. Chilana*, A-2628-09T1, 2012 WL 6652510 at *12 (N.J. Super. Ct. App. Div. Dec. 24, 2012).

Like most *inter se* rules in this act, this one is subject to the partnership agreement. For example, the partnership agreement has the power to provide for the buyout of a person's transferable interest in connection with the person's dissociation.

§ 603. **Dissociation as General Partner**

A person is dissociated as a general partner when:

(1)   the limited partnership knows or has notice of the person's express will to withdraw as a general partner, but, if the person has specified a withdrawal date later than the date the partnership knew or had notice, on that later date;

(2)   an event stated in the partnership agreement as causing the person's dissociation as a general partner occurs;

(3)   the person is expelled as a general partner pursuant to the partnership agreement;

(4)   the person is expelled as a general partner by the affirmative vote or consent of all the other partners if:

(A)   it is unlawful to carry on the limited partnership's activities and affairs with the person as a general partner;

(B)   there has been a transfer of all the person's transferable interest in the partnership, other than:

(i)   a transfer for security purposes; or

(ii)   a charging order in effect under Section 703 which has not been foreclosed;

(C)   the person is an entity and:

(i)   the partnership notifies the person that it will be expelled as a general partner because the person has filed a statement of dissolution or the equivalent, the person has been administratively dissolved, the person's charter or the equivalent has been revoked, or the person's right to conduct business has been suspended by the person's jurisdiction of formation; and

(ii)   not later than 90 days after the notification, the statement of dissolution or the equivalent has not been withdrawn, rescinded, or revoked, the person has not been reinstated, or the person's charter or the equivalent or right to conduct business has not been reinstated; or

(D)   the person is an unincorporated entity that has been dissolved and whose activities and affairs are being would up;

(5)   on application by the limited partnership or a partner in a direct action under Section 901, the person is expelled as a general partner by judicial order because the person:

(A)   has engaged or is engaging in wrongful conduct that has affected adversely and materially, or will affect adversely and materially, the partnership's activities and affairs;

(B)   has committed willfully or persistently, or is committing willfully or persistently, a material breach of the partnership agreement or a duty or obligation under Section 409; or

(C)   has engaged or is engaging in conduct relating to the partnership's activities and affairs which makes it not reasonably practicable to carry on the activities and affairs of the limited partnership with the person as a general partner;

(6)   in the case of an individual:

(A)   the individual dies;

(B)   a guardian or general conservator for the individual is appointed; or

(C)   a court orders that the individual has otherwise become incapable of performing the individual's duties as a general partner under this [act] or the partnership agreement;

(7)   the person:

(A)   becomes a debtor in bankruptcy;

(B)   executes an assignment for the benefit of creditors; or

(C)   seeks, consents to, or acquiesces in the appointment of a trustee, receiver, or liquidator of the person or of all or substantially all the person's property;

(8)   in the case of a person that is a testamentary or inter vivos trust or is acting as a general partner by virtue of being a trustee of such a trust, the trust's entire transferable interest in the limited partnership is distributed;

(9)   in the case of a person that is an estate or is acting as a general partner by virtue of being a personal representative of an estate, the estate's entire transferable interest in the limited partnership is distributed;

(10)   in the case of a person that is not an individual, the existence of the person terminates;

(11)   the limited partnership participates in a merger under [Article] 11 and:

(A)   the partnership is not the surviving entity; or

(B)   otherwise as a result of the merger, the person ceases to be a general partner;

(12)   the limited partnership participates in an interest exchange under [Article] 11 and, as a result of the interest exchange, the person ceases to be a general partner;

(13)   the limited partnership participates in a conversion under [Article] 11;

(14)   the limited partnership participates in a domestication under [Article] 11 and, as a result of the domestication, the person ceases to be a general partner; or

(15) the limited partnership dissolves and completes winding up.

COMMENT

This section mostly states default rules, which the limited partnership agreement may vary. However, it would make no sense to vary some of the rules—*e.g.*, to provide that death does *not* cause an individual's dissociation, Paragraph (6)(A), or that person (other than an individual) remains a general partner even *after* "the existence of the person terminates." Paragraph (10).

Paragraph (1)—Limited partnership agreements often require notice of dissociation to be in writing and to specify the effective date of the dissociation. The agreement cannot eliminate the power of a general partner to dissociate by express will, Section 105(c)(11) but can eliminate the right and thereby make the dissociation wrongful.

Paragraph (3)—Many partnership agreements provide for "no cause" expulsion, and courts considering such provisions have taken somewhat different approaches. *Compare Gelder Med. Grp. v. Webber*, 41 N.Y.2d 680, 684, 363 N.E.2d 573, 576 (1977) *with Winston & Strawn v. Nosal*, 279 Ill. App. 3d 231, 240, 664 N.E.2d 239, 245 (Ill. App. Ct. 1996). *See also* Section 409(d) and cmt. (stating and explaining the implied contractual covenant of good faith and fair dealing).

Paragraph (4)(B)—This paragraph permits expulsion when a general partner no longer has any "skin in the game." Under this paragraph (unless the partnership agreement provides otherwise), a general partner's transferee can protect itself from the vulnerability of "bare naked assignee" status, Section 107(b), cmt., by obligating the general partner/transferor to retain a 1% interest and exercise the partner's governance rights (including the right to bring a derivative suit) to protect the transferee's interests.

Paragraph (5)—The reference to "a direct action under Section 901" reflects the "separate entity" nature of a limited partnership. Section 901 limits a partner's standing to bring a direct action to circumstances in which the partner can "plead and prove an actual or threatened injury that is not solely the result of an injury suffered or threatened to be suffered by the limited partnership."

Example: General Partner Alpha breaches the limited partnership agreement by purporting to oust General Partner Beta from General Partner Beta's role in managing the limited partnership. General Partner Beta has a direct claim against General Partner Alpha, not only for breach of contract, but also for expulsion under Paragraph 5.

Example: General Partner Alpha breaches the limited partnership agreement (and also Section 409(c)) through grossly negligent conduct which harms the profitability of the limited partnership. Depending on the terms of the limited partnership agreement and the allocation of power among the partners, General Partner Beta may be able to cause the limited partnership to invoke Paragraph 5 and seek General Partner Alpha's expulsion. But General Partner Beta has no standing individually to seek General Partner Alpha's expulsion, except through a derivative claim. (The same is true for a claim of breach of contract. *See* Section 901(b), cmt.)

Paragraph (5)(C)—This provision has an analog among the causes for dissolution. *See* Section 801(a)(6)(B). For examples of conduct warranting an expulsion order, see *Della Ratta v. Dyas*, 183 Md. App. 344, 365–66, 961 A.2d 629, 642 (2008), aff'd, 414 Md. 556, 996 A.2d 382 (2010) (noting that "[t]he trial court expressly found that [two major capital] calls 'were issued in bad faith' . . . [and the] court also found that, '[by] another improper accounting movement' in [the partnership], $580,000 was taken 'for executive office expenses which was improper' ") (third bracket in original); *Brennan v. Brennan Associates*, 293 Conn. 60, 76–77, 977 A.2d 107, 117–18 (2009) (referring to the expelled partner's "moral turpitude and criminal fraud, and failure to be honest in court as to the extent of his criminal wrongdoing" and "his baseless claims of fraud" against a fellow partner; stating "he has rung the bell and it cannot be unrung").

For an analysis that helps distinguish Paragraph (5)(C) from Paragraphs (5)(A) and (B), see *All Saints Univ. of Med. Aruba v. Chilana*, A-2628-09T1, 2012 WL 6652510 at *15 (N.J. Super. Ct. App. Div. Dec. 24, 2012) (interpreting predecessor law and noting that the "not reasonably practicable standard" does not require a showing of wrongful conduct). *Cf. Dunnagan v. Watson*, 204 S.W.3d 30, 40 (Tex. App. 2006) (same issue in the context of dissolution).

Where grounds exist for both dissociation and dissolution, a court has the discretion to choose between the alternatives. *Robertson v. Jacobs Cattle Co.*, 285 Neb. 859, 870–72, 830 N.W.2d 191, 201–02 (2013) (discussing analogous provisions of UPA (1997)). "[T]here is no textual basis for imposing a higher burden of proof for dissociation than dissolution." *Brennan v. Brennan Associates*, 293 Conn. 60, 83, 977 A.2d 107, 121 (2009) (general partnership).

Paragraph (6)(B) and (C)—No comparable provisions appear in Section 601 (dealing with the dissociation of a limited partner), because, given the limited rights and duties of limited partners, the stated occurrences do not necessarily justify dissociation.

Paragraph 7(A)—This provision is subject to bankruptcy law. *See, e.g.,* 11 U.S.C.A. § 365(e) (invalidating "ipso facto" clauses, subject to some exceptions).

Paragraphs (8) and (9)—A change in trustee or personal representative does not cause dissociation.

Paragraph (10)—This provision is the entity analog to Paragraph (7)(A) (death of an individual). Although in theory the partnership agreement could change this rule, doing so would be nonsensical. *See* Section 803(a), cmt. (noting that a terminated limited partnership cannot rescind its dissolution because "a 'dead' entity lacks both the capacity and power to bring itself back from the dead"). *See also* Paragraph (15).

Paragraph (11)(A)—If a limited partnership disappears as part of a merger, no person can continue as a partner of the partnership. When the merger takes effect, the partners of the disappearing partnership are perforce dissociated. Depending on the plan of merger, those persons may become partners of a surviving limited partnership. In those circumstances, the merger will have dissociated them from one limited partnership and admitted them into partnership in the surviving limited partnership. *See* Section 401(b)(2).

Paragraph (11)(B)—It is possible for a plan of merger to "shuffle the equity" of the surviving entity, even to the extent of "taking out" some or all of the owners of the surviving entity. A reverse triangular merger involving a limited partnership as the surviving entity would dissociate all the pre-merger partners of the limited partnership.

Paragraph (13)—By definition, a limited partnership that converts ceases to be a limited partnership. *See* Section 1146. Thus, when the plan of conversion takes effect, all the partners of the converted entity are dissociated from that entity. In many cases, those persons will all be owners of the converted entity. In some cases, the conversion will "shuffle the equity" and "take out" some of the partners of the converting LLC.

Paragraph (14)—Domestication does not by itself dissociate a partner, because the domesticated entity remains both a limited partnership and "the same entity without interruption as the domesticating company." Section 1156(a)(1)(B). However, an "equity shuffle" could dissociate a general partner.

§ 604. Power to Dissociate as General Partner; Wrongful Dissociation

(a)   A person has the power to dissociate as a general partner at any time, rightfully or wrongfully, by withdrawing as a general partner by express will under Section 603(1).

(b)   A person's dissociation as a general partner is wrongful only if the dissociation:

　　(1)   is in breach of an express provision of the partnership agreement; or

　　(2)   occurs before the completion of the winding up of the limited partnership, and:

　　　　(A)   the person withdraws as a general partner by express will;

　　　　(B)   the person is expelled as a general partner by judicial order under Section 603(5);

　　　　(C)   the person is dissociated as a general partner under Section 603(7); or

　　　　(D)   in the case of a person that is not a trust other than a business trust, an estate, or an individual, the person is expelled or otherwise dissociated as a general partner because it willfully dissolved or terminated.

(c)   A person that wrongfully dissociates as a general partner is liable to the limited partnership and, subject to Section 901, to the other partners for damages caused by the dissociation. The liability is in addition to any debt, obligation, or other liability of the general partner to the partnership or the other partners.

COMMENT

Subsection (a)—The limited partnership agreement may not eliminate this power. *See* Section 105(c)(11). In this respect, a general partner in a limited partnership is analogous to a general partner in general partnership. *See* UPA (1997) (Last Amended 2013) § 105(c)(9).

Subsection (b)—This subsection list exhaustively ("only if") the dissociations that are "wrongful," but the list is a default rule. The limited partnership agreement can expand the list; *e.g.,* by making wrongful a dissociation that beaches the implied contractual covenant of good faith and fair dealing. In theory, the partnership agreement can provide for liquidated damages (subject to the requirements of contract law) and, in theory, can also contract or even eliminate the list of wrongful dissociations.

Subsection (b)(1)—The reference to "an express provision of the partnership agreement" means that a person's dissociation as a general partner in breach of the obligation of good faith and fair dealing is not wrongful dissociation for the purposes of this section. The breach might be actionable on other grounds.

Subsection (b)(2)—The reference to "before the termination of the limited partnership" reflects the expectation that each general partner will shepherd the limited partnership through winding up. *See* Section 406(f), cmt. A person's obligation to remain as general partner through winding up continues even if another general partner dissociates and even if that dissociation leads to the limited partnership's premature dissolution under Section 801(3)(A).

Subsection (b)(2)(C)—This subsection refers to Section 603(7), which involves *inter alia* dissociation on account of bankruptcy, which in turn is subject to bankruptcy law. *See, e.g.,* 11 U.S.C.A. § 365(e) (invalidating "ipso facto" clauses, subject to some exceptions).

Subsection (c)—A person who prematurely dissociates as a general partner risks liability for any resulting damages. For example, the limited partnership might incur substantial expenses in replacing the general partner's expertise, reputation, or creditworthiness.

In effect, this subsection equates wrongful dissociation with breach of contract. Accordingly, courts should look to contract law to determine what consequential damages are recoverable. *See Hadley v. Baxendale*, 9 Exch. 341 (1854); RESTATEMENT (SECOND) OF CONTRACTS § 351 (1981); *see also Williams v. Hildebrand*, 247 S.W.2d 356, 358 (Ark. 1952) (interpreting UPA (1914) § 38(2)(a)(II), pertaining to wrongful dissolution, and stating that "the measure of damages, when the partnership was to have continued for a fixed term, is the profits that the injured partner would have received").

The language "subject to Section 901" is intended to preserve the distinction between direct and derivative claims.

§ 605. Effect of Dissociation as General Partner

(a) If a person is dissociated as a general partner:

(1) the person's right to participate as a general partner in the management and conduct of the limited partnership's activities and affairs terminates;

(2) the person's duties and obligations as a general partner under Section 409 end with regard to matters arising and events occurring after the person's dissociation;

(3) the person may sign and deliver to the [Secretary of State] for filing a statement of dissociation pertaining to the person and, at the request of the limited partnership, shall sign an amendment to the certificate of limited partnership which states that the person has dissociated as a general partner; and

(4) subject to Section 704 and [Article] 11, any transferable interest owned by the person in the person's capacity as a general partner immediately before dissociation is owned by the person solely as a transferee.

(b) A person's dissociation as a general partner does not of itself discharge the person from any debt, obligation, or other liability to the limited partnership or the other partners which the person incurred while a general partner.

COMMENT

Subsection (a)(1)—Once a person dissociates as a general partner, the person loses all management rights as a general partner regardless of what happens to the limited partnership. This rule contrasts with UPA (1997) (Last Amended 2011) Section 603(b)(1), which permits a dissociated general partner to participate in winding up in some circumstances.

Subsection (a)(2)—This provision establishes a dividing line, separating out "matters arising and events occurring after the person's dissociation." If the limited partnership has continuing projects with clients, ongoing relationships with clients, or both, the dividing line requires special attention with regard to non-competition and partnership opportunities duties. *See* Section 409(b)(1) and (3).

Disputes involving law firms have generated much of the relevant case law. *See, e.g., Meehan v. Shaughnessy*, 404 Mass. 419, 422, 535 N.E.2d 1255, 1257 (1989); *Jewel v. Boxer*, 156 Cal. App. 3d 171, 175, 203 Cal. Rptr. 13, 15 (Ct. App. 1984). To a large extent, a well-drawn partnership agreement can delineate the parties' respective rights and responsibilities and thereby avoid problems. However, if the partnership becomes insolvent, the bankruptcy court may well scrutinize the partners' *inter se* arrangements. *See Geron v. Robinson & Cole LLP*, 476 B.R. 732, 743 (S.D.N.Y. 2012) (considering whether a law firm had "fraudulently transferred . . . assets when its partners adopted the Jewel Waiver [releasing rights recognized by *Jewel v. Boxer*] on the eve of dissolution without consideration").

This provision does not determine the effect of a person's dissociation as a general partner on the person's future obligations or rights under the partnership agreement. Some contractual obligations typically extend beyond dissociation—*e.g.*, non-competition provisions, buyout arrangements. To the extent provisions of the partnership agreement continue to apply, the common law obligation of good faith continues to apply as well. *See* 409(d), cmt. (explaining that the subsection "invokes the implied obligation that exists in every contract" as a matter of common law).

Subsection (a)(3)—Both records covered by this provision have the same effect under Section 103(d)— namely, to give constructive notice that the person has dissociated as a general partner. The notice benefits the person by curtailing any further personal liability under Sections 607, 805, and 1111. The notice benefits the limited partnership by curtailing any lingering power to bind under Sections 606, 804, and 1112.

The limited partnership is in any event obligated to amend its certificate of limited partnership to reflect the dissociation of a person as general partner. *See* Section 202(d)(2). In most circumstances, the amendment requires the signature of the person that has dissociated. Section 203(a)(5)(C). If that signature is required and the person refuses or fails to sign, the limited partnership may invoke Section 204 (Signing and Filing Pursuant to Judicial Order).

Subsection (a)(4)—As provided in Section 503(b), dissociation does not result in a distribution. In general, when a person dissociates as a general partner, the person's rights as a general partner disappear and, subject to Section 109 (Dual Capacity), the person's status degrades to that of a mere transferee—even when the dissociation comes in the form of expulsion. *All Saints Univ. of Med. Aruba v. Chilana*, A-2628-09T1, 2012 WL 6652510 at *12 (N.J. Super. Ct. App. Div. Dec. 24, 2012). On distinguishing between a person's rights of a general partner and as a limited partners, see Section 108(9)(C) (providing that, for any person that is both a general partner and a limited partner, the required information must state which transferable interest is owned in which capacity).

Like most *inter se* rules in this act, this one is subject to the partnership agreement. For example, the limited partnership agreement might provide for the buyout of a person's transferable interest in connection with the person's dissociation.

Section 704 provides additional information rights when an individual's death has caused dissociation. Article 11 covers organic transactions such as mergers and conversions.

Subsection (b)—A general partner's obligation to safeguard trade secrets and other confidential or proprietary information is incurred when the partner learns or otherwise obtains the information. This subsection preserves the obligation post-dissociation.

§ 606. Power to Bind and Liability of Person Dissociated as General Partner

(a) After a person is dissociated as a general partner and before the limited partnership is merged out of existence, converted, or domesticated under [Article] 11, or dissolved, the partnership is bound by an act of the person only if:

(1)   the act would have bound the partnership under Section 402 before the dissociation; and

(2)   at the time the other party enters into the transaction:

    (A)   less than two years has passed since the dissociation; and

    (B)   the other party does not know or have notice of the dissociation and reasonably believes that the person is a general partner.

(b)   If a limited partnership is bound under subsection (a), the person dissociated as a general partner which caused the partnership to be bound is liable:

(1)   to the partnership for any damage caused to the partnership arising from the obligation incurred under subsection (a); and

(2)   if a general partner or another person dissociated as a general partner is liable for the obligation, to the general partner or other person for any damage caused to the general partner or other person arising from the liability.

COMMENT

A person's dissociation as a general partner ends immediately the person's actual authority to act for the partnership. *See* Section 605(a)(1). However, the person's apparent authority may linger.

This section does not affect a person's power to bind a partnership in another capacity—*e.g.*, as an employee with actual authority.

Subsection (a)—This subsection codifies and constrains the lingering apparent authority of a person dissociated as a general partner. The constraint is in the phrase "only if."

The provision applies until the limited partnership dissolves or under [Article] 11 ceases to be governed by this act. Once a limited partnership dissolves, Section 804 applies.

Subsection (a)(1)—Section 402 states a general partner's statutory apparent authority. This provision causes the apparent authority to linger.

Subsection (a)(2)(A)—In any event, any lingering apparent authority ends two years after the dissociation.

Subsection (a)(2)(B)—A person might have notice under Section 103(d)(1) (statement of dissociation) as well as under Section 103(b)(1) (person "ha[ving] reason to know the fact from all the facts known to the person at the time in question").

Subsection (b)—The liability stated in this subsection is not exhaustive. For example, if a person dissociated as a general partner causes a limited partnership to be bound under Subsection (a) and, due to a guaranty, some other person—not a general partner nor dissociated as a general partner—is liable on the resulting obligation, that other person may have a claim under other law against the person dissociated as a general partner.

§ 607.   Liability of Person Dissociated as General Partner to Other Persons

(a)   A person's dissociation as a general partner does not of itself discharge the person's liability as a general partner for a debt, obligation, or other liability of the limited partnership incurred before dissociation. Except as otherwise provided in subsections (b) and (c), the person is not liable for a partnership obligation incurred after dissociation.

(b)   A person whose dissociation as a general partner results in a dissolution and winding up of the limited partnership's activities and affairs is liable on an obligation incurred by the partnership under Section 805 to the same extent as a general partner under Section 404.

(c)   A person that is dissociated as a general partner without the dissociation resulting in a dissolution and winding up of the limited partnership's activities and affairs is liable on a transaction entered into by the partnership after the dissociation only if:

(1)   a general partner would be liable on the transaction; and

(2)   at the time the other party enters into the transaction:

    (A)   less than two years has passed since the dissociation; and

987

    (B)   the other party does not have knowledge or notice of the dissociation and reasonably believes that the person is a general partner.

    (d)   By agreement with a creditor of a limited partnership and the partnership, a person dissociated as a general partner may be released from liability for a debt, obligation, or other liability of the partnership.

    (e)   A person dissociated as a general partner is released from liability for a debt, obligation, or other liability of the limited partnership if the partnership's creditor, with knowledge or notice of the person's dissociation as a general partner but without the person's consent, agrees to a material alteration in the nature or time of payment of the debt, obligation, or other liability.

COMMENT

To the extent a limited partnership has been a limited liability limited partnership throughout its existence, the liability rules stated in this section are moot. *See, e.g.*, subsection (c)(1).

Subsection (a)—A person's dissociation as a general partner does not categorically preclude the person being liable as a general partner for subsequently incurred obligations of the limited partnership. If the dissociation results in dissolution, Subsection (b) applies and the person will be liable as a general partner on any partnership obligation incurred under Section 805. If the dissociation does not result in dissolution, Subsection (c) applies.

The phrase "liability as a general partner for an obligation of the limited partnership" refers to liability under Section 404. As stated in Section 404(b) and (c), comments, other law determines when a partnership obligation is "incurred."

Subsection (b)—In these circumstances, a person's dissociation as a general partner has no effect on the person's liability exposure, even if any or all of the following occur:

- The certificate of limited partnership is amended to state that the person has dissociated as a general partner, as required by Section 202(d)(2).

- The person has filed a statement of dissociation, as permitted by Section 605(a)(3).

- The person was the sole general partner, and the limited partnership is wound up by someone else under Section 802(c) or (d).

However, amending the certificate of limited partnership to indicate dissolution would protect the person to the same extent as the amendment would protect the remaining general partners. *See* Sections 802(b)(2)(A) and 804.

Subsection (c)—The rule stated here for the "lingering liability" of a person dissociated as a general partner parallels the rule stated in Section 606 for the lingering apparent authority of a person dissociated as a general partner.

Subsection (c)(2)(B)—A person might have notice under Section 103(d)(1) as well as under Section 103(b)(1).

Subsections (c) and (d)—These provisions trace back to UPA (1914) § 36(2), (3).

[ARTICLE] 7.   TRANSFERABLE INTERESTS AND
RIGHTS OF TRANSFEREES AND CREDITORS

§ 701.   Nature of Transferable Interest

A transferable interest is personal property.

COMMENT

For the definition of transferable interest, see Section 102(25). Absent a contrary provision in the partnership agreement or the consent of the partners, a "transferable interest" is the only interest in a limited partnership that can be transferred to a person not already a partner. *See* Section 702. As to whether a partner may transfer governance rights to a fellow partner, the question is moot absent a provision in the partnership agreement changing the default rule. *See* Section 406(a) (allocating general partner governance rights *per capita*) and 406(b) (requiring unanimous agreement of all partners to take specified action). In the default mode, a general partner's transfer of governance rights to another general partner: (i) does not increase the transferee's governance rights;

(ii) eliminates the transferor's governance rights; and (iii) thereby changes the denominator but not the numerator in calculating governance rights

> **Example:** LCN Company is a limited partnership with three general partners, Laura, Charles, and Nora. The partnership agreement does not displace this act's default rule on the allocation of governance rights among general partners. Thus, each general partner has 1/3 of those rights. Laura transfers her entire ownership interest to Charles. The transfer does not increase Charles's governance rights but does eliminate Laura's. After the transfer, Laura has no governance rights (regardless of whether Charles and Nora agree to expel Laura under Section 603(4)(B)). As a result, Charles and Nora each have 1/2 of the governance rights.

Whether a transferable interest pledged as security is governed by Article 8 or 9 of the Uniform Commercial Code depends on the rules stated in those Articles.

§ 702. Transfer of Transferable Interest

(a) A transfer, in whole or in part, of a transferable interest:

    (1) is permissible;

    (2) does not by itself cause a person's dissociation as a partner or a dissolution and winding up of the limited partnership's activities and affairs; and

    (3) subject to Section 704, does not entitle the transferee to:

        (A) participate in the management or conduct of the partnership's activities and affairs; or

        (B) except as otherwise provided in subsection (c), have access to required information, records, or other information concerning the partnership's activities and affairs.

(b) A transferee has the right to receive, in accordance with the transfer, distributions to which the transferor would otherwise be entitled.

(c) In a dissolution and winding up of a limited partnership, a transferee is entitled to an account of the partnership's transactions only from the date of dissolution.

(d) A transferable interest may be evidenced by a certificate of the interest issued by a limited partnership in a record, and, subject to this section, the interest represented by the certificate may be transferred by a transfer of the certificate.

(e) A limited partnership need not give effect to a transferee's rights under this section until the partnership knows or has notice of the transfer.

(f) A transfer of a transferable interest in violation of a restriction on transfer contained in the partnership agreement is ineffective if the intended transferee has knowledge or notice of the restriction at the time of transfer.

(g) Except as otherwise provided in Sections 601(b)(4)(B) and 603(4)(B), if a general or limited partner transfers a transferable interest, the transferor retains the rights of a general or limited partner other than the transferable interest transferred and retains all the duties and obligations of a general or limited partner.

(h) If a general or limited partner transfers a transferable interest to a person that becomes a general or limited partner with respect to the transferred interest, the transferee is liable for the transferor's obligations under Sections 502 and 505 known to the transferee when the transferee becomes a partner.

COMMENT

One of the most fundamental characteristics of limited partnership law is its fidelity to the "pick your partner" principle. *See, e.g., Bynum v. Frisby*, 73 Nev. 145, 149–50, 311 P.2d 972, 975 (Nev. 1957) (stating: (i) "the assignment of a partnership interest from one partner to a stranger does not bring that stranger into fiduciary relationship with the remaining partners"; and (ii) absent consent by the remaining partners "[t]he stranger remains a stranger" with no rights to management or even information).

This section is the core of the act's provisions reflecting and protecting that principle. The provisions of this section apply regardless of whether the interest pertains to a general partner or a limited partner. A partner's rights in a limited partnership are bifurcated into economic rights (the transferable interest) and governance rights (including management rights, consent rights, rights to information, rights to seek judicial intervention). Unless the partnership agreement otherwise provides, a partner acting without the consent of all other partners lacks both the power and the right to: (i) bestow partnership on a non-partner, Sections 301(b)(3), 401(b)(3); or (ii) transfer to a non-partner anything other than some or all of the partner's transferable interest, Section 702(a)(3). The rights of a mere transferee are quite limited—*i.e.*, to receive distributions), Section 702(b), and, if the limited partnership dissolves and winds up, to receive specified information pertaining to the limited partnership from the date of dissolution. Section 702(c).

This section applies regardless of whether the transferor is a partner, a transferee of a partner, a transferee of a transferee, etc. *See* Section 102(25) (defining "transferable interest" in terms of a right "initially owned by a person in the person's capacity as a partner" regardless of "whether or not the person remains a partner or continues to own any part of the right").

This section does not directly consider whether a partner may transfer governance rights to another partner without obtaining consent from all the other partners. As noted above, Section 701, cmt., the question is moot under this act's default rule for allocating governance rights.

However, the question can be pivotal when the partnership agreement displaces the default rule on governance rights but does not determine whether transfer restrictions (whether contractual, statutory, or both) apply to transfers of governance rights from one partner to another. Case law is scant and pertains to LLCs. Nonetheless, the case law suggests that this act does not protect partners from control shifts that result from transfers among partners (as distinguished from transfers to non-partners who seek thereby to become partners). *Blythe v. Bell*, No. 11 CVS 933. 2012 WL 7807800, at ¶ 6 (N.C. Dist. Dec. 10, 2012) (holding in a case of "first impression in North Carolina" that "in the absence of articles of incorporation or an operating agreement to the contrary . . . the assignment of control [(*i.e.*, governance)] interests between members is effective without unanimous member consent"); *Achaian, Inc. v. Leemon Family L.L.C.*, 25 A.3d 800, 810 (Del. Ch. 2011) (Strine, Ch.) (holding that the terms of the LLC agreement did not preclude one member of a three-member LLC from transferring the member's entire interest (including governance rights) to a second member without first having the consent of the third member; stating that the third member's "argument relies on a very thinly sliced version of [the 'pick-your-partner principle, the strained version being] . . . that once one chooses his initial co-members, one continues to hold a veto over how much additional voting power they may acquire'; explaining that '[t]he problem for [the third member] is that nothing in the LLC Agreement supports [that member's] reading of it that would require an already admitted Member, like [the acquirer (*i.e.*, the second member)], to be become once, twice (or even three times) a Member each and every time that Member acquires an additional block of Interests' ").

Other law may affect the applicability of this section. *See* 11 U.S.C. § 541(c)(1) (providing that, initially at least, all property of a debtor becomes part of the bankruptcy estate regardless of restrictions on transfer); UCC §§ 9–406, 9–408 (overriding specified restrictions on assignment in specified circumstances, regardless of whether state law or a contract impose the restrictions).

In any event, this section does not apply to the transfer of ownership interests in a partner that is an entity.

Example: ABC, LP has three partners: one general partner—Ralph (an individual); and two limited partners—Alice, Inc. ("Alice"), and Norton, LLC ("Norton"). Section 702 applies to any attempt by Ralph, Alice, or Norton to transfer their respective partnership interest in ABC. Section 702 is inapplicable, however, to a change in control of Alice or Norton, or even a complete change in their respective ownership.

Subsection (a)—The definition of "transfer," Section 102(24), and this subsection's reference to "in whole or in part" combine to mean that this section encompasses not only unconditional, permanent, and complete transfers but also temporary, contingent, and partial ones. Thus, for example, a charging order under Section 703 effects a transfer of part of the judgment debtor's transferable interest, as does the pledge of a transferable interest as collateral for a loan and the gift of a life-interest in a partner's rights to distribution.

Subsection (a)(2)—The phrase "by itself" contemplates Sections 601(b)(4)(B) and 603(4)(B); each create a risk of dissociation via expulsion when a partner transfers all of the partner's transferable interest.

Subsection (a)(3)—Mere transferees have no right to participate in management or otherwise intrude as the partners carry on the affairs of the limited partnership and their activities as partners.

Because Section 102(24) defines "transfer" to include "a transfer by operation of law," this section affects the power of other law to effect transfers of a partner's ownership interest. For example, a divorce court lacks the power to award a partner's spouse anything beyond the partner's transferable interest. Nor does the partner have the power to enter into a property settlement purporting to effect any greater transfer.

For the divorce court, the best solution is to value the partner's complete ownership interest (*i.e.*, the transferable interest as enhanced by the management and information rights and the standing to sue) and: (i) if possible, award the partner's spouse marital property of equal value; or (ii) if not possible, award the partner's spouse a money judgment and a charging order to enforce the judgment.

Granting the non-partner any part of the partner's transferable interest is almost always imprudent; marital discord will almost inevitably carry over into the business relationship. Granting the partner's ex-spouse the entire transferable interest is rarely a viable alternative. If the partner is an active participant in the limited partnership, the approach is impossible. The partner's transferable interest will typically constitute much or all of the partner's remuneration for the partner's activity. Even if the partner is essentially passive, granting the transferable interest to the ex-spouse puts him or her at great risk as a "bare naked assignee." *See* Section 107(b), cmt.

When a partner dies, subject to the limited partnership agreement other law may effect a transfer of the partner's transferable interest to the partner's estate or personal representative. However, for the reasons just stated, other law lacks the power to transfer anything more than a transferable interest. (Section 704 does provide extra information rights for the purposes of settling the estate of the deceased partner.)

Subsection (a)(3)(B)—*See* Sections 304(i) and 407(i) (providing that the information rights stated in those sections do not apply to transferees).

Subsection (b)—Amounts due under this subsection are of course subject to offset for any amount owed to the limited partnership by the partner or person dissociated as a partner on whose account the distribution is made. Section 503(d). As to whether a limited partnership may properly offset for claims against a transferor that was never a partner is matter for other law, specifically the law of contracts dealing with assignments.

Subsection (c)—This very limited grant of information rights encompasses only transactions occurring at or after the date of the limited partnership's dissolution. The transferee has only the right to information as to the allocation of net assets among the limited partnership's creditors, partners, and transferees—and only from the date of dissolution.

This subsection does not prevent a transferee from contracting with a partner-transferor to require the partner-transferor to disclose further information to the transferee. Whether such an agreement would breach the limited partnership agreement, the implied contractual obligation of good faith and fair dealing, Section 409(d), or a fiduciary duty depends on the circumstances.

If a dissolved limited partnership rescinds its dissolution, Section 803, this subsection no longer applies.

Subsection (d)—The use of certificates can raise issues relating to Articles 8 and 9 of the Uniform Commercial Code.

Subsection (f)—This provision originated as UPA (1997) § 503(e), was then consistent with UCC section 9–318(3), and is now consistent with UCC section 9–406(a) (stating that "an account debtor . . . may discharge its obligation by paying the assignor until, but not after, the account debtor receives a notification, authenticated by the assignor or the assignee, that the amount due or to become due has been assigned and that payment is to be made to the assignee").

The term "notice" includes "reason to know," Section 103(b)(1), and ordinarily a potential transferee has reason to inquire about transfer restrictions that might be contained in the limited partnership agreement.

Subsection (g)—Under this subsection, a partner (whether general or limited) remains as such (with all attendant rights and obligations) even after permanently transferring the entirety of the transferable interest, unless: (i) the other partners opt for expulsion under Section 601(4)(B); or (ii) as otherwise provided in the partnership agreement.

§ 703. Charging Order

(a) On application by a judgment creditor of a partner or transferee, a court may enter a charging order against the transferable interest of the judgment debtor for the unsatisfied amount of the judgment. A charging order constitutes a lien on a judgment debtor's transferable interest and requires the limited partnership to pay over to the person to which the charging order was issued any distribution that otherwise would be paid to the judgment debtor.

(b) To the extent necessary to effectuate the collection of distributions pursuant to a charging order in effect under subsection (a), the court may:

(1)   appoint a receiver of the distributions subject to the charging order, with the power to make all inquiries the judgment debtor might have made; and

(2)   make all other orders necessary to give effect to the charging order.

(c)   Upon a showing that distributions under a charging order will not pay the judgment debt within a reasonable time, the court may foreclose the lien and order the sale of the transferable interest. The purchaser at the foreclosure sale obtains only the transferable interest, does not thereby become a partner, and is subject to Section 702.

(d)   At any time before foreclosure under subsection (c), the partner or transferee whose transferable interest is subject to a charging order under subsection (a) may extinguish the charging order by satisfying the judgment and filing a certified copy of the satisfaction with the court that issued the charging order.

(e)   At any time before foreclosure under subsection (c), a limited partnership or one or more partners whose transferable interests are not subject to the charging order may pay to the judgment creditor the full amount due under the judgment and thereby succeed to the rights of the judgment creditor, including the charging order.

(f)   This [act] does not deprive any partner or transferee of the benefit of any exemption law applicable to the transferable interest of the partner or transferee.

(g)   This section provides the exclusive remedy by which a person seeking in the capacity of a judgment creditor to enforce a judgment against a partner or transferee may satisfy the judgment from the judgment debtor's transferable interest.

COMMENT

The charging order concept dates back to the English Partnership Act of 1890 and in the United States has been a fundamental part of law of unincorporated business organizations since 1914. *See* UPA (1914) § 28. As much a remedy limitation as a remedy, the charging order is the sole method by which a person acting as judgment creditor of a partner or transferee can extract value from the partner's or transferee's ownership interest in a limited partnership. *See* Subsection (g), cmt.

Under this section, the judgment creditor of a partner or transferee is entitled to a charging order against the relevant transferable interest. While in effect, that order entitles the judgment creditor to whatever distributions would otherwise be due to the partner or transferee whose interest is subject to the order. However, the judgment creditor has no say in the timing or amount of those distributions. The charging order does not entitle the judgment creditor to accelerate any distributions or to otherwise interfere with the management and activities of the limited partnership.

This section applies regardless of whether the transferable interest at issue is owned by a person in the capacity of a general partner, limited partner, or transferee. The partnership agreement has no power to alter the provisions of this section to the prejudice of third parties. Section 105(c)(18).

By its terms, this section does not apply to foreign limited partnerships. *See* Section 102(12) (defining "[l]imited partnership" to mean "an entity *formed under this [act] or which becomes subject to this [act]*") (emphasis added); *see also Fannie Mae v. Heather Apartments Ltd. P'ship*, A13-0562, 2013 WL 6223564, at *6 (Minn. Ct. App. Dec. 2, 2013) (considering the remedies available to a judgment creditor with respect to the judgment debtor's interest in a Cook Islands LLC; rejecting the debtor's argument that the creditor's "only remedy is to obtain a charging order under" [the Minnesota LLC statute]; explaining that "this argument fails because that statute only applies to Minnesota limited liability companies," which that statute "defines . . . as 'a limited liability company, other than a foreign limited liability company, *organized or governed by this chapter*'") (emphasis added) (statutory citations omitted).

Subsection (a)—The phrase "judgment debtor" encompasses both partners and transferees. The lien pertains only to a distribution, which excludes "amounts constituting reasonable compensation for present or past service or payments made in the ordinary course of business under a bona fide retirement plan or other bona fide benefits program." Section 102(4)(B). A judgment creditor that wishes to levy on such amounts should use the appropriate creditor's remedy, such as garnishment (which may be subject to exemptions or exclusions not relevant to a charging order). *Cf. PB Real Estate, Inc. v. Dem II Props.*, 719 A.2d 73, 76 (Conn. 1998) (rejecting the contention of an LLC's two members that "payments of $28,000 to each of them" should be treated "as expenses for wages" rather than as distributions).

Whether an application for a charging order must be served on the limited partnership, the judgment debtor, or both is a matter for other law; principally, the law of remedies and civil procedure. The order itself must be served on the limited partnership. Whether the order must also be served on the judgment debtor is a matter for other law.

If a distribution consists of rights to acquire interests in a limited partnership, the charging order applies only to those rights within the definition of transferable interest. *See* Section 102(25) (defining transferable interest).

Subsection (b)—Paragraph (2) refers to "other orders" rather than "additional orders." Therefore, given appropriate circumstances, a court may invoke Paragraph (1), Paragraph (2), or both.

Subsection (b)(1)—The receiver contemplated here is emphatically not a receiver for the limited partnership, but rather a receiver for the distributions subject to the charging order. The principal advantage provided by this paragraph is an expanded right to information. However, that right goes no further than "the extent necessary to effectuate the collection of distributions pursuant to a charging order." For a correctly narrow reading of this provision, see *Wells Fargo Bank, Nat'l Ass'n v. Continuous Control Solutions, Inc.*, No. 11–1285, 2012 WL 3195759 (Iowa Ct. App. Aug. 8, 2012).

Subsection (b)(2)—This paragraph must be understood in the context of: (i) the very limited nature of the charging order; and (ii) the importance of preventing overreaching on behalf of a person that is not a judgment creditor of the limited partnership, has no claim on the limited partnership's assets, and has no right to interfere in the activities, affairs, and management of the limited partnership. In particular, the court's power to make "all other orders" is limited to "orders necessary to give effect to the charging order."

Example: A judgment creditor with a charging order believes that the limited partnership should invest less of its surplus in operations, leaving more funds for distributions. The creditor moves the court for an order directing the limited partnership to restrict re-investment. Subsection (b)(2) does not authorize the court to grant the motion.

Example: A judgment creditor with a judgment for $10,000 against a partner obtains a charging order against the partner's transferable interest. Having been properly served with the order, the limited partnership nonetheless fails to comply and makes a $3000 distribution to the partner. The court has the power to order the limited partnership to pay $3000 to the judgment creditor to "give effect to the charging order."

Under Subsection (b)(2), the court has the power to decide whether a particular payment is a distribution, because that decision determines whether the payment is part of a transferable interest subject to a charging order.

Example: General Partner A of ABC, LP has for some years received distributions form the limited partnership. However, when a judgment creditor of General Partner A obtains a charging order against General Partner A's transferable interest, the limited partnership ceases to make distributions to General Partner A and instead provides a salary to General Partner A equivalent to former distributions. A court might deem this salary a disguised distribution. (In any event, however, the salary will be subject to garnishment.)

This act has no specific rules for determining the fate or effect of a charging order when the limited partnership undergoes a merger, conversion, interest exchange, or domestication under [Article] 11. In the proper circumstances, such an organic change might trigger an order under Subsection (b)(2).

Subsection (c)—The phrase "that distributions under the charging order will not pay the judgment debt within a reasonable period of time" comes from case law. *See, e.g., Nigri v. Lotz*, 453 S.E.2d 780, 783 (Ga. Ct. App. 1995). *Stewart v. Lanier Park Med. Office Bldg., Ltd.*, 578 S.E.2d 572, 574 (Ga. Ct. App. 2003) ("Judicial sale may be appropriate where . . . it is apparent that distributions under the charging order will not pay the judgment debt within a reasonable amount of time."). A purchaser at a foreclosure sale obtains only the very limited rights of a mere transferee under Section 702 and is in some ways more vulnerable and less powerful than the holder of a charging order. After foreclosure and sale, Subsection (b) no longer applies. More generally, the court is no longer involved in the matter. For the vulnerability of a transferee, see Section 107(b), comment.

Subsection (d)—This provision allows the judgment debtor to end the charging order without need for a hearing.

Subsection (e)—Traditionally, charging order provisions referred to the possibility of "redeeming" an interest subject to a charging order. That usage was confusing, leaving several important questions unanswered.

This act substitutes a far simpler approach, contemplating the limited partnership or its partners buying the underlying judgment and thereby dispensing with any interference the judgment creditor might seek to inflict on the partnership.

In many circumstances, buying the judgment is superior to the mechanism provided by this subsection, because: (i) this subsection requires full satisfaction of the underlying judgment; and (ii) the limited partnership or the other partners might be able to buy the judgment for less than face value. On the other hand, this subsection operates without need for the judgment creditor's consent, so it remains a valuable protection in the event a judgment creditor seeks to do mischief to the limited partnership.

Whether a limited partnership should invoke this provision is a question for the general partners. Section 406(a). If the charging order pertains to the transferable interest of a general partner, subject to the partnership agreement, that partner should not be involved in deciding the question. *See* Section 409(b)(2).

Subsection (f)—This subsection preserves otherwise applicable exemptions but does not create any. *In re Foos*, 405 B.R. 604, 609 (Bankr. N.D. Ohio 2009) (interpreting the comparable provision in UPA (1997) and stating that "it is clear that [the provision] does not create an exemption").

Subsection (g)—This subsection does not override Uniform Commercial Code, Article 9, which may provide different remedies for a secured creditor acting in that capacity. A secured creditor with a judgment might decide to proceed under Article 9 alone, under this section alone, or under both Article 9 and this section. In the last-mentioned circumstance, the constraints of this section would apply to the charging order but not to the Article 9 remedies.

This subsection is not intended to prevent a court from effecting a "reverse pierce" where appropriate. In a reverse pierce, the court conflates the entity and its owner to hold the entity liable for a debt of the owner. *Cf. Trust, Inc. v. First Flight L.P.*, 580 S.E.2d 806, 810 (Va. 2003) (stating that "Virginia does recognize the concept of outsider reverse piercing and that this concept can be applied to a Virginia limited partnership"); *In re Burwell*, 391 B.R. 831, 837 (B.A.P. 8th Cir. 2008) (applying Minnesota law). Likewise, this subsection does not supplant fraudulent transfer law.

§ 704. Power of Legal Representative of Deceased Partner

If a partner dies, the deceased partner's legal representative may exercise:

(1)   the rights of a transferee provided in Section 702(c); and

(2)   for the purposes of settling the estate, the rights of a current limited partner under Section 304.

COMMENT

The estate and those claiming through the estate are transferees, and as such they have very limited rights to information. This section provides temporary, additional information rights to the legal representative of the estate. Sections 304 and 702(c) pertain only to information rights.

[ARTICLE] 8.   DISSOLUTION AND WINDING UP

§ 801. Events Causing Dissolution

(a)   A limited partnership is dissolved, and its activities and affairs must be wound up, upon the occurrence of any of the following:

(1)   an event or circumstance that the partnership agreement states causes dissolution;

(2)   the affirmative vote or consent of all general partners and of limited partners owning a majority of the rights to receive distributions as limited partners at the time the vote or consent is to be effective;

(3)   after the dissociation of a person as a general partner:

(A)   if the partnership has at least one remaining general partner, the affirmative vote or consent to dissolve the partnership not later than 90 days after the dissociation by partners owning a majority of the rights to receive distributions as partners at the time the vote or consent is to be effective; or

(B)   if the partnership does not have a remaining general partner, the passage of 90 days after the dissociation, unless before the end of the period:

(i)   consent to continue the activities and affairs of the partnership and admit at least one general partner is given by limited partners owning a majority of the rights to receive distributions as limited partners at the time the consent is to be effective; and

(ii)   at least one person is admitted as a general partner in accordance with the consent;

(4)   the passage of 90 consecutive days after the dissociation of the partnership's last limited partner, unless before the end of the period the partnership admits at least one limited partner;

(5)   the passage of 90 consecutive days during which the partnership has only one partner, unless before the end of the period:

(A)   the partnership admits at least one person as a partner;

(B)   if the previously sole remaining partner is only a general partner, the partnership admits the person as a limited partner; and

(C)   if the previously sole remaining partner is only a limited partner, the partnership admits a person as a general partner;

(6)   on application by a partner, the entry by [the appropriate court] of an order dissolving the partnership on the grounds that:

(A)   the conduct of all or substantially all the partnership's activities and affairs is unlawful; or

(B)   it is not reasonably practicable to carry on the partnership's activities and affairs in conformity with the certificate of limited partnership and partnership agreement; or

(7)   the signing and filing of a statement of administrative dissolution by the [Secretary of State] under Section 811.

(b)   If an event occurs that imposes a deadline on a limited partnership under subsection (a) and before the partnership has met the requirements of the deadline, another event occurs that imposes a different deadline on the partnership under subsection (a):

(1)   the occurrence of the second event does not affect the deadline caused by the first event; and

(2)   the partnership's meeting of the requirements of the first deadline does not extend the second deadline.

COMMENT

"Dissolution" has been a term of art in the law of unincorporated business organizations since at least the time of Roman law. JOSEPH STORY, COMMENTARIES ON THE LAW OF PARTNERSHIP § 266, at 408 (2d ed. 1850) ("The Roman law . . . declared, that partnership might be dissolved in various ways . . . ."). Dissolution does not end a limited partnership's existence but rather changes the purpose of that existence: "A dissolved limited partnership shall wind up its activities and affairs and . . . the partnership continues after dissolution only for the purpose of winding up." Section 802(a). The partnership may, but need not, amend its certificate of limited partnership to state that dissolution has occurred. Section 802(b)(2)(A). The limited partnership terminates when winding up is complete. The partnership may, but need not, file a statement of termination. Section 802(b)(2)(F).

Except for Paragraphs (a)(6) and (7), this section comprises default rules. Paragraph 7 is fully mandatory, Section 105(c)(3)(B); Paragraph 6 is mandatory only with regard to the stated grounds for dissolution. *See* Section 105(c)(12), cmt. Moreover, a partnership agreement can provide additional causes of dissolution. *See* Subsection (a)(1). Variations to the statutory causes of dissolution are commonplace.

Section 803 permits rescission of dissolution in some circumstances. In some circumstances, an amendment to the limited partnership agreement might avert dissolution—*e.g.,* by revising an agreed-upon deadline for selling the partnership assets and winding up the business. A retroactive amendment may also be possible. *See Kindred Ltd. P'ship v. Screen Actors Guild, Inc.,* CV082220PSGPJWX, 2009 WL 279080, at *5–6 (C.D. Cal. Feb. 3, 2009) (giving effect to an amendment that retroactively eliminated an event of dissolution; noting that UPA (1997) § 802(b) permitted a partnership to rescind dissolution).

Subsection (a)(2)—Although most actions involving limited partner consent require unanimous consent (*e.g.*, Section 406(b)), this provision requires only the specified majority consent. Rights to receive distributions owned by a person that is both a general and a limited partner figure into the limited partner determination only to the extent those rights are owned in the person's capacity as a limited partner. *See* Section 108(9)(C).

Example: XYZ is a limited partnership with three general partners, each of whom is also a limited partner, and five other limited partners. Rights to receive distributions are allocated as follows:

Partner #1 as general partner—3%

Partner #2 as general partner—2%

Partner #3 as general partner—1%

Partner #1 as limited partner—7%

Partner #2 as limited partner—3%

Partner #3 as limited partner—4%

Partner #4 as limited partner—5%

Partner #5 as limited partner—5%

Partner #6 as limited partner—5%

Partner #7 as limited partner—5%

Partner #8 as limited partner—5%

Several non-partner transferees, in the aggregate—55%

Distribution rights owned by persons as limited partners amount to 39% of total distribution rights. A majority is therefore anything greater than 19.5%. If only Partners 1, 2, 3, and 4 consent to dissolve, the limited partnership is not dissolved. Together these partners own as limited partners 19% of the distribution rights owned by persons as limited partners—just short of the necessary majority. For purposes of this calculation, distribution rights owned by non-partner transferees are irrelevant. So, too, are distribution rights owned by persons as general partners. (However, dissolution under this provision requires "the consent of all general partners.")

Subsection (a)(3)—Historically, the dissociation of any general partner from a limited partnership could lead to dissolution (subject of course to the partnership agreement). This provision continues that concept, albeit while modernizing the consent mechanisms.

Subsection (a)(3)(A)—Unlike Subsection (a)(2), this provision makes no distinction between distribution rights owned by persons as general partners and distribution rights owned by persons as limited partners. Distribution rights owned by non-partner transferees are irrelevant.

Subsection (a)(4) and (5)—These provisions reflect the number and type of partners required for a limited partnership to come into existence. Section 201(d).

Subsection (a)(6)—The partnership agreement cannot vary the causes of dissolution stated in this provision. However, the partnership agreement may contain a forum selection clause or change the forum from "the appropriate court" to binding arbitration. Section 105(c)(12), cmt.

As to whether the court of another jurisdiction can properly order dissolution of a limited partnership formed under this act, the majority rule is clearly no. "[T]he courts of several states have held that jurisdiction to dissolve a corporation rests only in the courts of the state of incorporation." *In re Blixseth*, 484 B.R. 360, 370 (B.A.P. 9th Cir. 2012) (citing cases, including a case involving an LLC). *But see In re Mercantile Guar. Co.*, 48 Cal. Rptr. 589, 591–93 (Cal. Ct. App. 1965) (explaining that "[w]e are . . . required to determine whether the courts of a state in which a foreign corporation has done business and in which its assets are there located have jurisdiction to wind up its affairs, even though the corporation was organized in another state," stating that "the question is not one of jurisdiction or power in the court of the state which is not the legal domicile of a foreign corporation, but it is a question . . . of the balance of convenience, of whether considerations of public policy, efficiency, expedience and justice to all parties interested demand that jurisdiction be retained in the foreign court, or that it be declined under the rule of forum non conveniens," and holding that "[t]he circumstances of the case at bench require a holding that the California courts assume jurisdiction of the winding up of [a Delaware corporation's] affairs preparatory to a dissolution").

Subsection (a)(6)(B)—For an analytic framework for applying this provision, see *Roth v. Laurus U.S. Fund, L.P.*, CIV.A. 5566-VCN, 2011 WL 808953, at *3 (Del. Ch. Feb. 25, 2011); *see also Mandell v. Centrum Frontier Corp.*, 407 N.E.2d 821, 829 (Ill. App. Ct. 1980) (upholding a decree dissolving a limited partnership ("[b]ecause the partnership had a negative cash flow during 15 months of the 17 months prior to filing this suit" and "find[ing] that the trial court properly decreed dissolution . . . on the ground that [the limited partnership] could only be carried on at a loss").

§ 802. Winding Up

(a)   A dissolved limited partnership shall wind up its activities and affairs and, except as otherwise provided in Section 803, the partnership continues after dissolution only for the purpose of winding up.

(b)   In winding up its activities and affairs, the limited partnership:

(1)   shall discharge the partnership's debts, obligations, and other liabilities, settle and close the partnership's activities and affairs, and marshal and distribute the assets of the partnership; and

(2)   may:

(A)   amend its certificate of limited partnership to state that the partnership is dissolved;

(B)   preserve the partnership activities, affairs, and property as a going concern for a reasonable time;

(C)   prosecute and defend actions and proceedings, whether civil, criminal, or administrative;

(D)   transfer the partnership's property;

(E)   settle disputes by mediation or arbitration;

(F)   deliver to the [Secretary of State] for filing a statement of termination stating the name of the partnership and that the partnership is terminated; and

(G)   perform other acts necessary or appropriate to the winding up.

(c)   If a dissolved limited partnership does not have a general partner, a person to wind up the dissolved partnership's activities and affairs may be appointed by the affirmative vote or consent of limited partners owning a majority of the rights to receive distributions as limited partners at the time the vote or consent is to be effective. A person appointed under this subsection:

(1)   has the powers of a general partner under Section 804 but is not liable for the debts, obligations, and other liabilities of the partnership solely by reason of having or exercising those powers or otherwise acting to wind up the dissolved partnership's activities and affairs; and

(2)   shall deliver promptly to the [Secretary of State] for filing an amendment to the partnership's certificate of limited partnership stating:

(A)   that the partnership does not have a general partner;

(B)   the name and street and mailing addresses of the person; and

(C)   that the person has been appointed pursuant to this subsection to wind up the partnership.

(d)   On the application of a partner, the [appropriate court] may order judicial supervision of the winding up of a dissolved limited partnership, including the appointment of a person to wind up the partnership's activities and affairs, if:

(1)   the partnership does not have a general partner and within a reasonable time following the dissolution no person has been appointed pursuant to subsection (c); or

(2)   the applicant establishes other good cause.

COMMENT

Under the default rules of this act, dissolution does not change governance arrangements. However, dissolution does change the context for determining for the purposes of Section 406(b)(3) whether to "sell, lease, exchange, or otherwise dispose of all, or substantially all, of the limited partnership's property, with or without the good will" is "other than in the usual and regular course of the limited partnership's activities and affairs."

Subsection (a)—*See* Section 801(a)(2), cmt.

Subsection (b)—The particular circumstances determine how long winding up may continue without giving "good cause" for court intervention under Section 702(d)(2). There is no "hard and fast" rule. *See, e.g., Mathis v. Meyeres*, 574 P.2d 447, 450 (Alaska 1978) (stating that we are aware of [no authority] requiring that deadlines be set in the winding up of a partnership"); *8182 Md. Assocs., Ltd. P'ship v. Sheehan*, 14 S.W.3d 576, 581 (Mo. 2000) ("The Uniform Partnership Law contemplates that dissolved partnerships may continue in business for a short, long or indefinite period of time . . . .") (quoting *Schoeller v. Schoeller*, 497 S.W.2d 860, 867 (Mo. Ct. App. 1973)).

"Winding up usually entails the time necessary for the partners to finish old business, collect and pay debts, and finally distribute remaining assets to the partners." *Gibson v. Deuth*, 270 N.W.2d 632, 635 (Iowa 1978). "Generally the best interests of the partnership will be served by winding up the partnership affairs as quickly as possible." *Doting v. Trunk*, 856 P.2d 536, 540 (Mont. 1993). However, in some circumstances, a long period of winding up is not only appropriate but necessary. *Lebanon Trotting Ass'n v. Battista*, 306 N.E.2d 769, 772 (Ohio Ct. App. 1972) ("[I]f the only means of availing the partners of the benefit of the value of the lease would be to continue to operate under such lease until its expiration, then such operation may continue as part of the winding up of the partnership affairs after dissolution. It is not necessary that a partnership, in the absence of the consent of all the partners, abandon a valuable asset upon dissolution merely because it may have no ready market value, but the value of such asset can continue to inure to the benefit of the partners through the continuation of the partnership after dissolution.").

Subsection (b)(2)(A) and (F)—For the constructive notice effect of the specified amendment and a statement of termination, see Sections 103(d)(2)(A) and (B).

Subsection (c)—Section 409 does not apply to a person appointed under this section. Such person will inevitably be an agent of the dissolved limited partnership, acting pursuant to a contract. Thus, agency and contract law will determine the person's duties.

Subsection (d)—Section 409 does not apply to a person appointed under this section. The applicable standards of conduct might come from any or all of these sources: the court order, the state law pertaining to receiverships, agency law, and contract law.

§ 803.   Rescinding Dissolution

(a)   A limited partnership may rescind its dissolution, unless a statement of termination applicable to the partnership has become effective, [the appropriate court] has entered an order under Section 801(a)(6) dissolving the partnership, or the [Secretary of State] has dissolved the partnership under Section 811.

(b)   Rescinding dissolution under this section requires:

(1)   the affirmative vote or consent of each partner; and

(2)   if the limited partnership has delivered to the [Secretary of State] for filing an amendment to the certificate of limited partnership stating that the partnership is dissolved and:

(A)   the amendment has not become effective, delivery to the [Secretary of State] for filing of a statement of withdrawal under Section 208 applicable to the amendment; or

(B)   the amendment has become effective, delivery to the [Secretary of State] for filing of an amendment to the certificate of limited partnership stating that dissolution has been rescinded under this section.

(c)   If a limited partnership rescinds its dissolution:

(1)   the partnership resumes carrying on its activities and affairs as if dissolution had never occurred;

(2)   subject to paragraph (3), any liability incurred by the partnership after the dissolution and before the rescission has become effective is determined as if dissolution had never occurred; and

(3)   the rights of a third party arising out of conduct in reliance on the dissolution before the third party knew or had notice of the rescission may not be adversely affected.

COMMENT

The Harmonization Project added this section.

Subsection (a)—The first exclusion results inevitably from the effect of a statement of termination—*i.e.*, the limited partnership ceases to exist as an entity. A "dead" entity lacks both the capacity and power to bring itself back from the dead.

The second and third exclusions pertain to dissolutions effected by outsiders—*i.e.*, the court and the filing office.

Subsections (b)(1)—The requirement of unanimous consent protects any vested rights of or reliance by partners. However, the partnership agreement may vary this provision.

Subsection (c)(3)—This paragraph protects third parties. *E.g.*, *Neurobehavorial Assocs., P.A. v. Cypress Creek Hosp., Inc.*, 995 S.W.2d 326, 331 (Tex. Ct. App. 1999) ("If the Hospital had the right to terminate the Agreement when it did because the Association was then dissolved, then even though the Association can revoke articles of dissolution and have that relate back to the date of dissolution, it would be grossly unfair to let the Association assert its *ex post facto* change as a defense. Surely the Association would be estopped from doing so, having created the very conditions that gave the Hospital the correct impression that it was then dissolved.").

§ 804.   Power to Bind Partnership After Dissolution

(a)   A limited partnership is bound by a general partner's act after dissolution which:

(1)   is appropriate for winding up the partnership's activities and affairs; or

(2)   would have bound the partnership under Section 402 before dissolution if, at the time the other party enters into the transaction, the other party does not know or have notice of the dissolution.

(b)   A person dissociated as a general partner binds a limited partnership through an act occurring after dissolution if:

(1)   at the time the other party enters into the transaction:

(A)   less than two years has passed since the dissociation; and

(B)   the other party does not know or have notice of the dissociation and reasonably believes that the person is a general partner; and

(2)   the act:

(A)   is appropriate for winding up the partnership's activities and affairs; or

(B)   would have bound the partnership under Section 402 before dissolution and at the time the other party enters into the transaction the other party does not know or have notice of the dissolution.

COMMENT

This section provides the "power to bind" rules applicable once dissolution occurs. The section originated in UPA (1997), which significantly departed from the approach of UPA (1914). ULPA (2001) accepted the UPA (1997) construct but revised the language for stylistic reasons. The Harmonization Project accepted the ULPA (2001) language.

In general, this section parallels Section 606 (power to bind of a person dissociated as general partner when dissolution does not result from the dissociation). However, one significant difference exists. Section 606(a)(2)(A) contains a provision analogous to a statute of repose. A person's power to bind the partnership terminates two years after the date of dissociation. Subsection (b) contains a comparable provision, but Subsection (a) does not.

Subsections (a) and (b)—Subsection (a) states the power-to-bind rules for persons still general partners when dissolution occurs. Subsection (b) pertains to persons dissociated as a general partner before dissolution, including a general partner whose dissociation results in dissolution.

Subsection (a)(1)—This paragraph states a rule of inherent agency power. *See* RESTATEMENT (SECOND) OF AGENCY § 8A (1958) defining "inherent agency power" as "the power of an agent which is derived not from authority, apparent authority or estoppel, but solely from the agency relation and exists for the protection of persons harmed by or dealing with a servant or other agent"). Thus, a general partner might act without actual or apparent authority and still bind the limited partnership. The partnership agreement cannot change the stated rule, because the rule pertains to the rights of third parties under this act. *See* Section 105(c)(18).

If a general partner's words or conduct trigger this paragraph, thereby binding the limited partnership, and the general partner lacks the actual authority to do so, the general partner breaches an agent's duty to act within authority, and is liable to the limited partnership for any resulting damages. RESTATEMENT (THIRD) OF AGENCY § 8.09(1) (2006) ("An agent has a duty to take action only within the scope of the agent's actual authority"). The general partner might also be liable for breach of the partnership agreement.

Subsection (a)(2)—A person might have notice under Section 103(d)(2)(A) (amendment of certificate of limited partnership to indicate dissolution) as well as under Section 103(b)(1) (reason to know).

Subsection (b)—This subsection deals with the post-dissolution power to bind of a person dissociated as a general partner. For the most part: (i) Paragraph 1 replicates Section 606, pertaining to the pre-dissolution power to bind of a person dissociated as a general partner; and (ii) Paragraph 2 replicates Subsection (a) of this section, which states the post-dissolution power to bind of a person who is still a general partner.

For a person dissociated as a general partner to bind a dissolved limited partnership:

- the person's dissociation must have:
  - been rightful; and
  - resulted in dissolution; and
- the person's act must satisfy both Paragraphs 1 and 2.

Subsection (b)(1)(B)—A person might have notice under Section 103(d)(1) (amendment to certificate of limited partnership indicating dissociation or statement of dissociation) as well as under Section 103(b)(1).

Subsection (b)(2)(B)—A person might have notice under Section 103(d)(2)(A) (amendment of certificate of limited partnership to indicate dissolution) as well as under Section 103(b)(1).

§ 805. Liability After Dissolution of General Partner and Person Dissociated as General Partner

(a) If a general partner having knowledge of the dissolution causes a limited partnership to incur an obligation under Section 804(a) by an act that is not appropriate for winding up the partnership's activities and affairs, the general partner is liable:

(1) to the partnership for any damage caused to the partnership arising from the obligation; and

(2) if another general partner or a person dissociated as a general partner is liable for the obligation, to that other general partner or person for any damage caused to that other general partner or person arising from the liability.

(b) If a person dissociated as a general partner causes a limited partnership to incur an obligation under Section 804(b), the person is liable:

(1) to the partnership for any damage caused to the partnership arising from the obligation; and

(2) if a general partner or another person dissociated as a general partner is liable for the obligation, to the general partner or other person for any damage caused to the general partner or other person arising from the obligation.

COMMENT

This section parallels Section 606(b). It is possible for more than one person to be liable under this section on account of the same limited partnership obligation. This act does not provide any rule for apportioning liability in that circumstance.

Subsection (a)(2)—If the limited partnership is not a limited liability limited partnership, the liability created by this paragraph includes liability under Sections 404(a), 607(b), and 607(c). The paragraph also applies when a partner or person dissociated as a general partner suffers damage due to a contract of guaranty.

Other law determines liability (if any) to a person that is neither a general partner nor dissociated as a general partner.

§ 806. Known Claims Against Dissolved Limited Partnership

(a) Except as otherwise provided in subsection (d), a dissolved limited partnership may give notice of a known claim under subsection (b), which has the effect provided in subsection (c).

(b) A dissolved limited partnership may in a record notify its known claimants of the dissolution. The notice must:

(1) specify the information required to be included in a claim;

(2) state that a claim must be in writing and provide a mailing address to which the claim is to be sent;

(3) state the deadline for receipt of a claim, which may not be less than 120 days after the date the notice is received by the claimant;

(4) state that the claim will be barred if not received by the deadline; and

(5) unless the partnership has been throughout its existence a limited liability limited partnership, state that the barring of a claim against the partnership will also bar any corresponding claim against any general partner or person dissociated as a general partner which is based on Section 404.

(c) A claim against a dissolved limited partnership is barred if the requirements of subsection (b) are met and:

(1) the claim is not received by the specified deadline; or

(2) if the claim is timely received but rejected by the partnership:

(A) the partnership causes the claimant to receive a notice in a record stating that the claim is rejected and will be barred unless the claimant commences an action against the partnership to enforce the claim not later than 90 days after the claimant receives the notice; and

(B) the claimant does not commence the required action not later than 90 days after the claimant receives the notice.

(d) This section does not apply to a claim based on an event occurring after the date of dissolution or a liability that on that date is contingent.

COMMENT

Sections 806, 807, and 808 provide rules under which a dissolved limited partnership may achieve finality with regard to claims.

Source: This section is derived almost verbatim from Model Business Corporation Act section 14.06.

Subsection (b)(5)—*See* Section 809, cmt.

§ 807. Other Claims Against Dissolved Limited Partnership

(a) A dissolved limited partnership may publish notice of its dissolution and request persons having claims against the partnership to present them in accordance with the notice.

(b) A notice under subsection (a) must:

(1) be published at least once in a newspaper of general circulation in the [county] in this state in which the dissolved limited partnership's principal office is located or, if the principal office is not located in this state, in the [county] in which the office of the partnership's registered agent is or was last located;

(2)   describe the information required to be contained in a claim, state that the claim must be in writing, and provide a mailing address to which the claim is to be sent;

(3)   state that a claim against the partnership is barred unless an action to enforce the claim is commenced not later than three years after publication of the notice; and

(4)   unless the partnership has been throughout its existence a limited liability limited partnership, state that the barring of a claim against the partnership will also bar any corresponding claim against any general partner or person dissociated as a general partner which is based on Section 404.

(c)   If a dissolved limited partnership publishes a notice in accordance with subsection (b), the claim of each of the following claimants is barred unless the claimant commences an action to enforce the claim against the partnership not later than three years after the publication date of the notice:

(1)   a claimant that did not receive notice in a record under Section 806;

(2)   a claimant whose claim was timely sent to the partnership but not acted on; and

(3)   a claimant whose claim is contingent at, or based on an event occurring after, the date of dissolution.

(d)   A claim not barred under this section or Section 806 may be enforced:

(1)   against the dissolved limited partnership, to the extent of its undistributed assets;

(2)   except as otherwise provided in Section 808, if assets of the partnership have been distributed after dissolution, against a partner or transferee to the extent of that person's proportionate share of the claim or of the partnership's assets distributed to the partner or transferee after dissolution, whichever is less, but a person's total liability for all claims under this paragraph may not exceed the total amount of assets distributed to the person after dissolution; and

(3)   against any person liable on the claim under Sections 404 and 607.

COMMENT

Source: This section is derived almost verbatim from Model Business Corporation Act section 14.07.

Subsection (b)(4)—*See* Section 809, cmt.

Subsection (d)(2)—Liability under this paragraph extends to those who have received distributions under a charging order. *See* Section 702(a), cmt. (explaining that the beneficiary of a charging order is a transferee). Unlike Section 505(b) (recapture of improper interim distributions), this paragraph contains no "knowledge" element.

§ 808.   Court Proceedings

(a)   A dissolved limited partnership that has published a notice under Section 807 may file an application with [the appropriate court] in the [county] where the partnership's principal office is located or, if the principal office is not located in this state, where the office of its registered agent is or was last located, for a determination of the amount and form of security to be provided for payment of claims that are contingent, have not been made known to the partnership, or are based on an event occurring after the date of dissolution but which, based on the facts known to the partnership, are reasonably expected to arise after the date of dissolution. Security is not required for any claim that is or is reasonably anticipated to be barred under Section 807.

(b)   Not later than 10 days after the filing of an application under subsection (a), the dissolved limited partnership shall give notice of the proceeding to each claimant holding a contingent claim known to the partnership.

(c)   In a proceeding brought under this section, the court may appoint a guardian ad litem to represent all claimants whose identities are unknown. The reasonable fees and expenses of the guardian, including all reasonable expert witness fees, must be paid by the dissolved limited partnership.

(d)   A dissolved limited partnership that provides security in the amount and form ordered by the court under subsection (a) satisfies the partnership's obligations with respect to claims that are contingent, have not been made known to the partnership, or are based on an event occurring after the date of dissolution, and such claims may not be enforced against a partner or transferee on account of assets received in liquidation.

COMMENT

Source: This section is derived almost verbatim from Model Business Corporation Act section 14.08.

§ 809.   Liability of General Partner and Person Dissociated as General Partner When Claim Against Limited Partnership Barred

If a claim against a dissolved limited partnership is barred under Section 806, 807, or 808, any corresponding claim under Section 404 or 607 is also barred.

COMMENT

A general partner's liability under Sections 404 and 607 is vicarious liability—liability solely by status and solely for the "debts, obligations, and other liabilities of the limited partnership." To the extent a claim pertaining to the underlying debt, obligation, or other liability is barred, a claim pertaining to the corresponding vicarious liability should likewise be barred.

§ 810.   Disposition of Assets in Winding Up; When Contributions Required

(a)   In winding up its activities and affairs, a limited partnership shall apply its assets, including the contributions required by this section, to discharge the partnership's obligations to creditors, including partners that are creditors.

(b)   After a limited partnership complies with subsection (a), any surplus must be distributed in the following order, subject to any charging order in effect under Section 703:

(1)   to each person owning a transferable interest that reflects contributions made and not previously returned, an amount equal to the value of the unreturned contributions; and

(2)   among persons owning transferable interests in proportion to their respective rights to share in distributions immediately before the dissolution of the partnership.

(c)   If a limited partnership's assets are insufficient to satisfy all of its obligations under subsection (a), with respect to each unsatisfied obligation incurred when the partnership was not a limited liability limited partnership, the following rules apply:

(1)   Each person that was a general partner when the obligation was incurred and that has not been released from the obligation under Section 607 shall contribute to the partnership for the purpose of enabling the partnership to satisfy the obligation. The contribution due from each of those persons is in proportion to the right to receive distributions in the capacity of a general partner in effect for each of those persons when the obligation was incurred.

(2)   If a person does not contribute the full amount required under paragraph (1) with respect to an unsatisfied obligation of the partnership, the other persons required to contribute by paragraph (1) on account of the obligation shall contribute the additional amount necessary to discharge the obligation. The additional contribution due from each of those other persons is in proportion to the right to receive distributions in the capacity of a general partner in effect for each of those other persons when the obligation was incurred.

(3)   If a person does not make the additional contribution required by paragraph (2), further additional contributions are determined and due in the same manner as provided in that paragraph.

(d)   A person that makes an additional contribution under subsection (c)(2) or (3) may recover from any person whose failure to contribute under subsection (c)(1) or (2) necessitated the additional contribution. A person may not recover under this subsection more than the amount additionally contributed. A person's liability under this subsection may not exceed the amount the person failed to contribute.

(e)   All distributions made under subsections (b) and (c) must be paid in money.

COMMENT

In some circumstances, this act requires a partner to make payments to the limited partnership. *See, e.g.,* Sections 502(b), 505(a), 505(b), 810(c). In other circumstances, this act requires a partner to make payments to other partners. *See, e.g.,* Sections 505(c), 810(d). In no circumstances does this act require a partner to make a payment for the purpose of equalizing or otherwise reallocating capital losses incurred by partners.

Example: XYZ Limited Partnership ("XYZ") has one general partner and four limited partners. As indicated by its name, XYZ is not a limited liability limited partnership. According to XYZ's required information, the value of each partner's contributions to XYZ are:

General partner—$5,000

Limited partner #1—$10,000

Limited partner #2—$15,000

Limited partner #3—$20,000

Limited partner #4—$25,000

XYZ is unsuccessful and eventually dissolves without ever having made a distribution to its partners. XYZ lacks any assets with which to return to the partners the value of their respective contributions. No partner is obliged to make any payment either to the limited partnership or to fellow partners to adjust these capital losses. These losses are not part of "the limited partnership's obligations to creditors." Section 810(a).

Example: Same facts, except that Limited Partner #4 loaned $25,000 to XYZ, and XYZ lacks the assets to repay the loan. The general partner must contribute to the limited partnership whatever funds are necessary to enable XYZ to satisfy the obligation owned to Limited Partner #4 on account of the loan. Section 810(a) and (c).

Subsection (a)—This subsection is non-waivable as to creditors who are not partners. *See* Section 105(c)(18) (stating that the partnership agreement may not "restrict the rights under this [act] of a person other than a partner "). However, if a creditor is willing, a dissolved limited partnership may certainly make agreements with the creditor specifying the terms under which the limited partnership will "discharge the partnership's obligations to" the creditor.

Subsection (b)—For the most part, this subsection states default rules. For example, partnership agreements often provide for different distribution rights upon liquidation than during operations. However, distributions under these subsections (or otherwise under the partnership agreement) are subject to charging orders, Section 703. As to the extent the partnership agreement can be amended to affect the distribution rights of persons already transferees, see Section 107(b).

Subsection (c)—This section applies obligation by obligation, because a person—*qua* general partner or person dissociated as a general partner—is required to contribute to the limited partnership to satisfy a partnership obligation only if, when the obligation was incurred: (i) the person was a general partner; and (ii) the limited partnership was not an LLLP. *See* Section 404(b), (c). As for when a limited partnership obligation is incurred, see Section 404(b) and (c), comments.

The partnership agreement can change the allocation *inter se* general partners and persons dissociated as general partners but cannot prejudice the rights of non-partner creditors.

Example: The A-B Limited Partnership (the "Partnership") owes Creditor $150, an obligation incurred when General Partners A and B were the only general partners, sharing distributions equally, and the Limited Partnership was not an LLLP. The Partnership has no funds to pay Creditor. Although Subsection (c)(1) would require Partners A and B each to contribute equally (*i.e.*, $75), the A-B Partnership Agreement provides that General Partner A has the entire contribution obligation and General Partner B has none. As between General Partners A and B, General Partner A is obligated to contribute $150 and General Partner B nothing. However, as to Creditor, General Partner B still has a contribution obligation of $75.

This formal distinction will have practical consequences only if General Partner A does not contribute the full $150. Also, Creditor may have problems establishing standing. *Cf.* Section 505, cmt.

Subsection (c)(2) and (3)—These provisions are analogous to buy-sell provisions that: (i) provide that an owner's effort to sell the ownership interest triggers an option to purchase allocated among all the other owners;

(ii) make the option conditional on the entire interest being purchased; and (iii) provide for successive allocations to take up any previous allocations that were not unexercised.

Subsection (e)—If a limited partnership has been a limited liability limited partnership throughout the partnership's existence, this subsection is consistent with this act's approach to loss sharing. If a partnership has been a limited liability limited partnership during only part of the partnership's existence, the issue of loss sharing upon dissolution: (i) can be exceedingly complicated, varying radically depending on the circumstances; (ii) is therefore not amenable to a statutory "gap filler"; and (iii) thus should always be addressed in the partnership agreement.

However, in case the partnership agreement does not address the issue, this act must provide a default rule. *See* Section 105(b), cmt. ("To the extent the partnership agreement does not determine an inter se matter, this act determines the matter."). This subsection applies to fill the gap. This approach has the virtues of simplicity and certainty but in no way resembles what "typical" partners might agree if they were to consider the matter *ab initio*, especially if the partnership was never a LLLP. *Cf.* Robert W. Hillman, *Private Ordering Within Partnerships*, 41 U. MIAMI L. REV. 425, 448 (1987) ("[T]he various norms established by the Act, applicable in the absence of agreements to the contrary, represent the supposed understandings partners most likely reach if they choose to bargain on the various issues.").

§ 811. Administrative Dissolution

(a) The [Secretary of State] may commence a proceeding under subsection (b) to dissolve a limited partnership administratively if the partnership does not:

(1) pay any fee, tax, interest, or penalty required to be paid to the [Secretary of State] not later than [six months] after it is due;

(2) deliver [an annual] [a biennial] report to the [Secretary of State] not later than [six months] after it is due; or

(3) have a registered agent in this state for [60] consecutive days.

(b) If the [Secretary of State] determines that one or more grounds exist for administratively dissolving a limited partnership, the [Secretary of State] shall serve the partnership with notice in a record of the [Secretary of State's] determination.

(c) If a limited partnership, not later than [60] days after service of the notice under subsection (b), does not cure or demonstrate to the satisfaction of the [Secretary of State] the nonexistence of each ground determined by the [Secretary of State], the [Secretary of State] shall administratively dissolve the partnership by signing a statement of administrative dissolution that recites the grounds for dissolution and the effective date of dissolution. The [Secretary of State] shall file the statement and serve a copy on the partnership pursuant to Section 121.

(d) A limited partnership that is administratively dissolved continues in existence as an entity but may not carry on any activities except as necessary to wind up its activities and affairs and liquidate its assets under Sections 802, 806, 807, 808, and 810, or to apply for reinstatement under Section 812.

(e) The administrative dissolution of a limited partnership does not terminate the authority of its registered agent.

COMMENT

Many failures to comply with statutory requirements that may give rise to administrative dissolution occur because of oversight or inadvertence and are usually corrected promptly when brought to the entity's attention. Subsections (b) and (c) therefore provide a mandatory notice by the filing office to each limited partnership subject to administrative dissolution and a sixty-day grace period following the notice before the statement of administrative dissolution may be filed.

In most instances, the issue whether the limited partnership is subject to administrative dissolution will not be controverted. If a limited partnership is administratively dissolved, it may petition the filing office for reinstatement under Section 812 and, if reinstatement is denied, the company may appeal to the courts under Section 813.

As a practical matter, administrative dissolution permits the filing office to clear the record of "dead wood" and free up names.

§ 812.   Reinstatement

(a)   A limited partnership that is administratively dissolved under Section 811 may apply to the [Secretary of State] for reinstatement [not later than [two] years after the effective date of dissolution]. The application must state:

(1)   the name of the partnership at the time of its administrative dissolution and, if needed, a different name that satisfies Section 114;

(2)   the address of the principal office of the partnership and the name and street and mailing addresses of its registered agent;

(3)   the effective date of the partnership's administrative dissolution; and

(4)   that the grounds for dissolution did not exist or have been cured.

(b)   To be reinstated, a limited partnership must pay all fees, taxes, interest, and penalties that were due to the [Secretary of State] at the time of the partnership's administrative dissolution and all fees, taxes, interest, and penalties that would have been due to the [Secretary of State] while the partnership was administratively dissolved.

(c)   If the [Secretary of State] determines that an application under subsection (a) contains the required information, is satisfied that the information is correct, and determines that all payments required to be made to the [Secretary of State] by subsection (b) have been made, the [Secretary of State] shall:

(1)   cancel the statement of administrative dissolution and prepare a statement of reinstatement that states the [Secretary of State's] determination and the effective date of reinstatement; and

(2)   file the statement of reinstatement and serve a copy on the limited partnership.

(d)   When reinstatement under this section has become effective, the following rules apply:

(1)   The reinstatement relates back to and takes effect as of the effective date of the administrative dissolution.

(2)   The limited partnership resumes carrying on its activities and affairs as if the administrative dissolution had not occurred.

(3)   The rights of a person arising out of an act or omission in reliance on the dissolution before the person knew or had notice of the reinstatement are not affected.

COMMENT

Some states require that reinstatement be sought within two years of administrative dissolution. Other states provide a longer time, or do not impose any time limit. Imposing no limit risks abuse by unscrupulous people seeking to reinstate and appropriate for improper ends a dormant limited partnership that has been abandoned by its partners. On the other hand, reinstatement is intended as a safety net for the inattentive (*i.e.*, for people in charge of a limited partnership who have neglected to file an annual report or otherwise subjected the limited partnership to administrative dissolution). If the deadline comes too soon, the safety net may be gone before the inattentive even learn that administrative dissolution has occurred.

Subsection (a)(1)—This provision will apply if, before the limited partnership is reinstated, another entity has taken the company's name. *See* Section 114(d).

Subsection (d)(3)—This paragraph provides an exception to the retroactive effect provided by this subsection's Paragraphs (1) and (2). The exception could preclude a reinstated limited partnership's use of its own name. *See* Section 114(d)(1) (indirectly permitting a limited partnership to use the name of a limited partnership that has been administratively dissolved). Comparable provisions exist in other uniform acts pertaining to entities. *E.g.*, UPA (1997) (Last Amended 2013) § 902(c)(2).

§ 813. Judicial Review of Denial of Reinstatement

(a) If the [Secretary of State] denies a limited partnership's application for reinstatement following administrative dissolution, the [Secretary of State] shall serve the partnership with a notice in a record that explains the reasons for the denial.

(b) A limited partnership may seek judicial review of denial of reinstatement in [the appropriate court] not later than [30] days after service of the notice of denial.

COMMENT

Because the grounds for administrative dissolution under Section 811 are limited and straight-forward, it is unlikely there will be a dispute about whether a limited partnership has corrected the reasons for its administrative dissolution. If a dissolved limited partnership disagrees with a determination by the filing office to deny the partnership's application for reinstatement, this section gives the partnership a limited right to seek judicial review of the denial of reinstatement.

[ARTICLE] 9.   ACTIONS BY PARTNERS

§ 901.   Direct Action by Partner

(a) Subject to subsection (b), a partner may maintain a direct action against another partner or the limited partnership, with or without an accounting as to the partnership's activities and affairs, to enforce the partner's rights and otherwise protect the partner's interests, including rights and interests under the partnership agreement or this [act] or arising independently of the partnership relationship.

(b) A partner maintaining a direct action under this section must plead and prove an actual or threatened injury that is not solely the result of an injury suffered or threatened to be suffered by the limited partnership.

(c) A right to an accounting on a dissolution and winding up does not revive a claim barred by law.

COMMENT

Subsection (a)—A partner's rights under this subsection are subject to the rule of standing stated in Subsection (b). The phrase "otherwise protect the partner's interests" pertains to remedies and creates no additional causes of action.

The last phrase of this subsection ("or arising independently . . . ") does not create any new rights, obligations, or remedies, and is included merely to emphasize that a person being a partner in a limited partnership does not preclude the person from enforcing rights existing "independently of the partnership relationship" (*e.g.*, as a creditor).

Subsection (b)—This subsection codifies the rule of standing that predominates in entity law. *See, e.g.,* *Mallia v. PaineWebber, Inc.*, 889 F. Supp. 277, 282 (S.D. Tex. 1995) ("[T]o bring a direct representative action against a general partner, a limited partner must demonstrate either direct injury or an injury that exists independently of the partnerships."); *Jones v. H. F. Ahmanson & Co.*, 460 P.2d 464, 470 (Cal. 1969) (stating that "the action is derivative, *i.e.*, in the corporate right, if the gravamen of the complaint is injury to the corporation, or to the whole body of its stock or property without any severance or distribution among individual holders, or if it seeks to recover assets for the corporation or to prevent the dissipation of its assets" (quoting *Gagnon Co., Inc. v. Nevada Desert Inn*, 289 P.2d 466, 471 (Cal. 1955) (internal quotation marks omitted)); *Litman v. Prudential-Bache Properties, Inc.*, 611 A.2d 12, 17 (Del. Ch. 1992) (stating that direct action by holders of interest in partnership is not permitted for indirect injuries from general partners' misconduct); *Tzolis v. Wolff*, 884 N.E.2d 1005, 1008 (N.Y. 2008) (holding that derivative actions exist under New York LLC law and referring to "the traditional line between direct and derivative claims"); *see also CML V, LLC v. Bax,* 6 A.3d 238, 245 (Del. Ch. 2010) (noting that issues of standing viz-a-viz direct and derivative claims are comparable regardless of whether the entity is a limited partnership, a limited liability company, or a corporation), *aff'd*, 28 A.3d 1037 (Del. 2011).

The distinction between direct and derivative claims protects the partnership agreement. If any partner can sue directly over any management issue, the mere threat of suit can interfere with the partners' agreed-upon arrangements.

Although in ordinary contractual situations it is axiomatic that each party to a contract has standing to sue for breach of that contract, within a limited partnership different circumstances typically exist. A partner does not have a direct claim against a general partner merely because the general partner has breached the partnership agreement. Likewise a general partner's violation of this act does not automatically create a direct claim for every other partner. To have standing in his, her, or its own right, a partner plaintiff must be able to show a harm that occurs independently of the harm caused or threatened to be caused to the limited partnership.

Example: Through grossly negligent conduct, in violation of Section 409(c), the general partner of a limited partnership reduces the net assets of the limited partnership by fifty percent, which in turns decreases the value of Limited Partner A's investment by $3,000,000. A has no standing to bring a direct claim; the damage is merely derivative of the damage first suffered by the limited partnership. The partner may, however, bring a derivative claim. Sections 902–906.

Example: Same facts, except in addition to violating Section 409(c), the general partner's conduct breaches an express provision of the partnership agreement to which Limited Partner A is a signatory. The analysis and the result are the same.

Example: A partnership agreement defines "distributable cash" and requires the limited partnership to periodically distribute that cash among all partners. The limited partnership's general partner fails to distribute the cash. Each partner has a direct claim against the general partner and the limited partnership.

The reference to "threatened injury" is to encompass potential claims for preventative relief, such as a temporary restraining order or preliminary injunction.

This section's standing rule is subject to reasonable alterations by the partnership agreement. *See* Section 105(c)(14), cmt.

Subsection (c)—This subsection originated as UPA (1997) § 405(c) and reversed the rule stated in UPA (1914) § 43. This subsection inevitably implies that other law governs the accrual of a claim under Subsection (b) as well as the statute of limitations applicable to those claims. As a result, partners must take care not to "to sit on their claims" waiting for the partnership to dissolve. *Veloski v. State Farm Mut. Auto Ins. Co.*, 719 N.E.2d 574, 576 (Ohio Ct. App. 1998).

§ 902.   Derivative Action

A partner may maintain a derivative action to enforce a right of a limited partnership if:

(1)   the partner first makes a demand on the general partners, requesting that they cause the partnership to bring an action to enforce the right, and the general partners do not bring the action within a reasonable time; or

(2)   a demand under paragraph (1) would be futile.

COMMENT

By its terms, this section permits a general partner as well as a limited partner to bring a derivative action, subject of course to Section 903.

Paragraph (1)—The demand requirement recognizes that, presumptively at least, the decision to cause a limited partnership to bring suit is a business decision, to be made by those who manage the business. Deborah A. DeMott, SHAREHOLDER DERIVATIVE ACTIONS: LAW AND PRACTICE § 5.9 (Westlaw, Nov. 4, 2012) (Demand on directors—Rationales for demand).

Paragraph (2)—Some jurisdictions have a "universal demand" requirement, but the approach stated here is by far the majority one. Deborah A. DeMott, SHAREHOLDER DERIVATIVE ACTIONS: LAW AND PRACTICE § 5.12 (Westlaw, Nov. 4, 2012).

§ 903.   Proper Plaintiff

A derivative action to enforce a right of a limited partnership may be maintained only by a person that is a partner at the time the action is commenced and:

(1)   was a partner when the conduct giving rise to the action occurred; or

(2)   whose status as a partner devolved on the person by operation of law or pursuant to the terms of the partnership agreement from a person that was a partner at the time of the conduct.

COMMENT

The rule stated here is conventional in both the law of unincorporated entities and corporate law. Persons dissociated as partners have no standing to bring a derivative action. *A fortiori*, mere transferees have no standing. *See* Sections 107(b), cmt., 702.

Paragraph (2)—This paragraph will be inapposite if the limited partnership has only two partners, one of whom is the derivative plaintiff. In that limited circumstance, the plaintiff's death would cause the derivative action to abate. The "pick your partner" principal enshrined in Section 702 would prevent the decedent's heirs from succeeding to plaintiff status in the derivative action (except in the unlikely event that the remaining partner consents to the heirs becoming partners). The analysis and result will be the same if the derivative plaintiff is an entity whose existence terminates.

This act takes no position on whether:

- the death of partner abates a direct claim against the limited partnership or a fellow partner; and

- bringing a direct claim precludes a person from being a proper plaintiff for a derivative claim.

As to the latter issue, *see, e.g., Cordts-Auth v. Crunk, L.L.C.*, 815 F. Supp. 2d 778, 793–94 (S.D.N.Y. 2011) (discussing the potential conflict of interest), *aff'd*, 479 F. App'x 375 (2d Cir. 2012).

§ 904.   Pleading

In a derivative action, the complaint must state with particularity:

(1)   the date and content of plaintiff's demand and the response to the demand by the general partner; or

(2)   why demand should be excused as futile.

COMMENT

This section parallels Section 902. The pleading requirement first appeared in a uniform act in 1976. ULPA (1976) § 1003.

§ 905.   Special Litigation Committee

(a)   If a limited partnership is named as or made a party in a derivative proceeding, the partnership may appoint a special litigation committee to investigate the claims asserted in the proceeding and determine whether pursuing the action is in the best interests of the partnership. If the partnership appoints a special litigation committee, on motion by the committee made in the name of the partnership, except for good cause shown, the court shall stay discovery for the time reasonably necessary to permit the committee to make its investigation. This subsection does not prevent the court from:

(1)   enforcing a person's right to information under Section 304 or 407; or

(2)   granting extraordinary relief in the form of a temporary restraining order or preliminary injunction.

(b)   A special litigation committee must be composed of one or more disinterested and independent individuals, who may be partners.

(c)   A special litigation committee may be appointed:

(1)   by a majority of the general partners not named as parties in the proceeding; or

(2)   if all general partners are named as parties in the proceeding, by a majority of the general partners named as defendants.

(d)   After appropriate investigation, a special litigation committee may determine that it is in the best interests of the limited partnership that the proceeding:

(1)   continue under the control of the plaintiff;

(2)   continue under the control of the committee;

(3)   be settled on terms approved by the committee; or

(4)   be dismissed.

(e)   After making a determination under subsection (d), a special litigation committee shall file with the court a statement of its determination and its report supporting its determination and shall serve each party with a copy of the determination and report. The court shall determine whether the members of the committee were disinterested and independent and whether the committee conducted its investigation and made its recommendation in good faith, independently, and with reasonable care, with the committee having the burden of proof. If the court finds that the members of the committee were disinterested and independent and that the committee acted in good faith, independently, and with reasonable care, the court shall enforce the determination of the committee. Otherwise, the court shall dissolve the stay of discovery entered under subsection (a) and allow the action to continue under the control of the plaintiff.

COMMENT

Although special litigation committees are best known in the corporate field, they are no more inherently corporate than derivative litigation or the notion that an organization is a person distinct from its owners. An "SLC" can serve as an ADR mechanism, help protect an agreed upon arrangement from strike suits, protect the interests of partners who are neither plaintiffs nor defendants (if any), and bring the benefits of a specially tailored business judgment to any judicial decision.

This section's approach corresponds to established law in most jurisdictions, modified to fit the typical governance structures of a limited partnership. Use of an SLC is optional. A partnership agreement can preclude the use of SLCs, rendering this section inapplicable, but cannot otherwise vary this section. *See* Section 105(c)(15).

Subsection (a)(1)—Sections 304 and 407 pertain to information rights. On the availability of these remedies pending the SLC's investigation, *compare* Section 410, *with Kaufman v. Computer Assoc. Int'l, Inc.*, No. Civ.A. 699-N, 2005 WL 3470589, at *1 (Del. Ch. Dec. 21, 2005) (presenting "the question of whether to stay a books and records action under 8 Del. C. § 220 at the request of a special litigation committee when a derivative action encompassing substantially the same allegations of wrongdoing filed by different plaintiffs is pending in another jurisdiction"; concluding "[f]or reasons that have much to do with the light burden imposed by the plaintiff's demand in this case . . . that the special litigation committee's motion to stay the books and records action should be denied").

Subsection (e)—The standard stated for judicial review of the SLC determination follows *Auerbach v. Bennett*, 393 N.E.2d 994 (N.Y. 1979) rather than *Zapata Corp. v. Maldonado*, 430 A.2d 779 (Del. 1981), because the latter's reference to a court's business judgment has generally not been followed in other states. In essence, an SLC is intended to function as a surrogate decision-maker, allowing the limited partnership to make what is fundamentally a business decision. If a court determines that "the members of the committee were disinterested and independent and [that] . . . the committee conducted its investigation and made its recommendation in good faith, independently, and with reasonable care, with the committee having the burden of proof," it makes no sense to substitute the court's legal judgment for the business judgment of the SLC.

Houle v. Low, 556 N.E.2d 51, 58 (Mass. 1990) contains an excellent explanation of the court's role in reviewing an SLC decision:

> The value of a special litigation committee is coextensive with the extent to which that committee truly exercises business judgment. In order to ensure that special litigation committees do act for the [entity]'s best interest, a good deal of judicial oversight is necessary in each case. At the same time, however, courts must be careful not to usurp the committee's valuable role in exercising business judgment. . . . [A] special litigation committee must be independent, unbiased, and act in good faith. Moreover, such a committee must conduct a thorough and careful analysis regarding the plaintiff's derivative suit. . . . The burden of proving that these procedural requirements have been met must rest, in all fairness, on the party capable of making that proof—the [entity].

For a discussion of how a court should approach the question of independence, see *Einhorn v. Culea*, 612 N.W.2d 78, 91 (Wis. 2000).

§ 906. Proceeds and Expenses

(a) Except as otherwise provided in subsection (b):

(1) any proceeds or other benefits of a derivative action, whether by judgment, compromise, or settlement, belong to the limited partnership and not to the plaintiff; and

(2) if the plaintiff receives any proceeds, the plaintiff shall remit them immediately to the partnership.

(b) If a derivative action is successful in whole or in part, the court may award the plaintiff reasonable expenses, including reasonable attorney's fees and costs, from the recovery of the limited partnership.

(c) A derivative action on behalf of a limited partnership may not be voluntarily dismissed or settled without the court's approval.

COMMENT

Subsection (c)—This provision is intended to prevent collusion.

[ARTICLE] 10.   FOREIGN LIMITED PARTNERSHIPS

§ 1001.   Governing Law

(a) The law of the jurisdiction of formation of a foreign limited partnership governs:

(1) the internal affairs of the partnership;

(2) the liability of a partner as partner for a debt, obligation, or other liability of the partnership; and

(3) the liability of a series of the partnership.

(b) A foreign limited partnership is not precluded from registering to do business in this state because of any difference between the law of its jurisdiction of formation and the law of this state.

(c) Registration of a foreign limited partnership to do business in this state does not authorize the foreign partnership to engage in any activities and affairs or exercise any power that a limited partnership may not engage in or exercise in this state.

COMMENT

Subsection (a)—This subsection provides that the laws of the jurisdiction of formation of a foreign limited partnership, rather than the laws of this state, govern both the internal affairs of the limited partnership and the liability of its partners for the obligations of the limited partnership. A partnership agreement cannot change this provision. Section 105(c)(18).

This subdivision parallels Section 104 (pertaining to the governing law for domestic limited partnerships). *See* Section 104, cmt.

Subsection (a)(3)—This act does not provide for series of the asset-partitioning type (as contemplated by Del. Code. Ann. tit. 6, § 17–218 (West 2014)). However, under this provision, the law of this state will respect the "internal shields" created under the series provisions of another jurisdiction's limited partnership statute. This provision does *not* address the myriad of other unsettled issues pertaining to series.

For an explanation of how the asset-partitioning concept of series differs from the traditional concept, see Section 1131, comment.

Subsections (b) and (c)—These sections together make clear that, although a foreign entity may not be denied registration simply because of a difference between the laws of its jurisdiction of formation and the laws of this state, the foreign limited partnership "may not engage in any activity or exercise any power that a limited partnership may not engage in or exercise in this state." Subsection (c).

§ 1002.   Registration to Do Business in This State

(a)   A foreign limited partnership may not do business in this state until it registers with the [Secretary of State] under this [article].

(b)   A foreign limited partnership doing business in this state may not maintain an action or proceeding in this state unless it is registered to do business in this state.

(c)   The failure of a foreign limited partnership to register to do business in this state does not impair the validity of a contract or act of the partnership or preclude it from defending an action or proceeding in this state.

(d)   A limitation on the liability of a general partner or limited partner of a foreign limited partnership is not waived solely because the partnership does business in this state without registering to do business in this state.

(e)   Section 1001(a) and (b) applies even if the foreign limited partnership fails to register under this [article].

COMMENT

Subsection (a)—Following a long-established tradition, this act does not state what constitutes "do[ing] business in this state." Instead, Section 1005 provides a non-exhaustive list of "[a]ctivities of a foreign limited partnership which do not constitute doing business in this state."

Subsection (b)—The purpose of this subsection is to induce foreign limited partnerships to register without imposing harsh or erratic sanctions. Often the failure to register is a result of inadvertence or bona fide disagreement as to the scope of Section 1005, which is necessarily imprecise. Thus, the imposition of harsh sanctions in those situations is inappropriate. The sanction of closing the courts of the state to suits brought by foreign limited partnerships that should have registered is not a punitive one. If a foreign limited partnership should have registered and failed to do so, it may still enforce its contractual and other rights simply by registering.

However, if a court dismisses a case under this subsection rather than staying the proceedings pending the foreign limited partnership's registration, a statute of limitations problem may occur. *See Corco, Inc. v. Ledar Transport, Inc.*, 946 P.2d 1009, 1010 (Kan. Ct. App. 1997) ("[T]he proper remedy was to dismiss [the unregistered entity's] counterclaim without prejudice rather than with prejudice. This would leave [the entity] the opportunity to comply with the statutes and then reassert its claim against [the defendant]. On the other hand, it would also leave the risk that the statute of limitations might run against [the entity].").

This subsection does not prevent a foreign limited partnership that has failed to register from "defending" an action or proceeding. The distinction between "maintaining" an action or proceeding under this subsection and "defending" an action or proceeding under Subsection (c) is determined on the basis of whether affirmative relief is sought. A nonregistered foreign limited partnership may interpose any defense or permissive or mandatory counterclaim to defeat a claimed recovery, but may not obtain an affirmative judgment based on the counterclaim without first registering.

Subsection (c)—In addition to permitting a non-registered foreign limited partnership doing business in this state to defend (but not maintain) an action or proceeding, this section makes clear that failure to register does not impair the validity of a foreign limited partnership's acts.

Subsection (d)—This subsection preserves the effectiveness of a foreign limited partnership's liability shield applicable under the limited partnership's governing law.

§ 1003.   Foreign Registration Statement

To register to do business in this state, a foreign limited partnership must deliver a foreign registration statement to the [Secretary of State] for filing. The statement must state:

(1)   the name of the partnership and, if the name does not comply with Section 114, an alternate name adopted pursuant to Section 1006(a);

(2)   that the partnership is a foreign limited partnership;

(3)   the partnership's jurisdiction of formation;

(4)   the street and mailing addresses of the partnership's principal office and, if the law of the partnership's jurisdiction of formation requires the partnership to maintain an office in that jurisdiction, the street and mailing addresses of the required office; and

(5)   the name and street and mailing addresses of the partnership's registered agent in this state.

COMMENT

The foreign registration statement provides certain basic information about the foreign limited partnership to ensure that citizens of the state have access to that information in their dealings with the foreign limited partnership. The statement also facilitates making the foreign limited partnership subject to the jurisdiction of the courts of the state.

Once registered, a foreign limited partnership must file an annual/biennial report. Section 212.

§ 1004.   Amendment of Foreign Registration Statement

A registered foreign limited partnership shall deliver to the [Secretary of State] for filing an amendment to its foreign registration statement if there is a change in:

(1)   the name of the partnership;

(2)   the partnership's jurisdiction of formation;

(3)   an address required by Section 1003(4); or

(4)   the information required by Section 1003(5).

COMMENT

This section works in tandem with the annual/biennial report required by Section 212 to keep up to date the information of record in the office of the filing office about a registered foreign limited partnership.

§ 1005.   Activities Not Constituting Doing Business

(a)   Activities of a foreign limited partnership which do not constitute doing business in this state under this [article] include:

(1)   maintaining, defending, mediating, arbitrating, or settling an action or proceeding;

(2)   carrying on any activity concerning its internal affairs, including holding meetings of its partners;

(3)   maintaining accounts in financial institutions;

(4)   maintaining offices or agencies for the transfer, exchange, and registration of securities of the partnership or maintaining trustees or depositories with respect to those securities;

(5)   selling through independent contractors;

(6)   soliciting or obtaining orders by any means if the orders require acceptance outside this state before they become contracts;

(7)   creating or acquiring indebtedness, mortgages, or security interests in property;

(8)   securing or collecting debts or enforcing mortgages or security interests in property securing the debts and holding, protecting, or maintaining property;

(9)   conducting an isolated transaction that is not in the course of similar transactions;

(10) owning, without more, property; and

(11) doing business in interstate commerce.

(b)   A person does not do business in this state solely by being a partner of a foreign limited partnership that does business in this state.

(c)   This section does not apply in determining the contacts or activities that may subject a foreign limited partnership to service of process, taxation, or regulation under law of this state other than this [act].

COMMENT

This act does not attempt to formulate an inclusive definition of what constitutes doing business in a state. Rather, the concept is defined in a negative fashion by Subsections (a) and (b), which state that certain activities do not constitute doing business.

In general terms, any conduct more regular, systematic, or extensive than that described in Subsection (a) constitutes doing business and requires the foreign limited partnership to register to do business. Typical conduct requiring registration includes maintaining an office to conduct local intrastate business, selling personal property not in interstate commerce, entering into contracts relating to the local business or sales, and owning or using real estate for general purposes. But the passive owning of real estate for investment purposes does not constitute doing business. *See* Subsection (a)(10).

The test of "doing business" defined in a negative way in Subsections (a) and (b) applies only to the question of whether a foreign limited partnership's contacts with the state are such that it must register under this section. The test is not applicable to other questions such as whether the foreign limited partnership is amenable to service of process under state "long-arm" statutes or liable for state or local taxes. A foreign limited partnership that has registered (or is required to register) will generally be subject to suit and state taxation in the state, while a foreign limited partnership that is subject to service of process or state taxation in a state will not necessarily be required to register.

Subsection (a)—The list of activities set forth in this subsection is not exhaustive.

Subsection (a)(1)—A foreign limited partnership is not "doing business" solely because it resorts to the courts of the state to recover an indebtedness, enforce an obligation, recover possession of personal property, obtain the appointment of a receiver, intervene in a pending proceeding, bring a petition to compel arbitration, file an appeal bond, or pursue appellate remedies. Similarly, a foreign limited partnership is not required to register merely because it files a complaint with a governmental agency or participates in an administrative proceeding within the state.

Subsection (a)(2)—A foreign limited partnership does not "do business" within a state under this section merely because some of its internal affairs occur within a state. Thus, a foreign limited partnership may hold meetings of its partners within a state without first registering. A foreign limited partnership also may maintain offices or agencies within a state relating solely to the transfer, exchange or registration of its interests without registering. Other activities relating to the internal affairs of the foreign limited partnership that do not constitute doing business under this section include having officers or representatives who reside within or are physically present in the state; while there, the officers or representatives may make executive decisions relating to the internal affairs of the foreign limited partnership without imposing on the foreign limited partnership the requirement that it register, if these activities are not so regular and systematic as to cause the residence to be viewed as a business office.

Subsection (a)(5)—Under this paragraph, a foreign limited partnership need not register if it sells goods in the state through independent contractors. These transactions are viewed as transactions by the independent contractors, not by the foreign limited partnership itself even though the foreign limited partnership sets some limits or ground rules for its contractors. If these controls are sufficiently pervasive, however, the foreign limited partnership may be deemed to be selling for itself in intrastate commerce, and not through the independent contractors and therefore engaged in doing business in the state.

Subsection (a)(7) and (8)—The mere act of making a loan by a foreign limited partnership that is not in the business of making loans does not constitute doing business in the state in which the loan is made. On the same theory, a foreign limited partnership may obtain security for the repayment of a loan, and foreclose or enforce the lien or security interest to collect the loan, without being deemed to be doing business. Similarly, a refunding or "roll over" of a loan or its adjustment or compromise does not involve doing business.

Subsection (a)(9)—The concept of "doing business" involves regular, repeated, and continuing business contacts of a local nature. A single agreement or isolated transaction within a state does not constitute doing business if there is no intention to repeat the transaction or engage in similar transactions. This act does not impose the limitation found in some statutes, such as section 15.01(b)(10) of the Model Business Corporation Act, that the isolated transaction be completed within thirty days. A foreign limited partnership should not be required to register simply because it engages in an isolated transaction that takes longer than thirty days to complete.

Subsection (a)(11)—A foreign limited partnership is not "doing business" within the meaning of this section if it is transacting business in interstate commerce. *See* Subsection (a)(6) (stating that soliciting or obtaining orders that must be accepted outside the state before they become contracts is not "doing business" within the meaning of this section).

These exclusions reflect the provisions of the United States Constitution that grant to the United States Congress exclusive power over interstate commerce, and preclude states from imposing restrictions or conditions upon this commerce. This subsection should be construed in a manner consistent with judicial decisions under the United States Constitution. Under those decisions, a foreign entity is not required to register even though it sells goods within the state if they are shipped to the purchasers in interstate commerce. Thus, a foreign limited partnership need not register even if it also does work and performs acts within the state incidental to the interstate business (*e.g.*, if it takes or enforces a security interest incidental to these transactions). Nor is it required to register merely because it sends traveling salespeople or solicitors into a state so long as contracts are not made within the state. Similarly, an office may be maintained by a foreign limited partnership in this state without registering if the office's functions relate solely to interstate commerce. Purchases of goods may of course be in interstate commerce as readily as sales. Thus, the purchase of personal property in this state by a foreign limited partnership for shipment in interstate commerce out of the state does not require the entity to register.

§ 1006. Noncomplying Name of Foreign Limited Partnership

(a)   A foreign limited partnership whose name does not comply with Section 114 may not register to do business in this state until it adopts, for the purpose of doing business in this state, an alternate name that complies with Section 114. A partnership that registers under an alternate name under this subsection need not comply with [this state's assumed or fictitious name statute]. After registering to do business in this state with an alternate name, a partnership shall do business in this state under:

(1)   the alternate name;

(2)   the partnership's name, with the addition of its jurisdiction of formation; or

(3)   a name the partnership is authorized to use under [this state's assumed or fictitious name statute].

(b)   If a registered foreign limited partnership changes its name to one that does not comply with Section 114, it may not do business in this state until it complies with subsection (a) by amending its registration to adopt an alternate name that complies with Section 114.

COMMENT

A foreign limited partnership must register under its true name if that name satisfies the requirements of Section 114. If the true name unavailable because it is not distinguishable upon the records of the filing office from a name already in use or reserved or registered, the foreign limited partnership may use an alternate name.

A foreign limited partnership that registers to do business in the state may do business under a fictitious name to the same extent as a domestic entity.

§ 1007. Withdrawal Deemed on Conversion to Domestic Filing Entity or Domestic Limited Liability Partnership

A registered foreign limited partnership that converts to a domestic limited liability partnership or to a domestic entity whose formation requires delivery of a record to the [Secretary of State] for filing is deemed to have withdrawn its registration on the effective date of the conversion.

COMMENT

When a registered foreign limited partnership has converted to a domestic "filing entity" or domestic limited liability partnership, information about the entity in its capacity as a domestic entity will continue to be of record in the office of the filing office. At that point, there is no further reason for the entity to be registered as a foreign limited partnership, and this section automatically treats its prior registration as withdrawn.

§ 1008. Withdrawal on Dissolution or Conversion to Nonfiling Entity Other than Limited Liability Partnership

(a)   A registered foreign limited partnership that has dissolved and completed winding up or has converted to a domestic or foreign entity whose formation does not require the public filing of a record, other than a limited liability partnership, shall deliver a statement of withdrawal to the [Secretary of State] for filing. The statement must state:

(1)   in the case of a partnership that has completed winding up:

(A)   its name and jurisdiction of formation;

(B)   that the partnership surrenders its registration to do business in this state; and

(2)   in the case of a partnership that has converted:

(A)   the name of the converting partnership and its jurisdiction of formation;

(B)   the type of entity to which the partnership has converted and its jurisdiction of formation;

(C)   that the converted entity surrenders the converting partnership's registration to do business in this state and revokes the authority of the converting partnership's registered agent to act as registered agent in this state on behalf of the partnership or the converted entity; and

(D)   a mailing address to which service of process may be made under subsection (b).

(b)   After a withdrawal under this section has become effective, service of process in any action or proceeding based on a cause of action arising during the time the foreign limited partnership was registered to do business in this state may be made pursuant to Section 121.

COMMENT

When a registered foreign limited partnership has dissolved and completed winding up, or has converted to a "nonfiling entity" other than a limited liability partnership, there is no further reason for information about the entity to appear in the records of the filing office. This section thus requires delivery of a statement of withdrawal for the purpose of removing the foreign limited partnership from the rolls of registered foreign entities.

Subsection (a)—The exclusion of limited liability partnerships from this provision is merely technical; Section 1007 covers conversion to a domestic LLP.

§ 1009.   Transfer of Registration

(a)   When a registered foreign limited partnership has merged into a foreign entity that is not registered to do business in this state or has converted to a foreign entity required to register with the [Secretary of State] to do business in this state, the foreign entity shall deliver to the [Secretary of State] for filing an application for transfer of registration. The application must state:

(1)   the name of the registered foreign limited partnership before the merger or conversion;

(2)   that before the merger or conversion the registration pertained to a foreign limited partnership;

(3)   the name of the applicant foreign entity into which the foreign limited partnership has merged or to which it has been converted and, if the name does not comply with Section 114, an alternate name adopted pursuant to Section 1006(a);

(4)   the type of entity of the applicant foreign entity and its jurisdiction of formation;

(5)   the street and mailing addresses of the principal office of the applicant foreign entity and, if the law of the entity's jurisdiction of formation requires the entity to maintain an office in that jurisdiction, the street and mailing addresses of that office; and

(6)   the name and street and mailing addresses of the applicant foreign entity's registered agent in this state.

(b)   When an application for transfer of registration takes effect, the registration of the foreign limited partnership to do business in this state is transferred without interruption to the foreign entity into which the partnership has merged or to which it has been converted.

COMMENT

The purpose of this section is to clarify the status of the foreign limited partnership in the public records of the state. A filing under this section has the two-fold effect of canceling the authority of the foreign limited partnership to do business in the state while at the same time reregistering the former foreign limited partnership as the new type of foreign entity. If the reregistered foreign entity subsequently wishes to cancel its registration to do business in the state, it may do so under the statute of this state pertaining the registration of the new type of foreign entity.

§ 1010.   Termination of Registration

(a)   The [Secretary of State] may terminate the registration of a registered foreign limited partnership in the manner provided in subsections (b) and (c) if the partnership does not:

(1)   pay, not later than [60] days after the due date, any fee, tax, interest, or penalty required to be paid to the [Secretary of State] under this [act] or law other than this [act];

(2)   deliver to the [Secretary of State] for filing, not later than [60] days after the due date, [an annual] [a biennial] report required under Section 212;

(3)   have a registered agent as required by Section 117; or

(4)   deliver to the [Secretary of State] for filing a statement of a change under Section 118 not later than [30] days after a change has occurred in the name or address of the registered agent.

(b)   The [Secretary of State] may terminate the registration of a registered foreign limited partnership by:

(1)   filing a notice of termination or noting the termination in the records of the [Secretary of State]; and

(2)   delivering a copy of the notice or the information in the notation to the partnership's registered agent or, if the partnership does not have a registered agent, to the partnership's principal office.

(c)   The notice must state or the information in the notation must include:

(1)   the effective date of the termination, which must be at least [60] days after the date the [Secretary of State] delivers the copy; and

(2)   the grounds for termination under subsection (a).

(d)   The authority of the registered foreign limited partnership to do business in this state ceases on the effective date of the notice of termination or notation under subsection (b), unless before that date the partnership cures each ground for termination stated in the notice or notation. If the partnership cures each ground, the [Secretary of State] shall file a record so stating.

COMMENT

This section is analogous to the procedures for administrative dissolution under Section 811.

§ 1011.   Withdrawal of Registration of Registered Foreign Limited Partnership

(a)   A registered foreign limited partnership may withdraw its registration by delivering a statement of withdrawal to the [Secretary of State] for filing. The statement of withdrawal must state:

(1)   the name of the partnership and its jurisdiction of formation;

(2)   that the partnership is not doing business in this state and that it withdraws its registration to do business in this state;

1017

(3)   that the partnership revokes the authority of its registered agent to accept service on its behalf in this state; and

(4)   an address to which service of process may be made under subsection (b).

(b)   After the withdrawal of the registration of a foreign limited partnership, service of process in any action or proceeding based on a cause of action arising during the time the partnership was registered to do business in this state may be made pursuant to Section 121.

COMMENT

The statement of withdrawal must set forth an address where service of process may be made on the foreign limited partnership pursuant to Section 121. There is no limit on how long the withdrawn entity must keep that address up to date.

§ 1012.   Action by [Attorney General]

The [Attorney General] may maintain an action to enjoin a foreign limited partnership from doing business in this state in violation of this [article].

COMMENT

The authority stated here has been part of corporate law for more than a century and has been carried over into the law of unincorporated business entities. Nowadays, the authority is rarely if ever invoked in either realm of entity law.

[ARTICLE] 11.   MERGER, INTEREST EXCHANGE, CONVERSION, AND DOMESTICATION

INTRODUCTORY COMMENT

This article deals comprehensively with both same-type and cross-type mergers and interest exchanges and with conversions and domestications. For this article to apply, at least one participant organization must be a domestic limited partnership. For a foreign organization to be involved, its organic law must permit the organization's participation.

Part 1 contains definitions specific to this article as well as provisions applicable to all transactions authorized by this article.

Part 2 governs mergers and is an amalgamation of existing entity law, both unincorporated and incorporated.

Part 3 governs interest exchanges, previously a feature only of corporate law. Part 3 is derived from the share exchange provisions in chapter 11 of the Model Business Corporation Act.

Part 4 governs conversions, a one-step procedure by which an entity changes from one type of entity to another type while nonetheless continuing in existence as the same legal entity.

Part 5 governs domestications, a procedure by a domestic limited partnership can become a foreign limited partnership or vice versa, in each instance with the company remaining the same legal entity.

Part 2 sets the paradigm for Parts 3, 4, and 5, because mergers are long established, and merger rules and concepts are familiar to business lawyers. Moreover, conversions and domestications could formerly be accomplished via mergers (with a new entity), and an interest exchange produces the same result as a triangular merger. The comments to Part 2 are thus relevant to understanding Parts 3, 4, and 5. This article contemplates transactions in which the surviving entity is neither a filing entity nor otherwise of record in the filing office (*e.g.*, the merger of a limited partnership into a non-LLP general partnership). As a result, a filing under this article may be the first time that a filing office takes cognizance of an entity's existence.

[PART] 1. GENERAL PROVISIONS

§ 1101. Definitions

In this [article]:

(1) "Acquired entity" means the entity, all of one or more classes or series of interests of which are acquired in an interest exchange.

(2) "Acquiring entity" means the entity that acquires all of one or more classes or series of interests of the acquired entity in an interest exchange.

(3) "Conversion" means a transaction authorized by [Part] 4.

(4) "Converted entity" means the converting entity as it continues in existence after a conversion.

(5) "Converting entity" means the domestic entity that approves a plan of conversion pursuant to Section 1143 or the foreign entity that approves a conversion pursuant to the law of its jurisdiction of formation.

(6) "Distributional interest" means the right under an unincorporated entity's organic law and organic rules to receive distributions from the entity.

(7) "Domestic", with respect to an entity, means governed as to its internal affairs by the law of this state.

(8) "Domesticated limited partnership" means the domesticating limited partnership as it continues in existence after a domestication.

(9) "Domesticating limited partnership" means the domestic limited partnership that approves a plan of domestication pursuant to Section 1153 or the foreign limited partnership that approves a domestication pursuant to the law of its jurisdiction of formation.

(10) "Domestication" means a transaction authorized by [Part] 5.

(11) "Entity":

    (A) means:

        (i) a business corporation;

        (ii) a nonprofit corporation;

        (iii) a general partnership, including a limited liability partnership;

        (iv) a limited partnership, including a limited liability limited partnership;

        (v) a limited liability company;

        [(vi) a general cooperative association;]

        (vii) a limited cooperative association;

        (viii) an unincorporated nonprofit association;

        (ix) a statutory trust, business trust, or common-law business trust; or

        (x) any other person that has:

            (I) a legal existence separate from any interest holder of that person; or

            (II) the power to acquire an interest in real property in its own name; and

    (B) does not include:

        (i) an individual;

        (ii) a trust with a predominantly donative purpose or a charitable trust;

        (iii) an association or relationship that is not an entity listed in subparagraph A and is not a partnership under the rules stated in [Section 202(c) of the Uniform Partnership Act (1997)

(Lasted Amended 2013)] [Section 7 of the Uniform Partnership Act (1914)] or a similar provision of the law of another jurisdiction;

    (iv) a decedent's estate; or

    (v) a government or a governmental subdivision, agency, or instrumentality.

(12) "Filing entity" means an entity whose formation requires the filing of a public organic record. The term does not include a limited liability partnership.

(13) "Foreign", with respect to an entity, means an entity governed as to its internal affairs by the law of a jurisdiction other than this state.

(14) "Governance interest" means a right under the organic law or organic rules of an unincorporated entity, other than as a governor, agent, assignee, or proxy, to:

    (A) receive or demand access to information concerning, or the books and records of, the entity;

    (B) vote for or consent to the election of the governors of the entity; or

    (C) receive notice of or vote on or consent to an issue involving the internal affairs of the entity.

(15) "Governor" means:

    (A) a director of a business corporation;

    (B) a director or trustee of a nonprofit corporation;

    (C) a general partner of a general partnership;

    (D) a general partner of a limited partnership;

    (E) a manager of a manager-managed limited liability company;

    (F) a member of a member-managed limited liability company;

    [(G) a director of a general cooperative association;]

    (H) a director of a limited cooperative association;

    (I) a manager of an unincorporated nonprofit association;

    (J) a trustee of a statutory trust, business trust, or common-law business trust; or

    (K) any other person under whose authority the powers of an entity are exercised and under whose direction the activities and affairs of the entity are managed pursuant to the organic law and organic rules of the entity.

(16) "Interest" means:

    (A) a share in a business corporation;

    (B) a membership in a nonprofit corporation;

    (C) a partnership interest in a general partnership;

    (D) a partnership interest in a limited partnership;

    (E) a membership interest in a limited liability company;

    [(F) a share in a general cooperative association;]

    (G) a member's interest in a limited cooperative association;

    (H) a membership in an unincorporated nonprofit association;

    (I) a beneficial interest in a statutory trust, business trust, or common-law business trust; or

    (J) a governance interest or distributional interest in any other type of unincorporated entity.

(17) "Interest exchange" means a transaction authorized by [Part] 3.

(18) "Interest holder" means:

(A) a shareholder of a business corporation;

(B) a member of a nonprofit corporation;

(C) a general partner of a general partnership;

(D) a general partner of a limited partnership;

(E) a limited partner of a limited partnership;

(F) a member of a limited liability company;

[(G) a shareholder of a general cooperative association;]

(H) a member of a limited cooperative association;

(I) a member of an unincorporated nonprofit association;

(J) a beneficiary or beneficial owner of a statutory trust, business trust, or common-law business trust; or

(K) any other direct holder of an interest.

(19) "Interest holder liability" means:

(A) personal liability for a liability of an entity which is imposed on a person:

(i) solely by reason of the status of the person as an interest holder; or

(ii) by the organic rules of the entity which make one or more specified interest holders or categories of interest holders liable in their capacity as interest holders for all or specified liabilities of the entity; or

(B) an obligation of an interest holder under the organic rules of an entity to contribute to the entity.

(20) "Merger" means a transaction authorized by [Part] 2.

(21) "Merging entity" means an entity that is a party to a merger and exists immediately before the merger becomes effective.

(22) "Organic law" means the law of an entity's jurisdiction of formation governing the internal affairs of the entity.

(23) "Organic rules" means the public organic record and private organic rules of an entity.

(24) "Plan" means a plan of merger, plan of interest exchange, plan of conversion, or plan of domestication.

(25) "Plan of conversion" means a plan under Section 1142.

(26) "Plan of domestication" means a plan under Section 1152.

(27) "Plan of interest exchange" means a plan under Section 1132.

(28) "Plan of merger" means a plan under Section 1122.

(29) "Private organic rules" means the rules, whether or not in a record, that govern the internal affairs of an entity, are binding on all its interest holders, and are not part of its public organic record, if any. The term includes:

(A) the bylaws of a business corporation;

(B) the bylaws of a nonprofit corporation;

(C) the partnership agreement of a general partnership;

(D) the partnership agreement of a limited partnership;

(E) the operating agreement of a limited liability company;

[(F) the bylaws of a general cooperative association;]

(G) the bylaws of a limited cooperative association;

(H) the governing principles of an unincorporated nonprofit association; and

(I) the trust instrument of a statutory trust or similar rules of a business trust or a common-law business trust.

(30) "Protected agreement" means:

(A) a record evidencing indebtedness and any related agreement in effect on [the effective date of this [act]];

(B) an agreement that is binding on an entity on [the effective date of this [act]];

(C) the organic rules of an entity in effect on [the effective date of this [act]]; or

(D) an agreement that is binding on any of the governors or interest holders of an entity on [the effective date of this [act]].

(31) "Public organic record" means the record the filing of which by the [Secretary of State] is required to form an entity and any amendment to or restatement of that record. The term includes:

(A) the articles of incorporation of a business corporation;

(B) the articles of incorporation of a nonprofit corporation;

(C) the certificate of limited partnership of a limited partnership;

(D) the certificate of organization of a limited liability company;

[(E) the articles of incorporation of a general cooperative association;]

(F) the articles of organization of a limited cooperative association; and

(G) the certificate of trust of a statutory trust or similar record of a business trust.

(32) "Registered foreign entity" means a foreign entity that is registered to do business in this state pursuant to a record filed by the [Secretary of State].

(33) "Statement of conversion" means a statement under Section 1145.

(34) "Statement of domestication" means a statement under Section 1155.

(35) "Statement of interest exchange" means a statement under Section 1135.

(36) "Statement of merger" means a statement under Section 1125.

(37) "Surviving entity" means the entity that continues in existence after or is created by a merger.

(38) "Type of entity" means a generic form of entity:

(A) recognized at common law; or

(B) formed under an organic law, whether or not some entities formed under that organic law are subject to provisions of that law that create different categories of the form of entity.

COMMENT

This section defines the terms that are used in this article. Many of the definitions describe attributes that are significant in some forms of entity and not in others. For example, the concept of separate "distributional" and "governance" interests are inherent in unincorporated entities but have no counterpart in corporations. In addition, because some statutes use different terms to describe the same transaction, the definitions are intended to be broad enough to encompass those similar transactions, regardless of how described. *See, e.g.,* Paragraph 10 (defining domestication).

"Acquired entity" [(1)]—This definition recognizes that an interest exchange may involve only the acquisition of a particular "class" or "series" of interests in an entity. Model Business Corporation Act section 6.01 does not expressly define "classes" or "series." Because the interests of members in an unincorporated business organization often tend to be distinctive, it may be that each member's interest will comprise a separate class or series. For an explanation of a new and different meaning of the word "series," see Section 1131, introductory comment. The term "acquired entity" does not encompass series under that new meaning.

"Acquiring entity" [(2)]—An "acquiring entity" is an entity that acquires the interests of the acquired entity in an interest exchange governed by Part 3 of this article.

"Conversion" [(3)]—The term "conversion" means a transaction authorized by Part 4 pursuant to which an entity of one type is converted into an entity of another type. As used in this act, the term "conversion" does not include a transaction in which an entity changes the jurisdiction in which it is organized but does not change to a different form of entity; that type of transaction is referred to in this act as a "domestication" and is governed by Part 5.

"Converted entity" [(4)]—This term is used in Part 4 to describe the entity that results from a conversion.

"Converting entity" [(5)]—A converting entity is the entity that becomes the converted entity under Part 4.

"Distributional interest" [(6)]—This term is similar to the concept of a "transferable interest" found in this act and the organic laws of several other types of unincorporated entities, but has a broader meaning because the scope of this act includes entities in addition to those whose organic law uses the term "transferable interest."

"Domestic" [(7)]—The term "domestic", when used in this article with respect to an entity, refers to an entity whose internal affairs are governed by the organic laws of this state. Except in the case of general partnerships and unincorporated nonprofit associations, this will mean an entity that is formed, organized, or incorporated under domestic law. In the case of a general partnership organized under UPA (1997) (Last Amended 2013), the term will mean a general partnership whose governing law under UPA (1997) § 104 is the law of the adopting state. Under that section, the governing law is determined by the location of the partnership's principal office, except for limited liability partnerships whose governing law is the law of the state where the LLP's statement of qualification is filed. It is a factual question whether the activities and organization of an unincorporated nonprofit association make it a domestic or foreign entity.

"Domesticated limited partnership" [(8)]—This term is used in Part 5 and means the entity that is domesticated pursuant to Part 5. By the nature of the transaction, the domesticated entity will be of the same type as the domesticating entity (*i.e.*, a limited partnership).

"Domesticating limited partnership" [(9)]—This term is used in Part 5 and means the entity that is domesticated pursuant to Part 5.

"Domestication" [(10)]—The term "domestication" means a transaction of the kind authorized by Part 5 pursuant to which an entity may change its *jurisdiction* of formation *but not its type* so long as the laws of the foreign jurisdiction permit the domestication. The legal effect of the domestication of a limited partnership out of this state will be governed by the laws of both this state and the foreign jurisdiction. Some statutes include what is described in this act as "domestication" in their definition of a "conversion." *See, e.g.*, COLO. REV. STAT. § 7–90–201. It is intended that the domestication provisions of this act will apply to a transaction that may be characterized under another act as a "conversion" if the transaction meets the definition of "domestication" under this act.

"Entity" [(11)]—This definition determines the overall scope of the act because only an "entity" may participate in the transactions authorized by Parts 2 (mergers), 3 (interest exchanges), 4 (conversions), and 5 (domestications). *See* Sections 1121 (authorization of mergers), 1131(authorization of interest exchanges), 1141(authorization of conversions), 1151(authorization of domestications).

Subparagraph (A)(x) is a "catch-all" provision that includes within the definition of "entity" any type of organization recognized under the law of this state, which is not listed specifically in the preceding paragraphs of this definition. Subparagraph (A)(x) is intended to include all forms of private organizations, regardless of whether organized for profit, and artificial legal persons other than those excluded by Subparagraph (B). This definition does not exclude regulated entities such as public utilities, banks, and insurance companies. Should a state desire to exclude certain types of regulated entities or any of the entities listed in Subparagraph (A)(i)–(x) from participating in transactions permitted by this act for policy reasons, that may be done by listing those types of entities in Section 1107(a), or by permitting those type of entities to engage in transactions under this act generally but prohibiting certain types of transactions by listing those transactions in Section 1107(b).

Unincorporated nonprofit associations are treated as a type of entity in Subparagraph (A)(viii) because section 5 of the Uniform Unincorporated Nonprofit Association Act (2008) (Last Amended 2013) specifically states that an unincorporated nonprofit association is an entity. In many states, the status of a nonprofit association may not be clear. Nevertheless, in most states a nonprofit association has the power to acquire an interest in real property in its own name and therefore would qualify as an "entity" under Subparagraph (A)(x). See Section 6 of the UUNAA, which gives an unincorporated nonprofit association the power to acquire in its own name an interest in real property.

Subparagraph (B)(i) of this definition excludes a sole proprietorship from the concept of an "entity."

Trusts with a predominately donative purpose, such as inter vivos and testamentary trusts and charitable trusts, are treated in many states as having a separate legal existence, but they have been excluded from the definition of "entity" (and thus are not within the scope of this article) under Subparagraph (B)(ii) because they should not be able to engage in transactions under this act as a matter of public policy. Trusts that carry on a business, however, such as business and statutory entity trusts, are "entities." *See* Subparagraph (A)(ix).

Subparagraph (B)(iii) of this definition excludes from the concept of an "entity" any form of co-ownership of property or sharing of returns from property that is not listed in Subparagraph (A) and is not a partnership under UPA (1997). In that connection, Section 202(c) of that act provides in part:

In determining whether a partnership is formed, the following rules apply:

(1)   Joint tenancy, tenancy in common, tenancy by the entireties, joint property, common property, or part ownership does not by itself establish a partnership, even if the co-owners share profits made by the use of the property.

(2)   The sharing of gross returns does not by itself establish a partnership, even if the persons sharing them have a joint or common right or interest in property from which the returns are derived.

Limited liability partnerships and limited liability limited partnerships are "entities" because they are general partnerships and limited partnerships respectively that have made the additional required election claiming LLP or LLLP status. A limited liability partnership is not, therefore, a separate type of entity from the underlying general or limited partnership that has elected limited liability partnership status. Thus, for example, the election of a general partnership to become a limited liability partnership is not a conversion subject to Article 4.

Under Subparagraph (B)(iv), decedent's estates are excluded from the definition of an entity for the same policy reason as trusts with a predominately donative purpose and charitable trusts.

This same public policy rationale is the justification for the exclusion of governmental subdivisions, agencies, or instrumentalities in Subparagraph (B)(v).

"Filing entity" [(12)]—Whether an entity is a filing entity is determined by reference to whether its legal existence requires the filing of a document with the state filing officer. To fit within this definition, the filing must be necessary but need not be sufficient to form the entity. *See, e.g.*, Section 201(d) ("A limited partnership is formed when the certificate of limited partnership becomes effective [*and*] at least two persons have become partners," one of them becoming a general partner and the other a limited partner) (emphasis added); ULLCA (2006) (Last Amended) § 201(d).

While the statute refers to the "formation" of an entity, the term is intended to encompass corporations that are "incorporated," as well as other filing entities whose statutes refer to them as being "organized." Business trusts present a special problem. In some states, a business trust could be a filing entity or a common law relationship, while in other states business trusts are only recognized at common law. A statutory trust entity formed under the Uniform Statutory Trust Entity Act (2009) (Last Amended 2013) section 201(a) is a filing entity, because a statutory trust entity is formed by the filing office filing a certificate of trust pertaining to the entity.

The term "filing entity" does not include a limited liability partnership because, while a filed document is a precondition to LLP status, that document (a statement of qualification under UPA (1997) (Last Amended 2013) § 901) does not form the underlying entity. A limited liability limited partnership, on the other hand, is a filing entity because the underlying limited partnership is formed by filing a certificate of limited partnership. ULPA (2001) (Last Amended 2013) § 201(a).

"Foreign" [(13)]—The term "foreign entity" includes any non-domestic entity of any type. Where a foreign entity is a filing entity, the entity is governed by the laws of the state of filing. A nonfiling foreign entity is governed by the laws governing its internal affairs. It is a factual question whether a general partnership whose internal affairs are governed by UPA (1914) is a domestic or foreign partnership. A UPA (1914) partnership will likely be deemed to be a domestic entity where the greatest nexus of contacts are found. The domestic or foreign characterization of partnerships under the UPA (1997) (Last Amended 2013) that have not become limited liability partnerships will be governed by Section 104(2) ("the law of the jurisdiction in which the partnership has its principal office") or the partnership agreement. (Section 104(2) is a default rule.)

"Governance interest" [(14)]—A governance interest is typically only part of the interest that a person will hold in an unincorporated entity and is usually coupled with a distributional interest (or economic rights). Memberships in some nonprofit corporations and unincorporated nonprofit associations consist solely of governance interests and memberships in other nonprofit entities may not include either governance interests or distributional interests. In some unincorporated business entities, including partnerships, there is a more limited right to transfer governance interests than there is to transfer distributional interests. An interest holder in such an unincorporated business entity who transfers only a distributional interest and retains the governance interest will also retain the status of an interest holder. Whether a transferee who acquires only a distributional interest will acquire the status of an interest holder is determined by the definition of "interest holder."

Governors of an entity have the kinds of rights listed in the definition of "governance interest" by reason of their position with the entity. For a governor to have a "governance interest," however, requires that the governor also have those rights for a reason other than the governor's status as such. A manager who is not a member in a limited liability company, for example, will not have a governance interest, but a manager who is a member will have a governance interest arising from the ownership of a membership interest.

"Governor" [(15)]—This term has been chosen to provide a way of referring to a person who has the authority under an entity's organic law to make management decisions regarding the entity that is different from any of the existing terms used in connection with particular types of entities. Depending on the type of entity or its organic rules, the governors of an entity may have the power to act on their own authority, or they may be organized as a board or similar group and only have the power to act collectively, and then only through a designated agent. In other words, a person having only the power to bind the organization pursuant to the instruction of the governors is not a governor. Under the organic rules, particularly those of unincorporated entities, most or all of the management decisions may be reserved to the members or partners. Thus, if a manager of a limited liability company were limited to having authority to execute management decisions made by the members and did not have any authority to make independent management decisions, the manager would not be a governor under this definition.

"Interest" [(16)]—In the usual case, the interest held by an interest holder will include both a governance interest and a distributional interest. Members in nonprofit corporations or unincorporated nonprofit associations generally do not have any distributional interest because they do not receive distributions, but they nonetheless may hold a governance interest in which case they would have the status of interest holders under this article.

"Interest exchange" [(17)]—The term "interest exchange" means a transaction authorized by Part 3 pursuant to which an entity may acquire interests in another entity. The consideration that may be provided to the interest holders whose interests are being acquired in an exchange may consist in whole or part of interests in a third party that is not one of the two parties to the exchange itself. *See* Section 1131(a).

"Interest holder" [(18)]—This act does not refer to "equity" interests or "equity" owners or holders because the term "equity" could be confusing in the case of a nonprofit entity whose members do not have an interest in the assets or results of operations of the entity but have only a right to vote on its internal affairs.

"Interest holder liability" [(19)]—This term is used to describe the vicarious liability of an interest holder, by virtue of being an interest holder, for liabilities of the entity. The term includes only personal liability of an interest holder for a debt of the entity imposed on the interest holder either by statute or by the organic rules to the extent authorized pursuant to the organic law. Liabilities that an interest holder incurs in any other fashion are not interest holder liabilities for purposes of this act. Thus, for example, if a state's business corporation law makes shareholders personally liable for unpaid wages because of their status as shareholders, that liability would be an "interest holder liability." If, on the other hand, a shareholder were to guarantee payment of an obligation of a corporation, that liability would not be an "interest holder liability" because it is a direct liability and not based on the status of being a shareholder. Similarly, the liability to return an improper distribution is not an interest holder liability because it is a direct liability of the interest holder based on receipt of the distribution.

"Merger" [(20)]—The term means a transaction in which two or more entities are combined into a single entity pursuant to a filing with the filing office. The term "merger" in this act includes the transaction known as a consolidation in which a new entity results from the combination of two or more pre-existing entities.

"Merging entity" [(21)]—The term "merging entity" refers to each entity that is in existence immediately before a merger and is a party to the merger. It will include the surviving entity if the surviving entity exists before the merger becomes effective. It does not include an entity that provides consideration to be received by interest holders if that entity is not a party to the merger.

"**Organic law**" **[(22)]**—Organic law means statutes that govern the internal affairs of an entity. For example, this act is the organic law of a limited partnership formed under this act.

Entity laws in a few states purport to require that some of their internal governance rules applicable to a domestic entity also apply to a foreign entity with significant ties to the state. *See, e.g.*, CAL. CORP. CODE § 2115 (Foreign Corporations); N.Y. NOT-FOR-PROFIT CORP. §§ 1318–21 (Liabilities of Directors and Officers of Foreign Corporations); 15 PA. CONS. STAT. § 6145 (Applicability of Certain Safeguards to Foreign Corporations). Such a "sticky fingers" law is not included within the definition of "organic law" for purposes of this act because those laws are not part of the law of the entity's jurisdiction of formation.

"**Organic rules**" **[(23)]**—The term "organic rules" means an entity's public organic record and the private organic rules. The organic rules, together with this act, the organic law, and the common law, provide the rules governing the internal affairs of the entity. For example, this act and the partnership agreement comprise the organic rules of a limited partnership formed under this act.

"**Plan**" **[(24)]**—The term "plan" is a short-hand way of referring to the plan of merger, interest exchange, conversion, or domestication, as the case may be, depending on which form of transaction is taking place. *See* Sections 1122 (plan of merger), 1132 (plan of interest exchange), 1142 (plan of conversion), 1152 (plan of domestication).

"**Private organic rules**" **[(29)]**—The term private "organic rules" is intended to include all governing rules of an entity that are binding on all of its interest holders, whether or not in record form, except for the provisions of the entity's public organic record, if any. The term is intended to include agreements in "record" form such as corporate bylaws, as well as oral partnership agreements and oral operating agreements among LLC members.

"**Protected agreement**" **[(30)]**—The term "protected agreement" refers to evidences of indebtedness and agreements binding on the entity or any of its governors or interest holders that are unpaid or executory in whole or in part on the effective date of the act. Thus, a revolving line of credit from a bank to a corporation would constitute a protected agreement even if advances were not made until after the effective date of the act. Likewise, a partnership agreement in effect under this act or a predecessor to this act is a "protected agreement."

If a protected agreement has provisions that apply if an entity merges, those provisions will apply if the entity enters into an interest exchange, conversion, or domestication even though the agreement does not mention those other types of transactions. *See* Sections 1131(c) (interest exchange), 1141(c) (conversion), 1151(c) (domestication).

"**Public organic record**" **[(31)]**—A "public organic record" is a record that is filed publicly to form, organize, incorporate, or otherwise create an entity. The term does not include a statement of authority filed under UPA (1997) (Last Amended 2013) § 303 or any of the other statements that may be filed under that act since those statements do not create a new entity. The same is true for statements filed under this act.

For the same reason, a statement of qualification filed under UPA (1997) (Last Amended 2013) § 1001 is not a "public organic record." The limited liability partnership that results from the filing is the same entity as the partnership that delivered the statement to the filing office. Similarly, the term does not include a statement of authority filed under section 7 of the Revised Uniform Unincorporated Nonprofit Association Act (2008) (Last Amended 2013), a statement appointing a registered agent filed under section 31 of that act, or any of the various statements filed under ULLCA (2006) (Last Amended 2013).

In those states where a deed of trust or other instrument is publicly filed to create a business trust, that filing will constitute a public organic record. But in those states where a business trust is not created by a public filing, the deed of trust or similar record will be part of the private organic rules of the business trust.

Where a public organic document has been amended or restated, the term means the public organic document as last amended or restated.

"**Registered foreign entity**" **[(32)]**—This term refers to a foreign entity that is registered to transact business in this state pursuant to a public filing.

"**Surviving entity**" **[(37)]**—The term "surviving entity" refers to either a merging entity that survives the merger or the new entity created by the merger.

"**Type of entity**" **[(38)]**—The term "type of entity" has been developed in an attempt to distinguish different legal forms of entities. It is sometimes difficult to decide whether one is dealing with a different form of entity or a variation of the same form. For example, a limited partnership, although it has long been characterized or even defined as a partnership, is a different type of entity from a general partnership, while a limited liability partnership is not a different type of entity from a general partnership. In some states cooperatives are categories of business corporations or nonprofit corporations, while in other states cooperatives are a separate type of entity.

§ 1102. Relationship of [Article] to Other Laws

(a) This [article] does not authorize an act prohibited by, and does not affect the application or requirements of, law other than this [article].

(b) A transaction effected under this [article] may not create or impair a right, duty, or obligation of a person under the statutory law of this state relating to a change in control, takeover, business combination, control-share acquisition, or similar transaction involving a domestic merging, acquired, converting, or domesticating business corporation unless:

(1) if the corporation does not survive the transaction, the transaction satisfies any requirements of the law; or

(2) if the corporation survives the transaction, the approval of the plan is by a vote of the shareholders or directors which would be sufficient to create or impair the right, duty, or obligation directly under the law.

COMMENT

This section preserves existing regulatory law in an adopting state in general terms. Adopting states should consider more carefully integrating this act with their various regulatory laws. For example, in some states certain professions are limited in their use of limited liability entities. *See* Section 1103.

Laws other than this act that will apply to transactions under the act include, for example, uniform fraudulent transfer and fraudulent conveyance acts, state insolvency statutes, federal bankruptcy law, and Articles 8 and 9 of the Uniform Commercial Code.

Subsection (b)—Many states have enacted "antitakeover" statutes intended to make it more difficult to acquire control of a publicly traded corporation. Those statutes often provide that their application to a particular corporation cannot be changed unless the corporation obtains certain specified approvals, such as a vote of disinterested directors or a supermajority vote by the shareholders. The purpose of the special requirements in this subsection on varying the application of an antitakeover statute is to protect against a hostile acquirer or group of shareholders seeking to use the act to avoid the application of the antitakeover statute.

This subsection protects the application of antitakeover statutes from being affected by a transaction under this act by requiring that the transaction be approved in a manner that would be sufficient to approve changing the application of the antitakeover statute. If a transaction is approved in that manner, there is no policy reason to prohibit the application of the antitakeover statute from being varied by a transaction under this act. If the application of an antitakeover statute cannot be varied by action of an entity subject to it, then a transaction under this act will be permissible only if the antitakeover provision continues to apply after the transaction or the transaction itself is permissible under the antitakeover statute.

§ 1103. Required Notice or Approval

(a) A domestic or foreign entity that is required to give notice to, or obtain the approval of, a governmental agency or officer of this state to be a party to a merger must give the notice or obtain the approval to be a party to an interest exchange, conversion, or domestication.

(b) Property held for a charitable purpose under the law of this state by a domestic or foreign entity immediately before a transaction under this [article] becomes effective may not, as a result of the transaction, be diverted from the objects for which it was donated, granted, devised, or otherwise transferred unless, to the extent required by or pursuant to the law of this state concerning cy pres or other law dealing with nondiversion of charitable assets, the entity obtains an appropriate order of [the appropriate court] [the Attorney General] specifying the disposition of the property.

(c) A bequest, devise, gift, grant, or promise contained in a will or other instrument of donation, subscription, or conveyance which is made to a merging entity that is not the surviving entity and which takes effect or remains payable after the merger inures to the surviving entity.

(d)   A trust obligation that would govern property if transferred to a nonsurviving entity applies to property that is transferred to the surviving entity under this section.

Legislative Note: As an alternative to enacting Subsection (a), a state may identify each of its regulatory laws that requires prior approval for a merger of a regulated entity, decide whether regulatory approval should be required for an interest exchange, conversion, or domestication, and make amendments as appropriate to those laws.

As with Subsection (a), an adopting state may choose to amend its various laws with respect to the nondiversion of charitable property to cover the various transactions authorized by this act as an alternative to enacting Subsection (b).

COMMENT

Subsection (a)—Because at least some of the provisions of this act will be new in most states, it is likely that existing state laws that require regulatory approval of transactions by businesses such as banks, insurance companies, or public utilities may not be worded in a fashion that will include at least some of the transactions authorized by this act. The purpose of this subsection is to ensure that transactions under this act will be subject to the same regulatory approval as mergers. This subsection is based on whether a merger by a regulated entity requires prior approval because the transactions authorized by this act may be effectuated indirectly in many cases under existing law by establishing a wholly owned subsidiary of the desired type and then merging into it.

The consequence of violating this subsection should be the same as in the case of a merger consummated without the required approval.

Subsection (b)—This act applies generally to nonprofit corporations and unincorporated nonprofit associations. As in the case of laws regulating particular industries, a state's laws governing the nondiversion of charitable property to other uses may not cover some of the transactions authorized by this act. To prevent the procedures in this act from being used to avoid restrictions on the use of property held by nonprofit entities, this subsection requires approval of the effect of transactions under this act by the appropriate arm of government having supervision of nonprofit entities.

An approval or order obtained under this section may impose conditions or specify the disposition of assets or liabilities in a manner different than would otherwise be the case. In such an instance, the approval or order will control over the provisions of this act specifying the effects of a transaction. *See* Sections 1126 (effect of merger), 1136 (effect of interest exchange), 1146 (effect of conversion), 1156 (effect of domestication).

Subsection (c)—This subsection clarifies the legal effect of a merger on bequests, etc. that were originally made to an entity that does not survive the merger. This issue does not arise in an interest exchange, conversion, or domestication transaction because the entity to which the bequest, etc. was made survives in some form after the transaction.

§ 1104.   Nonexclusivity

The fact that a transaction under this [article] produces a certain result does not preclude the same result from being accomplished in any other manner permitted by law other than this [article].

COMMENT

This section allows a transaction that has the same end result as one of the transactions governed by this act, but that is accomplished in a manner not within the scope of this act, to be exempt from this act. For example, a sale of assets and transfer of liabilities by two entities to a third entity followed by the liquidation of the two transferring entities can be accomplished pursuant to statutory provisions pertaining to sale of assets rather than under Part 2 of this article, even though the end result of the transaction is essentially the same as if the two entities had merged into a third entity.

§ 1105.   Reference to External Facts

A plan may refer to facts ascertainable outside the plan if the manner in which the facts will operate upon the plan is specified in the plan. The facts may include the occurrence of an event or a determination or action by a person, whether or not the event, determination, or action is within the control of a party to the transaction.

COMMENT

This section is based on, but more concise than, section 1.20(k) of the Model Business Corporation Act.

§ 1106. Appraisal Rights

An interest holder of a domestic merging, acquired, converting, or domesticating limited partnership is entitled to contractual appraisal rights in connection with a transaction under this [article] to the extent provided in:

(1)   the partnership agreement; or

(2)   the plan.

COMMENT

In corporate law, appraisal rights developed when corporate statutes were amended to permit mergers with less than unanimous consent of the shareholders. This article provides no appraisal rights, because, as a default rule, transactions under this article require the consent or affirmative vote of all the partners. Where the limited partnership agreement changes this default rule, parties may wish to consider contractual appraisal rights.

This subsection validates the grant of such contractual appraisal rights. *Cf.* 6 Del. Code §§ 15–120 (general partnerships), 17–212 (limited partnerships), 18–210 (limited liability companies) (validating "contractual appraisal rights"); MBCA § 13.02(5) (permitting the articles of incorporation, bylaws, or a resolution of the board of directors to confer appraisal rights in contexts in which they would otherwise not be available). Legislative authorization in this subsection of the grant of contractual appraisal rights removes any question as to whether a court would have jurisdiction to hear a case in which the parties were attempting to create jurisdiction in the court by private agreement.

In this section, the term "appraisal rights" refers to any arrangement, either in the limited partnership agreement or the plan, providing for the buy-out of partners that object to a

transaction under this article.

[§ 1107. Excluded Entities and Transactions

(a)   The following entities may not participate in a transaction under this [article]:

(1)

(2).

(b)   This [article] may not be used to effect a transaction that:

(1)

(2).]

Legislative Note: Subsection (a) may be used by states that have special statutes restricted to the organization of certain types of entities. A common example is banking statutes that prohibit banks from engaging in transactions other than pursuant to those statutes.

Nonprofit entities may participate in transactions under this act with for-profit entities, subject to compliance with Section 1103. If a state desires, however, to exclude entities with a charitable purpose or to exclude other types of entities from the scope of this act, that may be done by referring to those entities in Subsection (a).

Subsection (b) may be used to exclude certain types of transactions governed by more specific statutes. A common example is the conversion of an insurance company from mutual to stock form. There may be other types of transactions that vary greatly among the states.

[PART] 2.   MERGER

§ 1121.   Merger Authorized

(a)   By complying with this [part]:

(1)   one or more domestic limited partnerships may merge with one or more domestic or foreign entities into a domestic or foreign surviving entity; and

(2)   two or more foreign entities may merge into a domestic limited partnership.

(b)   By complying with the provisions of this [part] applicable to foreign entities, a foreign entity may be a party to a merger under this [part] or may be the surviving entity in such a merger if the merger is authorized by the law of the foreign entity's jurisdiction of formation.

COMMENT

The merger transaction authorized by this act involves the combination of one or more domestic limited partnerships with or into one or more other domestic or foreign entities. It also contemplates the consolidation of two or more foreign entities into a single domestic limited partnership. Upon the effective date of the merger, all the assets and liabilities of the constituent entities vest in the surviving entity as a matter of law. As such, mergers require the existence of

at least two separate entities before the transaction and only one entity may survive the merger. If independent existence of the constituent entities is desired following the conclusion of the transaction, a restructuring transaction other than a merger must be used to accomplish the transfer of assets and liabilities.

This act authorizes a merger for state entity law purposes. Federal law and other state law will independently determine how a merger transaction will be taxed.

Subsection (a)(1)—This paragraph states the general rule that subject to Subsection (b) one or more domestic limited partnerships may merge with or into a domestic or foreign surviving entity.

Subsection (a)(2)—This paragraph provides that two or more foreign entities may merge into a domestic surviving limited partnership so long as the requirements of Subsection (b) are met.

Subsection (b)—This subsection provides that a foreign entity may be a party to a merger or may be the surviving entity in a merger only if the merger is authorized by the laws of the foreign entity's jurisdiction of formation.

§ 1122.   Plan of Merger

(a)   A domestic limited partnership may become a party to a merger under this [part] by approving a plan of merger. The plan must be in a record and contain:

(1)   as to each merging entity, its name, jurisdiction of formation, and type of entity;

(2)   if the surviving entity is to be created in the merger, a statement to that effect and the entity's name, jurisdiction of formation, and type of entity;

(3)   the manner of converting the interests in each party to the merger into interests, securities, obligations, money, other property, rights to acquire interests or securities, or any combination of the foregoing;

(4)   if the surviving entity exists before the merger, any proposed amendments to:

(A)   its public organic record, if any; and

(B)   its private organic rules that are, or are proposed to be, in a record;

(5)   if the surviving entity is to be created in the merger:

(A)   its proposed public organic record, if any; and

(B)   the full text of its private organic rules that are proposed to be in a record;

(6)   the other terms and conditions of the merger; and

(7)   any other provision required by the law of a merging entity's jurisdiction of formation or the organic rules of a merging entity.

(b)   In addition to the requirements of subsection (a), a plan of merger may contain any other provision not prohibited by law.

COMMENT

Subsection (a)—This subsection states the requirements for the plan of merger. They are similar to plan of merger provisions in corporation statutes. *See* MBCA§ 11.02(c). The requirements stated in this subsection are mandatory. *See* Section 105(c)(16).

Subsection (a)(1)—This paragraph requires that the plan of merger identify the parties to the merger. The name of a merging entity as it appears in the plan of merger will be its name in its jurisdiction of formation.

Subsection (a)(3)—The language of this paragraph is similar to Model Business Corporation Act section 11.02(c)(3). What may be done under this paragraph with respect to providing for continuing interests in the surviving entity for some holders of interests of a class or series of a party to the merger while paying some other form of consideration to other holders of the same class or series of interests in that entity will vary depending on the type of entity involved and the extent to which its organic rules provide for non-uniform treatment of interest holders in a manner that is permissible under its organic law. Similarly, the ability to use a merger to reorganize the capital structure of the surviving entity will vary depending on the type of entity involved and whether the entity has appropriately adopted relevant provisions in its organic rules.

If the organic law and organic rules of an unincorporated entity permit a non-uniform "equity shuffle" to be accomplished in a merger involving the unincorporated entity, the minority owners of the unincorporated entity will not necessarily be entitled to the statutory appraisal rights currently afforded to minority stockholders in merging corporate entities. Any perceived unfairness in the shuffle would be addressed either: (i) under principles of fiduciary duties and the contractual obligations of good faith and fair dealing, assuming, of course, that such duties and obligations have not been contractually modified or eliminated to the extent permitted by the applicable organic law; or (ii) by the exercise of whatever rights the minority owners may have to veto the transaction or to withdraw or to dissociate and be paid the value of their interests.

The Model Business Corporation Act generally requires that shares of the same class or series be treated in the same manner in a merger unless the corporation has adopted an applicable provision of its articles of incorporation pursuant to section 6.01(e) of that act providing for variations in the treatment of holders of the same class or series of shares. Thus, a determination of what may be done by way of an equity shuffle in the case of a corporation will require reference to its organic law and organic rules.

The consideration paid to the interest holders of the merging parties may be supplied in whole or part by a person who is not a party to the merger.

Subsection (b)—This subsection provides the statutory authority for a merging party to include a provision in a plan of merger that is not specifically listed in Subsection (a). One such possibility is contractual appraisal rights as provided in Section 1106(2).

§ 1123. Approval of Merger

(a) A plan of merger is not effective unless it has been approved:

(1) by a domestic merging limited partnership, by all the partners of the partnership entitled to vote on or consent to any matter; and

(2) in a record, by each partner of a domestic merging limited partnership which will have interest holder liability for debts, obligations, and other liabilities that are incurred after the merger becomes effective, unless:

(A) the partnership agreement of the partnership provides in a record for the approval of a merger in which some or all of its partners become subject to interest holder liability by the affirmative vote or consent of fewer than all the partners; and

(B) the partner consented in a record to or voted for that provision of the partnership agreement or became a partner after the adoption of that provision.

(b) A merger involving a domestic merging entity that is not a limited partnership is not effective unless the merger is approved by that entity in accordance with its organic law.

(c) A merger involving a foreign merging entity is not effective unless the merger is approved by the foreign entity in accordance with the law of the foreign entity's jurisdiction of formation.

COMMENT

Subsection (a)—In the uniform acts pertaining to unincorporated business organizations, unanimity is the default rule for approving a merger. The limited partnership agreement certainly can change this rule, but care should be taken in doing so. For example, a merger can revise the partnership agreement. Section 1122(a)(4). Thus, if a merger requires less-than-unanimous consent, the partnership agreement is subject to amendment by the same quantum of consent. "Exit rights" also require consideration. This act does not provide appraisal rights, because such rights are inapposite when unanimous consent is required. *See* Section 1106, cmt.

Subsection (a)(2)—This provision is not a default rule, Section 105(c)(16), and deals with the situation in which a partner of a limited partnership that is a party to a merger will have vicarious liability for the liabilities of the surviving entity that are incurred after the merger has become effective. The special approval requirement in Subsection (a)(2) will be applicable; for example, to partners of a limited partnership that merges into a general partnership that is not a limited liability partnership if the partners become general partners of the surviving general partnership.

The consent of a partner required by Subsection (a)(2)(B) may be given either by: (i) signing or agreeing generally to the terms of a partnership agreement that includes the required provision permitting less than unanimous approval of a merger in which partners become subject to "interest holder liability"; or (ii) voting for or consenting to an amendment to the partnership agreement to add such a provision.

Subsection (b)—Where a domestic entity other than a limited partnership is a party to a merger under this act, this subsection defers to that entity's organic law for the requirements for approval of the merger by that entity.

Subsection (c)—Where a foreign entity is a party to a merger under this act, this subsection defers to the laws of the foreign jurisdiction for the requirements for approval of the merger by the foreign entity. Those laws will include the organic law of the foreign entity and other applicable laws. The laws of the foreign jurisdiction will also control the application of any special approval requirements found in the organic rules of the foreign entity.

§ 1124. Amendment or Abandonment of Plan of Merger

(a) A plan of merger may be amended only with the consent of each party to the plan, except as otherwise provided in the plan.

(b) A domestic merging limited partnership may approve an amendment of a plan of merger:

(1) in the same manner as the plan was approved, if the plan does not provide for the manner in which it may be amended; or

(2) by its partners in the manner provided in the plan, but a partner that was entitled to vote on or consent to approval of the merger is entitled to vote on or consent to any amendment of the plan that will change:

(A) the amount or kind of interests, securities, obligations, money, other property, rights to acquire interests or securities, or any combination of the foregoing, to be received by the interest holders of any party to the plan;

(B) the public organic record, if any, or private organic rules of the surviving entity that will be in effect immediately after the merger becomes effective, except for changes that do not require approval of the interest holders of the surviving entity under its organic law or organic rules; or

(C) any other terms or conditions of the plan, if the change would adversely affect the partner in any material respect.

(c) After a plan of merger has been approved and before a statement of merger becomes effective, the plan may be abandoned as provided in the plan. Unless prohibited by the plan, a domestic merging limited partnership may abandon the plan in the same manner as the plan was approved.

(d) If a plan of merger is abandoned after a statement of merger has been delivered to the [Secretary of State] for filing and before the statement becomes effective, a statement of abandonment, signed by a party to the plan, must be delivered to the [Secretary of State] for filing before the statement of merger becomes effective. The statement of abandonment takes effect on filing, and the merger is abandoned and does not become effective. The statement of abandonment must contain:

(1)   the name of each party to the plan of merger;

(2)   the date on which the statement of merger was filed by the [Secretary of State]; and

(3)   a statement that the merger has been abandoned in accordance with this section.

COMMENT

This section sets out the requirements for amending or abandoning the plan of merger. They are similar to provisions for amending or abandoning mergers found in existing corporation merger statutes. *See* MBCA §§ 11.02(e), 11.08.

§ 1125.   Statement of Merger; Effective Date of Merger

(a)   A statement of merger must be signed by each merging entity and delivered to the [Secretary of State] for filing.

(b)   A statement of merger must contain:

(1)   the name, jurisdiction of formation, and type of entity of each merging entity that is not the surviving entity;

(2)   the name, jurisdiction of formation, and type of entity of the surviving entity;

(3)   a statement that the merger was approved by each domestic merging entity, if any, in accordance with this [part] and by each foreign merging entity, if any, in accordance with the law of its jurisdiction of formation;

(4)   if the surviving entity exists before the merger and is a domestic filing entity, any amendment to its public organic record approved as part of the plan of merger;

(5)   if the surviving entity is created by the merger and is a domestic filing entity, its public organic record, as an attachment; and

(6)   if the surviving entity is created by the merger and is a domestic limited liability partnership, its statement of qualification, as an attachment.

(c)   In addition to the requirements of subsection (b), a statement of merger may contain any other provision not prohibited by law.

(d)   If the surviving entity is a domestic entity, its public organic record, if any, must satisfy the requirements of the law of this state, except that the public organic record does not need to be signed.

(e)   A plan of merger that is signed by all the merging entities and meets all the requirements of subsection (b) may be delivered to the [Secretary of State] for filing instead of a statement of merger and on filing has the same effect. If a plan of merger is filed as provided in this subsection, references in this [article] to a statement of merger refer to the plan of merger filed under this subsection.

(f)   If the surviving entity is a domestic limited partnership, the merger becomes effective when the statement of merger is effective. In all other cases, the merger becomes effective on the later of:

(1)   the date and time provided by the organic law of the surviving entity; and

(2)   when the statement is effective.

COMMENT

The filing of a statement of merger makes the transaction a matter of public record.

Subsection (a)—This subsection pertains to all merging entities involved in a merger, not merely any merging domestic limited partnership. Other filings may be required by the organic law of other entities participating in the merger.

Subsection (b)(1) and (2)—The names of foreign entities set forth in the statement of merger will generally be their names in their jurisdiction of formation, except that if a foreign entity has been required to adopt a different name in order to register to do business in this state, the foreign qualification statute will likely require that, when the entity does business in this state, the entity must use the name adopted for the purposes of registering to do business. Engaging in a merger under this act will be part of the business done by the entity in this state and the name of the entity set forth in the statement of merger will thus need to be the name under which the entity has registered to do business. Use of the name under which the entity has registered to do business will allow the records in the filing office to associate the registration of the entity to do business with the statement of merger.

Subsection (b)(3)—*See* Subsection (f), cmt.

Subsection (b)(4)—The statement in this paragraph that the plan of merger was approved by each entity in accordance with this article necessarily presupposes that the plan was approved in accordance with any valid, special requirements in the organic rules of each merging entity.

Subsection (b)(5) and (6)—The public organic record of a domestic surviving entity created by the merger that is attached to the statement of merger becomes the original, officially filed text of the public organic record of the surviving entity when the statement of merger takes effect. It is not necessary, or appropriate, to make any other filing to create the surviving entity.

Similarly, a statement of qualification for a domestic limited liability partnership created by the merger that is attached to the statement of merger does not need to be filed separately.

Subsection (d)—Organic laws typically require that an initial filing that creates an entity be signed by the person serving as the incorporator or other organizer. This subsection, however, provides that the public organic record of the surviving entity does not need to be signed since the record is attached to a signed record.

This subsection also permits the public organic record of the surviving entity to omit any provision that is not required to be included in a restatement of the public organic record. Pursuant to this provision, for example, the public organic record of a business corporation created as the surviving entity in the merger would not need to state the name and address of each incorporator even though that information would be required by section 2.02(a)(4) of the Model Business Corporation Act if the corporation were being incorporated outside the context of the merger.

Subsection (e)—A plan of merger that contains all the information required in the statement of merger may be filed instead of the statement of merger. The plan must be in a record and signed by each merging party.

Subsection (f)—A merger in which the surviving entity is a domestic limited partnership takes effect when the statement of merger takes effect. A merger in which the surviving entity is a foreign entity will usually also take effect when the statement of merger takes effect because the practice is to coordinate the filings that need to be made when a merger involves both a domestic entity and also a foreign entity so that the filings in each jurisdiction take effect at the same time.

However, when the surviving limited partnership is a foreign limited partnership, it is possible that the filing in the foreign jurisdiction will take effect at a different time. For that reason, this subsection provides that the merger will take effect at the later of: (i) when the statement of merger takes effect; and (ii) when the merger takes effect under the law of the foreign jurisdiction. This rule avoids the possibility that the merger will take effect in this state before it takes effect in the foreign jurisdiction, which would produce the undesirable result that the merging domestic limited partnership would cease to appear as an active entity on the records of this state before the records of the foreign jurisdiction reflect a completed merger.

It is only necessary for the filing office to record the effective date of the statement of merger and the filing office does not need to be concerned with the effective date of the merger itself. Persons wishing to determine the effective date of a merger involving both a domestic and a foreign entity will be able to do so by consulting the records of the filing offices in each jurisdiction.

§ 1126. Effect of Merger

(a) When a merger becomes effective:

(1) the surviving entity continues or comes into existence;

(2) each merging entity that is not the surviving entity ceases to exist;

(3)   all property of each merging entity vests in the surviving entity without transfer, reversion, or impairment;

(4)   all debts, obligations, and other liabilities of each merging entity are debts, obligations, and other liabilities of the surviving entity;

(5)   except as otherwise provided by law or the plan of merger, all the rights, privileges, immunities, powers, and purposes of each merging entity vest in the surviving entity;

(6)   if the surviving entity exists before the merger:

(A)   all its property continues to be vested in it without transfer, reversion, or impairment;

(B)   it remains subject to all its debts, obligations, and other liabilities; and

(C)   all its rights, privileges, immunities, powers, and purposes continue to be vested in it;

(7)   the name of the surviving entity may be substituted for the name of any merging entity that is a party to any pending action or proceeding;

(8)   if the surviving entity exists before the merger:

(A)   its public organic record, if any, is amended to the extent provided in the statement of merger; and

(B)   its private organic rules that are to be in a record, if any, are amended to the extent provided in the plan of merger;

(9)   if the surviving entity is created by the merger, its private organic rules become effective and:

(A)   if it is a filing entity, its public organic record becomes effective; and

(B)   if it is a limited liability partnership, its statement of qualification becomes effective; and

(10)   the interests in each merging entity which are to be converted in the merger are converted, and the interest holders of those interests are entitled only to the rights provided to them under the plan of merger and to any appraisal rights they have under Section 1106 and the merging entity's organic law.

(b)   Except as otherwise provided in the organic law or organic rules of a merging entity, the merger does not give rise to any rights that an interest holder, governor, or third party would have upon a dissolution, liquidation, or winding up of the merging entity.

(c)   When a merger becomes effective, a person that did not have interest holder liability with respect to any of the merging entities and becomes subject to interest holder liability with respect to a domestic entity as a result of the merger has interest holder liability only to the extent provided by the organic law of that entity and only for those debts, obligations, and other liabilities that are incurred after the merger becomes effective.

(d)   When a merger becomes effective, the interest holder liability of a person that ceases to hold an interest in a domestic merging limited partnership with respect to which the person had interest holder liability is subject to the following rules:

(1)   The merger does not discharge any interest holder liability under this [act] to the extent the interest holder liability was incurred before the merger became effective.

(2)   The person does not have interest holder liability under this [act] for any debt, obligation, or other liability that is incurred after the merger becomes effective.

(3)   This [act] continues to apply to the release, collection, or discharge of any interest holder liability preserved under paragraph (1) as if the merger had not occurred.

(4)   The person has whatever rights of contribution from any other person as are provided by this [act], law other than this [act], or the partnership agreement of the domestic merging limited

partnership with respect to any interest holder liability preserved under paragraph (1) as if the merger had not occurred.

(e)   When a merger becomes effective, a foreign entity that is the surviving entity may be served with process in this state for the collection and enforcement of any debts, obligations, or other liabilities of a domestic merging limited partnership as provided in Section 121.

(f)   When a merger becomes effective, the registration to do business in this state of any foreign merging entity that is not the surviving entity is canceled.

COMMENT

With the exception of Subsections (c) and (d), this section is similar to statutory provisions on the effect of a merger of a corporation with a corporation. *See* MBCA § 11.07.

Subsection (a)—This subsection states the general understanding that in a merger the assets and liabilities of the merging entities automatically vest in the surviving entity. The surviving entity becomes the owner of all real and personal property of the merged entities and is subject to all debts, obligations, and liabilities of the merging entities. A merger does not constitute a transfer, assignment, or conveyance of any property held by the merging entities before the merger. A merger also does not give rise to a claim that a contract with a merging entity is no longer in effect on the ground of nonassignability, unless the contract specifically provides that it does not survive a merger. The contract rights that are vested in the surviving entity include the right to enforce subscription agreements for interests and obligations to make capital contributions entered into or incurred before the merger. *See* Section 1103(c) (dealing with the surviving entity's rights in trust obligations of a nonsurviving party in a merger and transactions such as bequests made to a nonsurviving party to a merger that take effect after the merger).

After a merger becomes effective, the law of the surviving entity's jurisdiction of formation governs the surviving entity.

Sections 1103(a) and (b)modify the provisions of this section with respect to the effects of a merger to the extent a regulatory law provides otherwise or any of the parties holds property committed to charitable purposes.

Subsection (a)(2)—A merger cannot have the effect of making an interest holder of a domestic merging entity subject to interest holder liability for the debts, obligations, or other liabilities of any other person or entity unless the interest holder has signed a separate written consent to become subject to such liability or previously agreed to the effectuation of a transaction having that effect without the interest holder's consent. The partnership agreement cannot change this provision. Section 105(c)(16).

Subsection (a)(7)—All pending proceedings involving either the survivor or a party whose separate existence ceased as a result of the merger are continued. Under this paragraph, the name of the survivor may be, but need not be, substituted in any pending proceeding for the name of a party to the merger whose separate existence ceased as a result of the merger. The substitution may be made whether the survivor is a complainant or a respondent, and may be made at the instance of either the survivor or an opposing party. Such a substitution has no substantive effect because, whether or not the survivor's name is substituted, the survivor succeeds to the claims, and is subject to the liabilities, of any party to the merger whose separate existence ceased as a result of the merger.

Subsection (a)(8)(B)—The private organic rules of an unincorporated entity typically may be either oral or written. The plan of merger is not required to set forth amendments to oral provisions of the private organic rules of the surviving entity, and thus this provision is limited in scope to amendments to the private organic rules that are to be in a record, if any.

Subsection (a)(10)—*See* Section 1106, cmts.

Subsections (c) and (d)—These subsections set forth rules for two circumstances that typically do not exist in a merger where all the entities involved are corporations. Subsection (c) deals with the situation where an interest holder that does not have vicarious liability for the obligations of a merging entity before the merger has interest holder liability after the merger. An example would be a corporate shareholder who agrees to be the general partner in a limited partnership that is the surviving entity in a merger between a corporation and a limited partnership that is not a limited liability limited partnership. Subsection (d) deals with the situation where an interest holder has vicarious liability for the obligations of one of the merging parties before the merger but ceases to have any interest holder liability for the obligations of the surviving entity after the merger has become effective. An example would be a general partner in a general partnership that merges into a corporation.

The effects of Subsections (c) and (d) will depend on when a liability is incurred, which is determined by other law. For a discussion of the issue, see Section 404(c), cmt. (The Temporal Nexus—When Claim Incurred).

These subsections apply not only to merging domestic limited partnerships but also to any other domestic entity involved in the merger.

Subsection (c)—This subsection sets forth the general rule that an interest holder that was not liable for the liabilities of a merging entity before the merger but will have personal liability for the obligations of the surviving entity after the merger will be personally liable only for the liabilities of a domestic surviving entity that are incurred after the effective date of a merger.

Subsection (d)—This subsection provides four rules with respect to an interest holder who ceases to have interest holder liability after the effective date of the merger:

(1)   the interest holder remains personally liable for any obligations that were incurred before the effective date of the merger;

(2)   the interest holder does not have any personal liability for obligations of the surviving entity;

(3)   the pre-existing personal liability of the interest holder is enforced against the interest holder on the same basis as if the merger had not taken place; and

(4)   the interest holder has the same rights of contribution from other interest holders of the merging entity as the interest holder would have had if the merger had not occurred.

See Section 1146(d), cmt.

Subsection (e)—When a merger becomes effective, this subsection provides that a foreign entity that is the surviving entity may be served with process in this state. The proceedings covered by this subsection include a proceeding to enforce the rights of any interest holders of each domestic merging entity who are entitled to and exercise appraisal rights. One of the liabilities that a foreign surviving entity succeeds to is the obligation of a merging entity to pay the amount, if any, to which its interest holders who assert appraisal rights are entitled.

[PART] 3.   INTEREST EXCHANGE

§ 1131.   Interest Exchange Authorized

(a)   By complying with this [part]:

(1)   a domestic limited partnership may acquire all of one or more classes or series of interests of another domestic entity or a foreign entity in exchange for interests, securities, obligations, money, other property, rights to acquire interests or securities, or any combination of the foregoing; or

(2)   all of one or more classes or series of interests of a domestic limited partnership may be acquired by another domestic entity or a foreign entity in exchange for interests, securities, obligations, money, other property, rights to acquire interests or securities, or any combination of the foregoing.

(b)   By complying with the provisions of this [part] applicable to foreign entities, a foreign entity may be the acquiring or acquired entity in an interest exchange under this [part] if the interest exchange is authorized by the law of the foreign entity's jurisdiction of formation.

(c)   If a protected agreement contains a provision that applies to a merger of a domestic limited partnership but does not refer to an interest exchange, the provision applies to an interest exchange in which the domestic limited partnership is the acquired entity as if the interest exchange were a merger until the provision is amended after [the effective date of this [act]].

COMMENT

An interest exchange is the same type of transaction as the share exchange provided for in section 11.03 of the Model Business Corporation Act. The effect of an interest exchange is that: (i) the separate existence of the acquired entity is not affected; and (ii) the acquiring entity acquires all of the interests of one or more classes of the acquired entity. An interest exchange also allows an indirect acquisition through the use of consideration in the exchange that is not provided by the acquiring entity (*e.g.*, consideration from another or related entity).

Neither share exchanges nor interest exchanges are universally recognized in either corporation or unincorporated entity laws. The effect of an interest exchange can be achieved through a triangular merger in which the acquiring entity forms a new subsidiary and the acquired entity is then merged into the new subsidiary. Part 3 allows the interest exchange to be accomplished directly in a single step, rather than indirectly through the triangular merger route.

The "series" referenced in Subsection (a) are not the series contemplated by the Uniform Statutory Entity Trust Act §§ 401–405 and some LLC statutes. *See, e.g.*, Del. Code Ann. tit. 6, § 18–215 (2012); 805 ILL. COMP. STAT. 180/37–40 (2012). Instead, in this context "series" refers to a subset of a class, which is a meaning commonly found in corporation law. *See, e.g.*, MBCA § 6.2. Specific provisions authorizing classes and series are less common in unincorporated entity law but do exist. *See, e.g.*, MINN. STAT. § 322B.155 (2012). In any event, a partnership agreement certainly has the power to create classes and series as contemplated by this section.

Subsection (a)—For this section to apply, a domestic limited partnership must be either the acquiring or acquired entity.

The acquiring entity is not required to acquire all of the interests in the acquired entity. For example, assume that a limited partnership with three classes of limited partner interests enters into an interest exchange with an acquiring entity. The acquiring entity need only acquire all of the ownership interests of one or more classes of the limited partner interests.

Subsection (b)—This subsection allows a foreign entity to effectuate an interest exchange with a domestic limited partnership if the interest exchange is authorized by the organic law of the foreign entity.

Subsection (c)—This subsection deals with rights of parties to protected agreements (defined in Section 1101(30)) when an interest exchange takes place. Because the concept of an interest exchange is relatively new, a person contracting with a domestic limited partnership or loaning it money who drafted and negotiated special rights relating to the transaction before the enactment of this article should not be charged with the consequences of not having dealt with the concept of an interest exchange in the context of those special rights. Similarly, when the governance structure of an entity has been negotiated before the enactment of this act, the concept of an interest exchange may not have been reflected in any special governance arrangements; for example, special approval rights may have been provided for fundamental transactions, but those rights fail to include language that would make them applicable to an interest exchange.

Accordingly, this subsection provides a transitional rule that is intended to protect such special rights. If, for example, a limited partnership is a party to a contract that provides that the entity cannot participate in a merger without the consent of the other party to the contract, the requirement to obtain the consent of the other party will also apply to an interest exchange in which the entity is the acquired entity. If the limited partnership fails to obtain the consent, the result will be that the other party will have the same rights it would have had if the entity were to participate in a merger without the required consent.

The transitional rule in this subsection ceases to make sense at such time as the provisions of the agreement giving rise to the special rights are first amended after the effective date of this article because at that time the provision may be amended to address expressly an interest exchange. The transitional rule will continue to apply, however, if a provision other than the specific provisions giving rise to the special rights is amended.

§ 1132.   Plan of Interest Exchange

(a)   A domestic limited partnership may be the acquired entity in an interest exchange under this [part] by approving a plan of interest exchange. The plan must be in a record and contain:

    (1)   the name of the acquired entity;

    (2)   the name, jurisdiction of formation, and type of entity of the acquiring entity;

    (3)   the manner of converting the interests in the acquired entity into interests, securities, obligations, money, other property, rights to acquire interests or securities, or any combination of the foregoing;

    (4)   any proposed amendments to:

        (A)   the certificate of limited partnership of the acquired entity; and

        (B)   the partnership agreement of the acquired entity that are, or are proposed to be, in a record;

    (5)   the other terms and conditions of the interest exchange; and

(6)   any other provision required by the law of this state or the partnership agreement of the acquired entity.

(b)   In addition to the requirements of subsection (a), a plan of interest exchange may contain any other provision not prohibited by law.

COMMENT

This section sets forth the requirements for the plan of interest exchange, which must be approved by the acquired entity in accordance with Section 1131. The content of the plan of interest exchange is similar to the content of a plan of merger. *See* Section 1122.

The plan of interest exchange may, but need not, be filed instead of the statement of interest exchange, Section 1135, so long as the plan contains all the information required to be in the statement and is delivered to the filing office for filing after the plan has been adopted and approved. *See* Section 1135(d).

Subsection (a)—The requirements stated in this subsection are mandatory. *See* Section 105(c)(16).

Subsection (a)(3)—Under this paragraph, interest holders in the acquired entity may receive interests or securities of the acquiring entity or of a party other than the acquiring entity, obligations, rights to acquire interests or securities, cash, or other property. *See* Section 1122(a)(3), cmt.

Subsection (b)—This subsection authorizes the plan to contain any other provision the parties wish to include, unless the provision is prohibited by law.

§ 1133.   Approval of Interest Exchange

(a)   A plan of interest exchange is not effective unless it has been approved:

(1)   by all the partners of a domestic acquired limited partnership entitled to vote on or consent to any matter; and

(2)   in a record, by each partner of the domestic acquired limited partnership that will have interest holder liability for debts, obligations, and other liabilities that are incurred after the interest exchange becomes effective, unless:

(A)   the partnership agreement of the partnership provides in a record for the approval of an interest exchange or a merger in which some or all its partners become subject to interest holder liability by the affirmative vote or consent of fewer than all of the partners; and

(B)   the partner consented in a record to or voted for that provision of the partnership agreement or became a partner after the adoption of that provision.

(b)   An interest exchange involving a domestic acquired entity that is not a limited partnership is not effective unless it is approved by the domestic entity in accordance with its organic law.

(c)   An interest exchange involving a foreign acquired entity is not effective unless it is approved by the foreign entity in accordance with the law of the foreign entity's jurisdiction of formation.

(d)   Except as otherwise provided in its organic law or organic rules, the interest holders of the acquiring entity are not required to approve the interest exchange.

COMMENT

This section sets forth the required approval of an interest exchange. An interest exchange transaction governed by this article only requires approval by the acquired entity, unless the applicable organic law or the organic rules of the acquiring entity otherwise provide, Subsection (d), a condition that rarely exists.

Subsection (a)(2)—For an explanation of this interest holder liability provision, see Section 1123(a)(2), comment.

§ 1134.   Amendment or Abandonment of Plan of Interest Exchange

(a)   A plan of interest exchange may be amended only with the consent of each party to the plan, except as otherwise provided in the plan.

(b)   A domestic acquired limited partnership may approve an amendment of a plan of interest exchange:

(1)   in the same manner as the plan was approved, if the plan does not provide for the manner in which it may be amended; or

(2)   by its partners in the manner provided in the plan, but a partner that was entitled to vote on or consent to approval of the interest exchange is entitled to vote on or consent to any amendment of the plan that will change:

(A)   the amount or kind of interests, securities, obligations, money, other property, rights to acquire interests or securities, or any combination of the foregoing, to be received by any of the partners of the acquired partnership under the plan;

(B)   the certificate of limited partnership or partnership agreement of the acquired partnership that will be in effect immediately after the interest exchange becomes effective, except for changes that do not require approval of the partners of the acquired partnership under this [act] or the partnership agreement; or

(C)   any other terms or conditions of the plan, if the change would adversely affect the partner in any material respect.

(c)   After a plan of interest exchange has been approved and before a statement of interest exchange becomes effective, the plan may be abandoned as provided in the plan. Unless prohibited by the plan, a domestic acquired limited partnership may abandon the plan in the same manner as the plan was approved.

(d)   If a plan of interest exchange is abandoned after a statement of interest exchange has been delivered to the [Secretary of State] for filing and before the statement becomes effective, a statement of abandonment, signed by the acquired limited partnership, must be delivered to the [Secretary of State] for filing before the statement of interest exchange becomes effective. The statement of abandonment takes effect on filing, and the interest exchange is abandoned and does not become effective. The statement of abandonment must contain:

(1)   the name of the acquired partnership;

(2)   the date on which the statement of interest exchange was filed by the [Secretary of State]; and

(3)   a statement that the interest exchange has been abandoned in accordance with this section.

COMMENT

This section parallels provisions in Parts 2 (mergers), 4 (conversions), and 5 (domestications). *See* Sections 1124 (mergers), 1144 (conversions), 1154 (domestications).

§ 1135.   Statement of Interest Exchange; Effective Date of Interest Exchange

(a)   A statement of interest exchange must be signed by a domestic acquired limited partnership and delivered to the [Secretary of State] for filing.

(b)   A statement of interest exchange must contain:

(1)   the name of the acquired limited partnership;

(2)   the name, jurisdiction of formation, and type of entity of the acquiring entity;

(3)   a statement that the plan of interest exchange was approved by the acquired limited partnership in accordance with this [part]; and

(4)   any amendments to the acquired limited partnership's certificate of limited partnership approved as part of the plan of interest exchange.

(c)   In addition to the requirements of subsection (b), a statement of interest exchange may contain any other provision not prohibited by law.

(d)   A plan of interest exchange that is signed by a domestic acquired limited partnership and meets all the requirements of subsection (b) may be delivered to the [Secretary of State] for filing instead of a statement of interest exchange and on filing has the same effect. If a plan of interest exchange is filed as provided in this subsection, references in this [article] to a statement of interest exchange refer to the plan of interest exchange filed under this subsection.

(e)   An interest exchange becomes effective when the statement of interest exchange is effective.

COMMENT

This section applies only when the acquired entity is a domestic limited partnership. The filing makes the transaction a matter of public record.

This act has no filing requirement when the only domestic limited partnership involved is the acquiring entity.

Subsection (b)—This subsection states the requirements for a statement of interest exchange, which are essentially the same as the requirements for a statement of merger under Section 1125(b).

Subsection (d)—A plan of interest exchange can be used as a substitute for the statement of interest exchange so long as the plan satisfies the requirements in Subsection (b).

Subsection (e)—This subsection applies when the acquiring entity is a domestic limited partnership, and Section 207 determines when a record delivered for filing under this act becomes effective. A statement of interest exchange may specify a delayed effective time and date, subject to the ninety-day limit stated in Section 207(3) and (4).

If the acquiring entity is not a domestic limited partnership, the effectiveness of the interest exchange will occur when provided by the law of the jurisdiction of formation of the acquiring entity.

§ 1136.   Effect of Interest Exchange

(a)   When an interest exchange in which the acquired entity is a domestic limited partnership becomes effective:

(1)   the interests in the acquired partnership which are the subject of the interest exchange are converted, and the partners holding those interests are entitled only to the rights provided to them under the plan of interest exchange and to any appraisal rights they have under Section 1106;

(2)   the acquiring entity becomes the interest holder of the interests in the acquired partnership stated in the plan of interest exchange to be acquired by the acquiring entity;

(3)   the certificate of limited partnership of the acquired partnership is amended to the extent provided in the statement of interest exchange; and

(4)   the provisions of the partnership agreement of the acquired partnership that are to be in a record, if any, are amended to the extent provided in the plan of interest exchange.

(b)   Except as otherwise provided in the certificate of limited partnership or partnership agreement of a domestic acquired limited partnership, the interest exchange does not give rise to any rights that a partner or third party would have upon a dissolution, liquidation, or winding up of the acquired partnership.

(c)   When an interest exchange becomes effective, a person that did not have interest holder liability with respect to a domestic acquired limited partnership and becomes subject to interest holder liability with respect to a domestic entity as a result of the interest exchange has interest holder liability only to the extent provided by the organic law of the entity and only for those debts, obligations, and other liabilities that are incurred after the interest exchange becomes effective.

(d)   When an interest exchange becomes effective, the interest holder liability of a person that ceases to hold an interest in a domestic acquired limited partnership with respect to which the person had interest holder liability is subject to the following rules:

(1)   The interest exchange does not discharge any interest holder liability under this [act] to the extent the interest holder liability was incurred before the interest exchange became effective.

(2)   The person does not have interest holder liability under this [act] for any debt, obligation, or other liability that is incurred after the interest exchange becomes effective.

(3)   This [act] continues to apply to the release, collection, or discharge of any interest holder liability preserved under paragraph (1) as if the interest exchange had not occurred.

(4)   The person has whatever rights of contribution from any other person as are provided by this [act], law other than this [act], or the partnership agreement of the domestic acquired partnership with respect to any interest holder liability preserved under paragraph (1) as if the interest exchange had not occurred.

COMMENT

This section applies only when the *acquired* entity is a domestic limited partnership, and this part states no rule for the effect of an interest exchange when the only domestic limited partnership involved is the *acquiring* entity. For that situation, the other provisions of this act must be consulted, because this act is the organic law of the acquiring entity.

Subsection (a)—In contrast to a merger, an interest exchange does not in and of itself affect the separate existence of the parties, vest in the acquiring entity the assets of the acquired entity, or render the acquiring entity liable for the liabilities of the acquired entity. Thus, Subsection (a) is significantly simpler than Section 1126(a) with respect to the effects of a merger.

When an interest exchange becomes effective: (i) the interests of the acquired domestic limited partnership are exchanged, converted, or canceled as provided in the plan; (ii) the only rights of the former partners and transferees of the acquired limited partnership whose interests are affected by the interest exchange are those rights related to the exchange, conversion, or cancellation; (iii) the acquiring entity becomes the owner of the acquired limited partnership's interests as provided in the plan; (iv) the certificate of limited partnership of the acquired limited partnership is amended as provided in the statement of interest exchange, thus obviating the need for repetitive filings (*i.e.*, a filing as to the entity interest exchange and another filing to reflect amendments to certificate); and (v) the provisions of the partnership agreement of the acquired limited partnership that are to be in a record, if any, are amended to the extent provided in the plan of interest exchange.

Subsection (c)—This subsection provides the rule for future interest holder liability pertaining to domestic entities and parallels analogous provisions in Parts 2 (mergers), 4 (conversions), and 5 (domestications). *See* Section 1126, cmt.

Subsection (d)—This subsection provides the rule for past interest holder liability and parallels analogous provisions in Parts 2 (mergers), 4 (conversions), and 5 (domestications). *See* Sections 1126(d), cmt., 1146(d), cmt.

[PART] 4.   CONVERSION

§ 1141.   Conversion Authorized

(a)   By complying with this [part], a domestic limited partnership may become:

(1)   a domestic entity that is a different type of entity; or

(2)   a foreign entity that is a different type of entity, if the conversion is authorized by the law of the foreign entity's jurisdiction of formation.

(b)   By complying with the provisions of this [part] applicable to foreign entities, a foreign entity that is not a foreign limited partnership may become a domestic limited partnership if the conversion is authorized by the law of the foreign entity's jurisdiction of formation.

(c)   If a protected agreement contains a provision that applies to a merger of a domestic limited partnership but does not refer to a conversion, the provision applies to a conversion of the partnership as if the conversion were a merger until the provision is amended after [the effective date of this [act]].

COMMENT

This part of Article 11 permits an entity to change to a different type of entity. A transaction in which an entity changes its jurisdiction of organization but does not change its type is a domestication and is the subject of Part 5.

Subsection (a)(2)—For this provision to apply, this type of conversion must be authorized by the law of the foreign jurisdiction. If this is not the case, it may be possible to achieve the same result by forming an entity of the type desired in the foreign jurisdiction and then merging the domestic entity into the new foreign entity under Part 2 of Article 11.

Subsection (b)—This subsection allows a foreign entity to effectuate a conversion into a domestic limited partnership, but only if the conversion is permitted by the laws of the foreign entity's jurisdiction of formation. When a foreign entity becomes a domestic limited partnership pursuant to this part of Article 11, the effect of the conversion will be as provided in Section 1146. The procedures by which the conversion is approved, however, will be determined by the laws of the foreign entity's jurisdiction of formation. *See* Section 102(9) (defining "jurisdiction of formation").

Subsection (c)—*See* Section 1131(c), cmt.

§ 1142. Plan of Conversion

(a) A domestic limited partnership may convert to a different type of entity under this [part] by approving a plan of conversion. The plan must be in a record and contain:

(1) the name of the converting limited partnership;

(2) the name, jurisdiction of formation, and type of entity of the converted entity;

(3) the manner of converting the interests in the converting limited partnership into interests, securities, obligations, money, other property, rights to acquire interests or securities, or any combination of the foregoing;

(4) the proposed public organic record of the converted entity if it will be a filing entity;

(5) the full text of the private organic rules of the converted entity which are proposed to be in a record;

(6) the other terms and conditions of the conversion; and

(7) any other provision required by the law of this state or the partnership agreement of the converting limited partnership.

(b) In addition to the requirements of subsection (a), a plan of conversion may contain any other provision not prohibited by law.

COMMENT

This section sets forth the requirements for the plan of conversion, which must be approved by the converting entity in accordance with Section 1143. The content of a plan of conversion is similar to the content of a plan of merger. *See* Section 1122.

Subsection (a)—The requirements stated in this subsection are mandatory. *See* Section 105(c)(16).

Subsection (a)(3)—Interest holders in the converting entity may receive interests or other securities of the converted entity or of any other person, obligations, rights to acquire interests or other securities, cash, or other property. *See* Sections 1122(a)(3) (mergers), 1132(a)(3) (interest exchanges), 1152(a)(3) (domestications).

Subsection (b)—This subsection authorizes the plan to contain any other provision the parties wish to include, unless the provision is prohibited by law.

§ 1143. Approval of Conversion

(a) A plan of conversion is not effective unless it has been approved:

(1) by a domestic converting limited partnership, by all the partners of the limited partnership entitled to vote on or consent to any matter; and

(2) in a record, by each partner of a domestic converting limited partnership which will have interest holder liability for debts, obligations, and other liabilities that are incurred after the conversion becomes effective, unless:

(A)   the partnership agreement of the partnership provides in a record for the approval of a conversion or a merger in which some or all of its partners become subject to interest holder liability by the affirmative vote or consent of fewer than all the partners; and

(B)   the partner voted for or consented in a record to that provision of the partnership agreement or became a partner after the adoption of that provision.

(b)   A conversion involving a domestic converting entity that is not a limited partnership is not effective unless it is approved by the domestic converting entity in accordance with its organic law.

(c)   A conversion of a foreign converting entity is not effective unless it is approved by the foreign entity in accordance with the law of the foreign entity's jurisdiction of formation.

COMMENT

Subsection (a)(1)—This provision is a default rule, subject to change in the partnership agreement.

Subsection (a)(2)—This provision is not a default rule. Section 105(c)(16). For an explanation of this interest holder liability provision, see Section 1123(a)(2), comment.

§ 1144.   Amendment or Abandonment of Plan of Conversion

(a)   A plan of conversion of a domestic converting limited partnership may be amended:

(1)   in the same manner as the plan was approved, if the plan does not provide for the manner in which it may be amended; or

(2)   by its partners in the manner provided in the plan, but a partner that was entitled to vote on or consent to approval of the conversion is entitled to vote on or consent to any amendment of the plan that will change:

(A)   the amount or kind of interests, securities, obligations, money, other property, rights to acquire interests or securities, or any combination of the foregoing, to be received by any of the partners of the converting partnership under the plan;

(B)   the public organic record, if any, or private organic rules of the converted entity which will be in effect immediately after the conversion becomes effective, except for changes that do not require approval of the interest holders of the converted entity under its organic law or organic rules; or

(C)   any other terms or conditions of the plan, if the change would adversely affect the partner in any material respect.

(b)   After a plan of conversion has been approved by a domestic converting limited partnership and before a statement of conversion becomes effective, the plan may be abandoned as provided in the plan. Unless prohibited by the plan, a domestic converting limited partnership may abandon the plan in the same manner as the plan was approved.

(c)   If a plan of conversion is abandoned after a statement of conversion has been delivered to the [Secretary of State] for filing and before the statement becomes effective, a statement of abandonment, signed by the converting entity, must be delivered to the [Secretary of State] for filing before the statement of conversion becomes effective. The statement of abandonment takes effect on filing, and the conversion is abandoned and does not become effective. The statement of abandonment must contain:

(1)   the name of the converting limited partnership;

(2)   the date on which the statement of conversion was filed by the [Secretary of State]; and

(3)   a statement that the conversion has been abandoned in accordance with this section.

COMMENT

This section parallels analogous provisions in Parts 2 (mergers), 3 (interest exchanges), and 5 (domestications). *See* Sections 1124 (mergers), 1134 (interest exchanges), 1154 (domestications).

§ 1145. Statement of Conversion; Effective Date of Conversion

(a)   A statement of conversion must be signed by the converting entity and delivered to the [Secretary of State] for filing.

(b)   A statement of conversion must contain:

(1)   the name, jurisdiction of formation, and type of entity of the converting entity;

(2)   the name, jurisdiction of formation, and type of entity of the converted entity;

(3)   if the converting entity is a domestic limited partnership, a statement that the plan of conversion was approved in accordance with this [part] or, if the converting entity is a foreign entity, a statement that the conversion was approved by the foreign entity in accordance with the law of its jurisdiction of formation;

(4)   if the converted entity is a domestic filing entity, its public organic record, as an attachment; and

(5)   if the converted entity is a domestic limited liability partnership, its statement of qualification, as an attachment.

(c)   In addition to the requirements of subsection (b), a statement of conversion may contain any other provision not prohibited by law.

(d)   If the converted entity is a domestic entity, its public organic record, if any, must satisfy the requirements of the law of this state, except that the public organic record does not need to be signed.

(e)   A plan of conversion that is signed by a domestic converting limited partnership and meets all the requirements of subsection (b) may be delivered to the [Secretary of State] for filing instead of a statement of conversion and on filing has the same effect. If a plan of conversion is filed as provided in this subsection, references in this [article] to a statement of conversion refer to the plan of conversion filed under this subsection.

(f)   If the converted entity is a domestic limited partnership, the conversion becomes effective when the statement of conversion is effective. In all other cases, the conversion becomes effective on the later of:

(1)   the date and time provided by the organic law of the converted entity; and

(2)   when the statement is effective.

COMMENT

This section applies regardless of whether a domestic limited partnership is the converting or converted entity. A foreign entity seeking to convert to a domestic limited partnership must therefore comply with this section.

If either the converting or converted entity is a foreign entity, the organic law of the foreign entity's jurisdiction must also be consulted.

The filing of a statement of conversion makes the transaction a matter of public record.

Subsection (b)—This subsection sets forth the requirements for a statement of conversion. They are essentially the same as the requirements for a statement of merger in Section 1125.

Subsection (e)—A plan of conversion can be used as a substitute for the statement of conversion so long as the plan satisfies the requirements in Subsection (b).

Subsection (f)—Section 207 determines when a record delivered for filing under this act becomes effective. A statement of conversion may specify a delayed effective time and date, subject to the ninety-day limit stated in Section 207(3) and (4).

When the statement of conversion becomes effective under this subsection, the conversion transaction occurs if the converted entity is a domestic limited partnership. A conversion in which the converted entity is a foreign entity will usually also take effect when the statement of conversion takes effect because the best practice will be to coordinate the filings that need to be made when a conversion involves both a domestic entity and also a foreign entity so that the filings in each jurisdiction take effect at the same time.

However, when the converting limited partnership is a foreign limited partnership, it is possible that the filing in the foreign jurisdiction will take effect at a different time. For that reason, this subsection provides that the conversion will take effect at the later of: (i) when the statement of conversion takes effect; and (ii) when the conversion takes effect under the law of the foreign jurisdiction. This rule avoids the possibility that the conversion will take effect in this state before it takes effect in the foreign jurisdiction, which would produce the undesirable result that the converting domestic limited partnership would cease to appear as an active entity on the records of this state before appearing as its active, converted self on the records of the foreign jurisdiction.

It is only necessary for the filing office to record the effective date of the statement of conversion and the filing office does not need to be concerned with the effective date of the conversion itself. Persons wishing to determine the effective date of a conversion involving both a domestic limited partnership and a foreign entity will be able to do so by consulting the records of the filing offices in each jurisdiction.

§ 1146.   Effect of Conversion

(a)   When a conversion becomes effective:

(1)   the converted entity is:

(A)   organized under and subject to the organic law of the converted entity; and

(B)   the same entity without interruption as the converting entity;

(2)   all property of the converting entity continues to be vested in the converted entity without transfer, reversion, or impairment;

(3)   all debts, obligations, and other liabilities of the converting entity continue as debts, obligations, and other liabilities of the converted entity;

(4)   except as otherwise provided by law or the plan of conversion, all the rights, privileges, immunities, powers, and purposes of the converting entity remain in the converted entity;

(5)   the name of the converted entity may be substituted for the name of the converting entity in any pending action or proceeding;

(6)   the certificate of limited partnership of the converted entity becomes effective;

(7)   the provisions of the partnership agreement of the converted entity which are to be in a record, if any, approved as part of the plan of conversion become effective; and

(8)   the interests in the converting entity are converted, and the interest holders of the converting entity are entitled only to the rights provided to them under the plan of conversion and to any appraisal rights they have under Section 1106.

(b)   Except as otherwise provided in the partnership agreement of a domestic converting limited partnership, the conversion does not give rise to any rights that a partner or third party would have upon a dissolution, liquidation, or winding up of the converting entity.

(c)   When a conversion becomes effective, a person that did not have interest holder liability with respect to the converting entity and becomes subject to interest holder liability with respect to a domestic entity as a result of the conversion has interest holder liability only to the extent provided by the organic law of the entity and only for those debts, obligations, and other liabilities that are incurred after the conversion becomes effective.

(d)   When a conversion becomes effective, the interest holder liability of a person that ceases to hold an interest in a domestic converting limited partnership with respect to which the person had interest holder liability is subject to the following rules:

(1)   The conversion does not discharge any interest holder liability under this [act] to the extent the interest holder liability was incurred before the conversion became effective.

(2)   The person does not have interest holder liability under this [act] for any debt, obligation, or other liability that is incurred after the conversion becomes effective.

(3)   This [act] continues to apply to the release, collection, or discharge of any interest holder liability preserved under paragraph (1) as if the conversion had not occurred.

(4)   The person has whatever rights of contribution from any other person as are provided by this [act], law other than this [act], or the organic rules of the converting entity with respect to any interest holder liability preserved under paragraph (1) as if the conversion had not occurred.

(e)   When a conversion becomes effective, a foreign entity that is the converted entity may be served with process in this state for the collection and enforcement of any of its debts, obligations, and other liabilities as provided in Section 121.

(f)   If the converting entity is a registered foreign entity, its registration to do business in this state is canceled when the conversion becomes effective.

(g)   A conversion does not require the entity to wind up its affairs and does not constitute or cause the dissolution of the entity.

COMMENT

A converted entity is the same entity as it was before the conversion; the entity just has a different legal form.

Subsection (a)—This subsection states the principal legal effects of a conversion. The converted entity remains the owner of all real and personal property and remains subject to all the liabilities, actual or contingent, of the converted entity. A conversion is not a conveyance, transfer, or assignment. A conversion does not give rise to: (i) claims of reverter or impairment of title based on a prohibited conveyance or transfer; or (ii) to a claim that a contract with the converting entity is no longer in effect on the ground of nonassignability, unless the contract specifically provides that it does not survive a conversion. The contract rights that remain in the converted entity include, without limitation, the right to enforce subscription agreements for interests and obligations to make capital contributions entered into or incurred before the conversion.

When a conversion becomes effective, the internal affairs of the converting entity are no longer governed by its former organic law but instead by the organic law of the converted entity. As a result, filings that may have been made under the organic law of the converting entity, such as the following, will no longer be effective: a statement of qualification as a limited liability partnership under UPA (1997) (Last Amended 2013) § 901, a statement of partnership authority under section 303 of that act, a statement of authority under Section of the ULLCA (2006) (Last Amended 2013) § 302, or under Uniform Unincorporated Nonprofit Association Act (2008) (Last Amended 2013) § 7.

Subsection (a)(5)—All pending proceedings involving the converting entity are continued. The name of the converted entity may be, but need not be, substituted in any pending proceeding for the name of the converting entity.

Subsection (c)—This subsection provides the rule for future interest holder liability and parallels provisions in Parts 2 (mergers), 3 (interest exchanges), and 5 (domestications). *See* Section 1126(c), cmt.

Subsection (d)—Subsection (d) provides the rule for past interest holder liability and parallels analogous provisions in Parts 2 (mergers), 3 (interest exchanges), and 5 (domestications). *See* Section 1126(d), cmt.

Subsection (e)—For this provision to apply, the converting entity must have been a domestic limited partnership. When a domestic limited partnership becomes a foreign entity as a result of a conversion, some mechanism is needed to facilitate the enforcement of claims by the creditors and interest holders of the converting limited partnership. This subsection, which parallels analogous provisions in Parts 2 (mergers) and 5 (domestications), authorizes service of process for all such claims in this state.

Subsection (g)—When a conversion takes effect, the entity continues to exist—simply in a different form. This subsection thus makes clear that the conversion does not require the entity to wind up its affairs and does not constitute or cause the dissolution of the entity.

[PART] 5.   DOMESTICATION

§ 1151.   Domestication Authorized

(a)   By complying with this [part], a domestic limited partnership may become a foreign limited partnership if the domestication is authorized by the law of the foreign jurisdiction.

(b)　By complying with the provisions of this [part] applicable to foreign limited partnerships, a foreign limited partnership may become a domestic limited partnership if the domestication is authorized by the law of the foreign limited partnership's jurisdiction of formation.

(c)　If a protected agreement contains a provision that applies to a merger of a domestic limited partnership but does not refer to a domestication, the provision applies to a domestication of the limited partnership as if the domestication were a merger until the provision is amended after [the effective date of this [act]].

COMMENT

A domestication authorized by Part 5 of Article 11 differs from a conversion in that a domestication requires that the domesticating entity be the same type of entity as the domesticated entity. In a conversion, by contrast, the converting entity changes its type.

As with a conversion, all rights and privileges, debts, obligations and other liabilities, and actions or proceedings of a domesticating entity vest unimpaired in the domesticated entity. A domestication is not a sale, transfer, assignment, or conveyance and does not give rise to a claim of reverter or impairment of title. *See* Section 1146(a), cmt.

Part 5 of Article 11 governs the legal effect of a foreign limited partnership domesticating in this state. On the other hand, the organic laws of the foreign jurisdiction, and not Part 5, will govern the legal effect of most aspects of a domestication of a domestic limited partnership in another jurisdiction. In the latter scenario, Part 5 authorizes the domestication of the domestic entity in the foreign jurisdiction, but Part 5 does not create a right in the domestic entity to be received in the foreign jurisdiction. Similarly, this section does not provide a right on the part of a foreign limited partnership to become a domestic limited partnership if the domestication is not authorized by the laws of the foreign jurisdiction. If the foreign jurisdiction does not authorize a domestication transaction, the same results can be accomplished by forming a new limited partnership in this state and merging the existing foreign limited partnership into the new domestic limited partnership.

Subsection (c)—*See* Section 1131(c).

§ 1152.　Plan of Domestication

(a)　A domestic limited partnership may become a foreign limited partnership in a domestication by approving a plan of domestication. The plan must be in a record and contain:

(1)　the name of the domesticating limited partnership;

(2)　the name and jurisdiction of formation of the domesticated limited partnership;

(3)　the manner of converting the interests in the domesticating limited partnership into interests, securities, obligations, money, other property, rights to acquire interests or securities, or any combination of the foregoing;

(4)　the proposed certificate of limited partnership of the domesticated limited partnership;

(5)　the full text of the provisions of the partnership agreement of the domesticated limited partnership, that are proposed to be in a record;

(6)　the other terms and conditions of the domestication; and

(7)　any other provision required by the law of this state or the partnership agreement of the domesticating limited partnership.

(b)　In addition to the requirements of subsection (a), a plan of domestication may contain any other provision not prohibited by law.

COMMENT

This section sets forth the requirements for the plan of domestication for a domestic limited partnership seeking to become a limited partnership existing under the law of another jurisdiction. For a foreign limited partnership seeking to become a domestic limited partnership, the organic law of the foreign limited partnership governs the requirements for a plan of domestication. The content of a plan of domestication is similar to the content of a plan of merger. *See* Section 1122.

Subsection (a)—The requirements stated in this subsection are mandatory. *See* Section 105(c)(16).

Subsection (a)(3)—Interest holders in the domesticating limited partnership may receive interests or other securities of the domesticated limited partnership or any other entity, obligations, rights to acquire interests or other securities, cash, or other property. *See* Section 1122(a)(3), cmt.

Subsection (b)—This subsection authorizes the plan to contain any other provision the parties wish to include, unless the provision is prohibited by law.

§ 1153. Approval of Domestication

(a) A plan of domestication of a domestic domesticating limited partnership is not effective unless it has been approved:

    (1) by all the partners entitled to vote on or consent to any matter; and

    (2) in a record, by each partner that will have interest holder liability for debts, obligations, and other liabilities that are incurred after the domestication becomes effective, unless:

        (A) the partnership agreement of the domesticating partnership in a record provides for the approval of a domestication or merger in which some or all of its partners become subject to interest holder liability by the affirmative vote or consent of fewer than all the partners; and

        (B) the partner voted for or consented in a record to that provision of the partnership agreement or became a partner after the adoption of that provision.

(b) A domestication of a foreign domesticating limited partnership is not effective unless it is approved in accordance with the law of the foreign limited partnership's jurisdiction of formation.

COMMENT

Subsection (a)(1)—This provision is a default rule, subject to change in the partnership agreement.

Subsection (a)(2)—This provision is mandatory. Section 105(c)(16). For an explanation of the provision, see Section 1123(a)(2), comment.

Subsection (b)—In the case of a foreign limited partnership that is domesticating in this state, this subsection provides that the required approval is determined by the laws of the foreign limited partnership's jurisdiction of formation.

§ 1154. Amendment or Abandonment of Plan of Domestication

(a) A plan of domestication of a domestic domesticating limited partnership may be amended:

    (1) in the same manner as the plan was approved, if the plan does not provide for the manner in which it may be amended; or

    (2) by its partners in the manner provided in the plan, but a partner that was entitled to vote on or consent to approval of the domestication is entitled to vote on or consent to any amendment of the plan that will change:

        (A) the amount or kind of interests, securities, obligations, money, other property, rights to acquire interests or securities, or any combination of the foregoing, to be received by any of the partners of the domesticating limited partnership under the plan;

        (B) the certificate of limited partnership or partnership agreement of the domesticated limited partnership that will be in effect immediately after the domestication becomes effective, except for changes that do not require approval of the partners of the domesticated limited partnership under its organic law or partnership agreement; or

        (C) any other terms or conditions of the plan, if the change would adversely affect the partner in any material respect.

(b) After a plan of domestication has been approved by a domestic domesticating limited partnership and before a statement of domestication becomes effective, the plan may be abandoned as provided in the plan. Unless prohibited by the plan, a domestic domesticating limited partnership may abandon the plan in the same manner as the plan was approved.

(c)   If a plan of domestication is abandoned after a statement of domestication has been delivered to the [Secretary of State] for filing and before the statement becomes effective, a statement of abandonment, signed by the domesticating limited partnership, must be delivered to the [Secretary of State] for filing before the statement of domestication becomes effective. The statement of abandonment takes effect on filing, and the domestication is abandoned and does not become effective. The statement of abandonment must contain:

(1)   the name of the domesticating limited partnership;

(2)   the date on which the statement of domestication was filed by the [Secretary of State]; and

(3)   a statement that the domestication has been abandoned in accordance with this section.

COMMENT

This section parallels provisions in Parts 2 (mergers), 3 (interest exchanges), and 4 (conversions). *See* Sections 1124 (mergers), 1134 (interest exchanges), 1144 (conversions).

§ 1155.   Statement of Domestication; Effective Date of Domestication

(a)   A statement of domestication must be signed by the domesticating limited partnership and delivered to the [Secretary of State] for filing.

(b)   A statement of domestication must contain:

(1)   the name and jurisdiction of formation of the domesticating limited partnership;

(2)   the name and jurisdiction of formation of the domesticated limited partnership;

(3)   if the domesticating limited partnership is a domestic limited partnership, a statement that the plan of domestication was approved in accordance with this [part] or, if the domesticating limited partnership is a foreign limited partnership, a statement that the domestication was approved in accordance with the law of its jurisdiction of formation; and

(4)   the certificate of limited partnership of the domesticated limited partnership, as an attachment.

(c)   In addition to the requirements of subsection (b), a statement of domestication may contain any other provision not prohibited by law.

(d)   The certificate of limited partnership of a domesticated domestic limited partnership must satisfy the requirements of this [act], but the certificate does not need to be signed.

(e)   A plan of domestication that is signed by a domesticating domestic limited partnership and meets all the requirements of subsection (b) may be delivered to the [Secretary of State] for filing instead of a statement of domestication and on filing has the same effect. If a plan of domestication is filed as provided in this subsection, references in this [article] to a statement of domestication refer to the plan of domestication filed under this subsection.

(f)   If the domesticated entity is a domestic limited partnership, the domestication becomes effective when the statement of domestication is effective. If the domesticated entity is a foreign limited partnership, the domestication becomes effective on the later of:

(1)   the date and time provided by the organic law of the domesticated entity; and

(2)   when the statement is effective.

COMMENT

Regardless of whether a domestic limited partnership is the domesticating or domesticated entity:

- This section applies and, therefore, a foreign limited partnership seeking to domesticate and thereby become a domestic limited partnership must comply with this section.

- The organic law of the foreign limited partnership's jurisdiction must also be consulted.

The filing of a statement of domestication makes the transaction a matter of public record.

Subsection (b)—This subsection sets forth the requirements for a statement of domestication. They are essentially the same as the requirements for a statement of merger in Section 1125.

Subsection (e)—A plan of domestication can be used as a substitute for the statement of domestication so long as the plan satisfies the requirements in Subsection (b).

Subsection (f)—Section 207 determines when a record delivered for filing under this act becomes effective. A statement of domestication may specify a delayed effective time and date, subject to the ninety-day limit stated in Section 207(3) and (4).

When the statement of domestication becomes effective under this subsection, the domestication transaction occurs if the domesticated entity is a domestic limited partnership. A domestication in which the domesticated entity is a foreign limited partnership will usually also take effect when the statement of domestication takes effect because the best practice will be to coordinate the filings that need to be made in each jurisdiction so that they take effect at the same time.

However, when the domesticated limited partnership is a foreign limited partnership, it is possible that the filing in the foreign jurisdiction will take effect at a different time. For that reason, this subsection provides that the domestication will take effect at the later of: (i) when the statement of domestication takes effect; and (ii) when the domestication takes effect under the law of the foreign jurisdiction. This rule avoids the possibility that the domestication will take effect in this state before it takes effect in the foreign jurisdiction, which would produce the undesirable result that the domesticating domestic limited partnership would cease to appear as an active entity on the records of this state before appearing as its active, domesticated self on the records of the foreign jurisdiction.

It is only necessary for the filing office to record the effective date of the statement of domestication and the filing office does not need to be concerned with the effective date of the domestication itself. Persons wishing to determine the effective date of a domestication will be able to do so by consulting the records of the filing offices in each jurisdiction.

§ 1156. Effect of Domestication

(a) When a domestication becomes effective:

   (1) the domesticated entity is:

      (A) organized under and subject to the organic law of the domesticated entity[;] and

      (B) the same entity without interruption as the domesticating entity;

   (2) all property of the domesticating entity continues to be vested in the domesticated entity without transfer, reversion, or impairment;

   (3) all debts, obligations, and other liabilities of the domesticating entity continue as debts, obligations, and other liabilities of the domesticated entity;

   (4) except as otherwise provided by law or the plan of domestication, all the rights, privileges, immunities, powers, and purposes of the domesticating entity remain in the domesticated entity;

   (5) the name of the domesticated entity may be substituted for the name of the domesticating entity in any pending action or proceeding;

   (6) the certificate of limited partnership of the domesticated entity becomes effective;

   (7) the provisions of the partnership agreement of the domesticated entity that are to be in a record, if any, approved as part of the plan of domestication become effective; and

   (8) the interests in the domesticating entity are converted to the extent and as approved in connection with the domestication, and the partners of the domesticating entity are entitled only to the rights provided to them under the plan of domestication and to any appraisal rights they have under Section 1106.

(b)   Except as otherwise provided in the organic law or partnership agreement of the domesticating limited partnership, the domestication does not give rise to any rights that an partner or third party would have upon a dissolution, liquidation, or winding up of the domesticating partnership.

(c)   When a domestication becomes effective, a person that did not have interest holder liability with respect to the domesticating limited partnership and becomes subject to interest holder liability with respect to a domestic limited partnership as a result of the domestication has interest holder liability only to the extent provided by this [act] and only for those debts, obligations, and other liabilities that are incurred after the domestication becomes effective.

(d)   When a domestication becomes effective, the interest holder liability of a person that ceases to hold an interest in a domestic domesticating limited partnership with respect to which the person had interest holder liability is subject to the following rules:

(1)   The domestication does not discharge any interest holder liability under this [act] to the extent the interest holder liability was incurred before the domestication became effective.

(2)   A person does not have interest holder liability under this [act] for any debt, obligation, or other liability that is incurred after the domestication becomes effective.

(3)   This [act] continues to apply to the release, collection, or discharge of any interest holder liability preserved under paragraph (1) as if the domestication had not occurred.

(4)   A person has whatever rights of contribution from any other person as are provided by this [act], law other than this [act], or the partnership agreement of the domestic domesticating limited partnership with respect to any interest holder liability preserved under paragraph (1) as if the domestication had not occurred.

(e)   When a domestication becomes effective, a foreign limited partnership that is the domesticated partnership may be served with process in this state for the collection and enforcement of any of its debts, obligations, and other liabilities as provided in Section 121.

(f)   If the domesticating limited partnership is a registered foreign entity, the registration of the partnership is canceled when the domestication becomes effective.

(g)   A domestication does not require a domestic domesticating limited partnership to wind up its affairs and does not constitute or cause the dissolution of the partnership.

COMMENT

Subsection (a)(1)—The domesticated entity is the same entity as the domesticating entity; it has merely changed its jurisdiction of formation.

Subsection (a)(2)—A domestication is not a sale, conveyance, transfer, or assignment and does not give rise to claims of reverter or impairment of title that may be based on a prohibition on transfer, assignment, or conveyance.

Subsection (a)(4)—All pending proceedings involving the domesticating entity are continued. The name of the domesticated entity may be, but need not be, substituted in any pending proceeding for the name of the domesticating entity.

Subsection (a)(8)—The interests of the domesticating limited partnership are reclassified into whatever rights were negotiated in the domestication and the partners and transferees of the domesticating limited partnership are only entitled to those rights. Paragraph 8, on its face, allows for certain partners of the domesticating limited partnership to be entitled to a continuing equity interest in the domesticated limited partnership whereas other partners of the domesticating limited partnership may be cashed out as a result of the transaction.

Subsection (c)—This subsection provides the rule for future interest holder liability and parallels analogous provisions in Parts 2 (mergers), 3 (interest exchanges), and 4 (conversions).

See Section 1126(c), cmt.

Subsection (d)—This subsection provides the rule for past interest holder liability and parallels analogous provisions in Parts 2 (mergers), 3 (interest exchanges), and 4 (conversions). *See* Sections 1126(d), cmt., 1146(d), cmt.

Subsection (e)—When a domestic domesticating limited partnership becomes a foreign limited partnership as a result of a domestication, some mechanism is needed to facilitate the enforcement of claims by the creditors and interest holders of the domesticating limited partnership. This subsection, which parallels analogous provisions in Parts 2 (mergers) and 4 (conversions), authorizes service of process for all such claims in this state.

Subsection (g)—When a domestication takes effect, the entity continues to exist—simply as a domestic entity under the laws of a different state. This subsection thus makes clear that the domestication does not require the limited partnership to wind up its affairs and does not constitute or cause the dissolution of the limited partnership.

[ARTICLE] 12. MISCELLANEOUS PROVISIONS

§ 1201. Uniformity of Application and Construction

In applying and construing this uniform act, consideration must be given to the need to promote uniformity of the law with respect to its subject matter among states that enact it.

§ 1202. Relation to Electronic Signatures in Global and National Commerce Act

This [act] modifies, limits, and supersedes the Electronic Signatures in Global and National Commerce Act, 15 U.S.C. Section 7001 et seq., but does not modify, limit, or supersede Section 101(c) of that act, 15 U.S.C. Section 7001(c), or authorize electronic delivery of any of the notices described in Section 103(b) of that act, 15 U.S.C. Section 7003(b).

COMMENT

This section responds to specific language of the Electronic Signatures in Global and National Commerce Act and is designed to avoid preemption of state law under that federal legislation.

§ 1203. Savings Clause

This [act] does not affect an action commenced, proceeding brought, or right accrued before [the effective date of this [act]].

COMMENT

This section continues prior law after the effective date of this act with respect to rights accrued and proceedings. But for this section, the new law of this act would displace the old laws in some circumstances. The power of a new act to displace the old statute with respect to conduct occurring before the new act's enactment is substantial. Millard H. Ruud, *The Savings Clause—Some Problems in Construction and Drafting*, 33 TEX. L. REV. 285, 286–93 (1955). A court generally applies the law that exists at the time it acts.

Eventually, this act will apply all to pre-existing limited partnerships—whether by choice under Section 112(a)(2) (permitting an early opt-in), or without choice on the "all-inclusive date." Section 112(b). In this context, the phrase "before [the effective date of this [act]]" should be understood as referring to the date upon which this act becomes applicable to the particular limited partnership at issue.

§ 1204. Severability Clause

If any provision of this [act] or its application to any person or circumstance is held invalid, the invalidity does not affect other provisions or applications of this [act] which can be given effect without the invalid provision or application, and to this end the provisions of this [act] are severable.]

Legislative Note: Include this section only if this state lacks a general severability statute or decision by the highest court of this state stating a general rule of severability.

§ 1205.   Repeals

The following are repealed:

(1)   [the state limited partnership act as [amended, and as] in effect immediately before [the effective date of this [act]].

(2)   . . . .

(3)   . . . .

§ 1206.   Effective Date

This [act] takes effect. . . .

COMMENT

For the effect of the act's effective date on pre-existing limited partnerships, see Section 112.

DELAWARE REVISED UNIFORM LIMITED PARTNERSHIP ACT

(Delaware Code, Title 6, Chapter 17)

(Selected Provisions)

***

Table of Sections

***

§ 17–1101.   Construction and Application of Chapter and Partnership Agreement

(a)   This chapter shall be so applied and construed to effectuate its general purpose to make uniform the law with respect to the subject of this chapter among states enacting it.

(b)   The rule that statutes in derogation of the common law are to be strictly construed shall have no application to this chapter.

(c)   It is the policy of this chapter to give maximum effect to the principle of freedom of contract and to the enforceability of partnership agreements.

(d)   To the extent that, at law or in equity, a partner or other person has duties (including fiduciary duties) to a limited partnership or to another partner or to another person that is a party to or is otherwise bound by a partnership agreement, the partner's or other person's duties may be expanded or restricted or eliminated by provisions in the partnership agreement; provided that the partnership agreement may not eliminate the implied contractual covenant of good faith and fair dealing.

(e)   Unless otherwise provided in a partnership agreement, a partner or other person shall not be liable to a limited partnership or to another partner or to another person that is a party to or is otherwise bound by a partnership agreement for breach of fiduciary duty for the partner's or other person's good faith reliance on the provisions of the partnership agreement.

(f)   A partnership agreement may provide for the limitation or elimination of any and all liabilities for breach of contract and breach of duties (including fiduciary duties) of a partner or other person to a limited partnership or to another partner or to [another] person that is a party to or is otherwise bound by a partnership agreement; provided, that a partnership agreement may not limit or eliminate liability for any act or omission that constitutes a bad faith violation of the implied contractual covenant of good faith and fair dealing.

(g)   Sections 9–406 and 9–408 of this title do not apply to any interest in a limited partnership, including all rights, powers and interests arising under a partnership agreement or this chapter. This provision prevails over §§ 9–406 and 9–408 of this title.

(h)   Action validly taken pursuant to 1 provision of this chapter shall not be deemed invalid solely because it is identical or similar in substance to an action that could have been taken pursuant to some other provision of this chapter but fails to satisfy 1 or more requirements prescribed by such other provision.

(i)   A partnership agreement that provides for the application of Delaware law shall be governed by and construed under the laws of the State of Delaware in accordance with its terms.

§ 17–1105.   Cases Not Provided for in This Chapter

In any case not provided for in this chapter, the Delaware Uniform Partnership Law in effect on July 11, 1999 [6 Del. C. § 1501, et seq.] and the rules of law and equity, including the law merchant, shall govern.

UNIFORM LIMITED LIABILITY COMPANY ACT (1996)

Table of Sections

ARTICLE 1. GENERAL PROVISIONS

ARTICLE 2. ORGANIZATION

ARTICLE 3. RELATIONS OF MEMBERS AND MANAGERS TO PERSONS DEALING WITH LIMITED LIABILITY COMPANY

ARTICLE 4. RELATIONS OF MEMBERS TO EACH OTHER AND TO LIMITED LIABILITY COMPANY

UNIFORM LIMITED LIABILITY COMPANY ACT (1996)

PREFATORY NOTE

Borrowing from abroad, Wyoming initiated a national movement in 1977 by enacting this country's first limited liability company act. The movement started slowly as the Internal Revenue Service took more than ten years to announce finally that a Wyoming limited liability company would be taxed like a partnership. Since that time, every State has adopted or is considering its own distinct limited liability company act, many of which have already been amended one or more times.

The allure of the limited liability company is its unique ability to bring together in a single business organization the best features of all other business forms—properly structured, its owners obtain both a corporate-styled liability shield and the pass-through tax benefits of a partnership. General and limited partnerships do not offer their partners a corporate-styled liability shield. Corporations, including those having made a Subchapter Selection, do not offer their shareholders all the pass-through tax benefits of a partnership. All state limited liability company acts contain provisions for a liability shield and partnership tax status.

Despite these two common themes, state limited liability company acts display a dazzling array of diversity. Multistate activities of businesses are widespread. Recognition of out-of-state limited liability companies varies. Unfortunately, this lack of uniformity manifests itself in basic but fundamentally important questions, such as: may a company be formed and operated by only one owner; may it be formed for purposes other than to make a profit; whether owners have the power and right to withdraw from a company and receive a distribution of the fair value of their interests; whether a member's dissociation threatens a dissolution of the company; who has the apparent authority to bind the company and the limits of that authority; what are the fiduciary duties of owners and managers to a company and each other; how are the rights to manage a company allocated among its owners and managers; do the owners have the right to sue a company and its other owners in their own right as well as derivatively on behalf of the company; may general and limited partnerships be converted to limited liability companies and may limited liability companies merge with other limited liability companies and other business organizations; what is the law governing foreign limited liability companies; and are any or all of these and other rules simply default rules that may be modified by agreement or are they nonwaivable.

Practitioners and entrepreneurs struggle to understand the law governing limited liability companies organized in their own State and to understand the burgeoning law of other States. Simple questions concerning where to organize are increasingly complex. Since most state limited liability company acts are in their infancy, little if any interpretative case law exists. Even when case law develops, it will have limited precedential value because of the diversity of the state acts.

Accordingly, uniform legislation in this area of the law appeared to have become urgent.

After a Study Committee appointed by the National Conference of Commissioners in late 1991 recommended that a comprehensive project be undertaken, the Conference appointed a Drafting Committee which worked on a Uniform Limited Liability Company Act (ULLCA) from early 1992 until its adoption by the Conference at its Annual Meeting in August 1994. The Drafting Committee was assisted by a blue ribbon panel of national experts and other interested and affected parties and organizations. Many, if not all, of those assisting the Committee brought substantial experience from drafting limited liability company legislation in their own States. Many are also authors of leading treatises and articles in the field. Those represented in the drafting process included an American Bar Association (ABA) liaison, four advisors representing the three separate ABA Sections of Business Law, Taxation, and Real Property, Trust and Probate, the United States Treasury Department, the Internal Revenue Service, and many observers representing several other organizations, including the California Bar Association, the New York City Bar Association, the American College of Real Estate Lawyers, the National Association of Certified Public Accountants, the National Association of Secretaries of State, the Chicago and Lawyers Title Companies, the American Land Title Association, and several university law and business school faculty members.

The Committee met nine times and engaged in numerous national telephonic conferences to discuss policies, review over fifteen drafts, evaluate legal developments and consider comments by our many knowledgeable advisers and observers, as well as an ABA subcommittee's earlier work on a prototype. In examining virtually every aspect of each state limited liability company act, the Committee maintained a single policy vision—to draft a flexible act with a comprehensive set of default rules designed to substitute as the essence of the bargain for small entrepreneurs and others.

This Act is flexible in the sense that the vast majority of its provisions may be modified by the owners in a private agreement. Only limited and specific fundamental matters may not be altered by private agreement. To simplify, those nonwaivable provisions are set forth in a single subsection. Helped thereby, sophisticated parties will negotiate their own deal with the benefit of counsel.

The Committee also recognized that small entrepreneurs without the benefit of counsel should also have access to the Act. To that end, the great bulk of the Act sets forth default rules designed to operate a limited liability company without sophisticated agreements and to recognize that members may also modify the default rules by oral agreements defined in part by their own conduct. Uniquely, the Act combines two simple default structures which depend upon the presence of designations in the articles of organization. All default rules under the Act flow from these two designations.

First, unless the articles reflect that a limited liability company is a term company and the duration of that term, the company will be an at-will company. Generally, the owners of an at-will company may demand a payment of the fair value of their interests at any time. Owners of a term company must generally wait until the expiration of the term to obtain the value of their interests. Secondly, unless the articles reflect that a company will be managed by managers, the company will be managed by its members. This designation controls whether the members or managers have apparent agency authority, management authority, and the nature of fiduciary duties in the company.

In January of 1995 the Executive Committee of the Conference adopted an amendment to harmonize the Act with new and important Internal Revenue Service announcements, and the amendment was ratified by the National Conference at its Annual Meeting in August of 1995. Those Internal Revenue Service announcements generally provide that a limited liability company will not be taxed like a corporation regardless of its organizational structure. Freed from the old tax classification restraints, the amendment modifies the Act's dissolution provision by eliminating member dissociation as a dissolution event. This important amendment significantly increases the stability of a limited liability company and places greater emphasis on a limited liability company's required purchase of a dissociated member's interest.

The adoption of ULLCA will provide much needed consistency among the States, with flexible default rules, and multistate recognition of limited liability on the part of company owners. It will also promote the development of precedential case law.

[ARTICLE] 1
GENERAL PROVISIONS

§ 101.   Definitions

In this [Act]:

(1) "Articles of organization" means initial, amended, and restated articles of organization and articles of merger. In the case of a foreign limited liability company, the term includes all records serving a similar function required to be filed in the office of the [Secretary of State] or other official having custody of company records in the State or country under whose law it is organized.

(2) "At-will company" means a limited liability company other than a term company.

(3) "Business" includes every trade, occupation, profession, and other lawful purpose, whether or not carried on for profit.

(4) "Debtor in bankruptcy" means a person who is the subject of an order for relief under Title 11 of the United States Code or a comparable order under a successor statute of general application or a comparable order under federal, state, or foreign law governing insolvency.

(5) "Distribution" means a transfer of money, property, or other benefit from a limited liability company to a member in the member's capacity as a member or to a transferee of the member's distributional interest.

(6) "Distributional interest" means all of a member's interest in distributions by the limited liability company.

(7) "Entity" means a person other than an individual.

(8) "Foreign limited liability company" means an unincorporated entity organized under laws other than the laws of this State which afford limited liability to its owners comparable to the liability under Section 303 and is not required to obtain a certificate of authority to transact business under any law of this State other than this [Act].

(9) "Limited liability company" means a limited liability company organized under this [Act].

(10) "Manager" means a person, whether or not a member of a manager-managed company, who is vested with authority under Section 301.

(11) "Manager-managed company" means a limited liability company which is so designated in its articles of organization.

(12) "Member-managed company" means a limited liability company other than a manager-managed company.

(13) "Operating agreement" means the agreement under Section 103 concerning the relations among the members, managers, and limited liability company. The term includes amendments to the agreement.

(14) "Person" means an individual, corporation, business trust, estate, trust, partnership, limited liability company, association, joint venture, government, governmental subdivision, agency, or instrumentality, or any other legal or commercial entity.

(15) "Principal office" means the office, whether or not in this State, where the principal executive office of a domestic or foreign limited liability company is located.

(16) "Record" means information that is inscribed on a tangible medium or that is stored in an electronic or other medium and is retrievable in perceivable form.

(17) "Sign" means to identify a record by means of a signature, mark, or other symbol, with intent to authenticate it.

(18) "State" means a State of the United States, the District of Columbia, the Commonwealth of Puerto Rico, or any territory or insular possession subject to the jurisdiction of the United States.

(19) "Term company" means a limited liability company in which its members have agreed to remain members until the expiration of a term specified in the articles of organization.

(20) "Transfer" includes an assignment, conveyance, deed, bill of sale, lease, mortgage, security interest, encumbrance, and gift.

COMMENT

Uniform Limited Liability Company Act ("ULLCA") definitions, like the rest of the Act, are a blend of terms and concepts derived from the Uniform Partnership Act ("UPA"), the Uniform Partnership Act (1994) ("UPA 1994", also previously known as the Revised Uniform Partnership Act or "RUPA"), the Revised Uniform Limited Partnership Act ("RULPA"), the Uniform Commercial Code ("UCC"), and the Model Business Corporation Act ("MBCA"), or their revisions from time to time; some are tailored specially for this Act.

"Business." A limited liability company may be organized to engage in an activity either for or not for profit. The extent to which contributions to a nonprofit company may be deductible for Federal income tax purposes is determined by federal law. Other state law determines the extent of exemptions from state and local income and property taxes.

"Debtor in bankruptcy." The filing of a voluntary petition operates immediately as an "order for relief." See Sections 601(7)(i) and 602(b)(2)(iii).

"Distribution." This term includes all sources of a member's distributions including the member's capital contributions, undistributed profits, and residual interest in the assets of the company after all claims, including those of third parties and debts to members, have been paid.

"Distributional interest." The term does not include a member's broader rights to participate in the management of the company. See Comments to Article 5.

"Foreign limited liability company." The term is not restricted to companies formed in the United States.

"Manager." The rules of agency apply to limited liability companies. Therefore, managers may designate agents with whatever titles, qualifications, and responsibilities they desire. For example, managers may designate an agent as "President."

"Manager-managed company." The term includes only a company designated as such in the articles of organization. In a manager-managed company agency authority is vested exclusively in one or more managers and not in the members. See Sections 101(10) (manager), 203(a)(6) (articles designation), and 301(b) (agency authority of members and managers).

"Member-managed limited liability company." The term includes every company not designated as "manager-managed" under Section 203(a)(6) in its articles of organization.

"Operating agreement." This agreement may be oral. Members may agree upon the extent to which their relationships are to be governed by writings.

"Principal office." The address of the principal office must be set forth in the annual report required under Section 211(a)(3).

"Record." This Act is the first Uniform Act promulgated with a definition of this term. The definition brings this Act in conformity with the present state of technology and accommodates prospective future technology in the communication and storage of information other than by human memory. Modern methods of communicating and storing information employed in commercial practices are no longer confined to physical documents.

The term includes any writing. A record need not be permanent or indestructible, but an oral or other unwritten communication must be stored or preserved on some medium to qualify as a record. Information that has not been retained other than through human memory does not qualify as a record. A record may be signed or may be created without the knowledge or intent of a particular person. Other law must be consulted to determine admissibility in evidence, the applicability of statute of frauds, and other questions regarding the use of records. Under Section 206(a), electronic filings may be permitted and even encouraged.

§ 102. Knowledge and Notice

(a) A person knows a fact if the person has actual knowledge of it.

(b) A person has notice of a fact if the person:

(1) knows the fact;

(2) has received a notification of the fact; or

(3) has reason to know the fact exists from all of the facts known to the person at the time in question.

(c) A person notifies or gives a notification of a fact to another by taking steps reasonably required to inform the other person in ordinary course, whether or not the other person knows the fact.

(d) A person receives a notification when the notification:

(1) comes to the person's attention; or

(2) is duly delivered at the person's place of business or at any other place held out by the person as a place for receiving communications.

(e) An entity knows, has notice, or receives a notification of a fact for purposes of a particular transaction when the individual conducting the transaction for the entity knows, has notice, or receives a notification of the fact, or in any event when the fact would have been brought to the individual's attention had the entity exercised reasonable diligence. An entity exercises reasonable diligence if it maintains reasonable routines for communicating significant information to the individual conducting the transaction for the entity and there is reasonable compliance with the routines. Reasonable diligence does not require an individual acting for the entity to communicate information unless the communication is part of the individual's regular duties or the individual has reason to know of the transaction and that the transaction would be materially affected by the information.

COMMENT

Knowledge requires cognitive awareness of a fact, whereas notice is based on a lesser degree of awareness. The Act imposes constructive knowledge under limited circumstances. See Comments to Sections 301(c), 703, and 704.

§ 103. Effect of Operating Agreement; Nonwaivable Provisions

(a) Except as otherwise provided in subsection (b), all members of a limited liability company may enter into an operating agreement, which need not be in writing, to regulate the affairs of the company and the conduct of its business, and to govern relations among the members, managers, and company. To the extent the operating agreement does not otherwise provide, this [Act] governs relations among the members, managers, and company.

(b) The operating agreement may not:

(1) unreasonably restrict a right to information or access to records under Section 408;

(2) eliminate the duty of loyalty under Section 409(b) or 603(b)(3), but the agreement may:

(i) identify specific types or categories of activities that do not violate the duty of loyalty, if not manifestly unreasonable; and

(ii) specify the number or percentage of members or disinterested managers that may authorize or ratify, after full disclosure of all material facts, a specific act or transaction that otherwise would violate the duty of loyalty;

(3) unreasonably reduce the duty of care under Section 409(c) or 603(b)(3);

(4) eliminate the obligation of good faith and fair dealing under Section 409(d), but the operating agreement may determine the standards by which the performance of the obligation is to be measured, if the standards are not manifestly unreasonable;

(5)   vary the right to expel a member in an event specified in Section 601(6);

(6)   vary the requirement to wind up the limited liability company's business in a case specified in Section 801(3) or (4); or

(7)   restrict rights of a person, other than a manager, member, and transferee of a member's distributional interest, under this [Act].

COMMENT

The operating agreement is the essential contract that governs the affairs of a limited liability company. Since it is binding on all members, amendments must be approved by all members unless otherwise provided in the agreement. Although many agreements will be in writing, the agreement and any amendments may be oral or may be in the form of a record. Course of dealing, course of performance and usage of trade are relevant to determine the meaning of the agreement unless the agreement provides that all amendments must be in writing.

This section makes clear that the only matters an operating agreement may not control are specified in subsection (b). Accordingly, an operating agreement may modify or eliminate any rule specified in any section of this Act except matters specified in subsection (b). To the extent not otherwise mentioned in subsection (b), every section of this Act is simply a default rule, regardless of whether the language of the section appears to be otherwise mandatory. This approach eliminates the necessity of repeating the phrase "unless otherwise agreed" in each section and its commentary.

Under subsection (b)(1), an operating agreement may not unreasonably restrict the right to information or access to any records under Section 408. This does not create an independent obligation beyond Section 408 to maintain any specific records. Under subsections (b)(2) to (4), an irreducible core of fiduciary responsibilities survive any contrary provision in the operating agreement. Subsection (b)(2)(i) authorizes an operating agreement to modify, but not eliminate, the three specific duties of loyalty set forth in Section 409(b)(1) to (3) provided the modification itself is not manifestly unreasonable, a question of fact. Subsection (b)(2)(ii) preserves the common law right of the members to authorize future or ratify past violations of the duty of loyalty provided there has been a full disclosure of all material facts. The authorization or ratification must be unanimous unless otherwise provided in an operating agreement, because the authorization or ratification itself constitutes an amendment to the agreement. The authorization or ratification of specific past or future conduct may sanction conduct that would have been manifestly unreasonable under subsection (b)(2)(i).

§ 104.   Supplemental Principles of Law

(a)   Unless displaced by particular provisions of this [Act], the principles of law and equity supplement this [Act].

(b)   If an obligation to pay interest arises under this [Act] and the rate is not specified, the rate is that specified in [applicable statute].

COMMENT

Supplementary principles include, but are not limited to, the law of agency, estoppel, law merchant, and all other principles listed in UCC Section 1–103, including the law relative to the capacity to contract, fraud, misrepresentation, duress, coercion, mistake, bankruptcy, and other validating and invalidating clauses. Other principles such as those mentioned in UCC Section 1–205 (Course of Dealing and Usage of Trade) apply as well as course of performance. As with UPA 1994 Section 104, upon which this provision is based, no substantive change from either the UPA or the UCC is intended. Section 104(b) establishes the applicable rate of interest in the absence of an agreement among the members.

§ 105.   Name

(a)   The name of a limited liability company must contain "limited liability company" or "limited company" or the abbreviation "L.L.C.", "LLC", "L.C.", or "LC". "Limited" may be abbreviated as "Ltd.", and "company" may be abbreviated as "Co.".

(b)   Except as authorized by subsections (c) and (d), the name of a limited liability company must be distinguishable upon the records of the [Secretary of State] from:

(1)   the name of any corporation, limited partnership, or company incorporated, organized or authorized to transact business, in this State;

(2)   a name reserved or registered under Section 106 or 107;

(3)   a fictitious name approved under Section 1005 for a foreign company authorized to transact business in this State because its real name is unavailable.

(c)   A limited liability company may apply to the [Secretary of State] for authorization to use a name that is not distinguishable upon the records of the [Secretary of State] from one or more of the names described in subsection (b). The [Secretary of State] shall authorize use of the name applied for if:

(1)   the present user, registrant, or owner of a reserved name consents to the use in a record and submits an undertaking in form satisfactory to the [Secretary of State] to change the name to a name that is distinguishable upon the records of the [Secretary of State] from the name applied for; or

(2)   the applicant delivers to the [Secretary of State] a certified copy of the final judgment of a court of competent jurisdiction establishing the applicant's right to use the name applied for in this State.

(d)   A limited liability company may use the name, including a fictitious name, of another domestic or foreign company which is used in this State if the other company is organized or authorized to transact business in this State and the company proposing to use the name has:

(1)   merged with the other company;

(2)   been formed by reorganization with the other company; or

(3)   acquired substantially all of the assets, including the name, of the other company.

§ 106.   Reserved Name

(a)   A person may reserve the exclusive use of the name of a limited liability company, including a fictitious name for a foreign company whose name is not available, by delivering an application to the [Secretary of State] for filing. The application must set forth the name and address of the applicant and the name proposed to be reserved. If the [Secretary of State] finds that the name applied for is available, it must be reserved for the applicant's exclusive use for a nonrenewable 120-day period.

(b)   The owner of a name reserved for a limited liability company may transfer the reservation to another person by delivering to the [Secretary of State] a signed notice of the transfer which states the name and address of the transferee.

COMMENT

A foreign limited liability company that is not presently authorized to transact business in the State may reserve a fictitious name for a nonrenewable 120-day period. When its actual name is available, a company will generally register that name under Section 107 because the registration is valid for a year and may be extended indefinitely.

§ 107.   Registered Name

(a)   A foreign limited liability company may register its name subject to the requirements of Section 1005, if the name is distinguishable upon the records of the [Secretary of State] from names that are not available under Section 105(b).

(b)   A foreign limited liability company registers its name, or its name with any addition required by Section 1005, by delivering to the [Secretary of State] for filing an application:

(1)   setting forth its name, or its name with any addition required by Section 1005, the State or country and date of its organization, and a brief description of the nature of the business in which it is engaged; and

(2)   accompanied by a certificate of existence, or a record of similar import, from the State or country of organization.

(c)   A foreign limited liability company whose registration is effective may renew it for successive years by delivering for filing in the office of the [Secretary of State] a renewal application complying with subsection (b) between October 1 and December 31 of the preceding year. The renewal application renews the registration for the following calendar year.

(d)   A foreign limited liability company whose registration is effective may qualify as a foreign company under its name or consent in writing to the use of its name by a limited liability company later organized under this [Act] or by another foreign company later authorized to transact business in this State. The registered name terminates when the limited liability company is organized or the foreign company qualifies or consents to the qualification of another foreign company under the registered name.

§ 108.   Designated Office and Agent for Service of Process

(a)   A limited liability company and a foreign limited liability company authorized to do business in this State shall designate and continuously maintain in this State:

(1)   an office, which need not be a place of its business in this State; and

(2)   an agent and street address of the agent for service of process on the company.

(b)   An agent must be an individual resident of this State, a domestic corporation, another limited liability company, or a foreign corporation or foreign company authorized to do business in this State.

COMMENT

Limited liability companies organized under Section 202 or authorized to transact business under Section 1004 are required to designate and continuously maintain an office in the State. Although the designated office need not be a place of business, it most often will be the only place of business of the company. The company must also designate an agent for service of process within the State and the agent's street address. The agent's address need not be the same as the company's designated office address. The initial office and agent designations must be set forth in the articles of organization, including the address of the designated office. See Section 203(a)(2) to (3). The current office and agent designations must be set forth in the company's annual report. See Section 211(a)(2). See also Section 109 (procedure for changing the office or agent designations), Section 110 (procedure for an agent to resign), and Section 111(b) (the filing officer is the service agent for the company if it fails to maintain its own service agent).

§ 109.   Change of Designated Office or Agent for Service of Process

A limited liability company may change its designated office or agent for service of process by delivering to the [Secretary of State] for filing a statement of change which sets forth:

(1)   the name of the company;

(2)   the street address of its current designated office;

(3)   if the current designated office is to be changed, the street address of the new designated office;

(4)   the name and address of its current agent for service of process; and

(5)   if the current agent for service of process or street address of that agent is to be changed, the new address or the name and street address of the new agent for service of process.

§ 110.   Resignation of Agent for Service of Process

(a)   An agent for service of process of a limited liability company may resign by delivering to the [Secretary of State] for filing a record of the statement of resignation.

(b)   After filing a statement of resignation, the [Secretary of State] shall mail a copy to the designated office and another copy to the limited liability company at its principal office.

(c)   An agency is terminated on the 31st day after the statement is filed in the office of the [Secretary of State].

§ 111. Service of Process

(a)   An agent for service of process appointed by a limited liability company or a foreign limited liability company is an agent of the company for service of any process, notice, or demand required or permitted by law to be served upon the company.

(b)   If a limited liability company or foreign limited liability company fails to appoint or maintain an agent for service of process in this State or the agent for service of process cannot with reasonable diligence be found at the agent's address, the [Secretary of State] is an agent of the company upon whom process, notice, or demand may be served.

(c)   Service of any process, notice, or demand on the [Secretary of State] may be made by delivering to and leaving with the [Secretary of State], the [Assistant Secretary of State], or clerk having charge of the limited liability company department of the [Secretary of State's] office duplicate copies of the process, notice, or demand. If the process, notice, or demand is served on the [Secretary of State], the [Secretary of State] shall forward one of the copies by registered or certified mail, return receipt requested, to the company at its designated office. Service is effected under this subsection at the earliest of:

(1)   the date the company receives the process, notice, or demand;

(2)   the date shown on the return receipt, if signed on behalf of the company; or

(3)   five days after its deposit in the mail, if mailed postpaid and correctly addressed.

(d)   The [Secretary of State] shall keep a record of all processes, notices, and demands served pursuant to this section and record the time of and the action taken regarding the service.

(e)   This section does not affect the right to serve process, notice, or demand in any manner otherwise provided by law.

COMMENT

Service of process on a limited liability company and a foreign company authorized to transact business in the State must be made on the company's agent for service of process whose name and address should be on file with the filing office. If for any reason a company fails to appoint or maintain an agent for service of process or the agent cannot be found with reasonable diligence at the agent's address, the filing officer will be deemed the proper agent.

§ 112. Nature of Business and Powers

(a)   A limited liability company may be organized under this [Act] for any lawful purpose, subject to any law of this State governing or regulating business.

(b)   Unless its articles of organization provide otherwise, a limited liability company has the same powers as an individual to do all things necessary or convenient to carry on its business or affairs, including power to:

(1)   sue and be sued, and defend in its name;

(2)   purchase, receive, lease, or otherwise acquire, and own, hold, improve, use, and otherwise deal with real or personal property, or any legal or equitable interest in property, wherever located;

(3)   sell, convey, mortgage, grant a security interest in, lease, exchange, and otherwise encumber or dispose of all or any part of its property;

(4)   purchase, receive, subscribe for, or otherwise acquire, own, hold, vote, use, sell, mortgage, lend, grant a security interest in, or otherwise dispose of and deal in and with, shares or other interests in or obligations of any other entity;

(5)   make contracts and guarantees, incur liabilities, borrow money, issue its notes, bonds, and other obligations, which may be convertible into or include the option to purchase other securities of the limited liability company, and secure any of its obligations by a mortgage on or a security interest in any of its property, franchises, or income;

(6)   lend money, invest and reinvest its funds, and receive and hold real and personal property as security for repayment;

(7)   be a promoter, partner, member, associate, or manager of any partnership, joint venture, trust, or other entity;

(8)   conduct its business, locate offices, and exercise the powers granted by this [Act] within or without this State;

(9)   elect managers and appoint officers, employees, and agents of the limited liability company, define their duties, fix their compensation, and lend them money and credit;

(10) pay pensions and establish pension plans, pension trusts, profit sharing plans, bonus plans, option plans, and benefit or incentive plans for any or all of its current or former members, managers, officers, employees, and agents;

(11) make donations for the public welfare or for charitable, scientific, or educational purposes; and

(12) make payments or donations, or do any other act, not inconsistent with law, that furthers the business of the limited liability company.

COMMENT

A limited liability company may be organized for any lawful purpose unless the State has specifically prohibited a company from engaging in a specific activity. For example, many States require that certain regulated industries, such as banking and insurance, be conducted only by organizations that meet the special requirements. Also, many States impose restrictions on activities in which a limited liability company may engage. For example, the practice of certain professionals is often subject to special conditions.

A limited liability company has the power to engage in and perform important and necessary acts related to its operation and function. A company's power to enter into a transaction is distinguishable from the authority of an agent to enter into the transaction. See Section 301 (agency rules).

[ARTICLE] 2
ORGANIZATION

§ 201.   Limited Liability Company as Legal Entity

A limited liability company is a legal entity distinct from its members.

COMMENT

A limited liability company is legally distinct from its members who are not normally liable for the debts, obligations, and liabilities of the company. See Section 303. Accordingly, members are not proper parties to suits against the company unless an object of the proceeding is to enforce members' rights against the company or to enforce their liability to the company.

§ 202.   Organization

(a)   One or more persons may organize a limited liability company, consisting of one or more members, by delivering articles of organization to the office of the [Secretary of State] for filing.

(b)   Unless a delayed effective date is specified, the existence of a limited liability company begins when the articles of organization are filed.

(c)   The filing of the articles of organization by the [Secretary of State] is conclusive proof that the organizers satisfied all conditions precedent to the creation of a limited liability company.

COMMENT

Any person may organize a limited liability company by performing the ministerial act of signing and filing the articles of organization. The person need not be a member. As a matter of flexibility, a company may be organized and operated with only one member to enable sole proprietors to obtain the benefit of a liability shield. New and important Internal Revenue Service announcements clarify that a one-member limited liability company will not be taxed like a corporation. Nor will it be taxed like a partnership since it lacks at least two members. Rather, a one-member limited liability company is disregarded for Federal tax purposes and its operations are reported on the return of its single owner.

The existence of a company begins when the articles are filed. Therefore, the filing of the articles of organization is conclusive as to the existence of the limited liability shield for persons who enter into transactions on behalf of the company. Until the articles are filed, a firm is not organized under this Act and is not a "limited liability company" as defined in Section 101(9). In that case, the parties' relationships are not governed by this Act unless they have expressed a contractual intent to be bound by the provisions of the Act. Third parties would also not be governed by the provisions of this Act unless they have expressed a contractual intent to extend a limited liability shield to the members of the would-be limited liability company.

§ 203. Articles of Organization

(a) Articles of organization of a limited liability company must set forth:

(1) the name of the company;

(2) the address of the initial designated office;

(3) the name and street address of the initial agent for service of process;

(4) the name and address of each organizer;

(5) whether the company is to be a term company and, if so, the term specified;

(6) whether the company is to be manager-managed, and, if so, the name and address of each initial manager; and

(7) whether one or more of the members of the company are to be liable for its debts and obligations under Section 303(c).

(b) Articles of organization of a limited liability company may set forth:

(1) provisions permitted to be set forth in an operating agreement; or

(2) other matters not inconsistent with law.

(c) Articles of organization of a limited liability company may not vary the nonwaivable provisions of Section 103(b). As to all other matters, if any provision of an operating agreement is inconsistent with the articles of organization:

(1) the operating agreement controls as to managers, members, and members' transferees; and

(2) the articles of organization control as to persons, other than managers, members and their transferees, who reasonably rely on the articles to their detriment.

COMMENT

The articles serve primarily a notice function and generally do not reflect the substantive agreement of the members regarding the business affairs of the company. Those matters are generally reserved for an operating agreement which may be unwritten. Under Section 203(b), the articles may contain provisions permitted to be set forth in an operating agreement. Where the articles and operating agreement conflict, the operating agreement controls as to members but the articles control as to third parties. The articles may also contain any other matter not inconsistent with law. The most important is a Section 301(c) limitation on the authority of a member or manager to transfer interests in the company's real property.

A company will be at-will unless it is designated as a term company and the duration of its term is specified in its articles under Section 203(a)(5). The duration of a term company may be specified in any manner which sets forth a specific and final date for the dissolution of the company. For example, the period specified may be in the form of "50 years from the date of filing of the articles" or "the period ending on January 1, 2020." Mere specification of a particular undertaking of an uncertain business duration is not sufficient unless the particular undertaking is within a longer fixed period. An example of this type of designation would include "2020 or until the building is completed, whichever occurs first." When the specified period is incorrectly specified, the company will be an at-will company. Notwithstanding the correct specification of a term in the articles, a company will be an at-will company among the members under Section 203(c)(1) if an operating agreement so provides. A term company that continues after the expiration of its term specified in its articles will also be an at-will company.

A term company possesses several important default rule characteristics that differentiate it from an at-will company. An operating agreement may alter any of these rules. Generally, a member of an at-will company may rightfully dissociate at any time whereas a dissociation from a term company prior to the expiration of the specified term is wrongful. See Comments to Section 602(b). Accordingly, a dissociated member of an at-will company is entitled to have the company purchase that member's interest for its fair value determined as of the date of the member's dissociation. A dissociated member of a term company must generally await the expiration of the agreed term to withdraw the fair value of the interest determined at as of the date of the expiration of the agreed term. Thus, a dissociated member in an at-will company receives the fair value of their interest sooner than in a term company and also does not bear the risk of valuation changes for the remainder of the specified term. See Comments to Section 701(a).

A company will be member-managed unless it is designated as manager-managed under Section 203(a)(6). Absent further designation in the articles, a company will be a member-managed at-will company. The designation of a limited liability company as either member-or manager-managed is important because it defines who are agents and have the apparent authority to bind the company under Section 301. In a member-managed company, the members have the agency authority to bind the company. In a manager-managed company only the managers have that authority. New and important Internal Revenue Service announcements clarify that the agency structure of a limited liability company will not cause it to be taxed like a corporation. The agency designation relates only to agency and does not preclude members of a manager-managed company from participating in the actual management of company business. See Comments to Section 404(b).

§ 204.   Amendment or Restatement of Articles of Organization

(a)   Articles of organization of a limited liability company may be amended at any time by delivering articles of amendment to the [Secretary of State] for filing. The articles of amendment must set forth the:

(1)   name of the limited liability company;

(2)   date of filing of the articles of organization; and

(3)   amendment to the articles.

(b)   A limited liability company may restate its articles of organization at any time. Restated articles of organization must be signed and filed in the same manner as articles of amendment. Restated articles of organization must be designated as such in the heading and state in the heading or in an introductory paragraph the limited liability company's present name and, if it has been changed, all of its former names and the date of the filing of its initial articles of organization.

COMMENT

An amendment to the articles requires the consent of all the members unless an operating agreement provides for a lesser number. See Section 404(c)(3).

§ 205.   Signing of Records

(a)   Except as otherwise provided in this [Act], a record to be filed by or on behalf of a limited liability company in the office of the [Secretary of State] must be signed in the name of the company by a:

(1)   manager of a manager-managed company;

(2)   member of a member-managed company;

(3)   person organizing the company, if the company has not been formed; or

(4)   fiduciary, if the company is in the hands of a receiver, trustee, or other court-appointed fiduciary.

(b)   A record signed under subsection (a) must state adjacent to the signature the name and capacity of the signer.

(c)   Any person may sign a record to be filed under subsection (a) by an attorney-in-fact. Powers of attorney relating to the signing of records to be filed under subsection (a) by an attorney-in-fact need not be filed in the office of the [Secretary of State] as evidence of authority by the person filing but must be retained by the company.

COMMENT

Both a writing and a record may be signed. An electronic record is signed when a person adds a name to the record with the intention to authenticate the record. See Sections 101(16) ("record" definition) and 101(17) ("signed" definition).

Other provisions of this Act also provide for the filing of records with the filing office but do not require signing by the persons specified in clauses (1) to (3). Those specific sections prevail.

§ 206.   Filing in Office of [Secretary of State]

(a)   Articles of organization or any other record authorized to be filed under this [Act] must be in a medium permitted by the [Secretary of State] and must be delivered to the office of the [Secretary of State]. Unless the [Secretary of State] determines that a record fails to comply as to form with the filing requirements of this [Act], and if all filing fees have been paid, the [Secretary of State] shall file the record and send a receipt for the record and the fees to the limited liability company or its representative.

(b)   Upon request and payment of a fee, the [Secretary of State] shall send to the requester a certified copy of the requested record.

(c)   Except as otherwise provided in subsection (d) and Section 207(c), a record accepted for filing by the [Secretary of State] is effective:

(1)   at the time of filing on the date it is filed, as evidenced by the [Secretary of State's] date and time endorsement on the original record; or

(2)   at the time specified in the record as its effective time on the date it is filed.

(d)   A record may specify a delayed effective time and date, and if it does so the record becomes effective at the time and date specified. If a delayed effective date but no time is specified, the record is effective at the close of business on that date. If a delayed effective date is later than the 90th day after the record is filed, the record is effective on the 90th day.

COMMENT

The definition and use of the term "record" permits filings with the filing office under this Act to conform to technological advances that have been adopted by the filing office. However, since Section 206(a) provides that the filing "must be in a medium permitted by the [Secretary of State]", the Act simply conforms to filing changes as they are adopted.

§ 207.   Correcting Filed Record

(a)   A limited liability company or foreign limited liability company may correct a record filed by the [Secretary of State] if the record contains a false or erroneous statement or was defectively signed.

(b)   A record is corrected:

(1)   by preparing articles of correction that:

(i)   describe the record, including its filing date, or attach a copy of it to the articles of correction;

(ii)   specify the incorrect statement and the reason it is incorrect or the manner in which the signing was defective; and

(iii)   correct the incorrect statement or defective signing; and

(2)   by delivering the corrected record to the [Secretary of State] for filing.

(c)   Articles of correction are effective retroactively on the effective date of the record they correct except as to persons relying on the uncorrected record and adversely affected by the correction. As to those persons, articles of correction are effective when filed.

§ 208.   Certificate of Existence or Authorization

(a)   A person may request the [Secretary of State] to furnish a certificate of existence for a limited liability company or a certificate of authorization for a foreign limited liability company.

(b)   A certificate of existence for a limited liability company must set forth:

(1)   the company's name;

(2)   that it is duly organized under the laws of this State, the date of organization, whether its duration is at-will or for a specified term, and, if the latter, the period specified;

(3)   if payment is reflected in the records of the [Secretary of State] and if nonpayment affects the existence of the company, that all fees, taxes, and penalties owed to this State have been paid;

(4)   whether its most recent annual report required by Section 211 has been filed with the [Secretary of State];

(5)   that articles of termination have not been filed; and

(6)   other facts of record in the office of the [Secretary of State] which may be requested by the applicant.

(c)   A certificate of authorization for a foreign limited liability company must set forth:

(1)   the company's name used in this State;

(2)   that it is authorized to transact business in this State;

(3)   if payment is reflected in the records of the [Secretary of State] and if nonpayment affects the authorization of the company, that all fees, taxes, and penalties owed to this State have been paid;

(4)   whether its most recent annual report required by Section 211 has been filed with the [Secretary of State];

(5)   that a certificate of cancellation has not been filed; and

(6)   other facts of record in the office of the [Secretary of State] which may be requested by the applicant.

(d)   Subject to any qualification stated in the certificate, a certificate of existence or authorization issued by the [Secretary of State] may be relied upon as conclusive evidence that the domestic or foreign limited liability company is in existence or is authorized to transact business in this State.

§ 209.   Liability for False Statement in Filed Record

If a record authorized or required to be filed under this [Act] contains a false statement, one who suffers loss by reliance on the statement may recover damages for the loss from a person who signed the record or caused another to sign it on the person's behalf and knew the statement to be false at the time the record was signed.

§ 210.   Filing by Judicial Act

If a person required by Section 205 to sign any record fails or refuses to do so, any other person who is adversely affected by the failure or refusal may petition the [designate the appropriate court] to direct the signing of the record. If the court finds that it is proper for the record to be signed and that a person so designated has failed or refused to sign the record, it shall order the [Secretary of State] to sign and file an appropriate record.

§ 211.   Annual Report for [Secretary of State]

(a)   A limited liability company, and a foreign limited liability company authorized to transact business in this State, shall deliver to the [Secretary of State] for filing an annual report that sets forth:

(1)   the name of the company and the State or country under whose law it is organized;

(2)   the address of its designated office and the name and address of its agent for service of process in this State;

(3)   the address of its principal office; and

(4)   the names and business addresses of any managers.

(b)   Information in an annual report must be current as of the date the annual report is signed on behalf of the limited liability company.

(c)   The first annual report must be delivered to the [Secretary of State] between [January 1 and April 1] of the year following the calendar year in which a limited liability company was organized or a foreign company was authorized to transact business. Subsequent annual reports must be delivered to the [Secretary of State] between [January 1 and April 1] of the ensuing calendar years.

(d)   If an annual report does not contain the information required in subsection (a), the [Secretary of State] shall promptly notify the reporting limited liability company or foreign limited liability company and return the report to it for correction. If the report is corrected to contain the information required in subsection (a) and delivered to the [Secretary of State] within 30 days after the effective date of the notice, it is timely filed.

COMMENT

Failure to deliver the annual report within 60 days after its due date is a primary ground for administrative dissolution of the company under Section 809. See Comments to Sections 809 to 812.

[ARTICLE] 3
RELATIONS OF MEMBERS AND MANAGERS
TO PERSONS DEALING WITH LIMITED
LIABILITY COMPANY

§ 301.   Agency of Members and Managers

(a)   Subject to subsections (b) and (c):

(1)   Each member is an agent of the limited liability company for the purpose of its business, and an act of a member, including the signing of an instrument in the company's name, for apparently carrying on in the ordinary course the company's business or business of the kind carried on by the company binds the company, unless the member had no authority to act for the company in the particular matter and the person with whom the member was dealing knew or had notice that the member lacked authority.

(2)   An act of a member which is not apparently for carrying on in the ordinary course the company's business or business of the kind carried on by the company binds the company only if the act was authorized by the other members.

(b)   Subject to subsection (c), in a manager-managed company:

(1)   A member is not an agent of the company for the purpose of its business solely by reason of being a member. Each manager is an agent of the company for the purpose of its business, and an act of a manager, including the signing of an instrument in the company's name, for apparently carrying on in the ordinary course the company's business or business of the kind carried on by the company binds the company, unless the manager had no authority to act for the company in the particular matter and the person with whom the manager was dealing knew or had notice that the manager lacked authority.

(2) An act of a manager which is not apparently for carrying on in the ordinary course the company's business or business of the kind carried on by the company binds the company only if the act was authorized under Section 404.

(c) Unless the articles of organization limit their authority, any member of a member-managed company or manager of a manager-managed company may sign and deliver any instrument transferring or affecting the company's interest in real property. The instrument is conclusive in favor of a person who gives value without knowledge of the lack of the authority of the person signing and delivering the instrument.

COMMENT

Members of a member-managed and managers of manager-managed company, as agents of the firm, have the apparent authority to bind a company to third parties. Members of a manager-managed company are not as such agents of the firm and do not have the apparent authority, as members, to bind a company. Members and managers with apparent authority possess actual authority by implication unless the actual authority is restricted in an operating agreement. Apparent authority extends to acts for carrying on in the ordinary course the company's business and business of the kind carried on by the company. Acts beyond this scope bind the company only where supported by actual authority created before the act or ratified after the act.

Ordinarily, restrictions on authority in an operating agreement do not affect the apparent authority of members and managers to bind the company to third parties without notice of the restriction. However, the restriction may make a member or manager's conduct wrongful and create liability to the company for the breach. This rule is subject to three important exceptions. First, under Section 301(c), a limitation reflected in the articles of organization on the authority of any member or manager to sign and deliver an instrument affecting an interest in company real property is effective when filed, even to persons without knowledge of the agent's lack of authority. New and important Internal Revenue Service announcements clarify that the agency structure of a limited liability company will not cause it to be taxed like a corporation. Secondly, under Section 703, a dissociated member's apparent authority terminates two years after dissociation, even to persons without knowledge of the dissociation. Thirdly, under Section 704, a dissociated member's apparent authority may be terminated earlier than the two years by filing a statement of dissociation. The statement is effective 90 days after filing, even to persons without knowledge of the filing. Together, these three provisions provide constructive knowledge to the world of the lack of apparent authority of an agent to bind the company.

§ 302. Limited Liability Company Liable for Member's or Manager's Actionable Conduct

A limited liability company is liable for loss or injury caused to a person, or for a penalty incurred, as a result of a wrongful act or omission, or other actionable conduct, of a member or manager acting in the ordinary course of business of the company or with authority of the company.

COMMENT

Since a member of a manager-managed company is not as such an agent, the acts of the member are not imputed to the company unless the member is acting under actual or apparent authority created by circumstances other than membership status.

§ 303. Liability of Members and Managers

(a) Except as otherwise provided in subsection (c), the debts, obligations, and liabilities of a limited liability company, whether arising in contract, tort, or otherwise, are solely the debts, obligations, and liabilities of the company. A member or manager is not personally liable for a debt, obligation, or liability of the company solely by reason of being or acting as a member or manager.

(b) The failure of a limited liability company to observe the usual company formalities or requirements relating to the exercise of its company powers or management of its business is not a ground for imposing personal liability on the members or managers for liabilities of the company.

(c) All or specified members of a limited liability company are liable in their capacity as members for all or specified debts, obligations, or liabilities of the company if:

(1) a provision to that effect is contained in the articles of organization; and

(2)   a member so liable has consented in writing to the adoption of the provision or to be bound by the provision.

COMMENT

A member or manager, as an agent of the company, is not liable for the debts, obligations, and liabilities of the company simply because of the agency. A member or manager is responsible for acts or omissions to the extent those acts or omissions would be actionable in contract or tort against the member or manager if that person were acting in an individual capacity. Where a member or manager delegates or assigns the authority or duty to exercise appropriate company functions, the member or manager is ordinarily not personally liable for the acts or omissions of the officer, employee, or agent if the member or manager has complied with the duty of care set forth in Section 409(c).

Under Section 303(c), the usual liability shield may be waived, in whole or in part, provided the waiver is reflected in the articles of organization and the member has consented in writing to be bound by the waiver. The importance and unusual nature of the waiver consent requires that the consent be evidenced by a writing and not merely an unwritten record. See Comments to Section 205. New and important Internal Revenue Service announcements clarify that the owner liability structure of a limited liability company (other than a foreign limited liability company formed outside the United States) will not cause it to be taxed like a corporation.

[ARTICLE] 4
RELATIONS OF MEMBERS TO EACH OTHER
AND TO LIMITED LIABILITY COMPANY

§ 401.   Form of Contribution

A contribution of a member of a limited liability company may consist of tangible or intangible property or other benefit to the company, including money, promissory notes, services performed, or other agreements to contribute cash or property, or contracts for services to be performed.

COMMENT

Unless otherwise provided in an operating agreement, admission of a member and the nature and valuation of a would-be member's contribution are matters requiring the consent of all of the other members. See Section 404(c)(7). An agreement to contribute to a company is controlled by the operating agreement and therefore may not be created or modified without amending that agreement through the unanimous consent of all the members, including the member to be bound by the new contribution terms. See 404(c)(1).

§ 402.   Member's Liability for Contributions

(a)   A member's obligation to contribute money, property, or other benefit to, or to perform services for, a limited liability company is not excused by the member's death, disability, or other inability to perform personally. If a member does not make the required contribution of property or services, the member is obligated at the option of the company to contribute money equal to the value of that portion of the stated contribution which has not been made.

(b)   A creditor of a limited liability company who extends credit or otherwise acts in reliance on an obligation described in subsection (a), and without notice of any compromise under Section 404(c)(5), may enforce the original obligation.

COMMENT

An obligation need not be in writing to be enforceable. Given the informality of some companies, a writing requirement may frustrate reasonable expectations of members based on a clear oral agreement. Obligations may be compromised with the consent of all of the members under Section 404(c)(5), but the compromise is generally effective only among the consenting members. Company creditors are bound by the compromise only as provided in Section 402(b).

§ 403.   Member's and Manager's Rights to Payments and Reimbursement

(a)   A limited liability company shall reimburse a member or manager for payments made and indemnify a member or manager for liabilities incurred by the member or manager in the ordinary course of the business of the company or for the preservation of its business or property.

(b)   A limited liability company shall reimburse a member for an advance to the company beyond the amount of contribution the member agreed to make.

(c)   A payment or advance made by a member which gives rise to an obligation of a limited liability company under subsection (a) or (b) constitutes a loan to the company upon which interest accrues from the date of the payment or advance.

(d)   A member is not entitled to remuneration for services performed for a limited liability company, except for reasonable compensation for services rendered in winding up the business of the company.

COMMENT

The presence of a liability shield will ordinarily prevent a member or manager from incurring personal liability on behalf of the company in the ordinary course of the company's business. Where a member of a member-managed or a manager of a manager-managed company incurs such liabilities, Section 403(a) provides that the company must indemnify the member or manager where that person acted in the ordinary course of the company's business or the preservation of its property. A member or manager is therefore entitled to indemnification only if the act was within the member or manager's actual authority. A member or manager is therefore not entitled to indemnification for conduct that violates the duty of care set forth in Section 409(c) or for tortious conduct against a third party. Since members of a manager-managed company do not possess the apparent authority to bind the company, it would be more unusual for such a member to incur a liability for indemnification in the ordinary course of the company's business.

§ 404.   Management of Limited Liability Company

(a)   In a member-managed company:

     (1)   each member has equal rights in the management and conduct of the company's business; and

     (2)   except as otherwise provided in subsection (c), any matter relating to the business of the company may be decided by a majority of the members.

(b)   In a manager-managed company:

     (1)   each manager has equal rights in the management and conduct of the company's business;

     (2)   except as otherwise provided in subsection (c), any matter relating to the business of the company may be exclusively decided by the manager or, if there is more than one manager, by a majority of the managers; and

     (3)   a manager:

         (i)   must be designated, appointed, elected, removed, or replaced by a vote, approval, or consent of a majority of the members; and

         (ii)   holds office until a successor has been elected and qualified, unless the manager sooner resigns or is removed.

(c)   The only matters of a member or manager-managed company's business requiring the consent of all of the members are:

     (1)   the amendment of the operating agreement under Section 103;

     (2)   the authorization or ratification of acts or transactions under Section 103(b)(2)(ii) which would otherwise violate the duty of loyalty;

     (3)   an amendment to the articles of organization under Section 204;

     (4)   the compromise of an obligation to make a contribution under Section 402(b);

(5)   the compromise, as among members, of an obligation of a member to make a contribution or return money or other property paid or distributed in violation of this [Act];

(6)   the making of interim distributions under Section 405(a), including the redemption of an interest;

(7)   the admission of a new member;

(8)   the use of the company's property to redeem an interest subject to a charging order;

(9)   the consent to dissolve the company under Section 801(b)(2);

(10)   a waiver of the right to have the company's business wound up and the company terminated under Section 802(b);

(11)   the consent of members to merge with another entity under Section 904(c)(1); and

(12)   the sale, lease, exchange, or other disposal of all, or substantially all, of the company's property with or without goodwill.

(d)   Action requiring the consent of members or managers under this [Act] may be taken without a meeting.

(e)   A member or manager may appoint a proxy to vote or otherwise act for the member or manager by signing an appointment instrument, either personally or by the member's or manager's attorney-in-fact.

COMMENT

In a member-managed company, each member has equal rights in the management and conduct of the company's business unless otherwise provided in an operating agreement. For example, an operating agreement may allocate voting rights based upon capital contributions rather than the subsection (a) per capita rule. Also, member disputes as to any matter relating to the company's business may be resolved by a majority of the members unless the matter relates to a matter specified in subsection (c) (unanimous consent required). Regardless of how the members allocate management rights, each member is an agent of the company with the apparent authority to bind the company in the ordinary course of its business. See Comments to Section 301(a). A member's right to participate in management terminates upon dissociation. See Section 603(b)(1).

In a manager-managed company, the members, unless also managers, have no rights in the management and conduct of the company's business unless otherwise provided in an operating agreement. If there is more than one manager, manager disputes as to any matter relating to the company's business may be resolved by a majority of the managers unless the matter relates to a matter specified in subsection (c) (unanimous member consent required). Managers must be designated, appointed, or elected by a majority of the members. A manager need not be a member and is an agent of the company with the apparent authority to bind the company in the ordinary course of its business. See Sections 101(10) and 301(b).

To promote clarity and certainty, subsection (c) specifies those exclusive matters requiring the unanimous consent of the members, whether the company is member-or manager-managed. For example, interim distributions, including redemptions, may not be made without the unanimous consent of all the members. Unless otherwise agreed, all other company matters are to be determined under the majority of members or managers rules of subsections (a) and (b).

§ 405.   Sharing of and Right to Distributions

(a)   Any distributions made by a limited liability company before its dissolution and winding up must be in equal shares.

(b)   A member has no right to receive, and may not be required to accept, a distribution in kind.

(c)   If a member becomes entitled to receive a distribution, the member has the status of, and is entitled to all remedies available to, a creditor of the limited liability company with respect to the distribution.

COMMENT

Recognizing the informality of many limited liability companies, this section creates a simple default rule regarding interim distributions. Any interim distributions made must be in equal shares and approved by all members. See Section 404(c)(6). The rule assumes that: profits will be shared equally; some distributions will constitute a return of contributions that should be shared equally rather than a distribution of profits; and property contributors should have the right to veto any distribution that threatens their return of contributions on liquidation. In the simple case where the members make equal contributions of property or equal contributions of services, those assumptions avoid the necessity of maintaining a complex capital account or determining profits. Where some members contribute services and others property, the unanimous vote necessary to approve interim distributions protects against unwanted distributions of contributions to service contributors. Consistently, Section 408(a) does not require the company to maintain a separate account for each member, the Act does not contain a default rule for allocating profits and losses, and Section 806(b) requires that liquidating distributions to members be made in equal shares after the return of contributions not previously returned. See Comments to Section 806(b).

Section 405(c) governs distributions declared or made when the company was solvent. Section 406 governs distributions declared or made when the company is insolvent.

§ 406.   Limitations on Distributions

(a)   A distribution may not be made if:

(1)   the limited liability company would not be able to pay its debts as they become due in the ordinary course of business; or

(2)   the company's total assets would be less than the sum of its total liabilities plus the amount that would be needed, if the company were to be dissolved, wound up, and terminated at the time of the distribution, to satisfy the preferential rights upon dissolution, winding up, and termination of members whose preferential rights are superior to those receiving the distribution.

(b)   A limited liability company may base a determination that a distribution is not prohibited under subsection (a) on financial statements prepared on the basis of accounting practices and principles that are reasonable in the circumstances or on a fair valuation or other method that is reasonable in the circumstances.

(c)   Except as otherwise provided in subsection (e), the effect of a distribution under subsection (a) is measured:

(1)   in the case of distribution by purchase, redemption, or other acquisition of a distributional interest in a limited liability company, as of the date money or other property is transferred or debt incurred by the company; and

(2)   in all other cases, as of the date the:

(i)   distribution is authorized if the payment occurs within 120 days after the date of authorization; or

(ii)   payment is made if it occurs more than 120 days after the date of authorization.

(d)   A limited liability company's indebtedness to a member incurred by reason of a distribution made in accordance with this section is at parity with the company's indebtedness to its general, unsecured creditors.

(e)   Indebtedness of a limited liability company, including indebtedness issued in connection with or as part of a distribution, is not considered a liability for purposes of determinations under subsection (a) if its terms provide that payment of principal and interest are made only if and to the extent that payment of a distribution to members could then be made under this section. If the indebtedness is issued as a distribution, each payment of principal or interest on the indebtedness is treated as a distribution, the effect of which is measured on the date the payment is made.

COMMENT

This section establishes the validity of company distributions, which in turn determines the potential liability of members and managers for improper distributions under Section 407. Distributions are improper if the company is insolvent under subsection (a) at the time the distribution is measured under subsection (c). In recognition of the informality of many limited liability companies, the solvency determination under subsection (b) may be made on the basis of a fair valuation or other method reasonable under the circumstances.

The application of the equity insolvency and balance sheet tests present special problems in the context of the purchase, redemption, or other acquisition of a company's distributional interests. Special rules establish the time of measurement of such transfers. Under Section 406(c)(1), the time for measuring the effect of a distribution to purchase a distributional interest is the date of payment. The company may make payment either by transferring property or incurring a debt to transfer property in the future. In the latter case, subsection (c)(1) establishes a clear rule that the legality of the distribution is tested when the debt is actually incurred, not later when the debt is actually paid. Under Section 406(e), indebtedness is not considered a liability for purposes of subsection (a) if the terms of the indebtedness itself provide that payments can be made only if and to the extent that a payment of a distribution could then be made under this section. The effect makes the holder of the indebtedness junior to all other creditors but senior to members in their capacity as members.

§ 407. Liability for Unlawful Distributions

(a) A member of a member-managed company or a member or manager of a manager-managed company who votes for or assents to a distribution made in violation of Section 406, the articles of organization, or the operating agreement is personally liable to the company for the amount of the distribution which exceeds the amount that could have been distributed without violating Section 406, the articles of organization, or the operating agreement if it is established that the member or manager did not perform the member's or manager's duties in compliance with Section 409.

(b) A member of a manager-managed company who knew a distribution was made in violation of Section 406, the articles of organization, or the operating agreement is personally liable to the company, but only to the extent that the distribution received by the member exceeded the amount that could have been properly paid under Section 406.

(c) A member or manager against whom an action is brought under this section may implead in the action all:

(1) other members or managers who voted for or assented to the distribution in violation of subsection (a) and may compel contribution from them; and

(2) members who received a distribution in violation of subsection (b) and may compel contribution from the member in the amount received in violation of subsection (b).

(d) A proceeding under this section is barred unless it is commenced within two years after the distribution.

COMMENT

Whenever members or managers fail to meet the standards of conduct of Section 409 and vote for or assent to an unlawful distribution, they are personally liable to the company for the portion of the distribution that exceeds the maximum amount that could have been lawfully distributed. The recovery remedy under this section extends only to the company, not the company's creditors. Under subsection (a), members and managers are not liable for an unlawful distribution provided their vote in favor of the distribution satisfies the duty of care of Section 409(c).

Subsection (a) creates personal liability in favor of the company against members or managers who approve an unlawful distribution for the entire amount of a distribution that could not be lawfully distributed. Subsection (b) creates personal liability against only members who knowingly received the unlawful distribution, but only in the amount measured by the portion of the actual distribution received that was not lawfully made. Members who both vote for or assent to an unlawful distribution and receive a portion or all of the distribution will be liable, at the election of the company, under either but not both subsections.

A member or manager who is liable under subsection (a) may seek contribution under subsection (c)(1) from other members and managers who also voted for or assented to the same distribution and may also seek recoupment under subsection (c)(2) from members who received the distribution, but only if they accepted the payments knowing they were unlawful.

The two-year statute of limitations of subsection (d) is measured from the date of the distribution. The date of the distribution is determined under Section 406(c).

§ 408.   Member's Right to Information

(a)   A limited liability company shall provide members and their agents and attorneys access to its records, if any, at the company's principal office or other reasonable locations specified in the operating agreement. The company shall provide former members and their agents and attorneys access for proper purposes to records pertaining to the period during which they were members. The right of access provides the opportunity to inspect and copy records during ordinary business hours. The company may impose a reasonable charge, limited to the costs of labor and material, for copies of records furnished.

(b)   A limited liability company shall furnish to a member, and to the legal representative of a deceased member or member under legal disability:

(1)   without demand, information concerning the company's business or affairs reasonably required for the proper exercise of the member's rights and performance of the member's duties under the operating agreement or this [Act]; and

(2)   on demand, other information concerning the company's business or affairs, except to the extent the demand or the information demanded is unreasonable or otherwise improper under the circumstances.

(c)   A member has the right upon written demand given to the limited liability company to obtain at the company's expense a copy of any written operating agreement.

COMMENT

Recognizing the informality of many limited liability companies, subsection (a) does not require a company to maintain any records. In general, a company should maintain records necessary to enable members to determine their share of profits and losses and their rights on dissociation. If inadequate records are maintained to determine those and other critical rights, a member may maintain an action for an accounting under Section 410(a). Normally, a company will maintain at least records required by state or federal authorities regarding tax and other filings.

The obligation to furnish access includes the obligation to insure that all records, if any, are accessible in intelligible form. For example, a company that switches computer systems has an obligation either to convert the records from the old system or retain at least one computer capable of accessing the records from the old system.

The right to inspect and copy records maintained is not conditioned on a member or former member's purpose or motive. However, an abuse of the access and copy right may create a remedy in favor of the other members as a violation of the requesting member or former member's obligation of good faith and fair dealing. See Section 409(d).

Although a company is not required to maintain any records under subsection (a), it is nevertheless subject to a disclosure duty to furnish specified information under subsection (b)(1). A company must therefore furnish to members, without demand, information reasonably needed for members to exercise their rights and duties as members. A member's exercise of these duties justifies an unqualified right of access to the company's records. The member's right to company records may not be unreasonably restricted by the operating agreement. See Section 103(b)(1).

§ 409.   General Standards of Member's and Manager's Conduct

(a)   The only fiduciary duties a member owes to a member-managed company and its other members are the duty of loyalty and the duty of care imposed by subsections (b) and (c).

(b)   A member's duty of loyalty to a member-managed company and its other members is limited to the following:

(1) to account to the company and to hold as trustee for it any property, profit, or benefit derived by the member in the conduct or winding up of the company's business or derived from a use by the member of the company's property, including the appropriation of a company's opportunity;

(2) to refrain from dealing with the company in the conduct or winding up of the company's business as or on behalf of a party having an interest adverse to the company; and

(3) to refrain from competing with the company in the conduct of the company's business before the dissolution of the company.

(c) A member's duty of care to a member-managed company and its other members in the conduct of and winding up of the company's business is limited to refraining from engaging in grossly negligent or reckless conduct, intentional misconduct, or a knowing violation of law.

(d) A member shall discharge the duties to a member-managed company and its other members under this [Act] or under the operating agreement and exercise any rights consistently with the obligation of good faith and fair dealing.

(e) A member of a member-managed company does not violate a duty or obligation under this [Act] or under the operating agreement merely because the member's conduct furthers the member's own interest.

(f) A member of a member-managed company may lend money to and transact other business with the company. As to each loan or transaction, the rights and obligations of the member are the same as those of a person who is not a member, subject to other applicable law.

(g) This section applies to a person winding up the limited liability company's business as the personal or legal representative of the last surviving member as if the person were a member.

(h) In a manager-managed company:

(1) a member who is not also a manager owes no duties to the company or to the other members solely by reason of being a member;

(2) a manager is held to the same standards of conduct prescribed for members in subsections (b) through (f);

(3) a member who pursuant to the operating agreement exercises some or all of the rights of a manager in the management and conduct of the company's business is held to the standards of conduct in subsections (b) through (f) to the extent that the member exercises the managerial authority vested in a manager by this [Act]; and

(4) a manager is relieved of liability imposed by law for violation of the standards prescribed by subsections (b) through (f) to the extent of the managerial authority delegated to the members by the operating agreement.

COMMENT

Under subsections (a), (c), and (h), members and managers, and their delegatees, owe to the company and to the other members and managers only the fiduciary duties of loyalty and care set forth in subsections (b) and (c) and the obligation of good faith and fair dealing set forth in subsection (d). An operating agreement may not waive or eliminate the duties or obligation, but may, if not manifestly unreasonable, identify activities and determine standards for measuring the performance of them. See Section 103(b)(2) to (4).

Upon a member's dissociation, the duty to account for personal profits under subsection (b)(1), the duty to refrain from acting as or representing adverse interests under subsection (b)(2), and the duty of care under subsection (c) are limited to those derived from matters arising or events occurring before the dissociation unless the member participates in winding up the company's business. Also, the duty not to compete terminates upon dissociation. See Section 603(b)(3) and (b)(2). However, a dissociated member is not free to use confidential company information after dissociation. For example, a dissociated member of a company may immediately compete with the company for new clients but must exercise care in completing on-going client transactions and must account to the company for any fees from the old clients on account of those transactions. Subsection (c) adopts a gross negligence standard for the duty of care, the standard actually used in most partnerships and corporations.

Subsection (b)(2) prohibits a member from acting adversely or representing an adverse party to the company. The rule is based on agency principles and seeks to avoid the conflict of opposing interests in the mind of the member agent whose duty is to act for the benefit of the principal company. As reflected in subsection (f), the rule does not prohibit the member from dealing with the company other than as an adversary. A member may generally deal with the company under subsection (f) when the transaction is approved by the company.

Subsection (e) makes clear that a member does not violate the obligation of good faith under subsection (d) merely because the member's conduct furthers that member's own interest. For example, a member's refusal to vote for an interim distribution because of negative tax implications to that member does not violate that member's obligation of good faith to the other members. Likewise, a member may vote against a proposal by the company to open a shopping center that would directly compete with another shopping center in which the member owns an interest.

§ 410.   Actions by Members

(a)   A member may maintain an action against a limited liability company or another member for legal or equitable relief, with or without an accounting as to the company's business, to enforce:

     (1)   the member's rights under the operating agreement;

     (2)   the member's rights under this [Act]; and

     (3)   the rights and otherwise protect the interests of the member, including rights and interests arising independently of the member's relationship to the company.

(b)   The accrual, and any time limited for the assertion, of a right of action for a remedy under this section is governed by other law. A right to an accounting upon a dissolution and winding up does not revive a claim barred by law.

COMMENT

During the existence of the company, members have under this section access to the courts to resolve claims against the company and other members, leaving broad judicial discretion to fashion appropriate legal remedies. A member pursues only that member's claim against the company or another member under this section. Article 11 governs a member's derivative pursuit of a claim on behalf of the company.

A member may recover against the company and the other members under subsection (a)(3) for personal injuries or damage to the member's property caused by another member. One member's negligence is therefore not imputed to bar another member's action.

§ 411.   Continuation of Term Company After Expiration of Specified Term

(a)   If a term company is continued after the expiration of the specified term, the rights and duties of the members and managers remain the same as they were at the expiration of the term except to the extent inconsistent with rights and duties of members and managers of an at-will company.

(b)   If the members in a member-managed company or the managers in a manager-managed company continue the business without any winding up of the business of the company, it continues as an at-will company.

COMMENT

A term company will generally dissolve upon the expiration of its term unless either its articles are amended before the expiration of the original specified term to provide for an additional specified term or the members or managers simply continue the company as an at-will company under this section. Amendment of the articles specifying an additional term requires the unanimous consent of the members. See Section 404(c)(3). Therefore, any member has the right to block the amendment. Absent an amendment to the articles, a company may only be continued under subsection (b) as an at-will company. The decision to continue a term company as an at-will company does not require the unanimous consent of the members and is treated as an ordinary business matter with disputes resolved by a simple majority vote of either the members or managers. See Section 404. In that case, subsection (b) provides that the members' conduct amends or becomes part of an operating agreement to "continue" the company as an at-will company. The amendment to the operating agreement does not alter the rights of creditors who suffer detrimental reliance because the company does not liquidate after the expiration of its specified term. See Section 203(c)(2).

Preexisting operating-agreement provisions continue to control the relationship of the members under subsection (a) except to the extent inconsistent with the rights and duties of members of an at-will company with an operating agreement containing the same provisions. However, the members could agree in advance that, if the company's business continues after the expiration of its specified term, the company continues as a company with a new specified term or that the provisions of its operating agreement survive the expiration of the specified term.

[ARTICLE] 5
TRANSFEREES AND CREDITORS OF MEMBER

§ 501. Member's Distributional Interest

(a) A member is not a co-owner of, and has no transferable interest in, property of a limited liability company.

(b) A distributional interest in a limited liability company is personal property and, subject to Sections 502 and 503, may be transferred in whole or in part.

(c) An operating agreement may provide that a distributional interest may be evidenced by a certificate of the interest issued by the limited liability company and, subject to Section 503, may also provide for the transfer of any interest represented by the certificate.

COMMENT

Members have no property interest in property owned by a limited liability company. A distributional interest is personal property and is defined under Section 101(6) as a member's interest in distributions only and does not include the member's broader rights to participate in management under Section 404 and to inspect company records under Section 408.

Under Section 405(a), distributions are allocated in equal shares unless otherwise provided in an operating agreement. Whenever it is desirable to allocate distributions in proportion to contributions rather than per capita, certification may be useful to reduce valuation issues. New and important Internal Revenue Service announcements clarify that certification of a limited liability company will not cause it to be taxed like a corporation.

§ 502. Transfer of Distributional Interest

A transfer of a distributional interest does not entitle the transferee to become or to exercise any rights of a member. A transfer entitles the transferee to receive, to the extent transferred, only the distributions to which the transferor would be entitled.

COMMENT

Under Sections 501(b) and 502, the only interest a member may freely transfer is that member's distributional interest. A member's transfer of all of a distributional interest constitutes an event of dissociation. See Section 601(3). A transfer of less than all of a member's distributional interest is not an event of dissociation. A member ceases to be a member upon the transfer of all that member's distributional interest and that transfer is also an event of dissociation under Section 601(3). Relating the event of dissociation to the member's transfer of all of the member's distributional interest avoids the need for the company to track potential future dissociation events associated with a member no longer financially interested in the company. Also, all the remaining members may expel a member upon the transfer of "substantially all" the member's distributional interest. The expulsion is an event of dissociation under Section 601(5)(ii).

§ 503. Rights of Transferee

(a) A transferee of a distributional interest may become a member of a limited liability company if and to the extent that the transferor gives the transferee the right in accordance with authority described in the operating agreement or all other members consent.

(b)   A transferee who has become a member, to the extent transferred, has the rights and powers, and is subject to the restrictions and liabilities, of a member under the operating agreement of a limited liability company and this [Act]. A transferee who becomes a member also is liable for the transferor member's obligations to make contributions under Section 402 and for obligations under Section 407 to return unlawful distributions, but the transferee is not obligated for the transferor member's liabilities unknown to the transferee at the time the transferee becomes a member.

(c)   Whether or not a transferee of a distributional interest becomes a member under subsection (a), the transferor is not released from liability to the limited liability company under the operating agreement or this [Act].

(d)   A transferee who does not become a member is not entitled to participate in the management or conduct of the limited liability company's business, require access to information concerning the company's transactions, or inspect or copy any of the company's records.

(e)   A transferee who does not become a member is entitled to:

(1)   receive, in accordance with the transfer, distributions to which the transferor would otherwise be entitled;

(2)   receive, upon dissolution and winding up of the limited liability company's business:

(i)   in accordance with the transfer, the net amount otherwise distributable to the transferor;

(ii)   a statement of account only from the date of the latest statement of account agreed to by all the members;

(3)   seek under Section 801(5) a judicial determination that it is equitable to dissolve and wind up the company's business.

(f)   A limited liability company need not give effect to a transfer until it has notice of the transfer.

COMMENT

The only interest a member may freely transfer is the member's distributional interest. A transferee may acquire the remaining rights of a member only by being admitted as a member of the company by all of the remaining members. New and important Internal Revenue Service announcements clarify that the transferability of membership interests of a limited liability company in excess of these default rules will not cause it to be taxed like a corporation. In many cases a limited liability company will be organized and operated with only a few members. These default rules were chosen in the interest of preserving the right of existing members in such companies to determine whether a transferee will become a member.

A transferee not admitted as a member is not entitled to participate in management, require access to information, or inspect or copy company records. The only rights of a transferee are to receive the distributions the transferor would otherwise be entitled, receive a limited statement of account, and seek a judicial dissolution under Section 801(a)(5).

Subsection (e) sets forth the rights of a transferee of an existing member. Although the rights of a dissociated member to participate in the future management of the company parallel the rights of a transferee, a dissociated member retains additional rights that accrued from that person's membership such as the right to enforce Article 7 purchase rights. See and compare Sections 603(b)(1) and 801(a)(4) and Comments.

§ 504.   Rights of Creditor

(a)   On application by a judgment creditor of a member of a limited liability company or of a member's transferee, a court having jurisdiction may charge the distributional interest of the judgment debtor to satisfy the judgment. The court may appoint a receiver of the share of the distributions due or to become due to the judgment debtor and make all other orders, directions, accounts, and inquiries the judgment debtor might have made or which the circumstances may require to give effect to the charging order.

(b)   A charging order constitutes a lien on the judgment debtor's distributional interest. The court may order a foreclosure of a lien on a distributional interest subject to the charging order at any time. A purchaser at the foreclosure sale has the rights of a transferee.

(c)   At any time before foreclosure, a distributional interest in a limited liability company which is charged may be redeemed:

(1)   by the judgment debtor;

(2)   with property other than the company's property, by one or more of the other members; or

(3)   with the company's property, but only if permitted by the operating agreement.

(d)   This [Act] does not affect a member's right under exemption laws with respect to the member's distributional interest in a limited liability company.

(e)   This section provides the exclusive remedy by which a judgment creditor of a member or a transferee may satisfy a judgment out of the judgment debtor's distributional interest in a limited liability company.

COMMENT

A charging order is the only remedy by which a judgment creditor of a member or a member's transferee may reach the distributional interest of a member or member's transferee. Under Section 503(e), the distributional interest of a member or transferee is limited to the member's right to receive distributions from the company and to seek judicial liquidation of the company.

[ARTICLE] 6
MEMBER'S DISSOCIATION

§ 601.   Events Causing Member's Dissociation

A member is dissociated from a limited liability company upon the occurrence of any of the following events:

(1)   the company's having notice of the member's express will to withdraw upon the date of notice or on a later date specified by the member;

(2)   an event agreed to in the operating agreement as causing the member's dissociation;

(3)   upon transfer of all of a member's distributional interest, other than a transfer for security purposes or a court order charging the member's distributional interest which has not been foreclosed;

(4)   the member's expulsion pursuant to the operating agreement;

(5)   the member's expulsion by unanimous vote of the other members if:

(i)   it is unlawful to carry on the company's business with the member;

(ii)   there has been a transfer of substantially all of the member's distributional interest, other than a transfer for security purposes or a court order charging the member's distributional interest which has not been foreclosed;

(iii)   within 90 days after the company notifies a corporate member that it will be expelled because it has filed a certificate of dissolution or the equivalent, its charter has been revoked, or its right to conduct business has been suspended by the jurisdiction of its incorporation, the member fails to obtain a revocation of the certificate of dissolution or a reinstatement of its charter or its right to conduct business; or

(iv)   a partnership or a limited liability company that is a member has been dissolved and its business is being wound up;

(6)   on application by the company or another member, the member's expulsion by judicial determination because the member:

(i)   engaged in wrongful conduct that adversely and materially affected the company's business;

(ii)   willfully or persistently committed a material breach of the operating agreement or of a duty owed to the company or the other members under Section 409; or

(iii) engaged in conduct relating to the company's business which makes it not reasonably practicable to carry on the business with the member;

(7)   the member's:

(i)   becoming a debtor in bankruptcy;

(ii)   executing an assignment for the benefit of creditors;

(iii) seeking, consenting to, or acquiescing in the appointment of a trustee, receiver, or liquidator of the member or of all or substantially all of the member's property; or

(iv)   failing, within 90 days after the appointment, to have vacated or stayed the appointment of a trustee, receiver, or liquidator of the member or of all or substantially all of the member's property obtained without the member's consent or acquiescence, or failing within 90 days after the expiration of a stay to have the appointment vacated;

(8)   in the case of a member who is an individual:

(i)   the member's death;

(ii)   the appointment of a guardian or general conservator for the member; or

(iii) a judicial determination that the member has otherwise become incapable of performing the member's duties under the operating agreement;

(9)   in the case of a member that is a trust or is acting as a member by virtue of being a trustee of a trust, distribution of the trust's entire rights to receive distributions from the company, but not merely by reason of the substitution of a successor trustee;

(10) in the case of a member that is an estate or is acting as a member by virtue of being a personal representative of an estate, distribution of the estate's entire rights to receive distributions from the company, but not merely the substitution of a successor personal representative; or

(11) termination of the existence of a member if the member is not an individual, estate, or trust other than a business trust.

COMMENT

The term "dissociation" refers to the change in the relationships among the dissociated member, the company and the other members caused by a member's ceasing to be associated in the carrying on of the company's business. Member dissociation from either an at-will or term company, whether member-or manager-managed is not an event of dissolution of the company unless otherwise specified in an operating agreement. See Section 801(a)(1). However, member dissociation will generally trigger the obligation of the company to purchase the dissociated member's interest under Article 7.

A member may be expelled from the company under paragraph (5)(ii) by the unanimous vote of the other members upon a transfer of "substantially all" of the member's distributional interest other than for a transfer as security for a loan. A transfer of "all" of the member's distributional interest is an event of dissociation under paragraph (3).

Although a member is dissociated upon death, the effect of the dissociation where the company does not dissolve depends upon whether the company is at-will or term. Only the decedent's distributional interest transfers to the decedent's estate which does not acquire the decedent member's management rights. See Section 603(b)(1). Unless otherwise agreed, if the company was at-will, the estate's distributional interest must be purchased by the company at fair value determined at the date of death. However, if a term company, the estate and its transferees continue only as the owner of the distributional interest with no management rights until the expiration of the specified term that existed on the date of death. At the expiration of that term, the company must purchase the interest of a dissociated member if the company continues for an additional term by amending its articles or simply continues as an at-will company. See Sections 411 and 701(a)(2) and Comments. Before that time, the estate and its transferees have the right to make application for a judicial dissolution of the company under Section 801(b)(5) as successors in interest to a dissociated member. See Comments to Sections 801, 411, and 701. Where the members have allocated management rights on the basis of contributions rather than simply the number of members, a member's death will result in a transfer of management rights to the remaining members on a proportionate basis. This transfer of rights may be avoided by a provision in an operating agreement extending the Section 701(a)(1) at-will purchase right to a decedent member of a term company.

§ 602. Member's Power to Dissociate; Wrongful Dissociation

(a)   Unless otherwise provided in the operating agreement, a member has the power to dissociate from a limited liability company at any time, rightfully or wrongfully, by express will pursuant to Section 601(1).

(b)   If the operating agreement has not eliminated a member's power to dissociate, the member's dissociation from a limited liability company is wrongful only if:

(1)   it is in breach of an express provision of the agreement; or

(2)   before the expiration of the specified term of a term company:

(i)   the member withdraws by express will;

(ii)   the member is expelled by judicial determination under Section 601(6);

(iii)   the member is dissociated by becoming a debtor in bankruptcy; or

(iv)   in the case of a member who is not an individual, trust other than a business trust, or estate, the member is expelled or otherwise dissociated because it willfully dissolved or terminated its existence.

(c)   A member who wrongfully dissociates from a limited liability company is liable to the company and to the other members for damages caused by the dissociation. The liability is in addition to any other obligation of the member to the company or to the other members.

(d)   If a limited liability company does not dissolve and wind up its business as a result of a member's wrongful dissociation under subsection (b), damages sustained by the company for the wrongful dissociation must be offset against distributions otherwise due the member after the dissociation.

COMMENT

A member has the power to withdraw from both an at-will company and a term company although the effects of the withdrawal are remarkably different. See Comments to Section 601. At a minimum, the exercise of a power to withdraw enables members to terminate their continuing duties of loyalty and care. See Section 603(b)(2) to (3).

A member's power to withdraw by express will may be eliminated by an operating agreement. New and important Internal Revenue Service announcements clarify that alteration of a member's power to withdraw will not cause the limited liability company to be taxed like a corporation. An operating agreement may eliminate a member's power to withdraw by express will to promote the business continuity of an at-will company by removing member's right to force the company to purchase the member's distributional interest. See Section 701(a)(1). However, such a member retains the ability to seek a judicial dissolution of the company. See Section 801(a)(4).

If a member's power to withdraw by express will is not eliminated in an operating agreement, the withdrawal may nevertheless be made wrongful under subsection (b). All dissociations, including withdrawal by express will, may be made wrongful under subsection (b)(1) in both an at-will and term company by the inclusion of a provision in an operating agreement. Even where an operating agreement does not eliminate the power to withdraw by express will or make any dissociation wrongful, the dissociation of a member of a term company for the reasons specified under subsection (b)(2) is wrongful. The member is liable to the company and other members for damages caused by a wrongful dissociation under subsection (c) and, under subsection (d), the damages may be offset against all distributions otherwise due the member after the dissociation. Section 701(f) provides a similar rule permitting damages for wrongful dissociation to be offset against any company purchase of the member's distributional interest.

§ 603. Effect of Member's Dissociation

(a)   Upon a member's dissociation:

(1)   in an at-will company, the company must cause the dissociated member's distributional interest to be purchased under [Article] 7; and

(2)   in a term company:

(i)   if the company dissolves and winds up its business on or before the expiration of its specified term, [Article] 8 applies to determine the dissociated member's rights to distributions; and

(ii)   if the company does not dissolve and wind up its business on or before the expiration of its specified term, the company must cause the dissociated member's distributional interest to be purchased under [Article] 7 on the date of the expiration of the term specified at the time of the member's dissociation.

(b)   Upon a member's dissociation from a limited liability company:

(1)   the member's right to participate in the management and conduct of the company's business terminates, except as otherwise provided in Section 803, and the member ceases to be a member and is treated the same as a transferee of a member;

(2)   the member's duty of loyalty under Section 409(b)(3) terminates; and

(3)   the member's duty of loyalty under Section 409(b)(1) and (2) and duty of care under Section 409(c) continue only with regard to matters arising and events occurring before the member's dissociation, unless the member participates in winding up the company's business pursuant to Section 803.

COMMENT

Member dissociation is not an event of dissolution of a company unless otherwise specified in an operating agreement. See Section 801(a)(1). Dissociation from an at-will company that does not dissolve the company causes the dissociated member's distributional interest to be immediately purchased under Article 7. See Comments to Sections 602 and 603. Dissociation from a term company that does not dissolve the company does not cause the dissociated member's distributional interest to be purchased under Article 7 until the expiration of the specified term that existed on the date of dissociation.

Subsection (b)(1) provides that a dissociated member forfeits the right to participate in the future conduct of the company's business. Dissociation does not however forfeit that member's right to enforce the Article 7 rights that accrue by reason of the dissociation. Similarly, where dissociation occurs by death, the decedent member's successors in interest may enforce that member's Article 7 rights. See and compare Comments to Section 503(e).

Dissociation terminates the member's right to participate in management, including the member's actual authority to act for the company under Section 301, and begins the two-year period after which a member's apparent authority conclusively ends. See Comments to Section 703. Dissociation also terminates a member's continuing duties of loyalty and care, except with regard to continuing transactions, to the company and other members unless the member participates in winding up the company's business. See Comments to Section 409.

[ARTICLE] 7
MEMBER'S DISSOCIATION WHEN
BUSINESS NOT WOUND UP

§ 701.   Company Purchase of Distributional Interest

(a)   A limited liability company shall purchase a distributional interest of a:

(1)   member of an at-will company for its fair value determined as of the date of the member's dissociation if the member's dissociation does not result in a dissolution and winding up of the company's business under Section 801; or

(2)   member of a term company for its fair value determined as of the date of the expiration of the specified term that existed on the date of the member's dissociation if the expiration of the specified term does not result in a dissolution and winding up of the company's business under Section 801.

(b)   A limited liability company must deliver a purchase offer to the dissociated member whose distributional interest is entitled to be purchased not later than 30 days after the date determined under subsection (a). The purchase offer must be accompanied by:

(1)   a statement of the company's assets and liabilities as of the date determined under subsection (a);

(2)   the latest available balance sheet and income statement, if any; and

(3)   an explanation of how the estimated amount of the payment was calculated.

(c)   If the price and other terms of a purchase of a distributional interest are fixed or are to be determined by the operating agreement, the price and terms so fixed or determined govern the purchase unless the purchaser defaults. If a default occurs, the dissociated member is entitled to commence a proceeding to have the company dissolved under Section 801(4)(iv).

(d)   If an agreement to purchase the distributional interest is not made within 120 days after the date determined under subsection (a), the dissociated member, within another 120 days, may commence a proceeding against the limited liability company to enforce the purchase. The company at its expense shall notify in writing all of the remaining members, and any other person the court directs, of the commencement of the proceeding. The jurisdiction of the court in which the proceeding is commenced under this subsection is plenary and exclusive.

(e)   The court shall determine the fair value of the distributional interest in accordance with the standards set forth in Section 702 together with the terms for the purchase. Upon making these determinations, the court shall order the limited liability company to purchase or cause the purchase of the interest.

(f)   Damages for wrongful dissociation under Section 602(b), and all other amounts owing, whether or not currently due, from the dissociated member to a limited liability company, must be offset against the purchase price.

COMMENT

This section sets forth default rules regarding an otherwise mandatory company purchase of a distributional interest. Even though a dissociated member's rights to participate in the future management of the company are equivalent to those of a transferee of a member, the dissociation does not forfeit that member's right to enforce the Article 7 purchase right. Similarly, if the dissociation occurs by reason of death, the decedent member's successors in interest may enforce the Article 7 rights. See Comments to Sections 503(e) and 603(b)(1).

An at-will company must purchase a dissociated member's distributional interest under subsection (a)(1) when that member's dissociation does not result in a dissolution of the company under Section 801(a)(1). The purchase price is equal to the fair value of the interest determined as of the date of dissociation. Any damages for wrongful dissociation must be offset against the purchase price.

Dissociation from a term company does not require an immediate purchase of the member's interest but the operating agreement may specify that dissociation is an event of dissolution. See Section 801(a)(1). A term company must only purchase the dissociated member's distributional interest under subsection (a)(2) on the expiration of the specified term that existed on the date of the member's dissociation. The purchase price is equal to the fair value of the interest determined as of the date of the expiration of that specified term. Any damages for wrongful dissociation must be offset against the purchase price.

The valuation dates differ between subsections (a)(1) and (a)(2) purchases. The former is valued on the date of member dissociation whereas the latter is valued on the date of the expiration of the specified term that existed on the date of dissociation. A subsection (a)(2) dissociated member therefore assumes the risk of loss between the date of dissociation and the expiration of the then stated specified term. See Comments to Section 801 (dissociated member may file application to dissolve company under Section 801(a)(4)).

The default valuation standard is fair value. See Comments to Section 702. An operating agreement may fix a method or formula for determining the purchase price and the terms of payment. The purchase right may be modified. For example, an operating agreement may eliminate a member's power to withdraw from an at-will company which narrows the dissociation events contemplated under subsection (a)(1). See Comments to Section 602(a). However, a provision in an operating agreement providing for complete forfeiture of the purchase right may be unenforceable where the power to dissociate has not also been eliminated. See Section 104(a).

The company must deliver a purchase offer to the dissociated member within 30 days after the date determined under subsection (a). The offer must be accompanied by information designed to enable the dissociated member to evaluate the fairness of the offer. The subsection (b)(3) explanation of how the offer price was calculated need not be elaborate. For example, a mere statement of the basis of the calculation, such as "book value," may be sufficient.

The company and the dissociated member must reach an agreement on the purchase price and terms within 120 days after the date determined under subsection (a). Otherwise, the dissociated member may file suit within another 120 days to enforce the purchase under subsection (d). The court will then determine the fair value and terms of purchase under subsection (e). See Section 702. The member's lawsuit is not available under subsection (c) if the parties have previously agreed to price and terms in an operating agreement.

§ 702.   Court Action to Determine Fair Value of Distributional Interest

(a)   In an action brought to determine the fair value of a distributional interest in a limited liability company, the court shall:

(1)   determine the fair value of the interest, considering among other relevant evidence the going concern value of the company, any agreement among some or all of the members fixing the price or specifying a formula for determining value of distributional interests for any other purpose, the recommendations of any appraiser appointed by the court, and any legal constraints on the company's ability to purchase the interest;

(2)   specify the terms of the purchase, including, if appropriate, terms for installment payments, subordination of the purchase obligation to the rights of the company's other creditors, security for a deferred purchase price, and a covenant not to compete or other restriction on a dissociated member; and

(3)   require the dissociated member to deliver an assignment of the interest to the purchaser upon receipt of the purchase price or the first installment of the purchase price.

(b)   After the dissociated member delivers the assignment, the dissociated member has no further claim against the company, its members, officers, or managers, if any, other than a claim to any unpaid balance of the purchase price and a claim under any agreement with the company or the remaining members that is not terminated by the court.

(c)   If the purchase is not completed in accordance with the specified terms, the company is to be dissolved upon application under Section 801(b)(5)(iv). If a limited liability company is so dissolved, the dissociated member has the same rights and priorities in the company's assets as if the sale had not been ordered.

(d)   If the court finds that a party to the proceeding acted arbitrarily, vexatiously, or not in good faith, it may award one or more other parties their reasonable expenses, including attorney's fees and the expenses of appraisers or other experts, incurred in the proceeding. The finding may be based on the company's failure to make an offer to pay or to comply with Section 701(b).

(e)   Interest must be paid on the amount awarded from the date determined under Section 701(a) to the date of payment.

COMMENT

The default valuation standard is fair value. Under this broad standard, a court is free to determine the fair value of a distributional interest on a fair market, liquidation, or any other method deemed appropriate under the circumstances. A fair market value standard is not used because it is too narrow, often inappropriate, and assumes a fact not contemplated by this section—a willing buyer and a willing seller.

The court has discretion under subsection (a)(2) to include in its order any conditions the court deems necessary to safeguard the interests of the company and the dissociated member or transferee. The discretion may be based on the financial and other needs of the parties.

If the purchase is not consummated or the purchaser defaults, the dissociated member or transferee may make application for dissolution of the company under subsection (c). The court may deny the petition for good cause but the proceeding affords the company an opportunity to be heard on the matter and avoid dissolution. See Comments to Section 801(a)(4).

The power of the court to award all costs and attorney's fees incurred in the suit under subsection (d) is an incentive for both parties to act in good faith. See Section 701(c).

§ 703.   Dissociated Member's Power to Bind Limited Liability Company

For two years after a member dissociates without the dissociation resulting in a dissolution and winding up of a limited liability company's business, the company, including a surviving company under [Article] 9, is bound by an act of the dissociated member which would have bound the company under Section 301 before dissociation only if at the time of entering into the transaction the other party:

    (1)   reasonably believed that the dissociated member was then a member;

    (2)   did not have notice of the member's dissociation; and

    (3)   is not deemed to have had notice under Section 704.

COMMENT

Member dissociation will not dissolve the company unless otherwise specified in an operating agreement. See Section 801(a)(1). A dissociated member of a member-managed company does not have actual authority to act for the company. See Section 603(b)(1). Under Section 301(a), a dissociated member of a member-managed company has apparent authority to bind the company in ordinary course transactions except as to persons who knew or had notice of the dissociation. This section modifies that rule by requiring the person to show reasonable reliance on the member's status as a member provided a Section 704 statement has not been filed within the previous 90 days. See also Section 804 (power to bind after dissolution).

§ 704.   Statement of Dissociation

(a)   A dissociated member or a limited liability company may file in the office of the [Secretary of State] a statement of dissociation stating the name of the company and that the member is dissociated from the company.

(b)   For the purposes of Sections 301 and 703, a person not a member is deemed to have notice of the dissociation 90 days after the statement of dissociation is filed.

[ARTICLE] 8
WINDING UP COMPANY'S BUSINESS

§ 801.   Events Causing Dissolution and Winding up of Company's Business

A limited liability company is dissolved, and its business must be wound up, upon the occurrence of any of the following events:

    (1)   an event specified in the operating agreement;

    (2)   consent of the number or percentage of members specified in the operating agreement;

    (3)   an event that makes it unlawful for all or substantially all of the business of the company to be continued, but any cure of illegality within 90 days after notice to the company of the event is effective retroactively to the date of the event for purposes of this section;

    (4)   on application by a member or a dissociated member, upon entry of a judicial decree that:

        (i)   the economic purpose of the company is likely to be unreasonably frustrated;

        (ii)   another member has engaged in conduct relating to the company's business that makes it not reasonably practicable to carry on the company's business with that member;

        (iii) it is not otherwise reasonably practicable to carry on the company's business in conformity with the articles of organization and the operating agreement;

(iv)   the company failed to purchase the petitioner's distributional interest as required by Section 701; or

(v)   the managers or members in control of the company have acted, are acting, or will act in a manner that is illegal, oppressive, fraudulent, or unfairly prejudicial to the petitioner;

(5)   on application by a transferee of a member's interest, a judicial determination that it is equitable to wind up the company's business:

(i)   after the expiration of the specified term, if the company was for a specified term at the time the applicant became a transferee by member dissociation, transfer, or entry of a charging order that gave rise to the transfer; or

(ii)   at any time, if the company was at will at the time the applicant became a transferee by member dissociation, transfer, or entry of a charging order that gave rise to the transfer; or

(6)   the expiration of the term specified in the articles of organization.

COMMENT

The dissolution rules of this section are mostly default rules and may be modified by an operating agreement. However, an operating agreement may not modify or eliminate the dissolution events specified in subsection (a)(3) (illegal business) or subsection (a)(4) (member application). See Section 103(b)(6).

The relationship between member dissociation and company dissolution is set forth under subsection (a)(1). Unless member dissociation is specified as an event of dissolution in the operating agreement, such dissociation does not dissolve the company. New and important Internal Revenue Service announcements clarify that the failure of member dissociation to cause or threaten dissolution of a limited liability company will not cause the company to be taxed like a corporation.

A member or dissociated member whose interest is not required to be purchased by the company under Section 701 may make application under subsection (a)(4) for the involuntary dissolution of both an at-will company and a term company. A transferee may make application under subsection (a)(5). A transferee's application right, but not that of a member or dissociated member, may be modified by an operating agreement. See Section 103(b)(6). A dissociated member is not treated as a transferee for purposes of an application under subsections (a)(4) and (a)(5). See Section 603(b)(1). For example, this affords reasonable protection to a dissociated member of a term company to make application under subsection (a)(4) before the expiration of the term that existed at the time of dissociation. For purposes of a subsection (a)(4) application, a dissociated member includes a successor in interest, e.g., surviving spouse. See Comments to Section 601.

In the case of applications under subsections (a)(4) and (a)(5), the applicant has the burden of proving either the existence of one or more of the circumstances listed under subsection (a)(4) or that it is equitable to wind up the company's business under subsection (a)(5). Proof of the existence of one or more of the circumstances in subsection (a)(4), may be the basis of a subsection (a)(5) application. Even where the burden of proof is met, the court has the discretion to order relief other than the dissolution of the company. Examples include an accounting, a declaratory judgment, a distribution, the purchase of the distributional interest of the applicant or another member, or the appointment of a receiver. See Section 410.

A court has the discretion to dissolve a company under subsection (a)(4)(i) when the company has a very poor financial record that is not likely to improve. In this instance, dissolution is an alternative to placing the company in bankruptcy. A court may dissolve a company under subsections (a)(4)(ii), (a)(4)(iii), and (a)(4)(iv) for serious and protracted misconduct by one or more members. Subsection (a)(4)(v) provides a specific remedy for an improper squeeze-out of a member.

In determining whether and what type of relief to order under subsections (a)(4) and (a)(5) involuntary dissolution suits, a court should take into account other rights and remedies of the applicant. For example, a court should not grant involuntary dissolution of an at-will company if the applicant member has the right to dissociate and force the company to purchase that member's distributional interest under Sections 701 and 702. In other cases, involuntary dissolution or some other remedy such as a buy-out might be appropriate where, for example, one or more members have (i) engaged in fraudulent or unconscionable conduct, (ii) improperly expelled a member seeking an unfair advantage of a provision in an operating agreement that provides for a significantly lower price on expulsion than would be payable in the event of voluntary dissociation, or (iii) engaged in serious misconduct and the applicant member is a member of a term company and would not have a right to have the company purchase that member's distributional interest upon dissociation until the expiration of the company's specified term.

§ 802. Limited Liability Company Continues After Dissolution

(a)   Subject to subsection (b), a limited liability company continues after dissolution only for the purpose of winding up its business.

(b)   At any time after the dissolution of a limited liability company and before the winding up of its business is completed, the members, including a dissociated member whose dissociation caused the dissolution, may unanimously waive the right to have the company's business wound up and the company terminated. In that case:

(1)   the limited liability company resumes carrying on its business as if dissolution had never occurred and any liability incurred by the company or a member after the dissolution and before the waiver is determined as if the dissolution had never occurred; and

(2)   the rights of a third party accruing under Section 804(a) or arising out of conduct in reliance on the dissolution before the third party knew or received a notification of the waiver are not adversely affected.

COMMENT

The liability shield continues in effect for the winding up period because the legal existence of the company continues under subsection (a). The company is terminated on the filing of articles of termination. See Section 805.

§ 803. Right to Wind up Limited Liability Company's Business

(a)   After dissolution, a member who has not wrongfully dissociated may participate in winding up a limited liability company's business, but on application of any member, member's legal representative, or transferee, the [designate the appropriate court], for good cause shown, may order judicial supervision of the winding up.

(b)   A legal representative of the last surviving member may wind up a limited liability company's business.

(c)   A person winding up a limited liability company's business may preserve the company's business or property as a going concern for a reasonable time, prosecute and defend actions and proceedings, whether civil, criminal, or administrative, settle and close the company's business, dispose of and transfer the company's property, discharge the company's liabilities, distribute the assets of the company pursuant to Section 806, settle disputes by mediation or arbitration, and perform other necessary acts.

§ 804. Member's or Manager's Power and Liability as Agent After Dissolution

(a)   A limited liability company is bound by a member's or manager's act after dissolution that:

(1)   is appropriate for winding up the company's business; or

(2)   would have bound the company under Section 301 before dissolution, if the other party to the transaction did not have notice of the dissolution.

(b)   A member or manager who, with knowledge of the dissolution, subjects a limited liability company to liability by an act that is not appropriate for winding up the company's business is liable to the company for any damage caused to the company arising from the liability.

COMMENT

After dissolution, members and managers continue to have the authority to bind the company that they had prior to dissolution provided that the third party did not have notice of the dissolution. See Section 102(b) (notice defined). Otherwise, they have only the authority appropriate for winding up the company's business. See Section 703 (agency power of member after dissociation).

§ 805.   Articles of Termination

(a)   At any time after dissolution and winding up, a limited liability company may terminate its existence by filing with the [Secretary of State] articles of termination stating:

(1)   the name of the company;

(2)   the date of the dissolution; and

(3)   that the company's business has been wound up and the legal existence of the company has been terminated.

(b)   The existence of a limited liability company is terminated upon the filing of the articles of termination, or upon a later effective date, if specified in the articles of termination.

COMMENT

The termination of legal existence also terminates the company's liability shield. See Comments to Section 802 (liability shield continues in effect during winding up). It also ends the company's responsibility to file an annual report. See Section 211.

§ 806.   Distribution of Assets in Winding up Limited Liability Company's Business

(a)   In winding up a limited liability company's business, the assets of the company must be applied to discharge its obligations to creditors, including members who are creditors. Any surplus must be applied to pay in money the net amount distributable to members in accordance with their right to distributions under subsection (b).

(b)   Each member is entitled to a distribution upon the winding up of the limited liability company's business consisting of a return of all contributions which have not previously been returned and a distribution of any remainder in equal shares.

§ 807.   Known Claims Against Dissolved Limited Liability Company

(a)   A dissolved limited liability company may dispose of the known claims against it by following the procedure described in this section.

(b)   A dissolved limited liability company shall notify its known claimants in writing of the dissolution. The notice must:

(1)   specify the information required to be included in a claim;

(2)   provide a mailing address where the claim is to be sent;

(3)   state the deadline for receipt of the claim, which may not be less than 120 days after the date the written notice is received by the claimant; and

(4)   state that the claim will be barred if not received by the deadline.

(c)   A claim against a dissolved limited liability company is barred if the requirements of subsection (b) are met, and:

(1)   the claim is not received by the specified deadline; or

(2)   in the case of a claim that is timely received but rejected by the dissolved company, the claimant does not commence a proceeding to enforce the claim within 90 days after the receipt of the notice of the rejection.

(d)   For purposes of this section, "claim" does not include a contingent liability or a claim based on an event occurring after the effective date of dissolution.

COMMENT

A known claim will be barred when the company provides written notice to a claimant that a claim must be filed with the company no later than at least 120 days after receipt of the written notice and the claimant fails to file the claim. If the claim is timely received but is rejected by the company, the claim is nevertheless barred unless the claimant files suit to enforce the claim within 90 days after the receipt of the notice of rejection. A claim described in subsection (d) is not a "known" claim and is governed by Section 808. This section does not extend any other applicable statutes of limitation. See Section 104. Depending on the management of the company, members or managers must discharge or make provision for discharging all of the company's known liabilities before distributing the remaining assets to the members. See Sections 806(a), 406, and 407.

§ 808. Other Claims Against Dissolved Limited Liability Company

(a) A dissolved limited liability company may publish notice of its dissolution and request persons having claims against the company to present them in accordance with the notice.

(b) The notice must:

(1) be published at least once in a newspaper of general circulation in the [county] in which the dissolved limited liability company's principal office is located or, if none in this State, in which its designated office is or was last located;

(2) describe the information required to be contained in a claim and provide a mailing address where the claim is to be sent; and

(3) state that a claim against the limited liability company is barred unless a proceeding to enforce the claim is commenced within five years after publication of the notice.

(c) If a dissolved limited liability company publishes a notice in accordance with subsection (b), the claim of each of the following claimants is barred unless the claimant commences a proceeding to enforce the claim against the dissolved company within five years after the publication date of the notice:

(1) a claimant who did not receive written notice under Section 807;

(2) a claimant whose claim was timely sent to the dissolved company but not acted on; and

(3) a claimant whose claim is contingent or based on an event occurring after the effective date of dissolution.

(d) A claim not barred under this section may be enforced:

(1) against the dissolved limited liability company, to the extent of its undistributed assets; or

(2) if the assets have been distributed in liquidation, against a member of the dissolved company to the extent of the member's proportionate share of the claim or the company's assets distributed to the member in liquidation, whichever is less, but a member's total liability for all claims under this section may not exceed the total amount of assets distributed to the member.

COMMENT

An unknown claim will be barred when the company publishes notice requesting claimants to file claims with the company and stating that claims will be barred unless the claimant files suit to enforce the claim within five years after the date of publication. The procedure also bars known claims where the claimant either did not receive written notice described in Section 807 or received notice, mailed a claim, but the company did not act on the claim.

Depending on the management of the company, members or managers must discharge or make provision for discharging all of the company's known liabilities before distributing the remaining assets to the members. See Comment to Section 807. This section does not contemplate that a company will postpone member distributions until all unknown claims are barred under this section. In appropriate cases, the company may purchase insurance or set aside funds permitting a distribution of the remaining assets. Where winding up distributions have been made to members, subsection (d)(2) authorizes recovery against those members. However, a claimant's recovery against a member is limited to the lesser of the member's proportionate share of the claim or the amount received in the distribution. This section does not extend any other applicable statutes of limitation. See Section 104.

§ 809.   Grounds for Administrative Dissolution

The [Secretary of State] may commence a proceeding to dissolve a limited liability company administratively if the company does not:

    (1)   pay any fees, taxes, or penalties imposed by this [Act] or other law within 60 days after they are due; or

    (2)   deliver its annual report to the [Secretary of State] within 60 days after it is due.

COMMENT

Administrative dissolution is an effective enforcement mechanism for a variety of statutory obligations under this Act and it avoids the more expensive judicial dissolution process. When applicable, administrative dissolution avoids wasteful attempts to compel compliance by a company abandoned by its members.

§ 810.   Procedure for and Effect of Administrative Dissolution

    (a)   If the [Secretary of State] determines that a ground exists for administratively dissolving a limited liability company, the [Secretary of State] shall enter a record of the determination and serve the company with a copy of the record.

    (b)   If the company does not correct each ground for dissolution or demonstrate to the reasonable satisfaction of the [Secretary of State] that each ground determined by the [Secretary of State] does not exist within 60 days after service of the notice, the [Secretary of State] shall administratively dissolve the company by signing a certification of the dissolution that recites the ground for dissolution and its effective date. The [Secretary of State] shall file the original of the certificate and serve the company with a copy of the certificate.

    (c)   A company administratively dissolved continues its existence but may carry on only business necessary to wind up and liquidate its business and affairs under Section 802 and to notify claimants under Sections 807 and 808.

    (d)   The administrative dissolution of a company does not terminate the authority of its agent for service of process.

COMMENT

A company's failure to comply with a ground for administrative dissolution may simply occur because of oversight. Therefore, subsections (a) and (b) set forth a mandatory notice by the filing officer to the company of the ground for dissolution and a 60 day grace period for correcting the ground.

§ 811.   Reinstatement Following Administrative Dissolution

    (a)   A limited liability company administratively dissolved may apply to the [Secretary of State] for reinstatement within two years after the effective date of dissolution. The application must:

    (1)   recite the name of the company and the effective date of its administrative dissolution;

    (2)   state that the ground for dissolution either did not exist or have been eliminated;

    (3)   state that the company's name satisfies the requirements of Section 105; and

    (4)   contain a certificate from the [taxing authority] reciting that all taxes owed by the company have been paid.

    (b)   If the [Secretary of State] determines that the application contains the information required by subsection (a) and that the information is correct, the [Secretary of State] shall cancel the certificate of dissolution and prepare a certificate of reinstatement that recites this determination and the effective date of reinstatement, file the original of the certificate, and serve the company with a copy of the certificate.

    (c)   When reinstatement is effective, it relates back to and takes effect as of the effective date of the administrative dissolution and the company may resume its business as if the administrative dissolution had never occurred.

§812. Appeal from Denial of Reinstatement

(a) If the [Secretary of State] denies a limited liability company's application for reinstatement following administrative dissolution, the [Secretary of State] shall serve the company with a record that explains the reason or reasons for denial.

(b) The company may appeal the denial of reinstatement to the [name appropriate] court within 30 days after service of the notice of denial is perfected. The company appeals by petitioning the court to set aside the dissolution and attaching to the petition copies of the [Secretary of State's] certificate of dissolution, the company's application for reinstatement, and the [Secretary of State's] notice of denial.

(c) The court may summarily order the [Secretary of State] to reinstate the dissolved company or may take other action the court considers appropriate.

(d) The court's final decision may be appealed as in other civil proceedings.

[ARTICLE] 9
CONVERSIONS AND MERGERS

§901. Definitions

In this [article]:

(1) "Corporation" means a corporation under [the State Corporation Act], a predecessor law, or comparable law of another jurisdiction.

(2) "General partner" means a partner in a partnership and a general partner in a limited partnership.

(3) "Limited partner" means a limited partner in a limited partnership.

(4) "Limited partnership" means a limited partnership created under [the State Limited Partnership Act], a predecessor law, or comparable law of another jurisdiction.

(5) "Partner" includes a general partner and a limited partner.

(6) "Partnership" means a general partnership under [the State Partnership Act], a predecessor law, or comparable law of another jurisdiction.

(7) "Partnership agreement" means an agreement among the partners concerning the partnership or limited partnership.

(8) "Shareholder" means a shareholder in a corporation.

COMMENT

Section 907 makes clear that the provisions of Article 9 are not mandatory. Therefore, a partnership or a limited liability company may convert or merge in any other manner provided by law. However, if the requirements of Article 9 are followed, the conversion or merger is legally valid. Article 9 is not restricted to domestic business entities.

§902. Conversion of Partnership or Limited Partnership to Limited Liability Company

(a) A partnership or limited partnership may be converted to a limited liability company pursuant to this section.

(b) The terms and conditions of a conversion of a partnership or limited partnership to a limited liability company must be approved by all of the partners or by a number or percentage of the partners required for conversion in the partnership agreement.

(c) An agreement of conversion must set forth the terms and conditions of the conversion of the interests of partners of a partnership or of a limited partnership, as the case may be, into interests in the converted limited liability company or the cash or other consideration to be paid or delivered as a result of the conversion of the interests of the partners, or a combination thereof.

(d)   After a conversion is approved under subsection (b), the partnership or limited partnership shall file articles of organization in the office of the [Secretary of State] which satisfy the requirements of Section 203 and contain:

     (1)   a statement that the partnership or limited partnership was converted to a limited liability company from a partnership or limited partnership, as the case may be;

     (2)   its former name;

     (3)   a statement of the number of votes cast by the partners entitled to vote for and against the conversion and, if the vote is less than unanimous, the number or percentage required to approve the conversion under subsection (b); and

     (4)   in the case of a limited partnership, a statement that the certificate of limited partnership is to be canceled as of the date the conversion took effect.

(e)   In the case of a limited partnership, the filing of articles of organization under subsection (d) cancels its certificate of limited partnership as of the date the conversion took effect.

(f)   A conversion takes effect when the articles of organization are filed in the office of the [Secretary of State] or at any later date specified in the articles of organization.

(g)   A general partner who becomes a member of a limited liability company as a result of a conversion remains liable as a partner for an obligation incurred by the partnership or limited partnership before the conversion takes effect.

(h)   A general partner's liability for all obligations of the limited liability company incurred after the conversion takes effect is that of a member of the company. A limited partner who becomes a member as a result of a conversion remains liable only to the extent the limited partner was liable for an obligation incurred by the limited partnership before the conversion takes effect.

COMMENT

Subsection (b) makes clear that the terms and conditions of the conversion of a general or limited partnership to a limited liability company must be approved by all of the partners unless the partnership agreement specifies otherwise.

§ 903.   Effect of Conversion; Entity Unchanged

(a)   A partnership or limited partnership that has been converted pursuant to this [article] is for all purposes the same entity that existed before the conversion.

(b)   When a conversion takes effect:

     (1)   all property owned by the converting partnership or limited partnership vests in the limited liability company;

     (2)   all debts, liabilities, and other obligations of the converting partnership or limited partnership continue as obligations of the limited liability company;

     (3)   an action or proceeding pending by or against the converting partnership or limited partnership may be continued as if the conversion had not occurred;

     (4)   except as prohibited by other law, all of the rights, privileges, immunities, powers, and purposes of the converting partnership or limited partnership vest in the limited liability company; and

     (5)   except as otherwise provided in the agreement of conversion under Section 902(c), all of the partners of the converting partnership continue as members of the limited liability company.

COMMENT

A conversion is not a conveyance or transfer and does not give rise to claims of reverter or impairment of title based on a prohibited conveyance or transfer. Under subsection (b)(1), title to all partnership property, including real estate, vests in the limited liability company as a matter of law without reversion or impairment.

§ 904. Merger of Entities

(a)   Pursuant to a plan of merger approved under subsection (c), a limited liability company may be merged with or into one or more limited liability companies, foreign limited liability companies, corporations, foreign corporations, partnerships, foreign partnerships, limited partnerships, foreign limited partnerships, or other domestic or foreign entities.

(b)   A plan of merger must set forth:

(1)   the name of each entity that is a party to the merger;

(2)   the name of the surviving entity into which the other entities will merge;

(3)   the type of organization of the surviving entity;

(4)   the terms and conditions of the merger;

(5)   the manner and basis for converting the interests of each party to the merger into interests or obligations of the surviving entity, or into money or other property in whole or in part; and

(6)   the street address of the surviving entity's principal place of business.

(c)   A plan of merger must be approved:

(1)   in the case of a limited liability company that is a party to the merger, by all of the members or by a number or percentage of members specified in the operating agreement;

(2)   in the case of a foreign limited liability company that is a party to the merger, by the vote required for approval of a merger by the law of the State or foreign jurisdiction in which the foreign limited liability company is organized;

(3)   in the case of a partnership or domestic limited partnership that is a party to the merger, by the vote required for approval of a conversion under Section 902(b); and

(4)   in the case of any other entities that are parties to the merger, by the vote required for approval of a merger by the law of this State or of the State or foreign jurisdiction in which the entity is organized and, in the absence of such a requirement, by all the owners of interests in the entity.

(d)   After a plan of merger is approved and before the merger takes effect, the plan may be amended or abandoned as provided in the plan.

(e)   The merger is effective upon the filing of the articles of merger with the [Secretary of State], or at such later date as the articles may provide.

COMMENT

This section sets forth a "safe harbor" for cross-entity mergers of limited liability companies with both domestic and foreign: corporations, general and limited partnerships, and other limited liability companies. Subsection (c) makes clear that the terms and conditions of the plan of merger must be approved by all of the partners unless applicable state law specifies otherwise for the merger.

§ 905. Articles of Merger

(a)   After approval of the plan of merger under Section 904(c), unless the merger is abandoned under Section 904(d), articles of merger must be signed on behalf of each limited liability company and other entity that is a party to the merger and delivered to the [Secretary of State] for filing. The articles must set forth:

(1)   the name and jurisdiction of formation or organization of each of the limited liability companies and other entities that are parties to the merger;

(2)   for each limited liability company that is to merge, the date its articles of organization were filed with the [Secretary of State];

(3)   that a plan of merger has been approved and signed by each limited liability company and other entity that is to merge;

(4)   the name and address of the surviving limited liability company or other surviving entity;

(5)   the effective date of the merger;

(6)   if a limited liability company is the surviving entity, such changes in its articles of organization as are necessary by reason of the merger;

(7)   if a party to a merger is a foreign limited liability company, the jurisdiction and date of filing of its initial articles of organization and the date when its application for authority was filed by the [Secretary of State] or, if an application has not been filed, a statement to that effect; and

(8)   if the surviving entity is not a limited liability company, an agreement that the surviving entity may be served with process in this State and is subject to liability in any action or proceeding for the enforcement of any liability or obligation of any limited liability company previously subject to suit in this State which is to merge, and for the enforcement, as provided in this [Act], of the right of members of any limited liability company to receive payment for their interest against the surviving entity.

(b)   If a foreign limited liability company is the surviving entity of a merger, it may not do business in this State until an application for that authority is filed with the [Secretary of State].

(c)   The surviving limited liability company or other entity shall furnish a copy of the plan of merger, on request and without cost, to any member of any limited liability company or any person holding an interest in any other entity that is to merge.

(d)   Articles of merger operate as an amendment to the limited liability company's articles of organization.

§ 906.   Effect of Merger

(a)   When a merger takes effect:

(1)   the separate existence of each limited liability company and other entity that is a party to the merger, other than the surviving entity, terminates;

(2)   all property owned by each of the limited liability companies and other entities that are party to the merger vests in the surviving entity;

(3)   all debts, liabilities, and other obligations of each limited liability company and other entity that is party to the merger become the obligations of the surviving entity;

(4)   an action or proceeding pending by or against a limited liability company or other party to a merger may be continued as if the merger had not occurred or the surviving entity may be substituted as a party to the action or proceeding; and

(5)   except as prohibited by other law, all the rights, privileges, immunities, powers, and purposes of every limited liability company and other entity that is a party to a merger vest in the surviving entity.

(b)   The [Secretary of State] is an agent for service of process in an action or proceeding against the surviving foreign entity to enforce an obligation of any party to a merger if the surviving foreign entity fails to appoint or maintain an agent designated for service of process in this State or the agent for service of process cannot with reasonable diligence be found at the designated office. Upon receipt of process, the [Secretary of State] shall send a copy of the process by registered or certified mail, return receipt requested, to the surviving entity at the address set forth in the articles of merger. Service is effected under this subsection at the earliest of:

(1)   the date the company receives the process, notice, or demand;

(2)   the date shown on the return receipt, if signed on behalf of the company; or

(3)   five days after its deposit in the mail, if mailed postpaid and correctly addressed.

(c)   A member of the surviving limited liability company is liable for all obligations of a party to the merger for which the member was personally liable before the merger.

(d)   Unless otherwise agreed, a merger of a limited liability company that is not the surviving entity in the merger does not require the limited liability company to wind up its business under this [Act] or pay its liabilities and distribute its assets pursuant to this [Act].

(e)   Articles of merger serve as articles of dissolution for a limited liability company that is not the surviving entity in the merger.

§ 907.   [Article] Not Exclusive

This [article] does not preclude an entity from being converted or merged under other law.

[ARTICLE] 10
FOREIGN LIMITED LIABILITY COMPANIES

§ 1001.   Law Governing Foreign Limited Liability Companies

(a)   The laws of the State or other jurisdiction under which a foreign limited liability company is organized govern its organization and internal affairs and the liability of its managers, members, and their transferees.

(b)   A foreign limited liability company may not be denied a certificate of authority by reason of any difference between the laws of another jurisdiction under which the foreign company is organized and the laws of this State.

(c)   A certificate of authority does not authorize a foreign limited liability company to engage in any business or exercise any power that a limited liability company may not engage in or exercise in this State.

COMMENT

The law where a foreign limited liability company is organized, rather than this Act, governs that company's internal affairs and the liability of its owners. Accordingly, any difference between the laws of the foreign jurisdiction and this Act will not constitute grounds for denial of a certificate of authority to transact business in this State. However, a foreign limited liability company transacting business in this State by virtue of a certificate of authority is limited to the business and powers that a limited liability company may lawfully pursue and exercise under Section 112.

§ 1002.   Application for Certificate of Authority

(a)   A foreign limited liability company may apply for a certificate of authority to transact business in this State by delivering an application to the [Secretary of State] for filing. The application must set forth:

(1)   the name of the foreign company or, if its name is unavailable for use in this State, a name that satisfies the requirements of Section 1005;

(2)   the name of the State or country under whose law it is organized;

(3)   the street address of its principal office;

(4)   the address of its initial designated office in this State;

(5)   the name and street address of its initial agent for service of process in this State;

(6)   whether the duration of the company is for a specified term and, if so, the period specified;

(7)   whether the company is manager-managed, and, if so, the name and address of each initial manager; and

(8)   whether the members of the company are to be liable for its debts and obligations under a provision similar to Section 303(c).

(b)   A foreign limited liability company shall deliver with the completed application a certificate of existence or a record of similar import authenticated by the secretary of state or other official having custody of company records in the State or country under whose law it is organized.

COMMENT

As with articles of organization, the application must be signed and filed with the filing office. See Sections 105, 107 (name registration), 205, 206, 209 (liability for false statements), and 1005.

§ 1003.   Activities Not Constituting Transacting Business

(a)   Activities of a foreign limited liability company that do not constitute transacting business in this State within the meaning of this [article] include:

(1)   maintaining, defending, or settling an action or proceeding;

(2)   holding meetings of its members or managers or carrying on any other activity concerning its internal affairs;

(3)   maintaining bank accounts;

(4)   maintaining offices or agencies for the transfer, exchange, and registration of the foreign company's own securities or maintaining trustees or depositories with respect to those securities;

(5)   selling through independent contractors;

(6)   soliciting or obtaining orders, whether by mail or through employees or agents or otherwise, if the orders require acceptance outside this State before they become contracts;

(7)   creating or acquiring indebtedness, mortgages, or security interests in real or personal property;

(8)   securing or collecting debts or enforcing mortgages or other security interests in property securing the debts, and holding, protecting, and maintaining property so acquired;

(9)   conducting an isolated transaction that is completed within 30 days and is not one in the course of similar transactions of a like manner; and

(10)   transacting business in interstate commerce.

(b)   For purposes of this [article], the ownership in this State of income-producing real property or tangible personal property, other than property excluded under subsection (a), constitutes transacting business in this State.

(c)   This section does not apply in determining the contacts or activities that may subject a foreign limited liability company to service of process, taxation, or regulation under any other law of this State.

§ 1004.   Issuance of Certificate of Authority

Unless the [Secretary of State] determines that an application for a certificate of authority fails to comply as to form with the filing requirements of this [Act], the [Secretary of State], upon payment of all filing fees, shall file the application and send a receipt for it and the fees to the limited liability company or its representative.

§ 1005.   Name of Foreign Limited Liability Company

(a)   If the name of a foreign limited liability company does not satisfy the requirements of Section 105, the company, to obtain or maintain a certificate of authority to transact business in this State, must use a fictitious name to transact business in this State if its real name is unavailable and it delivers to the [Secretary of State] for filing a copy of the resolution of its managers, in the case of a manager-managed company, or of its members, in the case of a member-managed company, adopting the fictitious name.

(b)   Except as authorized by subsections (c) and (d), the name, including a fictitious name to be used to transact business in this State, of a foreign limited liability company must be distinguishable upon the records of the [Secretary of State] from:

(1)   the name of any corporation, limited partnership, or company incorporated, organized, or authorized to transact business in this State;

(2)   a name reserved or registered under Section 106 or 107; and

(3)   the fictitious name of another foreign limited liability company authorized to transact business in this State.

(c)   A foreign limited liability company may apply to the [Secretary of State] for authority to use in this State a name that is not distinguishable upon the records of the [Secretary of State] from a name described in subsection (b). The [Secretary of State] shall authorize use of the name applied for if:

(1)   the present user, registrant, or owner of a reserved name consents to the use in a record and submits an undertaking in form satisfactory to the [Secretary of State] to change its name to a name that is distinguishable upon the records of the [Secretary of State] from the name of the foreign applying limited liability company; or

(2)   the applicant delivers to the [Secretary of State] a certified copy of a final judgment of a court establishing the applicant's right to use the name applied for in this State.

(d)   A foreign limited liability company may use in this State the name, including the fictitious name, of another domestic or foreign entity that is used in this State if the other entity is incorporated, organized, or authorized to transact business in this State and the foreign limited liability company:

(1)   has merged with the other entity;

(2)   has been formed by reorganization of the other entity; or

(3)   has acquired all or substantially all of the assets, including the name, of the other entity.

(e)   If a foreign limited liability company authorized to transact business in this State changes its name to one that does not satisfy the requirements of Section 105, it may not transact business in this State under the name as changed until it adopts a name satisfying the requirements of Section 105 and obtains an amended certificate of authority.

§ 1006.   Revocation of Certificate of Authority

(a)   A certificate of authority of a foreign limited liability company to transact business in this State may be revoked by the [Secretary of State] in the manner provided in subsection (b) if:

(1)   the company fails to:

(i)   pay any fees, taxes, and penalties owed to this State;

(ii)   deliver its annual report required under Section 211 to the [Secretary of State] within 60 days after it is due;

(iii)   appoint and maintain an agent for service of process as required by this [article]; or

(iv)   file a statement of a change in the name or business address of the agent as required by this [article]; or

(2)   a misrepresentation has been made of any material matter in any application, report, affidavit, or other record submitted by the company pursuant to this [article].

(b)   The [Secretary of State] may not revoke a certificate of authority of a foreign limited liability company unless the [Secretary of State] sends the company notice of the revocation, at least 60 days before its effective date, by a record addressed to its agent for service of process in this State, or if the company fails to appoint and maintain a proper agent in this State, addressed to the office required to be maintained by Section 108. The notice must specify the cause for the revocation of the certificate of authority. The authority of the company to transact business in this State ceases on the effective date of the revocation unless the foreign limited liability company cures the failure before that date.

§ 1007.   Cancellation of Authority

A foreign limited liability company may cancel its authority to transact business in this State by filing in the office of the [Secretary of State] a certificate of cancellation. Cancellation does not terminate the authority of the [Secretary of State] to accept service of process on the company for [claims for relief] arising out of the transactions of business in this State.

§ 1008. Effect of Failure to Obtain Certificate of Authority

(a) A foreign limited liability company transacting business in this State may not maintain an action or proceeding in this State unless it has a certificate of authority to transact business in this State.

(b) The failure of a foreign limited liability company to have a certificate of authority to transact business in this State does not impair the validity of a contract or act of the company or prevent the foreign limited liability company from defending an action or proceeding in this State.

(c) Limitations on personal liability of managers, members, and their transferees are not waived solely by transacting business in this State without a certificate of authority.

(d) If a foreign limited liability company transacts business in this State without a certificate of authority, it appoints the [Secretary of State] as its agent for service of process for [claims for relief] arising out of the transaction of business in this State.

§ 1009. Action by [Attorney General]

The [Attorney General] may maintain an action to restrain a foreign limited liability company from transacting business in this State in violation of this [article].

[ARTICLE] 11
DERIVATIVE ACTIONS

§ 1101. Right of Action

A member of a limited liability company may maintain an action in the right of the company if the members or managers having authority to do so have refused to commence the action or an effort to cause those members or managers to commence the action is not likely to succeed.

COMMENT

A member may bring an action on behalf of the company when the members or managers having the authority to pursue the company recovery refuse to do so or an effort to cause them to pursue the recovery is not likely to succeed. See Comments to Section 411(a) (personal action of member against company or another member).

§ 1102. Proper Plaintiff

In a derivative action for a limited liability company, the plaintiff must be a member of the company when the action is commenced; and:

(1) must have been a member at the time of the transaction of which the plaintiff complains; or

(2) the plaintiff's status as a member must have devolved upon the plaintiff by operation of law or pursuant to the terms of the operating agreement from a person who was a member at the time of the transaction.

§ 1103. Pleading

In a derivative action for a limited liability company, the complaint must set forth with particularity the effort of the plaintiff to secure initiation of the action by a member or manager or the reasons for not making the effort.

There is no obligation of the company or its members or managers to respond to a member demand to bring an action to pursue a company recovery. However, if a company later decides to commence the demanded action or assume control of the derivative litigation, the member's right to commence or control the proceeding ordinarily ends.

§ 1104. Expenses

If a derivative action for a limited liability company is successful, in whole or in part, or if anything is received by the plaintiff as a result of a judgment, compromise, or settlement of an action or claim, the court may award the plaintiff reasonable expenses, including reasonable attorney's fees, and shall direct the plaintiff to remit to the limited liability company the remainder of the proceeds received.

[ARTICLE] 12
MISCELLANEOUS PROVISIONS

§ 1201. Uniformity of Application and Construction

This [Act] shall be applied and construed to effectuate its general purpose to make uniform the law with respect to the subject of this [Act] among States enacting it.

§ 1202. Short Title

This [Act] may be cited as the Uniform Limited Liability Company Act (1996).

§ 1203. Severability Clause

If any provision of this [Act] or its application to any person or circumstance is held invalid, the invalidity does not affect other provisions or applications of this [Act] which can be given effect without the invalid provision or application, and to this end the provisions of this [Act] are severable.

§ 1204. Effective Date

This [Act] takes effect [_____].

§ 1205. Transitional Provisions

(a) Before January 1, 199__, this [Act] governs only a limited liability company organized:

(1) after the effective date of this [Act], unless the company is continuing the business of a dissolved limited liability company under [Section of the existing Limited Liability Company Act]; and

(2) before the effective date of this [Act], which elects, as provided by subsection (c), to be governed by this [Act].

(b) On and after January 1, 199__, this [Act] governs all limited liability companies.

(c) Before January 1, 199__, a limited liability company voluntarily may elect, in the manner provided in its operating agreement or by law for amending the operating agreement, to be governed by this [Act].

Under subsection (a)(1), the application of the Act is mandatory for all companies formed after the effective date of the Act determined under Section 1204. Under subsection (a)(2), the application of the Act is permissive, by election under subsection (c), for existing companies for a period of time specified in subsection (b) after which application becomes mandatory. This affords existing companies and their members an opportunity to consider the changes effected by this Act and to amend their operating agreements, if appropriate. If no election is made, the Act becomes effective after the period specified in subsection (b). The period specified by adopting States may vary, but a period of five years is a common period in similar cases.

§ 1206.   Savings Clause

This [Act] does not affect an action or proceeding commenced or right accrued before the effective date of this [Act].

REVISED UNIFORM LIMITED LIABILITY COMPANY ACT (2006)

Table of Sections

[ARTICLE] 1
GENERAL PROVISIONS

[ARTICLE] 2
FORMATION; CERTIFICATE OF ORGANIZATION
AND OTHER FILINGS

[ARTICLE] 3
RELATIONS OF MEMBERS AND MANAGERS TO PERSONS
DEALING WITH LIMITED LIABILITY COMPANY

RULLCA (2006)

REVISED UNIFORM LIMITED
LIABILITY COMPANY ACT

PREFATORY NOTE

Background to this Act:
Developments since the Conference Considered and Approved
the Original Uniform Limited Liability Company Act (ULLCA)

The Uniform Limited Liability Company Act ("ULLCA") was conceived in 1992 and first adopted by the Conference in 1994. By that time nearly every state had adopted an LLC statute, and those statutes varied considerably in both form and substance. Many of those early statutes were based on the first version of the ABA Model Prototype LLC Act.

RULLCA (2006)

ULLCA's drafting relied substantially on the then recently adopted Revised Uniform Partnership Act ("RUPA"), and this reliance was especially heavy with regard to member-managed LLCs. ULLCA's provisions for manager-managed LLCs comprised an amalgam fashioned from the 1985 Revised Uniform Limited Partnership Act ("RULPA") and the Model Business Corporation Act ("MBCA"). ULLCA's provisions were also significantly influenced by the then-applicable federal tax classification regulations, which classified an unincorporated organization as a corporation if the organization more nearly resembled a corporation than a partnership. Those same regulations also made the tax classification of single-member LLCs problematic.

Much has changed. All states and the District of Columbia have adopted LLC statutes, and many LLC statutes have been substantially amended several times. LLC filings are significant in every U.S. jurisdiction, and in many states new LLC filings approach or even outnumber new corporate filings on an annual basis. Manager-managed LLCs have become a significant factor in non-publicly-traded capital markets, and increasing numbers of states provide for mergers and conversions involving LLCs and other unincorporated entities.

In 1997, the tax classification context changed radically, when the IRS' "check-the-box" regulations became effective. Under these regulations, an "unincorporated" business entity is taxed either as a partnership or disregarded entity (depending upon the number of owners) unless it elects to be taxed as a corporation. Exceptions exist (e.g., entities whose interests are publicly-traded), but, in general, tax classification concerns no longer constrain the structure of LLCs and the content of LLC statutes. Single-member LLCs, once suspect because novel and of uncertain tax status, are now popular both for sole proprietorships and as corporate subsidiaries.

In 1995, the Conference amended RUPA to add "full-shield" LLP provisions, and today every state has some form of LLP legislation (either through a RUPA adoption or shield-related revisions to a UPA-based statute). While some states still provide only a "partial shield" for LLPs, many states have adopted "full shield" LLP provisions. In full-shield jurisdictions, LLPs and member-managed LLCs offer entrepreneurs very similar attributes and, in the case of professional service organizations, LLPs may dominate the field.

ULLCA was revised in 1996 in anticipation of the "check the box" regulations and has been adopted in a number of states. In many non-ULLCA states, the LLC statute includes RUPA-like provisions. However, state LLC laws are far from uniform.

Eighteen years have passed since the IRS issued its gate-opening Revenue Ruling 88–76, declaring that a Wyoming LLC would be taxed as a partnership despite the entity's corporate-like liability shield. More than eight years have passed since the IRS opened the gate still further with the "check the box" regulations. It is an opportune moment to identify the best elements of the myriad "first generation" LLC statutes and to infuse those elements into a new, "second generation" uniform act.

Noteworthy Provisions of the New Act

The Revised Uniform Limited Company Act is drafted to replace a state's current LLC statute, whether or not that statute is based on ULLCA. The new Act's noteworthy provisions concern:

- the operating agreement

- fiduciary duty

- the ability to "pre-file" a certificate of organization without having a member at the time of the filing

- the power of a member or manager to bind the limited liability company

- default rules on management structure

- charging orders

- a remedy for oppressive conduct

- derivative claims and special litigation committees

- organic transactions—mergers, conversions, and domestications

RULLCA (2006)

The Operating Agreement: Like the partnership agreement in a general or limited partnership, an LLC's operating agreement serves as the foundational contract among the entity's owners. RUPA pioneered the notion of centralizing all statutory provisions pertaining to the foundational contract, and—like ULLCA and ULPA (2001)—the new Act continues that approach. However, because an operating agreement raises issues too numerous and complex to include easily in a single section, the new Act uses three related sections to address the operating agreement:

- Section 110—scope, function, and limitations;

- Section 111—effect on limited liability company and persons becoming members; preformation agreement; and

- Section 112—effect on third parties and relationship to records effective on behalf of limited liability company.

The new Act also contains a number of substantive innovations concerning the operating agreement, including:

- better delineating the extent to which the operating agreement can define, alter, or even eliminate aspects of fiduciary duty;

- expressly authorizing the operating agreement to relieve members and managers from liability for money damages arising from breach of duty, subject to specific limitations; and

- stating specific rules for applying the statutory phrase "manifestly unreasonable" and thereby providing clear guidance for courts considering whether to invalidate operating agreement provisions that address fiduciary duty and other sensitive matters.

Fiduciary Duty: RUPA also pioneered the idea of codifying partners' fiduciary duties in order to protect the partnership agreement from judicial second-guessing. This approach—to "cabin in" (or corral) fiduciary duty—was followed in ULLCA and ULPA (2001). In contrast, the new Act recognizes that, at least in the realm of limited liability companies:

- the "cabin in" approach creates more problems than it solves (e.g. . . . by putting inordinate pressure on the concept of "good faith and fair dealing"); and

- the better way to protect the operating agreement from judicial second-guessing is to:

  * increase and clarify the power of the operating agreement to define or re-shape fiduciary duties (including the power to eliminate aspects of fiduciary duties); and

  * provide some guidance to courts when a person seeks to escape an agreement by claiming its provisions are "manifestly unreasonable."

Accordingly, the new Act codifies major fiduciary duties but does not purport to do so exhaustively. *See* Section 409.

The Ability to "Pre-File" a Certificate of Organization: The Comments to Section 201 explain in detail how the new Act resolves the difficult question of the "shelf LLC"—i.e., an LLC formed without having at least one member upon formation. In short, the Act: (i) permits an organizer to file a certificate of organization without a person "waiting in the wings" to become a member upon formation; but (ii) provides that the LLC is not formed until and unless at least one person becomes a member and the organizer makes a second filing stating that the LLC has at least one member.

The Power of a Member or Manager to Bind the Limited Liability Company: In 1914, the original Uniform Partnership Act codified a particular type of apparent authority by position, providing that "[t]he act of every partner . . . for apparently carrying on in the usual way the business of the partnership binds the partnership. . . ." This concept of "statutory apparent authority" applies by linkage in the 1916 Uniform Limited Partnership Act and the 1976/85 Revised Uniform Limited Partnership Act and appears in RUPA, ULLCA, ULPA (2001), and almost every LLC statute in the United States.

RULLCA (2006)

The concept makes good sense for general and limited partnerships. A third party dealing with either type of partnership can know by the formal name of the entity and by a person's status as general or limited partner whether the person has the power to bind the entity.

The concept does not make sense for modern LLC law, because: (i) an LLC's status as member-managed or manager-managed is not apparent from the LLC's name (creating traps for unwary third parties); and (ii) although most LLC statutes provide templates for member-management and manager-management, variability of management structure is a key strength of the LLC as a form of business organization.

The new Act recognizes that "statutory apparent authority" is an attribute of partnership formality that does not belong in an LLC statute. Section 301(a) provides that "a member is not an agent of the limited liability company solely by reason of being a member." Other law—most especially the law of agency—will handle power-to-bind questions.

Although conceptually innovative, this approach will not significantly alter the commercial reality that exists between limited liability companies and third parties, because:

1. The vast majority of interactions between limited liability companies and "third parties" are quotidian and transpire without agency law issues being recognized by the parties, let alone disputed.

2. When a limited liability company enters into a major transaction with a sophisticated third party, the third party never relies on statutory apparent authority to determine that the person purporting to act for the limited liability company has the authority to do so.

3. Most LLCs use employees to carry out most of the LLC's dealings with third parties. In that context, the agency power of members and managers is usually irrelevant. (If an employee's authority is contested and the employee "reports to" a member or manager, the member or manager's authority will be relevant to determining the employee's authority. However, in that situation, agency law principles will suffice to delineate the manager or member's supervisory authority.)

4. Very few current LLC statutes contain rules for attributing to an LLC the wrongful acts of the LLC's members or managers. *Compare* RUPA § 305. In this realm, this Act merely acknowledges pre-existing reality.

5. As explained in detail in the Comments to section 301 and 407(c), agency law principles are well-suited to the tasks resulting from the "de-codification" of apparent authority by position.

The moment is opportune for this reform. The newly-issued Restatement (Third) of Agency gives substantial attention to the power of an enterprise's participants to bind the enterprise. In addition, the new Act has "souped up" RUPA's statement of authority to permit an LLC to publicly file a statement of authority for a position (not merely a particular person). Statements of authority will enable LLCs to provide reliable documentation of authority to enter into transactions without having to disclose to third parties the entirety of the operating agreement. (The new Act also has eliminated prolix provisions that sought to restate agency law rules on notice and knowledge.)

Default Rules on Management Structure: The new Act retains the manager-managed and member-managed constructs as options for members to use in configuring their *inter se* relationship, and the operating agreement is the vehicle by which the members make and state their choice of management structure. Given the elimination of statutory apparent authority, it is unnecessary and could be confusing to require the articles of organization to state the members' determination on this point.

Charging Orders: The charging order mechanism: (i) dates back to the 1914 Uniform Partnership Act and the English Partnership Act of 1890; and (ii) is an essential part of the "pick your partner" approach that is fundamental to the law of unincorporated businesses. The new Act continues the charging order mechanism, but modernizes the statutory language so that the language (and its protections against outside interference in an LLC's activities) can be readily understood.

A Remedy for Oppressive Conduct: Reflecting case law developments around the country, the new Act permits a member (but not a transferee) to seek a court order "dissolving the company on the grounds that the managers or those members in control of the company . . . have acted or are acting in a manner that is oppressive and was, is, or will be directly harmful to the [member]." Section 701(5)(B). This provision is necessary given the perpetual duration of an LLC formed under this Act, Section 104(c), and this Act's elimination of the "put right" provided by ULLCA, § 701.

Derivative Claims and Special Litigation Committees: The new Act contains modern provisions addressing derivative litigation, including a provision authorizing special litigation committees and subjecting their composition and conduct to judicial review.

Organic Transactions—Mergers, Conversions, and Domestications: The new Act has comprehensive, self-contained provisions for these transactions, including "inter-species" transactions.

No Provision for "Series" LLCs

The new Act also has a very noteworthy omission; it does not authorize "series LLCs." Under a series approach, a single limited liability company may establish and contain within itself separate series. Each series is treated as an enterprise separate from each other and from the LLC itself. Each series has associated with it specified members, assets, and obligations, and—due to what have been called "internal shields"—the obligations of one series are not the obligation of any other series or of the LLC.

Delaware pioneered the series concept, and the concept has apparently been quite useful in structuring certain types of investment funds and in arranging complex financing. Other states have followed Delaware's lead, but a number of difficult and substantial questions remain unanswered, including:

- *conceptual*—How can a series be—and expect to be treated as—a separate legal person for liability and other purposes if the series is defined as part of another legal person?

- *bankruptcy*—Bankruptcy law has not recognized the series as a separate legal person. If a series becomes insolvent, will the entire LLC and the other series become part of the bankruptcy proceedings? Will a bankruptcy court consolidate the assets and liabilities of the separate series?

- *efficacy of the internal shields in the courts of other states*—Will the internal shields be respected in the courts of states whose LLC statutes do not recognize series? Most LLC statutes provide that "foreign law governs" the liability of members of a foreign LLC. However, those provisions do not apply to the series question, because those provisions pertain to the liability of a member for the obligations of the LLC. For a series LLC, the pivotal question is entirely different—namely, whether some assets of an LLC should be immune from some of the creditors of the LLC.

- *tax treatment*—Will the IRS and the states treat each series separately? Will separate returns be filed? May one series "check the box" for corporate tax classification and the others not?

- *securities law*—Given the panoply of unanswered questions, what types of disclosures must be made when a membership interest is subject to securities law?

The Drafting Committee considered a series proposal at its February 2006 meeting, but, after serious discussion, no one was willing to urge adoption of the proposal, even for the limited purposes of further discussion. Given the availability of well-established alternate structures (e.g., multiple single member LLCs, an LLC "holding company" with LLC subsidiaries), it made no sense for the Act to endorse the complexities and risks of a series approach.

REVISED UNIFORM LIMITED
LIABILITY COMPANY ACT

[ARTICLE] 1
GENERAL PROVISIONS

§ 101. Short Title

This [act] may be cited as the Revised Uniform Limited Liability Company Act.

This Act is drafted to replace a state's current LLC statute, whether or not that statute is based on the original Uniform Limited Liability Company Act. Section 1104 contains transition provisions.

§ 102.   Definitions

In this [act]:

(1) "Certificate of organization" means the certificate required by Section 201. The term includes the certificate as amended or restated.

(2) "Contribution" means any benefit provided by a person to a limited liability company:

(A) in order to become a member upon formation of the company and in accordance with an agreement between or among the persons that have agreed to become the initial members of the company;

(B) in order to become a member after formation of the company and in accordance with an agreement between the person and the company; or

(C) in the person's capacity as a member and in accordance with the operating agreement or an agreement between the member and the company.

(3) "Debtor in bankruptcy" means a person that is the subject of:

(A) an order for relief under Title 11 of the United States Code or a successor statute of general application; or

(B) a comparable order under federal, state, or foreign law governing insolvency.

(4) "Designated office" means:

(A) the office that a limited liability company is required to designate and maintain under Section 113; or

(B) the principal office of a foreign limited liability company.

(5) "Distribution", except as otherwise provided in Section 405(g), means a transfer of money or other property from a limited liability company to another person on account of a transferable interest.

(6) "Effective", with respect to a record required or permitted to be delivered to the [Secretary of State] for filing under this [act], means effective under Section 205(c).

(7) "Foreign limited liability company" means an unincorporated entity formed under the law of a jurisdiction other than this state and denominated by that law as a limited liability company.

(8) "Limited liability company", except in the phrase "foreign limited liability company", means an entity formed under this [act].

(9) "Manager" means a person that under the operating agreement of a manager-managed limited liability company is responsible, alone or in concert with others, for performing the management functions stated in Section 407(c).

(10) "Manager-managed limited liability company" means a limited liability company that qualifies under Section 407(a).

(11) "Member" means a person that has become a member of a limited liability company under Section 401 and has not dissociated under Section 602.

(12) "Member-managed limited liability company" means a limited liability company that is not a manager-managed limited liability company.

(13) "Operating agreement" means the agreement, whether or not referred to as an operating agreement and whether oral, in a record, implied, or in any combination thereof, of all the members of a limited liability company, including a sole member, concerning the matters described in Section 110(a). The term includes the agreement as amended or restated.

(14) "Organizer" means a person that acts under Section 201 to form a limited liability company.

(15) "Person" means an individual, corporation, business trust, estate, trust, partnership, limited liability company, association, joint venture, public corporation, government or governmental subdivision, agency, or instrumentality, or any other legal or commercial entity.

(16) "Principal office" means the principal executive office of a limited liability company or foreign limited liability company, whether or not the office is located in this state.

(17) "Record" means information that is inscribed on a tangible medium or that is stored in an electronic or other medium and is retrievable in perceivable form.

(18) "Sign" means, with the present intent to authenticate or adopt a record:

(A) to execute or adopt a tangible symbol; or

(B) to attach to or logically associate with the record an electronic symbol, sound, or process.

(19) "State" means a state of the United States, the District of Columbia, Puerto Rico, the United States Virgin Islands, or any territory or insular possession subject to the jurisdiction of the United States.

(20) "Transfer" includes an assignment, conveyance, deed, bill of sale, lease, mortgage, security interest, encumbrance, gift, and transfer by operation of law.

(21) "Transferable interest" means the right, as originally associated with a person's capacity as a member, to receive distributions from a limited liability company in accordance with the operating agreement, whether or not the person remains a member or continues to own any part of the right.

(22) "Transferee" means a person to which all or part of a transferable interest has been transferred, whether or not the transferor is a member.

COMMENT

This Section contains definitions for terms used throughout the Act, while Section 1001 contains definitions specific to Article 10's provisions on mergers, conversions and domestications. Section 405(g) contains an exception to the definition of "distribution," which is specific to Section 405.

Paragraph (1) [Certificate of organization]—The original ULLCA and most other LLC statutes use "articles of organization" rather than "certificate of organization." This Act purposely uses the latter term to signal that: (i) the certificate merely reflects the existence of an LLC (rather than being the locus for important governance rules); and (ii) this document is significantly different from articles of *incorporation*, which have a substantially greater power to affect *inter se* rules for the corporate entity and its owners. For the relationship between the certificate of organization and the operating agreement, see Section 112(d).

Paragraph (2) [Contribution]—This definition serves to distinguish capital contributions from other circumstances under which a member or would-be member might provide benefits to a limited liability company (e.g., providing services to the LLC as an employee or independent contractor, leasing property to the LLC). The definition contemplates three typical situations in which contributions are made, and for each situation establishes two "markers" to identify capital contributions—the purpose for which the contributor makes the contribution and the agreement that contemplates the contribution:

circumstance	purpose/cause of providing benefits	the relevant agreement
pre-formation deal among would-be initial members [Paragraph 2(A)]	in order to become initial member(s)	agreement among would-be initial members
deal between an existing LLC and would-be member [Paragraph 2(B)]	in order to become a member	agreement between the LLC and the would-be member

| member contribution [Paragraph 2(C)] | in member's capacity as a member | operating agreement or an agreement between the member and the LLC |

This definition does not encompass capital raised from transferees, which is sometimes provided for in operating agreements. In such circumstances, the default rules for liquidating distributions should be altered accordingly. *See* Section 708(b)(1) ("referring to contributions made by a member and not previously returned").

Paragraph (7) [Foreign limited liability company]—Some statutes have elaborate definitions addressing the question of whether a non-U.S. entity is a "foreign limited liability company." The NY statute, for example, defines a "foreign limited liability company" as:

an unincorporated organization formed under the laws of any jurisdiction, including any foreign country, other than the laws of this state (i) that is not authorized to do business in this state under any other law of this state and (ii) of which some or all of the persons who are entitled (A) to receive a distribution of the assets thereof upon the dissolution of the organization or otherwise or (B) to exercise voting rights with respect to an interest in the organization have, or are entitled or authorized to have, under the laws of such other jurisdiction, limited liability for the contractual obligations or other liabilities of the organization.

N.Y. LIMIT LIAB. CO. LAW § 102(k) (McKinney 2006). ULLCA § 101(8) takes a similar but less complex approach ("an unincorporated entity organized under laws other than the laws of this State which afford limited liability to its owners comparable to the liability under Section 303 and is not required to obtain a certificate of authority to transact business under any law of this State other than this [Act]"). This Act follows Delaware's still simpler approach. DEL. CODE ANN. tit. 6, § 18–101(4) (2006) ("denominated as such").

Paragraph (8) [Limited liability company]—This definition makes no reference to a limited liability company having members upon formation, but Section 201 does. For a detailed discussion of the "shelf LLC" issue, see the Comment to Section 201.

Paragraph (9) [Manager]—The Act uses the word "manager" as a term of art, whose applicability is confined to manager-managed LLCs. The phrase "manager-managed" is itself a term of art, referring only to an LLC whose operating agreement refers to the LLC as such. Paragraph 10 (defining "manager-managed limited liability company"). Thus, for purposes of this Act, if the members of a *member*-managed LLC delegate plenipotentiary management authority to one person (whether or not a member), this Act's references to "manager" do not apply to that person.

This approach does have the potential for confusion, but confusion around the term "manager" is common to almost all LLC statutes. The confusion stems from the choice to define "manager" as a term of art in a way that can be at odds with other, common usages of the word. For example, a member-managed LLC might well have an "office manager" or a "property manager." Moreover, in a manager-managed LLC, the "property manager" is not likely to be a manager as the term is used in many LLC statutes. *See, e.g., Brown v. MR Group, LLC*, 278 Wis.2d 760, 768–9, 693 N.W.2d 138, 143 (Wis.App. 2005) (rejecting a party's urging to use the dictionary definition of "manager" in determining coverage of a policy applicable to a limited liability company and its "managers" and relying instead on the meaning of the term under the Wisconsin LLC act).

Under this Act, the category of "person" is not limited to individuals. Therefore, a "manager" need not be a natural person. After a person ceases to be a manager, the term "manager" continues to apply to the person's conduct while a manager. *See* Section 407(c)(7).

Paragraph (10) [Manager-managed]—This Act departs from most LLC statutes (including the original ULLCA) by authorizing a private agreement (the operating agreement) rather than a public document (certificate or articles of organization) to establish an LLC's status as a manager-managed limited liability company. Using the operating agreement makes sense, because under this Act managerial structure creates no statutory power to bind the entity. *See* Section 301 (eliminating statutory apparent authority). The only direct consequences of manager-managed status are *inter se*—principally the triggering of a set of rules concerning management structure, fiduciary duty, and information rights. Sections 407–410. The management structure rules are entirely default provisions—subject to change in whole or in part by the operating agreement. The operating agreement can also significantly affect the duty and rights provisions. Section 110.

For pre-existing limited liability companies that eventually become subject to this Act, Section 1104(c) provides that "language in the limited liability company's articles of organization designating the company's management structure will operate as if that language were in the operating agreement." For limited liability companies formed under this Act, the typical method to select manager-managed status will be an explicit provision of the operating agreement. However, a reference in the certificate of organization to manager-management might be evidence of the contents of the operating agreement. *See* Comment to Section 112(b).

An LLC that is "manager-managed" under this definition does not cease to be so simply because the members fail to designate anyone to act as a manager. In that situation, absent additional facts, the LLC is manager-managed and the manager position is vacant. Non-manager members who exercise managerial functions during the vacancy (or at any other time) will have duties as determined by other law, most particularly the law of agency.

Paragraph 10(A) and (B)—In these paragraphs, the phrases "manager-managed" and "managed by managers" are "magic words"—i.e., for either subparagraph to apply, the operating agreement must include precisely the required language. However, the word "expressly" does not mean "in writing" or "in a record." This Act permits operating agreements to be oral (in whole or in part), and an oral provision of an operating agreement could contain the magic words. This Act also recognizes that provisions of an operating agreement may be reflected in patterns of conduct.

Oral and implied agreements invite memory problems and "swearing matches." Section 110(a)(4) empowers the operating agreement to determine "the means and conditions for the amending the operating agreement."

Paragraph 10(C)—In contrast to Paragraphs 10(A) and (B), this provision does not contain "magic words" and considers instead all terms of the operating agreement that expressly refer to management by managers.

Paragraph 11 [Member]—After a person has been dissociated as a member, Section 602, the term "member" continues to apply to the person's conduct while a member. *See* Section 603(b).

Paragraph 12 [Member-managed limited liability company]—A limited liability company that does not effectively designate itself a manager-member limited liability company will operate, subject to any contrary provisions in the operating agreement, under statutory rules providing for management by the members. Section 407(a). For a discussion of potential confusion relating to the term "manager", see the Comment to Paragraph 9 (Manager).

Paragraph (13) [Operating Agreement]—This definition must be read in conjunction with Sections 110 through 112, which further describe the operating agreement. An operating agreement is a contract, and therefore all statutory language pertaining to the operating agreement must be understood in the context of the law of contracts.

The definition in Paragraph 13 is very broad and recognizes a wide scope of authority for the operating agreement: "the matters described in Section 110(a)." Those matters include not only all relations *inter se* the members and the limited liability company but also all "activities of the company and the conduct of those activities." Section 110(a)(3). Moreover, the definition puts no limits on the form of the operating agreement. To the contrary, the definition contains the phrase "whether oral, in a record, implied, or in any combination thereof".

This Act states no rule as to whether the statute of frauds applies to an oral operating agreement. Case law suggests that an oral agreement to form a partnership or joint venture with a term exceeding one year is within the statute. *E.g. Abbott v. Hurst*, 643 So.2d 589, 592 (Ala. 1994) ("Partnership agreements, like other contracts, are subject to the Statute of Frauds. A contract of partnership for a term exceeding one year is within the Statute of Frauds and is void unless it is in writing; however, a contract establishing a partnership terminable at the will of any partner is generally held to be capable of performance by its terms within one year of its making and, therefore, to be outside the Statute of Frauds.") (citations omitted); *Pemberton v. Ladue Realty & Const. Co.*, 362 Mo. 768, 770–71, 244 S.W.2d 62, 64 (Mo. 1951) (rejecting plaintiff's contention that mere part performance sufficed to take the oral agreement outside the statute and holding that partnership was therefore at will); *Ebker v. Tan Jay Int'l, Ltd.*, 739 F.2d 812, 827–28 (2d Cir.1984) (same analysis with regard to a joint venture). However, it is not possible to form an LLC without someone signing and delivering to the filing officer a certificate of organization in record form, Section 201(a), and the Act itself then establishes the LLC's duration. Subject to the operating agreement, that duration is perpetual. Section 104(c). An oral provision of an operating agreement calling for performance that extends beyond a year might be within the one-year provision—e.g., an oral agreement that a particular member will serve (and be permitted to serve) as manager for three years.

An oral provision of an operating agreement which involves the transfer of land, whether by or to the LLC, might come within the land provision of the statute of frauds. *Froiseth v. Nowlin*, 156 Wash. 314, 316, 287 P. 55. 56 (Wash. 1930) ("[The land provision] applies to an oral contract to transfer or convey partnership real property, and the interest of the other partners therein, to one partner as an individual, as well as to a parol contract by one of the parties to convey certain land owned by him individually to the partnership, or to another partner, or to put it into the partnership stock.") (quoting 27 CORPUS JURIS 220).").

In contrast, the fact that a limited liability company owns or deals in real property does not bring within the land provision agreements pertaining to the LLC's membership interests. Interests in a limited liability company are personal property and reflect no direct interest in the entity's assets. Re-ULLCA §§ 501 & 102(21). Thus, the real property issues pertaining to the LLC's ownership of land do not "flow through" to the members and membership interests. See, e.g., *Wooten v. Marshall*, 153 F. Supp. 759, 763–764 (S.D. N.Y. 1957) (involving an "oral agreement for a joint venture concerning the purchase, exploitation and eventual disposition of this 160 acre tract" and stating "[t]he real property acquired and dealt with by the venturers takes on the character of personal property as between the partners in the enterprise, and hence is not covered by [the Statute of Frauds]."

The operating agreement may comprise a number of separate documents (or records), however denominated, unless the operating agreement itself provides otherwise. Section 110(a)(4). Absent a contrary provision in the operating agreement, a threshold qualification for status as part of the "operating agreement" is the assent of all the persons then members. An agreement among less than all of the members might well be enforceable among those members as parties, but would not be part of the operating agreement.

An agreement to form an LLC is not itself an operating agreement. The term "operating agreement" presupposes the existence of members, and a person cannot have "member" status until the LLC exists. However, the Act's very broad definition of "operating agreement" means that, as soon as a limited liability company has any members, the limited liability company has an operating agreement. For example, suppose: (i) two persons orally and informally agree to join their activities in some way through the mechanism of an LLC, (ii) they form the LLC or cause it to be formed, and (iii) without further ado or agreement, they become the LLC's initial members. The LLC has an operating agreement. "[A]ll the members" have agreed on who the members are, and that agreement—no matter how informal or rudimentary—is an agreement "concerning the matters described in Section 110(a)." (To the extent the agreement does not provide the *inter se* "rules of the game," this Act "fills in the gaps." Section 110(b).)

The same result follows when a person becomes the sole initial member of an LLC. It is not plausible that the person would lack any understanding or intention with regard to the LLC. That understanding or intention constitutes an "agreement of all the members of the limited liability company, including a sole member."

It may seem oxymoronic to refer an "agreement of . . . a sole member," but this approach is common in LLC statutes. *See, e.g.,* ARIZ. REV. STAT. ANN. § 29–601 (14)(b) (2006) (defining operating agreement to mean "in the case of a limited liability company that has a single member, any written or oral statement of the member made in good faith"); COLO. REV. STAT. ANN. § 7–80–102 (11)(b)(I) (West 2006) (defining operating agreement to include, in the case of a single member LLC "[a]ny writing, without regard to whether such writing otherwise constitutes an agreement . . . signed by the sole member"; N.H. REV. STAT. ANN. § 304–c:1 (VI) (2006) (defining limited liability company agreement to include "a document adopted by the sole member"); OR. REV. STAT. ANN. § 63.431(2) (2005) (vesting the "power to adopt, alter, amend or repeal an operating agreement of . . . a single member limited liability company, in the sole member of the limited liability company"); R.I. GEN. LAWS § 7–16–2 (19) (2005) (stating that the term operating agreement "includes a document adopted by the sole member of a limited liability company that has only one member"); and WASH. REV. CODE ANN. § 25.15.005 (5) (West 2006) (defining limited liability company agreement to include "any written statement of the sole member").

This re-definition of "agreement" is a function of "path dependence." By the time single-member LLCs became widely accepted, almost all LLC statutes were premised on the LLC's key organic document being the operating agreement. Because a key function of the operating agreement is to override statutory default rules, it was necessary to make clear that a sole member could make an operating agreement. Such an agreement may also be of interest to third parties, because the operating agreement binds the LLC. Section 111(a).

In light of Paragraph 13's broad definition, it is possible to argue that any activity involving unanimous consent of the members becomes part of the operating agreement. For example, if pursuant to an operating agreement all the members consent to the redemption of one-half of the managing-member's transferable interest, does that action constitute an addition to the agreement?

Typically, such questions will turn on the practical issue of whether the unanimous consent pertained solely to a single event (now past) or also to future circumstances (now in controversy) rather than on the semantic question of whether the operating agreement has been amended. Occasionally, however, the amendment *vel non* question could have practical import. For example, if the operating agreement entitles a non-member to approve (or veto) amendments, see Section 112(a), the members and the non-member might see the matter quite differently.

Careful drafting of veto provisions can help avoid controversy—e.g., by defining with specificity the type of decisions subject to the veto. On the question of how far a written (or "in a record") operating agreement can go to prevent oral or implied-in-fact terms, see Section 110(a)(4).

If it is necessary for a court to decide whether the contents of a matter approved by unanimous consent have become part of the operating agreement, the court should rely on principles of contract interpretation and look:

- first, at the manifestations of the members, including:

  - the manifestations made to give the unanimous consent; and

  - any terms of the operating agreement (e.g., terms specifying how matters become part of the operating agreement); and

- second, at whether, viewed from the perspective of a reasonable person in the position of the members giving consent, the consent was intended to incorporate the matter into the ongoing "rules of the game" or merely take some particular action as already permitted by those rules.

Of course, if all the members have the same understanding, the reasonableness *vel non* of that understanding is irrelevant and the shared meaning governs. *See* RESTATEMENT (SECOND) OF CONTRACTS, § 201(1) (1981).

Paragraph (14) [Organizer]—If an LLC is to have one or more members when the filing officer files the certificate of organization, the organizer: (i) acts on behalf of the person or persons who will become the LLC's initial members, Section 401(a) and (b); and (ii) has no function other than to compose, sign, and deliver to the filing officer for filing the certificate of organization. Section 201(a). If an LLC is to have its first member sometime *after* the filing officer files the certificate of organization, the organizer has the power to admit the initial member or members, Section 401(c), and to sign and deliver for filing the notice of initial membership described in Section 201(e)(1). Whether in this latter category of circumstances the organizer acts on behalf of the initial member or members is determined under ordinary principles of agency law and depends on the facts of each situation.

Paragraph (20) [Transfer]—The reference to "transfer by operation of law" is significant in connection with Section 502 (Transfer of Transferable Interest). That section severely restricts a transferee's rights (absent the consent of the members), and this definition makes those restrictions applicable, for example, to transfers ordered by a family court as part of a divorce proceeding and transfers resulting from the death of a member. The restrictions also apply to transfers in the context of a member's bankruptcy, except to the extent that bankruptcy law supersedes this Act.

Paragraph (21) [Transferee]—"Transferee" has displaced "assignee" as the Conference's term of art.

§ 103. Knowledge; Notice

(a) A person knows a fact when the person:

    (1) has actual knowledge of it; or

    (2) is deemed to know it under subsection (d)(1) or law other than this [act].

(b) A person has notice of a fact when the person:

    (1) has reason to know the fact from all of the facts known to the person at the time in question; or

    (2) is deemed to have notice of the fact under subsection (d)(2).

(c) A person notifies another of a fact by taking steps reasonably required to inform the other person in ordinary course, whether or not the other person knows the fact.

(d) A person that is not a member is deemed:

    (1) to know of a limitation on authority to transfer real property as provided in Section 302(g); and

    (2) to have notice of a limited liability company's:

        (A) dissolution, 90 days after a statement of dissolution under Section 702(b)(2)(A) becomes effective;

(B)   termination, 90 days after a statement of termination Section 702(b)(2)(F) becomes effective; and

(C)   merger, conversion, or domestication, 90 days after articles of merger, conversion, or domestication under [Article] 10 become effective.

COMMENT

This section is substantially slimmer than the corresponding provisions of previous uniform acts pertaining to business organizations (RUPA, ULLCA, and ULPA (2001)). Each of those acts borrowed heavily from the comparable UCC provisions. For the most part, this Act relies instead on generally applicable principles of agency law, and therefore this section is mostly confined to rules specifically tailored to this Act.

Several facets of this section warrant particular note. First, and most fundamentally, because this Act does not provide for "statutory apparent authority," see Section 301, this section contains no special rules for attributing to an LLC information possessed, communicated to, or communicated by a member or manager.

Second, the section contains no generally applicable provisions determining when an organization is charged with knowledge or notice, because those imputation rules: (i) comprise core topics within the law of agency; (ii) are very complicated; (iii) should not have any different content under this Act than in other circumstances; and (iv) are the subject of considerable attention in the new Restatement (Third) of Agency.

Third, this Act does not define "notice" to include "knowledge." Although conceptualizing the latter as giving the former makes logical sense and has a long pedigree, that conceptualization is counter-intuitive for the non-*aficionado*. In ordinary usage, notice has a meaning separate from knowledge. This Act follows ordinary usage and therefore contains some references to "knowledge or notice."

Subsection (a)(2)—In this context, the most important source of "law other than this [act]" is the common law of agency.

Subsection (b)(1)—The "facts known to the person at the time in question" include facts the person is deemed to know under subsection (a)(2).

Subsection (d)(2)—Under this Act, the power to bind a limited liability company to a third party is primarily a matter of agency law. Section 301, Comment. The constructive notice provided under this paragraph will be relevant if a third party makes a claim under agency law that someone who purported to act on behalf of a limited liability company had the apparent authority to do so.

§ 104.   Nature, Purpose, and Duration of Limited Liability Company

(a)   A limited liability company is an entity distinct from its members.

(b)   A limited liability company may have any lawful purpose, regardless of whether for profit.

(c)   A limited liability company has perpetual duration.

Legislative Note: This state should consider whether to amend statutes protecting the public interest in organizations formed for charitable or similar purposes.

COMMENT

Subsection (a)—The "separate entity" characteristic is fundamental to a limited liability company and is inextricably connected to both the liability shield, Section 304, and the charging order provision, Section 503.

Subsection (b)—The phrase "any lawful purpose, regardless of whether for profit" means that: (i) a limited liability company need not have any business purpose; and (ii) the issue of profit *vel non* is irrelevant to the question of whether a limited liability company has been validly formed. Although some LLC statutes continue to require a business purpose, this Act follows the current trend and takes a more expansive approach.

The expansive approach comports both with the original ULLCA and with ULPA (2001). *See* ULLCA §§ 112(a) (captioned with reference to "Nature of Business" and permitting "any lawful purpose, subject to any law of this State governing or regulating business") and 101(3) (defining "Business" as including "every trade, occupation, profession, and other lawful purpose, whether or not carried on for profit"); ULPA (2001) § 104(b) (permitting a limited partnership to be organized for any "lawful" purpose). *Compare* UPA § 6 (defining a general partnership as organized for profit), RUPA § 101(6) (same), and RULPA (1976/85) § 106 (delineating the "Nature of [a limited partnership's] Business" by linking back to "any business that a partnership without limited partners may carry on").

The subsection does not bar a limited liability company from being organized to carry on charitable activities, and this act does not include any protective provisions pertaining to charitable purposes. Those protections must be (and typically are) found in other law, although sometimes that "other law" appears within a state's non-profit corporation statute. *See, e.g.,* MINN. STAT. § 317A.811 (2006) (providing restrictions on charitable organizations that seek to "dissolve, merge, or consolidate, or to transfer all or substantially all of their assets" but imposing those restrictions only on "corporations," which are elsewhere defined as corporations incorporated under the non-profit corporation act).

Subsection (c)—In this context, the word "perpetual" is a misnomer, albeit one commonplace in LLC statutes. Like all current LLC statutes, this Act provides several consent-based avenues to override perpetuity: a term specified in the operating agreement; an event specified in the operating agreement; member consent. Section 701 (events causing dissolution). In this context, "perpetuity" actually means that the Act does not require a definite term and creates no nexus between the dissociation of a member and the dissolution of the entity. (The dissociation of an LLC's last remaining member does threaten dissolution. Section 701(a)(3) (stating, as a default rule, that a limited liability company dissolves "upon . . . the passage of 90 consecutive days during which the limited liability company has no members").

An operating agreement is not a publicly-filed document, which means that the public record pertaining to a limited liability company will not necessarily reveal whether a limited liability company actually has a perpetual duration. *Accord* ULPA (2001) § 104, comment to subsection (c) ("The partnership agreement has the power to vary this subsection [which provides for perpetual duration], either by stating a definite term or by specifying an event or events which cause dissolution . . . . [The limited partnership act] also recognizes several other occurrences that cause dissolution. Thus, the public record pertaining to a limited partnership will not necessarily reveal whether the limited partnership actually has a perpetual duration.")

§ 105. Powers

A limited liability company has the capacity to sue and be sued in its own name and the power to do all things necessary or convenient to carry on its activities.

COMMENT

Following ULPA (2001), § 105, this Act omits as unnecessary any detailed list of specific powers. *Compare* ULLCA § 112 (containing a detailed list).

The capacity to sue and be sued is mentioned specifically so that Section 110(c)(1) can prohibit the operating agreement from varying that capacity. An LLC's standing to enforce the operating agreement is a separate matter, which is covered by Section 111(a) (stating, as a default rule, that the limited liability company "may enforce the operating agreement").

§ 106. Governing Law

The law of this state governs:

(1) the internal affairs of a limited liability company; and

(2) the liability of a member as member and a manager as manager for the debts, obligations, or other liabilities of a limited liability company.

COMMENT

Paragraph (1)—Like any other legal concept, "internal affairs" may be indeterminate at its edges. However, the concept certainly includes interpretation and enforcement of the operating agreement, relations among the members as members; relations between the limited liability company and a member as a member, relations between a manager-managed limited liability company and a manager, and relations between a manager of a manager-managed limited liability company and the members as members. *Compare* RESTATEMENT (SECOND) OF CONFLICT OF LAWS § 302, cmt. a (defining "internal affairs" with reference to a corporation as "the relations inter se of the corporation, its shareholders, directors, officers or agents").

The operating agreement cannot alter this provision. Section 110(c)(2). However, an operating agreement may lawfully incorporate by reference the provisions of another state's LLC statute. If done correctly, this incorporation makes the foreign statutory language part of the operating agreement, and the incorporated terms (together with the rest of the operating agreement) then govern the members (and those claiming through the members) to the extent not prohibited by this Act. *See* Section 110. This approach does <u>not</u> switch the limited liability company's governing law to that of another state, but instead takes the provisions of another state's law and incorporates them by reference into the contract among the members.

Paragraph (2)—This paragraph certainly encompasses Section 304 (the liability shield) but does not necessarily encompass a claim that a member or manager is liable to a third party for (i) having purported to bind a limited liability company to the third party; or (ii) having committed a tort against the third party while acting on the limited liability company's behalf or in the course of the company's business. That liability is not by status (i.e., not "as member . . . [or] as manager") but rather results from function or conduct. Contrast Section 301(b) (stating that, although this Act does not make a member as member the agent of a limited liability company, other law may make an LLC liable for the conduct of a member).

This paragraph is stated separately from Paragraph (1), because it can be argued that the liability of members and managers to third parties is not an internal affair. *See, e.g.,* RESTATEMENT (SECOND) OF CONFLICT OF LAWS, § 307 (treating shareholders' liability separately from the internal affairs doctrine). A few cases subsume owner/manager liability into internal affairs, but many do not. *See, e.g., Kalb, Voorhis & Co. v. American Fin. Corp.,* 8 F.3d 130, 132 (2nd Cir. 1993). In any event, the rule stated in this paragraph is correct. All sensible authorities agree that, except in extraordinary circumstances, "shield-related" issues should be determined according to the law of the state of organization.

§ 107.   Supplemental Principles of Law

Unless displaced by particular provisions of this [act], the principles of law and equity supplement this [act].

§ 108.   Name

(a)   The name of a limited liability company must contain the words "limited liability company" or "limited company" or the abbreviation "L.L.C.", "LLC", "L.C.", or "LC". "Limited" may be abbreviated as "Ltd.", and "company" may be abbreviated as "Co.".

(b)   Unless authorized by subsection (c), the name of a limited liability company must be distinguishable in the records of the [Secretary of State] from:

(1)   the name of each person that is not an individual and that is incorporated, organized, or authorized to transact business in this state;

(2)   the limited liability company name stated in each certificate of organization that contains the statement as provided in Section 201(b)(3) and that has not lapsed; and

(3)   each name reserved under Section 109 and [cite other state laws allowing the reservation or registration of business names, including fictitious or assumed name statutes].

(c)   A limited liability company may apply to the [Secretary of State] for authorization to use a name that does not comply with subsection (b). The [Secretary of State] shall authorize use of the name applied for if, as to each noncomplying name:

(1)   the present user, registrant, or owner of the noncomplying name consents in a signed record to the use and submits an undertaking in a form satisfactory to the [Secretary of State] to change the noncomplying name to a name that complies with subsection (b) and is distinguishable in the records of the [Secretary of State] from the name applied for; or

(2)   the applicant delivers to the [Secretary of State] a certified copy of the final judgment of a court establishing the applicant's right to use in this state the name applied for.

(d)   Subject to Section 805, this section applies to a foreign limited liability company transacting business in this state which has a certificate of authority to transact business in this state or which has applied for a certificate of authority.

COMMENT

Subsection (a) is taken verbatim from ULLCA § 105(a). Except for subsection (b)(2), the rest of the section is taken from ULPA (2001) § 108.

Subsection (b)(2)—This language is necessary to protect a name contained in a filed certificate of organization that has not become effective because there are no members. If a statement of membership is not thereafter timely filed, "the certificate lapses and is void," thereby freeing the name. Section 201(e)(1).

§ 109. Reservation of Name

(a) A person may reserve the exclusive use of the name of a limited liability company, including a fictitious or assumed name for a foreign limited liability company whose name is not available, by delivering an application to the [Secretary of State] for filing. The application must state the name and address of the applicant and the name proposed to be reserved. If the [Secretary of State] finds that the name applied for is available, it must be reserved for the applicant's exclusive use for a 120-day period.

(b) The owner of a name reserved for a limited liability company may transfer the reservation to another person by delivering to the [Secretary of State] for filing a signed notice of the transfer which states the name and address of the transferee.

COMMENT

Source: ULLCA, § 106.

Subsection (a)—Although 120-day reservation period is non-renewable, this subsection does not prevent a person from seeking successive 120-day periods of reservation.

§ 110. Operating Agreement; Scope, Function, and Limitations

(a) Except as otherwise provided in subsections (b) and (c), the operating agreement governs:

(1) relations among the members as members and between the members and the limited liability company;

(2) the rights and duties under this [act] of a person in the capacity of manager;

(3) the activities of the company and the conduct of those activities; and

(4) the means and conditions for amending the operating agreement.

(b) To the extent the operating agreement does not otherwise provide for a matter described in subsection (a), this [act] governs the matter.

(c) An operating agreement may not:

(1) vary a limited liability company's capacity under Section 105 to sue and be sued in its own name;

(2) vary the law applicable under Section 106;

(3) vary the power of the court under Section 204;

(4) subject to subsections (d) through (g), eliminate the duty of loyalty, the duty of care, or any other fiduciary duty;

(5) subject to subsections (d) through (g), eliminate the contractual obligation of good faith and fair dealing under Section 409(d);

(6) unreasonably restrict the duties and rights stated in Section 410;

(7) vary the power of a court to decree dissolution in the circumstances specified in Section 701(a)(4) and (5);

(8) vary the requirement to wind up a limited liability company's business as specified in Section 702(a) and (b)(1);

(9)   unreasonably restrict the right of a member to maintain an action under [Article] 9;

(10)   restrict the right to approve a merger, conversion, or domestication under Section 1014 to a member that will have personal liability with respect to a surviving, converted, or domesticated organization; or

(11)   except as otherwise provided in Section 112(b), restrict the rights under this [act] of a person other than a member or manager.

(d)   If not manifestly unreasonable, the operating agreement may:

(1)   restrict or eliminate the duty:

(A)   as required in Section 409(b)(1) and (g), to account to the limited liability company and to hold as trustee for it any property, profit, or benefit derived by the member in the conduct or winding up of the company's business, from a use by the member of the company's property, or from the appropriation of a limited liability company opportunity;

(B)   as required in Section 409(b)(2) and (g), to refrain from dealing with the company in the conduct or winding up of the company's business as or on behalf of a party having an interest adverse to the company; and

(C)   as required by Section 409(b)(3) and (g), to refrain from competing with the company in the conduct of the company's business before the dissolution of the company;

(2)   identify specific types or categories of activities that do not violate the duty of loyalty;

(3)   alter the duty of care, except to authorize intentional misconduct or knowing violation of law;

(4)   alter any other fiduciary duty, including eliminating particular aspects of that duty; and

(5)   prescribe the standards by which to measure the performance of the contractual obligation of good faith and fair dealing under Section 409(d).

(e)   The operating agreement may specify the method by which a specific act or transaction that would otherwise violate the duty of loyalty may be authorized or ratified by one or more disinterested and independent persons after full disclosure of all material facts.

(f)   To the extent the operating agreement of a member-managed limited liability company expressly relieves a member of a responsibility that the member would otherwise have under this [act] and imposes the responsibility on one or more other members, the operating agreement may, to the benefit of the member that the operating agreement relieves of the responsibility, also eliminate or limit any fiduciary duty that would have pertained to the responsibility.

(g)   The operating agreement may alter or eliminate the indemnification for a member or manager provided by Section 408(a) and may eliminate or limit a member or manager's liability to the limited liability company and members for money damages, except for:

(1)   breach of the duty of loyalty;

(2)   a financial benefit received by the member or manager to which the member or manager is not entitled;

(3)   a breach of a duty under Section 406;

(4)   intentional infliction of harm on the company or a member; or

(5)   an intentional violation of criminal law.

(h)   The court shall decide any claim under subsection (d) that a term of an operating agreement is manifestly unreasonable. The court:

(1)   shall make its determination as of the time the challenged term became part of the operating agreement and by considering only circumstances existing at that time; and

(2)   may invalidate the term only if, in light of the purposes and activities of the limited liability company, it is readily apparent that:

(A)   the objective of the term is unreasonable; or

(B)   the term is an unreasonable means to achieve the provision's objective.

COMMENT

The operating agreement is pivotal to a limited liability company, and Sections 110 through 112 are pivotal to this Act. They must be read together, along with Section 102(13) (defining the operating agreement).

One of the most complex questions in the law of unincorporated business organizations is the extent to which an agreement among the organization's owners can affect the law of fiduciary duty. This section gives special attention to that question and is organized as follows:

Subsection (a)	grants broad, *general* authority to the operating agreement
Subsection (b)	establishes this Act as comprising the "default rules" ("gap fillers") for matters within the purview of the operating agreement but not addressed by the operating agreement
Subsection (c)	states restrictions on the power of the operating agreement, especially but not exclusively with regard to fiduciary duties and the contractual obligation of good faith
Subsection (d)	contains *specific* grants of authority for the operating agreement with regard to fiduciary duty and the contractual obligation of good faith; expressed so as to state restrictions on those specific grants—including the "if not manifestly unreasonable" standard
Subsection (e)	specifically grants the operating agreement the power to provide mechanisms for approving or ratifying conduct that would otherwise violate the duty of loyalty; expressed so as to state restrictions on those mechanism—full disclosure and disinterested and independent decision makers
Subsection (f)	specifically authorizes the operating agreement to divest a member of fiduciary duty with regard to a matter if the operating agreement is also divesting the person of responsibility for the matter (and imposing that responsibility on one or more other members)
Subsection (g)	contains *specific* grants of authority for the operating agreement with regard to indemnification and exculpatory provisions; expressed so as to state restrictions on those specific grants
Subsection (h)	provides rules for applying the "not manifestly unreasonable" standard established by subsection (d)

A limited liability company is as much a creature of contract as of statute, and Section 102(13) delineates a very broad scope for "operating agreement." As a result, once an LLC comes into existence and has a member, the LLC necessarily has an operating agreement. *See* Comment to Section 102(13). Accordingly, this Act refers to "the operating agreement" rather than "an operating agreement."

This phrasing should not, however, be read to require a limited liability company or its members to take any formal action to adopt an operating agreement. *Compare* CAL. CORP. CODE § 17050(a) (West 2006) ("In order to form a limited liability company, one or more persons shall execute and file articles of organization with, and on a form prescribed by, the Secretary of State and, either before or after the filing of articles of organization, the members shall have entered into an operating agreement.")

The operating agreement is the exclusive consensual process for modifying this Act's various default rules pertaining to relationships *inter se* the members and between the members and the limited liability company. Section 110(b). The operating agreement also has power over "the rights and duties under this [act] of a person in the capacity of manager," subsection (a)(2), and "the obligations of a limited liability company and its members to a person in the person's capacity as a transferee or dissociated member." Section 112(b).

Subsection (a)—This section describes the very broad scope of a limited liability company's operating agreement, which includes all matters constituting "internal affairs." Compare Section 106(1) (using the phrase "internal affairs" in stating a choice of law rule). This broad grant of authority is subject to the restrictions stated in subsection (c), including the broad restriction stated in paragraph (c)(11) (concerning the rights under this Act of third parties).

Subsection (a)(1)—Under this Act, a limited liability company is emphatically an entity, and the members lack the power to alter that characteristic.

Subsection (a)(2)—Under this paragraph, the operating agreement has the power to affect the rights and duties of managers (including non-member managers). Because the term "[o]perating agreement. . . . includes the agreement as amended or restated," Section 102(13), this paragraph gives the members the ongoing power to define the role of an LLC's managers. Power is not the same as right, however, and exercising the power provided by this paragraph might constitute a breach of a separate contract between the LLC and the manager. A non-member manager might also have rights under Section 112(a).

Subsection (a)(4)—If the operating agreement does not address this matter, under subsection (b) this Act provides the rule. The rule appears in Section 407(b)(5) and 407(c)(4)(D) (unanimous consent).

This Act does not specially authorize the operating agreement to limit the sources in which terms of the operating agreement might be found or limit amendments to specified modes (e.g., prohibiting modifications except when consented to in writing). *Compare* UCC § 2–209(2) (authorizing such prohibitions in a "signed agreement" for the sale of goods). However, this Paragraph (a)(4) could be read to encompass such authorization. Also, under Section 107 the parol evidence rule will apply to a written operating agreement containing an appropriate merger provision.

Subsection (c)—If a person claims that a term of the operating agreement violates this subsection, as a matter of ordinary procedural law the burden is on the person making the claim.

Subsection (c)(4)—This limitation is less powerful than might first appear, because subsections (d) through (g) specifically authorize significantly alterations to fiduciary duty. The reference to "or any other fiduciary duty" is necessary because the Act has "un-cabined" fiduciary duty. *See* Comment to Section 409.

Subsection (c)(9)—Arbitration and forum selection provisions are commonplace in business agreements, and this paragraph's restrictions do not reflect any special hostility to or skepticism of such provisions.

Subsection (c)(10)—Under Section 1014:

- each member is protected from being merged, converted, or domesticated "into" the status of an unshielded general partner (or comparable position) without the member having *directly* consented to either:

  - the merger, conversion, or domestication; or

  - an operating agreement provision that permits such transactions to occur with less than unanimous consent of the members; and

- merely consenting to an operating agreement provision that permits amendment of the operating agreement with less than unanimous consent of the members does not qualify as the requisite direct consent.

The sole function of subsection (c)(10) is to protect Section 1014 by denying the operating agreement the power to restrict or otherwise undercut the protections of Section 1014.

Subsection (c)(11)—This limitation pertains only to "the rights under this[act] of" third parties. The extent to which an operating agreement can affect other rights of third parties is a question for other law, particularly the law of contracts.

Subsection (d)—Delaware recently amended its LLC statute to permit an operating agreement to fully "eliminate" fiduciary duty within an LLC. This Act rejects the ultra-contractarian notion that fiduciary duty within a business organization is merely a set of default rule and seeks instead to balance the virtues of "freedom of contract" against the dangers that inescapably exist when some have power over the interests of others. As one source has explained:

> The open-ended nature of fiduciary duty reflects the law's long-standing recognition that devious people can smell a loophole a mile away. For centuries, the law has assumed that (1) power creates opportunities for abuse and (2) the devious creativity of those in power may outstrip the prescience of those trying, through ex ante contract drafting, to constrain that combination of power and creativity.

CARTER G. BISHOP AND DANIEL S. KLEINBERGER, LIMITED LIABILITY COMPANIES: TAX AND BUSINESS LAW, ¶ 14.05[4][a][ii]

Subsection (h) contains rules for applying the "not manifestly unreasonable" standard.

Subsection (d)(1)—Subject to the "not manifestly unreasonable" standard, this paragraph empowers the operating agreement to eliminate <u>all</u> aspects of the duty of loyalty listed in Section 409. The contractual obligation of good faith would remain, see subsections(c)(5) and (d)(5), as would any other, uncodified aspects of the duty of loyalty. *See* Comment to Section 409 (explaining the decision to "un-cabin" fiduciary duty). *See also* subsection (d)(4) (empowering the operating agreement to "alter any other fiduciary duty, including eliminating particular aspects of that duty").

Subsection (d)(3)—The operating agreement's power to affect this Act's duty of care both parallels and differs from the agreement's power to affect this Act's duty of loyalty as well as any other fiduciary duties not codified in the statute. With regard to all fiduciary duties, the operating agreement is subject to the "manifestly unreasonable" standard. The differences concern: (i) the extent of the operating agreement's power to restrict the duty; and (ii) the power of the operating agreement to provide indemnity or exculpation for persons subject to the duty.

duty	extent of operating agreement's power to restrict the duty (subject to the "manifestly unreasonable" standard) § 110(d)(1), (3) and (4)	power of the operating agreement to provide indemnity or exculpation w/r/t breach of the duty § 110(g)
loyalty	restrict or completely eliminate	none
care	alter, but not eliminate; specifically may not authorize intentional misconduct or knowing violation of law	complete
other fiduciary duties, not codified in the statute	restrict or completely eliminate Section 110(4)	complete

Subsection (e)—Section 409(f) states the Act's default rule for authorization or ratification—unanimous consent. This subsection specifically empowers the operating agreement to provide alternate mechanisms but, in doing so, imposes significant restrictions—namely, any alternate mechanism must involve full disclosure to, and the disinterestedness and independence of, the decision makers. These restrictions are consonant with ordinary notions of authorization and ratification.

This Act provides four separate methods through which those with management power in a limited liability company can proceed with conduct that would otherwise violate the duty of loyalty:

Method	Statutory Authority
The operating agreement might eliminate the duty or otherwise permit the conduct, without need for further authorization or ratification.	Section 110(d)(1) and (2)
The conduct might be authorized or ratified by all the members after full disclosure.	Section 409(f)
The operating agreement might establish a mechanism other than the informed consent for authorizing or ratifying the conduct.	Section 110(e)
In the case of self-dealing the conduct might be successfully defended as being or having been fair to the limited liability company.	Section 409(e)

Subsection (f)—This subsection is intended to make clear that—regardless of the strictures stated elsewhere in this section—in the specified circumstances the operating agreement can entirely strip away the pertinent fiduciary duties.

Subsection (g)—This subsection specifically empowers the operating agreement to address matters of indemnification and exculpation but subjects that power to stated limitations. Those limitations are drawn from the raft of exculpatory provisions that sprung up in corporate statutes in response to *Smith v. Van Gorkum*, 488 A.2d 858 (Del. 1985). Delaware led the response with DEL. CODE ANN. tit. 8, § 102(b)(7) (2006), and a number of LLC statutes have similar provisions. *E.g.* GA. CODE ANN. § 14–11–305(4)(A) (West 2006); IDAHO CODE ANN. § 53–624(1) (2006). For an extreme example, see VA. CODE ANN. § 13.1–1025 (West 2006) (establishing limits of monetary liability as the default rule).

The restrictions stated in paragraphs (1) through (5) apply both to indemnification and exculpation. The power to "alter or eliminate the indemnification provided by Section 408(a)" includes the power to expand or reduce that indemnification.

Subsection (g)(4)—Due to this paragraph, an exculpatory provision cannot shield against a member's claim of oppression. *See* Section 701(a)(5)(B) and (b).

Subsection (h)—The "not manifestly unreasonable standard" became part of uniform business entity statutes when RUPA imported the concept from the Uniform Commercial Code. This subsection provides rules for applying that standard, which are necessary because:

- Determining unreasonableness *inter se* owners of an organization is a different task than doing so in a commercial context, where concepts like "usages of trade" are available to inform the analysis. Each business organization must be understood in its own terms and context.

- If loosely applied, the standard would permit a court to rewrite the members' agreement, which would destroy the balance this Act seeks to establish between freedom of contract and fiduciary duty.

- Case law research indicates that courts have tended to disregard the significance of the word "manifestly."

- Some decisions have considered reasonableness as of the time of the complaint, which means that a prospectively reasonable allocation of risk could be overturned because it functioned as agreed.

If a person claims that a term of the operating agreement in manifestly unreasonable under subsections (d) and (h), as a matter of ordinary procedural law the burden is on the person making the claim.

Subsection (h)(1)—The significance of the phrase "as of the time the term as challenged became part of the operating agreement" is best shown by example.

Example: An LLC's operating agreement as initially adopted includes a provision subjecting a matter to "the manager's sole, reasonable discretion." A year later, the agreement is amended to delete the word "reasonable." Later, a member claims that, without the word "reasonable," the provision is manifestly unreasonable. The relevant time under subsection (h)(1) is when the agreement was amended, not when the agreement was initially adopted.

Example: When a particular manager-managed LLC comes into existence, its business plan is quite unusual and its success depends on the willingness of a particular individual to serve as the LLC's sole manager. This individual has a rare combination of skills, experiences, and contacts, which are particularly appropriate for the LLC's start-up. In order to induce the individual to accept the position of sole manager, the members are willing to have the operating agreement significantly limit the manager's fiduciary duties. Several years later, when the LLC's operations have turned prosaic and the manager's talents and background are not nearly so crucial, a member challenges the fiduciary duty limitations as manifestly unreasonable. The relevant time under subsection (h)(1) is when the LLC began. Subsequent developments are not relevant, except as they might inferentially bear on the circumstances in existence at the relevant time.

§ 111. Operating Agreement; Effect on Limited Liability Company and Persons Becoming Members; Pre-Formation Agreement

(a) A limited liability company is bound by and may enforce the operating agreement, whether or not the company has itself manifested assent to the operating agreement.

(b) A person that becomes a member of a limited liability company is deemed to assent to the operating agreement.

(c) Two or more persons intending to become the initial members of a limited liability company may make an agreement providing that upon the formation of the company the agreement will become the operating agreement. One person intending to become the initial member of a limited liability company may assent to terms providing that upon the formation of the company the terms will become the operating agreement.

COMMENT

Subsection (a)—This subsection does not consider whether a limited liability company is an indispensable party to a suit concerning the operating agreement. That is a question of procedural law, which can determine whether federal diversity jurisdiction exists.

Subsection (b)—Given the possibility of oral and implied-in-fact components to the operating agreement, see Comment to Section 110(a)(4), a person becoming a member of an existing limited liability company should take precautions to ascertain fully the contents of the operating agreement.

Subsection (c)—The second sentence refers to "assent to terms" rather than "make an agreement" because, under venerable principles of contract law, an agreement presupposes at least two parties. This Act specifically defines the operating agreement to include a sole member, Section 102(13), but a preformation arrangement is not an operating agreement. An operating agreement is among "members," and, under this Act, the earliest a person can become a member is upon the formation of the limited liability company. Section 401.

§ 112. Operating Agreement; Effect on Third Parties and Relationship to Records Effective on Behalf of Limited Liability Company

(a) An operating agreement may specify that its amendment requires the approval of a person that is not a party to the operating agreement or the satisfaction of a condition. An amendment is ineffective if its adoption does not include the required approval or satisfy the specified condition.

(b) The obligations of a limited liability company and its members to a person in the person's capacity as a transferee or dissociated member are governed by the operating agreement. Subject only to any court order issued under Section 503(b)(2) to effectuate a charging order, an amendment to the operating agreement made after a person becomes a transferee or dissociated member is effective with regard to any debt, obligation, or other liability of the limited liability company or its members to the person in the person's capacity as a transferee or dissociated member.

(c) If a record that has been delivered by a limited liability company to the [Secretary of State] for filing and has become effective under this [act] contains a provision that would be ineffective under Section 110(c) if contained in the operating agreement, the provision is likewise ineffective in the record.

(d)   Subject to subsection (c), if a record that has been delivered by a limited liability company to the [Secretary of State] for filing and has become effective under this [act] conflicts with a provision of the operating agreement:

(1)   the operating agreement prevails as to members, dissociated members, transferees, and managers; and

(2)   the record prevails as to other persons to the extent they reasonably rely on the record.

COMMENT

Subsection (a)—This subsection, derived from DEL. CODE ANN. tit. 6, § 18–302(e), permits a non-member to have veto rights over amendments to the operating agreement. Such veto rights are likely to be sought by lenders but may also be attractive to non-member managers.

Example: A non-member manager enters into a management contract with the LLC, and that agreement provides in part that the LLC may remove the manager without cause only with the consent of members holding 2/3 of the profits interests. The operating agreement contains a parallel provision, but the non-member manager is not a party to the operating agreement. Later the LLC members amend the operating agreement to change the quantum to a simple majority and thereafter purport to remove the manager without cause. Although the LLC has undoubtedly breached its contract with the manager and subjected itself to a damage claim, the LLC has the power under Section 110(a)(2) to effect the removal—unless the operating agreement provided the non-member manager a veto right over changes in the quantum provision.

The subsection does not refer to member veto rights because, unless otherwise provided in the operating agreement, the consent of each member is necessary to effect an amendment. Section 407(b)(5) and (c)(4)(D).

Subsection (b)—The law of unincorporated business organizations is only beginning to grapple in a modern way with the tension between the rights of an organization's owners to carry on their activities as they see fit (or have agreed) and the rights of transferees of the organization's economic interests. (Such transferees can include the heirs of business founders as well as former owners who are "locked in" as transferees of their own interests. *See* Section 603(a)(3).).

If the law categorically favors the owners, there is a serious risk of expropriation and other abuse. On the other hand, if the law grants former owners and other transferees the right to seek judicial protection, that specter can "freeze the deal" as of the moment an owner leaves the enterprise or a third party obtains an economic interest.

Bauer v. Blomfield Co./Holden Joint Venture, 849 P2d 1365 (Alaska 1993) illustrates this point nicely. The case arose after all the partners had approved a commission arrangement with a third party and the arrangement dried up all the partnership profits. When an assignee of a partnership interest objected, the court majority flatly rejected not only the claim but also the assignee's right to assert the claim. A mere assignee "was not entitled to complain about a decision made with the consent of all the partners." *Id.* at 1367. A footnote explained, "We are unwilling to hold that partners owe a duty of good faith and fair dealing to assignees of a partner's interest." *Id.* at 1367, n. 2.

The dissent, invoking the law of contracts, asserted that the majority had turned the statutory protection of the partners' management prerogatives into an instrument for abuse of assignees:

It is a well-settled principle of contract law that an assignee steps into the shoes of an assignor as to the rights assigned. Today, the court summarily dismisses this principle in a footnote and leaves the assignee barefoot. . . .

As interpreted by the court, the [partnership] statute now allows partners to deprive an assignee of profits to which he is entitled by law for whatever outrageous motive or reason. The court's opinion essentially leaves the assignee of a partnership interest without remedy to enforce his right.

Id. at 1367–8 (Matthews, J., dissenting).

The *Bauer* majority is consistent with the limited but long-standing case law in this area (all of it pertaining to partnerships rather than LLCs). This subsection follows the *Bauer* majority and other cases by expressly subjecting transferees and dissociated members to operating agreement amendments made after the transfer or dissociation. *Compare* UPA § 32(2) (permitting an assignee to seek judicial dissolution of an at-will general partnership at any time and of a partnership for a term or undertaking if partnership continues in existence after the completion of the term or undertaking); RUPA § 801(6) (same except adding the requirement that the court determine that dissolution is equitable); ULLCA, § 801(5) (same as RUPA); ULLCA, § 801(4) (permitting a dissociated member to seek dissolution on the grounds *inter alia* of oppressive conduct). *See also* UCC §§ 9–405(a) and (b) and RESTATEMENT (SECOND) OF CONTRACTS § 338 (1981) (recognizing a duty of good faith applicable to the modification of a contract when an assignment of contract is in effect).

The issue of whether, in extreme and sufficiently harsh circumstances, transferees might be able to claim some type of duty or obligation to protect against expropriation, is a question for other law.

Subsection (d)—A limited liability company is a creature of contract as well as a creature of statute. It will be possible, albeit improvident, for the operating agreement to be inconsistent with the certificate of organization or other public filings pertaining to the limited liability company. For those circumstances, this subsection provides rules for determining which source of information prevails.

For members, managers and transferees, the operating agreement is paramount. For third parties seeking to invoke the public record, actual knowledge of that record is necessary and notice, deemed notice, and deemed knowledge under Section 103 are irrelevant. A third party wishing to enforce the public record over the operating agreement must show reasonable reliance on the public record, and reliance presupposes knowledge.

The mere fact that a term is present in a publicly-filed record and not in the operating agreement, or *vice versa*, does not automatically establish a conflict. This subsection does not expressly cover a situation in which (i) one of the specified filed records contains information in addition to, but not inconsistent with, the operating agreement, and (ii) a person, other than a member or transferee, reasonably relies on the additional information. However, the policy reflected in this subsection seems equally applicable to that situation.

Section 110(a)(4) might also be relevant to the subject matter of this subsection. Absent a contrary provision in the operating agreement, language in an LLC's certificate of organization might be evidence of the members' agreement and might thereby constitute or at least imply a term of the operating agreement.

This subsection does not apply to records delivered to the [Secretary of State] for filing on behalf of persons other than a limited liability company.

§ 113. Office and Agent for Service of Process

(a) A limited liability company shall designate and continuously maintain in this state:

  (1) an office, which need not be a place of its activity in this state; and

  (2) an agent for service of process.

(b) A foreign limited liability company that has a certificate of authority under Section 802 shall designate and continuously maintain in this state an agent for service of process.

(c) An agent for service of process of a limited liability company or foreign limited liability company must be an individual who is a resident of this state or other person with authority to transact business in this state.

COMMENT

Source—ULPA (2001), § 114.

§ 114. Change of Designated Office or Agent for Service of Process

(a) A limited liability company or foreign limited liability company may change its designated office, its agent for service of process, or the address of its agent for service of process by delivering to the [Secretary of State] for filing a statement of change containing:

  (1) the name of the company;

  (2) the street and mailing addresses of its current designated office;

  (3) if the current designated office is to be changed, the street and mailing addresses of the new designated office;

  (4) the name and street and mailing addresses of its current agent for service of process; and

  (5) if the current agent for service of process or an address of the agent is to be changed, the new information.

(b)   Subject to Section 205(c), a statement of change is effective when filed by the [Secretary of State].

COMMENT

Source—ULPA (2001) § 115, which is based on ULLCA § 109.

Subsection (a)—This subsection uses "may" rather than "shall" because other avenues exist. A limited liability company may also change the information by amending its certificate of organization, Section 202, or through its annual report. Section 209(e). A foreign limited liability company may use its annual report. Section 209(e). However, neither a limited liability company nor a foreign limited liability company may wait for the annual report if the information described in the public record becomes inaccurate. *See* Sections 207 (imposing liability for false information in record) and 116(b) (providing for substitute service).

§ 115.   Resignation of Agent for Service of Process

(a)   To resign as an agent for service of process of a limited liability company or foreign limited liability company, the agent must deliver to the [Secretary of State] for filing a statement of resignation containing the company name and stating that the agent is resigning.

(b)   The [Secretary of State] shall file a statement of resignation delivered under subsection (a) and mail or otherwise provide or deliver a copy to the designated office of the limited liability company or foreign limited liability company and another copy to the principal office of the company if the mailing addresses of the principal office appears in the records of the [Secretary of State] and is different from the mailing address of the designated office.

(c)   An agency for service of process terminates on the earlier of:

(1)   the 31st day after the [Secretary of State] files the statement of resignation;

(2) when a record designating a new agent for service of process is delivered to the [Secretary of State] for filing on behalf of the limited liability company and becomes effective.

COMMENT

Source—ULPA (2001) § 116, which is based on ULLCA § 110.

§ 116.   Service of Process

(a)   An agent for service of process appointed by a limited liability company or foreign limited liability company is an agent of the company for service of any process, notice, or demand required or permitted by law to be served on the company.

(b)   If a limited liability company or foreign limited liability company does not appoint or maintain an agent for service of process in this state or the agent for service of process cannot with reasonable diligence be found at the agent's street address, the [Secretary of State] is an agent of the company upon whom process, notice, or demand may be served.

(c)   Service of any process, notice, or demand on the [Secretary of State] as agent for a limited liability company or foreign limited liability company may be made by delivering to the [Secretary of State] duplicate copies of the process, notice, or demand. If a process, notice, or demand is served on the [Secretary of State], the [Secretary of State] shall forward one of the copies by registered or certified mail, return receipt requested, to the company at its designated office.

(d)   Service is effected under subsection (c) at the earliest of:

(1)   the date the limited liability company or foreign limited liability company receives the process, notice, or demand;

(2)   the date shown on the return receipt, if signed on behalf of the company; or

(3)   five days after the process, notice, or demand is deposited with the United States Postal Service, if correctly addressed and with sufficient postage.

(e)   The [Secretary of State] shall keep a record of each process, notice, and demand served pursuant to this section and record the time of, and the action taken regarding, the service.

(f)   This section does not affect the right to serve process, notice, or demand in any other manner provided by law.

COMMENT

Source—ULPA (2001) § 117, which is based on ULLCA § 111.

[ARTICLE] 2
FORMATION; CERTIFICATE OF ORGANIZATION AND OTHER FILINGS

§ 201.   Formation of Limited Liability Company; Certificate of Organization

(a)   One or more persons may act as organizers to form a limited liability company by signing and delivering to the [Secretary of State] for filing a certificate of organization.

(b)   A certificate of organization must state:

    (1)   the name of the limited liability company, which must comply with Section 108;

    (2)   the street and mailing addresses of the initial designated office and the name and street and mailing addresses of the initial agent for service of process of the company; and

    (3)   if the company will have no members when the [Secretary of State] files the certificate, a statement to that effect.

(c)   Subject to Section 112(c), a certificate of organization may also contain statements as to matters other than those required by subsection (b). However, a statement in a certificate of organization is not effective as a statement of authority.

(d)   Unless the filed certificate of organization contains the statement as provided in subsection (b)(3), the following rules apply:

    (1)   A limited liability company is formed when the [Secretary of State] has filed the certificate of organization and the company has at least one member, unless the certificate states a delayed effective date pursuant to Section 205(c).

    (2)   If the certificate states a delayed effective date, a limited liability company is not formed if, before the certificate takes effect, a statement of cancellation is signed and delivered to the [Secretary of State] for filing and the [Secretary of State] files the certificate.

    (3)   Subject to any delayed effective date and except in a proceeding by this state to dissolve a limited liability company, the filing of the certificate of organization by the [Secretary of State] is conclusive proof that the organizer satisfied all conditions to the formation of a limited liability company.

(e)   If a filed certificate of organization contains a statement as provided in subsection (b)(3), the following rules apply:

    (1)   The certificate lapses and is void unless, within [90] days from the date the [Secretary of State] files the certificate, an organizer signs and delivers to the [Secretary of State] for filing a notice stating:

        (A)   that the limited liability company has at least one member; and

        (B)   the date on which a person or persons became the company's initial member or members.

    (2)   If an organizer complies with paragraph (1), a limited liability company is deemed formed as of the date of initial membership stated in the notice delivered pursuant to paragraph (1).

(3)   Except in a proceeding by this state to dissolve a limited liability company, the filing of the notice described in paragraph (1) by the [Secretary of State] is conclusive proof that the organizer satisfied all conditions to the formation of a limited liability company.

Legislative Note: Enacting jurisdictions should consider revising their "name statutes" generally, to protect "the limited liability company name stated in each certificate of organization that contains the statement as provided in Section 201(b)(3)". Section 108(b)(2).

COMMENT

No topic received more attention or generated more debate in the drafting process for this Act than the question of the "shelf LLC"—i.e., an LLC formed without having at least one member upon formation. Reasonable minds differed (occasionally intensely) as to whether the "shelf" approach (i) is necessary to accommodate current business practices; and (ii) somehow does conceptual violence to the partnership antecedents of the limited liability company.

The 2006 Annual Meeting Draft provided for a "limited shelf"—a shelf that lacked capacity to conduct any substantive activities:

(a)   Except as otherwise provided in subsection (b), a limited liability company has the capacity to sue and be sued in its own name and the power to do all things necessary or convenient to carry on its activities.

(b)   Until a limited liability company has or has had at least one member, the company lacks the capacity to do any act or carry on any activity except:

(1)   delivering to the [Secretary of State] for filing a statement of change under Sections 114, an amendment to the certificate under Section 202, a statement of correction under Section 206, an annual report under section 209, and a statement of termination under Section 702(b)(2)(F);

(2)   admitting a member under section 401; and

(3)   dissolving under Section 701.

(c)   A limited liability company that has or has had at least one member may ratify an act or activity that occurred when the company lacked capacity under subsection (b).

However, when the Conference considered the 2006 Annual Meeting Draft, the Drafting Committee itself proposed an amendment, and the Conference agreed. A product of intense discussion and compromise with several ABA Advisors, the amendment substituted a double filing and "embryonic certificate" approach. An organizer may deliver for filing a certificate of organization without the company having any members and the filing officer will file the certificate, but:

- the certificate as delivered to the filing officer must acknowledge that situation, Subsection (a)(3);

- the limited liability company is not formed until and unless the organizer timely delivers to the filing officer a notice that the company has at least one member, Subsection (e)(1); and

- if the organizer does not timely deliver the required notice, the certificate lapses and is void. *Id.*

The Conference recommends a 90-day "window" for filing the notice, which must state "the date on which a person or persons became the company's initial member or members." When the filing officer files that notice, the company is deemed formed as of the date stated in the notice. Subsection (e)(2).

Thus under this Act, the delivery to the filing officer of a certificate of organization has different consequences, depending on whether the certificate contains the "no members" statement as provided by subsection (b)(3).

does the certificate contain the "no members" statement under subsection (b)(3)	by delivering the certificate for filing, what is the organizer affirming, per Section 207(c), about members	effect of the filing officer filing the certificate	logical relationship of the filed certificate to the formation of the LLC
no	that the LLC will have at least one member upon formation	LLC is formed, subject to any delayed effective date	necessary and sufficient
yes	that the LLC will have no members when the filing officer files the certificate	the document is part of the public record, protects the name, and starts the 90-day clock ticking	necessary but not sufficient

Subsection (b)—This Act does not require the certificate of organization to designate whether the limited liability company is manager-managed or member-managed. Under this Act, those characterizations pertain principally to *inter se* relations, and the Act therefore looks to the operating agreement to make the characterization. *See* Sections 102(10) and (12); 407(a).

Subsection (d)—This subsection states the "pathway" through which a limited liability company is formed if the certificate of organization does not contain a statement as provided in subsection (b)(3)—i.e., if the limited liability company will have at least one member when the filing officer files the certificate.

Subsection (e)—This subsection states the "pathway" through which a limited liability company is formed if the certificate of organization contains a statement as provided in subsection (b)(3)—i.e., if the limited liability company will not have at least one member when the filing officer files the certificate.

This pathway requires a second filing in order to form the limited liability company: "a notice stating (A) that the limited liability company has at least one member; and (B) the date on which a person or persons became the company's initial member or members." Subsection (e)(1).

In this pathway, a certificate of organization may not itself state a delayed effective date, Section 205(c), because:

- the reason to state a delayed effective date in a certificate of organization is to set the date on which the limited liability company is formed, Section 205(c); and

- when a certificate contains a statement as provided in subsection (b)(3), this Act mandates when (if at all) the limited liability company is deemed formed—i.e., "as of the date of initial membership stated in the notice delivered" to the filing officer as the second filing. Subsection (e)(2).

§ 202. Amendment or Restatement of Certificate of Organization

(a) A certificate of organization may be amended or restated at any time.

(b) To amend its certificate of organization, a limited liability company must deliver to the [Secretary of State] for filing an amendment stating:

(1) the name of the company;

(2) the date of filing of its certificate of organization; and

(3) the changes the amendment makes to the certificate as most recently amended or restated.

(c) To restate its certificate of organization, a limited liability company must deliver to the [Secretary of State] for filing a restatement, designated as such in its heading, stating:

(1) in the heading or an introductory paragraph, the company's present name and the date of the filing of the company's initial certificate of organization;

(2)   if the company's name has been changed at any time since the company's formation, each of the company's former names; and

(3)   the changes the restatement makes to the certificate as most recently amended or restated.

(d)   Subject to Sections 112(c) and 205(c), an amendment to or restatement of a certificate of organization is effective when filed by the [Secretary of State].

(e)   If a member of a member-managed limited liability company, or a manager of a manager-managed limited liability company, knows that any information in a filed certificate of organization was inaccurate when the certificate was filed or has become inaccurate owing to changed circumstances, the member or manager shall promptly:

(1)   cause the certificate to be amended; or

(2)   if appropriate, deliver to the [Secretary of State] for filing a statement of change under Section 114 or a statement of correction under Section 206.

COMMENT

Subsection (e)—This subsection is taken from ULPA (2001) § 202(c), which imposes the responsibility on general partners. The original ULLCA had no comparable provision.

This subsection imposes an obligation directly on the members and managers rather than on the limited liability company. A member or manager's failure to meet the obligation exposes the member or manager to liability to third parties under Section 207(a)(2) and might constitute a breach of the member or manager's duties under Section 409(c) and (g)(1). In addition, an aggrieved person may seek a remedy under Section 204 (Signing and Filing Pursuant to Judicial Order).

Like other provisions of the Act requiring records to be delivered to the filing officer for filing, this section is not subject to change by the operating agreement. *See* Section 110(c)(11) (precluding the operating agreement from "restrict[ing] the rights under this [act] of a person other than a member or manager").

§ 203.   Signing of Records to be Delivered for Filing to [Secretary of State]

(a)   A record delivered to the [Secretary of State] for filing pursuant to this [act] must be signed as follows:

(1)   Except as otherwise provided in paragraphs (2) through (4), a record signed on behalf of a limited liability company must be signed by a person authorized by the company.

(2)   A limited liability company's initial certificate of organization must be signed by at least one person acting as an organizer.

(3)   A notice under Section 201(e)(1) must be signed by an organizer.

(4)   A record filed on behalf of a dissolved limited liability company that has no members must be signed by the person winding up the company's activities under Section 702(c) or a person appointed under Section 702(d) to wind up those activities.

(5)   A statement of cancellation under Section 201(d)(2) must be signed by each organizer that signed the initial certificate of organization, but a personal representative of a deceased or incompetent organizer may sign in the place of the decedent or incompetent.

(6)   A statement of denial by a person under Section 303 must be signed by that person.

(7)   Any other record must be signed by the person on whose behalf the record is delivered to the [Secretary of State].

(b)   Any record filed under this [act] may be signed by an agent.

COMMENT

Subsection (b)—This subsection does not require that the agent's authority be memorialized in a writing or other record. However, a person signing as an agent "thereby affirms under penalties of perjury that [the assertion of agent status is] . . . accurate." Section 207(c).

§ 204.   **Signing and Filing Pursuant to Judicial Order**

(a) If a person required by this [act] to sign a record or deliver a record to the [Secretary of State] for filing under [this act] does not do so, any other person that is aggrieved may petition the [appropriate court] to order:

    (1) the person to sign the record;

    (2) the person to deliver the record to the [Secretary of State] for filing; or

    (3) the [Secretary of State] to file the record unsigned.

(b) If a petitioner under subsection (a) is not the limited liability company or foreign limited liability company to which the record pertains, the petitioner shall make the company a party to the action.

COMMENT

Source—ULPA (2001) § 205, which is based on RULPA § 205, which was the source of ULLCA § 210.

Subsection (a)(3)—A record filed under this paragraph is effective without being signed.

§ 205.   **Delivery to and Filing of Records by [Secretary of State]; Effective Time and Date**

(a) A record authorized or required to be delivered to the [Secretary of State] for filing under this [act] must be captioned to describe the record's purpose, be in a medium permitted by the [Secretary of State], and be delivered to the [Secretary of State]. If the filing fees have been paid, unless the [Secretary of State] determines that a record does not comply with the filing requirements of this [act], the [Secretary of State] shall file the record and:

    (1) for a statement of denial under Section 303, send a copy of the filed statement and a receipt for the fees to the person on whose behalf the statement was delivered for filing and to the limited liability company; and

    (2) for all other records, send a copy of the filed record and a receipt for the fees to the person on whose behalf the record was filed.

(b) Upon request and payment of the requisite fee, the [Secretary of State] shall send to the requester a certified copy of a requested record.

(c) Except as otherwise provided in Sections 115 and 206 and except for a certificate of organization that contains a statement as provided in Section 201(b)(3), a record delivered to the [Secretary of State] for filing under this [act] may specify an effective time and a delayed effective date. Subject to Sections 115, 201(d)(1), and 206, a record filed by the [Secretary of State] is effective:

    (1) if the record does not specify either an effective time or a delayed effective date, on the date and at the time the record is filed as evidenced by the [Secretary of State's] endorsement of the date and time on the record;

    (2) if the record specifies an effective time but not a delayed effective date, on the date the record is filed at the time specified in the record;

    (3) if the record specifies a delayed effective date but not an effective time, at 12:01 a.m. on the earlier of:

        (A) the specified date; or

        (B) the 90th day after the record is filed; or

    (4) if the record specifies an effective time and a delayed effective date, at the specified time on the earlier of:

        (A) the specified date; or

        (B) the 90th day after the record is filed.

COMMENT

Source—ULPA (2001) § 206, which was based on ULLCA § 206.

This Act uses the concept of "filing" to refer to the official act of the [Secretary of State], which is typically preceded by a person "delivering" some record "to the [Secretary of State] for filing."

Subsection (c)(3)(B) and 4(B)—If a person delivers to the Secretary of State for filing a record that contains an over-long delay in the effective date, the Secretary of State: (i) will not reject the record; and (ii) is neither required nor authorized to inform the person that this Act will truncate the period of delay specified in the record.

§ 206.   Correcting Filed Record

(a)   A limited liability company or foreign limited liability company may deliver to the [Secretary of State] for filing a statement of correction to correct a record previously delivered by the company to the [Secretary of State] and filed by the [Secretary of State], if at the time of filing the record contained inaccurate information or was defectively signed.

(b)   A statement of correction under subsection (a) may not state a delayed effective date and must:

     (1)   describe the record to be corrected, including its filing date, or attach a copy of the record as filed;

     (2)   specify the inaccurate information and the reason it is inaccurate or the manner in which the signing was defective; and

     (3)   correct the defective signature or inaccurate information.

(c)   When filed by the [Secretary of State], a statement of correction under subsection (a) is effective retroactively as of the effective date of the record the statement corrects, but the statement is effective when filed:

     (1)   for the purposes of Section 103(d); and

     (2)   as to persons that previously relied on the uncorrected record and would be adversely affected by the retroactive effect.

COMMENT

Source—ULPA (2001) § 207, which was based on ULLCA § 207.

§ 207.   Liability for Inaccurate Information in Filed Record

(a)   If a record delivered to the [Secretary of State] for filing under this [act] and filed by the [Secretary of State] contains inaccurate information, a person that suffers a loss by reliance on the information may recover damages for the loss from:

     (1)   a person that signed the record, or caused another to sign it on the person's behalf, and knew the information to be inaccurate at the time the record was signed; and

     (2)   subject to subsection (b), a member of a member-managed limited liability company or the manager of a manager-managed limited liability company, if:

         (A)   the record was delivered for filing on behalf of the company; and

         (B)   the member or manager had notice of the inaccuracy for a reasonably sufficient time before the information was relied upon so that, before the reliance, the member or manager reasonably could have:

            (i)   effected an amendment under Section 202;

            (ii)   filed a petition under Section 204; or

            (iii)   delivered to the [Secretary of State] for filing a statement of change under Section 114 or a statement of correction under Section 206.

(b)   To the extent that the operating agreement of a member-managed limited liability company expressly relieves a member of responsibility for maintaining the accuracy of information contained in records delivered on behalf of the company to the [Secretary of State] for filing under this [act] and imposes that responsibility on one or more other members, the liability stated in subsection (a)(2) applies to those other members and not to the member that the operating agreement relieves of the responsibility.

(c)   An individual who signs a record authorized or required to be filed under this [act] affirms under penalty of perjury that the information stated in the record is accurate.

COMMENT

Source—ULPA (2001) § 208, which expanded on ULLCA § 209.

Section (a)(2)(B)—This subparagraph implies that doing any of the acts listed in clauses (i) through (iii) will preclude liability arising from subsequent reliance. In this connection, Clause (a)(2)(B)(ii) warrants special attention, because that act (filing a petition in court) can occur without any immediate effect on the records relevant to a limited liability company maintained by the filing officer. The other clauses refer to acts that (assuming no filing backlog) affect that public record immediately.

§ 208.   Certificate of Existence or Authorization

(a)   The [Secretary of State], upon request and payment of the requisite fee, shall furnish to any person a certificate of existence for a limited liability company if the records filed in the [office of the Secretary of State] show that the company has been formed under Section 201 and the [Secretary of State] has not filed a statement of termination pertaining to the company. A certificate of existence must state:

(1)   the company's name;

(2)   that the company was duly formed under the laws of this state and the date of formation;

(3)   whether all fees, taxes, and penalties due under this [act] or other law to the [Secretary of State] have been paid;

(4)   whether the company's most recent annual report required by Section 209 has been filed by the [Secretary of State];

(5)   whether the [Secretary of State] has administratively dissolved the company;

(6)   whether the company has delivered to the [Secretary of State] for filing a statement of dissolution;

(7)   that a statement of termination has not been filed by the [Secretary of State]; and

(8)   other facts of record in the [office of the Secretary of State] which are specified by the person requesting the certificate.

(b)   The [Secretary of State], upon request and payment of the requisite fee, shall furnish to any person a certificate of authorization for a foreign limited liability company if the records filed in the [office of the Secretary of State] show that the [Secretary of State] has filed a certificate of authority, has not revoked the certificate of authority, and has not filed a notice of cancellation. A certificate of authorization must state:

(1)   the company's name and any alternate name adopted under Section 805(a) for use in this state;

(2)   that the company is authorized to transact business in this state;

(3)   whether all fees, taxes, and penalties due under this [act] or other law to the [Secretary of State] have been paid;

(4)   whether the company's most recent annual report required by Section 209 has been filed by the [Secretary of State];

(5)   that the [Secretary of State] has not revoked the company's certificate of authority and has not filed a notice of cancellation; and

    (6)   other facts of record in the [office of the Secretary of State] which are specified by the person requesting the certificate.

    (c)   Subject to any qualification stated in the certificate, a certificate of existence or certificate of authorization issued by the [Secretary of State] is conclusive evidence that the limited liability company is in existence or the foreign limited liability company is authorized to transact business in this state.

COMMENT

    Source—ULPA (2001), § 209, which was based on ULLCA, § 208.

    The information provided in a certificate of existence or authorization is, of course, current only as of the date of the certificate.

§ 209.   Annual Report for [Secretary of State]

    (a)   Each year, a limited liability company or a foreign limited liability company authorized to transact business in this state shall deliver to the [Secretary of State] for filing a report that states:

    (1)   the name of the company;

    (2)   the street and mailing addresses of the company's designated office and the name and street and mailing addresses of its agent for service of process in this state;

    (3)   the street and mailing addresses of its principal office; and

    (4)   in the case of a foreign limited liability company, the state or other jurisdiction under whose law the company is formed and any alternate name adopted under Section 805(a).

    (b)   Information in an annual report under this section must be current as of the date the report is delivered to the [Secretary of State] for filing.

    (c)   The first annual report under this section must be delivered to the [Secretary of State] between [January 1 and April 1] of the year following the calendar year in which a limited liability company was formed or a foreign limited liability company was authorized to transact business. A report must be delivered to the [Secretary of State] between [January 1 and April 1] of each subsequent calendar year.

    (d)   If an annual report under this section does not contain the information required in subsection (a), the [Secretary of State] shall promptly notify the reporting limited liability company or foreign limited liability company and return the report to it for correction. If the report is corrected to contain the information required in subsection (a) and delivered to the [Secretary of State] within 30 days after the effective date of the notice, it is timely delivered.

    (e)   If an annual report under this section contains an address of a designated office or the name or address of an agent for service of process which differs from the information shown in the records of the [Secretary of State] immediately before the annual report becomes effective, the differing information in the annual report is considered a statement of change under Section 114.

COMMENT

    Source—ULPA (2001) § 210, which was based on ULLCA § 211.

    A limited liability company that fails to comply with this section is subject to administrative dissolution. Section 705(a)(2). A foreign limited liability company that fails to comply with this section is subject to having its certificate of authority revoked. Section 806(a)(2).

[ARTICLE] 3
RELATIONS OF MEMBERS AND MANAGERS TO PERSONS DEALING WITH LIMITED LIABILITY COMPANY

§ 301.   No Agency Power of Member as Member

(a)   A member is not an agent of a limited liability company solely by reason of being a member.

(b)   A person's status as a member does not prevent or restrict law other than this [act] from imposing liability on a limited liability company because of the person's conduct.

COMMENT

Subsection (a)—Most LLC statutes, including the original ULLCA, provide for what might be termed "statutory apparent authority" for members in a member-managed limited liability company and managers in a manager-managed limited liability company. This approach codifies the common law notion of apparent authority by position and dates back at least to the original, 1914 Uniform Partnership Act. UPA, § 9 provided that "the act of every partner . . . for apparently carrying on in the usual way the business of the partnership . . . binds the partnership," and that formulation has been essentially followed by RUPA, § 301, ULLCA, § 301, ULPA (2001), § 402, and myriad state LLC statutes.

This Act rejects the statutory apparent authority approach, for reasons summarized in a "Progress Report on the Revised Uniform Limited Liability Company Act," published in the March 2006 issue of the newsletter of the ABA Committee on Partnerships and Unincorporated Business Organizations:

> The concept [of statutory apparent authority] still makes sense both for general and limited partnerships. A third party dealing with either type of partnership can know by the formal name of the entity and by a person's status as general or limited partner whether the person has the power to bind the entity.

> Most LLC statutes have attempted to use the same approach but with a fundamentally important (and problematic) distinction. An LLC's status as member-managed or manager-managed determines whether members or managers have the statutory power to bind. But an LLC's status as member- or manager-managed is not apparent from the LLC's name. A third party must check the public record, which may reveal that the LLC is manager-managed, which in turn means a member as member has no power to bind the LLC. As a result, a provision that originated in 1914 as a protection for third parties can, in the LLC context, easily function as a trap for the unwary. The problem is exacerbated by the almost infinite variety of management structures permissible in and used by LLCs.

> The new Act cuts through this problem by simply eliminating statutory apparent authority.

PUBOGRAM, Vol. XXIII, no. 2 at 9–10.

Codifying power to bind according to position makes sense only for organizations that have well-defined, well-known, and almost paradigmatic management structures. Because:

- flexibility of management structure is a hallmark of the limited liability company; and

- an LLC's name gives no signal as to the organization's structure,

it makes no sense to:

- require each LLC to publicly select between two statutorily preordained structures (i.e., manager-managed/member-managed); and then

- link a "statutory power to bind" to each of those two structures.

Under this Act, other law—most especially the law of agency—will handle power-to-bind questions. See the Comment to subsection (b).

This subsection does not address the power to bind of a manager in a manager-managed LLC, although this Act does consider a manager's management responsibilities. See Section 407(c) (allocating management authority, subject to the operating agreement). For a discussion of how agency law will approach the actual and apparent authority of managers, see Section 407(c), cmt.

Subsection (b)—As the "flip side" to subsection (a), this subsection expressly preserves the power of other law to hold an LLC directly or vicariously liable on account of conduct by a person who happens to be a member. For example, given the proper set of circumstances: (i) a member might have actual or apparent authority to bind an LLC to a contract; (ii) the doctrine of *respondeat superior* might make an LLC liable for the tortious conduct of a member (i.e., in some circumstances a member acts as a "servant" of the LLC); and (iii) an LLC might be liable for negligently supervising a member who is acting on behalf of the LLC. A person's status as a member does not weigh against these or any other relevant theories of law.

Moreover, subsection (a) does not prevent member status from being relevant to one or more elements of an "other law" theory. The most categorical example concerns the authority of a non-manager member of a manager-managed LLC.

Example: A vendor knows that an LLC is manager-managed but chooses to accept the signature of a person whom the vendor knows is merely a member of the LLC. Assuring the vendor that the LLC will stand by the member's commitment, the member states, "It's such a simple matter; no one will mind." The member genuinely believes the statement, and the vendor accepts the assurance.

The person's status as a mere member will undermine a claim of apparent authority. RESTATEMENT (THIRD) OF AGENCY § 2.03, cmt. d (2006) (explaining the "reasonable belief" element of a claim of apparent authority, and role played by context, custom, and the supposed agent's position in an organization). Likewise, the member will have no actual authority. Absent additional facts, section 407(c)(1) (vesting all management authority in the managers) renders the member's belief unreasonable. RESTATEMENT (THIRD) OF AGENCY § 2.01, cmt. c (2006) (explaining the "reasonable belief" element of a claim of actual authority).

In general, a member's actual authority to act for an LLC will depend fundamentally on the operating agreement.

Example: Rachael and Sam, who have known each other for years, decide to go into business arranging musical tours. They fill out and electronically sign a one page form available on the website of the Secretary of State and become the organizers of MMT, LLC. They are the only members of the LLC, and their understanding of who will do what in managing the enterprise is based on several lengthy, late-night conversations that preceded the LLC's formation. Sam is to "get the acts," and Rachael is to manage the tour logistics. There is no written operating agreement.

In the terminology of this Act, MMT, LLC is member-managed, Section 407(a), and the understanding reached in the late night conversations has become part of the LLC's operating agreement. Section 111(c). In agency law terms, the operating agreement constitutes a manifestation by the LLC to Rachael and Sam concerning the scope of their respective authority to act on behalf of the LLC. RESTATEMENT (THIRD) OF AGENCY § 2.01, cmt. c (2006) (explaining that a person's actual authority depends first on some manifestation attributable to the principal and stating: "Actual authority is a consequence of a principal's expressive conduct toward an agent, through which the principal manifests assent to be affected by the agent's action, and the agent's reasonable understanding of the principal's manifestation."

Circumstances outside the operating agreement can also be relevant to determining the scope of a member's actual authority.

Example: Homeworks, LLC is a manager-managed LLC with three members. The LLC's written operating agreement:

- specifies in considerable detail the management responsibilities of Margaret, the LLC's manager-member, and also states that Margaret is responsible for "the day-to-day operations" of the company;

- puts Garrett, a non-manager member, in charge of the LLC's transportation department; and

- specifies no management role for Brooksley, the third member.

When the LLC's chief financial officer quits suddenly, Margaret asks Brooksley, a CPA, to "step in until we can hire a replacement."

Under the operating agreement, Margaret's request to Brooksley is within Margaret's actual authority and is a manifestation attributable to the LLC. If Brooksley manifests assent to Margaret's request, Brooksley will have the actual authority to act as the LLC's CFO.

In the unlikely event that two or more people form a member-managed LLC without any understanding of how to allocate management responsibility between or among them, agency law, operating in the context the Act's "gap fillers" on management responsibility, will produce the following result:

A single member of a multi-member, member-managed LLC:

- has no actual authority to commit the LLC to any matter "outside the ordinary course of the activities of the company," section 407(b)(3); and

- has the actual authority to commit the LLC to any matter "in the ordinary course of the activities of the company," section 407(b)(2), unless the member has reason to know that other members might disagree or the member has some other reason to know that consultation with fellow members is appropriate.

For an explanation of this result, see Section 407(c), cmt., which provides a detailed agency law analysis in the context of a multi-manager, manager-managed LLC whose operating agreement is silent on the analogous question.

The common law of agency will also determine the apparent authority of a member of a member-managed LLC, and in that analysis what the particular third party knows or has reason to know about the management structure and business practices of the particular LLC will always be relevant. RESTATEMENT (THIRD) OF AGENCY § 3.03, cmt. b (2006) ("A principal may also make a manifestation by placing an agent in a defined position in an organization . . . . Third parties who interact with the principal through the agent will naturally and reasonably assume that the agent has authority to do acts consistent with the agent's position . . . unless they have notice of facts suggesting that this may not be so.")

Under section 301(a), however, the mere fact that a person is a member of a member-managed limited liability company cannot *by itself* establish apparent authority by position. A course of dealing, however, may easily change the analysis:

Example: David is a one of two members of DS, LLC, a member-managed LLC. David orders paper clips on behalf of the LLC, signing the purchase agreement, "David, as a member of DS, LLC." The vendor accepts the order, sends an invoice to the LLC's address, and in due course receives a check drawn on the LLC's bank account. When David next places an order with the vendor, the LLC's payment of the first order is a manifestation that the vendor may use in establishing David's apparent authority to place the second order.

§ 302. Statement of Authority

(a) A limited liability company may deliver to the [Secretary of State] for filing a statement of authority. The statement:

(1) must include the name of the company and the street and mailing addresses of its designated office;

(2) with respect to any position that exists in or with respect to the company, may state the authority, or limitations on the authority, of all persons holding the position to:

(A) execute an instrument transferring real property held in the name of the company; or

(B) enter into other transactions on behalf of, or otherwise act for or bind, the company; and

(3) may state the authority, or limitations on the authority, of a specific person to:

(A) execute an instrument transferring real property held in the name of the company; or

(B) enter into other transactions on behalf of, or otherwise act for or bind, the company.

(b) To amend or cancel a statement of authority filed by the [Secretary of State] under Section 205(a), a limited liability company must deliver to the [Secretary of State] for filing an amendment or cancellation stating:

(1) the name of the company;

(2) the street and mailing addresses of the company's designated office;

(3) the caption of the statement being amended or canceled and the date the statement being affected became effective; and

(4) the contents of the amendment or a declaration that the statement being affected is canceled.

(c) A statement of authority affects only the power of a person to bind a limited liability company to persons that are not members.

(d) Subject to subsection (c) and Section 103(d) and except as otherwise provided in subsections (f), (g), and (h), a limitation on the authority of a person or a position contained in an effective statement of authority is not by itself evidence of knowledge or notice of the limitation by any person.

(e) Subject to subsection (c), a grant of authority not pertaining to transfers of real property and contained in an effective statement of authority is conclusive in favor of a person that gives value in reliance on the grant, except to the extent that when the person gives value:

(1) the person has knowledge to the contrary;

(2) the statement has been canceled or restrictively amended under subsection (b); or

(3) a limitation on the grant is contained in another statement of authority that became effective after the statement containing the grant became effective.

(f) Subject to subsection (c), an effective statement of authority that grants authority to transfer real property held in the name of the limited liability company and that is recorded by certified copy in the office for recording transfers of the real property is conclusive in favor of a person that gives value in reliance on the grant without knowledge to the contrary, except to the extent that when the person gives value:

(1) the statement has been canceled or restrictively amended under subsection (b) and a certified copy of the cancellation or restrictive amendment has been recorded in the office for recording transfers of the real property; or

(2) a limitation on the grant is contained in another statement of authority that became effective after the statement containing the grant became effective and a certified copy of the later-effective statement is recorded in the office for recording transfers of the real property.

(g) Subject to subsection (c), if a certified copy of an effective statement containing a limitation on the authority to transfer real property held in the name of a limited liability company is recorded in the office for recording transfers of that real property, all persons are deemed to know of the limitation.

(h) Subject to subsection (i), an effective statement of dissolution or termination is a cancellation of any filed statement of authority for the purposes of subsection (f) and is a limitation on authority for the purposes of subsection (g).

(i) After a statement of dissolution becomes effective, a limited liability company may deliver to the [Secretary of State] for filing and, if appropriate, may record a statement of authority that is designated as a post-dissolution statement of authority. The statement operates as provided in subsections (f) and (g).

(j) Unless earlier canceled, an effective statement of authority is canceled by operation of law five years after the date on which the statement, or its most recent amendment, becomes effective. This cancellation operates without need for any recording under subsection (f) or (g).

(k) An effective statement of denial operates as a restrictive amendment under this section and may be recorded by certified copy for the purposes of subsection (f)(1).

COMMENT

This section is derived from and builds on RUPA, § 303, and, like that provision is conceptually divided into two realms: statements pertaining to the power to transfer interests in the LLC's real property and statements pertaining to other matters. In the latter realm, statements are filed only in the records of the [Secretary of State], operate only to the extent the statements are actually known. Section 302(d) and (e).

As to interests in real property, in contrast, this section: (i) requires double-filing—with the [Secretary of State] and in the appropriate land records; and (ii) provides for constructive knowledge of statements limiting authority. Thus, a properly filed and recorded statement can protect the limited liability company, Section 302(g), and, in order for a statement pertaining to real property to be a sword in the hands of a third party, the statement must have been both filed and properly recorded. Section 302(f).

Subsection (a)(2)—This paragraph permits a statement to designate authority by position (or office) rather than by specific person. This type of a statement will enable LLCs to provide evidence of ongoing authority to enter into transactions without having to disclose to third parties the entirety of the operating agreement.

Here and elsewhere in the section, the phrase "real property" includes interests in real property, such as mortgages, easements, etc.

Subsection (b)—For the requirement that the original statement, like any other record, be appropriately captioned, see Section 205(a).

Subsection (c)—This subsection contains a very important limitation—i.e., that this section's rules do not operate *viz a viz* members. The text of RUPA, § 303 makes this very important point only obliquely, but the Comment to that section is unequivocal:

> It should be emphasized that Section 303 concerns the authority of partners to bind the partnership to third persons. As among the partners, the authority of a partner to take any action is governed by the partnership agreement, or by the provisions of RUPA governing the relations among partners, and is not affected by the filing or recording of a statement of partnership authority.

RUPA § 303, comment 4.

However, like any other record delivered for filing on behalf of an LLC, a statement of authority might be some evidence of the contents of the operating agreement. *See* Comment to Section 112(d).

Subsection (d)—The phrase "by itself" is important, because the existence of a limitation could be evidence if, for example, the person in question reviewed the public record at a time when the limitation was of record.

Subsection (e)(1)—What happens if a statement of authority conflicts with the contents of an LLC's certificate of organization? The contents of the certificate are not statements of authority, Section 201(c), so the information in the certificate does not directly figure into the operation of this section. However, if the person claiming to rely on a statement of authority had read the certificate's conflicting information before giving value, that fact might be evidence that person gave value with "knowledge to the contrary" of the statement.

§ 303. Statement of Denial

A person named in a filed statement of authority granting that person authority may deliver to the [Secretary of State] for filing a statement of denial that:

(1) provides the name of the limited liability company and the caption of the statement of authority to which the statement of denial pertains; and

(2) denies the grant of authority.

COMMENT

For the effect of a statement of denial, see Section 302(k).

§ 304. Liability of Members and Managers

(a) The debts, obligations, or other liabilities of a limited liability company, whether arising in contract, tort, or otherwise:

(1) are solely the debts, obligations, or other liabilities of the company; and

(2) do not become the debts, obligations, or other liabilities of a member or manager solely by reason of the member acting as a member or manager acting as a manager.

(b) The failure of a limited liability company to observe any particular formalities relating to the exercise of its powers or management of its activities is not a ground for imposing liability on the members or managers for the debts, obligations, or other liabilities of the company.

COMMENT

Subsection (a)(2)—This paragraph shields members and managers only against the debts, obligations and liabilities of the limited liability company and is irrelevant to claims seeking to hold a member or manager directly liable on account of the member's or manager's own conduct.

Example: A manager personally guarantees a debt of a limited liability company. Subsection (a)(2) is irrelevant to the manager's liability as guarantor.

Example: A member purports to bind a limited liability company while lacking any agency law power to do so. The limited liability company is not bound, but the member is liable for having breached the "warranty of authority" (an agency law doctrine). Subsection (a)(2) does not apply. The liability is not *for* a "debt[ ], obligation[ ], [or] liabilit[y] of a limited liability company," but rather is the member's direct liability resulting because the limited liability company is *not* indebted, obligated or liable. RESTATEMENT (THIRD) OF AGENCY § 6.10 (2006).

Example: A manager of a limited liability company defames a third party in circumstances that render the limited liability company vicariously liable under agency law. Under subsection (a)(2), the third party cannot hold the manager accountable for the *company's* liability, but that protection is immaterial. The manager is the tortfeasor and in that role is directly liable to the third party.

Subsection (a)(2) pertains only to claims by third parties and is irrelevant to claims by a limited liability company against a member or manager and *vice versa. See e.g.* Sections 408 (pertaining to a limited liability company's obligation to indemnify a member or manager), 409 (pertaining to management duties) and 901 (pertaining to a member's rights to bring a direct claim against a limited liability company).

Subsection (b)—This subsection pertains to the equitable doctrine of "piercing the veil"—i.e., conflating an entity and its owners to hold one liable for the obligations of the other. The doctrine of "piercing the corporate veil" is well-established, and courts regularly (and sometimes almost reflexively) apply that doctrine to limited liability companies. In the corporate realm, "disregard of corporate formalities" is a key factor in the piercing analysis. In the realm of LLCs, that factor is inappropriate, because informality of organization and operation is both common and desired.

This subsection does not preclude consideration of another key piercing factor—disregard by an entity's owners of the entity's economic separateness from the owners.

Example: The operating agreement of a three-member, member-managed limited liability company requires formal monthly meetings of the members. Each of the members works in the LLC's business, and they consult each other regularly. They have forgotten or ignore the requirement of monthly meetings. Under subsection (b), that fact is irrelevant to a piercing claim.

Example: The sole owner of a limited liability company uses a car titled in the company's name for personal purposes and writes checks on the company's account to pay for personal expenses. These facts are relevant to a piercing claim; they pertain to economic separateness, not subsection (b) formalities.

This subsection has no relevance to a member's claim of oppression under Section 701(a)(5)(B). In some circumstances, disregard of agreed-upon formalities can be a "freeze out" mechanism. Likewise, this section has no relevance to a member's claim that the disregard of agreed-upon formalities is a breach of the operating agreement.

Provisions of regulatory law may impose liability by status on a member or manager. *See* CARTER G. BISHOP AND DANIEL S. KLEINBERGER, LIMITED LIABILITY COMPANIES: TAX AND BUSINESS LAW, ¶ 6.04(4) (Statutory Liability).

[ARTICLE] 4
RELATIONS OF MEMBERS TO EACH OTHER
AND TO LIMITED LIABILITY COMPANY

§ 401.   Becoming Member

(a)   If a limited liability company is to have only one member upon formation, the person becomes a member as agreed by that person and the organizer of the company. That person and the organizer may be, but need not be, different persons. If different, the organizer acts on behalf of the initial member.

(b)   If a limited liability company is to have more than one member upon formation, those persons become members as agreed by the persons before the formation of the company. The organizer acts on behalf of the persons in forming the company and may be, but need not be, one of the persons.

(c)   If a filed certificate of organization contains the statement required by Section 201(b)(3), a person becomes an initial member of the limited liability company with the consent of a majority of the organizers. The organizers may consent to more than one person simultaneously becoming the company's initial members.

(d)   After formation of a limited liability company, a person becomes a member:

   (1)   as provided in the operating agreement;

   (2)   as the result of a transaction effective under [Article] 10;

   (3)   with the consent of all the members; or

   (4)   if, within 90 consecutive days after the company ceases to have any members:

      (A)   the last person to have been a member, or the legal representative of that person, designates a person to become a member; and

      (B)   the designated person consents to become a member.

(e)   A person may become a member without acquiring a transferable interest and without making or being obligated to make a contribution to the limited liability company.

COMMENT

Most LLC statutes address in separate provisions: (i) how an LLC obtains its initial member or members; and (ii) how additional persons might later become members. This Act follows that approach. Subsections (a) and (b) address the most common circumstances under which a limited liability company is formed—with one or more persons becoming members upon formation. Subsection (c) addresses how a person becomes the initial member of an LLC whose certificate of organization was filed without there being any members. Subsection (d) addresses how persons become members after an LLC has had at least one member.

For a discussion of the concept of a "shelf LLC" and this Act's requirement that a limited liability company have at least one member upon formation, see the Comment to Section 201.

Subsection (d)(4)—The personal representative of the last member may designate her-, him-, or itself as the new member.

Subsection (e)—To accommodate business practices and also because a limited liability company need not have a business purpose, this subsection permits so-called "non-economic members."

§ 402.   Form of Contribution

A contribution may consist of tangible or intangible property or other benefit to a limited liability company, including money, services performed, promissory notes, other agreements to contribute money or property, and contracts for services to be performed.

COMMENT

Source—ULPA (2001) § 501, which derived from ULLCA § 401.

§ 403.   Liability for Contributions

(a)   A person's obligation to make a contribution to a limited liability company is not excused by the person's death, disability, or other inability to perform personally. If a person does not make a required contribution, the person or the person's estate is obligated to contribute money equal to the value of the part of the contribution which has not been made, at the option of the company.

(b)   A creditor of a limited liability company which extends credit or otherwise acts in reliance on an obligation described in subsection (a) may enforce the obligation.

Source—ULLCA § 402, which is taken from RULPA § 502(b), which also gave rise to ULPA (2001) § 502.

Subsection (a)—The reference to "perform personally" is not limited to individuals but rather may refer to any legal person (including an entity) that has a non-delegable duty.

§ 404.   Sharing of and Right to Distributions Before Dissolution

(a)   Any distributions made by a limited liability company before its dissolution and winding up must be in equal shares among members and dissociated members, except to the extent necessary to comply with any transfer effective under Section 502 and any charging order in effect under Section 503.

(b)   A person has a right to a distribution before the dissolution and winding up of a limited liability company only if the company decides to make an interim distribution. A person's dissociation does not entitle the person to a distribution.

(c)   A person does not have a right to demand or receive a distribution from a limited liability company in any form other than money. Except as otherwise provided in Section 708(c), a limited liability company may distribute an asset in kind if each part of the asset is fungible with each other part and each person receives a percentage of the asset equal in value to the person's share of distributions.

(d)   If a member or transferee becomes entitled to receive a distribution, the member or transferee has the status of, and is entitled to all remedies available to, a creditor of the limited liability company with respect to the distribution.

COMMENT

This Act follows both the original ULLCA and ULPA (2001) in omitting any default rule for allocation of losses. The Comment to ULPA (2001), § 503 explains that omission as follows:

> This Act has no provision allocating profits and losses among the partners. Instead, the Act directly apportions the right to receive distributions. Nearly all limited partnerships will choose to allocate profits and losses in order to comply with applicable tax, accounting and other regulatory requirements. Those requirements, rather than this Act, are the proper source of guidance for that profit and loss allocation.

Subsection (b)—The second sentence of this subsection accords with Section 603(a)(3)—upon dissociation a person is treated as a mere transferee of its own transferable interest. Like most *inter se* rules in this Act, this one is subject to the operating agreement. *See* Comment to Section 603(a)(3).

§ 405.   Limitations on Distribution

(a)   A limited liability company may not make a distribution if after the distribution:

(1)   the company would not be able to pay its debts as they become due in the ordinary course of the company's activities; or

(2)   the company's total assets would be less than the sum of its total liabilities plus the amount that would be needed, if the company were to be dissolved, wound up, and terminated at the time of the distribution, to satisfy the preferential rights upon dissolution, winding up, and termination of members whose preferential rights are superior to those of persons receiving the distribution.

(b)   A limited liability company may base a determination that a distribution is not prohibited under subsection (a) on financial statements prepared on the basis of accounting practices and principles that are reasonable in the circumstances or on a fair valuation or other method that is reasonable under the circumstances.

(c)   Except as otherwise provided in subsection (f), the effect of a distribution under subsection (a) is measured:

(1)   in the case of a distribution by purchase, redemption, or other acquisition of a transferable interest in the company, as of the date money or other property is transferred or debt incurred by the company; and

(2)　in all other cases, as of the date:

    (A)　the distribution is authorized, if the payment occurs within 120 days after that date; or

    (B)　the payment is made, if the payment occurs more than 120 days after the distribution is authorized.

(d)　A limited liability company's indebtedness to a member incurred by reason of a distribution made in accordance with this section is at parity with the company's indebtedness to its general, unsecured creditors.

(e)　A limited liability company's indebtedness, including indebtedness issued in connection with or as part of a distribution, is not a liability for purposes of subsection (a) if the terms of the indebtedness provide that payment of principal and interest are made only to the extent that a distribution could be made to members under this section.

(f)　If indebtedness is issued as a distribution, each payment of principal or interest on the indebtedness is treated as a distribution, the effect of which is measured on the date the payment is made.

(g)　In subsection (a), "distribution" does not include amounts constituting reasonable compensation for present or past services or reasonable payments made in the ordinary course of business under a bona fide retirement plan or other benefits program.

COMMENT

Source—ULPA (2001) § 508, which was derived from ULLCA § 406, which was in turn derived from MBCA § 6.40.

Subsection (b)—This subsection appears to involve a pure standard of ordinary care, in contrast with the more complicated approach stated in Section 409(c).

Subsection (g)—This exception applies only for the purposes of this section. *See* the Comment to Section 503(b)(2). The exception is derived from existing statutory provisions. *See, e.g.*, DEL. CODE ANN., tit. 6, § 18–607(a) (2006) and VA. CODE ANN. § 13.1–1035(E) (West 2006). *See also In re Tri-River Trading, LLC*, 329 B.R. 252, 266 (8th Cir. BAP 2005), aff'd. 452 F.3d 756 (8th Cir. 2006) ("We know of no principle of law which suggests that a manager of a company is required to give up agreed upon salary to pay creditors when business turns bad.")

§ 406.　Liability for Improper Distributions

(a)　Except as otherwise provided in subsection (b), if a member of a member-managed limited liability company or manager of a manager-managed limited liability company consents to a distribution made in violation of Section 405 and in consenting to the distribution fails to comply with Section 409, the member or manager is personally liable to the company for the amount of the distribution that exceeds the amount that could have been distributed without the violation of Section 405.

(b)　To the extent the operating agreement of a member-managed limited liability company expressly relieves a member of the authority and responsibility to consent to distributions and imposes that authority and responsibility on one or more other members, the liability stated in subsection (a) applies to the other members and not the member that the operating agreement relieves of authority and responsibility.

(c)　A person that receives a distribution knowing that the distribution to that person was made in violation of Section 405 is personally liable to the limited liability company but only to the extent that the distribution received by the person exceeded the amount that could have been properly paid under Section 405.

(d)　A person against which an action is commenced because the person is liable under subsection (a) may:

    (1)　implead any other person that is subject to liability under subsection (a) and seek to compel contribution from the person; and

    (2)　implead any person that received a distribution in violation of subsection (c) and seek to compel contribution from the person in the amount the person received in violation of subsection (c).

(e)   An action under this section is barred if not commenced within two years after the distribution.

COMMENT

Source—Same derivation as Section 405.

Liability under this section is not affected by a person ceasing to be a member, manager or transferee after the time that the liability attaches.

Subsection (b)—The operating agreement could not accomplish the "switch" in liability provided by this subsection, because the "switch" implicates the rights of third parties under this Act. Section 110(c)(11).

Subsections (c) and (d)(2)—Liability could apply to a person who receives a distribution under a charging order, but only if the person meets the knowledge requirement. That situation is very unlikely unless the person with the charging order is also a member or manager.

§ 407.   Management of Limited Liability Company

(a)   A limited liability company is a member-managed limited liability company unless the operating agreement:

   (1)   expressly provides that:

      (A)   the company is or will be "manager-managed";

      (B)   the company is or will be "managed by managers"; or

      (C)   management of the company is or will be "vested in managers"; or

   (2)   includes words of similar import.

(b)   In a member-managed limited liability company, the following rules apply:

   (1)   The management and conduct of the company are vested in the members.

   (2)   Each member has equal rights in the management and conduct of the company's activities.

   (3)   A difference arising among members as to a matter in the ordinary course of the activities of the company may be decided by a majority of the members.

   (4)   An act outside the ordinary course of the activities of the company may be undertaken only with the consent of all members.

   (5)   The operating agreement may be amended only with the consent of all members.

(c)   In a manager-managed limited liability company, the following rules apply:

   (1)   Except as otherwise expressly provided in this [act], any matter relating to the activities of the company is decided exclusively by the managers.

   (2)   Each manager has equal rights in the management and conduct of the activities of the company.

   (3)   A difference arising among managers as to a matter in the ordinary course of the activities of the company may be decided by a majority of the managers.

   (4)   The consent of all members is required to:

      (A)   sell, lease, exchange, or otherwise dispose of all, or substantially all, of the company's property, with or without the good will, outside the ordinary course of the company's activities;

      (B)   approve a merger, conversion, or domestication under [Article] 10;

      (C)   undertake any other act outside the ordinary course of the company's activities; and

      (D)   amend the operating agreement.

   (5)   A manager may be chosen at any time by the consent of a majority of the members and remains a manager until a successor has been chosen, unless the manager at an earlier time resigns,

is removed, or dies, or, in the case of a manager that is not an individual, terminates. A manager may be removed at any time by the consent of a majority of the members without notice or cause.

(6) A person need not be a member to be a manager, but the dissociation of a member that is also a manager removes the person as a manager. If a person that is both a manager and a member ceases to be a manager, that cessation does not by itself dissociate the person as a member.

(7) A person's ceasing to be a manager does not discharge any debt, obligation, or other liability to the limited liability company or members which the person incurred while a manager.

(d) An action requiring the consent of members under this [act] may be taken without a meeting, and a member may appoint a proxy or other agent to consent or otherwise act for the member by signing an appointing record, personally or by the member's agent.

(e) The dissolution of a limited liability company does not affect the applicability of this section. However, a person that wrongfully causes dissolution of the company loses the right to participate in management as a member and a manager.

(f) This [act] does not entitle a member to remuneration for services performed for a member-managed limited liability company, except for reasonable compensation for services rendered in winding up the activities of the company.

COMMENT

Subsection (a)—This subsection follows implicitly from the definitions of "manager-managed" and "member-managed" limited liability companies, Section 102(10) and (12), but is included here for the sake of clarity. Although this Act has eliminated the link between management structure and statutory apparent authority, Section 301, the Act retains the manager-managed and member-managed constructs as options for members to use to structure their *inter se* relationship.

Subsection (b)—The subsection states default rules that, under Section 110, are subject to the operating agreement.

Subsection (c)—Like subsection (b), this subsection states default rules that, under Section 110, are subject to the operating agreement. For example, a limited liability company's operating agreement might state "This company is manager-managed," Section 102(10)(i), while providing that managers must submit specified ordinary matters for review by the members.

The actual authority of an LLC's manager or managers is a question of agency law and depends fundamentally on the contents of the operating agreement and any separate management contract between the LLC and its manager or managers. These agreements are the primary source of the manifestations of the LLC (as principal) from which a manager (as agent) will form the reasonable beliefs that delimit the scope of the manager's actual authority. RESTATEMENT (THIRD) OF AGENCY § 3.01 (2006). *See also* RESTATEMENT (SECOND) OF AGENCY §§ 15, 26.

Other information may be relevant as well, such as the course of dealing within the LLC, unless the operating agreement effectively precludes consideration of that information. See Section 110(a)(4) (stating that the operating agreement governs "the means and conditions for amending the operating agreement") and the comment to that subparagraph, which states that:

[Although this] Act does not specially authorize the operating agreement to limit the sources in which terms of the operating agreement might be found or limit amendments to specified modes . . . Paragraph (a)(4) could be read to encompass such authorization. Also, under Section 107 the parol evidence rule will apply to a written operating agreement containing an appropriate merger provision.

If the operating agreement and a management contract conflict, the reasonable manager will know that the operating agreement controls the extent of the manager's rightful authority to act for the LLC—despite any contract claims the manager might have. *See* Section 111(a)(2) (stating that the operating agreement governs "the rights and duties under this [act] of a person in the capacity of manager") and the comment to that paragraph, which states:

Because the term "[o]perating agreement. . . . includes the agreement as amended or restated," Section 102(13), this paragraph gives the members the ongoing power to define the role of an LLC's managers. Power is not the same as right, however, and exercising the power provided by this paragraph might constitute a breach of a separate contract between the LLC and the manager.

See also RESTATEMENT (THIRD) OF AGENCY § 8.13, cmt. b (2006) and RESTATEMENT (SECOND) OF AGENCY, § 432, cmt. b (stating that, when a principal's instructions to an agent contravene a contract between the principal and agent, the agent may have a breach of contract claim but has no right to act contrary to the principal's instructions).

If (i) an LLC's operating agreement merely states that the LLC is manager-managed and does not further specify the managerial responsibilities, and (ii) the LLC has only one manager, the actual authority analysis is simple. In that situation, this subsection:

- serves as "gap filler" to the operating agreement; and thereby

- constitutes the LLC's manifestation to the manager as to the scope of the manager's authority; and thereby

- delimits the manager's actual authority, subject to whatever subsequent manifestations the LLC may make to the manager (e.g., by a vote of the members, or an amendment of the operating agreement).

If the operating agreement states only that the LLC is manager-managed and the LLC has more than one manager, the question of actual authority has an additional aspect. It is necessary to determine what actual authority any one manager has to act alone.

Paragraphs (c)(2), (3), and (4) combine to provide the answer. A single manager of a multi-manager LLC:

- has no actual authority to commit the LLC to any matter "outside the ordinary course of the activities of the company," paragraph (c)(4)(C), or any matter encompassed in paragraph (c)(4); and

- has the actual authority to commit the LLC to any matter "in the ordinary course of the activities of the company," paragraph (c)(3), unless the manager has reason to know that other managers might disagree or the manager has some other reason to know that consultation with fellow managers is appropriate.

The first point follows self-evidently from the language of paragraphs (c)(3) and (c)(4). In light of that language, no manager could reasonably believe to the contrary (unless the operating agreement provided otherwise).

The second point follows because:

- Subsection (c) serves as the gap-filler manifestation from the LLC to its managers, and subsection (c) does <u>not</u> require managers of a multi-manager LLC to act <u>only</u> in concert or after consultation.

- To the contrary, subject to the operating agreement:

    - paragraph (c)(2) expressly provides that "each manager has equal rights in the management and conduct of the activities of the company," and

    - paragraph (c)(3) suggests that several (as well as joint) activity is appropriate on ordinary matters, so long as the manager acting in the matter has no reason to believe that the matter will be controversial among the managers and therefore requires a decision under paragraph (c)(3).

While the individual members of a corporate board of directors lack actual authority to bind the corporation, 2 WILLIAM MEADE FLETCHER, FLETCHER CYCLOPEDIA OF THE LAW OF CORPORATIONS, § 392 (noting "the overwhelming weight of authority"), subsection (c) does not describe "board" management. Instead, subsection (c) provides management rules derived from those that govern the members of a general partnership and multiple general partners of a limited partnership. RUPA, § 401 and ULPA (2001), § 406.

The common law of agency will also determine the apparent authority of an LLC's manager or managers, and in that analysis what the particular third party knows or has reason to know about the management structure and business practices of the particular LLC will always be relevant. RESTATEMENT (THIRD) OF AGENCY § 3.03 cmt. d (2006) ("The nature of an organization's business or activity is relevant to whether a third party could reasonably believe that a [manager] is authorized to commit the organization to a particular transaction.").

As a general matter, however—i.e., as to the apparent authority of the position of LLC manager under this Act—courts may view the position as clothing its occupants with the apparent authority to take actions that reasonably appear within the ordinary course of the company's business. The actual authority analysis stated above supports that proposition; absent a reason to believe to the contrary, a third party could reasonably believe a manager to possess the authority contemplated by the gap-fillers of the statute. *But see* Section 102(9), cmt. (stating that "confusion around the term 'manager' is common to almost all LLC statutes").

Subsection (c)(5)—Under the default rule stated in this paragraph, dissolution of an entity that is a manager does not end the entity's status as manager. Contrast Section 602(4)(D) (referring to the expulsion of a member that is a partnership or limited liability company and authorizing the other members to expel, by unanimous consent, the dissolved partnership or limited liability company).

An LLC does not cease to be "manager-managed" simply because no managers are in place. In that situation, absent additional facts, the LLC is manager-managed and the manager position is vacant. Non-manager members who exercise managerial functions during the vacancy (or at any other time) will have duties as determined by other law, most particularly the law of agency.

Subsection (c)(7)—The obligation to safeguard trade secrets and other confidential or propriety information is incurred when the person is a manager, and a subsequent cessation does not entitle the person to usurp the information or use it to the prejudice of the LLC after the cessation.

Subsection (e)—Under the default rules of this Act, it is not possible for a person to wrongfully cause dissolution (as distinguished from wrongfully dissociating). Compare Section 701 with Section 601(b). However, the operating agreement might contemplate wrongful dissolution, and this subsection would then apply—unless the operating provides otherwise. Under the second sentence of this subsection, a person might lose the rights to act as a manager without automatically and formally ceasing to be denominated as a manager.

Subsection (f)—This provision traces back to the 1914 Uniform Partnership Act, § 18(f) and is included for fear that its absence might be misinterpreted as implying a contrary rule.

This Act does not provide for remuneration to a manager of a manager-managed LLC. That issue is for the operating agreement, or a separate agreement between the LLC and the manager. A manager seeking compensation will have the burden of proving an agreement. For a case demonstrating how *not* to establish an agreement, see Jandrain v. Lovald, 351 B.R. 679 (D. S.D. 2006).

§ 408. Indemnification and Insurance

(a) A limited liability company shall reimburse for any payment made and indemnify for any debt, obligation, or other liability incurred by a member of a member-managed company or the manager of a manager-managed company in the course of the member's or manager's activities on behalf of the company, if, in making the payment or incurring the debt, obligation, or other liability, the member or manager complied with the duties stated in Sections 405 and 409.

(b) A limited liability company may purchase and maintain insurance on behalf of a member or manager of the company against liability asserted against or incurred by the member or manager in that capacity or arising from that status even if, under Section 110(g), the operating agreement could not eliminate or limit the person's liability to the company for the conduct giving rise to the liability.

COMMENT

Subsection (a)—This subsection states a default rule, which corresponds to the default rules on management duties. In the default mode, the correspondence is appropriate, because otherwise the statutory rule on indemnification could undercut or even vitiate the statutory rules on duty. Both this subsection and the rules on duty are subject to the operating agreement.

This subsection does not expressly require a limited liability company to provide advances to cover expenses. However, in some jurisdictions the indemnity obligation might be interpreted to include an obligation to make advances.

This subsection concerns only managers of manager-managed limited liability companies and members of member-managed companies. The definite article in the phrases "the member's" [paragraph (1)] and "the member" [paragraph (2)] refers back to the original phrase "A limited liability company shall reimburse . . . and indemnify . . . a member of a member-managed company. . . ." A limited liability company's obligation, if any, to reimburse or indemnify others (including non-managing members of a manager-managed LLC and LLC employees) is a question for other law, including the law of agency.

      Subsection (b)—In contrast to subsection (a), this subsection encompasses all members, not just members in a member-managed LLC.

      This subsection's language is very broad and authorizes an LLC to purchase insurance to cover, e.g., a manager's intentional misconduct. It is unlikely that such insurance would be available. For restrictions on the power of an operating agreement to provide for indemnification, see Section 110, particularly subsection (g).

§ 409.   Standards of Conduct for Members and Managers

      (a)   A member of a member-managed limited liability company owes to the company and, subject to Section 901(b), the other members the fiduciary duties of loyalty and care stated in subsections (b) and (c).

      (b)   The duty of loyalty of a member in a member-managed limited liability company includes the duties:

         (1)   to account to the company and to hold as trustee for it any property, profit, or benefit derived by the member:

           (A)   in the conduct or winding up of the company's activities;

           (B)   from a use by the member of the company's property; or

           (C)   from the appropriation of a limited liability company opportunity;

         (2)   to refrain from dealing with the company in the conduct or winding up of the company's activities as or on behalf of a person having an interest adverse to the company; and

         (3)   to refrain from competing with the company in the conduct of the company's activities before the dissolution of the company.

      (c)   Subject to the business judgment rule, the duty of care of a member of a member-managed limited liability company in the conduct and winding up of the company's activities is to act with the care that a person in a like position would reasonably exercise under similar circumstances and in a manner the member reasonably believes to be in the best interests of the company. In discharging this duty, a member may rely in good faith upon opinions, reports, statements, or other information provided by another person that the member reasonably believes is a competent and reliable source for the information.

      (d)   A member in a member-managed limited liability company or a manager-managed limited liability company shall discharge the duties under this [act] or under the operating agreement and exercise any rights consistently with the contractual obligation of good faith and fair dealing.

      (e)   It is a defense to a claim under subsection (b)(2) and any comparable claim in equity or at common law that the transaction was fair to the limited liability company.

      (f)   All of the members of a member-managed limited liability company or a manager-managed limited liability company may authorize or ratify, after full disclosure of all material facts, a specific act or transaction that otherwise would violate the duty of loyalty.

      (g)   In a manager-managed limited liability company, the following rules apply:

         (1)   Subsections (a), (b), (c), and (e) apply to the manager or managers and not the members.

         (2)   The duty stated under subsection (b)(3) continues until winding up is completed.

         (3)   Subsection (d) applies to the members and managers.

         (4)   Subsection (f) applies only to the members.

         (5)   A member does not have any fiduciary duty to the company or to any other member solely by reason of being a member.

COMMENT

This section follows the structure of many LLC acts, first stating the duties of members in a member-managed limited liability company and then using that statement and a "switching" mechanism, subsection (g), to allocate duties in a manager-managed company. The duties stated in this section are subject to the operating agreement, but Section 110 contains important limitations on the power of the operating agreement to affect fiduciary duties and the obligation of good faith.

This section contains several noteworthy developments in the law of unincorporated business organizations:

- fiduciary duty is "uncabined"—see the Comment to subsections (a) and (b);

- the duty of care is not set at gross negligence—see the Comment to subsection (c); and

- the statutory endorsement of self-interest is omitted—see the Comment to section (e)

The standards, duties, and obligations of this Section are subject to delineation, restriction, and, to some extent, elimination by the operating agreement. See Section 110.

Subsections (a) and (b)—Until the promulgation of RUPA, it was almost axiomatic that: (i) fiduciary duties reflect judge-made law; and (ii) statutory formulations can express some of that law but do not exhaustively codify it. The original UPA was a prime example of this approach.

In an effort to respect freedom of contract, bolster predictability, and protect partnership agreements from second-guessing, the Conference decided that RUPA should fence or "cabin in" all fiduciary duties within a statutory formulation. That decision was followed without re-consideration in ULLCA and ULPA (2001).

This Act takes a different approach. After lengthy discussion in the drafting committee and on the floor of the 2006 Annual Meeting, the Conference decided that: (i) the "corral" created by RUPA does not fit in the very complex and variegated world of LLCs; and (ii) it is impracticable to cabin all LLC-related fiduciary duties within a statutory formulation.

As a result, this Act: (i) eschews "only" and "limited to"—the words RUPA used in an effort to exhaustively codify fiduciary duty; (ii) codifies the core of the fiduciary duty of loyalty; but (iii) does not purport to discern every possible category of overreaching. One important consequence is to allow courts to continue to use fiduciary duty concepts to police disclosure obligations in member-to-member and member-LLC transactions.

Subsection (c)—Although ULLCA, § 409(c) followed RUPA, § 404(c) and provided a gross negligence standard of care, at least a plurality of LLC statutes use an ordinary care standard. Sandra K. Miller, *The Role of the Court in Balancing Contractual Freedom With the Need For Mandatory Constraints on Opportunistic and Abusive Conduct in the LLC*, 152 U. PA. L. REV 1609, 1658 (May 2004) (containing two tables characterizing the standard of care under LLC statutes: 21 states with "good faith prudent person" language and 19 states using "gross negligence or willful misconduct" language); Elizabeth S. Miller and Thomas E. Rutledge, *The Duty of Finest Loyalty and Reasonable Decisions: The Business Judgment Rule in Unincorporated Business Organizations*, 30 DEL. J. CORP. L. 343, 366–368 (2005) (stating that "[a]pproximately eighteen state LLC statutes parallel language formerly used in the MBCA and require managers and managing members to act in good faith and exercise the care of an ordinarily prudent person in a like position under similar circumstances"). See also William J. Callison, *"The Law Does Not Perfectly Comprehend. . . .": The Inadequacy of the Gross Negligence Duty of Care Standard in Unincorporated Business Organizations*, 94 KY. L.J. 451, 452 (2005–2006) ("examin[ing] the gross negligence standard and find[ing] it wanting, particularly as it has intruded, largely unexamined and by drafting osmosis, into subsequent uniform acts governing limited partnerships and limited liability companies").

In some circumstances, an unadorned standard of ordinary care is appropriate for those in charge of a business organization or similar, non-business enterprise. In others, the proper application of the duty of care must take into account the difficulties inherent in establishing an enterprise's most fundamental policies, supervising the enterprise's overall activities, or making complex business judgments. Corporate law subdivides circumstances somewhat according to the formal role exercised by the person whose conduct is later challenged (e.g., distinguishing the duties of directors from the duties of officers). LLC law cannot follow that approach, because a hallmark of the LLC entity is its structural flexibility.

This subsection, therefore, seeks "the best of both worlds"—stating a standard of ordinary care but subjecting that standard to the business judgment rule to the extent circumstances warrant. The content and force of the business judgment rule vary across jurisdictions, and therefore the meaning of this subsection may vary from jurisdiction to jurisdiction.

That result is intended. In any jurisdiction, the business judgment rule's application will vary depending on the nature of the challenged conduct. There is, for example, very little (if any) judgment involved when a person with managerial power acts (or fails to act) on an essentially ministerial matter. Moreover, under the law of many jurisdictions, the business judgment rule applies similarly across the range of business organizations. That is, the doctrine is sufficiently broad and conceptual so that the formality of organizational choice is less important in shaping the application of the rule than are the nature of the challenged conduct and the responsibilities and authority of the person whose conduct is being challenged.

This Act seeks therefore to invoke rather than unsettle whatever may be each jurisdiction's approach to the business judgment rule.

Subsection (d)—This subsection refers to the *"contractual* obligation of good faith and fair dealing" to emphasize that the obligation is not an invitation to re-write agreements among the members. As explained in the Comment to ULPA (2001), § 305(b):

> The obligation of good faith and fair dealing is not a fiduciary duty, does not command altruism or self-abnegation, and does not prevent a partner from acting in the partner's own self-interest. Courts should not use the obligation to change ex post facto the parties' or this Act's allocation of risk and power. To the contrary, in light of the nature of a limited partnership, the obligation should be used only to protect agreed-upon arrangements from conduct that is manifestly beyond what a reasonable person could have contemplated when the arrangements were made. . . . In sum, the purpose of the obligation of good faith and fair dealing is to protect the arrangement the partners have chosen for themselves, not to restructure that arrangement under the guise of safeguarding it.

At first glance, it may seem strange to apply a contractual obligation to statutory duties and rights—i.e., duties and rights "under this [act]." However, for the most part those duties and rights apply to relationships *inter se* the members and the LLC and function only to the extent not displaced by the operating agreement. In the contract-based organization that is an LLC, those statutory default rules are intended to function like a contract. Therefore, applying the contractual notion of good faith makes sense.

As to whether the obligation stated in this subsection applies to transferees, see the Comment to Section 112(b).

Subsection (e)—Section 409 omits a noteworthy provision, which, beginning with RUPA, has been standard in the uniform business entity acts. RUPA, ULLCA, ULPA (2001) each placed the following language in the subsection following the formulation of the obligation of good faith:

> A member . . . does not violate a duty or obligation under this [act] or under the operating agreement merely because the member's conduct furthers the member's own interest.

This language is inappropriate in the complex and variegated world of LLCs. As a proposition of contract law, the language is axiomatic and therefore unnecessary. In the context of fiduciary duty, the language is at best incomplete, at worst wrong, and in any event confusing.

This Act's subsection (e) takes a very different approach, stating a well-established principle of judge-made law. Despite Section 107, the statement is not surplusage. Given this Act's very detailed treatment of fiduciary duties and especially the Act's very detailed treatment of the power of the operating agreement to modify fiduciary duties, the statement is important because its absence might be confusing. (An *ex post* fairness justification is not the same as an *ex ante* agreement to modify, but the topics are sufficiently close for a danger of the affirmative pregnant.)

This Act also omits, as anachronistic and potentially confusing, any provision resembling ULLCA, § 409(f) ("A member of a member-managed company may lend money to and transact other business with the company. As to each loan or transaction, the rights and obligations of the member are the same as those of a person who is not a member, subject to other applicable law.") *See also* ULPA (2001), § 112 ("A partner may lend money to and transact other business with the limited partnership and has the same rights and obligations with respect to the loan or other transaction as a person that is not a partner.")

Those provisions originated to combat the notion that debts to partners were categorically inferior to debts to non-partner creditors. That notion has never been part of LLC law, and so a modern uniform LLC act need not include language combating the notion. Moreover, to the uninitiated the language can be confusing, because the words might: (i) seem to undercut the duty of loyalty, which they do not; and (ii) deflect attention from bankruptcy law and the law of fraudulent transfer, which assuredly can look askance at transactions between an entity and an "insider."

Subsection (f)—The operating agreement can provide additional or different methods of authorization or ratification, subject to the strictures of Section 110(e). See the Comment to that subsection.

Subsection (g)—This is the "switching" mechanism, referred to in the introduction to this Comment.

Subsection (g)(2)—On the assumption that the members of a manager-managed LLC are dependent on the manager, this paragraph extends the duty longer than in a member-managed LLC.

Subsection (g)(5)—This paragraph merely negates a claim of fiduciary duty that is exclusively status-based and does not immunize misconduct.

Example: Although a limited liability company is manager-managed, one member who is not a manager owns a controlling interest and effectively, albeit indirectly, controls the company's activities. A member owning a minority interest brings an action for dissolution under Section 701(a)(5)(B) (oppression by "the managers or those members in control of the company"). The court wishes to understand a claim as one alleging a breach of fiduciary duty by the controlling member. Subsection (g)(5) does not preclude that approach.

§ 410. Right of Members, Managers, and Dissociated Members to Information

(a) In a member-managed limited liability company, the following rules apply:

(1) On reasonable notice, a member may inspect and copy during regular business hours, at a reasonable location specified by the company, any record maintained by the company regarding the company's activities, financial condition, and other circumstances, to the extent the information is material to the member's rights and duties under the operating agreement or this [act].

(2) The company shall furnish to each member:

(A) without demand, any information concerning the company's activities, financial condition, and other circumstances which the company knows and is material to the proper exercise of the member's rights and duties under the operating agreement or this [act], except to the extent the company can establish that it reasonably believes the member already knows the information; and

(B) on demand, any other information concerning the company's activities, financial condition, and other circumstances, except to the extent the demand or information demanded is unreasonable or otherwise improper under the circumstances.

(3) The duty to furnish information under paragraph (2) also applies to each member to the extent the member knows any of the information described in paragraph (2).

(b) In a manager-managed limited liability company, the following rules apply:

(1) The informational rights stated in subsection (a) and the duty stated in subsection (a)(3) apply to the managers and not the members.

(2) During regular business hours and at a reasonable location specified by the company, a member may obtain from the company and inspect and copy full information regarding the activities, financial condition, and other circumstances of the company as is just and reasonable if:

(A) the member seeks the information for a purpose material to the member's interest as a member;

(B) the member makes a demand in a record received by the company, describing with reasonable particularity the information sought and the purpose for seeking the information; and

(C) the information sought is directly connected to the member's purpose.

(3) Within 10 days after receiving a demand pursuant to paragraph (2)(B), the company shall in a record inform the member that made the demand:

(A) of the information that the company will provide in response to the demand and when and where the company will provide the information; and

(B)   if the company declines to provide any demanded information, the company's reasons for declining.

(4)   Whenever this [act] or an operating agreement provides for a member to give or withhold consent to a matter, before the consent is given or withheld, the company shall, without demand, provide the member with all information that is known to the company and is material to the member's decision.

(c)   On 10 days' demand made in a record received by a limited liability company, a dissociated member may have access to information to which the person was entitled while a member if the information pertains to the period during which the person was a member, the person seeks the information in good faith, and the person satisfies the requirements imposed on a member by subsection (b)(2). The company shall respond to a demand made pursuant to this subsection in the manner provided in subsection (b)(3).

(d)   A limited liability company may charge a person that makes a demand under this section the reasonable costs of copying, limited to the costs of labor and material.

(e)   A member or dissociated member may exercise rights under this section through an agent or, in the case of an individual under legal disability, a legal representative. Any restriction or condition imposed by the operating agreement or under subsection (g) applies both to the agent or legal representative and the member or dissociated member.

(f)   The rights under this section do not extend to a person as transferee.

(g)   In addition to any restriction or condition stated in its operating agreement, a limited liability company, as a matter within the ordinary course of its activities, may impose reasonable restrictions and conditions on access to and use of information to be furnished under this section, including designating information confidential and imposing nondisclosure and safeguarding obligations on the recipient. In a dispute concerning the reasonableness of a restriction under this subsection, the company has the burden of proving reasonableness.

COMMENT

This section is derived from ULPA (2001), §§ 304 (rights to information of limited partners and former limited partners) and 407 (same re: general partners and former general partners). The rules stated here are what might be termed "quasi-default rules"—subject to some change by the operating agreement. Section 110(c)(6) (prohibiting unreasonable restrictions on the information rights stated in this section).

Although the rights and duties stated in this section are extensive, they may not necessarily be exhaustive. In some situations, some courts have seen owners' information rights as reflecting a fiduciary duty of those with management power. This Act's statement of fiduciary duties is not exhaustive. *See* Comment to Section 409 (explaining that this Act does not seek to "cabin in" all fiduciary duties). In contrast, the operating agreement has considerable "cabining in" power of its own. Section 110(d)(4).

Subsection (a)—Paragraph 1 states the rule pertaining to information memorialized in "records maintained by the company". Paragraph 2 applies to information not in such a record. Appropriately, paragraph (2) sets a more demanding standard for those seeking information.

Subsection (a)(2) and (3)—In appropriate circumstances, violation of either or both of these provisions might cause a court to enjoin or even rescind action taken by the LLC, especially when the violation has interfered with an approval or veto mechanism involving member consent. *E.g. Blue Chip Emerald LLC v. Allied Partners Inc.*, 299 A.D.2d 278, 279–280 (N.Y. App. Div. 2002) (invoking partnership law precedent as reflecting a duty of full disclosure and holding that "[a]bsent such full disclosure, the transaction is voidable).

Subsection (a)(2)—Violation of this paragraph could give rise to a claim for damages against a member or manager [see subsection (b)(1)] who breaches the duties stated in Section 409 in causing or suffering the LLC to violate this paragraph.

Subsection (a)(3)—A member's violation of this paragraph is actionable in damages without need to show a violation of a duty stated in Section 409.

Subsection (b)(1)—This is a switching provision. A manager's violation of the duty stated in subsection (a)(3) is actionable in damages without need to show a violation of a duty stated in Section 409.

Subsection (b)(2)—This paragraph refers to "information" rather than "records maintained by the company"—compare subsection (a)—so in some circumstances the company might have an obligation to memorialize information. Such circumstances will likely be rare or at least unusual. Section 410 generally concerns providing existing information, not creating it. In any event, a member does not trigger the company's obligation under this paragraph merely by satisfying subparagraphs (A) through (C). The member must also satisfy the "just and reasonable" requirement.

Subsection (c)—This section does not control the rights of the estate of a member who dissociates by dying. In that circumstance, Section 504 controls.

Subsection (g)—The phrase "as a matter within the ordinary course of its activities" means that a mere majority consent is needed to impose a restriction or condition. *See* Section 407(b)(3) and (c)(3). This approach is necessary, lest a requesting member (or manager-member) have the power to block imposition of a reasonable restriction or condition needed to prevent the requestor from abusing the LLC.

The burden of proof under this subsection contrasts with the burden of proof when someone claims that a term of an operating agreement violates Section 110(c)(6). Under that subsection, as a matter of ordinary procedural law, the burden is on the person making the claim.

[ARTICLE] 5
TRANSFERABLE INTERESTS AND RIGHTS
OF TRANSFEREES AND CREDITORS

§ 501. Nature of Transferable Interest

A transferable interest is personal property.

COMMENT

Source—This Article most directly follows ULPA (2001), Article 7, because ULPA (2001) reflects the Conference's most recent thinking on the issues addressed here. However, ULPA (2001), Article 7 is quite similar in substance to ULLCA, Article 5, and both those Articles derive from Article 5 of RUPA.

Whether a transferable interest pledged as security is governed by Article 8 or 9 of the Uniform Commercial Code depends on the facts and the rules stated in those Articles.

This Act does not include ULLCA § 501(a), which provided: "A member is not a co-owner of, and has no transferable interest in, property of a limited liability company." That language was a vestige of the "aggregate" notion of the law of general partnerships, and in a modern LLC statute would be at least surplusage and perhaps confusing as well.

§ 502. Transfer of Transferable Interest

(a) A transfer, in whole or in part, of a transferable interest:

(1) is permissible;

(2) does not by itself cause a member's dissociation or a dissolution and winding up of the limited liability company's activities; and

(3) subject to Section 504, does not entitle the transferee to:

(A) participate in the management or conduct of the company's activities; or

(B) except as otherwise provided in subsection (c), have access to records or other information concerning the company's activities.

(b) A transferee has the right to receive, in accordance with the transfer, distributions to which the transferor would otherwise be entitled.

(c) In a dissolution and winding up of a limited liability company, a transferee is entitled to an account of the company's transactions only from the date of dissolution.

(d)   A transferable interest may be evidenced by a certificate of the interest issued by the limited liability company in a record, and, subject to this section, the interest represented by the certificate may be transferred by a transfer of the certificate.

(e)   A limited liability company need not give effect to a transferee's rights under this section until the company has notice of the transfer.

(f)   A transfer of a transferable interest in violation of a restriction on transfer contained in the operating agreement is ineffective as to a person having notice of the restriction at the time of transfer.

(g)   Except as otherwise provided in Section 602(4)(B), when a member transfers a transferable interest, the transferor retains the rights of a member other than the interest in distributions transferred and retains all duties and obligations of a member.

(h)   When a member transfers a transferable interest to a person that becomes a member with respect to the transferred interest, the transferee is liable for the member's obligations under Sections 403 and 406(c) known to the transferee when the transferee becomes a member.

COMMENT

One of the most fundamental characteristics of LLC law is its fidelity to the "pick your partner" principle. This section is the core of the Act's provisions reflecting and protecting that principle.

A member's rights in a limited liability company are bifurcated into economic rights (the transferable interest) and governance rights (including management rights, consent rights, rights to information, rights to seek judicial intervention). Unless the operating agreement otherwise provides, a member acting without the consent of all other members lacks both the power and the right to: (i) bestow membership on a non-member, Section 401(d); or (ii) transfer to a non-member anything other than some or all of the member's transferable interest. Section 502(a)(3). However, consistent with current law, a member may transfer governance rights to another member without obtaining consent from the other members. Thus, this Act does not itself protect members from control shifts that result from transfers among members (as distinguished from transfers to non-members who seek thereby to become members).

This section applies regardless of whether the transferor is a member, a transferee of a member, a transferee of a transferee, etc. *See* Section 102(21) (defining "transferable interest" in terms of a right "originally associated with a person's capacity as a member" regardless of "whether or not the person remains a member or continues to own any part of the right").

Subsection (a)—The definition of "transfer," Section 102(20), and this subsection's reference to "in whole or in part" combine to mean that this section encompasses not only unconditional, permanent, and complete transfers but also temporary, contingent, and partial ones as well. Thus, for example, a charging order under Section 504 effects a transfer of part of the judgment debtor's transferable interest, as does the pledge of a transferable interest as collateral for a loan and the gift of a life-interest in a member's rights to distribution.

Subsection (a)(2)—Section 602(4)(B) creates a risk of dissociation via expulsion when a member transfers all of the member's transferable interest.

Subsection (a)(3)—Mere transferees have no right to intrude as the members carry on their activities as members. When a member dies, other law may effect a transfer of the member's interest to the member's estate or personal representative. Section 504 contains special rules applicable to that situation.

Subsection (b)—Amounts due under this subsection are of course subject to offset for any amount owed to the limited liability company by the member or dissociated member on whose account the distribution is made. As to whether an LLC may properly offset for claims against a transferor that was never a member is matter for other law, specifically the law of contracts dealing with assignments.

Subsection (d)—The use of certificates can raise issues relating to Articles 8 and 9 of the Uniform Commercial Code.

§ 503.   Charging Order

(a)   On application by a judgment creditor of a member or transferee, a court may enter a charging order against the transferable interest of the judgment debtor for the unsatisfied amount of the judgment. A charging order constitutes a lien on a judgment debtor's transferable interest and requires the limited liability company to pay over to the person to which the charging order was issued any distribution that would otherwise be paid to the judgment debtor.

(b)   To the extent necessary to effectuate the collection of distributions pursuant to a charging order in effect under subsection (a), the court may:

(1)   appoint a receiver of the distributions subject to the charging order, with the power to make all inquiries the judgment debtor might have made; and

(2)   make all other orders necessary to give effect to the charging order.

(c)   Upon a showing that distributions under a charging order will not pay the judgment debt within a reasonable time, the court may foreclose the lien and order the sale of the transferable interest. The purchaser at the foreclosure sale obtains only the transferable interest, does not thereby become a member, and is subject to Section 502.

(d)   At any time before foreclosure under subsection (c), the member or transferee whose transferable interest is subject to a charging order under subsection (a) may extinguish the charging order by satisfying the judgment and filing a certified copy of the satisfaction with the court that issued the charging order.

(e)   At any time before foreclosure under subsection (c), a limited liability company or one or more members whose transferable interests are not subject to the charging order may pay to the judgment creditor the full amount due under the judgment and thereby succeed to the rights of the judgment creditor, including the charging order.

(f)   This [act] does not deprive any member or transferee of the benefit of any exemption laws applicable to the member's or transferee's transferable interest.

(g)   This section provides the exclusive remedy by which a person seeking to enforce a judgment against a member or transferee may, in the capacity of judgment creditor, satisfy the judgment from the judgment debtor's transferable interest.

COMMENT

Charging order provisions appear in various forms in UPA, ULPA, RULPA, RUPA, ULLCA, and ULPA (2001). This section builds on those acts, while: (i) modernizing the language: (ii) making explicit certain points that have been at best implicit; and (iii) seeking to delineate more precisely the types of extraordinary circumstances that would have to exist before a court enforcing a charging order would be justified in interfering with an LLC's management or activities.

This section balances the needs of a judgment creditor of a member or transferee with the needs of the limited liability company and the members. The section achieves that balance by allowing the judgment creditor to collect on the judgment through the transferable interest of the judgment debtor while prohibiting interference in the management and activities of the limited liability company.

Under this section, the judgment creditor of a member or transferee is entitled to a charging order against the relevant transferable interest. While in effect, that order entitles the judgment creditor to whatever distributions would otherwise be due to the member or transferee whose interest is subject to the order. However, the judgment creditor has no say in the timing or amount of those distributions. The charging order does not entitle the judgment creditor to accelerate any distributions or to otherwise interfere with the management and activities of the limited liability company.

The operating agreement has no power to alter the provisions of this section to the prejudice of third parties. Section 110(c)(11).

Subsection (a)—The phrase "judgment debtor" encompasses both members and transferees. As a matter of civil procedure and due process, an application for a charging order must be served both on the limited liability company and the member or transferee whose transferable interest is to be charged.

Subsection (b)—Paragraph (2) refers to "other orders" rather than "additional orders". Therefore, given appropriate circumstances, a court may invoke either paragraph (1) or (2) or both.

Subsection (b)(1)—The receiver contemplated here is not a receiver for the limited liability company, but rather a receiver for the distributions. The principal advantage provided by this paragraph is an expanded right to information. However, that right goes no further than "the extent necessary to effectuate the collections of distributions pursuant to a charging order."

Subsection (b)(2)—This paragraph must be understood in the context of the balance described in the introduction to this section's Comment. In particular, the court's power to make orders "that the circumstances may of the case may require" is limited to "giv[ing] effect to the charging order."

Example: A judgment creditor with a charging order believes that the limited liability company should invest less of its surplus in operations, leaving more funds for distributions. The creditor moves the court for an order directing the limited liability company to restrict re-investment. Subsection (b)(2) does not authorize the court to grant the motion.

Example: A judgment creditor with a judgment for $10,000 against a member obtains a charging order against the member's transferable interest. Having been properly served with the order, the limited liability company nonetheless fails to comply and makes a $3000 distribution to the member. The court has the power to order the limited liability company to pay $3000 to the judgment creditor to "give effect to the charging order."

Under subsection (b)(2), the court also has the power to decide whether a particular payment is a distribution, because that decision determines whether the payment is part of a transferable interest subject to a charging order. To the extent a payment is not a distribution, it is not part of the transferable interest and is not subject to subsection (g). The payment is therefore subject to whatever other creditor remedies may apply.

Section 405(g) states a special exception to the definition of "distribution," but that exception applies only "[f]or purposes of subsection (a)" of Section 405. Therefore, whether a charging order applies to "amounts constituting reasonable compensation for present or past services or reasonable payments made in the ordinary course of business under a bona fide retirement plan or other benefits program," Section 405(g), is a question determined under this section, without regard to Section 405(g). To date, case law is scant, but there is authority holding that compensation is a distribution. *PB Real Estate, Inc. v. Dem II Properties*, 719 A.2d 73, 75 (Conn. App. Ct. 1998) (rejecting the defendants' claim that the payments at issue were merely compensation for their services to their law firm, which was organized as an LLC; noting that the defendants' characterization was at odds with the firm's business records and tax returns; holding that the payments received were distributions subject to the charging order).

This Act has no specific rules for determining the fate or effect of a charging order when the limited liability company undergoes a merger, conversion, or domestication under [Article] 10. In the proper circumstances, such an organic change might trigger an order under subsection (b)(2).

Subsection (c)—The phrase "that distributions under the charging order will not pay the judgment debt within a reasonable period of time" comes from case law. *See, e.g., Nigri v. Lotz*, 453 S.E.2d 780, 783 (Ga. Ct. App. 1995).

Subsection (e)—This Act jettisons the confusing concept of redemption and substitutes an approach that more closely parallels the modern, real-world possibility of the LLC or its members buying the underlying judgment (and thereby dispensing with any interference the judgment creditor might seek to inflict on the LLC). When possible, buying the judgment remains superior to the mechanism provided by this subsection, because: (i) this subsection requires full satisfaction of the underlying judgment, (ii) while the LLC or the other members might be able to buy the judgment for less than face value. On the other hand, this subsection operates without need for the judgment creditor's consent, so it remains a valuable protection in the event a judgment creditor seeks to do mischief to the LLC.

Whether an LLC's decision to invoke this subsection is "ordinary course" or "outside the ordinary course," Section 407(b)(3) and (4) and (c)(3) and (4)(C), depends on the circumstances. However, the involvement of this subsection does not by itself make the decision "outside the ordinary course."

Subsection (g)—This subsection does not override Article 9, which may provide different remedies for a secured creditor acting in that capacity. A secured creditor with a judgment might decide to proceed under Article 9 alone, under this section alone, or under both Article 9 and this section. In the last-mentioned circumstance, the constraints of this section would apply to the charging order but not to the Article 9 remedies.

This subsection is not intended to prevent a court from effecting a "reverse pierce" where appropriate. In a reverse pierce, the court conflates the entity and its owner to hold the entity liable for a debt of the owner. *Litchfield Asset Mgmt. Corp. v. Howell*, 799 A.2d 298, 312 (Conn. App. Ct. 2002) (approving a reverse pierce where a judgment debtor had established a limited liability company in a patent attempt frustrate the judgment creditor).

§ 504. Power of Personal Representative of Deceased Member

If a member dies, the deceased member's personal representative or other legal representative may exercise the rights of a transferee provided in Section 502(c) and, for the purposes of settling the estate, the rights of a current member under Section 410.

COMMENT

Source—ULPA (2001) § 704.

Section 410 pertains only to information rights.

[ARTICLE] 6
MEMBER'S DISSOCIATION

§ 601. Member's Power to Dissociate; Wrongful Dissociation

(a)   A person has the power to dissociate as a member at any time, rightfully or wrongfully, by withdrawing as a member by express will under Section 602(1).

(b)   A person's dissociation from a limited liability company is wrongful only if the dissociation:

(1)   is in breach of an express provision of the operating agreement; or

(2)   occurs before the termination of the company and:

(A)   the person withdraws as a member by express will;

(B)   the person is expelled as a member by judicial order under Section 602(5);

(C)   the person is dissociated under Section 602(7)(A) by becoming a debtor in bankruptcy; or

(D)   in the case of a person that is not a trust other than a business trust, an estate, or an individual, the person is expelled or otherwise dissociated as a member because it willfully dissolved or terminated.

(c)   A person that wrongfully dissociates as a member is liable to the limited liability company and, subject to Section 901, to the other members for damages caused by the dissociation. The liability is in addition to any other debt, obligation, or other liability of the member to the company or the other members.

COMMENT

Source—ULPA (2001) § 604, which is based on RUPA Section 602. ULLCA § 602 is functionally identical in some respects but is not a good overall source, because that section presupposes the term/at-will paradigm.

§ 602. Events Causing Dissociation

A person is dissociated as a member from a limited liability company when:

(1)   the company has notice of the person's express will to withdraw as a member, but, if the person specified a withdrawal date later than the date the company had notice, on that later date;

(2)   an event stated in the operating agreement as causing the person's dissociation occurs;

(3)   the person is expelled as a member pursuant to the operating agreement;

(4)   the person is expelled as a member by the unanimous consent of the other members if:

(A)   it is unlawful to carry on the company's activities with the person as a member;

(B)   there has been a transfer of all of the person's transferable interest in the company, other than:

(i)   a transfer for security purposes; or

(ii)   a charging order in effect under Section 503 which has not been foreclosed;

(C)   the person is a corporation and, within 90 days after the company notifies the person that it will be expelled as a member because the person has filed a certificate of dissolution or the equivalent, its charter has been revoked, or its right to conduct business has been suspended by the jurisdiction of its incorporation, the certificate of dissolution has not been revoked or its charter or right to conduct business has not been reinstated; or

(D)   the person is a limited liability company or partnership that has been dissolved and whose business is being wound up;

(5)   on application by the company, the person is expelled as a member by judicial order because the person:

(A)   has engaged, or is engaging, in wrongful conduct that has adversely and materially affected, or will adversely and materially affect, the company's activities;

(B)   has willfully or persistently committed, or is willfully and persistently committing, a material breach of the operating agreement or the person's duties or obligations under Section 409; or

(C)   has engaged in, or is engaging, in conduct relating to the company's activities which makes it not reasonably practicable to carry on the activities with the person as a member;

(6)   in the case of a person who is an individual:

(A)   the person dies; or

(B)   in a member-managed limited liability company:

(i)   a guardian or general conservator for the person is appointed; or

(ii)   there is a judicial order that the person has otherwise become incapable of performing the person's duties as a member under [this act] or the operating agreement;

(7)   in a member-managed limited liability company, the person:

(A)   becomes a debtor in bankruptcy;

(B)   executes an assignment for the benefit of creditors; or

(C)   seeks, consents to, or acquiesces in the appointment of a trustee, receiver, or liquidator of the person or of all or substantially all of the person's property;

(8)   in the case of a person that is a trust or is acting as a member by virtue of being a trustee of a trust, the trust's entire transferable interest in the company is distributed;

(9)   in the case of a person that is an estate or is acting as a member by virtue of being a personal representative of an estate, the estate's entire transferable interest in the company is distributed;

(10)   in the case of a member that is not an individual, partnership, limited liability company, corporation, trust, or estate, the termination of the member;

(11)   the company participates in a merger under [Article] 10, if:

(A)   the company is not the surviving entity; or

(B)   otherwise as a result of the merger, the person ceases to be a member;

(12)   the company participates in a conversion under [Article] 10;

(13)   the company participates in a domestication under [Article] 10, if, as a result of the domestication, the person ceases to be a member; or

(14)   the company terminates.

COMMENT

Source—ULLCA § 601; RUPA Section 601; ULPA (2001) §§ 601 and 603.

Paragraph (4)(B)—Under this paragraph (unless the operating agreement provides otherwise), a member's transferee can protect itself from the vulnerability of "bare transferee" status by obligating the member/transferor to retain a 1% interest and then to exercise its governance rights (including the right to bring a derivative suit) to protect the transferee's interests.

§ 603.   Effect of Person's Dissociation as Member

(a)   When a person is dissociated as a member of a limited liability company:

(1)   the person's right to participate as a member in the management and conduct of the company's activities terminates;

(2)   if the company is member-managed, the person's fiduciary duties as a member end with regard to matters arising and events occurring after the person's dissociation; and

(3)   subject to Section 504 and [Article] 10, any transferable interest owned by the person immediately before dissociation in the person's capacity as a member is owned by the person solely as a transferee.

(b)   A person's dissociation as a member of a limited liability company does not of itself discharge the person from any debt, obligation, or other liability to the company or the other members which the person incurred while a member.

COMMENT

Source—ULPA (2001) § 605, which was drawn from RUPA Section 603(b).

Subsection (a)—This provision makes no reference to power-to-bind matters, because the Act provides that a member *qua* member has no power to bind the LLC. Section 301.

Subsection (a)(2)—This provision applies only when the limited liability company is member-managed, because in a manager-managed LLC these duties do not apply to a member *qua* member. Section 409(g)(5).

Subsection (a)(3)—This paragraph accords with Section 404(b)—dissociation does not entitle a person to any distribution. Like most *inter se* rules in this Act, this one is subject to the operating agreement. For example, the operating agreement has the power to provide for the buy out of a person's transferable interest in connection with the person's dissociation.

Subsection (b)—In a member-managed limited liability company, the obligation to safeguard trade secrets and other confidential or proprietary information is incurred when a person is a member. A subsequent dissociation does not entitle the person to usurp the information or use it to the prejudice of the LLC after the dissociation. (In a manager-managed LLC, any obligations of a non-manager member *viz a viz* proprietary information would be a matter for the operating agreement, the obligation of good faith, or other law.)

[ARTICLE] 7
DISSOLUTION AND WINDING UP

§ 701.   Events Causing Dissolution

(a)   A limited liability company is dissolved, and its activities must be wound up, upon the occurrence of any of the following:

(1)   an event or circumstance that the operating agreement states causes dissolution;

(2)   the consent of all the members;

(3)   the passage of 90 consecutive days during which the company has no members;

(4)   on application by a member, the entry by [appropriate court] of an order dissolving the company on the grounds that:

(A)   the conduct of all or substantially all of the company's activities is unlawful; or

(B)   it is not reasonably practicable to carry on the company's activities in conformity with the certificate of organization and the operating agreement; or

(5)   on application by a member, the entry by [appropriate court] of an order dissolving the company on the grounds that the managers or those members in control of the company:

(A)   have acted, are acting, or will act in a manner that is illegal or fraudulent; or

(B)   have acted or are acting in a manner that is oppressive and was, is, or will be directly harmful to the applicant.

(b)   In a proceeding brought under subsection (a)(5), the court may order a remedy other than dissolution.

COMMENT

Subsection(a)(4)—The standard stated here is conventional, and this subsection (a)(4) is non-waivable. Section 110(c)(7).

Subsection (a)(5)—ULLCA § 801(4)(v) contains a comparable provision, although that provision also gives standing to dissociated members. Even in non-ULLCA states, courts have begun to apply close corporation "oppression" doctrine to LLCs.

This provision's reference to "those members in control of the company" implies that such members have a duty to avoid acting oppressively toward fellow members.

Subsection (a)(5) is non-waivable. *See* Section 110(c)(7).

Subsection (b)—In the close corporation context, many courts have reached this position without express statutory authority, most often with regard to court-ordered buyouts of oppressed shareholders. This subsection saves courts and litigants the trouble of re-inventing that wheel in the LLC context. However, unlike, subsection (a)(4) and (5), subsection (b) can be overridden by the operating agreement. Thus, the members may agree to a restrict or eliminate a court's power to craft a lesser remedy, even to the extent of confining the court (and themselves) to the all-or-nothing remedy of dissolution.

§ 702.   Winding up

(a)   A dissolved limited liability company shall wind up its activities, and the company continues after dissolution only for the purpose of winding up.

(b)   In winding up its activities, a limited liability company:

(1)   shall discharge the company's debts, obligations, or other liabilities, settle and close the company's activities, and marshal and distribute the assets of the company; and

(2)   may:

(A)   deliver to the [Secretary of State] for filing a statement of dissolution stating the name of the company and that the company is dissolved;

(B)   preserve the company activities and property as a going concern for a reasonable time;

(C)   prosecute and defend actions and proceedings, whether civil, criminal, or administrative;

(D)   transfer the company's property;

(E)   settle disputes by mediation or arbitration;

(F)   deliver to the [Secretary of State] for filing a statement of termination stating the name of the company and that the company is terminated; and

(G)   perform other acts necessary or appropriate to the winding up.

(c)   If a dissolved limited liability company has no members, the legal representative of the last person to have been a member may wind up the activities of the company. If the person does so, the person has the powers of a sole manager under Section 407(c) and is deemed to be a manager for the purposes of Section 304(a)(2).

(d)   If the legal representative under subsection (c) declines or fails to wind up the company's activities, a person may be appointed to do so by the consent of transferees owning a majority of the rights to receive distributions as transferees at the time the consent is to be effective. A person appointed under this subsection:

(1)   has the powers of a sole manager under Section 407(c) and is deemed to be a manager for the purposes of Section 304(a)(2); and

(2)   shall promptly deliver to the [Secretary of State] for filing an amendment to the company's certificate of organization to:

(A)   state that the company has no members;

(B)   state that the person has been appointed pursuant to this subsection to wind up the company; and

(C)   provide the street and mailing addresses of the person.

(e)   The [appropriate court] may order judicial supervision of the winding up of a dissolved limited liability company, including the appointment of a person to wind up the company's activities:

(1)   on application of a member, if the applicant establishes good cause;

(2)   on the application of a transferee, if:

(A)   the company does not have any members;

(B)   the legal representative of the last person to have been a member declines or fails to wind up the company's activities; and

(C)   within a reasonable time following the dissolution a person has not been appointed pursuant to subsection (d); or

(3)   in connection with a proceeding under Section 701(a)(4) or (5).

COMMENT

Source—ULPA (2001) § 803, which was based on RUPA Sections 802 and 803.

Because under this Act the power to bind a limited liability company to a third party is primarily a matter of agency law, Section 301, Comment, this Act has no need of provisions delineating the effect of dissolution on a member or manager's power to bind.

Subsection (b)(2)(A) and (F)—For the constructive notice effect of a statement of dissolution or termination, see Section 103(d)(2)(A) and (B).

§ 703.   Known Claims Against Dissolved Limited Liability Company

(a)   Except as otherwise provided in subsection (d), a dissolved limited liability company may give notice of a known claim under subsection (b), which has the effect as provided in subsection (c).

(b)   A dissolved limited liability company may in a record notify its known claimants of the dissolution. The notice must:

(1)   specify the information required to be included in a claim;

(2)   provide a mailing address to which the claim is to be sent;

(3)   state the deadline for receipt of the claim, which may not be less than 120 days after the date the notice is received by the claimant; and

(4)   state that the claim will be barred if not received by the deadline.

(c)   A claim against a dissolved limited liability company is barred if the requirements of subsection (b) are met and:

(1)   the claim is not received by the specified deadline; or

(2)   if the claim is timely received but rejected by the company:

(A)   the company causes the claimant to receive a notice in a record stating that the claim is rejected and will be barred unless the claimant commences an action against the company to enforce the claim within 90 days after the claimant receives the notice; and

(B)   the claimant does not commence the required action within the 90 days.

(d)   This section does not apply to a claim based on an event occurring after the effective date of dissolution or a liability that on that date is contingent.

COMMENT

Source—ULPA (2001) § 806, which was based on ULLCA § 807, which in turn was based on MBCA § 14.06.

§ 704.   Other Claims Against Dissolved Limited Liability Company

(a)   A dissolved limited liability company may publish notice of its dissolution and request persons having claims against the company to present them in accordance with the notice.

(b)   The notice authorized by subsection (a) must:

(1)   be published at least once in a newspaper of general circulation in the [county] in this state in which the dissolved limited liability company's principal office is located or, if it has none in this state, in the [county] in which the company's designated office is or was last located;

(2)   describe the information required to be contained in a claim and provide a mailing address to which the claim is to be sent; and

(3)   state that a claim against the company is barred unless an action to enforce the claim is commenced within five years after publication of the notice.

(c)   If a dissolved limited liability company publishes a notice in accordance with subsection (b), unless the claimant commences an action to enforce the claim against the company within five years after the publication date of the notice, the claim of each of the following claimants is barred:

(1)   a claimant that did not receive notice in a record under Section 703;

(2)   a claimant whose claim was timely sent to the company but not acted on; and

(3)   a claimant whose claim is contingent at, or based on an event occurring after, the effective date of dissolution.

(d)   A claim not barred under this section may be enforced:

(1)   against a dissolved limited liability company, to the extent of its undistributed assets; and

(2)   if assets of the company have been distributed after dissolution, against a member or transferee to the extent of that person's proportionate share of the claim or of the assets distributed to the member or transferee after dissolution, whichever is less, but a person's total liability for all claims under this paragraph does not exceed the total amount of assets distributed to the person after dissolution.

COMMENT

Source—ULPA (2001) § 807, which was based on ULLCA § 808, which in turn was based on MBCA § 14.07.

Subsection (d)(2)—Liability under this paragraph extends to those who have received distributions under a charging order. *See* Comment to 502(a) (explaining that the beneficiary of a charging order is a transferee). Unlike Section 406(c) (recapture of improper interim distributions), this paragraph contains no "knowledge" element.

§ 705.   Administrative Dissolution

(a)   The [Secretary of State] may dissolve a limited liability company administratively if the company does not:

(1)   pay, within 60 days after the due date, any fee, tax, or penalty due to the [Secretary of State] under this [act] or law other than this [act]; or

(2)   deliver, within 60 days after the due date, its annual report to the [Secretary of State].

(b)   If the [Secretary of State] determines that a ground exists for administratively dissolving a limited liability company, the [Secretary of State] shall file a record of the determination and serve the company with a copy of the filed record.

(c)   If within 60 days after service of the copy pursuant to subsection (b) a limited liability company does not correct each ground for dissolution or demonstrate to the reasonable satisfaction of the [Secretary of State] that each ground determined by the [Secretary of State] does not exist, the [Secretary of State] shall dissolve the company administratively by preparing, signing, and filing a declaration of dissolution that states the grounds for dissolution. The [Secretary of State] shall serve the company with a copy of the filed declaration.

(d)   A limited liability company that has been administratively dissolved continues in existence but, subject to Section 706, may carry on only activities necessary to wind up its activities and liquidate its assets under Sections 702 and 708 and to notify claimants under Sections 703 and 704.

(e)   The administrative dissolution of a limited liability company does not terminate the authority of its agent for service of process.

COMMENT

Source—ULPA (2001) § 809, which was based on ULLCA §§ 809 and 810. *See also* RMBCA §§ 14.20 and 14.21.

§ 706.   Reinstatement Following Administrative Dissolution

(a)   A limited liability company that has been administratively dissolved may apply to the [Secretary of State] for reinstatement within two years after the effective date of dissolution. The application must be delivered to the [Secretary of State] for filing and state:

(1)   the name of the company and the effective date of its dissolution;

(2)   that the grounds for dissolution did not exist or have been eliminated; and

(3)   that the company's name satisfies the requirements of Section 108.

(b)   If the [Secretary of State] determines that an application under subsection (a) contains the required information and that the information is correct, the [Secretary of State] shall prepare a declaration of reinstatement that states this determination, sign and file the original of the declaration of reinstatement, and serve the limited liability company with a copy.

(c)   When a reinstatement becomes effective, it relates back to and takes effect as of the effective date of the administrative dissolution and the limited liability company may resume its activities as if the dissolution had not occurred.

COMMENT

Source—ULPA (2001) § 810, which was based on ULLCA § 811. *See also* RMBCA Section 14.22.

§ 707.   Appeal from Rejection of Reinstatement

(a)   If the [Secretary of State] rejects a limited liability company's application for reinstatement following administrative dissolution, the [Secretary of State] shall prepare, sign, and file a notice that explains the reason for rejection and serve the company with a copy of the notice.

(b)   Within 30 days after service of a notice of rejection of reinstatement under subsection (a), a limited liability company may appeal from the rejection by petitioning the [appropriate court] to set aside the dissolution. The petition must be served on the [Secretary of State] and contain a copy of the [Secretary of

State's] declaration of dissolution, the company's application for reinstatement, and the [Secretary of State's] notice of rejection.

(c)   The court may order the [Secretary of State] to reinstate a dissolved limited liability company or take other action the court considers appropriate.

COMMENT

Source—ULPA (2001) § 811, which was based on ULLCA § 812.

This section uses "rejection" rather than "denial" (the word used by both ULPA (2001) and ULLCA). The change is to avoid confusion with a "statement of denial" under Section 302.

§ 708.   Distribution of Assets in Winding up Limited Liability Company's Activities

(a)   In winding up its activities, a limited liability company must apply its assets to discharge its obligations to creditors, including members that are creditors.

(b)   After a limited liability company complies with subsection (a), any surplus must be distributed in the following order, subject to any charging order in effect under Section 503:

(1)   to each person owning a transferable interest that reflects contributions made by a member and not previously returned, an amount equal to the value of the unreturned contributions; and

(2)   in equal shares among members and dissociated members, except to the extent necessary to comply with any transfer effective under Section 502.

(c)   If a limited liability company does not have sufficient surplus to comply with subsection (b)(1), any surplus must be distributed among the owners of transferable interests in proportion to the value of their respective unreturned contributions.

(d)   All distributions made under subsections (b) and (c) must be paid in money.

COMMENT

Source—ULLCA § 806, restyled.

Subsection (a)—This section is mostly not a default rule. *See* Section 110(c)(11) (stating that "except as provided in Section 112(b), [the operating agreement may not] restrict the rights under this [act] of a person other than a member or manager"). However, if the creditors are willing, a dissolved limited liability company may certainly make agreements with them specifying the terms under which the LLC will "discharge its obligations to creditors."

Subsections (b), (c) and (d)—These subsection provide default rules. Distributions under these subsections (or otherwise under the operating agreement) are subject to Section 503 (charging orders).

[ARTICLE] 8
FOREIGN LIMITED LIABILITY COMPANIES

§ 801.   Governing Law

(a)   The law of the state or other jurisdiction under which a foreign limited liability company is formed governs:

(1)   the internal affairs of the company; and

(2)   the liability of a member as member and a manager as manager for the debts, obligations, or other liabilities of the company.

(b)   A foreign limited liability company may not be denied a certificate of authority by reason of any difference between the law of the jurisdiction under which the company is formed and the law of this state.

(c)   A certificate of authority does not authorize a foreign limited liability company to engage in any business or exercise any power that a limited liability company may not engage in or exercise in this state.

COMMENT

Subsection (a)—This Section parallels the formulation stated in Section 106 for a domestic limited liability company.

Subsection (a)(2)—This provision does not pertain to the "internal shields" of a foreign "series" LLC, because those shields do not concern the liability of members or managers for the obligations of the LLC. Instead, those shields seek to protect specified assets of the LLC (associated with one series) from being available to satisfy specified obligations of the LLC (associated with another series). See the Prefatory Note, *No Provision for "Series" LLCs.*

§ 802. Application for Certificate of Authority

(a)   A foreign limited liability company may apply for a certificate of authority to transact business in this state by delivering an application to the [Secretary of State] for filing. The application must state:

(1)   the name of the company and, if the name does not comply with Section 108, an alternate name adopted pursuant to Section 805(a);

(2)   the name of the state or other jurisdiction under whose law the company is formed;

(3)   the street and mailing addresses of the company's principal office and, if the law of the jurisdiction under which the company is formed requires the company to maintain an office in that jurisdiction, the street and mailing addresses of the required office; and

(4)   the name and street and mailing addresses of the company's initial agent for service of process in this state.

(b)   A foreign limited liability company shall deliver with a completed application under subsection (a) a certificate of existence or a record of similar import signed by the [Secretary of State] or other official having custody of the company's publicly filed records in the state or other jurisdiction under whose law the company is formed.

COMMENT

Source—ULPA (2001) § 902, which was based on ULLCA § 1002.

§ 803. Activities Not Constituting Transacting Business

(a)   Activities of a foreign limited liability company which do not constitute transacting business in this state within the meaning of this [article] include:

(1)   maintaining, defending, or settling an action or proceeding;

(2)   carrying on any activity concerning its internal affairs, including holding meetings of its members or managers;

(3)   maintaining accounts in financial institutions;

(4)   maintaining offices or agencies for the transfer, exchange, and registration of the company's own securities or maintaining trustees or depositories with respect to those securities;

(5)   selling through independent contractors;

(6)   soliciting or obtaining orders, whether by mail or electronic means or through employees or agents or otherwise, if the orders require acceptance outside this state before they become contracts;

(7)   creating or acquiring indebtedness, mortgages, or security interests in real or personal property;

(8)   securing or collecting debts or enforcing mortgages or other security interests in property securing the debts and holding, protecting, or maintaining property so acquired;

(9)   conducting an isolated transaction that is completed within 30 days and is not in the course of similar transactions; and

(10) transacting business in interstate commerce.

(b) For purposes of this [article], the ownership in this state of income-producing real property or tangible personal property, other than property excluded under subsection (a), constitutes transacting business in this state.

(c) This section does not apply in determining the contacts or activities that may subject a foreign limited liability company to service of process, taxation, or regulation under law of this state other than this [act].

COMMENT

Source—ULPA (2001) § 903, which was based on ULLCA § 1003.

§ 804. Filing of Certificate of Authority

Unless the [Secretary of State] determines that an application for a certificate of authority does not comply with the filing requirements of this [act], the [Secretary of State], upon payment of all filing fees, shall file the application of a foreign limited liability company, prepare, sign, and file a certificate of authority to transact business in this state, and send a copy of the filed certificate, together with a receipt for the fees, to the company or its representative.

COMMENT

Source—ULPA (2001) § 904, which was based on ULLCA § 1004 and RULPA § 903.

§ 805. Noncomplying Name of Foreign Limited Liability Company

(a) A foreign limited liability company whose name does not comply with Section 108 may not obtain a certificate of authority until it adopts, for the purpose of transacting business in this state, an alternate name that complies with Section 108. A foreign limited liability company that adopts an alternate name under this subsection and obtains a certificate of authority with the alternate name need not comply with [fictitious or assumed name statute]. After obtaining a certificate of authority with an alternate name, a foreign limited liability company shall transact business in this state under the alternate name unless the company is authorized under [fictitious or assumed name statute] to transact business in this state under another name.

(b) If a foreign limited liability company authorized to transact business in this state changes its name to one that does not comply with Section 108, it may not thereafter transact business in this state until it complies with subsection (a) and obtains an amended certificate of authority.

COMMENT

Source—ULPA (2001) § 905, which was based on ULLCA § 1005.

§ 806. Revocation of Certificate of Authority

(a) A certificate of authority of a foreign limited liability company to transact business in this state may be revoked by the [Secretary of State] in the manner provided in subsections (b) and (c) if the company does not:

(1) pay, within 60 days after the due date, any fee, tax, or penalty due to the [Secretary of State] under this [act] or law other than this [act];

(2) deliver, within 60 days after the due date, its annual report required under Section 209;

(3) appoint and maintain an agent for service of process as required by Section 113(b); or

(4) deliver for filing a statement of a change under Section 114 within 30 days after a change has occurred in the name or address of the agent.

(b) To revoke a certificate of authority of a foreign limited liability company, the [Secretary of State] must prepare, sign, and file a notice of revocation and send a copy to the company's agent for service of process in this state, or if the company does not appoint and maintain a proper agent in this state, to the company's designated office. The notice must state:

(1)   the revocation's effective date, which must be at least 60 days after the date the [Secretary of State] sends the copy; and

(2)   the grounds for revocation under subsection (a).

(c)   The authority of a foreign limited liability company to transact business in this state ceases on the effective date of the notice of revocation unless before that date the company cures each ground for revocation stated in the notice filed under subsection (b). If the company cures each ground, the [Secretary of State] shall file a record so stating.

COMMENT

Source—ULPA (2001) § 906, which was based on ULLCA § 1006.

§ 807.   Cancellation of Certificate of Authority

To cancel its certificate of authority to transact business in this state, a foreign limited liability company must deliver to the [Secretary of State] for filing a notice of cancellation stating the name of the company and that the company desires to cancel its certificate of authority. The certificate is canceled when the notice becomes effective.

§ 808.   Effect of Failure to Have Certificate of Authority

(a)   A foreign limited liability company transacting business in this state may not maintain an action or proceeding in this state unless it has a certificate of authority to transact business in this state.

(b)   The failure of a foreign limited liability company to have a certificate of authority to transact business in this state does not impair the validity of a contract or act of the company or prevent the company from defending an action or proceeding in this state.

(c)   A member or manager of a foreign limited liability company is not liable for the debts, obligations, or other liabilities of the company solely because the company transacted business in this state without a certificate of authority.

(d)   If a foreign limited liability company transacts business in this state without a certificate of authority or cancels its certificate of authority, it appoints the [Secretary of State] as its agent for service of process for rights of action arising out of the transaction of business in this state.

COMMENT

Source—ULPA (2001) § 907, which was based on RULPA § 907(d) and ULLCA § 1008.

§ 809.   Action by [Attorney General]

The [Attorney General] may maintain an action to enjoin a foreign limited liability company from transacting business in this state in violation of this [article].

COMMENT

Source—ULPA (2001) § 908, which was based on RULPA § 908 and ULLCA § 1009.

[ARTICLE] 9
ACTIONS BY MEMBERS

§ 901.   Direct Action by Member

(a)   Subject to subsection (b), a member may maintain a direct action against another member, a manager, or the limited liability company to enforce the member's rights and otherwise protect the member's interests, including rights and interests under the operating agreement or this [act] or arising independently of the membership relationship.

(b)   A member maintaining a direct action under this section must plead and prove an actual or threatened injury that is not solely the result of an injury suffered or threatened to be suffered by the limited liability company.

COMMENT

Subsection (a)—Source: ULPA (2001) § 1001(a), which was based on RUPA Section 405(b). The subsection has been somewhat re-styled from the ULPA version, and the phrase "for legal or equitable relief" has been deleted as unnecessary. ULPA's reference to "with or without an accounting" has been deleted because the reference: (i) was to the partnership remedy of accounting, which reflected the aggregate nature of a partnership and is inapposite for an *entity* such as an LLC; and (ii) generated some confusion with the equitable claim for an accounting (in the nature of a constructive trust). The "entity-analog" to the partnership-as-aggregate notion of an accounting is the distinction between a direct and derivative claim.

The last phrase of this subsection ("or arising independently . . . ") comes from RUPA § 405(b)(3), does not create any new rights, obligations, or remedies, and is included merely to emphasize that a person's membership in an LLC does not preclude the person from enforcing rights existing "independently or the membership relationship."

Subsection (b)—Source: ULPA (2001) § 1001(b). The Comment to that subsection explains:

In ordinary contractual situations it is axiomatic that each party to a contract has standing to sue for breach of that contract. Within a limited partnership, however, different circumstances may exist. A partner does not have a direct claim against another partner merely because the other partner has breached the operating agreement. Likewise a partner's violation of this Act does not automatically create a direct claim for every other partner. To have standing in his, her, or its own right, a partner plaintiff must be able to show a harm that occurs independently of the harm caused or threatened to be caused to the limited partnership.

§ 902.   Derivative Action

A member may maintain a derivative action to enforce a right of a limited liability company if:

(1)   the member first makes a demand on the other members in a member-managed limited liability company, or the managers of a manager-managed limited liability company, requesting that they cause the company to bring an action to enforce the right, and the managers or other members do not bring the action within a reasonable time; or

(2)   a demand under paragraph (1) would be futile.

COMMENT

Source—ULPA (2001) § 1002, which was a re-styled version RULPA § 1001.

§ 903.   Proper Plaintiff

(a)   Except as otherwise provided in subsection (b), a derivative action under Section 902 may be maintained only by a person that is a member at the time the action is commenced and remains a member while the action continues.

(b)   If the sole plaintiff in a derivative action dies while the action is pending, the court may permit another member of the limited liability company to be substituted as plaintiff.

COMMENT

This section abandons the traditional "contemporaneous ownership" rule, on the theory that the protections of that rule are unnecessary given the closely-held nature of most limited liability companies and the built-in, statutory restrictions on persons becoming members.

Subsection (b)—This subsection will be inapposite if the limited liability company has only two members, one of whom is the derivative plaintiff. In that limited circumstance, the plaintiff's death would cause the derivative action to abate. The "pick your partner" principal enshrined in Section 502 would prevent the decedent's heirs from succeeding to plaintiff status in the derivative action. This Act does not take a position on whether the death of member abates a <u>direct</u> claim against the LLC or a fellow member.

§904. Pleading

In a derivative action under Section 902, the complaint must state with particularity:

(1) the date and content of the plaintiff's demand and the response to the demand by the managers or other members; or

(2) if a demand has not been made, the reasons a demand under Section 902(1) would be futile.

COMMENT

Source—ULPA (2001) § 1004, which was a re-styled version RULPA § 1003.

§905. Special Litigation Committee

(a) If a limited liability company is named as or made a party in a derivative proceeding, the company may appoint a special litigation committee to investigate the claims asserted in the proceeding and determine whether pursuing the action is in the best interests of the company. If the company appoints a special litigation committee, on motion by the committee made in the name of the company, except for good cause shown, the court shall stay discovery for the time reasonably necessary to permit the committee to make its investigation. This subsection does not prevent the court from enforcing a person's right to information under Section 410 or, for good cause shown, granting extraordinary relief in the form of a temporary restraining order or preliminary injunction.

(b) A special litigation committee may be composed of one or more disinterested and independent individuals, who may be members.

(c) A special litigation committee may be appointed:

(1) in a member-managed limited liability company:

(A) by the consent of a majority of the members not named as defendants or plaintiffs in the proceeding; and

(B) if all members are named as defendants or plaintiffs in the proceeding, by a majority of the members named as defendants; or

(2) in a manager-managed limited liability company:

(A) by a majority of the managers not named as defendants or plaintiffs in the proceeding; and

(B) if all managers are named as defendants or plaintiffs in the proceeding, by a majority of the managers named as defendants.

(d) After appropriate investigation, a special litigation committee may determine that it is in the best interests of the limited liability company that the proceeding:

(1) continue under the control of the plaintiff;

(2) continue under the control of the committee;

(3) be settled on terms approved by the committee; or

(4) be dismissed.

(e) After making a determination under subsection (d), a special litigation committee shall file with the court a statement of its determination and its report supporting its determination, giving notice to the plaintiff. The court shall determine whether the members of the committee were disinterested and independent and whether the committee conducted its investigation and made its recommendation in good faith, independently, and with reasonable care, with the committee having the burden of proof. If the court finds that the members of the committee were disinterested and independent and that the committee acted in good faith, independently, and with reasonable care, the court shall enforce the determination of the committee. Otherwise, the court shall dissolve the stay of discovery entered under subsection (a) and allow the action to proceed under the direction of the plaintiff.

COMMENT

Although special litigation committees are best known in the corporate field, they are no more inherently corporate than derivative litigation or the notion that an organization is a person distinct from its owners. An "SLC" can serve as an ADR mechanism, help protect an agreed upon arrangement from strike suits, protect the interests of members who are neither plaintiffs nor defendants (if any), and bring to any judicial decision the benefits of a specially tailored business judgment.

This section's approach corresponds to established law in most jurisdictions, modified to fit the typical governance structures of a limited liability company.

Subsection (a)—On the availability of Section 410 remedies pending the SLC's investigation, compare *Kaufman v. Computer Assoc. Int'l., Inc.*, No. Civ.A. 699-N, 2005 WL 3470589 at *1 (Del.Ch. Dec. 21, 2005, as revised) (presenting "the question of whether to stay a books and records action under 8 Del. C. § 220 at the request of a special litigation committee when a derivative action encompassing substantially the same allegations of wrongdoing filed by different plaintiffs is pending in another jurisdiction;" concluding "[f]or reasons that have much to do with the light burden imposed by the plaintiff's demand in this case . . . that the special litigation committee's motion to stay the books and records action should be denied").

Subsection (d)—The standard stated for judicial review of the SLC determination follows *Auerbach v. Bennett*, 47 N.Y.2d 619, 419 N.Y.S.2d 920 (N.Y. 1979) rather than *Zapata Corp. v. Maldonado*, 430 A.2d 779 (Del. 1981), because the latter's reference to a court's business judgment has generally not been followed in other states.

Houle v. Low, 407 Mass. 810, 822, 556 N.E.2d 51, 58 (Mass. 1990) contains an excellent explanation of the court's role in reviewing an SLC decision:

> The value of a special litigation committee is coextensive with the extent to which that committee truly exercises business judgment. In order to ensure that special litigation committees do act for the [entity]'s best interest, a good deal of judicial oversight is necessary in each case. At the same time, however, courts must be careful not to usurp the committee's valuable role in exercising business judgment. . . . [A] special litigation committee must be independent, unbiased, and act in good faith. Moreover, such a committee must conduct a thorough and careful analysis regarding the plaintiff's derivative suit, . . . The burden of proving that these procedural requirements have been met must rest, in all fairness, on the party capable of making that proof—the [entity].

For a discussion of how a court should approach the question of independence, *see Einhorn v. Culea*, 612 N.W.2d 78, 91 (Wis.2000).

§ 906. Proceeds and Expenses

(a)   Except as otherwise provided in subsection (b):

(1)   any proceeds or other benefits of a derivative action under Section 902, whether by judgment, compromise, or settlement, belong to the limited liability company and not to the plaintiff; and

(2)   if the plaintiff receives any proceeds, the plaintiff shall remit them immediately to the company.

(b)   If a derivative action under Section 902 is successful in whole or in part, the court may award the plaintiff reasonable expenses, including reasonable attorney's fees and costs, from the recovery of the limited liability company.

COMMENT

Source—ULPA (2001) § 1005, which was a re-styled version RULPA § 1004.

[ARTICLE] 10
MERGER, CONVERSION, AND DOMESTICATION

§ 1001.   Definitions

In this [article]:

(1)   "Constituent limited liability company" means a constituent organization that is a limited liability company.

(2)   "Constituent organization" means an organization that is party to a merger.

(3)   "Converted organization" means the organization into which a converting organization converts pursuant to Sections 1006 through 1009.

(4)   "Converting limited liability company" means a converting organization that is a limited liability company.

(5)   "Converting organization" means an organization that converts into another organization pursuant to Section 1006.

(6)   "Domesticated company" means the company that exists after a domesticating foreign limited liability company or limited liability company effects a domestication pursuant to Sections 1010 through 1013.

(7)   "Domesticating company" means the company that effects a domestication pursuant to Sections 1010 through 1013.

(8)   "Governing statute" means the statute that governs an organization's internal affairs.

(9)   "Organization" means a general partnership, including a limited liability partnership, limited partnership, including a limited liability limited partnership, limited liability company, business trust, corporation, or any other person having a governing statute. The term includes a domestic or foreign organization regardless of whether organized for profit.

(10)   "Organizational documents" means:

(A)   for a domestic or foreign general partnership, its partnership agreement;

(B)   for a limited partnership or foreign limited partnership, its certificate of limited partnership and partnership agreement;

(C)   for a domestic or foreign limited liability company, its certificate or articles of organization and operating agreement, or comparable records as provided in its governing statute;

(D)   for a business trust, its agreement of trust and declaration of trust;

(E)   for a domestic or foreign corporation for profit, its articles of incorporation, bylaws, and other agreements among its shareholders which are authorized by its governing statute, or comparable records as provided in its governing statute; and

(F)   for any other organization, the basic records that create the organization and determine its internal governance and the relations among the persons that own it, have an interest in it, or are members of it.

(11)   "Personal liability" means liability for a debt, obligation, or other liability of an organization which is imposed on a person that co-owns, has an interest in, or is a member of the organization:

(A)   by the governing statute solely by reason of the person co-owning, having an interest in, or being a member of the organization; or

(B)   by the organization's organizational documents under a provision of the governing statute authorizing those documents to make one or more specified persons liable for all or specified debts, obligations, or other liabilities of the organization solely by reason of the person or persons co-owning, having an interest in, or being a member of the organization.

(12) "Surviving organization" means an organization into which one or more other organizations are merged whether the organization preexisted the merger or was created by the merger.

COMMENT

This article is based on Article 11 of ULPA (2001) and differs principally in treating domestications as a separate type of organic transaction rather than as a subset of conversions.

§ 1002.   Merger

(a)   A limited liability company may merge with one or more other constituent organizations pursuant to this section, Sections 1003 through 1005, and a plan of merger, if:

(1)   the governing statute of each of the other organizations authorizes the merger;

(2)   the merger is not prohibited by the law of a jurisdiction that enacted any of the governing statutes; and

(3)   each of the other organizations complies with its governing statute in effecting the merger.

(b)   A plan of merger must be in a record and must include:

(1)   the name and form of each constituent organization;

(2)   the name and form of the surviving organization and, if the surviving organization is to be created by the merger, a statement to that effect;

(3)   the terms and conditions of the merger, including the manner and basis for converting the interests in each constituent organization into any combination of money, interests in the surviving organization, and other consideration;

(4)   if the surviving organization is to be created by the merger, the surviving organization's organizational documents that are proposed to be in a record; and

(5)   if the surviving organization is not to be created by the merger, any amendments to be made by the merger to the surviving organization's organizational documents that are, or are proposed to be, in a record.

§ 1003.   Action on Plan of Merger by Constituent Limited Liability Company

(a)   Subject to Section 1014, a plan of merger must be consented to by all the members of a constituent limited liability company.

(b)   Subject to Section 1014 and any contractual rights, after a merger is approved, and at any time before articles of merger are delivered to the [Secretary of State] for filing under Section 1004, a constituent limited liability company may amend the plan or abandon the merger:

(1)   as provided in the plan; or

(2)   except as otherwise prohibited in the plan, with the same consent as was required to approve the plan.

§ 1004.   Filings Required for Merger; Effective Date

(a)   After each constituent organization has approved a merger, articles of merger must be signed on behalf of:

(1)   each constituent limited liability company, as provided in Section 203(a); and

(2)   each other constituent organization, as provided in its governing statute.

(b)   Articles of merger under this section must include:

(1)   the name and form of each constituent organization and the jurisdiction of its governing statute;

(2)   the name and form of the surviving organization, the jurisdiction of its governing statute, and, if the surviving organization is created by the merger, a statement to that effect;

(3)   the date the merger is effective under the governing statute of the surviving organization;

(4)   if the surviving organization is to be created by the merger:

(A)   if it will be a limited liability company, the company's certificate of organization; or

(B)   if it will be an organization other than a limited liability company, the organizational document that creates the organization that is in a public record;

(5)   if the surviving organization preexists the merger, any amendments provided for in the plan of merger for the organizational document that created the organization that are in a public record;

(6)   a statement as to each constituent organization that the merger was approved as required by the organization's governing statute;

(7)   if the surviving organization is a foreign organization not authorized to transact business in this state, the street and mailing addresses of an office that the [Secretary of State] may use for the purposes of Section 1005(b); and

(8)   any additional information required by the governing statute of any constituent organization.

(c)   Each constituent limited liability company shall deliver the articles of merger for filing in the [office of the Secretary of State].

(d)   A merger becomes effective under this [article]:

(1)   if the surviving organization is a limited liability company, upon the later of:

(A)   compliance with subsection (c); or

(B)   subject to Section 205(c), as specified in the articles of merger; or

(2)   if the surviving organization is not a limited liability company, as provided by the governing statute of the surviving organization.

§ 1005.   Effect of Merger

(a)   When a merger becomes effective:

(1)   the surviving organization continues or comes into existence;

(2)   each constituent organization that merges into the surviving organization ceases to exist as a separate entity;

(3)   all property owned by each constituent organization that ceases to exist vests in the surviving organization;

(4)   all debts, obligations, or other liabilities of each constituent organization that ceases to exist continue as debts, obligations, or other liabilities of the surviving organization;

(5)   an action or proceeding pending by or against any constituent organization that ceases to exist may be continued as if the merger had not occurred;

(6)   except as prohibited by other law, all of the rights, privileges, immunities, powers, and purposes of each constituent organization that ceases to exist vest in the surviving organization;

(7)   except as otherwise provided in the plan of merger, the terms and conditions of the plan of merger take effect; and

(8)   except as otherwise agreed, if a constituent limited liability company ceases to exist, the merger does not dissolve the limited liability company for the purposes of [Article] 7;

(9)   if the surviving organization is created by the merger:

(A)   if it is a limited liability company, the certificate of organization becomes effective; or

    (B) if it is an organization other than a limited liability company, the organizational document that creates the organization becomes effective; and

    (10) if the surviving organization preexisted the merger, any amendments provided for in the articles of merger for the organizational document that created the organization become effective.

  (b) A surviving organization that is a foreign organization consents to the jurisdiction of the courts of this state to enforce any debt, obligation, or other liability owed by a constituent organization, if before the merger the constituent organization was subject to suit in this state on the debt, obligation, or other liability. A surviving organization that is a foreign organization and not authorized to transact business in this state appoints the [Secretary of State] as its agent for service of process for the purposes of enforcing a debt, obligation, or other liability under this subsection. Service on the [Secretary of State] under this subsection must be made in the same manner and has the same consequences as in Section 116(c) and (d).

§ 1006.   Conversion

  (a) An organization other than a limited liability company or a foreign limited liability company may convert to a limited liability company, and a limited liability company may convert to an organization other than a foreign limited liability company pursuant to this section, Sections 1007 through 1009, and a plan of conversion, if:

    (1) the other organization's governing statute authorizes the conversion;

    (2) the conversion is not prohibited by the law of the jurisdiction that enacted the other organization's governing statute; and

    (3) the other organization complies with its governing statute in effecting the conversion.

  (b) A plan of conversion must be in a record and must include:

    (1) the name and form of the organization before conversion;

    (2) the name and form of the organization after conversion;

    (3) the terms and conditions of the conversion, including the manner and basis for converting interests in the converting organization into any combination of money, interests in the converted organization, and other consideration; and

    (4) the organizational documents of the converted organization that are, or are proposed to be, in a record.

§ 1007.   Action on Plan of Conversion by Converting Limited Liability Company

  (a) Subject to Section 1014, a plan of conversion must be consented to by all the members of a converting limited liability company.

  (b) Subject to Section 1014 and any contractual rights, after a conversion is approved, and at any time before articles of conversion are delivered to the [Secretary of State] for filing under Section 1008, a converting limited liability company may amend the plan or abandon the conversion:

    (1) as provided in the plan; or

    (2) except as otherwise prohibited in the plan, by the same consent as was required to approve the plan.

§ 1008.   Filings Required for Conversion; Effective Date

  (a) After a plan of conversion is approved:

    (1) a converting limited liability company shall deliver to the [Secretary of State] for filing articles of conversion, which must be signed as provided in Section 203(a) and must include:

      (A) a statement that the limited liability company has been converted into another organization;

(B)   the name and form of the organization and the jurisdiction of its governing statute;

(C)   the date the conversion is effective under the governing statute of the converted organization;

(D)   a statement that the conversion was approved as required by this [act];

(E)   a statement that the conversion was approved as required by the governing statute of the converted organization; and

(F)   if the converted organization is a foreign organization not authorized to transact business in this state, the street and mailing addresses of an office which the [Secretary of State] may use for the purposes of Section 1009(c); and

(2)   if the converting organization is not a converting limited liability company, the converting organization shall deliver to the [Secretary of State] for filing a certificate of organization, which must include, in addition to the information required by Section 201(b):

(A)   a statement that the converted organization was converted from another organization;

(B)   the name and form of that converting organization and the jurisdiction of its governing statute; and

(C)   a statement that the conversion was approved in a manner that complied with the converting organization's governing statute.

(b)   A conversion becomes effective:

(1)   if the converted organization is a limited liability company, when the certificate of organization takes effect; and

(2)   if the converted organization is not a limited liability company, as provided by the governing statute of the converted organization.

§ 1009.   Effect of Conversion

(a)   An organization that has been converted pursuant to this [article] is for all purposes the same entity that existed before the conversion.

(b)   When a conversion takes effect:

(1)   all property owned by the converting organization remains vested in the converted organization;

(2)   all debts, obligations, or other liabilities of the converting organization continue as debts, obligations, or other liabilities of the converted organization;

(3)   an action or proceeding pending by or against the converting organization may be continued as if the conversion had not occurred;

(4)   except as prohibited by law other than this [act], all of the rights, privileges, immunities, powers, and purposes of the converting organization remain vested in the converted organization;

(5)   except as otherwise provided in the plan of conversion, the terms and conditions of the plan of conversion take effect; and

(6)   except as otherwise agreed, the conversion does not dissolve a converting limited liability company for the purposes of [Article] 7.

(c)   A converted organization that is a foreign organization consents to the jurisdiction of the courts of this state to enforce any debt, obligation, or other liability for which the converting limited liability company is liable if, before the conversion, the converting limited liability company was subject to suit in this state on the debt, obligation, or other liability. A converted organization that is a foreign organization and not authorized to transact business in this state appoints the [Secretary of State] as its agent for service of process for purposes of enforcing a debt, obligation, or other liability under this subsection. Service on the

[Secretary of State] under this subsection must be made in the same manner and has the same consequences as in Section 116(c) and (d).

§ 1010.   Domestication

(a)   A foreign limited liability company may become a limited liability company pursuant to this section, Sections 1011 through 1013, and a plan of domestication, if:

(1)   the foreign limited liability company's governing statute authorizes the domestication;

(2)   the domestication is not prohibited by the law of the jurisdiction that enacted the governing statute; and

(3)   the foreign limited liability company complies with its governing statute in effecting the domestication.

(b)   A limited liability company may become a foreign limited liability company pursuant to this section, Sections 1011 through 1013, and a plan of domestication, if:

(1)   the foreign limited liability company's governing statute authorizes the domestication;

(2)   the domestication is not prohibited by the law of the jurisdiction that enacted the governing statute; and

(3)   the foreign limited liability company complies with its governing statute in effecting the domestication.

(c)   A plan of domestication must be in a record and must include:

(1)   the name of the domesticating company before domestication and the jurisdiction of its governing statute;

(2)   the name of the domesticated company after domestication and the jurisdiction of its governing statute;

(3)   the terms and conditions of the domestication, including the manner and basis for converting interests in the domesticating company into any combination of money, interests in the domesticated company, and other consideration; and

(4)   the organizational documents of the domesticated company that are, or are proposed to be, in a record.

§ 1011.   Action on Plan of Domestication by Domesticating Limited Liability Company

(a)   A plan of domestication must be consented to:

(1)   by all the members, subject to Section 1014, if the domesticating company is a limited liability company; and

(2)   as provided in the domesticating company's governing statute, if the company is a foreign limited liability company.

(b)   Subject to any contractual rights, after a domestication is approved, and at any time before articles of domestication are delivered to the [Secretary of State] for filing under Section 1012, a domesticating limited liability company may amend the plan or abandon the domestication:

(1)   as provided in the plan; or

(2)   except as otherwise prohibited in the plan, by the same consent as was required to approve the plan.

§ 1012.   Filings Required for Domestication; Effective Date

(a)   After a plan of domestication is approved, a domesticating company shall deliver to the [Secretary of State] for filing articles of domestication, which must include:

(1)   a statement, as the case may be, that the company has been domesticated from or into another jurisdiction;

(2)   the name of the domesticating company and the jurisdiction of its governing statute;

(3)   the name of the domesticated company and the jurisdiction of its governing statute;

(4)   the date the domestication is effective under the governing statute of the domesticated company;

(5)   if the domesticating company was a limited liability company, a statement that the domestication was approved as required by this [act];

(6)   if the domesticating company was a foreign limited liability company, a statement that the domestication was approved as required by the governing statute of the other jurisdiction; and

(7)   if the domesticated company was a foreign limited liability company not authorized to transact business in this state, the street and mailing addresses of an office that the [Secretary of State] may use for the purposes of Section 1013(b).

(b)   A domestication becomes effective:

(1)   when the certificate of organization takes effect, if the domesticated company is a limited liability company; and

(2)   according to the governing statute of the domesticated company, if the domesticated organization is a foreign limited liability company.

§1013.   Effect of Domestication

(a)   When a domestication takes effect:

(1)   the domesticated company is for all purposes the company that existed before the domestication;

(2)   all property owned by the domesticating company remains vested in the domesticated company;

(3)   all debts, obligations, or other liabilities of the domesticating company continue as debts, obligations, or other liabilities of the domesticated company;

(4)   an action or proceeding pending by or against a domesticating company may be continued as if the domestication had not occurred;

(5)   except as prohibited by other law, all of the rights, privileges, immunities, powers, and purposes of the domesticating company remain vested in the domesticated company;

(6)   except as otherwise provided in the plan of domestication, the terms and conditions of the plan of domestication take effect; and

(7)   except as otherwise agreed, the domestication does not dissolve a domesticating limited liability company for the purposes of [Article] 7.

(b)   A domesticated company that is a foreign limited liability company consents to the jurisdiction of the courts of this state to enforce any debt, obligation, or other liability owed by the domesticating company, if, before the domestication, the domesticating company was subject to suit in this state on the debt, obligation, or other liability. A domesticated company that is a foreign limited liability company and not authorized to transact business in this state appoints the [Secretary of State] as its agent for service of process for purposes of enforcing a debt, obligation, or other liability under this subsection. Service on the [Secretary of State] under this subsection must be made in the same manner and has the same consequences as in Section 116(c) and (d).

(c)   If a limited liability company has adopted and approved a plan of domestication under Section 1010 providing for the company to be domesticated in a foreign jurisdiction, a statement surrendering the company's certificate of organization must be delivered to the [Secretary of State] for filing setting forth:

    (1)   the name of the company;

    (2)   a statement that the certificate of organization is being surrendered in connection with the domestication of the company in a foreign jurisdiction;

    (3)   a statement the domestication was approved as required by this [act]; and

    (4)   the jurisdiction of formation of the domesticated foreign limited liability company.

§ 1014.   Restrictions on Approval of Mergers, Conversions, and Domestications

    (a)   If a member of a constituent, converting, or domesticating limited liability company will have personal liability with respect to a surviving, converted, or domesticated organization, approval or amendment of a plan of merger, conversion, or domestication is ineffective without the consent of the member, unless:

    (1)   the company's operating agreement provides for approval of a merger, conversion, or domestication with the consent of fewer than all the members; and

    (2)   the member has consented to the provision of the operating agreement.

    (b)   A member does not give the consent required by subsection (a) merely by consenting to a provision of the operating agreement that permits the operating agreement to be amended with the consent of fewer than all the members.

§ 1015.   [Article] Not Exclusive

    This [article] does not preclude an entity from being merged, converted, or domesticated under law other than this [act].

[ARTICLE] 11
MISCELLANEOUS PROVISIONS

§ 1101.   Uniformity of Application and Construction

    In applying and construing this uniform act, consideration must be given to the need to promote uniformity of the law with respect to its subject matter among states that enact it.

§ 1102.   Relation to Electronic Signatures in Global and National Commerce Act

    This [act] modifies, limits, and supersedes the federal Electronic Signatures in Global and National Commerce Act, 15 U.S.C. Section 7001 et seq., but does not modify, limit, or supersede Section 101(c) of that act, 15 U.S.C. Section 7001(c), or authorize electronic delivery of any of the notices described in Section 103(b) of that act, 15 U.S.C. Section 7003(b).

§ 1103.   Savings Clause

    This [act] does not affect an action commenced, proceeding brought, or right accrued before this [act] takes effect.

§ 1104.   Application to Existing Relationships

    (a)   Before [all-inclusive date], this [act] governs only:

    (1)   a limited liability company formed on or after [the effective date of this act]; and

    (2)   except as otherwise provided in subsection (c), a limited liability company formed before [the effective date of this act] which elects, in the manner provided in its operating agreement or by law for amending the operating agreement, to be subject to this [act].

    (b)   Except as otherwise provided in subsection (c), on and after [all-inclusive date] this [act] governs all limited liability companies.

(c)   For the purposes applying this [act] to a limited liability company formed before [the effective date of this act]:

(1)   the company's articles of organization are deemed to be the company's certificate of organization; and

(2)   for the purposes of applying Section 102(10) and subject to Section 112(d), language in the company's articles of organization designating the company's management structure operates as if that language were in the operating agreement.

Legislative Note: *It is recommended that the "all-inclusive" date should be at least one year after the date of enactment but no longer than two years.*

Each enacting jurisdiction should consider whether: (i) this Act makes material changes to the "default" (or "gap filler") rules of jurisdiction's predecessor statute; and (ii) if so, whether subsection (c) should carry forward any of those rules for pre-existing limited liability companies. In this assessment, the focus is on pre-existing limited liability companies that have left default rules in place, whether advisedly or not. The central question is whether, for such limited liability companies, expanding subsection (c) is necessary to prevent material changes to the members' "deal."

For an example of this type of analysis in the context of another business entity act, see the Uniform Limited Partnership Act (2001), § 1206(c).

Section 301 (de-codifying statutory apparent authority) does not require any special transition provisions, because: (i) applying the law of agency, as explained in the Comments to Sections 301 and 407, will produce appropriate results; and (ii) the notion of "lingering apparent authority" will protect any third party that has previously relied on the statutory apparent authority of a member of a particular member-managed LLC or a manager of a particular manager-managed LLC. RESTATEMENT (THIRD) OF AGENCY § 3.11, cmt. c (2006).

It is unnecessary to expand subsection (c) of this Act if the state's predecessor act is the original Uniform Limited Liability Company Act, revised to provide for perpetual duration.

COMMENT

Subsection (c)—When a pre-existing limited liability company becomes subject to this Act, the company ceases to be governed by the predecessor act, including whatever requirements that act might have imposed for the contents of the articles of organization.

§ 1105.   Repeals

Effective [all-inclusive date], the following acts and parts of acts are repealed: [the state limited liability company act, as amended, and in effect immediately before the effective date of this act].

§ 1106.   Effective Date

This [act] takes effect on. . . .

REVISED UNIFORM LIMITED LIABILITY COMPANY ACT (2013)

Table of Contents

[ARTICLE] 1

GENERAL PROVISIONS

[ARTICLE] 2

FORMATION; CERTIFICATE OF ORGANIZATION AND OTHER FILINGS

RULLCA (2013)

[ARTICLE] 3

RELATIONS OF MEMBERS AND MANAGERS TO PERSONS DEALING WITH LIMITED LIABILITY COMPANY

[ARTICLE] 4

RELATIONS OF MEMBERS TO EACH OTHER AND TO LIMITED LIABILITY COMPANY

[ARTICLE] 5

TRANSFERABLE INTERESTS AND RIGHTS OF TRANSFEREES AND CREDITORS

[ARTICLE] 6

DISSOCIATION

[ARTICLE] 7

DISSOLUTION AND WINDING UP

RULLCA (2013)

RULLCA (2013)

[PART] 3

INTEREST EXCHANGE

[PART] 4

CONVERSION

[PART] 5

DOMESTICATION

[ARTICLE] 11

MISCELLANEOUS PROVISIONS

* * *

PREFATORY NOTE TO 2011 AND 2013 HARMONIZATION AMENDMENTS

From 2009 to 2013, the Uniform Law Conference undertook an intensive effort to harmonize, to the extent possible, all uniform acts pertaining to unincorporated organizations. As part of that effort, the Uniform Limited Liability Company Act ("ULLCA") underwent four types of changes: substantive; major improvements in language; minor revisions in language for the sake of harmonization; and relocation within this particular "spoke" of provisions that are part of the "HUB" in the new Uniform Business Organizations Code ("UBOC").

RULLCA (2013)

Substantive Changes

The three most significant substantive changes are:

- eliminating the possibility of a shelf LLC (with the attendant, complex provision requiring two filings with the filing office) and providing instead that "[a] limited liability company is formed when the company's certificate of organization becomes effective and at least one person becomes a member," Section 201(d);

- replacing the "ordinary care/business judgment rule" standard with the duty to "refrain from engaging in grossly negligent or reckless conduct, willful or intentional misconduct, or knowing violation of law," Section 409(c);

- recognizing that, when an LLC has only one member, the "pick your partner" concept is inapposite and providing that, in that situation, the foreclosure of a charging order pertains to the entire ownership interest, not just the economic rights, Section 503(f).

Other substantive changes include: (i) providing a narrow exception to the rule that the amendments to the operating agreement control the rights of person dissociated as a members and of persons that had previously become transferees, Section 107(b)(2); (ii) eliminating the requirement that a domestic LLC designate and maintain an in-state office, Section 201; (iii) requiring that the annual report list the name of at least one member if the LLC is member-managed and one manager if the LLC is manger-managed, Section 212(a)(4) and (5); and (iv) expressly authorizing a limited liability company to provide advancements to a person entitled to indemnification, Section 408(c).

Substantial Improvements to Language

The most significant improvements in language appear in Section 105 (formerly Section 110), the first of three sections addressing the operating agreement. The structure of Section 105 is far less complicated than the structure of former Section 110.

Harmonization-Based Language Changes

Minor changes in language for the sake of harmonization appear throughout the act. For example, Section 202(b) is revised as follows:

(b)   To amend its certificate of organization, a limited liability company must deliver to the [Secretary of State] for filing an amendment stating:

(1)   the name of the company;

(2)   the date of filing of its initial certificate of organization; and

(3)   the changes the text of the amendment makes to the certificate as most recently amended or restated.

Relocation and Renumbering of HUB-Based Provisions

The Harmonization Project included both the harmonization of various stand-alone acts and the compilation of UBOC, which comprises a "HUB" (somewhat analogous to Article 1 of the Uniform Commercial Code) and various spokes. Each spoke pertains to a different type of organization (*e.g.*, limited liability company, statutory trust entity). Naturally, spokes in UBOC do not repeat the provisions from the HUB. In contrast, each stand-alone act includes provisions that appear in the HUB in the Code.

So that the section numbers of this "spoke" correspond with the spoke provisions in the Code, "HUB"-based provisions of this Act have been renumbered to appear at the end of articles. *See, e.g.*, Sections 112–21.

* * *

[ARTICLE] 1

GENERAL PROVISIONS

§ 101.   Short Title

This [act] may be cited as the Uniform Limited Liability Company Act.

COMMENT

This Act is drafted to replace a state's current limited liability company statute, regardless of whether that statute is based on ULLCA (1996), ULLCA (2006), or other source. Section 110 contains transition provisions.

§ 102.   Definitions

In this [act]:

(1)   "Certificate of organization" means the certificate required by Section 201. The term includes the certificate as amended or restated.

(2)   "Contribution", except in the phrase "right of contribution", means property or a benefit described in Section 402 which is provided by a person to a limited liability company to become a member or in the person's capacity as a member.

(3)   "Debtor in bankruptcy" means a person that is the subject of:

(A)   an order for relief under Title 11 of the United States Code or a comparable order under a successor statute of general application; or

(B)   a comparable order under federal, state, or foreign law governing insolvency.

(4)   "Distribution" means a transfer of money or other property from a limited liability company to a person on account of a transferable interest or in the person's capacity as a member. The term:

(A)   includes:

(i)   a redemption or other purchase by a limited liability company of a transferable interest; and

(ii)   a transfer to a member in return for the member's relinquishment of any right to participate as a member in the management or conduct of the company's activities and affairs or to have access to records or other information concerning the company's activities and affairs; and

(B)   does not include amounts constituting reasonable compensation for present or past service or payments made in the ordinary course of business under a bona fide retirement plan or other bona fide benefits program.

(5)   "Foreign limited liability company" means an unincorporated entity formed under the law of a jurisdiction other than this state which would be a limited liability company if formed under the law of this state.

(6)   "Jurisdiction", used to refer to a political entity, means the United States, a state, a foreign county, or a political subdivision of a foreign country.

(7)   "Jurisdiction of formation" means the jurisdiction whose law governs the internal affairs of an entity.

(8)   "Limited liability company", except in the phrase "foreign limited liability company" and in [Article] 10, means an entity formed under this [act] or which becomes subject to this [act] under [Article] 10 or Section 110.

(9)   "Manager" means a person that under the operating agreement of a manager-managed limited liability company is responsible, alone or in concert with others, for performing the management functions stated in Section 407(c).

(10) "Manager-managed limited liability company" means a limited liability company that qualifies under Section 407(a).

(11) "Member" means a person that:

(A) has become a member of a limited liability company under Section 401 or was a member in a company when the company became subject to this [act] under Section 110; and

(B) has not dissociated under Section 602.

(12) "Member-managed limited liability company" means a limited liability company that is not a manager-managed limited liability company.

(13) "Operating agreement" means the agreement, whether or not referred to as an operating agreement and whether oral, implied, in a record, or in any combination thereof, of all the members of a limited liability company, including a sole member, concerning the matters described in Section 105(a). The term includes the agreement as amended or restated.

(14) "Organizer" means a person that acts under Section 201 to form a limited liability company.

(15) "Person" means an individual, business corporation, nonprofit corporation, partnership, limited partnership, limited liability company, [general cooperative association,] limited cooperative association, unincorporated nonprofit association, statutory trust, business trust, common-law business trust, estate, trust, association, joint venture, public corporation, government or governmental subdivision, agency, or instrumentality, or any other legal or commercial entity.

(16) "Principal office" means the principal executive office of a limited liability company or foreign limited liability company, whether or not the office is located in this state.

(17) "Property" means all property, whether real, personal, or mixed or tangible or intangible, or any right or interest therein.

(18) "Record", used as a noun, means information that is inscribed on a tangible medium or that is stored in an electronic or other medium and is retrievable in perceivable form.

(19) "Registered agent" means an agent of a limited liability company or foreign limited liability company which is authorized to receive service of any process, notice, or demand required or permitted by law to be served on the company.

(20) "Registered foreign limited liability company" means a foreign limited liability company that is registered to do business in this state pursuant to a statement of registration filed by the [Secretary of State].

(21) "Sign" means, with present intent to authenticate or adopt a record:

(A) to execute or adopt a tangible symbol; or

(B) to attach to or logically associate with the record an electronic symbol, sound, or process.

(22) "State" means a state of the United States, the District of Columbia, Puerto Rico, the United States Virgin Islands, or any territory or insular possession subject to the jurisdiction of the United States.

(23) "Transfer" includes:

(A) an assignment;

(B) a conveyance;

(C) a sale;

(D) a lease;

(E) an encumbrance, including a mortgage or security interest;

(F) a gift; and

(G) a transfer by operation of law.

(24) "Transferable interest" means the right, as initially owned by a person in the person's capacity as a member, to receive distributions from a limited liability company, whether or not the person remains a member or continues to own any part of the right. The term applies to any fraction of the interest, by whomever owned.

(25) "Transferee" means a person to which all or part of a transferable interest has been transferred, whether or not the transferor is a member. The term includes a person that owns a transferable interest under Section 603(a)(3).

COMMENT

This Section contains definitions for terms used throughout the act, while Section 1001 contains definitions specific to Article 10's provisions on mergers, conversions, interest exchanges, and domestications.

"Certificate of organization" [(1)]—The original ULLCA and most other LLC statutes use "articles of organization" rather than "certificate of organization." This act purposely uses the latter term to signal that the certificate: (i) merely reflects the existence of an LLC (rather than being the locus for important governance rules); and (ii) is significantly different from articles of *incorporation*, which have a substantially greater power to affect *inter se* rules for the corporate entity and its owners. For the relationship between the certificate of organization and the operating agreement, see Section 107(d).

"Contribution" [(2)]—This definition serves to distinguish capital contributions from other circumstances under which a member or would-be member might provide benefits to a limited liability company (*e.g.*, providing services to the LLC as an employee or independent contractor, leasing property to the LLC).

This definition also distinguishes "contributions" from capital raised from transferees who invest; to be a contribution, the property or benefit must be "provided by a person . . . to become a partner or in the person's capacity as a partner." This distinction is ubiquitous in the law of unincorporated business organizations. *See, e.g.*, N.Y. LTD. LIAB. CO. LAW § 102(f) (McKinney 2013) (" 'Contribution' means any cash, property, services rendered, or a promissory note or other binding obligation to contribute cash or property or to render services that a member contributes to a limited liability company in his or her capacity as a member."); DEL. CODE ANN. tit. 6, § 17–101(2) (West 2013) (" 'Contribution' means any cash, property, services rendered or a promissory note or other obligation to contribute cash or property or to perform services, which a person contributes to a limited liability company in the person's capacity as a partner.").

In contrast, operating agreements sometimes provide for contributions from transferees. In such circumstances, the default rules for liquidating distributions should be altered accordingly. *See* Section 707(b)(1) (referring to distributions to be made "to each person owning a transferable interest that reflects *contributions* made and not previously returned") (emphasis added).

"Distribution" [(4)(A)—redemptions included]—This provision specifically refers to transactions between a limited liability company and one of its members, which in the corporate context would be labeled a "redemption." The paragraph has subparts because ownership interests in an LLC are conceptually bifurcated into economic rights ("transferable interest") and governance and information rights.

Under Section 404(a), "[a]ny distribution made by a limited liability company before its dissolution and winding up must be in equal shares among members and persons dissociated as members . . . ." Since a redemption is a distribution, absent authorization in the operating agreement an LLC may not redeem the interest of one member or transferee without redeeming (or at least offering to redeem) the interests of all other members and transferees to a comparable extent.

The law of close corporations has flirted with a similar notion. *See, e.g.*, *Donahue v. Rodd Electrotype Co. of New England, Inc.*, 367 Mass. 578, 598, 328 N.E.2d 505, 518 (1975) (stating, with regard to closely held corporations, "if the stockholder whose shares were purchased was a member of the controlling group, the controlling stockholders must cause the corporation to offer each stockholder an equal opportunity to sell a ratable number of his shares to the corporation at an identical price"); *Toner v. Baltimore Envelope Co.*, 304 Md. 256, 273, 498 A.2d 642, 650 (1985) (rejecting the "per se breach of duty" approach); *Wilkes v. Springside Nursing Home, Inc.*, 370 Mass. 842, 850, 353 N.E.2d 657, 663 (1976) (stating that "untempered application of the strict good faith standard enunciated in *Donahue* to . . . will result in the imposition of limitations on legitimate action by the controlling group in a close corporation which will unduly hamper its effectiveness in managing the corporation in the best interests of all concerned").

An operating agreement can override Section 404(a)'s equal treatment requirement without specifically mentioning redemptions.

Example: Ryan, LLC is a manager-managed limited liability company whose operating agreement: (i) includes a list (the "protected list") of decisions or actions that may be taken only with the consent of all members; and (ii) provides that all other decisions and acts may be taken as the manager determines. The protected list does not include redemptions. The operating agreement overrides the Section 404(a)'s equal treatment requirement.

[(4)(B)—exclusion]—This exclusion affects the reach of: (i) the charging order remedy under Section 503; and (ii) Section 405's clawback provision. The effect on the clawback provision reflects the law in several states, *see, e.g.*, DEL. CODE ANN., tit. 6, § 18–607(b) (2012) and VA. CODE ANN. § 13.1–1036 (2012), and makes sense conceptually and as a matter of policy. *See In re Tri-River Trading, LLC*, 329 B.R. 252, 266 (B.A.P. 8th Cir. 2005), *aff'd,* 452 F.3d 756 (8th Cir. 2006) ("We know of no principle of law which suggests that a manager of a company is required to give up agreed upon salary to pay creditors when business turns bad.").

"Foreign limited liability company" [(5)]—Some statutes have elaborate definitions addressing the question of whether an entity organized under the law of another jurisdiction is a "foreign limited liability company." The New York statute, for example, defines a "foreign limited liability company" as:

> an unincorporated organization formed under the laws of any jurisdiction, including any foreign country, other than the laws of this state (i) that is not authorized to do business in this state under any other law of this state and (ii) of which some or all of the persons who are entitled (A) to receive a distribution of the assets thereof upon the dissolution of the organization or otherwise or (B) to exercise voting rights with respect to an interest in the organization have, or are entitled or authorized to have, under the laws of such other jurisdiction, limited liability for the contractual obligations or other liabilities of the organization.

N.Y. LTD. LIAB. CO. LAW § 102(k) (McKinney 2012). In contrast, Delaware takes a succinct and entirely formalistic approach. DEL. CODE ANN. tit. 6, § 18–101(4) (2012) (stating that the foreign limited liability company is one that is "denominated as such").

This definition, in contrast, intends a flexible, comparative approach. If a particular type of foreign entity has key legal characteristics that approximate the essential legal characteristics of a domestic limited liability company, that particular type of foreign entity is a foreign limited liability company under this act.

"Jurisdiction of formation" [(7)]—This definition is not limited to United States jurisdictions.

"Limited liability company" [(8)]—This definition makes no reference to a limited liability company having members upon formation, but Section 201(d) does.

"Manager" [(9)]—The act uses "manager" as a term of art, whose applicability under this act is confined to manager-managed LLCs. The phrase "manager-managed" is itself a term of art, referring only to an LLC whose operating agreement refers to the LLC as such. *See* Paragraph 10 (defining "manager-managed limited liability company"). Thus, for purposes of this act, if the members of a *member*-managed LLC delegate plenipotentiary management authority to one person (whether or not a member), this act's references to "manager" do not apply to that person, even if the members or their operating agreement refers to the person as a "manager."

This approach has the potential for confusion, but confusion around the term "manager" is common to all LLC statutes. The confusion stems from the choice to define "manager" as a term of art in a way that can be at odds with other, common usages of the word. For example, a member-managed LLC might well have an "office manager" or a "property manager." Moreover, in a manager-managed LLC, the "property manager" is not likely to be a manager as the term is used in many LLC statutes. For this nomenclature problem, the best solution is to have the operating agreement carefully delineate who is and is not a manager as this act uses that label.

For cases exemplifying the complexity and problems, *see, e.g., In re Weddle*, 353 BR 892, 895 n.2 (Bankr. D. Idaho 2006) ("Plaintiff appears to argue that Debtors were managers of the LLC. However, Plaintiff's use of the term 'managers' to describe Debtors' duties under their employment agreement is not synonymous with 'manager' of the LLC within the use of that term in the operating agreement, the articles of incorporation, or chapter 6 of title 53 of the Idaho Code. The court views Debtors' 'management' role in the daily operation of the lodge as separate and distinct from management of the LLC."); *Brown v. MR Group, LLC*, 693 N.W.2d 138, 143 (Wis. App. 2005) (declining to use the dictionary definition of "manager" in determining coverage of a policy applicable to a limited liability company and its "managers" and relying instead on the meaning of the term under the Wisconsin LLC act); *Old Nat'l Villages, LLC v. Lenox Pine,' LLC*, 659 S.E. 2d 891, 893 (Ga. Ct. App. 2008) (treating the label "general manager" as a manager "under Georgia's LLC statute").

Under this act, the category of "person" is not limited to individuals. Therefore, a "manager" need not be a natural person. For example, one limited liability company can serve as the manager of another limited liability company.

After a person ceases to be a manager, the term "manager" continues to apply to the person's conduct while a manager. *See* Section 407(c)(6).

"Manager-managed limited liability company" [(10)]—This act authorizes a private agreement (the operating agreement) rather than a public document (certificate or articles of organization) to establish an LLC's status as a manager-managed limited liability company, thereby departing from most existing LLC statutes. Using the operating agreement makes sense, because under this act managerial structure creates no statutory power to bind the entity. *See* Section 301 (eliminating statutory apparent authority).

The only direct consequences of manager-managed status are *inter se*—principally the triggering of a set of rules concerning management structure, fiduciary duty, and information rights. *See* Sections 407–410. The rules on management structure are entirely default provisions—subject to change in whole or in part by the operating agreement. The operating agreement can also significantly affect the provisions on fiduciary duty and information rights. *See* Section 105.

An LLC that is "manager-managed" under this definition does not change its management structure simply because the members fail to designate anyone to act as a manager. In that situation, absent additional facts, the LLC is manager-managed and the manager position is vacant. Non-manager members who exercise managerial functions during the vacancy (or at any other time) will have duties as determined by other law, most particularly the law of agency.

"Member" [(11)]—After a person has been dissociated as a member under Section 602, the term "member" continues to apply to the person's conduct while a member. *See* Section 603(b).

"Member-managed limited liability company" [(12)]—Under this act, member-management is the default mode. *See* Section 407(a).

Some member-managed LLCs give important managerial responsibilities to one or more members. Because "manager" is a term of art under this act and applies only to manager-managed LLC, referring to such members as "managers" risks confusion. *See* the comment to Paragraph 9 (Manager). In contrast, "managing member" or some other designation such as Chief Executive Officer avoids the defined term of "manager" and thereby avoids confusion.

"Operating agreement" [(13)]—This definition must be read in conjunction with Sections 105 through 107, which further describe the operating agreement. In particular, although this definition refers to "the agreement . . . of all the members," the limited liability company itself is bound by and may enforce the agreement. Section 106(a).

An operating agreement is a contract, and therefore all statutory language pertaining to the operating agreement must be understood in the context of the law of contracts.

The definition in Paragraph 13 is very broad and recognizes a wide scope of authority for the operating agreement: "the matters described in Section 105(a)." Those matters include not only all relations *inter se* the members and the limited liability company but also all "activities and affairs of the company and the conduct of those activities and affairs." Section 105(a)(3). Moreover, the definition puts no limits on the form of the operating agreement. To the contrary, the definition contains the phrase "whether oral, implied, in a record, or in any combination thereof."

Unless the operating agreement itself provides otherwise:

- an operating agreement may comprise a number of separate documents (or records), however denominated; and

- subject to Section 106(b) (deeming new members to assent to the then-existing operating agreement), a document, record, understanding, etc. can be part of the operating agreement only with the assent of all persons then members.

An agreement among less than all members might well be enforceable among those members as parties, but would not be part of the operating agreement. However, under Section 105(a)(4), an amendment to an operating agreement can be made with less than unanimous consent if the operating agreement itself so provides.

An agreement to form an LLC is not itself an operating agreement. The term "operating agreement" presupposes at least one "member," and a person cannot be a member of an LLC before the LLC exists. However, as soon as a limited liability company has any members, the limited liability company perforce has an operating agreement. For example, suppose: (i) two persons orally and informally agree to join their activities in some way through the mechanism of an LLC; (ii) they form the LLC or cause it to be formed; and (iii) without further ado or agreement, they become the LLC's initial members. An operating agreement exists. In the words of Paragraph 13, "all the members" have agreed on who the members are, and that agreement—no matter how informal or rudimentary—is an agreement "concerning the matters described in Section 105(a)." To the extent the agreement does not provide the *inter se* "rules of the game," this act "fills in the gaps." Section 105(b).

The result is the same when a person becomes the sole initial member of an LLC, so long as the person has any understanding or intention with regard to the LLC. Any such understanding or intention constitutes an "agreement of all the members of the limited liability company, including a sole member." Paragraph 13.

It may seem oxymoronic to refer an "agreement of . . . a sole member," but this approach is common in LLC statutes. *See, e.g.*, ARIZ. REV. STAT. ANN. § 29–601 (14)(b) (2012) (defining operating agreement to mean "[i]n the case of a limited liability company that has a single member, any written or oral statement of the member made in good faith purporting to govern the affairs of a limited liability company or the conduct of its business as of the effective time of the statement"); WASH. REV. CODE ANN. § 25.15.005 (5) (2012) (defining limited liability company agreement to include "any written statement of the sole member").

This re-definition of "agreement" is a function of "path dependence." LLC statutes initially required an LLC to have at least two members, and almost all LLC statutes contemplated an agreement among members as an LLC's key organic document. Because LLC statutes make the operating agreement the principal way to override statutory default rules, the advent of single member LLCs made it necessary to provide that a sole member could make an operating agreement.

This act states no rule as to whether the statute of frauds applies to operating agreements. Case law suggests that the answer is yes. *Olson v. Halvorsen*, 986 A.2d 1150, 1161 (Del. 2009) ("The legislative history of the LLC Act does not demonstrate the General Assembly's intent to place LLC agreements outside of the statute of frauds.") (applying the one-year provision to an alleged oral buy-out agreement), *negated by* 2010 DEL. LAWS, ch. 287 (H.B. 372), §§ 1, 31 (pertaining to statutes of fraud generally).

The Delaware court decision is consistent with partnership cases.

Partnership agreements, like other contracts, are subject to the Statute of Frauds. A contract of partnership for a term exceeding one year is within the Statute of Frauds and is void unless it is in writing [and signed by the party to be bound]; however, a contract establishing a partnership terminable at the will of any partner is generally held to be capable of performance by its terms within one year of its making and, therefore, to be outside the Statute of Frauds.

Abbott v. Hurst, 643 So. 2d 589, 592 (Ala. 1994) (citations omitted).

Likewise, the land provision of the statute of frauds:

applies to an oral contract to transfer or convey partnership real property, and the interest of the other partners therein, to one partner as an individual, as well as to a parol contract by one of the parties to convey certain land owned by him individually to the partnership, or to another partner, or to put it into the partnership stock.

Froiseth v. Nowlin, 156 Wash. 314, 316, 287 P. 55, 56 (Wash. 1930) (quoting 27 C.J.S. § 220); *see also E. Piedmont 120 Associates, L.P. v. Sheppard*, 209 Ga. App. 664, 665, 434 S.E.2d 101, 102 (1993) (same, stating that "the fact that promises covered by the Statute of Frauds are made in the context of a partnership or joint venture agreement does not render the statute inapplicable"); *Filippi v. Filippi*, 818 A.2d 608, 618 (R.I. 2003) (applying the statute of frauds to an alleged oral agreement to transfer land owned by a limited partnership to one of its partners).

In contrast, the land provision does not apply to a member's ownership interest in an LLC, no matter how much the LLC owns or deals in real property. Interests in a limited liability company are personal property and reflect no direct interest in the entity's assets. *See* Sections 102(24), 501. Thus, the real property issues pertaining to the LLC's ownership of land do not "flow through" to the members and membership interests. *See, e.g., Wooten v. Marshall*, 153 F. Supp. 759, 763–64 (S.D. N.Y. 1957) (involving an "oral agreement for a joint venture concerning the purchase, exploitation and eventual disposition of this 160 acre tract" and stating "[t]he real property acquired and dealt with by the venturers takes on the character of personal property as between the partners in the enterprise, and hence is not covered by [the Statute of Frauds]"); *see also Wade v. DeHart*, 1926 WL 2944 (Ohio Com. Pl. 1926), *aff'd sub nom., Wade v. De Hart*, 26 Ohio App. 177, 159 N.E. 838 (1927) (same).

On the question of how far a written (or "in a record") operating agreement can go to prevent oral or implied-in-fact terms, see Section 105(a)(4), comment. For the effect of a pre-formation agreement, see Section 106(c). For the limited liability company's status viz-a-viz the operating agreement, see Section 106(a).

"Organizer" [(14)]—An organizer need not be a prospective member of the limited liability company. Unless the organizer will be the sole initial member of the limited liability company, as a matter of agency law and Section 401(a) and (b), the organizer is acting on behalf of the person or persons who have agreed to become the initial member or members of the limited liability company. The organizer does not act on behalf of the limited liability company, because a person cannot be an agent of an organization that does not yet exist. RESTATEMENT (THIRD) OF AGENCY § 4.04, cmt. c (2006) (Nonexistent Principals).

"Property" [(16)]—This definition encompasses every form of property.

"Transfer" [(23)]—The term "transfer" is broadly defined to include all types of conveyances of interests in property. The reference to "transfer by operation of law" is significant in connection with Section 502 (Transfer of Transferable Interest). That section severely restricts a transferee's rights (absent the consent of the members), and this definition makes those restrictions applicable, for example, to transfers ordered by a family court as part of a divorce proceeding and transfers resulting from the death of a member. The restrictions also apply to transfers in the context of a member's bankruptcy, except to the extent that bankruptcy law supersedes this act.

"Transferable interest" [(24)]—Absent a contrary provision in the operating agreement or the consent of the members, a "transferable interest" is the only interest in an LLC which can be transferred to a non-member. *See* the comment to Section 502.

This paragraph defines "transferable interest" as an interest "initially owned by a person in the person's capacity as a member," because this act does not contemplate an LLC directly creating interests that comprise only economic rights. *See* Sections 401 (addressing how a person becomes a member), 502 (addressing how a person becomes a transferee).

"Transferee" [(25)]—This definition should be read in light of Section 603(a)(3), which subject to limited exceptions provides that "any transferable interest owned by the person in the person's capacity as a member immediately before dissociation as a member is owned by the person solely as a transferee."

§ 103.   Knowledge; Notice

(a)   A person knows a fact if the person:

   (1)   has actual knowledge of it; or

   (2)   is deemed to know it under subsection (d)(1) or law other than this [act].

(b)   A person has notice of a fact if the person:

   (1)   has reason to know the fact from all the facts known to the person at the time in question; or

   (2)   is deemed to have notice of the fact under subsection (d)(2).

(c)   Subject to Section 210(f), a person notifies another person of a fact by taking steps reasonably required to inform the other person in ordinary course, whether or not those steps cause the other person to know the fact.

(d)   A person not a member is deemed:

   (1)   to know of a limitation on authority to transfer real property as provided in Section 302(g); and

   (2)   to have notice of a limited liability company's:

      (A)   dissolution 90 days after a statement of dissolution under Section 702(b)(2)(A) becomes effective;

      (B)   termination 90 days after a statement of termination under Section 702(b)(2)(F) becomes effective; and

(C) participation in a merger, interest exchange, conversion, or domestication, 90 days after articles of merger, interest exchange, conversion, or domestication under [Article] 10 become effective.

COMMENT

This section is substantially slimmer than the corresponding provisions of previous uniform acts pertaining to business organizations: UPA (1997), ULLCA (1996), and ULPA (2001). Each of those acts borrowed heavily from the comparable Uniform Commercial Code provision. This act relies instead on generally applicable principles of agency law, *see* Section 111; therefore, this section is confined mostly to rules specifically tailored to this act.

Several facets of this section warrant particular note. First, and most fundamentally, because this act does not provide for "statutory apparent authority," Section 301, this section contains no special rules for attributing to an LLC information possessed, communicated to, or communicated by a member or manager.

Second, the section contains no generally applicable provisions determining when an organization is charged with knowledge or notice, because those imputation rules: (i) comprise core topics within the law of agency; (ii) are very complicated; (iii) should not have any different content under this act than in other circumstances; and (iv) are the subject of considerable attention in the Restatement (Third) of Agency (2006).

Third, this act does not define "notice" to include "knowledge." Although conceptualizing the latter as giving the former makes logical sense and has a long pedigree, that conceptualization is counter-intuitive for the uninitiated. In ordinary usage, notice has a meaning separate from knowledge. This act follows ordinary usage and therefore contains some references to "knowledge or notice."

Subsection (a)(2)—In this context, the most important source of "law other than this [act]" is the common law of agency.

Subsection (b)(1)—The "facts known to the person at the time in question" include facts the person is deemed to know under Subsection (a)(2).

Subsection (c)—If a person "notifies" another person of a fact, the other person has "reason to know" the fact and therefore has notice under Subsection (b)(1). However, a person can have "notice" of a fact without having been "notifie[d]" of the fact.

Section 210(f) pertains to delivery of records *by* the filing office.

Subsection (d)—This subsection provides constructive notice of facts stated in specified filed public records.

Subsection (d)(2)—Under this act, the power to bind a limited liability company to a third party is primarily a matter of agency law. Section 301, cmt. The constructive notice provided under this paragraph will be relevant if a third party makes a claim under agency law that someone who purported to act on behalf of a limited liability company had the apparent authority to do so.

§ 104. Governing Law

The law of this state governs:

(1) the internal affairs of a limited liability company; and

(2) the liability of a member as member and a manager as manager for a debt, obligation, or other liability of a limited liability company.

COMMENT

Paragraph (1)—Like any other legal concept, "internal affairs" may be indeterminate at its edges. However, the concept certainly includes interpretation and enforcement of the operating agreement, relations among the members as members, relations between the limited liability company and a member as a member, relations between a manager-managed limited liability company and a manager, and relations between a manager of a manager-managed limited liability company and the members as members. *Compare* Paragraph 1, *with* RESTATEMENT (SECOND) OF CONFLICT OF LAWS § 302, cmt. a (1971) (defining "internal affairs" with reference to a corporation as "the relations inter se of the corporation, its shareholders, directors, officers or agents").

"Internal affairs" do not encompass the power *vel non* of a person to bind a limited liability company. RESTATEMENT (SECOND) OF CONFLICT OF LAWS § 292(2) (1971) ("The principal will be held bound by the agent's action if he would so be bound under the local law of the state where the agent dealt with the third person, provided at least that the principal had authorized the agent to act on his behalf in that state or had led the third person reasonably to believe that the agent had such authority."); *Id.* § 295(1) ("Whether a partnership is bound by action taken on its behalf by an agent in dealing with a third person is determined by the local law of the state selected by application of the rule of § 292."); RESTATEMENT (FIRST) OF CONFLICT OF LAWS § 345, cmt. c (1934) (Law Governing Effect of Act of Agent or Partner) ("If . . . the principal or partner sends the agent or other partner into a state to act on his behalf, he assumes the risk of liability not only for authorized but for unauthorized conduct of the agent or partner in accordance with the law of that state."). *See also Farm & Ranch Services, Ltd. v. LT Farm & Ranch, L.L.C.*, 779 F. Supp. 2d 949, 960 (S.D. Iowa 2011).

The operating agreement cannot alter this section. *See* Section 105(c)(1). This approach comports with the law of other businesses entities whose formation or legal status depends at least in part on a publicly-filed record. *See, e.g.,* ULPA (2001) (Last Amended 2013) § 104 (stating that the law of the state of formation is the domestic entity's governing law) and ULLCA (2006) (Last Amended 2013) § 104 (same).

However, an operating agreement may lawfully incorporate by reference the provisions of another state's LLC statute. If done correctly, this incorporation makes the foreign statutory language part of the operating agreement, and the incorporated terms (together with the rest of the operating agreement) then govern the members (and those claiming through the members) to the extent not prohibited by this act. *See* Section 105. This approach: (i) does *not* switch the limited liability company's governing law to that of another state; (ii) instead takes the provisions of another state's law and incorporates them by reference into the contract among the members; raises complex drafting issues—*e.g.,* how to address subsequent changes to the incorporated law (whether occurring by statutory amendment or court decision); and (iv) thus is rarely, if ever, a good idea.

Paragraph (2)—This paragraph obviously encompasses Section 304 (the liability shield) but does not necessarily encompass a claim that a member or manager is liable to a third party for: (i) having purported inaccurately to have the actual authority to bind a limited liability company to the third party; or (ii) having committed a tort against the third party while acting on the limited liability company's behalf or in the course of the company's business. That liability is not by status (*i.e.,* not "as member . . . [or] as manager") but rather results from function or conduct. *Compare* Paragraph 2, *with* Section 301(b) (stating that, although this act does not make a member as member the agent of a limited liability company, other law may make an LLC liable for the conduct of a member).

"Internal affairs" and the "liability of a member as a member" are mentioned separately because it can be argued that the liability of members and managers to third parties is not an internal affair. *See, e.g.,* RESTATEMENT (SECOND) OF CONFLICT OF LAWS § 307 (1971) (treating shareholders' liability separately from the internal affairs doctrine). A few cases subsume owner/manager liability into internal affairs, but many do not. *See, e.g., Kalb, Voorhis & Co. v. Am. Fin. Corp.*, 8 F.3d 130, 132 (2nd Cir. 1993) (holding that the corporation's "primary purpose is to insulate shareholders from legal liability" and therefore "the state of incorporation has the greater interest in determining when and if that insulation is to be stripped away") (quoting *Soviet Pan Am Travel Effort v. Travel Comm., Inc.*, 756 F. Supp. 126, 131 (S.D.N.Y. 1991) (internal quotation marks omitted).

In any event, most (if not all) LLC statutes follow the rule stated in this paragraph. *See, e.g.,* ARIZ. REV. STAT. ANN. § 29–801(A)(1) (2013) (stating that "[t]he laws of the state or another jurisdiction under which a foreign limited liability company is organized govern its organization and internal affairs and the liability of its members"); GA. CODE ANN. § 14–11–701 (West 2013)(a) (stating that "[t]he laws of the jurisdiction under which a foreign limited liability company is organized govern its organization and internal affairs and the liability of its managers, members, and other owners"); N.Y. LTD. LIAB. CO. LAW § 801(a) (McKinney 2013) (stating that "[t]he laws of the jurisdiction under which a foreign limited liability company is formed govern its organization and internal affairs and the liability of its members and managers").

Moreover, in the case law, "[t]he general rule is that a plaintiff's alter ego theory is governed by the law of the state in which the business at issue is organized." *Rual Trade Ltd. v. Viva Trade L.L.C.*, 549 F. Supp. 2d 1067, 1077 (E.D. Wis. 2008); *see also In re Gulf Fleet Holdings, Inc.*, 491 B.R. 747, 787 (Bankr. W.D. La. 2013) (stating both conceptual and policy rationales for choosing the law of the state of formation); *In re Saba Enterprises, Inc.*, 421 B.R. 626, 648–51 (Bankr. S.D.N.Y. 2009) (examining the issue in detail and applying the state of formation rule).

§ 105. Operating Agreement; Scope, Function, and Limitations

(a) Except as otherwise provided in subsections (c) and (d), the operating agreement governs:

(1) relations among the members as members and between the members and the limited liability company;

(2) the rights and duties under this [act] of a person in the capacity of manager;

(3) the activities and affairs of the company and the conduct of those activities and affairs; and

(4) the means and conditions for amending the operating agreement.

(b) To the extent the operating agreement does not provide for a matter described in subsection (a), this [act] governs the matter.

(c) An operating agreement may not:

(1) vary the law applicable under Section 104;

(2) vary a limited liability company's capacity under Section 109 to sue and be sued in its own name;

(3) vary any requirement, procedure, or other provision of this [act] pertaining to:

(A) registered agents; or

(B) the [Secretary of State], including provisions pertaining to records authorized or required to be delivered to the [Secretary of State] for filing under this [act];

(4) vary the provisions of Section 204;

(5) alter or eliminate the duty of loyalty or the duty of care, except as otherwise provided in subsection (d);

(6) eliminate the contractual obligation of good faith and fair dealing under Section 409(d), but the operating agreement may prescribe the standards, if not manifestly unreasonable, by which the performance of the obligation is to be measured;

(7) relieve or exonerate a person from liability for conduct involving bad faith, willful or intentional misconduct, or knowing violation of law;

(8) unreasonably restrict the duties and rights under Section 410, but the operating agreement may impose reasonable restrictions on the availability and use of information obtained under that section and may define appropriate remedies, including liquidated damages, for a breach of any reasonable restriction on use;

(9) vary the causes of dissolution specified in Section 701(a)(4);

(10) vary the requirement to wind up the company's activities and affairs as specified in Section 702(a), (b)(1), and (e);

(11) unreasonably restrict the right of a member to maintain an action under [Article] 8;

(12) vary the provisions of Section 805, but the operating agreement may provide that the company may not have a special litigation committee;

(13) vary the right of a member to approve a merger, interest exchange, conversion, or domestication under Section 1023(a)(2), 1033(a)(2), 1043(a)(2), or 1053(a)(2);

(14) vary the required contents of a plan of merger under Section 1022(a), plan of interest exchange under Section 1032(a), plan of conversion under Section 1042(a), or plan of domestication under Section 1052(a); or

(15) except as otherwise provided in Sections 106 and 107(b), restrict the rights under this [act] of a person other than a member or manager.

(d) Subject to subsection (c)(7), without limiting other terms that may be included in an operating agreement, the following rules apply:

(1) The operating agreement may:

(A)   specify the method by which a specific act or transaction that would otherwise violate the duty of loyalty may be authorized or ratified by one or more disinterested and independent persons after full disclosure of all material facts; and

(B)   alter the prohibition in Section 405(a)(2) so that the prohibition requires only that the company's total assets not be less than the sum of its total liabilities.

(2)   To the extent the operating agreement of a member-managed limited liability company expressly relieves a member of a responsibility that the member otherwise would have under this [act] and imposes the responsibility on one or more other members, the agreement also may eliminate or limit any fiduciary duty of the member relieved of the responsibility which would have pertained to the responsibility.

(3)   If not manifestly unreasonable, the operating agreement may:

(A)   alter or eliminate the aspects of the duty of loyalty stated in Section 409(b) and (i);

(B)   identify specific types or categories of activities that do not violate the duty of loyalty;

(C)   alter the duty of care, but may not authorize conduct involving bad faith, willful or intentional misconduct, or knowing violation of law; and

(D)   alter or eliminate any other fiduciary duty.

(e)   The court shall decide as a matter of law whether a term of an operating agreement is manifestly unreasonable under subsection (c)(6) or (d)(3). The court:

(1)   shall make its determination as of the time the challenged term became part of the operating agreement and by considering only circumstances existing at that time; and

(2)   may invalidate the term only if, in light of the purposes, activities, and affairs of the limited liability company, it is readily apparent that:

(A)   the objective of the term is unreasonable; or

(B)   the term is an unreasonable means to achieve the term's objective.

COMMENT

Principal Provisions of the Act Concerning the Operating Agreement

The operating agreement is pivotal to a limited liability company, and Sections 105 through 107 are pivotal to this act. They must be read together, along with Section 102(13) (defining the operating agreement).

This section performs five essential functions. Subsection (a) establishes the primacy of the operating agreement in establishing relations *inter se* the limited liability company, its member or members, and any manager. Subsection (b) recognizes this act as comprising mostly default rules—*i.e.*, gap fillers for issues as to which the operating agreement provides no rule. Subsection (c) lists the few mandatory provisions of the act. Subsection (d) lists some provisions frequently found in operating agreements, authorizing some unconditionally and others so long as "not manifestly unreasonable." Subsection (e) delineates in detail both the meaning of "not manifestly unreasonable" and the information relevant to a determining a claim that a provision of an operating agreement is manifestly unreasonable.

Section 106 details the effect of an operating agreement on the limited liability company and on persons becoming members of an LLC. Section 107 concerns the effect of an operating agreement on third parties.

Role and Inevitability of Operating Agreement

A limited liability company is as much a creature of contract as of statute, *TravelCenters of Am., L.L.C. v. Brog*, CIV.A. 3516-CC, 2008 WL 1746987, at *1 (Del. Ch. Apr. 3, 2008) (stating that "limited liability companies are creatures of contract"); *Gottsacker v. Monnier*, 281 Wis. 2d 361, 370, 697 N.W.2d 436, 440 (2005) (stating that "from the partnership form, the LLC borrows . . . internal governance by contract"), and Section 102(13) delineates a very broad scope for "operating agreement." As a result, once an LLC comes into existence and has a member, the LLC necessarily has an operating agreement. *See* the comment to Section 102(13). Accordingly, this act refers to "the operating agreement" rather than "an operating agreement." This phrasing should not, however, be read to require a limited liability company or its members to take any formal action to adopt an operating agreement.

The operating agreement is the exclusive consensual process for modifying this act's various default rules pertaining to relationships *inter se* the members and between the members and the limited liability company. Section 105(b). The operating agreement also has power over "the rights and duties under this [act] of a person in the capacity of manager," Subsection (a)(2), and "the obligations of a limited liability company and its members to a person in the person's capacity as a transferee or person dissociated as a member," Section 107(b). For the relationship between the operating agreement and certificate of formation, see Section 107(d).

The Operating Agreement and the Fiduciary and Other Duties of Those Who Manage

One of the most complex questions in the law of unincorporated business organizations is the extent to which an agreement among the organization's owners can affect the fiduciary and other duties of those who manage the organization (e.g., members in a member-managed LLC; managers in a manager-managed LLC). As explained in detail in the comment to Subsection (d)(3), this act rejects the notion that a contract can completely transform an inherently fiduciary relationship into a merely arm's length association. Within that limitation, however, this section provides substantial power to the operating agreement to reshape, limit, and eliminate fiduciary and other managerial duties.

Subsection (a) recognizes that the operating agreement is the map to the parties' deal and that any claim by a member of managerial misconduct must be assessed first under the relevant terms of the operating agreement. Subsection (d) specifically validates arrangements commonly used to reshape managerial duties and limit the consequences of breaching those duties. Subsection (c) contains relevant limitations, but those limitations: (i) must be read together with subsection (d); and (ii) do not preclude the operating agreement fundamentally redesigning the duties applicable to those who manage the organization. For the act's design of those duties, see Sections 409 and 410.

Subsection (a)—This section describes the very broad scope of a limited liability company's operating agreement, which includes all matters constituting "internal affairs." *Compare* Subsection (a), *with* Section 104(1) (using the phrase "internal affairs" in stating a choice of law rule). This broad grant of authority is subject to the restrictions stated in Subsection (c), including the broad restriction stated in Paragraph (c)(15) (concerning the rights of third parties under this act).

Subsection (a)(1)—This paragraph encompasses all the rights and duties of each member, including rights and duties pertaining to transactions under Article 10.

Subsection (a)(2)—Under this paragraph, the operating agreement has the power to affect the rights and duties of managers (including non-member managers). Because the term "[o]perating agreement . . . includes the agreement as amended or restated," Section 102(13), this paragraph gives the members the ongoing power to define the role of an LLC's managers. Power is not the same as right, however, and exercising the power provided by this paragraph might constitute a breach of a separate contract between the LLC and the manager. A non-member manager might also have rights under Section 107(a).

Subsection (a)(4)—Under this provision, the operating agreement can control both the quantum of consent required (*e.g.*, majority of members) and the means by which the consent is manifested (*e.g.*, prohibiting modifications except when consented to in writing). *See* the comment to Section 107(a).

If the operating agreement does not address the issue, this act provides the rule. Section 407(b)(4)(C) and 407(c)(3)(C) each require the affirmative vote or consent of all the members. Under Section 111 (supplemental principles of law), the parol evidence rule will apply to a written operating agreement when appropriate under contract law.

Subsection (b)—To the extent the operating agreement does not determine an inter se matter, this act determines the matter. The operating agreement may vary any provision of this act pertaining to *inter se* matters, except as provided in Subsections (c) and (d).

Sometimes—but not always—the Comments to this act refer to a variable provision as a "default rule" and a non-waivable provision as "mandatory." These references are merely to draw attention to the default/mandatory distinction in particular contexts and have neither the intent nor the power to affect the default/mandatory status of provisions of this act whose comments lack a comparable reference.

Subsection (c)—This subsection lists provisions of this act whose respective effects cannot be varied or may be varied subject to a stated limitation. For historical reasons, this subsection uses the words "vary" and "alter" interchangeably. No difference in meaning is intended.

If a person claims that a term of the operating agreement violates this subsection, as a matter of ordinary procedural law the burden of proof is on the person making the claim.

Subsection (c)(1)—Section 104 states that this act provides the law applicable to: (i) the internal affairs of an LLC formed under this act; and (ii) the liability of members and managers for obligations of the LLC. The organizers of an LLC make this choice of law by choosing to form an LLC under this act. Domestication to another jurisdiction will re-set the choice of law, see Sections 1051–56, but the operating agreement cannot, *see* the comment to Section 104(1).

Subsection (c) contains no parallel prohibition on varying Section 901 (stating the governing law for foreign limited liability companies), because a prohibition is unnecessary. As a matter of fundamental contract law, an agreement among members of one limited liability company is powerless to govern the affairs of another limited liability company.

Subsection (c)(2)—Under this act, a limited liability company is emphatically an entity, and the members lack the power to alter that characteristic.

Subsection (c)(3)—This prohibition is arguably implicit in Subsection (c)(15) (affecting rights of third parties under this act) but is specifically noted to avoid doubt.

Subsection (c)(4)—This provision means that the operating agreement cannot affect the right of an "aggrieved" person to seek the court's help when "a person required by this [act] to sign a record or deliver a record to the [Secretary of State] for filing under this [act] does not do so." Section 204(a).

Subsection (c)(5)—This limitation is less powerful than might first appear, because Subsection (d) specifically authorizes substantial alterations to the duties of loyalty and care, including restricting and substantially eliminating those duties.

Subsection (c)(6)—Section 409(d) refers to the "contractual obligation of good faith and fair dealing," which contract law implies in every contract. The operating agreement cannot eliminate this obligation, neither in whole (*i.e.*, generally) nor in part (*i.e.*, as applicable to specified situations).

However, an operating agreement may "prescribe the standards ... by which the performance of the obligation is to be measured."

Example: The operating agreement of a manager-managed LLC gives the manager the discretion to cause the LLC to enter into contracts with affiliates of the manager (so-called "Conflict Transactions"). The agreement further provides: "When causing the Company to enter into a Conflict Transaction, the manager complies with Section 409(d) of [this act] if a disinterested person, knowledgeable in the subject matter, states in writing that the terms and conditions of the Conflict Transaction are equivalent to the terms and conditions that would be agreed to by persons at arm's length in comparable circumstances." This provision "prescribe[s] the standards by which the performance of the [Section 409(d)] obligation is to be measured."

Example: Same facts as the previous example, except that, during the performance of a Conflict Transaction, the manager causes the LLC to waive material protections under the applicable contract. The standard stated in the previous example is inapposite to this conduct. Section 409(d) therefore applies to the conduct without any direct contractual delineation. (However, other terms of the agreement may be relevant to determining whether the conduct violates Section 409(d). See the comment to Section 409(d).)

Example: The operating agreement of a manager-managed LLC gives the manager "sole discretion" to make various decisions. The agreement further provides: "Whenever this agreement requires or permits a manager to make a decision that has the potential to benefit one class of members to the detriment of another class, the manager complies with Section 409(d) of [this act] if the manager makes the decision with:

    a.   the honest belief that the decision:

        i.   serves the best interests of the LLC; or

        ii. at least does not injure or otherwise disserve those interests; and

    b.   the reasonable belief that the decision breaches no member's rights under this agreement."

This provision "prescribe[s] the standards by which the performance of the [Section 409(d)] obligation is to be measured." *Compare* Section 105(c)(6), *with Nemec v. Shrader*, 991 A.2d 1120 (Del. 2010) (considering such a situation in the context of the right to call preferred stock and deciding by a 3–2 vote that exercising the call did not breach the implied covenant of good faith and fair dealing).

An operating agreement that seeks to prescribe standards for measuring the contractual obligation of good faith and fair dealing under Section 409(d) should expressly refer to the obligation. *See Gerber v. Enter. Prods.*

Hldgs., L.L.C., 67 A.3d 400, 418 (Del. 2013) (distinguishing between the implied contractual covenant and an express contractual obligation of "good faith" as stated in a limited partnership agreement).

For an explanation of the function and role of the covenant of good faith and fair dealing, see Section 409(d), comment. For the rules delimiting the "not manifestly unreasonable" requirement, see Subsection (e).

Subsection (c)(7)—These restrictions are ubiquitous in the law of business entities and, in conjunction with other provisions of this section, control the otherwise very broad power of an operating agreement to affect fiduciary and other duties. The restrictions are central to the raft of exculpatory provisions that sprung up in corporate statutes in response to *Smith v. Van Gorkum*, 488 A.2d 858 (Del. 1985), *overruled on other grounds by Gantler v. Stephens*, 965 A.2d 695 (Del. 2009). Delaware led the response with DEL. CODE ANN. tit. 8, § 102(b)(7), and a number of LLC statutes have similar provisions. *E.g.*, GA. CODE ANN. § 14–11–305(4)(A) (2011). For an extreme example, *see* VA. CODE ANN. § 13.1–1025 (B) (2012). In this context, "conduct" includes both acts and omissions. BLACK'S LAW DICTIONARY (9th ed. 2009) (defining conduct as "[p]ersonal behavior, whether by action or inaction").

The term "bad faith" has multiple meanings, and the context determines which meaning applies. In the context of the duty of loyalty, "bad faith" includes conduct motivated by ill will or other intent purposely to harm another person. The concept also includes conduct from which a person derives an improper personal benefit. *See, e.g., Mroz v. Hoaloha Na Eha, Inc.*, 410 F. Supp. 2d 919, 936–37 (D. Haw. 2005) (denying a motion to dismiss a claim that "the Majority Partners" were personally liable for the partnership's wrongful termination of the plaintiff; quoting the complaint as alleging that "the Majority Partners, individually and as a group, acted with malice and/or ill will, and/or with an intent to serve their own personal interests and/or without an intent to serve company interests, and/or outside of the scope of their authority and/or without justification"); *BOGNC, L.L.C. v. Cornelius NC Self-Storage L.L.C.*, 10 CVS 19072, 2013 WL 1867065, at *9 (N.C. Super. [Business Court] May 1, 2013) (noting that "no . . . [exculpatory] provision may limit a manager's liability for acts known to be in conflict with the interests of the limited liability company, or for acts from which the manager derived an improper personal benefit") (citing N.C. GEN. STAT. § 57C–3–32(b)); *Lasica v. Savers Grp. of Minn., L.L.C.*, A12-0092, 2012 WL 3553246, at *2 (Minn. Ct. App. Aug. 20, 2012) (noting that an "individual seeking indemnification [under statute providing for indemnification)] must have acted in good faith and must not have received an improper personal benefit") (citing MINN. STAT. § 322B.699, subdivs. 2(a)(2), (3) (2010)).

In the context of the duty of care, the concept of bad faith comes primarily from corporate law and means an extreme breach of the duty (i.e., "the failure to exercise "honest judgment in the lawful and legitimate furtherance of corporate purposes." *Deblinger v. Sani-Pine Products Co., Inc.*, 107 A.D.3d 659, 661, 967 N.Y.S.2d 394 (2013) (quoting *Auerbach v. Bennett*, 47 N.Y.2d 619, 629, 393 N.E.2d 994 (1979) (emphasis added) (internal quotation marks omitted).

Thus, when a plaintiff alleges bad faith as pertaining to the duty of care, "[t]he burden . . . is to show irrationality: a plaintiff must demonstrate that no reasonable business person could possibly authorize the action in good faith. Put positively, the decision must go so far beyond the bounds of reasonable business judgment that its only explanation is bad faith." *In re Tower Air, Inc.*, 416 F.3d 229, 238 (3d Cir. 2005) (discussing then prevailing Delaware law) (citation [omitted]); *see also KDW Restructuring & Liquidation Servs. LLC v. Greenfield*, 874 F. Supp. 2d 213, 226 (S.D.N.Y. 2012) (referring to a lack of "a rationale corporate purpose" and "a disregard for the duty to examine all available information—*information that was readily at hand*") (emphasis added).

With regard to both the duty of loyalty and the duty of care, "bad faith" is entirely distinct from the meaning of "good faith" in the contractual covenant of good faith and fair dealing. See the comment to Section 409(d).

Subsection (c)(7) pertains to indirect as well as direct efforts to "relieve or exonerate" and thus limits how far an operating agreement can go in providing for indemnification. *See* Section 408(b) (stating a default rule for indemnification). Also, in accordance with this paragraph, an exculpatory provision cannot shield against a member's claim of oppression. *See* Section 701(a)(4)(C).

Although this paragraph does not expressly address contracts between an LLC and a member or manager, the stated constraints must also apply to such contracts. If not, those constraints are effectively meaningless.

Example: A manager-managed LLC enters into a management contract with its sole manager, and the contract provides the manager exoneration for liability to the LLC even for willful and intentional misconduct. Most likely, contract law will treat the provision as against public policy and therefore unenforceable. RESTATEMENT (SECOND) OF CONTRACTS § 195(1) (1981) ("A term exempting a party from tort liability for harm caused intentionally or recklessly is unenforceable on grounds of public policy."). If not, a court should hold the provision unenforceable to avoid evisceration of Subsection (c)(7). (Or, the court could invoke the policy expressed in Subsection (c)(7) as grounds for holding the provision unenforceable under contract law.)

Subsection (c)(8)—Although phrased as a restriction, this provision grants substantial power to the operating agreement.

> **Example:** A law firm operates as a limited liability company, and the operating agreement provides that a "Compensation Committee" periodically decides each member's compensation. The agreement also states that only members who are on the Compensation Committee may have access to the Committee's compensation decisions pertaining to other members. This restriction is reasonable.

The act also empowers the LLC "as a matter within the ordinary course of its activities and affairs [to] impose reasonable restrictions and conditions on access to and use of information" obtained under Section 410. *See* Section 410(h).

In determining whether a restriction is reasonable, a court might consider: (i) the danger or other problem the restriction seeks to avoid; (ii) the purpose for which the information is sought; and (iii) whether, in light of both the problem and the purpose, the restriction is reasonably tailored. In addition, a restriction that is reasonable viz-a-viz a non-managing member in a manager-managed LLC might be unreasonable viz-a-viz a managing member or in the context of a member-managed LLC.

Subsection (c)(9)—The operating agreement may not change the stated grounds for judicial dissolution but may determine the forum in which a claim for dissolution under Section 701(a)(4) is determined. For example, arbitration and forum selection clauses are commonplace in business relationships in general and in operating agreements in particular.

The approach of this paragraph differs from the law of Delaware. *Huatuco v. Satellite Healthcare*, CV 8465-VCG, 2013 WL 6460898, at *1, n.2 (Del. Ch. Dec. 9, 2013) (stating that "the right to judicial dissolution is a default right which the parties may eschew by contract" but reserving the question of "[w]hether the parties may, by contract, divest this Court of its authority to order a dissolution in all circumstances, even where it appears manifest that equity so requires—leaving, for instance, irreconcilable members locked away together forever like some alternative entity version of Sartre's *Huis Clos*").

Subsection (c)(10)—The cited provisions comprise the non-waivable aspects of winding up a dissolved limited liability company. The other provisions of Section 702 are default rules.

Subsection (c)(11)—Article 8 delineates a member's rights to bring direct and derivative actions. It would be unreasonable to frustrate these rights but not unreasonable to channel their exercise. For example, the operating agreement might select a forum, require pre-suit mediation, provide for arbitration of both direct and derivative claims, or override Section 802 and require "universal demand" in all derivative cases. Similarly, it is not unreasonable to provide for liquidated damages consonant with the law of contracts. In contrast, it would be unreasonable for an operating agreement to both: (i) require a would-be derivative plaintiff to make demand regardless of futility; and (ii) bar taking the claim to court no matter how long the management group ponders the demand.

Subsection (c)(12)—An operating agreement may not alter the act's rules for a special litigation committee but may preclude entirely the use of such a committee.

Subsection (c)(13)—Section 1023(a)(1), 1033(a)(1), 1043(a)(1), and 1053(a)(1) each requires the consent or the affirmative vote of all members. The operating agreement may modify these requirements. In contrast, under the sections stated in this subsection:

- each member is protected from being merged, exchanged, converted, or domesticated "into" the status of a partner in a general partnership that is not a limited liability partnership (or a comparable "unshielded" position in some other organization) without the member having directly consented to either:

  o the merger, interest exchange, conversion, or domestication; or

  o an operating agreement provision that permits such transactions to occur with less than unanimous consent of the members; and

- merely consenting to an operating agreement provision that permits amendment of the agreement with less than unanimous consent of the members does not qualify as the requisite direct consent.

Subsection (c)(14)—Because these plans are the basic "deal documents" for each of the organic transactions contemplated in Article 10, the operating agreement may not vary the contents of these plans.

Subsection (c)(15)—This limitation pertains only to "the rights under this [act] of" third parties other than members and managers. Moreover, the limitation is subject to two substantial exceptions: Section 106 (pertaining to the operating agreement's relationship to the limited liability company itself and to persons becoming members) and Section 107(b) (pertaining to the operating agreement's power over the rights of transferees).

Subsection (d)—The operating agreement has plenipotentiary power over the matters described in Subsection (a), except as specifically limited by Subsections (c) and (d)(3). However, for the convenience of practitioners and the courts. Paragraphs 1 and 2 list various terms often found in operating agreements. No negative inference should be drawn about terms not listed; the listing is provided "without limiting other terms that may be included in an operating agreement."

Paragraph 3 lists terms subject to the "not manifestly unreasonable" standard. Subsection (e) delineates that standard. The same standard applies to terms of an operating agreement which seek to "prescribe the standards . . . by which the performance of the [Section 409(d)] obligation [of good faith and fair dealing] is to be measured." Subsection (c)(6).

Subsection (d)(1)(A)—An arrangement *not* involving "one or more disinterested and independent persons" acting "after full disclosure of all material facts" would "alter . . . the aspects of the duty of loyalty stated in Section 409(b) and (i)" and would therefore be subject to the "not manifestly unreasonable standard" of Subsection (d)(3)(A).

For the meaning of "material" as applied to information, see Section 409(f), comment.

Subsection (d)(1)(B)—Section 405(a)(2) prohibits distributions:

- *not merely* when, after the distribution, "the company's total assets would be less than the sum of its total liabilities,"

- *but also* when, after the distribution, the assets would less than the total liabilities "plus the amount that would be needed, if the company were to be dissolved and wound up at the time of the distribution, to satisfy the preferential rights upon dissolution and winding up of members and transferees whose preferential rights are superior to those of persons receiving the distribution."

The second part of the solvency test pertains to preferential rights to distributions, is thus a matter *inter se* the members and any transferees, and is therefore subject to change in the operating agreement.

In contrast, the first part of the solvency test protects third parties—creditors of the LLC—and therefore cannot be changed by the operating agreement. Subsection (c)(15). Likewise, the operating agreement cannot change the solvency test stated in Section 405(a)(1) (providing that "the company would not be able to pay its debts as they become due in the ordinary course of the company's activities and affairs").

Subsection (d)(2)—This provision is limited to member-managed limited liability companies on the premise that: (i) managers are collectively responsible; and (ii) managers may properly delegate a duty but the delegation does not discharge the duty. However, in a manager-managed LLC (as well as in a member-managed LLC), subject to Subsection (d)(3) the operating agreement may alter or even eliminate fiduciary duties.

Example: ABC LLC ("ABC") is a member-managed LLC. ABC has two entirely separate lines of business, the Alpha business and the Beta business. Under ABC's operating agreement:

- Member 1's responsibilities pertain exclusively to the Alpha business, while responsibility for:

  o the Beta business is allocated exclusively to Member 2; and

  o ABC's overall operations is allocated exclusively to Member 3.

- Member 2's responsibilities pertain exclusively to the Beta business, while responsibility for:

  o the Alpha business is allocated exclusively to Member 1; and

  o ABC's overall operations is allocated exclusively to Member 3.

- Member 1 has no fiduciary duties pertaining to the Beta business.

- Member 2 has no fiduciary duties pertaining to the Alpha business.

The elimination of Member 1's fiduciary duties with regard to the Beta business and Member 2's fiduciary duties with regard to the Alpha business are enforceable, without regard to the "manifestly unreasonable" standard of Subsection (d)(3).

Subsection (d)(3)—This act rejects the ultra-contractarian notion that fiduciary duty within a business organization is merely a set of default rules and seeks instead to balance the virtues of "freedom of contract" against the dangers that inescapably exist when some persons have power over the interests of others. *Cf.* Leo E. Strine, Jr. J. Travis Laster, *The Siren Song of Unlimited Contractual Freedom*, ELGAR HANDBOOK ON ALTERNATIVE ENTITIES (Eds. Mark Lowenstein and Robert Hillman), forthcoming 2014, Edward Elgar Publishing 2014) (noting that an "argument often made in favor of [Delaware] alternative entity statutes is that they allow for the elimination of fiduciary duties and the establishment of a purely contractual relationship between entity managers and investors" and stating that "[a]s judges who have seen our fair share of alternative entity disputes, we do not immediately grasp why this would be seen as a compelling advantage"); available at SSRN: http://ssrn.com/abstract=2481039, at 9–10 (footnote omitted).

Under this act, a properly drafted operating agreement may substantially alter and even eliminate fiduciary duties. However, two important limitations exist.

First, arrangements subject to this subsection may not be "manifestly unreasonable." See Subsection (e) (delineating this standard).

Second, the operating agreement may not transform the relationship inter se members, managers, and the LLC into an entirely arm's length arrangement. For example, displacement of fiduciary duties is effective only to the extent that the displacement is stated clearly and with particularity. This rule is fundamental in the jurisprudence of fiduciary duty. *See, e.g., Paige Capital Mgmt., L.L.C. v. Lerner Master Fund, L.L.C.*, Civ. A. No. 5502-CS, 2011 WL 3505355, at *31 (Del. Ch. Aug. 8, 2011) (Del. Ch. 2011) (stating that, even under a statute that "permits the waiver of fiduciary duties . . . such waivers must be set forth clearly"); *Kelly v. Blum*, Civ. A. No. 4516-VCP, 2010 WL 629850, at *10, n.70 (Del. Ch. Feb. 24, 2010) ("Having been granted great contractual freedom by the LLC Act, drafters of or parties to an LLC agreement should be expected to provide . . . clear and unambiguous provisions when they desire to expand, restrict or eliminate the operation of traditional fiduciary duties"). It would therefore be manifestly unreasonable for an operating agreement to negate this rule.

Although Subsection (d)(3) does not expressly address contracts between an LLC and a member or manager, the stated constraints must also apply to such contracts. If not, those constraints are effectively meaningless.

Example: A manager-managed LLC enters into a management contract with its sole manager, and the contract provides that the duties of loyalty stated in Section 409(b) and (i) are entirely eliminated. If the operating agreement were to so provide, the provision would be subject to the "manifestly unreasonable standard." Section 105(d)(3)(A). Absent the authorization provided by Section 105(d)(3)(A), the management contract's attempt to waive fiduciary duties may be unenforceable as a matter of public policy and contract law. *See Neubauer v. Goldfarb*, 108 Cal. App. 4th 47, 57, 133 Cal. Rptr. 2d 218 (2003) (stating that "waiver of corporate directors' and majority shareholders' fiduciary duties to minority shareholders in private close corporations is against public policy and a contract provision in a buy-sell agreement purporting to effect such a waiver is void"). If not, a court should hold the provision unenforceable nonetheless so as to avoid eviscerating Subsection (d)(3).

Subsection (d)(3)(A)—Subject to the "not manifestly unreasonable" standard, this paragraph empowers the operating agreement to eliminate *all* aspects of the duty of loyalty listed in Section 409(b). The obligation of good faith and fair dealing, Section 409(d), would remain. See Subsection (c)(6). As to any other, uncodified aspects of the duty of loyalty, see Subsection (d)(3)(D) (empowering the operating agreement to "alter or eliminate any other fiduciary duty").

Example: Joint Venture LLC ("JV") is a manager-managed limited liability company, with two members, Kappa, Inc. ("Kappa") and Lambda, LLC ("Lambda"). The operating agreement provides that:

- JV is managed by a "board of managers" consisting of one person appointed by Kappa and one person appointed by Lambda;

- each appointee:

  o owes fiduciary and any other duties exclusively to the member that made the appointment; and

  o owes no duties to the other member and the limited liability company.

The "not manifestly unreasonable" standard applies to these provisions under Subsection (d)(3)(A) and (D), and the provisions are not manifestly unreasonable. Note that the provisions do not affect the duties of Kappa and Lambda to:

- the limited liability company, under applicable case law (pertaining to the obligations of owners of an entity who control the entity indirectly); and

- each other, under applicable case law and Section 701(a)(4)(C)(ii) (providing for judicial dissolution when "the managers or those members in control of the company . . . have acted or are acting in a manner that is oppressive and was, is, or will be directly harmful to the [member seeking dissolution").

Example: ABC LLC ("ABC") is a manager-managed limited liability company with three managers and two entirely separate lines of business, the Alpha business and the Beta business. Under ABC's operating agreement:

- Manager 1's responsibilities pertain exclusively to the Alpha business; responsibility for:

  o the Beta business is allocated exclusively to Manager 2; and

  o ABC's overall operations is allocated exclusively to Manager 3.

- Manager 2's responsibilities pertain exclusively to the Beta business; responsibility for:

  o the Alpha business is allocated exclusively to Manager 1; and

  o ABC's overall operations is allocated exclusively to Manager 3.

- Manager 1 has no fiduciary duties pertaining to the Beta business.

- Manager 2 has no fiduciary duties pertaining to the Alpha business.

The "not manifestly unreasonable" standard applies to these provisions under Subsection (d)(3)(A) and (D), and the provisions are not manifestly unreasonable.

Subsection (d)(3)(B)—Under this paragraph, an operating agreement might provide that an affiliate of a manager of a manager-managed LLC will provide compensated services to the LLC at a price not exceeding market price, or that the manager may pursue opportunities that otherwise would be company opportunities. Such arrangements are commonplace and permissible.

Subsection (d)(3)(C)—In this context, "conduct" includes both acts and omissions. BLACK'S LAW DICTIONARY (9th ed. 2009) (defining conduct as "[p]ersonal behavior, whether by action or inaction"). Subject to the "not manifestly unreasonable" standard and the bedrock requirements stated here and in Subsection (c)(7), the operating agreement can reduce the duty of care substantially. In particular, the operating agreement can eliminate the aspects of the duty of care pertaining to gross negligence and recklessness.

This provision replicates in a particular context the general rule stated in Subsection (c)(7). For the meaning of "bad faith" in the context of the duty of care, see Subsection (c)(7), comment.

Subsection (e)—The "not manifestly unreasonable" concept became part of uniform business entity statutes when UPA (1997) imported the concept from the Uniform Commercial Code. (In the current version of the Uniform Commercial Code, the concept appears in Section 1–302(b).)

This subsection provides rules for applying the concept, specifying:

- who decides the issue of "manifestly unreasonable"

  ▪ "the court . . . as a matter of law," Subsection (e);

- the framework for determining the issue

  ▪ determination to be made "in light of the purposes, activities, and affairs of the limited liability company," Subsection (e)(2);

- the temporal setting for determining the issue

  ▪ "determination [to be made] as of the time the challenged term became part of the operating agreement," Subsection (e)(1); and

- what information is admissible for determining the issue

- "only circumstances existing" when "the challenged term became part of the operating agreement," Subsection (e)(1).

The subsection also provides a very demanding standard for persons claiming that a term of an operating agreement is "manifestly unreasonable." "The court . . . may invalidate the term only if, in light of the purposes, activities, and affairs of the limited liability company, it is *readily apparent* that: (A) the objective of the term is unreasonable; or (B) the term is an unreasonable means to achieve the term's objective." Subsection (e)(2) (emphasis added).

Subsection (e) is fundamental to this act, because: (i) this act generally defers to the agreement among the members; and (ii) Subsection (e) safeguards the operating agreement in at least four ways:

- Determining manifest unreasonableness *inter se* owners of an organization is a different task than doing so in a commercial context, where concepts like "usages of trade" are available to inform the analysis. Each business organization must be understood in its own terms and context.

- If loosely applied, the concept of "manifestly unreasonable" would permit a court to rewrite the members' agreement, which would destroy the balance this act seeks to establish between freedom of contract and fiduciary duty.

- Case law has not adequately delineated the concept. *See, e.g., In re Brobeck, Phleger & Harrison L.L.P.*, 408 B.R. 318, 335 (Bankr. N.D. Cal. 2009) ("RUPA [UPA (1997)] does not define what is 'manifestly unreasonable' and the parties have not cited, nor can the court locate, a decision that defines the term. Absent case law or even a dictionary definition, the court must rely on its common sense to recognize something as manifestly unreasonable.").

- In the context of statutes permitting stock transfer restrictions unless "manifestly unreasonable," courts have often ignored the word "manifestly." *See, e.g., Brandt v. Somerville*, 692 N.W.2d 144, 152 (N.D. 2005) (stating that "in close corporations, a majority of courts have sustained restrictions that are determined to be reasonable in light of the relevant circumstances"); *Roof Depot, Inc. v. Ohman*, 638 N.W.2d 782, 786 (Minn. Ct. App. 2002) (stating that "the restrictions [on share transfer] are not 'manifestly unreasonable' because they are reasonable means to ensure that the management and control of the business remains in the group of investors or with people well known to them"); *Castriota v. Castriota*, 633 A.2d 1024, 1027–28 (App. Div. 1993) ("We are obliged to apply the statute in a manner consonant with its essential purpose to permit reasonable restrictions upon alienation.").

Subsection (e)(1)—The significance of the phrase "as of the time the term as challenged became part of the operating agreement" is best shown by example.

Example: When a particular manager-managed LLC comes into existence, its business plan is quite unusual and its success depends on the willingness of a particular individual to serve as the LLC's sole manager. This individual has a rare combination of skills, experiences, and contacts, which are particularly appropriate for the LLC's start-up. In order to induce the individual to accept the position of sole manager, the members are willing to have the operating agreement significantly limit the manager's fiduciary duties. Several years later, when the LLC's operations have turned prosaic and the manager's talents and background are not nearly so crucial, a member challenges the fiduciary duty limitations as manifestly unreasonable. The relevant time under Subsection (e)(1) is when the LLC began. Subsequent developments are not relevant, except as they might inferentially bear on the circumstances in existence at the relevant time.

Example: As initially adopted, an operating agreement identifies a category of decisions ordinarily subject to the duty of loyalty and provides that "the manager's sole, reasonable discretion" satisfies the duty. A year later, the agreement is amended to delete the word "reasonable." Later, a member claims that, without the word "reasonable," the provision is manifestly unreasonable. The relevant time under Subsection (e)(1) is when the agreement was amended, not when the agreement was initially adopted.

Subsection (e)(2)—If a person claims that a term of the operating agreement is manifestly unreasonable under Subsections (c)(6) or (d)(3), as a matter of ordinary procedural law the person making the claim has the burden of proof.

§ 106.   Operating Agreement; Effect on Limited Liability Company and Person Becoming Member; Preformation Agreement

(a)   A limited liability company is bound by and may enforce the operating agreement, whether or not the company has itself manifested assent to the operating agreement.

(b)   A person that becomes a member is deemed to assent to the operating agreement.

(c)   Two or more persons intending to become the initial members of a limited liability company may make an agreement providing that upon the formation of the company the agreement will become the operating agreement. One person intending to become the initial member of a limited liability company may assent to terms providing that upon the formation of the company the terms will become the operating agreement.

COMMENT

Subsection (a)—This subsection resolves twin questions that have troubled some courts—namely, whether an unincorporated entity that has not signed its foundational agreement nonetheless is bound by and may enforce the agreement. The questions have been particularly troubling in the context of agreements to arbitrate. *See, e.g., Elkjer v. Scheef & Stone, L.L.P.*, 3:13-CV-1655-K, ___ F. Supp.2d ___, 2014 WL 1255844 at *5–6 (N.D. Tex. Mar. 27, 2014) (concluding that a limited liability partnership "is a party to the Partnership Agreement," even though the partnership itself never signed or otherwise assented to the agreement; enforcing arbitration provision to the benefit of the LLP). *Contra Trover v. 419 OCR, Inc.*, 397 Ill. App. 3d 403, 409, 921 N.E.2d 1249, 1255 (2010) (finding that "neither FODG [an LLC] nor the Golf Club [a related LLC] was a party to the operating agreements and that they are therefore not bound by the arbitration clauses therein").

Developments pertaining to the Virginia LLC Act further illustrate the difficulties. In *Mission Residential, L.L.C. v. Triple Net Properties, L.L.C.*, 654 S.E.2d 888, 891 (2008), the Virginia Supreme Court held that a member's derivative claim was not subject to the arbitration provision in the operating agreement, because: (i) the LLC was "the real party in interest"; (ii) the LLC had not signed the operating agreement; and (iii) requiring the claim to be arbitrated would "ignore[ ] the separate existence of Holdings [the LLC]." The Virginia legislature promptly disagreed and amended the LLC act to state: "A limited liability company is bound by its operating agreement whether or not the limited liability company executes the operating agreement." VA. CODE ANN. § 13.1–1023.A.1 (2012). The legislature left open the question of a limited liability company's power to enforce an operating agreement that the company has not executed.

This subsection answers the twin questions, categorically and in the affirmative.

This subsection does not consider whether a limited liability company is an indispensable party to a suit concerning the operating agreement. That question is one of procedural law, and the answer can determine whether federal diversity jurisdiction exists.

Subsection (b)—Given the possibility of oral and implied-in-fact terms in the operating agreement, a person becoming a member of an existing limited liability company should take precautions to ascertain fully the contents of the operating agreement. *See* the comment to Section 105(a)(4).

Subsection (c)—The second sentence refers to "assent to terms" rather than "make an agreement" because, under venerable principles of contract law, an agreement presupposes at least two parties, and Section 102(13) specifically contemplates an operating agreement in a single member LLC.

A pre-formation arrangement is not an operating agreement. An operating agreement presupposes at least one member, and, under this act, the earliest a person can become a member is upon the formation of the limited liability company. *See* Section 401.

§ 107.   Operating Agreement; Effect on Third Parties and Relationship to Records Effective on Behalf of Limited Liability Company

(a)   An operating agreement may specify that its amendment requires the approval of a person that is not a party to the agreement or the satisfaction of a condition. An amendment is ineffective if its adoption does not include the required approval or satisfy the specified condition.

(b)   The obligations of a limited liability company and its members to a person in the person's capacity as a transferee or a person dissociated as a member are governed by the operating agreement. Subject only to a court order issued under Section 503(b)(2) to effectuate a charging order, an amendment to the operating agreement made after a person becomes a transferee or is dissociated as a member:

(1) is effective with regard to any debt, obligation, or other liability of the limited liability company or its members to the person in the person's capacity as a transferee or person dissociated as a member; and

(2) is not effective to the extent the amendment imposes a new debt, obligation, or other liability on the transferee or person dissociated as a member.

(c) If a record delivered by a limited liability company to the [Secretary of State] for filing becomes effective and contains a provision that would be ineffective under Section 105(c) or (d)(3) if contained in the operating agreement, the provision is ineffective in the record.

(d) Subject to subsection (c), if a record delivered by a limited liability company to the [Secretary of State] for filing becomes effective and conflicts with a provision of the operating agreement:

(1) the agreement prevails as to members, persons dissociated as members, transferees, and managers; and

(2) the record prevails as to other persons to the extent they reasonably rely on the record.

COMMENT

Subsection (a)—This subsection, derived from DEL. CODE ANN. tit. 6, § 18–302(e), permits the operating agreement to: (i) accord a non-member veto rights over amendments to the agreement; and (ii) establish other preconditions for amendments. An amendment made in derogation of a veto right or precondition is ineffective.

Veto rights are likely to be sought by lenders but may also be attractive to non-member managers.

Example: A non-member manager enters into a management contract with an LLC, and that agreement provides in part that the LLC may remove the manager without cause only with the consent of members holding 2/3 of the profits interests. The operating agreement contains a parallel provision (the "operating agreement's quantum provision"), but the non-member manager is not a party to the operating agreement. Later, the LLC members amend the operating agreement's quantum provision to reduce the quantum to a simple majority of profits interests and thereafter purport to remove the manager without cause. Although the LLC has undoubtedly breached its contract with the manager and subjected itself to a damage claim, the LLC has the *power* under Section 105(a)(2) to effect the removal—unless the operating agreement provides the manager a veto right over changes in the operating agreement's quantum provision.

This subsection does not refer to member veto rights because, unless otherwise provided in the operating agreement, the consent of each member is necessary to effect an amendment. *See* Section 407(b)(4)(B), (c)(3)(B).

Because "[a]n operating agreement may specify that its amendment requires ... the satisfaction of a condition," an operating agreement can require that any amendment be made through a writing or a record signed by each member. *See* Section 105(a)(4) (empowering the operating agreement to determine "the means and conditions for amending the operating agreement").

Subsection (b)—The law of unincorporated business organizations is only beginning to grapple in a modern way with the tension between the rights of an organization's owners to carry on their activities as they see fit (or have agreed) and the rights of transferees of the organization's economic interests. Such transferees can include the heirs of business founders as well as former owners who are "locked in" as transferees of their own interests. *See* Section 603(a)(3).

If the law categorically favors the owners, there is a serious risk of expropriation and other abuse. On the other hand, if the law grants former owners and other transferees the right to seek judicial protection, that specter can "freeze the deal" as of the moment an owner leaves the enterprise or a third party obtains an economic interest.

There is little case law in this area, and almost all of it pertains to limited partnerships rather than LLCs. The partnership case law clearly favors the remaining owners over former owners and other transferees. *See, e.g., Bauer v. Blomfield Co./Holden Joint Venture*, 849 P.2d 1365, 1367, n.2 (Alaska 1993) (holding that a mere assignee "was not entitled to complain about a decision made with the consent of all the partners" and stating "[w]e are unwilling to hold that partners owe a duty of good faith and fair dealing to assignees of a partner's interest"); *Bynum v. Frisby*, 73 Nev. 145, 149–50, 311 P.2d 972, 975 (1957) ("[A]n assignment of a partnership interest from one partner to a stranger does not bring that stranger into fiduciary relationship with the remaining partners nor require them to resort to dissolution in order to prevent such a relationship from arising. The stranger remains a stranger entitled only to share in the partnership's worth and to demand an accounting upon dissolution.") (applying UPA (1914) § 27, pertaining to rights of an assignee). *See generally* Daniel S. Kleinberger, *The Plight of the Bare Naked Assignee*, 42 SUFFOLK L. REV. 587 (2009).

This subsection follows *Bauer* and other cases by expressly subjecting transferees (including a person dissociated as a member) to operating agreement amendments made after the transfer or dissociation, except amendments that increase obligations on transferees. For example, an amendment might extend the duration of a limited liability company but may not institute a new capital call obligation on transferees.

The question of whether, in extreme and sufficiently harsh circumstances, transferees might be able to claim some type of duty or obligation to protect against expropriation awaits development in the case law. An unreported LLC case suggests the answer might be yes, but the decision rests primarily on the wording of the LLC's operating agreement. In *Kohannim v. Katoli*, 08-11-00155-CV, 2013 WL 3943078, at *10–11 (Tex. App. July 24, 2013), the court: (i) noted that the LLC's "Regulations provide[ ] for the distribution of 'available cash' to members quarterly provided that the available cash is not needed for a reasonable working capital reserve"; (ii) also noted that "Jacob [the defendant member] paid himself $100,000 for management services that were not performed and failed to make any profit distributions to Mike [former member and ex-spouse of the plaintiff Parvaneh] or Parvaneh [ex-spouse of Mike, who became Mike's transferee as part of their divorce proceeding] even though more than $250,000 in undistributed profit had accumulated in the company's accounts since the mortgage on the property had been paid off in February 2007"; and (iii) concluded that "more than a scintilla of evidence supports the trial court's finding that Jacob failed to make profit distributions to Parvaneh." In essence, the court upheld a finding that Jacob had breached (or caused the LLC to breach) a contractual obligation to make distributions. But the court went further: "We also agree with the trial court's conclusion that the established facts demonstrated Jacob engaged in wrongful conduct and exhibited a lack of fair dealing in the company's affairs to the prejudice of Parvaneh." *Id.* at *11.

For the very limited rights of transferees, see Section 502.

Subsection (b)(1)—This provision is inapposite when "a member or transferee becomes entitled to receive a distribution." Section 404(d). In that circumstance:

- "the member or transferee has the status of . . . a creditor of the limited liability company with respect to the distribution," *Id.*; and

- the relevant obligation is not owed to "a person in the person's capacity as a transferee or person dissociated as a member," Subsection (b), but rather to the person in the person's capacity as a creditor.

Subsection (c)—This provision precludes using the certificate of organization to make an end run around the strictures of Section 105(c) and (d)(3).

Subsection (d)—It will be possible, albeit improvident, for a limited liability company's operating agreement to be inconsistent with the certificate of organization or other public filings pertaining to the company. For those circumstances, this subsection provides rules for determining which source of information prevails:

- For members, managers and transferees, the operating agreement is paramount.

- Third parties may invoke the public record upon a showing of reasonable reliance, which presupposes actual knowledge—*i.e.*, deemed knowledge under Section 103(d) does not suffice.

The mere fact that a term is present in a publicly filed record and not in the operating agreement, or *vice versa*, does not automatically establish a conflict. This subsection does not expressly cover a situation in which: (i) one of the specified filed records contains information in addition to, but not inconsistent with, the operating agreement; and (ii) a person, other than a member or transferee, reasonably relies on the additional information. However, the policy reflected in this subsection seems equally applicable to that situation. Moreover, to argue that the operating agreement prevails over the filed record is to argue that the additional term does conflict with the operating agreement, at least in effect.

Section 105(a)(4) might also be relevant to the subject matter of this subsection. Absent a contrary provision in the operating agreement, language in an LLC's certificate of organization or other record delivered to the filing office for filing on behalf of the LLC might be evidence of the members' agreement and might thereby constitute or at least imply a term of the operating agreement.

This subsection does not apply to records delivered to the filing office for filing on behalf of a person other than a limited liability company.

§ 108.   Nature, Purpose, and Duration of Limited Liability Company

(a)   A limited liability company is an entity distinct from its member or members.

(b)   A limited liability company may have any lawful purpose, regardless of whether for profit.

(c)   A limited liability company has perpetual duration.

COMMENT

Subsection (a)—The "separate entity" characteristic is fundamental to a limited liability company and is inextricably connected to both the liability shield, Section 304, and the inability of creditors of a member or transferee to reach the assets of the limited liability company absent a "reverse pierce" or a claim of fraudulent transfer. *See, e.g., Litchfield Asset Mgmt. Corp. v. Howell*, 799 A.2d 298 (Conn. Ct. App. 2002) (applying an "outside reverse pierce" to allow judgment creditor of member to reach assets of LLC) (overruled on other grounds by *Robinson v. Coughlin*, 830 A.2d 1114 (Conn. 2003)); *Egle v. Egle*, 817 So. 2d 136, 140 (La. Ct. App. 2002) (allowing plaintiff to proceed with claims that transfers made by her ex-spouse inter alia to an LLC were sham transactions).

Subsection (b)—Although some LLC statutes continue to require a business purpose, this act follows the current trend and takes a more expansive approach. The phrase "any lawful purpose, regardless of whether for profit" encompasses even charitable activities, but this act does not include any comprehensive protections pertaining to charitable assets and purposes. Section 1004(b) does contain a "nondiversion" provision, but the provision applies only to the organic transactions contemplated by Article 10. Comprehensive protections must be (and typically are) found in other law, although sometimes that "other law" appears within a state's non-profit corporation statute. *See, e.g.,* MINN. STAT. § 317A.811 (2012) (providing restrictions on charitable organizations that seek to "dissolve, merge, or consolidate, or to transfer all or substantially all of their assets" but imposing those restrictions only on "corporations," which are elsewhere defined as corporations incorporated under the non-profit corporation act).

Subsection (c)—The word "perpetual" is a misnomer, albeit one commonplace in LLC statutes. In this context, "perpetual" means merely that the act: (i) does not require a definite term; and (ii) creates no nexus between the dissociation of a member and the dissolution of the entity.

Moreover, the public record pertaining to a limited liability company will not necessarily reveal whether the company actually has a perpetual duration or has in fact dissolved, because: this act, like all LLC statutes, provides several consent-based methods to dissolve a limited liability company; and (ii) none of those methods involve a public filing. For example, dissolution and winding up of a limited liability company may result from a term specified in the operating agreement or the affirmative vote or consent of all members. *See* Sections 701 (events causing dissolution) and 702 (winding up required upon dissolution). An operating agreement is not a publicly filed document, and a member vote to dissolve a limited liability company is not a public event. A dissolved limited partnership may deliver to the filing office for filing a statement of dissolution, Section 702(b)(2)(A), and later a statement of termination, Section 702(b)(2)(F), or both, but the filing of such statements is permissive rather than mandatory, *id*.

Likewise, the public record will not reveal when (or even whether) a limited liability company has come into existence. *See* Section 201(d) ("A limited liability company is formed when the company's certificate of becomes effective and at least one person becomes a member.").

§ 109.   Powers

A limited liability company has the capacity to sue and be sued in its own name and the power to do all things necessary or convenient to carry on its activities and affairs.

COMMENT

Continuing the approach initiated in ULPA (2001) § 105, this act omits as unnecessary any detailed list of specific powers.

The operating agreement cannot vary a limited liability company's capacity to sue and be sued. Section 105(c)(2). An LLC's standing to enforce the operating agreement is a separate matter, which is covered by Section 106(a) (stating, as a default rule, that the limited liability company "may enforce the operating agreement").

§ 110. Application to Existing Relationships

(a) Before [all-inclusive date], this [act] governs only:

(1) a limited liability company formed on or after [the effective date of this [act]]; and

(2) except as otherwise provided in subsection (c), a limited liability company formed before [the effective date of this [act]] which elects, in the manner provided in its operating agreement or by law for amending the operating agreement, to be subject to this [act].

(b) Except as otherwise provided in subsection (c), on and after [all-inclusive date] this [act] governs all limited liability companies.

(c) For purposes of applying this [act] to a limited liability company formed before [the effective date of this [act]]:

(1) the company's articles of organization are deemed to be the company's certificate of organization; and

(2) for purposes of applying Section 102(10) and subject to Section 107(d), language in the company's articles of organization designating the company's management structure operates as if that language were in the operating agreement.

Legislative Note:

For states that have previously enacted ULLCA (2006):

For these states this section is unnecessary. There is no need for a delayed effective date, even with regard to pre-existing limited liability companies.

For states that have not previously enacted ULLCA (2006):

Each enacting jurisdiction should consider whether: (i) this act makes material changes to the "default" (or "gap filler") rules of a predecessor statute; and (ii) if so, whether Subsection (c) should carry forward any of those rules for pre-existing limited liability companies. In this assessment, the focus is on pre-existing limited liability companies that have left default rules in place, whether advisedly or not. The central question is whether, for such limited liability companies, expanding Subsection (c) is necessary to prevent material changes to the members' "deal."

Section 301 (de-codifying statutory apparent authority) does not require any special transition provisions, because: (i) applying the law of agency, as explained in the Comments to Sections 301 and 407, will produce appropriate results; and (ii) the notion of "lingering apparent authority" will protect any third party that has previously relied on the statutory apparent authority of a member of a particular member-managed LLC or a manager of a particular manager-managed LLC. RESTATEMENT (THIRD) OF AGENCY § 3.11, cmt. c (2006).

It is recommended that the "all-inclusive" date should be at least one year after the effective date of this act, Section 1106, but no more than two years.

COMMENT

Subsection (c)—When a pre-existing limited liability company becomes subject to this act, the company ceases to be governed by the predecessor act, including whatever requirements that act might have imposed for the contents of the articles of organization.

§ 111. Supplemental Principles of Law

Unless displaced by particular provisions of this [act], the principles of law and equity supplement this [act].

COMMENT

For this act, the common law rules of contract and agency are among the most important supplemental "principles of law." With regard to transactions under Article 10, noteworthy principles include the rights of creditors following leveraged buyouts, spinoffs, asset purchases, or other similar transactions; and creditors' rights under other laws.

§ 112.   Permitted Names

(a)   The name of a limited liability company must contain the phrase "limited liability company" or "limited company" or the abbreviation "L.L.C.", "LLC", "L.C.", or "LC". "Limited" may be abbreviated as "Ltd.", and "company" may be abbreviated as "Co.".

(b)   Except as otherwise provided in subsection (d), the name of a limited liability company, and the name under which a foreign limited liability company may register to do business in this state, must be distinguishable on the records of the [Secretary of State] from any:

(1)   name of an existing person whose formation required the filing of a record by the [Secretary of State] and which is not at the time administratively dissolved;

(2)   name of a limited liability partnership whose statement of qualification is in effect;

(3)   name under which a person is registered to do business in this state by the filing of a record by the [Secretary of State];

(4)   name reserved under Section 113 or other law of this state providing for the reservation of a name by the filing of a record by the [Secretary of State];

(5)   name registered under Section 114 or other law of this state providing for the registration of a name by the filing of a record by the [Secretary of State]; and

(6)   name registered under [this state's assumed or fictitious name statute].

(c)   If a person consents in a record to the use of its name and submits an undertaking in a form satisfactory to the [Secretary of State] to change its name to a name that is distinguishable on the records of the [Secretary of State] from any name in any category of names in subsection (b), the name of the consenting person may be used by the person to which the consent was given.

(d)   Except as otherwise provided in subsection (e), in determining whether a name is the same as or not distinguishable on the records of the [Secretary of State] from the name of another person, words, phrases, or abbreviations indicating a type of person, such as "corporation", "corp.", "incorporated", "Inc.", "professional corporation", "P.C.", "PC", "professional association", "P.A.", "PA", "Limited", "Ltd.", "limited partnership", "L.P.", "LP", "limited liability partnership", "L.L.P.", "LLP", "registered limited liability partnership", "R.L.L.P.", "RLLP", "limited liability limited partnership", "L.L.L.P.", "LLLP", "registered limited liability limited partnership", "R.L.L.L.P.", "RLLLP", "limited liability company", "L.L.C.", "LLC", "limited cooperative association", "limited cooperative", or "L.C.A.", or "LCA" may not be taken into account.

(e)   A person may consent in a record to the use of a name that is not distinguishable on the records of the [Secretary of State] from its name except for the addition of a word, phrase, or abbreviation indicating the type of person as provided in subsection (d). In such a case, the person need not change its name pursuant to subsection (c).

(f)   The name of a limited liability company or foreign limited liability company may not contain the words [insert prohibited word or words that may be used only with approval by an appropriate state agency].

(g)   A limited liability company or foreign limited liability company may use a name that is not distinguishable from a name described in subsection (b)(1) through (6) if the company delivers to the [Secretary of State] a certified copy of a final judgment of a court of competent jurisdiction establishing the right of the company to use the name in this state.

COMMENT

This section adopts the "distinguishable on the records" test for name availability and rejects the "deceptively similar" test widely used in the past.

For name requirements for foreign limited liability companies, see Section 906.

§ 113.   Reservation of Name

(a)   A person may reserve the exclusive use of a name that complies with Section 112 by delivering an application to the [Secretary of State] for filing. The application must state the name and address of the applicant and the name to be reserved. If the [Secretary of State] finds that the name is available, the [Secretary of State] shall reserve the name for the applicant's exclusive use for [120] days.

(b)   The owner of a reserved name may transfer the reservation to another person by delivering to the [Secretary of State] a signed notice in a record of the transfer which states the name and address of the person to which the reservation is being transferred.

COMMENT

This section does not provide for the renewal of a name reservation for successive 120-day periods. A new reservation may be filed upon the expiration of a reservation, but by requiring a new filing this section creates the possibility that another party may timely submit a reservation for the same name. It was considered appropriate to allow for that possibility so that the procedure in this section cannot be used to block a name indefinitely. *Compare* Section 113, *with* Section 114(d) (authorizing a renewable registration of certain names).

§ 114.   Registration of Name

(a)   A foreign limited liability company not registered to do business in this state under [Article] 9 may register its name, or an alternate name adopted pursuant to Section 906, if the name is distinguishable on the records of the [Secretary of State] from the names that are not available under Section 112.

(b)   To register its name or an alternate name adopted pursuant to Section 906, a foreign limited liability company must deliver to the [Secretary of State] for filing an application stating the company's name, the jurisdiction and date of its formation, and any alternate name adopted pursuant to Section 906. If the [Secretary of State] finds that the name applied for is available, the [Secretary of State] shall register the name for the applicant's exclusive use.

(c)   The registration of a name under this section is effective for [one year] after the date of registration.

(d)   A foreign limited liability company whose name registration is effective may renew the registration for successive [one-year] periods by delivering, not earlier than [three months] before the expiration of the registration, to the [Secretary of State] for filing a renewal application that complies with this section. When filed, the renewal application renews the registration for a succeeding [one-year] period.

(e)   A foreign limited liability company whose name registration is effective may register as a foreign limited liability company under the registered name or consent in a signed record to the use of that name by another person that is not an individual.

COMMENT

Unlike the reservation of a name under Section 113, a registration of a name under this section may be renewed for successive periods thus permitting a name to be protected for a period longer than the initial registration period. Use of the procedure in this section is limited, however, to the names of foreign limited liability companies that are not registered to do business in the state. The purpose of this section is to permit a foreign entity to make sure its name will be available if the entity should choose to register in the state in the future.

§ 115.   Registered Agent

(a)   Each limited liability company and each registered foreign limited liability company shall designate and maintain a registered agent in this state. The designation of a registered agent is an affirmation of fact by the limited liability company or registered foreign limited liability company that the agent has consented to serve.

(b)   A registered agent for a limited liability company or registered foreign limited liability company must have a place of business in this state.

(c)   The only duties under this [act] of a registered agent that has complied with this [act] are:

(1)   to forward to the limited liability company or registered foreign limited liability company at the address most recently supplied to the agent by the company or foreign company any process, notice, or demand pertaining to the company or foreign company which is served on or received by the agent;

(2)   if the registered agent resigns, to provide the notice required by Section 117(c) to the company or foreign company at the address most recently supplied to the agent by the company or foreign company; and

(3)   to keep current the information with respect to the agent in the certificate of organization or foreign registration statement.

COMMENT

This section is limited to prescribing the duties of a registered agent under this act. The operating agreement cannot vary this section. Section 105(c)(3)(A). However, an agent may undertake other responsibilities to a represented limited liability company or foreign limited liability company, such as by contract or course of dealing, but those duties will be determined under other law.

§ 116.   Change of Registered Agent or Address for Registered Agent by Limited Liability Company

(a)   A limited liability company or registered foreign limited liability company may change its registered agent or the address of its registered agent by delivering to the [Secretary of State] for filing a statement of change that states:

(1)   the name of the company or foreign company; and

(2)   the information that is to be in effect as a result of the filing of the statement of change.

(b)   The members or managers of a limited liability company need not approve the delivery to the [Secretary of State] filing of:

(1)   a statement of change under this section; or

(2)   a similar filing changing the registered agent or registered office, if any, of the company in any other jurisdiction.

(c)   A statement of change under this section designating a new registered agent is an affirmation of fact by the limited liability company or registered foreign limited liability company that the agent has consented to serve.

(d)   As an alternative to using the procedure in this section, a limited liability company may amend its certificate of organization.

COMMENT

A change in the identity of the registered agent of a LLC or foreign LLC or a change of the office address of a company's registered agent are usually routine matters that do not affect the rights of the members of the represented LLC. This section permits those changes to be made without: (i) amendment of an LLC's certificate of organization; (ii) formal approval by an LLC's managers (if any); and (iii) any approval by an LLC's members. For the registered agent's power to resign, see Section 117. For the registered agent's power to change its name, address, or both, see Section 118.

Subsection (c)—This subsection avoids the need to file with a statement of change consent of the new registered agent being designated.

Subsection (d)—This subsection makes clear that the procedures in this section are not exclusive. A common way in which a limited liability company changes its registered agent is to include the change in an amendment of its certificate of organization or in its annual/biennial report. *See* Section 212(e).

§ 117. Resignation of Registered Agent

(a)   A registered agent may resign as an agent for a limited liability company or registered foreign limited liability company by delivering to the [Secretary of State] for filing a statement of resignation that states:

(1)   the name of the company or foreign company;

(2)   the name of the agent;

(3)   that the agent resigns from serving as registered agent for the company or foreign company; and

(4)   the address of the company or foreign company to which the agent will send the notice required by subsection (c).

(b)   A statement of resignation takes effect on the earlier of:

(1)   the 31st day after the day on which it is filed by the [Secretary of State]; or

(2)   the designation of a new registered agent for the limited liability company or registered foreign limited liability company.

(c)   A registered agent promptly shall furnish to the limited liability company or registered foreign limited liability company notice in a record of the date on which a statement of resignation was filed.

(d)   When a statement of resignation takes effect, the registered agent ceases to have responsibility under this [act] for any matter thereafter tendered to it as agent for the limited liability company or registered foreign limited liability company. The resignation does not affect any contractual rights the company or foreign company has against the agent or that the agent has against the company or foreign company.

(e)   A registered agent may resign with respect to a limited liability company or registered foreign limited liability company whether or not the company or foreign company is in good standing.

COMMENT

Resignation under this section may be accomplished solely by action of the registered agent and does not require the cooperation or consent of the represented LLC or foreign LLC. Whether a resignation violates a contract between the registered agent and the company is beyond the scope of this act, and Subsection (d) preserves whatever claims a represented LLC may have against its registered agent for a wrongful termination. Even if a resignation were to violate such a contract, the resignation would still be effective if the provisions of this section were followed.

Subsection (b)—This subsection delays the effectiveness of a statement of resignation for thirty-one days to allow the notice of the resignation that must be sent under Subsection (c) to reach the represented LLC or registered foreign LLC and to allow the represented LLC to arrange for a substitute registered agent.

Subsection (e)—This subsection makes clear that a registered agent may resign with respect to LLC or registered foreign LLC that is not in good standing and supersedes the contrary administrative practice in some states of refusing to accept any filings with respect to an entity that is not in good standing until the problem with the entity's standing is cured.

§ 118. Change of Name or Address by Registered Agent

(a)   If a registered agent changes its name or address, the agent may deliver to the [Secretary of State] for filing a statement of change that states:

(1)   the name of the limited liability company or registered foreign limited liability company represented by the registered agent;

(2)   the name of the agent as currently shown in the records of the [Secretary of State] for the company or foreign company;

(3)   if the name of the agent has changed, its new name; and

(4)   if the address of the agent has changed, its new address.

(b)   A registered agent promptly shall furnish notice to the represented limited liability company or registered foreign limited liability company of the filing by the [Secretary of State] of the statement of change and the changes made by the statement.

Legislative Note: Many registered agents act in that capacity for many entities, and the Model Registered Agents Act (2006) (Last Amended 2013) provides a streamlined method through which a commercial registered agent can make a single filing to change its information for all represented entities. The single filing does not prevent an enacting state from assessing filing fees on the basis of the number of entity records affected. Alternatively the fees can be set on an incremental sliding fee or capitated amount based upon potential economies of costs for a bulk filing.

COMMENT

This section permits a registered agent to change the name and address of the agent that appears in the registered agent filing of an LLC or foreign LLC represented by the agent. This act does not provide for commercial registered agents. *Cf.* UBOC (2011) (Last Amended 2013) §§ 1–405, 1–406, 1–409. As a result, a registered agent will need to make a separate filing under this section for each LLC and foreign LLC represented by the agent, unless, if authorized by rule or administrative policy, the filing office establishes procedures for a bulk filing with one filing listing the names of all the registered agent's represented entities.

§ 119.   Service of Process, Notice, or Demand

(a)   A limited liability company or registered foreign limited liability company may be served with any process, notice, or demand required or permitted by law by serving its registered agent.

(b)   If a limited liability company or registered foreign limited liability company ceases to have a registered agent, or if its registered agent cannot with reasonable diligence be served, the company or foreign company may be served by registered or certified mail, return receipt requested, or by similar commercial delivery service, addressed to the company or foreign company at its principal office. The address of the principal office must be as shown on the company's or foreign company's most recent [annual] [biennial] report filed by the [Secretary of State]. Service is effected under this subsection on the earliest of:

(1)   the date the company or foreign company receives the mail or delivery by the commercial delivery service;

(2)   the date shown on the return receipt, if signed by the company or foreign company; or

(3)   five days after its deposit with the United States Postal Service, or with the commercial delivery service, if correctly addressed and with sufficient postage or payment.

(c)   If process, notice, or demand cannot be served on a limited liability company or registered foreign limited liability company pursuant to subsection (a) or (b), service may be made by handing a copy to the individual in charge of any regular place of business or activity of the company or foreign company if the individual served is not a plaintiff in the action.

(d)   Service of process, notice, or demand on a registered agent must be in a written record.

(e)   Service of process, notice, or demand may be made by other means under law other than this [act].

COMMENT

Subsection (b)—This subsection offers three alternative methods for establishing the date service is effected, a date important for determining the time within which an LLC or registered foreign LLC must respond to the process, notice, or demand served. Under Subsection (b)(1), service is effected on the date of receipt by the company of the mail or commercial delivery. Under Subsection (b)(2), service is effected on the date shown on the return receipt, if signed on behalf of the company. Under Subsection (b)(3), service is effected five days after it is deposited with the Postal Service or with a similar commercial delivery service, if correctly addressed and with correct postage or payment. Service is effective at the earliest of the three listed circumstances.

However, for the party effecting service there are difficulties of proof under the first two circumstances. Under Subsection (b)(1) the exact date of the receipt by the LLC or foreign LLC of mail or commercial delivery is peculiarly within the knowledge of the company. Under Subsection (b)(2) the return receipt must be signed on behalf of the company. That requirement is designed to assure that the service is actually received by the company, but the signature on the return receipt may not always show unambiguously that the signer was acting for the company and was authorized to do so. As a practical matter, therefore, parties effecting service under Subsection (b) may find it most convenient to rely on subsection (3) and to maintain their own records so that the date of deposit in the mails or with a commercial delivery service can easily be established.

Subsection (c)—This subsection provides a means for serving process on an LLC or foreign LLC that cannot be served under Subsection (a) or (b). Some LLC statutes require or permit service of process in that circumstance be made on the filing office

Subsection (e)—*See, e.g.*, Fed. R. Civ. P. 4(h)(1)(B) (authorizing service on "a domestic or foreign corporation, or a partnership or other unincorporated association that is subject to suit under a common name" to be made on "an officer, a managing or general agent, or any other agent authorized by appointment or by law to receive service of process").

§ 120.   Delivery of Record

(a)   Except as otherwise provided in this [act], permissible means of delivery of a record include delivery by hand, mail, conventional commercial practice, and electronic transmission.

(b)   Delivery to the [Secretary of State] is effective only when a record is received by the [Secretary of State].

COMMENT

Subsection (a)—Permissible means of delivery are not limited to those listed in this subsection, because this subsection by its terms is a non-exclusive list. Conventional commercial practice includes the use of private delivery or courier services. What constitutes conventional commercial practice may change over time.

Subsection (b)—This section lists permissible means of delivery but, except for delivery to the filing office, does not determine when delivery occurs. Delivery to the filing office is effective only upon actual receipt.

§ 121.   Reservation of Power to Amend or Repeal

The [legislature of this state] has power to amend or repeal all or part of this [act] at any time, and all limited liability companies and foreign limited liability companies subject to this [act] are governed by the amendment or repeal.

COMMENT

Provisions similar to this section have their genesis in *Trustees of Dartmouth College v. Woodward*, 17 U.S. (4 Wheat) 518 (1819), which held that the United States Constitution prohibited the application of newly enacted statutes to existing corporations while suggesting the efficacy of a reservation of power similar to this section. This section is a generalized form of the type of provision found in many entity organic laws, the purpose of which is to avoid any possible argument that an entity has contractual or vested rights in any specific statutory provision of its organic law and to ensure that the state may in the future modify its entity statutes as it deems appropriate and require existing entities to comply with the statutes as modified.

This section applies to changes in mandatory provisions of this act; the section does not pertain to changes in default rules.

Example: Having enacted this act, State A later amends Section 401(c)(3) (affirmative vote or consent of all members required for a person for a person to become a member) to reduce, as a default rule, the necessary quantum of consent to consent from members owning in the aggregate at least two-third of the interests in current profits owned by members at the time of the consent. XYZ, LLC is a limited liability company formed under State A's act before the amendment. XYZ's operating agreement is silent on this issue, leaving in place the act's default rule. Whether the act's amended default rule applies depends on whether the members initially: (i) agreed (whether expressly or implicitly) to accept the then-applicable default rule requiring unanimous consent; (ii) agreed (whether expressly or implicitly) to adopt whatever rule the act provided; or (iii) never considered the issue. In short, the change in a default rule occasions an inquiry into the members' express or implied agreement as to the role of the default rule in their mutual understanding. In the first instance, the old rule would continue in effect. In the second and third instances, the new rule would apply.

[ARTICLE] 2

FORMATION; CERTIFICATE OF ORGANIZATION AND OTHER FILINGS

§ 201.　Formation of Limited Liability Company; Certificate of Organization

(a)　One or more persons may act as organizers to form a limited liability company by delivering to the [Secretary of State] for filing a certificate of organization.

(b)　A certificate of organization must state:

(1)　the name of the limited liability company, which must comply with Section 112;

(2)　the street and mailing addresses of the company's principal office; and

(3)　the name and street and mailing addresses in this state of the company's registered agent.

(c)　A certificate of organization may contain statements as to matters other than those required by subsection (b), but may not vary or otherwise affect the provisions specified in Section 105(c) and (d) in a manner inconsistent with that section. However, a statement in a certificate of organization is not effective as a statement of authority.

(d)　A limited liability company is formed when the certificate of organization becomes effective and at least one person has become a member.

COMMENT

For a limited liability company to be formed (*i.e.*, to come into existence), two conditions must be met: (i) a certificate of organization must become effective; and (ii) at least one person must become a member.

By definition, the earliest a person can become a member is when the certificate of organization takes effect. *See* Section 102(11) (defining "member" as a person that "has become a member of a limited liability company"). However, a certificate of organization can take effect long before any person becomes a member, and the act does not require any public filing to indicate that a person has become a member. Therefore, the public record will not reflect when (and even whether) a limited liability company has come into existence. *See also* the comment to Section 211.

Subsection (b)—Consistent with the modern trend, this act requires only the most "bare bones" of disclosure.

Unlike many LLC statutes, this act does not require that the certificate of organization state whether the limited liability company is manager-managed or member-managed. Placing that information in a public record pertains primarily to "statutory apparent authority," which this act has eschewed. *See* the comment to Section 301(a). Under this act, the manager-managed and member-managed characterizations pertain principally to *inter se* relations, and the act therefore looks to the operating agreement to make the characterization. *See* Sections 102(10) and (12); Section 407(a).

Subsection (c)—This provision permits the certificate of organization to contain information beyond that required in Subsection (b). An LLC should have good reason, however, before choosing to include additional information. Such information: (i) is available to the public (including competitors); (ii) increases the chances of a conflict between the certificate of organization and the operating agreement, *see* Section 107(d); (iii) permits the argument that the additional information is part of the operating agreement, *see* the comment to Section 102(13) (stating that "[u]nless the operating agreement itself provides otherwise . . . an operating agreement may comprise a number of separate documents (or records), however denominated"); and (iv) can be confusing to the extent the information appears to delineate the power of persons to act for the LLC. (Subsection (c) states explicitly that information in a certificate of formation "is not effective as a statement of authority."). In any event, placing additional information in the certificate of formation does not enable an LLC to "end run" the provisions of Section 105(c) (limiting the power of the operating agreement to vary specified provisions of this act).

Subsection (d)—ULLCA (2006) flirted with the concept of a "shelf" LLC—*i.e.*, a limited liability company duly formed without having at least one member upon formation. As the Prefatory Note to ULLCA (2006) explains:

[T]he Act: (i) permits an organizer to file a certificate of organization without a person "waiting in the wings" to become a member upon formation; but (ii) provides that the LLC is not formed until and unless at least one person becomes a member and the organizer makes a second filing stating that the LLC has at least one member.

Prefatory Note, *The Ability to "Pre-File" a Certificate of Organization.*

Subsection (d) clearly precludes a "shelf" LLC, which is consistent with ULPA (2001) (Last Amended 2013) Section 201(d) (providing that a limited partnership is formed when the certificate of limited partnership becomes effective, at least two persons have become partners, at least one person has become a general partner, and at least one person has become a limited partner).

§ 202. Amendment or Restatement of Certificate of Organization

(a)   A certificate of organization may be amended or restated at any time.

(b)   To amend its certificate of organization, a limited liability company must deliver to the [Secretary of State] for filing an amendment stating:

(1)   the name of the company;

(2)   the date of filing of its initial certificate; and

(3)   the text of the amendment.

(c)   To restate its certificate of organization, a limited liability company must deliver to the [Secretary of State] for filing a restatement, designated as such in its heading.

(d)   If a member of a member-managed limited liability company, or a manager of a manager-managed limited liability company, knows that any information in a filed certificate of organization was inaccurate when the certificate was filed or has become inaccurate due to changed circumstances, the member or manager shall promptly:

(1)   cause the certificate to be amended; or

(2)   if appropriate, deliver to the [Secretary of State] for filing a statement of change under Section 116 or a statement of correction under Section 209.

COMMENT

Like other provisions of the act requiring records to be delivered to the filing officer for filing, this section is not subject to change by the operating agreement. See Section 105(c)(3). Except for Subsection (d), this section is essentially mechanical.

Subsection (d)—This subsection imposes an obligation directly on the members and managers rather than on the limited liability company. A member's or manager's failure to meet the obligation exposes the member or manager to liability to third parties under Section 205(a)(2) and might constitute a breach of the member or manager's duties under Section 409(c) and (i). In addition, an aggrieved person may seek a remedy under Sections 204 (Signing and Filing Pursuant to Judicial Order) and 205 (Liability for Inaccurate Information in Filed Record).

Like other provisions of the act requiring records to be delivered to the filing officer for filing, this section is not subject to change by the operating agreement. *See* Section 105(c)(3).

§ 203. Signing of Records to be Delivered for Filing to [Secretary of State]

(a)   A record delivered to the [Secretary of State] for filing pursuant to this [act] must be signed as follows:

(1)   Except as otherwise provided in paragraphs (2) and (3), a record signed by a limited liability company must be signed by a person authorized by the company.

(2)   A company's initial certificate of organization must be signed by at least one person acting as an organizer.

(3)   A record delivered on behalf of a dissolved company that has no member must be signed by the person winding up the company's activities and affairs under Section 702(c) or a person appointed under Section 702(d) to wind up the activities and affairs.

(4)   A statement of denial by a person under Section 303 must be signed by that person.

(5)   Any other record delivered on behalf of a person to the [Secretary of State] for filing must be signed by that person.

(b)   A record delivered for filing under this [act] may be signed by an agent. Whenever this [act] requires a particular individual to sign a record and the individual is deceased or incompetent, the record may be signed by a legal representative of the individual.

(c)   A person that signs a record as an agent or legal representative affirms as a fact that the person is authorized to sign the record.

COMMENT

Subsection (a)—Section 102(21) defines "sign" broadly, including "an electronic symbol, sound, or process."

Subsection (a)(1)—From the perspective of the filing office, it is not necessary that a record delivered for filing on behalf of a limited liability company be signed by a member or, in the case of a manager-managed LLC, a manager. The operating agreement can impose such a requirement as an *inter se* matter, but the requirement would not affect this provision. See Section 105(c)(3)(B) (stating that the operating agreement may not "vary any requirement, procedure, or other provision of this [act] pertaining to . . . the [Secretary of State], including provisions pertaining to records authorized or required to be delivered to the [Secretary of State] for filing under this [act]").

The filing office will not check whether a person who purports to be authorized to sign a record on behalf of an LLC actually has that authority, even if a statement of authority pertaining to the matter is in effect. Indeed, even if the filing office somehow "knows" of a statement limiting authority, the office lacks the authority to reject a record on that basis. *See* the comment to Section 206(a) (stating the requirements for filing and noting that the filing office's review is ministerial and limited to information pertaining to the stated requirements) and the comment to Section 302(c) (explaining why such a statement of authority does not affect the filing office).

Subsection (b)—The filing office will not check the bona fides of a person purporting to have signed a record in a representative capacity. This subsection expressly authorizes taking action through an agent so as to provide context for Subsection (c) and for the avoidance of doubt. No negative inference should be drawn about using agents to take other action under this act.

Subsection (c)—As a matter of agency law, a person who signs in a representative capacity gives a "warranty of authority." RESTATEMENT (THIRD) OF AGENCY § 6.10 (2006) (Agent's Implied Warranty of Authority). This subsection has criminal law implications.

§ 204.   Signing and Filing Pursuant to Judicial Order

(a)   If a person required by this [act] to sign a record or deliver a record to the [Secretary of State] for filing under this [act] does not do so, any other person that is aggrieved may petition [the appropriate court] to order:

(1)   the person to sign the record;

(2)   the person to deliver the record to the [Secretary of State] for filing; or

(3)   the [Secretary of State] to file the record unsigned.

(b)   If a petitioner under subsection (a) is not the limited liability company or foreign limited liability company to which the record pertains, the petitioner shall make the company or foreign company a party to the action.

(c)   A record filed under subsection (a)(3) is effective without being signed.

COMMENT

This section gives the court the flexibility to order either that a record be signed or that the record be filed by the filing office unsigned. The latter circumstance may arise, for example, in a situation where the person who should sign the record is not subject to the jurisdiction of the court. This section also makes clear that the court may order a person with control over a record that has been signed to deliver the record to the filing office for filing.

§ 205. Liability for Inaccurate Information in Filed Record

(a) If a record delivered to the [Secretary of State] for filing under this [act] and filed by the [Secretary of State] contains inaccurate information, a person that suffers loss by reliance on the information may recover damages for the loss from:

(1) a person that signed the record, or caused another to sign it on the person's behalf, and knew the information to be inaccurate at the time the record was signed; and

(2) subject to subsection (b), a member of a member-managed limited liability company or a manager of a manager-managed limited liability company if:

(A) the record was delivered for filing on behalf of the company; and

(B) the member or manager knew or had notice of the inaccuracy for a reasonably sufficient time before the information was relied upon so that, before the reliance, the member or manager reasonably could have:

(i) effected an amendment under Section 202;

(ii) filed a petition under Section 204; or

(iii) delivered to the [Secretary of State] for filing a statement of change under Section 116 or a statement of correction under Section 209.

(b) To the extent the operating agreement of a member-managed limited liability company expressly relieves a member of responsibility for maintaining the accuracy of information contained in records delivered on behalf of the company to the [Secretary of State] for filing under this [act] and imposes that responsibility on one or more other members, the liability stated in subsection (a)(2) applies to those other members and not to the member that the operating agreement relieves of the responsibility.

(c) An individual who signs a record authorized or required to be filed under this [act] affirms under penalty of perjury that the information stated in the record is accurate.

Subsection (a)—This subsection relates to liability to third parties for inaccurate information in a filed record. Paragraph 1 requires actual knowledge because the paragraph can inculpate a person who is neither a member of a member-managed limited liability company nor a manager of a manager-managed limited liability company. Under Paragraph 2(B), notice suffices, because: (i) the provision applies only to members of a member-managed LLC and managers of a manager-managed LLC; (ii) by status these persons have overall management authority; and (iii) therefore it is reasonable to impose liability when a person either knows or "has reason to know . . . from all the facts known to the person at the time in question." Section 103(b)(1) (defining notice). For the same reason, Paragraph 1 applies only to "information [known] to be inaccurate at the time the record was signed," while Paragraph 2 applies whenever a "member or manager knew or had notice of the inaccuracy for a reasonably sufficient time before the information was relied upon so that, before the reliance, the member or manager reasonably could have [taken corrective action]." Paragraph (2)(B).

Subsection (a)(2)—Although this act establishes the avoidance of gross negligence as the standard of care for those who manage a limited liability company, this provision encompasses liability to third parties. Accordingly, the standard here is more demanding. The phrases "reasonably sufficient time" and "reasonably could have" indicate a standard of ordinary care. "[N]otice of the inaccuracy" involves "reason to know." Section 103(b)(1)

Subsection (b)—Section 105(d)(2) authorizes the operating agreement to establish an analogous rule *inter se* the members. This subsection goes where the operating agreement cannot reach and affects the rights of third parties.

Subsection (c)—This subsection provides criminal liability. The elements of perjury are a matter for the criminal law of the jurisdiction.

§ 206.   Filing Requirements

(a)   To be filed by the [Secretary of State] pursuant to this [act], a record must be received by the [Secretary of State], comply with this [act], and satisfy the following:

(1)   The filing of the record must be required or permitted by this [act].

(2)   The record must be physically delivered in written form unless and to the extent the [Secretary of State] permits electronic delivery of records.

(3)   The words in the record must be in English, and numbers must be in Arabic or Roman numerals, but the name of an entity need not be in English if written in English letters or Arabic or Roman numerals.

(4)   The record must be signed by a person authorized or required under this [act] to sign the record.

(5)   The record must state the name and capacity, if any, of each individual who signed it, either on behalf of the individual or the person authorized or required to sign the record, but need not contain a seal, attestation, acknowledgment, or verification.

(b)   If law other than this [act] prohibits the disclosure by the [Secretary of State] of information contained in a record delivered to the [Secretary of State] for filing, the [Secretary of State] shall file the record if the record otherwise complies with this [act] but may redact the information.

(c)   When a record is delivered to the [Secretary of State] for filing, any fee required under this [act] and any fee, tax, interest, or penalty required to be paid under this [act] or law other than this [act] must be paid in a manner permitted by the [Secretary of State] or by that law.

(d)   The [Secretary of State] may require that a record delivered in written form be accompanied by an identical or conformed copy.

(e)   The [Secretary of State] may provide forms for filings required or permitted to be made by this [act], but, except as otherwise provided in subsection (f), their use is not required.

(f)   The [Secretary of State] may require that a cover sheet for a filing be on a form prescribed by the [Secretary of State].

COMMENT

The filing office's duty under this section is ministerial, Section 210(a), and the office's assessment of a record delivered for filing is limited to conformity with this section. The filing office *must* file a record delivered for filing if the record contains the information required by this act and is accompanied by the required filing fee. The filing office is authorized to provide forms but not require their use, and, as a result, may not reject records delivered for filing on the basis of form (except to the very limited extent permitted by Subsections (d) and (f)).

In view of the very limited discretion granted to the filing office under this section and Section 210(a), "[t]he filing of . . . a record does not create a presumption that the information contained in the record is correct. . . ." Section 210(e).

Subsection (a)—The first requisite for having a record filed is to cause the record actually to be received by the filing office. Section 120(b) reiterates this point.

Subsection (a)(2)—A record delivered for filing must be in typewritten or printed form unless the filing office permits delivery by electronic transmission. The types of electronic transmission that may be used will be determined by the filing office and is intended to include the evolving methods of electronic delivery, including facsimile transmissions, electronic transmissions between computers, and filings through delivery of storage media.

Subsection (a)(3)—The text of an entity filing must be in the English language, except to the limited extent permitted by this paragraph.

Subsection (a)(4)—To be filed a record must be signed by the appropriate person. *See* Section 102(21) (defining "sign" and manner in which a record may be "signed"). Who is an appropriate person is determined under Section 203, but the filing office will not check to determine whether a person purportedly authorized to sign is in fact authorized. *See* the comment to Section 203(a)–(c).

The requirement in some state statutes that records delivered for filing on behalf of an entity must be acknowledged or verified as a condition for filing has been rejected. These requirements serve little purpose in connection with entity filings. On the other hand, many organizations, like lenders or title companies, may desire that specific records include acknowledgements, verifications, or seals; Subsection (a)(4) does not prohibit the addition of these forms of execution and their use does not affect the eligibility of the record for filing.

Subsection (b)—Under this subsection, a confidentiality obligation does not affect the filing office's duty to file, and the filing office is authorized but not required to redact. This act does not affect any confidentiality-related obligations the filing office may have under other law.

§ 207. Effective Date and Time

Except as otherwise provided in Section 208 and subject to Section 209(d), a record filed under this [act] is effective:

(1) on the date and at the time of its filing by the [Secretary of State], as provided in Section 210(b);

(2) on the date of filing and at the time specified in the record as its effective time, if later than the time under paragraph (1);

(3) at a specified delayed effective date and time, which may not be more than 90 days after the date of filing; or

(4) if a delayed effective date is specified, but no time is specified, at 12:01 a.m. on the date specified, which may not be more than 90 days after the date of filing.

COMMENT

Records accepted for filing become effective at the date and time of filing as recorded by the filing office, or at another specified time on that date, unless a permissible delayed effective date is stated in the record.

Section 210(b) requires the filing office to maintain some means of recording the date and time of delivery of a record and requires that office to record that date and time as the date and time of filing. That provision gives express statutory authority to the common practice of most filing offices of ignoring processing time and treating a record as filed as of the date and time it is delivered for filing even though it may not be reviewed and accepted for filing until several days after delivery. That section contemplates that time of delivery, as well as the date, will be routinely recorded.

Paragraph (1)—In the absence of provision for a delayed effective date, a record delivered for filing becomes effective on the date and time of filing by the filing office. Since under 210(b) the date and time of filing is the recorded date and time of delivery of the record to the filing office (which under Section 210(b) is the date and time of actual receipt), together these provisions eliminate any doubt about situations involving same-day transactions in which a record, for example, a statement of merger, is delivered for filing on the morning of the day the merger is to become effective.

Paragraph (3)—This paragraph does not authorize or contemplate the retroactive establishment of an effective date before the date of filing.

Paragraphs (3) and (4)—A record that states an effective date beyond the 90-day limit is not a record that "satisfies this [act]," Section 210(a), and will properly be rejected by the filing office.

§ 208. Withdrawal of Filed Record Before Effectiveness

(a) Except as otherwise provided in Sections 1024, 1034, 1044, and 1054, a record delivered to the [Secretary of State] for filing may be withdrawn before it takes effect by delivering to the [Secretary of State] for filing a statement of withdrawal.

(b) A statement of withdrawal must:

(1) be signed by each person that signed the record being withdrawn, except as otherwise agreed by those persons;

(2) identify the record to be withdrawn; and

(3) if signed by fewer than all the persons that signed the record being withdrawn, state that the record is withdrawn in accordance with the agreement of all the persons that signed the record.

(c) On filing by the [Secretary of State] of a statement of withdrawal, the action or transaction evidenced by the original record does not take effect.

COMMENT

Only records that have not yet taken effect may be withdrawn under this section. If a record has taken effect, it may be corrected under Section 209 if the requirements of that section are satisfied. Otherwise, the record must be amended in accordance with this act or, if the record is a certificate of organization, the resulting limited liability company may be dissolved and terminated in accordance with Article 7.

Subsection (b)(1)—This provision is subject to Section 203(b) ("Whenever this [act] requires a particular individual to sign a record and the individual is deceased or incompetent, the record may be signed by a legal representative of the individual.").

§ 209.   Correcting Filed Record

(a) A person on whose behalf a filed record was delivered to the [Secretary of State] for filing may correct the record if:

(1) the record at the time of filing was inaccurate;

(2) the record was defectively signed; or

(3) the electronic transmission of the record to the [Secretary of State] was defective.

(b) To correct a filed record, a person on whose behalf the record was delivered to the [Secretary of State] must deliver to the [Secretary of State] for filing a statement of correction.

(c) A statement of correction:

(1) may not state a delayed effective date;

(2) must be signed by the person correcting the filed record;

(3) must identify the filed record to be corrected;

(4) must specify the inaccuracy or defect to be corrected; and

(5) must correct the inaccuracy or defect.

(d) A statement of correction is effective as of the effective date of the filed record that it corrects except for purposes of Section 103(d) and as to persons relying on the uncorrected filed record and adversely affected by the correction. For those purposes and as to those persons, the statement of correction is effective when filed.

COMMENT

This section permits making corrections in filed records without re-submitting the entire record.

Subsection (a)(1) and (2)—A filed record may be corrected because it contains an inaccuracy or because it was defectively signed (including defects in optional forms of execution that do not affect the eligibility of the original record for filing).

Subsection (a)(3)—In addition, a filed record may be corrected if its electronic transmission was defective— *i.e.*, where an electronic delivery is made but, due to a defect in transmission, the filed record is later discovered to be inconsistent with the record intended to be filed. If no delivery is made because of a defect in transmission, a statement of correction may not be used to effect a retroactive filing. Therefore, a limited liability company making an electronic delivery should take steps to confirm that the transmission was received by the filing office.

Subsection (c)—A provision in a filed record setting an effective date may be corrected under this section, but the corrected effective date must comply with Section 207, which limits delayed effective dates to within ninety days after filing. A corrected effective date is thus measured from the date of the original filing of the record being corrected, *i.e.*, it cannot be before the date of filing of the record or more than ninety days thereafter.

Subsection (d)—The correction relates back to the original effective date of the record being corrected, except as to persons relying on the original entity filing and adversely affected by the correction. As to these persons, the effective date of the statement of correction is the date the statement is filed.

§ 210. **Duty of [Secretary of State] to File; Review of Refusal to File; Delivery of Record by [Secretary of State]**

(a)   The [Secretary of State] shall file a record delivered to the [Secretary of State] for filing which satisfies this [act]. The duty of the [Secretary of State] under this section is ministerial.

(b)   When the [Secretary of State] files a record, the [Secretary of State] shall record it as filed on the date and at the time of its delivery. After filing a record, the [Secretary of State] shall deliver to the person that submitted the record a copy of the record with an acknowledgment of the date and time of filing and, in the case of a statement of denial, also to the limited liability company to which the statement pertains.

(c)   If the [Secretary of State] refuses to file a record, the [Secretary of State] shall, not later than [15] business days after the record is delivered:

(1)   return the record or notify the person that submitted the record of the refusal; and

(2)   provide a brief explanation in a record of the reason for the refusal.

(d)   If the [Secretary of State] refuses to file a record, the person that submitted the record may petition [the appropriate court] to compel filing of the record. The record and the explanation of the [Secretary of State] of the refusal to file must be attached to the petition. The court may decide the matter in a summary proceeding.

(e)   The filing of or refusal to file a record does not:

(1)   affect the validity or invalidity of the record in whole or in part; or

(2)   create a presumption that the information contained in the record is correct or incorrect.

(f)   Except as otherwise provided by Section 119 or by law other than this [act], the [Secretary of State] may deliver any record to a person by delivering it:

(1)   in person to the person that submitted it;

(2)   to the address of the person's registered agent;

(3)   to the principal office of the person; or

(4)   to another address the person provides to the [Secretary of State] for delivery.

COMMENT

Subsection (a)—Under this subsection the filing office is required to file a record if it "satisfies this [act]." The purpose of this language is to limit the discretion of the filing office to a ministerial role in reviewing the contents of records. If the record submitted is in the form prescribed, contains the information required by this act, and the appropriate filing fee is tendered, the filing office must file the record. Consistent with this approach, this subsection states explicitly that the filing duty of the filing office is ministerial. *See also* Subsection (e) (pertaining to presumptions not created).

Subsection (b)—This subsection provides that when the filing office files a record, the filing office records it as filed on the date and time of delivery to the filing office, retains the original record for the office's records, and delivers a copy of the record to the person who delivered the record for filing with an acknowledgement of the date and time of filing. In the case of a statement of denial, Section 303, the filing office will also send a copy of the record and acknowledgment to the limited liability company.

In the case of a record transmitted electronically to the filing office, that office may make delivery by electronic transmission. The copy returned will be the exact or conformed copy if one has been required by the filing office, or will be a copy made by the filing office if an exact or conformed copy was not required.

Under this subsection the acceptance of a filing is evidenced merely by the filing office's delivery of a copy of the record with an acknowledgment of the date and time of filing. The act does not provide for the filing office to issue a formal certificate of filing. A copy of the filed record together with an acknowledgment of the date and time of filing should sufficiently indicate that the filing has been accepted for filing and been filed.

Subsection (c)—Because of the simplification of formal filing requirements and the limited discretion granted to the filing office by this act, it is probable that rejection of records delivered to the filing office for filing will occur only rarely. This subsection provides that if the filing office does reject a record delivered for filing, the filing office must return the record to the person that submitted the filing within fifteen days together with a brief written explanation of the reason for rejection. In the case of a record delivered by electronic transmission, rejection of the record may be made electronically by the filing office or by a mailing to the person that submitted the record.

Subsection (e)—This subsection provides that the filing of a record by the filing office does not affect the validity or invalidity of any provision contained in the record and does not create any presumption with respect to any information in the record. Likewise, the refusal of the filing office to file a record creates no presumption that any of the information in the record is incorrect. Persons adversely affected by a statement in a filed record may contest the statement in a proceeding appropriate for that purpose, including a damage action under Section 205.

§ 211.   Certificate of Good Standing or Registration

(a)   On request of any person, the [Secretary of State] shall issue a certificate of good standing for a limited liability company or a certificate of registration for a registered foreign limited liability company.

(b)   A certificate under subsection (a) must state:

(1)   the limited liability company's name or the registered foreign limited liability company's name used in this state;

(2)   in the case of a limited liability company:

(A)   that a certificate of organization has been filed and has taken effect;

(B)   the date the certificate became effective;

(C)   the period of the company's duration if the records of the [Secretary of State] reflect that its period of duration is less than perpetual; and

(D)   that:

(i)   no statement of dissolution, statement of administrative dissolution, or statement of termination has been filed;

(ii)   the records of the [Secretary to State] do not otherwise reflect that the company has been dissolved or terminated; and

(iii)   a proceeding is not pending under Section 708;

(3)   in the case of a registered foreign limited liability company, that it is registered to do business in this state;

(4)   that all fees, taxes, interest, and penalties owed to this state by the limited liability company or foreign limited liability company and collected through the [Secretary of State] have been paid, if:

(A)   payment is reflected in the records of the [Secretary of State]; and

(B)   nonpayment affects the good standing or registration of the company or foreign company;

(5)   that the most recent [annual] [biennial] report required by Section 212 has been delivered to the [Secretary of State] for filing; and

(6)   other facts reflected in the records of the [Secretary of State] pertaining to the limited liability company or foreign limited liability company which the person requesting the certificate reasonably requests.

(c)   Subject to any qualification stated in the certificate, a certificate issued by the [Secretary of State] under subsection (a) may be relied on as conclusive evidence of the facts stated in the certificate.

COMMENT

This section establishes a procedure by which anyone may obtain a conclusive certificate from the filing office that, among other things, the records of the filing office either (i) do not indicate that a particular domestic limited liability company has ceased to exist; or (ii) indicate that a particular foreign limited liability company is registered to do business in the state. The certificate will probably be a standardized form. The filing office is to make those determinations from public records only and is neither expected nor permitted to make a more extensive investigation.

Thus, the certificate of good standing will state whether a certificate has been filed and become effective but not that the limited liability company has been formed. For two reasons, a certificate concerning a domestic limited liability company can never conclusively indicate whether the LLC has actually been formed and, if formed, whether the LLC has been dissolved. Formation depends in part on the occurrence of an act "not of record." *See* Section 201(d) ("A limited liability company is formed when the company's certificate of organization becomes effective and at least one person becomes a member."). Similarly, causes of dissolution are typically "not of record." *See* Section 701. A dissolved limited liability company may deliver for filing a statement of dissolution, Section 702(b)(2)(A), and the filing of such a statement would preclude the issuance of a certificate of good standing, Subsection (b)(2)(D)(i). However a statement of dissolution is permissive; so too is a statement of termination. *See* Section 702(b)(2)(F).

Subsection (b)(4)(B)—This provision refers only to fees, taxes, interest, and penalties collected by the filing office. In some states other agencies may report to the filing office that franchise or other taxes have been paid; in those states, this information may be included in the certificate. In states where this procedure does not unduly delay the issuance of certificates, this section may be revised appropriately. Subsection (b)(4)(B) limits the scope of the statement in the certificate that all fees, taxes, interest, and penalties have been paid to those where nonpayment affects the existence or authorization to do business of the entity.

§ 212.   [Annual] [Biennial] Report for [Secretary of State]

(a)   A limited liability company or registered foreign limited liability company shall deliver to the [Secretary of State] for filing [an annual] [a biennial] report that states:

     (1)   the name of the company or foreign company;

     (2)   the name and street and mailing addresses of its registered agent in this state;

     (3)   the street and mailing addresses of its principal office;

     (4)   if the company is member managed, the name of at least one member;

     (5)   if the company is manager managed, the name of at least one manager; and

     (6)   in the case of a foreign company, its jurisdiction of formation and any alternate name adopted under Section 906(a).

(b)   Information in the [annual] [biennial] report must be current as of the date the report is signed by the limited liability company or registered foreign limited liability company.

(c)   The first [annual] [biennial] report must be delivered to the [Secretary of State] for filing after [January 1] and before [April 1] of the year following the calendar year in which the limited liability company's certificate of organization became effective or the registered foreign limited liability company registered to do business in this state. Subsequent [annual] [biennial] reports must be delivered to the [Secretary of State] for filing after [January 1] and before [April 1] of each [second] calendar year thereafter.

(d)   If [an annual] [a biennial] report does not contain the information required by this section, the [Secretary of State] promptly shall notify the reporting limited liability company or registered foreign limited liability company in a record and return the report for correction.

apparent authority → 3rd party has knowledge that agent is working under the principal & binding

(e)   If [an annual] [a biennial] report contains the name or address of a registered agent which differs from the information shown in the records of the [Secretary of State] immediately before the report becomes effective, the differing information in the report is considered a statement of change under Section 116.

COMMENT

In some states, an annual or biennial report by a limited liability company or registered foreign limited liability company will be a new requirement.

Subsection (a)(4) and (5)—The requirement that the report include the name of at least one member of a member-managed LLC and one manager of a manager-managed LLC will be a new requirement in some states. There has been increasing pressure from law enforcement agencies for access to more information about the ownership and control of legal entities. This requirement will enable law enforcement to contact a person with some knowledge about the affairs of the limited liability company. Members of the public will also have that ability.

[ARTICLE] 3

RELATIONS OF MEMBERS AND MANAGERS TO PERSONS DEALING WITH LIMITED LIABILITY COMPANY

rejects the statutory apparent authority approach

§ 301.   No Agency Power of Member as Member

(a)   A member is not an agent of a limited liability company solely by reason of being a member.

(b)   A person's status as a member does not prevent or restrict law other than this [act] from imposing liability on a limited liability company because of the person's conduct.

COMMENT

Subsection (a)—Most LLC statutes, including the original ULLCA (1996), provide for what might be termed "statutory apparent authority" for members in a member-managed limited liability company and managers in a manager-managed limited liability company. This approach codifies the common law notion of apparent authority by position and dates back at least to the original Uniform Partnership Act. UPA (1914) § 9 provided that "the act of every partner ... for apparently carrying on in the usual way the business of the partnership ... binds the partnership," and that formulation has been essentially followed by UPA (1997) § 301, ULLCA (1996) § 301, ULPA (2001) § 402, and myriad state LLC statutes.

This act rejects the statutory apparent authority approach, for reasons summarized in a "Progress Report on the Revised Uniform Limited Liability Company Act," published in the March 2006 issue of the newsletter of the ABA Committee on Partnerships and Unincorporated Business Organizations:

The concept [of statutory apparent authority] still makes sense both for general and limited partnerships. A third party dealing with either type of partnership can know by the formal name of the entity and by a person's status as general or limited partner whether the person has the power to bind the entity.

Most LLC statutes have attempted to use the same approach but with a fundamentally important (and problematic) distinction. An LLC's status as member-managed or manager-managed determines whether members or managers have the statutory power to bind. But an LLC's status as member- or manager-managed is not apparent from the LLC's name. A third party must check the public record, which may reveal that the LLC is manager-managed, which in turn means a member as member has no power to bind the LLC. As a result, a provision that originated in 1914 as a protection for third parties can, in the LLC context, easily function as a trap for the unwary. The problem is exacerbated by the almost infinite variety of management structures permissible in and used by LLCs.

The new Act cuts through this problem by simply eliminating statutory apparent authority.

PUBOGRAM, Vol. XXIII, no. 2 at 9–10.

Codifying power to bind according to position makes sense only for organizations that have well-defined, well-known, and almost paradigmatic management structures. Because:

- flexibility of management structure is a hallmark of the limited liability company; and

- an LLC's name gives no signal as to the organization's structure, it makes no sense to:

- require each LLC to publicly select between two statutorily preordained structures (*i.e.*, manager-managed/member-managed); and then

- link a "statutory power to bind" to each of those two structures.

Under this act, other law—most especially the law of agency—will handle power-to-bind questions. Thus, LLCs formed under this act and corporations are subject to the same principles for attributing to the entity the conduct of those who act or purport to act on the entity's behalf. *See* RESTATEMENT (THIRD) AGENCY §§ 1.03, cmt. c (manifestations of authority by organizations); 2.01, cmt. e (actual authority); 2.03, cmts. (c)–(e) (apparent authority) (2006). Section 407 provides the default rules on the actual authority of those who manage an LLC.

This subsection does not address the power to bind of a manager in a manager-managed LLC, although this act does consider a manager's management responsibilities. *See* Section 407(c) (allocating management authority, subject to the operating agreement). For a discussion of how agency law will approach the actual and apparent authority of managers, see Section 407(c), comment.

Subsection (b)—As the "flip side" to Subsection (a), this subsection expressly preserves the power of other law to hold an LLC directly or vicariously liable on account of conduct by a person who happens to be a member. For example, given the proper set of circumstances: (i) a member might have actual or apparent authority to bind an LLC to a contract; (ii) the doctrine of *respondeat superior* might make an LLC liable for the tortious conduct of a member (*i.e.*, in some circumstances a member acts analogously to a "servant" or "employee" of the LLC); and (iii) an LLC might be liable for negligently supervising a member who is acting on behalf of the LLC. A person's status as a member does not weigh against these or any other relevant theories of law.

Moreover, subsection (a) does not prevent member status from being relevant to one or more elements of an "other law" theory. *See* Section 111. The most likely "other law" theory is the agency doctrine of apparent authority. Of course, if a member lacking actual authority binds an LLC through conduct within the member's apparent authority, the LLC has a claim against the member. RESTATEMENT (THIRD) OF AGENCY § 8.09 (2006) (Duty to Act Only Within Scope of Actual Authority and to Comply with Principal's Lawful Instructions). In contrast, if the member lacked even the power to bind the LLC, the member him, her, or itself will be liable to the vendor as a matter of agency law. RESTATEMENT (THIRD) OF AGENCY § 6.10 (2006) (Agent's Implied Warranty of Authority).

For example, the common law of agency will determine the apparent authority of a member to bind a member-managed LLC. In that analysis what the particular third party knows or has reason to know about the management structure and business practices of the particular LLC will always be relevant. RESTATEMENT (THIRD) OF AGENCY § 3.03, cmt. b (2006) ("A principal may also make a manifestation by placing an agent in a defined position in an organization . . . . Third parties who interact with the principal through the agent will naturally and reasonably assume that the agent has authority to do acts consistent with the agent's position . . . unless they have notice of facts suggesting that this may not be so.")

Under Section 301(a), however, the mere fact that a person is a member of a member-managed limited liability company cannot *by itself* establish apparent authority by position. A course of dealing, however, may easily change the analysis:

Example: David is a one of two members of DS, LLC, a member-managed LLC. David orders paper clips on behalf of the LLC, signing the purchase agreement, "David, as a member of DS, LLC." Absent further facts, David has no apparent authority to bind the LLC.

However, the vendor accepts the order, sends an invoice to the LLC's address, and in due course receives a check drawn on the LLC's bank account. When David next places an order with the vendor, the LLC's payment of the first order is a manifestation that the vendor may use in asserting that David had apparent authority to place the second order. A successful apparent authority claim also presupposes that: (i) the vendor believed that David was authorized; and (ii) the belief was reasonable. RESTATEMENT (THIRD) OF AGENCY § 3.03 (2006) (Creation of Apparent Authority).

In general, a member's actual authority to act for an LLC will depend fundamentally on the operating agreement. *See* the comment to Section 407(b).

§ 302. Statement of Limited Liability Company Authority

(a) A limited liability company may deliver to the [Secretary of State] for filing a statement of authority. The statement:

(1)   must include the name of the company and the name and street and mailing addresses of its registered agent;

(2)   with respect to any position that exists in or with respect to the company, may state the authority, or limitations on the authority, of all persons holding the position to:

    (A)   sign an instrument transferring real property held in the name of the company; or

    (B)   enter into other transactions on behalf of, or otherwise act for or bind, the company; and

(3)   may state the authority, or limitations on the authority, of a specific person to:

    (A)   sign an instrument transferring real property held in the name of the company; or

    (B)   enter into other transactions on behalf of, or otherwise act for or bind, the company.

(b)   To amend or cancel a statement of authority filed by the [Secretary of State], a limited liability company must deliver to the [Secretary of State] for filing an amendment or cancellation stating:

(1)   the name of the company;

(2)   the name and street and mailing addresses of the company's registered agent;

(3)   the date the statement being affected became effective; and

(4)   the contents of the amendment or a declaration that the statement is canceled.

(c)   A statement of authority affects only the power of a person to bind a limited liability company to persons that are not members.

(d)   Subject to subsection (c) and Section 103(d), and except as otherwise provided in subsections (f), (g), and (h), a limitation on the authority of a person or a position contained in an effective statement of authority is not by itself evidence of any person's knowledge or notice of the limitation.

(e)   Subject to subsection (c), a grant of authority not pertaining to transfers of real property and contained in an effective statement of authority is conclusive in favor of a person that gives value in reliance on the grant, except to the extent that when the person gives value:

(1)   the person has knowledge to the contrary;

(2)   the statement has been canceled or restrictively amended under subsection (b); or

(3)   a limitation on the grant is contained in another statement of authority that became effective after the statement containing the grant became effective.

(f)   Subject to subsection (c), an effective statement of authority that grants authority to transfer real property held in the name of the limited liability company, a certified copy of which statement is recorded in the office for recording transfers of the real property, is conclusive in favor of a person that gives value in reliance on the grant without knowledge to the contrary, except to the extent that when the person gives value:

(1)   the statement has been canceled or restrictively amended under subsection (b), and a certified copy of the cancellation or restrictive amendment has been recorded in the office for recording transfers of the real property; or

(2)   a limitation on the grant is contained in another statement of authority that became effective after the statement containing the grant became effective, and a certified copy of the later-effective statement is recorded in the office for recording transfers of the real property.

(g)   Subject to subsection (c), if a certified copy of an effective statement containing a limitation on the authority to transfer real property held in the name of a limited liability company is recorded in the office for recording transfers of that real property, all persons are deemed to know of the limitation.

(h)   Subject to subsection (i), an effective statement of dissolution or termination is a cancellation of any filed statement of authority for the purposes of subsection (f) and is a limitation on authority for the purposes of subsection (g).

(i)   After a statement of dissolution becomes effective, a limited liability company may deliver to the [Secretary of State] for filing and, if appropriate, may record a statement of authority that is designated as a post-dissolution statement of authority. The statement operates as provided in subsections (f) and (g).

(j)   Unless earlier canceled, an effective statement of authority is canceled by operation of law five years after the date on which the statement, or its most recent amendment, becomes effective. This cancellation operates without need for any recording under subsection (f) or (g).

(k)   An effective statement of denial operates as a restrictive amendment under this section and may be recorded by certified copy for purposes of subsection (f)(1).

COMMENT

This section is derived from and builds on UPA (1997) § 303, which was refined in ULLCA (2006) and further refined in the Harmonization Project. This section is conceptually divided into two realms: statements pertaining to the power to transfer interests in the LLC's real property and statements pertaining to other matters. In the latter realm, statements are filed only in the records of the filing office and operate only to the extent the statements are actually known and relied on by a third party. Section 302(d) and (e).

As to interests in real property, in contrast, this section: (i) requires double-filing—with the filing office and in the appropriate land records; and (ii) provides for constructive knowledge of statements limiting authority. Thus, a properly filed and recorded statement can protect the limited liability company, Section 302(g), and, in order for a statement pertaining to real property to be a sword in the hands of a third party, the statement must have been both filed and properly recorded. Section 302(f). Experience suggests that statements of authority will most often be used in connection with transactions in real estate.

By its terms, this section applies only to domestic limited liability companies. A foreign LLC cannot make use of this section even as to real property located in this state. The section refers throughout to "limited liability company," which this act defines as a domestic limited liability company. *See* Section 102(8) (" 'Limited liability company' . . . means an entity formed under this [act] or which becomes subject to this [act]"). *Cf. Fannie Mae v. Heather Apartments Ltd. P'ship*, A13-0562, 2013 WL 6223564 at *6 (Minn. Ct. App. Dec. 2, 2013) (considering the remedies available to a judgment creditor with respect to the judgment debtor's interest in a Cook Islands LLC; rejecting the debtor's argument that the creditor's "only remedy is to obtain a charging order under" [the Minnesota LLC statute]; explaining that "this argument fails because that statute only applies to Minnesota limited liability companies" which the Minnesota LLC statute "defines . . . as 'a limited liability company, other than a foreign limited liability company, *organized or governed by this chapter*' ") (emphasis added; statutory citations omitted).

Subsection (a)(2)—This paragraph permits a statement to designate authority by position (or office) rather than by specific person, thus avoiding the need to file anew whenever a new person assumes the position or the office. This type of a statement will enable LLCs to provide evidence of ongoing power to enter into transactions without having to disclose to third parties the entirety of the operating agreement.

Subsection (a)(2)(A) and (a)(3)(A)—The authority to "sign" an instrument includes the authority to commit the partnership to the transfer reflected in the agreement. *See* Subsection (f) (referring not merely to signing but also to "an effective statement of authority that grants authority to transfer real property").

Here and elsewhere in the section, the phrase "real property" includes all interests in real property, such as mortgages, easements, etc.

Subsection (c)—This subsection expresses a very important limitation—*i.e.*, that this section's rules do not operate viz-a-viz members. For members, the operating agreement is controlling. Section 107(d). However, like any other record delivered for filing on behalf of an LLC, a statement of authority might be some evidence of the contents of the operating agreement. *See* the comment to Section 107(d).

Another important limitation exists. The filing office is not affected by a statement of authority that purports to delineate the authority of persons to sign documents to be delivered for filing of behalf of a limited liability company. The act does define "[p]erson" to include a "government or governmental subdivision, agency, or instrumentality," Section 102(15), but "a limitation on the authority of a person or a position contained in an effective statement of authority is not by itself evidence of knowledge or notice of the limitation by any person." Subsection (d).

Moreover, even if an employee of the filing office happened to see that a statement of authority purported to delineate the authority of persons to sign records to be delivered on behalf of an LLC, that information would not pertain to a "fact [that] is material to the agent's duties to the principal" and therefore would not be attributed to the filing office. RESTATEMENT (THIRD) OF AGENCY § 5.03 (2006).

Subsection (d)—The phrase "by itself" is important, because the existence of a limitation of authority could be evidence if, for example, the person in question reviewed the public record at a time when the limitation was of record.

Subsection (e)(1)—What happens if a statement of authority conflicts with the contents of an LLC's certificate of organization? The contents of the certificate are not statements of authority, Section 201(c), so the information in the certificate does not directly figure into the operation of this section. However, if the person claiming to rely on a statement of authority had read the certificate's conflicting information before giving value, that fact might be evidence that person gave value with "knowledge to the contrary" of the statement.

Subsection (e)(2)—This paragraph by its terms does not affect a claim of lingering apparent authority. A person could: (i) assert knowledge of a statement of authority as the statement existed before a cancellation or restrictive amendment; and (ii) characterize the original statement as a manifestation of authority traceable to the limited liability company. RESTATEMENT (THIRD) OF AGENCY § 3.03, cmt. b (2006) ("Apparent authority is present only when a third party's belief is traceable to manifestations of the principal.").

However, for apparent authority to exist, the purported agent must *reasonably* appear to be authorized. RESTATEMENT (THIRD) OF AGENCY § 2.03 (2006) (stating that apparent authority can only exist when "a third party reasonably believes the actor has authority to act on behalf of the principal"). Given the possibility of cancellation or restrictive amendment, it might not be reasonable for a person to know of a statement of authority, let time pass, and then rely on the statement without re-checking the public record.

Subsections (f) through (h)—These subsections: (i) pertain to transactions in real property; (ii) provide a mechanism by which authority to transfer an LLC's real property can be made to appear in the real estate records; and (iii) thus address the principal concerns (raised by real estate lawyers) that led the drafters of UPA (1997) to provide for statements of authority.

Subsection (f)—This subsection provides a sword for a vendee of real property. If the vendee has "give[n] value in reliance on the grant without knowledge to the contrary," the statement of authority protects the vendee against claims that contradict the grant.

Subsection (f)(1) and (2)—As a claim of lingering apparent authority, see the comment to Section (e)(2). The analysis stated there applies even more strongly in the context of customary practices involving land transfers.

Subsection (g)—This subsection provides a shield for the limited liability company as alleged vendor. If a vendee's claim contradicts the stated limitation, constructive knowledge ("deemed to know") defeats the claim even if the vendee gave value and lacked actual knowledge.

Subsection (h)—This subsection integrates statements of dissolution and termination, Section 702, into the operation of this section.

The effect of a statement of dissolution depends on the circumstances.

Example: ABC, LLC has in effect a properly filed and recorded statement of authority authorizing ABC's CEO to transfer real estate owned by the LLC. The proper filing and recording by ABC of a statement of dissolution cancels the statement of authority. Subsequently, Buyer gives value in return for a deed signed by the CEO on behalf of ABC. Due to Subsections (h) and (f)(1), Subsection (f) does not protect Buyer. Moreover, under Subsections (g) and (h), Buyer is "deemed to know" of the dissolution. Whether that deemed knowledge functions to deprive the CEO of authority to bind ABC depends on agency law and additional facts. For example, the CEO might have had actual or apparent authority to transfer the real estate despite the dissolution of the LLC.

If properly filed with the filing office and properly recorded in the office for land records, a statement of termination eliminates the power of any person to transfer real property owned in the name of the LLC. No one can have the authority to act for a non-existent entity. *Cf.* RESTATEMENT (THIRD) OF AGENCY § 4.04(1)(a) (2006) (precluding ratification by a principal that did not exist at the time of the unauthorized act).

Subsection (i)—This provision permits an LLC to use statements of authority during winding up. As an additional protection for third parties, a statement must be "designated as a post-dissolution statement of authority" to be effective under this provision.

Subsection (k)—Presumably, when real property is involved, a person who obtains the filing of a statement of denial under Section 303 will cause a certified copy of the statement to be "recorded by certified copy for purposes of subsection (f)(1)" [undercutting constructive notice as to authority to transfer real property]. However, nothing in this subsection prevents the limited liability company from causing a certified copy to appear in the land records; due the section's use of the passive voice ("may be recorded"), the act does not delimit who has the authority to act under this subsection.

§ 303.   Statement of Denial

A person named in a filed statement of authority granting that person authority may deliver to the [Secretary of State] for filing a statement of denial that:

(1)   provides the name of the limited liability company and the caption of the statement of authority to which the statement of denial pertains; and

(2)   denies the grant of authority.

COMMENT

A person whose powers are delineated in the public record by another person should have the right to dissent from that delineation. This section takes an "all or nothing" approach; a person may not deny in part and confirm in part. For the effect of a statement of denial, see Section 302(k).

§ 304.   Liability of Members and Managers

(a)   A debt, obligation, or other liability of a limited liability company is solely the debt, obligation, or other liability of the company. A member or manager is not personally liable, directly or indirectly, by way of contribution or otherwise, for a debt, obligation, or other liability of the company solely by reason of being or acting as a member or manager. This subsection applies regardless of the dissolution of the company.

(b)   The failure of a limited liability company to observe formalities relating to the exercise of its powers or management of its activities and affairs is not a ground for imposing liability on a member or manager for a debt, obligation, or other liability of the company.

COMMENT

Derivation—ULLCA (2006) derived this section from UPA (1997) § 306, which was also the source for ULPA (2001) § 404. The Harmonization Project brought the two partnership acts and the limited liability company act into accord to the extent the three acts overlap.

Subsection (a)—This subsection provides a corporate-like liability shield to members and managers, protecting them against (and only against) the debts, obligations and liabilities of the limited liability company— *i.e.*, against a member's or manager's alleged vicarious liability for the obligations of the entity. The shield "applies regardless of the dissolution of the company" and thus continues in effect through the completion of winding up (*i.e.*, termination). The shield applies regardless of the law giving rise to a claim against a limited liability company.

Shield Applicable Regardless of the Identity of the Plaintiff

What makes the shield relevant is the nature of the claim. If the complaint seeks to hold a member vicariously liability for the LLC's obligations, the shield applies. If not, not. Thus, there is no distinction between a claim arising from an LLC's debt to a commercial creditor, a member's claim that the LLC has failed to return a contribution as required by the operating agreement, and a claim by a former member that the LLC has failed to follow through on a buy-out agreement. *See Rappaport v. Gelfand*, 197 Cal. App.4th 1213, 1230–1232, 129 Cal. Rptr. 3d 670, 682–84 (Cal. App. 2 Dist. 2011) (involving a claim by a former partner). *Accord Ederer v. Gursky*, 9 N.Y.3d 514, 526, 881 N.E.2d 204, 212–213 (N.Y. 2007) (Smith, J., dissenting).

Shield Inapposite for Claims Arising from a Member's or Manager's Own Conduct

Because the member or manager liability at issue is solely vicarious, the shield is irrelevant to claims seeking to hold a member or manager directly liable on account of the member's or manager's own conduct. Put another way, "[t]here is no question" that "the member-manager of a limited liability company who causes his business to breach common law and statutory duties may be held independently liable for his personal torts." *Dep't of Agric. v. Appletree Mktg., L.L.C.*, 485 Mich. 1, 4, 18, 779 N.W.2d 237, 239, 247 (2010).

A few judges have failed to understand this point. *See Puleo v. Topel*, 368 Ill. App. 3d 63, 68–69, 856 N.E.2d 1152, 1157 (Ill. App. Ct. 2006) (basing its holding on a legislative amendment that "removed . . . language which explicitly provided that a member or manager of an LLC could be held personally liable for his or her own actions or for the actions of the LLC to the same extent as a shareholder or director of a corporation could be held personally liable").

This mistaken view: (i) ignores the actual words of LLC shield provisions (which protect members and managers only against liability for obligations *of* an LLC and make no reference to direct obligations of a member or manager); and (ii) flouts public policy (which recoils from the idea of immunizing a person's misconduct solely because the person acts on behalf of an organization). Moreover, the mistaken view is contrary to the overwhelming weight of the case law. *See, e.g., Mbahaba v. Morgan*, 163 N.H. 561, 565, 44 A.3d 472, 476 (2012) ("When . . . a member or manager commits or participates in the commission of a tort, whether or not he acts on behalf of his LLC, he is liable to third persons injured thereby."); *Sturm v. Harb Dev., LLC*, 298 Conn. 124, 138, 2 A.3d 859, 870 (2010) (holding that the liability shield of an LLC is subject to "the common-law tort exception . . . [for] individual claims against LLC members); *Allen v. Dackman*, 413 Md. 132, 154, 991 A.2d 1216, 1229 (2010) ("An LLC member is liable for torts he or she personally commits, inspires, or participates in because he or she personally committed a wrong, not 'solely' because he or she is a member of the LLC."); *Weber v. U.S. Sterling Sec., Inc.*, 282 Conn. 722, 732–34, 924 A2d 816, 824–25 (2007) (stating that the Delaware LLC Act "does not preclude individual liability for members of a limited liability company if that liability is not based simply on the member's affiliation with the company" and holding, in particular, that the Act "does not bar the defendants' liability for tortious conduct").

Example: A manager personally guarantees a debt of a limited liability company. Subsection (a) is irrelevant to the manager's liability as guarantor.

Example: A member purports to bind a limited liability company while lacking any agency law power to do so. The limited liability company is not bound, but the member is liable for having breached the "warranty of authority" (an agency law doctrine). Subsection (a) does not apply. The liability is not *for* a debt, obligation, or other liability of the [limited liability] company, but rather is the member's own, direct liability. Indeed, the liability exists because the limited liability company is *not* indebted, obligated or liable. RESTATEMENT (THIRD) OF AGENCY § 6.10 (2006).

Example: A manager of a limited liability company defames a third party in circumstances that render the limited liability company vicariously liable under agency law. Under Subsection (a), the third party cannot hold the manager accountable for the *company's* liability, but that protection is immaterial. The manager is the tortfeasor and in that role is directly liable to the third party.

Example: A limited liability company provides professional services, and one of its members commits malpractice. The liability shield is irrelevant to the member's direct liability in tort. However, if the member's malpractice liability is attributed to the LLC under agency law principles, the liability shield will protect the other members of the LLC against a claim that they must make good on the LLC's liability.

Example: A single member limited liability company enters into a contract to build a home, and the member performs substantial amounts of the work. The homeowner sues both the LLC and the member for allegedly defective work, but the complaint sounds in contract rather than in tort. The LLC may be liable, but the member is not. *See Ogea v. Merritt* ___ So.3d ____, 2013 WL 6439355 at *24–25 (La. 2013).

Subsection (a) pertains only to claims based on the LLC's liability and is irrelevant to claims by a limited liability company against a member or manager and *vice versa. E.g.*, Sections 408 (pertaining to a limited liability company's obligation to indemnify a member or manager), 409 (pertaining to management duties) and 801 (pertaining to a member's rights to bring a direct claim against a limited liability company).

Shield Inapposite to Role Liability Claims

Provisions of regulatory law may impose liability on a member or manager due to a role the person plays in the LLC. *See, e.g., Food Team Intern., Ltd. v. Unilink, LLC*, 872 F. Supp. 2d 405, 424 (E.D Pa. 2012) (holding several individuals "subject to secondary individual liability under PACA [Perishable Agricultural Commodities Act]" because their roles within the LLC enabled them to control the relevant assets) (citing *Bear Mountain Orchards, Inc. v. Mich-Kim, Inc.*, 623 F.3d 163, 172 (3d Cir. 2010)).

The Shield and Dissolution.

The rule stated here is inherent in the nature of LLC dissolution. "[D]issolution does not end a limited liability company's existence but rather changes the purpose of that existence." Section 701, cmt. "A dissolved limited liability company shall wind up its activities and affairs and . . . continues after dissolution . . . for the purpose of winding up." Section 702(a). Put another way: dissolution and winding up are part of the life cycle of a limited liability company—sometimes the most complicated part. There is no logical reason to remove the shield during the last part of an LLC's life cycle.

This subsection makes this point expressly, because it is possible to misinterpret some outlying LLP cases as holding to the contrary. *See, e.g., Carolina Cas. Ins. Co. v. L.M. Ross Law Grp., LLP*, 151 Cal. Rptr. 3d 628, 635 (2012) (affirming the trial court's decision to hold an LLP's named partner liable for a judgment against his limited ability partnership; noting that "[c]entral to the decision to amend the judgment to add Ross [the named partner] as a judgment debtor . . . is the trial court's finding that Ross Law Group dissolved"; recognizing, however, that, before the partnership incurred the liability, Ross had signed and filed with the California Secretary of State a form stating that the law firm had "cease[d] to be a registered limited liability partnership and is hereby filing this notice with the California Secretary of State that [it] is no longer a registered limited partnership") (quotation marks omitted).

The Shield and Termination

This subsection does not expressly provide that, when a limited liability company's existence terminates, the liability shield remains in place as to any debt, obligation, or other liability of the LLC incurred before the termination. However, the point follows ineluctably from Subsection 304(a), which provides that the shield applies to any "debt, obligation, or other liability of a limited liability company." A debt, obligation or other liability of an LLC does not disappear merely because the LLC has terminated.

Moreover, any other result would: (i) create huge holes in the shield; (ii) put the law of unincorporated businesses at odds with the law of corporations; (iii) render surplus this act's distribution recapture provision, Section 406; and (iv) render nonsensical the otherwise logical extension of the equitable trust fund theory to limited liability companies. *Cf. Velasquez v. Franz*, 589 A.2d 143, 146 (N.J. 1991) (explaining that "the trust-fund doctrine . . . renders shareholders who receive distributed assets of the corporation liable as 'trustees' for claims of the corporation's creditors").

Dangers of Indemnification Provisions Inter Se the Members

Despite the phrase "by way of contribution or otherwise," the LLC shield has no effect on contribution or indemnification requirements running directly from member to member or from members to a manager. These obligations are not obligations of the LLC but rather personal to each member. Indirectly they pose a risk to the shield as to liability arising from the misconduct of a member or manager.

> **Example:** A law firm operates as a professional limited liability company. One practice area (the "Practice Area") brings in large fees but also exposes its practitioners (the "Practitioners") to liability risks substantially higher than the risks faced by other lawyers in the firm. Fees in the Practice Area are episodic, so it makes sense for the Practitioners to share profits with the rest of the firm, where returns are lower but more regular.
>
> The firm carries liability insurance, and the operating agreement provides broad indemnification rights to all the firm's lawyers. However, the Practitioners are mindful that the LLC liability shield sets a practical limit to the firm's indemnification obligations and that policies of insurance have limits. The Practitioners obtain a provision in the operating agreement by which each member of the LLC makes a personal promise of indemnification (subject to a cap).
>
> The tortious conduct of one of the Practitioners (the "Tortfeasor") results in a substantial judgment against the Tortfeasor and, per Section 305(a), against the LLC. For unrelated reasons, the LLC has become insolvent and its liability coverage is "maxed out." The Tortfeasor's right to indemnification from fellow members is an asset of the Tortfeasor. The judgment creditor can levy on that asset, thereby defeating the liability shield in effect if not in form.

Subsection (b)—This subsection pertains to the equitable doctrine of "piercing the veil" *i.e.*, conflating an entity and its owners to hold one liable for the obligations of the other. The doctrine of "piercing the corporate veil" is well-established, and courts regularly (and sometimes almost reflexively) apply that doctrine to limited liability companies. In the corporate realm, "disregard of corporate formalities" is a key factor in the piercing analysis. In the realm of LLCs, that factor is inappropriate, because informality of organization and operation is both common and desired. *See, e.g., In re Packer*, Bankruptcy No. 13–41304, 2014 WL 5100095 (Bankr. E.D. Tex. Oct. 10, 2014) (noting the informality of LLC governance, recognizing that "the disregard of corporate formalities . . . [is] one of the key factors in [corporate] veil-piercing determinations"; but holding that " 'it makes no sense to imperil the shield simply because the members do not undergo meaningless formalities such as formal meetings' ") (citing

Carter G. Bishop & Daniel S. Kleinberger, LIMITED LIABILITY COMPANIES: TAX AND BUSINESS LAW ¶ 6.3 at *3 (Thomson Reuters Tax and Accounting 2014)).

The formalities at issue are the process formalities of governance—both those few created by this act and however few or many might be created by the operating agreement.

Example: The operating agreement of a three-member, member-managed limited liability company requires formal monthly meetings of the members. Each of the members works in the LLC's business, and they consult each other regularly. They have forgotten or ignore the requirement of monthly meetings. Under Subsection (b), that fact is irrelevant to a piercing claim.

In contrast, this subsection is inapposite to another key piercing factor—disregard of the separateness between entity and owner. *E.g., Vanderford Co. v. Knudson*, 165 P.3d 261, 271 (Idaho 2007) (noting that managing member and "his accountant testified that the LLC's checking account was so confusing that the accountant could not be sure whose money was in the account at what times"); *Utzler v. Braca*, 972 A.2d 743 (Conn. App. 2009) (holding that veil piercing was appropriate under alter-ego theory when owner deposited LLC funds into a commingled bank account from which he made withdrawals for personal needs and unrelated projects).

Example: The sole owner of a limited liability company uses a car titled in the company's name for personal purposes and writes checks on the company's account to pay for personal expenses. These facts are relevant to a piercing claim; they pertain to economic separateness, not Subsection (b) formalities.

This subsection also is inapposite to a member's claim of oppression under Section 701(a)(4)(C)(ii). In some circumstances, disregard of agreed-upon formalities can be a "freeze out" mechanism. Likewise, this subsection has no relevance to a member's claim that the disregard of agreed-upon formalities is a breach of the operating agreement.

This subsection addresses claims to "impos[e] liability on a member or manager for a debt, obligation, or other liability of the company"—*i.e.*, for what is sometimes termed a "direct pierce." Whether the same approach should apply to claims for a "reverse pierce" is a question for the courts. *See Comm'r of Envtl. Prot. v. State Five Indus. Park, Inc.*, 304 Conn. 128, 140, 37 A.3d 724, 732–33 (2012) (stating that "[a]lthough some courts have adopted reverse veil piercing with little distinction as a logical corollary of traditional veil piercing, because the two share the same equitable goals, others wisely have recognized important differences between them").

[ARTICLE] 4

RELATIONS OF MEMBERS TO EACH OTHER AND TO LIMITED LIABILITY COMPANY

§ 401.   Becoming Member

(a)   If a limited liability company is to have only one member upon formation, the person becomes a member as agreed by that person and the organizer of the company. That person and the organizer may be, but need not be, different persons. If different, the organizer acts on behalf of the initial member.

(b)   If a limited liability company is to have more than one member upon formation, those persons become members as agreed by the persons before the formation of the company. The organizer acts on behalf of the persons in forming the company and may be, but need not be, one of the persons.

(c)   After formation of a limited liability company, a person becomes a member:

(1)   as provided in the operating agreement;

(2)   as the result of a transaction effective under [Article] 10;

(3)   with the affirmative vote or consent of all the members; or

(4)   as provided in Section 701(a)(3).

(d)   A person may become a member without:

(1)   acquiring a transferable interest; or

(2)   making or being obligated to make a contribution to the limited liability company.

COMMENT

Most LLC statutes address in separate provisions: (i) how an LLC obtains its initial member or members; and (ii) how additional persons might later become members. This act follows that approach.

Subsections (a) and (b)—These subsections make explicit the agency relationship between the person acting as organizer and the initial member or members.

Subsection (c)(3)—A limited liability company being in part a creature of contract, consent is determined on an objective basis (*i.e.,* contract law's "reasonable person" standard). Depending on the terms of an LLC's operating agreement, the members' manifestation of consent might involve detailed formalities, entirely informal activities, or anything in between. Moreover, the operating agreement might reduce the quantum of consent necessary or shift the consent right to a manager.

A limited liability company being a voluntary association, a person cannot become a member without manifesting consent to do so. That consent also is judged objectively.

Under Section 106(b), "[a] person that becomes a member of a limited liability company is deemed to assent to the operating agreement," and the agreement binds the member regardless of whether the member has actually indicated assent in any way.

Subsection (d)(1)—To accommodate business practices and also because a limited liability company need not have a business purpose, this provision permits so-called "non-economic members."

§ 402. Form of Contribution

A contribution may consist of property transferred to, services performed for, or another benefit provided to the limited liability company or an agreement to transfer property to, perform services for, or provide another benefit to the company.

COMMENT

This section is intentionally quite broad, encompassing past, present, and promised benefits. Comparable language exists in most, if not all, LLC statutes, and case law recognizes the intended broadness of this approach. *See, e.g., Belgard v. Manchac Technologies, LLC*, 92 So.3d 660, 664 (La.App. 3 Cir. 2012) (stating that "the creation of an obligation to establish a $1.8 million line of credit was valid consideration for the transfer of 24% of the membership interest in Manchac"); *In re Eight of Swords, LLC*, 96 A.D.3d 839, 840, 946 N.Y.S.2d 248, 249 Dept. 2012) (referring to "the petitioner's contributions to the LLC, which overwhelmingly consisted of services rendered to the LLC in the form of preparing and filing start-up documentation and performing activities associated with the renovation of the business's premises").

This act does not contain a statute of frauds specifically applicable to promised contributions. Generally applicable statutes of fraud might apply, however. For example, a promise to contribute land to the LLC would be subject to the statute of frauds pertaining to land transfers. Likewise, a promise that by its terms requires performance that extends beyond one year from the making of the contract would be subject to the one-year provision of the statute of frauds. *See* the comment to Section 102(13).

§ 403. Liability for Contributions

(a) A person's obligation to make a contribution to a limited liability company is not excused by the person's death, disability, termination, or other inability to perform personally.

(b) If a person does not fulfill an obligation to make a contribution other than money, the person is obligated at the option of the limited liability company to contribute money equal to the value of the part of the contribution which has not been made.

(c) The obligation of a person to make a contribution may be compromised only by the affirmative vote or consent of all the members. If a creditor of a limited liability company extends credit or otherwise acts in reliance on an obligation described in subsection (a) without knowledge or notice of a compromise under this subsection, the creditor may enforce the obligation.

COMMENT

Subsection (a)—Under common law principles of impracticability, an individual's death or incapacity will sometimes discharge a duty to render performance. RESTATEMENT (SECOND) OF CONTRACTS §§ 261 (Discharge by Supervening Impracticability), 262 (Death or Incapacity of Person Necessary For Performance). This subsection overrides those principles. Moreover, the reference to "perform personally" is not limited to individuals but rather may refer to any legal person (including an entity) that has a non-delegable duty.

Subsection (b)—This subsection is a statutory liquidated damage provision, exercisable at the option of the limited liability company, with the damage amount set according to the value of the promised, non-monetary contribution.

Example: In order to become a member, a person promises to contribute to the limited liability company various assets "free and clear," which the operating agreement values at $150,000. In return for the person's promise, and in light of the agreed value, the limited liability company admits the person as a member with a right to receive 25% of the LLC's distributions.

However, the promised assets are subject to a security agreement, and, before the member can contribute the assets, the secured party forecloses on the security interest and sells the assets at a public sale for $75,000. Even if the $75,000 reflects the actual fair market value of the assets, under this subsection the limited liability company has a claim against the member for "money equal to the value of the part of the contribution which has not been made"—*i.e.,* $150,000.

Example: Same facts as the previous example, except that the public sale brings $225,000. The limited liability company is neither obliged to invoke this subsection nor limited to the $150,000. The LLC may instead sue for breach of the promise to make the contribution, asserting the $225,000 figure as evidence of the actual loss suffered as a result of the breach.

Subsection (c)—The unanimity requirement expressed in the first sentence might indirectly benefit creditors, but the requirement is nonetheless a default rule and therefore may be varied by operating agreement. The right of each member to consent is not a "right[ ] under this [act] of a person other than a member or manager." *See* Section 105(c)(15) (preventing the operating agreement from affecting such rights). In contrast, the creditor right stated in the second sentence fits squarely within Section 105(c)(15) and therefore may not be varied by the operating agreement.

§ 404. Sharing of and Right to Distributions Before Dissolution

(a) Any distribution made by a limited liability company before its dissolution and winding up must be in equal shares among members and persons dissociated as members, except to the extent necessary to comply with a transfer effective under Section 502 or charging order in effect under Section 503.

(b) A person has a right to a distribution before the dissolution and winding up of a limited liability company only if the company decides to make an interim distribution. A person's dissociation does not entitle the person to a distribution.

(c) A person does not have a right to demand or receive a distribution from a limited liability company in any form other than money. Except as otherwise provided in Section 707(d), a company may distribute an asset in kind only if each part of the asset is fungible with each other part and each person receives a percentage of the asset equal in value to the person's share of distributions.

(d) If a member or transferee becomes entitled to receive a distribution, the member or transferee has the status of, and is entitled to all remedies available to, a creditor of the limited liability company with respect to the distribution. However, the company's obligation to make a distribution is subject to offset for any amount owed to the company by the member or a person dissociated as a member on whose account the distribution is made.

COMMENT

Past uniform unincorporated entity acts and many current LLC acts provide default rules for allocation of profits, and UPA (1997) even provided a default structure for maintaining capital accounts. For the following reasons, this act, incorporating changes made by the Harmonization Project, provides a default rule only for rights to share in distributions:

- Capital accounts are maintained for one purpose, to determine how distributions will be made to members. The rules for maintenance of capital accounts can be very complex. Generally, however, profits increase capital account balances (and increase the amounts that will be distributed to the members) and losses reduce capital account balances (and reduce the amounts that will be distributed to the members). If the statute has a simple default rule for how distributions are to be made to the members, providing an additional set of default profit and loss allocation provisions and capital account rules will be, at best, duplicative and, at worse, inconsistent with the distribution rules.

- Some argue that capital account rules and profit and loss allocation provisions are necessary to comply with tax requirements. Tax income or loss is allocated to "partners" (including members of an LLC taxed as a partnership) according to the partners' economic interests in the LLC, and these interests are based on distributions that would be made to partners on liquidation of the LLC. By including default distribution provisions, the act includes the information necessary to make these tax determinations. To the extent the tax law allows partners to make further tax elections or satisfy alternative safe harbors, the partners may look to the tax law for guidance and include necessary provisions in their agreements.

Subsection (a)—The rule stated applies to redemptions as well as operating distributions but is a default rule in both contexts. *See* the comment to Section 102(4)(A).

Subsection (b)—The second sentence of this subsection accords with Section 603(a)(3)—upon dissociation a person is treated as a mere transferee of its own transferable interest. Like most *inter se* rules in this act, this one is subject change by the operating agreement. *See* the comment to Section 603(a)(3).

Subsection (d)—*See also* Section 405(d) (pertaining to the rights of members and transferees that receive a distribution in the form of indebtedness) and 405(e) (pertaining to solvency testing for payments on indebtedness issued to redeem an interest).

§ 405. Limitations on Distributions

(a) A limited liability company may not make a distribution, including a distribution under Section 707, if after the distribution:

(1) the company would not be able to pay its debts as they become due in the ordinary course of the company's activities and affairs; or

(2) the company's total assets would be less than the sum of its total liabilities plus the amount that would be needed, if the company were to be dissolved and wound up at the time of the distribution, to satisfy the preferential rights upon dissolution and winding up of members and transferees whose preferential rights are superior to the rights of persons receiving the distribution.

(b) A limited liability company may base a determination that a distribution is not prohibited under subsection (a) on:

(1) financial statements prepared on the basis of accounting practices and principles that are reasonable in the circumstances; or

(2) a fair valuation or other method that is reasonable under the circumstances.

(c) Except as otherwise provided in subsection (e), the effect of a distribution under subsection (a) is measured:

(1) in the case of a distribution as defined in Section 102(4)(A), as of the earlier of:

(A) the date money or other property is transferred or debt is incurred by the limited liability company; or

(B) the date the person entitled to the distribution ceases to own the interest or right being acquired by the company in return for the distribution;

(2) in the case of any other distribution of indebtedness, as of the date the indebtedness is distributed; and

(3) in all other cases, as of the date:

    (A)   the distribution is authorized, if the payment occurs not later than 120 days after that date; or

    (B)   the payment is made, if the payment occurs more than 120 days after the distribution is authorized.

(d)   A limited liability company's indebtedness to a member or transferee incurred by reason of a distribution made in accordance with this section is at parity with the company's indebtedness to its general, unsecured creditors, except to the extent subordinated by agreement.

(e)   A limited liability company's indebtedness, including indebtedness issued as a distribution, is not a liability for purposes of subsection (a) if the terms of the indebtedness provide that payment of principal and interest is made only if and to the extent that payment of a distribution could then be made under this section. If the indebtedness is issued as a distribution, each payment of principal or interest is treated as a distribution, the effect of which is measured on the date the payment is made.

(f)   In measuring the effect of a distribution under Section 707, the liabilities of a dissolved limited liability company do not include any claim that has been disposed of under Section 704, 705, or 706.

COMMENT

Both this section and Section 406 were derived essentially from the Model Business Corporation Act section 6.40. Both sections are necessary and appropriate because a limited liability company provides its members and managers a corporate-like liability shield. With the exception noted in the comment to Subsection (a)(2), the provisions of this section are nonwaivable. Section 105(c)(15).

"Distribution" does not include "amounts constituting reasonable compensation for present or past service or payments made in the ordinary course of business under a bona fide retirement plan or other bona fide benefits program." Section 102(4)(B).

Subsection (a)—Insolvency is a fundamental issue under this section, and this subsection provides two tests of insolvency. The tests are disjunctive; a distribution violates this section if after the distribution the LLC fails either of the tests. The subsection applies both to interim and liquidating distributions.

Solvency is also a fundamental issue under bankruptcy and fraudulent transfer law, which provide their own respective definitions of the concept.

Subsection (a)(2)—The reference to "preferential rights upon dissolution and winding up" is a default rule, because removing this protection for preferred members or transferees is an *inter se* matter. *See* Section 105(d)(1)(B). The rest of the section is not subject to change in the operating agreement. Section 105(c)(15).

Subsection (b)—This subsection states a standard of ordinary care, in contrast with the generally-applicable standard stated in Section 409(c) (gross negligence).

Subsection (b)(2)—This alternative valuation provision is likely to be both useful and fair when the limited liability company has appreciated assets but for accounting purposes these assets are valued at book value less depreciation.

Subsection (c)—This subsection provides three alternative rules for determining the point(s) in time of as which to apply the Subsection (a) solvency tests. The timing depends on which of three categories encompasses a distribution: (i) a distribution in the nature of a redemption (regardless of whether the distribution includes a distribution of indebtedness); (ii) any distribution of indebtedness other than a distribution in the nature of a redemption; and (iii) any distribution that involves neither a redemption nor a distribution of indebtedness. A requirement for additional solvency testing pertaining to distributions of indebtedness appears in Subsection (e).

Subsection (c)(1)—Section 102(4)(A) encompasses distributions in the nature of a redemption.

Subsection (c)(1)(A) and (B)—Under Subparagraph (A), any beginning of payment activity triggers the rule and sets the date as of when to apply the solvency tests. Under Subparagraph (B), the LLC's complete acquisition of the rights is necessary to trigger the rule.

Subsection (c)(2)—This provision states the general rule for distributions in the form of debt which are not connected with a redemption.

Subsection (c)(3)—This provision states alternative rules for all distributions of money or property (*i.e.*, not debt). The measuring date depends on the length of time between the authorization and payment of the distribution.

Subsection (d)—*Compare* Subsection (d), *with* Section 404(d) (characterizing as a creditor a person who has become entitled to receive a distribution).

Subsection (e)—This subsection contains two rules pertaining to indebtedness issued as part of a distribution and the solvency tests of Subsection (a). The first sentence states the sensible rule that indebtedness that is essentially subordinated to the solvency requirement—*i.e.*, not payable if making payment would transgress that requirement—is not counted in determining liabilities for purposes of the solvency tests. The second sentence applies the solvency tests to each payment of principal and interest on any indebtedness issued as a distribution, in addition to any previous testing required by Subsection (c)(1)(A) or (c)(2).

Example: An LLC and one of its members agree that the LLC will buy out the member's entire ownership interest in the LLC in return for a promissory note from the LLC, payable in installments. Under the redemption agreement, the member surrenders all its interests and rights on January 15 and the LLC signs and delivers the note to the person dissociated as a member on February 15. Under the note, payment of interest is due monthly beginning March 15, with a balloon payment of the principal due December 30.

Under Subsection (c)(1)(B), the solvency tests are applied as of January 15. Under Subsection (e), the solvency tests are again applied on the March 15, April 15, etc., and again on December 30.

Subsection (f)—The cited sections provide methods for extinguishing or limiting the debts of an LLC that is winding up its affairs and activities and thus any debt affected by any of the cited sections is irrelevant for purposes of solvency testing.

§ 406. Liability for Improper Distributions

(a) Except as otherwise provided in subsection (b), if a member of a member-managed limited liability company or manager of a manager-managed limited liability company consents to a distribution made in violation of Section 405 and in consenting to the distribution fails to comply with Section 409, the member or manager is personally liable to the company for the amount of the distribution which exceeds the amount that could have been distributed without the violation of Section 405.

(b) To the extent the operating agreement of a member-managed limited liability company expressly relieves a member of the authority and responsibility to consent to distributions and imposes that authority and responsibility on one or more other members, the liability stated in subsection (a) applies to the other members and not the member that the operating agreement relieves of the authority and responsibility.

(c) A person that receives a distribution knowing that the distribution violated Section 405 is personally liable to the limited liability company but only to the extent that the distribution received by the person exceeded the amount that could have been properly paid under Section 405.

(d) A person against which an action is commenced because the person is liable under subsection (a) may:

(1) implead any other person that is liable under subsection (a) and seek to enforce a right of contribution from the person; and

(2) implead any person that received a distribution in violation of subsection (c) and seek to enforce a right of contribution from the person in the amount the person received in violation of subsection (c).

(e) An action under this section is barred unless commenced not later than two years after the distribution.

COMMENT

This section and Section 405 were derived essentially from Model Business Corporation Act section 6.40. As with Section 405, this section is appropriate and necessary due to the liability shield of a limited liability company. The provisions of this section are non-waivable. Section 105(c)(15).

This section contemplates two categories of liability: liability of those who have authorized improper distributions, Subsection (a), and the liability of those who have received improper distributions, Subsection (c).

Liability that has accrued under this section is not affected by a person subsequently ceasing to be a member, manager or transferee.

The liability is to the LLC, not to the creditors of an insolvent LLC. *Weinstein v. Colborne Foodbotics, LLC*, 302 P.3d 263, 268 (2013); *Rev O, Inc. v. Woo*, 725 S.E.2d 45, 52 (N.C. Ct. App. 2012).

This section does not preclude or interfere with claims for fraudulent transfer. *See* the comment to Subsection (e).

Subsection (a)—The liability is not strict liability but rather attaches only to the extent a decision maker has failed to comply with the duties stated in Section 409. To the extent those duties have been permissibly revised by the operating agreement, the revised standards apply to this subsection. *See also* Section 405(b)(1) (permitting reasonable reliance on specified financial information).

Subsection (b)—*Compare* Subsection (b), *with* Section 105(d)(2) (generally permitting provisions of this type).

Subsection (c)—Actual knowledge is necessary to impose liability. Reason to know does not suffice. *Compare* Subsection (c), *with* Section 103(a)–(b).

Subsections (c) and (d)(2)—Liability could apply to a person who receives a distribution under a charging order, but only if the person meets the knowledge requirement. That situation is very unlikely unless the person with the charging order is also a member or manager.

Subsection (e)—When the distribution is in the form of indebtedness, the distribution may occur on several different dates. *See* the comment to Section 405(e).

This statute of limitations applies only to actions "under this section" and does not affect claims under other applicable law, which most often is fraudulent transfer law. For a different approach, see DEL. CODE ANN. tit. 6, § 17–607(c) (West 2013) (applying a 3-year statute of limitations to claims "under this chapter or other applicable law"); NY LTD. LIAB. CO. § 508(c) (McKinney 2013) (same). *But see, e.g., In re The Heritage Org., LLC*, 413 BR 438, 461 (Bankr. ND Tex. 2009) (invoking the Texas Uniform Fraudulent Act [TUFTA] to recover distributions made by a Delaware LLC headquartered in Texas; rejecting DEL. CODE ANN. tit. 6, § 18–607(c) on choice of law grounds; stating that "the Delaware legislature cannot limit the reach of TUFTA").

§ 407. Management of Limited Liability Company [*Default → member-managed*]

(a) A limited liability company is a member-managed limited liability company unless the operating agreement: [*default "Type #1" of LLC*]

(1) expressly provides that:

(A) the company is or will be "manager-managed";

(B) the company is or will be "managed by managers"; or

(C) management of the company is or will be "vested in managers"; or

(2) includes words of similar import.

(b) In a member-managed limited liability company, the following rules apply:

(1) Except as expressly provided in this [act], the management and conduct of the company are vested in the members.

(2) Each member has equal rights in the management and conduct of the company's activities and affairs.

(3) A difference arising among members as to a matter in the ordinary course of the activities and affairs of the company may be decided by a majority of the members. [*majority vote for*]

(4) The affirmative vote or consent of all the members is required to: [*Affirmative vote for*]

(A) undertake an act outside the ordinary course of the activities and affairs of the company; or

(B) amend the operating agreement.

(c)   In a manager-managed limited liability company, the following rules apply:

(1)   Except as expressly provided in this [act], any matter relating to the activities and affairs of the company is decided exclusively by the manager, or, if there is more than one manager, by a majority of the managers.

(2)   Each manager has equal rights in the management and conduct of the company's activities and affairs.

(3)   The affirmative vote or consent of all members is required to:

(A)   undertake an act outside the ordinary course of the company's activities and affairs; or

(B)   amend the operating agreement.

(4)   A manager may be chosen at any time by the affirmative vote or consent of a majority of the members and remains a manager until a successor has been chosen, unless the manager at an earlier time resigns, is removed, or dies, or, in the case of a manager that is not an individual, terminates. A manager may be removed at any time by the affirmative vote or consent of a majority of the members without notice or cause.

(5)   A person need not be a member to be a manager, but the dissociation of a member that is also a manager removes the person as a manager. If a person that is both a manager and a member ceases to be a manager, that cessation does not by itself dissociate the person as a member.

(6)   A person's ceasing to be a manager does not discharge any debt, obligation, or other liability to the limited liability company or members which the person incurred while a manager.

(d)   An action requiring the vote or consent of members under this [act] may be taken without a meeting, and a member may appoint a proxy or other agent to vote, consent, or otherwise act for the member by signing an appointing record, personally or by the member's agent.

(e)   The dissolution of a limited liability company does not affect the applicability of this section. However, a person that wrongfully causes dissolution of the company loses the right to participate in management as a member and a manager.

(f)   A limited liability company shall reimburse a member for an advance to the company beyond the amount of capital the member agreed to contribute.

(g)   A payment or advance made by a member which gives rise to a limited liability company obligation under subsection (f) or Section 408(a) constitutes a loan to the company which accrues interest from the date of the payment or advance.

(h)   A member is not entitled to remuneration for services performed for a member-managed limited liability company, except for reasonable compensation for services rendered in winding up the activities of the company.

COMMENT

Subsection (a)—This subsection follows implicitly from the definitions of "manager-managed" and "member-managed" limited liability companies, Section 102(10) and (12), but is included here for the sake of clarity. Although this act has eliminated the link between management structure and statutory apparent authority, the act retains the manager-managed and member-managed constructs as options for members to use to structure their *inter se* relationship. *See also* the comments to Sections 301 (No Agency Power of Member as Member), and 409 (Standards of Conduct).

Subsection (b)—The subsection follows essentially the long-standing default paradigm for management rights of general partners. *See* UPA (1914) § 18; UPA (1997) (Last Amended 2013) § 401. The stated rules are subject to change by the operating agreement. Section 105.

In general, a member's actual authority to act for an LLC will depend fundamentally on the operating agreement.

Example: Rachael and Sam, who have known each other for years, decide to go into business arranging musical tours. They fill out and electronically sign a one page form available on the website of the filing office and become the organizers of MMT, LLC. They are the only members of the LLC, and their understanding of who will do what in managing the enterprise is based on several lengthy, late-night conversations that preceded the LLC's formation. Sam is to "get the acts," and Rachael is to manage the tour logistics. There is no written operating agreement.

In the terminology of this act, MMT, LLC is member-managed, Section 407(a), and the understanding reached in the late night conversations has become part of the LLC's operating agreement, Section 102(13). In the terminology of agency law, the operating agreement constitutes a manifestation by the LLC to Rachael and Sam concerning the scope of their respective authority to act on behalf of the LLC. RESTATEMENT (THIRD) OF AGENCY § 2.01, cmt. c (2006) (explaining that a person's actual authority depends first on some manifestation attributable to the principal and stating: "[a]ctual authority is a consequence of a principal's expressive conduct toward an agent, through which the principal manifests assent to be affected by the agent's action, and the agent's reasonable understanding of the principal's manifestation").

Circumstances outside the operating agreement can also be relevant to determining the scope of a member's actual authority.

Example: Homeworks, LLC is a manager-managed LLC with three members. The LLC's written operating agreement:

- specifies in considerable detail the management responsibilities of Margaret, the LLC's manager-member, and also states that Margaret is responsible for "the day-to-day operations" of the company;

- puts Garrett, a non-manager member, in charge of the LLC's transportation department; and

- specifies no management role for Brooksley, the third member.

When the LLC's chief financial officer quits suddenly, Margaret asks Brooksley, a CPA, to "step in until we can hire a replacement."

Under the operating agreement, Margaret's request to Brooksley is within Margaret's actual authority and is a manifestation attributable to the LLC. If Brooksley manifests assent to Margaret's request, Brooksley will have the actual authority to act as the LLC's chief financial officer.

In the unlikely event that two or more people form a member-managed LLC without any understanding of how to allocate management responsibility, agency law, operating in the context the act's "gap fillers" on management responsibility, will produce the following result:

A single member of a multi-member, member-managed LLC:

- has no actual authority to bind the LLC to any matter "outside the ordinary course of the activities of the company," Section 407(b)(3); and

- has the actual authority to bind the LLC to any matter "in the management and conduct of the company's [ordinary course of] activities and affairs," Section 407(b)(2), unless the member has reason to know that other members might disagree or the member has some other reason to know that consultation with fellow members is appropriate.

For an explanation of this result, see Section 407(c), comment, which provides a detailed analysis in the context of a multi-manager LLC whose operating agreement is silent on the analogous question.

For a discussion of the apparent authority of a member to bind an LLC, see Section 301(b), comment.

Subsection (b)(4)—This list is not exhaustive. Other approval rights appear in the context of the provisions to which the rights apply. *E.g.*, Section 401(c)(3) (providing that "[a]fter formation of a limited liability company, a person becomes a member ... with the affirmative vote or consent of all the members"); Section 703(b)(1) requiring "the affirmative vote or consent of each member" to rescind dissolution); Sections 1023, 1033, 1043, 1053 (same with regard to Article 10 transactions).

Subsection (c)—Like Subsection (b), this subsection states default rules that, under Section 105, are subject to the operating agreement. For example, a limited liability company's operating agreement might state "This company is manager-managed," Sections 102(10) and 407(a), while providing that managers must submit specified ordinary matters for review by the members.

The actual authority of an LLC's manager or managers is a question of agency law and depends fundamentally on the contents of the operating agreement and any separate management contract between the LLC and its manager or managers. These agreements are the primary source of the manifestations of the LLC (as principal) from which a manager (as agent) will form the reasonable beliefs that delimit the scope of the manager's actual authority. RESTATEMENT (THIRD) OF AGENCY § 3.01 (2006). *See also* RESTATEMENT (SECOND) OF AGENCY §§ 15, 26 (1958).

Other information may be relevant as well, such as the course of dealing within the LLC, unless the operating agreement effectively precludes consideration of that information. *See* the comment to Section 105(a)(4) (stating that the operating agreement governs "the means and conditions for amending the operating agreement").

If the operating agreement and a management contract conflict, the reasonable manager will know that the operating agreement controls the extent of the manager's rightful authority to act for the LLC—despite any contract claims the manager might have. *See* the comment to Section 105(a)(2) (stating that the operating agreement governs "the rights and duties under this [act] of a person in the capacity of manager"). *See also* RESTATEMENT (THIRD) OF AGENCY § 8.13, cmt. b (2006) and RESTATEMENT (SECOND) OF AGENCY § 432, cmt. b (1958) (stating that, when a principal's instructions to an agent contravene a contract between the principal and agent, the agent may have a breach of contract claim but has no right to act contrary to the principal's instructions).

If: (i) an LLC's operating agreement merely states that the LLC is manager-managed and does not further specify the managerial responsibilities; and (ii) the LLC has only one manager, the actual authority analysis is simple. In that situation, this subsection:

- serves as "gap filler" to the operating agreement; and thereby

- constitutes the LLC's manifestation to the manager as to the scope of the manager's authority; and thereby

- delimits the manager's actual authority, subject to whatever subsequent manifestations the LLC may make to the manager (*e.g.,* by a vote of the members, or an amendment of the operating agreement).

If the operating agreement states only that the LLC is manager-managed and the LLC has more than one manager, the question of actual authority has an additional aspect. It is necessary to determine what actual authority any one manager has to act alone.

Paragraphs (c)(1)–(3), combine to provide the answer. A single manager of a multi-manager LLC:

- has no actual authority to commit the LLC to any matter encompassed in Paragraph (c)(3) or for which this act elsewhere requires unanimity;

- has the actual authority to commit the LLC to usual and customary matters, unless the manager has reason to know that: (i) other managers might disagree; or (ii) for some other reason consultation with fellow managers is appropriate; and

- has no actual authority to take unusual or non-customary actions that will have a substantial effect on the LLC.

The first point follows self-evidently from the language of Paragraph (c)(3) and other provisions requiring the affirmative vote or consent of the members, which reserves specified matters to the members. Given that language, no manager could reasonably believe to the contrary (unless the operating agreement provided otherwise).

The second point follows because:

Subsection (c) serves as the gap-filler manifestation from the LLC to its managers and does *not* require managers of a multi-manager LLC to act *only* in concert or after consultation. To the contrary, subject to the operating agreement Subsection (c)(2) expressly provides that "each manager has equal rights in the management and conduct of the company's activities and affairs."

- It would be impractical to require collective action on even the smallest of decisions.

- However, to the extent a manager has reason to know of a possible difference of opinion among the managers, Paragraph (c)(1) requires decision by "a majority of the managers."

The third point is a matter of common sense. The more serious the matter, the less likely it is that a manager has actual authority to act unilaterally. *Cf.* RESTATEMENT (THIRD) OF AGENCY § 3.03, cmt. c (2006) (noting the unreasonableness of believing, without more facts, that an individual has "an unusual degree of unilateral authority over a matter fraught with enduring consequences for the institution" and stating that "[t]he gravity of the matter from the standpoint of the organization is relevant to whether a third party could reasonably believe that the manager has authority to proceed unilaterally").

The common law of agency will also determine the apparent authority of an LLC's manager or managers, and in that analysis what the particular third party knows or has reason to know about the management structure and business practices of the particular LLC will always be relevant. RESTATEMENT (THIRD) OF AGENCY § 3.03, cmt. d (2006) ("The nature of an organization's business or activity is relevant to whether a third party could reasonably believe that a [manager] is authorized to commit the organization to a particular transaction.").

As a general matter, absent countervailing facts, courts may see the position of manager as clothing its occupants with the apparent authority to take actions that reasonably appear within the ordinary course of the company's business. The actual authority analysis stated above supports that proposition; absent a reason to believe to the contrary, a third party could reasonably believe that a manager possesses the authority contemplated by the gap-fillers of this act. *But see* the comment to Section 102(9) (stating that "confusion around the term 'manager' is common to almost all LLC statutes").

Subsection (c)(1)—For limited liability companies that have more than one manager, this act provides that in most circumstances a "matter relating to the activities and affairs of the company is decided . . . by a majority of the managers." However, unlike corporate statutes, this act does not provide a rule for the quantum of participation necessary to constitute "a majority." *Cf., e.g.,* MINN. STAT. § 302A.237 (2014) (providing rules for determining the votes need to constitute "an act of the board"). If a manager-managed LLC has more than one manager, the operating agreement should consider what "a majority" means in the event a manager position is vacant.

Subsection (c)(3)—This list is not exhaustive. *See* the comment to Subsection (b)(4).

Subsection (c)(4)—Under the default rule stated in this paragraph, dissolution of an entity that is a manager of an LLC does not end the entity's status as manager. Likewise, dissolution of entity that is a member does not cause the entity to dissociate. *See* Section 602(11) (providing that termination of such an entity causes dissociation).

An LLC does not cease to be "manager-managed" simply because no managers are in place. In that situation, absent additional facts, the LLC is manager-managed and the manager position is vacant. Non-manager members who exercise managerial functions during the vacancy (or at any other time) will have duties as determined by other law, most particularly the law of agency.

Subsection (c)(6)—For example, the obligation to safeguard trade secrets and other confidential or propriety information learned when the person is a manager remains in force after the person ceases to be a manager.

Subsection (d)—In this context, the doctrine of *noscitur a sociis* limits the authorized extent of a proxy holder or other agent. (The doctrine of *noscitur a sociis* holds "that the meaning of an unclear word or phrase should be determined by the words immediately surrounding it." BLACK'S LAW DICTIONARY (9th ed. 2009).

In particular, unless the operating agreement so provides, neither a proxy nor other agent may be used to circumvent the transfer restrictions that are fundamental to the law of limited liability companies. *See* Article 5 and RESTATEMENT (SECOND) OF CONTRACTS § 318(2) (1981) (stating that "a promise requires performance by a particular person . . . to the extent that the obligee has a substantial interest in having that person perform or control the acts promised").

Subsection (e), second sentence—The default rules of this act do not contemplate a person wrongfully causing dissolution, as distinguished from wrongfully dissociating. *Compare* Section 701, *with* Section 601(b). However, the operating agreement might contemplate wrongful dissolution, and then the second sentence of this subsection would apply unless the operating agreement provided otherwise.

Subsection (h)—This provision traces back to the UPA (1914) § 18(f) and is included to avoid its absence being misinterpreted as implying a contrary rule.

This act does not provide for remuneration to a manager of a manager-managed LLC. That issue is for the operating agreement, or a separate agreement between the LLC and the manager. A manager may also have a common law right to compensation. RESTATEMENT (THIRD) AGENCY § 8.13, cmt. d (2006) ("Unless an agreement between a principal and an agent indicates otherwise, a principal has a duty to pay compensation to an agent for services that the agent provides.").

§ 408. Reimbursement; Indemnification; Advancement; and Insurance

(a) A limited liability company shall reimburse a member of a member-managed company or the manager of a manager-managed company for any payment made by the member or manager in the course of the member's or manager's activities on behalf of the company, if the member or manager complied with Sections 405, 407, and 409 in making the payment.

(b) A limited liability company shall indemnify and hold harmless a person with respect to any claim or demand against the person and any debt, obligation, or other liability incurred by the person by reason of the person's former or present capacity as a member or manager, if the claim, demand, debt, obligation, or other liability does not arise from the person's breach of Section 405, 407, or 409.

(c) In the ordinary course of its activities and affairs, a limited liability company may advance reasonable expenses, including attorney's fees and costs, incurred by a person in connection with a claim or demand against the person by reason of the person's former or present capacity as a member or manager, if the person promises to repay the company if the person ultimately is determined not to be entitled to be indemnified under subsection (b).

(d) A limited liability company may purchase and maintain insurance on behalf of a member or manager against liability asserted against or incurred by the member or manager in that capacity or arising from that status even if, under Section 105(c)(7), the operating agreement could not eliminate or limit the person's liability to the company for the conduct giving rise to the liability.

COMMENT

Subsections (a) and (b)—A limited liability company's obligation, if any, to reimburse or indemnify others (*e.g.*, employees, independent contractors, other agents) is a question for other law, including the law of agency, contract and restitution. The fact a person has dissociated as a member or ceased to be a manager does not affect any obligations incurred by the limited liability company under these subsections for conduct occurring before the dissociation or cessation.

Subsection (a)—The reimbursement obligation stated here is a default rule and roughly parallels a rule of agency law. RESTATEMENT (THIRD) OF AGENCY § 8.14(2)(a) (2006) (stating that "[a] principal has a duty to indemnify an agent . . . when the agent makes a payment (i) within the scope of the agent's actual authority, or (ii) that is beneficial to the principal, unless the agent acts officiously in making the payment").

This subsection applies only to managers of manager-managed limited liability companies and members of member-managed companies. The definite article in the phrase "the member or manager" and "the member's" refers back to the original phrase: "A limited liability company shall reimburse a member of a member-managed company or the manager of a manger-managed company . . . ."

A limited liability company's obligation, if any, to reimburse others (including LLC employees and non-managing members of a manager-managed LLC) is a question for other law, including the law of agency and restitution. The fact a person has ceased to be a member of a member-managed LLC or a manager of a manager-managed LLC does not affect any obligations incurred by the LLC under this subsection for payments made before the cessation.

To the extent an operating agreement modifies or displaces the default rules stated in Sections 407 and 409, the agreement should also address this section. For example, if the operating agreement establishes a duty of ordinary care (modifying Section 409(c)), the agreement should specify which level of care is necessary to satisfy this subsection. It is not necessary that the levels of care be the same, only that the operating agreement make the situation clear and thereby avoid difficult issues of interpretation.

Subsection (b)—This subsection provides for indemnification but only as a default rule. Subject only to Section 105(c)(7), the operating agreement can relax these preconditions substantially. The agreement can also impose stricter preconditions.

The rule's eligibility requirements correspond to the default rules on management duties, which is appropriate because otherwise the statutory default rule on indemnification could undercut or even vitiate the statutory default rules on duty. To the extent an operating agreement modifies or displaces the default rules stated in Sections 405, 407, or 409, the agreement should also address this section. *See* the comment to Subsection (a).

Although referring broadly to any "person," this subsection is actually limited to present and former members or managers. The indemnification obligation applies only to a "debt, obligation, or other liability incurred by the

1251

person by reason of the person's former or present capacity as a member or manager." Thus, by its terms this subsection does not apply to a person in the capacity of an "officer," unless being an officer constitutes being a manager. For a discussion of the vagaries of the term "manager," see Section 102(9), comment.

Of course, the operating agreement may mandate indemnification to officers, employees, and other persons providing services to or acting for the limited liability company. Within the limitations stated in Section 105(c)(7), the operating agreement may obligate an LLC to indemnify a person even when the person has breached a managerial duty or the operating agreement itself.

Subsection (c)—This subsection authorizes but does not require a limited liability company to provide advances to cover expenses. *Cf. Majkowski v. American Imaging Mgmt. Servs., LLC*, 913 A.2d 572, 589 (Del. Ch. 2006) ("Because rights to indemnification and advancement differ in important ways, our courts have refused to recognize claims for advancement not granted in specific language clearly suggesting such rights."). The phrase "hold harmless" likewise does not encompass advances. *Id* The authorization applies only to those persons eligible for indemnification under Subsection (b), but the operating agreement certainly can authorize a broader scope and also make advances obligatory.

The reference to "ordinary course" pertains to Section 407(b)(3) (stating that any "difference arising among members [in a member-managed LLC] as to a matter in the ordinary course of the activities of the company may be decided by a majority of the members"). As for a manager-managed LLC, see Section 407(c)(1) ("Except as expressly provided in this [act], *any* matter relating to the activities and affairs of the [manager-managed] company is decided exclusively by the manager, or, if there is more than one manager, by a majority of the managers.") (emphasis added).

Subsection (d)—This subsection's language is very broad and authorizes an LLC to purchase insurance to cover, *e.g.,* a manager's intentional misconduct. It is unlikely that such insurance would be available. In contrast to Subsection (a), this subsection encompasses all members, not just members in a member-managed LLC. This authorization comes from the act, not the operating agreement, and therefore is not subject to Section 105(c)(7).

§ 409.   Standards of Conduct for Members and Managers

(a)   A member of a member-managed limited liability company owes to the company and, subject to Section 801, the other members the duties of loyalty and care stated in subsections (b) and (c).

(b)   The fiduciary duty of loyalty of a member in a member-managed limited liability company includes the duties:

(1)   to account to the company and hold as trustee for it any property, profit, or benefit derived by the member:

(A)   in the conduct or winding up of the company's activities and affairs;

(B)   from a use by the member of the company's property; or

(C)   from the appropriation of a company opportunity;

(2)   to refrain from dealing with the company in the conduct or winding up of the company's activities and affairs as or on behalf of a person having an interest adverse to the company; and

(3)   to refrain from competing with the company in the conduct of the company's activities and affairs before the dissolution of the company.

(c)   The duty of care of a member of a member-managed limited liability company in the conduct or winding up of the company's activities and affairs is to refrain from engaging in grossly negligent or reckless conduct, willful or intentional misconduct, or knowing violation of law.

(d)   A member shall discharge the duties and obligations under this [act] or under the operating agreement and exercise any rights consistently with the contractual obligation of good faith and fair dealing.

(e)   A member does not violate a duty or obligation under this [act] or under the operating agreement solely because the member's conduct furthers the member's own interest.

(f)   All the members of a member-managed limited liability company or a manager-managed limited liability company may authorize or ratify, after full disclosure of all material facts, a specific act or transaction that otherwise would violate the duty of loyalty.

(g) It is a defense to a claim under subsection (b)(2) and any comparable claim in equity or at common law that the transaction was fair to the limited liability company.

(h) If, as permitted by subsection (f) or (i)(6) or the operating agreement, a member enters into a transaction with the limited liability company which otherwise would be prohibited by subsection (b)(2), the member's rights and obligations arising from the transaction are the same as those of a person that is not a member.

(i) In a manager-managed limited liability company, the following rules apply:

(1) Subsections (a), (b), (c), and (g) apply to the manager or managers and not the members.

(2) The duty stated under subsection (b)(3) continues until winding up is completed.

(3) Subsection (d) applies to managers and members.

(4) Subsection (e) applies only to members.

(5) The power to ratify under subsection (f) applies only to the members.

(6) Subject to subsection (d), a member does not have any duty to the company or to any other member solely by reason of being a member.

COMMENT

This section states some of the core aspects of the fiduciary duty of loyalty, provides a duty of care, and incorporates the contractual obligation of good faith and fair dealing. The section follows the structure of many LLC acts, first stating the duties of members in a member-managed limited liability company and then using that statement and a "switching" mechanism, Subsection (i), to allocate duties in a manager-managed company. The duties stated in this section are subject to the operating agreement, but Section 105(c) and (d) contain important limitations on the power of the operating agreement to affect fiduciary and other duties and the obligation of good faith and fair dealing.

For the effect of dissociation on a person's duties under this section, see Section 603(a)(2).

Subsection (a)—This subsection recognizes two core managerial duties but, unlike some earlier uniform acts, does not purport to state all managerial duties. Indeed, many cases characterize a manager's duty to disclose as a fiduciary duty. *E.g., Salm v. Feldstein*, 20 A.D.3d 469, 470, 799 N.Y.S.2d 104, 105 (N.Y. App. Div. 2005) (stating that, "[a]s the managing member of the [limited liability] company and as a co-member with the plaintiff, the defendant owed the plaintiff a fiduciary duty to make full disclosure of all material facts"); *Metro Commc'n Corp. BVI v. Advanced Mobilecomm Technologies Inc.*, 854 A.2d 121, 156 n. 78 (Del. Ch. 2004) (referring to "certain standards governing the disclosure-related duties of the fiduciaries of Delaware business entities;" noting that "[t]hese standards have been mostly articulated in the corporate context but the corporate standards often serve as the default rule in the alternative entity context").

Subsection (b)—This subsection states three core aspects of the fiduciary duty of loyalty: (i) not "usurping" company opportunities or otherwise wrongly benefiting from the company's operations or property; (ii) avoiding conflict of interests in dealing with the company (whether directly or on behalf of another); and (iii) refraining from competing with the company. Essentially the same duties exist in agency law and under the law of all types of business organizations.

The subsection applies beginning with "the conduct of the company's activities and affairs," which by definition cannot exist before the company exists; thus the stated duties do not apply to pre-formation activities. In some circumstances, comparable duties might arise from other law, particular the law of agency. *See, e.g.,* Section 401(a) and (b) (stating that the organizer acts "on behalf of others").

The stated duties comprise a default rule. Under Section 105(d)(3)(A): "If not manifestly unreasonable, the operating agreement may . . . alter or eliminate the aspects of the duty of loyalty stated in Section 409(b)."

Subsection (b)(1)—The phrase "hold as trustee" dates back to UPA (1914) § 21 and reflects the availability of disgorgement remedies, such as a constructive trust. In contrast to an actual trustee, a person subject to this duty does not: (i) face the special obstacles to consent characteristic of trust law; or (ii) enjoy protection for decisions taken in reliance on the governing instrument and other sources of information. *Cf.* UNIFORM STATUTORY TRUST ENTITY ACT (2009) (Last Amended 2013) § 506 ("A trustee [of a statutory trust] . . . is not liable to the trust or to a beneficial owner for breach of any duty, *including a fiduciary duty*, to the extent the breach results from reasonable reliance on: (i) a term of the governing instrument; (ii) a record of the statutory trust; or (iii) an opinion, report, or statement of another person that the person to which the opinion, report, or statement is made or delivered reasonably believes is within the other person's professional or expert competence and is made or delivered to the trustee . . . .") (emphasis added).

Subsection (b)(1)(A)—This provision is consistent with a basic principle of agency law—namely, that an agent may not benefit at all from the performance of the agency unless the principal consents. RESTATEMENT (THIRD) OF AGENCY § 8.06, cmt. c (2006). Typically, however, the operating agreement will legitimize particular benefits—*e.g.*, a management fee paid to a managing member in addition to that member's share of distributions. Also, an agreed allocation of distributions takes those benefits outside the reach of this provision.

Subsection (b)(1)(B)—For the expansive meaning of "property," see Section 102(17). The term includes confidential information.

Subsection (b)(1)(C)—This act does not specify what constitutes "a company opportunity," but ample case law exists. *See, e.g., Ebenezer United Methodist Church v. Riverwalk Development Phase, II, LLC*, 45 A.3d 883, 887 (Md. App. 2012) (discussing the "interest or reasonable expectancy test"); *In re McCook Metals, L.L.C.*, 319 B.R. 570, 596 (Bkrtcy. N.D.Ill. 2005) (discussing the "line of business test").

This duty continues through winding up, although in that context the scope of company opportunities inevitably narrows.

In most, if not all, situations, usurping a company opportunity also breaches the duty not to compete, Paragraph (b)(3), but not vice versa.

Subsection (b)(2)—In this context, the phrase "adverse interest" is a term of art, meaning "to be on the other side of the table" in some dealing with the limited liability company. Absent informed consent by the LLC, this duty is breached by the mere existence of the conflict of interest; the LLC need not prove that the outcome of the dealing was adverse to the LLC. *But see* Subsection (g) (permitting the defense of fairness). This duty continues through winding up.

Subsection (b)(3)—Although competition is often thought of in terms of potential customers, this duty applies equally to competition for resources, including employees. The duty not to compete continues longer in a manager-managed LLC. *See* Subsection (i)(2).

Subsection (c)—ULLCA (2006) § 409(c) stated a different rule: "Subject to the business judgment rule, the duty of care of a member of a member-managed limited liability company in the conduct and winding up of the company's activities is to act with the care that a person in a like position would reasonably exercise under similar circumstances and in a manner the member reasonably believes to be in the best interests of the company." As part of the Harmonization Project, the ULLCA duty of care was conformed to the duty of care stated in ULPA (2001) and UPA (1997).

Neither this act nor the two harmonized partnership acts refer to the duty of care as a fiduciary duty, because: (i) the duty of care applies in many non-fiduciary situations; and (ii) breach of the duty of care is remediable only in damages while breach of a fiduciary duty gives rise also to equitable remedies, including disgorgement, constructive trust, and rescission. *See* ULPA (2001) (Last Amended 2013) § 409(c) and UPA (1997) (Last Amended 2013) § 409(c).

The change in label is consistent with the RESTATEMENT (THIRD) OF AGENCY § 8.02 (2006), which refers to the agent's "fiduciary duty to act loyally, but eschews the word "fiduciary" when stating the agent's duties of "care, competence, and diligence." *Id.* § 8.08. However, the change in label is merely semantics; no change in the law is intended.

The operating agreement can raise the standard of care, or subject to Sections 105(c)(7) and (d)(3)(C), lower it. A person's practical exposure for breaching the duty of care involves not only the standard of care but also any operating agreement provision that: (i) exonerates the person from liability for breach of the duty of care, Section 105(c)(7); or (ii) entitles the person to indemnification despite such breach, Section 408(b), comment.

Subsection (d)—This subsection refers to the "contractual obligation of good faith and fair dealing" (emphasis added) and thereby invokes the implied obligation that exists in every contract. *See* RESTATEMENT (SECOND) CONTRACTS § 205 (1981) ("Every contract imposes upon each party a duty of good faith and fair dealing in its performance and its enforcement."). The adjective ("contractual") should help avoid decisions like *Phelps v. Frampton*, 2007 MT 263, 339 Mont. 330, 342–43, 170 P.3d 474, 483 (2007) (holding that Montana's version of UPA (1997) creates a statutory obligation of good faith and fair dealing separate from the implied contractual covenant).

At first glance, it may seem strange to apply a contractual obligation to statutory duties and rights—*i.e.*, duties and rights "under this [act]." However, for the most part those duties and rights apply to relationships *inter se* the members and the LLC and function only to the extent not displaced by the operating agreement. These statutory default rules are intended in essence to function like a contract; applying the contractual notion of good faith and fair dealing therefore makes sense.

The contractual obligation of "good faith" has nothing to do with the corporate concept of good faith that for years bedeviled courts and attorneys trying to understand: (i) Delaware's famous corporate law exoneration provision; and (ii) that provision's exception "for acts or omissions not in good faith." DEL. CODE ANN. tit. 8, § 102(b)(7) (2012). In that context, good faith is an aspect of the duty of loyalty. *See Stone ex rel. AmSouth Bancorporation v. Ritter*, 911 A.2d 362, 369–70 (Del. 2006).

Likewise, the contractual obligation of good faith and fair dealing has nothing to do with the "utmost good faith" sometimes used to describe the fiduciary duties that owners of closely held businesses owe each other. *See, e.g., Meinhard v. Salmon*, 249 N.Y. 458, 477, 164 N.E. 545, 551 (1928) ("[W]here parties engage in a joint enterprise each owes to the other the duty of the utmost good faith in all that relates to their common venture. Within its scope they stand in a fiduciary relationship."); *Donahue v. Rodd Electrotype Co. of New England, Inc.*, 367 Mass. 578, 593, 328 N.E.2d 505, 515 (1975) ("[S]tockholders in the close corporation owe one another substantially the same fiduciary duty in the operation of the enterprise1 that partners owe to one another. In our previous decisions, we have defined the standard of duty owed by partners to one another as the utmost good faith and loyalty.") (footnotes omitted) (citations omitted) (internal quotations omitted).

To the contrary, the contractual obligation of good faith and fair dealing is not a fiduciary duty, does not command altruism or self-abnegation, and does not prevent a member from acting in the member's own self-interest:

"Fair dealing" is not akin to the fair process component of entire fairness, *i.e.*, whether the fiduciary acted fairly when engaging in the challenged transaction as measured by duties of loyalty and care . . . . It is rather a commitment to deal "fairly" in the sense of consistently with the terms of the parties' agreement and its purpose. Likewise "good faith" does not envision loyalty to the contractual counterparty, but rather faithfulness to the scope, purpose, and terms of the parties' contract. Both necessarily turn on the contract itself and what the parties would have agreed upon had the issue arisen when they were bargaining originally.

Gerber v. Enter. Products Holdings, LLC, 67 A.3d 400, 418–19 (Del. 2013) (quoting *ASB Allegiance Real Estate Fund v. Scion Breckenridge Managing Member, LLC*, 50 A.3d 434, 440–42 (Del. Ch. 2012), *aff'd in part, rev'd in part on other grounds*, 68 A.3d 665 (Del. 2013)) (footnotes omitted) (citations omitted) (internal quotations omitted without ellipsis by *Gerber*). *See also* Subsection (e).

Courts should not use the contractual obligation to change *ex post facto* the parties' or this act's allocation of risk and power. To the contrary, the obligation should be used only to protect agreed-upon arrangements from conduct that is manifestly beyond what a reasonable person could have contemplated when the arrangements were made.

The operating agreement or this act may grant discretion to a member or manager, and the contractual obligation of good faith and fair dealing is especially salient when discretion is at issue. However, a member or manager may properly exercise discretion even though another member suffers as a consequence. Conduct does not violate the obligation of good faith and fair dealing merely because that conduct substantially prejudices a party. Indeed, parties allocate risk precisely because prejudice may occur.

The exercise of discretion constitutes a breach of the obligation of good faith and fair dealing only when the party claiming breach shows that the conduct has no honestly-held purpose that legitimately comports with the parties' agreed-upon arrangements:

An implied covenant claim . . . looks to the past. It is not a free-floating duty unattached to the underlying legal documents. It does not ask what duty the law should impose on the parties given their relationship at the time of the wrong, but *rather what the parties would have agreed to themselves had they considered the issue in their original bargaining positions at the time of contracting.*

Gerber v. Enter. Prods. Holdings, LLC, 67 A.3d 400, 418 (Del. 2013) (quoting *ASB Allegiance Real Estate Fund v. Scion Breckenridge Managing Member, LLC*, 50 A.3d 434, 440–42 (Del. Ch. 2012), *aff'd in part, rev'd in part on other grounds*, 68 A.3d 665 (Del. 2013)) (emphasis added) (footnotes omitted) (citations omitted) (internal quotations omitted without ellipsis by *Gerber*).

In sum, the purpose of the contractual obligation of good faith and fair dealing is to protect the arrangement the members have chosen for themselves, not to restructure that arrangement under the guise of safeguarding it.

As to the power of the operating agreement to affect the contractual obligation of good faith and fair dealing, see Section 105(c)(6) (prohibiting elimination but allowing the agreement to "prescribe standards, if not manifestly unreasonable, by which the performance of the obligation is to be measured"). For examples, see Section 105(c)(6), comment. As to whether the obligation stated in this subsection applies to transferees, see Section 107(b), comment.

Subsection (e)—A member in a member-managed LLC has at least two different roles: (i) as a party to the operating agreement, with rights and obligations under that agreement; and (ii) as manager or co-manager of the enterprise. This provision pertains to the first role. A member's exercise of rights under the operating agreement is subject to the obligation of good faith and fair dealing, Subsection (d), but a person does not breach that contractual obligation "solely because the [person's exercise of rights] furthers the [person's] own interest." In contrast, this provision is ineffective with regard to a member's duties as manager or co-manager. For example, a member's liability under Section 409(b)(3) (prohibiting competition) is not "solely because the member's conduct furthers the member's own interest." Rather, the liability results from the breach of a specific obligation—*i.e.*, the codified aspect of the duty of loyalty that prohibits competition.

With regard to a manager-managed LLC: (i) the same analysis applies to a member that is a manager; and (ii) with regard to a non-managing member the analysis as to contractual rights applies and the analysis as to managerial duties is inapposite.

Subsection (f)—Here and elsewhere in this act, information "is material if there is a substantial likelihood that a reasonable [decision maker] would consider it important in deciding how to vote" or take other action under this act or the operating agreements. *TSC Industries, Inc. v. Northway, Inc.*, 426 U.S. 438, 449, 96 S.Ct. 2126, 2132 (1976).

The operating agreement can provide additional or different methods of authorization or ratification, subject to the strictures of Section 105(c)(5), (d)(1), and (d)(3)(A)(B) and (D).

Subsection (g)—This subsection codifies judge-made law applicable to all business entities. *See, e.g., Gottsacker v. Monnier*, 281 Wis. 2d 361, 379, 697 N.W.2d 436, 444 (Wisc. 2005) (referring to "a willful failure to deal fairly with the LLC or its other members"); *Lonergan v. EPE Holdings, LLC*, 5 A.3d 1008, 1019 (Del. Ch. 2010) (discussing "entire fairness" in the context of a limited partnership"); *Kahn v. Lynch Commc'n Sys., Inc.*, 638 A.2d 1110, 1116 (Del. 1994) (discussing "entire fairness" in the context of a corporation's merger with an affiliate); *Lonergan v. EPE Holdings, LLC*, 5 A.3d 1008, 1019 (Del. Ch. 2010) (discussing "entire fairness" in the context of a limited partnership").

Subsection (h)—This subsection is the modern, reformulated version of a language that sought to overturn the now-defunct notion that debts to owners were categorically inferior to debts to non-owner creditors. *See, e.g.,* ULPA (2001) § 112 ("A partner may lend money to and transact other business with the limited partnership and has the same rights and obligations with respect to the loan or other transaction as a person that is not a partner."). The reformulation makes clear that this provision has nothing to do with the fiduciary duty pertaining to conflict of interests. *See BT-I v. Equitable Life Assurance Soc'y of the United States*, 75 Cal. App. 4th 1406, 1415, 89 Cal. Rptr. 2d 811 (1999) (examining the prior formulation, explaining its history and stating "[w]e cannot discern anything in the purpose of [the prior formulation] that suggests an intent to affect a general partner's fiduciary duty to limited partners").

This subsection states a default rule. The operating agreement may provide that debt to a member (or members generally) is subordinate to other limited liability company obligations. The agreement that creates the debt may do likewise.

Subsection (i)—This is the "switching" mechanism, referred to in the introduction to this comment. The list does not include Subsection (h).

Subsection (i)(1)—This provision switches most managerial duties to the managers and away from members. Of course, if a member is a manager, the duties apply to the member-manager in the person's capacity of manager.

Subsection (i)(2)—On the assumption that the members of a manager-managed LLC are dependent on the manager, this paragraph extends the duty not to compete longer than in a member-managed LLC.

Subsection (i)(3)—The contractual obligation of good faith and fair dealing applies to members regardless of whether they are managers; non-managing members have rights and perhaps duties under the operating agreement and under this act. As to non-member managers, the operating agreement (and the corresponding obligation of good faith and fair dealing) are relevant regardless of whether the manager is party to the agreement. *See* Section 105(a)(2) (stating that the operating agreement "governs . . . the rights and duties under this [act] of a person in the capacity of manager"). Also, non-member managers will have rights and obligations under this act, which per Subsection (d) are also subject to the obligation of good faith and fair dealing.

Subsection (i)(4)—As explained in the comment to Subsection (e), that provision does not apply to the managerial function.

Subsection (i)(5)—The power to ratify belongs to the entity's owners; thus Subsection (f) does not switch from members to managers.

Subsection (i)(6)—This paragraph merely negates a claim of fiduciary duty that is exclusively status-based and does not immunize misconduct.

Example: Although a limited liability company is manager-managed, one member who is not a manager owns a controlling interest and effectively, albeit indirectly, controls the company's activities. A member owning a minority interest brings an action for dissolution under Section 701(a)(4)(C)(ii) (oppression by "the managers or those members in control of the company"). This paragraph does not prevent the court from construing the claim as alleging a breach of fiduciary duty by the controlling member.

§ 410. Rights to Information of Member, Manager, and Person Dissociated as Member

(a) In a member-managed limited liability company, the following rules apply:

(1) On reasonable notice, a member may inspect and copy during regular business hours, at a reasonable location specified by the company, any record maintained by the company regarding the company's activities, affairs, financial condition, and other circumstances, to the extent the information is material to the member's rights and duties under the operating agreement or this [act].

(2) The company shall furnish to each member:

(A) without demand, any information concerning the company's activities, affairs, financial condition, and other circumstances which the company knows and is material to the proper exercise of the member's rights and duties under the operating agreement or this [act], except to the extent the company can establish that it reasonably believes the member already knows the information; and

(B) on demand, any other information concerning the company's activities, affairs, financial condition, and other circumstances, except to the extent the demand for the information demanded is unreasonable or otherwise improper under the circumstances.

(3) The duty to furnish information under paragraph (2) also applies to each member to the extent the member knows any of the information described in paragraph (2).

(b) In a manager-managed limited liability company, the following rules apply:

(1) The informational rights stated in subsection (a) and the duty stated in subsection (a)(3) apply to the managers and not the members.

(2) During regular business hours and at a reasonable location specified by the company, a member may inspect and copy information regarding the activities, affairs, financial condition, and other circumstances of the company as is just and reasonable if:

(A) the member seeks the information for a purpose reasonably related to the member's interest as a member;

(B) the member makes a demand in a record received by the company, describing with reasonable particularity the information sought and the purpose for seeking the information; and

(C) the information sought is directly connected to the member's purpose.

(3) Not later than 10 days after receiving a demand pursuant to paragraph (2)(B), the company shall inform in a record the member that made the demand of:

(A)   what information the company will provide in response to the demand and when and where the company will provide the information; and

(B)   the company's reasons for declining, if the company declines to provide any demanded information.

(4)   Whenever this [act] or an operating agreement provides for a member to vote on or give or withhold consent to a matter, before the vote is cast or consent is given or withheld, the company shall, without demand, provide the member with all information that is known to the company and is material to the member's decision.

(c)   Subject to subsection (h), on 10 days' demand made in a record received by a limited liability company, a person dissociated as a member may have access to the information to which the person was entitled while a member if:

(1)   the information pertains to the period during which the person was a member;

(2)   the person seeks the information in good faith; and

(3)   the person satisfies the requirements imposed on a member by subsection (b)(2).

(d)   A limited liability company shall respond to a demand made pursuant to subsection (c) in the manner provided in subsection (b)(3).

(e)   A limited liability company may charge a person that makes a demand under this section the reasonable costs of copying, limited to the costs of labor and material.

(f)   A member or person dissociated as a member may exercise the rights under this section through an agent or, in the case of an individual under legal disability, a legal representative. Any restriction or condition imposed by the operating agreement or under subsection (h) applies both to the agent or legal representative and to the member or person dissociated as a member.

(g)   Subject to Section 504, the rights under this section do not extend to a person as transferee.

(h)   In addition to any restriction or condition stated in its operating agreement, a limited liability company, as a matter within the ordinary course of its activities and affairs, may impose reasonable restrictions and conditions on access to and use of information to be furnished under this section, including designating information confidential and imposing nondisclosure and safeguarding obligations on the recipient. In a dispute concerning the reasonableness of a restriction under this subsection, the company has the burden of proving reasonableness.

COMMENT

This section is derived from the Uniform Limited Partnership Act (2001) §§ 304 (rights to information of limited partners and former limited partners) and 407 (rights to information of general partners and former general partners). The rules stated here are what might be termed "quasi-default rules"—subject to some change by the operating agreement. *See* Section 105(c)(8) (prohibiting unreasonable restrictions on the information rights stated in this section).

Although the rights and duties stated in this section are extensive, they are not necessarily all-inclusive. This act's statement of fiduciary duties is not exhaustive, *see* the comment to Section 409(a), and some cases characterize owners' information rights as reflecting a fiduciary duty of those with management power. *E.g., Bakerman v. Sidney Frank Importing Co., Inc.*, No. Civ.A. 1844-N, 2006 WL 3927242 at *14 (Del. Ch. Oct. 16, 2006) (holding that an LLC manager owed "certain duties to members of the LLC" and stating that "[w]hen fiduciaries communicate with their beneficiaries in the context of asking the beneficiary to make a discretionary decision—such as whether to consent to a sale of substantially all the assets of an LLC—the fiduciary has a duty to disclose all material facts bearing on the decision at issue") (citing *Loudon v. Archer-Daniels-Midland Co.*, 700 A.2d 135, 137 (Del.1997)). Also, the rights stated in this section are in addition to whatever discovery rights a party has in a civil suit.

Subsection (a)—Paragraph 1 states the rule pertaining to information memorialized in "any record maintained by the company." Paragraph 2 applies to information not in such a record. Appropriately, Paragraph (2) sets a more demanding standard for those seeking such information.

Subsection (a)(2) and (3)—In appropriate circumstances, violation of either or both of these provisions might cause a court to enjoin or even rescind action taken by the LLC, especially when the violation has interfered with an approval or veto mechanism involving member consent. *E.g., Blue Chip Emerald LLC v. Allied Partners Inc.*, 299 A.D.2d 278, 279–80 (N.Y. App. Div. 2002) (invoking partnership law precedent as reflecting a duty of full disclosure and holding that "[a]bsent such full disclosure, the transaction is voidable").

Subsection (a)(2)—This paragraph imposes a duty on the limited liability company, not the members who manage the LLC. However, a member could be liable in damages if the member were to: (i) breach a duty under Section 409 or the operating agreement; and (ii) in doing so cause or suffer the LLC to breach the duty stated in this paragraph.

Subsection (a)(2)(A)—For the meaning of "material" as applied to information, see Section 409(f), comment.

Subsection (a)(3)—This paragraph imposes a duty directly on each member. Therefore, a member's violation of this paragraph is actionable in damages without need to show a violation of a duty stated in Section 409.

Subsection (b)(1)—This is a switching provision. The comments to Paragraph (a)(2) and (3) apply here by analogy.

Subsection (b)(2)—This paragraph refers to "information" rather than "records maintained by the company" so in some circumstances the company might have an obligation to memorialize information. *Compare* Subsection (b)(2), *with* Subsection (a). Such circumstances will likely be rare or at least unusual. This section generally concerns providing existing information, not creating it. In any event, a member does not trigger the company's obligation under this paragraph merely by satisfying Subparagraphs (A) through (C). The member must also satisfy the "just and reasonable" requirement.

Subsection (b)(4)—For the meaning of "material" as applied to information, see Section 409(f), comment.

Subsection (c)—When a member dies, Section 504 provides information rights to the legal representative of the deceased member.

Subsection (c)(1)—A person dissociated as a member has information rights in that capacity only as to the period during which the person was a member. To the extent that further information is accessible under Section 504(2) (providing access to the legal representative of a deceased partner), that access is limited both in purpose ("for purposes of settling the estate") and in scope ("the rights the deceased partner had under Section 410").

Subsection (f)—Some old cases involved conflicts over whether a shareholder could exercise inspection rights through another person. *White v. Coeur D'Alene Big Creek Mining Co.*, 55 P.2d 720, 723 (Idaho 1936) (stating that "[t]he refusal to permit respondent [shareholder] to appoint his own attorney or agent to make the examination [of the corporation's books] was in effect a denial of his right" of inspection); *State v. Monida & Yellowstone Stage Co.*, 124 N.W. 971, 972 (Minn. 1910) (upholding a trial court's mandamus order, "which shall provide that [the shareholder complainant], or such attorney or agent as he may select, . . . shall be allowed to inspect the books, records, and papers of the defendant [corporation]"). In light of that history, for the avoidance of doubt, this subsection expressly authorizes taking action through an agent. No negative inference should be drawn about using agents to take other action under this act.

Subsection (h)—This provision provides fallback protection for gaps in the operating agreement. For example, those managing an LLC may protect trade secrets from disclosure prohibit various misuses of confidential information even if the operating agreement omits to do so.

The reference to "ordinary course" pertains to Section 407(b)(3) (stating that any "difference arising among members [in a member-managed LLC] as to a matter in the ordinary course of the activities of the company may be decided by a majority of the members"). As for a manager-managed LLC, see Section 407(c)(1) ("Except as expressly provided in this [act], *any* matter relating to the activities and affairs of the [manager-managed] company is decided exclusively by the manager, or, if there is more than one manager, by a majority of the managers.") (emphasis added). This approach is necessary, lest a requesting member (or manager-member) have the power to block imposition of a reasonable restriction or condition needed to prevent the requestor from abusing the LLC.

The burden of persuasion under this subsection contrasts with the burden of persuasion under Section 105(c)(8) (prohibiting unreasonable limitations on the information rights provided by this section). Under that subsection, as a matter of ordinary procedural law the burden is on the person making the claim.

[ARTICLE] 5

TRANSFERABLE INTERESTS AND RIGHTS
OF TRANSFEREES AND CREDITORS

§ 501.   Nature of Transferable Interest

A transferable interest is personal property.

COMMENT

For the definition of transferable interest, see Section 102(24). Absent a contrary provision in the operating agreement or the consent of the members, a "transferable interest" is the only interest in an LLC which can be transferred to a person who is not already a member. *See* Section 502. As to whether a member may transfer governance rights to a fellow member, the question is moot absent a provision in the operating agreement changing the default rule, *see* Section 407(b)(2) (allocating governance rights *per capita*). In the default mode, a member's transfer of governance rights to another member: (i) does not increase the transferee's governance rights; (ii) eliminates the transferor's governance rights; and (iii) thereby changes that denominator but not the numerator in calculating governance rights.

> **Example:** LCN Company, LLC is a member-managed limited liability company with three members, Laura, Charles, and Nora. The operating agreement does not displace this act's default rule on the allocation of governance rights among members. Thus, each member has 1/3 of those rights. Laura transfers her entire ownership interest to Charles. The transfer does not increase Charles's governance rights but does eliminate Laura's. After the transfer, Laura has no governance rights (regardless of whether Charles and Nora agree to expel Laura under Section 602(5)(B)). As a result, Charles and Nora each have 1/2 of the governance rights.

Whether a transferable interest pledged as security is governed by Article 8 or 9 of the Uniform Commercial Code depends on the rules stated in those articles.

§ 502.   Transfer of Transferable Interest

(a)   Subject to Section 503(f), a transfer, in whole or in part, of a transferable interest:

(1)   is permissible;

(2)   does not by itself cause a person's dissociation as a member or a dissolution and winding up of the limited liability company's activities and affairs; and

(3)   subject to Section 504, does not entitle the transferee to:

(A)   participate in the management or conduct of the company's activities and affairs; or

(B)   except as otherwise provided in subsection (c), have access to records or other information concerning the company's activities and affairs.

(b)   A transferee has the right to receive, in accordance with the transfer, distributions to which the transferor would otherwise be entitled.

(c)   In a dissolution and winding up of a limited liability company, a transferee is entitled to an account of the company's transactions only from the date of dissolution.

(d)   A transferable interest may be evidenced by a certificate of the interest issued by a limited liability company in a record, and, subject to this section, the interest represented by the certificate may be transferred by a transfer of the certificate.

(e)   A limited liability company need not give effect to a transferee's rights under this section until the company knows or has notice of the transfer.

(f)   A transfer of a transferable interest in violation of a restriction on transfer contained in the operating agreement is ineffective if the intended transferee has knowledge or notice of the restriction at the time of transfer.

(g)　Except as otherwise provided in Section 602(5)(B), if a member transfers a transferable interest, the transferor retains the rights of a member other than the transferable interest transferred and retains all the duties and obligations of a member.

(h)　If a member transfers a transferable interest to a person that becomes a member with respect to the transferred interest, the transferee is liable for the member's obligations under Sections 403 and 406 known to the transferee when the transferee becomes a member.

COMMENT

One of the most fundamental characteristics of LLC law is its fidelity to the "pick your partner" principle. *See, e.g., Bynum v. Frisby*, 73 Nev. 145, 149–50, 311 P.2d 972, 975 (1957) (stating that (i) "the assignment of a partnership interest from one partner to a stranger does not bring that stranger into fiduciary relationship with the remaining partners" and (ii) absent consent by the remaining partners "[t]he stranger remains a stranger" with no rights to management or even information).

This section is the core of the act's provisions reflecting and protecting that principle. A member's rights in a limited liability company are bifurcated into economic rights (the transferable interest) and governance rights (including management rights, consent rights, rights to information, rights to seek judicial intervention). Unless the operating agreement otherwise provides, a member acting without the consent of all other members lacks both the power and the right to: (i) bestow membership on a non-member, Section 401(d); or (ii) transfer to a non-member anything other than some or all of the member's transferable interest, Section 502(a)(3). The rights of a mere transferee are quite limited—*i.e.*, to receive distributions, Section 502(b), and, if the LLC dissolves and winds up, to receive specified information pertaining to the LLC from the date of dissolution. Section 502(c).

This section applies regardless of whether the transferor is a member, a transferee of a member, a transferee of a transferee, etc. *See* Section 102(24) (defining "transferable interest" in terms of a right "initially owned by a person in the person's capacity as a member" regardless of "whether or not the person remains a member or continues to own any part of the right").

This section does not directly consider whether a member may transfer governance rights to another member without obtaining consent from all the other members. As noted above, Section 501, cmt., the question is moot under this act's default rule for allocating governance rights.

However, the question can be pivotal when the operating agreement displaces the default rule on governance rights but does not determine whether transfer restrictions (whether contractual, statutory, or both) apply to transfers of governance rights from one member to another. Case law is scant but suggests that this act does not protect members from control shifts that result from transfers among members (as distinguished from transfers to non-members who seek thereby to become members). *Blythe v. Bell*, No. 11 CVS 933, 2012 WL 7807800, at ¶ 6 (N.C.Dist. Dec. 10, 2012) (holding in a case of "first impression in North Carolina" that "in the absence of articles of incorporation or an operating agreement to the contrary . . . the assignment of control (*i.e.*, governance) interests between members is effective without unanimous member consent;" *Achaian, Inc. v. Leemon Family L.L.C.*, 25 A.3d 800, 810 (Del. Ch. 2011) (Strine, Ch.) (holding that the terms of the LLC agreement did not preclude one member of a three-member LLC from transferring the member's entire interest (including governance rights) to a second member without first having the consent of the third member; stating that the third member's "argument relies on a very thinly sliced version of [the "pick-your-partner principle, the strained version being] . . . that once one chooses his initial co-members, one continues to hold a veto over how much additional voting power they may acquire;" explaining that "[t]he problem for [the third member] is that nothing in the LLC Agreement supports [that member's] reading of it that would require an already admitted Member, like [the acquirer—*i.e.*, the second member], to be become once, twice (or even three times) a Member each and every time that Member acquires an additional block of Interests").

Other law may affect the applicability of this section. *See* 11 U.S.C. § 541(c)(1) (providing that, initially at least, all property of a debtor becomes part of the bankruptcy estate regardless of restrictions on transfer); UCC §§ 9–406, 9–408 (overriding specified restrictions on assignment in specified circumstances, regardless of whether state law or a contract imposes the restrictions).

In any event, this section does not apply to the transfer of ownership interests in a member that is an entity.

Example: ABC, LLC has three members: Ralph (an individual), Alice, Inc. ("Alice"), and Norton, LLC ("Norton"). Section 502 applies to any attempt by Ralph, Alice, or Norton to transfer their respective membership interest in ABC. Section 502 is inapplicable, however, to a change in control of Alice or Norton or even a complete change in their respective membership.

Subsection (a)—The definition of "transfer," Section 102(23), and this subsection's reference to "in whole or in part" combine to mean that this section encompasses not only unconditional, permanent, and complete transfers but also temporary, contingent, and partial ones. Thus, for example, a charging order under Section 503 effects a transfer of part of the judgment debtor's transferable interest, as does the pledge of a transferable interest as collateral for a loan and the gift of a life-interest in a member's rights to distribution.

Subsection (a)(2)—The phrase "by itself" contemplates Section 602(5)(B), which creates a risk of dissociation via expulsion when a member transfers all of the member's transferable interest.

Subsection (a)(3)—Mere transferees have no right to participate in management or otherwise intrude as the members carry on the affairs of the limited liability company and their activities as members.

Because Section 102(22)(G) defines "transfer" to include "a transfer by operation of law," this section affects the power of other law to effect transfers of a member's ownership interest. For example, a divorce court lacks the power to award a member's spouse anything beyond the member's transferable interest. Nor does the member have the power to enter into a property settlement purporting to effect any greater transfer.

For the divorce court, the best solution is to value the member's complete ownership interest (*i.e.*, the transferable interest as enhanced by the management and information rights and the standing to sue) and: (i) if possible, award the member's spouse marital property of equal value; or (ii) if not possible, award the member's spouse a money judgment and a charging order to enforce the judgment.

Granting the non-member any part of member's transferable interest is almost always imprudent; marital discord will almost inevitably carry over into the business relationship. Granting the member's ex-spouse the entire transferable interest is rarely a viable alternative. If the member is an active participant in the limited liability company, the approach is impossible. The member's transferable interest will typically constitute much or all of the member's remuneration for the partner's activity. Even if the member is essentially passive, granting the transferable interest to the ex-spouse puts him or her at great risk as a "bare naked assignee." *See* the comment to Section 107(b).

When a member dies, subject to the operating agreement other law may effect a transfer of the member's transferable interest to the member's estate or personal representative. However, for the reasons just stated, other law lacks the power to transfer anything more than a transferable interest. (Section (504) does provide extra information rights for the purposes of settling the estate of the deceased member.)

Subsection (a)(3)(B)—*See* Section 410(g) (providing that that section's information rights do not apply to transferees).

Subsection (b)—Amounts due under this subsection are of course subject to offset for any amount owed to the limited liability company by the member or person dissociated as a member on whose account the distribution is made. Section 404(d). As to whether an LLC may properly offset for claims against a transferor that was never a member is matter for other law, specifically the law of contracts dealing with assignments.

Subsection (c)—This very limited grant of information rights encompasses only transactions occurring at or after the date of the LLC's dissolution. The transferee has only the right to information as to the allocation of net assets among the LLC's creditors, members, and transferees—and only from the date of dissolution.

This subsection does not prevent a transferee from contracting with a member-transferor to require the member-transferor to disclose further information to the transferee. Whether such an agreement would breach the operating agreement, the implied contractual obligation of good faith and fair dealing, Section 409(d), or a fiduciary duty depends on the circumstances.

If a dissolved LLC rescinds its dissolution, Section 703, this subsection no longer applies.

Subsection (d)—The use of certificates can raise issues relating to Articles 8 and 9 of the Uniform Commercial Code.

Subsection (f)—This provision originated as UPA (1997) § 503(e), was then consistent with U.C.C section 9–318(3), and is now consistent with U.C.C section 9–406(a) (stating that "an account debtor . . . may discharge its obligation by paying the assignor until, but not after, the account debtor receives a notification, authenticated by the assignor or the assignee, that the amount due or to become due has been assigned and that payment is to be made to the assignee").

The term "notice" includes "reason to know," Section 103(b)(1), and ordinarily a potential transferee has reason to inquire about transfer restrictions that might be contained in the operating agreement.

Subsection (g)—Under this subsection, a member remains a member (with all attendant rights and obligations) even after permanently transferring the entirety of the transferable interest, unless: (i) the other members opt for expulsion under Section 602(5)(B); or (ii) as otherwise provided in the operating agreement.

§ 503. Charging Order

(a) On application by a judgment creditor of a member or transferee, a court may enter a charging order against the transferable interest of the judgment debtor for the unsatisfied amount of the judgment. Except as otherwise provided in subsection (f), a charging order constitutes a lien on a judgment debtor's transferable interest and requires the limited liability company to pay over to the person to which the charging order was issued any distribution that otherwise would be paid to the judgment debtor.

(b) To the extent necessary to effectuate the collection of distributions pursuant to a charging order in effect under subsection (a), the court may:

(1) appoint a receiver of the distributions subject to the charging order, with the power to make all inquiries the judgment debtor might have made; and

(2) make all other orders necessary to give effect to the charging order.

(c) Upon a showing that distributions under a charging order will not pay the judgment debt within a reasonable time, the court may foreclose the lien and order the sale of the transferable interest. Except as otherwise provided in subsection (f), the purchaser at the foreclosure sale obtains only the transferable interest, does not thereby become a member, and is subject to Section 502.

(d) At any time before foreclosure under subsection (c), the member or transferee whose transferable interest is subject to a charging order under subsection (a) may extinguish the charging order by satisfying the judgment and filing a certified copy of the satisfaction with the court that issued the charging order.

(e) At any time before foreclosure under subsection (c), a limited liability company or one or more members whose transferable interests are not subject to the charging order may pay to the judgment creditor the full amount due under the judgment and thereby succeed to the rights of the judgment creditor, including the charging order.

(f) If a court orders foreclosure of a charging order lien against the sole member of a limited liability company:

(1) the court shall confirm the sale;

(2) the purchaser at the sale obtains the member's entire interest, not only the member's transferable interest;

(3) the purchaser thereby becomes a member; and

(4) the person whose interest was subject to the foreclosed charging order is dissociated as a member.

(g) This [act] does not deprive any member or transferee of the benefit of any exemption law applicable to the transferable interest of the member or transferee.

(h) This section provides the exclusive remedy by which a person seeking in the capacity of judgment creditor to enforce a judgment against a member or transferee may satisfy the judgment from the judgment debtor's transferable interest.

COMMENT

The charging order concept dates back to the English Partnership Act of 1890 and in the United States has been a fundamental part of law of unincorporated business organizations since 1914. *See* UPA (1914) § 28. As much a remedy limitation as a remedy, the charging order is the sole method by which a person acting as judgment creditor of a member or transferee can extract value from the member's or transferee's ownership interest in a limited liability company. *See* the comment to Subsection (h).

Under this section, the judgment creditor of a member or transferee is entitled to a charging order against the relevant transferable interest. While in effect, that order entitles the judgment creditor to whatever distributions would otherwise be due to the member or transferee whose interest is subject to the order. However, the judgment creditor has no say in the timing or amount of those distributions. The charging order does not entitle the judgment creditor to accelerate any distributions or to otherwise interfere with the management and activities of the limited liability company.

By its terms, this section does not apply to foreign limited liability companies. *See* Section 102(8) (defining "[l]imited liability company" to mean "an entity *formed under this [act] or which becomes subject to this [act]*") (emphasis added); *see also Fannie Mae v. Heather Apartments Ltd. P'ship*, A13-0562, 2013 WL 6223564, at *6 (Minn. Ct. App. Dec. 2, 2013) (considering the remedies available to a judgment creditor with respect to the judgment debtor's interest in a Cook Islands LLC; rejecting the debtor's argument that the creditor's "only remedy is to obtain a charging order under" [the Minnesota LLC statute]; explaining that "this argument fails because that statute only applies to Minnesota limited liability companies" which that statute "defines . . . as 'a limited liability company, other than a foreign limited liability company, *organized or governed by this chapter*'") (emphasis added) (statutory citations omitted).

The operating agreement has no power to alter the provisions of this section to the prejudice of third parties. Section 105(c)(15).

Subsection (a)—The phrase "judgment debtor" encompasses both members and transferees. The lien pertains only to a distribution, which excludes "amounts constituting reasonable compensation for present or past service or payments made in the ordinary course of business under a bona fide retirement plan or other bona fide benefits program." Section 102(4)(B). A judgment creditor that wishes to levy on such amounts should use the appropriate creditor's remedy, such as garnishment (which may be subject to exemptions or exclusions not relevant to a charging order). *Cf. PB Real Estate, Inc. v. Dem II Props.*, 719 A.2d 73, 76 (Conn. 1998) (rejecting the contention of an LLC's two members that "payments of $28,000 to each of them" should be treated "as expenses for wages" rather than as distributions).

Whether an application for a charging order must be served on the limited liability company, the judgment debtor, or both is a matter for other law, principally the law of remedies and civil procedure. The order itself must be served on the limited liability company. Whether the order must also be served on the judgment debtor is a matter for other law.

If a distribution consists of rights to acquire interests in a limited liability company, the charging order applies only to those rights within the definition of transferable interest. *See* Section 102(24) (defining transferable interest).

Subsection (b)—Paragraph (2) refers to "other orders" rather than "additional orders." Therefore, given appropriate circumstances, a court may invoke Paragraph (1), Paragraph (2), or both.

Subsection (b)(1)—The receiver contemplated here is emphatically not a receiver for the limited liability company, but rather a receiver for the distributions subject to the charging order. The principal advantage provided by this paragraph is an expanded right to information. However, that right goes no further than "the extent necessary to effectuate the collections of distributions pursuant to a charging order." For a correctly narrow reading of this provision, see *Wells Fargo Bank, Nat. Ass'n v. Continuous Control Solutions, Inc.*, No. 11–1285, 2012 WL 3195759 (Iowa Ct. App. Aug. 8, 2012).

Subsection (b)(2)—This paragraph must be understood in the context of: (i) the very limited nature of the charging order; and (ii) the importance of preventing overreaching on behalf of a person that is not a judgment creditor of the LLC, has no claim on the LLC's assets, and has no right to interfere in the activities, affairs, and management of the LLC. In particular, the court's power to make "all other orders" is limited to "orders necessary to give effect to the charging order."

Example: A judgment creditor with a charging order believes that the limited liability company should invest less of its surplus in operations, leaving more funds for distributions. The creditor moves the court for an order directing the limited liability company to restrict re-investment. Subsection (b)(2) does not authorize the court to grant the motion.

Example: A judgment creditor with a judgment for $10,000 against a member obtains a charging order against the member's transferable interest. Having been properly served with the order, the limited liability company nonetheless fails to comply and makes a $3000 distribution to the member. The court has the power to order the limited liability company to pay $3000 to the judgment creditor to "give effect to the charging order."

Under Subsection (b)(2), the court has the power to decide whether a particular payment is a distribution, because that decision determines whether the payment is part of a transferable interest subject to a charging order.

Example: Member A of ABC, LLC has for some years received distributions form the LLC. However, when a judgment creditor of Member A obtains a charging order against Member A's transferable interest, the LLC ceases to make distributions to Member A and instead provides a salary to Member A equivalent to former distributions. A court might deem this salary a disguised distribution. (In any event, however, the salary will be subject to garnishment.)

This act has no specific rules for determining the fate or effect of a charging order when the limited liability company undergoes a merger, conversion, interest exchange, or domestication under [Article] 10. In the proper circumstances, such an organic change might trigger an order under Subsection (b)(2).

Subsection (c)—The phrase "that distributions under the charging order will not pay the judgment debt within a reasonable period of time" comes from case law. *See, e.g., Stewart v. Lanier Park Med. Office Bldg.*, Ltd., 578 S.E.2d 572, 574 (Ga. Ct. App. 2003) ("Judicial sale may be appropriate where . . . it is apparent that distributions under the charging order will not pay the judgment debt within a reasonable amount of time."); *Nigri v. Lotz*, 453 S.E.2d 780, 783 (Ga. Ct. App. 1995).). A purchaser at a foreclosure sale obtains only the very limited rights of a transferee under Section 502 and is in some ways more vulnerable and less powerful than the holder of a charging order. After foreclosure and sale, Subsection (b) no longer applies. More generally, the court is no longer involved in the matter. For the vulnerability of a transferee, see Section 107(b), comment.

Subsection (d)—This provision allows the judgment debtor to end the charging order without need for a hearing.

Subsection (e)—Traditionally, charging order provisions referred to the possibility of "redeeming" an interest subject to a charging order. That usage was confusing, leaving several important questions unanswered. This act substitutes a far simpler approach, contemplating the limited partnership or its members buying the underlying judgment and thereby dispensing with any interference the judgment creditor might seek to inflict on the partnership.

In many circumstances, buying the judgment is superior to the mechanism provided by this subsection, because: (i) this subsection requires full satisfaction of the underlying judgment; and (ii) the LLC or the other members might be able to buy the judgment for less than face value. On the other hand, this subsection operates without need for the judgment creditor's consent, so it remains a valuable protection in the event a judgment creditor seeks to do mischief to the LLC.

Whether a member-managed LLC's decision to invoke this subsection is "ordinary course" or "outside the ordinary course," Section 407(b)(3) and (4)(A), depends on the circumstances. However, the involvement of this subsection does not by itself make the decision "outside the ordinary course." For a manager-managed LLC, the distinction is irrelevant. Section 407(c)(1).

Subsection (f)—The charging order remedy—and, more particularly, the exclusiveness of the remedy—protect the "pick your partner" principle. That principle is inapposite when a limited liability company has only one member. The exclusivity of the charging order remedy was never intended to protect a judgment debtor, but rather only to protect the interests of the judgment debtor's co-owners.

Put another way, the charging order remedy was never intended as an "asset protection" device for judgment debtors. *See Olmstead v. F.T.C.*, 44 So. 3d 76, 83 (Fla. 2010) (recognizing "the full scope of a judgment creditor's rights with respect to a judgment debtor's freely alienable membership interest in a single-member LLC"); *In re Albright*, 291 B.R. 538, 540 (Bankr. D. Colo. 2003) (holding that, "[b]ecause there are no other members in the LLC, . . . the Debtor's bankruptcy filing effectively assigned her entire membership interest in the LLC to the bankruptcy estate, and the Trustee obtained all her rights, including the right to control the management of the LLC"). Accordingly, when a charging order against an LLC's sole member is foreclosed, the member's entire ownership interest is sold and the buyer replaces the judgment debtor as the LLC's sole member.

This subsection was added during the Harmonization Project but not for the purposes of harmonization. The subsection addresses an issue that does not exist with partnerships; neither a general nor a limited partnership can continue perpetually in existence with only one partner. *See* ULPA (2001) (Last Amended 2013) § 801(a)(5) (stating that dissolution is caused upon "the passage of 90 consecutive days during which the partnership has only one partner"); UPA (1997) (Last Amended 2013) § 801(6) (stating that dissolution is caused upon "the passage of 90 consecutive days during which the partnership does not have at least two partners").

Subsection (g)—This subsection preserves otherwise applicable exemptions but does not create any. *In re Foos*, 405 B.R. 604, 609 (Bankr. N.D. Ohio 2009) (interpreting the comparable provision in UPA (1997) and stating, "it is clear that [the provision] does not create an exemption").

Subsection (h)—This subsection does not override Uniform Commercial Code, Article 9, which may provide different remedies for a secured creditor acting in that capacity. A secured creditor with a judgment might decide to proceed under Article 9 alone, under this section alone, or under both Article 9 and this section. In the last-mentioned circumstance, the constraints of this section would apply to the charging order but not to the Article 9 remedies.

This subsection is not intended to prevent a court from effecting a "reverse pierce" where appropriate. In a reverse pierce, the court conflates the entity and its owner to hold the entity liable for a debt of the owner. *Litchfield Asset Mgmt. Corp. v. Howell*, 799 A.2d 298, 312 (Conn. App. Ct. 2002) (approving a reverse pierce where a judgment debtor had established a limited liability company in a patent attempt to frustrate the judgment creditor), *overruled on other grounds by*, *Robinson v. Coughlin*, 830 A.2d 1114 (Conn. 2003). Likewise, this subsection does not supplant fraudulent transfer law.

§ 504. Power of Legal Representative of Deceased Member

If a member dies, the deceased member's legal representative may exercise:

(1) the rights of a transferee provided in Section 502(c); and

(2) for the purposes of settling the estate, the rights the deceased member had under Section 410.

COMMENT

The estate and those claiming through the estate are transferees, and as such they have very limited rights to information. This section provides temporary, additional information rights to the legal representative of the estate. Sections 410 and 502(c) pertain only to information rights.

[ARTICLE] 6

DISSOCIATION

§ 601. Power to Dissociate as Member; Wrongful Dissociation

(a) A person has the power to dissociate as a member at any time, rightfully or wrongfully, by withdrawing as a member by express will under Section 602(1).

(b) A person's dissociation as a member is wrongful only if the dissociation:

(1) is in breach of an express provision of the operating agreement; or

(2) occurs before the completion of the winding up of the limited liability company and:

(A) the person withdraws as a member by express will;

(B) the person is expelled as a member by judicial order under Section 602(6);

(C) the person is dissociated under Section 602(8); or

(D) in the case of a person that is not a trust other than a business trust, an estate, or an individual, the person is expelled or otherwise dissociated as a member because it willfully dissolved or terminated.

(c) A person that wrongfully dissociates as a member is liable to the limited liability company and, subject to Section 801, to the other members for damages caused by the dissociation. The liability is in addition to any debt, obligation, or other liability of the member to the company or the other members.

COMMENT

This article deals with the dissociation of a person as a member. Article 7 deals with the dissolution of a limited liability company.

Subsection (a)—The operating agreement can vary this provision, even to the extent of negating a member's power to dissociate. Doing so, however, is fundamentally at odds with the concept of a limited liability company as a creature of contract. *See* the comment to Section 105 (Role and Inevitability of Operating Agreement). Only in exceptional circumstances does a party to a contract lack the power to breach, and courts will not enjoin a person to remain in an ongoing contractual relationship that involves trust and confidence. E. ALLAN FARNSWORTH, CONTRACTS § 12.7, at 781 (3d ed. 1999) ("A court will not grant specific performance of a contract to provide a service that is personal in nature. This refusal . . . is based [in part] of the undesirability of compelling the continuance of personal relations after disputes have arisen and confidence and loyalty have been shaken and the undesirability, in some instances, of imposing what might seem like involuntary servitude.") (footnote omitted). Moreover, eliminating or even substantially restricting a member's power to dissociate may have dreadful practical consequences.

Subsection (b)—This subsection list exhaustively ("only if") the dissociations that are "wrongful," but the list is a default rule. The operating agreement can expand the list; *e.g.*, by making wrongful a dissociation that beaches the implied contractual covenant of good faith and fair dealing. In theory, the operating agreement can provide for liquidated damages (subject to the requirements of contract law) and, in theory, can also contract or even eliminate the list of wrongful dissociations.

Subsection (b)(1)—The reference to "an express provision of the operating agreement" means that a person's dissociation as a member in breach of the obligation of good faith and fair dealing is not wrongful dissociation for the purposes of this section. The breach might be actionable on other grounds.

Subsection (b)(2)(C)—This subsection refers to Section 602(8), which involves *inter alia* dissociation on account of bankruptcy, which in turn is subject to bankruptcy law. *See, e.g.*, 11 U.S.C.A. § 365(e) (invalidating "ipso facto" clauses, subject to some exceptions).

Subsection (c)—A person who prematurely dissociates as a member risks liability for any resulting damages. For example, the limited liability company might incur substantial expenses in replacing the member's expertise, reputation, or creditworthiness.

In effect, this subsection equates wrongful dissociation with breach of contract. Accordingly, courts should look to contract law to determine what consequential damages are recoverable. *See Hadley v. Baxendale*, 9 Exch. 341 (1854); RESTATEMENT (SECOND) OF CONTRACTS § 351 (1981); *see also Williams v. Hildebrand*, 247 S.W.2d 356, 358 (Ark. 1952) (interpreting UPA (1914) § 38(2)(a)(II), pertaining to wrongful dissolution, and stating that "the measure of damages, when the partnership was to have continued for a fixed term, is the profits that the injured partner would have received").

§ 602. Events Causing Dissociation

A person is dissociated as a member when:

(1)   the limited liability company knows or has notice of the person's express will to withdraw as a member, but, if the person has specified a withdrawal date later than the date the company knew or had notice, on that later date;

(2)   an event stated in the operating agreement as causing the person's dissociation occurs;

(3)   the person's entire interest is transferred in a foreclosure sale under Section 503(f);

(4)   the person is expelled as a member pursuant to the operating agreement;

(5)   the person is expelled as a member by the affirmative vote or consent of all the other members if:

(A)   it is unlawful to carry on the limited liability company's activities and affairs with the person as a member;

(B)   there has been a transfer of all the person's transferable interest in the company, other than:

(i)   a transfer for security purposes; or

(ii)   a charging order in effect under Section 503 which has not been foreclosed;

(C)   the person is an entity and:

(i)   the company notifies the person that it will be expelled as a member because the person has filed a statement of dissolution or the equivalent, the person has been administratively dissolved, the person's charter or the equivalent has been revoked, or the person's right to conduct business has been suspended by the person's jurisdiction of formation; and

(ii) not later than 90 days after the notification, the statement of dissolution or the equivalent has not been withdrawn, rescinded, or revoked, the person has not been reinstated, or the person's charter or the equivalent or right to conduct business has not been reinstated; or

(D) the person is an unincorporated entity that has been dissolved and whose activities and affairs are being wound up;

(6) on application by the limited liability company or a member in a direct action under Section 801, the person is expelled as a member by judicial order because the person:

(A) has engaged or is engaging in wrongful conduct that has affected adversely and materially, or will affect adversely and materially, the company's activities and affairs;

(B) has committed willfully or persistently, or is committing willfully or persistently, a material breach of the operating agreement or a duty or obligation under Section 409; or

(C) has engaged or is engaging in conduct relating to the company's activities and affairs which makes it not reasonably practicable to carry on the activities and affairs with the person as a member;

(7) in the case of an individual:

(A) the individual dies; or

(B) in a member-managed limited liability company:

(i) a guardian or general conservator for the individual is appointed; or

(ii) a court orders that the individual has otherwise become incapable of performing the individual's duties as a member under this [act] or the operating agreement;

(8) in a member-managed limited liability company, the person:

(A) becomes a debtor in bankruptcy;

(B) signs an assignment for the benefit of creditors; or

(C) seeks, consents to, or acquiesces in the appointment of a trustee, receiver, or liquidator of the person or of all or substantially all the person's property;

(9) in the case of a person that is a testamentary or inter vivos trust or is acting as a member by virtue of being a trustee of such a trust, the trust's entire transferable interest in the limited liability company is distributed;

(10) in the case of a person that is an estate or is acting as a member by virtue of being a personal representative of an estate, the estate's entire transferable interest in the limited liability company is distributed;

(11) in the case of a person that is not an individual, the existence of the person terminates;

(12) the limited liability company participates in a merger under [Article] 10 and:

(A) the company is not the surviving entity; or

(B) otherwise as a result of the merger, the person ceases to be a member;

(13) the limited liability company participates in an interest exchange under [Article] 10 and, as a result of the interest exchange, the person ceases to be a member;

(14) the limited liability company participates in a conversion under [Article] 10;

(15) the limited liability company participates in a domestication under [Article] 10 and, as a result of the domestication, the person ceases to be a member; or

(16) the limited liability company dissolves and completes winding up.

COMMENT

This section mostly states default rules, which the operating agreement may vary. However, it would make no sense to vary some of the rules—*e.g.,* to provide that the death of a member who is an individual does not cause the individual's dissociation as a member, Paragraph (7)(A), or that an entity remains a member even *after* the existence of the person has terminated. Paragraph (11).

Paragraph (1)—Operating agreements often require notice of dissociation to be in writing and to specify the effective date of the dissociation.

Paragraph (3)—The cited section pertains to a charging order against the transferable interest of the sole member of a limited liability company.

Paragraph (4)—Many operating agreements provide for "no cause" expulsion, and courts considering such provisions will likely look to cases addressing the issue in the context of partnerships. In that context, courts have taken somewhat different approaches. *Compare Gelder Med. Grp. v. Webber,* 363 N.E.2d 573, 576 (N.Y. 1977), *with Winston & Strawn v. Nosal,* 664 N.E.2d 239, 245 (Ill. App. Ct. 1996). *See also* the comment to Section 409(d) (stating and explaining the implied contractual covenant of good faith and fair dealing).

Paragraph (5)(B)—This paragraph permits expulsion when a member no longer has any "skin in the game." Under this paragraph (unless the operating agreement provides otherwise), a member's transferee can protect itself from the vulnerability of "bare naked assignee" status, Section 107(b), cmt., by obligating the member/transferor to retain a one-percent interest and exercise the member's governance rights (including the right to bring a derivative suit) to protect the transferee's interests.

Paragraph (6)—The reference to "a direct action under Section 801(b)" reflects the "separate entity" nature of a limited liability company. Section 801(b) limits a member's standing to bring a direct action to circumstances in which the member can "plead and prove an actual or threatened injury that is not solely the result of an injury suffered or threatened to be suffered by the limited liability company." For example, a member might invoke Paragraph (6)(B) if another member's breach of the operating agreement harmed the first member directly. If a member has suffered only indirect harm, the Paragraph (6)(B) claim belongs to the LLC and not the member. If the LLC fails to bring suit, the member may assert the claim derivatively. *See* Sections 802–06.

Although the operating agreement can revise or eliminate the possibility of judicial expulsion, doing so requires careful planning. *Cf. Huatuco v. Satellite Healthcare,* CV 8465-VCG, 2013 WL 6460898, at *1, n.2 (Del. Ch. Dec. 9, 2013) (stating that "the right to judicial dissolution is a default right which the parties may eschew by contract" while reserving the question of "[w]hether the parties may, by contract, divest this Court of its authority to order a dissolution in all circumstances, even where it appears manifest that equity so requires—leaving, for instance, irreconcilable members locked away together forever like some alternative entity version of Sartre's Huis Clos").

For examples of conduct warranting an expulsion order, see *All Saints Univ. of Med. Aruba v. Chilana,* A-2628-09T1, 2012 WL 6652510 (N.J. Super. Ct. App. Div. Dec. 24, 2012) (discussing a pattern of conduct); *Sherwood Park Bus. Ctr., L.L.C. v. Taggart,* 323 P.3d 551, 561 (Or. Ct. App. 2014) (upholding expulsion of a member who "had stolen a large amount of money from [the limited liability company], had intentionally failed to provide financial information, and had made himself unavailable to carry on the business"); *CCD, L.C. v. Millsap,* 116 P.3d 366, 373 (Utah 2005) (holding that a member's "misappropriat[ion of] trust account funds totaling at least $11,540.06 for his personal use" warranted expulsion, where the member's "misconduct continued the pattern of behavior that [had previously] resulted in losses to the company of $625,000[, where the new misconduct] . . . took place after [the member's] prior wrongdoing had been discovered and after [the limited liability company] had assented to permit [the member] to atone for his misdeeds by fulfilling the terms of the amended operating agreement").

For an analysis that helps distinguish Paragraph (6)(C) from Paragraphs (6)(A) and (B), see *All Saints Univ. of Med. Aruba v. Chilana,* A-2628-09T1, 2012 WL 6652510, at *15 (N.J. Super. Ct. App. Div. Dec. 24, 2012) (interpreting predecessor law and noting that the "not reasonably practicable standard" does not require a showing of wrongful conduct). *Cf. Dunnagan v. Watson,* 204 S.W.3d 30, 40 (Tex. Ct. App. 2006) (same issue in the context of dissolution). Where grounds exist for both dissociation and dissolution, a court has the discretion to choose between the alternatives. *Robertson v. Jacobs Cattle Co.,* 830 N.W.2d 191, 201–02 (Neb. 2013) (discussing analogous provisions of UPA (1997)). "[T]here is no textual basis for imposing a higher burden of proof for dissociation than dissolution." *Brennan v. Brennan Assocs.,* 977 A.2d 107, 121 (Conn. 2009) (general partnership).

Paragraph (6)(C)—This provision has an analog among the causes for dissolution. *See* Section 701(a)(4)(B).

Paragraph (7)(B)—This provision does not apply to a manager-managed limited liability company because, given the limited rights of non-manager members, the stated occurrences do not necessarily justify dissociation. For a parallel provision approach under the uniform limited partnership act, see ULPA §§ 601(b)(6) (2001) (Last Amended 2013) (limited partner), 603(6)(B) and (C) (general partner). As for the effect of the stated occurrences on a person's role as a manager, see Section 407(c)(4) (permitting the removal of a manager "at any time by the affirmative vote or consent of a majority of the members without notice or cause").

Paragraph 8(A)—This provision is subject to bankruptcy law. *See, e.g.,* 11 U.S.C.A. § 365(e) (invalidating "ipso facto" clauses, subject to some exceptions).

Paragraphs (9) and (10)—A change in trustee or personal representation does not cause dissociation.

Paragraph (11)—This provision is the entity analog to Paragraph (7)(A) (death of an individual). Although in theory the operating agreement could change this rule, doing so would be nonsensical. *See* the comment to Section 703(a) (noting that a terminated limited liability company cannot rescind its dissolution because "a 'dead' entity lacks both the capacity and power to bring itself back from the dead").

Paragraph (12)(A)—If a limited liability company disappears as part of a merger, no person can continue as a member of the company. When the merger takes effect, the members of the disappearing company are perforce dissociated. Depending on the plan of merger, those persons may become members of a surviving limited liability company. In those circumstances, the merger will have dissociated them from one LLC and admitted them into membership in the surviving LLC. *See* Sections 401(c)(2), 1026(c)(10).

Paragraph (12)(B)—It is possible for a plan of merger to "shuffle the equity" of the surviving entity, even to the extent of "taking out" some or all of the owners of the surviving entity. A reverse triangular merger involving a limited liability company as the surviving entity would dissociate all the members of the LLC.

Paragraph (14)—By definition, a limited liability company that converts ceases to be a limited liability company. *See* Section 1046. Thus, when the plan of conversion takes effect, all the members of the converted entity are dissociated from that entity. In many cases, those persons will all be owners of the converted entity. In some cases, the conversion will "shuffle the equity" and "take out" some of the members of the converting LLC.

Paragraph (15)—Domestication does not by itself dissociate a member, because the domesticated entity remains both a limited liability company and "the same entity without interruption as the domesticating company." Section 1056(a)(1)(B). However, an "equity shuffle" could dissociate a member.

§ 603.   Effect of Dissociation

(a)   If a person is dissociated as a member:

    (1)   the person's right to participate as a member in the management and conduct of the limited liability company's activities and affairs terminates;

    (2)   the person's duties and obligations under Section 409 as a member end with regard to matters arising and events occurring after the person's dissociation; and

    (3)   subject to Section 504 and [Article] 10, any transferable interest owned by the person in the person's capacity as a member immediately before dissociation is owned by the person solely as a transferee.

(b)   A person's dissociation as a member does not of itself discharge the person from any debt, obligation, or other liability to the limited liability company or the other members which the person incurred while a member.

COMMENT

Subsection (a)—This provision makes no reference to power-to-bind matters, because the act provides that a member *qua* member has no power to bind the LLC. Section 301.

Subsection (a)(2)—This provision establishes a dividing line, separating out "matters arising and events occurring after the person's dissociation." If the limited liability company has continuing projects with clients, ongoing relationships with clients, or both, the dividing line requires special attention with regard to non-competition and partnership opportunities duties. *See* Section 409(b)(1), (3).

Disputes involving law firms have generated much of the relevant case law. *See, e.g., Jewel v. Boxer,* 156 Cal. App. 3d 171, 175 (Cal. Ct. App. 1984); *Meehan v. Shaughnessy,* 535 N.E. 1255, 1257 (Mass. 1989). To a large extent, a well-drawn operating agreement can delineate the parties' respective rights and responsibilities and thereby avoid problems. However, if the company becomes insolvent, the bankruptcy court may well scrutinize the members' *inter se* arrangements. *See Geron v. Robinson & Cole L.L.P.*, 476 B.R. 732, 743 (S.D.N.Y. 2012) (considering whether a law firm had "fraudulently transferred . . . assets when its partners adopted the Jewel Waiver [releasing rights recognized by *Jewel v. Boxer*] on the eve of dissolution without consideration").

This provision applies regardless of whether the limited liability company is member-managed or manager-managed. However, in the latter case, the pre-dissociation duties will be much narrower, because in a manager-managed LLC a member *qua* member has no management duties. Section 409(i)(1). But each member remains subject to the obligation of good faith and fair dealing. Section 409(i)(3).

This provision does not determine the effect of a person's dissociation as a member on the person's future obligations or rights under the operating agreement. Some contractual obligations typically extend beyond dissociation—*e.g.*, non-competition provisions, buyout arrangements. To the extent provisions of the operating agreement continue to apply, the common law obligation of good faith continues to apply as well. *See* the comment to Section 409(d) (explaining that the subsection "invokes the implied obligation that exists in every contract" as a matter of common law).

Subsection (a)(3)—This paragraph accords with Section 404(b)—dissociation does not result in a distribution. In general, when a person dissociates as a member, the person's rights as a member disappear and the person's status degrades to that of a mere transferee—even when the dissociation takes the form of expulsion. *All Saints Univ. of Med. Aruba v. Chilana*, A-2628-09T1, 2012 WL 6652510, at *12 (N.J. Super. Ct. App. Div. Dec. 24, 2012).

Like most *inter se* rules in this act, this one is subject to the operating agreement. For example, the operating agreement has the power to provide for the buyout of a person's transferable interest in connection with the person's dissociation.

Section 504 provides additional information rights when an individual's death has caused dissociation. Article 10 covers organic transactions such as mergers and conversions.

Subsection (b)—In a member-managed limited liability company, a member's obligation to safeguard trade secrets and other confidential or proprietary information is incurred when the member learns or otherwise obtains the information. This subsection preserves the obligation post-dissociation. (In a manager-managed LLC, any obligations of a non-manager member viz-a-viz proprietary information would be a matter for the operating agreement, the obligation of good faith and fair dealing, or other law.)

[ARTICLE] 7

DISSOLUTION AND WINDING UP

§ 701. Events Causing Dissolution

(a) A limited liability company is dissolved, and its activities and affairs must be wound up, upon the occurrence of any of the following:

(1) an event or circumstance that the operating agreement states causes dissolution;

(2) the affirmative vote or consent of all the members;

(3) the passage of 90 consecutive days during which the company has no members unless before the end of the period:

(A) consent to admit at least one specified person as a member is given by transferees owning the rights to receive a majority of distributions as transferees at the time the consent is to be effective; and

(B) at least one person becomes a member in accordance with the consent;

(4) on application by a member, the entry by [the appropriate court] of an order dissolving the company on the grounds that:

(A) the conduct of all or substantially all the company's activities and affairs is unlawful;

(B) it is not reasonably practicable to carry on the company's activities and affairs in conformity with the certificate of organization and the operating agreement; or

    (C)   the managers or those members in control of the company:

        (i)   have acted, are acting, or will act in a manner that is illegal or fraudulent; or

        (ii)   have acted or are acting in a manner that is oppressive and was, is, or will be directly harmful to the applicant; or

    (5)   the signing and filing of a statement of administrative dissolution by the [Secretary of State] under Section 708.

    (b)   In a proceeding brought under subsection (a)(4)(C), the court may order a remedy other than dissolution.

COMMENT

    "Dissolution" has been a term of art in the law of unincorporated business organizations since at least the time of Roman law. JOSEPH STORY, COMMENTARIES ON THE LAW OF PARTNERSHIP § 266, at 408 (2d ed. 1850) ("The Roman law . . . declared, that partnership might be dissolved in various ways . . . ."). Dissolution does not end a limited liability company's existence but rather changes the purpose of that existence: "A dissolved limited liability company shall wind up its activities and affairs and . . . the company continues after dissolution only for the purpose of winding up." Section 702(a). The company may, but need not, filed a statement of dissolution. Section 702(b)(2)(A). The limited liability company terminates when winding up is complete. The company may, but need not, file a statement of termination. Section 702(b)(2)(F).

    Except for Paragraphs (a)(4) and (5), this section comprises default rules. Paragraph 5 is fully mandatory, Section 105(c)(3)(B); Paragraph 4 is mandatory only with regard to the stated grounds for dissolution. *See* the comment to Section 105(c)(9). Moreover, an operating agreement can provide additional causes of dissolution. *See* Subsection (a)(1). Variations to the statutory causes of dissolution are commonplace.

    Section 703 permits rescission of dissolution in some circumstances. In some circumstances, an amendment to the operating agreement might avert dissolution (*e.g.*, by revising an agreed-upon deadline for selling the LLC's assets and winding up the business). A retroactive amendment may also be possible. *See Kindred Ltd. P'ship v. Screen Actors Guild, Inc.*, CV082220PSGPJWX, 2009 WL 279080, at *5–6 (C.D. Cal. Feb. 3, 2009) (giving effect to an amendment that retroactively eliminated an event of dissolution; noting that UPA (1997) § 802(b) permitted a partnership to rescind dissolution).

    Subsection (a)(4)—The operating agreement cannot vary the causes of dissolution stated in this provision. However, the operating agreement may contain a forum selection clause or change the forum from "the appropriate court" to binding arbitration. Section 105(c)(9), cmt.

    As to whether the court of another jurisdiction can properly order dissolution of a limited liability company formed under this act, the majority rule is clearly no. "[T]he courts of several states have held that jurisdiction to dissolve a corporation rests only in the courts of the state of incorporation." *In re Blixseth*, 484 B.R. 360, 370 (B.A.P. 9th Cir. 2012) (citing cases, including a case involving an LLC). *But see In re Mercantile Guar. Co.*, 238 Cal. App. 2d 426, 430–33 (Cal. Ct. App. 1965) (explaining that "[w]e are . . . required to determine whether the courts of a state in which a foreign corporation has done business and in which its assets are there located have jurisdiction to wind up its affairs, even though the corporation was organized in another state," stating that "the question is not one of jurisdiction or power in the court of the state which is not the legal domicile of a foreign corporation, but it is a question . . . of the balance of convenience, of whether considerations of public policy, efficiency, expedience and justice to all parties interested demand that jurisdiction be retained in the foreign court, or that it be declined under the rule of forum *non conveniens*," and holding that "[t]he circumstances of the case at bench require a holding that the California courts assume jurisdiction of the winding up of [a Delaware corporation's] affairs preparatory to a dissolution").

    Subsection (a)(4)(B)—The standard stated here is conventional, deriving originally from the law of limited partnerships. *See, e.g., Kirksey v. Grohmann*, 754 N.W.2d 825, 828–30 (S.D 2008) (discussing cases and noting that "cases interpreting language similar to our statutory terminology, whether involving a partnership or a limited liability company, are instructive"). For discussion of the meaning of the standard, see *Venture Sales, L.L.C. v. Perkins*, 86 So. 3d 910, 914–15 (Miss. 2012) (discussing cases); *In re 1545 Ocean Ave., LLC*, 72 A.D.3d 121, 129–30 (N.Y. 2010) (same).

    The court-ordered expulsion of a miscreant member can negate a claim for dissolution. *Dunbar Grp., LLC v. Tignor*, 267 Va. 361, 367–68, 593 S.E.2d 216, 219 (2004) ("Although Tignor's actions in [the] capacities [of member and manager of Xpert] had created numerous problems in the operation of Xpert, his expulsion as a member changed his role from one of an active participant in the management of Xpert to the more passive role of an investor in the company. The record fails to show that after this change in the daily management of Xpert, it would not be reasonably practicable for Xpert to carry on its business pursuant to its operating authority.").

However, where grounds exist for both dissociation and dissolution, a court has the discretion to choose between the alternatives. *Robertson v. Jacobs Cattle Co.*, 830 N.W.2d 191 201–02 (Neb. 2013). "[T]here is no textual basis for imposing a higher burden of proof for dissociation than dissolution." *Brennan v. Brennan Assocs.*, 977 A.2d 107, 121 (Conn. 2009) (general partnership).

This provision has an analog among the grounds for dissociation. *See* Section 602(6)(c).

Subsection (a)(4)(C)—The provision's reference to "those members in control of the company" implies that such members have a duty to avoid acting oppressively toward fellow members.

The act does not define "oppressively," but "oppression" is a concept well-grounded in the law of close corporations. *See, e.g., Kiriakides v. Atlas Food Sys. & Servs., Inc.*, 541 S.E.2d 257, 264–66 (S.C. 2001); Robert B. Thompson, *The Shareholder's Cause of Action for Oppression*, 48 BUS. LAW. 69, 70 (1993) (referring to then "evolving cause of action of shareholder oppression"). In many jurisdictions the concept equates to or at least includes the frustration of the plaintiff's reasonable expectations. *Baur v. Baur Farms, Inc.*, 832 N.W.2d 663, 670 (Iowa 2013) (stating that "perhaps the most widely adopted [approach] links oppression to the frustration of the reasonable expectations of the corporation's shareholders"). (This concept of reasonable expectations is entirely separate from the "fruits of the bargain" and "reasonable expectations" language sometimes used in explaining the implied contractual obligation of good faith and fair dealing.)

Courts have extrapolated close corporation doctrine to unincorporated organizations. *See, e.g., Alloy v. Wills Family Trust*, 944 A.2d 1234, 1262–64 (Md. Ct. Spec. App. 2008) (discussing cases). Indeed many cases simply conflate the two contexts. *E.g. Kohannim v. Katoli*, 08-11-00155-CV, 2013 WL 3943078, at *9 (Tex. Ct. App. July 24, 2013) ("A member oppression claim may exist when: (i) a majority shareholder's conduct substantially defeats the minority's expectations that objectively viewed, were both reasonable under the circumstances and central to the minority shareholder's decision to join the venture; or (ii) burdensome, harsh, or wrongful conduct, a lack of probity and fair dealing in the company's affairs to the prejudice of some members, or a visible departure from the standards of fair dealing, and a violation of fair play on which every shareholder who entrusts his money to a company is entitled to rely."); *Pinnacle Data Servs., Inc. v. Gillen*, 104 S.W.3d 188, 196 (Tex. Ct. App. 2003) (explaining oppression of "members" in terms of shareholder oppression).

However, applying close corporation law to limited liability companies requires some caution. Close corporation law developed in part because the standard corporate governance structure exalts majority power and does not presuppose contractual relationships among the shareholders.

In contrast, while an LLC depends on the sovereign for legal existence and the all-important liability shield, LLC governance is fundamentally contractual. Therefore, in most situations, the operating agreement should reflect and comprise members' reasonable expectations. As a result, a court considering a claim of oppression by an LLC member should consider, with regard to each reasonable expectation invoked by the plaintiff, whether the expectation: (i) contradicts any term of the operating agreement or any reasonable implication of any term of that agreement; (ii) was central to the plaintiff's decision to become a member of the limited liability company or for a substantial time has been centrally important in the member's continuing membership; (iii) was known to other members, who expressly or impliedly acquiesced in it; (iv) is consistent with the reasonable expectations of all the members, including expectations pertaining to the plaintiff's conduct; and (v) is otherwise reasonable under the circumstances. *See* the comment to Sections 102(13) ("[T]he definition [of 'operating agreement'] puts no limits on the form of the operating agreement. To the contrary, the definition contains the phrase 'whether oral, implied, in a record, or in any combination thereof.' "), Section 105(a)(4), cmt. (explaining how a written operating agreement, if properly drafted, can provide that amendments must be in writing and signed to be effective).

Example: From its formation, Work-Here, LLC has had three members, been member-managed, involved all three members in company operations, and allocated distributions in part in reference to the members' work for the company. The operating agreement is brief, informal, contains no integration clause, and makes no reference to a member's right to work for the company.

After ten years, two of the members: (i) take a vote; (ii) purport to oust the third member from any continuing role in company operations; and (iii) announce that the third member's distributions will be substantially reduced.

The ousted member has at least three theories of recovery:

- breach of an implied-in-fact term of the operating agreement, under which each member is entitled to work for the company and be compensated for the work;

- violation of Section 407(b)(4)(A) (requiring "[t]he affirmative vote or consent of all the members . . . to . . . undertake an act outside the ordinary course of the activities and affairs of the company"); and

- oppression under Section 701(4)(C)(ii).

On the limited facts stated, these theories are undoubtedly plausible, although of course not necessarily persuasive. *See* Section 409(d) (incorporating "the contractual obligation of good faith and fair dealing").

Subsection (a)(5)—The operating agreement may not vary this provision.

Subsection (b)—In the close corporation context, many courts have reached this position without express statutory authority, most often with regard to court-ordered buyouts of oppressed shareholders. *See, e.g., Kirtz v. Grossman*, 463 S.W.2d 541, 545 (Mo. Ct. App. 1971) (per curiam); *Brenner v. Berkowitz*, 634 A.2d 1019, 1031 (N.J. 1993); *N.D. ex rel. Heitkamp v. Family Life Servs.*, 616 N.W.2d 826, 838 (N.D. 2000); *Baker v. Commercial Body Builders, Inc.*, 507 P.2d 387, 394–96 (Or. 1973); *Davis v. Sheerin*, 754 S.W.2d 375, 380 (Tex. Ct. App. 1988). *Contra White v. Perkins*, 189 S.E.2d 315, 320 (Va. 1972).

This subsection saves courts and litigants the trouble of re-inventing that wheel in the LLC context. However, unlike Subsection (a)(4), Subsection (b) can be overridden by the operating agreement. Thus, the members may agree to restrict or eliminate a court's power to craft a lesser remedy, even to the extent of confining the court (and themselves) to the all-or-nothing remedy of dissolution.

§ 702.   Winding Up

(a)   A dissolved limited liability company shall wind up its activities and affairs and, except as otherwise provided in Section 703, the company continues after dissolution only for the purpose of winding up.

(b)   In winding up its activities and affairs, a limited liability company:

(1)   shall discharge the company's debts, obligations, and other liabilities, settle and close the company's activities and affairs, and marshal and distribute the assets of the company; and

(2)   may:

(A)   deliver to the [Secretary of State] for filing a statement of dissolution stating the name of the company and that the company is dissolved;

(B)   preserve the company activities, affairs, and property as a going concern for a reasonable time;

(C)   prosecute and defend actions and proceedings, whether civil, criminal, or administrative;

(D)   transfer the company's property;

(E)   settle disputes by mediation or arbitration;

(F)   deliver to the [Secretary of State] for filing a statement of termination stating the name of the company and that the company is terminated; and

(G)   perform other acts necessary or appropriate to the winding up.

(c)   If a dissolved limited liability company has no members, the legal representative of the last person to have been a member may wind up the activities and affairs of the company. If the person does so, the person has the powers of a sole manager under Section 407(c) and is deemed to be a manager for the purposes of Section 304(a).

(d)   If the legal representative under subsection (c) declines or fails to wind up the limited liability company's activities and affairs, a person may be appointed to do so by the consent of transferees owning a majority of the rights to receive distributions as transferees at the time the consent is to be effective. A person appointed under this subsection:

(1)   has the powers of a sole manager under Section 407(c) and is deemed to be a manager for the purposes of Section 304(a); and

(2)   shall deliver promptly to the [Secretary of State] for filing an amendment to the company's certificate of organization stating:

(A)   that the company has no members;

(B)   the name and street and mailing addresses of the person; and

(C)   that the person has been appointed pursuant to this subsection to wind up the company.

(e)   [The appropriate court] may order judicial supervision of the winding up of a dissolved limited liability company, including the appointment of a person to wind up the company's activities and affairs:

(1)   on the application of a member, if the applicant establishes good cause;

(2)   on the application of a transferee, if:

(A)   the company does not have any members;

(B)   the legal representative of the last person to have been a member declines or fails to wind up the company's activities; and

(C)   within a reasonable time following the dissolution a person has not been appointed pursuant to subsection (c); or

(3)   in connection with a proceeding under Section 701(a)(4).

COMMENT

Under the default rules of this act, dissolution does not change governance arrangements. However, dissolution does change the context for determining, with regard to a member-managed LLC, whether a matter is in or outside "the ordinary course of the activities of the company." Section 407(b)(3), (4).

As for determining the post-dissolution power of a member or manager to bind the LLC, other law, primarily agency law, supplies the rules. Thus, dissolution does not change the applicable source of law for determining actual and apparent authority. Section 301, cmt.

Subsection (a)—*See* the comment to Section 701(a).

Subsection (b)—The particular circumstances determine how long winding up may continue without giving "good cause" for court intervention under Section 702(e). The case law is partnership law and applies by analogy. There is no "hard and fast" rule. *See, e.g., Mathis v. Meyeres,* 574 P.2d 447, 450 (Alaska 1978) (stating that we are aware of [no authority] requiring that deadlines be set in the winding up of a partnership"); *8182 Md. Assocs., Ltd. P'ship v. Sheehan,* 14 S.W.3d 576, 581 (Mo. 2000) ("The Uniform Partnership Law contemplates that dissolved partnerships may continue in business for a short, long or indefinite period of time . . . .") (quoting *Schoeller v. Schoeller,* 497 S.W.2d 860, 867 (Mo. Ct. App. 1973)).

"Winding up usually entails the time necessary for the partners to finish old business, collect and pay debts, and finally distribute remaining assets to the partners." *Gibson v. Deuth,* 270 N.W.2d 632, 635 (Iowa 1978). "Generally the best interests of the partnership will be served by winding up the partnership affairs as quickly as possible." *Doting v. Trunk,* 259 Mont. 343, 349, 856 P.2d 536, 540 (1993). However, in some circumstances, a long period of winding up is not only appropriate but necessary. *Lebanon Trotting Ass'n v. Battista,* 306 N.E.2d 769, 772 (Ohio Ct. App. 1972) ("[I]f the only means of availing the partners of the benefit of the value of the lease would be to continue to operate under such lease until its expiration, then such operation may continue as part of the winding up of the partnership affairs after dissolution. It is not necessary that a partnership, in the absence of the consent of all the partners, abandon a valuable asset upon dissolution merely because it may have no ready market value, but the value of such asset can continue to inure to the benefit of the partners through the continuation of the partnership after dissolution.")

Subsection (b)(2)(A) and (F)—For the constructive notice effect of a statement of dissolution or termination, see Sections 103(d)(2)(A) and (B) and 302(h).

Subsection (c)—Section 304 provides a shield for managers as well members against automatic, vicarious liability for an LLC's debts, obligations, and other liabilities. Section 407 provides default rules for a manager's actual authority. Some of those rules provide for consent by members. *See* Section 407(c)(3). Those rules are inapposite in the circumstances contemplated by this subsection.

Section 409 does not apply to a person appointed under this section. Such person will inevitably be an agent of the dissolved limited liability company, acting pursuant to a contract. Thus, agency and contract law will determine the person's duties.

Subsection (d)(1)—See the comment to Subsection (c).

Subsection (e)—Section 409 does not apply to a person appointed under this section. The applicable standards of conduct might come from any or all of these sources: the court order, state law pertaining to receiverships, agency law, and contract law.

Subsection (e)(1)—Managers do not have standing under this provision. If a non-member manager has so lost control of the limited liability company as to desire dissolution, the non-manager's remedy is to: (i) seek court enforcement of the relevant provisions of the operating agreement, management agreement, or both; or (ii) resign.

§ 703. Rescinding Dissolution

(a) A limited liability company may rescind its dissolution, unless a statement of termination applicable to the company has become effective, [the appropriate court] has entered an order under Section 701(a)(4) dissolving the company, or the [Secretary of State] has dissolved the company under Section 708.

(b) Rescinding dissolution under this section requires:

(1) the affirmative vote or consent of each member; and

(2) if the limited liability company has delivered to the [Secretary of State] for filing a statement of dissolution and:

(A) the statement has not become effective, delivery to the [Secretary of State] for filing of a statement of withdrawal under Section 208 applicable to the statement of dissolution; or

(B) if the statement of dissolution has become effective, delivery to the [Secretary of State] for filing of a statement of rescission stating the name of the company and that dissolution has been rescinded under this section.

(c) If a limited liability company rescinds its dissolution:

(1) the company resumes carrying on its activities and affairs as if dissolution had never occurred;

(2) subject to paragraph (3), any liability incurred by the company after the dissolution and before the rescission has becomes effective is determined as if dissolution had never occurred; and

(3) the rights of a third party arising out of conduct in reliance on the dissolution before the third party knew or had notice of the rescission may not be adversely affected.

COMMENT

The Harmonization Project added this section, which is based on UPA (1997) § 802(b)(1) permitting the partners to "waive the right to have the partnership's business wound up and the partnership terminated" after which "the partnership resumes carrying on its business as if dissolution had never occurred").

Subsection (a)—The first exclusion results inevitably from the effect of a statement of termination (*i.e.*, the limited liability company ceases to exist). A "dead" entity lacks both the capacity and power to bring itself back from the dead.

The second and third exclusions pertain to dissolutions affected by outsiders (*i.e.*, the court and the filing office).

Subsections (b)(1)—The requirement of unanimous consent protects any vested rights of, or reliance by, members. However, the operating agreement may vary this provision.

Subsection (c)(3)—This paragraph protects third parties. *E.g.*, *Neurobehavorial Assocs., P.A. v. Cypress Creek Hosp., Inc.*, 995 S.W.2d 326, 331 (Tex. Ct. App. 1999) ("If the Hospital had the right to terminate the Agreement when it did because the Association was then dissolved, then even though the Association can revoke articles of dissolution and have that relate back to the date of dissolution, it would be grossly unfair to let the Association assert its ex post facto change as a defense. Surely the Association would be estopped from doing so, having created the very conditions that gave the Hospital the correct impression that it was then dissolved.").

§ 704. Known Claims Against Dissolved Limited Liability Company

(a) Except as otherwise provided in subsection (d), a dissolved limited liability company may give notice of a known claim under subsection (b), which has the effect provided in subsection (c).

(b) A dissolved limited liability company may in a record notify its known claimants of the dissolution. The notice must:

(1) specify the information required to be included in a claim;

(2) state that a claim must be in writing and provide a mailing address to which the claim is to be sent;

(3) state the deadline for receipt of a claim, which may not be less than 120 days after the date the notice is received by the claimant; and

(4) state that the claim will be barred if not received by the deadline.

(c) A claim against a dissolved limited liability company is barred if the requirements of subsection (b) are met and:

(1) the claim is not received by the specified deadline; or

(2) if the claim is timely received but rejected by the company:

(A) the company causes the claimant to receive a notice in a record stating that the claim is rejected and will be barred unless the claimant commences an action against the company to enforce the claim not later than 90 days after the claimant receives the notice; and

(B) the claimant does not commence the required action not later than 90 days after the claimant receives the notice.

(d) This section does not apply to a claim based on an event occurring after the date of dissolution or a liability that on that date is contingent.

COMMENT

Sections 704 through 706 provide rules under which a dissolved limited liability company may achieve finality with regard to claims.

This section is derived almost verbatim from Model Business Corporation Act section 14.06.

§ 705. Other Claims Against Dissolved Limited Liability Company

(a) A dissolved limited liability company may publish notice of its dissolution and request persons having claims against the company to present them in accordance with the notice.

(b) A notice under subsection (a) must:

(1) be published at least once in a newspaper of general circulation in the [county] in this state in which the dissolved limited liability company's principal office is located or, if the principal office is not located in this state, in the [county] in which the office of the company's registered agent is or was last located;

(2) describe the information required to be contained in a claim, state that the claim must be in writing, and provide a mailing address to which the claim is to be sent; and

(3) state that a claim against the company is barred unless an action to enforce the claim is commenced not later than three years after publication of the notice.

(c)   If a dissolved limited liability company publishes a notice in accordance with subsection (b), the claim of each of the following claimants is barred unless the claimant commences an action to enforce the claim against the company not later than three years after the publication date of the notice:

     (1)   a claimant that did not receive notice in a record under Section 704;

     (2)   a claimant whose claim was timely sent to the company but not acted on; and

     (3)   a claimant whose claim is contingent at, or based on an event occurring after, the date of dissolution.

(d)   A claim not barred under this section or Section 704 may be enforced:

     (1)   against a dissolved limited liability company, to the extent of its undistributed assets; and

     (2)   except as otherwise provided in Section 706, if assets of the company have been distributed after dissolution, against a member or transferee to the extent of that person's proportionate share of the claim or of the company's assets distributed to the member or transferee after dissolution, whichever is less, but a person's total liability for all claims under this paragraph may not exceed the total amount of assets distributed to the person after dissolution.

COMMENT

This section is derived almost verbatim from Model Business Corporation Act section 14.07.

Subsection (d)(2)—Liability under this paragraph extends to those who have received distributions under a charging order. *See* the comment to Section 502(a) (explaining that the beneficiary of a charging order is a transferee). Unlike Section 406(c) (recapture of improper distributions), this paragraph contains no "knowledge" element.

§ 706.   Court Proceedings

(a)   A dissolved limited liability company that has published a notice under Section 705 may file an application with [the appropriate court] in the [county] where the company's principal office is located or, if the principal office is not located in this state, where the office of its registered agent is or was last located, for a determination of the amount and form of security to be provided for payment of claims that are reasonably expected to arise after the date of dissolution based on facts known to the company and:

     (1)   at the time of application:

         (A)   are contingent; or

         (B)   have not been made known to the company; or

     (2)   are based on an event occurring after the date of dissolution.

(b)   Security is not required for any claim that is or is reasonably anticipated to be barred under Section 705.

(c)   Not later than 10 days after the filing of an application under subsection (a), the dissolved limited liability company shall give notice of the proceeding to each claimant holding a contingent claim known to the company.

(d)   In a proceeding under this section, the court may appoint a guardian ad litem to represent all claimants whose identities are unknown. The reasonable fees and expenses of the guardian, including all reasonable expert witness fees, must be paid by the dissolved limited liability company.

(e)   A dissolved limited liability company that provides security in the amount and form ordered by the court under subsection (a) satisfies the company's obligations with respect to claims that are contingent, have not been made known to the company, or are based on an event occurring after the date of dissolution, and such claims may not be enforced against a member or transferee on account of assets received in liquidation.

COMMENT

This section is derived almost verbatim from Model Business Corporation Act section 14.08.

§ 707. Disposition of Assets in Winding Up

(a)   In winding up its activities and affairs, a limited liability company shall apply its assets to discharge the company's obligations to creditors, including members that are creditors.

(b)   After a limited liability company complies with subsection (a), any surplus must be distributed in the following order, subject to any charging order in effect under Section 503:

(1)   to each person owning a transferable interest that reflects contributions made and not previously returned, an amount equal to the value of the unreturned contributions; and

(2)   among persons owning transferable interests in proportion to their respective rights to share in distributions immediately before the dissolution of the company.

(c)   If a limited liability company does not have sufficient surplus to comply with subsection (b)(1), any surplus must be distributed among the owners of transferable interests in proportion to the value of the respective unreturned contributions.

(d)   All distributions made under subsections (b) and (c) must be paid in money.

COMMENT

Subsection (a)—This subsection is non-waivable as to creditors who are not members. *See* Section 105(c)(15) (stating that the operating agreement may not "restrict the rights under this [act] of a person other than a member or manager"). However, if a creditor is willing, a dissolved limited liability company may certainly make agreements with the creditor specifying the terms under which the LLC will "discharge its obligations" to the creditor.

Subsections (b), (c) and (d)—For the most part, these subsections state default rules. For example, operating agreements often provide for different distribution rights upon liquidation than during operations. However, distributions under these subsections (or otherwise under the operating agreement) are subject to Section 503 (charging orders). As to the extent the operating agreement can be amended to affect the distribution rights of persons already transferees, see Section 107(b).

§ 708. Administrative Dissolution

(a)   The [Secretary of State] may commence a proceeding under subsection (b) to dissolve a limited liability company administratively if the company does not:

(1)   pay any fee, tax, interest, or penalty required to be paid to the [Secretary of State] not later than [six months] after it is due;

(2)   deliver [an annual] [a biennial] report to the [Secretary of State] not later than [six months] after it is due; or

(3)   have a registered agent in this state for [60] consecutive days.

(b)   If the [Secretary of State] determines that one or more grounds exist for administratively dissolving a limited liability company, the [Secretary of State] shall serve the company with notice in a record of the [Secretary of State's] determination.

(c)   If a limited liability company, not later than [60] days after service of the notice under subsection (b), does not cure or demonstrate to the satisfaction of the [Secretary of State] the nonexistence of each ground determined by the [Secretary of State], the [Secretary of State] shall administratively dissolve the company by signing a statement of administrative dissolution that recites the grounds for dissolution and the effective date of dissolution. The [Secretary of State] shall file the statement and serve a copy on the company pursuant to Section 210.

(d)   A limited liability company that is administratively dissolved continues in existence as an entity but may not carry on any activities except as necessary to wind up its activities and affairs and liquidate its assets under Sections 702, 704, 705, 706, and 707, or to apply for reinstatement under Section 709.

(e)   The administrative dissolution of a limited liability company does not terminate the authority of its registered agent.

COMMENT

Many failures to comply with statutory requirements that may give rise to administrative dissolution occur because of oversight or inadvertence and are usually corrected promptly when brought to the entity's attention. Subsections (b) and (c) therefore provide a mandatory notice by the filing office to each limited liability company subject to administrative dissolution and a sixty-day grace period following the notice before the statement of administrative dissolution may be filed.

In most instances, the issue whether the limited liability company is subject to administrative dissolution will not be controverted. If a limited liability company is administratively dissolved, it may petition the filing office for reinstatement under Section 709 and, if reinstatement is denied, the company may appeal to the courts under Section 710.

As a practical matter, administrative dissolution permits the filing office to clear the record of "dead wood" and free up names.

§ 709. Reinstatement

(a) A limited liability company that is administratively dissolved under Section 708 may apply to the [Secretary of State] for reinstatement [not later than [two] years after the effective date of dissolution]. The application must state:

(1) the name of the company at the time of its administrative dissolution and, if needed, a different name that satisfies Section 112;

(2) the address of the principal office of the company and the name and street and mailing addresses of its registered agent;

(3) the effective date of the company's administrative dissolution; and

(4) that the grounds for dissolution did not exist or have been cured.

(b) To be reinstated, a limited liability company must pay all fees, taxes, interest, and penalties that were due to the [Secretary of State] at the time of the company's administrative dissolution and all fees, taxes, interest, and penalties that would have been due to the [Secretary of State] while the company was administratively dissolved.

(c) If the [Secretary of State] determines that an application under subsection (a) contains the required information, is satisfied that the information is correct, and determines that all payments required to be made to the [Secretary of State] by subsection (b) have been made, the [Secretary of State] shall:

(1) cancel the statement of administrative dissolution and prepare a statement of reinstatement that states the [Secretary of State's] determination and the effective date of reinstatement; and

(2) file the statement of reinstatement and serve a copy on the limited liability company.

(d) When reinstatement under this section has become effective, the following rules apply:

(1) The reinstatement relates back to and takes effect as of the effective date of the administrative dissolution.

(2) The limited liability company resumes carrying on its activities and affairs as if the administrative dissolution had not occurred.

(3) The rights of a person arising out of an act or omission in reliance on the dissolution before the person knew or had notice of the reinstatement are not affected.

COMMENT

Some states require that reinstatement be sought within two years of administrative dissolution. Other states provide a longer time, or do not impose any time limit. Imposing no limit risks abuse by unscrupulous people seeking to reinstate and appropriate for improper ends a dormant limited liability company that has been abandoned by its members. On the other hand, reinstatement is intended as a safety net for the inattentive (*i.e.*, for people in charge of a limited liability company who have neglected to file an annual report or otherwise subjected the LLC to administrative dissolution). If the deadline comes too soon, the safety net may be gone before the inattentive even learn that administrative dissolution has occurred.

Subsection (a)(1)—This provision will apply if, before the limited liability company is reinstated, another entity has taken the company's name. *See* Section 112(b)(1).

Subsection (d)(3)—This paragraph provides an exception to the retroactive effect provided by this subsection's Paragraphs (1) and (2). The exception could preclude a reinstated LLC's use of its own name. *See* Section 112(b)(1) (indirectly permitting a limited liability company to use the name of an LLC that has been administratively dissolved). Comparable provisions exist in other uniform acts pertaining to entities. *E.g.*, UPA (1997) (Last Amended 2013) § 902(c)(2).

§ 710.   Judicial Review of Denial of Reinstatement

(a)   If the [Secretary of State] denies a limited liability company's application for reinstatement following administrative dissolution, the [Secretary of State] shall serve the company with a notice in a record that explains the reasons for the denial.

(b)   A limited liability company may seek judicial review of denial of reinstatement in [the appropriate court] not later than [30] days after service of the notice of denial.

COMMENT

Because the grounds for administrative dissolution under Section 708 are limited and straight-forward, it is unlikely there will be a dispute about whether a limited liability company has corrected the reasons for its administrative dissolution. If a dissolved limited liability company disagrees with a determination by the filing office to deny the company's application for reinstatement, this section gives the company a limited right to seek judicial review of the denial of reinstatement.

[ARTICLE] 8
ACTIONS BY MEMBERS

§ 801.   Direct Action by Member

(a)   Subject to subsection (b), a member may maintain a direct action against another member, a manager, or the limited liability company to enforce the member's rights and protect the member's interests, including rights and interests under the operating agreement or this [act] or arising independently of the membership relationship.

(b)   A member maintaining a direct action under this section must plead and prove an actual or threatened injury that is not solely the result of an injury suffered or threatened to be suffered by the limited liability company.

COMMENT

Subsection (a)—A member's rights under this subsection are subject to the rule of standing stated in Subsection (b). The phrase "otherwise protect the member's interests" pertains to remedies and creates no additional causes of action.

The last phrase of this subsection ("or arising independently . . . ") does not create any new rights, obligations, or remedies, and is included merely to emphasize that a person's membership in an LLC does not preclude the person from enforcing rights existing "independently of the membership relationship" (*e.g.*, as a creditor).

Subsection (b)—This subsection codifies the rule of standing that predominates in entity law. *See, e.g.*, *PacLink Commc'ns Int'l, Inc. v. Superior Court*, 109 Cal. Rptr. 2d 436, 441 (Cal. Ct. App. 2001) (noting that, "[i]n determining whether an individual action as opposed to a derivative action lies, a court looks at 'the gravamen of the wrong alleged in the pleadings' "; holding that "[a] contextual reading of [plaintiffs'] complaint makes clear that they are not suing based upon a claim that as members of the LLC they were entitled to a distribution which was not made, but instead are suing for financial injury caused by fraudulent transfer of the company's assets") (quoting *Nelson v. Anderson*, 84 Cal. Rptr. 2d 753. (Cal. Ct. App. 1999)); *Mallia v. PaineWebber, Inc.*, 889 F. Supp. 277, 282 (S.D. Tex. 1995) ("[T]o bring a direct representative action against a general partner, a limited partner must demonstrate either direct injury or an injury that exists independently of the partnerships.' "); *Tooley v. Donaldson, Lufkin, & Jenrette, Inc.*, 845 A.2d 1031, 1039 (Del. 2004) (expressly disapproving "both the concept of 'special injury' and the concept that a claim is necessarily derivative if it affects all stockholders equally;" stating that "a court should look to the nature of the wrong and to whom the relief should go;" requiring that any "claimed direct injury . . . be independent of any alleged injury to the [entity]"); *Tzolis v. Wolff*, 884 N.E.2d 1005, 1008 (N.Y. 2008) (holding that derivative actions exist under New York LLC law and referring to "the traditional line between direct and derivative claims"); *see also CML V, LLC v. Bax* 6 A.3d 238, 245 (Del. Ch. 2010) (noting that issues of standing viz-a-viz direct and derivative claims are comparable regardless of whether the entity is a limited partnership, a limited liability company, or a corporation), *aff'd*, 28 A.3d 1037 (Del. 2011).

The distinction between direct and derivative claims protects the operating agreement. If any member can sue directly over any management issue, the mere threat of suit can interfere with the members' agreed-upon arrangements.

Although in ordinary contractual situations it is axiomatic that each party to a contract has standing to sue for breach of that contract, within a limited liability company different circumstances typically exist. A member does not have a direct claim against a manager or another member merely because the manager or other member has breached the operating agreement. Likewise a member's violation of this act does not automatically create a direct claim for every other member. To have standing in his, her, or its own right, a member plaintiff must be able to show a harm that occurs independently of the harm caused or threatened to be caused to the limited liability company.

Example: Through grossly negligent conduct, in violation of Section 409(c), the manager of a manager-managed LLC reduces the net assets of an LLC by fifty percent, which in turns decreases the value of Member A's investment by $3,000,000. Member A has no standing to bring a direct claim; the damage is merely derivative of the damage first suffered by the LLC. Member A may, however, bring a derivative claim. Sections 802–806.

Example: Same facts, except in addition to violating Section 409(c), the manager's conduct breaches an express provision of the operating agreement to which Member A is a signatory. The analysis and the result are the same.

Example: An operating agreement defines "distributable cash" and requires the LLC to periodically distribute that cash among all members. The LLC's manager fails to distribute the cash. Each member has a direct claim against the manager and the LLC.

The reference to "threatened injury" is to encompass potential claims for preventative relief, such as a temporary restraining order or preliminary injunction.

This section's standing rule is subject to reasonable alterations by the operating agreement. *See* the comment to Section 105(c)(11).

§ 802. Derivative Action

A member may maintain a derivative action to enforce a right of a limited liability company if:

(1)   the member first makes a demand on the other members in a member-managed limited liability company, or the managers of a manager-managed limited liability company, requesting that they cause the company to bring an action to enforce the right, and the managers or other members do not bring the action within a reasonable time; or

(2)   a demand under paragraph (1) would be futile.

COMMENT

Paragraph (1)—The demand requirement recognizes that, presumptively at least, the decision to cause a limited liability company to bring suit is a business decision, to be made by those who manage the business. Deborah A. DeMott, SHAREHOLDER DERIVATIVE ACTIONS: LAW AND PRACTICE § 5.9 (Westlaw, November 4, 2012) (Demand on directors—Rationales for demand).

Paragraph (2)—Some jurisdictions have a "universal demand" requirement, but the approach stated here is by far the majority one. Deborah A. DeMott, SHAREHOLDER DERIVATIVE ACTIONS: LAW AND PRACTICE § 5.12 (Westlaw, November 4, 2012).

§ 803. Proper Plaintiff

A derivative action to enforce a right of a limited liability company may be maintained only by a person that is a member at the time the action is commenced and:

(1) was a member when the conduct giving rise to the action occurred; or

(2) whose status as a member devolved on the person by operation of law or pursuant to the terms of the operating agreement from a person that was a member at the time of the conduct.

COMMENT

The rule stated here is conventional in both the law of unincorporated entities and corporate law. Persons dissociated as members have no standing to bring a derivative action. *A fortiori*, mere transferees have no standing. *See* the comments to Sections 107(b) and 502.

Paragraph (2)—This paragraph will be inapposite if the limited liability company has only two members, one of whom is the derivative plaintiff. In that limited circumstance, the plaintiff's death would cause the derivative action to abate. The "pick your partner" principal enshrined in Section 502 would prevent the decedent's heirs from succeeding to plaintiff status in the derivative action (except in the unlikely event that the remaining member consents to the heirs becoming members). The analysis and result will be the same if the derivative plaintiff is an entity whose existence terminates.

This act takes no position on whether:

- the death of member abates a direct claim against the LLC or a fellow member; and

- bringing a direct claim precludes a person from being a proper plaintiff for a derivative claim.

As to the latter issue, *see, e.g., Cordts-Auth v. Crunk, L.L.C.*, 815 F. Supp. 2d 778, 793–94 (S.D.N.Y. 2011) (discussing the potential conflict of interest), *aff'd*, 479 F. App'x 375 (2d Cir. 2012).

§ 804. Pleading

In a derivative action, the complaint must state with particularity:

(1) the date and content of plaintiff's demand and the response to the demand by the managers or other members; or

(2) why demand should be excused as futile.

COMMENT

This section parallels Section 802. The pleading requirement first appeared in a uniform act in 1976. ULPA (1976) § 1003.

§ 805. Special Litigation Committee

(a) If a limited liability company is named as or made a party in a derivative proceeding, the company may appoint a special litigation committee to investigate the claims asserted in the proceeding and determine whether pursuing the action is in the best interests of the company. If the company appoints a special litigation committee, on motion by the committee made in the name of the company, except for good cause shown, the court shall stay discovery for the time reasonably necessary to permit the committee to make its investigation. This subsection does not prevent the court from:

(1) enforcing a person's right to information under Section 410; or

(2) granting extraordinary relief in the form of a temporary restraining order or preliminary injunction.

(b) A special litigation committee must be composed of one or more disinterested and independent individuals, who may be members.

(c)   A special litigation committee may be appointed:

    (1)   in a member-managed limited liability company:

        (A)   by the affirmative vote or consent of a majority of the members not named as parties in the proceeding; or

        (B)   if all members are named as parties in the proceeding, by a majority of the members named as defendants; or

    (2)   in a manager-managed limited liability company:

        (A)   by a majority of the managers not named as parties in the proceeding; or

        (B)   if all managers are named as parties in the proceeding, by a majority of the managers named as defendants.

(d)   After appropriate investigation, a special litigation committee may determine that it is in the best interests of the limited liability company that the proceeding:

    (1)   continue under the control of the plaintiff;

    (2)   continue under the control of the committee;

    (3)   be settled on terms approved by the committee; or

    (4)   be dismissed.

(e)   After making a determination under subsection (d), a special litigation committee shall file with the court a statement of its determination and its report supporting its determination and shall serve each party with a copy of the determination and report. The court shall determine whether the members of the committee were disinterested and independent and whether the committee conducted its investigation and made its recommendation in good faith, independently, and with reasonable care, with the committee having the burden of proof. If the court finds that the members of the committee were disinterested and independent and that the committee acted in good faith, independently, and with reasonable care, the court shall enforce the determination of the committee. Otherwise, the court shall dissolve the stay of discovery entered under subsection (a) and allow the action to continue under the control of the plaintiff.

COMMENT

Although special litigation committees are best known in the corporate field, they are no more inherently corporate than derivative litigation or the notion that an organization is a person distinct from its owners. An "SLC" can serve as an ADR mechanism, help protect an agreed upon arrangement from strike suits, protect the interests of members who are neither plaintiffs nor defendants (if any), and bring the benefits of a specially tailored business judgment to any judicial decision.

This section's approach corresponds to established law in most jurisdictions, modified to fit the typical governance structures of a limited liability company. Use of an SLC is optional. An operating agreement can preclude the use of SLCs, rendering this section inapplicable, but cannot otherwise vary this section. *See* Section 105(c)(12).

Subsection (a)(1)—Section 410 pertains to information rights. On the availability of remedies pending the SLC's investigation, *compare* Section 410, *with Kaufman v. Computer Assocs. Int'l, Inc.*, No. Civ.A. 699-N, 2005 WL 3470589, at *1 (Del. Ch. Dec. 21, 2005) (presenting "the question of whether to stay a books and records action under 8 Del. C. § 220 at the request of a special litigation committee when a derivative action encompassing substantially the same allegations of wrongdoing filed by different plaintiffs is pending in another jurisdiction"; concluding "[f]or reasons that have much to do with the light burden imposed by the plaintiff's demand in this case . . . that the special litigation committee's motion to stay the books and records action should be denied").

Subsection (e)—The standard stated for judicial review of the SLC determination follows *Auerbach v. Bennett*, 393 N.E.2d 994 (N.Y. 1979) rather than *Zapata Corp. v. Maldonado*, 430 A.2d 779 (Del. 1981), because the latter's reference to a court's business judgment has generally not been followed in other states. In essence, an SLC is intended to function as a surrogate decision-maker, allowing the limited liability company to make what is fundamentally a business decision. If a court determines that "the members of the committee were disinterested and independent and whether the committee conducted its investigation and made its recommendation in good faith, independently, and with reasonable care, with the committee having the burden of proof," it makes no sense to substitute the court's legal judgment for the business judgment of the SLC.

Houle v. Low, 556 N.E.2d 51, 58 (Mass. 1990) contains an excellent explanation of the court's role in reviewing an SLC decision:

> The value of a special litigation committee is coextensive with the extent to which that committee truly exercises business judgment. In order to ensure that special litigation committees do act for the [entity]'s best interest, a good deal of judicial oversight is necessary in each case. At the same time, however, courts must be careful not to usurp the committee's valuable role in exercising business judgment. . . . [A] special litigation committee must be independent, unbiased, and act in good faith. Moreover, such a committee must conduct a thorough and careful analysis regarding the plaintiff's derivative suit. . . . The burden of proving that these procedural requirements have been met must rest, in all fairness, on the party capable of making that proof—the [entity].

For an extensive discussion of how a court should approach the question of independence, see *Einhorn v. Culea*, 612 N.W.2d 78, 91 (Wis. 2000).

§ 806. Proceeds and Expenses

(a) Except as otherwise provided in subsection (b):

(1) any proceeds or other benefits of a derivative action, whether by judgment, compromise, or settlement, belong to the limited liability company and not to the plaintiff; and

(2) if the plaintiff receives any proceeds, the plaintiff shall remit them immediately to the company.

(b) If a derivative action is successful in whole or in part, the court may award the plaintiff reasonable expenses, including reasonable attorney's fees and costs, from the recovery of the limited liability company.

(c) A derivative action on behalf of a limited liability company may not be voluntarily dismissed or settled without the court's approval.

COMMENT

Subsection (c)—This provision is intended to prevent collusion.

[ARTICLE] 9

FOREIGN LIMITED LIABILITY COMPANIES

§ 901. Governing Law

(a) The law of the jurisdiction of formation of a foreign limited liability company governs:

(1) the internal affairs of the company;

(2) the liability of a member as member and a manager as manager for a debt, obligation, or other liability of the company; and

(3) the liability of a series of the company.

(b) A foreign limited liability company is not precluded from registering to do business in this state because of any difference between the law of its jurisdiction of formation and the law of this state.

(c) Registration of a foreign limited liability company to do business in this state does not authorize the foreign company to engage in any activities and affairs or exercise any power that a limited liability company may not engage in or exercise in this state.

COMMENT

Subsection (a)—This subsection provides that the laws of the jurisdiction of formation of a foreign limited liability company, rather than the laws of this state, govern both the internal affairs of the foreign LLC and the liability of its members and managers for the obligations of the LLC. An operating agreement cannot change this provision. Section 105(c)(15).

This subdivision parallels Section 104 (pertaining to the governing law for domestic LLCs). *See* the comment to Section 104.

Subsection (a)(3)—The LLC statutes of several states authorize limited liability companies to have asset-partitioning series. According to those statutes, if series are properly created, a debt, obligation, or liability associated with the property of a particular series is enforceable only against property of that series, and not against the property of the LLC generally or any other series thereof.

This act does not provide for asset-partitioning series. However, under this provision, the law of this state will respect the "internal shields" created under the series provisions of another jurisdiction's limited liability company statute. This provision does *not* address the myriad of other unsettled issues pertaining to series.

For an explanation of how the asset-partitioning concept of series differs from the traditional concept, see Section 1031, comment.

Subsections (b) and (c)—These sections together make clear that, although a foreign limited liability company may not be denied registration simply because of a difference between the laws of its jurisdiction of formation and the laws of this state, the foreign limited liability company "may not engage in any activity or exercise any power that a limited liability company may not engage in or exercise in this state." Subsection (c).

§ 902.   Registration to do Business in This State

(a)   A foreign limited liability company may not do business in this state until it registers with the [Secretary of State] under this [article].

(b)   A foreign limited liability company doing business in this state may not maintain an action or proceeding in this state unless it is registered to do business in this state.

(c)   The failure of a foreign limited liability company to register to do business in this state does not impair the validity of a contract or act of the company or preclude it from defending an action or proceeding in this state.

(d)   A limitation on the liability of a member or manager of a foreign limited liability company is not waived solely because the company does business in this state without registering to do business in this state.

(e)   Section 901(a) and (b) applies even if a foreign limited liability company fails to register under this [article].

COMMENT

Subsection (a)—Following a long-established tradition, this act does not state what constitutes "do[ing] business in this state." Instead, Section 905 provides a non-exhaustive list of "[a]ctivities of a foreign limited liability company which do not constitute doing business in this state."

Subsection (b)—The purpose of this subsection is to induce foreign limited liability companies to register without imposing harsh or erratic sanctions. Often the failure to register is a result of inadvertence or bona fide disagreement as to the scope of Section 905, which is necessarily imprecise. Thus, the imposition of harsh sanctions in those situations is inappropriate. The sanction of closing the courts of the state to suits brought by foreign LLCs that should have registered is not a punitive one. If a foreign LLC should have registered and failed to do so, it may still enforce its contractual and other rights simply by registering.

However, if a court dismisses a case under this subsection rather than staying the proceedings pending the foreign LLC's registration, a statute of limitations problem may occur. *See Corco, Inc. v. Ledar Transport, Inc.* 946 P.2d 1009, 1010 (Kan. Ct. App. 1997) ("[T]he proper remedy was to dismiss [the unregistered entity's] counterclaim without prejudice rather than with prejudice. This would leave [the entity] the opportunity to comply with the statutes and then reassert its claim against [the defendant]. On the other hand, it would also leave the risk that the statute of limitations might run against [the entity].").

This subsection does not prevent a foreign LLC that has failed to register from "defending" an action or proceeding. The distinction between "maintaining" an action or proceeding under this subsection and "defending" an action or proceeding under Subsection (c) is determined on the basis of whether affirmative relief is sought. A nonregistered foreign LLC may interpose any defense or permissive or mandatory counterclaim to defeat a claimed recovery, but may not obtain an affirmative judgment based on the counterclaim without first registering.

Subsection (c)—In addition to permitting a non-registered foreign LLC doing business in this state to defend (but not maintain) an action or proceeding, this section makes clear that failure to register does not impair the validity of a foreign LLC's acts.

Subsection (d)—This subsection preserves the effectiveness of a foreign LLC's liability shield applicable under the LLC's governing law.

§ 903. Foreign Registration Statement

To register to do business in this state, a foreign limited liability company must deliver a foreign registration statement to the [Secretary of State] for filing. The statement must state:

(1) the name of the company and, if the name does not comply with Section 112, an alternate name adopted pursuant to Section 906(a);

(2) that the company is a foreign limited liability company;

(3) the company's jurisdiction of formation;

(4) the street and mailing addresses of the company's principal office and, if the law of the company's jurisdiction of formation requires the company to maintain an office in that jurisdiction, the street and mailing addresses of the required office; and

(5) the name and street and mailing addresses of the company's registered agent in this state.

COMMENT

The foreign registration statement provides certain basic information about the foreign limited liability company to ensure that citizens of the state have access to that information in their dealings with the foreign limited liability company. The statement also facilitates making the foreign company subject to the jurisdiction of the courts of the state.

Once registered, a foreign limited liability company must file an annual/biennial report. Section 212.

§ 904. Amendment of Foreign Registration Statement

A registered foreign limited liability company shall deliver to the [Secretary of State] for filing an amendment to its foreign registration statement if there is a change in:

(1) the name of the company;

(2) the company's jurisdiction of formation;

(3) an address required by Section 903(4); or

(4) the information required by Section 903(5).

COMMENT

This section works in tandem with the annual/biennial report required by Section 212 to keep up to date the information of record in the office of the filing office about a registered foreign limited liability company.

§ 905. Activities Not Constituting Doing Business

(a) Activities of a foreign limited liability company which do not constitute doing business in this state under this [article] include:

(1) maintaining, defending, mediating, arbitrating, or settling an action or proceeding;

(2) carrying on any activity concerning its internal affairs, including holding meetings of its members or managers;

(3) maintaining accounts in financial institutions;

(4) maintaining offices or agencies for the transfer, exchange, and registration of securities of the company or maintaining trustees or depositories with respect to those securities;

(5)   selling through independent contractors;

(6)   soliciting or obtaining orders by any means if the orders require acceptance outside this state before they become contracts;

(7)   creating or acquiring indebtedness, mortgages, or security interests in property;

(8)   securing or collecting debts or enforcing mortgages or security interests in property securing the debts and holding, protecting, or maintaining property;

(9)   conducting an isolated transaction that is not in the course of similar transactions;

(10) owning, without more, property; and

(11) doing business in interstate commerce.

(b)   A person does not do business in this state solely by being a member or manager of a foreign limited liability company that does business in this state.

(c)   This section does not apply in determining the contacts or activities that may subject a foreign limited liability company to service of process, taxation, or regulation under law of this state other than this [act].

COMMENT

This act does not attempt to formulate an inclusive definition of what constitutes doing business in a state. Rather, the concept is defined in a negative fashion by Subsections (a) and (b), which state that certain activities do not constitute doing business.

In general terms, any conduct more regular, systematic, or extensive than that described in Subsection (a) constitutes doing business and requires the foreign limited liability company to register to do business. Typical conduct requiring registration includes maintaining an office to conduct local intrastate business, selling personal property not in interstate commerce, entering into contracts relating to the local business or sales, and owning or using real estate for general purposes. But the passive owning of real estate for investment purposes does not constitute doing business. *See* Subsection (a)(10).

The test of "doing business" defined in a negative way in Subsections (a) and (b) applies only to the question whether a foreign limited liability company's contacts with the state are such that it must register under this section. The test is not applicable to other questions such as whether the foreign LLC is amenable to service of process under state "long-arm" statutes or liable for state or local taxes. A foreign LLC that has registered (or is required to register) will generally be subject to suit and state taxation in the state, while a foreign LLC that is subject to service of process or state taxation in a state will not necessarily be required to register.

Subsection (a)—The list of activities set forth in this subsection is not exhaustive.

Subsection (a)(1)—A foreign limited liability company is not "doing business" solely because it resorts to the courts of the state to recover an indebtedness, enforce an obligation, recover possession of personal property, obtain the appointment of a receiver, intervene in a pending proceeding, bring a petition to compel arbitration, file an appeal bond, or pursue appellate remedies. Similarly, a foreign LLC is not required to register merely because it files a complaint with a governmental agency or participates in an administrative proceeding within the state.

Subsection (a)(2)—A foreign limited liability company does not "do business" within a state under this section merely because some of its internal affairs occur within a state. Thus, a foreign LLC may hold meetings of its managers or members within a state without first registering. A foreign LLC also may maintain offices or agencies within a state relating solely to the transfer, exchange or registration of its interests without registering. Other activities relating to the internal affairs of the foreign LLC that do not constitute doing business under this section include having officers or representatives who reside within or are physically present in the state; while there, the officers or representatives may make executive decisions relating to the internal affairs of the foreign LLC without imposing on the foreign LLC the requirement that it register, if these activities are not so regular and systematic as to cause the residence to be viewed as a business office.

Subsection (a)(5)—Under this paragraph, a foreign limited liability company need not register if it sells goods in the state through independent contractors. These transactions are viewed as transactions by the independent contractors, not by the foreign LLC itself even though the foreign LLC sets some limits or ground rules for its contractors. If these controls are sufficiently pervasive, however, the foreign LLC may be deemed to be selling for itself in intrastate commerce, and not through the independent contractors and therefore engaged in doing business in the state.

Subsection (a)(7) and (8)—The mere act of making a loan by a foreign limited liability company that is not in the business of making loans does not constitute doing business in the state in which the loan is made. On the same theory, a foreign LLC may obtain security for the repayment of a loan, and foreclose or enforce the lien or security interest to collect the loan, without being deemed to be doing business. Similarly, a refunding or "roll over" of a loan or its adjustment or compromise does not involve doing business.

Subsection (a)(9)—The concept of "doing business" involves regular, repeated, and continuing business contacts of a local nature. A single agreement or isolated transaction within a state does not constitute doing business if there is no intention to repeat the transaction or engage in similar transactions. This act does not impose the limitation found in some statutes, such as section 15.01(b)(10) of the Model Business Corporation Act, that the isolated transaction be completed within thirty days. A foreign LLC should not be required to register simply because it engages in an isolated transaction that takes longer than thirty days to complete.

Subsection (a)(11)—A foreign limited liability company is not "doing business" within the meaning of this section if it is transacting business in interstate commerce. *See* Subsection (a)(6) (stating that soliciting or obtaining orders that must be accepted outside the state before they become contracts is not "doing business" within the meaning of this section).

These exclusions reflect the provisions of the United States Constitution that grant to the United States Congress exclusive power over interstate commerce, and preclude states from imposing restrictions or conditions upon this commerce. This subsection should be construed in a manner consistent with judicial decisions under the United States Constitution. Under those decisions, a foreign entity is not required to register even though it sells goods within the state if they are shipped to the purchasers in interstate commerce. Thus, a foreign LLC need not register even if it also does work and performs acts within the state incidental to the interstate business (*e.g.*, if it takes or enforces a security interest incidental to these transactions). Nor is it required to register merely because it sends traveling salespeople or solicitors into a state so long as contracts are not made within the state. Similarly, an office may be maintained by a foreign LLC in this state without registering if the office's functions relate solely to interstate commerce. Purchases of goods may of course be in interstate commerce as readily as sales. Thus, the purchase of personal property in this state by a foreign limited liability company for shipment in interstate commerce out of the state does not require the entity to register.

§ 906. Noncomplying Name of Foreign Limited Liability Company

(a)   A foreign limited liability company whose name does not comply with Section 112 may not register to do business in this state until it adopts, for the purpose of doing business in this state, an alternate name that complies with Section 112. A company that registers under an alternate name under this subsection need not comply with [this state's assumed or fictitious name statute]. After registering to do business in this state with an alternate name, a company shall do business in this state under:

(1)   the alternate name;

(2)   the company's name, with the addition of its jurisdiction of formation; or

(3)   a name the company is authorized to use under [this state's assumed or fictitious name statute].

(b)   If a registered foreign limited liability company changes its name to one that does not comply with Section 112, it may not do business in this state until it complies with subsection (a) by amending its registration to adopt an alternate name that complies with Section 112.

COMMENT

A foreign limited liability company must register under its true name if that name satisfies the requirements of Section 112. If the true name is unavailable because it is not distinguishable upon the records of the filing office from a name already in use or reserved or registered, the foreign LLC may use an alternate name.

A foreign limited liability company that registers to do business in the state may do business under a fictitious name to the same extent as a domestic entity.

§ 907.   Withdrawal Deemed on Conversion to Domestic Filing Entity or Domestic Limited Liability Partnership

A registered foreign limited liability company that converts to a domestic limited liability partnership or to a domestic entity whose formation requires delivery of a record to the [Secretary of State] for filing is deemed to have withdrawn its registration on the effective date of the conversion.

COMMENT

When a registered foreign limited liability company has converted to a domestic "filing entity" or domestic limited liability partnership, information about the entity in its capacity as a domestic entity will continue to be of record in the filing office. At that point, there is no further reason for the entity to be registered as a foreign LLC, and this section automatically treats its prior registration as withdrawn.

§ 908.   Withdrawal on Dissolution or Conversion to Nonfiling Entity Other than Limited Liability Partnership

(a)   A registered foreign limited liability company that has dissolved and completed winding up or has converted to a domestic or foreign entity whose formation does not require the public filing of a record, other than a limited liability partnership, shall deliver a statement of withdrawal to the [Secretary of State] for filing. The statement must state:

   (1)   in the case of a company that has completed winding up:

      (A)   its name and jurisdiction of formation;

      (B)   that the company surrenders its registration to do business in this state; and

   (2)   in the case of a company that has converted:

      (A)   the name of the converting company and its jurisdiction of formation;

      (B)   the type of entity to which the company has converted and its jurisdiction of formation;

      (C)   that the converted entity surrenders the converting company's registration to do business in this state and revokes the authority of the converting company's registered agent to act as registered agent in this state on behalf of the company or the converted entity; and

      (D)   a mailing address to which service of process may be made under subsection (b).

(b)   After a withdrawal under this section has become effective, service of process in any action or proceeding based on a cause of action arising during the time the foreign limited liability company was registered to do business in this state may be made pursuant to Section 119.

COMMENT

When a registered foreign limited liability company has dissolved and completed winding up, or has converted to a "nonfiling entity" other than a limited liability partnership, there is no further reason for information about the entity to appear in the records of the filing office. This section thus requires delivery of a statement of withdrawal for the purpose of removing the foreign LLC from the rolls of registered foreign entities.

Subsection (a)—The exclusion of limited liability partnerships from this provision is merely technical; Section 907 covers conversion to a domestic LLP.

§ 909.   Transfer of Registration

(a)   When a registered foreign limited liability company has merged into a foreign entity that is not registered to do business in this state or has converted to a foreign entity required to register with the [Secretary of State] to do business in this state, the foreign entity shall deliver to the [Secretary of State] for filing an application for transfer of registration. The application must state:

   (1)   the name of the registered foreign limited liability company before the merger or conversion;

   (2)   that before the merger or conversion the registration pertained to a foreign limited liability company;

(3)   the name of the applicant foreign entity into which the foreign limited liability company has merged or to which it has been converted and, if the name does not comply with Section 112, an alternate name adopted pursuant to Section 906(a);

(4)   the type of entity of the applicant foreign entity and its jurisdiction of formation;

(5)   the street and mailing addresses of the principal office of the applicant foreign entity and, if the law of the entity's jurisdiction of formation requires the entity to maintain an office in that jurisdiction, the street and mailing addresses of that office; and

(6)   the name and street and mailing addresses of the applicant foreign entity's registered agent in this state.

(b)   When an application for transfer of registration takes effect, the registration of the foreign limited liability company to do business in this state is transferred without interruption to the foreign entity into which the company has merged or to which it has been converted.

COMMENT

The purpose of this section is to clarify the status of the foreign limited liability company in the public records of the state. A filing under this section has the two-fold effect of canceling the authority of the foreign LLC to do business in the state while at the same time reregistering the former foreign LLC as the new type of foreign entity. If the reregistered foreign entity subsequently wishes to cancel its registration to do business in the state, it may do so under the statute of this state pertaining to the registration of the new type of foreign entity.

§ 910.   Termination of Registration

(a)   The [Secretary of State] may terminate the registration of a registered foreign limited liability company in the manner provided in subsections (b) and (c)   if the company does not:

(1)   pay, not later than [60] days after the due date, any fee, tax, interest, or penalty required to be paid to the [Secretary of State] under this [act] or law other than this [act];

(2)   deliver to the [Secretary of State] for filing, not later than [60] days after the due date, [an annual] [a biennial] report required under Section 212;

(3)   have a registered agent as required by Section 115; or

(4)   deliver to the [Secretary of State] for filing a statement of a change under Section 116 not later than [30] days after a change has occurred in the name or address of the registered agent.

(b)   The [Secretary of State] may terminate the registration of a registered foreign limited liability company by:

(1)   filing a notice of termination or noting the termination in the records of the [Secretary of State]; and

(2)   delivering a copy of the notice or the information in the notation to the company's registered agent or, if the company does not have a registered agent, to the company's principal office.

(c)   The notice must state or the information in the notation must include:

(1)   the effective date of the termination, which must be at least [60] days after the date the [Secretary of State] delivers the copy; and

(2)   the grounds for termination under subsection (a).

(d)   The authority of a registered foreign limited liability company to do business in this state ceases on the effective date of the notice of termination or notation under subsection (b), unless before that date the company cures each ground for termination stated in the notice or notation. If the company cures each ground, the [Secretary of State] shall file a record so stating.

COMMENT

This section is analogous to the procedures for administrative dissolution under Section 708.

§ 911.   Withdrawal of Registration of Registered Foreign Limited Liability Company

(a)   A registered foreign limited liability company may withdraw its registration by delivering a statement of withdrawal to the [Secretary of State] for filing. The statement of withdrawal must state:

(1)   the name of the company and its jurisdiction of formation;

(2)   that the company is not doing business in this state and that it withdraws its registration to do business in this state;

(3)   that the company revokes the authority of its registered agent to accept service on its behalf in this state; and

(4)   an address to which service of process may be made under subsection (b).

(b)   After the withdrawal of the registration of a foreign limited liability company, service of process in any action or proceeding based on a cause of action arising during the time the company was registered to do business in this state may be made pursuant to Section 119.

COMMENT

The statement of withdrawal must set forth an address where service of process may be made on the foreign limited liability company pursuant to Section 119. There is no limit on how long the withdrawn company must keep that address up to date.

§ 912.   Action by [Attorney General]

The [Attorney General] may maintain an action to enjoin a foreign limited liability company from doing business in this state in violation of this [article].

COMMENT

The authority stated here has been part of corporate law for more than a century and has been carried over into the law of unincorporated business entities. Nowadays, the authority is rarely if ever invoked in either realm of entity law.

[ARTICLE] 10

MERGER, INTEREST EXCHANGE, CONVERSION, AND DOMESTICATION

INTRODUCTORY COMMENT

This article deals comprehensively with both same-type and cross-type mergers and interest exchanges and with conversions and domestications. For this article to apply, at least one participant organization must be a domestic limited liability company. For a foreign organization to be involved, its organic law must permit the organization's participation.

Part 1 contains definitions specific to this article as well as provisions applicable to all transactions authorized by this article.

Part 2 governs mergers and is an amalgamation of existing entity law, both unincorporated and incorporated.

Part 3 governs interest exchanges, previously a feature only of corporate law. Part 3 is derived from the share exchange provisions in chapter 11 of the Model Business Corporation Act.

Part 4 governs conversions, a one-step procedure by which an entity changes from one type of entity to another type while nonetheless continuing in existence as the same legal entity.

Part 5 governs domestications, a procedure by a domestic limited liability company can become a foreign limited liability company or vice versa, in each instance with the company remaining the same legal entity.

Part 2 sets the paradigm for Parts 3, 4, and 5, because mergers are long-established and merger rules and concepts are familiar to business lawyers. Moreover, conversions and domestications could formerly be accomplished via mergers (with a new entity), and an interest exchange produces the same result as a triangular merger. The comments to Part 2 are thus relevant to understanding Parts 3, 4, and 5.

This article contemplates transactions in which the surviving entity is neither a filing entity nor otherwise of record in the filing office (*e.g.*, the merger of an LLC into a non-LLP general partnership). As a result, a filing under this article may be the first time that a filing office takes cognizance of an entity's existence.

[PART] 1

GENERAL PROVISIONS

§ 1001. Definitions

In this [article]:

(1)   "Acquired entity" means the entity, all of one or more classes or series of interests of which are acquired in an interest exchange.

(2)   "Acquiring entity" means the entity that acquires all of one or more classes or series of interests of the acquired entity in an interest exchange.

(3)   "Conversion" means a transaction authorized by [Part] 4.

(4)   "Converted entity" means the converting entity as it continues in existence after a conversion.

(5)   "Converting entity" means the domestic entity that approves a plan of conversion pursuant to Section 1043 or the foreign entity that approves a conversion pursuant to the law of its jurisdiction of formation.

(6)   "Distributional interest" means the right under an unincorporated entity's organic law and organic rules to receive distributions from the entity.

(7)   "Domestic", with respect to an entity, means governed as to its internal affairs by the law of this state.

(8)   "Domesticated limited liability company" means the domesticating limited liability company as it continues in existence after a domestication.

(9)   "Domesticating limited liability company" means the domestic limited liability company that approves a plan of domestication pursuant to Section 1053 or the foreign limited liability company that approves a domestication pursuant to the law of its jurisdiction of formation.

(10) "Domestication" means a transaction authorized by [Part] 5.

(11) "Entity":

(A)   means:

(i)   a business corporation;

(ii)   a nonprofit corporation;

(iii) a general partnership, including a limited liability partnership;

(iv)   a limited partnership, including a limited liability limited partnership;

(v)   a limited liability company;

[(vi) a general cooperative association;]

(vii) a limited cooperative association;

(viii) an unincorporated nonprofit association;

(ix)   a statutory trust, business trust, or common-law business trust; or

(x)   any other person that has:

(I)   a legal existence separate from any interest holder of that person; or

1293

(II) the power to acquire an interest in real property in its own name; and

(B) does not include:

(i) an individual;

(ii) a trust with a predominantly donative purpose or a charitable trust;

(iii) an association or relationship that is not an entity listed in subparagraph A and is not a partnership under the rules stated in [Section 202(c) of the Uniform Partnership Act (1997) (Last Amended 2013)] [Section 7 of the Uniform Partnership Act (1914)] or a similar provision of the law of another jurisdiction;

(iv) a decedent's estate; or

(v) a government or a governmental subdivision, agency, or instrumentality.

(12) "Filing entity" means an entity whose formation requires the filing of a public organic record. The term does not include a limited liability partnership.

(13) "Foreign", with respect to an entity, means an entity governed as to its internal affairs by the law of a jurisdiction other than this state.

(14) "Governance interest" means a right under the organic law or organic rules of an unincorporated entity, other than as a governor, agent, assignee, or proxy, to:

(A) receive or demand access to information concerning, or the books and records of, the entity;

(B) vote for or consent to the election of the governors of the entity; or

(C) receive notice of or vote on or consent to an issue involving the internal affairs of the entity.

(15) "Governor" means:

(A) a director of a business corporation;

(B) a director or trustee of a nonprofit corporation;

(C) a general partner of a general partnership;

(D) a general partner of a limited partnership;

(E) a manager of a manager-managed limited liability company;

(F) a member of a member-managed limited liability company;

[(G) a director of a general cooperative association;]

(H) a director of a limited cooperative association;

(I) a manager of an unincorporated nonprofit association;

(J) a trustee of a statutory trust, business trust, or common-law business trust; or

(K) any other person under whose authority the powers of an entity are exercised and under whose direction the activities and affairs of the entity are managed pursuant to the organic law and organic rules of the entity.

(16) "Interest" means:

(A) a share in a business corporation;

(B) a membership in a nonprofit corporation;

(C) a partnership interest in a general partnership;

(D) a partnership interest in a limited partnership;

(E) a membership interest in a limited liability company;

[(F) a share in a general cooperative association;]

(G) a member's interest in a limited cooperative association;

(H)   a membership in an unincorporated nonprofit association;

(I)   a beneficial interest in a statutory trust, business trust, or common-law business trust; or

(J)   a governance interest or distributional interest in any other type of unincorporated entity.

(17) "Interest exchange" means a transaction authorized by [Part] 3.

(18) "Interest holder" means:

(A)   a shareholder of a business corporation;

(B)   a member of a nonprofit corporation;

(C)   a general partner of a general partnership;

(D)   a general partner of a limited partnership;

(E)   a limited partner of a limited partnership;

(F)   a member of a limited liability company;

[(G)   a shareholder of a general cooperative association;]

(H)   a member of a limited cooperative association;

(I)   a member of an unincorporated nonprofit association;

(J)   a beneficiary or beneficial owner of a statutory trust, business trust, or common-law business trust; or

(K)   any other direct holder of an interest.

(19) "Interest holder liability" means:

(A)   personal liability for a liability of an entity which is imposed on a person:

(i)   solely by reason of the status of the person as an interest holder; or

(ii)   by the organic rules of the entity which make one or more specified interest holders or categories of interest holders liable in their capacity as interest holders for all or specified liabilities of the entity; or

(B)   an obligation of an interest holder under the organic rules of an entity to contribute to the entity.

(20) "Merger" means a transaction authorized by [Part] 2.

(21) "Merging entity" means an entity that is a party to a merger and exists immediately before the merger becomes effective.

(22) "Organic law" means the law of an entity's jurisdiction of formation governing the internal affairs of the entity.

(23) "Organic rules" means the public organic record and private organic rules of an entity.

(24) "Plan" means a plan of merger, plan of interest exchange, plan of conversion, or plan of domestication.

(25) "Plan of conversion" means a plan under Section 1042.

(26) "Plan of domestication" means a plan under Section 1052.

(27) "Plan of interest exchange" means a plan under Section 1032.

(28) "Plan of merger" means a plan under Section 1022.

(29) "Private organic rules" means the rules, whether or not in a record, that govern the internal affairs of an entity, are binding on all its interest holders, and are not part of its public organic record, if any. The term includes:

(A)   the bylaws of a business corporation;

(B)   the bylaws of a nonprofit corporation;

(C)   the partnership agreement of a general partnership;

(D)   the partnership agreement of a limited partnership;

(E)   the operating agreement of a limited liability company;

[(F)   the bylaws of a general cooperative association;]

(G)   the bylaws of a limited cooperative association;

(H)   the governing principles of an unincorporated nonprofit association; and

(I)   the trust instrument of a statutory trust or similar rules of a business trust or common-law business trust.

(30)   "Protected agreement" means:

(A)   a record evidencing indebtedness and any related agreement in effect on [the effective date of this [act]];

(B)   an agreement that is binding on an entity on [the effective date of this [act]];

(C)   the organic rules of an entity in effect on [the effective date of this [act]]; or

(D)   an agreement that is binding on any of the governors or interest holders of an entity on [the effective date of this [act]].

(31)   "Public organic record" means the record the filing of which by the [Secretary of State] is required to form an entity and any amendment to or restatement of that record. The term includes:

(A)   the articles of incorporation of a business corporation;

(B)   the articles of incorporation of a nonprofit corporation;

(C)   the certificate of limited partnership of a limited partnership;

(D)   the certificate of organization of a limited liability company;

[(E)   the articles of incorporation of a general cooperative association;]

(F)   the articles of organization of a limited cooperative association; and

(G)   the certificate of trust of a statutory trust or similar record of a business trust.

(32)   "Registered foreign entity" means a foreign entity that is registered to do business in this state pursuant to a record filed by the [Secretary of State].

(33)   "Statement of conversion" means a statement under Section 1045.

(34)   "Statement of domestication" means a statement under Section 1055.

(35)   "Statement of interest exchange" means a statement under Section 1035.

(36)   "Statement of merger" means a statement under Section 1025.

(37)   "Surviving entity" means the entity that continues in existence after or is created by a merger.

(38)   "Type of entity" means a generic form of entity:

(A)   recognized at common law; or

(B)   formed under an organic law, whether or not some entities formed under that organic law are subject to provisions of that law that create different categories of the form of entity.

COMMENT

This section defines the terms that are used in this article. Many of the definitions describe attributes that are significant in some forms of entity and not in others. For example, the concept of separate "distributional" and "governance" interests are inherent in unincorporated entities but have no counterpart in corporations. In addition, because some statutes use different terms to describe the same transaction, the definitions are intended to be broad enough to encompass those similar transactions, regardless of how described. *See, e.g.,* Paragraph 10 (defining "domestication").

"Acquired entity" [(1)]—This definition recognizes that an interest exchange may involve only the acquisition of a particular "class" or "series" of interests in an entity. Model Business Corporation Act section 6.01 does not expressly define "classes" or "series." Because the interests of members in an unincorporated business organization often tend to be distinctive, it may be that each member's interest will comprise a separate class or series. For an explanation of a new and different meaning of the word "series," see Section 1031, introductory comment. The term "acquired entity" does not encompass series under that new meaning.

"Acquiring entity" [(2)]—An "acquiring entity" is an entity that acquires the interests of the acquired entity in an interest exchange governed by Part 3 of this article.

"Conversion" [(3)]—The term "conversion" means a transaction authorized by Part 4 pursuant to which an entity of one type is converted into an entity of another type. As used in this act, the term "conversion" does not include a transaction in which an entity changes the jurisdiction in which it is organized but does not change to a different form of entity; that type of transaction is referred to in this act as a "domestication" and is governed by Part 5.

"Converted entity" [(4)]—This term is used in Part 4 to describe the entity that results from a conversion.

"Converting entity" [(5)]—A converting entity is the entity that becomes the converted entity under Part 4.

"Distributional interest" [(6)]—This term is similar to the concept of a "transferable interest" found in this act and the organic laws of several other types of unincorporated entities, but has a broader meaning because the scope of this act includes entities in addition to those whose organic law uses the term "transferable interest."

"Domestic" [(7)]—The term "domestic", when used in this article with respect to an entity, refers to an entity whose internal affairs are governed by the organic laws of this state. Except in the case of general partnerships and unincorporated nonprofit associations, this will mean an entity that is formed, organized, or incorporated under domestic law. In the case of a general partnership organized under UPA (1997) (Last Amended 2013), the term will mean a general partnership whose governing law under UPA (1997) § 104 is the law of the adopting state. Under that section, the governing law is determined by the location of the partnership's principal office, except for limited liability partnerships whose governing law is the law of the state where the LLP's statement of qualification is filed. It is a factual question whether the activities and organization of an unincorporated nonprofit association make it a domestic or foreign entity.

"Domesticated limited liability company" [(8)]—This term is used in Part 5 and means the entity that is domesticated pursuant to Part 5. By the nature of the transaction, the domesticated entity will be of the same type as the domesticating entity (*i.e.,* an LLC).

"Domesticating limited liability company" [(9)]—This term is used in Part 5 and means the entity that is domesticated pursuant to Part 5.

"Domestication" [(10)]—The term "domestication" means a transaction of the kind authorized by Part 5 pursuant to which an entity may change its *jurisdiction* of formation *but not its type* so long as the laws of the foreign jurisdiction permit the domestication. The legal effect of the domestication of a limited liability company out of this state will be governed by the laws of both this state and the foreign jurisdiction. Some statutes include what is described in this act as "domestication" in their definition of a "conversion." *See, e.g.,* COLO. REV. STAT. § 7–90–201. It is intended that the domestication provisions of this act will apply to a transaction that may be characterized under another act as a "conversion" if the transaction meets the definition of "domestication" under this act.

"Entity" [(11)]—This definition determines the overall scope of the act because only an "entity" may participate in the transactions authorized by Parts 2 (mergers), 3 (interest exchanges), 4 (conversions), and 5 (domestications). *See* Sections 1021 (authorization of mergers), 1031(authorization of interest exchanges), 1041(authorization of conversions), 1051(authorization of domestications).

Subparagraph (A)(x) is a "catch-all" provision that includes within the definition of "entity" any type of organization recognized under the law of this state, which is not listed specifically in the preceding paragraphs of this definition. Subparagraph (A)(x) is intended to include all forms of private organizations, regardless of whether organized for profit, and artificial legal persons other than those excluded by Subparagraph (B). This definition does not exclude regulated entities such as public utilities, banks, and insurance companies. Should a state desire to exclude certain types of regulated entities or any of the entities listed in Subparagraph (A)(i)–(x) from participating in transactions permitted by this act for policy reasons, that may be done by listing those types of entities in Section 1007(a), or by permitting those type of entities to engage in transactions under this act generally but prohibiting certain types of transactions by listing those transactions in Section 1007(b).

Unincorporated nonprofit associations are treated as a type of entity in Subparagraph (A)(viii) because section 5 of the Uniform Unincorporated Nonprofit Association Act (2008) (Last Amended 2013) specifically states that an unincorporated nonprofit association is an entity. In many states, the status of a nonprofit association may not be clear. Nevertheless, in most states a nonprofit association has the power to acquire an interest in real property in its own name and therefore would qualify as an "entity" under Subparagraph (A)(x). See Section 6 of the UUNAA, which gives an unincorporated nonprofit association the power to acquire in its own name an interest in real property.

Subparagraph (B)(i) of this definition excludes a sole proprietorship from the concept of an "entity."

Trusts with a predominately donative purpose, such as inter vivos and testamentary trusts and charitable trusts, are treated in many states as having a separate legal existence, but they have been excluded from the definition of "entity" (and thus are not within the scope of this article) under Subparagraph (B)(ii) because they should not be able to engage in transactions under this act as a matter of public policy. Trusts that carry on a business, however, such as business and statutory entity trusts, are "entities." *See* Subparagraph (A)(ix).

Subparagraph (B)(iii) of this definition excludes from the concept of an "entity" any form of co-ownership of property or sharing of returns from property that is not listed in Subparagraph (A) and is not a partnership under UPA (1997). In that connection, Section 202(c) of that act provides in part:

In determining whether a partnership is formed, the following rules apply:

(1)   Joint tenancy, tenancy in common, tenancy by the entireties, joint property, common property, or part ownership does not by itself establish a partnership, even if the co-owners share profits made by the use of the property.

(2)   The sharing of gross returns does not by itself establish a partnership, even if the persons sharing them have a joint or common right or interest in property from which the returns are derived.

Limited liability partnerships and limited liability limited partnerships are "entities" because they are general partnerships and limited partnerships respectively that have made the additional required election claiming LLP or LLLP status. A limited liability partnership is not, therefore, a separate type of entity from the underlying general or limited partnership that has elected limited liability partnership status. Thus, for example, the election of a general partnership to become a limited liability partnership is not a conversion subject to Article 4.

Under Subparagraph (B)(iv), decedent's estates are excluded from the definition of an entity for the same policy reason as trusts with a predominately donative purpose and charitable trusts.

This same public policy rationale is the justification for the exclusion of governmental subdivisions, agencies, or instrumentalities in Subparagraph (B)(v).

"Filing entity" [(12)]—Whether an entity is a filing entity is determined by reference to whether its legal existence requires the filing of a document with the state filing officer. To fit within this definition, the filing must be necessary but need not be sufficient to form the entity. *See, e.g.*, Section 201(d) ("A limited liability company is formed when the company's certificate of organization becomes effective *and* at least one person becomes a member.") (emphasis added).

While the statute refers to the "formation" of an entity, the term is intended to encompass corporations that are "incorporated," as well as other filing entities whose statutes refer to them as being "organized." Business trusts present a special problem. In some states, a business trust could be a filing entity or a common law relationship, while in other states business trusts are only recognized at common law. A statutory trust entity formed under the Uniform Statutory Trust Entity Act (2009) (Last Amended 2013) § 201(a) is a filing entity, because a statutory trust entity is formed by the filing office filing a certificate of trust pertaining to the entity.

The term "filing entity" does not include a limited liability partnership because, while a filed document is a precondition to LLP status, that document (a statement of qualification under UPA (1997) (Last Amended 2013) § 901) does not form the underlying entity. A limited liability limited partnership, on the other hand, is a filing entity because the underlying limited partnership is formed by filing a certificate of limited partnership. ULPA (2001) (Last Amended 2013) § 201(a).

"Foreign" [(13)]—The term "foreign entity" includes any non-domestic entity of any type. Where a foreign entity is a filing entity, the entity is governed by the laws of the state of filing. A nonfiling foreign entity is governed by the laws governing its internal affairs. It is a factual question whether a general partnership whose internal affairs are governed by UPA (1914) is a domestic or foreign partnership. A UPA (1914) partnership will likely be deemed to be a domestic entity where the greatest nexus of contacts are found. The domestic or foreign characterization of partnerships under the UPA (1997) (Last Amended 2013) that have not become limited liability partnerships will be governed by Section 104(2) ("the law of the jurisdiction in which the partnership has its principal office") or the partnership agreement. (Section 104(2) is a default rule.)

"Governance interest" [(14)]—A governance interest is typically only part of the interest that a person will hold in an unincorporated entity and is usually coupled with a distributional interest (or economic rights). Memberships in some nonprofit corporations and unincorporated nonprofit associations consist solely of governance interests and memberships in other nonprofit entities may not include either governance interests or distributional interests. In some unincorporated business entities, including limited liability companies, there is a more limited right to transfer governance interests than there is to transfer distributional interests. An interest holder in such an unincorporated business entity who transfers only a distributional interest and retains the governance interest will also retain the status of an interest holder. Whether a transferee who acquires only a distributional interest will acquire the status of an interest holder is determined by the definition of "interest holder."

Governors of an entity have the kinds of rights listed in the definition of "governance interest" by reason of their position with the entity. For a governor to have a "governance interest," however, requires that the governor also have those rights for a reason other than the governor's status as such. A manager who is not a member in a limited liability company, for example, will not have a governance interest, but a manager who is a member will have a governance interest arising from the ownership of a membership interest.

"Governor" [(15)]—This term has been chosen to provide a way of referring to a person who has the authority under an entity's organic law to make management decisions regarding the entity that is different from any of the existing terms used in connection with particular types of entities. Depending on the type of entity or its organic rules, the governors of an entity may have the power to act on their own authority, or they may be organized as a board or similar group and only have the power to act collectively, and then only through a designated agent. In other words, a person having only the power to bind the organization pursuant to the instruction of the governors is not a governor. Under the organic rules, particularly those of unincorporated entities, most or all of the management decisions may be reserved to the members or partners. Thus, if a manager of a limited liability company were limited to having authority to execute management decisions made by the members and did not have any authority to make independent management decisions, the manager would not be a governor under this definition.

"Interest" [(16)]—In the usual case, the interest held by an interest holder will include both a governance interest and a distributional interest. Members in nonprofit corporations or unincorporated nonprofit associations generally do not have any distributional interest because they do not receive distributions, but they nonetheless may hold a governance interest in which case they would have the status of interest holders under this article.

"Interest exchange" [(17)]—The term "interest exchange" means a transaction authorized by Part 3 pursuant to which an entity may acquire interests in another entity. The consideration that may be provided to the interest holders whose interests are being acquired in an exchange may consist in whole or part of interests in a third party that is not one of the two parties to the exchange itself. *See* Section 1031(a).

"Interest holder" [(18)]—This act does not refer to "equity" interests or "equity" owners or holders because the term "equity" could be confusing in the case of a nonprofit entity whose members do not have an interest in the assets or results of operations of the entity but have only a right to vote on its internal affairs.

"Interest holder liability" [(19)]—This term is used to describe the vicarious liability of an interest holder, by virtue of being an interest holder, for liabilities of the entity. The term includes only personal liability of an interest holder for a debt of the entity imposed on the interest holder either by statute or by the organic rules to the extent authorized pursuant to the organic law. Liabilities that an interest holder incurs in any other fashion are not interest holder liabilities for purposes of this act. Thus, for example, if a state's business corporation law makes shareholders personally liable for unpaid wages because of their status as shareholders, that liability would be an "interest holder liability." If, on the other hand, a shareholder were to guarantee payment of an obligation of a corporation, that liability would not be an "interest holder liability" because it is a direct liability and not based on the status of being a shareholder. Similarly, the liability to return an improper distribution is not an interest holder liability because it is a direct liability of the interest holder based on receipt of the distribution.

"Merger" [(20)]—The term means a transaction in which two or more entities are combined into a single entity pursuant to a filing with the filing office. The term "merger" in this act includes the transaction known as a consolidation in which a new entity results from the combination of two or more pre-existing entities.

"Merging entity" [(21)]—The term "merging entity" refers to each entity that is in existence immediately before a merger and is a party to the merger. It will include the surviving entity if the surviving entity exists before the merger becomes effective. It does not include an entity that provides consideration to be received by interest holders if that entity is not a party to the merger.

"Organic law" [(22)]—Organic law means statutes that govern the internal affairs of an entity. For example, this act is the organic law of a limited liability company formed under this act.

Entity laws in a few states purport to require that some of their internal governance rules applicable to a domestic entity also apply to a foreign entity with significant ties to the state. *See, e.g.*, CAL. CORP. CODE § 2115 (Foreign Corporations); N.Y. NOT-FOR-PROFIT-CORP. §§ 1318–21 (Liabilities of Directors and Officers of Foreign Corporations); 15 PA. CONS. STAT. § 6145 (Applicability of Certain Safeguards to Foreign Corporations). Such a "sticky fingers" law is not included within the definition of "organic law" for purposes of this act because those laws are not part of the law of the entity's jurisdiction of formation.

"Organic rules" [(23)]—The term "organic rules" means an entity's public organic record and the private organic rules. The organic rules, together with this act, the organic law, and the common law, provide the rules governing the internal affairs of the entity. For example, this act and the operating agreement comprise the organic rules of a limited liability company formed under this act.

"Plan" [(24)]—The term "plan" is a short-hand way of referring to the plan of merger, interest exchange, conversion, or domestication, as the case may be, depending on which form of transaction is taking place. *See* Sections 1022 (plan of merger), 1032 (plan of interest exchange), 1042 (plan of conversion), 1052 (plan of domestication).

"Private organic rules" [(29)]—The term private "organic rules" is intended to include all governing rules of an entity that are binding on all of its interest holders, whether or not in record form, except for the provisions of the entity's public organic record, if any. The term is intended to include agreements in "record" form such as corporate bylaws, as well as oral partnership agreements and oral operating agreements among LLC members.

"Protected agreement" [(30)]—The term "protected agreement" refers to evidences of indebtedness and agreements binding on the entity or any of its governors or interest holders that are unpaid or executory in whole or in part on the effective date of the act. Thus, a revolving line of credit from a bank to a corporation would constitute a protected agreement even if advances were not made until after the effective date of the act. Likewise, an operating agreement in effect under this act or a predecessor to this act is a "protected agreement."

If a protected agreement has provisions that apply if an entity merges, those provisions will apply if the entity enters into an interest exchange, conversion, or domestication even though the agreement does not mention those other types of transactions. *See* Sections 1031(c) (interest exchange), 1041(c) (conversion), 1051(c) (domestication).

"Public organic record" [(31)]—A "public organic record" is a record that is filed publicly to form, organize, incorporate, or otherwise create an entity. The term does not include a statement of authority filed under UPA (1997) (Last Amended 2013) § 303 or any of the other statements that may be filed under that act since those statements do not create a new entity. The same is true for statements filed under this act.

For the same reason, a statement of qualification filed under UPA (1997) (Last Amended 2013) § 1001 is not a "public organic record." The limited liability partnership that results from the filing is the same entity as the partnership that delivered the statement to the filing office. Similarly, the term does not include a statement of authority filed under section 7 of the Revised Uniform Unincorporated Nonprofit Association Act (2008) (Last Amended 2013), a statement appointing a registered agent filed under section 31 of that act, or any of the various statements filed under this act.

In those states where a deed of trust or other instrument is publicly filed to create a business trust, that filing will constitute a public organic record. But in those states where a business trust is not created by a public filing, the deed of trust or similar record will be part of the private organic rules of the business trust.

Where a public organic document has been amended or restated, the term means the public organic document as last amended or restated.

"**Registered foreign entity**" **[(32]**—This term refers to a foreign entity that is registered to transact business in this state pursuant to a public filing.

"**Surviving entity**" **[(37)]**—The term "surviving entity" refers to either a merging entity that survives the merger or the new entity created by the merger.

"**Type of entity**" **[(38]**—The term "type of entity" has been developed in an attempt to distinguish different legal forms of entities. It is sometimes difficult to decide whether one is dealing with a different form of entity or a variation of the same form. For example, a limited partnership, although it has long been characterized or even defined as a partnership, is a different type of entity from a general partnership, while a limited liability partnership is not a different type of entity from a general partnership. In some states cooperatives are categories of business corporations or nonprofit corporations, while in other states cooperatives are a separate type of entity.

§ 1002. Relationship of [Article] to Other Laws

(a)   This [article] does not authorize an act prohibited by, and does not affect the application or requirements of, law other than this [article].

(b)   A transaction effected under this [article] may not create or impair a right, duty or obligation of a person under the statutory law of this state other than this [article] relating to a change in control, takeover, business combination, control-share acquisition, or similar transaction involving a domestic merging, acquired, converting, or domesticating business corporation unless:

(1)   if the corporation does not survive the transaction, the transaction satisfies any requirements of the law; or

(2)   if the corporation survives the transaction, the approval of the plan is by a vote of the shareholders or directors which would be sufficient to create or impair the right, duty, or obligation directly under the law.

COMMENT

This section preserves existing regulatory law in an adopting state in general terms. Adopting states should consider more carefully integrating this act with their various regulatory laws. For example, in some states certain professions are limited in their use of limited liability entities. *See* Section 1003.

Laws other than this act that will apply to transactions under this act include, for example, fraudulent transfer and fraudulent conveyance acts, state insolvency statutes, federal bankruptcy law, and Articles 8 and 9 of the Uniform Commercial Code.

Subsection (b)—Many states have enacted "antitakeover" statutes intended to make it more difficult to acquire control of a publicly traded corporation. Those statutes often provide that their application to a particular corporation cannot be changed unless the corporation obtains certain specified approvals, such as a vote of disinterested directors or a supermajority vote by the shareholders. The purpose of the special requirements in this subsection on varying the application of an antitakeover statute is to protect against a hostile acquirer or group of shareholders seeking to use the act to avoid the application of the antitakeover statute.

This subsection protects the application of antitakeover statutes from being affected by a transaction under this act by requiring that the transaction be approved in a manner that would be sufficient to approve changing the application of the antitakeover statute. If a transaction is approved in that manner, there is no policy reason to prohibit the application of the antitakeover statute from being varied by a transaction under this act. If the application of an antitakeover statute cannot be varied by action of an entity subject to it, then a transaction under this act will be permissible only if the antitakeover provision continues to apply after the transaction or the transaction itself is permissible under the antitakeover statute.

§ 1003. Required Notice or Approval

(a)   A domestic or foreign entity that is required to give notice to, or obtain the approval of, a governmental agency or officer of this state to be a party to a merger must give the notice or obtain the approval to be a party to an interest exchange, conversion, or domestication.

(b)   Property held for a charitable purpose under the law of this state by a domestic or foreign entity immediately before a transaction under this [article] becomes effective may not, as a result of the transaction, be diverted from the objects for which it was donated, granted, devised, or otherwise transferred unless, to the extent required by or pursuant to the law of this state concerning cy pres or other law dealing with nondiversion of charitable assets, the entity obtains an appropriate order of [the appropriate court] [the Attorney General] specifying the disposition of the property.

(c)   A bequest, devise, gift, grant, or promise contained in a will or other instrument of donation, subscription, or conveyance which is made to a merging entity that is not the surviving entity and which takes effect or remains payable after the merger inures to the surviving entity.

(d)   A trust obligation that would govern property if transferred to a nonsurviving entity applies to property that is transferred to the surviving entity under this section.

Legislative Note: As an alternative to enacting Subsection (a), a state may identify each of its regulatory laws that requires prior approval for a merger of a regulated entity, decide whether regulatory approval should be required for an interest exchange, conversion, or domestication, and make amendments as appropriate to those laws.

As with Subsection (a), an adopting state may choose to amend its various laws with respect to the nondiversion of charitable property to cover the various transactions authorized by this act as an alternative to enacting Subsection (b).

COMMENT

Subsection (a)—Because at least some of the provisions of this act will be new in most states, it is likely that existing state laws that require regulatory approval of transactions by businesses such as banks, insurance companies, or public utilities may not be worded in a fashion that will include at least some of the transactions authorized by this act. The purpose of this subsection is to ensure that transactions under this act will be subject to the same regulatory approval as mergers. This subsection is based on whether a merger by a regulated entity requires prior approval because the transactions authorized by this act may be effectuated indirectly in many cases under existing law by establishing a wholly-owned subsidiary of the desired type and then merging into it.

The consequence of violating this subsection should be the same as in the case of a merger consummated without the required approval.

Subsection (b)—This act applies generally to nonprofit corporations and unincorporated nonprofit associations. As in the case of laws regulating particular industries, a state's laws governing the nondiversion of charitable property to other uses may not cover some of the transactions authorized by this act. To prevent the procedures in this act from being used to avoid restrictions on the use of charitable property held by nonprofit entities, this subsection requires approval of the effect of transactions under this act by the appropriate arm of government having supervision of nonprofit entities.

An approval or order obtained under this section may impose conditions or specify the disposition of assets or liabilities in a manner different than would otherwise be the case. In such an instance, the approval or order will control over the provisions of this act specifying the effects of a transaction. *See* Sections 1026 (effect of merger), 1036 (effect of interest exchange), 1046 (effect of conversion), 1056 (effect of domestication).

Subsection (c)—This subsection clarifies the legal effect of a merger on bequests, etc. that were originally made to an entity that does not survive the merger. This issue does not arise in an interest exchange, conversion, or domestication transaction because the entity to which the bequest, etc. was made survives in some form after the transaction.

§ 1004.   Nonexclusivity

The fact that a transaction under this [article] produces a certain result does not preclude the same result from being accomplished in any other manner permitted by law other than this [article].

COMMENT

This section allows a transaction that has the same end result as one of the transactions governed by this act, but that is accomplished in a manner not within the scope of this act, to be exempt from this act. For example, a sale of assets and transfer of liabilities by two entities to a third entity followed by the liquidation of the two transferring entities can be accomplished pursuant to statutory provisions pertaining to sale of assets rather than under Part 2 of this article, even though the end result of the transaction is essentially the same as if the two entities had merged into a third entity.

§ 1005. Reference to External Facts

A plan may refer to facts ascertainable outside the plan if the manner in which the facts will operate upon the plan is specified in the plan. The facts may include the occurrence of an event or a determination or action by a person, whether or not the event, determination, or action is within the control of a party to the transaction.

COMMENT

This section is based on, but more concise than, section 1.20(k) of the Model Business Corporation Act.

§ 1006. Appraisal Rights

An interest holder of a domestic merging, acquired, converting, or domesticating limited liability company is entitled to contractual appraisal rights in connection with a transaction under this [article] to the extent provided in:

(1)   the operating agreement; or

(2)   the plan.

COMMENT

In corporate law, appraisal rights developed when corporate statutes were amended to permit mergers with less than unanimous consent of the shareholders. This article provides no appraisal rights, because, as a default rule, transactions under this article require the consent or affirmative vote of all the members. Where the operating agreement changes this default rule, parties may wish to consider contractual appraisal rights.

This subsection validates the grant of such contractual appraisal rights. *Cf.* 6 DEL. CODE §§ 15–120 (general partnerships), 17–212 (limited partnerships), 18–210 (limited liability companies) (validating "contractual appraisal rights"); MBCA § 13.02(5) (permitting the articles of incorporation, bylaws, or a resolution of the board of directors to confer appraisal rights in contexts in which they would otherwise not be available). Legislative authorization in this subsection of the grant of contractual appraisal rights removes any question as to whether a court would have jurisdiction to hear a case in which the parties were attempting to create jurisdiction in the court by private agreement.

In this section, the term "appraisal rights" refers to any arrangement, either in the operating agreement or the plan, providing for the buy-out of members that object to a transaction under this article.

[§ 1007. Excluded Entities and Transactions

(a)   The following entities may not participate in a transaction under this [article]:

(1)

(2).

(b)   This [article] may not be used to effect a transaction that:

(1)

(2).]

Legislative Note: Subsection (a) may be used by states that have special statutes restricted to the organization of certain types of entities. A common example is banking statutes that prohibit banks from engaging in transactions other than pursuant to those statutes.

Nonprofit entities may participate in transactions under this act with for-profit entities, subject to compliance with Section 1003. If a state desires, however, to exclude entities with a charitable purpose or to exclude other types of entities from the scope of this article, that may be done by referring to those entities in Subsection (a).

Subsection (b) may be used to exclude certain types of transactions governed by more specific statutes. A common example is the conversion of an insurance company from mutual to stock form. There may be other types of transactions that vary greatly among the states.

[PART] 2

MERGER

§ 1021. Merger Authorized

(a) By complying with this [part]:

(1) one or more domestic limited liability companies may merge with one or more domestic or foreign entities into a domestic or foreign surviving entity; and

(2) two or more foreign entities may merge into a domestic limited liability company.

(b) By complying with the provisions of this [part] applicable to foreign entities, a foreign entity may be a party to a merger under this [part] or may be the surviving entity in such a merger if the merger is authorized by the law of the foreign entity's jurisdiction of formation.

COMMENT

The merger transaction authorized by this act involves the combination of one or more domestic limited liability companies with or into one or more other domestic or foreign entities. It also contemplates the consolidation of two or more foreign entities into a single domestic limited liability company. Upon the effective date of the merger, all the assets and liabilities of the constituent entities vest in the surviving entity as a matter of law. As such, mergers require the existence of at least two separate entities before the transaction and only one entity may survive the merger. If independent existence of the constituent entities is desired following the conclusion of the transaction, a restructuring transaction other than a merger must be used to accomplish the transfer of assets and liabilities.

This act authorizes a merger for state entity law purposes. Federal law and other state law will independently determine how a merger transaction will be taxed.

Subsection (a)(1)—This paragraph states the general rule that subject to Subsection (b) one or more domestic limited liability companies may merge with or into a domestic or foreign surviving entity.

Subsection (a)(2)—This paragraph provides that two or more foreign entities may merge into a domestic surviving limited liability company so long as the requirements of Subsection (b) are met.

Subsection (b)—This subsection provides that a foreign entity may be a party to a merger or may be the surviving entity in a merger only if the merger is authorized by the laws of the foreign entity's jurisdiction of formation.

§ 1022. Plan of Merger

(a) A domestic limited liability company may become a party to a merger under this [part] by approving a plan of merger. The plan must be in a record and contain:

(1) as to each merging entity, its name, jurisdiction of formation, and type of entity;

(2) if the surviving entity is to be created in the merger, a statement to that effect and the entity's name, jurisdiction of formation, and type of entity;

(3) the manner of converting the interests in each party to the merger into interests, securities, obligations, money, other property, rights to acquire interests or securities, or any combination of the foregoing;

(4) if the surviving entity exists before the merger, any proposed amendments to:

(A) its public organic record, if any; and

(B) its private organic rules that are, or are proposed to be, in a record;

(5) if the surviving entity is to be created in the merger:

(A) its proposed public organic record, if any; and

(B) the full text of its private organic rules that are proposed to be in a record;

(6) the other terms and conditions of the merger; and

(7)   any other provision required by the law of a merging entity's jurisdiction of formation or the organic rules of a merging entity.

(b)   In addition to the requirements of subsection (a), a plan of merger may contain any other provision not prohibited by law.

COMMENT

Subsection (a)—This subsection states the requirements for the plan of merger. They are similar to plan of merger provisions in corporation statutes. *See* MBCA § 11.02(c). The requirements stated in this subsection are mandatory. *See* Section 105(c)(14).

Subsection (a)(1)—This paragraph requires that the plan of merger identify the parties to the merger. The name of a merging entity as it appears in the plan of merger will be its name in its jurisdiction of formation.

Subsection (a)(3)—The language of this paragraph is similar to Model Business Corporation Act section 11.02(c)(3). What may be done under this paragraph with respect to providing for continuing interests in the surviving entity for some holders of interests of a class or series of a party to the merger while paying some other form of consideration to other holders of the same class or series of interests in that entity will vary depending on the type of entity involved and the extent to which its organic rules provide for non-uniform treatment of interest holders in a manner that is permissible under its organic law. Similarly, the ability to use a merger to reorganize the capital structure of the surviving entity will vary depending on the type of entity involved and whether the entity has appropriately adopted relevant provisions in its organic rules.

If the organic law and organic rules of an unincorporated entity permit a non-uniform "equity shuffle" to be accomplished in a merger involving the unincorporated entity, the minority owners of the unincorporated entity will not necessarily be entitled to the statutory appraisal rights currently afforded to minority stockholders in merging corporate entities. Any perceived unfairness in the shuffle would be addressed either: (i) under principles of fiduciary duties and the contractual obligations of good faith and fair dealing, assuming, of course, that such duties and obligations have not been contractually modified or eliminated to the extent permitted by the applicable organic law; or (ii) by the exercise of whatever rights the minority owners may have to veto the transaction or to withdraw or to dissociate and be paid the value of their interests.

The Model Business Corporation Act generally requires that shares of the same class or series be treated in the same manner in a merger unless the corporation has adopted an applicable provision of its articles of incorporation pursuant to section 6.01(e) of that act providing for variations in the treatment of holders of the same class or series of shares. Thus a determination of what may be done by way of an equity shuffle in the case of a corporation will require reference to its organic law and organic rules.

The consideration paid to the interest holders of the merging parties may be supplied in whole or part by a person who is not a party to the merger.

Subsection (b)—This subsection provides the statutory authority for a merging party to include a provision in a plan of merger that is not specifically listed in Subsection (a). One such possibility is contractual appraisal rights as provided in Section 1006(b).

§ 1023. Approval of Merger

(a)   A plan of merger is not effective unless it has been approved:

(1)   by a domestic merging limited liability company, by all the members of the company entitled to vote on or consent to any matter; and

(2)   in a record, by each member of a domestic merging limited liability company which will have interest holder liability for debts, obligations, and other liabilities that are incurred after the merger becomes effective, unless:

(A)   the operating agreement of the company provides in a record for the approval of a merger in which some or all of its members become subject to interest holder liability by the affirmative vote or consent of fewer than all the members; and

(B)   the member consented in a record to or voted for that provision of the operating agreement or became a member after the adoption of that provision.

(b)   A merger involving a domestic merging entity that is not a limited liability company is not effective unless the merger is approved by that entity in accordance with its organic law.

(c)   A merger involving a foreign merging entity is not effective unless the merger is approved by the foreign entity in accordance with the law of the foreign entity's jurisdiction of formation.

COMMENT

Subsection (a)—In the uniform acts pertaining to unincorporated business organizations, unanimity is the default rule for approving a merger. The operating agreement certainly can change this rule, but care should be taken in doing so. For example, a merger can revise the operating agreement. Section 1022(a)(4). Thus, if a merger requires less-than-unanimous consent, the operating agreement is subject to amendment by the same quantum of consent. "Exit rights" also require consideration. This act does not provide appraisal rights, because such rights are inapposite when unanimous consent is required. *See* the comment to Section 1006.

Subsection (a)(2)—This provision is not a default rule, Section 105(c)(14), and deals with the situation in which a member of an LLC that is a party to a merger will have vicarious liability for the liabilities of the surviving entity that are incurred after the merger becomes effective. The special approval requirement in Subsection (a)(2) will be applicable; for example, to members of an LLC that merges into a general partnership that is not a limited liability partnership if the members become general partners of the surviving general partnership.

The consent of a member required by Subsection (a)(2)(B) may be given either by: (i) signing or agreeing generally to the terms of an operating agreement that includes the required provision permitting less than unanimous approval of a merger in which members become subject to "interest holder liability"; or (ii) voting for or consenting to an amendment to the operating agreement to add such a provision.

Subsection (b)—Where a domestic entity other than a limited liability company is a party to a merger under this act, this subsection defers to that entity's organic law for the requirements for approval of the merger by that entity.

Subsection (c)—Where a foreign entity is a party to a merger under this act, this subsection defers to the laws of the foreign jurisdiction for the requirements for approval of the merger by the foreign entity. Those laws will include the organic law of the foreign entity and other applicable laws. The laws of the foreign jurisdiction will also control the application of any special approval requirements found in the organic rules of the foreign entity.

§ 1024.   Amendment or Abandonment of Plan of Merger

(a)   A plan of merger may be amended only with the consent of each party to the plan, except as otherwise provided in the plan.

(b)   A domestic merging limited liability company may approve an amendment of a plan of merger:

(1)   in the same manner as the plan was approved, if the plan does not provide for the manner in which it may be amended; or

(2)   by its managers or members in the manner provided in the plan, but a member that was entitled to vote on or consent to approval of the merger is entitled to vote on or consent to any amendment of the plan that will change:

(A)   the amount or kind of interests, securities, obligations, money, other property, rights to acquire interests or securities, or any combination of the foregoing, to be received by the interest holders of any party to the plan;

(B)   the public organic record, if any, or private organic rules of the surviving entity that will be in effect immediately after the merger becomes effective, except for changes that do not require approval of the interest holders of the surviving entity under its organic law or organic rules; or

(C)   any other terms or conditions of the plan, if the change would adversely affect the member in any material respect.

(c)   After a plan of merger has been approved and before a statement of merger becomes effective, the plan may be abandoned as provided in the plan. Unless prohibited by the plan, a domestic merging limited liability company may abandon the plan in the same manner as the plan was approved.

(d)   If a plan of merger is abandoned after a statement of merger has been delivered to the [Secretary of State] for filing and before the statement becomes effective, a statement of abandonment, signed by a party to the plan, must be delivered to the [Secretary of State] for filing before the statement of merger becomes effective. The statement of abandonment takes effect on filing, and the merger is abandoned and does not become effective. The statement of abandonment must contain:

(1)   the name of each party to the plan of merger;

(2)   the date on which the statement of merger was filed by the [Secretary of State]; and

(3)   a statement that the merger has been abandoned in accordance with this section.

COMMENT

This section sets out the requirements for amending or abandoning the plan of merger. They are similar to provisions for amending or abandoning mergers found in existing corporation merger statutes. *See* MBCA §§ 11.02(e), 11.08.

§ 1025.   Statement of Merger; Effective Date of Merger

(a)   A statement of merger must be signed by each merging entity and delivered to the [Secretary of State] for filing.

(b)   A statement of merger must contain:

(1)   the name, jurisdiction of formation, and type of entity of each merging entity that is not the surviving entity;

(2)   the name, jurisdiction of formation, and type of entity of the surviving entity;

(3)   a statement that the merger was approved by each domestic merging entity, if any, in accordance with this [part] and by each foreign merging entity, if any, in accordance with the law of its jurisdiction of formation;

(4)   if the surviving entity exists before the merger and is a domestic filing entity, any amendment to its public organic record approved as part of the plan of merger;

(5)   if the surviving entity is created by the merger and is a domestic filing entity, its public organic record, as an attachment; and

(6)   if the surviving entity is created by the merger and is a domestic limited liability partnership, its statement of qualification, as an attachment.

(c)   In addition to the requirements of subsection (b), a statement of merger may contain any other provision not prohibited by law.

(d)   If the surviving entity is a domestic entity, its public organic record, if any, must satisfy the requirements of the law of this state, except that the public organic record does not need to be signed.

(e)   A plan of merger that is signed by all the merging entities and meets all the requirements of subsection (b) may be delivered to the [Secretary of State] for filing instead of a statement of merger and on filing has the same effect. If a plan of merger is filed as provided in this subsection, references in this [article] to a statement of merger refer to the plan of merger filed under this subsection.

(f)   If the surviving entity is a domestic limited liability company, the merger becomes effective when the statement of merger is effective. In all other cases, the merger becomes effective on the later of:

(1)   the date and time provided by the organic law of the surviving entity; and

(2)   when the statement is effective.

COMMENT

The filing of a statement of merger makes the transaction a matter of public record.

Subsection (a)—This subsection pertains to all merging entities involved in a merger, not merely any merging domestic limited liability company. Other filings may be required by the organic law of other entities participating in the merger.

Subsection (b)(1) and (2)—The names of foreign entities set forth in the statement of merger will generally be their names in their jurisdiction of formation, except that if a foreign entity has been required to adopt a different name in order to register to do business in this state, the foreign qualification statute will likely require that, when the entity does business in this state, the entity must use the name adopted for the purposes of registering to do business. Engaging in a merger under this act will be part of the business done by the entity in this state and the name of the entity set forth in the statement of merger will thus need to be the name under which the entity has registered to do business. Use of the name under which the entity has registered to do business will allow the records in the filing office to associate the registration of the entity to do business with the statement of merger.

Subsection (b)(3)—*See* the comment to Subsection (f).

Subsection (b)(4)—The statement in this paragraph that the plan of merger was approved by each entity in accordance with this article necessarily presupposes that the plan was approved in accordance with any valid, special requirements in the organic rules of each merging entity.

Subsection (b)(5) and (6)—The public organic record of a domestic surviving entity created by the merger that is attached to the statement of merger becomes the original, officially filed text of the public organic record of the surviving entity when the statement of merger takes effect. It is not necessary, or appropriate, to make any other filing to create the surviving entity.

Similarly, a statement of qualification for a domestic limited liability partnership created by the merger that is attached to the statement of merger does not need to be filed separately.

Subsection (d)—Organic laws typically require that an initial filing that creates an entity be signed by the person serving as the incorporator or other organizer. This subsection, however, provides that the public organic record of the surviving entity does not need to be signed since the record is attached to a signed record.

This subsection also permits the public organic record of the surviving entity to omit any provision that is not required to be included in a restatement of the public organic record. Pursuant to this provision, for example, the public organic record of a business corporation created as the surviving entity in the merger would not need to state the name and address of each incorporator even though that information would be required by the Model Business Corporation Act section 2.02(a)(4) if the corporation were being incorporated outside the context of the merger.

Subsection (e)—A plan of merger that contains all the information required in the statement of merger may be filed instead of the statement of merger. The plan must be in a record and signed by each merging party.

Subsection (f)—A merger in which the surviving entity is a domestic limited liability company takes effect when the statement of merger takes effect. A merger in which the surviving entity is a foreign entity will usually also take effect when the statement of merger takes effect because the practice is to coordinate the filings that need to be made when a merger involves both a domestic entity and also a foreign entity so that the filings in each jurisdiction take effect at the same time.

However, when the surviving limited liability company is a foreign limited liability company, it is possible that the filing in the foreign jurisdiction will take effect at a different time. For that reason, this subsection provides that the merger will take effect at the later of: (i) when the statement of merger takes effect; and (ii) when the merger takes effect under the law of the foreign jurisdiction. This rule avoids the possibility that the merger will take effect in this state before it takes effect in the foreign jurisdiction, which would produce the undesirable result that the merging domestic limited liability company would cease to appear as an active entity on the records of this state before the records of the foreign jurisdiction reflect a completed merger.

It is only necessary for the filing office to record the effective date of the statement of merger and the filing office does not need to be concerned with the effective date of the merger itself. Persons wishing to determine the effective date of a merger involving both a domestic and a foreign entity will be able to do so by consulting the records of the filing offices in each jurisdiction.

§ 1026. Effect of Merger

(a) When a merger becomes effective:

(1) the surviving entity continues or comes into existence;

(2) each merging entity that is not the surviving entity ceases to exist;

(3) all property of each merging entity vests in the surviving entity without transfer, reversion, or impairment;

(4) all debts, obligations, and other liabilities of each merging entity are debts, obligations, and other liabilities of the surviving entity;

(5) except as otherwise provided by law or the plan of merger, all the rights, privileges, immunities, powers, and purposes of each merging entity vest in the surviving entity;

(6) if the surviving entity exists before the merger:

(A) all its property continues to be vested in it without transfer, reversion, or impairment;

(B) it remains subject to all its debts, obligations, and other liabilities; and

(C) all its rights, privileges, immunities, powers, and purposes continue to be vested in it;

(7) the name of the surviving entity may be substituted for the name of any merging entity that is a party to any pending action or proceeding;

(8) if the surviving entity exists before the merger:

(A) its public organic record, if any, is amended to the extent provided in the statement of merger; and

(B) its private organic rules that are to be in a record, if any, are amended to the extent provided in the plan of merger;

(9) if the surviving entity is created by the merger, its private organic rules are effective and:

(A) if it is a filing entity, its public organic record becomes effective; and

(B) if it is a limited liability partnership, its statement of qualification becomes effective; and

(10) the interests in each merging entity which are to be converted in the merger are converted, and the interest holders of those interests are entitled only to the rights provided to them under the plan of merger and to any appraisal rights they have under Section 1006 and the merging entity's organic law.

(b) Except as otherwise provided in the organic law or organic rules of a merging entity, the merger does not give rise to any rights that an interest holder, governor, or third party would have upon a dissolution, liquidation, or winding up of the merging entity.

(c) When a merger becomes effective, a person that did not have interest holder liability with respect to any of the merging entities and becomes subject to interest holder liability with respect to a domestic entity as a result of the merger has interest holder liability only to the extent provided by the organic law of that entity and only for those debts, obligations, and other liabilities that are incurred after the merger becomes effective.

(d) When a merger becomes effective, the interest holder liability of a person that ceases to hold an interest in a domestic merging limited liability company with respect to which the person had interest holder liability is subject to the following rules:

(1) The merger does not discharge any interest holder liability under this [act] to the extent the interest holder liability was incurred before the merger became effective.

(2) The person does not have interest holder liability under this [act] for any debt, obligation, or other liability that is incurred after the merger becomes effective.

(3) This [act] continues to apply to the release, collection, or discharge of any interest holder liability preserved under paragraph (1) as if the merger had not occurred.

(4) The person has whatever rights of contribution from any other person as are provided by this [act], law other than this [act], or the operating agreement of the domestic merging limited liability company with respect to any interest holder liability preserved under paragraph (1) as if the merger had not occurred.

(e) When a merger becomes effective, a foreign entity that is the surviving entity may be served with process in this state for the collection and enforcement of any debts, obligations, or other liabilities of a domestic merging limited liability company as provided in Section 119.

(f) When a merger becomes effective, the registration to do business in this state of any foreign merging entity that is not the surviving entity is canceled.

COMMENT

With the exception of Subsections (c) and (d), this section is similar to statutory provisions on the effect of a merger of a corporation with a corporation. *See* MBCA § 11.07.

Subsection (a)—This subsection states the general understanding that in a merger the assets and liabilities of the merging entities automatically vest in the surviving entity. The surviving entity becomes the owner of all real and personal property of the merged entities and is subject to all debts, obligations, and liabilities of the merging entities. A merger does not constitute a transfer, assignment, or conveyance of any property held by the merging entities before the merger. A merger also does not give rise to a claim that a contract with a merging entity is no longer in effect on the ground of nonassignability, unless the contract specifically provides that it does not survive a merger. The contract rights that are vested in the surviving entity include the right to enforce subscription agreements for interests and obligations to make capital contributions entered into or incurred before the merger. *See* Section 1003(c) (dealing with the surviving entity's rights in trust obligations of a nonsurviving party in a merger and transactions such as bequests made to a nonsurviving party to a merger that take effect after the merger).

After a merger becomes effective, the law of the surviving entity's jurisdiction of formation governs the surviving entity.

Sections 1003(a) and (b), modify the provisions of this section with respect to the effects of a merger to the extent a regulatory law provides otherwise or any of the parties holds property committed to charitable purposes.

Subsection (a)(2)—A merger cannot have the effect of making an interest holder of a domestic merging entity subject to interest holder liability for the debts, obligations, or other liabilities of any other person or entity unless the interest holder has signed a separate written consent to become subject to such liability or previously agreed to the effectuation of a transaction having that effect without the interest holder's consent. The operating agreement cannot change this provision. Section 105(c)(14).

Subsection (a)(7)—All pending proceedings involving either the survivor or a party whose separate existence ceased as a result of the merger are continued. Under this paragraph, the name of the survivor may be, but need not be, substituted in any pending proceeding for the name of a party to the merger whose separate existence ceased as a result of the merger. The substitution may be made whether the survivor is a complainant or a respondent, and may be made at the instance of either the survivor or an opposing party. Such a substitution has no substantive effect because, whether or not the survivor's name is substituted, the survivor succeeds to the claims, and is subject to the liabilities, of any party to the merger whose separate existence ceased as a result of the merger.

Subsection (a)(8)(B)—The private organic rules of an unincorporated entity typically may be either oral or written. The plan of merger is not required to set forth amendments to oral provisions of the private organic rules of the surviving entity, and thus this provision is limited in scope to amendments to the private organic rules that are to be in a record, if any.

Subsection (a)(10)—*See* the comments to Section 1006.

Subsections (c) and (d)—These subsections set forth rules for two circumstances that typically do not exist in a merger where all the entities involved are corporations. Subsection (c) deals with the situation where an interest holder that does not have vicarious liability for the obligations of a merging entity before the merger has interest holder liability after the merger. An example would be a corporate shareholder who agrees to be the general partner in a limited partnership that is the surviving entity in a merger between a corporation and a limited partnership that is not a limited liability limited partnership. Subsection (d) deals with the situation where an interest holder has vicarious liability for the obligations of one of the merging parties before the merger but ceases to have any interest holder liability for the obligations of the surviving entity after the merger becomes effective. An example would be a general partner in a general partnership that merges into a corporation.

The effects of Subsections (c) and (d) will depend on when a liability is incurred, which is determined by other law. For a discussion of the issue in a related context, see UPA (1997) (Last Amended 2013) § 306(c), cmt. (The Temporal Nexus—When Claim Incurred).

These subsections apply not only to merging domestic limited liability companies but also to any other domestic entity involved in the merger.

Subsection (c)—This subsection sets forth the general rule that an interest holder that was not liable for the liabilities of a merging entity before the merger but will have personal liability for the obligations of the surviving entity after the merger will be personally liable only for the liabilities of a domestic surviving entity that are incurred after the effective date of a merger. When a liability is incurred will be determined by other applicable law.

Subsection (d)—This subsection provides four rules with respect to an interest holder who ceases to have interest holder liability after the effective date of the merger:

(1)   the interest holder remains personally liable for any obligations that were incurred before the effective date of the merger;

(2)   the interest holder does not have any personal liability for obligations of the surviving entity;

(3)   the pre-existing personal liability of the interest holder is enforced against the interest holder on the same basis as if the merger had not taken place; and

(4)   the interest holder has the same rights of contribution from other interest holders of the merging entity as the interest holder would have had if the merger had not occurred.

See the comment to Section 1046(d).

Subsection (e)—When a merger becomes effective, this subsection provides that a foreign entity that is the surviving entity may be served with process in this state. The proceedings covered by this subsection include a proceeding to enforce the rights of any interest holders of each domestic merging entity who are entitled to and exercise appraisal rights. One of the liabilities that a foreign surviving entity succeeds to is the obligation of a merging entity to pay the amount, if any, to which its interest holders who assert appraisal rights are entitled.

[PART] 3

INTEREST EXCHANGE

§ 1031.   Interest Exchange Authorized

(a)   By complying with this [part]:

(1)   a domestic limited liability company may acquire all of one or more classes or series of interests of another domestic entity or a foreign entity in exchange for interests, securities, obligations, money, other property, rights to acquire interests or securities, or any combination of the foregoing; or

(2)   all of one or more classes or series of interests of a domestic limited liability company may be acquired by another domestic entity or a foreign entity in exchange for interests, securities, obligations, money, other property, rights to acquire interests or securities, or any combination of the foregoing.

(b)   By complying with the provisions of this [part] applicable to foreign entities, a foreign entity may be the acquiring or acquired entity in an interest exchange under this [part] if the interest exchange is authorized by the law of the foreign entity's jurisdiction of formation.

(c)   If a protected agreement contains a provision that applies to a merger of a domestic limited liability company but does not refer to an interest exchange, the provision applies to an interest exchange in which the domestic limited liability company is the acquired entity as if the interest exchange were a merger until the provision is amended after [the effective date of this [act]].

COMMENT

An interest exchange is the same type of transaction as the share exchange provided for in section 11.03 of the Model Business Corporation Act. The effect of an interest exchange is that: (i) the separate existence of the acquired entity is not affected; and (ii) the acquiring entity acquires all of the interests of one or more classes of the acquired entity. An interest exchange also allows an indirect acquisition through the use of consideration in the exchange that is not provided by the acquiring entity (*e.g.*, consideration from another or related entity).

Neither share exchanges nor interest exchanges are universally recognized in either corporation or unincorporated entity laws. The effect of an interest exchange can be achieved through a triangular merger in which the acquiring entity forms a new subsidiary and the acquired entity is then merged into the new subsidiary. Part 3 allows the interest exchange to be accomplished directly in a single step, rather than indirectly through the triangular merger route.

The "series" referenced in Subsection (a) are not the series contemplated by the Uniform Statutory Entity Trust Act §§ 401–05 and some LLC statutes. *See, e.g.*, DEL. CODE ANN. tit. 6, § 18–215 (2012); 805 ILL. COMP. STAT. 180/37–40 (2012). Instead, in this context "series" refers to a subset of a class, which is a meaning commonly found in corporation law. *See, e.g.*, MBCA § 6.02. Specific provisions authorizing classes and series are less common in unincorporated entity law but do exist. *See, e.g.*, MINN. STAT. § 322B.155 (2012). In any event, an operating agreement certainly has the power to create classes and series as contemplated by this section.

Subsection (a)—For this section to apply, a domestic limited liability company must be either the acquiring or acquired entity.

The acquiring entity is not required to acquire all of the interests in the acquired entity. For example, assume that an LLC with three classes of membership interests enters into an interest exchange with an acquiring entity. The acquiring entity need only acquire all of the ownership interests of one or more classes of the LLC membership interests.

Subsection (b)—This subsection allows a foreign entity to effectuate an interest exchange with a domestic limited liability company if the interest exchange is authorized by the organic law of the foreign entity.

Subsection (c)—This subsection deals with rights of parties to protected agreements (defined in Section 1001(30)) when an interest exchange takes place. Because the concept of an interest exchange is relatively new, a person contracting with a domestic limited liability company or loaning it money who drafted and negotiated special rights relating to the transaction before the enactment of this article should not be charged with the consequences of not having dealt with the concept of an interest exchange in the context of those special rights. Similarly, when the governance structure of an entity has been negotiated before the enactment of this act, the concept of an interest exchange may not have been reflected in any special governance arrangements; for example, special approval rights may have been provided for fundamental transactions, but those rights fail to include language that would make them applicable to an interest exchange.

Accordingly, this subsection provides a transitional rule that is intended to protect such special rights. If, for example, a limited liability company is a party to a contract that provides that the company cannot participate in a merger without the consent of the other party to the contract, the requirement to obtain the consent of the other party will also apply to an interest exchange in which the entity is the acquired entity. If the limited liability company fails to obtain the consent, the result will be that the other party will have the same rights it would have had if the entity were to participate in a merger without the required consent.

The transitional rule in this subsection ceases to make sense at such time as the provisions of the agreement giving rise to the special rights are first amended after the effective date of this article because at that time the provision may be amended to address expressly an interest exchange. The transitional rule will continue to apply, however, if a provision other than the specific provisions giving rise to the special rights is amended.

§ 1032. Plan of Interest Exchange

(a)   A domestic limited liability company may be the acquired entity in an interest exchange under this [part] by approving a plan of interest exchange. The plan must be in a record and contain:

  (1)   the name of the acquired entity;

  (2)   the name, jurisdiction of formation, and type of entity of the acquiring entity;

(3)   the manner of converting the interests in the acquired entity into interests, securities, obligations, money, other property, rights to acquire interests or securities, or any combination of the foregoing;

(4)   any proposed amendments to:

(A)   the certificate of organization of the acquired entity; and

(B)   the operating agreement of the acquired entity that are, or are proposed to be, in a record;

(5)   the other terms and conditions of the interest exchange; and

(6)   any other provision required by the law of this state or the operating agreement of the acquired entity.

(b)   In addition to the requirements of subsection (a), a plan of interest exchange may contain any other provision not prohibited by law.

COMMENT

This section sets forth the requirements for the plan of interest exchange, which must be approved by the acquired entity in accordance with Section 1031. The content of the plan of interest exchange is similar to the content of a plan of merger. *See* Section 1022.

The plan of interest exchange may, but need not, be filed instead of the statement of interest exchange, Section 1035, so long as the plan contains all the information required to be in the statement and is delivered to the filing office for filing after the plan has been adopted and approved. *See* Section 1035(d).

Subsection (a)—The requirements stated in this subsection are mandatory. *See* Section 105(c)(14).

Subsection (a)(3)—Under this paragraph, interest holders in the acquired entity may receive interests or securities of the acquiring entity or of a party other than the acquiring entity, obligations, rights to acquire interests or securities, cash, or other property. *See* the comment to Section 1022(a)(3).

Subsection (b)—This subsection authorizes the plan to contain any other provision the parties wish to include, unless the provision is prohibited by law.

§ 1033.   Approval of Interest Exchange

(a)   A plan of interest exchange is not effective unless it has been approved:

(1)   by all the members of a domestic acquired limited liability company entitled to vote on or consent to any matter; and

(2)   in a record, by each member of the domestic acquired limited liability company that will have interest holder liability for debts, obligations, and other liabilities that are incurred after the interest exchange becomes effective, unless:

(A)   the operating agreement of the company provides in a record for the approval of an interest exchange or a merger in which some or all of its members become subject to interest holder liability by the affirmative vote or consent of fewer than all the members; and

(B)   the member consented in a record to or voted for that provision of the operating agreement or became a member after the adoption of that provision.

(b)   An interest exchange involving a domestic acquired entity that is not a limited liability company is not effective unless it is approved by the domestic entity in accordance with its organic law.

(c)   An interest exchange involving a foreign acquired entity is not effective unless it is approved by the foreign entity in accordance with the law of the foreign entity's jurisdiction of formation.

(d)   Except as otherwise provided in its organic law or organic rules, the interest holders of the acquiring entity are not required to approve the interest exchange.

This section sets forth the required approval of an interest exchange. An interest exchange transaction governed by this article only requires approval by the acquired entity, unless the applicable organic law or the organic rules of the acquiring entity otherwise provide, Subsection (d), a condition that rarely exists.

Subsection (a)(2)—For an explanation of this interest holder liability provision, see Section 1023(a)(2), comment.

§ 1034. Amendment or Abandonment of Plan of Interest Exchange

(a)   A plan of interest exchange may be amended only with the consent of each party to the plan, except as otherwise provided in the plan.

(b)   A domestic acquired limited liability company may approve an amendment of a plan of interest exchange:

(1)   in the same manner as the plan was approved, if the plan does not provide for the manner in which it may be amended; or

(2)   by its managers or members in the manner provided in the plan, but a member that was entitled to vote on or consent to approval of the interest exchange is entitled to vote on or consent to any amendment of the plan that will change:

(A)   the amount or kind of interests, securities, obligations, money, other property, rights to acquire interests or securities, or any combination of the foregoing, to be received by any of the members of the acquired company under the plan;

(B)   the certificate of organization or operating agreement of the acquired company that will be in effect immediately after the interest exchange becomes effective, except for changes that do not require approval of the members of the acquired company under this [act] or the operating agreement; or

(C)   any other terms or conditions of the plan, if the change would adversely affect the member in any material respect.

(c)   After a plan of interest exchange has been approved and before a statement of interest exchange becomes effective, the plan may be abandoned as provided in the plan. Unless prohibited by the plan, a domestic acquired limited liability company may abandon the plan in the same manner as the plan was approved.

(d)   If a plan of interest exchange is abandoned after a statement of interest exchange has been delivered to the [Secretary of State] for filing and before the statement becomes effective, a statement of abandonment, signed by the acquired limited liability company, must be delivered to the [Secretary of State] for filing before the statement of interest exchange becomes effective. The statement of abandonment takes effect on filing, and the interest exchange is abandoned and does not become effective. The statement of abandonment must contain:

(1)   the name of the acquired company;

(2)   the date on which the statement of interest exchange was filed by the [Secretary of State]; and

(3)   a statement that the interest exchange has been abandoned in accordance with this section.

This section parallels provisions in Parts 2 (mergers), 4 (conversions), and 5 (domestications). *See* Sections 1024 (mergers), 1044 (conversions), 1054 (domestications).

§ 1035. Statement of Interest Exchange; Effective Date of Interest Exchange

(a)   A statement of interest exchange must be signed by a domestic acquired limited liability company and delivered to the [Secretary of State] for filing.

(b)　A statement of interest exchange must contain:

(1)　the name of the acquired limited liability company;

(2)　the name, jurisdiction of formation, and type of entity of the acquiring entity;

(3)　a statement that the plan of interest exchange was approved by the acquired company in accordance with this [part]; and

(4)　any amendments to the acquired company's certificate of organization approved as part of the plan of interest exchange.

(c)　In addition to the requirements of subsection (b), a statement of interest exchange may contain any other provision not prohibited by law.

(d)　A plan of interest exchange that is signed by a domestic acquired limited liability company and meets all the requirements of subsection (b) may be delivered to the [Secretary of State] for filing instead of a statement of interest exchange and on filing has the same effect. If a plan of interest exchange is filed as provided in this subsection, references in this [article] to a statement of interest exchange refer to the plan of interest exchange filed under this subsection.

(e)　An interest exchange becomes effective when the statement of interest exchange is effective.

COMMENT

This section applies only when the acquired entity is a domestic limited liability company. The filing makes the transaction a matter of public record.

This act has no filing requirement when the only domestic limited liability company involved is the acquiring entity.

Subsection (b)—This subsection states the requirements for a statement of interest exchange, which are essentially the same as the requirements for a statement of merger under Section 1025(b).

Subsection (d)—A plan of interest exchange can be used as a substitute for the statement of interest exchange so long as the plan satisfies the requirements in Subsection (b).

Subsection (e)—This subsection applies when the acquiring entity is a domestic limited liability company, and Section 207 determines when a record delivered for filing under this act becomes effective. A statement of interest exchange may specify a delayed effective time and date, subject to the ninety-day limit stated in Section 207(3) and (4).

If the acquiring entity is not a domestic limited liability company, the effectiveness of the interest exchange will occur when provided by the law of the jurisdiction of formation of the acquiring entity.

§ 1036.　Effect of Interest Exchange

(a)　When an interest exchange in which the acquired entity is a domestic limited liability company becomes effective:

(1)　the interests in the acquired company which are the subject of the interest exchange are converted, and the members holding those interests are entitled only to the rights provided to them under the plan of interest exchange and to any appraisal rights they have under Section 1006;

(2)　the acquiring entity becomes the interest holder of the interests in the acquired company stated in the plan of interest exchange to be acquired by the acquiring entity;

(3)　the certificate of organization of the acquired company is amended to the extent provided in the statement of interest exchange; and

(4)　the provisions of the operating agreement of the acquired company that are to be in a record, if any, are amended to the extent provided in the plan of interest exchange.

(b)　Except as otherwise provided in the operating agreement of a domestic acquired limited liability company, the interest exchange does not give rise to any rights that a member, manager, or third party would have upon a dissolution, liquidation, or winding up of the acquired company.

(c)   When an interest exchange becomes effective, a person that did not have interest holder liability with respect to a domestic acquired limited liability company and becomes subject to interest holder liability with respect to a domestic entity as a result of the interest exchange has interest holder liability only to the extent provided by the organic law of the entity and only for those debts, obligations, and other liabilities that are incurred after the interest exchange becomes effective.

(d)   When an interest exchange becomes effective, the interest holder liability of a person that ceases to hold an interest in a domestic acquired limited liability company with respect to which the person had interest holder liability is subject to the following rules:

(1)   The interest exchange does not discharge any interest holder liability under this [act] to the extent the interest holder liability was incurred before the interest exchange became effective.

(2)   The person does not have interest holder liability under this [act] for any debt, obligation, or other liability that is incurred after the interest exchange becomes effective.

(3)   This [act] continues to apply to the release, collection, or discharge of any interest holder liability preserved under paragraph (1) as if the interest exchange had not occurred.

(4)   The person has whatever rights of contribution from any other person as are provided by this [act], law other than this [act], or the operating agreement of the acquired company with respect to any interest holder liability preserved under paragraph (1) as if the interest exchange had not occurred.

COMMENT

This section applies only when the *acquired* entity is a domestic limited liability company, and this part states no rule for the effect of an interest exchange when the only domestic limited liability company involved is the *acquiring* entity. For that situation, the other provisions of this act must be consulted, because this act is the organic law of the acquiring entity.

Subsection (a)—In contrast to a merger, an interest exchange does not in and of itself affect the separate existence of the parties, vest in the acquiring entity the assets of the acquired entity, or render the acquiring entity liable for the liabilities of the acquired entity. Thus, Subsection (a) is significantly simpler than Section 1026(a) with respect to the effects of a merger.

When an interest exchange becomes effective: (i) the interests of the acquired domestic limited liability company are exchanged, converted, or canceled as provided in the plan; (ii) the only rights of the former members and transferees of the acquired LLC whose interests are affected by the interest exchange are those rights related to the exchange, conversion, or cancellation; (iii) the acquiring entity becomes the owner of the acquired LLC's interests as provided in the plan; (iv) the certificate of organization of the acquired LLC is amended as provided in the statement of interest exchange, thus obviating the need for repetitive filings (*i.e.*, a filing as to the entity interest exchange and another filing to reflect amendments to certificate); and (v) the provisions of the operating agreement of the acquired LLC that are to be in a record, if any, are amended to the extent provided in the plan of interest exchange.

Subsection (c)—This subsection provides the rule for future interest holder liability pertaining to domestic entities and parallels analogous provisions in Parts 2 (mergers), 4 (conversions), and 5 (domestications). *See* the comment to Section 1026.

Subsection (d)—This subsection provides the rule for past interest holder liability and parallels analogous provisions in Parts 2 (mergers), 4 (conversions), and 5 (domestications). *See* the comments to Sections 1026(d) and 1046(d).

[PART] 4

CONVERSION

§ 1041.   Conversion Authorized

(a)   By complying with this [part], a domestic limited liability company may become:

(1)   a domestic entity that is a different type of entity; or

(2)   a foreign entity that is a different type of entity, if the conversion is authorized by the law of the foreign entity's jurisdiction of formation.

(b)   By complying with the provisions of this [part] applicable to foreign entities, a foreign entity that is not a foreign limited liability company may become a domestic limited liability company if the conversion is authorized by the law of the foreign entity's jurisdiction of formation.

(c)   If a protected agreement contains a provision that applies to a merger of a domestic limited liability company but does not refer to a conversion, the provision applies to a conversion of the company as if the conversion were a merger until the provision is amended after [the effective date of this [act]].

COMMENT

This part of Article 10 permits an entity to change to a different type of entity in its jurisdiction of formation or in a foreign jurisdiction. A transaction in which an entity changes its jurisdiction of organization but does not change its type is a domestication and is the subject of Part 5.

Subsection (a)(2)—For this provision to apply, this type of conversion must be authorized by the law of the foreign jurisdiction. If this is not the case, it may be possible to achieve the same result by forming an entity of the type desired in the foreign jurisdiction and then merging the domestic entity into the new foreign entity under Part 2 of Article 10.

Subsection (b)—This subsection allows a foreign entity to effectuate a conversion into a domestic limited liability company, but only if the conversion is permitted by the laws of the foreign entity's jurisdiction of formation. When a foreign entity becomes a domestic limited liability company pursuant to this part of Article 10, the effect of the conversion will be as provided in Section 1046. The procedures by which the conversion is approved, however, will be determined by the laws of the foreign entity's jurisdiction of formation. *See* Section 102(7) (defining "jurisdiction of formation").

Subsection (c)—*See* the comment to Section 1031(c).

§ 1042.   Plan of Conversion

(a)   A domestic limited liability company may convert to a different type of entity under this [part] by approving a plan of conversion. The plan must be in a record and contain:

(1)   the name of the converting limited liability company;

(2)   the name, jurisdiction of formation, and type of entity of the converted entity;

(3)   the manner of converting the interests in the converting limited liability company into interests, securities, obligations, money, other property, rights to acquire interests or securities, or any combination of the foregoing;

(4)   the proposed public organic record of the converted entity if it will be a filing entity;

(5)   the full text of the private organic rules of the converted entity which are proposed to be in a record;

(6)   the other terms and conditions of the conversion; and

(7)   any other provision required by the law of this state or the operating agreement of the converting limited liability company.

(b)   In addition to the requirements of subsection (a), a plan of conversion may contain any other provision not prohibited by law.

COMMENT

This section sets forth the requirements for the plan of conversion, which must be approved by the converting entity in accordance with Section 1043. The content of a plan of conversion is similar to the content of a plan of merger. *See* Section 1022.

Subsection (a)—The requirements stated in this subsection are mandatory. *See* Section 105(c)(14).

Subsection (a)(3)—Interest holders in the converting entity may receive interests or other securities of the converted entity or of any other person, obligations, rights to acquire interests or other securities, cash, or other property. *See* Sections 1022(a)(3) (mergers), 1032(a)(3) (interest exchanges), 1052(a)(3) (domestications).

Subsection (b)—This subsection authorizes the plan to contain any other provision the parties wish to include, unless the provision is prohibited by law.

§ 1043.   Approval of Conversion

(a)   A plan of conversion is not effective unless it has been approved:

(1)   by a domestic converting limited liability company, by all the members of the limited liability company entitled to vote on or consent to any matter; and

(2)   in a record, by each member of a domestic converting limited liability company which will have interest holder liability for debts, obligations, and other liabilities that are incurred after the conversion becomes effective, unless:

(A)   the operating agreement of the company provides in a record for the approval of a conversion or a merger in which some or all of its members become subject to interest holder liability by the affirmative vote or consent of fewer than all the members; and

(B)   the member voted for or consented in a record to that provision of the operating agreement or became a member after the adoption of that provision.

(b)   A conversion involving a domestic converting entity that is not a limited liability company is not effective unless it is approved by the domestic converting entity in accordance with its organic law.

(c)   A conversion of a foreign converting entity is not effective unless it is approved by the foreign entity in accordance with the law of the foreign entity's jurisdiction of formation.

COMMENT

Subsection (a)(1)—This provision is a default rule, subject to change in the operating agreement.

Subsection (a)(2)—This provision is not a default rule. Section 105(c)(14). For an explanation of this interest holder liability provision, see Section 1023(a)(2), comment.

§ 1044.   Amendment or Abandonment of Plan of Conversion

(a)   A plan of conversion of a domestic converting limited liability company may be amended:

(1)   in the same manner as the plan was approved, if the plan does not provide for the manner in which it may be amended; or

(2)   by its managers or members in the manner provided in the plan, but a member that was entitled to vote on or consent to approval of the conversion is entitled to vote on or consent to any amendment of the plan that will change:

(A)   the amount or kind of interests, securities, obligations, money, other property, rights to acquire interests or securities, or any combination of the foregoing, to be received by any of the members of the converting company under the plan;

(B)   the public organic record, if any, or private organic rules of the converted entity which will be in effect immediately after the conversion becomes effective, except for changes that do not require approval of the interest holders of the converted entity under its organic law or organic rules; or

(C)   any other terms or conditions of the plan, if the change would adversely affect the member in any material respect.

(b)   After a plan of conversion has been approved by a domestic converting limited liability company and before a statement of conversion becomes effective, the plan may be abandoned as provided in the plan. Unless prohibited by the plan, a domestic converting limited liability company may abandon the plan in the same manner as the plan was approved.

(c)   If a plan of conversion is abandoned after a statement of conversion has been delivered to the [Secretary of State] for filing and before the statement becomes effective, a statement of abandonment, signed by the converting entity, must be delivered to the [Secretary of State] for filing before the statement of conversion becomes effective. The statement of abandonment takes effect on filing, and the conversion is abandoned and does not become effective. The statement of abandonment must contain:

(1)   the name of the converting limited liability company;

(2)   the date on which the statement of conversion was filed by the [Secretary of State]; and

(3)   a statement that the conversion has been abandoned in accordance with this section.

COMMENT

This section parallels analogous provisions in Parts 2 (mergers), 3 (interest exchanges), and 5 (domestications). *See* Sections 1024 (mergers), 1034 (interest exchanges), 1054 (domestications).

§ 1045.   Statement of Conversion; Effective Date of Conversion

(a)   A statement of conversion must be signed by the converting entity and delivered to the [Secretary of State] for filing.

(b)   A statement of conversion must contain:

(1)   the name, jurisdiction of formation, and type of entity of the converting entity;

(2)   the name, jurisdiction of formation, and type of entity of the converted entity;

(3)   if the converting entity is a domestic limited liability company, a statement that the plan of conversion was approved in accordance with this [part] or, if the converting entity is a foreign entity, a statement that the conversion was approved by the foreign entity in accordance with the law of its jurisdiction of formation;

(4)   if the converted entity is a domestic filing entity, its public organic record, as an attachment; and

(5)   if the converted entity is a domestic limited liability partnership, its statement of qualification, as an attachment.

(c)   In addition to the requirements of subsection (b), a statement of conversion may contain any other provision not prohibited by law.

(d)   If the converted entity is a domestic entity, its public organic record, if any, must satisfy the requirements of the law of this state, except that the public organic record does not need to be signed.

(e)   A plan of conversion that is signed by a domestic converting limited liability company and meets all the requirements of subsection (b) may be delivered to the [Secretary of State] for filing instead of a statement of conversion and on filing has the same effect. If a plan of conversion is filed as provided in this subsection, references in this [article] to a statement of conversion refer to the plan of conversion filed under this subsection.

(f)   If the converted entity is a domestic limited liability company, the conversion becomes effective when the statement of conversion is effective. In all other cases, the conversion becomes effective on the later of:

(1)   the date and time provided by the organic law of the converted entity; and

(2)   when the statement is effective.

COMMENT

This section applies regardless of whether a domestic limited liability company is the converting or converted entity. A foreign entity seeking to convert to a domestic LLC must therefore comply with this section.

If either the converting or converted entity is a foreign entity, the organic law of the foreign entity's jurisdiction must also be consulted.

The filing of a statement of conversion makes the transaction a matter of public record.

Subsection (b)—This subsection sets forth the requirements for a statement of conversion. They are essentially the same as the requirements for a statement of merger in Section 1025.

Subsection (e)—A plan of conversion can be used as a substitute for the statement of conversion so long as the plan satisfies the requirements in Subsection (b).

Subsection (f)—Section 207 determines when a record delivered for filing under this act becomes effective. A statement of conversion may specify a delayed effective time and date, subject to the ninety-day limit stated in Section 207(3) and (4).

When the statement of conversion becomes effective under this subsection, the conversion transaction occurs if the converted entity is a domestic limited liability company. A conversion in which the converted entity is a foreign entity will usually also take effect when the statement of conversion takes effect because the best practice will be to coordinate the filings that need to be made when a conversion involves both a domestic entity and also a foreign entity so that the filings in each jurisdiction take effect at the same time.

However, when the converting limited liability company is a foreign limited liability company, it is possible that the filing in the foreign jurisdiction will take effect at a different time. For that reason, this subsection provides that the conversion will take effect at the later of: (i) when the statement of conversion takes effect; and (ii) when the conversion takes effect under the law of the foreign jurisdiction. This rule avoids the possibility that the conversion will take effect in this state before it takes effect in the foreign jurisdiction, which would produce the undesirable result that the converting domestic limited liability company would cease to appear as an active entity on the records of this state before appearing as its active, converted self on the records of the foreign jurisdiction.

It is only necessary for the filing office to record the effective date of the statement of conversion and the filing office does not need to be concerned with the effective date of the conversion itself. Persons wishing to determine the effective date of a conversion involving both a domestic limited liability company and a foreign entity will be able to do so by consulting the records of the filing offices in each jurisdiction.

§ 1046.   Effect of Conversion

(a)   When a conversion becomes effective:

    (1)   the converted entity is:

        (A)   organized under and subject to the organic law of the converted entity; and

        (B)   the same entity without interruption as the converting entity;

    (2)   all property of the converting entity continues to be vested in the converted entity without transfer, reversion, or impairment;

    (3)   all debts, obligations, and other liabilities of the converting entity continue as debts, obligations, and other liabilities of the converted entity;

    (4)   except as otherwise provided by law or the plan of conversion, all the rights, privileges, immunities, powers, and purposes of the converting entity remain in the converted entity;

    (5)   the name of the converted entity may be substituted for the name of the converting entity in any pending action or proceeding;

    (6)   the certificate of organization of the converted entity becomes effective;

    (7)   the provisions of the operating agreement of the converted entity which are to be in a record, if any, approved as part of the plan of conversion become effective; and

    (8)   the interests in the converting entity are converted, and the interest holders of the converting entity are entitled only to the rights provided to them under the plan of conversion and to any appraisal rights they have under Section 1006.

(b)   Except as otherwise provided in the operating agreement of a domestic converting limited liability company, the conversion does not give rise to any rights that a member, manager, or third party would have upon a dissolution, liquidation, or winding up of the converting entity.

(c)   When a conversion becomes effective, a person that did not have interest holder liability with respect to the converting entity and becomes subject to interest holder liability with respect to a domestic entity as a result of the conversion has interest holder liability only to the extent provided by the organic law of the entity and only for those debts, obligations, and other liabilities that are incurred after the conversion becomes effective.

(d)   When a conversion becomes effective, the interest holder liability of a person that ceases to hold an interest in a domestic converting limited liability company with respect to which the person had interest holder liability is subject to the following rules:

(1)   The conversion does not discharge any interest holder liability under this [act] to the extent the interest holder liability was incurred before the conversion became effective;

(2)   The person does not have interest holder liability under this [act] for any debt, obligation, or other liability that arises after the conversion becomes effective.

(3)   This [act] continues to apply to the release, collection, or discharge of any interest holder liability preserved under paragraph (1) as if the conversion had not occurred.

(4)   The person has whatever rights of contribution from any other person as are provided by this [act], law other than this [act], or the organic rules of the converting entity with respect to any interest holder liability preserved under paragraph (1) as if the conversion had not occurred.

(e)   When a conversion becomes effective, a foreign entity that is the converted entity may be served with process in this state for the collection and enforcement of any of its debts, obligations, and other liabilities as provided in Section 119.

(f)   If the converting entity is a registered foreign entity, its registration to do business in this state is canceled when the conversion becomes effective.

(g)   A conversion does not require the entity to wind up its affairs and does not constitute or cause the dissolution of the entity.

COMMENT

A converted entity is the same entity as it was before the conversion; the entity just has a different legal form.

Subsection (a)—This subsection states the principal legal effects of a conversion. The converted entity remains the owner of all real and personal property and remains subject to all the liabilities, actual or contingent, of the converted entity. A conversion is not a conveyance, transfer, or assignment. A conversion does not give rise to: (i) claims of reverter or impairment of title based on a prohibited conveyance or transfer; or (ii) to a claim that a contract with the converting entity is no longer in effect on the ground of nonassignability, unless the contract specifically provides that it does not survive a conversion. The contract rights that remain in the converted entity include, without limitation, the right to enforce subscription agreements for interests and obligations to make capital contributions entered into or incurred before the conversion.

When a conversion becomes effective, the internal affairs of the converting entity are no longer governed by its former organic law but instead by the organic law of the converted entity. As a result, filings that may have been made under the organic law of the converting entity, such as the following, will no longer be effective: a statement of qualification as a limited liability partnership under UPA (1997) (Last Amended 2013) § 901, a statement of partnership authority under section 303 of that act, a statement of authority under ULLCA (2006) (Last Amended 2013) § 302, or under Uniform Unincorporated Nonprofit Association Act (2008) (Last Amended 2013) § 7.

Subsection (a)(5)—All pending proceedings involving the converting entity are continued. The name of the converted entity may be, but need not be, substituted in any pending proceeding for the name of the converting entity.

Subsection (c)—This subsection provides the rule for future interest holder liability and parallels provisions in Parts 2 (mergers), 3 (interest exchanges), and 5 (domestications). *See* the comment to Section 1026(c).

Subsection (d)—Subsection (d) provides the rule for past interest holder liability and parallels analogous provisions in Parts 2 (mergers), 3 (interest exchanges), and 5 (domestications). *See* the comment to Section 1026(d).

At first glance, this subsection might seem to apply to the null set; members of an LLC typically do not have interest holder liability. However, the definition of interest holder liability also includes "personal liability for a liability of an entity which is imposed on a person . . . by the organic rules of the entity which make one or more specified interest holders or categories of interest holders liable in their capacity as interest holders for all or specified liabilities of the entity." Section 1001(19)(A)(ii).

Subsection (e)—For this provision to apply, the converting entity must have been a domestic limited liability company. When a domestic LLC becomes a foreign entity as a result of a conversion, some mechanism is needed to facilitate the enforcement of claims by the creditors and interest holders of the converting LLC. This subsection, which parallels analogous provisions in Parts 2 (mergers) and 5 (domestications), authorizes service of process for all such claims in this state.

Subsection (g)—When a conversion takes effect, the entity continues to exist—simply in a different form. This subsection thus makes clear that the conversion does not require the entity to wind up its affairs and does not constitute or cause the dissolution of the entity.

[PART] 5

DOMESTICATION

§ 1051. Domestication Authorized

(a) By complying with this [part], a domestic limited liability company may become a foreign limited liability company if the domestication is authorized by the law of the foreign jurisdiction.

(b) By complying with the provisions of this [part] applicable to foreign limited liability companies, a foreign limited liability company may become a domestic limited liability company if the domestication is authorized by the law of the foreign limited liability company's jurisdiction of formation.

(c) If a protected agreement contains a provision that applies to a merger of a domestic limited liability company but does not refer to a domestication, the provision applies to a domestication of the limited liability company as if the domestication were a merger until the provision is amended after [the effective date of this [act]].

COMMENT

A domestication authorized by Part 5 of Article 10 differs from a conversion in that a domestication requires that the domesticating entity be the same type of entity as the domesticated entity. In a conversion, by contrast, the converting entity changes its type.

As with a conversion, all rights and privileges, debts, obligations and other liabilities, and actions or proceedings of a domesticating entity vest unimpaired in the domesticated entity. A domestication is not a sale, transfer, assignment, or conveyance and does not give rise to a claim of reverter or impairment of title.

Part 5 of Article 10 governs the legal effect of a foreign limited liability company domesticating in this state. On the other hand, the organic laws of the foreign jurisdiction, and not Part 5, will govern the legal effect of most aspects of a domestication of a domestic limited liability company in another jurisdiction. In the latter scenario, Part 5 authorizes the domestication of the domestic entity in the foreign jurisdiction, but Part 5 does not create a right in the domestic entity to be received in the foreign jurisdiction. Similarly, this section does not provide a right on the part of a foreign limited liability company to become a domestic limited liability company if the domestication is not authorized by the laws of the foreign jurisdiction. If the foreign jurisdiction does not authorize a domestication transaction, the same results can be accomplished by forming a new limited liability company in this state and merging the existing foreign limited liability company into the new domestic limited liability company.

Subsection (c)—*See* Section 1031(c).

§ 1052. Plan of Domestication

(a) A domestic limited liability company may become a foreign limited liability company in a domestication by approving a plan of domestication. The plan must be in a record and contain:

(1) the name of the domesticating limited liability company;

(2)   the name and jurisdiction of formation of the domesticated limited liability company;

(3)   the manner of converting the interests in the domesticating limited liability company into interests, securities, obligations, money, other property, rights to acquire interests or securities, or any combination of the foregoing;

(4)   the proposed certificate of organization of the domesticated limited liability company;

(5)   the full text of the provisions of the operating agreement of the domesticated limited liability company that are proposed to be in a record;

(6)   the other terms and conditions of the domestication; and

(7)   any other provision required by the law of this state or the operating agreement of the domesticating limited liability company.

(b)   In addition to the requirements of subsection (a), a plan of domestication may contain any other provision not prohibited by law.

COMMENT

This section sets forth the requirements for the plan of domestication for a domestic limited liability company seeking to become a limited liability company existing under the law of another jurisdiction. For a foreign limited liability company seeking to become a domestic limited liability company, the organic law of the foreign limited liability company governs the requirements for a plan of domestication. The content of a plan of domestication is similar to the content of a plan of merger. *See* Section 1022.

Subsection (a)—The requirements stated in this subsection are mandatory. *See* Section 105(c)(14).

Subsection (a)(3)—Interest holders in the domesticating limited liability company may receive interests or other securities of the domesticated limited liability company or any other entity, obligations, rights to acquire interests or other securities, cash, or other property. *See* the comment to Section 1022(a)(3).

Subsection (b)—This subsection authorizes the plan to contain any other provision the parties wish to include, unless the provision is prohibited by law.

§ 1053.   Approval of Domestication

(a)   A plan of domestication of a domestic domesticating limited liability company is not effective unless it has been approved:

(1)   by all the members entitled to vote on or consent to any matter; and

(2)   in a record, by each member that will have interest holder liability for debts, obligations, and other liabilities that are incurred after the domestication becomes effective, unless:

(A)   the operating agreement of the domesticating company in a record provides for the approval of a domestication or merger in which some or all of its members become subject to interest holder liability by the affirmative vote or consent of fewer than all the members; and

(B)   the member voted for or consented in a record to that provision of the operating agreement or became a member after the adoption of that provision.

(b)   A domestication of a foreign domesticating limited liability company is not effective unless it is approved in accordance with the law of the foreign limited liability company's jurisdiction of formation.

COMMENT

Subsection (a)(1)—This provision is a default rule, subject to change in the operating agreement.

Subsection (a)(2)—This provision is mandatory. Section 105(c)(14). For an explanation of the provision, see Section 1023(a)(2), comment.

Subsection (b)—In the case of a foreign limited liability company that is domesticating in this state, this subsection provides that the required approval is determined by the laws of the foreign limited liability company's jurisdiction of formation.

§ 1054. Amendment or Abandonment of Plan of Domestication

(a) A plan of domestication of a domestic domesticating limited liability company may be amended:

(1) in the same manner as the plan was approved, if the plan does not provide for the manner in which it may be amended; or

(2) by its managers or members in the manner provided in the plan, but a member that was entitled to vote on or consent to approval of the domestication is entitled to vote on or consent to any amendment of the plan that will change:

(A) the amount or kind of interests, securities, obligations, money, other property, rights to acquire interests or securities, or any combination of the foregoing, to be received by any of the members of the domesticating limited liability company under the plan;

(B) the certificate of organization or operating agreement of the domesticated limited liability company that will be in effect immediately after the domestication becomes effective, except for changes that do not require approval of the members of the domesticated limited liability company under its organic law or operating agreement; or

(C) any other terms or conditions of the plan, if the change would adversely affect the member in any material respect.

(b) After a plan of domestication has been approved by a domestic domesticating limited liability company and before a statement of domestication becomes effective, the plan may be abandoned as provided in the plan. Unless prohibited by the plan, a domestic domesticating limited liability company may abandon the plan in the same manner as the plan was approved.

(c) If a plan of domestication is abandoned after a statement of domestication has been delivered to the [Secretary of State] for filing and before the statement becomes effective, a statement of abandonment, signed by the domesticating limited liability company, must be delivered to the [Secretary of State] for filing before the statement of domestication becomes effective. The statement of abandonment takes effect on filing, and the domestication is abandoned and does not become effective. The statement of abandonment must contain:

(1) the name of the domesticating limited liability company;

(2) the date on which the statement of domestication was filed by the [Secretary of State]; and

(3) a statement that the domestication has been abandoned in accordance with this section.

COMMENT

This section parallels provisions in Parts 2 (mergers), 3 (interest exchanges), and 4 (conversions). *See* Sections 1024 (mergers), 1034 (interest exchanges), 1044 (conversions).

§ 1055. Statement of Domestication; Effective Date of Domestication

(a) A statement of domestication must be signed by the domesticating limited liability company and delivered to the [Secretary of State] for filing.

(b) A statement of domestication must contain:

(1) the name and jurisdiction of formation of the domesticating limited liability company;

(2) the name and jurisdiction of formation of the domesticated limited liability company;

(3) if the domesticating limited liability company is a domestic limited liability company, a statement that the plan of domestication was approved in accordance with this [part] or, if the domesticating limited liability company is a foreign limited liability company, a statement that the domestication was approved in accordance with the law of its jurisdiction of formation; and

(4) the certificate of organization of the domesticated limited liability company, as an attachment.

(c) In addition to the requirements of subsection (b), a statement of domestication may contain any other provision not prohibited by law.

(d) The certificate of organization of a domestic domesticated limited liability company must satisfy the requirements of this [act], but the certificate does not need to be signed.

(e) A plan of domestication that is signed by a domesticating domestic limited liability company and meets all the requirements of subsection (b) may be delivered to the [Secretary of State] for filing instead of a statement of domestication and on filing has the same effect. If a plan of domestication is filed as provided in this subsection, references in this [article] to a statement of domestication refer to the plan of domestication filed under this subsection.

(f) If the domesticated entity is a domestic limited liability company, the domestication becomes effective when the statement of domestication is effective. If the domesticated entity is a foreign limited liability company, the domestication becomes effective on the later of:

(1) the date and time provided by the organic law of the domesticated entity; and

(2) when the statement is effective.

COMMENT

Regardless of whether a domestic limited liability company is the domesticating or domesticated entity:

- This section applies and, therefore, a foreign limited liability company seeking to domesticate and thereby become a domestic LLC must comply with this section.

- The organic law of the foreign LLC's jurisdiction must also be consulted.

The filing of a statement of domestication makes the transaction a matter of public record.

Subsection (b)—This subsection sets forth the requirements for a statement of domestication. They are essentially the same as the requirements for a statement of merger in Section 1025.

Subsection (e)—A plan of domestication can be used as a substitute for the statement of domestication so long as the plan satisfies the requirements in Subsection (b).

Subsection (f)—Section 207 determines when a record delivered for filing under this act becomes effective. A statement of domestication may specify a delayed effective time and date, subject to the ninety-day limit stated in Section 207(3) and (4).

When the statement of domestication becomes effective under this subsection, the domestication transaction occurs if the domesticated entity is a domestic limited liability company. A domestication in which the domesticated entity is a foreign limited liability company will usually also take effect when the statement of domestication takes effect because the best practice will be to coordinate the filings that need to be made in each jurisdiction so that they take effect at the same time.

However, when the domesticated limited liability company is a foreign limited liability company, it is possible that the filing in the foreign jurisdiction will take effect at a different time. For that reason, this subsection provides that the domestication will take effect at the later of: (i) when the statement of domestication takes effect; and (ii) when the domestication takes effect under the law of the foreign jurisdiction. This rule avoids the possibility that the domestication will take effect in this state before it takes effect in the foreign jurisdiction, which would produce the undesirable result that the domesticating domestic limited liability company would cease to appear as an active entity on the records of this state before appearing as its active, domesticated self on the records of the foreign jurisdiction.

It is only necessary for the filing office to record the effective date of the statement of domestication and the filing office does not need to be concerned with the effective date of the domestication itself. Persons wishing to determine the effective date of a domestication will be able to do so by consulting the records of the filing offices in each jurisdiction.

§ 1056. Effect of Domestication

(a) When a domestication becomes effective:

(1) the domesticated entity is:

(A)   organized under and subject to the organic law of the domesticated entity; and

(B)   the same entity without interruption as the domesticating entity;

(2)   all property of the domesticating entity continues to be vested in the domesticated entity without transfer, reversion, or impairment;

(3)   all debts, obligations, and other liabilities of the domesticating entity continue as debts, obligations, and other liabilities of the domesticated entity;

(4)   except as otherwise provided by law or the plan of domestication, all the rights, privileges, immunities, powers, and purposes of the domesticating entity remain in the domesticated entity;

(5)   the name of the domesticated entity may be substituted for the name of the domesticating entity in any pending action or proceeding;

(6)   the certificate of organization of the domesticated entity becomes effective;

(7)   the provisions of the operating agreement of the domesticated entity that are to be in a record, if any, approved as part of the plan of domestication become effective; and

(8)   the interests in the domesticating entity are converted to the extent and as approved in connection with the domestication, and the members of the domesticating entity are entitled only to the rights provided to them under the plan of domestication and to any appraisal rights they have under Section 1006.

(b)   Except as otherwise provided in the organic law or operating agreement of the domesticating limited liability company, the domestication does not give rise to any rights that a member, manager, or third party would otherwise have upon a dissolution, liquidation, or winding up of the domesticating company.

(c)   When a domestication becomes effective, a person that did not have interest holder liability with respect to the domesticating limited liability company and becomes subject to interest holder liability with respect to a domestic company as a result of the domestication has interest holder liability only to the extent provided by this [act] and only for those debts, obligations, and other liabilities that are incurred after the domestication becomes effective.

(d)   When a domestication becomes effective, the interest holder liability of a person that ceases to hold an interest in a domestic domesticating limited liability company with respect to which the person had interest holder liability is subject to the following rules:

(1)   The domestication does not discharge any interest holder liability under this [act] to the extent the interest holder liability was incurred before the domestication became effective.

(2)   A person does not have interest holder liability under this [act] for any debt, obligation, or other liability that is incurred after the domestication becomes effective.

(3)   This [act] continues to apply to the release, collection, or discharge of any interest holder liability preserved under paragraph (1) as if the domestication had not occurred.

(4)   A person has whatever rights of contribution from any other person as are provided by this [act], law other than this [act], or the operating agreement of the domestic domesticating limited liability company with respect to any interest holder liability preserved under paragraph (1) as if the domestication had not occurred.

(e)   When a domestication becomes effective, a foreign limited liability company that is the domesticated company may be served with process in this state for the collection and enforcement of any of its debts, obligations, and other liabilities as provided in Section 119.

(f)   If the domesticating limited liability company is a registered foreign entity, the registration of the company is canceled when the domestication becomes effective.

(g)   A domestication does not require a domestic domesticating limited liability company to wind up its affairs and does not constitute or cause the dissolution of the company.

COMMENT

Subsection (a)(1)—The domesticated entity is the same entity as the domesticating entity; it has merely changed its jurisdiction of formation.

Subsection (a)(2)—A domestication is not a sale, conveyance, transfer, or assignment and does not give rise to claims of reverter or impairment of title that may be based on a prohibition on transfer, assignment, or conveyance.

Subsection (a)(4)—All pending proceedings involving the domesticating entity are continued. The name of the domesticated entity may be, but need not be, substituted in any pending proceeding for the name of the domesticating entity.

Subsection (a)(8)—The interests of the domesticating limited liability company are reclassified into whatever rights were negotiated in the domestication and the members and transferees of the domesticating LLC are only entitled to those rights. Paragraph 8, on its face, allows for certain members of the domesticating LLC to be entitled to a continuing equity interest in the domesticated LLC whereas other members of the domesticating LLC may be cashed out as a result of the transaction.

Subsection (c)—This subsection provides the rule for future interest holder liability and parallels analogous provisions in Parts 2 (mergers), 3 (interest exchanges), and 4 (conversions). *See* the comment to Section 1026(c).

Subsection (d)—This subsection provides the rule for past interest holder liability and parallels analogous provisions in Parts 2 (mergers), 3 (interest exchanges), and 4 (conversions). *See* the comments to Sections 1026(d) and 1046(d).

Subsection (e)—When a domestic domesticating limited liability company becomes a foreign LLC as a result of a domestication, some mechanism is needed to facilitate the enforcement of claims by the creditors and interest holders of the domesticating LLC. This subsection, which parallels analogous provisions in Parts 2 (mergers) and 4 (conversions), authorizes service of process for all such claims in this state.

Subsection (g)—When a domestication takes effect, the entity continues to exist—simply as a domestic entity under the laws of a different state. This subsection thus makes clear that the domestication does not require the limited liability company to wind up its affairs and does not constitute or cause the dissolution of the limited liability company.

[ARTICLE] 11

MISCELLANEOUS PROVISIONS

§ 1101. Uniformity of Application and Construction

In applying and construing this uniform act, consideration must be given to the need to promote uniformity of the law with respect to its subject matter among states that enact it.

§ 1102. Relation to Electronic Signatures in Global and National Commerce Act

This [act] modifies, limits, and supersedes the Electronic Signatures in Global and National Commerce Act, 15 U.S.C. Section 7001 et seq., but does not modify, limit, or supersede Section 101(c) of that act, 15 U.S.C. Section 7001(c), or authorize electronic delivery of any of the notices described in Section 103(b) of that act, 15 U.S.C. Section 7003(b).

COMMENT

This section responds to specific language of the Electronic Signatures in Global and National Commerce Act and is designed to avoid preemption of state law under that federal legislation.

§ 1103. Savings Clause

This [act] does not affect an action commenced, proceeding brought, or right accrued before [the effective date of this [act]].

COMMENT

This section continues prior law after the effective date of this act with respect to rights accrued and proceedings. But for this section, the new law of this act would displace the old laws in some circumstances. The power of a new act to displace the old statute with respect to conduct occurring before the new act's enactment is substantial. Millard H. Ruud, *The Savings Clause—Some Problems in Construction and Drafting*, 33 TEX. L. REV. 285, 286–93 (1955). A court generally applies the law that exists at the time it acts.

Eventually, this act will apply all to pre-existing limited liability companies—whether by choice under Section 110(a)(2) (permitting an early opt-in), or without choice on the "all-inclusive date." Section 110(b). In this context, the phrase "before [the effective date of this [act]]" should be understood as referring to the date upon which this act became applicable to the particular limited liability company at issue.

§ 1104. Severability Clause

If any provision of this [act] or its application to any person or circumstance is held invalid, the invalidity does not affect other provisions or applications of this [act] which can be given effect without the invalid provision or application, and to this end the provisions of this [act] are severable.]

Legislative Note: *Include this section only if this state lacks a general severability statute or decision by the highest court of this state stating a general rule of severability.*

§ 1105. Repeals

The following are repealed:

(1) [the state limited liability company act, as [amended, and as] in effect immediately before [the effective date of this [act]];

(2) . . . .

(3) . . . .

§ 1106. Effective Date

This [act] takes effect . . . .

COMMENT

For the effect of the act's effective date on pre-existing limited liability companies, see Section 110.

DELAWARE LIMITED LIABILITY COMPANY ACT

Delaware Code, Title 6, Chapter 18

Table of Contents

SUBCHAPTER I.   GENERAL PROVISIONS

SUBCHAPTER II.   FORMATION; CERTIFICATE OF FORMATION

DLLCA

––––––––––

SUBCHAPTER I.   GENERAL PROVISIONS

§ 18–101.   Definitions.

As used in this chapter unless the context otherwise requires:

(1) "Bankruptcy" means an event that causes a person to cease to be a member as provided in § 18–304 of this title.

(2) "Certificate of formation" means the certificate referred to in § 18–201 of this title, and the certificate as amended.

(3) "Contribution" means any cash, property, services rendered or a promissory note or other obligation to contribute cash or property or to perform services, which a person contributes to a limited liability company in the person's capacity as a member.

(4) "Document" means:

    a. Any tangible medium on which information is inscribed, and includes handwritten, typed, printed or similar instruments, and copies of such instruments; and

    b. An electronic transmission.

(5) "Electronic transmission" means any form of communication not directly involving the physical transmission of paper, including the use of, or participation in, 1 or more electronic networks or databases (including 1 or more distributed electronic networks or databases), that creates a record that may be retained, retrieved and reviewed by a recipient thereof and that may be directly reproduced in paper form by such a recipient through an automated process.

(6) "Foreign limited liability company" means a limited liability company formed under the laws of any state or under the laws of any foreign country or other foreign jurisdiction. When used in this title in reference to a foreign limited liability company, the terms "limited liability company agreement," "limited liability company interest," "manager" or "member" shall mean a limited liability company agreement, limited liability company interest, manager or member, respectively, under the laws of the state or foreign country or other foreign jurisdiction under which the foreign limited liability company is formed.

(7) "Knowledge" means a person's actual knowledge of a fact, rather than the person's constructive knowledge of the fact.

(8) "Limited liability company" and "domestic limited liability company" means a limited liability company formed under the laws of the State of Delaware and having 1 or more members.

(9) "Limited liability company agreement" means any agreement (whether referred to as a limited liability company agreement, operating agreement or otherwise), written, oral or implied, of the member or members as to the affairs of a limited liability company and the conduct of its business. A member or manager of a limited liability company or an assignee of a limited liability company interest is bound by the limited liability company agreement whether or not the member or manager or assignee executes the limited liability company agreement. A limited liability company is not required to execute its limited liability company agreement. A limited liability company is bound by its limited liability company agreement whether or not the limited liability company executes the limited liability company agreement. A limited liability company agreement of a limited liability company having only 1 member shall not be unenforceable by reason of there being only 1 person who is a party to the limited liability company agreement. A limited liability company agreement is not subject to any statute of frauds (including § 2714 of this title). A limited liability company agreement may provide rights to any person, including a person who is not a party to the limited liability company agreement, to the extent set forth therein. A written limited liability company agreement or another written agreement or writing:

    a. May provide that a person shall be admitted as a member of a limited liability company, or shall become an assignee of a limited liability company interest or other rights or powers of a member to the extent assigned:

        1. If such person (or a representative authorized by such person orally, in writing or by other action such as payment for a limited liability company interest) executes the limited liability company agreement or any other writing evidencing the intent of such person to become a member or assignee; or

2. Without such execution, if such person (or a representative authorized by such person orally, in writing or by other action such as payment for a limited liability company interest) complies with the conditions for becoming a member or assignee as set forth in the limited liability company agreement or any other writing; and

b. Shall not be unenforceable by reason of its not having been signed by a person being admitted as a member or becoming an assignee as provided in paragraph (7)a. of this section, or by reason of its having been signed by a representative as provided in this chapter.

(10) "Limited liability company interest" means a member's share of the profits and losses of a limited liability company and a member's right to receive distributions of the limited liability company's assets.

(11) "Liquidating trustee" means a person carrying out the winding up of a limited liability company.

(12) "Manager" means a person who is named as a manager of a limited liability company in, or designated as a manager of a limited liability company pursuant to, a limited liability company agreement or similar instrument under which the limited liability company is formed, and includes a manager of the limited liability company generally and a manager associated with a series of the limited liability company. Unless the context otherwise requires, references in this chapter to a manager (including references in this chapter to a manager of a limited liability company) shall be deemed to be references to a manager of the limited liability company generally and to a manager associated with a series with respect to such series.

(13) "Member" means a person who is admitted to a limited liability company as a member as provided in § 18–301 of this title, and includes a member of the limited liability company generally and a member associated with a series of the limited liability company. Unless the context otherwise requires, references in this chapter to a member (including references in this chapter to a member of a limited liability company) shall be deemed to be references to a member of the limited liability company generally and to a member associated with a series with respect to such series.

(14) "Person" means a natural person, partnership (whether general or limited), limited liability company, trust (including a common law trust, business trust, statutory trust, voting trust or any other form of trust), estate, association (including any group, organization, co-tenancy, plan, board, council or committee), corporation, government (including a country, state, county or any other governmental subdivision, agency or instrumentality), custodian, nominee or any other individual or entity (or series thereof) in its own or any representative capacity, in each case, whether domestic or foreign.

(15) "Personal representative" means, as to a natural person, the executor, administrator, guardian, conservator or other legal representative thereof and, as to a person other than a natural person, the legal representative or successor thereof.

(16) "Protected series" means a designated series of members, managers, limited liability company interests or assets that is established in accordance with § 18–215(b) of this title.

(17) "Registered series" means a designated series of members, managers, limited liability company interests or assets that is formed in accordance with § 18–218 of this title.

(18) "Series" means a designated series of members, managers, limited liability company interests or assets that is a protected series or a registered series, or that is neither a protected series nor a registered series.

(19) "State" means the District of Columbia or the Commonwealth of Puerto Rico or any state, territory, possession or other jurisdiction of the United States other than the State of Delaware.

§ 18–102. Name set forth in certificate.

The name of each limited liability company as set forth in its certificate of formation:

(1) Shall contain the words "Limited Liability Company" or the abbreviation "L.L.C." or the designation "LLC";

(2) May contain the name of a member or manager;

(3) Must be such as to distinguish it upon the records in the office of the Secretary of State from the name on such records of any corporation, partnership, limited partnership, statutory trust, limited liability company, registered series of a limited liability company or registered series of a limited partnership reserved, registered, formed or organized under the laws of the State of Delaware or qualified to do business or registered as a foreign corporation, foreign limited partnership, foreign statutory trust, foreign partnership, or foreign limited liability company in the State of Delaware; provided however, that a limited liability company may register under any name which is not such as to distinguish it upon the records in the office of the Secretary of State from the name on such records of any domestic or foreign corporation, partnership, limited partnership, statutory trust, registered series of a limited liability company, registered series of a limited partnership or foreign limited liability company reserved, registered, formed or organized under the laws of the State of Delaware with the written consent of the other corporation, partnership, limited partnership, statutory trust, registered series of a limited liability company, registered series of a limited partnership or foreign limited liability company, which written consent shall be filed with the Secretary of State; provided further, that, if on July 31, 2011, a limited liability company is registered (with the consent of another limited liability company) under a name which is not such as to distinguish it upon the records in the office of the Secretary of State from the name on such records of such other domestic limited liability company, it shall not be necessary for any such limited liability company to amend its certificate of formation to comply with this subsection;

(4) May contain the following words: "Company," "Association," "Club," "Foundation," "Fund," "Institute," "Society," "Union," "Syndicate," "Limited", "Public Benefit" or "Trust" (or abbreviations of like import); and

(5) Shall not contain the word "bank," or any variation thereof, except for the name of a bank reporting to and under the supervision of the State Bank Commissioner of this State or a subsidiary of a bank or savings association (as those terms are defined in the Federal Deposit Insurance Act, as amended, at 12 U.S.C. § 1813), or a limited liability company regulated under the Bank Holding Company Act of 1956, as amended, 12 U.S.C. § 1841 et seq., or the Home Owners' Loan Act, as amended, 12 U.S.C. § 1461 et seq.; provided, however, that this section shall not be construed to prevent the use of the word "bank," or any variation thereof, in a context clearly not purporting to refer to a banking business or otherwise likely to mislead the public about the nature of the business of the limited liability company or to lead to a pattern and practice of abuse that might cause harm to the interests of the public or this State as determined by the Division of Corporations in the Department of State.

§ 18–103.   Reservation of name.

(a) The exclusive right to the use of a name may be reserved by:

(1) Any person intending to organize a limited liability company under this chapter and to adopt that name;

(2) Any person intending to form a registered series of a limited liability company under this chapter and to adopt that name in accordance with § 18–218(e) of this title;

(3) Any domestic limited liability company or any foreign limited liability company registered in the State of Delaware which, in either case, proposes to change its name;

(4) Any foreign limited liability company intending to register in the State of Delaware and adopt that name; and

(5) Any person intending to organize a foreign limited liability company and intending to have it register in the State of Delaware and adopt that name.

(b) The reservation of a specified name shall be made by filing with the Secretary of State an application, executed by the applicant, specifying the name to be reserved and the name and address of the applicant. If the Secretary of State finds that the name is available for use by a domestic or foreign limited liability company, the Secretary shall reserve the name for the exclusive use of the applicant for a period of

120 days. Once having so reserved a name, the same applicant may again reserve the same name for successive 120-day periods. The right to the exclusive use of a reserved name may be transferred to any other person by filing in the office of the Secretary of State a notice of the transfer, executed by the applicant for whom the name was reserved, specifying the name to be transferred and the name and address of the transferee. The reservation of a specified name may be canceled by filing with the Secretary of State a notice of cancellation, executed by the applicant or transferee, specifying the name reservation to be canceled and the name and address of the applicant or transferee. Unless the Secretary of State finds that any application, notice of transfer, or notice of cancellation filed with the Secretary of State as required by this subsection does not conform to law, upon receipt of all filing fees required by law the Secretary shall prepare and return to the person who filed such instrument a copy of the filed instrument with a notation thereon of the action taken by the Secretary of State.

(c) A fee as set forth in § 18–1105(a)(1) of this title shall be paid at the time of the initial reservation of any name, at the time of the renewal of any such reservation and at the time of the filing of a notice of the transfer or cancellation of any such reservation.

§ 18–104. Registered office; registered agent.

(a) Each limited liability company shall have and maintain in the State of Delaware:

(1) A registered office, which may but need not be a place of its business in the State of Delaware; and

(2) A registered agent for service of process on the limited liability company, having a business office identical with such registered office, which agent may be any of:

a. The limited liability company itself,

b. An individual resident in the State of Delaware,

c. A domestic limited liability company (other than the limited liability company itself), a domestic corporation, a domestic partnership (whether general (including a limited liability partnership) or limited (including a limited liability limited partnership)), or a domestic statutory trust, or

d. A foreign corporation, a foreign partnership (whether general (including a limited liability partnership) or limited (including a limited liability limited partnership)), a foreign limited liability company, or a foreign statutory trust.

(b) A registered agent may change the address of the registered office of the limited liability company(ies) for which it is registered agent to another address in the State of Delaware by paying a fee as set forth in § 18–1105(a)(2) of this title and filing with the Secretary of State a certificate, executed by such registered agent, setting forth the address at which such registered agent has maintained the registered office for each of the limited liability companies for which it is a registered agent, and further certifying to the new address to which each such registered office will be changed on a given day, and at which new address such registered agent will thereafter maintain the registered office for each of the limited liability companies for which it is a registered agent. Upon the filing of such certificate, the Secretary of State shall furnish to the registered agent a certified copy of the same under the Secretary's hand and seal of office, and thereafter, or until further change of address, as authorized by law, the registered office in the State of Delaware of each of the limited liability companies for which the agent is a registered agent shall be located at the new address of the registered agent thereof as given in the certificate. In the event of a change of name of any person acting as a registered agent of a limited liability company, such registered agent shall file with the Secretary of State a certificate executed by such registered agent setting forth the new name of such registered agent, the name of such registered agent before it was changed, and the address at which such registered agent has maintained the registered office for each of the limited liability companies for which it is a registered agent, and shall pay a fee as set forth in § 18–1105(a)(2) of this title. Upon the filing of such certificate, the Secretary of State shall furnish to the registered agent a certified copy of the certificate under the Secretary of State's own hand and seal of office. A change of name of any person acting as a registered agent of a limited liability company as a result of a merger or consolidation of the registered agent with or into another person which succeeds to its assets and liabilities by operation of law shall be deemed a change of name for purposes of this section. Filing a certificate under this section shall be deemed to be an amendment of the certificate of formation of each limited liability company affected thereby, and each such limited liability company shall not be required to take any further action with respect thereto to amend its certificate of formation under § 18–202 of this title. Any registered agent filing a certificate under this section shall promptly, upon such filing, deliver a copy of any such certificate to each limited liability company affected thereby.

(c)   The registered agent of 1 or more limited liability companies may resign and appoint a successor registered agent by paying a fee as set forth in § 18–1105(a)(2) of this title and filing a certificate with the Secretary of State stating that it resigns and the name and address of the successor registered agent. There shall be attached to such certificate a statement of each affected limited liability company ratifying and approving such change of registered agent. Upon such filing, the successor registered agent shall become the registered agent of such limited liability companies as have ratified and approved such substitution, and the successor registered agent's address, as stated in such certificate, shall become the address of each such limited liability company's registered office in the State of Delaware. The Secretary of State shall then issue a certificate that the successor registered agent has become the registered agent of the limited liability companies so ratifying and approving such change and setting out the names of such limited liability companies. Filing of such certificate of resignation shall be deemed to be an amendment of the certificate of formation of each limited liability company affected thereby, and each such limited liability company shall not be required to take any further action with respect thereto to amend its certificate of formation under § 18–202 of this title.

(d)   The registered agent of a limited liability company, including a limited liability company whose certificate of formation has been cancelled pursuant to § 18–1108 of this title, may resign without appointing a successor registered agent by paying a fee as set forth in § 18–1105(a)(2) of this title and filing a certificate of resignation with the Secretary of State, but such resignation shall not become effective until 30 days after the certificate is filed. The certificate shall contain a statement that written notice of resignation was given to the limited liability company at least 30 days prior to the filing of the certificate by mailing or delivering such notice to the limited liability company at its address last known to the registered agent and shall set forth the date of such notice. The certificate shall include such information last provided to the registered agent pursuant to subsection (g) of this section of this title for a communications contact for the limited liability company. Such information regarding the communications contact shall not be deemed public. A certificate filed pursuant to this subsection must be on the form prescribed by the Secretary of State. After receipt of the notice of the resignation of its registered agent, the limited liability company for which such registered agent was acting shall obtain and designate a new registered agent, to take the place of the registered agent so resigning. If such limited liability company fails to obtain and designate a new registered agent as aforesaid prior to the expiration of the period of 30 days after the filing by the registered agent of the certificate of resignation, the certificate of formation of such limited liability company shall be canceled. After the resignation of the registered agent shall have become effective as provided in this section and if no new registered agent shall have been obtained and designated in the time and manner aforesaid, service of legal process against each limited liability company (and each protected series and each registered series thereof) for which the resigned registered agent had been acting shall thereafter be upon the Secretary of State in accordance with § 18–105 of this title.

(e)   Every registered agent shall:

(1)   If an entity, maintain a business office in the State of Delaware which is generally open, or if an individual, be generally present at a designated location in the State of Delaware, at sufficiently frequent times to accept service of process and otherwise perform the functions of a registered agent;

(2)   If a foreign entity, be authorized to transact business in the State of Delaware;

(3)   Accept service of process and other communications directed to the limited liability companies (and any protected series or registered series thereof) and foreign limited liability companies for which it serves as registered agent and forward same to the limited liability company or foreign limited liability company to which the service or communication is directed;

(4)   Forward to the limited liability companies and foreign limited liability companies for which it serves as registered agent the statement for the annual tax for such limited liability company (and each registered series thereof) or such foreign limited liability company, as applicable, as described in

§ 18–1107 of this title or an electronic notification of same in a form satisfactory to the Secretary of State; and

(5) Satisfy and adhere to regulations established by the Secretary regarding the verification of both the identity of the entity's contacts and individuals for which the registered agent maintains a record for the reduction of risk of unlawful business purposes.

(f) Any registered agent who at any time serves as registered agent for more than 50 entities (a "commercial registered agent"), whether domestic or foreign, shall satisfy and comply with the following qualifications:

(1) A natural person serving as a commercial registered agent shall:

a. Maintain a principal residence or a principal place of business in the State of Delaware;

b. Maintain a Delaware business license;

c. Be generally present at a designated location within the State of Delaware during normal business hours to accept service of process and otherwise perform the functions of a registered agent as specified in subsection (e) of this section;

d. Provide the Secretary of State upon request with such information identifying and enabling communication with such commercial registered agent as the Secretary of State shall require; and

e. Satisfy and adhere to regulations established by the Secretary regarding the verification of both the identity of the entity's contacts and individuals for which the natural person maintains a record for the reduction of risk of unlawful business purposes.

(2) A domestic or foreign corporation, a domestic or foreign partnership (whether general (including a limited liability partnership) or limited (including a limited liability limited partnership)), a domestic or foreign limited liability company, or a domestic or foreign statutory trust serving as a commercial registered agent shall:

a. Have a business office within the State of Delaware which is generally open during normal business hours to accept service of process and otherwise perform the functions of a registered agent as specified in subsection (e) of this section;

b. Maintain a Delaware business license;

c. Have generally present at such office during normal business hours an officer, director or managing agent who is a natural person;

d. Provide the Secretary of State upon request with such information identifying and enabling communication with such commercial registered agent as the Secretary of State shall require; and

e. Satisfy and adhere to regulations established by the Secretary regarding the verification of both the identity of the entity's contacts and individuals for which it maintains a record for the reduction of risk of unlawful business purposes.

(3) For purposes of this subsection and paragraph (i)(2)a. of this section, a commercial registered agent shall also include any registered agent which has an officer, director or managing agent in common with any other registered agent or agents if such registered agents at any time during such common service as officer, director or managing agent collectively served as registered agents for more than 50 entities, whether domestic or foreign.

(g) Every domestic limited liability company and every foreign limited liability company qualified to do business in the State of Delaware shall provide to its registered agent and update from time to time as necessary the name, business address and business telephone number of a natural person who is a member, manager, officer, employee or designated agent of the domestic or foreign limited liability company who is then authorized to receive communications from the registered agent. Such person shall be deemed the communications contact for the domestic or foreign limited liability company. A domestic limited liability company, upon receipt of a request by the communications contact delivered in writing or by electronic transmission, shall provide the communications contact with the name, business address and business telephone number of a natural person who has access to the record required to be maintained pursuant to § 18–305(h) of this title. Every registered agent shall retain (in paper or electronic form) the above information concerning the current communications contact for each domestic limited liability company and each foreign limited liability company for which that registered agent serves as registered agent. If the domestic or foreign limited liability company fails to provide the registered agent with a current communications contact, the registered agent may resign as the registered agent for such domestic or foreign limited liability company pursuant to this section.

(h) The Secretary of State is fully authorized to issue such regulations, as may be necessary or appropriate to carry out the enforcement of subsections (e), (f) and (g) of this section, and to take actions reasonable and necessary to assure registered agents' compliance with subsections (e), (f) and (g) of this section. Such actions may include refusal to file documents submitted by a registered agent, including the refusal to file any documents regarding an entity's formation.

(i) Upon application of the Secretary of State, the Court of Chancery may enjoin any person or entity from serving as a registered agent or as an officer, director or managing agent of a registered agent.

(1) Upon the filing of a complaint by the Secretary of State pursuant to this section, the court may make such orders respecting such proceeding as it deems appropriate, and may enter such orders granting interim or final relief as it deems proper under the circumstances.

(2) Any 1 or more of the following grounds shall be a sufficient basis to grant an injunction pursuant to this section:

a. With respect to any registered agent who at any time within 1 year immediately prior to the filing of the Secretary of State's complaint is a commercial registered agent, failure after notice and warning to comply with the qualifications set forth in subsection (e) of this section and/or the requirements of subsection (f) or (g) of this section above;

b. The person serving as a registered agent, or any person who is an officer, director or managing agent of an entity registered agent, has been convicted of a felony or any crime which includes an element of dishonesty or fraud or involves moral turpitude; or

c. The registered agent has engaged in conduct in connection with acting as a registered agent that is intended to or likely to deceive or defraud the public.

(3) With respect to any order the court enters pursuant to this section with respect to an entity that has acted as a registered agent, the Court may also direct such order to any person who has served as an officer, director or managing agent of such registered agent. Any person who, on or after January 1, 2007, serves as an officer, director or managing agent of an entity acting as a registered agent in the State of Delaware shall be deemed thereby to have consented to the appointment of such registered agent as agent upon whom service of process may be made in any action brought pursuant to this section, and service as an officer, director or managing agent of an entity acting as a registered agent in the State of Delaware shall be a signification of the consent of such person that any process when so served shall be of the same legal force and validity as if served upon such person within the State of Delaware, and such appointment of the registered agent shall be irrevocable.

(4) Upon the entry of an order by the Court enjoining any person or entity from acting as a registered agent, the Secretary of State shall mail or deliver notice of such order to each affected domestic or foreign limited liability company:

a. That has specified the address of a place of business in a record of the Secretary of State, to the address specified, or

b. An address of which the Secretary of State has obtained from the domestic or foreign limited liability company's former registered agent, to the address obtained.

If such a domestic limited liability company fails to obtain and designate a new registered agent within 30 days after such notice is given, the certificate of formation of such limited liability company shall be canceled. If such a foreign limited liability company fails to obtain and designate a new registered agent within 30 days after such notice is given, such foreign limited liability company shall not be permitted to do business in the State of Delaware and its registration shall be canceled. If any other affected domestic limited liability company fails to obtain and designate a new registered agent within 60 days after entry of an order by the Court enjoining such limited liability company's registered agent from acting as a registered agent, the certificate of formation of such limited liability company shall be canceled. If any other affected foreign limited liability company fails to obtain and designate a new registered agent within 60 days after entry of an order by the Court enjoining such foreign limited liability company's registered agent from acting as a registered agent, such foreign limited liability company shall not be permitted to do business in the State of Delaware and its registration shall be canceled. If the Court enjoins a person or entity from acting as a registered agent as provided in this section and no new registered agent shall have been obtained and designated in the time and manner aforesaid, service of legal process against the domestic or foreign limited liability company for which the registered agent had been acting shall thereafter be upon the Secretary of State in accordance with § 18–105 or § 18–911 of this title. The Court of Chancery may, upon application of the Secretary of State on notice to the former registered agent, enter such orders as it deems appropriate to give the Secretary of State access to information in the former registered agent's possession in order to facilitate communication with the domestic and foreign limited liability companies the former registered agent served.

(j)   The Secretary of State is authorized to make a list of registered agents available to the public, and to establish such qualifications and issue such rules and regulations with respect to such listing as the Secretary of State deems necessary or appropriate.

(k)   As contained in any certificate of formation, application for registration as a foreign limited liability company, or other document filed in the office of the Secretary of State under this chapter, the address of a registered agent or registered office shall include the street, number, city and postal code.

§ 18–105.   Service of process on domestic limited liability companies and protected series or registered series thereof.

(a)   Service of legal process upon any domestic limited liability company or any protected series or registered series thereof shall be made by delivering a copy personally to any manager of the limited liability company in the State of Delaware, or the registered agent of the limited liability company in the State of Delaware, or by leaving it at the dwelling house or usual place of abode in the State of Delaware of any such manager or registered agent (if the registered agent be an individual), or at the registered office or other place of business of the limited liability company in the State of Delaware. If service of legal process is made upon the registered agent of the limited liability company in the State of Delaware on behalf of any such protected series or registered series, such process shall include the name of the limited liability company and the name of such protected series or registered series. If the registered agent be a corporation, service of process upon it as such may be made by serving, in the State of Delaware, a copy thereof on the president, vice-president, secretary, assistant secretary or any director of the corporate registered agent. Service by copy left at the dwelling house or usual place of abode of a manager or registered agent, or at the registered office or other place of business of the limited liability company in the State of Delaware, to be effective, must be delivered thereat at least 6 days before the return date of the process, and in the presence of an adult person, and the officer serving the process shall distinctly state the manner of service in the officer's return thereto. Process returnable forthwith must be delivered personally to the manager or registered agent.

(b)   In case the officer whose duty it is to serve legal process cannot by due diligence serve the process in any manner provided for by subsection (a) of this section, it shall be lawful to serve the process against the limited liability company or any protected series or registered series thereof upon the Secretary of State, and such service shall be as effectual for all intents and purposes as if made in any of the ways provided for in subsection (a) of this section. If service of legal process is made upon the Secretary of State on behalf of any such protected series or registered series, such process shall include the name of the limited liability company and the name of such protected series or registered series. Process may be served upon the Secretary of State under this subsection by means of electronic transmission but only as prescribed by the Secretary of State. The Secretary of State is authorized to issue such rules and regulations with respect to such service as the Secretary of State deems necessary or appropriate. In the event that service is effected through the Secretary of State in accordance with this subsection, the Secretary of State shall forthwith notify the limited liability company by letter, directed to the limited liability company at its address as it appears on the records relating to such limited liability company on file with the Secretary of State or, if no such address appears, at its last registered office. Such letter shall be sent by a mail or courier service that includes a record of mailing or deposit with the courier and a record of delivery evidenced by the signature of the recipient. Such letter shall enclose a copy of the process and any other papers served on the Secretary of State pursuant to this subsection. It shall be the duty of the plaintiff in the event of such service to serve process and any other papers in duplicate, to notify the Secretary of State that service is being effected pursuant to this subsection, and to pay the Secretary of State the sum of $50 for the use of the State of Delaware, which sum shall be taxed as part of the costs in the proceeding if the plaintiff shall prevail therein. The Secretary of State shall maintain an alphabetical record of any such service setting forth the name of the plaintiff and defendant, the title, docket number and nature of the proceeding in which process has been served upon the Secretary, the fact that service has been effected pursuant to this subsection, the return date thereof, and the day and hour when the service was made. The Secretary of State shall not be required to retain such information for a period longer than 5 years from the Secretary's receipt of the service of process.

§ 18–106. Nature of business permitted; powers.

(a) A limited liability company may carry on any lawful business, purpose or activity, whether or not for profit, with the exception of the business of banking as defined in § 126 of Title 8.

(b) A limited liability company shall possess and may exercise all the powers and privileges granted by this chapter or by any other law or by its limited liability company agreement, together with any powers incidental thereto, including such powers and privileges as are necessary or convenient to the conduct, promotion or attainment of the business, purposes or activities of the limited liability company.

(c) Notwithstanding any provision of this chapter to the contrary, without limiting the general powers enumerated in subsection (b) of this section, a limited liability company shall, subject to such standards and restrictions, if any, as are set forth in its limited liability company agreement, have the power and authority to make contracts of guaranty and suretyship and enter into interest rate, basis, currency, hedge or other swap agreements or cap, floor, put, call, option, exchange or collar agreements, derivative agreements, or other agreements similar to any of the foregoing.

(d) Unless otherwise provided in a limited liability company agreement, a limited liability company has the power and authority to grant, hold or exercise a power of attorney, including an irrevocable power of attorney.

§ 18–107. Business transactions of member or manager with the limited liability company.

Except as provided in a limited liability company agreement, a member or manager may lend money to, borrow money from, act as a surety, guarantor or endorser for, guarantee or assume 1 or more obligations of, provide collateral for, and transact other business with, a limited liability company and, subject to other applicable law, has the same rights and obligations with respect to any such matter as a person who is not a member or manager.

§ 18–108. Indemnification.

Subject to such standards and restrictions, if any, as are set forth in its limited liability company agreement, a limited liability company may, and shall have the power to, indemnify and hold harmless any member or manager or other person from and against any and all claims and demands whatsoever.

§ 18–109. Service of process on managers and liquidating trustees.

(a) A manager or a liquidating trustee of a limited liability company may be served with process in the manner prescribed in this section in all civil actions or proceedings brought in the State of Delaware involving or relating to the business of the limited liability company or a violation by the manager or the liquidating trustee of a duty to the limited liability company or any member of the limited liability company, whether or not the manager or the liquidating trustee is a manager or a liquidating trustee at the time suit is commenced. A manager's or a liquidating trustee's serving as such constitutes such person's consent to the appointment of the registered agent of the limited liability company (or, if there is none, the Secretary of State) as such person's agent upon whom service of process may be made as provided in this section. Such service as a manager or a liquidating trustee shall signify the consent of such manager or liquidating trustee that any process when so served shall be of the same legal force and validity as if served upon such manager or liquidating trustee within the State of Delaware and such appointment of the registered agent (or, if there is none, the Secretary of State) shall be irrevocable. As used in this subsection (a) and in subsections (b), (c) and (d) of this section, the term "manager" refers (i) to a person who is a manager as defined in § 18–101 of this title and (ii) to a person, whether or not a member of a limited liability company, who, although not a "manager" as defined in § 18–101 of this title, participates materially in the management of the limited liability company; provided however, that the power to elect or otherwise select or to participate in the election or selection of a person to be a "manager" as defined in § 18–101 of this title shall not, by itself, constitute participation in the management of the limited liability company.

(b)   Service of process shall be effected by serving the registered agent (or, if there is none, the Secretary of State) with 1 copy of such process in the manner provided by law for service of writs of summons. In the event service is made under this subsection upon the Secretary of State, the plaintiff shall pay to the Secretary of State the sum of $50 for the use of the State of Delaware, which sum shall be taxed as part of the costs of the proceeding if the plaintiff shall prevail therein. In addition, the Prothonotary or the Register in Chancery of the court in which the civil action or proceeding is pending shall, within 7 days of such service, deposit in the United States mails, by registered mail, postage prepaid, true and attested copies of the process, together with a statement that service is being made pursuant to this section, addressed to such manager or liquidating trustee at the registered office of the limited liability company and at the manager's or liquidating trustee's address last known to the party desiring to make such service.

(c)   In any action in which any such manager or liquidating trustee has been served with process as hereinabove provided, the time in which a defendant shall be required to appear and file a responsive pleading shall be computed from the date of mailing by the Prothonotary or the Register in Chancery as provided in subsection (b) of this section; however, the court in which such action has been commenced may order such continuance or continuances as may be necessary to afford such manager or liquidating trustee reasonable opportunity to defend the action.

(d)   In a written limited liability company agreement or other writing, a manager or member may consent to be subject to the nonexclusive jurisdiction of the courts of, or arbitration in, a specified jurisdiction, or the exclusive jurisdiction of the courts of the State of Delaware, or the exclusivity of arbitration in a specified jurisdiction or the State of Delaware, and to be served with legal process in the manner prescribed in such limited liability company agreement or other writing. Except by agreeing to arbitrate any arbitrable matter in a specified jurisdiction or in the State of Delaware, a member who is not a manager may not waive its right to maintain a legal action or proceeding in the courts of the State of Delaware with respect to matters relating to the organization or internal affairs of a limited liability company.

(e)   Nothing herein contained limits or affects the right to serve process in any other manner now or hereafter provided by law. This section is an extension of and not a limitation upon the right otherwise existing of service of legal process upon nonresidents.

(f)   The Court of Chancery and the Superior Court may make all necessary rules respecting the form of process, the manner of issuance and return thereof and such other rules which may be necessary to implement this section and are not inconsistent with this section.

§ 18–110.   Contested matters relating to managers; contested votes.

(a)   Upon application of any member or manager, the Court of Chancery may hear and determine the validity of any admission, election, appointment, removal or resignation of a manager of a limited liability company, and the right of any person to become or continue to be a manager of a limited liability company, and, in case the right to serve as a manager is claimed by more than 1 person, may determine the person or persons entitled to serve as managers; and to that end make such order or decree in any such case as may be just and proper, with power to enforce the production of any books, papers and records of the limited liability company relating to the issue. In any such application, the limited liability company shall be named as a party and service of copies of the application upon the registered agent of the limited liability company shall be deemed to be service upon the limited liability company and upon the person or persons whose right to serve as a manager is contested and upon the person or persons, if any, claiming to be a manager or claiming the right to be a manager; and the registered agent shall forward immediately a copy of the application to the limited liability company and to the person or persons whose right to serve as a manager is contested and to the person or persons, if any, claiming to be a manager or the right to be a manager, in a postpaid, sealed, registered letter addressed to such limited liability company and such person or persons at their post-office addresses last known to the registered agent or furnished to the registered agent by the applicant member or manager. The Court may make such order respecting further or other notice of such application as it deems proper under these circumstances.

(b)   Upon application of any member or manager, the Court of Chancery may hear and determine the result of any vote of members or managers upon matters as to which the members or managers of the limited liability company, or any class or group of members or managers, have the right to vote pursuant to the limited liability company agreement or other agreement or this chapter (other than the admission, election, appointment, removal or resignation of managers). In any such application, the limited liability company shall be named as a party and service of the application upon the registered agent of the limited liability company shall be deemed to be service upon the limited liability company, and no other party need be joined in order for the Court to adjudicate the result of the vote. The Court may make such order respecting further or other notice of such application as it deems proper under these circumstances.

(c)   As used in this section, the term "manager" refers to a person:

(1)   Who is a "manager" as defined in § 18–101 of this title; and

(2)   Whether or not a member of a limited liability company, who, although not a "manager" as defined in § 18–101 of this title, participates materially in the management of the limited liability company;

provided however, that the power to elect or otherwise select or to participate in the election or selection of a person to be a "manager" as defined in § 18–101 of this title shall not, by itself, constitute participation in the management of the limited liability company.

(d)   Nothing herein contained limits or affects the right to serve process in any other manner now or hereafter provided by law. This section is an extension of and not a limitation upon the right otherwise existing of service of legal process upon nonresidents.

§ 18–111.   Interpretation and enforcement of limited liability company agreement.

Any action to interpret, apply or enforce the provisions of a limited liability company agreement, or the duties, obligations or liabilities of a limited liability company to the members or managers of the limited liability company, or the duties, obligations or liabilities among members or managers and of members or managers to the limited liability company, or the rights or powers of, or restrictions on, the limited liability company, members or managers, or any provision of this chapter, or any other instrument, document, agreement or certificate contemplated by any provision of this chapter, may be brought in the Court of Chancery.

As used in this section, the term "manager" refers to a person:

(1)   Who is a "manager" as defined in § 18–101 of this title; and

(2)   Whether or not a member of a limited liability company, who, although not a "manager" as defined in § 18–101 of this title, participates materially in the management of the limited liability company;

provided however, that the power to elect or otherwise select or to participate in the election or selection of a person to be a "manager" as defined in § 18–101 of this title shall not, by itself, constitute participation in the management of the limited liability company.

§ 18–112.   Judicial cancellation of certificate of formation; proceedings.

(a)   Upon motion by the Attorney General, the Court of Chancery shall have jurisdiction to cancel the certificate of formation of any domestic limited liability company for abuse or misuse of its limited liability company powers, privileges or existence. The Attorney General shall proceed for this purpose in the Court of Chancery.

(b)   The Court of Chancery shall have power, by appointment of trustees, receivers or otherwise, to administer and wind up the affairs of any domestic limited liability company whose certificate of formation shall be canceled by the Court of Chancery under this section, and to make such orders and decrees with respect thereto as shall be just and equitable respecting its affairs and assets and the rights of its members and creditors.

§ 18–113.   Document form, signature and delivery.

(a)   Except as provided in subsection (b) of this section, without limiting the manner in which any act or transaction may be documented, or the manner in which a document may be signed or delivered:

(1)   Any act or transaction contemplated or governed by this chapter or the limited liability company agreement may be provided for in a document, and an electronic transmission is the equivalent of a written document.

(2)   Whenever this chapter or the limited liability company agreement requires or permits a signature, the signature may be a manual, facsimile, conformed or electronic signature. "Electronic signature" means an electronic symbol or process that is attached to, or logically associated with, a document and executed or adopted by a person with an intent to authenticate or adopt the document.

(3)   Unless otherwise provided in the limited liability company agreement or agreed between the sender and recipient, an electronic transmission is delivered to a person for purposes of this chapter and the limited liability company agreement when it enters an information processing system that the person has designated for the purpose of receiving electronic transmissions of the type delivered, so long as the electronic transmission is in a form capable of being processed by that system and such person is able to retrieve the electronic transmission. Whether a person has so designated an information processing system is determined by the limited liability company agreement or from the context and surrounding circumstances, including the parties' conduct. An electronic transmission is delivered under this section even if no person is aware of its receipt. Receipt of an electronic acknowledgement from an information processing system establishes that an electronic transmission was received but, by itself, does not establish that the content sent corresponds to the content received.

This chapter shall not prohibit 1 or more persons from conducting a transaction in accordance with Chapter 12A of this title so long as the part or parts of the transaction that are governed by this chapter are documented, signed and delivered in accordance with this subsection or otherwise in accordance with this chapter. This subsection shall apply solely for purposes of determining whether an act or transaction has been documented, and the document has been signed and delivered, in accordance with this chapter and the limited liability company agreement.

(b)   Subsection (a) of this section shall not apply to:

(1)   A document filed with or submitted to the Secretary of State, the Register in Chancery, or a court or other judicial or governmental body of this State;

(2)   A certificate of limited liability company interest; and

(3)   An act or transaction effected pursuant to § 18–104, § 18–105, or § 18–109 or subchapter IX or X of this title.

The foregoing shall not create any presumption about the lawful means to document a matter addressed by this subsection, or the lawful means to sign or deliver a document addressed by this subsection. A provision of the limited liability company agreement shall not limit the application of subsection (a) of this section unless the provision expressly restricts one or more of the means of documenting an act or transaction, or of signing or delivering a document, permitted by subsection (a) of this section.

(c)   In the event that any provision of this chapter is deemed to modify, limit or supersede the Electronic Signatures in Global and National Commerce Act, 15 U.S.C. § 7001 et. seq., the provisions of this chapter shall control to the fullest extent permitted by § 7002(a)(2) of such act [15 U.S.C. § 7002(a)(2)].

SUBCHAPTER II.   FORMATION; CERTIFICATE OF FORMATION

§ 18–201.   Certificate of formation.

(a)   In order to form a limited liability company, 1 or more authorized persons must execute a certificate of formation. The certificate of formation shall be filed in the office of the Secretary of State and set forth:

(1)   The name of the limited liability company;

(2)   The address of the registered office and the name and address of the registered agent for service of process required to be maintained by § 18–104 of this title; and

(3)   Any other matters the members determine to include therein.

(b)   A limited liability company is formed at the time of the filing of the initial certificate of formation in the office of the Secretary of State or at any later date or time specified in the certificate of formation if, in either case, there has been substantial compliance with the requirements of this section. A limited liability company formed under this chapter shall be a separate legal entity, the existence of which as a separate legal entity shall continue until cancellation of the limited liability company's certificate of formation.

(c)   The filing of the certificate of formation in the office of the Secretary of State shall make it unnecessary to file any other documents under Chapter 31 of this title.

(d)   A limited liability company agreement shall be entered into or otherwise existing either before, after or at the time of the filing of a certificate of formation and, whether entered into or otherwise existing before, after or at the time of such filing, may be made effective as of the effective time of such filing or at such other time or date as provided in or reflected by the limited liability company agreement.

(e)   A certificate of formation substantially complies with § 18–201(a)(2) of this title if it contains the name of the registered agent and the address of the registered office even if the certificate of formation does not expressly designate such person as the registered agent or such address as the registered office or the address of the registered agent.

§ 18–202.   Amendment to certificate of formation.

(a)   A certificate of formation is amended by filing a certificate of amendment thereto in the office of the Secretary of State. The certificate of amendment shall set forth:

(1)   The name of the limited liability company; and

(2)   The amendment to the certificate of formation.

(b)   A manager or, if there is no manager, then any member who becomes aware that any statement in a certificate of formation was false when made, or that any matter described has changed making the certificate of formation false in any material respect, shall promptly amend the certificate of formation.

(c)   A certificate of formation may be amended at any time for any other proper purpose.

(d)   Unless otherwise provided in this chapter or unless a later effective date or time (which shall be a date or time certain) is provided for in the certificate of amendment, a certificate of amendment shall be effective at the time of its filing with the Secretary of State.

§ 18–203.   Cancellation of certificate.

(a)   A certificate of formation shall be canceled upon the dissolution and the completion of winding up of a limited liability company, or as provided in § 18–104(d), § 18–104 (i)(4), § 18–112 or § 18–1108 of this title, or upon the filing of a certificate of merger or consolidation or a certificate of ownership and merger if the limited liability company is not the surviving or resulting entity in a merger or consolidation or upon the future effective date or time of a certificate of merger or consolidation or a certificate of ownership and merger if the limited liability company is not the surviving or resulting entity in a merger or consolidation, or upon the filing of a certificate of transfer or upon the future effective date or time of a certificate of transfer, or upon the filing of a certificate of conversion to non-Delaware entity or upon the future effective date or time of a certificate of conversion to non-Delaware entity or upon the filing of a certificate of division if the limited liability company is a dividing company that is not a surviving company or upon the future effective date or time of a certificate of division if the limited liability company is a dividing company that is not a surviving company. A certificate of cancellation shall be filed in the office of the Secretary of State to accomplish the cancellation of a certificate of formation upon the dissolution and the completion of winding up of a limited liability company and shall set forth:

(1)   The name of the limited liability company;

(2)   The date of filing of its certificate of formation;

(3)   If the limited liability company has formed 1 or more registered series whose certificate of registered series has not been canceled prior to the filing of the certificate of cancellation, the name of each such registered series;

(4)   The future effective date or time (which shall be a date or time certain) of cancellation if it is not to be effective upon the filing of the certificate; and

(5)   Any other information the person filing the certificate of cancellation determines.

(b)   A certificate of cancellation that is filed in the office of the Secretary of State prior to the dissolution or the completion of winding up of a limited liability company may be corrected as an erroneously executed certificate of cancellation by filing with the office of the Secretary of State a certificate of correction of such certificate of cancellation in accordance with § 18–211 of this title.

(c)   The Secretary of State shall not issue a certificate of good standing with respect to a limited liability company (or any registered series thereof) if its certificate of formation is canceled.

§ 18–204.   Execution.

(a)   Each certificate required by this subchapter to be filed in the office of the Secretary of State shall be executed by 1 or more authorized persons or, in the case of a certificate of conversion to limited liability company or certificate of limited liability company domestication, by any person authorized to execute such certificate on behalf of the other entity or non-United States entity, respectively, except that a certificate of merger or consolidation filed by a surviving or resulting other business entity shall be executed by any person authorized to execute such certificate on behalf of such other business entity.

(b)   Unless otherwise provided in a limited liability company agreement, any person may sign any certificate or amendment thereof or enter into a limited liability company agreement or amendment thereof by an agent, including an attorney-in-fact. An authorization, including a power of attorney, to sign any certificate or amendment thereof or to enter into a limited liability company agreement or amendment thereof need not be in writing, need not be sworn to, verified or acknowledged, and need not be filed in the office of the Secretary of State, but if in writing, must be retained by the limited liability company.

(c)   For all purposes of the laws of the State of Delaware, unless otherwise provided in a limited liability company agreement, a power of attorney or proxy with respect to a limited liability company granted to any person shall be irrevocable if it states that it is irrevocable and it is coupled with an interest sufficient in law to support an irrevocable power or proxy. Such irrevocable power of attorney or proxy, unless otherwise provided therein or in a limited liability company agreement, shall not be affected by subsequent death, disability, incapacity, dissolution, termination of existence or bankruptcy of, or any other event concerning, the principal. A power of attorney or proxy with respect to matters relating to the organization, internal affairs or termination of a limited liability company or granted by a person as a member or an assignee of a limited liability company interest or by a person seeking to become a member or an assignee of a limited liability company interest and, in either case, granted to the limited liability company, a manager or member thereof, or any of their respective officers, directors, managers, members, partners, trustees, employees or agents shall be deemed coupled with an interest sufficient in law to support an irrevocable power or proxy. The provisions of this subsection shall not be construed to limit the enforceability of a power of attorney or proxy that is part of a limited liability company agreement.

(d)   The execution of a certificate by a person who is authorized by this chapter to execute such certificate constitutes an oath or affirmation, under the penalties of perjury in the third degree, that, to the best of such person's knowledge and belief, the facts stated therein are true.

§ 18–205.   Execution, amendment or cancellation by judicial order.

(a)   If a person required to execute a certificate required by this subchapter fails or refuses to do so, any other person who is adversely affected by the failure or refusal may petition the Court of Chancery to direct the execution of the certificate. If the Court finds that the execution of the certificate is proper and that any person so designated has failed or refused to execute the certificate, it shall order the Secretary of State to record an appropriate certificate.

(b)   If a person required to execute a limited liability company agreement or amendment thereof fails or refuses to do so, any other person who is adversely affected by the failure or refusal may petition the Court of Chancery to direct the execution of the limited liability company agreement or amendment thereof. If the Court finds that the limited liability company agreement or amendment thereof should be executed and that any person required to execute the limited liability company agreement or amendment thereof has failed or refused to do so, it shall enter an order granting appropriate relief.

§ 18–206.   Filing.

(a)   The signed copy of any certificate authorized to be filed under this chapter shall be delivered to the Secretary of State. A person who executes a certificate as an agent or fiduciary need not exhibit evidence of that person's authority as a prerequisite to filing. Any signature on any certificate authorized to be filed with the Secretary of State under any provision of this chapter may be a facsimile, a conformed signature or an electronically transmitted signature. Upon delivery of any certificate, the Secretary of State shall record the date and time of its delivery. Unless the Secretary of State finds that any certificate does not conform to law, upon receipt of all filing fees required by law the Secretary of State shall:

(1)   Certify that any certificate authorized to be filed under this chapter has been filed in the Secretary of State's office by endorsing upon the signed certificate the word "Filed," and the date and time of the filing. This endorsement is conclusive of the date and time of its filing in the absence of actual fraud. Except as provided in paragraph (a)(5) or (a)(6) of this section, such date and time of filing of a certificate shall be the date and time of delivery of the certificate;

(2)   File and index the endorsed certificate;

(3)   Prepare and return to the person who filed it or that person's representative a copy of the signed certificate, similarly endorsed, and shall certify such copy as a true copy of the signed certificate; and

(4)   Cause to be entered such information from the certificate as the Secretary of State deems appropriate into the Delaware Corporation Information System or any system which is a successor thereto in the office of the Secretary of State, and such information and a copy of such certificate shall be permanently maintained as a public record on a suitable medium. The Secretary of State is authorized to grant direct access to such system to registered agents subject to the execution of an operating agreement between the Secretary of State and such registered agent. Any registered agent granted such access shall demonstrate the existence of policies to ensure that information entered into the system accurately reflects the content of certificates in the possession of the registered agent at the time of entry.

(5)   Upon request made upon or prior to delivery, the Secretary of State may, to the extent deemed practicable, establish as the date and time of filing of a certificate a date and time after its delivery. If the Secretary of State refuses to file any certificate due to an error, omission or other imperfection, the Secretary of State may hold such certificate in suspension, and in such event, upon delivery of a replacement certificate in proper form for filing and tender of the required fees within 5 business days after notice of such suspension is given to the filer, the Secretary of State shall establish as the date and time of filing of such certificate the date and time that would have been the date and

time of filing of the rejected certificate had it been accepted for filing. The Secretary of State shall not issue a certificate of good standing with respect to any limited liability company or registered series with a certificate held in suspension pursuant to this subsection. The Secretary of State may establish as the date and time of filing of a certificate the date and time at which information from such certificate is entered pursuant to paragraph (a)(4) of this section if such certificate is delivered on the same date and within 4 hours after such information is entered.

(6) If:

a. Together with the actual delivery of a certificate and tender of the required fees, there is delivered to the Secretary of State a separate affidavit (which in its heading shall be designated as an affidavit of extraordinary condition) attesting, on the basis of personal knowledge of the affiant or a reliable source of knowledge identified in the affidavit, that an earlier effort to deliver such certificate and tender such fees was made in good faith, specifying the nature, date and time of such good faith effort and requesting that the Secretary of State establish such date and time as the date and time of filing of such certificate; or

b. Upon the actual delivery of a certificate and tender of the required fees, the Secretary of State in the Secretary of State's own discretion provides a written waiver of the requirement for such an affidavit stating that it appears to the Secretary of State that an earlier effort to deliver such certificate and tender such fees was made in good faith and specifying the date and time of such effort; and

c. The Secretary of State determines that an extraordinary condition existed at such date and time, that such earlier effort was unsuccessful as a result of the existence of such extraordinary condition, and that such actual delivery and tender were made within a reasonable period (not to exceed 2 business days) after the cessation of such extraordinary condition, then the Secretary of State may establish such date and time as the date and time of filing of such certificate. No fee shall be paid to the Secretary of State for receiving an affidavit of extraordinary condition. For purposes of this subsection, an extraordinary condition means: any emergency resulting from an attack on, invasion or occupation by foreign military forces of, or disaster, catastrophe, war or other armed conflict, revolution or insurrection or rioting or civil commotion in, the United States or a locality in which the Secretary of State conducts its business or in which the good faith effort to deliver the certificate and tender the required fees is made, or the immediate threat of any of the foregoing; or any malfunction or outage of the electrical or telephone service to the Secretary of State's office, or weather or other condition in or about a locality in which the Secretary of State conducts its business, as a result of which the Secretary of State's office is not open for the purpose of the filing of certificates under this chapter or such filing cannot be effected without extraordinary effort. The Secretary of State may require such proof as it deems necessary to make the determination required under this paragraph (a)(6)c., and any such determination shall be conclusive in the absence of actual fraud. If the Secretary of State establishes the date and time of filing of a certificate pursuant to this subsection, the date and time of delivery of the affidavit of extraordinary condition or the date and time of the Secretary of State's written waiver of such affidavit shall be endorsed on such affidavit or waiver and such affidavit or waiver, so endorsed, shall be attached to the filed certificate to which it relates. Such filed certificate shall be effective as of the date and time established as the date and time of filing by the Secretary of State pursuant to this subsection, except as to those persons who are substantially and adversely affected by such establishment and, as to those persons, the certificate shall be effective from the date and time endorsed on the affidavit of extraordinary condition or written waiver attached thereto.

(b) Notwithstanding any other provision of this chapter, any certificate filed under this chapter shall be effective at the time of its filing with the Secretary of State or at any later date or time (not later than a time on the one hundred and eightieth day after the date of its filing if such date of filing is on or after January 1, 2012) specified in the certificate. Upon the filing of a certificate of amendment (or judicial decree of amendment), certificate of correction, corrected certificate or restated certificate in the office of the Secretary of State, or upon the future effective date or time of a certificate of amendment (or judicial decree thereof) or restated certificate, as provided for therein, the certificate of formation or certificate of registered series, as applicable, shall be amended, corrected or restated as set forth therein. Upon the filing of a certificate of cancellation (or a judicial decree thereof), a certificate of merger or consolidation or a certificate of ownership and merger or a certificate of division which acts as a certificate of cancellation, a certificate of transfer, a certificate of conversion to a non-Delaware entity, or a certificate of conversion of registered series to protected series, or upon the future effective date or time of a certificate of cancellation (or a judicial decree thereof), a certificate of merger or consolidation or a certificate of ownership and merger or a certificate of division which acts as a certificate of cancellation, a certificate of transfer, a certificate of conversion to a non-Delaware entity, or a certificate of conversion of registered series to protected series, as provided for therein, or as specified in § 18–104(d), § 18–104(i)(4), § 18–112 or § 18–1108 of this title, the certificate of formation or certificate of registered series, as applicable, is canceled. Upon the filing of a certificate of limited liability company domestication or upon the future effective date or time of a certificate of limited liability company domestication, the entity filing the certificate of limited liability company domestication is domesticated as a limited liability company with the effect provided in § 18–212 of this title. Upon the filing of a certificate of conversion to limited liability company or upon the future effective date or time of a certificate of conversion to limited liability company, the entity filing the certificate of conversion to limited liability company is converted to a limited liability company with the effect provided in § 18–214 of this title. Upon the filing of a certificate of conversion of protected series to registered series, or upon the future effective date or time of a certificate of conversion of protected series to registered series, the protected series with respect to which such filing is made is converted to a registered series with the effect provided in § 18–219 of this title. Upon the filing of a certificate of conversion of registered series to protected series, or upon the future effective date or time of a certificate of conversion of registered series to protected series, the registered series filing such certificate is converted to a protected series with the effect provided in § 18–220 of this title. Upon the filing of a certificate of revival, a limited liability company or a registered series is revived with the effect provided in § 18–1109 or § 18–1110 of this title. Upon the filing of a certificate of transfer and domestic continuance, or upon the future effective date or time of a certificate of transfer and domestic continuance, as provided for therein, the limited liability company filing the certificate of transfer and domestic continuance shall continue to exist as a limited liability company of the State of Delaware with the effect provided in § 18–213 of this title.

(c) If any certificate filed in accordance with this chapter provides for a future effective date or time and if, prior to such future effective date or time set forth in such certificate, the transaction is terminated or its terms are amended to change the future effective date or time or any other matter described in such certificate so as to make such certificate false or inaccurate in any respect, such certificate shall, prior to the future effective date or time set forth in such certificate, be terminated or amended by the filing of a certificate of termination or certificate of amendment of such certificate, executed in accordance with § 18–204 of this title, which shall identify the certificate which has been terminated or amended and shall state that the certificate has been terminated or the manner in which it has been amended. Upon the filing of a certificate of amendment of a certificate with a future effective date or time, the certificate identified in such certificate of amendment is amended. Upon the filing of a certificate of termination of a certificate with a future effective date or time, the certificate identified in such certificate of termination is terminated.

(d) A fee as set forth in § 18–1105(a)(3) of this title shall be paid at the time of the filing of a certificate of formation, a certificate of registered series, a certificate of amendment, a certificate of correction, a certificate of amendment of a certificate with a future effective date or time, a certificate of termination of a certificate with a future effective date or time, a certificate of cancellation, a certificate of merger or consolidation, a certificate of ownership and merger, a restated certificate, a corrected certificate, a certificate of conversion to limited liability company, a certificate of conversion to a non-Delaware entity, a certificate of conversion of protected series to registered series, a certificate of conversion of registered series to protected series, a certificate of transfer, a certificate of transfer and domestic continuance, a certificate of limited liability company domestication, a certificate of division or a certificate of revival.

(e) The Secretary of State, acting as agent, shall collect and deposit in a separate account established exclusively for that purpose, a courthouse municipality fee with respect to each filed instrument and shall thereafter monthly remit funds from such account to the treasuries of the municipalities designated in § 301 of Title 10. Said fees shall be for the purposes of defraying certain costs incurred by such municipalities in hosting the primary locations for the Delaware Courts. The fee to such municipalities shall be $ 20 for each instrument filed with the Secretary of State in accordance with this section. The municipality to receive the fee shall be the municipality designated in § 301 of Title 10 in the county in which the limited liability company's registered office in this State is, or is to be, located, except that a fee shall not be charged for a document filed in accordance with subchapter IX of this chapter.

(f)   A fee as set forth in § 18–1105(a)(4) of this title shall be paid for a certified copy of any paper on file as provided for by this chapter, and a fee as set forth in § 18–1105(a)(5) of this title shall be paid for each page copied.

(g)   Notwithstanding any other provision of this chapter, it shall not be necessary for any limited liability company or foreign limited liability company to amend its certificate of formation, its application for registration as a foreign limited liability company, or any other document that has been filed in the office of the Secretary of State prior to August 1, 2011, to comply with § 18–104(k) of this title; notwithstanding the foregoing, any certificate or other document filed under this chapter on or after August 1, 2011, and changing the address of a registered agent or registered office shall comply with § 18–104(k) of this title.

§ 18–207.   Notice.

The fact that a certificate of formation is on file in the office of the Secretary of State is notice that the entity formed in connection with the filing of the certificate of formation is a limited liability company formed under the laws of the State of Delaware and is notice of all other facts set forth therein which are required to be set forth in a certificate of formation by § 18–201(a)(1) and (2) or § 18–1202 of this title and which are permitted to be set forth in a certificate of formation by § 18–215(b) or § 18–218(b) of this title. The fact that a certificate of registered series is on file in the office of the Secretary of State is notice that the registered series named in such certificate of registered series has been formed pursuant to § 18–218 of this title and is notice of all other facts set forth therein which are required to be set forth in a certificate of registered series by § 18–218(d) of this title.

§ 18–208.   Restated certificate.

(a)   *Restated certificate of formation.—*

(1)   A limited liability company may, whenever desired, integrate into a single instrument all of the provisions of its certificate of formation which are then in effect and operative as a result of there having theretofore been filed with the Secretary of State 1 or more certificates or other instruments pursuant to any of the sections referred to in this subchapter, and it may at the same time also further amend its certificate of formation by adopting a restated certificate of formation.

(2)   If a restated certificate of formation merely restates and integrates but does not further amend the initial certificate of formation, as theretofore amended or supplemented by any instrument that was executed and filed pursuant to any of the sections in this subchapter, it shall be specifically designated in its heading as a "Restated Certificate of Formation" together with such other words as the limited liability company may deem appropriate and shall be executed by an authorized person and filed as provided in § 18–206 of this title in the office of the Secretary of State. If a restated certificate restates and integrates and also further amends in any respect the certificate of formation, as theretofore amended or supplemented, it shall be specifically designated in its heading as an "Amended and Restated Certificate of Formation" together with such other words as the limited liability company may deem appropriate and shall be executed by at least 1 authorized person, and filed as provided in § 18–206 of this title in the office of the Secretary of State.

(3)   A restated certificate of formation shall state, either in its heading or in an introductory paragraph, the limited liability company's present name, and, if it has been changed, the name under which it was originally filed, and the date of filing of its original certificate of formation with the Secretary of State, and the future effective date or time (which shall be a date or time certain) of the restated certificate if it is not to be effective upon the filing of the restated certificate. A restated certificate shall also state that it was duly executed and is being filed in accordance with this section. If a restated certificate only restates and integrates and does not further amend a limited liability company's certificate of formation as theretofore amended or supplemented and there is no discrepancy between those provisions and the restated certificate, it shall state that fact as well.

(4)   Upon the filing of a restated certificate of formation with the Secretary of State, or upon the future effective date or time of a restated certificate of formation as provided for therein, the initial

certificate of formation, as theretofore amended or supplemented, shall be superseded; thenceforth, the restated certificate of formation, including any further amendment or changes made thereby, shall be the certificate of formation of the limited liability company, but the original effective date of formation shall remain unchanged.

(5)   Any amendment or change effected in connection with the restatement and integration of the certificate of formation shall be subject to any other provision of this chapter, not inconsistent with this section, which would apply if a separate certificate of amendment were filed to effect such amendment or change.

(b)   *Restated certificate of registered series.—*

(1)   A registered series of a limited liability company may, whenever desired, integrate into a single instrument all of the provisions of its certificate of registered series which are then in effect and operative as a result of there having theretofore been filed with the Secretary of State 1 or more certificates or other instruments pursuant to any of the sections referred to in this subchapter, and it may at the same time also further amend its certificate of registered series by adopting a restated certificate of registered series.

(2)   If a restated certificate of registered series merely restates and integrates but does not further amend the initial certificate of registered series, as theretofore amended or supplemented by any instrument that was executed and filed pursuant to any of the sections in this subchapter, it shall be specifically designated in its heading as a "Restated Certificate of Registered Series" together with such other words as the registered series may deem appropriate and shall be executed by an authorized person and filed as provided in § 18–206 of this title in the office of the Secretary of State. If a restated certificate restates and integrates and also further amends in any respect the certificate of registered series as theretofore amended or supplemented, it shall be specifically designated in its heading as an "Amended and Restated Certificate of Registered Series" together with such other words as the registered series may deem appropriate and shall be executed by at least 1 authorized person, and filed as provided in § 18–206 of this title in the office of the Secretary of State.

(3)   A restated certificate of registered series shall state, either in its heading or in an introductory paragraph, the name of the limited liability company, the present name of the registered series, and, if the name of the registered series has been changed, the name under which it was originally filed, and the date of filing of its original certificate of registered series with the Secretary of State, and the future effective date or time (which shall be a date or time certain) of the restated certificate of registered series if it is not to be effective upon the filing of the restated certificate of registered series. A restated certificate shall also state that it was duly executed and is being filed in accordance with this section. If a restated certificate only restates and integrates and does not further amend a certificate of registered series, as theretofore amended or supplemented and there is no discrepancy between those provisions and the restated certificate, it shall state that fact as well.

(4)   Upon the filing of a restated certificate of registered series with the Secretary of State, or upon the future effective date or time of a restated certificate of registered series as provided for therein, the initial certificate of registered series, as theretofore amended or supplemented, shall be superseded; thenceforth, the restated certificate of registered series, including any further amendment or changes made thereby, shall be the certificate of registered series of such registered series, but the original effective date of formation of the registered series, as applicable, shall remain unchanged.

(5)   Any amendment or change effected in connection with the restatement and integration of a certificate of registered series shall be subject to any other provision of this chapter, not inconsistent with this section, which would apply if a separate certificate of amendment were filed to effect such amendment or change.

§ 18–209.   Merger and consolidation.

(a)   As used in this section and in §§ 18–204, 18–217, 18–219, 18–220 and 18–221 of this title, "other business entity" means a corporation, a statutory trust, a business trust, an association, a real estate investment trust, a common-law trust, or any other incorporated or unincorporated business or entity, including a partnership (whether general (including a limited liability partnership) or limited (including a limited liability limited partnership)), and a foreign limited liability company, but excluding a domestic limited liability company. As used in this section and in §§ 18–210 and 18–301 of this title, "plan of merger" means a writing approved by a domestic limited liability company, in the form of resolutions or otherwise, that states the terms and conditions of a merger under subsection (i) of this section.

(b)   Pursuant to an agreement of merger or consolidation, 1 or more domestic limited liability companies may merge or consolidate with or into 1 or more domestic limited liability companies or 1 or more other business entities formed or organized under the laws of the State of Delaware or any other state or the United States or any foreign country or other foreign jurisdiction, or any combination thereof, with such domestic limited liability company or other business entity as the agreement shall provide being the surviving or resulting domestic limited liability company or other business entity. Unless otherwise provided in the limited liability company agreement, an agreement of merger or consolidation or a plan of merger shall be approved by each domestic limited liability company which is to merge or consolidate by members who own more than 50 percent of the then current percentage or other interest in the profits of the domestic limited liability company owned by all of the members. In connection with a merger or consolidation hereunder, rights or securities of, or interests in, a domestic limited liability company or other business entity which is a constituent party to the merger or consolidation may be exchanged for or converted into cash, property, rights or securities of, or interests in, the surviving or resulting domestic limited liability company or other business entity or, in addition to or in lieu thereof, may be exchanged for or converted into cash, property, rights or securities of, or interests in, a domestic limited liability company or other business entity which is not the surviving or resulting limited liability company or other business entity in the merger or consolidation, may remain outstanding or may be canceled. Notwithstanding prior approval, an agreement of merger or consolidation or a plan of merger may be terminated or amended pursuant to a provision for such termination or amendment contained in the agreement of merger or consolidation or plan of merger. Unless otherwise provided in a limited liability company agreement, a limited liability company whose original certificate of formation was filed with the Secretary of State and effective on or prior to July 31, 2015, shall continue to be governed by the second sentence of this subsection as in effect on July 31, 2015.

(c)   Except in the case of a merger under subsection (i) of this section, if a domestic limited liability company is merging or consolidating under this section, the domestic limited liability company or other business entity surviving or resulting in or from the merger or consolidation shall file a certificate of merger or consolidation executed by 1 or more authorized persons on behalf of the domestic limited liability company when it is the surviving or resulting entity in the office of the Secretary of State. The certificate of merger or consolidation shall state:

(1)   The name, jurisdiction of formation or organization and type of entity of each of the domestic limited liability companies and other business entities which is to merge or consolidate;

(2)   That an agreement of merger or consolidation has been approved and executed by each of the domestic limited liability companies and other business entities which is to merge or consolidate;

(3)   The name of the surviving or resulting domestic limited liability company or other business entity;

(4)   In the case of a merger in which a domestic limited liability company is the surviving entity, such amendments, if any, to the certificate of formation of the surviving domestic limited liability company to change its name, registered office or registered agent as are desired to be effected by the merger;

(5)   The future effective date or time (which shall be a date or time certain) of the merger or consolidation if it is not to be effective upon the filing of the certificate of merger or consolidation;

(6)   That the agreement of merger or consolidation is on file at a place of business of the surviving or resulting domestic limited liability company or other business entity, and shall state the address thereof;

(7)   That a copy of the agreement of merger or consolidation will be furnished by the surviving or resulting domestic limited liability company or other business entity, on request and without cost, to any member of any domestic limited liability company or any person holding an interest in any other business entity which is to merge or consolidate; and

(8) If the surviving or resulting entity is not a domestic limited liability company, or a corporation, partnership (whether general (including a limited liability partnership) or limited (including a limited liability limited partnership)) or statutory trust organized under the laws of the State of Delaware, a statement that such surviving or resulting other business entity agrees that it may be served with process in the State of Delaware in any action, suit or proceeding for the enforcement of any obligation of any domestic limited liability company which is to merge or consolidate, irrevocably appointing the Secretary of State as its agent to accept service of process in any such action, suit or proceeding and specifying the address to which a copy of such process shall be mailed to it by the Secretary of State. Process may be served upon the Secretary of State under this subsection by means of electronic transmission but only as prescribed by the Secretary of State. The Secretary of State is authorized to issue such rules and regulations with respect to such service as the Secretary of State deems necessary or appropriate. In the event of service hereunder upon the Secretary of State, the procedures set forth in § 18–911(c) of this title shall be applicable, except that the plaintiff in any such action, suit or proceeding shall furnish the Secretary of State with the address specified in the certificate of merger or consolidation provided for in this section and any other address which the plaintiff may elect to furnish, together with copies of such process as required by the Secretary of State, and the Secretary of State shall notify such surviving or resulting other business entity at all such addresses furnished by the plaintiff in accordance with the procedures set forth in § 18–911(c) of this title.

(d) Unless a future effective date or time is provided in a certificate of merger or consolidation, or in the case of a merger under subsection (i) of this section in a certificate of ownership and merger, in which event a merger or consolidation shall be effective at any such future effective date or time, a merger or consolidation shall be effective upon the filing in the office of the Secretary of State of a certificate of merger or consolidation or a certificate of ownership and merger.

(e) A certificate of merger or consolidation or a certificate of ownership and merger shall act as a certificate of cancellation for a domestic limited liability company which is not the surviving or resulting entity in the merger or consolidation. A certificate of merger that sets forth any amendment in accordance with paragraph (c)(4) of this section shall be deemed to be an amendment to the certificate of formation of the limited liability company, and the limited liability company shall not be required to take any further action to amend its certificate of formation under § 18–202 of this title with respect to such amendments set forth in the certificate of merger. Whenever this section requires the filing of a certificate of merger or consolidation, such requirement shall be deemed satisfied by the filing of an agreement of merger or consolidation containing the information required by this section to be set forth in the certificate of merger or consolidation.

(f) An agreement of merger or consolidation or a plan of merger approved in accordance with subsection (b) of this section may:

(1) Effect any amendment to the limited liability company agreement; or

(2) Effect the adoption of a new limited liability company agreement, for a limited liability company if it is the surviving or resulting limited liability company in the merger or consolidation.

Any amendment to a limited liability company agreement or adoption of a new limited liability company agreement made pursuant to the foregoing sentence shall be effective at the effective time or date of the merger or consolidation and shall be effective notwithstanding any provision of the limited liability company agreement relating to amendment or adoption of a new limited liability company agreement, other than a provision that by its terms applies to an amendment to the limited liability company agreement or the adoption of a new limited liability company agreement, in either case, in connection with a merger or consolidation. The provisions of this subsection shall not be construed to limit the accomplishment of a merger or of any of the matters referred to herein by any other means provided for in a limited liability company agreement or other agreement or as otherwise permitted by law, including that the limited liability company agreement of any constituent limited liability company to the merger or consolidation (including a limited liability company formed for the purpose of consummating a merger or consolidation) shall be the limited liability company agreement of the surviving or resulting limited liability company.

(g) When any merger or consolidation shall have become effective under this section, for all purposes of the laws of the State of Delaware, all of the rights, privileges and powers of each of the domestic limited liability companies and other business entities that have merged or consolidated, and all property, real, personal and mixed, and all debts due to any of said domestic limited liability companies and other business entities, as well as all other things and causes of action belonging to each of such domestic limited liability companies and other business entities, shall be vested in the surviving or resulting domestic limited liability company or other business entity, and shall thereafter be the property of the surviving or resulting domestic limited liability company or other business entity as they were of each of the domestic limited liability companies and other business entities that have merged or consolidated, and the title to any real property vested by deed or otherwise, under the laws of the State of Delaware, in any of such domestic limited liability companies and other business entities, shall not revert or be in any way impaired by reason of this chapter; but all rights of creditors and all liens upon any property of any of said domestic limited liability companies and other business entities shall be preserved unimpaired, and all debts, liabilities and duties of each of the said domestic limited liability companies and other business entities that have merged or consolidated shall thenceforth attach to the surviving or resulting domestic limited liability company or other business entity, and may be enforced against it to the same extent as if said debts, liabilities and duties had been incurred or contracted by it. Unless otherwise agreed, a merger or consolidation of a domestic limited liability company, including a domestic limited liability company which is not the surviving or resulting entity in the merger or consolidation, shall not require such domestic limited liability company to wind up its affairs under § 18–803 of this title or pay its liabilities and distribute its assets under § 18–804 of this title, and the merger or consolidation shall not constitute a dissolution of such limited liability company.

(h) A limited liability company agreement may provide that a domestic limited liability company shall not have the power to merge or consolidate as set forth in this section.

(i) In any case in which (i) at least 90% of the outstanding shares of each class of the stock of a corporation or corporations (other than a corporation which has in its certificate of incorporation the provision required by § 251(g)(7)(i) of Title 8), of which class there are outstanding shares that, absent § 267(a) of Title 8, would be entitled to vote on such merger, is owned by a domestic limited liability company, (ii) 1 or more of such corporations is a corporation of the State of Delaware, and (iii) any corporation that is not a corporation of the State of Delaware is a corporation of any other state or the District of Columbia or another jurisdiction, the laws of which do not forbid such merger, the domestic limited liability company having such stock ownership may either merge the corporation or corporations into itself and assume all of its or their obligations, or merge itself, or itself and 1 or more of such corporations, into 1 of the other corporations, pursuant to a plan of merger. If a domestic limited liability company is causing a merger under this subsection, the domestic limited liability company shall file a certificate of ownership and merger executed by 1 or more authorized persons on behalf of the domestic limited liability company in the office of the Secretary of State. The certificate of ownership and merger shall certify that such merger was authorized in accordance with the domestic limited liability company's limited liability company agreement and this chapter, and if the domestic limited liability company shall not own all the outstanding stock of all the corporations that are parties to the merger, shall state the terms and conditions of the merger, including the securities, cash, property, or rights to be issued, paid, delivered or granted by the surviving domestic limited liability company or corporation upon surrender of each share of the corporation or corporations not owned by the domestic limited liability company, or the cancellation of some or all of such shares. If a corporation surviving a merger under this subsection is not a corporation organized under the laws of the State of Delaware, then the terms and conditions of the merger shall obligate such corporation to agree that it may be served with process in the State of Delaware in any proceeding for enforcement of any obligation of the domestic limited liability company or any obligation of any constituent corporation of the State of Delaware, as well as for enforcement of any obligation of the surviving corporation, including any suit or other proceeding to enforce the right of any stockholders as determined in appraisal proceedings pursuant to § 262 of Title 8, and to irrevocably appoint the Secretary of State as its agent to accept service of process in any such suit or other proceedings, and to specify the address to which a copy of such process shall be mailed by the Secretary of State. Process may be served upon the Secretary of State under this subsection by means of electronic transmission but only as prescribed by the Secretary of State. The Secretary of State is authorized to issue such rules and regulations with respect to such service as the Secretary of State deems necessary or appropriate. In the event of such service upon the Secretary of State in accordance with this subsection, the Secretary of State shall forthwith notify such surviving corporation thereof by letter, directed to such surviving corporation at its address so specified, unless such surviving corporation shall have designated in writing to the Secretary of State a different address for such purpose, in which case it shall be mailed to the last address so designated. Such letter shall be sent by a mail or courier service that includes a record of mailing or deposit with the courier and a record of delivery evidenced by the signature of the recipient. Such letter shall enclose a copy of the process and any other papers served on the Secretary of State pursuant to this subsection. It shall be the duty of the plaintiff in the event of such service to serve process and any other papers in duplicate, to notify the Secretary of State that service is being effected pursuant to this subsection and to pay the Secretary of State the sum of $50 for the use of the State of Delaware, which sum shall be taxed as part of the costs in the proceeding, if the plaintiff shall prevail therein. The Secretary of State shall maintain an alphabetical record of any such service setting forth the name of the plaintiff and the defendant, the title, docket number and nature of the proceeding in which process has been served, the fact that service has been effected pursuant to this subsection, the return date thereof, and the day and hour service was made. The Secretary of State shall not be required to retain such information longer than 5 years from receipt of the service of process.

§ 18–210. Contractual appraisal rights.

A limited liability company agreement or an agreement of merger or consolidation or a plan of merger or a plan of division may provide that contractual appraisal rights with respect to a limited liability company interest or another interest in a limited liability company shall be available for any class or group or series of members or limited liability company interests in connection with any amendment of a limited liability company agreement, any merger or consolidation in which the limited liability company or a registered series of the limited liability company is a constituent party to the merger or consolidation, any division of the limited liability company, any conversion of the limited liability company to another business form, any conversion of a protected series of the limited liability company to a registered series of such limited liability company, any conversion of a registered series of the limited liability company to a protected series of such limited liability company, any transfer to or domestication or continuance in any jurisdiction by the limited liability company, or the sale of all or substantially all of the limited liability company's assets. The Court of Chancery shall have jurisdiction to hear and determine any matter relating to any such appraisal rights.

§ 18–211. Certificate of correction.

(a) Whenever any certificate authorized to be filed with the office of the Secretary of State under any provision of this chapter has been so filed and is an inaccurate record of the action therein referred to, or was defectively or erroneously executed, such certificate may be corrected by filing with the office of the Secretary of State a certificate of correction of such certificate. The certificate of correction shall specify the inaccuracy or defect to be corrected, shall set forth the portion of the certificate in corrected form, and shall be executed and filed as required by this chapter. The certificate of correction shall be effective as of the date the original certificate was filed, except as to those persons who are substantially and adversely affected by the correction, and as to those persons the certificate of correction shall be effective from the filing date.

(b) In lieu of filing a certificate of correction, a certificate may be corrected by filing with the Secretary of State a corrected certificate which shall be executed and filed as if the corrected certificate were the certificate being corrected, and a fee equal to the fee payable to the Secretary of State for a certificate of correction as prescribed by § 18–1105 of this title shall be paid and collected by the Secretary of State for the use of the State of Delaware in connection with the filing of the corrected certificate. The corrected certificate shall be specifically designated as such in its heading, shall specify the inaccuracy or defect to be corrected and shall set forth the entire certificate in corrected form. A certificate corrected in accordance with this section shall be effective as of the date the original certificate was filed, except as to those persons who are substantially and adversely affected by the correction and as to those persons the certificate as corrected shall be effective from the filing date.

§ 18–212. Domestication of non-United States entities.

(a) As used in this section and in § 18–204 of this title, "non-United States entity" means a foreign limited liability company (other than 1 formed under the laws of a state) or a corporation, a statutory trust, a business trust, an association, a real estate investment trust, a common-law trust or any other incorporated or unincorporated business or entity, including a partnership (whether general (including a limited liability partnership) or limited (including a limited liability limited partnership)) formed, incorporated, created or that otherwise came into being under the laws of any foreign country or other foreign jurisdiction (other than any state).

(b)   Any non-United States entity may become domesticated as a limited liability company in the State of Delaware by complying with subsection (g) of this section and filing in the office of the Secretary of State in accordance with § 18–206 of this title:

(1)   A certificate of limited liability company domestication that has been executed in accordance with § 18–204 of this title; and

(2)   A certificate of formation that complies with § 18–201 of this title and has been executed by 1 or more authorized persons in accordance with § 18–204 of this title.

Each of the certificates required by this subsection (b) shall be filed simultaneously in the office of the Secretary of State and, if such certificates are not to become effective upon their filing as permitted by § 18–206(b) of this title, then each such certificate shall provide for the same effective date or time in accordance with § 18–206(b) of this title.

(c)   The certificate of limited liability company domestication shall state:

(1)   The date on which and jurisdiction where the non-United States entity was first formed, incorporated, created or otherwise came into being;

(2)   The name of the non-United States entity immediately prior to the filing of the certificate of limited liability company domestication;

(3)   The name of the limited liability company as set forth in the certificate of formation filed in accordance with subsection (b) of this section;

(4)   The future effective date or time (which shall be a date or time certain) of the domestication as a limited liability company if it is not to be effective upon the filing of the certificate of limited liability company domestication and the certificate of formation;

(5)   The jurisdiction that constituted the seat, siege social, or principal place of business or central administration of the non-United States entity, or any other equivalent thereto under applicable law, immediately prior to the filing of the certificate of limited liability company domestication; and

(6)   That the domestication has been approved in the manner provided for by the document, instrument, agreement or other writing, as the case may be, governing the internal affairs of the non-United States entity and the conduct of its business or by applicable non-Delaware law, as appropriate.

(d)   Upon the filing in the office of the Secretary of State of the certificate of limited liability company domestication and the certificate of formation or upon the future effective date or time of the certificate of limited liability company domestication and the certificate of formation, the non-United States entity shall be domesticated as a limited liability company in the State of Delaware and the limited liability company shall thereafter be subject to all of the provisions of this chapter, except that notwithstanding § 18–201 of this title, the existence of the limited liability company shall be deemed to have commenced on the date the non-United States entity commenced its existence in the jurisdiction in which the non-United States entity was first formed, incorporated, created or otherwise came into being.

(e)   The domestication of any non-United States entity as a limited liability company in the State of Delaware shall not be deemed to affect any obligations or liabilities of the non-United States entity incurred prior to its domestication as a limited liability company in the State of Delaware, or the personal liability of any person therefor.

(f)   The filing of a certificate of limited liability company domestication shall not affect the choice of law applicable to the non-United States entity, except that from the effective date or time of the domestication, the law of the State of Delaware, including the provisions of this chapter, shall apply to the non-United States entity to the same extent as if the non-United States entity had been formed as a limited liability company on that date.

(g)   Prior to the filing of a certificate of limited liability company domestication with the Office of the Secretary of State, the domestication shall be approved in the manner provided for by the document, instrument, agreement or other writing, as the case may be, governing the internal affairs of the non-United States entity and the conduct of its business or by applicable non-Delaware law, as appropriate, and a limited liability company agreement shall be approved by the same authorization required to approve the domestication.

(h)   When any domestication shall have become effective under this section, for all purposes of the laws of the State of Delaware, all of the rights, privileges and powers of the non-United States entity that has been domesticated, and all property, real, personal and mixed, and all debts due to such non-United States entity, as well as all other things and causes of action belonging to such non-United States entity, shall remain vested in the domestic limited liability company to which such non-United States entity has been domesticated (and also in the non-United States entity, if and for so long as the non-United States entity continues its existence in the foreign jurisdiction in which it was existing immediately prior to the domestication) and shall be the property of such domestic limited liability company (and also of the non-United States entity, if and for so long as the non-United States entity continues its existence in the foreign jurisdiction in which it was existing immediately prior to the domestication), and the title to any real property vested by deed or otherwise in such non-United States entity shall not revert or be in any way impaired by reason of this chapter; but all rights of creditors and all liens upon any property of such non-United States entity shall be preserved unimpaired, and all debts, liabilities and duties of the non-United States entity that has been domesticated shall remain attached to the domestic limited liability company to which such non-United States entity has been domesticated (and also to the non-United States entity, if and for so long as the non-United States entity continues its existence in the foreign jurisdiction in which it was existing immediately prior to the domestication), and may be enforced against it to the same extent as if said debts, liabilities and duties had originally been incurred or contracted by it in its capacity as a domestic limited liability company. The rights, privileges, powers and interests in property of the non-United States entity, as well as the debts, liabilities and duties of the non-United States entity, shall not be deemed, as a consequence of the domestication, to have been transferred to the domestic limited liability company to which such non-United States entity has domesticated for any purpose of the laws of the State of Delaware.

(i)   When a non-United States entity has become domesticated as a limited liability company pursuant to this section, for all purposes of the laws of the State of Delaware, the limited liability company shall be deemed to be the same entity as the domesticating non-United States entity and the domestication shall constitute a continuation of the existence of the domesticating non-United States entity in the form of a domestic limited liability company. Unless otherwise agreed, for all purposes of the laws of the State of Delaware, the domesticating non-United States entity shall not be required to wind up its affairs or pay its liabilities and distribute its assets, and the domestication shall not be deemed to constitute a dissolution of such non-United States entity. If, following domestication, a non-United States entity that has become domesticated as a limited liability company continues its existence in the foreign country or other foreign jurisdiction in which it was existing immediately prior to domestication, the limited liability company and such non-United States entity shall, for all purposes of the laws of the State of Delaware, constitute a single entity formed, incorporated, created or otherwise having come into being, as applicable, and existing under the laws of the State of Delaware and the laws of such foreign country or other foreign jurisdiction.

(j)   In connection with a domestication hereunder, rights or securities of, or interests in, the non-United States entity that is to be domesticated as a domestic limited liability company may be exchanged for or converted into cash, property, rights or securities of, or interests in, such domestic limited liability company or, in addition to or in lieu thereof, may be exchanged for or converted into cash, property, rights or securities of, or interests in, another domestic limited liability company or other entity, may remain outstanding or may be canceled.

§ 18–213.   Transfer or continuance of domestic limited liability companies.

(a)   Upon compliance with this section, any limited liability company may transfer to or domesticate or continue in any jurisdiction, other than any state, and, in connection therewith, may elect to continue its existence as a limited liability company in the State of Delaware.

(b)   If the limited liability company agreement specifies the manner of authorizing a transfer or domestication or continuance described in subsection (a) of this section, the transfer or domestication or continuance shall be authorized as specified in the limited liability company agreement. If the limited liability company agreement does not specify the manner of authorizing a transfer or domestication or continuance described in subsection (a) of this section and does not prohibit such a transfer or domestication or continuance, the transfer or domestication or continuance shall be authorized in the same manner as is specified in the limited liability company agreement for authorizing a merger or consolidation that involves the limited liability company as a constituent party to the merger or consolidation. If the limited liability company agreement does not specify the manner of authorizing a transfer or domestication or continuance described in subsection (a) of this section or a merger or consolidation that involves the limited liability company as a constituent party and does not prohibit such a transfer or domestication or continuance, the transfer or domestication or continuance shall be authorized by the approval by members who own more than 50 percent of the then current percentage or other interest in the profits of the domestic limited liability company owned by all of the members. If a transfer or domestication or continuance described in subsection (a) of this section shall be authorized as provided in this subsection (b), a certificate of transfer if the limited liability company's existence as a limited liability company of the State of Delaware is to cease, or a certificate of transfer and domestic continuance if the limited liability company's existence as a limited liability company in the State of Delaware is to continue, executed in accordance with § 18–204 of this title, shall be filed in the office of the Secretary of State in accordance with 18–206 of this title. The certificate of transfer or the certificate of transfer and domestic continuance shall state:

(1) The name of the limited liability company and, if it has been changed, the name under which its certificate of formation was originally filed;

(2) The date of the filing of its original certificate of formation with the Secretary of State;

(3) The jurisdiction to which the limited liability company shall be transferred or in which it shall be domesticated or continued and the name of the entity or business form formed, incorporated, created or that otherwise comes into being as a consequence of the transfer of the limited liability company to, or its domestication or continuance in, such foreign jurisdiction;

(4) The future effective date or time (which shall be a date or time certain) of the transfer to or domestication or continuance in the jurisdiction specified in paragraph (b)(3) of this section if it is not to be effective upon the filing of the certificate of transfer or the certificate of transfer and domestic continuance;

(5) That the transfer or domestication or continuance of the limited liability company has been approved in accordance with this section;

(6) In the case of a certificate of transfer, (i) that the existence of the limited liability company as a limited liability company of the State of Delaware shall cease when the certificate of transfer becomes effective, and (ii) the agreement of the limited liability company that it may be served with process in the State of Delaware in any action, suit or proceeding for enforcement of any obligation of the limited liability company arising while it was a limited liability company of the State of Delaware, and that it irrevocably appoints the Secretary of State as its agent to accept service of process in any such action, suit or proceeding;

(7) The address (which may not be that of the limited liability company's registered agent without the written consent of the limited liability company's registered agent, such consent to be filed with the certificate of transfer) to which a copy of the process referred to in paragraph (b)(6) of this section shall be mailed to it by the Secretary of State. Process may be served upon the Secretary of State under paragraph (b)(6) of this section by means of electronic transmission but only as prescribed by the Secretary of State. The Secretary of State is authorized to issue such rules and regulations with respect to such service as the Secretary of State deems necessary or appropriate. In the event of service hereunder upon the Secretary of State, the procedures set forth in § 18–911(c) of this title shall be applicable, except that the plaintiff in any such action, suit or proceeding shall furnish the Secretary of State with the address specified in this subsection and any other address that the plaintiff may elect to furnish, together with copies of such process as required by the Secretary of State, and the Secretary of State shall notify the limited liability company that has transferred or domesticated or continued out of the State of Delaware at all such addresses furnished by the plaintiff in accordance with the procedures set forth in § 18–911(c) of this title; and

(8)   In the case of a certificate of transfer and domestic continuance, that the limited liability company will continue to exist as a limited liability company of the State of Delaware after the certificate of transfer and domestic continuance becomes effective.

Unless otherwise provided in a limited liability company agreement, a limited liability company whose original certificate of formation was filed with the Secretary of State and effective on or prior to July 31, 2015, shall continue to be governed by the third sentence of this subsection as in effect on July 31, 2015.

(c)   Upon the filing in the office of the Secretary of State of the certificate of transfer or upon the future effective date or time of the certificate of transfer and payment to the Secretary of State of all fees prescribed in this chapter, the Secretary of State shall certify that the limited liability company has filed all documents and paid all fees required by this chapter, and thereupon the limited liability company shall cease to exist as a limited liability company of the State of Delaware. Such certificate of the Secretary of State shall be prima facie evidence of the transfer or domestication or continuance by such limited liability company out of the State of Delaware.

(d)   The transfer or domestication or continuance of a limited liability company out of the State of Delaware in accordance with this section and the resulting cessation of its existence as a limited liability company of the State of Delaware pursuant to a certificate of transfer shall not be deemed to affect any obligations or liabilities of the limited liability company incurred prior to such transfer or domestication or continuance or the personal liability of any person incurred prior to such transfer or domestication or continuance, nor shall it be deemed to affect the choice of law applicable to the limited liability company with respect to matters arising prior to such transfer or domestication or continuance. Unless otherwise agreed, the transfer or domestication or continuance of a limited liability company out of the State of Delaware in accordance with this section shall not require such limited liability company to wind up its affairs under § 18–803 of this title or pay its liabilities and distribute its assets under § 18–804 of this title and shall not be deemed to constitute a dissolution of such limited liability company.

(e)   If a limited liability company files a certificate of transfer and domestic continuance, after the time the certificate of transfer and domestic continuance becomes effective, the limited liability company shall continue to exist as a limited liability company of the State of Delaware, and the laws of the State of Delaware, including this chapter, shall apply to the limited liability company to the same extent as prior to such time. So long as a limited liability company continues to exist as a limited liability company of the State of Delaware following the filing of a certificate of transfer and domestic continuance, the continuing domestic limited liability company and the entity or business form formed, incorporated, created or that otherwise came into being as a consequence of the transfer of the limited liability company to, or its domestication or continuance in, a foreign country or other foreign jurisdiction shall, for all purposes of the laws of the State of Delaware, constitute a single entity formed, incorporated, created or otherwise having come into being, as applicable, and existing under the laws of the State and the laws of such foreign country or other foreign jurisdiction.

(f)   In connection with a transfer or domestication or continuance of a domestic limited liability company to or in another jurisdiction pursuant to subsection (a) of this section, rights or securities of, or interests in, such limited liability company may be exchanged for or converted into cash, property, rights or securities of, or interests in, the entity or business form in which the limited liability company will exist in such other jurisdiction as a consequence of the transfer or domestication or continuance or, in addition to or in lieu thereof, may be exchanged for or converted into cash, property, rights or securities of, or interests in, another entity or business form, may remain outstanding or may be canceled.

(g)   When a limited liability company has transferred or domesticated or continued out of the State of Delaware pursuant to this section, the transferred or domesticated or continued entity or business form shall, for all purposes of the laws of the State of Delaware, be deemed to be the same entity as the limited liability company and shall constitute a continuation of the existence of such limited liability company in the form of the transferred or domesticated or continued entity or business form. When any transfer or domestication or continuance of a limited liability company out of the State of Delaware shall have become effective under this section, for all purposes of the laws of the State of Delaware, all of the rights, privileges and powers of the limited liability company that has transferred or domesticated or continued, and all property, real, personal and mixed, and all debts due to such limited liability company, as well as all other things and causes of action belonging to such limited liability company, shall remain vested in the transferred or domesticated or continued entity or business form (and also in the limited liability company that has transferred, domesticated or continued, if and for so long as such limited liability company continues its existence as a domestic limited liability company) and shall be the property of such transferred or domesticated or continued entity or business form (and also of the limited liability company that has transferred, domesticated or continued, if and for so long as such limited liability company continues its existence as a domestic limited liability company), and the title to any real property vested by deed or otherwise in such limited liability company shall not revert or be in any way impaired by reason of this chapter; but all rights of creditors and all liens upon any property of such limited liability company shall be preserved unimpaired, and all debts, liabilities and duties of the limited liability company that has transferred or domesticated or continued shall remain attached to the transferred or domesticated or continued entity or business form (and also to the limited liability company that has transferred, domesticated or continued, if and for so long as such limited liability company continues its existence as a domestic limited liability company), and may be enforced against it to the same extent as if said debts, liabilities and duties had originally been incurred or contracted by it in its capacity as the transferred or domesticated or continued entity or business form. The rights, privileges, powers and interests in property of the limited liability company that has transferred or domesticated or continued, as well as the debts, liabilities and duties of such limited liability company, shall not be deemed, as a consequence of the transfer or domestication or continuance out of the State of Delaware, to have been transferred to the transferred or domesticated or continued entity or business form for any purpose of the laws of the State of Delaware.

(h)   A limited liability company agreement may provide that a domestic limited liability company shall not have the power to transfer, domesticate or continue as set forth in this section.

§ 18–214.   Conversion of certain entities to a limited liability company.

(a)   As used in this section and in § 18–204 of this title, the term "other entity" means a corporation, a statutory trust, a business trust, an association, a real estate investment trust, a common-law trust or any other incorporated or unincorporated business or entity, including a partnership (whether general (including a limited liability partnership) or limited (including a limited liability limited partnership)) or a foreign limited liability company.

(b)   Any other entity may convert to a domestic limited liability company by complying with subsection (h) of this section and filing in the office of the Secretary of State in accordance with § 18–206 of this title:

(1)   A certificate of conversion to limited liability company that has been executed in accordance with § 18–204 of this title; and

(2)   A certificate of formation that complies with § 18–201 of this title and has been executed by 1 or more authorized persons in accordance with § 18–204 of this title.

Each of the certificates required by this subsection (b) shall be filed simultaneously in the office of the Secretary of State and, if such certificates are not to become effective upon their filing as permitted by § 18–206(b) of this title, then each such certificate shall provide for the same effective date or time in accordance with § 18–206(b) of this title.

(c)   The certificate of conversion to limited liability company shall state:

(1)   The date on which and jurisdiction where the other entity was first created, incorporated, formed or otherwise came into being and, if it has changed, its jurisdiction immediately prior to its conversion to a domestic limited liability company;

(2)   The name and type of entity of the other entity immediately prior to the filing of the certificate of conversion to limited liability company;

(3)   The name of the limited liability company as set forth in its certificate of formation filed in accordance with subsection (b) of this section; and

(4)   The future effective date or time (which shall be a date or time certain) of the conversion to a limited liability company if it is not to be effective upon the filing of the certificate of conversion to limited liability company and the certificate of formation.

(d)   Upon the filing in the office of the Secretary of State of the certificate of conversion to limited liability company and the certificate of formation or upon the future effective date or time of the certificate of conversion to limited liability company and the certificate of formation, the other entity shall be converted into a domestic limited liability company and the limited liability company shall thereafter be subject to all of the provisions of this chapter, except that notwithstanding § 18–201 of this title, the existence of the limited liability company shall be deemed to have commenced on the date the other entity commenced its existence in the jurisdiction in which the other entity was first created, formed, incorporated or otherwise came into being.

(e)   The conversion of any other entity into a domestic limited liability company shall not be deemed to affect any obligations or liabilities of the other entity incurred prior to its conversion to a domestic limited liability company or the personal liability of any person incurred prior to such conversion.

(f)   When any conversion shall have become effective under this section, for all purposes of the laws of the State of Delaware, all of the rights, privileges and powers of the other entity that has converted, and all property, real, personal and mixed, and all debts due to such other entity, as well as all other things and causes of action belonging to such other entity, shall remain vested in the domestic limited liability company to which such other entity has converted and shall be the property of such domestic limited liability company, and the title to any real property vested by deed or otherwise in such other entity shall not revert or be in any way impaired by reason of this chapter; but all rights of creditors and all liens upon any property of such other entity shall be preserved unimpaired, and all debts, liabilities and duties of the other entity that has converted shall remain attached to the domestic limited liability company to which such other entity has converted, and may be enforced against it to the same extent as if said debts, liabilities and duties had originally been incurred or contracted by it in its capacity as a domestic limited liability company. The rights, privileges, powers and interests in property of the other entity, as well as the debts, liabilities and duties of the other entity, shall not be deemed, as a consequence of the conversion, to have been transferred to the domestic limited liability company to which such other entity has converted for any purpose of the laws of the State of Delaware.

(g)   Unless otherwise agreed, for all purposes of the laws of the State of Delaware, the converting other entity shall not be required to wind up its affairs or pay its liabilities and distribute its assets, and the conversion shall not be deemed to constitute a dissolution of such other entity. When an other entity has been converted to a limited liability company pursuant to this section, for all purposes of the laws of the State of Delaware, the limited liability company shall be deemed to be the same entity as the converting other entity and the conversion shall constitute a continuation of the existence of the converting other entity in the form of a domestic limited liability company.

(h)   Prior to filing a certificate of conversion to limited liability company with the office of the Secretary of State, the conversion shall be approved in the manner provided for by the document, instrument, agreement or other writing, as the case may be, governing the internal affairs of the other entity and the conduct of its business or by applicable law, as appropriate and a limited liability company agreement shall be approved by the same authorization required to approve the conversion.

(i)   In connection with a conversion hereunder, rights or securities of or interests in the other entity which is to be converted to a domestic limited liability company may be exchanged for or converted into cash, property, or rights or securities of or interests in such domestic limited liability company or, in addition to or in lieu thereof, may be exchanged for or converted into cash, property, or rights or securities of or interests in another domestic limited liability company or other entity, may remain outstanding or may be canceled.

(j)   The provisions of this section shall not be construed to limit the accomplishment of a change in the law governing, or the domicile of, an other entity to the State of Delaware by any other means provided for in a limited liability company agreement or other agreement or as otherwise permitted by law, including by the amendment of a limited liability company agreement or other agreement.

§ 18–215.   Series of members, managers, limited liability company interests or assets.

(a)   A limited liability company agreement may establish or provide for the establishment of 1 or more designated series of members, managers, limited liability company interests or assets. Any such series may have separate rights, powers or duties with respect to specified property or obligations of the limited liability company or profits and losses associated with specified property or obligations, and any such series may have a separate business purpose or investment objective. No provision of subsection (b) of this section or § 18–218 of this title shall be construed to limit the application of the principle of freedom of contract to a series that is not a protected series or a registered series. Other than pursuant to §§ 18–219, 18–220 and 18–221, a series may not merge, convert or consolidate pursuant to any section of this title or any other statute of this State.

(b)   A series established in accordance with the following sentence is a protected series. Notwithstanding anything to the contrary set forth in this chapter or under other applicable law, in the event that a limited liability company agreement establishes or provides for the establishment of 1 or more series, and to the extent the records maintained for any such series account for the assets associated with such series separately from the other assets of the limited liability company, or any other series thereof, and if the limited liability company agreement so provides, and if notice of the limitation on liabilities of a series as referenced in this subsection is set forth in the certificate of formation of the limited liability company, then the debts, liabilities, obligations and expenses incurred, contracted for or otherwise existing with respect to such series shall be enforceable against the assets of such series only, and not against the assets of the limited liability company generally or any other series thereof, and, unless otherwise provided in the limited liability company agreement, none of the debts, liabilities, obligations and expenses incurred, contracted for or otherwise existing with respect to the limited liability company generally or any other series thereof shall be enforceable against the assets of such series. Neither the preceding sentence nor any provision pursuant thereto in a limited liability company agreement or certificate of formation shall (i) restrict a protected series or limited liability company on behalf of a protected series from agreeing in the limited liability company agreement or otherwise that any or all of the debts, liabilities, obligations and expenses incurred, contracted for or otherwise existing with respect to the limited liability company generally or any other series thereof shall be enforceable against the assets of such protected series or (ii) restrict a limited liability company from agreeing in the limited liability company agreement or otherwise that any or all of the debts, liabilities, obligations and expenses incurred, contracted for or otherwise existing with respect to a protected series shall be enforceable against the assets of the limited liability company generally. A limited liability company agreement does not need to use the term protected when referencing series or refer to this section. Assets associated with a protected series may be held directly or indirectly, including in the name of such series, in the name of the limited liability company, through a nominee or otherwise. Records maintained for a protected series that reasonably identify its assets, including by specific listing, category, type, quantity, computational or allocational formula or procedure (including a percentage or share of any asset or assets) or by any other method where the identity of such assets is objectively determinable, will be deemed to account for the assets associated with such series separately from the other assets of the limited liability company, or any other series thereof. Notice in a certificate of formation of the limitation on liabilities of a protected series as referenced in this subsection shall be sufficient for all purposes of this subsection whether or not the limited liability company has established any protected series when such notice is included in the certificate of formation, and there shall be no requirement that (i) any specific protected series of the limited liability company be referenced in such notice, or (ii) such notice use the term protected when referencing series or include a reference to this section. The fact that a certificate of formation that contains the foregoing notice of the limitation on liabilities of a protected series is on file in the office of the Secretary of State shall constitute notice of such limitation on liabilities of a protected series. As used in this chapter, a reference to assets of a protected series includes assets associated with such series, a reference to assets associated with a protected series includes assets of such series, a reference to members or managers of a protected series includes members or managers associated with such series, and a reference to members or managers associated with a protected series includes members or managers of such series. The following shall apply to a protected series:

(1)   A protected series may carry on any lawful business, purpose or activity, whether or not for profit, with the exception of the business of banking as defined in § 126 of Title 8. Unless otherwise provided in a limited liability company agreement, a protected series shall have the power and capacity to, in its own name, contract, hold title to assets (including real, personal and intangible property), grant liens and security interests, and sue and be sued.

(2)   Except as otherwise provided by this chapter, no member or manager of a protected series shall be obligated personally for any debt, obligation or liability of such series, whether arising in contract, tort or otherwise, solely by reason of being a member or acting as manager of such series.

Notwithstanding the preceding sentence, under a limited liability company agreement or under another agreement, a member or manager may agree to be obligated personally for any or all of the debts, obligations and liabilities of 1 or more protected series.

(3)   A limited liability company agreement may provide for classes or groups of members or managers associated with a protected series having such relative rights, powers and duties as the limited liability company agreement may provide, and may make provision for the future creation in the manner provided in the limited liability company agreement of additional classes or groups of members or managers associated with such series having such relative rights, powers and duties as may from time to time be established, including rights, powers and duties senior to existing classes and groups of members or managers associated with such series. A limited liability company agreement may provide for the taking of an action, including the amendment of the limited liability company agreement, without the vote or approval of any member or manager or class or group of members or managers, including an action to create under the provisions of the limited liability company agreement a class or group of a protected series of limited liability company interests that was not previously outstanding. A limited liability company agreement may provide that any member or class or group of members associated with a protected series shall have no voting rights.

(4)   A limited liability company agreement may grant to all or certain identified members or managers or a specified class or group of the members or managers associated with a protected series the right to vote separately or with all or any class or group of the members or managers associated with such series, on any matter. Voting by members or managers associated with a protected series may be on a per capita, number, financial interest, class, group or any other basis.

(5)   Unless otherwise provided in a limited liability company agreement, the management of a protected series shall be vested in the members associated with such series in proportion to the then current percentage or other interest of members in the profits of such series owned by all of the members associated with such series, the decision of members owning more than 50 percent of the said percentage or other interest in the profits controlling; provided, however, that if a limited liability company agreement provides for the management of a protected series, in whole or in part, by a manager, the management of such series, to the extent so provided, shall be vested in the manager who shall be chosen in the manner provided in the limited liability company agreement. The manager of a protected series shall also hold the offices and have the responsibilities accorded to the manager as set forth in a limited liability company agreement. A protected series may have more than 1 manager. Subject to § 18–602 of this title, a manager shall cease to be a manager with respect to a protected series as provided in a limited liability company agreement. Except as otherwise provided in a limited liability company agreement, any event under this chapter or in a limited liability company agreement that causes a manager to cease to be a manager with respect to a protected series shall not, in itself, cause such manager to cease to be a manager of the limited liability company or with respect to any other series thereof.

(6)   Notwithstanding § 18–606 of this title, but subject to paragraphs (b)(7) and (b)(10) of this section, and unless otherwise provided in a limited liability company agreement, at the time a member of a protected series becomes entitled to receive a distribution with respect to such series, the member has the status of, and is entitled to all remedies available to, a creditor of such series, with respect to the distribution. A limited liability company agreement may provide for the establishment of a record date with respect to allocations and distributions with respect to a protected series.

(7)   Notwithstanding § 18–607(a) of this title, a limited liability company may make a distribution with respect to a protected series. A limited liability company shall not make a distribution with respect to a protected series to a member to the extent that at the time of the distribution, after giving effect to the distribution, all liabilities of such series, other than liabilities to members on account of their limited liability company interests with respect to such series and liabilities for which the recourse of creditors is limited to specified property of such series, exceed the fair value of the assets associated with such series, except that the fair value of property of such series that is subject to a liability for which the recourse of creditors is limited shall be included in the assets associated with such series only to the extent that the fair value of that property exceeds that liability. For purposes of the immediately preceding sentence, the term "distribution" shall not include amounts constituting reasonable compensation for present or past services or reasonable payments made in the

ordinary course of business pursuant to a bona fide retirement plan or other benefits program. A member who receives a distribution in violation of this paragraph (b)(7), and who knew at the time of the distribution that the distribution violated this paragraph (b)(7), shall be liable to the protected series for the amount of the distribution. A member who receives a distribution in violation of this paragraph (b)(7), and who did not know at the time of the distribution that the distribution violated this paragraph (b)(7), shall not be liable for the amount of the distribution. Subject to § 18–607(c) of this title, which shall apply to any distribution made with respect to a protected series under this paragraph (b)(7), this paragraph (b)(7) shall not affect any obligation or liability of a member under an agreement or other applicable law for the amount of a distribution.

(8)   Unless otherwise provided in the limited liability company agreement, a member shall cease to be associated with a protected series and to have the power to exercise any rights or powers of a member with respect to such series upon the assignment of all of the member's limited liability company interest with respect to such series. Except as otherwise provided in a limited liability company agreement, any event under this chapter or a limited liability company agreement that causes a member to cease to be associated with a protected series shall not, in itself, cause such member to cease to be associated with any other series or terminate the continued membership of a member in the limited liability company or cause the termination of the protected series, regardless of whether such member was the last remaining member associated with such series.

(9)   Subject to § 18–801 of this title, except to the extent otherwise provided in the limited liability company agreement, a protected series may be terminated and its affairs wound up without causing the dissolution of the limited liability company. The termination of a protected series shall not affect the limitation on liabilities of such series provided by this subsection (b). A protected series is terminated and its affairs shall be wound up upon the dissolution of the limited liability company under § 18–801 of this title or otherwise upon the first to occur of the following:

a.   At the time specified in the limited liability company agreement;

b.   Upon the happening of events specified in the limited liability company agreement;

c.   Unless otherwise provided in the limited liability company agreement, upon the vote or consent of members associated with such series who own more than 2/3 of the then-current percentage or other interest in the profits of such series of the limited liability company owned by all of the members associated with such series; or

d.   The termination of such series under paragraph (b)(11) of this section.

Unless otherwise provided in a limited liability company agreement, a limited liability company whose original certificate of formation was filed with the Secretary of State and effective on or prior to July 31, 2015, shall continue to be governed by paragraph (k)(3) of this section as in effect on July 31, 2015 (except that "affirmative" and "written" shall be deleted from such paragraph (k)(3) of this section).

(10) Notwithstanding § 18–803(a) of this title, unless otherwise provided in the limited liability company agreement, a manager associated with a protected series who has not wrongfully terminated such series or, if none, the members associated with such series or a person approved by the members associated with such series, in either case, by members who own more than 50 percent of the then current percentage or other interest in the profits of such series owned by all of the members associated with such series, may wind up the affairs of such series; but the Court of Chancery, upon cause shown, may wind up the affairs of a protected series upon application of any member or manager associated with such series, or the member's personal representative or assignee, and in connection therewith, may appoint a liquidating trustee. The persons winding up the affairs of a protected series may, in the name of the limited liability company and for and on behalf of the limited liability company and such series, take all actions with respect to such series as are permitted under § 18–803(b) of this title. The persons winding up the affairs of a protected series shall provide for the claims and obligations of such series and distribute the assets of such series as provided in § 18–804 of this title, which section shall apply to the winding up and distribution of assets of a protected series. Actions taken in accordance with this paragraph (b)(10)shall not affect the liability of members and shall not impose liability on a liquidating trustee. Unless otherwise provided in a limited liability company agreement, a limited

liability company whose original certificate of formation was filed with the Secretary of State and effective on or prior to July 31, 2015, shall continue to be governed by the first sentence of this paragraph (b)(10) as in effect on July 31, 2015.

(11) On application by or for a member or manager associated with a protected series, the Court of Chancery may decree termination of such series whenever it is not reasonably practicable to carry on the business of such series in conformity with a limited liability company agreement.

(12) For all purposes of the laws of the State of Delaware, a protected series is an association, regardless of the number of members or managers, if any, of such series.

(c) If a foreign limited liability company that is registering to do business in the State of Delaware in accordance with § 18–902 of this title is governed by a limited liability company agreement that establishes or provides for the establishment of designated series of members, managers, limited liability company interests or assets having separate rights, powers or duties with respect to specified property or obligations of the foreign limited liability company or profits and losses associated with specified property or obligations, that fact shall be so stated on the application for registration as a foreign limited liability company. In addition, the foreign limited liability company shall state on such application whether the debts, liabilities and obligations incurred, contracted for or otherwise existing with respect to a particular series, if any, shall be enforceable against the assets of such series only, and not against the assets of the foreign limited liability company generally or any other series thereof, and whether any of the debts, liabilities, obligations and expenses incurred, contracted for or otherwise existing with respect to the foreign limited liability company generally or any other series thereof shall be enforceable against the assets of such series.

§ 18–216.   Approval of conversion of a limited liability company.

(a) Upon compliance with this section, a domestic limited liability company may convert to a corporation, a statutory trust, a business trust, an association, a real estate investment trust, a common-law trust or any other incorporated or unincorporated business or entity, including a partnership (whether general (including a limited liability partnership) or limited (including a limited liability limited partnership)) or a foreign limited liability company.

(b) If the limited liability company agreement specifies the manner of authorizing a conversion of the limited liability company, the conversion shall be authorized as specified in the limited liability company agreement. If the limited liability company agreement does not specify the manner of authorizing a conversion of the limited liability company and does not prohibit a conversion of the limited liability company, the conversion shall be authorized in the same manner as is specified in the limited liability company agreement for authorizing a merger or consolidation that involves the limited liability company as a constituent party to the merger or consolidation. If the limited liability company agreement does not specify the manner of authorizing a conversion of the limited liability company or a merger or consolidation that involves the limited liability company as a constituent party and does not prohibit a conversion of the limited liability company, the conversion shall be authorized by the approval by members who own more than 50 percent of the then current percentage or other interest in the profits of the domestic limited liability company owned by all of the members. Unless otherwise provided in a limited liability company agreement, a limited liability company whose original certificate of formation was filed with the Secretary of State and effective on or prior to July 31, 2015, shall continue to be governed by the third sentence of this subsection as in effect on July 31, 2015.

(c) Unless otherwise agreed, the conversion of a domestic limited liability company to another entity or business form pursuant to this section shall not require such limited liability company to wind up its affairs under § 18–803 of this title or pay its liabilities and distribute its assets under § 18–804 of this title, and the conversion shall not constitute a dissolution of such limited liability company. When a limited liability company has converted to another entity or business form pursuant to this section, for all purposes of the laws of the State of Delaware, the other entity or business form shall be deemed to be the same entity as the converting limited liability company and the conversion shall constitute a continuation of the existence of the limited liability company in the form of such other entity or business form.

(d) In connection with a conversion of a domestic limited liability company to another entity or business form pursuant to this section, rights or securities of or interests in the domestic limited liability company which is to be converted may be exchanged for or converted into cash, property, rights or securities of or interests in the entity or business form into which the domestic limited liability company is being converted or, in addition to or in lieu thereof, may be exchanged for or converted into cash, property, rights or securities of or interests in another entity or business form, may remain outstanding or may be canceled.

(e) If a limited liability company shall convert in accordance with this section to another entity or business form organized, formed or created under the laws of a jurisdiction other than the State of Delaware, a certificate of conversion to non-Delaware entity executed in accordance with § 18–204 of this title, shall be filed in the office of the Secretary of State in accordance with § 18–206 of this title. The certificate of conversion to non-Delaware entity shall state:

(1) The name of the limited liability company and, if it has been changed, the name under which its certificate of formation was originally filed;

(2) The date of filing of its original certificate of formation with the Secretary of State;

(3) The jurisdiction in which the entity or business form, to which the limited liability company shall be converted, is organized, formed or created, and the name of such entity or business form;

(4) The future effective date or time (which shall be a date or time certain) of the conversion if it is not to be effective upon the filing of the certificate of conversion to non-Delaware entity;

(5) That the conversion has been approved in accordance with this section;

(6) The agreement of the limited liability company that it may be served with process in the State of Delaware in any action, suit or proceeding for enforcement of any obligation of the limited liability company arising while it was a limited liability company of the State of Delaware, and that it irrevocably appoints the Secretary of State as its agent to accept service of process in any such action, suit or proceeding;

(7) The address to which a copy of the process referred to in paragraph (e)(6) of this section shall be mailed to it by the Secretary of State. Process may be served upon the Secretary of State under paragraph (e)(6) of this section by means of electronic transmission but only as prescribed by the Secretary of State. The Secretary of State is authorized to issue such rules and regulations with respect to such service as the Secretary of State deems necessary or appropriate. In the event of service hereunder upon the Secretary of State, the procedures set forth in § 18–911(c) of this title shall be applicable, except that the plaintiff in any such action, suit or proceeding shall furnish the Secretary of State with the address specified in this subdivision and any other address that the plaintiff may elect to furnish, together with copies of such process as required by the Secretary of State, and the Secretary of State shall notify the limited liability company that has converted out of the State of Delaware at all such addresses furnished by the plaintiff in accordance with the procedures set forth in § 18–911(c) of this title.

(f) Upon the filing in the office of the Secretary of State of the certificate of conversion to non-Delaware entity or upon the future effective date or time of the certificate of conversion to non-Delaware entity and payment to the Secretary of State of all fees prescribed in this chapter, the Secretary of State shall certify that the limited liability company has filed all documents and paid all fees required by this chapter, and thereupon the limited liability company shall cease to exist as a limited liability company of the State of Delaware. Such certificate of the Secretary of State shall be prima facie evidence of the conversion by such limited liability company out of the State of Delaware.

(g) The conversion of a limited liability company out of the State of Delaware in accordance with this section and the resulting cessation of its existence as a limited liability company of the State of Delaware pursuant to a certificate of conversion to non-Delaware entity shall not be deemed to affect any obligations or liabilities of the limited liability company incurred prior to such conversion or the personal liability of any person incurred prior to such conversion, nor shall it be deemed to affect the choice of law applicable to the limited liability company with respect to matters arising prior to such conversion.

(h) When any conversion shall have become effective under this section, for all purposes of the laws of the State of Delaware, all of the rights, privileges and powers of the limited liability company that has converted, and all property, real, personal and mixed, and all debts due to such limited liability company, as well as all other things and causes of action belonging to such limited liability company, shall remain vested in the other entity or business form to which such limited liability company has converted and shall be the property of such other entity or business form, and the title to any real property vested by deed or otherwise in such limited liability company shall not revert or be in any way impaired by reason of this chapter; but all rights of creditors and all liens upon any property of such limited liability company shall be preserved unimpaired, and all debts, liabilities and duties of the limited liability company that has converted shall remain attached to the other entity or business form to which such limited liability company has converted, and may be enforced against it to the same extent as if said debts, liabilities and duties had originally been incurred or contracted by it in its capacity as such other entity or business form. The rights, privileges, powers and interests in property of the limited liability company that has converted, as well as the debts, liabilities and duties of such limited liability company, shall not be deemed, as a consequence of the conversion, to have been transferred to the other entity or business form to which such limited liability company has converted for any purpose of the laws of the State of Delaware.

(i)   A limited liability company agreement may provide that a domestic limited liability company shall not have the power to convert as set forth in this section.

§ 18–217.   Division of a limited liability company.

(a)   As used in this section and §§ 18–203, 18–301 and 18–1203:

(1)   "Dividing company" means the domestic limited liability company that is effecting a division in the manner provided in this section.

(2)   "Division" means the division of a dividing company into 2 or more domestic limited liability companies in accordance with this section.

(3)   "Division company" means a surviving company, if any, and each resulting company.

(4)   "Division contact" means, in connection with any division, a natural person who is a Delaware resident, any division company in such division or any other domestic limited liability company or other business entity as defined in § 18–209 of this title formed or organized under the laws of the State of Delaware, which division contact shall maintain a copy of the plan of division for a period of 6 years from the effective date of the division and shall comply with paragraph (g)(3) of this section.

(5)   "Organizational documents" means the certificate of formation and limited liability company agreement of a domestic limited liability company.

(6)   "Resulting company" means a domestic limited liability company formed as a consequence of a division.

(7)   "Surviving company" means a dividing company that survives the division.

(b)   Pursuant to a plan of division, any domestic limited liability company may, in the manner provided in this section, be divided into 2 or more domestic limited liability companies. The division of a domestic limited liability company in accordance with this section and, if applicable, the resulting cessation of the existence of the dividing company pursuant to a certificate of division shall not be deemed to affect the personal liability of any person incurred prior to such division with respect to matters arising prior to such division, nor shall it be deemed to affect the validity or enforceability of any obligations or liabilities of the dividing company incurred prior to such division; provided, that the obligations and liabilities of the dividing company shall be allocated to and vested in, and valid and enforceable obligations of, such division company or companies to which such obligations and liabilities have been allocated pursuant to the plan of division, as provided in subsection (*l*) of this section. Each resulting company in a division shall be formed in compliance with the requirements of this chapter and subsection (i) of this section.

(c)   If the limited liability company agreement of the dividing company specifies the manner of adopting a plan of division, the plan of division shall be adopted as specified in the limited liability company agreement. If the limited liability company agreement of the dividing company does not specify the manner of adopting a plan of division and does not prohibit a division of the limited liability company, the plan of division shall be adopted in the same manner as is specified in the limited liability company agreement for authorizing a merger or consolidation that involves the limited liability company as a constituent party to the merger or consolidation. If the limited liability company agreement of the dividing company does not specify the manner of adopting a plan of division or authorizing a merger or consolidation that involves the limited liability company as a constituent party and does not prohibit a division of the limited liability company, the adoption of a plan of division shall be authorized by the approval by members who own more than 50 percent of the then current percentage or other interest in the profits of the dividing company owned by all of the members. Notwithstanding prior approval, a plan of division may be terminated or amended pursuant to a provision for such termination or amendment contained in the plan of division.

(d)   Unless otherwise provided in a plan of division, the division of a domestic limited liability company pursuant to this section shall not require such limited liability company to wind up its affairs under § 18–803 of this title or pay its liabilities and distribute its assets under § 18–804 of this title, and the division shall not constitute a dissolution of such limited liability company.

(e)   In connection with a division under this section, rights or securities of, or interests in, the dividing company may be exchanged for or converted into cash, property, rights or securities of, or interests in, the surviving company or any resulting company or, in addition to or in lieu thereof, may be exchanged for or converted into cash, property, rights or securities of, or interests in, a domestic limited liability company or any other business entity which is not a division company or may be canceled or remain outstanding (if the dividing company is a surviving company).

(f)   A plan of division adopted in accordance with subsection (c) of this section:

(1)   May effect any amendment to the limited liability company agreement of the dividing company if it is a surviving company in the division; or

(2)   May effect the adoption of a new limited liability company agreement for the dividing company if it is a surviving company in the division; and

(3)   Shall effect the adoption of a limited liability company agreement for each resulting company.

Any amendment to a limited liability company agreement or adoption of a new limited liability company agreement for the dividing company, if it is a surviving company in the division, or adoption of a limited liability company agreement for each resulting company made pursuant to the foregoing sentence shall be effective at the effective time or date of the division. Any amendment to a limited liability company agreement or adoption of a limited liability company agreement for the dividing company, if it is a surviving company in the division, shall be effective notwithstanding any provision in the limited liability company agreement of the dividing company relating to amendment or adoption of a new limited liability company agreement, other than a provision that by its terms applies to an amendment to the limited liability company agreement or the adoption of a new limited liability company agreement, in either case, in connection with a division, merger or consolidation.

(g)   If a domestic limited liability company is dividing under this section, the dividing company shall adopt a plan of division which shall set forth:

(1)   The terms and conditions of the division, including:

a.   Any conversion or exchange of the limited liability company interests of the dividing company into or for limited liability company interests or other securities or obligations of any division company or cash, property or rights or securities or obligations of or interests in any other business entity or domestic limited liability company which is not a division company, or that the limited liability company interests of the dividing company shall remain outstanding or be canceled, or any combination of the foregoing; and

b.   The allocation of assets, property, rights, series, debts, liabilities and duties of the dividing company among the division companies;

(2)   The name of each resulting company and, if the dividing company will survive the division, the name of the surviving company;

(3)   The name and business address of a division contact which shall have custody of a copy of the plan of division. The division contact, or any successor division contact, shall serve for a period of 6 years following the effective date of the division. During such 6-year period the division contact shall provide, without cost, to any creditor of the dividing company, within 30 days following the division

contact's receipt of a written request from any creditor of the dividing company, the name and business address of the division company to which the claim of such creditor was allocated pursuant to the plan of division; and

    (4)   Any other matters that the dividing company determines to include therein.

    (h)   If a domestic limited liability company divides under this section, the dividing company shall file a certificate of division executed by 1 or more authorized persons on behalf of such dividing company in the office of the Secretary of State in accordance with § 18–204 of this title and a certificate of formation that complies with § 18–201 of this title for each resulting company executed by 1 or more authorized persons in accordance with § 18–204 of this title. The certificate of division shall state:

    (1)   The name of the dividing company and, if it has been changed, the name under which its certificate of formation was originally filed and whether the dividing company is a surviving company;

    (2)   The date of filing of the dividing company's original certificate of formation with the Secretary of State;

    (3)   The name of each division company;

    (4)   The name and business address of the division contact required by paragraph (g)(3) of this section;

    (5)   The future effective date or time (which shall be a date or time certain) of the division if it is not to be effective upon the filing of the certificate of division;

    (6)   That the division has been approved in accordance with this section;

    (7)   That the plan of division is on file at a place of business of such division company as is specified therein, and shall state the address thereof; and

    (8)   That a copy of the plan of division will be furnished by such division company as is specified therein, on request and without cost, to any member of the dividing company.

    (i)   The certificate of division and each certificate of formation for each resulting company required by subsection (h) of this section shall be filed simultaneously in the office of the Secretary of State and, if such certificates are not to become effective upon their filing as permitted by § 18–206(b) of this title, then each such certificate shall provide for the same effective date or time in accordance with § 18–206(b) of this title. Concurrently with the effective date or time of a division, the limited liability company agreement of each resulting company shall become effective.

    (j)   A certificate of division shall act as a certificate of cancellation for a dividing company which is not a surviving company.

    (k)   A limited liability company agreement may provide that a domestic limited liability company shall not have the power to divide as set forth in this section.

    (*l*)   Upon the division of a domestic limited liability company becoming effective:

    (1)   The dividing company shall be divided into the distinct and independent resulting companies named in the plan of division, and, if the dividing company is not a surviving company, the existence of the dividing company shall cease.

    (2)   For all purposes of the laws of the State of Delaware, all of the rights, privileges and powers, and all the property, real, personal and mixed, of the dividing company and all debts due on whatever account to it, as well as all other things and other causes of action belonging to it, shall without further action be allocated to and vested in the applicable division company in such a manner and basis and with such effect as is specified in the plan of division, and the title to any real property or interest therein allocated to and vested in any division company shall not revert or be in any way impaired by reason of the division.

    (3)   Each division company shall, from and after effectiveness of the certificate of division, be liable as a separate and distinct domestic limited liability company for such debts, liabilities and duties of the dividing company as are allocated to such division company pursuant to the plan of division in the manner and on the basis provided in paragraph (g)(1)b. of this section.

(4)   Each of the debts, liabilities and duties of the dividing company shall without further action be allocated to and be the debts, liabilities and duties of such division company as is specified in the plan of division as having such debts, liabilities and duties allocated to it, in such a manner and basis and with such effect as is specified in the plan of division, and no other division company shall be liable therefor, so long as the plan of division does not constitute a fraudulent transfer under applicable law, and all liens upon any property of the dividing company shall be preserved unimpaired, and all debts, liabilities and duties of the dividing company shall remain attached to the division company to which such debts, liabilities and duties have been allocated in the plan of division, and may be enforced against such division company to the same extent as if said debts, liabilities and duties had originally been incurred or contracted by it in its capacity as a domestic limited liability company.

(5)   In the event that any allocation of assets, debts, liabilities and duties to division companies in accordance with a plan of division is determined by a court of competent jurisdiction to constitute a fraudulent transfer, each division company shall be jointly and severally liable on account of such fraudulent transfer notwithstanding the allocations made in the plan of division; provided, however, the validity and effectiveness of the division are not otherwise affected thereby.

(6)   Debts and liabilities of the dividing company that are not allocated by the plan of division shall be the joint and several debts and liabilities of all of the division companies.

(7)   It shall not be necessary for a plan of division to list each individual asset, property, right, series, debt, liability or duty of the dividing company to be allocated to a division company so long as the assets, property, rights, series, debts, liabilities or duties so allocated are reasonably identified by any method where the identity of such assets, property, rights, series, debts, liabilities or duties is objectively determinable.

(8)   The rights, privileges, powers and interests in property of the dividing company that have been allocated to a division company, as well as the debts, liabilities and duties of the dividing company that have been allocated to such division company pursuant to a plan of division, shall remain vested in each such division company and shall not be deemed, as a result of the division, to have been assigned or transferred to such division company for any purpose of the laws of the State of Delaware.

(9)   Any action or proceeding pending against a dividing company may be continued against the surviving company as if the division did not occur, but subject to paragraph (*l*)(4) of this section, and against any resulting company to which the asset, property, right, series, debt, liability or duty associated with such action or proceeding was allocated pursuant to the plan of division by adding or substituting such resulting company as a party in the action or proceeding.

(m)   In applying the provisions of this chapter on distributions, a direct or indirect allocation of property or liabilities in a division is not deemed a distribution for purposes of this chapter.

(n)   The provisions of this section shall not be construed to limit the means of accomplishing a division by any other means provided for in a limited liability company agreement or other agreement or as otherwise permitted by this chapter or as otherwise permitted by law.

(*o*)   All limited liability companies formed on or after August 1, 2018, shall be governed by this section. All limited liability companies formed prior to August 1, 2018, shall be governed by this section; provided, that if the dividing company is a party to any written contract, indenture or other agreement entered into prior to August 1, 2018, that, by its terms, restricts, conditions or prohibits the consummation of a merger or consolidation by the dividing company with or into another party, or the transfer of assets by the dividing company to another party, then such restriction, condition or prohibition shall be deemed to apply to a division as if it were a merger, consolidation or transfer of assets, as applicable.

§ 18–218.   Registered series of members, managers, limited liability company interests or assets.

(a)   If a limited liability company agreement provides for the establishment or formation of 1 or more series, then a registered series may be formed by complying with this § 18–218. A limited liability company agreement does not need to use the term registered when referencing series or refer to this § 18–218, and a reference in a limited liability company agreement for a registered series, including a registered series resulting from the conversion of a protected series to a registered series, may continue to refer to § 18–215 of this title, which reference shall be deemed a reference to this § 18–218 with respect to such registered series. A registered series is formed by the filing of a certificate of registered series in the office of the Secretary of State.

(b)   Notice of the limitation on liabilities of a registered series as referenced in subsection (c) of this section shall be set forth in the certificate of formation of the limited liability company. Notice in a certificate of formation of the limitation on liabilities of a registered series as referenced in subsection (c) of this section shall be sufficient for all purposes of this subsection whether or not the limited liability company has formed any registered series when such notice is included in the certificate of formation, and there shall be no requirement that (i) any specific registered series of the limited liability company be referenced in such notice, (ii) such notice use the term registered when referencing series or include a reference to this § 18–218, or (iii) the certificate of formation be amended if it includes a reference to § 18–215 of this title. Any reference to § 18–215 of this title in a certificate of formation of a limited liability company that has one or more registered series shall be deemed a reference to this § 18–218 with respect to such registered series. The fact that a certificate of formation that contains the foregoing notice of the limitation on liabilities of a series is on file in the office of the Secretary of State shall constitute notice of such limitation on liabilities of a registered series.

(c)   Notwithstanding anything to the contrary set forth in this chapter or under other applicable law, to the extent the records maintained for a registered series account for the assets associated with such series separately from the other assets of the limited liability company, or any other series thereof, then the debts, liabilities, obligations and expenses incurred, contracted for or otherwise existing with respect to such series shall be enforceable against the assets of such series only, and not against the assets of the limited liability company generally or any other series thereof, and, unless otherwise provided in the limited liability company agreement, none of the debts, liabilities, obligations and expenses incurred, contracted for or otherwise existing with respect to the limited liability company generally or any other series thereof shall be enforceable against the assets of such series. Neither the preceding sentences nor any provision pursuant thereto in a limited liability company agreement, certificate of formation or certificate of registered series shall (i) restrict a registered series or limited liability company on behalf of a registered series from agreeing in the limited liability company agreement or otherwise that any or all of the debts, liabilities, obligations and expenses incurred, contracted for or otherwise existing with respect to the limited liability company generally or any other series thereof shall be enforceable against the assets of such registered series or (ii) restrict a limited liability company from agreeing in the limited liability company agreement or otherwise that any or all of the debts, liabilities, obligations and expenses incurred, contracted for or otherwise existing with respect to a registered series shall be enforceable against the assets of the limited liability company generally. Assets associated with a registered series may be held directly or indirectly, including in the name of such series, in the name of the limited liability company, through a nominee or otherwise. Records maintained for a registered series that reasonably identify its assets, including by specific listing, category, type, quantity, computational or allocational formula or procedure (including a percentage or share of any asset or assets) or by any other method where the identity of such assets is objectively determinable, will be deemed to account for the assets associated with such series separately from the other assets of the limited liability company, or any other series thereof. As used in this chapter, a reference to assets of a registered series includes assets associated with such series, a reference to assets associated with a registered series includes assets of such series, a reference to members or managers of a registered series includes members or managers associated with such series, and a reference to members or managers associated with a registered series includes members or managers of such series. The following shall apply to a registered series:

(1)   A registered series may carry on any lawful business, purpose or activity, whether or not for profit, with the exception of the business of banking as defined in § 126 of Title 8. Unless otherwise provided in a limited liability company agreement, a registered series shall have the power and capacity to, in its own name, contract, hold title to assets (including real, personal and intangible property), grant liens and security interests, and sue and be sued.

(2)   Except as otherwise provided by this chapter, no member or manager of a registered series shall be obligated personally for any debt, obligation or liability of such series, whether arising in contract, tort or otherwise, solely by reason of being a member or acting as manager of such series. Notwithstanding the preceding sentence, under a limited liability company agreement or under

another agreement, a member or manager may agree to be obligated personally for any or all of the debts, obligations and liabilities of 1 or more registered series.

(3)   A limited liability company agreement may provide for classes or groups of members or managers associated with a registered series having such relative rights, powers and duties as the limited liability company agreement may provide, and may make provision for the future creation in the manner provided in the limited liability company agreement of additional classes or groups of members or managers associated with such series having such relative rights, powers and duties as may from time to time be established, including rights, powers and duties senior to existing classes and groups of members or managers associated with such series. A limited liability company agreement may provide for the taking of an action, including the amendment of the limited liability company agreement, without the vote or approval of any member or manager or class or group of members or managers, including an action to create under the provisions of the limited liability company agreement a class or group of a registered series of limited liability company interests that was not previously outstanding. A limited liability company agreement may provide that any member or class or group of members associated with a registered series shall have no voting rights.

(4)   A limited liability company agreement may grant to all or certain identified members or managers or a specified class or group of the members or managers associated with a registered series the right to vote separately or with all or any class or group of the members or managers associated with such series, on any matter. Voting by members or managers associated with a registered series may be on a per capita, number, financial interest, class, group or any other basis.

(5)   Unless otherwise provided in a limited liability company agreement, the management of a registered series shall be vested in the members associated with such series in proportion to the then current percentage or other interest of members in the profits of such series owned by all of the members associated with such series, the decision of members owning more than 50 percent of the said percentage or other interest in the profits controlling; provided, however, that if a limited liability company agreement provides for the management of a registered series, in whole or in part, by a manager, the management of such series, to the extent so provided, shall be vested in the manager who shall be chosen in the manner provided in the limited liability company agreement. The manager of a registered series shall also hold the offices and have the responsibilities accorded to the manager as set forth in a limited liability company agreement. A registered series may have more than 1 manager. Subject to § 18–602 of this title, a manager shall cease to be a manager with respect to a registered series as provided in a limited liability company agreement. Except as otherwise provided in a limited liability company agreement, any event under this chapter or in a limited liability company agreement that causes a manager to cease to be a manager with respect to a registered series shall not, in itself, cause such manager to cease to be a manager of the limited liability company or with respect to any other series thereof.

(6)   Notwithstanding § 18–606 of this title, but subject to paragraphs (c)(7) and (c)(10) of this section, and unless otherwise provided in a limited liability company agreement, at the time a member of a registered series becomes entitled to receive a distribution with respect to such series, the member has the status of, and is entitled to all remedies available to, a creditor of such series, with respect to the distribution. A limited liability company agreement may provide for the establishment of a record date with respect to allocations and distributions with respect to a registered series.

(7)   Notwithstanding § 18–607(a) of this title, a limited liability company may make a distribution with respect to a registered series. A limited liability company shall not make a distribution with respect to a registered series to a member to the extent that at the time of the distribution, after giving effect to the distribution, all liabilities of such series, other than liabilities to members on account of their limited liability company interests with respect to such series and liabilities for which the recourse of creditors is limited to specified property of such series, exceed the fair value of the assets associated with such series, except that the fair value of property of such series that is subject to a liability for which the recourse of creditors is limited shall be included in the assets associated with such series only to the extent that the fair value of that property exceeds that liability. For purposes of the immediately preceding sentence, the term "distribution" shall not include amounts constituting reasonable compensation for present or past services or reasonable payments made in the ordinary course of business pursuant to a bona fide retirement plan or other benefits program. A

member who receives a distribution in violation of this subsection, and who knew at the time of the distribution that the distribution violated this subsection, shall be liable to the registered series for the amount of the distribution. A member who receives a distribution in violation of this subsection, and who did not know at the time of the distribution that the distribution violated this subsection, shall not be liable for the amount of the distribution. Subject to § 18–607(c) of this title, which shall apply to any distribution made with respect to a registered series under this subsection, this subsection shall not affect any obligation or liability of a member under an agreement or other applicable law for the amount of a distribution.

(8) Unless otherwise provided in the limited liability company agreement, a member shall cease to be associated with a registered series and to have the power to exercise any rights or powers of a member with respect to such series upon the assignment of all of the member's limited liability company interest with respect to such series. Except as otherwise provided in a limited liability company agreement, any event under this chapter or a limited liability company agreement that causes a member to cease to be associated with a registered series shall not, in itself, cause such member to cease to be associated with any other series or terminate the continued membership of a member in the limited liability company or cause the dissolution of the registered series, regardless of whether such member was the last remaining member associated with such series.

(9) Subject to § 18–801 of this title, except to the extent otherwise provided in the limited liability company agreement, a registered series may be dissolved and its affairs wound up without causing the dissolution of the limited liability company. The dissolution of a registered series shall not affect the limitation on liabilities of such series provided by this subsection (c). A registered series is dissolved and its affairs shall be wound up upon the dissolution of the limited liability company under § 18–801 of this title or otherwise upon the first to occur of the following:

    a. At the time specified in the limited liability company agreement;

    b. Upon the happening of events specified in the limited liability company agreement;

    c. Unless otherwise provided in the limited liability company agreement, upon the vote or consent of members associated with such series who own more than 2/3 of the then-current percentage or other interest in the profits of such series of the limited liability company owned by all of the members associated with such series; or

    d. The dissolution of such series under paragraph (c)(11) of this section.

(10) Notwithstanding § 18–803(a) of this title, unless otherwise provided in the limited liability company agreement, a manager associated with a registered series who has not wrongfully dissolved such series or, if none, the members associated with such series or a person approved by the members associated with such series, in either case, by members who own more than 50 percent of the then current percentage or other interest in the profits of such series owned by all of the members associated with such series, may wind up the affairs of such series; but the Court of Chancery, upon cause shown, may wind up the affairs of a registered series upon application of any member or manager associated with such series, or the member's personal representative or assignee, and in connection therewith, may appoint a liquidating trustee. The persons winding up the affairs of a registered series may, in the name of the limited liability company and for and on behalf of the limited liability company and such series, take all actions with respect to such series as are permitted under § 18–803(b) of this title. The persons winding up the affairs of a registered series shall provide for the claims and obligations of such series and distribute the assets of such series as provided in § 18–804 of this title, which section shall apply to the winding up and distribution of assets of a registered series. Actions taken in accordance with this subsection shall not affect the liability of members and shall not impose liability on a liquidating trustee.

(11) On application by or for a member or manager associated with a registered series, the Court of Chancery may decree dissolution of such series whenever it is not reasonably practicable to carry on the business of such series in conformity with a limited liability company agreement.

(12) For all purposes of the laws of the State of Delaware, a registered series is an association, regardless of the number of members or managers, if any, of such series.

(d)   In order to form a registered series of a limited liability company, a certificate of registered series must be filed in accordance with this subsection.

(1)   A certificate of registered series:

a.   Shall set forth:

1.   The name of the limited liability company; and

2.   The name of the registered series.

b.   May include any other matter that the members of such registered series determine to include therein.

(2)   A certificate of registered series shall be executed in accordance with § 18–204 of this title and shall be filed in the office of the Secretary of State in accordance with § 18–206 of this title. A certificate of registered series shall be effective as of the effective time of such filing unless a later effective date or time (which shall be a date or time certain) is provided for in the certificate of registered series. A certificate of registered series is not an amendment to the certificate of formation of the limited liability company. The filing of a certificate of registered series in the office of the Secretary of State shall make it unnecessary to file any other documents under Chapter 31 of this title.

(3)   A certificate of registered series is amended by filing a certificate of amendment thereto in the office of the Secretary of State. The certificate of amendment of certificate of registered series shall set forth:

a.   The name of the limited liability company;

b.   The name of the registered series; and

c.   The amendment to the certificate of registered series.

(4)   A manager of a registered series or, if there is no manager, then any member of a registered series who becomes aware that any statement in a certificate of registered series filed with respect to such registered series was false when made, or that any matter described therein has changed making the certificate of registered series false in any material respect, shall promptly amend the certificate of registered series.

(5)   A certificate of registered series may be amended at any time for any other proper purpose.

(6)   Unless otherwise provided in this chapter or unless a later effective date or time (which shall be a date or time certain) is provided for in the certificate of amendment of certificate of registered series, a certificate of amendment of certificate of registered series shall be effective at the time of its filing with the Secretary of State.

(7)   A certificate of registered series shall be canceled upon the cancellation of the certificate of formation of the limited liability company named in the certificate of registered series, or upon the filing of a certificate of cancellation of the certificate of registered series or upon the future effective date or time of a certificate of cancellation of the certificate of registered series, or as provided in § 18–1108(b) of this title, or upon the filing of a certificate of merger or consolidation of registered series if the registered series is not the surviving or resulting registered series in a merger or consolidation or upon the future effective date or time of a certificate of merger or consolidation of registered series if the registered series is not the surviving or resulting registered series in a merger or consolidation, or upon the filing of a certificate of conversion of registered series to protected series or upon the future effective date or time of a certificate of conversion of registered series to protected series. A certificate of cancellation of the certificate of registered series may be filed at any time, and shall be filed, in the office of the Secretary of State to accomplish the cancellation of a certificate of registered series upon the dissolution of a registered series for which a certificate of registered series was filed and completion of the winding up of such registered series. A certificate of cancellation of the certificate of registered series shall set forth:

a.   The name of the limited liability company;

b.   The name of the registered series;

    c.   The date of filing of the certificate of registered series;

    d.   The future effective date or time (which shall be a date or time certain) of cancellation if it is not to be effective upon the filing of the certificate of cancellation; and

    e.   Any other information the person filing the certificate of cancellation of the certificate of registered series determines.

    (8)   A certificate of cancellation of the certificate of registered series that is filed in the office of the Secretary of State prior to the dissolution or the completion of winding up of a registered series may be corrected as an erroneously executed certificate of cancellation of the certificate of registered series by filing with the office of the Secretary of State a certificate of correction of such certificate of cancellation of the certificate of registered series in accordance with § 18–211 of this title.

    (9)   The Secretary of State shall not issue a certificate of good standing with respect to a registered series if its certificate of registered series is canceled or the limited liability company has ceased to be in good standing.

(e)   The name of each registered series as set forth in its certificate of registered series:

    (1)   Shall begin with the name of the limited liability company, including any word, abbreviation or designation required by § 18–102 of this title;

    (2)   May contain the name of a member or manager;

    (3)   Must be such as to distinguish it upon the records in the office of the Secretary of State from the name on such records of any corporation, partnership, limited partnership, statutory trust, limited liability company or registered series reserved, registered, formed or organized under the laws of the State of Delaware or qualified to do business or registered as a foreign corporation, foreign limited partnership, foreign statutory trust, foreign partnership or foreign limited liability company in the State of Delaware; provided, however, that a registered series may register under any name which is not such as to distinguish it upon the records in the office of the Secretary of State from the name on such records of any domestic or foreign corporation, partnership, limited partnership, statutory trust, registered series or foreign limited liability company reserved, registered, formed or organized under the laws of the State of Delaware with the written consent of the other corporation, partnership, limited partnership, statutory trust, registered series or foreign limited liability company, which written consent shall be filed with the Secretary of State;

    (4)   May contain the following words: "Company," "Association," "Club," "Foundation," "Fund," "Institute," "Society," "Union," "Syndicate," "Limited," "Public Benefit" or "Trust" (or abbreviations of like import); and

    (5)   Shall not contain the word "bank," or any variation thereof, except for the name of a bank reporting to and under the supervision of the State Bank Commissioner of this State or a subsidiary of a bank or savings association (as those terms are defined in the Federal Deposit Insurance Act, as amended, at 12 U.S.C. § 1813), or a limited liability company regulated under the Bank Holding Company Act of 1956, as amended, 12 U.S.C. § 1841 et seq., or the Home Owners' Loan Act, as amended, 12 U.S.C. § 1461 et seq.; provided, however, that this section shall not be construed to prevent the use of the word "bank," or any variation thereof, in a context clearly not purporting to refer to a banking business or otherwise likely to mislead the public about the nature of the business of the limited liability company or the registered series, or to lead to a pattern and practice of abuse that might cause harm to the interests of the public or this State as determined by the Division of Corporations in the Department of State.

§ 18–219.   Approval of conversion of a protected series of a domestic limited liability company to a registered series of such domestic limited liability company.

(a)   A protected series of a domestic limited liability company may convert to a registered series of such domestic limited liability company by complying with this section and filing in the office of the Secretary of State in accordance with § 18–206 of this title:

(1) A certificate of conversion of protected series to registered series that has been executed in accordance with § 18–204 of this title; and

(2) A certificate of registered series that complies with § 18–218(d) of this title and has been executed by 1 or more authorized persons in accordance with § 18–204 of this title.

Each of the certificates required by this subsection (a) shall be filed simultaneously in the office of the Secretary of State and, if such certificates are not to become effective upon their filing as permitted by § 18–206(b) of this title, then each such certificate shall provide for the same effective date or time in accordance with § 18–206(b) of this title.

An existing series may not become a registered series other than pursuant to this section.

(b) If the limited liability company agreement specifies the manner of authorizing a conversion of a protected series of such limited liability company to a registered series of such limited liability company, the conversion of a protected series to a registered series shall be authorized as specified in the limited liability company agreement. If the limited liability company agreement does not specify the manner of authorizing a conversion of a protected series of such limited liability company to a registered series of such limited liability company and does not prohibit a conversion of a protected series to a registered series, the conversion shall be authorized by members of such protected series who own more than 50 percent of the then current percentage or other interest in the profits of such protected series owned by all of the members of such protected series.

(c) Unless otherwise agreed, the conversion of a protected series of a limited liability company to a registered series of such limited liability company pursuant to this section shall not require such limited liability company or such protected series of such limited liability company to wind up its affairs under § 18–803 or § 18–215 of this title or pay its liabilities and distribute its assets under § 18–804 or § 18–215 of this title, and the conversion of a protected series of a limited liability company to a registered series of such limited liability company shall not constitute a dissolution of such limited liability company or a termination of such protected series. When a protected series of a limited liability company has converted to a registered series of such limited liability company pursuant to this section, for all purposes of the laws of the State of Delaware, the registered series shall be deemed to be the same series as the converting protected series and the conversion shall constitute a continuation of the existence of the protected series in the form of such registered series.

(d) In connection with a conversion of a protected series of a limited liability company to a registered series of such limited liability company pursuant to this section, rights or securities of or interests in the protected series which is to be converted may be exchanged for or converted into cash, property, rights or securities of or interests in the registered series into which the protected series is being converted or, in addition to or in lieu thereof, may be exchanged for or converted into cash, property, rights or securities of or interests in any other business entity, may remain outstanding or may be canceled.

(e) If a protected series shall convert to a registered series in accordance with this section, a certificate of conversion of protected series to registered series executed in accordance with § 18–204 of this title shall be filed in the office of the Secretary of State in accordance with § 18–206 of this title. The certificate of conversion of protected series to registered series shall state:

(1) The name of the limited liability company and, if it has been changed, the name under which its certificate of formation was originally filed;

(2) The name of the protected series and, if it has been changed, the name of the protected series as originally established;

(3) The name of the registered series as set forth in its certificate of registered series filed in accordance with subsection (a) of this section;

(4) The date of filing of the original certificate of formation of the limited liability company with the Secretary of State;

(5) The date on which the protected series was established;

(6)   The future effective date or time (which shall be a date or time certain) of the conversion if it is not to be effective upon the filing of the certificate of conversion of protected series to registered series; and

(7)   That the conversion has been approved in accordance with this section.

(f)   A copy of the certificate of conversion of protected series to registered series certified by the Secretary of State shall be prima facie evidence of the conversion by such protected series to a registered series of such limited liability company.

(g)   When any conversion shall have become effective under this section, for all purposes of the laws of the State of Delaware, all of the rights, privileges and powers of the protected series that has converted, and all property, real, personal and mixed, and all debts due to such protected series, as well as all other things and causes of action belonging to such protected series, shall remain vested in the registered series to which such protected series has converted and shall be the property of such registered series, and the title to any real property vested by deed or otherwise in such protected series shall not revert or be in any way impaired by reason of this chapter; but all rights of creditors and all liens upon any property of such protected series shall be preserved unimpaired, and all debts, liabilities and duties of the protected series that has converted shall remain attached to the registered series to which such protected series has converted, and may be enforced against it to the same extent as if said debts, liabilities and duties had originally been incurred or contracted by it in its capacity as such registered series. The rights, privileges, powers and interests in property of the protected series that has converted, as well as the debts, liabilities and duties of such protected series, shall not be deemed, as a consequence of the conversion, to have been transferred to the registered series to which such protected series of such limited liability company has converted for any purpose of the laws of the State of Delaware.

(h)   A limited liability company agreement may provide that a protected series of a limited liability company shall not have the power to convert to a registered series of such limited liability company as set forth in this section.

§ 18–220.   Approval of conversion of a registered series of a domestic limited liability company to a protected series of such domestic limited liability company.

(a)   Upon compliance with this section, a registered series of a domestic limited liability company may convert to a protected series of such domestic limited liability company. An existing registered series may not become a protected series other than pursuant to this section.

(b)   If the limited liability company agreement specifies the manner of authorizing a conversion of a registered series of such limited liability company to a protected series of such limited liability company, the conversion of a registered series to a protected series shall be authorized as specified in the limited liability company agreement. If the limited liability company agreement does not specify the manner of authorizing a conversion of a registered series of such limited liability company to a protected series of such limited liability company and does not prohibit a conversion of a registered series to a protected series, the conversion shall be authorized by members of such registered series who own more than 50 percent of the then current percentage or other interest in the profits of such registered series owned by all of the members of such registered series.

(c)   Unless otherwise agreed, the conversion of a registered series of a limited liability company to a protected series of such limited liability company pursuant to this section shall not require such limited liability company or such registered series of such limited liability company to wind up its affairs under § 18–803 or § 18–218 of this title or pay its liabilities and distribute its assets under § 18–804 or § 18–218 of this title, and the conversion of a registered series of a limited liability company to a protected series of such limited liability company shall not constitute a dissolution of such limited liability company or of such registered series. When a registered series of a limited liability company has converted to a protected series of such limited liability company pursuant to this section, for all purposes of the laws of the State of Delaware, the protected series shall be deemed to be the same series as the converting registered series and the conversion shall constitute a continuation of the existence of the registered series in the form of such protected series.

(d)   In connection with a conversion of a registered series of a limited liability company to protected series of such limited liability company pursuant to this section, rights or securities of or interests in the registered series which is to be converted may be exchanged for or converted into cash, property, rights or securities of or interests in the protected series into which the registered series is being converted or, in addition to or in lieu thereof, may be exchanged for or converted into cash, property, rights or securities of or interests in any other business entity, may remain outstanding or may be canceled.

(e)   If a registered series shall convert to a protected series in accordance with this section, a certificate of conversion of registered series to protected series executed in accordance with § 18–204 of this title shall be filed in the office of the Secretary of State in accordance with § 18–206 of this title. The certificate of conversion of registered series to protected series shall state:

(1)   The name of the limited liability company and, if it has been changed, the name under which its certificate of formation was originally filed;

(2)   The date of filing of the original certificate of formation of the limited liability company with the Secretary of State;

(3)   The name of the registered series and, if it has been changed, the name under which its certificate of registered series was originally filed;

(4)   The date of filing of its original certificate of registered series with the Secretary of State;

(5)   The future effective date or time (which shall be a date or time certain) of the conversion if it is not to be effective upon the filing of the certificate of conversion of registered series to protected series; and

(6)   That the conversion has been approved in accordance with this section.

(f)   Upon the filing in the office of the Secretary of State of the certificate of conversion of registered series to protected series or upon the future effective date or time of the certificate of conversion of registered series to protected series and payment to the Secretary of State of all fees prescribed in this chapter, the Secretary of State shall certify that the registered series has filed all documents and paid all fees required by this chapter. Such certificate of the Secretary of State shall be prima facie evidence of the conversion by such registered series to a protected series of such limited liability company.

(g)   When any conversion shall have become effective under this section, for all purposes of the laws of the State of Delaware, all of the rights, privileges and powers of the registered series that has converted, and all property, real, personal and mixed, and all debts due to such registered series, as well as all other things and causes of action belonging to such registered series, shall remain vested in the protected series to which such registered series has converted and shall be the property of such protected series, and the title to any real property vested by deed or otherwise in such registered series shall not revert or be in any way impaired by reason of this chapter; but all rights of creditors and all liens upon any property of such registered series shall be preserved unimpaired, and all debts, liabilities and duties of the registered series that has converted shall remain attached to the protected series to which such registered series has converted, and may be enforced against it to the same extent as if said debts, liabilities and duties had originally been incurred or contracted by it in its capacity as such protected series. The rights, privileges, powers and interests in property of the registered series that has converted, as well as the debts, liabilities and duties of such registered series, shall not be deemed, as a consequence of the conversion, to have been transferred to the protected series to which such registered series of such limited liability company has converted for any purpose of the laws of the State of Delaware.

(h)   A limited liability company agreement may provide that a registered series of a limited liability company shall not have the power to convert to a protected series of such limited liability company as set forth in this section.

§ 18–221.   Merger and consolidation of registered series.

(a)   Pursuant to an agreement of merger or consolidation, 1 or more registered series may merge or consolidate with or into 1 or more other registered series of the same limited liability company with such registered series as the agreement shall provide being the surviving or resulting registered series. Unless otherwise provided in the limited liability company agreement, an agreement of merger or consolidation shall be approved by each registered series which is to merge or consolidate by members of such registered series who own more than 50 percent of the then current percentage or other interest in the profits of such registered series owned by all of the members of such registered series. In connection with a merger or consolidation hereunder, rights or securities of, or interests in, a registered series which is a constituent party to the merger or consolidation may be exchanged for or converted into cash, property, rights or securities of, or interests in, the surviving or resulting registered series or, in addition to or in lieu thereof, may be exchanged for or converted into cash, property, rights or securities of, or interests in, a domestic limited liability company or other business entity which is not the surviving or resulting registered series in the merger or consolidation, may remain outstanding or may be canceled. Notwithstanding prior approval, an agreement of merger or consolidation may be terminated or amended pursuant to a provision for such termination or amendment contained in the agreement of merger or consolidation.

(b)   If a registered series is merging or consolidating under this section, the registered series surviving or resulting in or from the merger or consolidation shall file a certificate of merger or consolidation of registered series executed by 1 or more authorized persons on behalf of the registered series when it is the surviving or resulting registered series in the office of the Secretary of State. The certificate of merger or consolidation of registered series shall state:

(1)   The name of each registered series which is to merge or consolidate and the name of the limited liability company that formed such registered series;

(2)   That an agreement of merger or consolidation has been approved and executed by or on behalf of each registered series which is to merge or consolidate;

(3)   The name of the surviving or resulting registered series;

(4)   Such amendment, if any, to the certificate of registered series of the registered series that is the surviving registered series to change the name of the surviving registered series, as is desired to be effected by the merger;

(5)   The future effective date or time (which shall be a date or time certain) of the merger or consolidation if it is not to be effective upon the filing of the certificate of merger or consolidation of registered series;

(6)   That the agreement of merger or consolidation is on file at a place of business of the surviving or resulting registered series or the limited liability company that formed such registered series, and shall state the address thereof; and

(7)   That a copy of the agreement of merger or consolidation will be furnished by the surviving or resulting registered series, on request and without cost, to any member of any registered series which is to merge or consolidate.

(c)   Unless a future effective date or time is provided in a certificate of merger or consolidation of registered series, a merger or consolidation pursuant to this section shall be effective upon the filing in the office of the Secretary of State of a certificate of merger or consolidation of registered series.

(d)   A certificate of merger or consolidation of registered series shall act as a certificate of cancellation of the certificate of registered series of the registered series which is not the surviving or resulting registered series in the merger or consolidation. A certificate of merger or consolidation of registered series that sets forth any amendment in accordance with paragraph (b)(4) of this section shall be deemed to be an amendment to the certificate of registered series of the surviving registered series, and no further action shall be required to amend the certificate of registered series of the surviving registered series under § 18–218 of this title with respect to such amendments set forth in such certificate of merger or consolidation. Whenever this section requires the filing of a certificate of merger or consolidation of registered series, such requirement shall be deemed satisfied by the filing of an agreement of merger or consolidation containing the information required by this section to be set forth in such certificate of merger or consolidation.

(e)   An agreement of merger or consolidation approved in accordance with subsection (a) of this section may effect any amendment to the limited liability company agreement relating solely to the registered series that are constituent parties to the merger or consolidation.

Any amendment to a limited liability company agreement relating solely to the registered series that are constituent parties to the merger or consolidation made pursuant to the foregoing sentence shall be effective at the effective time or date of the merger or consolidation and shall be effective notwithstanding any provision of the limited liability company agreement relating to amendment of the limited liability company agreement, other than a provision that by its terms applies to an amendment to the limited liability company agreement in connection with a merger or consolidation. The provisions of this subsection shall not be construed to limit the accomplishment of a merger or of any of the matters referred to herein by any other means provided for in a limited liability company agreement or other agreement or as otherwise permitted by law, including that the limited liability company agreement relating to any constituent registered series to the merger or consolidation (including a registered series formed for the purpose of consummating a merger or consolidation) shall be the limited liability company agreement of the surviving or resulting registered series.

(f) When any merger or consolidation shall have become effective under this section, for all purposes of the laws of the State of Delaware, all of the rights, privileges and powers of each of the registered series that have merged or consolidated, and all property, real, personal and mixed, and all debts due to any of said registered series, as well as all other things and causes of action belonging to each of such registered series, shall be vested in the surviving or resulting registered series, and shall thereafter be the property of the surviving or resulting registered series as they were of each of the registered series that have merged or consolidated, and the title to any real property vested by deed or otherwise, under the laws of the State of Delaware, in any of such registered series, shall not revert or be in any way impaired by reason of this chapter; but all rights of creditors and all liens upon any property of any of said registered series shall be preserved unimpaired, and all debts, liabilities and duties of each of the said registered series that have merged or consolidated shall thenceforth attach to the surviving or resulting registered series, and may be enforced against it to the same extent as if said debts, liabilities and duties had been incurred or contracted by it. Unless otherwise agreed, a merger or consolidation of a registered series of a limited liability company, including a registered series which is not the surviving or resulting registered series in the merger or consolidation, shall not require such registered series to wind up its affairs under § 18–218 of this title, or pay its liabilities and distribute its assets under § 18–218 of this title and the merger or consolidation shall not constitute a dissolution of such registered series.

(g) A limited liability company agreement may provide that a registered series of such limited liability company shall not have the power to merge or consolidate as set forth in this section.

SUBCHAPTER III. MEMBERS

§ 18–301. Admission of members.

(a) In connection with the formation of a limited liability company, a person is admitted as a member of the limited liability company upon the later to occur of:

(1) The formation of the limited liability company; or

(2) The time provided in and upon compliance with the limited liability company agreement or, if the limited liability company agreement does not so provide, when the person's admission is reflected in the records of the limited liability company.

(b) After the formation of a limited liability company, a person is admitted as a member of the limited liability company:

(1) In the case of a person who is not an assignee of a limited liability company interest, including a person acquiring a limited liability company interest directly from the limited liability company and a person to be admitted as a member of the limited liability company without acquiring a limited liability company interest in the limited liability company at the time provided in and upon compliance with the limited liability company agreement or, if the limited liability company agreement does not so provide, upon the consent of all members and when the person's admission is reflected in the records of the limited liability company;

(2) In the case of an assignee of a limited liability company interest, as provided in § 18–704(a) of this title and at the time provided in and upon compliance with the limited liability company

agreement or, if the limited liability company agreement does not so provide, when any such person's permitted admission is reflected in the records of the limited liability company;

(3)   In the case of a person being admitted as a member of a surviving or resulting limited liability company pursuant to a merger or consolidation approved in accordance with § 18–209(b) of this title, as provided in the limited liability company agreement of the surviving or resulting limited liability company or in the agreement of merger or consolidation or plan of merger, and in the event of any inconsistency, the terms of the agreement of merger or consolidation or plan of merger shall control; and in the case of a person being admitted as a member of a limited liability company pursuant to a merger or consolidation in which such limited liability company is not the surviving or resulting limited liability company in the merger or consolidation, as provided in the limited liability company agreement of such limited liability company; or

(4)   In the case of a person being admitted as a member of a division company pursuant to a division approved in accordance with § 18–217(c) of this title, as provided in the limited liability company agreement of such division company or in the plan of division, and in the event of any inconsistency, the terms of the plan of division shall control; and in the case of a person being admitted as a member of a limited liability company pursuant to a division in which such limited liability company is not a division company in the division, as provided in the limited liability company agreement of such limited liability company.

(c)   In connection with the domestication of a non-United States entity (as defined in § 18–212 of this title) as a limited liability company in the State of Delaware in accordance with § 18–212 of this title or the conversion of an other entity (as defined in § 18–214 of this title) to a domestic limited liability company in accordance with § 18–214 of this title, a person is admitted as a member of the limited liability company as provided in the limited liability company agreement.

(d)   A person may be admitted to a limited liability company as a member of the limited liability company and may receive a limited liability company interest in the limited liability company without making a contribution or being obligated to make a contribution to the limited liability company. Unless otherwise provided in a limited liability company agreement, a person may be admitted to a limited liability company as a member of the limited liability company without acquiring a limited liability company interest in the limited liability company. Unless otherwise provided in a limited liability company agreement, a person may be admitted as the sole member of a limited liability company without making a contribution or being obligated to make a contribution to the limited liability company or without acquiring a limited liability company interest in the limited liability company.

(e)   Unless otherwise provided in a limited liability company agreement or another agreement, a member shall have no preemptive right to subscribe to any additional issue of limited liability company interests or another interest in a limited liability company.

§ 18–302.   Classes and voting.

(a)   A limited liability company agreement may provide for classes or groups of members having such relative rights, powers and duties as the limited liability company agreement may provide, and may make provision for the future creation in the manner provided in the limited liability company agreement of additional classes or groups of members having such relative rights, powers and duties as may from time to time be established, including rights, powers and duties senior to existing classes and groups of members. A limited liability company agreement may provide for the taking of an action, including the amendment of the limited liability company agreement, without the vote or approval of any member or class or group of members, including an action to create under the provisions of the limited liability company agreement a class or group of limited liability company interests that was not previously outstanding. A limited liability company agreement may provide that any member or class or group of members shall have no voting rights.

(b)   A limited liability company agreement may grant to all or certain identified members or a specified class or group of the members the right to vote separately or with all or any class or group of the members or managers, on any matter. Voting by members may be on a per capita, number, financial interest, class, group or any other basis.

(c)   A limited liability company agreement may set forth provisions relating to notice of the time, place or purpose of any meeting at which any matter is to be voted on by any members, waiver of any such notice, action by consent without a meeting, the establishment of a record date, quorum requirements, voting in person or by proxy, or any other matter with respect to the exercise of any such right to vote.

(d)   Unless otherwise provided in a limited liability company agreement, meetings of members may be held by means of conference telephone or other communications equipment by means of which all persons participating in the meeting can hear each other, and participation in a meeting pursuant to this subsection shall constitute presence in person at the meeting. Unless otherwise provided in a limited liability company agreement, on any matter that is to be voted on, consented to or approved by members, the members may take such action without a meeting, without prior notice and without a vote if consented to or approved, in writing, by electronic transmission or by any other means permitted by law, by members having not less than the minimum number of votes that would be necessary to authorize or take such action at a meeting at which all members entitled to vote thereon were present and voted. Unless otherwise provided in a limited liability company agreement, if a person (whether or not then a member) consenting as a member to any matter provides that such consent will be effective at a future time (including a time determined upon the happening of an event), then such person shall be deemed to have consented as a member at such future time so long as such person is then a member. Unless otherwise provided in a limited liability company agreement, on any matter that is to be voted on by members, the members may vote in person or by proxy, and such proxy may be granted in writing, by means of electronic transmission or as otherwise permitted by applicable law. Unless otherwise provided in a limited liability company agreement, a consent transmitted by electronic transmission by a member or by a person or persons authorized to act for a member shall be deemed to be written and signed for purposes of this subsection.

(e)   If a limited liability company agreement provides for the manner in which it may be amended, including by requiring the approval of a person who is not a party to the limited liability company agreement or the satisfaction of conditions, it may be amended only in that manner or as otherwise permitted by law, including as permitted by § 18–209(f) of this title (provided that the approval of any person may be waived by such person and that any such conditions may be waived by all persons for whose benefit such conditions were intended). Unless otherwise provided in a limited liability company agreement, a supermajority amendment provision shall only apply to provisions of the limited liability company agreement that are expressly included in the limited liability company agreement. As used in this section, "supermajority amendment provision" means any amendment provision set forth in a limited liability company agreement requiring that an amendment to a provision of the limited liability company agreement be adopted by no less than the vote or consent required to take action under such latter provision.

(f)   If a limited liability company agreement does not provide for the manner in which it may be amended, the limited liability company agreement may be amended with the approval of all of the members or as otherwise permitted by law, including as permitted by § 18–209(f) of this title. This subsection shall only apply to a limited liability company whose original certificate of formation was filed with the Secretary of State on or after January 1, 2012.

§ 18–303.   Liability to third parties.

(a)   Except as otherwise provided by this chapter, the debts, obligations and liabilities of a limited liability company, whether arising in contract, tort or otherwise, shall be solely the debts, obligations and liabilities of the limited liability company, and no member or manager of a limited liability company shall be obligated personally for any such debt, obligation or liability of the limited liability company solely by reason of being a member or acting as a manager of the limited liability company.

(b)   Notwithstanding the provisions of subsection (a) of this section, under a limited liability company agreement or under another agreement, a member or manager may agree to be obligated personally for any or all of the debts, obligations and liabilities of the limited liability company.

§ 18–304.   Events of bankruptcy.

A person ceases to be a member of a limited liability company upon the happening of any of the following events:

(1)   Unless otherwise provided in a limited liability company agreement, or with the consent of all members, a member:

      a.   Makes an assignment for the benefit of creditors;

      b.   Files a voluntary petition in bankruptcy;

      c.   Is adjudged a bankrupt or insolvent, or has entered against the member an order for relief, in any bankruptcy or insolvency proceeding;

      d.   Files a petition or answer seeking for the member any reorganization, arrangement, composition, readjustment, liquidation, dissolution or similar relief under any statute, law or regulation;

      e.   Files an answer or other pleading admitting or failing to contest the material allegations of a petition filed against the member in any proceeding of this nature;

      f.   Seeks, consents to or acquiesces in the appointment of a trustee, receiver or liquidator of the member or of all or any substantial part of the member's properties; or

(2)   Unless otherwise provided in a limited liability company agreement, or with the consent of all members, 120 days after the commencement of any proceeding against the member seeking reorganization, arrangement, composition, readjustment, liquidation, dissolution or similar relief under any statute, law or regulation, if the proceeding has not been dismissed, or if within 90 days after the appointment without the member's consent or acquiescence of a trustee, receiver or liquidator of the member or of all or any substantial part of the member's properties, the appointment is not vacated or stayed, or within 90 days after the expiration of any such stay, the appointment is not vacated.

§ 18–305.   Access to and confidentiality of information; records.

(a)   Each member of a limited liability company, in person or by attorney or other agent, has the right, subject to such reasonable standards (including standards governing what information and documents are to be furnished at what time and location and at whose expense) as may be set forth in a limited liability company agreement or otherwise established by the manager or, if there is no manager, then by the members, to obtain from the limited liability company from time to time upon reasonable demand for any purpose reasonably related to the member's interest as a member of the limited liability company:

(1)   True and full information regarding the status of the business and financial condition of the limited liability company;

(2)   Promptly after becoming available, a copy of the limited liability company's federal, state and local income tax returns for each year;

(3)   A current list of the name and last known business, residence or mailing address of each member and manager;

(4)   A copy of any written limited liability company agreement and certificate of formation and all amendments thereto, together with executed copies of any written powers of attorney pursuant to which the limited liability company agreement and any certificate and all amendments thereto have been executed;

(5)   True and full information regarding the amount of cash and a description and statement of the agreed value of any other property or services contributed by each member and which each member has agreed to contribute in the future, and the date on which each became a member; and

(6)   Other information regarding the affairs of the limited liability company as is just and reasonable.

(b)   Each manager shall have the right to examine all of the information described in subsection (a) of this section for a purpose reasonably related to the position of manager.

(c)   The manager of a limited liability company shall have the right to keep confidential from the members, for such period of time as the manager deems reasonable, any information which the manager reasonably believes to be in the nature of trade secrets or other information the disclosure of which the manager in good faith believes is not in the best interest of the limited liability company or could damage the limited liability company or its business or which the limited liability company is required by law or by agreement with a third party to keep confidential.

(d) A limited liability company may maintain its records in other than a written form, including on, by means of, or in the form of any information storage device, method, or 1 or more electronic networks or databases (including 1 or more distributed electronic networks or databases), if such form is capable of conversion into written form within a reasonable time.

(e) Any demand under this section shall be in writing and shall state the purpose of such demand. In every instance where an attorney or other agent shall be the person who seeks the right to obtain the information described in subsection (a) of this section, the demand shall be accompanied by a power of attorney or such other writing which authorizes the attorney or other agent to so act on behalf of the member.

(f) Any action to enforce any right arising under this section shall be brought in the Court of Chancery. If the limited liability company refuses to permit a member, or attorney or other agent acting for the member, to obtain or a manager to examine the information described in subsection (a) of this section or does not reply to the demand that has been made within 5 business days (or such shorter or longer period of time as is provided for in a limited liability company agreement but not longer than 30 business days) after the demand has been made, the demanding member or manager may apply to the Court of Chancery for an order to compel such disclosure. The Court of Chancery is hereby vested with exclusive jurisdiction to determine whether or not the person seeking such information is entitled to the information sought. The Court of Chancery may summarily order the limited liability company to permit the demanding member to obtain or manager to examine the information described in subsection (a) of this section and to make copies or abstracts therefrom, or the Court of Chancery may summarily order the limited liability company to furnish to the demanding member or manager the information described in subsection (a) of this section on the condition that the demanding member or manager first pay to the limited liability company the reasonable cost of obtaining and furnishing such information and on such other conditions as the Court of Chancery deems appropriate. When a demanding member seeks to obtain or a manager seeks to examine the information described in subsection (a) of this section, the demanding member or manager shall first establish:

(1) That the demanding member or manager has complied with the provisions of this section respecting the form and manner of making demand for obtaining or examining of such information, and

(2) That the information the demanding member or manager seeks is reasonably related to the member's interest as a member or the manager's position as a manager, as the case may be.

The Court of Chancery may, in its discretion, prescribe any limitations or conditions with reference to the obtaining or examining of information, or award such other or further relief as the Court of Chancery may deem just and proper. The Court of Chancery may order books, documents and records, pertinent extracts therefrom, or duly authenticated copies thereof, to be brought within the State of Delaware and kept in the State of Delaware upon such terms and conditions as the order may prescribe.

(g) The rights of a member or manager to obtain information as provided in this section may be restricted in an original limited liability company agreement or in any subsequent amendment approved or adopted by all of the members or in compliance with any applicable requirements of the limited liability company agreement. The provisions of this subsection shall not be construed to limit the ability to impose restrictions on the rights of a member or manager to obtain information by any other means permitted under this chapter.

(h) A limited liability company shall maintain a current record that identifies the name and last known business, residence or mailing address of each member and manager.

§ 18–306. Remedies for breach of limited liability company agreement by member.

A limited liability company agreement may provide that:

(1)   A member who fails to perform in accordance with, or to comply with the terms and conditions of, the limited liability company agreement shall be subject to specified penalties or specified consequences; and

(2)   At the time or upon the happening of events specified in the limited liability company agreement, a member shall be subject to specified penalties or specified consequences.

Such specified penalties or specified consequences may include and take the form of any penalty or consequence set forth in § 18–502(c) of this title.

SUBCHAPTER IV.   MANAGERS

§ 18–401.   Admission of managers.

A person may be named or designated as a manager of the limited liability company as provided in § 18–101(12) of this title.

§ 18–402.   Management of limited liability company.

Unless otherwise provided in a limited liability company agreement, the management of a limited liability company shall be vested in its members in proportion to the then current percentage or other interest of members in the profits of the limited liability company owned by all of the members, the decision of members owning more than 50 percent of the said percentage or other interest in the profits controlling; provided however, that if a limited liability company agreement provides for the management, in whole or in part, of a limited liability company by a manager, the management of the limited liability company, to the extent so provided, shall be vested in the manager who shall be chosen in the manner provided in the limited liability company agreement. The manager shall also hold the offices and have the responsibilities accorded to the manager by or in the manner provided in a limited liability company agreement. Subject to § 18–602 of this title, a manager shall cease to be a manager as provided in a limited liability company agreement. A limited liability company may have more than 1 manager. Unless otherwise provided in a limited liability company agreement, each member and manager has the authority to bind the limited liability company.

§ 18–403.   Contributions by a manager.

A manager of a limited liability company may make contributions to the limited liability company and share in the profits and losses of, and in distributions from, the limited liability company as a member. A person who is both a manager and a member has the rights and powers, and is subject to the restrictions and liabilities, of a manager and, except as provided in a limited liability company agreement, also has the rights and powers, and is subject to the restrictions and liabilities, of a member to the extent of the manager's participation in the limited liability company as a member.

§ 18–404.   Classes and voting.

(a)   A limited liability company agreement may provide for classes or groups of managers having such relative rights, powers and duties as the limited liability company agreement may provide, and may make provision for the future creation in the manner provided in the limited liability company agreement of additional classes or groups of managers having such relative rights, powers and duties as may from time to time be established, including rights, powers and duties senior to existing classes and groups of managers. A limited liability company agreement may provide for the taking of an action, including the amendment of the limited liability company agreement, without the vote or approval of any manager or class or group of managers, including an action to create under the provisions of the limited liability company agreement a class or group of limited liability company interests that was not previously outstanding.

(b)   A limited liability company agreement may grant to all or certain identified managers or a specified class or group of the managers the right to vote, separately or with all or any class or group of managers or members, on any matter. Voting by managers may be on a per capita, number, financial interest, class, group or any other basis.

(c)   A limited liability company agreement may set forth provisions relating to notice of the time, place or purpose of any meeting at which any matter is to be voted on by any manager or class or group of managers, waiver of any such notice, action by consent without a meeting, the establishment of a record date, quorum requirements, voting in person or by proxy, or any other matter with respect to the exercise of any such right to vote.

(d)   Unless otherwise provided in a limited liability company agreement, meetings of managers may be held by means of conference telephone or other communications equipment by means of which all persons participating in the meeting can hear each other, and participation in a meeting pursuant to this subsection shall constitute presence in person at the meeting. Unless otherwise provided in a limited liability company agreement, on any matter that is to be voted on, consented to or approved by managers, the managers may take such action without a meeting, without prior notice and without a vote if consented to or approved, in writing, by electronic transmission or by any other means permitted by law, by managers having not less than the minimum number of votes that would be necessary to authorize or take such action at a meeting at which all managers entitled to vote thereon were present and voted. Unless otherwise provided in a limited liability company agreement, if a person (whether or not then a manager) consenting as a manager to any matter provides that such consent will be effective at a future time (including a time determined upon the happening of an event), then such person shall be deemed to have consented as a manager at such future time so long as such person is then a manager. Unless otherwise provided in a limited liability company agreement, on any matter that is to be voted on by managers, the managers may vote in person or by proxy, and such proxy may be granted in writing, by means of electronic transmission or as otherwise permitted by applicable law. Unless otherwise provided in a limited liability company agreement, a consent transmitted by electronic transmission by a manager or by a person or persons authorized to act for a manager shall be deemed to be written and signed for purposes of this subsection.

§ 18–405.   Remedies for breach of limited liability company agreement by manager.

A limited liability company agreement may provide that:

(1)   A manager who fails to perform in accordance with, or to comply with the terms and conditions of, the limited liability company agreement shall be subject to specified penalties or specified consequences; and

(2)   At the time or upon the happening of events specified in the limited liability company agreement, a manager shall be subject to specified penalties or specified consequences.

§ 18–406.   Reliance on reports and information by member or manager.

A member, manager or liquidating trustee of a limited liability company shall be fully protected in relying in good faith upon the records of the limited liability company and upon information, opinions, reports or statements presented by another manager, member or liquidating trustee, an officer or employee of the limited liability company, or committees of the limited liability company, members or managers, or by any other person as to matters the member, manager or liquidating trustees reasonably believes are within such other person's professional or expert competence, including information, opinions, reports or statements as to the value and amount of the assets, liabilities, profits or losses of the limited liability company, or the value and amount of assets or reserves or contracts, agreements or other undertakings that would be sufficient to pay claims and obligations of the limited liability company or to make reasonable provision to pay such claims and obligations, or any other facts pertinent to the existence and amount of assets from which distributions to members or creditors might properly be paid.

§ 18–407.   Delegation of rights and powers to manage.

Unless otherwise provided in the limited liability company agreement, a member or manager of a limited liability company has the power and authority to delegate to 1 or more other persons any or all of the member's or manager's, as the case may be, rights, powers and duties to manage and control the business and affairs of the limited liability company. Any such delegation may be to agents, officers and employees of a member or manager or the limited liability company, and by a management agreement or another agreement with, or otherwise to, other persons. Unless otherwise provided in the limited liability company agreement, such delegation by a member or manager shall be irrevocable if it states that it is irrevocable.

Unless otherwise provided in the limited liability company agreement, such delegation by a member or manager of a limited liability company shall not cause the member or manager to cease to be a member or manager, as the case may be, of the limited liability company or cause the person to whom any such rights, powers and duties have been delegated to be a member or manager, as the case may be, of the limited liability company. No other provision of this chapter shall be construed to restrict a member's or manager's power and authority to delegate any or all of its rights, powers and duties to manage and control the business and affairs of the limited liability company.

SUBCHAPTER V. FINANCE

§ 18–501.   Form of contribution.

The contribution of a member to a limited liability company may be in cash, property or services rendered, or a promissory note or other obligation to contribute cash or property or to perform services.

§ 18–502.   Liability for contribution.

(a)   Except as provided in a limited liability company agreement, a member is obligated to a limited liability company to perform any promise to contribute cash or property or to perform services, even if the member is unable to perform because of death, disability or any other reason. If a member does not make the required contribution of property or services, the member is obligated at the option of the limited liability company to contribute cash equal to that portion of the agreed value (as stated in the records of the limited liability company) of the contribution that has not been made. The foregoing option shall be in addition to, and not in lieu of, any other rights, including the right to specific performance, that the limited liability company may have against such member under the limited liability company agreement or applicable law.

(b)   Unless otherwise provided in a limited liability company agreement, the obligation of a member to make a contribution or return money or other property paid or distributed in violation of this chapter may be compromised only by consent of all the members. Notwithstanding the compromise, a creditor of a limited liability company who extends credit, after the entering into of a limited liability company agreement or an amendment thereto which, in either case, reflects the obligation, and before the amendment thereof to reflect the compromise, may enforce the original obligation to the extent that, in extending credit, the creditor reasonably relied on the obligation of a member to make a contribution or return. A conditional obligation of a member to make a contribution or return money or other property to a limited liability company may not be enforced unless the conditions of the obligation have been satisfied or waived as to or by such member. Conditional obligations include contributions payable upon a discretionary call of a limited liability company prior to the time the call occurs.

(c)   A limited liability company agreement may provide that the interest of any member who fails to make any contribution that the member is obligated to make shall be subject to specified penalties for, or specified consequences of, such failure. Such penalty or consequence may take the form of reducing or eliminating the defaulting member's proportionate interest in a limited liability company, subordinating the member's limited liability company interest to that of nondefaulting members, a forced sale of that limited liability company interest, forfeiture of the defaulting member's limited liability company interest, the lending by other members of the amount necessary to meet the defaulting member's commitment, a fixing of the value of the defaulting member's limited liability company interest by appraisal or by formula and redemption or sale of the limited liability company interest at such value, or other penalty or consequence.

§ 18–503.   Allocation of profits and losses.

The profits and losses of a limited liability company shall be allocated among the members, and among classes or groups of members, in the manner provided in a limited liability company agreement. If the limited liability company agreement does not so provide, profits and losses shall be allocated on the basis of the agreed value (as stated in the records of the limited liability company) of the contributions made by each member to the extent they have been received by the limited liability company and have not been returned.

§18–504. Allocation of distributions.

Distributions of cash or other assets of a limited liability company shall be allocated among the members, and among classes or groups of members, in the manner provided in a limited liability company agreement. If the limited liability company agreement does not so provide, distributions shall be made on the basis of the agreed value (as stated in the records of the limited liability company) of the contributions made by each member to the extent they have been received by the limited liability company and have not been returned.

§18–505. Defense of usury not available.

No obligation of a member or manager of a limited liability company to the limited liability company, or to a member or manager of the limited liability company, arising under the limited liability company agreement or a separate agreement or writing, and no note, instrument or other writing evidencing any such obligation of a member or manager, shall be subject to the defense of usury, and no member or manager shall interpose the defense of usury with respect to any such obligation in any action.

SUBCHAPTER VI.   DISTRIBUTIONS AND RESIGNATION

§18–601. Interim distributions.

Except as provided in this subchapter, to the extent and at the times or upon the happening of the events specified in a limited liability company agreement, a member is entitled to receive from a limited liability company distributions before the member's resignation from the limited liability company and before the dissolution and winding up thereof.

§18–602. Resignation of manager.

A manager may resign as a manager of a limited liability company at the time or upon the happening of events specified in a limited liability company agreement and in accordance with the limited liability company agreement. A limited liability company agreement may provide that a manager shall not have the right to resign as a manager of a limited liability company. Notwithstanding that a limited liability company agreement provides that a manager does not have the right to resign as a manager of a limited liability company, a manager may resign as a manager of a limited liability company at any time by giving written notice to the members and other managers. If the resignation of a manager violates a limited liability company agreement, in addition to any remedies otherwise available under applicable law, a limited liability company may recover from the resigning manager damages for breach of the limited liability company agreement and offset the damages against the amount otherwise distributable to the resigning manager.

§18–603. Resignation of member.

A member may resign from a limited liability company only at the time or upon the happening of events specified in a limited liability company agreement and in accordance with the limited liability company agreement. Notwithstanding anything to the contrary under applicable law, unless a limited liability company agreement provides otherwise, a member may not resign from a limited liability company prior to the dissolution and winding up of the limited liability company. Notwithstanding anything to the contrary under applicable law, a limited liability company agreement may provide that a limited liability company interest may not be assigned prior to the dissolution and winding up of the limited liability company.

Unless otherwise provided in a limited liability company agreement, a limited liability company whose original certificate of formation was filed with the Secretary of State and effective on or prior to July 31, 1996, shall continue to be governed by this section as in effect on July 31, 1996.

§18–604. Distribution upon resignation.

Except as provided in this subchapter, upon resignation any resigning member is entitled to receive any distribution to which such member is entitled under a limited liability company agreement and, if not otherwise provided in a limited liability company agreement, such member is entitled to receive, within a reasonable time after resignation, the fair value of such member's limited liability company interest as of the date of resignation based upon such member's right to share in distributions from the limited liability company.

§ 18–605.   Distribution in kind.

Except as provided in a limited liability company agreement, a member, regardless of the nature of the member's contribution, has no right to demand and receive any distribution from a limited liability company in any form other than cash. Except as provided in a limited liability company agreement, a member may not be compelled to accept a distribution of any asset in kind from a limited liability company to the extent that the percentage of the asset distributed exceeds a percentage of that asset which is equal to the percentage in which the member shares in distributions from the limited liability company. Except as provided in the limited liability company agreement, a member may be compelled to accept a distribution of any asset in kind from a limited liability company to the extent that the percentage of the asset distributed is equal to a percentage of that asset which is equal to the percentage in which the member shares in distributions from the limited liability company.

§ 18–606.   Right to distribution.

Subject to §§ 18–607 and 18–804 of this title, and unless otherwise provided in a limited liability company agreement, at the time a member becomes entitled to receive a distribution, the member has the status of, and is entitled to all remedies available to, a creditor of a limited liability company with respect to the distribution. A limited liability company agreement may provide for the establishment of a record date with respect to allocations and distributions by a limited liability company.

§ 18–607.   Limitations on distribution.

(a)   A limited liability company shall not make a distribution to a member to the extent that at the time of the distribution, after giving effect to the distribution, all liabilities of the limited liability company, other than liabilities to members on account of their limited liability company interests and liabilities for which the recourse of creditors is limited to specified property of the limited liability company, exceed the fair value of the assets of the limited liability company, except that the fair value of property that is subject to a liability for which the recourse of creditors is limited shall be included in the assets of the limited liability company only to the extent that the fair value of that property exceeds that liability. For purposes of this subsection (a), the term "distribution" shall not include amounts constituting reasonable compensation for present or past services or reasonable payments made in the ordinary course of business pursuant to a bona fide retirement plan or other benefits program.

(b)   A member who receives a distribution in violation of subsection (a) of this section, and who knew at the time of the distribution that the distribution violated subsection (a) of this section, shall be liable to a limited liability company for the amount of the distribution. A member who receives a distribution in violation of subsection (a) of this section, and who did not know at the time of the distribution that the distribution violated subsection (a) of this section, shall not be liable for the amount of the distribution. Subject to subsection (c) of this section, this subsection shall not affect any obligation or liability of a member under an agreement or other applicable law for the amount of a distribution.

(c)   Unless otherwise agreed, a member who receives a distribution from a limited liability company shall have no liability under this chapter or other applicable law for the amount of the distribution after the expiration of 3 years from the date of the distribution unless an action to recover the distribution from such member is commenced prior to the expiration of the said 3-year period and an adjudication of liability against such member is made in the said action.

SUBCHAPTER VII.   ASSIGNMENT OF LIMITED LIABILITY COMPANY INTERESTS

§ 18–701.   Nature of limited liability company interest.

A limited liability company interest is personal property. A member has no interest in specific limited liability company property.

§ 18–702.   Assignment of limited liability company interest.

(a)   A limited liability company interest is assignable in whole or in part except as provided in a limited liability company agreement. The assignee of a member's limited liability company interest shall have no right to participate in the management of the business and affairs of a limited liability company except as provided in a limited liability company agreement or, unless otherwise provided in the limited liability company agreement, upon the vote or consent of all of the members of the limited liability company.

(b)   Unless otherwise provided in a limited liability company agreement:

(1)   An assignment of a limited liability company interest does not entitle the assignee to become or to exercise any rights or powers of a member;

(2)   An assignment of a limited liability company interest entitles the assignee to share in such profits and losses, to receive such distribution or distributions, and to receive such allocation of income, gain, loss, deduction, or credit or similar item to which the assignor was entitled, to the extent assigned; and

(3)   A member ceases to be a member and to have the power to exercise any rights or powers of a member upon assignment of all of the member's limited liability company interest. Unless otherwise provided in a limited liability company agreement, the pledge of, or granting of a security interest, lien or other encumbrance in or against, any or all of the limited liability company interest of a member shall not cause the member to cease to be a member or to have the power to exercise any rights or powers of a member.

(c)   Unless otherwise provided in a limited liability company agreement, a member's interest in a limited liability company may be evidenced by a certificate of limited liability company interest issued by the limited liability company. A limited liability company agreement may provide for the assignment or transfer of any limited liability company interest represented by such a certificate and make other provisions with respect to such certificates. A limited liability company shall not have the power to issue a certificate of limited liability company interest in bearer form.

(d)   Unless otherwise provided in a limited liability company agreement and except to the extent assumed by agreement, until an assignee of a limited liability company interest becomes a member, the assignee shall have no liability as a member solely as a result of the assignment.

(e)   Unless otherwise provided in the limited liability company agreement, a limited liability company may acquire, by purchase, redemption or otherwise, any limited liability company interest or other interest of a member or manager in the limited liability company. Unless otherwise provided in the limited liability company agreement, any such interest so acquired by the limited liability company shall be deemed canceled.

§ 18–703.   Member's limited liability company interest subject to charging order.

(a)   On application by a judgment creditor of a member or of a member's assignee, a court having jurisdiction may charge the limited liability company interest of the judgment debtor to satisfy the judgment. To the extent so charged, the judgment creditor has only the right to receive any distribution or distributions to which the judgment debtor would otherwise have been entitled in respect of such limited liability company interest.

(b)   A charging order constitutes a lien on the judgment debtor's limited liability company interest.

(c)   This chapter does not deprive a member or member's assignee of a right under exemption laws with respect to the judgment debtor's limited liability company interest.

(d)   The entry of a charging order is the exclusive remedy by which a judgment creditor of a member or a member's assignee may satisfy a judgment out of the judgment debtor's limited liability company interest and attachment, garnishment, foreclosure or other legal or equitable remedies are not available to the judgment creditor, whether the limited liability company has 1 member or more than 1 member.

(e)   No creditor of a member or of a member's assignee shall have any right to obtain possession of, or otherwise exercise legal or equitable remedies with respect to, the property of the limited liability company.

(f)   The Court of Chancery shall have jurisdiction to hear and determine any matter relating to any such charging order.

§ 18–704.   Right of assignee to become member.

(a)   An assignee of a limited liability company interest becomes a member:

(1)   As provided in the limited liability company agreement;

(2)   Unless otherwise provided in the limited liability company agreement, upon the vote or consent of all of the members of the limited liability company; or

(3)   Unless otherwise provided in the limited liability company agreement by a specific reference to this subsection or otherwise provided in connection with the assignment, upon the voluntary assignment by the sole member of the limited liability company of all of the limited liability company interests in the limited liability company to a single assignee. An assignment will be voluntary for purposes of this subsection if it is consented to by the member at the time of the assignment and is not effected by foreclosure or other similar legal process.

(b)   An assignee who has become a member has, to the extent assigned, the rights and powers, and is subject to the restrictions and liabilities, of a member under a limited liability company agreement and this chapter. Notwithstanding the foregoing, unless otherwise provided in a limited liability company agreement, an assignee who becomes a member is liable for the obligations of the assignor to make contributions as provided in § 18–502 of this title, but shall not be liable for the obligations of the assignor under subchapter VI of this chapter. However, the assignee is not obligated for liabilities, including the obligations of the assignor to make contributions as provided in § 18–502 of this title, unknown to the assignee at the time the assignee became a member and which could not be ascertained from a limited liability company agreement.

(c)   Whether or not an assignee of a limited liability company interest becomes a member, the assignor is not released from liability to a limited liability company under subchapters V and VI of this chapter.

§ 18–705.   Powers of estate of deceased or incompetent member.

If a member who is an individual dies or a court of competent jurisdiction adjudges the member to be incompetent to manage the member's person or property, the member's personal representative may exercise all of the member's rights for the purpose of settling the member's estate or administering the member's property, including any power under a limited liability company agreement of an assignee to become a member. If a member is a corporation, trust or other entity and is dissolved or terminated, the powers of that member may be exercised by its personal representative.

SUBCHAPTER VIII.   DISSOLUTION

§ 18–801.   Dissolution.

(a)   A limited liability company is dissolved and its affairs shall be wound up upon the first to occur of the following:

(1)   At the time specified in a limited liability company agreement, but if no such time is set forth in the limited liability company agreement, then the limited liability company shall have a perpetual existence;

(2)   Upon the happening of events specified in a limited liability company agreement;

(3)   Unless otherwise provided in a limited liability company agreement, upon the vote or consent of members who own more than 2/3 of the then-current percentage or other interest in the profits of the limited liability company owned by all of the members;

(4)   At any time there are no members; provided, that the limited liability company is not dissolved and is not required to be wound up if:

a. Unless otherwise provided in a limited liability company agreement, within 90 days or such other period as is provided for in the limited liability company agreement after the occurrence of the event that terminated the continued membership of the last remaining member, the personal representative of the last remaining member agrees to continue the limited liability company and to the admission of the personal representative of such member or its nominee or designee to the limited liability company as a member, effective as of the occurrence of the event that terminated the continued membership of the last remaining member; provided, that a limited liability company agreement may provide that the personal representative of the last remaining member shall be obligated to agree to continue the limited liability company and to the admission of the personal representative of such member or its nominee or designee to the limited liability company as a member, effective as of the occurrence of the event that terminated the continued membership of the last remaining member, or

b. A member is admitted to the limited liability company in the manner provided for in the limited liability company agreement, effective as of the occurrence of the event that terminated the continued membership of the last remaining member, within 90 days or such other period as is provided for in the limited liability company agreement after the occurrence of the event that terminated the continued membership of the last remaining member, pursuant to a provision of the limited liability company agreement that specifically provides for the admission of a member to the limited liability company after there is no longer a remaining member of the limited liability company.

(5) The entry of a decree of judicial dissolution under § 18–802 of this title.

Unless otherwise provided in a limited liability company agreement, a limited liability company whose original certificate of formation was filed with the Secretary of State and effective on or prior to July 31, 2015, shall continue to be governed by paragraph (a)(3) of this section as in effect on July 31, 2015 (except that "affirmative" and "written" shall be deleted from such paragraph (a)(3) of this section).

(b) Unless otherwise provided in a limited liability company agreement, the death, retirement, resignation, expulsion, bankruptcy or dissolution of any member or the occurrence of an event that terminates the continued membership of any member shall not cause the limited liability company to be dissolved or its affairs to be wound up, and upon the occurrence of any such event, the limited liability company shall be continued without dissolution.

§ 18–802. Judicial dissolution.

On application by or for a member or manager the Court of Chancery may decree dissolution of a limited liability company whenever it is not reasonably practicable to carry on the business in conformity with a limited liability company agreement.

§ 18–803. Winding up.

(a) Unless otherwise provided in a limited liability company agreement, a manager who has not wrongfully dissolved a limited liability company or, if none, the members or a person approved by the members, in either case, by members who own more than 50 percent of the then current percentage or other interest in the profits of the limited liability company owned by all of the members, may wind up the limited liability company's affairs; but the Court of Chancery, upon cause shown, may wind up the limited liability company's affairs upon application of any member or manager, or the member's personal representative or assignee, and in connection therewith, may appoint a liquidating trustee. Unless otherwise provided in a limited liability company agreement, a limited liability company whose original certificate of formation was filed with the Secretary of State and effective on or prior to July 31, 2015, shall continue to be governed by this subsection as in effect on July 31, 2015.

(b) Upon dissolution of a limited liability company and until the filing of a certificate of cancellation as provided in § 18–203 of this title, the persons winding up the limited liability company's affairs may, in the name of, and for and on behalf of, the limited liability company, prosecute and defend suits, whether civil, criminal or administrative, gradually settle and close the limited liability company's business, dispose of and convey the limited liability company's property, discharge or make reasonable provision for the limited liability company's liabilities, and distribute to the members any remaining assets of the limited liability company, all without affecting the liability of members and managers and without imposing liability on a liquidating trustee.

§ 18–804.   Distribution of assets.

(a)   Upon the winding up of a limited liability company, the assets shall be distributed as follows:

(1)   To creditors, including members and managers who are creditors, to the extent otherwise permitted by law, in satisfaction of liabilities of the limited liability company (whether by payment or the making of reasonable provision for payment thereof) other than liabilities for which reasonable provision for payment has been made and liabilities for distributions to members and former members under § 18–601 or § 18–604 of this title;

(2)   Unless otherwise provided in a limited liability company agreement, to members and former members in satisfaction of liabilities for distributions under § 18–601 or § 18–604 of this title; and

(3)   Unless otherwise provided in a limited liability company agreement, to members first for the return of their contributions and second respecting their limited liability company interests, in the proportions in which the members share in distributions.

(b)   A limited liability company which has dissolved:

(1)   Shall pay or make reasonable provision to pay all claims and obligations, including all contingent, conditional or unmatured contractual claims, known to the limited liability company;

(2)   Shall make such provision as will be reasonably likely to be sufficient to provide compensation for any claim against the limited liability company which is the subject of a pending action, suit or proceeding to which the limited liability company is a party; and

(3)   Shall make such provision as will be reasonably likely to be sufficient to provide compensation for claims that have not been made known to the limited liability company or that have not arisen but that, based on facts known to the limited liability company, are likely to arise or to become known to the limited liability company within 10 years after the date of dissolution.

If there are sufficient assets, such claims and obligations shall be paid in full and any such provision for payment made shall be made in full. If there are insufficient assets, such claims and obligations shall be paid or provided for according to their priority and, among claims of equal priority, ratably to the extent of assets available therefor. Unless otherwise provided in the limited liability company agreement, any remaining assets shall be distributed as provided in this chapter. Any liquidating trustee winding up a limited liability company's affairs who has complied with this section shall not be personally liable to the claimants of the dissolved limited liability company by reason of such person's actions in winding up the limited liability company.

(c)   A member who receives a distribution in violation of subsection (a) of this section, and who knew at the time of the distribution that the distribution violated subsection (a) of this section, shall be liable to the limited liability company for the amount of the distribution. For purposes of the immediately preceding sentence, the term "distribution" shall not include amounts constituting reasonable compensation for present or past services or reasonable payments made in the ordinary course of business pursuant to a bona fide retirement plan or other benefits program. A member who receives a distribution in violation of subsection (a) of this section, and who did not know at the time of the distribution that the distribution violated subsection (a) of this section, shall not be liable for the amount of the distribution. Subject to subsection (d) of this section, this subsection shall not affect any obligation or liability of a member under an agreement or other applicable law for the amount of a distribution.

(d)   Unless otherwise agreed, a member who receives a distribution from a limited liability company to which this section applies shall have no liability under this chapter or other applicable law for the amount of the distribution after the expiration of 3 years from the date of the distribution unless an action to recover the distribution from such member is commenced prior to the expiration of the said 3-year period and an adjudication of liability against such member is made in the said action.

(e)   Section 18–607 of this title shall not apply to a distribution to which this section applies.

§ 18–805. Trustees or receivers for limited liability companies; appointment; powers; duties.

When the certificate of formation of any limited liability company formed under this chapter shall be canceled by the filing of a certificate of cancellation pursuant to § 18–203 of this title, the Court of Chancery, on application of any creditor, member or manager of the limited liability company, or any other person who shows good cause therefor, at any time, may either appoint 1 or more of the managers of the limited liability company to be trustees, or appoint 1 or more persons to be receivers, of and for the limited liability company, to take charge of the limited liability company's property, and to collect the debts and property due and belonging to the limited liability company, with the power to prosecute and defend, in the name of the limited liability company, or otherwise, all such suits as may be necessary or proper for the purposes aforesaid, and to appoint an agent or agents under them, and to do all other acts which might be done by the limited liability company, if in being, that may be necessary for the final settlement of the unfinished business of the limited liability company. The powers of the trustees or receivers may be continued as long as the Court of Chancery shall think necessary for the purposes aforesaid.

§ 18–806. Revocation of dissolution.

If a limited liability company agreement provides the manner in which a dissolution may be revoked, it may be revoked in that manner and, unless a limited liability company agreement prohibits revocation of dissolution, then notwithstanding the occurrence of an event set forth in § 18–801(a)(1), (2), (3) or (4) of this title, the limited liability company shall not be dissolved and its affairs shall not be wound up if, prior to the filing of a certificate of cancellation in the office of the Secretary of State, the limited liability company is continued, effective as of the occurrence of such event:

(1) In the case of dissolution effected by the vote or consent of the members or other persons, pursuant to such vote or consent (and the approval of any members or other persons whose approval is required under the limited liability company agreement to revoke a dissolution contemplated by this paragraph);

(2) In the case of dissolution under § 18–801(a)(1) or (2) of this title (other than a dissolution effected by the vote or consent of the members or other persons or the occurrence of an event that causes the last remaining member to cease to be a member), pursuant to such vote or consent that, pursuant to the terms of the limited liability company agreement, is required to amend the provision of the limited liability company agreement effecting such dissolution (and the approval of any members or other persons whose approval is required under the limited liability company agreement to revoke a dissolution contemplated by this paragraph); and

(3) In the case of dissolution effected by the occurrence of an event that causes the last remaining member to cease to be a member, pursuant to the vote or consent of the personal representative of the last remaining member of the limited liability company or the assignee of all of the limited liability company interests in the limited liability company (and the approval of any other persons whose approval is required under the limited liability company agreement to revoke a dissolution contemplated by this paragraph).

If there is no remaining member of the limited liability company and the personal representative of the last remaining member or the assignee of all of the limited liability company interests in the limited liability company votes in favor of or consents to the continuation of the limited liability company, such personal representative or such assignee, as applicable, shall be required to agree to the admission of a nominee or designee as a member, effective as of the occurrence of the event that terminated the continued membership of the last remaining member. The provisions of this section shall not be construed to limit the accomplishment of a revocation of dissolution by other means permitted by law.

SUBCHAPTER IX. FOREIGN LIMITED LIABILITY COMPANIES

§ 18–901. Law governing.

(a) Subject to the Constitution of the State of Delaware:

(1)   The laws of the state, territory, possession, or other jurisdiction or country under which a foreign limited liability company is organized govern its organization and internal affairs and the liability of its members and managers; and

(2)   A foreign limited liability company may not be denied registration by reason of any difference between those laws and the laws of the State of Delaware.

(b)   A foreign limited liability company shall be subject to § 18–106 of this title.

§ 18–902. Registration required; application.

Before doing business in the State of Delaware, a foreign limited liability company shall register with the Secretary of State. In order to register, a foreign limited liability company shall submit to the Secretary of State:

(1)   A copy executed by an authorized person of an application for registration as a foreign limited liability company, setting forth:

   a.   The name of the foreign limited liability company and, if different, the name under which it proposes to register and do business in the State of Delaware;

   b.   The state, territory, possession or other jurisdiction or country where formed, the date of its formation and a statement from an authorized person that, as of the date of filing, the foreign limited liability company validly exists as a limited liability company under the laws of the jurisdiction of its formation;

   c.   The nature of the business or purposes to be conducted or promoted in the State of Delaware;

   d.   The address of the registered office and the name and address of the registered agent for service of process required to be maintained by § 18–904(b) of this title;

   e.   A statement that the Secretary of State is appointed the agent of the foreign limited liability company for service of process under the circumstances set forth in § 18–910(b) of this title; and

   f.   The date on which the foreign limited liability company first did, or intends to do, business in the State of Delaware.

(2)   A certificate, as of a date not earlier than 6 months prior to the filing date, issued by an authorized officer of the jurisdiction of its formation evidencing its existence. If such certificate is in a foreign language, a translation thereof, under oath of the translator, shall be attached thereto.

(3)   A fee as set forth in § 18–1105(a)(6) of this title shall be paid.

§ 18–903. Issuance of registration.

(a)   If the Secretary of State finds that an application for registration conforms to law and all requisite fees have been paid, the Secretary shall:

(1)   Certify that the application has been filed by endorsing upon the original application the word "Filed", and the date and hour of the filing. This endorsement is conclusive of the date and time of its filing in the absence of actual fraud;

(2)   File and index the endorsed application.

(b)   The Secretary of State shall prepare and return to the person who filed the application or the person's representative a copy of the original signed application, similarly endorsed, and shall certify such copy as a true copy of the original signed application.

(c)   The filing of the application with the Secretary of State shall make it unnecessary to file any other documents under Chapter 31 of this title.

§ 18–904. Name; registered office; registered agent.

(a)   A foreign limited liability company may register with the Secretary of State under any name (whether or not it is the name under which it is registered in the jurisdiction of its formation) that includes the words "Limited Liability Company" or the abbreviation "L.L.C." or the designation "LLC" and that could be registered by a domestic limited liability company; provided however, that a foreign limited liability company may register under any name which is not such as to distinguish it upon the records in the office of the Secretary of State from the name on such records of any domestic or foreign corporation, partnership, statutory trust, limited liability company or limited partnership reserved, registered, formed or organized under the laws of the State of Delaware with the written consent of the other corporation, partnership, statutory trust, limited liability company or limited partnership, which written consent shall be filed with the Secretary of State.

(b)   Each foreign limited liability company shall have and maintain in the State of Delaware:

(1)   A registered office which may but need not be a place of its business in the State of Delaware; and

(2)   A registered agent for service of process on the foreign limited liability company, having a business office identical with such registered office, which agent may be any of:

a.   An individual resident in the State of Delaware,

b.   A domestic limited liability company, a domestic corporation, a domestic partnership (whether general (including a limited liability partnership) or limited (including a limited liability limited partnership)), or a domestic statutory trust, or

c.   A foreign corporation, a foreign partnership (whether general (including a limited liability partnership) or limited (including a limited liability limited partnership)), a foreign limited liability company (other than the foreign limited liability company itself), or a foreign statutory trust.

(c)   A registered agent may change the address of the registered office of the foreign limited liability company or companies for which the agent is registered agent to another address in the State of Delaware by paying a fee as set forth in § 18–1105(a)(7) of this title and filing with the Secretary of State a certificate, executed by such registered agent, setting forth the address at which such registered agent has maintained the registered office for each of the foreign limited liability companies for which it is a registered agent, and further certifying to the new address to which each such registered office will be changed on a given day, and at which new address such registered agent will thereafter maintain the registered office for each of the foreign limited liability companies for which it is registered agent. Upon the filing of such certificate, the Secretary of State shall furnish to the registered agent a certified copy of the same under the Secretary's hand and seal of office, and thereafter, or until further change of address, as authorized by law, the registered office in the State of Delaware of each of the foreign limited liability companies for which the agent is a registered agent shall be located at the new address of the registered agent thereof as given in the certificate. In the event of a change of name of any person acting as a registered agent of a foreign limited liability company, such registered agent shall file with the Secretary of State a certificate, executed by such registered agent, setting forth the new name of such registered agent, the name of such registered agent before it was changed and the address at which such registered agent has maintained the registered office for each of the foreign limited liability companies for which it is registered agent, and shall pay a fee as set forth in § 18–1105(a)(7) of this title. Upon the filing of such certificate, the Secretary of State shall furnish to the registered agent a certified copy of the same under the Secretary of State's own hand and seal of office. A change of name of any person acting as a registered agent of a foreign limited liability company as a result of the merger or consolidation of the registered agent with or into another person which succeeds to its assets and liabilities by operation of law shall be deemed a change of name for purposes of this section. Filing a certificate under this section shall be deemed to be an amendment of the application of each foreign limited liability company affected thereby and each such foreign limited liability company shall not be required to take any further action with respect thereto to amend its application under § 18–905 of this title. Any registered agent filing a certificate under this section shall promptly, upon such filing, deliver a copy of any such certificate to each foreign limited liability company affected thereby.

(d)   The registered agent of 1 or more foreign limited liability companies may resign and appoint a successor registered agent by paying a fee as set forth in § 18–1105(a)(7) of this title and filing a certificate with the Secretary of State stating that it resigns and the name and address of the successor registered agent. There shall be attached to such certificate a statement of each affected foreign limited liability company ratifying and approving such change of registered agent. Upon such filing, the successor registered agent shall become the registered agent of such foreign limited liability companies as have ratified and approved such substitution and the successor registered agent's address, as stated in such certificate, shall become the address of each such foreign limited liability company's registered office in the State of Delaware. The Secretary of State shall then issue a certificate that the successor registered agent has become the registered agent of the foreign limited liability companies so ratifying and approving such change and setting out the names of such foreign limited liability companies. Filing of such certificate of resignation shall be deemed to be an amendment of the application of each foreign limited liability company affected thereby and each such foreign limited liability company shall not be required to take any further action with respect thereto to amend its application under § 18–905 of this title.

(e)   The registered agent of 1 or more foreign limited liability companies may resign without appointing a successor registered agent by paying a fee as set forth in § 18–1105(a)(7) of this title and filing a certificate of resignation with the Secretary of State, but such resignation shall not become effective until 30 days after the certificate is filed. The certificate shall contain a statement that written notice of resignation was given to each affected foreign limited liability company at least 30 days prior to the filing of the certificate by mailing or delivering such notice to the foreign limited liability company at its address last known to the registered agent and shall set forth the date of such notice. After receipt of the notice of the resignation of its registered agent, the foreign limited liability company for which such registered agent was acting shall obtain and designate a new registered agent to take the place of the registered agent so resigning. If such foreign limited liability company fails to obtain and designate a new registered agent as aforesaid prior to the expiration of the period of 30 days after the filing by the registered agent of the certificate of resignation, such foreign limited liability company shall not be permitted to do business in the State of Delaware and its registration shall be canceled. After the resignation of the registered agent shall have become effective as provided in this section and if no new registered agent shall have been obtained and designated in the time and manner aforesaid, service of legal process against each foreign limited liability company for which the resigned registered agent had been acting shall thereafter be upon the Secretary of State in accordance with § 18–911 of this title.

§ 18–905.   Amendments to application.

If any statement in the application for registration of a foreign limited liability company was false when made or any arrangements or other facts described have changed, making the application false in any respect, the foreign limited liability company shall promptly file in the office of the Secretary of State a certificate, executed by an authorized person, correcting such statement, together with a fee as set forth in § 18–1105(a)(6) of this title.

§ 18–906.   Cancellation of registration.

A foreign limited liability company may cancel its registration by filing with the Secretary of State a certificate of cancellation, executed by an authorized person, together with a fee as set forth in § 18–1105(a)(6) of this title. The registration of a foreign limited liability company shall be canceled as provided in §§ 18–104(i)(4), 18–904(e) and 18–1107(h) of this title. A cancellation does not terminate the authority of the Secretary of State to accept service of process on the foreign limited liability company with respect to causes of action arising out of the doing of business in the State of Delaware.

§ 18–907.   Doing business without registration.

(a)   A foreign limited liability company doing business in the State of Delaware may not maintain any action, suit or proceeding in the State of Delaware until it has registered in the State of Delaware, and has paid to the State of Delaware all fees and penalties for the years or parts thereof, during which it did business in the State of Delaware without having registered.

(b)   The failure of a foreign limited liability company to register in the State of Delaware does not impair:

(1)   The validity of any contract or act of the foreign limited liability company;

(2)   The right of any other party to the contract to maintain any action, suit or proceeding on the contract; or

(3)   Prevent the foreign limited liability company from defending any action, suit or proceeding in any court of the State of Delaware.

(c)   A member or a manager of a foreign limited liability company is not liable for the obligations of the foreign limited liability company solely by reason of the limited liability company's having done business in the State of Delaware without registration.

(d)   Any foreign limited liability company doing business in the State of Delaware without first having registered shall be fined and shall pay to the Secretary of State $200 for each year or part thereof during which the foreign limited liability company failed to register in the State of Delaware.

§ 18–908.   Foreign limited liability companies doing business without having qualified; injunctions.

The Court of Chancery shall have jurisdiction to enjoin any foreign limited liability company, or any agent thereof, from doing any business in the State of Delaware if such foreign limited liability company has failed to register under this subchapter or if such foreign limited liability company has secured a certificate of the Secretary of State under § 18–903 of this title on the basis of false or misleading representations. Upon the motion of the Attorney General or upon the relation of proper parties, the Attorney General shall proceed for this purpose by complaint in any county in which such foreign limited liability company is doing or has done business.

§ 18–909.   Execution; liability.

Section 18–204(d) of this title shall be applicable to foreign limited liability companies as if they were domestic limited liability companies.

§ 18–910.   Service of process on registered foreign limited liability companies.

(a)   Service of legal process upon any foreign limited liability company shall be made by delivering a copy personally to any managing or general agent or manager of the foreign limited liability company in the State of Delaware or the registered agent of the foreign limited liability company in the State of Delaware, or by leaving it at the dwelling house or usual place of abode in the State of Delaware of any such managing or general agent, manager or registered agent (if the registered agent be an individual), or at the registered office or other place of business of the foreign limited liability company in the State of Delaware. If the registered agent be a corporation, service of process upon it as such may be made by serving, in the State of Delaware, a copy thereof on the president, vice-president, secretary, assistant secretary or any director of the corporate registered agent. Service by copy left at the dwelling house or usual place of abode of any managing or general agent, manager or registered agent, or at the registered office or other place of business of the foreign limited liability company in the State of Delaware, to be effective must be delivered thereat at least 6 days before the return date of the process, and in the presence of an adult person, and the officer serving the process shall distinctly state the manner of service in the officer's return thereto. Process returnable forthwith must be delivered personally to the managing or general agent, manager or registered agent.

(b)   In case the officer whose duty it is to serve legal process cannot by due diligence serve the process in any manner provided for by subsection (a) of this section, it shall be lawful to serve the process against the foreign limited liability company upon the Secretary of State, and such service shall be as effectual for all intents and purposes as if made in any of the ways provided for in subsection (a) of this section. Process may be served upon the Secretary of State under this subsection by means of electronic transmission but only as prescribed by the Secretary of State. The Secretary of State is authorized to issue such rules and regulations with respect to such service as the Secretary of State deems necessary or appropriate. In the event that service is effected through the Secretary of State in accordance with this subsection, the Secretary of State shall forthwith notify the foreign limited liability company by letter, directed to the foreign limited liability company at its last registered office. Such letter shall be sent by a mail or courier service that includes a record of mailing or deposit with the courier and a record of delivery evidenced by the signature of the recipient. Such letter shall enclose a copy of the process and any other papers served on the Secretary of State pursuant to this subsection. It shall be the duty of the plaintiff in the event of such service to serve process and any other papers in duplicate, to notify the Secretary of State that service is being effected pursuant to this subsection, and to pay to the Secretary of State the sum of $50 for the use of the State of Delaware, which sum shall be taxed as a part of the costs in the proceeding if the plaintiff shall prevail therein. The Secretary of State shall maintain an alphabetical record of any such service setting forth the name of the plaintiff and defendant, the title, docket number and nature of the proceeding in which process has been served upon the Secretary, the fact that service has been effected pursuant to this subsection, the return date thereof and the day and hour when the service was made. The Secretary of State shall not be required to retain such information for a period longer than 5 years from the Secretary's receipt of the service of process.

§ 18–911. Service of process on unregistered foreign limited liability companies.

(a) Any foreign limited liability company which shall do business in the State of Delaware without having registered under § 18–902 of this title shall be deemed to have thereby appointed and constituted the Secretary of State of the State of Delaware its agent for the acceptance of legal process in any civil action, suit or proceeding against it in any state or federal court in the State of Delaware arising or growing out of any business done by it within the State of Delaware. The doing of business in the State of Delaware by such foreign limited liability company shall be a signification of the agreement of such foreign limited liability company that any such process when so served shall be of the same legal force and validity as if served upon an authorized manager or agent personally within the State of Delaware. Process may be served upon the Secretary of State under this subsection by means of electronic transmission but only as prescribed by the Secretary of State. The Secretary of State is authorized to issue such rules and regulations with respect to such service as the Secretary of State deems necessary or appropriate.

(b) Whenever the words "doing business," "the doing of business" or "business done in this State," by any such foreign limited liability company are used in this section, they shall mean the course or practice of carrying on any business activities in the State of Delaware, including, without limiting the generality of the foregoing, the solicitation of business or orders in the State of Delaware.

(c) In the event of service upon the Secretary of State in accordance with subsection (a) of this section, the Secretary of State shall forthwith notify the foreign limited liability company thereof by letter, directed to the foreign limited liability company at the address furnished to the Secretary of State by the plaintiff in such action, suit or proceeding. Such letter shall be sent by a mail or courier service that includes a record of mailing or deposit with the courier and a record of delivery evidenced by the signature of the recipient. Such letter shall enclose a copy of the process and any other papers served upon the Secretary of State. It shall be the duty of the plaintiff in the event of such service to serve process and any other papers in duplicate, to notify the Secretary of State that service is being made pursuant to this subsection, and to pay to the Secretary of State the sum of $50 for the use of the State of Delaware, which sum shall be taxed as part of the costs in the proceeding, if the plaintiff shall prevail therein. The Secretary of State shall maintain an alphabetical record of any such process setting forth the name of the plaintiff and defendant, the title, docket number and nature of the proceeding in which process has been served upon the Secretary, the return date thereof, and the day and hour when the service was made. The Secretary of State shall not be required to retain such information for a period longer than 5 years from the receipt of the service of process.

§ 18–912. Activities not constituting doing business.

(a) Activities of a foreign limited liability company in the State of Delaware that do not constitute doing business for the purpose of this subchapter include:

(1) Maintaining, defending or settling an action or proceeding;

(2) Holding meetings of its members or managers or carrying on any other activity concerning its internal affairs;

(3) Maintaining bank accounts;

(4) Maintaining offices or agencies for the transfer, exchange or registration of the limited liability company's own securities or maintaining trustees or depositories with respect to those securities;

(5) Selling through independent contractors;

(6) Soliciting or obtaining orders, whether by mail or through employees or agents or otherwise, if the orders require acceptance outside the State of Delaware before they become contracts;

(7) Selling, by contract consummated outside the State of Delaware, and agreeing, by the contract, to deliver into the State of Delaware, machinery, plants or equipment, the construction, erection or installation of which within the State of Delaware requires the supervision of technical engineers or skilled employees performing services not generally available, and as part of the contract of sale agreeing to furnish such services, and such services only, to the vendee at the time of construction, erection or installation;

(8) Creating, as borrower or lender, or acquiring indebtedness with or without a mortgage or other security interest in property;

(9) Collecting debts or foreclosing mortgages or other security interests in property securing the debts, and holding, protecting and maintaining property so acquired;

(10) Conducting an isolated transaction that is not 1 in the course of similar transactions;

(11) Doing business in interstate commerce; and

(12) Doing business in the State of Delaware as an insurance company.

(b) A person shall not be deemed to be doing business in the State of Delaware solely by reason of being a member or manager of a domestic limited liability company or a foreign limited liability company.

(c) This section does not apply in determining whether a foreign limited liability company is subject to service of process, taxation or regulation under any other law of the State of Delaware.

SUBCHAPTER X. DERIVATIVE ACTIONS

§ 18–1001. Right to bring action.

A member or an assignee of a limited liability company interest may bring an action in the Court of Chancery in the right of a limited liability company to recover a judgment in its favor if managers or members with authority to do so have refused to bring the action or if an effort to cause those managers or members to bring the action is not likely to succeed.

§ 18–1002. Proper plaintiff.

In a derivative action, the plaintiff must be a member or an assignee of a limited liability company interest at the time of bringing the action and:

(1) At the time of the transaction of which the plaintiff complains; or

(2) The plaintiff's status as a member or an assignee of a limited liability company interest had devolved upon the plaintiff by operation of law or pursuant to the terms of a limited liability company agreement from a person who was a member or an assignee of a limited liability company interest at the time of the transaction.

§ 18–1003. Complaint.

In a derivative action, the complaint shall set forth with particularity the effort, if any, of the plaintiff to secure initiation of the action by a manager or member or the reasons for not making the effort.

§ 18–1004.   Expenses.

If a derivative action is successful, in whole or in part, as a result of a judgment, compromise or settlement of any such action, the court may award the plaintiff reasonable expenses, including reasonable attorney's fees, from any recovery in any such action or from a limited liability company.

SUBCHAPTER XI.   MISCELLANEOUS

§ 18–1101.   Construction and application of chapter and limited liability company agreement.

(a)   The rule that statutes in derogation of the common law are to be strictly construed shall have no application to this chapter.

(b)   It is the policy of this chapter to give the maximum effect to the principle of freedom of contract and to the enforceability of limited liability company agreements.

(c)   To the extent that, at law or in equity, a member or manager or other person has duties (including fiduciary duties) to a limited liability company or to another member or manager or to another person that is a party to or is otherwise bound by a limited liability company agreement, the member's or manager's or other person's duties may be expanded or restricted or eliminated by provisions in the limited liability company agreement; provided, that the limited liability company agreement may not eliminate the implied contractual covenant of good faith and fair dealing.

(d)   Unless otherwise provided in a limited liability company agreement, a member or manager or other person shall not be liable to a limited liability company or to another member or manager or to another person that is a party to or is otherwise bound by a limited liability company agreement for breach of fiduciary duty for the member's or manager's or other person's good faith reliance on the provisions of the limited liability company agreement.

(e)   A limited liability company agreement may provide for the limitation or elimination of any and all liabilities for breach of contract and breach of duties (including fiduciary duties) of a member, manager or other person to a limited liability company or to another member or manager or to another person that is a party to or is otherwise bound by a limited liability company agreement; provided, that a limited liability company agreement may not limit or eliminate liability for any act or omission that constitutes a bad faith violation of the implied contractual covenant of good faith and fair dealing.

(f)   Unless the context otherwise requires, as used herein, the singular shall include the plural and the plural may refer to only the singular. The use of any gender shall be applicable to all genders. The captions contained herein are for purposes of convenience only and shall not control or affect the construction of this chapter.

(g)   Sections 9–406 and 9–408 of this title do not apply to any interest in a limited liability company, including all rights, powers and interests arising under a limited liability company agreement or this chapter. This provision prevails over §§ 9–406 and 9–408 of this title.

(h)   Action validly taken pursuant to 1 provision of this chapter shall not be deemed invalid solely because it is identical or similar in substance to an action that could have been taken pursuant to some other provision of this chapter but fails to satisfy 1 or more requirements prescribed by such other provision.

(i)   A limited liability company agreement that provides for the application of Delaware law shall be governed by and construed under the laws of the State of Delaware in accordance with its terms.

(j)   The provisions of this chapter shall apply whether a limited liability company has 1 member or more than 1 member.

§ 18–1102.   Short title.

This chapter may be cited as the "Delaware Limited Liability Company Act."

§ 18–1103.   Severability.

If any provision of this chapter or its application to any person or circumstances is held invalid, the invalidity does not affect other provisions or applications of the chapter which can be given effect without the invalid provision or application, and to this end, the provisions of this chapter are severable.

§ 18–1104.   Cases not provided for in this chapter.

In any case not provided for in this chapter, the rules of law and equity, including the rules of law and equity relating to fiduciary duties and the law merchant, shall govern.

§ 18–1105.   Fees.

(a)   No document required to be filed under this chapter shall be effective until the applicable fee required by this section is paid. The following fees shall be paid to and collected by the Secretary of State for the use of the State of Delaware:

(1)   Upon the receipt for filing of an application for reservation of name, an application for renewal of reservation or a notice of transfer or cancellation of reservation pursuant to § 18–103(b) of this title, a fee in the amount of $75.

(2)   Upon the receipt for filing of a certificate under § 18–104(b) of this title, a fee in the amount of $200, upon the receipt for filing of a certificate under § 18–104(c) of this title, a fee in the amount of $200, and upon the receipt for filing of a certificate under § 18–104(d) of this title, a fee in the amount of $2.00 for each limited liability company whose registered agent has resigned by such certificate.

(3)   Upon the receipt for filing of a certificate of formation under § 18–201 of this title or a certificate of registered series under § 18–218 of this title, a fee in the amount of $70 and upon the receipt for filing of a certificate of limited liability company domestication under § 18–212 of this title, a certificate of transfer or a certificate of transfer and domestic continuance under § 18–213 of this title, a certificate of conversion to limited liability company under § 18–214 of this title, a certificate of conversion to a non-Delaware entity under § 18–216 of this title, a certificate of amendment under § 18–202 or § 18–218(d)(3) of this title (except as otherwise provided in paragraph (a)(11) of this section), a certificate of cancellation under § 18–203 or § 18–218(d)(7) of this title, a certificate of merger or consolidation or a certificate of ownership and merger under § 18–209 of this title, a restated certificate of formation or a restated certificate of registered series under § 18–208 of this title, a certificate of amendment of a certificate with a future effective date or time under § 18–206(c) of this title, a certificate of termination of a certificate with a future effective date or time under § 18–206(c) of this title, a certificate of correction under § 18–211 of this title, a certificate of division under § 18–217 of this title, a certificate of conversion of protected series to registered series under § 18–219 of this title, a certificate of conversion of registered series to protected series under § 18–220 of this title, a certificate of merger or consolidation of registered series under § 18–221 of this title or a certificate of revival under § 18–1109 or § 18–1110 of this title, a fee in the amount of $180, plus, in the case of a certificate of cancellation under § 18–203 of this title, a fee in the amount of $50 for each registered series of the limited liability company named in the certificate of cancellation.

(4)   For certifying copies of any paper on file as provided for by this chapter, a fee in the amount of $50 for each copy certified. In addition, a fee of $2.00 per page shall be paid in each instance where the Secretary of State provides the copies of the document to be certified.

(5)   The Secretary of State may issue photocopies or electronic image copies of instruments on file, as well as instruments, documents and other papers not on file, and for all such photocopies or electronic image copies which are not certified by the Secretary of State, a fee of $10 shall be paid for the first page and $2.00 for each additional page. Notwithstanding Delaware's Freedom of Information Act (Chapter 100 of Title 29) or other provision of law granting access to public records, the Secretary of State upon request shall issue only photocopies or electronic image copies of public records in exchange for the fees described in this section, and in no case shall the Secretary of State be required to provide copies (or access to copies) of such public records (including without limitation bulk data, digital copies of instruments, documents and other papers, databases or other information) in an electronic medium or in any form other than photocopies or electronic image copies of such public

records in exchange, as applicable, for the fees described in this section or § 2318 of Title 29 for each such record associated with a file number.

(6) Upon the receipt for filing of an application for registration as a foreign limited liability company under § 18–902 of this title, a certificate under § 18–905 of this title or a certificate of cancellation under § 18–906 of this title, a fee in the amount of $200.

(7) Upon the receipt for filing of a certificate under § 18–904(c) of this title, a fee in the amount of $200, upon the receipt for filing of a certificate under § 18–904(d) of this title, a fee in the amount of $200, and upon the receipt for filing of a certificate under § 18–904(e) of this title, a fee in the amount of $2.00 for each foreign limited liability company whose registered agent has resigned by such certificate.

(8) For preclearance of any document for filing, a fee in the amount of $250.

(9) For preparing and providing a written report of a record search, a fee of up to $100.

(10) For issuing any certificate of the Secretary of State, including but not limited to a certificate of good standing with respect to a limited liability company or a registered series thereof, other than a certification of a copy under paragraph (a)(4) of this section, a fee in the amount of $50, except that for issuing any certificate of the Secretary of State that recites all of the filings with the Secretary of State of a limited liability company or all of the filings of any registered series or that lists all of the registered series formed by a limited liability company, a fee of $175 shall be paid for each such certificate. For issuing any certificate via the Secretary of State's online services, a fee of up to $175 shall be paid for each certificate.

(11) For receiving and filing and/or indexing any certificate, affidavit, agreement or any other paper provided for by this chapter, for which no different fee is specifically prescribed, a fee in the amount of $200. For filing any instrument submitted by a limited liability company or foreign limited liability company that only changes the registered office or registered agent and is specifically captioned as a certificate of amendment changing only the registered office or registered agent, a fee in the amount of $50 provided that no fee shall be charged pursuant to § 18–206(e) of this title.

(12) The Secretary of State may in the Secretary of State's own discretion charge a fee of $60 for each check received for payment of any fee that is returned due to insufficient funds or the result of a stop payment order.

(b) In addition to those fees charged under subsection (a) of this section, there shall be collected by and paid to the Secretary of State the following:

(1) For all services described in subsection (a) of this section that are requested to be completed within 30 minutes on the same day as the day of the request, an additional sum of up to $7,500 and for all services described in subsection (a) of this section that are requested to be completed within 1 hour on the same day as the day of the request, an additional sum of up to $1,000 and for all services described in subsection (a) of this section that are requested to be completed within 2 hours on the same day of the request, an additional sum of up to $500;

(2) For all services described in subsection (a) of this section that are requested to be completed within the same day as the day of the request, an additional sum of up to $300; and

(3) For all services described in subsection (a) of this section that are requested to be completed within a 24-hour period from the time of the request, an additional sum of up to $150.

The Secretary of State shall establish (and may from time to time amend) a schedule of specific fees payable pursuant to this subsection.

(c) The Secretary of State may in his or her discretion permit the extension of credit for the fees required by this section upon such terms as the secretary shall deem to be appropriate.

(d) The Secretary of State shall retain from the revenue collected from the fees required by this section a sum sufficient to provide at all times a fund of at least $500, but not more than $1,500, from which the secretary may refund any payment made pursuant to this section to the extent that it exceeds the fees required by this section. The funds shall be deposited in a financial institution which is a legal depository of State of Delaware moneys to the credit of the Secretary of State and shall be disbursable on order of the Secretary of State.

(e)   Except as provided in this section, the fees of the Secretary of State shall be as provided in § 2315 of Title 29.

§ 18–1106.   Reserved power of State of Delaware to alter or repeal chapter.

All provisions of this chapter may be altered from time to time or repealed and all rights of members and managers are subject to this reservation. Unless expressly stated to the contrary in this chapter, all amendments of this chapter shall apply to limited liability companies and members and managers whether or not existing as such at the time of the enactment of any such amendment.

§ 18–1107.   Taxation of limited liability companies and registered series.

(a)   For purposes of any tax imposed by the State of Delaware or any instrumentality, agency or political subdivision of the State of Delaware, a domestic limited liability company or a foreign limited liability company qualified to do business in the State of Delaware shall be classified as a partnership unless classified otherwise for federal income tax purposes, in which case the domestic or foreign limited liability company shall be classified in the same manner as it is classified for federal income tax purposes. For purposes of any tax imposed by the State of Delaware or any instrumentality, agency or political subdivision of the State of Delaware, a member or an assignee of a member of a domestic limited liability company or a foreign limited liability company qualified to do business in the State of Delaware shall be treated as either a resident or nonresident partner unless classified otherwise for federal income tax purposes, in which case the member or assignee of a member shall have the same status as such member or assignee of a member has for federal income tax purposes.

(b)   Every domestic limited liability company and every foreign limited liability company registered to do business in the State of Delaware shall pay an annual tax, for the use of the State of Delaware, in the amount of $300. There shall be paid by or on behalf of each registered series of a domestic limited liability company an annual tax, for use of the State of Delaware, in the amount of $75 per registered series.

(c)   The annual tax for a domestic limited liability company shall be due and payable on the first day of June following the close of the calendar year or upon the cancellation of a certificate of formation. The annual tax for a registered series shall be due and payable on the first day of June following the close of the calendar year or upon the cancellation of a certificate of registered series. The annual tax for a foreign limited liability company shall be due and payable on the first day of June following the close of the calendar year or upon the cancellation of the certificate of registration. The Secretary of State shall receive the annual tax and pay over all taxes collected to the Department of Finance of the State of Delaware. If the annual tax remains unpaid after the due date, the tax shall bear interest at the rate of 1 and one-half percent for each month or portion thereof until fully paid.

(d)   The Secretary of State shall, at least 60 days prior to June 1 of each year, cause to be mailed to each domestic limited liability company and each registered series thereof and each foreign limited liability company required to comply with the provisions of this section in care of its registered agent in the State of Delaware an annual statement for the tax to be paid hereunder.

(e)   In the event of neglect, refusal or failure on the part of any domestic limited liability company, registered series or foreign limited liability company to pay the annual tax to be paid hereunder on or before June 1 in any year, such domestic limited liability company or foreign limited liability company shall pay the sum of $200, and such registered series shall pay the sum of $50, to be recovered by adding that amount to the annual tax and such additional sum shall become a part of the tax and shall be collected in the same manner and subject to the same penalties.

(f)   In case any domestic limited liability company, registered series or foreign limited liability company shall fail to pay the annual tax due within the time required by this section, and in case the agent in charge of the registered office of any domestic limited liability company or foreign limited liability company upon whom process against such domestic limited liability company or any protected series or registered series thereof or foreign limited liability company may be served shall die, resign, refuse to act as such, remove from the State of Delaware or cannot with due diligence be found, it shall be lawful while default continues to serve process against such domestic limited liability company or any protected series or registered series thereof or foreign limited liability company upon the Secretary of State. Such service upon the Secretary of State shall be made in the manner and shall have the effect stated in § 18–105 of this title in the case of a domestic limited liability company or any protected series or registered series thereof and § 18–910 of this title in the case of a foreign limited liability company and shall be governed in all respects by said sections.

(g) The annual tax shall be a debt due from a domestic limited liability company, registered series or foreign limited liability company to the State of Delaware, for which an action at law may be maintained after the same shall have been in arrears for a period of 1 month. The tax shall also be a preferred debt in the case of insolvency.

(h) A domestic limited liability company that neglects, refuses or fails to pay the annual tax when due shall cease to be in good standing as a domestic limited liability company and all registered series thereof shall also cease to be in good standing. A registered series that neglects, refuses or fails to pay the annual tax when due shall cease to be in good standing as a registered series. A foreign limited liability company that neglects, refuses or fails to pay the annual tax when due shall cease to be registered as a foreign limited liability company in the State of Delaware.

(i) A domestic limited liability company or registered series that has ceased to be in good standing or a foreign limited liability company that has ceased to be registered by reason of the failure by the limited liability company, registered series or foreign limited liability company to pay an annual tax shall be restored to and have the status of a domestic limited liability company or registered series in good standing or a foreign limited liability company that is registered in the State of Delaware upon the payment of the annual tax and all penalties and interest thereon for each year for which such domestic limited liability company, registered series or foreign limited liability company neglected, refused or failed to pay an annual tax.

(j) On the motion of the Attorney General or upon request of the Secretary of State, whenever any annual tax due under this chapter from any domestic limited liability company, registered series or foreign limited liability company shall have remained in arrears for a period of 3 months after the tax shall have become payable, the Attorney General may apply to the Court of Chancery, by petition in the name of the State of Delaware, on 5 days' notice to such domestic limited liability company, registered series or foreign limited liability company, which notice may be served in such manner as the Court may direct, for an injunction to restrain such domestic limited liability company, registered series or foreign limited liability company from the transaction of any business within the State of Delaware or elsewhere, until the payment of the annual tax, and all penalties and interest due thereon and the cost of the application which shall be fixed by the Court. The Court of Chancery may grant the injunction, if a proper case appears, and upon granting and service of the injunction, such domestic limited liability company, registered series or foreign limited liability company thereafter shall not transact any business until the injunction shall be dissolved.

(k) A domestic limited liability company that has ceased to be in good standing by reason of the domestic limited liability company's neglect, refusal or failure to pay an annual tax shall remain a domestic limited liability company formed under this chapter, and each registered series thereof shall remain a registered series formed under this chapter, and each protected series thereof shall remain a protected series established under this chapter. A registered series that has ceased to be in good standing by reason of the registered series' neglect, refusal or failure to pay an annual tax shall remain a registered series formed under this chapter. The Secretary of State shall not accept for filing any certificate (except a certificate of resignation of a registered agent when a successor registered agent is not being appointed) required or permitted by this chapter to be filed in respect of any domestic limited liability company, registered series or foreign limited liability company if such domestic limited liability company, registered series or foreign limited liability company has neglected, refused or failed to pay an annual tax, and shall not issue any certificate of good standing with respect to such domestic limited liability company, registered series or foreign limited liability company, unless or until such domestic limited liability company, registered series or foreign limited liability company shall have been restored to and have the status of a domestic limited liability company or registered series in good standing or a foreign limited liability company duly registered in the State of Delaware.

(*l*)   A domestic limited liability company that has ceased to be in good standing (and each protected series and registered series thereof), a registered series that has ceased to be in good standing, or a foreign limited liability company that has ceased to be registered in the State of Delaware by reason of the domestic limited liability company's, registered series' or foreign limited liability company's neglect, refusal or failure to pay an annual tax may not maintain any action, suit or proceeding in any court of the State of Delaware until such domestic limited liability company, registered series or foreign limited liability company has been restored to and has the status of a domestic limited liability company, registered series or foreign limited liability company in good standing or duly registered in the State of Delaware. An action, suit or proceeding may not be maintained in any court of the State of Delaware by any successor or assignee of such domestic limited liability company (or any protected series or registered series thereof), registered series, or foreign limited liability company on any right, claim or demand arising out the transaction of business by such domestic limited liability company (or any protected series or registered series thereof) or registered series after the domestic limited liability company or registered series has ceased to be in good standing or a foreign limited liability company that has ceased to be registered in the State of Delaware until such domestic limited liability company, registered series or foreign limited liability company, or any person that has acquired all or substantially all of its assets, has paid any annual tax then due and payable, together with penalties and interest thereon.

(m)   The neglect, refusal or failure of a domestic limited liability company, registered series or foreign limited liability company to pay an annual tax shall not impair the validity of any contract, deed, mortgage, security interest, lien or act of such domestic limited liability company or any protected series or registered series thereof or foreign limited liability company or prevent such domestic limited liability company or any protected series or registered series thereof or foreign limited liability company from defending any action, suit or proceeding with any court of the State of Delaware.

(n)   A member or manager of a domestic limited liability company, registered series or foreign limited liability company is not liable for the debts, obligations or liabilities of such domestic limited liability company, registered series or foreign limited liability company solely by reason of the neglect, refusal or failure of such domestic limited liability company, registered series or foreign limited liability company to pay an annual tax or by reason of such domestic limited liability company, registered series or foreign limited liability company ceasing to be in good standing or duly registered. A protected series or registered series of a domestic limited liability company is not liable for the debts, obligations or liabilities of such domestic limited liability company or any other series thereof solely by reason of the neglect, refusal or failure of such domestic limited liability company or other series to pay an annual tax or by reason of such domestic limited liability company or other series ceasing to be in good standing.

§ 18–1108.   Cancellation of certificate of formation or certificate of registered series for failure to pay taxes.

(a)   The certificate of formation of a domestic limited liability company shall be canceled if the annual tax due under § 18–1107 of this title for the domestic limited liability company is not paid for a period of 3 years from the date it is due, such cancellation to be effective on the third anniversary of such due date.

(b)   The certificate of registered series shall be canceled if the annual tax due under § 18–1107 of this title is not paid for a period of 3 years from the date it is due, such cancellation to be effective on the third anniversary of such due date.

(c)   A list of those domestic limited liability companies and registered series whose certificates of formation or certificates of registered series were canceled on June 1 of such calendar year pursuant to § 18–1108(a) or § 18–1108(b) of this title shall be filed in the office of the Secretary of State. On or before October 31 of each calendar year, the Secretary of State shall publish such list on the Internet or on a similar medium for a period of 1 week and shall advertise the website or other address where such list can be accessed in at least 1 newspaper of general circulation in the State of Delaware.

§ 18–1109.   Revival of domestic limited liability company.

(a)   A domestic limited liability company whose certificate of formation has been canceled pursuant to § 18–104(d) or (i)(4) or § 18–1108(a) of this title may be revived by filing in the office of the Secretary of State a certificate of revival accompanied by the payment of the fee required by § 18–1105(a)(3) of this title and payment of the annual tax due under § 18–1107 of this title and all penalties and interest thereon due at the time of the cancellation of its certificate of formation. The certificate of revival shall set forth:

(1) The name of the limited liability company at the time its certificate of formation was canceled and, if such name is not available at the time of revival, the name under which the limited liability company is to be revived;

(2) The date of filing of the original certificate of formation of the limited liability company;

(3) The address of the limited liability company's registered office in the State of Delaware and the name and address of the limited liability company's registered agent in the State of Delaware;

(4) A statement that the certificate of revival is filed by 1 or more persons authorized to execute and file the certificate of revival to revive the limited liability company; and

(5) Any other matters the persons executing the certificate of revival determine to include therein.

(b) The certificate of revival shall be deemed to be an amendment to the certificate of formation of the limited liability company, and the limited liability company shall not be required to take any further action to amend its certificate of formation under § 18–202 of this title with respect to the matters set forth in the certificate of revival.

(c) Upon the filing of a certificate of revival, a limited liability company and all registered series thereof that have been formed and whose certificate of registered series has not been canceled prior to the cancellation of the certificate of formation shall be revived with the same force and effect as if its certificate of formation had not been canceled pursuant to § 18–104(d), § 18–104(i)(4) or § 18–1108(a) of this title. Such revival shall validate all contracts, acts, matters and things made, done and performed by the limited liability company, its members, managers, employees and agents during the time when its certificate of formation was canceled pursuant to § 18–104(d), § 18–104(i)(4) or § 18–1108(a) of this title, with the same force and effect and to all intents and purposes as if the certificate of formation had remained in full force and effect. All real and personal property, and all rights and interests, which belonged to the limited liability company at the time its certificate of formation was canceled pursuant to § 18–104(d), § 18–104(i)(4) or § 18–1108(a) of this title or which were acquired by the limited liability company following the cancellation of its certificate of formation pursuant to § 18–104(d), § 18–104(i)(4) or § 18–1108(a) of this title, and which were not disposed of prior to the time of its revival, shall be vested in the limited liability company after its revival as fully as they were held by the limited liability company at, and after, as the case may be, the time its certificate of formation was canceled pursuant to § 18–104(d), § 18–104(i)(4) or § 18–1108(a) of this title. After its revival, the limited liability company shall be as exclusively liable for all contracts, acts, matters and things made, done or performed in its name and on its behalf by its members, managers, employees and agents prior to its revival as if its certificate of formation had at all times remained in full force and effect.

§ 18–1110.   Revival of a registered series.

(a) A registered series whose certificate of registered series has been canceled pursuant to § 18–1108(b) of this title may be revived by filing in the office of the Secretary of State a certificate of revival of registered series accompanied by the payment of the fee required by § 18–1105(a)(3) of this title and payment of the annual tax due under § 18–1107 of this title and all penalties and interest thereon due at the time of the cancellation of its certificate of registered series. The certificate of revival of registered series shall set forth:

(1) The name of the limited liability company at the time the certificate of registered series was canceled and, if such name has changed, the name of the limited liability company at the time of revival of the registered series;

(2) The name of the registered series at the time the certificate of registered series was canceled and, if such name is not available at the time of revival, the name under which the registered series is to be revived;

(3) The date of filing of the original certificate of registered series;

(4)   A statement that the certificate of revival of registered series is filed by 1 or more persons authorized to execute and file such certificate of revival to revive the registered series; and

(5)   Any other matters the persons executing the certificate of revival of registered series determine to include therein.

(b)   The certificate of revival of registered series shall be deemed to be an amendment to the certificate of registered series, and no further actions shall be required to amend its certificate of registered series under § 18–218(d)(3) of this title with respect to the matters set forth in such certificate of revival.

(c)   Upon the filing of a certificate of revival of registered series, a registered series shall be revived with the same force and effect as if its certificate of registered series had not been canceled pursuant to § 18–1108(b) of this title. Such revival shall validate all contracts, acts, matters and things made, done and performed by the registered series, its members, managers, employees and agents during the time when its certificate of registered series was canceled pursuant to § 18–1108(b) of this title, with the same force and effect and to all intents and purposes as if the certificate of registered series had remained in full force and effect. All real and personal property, and all rights and interests, which belonged to the registered series at the time its certificate of registered series was canceled pursuant to § 18–1108(b) of this title or which were acquired by the registered series following the cancellation of its certificate of registered series pursuant to § 18–1108(b) of this title, and which were not disposed of prior to the time of its revival, shall be vested in the registered series after its revival as fully as they were held by the registered series at, and after, as the case may be, the time its certificate of registered series was canceled pursuant to § 18–1108(b) of this title. After its revival, the registered series shall be as exclusively liable for all contracts, acts, matters and things made, done or performed in its name and on its behalf by its members, managers, employees and agents prior to its revival as if its certificate of registered series had at all times remained in full force and effect.

SUBCHAPTER XII.   STATUTORY PUBLIC BENEFIT LIMITED LIABILITY COMPANIES

§ 18–1201.   Law applicable to statutory public benefit limited liability companies; how formed.

This subchapter applies to all statutory public benefit limited liability companies, as defined in § 18–1202 of this title. If a limited liability company elects to become a statutory public benefit limited liability company under this subchapter in the manner prescribed in this subchapter, it shall be subject in all respects to the provisions of this chapter, except to the extent this subchapter imposes additional or different requirements, in which case such requirements shall apply, and notwithstanding § 18–1101 of this title or any other provision of this title, such requirements imposed by this subchapter may not be altered in the limited liability company agreement.

§ 18–1202.   Statutory public benefit limited liability company defined; contents of certificate of formation and limited liability company agreement.

(a)   A "statutory public benefit limited liability company" is a for-profit limited liability company formed under and subject to the requirements of this chapter that is intended to produce a public benefit or public benefits and to operate in a responsible and sustainable manner. To that end, a statutory public benefit limited liability company shall be managed in a manner that balances the members' pecuniary interests, the best interests of those materially affected by the limited liability company's conduct, and the public benefit or public benefits set forth in its certificate of formation. A statutory public benefit limited liability company shall state in the heading of its certificate of formation that it is a statutory public benefit limited liability company and shall set forth 1 or more specific public benefits to be promoted by the limited liability company in its certificate of formation. The limited liability company agreement of a statutory public benefit limited liability company may not contain any provision inconsistent with this subchapter.

(b)   "Public benefit" means a positive effect (or reduction of negative effects) on 1 or more categories of persons, entities, communities or interests (other than members in their capacities as members) including, but not limited to, effects of an artistic, charitable, cultural, economic, educational, environmental, literary, medical, religious, scientific or technological nature. "Public benefit provisions" means the provisions of a limited liability company agreement contemplated by this subchapter.

§ 18–1203.   Certain amendments and mergers; votes required.

Notwithstanding any other provision of this chapter, a statutory public benefit limited liability company may not, without the approval of members who own at least 2/3 of the then-current percentage or other interest in the profits of the limited liability company owned by all members:

(1)   Amend its certificate of formation to delete or amend a provision required by § 18–1202(a) of this title;

(2)   Merge or consolidate with or into another entity or divide into 2 or more domestic limited liability companies if, as a result of such merger, consolidation or division, the limited liability company interests in such limited liability company would become, or be converted into or exchanged for the right to receive, limited liability company interests or other equity interests in a domestic or foreign limited liability company or other entity that is not a statutory public benefit limited liability company or similar entity, the certificate of formation or limited liability company agreement (or similar governing document) of which does not contain provisions identifying a public benefit or public benefits comparable in all material respects to those set forth in the certificate of formation of such limited liability company as contemplated by § 18–1202(a) of this title; or

(3)   Cease to be a statutory public benefit limited liability company under the provisions of this subchapter.

§ 18–1204.   Duties of members or managers.

(a)   The members or managers or other persons with authority to manage or direct the business and affairs of a statutory public benefit limited liability company shall manage or direct the business and affairs of the statutory public benefit limited liability company in a manner that balances the pecuniary interests of the members, the best interests of those materially affected by the limited liability company's conduct, and the specific public benefit or public benefits set forth in its certificate of formation. Unless otherwise provided in a limited liability company agreement, no member, manager or other person with authority to manage or direct the business and affairs of the statutory public benefit limited liability company shall have any liability for monetary damages for the failure to manage or direct the business and affairs of the statutory public benefit limited liability company as provided in this subsection.

(b)   A member or manager of a statutory public benefit limited liability company or any other person with authority to manage or direct the business and affairs of the statutory public benefit limited liability company shall not, by virtue of the public benefit provisions or § 18–1202(a) of this title, have any duty to any person on account of any interest of such person in the public benefit or public benefits set forth in its certificate of formation or on account of any interest materially affected by the limited liability company's conduct and, with respect to a decision implicating the balance requirement in subsection (a) of this section, will be deemed to satisfy such person's fiduciary duties to members and the limited liability company if such person's decision is both informed and disinterested and not such that no person of ordinary, sound judgment would approve.

§ 18–1205.   Periodic statements and third-party certification.

A statutory public benefit limited liability company shall no less than biennially provide its members with a statement as to the limited liability company's promotion of the public benefit or public benefits set forth in its certificate of formation and as to the best interests of those materially affected by the limited liability company's conduct. The statement shall include:

(1)   The objectives that have been established to promote such public benefit or public benefits and interests;

(2)   The standards that have been adopted to measure the limited liability company's progress in promoting such public benefit or public benefits and interests;

(3)   Objective factual information based on those standards regarding the limited liability company's success in meeting the objectives for promoting such public benefit or public benefits and interests; and

(4)   An assessment of the limited liability company's success in meeting the objectives and promoting such public benefit or public benefits and interests.

§ 18–1206.   Derivative suits.

Members of a statutory public benefit limited liability company or assignees of limited liability company interests in a statutory public benefit limited liability company owning individually or collectively, as of the date of instituting such derivative suit, at least 2% of the then-current percentage or other interest in the profits of the limited liability company or, in the case of a limited liability company with limited liability company interests listed on a national securities exchange, the lesser of such percentage or limited liability company interests of at least $2,000,000 in market value, may maintain a derivative lawsuit to enforce the requirements set forth in § 18–1204(a) of this title.

§ 18–1207.   No effect on other limited liability companies.

This subchapter shall not affect a statute or rule of law that is applicable to a limited liability company that is not a statutory public benefit limited liability company.

§ 18–1208.   Accomplishment by other means.

The provisions of this subchapter shall not be construed to limit the accomplishment by any other means permitted by law of the formation or operation of a limited liability company that is formed or operated for a public benefit (including a limited liability company that is designated as a public benefit limited liability company) that is not a statutory public benefit limited liability company.